Como utilizar el DICCIONARIO WILLIAMS
editado por Bantam Books

Lea toda la entrada para encontrar el significado exacto:
- Tome nota de los DIFERENTES SIGNIFICADOS. P.ej. al traducir **hoja** ¿usted desea decir "sheet" *(de papel)* o "blade" *(de cuchillo)* o "pad" *(de planta acuática)*?
- Tome nota de las CATEGORÍAS. P.ej. **order** cuando lleva la categoría (com) comercial, significa "pedido," pero en la categoría (mil) militar, significa "orden."
- Tome nota de los NIVELES DE USO. P.ej. **buck** significa "dólar" en el lenguaje popular (slang).

Las categorías y los niveles de uso figuran en las págs. 3-4 de la sección Inglés-Español. La lista incluye también 22 REGIONALISMOS, *p.ej.* (Arg), (Chile), (Col), (Mex), *entre otros.*

Luego de leer una entrada, vea LA OTRA SECCIÓN del diccionario para encontrar más información sobre el significado de las palabras. Véase, p.ej., **fuerza** y **force.**

Se citan las INFLEXIONES IRREGULARES de los substantivos, verbos y adjetivos ingleses.

Un PUNTO DIVISORIO señala la sílaba que debe separarse antes de añadir las sílabas de la infexión irregular, p.ej. **pic•nic . . . -nicked, -nicking.**

Una COMA separa las palabras con significados muy similares. El PUNTO Y COMA separa las palabras con significados diferentes. BARRAS PARALELAS (‖) separan las partes de la oración. Véase, p.ej., **orderly.**

Nótese que incluímos estas características nuevas en la sección GRAMÁTICA INGLESA:
- Una tabla de verbos irregulares que da información sobre el gerundio y otras formas verbales.
- La pronunciación de los participios pasados, p.ej. *hissed* [hɪst].
- La **s** de "posesión," p.ej. *a month's vacation.*
- Las contracciones corrientes, p.ej. *who'd, they'll.*

Y muchas otras características útiles.

THE BANTAM NEW
COLLEGE DICTIONARY SERIES

Edwin B. Williams, General Editor

Edwin B. Williams, A.B., A.M., Ph.D., Doct. d'Univ., LL.D, L.H.D. was chairman of the Department of Romance Languages, dean of the Graduate School, and provost of the University of Pennsylvania. He was a member of the American Philosophical Society and the Hispanic Society of America and the author of *The Bantam New College Spanish & English Dictionary* and the Scribner's (formerly the Holt) *Spanish and English Dictionary* and many other works on the Spanish, Portuguese and French languages.

THE BANTAM NEW COLLEGE
SPANISH & ENGLISH
DICTIONARY

DICCIONARIO
INGLÉS y ESPAÑOL

BY EDWIN B. WILLIAMS
Professor of Romance Languages
University of Pennsylvania

BANTAM BOOKS
TORONTO · NEW YORK · LONDON · SYDNEY

THE BANTAM NEW COLLEGE
SPANISH & ENGLISH DICTIONARY

A Bantam Book / November 1968
33 printings through July 1980
Bantam export edition / July 1980
2nd printing .... November 1980
3rd printing .... April 1981

Library of Congress Catalog Card Number: 68-29099

ISBN 0-553-17048-1

Published simultaneously in the United States and Canada

Bantam Books are published by Bantam Books, Inc. Its trade-
mark, consisting of the words "Bantam Books" and the por-
trayal of a bantam, is Registered in U.S. Patent and Trademark
Office, and in other countries. Marca Registrada. Bantam
Books, Inc., 666 Fifth Avenue, New York, New York 10103.

PRINTED IN THE UNITED STATES OF AMERICA

12 11

CONTENTS

PREFACE

This book is based on primary spoken and written sources. It is designed for speakers of either language who wish to find words or the meanings of words in the foreign language. Its purpose is, therefore, fourfold. It gives to the English-speaking user (1) the Spanish words he needs to express his thoughts in Spanish and (2) the English meanings of Spanish words he needs to understand Spanish, and to the Spanish-speaking user (3) the English words he needs to express his thoughts in English and (4) the Spanish meanings of English words he needs to understand English.

In order to accomplish the purpose of (1) and (3), discriminations are provided in the source language except that, because of the special facility with which the subject of the verb can be shown in Spanish and because of the convenience of showing the object with personal **a,** discriminations in the form of subject and/or object are given in Spanish on the English-Spanish side as well as on the Spanish-English side. For the purpose of (2) and (4) discriminations are not needed and are not given because the user will always have the context of what he hears or reads to guide him. However, some glosses whose purpose is not to show discrimination but rather to elaborate on the meaning of what may be judged to be an unfamiliar or obscure word or expression in the user's native language are provided in that language.

All words are treated in a fixed order according to the parts of speech and the functions of verbs; and meanings with subject, usage, and regional labels come after more general meanings.

In order to facilitate the finding of the meaning and use sought for, changes within a vocabulary entry in part of speech and function of verb, in irregular inflection, in the gender of Spanish nouns, and in the pronunciation of English words are marked with parallels instead of the usual semicolons.

Periods are omitted after labels and grammatical abbreviations and at the end of vocabulary entries.

The feminine form of a Spanish adjective used as a noun (or a Spanish feminine noun having identical spelling with the feminine form of an adjective) which falls alphabetically in a separate position from the adjective is treated in that position and is listed again as a cross reference under the adjective.

PRÓLOGO

Hemos basado este libro en fuentes originales del lenguaje hablado y escrito. Está destinado a los hablantes de uno u otro idioma que buscan palabras o significados de palabras en el idioma extranjero. Tiene, por lo tanto, los cuatro siguientes propósitos: al usuario de habla inglesa le suministra (1) las palabras españolas que necesita para expresar su pensamiento en español y (2) los significados ingleses de las palabras españolas que necesita para comprender el español; y al usuario de habla española le suministra (3) las palabras inglesas que necesita para expresar su pensamiento en inglés y (4) los significados españoles de las palabras inglesas que necesita para comprender el inglés.

Para lograr los propósitos indicados bajo los números (1) y (3), se suministran diferenciaciones (es decir, distinciones entre dos o más significados de una palabra) en la lengua-fuente; pero, dada la facilidad con que el sujeto del verbo puede indicarse en español y dada la conveniencia de destacar el objeto del verbo con la preposición **a**, las diferenciaciones consistentes en el sujeto o el objeto, o ambos, se dan en español tanto en la parte de inglés-español como en la parte de español-inglés. Para los propósitos indicados bajo los números (2) y (4) no se necesitan diferenciaciones y no se dan, porque el usuario siempre tendrá como guía el contexto de lo que oye o lee. Con todo, algunas glosas que no tienen por objeto indicar diferenciaciones sino más bien dilucidar el sentido de lo que parece ser una palabra o expresión raras u obscuras en la lengua nativa del usuario, se indican en esta lengua.

Los vocablos se tratan consecutivamente de acuerdo con las partes de la oración y las funciones verbales; y los significados marcados con calificativos de tema, uso y país van después de los significados más generales.

Para facilitar la búsqueda del significado y el uso deseados, los cambios en la parte de la oración y función verbal, en la flexión, en el género de los nombres españoles y en la pronunciación de las palabras inglesas van señalados con doble raya vertical, en vez del punto y coma de costumbre.

Se han omitido los puntos después de los calificativos y abreviaturas gramaticales y al fin de los artículos.

La forma femenina de un adjetivo español usado como sustan-

The gender of Spanish nouns is shown on both sides of the Dictionary except that the gender of masculine nouns ending in **-o**, feminine nouns ending in **-a, -dad, -tad, -tud, -ión,** and **-umbre,** masculine nouns modified by an adjective ending in **-o,** and feminine nouns modified by an adjective ending in **-a** is not shown on the English-Spanish side.

Numbers referring to the model conjugations of Spanish verbs are placed before the abbreviations indicating the part of speech. The complete list of model verbs includes models of all verbs that show a combination of two types of irregularity, e.g., **esforzar, seguir, teñir.**

Proper nouns and abbreviations are listed in their alphabetical position in the main body of the Dictionary. Thus **España** and **español** do not have to be looked up in two different parts of the book. And all subentries are listed in strictly alphabetical order.

The centered period is used in vocabulary entries of irregularly inflected words to mark off the final syllable that has to be detached before the syllable showing the inflection is added, e.g., **lá·piz** *m* (*pl* **-pices**) and **falsi·fy** ['fɔlsɪ ˌfaɪ] *v* (*pret & pp* **-fied**).

There are three kinds of compound words in English: (1) solid, e.g., **steamboat,** (2) hyphenated, e.g., **long-range,** and (3) spaced, e.g., **high school.** In this Dictionary the pronunciation of all English simple words is shown in a new adaptation of the symbols of the International Phonetic Alphabet and in brackets. The pronunciation of English compound words is not shown provided the pronunciation of the components is shown where they appear as independent vocabulary entries, except that the accentuation of solid and hyphenated compounds is indicated in the vocabulary entry itself, e.g., **fall'out',** the IPA pronunciation of **fall** and **out** being shown where these words appear as independent vocabulary entries.

Since vocabulary entries are not determined on the basis of etymology, homographs are included in a single entry. When the pronunciation of an English homograph changes, this is shown in the proper place after parallels.

E.B.W.

The author wishes to express his gratitude to many persons who have worked with him in lexicographical research and development and who helped him directly in the compilation of this book and particularly to the following: Paul Aguilar, William Beigel, Henry H. Carter, Eugenio Chang-Rodríguez, R. Thomas Douglass, David Louis Gold, Allison Gronberg, James E. Iannucci, Christopher Stavrou, Roger J. Steiner, John C. Traupman, and José Vidal.

tivo (o de un sustantivo femenino que se escribe lo mismo que la forma femenina de un adjetivo), que cae alfabéticamente en lugar apartado del adjetivo, se trata en este lugar y se consigna otra vez bajo el adjetivo con una referencia a la palabra traducida anteriormente.

El género de los nombres españoles aparece en ambas partes del Diccionario; pero no aparece en la parte de inglés-español el género de los nombres masculinos que terminan en **-o**, los nombres femeninos que terminan en **-a, -dad, -tad, -tud, -ión** y **-umbre,** los nombres masculinos modificados por un adjetivo que termina en **-o** ni los nombres femeninos modificados por un adjetivo que termina en **-a.**

Los números que se refieren a los modelos de conjugación de los verbos españoles van antes de las abreviaturas que indican la parte de la oración. La lista completa de los modelos de conjugación incluye muchos que muestran una combinación de dos irregularidades, p.ej., **esforzar, seguir, teñir.**

Los nombres propios y las abreviaturas se consignan en su propio lugar alfabético en el texto del Diccionario. No hay, pues, que buscar **España** y **español** en dos partes distintas del libro. Y todos los artículos secundarios van colocados en riguroso orden alfabético.

Se usa el punto divisorio en los artículos de palabras de flexión irregular para señalar la sílaba final que debe separarse antes de agregar la sílaba que denota la flexión, p.ej., **lá·piz** (*pl* **-pices**) y **falsi·fy** [ˈfɔlsɪ‚faɪ] *v* (*pret & pp* **-fied**).

Hay tres clases de palabras compuestas en inglés: (1) las sólidas, p.ej., **steamboat,** (2) las escritas con guión, p.ej., **long-range** y (3) las separadas en dos o más elementos, p.ej., **high school.** En este Diccionario se muestra la pronunciación de todas las palabras inglesas simples por medio de una nueva adaptación de los símbolos del Alfabeto fonético internacional y entre corchetes. No se muestra la pronunciación de las palabras inglesas compuestas cuando la pronunciación de los componentes consta en los lugares donde aparecen como artículos independientes, si bien la acentuación de las palabras compuestas sólidas y las escritas con guión se indica en la voz alfabetizada misma, p.ej., **fall'out′,** pues la pronunciación de **fall** y **out** va indicada según el Alfabeto fonético internacional en los lugares donde estas palabras aparecen como artículos independientes.

Como la constitución de los artículos no se ha determinado a base de su etimología, se incluyen bajo un mismo artículo todos los homógrafos de una palabra. Cuando varía la pronunciación de un homógrafo inglés, se indica en su propio lugar después de la doble raya vertical.

E.B.W.

Labels and Grammatical Abbreviations
Calificativos y abreviaturas gramaticales

abbr abbreviation—abreviatura

(acronym) acrónimo—a word formed from the initial letters or syllables of a series of words—palabra formada de las letras o sílabas iniciales de una serie de palabras

adj adjective—adjetivo

adv adverb—adverbio

(aer) aeronautics—aeronáutica

(agr) agriculture—agricultura

(alg) algebra—álgebra

(Am) Spanish American—hispano-americano

(anat) anatomy—anatomía

(archaic) arcaico

(archeol) archeology—arqueología

(archit) architecture—arquitectura

(Arg) Argentine—argentino

(arith) arithmetic—aritmética

art article—artículo

(arti) artillery—artillería

(astr) astronomy—astronomía

(aut) automobiles—automóviles

(bact) bacteriology—bacteriología

(bb) bookbinding—encuadernación

(Bib) Biblical—bíblico

(billiards) billar

(biochem) biochemistry—bioquímica

(biol) biology—biología

(Bol) Bolivian—boliviano

(bowling) bolos

(bot) botany—botánica

(box) boxing—boxeo

(Brit) British—británico

(CAm) Central American—centroamericano

(cards) naipes

(carp) carpentry—carpintería

(chem) chemistry—química

(chess) ajedrez

(Chile) Chilean—chileno

(Col) Colombian—colombiano

(coll) colloquial—familiar

(com) commercial—comercial

comp comparative—comparativo

cond conditional—condicional

conj conjunction—conjunción

(C-R) Costa Rican—costarriqueño

(Cuba) Cuban—cubano

(culin) cooking—cocina

def definite—definido

dem demonstrative—demostrativo

(dent) dentistry—odontología

(dial) dialectal—dialectal

(eccl) ecclesiastical—eclesiástico

(econ) economics—economía

(Ecuad) Ecuadorian—ecuatoriano

(educ) education—educación

(elec) electricity—electricidad

(electron) electronics—electrónica

(El Salv) El Salvador

(ent) entomology—entomología

f feminine noun—nombre femenino

(fa) fine arts—bellas artes

fem feminine—femenino

(fencing) esgrima

(feud) feudalism—feudalismo

(fig) figurative—figurado

fpl feminine noun plural—nombre femenino plural

fsg feminine noun singular—nombre femenino singular

fut future—futuro

(geog) geography—geografía

(geol) geology—geología

(geom) geometry—geometría

ger gerund—gerundio

(gram) grammar—gramática

(Guat) Guatemalan—guatemalteco

(heral) heraldry—heráldica

(hist) history—historia

(Hond) Honduran—hondureño

(hort) horticulture—horticultura

(hum) humorous—jocoso

(hunt) hunting—caza

(ichth) ichthyology—ictiología

imperf imperfect—imperfecto

impers impersonal—impersonal

impv imperative—imperativo

ind indicative—indicativo

indecl indeclinable—indeclinable

indef indefinite—indefinido

inf infinitive—infinitivo

(ins) insurance—seguros

interj interjection—interjección

interr interrogative—interrogativo

intr intransitive verb—verbo intransitivo

invar invariable—invariable

(iron) ironical—irónico

(Lat) Latin—latín

(law) derecho

(letterword) a word in the form of an abbreviation which is pronounced by sounding the names of its letters in succession and which functions as a part of speech—palabra en forma de abreviatura la cual se pronuncia haciendo sonar el nombre de cada letra consecutivamente y que funciona como parte del discurso

(log) logic—lógica

m masculine noun—nombre masculino

(mach) machinery—maquinaria

(mas) masonry—albañilería

masc masculine—masculino

(math) mathematics—matemática

(mech) mechanics—mecánica

(med) medicine—medicina

(metal) metallurgy—metalurgia

(meteor) meteorology—meteorología

(Mex) Mexican—mejicano

mf masculine or feminine noun according to sex—nombre masculino o nombre femenino según el sexo

(mil) military—militar

(min) mining—minería

(mineral) mineralogy—mineralogía

(mountaineering) alpinismo

(mov) moving pictures—cine

mpl masculine noun plural—nombre masculino plural

msg masculine noun singular—nombre masculino singular

(mus) music—música

(myth) mythology—mitología

m & f masculine and feminine noun without regard to sex—nombre masculino y femenino sin tener en cuenta el sexo
(naut) nautical—náutico
(nav) naval—naval militar
neut neuter—neutro
(obs) obsolete—desusado
(obstet) obstetrics—obstetricia
(opt) optics—óptica
(orn) ornithology—ornitología
(paint) painting—pintura
(Pan) Panamanian—panameño
(Para) Paraguayan—paraguayo
(pathol) pathology—patología
pers personal—personal
(Peru) Peruvian—peruano
(pharm) pharmacy—farmacia
(philol) philology—filología
(philos) philosophy—filosofía
(phonet) phonetics—fonética
(phot) photography—fotografía
(phys) physics—física
(physiol) physiology—fisiología
pl plural—plural
(poet) poetical—poético
(pol) politics—política
poss possessive—posesivo
pp past participle—participio pasado
(P-R) Puerto Rican—puertorriqueño
prep preposition—preposición
pres present—presente
pret preterit—pretérito
pron pronoun—pronombre
(psychol) psychology—sicología
(rad) radio—radio
ref reflexive verb—verbo reflexivo
reflex reflexive—reflexivo
rel relative—relativo

(rhet) rhetoric—retórica
(rr) railway—ferrocarril
s substantive—substantivo
(SAm) South American—sudamericano
(scornful) despreciativo
(sculp) sculpture—escultura
(S-D) Santo Domingo—República Dominicana
(sew) sewing—costura
sg singular—singular
(slang) jerga
spl substantive plural—substantivo plural
ssg substantive singular—substantivo singular
subj subjunctive—subjuntivo
super superlative—superlativo
(surg) surgery—cirugía
(surv) surveying—agrimensura
(taur) bullfighting—tauromaquia
(telg) telegraphy—telegrafía
(telp) telephony—telefonía
(telv) television—televisión
(tennis) tenis
(theat) theater—teatro
(theol) theology—teología
tr transitive verb—verbo transitivo
(typ) printing—imprenta
(Urug) Uruguayan—uruguayo
v verb—verbo
var variant—variante
v aux auxiliary verb—verbo auxiliar
(Ven) Venezuelan—venezolano
(vet) veterinary medicine—veterinaria
(vulg) vulgar—grosero
(W-I) West Indian—antillano
(zool) zoology—zoología

PART ONE

Spanish-English

Spanish Pronunciation

The Spanish alphabet has twenty-eight letters. Note that **ch**, **ll**, and **ñ** are considered to be separate single letters and are so treated in the alphabetization of Spanish words. While **rr** is considered to be a distinct sign for a particular sound, it is not included in the alphabet and, except in syllabification—notably for the division of words at the end of a line—, is not treated as a separate letter, perhaps because words never begin with it.

These twenty-eight letters plus the sign **rr** are listed below with their names and a description of their sounds.

LETTER	NAME	SOUND
a	a	Like a in English **father**, e.g., **casa, fácil**.
b	be	When initial or preceded by **m**, like b in English **book**, e.g., **boca, combate**. When standing between two vowels and when preceded by a vowel and followed by **l** or **r**, like v in English **voodoo** except that it is formed with both lips, e.g., **saber, hablar, sobre**. It is generally silent before **s** plus a consonant and often dropped in spelling, e.g., **oscuro** for **obscuro**.
c	ce	When followed by **e** or **i**, like th in English **think** in Castilian and like c in English **cent** in American Spanish, e.g., **acento, cinco**. When followed by **a, o, u**, or a consonant, like c in English **come**, e.g., **cantar, como, cubo, acto, creer**.
ch	che	Like ch in English **much**, e.g., **escuchar**.
d	de	Generally, like d in **dog**, e.g., **diente, rendir**. When standing between two vowels, when preceded by a vowel and followed by **r**, and when final, like th in English **this**, e.g., **miedo, piedra, libertad**.
e	e	At the end of a syllable, like a in English **fate**, but without the glide the English sound sometimes has, e.g., **beso, menos**. When followed by a consonant in the same syllable, like e in English **met**, e.g., **perla, selva**.
f	efe	Like f in English **five**, e.g., **flor, efecto**.
g	ge	When followed by **e** or **i**, somewhat like h in English **home**, e.g., **gente, giro**. When followed by **a, o, u**, or a consonant, like g in English **go**, e.g., **gato, agudo, grande**.
h	hache	Always silent, e.g., **hombre, alcohol**.
i	i	Like i in English **machine**, e.g., **camino, ida**. When preceded or followed by another vowel, it has the sound of English **y**, e.g., **tierra, reina**.
j	jota	Somewhat like h in English **home**, e.g., **jardín**.
k	ka	Like English k, e.g., **kilociclo**.
l	ele	Like l in English **laugh**, e.g., **lado, ala**.
ll	elle	Somewhat like lli in **William** in Castilian and like y in English **yes** in American Spanish, e.g., **silla, llamar**.

3

LETTER	NAME	SOUND
m	eme	Like **m** in English **man**, e.g., **mesa, amar.**
n	ene	Generally, like **n** in English **name**, e.g., **andar, nube.** Before **v**, like **m** in English **man**, e.g., **invierno, enviar.** Before **c** [k] and **g** [g], like **n** in English **drink**, e.g., **finca, manga.**
ñ	eñe	Somewhat like **ni** in English **onion**, e.g., **año, enseñar.**
o	o	At the end of a syllable, like **o** in English **note**, but without the glide the English sound sometimes has, e.g., **boca, como.** When followed by a consonant in the same syllable, like **o** in English **organ**, e.g., **poste, norte.**
p	pe	Like **p** in English **pen**, e.g., **poco, aplicar.** It is often silent in **septiembre** and **séptimo.**
q	cu	Like **c** in English **come** It is always followed by **ue** or **ui**, in which the **u** is silent, e.g., **querer, quitar.** The sound of English **qu** is represented in Spanish by **cu**, e.g., **frecuente.**
r	ere	Strongly trilled, when initial and when preceded by **l, n,** or **s**, e.g., **rico, alrededor, honra, israelí.** Pronounced with a single tap of the tongue in all other positions, e.g., **caro, grande, amar.**
rr	erre	Strongly trilled, e.g., **carro, tierra.**
s	ese	Generally, like **s** in English **say**, e.g., **servir, casa, este.** Before a voiced consonant (**b, d, g** [g], **l, r, m, n**), like **z** in English **zero**, e.g., **esbelto, desde, rasgar, eslabón, mismo, asno.**
t	te	Like **t** in English **stamp**, e.g., **tiempo, matar.**
u	u	Like **u** in English **rude**, e.g., **mudo, puño.** It is silent in **gue, gui, que,** and **qui,** but not in **güe** and **güi**, e.g., **guerra, guisa, querer, quitar,** but **agüero, lingüístico.** When preceded or followed by another vowel, it has the sound of English **w**, e.g., **fuego, deuda.**
v	ve or uve	Like Spanish **b** in all positions, e.g., **vengo, invierno, uva, huevo.**
x	equis	When followed by a consonant, like **s** in English **say**, e.g., **expresar, sexto.** Between two vowels, like **gs**, e.g., **examen, existencia, exótico;** and in some words, like **s** in **say**, e.g., **auxilio, exacto.** In **México** (for **Méjico**), like Spanish **j.**
y	ye or i griega	In the conjunction **y**, like **i** in English **machine.** When standing next to a vowel or between two vowels, like **y** in English **yes**, e.g., **yo, hoy, vaya.**
z	zeda or zeta	Like **th** in English **think** in Castilian and like **c** in English **cent** in American Spanish, e.g., **zapato, zona.**

4

SPANISH–ENGLISH

a
ab

A

A, a (a) *f* first letter of the Spanish alphabet

a *prep* at; for, to; on, upon; in, into; by; from; **a decir verdad** to tell the truth; **a la española** in the Spanish manner; **a lo que parece** as it seems; **a no ser por** if it weren't for; **a saberlo yo** if I had known it; **oler a** to smell of

abacería *f* grocery store

abace·ro -ra *mf* grocer

abad *m* abbot

abadejo *m* codfish; (orn) kinglet; (ent) Spanish fly

abadesa *f* abbess

abadía *f* abbacy; abbey

abaje·ño -ña *adj* (Mex) coastal, lowland ‖ *mf* (Mex) lowlander

abaje·ro -ra *adj* (Arg) lower, under ‖ *f* (Arg) bellyband, bellystrap; (Arg) saddlecloth

abaji·no -na *adj* (Col, Chile) northern ‖ *mf* (Col, Chile) northerner

abajo *adv* down, underneath; downwards; downstairs; **abajo de** down; **más abajo** lower down; **río abajo** downstream ‖ *interj* down with . . .!

abalanzar §60 *tr* to hurl ‖ *ref* to rush; to venture; (*un caballo*) to rear

abalizar §60 *tr* to mark with buoys ‖ *ref* (naut) to take bearings

abalorio *m* glass bead

abaluartar *tr* to bulwark

abanderado *m* colorbearer

abanderar *tr* (*un buque*) to register

abanderizar §60 *tr* to organize into bands ‖ *ref* to band together; (Chile, Peru) to join up

abandonar *tr* to abandon, to forsake ‖ *intr* to give up ‖ *ref* to abandon oneself; to give up

abandonismo *m* defeatism

abandonista *adj* & *mf* defeatist

abandono *m* abandon, abandonment; neglect; forlornness; yielding, giving up

abanicar §73 *tr* to fan

abanico *m* fan; fanlight; (coll) sword; **abanico de chimenea** fire screen

abaniquear *tr* to fan

abaniqueo *m* fanning; gesticulations

abanto *adj* skittish (*bull*)

abaratar *tr* to cheapen; (*precios*) to lower ‖ *intr* & *ref* to get cheap

abarca *f* sandal

abarcar §73 *tr* to embrace; to encompass; to surround; (Am) to corner, monopolize

abarloar *tr* (naut) to bring alongside ‖ *ref* to snuggle up

abarquillar *tr* & *ref* to curl up

abarrotar *tr* to bar; to bind, to fasten; to jam, to pack, to stuff; to overstock ‖ *ref* (Am) to become a glut on the market

abarrote *m* (naut) packing; **abarrotes** (Am) groceries; (Am) hardware

abarrotería *f* (Guat) grocery store; (CAm) hardware store

abarrote·ro -ra *mf* (Am) grocer

abastecer §22 *tr* to supply, to provide

abastecimiento *m* supplying; supplies, provisions

abasto *m* supply; abundance; **dar abasto** to be sufficient

abatanar *tr* to full

abatí *m* (Arg, Para) corn; (Arg, Para) corn whiskey

abati·do -da *adj* downcast; abject, contemptible ‖ *f* abatis

abatir *tr* to lower; to knock down; to shoot down; to take apart; to humble; to discourage ‖ *intr* (aer) to drift; (naut) to have leeway ‖ *ref* to be discouraged; to be humbled; to drop, fall; to swoop down

abdicar §73 *tr* & *intr* to abdicate

abdomen *m* abdomen

abecé *m* A B C

abecedario *m* A B C's

abedul *m* birch

abeja *f* bee; **abeja maestra** or **abeja reina** queen bee

abejar *m* apiary, beehive

abejarrón *m* bumblebee

abeje·ro -ra *mf* beekeeper

abejorro *m* bumblebee

abertura *f* aperture; opening; crack, slit; cove; openness, frankness

abeto *m* fir tree; hemlock; **abeto del Norte, abeto falso** spruce tree

abier·to -ta *adj* open; frank

abigarra·do -da *adj* motley, variegated

abigeo *m* horse thief, cattle thief

abijar *tr* (Col) to sic

abiselar *tr* to bevel

abismar *tr* to cast down; to humble; to spoil, ruin ‖ *ref* to sink; to cave in; to be humbled; to give in; to lose oneself; (Am) to be surprised

abismo *m* abyss, chasm

ablandabre·vas *m* (*pl* -vas) or **ablandahi·gos** *m* (*pl* -gos) good-for-nothing

ablandar *tr* to soften; to soften up; to soothe; to loosen ‖ *intr* (*el tiempo*) to moderate ‖ *ref* to soften; to relent; (*el tiempo*) to moderate

ablativo *m* ablative

aboba·do -da *adj* stupid, stupid-looking

abobar *tr* to make stupid ‖ *ref* to grow stupid

aboca·do -da *adj* (*vino*) mild, smooth; vulnerable; **abocado a** verging on

abocar §73 *tr* to bite; to pour; to bring near ‖ *intr* to enter ‖ *ref* to approach; to have an interview

abocinar *tr* to give a flare to ‖ *intr* to fall on the face ‖ *ref* to flare

abochornar *tr* to overheat; to make blush ‖ *ref* to blush; to wilt

abofetear *tr* to slap in the face

abogacía *f* law, legal profession

abogaderas *fpl* (CAm) specious arguments

abogado *m* lawyer; **abogado de secano** quack lawyer; **abogado firmón** lawyer who will sign anything; **abogado trampista** shyster

abogar §44 *intr* to plead; **abogar por** to advocate, to back

abolengo *m* ancestry, descent; inheritance

abolir §1 *tr* to revoke, to repeal

abolladura *f* dent; bump, bruise; embossing

abollar *tr* to bump, to bruise; to dent; to stun; to emboss ‖ *ref* to get bumped, get bruised; to dent, be dented

abollonar *tr* to emboss

abombar *tr* to make convex; (coll) to stun, confound ‖ *ref* to rot, to decompose

abominación *f* abomination

abominar *tr* to detest, abominate ‖ *intr* — **abominar de** to abominate

abona·do -da *adj* trustworthy; apt, likely ‖ *mf* subscriber; (*al gas, electricidad, etc.*) consumer; (*a una localidad en el teatro*) season-ticket holder; (*al ferrocarril*) commuter

abonanzar §60 *intr* (*el tiempo*) to clear up; (*el viento*) to abate

abonar *tr* to vouch for; to certify; to improve; to fertilize; **abonar en cuenta** a credit to the account of ‖ *intr* (*el tiempo*) to clear up ‖ *ref* to subscribe

abonaré *m* promissory note

abono *m* subscription; credit; installment; voucher; fertilizer; manure

abordar *tr* to approach; to accost; to undertake, to plan; (naut) to board; (naut) to run afoul of; (naut) to dock ‖ *intr* to run afoul; (naut) to put into port

aborígenes *mpl* aborigines

aborrascarse §73 *ref* to get stormy

aborrecer §22 *tr* to abhor, detest, hate; to bore ‖ *ref* to get bored

aborrecible *adj* abhorrent, hateful

aborrega·do -da *adj* (*nubes*) fleecy; (*cielo*) mackerel

abortar *tr* & *intr* to abort

aborto *m* abortion

abotagar §44 *ref* to become bloated, to swell up

abotonador *m* buttonhook

abotonar *tr* to button ‖ *intr* to bud

abovedar *tr* to arch, to vault

abozalar *tr* to muzzle

abra *f* cove; vale; fissure; (Mex) clearing

abrasar *tr* to set fire to, to burn; to

parch; to nip; to squander; to shame ‖ *intr* to burn ‖ *ref* to burn; to become parched; (fig) to be burning up

abrasi·vo -va *adj* & *m* abrasive

abrazadera *f* clasp, clip, clamp; (typ) bracket

abrazar §60 *tr* to embrace, to clasp; to include; to take in ‖ *ref* (*dos personas*) to embrace

abrazo *m* embrace, hug

abrebo·cas *m* (*pl* -cas) mouth prop, mouth gag

abrebote·llas *m* (*pl* -llas) bottle opener

abrecar·tas *m* (*pl* -tas) knife, letter opener

abreco·ches *m* (*pl* -ches) doorman

abrela·tas *m* (*pl* -tas) can opener

abreos·tras *m* (*pl* -tras) oyster knife

abrevadero *m* watering place, drinking trough

abrevar *tr* to water; to wet, soak; to irrigate; to size ‖ *ref* to drink

abreviación *f* abridgment, abbreviation, shortening; hastening

abreviar *tr* to abridge; to abbreviate; to shorten; to hasten ‖ *intr* to be quick; **abreviar con** to make short work of

abreviatura *f* abbreviation; **en abreviatura** (coll) in a hurry

abridor *m* opener; grafting knife; **abridor de guantes** glove stretcher

abrigadero *m* windbreak

abrigar §44 *tr* to shelter; to protect; (*esperanzas, sospechas*) to harbor ‖ *ref* to take shelter; to wrap oneself up

abrigo *m* shelter; aid, support; cover, wrap; overcoat; (naut) harbor; **abrigo antiaéreo** air-raid shelter; **abrigo de entretiempo** topcoat, spring-and-fall coat; **al abrigo de** sheltered from, protected from; sheltered by, protected by; (*ropa*) **de mucho abrigo** heavy

abril *m* April

abrir *m* opening; **en un abrir y cerrar de ojos** (coll) in the twinkling of an eye ‖ §83 *tr* to open; to unlock, unfasten; (*el apetito*) to whet; (*el bosque*) (Am) to clear ‖ *intr* to open ‖ *ref* to open; **abrirse a** or **con** to unbosom oneself to

abrochador *m* buttonhook

abrochar *tr* to button, to hook; to fasten

abrojo *m* thistle, thorn; **abrojos** reef, hidden rocks

abrótano *m* southernwood

abruma·dor -dora *adj* crushing, oppressing; overwhelming

abrumar *tr* to crush, oppress; to overwhelm; to annoy ‖ *ref* to become foggy

abrup·to -ta *adj* abrupt, steep; rough, rugged

absceso *m* abscess

absenta *f* absinth

ábsida *f* or **ábside** *m* apse

absoluta *f* dogmatic statement; (mil) discharge

absolutamente *adv* absolutely; (Am) by no means

absolu·to -ta *adj* absolute; (coll) arbitrary ‖ *m* absolute; **en absoluto** absolutely not ‖ *f* see **absoluta**

absolvederas *fpl* — **tener buenas absolvederas** (coll) to be an indulgent confessor

absolver §47 & §83 *tr* to absolve; to solve, to answer

absorbente *adj* absorbent; (*interesante*) absorbing

absorber *tr* to absorb; to use up; to attract

absor·to -ta *adj* absorbed; entranced

abste·mio -mia *adj* abstemious

abstener §71 *ref* to abstain

abstinente *adj* abstinent

abstracción *f* abstraction; absorption, deep thought; **hacer abstracción de** to leave out, to disregard

abstrac·to -ta *adj* abstract

abstraer §75 *tr* to abstract ‖ *intr* — **abstraer de** to do without, leave aside ‖ *ref* to be abstracted or absorbed; **abstraerse de** to do without, leave aside

abstraí·do -da *adj* absorbed in thought; withdrawn

abstru·so -sa *adj* abstruse

absurdidad *f* absurdity

absur·do -da *adj* absurd ‖ *m* absurdity

abuchear *tr* & *intr* to boo, to hoot

abuela *f* grandmother; **cuéntaselo a su abuela** (coll) tell that to the marines

abuelo *m* grandparent; grandfather; **abuelos** grandparents; ancestors

abulta·do -da *adj* bulky, massive

abultar *tr* to enlarge; to exaggerate ‖ *intr* to be bulky

abundamiento *m* abundance; **a mayor abundamiento** with greater reason

abundante *adj* abundant

abundar *intr* to abound

abur *interj* (coll) good-bye!, so long!

aburri·do -da *adj* bored; tiresome

aburrir *tr* to bore, tire ‖ *ref* to become bored

abusar *intr* to go too far; **abusar de** to abuse; to impose on; to overindulge in

abusión *f* superstition

abusi·vo -va *adj* abusive

abuso *m* abuse; imposition

abyec·to -ta *adj* abject

A.C. *abbr* **año de Cristo**

acá *adv* here, around here; **acá y allá** here and there; **de ayer acá** since yesterday; **¿de cuándo acá?** since when?; **desde entonces acá** since then; **más acá** here closer; **muy acá** right here

acaba·do -da *adj* complete, perfect; worn-out, exhausted ‖ *m* finish

acabar *tr* to end, finish, complete ‖ *intr* to end; to die; **acabar con** to put an end to; to end in; **acabar de** to finish; to have just, e.g., **acaba de salir** he has just left; **acababa de salir** he had just left; **acabar por** to end in; to end by; **no acabar de decidirse** to be unable to make up one's mind ‖ *ref* to end; to be ex-

hausted; to be all over; to run out of, e.g., **se me acabó el café** I have run out of coffee

acabóse *m* (coll) limit, last straw

acacia *f* acacia; **acacia falsa** locust tree

academia *f* academy

académi·co -ca *adj* academic ‖ *mf* academician

acaecer §22 *intr* to happen, to occur

acaecimiento *m* happening, occurrence

acalora·do -da *adj* heated; warm; fiery, excited

acalorar *tr* to heat, to warm; to incite, to encourage; to stir up ‖ *ref* to become heated; to warm up

acallar *tr* to quiet, to silence; to pacify

acampada *f* camp

acamar *tr* (*las mieses la lluvia o el viento*) to beat down, to blow over

acampamento *m* camp, encampment

acampana·do -da *adj* bell-shaped

acampar *tr, intr* & *ref* to encamp

acanalar *tr* to groove; to flute; to channel; to corrugate

acantila·do -da *adj* rocky; steep, precipitous ‖ *m* cliff, bluff

acantonamiento *m* cantonment

acantonar *tr* to canton, to quarter ‖ *ref* to be quartered; **acantonarse en** to limit one's activities to

acaparar *tr* to corner; to monopolize; to hoard

acaramela·do -da *adj* candied; (coll) smooth, honey-tongued

acarar *tr* to bring face to face

acarear *tr* to bring face to face; to face, to brave

acariciar *tr* to caress; (*una ilusión*) to cherish

acarraladura *f* (Chile, Peru) run (*in stockings*)

acarreadi·zo -za *adj* transportable

acarrear *tr* to cart, transport, carry along; to cause, occasion ‖ *ref* to incur, to bring upon oneself

acarreo *m* cartage, drayage; conveyance

acartonar *ref* (coll) to shrivel up, become wizened

acasera·do -da *adj* (Chile, Peru) home-loving; (*parroquiano*) (Chile, Peru) regular ‖ *mf* (Chile, Peru) stay-at-home, homebody; (Chile, Peru) regular customer

acaso *m* chance, accident; **al acaso** at random ‖ *adv* maybe, perhaps; **por si acaso** in case of need, just in case

acatar *tr* to respect, to hold in awe; to observe

acatarrar *tr* to chill, give a cold to; (Chile, Mex) to bother, annoy ‖ *ref* to catch cold; (Am) to get tipsy

acaudala·do -da *adj* rich, well-to-do

acaudalar *tr* to acquire, to accumulate

acaudillar *tr* to lead, to command; to direct

acceder *intr* to accede; to agree

accesible *adj* accesible

accesión *f* accession; acquiescence; access, entry

accésit *m* second prize, honorable mention

acceso *m* access, approach; attack, fit, spell; **acceso prohibido** no admittance

acceso·rio -ria *adj* accessory ‖ *m* accessory, fixture, attachment; **accesorios** (theat) properties

accidenta·do -da *adj* agitated; restless; rough, uneven ‖ *mf* victim, casualty

accidental *adj* accidental; acting, pro-tempore, temporary

accidentar *tr* to injure, hurt ‖ *ref* to faint

accidente *m* accident; (*del terreno*) roughness, unevenness; fainting spell

acción *f* action; gesture; (*parte del capital de una sociedad*) share; stock certificate; **acción crecedera** growth stock; **acción de gracias** thanksgiving; **acción liberada** stock dividend

accionar *tr* to drive ‖ *intr* to gesticulate

accionista *mf* shareholder, stockholder

acebo *m* holly tree

acebuche *m* wild olive

acecinar *tr* to dry-cure, to dry-salt; (*el salmón o el arenque*) to kipper ‖ *intr* to shrivel up

acechar *tr* to watch, to spy on

acecho *m* watching, spying; **al acecho** or **en acecho** on the watch, spying

acedar *tr* to turn sour; to embitter ‖ *ref* to turn sour; to wither

acedía *f* sourness; crabbedness; heartburn

ace·do -da *adj* sour, tart; crabbed

aceitar *tr* to oil; to grease

aceite *m* oil; olive oil; **aceite de hígado de bacalao** cod-liver oil; **aceite de linaza** linseed oil; **aceite de pie de buey** neat's-foot oil; **aceite de ricino** castor oil; **aceite mineral** coal oil

aceite·ro -ra *adj* oil ‖ *mf* oiler; oil dealer ‖ *f* oilcan; oil cup; **aceiteras** cruet stand

aceito·so -sa *adj* oily, greasy

aceituna *f* olive

aceituno *m* olive tree

acelerador *m* accelerator

acelerar *tr & ref* to accelerate; to hasten, hurry

acelga *f* Swiss chard

acémila *f* beast of burden, pack animal; (coll) dolt; (coll) drudge

acendra·do -da *adj* refined; stainless, spotless

acendrar *tr* to refine; to purify, make stainless

acento *m* accent; **acento de altura** pitch accent; **acento ortográfico** written accent, accent mark; **acento prosódico** stress accent, tonic accent

acentuar §21 *tr* to accent; to accentuate, emphasize

aceña *f* water-driven flour mill

acepción *f* meaning

acepillar *tr* to plane; to brush; to smooth

aceptable *adj* acceptable

aceptación *f* acceptance

aceptar *tr* to accept; to agree

acequia *f* irrigation ditch; (Bol, Col, Peru) stream, rivulet

acera *f* sidewalk

acera·do -da *adj* steel, steely; (fig) cutting, biting, sharp

acerar *tr* to steel, to harden; to line with a sidewalk ‖ *ref* to harden; to steel oneself

acer·bo -ba *adj* sour, bitter; harsh

acerca *adv* — **acerca de** about, with regard to

acercamiento *m* approach, rapprochement

acercar §73 *tr* to bring near or nearer ‖ *ref* to approach, to come near or nearer

acería *f* steel mill

acerico *m* small cushion; pincushion

acero *m* steel; sword; courage, spirit

acérri·mo -ma *adj* all-out; (*enemigo*) bitter

acerrojar *tr* to bolt

acerta·do -da *adj* fit, right; skillful, sure; well-aimed

acertante *mf* winner

acertar §2 *tr* to hit; to hit upon; to figure out correctly; to find; to do right ‖ *intr* to be right; to succeed; to guess right; **acertar a** to happen to; to succeed in; **acertar con** to come upon; to find

acertijo *m* conundrum, riddle

acervo *m* heap; assets, estate; shoal; store, fund, hoard

acetato *m* acetate

acéti·co -ca *adj* acetic

acetificar §73 *tr & ref* to acetify

acetileno *m* acetylene

acetona *f* acetone

acia·go -ga *adj* unlucky, ill-fated, evil

acíbar *m* aloes; bitterness, sorrow

acicalar *tr* to polish, to burnish; to dress, to dress up ‖ *ref* to get all dressed up

acicate *m* long-pointed spur; incentive, stimulus

acidez *f* acidity

acidificar §73 *tr & ref* to acidify

áci·do -da *adj* acid, tart, sour ‖ *m* acid

acierto *m* lucky hit, good shot; good guess; tact, prudence; ability, skill; accuracy; success

aci·mut *m* (*pl* **-muts**) azimut

aclamación *f* acclaim, applause

aclamar *tr & intr* to acclaim, to hail, to cheer

aclarar *tr* to brighten, to clear; to rinse; to explain ‖ *intr* to get bright; to clear up; to dawn

aclarato·rio -ria *adj* explanatory

aclimatar *tr & ref* to acclimate

acobardar *tr* to cow, intimidate ‖ *ref* to be frightened

acocear *tr* to kick; to trample upon, to ill-treat

acocil *m* Mexican crayfish; **estar como un acocil** (Mex) to blush, to be abashed

acoda·do -da *adj* elbow-shaped

acodar *tr* (*el brazo*) to lean; to prop; (hort) to layer ‖ *ref* to lean

acodillar *tr* to bend at an angle ‖ *ref* to double up; to bend, to crumple

acoger §17 *tr* to receive, to welcome;

to accept ‖ *ref* to take refuge; to resort

acogida *f* reception, welcome; meeting place, confluence; refuge, shelter; **dar acogida a** (com) to honor

acolada *f* accolade

acolchar *tr* to quilt, to pad

acolchí *m* (Mex) red-winged blackbird

acólito *m* acolyte; altar boy

acollador *m* (naut) lanyard

acomedi·do -da *adj* (Am) obliging

acometer *tr* to attack; to undertake; (*el sueño, la enfermedad, el deseo a una persona*) to overcome

acometida *f* attack; (*p.ej., de una línea eléctrica*) house connection

acomodación *f* accommodation

acomodadi·zo -za *adj* accommodating, obliging

acomoda·do -da *adj* convenient, suitable; comfort-loving; well-to-do

acomoda·dor -dora *adj* accommodating, obliging ‖ *mf* usher

acomodar *tr* to accommodate; to usher; to reconcile; to suit; to furnish, to supply ‖ *intr* to be suitable, be convenient ‖ *ref* to comply; to come to terms; to hire out; to make oneself comfortable

acomodo *m* arrangement, adjustment; lodgings; job, position; (Chile) neatness, tidiness

acompañamiento *m* accompaniment; escort, retinue; (theat) extras, supernumeraries

acompañanta *f* female companion or escort; accompanist

acompañante *m* companion; accompanist

acompañar *tr* to accompany; to escort; to enclose; to sympathize with

acompasa·do -da *adj* rhythmic; slow; easy-going; cautious

aconchar *tr* to push to safety; (naut) to beach, run aground ‖ *ref* to take shelter; (naut) to run aground; (Chile) to form a deposit

acondiciona·do -da *adj* conditioned; **bien acondicionado** well-disposed; in good condition; **mal acondicionado** ill-disposed; in bad condition

acondicionador *m* conditioner; **acondicionador de aire** air conditioner

acondicionamiento *m* conditioning; **acondicionamiento del aire** air conditioning

acondicionar *tr* to condition; to put in condition; to repair; to season ‖ *ref* to qualify; to find a job

acongojar *tr* to grieve, to afflict ‖ *ref* to grieve

aconsejable *adj* advisable

aconsejar *tr* to advise, to counsel, to warn ‖ *ref* to seek advice, to get advice

acontecer §22 *intr* to happen, to occur

acontecimiento *m* happening, event

acopiar *tr* to gather together

acopio *m* gathering; stock; abundance

acoplado *m* (Arg, Chile, Urug) trailer trolley car

acoplamiento *m* coupling; joint; connection

acoplar *tr* to couple; to join; to connect; to hitch; to reconcile ‖ *ref* to be reconciled; to mate; to be intimate

acoquinar *tr* to intimidate

acoraza·do -da *adj* armored, armorplated; (coll) contrary ‖ *m* battleship

acorazar §60 *tr* to armor-plate

acorchar *tr* to line with cork; to turn into cork ‖ *ref* to get spongy; to wither, shrivel; to become corky or pithy; to get numb

acorchetar *tr* to bracket

acordar §61 *tr* to agree upon; to authorize; to reconcile; to make level or flush; to remind of; to tune ‖ *intr* to agree; to blend ‖ *ref* to be agreed, come to an agreement; to remember; **acordarse de** to remember

acorde *adj* agreed, in accord; in tune ‖ *m* accord; (mus) chord

acordeón *m* accordion

acordonar *tr* to cord, to lace; (*monedas*) to knurl, to mill; to rope off

acornar §61 *tr* gore; to butt

acornear *tr* to gore; to butt

acorralar *tr* to corral, to corner; to intimidate

acortar *tr* to shorten; to reduce; to slow down; to check, to stop ‖ *ref* to become shorter; to hold back; to be timid; to slow down; to shrink

acosar *tr* to harass; to pester

acostar §61 *tr* to lay down; to put to bed; (naut) to bring alongside ‖ *ref* to lie down; to go to bed

acostumbra·do -da *adj* accustomed; customary, usual

acostumbrar *tr* to accustom ‖ *intr* to be accustomed ‖ *ref* to accustom oneself; to become accustomed

acotación *f* boundary mark; marginal note; elevation mark

acotamiento *m* boundary mark; marginal note; elevation mark; stage direction

acotar *tr* to mark off, to map; to annotate; to admit, to accept; to check; to vouch for; to select; to mark elevations on

acotillo *m* sledge hammer

acre *adj* acrid; austere; biting, mordant

acrecentamiento *m* increase, growth; promotion

acrecentar §2 *tr* to increase; to promote ‖ *ref* to increase; to bud, to blossom

acreditar *tr* to accredit; to credit; to get a reputation for ‖ *ref* to get a reputation, to prove oneself

acree·dor -dora *adj* accrediting; deserving ‖ *mf* creditor; **acreedor hipotecario** mortgagee

acribar *tr* to sift; to riddle

acribillar *tr* to riddle; (coll) to harass, to plague, to pester

acriminar *tr* to incriminate; to exaggerate

acrimonio·so -sa *adj* acrid; acrimonious

acriollar *ref* (Am) to acquire Spanish American ways

acrisolar *tr* to purify, to refine; to reveal, to bring out

acrobacia *f* acrobatics

acróbata *mf* acrobat

acrobatismo *m* acrobatics

acrónimo *m* acronym

acrópo·lis *f* (*pl* -lis) acropolis

acróstico *m* acrostic

acta *f* minutes; certificate; **acta notarial** affidavit; **actas** proceedings, transactions; **levantar acta** to write up the minutes

actitud *f* attitude; **en actitud de** getting ready to

activar *tr* to activate; to hasten, to expedite

actividad *f* activity

acti·vo -va *adj* active ‖ *m* (com) assets; (com) credit side

acto *m* act; ceremony, function; commencement; thesis; **acto continuo** right afterward; **acto seguido** right afterward; **acto seguido de** right after; **hacer acto de presencia** to honor with one's presence

actor *m* actor; agent; **primer actor** leading man

ac·triz *f* (*pl* -trices) actress; **primera actriz** leading lady

actuación *f* acting, performance; action; operation; behavior

actual *adj* present, present-day; up-to-date ‖ *m* current month

actualidad *f* present time; timeliness; **actualidades** current events; newsreel; **actualidad escénica** theater news; **actualidad gráfica** news in pictures

actualizar §60 *tr* to bring up to date

actualmente *adv* at present, at the present time

actuante *mf* participant

actuar §21 *tr* to actuate ‖ *intr* to act; to perform

actua·rio -ria *mf* actuary

acuaplano *m* aquaplane

acuarela *f* water color

acuario *m* aquarium

acuartelar *tr* to billet, to quarter

acuáti·co -ca *adj* aquatic

acuatizaje *m* (aer) alighting on water; (*de nave espacial*) splashdown

acuatizar §60 *intr* (aer) to alight on water

acucia *f* zeal, diligence; yearning

acuciar *tr* to goad, to prod; to harass; to yearn for

acuclillar *ref* to squat, to crouch

acuchilla·do -da *adj* knife-shaped; schooled by experienced; (*vestido*) slashed

acuchillar *tr* to stab; to stab to death; to slash

acudir *intr* to come up, to respond; to apply; to hang around; to come to the rescue

acueducto *m* aqueduct

acuerdo *m* accord; agreement; memory; **de acuerdo con** in accord with; **de común acuerdo** with one accord; **estar en su acuerdo** to be in one's

right mind; **ponerse de acuerdo** to come to an agreement; **recobrar su acuerdo** to come to; **tomar un acuerdo** to make a decision; **volver en su acuerdo** to come to; to change one's mind

acuitar *tr & intr* to grieve

acullá *adv* yonder, over there

acumulador *m* storage battery

acumular *tr* to accumulate, to gather; to store up ‖ *intr & ref* to accumulate, to gather

acunar *tr* to rock; to cradle

acuñación *f* coining, minting; wedging

acuñar *tr* to coin, to mint; to wedge; to key, to lock; (typ) to quoin

acuo·so -sa *adj* watery; juicy

acurrucar §73 *ref* to squat, to crouch; to huddle

acusación *f* accusation

acusa·do -da marked ‖ *mf* accused

acusar *tr* to accuse; to show; (*recibo de una carta*) to acknowledge ‖ *ref* to confess

acusati·vo -va *adj & m* accusative

acuse *m* acknowledgment

acústi·co -ca *adj* acoustic ‖ *f* acoustics

achacar §73 *tr* to impute, to attribute

achaco·so -sa *adj* ailing, sickly

achaparra·do -da *adj* stocky; stubby; chubby

achaparrar *tr* to become stunted

achaque *m* sickliness, indisposition; excuse, pretext; matter, subject; weakness; (coll) monthlies

achatar *tr* to flatten

achica·do -da *adj* childish; abashed, disconcerted

achicador *m* scoop

achicar §73 *tr* to make smaller; to humble; to bail, to bail out

achicoria *f* chicory

achicharrar *tr* to scorch; to bedevil ‖ *ref* to get scorched

achispa·do -da *adj* tipsy

achispar *tr* to make tipsy ‖ *ref* to get tipsy

achuchar *tr* to incite; to crumple, crush; to jostle ‖ *ref* (Arg, Urug) to shiver, have a chill

adagio *m* adage

adalid *m* chief; guide, leader; champion

adama·do -da *adj* womanish; chic, stylish

adamar *ref* to become effeminate

adán *m* (coll) dirty, ragged fellow, lazy, careless fellow ‖ **Adán** *m* Adam

adaptación *f* adaptation

adaptar *tr* to adapt

adarga *f* oval or heart-shaped leather shield

adarvar *tr* to bewilder, to stun

A. de C. *abbr* año de Cristo

adecentar *tr* to clean up, to tidy up ‖ *ref* (coll) to put on a clean shirt, to dress up

adecua·do -da *adj* fitting, suitable

adecuar *tr* to fit, to adapt

adefesio *m* (coll) nonsense; (coll) outlandish outfit; (coll) queer-looking fellow

adehala *f* gratuity, extra
adehesar *tr* to convert into pasture
adelanta·do -da *adj* precocious; bold, forward; *(reloj)* fast; **por adelantado** in advance || *m* provincial governor
adelantamiento *m* anticipation; advancement, promotion, progress
adelantar *tr* to move forward; to outstrip, get ahead of; to advance; to promote; to improve || *intr* to advance; to improve; to be fast || *ref* to move forward; to gain, be fast
adelante *adv* ahead; forward; **más adelante** farther on; later || *interj* go ahead!; come in!
adelanto *m* advance, progress, improvement; advancement; payment in advance
adelfa *f* oleander
adelgazar §60 *tr* to make thin; to taper; to purify; to argue subtly about; to weaken, lessen || *intr & ref* to get thin; to taper
ademán *m* attitude; gesture; ademanes manners; **en ademán de** getting ready to; **hacer ademán de** to make a move to
además *adv* moreover, besides; **además de** in addition to, besides
adentellar *tr* to sink one's teeth into
adentrar *intr & ref* to go in; **adentrarse en el mar** to go farther out to sea
adentro *adv* inside; **mar adentro** out at sea; **ser muy de adentro** to be like a member of the family; **tierra adentro** inland || **adentros** *mpl* inmost being, inmost thoughts; **en o para sus adentros** to oneself, to himself, etc.
adep·to -ta *adj* initiated || *mf* follower
aderezar §60 *tr* to dress, adorn; to cook; *(una tela)* to starch; to season; to repair; to lead; *(bebidas)* to mix; *(vinos)* to blend || *ref* to dress, get ready
aderezo *m* dressing; seasoning, condiment; starch; finery; equipment; set of jewelry
adestrar §2 *tr & ref* var of adiestrar
adeuda·do -da *adj* indebted, in debt
adeudar *tr* to owe; to be liable for; to charge || *intr* to become related by marriage || *ref* to run into debt
adeudo *m* debt, indebtedness; customs duty; charge, debit
adherencia *f* adhesion; **tener adherencias** to have connections
adherente *adj* adherent || *m* adherent; adherentes accessories
adherir §68 *intr & ref* to adhere; to stick
adhesión *f* adherence, adhesion
adhesi·vo -va *adj* adhesive
adición *f* addition; *(en un café o restaurante)* check
adicionar *tr* to add; to add to
adic·to -ta *adj* devoted; supporting || *mf* supporter, follower
adiestrar *tr* to train; to teach; to lead, to guide || *ref* to train, to practice
adietar *tr* to put on a diet

adinera·do -da *adj* wealthy, well-to-do
adiós *m* adieu, good-bye || *interj* adieu!, good-bye!
aditamento *m* addition; accessory
aditi·vo -va *adj & m* additive
adivinación *f* prophecy; guessing, divination; **adivinación del pensamiento** mind reading
adivina·dor -dora *mf* guesser; good guesser; **adivinador del pensamiento** mind reader
adivinaja *f* (coll) riddle, puzzle
adivinanza *f* riddle; guess
adivinar *tr* to prophesy; to guess, to divine; *(un enigma)* to solve; *(el pensamiento ajeno)* to read
adivi·no -na *mf* fortuneteller; guesser
adjetivo *m* adjective
adjudicar §73 *tr* to adjudge, to award || *ref* to appropriate
adjuntar *tr* to join, connect; to add; to enclose
adjun·to -ta *adj* added, attached; enclosed || *mf* associate || *m* adjunct; adjective
adminículo *m* aid, auxiliary; gadget; meddler; **adminículos** emergency equipment
administración *f* administration, management; headquarters
administra·dor -dora *mf* administrator, manager; **administrador de correos** postmaster
administrar *tr* to administer, to manage
admiración *f* admiration; wonder; exclamation mark
admira·dor -dora *mf* admirer
admirar *tr* to admire; to surprise || *ref* to wonder; **admirarse de** to wonder at
admisible *adj* admissible
admisión *f* admission; (mach) intake
admitir *tr* to admit; to allow; to accept, recognize; to agree to
adobar *tr* to repair, restore; to dress, prepare; to cook, stew; *(carne, pescado)* to pickle; *(pieles)* to tan
adobe *m* adobe
adobo *m* repairing; dressing; cooking; pickling; tanning; pickled meat or fish
adocena·do -da common, ordinary
adoctrinar *tr* to indoctrinate, to teach, to instruct
adolecer §22 *intr* to fall sick; **adolecer de** to suffer from || *ref* — **adolecerse de** (archaic) to sympathize with, feel sorry for
adolescencia *f* adolescence
adolescente *adj & mf* adolescent
adonde *conj* where, whither
adónde *adv* where, whither
adopción *f* adoption
adoptar *tr* to adopt
adoquín *m* paving stone, paving block; (coll) blockhead
adoquina·do -da *adj* paved with cobblestones || *m* cobblestone paving
adorable *adj* adorable
adoración *f* adoration, worship; **Adoración de los Reyes** Epiphany

adora·dor -dora *mf* adorer, worshiper || *m* suitor
adorar *tr & intr* to adore, to worship
adormecer §22 *tr* to put to sleep || *ref* to go to sleep; to get sleepy
adormeci·do -da *adj* sleepy, drowsy; numb; calm
adormilar *ref* to doze, to drowse
adornar *tr* to adorn; (*un cuento*) to embroider
adornista *mf* decorator
adorno *m* adornment, decoration; **adorno de escaparate** window dressing
adosar *tr* to lean; to push close
adquirir §40 *tr* to acquire; **adquirir en propiedad** to buy, to purchase
adquisición *f* acquisition
adrede *adv* on purpose
Adriáti·co -ca *adj & m* Adriatic
adscribir §83 *tr* to attribute; to assign
adscripción *f* attribution; assignment
aduana *f* customhouse; **aduana seca** inland customhouse
aduane·ro -ra *adj* customhouse; customs || *m* customhouse officer, customs inspector
aduar *m* Arab settlement; gipsy camp; Indian ranch
adueñar *ref* to take possession
adujar *tr* (naut) to coil || *ref* (naut) to curl up
adular *tr* to flatter, to fawn on
adu·lón -lona *adj* (coll) fawning, groveling || *mf* (coll) fawner
adúltera *f* adulteress
adulterar *tr* to adulterate || *intr* to commit adultery || *ref* to become adulterated, to spoil
adulterio *m* adultery
adúlte·ro -ra *adj* adulterous || *m* adulterer || *f* see **adúltera**
adul·to -ta *adj & mf* adult
adulzar §60 *tr* to sweeten; (*metales*) to soften
adunar *tr* to join, bring together
adus·to -ta *adj* grim, stern, gloomy; scorching hot
advenedi·zo -za *adj* strange; foreign || *mf* stranger; foreigner; outsider; parvenu, upstart; nouveau riche
advenimiento *m* advent, coming; accession; **esperar el santo advenimiento** (coll) to wait in vain
advenir §79 *intr* to come, arrive; to happen
adverbio *m* adverb
adversa·rio -ria *mf* adversary
adversidad *f* adversity
advertencia *f* observation; notice, remark; warning; preface
adverti·do -da *adj* capable, clever, wide-awake
advertir §68 *tr* to notice, observe; to notify, warn; to point out || *ref* to become aware
Adviento *m* (eccl) Advent
adyacente *adj* adjacent
aeración *f* aeration; ventilation; air conditioning
aére·o -a *adj* air, aerial; overhead, elevated; airy, light, fanciful
aeroatómi·co -ca *adj* air-atomic

aerodinámi·co -ca *adj* aerodynamic || *f* aerodynamics
aeródromo *m* aerodrome, airdrome; **aeródromo de urgencia** emergency-landing field
aeroespacial *adj* aerospace
aerofumigación *f* crop dusting
aeromedicina *f* aviation medicine
aeromodelismo *m* model-airplane building
aeromodelista *mf* model-airplane builder
aeromodelo *m* model airplane
aeromotor *m* windmill; airplane motor
aeromoza *f* air hostess, stewardess
aeronauta *mf* aeronaut
aeronáuti·co -ca *adj* aeronautic || *f* aeronautics
aeronave *f* airship; **aeronave cohete** rocket ship
aeropista *f* landing strip
aeroplano *m* aeroplane
aeroposta *f* air mail
aeropostal *adj* air-mail
aeropropulsor *m* airplane engine; **aeropropulsor por reacción** jet engine
aeropuerto *m* airport
aeroscala *f* transit point
aerosol *m* aerosol
aeroste·ro -ra *adj* aviation || *m* flyer; airman
aeroterrestre *adj* air-ground
aerovía *f* airway
afable *adj* affable, friendly, agreeable
afama·do -da *adj* noted, famous
afamar *tr* to make famous || *ref* to become famous
afán *m* hard work; eagerness, zeal; task; worry
afanar *tr* to press, hurry || *intr* to strive, toil || *ref* to strive, toil; to busy oneself
afano·so -sa *adj* hard, laborious; hardworking
afarolar *ref* (Am) to make a fuss, to get excited
afear *tr* to deface, to disfigure; to blame
afeblecer §22 *intr* to grow feeble, to get thin
afección *f* affection, fondness; (med) affection
afectación *f* affectation
afecta·do -da *adj* affected; **estar afectado de** (*p.ej., los riñones*) to have (*e.g., kidney*) trouble
afectar *tr* to affect; (Am) to hurt, to injure || *ref* to be moved, be stirred
afecti·vo -va *adj* emotional
afec·to -ta *adj* fond; kind; affected; **afecto a** fond of; (*un empleo, un servicio, etc.*) attached to; **afecto de** suffering from || *m* affection, fondness; emotion
afectuo·so -sa *adj* affectionate; kind
afeitado *m* shave; **afeitado a ras** close shave
afeitar *tr* to shave; to adorn; (*la cara*) to paint || *ref* to shave; to paint
afeite *m* cosmetics, rouge, make-up
afeminación *f* effeminacy
afemina·do -da *adj* effeminate

ad
ag

afeminar *tr* to effeminate ǁ *ref* to become effeminate

aferra·do -da *adj* stubborn, obstinate

aferrar *tr* to seize; to catch; to hook; (naut) to moor; (naut) to furl ǁ *ref* to interlock, hook together; to cling; to insist

Afganistán, el Afghanistan

afga·no -na *adj & mf* Afghan

afianzar §60 *tr* to guarantee, vouch for; to bail; to fasten; to prop up; to grasp; to support ǁ *ref* to hold fast, to steady oneself

afición *f* fondness, liking, taste; ardor, zeal; fans, public

aficiona·do -da *adj* fond; amateur; **aficionado a** fond of ǁ *mf* amateur; fan, follower

aficionar *tr* to win, to win the attachment of ǁ *ref* — **aficionarse a** or **de** to become fond of; to become a follower of, become a fan of

afiebra·do -da *adj* feverish

afi·jo -ja *adj* affixed ǁ *m* affix

afila·do -da *adj* sharp; tapering; pointed; peaked

afilador *m* grinder, sharpener; razor strop

afilápi·ces *m (pl -ces)* pencil sharpener

afilar *tr* to grind, to sharpen; *(una navaja de afeitar)* to strop; (Arg & Urug) to flirt with ǁ *ref* to sharpen, get sharp; to taper, get thin

afiliar §77 & *regular tr* to affiliate, take in ǁ *ref* — **afiliarse a** to join

afiligranar *tr* to filigree; to adorn, embellish

afilón *m* knife sharpener; razor strop

afín *adj* near, bordering; like, similar; related ǁ *mf* relative by marriage

afinador *m* tuner; tuning hammer, tuning key

afinar *tr* to purify, refine, perfect; to trim; to tune

afincar §73 *intr & ref* to buy up real estate

afinidad *f* affinity; **por afinidad** by marriage

afirmar *tr* to strengthen, secure, fasten; to assert ǁ *ref* to hold fast; to steady oneself

afirmati·vo -va *adj & f* affirmative

aflicción *f* affliction; sorrow, grief

afligir §27 *tr* to afflict, to grieve ǁ *ref* to grieve

aflojar *tr* to slacken, to let go; to loosen ǁ *intr* to slacken, to slow up; to abate, lessen ǁ *ref* to come loose; to slacken

aflora·do -da *adj* flour; fine, elegant

aflorar *tr* to sift ǁ *intr* to crop out

afluencia *f* flowing; affluence, abundance; crowd, jam, rush; fluency

afluente *adj* flowing; abundant; fluent ǁ *m* tributary

afluir §20 *intr* to flow; to pour, to flock

afmo. *abbr* **afectísimo**

afofar *tr* to make fluffy, make spongy

afonizar §60 *tr & ref* to unvoice

aforar *tr* to gauge, to measure; to appraise

aforismo *m* aphorism

afortuna·do -da *adj* fortunate; happy

afrancesa·do -da *adj & mf* Francophile

afrecho *m* bran

afrenta *f* affront

afrentar *tr* to affront ǁ *ref* to be ashamed

África *f* Africa

africa·no -na *adj & mf* African

afrodisía·co -ca *adj & m* aphrodisiac

afrontar *tr* to bring face to face; to defy ǁ *ref* — **afrontarse con** to confront, to meet face to face

afuera *adv* outside ǁ *interj* clear the way!, look out! ǁ **afueras** *fpl* outskirts, environs

agachadiza *f* snipe; **hacer la agachadiza** (coll) to duck

agachar *tr* to lower, bend down ǁ *ref* to crouch, to squat; to cower; (SAm) to give in, yield

agalla *f* gallnut; *(de pez)* gill; *(de ave)* ear lobe; **agallas** (coll) courage, guts

ágape *m* banquet, love feast

agarrada *f* (coll) brawl, fight, scrap

agarra·do -da *adj* (coll) stingy, tight ǁ *f* see **agarrada**

agarrar *tr* to grab, to grasp; to take hold of; (coll) to get, obtain ǁ *intr* to take hold; to take root; to stick ǁ *ref* to grapple; to have a good hold; to worry; **agarrarse a** to take hold of, to cling to

agarrochar *tr* to jab with a goad

agarrotar *tr* to garrote; to bind, to tie up ǁ *ref* to become numb

agasajar *tr* to regale, to lionize, to make a fuss over

agasajo *m* kindness, attention; lionization; favor, gift; treat; party

agavillar *tr* to bind or tie in sheaves ǁ *ref* to band together

agazapar *tr* (coll) to grab, to nab ǁ *ref* (coll) to crouch; (coll) to hide

agencia *f* agency; bureau; (Chile) pawn shop; **agencia de noticias** news agency

agenciar *tr* to manage to bring about; to promote ǁ *ref* to manage

agenda *f* notebook

agente *m* agent; policeman; **agente de policía** policeman; **agente viajero** traveling salesman, commercial traveler

agigantar *tr* to make huge ǁ *ref* to become huge

ágil *adj* agile; flexible, light

agilitar *tr & ref* to limber up

agita·do -da *adj* agitated, excited; *(mar)* rough; exalted

agitar *tr* to agitate; to shake; to wave; to stir ǁ *intr* to agitate ǁ *ref* to be agitated; to shake; to wave; to get excited; *(el mar)* to get rough

aglomeración *f* agglomeration; crowd; built-up area

aglomerado *m* briquet, coal briquet

aglutinar *tr* to stick together ǁ *ref* to cake

agnósti·co -ca *adj & mf* agnostic

agobiar *tr* to overburden; to exhaust, oppress

agolpar *ref* to flock, to throng

agonía *f* agony, throes of death; agony, anguish; yearning; craving

agonizar §60 *tr* (*al moribundo*) to assist, to attend; (coll) to harass || *intr* to be in the throes of death

agorar §3 *tr* to augur, foretell

agore·ro -ra *adj* fortunetelling; ill-omened; superstitious || *mf* fortune-teller

agostar *tr* to burn up, to parch || *ref* to dry up; (*la esperanza, la felicidad*) to fade away

agostero *m* harvest helper

agosto *m* August; harvest; harvest time; **hacer su agosto** to make hay while the sun shines

agota·do -da *adj* exhausted; sold out; out of print

agotar *tr* to exhaust, to wear out, to use up || *ref* to become exhausted, to be used up; to go out of print; to run out

agracia·do -da *adj* charming, graceful; nice, pretty || *mf* winner

agradable *adj* agreeable

agradar *tr* to please || *intr* to be pleasing || *ref* to be pleased

agradecer §22 *tr* to thank; **agradecerle a uno una cosa** to thank someone for something

agradeci·do -da *adj* thankful, grateful; rewarding

agradecimiento *m* thanks, gratitude

agrado *m* agreeableness, graciousness; pleasure, liking

agrandar *tr* to enlarge || *ref* to grow larger

agranelar *tr* (*cuero*) to grain, to pebble

agrapar *tr* to clamp

agrariense *adj* & *mf* agrarian

agra·rio -ria *adj* agrarian

agravar *tr* to weigh down; to aggravate; to exaggerate; to oppress || *ref* to get worse

agraviar *tr* to wrong, offend || *ref* to take offense

agravio *m* wrong, offense; **agravios de hecho** assault and battery

agravio·so -sa *adj* offensive, insulting

agraz *m* (*pl* **agraces**) sour grape; sour-grape juice; (coll) bitterness, displeasure; **en agraz** prematurely

agredir §1 *tr* to attack, assault

agregado *m* aggregate; concrete block; attaché; (Arg) tenant farmer

agregar §44 *tr* to add; to attach; to appoint || *ref* to join

agremiado *m* union member

agremiar *tr* to unionize

agresión *f* aggression

agresi·vo -va *adj* aggressive

agre·sor -sora *adj* aggressive || *mf* aggressor

agreste *adj* country, rustic; wild, rough; uncouth

agriar §77 & *regular tr* to make sour; to exasperate || *ref* to turn sour; to become exasperated

agrícola *adj* agricultural || *mf* farmer

agricultura *f* agriculture

agridulce *adj* bittersweet

agriera *f* (Chile) heartburn; **agrieras** (Col) cruet stand

agrietar *tr* & *ref* to crack

agrimensor *m* surveyor

agrimensura *f* surveying

agringar §44 *ref* (Am) to act like a gringo

a·grio -gria *adj* sour, acrid; uneven, rough; brittle || **agrios** *mpl* citrus fruit

agronomía *f* agronomy

agropecua·rio -ria *adj* land-and-cattle, farm

agrumar *tr* & *ref* to curd, to clot

agrupar *tr* & *ref* to group, to cluster

agrura *f* sourness; unpleasantness; **agruras** citrus fruit

agua *f* water; (*de un tejado*) slope; **agua abajo** downstream; **agua arriba** upstream; **agua bendita** holy water; **agua corriente** running water; **agua de Colonia** eau de Cologne; **agua de marea** tidewater; **agua gaseosa** carbonated water; **agua oxigenada** hydrogen peroxide; **aguas** mineral springs; (*de sedas; de piedras preciosas*) water, sparkle; **aguas mayores** equinoctial tide; feces; **aguas menores** ordinary tide; urination; **cubrir aguas** to have under roof; **entre dos aguas** under water, under the surface of the water; (coll) undecided

aguacate *m* avocado, alligator pear

aguacero *m* shower

aguada *f* source of water; water color; watering station

aguade·ro -ra *adj* water || *m* watering place

agua·do -da *adj* watery; thin, watered; (Am) weak, washed out, limp; (Am) dull, insipid || *f* see **aguada**

agua·dor -dora *mf* water carrier || *m* paddle, bucket

aguafies·tas *mf* (*pl* **-tas**) kill-joy, wet blanket, crapehanger

aguafortista *mf* etcher

aguafuerte *f* etching; **grabar al aguafuerte** to etch

aguaje *m* watering place; tidal wave; strong current; (*de buque*) wake

aguamala *f* jellyfish

aguamanil *m* ewer, wash pitcher; washstand

aguama·nos *m* (*pl* **-nos**) water for washing hands; washstand

aguamarina *f* aquamarine

aguanie·ves *f* (*pl* **-ves**) wagtail

aguano·so -sa *adj* watery, soaked

aguantar *tr* to hold up, sustain; to bear, endure, tolerate; to hold back, control || *intr* to last; to hold out || *ref* to restrain oneself; to keep quiet; **aguantarse las lágrimas** to swallow one's tears

aguante *m* patience, endurance; strength, vigor

aguar §10 *tr* to water; to spoil, to mar || *ref* to become watery; to fill up with water; to be spoiled

aguardar *tr* to await, to wait for; to grant time to || *intr* to wait; **aguardar a que** to wait until

aguardentera *f* liquor bottle, brandy flask

aguardentería *f* liquor store

aguardento·so -sa *adj* brandy; (*voz*) whiskey

aguardiente *m* brandy; spirituous liquor; **aguardiente de caña** rum; **aguardiente de manzana** applejack

aguardo *m* hunter's blind

aguasar *ref* (Arg & Chile) to become countrified

aguazal *m* swamp, pool

agudeza *f* acuteness, acuity; sharpness; witticism; **agudeza visual** visual acuity

agu·do -da *adj* acute; keen; witty

agüero *m* augury; omen; forecast

aguerri·do -da *adj* inured, hardened

aguijada *f* goad, spur; prod

aguijar *tr* to goad, spur, prod ‖ *intr* to hurry along

aguijón *m* goad, spur; sting; thorn; stimulus; **dar coces contra el aguijón** to kick against the pricks

aguijonear *tr* to goad, incite; to sting

águila *f* eagle; **ser un águila** to be wide-awake, be a wizard

aguile·ño -ña *adj* aquiline; sharp-featured

aguilón *m* (*de grúa*) boom, jib; (*del tejado*) gable

aguinaldo *m* Christmas gift, Epiphany gift; Christmas carol

aguja *f* needle; hatpin; steeple; spire; (*del reloj*) hand; **aguja de gancho** crochet needle; **aguja de hacer media** knitting needle; **aguja de zurcir** darning needle; **agujas** (rr) switch; **buscar una aguja en un pajar** to look for a needle in a haystack

agujerear *tr* to make a hole in, to pierce; to perforate

agujero *m* hole; pincushion; **agujero negro** (astr) black hole

agujeta *f* (*de la jeringa*) needle; shoestring; **agujetas** stitches, twinges

agusanar *ref* to get wormy; to become worm-eaten

aguzanie·ves *f* (*pl* -ves) wagtail

aguzar §60 *tr* to sharpen; to incite, stir up; to stare at; (*las orejas*) to prick up

ah-chís *interj* kerchoo!

aherrojar *tr* to fetter, to shackle; to oppress

aherrumbrar *tr & ref* to rust

ahí *adv* there; **de ahí que** hence; **por ahí** that way

ahija·do -da *mf* godchild; protégé ‖ *m* godson ‖ *f* goddaughter

ahilar *ref* to faint from hunger; to waste away; to grow poorly; to turn sour

ahincar §73 *tr* to urge, press; to importune ‖ *ref* to hasten

ahínco *m* earnestness, zeal, eagerness

ahitar *tr* to cloy, to surfeit, to stuff

ahí·to -ta *adj* surfeited, stuffed; fed up, disgusted ‖ *m* surfeit; indigestion

ahoga·do -da *adj* drowned; smothered; sunk; close, unventilated; **mate ahogado** stalemate; **perecer ahogado** to

drown; **verse ahogado** (coll) to be swamped

ahogar §44 *tr* to drown; to suffocate, smother; (*cal*) to slake; (*plantas*) to soak; to oppress; to extinguish; to stalemate ‖ *ref* to drown; to suffocate; to drown oneself

ahogo *m* shortness of breath; great sorrow; stringency

ahondar *tr* to make deeper; to go deep into ‖ *intr* to go deep, go deeper

ahora *adv* now; presently; **ahora bien** now then, so then; **ahora mismo** right now; **por ahora** for the present

ahorcajar *ref* to sit astride

ahorcar §73 *tr* to hang ‖ *ref* to hang, be hanged; to hang oneself

ahorra·do -da *adj* saving, thrifty

ahorrar *tr* to save; to spare ‖ *ref* to save or spare oneself

ahorrati·vo -va *adj* saving, thrifty; stingy ‖ *f* economy

ahorro *m* economy; **ahorros** savings

ahuchar *tr* to hoard

ahuecar §73 *tr* to hollow, hollow out; to loosen, fluff up; **ahuecar la voz** to speak in deep and solemn tones ‖ *ref* to be puffed up

ahumar *tr* to smoke ‖ *intr* to be smoky ‖ *ref* to get smoked up; to look or taste smoky; (coll) to get drunk

ahusar *tr & ref* to taper

ahuyentar *tr* to put to flight; to scare away ‖ *ref* to flee, run away

aira·do -da *adj* angry; wild; depraved

airar §4 *tr* to anger ‖ *ref* to get angry

aire *m* air; **al aire libre** in the open air; **darse aires** to put on airs

airear *tr* to air, aerate, ventilate ‖ *ref* to get aired; to catch cold

airón *m* aigrette, panache; gray heron

airo·so -sa *adj* airy; drafty; graceful, light; resplendent; successful

aislación *f* insulation

aislacionista *adj & mf* isolationist

aislador *m* insulator

aislamiento *m* isolation; (elec) insulation

aislar §4 *tr* to isolate; to detach, separate; (elec) to insulate ‖ *ref* to live in seclusion

ajar *m* garlic field ‖ *tr* to crumple, to muss; (*marchitar*) to wither; to tamper with; to abuse, ill-treat ‖ *ref* to get mussed; to wither

ajedrea *f* (bot) savory

ajedrecista *mf* chess player

ajedrez *m* chess; chess set

ajenjo *m* (*Artemisia*) wormwood; (*licor*) absinthe; (*sinsabores y penas*) (fig) wormwood, bitterness; **ajenjo del campo** or **ajenjo mayor** (*Artemisia absinthium*) wormwood

aje·no -na *adj* another's; extraneous, foreign; different; contrary; free; insane; uninformed; **lo ajeno** what belongs to someone else

ajetrear *tr* to drive, harass ‖ *ref* to bustle about; to fidget

ajetreo *m* bustle, fuss

ají *m* (*pl* ajíes) chili; chili sauce; **po-**

nerse como un ají (Chile) to turn red as a tomato

aji·mez m (pl **-meces**) mullioned window

ajo m garlic; garlic clove; garlic sauce

ajorca f bracelet, anklet

ajornalar tr to hire by the day ‖ ref to hire out by the day

ajuar m housefurnishings; trousseau

ajuiciar tr to bring to one's senses ‖ ref to come to one's senses

ajusta·do -da adj just, right; tight, close-fitting

ajustar tr to adapt, to fit, to adjust; to hire; to arrange; to reconcile; to fasten; to settle ‖ intr to fit ‖ ref to fit; to hire out; to be hired; to come to an agreement

ajuste m fit; fitting, adjustment; hiring; arrangement; reconciliation; settlement; agreement

ajusticiar tr to execute, to put to death

ala f wing; (del sombrero) brim; (de puerta, mesa, etc.) leaf; (de pez) fin; (de hélice) blade; (football) end; **ahuecar el ala** (coll) to beat it; **ala en flecha** (aer) sweptback wing; **alas** boldness, courage; **volar con sus propias alas** to stand on one's own feet

Alá m Allah

alabanza f praise

alabar tr to praise ‖ ref to boast

alabarda f halberd

alabardero m halberdier; hired applauder, claqueur

alabastro m alabaster

álabe m drooping branch; bucket, paddle; cog

alabear tr & ref to warp

alacena f cupboard, wall closet; (naut) locker; (Mex) booth, stall

alacrán m scorpion

ala·do -da adj winged

alamar m frog (button and loop on a garment)

alambica·do -da adj precious, over-subtle, fine-spun; begrudged

alambicar §73 tr to distill; to refine to excess

alambique m still, alembic; (de laboratorio) retort; **por alambique** sparingly

alambrada f chicken wire; wire mesh; (mil) barbed wire; (elec) wiring

alambrado m chicken wire; wire mesh; wire fence; (elec) wiring; (mil) wire entanglement

alambraje m (elec) wiring

alambrar tr to fence with wire; to string with wire; to wire

alambre m wire; **alambre cargado** live wire; **alambre de púas** barbed wire; **alambre sin aislar** bare wire

alambrera f wire screen; wire cover

alameda f poplar grove; mall, shaded walk

álamo m poplar; **álamo de Italia** Lombardy poplar; **álamo negro** black poplar; **álamo temblón** aspen

alampar ref to have a craving

alancear tr to lance, to spear

alano m mastiff, great Dane

alarde m display, ostentation; (mil) review; **hacer alarde de** to make a show of; to boast of

alardear intr to boast, brag, show off

alardo·so -sa adj showy, ostentatious

alargar §44 tr to extend, lengthen, stretch; to hand; to increase; to let out ‖ ref to go away, withdraw; to grow longer; to be long-winded

alarido m howl, shout, yell, whoop

alarma f alarm; (aer) alert; **alarma aérea** air-raid warning; **alarma de incendios** fire alarm; **alarma de ladrones** burglar alarm

alarmar tr to alarm; to alert ‖ ref to become alarmed

alarmista mf alarmist

alastrar tr (las orejas) to throw back; (naut) to ballast ‖ ref to lie flat, to cower

ala·zán -zana adj sorrel, reddish-brown ‖ mf sorrel horse

alba f dawn, daybreak

albacea m executor ‖ f executrix

albahaquero m flowerpot

alba·nés -nesa adj & mf Albanian

albañal m sewer, drain

albañil m mason, bricklayer

albañilería f masonry

albarán m rent sign; bulletin; (com) check list

albarca f sandal

albarda f packsaddle

albardilla f (tejadillo sobre los muros) coping; shoulder pad

albaricoque m apricot

albaricoquero m apricot tree

alba·tros m (pl **-tros**) albatross

albayalde m white lead

albear intr to turn white; (Arg) to get up at dawn

albedrío m free will; fancy, caprice, pleasure; **libre albedrío** free will

albéitar m veterinarian

alberca f pond, pool; tank, reservoir; **en alberca** roofless

albérchigo m clingstone peach

albergar §44 tr to shelter, to harbor; to house ‖ intr & ref to take shelter; to take lodgings

albergue m shelter, refuge; lodging; den, lair

albero m dishcloth, dishrag; white earth

al·bo -ba adj (poet) white ‖ f see **alba**

albóndiga f meat ball, fish ball

albor m whiteness; dawn

alborada f dawn; morning serenade; reveille

alborear intr to dawn

albor·noz m (pl **-noces**) terry cloth; burnoose; cardigan; beach robe

alborota·do -da adj hasty, rash; noisy; rough

alborota·dor -dora mf agitator, rioter

alborotapue·blos mf (pl **-blos**) (coll) rabble rouser; (coll) gay noisy person

alborotar tr to agitate, arouse, stir up ‖ intr to make a racket ‖ ref to get excited; to riot; (la mar) to get rough

alboroto m agitation, disturbance;

noise, riot; **alborotos** (CAm) candied popcorn; **armar un alboroto**
to raise a racket
alborozar §60 *tr* to gladden, to cheer,
to overjoy, to elate
alborozo *m* joy, merriment, elation
albricias *fpl* reward for good news;
reward given on the occasion of
some happy event; **en albricias de**
as a token of || *interj* good news!,
congratulations!
albufera *f* saltwater lagoon
ál·bum *m* (*pl* -**bumes**) album; **álbum
de recortes** scrapbook
albumen *m* albumen
albúmina *f* albumin
albuminar *tr* (phot) to emulsify
albur *m* risk, chance
alcachofa *f* artichoke
alcahue·te -ta *mf* bawd, procurer, go-
between; screen, fence; (coll)
schemer; (coll) gossip
alcahuetear *tr* to procure; to harbor ||
intr to pander
alcaide *m* governor, warden, jailer
alcalde *m* mayor, chief burgess; **alcalde de monterilla** small-town may-
or
alcaldesa *f* mayoress
álcali *m* alkali
alcali·no -na *adj* alkaline
alcallería *f* pottery
alcana *f* henna
alcance *m* reach, scope, extent; range;
pursuit; capacity; late news; import; coverage; brains, intelligence;
al alcance de within reach of, within
range of; **alcance de la vista** eye-
sight, eyeshot; **alcance del oído** earshot; **dar alcance a** to catch up with
alcancía *f* child's bank; bin, hopper
alcanfor *m* camphor
alcantarilla *f* sewer; culvert
alcantarillar *tr* to sewer
alcanza·do -da *adj* needy, hard up
alcanzar §60 *tr* to reach; to overtake,
catch up to; to grasp; to obtain;
to understand; to live through || *intr*
to succeed; (*un arma de fuego*) to
carry; to manage; to suffice
alcaravea *f* caraway
alcázar *m* fortress; castle, royal palace; quarterdeck
alce *m* elk, moose
alcista *adj* bullish || *mf* (fig) bull
alcoba *f* bedroom; **alcoba de respeto**
master bedroom
alcohol *m* alcohol
alcohóli·co -ca *adj & mf* alcoholic
alconafta *f* gasohol
alcor *m* hill, elevation, eminence
alcornoque *m* cork oak; (coll) blockhead
alcorque *m* cork-soled shoe; trench
for water around a tree
alcorza *f* sugar paste, sugar icing; **ser
una alcorza** (Arg) to be highly emotional
alcurnia *f* ancestry, lineage
alcuza *f* olive-oil can
aldaba *f* knocker, door knocker; bolt,
crossbar; latch; hitching ring; **aldaba**

dormida deadlatch; **tener buenas
aldabas** to have pull
aldabonazo *m* knock on the door
aldea *f* village, hamlet
aldea·no -na *adj* village; rustic || *mf*
villager
aleación *f* alloy
alear *tr* to alloy || *intr* to flap the
wings; to flap one's arms; to convalesce
aleccionar *tr* to teach, instruct; to
train, to coach
aleda·ño -ña *adj* bordering || *m* bor-
der, boundary
alegar §44 *tr* to allege; to declare, as-
sert || *intr* (Col, Hond) to quarrel
alegoría *f* allegory
alegóri·co -ca *adj* allegoric(al)
alegrar *tr* to cheer, gladden; (*un
fuego*) to stir || *ref* to be glad, to re-
joice; (coll) to get tipsy
alegre *adj* glad; bright, gay; cheerful,
light-hearted; careless; fast, spicy;
alegre de cascos scatterbrained
alegría *f* cheer, joy, gladness; brightness, gaiety
aleja·do -da *adj* distant, remote
alejandri·no -na *adj & mf* Alexandrine
alejar *tr & ref* to move aside, to move
away
alelar *tr* to make stupid || *ref* to grow
stupid
aleluya *m & f* hallelujah || *m* Easter
time || *f* doggerel; daub; **aleluya
navideña** Christmas card || *interj*
hallelujah!
ale·mán -mana *adj & mf* German
Alemania *f* Germany
alenta·do -da *adj* brave, spirited;
proud, haughty; (Am) well, healthy
|| *f* deep breath
alentar §2 *tr* to encourage, to cheer
up || *intr* to breathe || *ref* to take
heart; to get well, to recover
alerce *m* larch
alergia *f* allergy
alero *m* eaves
alerón *m* aileron
alerta *adv* on the alert || *interj* watch
out!, look out! || *m* (mil) alert; (mil)
watchword
alertar *tr* to alert
aler·to -ta *adj* alert, watchful, vigilant
alesaje *m* bore
alesna *f* awl
aleta *f* small wing; (*de pez*) fin; (*de
hélice*) blade
aletargar §44 *tr* to benumb; to put
to sleep || *ref* to get drowsy, fall
asleep
aletear *intr* to flap the wings; to flap,
flip, flutter
aleve *adj* treacherous, perfidious
alevosía *f* treachery, perfidy
alevo·so -sa *adj* treacherous, perfidious
alfabetizar §60 *tr* to alphabetize; **to
teach reading and writing to**
alfabeto *m* alphabet
alfaneque *m* buzzard
alfanje *m* cutlass
alfarería *f* pottery
alfarero *m* potter**

alféizar *m* splay; embrasure
alfeñicar §73 *tr* to candy, to ice ‖ *ref* (coll) to grow thin; (coll) to be affected, to be finical
alfeñique *m* almond-flavored sugar paste; (coll) affectation, prudery; (coll) thin, delicate person, weakling
alfé·rez *m* (*pl* **-reces**) (mil) second lieutenant; (mil) subaltern (Brit); **alférez de fragata** (nav) ensign; **alférez de navío** (nav) lieutenant (j.g.)
alfil *m* bishop
alfiler *m* pin; **alfiler de corbata** stickpin, scarfpin; **alfiler de madera** clothespin; **alfiler de seguridad** safety pin; **alfileres** pin money
alfilerar *tr* to pin, to pin up
alfiletero *m* pincase, needlecase
alfombra *f* carpet; rug
alfombrar *tr* to carpet
alforfón *m* buckwheat
alforja *f* shoulder bag; traveling supplies; **pasarse a la otra alforja** (coll) to go too far, take too much liberty
alforza *f* pleat, tuck
al·foz *m* (*pl* **-foces**) outskirts; dependence; mountain pass
alga *f* alga; **alga marina** seaweed; **algas algae**
algaida *f* brush, thicket; sandbank
algalia *f* civet; catheter
algarabía *f* Arabic; (coll) gibberish, jabber; (coll) hubbub, uproar
algarada *f* outcry; uproar
algarroba *f* carob bean
algarrobo *m* carob
algazara *f* Moorish battle cry; din, uproar
álgebra *f* algebra
algebrai·co -ca *adj* algebraic
álgi·do -da *adj* cold, icy, frigid
algo *pron indef* something; anything; **algo por el estilo** something of the sort ‖ *adv* somewhat, a little, rather
algodón *m* cotton; **algodón pólvora** guncotton; **estar criado entre algodones** to be brought up in comfort
algodoncillo *m* milkweed
algodono·so -sa *adj* cottony
alguacil *m* bailiff; mounted police officer at the head of the processional entrance of the bullfighters
alguien *pron indef* somebody, someone
algún *adj indef* apocopated form of **alguno**, used only before masculine singular nouns and adjectives
algu·no -na *adj indef* some, any; not any; **alguna vez** sometimes; ever ‖ *pron indef* someone; **algunos** some
alhaja *f* jewel, gem; **buena alhaja** a bad egg, a sly fellow
alharaca *f* fuss, ado, ballyhoo; **hacer alharacas** to make a fuss
alharaquien·to -ta *adj* fussy, noisy
alhe·lí *m* (*pl* **-líes**) gillyflower (*Matthiola incana*); wallflower (*Cheiranthus*)
alheña *f* henna; blight, mildew
alheñar *tr* to henna; to blight, mildew ‖ *ref* (*el pelo*) to henna

alhucema *f* lavender
alhumajo *m* pine needles
alia·do -da *adj* allied ‖ *mf* ally
aliaga *f* furze, gorse
alianza *f* alliance; wedding ring; (Bib) covenant
aliar §77 *tr* to ally ‖ *ref* to ally, become allied; to form an alliance
alias *adv* & *m* alias
alicaí·do -da *adj* failing, weak; (coll) crestfallen, discouraged
alicates *mpl* pliers
aliciente *m* inducement, incentive
alienar *tr* to alienate; to enrapture
aliento *m* breath, breathing; courage, spirit; **dar aliento a** to encourage; **de mucho aliento** arduous, difficult, endless; **nuevo aliento** second wind; **sin aliento** out of breath
alifafe *m* (coll) complaint, indisposition
aligerar *tr* to lighten; to alleviate, to ease; to hasten; to shorten
aligustre *m* privet
alijador *m* lighter; lighterman; sander
alijar *tr* to unload, to lighten; to sandpaper
alimaña *f* varmint, small predacious animal
alimentar *tr* to feed, nourish; (*p.ej., esperanzas*) to cherish, foster ‖ *ref* to feed, to nourish oneself
alimenti·cio -cia *adj* alimentary, nourishing
alimento *m* food, nourishment; encouragement; **alimentos** foodstuffs; allowance; alimony
alindar *tr* to mark off; to embellish, to prettify ‖ *intr* to border, be contiguous
alinear *tr* & *ref* to align, to line up
aliñar *tr* to dress, to season
aliño *m* dressing, seasoning
aliquebra·do -da *adj* (coll) crestfallen
alisar *tr* to smooth; to polish, to sleek; to iron lightly
aliso *m* alder tree
alistar *tr* to list; to enlist, to enroll; to stripe ‖ *ref* to enlist, to enroll; to get ready
aliteración *f* alliteration
aliviar *tr* to alleviate, to relieve, to soothe; to remedy; to lighten; to hasten ‖ *ref* to get better, to recover
alivio *m* alleviation, relief; remedy
aljaba *f* quiver
aljama *f* mosque; synagogue; Moorish quarter; ghetto
aljamía *f* Spanish of Moors and Jews; Spanish written in Arabic characters
aljez *m* gypsum
aljibe *m* water tender, tank barge; oil tanker; cistern
aljófar *m* imperfect pearl; (fig) dewdrops
aljofifa *f* floor mop
aljofifar *tr* to mop
alma *f* soul, heart, spirit; (*persona*) living soul, crux, heart; sweetheart; (*de carril*) web; (*de cañón*) bore; (*de escalera*) newel; **dar el alma,**

entregar el alma, rendir el alma to give up the ghost
almacén *m* warehouse; store, department store; storehouse; (phot) magazine
almacenaje *m* storage
almacenar *tr* to store; to store up, to hoard .
almacenista *mf* storekeeper ‖ *m* warehouseman
almáciga *f* seedbed, tree nursery
almádana *f* spalling hammer
almagre *m* red ocher
almajara *f* (hort) hotbed
almanaque *m* almanac; calendar
almeja *f* clam
almena *f* merlon
almenaje *m* battlement
almendra *f* almond; (*de cualquier fruto drupáceo*) kernel; **almendra amarga** bitter almond; **almendra de Málaga** Jordan almond; **almendra tostada** burnt almond
almendrado *m* macaroon
almendro *m* almond tree
almiar *m* haystack, hayrick
almíbar *m* simple syrup; fruit juice; **estar hecho un almíbar** (coll) to be as sweet as pie
almibarar *tr* to preserve in syrup; (*sus palabras*) to honey ‖ *intr* to candy
almidón *m* starch; (Am) paste; **almidón de maíz** cornstarch
almidona·do -da *adj* starched; (coll) spruce, dapper; (coll) stiff, prim
almidonar *tr* to starch
alminar *m* minaret
almiranta *f* admiral's wife; flagship
almirante *m* admiral
almi·rez *m* (*pl* **-reces**) brass mortar
almizcle *m* musk
almizclera *f* muskrat
almizclero *m* musk deer
almohada *f* pillow; **consultar con la almohada** to sleep it over
almohadilla *f* cushion; pad; (Chile) pincushion
almohaza *f* currycomb
almohazar §60 *tr* to currycomb
almoneda *f* auction; clearance sale
almonedar *tr* to auction
almorranas *fpl* piles, hemorrhoids
almorta *f* grass pea
almorzar §35 *tr* to lunch on ‖ *intr* to lunch, have lunch
almuecín *m* or **almuédano** *m* muezzin
almuerzo *m* lunch
alna·do -da *mf* stepchild
aloca·do -da *adj* mad, wild, reckless ‖ *mf* madcap
alocar §73 *tr* to drive crazy
alocución *f* address, speech
áloe *m* or **aloe** *m* aloe; aloes
alojar *tr* to lodge; to quarter, billet ‖ *intr* & *ref* to lodge; to be quartered or billeted
alondra *f* lark
aloquecer §22 *ref* to go crazy, to lose one's mind
alosa *f* shad
alpargata *f* hemp sandal, espadrille
alpende *m* tool shed; lean-to, penthouse

Alpes *mpl* Alps
alpestre *adj* alpine
alpinismo *m* mountain climbing
alpi·no -na *adj* alpine
alpiste *m* canary seed, birdseed; **quedarse alpiste** (coll) to be disappointed
alquería *f* farmhouse
alquibla *f* kiblah
alquiladi·zo -za *adj* & *mf* hireling
alquilar *tr* to rent, to let, to hire ‖ *ref* to hire out; to be for rent
alquiler *m* rent, rental; hire; **alquiler de coches** car-rental service; **alquiler sin chófer** drive-yourself service; **de alquiler** for rent, for hire
alquilona *f* cleaning woman, charwoman
alquimia *f* alchemy
alquitarar *tr* to distill
alquitrán *m* tar; **alquitrán de hulla** coal tar
alquitranado *m* tarpaulin
alquitranar *tr* to tar
alrededor *adv* around; **alrededor de** around; about, approximately ‖ **alrededores** *mpl* environs, surroundings, outskirts
Alsacia *f* Alsace
alsacia·no -na *adj* & *mf* Alsatian
alta *f* discharge from hospital; (mil) certificate of induction into active service; **dar de alta** to discharge from the hospital; **darse de alta** to join, be admitted; (mil) to report for duty
altane·ro -ra *adj* towering; arrogant, haughty
altar *m* altar; **altar mayor** high altar; **conducir al altar** to lead to the altar
alta·voz *m* (*pl* **-voces**) loudspeaker
altea *f* (bot) marsh mallow
alteración *f* alteration; disturbance; uneven pulse; altercation, quarrel
alterar *tr* to alter; to disturb; to agitate, upset; to falsify; to lessen ‖ *ref* to alter; to be disturbed; to be agitated; to lessen; (*el pulso*) to flutter
altercación *f* or **altercado** *m* argument, wrangle, bickering
altercar §73 *intr* to argue, bicker, wrangle
alternar *tr* & *intr* to alternate; **alternar con** to go around with
alternativa *f* choice, option; admission as a matador; **no tener alternativa** to have no choice
alter·no -na *adj* alternate
alteza *f* sublimity ‖ **Alteza** *f* (*tratamiento*) Highness
altibajo *m* downward thrust; **altibajos** uneven ground; ups and downs
altillo *m* hillock; (*oficina en una tienda o taller*) balcony; (Arg, Ecuad) attic, garret
altimetría *f* altimetry
altiplanicie *f* tableland
altitud *f* altitude; height
altivez *f* or **altiveza** *f* arrogance, haughtiness, pride
alti·vo -va *adj* haughty, proud; high; lofty
al·to -ta *adj* high; upper; top; loud;

(*horas*) late; **ponerse tan alto** to take offense, to be hoity-toity ‖ *m* height, altitude; story, floor; stop, halt; **de alto a bajo** from top to bottom; **hacer alto** to stop; **pasar por alto** to overlook, disregard ‖ *f see* **alta** ‖ **alto** *adv* high up; loud; aloud ‖ **alto** *interj* halt!

altoparlante *m* loudspeaker

altozanero *m* (Col) public errand boy

altozano *m* hill, knoll; upper part of town; (CAm, Col, Ven) parvis

altruísta *adj* altruistic ‖ *mf* altruist

altura *f* height, altitude; high seas; juncture, point, stage; (mus) pitch; (naut) latitude; **a estas alturas** at this juncture; **a la altura de** (naut) off; **estar a la altura de** to be up to, to be equal to; to be abreast of; **por estas alturas** (coll) around here

alucinación *f* hallucination

alud *m* avalanche

aludi·do -da *adj* above-mentioned

aludir *intr* to allude

alumbra·do -da *adj* lighted; enlightened; (coll) tipsy ‖ *m* lighting; lighting system

alumbramiento *m* lighting; childbirth, accouchement

alumbrar *tr* to light, illuminate; (*a los ciegos*) to give sight to; to enlighten; (*aguas subterráneas*) to discover and bring to the surface ‖ *intr* to have a child ‖ *ref* (coll) to get tipsy

alumbre *m* alum

aluminio *m* aluminum

alumnado *m* student body

alum·no -na *mf* (*niño criado como si fuera hijo*) foster child; (*discípulo*) pupil, student; **alumno mimado** teacher's pet

alunizaje *m* lunar landing

alunizar §60 *intr* to land on the moon

alusión *f* allusion

álveo *m* bed of a stream, river bed

alvéolo *m* alveolus; (*de diente*) socket; (*de rueda de agua*) bucket

alza *f* rise, advance, increase; **jugar al alza** to bull the market

alzada *f* height (*e.g., of a horse*)

alzado *m* lump sum, cash settlement; front elevation; (bb) quire, gathering

alzapaño *m* curtain holder; tieback

alzapié *m* snare, trap

alzaprima *f* crowbar, lever; (*de instrumento de arco*) (mus) bridge

alzaprimar *tr* to pry, pry up; to arouse, stir up

alzapuer·tas *m* (*pl* -tas) (archaic) dumb player, supernumerary

alzar §60 *tr* to raise, lift, hoist; to pick up; (*la hostia*) to elevate; to hide, lock up; (*naipes*) to cut; (bb) to gather ‖ *ref* to rise, to get up; to revolt; **alzarse con** to abscond with

alzaválvu·las *m* (*pl* -las) tappet

allá *adv* there, over there; back there; **allá en** over in; back in; **el más allá** the beyond; **más allá** farther on, farther away; **más allá de** beyond; **por allá** thereabouts; that way

allanar *tr* to level, smooth, flatten;

(*una dificultad*) to iron out, to overcome, to get around; (*una casa*) to break into; the subdue ‖ *intr* to level off ‖ *ref* to tumble down; to yield, to submit; to humble oneself

allega·do -da *adj* near, close; related; partisan ‖ *mf* relative; partisan

allegar §44 *tr* to collect, gather; to reap ‖ *intr* to approach ‖ *ref* to approach; to be attached, be a follower, agree

allende *adv* beyond; **allende de** besides, in addition to ‖ *prep* beyond

allí *adv* there; **allí dentro** in there; **por allí** that way; around there

ama *f* housekeeper; housewife, lady of the house; landlady, proprietress; **ama de casa** housewife; **ama de cría** or **de leche** wet nurse; **ama de llaves** housekeeper; **ama seca** dry nurse

amable *adj* amiable, kind, obliging; (*digno de ser amado*) lovable

ama·do -da *adj & mf* beloved

amador -dora *adj* fond, loving ‖ *mf* lover

amadrigar §44 *tr* to welcome, receive with open arms ‖ *ref* to burrow; to go into seclusion

amaestrar *tr* to teach, to coach; (*a los animales*) to train

amagar §44 *tr* to show signs of, to threaten; to feint ‖ *intr* to look threatening

amago *m* threat, menace; sign, indication; feint

amainar *tr* to lessen; (naut) to lower, shorten ‖ *intr* to subside, die down; to lessen; to yield ‖ *ref* to lessen; to yield

amalgama *f* amalgam

amalgamar *tr & ref* to amalgamate

amamantar *tr* to nurse, to suckle

amancebamiento *m* cohabitation, concubinage, liaison

amancebar *ref* to cohabit, to live in concubinage

amancillar *tr* to stain, spot; to sully, to tarnish

amanecer *m* dawn, daybreak ‖ *v* §22 *intr* to dawn, to begin to get light; to begin to appear; to get awake, to start the day

amanecida *f* dawn, daybreak

amanera·do -da *adj* mannered, affected

amansar *tr* (*a un animal*) to tame; (*a un caballo*) to break; to soothe, to appease

amante *adj* fond, loving ‖ *mf* lover

amaño *m* skill, cleverness, dexterity; trick; **amaños** tools, implements

amapola *f* poppy

amar *tr* to love

amaraje *m* alighting on water

amarar *intr* to alight on water

amargar §44 *tr* to make bitter; to embitter; (*una tertulia, una velada*) to spoil ‖ *intr & ref* to become bitter; to become embittered

amar·go -ga *adj* bitter; sour; distressing ‖ **amargos** *mpl* bitters

amargura *f* bitterness; sorrow, grief

amarillear *intr* to turn yellow, to show yellow

amarillecer §22 *intr* to become yellow

amarillen·to -ta *adj* yellowish

amarillez *f* yellowness

amari·llo -lla *adj* & *m* yellow

amarra *f* mooring cable; **amarras** support, protection; **soltar las amarras** (naut) to cast off

amarrar *tr* to moor; to lash, to tie up; (*las cartas*) to stack

amartelar *tr* to make love to; to make jealous || *ref* to fall in love; to become jealous

amartillar *tr* to hammer; (*un arma de fuego*) to cock

amasar *tr* to knead; to mix; to massage; (*dinero*) to amass; to concoct

amatista *f* amethyst

amazonas *m* Amazon

ambages *mpl* ambiguity, quibbling; **sin ambages** straight to the point

ambar *m* amber

amberes *f* Antwerp

ambición *f* ambition

ambicionar *tr* to strive for, to be eager for

ambicio·so -sa *adj* ambitious; eager; **ambicioso de figurar** social climber

ambiente *m* atmosphere

ambi·gú *m* (*pl* -gúes*) buffet supper; bar, refreshment bar

ambigüedad *f* ambiguity

ambi·guo -gua *adj* ambiguous; (*género*) (gram) common

ambito *m* boundary, limit; compass, scope

ambladura *f* amble

amblar *intr* to amble

am·bos -bas *adj* & *pron indef* both; **ambos a dos** both, both together

ambrosía *f* ragweed

ambulancia *f* ambulance; **ambulancia de correos** mail car, railway post office

ambulante *adj* itinerant, traveling || *m* railway mail clerk

amedrentar *tr* to frighten, to scare

amelona·do -da *adj* melon-shaped; (coll) mentally retarded; (coll) lovesick

amén *interj* amen! || *m* amen || *adv* — **amén de** (coll) aside from; (coll) in addition to

amenaza *f* threat, menace

amenazar §60 *tr* to threaten, menace

amenguar §10 *tr* to lessen, to diminish; to belittle; to dishonor

amenidad *f* amenity

amenizar §60 *tr* to make pleasant, to brighten, to cheer

ame·no -na *adj* agreeable, pleasant

amento *m* catkin

américa *f* America; **la América Central** Central America; **la América del Norte** North America; **la América del Sur** South America; **la América Latina** Latin America

americana *f* sack coat, jacket

americanizar §60 *tr* to Americanize

america·no -na *adj* & *mf* American; Spanish American || *f* see **americana**

amerizar §60 *intr* to alight on water

ametralladora *f* machine gun

ametrallar *tr* to machine-gun

amiba *f* amoeba

amiga *f* friend; mistress; schoolmistress; girls' school

amigable *adj* amicable, friendly

amigacho *m* (coll) chum, crony, pal

amígdala *f* tonsil

amigdalitis *f* tonsillitis

ami·go -ga *adj* friendly; fond || *mf* friend; sweetheart; **amigo del alma** bosom friend || *f* see **amiga**

amigote *m* (coll) chum, crony, pal

amilanar *tr* to terrify, intimidate

aminorar *tr* to lessen, to diminish

amistad *f* friendship; liaison; **hacer las amistades** (coll) to make up; **romper las amistades** (coll) to fall out, become enemies

amistar *tr* to bring together || *ref* to become friends

amisto·so -sa *adj* friendly

amnistía *f* amnesty

amnistiar §77 *tr* to amnesty, to grant amnesty to

amo *m* head of family; landlord, proprietor; boss; **ser el amo del cotarro** (coll) to rule the roost

amoblar §61 *tr* to furnish

amodorrar *ref* to get drowsy; to fall asleep; to grow numb

amohinar *tr* to annoy, irritate, vex

amojonar *tr* to mark off with landmarks

amoladera *f* grindstone, whetstone

amolar §61 *tr* to grind, sharpen; (coll) to bore, to annoy

amoldar *tr* to mold; to model, to pattern, to fashion; to adjust, adapt

amonestación *f* admonition; marriage banns

amonestar *tr* to admonish, to warn; to publish the banns of

amoníaco *m* ammonia

amontonar *tr* to heap, pile; to accumulate; to hoard || *ref* to collect, to gather; to crowd; (coll) to get angry; (Mex) to gang up

amor *m* love; **al amor del agua** with the current; obligingly; **al amor de la lumbre** by the fire, in the warmth of the fire; **amores** love affair; **amor propio** amour-propre; conceit; **por amor de** for the sake of

amorata·do -da *adj* livid, black-and-blue

amordazar §60 *tr* to muzzle; to gag

amorío *m* (coll) love-making; (coll) love affair

amoro·so -sa *adj* loving, affectionate, amorous

amortajar *tr* to shroud; (carp) to mortise

amortecer §22 *tr* to deaden, to muffle || *ref* to die away, become faint

amortiguador *m* shock absorber; door check; (*de automóvil*) bumper; **amortiguador de luz** dimmer; **amortiguador de ruido** muffler

amortiguar §10 *tr* to deaden, to muffle; to soften, tone down; to dim; to damp; (*un golpe*) to cushion; (*ondas electromagnéticas*) to damp

amortizar §60 *tr* to amortize; (*una deuda*) to pay off

amoscar §73 *ref* (coll) to get peeved; (Mex) to blush, be embarrassed

amotina·do -da *adj* mutinous, rebellious ‖ *mf* mutineer, rebel, rioter

amotinar *tr* to stir up; to incite to mutiny ‖ *ref* to rise up, mutiny, rebel

amover §47 *tr* to discharge, dismiss

amovible *adj* removable, detachable

amparar *tr* to shelter, protect ‖ *ref* to seek shelter; to protect oneself

amparo *m* shelter, protection, refuge; stall; aid, favor

amperio *m* ampere

amperio-hora *m* (*pl* **amperios-hora**) ampere-hour

ampliación *f* amplification; (phot) enlargement

ampliar §77 *tr* to amplify, enlarge; to widen; (phot) to enlarge

amplificador *m* amplifier

amplificar §73 *tr* to amplify; to expand, enlarge; to magnify

am·plio -plia *adj* ample; spacious, roomy

amplitud *f* amplitude; roominess

ampo *m* dazzling white; snowflake

ampolla *f* blister; bubble; cruet; bulb, light bulb

ampollar *tr* & *ref* to blister

ampolleta *f* vial; sandglass, hourglass; bulb, light bulb; cruet

ampulosidad *f* bombast, pomposity

ampulo·so -sa *adj* bombastic, pompous

amputar *tr* to amputate

amueblar *tr* to furnish

amujera·do -da *adj* effeminate

amuleto *m* amulet, charm

amurallar *tr* to wall, to wall in

amurcar §73 *tr* to gore

amusgar §44 *tr* (*las orejas el toro, el caballo*) to throw back

anacardo *m* cashew; cashew nut

anacronismo *m* anachronism

ánade *mf* duck

anadear *intr* to waddle

anadeo *m* waddle, waddling

anales *mpl* annals

analfabetismo *m* illiteracy

analfabe·to -ta *adj* & *mf* illiterate

análi·sis *m* & *f* (*pl* -sis) analysis; **análisis gramatical** parsing; **análisis ocupacional** job analysis

analista *mf* analyst; annalist

analíti·co -ca *adj* analytic(al)

analizar §60 *tr* to analyze; **analizar gramaticalmente** to parse

analogía *f* analogy; similarity

análo·go -ga *adj* analogous; similar

ana·ná *m* (*pl* -naes) pineapple

ananás *m* pineapple

anaquel *m* shelf

anaranja·do -da *adj* & *m* (*color*) orange

anarquía *f* anarchy

anárqui·co -ca *adj* anarchic(al)

anarquista *mf* anarch, anarchist

anatema *m* & *f* anathema; curse

anatomía *f* anatomy

anatómi·co -ca *adj* anatomic(al) ‖ *m* anatomist

anatomista *mf* anatomist

anca *f* croup, haunch; buttock; rump; **a ancas** or **a las ancas** mounted behind another person

ancianidad *f* old age

ancia·no -na *adj* old, aged ‖ *m* old man; (eccl) elder ‖ *f* old woman

ancla *f* anchor; **echar anclas** to cast anchor; **levar anclas** to weigh anchor

anclar *intr* to anchor

anclote *m* kedge, kedge anchor

ancón *m* bay, cove

áncora *f* anchor

ancorar *intr* to anchor

an·cho -cha *adj* wide, broad; full; ample; loose, loose-fitting ‖ *m* width, breadth

anchoa *f* anchovy

anchura *f* width, breadth; fullness, ampleness; looseness; comfort, ease

anchuro·so -sa *adj* wide, broad; spacious, roomy

andada *f* thin, hard-baked cracker; **andadas** (*de conejos y otros animales*) tracks; **volver a los andadas** to revert to one's old tricks

andaderas *fpl* gocart, walker

anda·do -da *adj* gone by, elapsed; frequented, trodden; worn, used; ordinary ‖ *m* (Am) gait ‖ *f* see **andada**

andadores *mpl* leading strings

andadura *f* pace, gait; amble; (Mex) mount

Andalucía *f* Andalusia

anda·luz -luza *adj* & *mf* Andalusian

andaluzada *f* (coll) tall story, exaggeration, fish story

andamiaje *m* scaffolding

andamio *m* scaffold; platform

andanada *f* (naut) broadside; (taur) covered upper section; (coll) scolding; (fig) fusillade

andante *adj* walking; errant, wandering

andanza *f* wandering, rambling; fate, fortune

andar *m* gait, pace, walk ‖ §5 *tr* (*p.ej., dos millas*) to go; (*un camino*) to go down or up ‖ *intr* to go, to walk to run; to travel; to act, to behave (*p.ej., un reloj*) to go, to run, to work; to be, to feel; to go by, to pass, to elapse; to go (*to bear up, to last*), e.g., **anduve diez horas sin comer** I went ten hours without eating ‖ *ref* to go by, to pass, to elapse; to go away; **andarse sin** to go without

andarie·go -ga *adj* wandering, roving; swift, fleet

andas *fpl* litter; stretcher; bier

andén *m* railway platform; quay; footpath

Andes *mpl* Andes

andi·no -na *adj* Andean

andraje·ro -ra *mf* ragpicker

andrajo *m* rag, tatter; ragamuffin; scalawag

andrajo·so -sa *adj* ragged, raggedy, in tatters

andurriales *mpl* byways, out-of-the-way place

anea *f* cattail, bulrush

aneblar §2 *tr* to cloud; to becloud ‖ *ref* to become clouded; to get dark

anécdota *f* anecdote

anegar §44 *tr* to flood; to drown ‖ *ref* to become flooded; to drown

ane·jo -ja *adj* annexed; accessory ‖ *m* annex; dependency; supplement

anemia *f* anaemia

anémi·co -ca *adj* anaemic

anestesia *f* anaesthesia

anestesiar *tr* anaesthetize

anestési·co -ca *adj* & *m* anaesthetic

aneurisma *m* & *f* aneurysm

anexar *tr* to annex

ane·xo -xa *adj* annexed; accessory ‖ *m* annex; dependency

anfi·bio -bia *adj* amphibious

anfiteatro *m* amphitheater

anfitrión *m* (coll) host

anfitriona *f* (coll) hostess

ánfora *f* (Am) voting urn, ballot box

anfractuo·so -sa *adj* winding, tortuous

angarillas *fpl* handbarrow; panniers; cruet stand

ángel *m* angel; **ángel custodio** or **de la guarda** guardian angel; **ángel patudo** (coll) wolf in sheep's clothing; **tener ángel** to have great charm

angelical or **angéli·co -ca** *adj* angelic(al)

angina *f* angina; **angina de pecho** angina pectoris

angloparlante *adj* English-speaking ‖ *mf* speaker of English

anglosa·jón -jona *adj* & *mf* Anglo-Saxon

angos·to -ta *adj* narrow

anguila *f* eel; **anguilas** (*para botar un barco al agua*) ways; **escurrirse como una anguila** to be as slippery as an eel

angular *adj* angular

ángulo *m* angle; corner

angulo·so -sa *adj* (*facciones*) angular

angustia *f* anguish, distress, grief

angustia·do -da *adj* distressed, grieved

angustiar *tr* to distress, afflict, grieve

angustio·so -sa *adj* distressed, grieved; worrisome

anhelar *tr* to crave, to want badly ‖ *intr* to pant; to yearn; **anhelar por** to long for

anhélito *m* hard breathing

anhelo *m* craving; yearning, longing

anhelo·so -sa *adj* eager, yearning; breathless, panting

anhi·dro -dra *adj* anhydrous

Aníbal *m* Hannibal

anidar *tr* to harbor, to shelter ‖ *intr* & *ref* to nestle, make a nest; to live

anilina *f* aniline

anilla *f* curtain ring; (*en la gimnasia*) ring; hoop

anillo *m* ring; cigar band; **anillo de compromiso** or **de pedida** engagement ring; **anillo sigilar** signet ring

ánima *f* soul; (*de arma de fuego*) bore

animación *f* animation; liveliness; bustle, movement

anima·do -da *adj* animated, lively

animador *m* (*de un café-cantante*) master of ceremonies

animal *adj* & *m* animal

animar *tr* to enliven; to encourage; to strengthen; to drive ‖ *ref* to take heart, feel encouraged

ánimo *m* mind, spirit; courage, valor, energy; attention, thought

animosidad *f* animosity, ill will

animo·so -sa *adj* brave, courageous; spirited; ready, disposed

aniña·do -da *adj* babyish, childish

anión *m* anion

aniquilar *tr* to annihilate, destroy ‖ *ref* to be annihilated; to decline, waste away; to be humbled

anís *m* anise; anise-flavored brandy

aniversa·rio -ria *adj* & *m* anniversary

anoche *adv* last night

anochecer *m* nightfall, dusk ‖ *v* §22 *intr* to grow dark; to arrive or happen at nightfall; to end the day; to go to sleep ‖ *ref* to get dark; to get cloudy; (coll) to slip away

anochecida *f* nightfall, dusk

anodi·no -na *adj* innocuous, ineffective, harmless

ánodo *m* anode

anomalía *f* anomaly

anóma·lo -la *adj* anomalous

anonadar *tr* to annihilate, destroy; to overwhelm; to humble

anóni·mo -ma *adj* anonymous ‖ *m* anonymity; **guardar** or **conservar el anónimo** to preserve one's anonymity

anormal *adj* abnormal

anotar *tr* to annotate; to note, jot down; to point out

anquilosa·do -da *adj* stiff-jointed; old-fashioned

ánsar *m* goose; wild goose

ansia *f* anxiety, anguish; eagerness; **ansias** (Ven) nausea

ansiar §77 & **regular** *tr* to long for, yearn for ‖ *intr* to be madly in love

ansiedad *f* anxiety, worry; pain

ansio·so -sa *adj* anxious; anguished; longing; covetous

ant. *abbr* **anticuado**

anta *f* elk

antagonismo *m* antagonism

antaño *adv* last year; of yore, long ago

antárti·co -ca *adj* antarctic

ante *prep* before, in the presence of; in front of; at, with ‖ *m* elk; buff

antea·do -da *adj* buff; (Mex) damaged, shopworn

anteanoche *adv* the night before last

anteayer *adv* the day before yesterday

antebrazo *m* forearm

antecámara *f* antechamber, anteroom

antecedente *adj* antecedent ‖ *m* antecedent; **antecedentes** antecedents

anteceder *tr* to precede, to go before

antece·sor -sora *mf* predecessor; ancestor

antedatar *tr* to antedate

antedi·cho -cha *adj* aforesaid, above-mentioned

antelación *f* previousness, anticipation

antemano — de antemano in advance, beforehand

am
an

antena f (ent) antenna; (rad) antenna, aerial; **antena de conejo** (coll) rabbit ears; **en antena** on the air; **llevar a las antenas** to put on the air

antenombre m title, honorific

anteojera f spectacle case; blinker, blinder

anteojo m eyeglass; spyglass; **anteojos** eyeglasses; binoculars; blinkers

antepasa·do -da adj before last ‖ **antepasados** mpl ancestors

antepecho m railing, guardrail; parapet; window sill

antepenúltima f antepenult

anteponer §54 tr to place in front; to prefer

anteportada f half title, bastard title

anteportal m porch, vestibule

antepuerta f portière

antepuerto m entrance to a mountain pass; (naut) outer harbor

anterior adj front; previous; earlier

antes adv before; sooner, soonest; rather; previously; **antes bien** rather; on the contrary; **antes de** before; **antes (de) que** before; **cuanto antes** as soon as possible

antesala f antechamber; (p.ej., de médico) waiting room; **hacer antesala** to dance attendance

antiaére·o -a adj anti-aircraft

antiartísti·co -ca adj inartistic

antibéli·co -ca adj antiwar

anticartel adj antitrust

anticientífi·co -ca adj unscientific

anticipación f preparation, anticipation; **con anticipación** in advance

anticipa·do -da adj future; advance; **por anticipado** in advance

anticipar tr to anticipate, hasten; to move ahead ‖ ref to happen early; **anticiparse a** to anticipate, to get ahead of

anticipo m anticipation; advance payment, down payment; retaining fee

anticoncepti·vo -va adj & m contraceptive

anticongelante m antifreeze

anticonstitucional adj unconstitutional

anticua·do -da adj antiquated; old-fashioned; obsolete

anticua·rio -ria adj antiquarian ‖ m antiquarian, antiquary; antique dealer

anticuerpo m antibody

antideporti·vo -va adj unsportsmanlike

antiderrapante adj nonskid

antideslizante adj nonskid

antideslumbrante adj antiglare

antidetonante adj & m antiknock

antídoto m antidote

antieconómi·co -ca adj uneconomic(al)

antier adv (coll) the day before yesterday

antiesclavista adj antislavery ‖ mf abolitionist

anti·faz m (pl -faces) veil, mask

antífona f anthem

antigás adj invar gas (e.g., mask, shelter)

antigramatical adj ungrammatical

antigualla f antique; (coll) relic, antique; (coll) has-been

antiguar §10 intr & ref to attain seniority

antigüedad f antiquity; seniority; (mueble u otro objeto de arte antiguos) antique; **antigüedades** antiquities; antiques

anti·guo -gua adj old; ancient; antique; former ‖ mf veteran; senior

antihigiéni·co -ca adj unsanitary

antílope m antelope

antilla·no -na adj & mf West Indian

Antillas fpl Antilles

antimonio m antimony

antiobre·ro -ra adj antilabor

antiparras spl (coll) spectacles

antipatía f dislike, antipathy

antipáti·co -ca adj disagreeable, uncongenial

antipatrióti·co -ca adj unpatriotic

antiproyectil adj antimissile

antirresbaladi·zo -za adj nonskid

antisemíti·co -ca adj anti-Semitic

antisépti·co -ca adj & m antiseptic

antisono·ro -ra adj soundproof

antisoviéti·co -ca adj anti-Soviet

antitanque adj antitank

antíte·sis f (pl -sis) antithesis

antitoxina f antitoxin

antojadi·zo -za adj capricious, whimsical

antojar ref to seem; to fancy; to seem likely; to have a notion to + inf; to take a fancy to + inf

antojo m caprice, fancy, whim; snap judgment; birthmark; **antojos** moles, warts; **a su antojo** as one pleases

antología f anthology

antónimo m antonym

antorcha f torch; **antorcha a soplete** blowtorch

antracita f anthracite

ántrax m anthrax

antro m cave, cavern; (fig) den

antropología f anthropology

antruejo m carnival

anual adj annual

anualidad f annuity; year's pay; annual occurrence

anuario m yearbook; directory; bulletin, catalogue; **anuario telefónico** telephone directory

anublar tr to cloud; to dim, darken; to blight, to wither ‖ ref to become cloudy; to be withered; (las esperanzas de uno) to fade away

anudar tr to tie, fasten, knot; to unite; to resume ‖ ref to get knotted; to be united; to fade away, to wilt, to fail

anuente adj consenting

anular tr to annul; to nullify; to remove, to discharge ‖ ref to be passed over

anunciar tr to announce; to advertise ‖ intr to advertise

anunciante mf advertiser

anuncio m announcement; advertisement

anverso m obverse

anzuelo m fishhook; **picar en el anzuelo** or **tragar el anzuelo** to swallow the bait, swallow the hook

añadi·do -da *adj* additional ‖ *m* false hair, switch

añadidura *f* addition; extra weight, extra measure; **de añadidura** extra, in the bargain; **por añadidura** besides

añadir *tr* to add; to increase

añafil *m* straight Moorish trumpet

añagaza *f* bird call; decoy, lure; trap, trick

añe·jo -ja *adj* aged; stale; musty, rancid

añicos *mpl* bits, pieces; **hacer añicos** to tear to pieces, to break to pieces; **hacerse añicos** (coll) to wear oneself out

añil *m* indigo; bluing

añilar *tr* to dye with indigo; (*la ropa blanca*) to blue

año *m* year; **año bisiesto** leap year; **año económico** fiscal year; **año lectivo** school year; **año luz** (*pl* **años luz**) light-year; **años** birthday; **cumplir . . . años** to be . . . years old

añoranza *f* longing, sorrow

añorar *tr* to long for, to sorrow for; to grieve over ‖ *intr* to yearn; to sorrow, to grieve

año·so -sa *adj* aged, old

aojada *f* (Col) skylight; (Col) transom

aojar *tr* to cast the evil eye on, to jinx

aojo *m* evil eye, jinx

aovar *intr* to lay eggs

ap. *abbr* **aparte, apóstol**

apabilar *tr* to trim

apabullar *tr* (coll) to mash, crush; (coll) to squelch

apacentar §2 *tr* & *ref* to pasture, to graze; to feed

apacible *adj* gentle, mild; calm

apaciguamiento *m* pacification, appeasement

apaciguar §10 *tr* to pacify, to appease ‖ *ref* to calm down

apachurrar *tr* to crush, squash, mash

apadrinar *tr* to sponsor; to act as godfather for; to back, support; to second

apagabron·cas *m* (*pl* **-cas**) bouncer

apagador *m* extinguisher; (*de piano*) damper

apagaincen·dios *m* (*pl* **-dios**) fire extinguisher

apagar §44 *tr* to extinguish, to put out; (*la luz, la radio*) to turn off; (*la cal*) to slake; (*el sonido*) to damp, to muffle; (*el fuego del enemigo*) to silence; (*la sed*) to quench; (*el dolor*) to deaden ‖ *ref* to go out; to subside, calm down, fade away

apagón *m* blackout

apalabrar *tr* to bespeak; to consider ‖ *ref* to agree

apalancar §73 *tr* to raise with a lever or crowbar

apalear *tr* to shovel; to beat; to pile up

apandar *tr* (coll) to steal

apantallar *tr* (elec) to shield, to screen; (Am) to dazzle, amaze

apañar *tr* to grasp; to pick up; to steal; to repair, to mend; (coll) to wrap up ‖ *ref* (coll) to be handy

apañuscar §73 *tr* (coll) to crumple, to

rumple; (coll) to steal; (CAm, Col, Ven) to jam, to crowd

aparador *m* sideboard, buffet; showcase; workshop

aparar *tr* to prepare; to adorn; to block; (*las manos, la falda, el pañuelo, la capa*) to hold out

aparato *m* apparatus; ostentation, show; exaggeration; radio set; television set; telephone; airplane; camera; bandage, application; (theat) scenery, properties; **aparato auditivo** hearing aid; **aparato de relojería** clockwork; **aparatos sanitarios** bathroom fixtures; **ponerse al aparato** to go or to come to the phone

aparato·so -sa *adj* showy, pompous, ostentatious

aparcamiento *m* parking; parking space

aparcar §44 *tr* & *intr* to park

aparcería *f* partnership, sharecropping

aparce·ro -ra *mf* partner, sharecropper; (Arg) customer

aparear *tr* to pair, to match; to mate ‖ *ref* to pair; to mate

aparecer §22 *intr* & *ref* to appear; to show up

aparecido *m* ghost, specter

aparejador *m* builder

aparejar *tr* to prepare; to prime; to size; to harness

aparejo *m* preparation; harness; set, kit; priming; sizing; (mas) bond; **aparejos** tools, implements, equipment

aparentar *tr* to feign, pretend; to look, to look to be

aparente *adj* apparent, seeming; evident; right, proper

aparición *f* apparition

apariencia *f* appearance, aspect; sign, indication; **salvar las apariencias** to save face

aparqueamiento *m* parking

aparquear *tr* & *intr* to park

aparqueo *m* parking

aparragar §44 *ref* (Am) to crouch, to squat; (CAm) to loll, to sprawl

apartadero *m* siding, side track; turnout

aparta·do -da *adj* distant, remote; aloof; (*camino*) side, back; different ‖ *m* side room; post-office box; vocabulary entry; section

apartamento *m* apartment, apartment house

apartar *tr* to take aside; to separate; to push away; to shunt; (*el ganado*) to sort ‖ *ref* to separate; to move away, keep away, stand aside; to withdraw; to get divorced; to give up

aparte *adv* apart, aside; **aparte de** apart from ‖ *prep* apart from ‖ *m* (theat) aside

apasiona·do -da *adj* passionate; devoted, tender, loving; sore

apasionar *tr* to impassion, appeal deeply to; to afflict ‖ *ref* to become impassioned; to be stirred up; to fall madly in love

apatía *f* apathy

apáti·co -ca adj apathetic
apatusco m (coll) ornament, finery
apdo. abbr **apartado**
apeadero m horse block; flag stop, wayside station; platform; temporary quarters
apear tr to help dismount, to help down; to bring down; to remove; to overcome; to prop up || ref to dismount, get off; to back down; to stop, to put up
apechugar §44 intr to push with the chest; **apechugar con** (coll) to make the best of
apedazar §60 tr to mend, to patch; to cut or tear to pieces
apedrear tr to stone; to stone to death; to pit; to speckle || intr to hail || ref to be damaged by hail; to be pitted
apegar §44 ref to become attached, grow fond
apego m attachment, fondness
apelación f (coll) medical consultation; (coll) remedy, help; (law) appeal
apelar tr to appeal, make an appeal; to have recourse; to refer
apeldar tr — **apeldarlas** (coll) to flee, run away
apelmazar §60 tr to squeeze, compress || ref to cake
apelotonar tr to form into a ball || ref to form a ball; to curl up
apellidar tr to call, to name; to proclaim
apellido m name; surname, last name, family name; **apellido de soltera** maiden name
apenar tr & ref to grieve
apenas adv hardly, scarcely; **apenas si** hardly, scarcely || conj no sooner, as soon as
apéndice m appendage; (anat) appendix
apendicitis f appendicitis
apercancar §73 ref (Chile) to get moldy, to mildew
apercibir tr to prepare; to provide; to warn; to perceive; (coll) to collect || ref to get ready; to be provided; **apercibirse de** to notice
apergaminar ref (coll) to dry up, to become yellow and wrinkled
aperitivo m appetizer
aperla·do -da adj pearly
apero m tools, equipment, outfit; (Am) riding gear
aperrear tr to set the dogs on; to harass, plague, pester
apersogar §44 tr to tether
apersona·do -da adj — **bien apersonado** presentable; **mal apersonado** unpresentable
apersonar ref to appear in person; to have an interview
apertura f opening
apesadumbrar or **apesarar** tr & ref to grieve
apestar tr to infect with the plague; to corrupt; (coll) to sicken, to nauseate; to infest || intr to stink || ref to be infected with the plague

apesto·so -sa adj stinking, foul-smelling; pestilent; sickening
apetecer §22 tr to hunger for, to thirst for, to crave
apetecible adj desirable, tempting
apetencia f hunger, appetite, craving
apetito m appetite
apetito·so -sa adj tasty; tempting; gourmand
ápex m apex
apiadar tr to move to pity; to take pity on || ref to have pity
ápice m apex; bit, whit; crux; **estar en los ápices de** (coll) to be up in
apilar tr & ref to pile, to pile up
apimpollar ref to sprout, to put forth shoots
apiñar tr & ref to crowd, to jam
apio m celery
apisonadora f road roller
apisonar tr to tamp; to roll
aplacar §73 tr to placate, appease, pacify; (la sed) to quench
aplanar tr to smooth, make even; (coll) to astonish || ref to collapse; to become discouraged
aplanchar tr to iron
aplanetizar §60 intr to land on another planet
aplastar tr to flatten, crush, smash; (coll) to dumbfound
aplaudir tr & intr to applaud
aplauso m applause; **aplausos** applause
aplazar §60 tr to postpone; to convene; to summon
aplicación f appliance, application; diligence
aplica·do -da adj industrious, studious; applied
aplicar §73 tr to apply; to attribute || ref to apply; to apply oneself
aplomar tr to plumb; to make straight or vertical || intr to be vertical || ref to collapse; (Chile) to be embarrassed; (Mex) to be slow, be backward
aplomo m aplomb, poise, self-possession; gravity
apoca·do -da adj diffident, timid, irresolute; humble, lowly
apocar §73 tr to cramp, contract; to narrow; to humble, belittle
apodar tr to nickname; to make fun of
apodera·do -da adj empowered, authorized || m proxy; attorney
apoderar tr to empower, to authorize || ref — **apoderarse de** to seize, grasp; to take possession of
apodo m nickname
apofonía f ablaut
apogeo m apogee; (fig) height, apogee
apolilla·do -da adj moth-eaten, mothy
apolilladura f moth hole
apolillar tr (la polilla, p.ej., las ropas) to eat || ref to become moth-eaten
apología f eulogy
apoltronar ref to loaf around; to loll, to sprawl
apontizaje m deck-landing
apontizar §60 intr to deck-land
apoplejía f apoplexy
apopléti·co -ca adj & mf apoplectic
aporcar §73 tr (las hortalizas) to hill

aporrear *tr* to beat, to club, to cudgel; to annoy ‖ *ref* to drudge, to slave
aportación *f* contribution; dowry
aportar *tr* to contribute; to bring; to lead; (*como dote*) to bring ‖ *intr* to show up; to reach port
aporte *m* contribution
aposentar *tr* to put up, to lodge ‖ *ref* to take lodging
aposento *m* lodging; room; inn
apostadero *m* stand, post; naval station
apostar *tr* to post, to station ‖ §61 *tr* to bet, to wager ‖ *intr* to bet; to compete
apostilla *f* note, comment
apóstol *m* apostle
apóstrofe *m* & *f* apostrophe (*words addressed to absent person*)
apóstrofo *m* apostrophe (*written sign*)
apostura *f* neatness, spruceness; bearing, carriage
apoyabra·zos *m* (*pl* -zos) armrest
apoyali·bros *m* (*pl* -bros) book end
apoyar *tr* to support, hold up; to lean, rest; to abet, back ‖ *intr* & *ref* to lean, rest, be supported
apoyatura *f* (mus) grace note
apoyo *m* support, prop; backing, approval
apreciable *adj* appreciable; estimable
apreciación *f* appraisal
apreciar *tr* to appreciate; to appraise; to esteem
aprecio *m* appreciation, esteem
aprehender *tr* to apprehend, catch; to think, conceive
aprehensión *f* apprehension
aprehensi·vo -va *adj* apprehensive
aprehensor *m* captor
apremiar *tr* to press, urge; to compel, force; to hurry; to harass; (*a un deudor*) to dun ‖ *intr* to be urgent
apremio *m* pressure; urgency; compulsion; oppression; surtax for late payment; (*demanda de pago*) dun
aprender *tr* & *intr* to learn
apren·diz -diza *mf* apprentice; **aprendiz de imprenta** printer's devil
aprendizaje *m* apprenticeship; **pagar el aprendizaje** (coll) to pay for one's inexperience
aprensar *tr* to press; to oppress
aprensión *f* apprehension; misgiving, prejudice
aprensi·vo -va *adj* apprehensive
apresar *tr* to grasp, to seize; to capture
aprestador *m* primer
aprestar *tr* to prepare; (*tejidos*) to process; to prime; to size ‖ *ref* to get ready
apresto *m* preparation; equipment; priming; sizing
apresurar *tr* & *ref* to hurry, to hasten
apretadera *f* strap, rope; **apretaderas** (coll) pressure
apreta·do -da *adj* compact, tight; close, intimate; dense, thick; difficult, dangerous; (coll) mean, stingy; **estar muy apretado** (coll) to be in a bad way
apretar §2 *tr* to tighten; to squeeze; to

pinch; to hug; to harass, to importune; to afflict, to beset; (*un botón*) to press; (*los puños*) to clench; (*los dientes*) to grit; (*la mano*) to shake ‖ *intr* to pinch; to insist; to get worse; to push hard, press forward; **apretar a correr** to start running; **apretar con** (coll) to close in on ‖ *ref* to grieve, be distressed; to crowd
apretón *m* pressure, squeeze; struggle; dash, run; **apretón de manos** handshake
apretura *f* crush, jam; tightness; fix, trouble; need, want
aprietarropa *m* clothespin
aprieto *m* crush, jam; fix
aprisa *adv* fast, quickly
aprisco *m* sheepfold
aprisionar *tr* to imprison; to bind, tie; to shackle
aprobación *f* approbation, approval; pass, passing grade
aproba·do -da *adj* excellent ‖ *m* pass
aprobar §61 *tr* & *intr* to approve; to pass
aprontar *tr* to hand over without delay; to expedite
apropia·do -da *adj* appropriate, fitting, proper
apropiar *tr* to hand over; to fit, adapt ‖ *ref* to appropriate; to preëmpt
aprovechable *adj* available, usable
aprovecha·do -da *adj* thrifty; stingy; diligent; well-spent ‖ *mf* opportunist
aprovechar *tr* to make good use of, take advantage of; (*una caída de agua*) to harness ‖ *intr* to be useful; to progress, improve ‖ *ref* — **aprovecharse de** to avail oneself of, to take advantage of
aprovisionar *tr* to provision, supply, furnish
aproxima·do -da *adj* approximate, rough
aproximar *tr* to bring near; to approximate ‖ *ref* to come near; to approximate
aptitud *f* aptitude; suitability
ap·to -ta *adj* apt; suitable
apuesta *f* bet, wager
apues·to -ta *adj* neat, spruce, elegant ‖ *f* see **apuesta**
apulgarar *ref* to become mildewed
apuntador *m* (theat) prompter
apuntalar *tr* to prop up, underpin
apuntar *tr* to point; to point at; to aim; to aim at; to take note of; to sharpen; to stitch, to darn, to patch; to correct; to prompt; to stake, to put up; (theat) to prompt ‖ *intr* to begin to appear; to dawn ‖ *ref* (*el vino*) to begin to turn sour; to register; (coll) to get tipsy
apunte *m* note; rough sketch; stake; (coll) rogue, rascal; (theat) cue
apuñalar *tr* & *intr* to stab
apuñear *tr* to punch
apura·do -da *adj* needy, hard up; difficult, dangerous; (coll) hurried, rushed
apurar *tr* to purify, refine; to clear up, verify; to finish; to drain, use up,

exhaust; to hurry, press; to annoy || *ref* to worry, grieve; to exert oneself, to strive

apuro *m* need, want; grief, sorrow; (Am) haste, urgency; **apuros** financial embarrassment

aquejar *tr* to grieve, afflict

aquel, aquella *adj dem* (*pl* **aquellos, aquellas**) that, that . . . yonder

aquél, aquélla *pron dem* (*pl* **aquéllos, aquéllas**) that; that one, that one yonder; the one; the former || *m* (coll) charm, appeal

aquelarre *m* witches' Sabbath

aquello *pron dem* that; that thing, that matter

aquende *adv* on this side || *prep* on this side of

aquerenciar *ref* to become fond or attached

aquí *adv* here; **aquí dentro** in here; **de aquí en adelante** from now on; **por aquí** this way

aquiescencia *f* acquiescence

aquietar *tr* to quiet, to calm

aquilatar *tr* to assay; to check; to refine

Aquiles *m* Achilles

aquilón *m* north wind

ara *f* altar; altar slab; **en aras de** for the sake of

árabe *adj* Arab, Arabian; (archit) Moresque || *mf* Arab, Arabian || *m* (idioma) Arabic

Arabia, la Arabia

arábi·go -ga *adj* Arabian, Arabic || *m* (idioma) Arabic; **estar en arábigo** (coll) to be Greek

aracanga *f* macaw

arado *m* plow

Aragón *m* Aragon

arago·nés -nesa *adj & mf* Aragonese

arancel *m* tariff

arancela·rio -ria *adj* tariff, customs

arándano *m* whortleberry; **arándano agrio** cranberry

arandela *f* bobèche; (mach) washer

araña *f* spider; chandelier

arañar *tr* to scratch; to scrape; (coll) to scrape together

arañazo *m* scratch

araño *m* scratching

aráquida *f* peanut

arar *tr* to plow

arbitraje *m* arbitration

arbitrar *tr & intr* to arbitrate; to referee; to umpire

arbitra·rio -ria *adj* arbitrary

arbitrio *m* free will; means, ways; **arbitrios** excise taxes

arbitrista *mf* wild-eyed dreamer

árbi·tro -tra *mf* arbiter; referee || *m* umpire

árbol *m* tree; axle, shaft; **árbol del caucho** rubber plant; **árbol de levas** camshaft; **árbol de mando** drive shaft; **árbol de Navidad** Christmas tree; **árbol motor** drive shaft

arbola·do -da *adj* wooded; (mar) high || *m* woodland

arboleda *f* grove

arbollón *m* sewer, drain

arbotante *m* flying buttress

arbusto *m* shrub

arca *f* chest, coffer; tank; ark; **arca de agua** water tower; **arca de la alianza** ark of the covenant; **arca de Noé** ark, Noah's ark

arcada *f* arcade; archway; stroke of bow; **arcadas** retching

arcai·co -ca *adj* archaic

arcaísmo *m* archaism

arcaizante *adj* obsolescent

arcángel *m* archangel

arca·no -na *adj & m* secret

arcar §73 *tr* to arch

arce *m* maple tree

arcilla *f* clay; **arcilla figulina** potter's clay

arco *m* arch; (*de cuna o mecedor*) rocker; (elec, geom) arc; (mus) bow; **arco iris** rainbow; **arco triunfal** triumphal arch; memorial arch

arcón *m* large chest; bin, bunker

archiduque *m* archduke

archienemigo *m* archenemy

archipiélago *m* archipelago; (coll) mass, entanglement || **Archipiélago** *m* Aegean Sea

archiva·dor -dora *mf* file clerk || *m* filing cabinet; letter file

archivar *tr* to file; to file away; (coll) to hide away

archivero *m* city clerk

archivo *m* archives; files; filing; (Col) office

ardentía *f* heartburn; (*en las olas de la mar*) phosphorescence

arder *tr* to burn || *intr* to burn; to blaze; **estar que arde** to be coming to a head || *ref* to burn up

ardid *m* artifice, trick, wile

ardi·do -da *adj* burnt-up; bold, intrepid; (Am) angry

ardiendo *adj invar* burning

ardiente *adj* ardent; fiery, passionate; burning, hot

ardilla *f* squirrel; **ardilla de tierra** gopher; **ardilla ladradora** prairie dog; **ardilla listada** chipmunk

ardillón *m* gopher

ardite *m* old Spanish coin of little value; **no me importa un ardite** (coll) I don't care a hang; **no valer un ardite** (coll) to be not worth a straw

ardor *m* ardor; eagerness, fervor, zeal; vehemence; courage, dash

ardoro·so -sa *adj* fiery, enthusiastic; balky, restive

ar·duo -dua *adj* arduous, difficult

área *f* area; small plot

arena *f* sand; grit; arena; **arena movediza** quicksand; **arenas** arena; (pathol) stones

arenal *m* sandy place; quicksand

arenga *f* harangue

arengar *tr & intr* to harangue

arenis·co -ca *adj* sandy, gritty; sand || *f* sandstone

areno·so -sa *adj* sandy

arenque *m* herring

areómetro *m* hydrometer

arepa *f* (Am) corn griddle cake

arete *m* eardrop, earring

arfada *f* (naut) pitching

arfar *intr* (naut) to pitch

argadijo or **argadillo** *m* bobbin, reel; (coll) restless fellow

argado *m* prank, trick, artifice

argamasa *f* mortar

argamasar *tr* to mortar, to plaster; *(los materiales de construcción)* to mix

árgana *f* (mach) crane; **árganas** panniers

Argel *f* Algiers

Argelia *f* Algeria

argeli·no -na *adj* & *mf* Algerian

argentar *tr* to silver

argenti·no -na *adj* & *mf* Argentine, Argentinean || **la Argentina** Argentina, the Argentine

argolla *f* large iron ring; *(que se pone en la nariz a un animal)* ring; (Am) engagement ring

argonauta *m* Argonaut

argucia *f* subtlety; trick

argüir §6 *tr* to argue, argue for; to prove; to accuse || *ref* to argue, to dispute

argumenta·dor -dora *adj* argumentative || *mf* arguer

argumentar *tr* to argue for; to prove || *intr* & *ref* to argue, dispute

argumento *m* argument

aria *f* (mus) aria

aridez *f* aridity, dryness

ári·do -da *adj* arid; *(aburrido, falto de interés)* dry

ariete *m* battering ram; **ariete hidráulico** hydraulic ram

arimez *m* projection

a·rio -ria *adj* & *mf* Aryan || *f* see **aria**

aris·co -ca *adj* churlish, surly, evasive; *(caballo)* vicious

arista *f* edge; *(intersección de dos planos)* ridge; *(del grano de trigo)* beard; **arista de encuentro** (archit) groin

aristocracia *f* aristocracy

aristócrata *mf* aristocrat

aristocráti·co -ca *adj* aristocratic

Aristóteles *m* Aristotle

aristotéli·co -ca *adj* & *mf* Aristotelian

aritméti·co -ca *adj* arithmetical || *mf* arithmetician || *f* arithmetic

arlequín *m* harlequin

arma *f* arm, weapon; **alzarse en armas** to rise up, rebel; **arma blanca** steel blade; **arma corta** pistol; **arma de fuego** firearm; **jugar a las armas** to fence; **sobre las armas** under arms

armada *f* fleet, armada; navy

armadía *f* raft, float

armadijo *m* trap, snare

arma·do -da *adj* armed; *(hormigón)* reinforced || *f* see **armada**

arma·dor -dora *m* assembler || *m* recruiter of fishermen and whalers

armadura *f* armor; framework; skeleton; (elec) armature; *(de imán)* keeper

armamento *m* armament

armar *tr* to arm; *(un arma)* to load; *(una bayoneta)* to fix; to mount, assemble; to build; to equip; *(el hormigón)* to reinforce; *(una nave)* to fit out; *(caballero)* to dub; (coll) to start, stir up; **armarla** (coll) to start

a row || *ref* to arm oneself; to get ready; (Am) to balk

armario *m* closet, wardrobe; **armario botiquín** medicine cabinet; **armario de luna** wardrobe with mirror; **armario frigorífico** refrigerator

armatoste *m* hulk

armazón *f* frame; assemblage; skeleton

armella *f* screw eye, eyebolt

arme·nio -nia *adj* & *mf* Armenian || **Armenia** *f* Armenia

armería *f* arms shop; arms museum; arms

armero *m* gunsmith; *(para las armas)* rack

armiño *m* ermine

armisticio *m* armistice

armonía *f* harmony

armóni·co -ca *adj* & *m* harmonic || *f* harmonica; **armónica de boca** mouth organ

armonio·so -sa *adj* harmonious

armonizar §60 *tr* & *intr* to harmonize

arnés *m* armor, coat of mail; harness; **arneses** harness, trappings; outfit, equipment; accessories

aro *m* hoop; rim; **aro de émbolo** piston ring

aroma *m* aroma, fragrance

aromáti·co -ca *adj* aromatic

arpa *f* harp

arpar *tr* to claw, scratch; to tear, rend

arpegio *m* arpeggio

arpeo *m* grappling iron

arpía *f* harpy; (coll) shrew, jade

arpillera *f* burlap, sackcloth

arpista *mf* harpist

arpón *m* harpoon

arponear *tr* & *intr* to harpoon

arqueada *f* (mus) bow

arquear *tr* to arch; *(la lana)* to beat; *(una nave)* to gauge; to audit || *intr* to retch || *ref* to bow

arqueología *f* archeology

arquería *f* arcade

arquero *m* archer, bowman

arquitecto *m* architect

arquitectóni·co -ca *adj* architectural

arquitectura *f* architecture

arrabal *m* suburb; **arrabales** outskirts

arracada *f* earring with pendant

arracimar *ref* to cluster, to bunch

arraiga·do -da *adj* deep-rooted; property-owning, landed

arraigar §44 *tr* to establish, to strengthen || *intr* to take root || *ref* to take root; to become settled

arraigo *m* taking root; stability; property, real estate

arramblar *tr* to cover with sand or gravel; to sweep away

arrancadero *m* starting point

arrancar §73 *tr* to root up, pull out, pull up; to snatch, to wrest; *(lágrimas)* to draw forth || *intr* to start; to set sail; (coll) to leave; to originate

arranque *m* pull; fit, impulse; jerk, sudden start; sally, outburst; (aut) start, starter; **arranque a mano** (aut) hand cranking; **arranque automático** (aut) self-starter

arrapiezo *m* rag, tatter; (coll) whippersnapper

arras *fpl* earnest money, pledge; dowry

arrasar *tr* to level; to wreck, to demolish; to fill to the brim || *intr* to clear up || *ref* to clear up; to fill up

arrastra·do -da *adj* (coll) mean, crooked || *mf* (coll) wretch, crook

arrastrar *tr* to drag, drag along; to drag down; to impel || *intr* to drag, to trail; to crawl, creep || *ref* to drag, to trail; to crawl, creep; to drag on; to cringe

arrastre *m* drag; crawl; washout; influence; haulage; (*influencia política y social*) (Cuba, Mex) drag

arrayán *m* myrtle

arre *interj* gee!, get up!

arreador *m* muleteer; (SAm) whip

arrear *tr* to drive || *intr* (coll) to hurry || *ref* to lose all one's money

arrebata·do -da *adj* rash, reckless; (*color del rostro*) flushed, ruddy

arrebatar *tr* to snatch; to carry away; to attract; to move, to stir || *ref* to be carried away, to be overcome

arrebatiña *f* scuffle, scramble; **andar a la arrebatiña** (coll) to scramble

arrebato *m* rage, fury; ecstasy, rapture

arrebol *m* (*de las nubes*) red; (*de las mejillas*) rosiness; (*afeite*) rouge; **arreboles** red clouds

arrebozar §60 *tr* to muffle || *ref* to muffle one's face

arrebujar *tr* to jumble together; to wrap || *ref* to wrap oneself up

arreciar *intr & ref* to grow worse; to become more violent; to grow stronger

arrecife *m* stone-paved road; dike; reef; **arrecife de coral** coral reef

arredrar *tr* to drive back; to frighten || *ref* to draw back; to shrink; to be frightened

arregazar §60 *tr* to tuck up

arreglar *tr* to adjust, regulate, settle; to arrange; to fix, repair || *ref* to adjust, settle; to arrange; to conform; **arreglárselas** (coll) to manage, to make out

arreglo *m* adjustment, regulation, settlement; arrangement; order, rule; agreement; **con arreglo a** in accordance with

arregostar *ref* (coll) to take a liking

arregosto *m* (coll) liking, taste

arrellanar *ref* to loll, to sprawl; to like one's work

arremangar *tr* (*las mangas*) to turn up; (*la ropa*) to tuck up || *ref* to turn up one's sleeves; to tuck up one's dress; (coll) to take a firm stand

arremeter *tr* to attack, assail; (*un caballo*) to spur || *intr* to attack; to be offensive to look at; **arremeter contra** to light into, sail into

arremetida *f* attack; (*de un caballo*) sudden start; push; short, wild run

arremolinar *ref* to crowd, mill around; to whirl

arrendajo *m* (orn) jay; (coll) mimic

arrendar §2 *tr* to rent; (*una caballería*) to tie || *ref* to rent, be rented

arreo *m* adornment; (SAm) drove; **arreos** harness, trappings

arrepenti·do -da *adj* repentant || *mf* penitent

arrepentimiento *m* repentance

arrepentir §68 *ref* to repent, be repentant; **arrepentirse de** (*p.ej., un pecado*) to repent

arrequives *mpl* finery; (coll) attendant circumstances

arresta·do -da *adj* bold, daring

arrestar *tr* to arrest || *ref* to rush boldly

arresto *m* arrest; boldness, daring; **bajo arresto** under arrest

arrezagar §44 *tr* to tuck up

arriada *f* flood

arriar §77 *tr* to flood; (naut) to lower, to strike; (naut) to slacken || *ref* to be flooded

arriba *adv* up, upward; above; upstairs; uptown; on top; **arriba de** up; **de arriba abajo** from top to bottom; from beginning to end; superciliously; **más arriba** farther up; **río arriba** upstream || *interj* up with . . .!

arribada *f* arrival (*by sea*); **de arribada** (naut) emergency

arribar *intr* to put into port; to arrive; (naut) to fall off to leeward; to recover, make a comeback

arribista *adj & mf* parvenu, upstart

arribo *m* arrival

arricete *m* shoal, bar

arriendo *m* rent, rental; lease

arriero *m* muleteer

arriesga·do -da *adj* dangerous, risky; bold, daring

arriesgar §44 *tr* to risk, jeopardize || *ref* to take a risk

arrimadillo *m* wainscot

arrimar *tr* to bring close, move up; (*un golpe*) to give; to abandon, neglect; to give up; to get rid of || *ref* to come close, move up; to snuggle up; to lean; to depend

arrinconar *tr* to corner; to put aside; to abandon, neglect; to get rid of || *ref* to live in seclusion

arrisca·do -da *adj* enterprising; brisk, spirited; craggy

arriscar §73 *tr* to risk || *ref* to take a risk; (*las reses*) to plunge over a cliff

arrisco *m* risk

arrivista *adj & mf* parvenu, upstart

arrizar §60 *tr* to reef

arroba *f* Spanish weight of about 25 pounds

arrobar *tr* to entrance, to enrapture || *ref* to be enraptured

arrobo *m* ecstasy, rapture

arroce·ro -ra *adj* rice || *mf* rice grower; rice merchant

arrocinar *tr* to bestialize || *ref* to become bestialized; to fall madly in love

arrodajar *ref* (CAm) to squat down with one's legs crossed

arrodillar *ref* to kneel, to kneel down

arrogancia *f* arrogance

arrogante adj arrogant

arrogar §44 tr to adopt || ref to arrogate to oneself

arrojadi·zo -za adj for throwing, projectile

arroja·do -da adj bold, fearless, rash

arrojalla·mas m (pl **-mas**) flame thrower

arrojar tr to throw, to hurl; to emit; to bring forth; to yield || ref to rush, rush forward

arrojo m boldness, fearlessness, rashness

arrollado m (elec) coil

arrolla·dor -dora adj sweeping, devastating

arrollamiento m winding

arrollar tr to roll; to roll up; to wind, to coil; (al enemigo) to rout; to dumbfound; (coll) to knock down, to run over

arropar tr to wrap, to wrap up || ref to bundle up

arrope m grape syrup; honey syrup

arropía f taffy

arrostrar tr to face; to like || intr — **arrostrar con** or **por** to face, to resist || ref to rush into the fight

arroyada f gully; flood, freshet

arroyo m stream, brook; gutter; street; (de lágrimas, sangre, etc.) stream

arroz m rice

arrufar tr to sic, to incite

arruga f wrinkle; crease, rumple

arrugar §44 tr to wrinkle; to crease, rumple; (la frente) to knit || ref to wrinkle; to crease, rumple; to shrink, shrivel

arruinar tr to ruin || ref to go to ruin

arrullar tr to sing to sleep, to lull to sleep; (coll) to court, to woo || intr to coo || ref to coo; (las palomas) to bill

arrullo m billing and cooing; lullaby

arrumaje m stowage; ballast

arrumar tr to stow || ref to become overcast

arrumbar tr to cast aside, to neglect; to silence; (una costa) to determine the lay of || intr (naut) to take bearings || ref to get seasick; (naut) to take bearings

arsenal m arsenal, armory; dockyard, shipyard

arsénico m arsenic

art. abbr **artículo**

arte m & f art; trick; knack; fishing gear; **artes y oficios** arts and crafts; **bellas artes** fine arts; **no tener arte ni parte en** to have nothing to do with

artefacto m artifact; appliance, device, contrivance; **artefactos de alumbrado** lighting fixtures; **artefactos sanitarios** bathroom fixtures

artemisa f sagebrush

arteria f artery

artería f craftiness, cunning

arte·ro -ra adj crafty, cunning, sly

artesa f trough; Indian canoe

artesanía f craftsmanship

artesa·no -na mf artisan, craftsman || f craftswoman

artesón m kitchen tub; coffer, caisson (in ceiling)

árti·co -ca adj arctic

articulación f articulation; (de huesos) joint; **articulación universal** universal joint

articular tr to articulate

articulista mf feature writer

artículo m article; item; joint; (en un diccionario) entry; **artículo de fondo** leader, editorial; **artículos de consumo** consumers' goods; **artículos de deporte** sporting goods; **artículos de primera necesidad** basic commodities; **artículos para caballeros** men's furnishings

artífice mf artificer; craftsman

artificial adj artificial

artificio m artifice; workmanship; appliance, device; cunning; trick, ruse

artificio·so -sa adj ingenious, skillful; cunning, scheming, deceptive

artilugio m (coll) contraption, jigger

artillería f artillery

artillero m artilleryman, gunner

artimaña f trap; (coll) trick, cunning

artista mf artist

artísti·co -ca adj artistic

artolas fpl mule chair, cacolet

artríti·co -ca adj & mf arthritic

artritis f arthritis

arúspice m diviner, soothsayer

arveja f vetch, tare; (Chile) pea

arzobispo m archbishop

arzón m saddletree; **arzón delantero** saddlebow; **arzón trasero** cantle

as m ace; **as de fútbol** football star; **as de la pantalla** movie star; **as del volante** speed king

asa f handle; juice; **en asas** with arms akimbo

asa·do -da adj roasted; **bien asado** well done; **poco asado** rare || m roast

asador m spit

asadura f entrails

asalaria·do -da mf wage earner

asaltar tr to assail, to assault, to storm; to overtake, overcome

asalto m assault, attack; (box) round; (mil) storm; **tomar por asalto** to take by storm

asamblea f assembly

asar tr to roast || ref to be burning up

asbesto m asbestos

ascendencia f ancestry

ascendente adj ascending; up

ascender §51 tr to promote || intr to ascend, go up; to be promoted; **ascender a** to amount to

ascendiente adj ascending; up || mf ancestor || m ascendancy, upper hand

ascensión f ascension, ascent

ascenso m ascent; promotion

ascensor m elevator; freight elevator

ascensorista mf elevator operator

asceta mf ascetic

ascéti·co -ca adj ascetic

asco m disgust, nausea, loathing; **dar asco** (coll) to turn the stomach; **estar hecho un asco** (coll) to be filthy; **hacer ascos de** (coll) to turn one's nose up at; **ser un asco** (coll) to be contemptible; (coll) to be worthless

ascua f ember, live coal; **estar sobre ascuas** (coll) to be on needles and pins || **ascuas** interj (coll) ouch!

asea·do -da adj clean, neat, tidy

asear tr & ref to clean up, tidy up

asechamiento m or **asechanza** f snare, trap

asechar tr to set a trap for

asediar tr to besiege; to harass

asedio m siege

asegundar tr to repeat right away

aseguración f insurance policy

asegura·dor -dora mf insurer, underwriter

asegurar tr to fasten, secure; to assure; to assert; to seize; to imprison; (garantizar por un precio contra determinado accidente o pérdida) to insure || ref to make sure; to take out insurance

asemejar tr to make like; to compare; to resemble || ref to be similar

asenso m assent; **dar asenso a** to believe

asentada f sitting; **de una asentada** at one sitting

asentaderas fpl (coll) buttocks

asentadillas — a asentadillas sidesaddle

asenta·do -da adj sedate; stable || f see **asentada**

asentador m strap, razor strap

asentar §2 tr to seat; to place; to establish; to tamp down, to level; to hone, sharpen; to note down; (un golpe) to impart; (en la mente de uno) to impress; to affirm; to suppose || intr to be becoming || ref to sit down; to be established, to establish oneself; to settle

asentimiento m assent

asentir §68 intr to assent

aseo m cleanliness, neatness, tidiness; care; toilet

asépti·co -ca adj aseptic

aseptizar §60 tr to purify, make aseptic

asequible adj accessible, obtainable

aserción f assertion

aserradero m sawmill

aserra·dor -dora mf sawyer; (coll) fiddler || f power saw

aserraduras fpl sawdust

aserrar §2 tr to saw

aserrín m sawdust

aserto m assertion

asesinar tr to assassinate, to murder

asesinato m assassination, murder

asesi·no -na adj murderous || mf assassin, murderer

asesorar tr to advise || ref to seek advice; to get advice

asestar tr to aim; to shoot; (un golpe) to deal

aseveración f assertion, declaration

aseverar tr to assert, to declare

asfaltar tr to asphalt

asfalto m asphalt

asfixia f asphyxiation

asfixiar tr to asphyxiate

así adv so, thus; **así . . . como** both . . . and; **así como** as soon as; as well as;

así que as soon as; with the result that; **así y todo** even so, anyhow; **por decirlo así** so to speak; **y así sucesivamente** and so on

Asia f Asia; **el Asia Menor** Asia Minor

asiáti·co -ca adj & mf Asian, Asiatic

asidero m handle; occasion, pretext

así·duo -dua adj assiduous; frequent, persistent

asiento m seat; site; (de un edificio) settling; (de una botella, una silla, etc.) bottom; sediment; list, roll; wisdom, maturity; **asiento de rejilla** cane seat; **asiento lanzable** (aer) ejection seat; **asientos** buttocks; **planchar el asiento** (Am) to be a wallflower; **tome Vd. asiento** have a seat

asignación f assignment; salary; allowance

asignar tr to assign

asignatura f course, subject

asila·do -da mf inmate

asilar tr to shelter; to place in an asylum; to silo || ref to take refuge; to be placed in an asylum

asilo m asylum; shelter, refuge; (para menesterosos) home; **asilo de huérfanos** orphan asylum; **asilo de locos** insane asylum; **asilo de pobres** poorhouse

asilla f fastener; collarbone; **asillas** shoulder pole

asimetría f asymmetry

asimilar tr to compare; to take in || intr to be alike || ref to assimilate; **asimilarse a** to resemble

asimismo adv also, likewise

asir §7 tr to grasp, seize || intr to take root || ref to take hold; to fight, to grapple; **asirse a** or **de** to cling to

Asiria f Assyria

asi·rio -ria adj & mf Assyrian

asistencia f attendance; assistence; reward; audience, persons present; welfare, social work; (Mex) sitting room, parlor; **asistencias** allowance, support

asistenta f charwoman, cleaning woman

asistente adj attendant; present || m assistant, helper; bystander, spectator, person present; (mil) orderly

asistir tr to assist, help; to attend; to serve, wait on || intr to be present; **asistir a** to be present at, to attend

asma f asthma

asna f she-ass, jenny ass; **asnas** rafters

asnal adj donkey; (coll) brutish

asno m ass, donkey, jackass

asociación f association

asocia·do -da adj associated; associate || mf associate, partner

asociar tr to associate; to take as partner || ref to become associated; to become a partner; to become partners

asolamiento m razing, destruction

asolar tr to parch, burn || ref to become parched || §61 tr to raze, destroy

asolear tr to sun || ref to bask; to get sunburned

asomar *tr* (*p.ej.*, *la cabeza*) to show, to stick out ‖ *intr* to begin to show or appear; to show ‖ *ref* to show, to appear; to stick out; to get tipsy

asombradi·zo -za *adj* timid, shy

asombrar *tr* to shade; (*un color*) to darken; to frighten; to astonish, amaze ‖ *ref* to be frightened; to be astonished, be amazed

asombro *m* fright; astonishment

asombro·so -sa *adj* astonishing, amazing

asomo *m* mark, token, sign; appearance; **ni por asomo** nothing of the kind, not by a long shot

asordar *tr* to deafen

aspa *f* X-shaped figure; reel; (*de molino de viento*) wheel, vane; propeller blade

aspar *tr* to reel; to crucify; to annoy, harass ‖ *ref* to writhe; to take great pains

aspaviento *m* fuss, excitement

aspecto *m* aspect

aspereza *f* harshness; roughness; bitterness, sourness; gruffness

asperjar *tr* to sprinkle; to sprinkle with holy water

áspe·ro -ra *adj* harsh; rough; bitter; gruff

áspid *m* asp

aspirador *m* vacuum cleaner; **aspirador de gasolina** (aut) vacuum tank

aspirante *m* applicant, candidate; **aspirante a cabo** private first class; **aspirante a marina** midshipman

aspirar *tr* to suck in, draw in; to inhale ‖ *intr* to aspire; to inhale, to breathe in

aspirina *f* aspirin

asquear *tr* to loathe ‖ *ref* to be nauseated

asquero·so -sa *adj* disgusting, loathsome; nauseating; squeamish

asta *f* spear; shaft; flagpole, staff, mast; antler; (*de toro*) horn; **a media asta** at half-mast; **dejar en las astas del toro** (coll) to leave high and dry

asta·do -da *adj* horned ‖ *m* bull

ástato *m* astatine

aster *m* aster

asterisco *m* asterisk

astil *m* handle; shaft

astilla *f* chip, splinter

astillar *tr & ref* to chip, splinter

Astillejos *mpl* (astr) Castor and Pollux

astillero *m* dockyard, shipyard

astro *m* star, heavenly body; (fig) star, leading light

astrología *f* astrology

astronauta *m* astronaut

astronáuti·co -ca *adj* astronautic ‖ *f* astronautics

astronave *f* spaceship; **astronave tripulada** manned spaceship

astronomía *f* astronomy

astronómi·co -ca *adj* astronomic(al)

astróno·mo -ma *mf* astronomer

astro·so -sa *adj* ill-fated; vile, contemptible; (coll) ragged, shabby

astucia *f* cunning, craftiness; trick

asturia·no -na *adj & mf* Asturian

astu·to -ta *adj* astute, cunning; tricky

asueto *m* day off; (coll) leisure

asumir *tr* to assume, take on

asunción *f* assumption

asunto *m* subject, matter; affair, business; theme; **asuntos internacionales** world affairs

asurar *tr* to burn; to parch; to harass, worry

asurcar §73 *tr* to furrow, to plow

asustadi·zo -za *adj* scary, skittish

asustar *tr* to scare, frighten

atabal *m* kettledrum; timbrel

ataca·do -da *adj* irresolute, undecided; mean, stingy

atacar §73 *tr* to attack; to attach, fasten; to pack, jam; (*un barreno*) to tamp; to corner, to contradict ‖ *intr* to attack

ata·do -da *adj* timid, shy; weak, irresolute; insignificant; cramped ‖ *m* pack, bundle, roll

ataguía *f* cofferdam

atajar *tr* to stop, intercept, interrupt; to partition off ‖ *intr* to take a short cut ‖ *ref* to be abashed

atajo *m* short cut; (*en un escrito*) cut

atalaya *m* guard, lookout ‖ *f* watchtower; elevation

atalayar *tr* to watch from a watchtower; to spy on

atanquía *f* depilatory ointment

atañer §70 *tr* to concern

ataque *m* attack

atar *tr* to tie, fasten

ataracea *f* marquetry, inlaid work

atarantar *tr* to stun, daze

atardecer *m* late afternoon ‖ *v* §22 *intr* to draw toward evening; to happen in the late afternoon

atarea·do -da *adj* busy

atarear *tr* to give an assignment to; to overload with work ‖ *ref* to toil, to work hard, to keep busy

atarjea *f* sewer

atarugar §44 *tr* to peg, to wedge; to plug; to stuff, to fill; (coll) to silence, shut up ‖ *ref* (coll) to become confused

atasajar *tr* to slash, hack; (*carne*) to jerk

atascadero *m* mudhole; (fig) pitfall

atascar §73 *tr* to stop, to stop up, clog, obstruct ‖ *ref* to get stuck; to stuff oneself; to clog, get clogged

atasco *m* sticking, clogging; obstruction

ataúd *m* casket, coffin

ataujía *f* damascene work

ataujiar §77 *tr* to damascene

ataviar §77 *tr* to dress, adorn, deck out

atavío *m* dress, adornment; **atavíos** finery, frippery, chiffons

atediar *tr* to tire, bore

ateísmo *m* atheism

ateísta *mf* atheist

ataleje *m* harness

atemorizar §60 *tr* to frighten

atemperar *tr* to soften, moderate, temper; to adjust, adapt

Atenas *f* Athens

atención *f* attention; **en atención a** in view of

atender §51 *tr* to attend to; to heed, pay attention to; to take care of; (*a los parroquianos*) to wait on

atener §71 *ref* — **atenerse a** to abide by, to rely on

ateniense *adj & mf* Athenian

atenta·do -da *adj* moderate, prudent; cautious ‖ *m* attempt, assault

atentar *tr* to attempt, to try to commit ‖ *intr* — **atentar a** or **contra** (*p.ej., la vida de una persona*) to attempt ‖ §2 *ref* to grope

aten·to -ta *adj* attentive; courteous, polite ‖ *f* favor (*letter*)

atenuar §21 *tr* to extenuate

ate·o -a *adj & mf* atheist

aterciopela·do -da *adj* velvety

ateri·do -da *adj* stiff, numb with cold

aterrada *f* landfall

aterrajar *tr* to thread, to tap

aterraje *m* landing

aterrar *tr* to terrify ‖ §2 *tr* to destroy, demolish; to cover with earth ‖ *intr* to land ‖ *ref* to stand inshore

aterrizaje *m* landing; **aterrizaje a ciegas** blind landing; **aterrizaje aplastado** or **en desplome** pancake landing; **aterrizaje forzoso** emergency landing

aterrizar §60 *intr* to land

aterronar *tr* to make lumpy ‖ *ref* to cake, to lump

aterrorizar §60 *tr* to terrify

atesorar *tr* to treasure; to hoard; (*virtudes, perfecciones*) to possess

atesta·do -da *adj* stuffed, jammed; obstinate, stubborn ‖ *m* certificate

atestar *tr* (law) to attest ‖ §2 & *regular tr* to jam, pack, stuff, cram; (coll) to stuff

atestiguar §10 *tr* to attest, testify, depose

atezar §60 *tr* to tan; to blacken ‖ *ref* to become tanned, become sun-burned

atiborrar *tr* to stuff ‖ *ref* (coll) to stuff, stuff oneself

atiesar *tr* to stiffen; to tighten ‖ *ref* to become stiff; to become tight

atildar *tr* to mark with a tilde, dash, or accent mark; to point out; to find fault with; to tidy up, to trim, to adorn

atina·do -da *adj* careful, keen, wise

atinar *tr* to find, come upon ‖ *intr* to guess, guess right; to be right; to manage

atisbadero *m* peephole

atisbar *tr* to watch, spy on

atisbo *m* glimpse, look, peek

atizar §60 *tr* to stir, to poke; to snuff; to rouse; (*p.ej., un puntapié*) to let go

Atlánti·co -ca *adj & m* Atlantic

at·las *m* (*pl* **-las**) atlas

atleta *mf* athlete

atleticismo *m* athletics

atléti·co -ca *adj* athletic ‖ *f* athletics

atmósfera *f* atmosphere

atmosféri·co -ca *adj* atmospheric

atoar *tr* (naut) to tow

atocinar *tr* (*un cerdo*) to cut up; to make into bacon; (coll) to murder ‖

ref to get angry; to fall madly in love

atocha *f* esparto

atolondra·do -da *adj* confused; scatterbrained

atolondrar *tr* to confuse, bewilder

atolladero *m* mudhole; obstacle, difficulty

atollar *intr & ref* to get stuck, to get stuck in the mud

atómi·co -ca *adj* atomic

átomo *m* atom

atóni·to -ta *adj* astounded, aghast

atontar *tr* to stun; to confuse, bewilder

atorar *tr* to clog, obstruct ‖ *intr & ref* to stick, get stuck; to choke

atormentar *tr* to torment; to torture

atornillar *tr* to screw, screw on

atortolar *tr* to rattle, scare, intimidate

atosigar §44 *tr* to poison; to harass ‖ *ref* to be in a hurry

atrabanca·do -da *adj* overworked; (Mex) hasty, rash; (Ven) deep in debt

atrabancar §73 *tr & intr* to rush through

atrabilia·rio -ria *adj* irascible, grouchy

atracador *m* hold-up man

atracar §73 *tr* to hold up; to bring up; (naut) to bring alongside, to dock; (coll) to stuff ‖ *intr* (naut) to come alongside, to dock ‖ *ref* (coll) to stuff; (Am) to quarrel

atracción *f* attraction; amusement

atraco *m* holdup

atracón *m* (coll) stuffing, gluttony; (Am) fight; (Am) push, shove

atracti·vo -va *adj* attractive ‖ *m* attraction; attractiveness

atraer §75 *tr* to attract

atragantar *tr* to choke down ‖ *ref* to choke; **atragantarse con** to choke on

atraillar §4 *tr* to leash; to master, subdue

atrampar *ref* to fall into a trap; to be stopped up; to stick; to get stuck

atrancar §73 *tr* to bar; to obstruct ‖ *intr* (coll) to stride; (coll) to read falteringly ‖ *ref* to get stuck; (*una ventana*) to stick; (Mex) to stick to one's opinion

atrapamos·cas *m* (*pl* **-cas**) flytrap; (bot) Venus's-flytrap

atrapar *tr* (coll) to trap, to catch; to get, to land; to net

atrás *adv* back, backward; behind; before; previously; **atrás de** back of, behind; **hacerse atrás** to back up, move back; **hacia atrás** backwards; the other way

atrasa·do -da *adj* late; (*reloj*) slow; needy; back; retarded; in arrears; **atrasado de medios** short of funds; **atrasado de noticias** behind the times

atrasar *tr* to slow down; to retard; to set back, to turn back; to delay; to leave behind; to postdate ‖ *intr* to be slow ‖ *ref* to be slow; to lose time; to lag, to stay behind; to be late; to be in debt

atraso *m* delay, slowness; backwardness; lag; **atrasos** arrears, delinquency

atravesar §2 *tr* to cross, to go across; to pierce; to pass through, go through; to put crosswise; to stake, wager ‖ *ref* to butt in; to fight, wrangle; to get stuck

atrayente *adj* attractive

atreguar §10 *tr* to give a truce to; to grant an extension to ‖ *ref* to agree to a truce

atrever *ref* to dare; **atreverse con** or **contra** to be impudent toward

atrevi·do -da *adj* bold, daring; impudent

atrevimiento *m* boldness, daring; impudence

atribuir §20 *tr* to attribute, ascribe ‖ *ref* to assume

atribular *tr* & *ref* to grieve

atributo *m* attribute

atril *m* lectern; music stand

atrincherar *tr* to entrench ‖ *ref* to dig in

atrio *m* hall, vestibule; court, courtyard; parvis

atri·to -ta *adj* contrite

atrocidad *f* atrocity; (coll) enormity

atrofia *f* atrophy

atrofiar *tr* & *ref* to atrophy

atrojar *tr* (*granos*) to garner; (Mex) to befuddle

atrona·do -da *adj* reckless, thoughtless

atronar §61 *tr* to deafen; to stun ‖ *intr* to thunder

atropella·do -da *adj* brusk, violent; hasty; tumultuous

atropellar *tr* to trample; to knock down; to run over; to disregard; to do hurriedly ‖ *intr* & *ref* to act hastily or recklessly

atropello *m* trampling; knocking down; running over; abuse, insult; outrage

a·troz *adj* (*pl* **-troces**) atrocious; (coll) huge, enormous

atto. *abbr* atento

atufar *tr* to anger, irritate ‖ *ref* to get angry; (*el vino*) to turn sour

atún *m* tuna

aturdi·do -da *adj* reckless, harebrained

aturdir *tr* to stun; to perplex, bewilder

atusar *tr* to trim; to smooth ‖ *ref* to dress fancily; (*el bigote*) to twist

audacia *f* audacity

au·daz *adj* (*pl* **-daces**) audacious

audición *f* audition; hearing; concert; listening

audiencia *f* audience, hearing; audience chamber; royal tribunal; provincial high court

audífono *m* hearing aid; earphone

audiofrecuencia *f* audio frequency

audiómetro *m* audiometer

auditor *m* judge advocate; **auditor de guerra** judge advocate (*in army*); **auditor de marina** judge advocate (*in navy*)

auditorio *m* (*concurso de oyentes*) audience; (*local*) auditorium

auge *m* height, acme; boom; vogue; **estar en auge** to be booming

augur *m* augur

augurar *tr* to augur; (Am) to wish ‖ *intr* to augur

augurio *m* augury; (Am) wish

augus·to -ta *adj* august

aula *f* classroom, lecture room; **aula magna** assembly hall

aulaga *f* gorse, furze

aullar §8 *intr* to howl

aullido *m* howl, howling

aúllo *m* howl

aumentar *tr* to augment, increase, enlarge; to promote; (coll) to exaggerate ‖ *intr* & *ref* to augment, increase

aumento *m* augmentation, increase, enlargement; promotion; **ir en aumento** to be on the increase

aun *adv* even; **aun cuando** although

aún *adv* still, yet

aunar §8 *tr* & *ref* to join, unite; to combine, mix

aunque *conj* although, though

aúpa *interj* up!; **de aúpa** (coll) swanky; **los de aúpa** (taur) the picadors

aupar §8 *tr* (coll) to help up; (coll) to extol

aura *f* gentle breeze; breath; popularity; turkey vulture

áure·o -a *adj* gold, golden

aureola *f* halo, aureole

auricular *m* earpiece, receiver; **auricular de casco** headpiece

auriga *m* (poet) coachman, charioteer

aurora *f* aurora, dawn; roseate hue

ausencia *f* absence

ausentar *tr* to send away ‖ *ref* to absent oneself

ausente *adj* absent; absent-minded ‖ *mf* absentee

auspiciar *tr* (Am) to sponsor, foster, back

auspicio *m* auspice; **bajo los auspicios de** under the auspices of

auste·ro -ra *adj* austere; harsh; honest; penitent

Australia *f* Australia

australia·no -na *adj* & *mf* Australian

Austria *f* Austria

austria·co -ca *adj* & *mf* Austrian

austro *m* south wind

auténtica *f* certificate; certification

autenticar §73 *tr* to authenticate

autén·ti·co -ca *adj* authentic; real ‖ *f* see **auténtica**

autillo *m* tawny owl

auto *m* edict; short Biblical play; miracle play; auto; **auto de prisión** commitment, warrant for arrest; **auto sacramental** play in honor of the Sacrament

autoamortizable *adj* self-liquidating

autobanco *m* drive-in bank

autobiografía *f* autobiography

autobombo *m* self-glorification

autobús *m* autobus, bus

autocamión *m* motor truck

autocráti·co -ca *adj* autocratic(al)

autócto·no -na *adj* native, indigenous

autodefensa *f* self-defense

autodeterminación *f* self-determination

autodidac·to -ta *adj* self-taught

autodisciplina *f* self-discipline

autódromo *m* automobile race track

auto-escuela *f* driving school

autógena *f* welding

autogobierno *m* self-government

autografiar §77 *tr* to autograph
autógra·fo -fa *adj & m* autograph
autoguia·do -da *adj* self-guided, homing
automación *f* automation
autómata *m* automaton
automáti·co -ca *adj* automatic
automatización *f* automation
automóvil *m* automobile
automovilista *mf* motorist
autonomía *f* autonomy; cruising radius
autóno·mo -ma *adj* autonomous, independent
autopiano *m* player piano
autopista *f* turnpike, automobile road
autopsia *f* autopsy
au·tor -tora *mf* author; (*de un crimen*) perpetrator || *f* authoress
autoridad *f* authority; pomp, display
autorita·rio -ria *adj & mf* authoritarian
autoriza·do -da *adj* authoritative
autorizar §60 *tr* to authorize; to legalize; to exalt
autorretrato *m* self-portrait
autoservicio *m* self-service
autostop *m* hitchhiking; **viajar en autostop** to hitchhike
autostopista *mf* hitchhiker
auto-teatro *m* drive-in movie theater
autovía *m* railway motor coach || *f* turnpike, automobile road
auxiliar *adj* auxiliary || *mf* auxiliary; aid, helper; substitute teacher || *v* §77 & **regular** *tr* to aid, help, assist; (*a un moribundo*) to attend
auxilio *m* aid, help, assistance; **acudir en auxilio a** or **de** to come to the aid of; **auxilio en carretera** road service; **primeros auxilios** first aid
avahar *tr* to steam; to breathe warmth on || *intr* to steam, give off vapor || *ref* to steam, give off vapor; to warm one's hands with one's breath
aval *m* indorsement; countersignature
avalancha *f* avalanche
avalorar *tr* to estimate; to encourage
avaluación *f* appraisal, valuation
avaluar §21 *tr* to appraise, to estimate
avalúo *m* appraisal, valuation
avance *m* advance; advance payment; (com) balance; (com) estimate; (mov) preview; **avance rápido** (mach, mov) fast forward
avante *adv* (naut) fore
avanza·do -da *adj* advanced; **avanzado de edad** advanced in years || *f* outpost, advance guard
avanzar §60 *tr* to advance, extend; to propose || *intr & ref* to advance; to approach
avanzo *m* balance sheet; estimate
avaricia *f* avarice
avaricio·so -sa *adj* avaricious
avarien·to -ta *adj* avaricious || *mf* miser
ava·ro -ra *adj* miserly || *mf* miser
avasallar *tr* to subject, subjugate, enslave || *ref* to submit
ave *f* bird; fowl; **ave canora** songbird; **ave de corral** barnyard fowl; **ave de mal agüero** Jonah, jinx; **ave de paso** bird of passage; **ave de rapiña** bird of prey; **ave fría** lapwing

avecinar *tr* to bring near || *ref* to approach; to take up residence
avecindar *tr* to domicile || *ref* to become a resident
avejentar *tr & ref* to age prematurely
avejigar §44 *tr, intr & ref* to blister
avellana *f* hazelnut
avellanar *tr* to countersink || *ref* to shrivel, shrivel up
avellano *m* hazel, hazel tree
avemaría *f* Hail Mary, Ave Maria; **al avemaría** at sunset; **en un avemaría** (coll) in a jiffy; **saber como el avemaría** (coll) to have a thorough knowledge of
avena *f* oats
avenar *tr* to drain
avenate *m* gruel, oatmeal gruel
avenencia *f* agreement; deal, bargain
avenida *f* avenue; allée; flood, freshet; gathering, assemblage
aveni·do -da *adj* — **bien avenido** in agreement; **mal avenido** in disagreement || *f* see **avenida**
avenimiento *m* agreement; reconciliation
avenir §79 *tr* to reconcile, bring together || *ref* to be reconciled, to agree; to compromise; to correspond
aventa·dor -dora *mf* winnower || *m* fan
aventaja·do -da *adj* excellent, outstanding; advantageous
aventajar *tr* to advance; to put ahead; to excel || *ref* to advance, win an advantage; to excel
aventar §2 *tr* to fan; to winnow; to scatter to the winds; to blow; (coll) to drive away || *ref* to swell up; (coll) to flee, run away
aventón *m* (Guat, Mex, Peru) push, shove; (*llevada gratuita*) (Mex) free ride; **pedir aventón** (Mex) to hitchhike
aventura *f* adventure; danger, risk
aventura·do -da *adj* hazardous, venturesome
aventurar *tr* to adventure, to venture, to hazard || *ref* to adventure, to take a risk; to venture, to risk
aventure·ro -ra *adj* adventuresome, adventurous || *m* adventurer, soldier of fortune || *f* adventuress
avergonzar §9 *tr* to shame; to embarrass || *ref* to be ashamed; to be embarrassed
avería *f* aviary; breakdown, failure; (com) damage; (naut) average
averiar §77 *tr* to damage || *ref* to suffer damage; to break down
averiguable *adj* ascertainable
averiguar §10 *tr* to ascertain, to find out
aversión *f* aversion, dislike; **cobrar aversión a** to take a dislike for
aves·truz *m* (*pl* **-truces**) ostrich
avezar §60 *tr* to accustom || *ref* to become accustomed
aviación *f* aviation
avia·dor -dora *mf* aviator, flyer || *m* aviator, airman; (mil) airman; **aviador postal** air-mail pilot || *f* aviatrix, airwoman
aviar §77 *tr* to make ready, prepare;

(coll) to equip, provide; **estar, encontrarse** or **quedar aviado** (coll) to be in a mess, be in a jam || *ref* to hurry; (aer) to take off

avia·triz (*pl* **-trices**) aviatrix

avidez *f* avidity, greediness

ávi·do -da *adj* avid, greedy, eager

aviejar *tr* & *ref* to age prematurely

aviento *m* winnowing fork, pitchfork

avie·so -sa *adj* crooked, distorted; evil-minded, perverse

avilantar *ref* to be insolent

avilantez *f* insolence; meanness

avillana·do -da *adj* rustic, boorish

avillanar *tr* to debase, make boorish || *ref* to become boorish

avinagra·do -da *adj* (coll) vinegarish, sour, crabbed

avinagrar *tr* to sour || *ref* to become sour; to turn into vinegar

avío *m* provision; arrangement; (Am) load; **¡al avío!** let's go!; **avíos** equipment, tools, outfit; **avíos de pescar** fishing tackle

avión *m* airplane; (orn) martin; **avión birreactor** twin-jet plane; **avión de caza** pursuit plane; **avión a chorro,** **avión de propulsión a chorro** or **a reacción** jet plane

avión-correo *m* mailplane

avioneta *f* small plane; **avioneta de alquiler** taxiplane

avisaco·ches *m* (*pl* **-ches**) car caller

avisa·do -da *adj* prudent, wise; **mal avisado** rash, thoughtless

avisa·dor -dora *adj* warning || *mf* informer; adviser || *m* electric bell; **avisador de incendio** fire alarm

avisar *tr* to advise, inform; to warn; to report on

aviso *m* advice, information; warning; care, prudence; dispatch boat; (Am) advertisement; **sobre aviso** on the lookout

avispa *f* wasp

avispa·do -da *adj* (coll) brisk, wide-awake

avispar *tr* to spur; (coll) to stir up || *ref* to fret, worry

avispón *m* hornet

avistar *tr* to descry || *ref* to meet, have an interview

avituallar *tr* to supply, provision || *ref* to take in supplies

avivar *tr* to brighten, enlive, revive || *intr* & *ref* to brighten, revive

avizor *adj* watchful, alert || *m* watcher; **avizores** (slang) eyes

avizorar *tr* to watch, spy on || *ref* to hide and watch, to spy

ax *interj* ouch!, ow!

axioma *m* axiom

axiomáti·co -ca *adj* axiomatic

ay *interj* ay!, alas! **¡ay de mí!** woe is me! || *m* sigh

aya *f* nurse, governess

ayer *adj* & *m* yesterday

ayo *m* tutor

ayuda *m* valet; **ayuda de cámara** valet de chambre || *f* help, aid; enema

ayudanta *f* assistant; **ayudanta de cocina** kitchenmaid

ayudante *m* aid, assistant; adjutant; **ayudante de campo** aide-de-camp

ayudar *tr* to aid, help, assist

ayunar *intr* to fast

ayu·no -na *adj* fasting; uninformed; **en ayunas** or **en ayuno** fasting; before breakfast; uninformed; missing the point || *m* fast, fasting

ayuntamiento *m* town or city council; town or city hall; sexual intercourse

azabacha·do -da *adj* jet, jet-black

azabache *m* jet; **azabaches** jet trinkets

aza·cán -cana *adj* menial || *mf* drudge || *m* water carrier

azada *f* hoe

azadón *m* hoe; grub hoe; **azadón de peto** or **de pico** mattock

azadonar *tr* to hoe

azafata *f* air hostess, stewardess; lady of the queen's wardrobe

azafate *m* wicker tray

azafrán *m* saffron

azafrana·do -da *adj* saffron

azafranar *tr* to saffron

azahar *m* orange or lemon blossom

azar *m* chance, hazard; accident, misfortune; fate, destiny; losing card; losing throw; (*persona o cosa que traen mala suerte*) Jonah

azarar *ref* to go awry; to get rattled

azaro·so -sa *adj* hazardous, risky; unlucky

ázi·mo -ma *adj* unleavened

azófar *m* brass

azoga·do -da *adj* fidgety, restless || *m* quicksilver foil; **temblar como un azogado** (coll) to shake like a leaf

azogar §44 *tr* (*un espejo*) to silver || *ref* to have mercury poisoning; (coll) to shake, become agitated

azogue *m* quicksilver; market place; (coll) mirror

azor *m* goshawk

azorar *tr* to abash; to excite, stir up

Azores *fpl* Azores

azotar *tr* to whip, to scourge; to beat; to flail; to beat down upon

azote *m* whip; lash; (fig) scourge; **azotes y galeras** (coll) tiresome fare

azotea *f* flat roof, roof terrace

azteca *adj* & *mf* Aztec

azúcar *m* sugar; **azúcar de caña** cane sugar; **azúcar de remolacha** beet sugar

azucarar *tr* to sugar, to sugarcoat; (coll) to sugar over

azucare·ro -ra *adj* sugar || *m* sugar bowl

azucena *f* Madonna lily, white lily

azufrar *tr* to sulphur

azufre *m* sulfur; brimstone

azul *adj* & *m* blue; **azul marino** navy blue

azular *tr* to color blue, to dye blue

azulear *intr* to turn blue

azulejar *tr* to tile, to cover with tiles

azulejo *m* glazed colored tile; (orn) roller; (orn) indigo bunting; (orn) bee eater

azuzar §60 *tr* to sic; (coll) to tease, incite

B, b (be) *f* second letter of the Spanish alphabet

B. *abbr* Beato, **Bueno**

baba *f* drivel, spittle, slobber; *(de culebras, peces, etc.)* slime

babear *intr* to slobber, to drivel; to froth, foam

babel *m & f* (coll) bedlam, confusion; **estar en babel** (coll) to be daydreaming

babero *m* bib

Babia *f* — **estar en Babia** (coll) to be daydreaming

babieca *adj* (coll) silly, simple ‖ *mf* (coll) simpleton

Babilonia *f* (*imperio*) Babylonia; *(ciudad)* Babylon

babilóni·co -ca *adj* Babylonian

babilo·nio -nia *adj & mf* Babylonian ‖ *f* see **Babilonia**

bable *m* Asturian dialect; patois

babor *m* (naut) port

babosa *f* slug

babosear *tr* to slobber over ‖ *intr* to slobber

babo·so -sa *adj* slobbery; *(con las damas)* (coll) mushy ‖ *m* (CAm) scoundrel ‖ *f* see **babosa**

babucha *f* slipper, mule

babuino *m* baboon

bacalao or **bacallao** *m* codfish

baceta *f* (cards) widow

bacía *f* basin, vessel; shaving dish

bacilo *m* bacillus

bacín *m* chamber pot

Baco *m* Bacchus

bacteria *f* bacterium

bacteria·no -na *adj* bacterial

bacteriología *f* bacteriology

bacteriólo·go -ga *mf* bacteriologist

báculo *m* staff; crook; (fig) staff, comfort; **báculo pastoral** crozier

bache *m* hole, rut; blip; **bache aéreo** air pocket

bachi·ller -llera *adj* garrulous ‖ *mf* garrulous person ‖ **bachiller** *m* bachelor

bachillerar *tr* to confer the bachelor's degree on ‖ *ref* to receive the bachelor's degree

bachillerato *m* baccalaureate, bachelor's degree

bachillerear *intr* (coll) to babble, prattle

bachillería *f* (coll) babble, prattle; (coll) gossip

badajo *m* clapper

badana *f* (dressed) sheepskin; **zurrarle a uno la badana** (coll) to tan someone's hide

badén *m* gully, gutter

badil *m* fire shovel

badulaque *m* (coll) nincompoop

bagaje *m* beast of burden; (mil) baggage

bagatela *f* trinket; triviality; (Chile, Peru) pinball

bagazo *m* waste pulp, bagasse

bagre *adj* (Bol, Col) showy, gaudy; (CAm) sly, slick; (SAm) coarse, ill-bred; (Mex) stupid ‖ *m* catfish

bahía *f* bay

bahorrina *f* (coll) slop; (coll) riffraff

bailable *adj* for dancing ‖ *m* ballet

bailadero *m* dance floor, dance hall

baila·dor -dora *mf* dancer

bailar *tr* (*p.ej., un vals*) to dance; *(un trompo)* to spin ‖ *intr* to dance; to spin; to wobble

baila·rín -rina *mf* dancer ‖ *f* ballerina; **bailarina ombliguista** (coll) belly dancer

baile *m* dance; ball; ballet; **baile de etiqueta** dress ball, formal dance; **baile de los globos** bubble dance; **baile de máscaras** masked ball, masquerade ball; **baile de San Vito** (pathol) Saint Vitus's dance; **baile de trajes** costume ball, fancy-dress ball

baja *f* (*de los precios*) fall, drop; (*en la guerra*) casualty; **dar baja** to go down, decline; **dar de baja** to drop; (mil) to mark absent; **darse de baja** to drop out; **jugar a la baja** to bear the market

bajaca *f* (Ecuad) hair ribbon

bajada *f* descent; slope; downspout; (rad) lead-in wire

bajagua *f* (Mex) cheap tobacco

bajamar *f* low tide

bajar *tr* to lower, take down; to bring down; (*la escalera*) to go down, descend; to humble ‖ *intr* to come down, to go down; to get off ‖ *ref* to bend down; to get off; to humble oneself

bajel *m* ship, vessel

bajeza *f* humbleness, lowliness; meanness, baseness

bajío *m* shoal, sandbank; pitfall; (Am) lowland

bajista *adj* bearish ‖ *mf* (fig) bear

ba·jo -ja *adj* low, under, lower; short; mean, base; lowly, humble; (mus) bass ‖ *m* shoal, sandbank; (mus) bass ‖ *f* see **baja** ‖ **bajo** *adv* down; low, in a low voice ‖ **bajo** *prep* under

bajón *m* bassoon; (*en el caudal, la salud, etc.*) (coll) decline, loss

bajonista *mf* bassoon player

bajorrelieve *m* bas-relief

bala *f* bullet; bale; **bala fría** spent bullet; **bala perdida** stray bullet

balaca *f* (Am) boasting, show

balada *f* ballad; (mus) ballade

bala·dí *adj* (*pl* -**díes**) trivial, paltry

baladro *m* scream, shout, outcry

baladronada *f* boast, boasting

baladronear *intr* to boast, to brag

bálago *m* chaff

balance *m* balance, balance sheet; rocking, swinging; hesitation; doubt; (*de una nave*) rolling

balancear *tr* to balance ‖ *intr & ref* to rock, to swing; to hesitate, to waver; (*la nave*) to roll

balancín *m* balance beam; singletree; rocker arm; seesaw

balandra *f* sloop
balandrán *m* cassock
balanza *f* scales, balance; comparison, judgment; **balanza de pagos** balance of payments
balar *intr* to bleat; (coll) to pine
balastar *tr* to ballast
balasto *m* ballast
balaustre *m* baluster, banister
balay *m* (Am) wicker basket
balazo *m* shot; bullet wound
balbucear *tr* to stammer || *intr* to stammer, stutter; to babble, to prattle
balbucir §1 *tr* & *intr* var of **balbucear**
Balcanes, los the Balkans
balcarrotas *fpl* (SAm) sideburns; (Mex) locks falling over sides of face
balcón *m* balcony
baldar *tr* to cripple; to incapacitate; to inconvenience; to trump
balde *m* bucket, pail; **de balde** free, gratis; over, in excess; **en balde** in vain
baldear *tr* to wash with pails of water; (*una excavación*) to bail out
baldí·o -a *adj* uncultivated; idle, lazy; careless; useless, vain; unfounded || *m* untilled land
baldón *m* insult; blot, disgrace
baldonar *tr* to insult; to stain, disgrace
baldosa *f* floor tile, paving tile; flagstone
baldra·gas *m* (*pl* **-gas**) (coll) jellyfish
balduque *s* red tape, wrapping tape
balear *adj* Balearic || *tr* to shoot at, to shoot, to shoot to death
balido *m* bleat, bleating
balísti·co -ca *adj* ballistic
baliza *f* buoy, beacon; danger signal
balizaje *m* (aer) airway lighting; (naut) buoys
balizar §60 *tr* to mark with buoys; to mark off
balnea·rio -ria *adj* bathing || *m* watering place, spa
balompié *m* football, soccer
balón *m* football; bale; balloon
baloncesto *m* basketball
balota *f* ballot
balotar *intr* to ballot
balsa *f* pool, puddle; raft; float; corkwood; **balsa salvavidas** life float
bálsamo *m* balsam, balm
balsear *tr* to cross by raft; to ferry across
balsero *m* ferryman
bálti·co -ca *adj* Baltic
baluarte *m* bulwark
ballena *f* whale; whalebone; (*de corsé*) stay
ballesta *f* crossbow; spring, auto spring
ba·llet *m* (*pl* **-llets**) ballet
bambalinas *fpl* (theat) flies, borders
bambolear *intr* to sway, reel, wobble
bambolla *f* (coll) hulk; (coll) show, sham; (coll) show-off
bam·bú *m* (*pl* **-búes**) bamboo
banana *f* banana; (rad) plug
banane·ro -ra *adj* banana || *m* banana tree
banano *m* banana tree
banas *fpl* (Mex) banns
banasta *f* hamper, large basket

banca *f* bench; banking; stand, fruit stand; (*en el juego*) bank; **banca de hielo** iceberg; **hacer saltar la banca** to break the bank
banca·rio -ria *adj* banking, bank
bancarrota *f* bankruptcy; **hacer bancarrota** to go bankrupt
bancarrote·ro -ra *adj* & *mf* bankrupt
banco *m* bench; bank; (*de peces*) school; **banco de ahorros** savings bank; **banco de datos** data bank; **banco de hielo** iceberg; **banco de liquidación** clearing house
banda *f* band; ribbon; faction, party; flock; border, edge; bank, shore; (*de la mesa de billar*) cushion; **banda ciudadana** citizens band, CB; **banda de rodamiento** (aut) tread; **banda de tambores** drum corps; **irse a la banda** (naut) to list
bandada *f* flock, covey; (*de gente*) (coll) flock
bandaje *m* tire
bandazo *m* swerving; (naut) lurch
bandear *tr* (Am) to go through, to pierce; (Am) to pursue; (Am) to make love to || *ref* to manage
bandeja *f* tray; (Am) dish, platter
bandera *f* flag, banner; **con banderas desplegadas** with flying colors
banderilla *f* (taur) banderilla; **poner una banderilla a** (coll) to taunt; (coll) to hit for a loan
banderín *m* (mil) color corporal; recruiting post
banderola *f* streamer, pennant; (Am) transom
bandido *m* bandit
bando *m* proclamation; faction, side
bandolera *f* bandoleer; female bandit; **en bandolera** across the shoulders
bandolero *m* highwayman, brigand
bandurria *f* Spanish lute
banquero *m* banker
banqueta *f* stool, footstool; (Guat, Mex) sidewalk
banquete *m* banquet
banquetear *tr, intr* & *ref* to banquet
banquisa *f* floe, iceberg
bañadera *f* (Am) bathtub
bañado *m* chamber pot; (Am) marshland
baña·dor -dora *adj* bathing || *mf* bather || *m* bathing suit
bañar *tr* to bathe; to dip; to coat by dipping || *ref* to bathe
bañera *f* bathtub
bañista *mf* bather
baño *m* bath; bathing; bathroom; bathtub; **baño de asiento** sitz bath; **baño de ducha** shower bath
bao *m* (naut) beam
baptista *adj* & *mf* Baptist
baptisterio *m* baptistery
baque *m* thud, thump; bump, bruise
baquelita *f* bakelite
ba·quet *m* (*pl* **-quets**) bucket seat
baqueta *f* ramrod; drumstick; **correr baquetas** or **pasar por baquetas** to run the gauntlet
baquía *f* (Am) knowledge of the road, paths, rivers, etc. of a region; (Am) manual skill

baquia·no -na *adj* (Am) skillful, expert ǁ *mf* (Am) scout, pathfinder, guide

báqui·co -ca *adj* Bacchic

bar *m* bar; cocktail bar

barahunda *f* uproar, tumult

baraja *f* (*de naipes*) deck, pack; gang, mob; confusion, mix-up

barajadura *f* shuffling; dispute, quarrel

barajar *tr* (*naipes*) to shuffle; to jumble, to mix ǁ *intr* to shuffle; to fight, quarrel ǁ *ref* to get jumbled or mixed

baranda *f* railing; (*de la mesa de billar*) cushion

barandilla *f* balustrade, railing

barata *f* cheapness; barter; (Mex) bargain sale; (Chile, Peru) cockroach

baratija *f* trinket

baratillo *m* second-hand goods; second-hand shop; bargain counter

bara·to -ta *adj* cheap ǁ *m* bargain sale; **dar de barato** (coll) to admit for the sake of argument; **de barato** gratis, free ǁ *f* see **barata** ǁ **barato** *adv* cheap

bárratro *m* (poet) hell

baratura *f* cheapness

baraúnda *f* uproar, tumult

barba *f* (*parte de la cara*) chin; (*pelo en ella*) beard; (*del papel*) deckle edge; (*de ave*) gill, wattle; **barba española** Spanish moss; **barbas** whiskers; **hacer la barba a** to shave; to bore, annoy; (Mex) to fawn on; **llevar por la barba** to lead by the nose; **mentir por la barba** (coll) to tell fish stories ǁ *m* (theat) old man

barbacoa *f* barbecue; (Col) kitchen cupboard; (Peru) attic

barbada *f* lower jaw of horse; bridle curb ǁ **la Barbada** Barbados

barbar *intr* to grow a beard; to strike root

barbaridad *f* barbarism; outrage; piece of folly; (coll) large amount; ¡**qué barbaridad!** how awful!, what nonsense!

barbarie *f* barbarity, barbarism

barbarismo *m* illiteracy; outrage; (gram) barbarism

bárba·ro -ra *adj* barbaric; barbarous ǁ *mf* barbarian

barbear *tr* to reach with the chin; to be as high as ǁ *intr* to reach the same height; **barbear con** to be as high as

barbechar *tr* to plow for seeding; to fallow

barbecho *m* fallow; **firmar como en un barbecho** (coll) to sign with one's eyes closed

barbería *f* barber shop

barberil *adj* barber

barbe·ro -ra *mf* barber; (Mex) flatterer

barbilampi·ño -ña *adj* smooth-faced, beardless; beginning, green

barbilla *f* tip of chin; (*de pluma*) barb; (*de pez*) wattle

bar·bón -bona *adj* bearded ǁ *m* greybeard; solemn old fellow; billy goat

barboquejo *m* chin strap

barbotar *tr & intr* to mutter, to mumble

barbu·do -da *adj* bearded, longbearded, heavy-bearded ǁ *m* shoot, sucker

barbullar *tr & intr* to blabber

barca *f* small boat; bark

barcia *f* chaff

barco *m* boat, ship; **barco de carga** cargo boat; **barco náufrago** shipwreck

barchi·lón -lona *mf* (Ecuad, Peru) nurse, orderly; (Arg, Bol, Peru) quack

barda *f* thatch; bard, horse armor

bardana *f* burdock

bardar *tr* to thatch; (*un caballo*) to bard

bardo *m* bard

bargueño *m* carved inlaid secretary

bario *m* barium

barjuleta *f* haversack

barloventear *intr* to wander around; to turn to windward

barlovento *m* windward

bar·niz *m* (*pl* -**nices**) varnish; (*de la loza, la porcelana, etc.*) glaze; gloss, polish; (*conocimientos superficiales*) smattering; (aer) dope

barnizar §60 *tr* to varnish

barómetro *m* barometer; **barómetro aneroide** aneroid barometer

barón *m* baron

baronesa *f* baroness

barquero *m* boatman

barquilla *f* (naut) log; (naut) log chip; (aer) nacelle

barquillero *m* waffle iron; harbor boatman

barquillo *m* cone; waffle

barquín *m* bellows

barra *f* bar; (*de dinamita*) stick; (*en el tribunal*) bar, railing; **barra colectora** (elec) bus bar; **barra de labios** or **para los labios** lipstick; **barra imantada** bar magnet; **barras paralelas** (sport) parallel bars

barrabasada *f* (coll) fiendish prank, mean trick

barraca *f* cabin, hut; cottage; (Am) storage shed

barracón *m* barracks; fair booth

barragana *f* concubine

barranca *f* gorge, ravine, gully

barranco *m* gorge, ravine, gully; difficulty, obstruction; (Am) cliff, precipice

barrar *tr* to daub, to smear

barrear *tr* to barricade; to bar shut

barredera *f* street sweeper

barre·dor -dora *mf* sweeper; **barredora de alfombras** carpet sweeper; **barredora de nieve** snowplow

barredura *f* sweeping; **barreduras** sweepings

barremi·nas *m* (*pl* -**nas**) mine sweeper

barrena *f* auger, drill, gimlet; (*espiga para taladrar*) bit; (aer) spin; **barrena picada** (aer) tail spin; **entrar en barrena** (aer) to go into a spin

barrenar *tr* to drill; (*un buque*) to scuttle; to blast; to upset, to frustrate; to violate

barrende·ro -ra *mf* sweeper

barreno *m* large drill; drill hole; blast

hole; pride, vanity; (Chile) mania, pet idea; **dar barreno a** (*un buque*) to scuttle

barreño *m* earthen dishpan

barrer *tr* to sweep, to sweep away; to graze ‖ *intr* to sweep; **barrer hacia dentro** to look out for oneself

barrera *f* barrier; barricade; (mil) barrage; crockery cupboard; tollgate; (rr) crossing gate; (taur) fence around inside of ring; (taur) first row of seats; **barrera de arrecifes** barrier reef; **barrera de paso a nivel** (rr) crossing gate

barriada *f* district, quarter

barrica *f* cask, barrel

barriga *f* belly; (*de una vasija, una pared, etc.*) bulge

barri·gón -gona or **barrigu·do -da** *adj* big-bellied

barril *m* barrel

barrilero *m* cooper, barrel maker

barrio *m* ward, quarter; suburb; **barrio bajo** slums; **barrio comercial** shopping district, business district; **el otro barrio** the other world; **estar vestido de barrio** (coll) to be dressed in house clothes

barro *m* mud; clay; earthenware; pimple; (coll) money; (Arg, Urug) blunder

barro·co -ca *adj & m* baroque

barro·so -sa *adj* muddy; pimply

barrote *m* heavy bar; bolt; cross brace

barruntar *tr* to guess; to sense

barrunto *m* guess, conjecture; sign, token, foreboding

bartola *f* (coll) belly; **a la bartola** lazily

bartolina *f* (CAm, W-I) jail, dungeon

bártulos *mpl* household tools; **liar los bártulos** (coll) to pack up one's belongings

barullo *m* confusion, tumult

basar *tr* to base; to build ‖ *ref* — **basarse en** to base one's judgment on, to rely on

basca *f* nausea, squeamishness; (coll) fit of temper, tantrum

basco·so -sa *adj* nauseated, squeamish

báscula *f* scales; platform scale

base *f* base; basis; **a base de** on the basis of

bási·co -ca *adj* basic

Basilea *f* Basle, Basel

basílica *f* basilica

basilisco *m* basilisk; **estar hecho un basilisco** (coll) to be in a rage

basquear *intr* to be nauseated

bastante *adj* enough ‖ *adv* enough; fairly, rather ‖ *m* enough

bastar *intr* to be enough, to suffice; to abound, be more than enough ‖ *ref* to be self-sufficient

bastardilla *f* italics

bastar·do -da *adj & mf* bastard

bastidor *m* frame; stretcher; (theat) wing; **entre bastidores** behind the scenes

bastilla *f* hem

bastillar *tr* to hem

bas·to -ta *adj* coarse, rough; uncouth

‖ *m* packsaddle; (*naipe*) club; **el basto** the ace of clubs

bastón *m* stick, staff; cane, walking stick; baton; **bastón de esquiar** ski pole or stick

bastoncillo *m* small stick; (*de la retina*) rod

bastonear *tr* to cane, to beat

basura *f* sweepings; rubbish, litter, refuse; horse manure

basurero *m* trash can; rubbish dump; rubbish collector

bata *f* smock; dressing gown, wrapper; **bata de baño** bathrobe

batacazo *m* thud, bump

bataclán *m* (Cuba) burlesque show

bataclana *f* (Cuba) showgirl, stripteaser

batahola *f* (coll) racket, hubbub

batalla *f* battle; (*de un vehículo*) wheel base; (*de la silla de montar*) seat; (paint) battle piece; **batalla campal** pitched battle; **librar batalla** to do battle

batallar *intr* to battle, to fight; to hesitate, to waver

bata·llón -llona *adj* (*cuestión*) controversial, moot ‖ *m* battalion

batata *f* sweet potato; (Arg) timidity

bate *m* baseball bat

batea *f* tray; flat-bottomed boat; (rr) flatcar

bateador *m* batter

batear *tr & intr* to bat

batel *m* small boat

batelero *m* boatman

batería *f* battery; footlights; **batería de cocina** kitchen utensils

bati·do -da *adj* (*camino*) beaten; (*tejido*) moiré ‖ *m* batter; milk shake; (rad) beat ‖ *f* battue; combing, search

batidor *m* beater; scout, ranger; **batidor de huevos** egg beater; **batidor de oro** goldbeater

batidora *f* beater, mixer

batiente *m* jamb; (*hoja de puerta*) leaf, door; (*de piano*) damper; wash, place where surf breaks

batihoja *m* goldbeater; sheet-metal worker

batimiento *m* beating; (phys) beat

batín *m* smoking jacket

batintín *m* Chinese gong

batir *tr* to beat; to batter, beat down; (*las alas*) to flap; (*manos*) to clap; (*las olas*) to ply; **batir tiendas** (mil) to strike camp

bato *m* simpleton, rustic

batuque *m* (Arg) uproar, rumpus, jamboree; **armar un batuque** (Arg) to raise a rumpus

baturrillo *m* hodgepodge

batuta *f* (mus) baton; **llevar la batuta** (coll) to boss the show

baúl *m* trunk; **baúl mundo** large trunk; **baúl ropero** wardrobe trunk

bauprés *m* bowsprit

bautismo *m* baptism; **bautismo de aire** first flight

bautista *adj* Baptist ‖ *mf* Baptist; baptizer; **el Bautista** John the Baptist

bautisterio *m* baptistery

bautizar §60 *tr* to baptize; (*el vino*) (coll) to water

bautizo *m* baptism; christening party

báva·ro -ra *adj & mf* Bavarian

Baviera *f* Bavaria

baya *f* berry

bayeta *f* baize

ba·yo -ya *adj* bay || *m* bay horse || *f* see **baya**

bayoneta *f* bayonet

bayonetear *tr* (Am) to bayonet

baza *f* trick; **meter baza en** (coll) to butt into

bazar *m* bazaar

ba·zo -za *adj* yellowish-brown || *m* yellowish brown; spleen || *f* see **baza**

bazofia *f* refuse, offal, garbage

bazuca *f* bazooka

bazucar §73 *tr* to stir, to shake; to tamper with

be *m* baa

beata *f* lay sister

beatería *f* cant, hypocrisy

beatificar §73 *tr* to beatify

beatísi·mo -ma *adj* most holy

bea·to -ta *adj* blessed; pious, devout; bigoted, prudish || *mf* beatified person; devout person; bigot; (coll) churchgoer || *f* see **beata**

bebé *m* baby; doll

bebede·ro -ra *adj* (archaic) drinkable || *m* watering place; (Col, Ecuad, Mex) watering trough

bebedi·zo -za *adj* drinkable || *m* potion, philter

bebe·dor -dora *adj* drinking || *mf* drinker; hard drinker

beber *m* drink, drinking || *tr & intr* to drink; **beber de** or **en** to drink out of || *ref* to drink, drink up; (*p.ej., un libro*) to drink in

bebestible *adj* drinkable || *m* drink

bebezón *f* (Col) drunk, spree

bebible *adj* drinkable

bebi·do -da *adj* tipsy, unsteady || *f* drink

bebistrajo *m* (coll) dose, mixture

beborrotear *intr* (coll) to tipple

beca *f* scholarship, fellowship; (*de los colegiales*) sash

becacín *m* snipe, whole snipe

becacina *f* snipe, great snipe

becada *f* woodcock

beca·rio -ria *mf* scholar, fellow

becerra *f* snapdragon

becerrillo *m* calfskin

bece·rro -rra *mf* yearling calf || *m* calfskin || *f* see **becerra**

becuadro *m* (mus) natural sign

bedel *m* beadle

befa *f* jeer, flout, scoff

befar *tr* to jeer at, to scoff at || *intr* (*un caballo*) to move the lips

be·fo -fa *adj* blobber-lipped; knock-kneed || *m* (*de animal*) lip || *f* see **befa**

béisbol *m* baseball

bejuco *m* cane, liana

beldad *f* beauty

beldar §2 *tr* to winnow

belén *m* crèche; (coll) bedlam, confusion; (coll) madhouse; (coll) gossip || **Belén** Bethlehem

bel·fo -fa *adj* (*labio*) blobber; blobber-lipped || *m* (*de animal*) lip; blobber lip

belga *adj & mf* Belgian

Bélgica *f* Belgium

bélgi·co -ca *adj* Belgian || *f* see **Bélgica**

belicista *mf* warmonger

béli·co -ca *adj* warlike

belico·so -sa *adj* bellicose

beligerante *adj & mf* belligerent

belitre *adj* low, mean || *m* scoundrel

bella·co -ca *adj* cunning, sly; wicked || *mf* scoundrel

bellaquear *intr* to cheat, be crooked; (SAm) to be stubborn; (SAm) to rear

bellaquería *f* cunning, slyness; wickedness

belleza *f* beauty; **belleza exótica** glamour girl

be·llo -lla *adj* beautiful, fair

bellota *f* acorn; carnation bud

bem·bo -ba *adj* (Am) thick-lipped; (Mex) simple, silly || *mf* (*persona*) (Am) thicklips

bemol *adj & m* (mus) flat; **tener bemoles** (coll) to be a tough job

bencina *f* benzine

bendecir §11 *tr* to bless; to consecrate; **bendecir la mesa** to say grace

bendición *f* benediction, blessing; godsend; (*en la mesa*) grace; **bendiciones** wedding ceremony; **echar la bendición a** (coll) to have nothing more to do with

bendi·to -ta *adj* blessed, saintly; simple, silly; happy; (*agua*) holy; **como el pan bendito** (coll) as easy as pie || *m* simple-minded soul

benedícite *m* grace; **rezar el benedícite** to say grace

benedicti·no -na *adj & mf* Benedictine || *m* benedictine

beneficencia *f* beneficence; charity, welfare; social service

beneficia·do -da *mf* person or charity receiving the proceeds of a benefit performance

beneficiar *tr* to benefit; (*la tierra*) to cultivate; (*una mina*) to work, to exploit; (*minerales*) to process, to reduce; (*una región del país*) to serve; to season; (Am) to slaughter || *ref* — **beneficiarse de** to take advantage of

beneficia·rio -ria *mf* beneficiary

beneficio *m* benefit; profit, gain, yield; (*de una mina*) exploitation; smelting, ore reduction; benefit performance; **a beneficio de** for the benefit of; on the strength of

beneficio·so -sa *adj* beneficial, profitable

benéfi·co -ca *adj* charitable, benevolent

benemérí·to -ta *adj & mf* worthy; **benemérito de la patria** national hero

beneplácito *m* approval, consent

benevolencia *f* benevolence

benévo·lo -la *adj* benevolent, kindhearted

bengala *f* Bengal light; (aer) flare

benignidad *f* benignity, mildness, kindness; (*del tiempo*) mildness
benig·no -na *adj* benign, mild, kind; (*tiempo*) clement, mild
benjamín *m* baby (*the youngest child*)
beodez *f* drunkenness
beo·do -da *adj & mf* drunk
berbi·quí *m* (*pl* **-quíes**) brace; **berbiquí y barrena** brace and bit
berenjena *f* eggplant
berenjenal *m* eggplant patch; (coll) predicament, jam, fix
bergante *m* scoundrel, rascal
bergantín *m* (naut) brig; **bergantín goleta** (naut) brigantine
berilio *m* beryllium
berkelio *m* berkelium
berli·nés -nesa *adj* Berlin ǁ *mf* Berliner
bermejear *intr* to turn bright red; to look bright red
berme·jo -ja *adj* vermilion, bright-red
berme·jón -jona *adj* red, reddish
bermellón *m* vermilion
berrear *intr* to bellow, to low; to bawl, yowl
berrenchín *m* (coll) rage, tantrum
berrido *m* bellow; scream, yowl
berrín *m* (coll) touchy person, cross child
berrinche *m* (coll) tantrum, conniption
berro *m* water cress
berza *f* cabbage
berzal *m* cabbage patch
besalamano *m* announcement, written in the third person and marked B.L.M. (*kisses your hand*)
besamanos *m* levee, reception at court; throwing kisses
besar *tr* to kiss; (coll) to graze ǁ *ref* (coll) to bump heads together
beso *m* kiss; **beso sonado** buss
bestia *adj* stupid ǁ *mf* dunce ǁ *f* beast; **bestia de carga** beast of burden
bestial *adj* beastly; (coll) terrific
besucar §73 *tr & intr* (coll) to keep on kissing
besu·cón -cona *adj* (coll) kissing ǁ *mf* (coll) kisser
besuquear *tr & intr* (coll) to keep on kissing
betabel *m* (Mex) beet
betún *m* bitumen, pitch; shoe polish
bezo *m* blubber lip; proud flesh
bezu·do -da *adj* thick-lipped
biberón *m* nursing bottle
Biblia *f* Bible
bíbli·co -ca *adj* Biblical
bibliófi·lo -la *mf* bibliophile
bibliografía *f* bibliography
bibliógra·fo -fa *mf* bibliographer
biblioteca *f* library; **biblioteca de consulta** reference library; **biblioteca de préstamo** lending library
biblioteca·rio -ria *mf* librarian
bibliotecnia *f* bookmaking
bicameral *adj* bicameral
bicarbonato *m* bicarbonate
bicicleta *f* bicycle
bichero *m* boat hook
bicho *m* bug, insect; vermin; animal;

fighting bull; simpleton; brat; **bicho viviente** (coll) living soul; **mal bicho** scoundrel; ferocious bull
bidón *m* (*bote, lata*) can; (*tonel de metal*) drum
biela *f* connecting rod
bielda *f* winnowing rack; winnowing
bieldar *tr* to winnow
bien *adv* well; readily; very; indeed; **ahora bien** now then; **bien como** just as; **bien que** although; **más bien** rather; somewhat; **no bien** as soon as; scarcely ǁ *s* welfare; property; darling; **bienes** wealth, riches, possessions; **bienes de fortuna** worldly possessions; **bienes dotales** dower; **bienes inmuebles** real estate; **bienes muebles** personal property; **bienes raíces** real estate; **bienes relictos** estate; **bienes semovientes** livestock; **bien público** commonweal; **en bien de** for the sake of
bienal *adj* biennial
bienama·do -da *adj* dearly beloved
bienandanza *f* happiness, prosperity
bienaventura·do -da *adj* happy, blissful; blessed; simple
bienaventuranza *f* happiness, bliss; blessedness
bienestar *m* well-being, welfare
bienhabla·do -da *adj* well-spoken
bienhada·do -da *adj* fortunate, lucky
bienhe·chor -chora *adj* beneficent ǁ *m* benefactor ǁ *f* benefactress
bienintenciona·do -da *adj* well-meaning
bienio *m* biennium
bienquerencia *f* affection, fondness
bienquistar *tr* to bring together, reconcile
bienvenida *f* safe arrival; welcome; **dar la bienvenida a** to welcome
bienveni·do -da *adj* welcome ǁ *f* see **bienvenida**
bienvivir *intr* to live in comfort; to live decently, properly
bif·tec *m* (*pl* **-tecs**) beefsteak
bifurcar §73 *ref* to branch, to fork
bigamia *f* bigamy
bíga·mo -ma *adj* bigamous ǁ *mf* bigamist
bigornia *f* two-horn anvil
bigote *m* mustache; **bigotes** (*del gato*) whiskers; **tener bigotes** (coll) to have a mind of one's own
bilingüe *adj* bilingual
bilis *f* bile; **descargar la bilis** to vent one's spleen
billar *m* billiards; billiard table; billiard room; **billar romano** pinball
billete *m* ticket; note, bill; **billete de abono** season ticket; commutation ticket; **billete de banco** bank note; **billete de ida y vuelta** round-trip ticket; **billete kilométrico** mileage ticket; **medio billete** half fare
billetero *m* billfold; ticket agent
billón *m* (U.S.A.) trillion; (Brit) billion
bimotor *adj* twin-motor ǁ *m* twin-motor plane
biodegradable *adj* biodegradable
biofísi·co -ca *adj* biophysical ǁ *f* biophysics

biografía f biography
biógra·fo -fa mf biographer
biología f biology
biólo·go -ga mf biologist
biombo m folding screen
bióxido m dioxide
bioquími·co -ca adj biochemical ‖ mf biochemist ‖ f biochemistry
bipartición f fission, splitting
biplano m biplane
biplaza m (aer) two-seater
birimbao m jews'-harp
birlar tr to knock down, to shoot down; (coll) to outwit; **birlar algo a alguien** (coll) to snitch something from someone
birlocha f kite
Birmania f Burma
birma·no -na adj & mf Burmese
birreta f biretta, red biretta
birrete m mortarboard, academic cap
bis interj encore! ‖ m encore
bisabue·lo -la mf great-grandparent ‖ m great-grandfather ‖ f great-grand-mother
bisagra f hinge
bisar tr to repeat
bisbisar tr (coll) to mutter, mumble
bisecar §73 tr to bisect
bisel m bevel edge
biselar tr to bevel
bisies·to -ta adj leap
bismuto m bismuth
bisnie·to -ta mf great-grandchild ‖ m great-grandson ‖ f great-grand-daughter
biso·jo -ja adj squint-eyed, cross-eyed
bisonte m bison; buffalo
biso·ño -ña adj green, inexperienced ‖ mf greenhorn, rookie
bisté m or **bistec** m beefsteak
bisun·to -ta adj dirty, greasy
bisutería f costume jewelry
bitácora f binnacle
bitoque m bung; (CAm) sewer; (Mex) spigot
Bizancio Byzantium
bizanti·no -na adj & mf Byzantine
bizarría f gallantry, bravery; magnanimity
biza·rro -rra adj gallant, brave; magnanimous
bizcar §73 tr to wink ‖ intr to squint
biz·co -ca adj squint-eyed, cross-eyed
bizcocho m biscuit; cake, sponge cake; hardtack; bisque
bizma f poultice
bizmar tr to poultice
biznie·to -ta mf var of **bisnieto**
bizquear intr to squint
bizquera f squint
blanca f steel blade; **sin blanca** (coll) penniless
blanca·zo -za adj (coll) whitish
blan·co -ca adj white; (tez) fair; (fuerza) water; (arma) steel; (cobarde) (coll) yellow; blank ‖ m (persona) white; (coll) coward ‖ m (color) white; blank; target; aim, object; interval; white heat; blank form; **en blanco** (hoja) blank; **hacer blanco** to hit the mark; **quedarse en**

blanco to not get the point; to be disappointed ‖ f see **blanca**
blancor m whiteness
blancura f whiteness; purity
blancuz·co -ca adj whitish; dirty-white
blandear tr to persuade; to brandish ‖ intr & ref to yield, give in
blandengue adj (coll) soft, colorless
blandir §1 tr, intr & ref to brandish
blan·do -da adj bland, soft; indulgent; flabby; sensual; (coll) cowardly; (ojos) (coll) tender
blandón m wax candle; candlestick
blandura f blandness, softness; tolerance; flabbiness; sensuality; flattery; mild weather; (coll) cowardice
blanquear tr to whiten, bleach; to blanch; to whitewash; to tin ‖ intr to turn white
blanqueci·no -na adj whitish
blanqui·llo -lla adj white, whitish ‖ m (Guat, Mex) egg; (Chile, Peru) white peach
blanqueci·no -na adj whitish
blasfemar intr to blaspheme, to curse
blasfemia f blasphemy
blasfe·mo -ma adj blasphemous ‖ mf blasphemer
blasón m (ciencia de los escudos de armas; escudo de armas) heraldry; (heral) charge; (fig) glory, honor
blasonar tr to emblazon; (fig) to emblazon, to extol ‖ intr to boast; **blasonar de** to boast of being
bledo m straw; **no me importa un bledo** or **no se me da un bledo de ello** that doesn't matter a rap to me
blindaje m armor; (elec) shield
blindar tr to armor, armor-plate; (elec) to shield
b.l.m. abbr **besa la mano**
bloc m (pl **bloques**) pad
blon·do -da adj blond, fair, flaxen, light; (Arg) curly ‖ f blond lace
bloque m block; (de papel) pad; **bloque de hormigón** concrete block
bloquear tr to blockade; (un coche, un tren) to brake; (créditos) to freeze
bloqueo m blockade; (de crédito) freezing; **bloqueo vertical** (telv) vertical hold
b.l.p. abbr **besa los pies**
blusa f blouse, smock; (de mujer) shirt-waist; (Col) jacket
boardilla f dormer window; garret
boato m show, pomp
bobada f folly, piece of folly
bobalías mf (coll) simpleton, dunce
bobali·cón -cona adj simple, silly ‖ mf simpleton, nitwit
bobear intr to talk nonsense; to dawdle, loiter around
bobería f folly, nonsense
bóbilis: de bóbilis (coll) free, for nothing; (coll) without effort
bobina f bobbin; (elec) coil; **bobina de chispas** spark coil; **bobina de encendido** ignition coil, spark coil; **bobina de sintonía** tuning coil
bobinar tr to wind
bo·bo -ba adj simple, foolish, stupid ‖ mf simpleton, fool ‖ m (archaic) clown, jester

boca *f* mouth; speech; taste, flavor; (*del estómago*) pit; **a boca de jarro** immoderately; at close range; **boca de agua** hydrant; **boca de dragón** (bot) snapdragon; **boca de riego** hydrant; **buscarle a uno la boca** to draw someone out; **decir con la boca chica** (coll) to offer as a mere formality; **no decir esta boca es mía** (coll) to not say a word

bocacalle *f* street entrance

boca·caz *m* (*pl* -**caces**) spillway

bocadillo *m* tape, ribbon; snack, bite; farmer's snack in the field; sandwich

bocadito *m* little bit; (Cuba) cigarillo (*cigaret wrapped in tobacco*)

bocado *m* bite, morsel; bit; **bocado de Adán** Adam's apple; **no tener para un bocado** (coll) to not have a cent

bocal *m* narrow-mouthed pitcher; (*de un puerto*) narrows

bocallave *f* keyhole

bocamanga *f* cuff, wristband

bocanada *f* (*de líquido*) swallow; (*de humo*) puff; (*de viento*) gust; boasting

bocartear *tr* to crush, to stamp

bocera *f* smear on lips

boceto *m* sketch, outline; wax model, clay model

bocina *f* horn, trumpet; auto horn; phonograph horn; (Am) ear trumpet

bocio *m* goiter

bocoy *m* large barrel

bocha *f* bowling ball

boche *m* small hole in ground for boys' game; (Ven) slight, snub

bochinche *m* uproar, tumult, row

bochorno *m* sultry weather; blush, embarrassment, shame

bochorno·so -sa *adj* sultry, stuffy; embarrassing, shameful

boda *f* marriage, wedding; **bodas de Camacho** banquet, lavish feast

bodega *f* wine cellar; dock warehouse; granary; (*de nave*) hold; (coll) cellar; (*hombre que bebe mucho*) (coll) tank; (Am) grocery store

bodegón *m* hash house, beanery; saloon; still life

bodegue·ro -ra *mf* cellarer; (Am) grocer

bodijo *m* (coll) unequal match; (coll) simple wedding

bodoque *m* lump; (coll) dunce, dolt; (Mex) bump, lump

bodoquera *f* peashooter

bóer *mf* Boer

bofe *m* (coll) lung; (P-R) cinch, snap; **echar el bofe** or **los bofes** (coll) to drudge, to grind; **bofes** lights (*of sheep, etc.*)

bofetada *f* slap in the face

boga *mf* rower ‖ *f* vogue, fashion; rowing

bogar §44 *intr* to row

bogavante *m* lobster

bohardilla *f* dormer window; garret

bohe·mio -mia *adj & mf* Bohemian

bohío *m* (Am) hut, shack

boicotear *tr* to boycott

boicoteo *m* boycott, boycotting

boina *f* beret

boj *m* boxwood

boja *f* southernwood

bojar *tr* to measure the perimeter of; (*el cuero*) to scrape clean ‖ *intr* to measure

bola *f* ball; marble; bowling; shoe polish; shoeshine; (cards) slam; lie, deceit; (Mex) brawl, riot; **bola de alcanfor** moth ball; **bola de cristal** crystal ball; **bola de nieve** snowball; **bola rompedora** wrecking ball; **bolas** Gaucho lasso tipped with balls; **dejar que ruede la bola** to let things take their course; **raspar la bola** (Chile) to clear out, beat it

bolada *f* (*de una bola*) throw; (Am) luck, opportunity; (Arg) billiard stroke; (Chile) dainty, tidbit; (Guat, Mex) lie, fib

bolazo *m* hit with a ball; **de bolazo** (coll) hurriedly, right away; (Mex) at random

bolchevique *adj & mf* Bolshevik

bolchevismo *m* Bolshevism

boleada *f* (Arg) hunting with bolas; (Mex) shoeshine; (Peru) flunking

bolear *tr* (coll) to throw; (Arg) to catch with bolas; (*zapatos*) (Mex) to shine; (SAm) to kick out, to flunk ‖ *intr* to play for fun; to lie; to boast ‖ *ref* (Arg, Urug) to rear and fall backwards; (Arg, Urug) to upset; (Arg, Urug) to blush

bole·ro -ra *mf* bolero dancer ‖ *m* bolero (*dance; music; jacket*); (Mex) bootblack ‖ *f* bowling alley; **bolera encespada** bowling green

boleta *f* pass, permit, admission ticket; (mil) billet; (Am) ballot

boletería *f* (Am) ticket office

boletín *m* bulletin; ticket; form; press release

boleto *m* (Am) ticket

boliche *m* bowling; bowling alley; (SAm) hash house

bólido *m* fireball, bolide

bolígrafo *m* ball-point pen

bolillo *m* bobbin for making lace; frame for stiffening lace cuffs

Bolivia *f* Bolivia

bolivia·no -na *adj & mf* Bolivian

bolo *m* ninepin, tenpin; dunce, blockhead; (*de escalera*) newel; (cards) slam; **bolos** bowling, ninepins, tenpins; **jugar a los bolos** to bowl

bolsa *f* purse, pocketbook; pouch; stock exchange, stock market; (*en el vestido*) bag, pucker; grant, award; **bolsa de agua caliente** hot-water bottle; **bolsa de hielo** ice bag; **bolsa de trabajo** employment bureau; **hacer bolsa** (*un vestido*) to bag; **jugar a la bolsa** to play the market

bolsear *tr* (Arg, Bol, Urug) to jilt; (Am) to pick the pocket of; (Chile) to sponge on

bolsacalculadora *f* pocket calculator

bolsillo *m* pocket; purse; pocketbook

bolsista *m* broker, stockbroker; (CAm, Mex) pickpocket

bi
bo

bolso *m* purse, pocketbook; **bolso de mano** handbag

bollo *m* bun, roll; bump, lump; dent; (*en un vestido*) puff; (*en adorno de tapicería*) tuft; **bollo de crema** cream puff

bomba *f* pump; bomb; fire engine; lamp globe; high hat; firecracker; soap bubble; bombshell; **a prueba de bombas** bombproof; **bomba atómica** atomic bomb; **bomba cohete** rocket bomb; **bomba de hidrógeno** hydrogen bomb; **bomba de incendios** fire engine; **bomba de profundidad** depth bomb; **bomba de sentina** bilge pump; **bomba rompedora** block-buster; **bomba volante** buzz bomb; **caer como una bomba** (coll) to fall like a bombshell; (coll) to burst in unexpectedly

bombachas *fpl* loose-fitting baggy trousers

bombardear *tr* & *intr* to bomb; to bombard; **bombardear en picado** to dive-bomb

bombardeo *m* bombing; bombarding; **bombardeo en picado** dive bombing

bombardero *m* bomber; bombardier

bomba-reloj *f* time bomb

bombazo *m* bomb explosion; bomb hit; bomb damage

bombear *tr* to bomb; to ballyhoo, to puff up; (Am) to pump; (SAm) to reconnoiter; (Col) to fire, dismiss || *ref* to camber, bulge

bombero *m* fireman; pumpman

bombilla *f* bulb, light bulb; lamp chimney; (Am) tube for sucking up maté; **bombilla de destello** flash bulb

bombillo *m* trap, stench trap; (naut) pump

bombista *m* lamp maker; (*el que da bombos*) (coll) booster

bom·bo -ba *adj* (coll) astounded, stunned; (W-I) lukewarm || *m* bass drum; ballyhoo; (naut) barge, lighter; **dar bombo a** (coll) to ballyhoo, puff up; **irse al bombo** (Arg) to fail || *f* see **bomba**

bombón *m* bonbon, candy

bombona *f* carboy

bombonera *f* candy box

bona·chón -chona *adj* (coll) good-natured, kind, simple

bonancible *adj* (*tiempo*) fair; (*mar*) calm; (*viento*) moderate

bonanza *f* fair weather, calm seas; prosperity, boom; rich ore pocket

bona·zo -za *adj* (coll) kind-hearted

bondad *f* kindness; favor; **tener la bondad de** to have the kindness to

bondado·so -sa *adj* kind, generous

bonete *m* cap, hat; candy bowl

boniato *m* sweet potato

bonificar §73 *tr* to improve; to give a discount on

boni·to -ta *adj* pretty, nice; pretty good

bono *m* bond; food voucher

boñiga *f* manure, cow dung

boqueada *f* gasp of death

boquear *tr* to pronounce, utter || *intr* to gasp

boquerel *m* nozzle

boquete *m* gap, breach, opening

boquiabier·to -ta *adj* open-mouthed

boquian·cho -cha *adj* wide-mouthed

boquiangos·to -ta *adj* narrow-mouthed

boquihundi·do -da *adj* hollow-mouthed

boquilla *f* (*de instrumento de viento*) mouthpiece; (*de pipa*) stem; (*de cigarro*) tip; (*de aparato de alumbrado*) burner; cigar holder, cigarette holder; (*de manguera*) nozzle; opening in irrigation canal; opening at bottom of trouser leg

boquirro·to -ta *adj* (coll) garrulous

boquiverde *adj* (coll) obscene, smutty

bórax *m* borax

borbollar or **borbollear** *intr* to bubble up

borbollón *m* bubbling; **a borbollones** impetuously

borborigmos *mpl* rumbling of the bowels

borbotar *intr* to bubble up, bubble over

borce·guí *m* (*pl* **-guíes**) high shoe

borda *f* hut; (naut) gunwale; **arrojar, echar** or **tirar por la borda** to throw overboard

bordada *f* (naut) tack; **dar bordadas** (naut) to tack; to pace to and fro

bordado *m* embroidery

bordadura *f* embroidery

bordar *tr* to embroider

borde *m* border, edge; fringe; rim; **borde de la acera** curb; **borde del mar** seaside

bordear *tr* to border || *intr* to go on the edge; (naut) to tack

bordo *m* (naut) board; (naut) side; (naut) tack; (Guat, Mex) dam, dike; **a bordo** (naut) on board; **al bordo** (naut) alongside; **de alto bordo** seagoing; distinguished, important

bordón *m* (*de tambor*) snare; pilgrim's staff; pet word; burden, refrain

bordonear *intr* to grope along with a stick; to go around begging

borgoña *m* Burgundy (*wine*) || **la Borgoña** Burgundy

borgo·ñón -ñona *adj* & *mf* Burgundian

boricua or **borinque·ño -ña** *adj* & *mf* Puerto Rican

borla *f* tassel; powder puff; **tomar la borla** to take a higher degree, to take the doctor's degree

borne *m* binding post; (*de la lanza*) tip

bornear *tr* to bend, to twist; (*sillares pesados*) to set in place || *intr* to swing at anchor || *ref* to warp

borra *f* fuzz, nap, lint

borrachera *f* drunkenness; spree, binge; great exaltation; (coll) piece of folly; **pegarse una borrachera** to go on a binge

borrachín *m* drunkard

borra·cho -cha *adj* drunk; (*habitualmente*) drinking || *mf* drunkard

borrador *m* blotter, day book; rough draft; (Am) eraser

borradura *f* striking out, scratching out

borraj *m* borax

borrajear *tr* & *intr* to scribble; to doodle

borrar *tr* to scratch out, cross out; to erase, rub out; to darken, obscure; to blot, to smear

borrasca *f* storm, tempest; upset, setback

borrasco·so -sa *adj* stormy

borregos *mpl* (coll) fleecy clouds

borrica *f* she-ass; (coll) stupid woman

borrico *m* ass, donkey; sawhorse; (coll) stupid fellow, ass

borricón *m* or **borricote** *m* (coll) drudge

borrón *m* blot; rough draft; blemish; (fig) blot, stain

borronear *tr* to scribble

borro·so -sa *adj* blurred, smudgy, fuzzy; muddy, thick

boruca *f* noise, clamor, uproar

borujo *m* lump, clump

boscaje *m* forest, woodland; (paint) woodland scene

bosque *m* forest, woodland; **bosque maderable** timberland

bosquejar *tr* to sketch, to outline; to make a rough model of

bosquejo *m* sketch, outline; rough model

bostezar §60 *intr* to yawn, gape

bostezo *m* yawn, yawning

bota *f* shoe, boot; leather wine bag; liquid measure (*125 gallons or 516 liters*); **bota de agua** gum boot; **bota de montar** riding boot; **ponerse las botas** (coll) to hit the jack pot, come out on top

botador *m* boat pole; punch, nailset

botadura *f* launching

botafuego *m* (coll) hothead, firebrand

botalón *m* (naut) boom; **botalón de foque** (naut) jib boom

botáni·co -ca *adj* botanical ‖ *mf* botanist ‖ *f* botany

botanista *mf* botanist

botar *tr* to throw, hurl; to throw away, throw out; (*un buque*) to launch; (*el timón*) to shift; (Am) to fire, dismiss; (Am) to squander ‖ *intr* to jump; to bounce ‖ *ref* (*un caballo*) to buck

botarate *m* madcap, wild man; (Am) spendthrift

bote *m* boat, small boat; can, jar, pot; bounce; blow, thrust; (Mex) jug, jail; **bote de paso** ferryboat; **bote de porcelana** apothecary's jar; **bote de remos** rowboat; **bote de salvamento** or **bote salvavidas** lifeboat; **bote en bote** (coll) crowded, jammed; **de bote y voleo** (coll) thoughtlessly

botella *f* bottle

botica *f* drug store; medicine

botica·rio -ria *mf* druggist, apothecary

botija *f* earthenware jug with short narrow neck; (CAm, Ven) hidden treasure; **decirle a uno botija verde** (Cuba) to let someone have it, to tell someone off; **estar hecho una botija** (*un niño*) (coll) to be cross and scream; (*una persona*) (coll) to be fat, be pudgy

botijo *m* earthenware jar with spout and handle

botín *m* booty, plunder, spoils; spat, legging; (Chile) sock

botina *f* shoe, high shoe

botiquín *m* medicine kit, first-aid kit; medicine chest; first-aid station; (Ven) saloon

bo·to -ta *adj* (*sin filo o punta*) blunt, dull; (fig) dull, slow ‖ *m* leather bag ‖ *f* see **bota**

botón *m* button; (*de mueble o puerta*) knob; (*de reloj de bolsillo*) stem; (bot) bud; (elec) push button; **botón de oro** buttercup; **botón de puerta** doorknob; **botones** *msg* bellboy, bellhop

bou *m* fishing with a dragnet between two boats

bóveda *f* dome, vault; crypt; (aut) cowl; **bóveda celeste** canopy of heaven

boxeador *m* boxer; (Mex) brass knuckles

boxear *intr* to box

boxeo *m* boxing

bóxer *m* brass knuckles

boxibalón *m* punching bag

boya *f* buoy; **boya salvavidas** life buoy

boyante *adj* buoyant; lucky, successful; (*que no cala lo que debe calar*) (naut) light

boyera or **boyeriza** *f* ox stable

boyerizo or **boyero** *m* ox driver

bozal *adj* simple, stupid; (*negro*) just brought in ‖ *m* muzzle; head-harness bells; (Am) headstall

bozo *m* down on upper lip; lips, mouth; headstall

B.p. *abbr* **Bendición papal**

Br. *abbr* **bachiller**

bracear *intr* to swing the arms; to swim with overhead strokes; to struggle

brace·ro -ra *adj* arm, hand; thrown with the hand ‖ *m* man who offers his arm to a lady; day laborer; **de bracero** arm in arm

bra·co -ca *adj* pug-nosed

braga *f* diaper, clout; hoisting rope; **bragas** panties, step-ins; breeches; **calzarse las bragas** (coll) to wear the pants

bragadura *f* crotch

braga·zas *m* (*pl* **-zas**) (coll) easy mark, henpecked fellow

braguero *m* (*para hernias*) truss; (*entrepiernas*) crotch

bragueta *f* fly

bragui·llas *m* (*pl* **-llas**) (coll) brat

brama *f* rut, mating, mating time

bramante *adj* bellowing, roaring ‖ *m* packthread, twine

bramar *intr* to bellow, roar; (*el viento*) to howl; to rage, storm

bramido *m* bellow, roar; howling; raging

brasa *f* live coal, red-hot coal

brasero *m* brazier; (Col) bonfire; (Mex) hearth, fireplace

Brasil, el Brazil

brasile·ño -ña *adj* & *mf* Brazilian

bravata *f* bravado, bragging; **echar bravatas** to talk big

bravear *intr* to talk big, to four-flush

braveza *f* bravery; ferocity; (*de los elementos*) fury, violence

braví·o -a *adj* ferocious; wild, untamed, uncultivated; crude, unpolished; (*mar*) rough, wild; (*terreno*) rough, rugged

bra·vo -va *adj* (*valiente*) brave; fine, excellent; fierce, savage, wild; (*mar*) rough; magnificent; angry, mad; (*perro*) vicious; (*toro*) game; (coll) boasting; (*chili*) (coll) strong || *interj* bravo!

bravu·cón -cona *adj* (coll) four-flushing || *mf* (coll) fourflusher

bravura *f* bravery; fierceness; gameness; bravado, boasting

braza *f* fathom

brazada *f* stroke, pull (*with the arm*); **brazada de pecho** breast stroke

brazado *m* armful, armload

brazal *m* arm band; **brazal de luto** mourning band

brazalete *m* bracelet

brazo *m* arm; (*de animal*) foreleg; **a brazo partido** hand to hand (*i.e., without weapons*); **asidos del brazo** arm in arm; **brazo derecho** righthand man; **brazos** hands, workmen; backers; **hecho un brazo de mar** dressed to kill

brea *f* tar, wood tar; calking substance; packing canvas; **brea seca** rosin

brear *tr* to annoy, mistreat, beat; to tar

brebaje *m* beverage, drink

brécol *m* or **brécoles** *mpl* broccoli

brecha *f* opening; (*en un muro*) breach; breakthrough

brega *f* fight, struggle, quarrel; trickery; drudgery

bregar §44 *intr* to strive, struggle, toil

breña *f*, **breñal** *m* or **breñar** *m* rocky thicket

bresca *f* honeycomb

Bretaña *f* Brittany; **la Gran Bretaña** Great Britain

brete *m* fetters, shackles; tight squeeze, fix

bretones *mpl* Brussels sprouts

breva *f* early fig; cinch, snap

breval *m* early-fig tree

breve *adj* brief, short; **en breve** shortly, soon

brevedad *f* brevity, shortness; **a la mayor brevedad** as soon as possible

brevete *m* note, mark

brezal *m* heath, moor

brezo *m* heath, heather

briba *f* loafing; **andar a la briba** to loaf around

bri·bón -bona *adj* loafing, crooked || *mf* loafer, crook

bribonada *f* loafing, crookedness

bribonear *intr* to loaf around, to be crooked

brida *f* bridle

brigada *f* brigade; gang, squad; warrant officer

brillante *adj* bright, brilliant, shining || *m* diamond, gem

brillantez *f* brilliance

brillar *intr* to shine; to sparkle

brillazón *f* (Arg, Bol, Urug) pampa mirage

brillo *m* brightness, brilliance; sparkle; **sacar brillo a** to shine

brillo·so -sa *adj* (*que brilla por el mucho uso*) shiny; (Am) shining, brilliant

brin *m* canvas

brincar §73 *tr* to bounce up and down; to skip, skip over || *intr* to jump, to leap; (coll) to be touchy, get angry easily

brinco *m* bounce; jump, leap; **en dos brincos** or **en un brinco** in an instant

brindador *m* toaster

brindar *tr* to invite; to offer; **brindar a uno con una cosa** to offer someone something || *intr* — **brindar a** or **por** to drink to, to toast || *ref* — **brindarse a** to offer to

brin·dis *m* (*pl* **-dis**) invitation, treat; toast

brío *m* spirit, enterprise; elegance; **cortar los bríos a** to cut the wings of

brio·so -sa *adj* spirited, lively, enterprising; elegant

brisa *f* breeze; residue of pressed grapes

brisera *f* or **brisero** *m* (Am) glass lamp shade (*for candles*)

británi·co -ca *adj* British, Britannic

brita·no -na *adj* British || *mf* Briton, Britisher

brizna *f* chip, particle; (Ven) drizzle

brl. *abbr* barril

broca *f* reel, spindle; drill, bit

brocado *m* brocade

brocal *m* (*de pozo*) curbstone; (*de bota*) mouthpiece; (*de banqueta*) (Mex) curb

brocamantón *m* diamond brooch

bróculi *m* broccoli

brocha *f* brush; loaded dice; **de brocha gorda** house (*painter*); (coll) crude, heavy-handed

brochada *f* stroke with a brush; rough sketch

brochazo *m* stroke with a brush

broche *m* clasp, clip, fastener; (*conjunto de dos piezas*) hook and eye; (Chile) paper clip; **broche de oro** punch line; **broche de presión** snap, catch; **broches** (Ecuad) cuff buttons

brocheta *f* skewer

broma *f* joke, jest; fun; shipworm; **bromas aparte** joking aside; **en broma** in fun, jokingly; **gastar una broma a** to play a joke on

bromear *intr & ref* to joke, jest; to have a good time

bromhídri·co -ca *adj* hydrobromic

bromista *adj* joking || *mf* joker

bromo *m* bromine

bromuro *m* bromide

bronca *f* (coll) row, quarrel; (coll) rough joke, poor joke; **armar una bronca** (coll) to start a row

bronce *m* bronze; **bronce de cañón** gun metal

broncea·do -da *adj* bronze; tanned, sunburned || *m* bronzing; bronze finish; tan, sunburn

broncear tr, intr & ref to bronze; to tan, sunburn
bron·co -ca adj coarse, rough; gruff; crude; (voz) harsh, hoarse || f see **bronca**
bronquitis f bronchitis
broquel m buckler, shield; (fig) shield
broqueta f skewer
brota f bud, shoot
brotadura f budding, sprouting; gushing; (de la piel) eruption, rash
brotar tr to bring forth, to produce || intr to bud, sprout; to gush; (la piel) to break out
brote m bud, shoot; outbreak; (de petróleo) gush, spurt
broza f (maleza) underbrush; (hojas, ramas, cortezas) brushwood; (desperdicio) trash, rubbish; printer's brush
bruces — dar or caer de bruces to fall on one's face
bruja f witch, sorceress; barn owl; (mujer fea) hag; (mujer de mala vida) prostitute; (W-I) spook
brujear tr (bestias salvajes) (Ven) to hunt || intr to practice witchcraft
brujería f witchcraft, sorcery, magic
brujo m sorcerer, wizard
brújula f (flechilla) magnetic needle; (instrumento) compass; (agujero para la puntería) sight; **perder la brújula** to lose one's touch
brujulear tr (las cartas) to uncover gradually; (coll) to suspect
brulote m fire ship; (Arg, Chile, Bol) vulgarity, insult
bruma f fog, mist
brumo·so -sa adj foggy, misty
bruñido m burnish, polish; burnishing
bruñir §12 tr to burnish, to polish; to put rouge on; (CAm) to annoy
brus·co -ca adj brusque, gruff; sudden; (curva) sharp
bruselas fpl tweezers || **Bruselas** Brussels
brusquedad f brusqueness, gruffness; suddenness; (de una curva) sharpness
brutal adj brutal; sudden; (coll) huge, terrific; (coll) stunning
brutalidad f brutality; stupidity; (coll) tremendous amount
bruteza f brutality; (archaic) roughness
bru·to -ta adj brute; rough, coarse; stupid; gross || mf (persona) brute; blockhead || m (animal) brute
bu m (pl **búes**) (coll) bugaboo; **hacer el bu a** (coll) to scare, frighten
bucear intr to dive, be a diver; to delve, search
buceo m diving
bucle m curl, lock
buche m (de ave) craw, crop, maw; (de líquido) mouthful; (del vestido) bag, pucker; (para secretos) bosom; (coll) belly; (Ecuad) high hat; (Guat, Mex) goiter; **sacar el buche a** (coll) to make (someone) open up
budín m pudding
buen adj var of **bueno**, used before masculine singular nouns

buenamente adv with ease; gladly, willingly; conveniently
buenaventura f fortune, good luck; (adivinación) fortune; **decirle a uno la buenaventura** to tell someone his fortune
bue·no -na adj good; kind; (sano) well; (tiempo) good, fine; **a buenas** willingly; **¡buena es ésa** (or **ésta**)! (coll) that's a good one; **de buenas a primeras** all of a sudden; from the start; **¿de dónde bueno?** (coll) where have you been?, what's new?
buey m ox, bullock, steer
búfa·lo -la mf buffalo
bufanda f muffler, scarf
bufar intr to snort
bufete m writing desk; law office; (de un abogado) clients; law practice; (Am) refreshment; (Col) bedpan; **abrir bufete** to open a law office
bufido m snort
bu·fo -fa adj comic; (Ven) spongy || mf buffoon
bu·fón -fona adj clownish || m clown, buffoon; jester; peddler
bufonada f buffoonery; sarcasm
bufonería f buffoonery; peddling
bufones·co -ca adj clownish; coarse, crude
bugui-bugui m boogie-woogie
buharda f dormer; dormer window; garret
buhardilla f dormer window; garret
buho m eagle owl; (coll) shy fellow
buhonería f peddler's kit; peddler's wares
buhonero m peddler, hawker
buitre m vulture
buje m axle box, bushing
bujería f gewgaw, trinket
bujía f candle; candlestick; candle power; (de motor de explosión) spark plug
bulbo m bulb
bulevar m boulevard
bulevardero m boulevardier, man about town
Bulgaria f Bulgaria
búlga·ro -ra adj & mf Bulgarian
bulto m bulk, volume; bust, statue; parcel, piece of baggage; bump, swelling; pillowcase; form, mass; **a bulto** broadly, by guess; **buscar el bulto a** (coll) to keep after; **de bulto** evident; **escurrir** or **huir el bulto** (coll) to duck
bulla f noise; crowd; loud argument
bullaje m crush, mob (of people)
bullanga f racket, disturbance
bullebulle mf (coll) busybody, bustler
bullicio m brawl, riot, uprising; (rumor que hace mucha gente) rumble
bullicio·so -sa adj brawling, riotous; rumbling || mf rioter
bullir §13 tr to move || intr to boil; to abound; to bustle, to hustle; to swarm; to move, to stir; (coll) to be restless || ref to move, to stir
buniato m sweet potato
buñuelo m cruller, fritter, bun; (coll) botch, bungle
buque m ship, vessel; (de una nave)

hull; (*de cualquier cosa*) capacity; (C-R) doorframe; **buque almirante** admiral; **buque cisterna** tanker; **buque de guerra** warship; **buque de vapor** steamer, steamship; **buque de vela** sailboat; **buque escucha** vedette; **buque escuela** training ship; **buque fanal** or **buque faro** lightship; **buque mercante** merchantman, merchant vessel; **buque portaminas** mine layer; **buque tanque** tanker; **buque velero** sailing vessel

burbuja *f* bubble
burbujear *intr* to bubble
burdégano *m* hinny
burdel *m* brothel, disorderly house
Burdeos Bordeaux
bur·do -da *adj* coarse, rough
burear *tr* (Col) to fool || *intr* to have fun
burga *f* hot springs
bur·gués -guesa *adj* middle-class, bourgeois; (*antiartístico*) bourgeois || *m* middle-class man || *f* middle-class woman
burguesía *f* middle class, bourgeoisie; **alta burguesía** upper middle class; **pequeña burguesía** lower middle class
burla *f* hoax, trick; joke; ridicule; **burlas aparte** joking aside; **de burlas** in fun, for fun
burladero *m* safety island, safety zone; (*en las plazas de toros*) covert; (*en los túneles*) safety niche; hiding place
burla·dor -dora *adj* joking; deceptive || *mf* wag, prankster, practical joker || *m* seducer, libertine
burlar *tr* to make fun of; to deceive; to disappoint; to outwit, frustrate; (*a una mujer*) to seduce || *intr* to scoff || *ref* to joke; **burlarse de** to make fun of
burlería *f* derision, mockery; deception, trick; scorn, derision; fish story
burles·co -ca *adj* (coll) funny, comic, burlesque
burlete *m* weather stripping
bur·lón -lona *adj* joking || *mf* joker || *m* mockingbird
bu·ró *m* (*pl* -rós) writing desk; (Mex) night table
burócrata *mf* jobholder, bureaucrat
burra *f* she-ass; stupid woman; drudge (*woman*)

burrajear *tr & intr* to scribble; to doodle
burra·jo -ja *adj* (Mex) coarse, stupid || *m* dung (*used as fuel*)
bu·rro -rra *adj* (coll) stupid, asinine || *m* donkey; jackass; sawbuck, sawhorse; (Mex) stepladder; **burro cargado de letras** (coll) learned jackass; **burro de carga** (coll) drudge || *f* see **burra**
bursátil *adj* stock-market
busca *f* search; **en busca de** in search of
buscani·guas *m* (*pl* -guas) (Col) snake
buscapié *m* (*para dar a entender algo*) hint; (*para averiguar algo*) feeler || **busca·piés** *m* (*pl* -piés) snake
buscaplei·tos *mf* (*pl* -tos) (Am) troublemaker
buscar §73 *tr* to seek, to hunt, to look for; (Mex) to provoke; **buscar tres pies al gato** to be looking for trouble || *ref* to take care of oneself; **buscársela** (coll) to manage to get along; (coll) to ask for it
buscareta *f* wren
buscarrui·dos *mf* (*pl* -dos) (coll) troublemaker
buscavi·das *mf* (*pl* -das) (coll) snoop, busybody; (coll) go-getter
bus·cón -cona *adj* searching; cheating || *mf* seeker; thief, cheat; (min) prospector || *f* loose woman
busi·lis *m* (*pl* -lis) (coll) trouble; **ahí está el busilis** (coll) that's the trouble; **dar en el busilis** (coll) to hit the nail on the head
búsqueda *f* search, hunt
busto *m* bust
butaca *f* armchair, easy chair; orchestra seat
butifarra *f* Catalonian sausage; (coll) loose sock, loose stocking; (Peru) ham and salad sandwich
bution·do -da *adj* lewd, lustful
buz *m* (*pl* buces) kiss of gratitude and reverence; lip; **hacer el buz** (archaic) to bow and scrape
buzo *m* diver
buzón *m* plug, stopper; mailbox, letter box; (*agujero para echar las cartas*) slot, letter drop; **buzón de alcance** special-delivery box; late-collection slot

C

C, c (ce) *f* third letter of the Spanish alphabet
c. *abbr* **capítulo, compañía, corriente, cuenta**
c *abbr* **caja, cargo, contra, corriente**
cabal *adj* exact; full, complete, perfect; **no estar en sus cabales** to be not in one's right mind || *adv* exactly; completely || *interj* right!

cábala *f* intrigue; divination
cabalgada *f* raid on horseback; gathering of riders
cabalgador *m* rider, horseman
cabalgadura *f* mount, horse; beast of burden
cabalgar §44 *intr* to go horseback riding
cabalgata *f* cavalcade

caballa *f* mackerel

caballada *f* drove of horses; (Am) nonsense, stupidity

caballaje *m* stud service

caballazo *m* (Am) collision of two horses, trampling by a horse; (Chile, Peru) bitter attack

caballerango *m* (Mex) stableman

caballeres‧co -ca *adj* chivalric, knightly; gentlemanly

caballerete *m* (coll) dude

caballería *f* mount, horse, mule; cavalry; chivalry, knighthood; **andarse en caballerías** (coll) to fall all over oneself in compliments; **caballería andante** knight-errantry; **caballería mayor** horse, mule; **caballería menor** ass, donkey

caballeriza *f* stable; stable hands

caballerizo *m* groom, stableman

caballe‧ro -ra *adj* riding, mounted; stubborn ‖ *m* knight, nobleman; gentleman; mister; horseman, cavalier, rider; **armar caballero** to knight; **caballero andante** knight errant; **caballero de industria** crook, adventurer, sharper; **Caballero de la triste figura** Knight of the Rueful Countenance (*Don Quijote*); **ir caballero en** to ride

caballerosidad *f* chivalry, gentlemanliness

caballerote *m* boorish fellow, cad

caballete *m* (*bastidor para sostener un cuadro o pizarra*) easel; (*de tejado*) ridge, hip; (*lomo de tierra*) ridge; (*artificio usado como soporte*) trestle, sawbuck, horse; (*de la nariz*) bridge; chimney cap; (*del ave*) breastbone; little horse

caballista *m* horseman; mounted smuggler ‖ *f* horsewoman

caballito *m* little horse; merry-go-round; **caballito del diablo** dragonfly

caballo *m* horse; (*en ajedrez*) knight; playing card (*figure on horseback equivalent to queen*); **a caballo** on horseback; **a caballo de** astride; **a caballo regalado no se le mira el diente** never look a gift horse in the mouth; **caballo blanco** (*persona que da dinero para una empresa dudosa*) angel; **caballo de batalla** battle horse; (*de una controversia*) gist, main point; (*aquello en que uno sobresale*) forte, strong point; **caballo de carreras** race horse; **caballo de fuerza** French horsepower, metric horsepower; **caballo de tiro** draft horse; **caballo de Troya** Trojan horse; **caballo de vapor** French horsepower, metric horsepower; **caballo de vapor inglés** horsepower; **caballo mecedor** rocking horse, hobbyhorse; **caballo padre** stallion; **caballo semental** stallion

caballu‧no -na *adj* horse, horselike

cabaña *f* cabin, hut; drove, flock; livestock; pastoral scene; (Arg) cattle-breeding ranch

cabañuelas *fpl* (Arg, Bol) first summer rains; (Mex) winter rains

caba‧ret *m* (*pl* **-rets**) cabaret

cabecear *tr* (*un libro*) to put a headband on; (*el vino*) to head; (*una media*) to put a new foot on ‖ *intr* to nod; to bob the head; (*en señal de negación*) to shake the head; (*los caballos*) to toss the head; (*la caja de un carruaje*) to lurch; (*un buque*) to pitch

cabeceo *m* (*de la cabeza*) nod, bob, shake; (*de la caja del carruaje*) lurching; (*del buque*) pitch, pitching

cabecera *f* (*de cama, mesa, etc.*) head; bedside; headboard; headwaters; (*de una casa, un campo*) end; (*del capítulo de un libro*) heading; (*del periódico*) headline; capital, county seat; bolster, pillow; (typ) headpiece, vignette; **cabecera de cartel** top billing; **cabecera de puente** (mil) bridgehead

cabecilla *mf* (coll) scalawag ‖ *m* ringleader ‖ *f* **cabecilla de alfiler** pinhead

cabellar *intr* to grow hair; to put on false hair ‖ *ref* to put on false hair

cabellera *f* head of hair; foliage; (*del cometa*) coma; (bot) mistletoe

cabello *m* hair; **cabello de Venus** maidenhair; **cabellos de ángel** cotton candy; **en cabello** with the hair down; **en cabellos** bareheaded; **traído por los cabellos** far-fetched

cabellu‧do -da *adj* hairy

caber §14 *intr* to fit, to go; to have enough room; to be possible; to happen, to befall; **no cabe duda** there is no doubt; **no cabe más** that's the limit; **no caber de** to be bursting with; **no caber en sí** to be beside oneself; to be puffed up with pride; **todo cabe en** anything can be expected of

cabestrar *tr* to put a halter on

cabestrillo *m* sling

cabestro *m* halter; **llevar** or **traer del cabestro** (coll) to lead by the halter; (fig) to lead by the nose

cabeza *f* head; chief city, capital; **cabeza de chorlito** (coll) scatterbrains; (Arg) forgetful person; **cabeza de motín** ringleader; **cabeza de playa** beachhead; **cabeza de puente** bridgehead; **cabeza de turco** butt, scapegoat; **cabeza mayor** head of cattle; **cabeza menor** head of sheep, goats, etc.; **de cabeza** headfirst; on end; on one's own; by heart; **ir cabeza abajo** (coll) to go downhill; **irse de la cabeza** to go out of one's mind; **mala cabeza** headstrong person; **por su cabeza** on one's own; **romperse la cabeza** (coll) to rack one's brains

cabezada *f* butt with the head; blow on the head; (*de buque*) pitch, pitching; (*de bota*) instep; (*de libro*) headband; **dar cabezadas** to nod; (*un buque*) to pitch

cabezal *m* pillow, cushion; bolster

cabezo *m* hillock; summit, peak; reef

cabe‧zón -zona *adj* big-headed; stubborn; (*licor*) (Chile) strong ‖ *m* (*en la ropa*) hole for the head; tax register

cabezonada *f* (coll) stubbornness

cabezu·do -da *adj* big-headed; (coll) headstrong; (*vino*) heady
cabezuela *f* little head; (*harina gruesa del trigo*) middling; cornflower
cabida *f* room, space, capacity; influence, pull; tener cabida en to be included in
cabildear *intr* to lobby
cabildeo *m* lobbying
cabildero *m* lobbyist
cabildo *m* chapter (*of a cathedral*); chapter meeting; town hall
cabina *f* cabin; (*locutorio del teléfono*) booth; bathhouse, dressing room
cabio *m* rafter; joist
cabizba·jo -ja *adj* crestfallen, downcast
cable *m* cable; rope, hawser; cable de remolque towline; cable de retén guy wire
cablegrafiar §77 *tr* & *intr* to cable
cablegráfi·co -ca *adj* cable
cablegrama *m* cablegram
cabo *m* end, tip; (*punta de tierra que penetra en el mar*) cape; (*mango*) handle; small bundle; small piece; boss, foreman; cord, rope, cable; (mil) corporal; al cabo finally, at last; al cabo de at the end of; atar cabos (coll) to put two and two together; Cabo de Buena Esperanza Cape of Good Hope; Cabo de Hornos Cape Horn; cabos (*de caballo*) paws, nose, and mane; eyes, eyebrows, and hair; clothing; cabo suelto (coll) loose end; estar al cabo de (coll) to be well informed about; llevar a cabo to carry out, to accomplish
cabotaje *m* coasting trade
cabra *f* goat; nanny goat; (Chile) light two-wheel carriage; (Chile) sawbuck; (Col, Cuba, Ven) trick, gyp, loaded dice; cabras light clouds
cabrahigo wild fig
cabrería *f* goat stable; goat-milk dairy
cabre·ro -ra *mf* goatherd
cabrestante *m* capstan
cabrilla *f* sawbuck, sawhorse; (ichth) grouper; cabrillas skipping stones; (*olas blancas en el mar*) whitecaps
cabrillear *intr* (*el mar*) to be covered with whitecaps; to shimmer
cabrio *m* rafter; joist
cabrí·o -a *adj* goat; goatish || *m* herd of goats
cabriola *f* caper; somersault; dar cabriolas to cut capers
cabriolear *intr* to caper, frisk, prance
cabritilla *f* kid, kidskin
cabrito *m* kid; cabritos (Chile) popcorn
cabrón *m* buck, billy goat; (coll) complaisant cuckold; (Chile) pimp
cabronada *f* (coll) shamelessness; (coll) shameless forbearance
cabru·no -na *adj* goat
cacahuate *adj* (Mex) pocked || *m* peanut
cacahuete *m* peanut
cacahuete·ro -ra *mf* peanut vendor
cacalote *m* (Mex) raven; (CAm, Mex) candied popcorn; (Cuba) break, blunder

cacao *m* chocolate tree; cocoa, chocolate; pedir cacao (Am) to call quits; tener mucho cacao (Guat) to have a lot of pep
cacaraña *f* pit, pock
cacarear *tr* (coll) to crow over, boast of || *intr* (*la gallina*) to cackle; (*el gallo*) to crow
cacareo *m* (*de la gallina*) cackling; (*del gallo*) crowing; (*de una persona*) (coll) crowing, boasting
cacatúa *f* cockatoo
cacea *f* trolling; pescar a la cacea to troll
cacear *tr* to stir with a dipper or ladle || *intr* to troll
cacería *f* hunting; hunting party; (*animales cobrados en la caza*) bag; hunting scene
cacerola *f* casserole, saucepan
cacique *m* Indian chief; bossy fellow; (*en asuntos políticos*) (coll) boss; (Chile) lazy lummox; cacique veranero Baltimore oriole, hangbird
caciquismo *m* bossism
caco *m* thief, pickpocket; (coll) coward
cacto *m* cactus
cacumen *m* summit; acumen, keen insight
cacha·co -ca *adj* (SAm) sporty || *m* (SAm) sport, dude
cachada *f* (Am) thrust or wound made with the horns
cachalote *m* sperm whale
cachar *tr* to break to pieces; (*la madera*) to slit, split; (Arg, Ecuad, Urug) to make fun of; (Am) to butt with the horns; (Chile) to grasp, understand
cacharpari *m* (Arg, Bol, Peru) send-off party
cacharro *m* crock, earthen pot; piece of crockery; piece of junk; (CAm, W-I) jail; (Col) trinket
cachaza *f* (coll) sloth, phlegm; rum; (Am) first froth on cane juice when boiled
cachazu·do -da *adj* (coll) slothful, phlegmatic || *mf* (coll) sluggard
cachear *tr* to frisk
cacheo *m* frisking
cachete *m* slap in the face; cheek, swollen cheek; dagger
cachetero *m* dagger; dagger man
cachetina *f* (coll) brawl, fistfight
cachicuer·no -na *adj* horn-handled
cachillada *f* brood, litter
cachimba *f* (*para fumar*) (Am) pipe; (Arg, Urug) well, spring; (Chile) revolver
cachimbo *m* (*para fumar*) (Am) pipe; (Cuba) sugar mill; chupar cachimbo (Ven) to smoke a pipe; (*un niño*) (Ven) to suck its finger
cachiporra *f* billy, bludgeon
cachivache *m* good-for-nothing; cachivaches broken pottery; pots and pans; junk, trash
cacho *m* slice, piece; (*mercadería que no se vende*) (Chile) drug on the market

cachón *m* (*ola de agua*) breaker; splash of water; **cachones** surf

cachon·do -da *adj* (*perra*) in rut; sexy

cacho·rro -rra *mf* cub, whelp, pup ‖ *m* little pistol

cachucha *f* rowboat; cap; Andalusian dance

cachuela *f* gizzard; fricassee of pork

cachu·pín -pina *mf* (CAm, Mex) Spanish settler in Latin America

cada *adj* each; every; **cada vez más** more and more; **cada vez que** whenever

cadalso *m* stand, platform; (*para la ejecución de un reo*) scaffold

cadarzo *m* floss, floss silk

cadáver *m* corpse, cadaver

cadavéri·co -ca *adj* cadaverous

cadena *f* chain; **cadena de presidiarios** chain gang; **cadena perpetua** life imprisonment

cadencia *f* cadence, rhythm

cadencio·co -sa *adj* rhythmical

cadenero *m* (surv) lineman

cadera *f* hip

cadete *m* (mil) cadet; (Arg, Bol) apprentice (*without pay*), errand boy

cadillo *m* burdock

cadmio *m* cadmium

caducar §73 *intr* to be in one's dotage; to be worn out; to lapse, expire

caedi·zo -za *adj* tottery, ready to fall over ‖ *m* (Am) lean-to

caer §15 *intr* to fall; to droop; to fall due; to be, be found; to fade; (*el sol, el día, el viento*) to decline; to happen; **caer a** to face, overlook; **caer bien** to fit; to be becoming; (coll) to make a hit; **caer de plano** to fall flat; **caer en** (*cierto día*) to come on, fall on, happen on; (*cierta página*) to be found on; **caer en cama** to fall ill; **caer en favor** to be in favor; **caer en la cuenta** to catch on, get the point; **caer en que** to realize that; **caer mal** to fit badly; to be unbecoming; (coll) to fall flat; **no caigo** (coll) I don't get it ‖ *ref* to fall, fall down; to be, be found; **caerse de su peso**, **caerse de suyo** to be self-evident; **caerse muerto de** (*p.ej., alegría, miedo, risa*) to be overcome with

café *adj* (Am) tan ‖ *m* coffee; coffee tree; coffee house; café; (Arg) reprimand; (Mex) tantrum; **café cantante** night club; **café de maquinilla** drip coffee; **café solo** black coffee

cafetal *m* coffee plantation

cafetera *f* coffee pot; (Arg) jalopy; **cafetera elétrica** electric percolator

cafetería *f* cafeteria

cafete·ro -ra *adj* coffee ‖ *mf* coffee dealer; coffee-bean picker ‖ *f* see **cafetera**

cafeto *m* coffee tree

cagar §44 *tr* (coll) to spot, stain, spoil ‖ *intr* to defecate ‖ *ref* to defecate; to be scared

cagatin·ta *m* or **cagatin·tas** *m* (*pl* -tas) office drudge, penpusher

ca·gón -gona *adj* (coll) cowardly ‖ *mf* (coll) coward

caída *f* fall; spill, tumble; drop; failure; blunder, slip; (*de una cortina*) hang; **a la caída de la noche** at nightfall; **a la caída del sol** at sunset; **caída de agua** waterfall; **caída radiactiva** fallout; **caídas** coarse wool; (coll) witticisms

caí·do -da *adj* fallen; (*cuello*) turndown; (*párpado, hombro*) drooping; dejected, crestfallen; **caído en desuso** obsolete ‖ **caídos** *mpl* interest due; **los caídos** (*en la guerra*) the fallen ‖ *f* see **caída**

caimán *m* alligator; (coll) schemer

Caín *m* Cain; **pasar las de Caín** (coll) to have a frightful time

Cairo, El Cairo

caja *f* box; case, chest, coffer; (*de caudales*) safe, strongbox; (*para dinero contante*) cashbox; (*dinero contante*) cash; (*ataúd*) casket, coffin; (*de reloj de bolsillo*) case; (*donde se pagan las cuentas en los hoteles*) desk; cashier's desk; (*del aparato de radio o televisión*) cabinet; (*de coche*) body; (*tambor*) drum; (*de fusil*) stock; (*de ascensor, de escalera*) shaft, well; (mach) housing; (typ) case; **caja alta** upper case; **caja baja** lower case; **caja clara** snare drum; **caja de ahorros** savings bank; **caja de cambio de marchas** transmission-gear box; **caja de caudales** safe; **caja de cigüeñal** crankcase; **caja de colores** paintbox; **caja de embalaje** packing box or case; **caja de enchufe** (elec) outlet; **caja de engranajes** gear case; **caja de fuego** firebox; **caja de fusibles** fuse box; **caja de ingletes** miter box; **caja de menores** petty cash; **caja de registro** manhole; **caja de reloj** watchcase; **caja de seguridad** safe; safe-deposit box; **caja de sorpresa** jack-in-the-box; **caja de velocidades** transmission-gear box; **caja fuerte** safe, bank vault; **caja postal de ahorros** postal savings bank; **caja registradora** cash register; **despedir** or **echar con cajas destempladas** (coll) to send packing, to give the gate

caje·ro -ra *mf* boxmaker; (*en un banco*) cashier, teller; (*en un hotel*) desk clerk

cajeta *f* little box; tobacco box; **de cajeta** (CAm, Mex) fine

cajetilla *f* pack (*of cigarettes*)

cajetín *m* rubber stamp; (typ) box

cajista *mf* compositor

cajón *m* large box, bin; (*caja movible de un mueble*) drawer; (*que se cierra con llave*) locker; (*que sirve de tienda*) booth, stall; (Chile) long gully; (Mex) dry-goods store; (SAm) coffin; **cajón de aire comprimido** caisson; **cajón de sastre** (coll) odds and ends; (coll) muddlehead; **ser de cajón** (coll) to be in vogue, be the thing

cal *f* lime; **cal apagada** slaked lime; **cal viva** quicklime; **de cal y canto** (coll) strong, tough

cala *f* calla lily; cove, inlet; (*de fruta*)

sample slice; (*de buque*) hold; suppository

calabacear *tr* (*a un alumno*) (coll) to flunk; (*una mujer a un pretendiente*) (coll) to jilt

calabacera *f* calabash, pumpkin, squash

calabaza *f* calabash, gourd, pumpkin, squash; (coll) dolt; **dar calabaza a** (*un alumno*) (coll) to flunk; (*un pretendiente*) (coll) to jilt

calabo·bos *m* (*pl* **-bos**) (coll) steady drizzle

calabocero *m* jailer, warden

calabozo *m* dungeon; cell, prison cell

calada *f* soaking; (*del ave de rapiña*) swoop; (coll) scolding

calado *m* openwork, drawn work; fretwork; (*del agua*) depth; (naut) draught

calafatear *tr* to calk

calafateo *m* calking

calamar *m* squid

calambre *m* cramp

calamidad *f* calamity

calamita *f* magnetic needle

calamito·so -sa *adj* calamitous

cálamo *m* reed, stalk; (poet) pen; (poet) flute, reed

calamoca·no -na *adj* (*algo embriagado*) (coll) tipsy; (*chocho*) (coll) doddering

calaña *f* nature, kind; pattern; fan

calar *tr* to pierce; to soak; to wedge; to cut open work in; (*un melón*) to cut a plug in; (*la bayoneta*) to fix; (*un puente levadizo*) to lower; (*las redes de pesca*) to lower in the water; (*un buque cierta profundidad*) to draw; (*a una persona o las intenciones de una persona*) to size up, to see through; (Arg) to stare at ‖ *ref* to get soaked, get drenched; (*introducirse*) to slip in; (*el ave de rapiña*) to swoop down; to miss fire; (*el sombrero*) to pull down tight; (*las gafas*) to stick on; **calarse hasta los huesos** to get soaked to the skin

cala·to -ta *adj* (Peru) naked; (Peru) penniless

calavera *m* daredevil; libertine ‖ *f* skull; (*imitación de la calavera*) death's-head; (Mex) tail light

calaverada *f* recklessness, daredeviltry; (Am) escapade

calaverear *tr* to spoil, make ugly ‖ *intr* (coll) to act recklessly; (Am) to go on a spree

calcado *m* tracing

calcañal *m* or **calcañar** *m* heel

calcar §73 *tr* to trace; to copy, imitate; to tread on

calce *m* wedge; iron tire; iron tip; (*de un documento*) (CAm, Mex, P-R) bottom, foot

calceta *f* stocking; fetter, shackle; **hacer calceta** to knit

calcetería *f* hosiery; hosiery shop

calcete·ro -ra *mf* hosier; stocking mender

calcetín *m* sock

calcificar §73 *tr & ref* to calcify

calcio *m* calcium

calco *m* tracing; copy, imitation

calcula·dor -dora *adj* calculating; (*egoísta, interesado*) (fig) calculating ‖ *mf* calculator ‖ *f* calculating machine; **calculadora de bolsillo** pocket calculator

calcular *tr & intr* to calculate; (*suponer*) (fig) to calculate

cálculo *m* calculation; (math, pathol) calculus; **cálculo biliar** gallstone; **cálculo renal** kidney stone

calchona *f* (Chile) goblin, bogey; (Chile) witch, old hag

calda *f* heating, warming; **caldas** hot springs

caldeamiento *m* heating

caldear *tr* to heat; to weld ‖ *ref* to get hot; to get overheated

caldeo *m* heating; welding

caldera *f* boiler; pot, kettle; (Arg) coffee pot, teapot

calderero *m* boilermaker

calderilla *f* holy-water vessel; copper coin; small change; mountain currant

caldero *m* kettle, pot; (*reloj de bolsillo*) (Arg) turnip

calderón *m* caldron; (*signo*) (mus) pause, hold

caldo *m* broth; sauce, gravy, dressing; salad dressing; (Mex) syrup; (Mex) sugar-cane juice; **caldo de la reina** eggnog; **caldos** wet goods

calefacción *f* heating; **calefacción por agua caliente** hot-water heat; **calefacción por aire caliente** hot-air heat

calefactor *m* heater man; (electron) heater, heater element

calefón *m* (Arg) hot-water heater

calendar *tr* to date

calendario *m* calendar; **hacer calendarios** (coll) to meditate; (coll) to make wild predictions

calenta·dor -dora *adj* heating ‖ *m* heater; warming pan; (*reloj de bolsillo*) (coll) turnip; **calentador a gas** gas heater; **calentador de agua** water heater

calentamiento *m* heating

calentar §2 *tr* to heat; to warm; to beat; (Chile) to bore, annoy; **calentar la silla** (*detenerse demasiado*) to warm a chair ‖ *ref* to heat up, run hot; to warm oneself; to warm up; (*estar en celo las bestias*) to be in heat; (Chile, Ven) to become annoyed, get angry

calentón *m* (coll) warm-up; **darse un calentón** (coll) to stop and warm up

calentura *f* fever, temperature

calenturien·to -ta *adj* feverish; exalted

calenturón *m* high fever

calenturo·co -sa *adj* feverish

calera *f* limekiln; limestone quarry

calesa *f* chaise

caleta *f* cove, inlet

caletre *m* (coll) judgment, acumen

calibrador *m* calipers; **calibrador de alambre** wire gauge

calibrar *tr* to calibrate; to gauge

calibre *m* caliber; gauge; bore, diameter

calicanto *m* rubble masonry

cali·có *m* (*pl* **-cós**) calico
calidad *f* quality; condition, term; rank, nobility; importance; **a calidad de que** provided that; **en calidad de** in the capacity of
cáli·do -da *adj* warm, hot
calidoscopio *m* kaleidoscope
calientaca·mas *m* (*pl* **-mas**) bed warmer
calienta·piés *m* (*pl* **-piés**) foot warmer
caliente *adj* hot; fiery, vehement; (*en celo*) hot; **caliente de cascos** hot-headed; **en caliente** while hot; at once
califa *m* caliph
califato *m* caliphate
calificación *f* qualification; (*nota en un examen*) grade, mark; rating, standing
calificar §73 *tr* to qualify; to certify; to ennoble; (*un examen*) to mark; (*en los registros electorales*) (Chile) to register || *ref* (archaic) to prove one's noble birth; (*en los registros electorales*) (Chile) to register
calificati·vo -va *adj* qualifying || *m* (*nota en la escuela*) grade, mark; (*en un diccionario*) usage label
California *f* California; **la Baja California** Lower California
caligrafía *f* penmanship
calina *f* haze
calino·so -sa *adj* hazy
Calíope *f* Calliope
calipso *m* calypso || **Calipso** *f* Calypso
calistenia *f* calisthenics
calisténi·co -ca *adj* calisthenic
cá·liz *m* (*pl* **-lices**) chalice; **cáliz de dolor** cup of sorrow
cali·zo -za *adj* lime, limestone || *f* limestone
calma *f* calm; calm weather; quiet, tranquility; slowness; (*cesación*) letup, suspension; **calma chicha** dead calm; **calmas ecuatoriales** doldrums; **en calma** in suspension; (*mercado*) steady; (*mar*) calm, smooth
calmante *adj* soothing; pain-relieving || *m* sedative
calmar *tr* to calm, sooth || *intr* to grow calm; to abate || *ref* to calm down
calmazo *m* dead calm
cal·mo -ma *adj* barren, treeless; fallow, uncultivated || *f* see **calma**
calmo·so -sa *adj* calm; (coll) slow, lazy
calmu·do -da *adj* calm; (*viento*) (naut) light; (*tiempo*) (naut) mild
caló *m* gypsy slang, underworld slang
calofriar §77 *ref* to become chilled
calofrío *m* chill
calor *m* heat; warmth; (fig) warmth, enthusiasm; **hace calor** it is hot, it is warm; **tener calor** (*una persona*) to be hot, be warm
calorífe·ro -ra *adj* heat || *m* heater, furnace; heating system; foot warmer
calorífu·go -ga *adj* heatproof; fireproof
caloro·so -sa *adj* warm, hot; (fig) warm, enthusiastic, hearty
calotear *tr* (Arg) to gyp, cheat
calpul *m* (Guat) gathering, meeting; (Hond) Indian mound
caluma *f* (Peru) gorge in the Andes; (Peru) Indian hamlet

calumnia *f* calumny, slander
calumniar *tr* to slander
calumnio·so -sa *adj* slanderous
caluro·so -sa *adj* warm, hot; (fig) warm, enthusiastic, hearty
calva *f* bald spot; bare spot, clearing; (*en un tejido*) worn spot
calvario *m* (*sufrimiento moral*) cross; (coll) series of misfortunes; (coll) string of debts || **Calvario** *m* Calvary; Stations of the Cross
calvero *m* clearing; clay pit
calvez *f* or **calvicie** *f* baldness
cal·vo -va *adj* bald; barren, bare || *f* see **calva**
calza *f* wedge; (coll) stocking; **calzas** hose, breeches, tights; **en calzas prietas** (coll) in a tight fix
calzada *f* highway, causeway; (S-D) sidewalk
calzado *m* footwear, shoes
calzador *m* shoehorn
calzar §60 *tr* to shoe, put shoes on; to provide with shoes; (*cierto tamaño de zapatos, guantes, etc.*) to wear, to take; (*un zapato a una persona*) to fit; to wedge; (*una rueda*) to block, scotch; (*la pata de una mesa*) to block up; to tip or trim with iron; (*plantas*) (hort) to hill || *intr* (Arg) to get the place sought; **calzar bien** to wear good footwear; **calzar mal** to wear poor footwear || *ref* to get; (*zapatos, guantes*) to put on, to wear; to put one's shoes on; (*a una persona*) (coll) to dominate, to manage
calzo *m* wedge; chock, skid
calzón *m* trousers, pants; **calzones** trousers, breeches; **calzarse los calzones** to wear the pants
calzonarias *fpl* (Col) suspenders
calzona·zos *m* (*pl* **-zos**) (coll) jellyfish; (coll) henpecked husband
calzoncillos *mpl* underdrawers
callada *f* (naut) abatement, lull; **a las calladas** or **de callada** (coll) on the quiet; **dar la callada por respuesta** to give no answer
calla·do -da *adj* silent; mysterious, secret || *f* see **callada**
callampa *f* (Chile) felt hat; (Chile) large ear; (Chile) mushroom
callana *f* (SAm) Indian baking bowl; (*reloj de bolsillo*) (Chile) turnip; (Chile) behind; (Chile, Peru) flowerpot
callao *m* pebble
callar *tr* to silence; to not mention; (*un secreto*) to keep; to calm, quiet || *intr* & *ref* to become silent, keep silent; to keep quiet, keep still; **callarse la boca** (coll) to shut up, to clam up
calle *f* street; **calle de travesía** cross street; **calle mayor** main street; **dejar en la calle** (coll) to deprive of one's livelihood
calleja *f* side street, alley; (coll) subterfuge, pretext
callejear *intr* to walk around the streets, to ramble around
calleje·ro -ra *adj* street; gadabout || *m*

street guide; list of addresses of newspaper subscribers

callejón *m* alley, lane; **callejón sin salida** blind alley

callejuela *f* side street, alley; (coll) subterfuge, pretext

callicida *m* corn cure

callo *m* callus; (*en el pie*) corn; **callos** tripe

callo·so -sa *adj* callous

cama *f* bed; (*para las bestias*) bedding, litter; **cama imperial** four-poster; **cama turca** day bed; **guardar cama** to be sick in bed

camachuelo *m* (orn) bullfinch

camada *f* brood, litter; layer, stratum; (*de ladrones*) den

camafeo *m* cameo

camaleón *m* chameleon

cámara *f* chamber; hall; (*cuerpo legislador*) house, chamber; (*aparato fotográfico*) camera; (*tubo de goma del neumático*) inner tube; (*del arma de fuego*) chamber, breech; (*para cartuchos*) magazine; board, council; (*mueble donde se conservan los alimentos*) icebox; (*evacuación*) bowels; (aer) cockpit; **cámara agrícola** grange; **cámara ardiente** funeral chamber; **cámara de compensación** clearing house; **cámara de fuelle** folding camera; **cámara de las máquinas** (naut) engine room; **Cámara de los Comunes** House of Commons; **Cámara de los Lores** House of Lords; **cámara de oxígeno** oxygen tent; **Cámara de Representantes** House of Representatives; **cámara frigorífica** cold-storage room; **cámara indiscreta** candid camera; **cámaras** loose bowels

camarada *m* comrade

camarera *f* waitress; chambermaid, maid; (*en los barcos*) stewardess; (*que sirve a una reina o princesa*) lady in waiting

camarero *m* waiter; valet; (*en un barco o avión*) steward

camarilla *f* clique, coterie, cabal; palace coterie

camarín *m* boudoir; (theat) dressing room

cámaro *m* var of **camarón**

camarógrafo *m* cameraman

camarón *m* shrimp, prawn; (CAm, Col) tip, gratuity; (Ven) nap; **ponerse como un camarón** (Am) to blush

camarote *m* stateroom, cabin

camasquin·ce *mf* (*pl* -ce) (coll) meddlesome person, kibitzer

cambalachar *tr & intr* var of **cambalachear**

cambalache *m* exchange, swap; (Arg) second-hand shop

cambalachear *tr* to swap, exchange, trade off ‖ *intr* to swap, exchange

cambiadis·cos *m* (*pl* -cos) record changer

cambiante *adj* changing; fickle; iridescent ‖ **cambiantes** *mpl* iridescence

cambiar *tr* to change; to exchange ‖ *intr* to change; **cambiar de** (*p.ej.*, *sombreros, ropa, trenes*) to change; **cambiar de marcha** to shift gears ‖ *ref* to change

cambiavía *m* (Am) switch; (Am) switchman

cambio *m* change; exchange; rate of exchange; (aut) shift; (rr) switch; **cambio de marchas, cambio de velocidades** gearshift; **en cambio** on the other hand

cambista *mf* moneychanger; banker ‖ *m* (Arg) switchman

cambullón *m* (Mex, Col, Ven) barter, exchange; (Chile) subversion; (Peru) scheming, trickery

camelar *tr* (coll) to flirt with; (coll) to cajole, to tease

camelo *m* (coll) flirtation; (coll) joke; (coll) false rumor

camellero *m* camel driver

camello *m* camel

camellón *m* drinking trough; flower bed

came·ro -ra *adj* bed ‖ *mf* maker of bedding ‖ *m* (Col) highway

camilla *f* stretcher; couch; round table with heater underneath; (Mex) clothing store

camillero *m* stretcher-bearer

caminante *mf* walker; traveler on foot ‖ *m* groom attending his master's horse

caminar *tr* (*cierta distancia*) to walk ‖ *intr* to walk; to go; to travel, to journey; to behave

caminata *f* (coll) long walk, hike; (coll) outing, jaunt

camine·ro -ra *adj* road, highway

camino *m* road, way; (*viaje*) journey; (*tira larga que se pone en mesas o pisos*) (SAm) runner; **a medio camino** (entre) halfway (between); **camino de** on the way to; **camino de herradura** bridle path; **camino de hierro** railway; **camino de ruedas** wagon road; **Camino de Santiago** Way of St. James (*Milky Way*); **camino de sirga** towpath; **camino de tierra** dirt road; **camino real** highroad; **camino trillado** beaten path; **echar camino adelante** to strike out

camión *m* truck, motor truck; (Mex) bus; **camión volquete** dump truck

camionaje *m* trucking

camione·ro -ra *adj* truck ‖ *m* trucker, teamster

camioneta *f* light truck

camión-grúa *m* tow truck

camionista *m* trucker, teamster

camisa *f* (*de hombre*) shirt; (*de mujer*) chemise; (*de la culebra*) slough; (*de un libro*) jacket; (*para papeles*) folder; (*de una pieza mecánica*) jacket, casing; (*de un horno de fundición*) lining; **camisa de agua** water jacket; **camisa de dormir** nightshirt; **camisa de fuerza** strait jacket; **cambiarse la camisa** to become a turncoat

camisería *f* haberdashery; shirt factory

camise·ro -ra *mf* haberdasher; shirt maker

camiseta *f* undershirt; *(de traje de baño)* top

camisola *f* stiff shirt

camisolín *m* dickey, shirt front

camón *m* bay window; **camón de vidrios** glass partition

camorra *f* (coll) quarrel, row; **armar camorra** (coll) to raise Cain, to raise a row; **buscar camorra** (coll) to be looking for trouble

camorrista *adj* (coll) quarrelsome ‖ *mf* (coll) quarrelsome person

camote *m* (Mex) sweet potato; (Am) onion; (Chile) lie, fib; (Chile, Peru) sweetheart; (Arg, Ecuad) blockhead; (Mex) churl; (El Salv) black-and-blue mark; **tomar un camote** (Am) to become infatuated

camotear *tr* (Arg) to filch, to snitch; (Guat) to bother ‖ *intr* (Mex) to wander around aimlessly

campal *adj* pitched *(battle)*

campamento *m* camp; encampment

campana *f* bell; *(para la protección de plantas)* bell glass, bell jar; *(de las guarniciones de alumbrado eléctrico)* canopy; **campana de buzo** diving bell; **por campana de vacante** (Mex) rarely, seldom

campanada *f* stroke of a bell, ring of a bell; scandal

campanario *m* belfry, steeple

campanear *tr* *(las campanas)* to ring ‖ *intr* to ring the bells ‖ *ref* (coll) to strut

campanero *m* bell ringer; bell founder

campanil *adj* bell ‖ *m* belfry, bell tower

campanilla *f* hand bell; door bell; bubble; (anat) uvula; **de (muchas) campanillas** (coll) of great importance

campano *m* cowbell

campante *adj* (coll) proud, satisfied; (coll) outstanding

campanu·do -da *adj* bell-shaped; pompous, high-sounding

campaña *f* campaign; cruise; countryside

campar *intr* to camp; to excel, stand out

campear *intr* to go to pasture; *(las sementeras)* to turn green; to stand out, excel; to reconnoiter; (Am) to ride through the fields to check the cattle

campecha·no -na *adj* (coll) frank, good-natured, cheerful ‖ *f* (Mex) mixed drink; (Ven) hammock

campeche *m* logwood

campeón *m* champion; **campeón de venta** best seller

campeona *f* championess

campeonato *m* championship

campe·ro -ra *adj* unsheltered, in the open

campesi·no -na *adj* country, rural, peasant ‖ *mf* peasant, farmer ‖ *m* countryman ‖ *f* countrywoman

campestre *adj* country, rural

campiña *f* countryside, open country

campo *m* *(terreno sembradío; sitio o foco de varias actividades)* field; *(en oposición a la ciudad)* country; ground, background; *(campamento)* (mil) camp; **a campo traviesa** across country; **campo de batalla** battlefield; **campo de juego** playground; **campo de tiro** range, shooting range; **campo santo** cemetery; **levantar el campo** (mil) to break camp; **quedar en el campo** to fall in battle

camposanto *m* cemetery

camuesa *f* pippin *(apple)*

camueso *m* pippin *(tree)*

camuflaje *m* camouflage

camuflar *tr* to camouflage

can *m* dog; *(de arma de fuego)* trigger

cana *f* grey hair; **echar una cana al aire** (coll) to cut loose, to step out; **peinar canas** (coll) to be getting old

Canadá, el Canada

canadiense *adj & mf* Canadian

canal *m (cauce artificial)* canal; *(estrecho en el mar)* channel; (anat) duct, canal; (telv) channel; **Canal de la Mancha** English Channel; **Canal de Panamá** Panama Canal; **Canal de Suez** Suez Canal; **canal alimenticio** alimentary canal ‖ *f* channel; *(conducto del tejado)* gutter; *(estría)* flute, groove; pipe; *(de un libro)* fore edge

canalización *f (de agua o gas)* mains, pipes; ductwork; (elec) wiring; **canalización de consumo** (elec) house current

canalizar §60 to channel; to pipe; (elec) to wire

canalizo *m* (naut) waterway, fairway

canalón *m* rain-water spout; shovel hat; **canalones** ravioli

canalla *m* (coll) churl, scoundrel ‖ *f* (coll) riffraff, canaille

canallada *f* (coll) dirty trick, meanness

canana *f* cartridge belt

canapé *m* sofa, couch

Canarias *fpl* Canaries

cana·rio -ria *adj & mf* Canarian ‖ *m* canary, canary bird ‖ *fpl* see **Canarias**

canasta *f* basket, hamper

canastilla *f* basket; *(ropa para el niño que ha de nacer)* layette; *(equipo de novia)* (dial) trousseau

canastillo *m* basket-weave tray

canasto *m* hamper ‖ **canastos** *interj* confound it!

cáncamo *m* eyebolt; **cáncamo de argolla** ringbolt

cancanear *intr* (coll) to loaf around; (Am) to stammer

cancel *m* storm door; (Am) folding screen

cancela *f* door of ironwork

cancelar *tr* to cancel; *(una deuda)* to pay off

cáncer *m* cancer

cance·ro·so -sa *adj* cancerous

cancilla *f* lattice gate

canciller *m* chancellor

cancillería *f* chancellery

canción *f* song; poem, lyric poem; **canción de amor** love song; **canción de cuna** cradlesong, lullaby; **canción típica** folk song; **volver a la misma canción** to sing the same old song

cancionero *m* songbook; anthology

cancionista *mf* popular singer
canco *m* (Chile) flowerpot; (Chile) earthen jug; (Chile) chamber pot; (Bol) buttock; **cancos** (Chile) woman's broad hips
cancón *m* (coll) bugaboo; **hacer un cancón a** (Mex) to try to bluff
cancha *f* field, ground; race track; golf links; tennis court; cockpit; (Urug) path, way; **estar en su cancha** (Arg, Chile, Urug) to be in one's element; **tener cancha** (Arg) to have pull || *interj* gangway!
canche *adj* (Col) tasteless, poorly seasoned; (CAm) blond
candado *m* padlock
candar *tr* to lock, to padlock
candela *f* candle; candlestick; fire, light; **con la candela en la mano at** death's door
candelabro *m* candelabrum
candelecho *m* elevated hut for watching the vineyard
candelero *m* candlestick; brass olive-oil lamp; fishing torch
candelilla *f* catkin; (Arg, Chile) will-o'-the-wisp; (Am) glowworm
candida·to -ta *mf* candidate
candidatura *f* candidacy; list of candidates; voting paper
candidez *f* whiteness; innocence
cándi·do -da *adj* white; simple, innocent
candil *m* open olive-oil lamp
candilejas *fpl* footlights
candon·go -ga *adj* fawning, slick; loafing, shirking || *mf* fawner, flatterer; loafer, shirker || *f* fawning; teasing
candonguear *tr* (coll) to kid, tease || *intr* (coll) to scheme to get out of work
candor *m* innocence, ingenuousness
caneca *f* glazed earthen bottle
cane·co -ca *adj* (Arg, Bol) tipsy || *f* see **caneca**
canela *f* cinnamon; (*cosa fina*) (coll) peach
canela·do -da *adj* cinnamon-colored
cane·lo -la *adj* cinnamon || *m* (*árbol*) cinnamon || *f* see **canela**
canelón *m* rain-water spout; large icicle; cinnamon candy
cane·sú *m* (*pl* -**súes**) (*prenda*) guimpe; (*pieza de una prenda*) yoke
cangilón *m* jug, jar, bucket; (*de draga*) bucket, scoop; (Am) rut, track
cangrejo *m* crab
cangrena *f* gangrene
cangrenar *ref* to have gangrene
canguro *m* kangaroo
caníbal *adj* & *mf* cannibal
canica *f* (*bolita*) marble; (*juego*) marbles
canicie *f* whiteness (*of hair*)
canícula *f* dog days || **Canícula** *f* Dog Star
caniculares *mpl* dog days
cani·jo -ja *adj* (coll) weak, sickly || *mf* (coll) weakling
canilla *f* shank (*of leg*); (*espita, grifo*) tap; bobbin, spool; (Mex) strength
cani·no -na *adj* canine || *m* canine, canine tooth || *f* excrement of dogs
canje *m* exchange
canjear *tr* to exchange

ca·no -na *adj* gray; gray-haired; hoary, old || *f* see **cana**
canoa *f* canoe; launch
canoe·ro -ra *mf* canoeist
canon *m* canon
canóni·co -ca *adj* canonical || *f* rules of canonical life
canóniga *f* (coll) nap before eating; (coll) drunk
canónigo *m* canon
canonizar §60 *tr* to canonize; to approve
canonjía *f* (coll) sinecure
cano·ro -ra *adj* (*voz*) melodious; (*ave*) song, sweet-singing
cano·so -sa *adj* gray-haired
canotié *m* straw hat, skimmer
cansa·do -da *adj* tired, weary; exhausted, worn-out; tiresome
cansancio *m* tiredness, fatigue
cansar *tr* to tire, weary; to bore || *intr* be tiresome || *ref* to tire, get tired
cantable *adj* tuneful, singable || *m* (*del libreto de una zarzuela*) lyric; (*de una zarzuela*) musical passage
canta·dor -dora *mf* singer of popular songs
cantaletear *tr* (Am) to say over and over again; (Am) to make fun of
cantalupo *m* cantaloupe
cantante *adj* singing || *mf* singer
cantar *m* song, singing; chant; **Cantar de los Cantares** Song of Songs || *tr* to sing; to chant; to sing of; **cantarlas claras** (coll) to speak out || *intr* to sing; to chant; (coll) to creak, squeak; (coll) to squeal, to peach; **cantar de plano** (coll) to make a full confession
cántara *f* jug, pitcher
cantárida *f* Spanish fly
canta·rín -rina *adj* (*voz*) melodious; (coll) fond of singing || *mf* singer || *m* professional singer
cántaro *m* jug, pitcher; jugful; ballot box; **llover a cántaros** to rain pitchforks
canta·triz *f* (*pl* -**trices**) singer
cantera *f* quarry; talent, genius
cántico *m* canticle
cantidad *f* quantity; amount; sum; **cantidad de movimiento** (mech) momentum
cantiga *f* poem of the troubadours
cantilena *f* ballad, song; **salir con la misma cantilena** (coll) to sing the same old song
cantimplora *f* siphon; carafe, decanter; (*frasco para llevar bebida*) canteen; (Col) powder flask; (Guat) mumps
cantina *f* cantine; lunchroom, station restaurant; (Am) barroom
cantinera *f* camp follower
cantinero *m* bartender
canto *m* song; singing; (*división del poema épico*) canto; (*de notas iguales y uniformes*) chant; (*extremidad*) edge; (*esquina*) corner; (*de cuchillo*) back; (*de pan*) crust; stone, pebble; **canto de corte** cutting edge; **canto del cisne** swan song
cantonera *f* corner reinforcement; corner table, corner shelf; streetwalker

cantonero *m* corner loafer
can·tor -tora *adj* singing; (*pájaro*) song ‖ *mf* singer ‖ *m* chanter; minstrel; poet, bard
canto·so -sa *adj* rocky, stony
canturrear *tr & intr* to hum
canturreo *m* hum, humming
canzonetista *mf* popular singer
caña *f* cane; reed; stalk, stem; (*del brazo o la pierna*) long bone; (*de bota o media*) leg; wineglass; **caña de azúcar** sugar cane; **caña de pescar** fishing rod
cañada *f* glen, ravine, gully; cattle path; (Am) brook
cañamazo *m* canvas, burlap; embroidered canvas
cañamiel *f* sugar cane
cáñamo *m* hemp
cañamones *mpl* birdseed
cañaveral *m* canebrake; sugar-cane plantation
cañería *f* pipe; pipe line; piping; **cañería maestra** gas main, water main
cañero *m* pipe fitter, plumber; (Am) sugar-cane dealer; (SAm) cheat; (SAm) bluffer
cañista *m* pipe fitter, plumber
caño *m* pipe, tube; gutter, sewer; ditch; (*chorro*) spurt, jet; (*canal angosto*) channel; organ pipe; (*río pequeño*) (Col) stream
cañón *m* (*pieza de artillería*) cannon; (*valle estrecho*) canyon; (*de arma de fuego; de pluma*) barrel; (*pluma de ave*) quill; (*de escalera*) well; (*de columna; de ascensor*) shaft; organ pipe; (Col) trunk of tree; **cañón de campaña** fieldpiece; **cañón de chimenea** flue, chimney flue; **cañón obús** howitzer
cañonear *tr* to cannonade, to shell
cañutazo *m* (coll) gossip
caoba *f* mahogany
caos *m* chaos
caóti·co -ca *adj* chaotic
cap. *abbr* **capitán, capítulo**
capa *f* cloak, cape, mantle; (*de pintura*) coat; (*lo que cubre*) bed, layer; (*apariencia, pretexto*) (fig) cloak, mask; **capa del cielo** canopy of heaven; **andar de capa caída** to be on the decline, be in a bad way; (*comedia*) **de capa y espada** cloak-and-sword; (*intriga, espionaje*) **de capa y espada** cloak-and-dagger; **so capa de** under the guise of
capacidad *f* capacity
capacitar *tr* to enable, qualify; to empower ‖ *ref* to become qualified
capacha *f* fruit basket; (SAm) jail
capacho *m* fruit basket; hamper; (*de albañil*) hod
capar *tr* to geld, castrate; to curtail
caparazón *m* caparison; horse blanket; nose bag; (*de crustáceo*) shell
caparrosa *f* vitriol
capa·taz *m* (*pl* **-taces**) overseer, foreman, boss
ca·paz *adj* (*pl* **-paces**) (*grande*) capacious, spacious; (*que tiene cierta aptitud; diestro, instruído*) capable; **capaz de** capable of; with a capacity

of; **capaz para** competent in; qualified for; with room for
capcio·so -sa *adj* crafty, deceptive
capea *f* amateur free-for-all bullfight
capear *tr* (*al toro*) to challenge; (*el mal tiempo*) to weather; (coll) to deceive, take in ‖ *intr* (naut) to lay to; (Guat) to play hooky
capellán *m* chaplain
capeo *m* capework (*of bullfighter*)
caperucita *f* little pointed hood; **Caperucita Roja** Little Red Ridinghood
caperuza *f* pointed hood; chimney cap
capilla *f* (*parte de una iglesia con altar*) chapel; (*de los reos de muerte*) death house; (*pliego suelto*) proof sheet; cowl, hood, cape; **estar en capilla** to be in the death house; (coll) to be on pins and needles; **estar expuesto en capilla ardiente** to be on view, to lie in state
capiller *m* churchwarden, sexton
capillo *m* baby cap; baptismal cap; hood; cocoon; (*del cigarro*) filler
capirotazo *m* fillip
capirote *m* hood; doctor's cap and hood; cardboard or paper cone (*worn on head*); fillip
capitación *f* poll tax
capital *adj* capital; main, principal; paramount; (*enemigo*) mortal ‖ *m* (*dinero que produce renta*) capital; (*dinero que se presta para producir renta*) principal ‖ *f* capital
capitalismo *m* capitalism
capitalista *adj* capitalistic ‖ *mf* capitalist; shareholder, investor
capitalizar §60 *tr* to capitalize; (*los intereses devengados*) to compound
capitán *m* captain; leader; **capitán de bandera** flag captain; **capitán de corbeta** (nav) lieutenant commander; **capitán del puerto** harbor master
capitana *f* flagship
capitanear *tr* to captain; to lead, to command
capitanía *f* captaincy; (mil) company
capitel *m* (*de una iglesia*) spire; (*de una columna*) capital
capitolio *m* capitol
capítula *f* chapter (*of Scriptures*)
capitular *tr* to accuse; to agree on ‖ *intr* to capitulate
capitulear *intr* (Arg, Chile, Peru) to lobby
capituleo *m* (Arg, Chile, Peru) lobbying
capitulero *m* (Arg, Chile, Peru) political henchman, lobbyist
capítulo *m* chapter; chapter house; subject, matter; errand; main point; **ganar capítulo** (coll) to win one's point; **llamar a capítulo** to take to task, call to account; **perder capítulo** (coll) to lose one's point
ca·pó *m* (*pl* **-pós**) hood (*of auto*)
capolar *tr* to cut to pieces, chop up
ca·pón -pona *adj* castrated ‖ *m* eunuch; (*pollo*) capon; bundle of firewood; (*golpe*) (coll) fillip ‖ *f* shoulder strap
caponera *f* coop for fattening capons; place of welcome; (*cárcel*) (coll) coop, jail

ca
ca

caporal *m* chief, leader; (Am) foreman (*on cattle ranch*)

capota *f* bonnet; (aer) cowling; (aut) top

capotaje *m* (aer) nosing over

capotar *intr* to upset; (aer) to nose over

capote *m* cape, cloak; (coll) frown, scowl; (Chile, Mex) beating; **capote de monte** poncho; **de capote** (Mex) on the sly; **dar capote a** (coll) to flabbergast; (*un rezagado*) (coll) to leave hungry; **decir para su capote** to say to oneself; **echar un capote** (coll) to turn the conversation

capotear *tr* (*al toro*) to challenge; (*dificultades*) to evade, duck; (coll) to beguile, take in; (*una obra teatral*) to cut, make cuts in

Capricornio *m* Capricorn

capricho *m* caprice, whim, fancy

caprichoso -sa *adj* capricious, whimsical; willful

caprichudo -da *adj* (coll) capricious, whimsical

cápsula *f* capsule; (*de botella*) cap

capsular *tr* to cap

captación *f* capture; (*de las aguas de un río*) harnessing; (rad) tuning in, picking up

captar *tr* to catch; (*la confianza de una persona*) to win; (*las aguas de un río*) to harness; (*las ondas radiofónicas*) to tune in, to pick up; (*lo que uno dice*) to get, grasp ‖ *ref* to attract, win

captura *f* capture, catch

capturar *tr* to capture, catch

capucha *f* cowl, hood; circumflex accent

capuchina *f* garden nasturtium, Indian cress; Capuchin nun; confection of egg yolks

capucho *m* cowl, hood

capuchón *m* lady's cloak and hood; (*de una plumafuente*) cap; (aut) valve cap

capullo *m* cocoon; coarse spun silk; bud; **capullo de rosa** rosebud

capuzar §60 *tr* to throw in headfirst; (*un buque*) to overload at the bow

caqui *adj* khaki ‖ *m* khaki; Japanese persimmon

caquinos *mpl* (Mex) guffaw, outburst of laughter

cara *f* face; look, countenance; façade, front; (*de disco de fonógrafo*) side; **a cara descubierta** openly; **a cara o cruz** heads or tails; **cara a** facing; **cara al público** with an audience; **cara de acelga** (coll) sallow face; **cara de ajo** (coll) vinegar face; **cara de hereje** (*persona de feo aspecto*) (coll) fright, baboon; **cara de vinagre** (coll) vinegar face; **dar la cara** to take the consequences; **de cara** in the face; facing; **echar a cara o cruz** to flip a coin; **hacer cara a** to stand up to; **tener buena cara** to look well, to look good; **tener mala cara** to look ill, to look bad

cárabe *m* amber

carabina *f* carbine; (coll) chaperon

caracol *m* snail; snail shell; (*de pelo*) curl; (*trazado en espiral*) spiral; (*del oído*) cochlea

carácter *m* (*pl* **caracteres**) character; (*marca que se pone a las reses*) brand

característ·i·co -ca *adj* characteristic ‖ *m* (theat) old man ‖ *f* characteristic; (theat) old woman

caracteriza·do -da *adj* distinguished

caracterizar §60 *tr* to characterize; to confer a distinction on; (*un personaje en la escena*) to interpret ‖ *ref* to dress and make up for a role

caramba *interj* confound it!; upon my word!

carámbano *m* icicle

carambola *f* carom; (coll) double shot; (coll) trick, cheating

carambolear *intr* to carom ‖ *ref* (coll) to get tipsy

caramelo *m* caramel; drop, lozenge

carantamaula *f* (coll) ugly false face; (*persona*) (coll) ugly mug

carantoña *f* (coll) ugly false face; **carantoñas** (coll) adulation, fawning

carátula *f* mask; (*profesión de actor*) stage, theater; (Am) title page; (*de reloj*) (Mex, Guat) face

caravana *f* caravan; (*casa rodante*) trailer

caravanera *f* caravansary

caray *m* var of **carey**

carbohielo *m* dry ice

carbóli·co -ca *adj* carbolic

carbón *m* (*de leña*) charcoal; (*de piedra*) coal; (*electrodo de carbono de la lámpara de arco o la pila*) carbon; black crayon; (*honguillo parásito*) smut; **carbón de bujía** cannel coal, jet coal; **carbón tal como sale** run-of-mine coal

carboncillo *m* charcoal, charcoal pencil

carbonera *f* bunker, coal bunker; coalbin; (Col) coal mine

carbonería *f* coalyard

carbone·ro -ra *adj* coal, charcoal; coaling ‖ *mf* coaldealer; charcoal burner ‖ *f* see **carbonera**

carbonilla *f* fine coal; (*en los cilindros*) carbon

carbonizar §60 *tr* to char

carbono *m* carbon

carbunclo *m* (*piedra*) carbuncle; (pathol) carbuncle

carbunco *m* (pathol) carbuncle

carbúnculo *m* (*piedra*) carbuncle

carburador *m* carburetor

carburo *m* carbide

carcacha *f* (Mex) jalopy

carcaj *m* quiver

carcajada *f* outburst of laughter

cárcel *f* jail, prison; (*para oprimir dos piezas de madera encoladas*) clamp

carcele·ro -ra *adj* jail ‖ *m* jailer, warden

carcoma *f* woodworm, borer; anxiety, worry; spendthrift

carcomer *tr* to bore, gnaw away at; to undermine, to harass ‖ *ref* to become worm-eaten

cardán *m* universal joint

cardenal *m* cardinal; cardinal bird; black-and-blue mark

cardenillo *m* verdigris

cárde·no -na *adj* purple; dapple-gray; *(agua)* opaline

cardia·co -ca *adj* cardiac ‖ *mf* (*persona que padece del corazón*) cardiac ‖ *m* (*remedio*) cardiac

cardinal *adj* cardinal

cardo *m* thistle

cardume *m* school (*of fish*)

carear *tr* to bring face to face; to compare ‖ *intr* — **carear a** to overlook ‖ *ref* to meet face to face

carecer §22 *intr* — **carecer de** to lack, need, be in want of

carecimiento *m* lack, need, want

carencia *f* lack, need, want

carente *adj* — **carente de** lacking

careo *m* meeting; confrontation

care·ro -ra *adj* (coll) dear, expensive

carestía *f* scarcity, want, dearth; high prices; **carestía de la vida** high cost of living

careta *f* mask; **careta antigás** gas mask

carey *m* hawksbill turtle; tortoise shell

carga *f* load, loading; (*mercancías que se transportan*) freight, cargo; (*peso u obligación que pesan sobre una persona*) burden; (*de substancia explosiva, de electricidad, de soldados contra el enemigo*) charge; charge, responsibility, obligation; **carga de familia** dependent; **carga de punta** (elec) peak load; **carga útil** pay load; **echar la carga a** to put the blame on; **volver a la carga** to keep at it

cargaderas *fpl* (Col) suspenders

cargadero *m* loading platform; freight station

carga·do -da *adj* loaded; (*cielo*) overcast, cloudy; (*atmósfera, tiempo*) close, sultry; (*alambre eléctrico*) hot, charged; (*café, té*) strong; (*rato, hora*) busy; **cargado de años** along in years; **cargado de espaldas** round-shouldered, stoop-shouldered

cargador *m* loader, stevedore; carrier, porter; (*de acumulador*) charger

cargamento *m* load; (naut) loading; (naut) cargo, shipment

cargante *adj* (coll) boring, annoying, tiresome

cargar §44 *tr* (*un peso, mercancías; un carro, un mulo, un barco; un horno; un arma de fuego; a una persona*) to load; (*a una persona con un peso u obligación*) to burden; (*un acumulador; al enemigo*) to charge; (*a una persona*) to charge with; to entrust with; (coll) to annoy, bore, weary; **cargar en cuenta a** (*una persona*) to charge to the account of; **cargar** (*a una persona*) **de** to charge with; to burden with ‖ *intr* to load; (*el viento*) to turn; to crowd; to incline, tip; (*el acento*) to fall; (coll) to eat too much, drink too much; **cargar con** to pick up; to walk away with; (*un fusil*) to shoulder; to take on; **cargar sobre** to rest on; to bother, pester; to devolve on ‖ *ref* (*el cielo*) to become overcast; (*el viento*) to turn; (coll) to become an-

noyed, be bored; **cargarse de** to have a lot of; (*lágrimas*) to be bathed in

cargaréme *m* receipt, voucher

cargazón *f* loading; (*en el estómago, la cabeza, etc.*) heaviness; mass of heavy clouds; (Arg) clumsy job; (Chile) good crop

cargo *m* job, position; duty, responsibility; burden, weight; management; (*falta que se atribuye a uno; cantidad que uno debe y la acción de anotarla*) charge; **a cargo de** in charge of; **cargo de conciencia** sense of guilt; **girar a cargo de** to draw on; **hacerse cargo de** to take charge of; to realize, become aware of; to look into; **librar a cargo de** to draw on; **vestir el cargo** to look the part

cargosear *tr* (Arg, Chile) to pester

cargo·so -sa *adj* annoying, bothersome; onerous, costly

carguero *m* (naut) freighter; (Arg, Urug) beast of burden

cariaconteci·do -da *adj* (coll) downcast, woebegone

cariar §77 *tr & intr* to decay

cariátide *f* caryatid

Caribdis *f* Charybdis

caribe *adj* Caribbean ‖ *m* savage, brute

caricatura *f* (*descripción o figura grotescas; retrato festivo*) caricature; (*retrato festivo*) cartoon

caricaturista *mf* caricaturist; cartoonist

caricaturizar §60 *tr* to caricature; to cartoon

caricia *f* caress; endearment

caridad *f* charity; **la caridad bien ordenada empieza por uno mismo** charity begins at home

caries *f* decay, tooth decay; caries

carilla *f* (*de colmenero*) mask; (*de libro*) page

carille·no -na *adj* full-faced

carillón *m* carillon

cari·ne·gro -gra *adj* swarthy

cariño *m* love, affection; loved one; (Chile) gift, present; **cariños** caresses, endearments; (Arg) greetings

cariño·so -sa *adj* loving, affectionate

caripare·jo -ja *adj* (coll) stone-faced, impassive

carirraí·do -da *adj* brazen-faced, shameless

carita *f* little face; **dar** or **hacer carita** (*una mujer coqueta*) (Mex) to smile back

caritati·vo -va *adj* charitable

cariz *m* (*de la atmósfera, el tiempo*) appearance, look; (*de un asunto*) (coll) look, outlook; (*de la cara de uno*) (coll) look; **mal cariz** black look, scowl

carlinga *f* (aer) cockpit

Carlomagno *m* Charlemagne

Carlos *m* Charles

carlota *f* pudding; **carlota rusa** charlotte russe ‖ **Carlota** *f* Charlotte

carmen *m* song, poem; house and garden (*in Granada*)

carmesí (*pl* -síes) *adj & m* crimson

carnada *f* bait; (coll) bait, trap

carnal *adj* carnal; (*hermano*) full; (*primo*) first

carne f (*parte blanda del cuerpo humano y del animal*) flesh; (*la comestible del animal*) meat; **carne de cañón** cannon fodder; **carne de cerdo asada** roast pork; **carne de cordero** lamb; **carne de gallina** goose flesh; **carne de horca** gallows bird; **carne de res** beef; **carne de ternera** veal; **carne de vaca asada** roast of beef; **carne de venado** venison; **carne fiambre** cold meat; **carne sin hueso** (coll) cinch, snap; **carne y sangre** flesh and blood; **cobrar carnes** (coll) to put on flesh; **en carnes** naked; **en vivas carnes** stark-naked

carnear tr (Arg, Chile, Urug) to butcher, slaughter; (Arg, Urug) to stab; (Chile) to take in, swindle

carnero m sheep; (*carne de este animal*) mutton; (*osario*) charnel house; family vault; (*persona que no tiene voluntad propia*) (Arg, Chile) sheep; **cantar para el carnero** (Arg, Bol, Urug) to die; **no hay tales carneros** there's no truth to it

car·net m (pl **-nets**) notebook; membership card; (Arg) dance card; **carnet de chófer** driver's license; **carnet de identidad** identification card

carnicería f butcher shop, meat market; (fig) carnage, massacre

carnice·ro -ra adj carnivorous; bloodthirsty || mf butcher

carnosidad f fleshiness, corpulence; (*excrecencia carnosa anormal*) proud flesh

carno·so -sa adj fleshy; meaty, fat

ca·ro -ra adj (*de subido precio; amado, querido*) dear || f see **cara** || **caro** adv dear

carpa f carp; (Am) awning, tent; (Am) stand at a fair; **carpa dorada** goldfish

carpanta f (coll) raging hunger

carpeta f (*cubierta para mesas*) table cover; (*par de cubiertas para documentos*) letter file, portfolio; (*factura*) invoice; (Col) accounting department; (Peru) writing desk

carpintería f carpentry; **carpintería de taller** millwork

carpintero m carpenter; woodpecker; **carpintero de carreta** wheelwright

carra·co -ca adj (coll) old, decrepit || f (*barco viejo*) tub, hulk; (*instrumento de madera para producir un ruido desapacible*) rattle; (*berbiquí*) ratchet drill || **la Carraca** Cádiz navy yard

carraspear intr to be hoarse

carraspera f hoarseness

carrera f (*paso del que corre*) run; (*lucha de velocidad*) race; (*sitio para correr*) race track; (*espacio recorrido corriendo*) course, stretch; (*curso de la vida, profesión*) career; (*calle*) avenue, boulevard; (*raya, crencha*) part (*in hair*); (*en las medias*) run; (*hilera*) row, line; (*viga*) rafter, girder; (*movimiento del émbolo del motor*) stroke; **a carrera abierta** at full speed; **carrera a pie** foot race; **carrera ascendente** upstroke; **carrera de baquetas** gantlet; **carrera de caballos** horse race; **carrera de campanario** steeplechase; **carrera de obstáculos** obstacle race; steeplechase; **carrera de relevos** relay race; **carrera descendente** downstroke; **carrera de vallas** hurdle race; **carreras** horse racing, turf

carrerista adj horsy || mf racegoer; auto racer; bicycle racer || m outrider || f (slang) streetwalker

carreta f cart; **carreta de bueyes** oxcart

carrete m reel, spool; fishing reel; (elec) coil

carretear tr to cart, haul; (*un carro, una carreta*) to drive; (aer) to taxi || intr (aer) to taxi

carretera f highway, road; **carretera de peaje** turnpike; **carretera de vía libre** expressway, limited-access highway

carretería f carts; wagon work; carting business; wagon shop

carrete·ro -ra adj wagon, carriage || m wheelwright; teamster; charioteer; **jurar como un carretero** (coll) to swear like a trooper || f see **carretera**

carretilla f wheelbarrow; baggage truck; (*para enseñar a los niños a andar*) gocart; (*buscapiés*) snake, serpent; (Arg, Chile, Urug) jaw; **carretilla de mano** handcart; **carretilla elevadora** lift truck; **de carretilla** (coll) offhand

carretón m cart, wagon, dray; gocart; (rr) truck; (Am) covered wagon

carricoche m covered wagon

carricuba f street sprinkler

carril m (*barra de acero en el ferrocarril*) rail, track; (*huella*) track, rut; (*hecho por el arado*) furrow; lane, path; (Chile) train; (Chile, P-R) railroad; **carril de toma** third rail

carrilera f track, rut

carrilero m (Peru) railroader

carrillera f jaw; chin strap

carrillo m cheek, jowl; pulley; **comer a dos carrillos** (coll) to eat like a glutton; (coll) to have two sources of income; (coll) to play both sides

carrizo m ditch reed

carro m cart, wagon; (mach) carriage; (Am) car, auto; **carro alegórico** float; **carro blindado** armored car; **carro correo** mail car; **carro de asalto** tank; **carro de combate** combat car, tank; **carro de equipajes** baggage car; **carro de mudanza** moving van; **carro de riego** street sprinkler; **carro frigorífero** refrigerator car; **carro fúnebre** hearse; **Carro mayor** Big Dipper; **Carro menor** Little Dipper; **carro romano** chariot; **pare Vd. el carro** hold your horses

ca·rró m (pl **-rrós**) diamond

carrocería f (*de automóvil*) body

carrocha f eggs (*of insect*)

carromato m covered wagon

carro·ño -ña adj & f carrion

carroza f coach, carriage; **carroza alegórica** float; **carroza fúnebre** hearse

carruaje m carriage

carta *f* (*comunicación escrita*) letter; (*constitución escrita de un país*) charter; (*naipe*) card, playing card; map; **carta aérea** air-mail letter; **carta blanca** carte blanche; **carta certificada** registered letter; **carta de marear** (naut) chart; **carta de naturaleza** naturalization papers; **carta general** form letter; **carta por avión** air-mail letter; **poner las cartas boca arriba** to put one's cards on the table

cartabón *m* carpenter's square

cartagi·nés -nesa *adj & mf* Carthaginian

Cartago *f* Carthage

cartapacio *m* notebook; schoolboy's satchel; writing book; (*papeles contenidos en una carpeta*) file, dossier

cartear *intr* to play low cards (*in order to see how the game stands*) ‖ *ref* to write to each other

cartel *m* show bill, poster, placard; cartel, trust; (*pasquín*) lampoon; (*de toreros*) bill, line-up; (*del torero*) fame, reputation; **cartel de teatro** bill, show bill; **dar cartel a** (coll) to headline; **se prohíbe fijar carteles** post no bills; **tener cartel** (coll) to be the rage

cartela *f* card; bracket

cartelera *f* billboard; (*en los periódicos*) amusement page, theater section

cartelero *m* billposter

cartelón *m* show bill

carteo *m* finessing; exchange of letters

cárter *m* (mach) housing; **cárter de engranajes** gearcase; **cárter del cigüeñal** crankcase

cartera *f* portfolio; pocket flap; **cartera de bolsillo** billfold, wallet

cartería *f* sorting room

carterista *m* pickpocket, purse snatcher

cartero *m* letter carrier, postman

cartilagino·so -sa *adj* gristly

cartílago *m* gristle

cartilla *f* primer, speller, reader; notebook; (*de la caja de ahorros*) deposit book; **cartilla de racionamiento** ration book

cartivana *f* (bb) hinge, joint

cartón *m* cardboard, pasteboard; cardboard box; **cartón de yeso y fieltro** plasterboard; **cartón picado** stencil; **cartón tabla** wallboard

cartoné — en cartoné (bb) in boards, bound in boards

cartucho *m* cartridge

cartulina *f* fine cardboard

casa *f* (*edificio para habitar*) house; (*hogar, domicilio*) home; (*establecimiento comercial o industrial*) firm, concern; (*familia*) household; (*escaque*) square; **a casa** home, homeward; **casa consistorial** town hall, city hall; **casa de azotea** penthouse; **casa de campo** country house; **casa de caridad** poorhouse; **casa de citas** house of assignation; **casa de correos** post office; **casa de empeños** pawnshop; **casa de expósitos** foundling home; **casa de fieras** menagerie; **casa**

de huéspedes boarding house; **casa de juego** gambling house; **casa de locos** madhouse; **casa de modas** dress shop; **casa de moneda** mint; **casa de préstamos** pawnshop; **casa de salud** private hospital; **casa de socorro** first-aid station; **casa de vecindad** or **de vecinos** apartment house, tenement house; **casa editorial** publishing house; **casa matriz** main office; **casa pública** brothel; **casa real** royal palace; royal family; **casas baratas** low-cost housing; **casa solar** or **solariega** ancestral mansion, manor house; **casa y comida** board and lodging; **¡convida la casa!** the drinks are on the house!; **en casa** home, at home; **ir a buscar casa** to go house hunting; **poner casa** to set up housekeeping

casaca *f* dress coat; (coll) marriage contract; (Guat, Hond) lively whispered conversation; **volver la casaca** (coll) to become a turncoat

casade·ro -ra *adj* marriageable

casa·do -da *adj* married ‖ *mf* married person

casal *m* country place; (Arg) pair, couple

casamente·ro -ra *adj* matchmaking ‖ *mf* matchmaker

casamiento *m* marriage; wedding

casapuerta *f* entrance hall, vestibule

casaquilla *f* jacket

casar *tr* to marry; to marry off; to match; to harmonize; (law) to annul, repeal ‖ *intr* to marry, get married ‖ *ref* to marry, get married; **no casarse con nadie** (coll) to get tied up with nobody

casatienda *f* store and home combined

cascabel *m* sleigh bell, jingle bell; rattlesnake; **ponerle cascabel al gato** (coll) to bell the cat

cascabelear *intr* to jingle; (coll) to act tactlessly

cascabeleo *m* jingle

cascabele·ro -ra *adj* (coll) tactless, thoughtless ‖ *mf* (coll) featherbrain ‖ *m* baby's rattle

cascabillo *m* jingle bell; chaff, husk; cup of acorn

cascada *f* cascade, waterfall

cascajo *m* pebble; gravel, rubble; (coll) broken jar; (coll) piece of junk; **estar hecho un cascajo** (coll) to be old and worn-out, to be a wreck

cascanue·ces *m* (*pl* -ces) nutcracker

cascar §73 *tr* to crack, break, split; (coll) to beat, strike, hit ‖ *ref* to crack, break, split

cáscara *f* hull, peel, rind, shell; bark, crust; **cáscara rueda** (Arg) ring-around-a-rosy; **ser de la cáscara amarga** (coll) to be wild and flighty; (coll) to hold advanced views; (Mex) to be determined

cascarón *m* eggshell

cascarra·bias *mf* (*pl* -bias) (coll) crab, grouch

casco *m* (*pieza que sirve para proteger la cabeza del soldado, el bombero, etc.*) helmet; (*uña de las caba-*

llerías) hoof; (*pedazo de vasija rota*) potsherd; (*capa de la cebolla*) coat, shell; (*del sombrero*) crown; (*cuerpo de la nave*) hull; (*de un barco inservible*) hulk; (*barril, pipa*) barrel, tank, cask, vat; (*pieza del teléfono*) headset, headpiece; bottle; (mach) shell, casing; (*gajo de la naranja*) (Arg, Col, Chile) slice; (Peru) chest, breast; **casco de población** or **casco urbano** city limits; **romperse los cascos** (coll) to rack one's brain

casera *f* landlady; housekeeper

casería *f* country place; (Am) customers

caserío *m* country house; small settlement, hamlet

case·ro -ra *adj* homemade; home-loving; (*remedio*) household; house, home; (*sencillo*) homely || *mf* owner, proprietor; renter; caretaker; janitor; (Am) huckster; (Am) vendor || *m* landlord || *f* see **casera**

caseta *f* (*casa sin piso alto*) cottage; (*de una feria*) stall, booth; bathhouse

casi *adv* almost, nearly; **casi nada** next to nothing; **casi nunca** hardly ever

casilla *f* hut, shack, shed; cabin, lodge; stall, booth; (*escaque*) square; (*compartimiento en un mueble*) pigeon-hole; (*división del papel rayado*) column, square; (*taquilla*) ticket office; (*de locomotora o camión*) cab; (Bol, Chile, Peru, Urug) post-office box; (Ecuad) water closet; (Cuba) bird trap; **sacarle a uno de sus casillas** (coll) to jolt someone out of his old habits; (coll) to drive someone crazy

casille·ro -ra *mf* (rr) crossing guard || *m* filing cabinet, set of pigeonholes

casino *m* casino; club; clubhouse

caso *m* case; chance; event; **caso de conformidad** in case you agree; **caso que** in case; **de caso pensado** deliberately, on purpose; **en todo caso** at all events; **hacer al caso** (coll) to be to the purpose; **hacer caso de** (coll) to take into account, pay attention to; **hacer caso omiso de** to pass over in silence, not mention; **no venir al caso** to be beside the point; **poner por caso** to take as an example; **venir al caso** to be just the thing

casorio *m* (coll) hasty marriage, unwise marriage

caspa *f* dandruff, scurf

cáspita *interj* well, well!, upon my word!

caspo·so -sa *adj* full of dandruff

casquete *m* (*cubierta que se ajusta al casco de la cabeza*) skullcap; skull, cranium; (*pieza de la armadura que cubre el casco de la cabeza*) helmet; (*pieza del teléfono*) headset

casquillo *m* butt, cap, tip; bushing, sleeve; ferrule; (Am) horseshoe

casquiva·no -na *adj* (coll) scatterbrained

casta *f* caste; kind, quality; breed, race

castaña *f* chestnut; (*moño*) knot, chignon; demijohn; **castaña de Indias** horse chestnut; **castaña de Pará** Brazil nut

castañeta *f* castanet; snapping of the fingers

castañetear *tr* (*los dedos*) to snap, to click; (*p.ej., una seguidilla*) to click off with the castanets || *intr* to click; (*los dientes*) to chatter

casta·ño -ña *adj* chestnut, chestnut-colored; (*p.ej., pelo*) brown; (*p.ej., ojos*) hazel || *m* chestnut tree; **castaño de Indias** horse chestnut || *f* see **castaña**

castañuela *f* castanet; **estar como unas castañuelas** (coll) to be bubbling over with joy

castella·no -na *adj & mf* Castilian || *m* Castilian, Spanish (*language*) || *f* chatelaine

casticidad *f* purity, correctness (*in language*)

casticismo *m* purism

castidad *f* chastity

castiga·dor -dora *mf* punisher || *m* (coll) seducer, Don Juan

castigar §44 *tr* to punish, chastise; (*la carne*) to mortify; (*los gastos*) to cut down, curtail; (*obras, escritos*) to correct, emend; (*un tornillo*) (Mex) to tighten

castigo *m* punishment, chastisement

Castilla *f* Castile; **Castilla la Nueva** New Castile; **Castilla la Vieja** Old Castile

castillo *m* castle; (*montura sobre un elefante*) howdah; **castillo en el aire** castle in Spain, castle in the air; **castillo de naipes** house of cards; **castillo de proa** forecastle

casti·zo -za *adj* chaste, pure, correct; pure-blooded; real, regular

cas·to -ta *adj* chaste, pure || *f* see **casta**

castor *m* beaver

castrar *tr* to castrate; (*una planta*) to prune, cut back; to weaken

casual *adj* casual, accidental, chance

casualidad *f* accident; chance; chance event; **por casualidad** by chance

casuca or **casucha** *f* shack, shanty

casulla *f* chasuble

cata *f* tasting; taste, sample

catacul·dos *mf* (*pl* -**dos**) (coll) rolling stone; (coll) busybody

catacumba *f* catacomb

cata·lán -lana *adj & mf* Catalan, Catalonian

catalejo *m* spyglass

catalogar §44 *tr* to catalogue

catálogo *m* catalogue

Cataluña *f* Catalonia

cataplasma *f* poultice; **cataplasma de mostaza** mustard plaster

catapulta *f* catapult

catapultar *tr* to catapult

catar *tr* to taste, sample; to check, examine; to be on the look out for

catarata *f* cataract, waterfall; (pathol) cataract

catarro *m* (*inflamación de las membranas mucosas*) catarrh; (*resfriado*) head cold

catástrofe *f* catastrophe

catavino *m* cup for tasting wine
catavi·nos *m* (*pl* **-nos**) winetaster; (*borracho*) (coll) rounder
catear *tr* to hunt, look for; (*a un alumno*) to flunk; (Am) to explore; (*una casa*) (Am) to search
catecismo *m* catechism
cátedra *f* chair, professorship; academic subject; teacher's desk; classroom; **poner cátedra** to hold forth
catedral *f* cathedral
catedrático *m* university professor
categoría *f* category; status, standing; class, kind; condition, quality; **de categoría** prominent
caterva *f* throng, crowd
catéter *m* catheter
cateterizar §60 *tr* to catheterize
cátodo *m* cathode
católi·co -ca *adj* catholic; Catholic; **no estar muy católico** (coll) to be under the weather || *mf* Catholic; **católico romano** Roman Catholic
catorce *adj* & *pron* fourteen || *m* fourteen; (*en las fechas*) fourteenth
catorcea·vo -va *adj* & *m* fourteenth
catorza·vo -va *adj* & *m* fourteenth
catre *m* cot; **catre de tijera** folding cot
catrecillo *m* campstool, folding canvas chair
ca·trín -trina *adj* (CAm, Mex) sporty, swell || *mf* (CAm, Mex) sport, dude
caucasia·no -na or **caucási·co -ca** *adj* & *mf* Caucasian
Cáucaso *m* Caucasus
cauce *m* river bed; channel, ditch, trench
caución *f* precaution; (law) bail, security
caucionar *tr* to guard against; (law) to give bail for
cauchal *m* rubber plantation
caucho *m* rubber; rubber plant; (Col) rubber raincoat; **caucho esponjoso** foam rubber; **cauchos** (*chanclos*) (Am) rubbers
caudal *adj* of great volume || *m* (*de agua*) volume; abundance; wealth
caudalo·so -sa *adj* of great volume; abundant; rich, wealthy
caudillo *m* chief, leader; military leader; caudillo, head of state
causa *f* cause; (law) suit, trial; (Chile) bite, snack; (Peru) potato salad; **a** or **por causa de** on account of, because of
causa·dor -dora *adj* causing || *mf* (*persona*) cause
causante *mf* (*persona*) cause; (law) principal, constituent; (Mex) taxpayer
causar *tr* to cause
causear *tr* (Chile) to get the best of || *intr* (Chile) to have a bite
causeo *m* (Chile) bite, snack
cáusti·co -ca *adj* caustic
cautela *f* caution
cautelo·so -sa *adj* cautious, guarded
cauterizar §60 *tr* to cauterize
cautín *m* soldering iron
cautivar *tr* to take prisoner; to attract, win over; (*encantar*) to captivate
cautiverio *m* or **cautividad** *f* captivity

cauti·vo -va *adj* & *mf* captive
cau·to -ta *adj* cautious
cavar *tr* to dig, dig up || *intr* (*una herida*) to go deep; (*el caballo*) to paw; **cavar en** to study thoroughly, to delve into
caverna *f* cavern, cave
cavidad *f* cavity
cavilar *tr* to brood over || *intr* to worry, fret
cavilo·so -sa *adj* suspicious, mistrustful; (CAm) gossipy; (Col) touchy
cayado *m* (*de pastor*) crook; (*de obispo*) crozier
cayo *m* key, reef; **Cayo Hueso** Key West; **Cayos de la Florida** Florida Keys
caz *m* (*pl* **caces**) flume, millrace
caza *m* pursuit plane, fighter; **caza de reacción** jet fighter || *f* chase, hunt; hunting; (*animales que se cazan*) game; **a caza de** on the hunt for; **caza al hombre** man hunt; **caza de grillos** fool's errand, wild-goose chase; **ir de caza** to go hunting
cazaautógra·fos *mf* (*pl* **-fos**) autograph seeker
caza·dor -dora *adj* hunting || *m* hunter; huntsman; **cazador de alforja** trapper; **cazador de cabezas** head-hunter; **cazador de dotes** fortune hunter; **cazador furtivo** poacher || *f* huntress; hunting jacket; jacket
cazanoti·cias (*pl* **-cias**) *m* newshawk || *f* newshen
cazar §60 *tr* to chase; to hunt; to catch; (*en un descuido o error*) (coll) to catch up; (*un descuido o error*) (coll) to catch; (*adquirir con maña*) (coll) to wangle; (*con halagos o engaños*) to take in || *intr* to hunt
cazarreactor *m* jet fighter
cazcalear *intr* (coll) to buzz around
cazo *m* dipper, ladle; glue pot; (*de cuchillo*) back
cazuela *f* earthen casserole; stew; (*archaic*) gallery for women; (SAm) chicken stew
cazu·rro -rra *adj* (coll) sullen, surly
cazuz *m* ivy
C. de J. *abbr* **Compañía de Jesús**
cebada *f* barley
cebadera *f* nose bag
cebador *m* (mach) primer
cebar *tr* (*a un animal*) to fatten; (*un horno*) to feed; (*un arma de fuego, una bomba, un carburador*) to prime; (*una pasión, la esperanza*) to nourish; (*atraer*) to lure; (*un clavo, un tornillo*) to make catch, make take hold; (*un anzuelo*) to bait || *intr* (*un clavo, un tornillo*) to catch, take hold || *ref* (*una enfermedad, una epidemia*) to rage; **cebarse en** to be absorbed in; to vent one's fury on
cebo *m* fattening; feed; bait; lure; (*carga de un arma de fuego*) primer; priming
cebolla *f* onion; bulb; (*del velón*) oil receptacle
cebra *f* zebra
ce·bú *m* (*pl* **-búes**) zebu

ceca f mint; **de Ceca en Meca** or **de la Ceca a la Meca** hither and thither, from pillar to post

cecear intr to lisp

ceceo m lisp, lisping

cecina f dried beef

cedazo m sieve

ceder tr to yield, cede, give up ‖ intr to yield, give way, give in; to slacken, relax; to go down, decline

cedro m cedar; **cedro de Virginia** juniper, red cedar

cédula f (de papel) slip; form, blank; rent sign; certificate, document; **cédula de vecindad** or **cédula personal** identification papers

cedulón m proclamation, public notice; (pasquín) lampoon

céfiro m zephyr

cegar §66 tr to blind; (un agujero) to plug, stop up; (una puerta, una ventana) to wall up ‖ intr to go blind; to be blinded ‖ ref to be blinded

cega·to -ta adj (coll) dim-sighted, weak-eyed

ceguedad f blindness

ceguera f blindness

Ceilán Ceylon

ceila·nés -nesa adj & mf Ceylonese

ceja f (pelo sobre la cuenca del ojo) eyebrow; edge, rim; cloud cap; (Am) clearing for a road; **arquear las cejas** to raise one's eyebrows; **fruncir las cejas** to knit one's brow; **quemarse las cejas** to burn the midnight oil

cejar intr to back up; to turn back; to slacken

cejijun·to -ta or **ceju·do -da** adj beetle-browed; (coll) scowling

celada f ambush; trap, trick

celador m guard (e.g., in a museum); (elec) lineman; (Urug) policeman

celaje m cloud effect; skylight, transom; (Am) ghost

celar tr to see to; to watch over, to keep an eye on; to hide; to carve

celda f cell; **celda de castigo** solitary confinement

celdilla f cell; niche

celebración f celebration; applause; (de una reunión) holding

celebrante m (sacerdote) celebrant

celebrar tr to celebrate; (una reunión) to hold; (aprobar) to welcome; (un matrimonio) to perform; (misa) to say ‖ intr (decir misa) to celebrate; to be glad ‖ ref to take place, be held; to be celebrated

célebre adj celebrated, famous; (coll) funny, witty; (Am) pretty

celebridad f (fama; persona) celebrity

celeridad f speed, swiftness

celeste adj celestial; sky-blue

celestial adj celestial, heavenly; (coll) stupid, silly

celestina f procuress, bawd

celestinaje m procuring, pandering

celibato m celibacy; (coll) bachelor

célibe adj celibate, single, unmarried ‖ mf celibate, single person ‖ m bachelor ‖ f spinster

celinda f mock orange

celo m zeal; envy; (impulso reproductivo en las bestias) heat, rut; **celos** jealousy

celofán m or **celofana** f cellophane

celosía f (celotipia) jealousy; (enrejado de listoncillos) lattice window, jalousie

celo·so -sa adj (que tiene celo) zealous; (que tiene celos) jealous; fearful, distrustful; (naut) unsteady

celotipia f jealousy

celta adj Celtic ‖ mf Celt ‖ m (idioma) Celtic

célti·co -ca adj Celtic

célula f cell

celuloide m celluloid; **llevar al celuloide** to put on the screen

cellisca f sleet, sleet storm

cellisquear intr to sleet

cementerio m cemetery

cemento m cement; concrete; **cemento armado** reinforced concrete

cena f supper; dinner ‖ **la Cena** the Last Supper

cena·dor -dora mf diner-out ‖ m arbor, bower, summerhouse

cenaduría f (Mex) supper club

cenagal m quagmire

cenago·so -sa adj muddy, miry

cenaoscu·ras mf (pl -ras) (coll) recluse; (coll) skinflint

cenar tr to have for supper, have for dinner ‖ intr to have supper, have dinner

cencerrada f tin-pan serenade

cencerrear intr to keep jingling; to rattle, jangle; (coll) to play out of tune

cencerro m cowbell; **a cencerros tapados** (coll) cautiously

cendal m gauze, sendal

cenefa f edging, trimming, border

cenicero m ash tray

cenicien·to -ta adj ashen, ash-gray ‖ **la Cenicienta** Cinderella

cenit m zenith

ceniza f ash; ashes; **cenizas** ashes; **huir de las cenizas y caer en las brasas** to jump from the frying pan into the fire

ceni·zo -za adj ashen, ash-gray ‖ f see ceniza

cenojil m garter

cenote m (Mex) deep underground water reservoir

censo m census; **levantar el censo** to take the census

censor m censor; **censor jurado de cuentas** certified public accountant

censura f censure; censoring; gossip; **censura de cuentas** auditing

censurar tr (criticar, reprobar) to censure; (formar juicio de) to censor

centauro m centaur

centa·vo -va adj hundredth ‖ m hundredth; cent

centella f flash of lightning; flash of light; spark; (de ingenio, de ira) (fig) spark, flash

centellar or **centellear** intr to flash, to spark; to glimmer, gleam, twinkle

centenar m hundred; **a centenares** by the hundreds

centena·rio -ria *adj* centennial ‖ *mf* centenarian ‖ *m* centennial
cente·no -na *adj* hundredth ‖ *m* rye
centési·mo -ma *adj & m* hundredth
centígra·do -da *adj* centigrade
centímetro *m* centimeter
cénti·mo -ma *adj* hundredth ‖ *m* hundredth; centime
centinela *mf* (*persona*) watch, guard ‖ *m & f* (*soldado*) sentinel, sentry; **hacer de centinela** to stand sentinel
centípedo *m* centipede
central *adj* central ‖ *m* sugar mill, sugar refinery ‖ *f* headquarters, main office; powerhouse; (*telp*) exchange, central; **central de correos** main post office; **central de teléfonos** telephone exchange
centralizar §60 *tr & ref* to centralize
centrar *tr* to center
céntri·co -ca *adj* center, central; (*próximo al centro de la ciudad*) downtown
centro *m* center; middle; business district, downtown; club; object, goal, purpose; **centro de mesa** centerpiece; **centro docente** educational institution; **pegar centro** (CAm) to hit the bull's-eye
Centro América *f* Central America
centroamerica·no -na *adj & mf* Central American
cénts. *abbr* céntimos
ceñi·do -da *adj* tight, tight-fitting; lithe, svelte; thrifty
ceñidor *m* belt, girdle, sash
ceñir §72 *tr* to gird; to girdle; to fasten around the waist; to fasten, to tie; to abridge, shorten; to surround; (*la espada*) to gird on; (*mil*) to besiege ‖ *ref* (*reducirse en los gastos*) to tighten one's belt; (*a pocas palabras*) to restrict oneself; to adapt oneself; **ceñirse a** (*p.ej., un muro*) to hug, keep close to
ceño *m* frown; (*del cielo, las nubes, el mar*) threatening look; (*cerco, aro*) hoop, ring, band; **arrugar el ceño** to knit one's brow; **mirar con ceño** to frown at
ceño·so -sa or **ceñu·do -da** *adj* beetle-browed; frowning, grim, gruff
cepa *f* (*de árbol*) stump; (*de la cola del animal*) stub; (*de la vid*) vine-stalk; (*de una famila o linaje*) strain; **de buena cepa** of well-known quality
cepillar *tr* to plane; to brush; to smooth
cepillo *m* (*instrumento para alisar la madera*) plane; (*utensilio para limpieza*) brush; (*cepo para limosnas*) charity box, poor box; (CAm, Mex) flatterer; **cepillo de cabeza** hairbrush; **cepillo de dientes** toothbrush; **cepillo de ropa** clothesbrush; **cepillo de uñas** nail brush
cepo *m* (*de limosnas*) poor box; (*rama de árbol*) bough, branch; (*trampa*) snare, trap; (*del yunque*) stock; (*para devanar la seda*) reel; clamp, vise; (*para asegurar a un reo*) stocks, pillory; **¡cepos quedos!** (coll) quiet!, stop it!
cera *f* wax; **cera de abejas** beeswax;

cera de los oídos earwax; **cera de lustrar** polishing wax; **cera de pisos** floor wax; **ceras** honeycomb; **se como una cera** to be wax in one's hands
cerámi·co -ca *adj* ceramic
cerbatana *f* peashooter; ear trumpet; (coll) spokesman, go-between
cerca *m* (coll) close-up; **tener buen cerca** (coll) to look good at close quarters ‖ *f* fence, wall; **cerca viva** hedge ‖ *adv* near; **cerca de** near, close to; about; to, at the court of; **de cerca** closely; at close range
cercado *m* fence, wall; walled-in garden or field
cercanía *f* nearness, proximity; **cercanías** neighborhood, vicinity
cerca·no -na *adj* close, near; adjoining, neighboring; (*que debe acontecer en breve*) early
cercar §73 *tr* to fence in, wall in; to encircle, surround; to crowd around; (*mil*) to besiege
cercenar *tr* to clip, trim; to curtail; to cut out
cerciorar *tr* to inform, assure ‖ *ref* to find out; **cerciorarse de** to ascertain, find out about
cerco *m* (*aro, anillo*) hoop, ring; (*marco de puerta o ventana*) casing, frame; (*círculo que aparece alrededor del sol o la luna*) halo; (*reunión de personas*) circle, group; fence, wall; (*mil*) siege; **poner cerco a** (*mil*) to lay siege to
cerda *f* bristle, horsehair; (*hembra del cerdo*) sow
cerdear *intr* to be weak in the forelegs; (*las cuerdas de un instrumento*) to rasp, to grate; (coll) to hold back, look for excuses
Cerdeña *f* Sardinia
cerdo *m* hog; (*persona sucia*) (coll) pig, swine; (*hombre sin cortesía*) (coll) cad, ill-bred fellow; **cerdo de muerte** pig to be slaughtered; **cerdo de vida** pig not old enough to be slaughtered; **cerdo marino** porpoise
cerdo·so -sa *adj* bristly
cereal *adj & m* cereal
cerebro *m* brain; (*seso, inteligencia*) brain, brains
ceremonia *f* ceremony; formality; **de ceremonia** formal; **hacer ceremonias** to stand on ceremony; **por ceremonia** as a matter of form
ceremonio·so -sa *adj* ceremonious, punctilious; (*que gusta de ceremonias*) formal
cereza *f* cherry
cerezo *m* cherry tree
cerilla *f* wax taper; wax match
cerillera *f* or **cerillero** *m* match box
cerneja *f* fetlock
cerner §51 *tr* to sift; (*el horizonte*) to scan ‖ *intr* to bud, blossom; to drizzle ‖ *ref* to waddle; (*el ave*) to soar, to hover; (*un mal*) to threaten; **cernerse sobre** (*amenazar*) to hang over
cernícalo *m* (orn) sparrow hawk; (coll) ignoramus; (coll) jag, drunk

cernir §28 *tr* to sift
cero *m* zero; **ser un cero a la izquierda** (coll) to not count, to be a nobody
cerote *m* shoemaker's wax; (coll) fear
cerotear *tr* (*el hilo*) to wax ‖ *intr* (Chile) to drip
cerra·do -da *adj* closed; close; incomprehensible; (*cielo*) cloudy, overcast; (*barba*) thick; (*curva*) sharp; (coll) quiet, reserved, secretive; (coll) dense, stupid
cerradura *f* lock; closing, locking; **cerradura embutida** mortise lock
cerrajería *f* locksmith business; hardware; hardware store
cerrajero *m* locksmith; hardware dealer; (*el que trabaja el hierro frío*) ironworker
cerrar §2 *tr* to close, shut; to lock; to bolt; (*el puño*) to clench; to enclose; (*la radio*) to turn off; **cerrar con llave** to lock ‖ *intr* to close, to shut; (*la noche*) to fall; **cerrar con** (*el enemigo*) to close in on; **cerrar en falso** (*una puerta, cerradura, etc.*) to not catch ‖ *ref* to close, to shut; to lock; **cerrarse en falso** to not heal right
cerrazón *f* gathering storm clouds; (Arg) heavy fog
cerre·ro -ra *adj* free, loose; untamed; haughty; (Mex) rough, unpolished; (*café*) (Ven) bitter
cerril *adj* rough, uneven; wild, untamed; (coll) boorish, rough
cerrillar *tr* to knurl, to mill
cerro *m* hill, hillock; (*entre dos surcos*) ridge; (*espinazo*) backbone; (*del animal*) neck; **en cerro** bareback; **echar por los cerros de Úbeda** (coll) to talk nonsense; **por los cerros de Úbeda** (coll) off the beaten path
cerrojo *m* bolt; **cerrojo dormido** dead bolt
certamen *m* literary competition; contest, match
certe·ro -ra *adj* certain, sure, accurate; well-informed; (*tiro*) well-aimed; (*tirador*) good, crack
certeza *f* certainty
certidumbre *f* certainty; sureness
certificación *f* certification; certificate
certifica·do -da *adj* registered ‖ *m* registered letter, registered package; certificate; **certificado de estudios** transcript
certificar §73 *tr* to certify; (*una carta*) to register
certitud *f* certainty
cerval *adj* deer; (*miedo*) intense
cervato *m* fawn
cervecería *f* brewery; beer saloon
cervece·ro -ra *adj* beer ‖ *mf* brewer
cerveza *f* beer; **cerveza a presión** draught beer; **cerveza de marzo** bock beer
cer·viz *f* (*pl* **-vices**) cervix; nape of the neck; **bajar** or **doblar la cerviz** to humble oneself; **levantar la cerviz** to raise one's head, become proud; **ser de dura cerviz** to be ungovernable
cesación *f* cessation, suspension

cesante *adj* retired, out of office ‖ *mf* pensioner
cesantía *f* retirement; dismissal (*of a public official*)
cesar *intr* to stop, cease
César *m* Caesar
cese *m* ceasing; notice of retirement; **cese de alarma** all-clear; **cese de fuego** ceasefire
césped *m* lawn, sward; sod, turf
cesta *f* basket; (*para jugar a la pelota*) wicker scoop; **cesta de costura** sewing basket; **cesta para compras** market basket
cesto *m* basket; washbasket; **cesto de la colada** clothesbasket, washbasket; **estar hecho un cesto** (coll) to be overcome with sleep; **ser un cesto** (coll) to be crude and ignorant
cetrería *f* falconry
cetrero *m* falconer
cetri·no -na *adj* (*tez*) sallow; jaundiced, melancholy
cetro *m* scepter; (*para aves*) perch, roost; (eccl) verge; **cetro de bufón** bauble; **cetro de locura** fool's scepter; **empuñar el cetro** to ascend the throne
cf. *abbr* confesor
cg. *abbr* centigramo
C.I. *abbr* cociente intelectual
cía. *abbr* compañía
cía *f* hipbone
cianamida *f* cyanamide
cianuro *m* cyanide
ciar §77 *intr* to back up; to back water; to ease up
ciborio *m* ciborium
cicatear *intr* (coll) to be stingy
cicate·ro -ra *adj* (coll) stingy ‖ *mf* (coll) miser, niggard
cica·triz *f* (*pl* **-trices**) scar
cicatrizar §60 *tr* to heal; (*una impresión dolorosa*) (Arg) to heal ‖ *ref* to heal; to scar
Cicerón *m* Cicero
ciclamor *m* Judas tree; **ciclamor del Canadá** redbud
cícli·co -ca *adj* cyclic(al)
ciclismo *m* bicycle racing
ciclista *mf* bicyclist; bicycle racer
ciclo *m* cycle; series (of lectures); (*en las escuelas*) (Arg, Urug) term
ciclón *m* cyclone
cicuta *f* hemlock
cidra *f* citron (*fruit*)
cidrada *f* citron (*candied rind*)
cidro *m* citron (*tree or shrub*)
cie·go -ga *adj* blind; blocked, stopped up; **más ciego que un topo** blind as a bat ‖ *mf* blind person ‖ *m* blind man ‖ *f* blind woman; **a ciegas** blindly; thoughtlessly; without looking
cielo *m* sky, heavens; (*clima, tiempo*) skies, climate, weather; (*de una cama*) canopy; (*mansión de los bienaventurados*) Heaven; **a cielo abierto** in the open air, outdoors; **a cielo descubierto** openly; **a cielo raso** in the open air, outdoors; in the country; **cielo de la boca** roof of the mouth; **cielo máximo** (aer) ceiling;

cielo raso ceiling; **llovido del cielo** heaven-sent, manna from heaven
cielorraso *m* ceiling
ciem•piés *m* (*pl* **-piés**) centipede
cien *adj* hundred, a hundred, one hundred
ciénaga *f* swamp, marsh, mudhole
ciencia *f* science; knowledge; learning; **a ciencia cierta** with certainty
cieno *m* mud, mire, silt
cieno•so -sa *adj* muddy, miry, silty
ciento *adj & m* hundred, a hundred, one hundred; **por ciento** per cent
cierne *m* budding, blossoming; **en cierne** in blossom; only beginning
cierrarrenglón *m* marginal stop
cierre *m* closing; shutting; snap, clasp, fastener; latch, lock; (*de una tienda, de la Bolsa*) close; (*paro de trabajo*) shutdown; **cierre cremallera** zipper; **cierre de portada** metal shutter (*of store front*); **cierre de puerta** door check; **cierre hermético** weather stripping; **cierre relámpago** zipper
cierro *m* closing; shutting; (Chile) fence, wall; (Chile) envelope
cier•to -ta *adj* certain; a certain; (*acertado, verdadero*) true; (*seguro*) sure; **por cierto** for sure || **cierto** *adv* surely, certainly
cierva *f* hind
ciervo *m* deer, stag, hart
cierzo *m* cold north wind
cifra *f* (*número*) cipher; (*escritura secreta*) code; (*enlace de dos o más letras empleado en sellos*) device, monogram, emblem; abbreviation; amount, sum; **en cifra** in code; in brief; mysteriously
cifrar *tr* to cipher, to code; to abridge; to calculate; **cifrar la dicha en** to base one's happiness in; **cifrar la esperanza en** to place one's hope in || *ref* to be abridged; **cifrarse en** to be based on
cifrario *m* (com) code
cigarra *f* harvest fly, locust
cigarrera *f* cigar case; cigar girl
cigarrería *f* cigar store, tobacco store
cigarre•ro -ra *mf* cigar maker; cigar dealer || *f* see **cigarrera**
cigarrillo *m* cigarette; **cigarrillo con filtro** filter cigarette
cigarro *m* cigar; **cigarro de papel** cigarette; **cigarro puro** cigar
cigoñal *m* well sweep; (*del motor de explosión*) crankshaft
cigüeña *f* stork; crank, winch
cigüeñal *m* var of **cigoñal**
cilicio *m* haircloth, hair shirt
cilindrada *f* piston displacement
cilindrar *tr* to roll
cilíndri•co -ca *adj* cylindrical
cilindro *m* cylinder; roll, roller; (Mex) barrel organ, hand organ
cima *f* (*de árbol*) top; (*de montaña*) top, summit; **dar cima a** to complete, to carry out; **por cima** (coll) at the very top
cimarra *f* — **hacer cimarra** (Arg, Chile) to play hooky
cima•rrón -rrona *adj* (*animal*) (Am) wild, untamed; (*planta*) (Am) wild; (*esclavo*) (Am) fugitive; (*marinero*) (Am) lazy; (*mate*) (Arg, Urug) black, bitter
cimarronear *intr* (Arg, Urug) to drink black maté || *ref* (*el esclavo*) (Am) to flee, run away
címbalo *m* cymbal
cimbel *m* decoy pigeon, stool pigeon
cimborio or **cimborrio** *m* dome
cimbrar or **cimbrear** *tr* to brandish; to swing, sway; to bend; (coll) to thrash, beat || *ref* to swing, sway; to shake
cimbre•ño -ña *adj* flexible, pliant; lithe, willowy
cimentar §2 *tr* to found, establish; to lay the foundations of
cime•ro -ra *adj* top, uppermost
cimiento *m* foundation, groundwork; basis, source
cimitarra *f* scimitar
cinabrio *m* cinnabar
cinanquia *f* quinsy
cinc *m* (*pl* **cinces**) zinc
cincel *m* chisel, graver
cincelar *tr* to chisel, engrave
cinco *adj & pron* five; **las cinco** five o'clock || *m* five; (*en las fechas*) fifth; **¡choque Vd. esos cinco!** or **¡vengan esos cinco!** put it here!, shake!; **decirle a uno cuántas son cinco** (coll) to tell someone what's what
cincograbado *m* zinc etching
cincuenta *adj, pron & m* fifty
cincuenta•vo -va *adj & m* fiftieth
cincha *f* cinch; **a revienta cinchas** at breakneck speed; (Am) reluctantly
cinchar *tr* to cinch; to band, to hoop
cincho *m* girdle, sash; iron hoop; iron tire
cine *m* movie; **cine en colores** color movies; **cine hablado** talkie; **cine mudo** silent movie; **cine parlante** talkie; **cine sonoro** sound movie
cineasta *mf* motion-picture producer; movie fan || *m* movie actor || *f* movie actress
cinedrama *m* screenplay
cinelandia *f* (coll) movieland
cinema *m* var of **cine**
cinematografiar §77 *tr & intr* to cinematograph, to film
cinematógrafo *m* cinematograph; motion picture; motion-picture projector; motion-picture theater
cinematurgo *m* scriptwriter
cinescopio (telv) *m* kinescope
cineteatro *m* movie house
cinéti•co -ca *adj* kinetic || *f* kinetics
cínga•ro -ra *adj & mf* gypsy
cíni•co -ca *adj* cynical; impudent; slovenly, untidy || *mf* cynic || *m* Cynic
cinismo *m* cynicism; impudence
cinta *f* ribbon; (*tira de papel, celuloide, etc.*) tape; film; measuring tape; (*borde de la acera*) curb; fillet, scroll; **cinta aislante** electric tape, friction tape; **cinta de medir** tape measure; **cinta de teleimpresor** ticker tape; **cinta grabada de televisión** video tape; **cinta perforada** punched tape

cintillo *m* hatband; fancy hat cord; ring set with a gem; (*borde de la acera*) (P-R) curb; (Am) hair ribbon

cinto *m* belt, girdle; waist

cintura *f* (*parte estrecha del cuerpo humano sobre las caderas*) waist; waistline; (*de una chimenea*) throat; **meter en cintura** (coll) to bring to reason

cinturón *m* belt, sash; sword belt; **cinturón de asiento** seat belt; **cinturón salvavidas** (naut) safety belt

cipo *m* milestone; signpost; memorial pillar

cipote *adj* (Col, Ven) stupid; (Guat) chubby || *mf* (Hond, El Salv, Ven) brat

ciprés *m* cypress

circo *m* circus

circón *m* zircon

circonio *m* zirconium

circuito *m* circuit; (*de carreteras, ferrocarriles, etc.*) network; race track; **corto circuito** (elec) short circuit

circulación *f* circulation; traffic; **circulación rodada** vehicular traffic

circular *adj* circular || *f* circular, circular letter || *tr & intr* to circulate

círculo *m* circle; club; clubhouse

circuncidar *tr* to circumcise; to clip, curtail

circundante *adj* surrounding

circundar *tr* to surround, go around

circunferencia *f* circumference

circunfle·jo -ja *adj* circumflex

circunlocución *f* or **circunloquio** *m* circumlocution

circunnavegación *f* circumnavigation

circunnavegar §44 *tr* to circumnavigate

circunscribir §83 *tr* to circumscribe || *ref* to hold oneself down; to be held down

circunscripción *f* circumscription; district, subdivision

circunspec·to -ta *adj* circumspect

circunstancia *f* circumstance

circunstancia·do -da *adj* circumstantial, detailed

circunstancial *adj* circumstantial

circunstanciar *tr* to circumstantiate, to describe in detail

circunstante *adj* surrounding; present || *mf* bystander, onlooker

circunveci·no -na *adj* neighboring

circunvolar §61 *tr* to fly around

cirial *m* (eccl) processional candlestick

ciriga·llo -lla *mf* gadabout

ciríli·co -ca *adj* Cyrillic

cirio *m* wax candle

Ciro *m* Cyrus

ciruela *f* plum; **ciruela claudia** greengage; **ciruela pasa** prune

ciruelo *m* plum, plum tree; (coll) stupid fellow

cirugía *f* surgery; **cirugía cosmética, decorativa** or **estética** face lifting

ciruja·no -na *mf* surgeon

ciscar §73 *tr* (coll) to soil, dirty || *ref* (coll) to soil one's clothes, to have an accident

cisco *m* culm; (coll) row, disturbance

cisma *m* schism; discord, disagree-

ment; (Arg) worry, concern; (Col) gossip; (Col) fastidiousness

cismáti·co -ca *adj* schismatic; dissident; (Col) gossipy; (Col) fastidious || *mf* schismatic; dissident

cisne *m* swan; (Arg) powder puff

cisterna *f* cistern; reservoir

cita *f* date, appointment, engagement; (*mención, pasaje textual*) citation, quotation; **cita a ciegas** blind date; **cita previa** by appointment; **darse cita** to make a date

citación *f* citation, quotation; (*ante un juez*) citation, summons

citar *tr* to make a date with, have an appointment with; to cite, to quote; (*ante un juez*) to cite, to summon; (*al toro*) to incite, provoke || *ref* to make a date, have an appointment

cítara *f* (mus) zither

ciudad *f* city; city council; **la ciudad Condal** Barcelona; **la ciudad del Apóstol** Santiago de Compostela; **la ciudad del Betis** Seville; **la ciudad del Cabo** Capetown or Cape Town; **la ciudad de los Califas** Cordova; **la ciudad de los Reyes** Lima, Peru; **la ciudad de María Santísima** Seville; **la ciudad Imperial** or **Imperial ciudad** Toledo

ciudadanía *f* citizenship

ciudada·no -na *adj* city; citizen; civic || *mf* citizen; urbanite

ciudadela *f* citadel; (Cuba) tenement house

cívi·co -ca *adj* civic; city; domestic; public-spirited

civil *adj* civil; civilian || *mf* civilian || *m* guard, policeman

civilidad *f* civility

civilista *adj* civil-law || *mf* authority on civil law; (Chile) antimilitarist

civilización *f* civilization

civilizar §60 *tr* to civilize

civismo *m* good citizenship

cizalla *f* shears; metal shaving, metal clipping; **cizalla de guillotina** gate shears, guillotine shears; **cizallas** shears

cizallar *tr* to shear

cizaña *f* darnel; contamination, corruption; discord; **sembrar cizaña** to sow discord

clac *m* (*pl* **claques**) opera hat, claque, crush hat; (*sombrero de tres picos*) cocked hat

clamar *tr* to cry out for || *intr* to cry out; **clamar contra** to cry out against; **clamar por** to cry out for

clamor *m* clamor, outcry; (*toque de difuntos*) knell, toll; fame

clamorear *tr* to clamor for || *intr* to clamor; (*tocar a muerto*) to toll

clamoreo *m* clamoring; tolling

clamoro·so -sa *adj* clamorous; loud, noisy

clan *m* clan

clandestinista *mf* (Guat) bootlegger

clandesti·no -na *adj* clandestine

claque *f* claque, hired clappers

clara *f* white of egg; bald spot; (*de un trozo de tela*) thin spot; (*en el tiempo lluvioso*) break, let-up

claraboya f (*ventana en el techo*) skylight; (*en la parte alta de la pared*) transom; (*esp. en las iglesias la parte superior de la nave que tiene una serie de ventanas*) clerestory

clarear tr to brighten, light up ‖ intr (*empezar a amanecer*) to get light, to dawn; (*el mal tiempo*) to clear up ‖ ref (*una tela*) to show through; (coll) to show one's hand

clarecer §22 ref to dawn

clarete m claret

claridad f clarity; clearness; brightness; fame, glory; blunt remark; **claridades** plain language

clarido·so -sa adj (CAm, Mex) blunt, rude, plain-spoken

clarificar §73 tr to clarify; to brighten, light up; (*lo que estaba turbio*) to clear

clarín m clarion; fine cambric; (Chile) sweet pea

clarinada f clarion call; (coll) uncalled-for remark

clarinete m clarinet

clarión m chalk

clarividencia f clairvoyance; clear-sightedness

clarividente adj clairvoyant; clear-sighted ‖ mf clairvoyant

cla·ro -ra adj clear; (*de color*) light; (*pelo*) thin, sparse; (*té*) weak; famous, illustrious; (*cerveza*) light; **a las claras** publicly, openly, frankly ‖ m gap; (*en el bosque*) glade, clearing; space, interval; (*ventana u otra abertura*) light; (*claraboya*) skylight; (*en las nubes*) break; **claro de luna** brief moonlight; **de claro en claro** evidently; from one end to the other; **pasar la noche de claro en claro** to not sleep all night; **poner** or **sacar en claro** to explain, clear up; (*un borrador*) to copy ‖ f see **clara** ‖ adv clearly ‖ **claro** interj sure!, of course!; **¡claro está!, ¡claro que sí!** sure!, of course!

claror m brightness; **claror de luna** moonlight, moonglow

claru·cho -cha adj (coll) watery, thin

clase f class; classroom; **clase alta** upper class; **clase baja** lower class; **clase media** middle class; **clase obrera** working class; **clases no-commissioned** officers, warrant officers; **clases pasivas** pensioners

clasicista mf classicist

clási·co -ca adj classical ‖ mf classicist ‖ m classic

clasificador m filing cabinet

clasificar §73 tr to classify; to class; to sort; to file ‖ ref to class

clasismo m segregation

clasista mf segregationist

claudicar §73 intr (*cojear*) to limp; (*obrar defectuosamente*) to bungle; (coll) to back down

claustral adj cloistral

claustro m cloister; (*junta de la universidad*) faculty

cláusula f (*de un contrato u otro documento*) clause; (gram) sentence

clausula·do -da adj (*estilo*) choppy ‖ m series of clauses

clausular tr to close, finish, conclude

clausura f confinement; seclusion; enclosure; adjournment

clausurar tr (*una asamblea, un tribunal, etc.*) to close, to adjourn; (*un comercio por orden gubernativa*) to suspend, to close up

clava f club

clavadista mf (Mex) diver

clava·do -da adj studded with nails; exact, precise; (*reloj*) stopped; sharp, e.g., **a las siete clavadas** at seven o'clock sharp ‖ m (Mex) dive

clavar tr to nail; (*un clavo*) to drive; (*una daga, un punzón*) to stick; (*una piedra preciosa*) to set; (*los ojos, una atención*) to fix; (a *un caballo al herrarlo*) to prick; (coll) to cheat ‖ ref to prick oneself; (coll) to get cheated; (Mex) to dive; **clavárselas** (CAm) to get drunk

clave m harpsichord ‖ f (*de un enigma, código, etc.*) key; (*piedra con que se cierra el arco*) (archit) keystone; (mus) clef

clavel m carnation, pink; **clavel de ramillete** sweet william; **clavel reventón** double-flowered carnation

clavelón m marigold

clavelina f carnation, pink

clave·ro -ra mf keeper of the keys ‖ m clove tree ‖ f nail hole

claveta f peg, wooden peg

clavetear tr to stud; to tip, put a tip on; to wind up, settle

clavicordio m clavichord

clavícula f clavicle, collarbone

clavija f pin, peg, dowel; (elec) plug; (mus) peg; **apretarle a uno las clavijas** (coll) to put the screws on someone

clavillo or **clavito** m brad, tack; (*que sujeta las hojas de unas tijeras*) pin, rivet; clove

clavo m nail; (*capullo seco de la flor del clavero*) clove; migraine; keen sorrow; (*artículo que no se vende*) (Arg, Bol, Chile) drug on the market; (Col) bad deal; (Hond, Mex) rich vein of ore; (Ven) heartburn; **clavo de alambre** wire nail; **clavo de especia** (flor) clove; **clavo de herrar** horseshoe nail; **dar en el clavo** (coll) to hit the nail on the head

clemátide f clematis

clemencia f clemency

clemente adj clement, merciful

cleptóma·no -na mf kleptomaniac

clerecía f clergy

clerical adj & m clerical

clericato m or **clericatura** f priesthood

clerigalla f (contemptuous) priests

clérigo m cleric, priest; **clérigo de misa y olla** (coll) priestlet

clerizonte m shabby-looking priest; fake priest

clero m clergy

clerófo·bo -ba adj priest-hating ‖ mf priest hater

cliché m (*lugar común*) cliché

cliente mf (*parroquiano de una tienda*)

customer; (*de un abogado*) client; (*de un médico*) patient; (*de un hotel*) guest

clientela *f* customers; clientele; patronage, protection; practice

clima *m* climate; country, region; **clima artificial** air conditioning

climatizar §60 *tr* to air-condition

clíni·co -ca *adj* clinical ‖ *mf* clinician ‖ *f* clinic; private hospital; **clínica de reposo** nursing home, convalescent home

cliqueteo *m* clicking

clisar *tr* (typ) to plate

clisé *m* (*plancha clisada*) cliché, plate; (phot) plate; (*lugar común*) cliché

clo *m* cluck; **decir clo** (Chile) to kick the bucket; **hacer clo clo** (*la gallina clueca*) to cluck

cloaca *f* sewer

clocar §81 *intr* to cluck

cloquear *intr* to cluck

cloqueo *m* cluck, clucking

clorhídri·co -ca *adj* hydrochloric

cloro *m* chlorine

clorofila *f* chlorophyll

cloroformizar §60 *tr* to chloroform

cloroformo *m* chloroform

cloruro *m* chloride

club *m* (*pl* **clubs**) club; **club náutico** yacht club

clubista *mf* club member

clue·co -ca *adj* broody; (coll) decrepit

c.m.b., C.M.B. *abbr* **cuyas manos beso**

coa *f* (Mex) hoe; (Chile) thieves' jargon

coacción *f* coercion, compulsion

coaccionar *tr* to coerce, compel

coacervar *tr* to pile up

coactar *tr* to coerce, compel

coadunar *tr & ref* to mix together

coadyuvar *tr & intr* to help, aid, assist

coagular *tr & ref* (*la sangre*) to coagulate; (*la leche*) to curdle

coágulo *m* clot

coalición *f* coalition

coalla *f* woodcock

coartada *f* alibi

coartar *tr* to limit, restrict

coba *f* (coll) hoax; (coll) flattery

cobalto *m* cobalt

cobarde *adj* cowardly; timid; (*vista*) dim, weak ‖ *mf* coward

cobardear *intr* to act cowardly; to be timid

cobardía *f* cowardice; timidity

cobayo *m* guinea pig

cobertera *f* lid; bawd, procuress

cobertizo *m* shed; (*tejado saledizo*) covered balcony, penthouse

cobertor *m* bedcover, bedspread; lid

cobertura *f* cover; covering; (*garantía metálica*) coverage

cobija *f* curved tile; top, lid; short mantilla; (W-I) guano roof; **cobijas** (Am) bedclothes

cobijar *tr* to cover; to shelter, protect

cobijo *m* covering; shelter, protection; (*hospedaje sin manutención*) lodging

cobra *f* team of mares used in threshing; (hunt) retrieval

cobra·dor -dora *adj* (*perro*) retrieving ‖ *mf* collector; trolley conductor

cobranza *f* collecting; (hunt) retrieval

cobrar *tr* (*lo perdido*) to recover; (*lo que otro le debe*) to collect; (*un cheque*) to cash; (*cierto precio*) to charge; to acquire, get; (*una cuerda*) to pull in; (hunt) to retrieve; (*pedir, reclamar*) (Am) to dun; **cobrar afición a** to take a liking for; **cobrar al número llamado** (telp) to reverse the charges; **cobrar ánimo** to take courage; **cobrar carnes** to put on flesh; **cobrar fuerzas** to gain strength ‖ *intr* to get hit ‖ *ref* to recover, to come to

cobre *m* copper; copper or brass kitchen utensils; **batir el cobre** (coll) to hustle, to work with a will; **cobres** (mus) brasses

cobre·ño -ña *adj* copper

cobrero *m* coppersmith

cobri·zo -za *adj* coppery

cobro *m* collection; recovery; **cobro contra entrega** collect on delivery; **en cobro** in a safe place

coca *f* (*en una cuerda*) kink; (coll) head; **de coca** (Mex) free; (Mex) in vain

cocaína *f* cocaine

cocción *f* cooking, baking; (*de objetos cerámicos*) baking, burning

cocear *intr* to kick; (*resistir*) (coll) to balk, rebel

cocer §16 *tr* to cook; to boil; (*pan; ladrillos*) to bake; to digest ‖ *intr* to cook; to boil; to ferment ‖ *ref* to suffer a long time

coci·do -da *adj* cooked ‖ *m* Spanish stew

cociente *m* quotient; **cociente intelectual** intelligence quotient

cocina *f* (*pieza*) kitchen; (*arte*) cooking, cuisine; (*aparato*) stove; **cocina de presión** pressure cooker; **cocina económica** kitchen range

cocinar *tr* to cook ‖ *intr* to meddle

cocine·ro -ra *mf* cook

cocinilla *m* (coll) meddler ‖ *f* kitchenette; chafing dish; **cocinilla sin fuego** fireless cooker

coco *m* cocoanut; (*moño*) topknot, chignon; (*duende*) (coll) bogeyman; (*gesto, mueca*) (coll) face, grimace; (*sombrero hongo*) (Col, Ecuad) derby hat; **hacer cocos** (coll) to make a face; (*los enamorados*) (coll) to make eyes

cocodrilo *m* crocodile

cócora *adj* (coll) boring, tiresome ‖ *mf* (coll) bore, pest

coco·so -sa *adj* worm-eaten

cocotero *m* cocoanut palm or tree

coctel *m* or **cóctel** *m* cocktail; cocktail party

coctelera *f* cocktail shaker

cocuma *f* (Peru) roast corn on the cob

cochambre *m* (coll) dirty, stinking thing, pigsty

cochambro·so -sa *adj* (coll) dirty, stinking

coche *m* carriage; coach; car; taxi; (*puerco*) hog; **caminar en el coche de San Francisco** to go or to ride on shank's mare; **coche bar** (rr) club

car; **coche bomba** fire engine; **coche celular** Black Maria, prison van; **coche de alquiler** cab, hack; **coche de carreras** racing car; **coche de correos** mail car; **coche de plaza** or **de punto** cab, hack; **coche de serie** (aut) stock car; **coche fúnebre** hearse
coche-cama m (pl **coches-camas**) sleeping car
cochecillo m baby carriage; **cochecillo para inválidos** wheelchair; **cochecillo para niños** baby carriage
coche-comedor m (pl **coches-comedores**) (rr) diner, dining car
coche-correo m (pl **coches-correo**) (rr) mail car
coche-fumador m (pl **coches-fumadores**) (rr) smoker, smoking car
coche-habitación m (pl **coches-habitación**) trailer
cochera f coach house; livery stable; carbarn; garage
cochería f (Arg, Chile) livery stable
coche•ro -ra adj easy to cook || m coachman, driver; **cochero de punto** cabby, hackman || f see **cochera**
cocherón m coach house; (depósito de locomotoras) roundhouse
coche-salón m (pl **coches-salón**) (rr) parlor car
cochevira f lard
cochina f sow; (mujer sucia y desaliñada) trollop
cochinada f (coll) piggishness, filthiness; (coll) dirty trick
cochinillo m sucking pig
cochi•no -na adj (coll) piggish, filthy; (tacaño) (coll) stingy; (Ven) cowardly || mf hog; (persona muy sucia) (coll) pig, dirty person || f see **cochina**
cochite hervite adj, adv & m (coll) helter-skelter
cochitril m pigsty; (coll) den, hovel
cochura f batch of dough
codadura f (hort) layer
codal adj elbow || m prop, shoring
codazo m poke, nudge; **dar codazo a** (Mex) to tip off
codear tr (SAm) to sponge on || intr to elbow, elbow one's way || ref to hobnob, to rub elbows
codelincuencia f complicity
codor•niz f (pl **-nices**) quail
codelincuente mf accomplice
codera f elbow patch; elbow itch
códice m codex
codicia f covetousness, greed, cupidity
codiciar tr to covet
codicilo m codicil
codicio•so -sa adj covetous, greedy; (laborioso) hard-working
codificar §73 tr to codify
código m code; **código penal** criminal code
codillo m (de animal) knee; (estribo) stirrup; (de un tubo) elbow; (de la rama cortada) stump
codo m elbow; **dar de codo a** to nudge; (coll) to spurn; **empinar el codo** (coll) to crook the elbow; **hablar por los codos** (coll) to talk too much
coeducación f coeducation

coeficiente adj & m coefficient
coetáne•o -a adj & mf contemporary
coexistencia f coexistence
coexistir intr to coexist
cofa f (naut) top; **cofa de vigía** (naut) crow's-nest
cofrade mf member, fellow member || m brother || f sister
cofradía f brotherhood, sisterhood; association, fraternity
cofre m coffer, chest, trunk
cogedor m dustpan; coal shovel, ash shovel
coger §17 tr to catch, seize, take hold of: to collect, gather, pick; to overtake; to surprise; to hold || intr to be, be located; to fit || ref to get caught; to cling; to get involved
cogida f (coll) collecting, gathering, picking; (taur) hook
cogollo m (de la lechuga) heart; (de la berza) head; (de una planta) shoot; (del árbol) top; (lo mejor) cream, pick
cogote m back of the neck
cogotera f havelock
cogotu•do -da adj thick-necked; (coll) proud, stiff-necked; (SAm) moneyed
cogulla f cowl, frock; **cogulla de fraile** (bot) monkshood
cohabitar intr to live together; (el hombre y la mujer) to cohabit
cohechar tr to bribe; to plow just before sowing || intr to take a bribe
cohecho m bribe
coherede•ro -ra mf coheir || f coheiress
coherente adj coherent
cohesión f cohesion
cohete m (fuego artificial) rocket, sky-rocket; (motor a reacción) rocket; (coll) fidgety person; **cohete de señales** (aer) flare; **cohete lanzador** booster rocket
cohibente adj (elec) nonconducting
cohibi•do -da adj timid, self-conscious
cohibir tr to check, restrain, inhibit; (Mex) to oblige
cohombro m cucumber
cohonestar tr to gloss over, to rationalize
coima f rake-off paid to operator of a gambling table; concubine; (SAm) bribe
coincidencia f coincidence
coincidir intr to coincide; to happen at the same time; to be at the same time (at a given place); to agree
coito m coition, coitus
coja f lame woman; (coll) lewd woman
cojear intr to limp; (una mesa, una silla) to wobble; (adolecer de algún vicio) to slip, lapse, have a weakness
cojera f (anormalidad del que cojea) lameness; (movimiento del que cojea) limp
cojijo m bug, insect; (coll) peeve
cojijo•so -sa adj peevish
cojín m cushion
cojincillo m pad
cojinete m cushion; sewing cushion; (mach) bearing; **cojinete de bolas** ball bearing; **cojinete de rodillos** roller bearing

co·jo -ja *adj* lame, crippled; *(mesa, silla)* wobbly; *(pierna)* game ‖ *mf* lame person, cripple ‖ *f* see **coja**

cojón *m* testicle

cok *m* var of **coque**

col. *abbr* **colonia, columna**

col *f* cabbage; **col de Bruselas** Brussels sprouts

cola *f* *(de animal, de ave, de cometa)* tail; *(de un vestido)* train, trail; *(de personas que esperan turno)* queue; *(extremidad posterior)* tail end, rear end; *(de una clase de alumnos)* bottom; *(pasta fuerte)* glue; **cola del pan** bread line; **cola de milano** or **de pato** dovetail; **cola de pescado** isinglass; **cola de retazo** size, sizing; **hacer cola** to queue, to stand in line

colaboración *f* collaboration; *(en un periódico, coloquio, etc.)* contribution

colaboracionista *mf* collaborationist

colabora·dor -dora *adj* collaborating ‖ *mf* collaborator; contributor

colaborar *intr* to collaborate; *(en un periódico, coloquio, etc.)* to contribute

colación *f* *(cotejo; refacción ligera)* collation; *(de un grado de universidad)* conferring; parish land; **sacar a colación** to mention, bring up; **traer a colación** to bring up; to adduce as proof; to bring up irrelevantly

colacionar *tr* to collate; to compare; *(un beneficio)* to confer

colactánea *f* foster sister

colactáneo *m* foster brother

colada *f* washing powder; wash; *(garganta entre montañas)* gulch; cattle run; **todo saldrá en la colada** (coll) it will all come out in the wash; (coll) the day of reckoning will come

coladera *f* strainer; (Mex) sewer

coladero *m* strainer; cattle run; narrow pass

colador *m* strainer, colander

colapez *f* or **colapiscis** *f* isinglass

colapso *m* breakdown, collapse; **colapso nervioso** nervous breakdown

colar *tr* *(un grado universitario)* to confer ‖ §61 *tr* *(un líquido)* to strain; to bleach in hot lye, to buck; *(metales)* to cast; *(una moneda falsa)* (coll) to pass off; **colar el hueso por** (coll) to squeeze through ‖ *intr* to run, to ooze; to squeeze through; to come in, slip in; (coll) to drink wine; **colar a fondo** to sink; **no colar** *(una cosa)* (coll) to not be believed ‖ *ref* to seep, seep through; to slip in, slip through; to make a slip; to lie; **colarse de gorra** (coll) to crash the gate

colateral *adj* collateral ‖ *mf* *(pariente)* collateral ‖ *m* (com) collateral

colcrén *m* cold cream

colcha *f* quilt, counterpane, bedspread

colchón *m* mattress; **colchón de aire** air mattress; **colchón de muelles** bedspring, spring mattress; **colchón de plumas** feather bed

coleada *f* wag *(of the tail)*; (Mex, Ven) throwing the bull by twisting its tail

colear *tr* (taur) to grab by the tail; *(la res)* (Mex, Ven) to throw by twisting the tail; (Col, Ven) to nag, harass; (Guat) to trail after; *(reprobar en un examen)* (Chile) to flunk ‖ *intr* to wag the tail; (aer) to fishtail; (coll) to stay alive, to keep going; *(los últimos vagones de un tren)* (Am) to sway; **colear en** *(cierta edad)* (CAm, W-I) to border on, be close to; **todavía colea** (coll) it's not over yet

colección *f* collection

coleccionar *tr* to collect

coleccionista *mf* collector

colecta *f* collection for charity; (eccl) collect

colectar *tr* to collect; *(obras antes sueltas)* to collect in one volume

colecti·cio -cia *adj* new, untrained, green; *(tomo)* omnibus

colecti·vo -va *adj* collective

colector *m* collector; catch basin; (elec) commutator; (aut) manifold

colega *mf* colleague ‖ *m* confrere

colegial *m* schoolboy

colegiala *f* schoolgirl

colegiatura *f* scholarship; (Mex) tuition

colegio *m* school, academy; *(sociedad de hombres de una misma profesión)* college *(e.g., of cardinals, electors)*

colegir §57 *tr* to gather, collect; to conclude, infer

cólera *m* cholera ‖ *f* anger, wrath; *(bilis)* bile; **montar en cólera** to fly into a rage

coléri·co -ca *adj* choleric, irascible

colesterol *m* cholesterol

coleta *f* pigtail; *(del torero)* cue, queue; (coll) postscript; **cortarse la coleta** to quit the bull ring; to quit, retire; **tener** or **traer coleta** to have serious consequences

coletero *m* wren

coleto *m* buff jacket; (coll) body, one's body, oneself; **decir para su coleto** (coll) to say to oneself; **echarse al coleto** (coll) to eat up, drink up; (coll) to read from cover to cover

colgadero *m* hanger, hook; clothes rack

colgadizo *m* lean-to, penthouse; projection over a door, canopy

colga·do -da *adj* pending, unsettled; **dejar colgado** (coll) to disappoint, frustrate; **quedarse colgado** (coll) to be disappointed, frustrated

colgador *m* clothes hanger, coat hanger

colgajo *m* rag, tatter

colgante *adj* hanging, dangling; *(puente)* suspension ‖ *m* drop, pendant; (archit) festoon; (P-R) watch fob

colgar §63 *tr* to hang; to impute, attribute; *(a un alumno)* to flunk; *(a un reo)* (coll) to hang ‖ *intr* to hang, hang down, dangle; to droop; (telp) to hang up; **colgar de** to hang from, hang on; to depend on

colibrí *m* *(pl* **-bríes)** humming bird

cóli·co -ca *adj & m* colic ‖ *f* upset stomach

coliche *m* (coll) at-home, open house

coliflor *f* cauliflower

coligar §44 *ref* to join forces, make common cause
colilla *f* butt, stump, stub
co·lín -lina *adj* (*caballo o yegua*) bobtailed ‖ *m* bobwhite; **colín de Virginia** bobwhite ‖ *f* see **colina**
colina *f* hill, knoll
colindante *adj* adjacent, contiguous
colindar *intr* to be adjacent
colino·so -sa *adj* hilly
colirio *m* eyewash
coliseo *m* coliseum
colisión *f* collision; bruise, bump
colista *mf* (coll) person standing in line
colma·do -da *adj* abundant, plentiful ‖ *m* food store, grocery store; seafood restaurant
colmar *tr* to fill up; (*las esperanzas de uno*) to fulfill; to overwhelm; **colmar de** to shower with, overwhelm with
colmena *f* beehive
colmenar *m* apiary
colmene·ro -ra *mf* beekeeper
colmillo *m* eyetooth, canine tooth; (*del elefante*) tusk; **tener el colmillo retorcido** (coll) to cut one's eyeteeth
col·mo -ma *adj* brimful, overflowing ‖ *m* overflow; thatch, thatch roof; (*de un sorbete*) topping; **eso es el colmo** (coll) that's the limit; **para colmo de** to top off
colocación *f* (*acción de poner una persona o cosa en un lugar*) location; (*disposición de una cosa respecto del lugar que ocupa*) placement; (*inversión de dinero*) investment; (*empleo*) position, employment, job
colocar §73 *tr* to place, put; (*una trampa*) to set ‖ *ref* to get placed, find a job; (*venderse*) to sell
colodra *f* milk bucket; drinking horn; (*bebedor de vino*) (coll) toper
colofón *m* colophon
colofonia *f* rosin
coloide *adj & m* colloid
colon *m* colon; (gram) main clause
Colón *m* Columbus
colonia *f* colony; cologne; silk ribbon; housing development; (W-I) sugar plantation ‖ **Colonia** *f* Cologne; **la Colonia del Cabo** Cape Colony
colonial *adj* colonial; overseas ‖ **coloniales** *mpl* imported foods
colonizar §60 *tr & intr* to colonize
colono *m* colonist, settler; tenant farmer; (W-I) owner of sugar plantation
coloquial *adj* colloquial
coloquialismo *m* colloquialism
coloquio *m* colloquy, talk, conference
color *m* color; (*substancia para pintar*) paint; (*para pintarse el rostro*) rouge; **colores** (*bandera*) colors; (*persona*) **de color** colored; (*zapatos*) tan; **sacar los colores** to make blush; **so color de** under color of, under pretext of; **verlo todo de color de rosa** to see everything through rose-colored glasses
colora·do -da *adj* red, reddish; (*libre, obsceno*) off-color; (*aparentemente justo y razonable*) specious; **ponerse colorado** to blush

colorado·te -ta *adj* (coll) ruddy, sanguine
colorante *adj & m* coloring
colorar *tr* to color; to dye; to stain
colorear *tr* to color; (fig) to color, excuse, palliate ‖ *ref* (*la cereza, el tomate, etc.*) to redden, turn red
colorete *m* rouge; **ponerse colorete** to put on rouge
colorir §1 *tr* to color; (fig) to color, to palliate ‖ *intr* to take on color
colosal *adj* colossal
coloso *m* colossus
columbrar *tr* to discern, descry, glimpse; to guess
columna *f* column; **quinta columna** fifth column
columnata *f* colonnade
columnista *mf* columnist
columpiar *tr* to swing ‖ *ref* to swing; to seesaw; (coll) to swing, swagger
columpio *m* swing; **columpio de tabla** seesaw
colusión *f* collusion
collada *f* mountain pass; (naut) steady blow
collado *m* hill, height
collar *m* necklace; dog collar; horse collar; (*aro de hierro asegurado al cuello del malhechor*) collar, band; (*plumas del cuello de ciertas aves*) frill, ring; (*cadena que rodea el cuello como insignia*) cord, chain; (mach) collar
collera *f* horse collar; chain gang; **colleras** (Arg, Chile) cuff links
co·llón -llona *adj* (coll) cowardly ‖ *mf* (coll) coward
coma *m* (pathol) coma ‖ *f* comma; (*en inglés se emplea el punto en aritmética para separar los enteros de las fracciones decimales*) decimal point
comadre *f* mother or godmother (*with respect to each other*); gossip (*woman*); friend, neighbor (*woman*)
comadrear *intr* (coll) to gossip, go around gossiping
comadreja *f* weasel
comadrería *f* (coll) gossip, idle gossip
comadre·ro -ra *adj* (coll) gossipy ‖ *mf* (coll) gossip
comadrón *m* accoucheur
comadrona *f* midwife
comandancia *f* command; commander's headquarters; (mil) majority
comandante *m* commander, commandant; (mil) major
comandar *tr* (mil, nav) to command
comando *m* (mil) command; **comando a distancia** remote control
comarca *f* district, region, country
comarcar §73 *tr* to plant in a line at regular intervals ‖ *intr* to border, be contiguous
comato·so -sa *adj* comatose
comba *f* bend, curve; warp, bulge; skipping rope; **saltar a la comba** to jump rope, to skip rope
combar *tr* to bend, curve ‖ *ref* to bend, curve; to warp, bulge; to sag
combate *m* combat, fight; **combate revancha** (box) return bout; **fuera de**

combate hors de combat; (box) knockout
combatiente *adj & m* combatant
combatir *tr* to combat, fight; to beat, beat upon ‖ *intr & ref* to combat, fight, struggle
combinación *f* combination; (*de trenes*) connection
combinar *tr & ref* to combine
com·bo -ba *adj* bent, curved, crooked; warped ‖ *m* trunk or rock to stand wine casks on ‖ *f see* **comba**
combustible *adj* combustible ‖ *m* (*substancia que arde con facilidad*) combustible; (*substancia que sirve para calentar, cocinar, etc.*) fuel
combustión *f* combustion
comede·ro -ra *adj* eatable ‖ *m* manger, feed trough; (Mex) haunt, hangout; **limpiarle a uno el comedero** (coll) to deprive someone of his bread and butter
comedia *f* drama, play; theater; comedy; (fig) farce; **comedia cómica** (*drama de desenlace festivo*) comedy; **hacer la comedia** (coll) to pretend, make believe
comedian·te -ta *mf* (coll) hypocrite ‖ *m* actor, comedian ‖ *f* actress, comedienne
comedi·do -da *adj* courteous, polite; moderate; (Am) obliging, accommodating
comedimiento *m* courtesy, politeness; moderation
comediógra·fo -fa *mf* playwright
comedir §50 *ref* to be courteous; to restrain oneself, be moderate; (Am) to be obliging; **comedirse a** (Am) to offer to, to volunteer to
comedón *m* blackhead
come·dor -dora *adj* heavy-eating ‖ *m* dining room; restaurant, eating place; dining-room suite; **comedor de beneficencia** soup kitchen
comején *m* termite
comendador *m* prelate, prior; knight commander; (*de una orden militar*) commander
comensal *mf* dependent, servant; table companion
comentar *tr* to comment on ‖ *intr* to comment; (coll) to gossip
comentario *m* comment, commentary; **comentarios** (coll) talk, gossip
comentarista *mf* commentator
comento *m* comment, commentary; deceit, falsehood
comenzar §18 *tr & intr* to commence, begin, start
comer *m* eating, food ‖ *tr* to eat; to feed on; to gnaw away; to consume; (*alguna renta*) to enjoy; to itch; (*una pieza en el juego de damas*) to take; **comer vivo** (coll) to have it in for; **sin comerlo ni beberlo** (coll) without having anything to do with it; **tener qué comer** (coll) to have enough to live on ‖ *intr* to eat; to dine, to have dinner; to itch ‖ *ref* to eat up; (*las uñas*) to bite; (*el dinero*) (coll) to consume, eat up; (*omitir*) to skip,

skip over; **comerse unos a otros** (coll) to be at loggerheads
comerciable *adj* marketable; sociable
comercial *adj* commercial, business
comerciante *mf* merchant, trader, dealer; **comerciante al por mayor** wholesaler; **comerciante al por menor** retailer
comerciar *intr* to trade, to deal
comercio *m* commerce, trade, business; store, shop; business center; commerce, intercourse; **comercio de artículos de regalo** gift shop; **comercio exterior** foreign trade
comestible *adj* eatable ‖ *m* food, foodstuff
cometa *m* comet ‖ *f* kite
cometer *tr* (*un crimen, una falta*) to commit; (*un negocio a una persona*) to commit, to entrust; (*figuras retóricas*) to employ
cometido *m* assignment, duty; commitment
comezón *f* itch
comicastro *m* ham, ham actor
comicios *mpl* polls; **acudir a los comicios** to go to the polls
cómi·co -ca *adj* comic, comical; dramatic ‖ *mf* actor; comedian; **cómico de la legua** strolling player, barnstormer ‖ *f* actress; comedienne
comida *f* (*alimento*) food; (*el que se toma a horas señaladas*) meal; (*el principal de cada día*) dinner; **comida corrida** (Mex) table d'hôte
comidilla *f* (coll) hobby; **la comidilla del pueblo** (coll) the talk of the town
comienzo *m* beginning, start; **a comienzos de** around the beginning of
comilitona *f* (coll) spread, feast
comi·lón -lona *adj* (coll) heavy-eating ‖ *mf* (coll) hearty eater ‖ *f* (coll) hearty meal, spread
comillas *fpl* quotation marks
cominear *intr* (*el hombre*) (coll) to fuss around like a woman
comiquear *intr* to put on amateur plays
comiquillo *m* ham, ham actor
comisar *tr* to seize, confiscate
comisario *m* commissary; commissioner; **comisario de a bordo** purser
comisión *f* commission; committee; (*recado*) errand
comisiona·do -da *mf* commissioner ‖ *m* committeeman
comisionar *tr* to commission
comiso *m* seizure, confiscation; confiscated goods
comisura *f* corner (*e.g., of lips*)
comité *m* committee
comitente *mf* constituent
comitiva *f* retinue, suite; procession
como *adv* as, like; so to speak, as it were ‖ *conj* as; when; if; so that; as soon as; as long as; inasmuch as; **así como** as soon as; **como no** unless; **como que** because, inasmuch as; **como quien dice** so to speak; **tan luego como** as soon as
cómo *adv* how; why; what; **¿a cómo es . . .?** how much is . . .?; **¿cómo no?** why not?
cómoda *f* bureau, commode, chest

comodidad _f_ comfort; convenience; advantage, interest

comodín _m_ joker, wild card; gadget, jigger; excuse, alibi

có·mo·do -da _adj_ handy, convenient; comfortable ‖ _f_ see **cómoda**

como·dón -dona _adj_ (coll) comfort-loving, self-indulgent, easy-going

compac·to -ta _adj_ compact

compadecer §22 _tr_ to pity, feel sorry for ‖ _ref_ to harmonize; **compadecerse con** to harmonize with; **compadecerse de** to pity, feel sorry for

compadraje _m_ clique, cabal

compadrar _intr_ to become a godfather; to become friends

compadre _m_ father or godfather (_with respect to each other_); friend, companion

compadrear _intr_ (coll) to be close friends; (Arg, Urug) to brag, show off

compadrería _f_ close companionship

compadrito _m_ (Arg) bully

compaginar _tr_ to arrange, put in order ‖ _ref_ to fit, agree; to blend

companage _m_ snacks, cold cuts

compañerismo _m_ companionship

compañe·ro -ra _mf_ companion; partner; mate; **compañero de cama** bedfellow; **compañero de cuarto** roommate; **compañero de juego** playmate; **compañero de viaje** fellow traveler ‖ _f_ (_esposa_) helpmeet

compañía _f_ company; society; **compañía de desembarco** (nav) landing force; **hacerle compañía a una persona** to keep someone company

compañón _m_ testicle; **compañón de perro** orchid

comparación _f_ comparison

comparar _tr_ to compare

comparati·vo -va _adj_ comparative

comparecencia _f_ (law) appearance

comparecer §22 _intr_ (law) to appear

comparendo _m_ (law) summons

comparsa _mf_ (theat) supernummerary, extra ‖ _f_ supernummeraries, extras

compartimiento _m_ distribution, division; compartment

compartir _tr_ to distribute, divide; to share

compás _m_ (_brújula_) compass; (_instrumento para trazar curvas_) compass or compasses; rule, measure; (mus) time, measure; (mus) bar, measure; (mus) beat; **a compás** (mus) in time; **compás de calibres** calipers; **compás de división** dividers; **llevar el compás** (mus) to keep time

compasible _adj_ compassionate; pitiful

compasión _f_ compassion; **¡por compasión!** for pity's sake!

compasi·vo -va _adj_ compassionate

compatri·cio -cia or **compatriota** _mf_ fellow countryman, compatriot

compeler _tr_ to compel

compendiar _tr_ to condense, to summarize

compendio _m_ compendium; **en compendio** in a word

compendio·so -sa _adj_ compendious

compensación _f_ compensation; (com) clearing, clearance

compensar _tr_ to compensate; to compensate for ‖ _intr_ to compensate ‖ _ref_ to be compensated for

competencia _f_ (_aptitud_) competence; (_rivalidad_) competition; dispute; area, field; **de la competencia de** in the domain of; **sin competencia** unmatched (_prices_)

competente _adj_ competent; reliable

competer _intr_ to be incumbent

competición _f_ competition

competi·dor -dora _adj_ competing ‖ _mf_ competitor

competir §50 _intr_ to compete

compilación _f_ compilation

compilar _tr_ to compile

compinche _mf_ (coll) chum, crony, pal

complacencia _f_ complacency

complacer §22 _tr_ to please, to humor ‖ _ref_ to be pleased, take pleasure

complaciente _adj_ obliging; indulgent

comple·jo -ja _adj_ & _m_ complex; **complejo de inferioridad** inferiority complex

complementar _tr_ to complement

complemento _m_ complement; completion; perfection; accessory; **complemento directo** (gram) direct object

completar _tr_ to complete; to perfect

comple·to -ta _adj_ complete; (_autobús, tranvía_) full

complexión _f_ constitution

complexiona·do -da _adj_ — **bien complexionado** strong, robust; **mal complexionado** weak, frail

comple·xo -xa _adj_ complex

complica·do -da _adj_ complicated, complex

complicar §73 _tr_ to complicate; to involve ‖ _ref_ to become complicated; to become involved

cómplice _mf_ accomplice, accessory

complicidad _f_ complicity

com·plot _m_ (_pl_ -plots) plot, intrigue

compone·dor -dora _mf_ composer, compositor; typesetter; arbitrator; repairer ‖ _m_ stick, composing stick; **amigable componedor** mediator, umpire

componenda _f_ compromise, settlement, reconciliation

componente _adj_ component, constituent ‖ _m_ component, constituent; member ‖ _f_ (mech) component

componer §54 _tr_ to compose; to compound; to mend, repair; to pacify, reconcile; to arrange, put in order; (coll) to restore, strengthen; (_huesos dislocados_) (Am) to set; (Col) to bewitch ‖ _ref_ to compose oneself; to get dressed; to make up, become friends again; (_pintarse el rostro_) to make up; **componérselas** (coll) to make out, to manage

comportable _adj_ bearable, tolerable

comportamiento _m_ behavior, conduct

comportar _tr_ to support; (Am) to bring about, entail ‖ _ref_ to act, behave

comporte _m_ behavior; carriage, bearing

composición _f_ composition; agreement; (_circunspección_) composure, restraint; **hacer una composición de lugar** to carefully lay one's plans

compositi·vo -va *adj* (gram) combining

composi·tor -tora *mf* composer || *m* (Arg, Urug) horse trainer, trainer of fighting cocks

compostura *f* composition; agreement; (*circunspección*) composure, restraint; repair, repairing, mending; (*aseo*) neatness; adulteration; (Arg, Urug) training

compota *f* compote, preserves; **compota de frutas** stewed fruit; **compota de manzanas** applesauce

compotera *f* (*vasija*) compote

compra *f* purchase, buy; shopping; **compra al contado** cash purchase; **compra a plazos** installment buying; **hacer compras, ir de compras** to go shopping

compra·dor -dora *mf* buyer; shopper

comprar *tr* to purchase, to buy; (*sobornar*) to buy off || *intr* to shop

compraventa *f* dealing, business, bargain, trading; resale

comprender *tr* (*entender*) to understand; (*entender; abrazar*) to comprehend; (*contener, incluir*) to comprise

comprensible *adj* comprehensible, understandable

comprensión *f* understanding, comprehension; inclusion

comprensi·vo -va *adj* understanding; comprehensive; **comprensivo de** inclusive of

compresa *f* (med) compress; **compresa higiénica** sanitary napkin

compresión *f* compression

comprimido *m* tablet

comprimir *tr* to compress; to restrain, repress; to flatten

comprobación *f* checking, verification; proof

comprobante *adj* proving || *m* certificate, voucher, warrant; proof; claim check

comprobar §61 *tr* to check, verify; to prove

comprometer *tr* to compromise, endanger, jeopardize; to force, to oblige; (*un negocio a un tercero*) to entrust || *ref* to promise; to commit oneself; to become engaged

comprometi·do -da *adj* awkward, embarrassing; engaged to be married

comprometimiento *m* commitment, promise; predicament, awkward situation; compromise

compromiso *m* commitment, promise; appointment, engagement; predicament, awkward situation; betrothal

compuerta *f* hatch, half door; floodgate, sluice

compues·to -ta *adj* & *m* composite, compound

compulsar *tr* to collate; to make an authentic copy of

compungi·do -da *adj* remorseful

compungir §27 *tr* to make remorseful || *ref* to feel remorse

compurgar §44 *tr* (*el reo la pena*) (Mex) to finish serving

compudador *m* or **computadora** computer; (coll) hardware

computar *tr* & *intr* to compute

cómputo *m* computation, calculation

comulgante *mf* (eccl) communicant

comulgar §44 *tr* to administer communion to || *intr* to take communion

comulgatorio *m* communion rail, altar rail

común *adj* common || *m* community; water closet; toilet; **el común de las gentes** the general run of people; **por lo común** commonly

comunal *adj* common; community || *m* community

comune·ro -ra *adj* popular || *m* shareholder

comunicación *f* communication; connection

comunicado *m* communiqué; letter to the editor; official announcement

comunica·dor -dora *adj* communicating

comunicante *mf* communicant, informant

comunicar §73 *tr* to communicate; to notify, inform; to connect, put into communication || *intr* to communicate || *ref* to communicate; to communicate with each other

comunicati·vo -va *adj* communicative

comunidad *f* community

comunión *f* communion; political party; sect

comunismo *m* communism

comunista *mf* communist

comunistizar §60 *tr* to convert to communism || *ref* to become communistic

comunizar §60 *tr* to communize

con *prep* with; to, towards; in spite of; **con que** and so; whereupon; **con tal (de) que** provided that; **con todo** however, nevertheless

conato *m* effort, endeavor; (*delito que no llegó a consumarse*) attempt

cónca·vo -va *adj* concave

concebible *adj* conceivable

concebir §50 *tr* & *intr* to conceive

conceder *tr* to concede, admit; to grant

concejal *m* alderman, councilman; **concejales** city fathers

concejo *m* town council; town hall; council meeting; (*expósito*) foundling

concentrar *tr* & *ref* to concentrate

concéntri·co -ca *adj* concentric

concepción *f* conception

concepto *m* concept; opinion, judgment; (*dicho ingenioso*) conceit, witticism; point of view; **en concepto de** under the head of; **tener buen concepto de** or **tener en buen concepto** to have a high opinion of, to hold in high esteem

conceptuar §21 *tr* to deem, to judge, to regard

conceptuo·so -sa *adj* witty, epigrammatic

concerniente *adj* relative

concernir §28 *tr* to concern

concertar §2 *tr* to concert; to mend, repair; (*un casamiento; la paz*) to arrange; (*huesos dislocados*) to set; (*poner de acuerdo*) to reconcile; (*un pacto*) to conclude; to harmonize || *intr* to concert; to agree || *ref* to come to terms, become reconciled; to agree

concertino *m* concertmaster

concertista *mf* (mus) manager; (mus) performer, soloist

concesión *f* concession, admission; grant

concesionario *m* licensee; (*comerciante*) dealer

concesi·vo -va *adj* concessive

conciencia *f* (*conocimiento que uno tiene de su propia existencia*) consciousness; (*sentimiento del bien y del mal*) conscience; (*conocimiento*) awareness; **cobrar conciencia de** to become aware of; **en conciencia** in all conscience

concienzu·do -da *adj* conscientious; thorough

concierto *m* concert, harmony; (*función de música*) concert; (*composición de música*) concerto

concilia·dor -dora *adj* conciliatory

conciliar *tr* to conciliate, to reconcile ǁ *ref* (*el respeto, la estima, etc.*) to conciliate, to win

concilio *m* (eccl) council

conci·so -sa *adj* concise

concitar *tr* to stir up, incite, agitate

conciudada·no -na *mf* fellow citizen

concluir §20 *tr* to conclude; to convince ǁ *intr & ref* to conclude, to end

conclusión *f* conclusion

concluyente *adj* conclusive, convincing

concomitar *tr* to accompany, go with

concordancia *f* concordance; (gram, mus) concord

concordar §61 *tr* to harmonize; to reconcile; to make agree ǁ *intr* to agree

concordia *f* concord; **de concordia** by common consent

concre·to -ta *adj* concrete

concubina *f* concubine

concubio *m* (archaic) bedtime

concuñada *f* sister-in-law

concuñado *m* brother-in-law

concurrencia *f* (*acaecimiento de varios sucesos en un mismo tiempo*) concurrence; (*competencia comercial*) competition; (*ayuda*) assistance; crowd, gathering, attendance

concurrente *adj* concurrent; competing ǁ *mf* competitor, contender, entrant

concurri·do -da *adj* crowded, full of people; well-attended

concurrir *intr* to concur; to gather, meet, come together; to compete, contend; to coincide; **concurrir con** (*p.ej., dinero*) to contribute

concursante *mf* contender

concursar *tr* to declare insolvent ǁ *intr* to contend, to compete

concurso *m* contest, competition; (*de gente*) concourse, crowd, throng; backing, coöperation; show, exhibition; **concurso de acreedores** meeting of creditors; **concurso de belleza** beauty contest; **concurso hípico** horse show

concusión *f* concussion; extortion, shakedown

concha *f* (*de molusco o crustáceo*) shell; (*cada una de las dos partes*

del caparazón de los moluscos bivalvos) half shell; (*en que se sirve el pescado*) scallop; (*carey*) tortoise shell; oyster; shellfish; horseshoe bay; (theat) prompter's box; **concha de peregrino** scallop shell; (zool) scallop; (*ostras*) **en su concha** on the half shell; **tener muchas conchas** (coll) to be sly, cunning

conchabanza *f* comfort; (coll) collusion, cabal

conchabar *tr* to join, unite; (Am) to hire ǁ *ref* (coll) to gang up; (Am) to hire out

conchabero *m* (Col) pieceworker

condado *m* county; earldom

conde *m* count, earl; gypsy chief

condecoración *f* decoration

condecorar *tr* to decorate

condena *f* sentence; penalty, jail term; **condena judicial** conviction

condenación *f* condemnation; (*la eterna*) damnation

condena·do -da *adj* condemned; damned; (Chile) shrewd, clever ǁ *mf* sentenced person; **los condenados** the damned

condenar *tr* to condemn; to convict; (*a la pena eterna*) to damn; (*p.ej., una ventana*) to shut off, to block up; (*una habitación*) to padlock ǁ *ref* to condemn oneself, confess one's guilt; (*a la pena eterna*) to be damned

condensar *tr* to condense ǁ *ref* to condense, be condensed

condesa *f* countess

condescendencia *f* acquiescence, compliance

condescender §51 *intr* to acquiesce, comply; **condescender a** to accede to

condescendiente *adj* acquiescent, obliging

condición *f* condition, state; position, situation; standing; nature, character, temperament; **a condición (de) que** on condition that; **en buenas condiciones** in good condition, in good shape; **tener condición** to have a bad temper

condicional *adj* conditional

condimentar *tr* to season

condimento *m* condiment, seasoning

condiscípulo *m* fellow student

condolencia *f* condolence

condoler §47 *ref* to condole; **condolerse de** to sympathize with, feel sorry for, commiserate with

condonar *tr* to condone, overlook

conducción *f* conveyance, transportation; guiding, leading; (aut) drive, driving; **conducción a la derecha** right-hand drive; **conducción a la izquierda** left-hand drive; **conducción interior** closed car

conducente *adj* conducive

conducir §19 *tr* to conduct; to manage, direct; to guide, lead; to convey, transport; to drive; to employ, hire ǁ *intr* to lead; to conduce ǁ *ref* to conduct oneself, behave

conducta *f* conduct; management, direction; guidance; conveyance; conduct, behavior

conducto m pipe; conduit; (anat) duct, canal; agency, intermediary, channel; **por conducto de** through

conduc·tor -tora adj conducting ‖ mf driver, motorist; (cobrador en un vehículo público) (Am) conductor ‖ m & f (elec & phys) conductor; **buen conductor, buena conductora** good conductor; **mal conductor, mala conductora** bad or poor conductor ‖ m (rr) engineman, engine driver

conectar tr to connect

conejera f burrow, warren; (coll) joint, dive

conejillo m young rabbit; **conejillo de Indias** guinea pig

conejo m rabbit

conexión f connection

conexionar tr to connect; to put in touch ‖ ref to connect; to make contacts

confabulación f collusion, connivance

confabular ref to connive, scheme, plot

confección f making, preparation, confection; tailoring; ready-made suit; **confección a medida** suit made to order; **de confección** ready-made

confeccionar tr (ropa) to make; (una receta) to make up, concoct

confeccionista mf ready-made clothier

confederación f confederacy; alliance

confedera·do -da adj & mf confederate

confederar tr & ref to confederate

conferencia f (reunión para tratar asuntos internacionales, etc.) conference; (plática para tratar de algún negocio) interview; (disertación en público o en la universidad) lecture; **conferencia telefónica** (telp) long-distance call

conferenciante mf conferee; lecturer

conferenciar intr to confer, hold an interview

conferencista mf (Arg) lecturer

conferir §68 tr to confer, award, bestow; to discuss; to compare ‖ intr to confer

confesante mf confessor

confesar §2 tr, intr & ref to confess

confesión f confession; denomination, faith, religion

confe·so -sa adj confessed; (judío) converted ‖ mf converted Jew ‖ m lay brother

confesonario m confessional

confesor m confessor

confiable adj reliable, dependable

confia·do -da adj unsuspecting; haughty, self-confident

confianza f confidence; self-confidence, self-assurance; familiarity; secret deal; **de confianza** reliable

confianzu·do -da adj (coll) overconfident; (Am) overfamiliar

confiar §77 tr to confide, entrust; to strengthen the confidence of ‖ intr & ref to confide, trust; **confiar** or **confiarse de** or **en** to confide in, trust in; to rely on

confidencia f confidence; secret

confidencial adj confidential

confiden·te -ta adj trustworthy, faithful ‖ mf confident ‖ m spy; informer; secret agent; love seat

configurar tr to shape, form

confín m confine, border, boundary; **los confines** the confines

confina·do -da adj exiled ‖ m prisoner

confinamiento m confinement; abutment

confinar tr to exile; to confine ‖ intr to border

confirmar tr to confirm

confiscar §73 tr to confiscate

confita·do -da adj hopeful, confident; (bañado de azúcar) candied

confitar tr (frutas) to candy; (en almíbar) to preserve; (endulzar) to sweeten

confite m candy, bonbon, confection; **confites** confectionery

confitera f candy box; candy jar

confitería f confectionery; confectionery store

confite·ro -ra mf confectioner ‖ f see **confitera**

confitura f preserves, confiture; **confituras** confectionery

conflagración f conflagration

conflagrar tr to set fire to

conflicto m conflict; (apuro) fix, jam

confluencia f confluence

confluir §20 intr to flow together; to crowd, gather

conformador m hat block

conformar tr to shape; (un sombrero) to block ‖ intr & ref to conform, to comply, to yield, to agree

conforme adj in agreement ‖ adv depending on circumstances; fine, O.K.; **conforme a** according to ‖ conj as, in proportion as; as soon as ‖ m approval

conformidad f conformance, conformity; resignation

confort m comfort

confortable adj comfortable; comforting

confortante adj comforting; tonic ‖ mf comforter ‖ m tonic

confr. abbr **confesor**

confricar tr to rub

confrontar tr (poner en presencia; cotejar) to confront ‖ intr to border; to agree ‖ ref to get along, to agree; **confrontarse con** (hacer frente a) to confront

confundir tr to confuse; (turbar, dejar desarmado) to confound ‖ ref to become confused; (en la muchedumbre) to get lost

confusión f confusion

confutar tr to confute

congelador m freezer

congelar tr to congeal, freeze; (créditos) (fig) to freeze ‖ ref to congeal, freeze

congenial adj congenial (having the same nature)

congeniar intr to be congenial, to get along well

congéni·to -ta adj congenital

congestión f congestion

congestionar tr to congest ‖ ref to congest, become congested

conglobar *tr* to lump together
congoja *f* anguish, grief
congojo·so -sa *adj* distressing; distressed
congosto *m* narrow mountain pass
congraciar *tr* to win over ‖ *ref* to ingratiate oneself; **congraciarse con** to get into the good graces of
congratulación *f* congratulation
congratular *tr* to congratulate ‖ *ref* to congratulate oneself, to rejoice
congregación *f* congregation; **la Congregación de los fieles** the Roman Catholic Church
congregar §44 *tr* to bring together ‖ *ref* to congregate, to come together
congresal *m* (Arg, Chile) congressman
congresista *mf* delegate; member of congress ‖ *m* congressman
congreso *m* (*asamblea legislativa*) congress; (*reunión para deliberar sobre intereses comunes*) meeting, convention
congrio *m* conger eel
cóni·co -ca *adj* conical
conjetura *f* conjecture, guess
conjeturar *tr* & *intr* to conjecture, guess
conjugación *f* conjugation
conjugar §44 *tr* to conjugate; to combine
conjunción *f* conjunction; combination
conjuntamente *adv* together
conjuntista *m* chorus man ‖ *f* chorus girl
conjunti·vo -va *adj* conjunctive; subjunctive
conjun·to -ta *adj* joined, combined, united ‖ *m* whole, entirety, ensemble; unit; group; (theat) chorus; **de conjunto** general; **en conjunto** as a whole; **en su conjunto** in its entirety
conjura or **conjuración** *f* conspiracy, plot
conjuramentar *tr* to swear in ‖ *ref* to take an oath
conjurar *tr* to swear in; to conjure, entreat; to conjure away, to exorcise ‖ *intr* to conspire, plot ‖ *ref* to conspire, join in a conspiracy
conjuro *m* (*invocación supersticiosa*) conjuration; adjuration, entreaty
conllevar *tr* (*los trabajos*) to share in bearing; (*a una persona*) to tolerate, stand for; (*las adversidades*) to suffer
conmemorar *tr* to commemorate, memorialize
conmigo *pron* with me, with myself
conmilitón *m* fellow soldier
conminar *tr* to threaten
conmoción *f* commotion; concussion, shock
conmove·dor -dora *adj* touching, moving, stirring
conmover §47 *tr* to touch, move, affect; to stir, stir up; to shake, upset ‖ *ref* to be touched, be moved
conmutación *f* commutation
conmutador *m* (elec) change-over switch
conmutar *tr* to commute
connivencia *f* connivance; **estar en connivencia** to connive

cono *m* cone; **cono de proa** nose cone; **cono de viento** (aer) wind cone, wind sock
conoce·dor -dora *adj* knowledgeable ‖ *mf* expert. connoisseur
conocer §22 *tr* to know; to meet, get to know; to tell, to distinguish; (law) to try ‖ *intr* to know; **conocer de** or **en** to know, have knowledge of ‖ *ref* to know oneself; to know each other; to meet, meet each other
conoci·do -da *adj* known, well-known, familiar; distinguished, prominent ‖ *mf* acquaintance
conocimiento *m* knowledge; understanding; acquaintance; consciousness; (com) bill of lading; **con conocimiento de causa** knowingly, with full knowledge; **conocimiento de embarque** (com) bill of lading; **conocimientos** knowledge; **hablar con pleno conocimiento de causa** to know what one is talking about; **perder el conocimiento** to lose consciousness; **por su real conocimiento** (Arg) for real money; **recobrar el conocimiento** to regain consciousness; **venir en conocimiento de** to come to know
conque *adv* and so ‖ *m* (coll) condition, terms
conquista *f* conquest
conquista·dor -dora *adj* conquering ‖ *m* conqueror; (*ladrón de corazones*) lady-killer
conquistar *tr* to conquer; (*ganar la voluntad de*) to win over
consabi·do -da *adj* well-known; above-mentioned
consagrar *tr* to consecrate; to devote; to dedicate; (*una nueva palabra*) to authorize ‖ *ref* to devote oneself; to make a name for oneself
consciente *adj* conscious
conscripción *f* conscription
conscripto *m* conscript, draftee
consecución *f* obtaining, getting
consecuencia *f* (*correspondencia lógica entre sus elementos*) consistency; (*acontecimiento que resulta necesariamente de otro*) consequence; **en consecuencia** accordingly; **guardar consecuencia** to remain consistent; **traer a consecuencia** to bring in
consecuente *adj* (*que tiene proporción consigo mismo*) consistent; (*que sigue en orden a otra cosa*) consecutive
consecuti·vo -va *adj* consecutive
conseguir §67 *tr* to get, obtain; **conseguir + inf** to succeed in + **ger**
conseja *f* story, fairy tale; cabal.
conseje·ro -ra *adj* advisory ‖ *mf* advisor, counselor; councilor
consejo *m* advice, counsel; board; council; **consejos** advice; **un consejo** a piece of advice
consenso *m* consensus
consenti·do -da *adj* spoiled, pampered; (*marido*) indulgent
consenti·dor -dora *adj* acquiescent; pampering ‖ *mf* acquiescent person; (*de niños*) pamperer ‖ *m* cuckold

co
co

consentimiento m consent

consentir §68 tr to allow; to admit; to pamper, to spoil || intr to consent; to come loose; **consentir** + inf to think that + ind; **consentir con** to be indulgent toward; **consentir en** to consent to || ref to begin to crack up; (Arg) to be proud

conserva f preserves; preserved food; **conserje** m janitor, concierge pickles; (naut) convoy; **conservas alimenticias** canned goods; **llevar en su conserva** (naut) to convoy; **navegar en (la) conserva** (naut) to sail in a convoy

conservación f conservation; preservation; self-preservation; maintenance, upkeep

conserva·dor -dora adj preservative; (pol) conservative || mf conservative || m curator

conservar tr to conserve, keep, maintain; to preserve || ref to take good care of oneself; to keep

conservati·vo -va adj conservative, preservative

conservatorio m (p.ej., de música) conservatory; (Arg) private school; (Chile) hothouse, greenhouse

conservera f cannery; (Mex) preserve dish

conservería f canning

conserve·ro -ra adj canning || mf canner || f see **conservera**

considerable adj considerable; large, great, important

consideración f consideration; **ser de consideración** to be of importance, be of concern; **someter a consideración** to take under advisement

considera·do -da adj (que guarda consideración a los demás) considerate; (digno de respeto) respected, esteemed; (que obra con reflexión) cautious, prudent

considerando conj & m whereas

considerar tr to consider; to treat with consideration

consigna f slogan; watchword; (mil) orders; (rr) checkroom

consignación f consignment

consignar tr to consign; to assign; to state in writing, to set forth

consignatario m consignee

consigo pron with him, with her, with them, with you; with himself, with herself, with themselves, with yourself or yourselves

consiguiente adj consequential; **ir or proceder consiguiente** to act consistently || m consequence; **por consiguiente** consequently, therefore

consilia·rio -ria mf advisor, counselor

consistencia f consistence, consistency

consistente adj consistent

consistir intr to consist; **consistir en** (estar compuesto de) to consist of; (residir en) to consist in

consistorio m consistory; town council; town hall

conso·cio -cia mf copartner; companion, fellow member

consola f console, console table; bracket

consolación f consolation

consolar §61 tr to console

consolidar tr to fund, refund; to strengthen; to repair

consommé m consommé

consonancia f consonance; rhyme

consonante adj consonantal; rhyming || m rhyme || f consonant

consonar §61 intr to be in harmony; to rhyme

cónsone adj harmonious || m (mus) chord

consorcio m consortium; partnership; fellowship

consorte mf consort, mate, spouse; partner, companion; **consortes** (law) colitigants; (law) accomplices

conspi·cuo -cua adj outstanding, prominent

conspiración f conspiracy

conspirar intr to conspire

constancia f constancy; certainty, proof

constante adj constant; steady, regular; sure, certain || f constant

constar intr to be clear, be certain; to be on record; to have the right rhythm; **constar de** to consist of; **hacer constar** to state, make known; **y para que conste** in witness whereof

constatación f proof

constatar tr to prove, establish, show

constelación f constellation; climate, weather; epidemic

consternar tr to depress, dismay

constipación f or **constipado** m cold, cold in the head

constipar tr (los poros) to stop up || ref to catch cold

constitución f constitution

constituir §20 tr to constitute; to establish, found; **constituir en** to force into || ref — **constituirse en** to set oneself up as

constituti·vo -va adj & m constituent

constituyente adj (para dictar o reformar la constitución) constituent

constreñir §72 tr to constrain, force, compel; to constrict, compress

construcción f construction; building, structure; **construcción de buques** shipbuilding

construc·tor -tora adj construction || mf builder, constructor; **constructor de buques** shipbuilder

construir §20 tr to build, to construct

consuegro m fellow father-in-law (with respect to the father of one's son-in-law or daughter-in-law), father-in-law of one's child

consuelda f comfrey; **consuelda real** field larkspur; **consuelda sarracena** goldenrod

consuelo m consolation; joy, delight; **sin consuelo** inconsolably; (coll) to excess

consueta m (theat) prompter

consuetudina·rio -ria adj customary, usual

cónsul m consul

consulado m consulate, consulship; (casa u oficina) consulate

consular *adj* consular

consulta *f* consultation; opinion; reference

consultación *f* consultation

consultar *tr* to consult; to take up, discuss; to advise ‖ *intr* to consult, confer

consulti·vo -va *adj* advisory

consul·tor -tora *mf* consultant

consultorio *m* doctor's office

consuma·do -da *adj* consummate ‖ *m* consommé

consumar *tr* to consummate; to fulfill, carry out

consumerismo *m* consumerism

consumición *f* consumption; drink (*in bar or restaurant*)

consumi·do -da *adj* (coll) thin, weak, emaciated; (coll) fretful

consumi·dor -dora *mf* consumer; customer (*in bar or restaurant*)

consumir *tr* to consume; to exhaust; (coll) to harass, wear down ‖ *ref* to consume, waste away; to long, yearn

consumo *m* consumption; drink (*in bar or restaurant*); customers; **consumos** octroi

consunción *f* consumption; (pathol) consumption

consuno *adv* — **de consuno** together, in accord

consunti·vo -va *adj* consumptive; (*crédito*) consumer

contabilidad *f* accounting, bookkeeping

contabilista *mf* accountant, bookkeeper

contabilizadora *f* computer

contabilizar §60 *tr* to enter in the ledger

contable *adj* countable ‖ *mf* accountant, bookkeeper

contactar *intr* to contact, be in contact

contacto *m* contact; **ponerse en contacto con** to get in touch with

conta·do -da *adj* scarce, rare; **al contado** cash, for cash; **contados** a few; **de contado** right away; **por de contado** of course

contador *m* counter; accountant; (*que mide el agua, gas, electricidad*) meter; (law) receiver; **contador de abonado** house meter; **contador kilométrico** speedometer; **contador público titulado** certified public accountant

contaduría *f* accountancy; accountant's office; box office for advanced sales

contagiar *tr* to infect; to corrupt

contagio *m* contagion

contagio·so -sa *adj* contagious

contaminación *f* contamination

contaminante *m* pollutant

contaminar *tr* to contaminate; (*un texto*) to corrupt; (*la ley de Dios*) to break

contante *adj* (*dinero*) ready

contar §61 *tr* to count; to regard, consider; to tell, relate; **contar . . . años** to be . . . years old; **dejarse contar diez** (box) to take the count; **tiene sus horas contadas** his days are numbered ‖ *intr* to count; **a contar desde** beginning with; **contar con** to count on, rely on; to reckon with

contemplación *f* contemplation; leniency, condescension

contemplar *tr* to contemplate; to be lenient to ‖ *intr* to contemplate

contemporáne·o -a *adj* contemporaneous, contemporary ‖ *mf* contemporary

contemporizar §60 *intr* to temporize

contención *f* containment; contention, strife; (law) suit, litigation

contencio·so -sa *adj* contentious

contender §51 *intr* to contend

contendiente *mf* contender, contestant

contener §71 *tr* to contain ‖ *ref* to contain oneself

conteni·do -da *adj* moderate, restrained ‖ *m* content, contents

contenta *f* gift or treat; indorsement; (mil) certificate of good conduct; (law) release

contentadi·zo -za *adj* easy to please

contentamiento *m* contentment

contentar *tr* to content; (com) to indorse; (Am) to reconcile

conten·to -ta *adj* content, contented, glad ‖ *m* content, contentment; **a contento** to one's satisfaction; **no caber de contento** (coll) to be beside oneself with joy ‖ *f* see **contenta**

contera *f* tip, metal tip

contesta *f* (Am) answer; (Mex) chat

contestación *f* answer; argument, debate; **mala contestación** (coll) back talk

contestar *tr* to answer ‖ *intr* to answer; to agree

contexto *m* interweaving; context

conticinio *m* dead of night

contienda *f* contest, dispute, fight

contigo *pron* with thee, with you

conti·guo -gua *adj* contiguous

continencia *f* continence

continental *adj* continental

continente *adj* continent ‖ *m* (*cosa que contiene en sí a otra*) container; (*aire del semblante, compostura del cuerpo*) mien, bearing; (*gran extensión de tierra rodeada por los océanos*) continent

contingencia *f* contingency

contingente *adj* contingent ‖ *m* contingent; share, quota

continuar §21 *tr* & *intr* to continue; **continuará** to be continued

continuidad *f* continuity

conti·nuo -nua *adj* continuous, continual; (mach) endless ‖ **continuo** *adv* continuously

contonear *ref* to strut, swagger

contoneo *m* strut, swagger

contorcer §74 *ref* to writhe

contorno *m* contour, outline; **contornos** environs, neighborhood

contorsión *f* contorsion

contra *prep* against; toward, facing ‖ *m* (*concepto opuesto*) con ‖ *f* trouble, inconvenience; (*al comprador*) (Cuba) gift, extra; (Chile) antidote; **llevar la contra a** (coll) to disagree with

contraalmirante *m* rear admiral

contraatacar §73 *tr* & *intr* to counterattack

contraataque *m* counterattack

contrabajo *m* contrabass, double bass

contrabajón *m* double bassoon

contrabalancear *tr* to counterbalance

contrabalanza *f* counterbalance

contrabandear *intr* to smuggle

contrabandista *adj* smuggling; contraband ‖ *mf* smuggler, contrabandist

contrabando *m* smuggling, contraband; **meter de contrabando** to smuggle, smuggle in

contrabarrera *f* second row of seats (*in bull ring*)

contracalle *f* parallel side street

contracarril *m* (rr) guardrail

contracción *f* contraction; (*reducción del ritmo normal de los negocios*) recession; (*al estudio*) (Chile, Peru) concentration

contracepti·vo -va *adj & m* contraceptive

contracorriente *f* countercurrent, crosscurrent; (*entre aguas*) undertow

contrachapado *m* plywood

contradecir §24 *tr* to contradict

contradicción *f* contradiction

contradic·tor -tora *adj* contradictory ‖ *mf* contradicter

contradicto·rio -ria *adj* contradictory

contraer §75 *tr* to contract; (*deudas*) to incur; (*el discurso o idea*) to condense ‖ *ref* to contract; to shrink; (Chile, Peru) to concentrate, apply oneself

contraescalón *m* riser (*of stairway*)

contraespía *mf* counterspy

contraespionaje *m* counterespionage

contrafallar *tr & intr* to overtrump

contrafallo *m* overtrump

contrafigura *f* counterpart

contrafuero *m* infringement, violation

contrafuerte *m* abutment, buttress

contragolpe *m* counterstroke; kickback; (box) counter

contrahace·dor -dora *adj* counterfeiting; fake ‖ *mf* counterfeiter; fake; impersonator

contrahacer §39 *tr* to counterfeit, copy, imitate; to fake; to impersonate; (*un libro*) to pirate ‖ *ref* to pretend to be

contra·haz *f* (*pl* **-haces**) wrong side

contrahe·cho -cha *adj* counterfeit, fake; deformed

contrahechura *f* counterfeit, fake

contrahuella *f* riser (*of stairway*)

contralor *m* comptroller

contralto *mf* contralto (*person*) ‖ *m* contralto (*voice*)

contraluz *f* view against the light; **a contraluz** against the light

contramaestre *m* foreman; (naut) boatswain; **segundo contramaestre** boatswain's mate

contramandar *tr* to countermand

contramandato *m* countermand

contramano *adv* — **a contramano** in the wrong direction, the wrong way

contramarcha *f* countermarch; reverse

contramarchar *intr* to countermarch; to go in reverse

contraofensiva *f* counteroffensive

contraorden *f* cancellation

contraparte *f* counterpart

contrapasar *intr* to go over to the other side

contrapelo *adv* — **a contrapelo** against the hair, against the grain; the wrong way; **a contrapelo de** against, counter to

contrapesar *tr* to offset, counterbalance

contrapeso *m* counterweight; counterbalance; (*para completar el peso de carne, etc.*) makeweight

contraponer §54 *tr* to set opposite; to oppose; to compare

contraportada del disco *f* flip side

contraproducente *adj* self-defeating, unproductive

contraprueba *f* second proof

contrapuerta *f* storm door; vestibule door

contrapuntear *tr* to sing in counterpoint; to taunt, be sarcastic to ‖ *ref* to taunt each other

contrapunto *m* counterpoint

contrapunzón *m* nailset, punch

contrariar §77 *tr* to counteract, to oppose; to annoy, provoke

contrariedad *f* opposition; interference; annoyance, bother

contra·rio -ria *adj* opposite, contrary; harmful ‖ *mf* enemy, opponent, rival ‖ *m* opposite, contrary; **al contrario** on the contrary; **de lo contrario** otherwise

contrarreferencia *f* cross reference

Contrarreforma *f* Counter Reformation

contrarregistro *m* (*para comprobar si algún género ha pasado por la frontera*) double check; (*de una experiencia científica*) control

contrarréplica *f* (law) rejoinder

contrarrestar *tr* to resist, counteract; (*la pelota*) to return

contrarrevolución *f* counterrevolution

contrasentido *m* misinterpretation; mistranslation; nonsense

contraseña *f* countersign; baggage check; **contraseña de salida** (mov, theat) check

contrastar *tr* to resist; (*las pesas y medidas*) to check ‖ *intr* to resist; to contrast

contraste *m* resistance; contrast; assayer; assayer's office; (naut) sudden shift in the wind

contratar *tr* to contract for; to hire

contratiempo *m* misfortune, disappointment, setback

contratista *mf* contractor

contrato *m* contract

contratreta *f* counterplot

contratuerca *f* lock nut, jam nut

contraveneno *m* counterpoison, antidote

contravenir §79 *intr* to act contrary; **contravenir a** to contravene, act counter to

contraventana *f* window shutter

contravidriera *f* storm sash

contrayente *mf* contracting party (*to a marriage*)

contribución *f* contribution; tax; **contribución de sangre** military service;

contribución industrial excise tax; **contribución territorial** land tax

ontribui·dor -dora *mf* contributor; taxpayer

ontribuir §20 *tr & intr* to contribute

ontribuyente *mf* contributor; taxpayer

ontrición *f* contrition

ontrincante *m* competitor, rival; fellow candidate

ontristar *tr* to sadden

ontri·to -ta *adj* contrite

ontrol *m* control, check

ontrolar *tr* to control, check

ontroversia *f* controversy

ontrovertible *adj* controversial, controvertible

ontrovertir §68 *tr* to controvert

ontubernio *m* cohabitation; evil alliance

ontumacia *f* contumacy; (law) contempt

ontu·maz *adj* (*pl* **-maces**) contumacious; germ-bearing; (law) guilty of contempt of court

ontumelia *f* contumely

ontundente *adj* bruising; impressive, convincing

ontundir *tr* to bruise

onturbar *tr* to trouble, worry, upset

ontusión *f* contusion

ontusionar *tr* (Chile) to bruise

onvalecencia *f* convalescence

onvalecer §22 *intr* to convalesce, recover

onvaleciente *adj & mf* convalescent

onvalidar *tr* to confirm

onveci·no -na *adj* neighboring || *mf* neighbor

onvencer §78 *tr* to convince

onvencimiento *m* conviction

onvención *f* (*acuerdo; conformidad; asamblea*) convention; (Am) political convention

onvencional *adj* conventional

onvenible *adj* docile, compliant; (*precio*) fair, reasonable

onveniencia *f* (*comodidad*) convenience; (*acuerdo, convenio*) agreement; fitness, suitability; (*formas sociales*) propriety; domestic employment; **conveniencias** income, property

onveniencie·ro -ra *adj* (coll) comfortloving

onveniente *adj* (*cómodo*) convenient; fit, suitable; advantageous; proper

onvenio *m* pact, covenant, treaty

onvenir §79 *intr* to agree; (*concurrir, juntarse*) to convene; to be suitable, be becoming; to be important, to be necessary; **conviene a saber** to wit, namely || *ref* to agree, come to an agreement

onventillo *m* (SAm) tenement house

onvento *m* convent, monastery; **convento de religiosas** convent

onverger §17 or **convergir** §27 *intr* to converge; to concur

onversa *f* (coll) chat, conversation

onversación *f* conversation

onversacional *adj* conversational

conversar *intr* to converse; to live, dwell

conversión *f* conversion

conver·so -sa *adj* converted || *mf* convert || *m* lay brother || *f* see **conversa**

convertible *adj* convertible || *m* (aut) convertible

convertir §68 *tr* to convert; to turn || *ref* to convert; to be converted; **convertirse en** to turn into, become

conve·xo -xa *adj* convex

convic·to -ta *adj* convicted, found guilty

convida·do -da *mf* guest || *f* (coll) treat

convidar *tr* to invite; to treat; to move, incite; **convidarle a uno con alguna cosa** to treat someone to something || *ref* to offer one's services

convincente *adj* convincing

convite *m* invitation; treat, banquet, party; **convite a escote** Dutch treat

convivir *intr* to live together

convocar §73 *tr* to convoke, call together; (*p.ej., una huelga*) to call; to acclaim

convoy *m* convoy; escort; cruet stand; (rr) train

convoyar *tr* to convoy

convulsionar *tr* to convulse

conyugal *adj* conjugal

cónyuge *mf* spouse, consort || **cónyuges** *mpl* couple, husband and wife

co·ñac *m* (*pl* **-ñacs** or **-ñaques**) cognac

cooperación *f* coöperation

cooperar *intr* to coöperate

cooperati·vo -va *adj* coöperative

coordena·do -da *adj* coördinate || *f* (math) coördinate

coordinante *adj* (gram) coördinating

coordinar *tr & intr* to coördinate

copa *f* goblet, wineglass; (*del sombrero*) crown; brazier; vase; drink; sundae; playing card, representing a bowl, equivalent to heart; (*del dolor*) (fig) cup; (sport) cup

copar *tr* (*la puesta equivalente a todo el dinero de la banca*) to cover; (*todos los puestos en una elección*) to sweep; (mil) to cut off and capture

coopartícipe *mf* copartner, joint partner

copear *intr* to sell wine or liquor by the glass; (coll) to tipple

copero *m* cabinet for wineglasses

copete *m* (*cabello levantado sobre la frente*) pompadour; (*de plumas; de una montaña*) crest; (*de un caballo*) forelock; (*de lana, cabello, plumas, etc.*) tuft; (*de un mueble*) top, finial; (*de un sorbete*) topping; **de alto copete** aristocratic, important; **tener mucho copete** to be high-hat

copetu·do -da *adj* tufted; high, lofty; (coll) high-hat

copia *f* plenty, abundance; copy; **copia al carbón** carbon copy; **copia fiel** true copy

copiador *m* copier, copying machine

copiante *mf* copier, copyist

copiar *tr* to copy, copy down

copiloto *m* copilot

copio·so -sa *adj* copious, abundant

copista *mf* copier, copyist

copla *f* couplet; ballad, popular song; **coplas** (coll) verse, poetry; **coplas de ciego** (coll) doggerel

cople·ro -ra *mf* vendor of ballads; poetaster

coplista *mf* poetaster

copo *m* bundle of cotton, flax, hemp, etc. to be spun; **copo de nieve** snowflake; **copos de jabón** soap flakes

copón *m* ciborium, pyx

copo·so -sa *adj* bushy; flaky, woolly

copu·do -da *adj* bushy, thick

copular *ref* to copulate

coque *m* coke

coqueluche *f* whooping cough

coqueta *adj* coquettish ‖ *f* coquette, flirt; (W-I) dressing table

coquetear *intr* to coquette, to flirt; to try to please everybody

coquetería *f* coquetry, flirting; affectation

coque·tón -tona *adj* (coll) coquettish, kittenish ‖ *m* (coll) flirt, lady-killer

coracha *f* leather bag

coraje *m* anger; mettle, spirit

coraju·do -da *adj* (coll) ill-tempered; (Arg) brave, courageous

coral *adj* (mus) choral ‖ *m* (mus) chorale; (zoófito; esqueleto calizo del zoófito; color) coral; **corales** coral beads

corambre *f* hides, skins

Corán *m* Koran

coranvo·bis *m* (pl **-bis**) (coll) fat solemn look

coraza *f* armor; cuirass; (sport) guard

corazón *m* heart; (centro de una cosa) core; **de corazón** heartily; **hacer de tripas corazón** to pluck up courage

corazonada *f* impulsiveness; hunch, presentiment; (coll) entrails

corbata *f* necktie, cravat; scarf; **corbata de mariposa, corbata de lazo** bow tie; **corbata de nudo corredizo** four-in-hand tie

corbatín *m* bow tie

corbeta *f* corvette

Córcega *f* Corsica

corcel *m* steed, charger

corcova *f* hump, hunch

corcova·do -da *adj* humpbacked, hunchbacked ‖ *mf* humpback, hunchback

corcovar *tr* to bend

corcovear *intr* to buck; (Am) to grumble; (Mex) to be afraid

corcha *f* cork bark; cork bucket (for cooling wine)

corchea *f* (mus) quaver, eighth note

corche·ro -ra *adj* cork ‖ *f* cork bucket (for cooling wine)

corcheta *f* eye (of hook and eye)

corchete *m* snap; hook and eye; hook (of hook and eye); (signo) bracket; **corchete de presión** snap fastener

corcho *m* cork; cork, cork stopper; cork wine cooler; cork box; cork mat; **corcho bornizo, corcho virgen** virgin cork

cordada *f* (mountaineering) party of two or three men roped together

cordaje *m* cordage; (naut) rigging

cordal *adj* wisdom (tooth) ‖ *m* (mus) tailpiece

cordel *m* cord, string; (distance of five steps; cattle run; **a cordel** in straight line

cordelejo *m* string; **dar cordelejo a** to make fun of; (Mex) to keep putting off

cordera *f* ewe lamb; (mujer dócil y humilde) (fig) lamb

cordería *f* cordage

corderillo *m* lambskin

corderi·no -na *adj* lamb ‖ *f* lambskin

cordero *m* lamb; lambskin; (hombre dócil y humilde) (fig) lamb

corderuna *f* lambskin

cordial *adj* cordial; (dedo) middle ‖ *m* cordial

cordialidad *f* cordiality

cordillera *f* chain of mountains

cordobana *f* — **andar a la cordobana** (coll) to go naked

cordón *m* lace; (de cuerda o alambre) strand; cordon; milled edge of coin; (de monje) rope belt; **cordón umbilical** umbilical cord

cordoncillo *m* rib, ridge; braid; (de monedas) milling

cordura *f* prudence, wisdom

Corea *f* Korea; **la Corea del Norte** North Korea; **la Corea del Sur** South Korea

corea·no -na *adj* & *mf* Korean

corear *tr* to compose for a chorus; to accompany with a chorus; to join in singing; to agree obsequiously with

coreografía *f* choreography

coriáce·o -a *adj* leathery

Corinto *f* Corinth

corista *m* choir priest; (theat) chorus man ‖ *f* chorus girl, chorine

cori·to -ta *adj* naked; bashful, timid

cormorán *m* cormorant

cor·nac *m* (pl **-nacs**) or **cornaca** *m* mahout

cornada *f* hook with horns; goring; (en la esgrima) upward thrust

cornadura or **cornamenta** *f* (del toro, la vaca, etc.) horns; (del ciervo) antlers

cornamusa *f* bagpipe

córnea *f* cornea

cornear *tr* to butt; to gore

corneja *f* daw, crow

cornejo *m* dogwood

córne·o -a *adj* horn, horny ‖ *f* sec córnea

corneta *f* bugle; swineherd's horn; **corneta acústica** ear trumpet; **corneta de llaves** cornet, cornet-à-pistons; **corneta de monte** hunting horn

cornisa *f* cornice

cornisamento *m* (archit) entablature

corno *m* horn; dogwood; **corno inglé** (mus) English horn

Cornualles Cornwall

cornucopia *f* cornucopia; sconce with mirror

cornu·do -da *adj* horned, antlered cuckold ‖ *m* cuckold

coro *m* chorus; choir; choir loft; a

coros alternately; **de coro** by heart; **hacer coro a** to echo

corolario *m* corollary

corona *f* (*cerco de metal; moneda; dignidad real; parte visible de una muela*) crown; (*cerco de flores*) garland, wreath; (*aureola*) halo; (*de eclesiástico*) tonsure; (*la que corresponde a un título nobiliario*) coronet; **corona nupcial** bridal wreath

coronación *f* coronation

coronamento or **coronamiento** *m* coronation; completion, termination; (archit) coping; (naut) taffrail

coronar *tr* to crown; to complete, finish; to top, surmount; (checkers) to crown

coronel *m* colonel

coronelía *f* colonelcy

coronilla *f* (*de la cabeza*) crown; **andar** or **bailar de coronilla** (coll) to be hard at it; **estar hasta la coronilla** (coll) to be fed up

corpiño *m* bodice, waist; (Arg) brassière

corporación *f* corporation

corporal *adj* corporal, bodily

corpu·do -da *adj* corpulent

corpulen·to -ta *adj* corpulent

corpúsculo *m* corpuscle; particle

corral *m* corral, stockyard; barnyard; fishpound; theater; **corral de madera** lumberyard; **corral de vacas** (coll) pigpen; **hacer corrales** (coll) to play hooky

correa *f* strap, thong; (aer, mach) belt; **besar la correa** (coll) to eat humble pie; **correa de seguridad** (aer, aut) safety belt

corrección *f* (*acción de corregir; reprensión*) correction; (*calidad de correcto*) correctness

correcti·vo -va *adj & m* corrective

correc·to -ta *adj* correct

correc·tor -tora *mf* corrector; **corrector de pruebas** proofreader

corredera *f* track, slide; slide valve; (*del trombón*) slide; (naut) log; (naut) log line; (*puerta*) **de corredera** sliding

corredi·zo -za *adj* slide; sliding; (*nudo*) slip

corre·dor -dora *adj* running || *mf* runner || *m* corridor; porch, gallery; (*el que interviene en compras y ventas de efectos comerciales, etc.*) broker; (mil) scout; **corredor de apuestas** bookmaker

corregidor *m* Spanish magistrate; chief magistrate of Spanish town

corregir §57 *tr* to correct; to temper, moderate || *intr* (W-I) to have a bowel movement || *ref* to mend one's ways

correlación *f* correlation

correlacionar *tr & intr* to correlate

correlati·vo -va *adj & m* correlative

correncia *f* bashfulness; (coll) looseness of the bowels

corrienti·o -a *adj* running; (coll) free, easy || *f* (coll) looseness of the bowels

corren·tón -tona *adj* jolly, full of fun

corrento·so -sa *adj* (Am) swift, rapid

correo *m* mail; post office; mail train; postman; courier; **correo aéreo** air mail; **correo urgente** special delivery; **echar al correo** to mail, to post

correo·so -sa *adj* leathery, tough

correr *tr* (*un caballo*) to run, to race; (*un riesgo*) to run; to travel over; to overrun; (*una cortina*) to draw; (*un toro*) to fight; to chase, pursue; to auction; to confuse; ·(Am) to throw out; **correrla** (coll) to run around all night || *intr* to run; to race; to pass, elapse; to circulate, be common talk; to be current; **a todo correr** at full speed; **correr a** to sell for; **correr a cargo de** or **por cuenta de** to be the business of; **correr con** to be on good terms with; to be in charge of; (*mes*) **que corre** current || *ref* (*a derecha o a izquierda*) to turn; to be confused; to be embarrassed, be ashamed; to slide, glide; (*una bujía, un color*) to run; to go too far

correría *f* short trip, excursion; foray, raid

correspondencia *f* correspondence; contact, communication; agreement, harmony; (*en el metro*) connection; (*en una carretera*) interchange

corresponder *intr* to correspond; (*dos habitaciones*) to communicate; **corresponder a** (*un beneficio, el afecto de una persona*) to return, reciprocate; to concern; to be up to || *ref* (*comunicarse por escrito*) to correspond; (*dos cosas*) to correspond with each other; to be in agreement; to be attached to each other

correspondiente *adj* corresponding; correspondent; respective || *mf* correspondent

corresponsal *mf* correspondent

corretaje *m* brokerage

corretear *tr* (Am) to harass, pursue; (CAm) to drive away; (Chile) to speed up || *intr* (coll) to race around

correveidi·le *mf* (*pl* -**le**) (coll) gossip; (coll) go-between

corrida *f* run; bullfight; (*carrera de entrenamiento de un caballo*) (Am) trial run; **corrida de banco** (Am) run on the bank; **corrida de toros** bullfight

corri·do -da *adj* (*peso, medida*) in excess; (*letra*) cursive; continued, unbroken; abashed, ashamed; (coll) worldly-wise, sophisticated || *m* overhang; (Am) street ballad || *f* see **corrida**

corriente *adj* (*agua*) running; (*actual*) current; common, ordinary; regular; well-known; fluent || *adv* all right, O.K. || *m* current month; **al corriente** on time; informed, aware, posted || *f* current, stream; (elec) current; **corriente de aire** draft; **Corriente del Golfo** Gulf Stream; **ir contra la corriente** to go against the tide

corrillo *m* circle, clique

corrimiento *m* running; sliding; watery

discharge; embarrassment, shyness; landslide; (Am) rheumatism

corro *m* (*cerco de gente; espacio circular*) ring; (*juego de niñas*) ring-around-a-rosy; **corro de brujas** fairy ring; **hacer corro** to make room

corroborar *tr* to corroborate; to strengthen

corroer §62 *tr* & *ref* to corrode

corromper *tr* to corrupt; to spoil; to rot; to seduce; to bribe; (coll) to annoy || *intr* to smell bad || *ref* to become corrupted; to spoil; to rot

corrosión *f* corrosion

corrosi·vo -va *adj* & *m* corrosive

corrugar §44 *tr* to shrink; to wrinkle

corrupción *f* corruption; seduction; bribery; stench

corruptela *f* corruption

corruptible *adj* corruptible; (*p.ej., frutas*) perishable

corrusco *m* (coll) crust of bread

corsa *f* (naut) day's run

corsario *m* corsair

corsé *m* corset

cor·so -sa *adj* & *mf* Corsican || *m* (naut) privateering; (SAm) drive, promenade || *f* see **corsa**

corta *f* clearing, cutting, felling

cortaalam·bres *m* (*pl* -bres) wire cutter

cortabol·sas *m* (*pl* -sas) (coll) pickpocket

cortacésped *m* lawn mower

cortaciga·rros *m* (*pl* -rros) cigar cutter

cortacircui·tos *m* (*pl* -tos) (elec) fuse

cortacorriente *m* (elec) change-over switch

cortada *f* (Am) cut, cutting

cortadillo *m* drinking cup

corta·do -da *adj* (*estilo*) choppy; (SAm) hard up || *f* see **cortada**

corta·dor -dora *adj* cutting || *mf* cutter || *m* butcher || *f* cutting machine

cortafrío *m* cold chisel

cortafuego *s* fire wall

cortahie·los *m* (*pl* -los) icebreaker

cortalápi·ces *m* (*pl* -ces) pencil sharpener

cortante *adj* cutting, sharp || *m* butcher; butcher knife

cortapape·les *m* (*pl* -les) paper cutter

cortapi·cos *m* (*pl* -cos) (ent) earwig; **cortapicos y callares** (coll) little children should be seen and not heard

cortaplu·mas *m* (*pl* -mas) penknife

cortapu·ros *m* (*pl* -ros) cigar cutter

cortar *tr* to cut; to trim; to chop; to cut off; to rout, omit; to cut short; to cut up; to carve; (*la corriente; la ignición*) to cut off || *intr* to cut; (*el viento, el frío*) to be cutting; **cortar de vestir** to cut cloth; (coll) to gossip || *ref* to become speechless; (*la leche*) to curdle, turn sour; (*la piel*) to chap, to crack

cortarrenglón *m* marginal stop

cortau·ñas *m* (*pl* -ñas) nail clipper

cortavi·drios *m* (*pl* -drios) glass cutter

cortaviento *m* windshield

corte *m* cut; cutting; (*filo de un arma, cuchillo, etc.; borde de un libro*) edge; cross section; (*de un vestido*) cut, fit; piece of material; **corte de pelo** haircut; **corte de pelo a cepillo** crew cut; **corte de traje** suiting || *f* (*de un rey*) court; (*corral*) yard; stable, fold; (*tribunal de justicia*) (Am) court; **Cortes** Parliament; **darse cortes** (SAm) to put on airs; **hacer la corte a** to pay court to; **la Corte** the Capital (*Madrid*)

cortedad *f* shortness; smallness; lack; bashfulness

cortejar *tr* to escort, attend, court; to court, to woo

cortejo *m* courting; courtship; (*séquito*) cortege; gift, treat; (coll) beau

cortera *f* (Chile) streetwalker

cortero *m* (Chile) day laborer

cortés *adj* courteous, polite, courtly

cortesana *f* courtesan

cortesana·zo -za *adj* overpolite, obsequious

cortesanía *f* courtliness

cortesa·no -na *adj* courtly, courteous || *m* courtier || *f* see **cortesana**

cortesía *f* courtesy, politeness, courtliness; gift, favor; (*inclinación de la cabeza o el cuerpo en señal de respeto*) curtsy; (*de una carta*) conclusion; **hacer una cortesía** to make a bow; to curtsy

corteza *f* bark; peel, rind, skin; (*de pan*) crust; coarseness; (*envoltura exterior de un órgano*) cortex; **corteza cerebral** cortex

cortijo *m* farm, farmhouse

cortil *m* barnyard

cortina *f* curtain; **correr la cortina** to pull the curtain aside; **cortina de hierro** iron curtain; **cortina de humo** smoke screen

cortinal *m* fenced-in field

cortinilla *f* shade, window shade

cortisona *f* cortisone

cor·to -ta *adj* short; dull; bashful, shy; speechless; **a la corta o a la larga** sooner or later; **desde muy corta edad** from earliest childhood || *f* see **corta**

cortocircuitar *tr* & *ref* (elec) to short-circuit

cortocircuito *m* (elec) short circuit

cortometraje *m* (mov) short

corva *f* ham, back of knee; (vet) curb

corvejón *m* gambrel, hock; (orn) cormorant

cor·vo -va *adj* arched, bent, curved || *m* hook || *f* see **corva**

cor·zo -za *mf* roe deer

cosa *f* thing; **cosa de** a matter of; **cosa de cajón** a matter of course; **cosa de mieles** (coll) something fine; **cosa de nunca acabar** endless bore; **cosa de oír** something worth hearing; **cosa de ver** something worth seeing; **cosa de risa** something to laugh at; **cosa nunca vista** (coll) something unheard-of; **cosa que** (Am coll) so that; **cosa rara** strange to say; **como si tal cosa** (coll) as if nothing had happened; **en cosa de** in a matter of; **no . . . gran cosa** not much; **no haber**

tal cosa to be not so; **otra cosa** something else; **¿qué cosa?** what's new?

cosa·co -ca adj & mf Cossack ‖ m Cossack (horseman)

coscolina f (Mex) loose woman

cos·cón -cona adj sly, crafty

cosecha f crop, harvest; harvest time; **cosecha de vino** vintage; **de su cosecha** (coll) out of one's own head

cosechar tr to harvest, reap ‖ intr to harvest

coseche·ro -ra mf harvester, reaper; vintner

cose-pape·les m (pl -les) stapler

coser tr to sew; to join, unite closely; **coser a preguntas** to riddle with questions; **coser a puñaladas** to cut to pieces ‖ intr to sew; **ser coser y cantar** (coll) to be a cinch ‖ ref — **coserse con** or **contra** to be closely attached to

cosméti·co -ca adj & m cosmetic

cósmi·co -ca adj cosmic

cosmonauta mf cosmonaut

cosmopolita adj & mf cosmopolitan

cosmos m cosmos; (bot) cosmos

coso m enclosure for bullfighting

cosquillas fpl tickling, ticklishness; **buscarle a uno las cosquillas** (coll) to try to irritate a person; **no sufrir cosquillas** or **tener malas cosquillas** (coll) to be touchy

cosquillear tr to tickle; to tease, taunt; to stir up the curiosity of; to scare ‖ intr to tickle ‖ ref to be curious; to enjoy oneself

cosquilleo m tickling, tickling sensation

cosquillo·so -sa adj ticklish; (que se ofende fácilmente) touchy

costa f coast, shore; cost, price; **a toda costa** at all costs; **Costa Brava** Mediterranean coast in province of Gerona, Spain; **Costa Firme** Spanish Main; **costa marítima** seacoast; **costas** (law) costs

costado m side; (del ejército) flank; (Mex) station platform; **costados** ancestors, stock

costal m bag, sack; **costal de los pecados** human body (full of sin); **estar hecho un costal de huesos** (coll) to be nothing but skin and bones

costanera f slope; **costaneras** rafters

costane·ro -ra adj sloping; coastal ‖ f see costanera

costanilla f short steep street

costar §61 intr to cost; **cueste lo que cueste** cost what it may

costarricense or **costarrique·ño -ña** adj & mf Costa Rican

coste m cost; **a coste y costas** at cost

costear tr to pay for, to defray the cost of; to sail along the coast of ‖ intr to sail along the coast ‖ ref to pay; to pay one's way

coste·ño -ña adj sloping; coastal

coste·ro -ra adj coastal

costilla f rib; (coll) wealth; **costillas** back, shoulders

costillu·do -da adj heavy-set, broad-shouldered

costo m cost; **costo de la vida** cost of living; **costo, seguro y flete** cost, insurance, and freight

costo·so -sa adj costly, expensive; grievous

costra f scab, scale; (moco de una vela) snuff

costro·so -sa adj scabby, scaly

costumbre f custom, habit; **de costumbre** usual; usually; **tener por costumbre** to be in the habit of

costumbrista mf critic of manners and customs

costura f sewing, needlework; dressmaking; (unión de dos piezas cosidas) seam; **alta costura** fashion designing, haute couture

costurera f seamstress, dressmaker

costurero m sewing table

cota f coat of arms; coat of mail

cotarrera f (coll) gossipy woman

cotarro m night shelter (for beggars and tramps); **alborotar el cotarro** (coll) to raise a row

cotejar tr to compare, collate

cotejo m comparison, collation

cotidia·no -na adj daily, everyday

cotilla f (coll) gossip, tattletale

cotín m (sport) backstroke

cotización f quotation; dues

cotizante adj dues-paying

cotizar §60 tr to quote; to prorate ‖ intr to collect dues; to pay dues

coto m price; fixed price; term, limit

cotón m printed cotton

cotona f (Am) work shirt

cotonía f dimity

cotorra f parrot; parakeet; magpie; (coll) chatterbox; (Mex) night shelter

cotorrear intr (coll) to gossip, gabble

cotufa f Jerusalem artichoke; delicacy, tidbit; **hacer cotufas** (Bol) to be fastidious; **pedir cotufas en el golfo** (coll) to ask for the moon

coturno m buskin

covacha f cave; (Am) cubbyhole; (Am) shanty; (Am) doghouse

covachuelista m (coll) clerk, government clerk

coxcojita f hopscotch; **a coxcojita** hippety-hop

coy m (naut) hammock

coyunda f strap for yoking oxen; sandal string; marriage; tyranny

coyuntura f joint, articulation; (sazón, oportunidad) juncture

coz f (pl coces) kick; big end; ebb; (coll) insult; **dar coces contra el aguijón** to kick against the pricks

c.p.b., C.P.B. abbr **cuyos pies beso**

cps. abbr **compañeros**

crabrón m hornet

crac m (ruido seco) crack; crash; **hacer crac** to crash, to fail

cráneo m cranium, skull

crápula f drunkenness, debauchery; riffraff

crapulo·so -sa adj drunken; vicious, evil

crascitar intr to crow, croak

co
cr

cra·so -sa *adj* fat, greasy, thick; (*ignorancia*) crass, gross

cráter *m* crater

creación *f* creation

crea·dor -dora *adj* creative || *mf* creator

crear *tr* to create; to appoint; to found || *ref* to make for oneself, to build up; to trump up

creati·vo -va *adj* creative

crecede·ro -ra *adj* growth; large enough to allow for growth

crecepelo *m* hair restorer

crecer §22 *intr* to grow; to increase; (*el río*) to rise, swell; (*la luna*) to wax || *ref* to grow; to take on more authority; to get bolder

creces *fpl* growth, increase; excess, extra; **con creces** amply, in abundance

crecida *f* freshet, flood

creciente *adj* growing, increasing || *f* — **creciente de la luna** waxing of the moon, crescent; **creciente del mar** high tide, flood tide

crecimiento *m* growth, increase

credenciales *fpl* credentials

crédito *m* credit

credo *m* creed; credo; **con el credo en la boca** (coll) with one's heart in one's mouth; **en un credo** (coll) in a trice

crédu·lo -la *adj* credulous

creederas *fpl* — **tener buenas creederas** (coll) to be gullible

creencia *f* belief; (*crédito que se presta a un hecho*) credence; (*secta*) creed

creer §43 *tr & intr* to believe; **¡ya lo creo!** (coll) I should say so! || *ref* to believe; to believe oneself to be

creíble *adj* believable, credible

crema *f* cream; cold cream; shoe polish; (*gram*) diaeresis; **crema de menta** crème de menthe; **crema desvanecedora** vanishing cream

cremación *f* cremation

cremallera *f* rack; zipper

cremato·rio -ria *adj & m* crematory

crémor *m* cream of tartar

cremo·so -sa *adj* creamy

crencha *f* part (*in hair*); hair on each side of part

crepitar *intr* to crackle

crepuscular *adj* twilight

crepúsculo *m* twilight

cresa *f* maggot

crespar *tr & ref* to curl

cres·po -pa *adj* curly; curled; angry, irritated; stylish, conceited; (*estilo*) turgid || *m* (Am) curl

crespón *m* crape; **crespón fúnebre** crape; mourning band

cresta *f* crest; **cresta de gallo** cockscomb; (bot) cockscomb

creta *f* chalk || **Creta** *f* Crete

cretense *adj & mf* Cretan

cretona *f* cretonne

creyente *adj* believing || *mf* believer

creyón *m* crayon

cría *f* brood, litter; breeding; raising, rearing; nursing

criada *f* female servant, maid; **criada de casa, criada de servir** housemaid

criadero *m* nursery, tree nursery; fish hatchery; oyster bed

criadilla *f* testicle; potato

cria·do -da *adj* — **bien criado** wellbred; **mal criado** ill-bred || *mf* servant || *f* see **criada**

cria·dor -dora *adj* breeder || *f* wet nurse

criamiento *m* care, upkeep

crianza *f* raising, rearing; nursing; (*urbanidad*) breeding, manners; **buena crianza** good breeding; **mala crianza** bad breeding

criar §77 *tr* to raise, rear, bring up; to breed; to grow; to nurse, nourish; to fatten; to create; to foster

criatura *f* (*toda cosa creada; persona que debe su cargo o situación a otra*) creature; little child, little creature

criba *f* screen, sieve

cribar *tr* to screen, sieve

cribo *m* screen, sieve

cric *m* (*pl* **crics**) jack

crimen *m* crime; **crimen de lesa majestad** lese majesty

criminal *adj & mf* criminal

criminar *tr* to accuse, incriminate

crimino·so -sa *adj & mf* criminal

crines *fpl* mane

crío *m* (coll) baby, infant

crio·llo -lla *adj & mf* Creole

cripta *f* crypt

crisálida *f* chrysalis

crisantemo *m* chrysanthemum

cri·sis *f* (*pl* **-sis**) crisis; (*pánico económico*) depression, slump; mature judgment; **crisis del servicio doméstico** servant problem; **crisis de llanto** crying fit; **crisis de vivienda** housing shortage; **crisis ministerial** cabinet crisis; **crisis nerviosa** fit of nerves

crisma *f* (coll) head, bean

crisol *m* crucible

crispar *tr* to cause to twitch || *ref* to twitch

crispatura *f* twitch, twitching

crispir *tr* to grain, to marble

cristal *m* crystal; glass; pane of glass; mirror, looking glass; **cristal cilindrado** plate glass; **cristal de reloj** watch crystal; **cristal de roca** rock crystal; **cristal hilado** glass wool, spun glass; **cristal tallado** cut glass

cristalera *f* China closet; sideboard; glass door

cristalería *f* glassworks, glass store; glassware; glass cabinet

cristali·no -na *adj* crystalline || *m* lens, crystalline lens

cristalizer §60 *tr & ref* to crystallize

cristianar *tr* (coll) to baptize, christen

cristiandad *f* Christendom

cristianismo *m* Christianity

cristianizar §60 *tr* to Christianize

cristia·no -na *adj & mf* Christian || *m* soul, person; Spanish; (coll) watered wine

Cristo *m* Christ; crucifix; **donde Cristo dió las tres voces** (coll) in the middle of nowhere

Cristóbal *m* Christopher

criterio *m* criterion

crítica *f* (*juicio sobre una obra literaria, etc.; censura de la conducta de al-*

guno) criticism; (*arte de juzgar una obra literaria, etc.*) critique; gossip
criticar §73 *tr* & *intr* to criticize
críti·co -ca *adj* critical; (*criticón*) (Am) critical (*faultfinding*) || *mf* critic || *f* see **crítica**
criti·cón -cona *adj* (coll) critical, faultfinding || *mf* (coll) critic, faultfinder
criticquizar §60 *tr* to overcriticize
crizneja *f* braid of hair
croar *intr* to croak
croata *adj* & *mf* Croatian
crocante *m* almond brittle, peanut brittle
crocitar *intr* to crow, croak
croco *m* crocus
croché *m* crochet
crochet *m* (box) hook
croma·do -da *adj* chrome || *m* chromium plating
cromar *tr* to chrome
cromo *m* chromium
cromosoma *m* chromosome
crónica *f* chronicle; news chronicle, feature story
cróni·co -ca *adj* chronic; longstanding; (*vicio*) inveterate || *f* see **crónica**
cronista *mf* chronicler; reporter, feature writer; **cronista de radio** newscaster
cronología *f* chronology
cronometra·dor -dora *mf* (sport) timekeeper
cronometraje *m* (sport) clocking, timing
cronómetro *m* chronometer; stop watch
croqueta *f* croquette
cro·quis *m* (*pl* -quis) sketch
croscitar *intr* to crow, croak
crótalo *m* rattlesnake; castanet
cruce *m* crossing; crossroads, intersection; exchange (*e.g., of letters*); (*avería*) (elec) crossed wires, short circuit; **cruce a nivel** grade crossing; **cruce en trébol** cloverleaf intersection
crucero *m* crossroads; railroad crossing; (archit) transept; (aer, naut) cruise, cruising; (nav) cruiser; **crucero a nivel** grade crossing
crucial *adj* crucial
crucificar §73 *tr* to crucify
crucifijo *m* crucifix
crucifixión *f* crucifixion
crucigrama *m* crossword puzzle
cruda *f* (Mex) hangover
crudeza *f* crudeness, rawness; (*del agua*) hardness; harshness, roughness; (coll) blustering; **crudezas** undigested food
cru·do -da *adj* crude, raw; (*agua*) hard; harsh, rough; (*tiempo*) raw; (*lienzo*) unbleached; **estar crudo** (P-R) to be rusty; (Mex) to have a hangover || *f* see **cruda**
cruel *adj* cruel
crueldad *f* cruelty
cruen·to -ta *adj* bloody
crujía *f* corridor, hall; hospital ward; block of houses; (naut) midship gangway; **crujía de piezas** suite of

rooms; **sufrir una crujía** (coll) to have a hard time of it
crujido *m* creak; crackle; clatter; chatter; rustle
crujir *intr* to creak; to crackle; to clatter; to chatter; to rustle; to crunch
crup *m* croup
crustáce·o -a *adj* crustaceous || *m* crustacean
cruz *f* (*pl* cruces) cross; (*de una moneda*) tails; (typ) dagger; **Cruz del Sur** Southern Cross; **¡cruz y raya!** (coll) that's enough!; **de la cruz a la fecha** from beginning to end
cruzada *f* (*expedición contra los infieles; propaganda contra un vicio*) crusade; crossroads, intersection
cruza·do -da *adj* crossed; (*de raza mixta*) cross; double-breasted || *m* (*el que toma parte en una cruzada*) crusader; (*caballero de una orden militar*) knight; twill || *f* see **cruzada**
cruzar §60 *tr* to cross; (*la tela*) to twill; (*cartas*) to exchange; to crossbreed; (naut) to cruise, cruise over || *intr* to cross; to cruise || *ref* to cross each other, to cross one's another's path; (*alistarse para una cruzada*) to take the cross; **cruzarse con** (*otro automóvil*) to pass; **cruzarse de brazos** (*estar ocioso*) to cross one's arms
cs. *abbr* **céntimos, cuartos**
cte. *abbr* **corriente**
c/u *abbr* **cada uno**
cuad. *abbr* **cuadrado**
cuaderna *f* (naut) frame
cuaderno *m* notebook; folder; **cuaderno de bitácora** (naut) logbook; **cuaderno de hojas cambiables** or **sueltas** loose-leaf notebook
cuadra *f* hall, large room; stable; dormitory, ward; croup, rump; (Am) block
cuadra·do -da *adj* square; square-shouldered; perfect || *m* square; (*regla*) ruler; (*en las medias*) clock; **de cuadrado** perfectly; (*que se mira frente a frente*) full-faced
cuadragési·mo -ma *adj* & *m* fortieth
cuadrangular *adj* quadrangular || *m* home run
cuadrángu·lo -la *adj* quadrangular || *m* quadrangle
cuadrante *m* quadrant; (*de reloj*) face, dial; **cuadrante solar** sundial
cuadrar *tr* to square; to please; (*al toro*) (taur) to square off, to line up || *ref* to square; to stand at attention; (coll) to take on a serious air
cuadrilla *f* group, party; crew, gang
cuadrillazo *m* (SAm) surprise attack
cuadrillo *m* (*saeta*) bolt (*arrow*)
cuadrimotor *m* four-motor plane
cua·dro -dra *adj* square || *m* square; (*lienzo, pintura*) painting, picture; (*marco de pintura, ventana, etc.*) frame; (*de jardín*) patch, flower bed; staff, personnel; (mil) cadre; (sport) team; (theat) scene; (coll) sight, mess; **a cuadros** checked; **cuadro de costumbres** sketch of manners and customs; **cuadro de distribución** switchboard; **cuadro indicador** score

board; **cuadro vivo** tableau; **en cuadro** square, e.g., **ocho pulgadas en cuadro** eight inches square; (coll) topsy-turvy; **quedarse en cuadro** to be all alone in the world; (mil) to be skeletonized || *f* see **cuadra**

cuadrúpe·do -da *adj & m* quadruped

cuádruple *adj & m* quadruple

cuadruplicar §73 *tr & ref* to quadruple

cuajada *f* curd

cuajado *m* mincemeat

cuajar *tr* to curd, curdle, thicken, jelly; (coll) to please, to suit || *intr* (coll) to take hold, catch on, jell, take shape; (Mex) to chatter, prattle || *ref* to curd, curdle, thicken, jelly; to sleep sound; (coll) to become crowded

cuajo *m* curd; (Mex) chatter, prattle; (*en la escuela*) (Mex) recess

cual *adj rel & pron rel* such as; **el cual** which; who; **lo cual** which; **por lo cual** for which reason || *adv* as || *prep* like

cuál *adj interr & pron interr* which, what; which one

cualidad *f* quality, characteristic, trait

cualquier *adj indef* (*pl* **cualesquier**) apocopated form of **cualquiera**, used only before masculine nouns and adjectives

cualquiera (*pl* **cualesquiera**) *pron indef* anyone; **cualquiera que** whichever; whoever || *adj indef* any || *adj rel* whichever || *m* (*persona poco importante*) nobody

cuan *adv* as

cuán *adv* how, how much

cuando *conj* when; although; in case; since; **aun cuando** even if, even though; **cuando más** at most; **cuando menos** at least; **cuando mucho** at most; **cuando quiera** whenever; **de cuando en cuando** from time to time || *prep* (coll) at the time of

cuándo *adv* when; **cuándo . . . cuándo** sometimes . . . sometimes; **¿de cuándo acá?** since when?; how come?

cuantía *f* quantity; importance; **delito de mayor cuantía** felony; **delito de menor cuantía** misdemeanor; **de mayor cuantía** first-rate; **de menor cuantía** second-rate, of little importance

cuantiar §77 *tr* to estimate, appraise

cuánti·co -ca *adj* quantum

cuantio·so -sa *adj* large, substantial

cuan·to -ta *adj rel & pron rel* as much as, whatever, all that which; **cuantos** as many as, all those who, everybody who; **unos cuantos** some few || **cuanto** *adv* as soon as; as long as; **cuanto antes** as soon as possible; **cuanto más . . . tanto más** the more . . . the more; **cuanto más que** all the more because; **en cuanto** as soon as; while; insofar as; **en cuanto a** as to, as for; **por cuanto** inasmuch as; **por cuanto . . . por tanto** inasmuch as . . . therefore || **cuan·to** *m* (*pl* -ta) quantum

cuán·to -ta *adj interr & pron interr* how much; **cuántos** how many ||

cuánto *adv* how, how much; how long; how long ago; **cada cuánto** how often

cuáque·ro -ra *adj & mf* Quaker

cuarenta *adj, pron & m* forty

cuarenta·vo -va *adj & m* fortieth

cuarentena *f* forty; quarantine; forty days, forty months, forty years; **poner en cuarentena** to quarantine; to withhold one's credence in

cuaresma *f* Lent

cuaresmal *adj* Lenten

cuarta *f* fourth, fourth part; (*de la mano*) span; (CAm, W-I) horse whip

cuartago *m* nag, pony

cuartear *tr* to divide in four parts; to divide; (*la aguja*) (naut) to box; (CAm, W-I) to whip || *ref* to crack, split; (taur) to step aside, dodge

cuartel *m* quarter; (*de una ciudad*) section, ward; (*terreno*) lot; flower bed; (mil) barracks; (*buen trato*) (mil) quarter; (*armazón de tablas para cerrar la escotilla*) (naut) hatch; (coll) house, home; **cuartel de bomberos** engine house, firehouse; **cuarteles** (mil) quarters; **cuartel general** (mil) headquarters

cuartelada *f* mutiny, military uprising

cuarte·rón -rona *mf* quadroon || *m* quarter; (*de puerta*) panel; (*de ventana*) shutter

cuarteto *m* quartet

cuartilla *f* sheet of paper

cuar·to -ta *adj* fourth; quarter || *m* fourth; quarter; room, bedroom; quarter-hour; **cuarto creciente** (*de la luna*) first quarter; **cuarto de aseo** lavatory; **cuarto de baño** bathroom; **cuarto de dormir** bedroom; **cuarto de estar** living room; **cuarto delantero** (*de la res*) forequarter; **cuarto de los niños** nursery; **cuarto de luna** quarter; **cuarto menguante** (*de la luna*) last quarter; **cuarto obscuro** (phot) darkroom; **cuartos** (coll) money, cash; **cuarto trasero** (*p.ej., de vaca*) rump || *f* see **cuarta**

cuarzo *m* quartz

cuate *adj* (Mex) twin; (Mex) like || *mf* (Mex) twin; (Mex) pal

cuatrilli·zo -za *mf* quadruplet

cuatrinca *f* foursome

cuatro *adj & pron* four; **las cuatro** four o'clock || *m* four; (*en las fechas*) fourth; (*de voces*) quartet; **más de cuatro** (coll) quite a number

cuatrocien·tos -tas *adj & pron* four hundred || **cuatrocientos** *m* four hundred

cuba *f* cask, barrel; tub, vat; (*persona de mucho vientre*) (coll) tub; (*persona que bebe mucho*) (coll) toper; **cuba de riego** street sprinkler

cuba·no -na *adj & mf* Cuban

cubeta *f* keg, cask; pail; bowl, toilet bowl; (*del termómetro*) cup; (chem, phot) tray; (Mex) high hat

cubicaje *m* piston displacement, cylinder capacity

cubicar *tr* (*elevar al cubo*) to cube; to measure the volume of; to have a piston displacement of

cúbi·co -ca adj cubic; (raíz) cube
cubierta f cover; envelope; roof; (de un libro) paper cover; (de un neumático) casing, shoe; (del motor de un coche) hood; (naut) deck; **bajo cubierta** under separate cover; **cubierta separada** under separate cover; **cubierta de aterrizaje** (nav) flight deck; **cubierta de cama** bedcover; **cubierta de mesa** table cover; **cubierta de paseo** (naut) promenade deck; **cubierta de vuelo** (nav) flight deck; **cubierta principal** (naut) main deck; **entre cubiertas** (naut) between decks
cubiertamente adv secretly
cubier·to -ta adj covered; (cielo) overcast ‖ m cover, roof, shelter; (servicio de mesa para una persona) cover; knife, fork, and spoon; table d'hôte, prix fixe; **a cubierto de** under cover of; protected from; **bajo cubierto** under cover, indoors ‖ f see **cubierta**
cubil m (de fieras) lair, den; (de arroyo) bed
cubilete m (de cocinero) copper mold; dicebox; mince pie; (Am) high hat; (SAm) scheming, wirepulling
cubo m bucket; (de rueda) hub; (de un candelero; de una llave de caja) socket; cube; (mach) barrel, drum; (math) cube; (Arg) finger bowl
cubreasiento m seat cover
cubrecama f counterpane, bedcover
cubrecorsé m corset cover
cubrefuego m curfew
cubrelibro m jacket
cubrenuca f havelock
cubrerrueda f mudguard
cubresexo m G-string
cubretablero m (aut) cowl
cubretetera f cozy, tea cozy
cubrir §83 tr to cover, cover over, cover up ‖ ref to cover oneself; to be covered; to put one's hat on; (el cielo) to become overcast; (satisfacer una deuda) to cover
cucaña f greased pole to be climbed as a game; (coll) cinch
cucañe·ro -ra mf (coll) loafer, parasite
cucar §73 tr to wink; to make fun of; (la caza) to sight; (Am) to incite, stir up ‖ intr (el ganado) to go off on a run (when bitten by flies)
cucaracha f roach, cockroach
cucarache·ro -ra adj (W-I) sly, tricky; (W-I) amorous, lecherous
cucarda f cockade
cuclillas — **en cuclillas** squatting, crouching
cuclillo m cuckoo; (coll) cuckold
cu·co -ca adj sly, tricky; (coll) cute ‖ mf (coll) sly person ‖ m bogeyman; cuckoo
cu·cú m (pl -cúes) cuckoo (call)
cuculla f cowl, hood
cucurucho m paper cone, ice-cream cone; **hacer cucurucho a** (Chile) to deceive, take in
cuchara f spoon; (cazo) dipper, ladle; (para áridos; para achicar el agua en los botes) scoop; (de albañil) trowel; (Mex) pickpocket; **cuchara de sopa** tablespoon; **media cuchara**

(coll) ordinary fellow; (Am) fellow with heavy accent; (Mex) mason's helper; **meter su cuchara** to butt in
cucharada f spoonful; ladleful; scoop
cucharear tr to spoon, ladle out
cucharetear intr (coll) to stir the pot, stir with a spoon; (coll) to meddle
cucharilla f teaspoon; (de soldador) ladle
cucharón m large spoon; soup ladle; dipper; scoop; **despacharse con el cucharón** (coll) to look out for number one
cuchichear intr to whisper
cuchilla f knife; (hoja de arma blanca de corte) blade; (de patín de hielo) runner; (cerro escarpado) hogback; (de interruptor) (elec) blade; (poet) sword; **cuchilla de carnicero** butcher knife, cleaver
cuchillada f slash, gash, hack; **cuchilladas** fight, quarrel; **dar cuchillada** (un actor o un teatro) (coll) to be the hit of the town
cuchillería f cutlery; cutler's shop
cuchillero m cutler
cuchillo m knife; (en un vestido) gore; (naut) triangular sail; **cuchillo de trinchar** carving knife; **cuchillo de vidriero** putty knife; **pasar a cuchillo** to put to the sword
cuchitril m hovel, den
cuchufleta f (coll) joke, fun, wisecrack
cuchufletear intr (coll) to joke, make fun, wisecrack
cuelga f fruit hung up for keeping; (coll) birthday present
cuelgaca·pas m (pl -pas) cloak hanger
cuello m (del cuerpo) neck; (de una prenda) collar; shirt collar; **cuello almidonado** stiff collar; **cuello de camisa** shirtband; **cuello de cisne** gooseneck; **cuello de pajarita** or **doblado** wing collar; **levantar el cuello** (coll) to get back on one's feet again
cuenca f wooden bowl; (del ojo) socket; basin, river basin; **cuenca de polvo** dust bowl
cuenco m earthen bowl; hollow
cuenta f count, calculation; account; (factura) bill; (en un restaurante) check; (del rosario) bead; **abonar en cuenta a** to credit to the account of; **a cuenta** or **a buena cuenta** on account; **adeudar en cuenta a** to charge to the account of; **a fin de cuentas** after all; **caer en la cuenta** (coll) to get the point; **cargar en cuenta a** to charge to the account of; **correr por cuenta de** to be the responsibility of, to be under the administration of; **cuenta corriente** current account; **cuenta de gastos** expense account; **cuenta de la vieja** (coll) counting on one's fingers; **cuentas del gran capitán** overdrawn account; **cuentas galanas** (coll) illusions; **darse cuenta de** to realize, become aware of; **de cuenta** of importance; **más de la cuenta** too long; too much; **pedir cuentas a** to bring to account; **por la cuenta** apparently;

por mi cuenta to my way of thinking; **tomar por su cuenta** to take upon oneself; **vamos a cuentas** (coll) let's settle this

cuentacorrentista *mf* depositor

cuentago·tas *m* (*pl* -**tas**) dropper, medicine dropper

cuentakiló·metros *m* (*pl* -**tros**) odometer

cuente·ro -ra *adj* (coll) gossipy ‖ *mf* (coll) gossip

cuentista *adj* (coll) gossipy ‖ *mf* story teller; short-story writer; (coll) gossip

cuento *m* story, tale; short story; prop, support; tip, point; (*cómputo*) count; (coll) gossip, evil talk; (coll) disagreement; **cuento de hadas** fairy tale; **cuento del tío** (SAm) gyp, swindle; **cuento de nunca acabar** (coll) endless affair; **cuento de penas** (coll) hard-luck story; **cuento de viejas** old wives' tale; **Cuentos de Calleja** collection of nursery stories; **dejarse de cuentos** (coll) to come to the point; **estar en el cuento** to be well-informed; **¡puro cuento!** pure fiction!; **sin cuento** countless; **traer a cuento** to bring up; **venir a cuento** (coll) to be opportune; **vivir del cuento** to live by one's wits

cuerda *f* cord, rope; watch spring; winding a watch or clock; (*acción de ahorcar*) hanging; fishing line; (aer, anat, geom) chord; (mus) string; **acabarse la cuerda** to run down, e.g., **se acabó la cuerda** the watch ran down; **bajo cuerda** secretly, underhandedly; **cuerda de presos** chain gang; **cuerda de remolcar** tow rope; **cuerda de tripa** (mus) catgut; **cuerda tirante** tight rope; **dar cuerda a** to give free rein to; (*un reloj*) to wind; **sin cuerda** unwound, run-down

cuer·do -da *adj* wise, prudent; sane ‖ *f* see **cuerda**

cuerna *f* antler; horns

cuerno *m* horn; (mus) horn; **cuerno de caza** huntinghorn; **cuerno inglés** (mus) English horn

cuero *m* (*pellejo de buey*) hide; (*después de curtido*) leather; wineskin; **cuero cabelludo** scalp; **cuero en verde** rawhide; **en cueros** stark-naked

cuerpear *intr* (Arg) to duck, dodge

cuerpo *m* body; (*parte del vestido hasta la cintura*) waist; (*talle, aspecto*) build; (*de escritos, leyes, etc.*) corpus; corps, staff; (mil) corps; **cuerpo a cuerpo** hand to hand; **cuerpo celeste** heavenly body; **cuerpo compuesto** (chem) compound; **cuerpo de aviación** air corps; **cuerpo de baile** corps of ballet; **cuerpo de bomberos** fire brigade, fire company; **cuerpo de ejército** army corps; **cuerpo de redacción** editorial staff; **cuerpo simple** (chem) simple substance; **dar con el cuerpo en tierra** (coll) to fall flat on the ground; **de cuerpo entero** full-length; **de medio**

cuerpo half-length; **descubrir el cuerpo** to drop one's guard; **en cuerpo or en cuerpo de camisa** in shirt sleeves; **estar de cuerpo presente** to be on view, to lie in state; **hacer del cuerpo** (coll) to have a movement of the bowels

cueru·do -da *adj* (Am) thick-skinned; (Am) annoying, boring; (Am) bold, shameless

cuervo *m* raven; **cuervo marino** cormorant; **cuervo merendero** rook

cuesco *m* (*de la fruta*) stone; (*del molino de aceite*) millstone; (coll) windiness

cuesta *f* hill, slope, grade; charity drive; **cuesta abajo** downhill; **cuesta arriba** uphill; **llevar a cuestas** (coll) to be burdened with

cuestión *f* question; dispute, quarrel; matter; **cuestión batallona** much-debated question; **cuestión palpitante** burning question; **en cuestión de** in a matter of

cuestionable *adj* questionable

cuestionar *tr* to question ‖ *intr* (Arg) to argue

cuestionario *m* questionnaire

cuestua·rio -ria or **cuestuo·so -sa** *adj* profitable, lucrative

cuetear *ref* (Col) to blow up, explode; (Col) to die, kick the bucket; (Mex) to get drunk

cueva *f* cave; cellar; (*de ladrones, fieras, etc.*) den

cufi·fo -fa *adj* (Chile) tipsy

cugulla *f* cowl

cui·co -ca *adj* (Am) foreign, outside ‖ *m* (Mex) cop, policeman

cuidado *m* care, concern, worry; **¡cuidado con . . .!** beware of . . .!, look out for!; **de cuidado** dangerously; **estar de cuidado** (coll) to be dangerously ill; **pierda Vd. cuidado** don't worry; **salir de su cuidado** (*una mujer*) to be delivered; **tener cuidado** to beware, be careful

cuidadora *f* (Mex) governess, chaperon

cuidado·so -sa *adj* careful, concerned, worried; watchful

cuidar *tr* to take care of, to watch over ‖ *intr* — **cuidar de** to take care of, to care for; to care to ‖ *ref* to take care of oneself; **cuidarse de** to care about; to be careful to

cuita *f* trouble, worry; longing, yearning

cuja *f* bedstead

culata *f* buttock, haunch; (*de la escopeta*) butt; (*de imán*) keeper, yoke; **culata de cilindro** cylinder head

culatazo *m* kick, recoil

culebra *f* snake; (*del alambique*) coil; **culebra de anteojos** cobra; **culebra de cascabel** rattlesnake; **saber más que las culebras** (coll) to be foxy

culebrear *intr* to wriggle; to wind, meander; to zigzag

culebrón *m* (coll) foxy fellow; (Mex) poor farce

cule·co -ca *adj* (Am) self-satisfied; (Am) madly in love

cu·lí *m* (*pl* -**líes**) coolie

culina·rio -ria *adj* culinary
culipandear *intr* & *ref* (CAm, W-I) to welsh, be evasive
culminar *intr* to culminate
culo *m* seat, behind, backside; (*de animal*) buttocks; (*de un vaso*) bottom; **culo de mal asiento** (coll) fidgety person; **volver el culo** (coll) to run away
culote *m* base
culpa *f* blame, guilt, fault; **echar la culpa a** to put the blame on; **tener la culpa** to be wrong, to be to blame
culpable *adj* blamable, guilty, culpable
culpa·do -da *adj* guilty || *mf* culprit
culpar *tr* to blame, censure, accuse || *ref* to take the blame
cultedad *f* fustian, affectation
culteranismo *m* euphuism, Gongorism
cultiparlar *intr* to speak in a euphuistic manner
cultismo *m* learned word; cultism, Gongorism
cultivar *tr* to cultivate; to till
cultivo *m* cultivation; **cultivo de secano** dry farming
cul·to -ta *adj* cultivated, cultured; (*vocablo*) learned || *m* worship; cult; **culto a la personalidad** personality cult
cultura *f* culture, cultivation
culturar *tr* to cultivate, to till
cumbre *adj* top, greatest || *f* summit; acme, pinnacle
cúmel *m* kümmel
cumiche *m* (CAm) baby (*youngest member of family*)
cúmplase *m* approval, O.K.
cumplea·ños *m* (*pl* **-ños**) birthday
cumpli·do -da *adj* full; perfect; (*en muestras de urbanidad*) correct || *m* correctness; courtesy; present
cumplimentar *tr* to compliment; to pay a complimentary visit to; to carry out, execute; (*un cuestionario*) to fill out
cumplimente·ro -ra *adj* (coll) effusive, obsequious
cumplimiento *m* (*muestra de urbanidad*) compliment; (*conducta decorosa*) correctness; fulfillment; perfection; **por cumplimiento** as a matter of pure formality
cumplir *tr* to fulfill, perform, execute; **cumplir años** to have a birthday; **cumplir . . . años** to be . . . years old || *intr* to fall due; to expire; to keep one's promise; to finish one's service in the army; **cumplir con** to fulfill; to fulfill one's obligation to; **cumplir por** to act on behalf of; to pay the respects of || *ref* to be fulfilled, to come true; to fall due; **cúmplase** approved
cumquibus *m* (coll) wherewithal
cúmulo *m* heap, pile, lot
cuna *f* cradle
cundido *m* olive, vinegar, and salt for shepherds; olive oil, cheese, and honey to make children eat
cundir *tr* to spread; to swell, puff up; to increase

cunear *tr* to cradle, rock in a cradle || *intr* (coll) to rock, swing, sway
cune·co -ca *mf* (Ven) baby (*youngest member of family*)
cuneta *f* gutter, ditch
cuña *f* wedge; (typ) quoin; **ser buena cuña** (coll) to take up a lot of room
cuñada *f* sister-in-law
cuñado *m* brother-in-law
cuñete *m* keg
cuño *m* die; stamp; mark
cuota *f* quota, share; fee, dues; tuition fee
cupé *m* coupé
cupo *m* quota, share; (Mex) capacity
cupón *m* coupon
cúpula *f* cupola; dome
cuquillo *m* cuckoo
cura *m* curate; (coll) priest; **este cura** (*yo*) (coll) yours truly (*I*) || *f* cure; care, treatment; **cura de aguas** water cure; **cura de almas** care of souls; **cura de hambre** starvation diet; **cura de reposo** rest cure; **cura de urgencia** first aid; **no tener cura** (coll) to be hopeless, be incorrigible
curaca *m* (SAm) boss, chief || *f* (Bol, Peru) priest's housekeeper
curación *f* cure, treatment
curade·ro -ra *mf* caretaker || *m* (law) guardian
curande·ro -ra *mf* quack, healer
curar *tr* (*a un enfermo*) to treat; (*sanar*) to cure, to heal; (*curtir*) to cure; (*la madera*) to season; (*una herida*) to dress || *intr* to cure; to recover; **curar de** to take care of; to recover from; to mind, pay attention to || *ref* to cure; to cure oneself; to get well, to recover; (Am) to get drunk; **curarse de** to recover from, get over; **curarse en salud** to be forewarned
curati·vo -va *adj* & *f* curative
curda *f* (coll) jag, drunk
cureña *f* gun carriage
curia *f* (hist) curia; (*de rey*) court; (*conjunto de abogados*) bar
curiales·co -ca *adj* hairsplitting, legalistic
curiosear *tr* (coll) to pry into || *intr* (coll) to snoop; (coll) to browse around
curiosidad *f* curiosity; (*objeto de arte raro y curioso*) curio; neatness, tidiness; care, carefulness
curio·so -sa *adj* curious; neat, tidy; careful || *mf* busybody || *m* (Ven) healer, medical man
currinche *m* (coll) cub reporter; (coll) hit playwright
cu·rro -rra *adj* (coll) flashy, sporty || *m* (coll) sport, dandy
curruca *f* (orn) whitethroat; **curruca de cabeza negra** blackcap, warbler
curruta·co -ca *adj* (coll) dudish, sporty; (Am) chubby || *m* (coll) dude, sport || *f* (coll) chic dame
cursa·do -da *adj* skilled, experienced; (*asignatura*) taken
cursante *mf* student
cursar *tr* (*una materia, estudios*) to take, to study; (*conferencias*) to attend; (*una carta*) to forward; (*un*

paraje) to frequent, to haunt ‖ *intr* to study; to be current

cursería *f* cheapness, flashiness, vulgarity; flashy lot of people

cursi *adj* cheap, flashy, vulgar, loud ‖ *m* sporty guy ‖ *f* flashy dame

cursien·to -ta *adj* (Am) diarrheic

cursilería *f* cheapness, flashiness, vulgarity; flashy lot of people

cursillo *m* refresher course; short course of lectures

cursi·vo -va *adj* cursive; italic ‖ *f* cursive; italics

curso *m* course; academic year, school year; price, quotation, current rate; **curso académico** academic year; **curso legal** legal tender; **cursos loose bowels; dar curso a** to give way to; to forward

cursor *m* slide; sliding contact; **cursor de procesiones** marshal

curtiduría *f* tannery

curtiembre *f* (Am) tannery

curtir *tr* (*las pieles*) to tan; (*el cutis de una persona*) to tan, sunburn; to

harden, to inure; **estar curtido en** to be skilled in, be expert in ‖ *ref* to become tanned, sunburned; to become hardened; to be weather-beaten

curva *f* curve; bend

curvadura *f* painful exhaustion

cur·vo -va *adj* curved, bent ‖ *f* see **curva**

cusca *f* (Col) jag, drunk; (Mex) prostitute, slut

cúspide *f* (*de montaña*) peak; (*de diente*) cusp; apex, tip, top

custodia *f* custody, care; (*de un preso*) guard; (eccl) monstrance

custodiar *tr* to guard, watch over

custodio *m* custodian; guard

cususa *f* (CAm) rum

cu·tí *m* (*pl* -**tíes**) bedtick, ticking

cutícula *f* cuticle

cutio *m* work, labor

cu·tis *m* (& *f*) (*pl* -**tis**) skin, complexion; **cutis anserina** goose flesh

cu·yo -ya *adj rel* whose

c/v *abbr* **cuenta de venta**

Ch

Ch, ch (che) *f* fourth letter of the Spanish alphabet

chabacanada or **chabacanería** *f* crudeness, coarseness, vulgarity

chabaca·no -na *adj* crude, coarse, vulgar ‖ *m* (Mex) apricot tree

chabola *f* shack, shanty; (mil) foxhole

chacal *m* jackal

chacanear *tr* (Chile) to spur, goad on; (Chile) to annoy, bother

chacare·ro -ra *mf* (SAm) farm laborer, field worker; (Col) quack doctor; (Urug) gossip

chacarrachaca *f* (coll) row, racket

chacolotear *intr* to clatter

chacota *f* laughter, racket; **hacer chacota de** (coll) to make fun of

chacotear *intr* to laugh and make a racket

chacra *f* (Am) farm house; (Am) small farm; (Am) sown field

chacua·co -ca *adj* (Am) ugly, crude, boorish ‖ *m* (CAm) cigar butt; (CAm) cheap cigar

cháchara *f* (coll) chatter, idle talk; **chácharas** (coll) trinkets, junk

chacharear *intr* (coll) to chatter

chafallar *tr* (coll) to botch

chafandín *m* conceited ass

chafar *tr* to rumple, muss; to flatten; (coll) to cut short; (Chile) to dismiss, send off

chafarrinar *tr* to blot, stain

chafarrinón *m* blot, stain; **echar un chafarrinón a** (coll) to insult, throw mud at

chaflán *m* chamfer

chaflanar *tr* to chamfer

chal *m* shawl

cha·lán -lana *adj* horse-dealing ‖ *mf*

horse dealer; horse trader ‖ *m* (Am) broncobuster, horsebreaker ‖ *f* scow, flatboat

chalanear *tr* (*un negocio*) to pull off shrewdly; (*un caballo*) (Am) to break; (Arg) to take advantage of ‖ *intr* to horse-trade

chalanería *f* horse trading

chalanes·co -ca *adj* horse-trading

chaleco *m* vest, waistcoat

chalupa *f* small two-master; launch, lifeboat; (Mex) corncake

chama·co -ca *mf* (Mex) youngster, urchin

chamago·so -sa *adj* (Mex) dirty, filthy; (Mex) botched

chamarasca *f* brushwood; brush fire

chamarille·ro -ra *mf* junk dealer, second-hand dealer ‖ *m* gambler

chamari·llón -llona *mf* poor card player

chamarra *f* sheepskin jacket

chamarreta *f* loose jacket; (Am) square poncho

chamba *f* fluke, scratch

chambelán *m* chamberlain; (Mex) atomizer, spray

chambergo *m* (orn) bobolink; (Arg) soft hat

chambe·rí *adj* (*pl* -**ríes**) (Peru) showy, flashy

cham·bón -bona *adj* (coll) awkward, clumsy; (coll) lucky

chambonada *f* (coll) awkwardness, clumsiness; (coll) stroke of luck

chambonear *intr* to foozle

chambra *f* blouse; (Ven) din, uproar

chambrana *f* trim (*around a door*)

chamburgo *m* (Col) stagnant water, puddle

chamico *m* jimson weed; **dar chamico a** (SAm) to bewitch

chamorrar *tr* (coll) to shear

champán *m* sampan; (coll) champagne

champaña *m* champagne

cham·pú *m* (*pl* **-púes**) shampoo

chamuscar §73 *tr* to singe, scorch; (Mex) to undersell

chamusco *m* singe, scorch

chamusquina *f* singeing; (coll) fight, row, quarrel; **oler a chamusquina** (coll) to look like a fight; (coll) to smack of heresy

chancar §73 *tr* (Am) to crush; (Am) to beat, beat up; (Am) to botch

chancear *intr & ref* to joke, jest

chance·ro -ra *adj* joking, jesting

canciller *m* chancellor

chancla *f* old shoe; house slipper

chancleta *mf* (coll) good-for-nothing || *f* slipper; (Ven) accelerator

chanclo *m* overshoe, rubber

chancha *f* cheat, lie; (Chile) slut; **hacer la chancha** (Bol, Col, Chile) to play hooky

chanche·ro -ra *mf* (Arg, Chile) pork butcher

chan·cho -cha *adj* (Am) dirty, filthy || *m* (Am) pig || *f* see **chancha**

chanchulle·ro -ra *mf* (coll) crook

changador *m* (SAm) errand boy

changarro *m* (Mex) small shop

chan·go -ga *adj* (Chile) dull, stupid; (Mex) sly, crafty || *mf* (Mex) monkey || *m* (Arg) house boy

chan·guí *m* (*pl* **-guíes**) (coll) trick, deception

chantaje *m* blackmail

chantajista *mf* blackmailer

chantar *tr* to put on; (SAm) to throw hard; (Urug) to keep waiting || *ref* (*p.ej.*, *el sombrero*) to clap on

chantre *m* cantor, precentor

chanza *f* joke, jest

chapa *f* sheet, plate; (*hoja fina de madera*) veneer; (*en las mejillas*) flush; (coll) good sense, judgment; (Chile) lock, bolt; **chapa de circulación** (aut) license plate; **chapas** flipping coins

chapa·do -da *adj* plated; veneered; **chapado a la antigua** old-fashioned

chapalear *intr* (*el agua; las manos y los pies en el agua*) to splash; (*la herradura floja*) to clatter

chapar *tr* to cover or line with sheets of metal; to veneer

chaparrear *intr* to pour

chapa·rro -rra *mf* (Mex) child, little one; (Mex) runt || *m* scrub oak

chaparrón *m* downpour

chapea·do -da *adj* lined with sheets of metal; veneered || *m* plywood; veneer

chapear *tr* to cover or line with sheets of metal; to veneer

chapista *m* tinsmith, tinman

chapitel *m* (*remate de torre*) spire; (*capitel de columna*) capital

chapodar *tr* to trim, clear of branches; to curtail

chapotear *tr* to sponge, moisten || *intr* to splash

chapucear *tr & intr* to botch, bungle

chapuce·ro -ra *adj* crude, rough;

clumsy, bungling || *mf* bungler; amateur || *m* blacksmith; junk dealer

chapurrar *tr & intr* to jabber

chapurreo *m* jabber

cha·puz *m* (*pl* **-puces**) duck, ducking

chapuzar §60 *tr*, *intr & ref* to duck

chaqué *m* cutaway coat, morning coat

chaqueta *f* jacket

chaquetilla *f* short jacket; (Ecuad) lady's vest

chaquetón *m* reefer, pea jacket

charamusca *f* (Am) brushwood, firewood; (Mex) candy twist

charanga *f* (mil) brass band

charangue·ro -ra *adj* crude, rough; bungling, clumsy || *mf* bungler

charca *f* pool

charco *m* puddle

charla *f* (coll) talk, chat; (coll) talk, lecture; (coll) chatter, prattle

charla·dor -dora *adj* (coll) garrulous; (coll) gossipy || *mf* (coll) chatterbox; (coll) gossip

charlar *intr* (coll) to talk, chat; (coll) to chatter, prattle

charla·tán -tana *adj* garrulous; gossipy || *mf* chatterbox; gossip; charlatan

charlatanería *f* garrulity, loquacity

charlatanismo *m* charlatanism; garrulity, loquacity

charnela *f* (*de puerta; de molusco*) hinge; (mach) knuckle

charol *m* varnish; patent leather; (Am) lacquered tray; **calzarse las de charol** (Arg, Urug) to hit the jackpot; **darse charol** (coll) to blow one's own horn

charola·do -da *adj* shiny

charolar *tr* to varnish, to lacquer

charpa *f* pistol belt; (*cabestrillo*) sling

charquear *tr* (*carne de vaca*) (Am) to jerk; (Am) to slash, cut to pieces

charqui *m* (Am) jerked beef

charrada *f* country dance; boorishness; (coll) tawdry ornamentation

charretera *f* epaulet; garter; (*del aguador*) (coll) shoulder pad

charriada *f* (Mex) rodeo

cha·rro -rra *adj* coarse, ill-bred; flashy, loud, showy; Salamanca || *mf* peasant; Salamanca peasant || *m* broad-brimmed hat; Mexican cowboy

chasca *f* brushwood

chascar §73 *tr* (*la lengua*) to click; (*algún manjar*) to crunch; (*engullir*) to swallow || *intr* to crack, crackle

chascarrillo *m* (coll) funny story

chas·co -ca *adj* (Arg, Bol) crinkly, crinkly-haired || *m* joke, trick; disappointment; **dar un chasco a** to play a trick on; **llevar** or **llevarse (un) chasco** to be disappointed

chas·cón -cona *adj* (Bol, Chile) disheveled; (Bol, Chile) bushy-haired; (Bol, Chile) clumsy, unskilled

cha·sis *m* (*pl* **-sis**) chassis

chasquear *tr* (*un látigo*) to crack; to play a trick on; to disappoint || *intr* to crack || *ref* to be disappointed

chasqui *m* (SAm) messenger, courier

chasquido *m* crack; crackle

chata *f* barge, scow; flatcar; bedpan

chatarra *f* iron slag; junk, scrap iron

cu
ch

chatarrería *f* junk yard

chatarre·ro -ra *mf* junk dealer, scrap-iron dealer

cha·to -ta *adj* flat; flat-nosed; blunt; (Am) commonplace; (Am) disappointed || *m* (coll) wineglass || *f* see **chata**

chatre *adj* (Chile, Ecuad) all dressed up

cha·val -vala *adj* (coll) young || *m* (coll) lad || *f* (coll) lass

chaveta *f* cotter pin; **perder la chaveta** (coll) to go out of one's head

chayote *m* (Am) chayote, vegetable pear; (Am) dunce, fool

chazar §60 *tr* (*la pelota*) to stop; (*el sitio donde paró la pelota*) to mark

che *interj* (SAm) say!, hey!

che·co -ca *adj & mf* Czech

checoeslova·co -ca *adj & mf* Czecho-Slovak

Checoeslovaquia *f* Czecho-Slovakia

checoslova·co -ca *adj & mf* Czecho-Slovak

Checoslovaquia *f* Czecho-Slovakia

chechén *m* (Mex) poison ivy

chécheres *mpl* (Am) trinkets, junk

chelín *m* shilling

cheque *m* check; **cheque de viajeros** traveler's check

chica *f* lass, little girl; girl; (coll) my dear; **chica de cita** call girl; **chica de la vida alegre** party girl

chicalote *m* Mexican poppy

chicle *m* (Am) chewing gum

chiclear *intr* (Mex) to chew gum

chi·co -ca *adj* small, little; young || *mf* child, youngster || *m* lad, little boy; (coll) young fellow; (coll) old man; (Am) hand, turn || *f* see **chica**

chicolear *intr* to pay compliments, to flirt || *ref* (Arg, Peru) to enjoy oneself

chico·te -ta *mf* husky youngster || *m* (coll) cigar; (Am) cigar stub; (Am) whip

chicue·lo -la *adj* small, little || *m* little boy || *f* little girl

chicha *f* corn liquor; **no ser ni chicha ni limonada** (coll) to be good for nothing

chícharo *m* (Am) pea; (Col) poor cigar; (Mex) apprentice

chicharra *f* harvest fly; (coll) chatterbox; **cantar la chicharra** (coll) to be hot and sultry

chicharrón *m* residue of hog's fat; burnt meat; (coll) sunburned person; (Am) wrinkled person

chichear *tr & intr* to hiss

chi·chón -chona *adj* (CAm) easy; (SAm) joking; (Guat) large-breasted || *m* lump, bump on the head

chifla *f* hissing, whistling; paring knife; **estar de chifla** (Mex) to be in a bad humor

chifla·do -da *adj* (coll) daffy, nutty || *mf* (coll) crackbrain, nut

chifladura *f* (coll) daffiness, nuttiness; (coll) whim, wild idea

chiflar *tr* (*un actor*) to hiss; (*vino o licor*) to gulp down; (*el cuero*) to pare || *intr* to whistle; (*las aves*) (Guat, Mex) to sing || *ref* to go crazy

chifle *m* whistle; (*para cazar aves*) bird call; powder flask

chiflido *m* whistle, hiss

chiflón *m* (SAm) cold blast of air; (Am) rapids; (Am) slide of loose stone

chilaba *f* jelab, jellaba

Chile *m* Chile

chile·no -na *adj & mf* Chilean

chilla *f* fox call, hare call; clapboard; (Chile) small fox; (Mex) top gallery

chillar *intr* to shriek; to squeak; to hiss, sizzle; (*los colores*) to scream || *ref* (Am) to take offense

chillido *m* shriek, scream

chi·llón -llona *adj* shrill, high-pitched; (coll) screaming; (*color*) loud

chimenea *f* chimney, smokestack; fireplace, hearth; stovepipe hat; (naut) funnel

chimpancé *m* chimpanzee

china *f* Chinese woman; china, porcelain; pebble; (Am) nursemaid; (Col) spinning top || **China** *f* China

chinche *mf* (coll) bore, tiresome person || *m* (*clavito de cabeza chata*) thumbtack || *f* (*insecto*) bedbug; **caer** or **morir como chinches** to die like flies

chinchorre·ro -ra *adj* (coll) gossipy, mischievous

chincho·so -sa *adj* (coll) boring, tiresome

chinero *m* china closet

chines·co -ca *adj* Chinese || **chinescos** *mpl* (mus) bell tree

chingar §44 *tr* (coll) to tipple; (CAm) to bob, dock; (CAm, Mex) to bother, annoy || *ref* (coll) to tipple; (Am) to fail

chin·go -ga *adj* (CAm) short; (CAm) dull, blunt; (CAm) naked

chinguirito *m* (Am) cheap rum; (Am) swig of liquor

chi·no -na *adj & mf* Chinese || *m* (*idioma*) Chinese; (Col) boy, newsboy; (Mex) curl || *f* see **china**

chipichipi *m* (Am) drizzle, mist

Chipre *f* Cyprus

chiquero *m* pigsty; bull pen

chiquillada *f* childish prank

chiqui·to -ta *adj* small, little || *mf* little one || *m* (*de vino*) snifter; (Arg) moment, instant || *f* five cents; **no andarse con** or **en chiquitas** (coll) to talk right off the shoulder

chiribita *f* spark; daisy; **chiribitas** (coll) spots before the eyes

chiribitil *m* garret; cubbyhole

chirimbolos *mpl* (coll) utensils, vessels

chirimía *f* hornpipe

chiripa *f* (billiards) fluke, scratch; (coll) stroke of luck

chirivía *f* parsnip

chirle *adj* (coll) insipid, tasteless

chirlo *m* slash or scar on the face

chirlota *f* (Mex) meadow lark

chirona *f* (coll) jail, jug

chirriar §77 *intr* to creak, squeak; to shriek; to hiss, sizzle; to sing or play out of tune || *ref* (Col) to go on a spree; (Col) to shiver

chirrido *m* creak, squeak; shriek; hiss, sizzle

chis *interj* sh-sh!; ¡chis, chis! pst!

chischás *m* clash of swords

chisguete *m* (coll) swig of wine; (coll) squirt

chisme *m* piece of gossip; (coll) trinket; **chisme de vecindad** (coll) idle talker; **chismes** gossip; articles; **chismes de aseo** toilet articles

chismear *intr* to gossip

chismo·so -sa *adj* gossipy, catty ‖ *mf* gossip

chispa *f* spark; (*pequeña cantidad*) drop; lightning; (fig) sparkle, wit; (coll) drunk, spree; (Col) rumor; **coger una chispa** (coll) to go on a drunk; **chispa de entrehierro** (elec) jump spark; **chispas sprinkle** (*of rain*); **dar chispa** (Guat, Mex) to work, to click; **echar chispas** (coll) to blow up, hit the ceiling

chispeante *adj* sparkling

chispear *intr* to spark; to sparkle; to drizzle, to sprinkle

chis·po -pa *adj* (coll) tipsy ‖ *m* (coll) swallow, drink ‖ *f* see **chispa**

chisporrotear *intr* (coll) to spark, to sputter

chispo·so -sa *adj* sputtering, sparking

chisquero *m* pocket lighter

chistar *intr* to speak, say something; **no chistar** to not say a word

chiste *m* joke; witticism; **caer en el chiste** (coll) to get the point; **dar en el chiste** (coll) to hit the nail on the head

chistera *f* fish basket; (coll) top hat

chisto·so -sa *adj* funny; witty ‖ *mf* funny person; wit

chita *f* anklebone; quoits; **a la chita callando** (coll) quietly, secretly; **dar en la chita** (coll) to hit the nail on the head

chiticalla *mf* (*persona que no revela lo que sabe*) (coll) clam ‖ *f* (coll) secret

chito *interj* hush!, sh-sh!

chivato *m* kid, young goat; (*soplón*) (coll) squealer; (Bol) apprentice, helper; (Chile) cheap rum

chi·vo -va *mf* kid ‖ *m* billy goat ‖ *f* nanny goat

chocante *adj* shocking; coarse, crude; (Col) annoying; (Mex) disagreeable

chocar §73 *tr* to shock, annoy, irritate; to surprise; (*vasos*) to clink; (coll) to please; ¡choque Vd. esos cinco! (coll) shake! ‖ *intr* to shock; to collide; to clash, fight

chocarre·ro -ra *adj* coarse, crude ‖ *mf* crude joker

choclo *m* wooden overshoe; (Mex) low shoe; (SAm) tender ear of corn

chocolate *m* chocolate

chocha *f* woodcock

chochear *intr* to be in one's dotage; (coll) to dote, be infatuated

chochera *f* dotage; (Arg, Peru) favorite

cho·chez *f* (*pl* -checes) dotage; doting act or remark

cho·cho -cha *adj* doting; doddering ‖ *m* stick of cinnamon candy; **chochos** candy to quiet a child ‖ *f* see **chocha**

chófer *m* chauffeur

chofeta *f* fire pan (*for lighting cigars*)

cho·lo -la *adj* (Am) half-breed (*Indian and white*); (Am) half-civilized (*Indian*) ‖ *mf* (Am) Indian; (Am) half-breed; (Am) half-civilized Indian; (Chile) coward; (SAm) darling

cholla *f* (coll) noodle, head; (coll) ability, brains

chomite *m* (Mex) coarse wool; (Mex) woolen skirt

chopo *m* black poplar; (coll) gun, rifle; **chopo de Italia** Lombardy poplar; **chopo del Canadá** or **de Virginia** cottonwood; **chopo lombardo** Lombardy poplar

choque *m* shock; collision, impact; clash, conflict, skirmish; (elec) choke, choke coil

choricería *f* sausage shop

chorizo *m* smoked pork sausage

chorlito *m* plover, golden plover; (coll) scatterbrains

chorrear *intr* to gush, spurt, spout; to drip; to trickle

chorrera *f* spout, channel; cut, gulley; rapids; lace front, jabot; (Arg) string, stream

chorrillo *m* constant stream; **irse por el chorrillo** (coll) to follow the current; **tomar el chorrillo de** (coll) to get the habit of

chorro *m* jet, spurt; stream, flow; **a chorros** in abundance; **chorro de arena** sandblast

chotaca·bras *m* (*pl* -bras) goatsucker

chotear *tr* (Am) to make fun of; (Guat) to keep an eye on

choteo *m* (Am) jeering, mocking

choza *f* hut, cabin, lodge

chubasco *m* squall, shower; (fig) temporary setback; **chubasco de agua** rainstorm; **chubasco de nieve** blizzard

chubasco·so -sa *adj* stormy, threatening

chucruta *f* sauerkraut

chucha *f* (coll) female dog, bitch; (coll) drunk, jag; (Col) opossum; (Col) body odor

chuchaque *m* (Ecuad) hangover

chuchear *tr* (*caza menor*) to trap ‖ *intr* to whisper

chuchería *f* knickknack, trinket; delicacy, tidbit

chu·cho -cha *adj* (CAm) mean, stingy; (*fruto*) (Col) watery; (Col) wrinkled ‖ *m* (coll) dog ‖ *f* see **chucha**

chue·co -ca *adj* (Mex) twisted, bent; (SAm) bow-legged; (Mex) crippled ‖ *m* (Mex) dealing in stolen goods ‖ *f* stump; hockey; hockey ball

chufa *f* groundnut

chufletear *intr* (coll) to joke, jest

chula *f* flashy dame (*in lower classes of Madrid*)

chulada *f* light-hearted remark; vulgarity

chul·co -ca *mf* (Bol) baby (*youngest child*)

chulear *tr* to tease; (Mex) to flirt with

chuleta *f* chop, cutlet; (coll) slap, smack; (*de los estudiantes*) (coll) crib, pony; **chuleta de cerdo** pork chop; **chuleta de ternera** veal chop; **chuletas** sideburns, side whiskers

chu·lo -la adj flashy, sporty; foxy, slick; (Guat, Mex) pretty, cute || m sporty fellow (in lower classes of Madrid); pimp, procurer; gigolo; butcher's helper; (taur) attendant on foot || f see **chula**

chumbera f prickly pear

chunga f (coll) jest, fun

chunguear ref (coll) to jest, joke

chupa f frock, coat; (Arg) drunk, jag; (Arg) tobacco pouch

chupa·do -da adj (coll) thin, skinny; (Am) drunk; (falda) (Am) tight || f suck; pull (on a cigar)

chupador m teething ring, pacifier

chupaflor m (Mex, Ven) hummingbird

chupamirto m (Mex) hummingbird

chupar tr to suck; (la hacienda ajena) to milk, sap; (coll) to absorb || intr to suck || ref to get thin, lose strength; (los labios) to smack

chupatin·tas mf (pl -tas) (coll) office drudge

chupete m (para un niño) pacifier; (Am) lollipop; **de chupete** (coll) fine, splendid

chu·pón -pona mf (coll) swindler || m

(bot) sucker, shoot; (mach) plunger

chupópte·ro -ra mf (coll) sponger

chuquisa f (Chile, Peru) prostitute

churrasco m (Am) barbecue

churrasquear tr (Am) to barbecue

churre m (coll) filth, dirt, grease

churrete m dirty spot (on hands or face)

churrigueres·co -ca adj churrigueresque; loud, flashy, tawdry

chu·rro -rra adj (lana) coarse; (carnero) coarse-wooled || m coarse-wooled sheep; fritter; (coll) botch

churrulle·ro -ra adj gossipy, loquacious || mf gossip, chatterbox

churrusco m burnt piece of bread

churumbela f hornpipe, flageolet; (Am) maté cup; (Col) worry, anxiety; (Col, Ecuad) pipe

churumo m (coll) substance (money, brains, etc.)

chus interj here! (to call a dog); **no decir chus ni mus** (coll) to not say boo

chus·co -ca adj droll, funny; (Peru) ill-mannered; (perro) (Peru) mongrel

chusma f galley slaves; mob, rabble

chuza f (Mex) strike (in bowling)

D

D, d (de) f fifth letter of the Spanish alphabet

D. abbr don

D.ª abbr doña

daca give me, hand over; **andar al daca y toma** (coll) to be at cross purposes

dactilógra·fo -fa mf typist, typewriter || m typewriter

dactilograma m fingerprint

dádiva f gift, present

dadivo·so -sa adj liberal, generous

da·do -da adj given; **dado que** provided, as long as || m die; **cargar los dados** to load the dice; **dados** dice; **el dado está tirado** the die is cast

daga f dagger

dalia f dahlia

dama f lady, dame; maid-in-waiting; (en el juego de damas) king; (en el ajedrez y los naipes) queen; (theat) leading lady; concubine, mistress; **dama joven** (theat) young lead; **damas** checkers; **señalar dama** (en el juego de damas) to crown a man

damajuana f demijohn

damasquina·do -da adj & m damascene

damasquinar tr to damascene

damasqui·no -na adj damascene

damero m checkerboard

damisela f young lady; courtesan

damnación f damnation

damnificar §73 tr to damage, hurt

da·nés -nesa adj Danish || mf Dane || m (idioma) Danish

dáni·co -ca adj Danish

Danubio m Danube

danza f dance; dancing; dance team; **danza de cintas** Maypole dance; **danza de figuras** square dance; **meter en la danza** (coll) to drag in, involve

danza·dor -dora mf dancer

danzar §60 tr to dance || intr to dance; (coll) to butt in

danza·rín -rina f dancer; (coll) meddler, scatterbrain

dañable adj harmful; reprehensible

daña·do -da adj bad, wicked; spoiled

dañar tr to hurt, damage, injure; to spoil || ref to be damaged; to spoil

dañi·no -na adj harmful, destructive, noxious; wicked

daño m damage, harm; (Arg) witchcraft; **a daño de** on the responsibility of; **daños y perjuicios** (law) damages; **en daño de** to the detriment of; **hacer daño** to be harmful; **hacer daño a** to hurt; **hacerse daño** to hurt oneself; to get hurt

daño·so -sa adj harmful, injurious

dar §23 tr to give; to cause; to hit, strike; (el reloj la hora) to strike; (cartas) to deal; (un paseo) to take; (los buenos días) to wish; (un film) to show; (una capa de pintura) to put on, apply; **dar a conocer** to make known; **dar a luz** to bring out, publish; **dar cuerda a** (un reloj) to wind; **dar curso a** to circulate; **dar de beber a** to give something to drink to; **dar de comer a** to give something to eat to; **dar la razón a** to admit that (*someone*) is right; **dar prestado** to lend; **dar palmadas** to clap the hands; **dar por** to consider as; **dar que hablar** to cause talk; to stir up criticism; **dar que hacer** to cause annoyance or trouble; **dar que pensar** to give food for thought; to give rise to suspicion ‖ *intr* to take place; to hit, strike; (*el reloj; dos, tres, etc. horas*) to strike; to tell, intimate; **dar a** to overlook; **dar con** to run into; **dar contra** to run against, strike against; **dar de sí** to stretch; to give; **dar en** to overlook; to hit; to run into; to fall into; to be bent on; (*un chiste*) to catch on to; **dar sobre** to overlook; **dar tras** to pursue hotly ‖ *ref* to give oneself up; to give in, yield; to occur, be found; **darse a** to devote oneself to; **darse a conocer** to make a name for oneself, make oneself known; to get to know each other; **darse cuenta de** to realize, become aware of; **darse la mano** to shake hands; **dárselas de** to pose as; **darse por aludido** to take the hint; **darse por entendido** to show an understanding; to show appreciation; **darse por ofendido** to take offense; **darse por vencido** to give up, to acknowledge defeat

dardo *m* dart; cutting remark

dares y tomares *mpl* (coll) quarrels, disputes

dársena *f* basin, dock, inner harbor

data *f* date; (*en una cuenta*) item; **de larga data** of long standing; **estar de mala data** (coll) to be in a bad humor

datar *tr & intr* to date; **datar de** to date from

dátil *m* date

datilera *f* date, date palm

dativo -va *adj & m* dative

dato *m* datum; basis, foundation

de *prep* of; from; about; **acompañado de** accompanied by; **cubierto de** covered with; **de noche** in the nighttime; **de no llegar nosotros a la hora** if we do not arrive on time; **más de** more than; **tratar de** to try to

deán *m* (eccl) dean

debajo *adv* below, underneath; **debajo de** below, under

debate *m* debate; altercation, argument

debatir *tr & intr* to debate; to fight, argue ‖ *ref* to struggle

debe *m* debit

debelar *tr* to conquer, vanquish

deber *m* duty; (*deuda*) debt; homework, school work; **últimos deberes** last rites ‖ *tr* to owe ‖ *v aux* to have to, ought to, must, should; **deber de** must, most likely ‖ *ref* to be committed; **deberse a** to be due to

debidamente *adv* duly

debi-do -da *adj* due, owed; proper, right; **debido a** due to

débil *adj* weak

debilidad *f* weakness, debility

debilitar *tr & ref* to weaken

débito *m* debt, debit; responsibility

debutar *intr* to make one's start, appear for the first time

década *f* decade

decadencia *f* decadence

decadente *adj & mf* decadent

decaer §15 *intr* to decay, decline, fail, weaken; (naut) to drift from the course

decampar *intr* (mil) to decamp

decanato *m* deanship

decano *m* dean

decanta-do -da *adj* puffed-up, overrated

decapitar *tr* to decapitate

decelerar *tr, intr, & ref* to decelerate

decencia *f* decency

decenio *m* decade

dece-no -na *adj & m* tenth

decentar §2 *tr* to cut the first slice of; to begin to damage ‖ *ref* to get bedsores

decente *adj* decent, proper; decent-looking

decepción *f* disappointment

decepcionar *tr* to disappoint

decidi-do -da *adj* decided, determined

decidir *tr* to decide; to persuade ‖ *intr & ref* to decide

deci-dor -dora *adj* facile, fluent, witty

decimal *adj & m* decimal

déci-mo -ma *adj & m* tenth

decimocta-vo -va *adj* eighteenth

decimocuar-to -ta *adj* fourteenth

decimono-no -na *adj* nineteenth

decimonove-no -na *adj* nineteenth

decimoquin-to -ta *adj* fifteenth

decimosépti-mo -ma *adj* seventeenth

decimosex-to -ta *adj* sixteenth

decimoterce-ro -ra *adj* thirteenth

decimoter-cio -cia *adj* thirteenth

decir *m* say-so; **al decir de** according to ‖ §24 *tr* to say; to tell; (*disparates*) to talk; **como si dijéramos** so to speak, in a manner of speaking; **decir entre sí** to say to oneself; **decirle a uno cuántas son cinco** (coll) to tell a person what's what; **decir para sí** to say to oneself; **decir por decir** to talk for talk's sake; **decir que no** to say no; **decir que sí** to say yes; **decírselo a una persona deletreado** (coll) to spell it out to a person; **es decir** that is to say; **mejor dicho** rather; **¡por algo te lo dije!** I told you so!; **por decirlo así** so to speak ‖ *intr* to suit, fit; **¡diga!** (al contestar el teléfono) hello! ‖ *ref* to be said; to be called; **se dice** it is said

decisión *f* decision

decisi-vo -va *adj* decisive

declamar *tr & intr* to declaim

declaración *f* declaration; (en bridge) bid

declarante *mf* declarant, deponent; (en el juego de bridge) bidder

declarar *tr* to declare; (en bridge) to bid; (law) to depose ‖ *ref* to declare oneself; to break out, take place

declarati-vo -va *adj* declarative

declinación *f* declination; fall, drop; decline; (gram) declension

declinar *tr & intr* to decline

declive *m* descent, declivity, slope

ch
de

declividad *f* declivity
decollaje *m* (aer) take-off
decollar *intr* (aer) to take off
decomisar *tr* to seize, confiscate
decomiso *m* seizure, confiscation
decoración *f* decoration; memorizing; (theat) set, scenery; **decoraciones** (theat) scenery; **decoración interior** interior decoration
decorado *m* decoration; (theat) décor, scenery; memorizing
decora•dor -dora *mf* decorator
decorar *tr* to decorate; to memorize
decoro *m* decorum; honor, respect; decency, propriety
decoro•so -sa *adj* decorous; respectful; decent
decrecer §22 *intr* to decrease, grow smaller, grow shorter
decrepitar *intr* to crackle
decrépi•to -ta *adj* decrepit
decretar *tr* to decree
decreto *m* decree
decurso *m* course; **en el decurso de** in the course of
dechado *m* sample, model, example; (*labor de las niñas*) sampler
dedada *f* touch, spot; **dar una dedada de miel a** (coll) to feed the hopes of
dedal *m* thimble
dedalera *f* foxglove
dedeo *m* (mus) finger dexterity
dedicación *f* dedication
dedicar §73 *tr* to dedicate; to devote; to autograph ‖ *ref* to devote oneself
dedicatoria *f* dedication
dedil *m* fingerstall
dedillo *m* little finger; **saber** or **tener al dedillo** (coll) to have at one's finger tips, to have a thorough knowledge of
dedo *m* finger; toe; (coll) bit; **alzar el dedo** (*en señal de dar palabra*) (coll) to raise one's hand; **cogerse los dedos** (coll) to burn one's fingers; **dedo auricular** little finger; **dedo cordial, de en medio,** or **del corazón** middle finger; **dedo gordo** thumb; big toe; **dedo índice** index finger, forefinger; **dedo meñique** little finger; **dedo mostrador** forefinger; **dedo pulgar** thumb; big toe; **estar a dos dedos de** (coll) to be within an ace of; **irse de entre los dedos** (coll) to slip between the fingers; **tener en la punta de los dedos** (coll) to have at one's finger tips
deducción *f* deduction; drawing off
deducir §19 *tr* (*concluir*) to deduce; (*rebajar*) to deduct; (law) to allege
defecar §73 *intr* to defecate
defección *f* defection
defeccionar *intr* & *ref* (Chile) to defect
defecti•vo -va *adj* defective
defecto *m* defect; shortage, lack; **en defecto de** for lack of
defectuo•so -sa *adj* defective; lacking
defender §51 *tr* to defend; to protect; to delay, interfere with
defensa *f* defense; fender, guard; (*del toro*) horn; (*del elefante*) tusk; (*del automóvil*) (Am) bumper; **defensa marítima** (Arg) sea wall; **defensa propia** self-defense

defensi•vo -va *adj* & *f* defensive
defen•sor -sora *adj* defending ‖ *mf* defender; (law) counsel for the defense
deferencia *f* deference
deferente *adj* deferential
deferir §68 *tr* to delegate ‖ *intr* to defer
deficiencia *f* deficiency
deficiente *adj* deficient
défi•cit *m* (*pl* -cits) deficit
deficita•rio -ria *adj* deficit
definición *f* definition; decision, verdict
defini•do -da *adj* definite; sharp, defined
definir *tr* to define; to settle, determine
definiti•vo -va *adj* definitive; **en definitiva** after all, in short
deflación *f* deflation
deflector *m* baffle
deformación *f* deformation; (rad) distortion
deformar *tr* to deform; to disfigure; to distort
deforme *adj* deformed
deformidad *f* deformity; gross error
defraudar *tr* to defraud, to cheat; (*las esperanzas de una persona*) to defeat; (*la claridad del día*) to cut off
defuera *adv* outside; **por defuera** on the outside
defunción *f* decease, demise
degeneración *f* (*acción y efecto de degenerar*) degeneration; (*estado de degenerado; depravación*) degeneracy
degenera•do -da *adj* & *mf* degenerate
degenerar *intr* to degenerate
deglutir *tr* & *intr* to swallow
degollar §3 *tr* to cut the throat of; to kill, massacre; (*un vestido*) to cut low in the neck; (*el actor una obra dramática*) to butcher, to murder; (coll) to become obnoxious to
degradante *adj* degrading
degradar *tr* to degrade; (mil) to break
degüello *m* throat-cutting; massacre; (*de un arma*) neck; **tirar a degüello** (coll) to try to harm
degustar *tr* (*probar*) to taste; (*percibir con deleite el sabor de*) to savor
dehesa *f* pasture land, meadow; (taur) range
deidad *f* deity
deificar §73 *tr* to deify
dejación *f* abandonment; (CAm, Chile, Col) negligence
dejadez *f* laziness; negligence; slovenliness; low spirits
deja•do -da *adj* lazy; negligent; slovenly; dejected
dejamiento *m* laziness; negligence; indolence, languor, indifference
dejar *tr* to leave; to abandon; to let, allow, permit; **dejar caer** to drop, let fall; **dejar feo** (coll) to slight; **dejar fresco** (coll) to leave in the lurch; **dejar por** + *inf* or **que** + *inf* to leave (*something*) to be + *pp*, e.g., **hemos dejado dos manuscritos por corregir** or **que corregir** we left two manuscripts to be corrected ‖ *intr* to stop; **dejar de** to stop, to cease; to fail to ‖ *ref* to be slovenly, to neglect oneself; (*una barba*) to grow; **dejarse de**

(*disparates*) to cut out; (*preguntas*) to stop asking; (*dudas*) to put aside; **dejarse ver** to show up; to be evident

dejillo *m* (*gusto que deja alguna comida*) aftertaste; (*acento regional*) local accent

dejo *m* (*gusto que deja alguna comida*) aftertaste; abandonment; slovenliness, neglect; local accent; (*placer o disgusto que queda después de hecha una cosa*) (fig) aftertaste

delación *f* accusation, denunciation

delantal *m* apron

delante *adv* before, ahead, in front; **delante de** before, ahead of, in front of

delantera *f* front; front row; advantage, lead; cowcatcher; **coger** or **tomar la delantera a** to get ahead of; to get a start on; **delanteras** overalls

delante·ro -ra *adj* front, foremost, first ‖ *f* see **delantera**

delatar *tr* to accuse, denounce

delega·do -da *mf* delegate

delegar §44 *tr* to delegate

deleitable *adj* delectable, enjoyable

deleitar *tr & ref* to delight

deleite *m* delight

deleito·so -sa *adj* delightful

deletrear *tr & intr* to spell; to decipher

deletreo *m* spelling

deleznable *adj* (*poco durable*) perishable; (*que se rompe fácilmente*) crumbly, fragile; (*que se desliza con facilidad*) slippery

delfín *m* (*primogénito del rey de Francia*) dauphin; (*mamífero cetáceo*) dolphin

delgadez *f* thinness, leanness; delicateness, lightness; perspicacity

delga·do -da *adj* thin, lean; delicate, light; sharp, perspicacious; (*terreno*) poor, exhausted ‖ *adv* — **hilar delgado** (coll) to hew close to the line; (coll) to split hairs

deliberar *tr & intr* to deliberate

delicadeza *f* delicacy, delicateness; scrupulousness

delica·do -da *adj* delicate; scrupulous

delicia *f* delight

delicio·so -sa *adj* delicious, delightful

delincuencia *f* guilt, criminality

delincuente *adj* guilty, criminal ‖ *mf* criminal

delineante *mf* designer ‖ *m* draughtsman

delinquir §25 *intr* to transgress, be guilty

deliquio *m* faint, swoon; weakening

delirante *adj* delirious

delirar *intr* to be delirious, rant, rave; to talk nonsense

delirio *m* delirium; nonsense

delito *m* crime; **delito de incendio** arson; **delito de lesa majestad** lese majesty; **delito de mayor cuantía** (law) felony; **delito de menor cuantía** (law) misdemeanor

deludir *tr* to delude

demacra·do -da *adj* emaciated, wasted, thin

demago·go -ga *mf* demagogue

demanda *f* demand, petition; charity box; lawsuit; undertaking; (*del Santo*

Grial) quest; **en demanda de** in search of; **tener demanda** to be in demand

demanda·do -da *mf* (law) defendant

demandante *mf* (law) complainant, plaintiff

demandar *tr* to ask for, request; (law) to sue ‖ *intr* (law) to sue, bring suit

demarcar §73 *tr* to demarcate

demás *adj* — **el demás . . .** the other **. . . , the rest of the . . . ; estar demás** to be useless, to be in the way; **lo demás** the rest; **por lo demás** furthermore, besides ‖ *pron* others; **los demás** the others, the rest ‖ *adv* besides; **por demás** in vain; too, too much

demasía *f* excess, surplus; daring, boldness; evil, guilt, wrong; insolence; **en demasía** excessively, too much

demasia·do -da *adj & pron* too much; **demasia·dos -das** too many ‖ **demasiado** *adv* too, too much, too hard

demasiar §77 *intr* (coll) to go too far

demediar *tr* to divide in half; to use up half of; to reach the middle of ‖ *intr* to be divided in half

demente *adj* insane ‖ *mf* lunatic

democracia *f* democracy

demócrata *mf* democrat

democráti·co -ca *adj* democratic

demoler §47 *tr* to demolish

demolición *f* demolition

demonía·co -ca *adj* demoniacal

demonio *m* demon, devil; **estudiar con el demonio** (coll) to be full of devilishness

demora *f* delay

demorar *tr & ref* to delay

demostración *f* demonstration

demostra·dor -dora *mf* demonstrator ‖ *m* hand (*of clock*)

demostrar §61 *tr* to demonstrate

demostrati·vo -va *adj* demonstrative

demudar *tr* to change, alter; to disguise, cloak ‖ *ref* to change countenance, to color

denegación *f* denial, refusal

denegar §66 *tr* to deny, to refuse

denegrecer §22 *tr* to blacken ‖ *ref* to turn black

dengo·so -sa *adj* affected, finicky, overnice; (Col) strutting

dengue *m* affectation, finickiness, overniceness; (Col) strut, swagger

denguear *ref* (Col) to strut, swagger

denigrar *tr* to defame, revile; to insult

denominación *f* denomination

denoda·do -da *adj* bold, daring

denostar §61 *tr* to abuse, insult, mistreat

denotar *tr* to denote

densidad *f* density; darkness, confusion

den·so -sa *adj* dense; dark, confused; crowded, thick, close

denta·do -da *adj* toothed; (*sello de correo*) perforated ‖ *m* gear; teeth

dentadura *f* set of teeth; **dentadura artificial** or **postiza** denture

dental *adj & f* dental

dentellada *f* bite; tooth mark

dentellar *intr* (*los dientes*) to chatter

dentellear *tr* to nibble, nibble at

dentera *f* (coll) envy; (coll) eagerness;

dar dentera to set the teeth on edge; to make the mouth water

dentición f teething

dentífri·co -ca adj (pasta, polvos) tooth || m dentifrice

dentista mf dentist

dentistería f dentistry

dentística f (Chile) dentistry

dentro adv inside, within; **dentro de** inside, within; **dentro de poco** shortly; **por dentro** on the inside

denuedo m bravery, courage, daring

denuesto m abuse, insult, mistreatment

denuncia f denunciation; report; proclamation

denunciar tr to denounce; to report; (la guerra) to proclaim

deparar tr to furnish, provide; to offer, present

departamento m department; (rr) compartment; (piso) (Am) apartment; naval district (in Spain)

departir intr to chat, converse

depauperación f impoverishment; exhaustion, weakening

depauperar tr to impoverish; to exhaust, weaken

dependencia f dependence, dependency; branch, branch office; relationship, friendship; accessory; personnel

depender intr to depend; **depender de** to depend on; to be attached to, to belong to

dependienta f female employee, clerk

dependiente adj dependent; branch || mf employee, clerk

deplorable adj deplorable

deplorar tr to deplore

deponer §54 tr to depose; to set aside, remove; (las armas) to lay down || intr to depose; (evacuar el vientre) to have a movement; (CAm, Mex) to vomit

deportación f deportation

deporta·do -da mf deportee

deportar tr to deport

deporte m sport; outdoor recreation

deportista mf sport fan || m sportsman || f sportswoman

deporti·vo -va adj sport, sports

depositante mf depositor

depositar tr to deposit; (la esperanza, la confianza) to put, place; (el equipaje) to check; (a una persona en seguro) to commit; to store || ref to deposit, settle

deposita·rio -ria mf trustee; (de un secreto) repository || m public treasurer

depósito m deposit; depot, warehouse; tank, reservoir; (de libros en una biblioteca) stack; (mil) depot; **depósito comercial** bonded warehouse; **depósito de agua** reservoir; **depósito de cadáveres** morgue; **depósito de cereales** grain elevator; **depósito de equipajes** (rr) checkroom; **depósito de gasolina** (aut) gas tank; **depósito de locomotoras** roundhouse; **depósito de municiones** munition dump

depravación f depravity, depravation

deprava·do -da adj depraved

depravar tr to deprave || ref to become depraved

deprecar §73 tr to entreat, implore

depreciación f depreciation

depreciar tr & ref to depreciate

depresión f depression; drop, dip; (en un muro) recess

deprimir tr to depress; to press down; to push in; to belittle; to humiliate || ref to be depressed; (la frente de una persona) to recede

depurar tr to purify, cleanse; to purge

derecha f right hand; right-hand side; (pol) right; **a la derecha** on the right, to the right

derechamente adv rightly; straight, direct; properly; wisely

derechazo m blow with the right; (box) right

derece·ro -ra adj right, just

derechista adj rightist || mf rightist, right-winger

dere·cho -cha adj right; right-hand; right-handed; straight; upright, standing || m right; law; exemption, privilege; road, path; (de tela, papel, tabla) right side; **derecho consuetudinario** common law; **derecho de gentes** law of nations, international law; **derecho de subscripción** (a una nueva emisión de acciones) (com) right; **derecho de tránsito** or **paso** right of way; **derecho internacional** international law; **derecho penal** criminal law; **derechos** dues, fees, taxes; (de aduana) duties; **derechos de almacenaje** storage, cost of storage; **derechos de autor** royalty; **derechos del hombre** rights of man; **derechos de propiedad literaria** or **derechos reservados** copyright; **según derecho** by right, by rights || f see **derecha** || **derecho** adv straight, direct; rightly

deriva (aer, naut) drift; **ir a la deriva** (naut) to drift, to be adrift

derivado m by-product

derivar tr to derive || intr & ref to derive, be derived; (aer, naut) to drift

derogar §44 tr to abolish, destroy, repeal

derrabar tr to dock, cut off the tail of

derrama·do -da adj extravagant, lavish

derramamiento m pouring, spilling; shedding; spreading; lavishing, wasting

derramar tr to pour, to spill; (sangre) to shed; to spread, publish abroad; (dinero) to lavish, waste || ref to run over, overflow; to spread, scatter; (una corriente, un río) to open, empty; (la plumafuente) to leak

derrame m pouring, spilling; (de sangre) shed, shedding; spread, scattering; lavishing, wasting; overflow; leakage; slope; chamfering; (pathol) discharge, effusion

derredor m circumference; **al** or **en derredor** around, round about

derrelicto m derelict

derrelinquir §25 tr to abandon, forsake

derrenga·do -da adj crooked, out of shape; crippled, lame

derrengar §44 or §66 tr to bend, make crooked; to cripple

derreniego *m* (coll) curse
derreti·do -da *adj* madly in love; (*mantequilla*) drawn || *m* concrete
derretimiento *m* thawing, melting; intense love, passion
derretir §50 *tr* to thaw, melt; (*la mantequilla*) to draw; (*la hacienda*) to squander || *ref* to thaw, melt; to fall madly in love; to be quite susceptible; (coll) to be worried, be impatient
derribar *tr* to destroy, tear down, knock down; to wreck; (*un árbol*) to fell; to bring down, shoot down; to overthrow; to humiliate || *ref* to fall down, tumble down; to throw oneself on the ground
derribo *m* demolition, wrecking; (*de un árbol*) felling; overthrow; (*de un avión enemigo*) bringing down; **derribos** debris, rubble
derrocadero *m* rocky precipice
derrocar §73 or §81 *tr* to throw or hurl from a height; to ruin, wreck, tear down; to bring down, humble, overthrow
derrocha·dor -dora *mf* wastrel, squanderer
derrochar *tr* to waste, squander
derroche *m* wasting, squandering, extravagance
derrota *f* defeat, rout; road, route, way; (*de embarcación*) course
derrotadamente *adv* shabbily, poorly
derrotar *tr* to rout, put to flight; to wear out; to ruin || *ref* (naut) to drift from the course
derrotero *m* course, route; ship's course
derrotismo *m* defeatism
derrotista *adj* & *mf* defeatist
derrubiar *tr* & *ref* to wash away, wear away
derrubio *m* washout
derruir §20 *tr* to tear down, demolish
derrumbadero *m* crag, precipice; hazard, risky business
derrumbamiento *m* headlong plunge; cave-in, collapse; **derrumbamiento de tierra** landslide
derrumbar *tr* to throw headlong || *ref* to plunge headlong; to collapse, cave in, crumble
derrumbe *m* precipice; landslide; cave-in
derviche *m* dervish
desabonar *ref* to drop one's subscription
desabono *m* cancellation of subscription; discredit, disparagement
desabor *m* insipidity, tastelessness
desabotonar *tr* to unbutton || *intr* to blossom, bloom
desabri·do -da *adj* insipid, tasteless; gruff, surly; (*tiempo*) unsettled
desabrigar §44 *tr* to uncover, bare || *ref* to bare oneself; to undress
desabrir *tr* to give a bad taste to; to displease, to embitter
desabrochar *tr* to unclasp, unbutton, unfasten || *ref* (coll) to unbosom oneself
desacalorar *ref* to cool off
desacatamiento *m* incivility, disrespect
desacatar *tr* to treat disrespectfully

desacato *m* incivility, disrespect, contempt; (*para con las cosas sagradas*) profanation
desacelerar *tr* & *ref* to decelerate
desacerta·do -da *adj* mistaken, wrong
desacertar §2 *intr* to be mistaken, be wrong
desacierto *m* error, mistake, blunder
desacomoda·do -da *adj* inconvenient; out of work; in straightened circumstances
desacomodar *tr* to inconvenience; to discharge, dismiss
desacomodo *m* discharge, dismissal
desaconseja·do -da *adj* ill-advised
desaconsejar *tr* to dissuade
desacordar §61 *tr* to put out of tune || *ref* to get out of tune; to become forgetful
desacorde *adj* out of tune; incongruous
desacostumbra·do -da *adj* unusual
desacostumbrar *tr* to break of a habit
desacreditar *tr* to discredit; to disparage
desacuerdo *m* discord, disagreement; error, mistake; unconsciousness; forgetfulness
desadaptación *f* maladjustment
desadeudar *tr* to free of debt || *ref* to get out of debt
desadormecer §22 *tr* to awaken; to free of numbness || *ref* to get awake; to shake off the numbness
desadorna·do -da *adj* unadorned, plain; bare, uncovered
desadverti·do -da *adj* unnoticed; inattentive
desadvertimiento *m* inadvertence
desafección *f* dislike
desafec·to -ta *adj* adverse, hostile; opposed || *m* dislike
desaferrar *tr* to unfasten, loosen; to make (*a person*) change his mind; (*las áncoras*) to weigh
desafiar §77 *tr* to challenge, defy, dare; to rival, compete with
desafición *f* dislike
desaficionar *tr* to cause to dislike
desafilar *tr* to make dull || *ref* to become dull
desafina·do -da *adj* flat, out of tune
desafío *m* challenge, dare; rivalry, competition
desafora·do -da *adj* colossal, huge; disorderly, outrageous
desafortuna·do -da *adj* unfortunate
desafuero *m* excess, outrage
desagracia·do -da *adj* ungraceful, graceless
desagradable *adj* disagreeable
desagradar *tr* & *intr* to displease || *ref* to be displeased
desagradeci·do -da *adj* ungrateful
desagradecimiento *m* ungratefulness
desagrado *m* displeasure
desagraviar *tr* to make amends to, to indemnify
desagravio *m* amends, indemnification
desagregación *f* disintegration
desagregar §44 *ref* to disintegrate
desaguadero *m* drain, outlet; (*ocasión de continuo gasto*) (fig) drain
desaguar §10 *tr* to drain, empty; to

de
de

squander, waste || *intr* to flow, empty
|| *ref* to drain, be drained

desagüe *m* drainage, sewerage; drain,
outlet

desaguisa·do -da *adj* illegal || *m* offense, outrage, wrong

desahijar *tr* (*las crías del ganado*) to
wean || *ref* (*las abejas*) to swarm

desahogadamente *adv* freely; comfortably, easily; impudently

desahoga·do -da *adj* brazen, forward;
roomy; in comfortable circumstances

desahogar §44 *tr* to relieve, comfort;
(*deseos, pasiones*) to give free rein to
|| *ref* to take it easy, get comfortable;
to unbosom oneself, open up one's
heart; to get out of debt; **desahogarse
en** (*denuestos*) to burst forth in

desahogo *m* brazenness; ample room;
comfort; outlet; relief; comfortable
circumstances

desahuciar *tr* to deprive of hope; to
evict, oust, dispossess || *ref* to lose
all hope

desahucio *m* eviction, ousting, dispossession

desaira·do -da *adj* unattractive, unprepossessing; unsuccessful

desairar *tr* to slight, snub, disregard

desaire *m* slight, snub, disregard; unattractiveness, lack of charm

desajustar *tr* to put out of order || *ref* to
get out of order; to disagree

desalabanza *f* belittling, disparagement

desalabar *tr* to belittle, disparage

desala·do -da *adj* eager, in a hurry

desalar *tr* to desalt; to clip the wings
of || *ref* to hasten, rush; **desalarse por**
to be eager to

desalentar §2 *tr* to put out of breath; to
discourage || *ref* to become discouraged

desalforjar *ref* to loosen one's clothing

desaliento *m* discouragement

desalinización *f* desalinization

desaliña·do -da *adj* slovenly, untidy;
careless, slipshod

desaliño *m* slovenliness, untidiness;
carelessness, neglect

desalma·do -da *adj* cruel, inhuman

desalojar *tr* to oust, evict; (*al enemigo*)
to dislodge; (*el camino*) to clear ||
intr to leave, move away, move out

desalquila·do -da *adj* vacant, unrented

desalterar *tr* to calm, quiet

desalumbra·do -da *adj* dazzled, blinded;
confused, unsure of oneself

desamable *adj* unlikeable, unlovable

desamar *tr* to dislike, hate, detest

desamarrar *tr* to untie, unfasten; (naut)
to unmoor

desamistar *ref* to fall out, become estranged

desamor *m* dislike, coldness; hatred

desamorrar *tr* to make (*a person*) talk

desamparar *tr* to abandon, forsake; to
give up

desamparo *m* abandonment, desertion;
helplessness

desamuebla·do -da *adj* unfurnished

desandar §5 *tr* to retrace, go back over

desandraja·do -da *adj* ragged, in tatters

desangrar *tr* to bleed; to drain; (fig) to

bleed, impoverish || *ref* to lose a lot
of blood

desanimación *f* discouragement, downheartedness

desanima·do -da *adj* discouraged, downhearted; (*reunión*) lifeless, dull

desanimar *tr* to discourage, dishearten
|| *ref* to become discouraged

desánimo *m* discouragement

desanublar *tr* & *ref* to clear up, brighten
up

desanudar *tr* to untie; to disentangle

desapacible *adj* unpleasant, disagreeable

desapadrinar *tr* to disavow; to disapprove

desaparecer §22 *intr* & *ref* to disappear

desapareci·do -da *adj* missing; extinct
|| **desaparecidos** *mpl* missing persons

desaparecimiento *m* disappearance

desaparejar *tr* to unharness, unhitch;
(naut) to unrig

desaparición *f* disappearance; (Ven)
death

desapasiona·do -da *adj* dispassionate,
impartial

desapego *m* dislike, coolness, indifference

desapercibi·do -da *adj* unprepared;
wanting; unnoticed

desapiada·do -da *adj* merciless, pitiless

desaplica·do -da *adj* idle, lazy

desapodera·do -da *adj* headlong, impetuous; violent, wild; excessive

desapoderar *tr* to dispossess; to deprive of power || *ref* — **desapoderarse de** to lose possession of, give up
possession of

desapolillar *tr* to free of moths || *ref*
(coll) to expose oneself to the weather

desapreciar *tr* to depreciate

desaprecio *m* depreciation

desaprender *tr* to unlearn

desaprensión *f* composure, nonchalance

desapretar §2 *tr* to slacken, loosen;
(typ) to unlock

desaprobación *f* disapproval

desaprobar §61 *tr* & *intr* to disapprove

desapropiar *tr* to divest || *ref* — **desapropiarse de** to divest oneself of

desaprovecha·do -da *adj* unproductive,
indifferent, lackadaisical

desaprovechar *tr* to not take advantage
of || *intr* to slip back

desarmable *adj* dismountable

desarmador *m* hammer (*of gun*); (Mex)
screwdriver

desarmar *tr* to disarm; to dismount, dismantle, take apart; (*la cólera*) to
temper, calm || *intr* & *ref* to disarm

desarme *m* disarmament; dismantling,
dismounting

desarraigar §44 *tr* to uproot, dig up; to
expel, drive out

desarregla·do -da *adj* out of order; slovenly, disorderly; intemperate

desarrollar *tr* & *intr* to develop; to unroll, unfold || *ref* to develop; to unroll, unfold; to take place

desarrollo *m* development; unrolling,
unfolding

desarropar *tr* & *ref* to undress

desarrugar §44 *tr* & *ref* to unwrinkle

desarzonar *tr* to unsaddle, unhorse

desasea·do -da *adj* dirty, unclean, slovenly

desasentar §2 *tr* to remove; to displease || *ref* to stand up

desaseo *m* dirtiness, uncleanliness, slovenliness

desasir §7 *tr* to let go, let go of || *ref* to come loose; to let go; **desasirse de** to let go of; to give up, get free of

desasosegar §66 *tr* to disquiet, worry, disturb

desasosiego *m* disquiet, worry

desastra·do -da *adj* disastrous; unfortunate, wretched; ragged, shabby

desastre *m* disaster; **ir al desastre** to go to rack and ruin

desastro·so -sa *adj* disastrous

desatacar §73 *tr* to unbuckle, untie

desatar *tr* to untie, undo, unfasten; to solve, unravel || *ref* to come loose; to free oneself; *(la tempestad)* to break loose; to forget oneself, go too far; **desatarse en** *(denuestos)* to burst forth in

desatascar §73 *tr* to pull out of the mud; *(un conducto obstruído)* to unclog; *(a una persona de un apuro)* to extricate

desataviar §77 *tr* to disarray, undress

desatavío *m* disarray, undress, slovenliness

desate *m (de palabras)* flood; **desate del vientre** loose bowels

desatención *f* inattention; discourtesy, disrespect

desatender §51 *tr* to slight, disregard, pay no attention to

desatenta·do -da *adj* wild, disorderly; extreme

desaten·to -ta *adj* inattentive; discourteous, disrespectful

desatina·do -da *adj* wild, disorderly; foolish, nonsensical || *mf* fool

desatinar *tr* to bewilder, confuse || *intr* to talk nonsense, to act foolishly; to lose one's bearings

desatino *m* folly, nonsense; awkwardness, loss of touch

desatolondrar *tr* to bring to || *ref* to come to one's senses

desatollar *tr* to pull out of the mud

desatornillar *tr* to unscrew

desatraillar §4 *tr* to unleash

desatrampar *tr* to unclog

desatrancar §73 *tr* to unbar, unbolt; to unclog

desatufar *ref* to get out of the close air; to cool off, quiet down

desautoriza·do -da *adj* unauthorized

desavenencia *f* disagreement, discord

desavenir §79 *tr* to cause disagreement among || *ref* to disagree; **desavenirse con** to differ with, disagree with

desaventura *f* misfortune

desaviar §77 *tr* to mislead, lead astray

desayuna·do -da *adj* — **estar desayunado** to have had breakfast

desayunar *intr* to breakfast || *ref* to breakfast; **desayunarse con** to have breakfast on; **desayunarse de** to get the first news of

desayuno *m* breakfast

desazón *f* insipidity, tastelessness; annoyance, displeasure; discomfort

desazonar *tr* to make tasteless; to annoy, displease || *ref* to feel ill

desbancar §73 *tr* to win the bank from; to cut out, to supplant

desbandada *f* — **a la desbandada** helter-skelter, in confusion

desbandar *ref* to run away; to disband; to desert

desbarajustar *tr* to put out of order || *ref* to get out of order, break down

desbarata·do -da *adj* (coll) debauched, corrupt || *mf* (coll) libertine

desbaratar *tr* to destroy, spoil, ruin; to squander, waste; (mil) to rout, throw into confusion || *intr* to talk nonsense || *ref* to be unbalanced

desbarrancadero *m* (Am) precipice

desbastar *tr* to smooth off; to waste, weaken; *(a una persona inculta)* to polish || *ref* to become polished

desbautizar §60 *ref* (coll) to lose one's temper

desbeber *intr* (coll) to urinate

desbloquear *tr* to relieve the blockade of; *(crédito)* to unfreeze

desboca·do -da *adj (pieza de artillería)* wide-mouthed; *(herramienta)* nicked; *(caballo)* runaway; *(persona)* (coll) foul-mouthed

desbocar §73 *tr* to break the mouth of, break the spout of || *intr (un río)* to empty; *(una calle)* to run, open, end || *ref (un caballo)* to run away, to break loose; to curse, swear

desbordamiento *m* overflow

desbordar *tr* to overwhelm || *intr & ref* to overflow

desbozalar *tr* to unmuzzle

desbravar *tr* to tame, break in || *intr & ref* to abate, moderate; to cool off, calm down

desbrozar §60 *tr* to clear of underbrush, to clear of rubbish

desbulla *f* oyster shell

desbulla·dor -dora *mf* oyster opener || *m* oyster fork

desbullar *tr (la ostra)* to open

descabal *adj* incomplete, imperfect

descabalgar §44 *intr* to dismount, alight from a horse

descabella·do -da *adj* disheveled; rash, wild

descabellar *tr* to muss, dishevel

descabeza·do -da *adj* crazy, rash, wild

descabezar §60 *tr* to behead; *(un árbol)* to top; *(una dificultad)* (coll) to get the best off; **descabezar el sueño** to doze, snooze || *intr* to border || *ref* to rack one's brains

descabullir §13 *ref* to sneak out, slip away; to refuse to face the facts

descacharra·do -da *adj* (CAm) dirty, slovenly, ragged

descaecer §22 *intr* to decline, lose ground

descaecimiento *m* weakness; depression, despondency

descalabazar §60 *ref* (coll) to rack one's brain

descalabra·do -da *adj* banged on the

head; **salir descalabrado** to come out the loser, to be worsted

descalabrar tr to bang on the head; to knock down ‖ ref to bang one's head

descalabro m misfortune, setback, loss

descalificar §73 tr to disqualify

descalzar §60 tr (las botas, los guantes) to take off; (a una persona) to take the shoes or stockings off; to undermine ‖ ref to take one's shoes or stockings off; to take one's gloves off; (las botas, los guantes) to take off; (el caballo) to lose a shoe

descal·zo -za adj barefooted; seedy, down at the heel

descamar ref to scale, scale off

descaminadamente adv off the road, on the wrong track

descaminar tr to mislead, lead astray ‖ ref to get lost; to run off the road

descamino m going astray; leading astray; nonsense; contraband, smuggled goods

descamisa·do -da adj shirtless, ragged ‖ m wretch, ragamuffin

descampa·do -da adj free, open ‖ m open country

descansadero m resting place, stopping place

descansa·do -da adj rested, refreshed; calm, restful

descansar tr to rest, relieve; (la cabeza, el brazo) to rest, lean ‖ intr to rest; to lean; to not worry; (yacer en el sepulcro) to rest; **descansar en** to trust in

descanso m rest; peace, quiet; (de la escalera) landing; (theat) intermission; (Chile) toilet

descantillar tr to chip off; to deduct

descañonar tr to pluck; to shave against the grain; (coll) to gyp

descapiruzar §60 tr (Col) to muss, rumple, crumple

descapotable adj & m (aut) convertible

descara·do -da adj barefaced, brazen, saucy

descarar ref to be impudent; **descararse a** to have the nerve to

descarga f unloading; (de un arma de fuego) discharge; (com) discount; (elec) discharge; **descarga de aduana** customhouse clearance

descargar §44 tr to unload; (de una deuda u obligación) to free; (un arma de fuego) to discharge; (un golpe) to strike, to deal; (elec) to discharge ‖ intr to unload; (un río) to empty; (una calle, paseo) to open; (una nube en lluvia) to burst ‖ ref to unburden oneself; to resign; **descargarse con** or **en uno de algo** to unload something on someone; **descargarse de** to get rid of; to resign from; (una imputación, un cargo) to clear oneself of

descargo m unloading; (de una obligación) discharge; (del cargo que se hace a uno) release, acquittal; receipt

descargue m unloading

descariño m coolness, indifference

descarnadamente adv right off the shoulder, bluntly

descarnar tr to remove the flesh from; to chip; to wear away; to detach from earthly matters ‖ ref to lose flesh

descaro m brazenness, effrontery

descarriar §77 tr to mislead, to lead astray ‖ ref to go wrong, to go astray

descarrilamiento m derailment

descarrilar intr to jump the track; (coll) to wander from the point ‖ ref to jump the track

descartable adj disposable

descartar tr to cast aside, reject; to discard ‖ ref to shirk, evade; **descartarse de** (un compromiso) to shirk, evade

descarte m casting aside, rejection; discarding; (cartas desechadas) discard; shirking, evasion

descasar tr to divorce; to disturb, disarrange

descascar §73 tr to husk, shell, peel ‖ ref to break to pieces; to jabber, talk too much

descascarar tr to shell, peel ‖ ref to shell off, peel off

descascarillar tr & ref to shell, peel

descasta·do -da adj ungrateful, ungrateful to one's family

descaudala·do -da adj ruined, penniless

descendencia f descent

descendente adj descendent, descending; (tren) down

descender §51 tr to bring down, lower; (la escalera) to descend, to go down ‖ intr to descend, go down; to flow, run; to decline

descendiente mf descendant

descenso m descent; (de temperatura) drop; decline

descentralizar §60 tr to decentralize

desceñi·do -da adj loose-fitting, loose

descepar tr to pull up by the roots; to extirpate, exterminate

descerebrar tr to brain

descerraja·do -da adj (coll) corrupt, evil, wicked

descifrar tr to decipher, to decode, to figure out

desclasificar §73 tr to disqualify

descocer §16 tr to digest

descoco m (coll) impudence, insolence

descocholla·do -da adj (Chile) ragged

descolar tr to dock, crop; (a un empleado) (CAm) to discharge, fire; (Mex) to slight, snub

descolgar §63 tr to unhook; to take down, lower; (el auricular) to pick up ‖ ref to come down, come off; to show up suddenly; **descolgarse con** (coll) to blurt out

descolón m (Mex) slight, snub

descolorar tr & ref to discolor, to fade

descolori·do -da adj faded, off color

descollante adj prominent, outstanding; chief, main

descollar §61 intr to tower, stand out; (fig) to excel, stand out

descomedi·do -da adj immoderate, excessive; rude, discourteous

descomedir §50 ref to be rude, be discourteous

descomer intr to have a bowel movement

descómo·do -da adj inconvenient

descompasa·do -da adj extreme, excessive

descompletar tr to break (a set or series)

descomponer §54 tr to decompose; to disturb, disorganize; to put out of order; to set at odds ‖ ref to decompose; (una persona, la salud de una persona) to fall to pieces; (el tiempo) to change for the worse; (el rostro) to become distorted; (un aparato) to get out of order; to lose one's temper; **descomponerse con** to get angry with

descomposición f decomposition; disorder, disorganization; discord

descompostura f decomposition; disorder, untidiness; brazenness

descompresión f decompression

descompues·to -ta adj out of order; brazen, discourteous; irritated; (Am) drunk

descomulgar §44 tr to excommunicate

descomunal adj huge, colossal, enormous, extraordinary

desconcerta·do -da adj out of order; disconcerted, baffled, bewildered; slovenly; unbridled

desconcertar §2 tr to put out of order; to disturb, upset; (un hueso) to dislocate; to disconcert, bewilder

desconcierto m disrepair; disorder; mismanagement; confusion; discomfiture; disagreement; lack of restraint; loose bowels

desconchabar tr (Am) to dislocate ‖ ref (Am) to become dislocated; (Am) to disagree, fall out

desconchado m scaly part of wall; (en la porcelana) chip

desconchar tr & ref to chip, chip off; to scale off

desconectar tr to detach; to disconnect

desconfia·do -da adj distrustful, suspicious

desconfianza f distrust

desconfiar §77 intr to lose confidence; **desconfiar de** to lose confidence in, to distrust

desconformar intr to dissent, disagree ‖ ref to not go well together

descongelar tr to melt; to defrost; (com) to unfreeze

desconocer §22 tr to not know; to disavow, disown; to not recognize; to slight, ignore; to not see ‖ ref to be unknown; to be quite changed, be unrecognizable

desconocidamente adv unknowingly

desconoci·do -da adj unknown; strange, unfamiliar; ungrateful ‖ mf unknown, unknown person

desconsentir §68 tr to not consent to

desconsidera·do -da adj ill-considered; inconsiderate

desconsola·do -da adj disconsolate, downhearted; (estómago) weak

desconsuelo m disconsolateness, grief; upset stomach

descontaminación f decontamination

descontar §61 tr to discount; to deduct;

to take for granted; **dar por descontado que** to take for granted that

descontentadi·zo -za adj hard to please

desconten·to -ta adj & m discontent

descontinuar §21 tr to discontinue

desconvenir §79 intr to disagree; to not go together, to not match; to not be suitable ‖ ref to disagree

desconvidar tr to cancel an invitation to; (lo prometido) to take back

descopar tr to top (a tree)

descorazonar tr to discourage

descorchar tr to remove the bark from; (una botella) to uncork; to break into

descornar §61 tr to dehorn ‖ ref (coll) to rack one's brains

descorrer tr to run back over; (una cortina, un cerrojo) to draw ‖ intr & ref to flow, run off

descortés adj discourteous, impolite

descortesía f discourtesy, impoliteness

descortezar §60 tr to strip the bark from; to take the crust off; (coll) to polish ‖ ref (coll) to become polished

descoser tr to unstitch, to rip ‖ ref to loose one's tongue; (coll) to break wind

descosi·do -da adj disorderly, wild; indiscreet; desultory ‖ m wild man; rip, open seam

descote m low neck

descoyuntar tr to dislocate; to bore, annoy ‖ ref (p.ej., el brazo) to throw out of joint

descrédito m discredit

descreer §43 tr to disbelieve; to discredit ‖ intr to disbelieve

descreí·do -da adj disbelieving, unbelieving ‖ mf disbeliever, unbeliever

descriar §77 tr to spoil; to waste away

describir §83 tr to describe

descripción f description

descripti·vo -va adj descriptive

descto. abbr **descuento**

descuadrar intr to disagree; **descuadrar con** (Mex) to displease

descuajar tr to liquefy, dissolve; to uproot; to discourage ‖ ref to liquefy; to drudge

descuartizar §60 tr to tear to pieces; to quarter

descubierta f open pie; inspection; reconnoitering; (naut) scanning the horizon; **a la descubierta** openly; in the open; reconnoitering

descubiertamente adv clearly, openly

descubier·to -ta adj bareheaded; (campo) bare, barren; (expuesto a reconvenciones) under fire ‖ m deficiency, shortage; exposition of the Holy Sacrament; **al descubierto** in the open; unprotected; (sin tener disponibles las acciones que se venden) short, e.g., **vender al descubierto** to sell short ‖ f see **descubierta**

descubri·dor -dora mf discoverer ‖ m (mil) scout

descubrimiento m discovery

descubrir §83 tr to discover; to uncover, lay open, reveal; to invent; (p.ej., una estatua) to unveil ‖ ref to take off one's hat, uncover; to be discovered; to open one's heart

descuello *m* excellence, superiority; great height; haughtiness

descuento *m* discount; deduction, rebate

descuerar *tr* (Chile) to skin, flay; (Chile) to discredit, flay

descuerno *m* (coll) slight, snub

descuida·do -da *adj* careless, negligent; slovenly, dirty; off guard

descuidar *tr* to overlook, neglect; to divert, distract, relieve ‖ *ref* to be careless, not bother; to be diverted

descuide·ro -ra *mf* sneak thief

descuido *m* carelessness, negligence, neglect; slip, mistake, blunder; oversight; **al descuido** with studied carelessness; **en un descuido** (Am) when least expected

descuita·do -da *adj* carefree

desde *prep* since, from; after; **desde ahora** from now on; **desde entonces** since then, ever since; **desde hace** for, e.g., **estoy aquí desde hace cinco días** I've been here for five days; **desde luego** at once; of course; **desde que** since

desdecir §24 *intr* to slip back; to be out of harmony ‖ *ref* — **desdecirse de** to take back, retract

desdén *m* scorn, disdain; **al desdén** with studied neglect

desdenta·do -da *adj* toothless

desdeñar *tr* to scorn, disdain ‖ *ref* to be disdainful; **desdeñarse de** to loathe, despise; to not deign to

desdeño·so -sa *adj* scornful, disdainful

desdicha *f* misfortune; indigence

desdicha·do -da *adj* unfortunate, unlucky; poor, wretched; (coll) backward, timid

desdinerar *tr* to impoverish

desdoblar *tr & intr* to unfold, spread open; to split, divide

desdorar *tr* to remove the gold or gilt from; to tarnish, sully; to disparage

desdoro *m* tarnish, blemish, blot; disparagement

deseable *adj* desirable

desear *tr* to desire, wish

desecar §73 *tr & ref* to dry; to drain

desechable *adj* disposable

desechar *tr* to discard, to throw out, to cast aside; to underrate; to blame, censure; (la llave de una puerta) to turn

desecho *m* remainder; offal, rubbish; castoff; scorn, contempt; (Am) short cut; **desecho de hierro** scrap iron

desegregación *f* desegregation

desellar *tr* to unseal

desembalaje *m* unpacking

desembalar *tr* to unpack

desembarazar §60 *tr* to free, clear, empty, open ‖ *ref* to free oneself; to be cleared, be emptied; **desembarazarse de** to get rid of

desembarazo *m* naturalness, lack of restraint; (Am) delivery, childbirth; **con desembarazo** naturally, readily

desembarcadero *m* wharf, pier, landing

desembarcar §73 *tr* to unload, debark, disembark ‖ *intr* to land, debark, disembark; (de un carruaje) to get out,

alight; (la escalera al plano bajo) to end ‖ *ref* to land, debark, disembark

desembarco *m* landing, debarkation, disembarkation; (de la escalera) landing

desembarque *m* unloading, debarkation, disembarkation

desembocadura *f* (de una calle) opening, outlet; (de un río) mouth

desembocar §73 *intr* (una calle) open, to end; (un río) to flow, empty

desembolsar *tr* to disburse, pay out

desembolso *m* disbursement, payment

desembragar §44 *tr* (el motor) to disengage ‖ *intr* to throw the clutch out

desembrague *m* disengagement, clutch release

desembravecer §22 *tr* to tame; to calm, quiet, pacify

desembriagar §44 *tr & ref* to sober up

desembrollar *tr* to untangle, unravel

desemejante *adj* — **desemejante de** dissimilar from or to, unlike; **desemejantes** dissimilar, unlike

desemejar *tr* to change, disfigure ‖ *intr* to be different, not look alike

desempacar §73 *tr* to unpack, unwrap ‖ *ref* to cool off, calm down

desempalagar §44 *tr* to rid of nausea ‖ *ref* to get rid of nausea

desempañar *tr* (el vidrio) to wipe the steam or smear from; to take the diaper off

desempapelar *tr* to unwrap; (una pared, una habitación) to scrape the wallpaper from

desempaquetar *tr* to unpack; to unwrap

desempatar *tr* to break the tie between; (los votos) to break the tie in

desempate *m* breaking a tie

desempedrar §2 *tr* to remove the paving stones from; (un sitio empedrado) (coll) to pound; **ir desempedrando la calle** (coll) to dash down the street

desempeñar *tr* (un papel) to play (a rôle); (un cargo) to fill, perform; (a uno de un empeño) to disengage; (un deber) to discharge; to free of debt; to take out of hock ‖ *ref* to get out of a jam; to get out of debt

desempeño *m* acting, performance; disengagement; (de un deber) discharge; payment of a debt; taking out of hock

desempernar *tr* to unbolt

desemplea·do -da *adj & mf* unemployed

desempleo *m* unemployment

desempolvar *tr* to dust; to renew, take up again ‖ *ref* to brush up

desempolvorar *tr* to dust, dust off

desencadenar *tr* to unchain, unleash ‖ *ref* to break loose

desencajar *tr* to dislocate; to disconnect ‖ *ref* to get out of joint; (el rostro) to be contorted

desencaminar *tr* to lead astray, mislead

desencantamiento *m* disenchantment, disillusion

desencantar *tr* to disenchant, disillusion

desencantarar *tr* (nombres o números) to draw; (un nombre o nombres) to exclude from balloting

desencanto *m* disenchantment, disillusion

desencarecer §22 *tr* to lower the price of ‖ *intr* & *ref* to come down in price

desencerrar §2 *tr* to release, set free; to disclose, reveal

desencoger §17 *tr* to unfold, spread out ‖ *ref* to relax, shake off one's timidity

desencolar *tr* to unglue ‖ *ref* to become unglued

desenconar *tr* to take the soreness out of; to calm down

desenchufar *tr* to unplug, to disconnect

desendiosar *tr* to bring down a peg

desenfadaderas *fpl* — **tener buenas desenfadaderas** (coll) to be resourceful

desenfada·do -da *adj* free, easy, unconstrained

desenfado *m* ease, naturalness; relaxation, calmness

desenfoca·do -da *adj* out of focus

desenfrena·do -da *adj* unbridled, wanton, licentious

desenfrenar *tr* to unbridle ‖ *ref* to yield to temptation; to fly into a passion; (*la tempestad, el viento*) to break loose

desenfreno *m* unruliness, wantonness, licentiousness

desenfundar *tr* to take out of its sheath, bag, pillowcase, etc.

desenganchar *tr* to unhook, uncouple, unfasten, disengage; to unhitch

desenganche *m* unhooking, disengaging; unhitching

desengañar *tr* to disabuse, undeceive; to disillusion; to disappoint

desengaño *m* disabusing; disillusionment; disappointment; plain fact, plain truth

desengrana·do -da *adj* out of gear

desengranar *tr* to unmesh; to disengage, throw out of gear

desengraso *m* (Chile) dessert

desenlace *m* outcome, result; (*de un drama, novela, etc.*) dénouement

desenlazar §60 *tr* to untie; to solve; (*el nudo de un drama*) to unravel

desenmarañar *tr* to disentangle; (*una cosa obscura*) to unravel

desenmascarar *tr* to unmask ‖ *ref* to take one's mask off

desenojar *tr* to appease, to free of anger ‖ *ref* to calm down; to be amused

desenredar *tr* to disentangle; to clear up ‖ *ref* to extricate oneself

desenredo *m* disentanglement; (*de un drama, novela, etc.*) dénouement

desenrollar *tr* to unroll, unwind, unreel

desensartar *tr* to unstring, unthread

desensillar *tr* to unsaddle (*a horse*)

desentablar *tr* to disrupt; to break off (*a bargain, friendship, etc.*)

desentender §51 *ref* — **desentenderse de** to take no part in, to not participate in; to affect ignorance of, pretend to be unaware of

desenterrar §2 *tr* to dig up; to disinter; (fig) to unearth, dig up; (fig) to recall to mind

desentona·do -da *adj* out of tune, flat

desentonar *tr* to humble, bring down a peg ‖ *intr* to be out of tune; to be out of harmony ‖ *ref* to talk loud and disrespectfully

desentono *m* dissonance, false note; loud tone of voice

desentornillar *tr* to unscrew

desentrampar *ref* (coll) to get out of debt

desentrañar *tr* to disembowel; to figure out, unravel ‖ *ref* to give away all that one has

desentrena·do -da *adj* out of training

desentronizar §60 *tr* to dethrone; to strip of influence

desentumecer §22 *tr* to relieve of numbness ‖ *ref* to be relieved of numbness

desenvainar *tr* to unsheathe; (*las uñas el animal*) to show, stretch out; (coll) to bare, uncover, show

desenvoltura *f* naturalness, ease of manner, offhandedness; fluency; lewdness, boldness (*chiefly in women*)

desenvolver §47 & §83 *tr* to unfold, unroll, unwrap; to unwind; to unravel, clear up; to develop ‖ *ref* to unroll; to unwind; to develop, evolve; to extricate oneself; to be forward

desenvuel·to -ta *adj* free and easy, offhand; fluent; brazen, bold, lewd

deseo *m* desire, wish

deseo·so -sa *adj* desirous, anxious

desequilibra·do -da *adj* unbalanced

desequilibrar *tr* to unbalance ‖ *ref* to become unbalanced

desequilibrio *m* disequilibrium, imbalance; derangement, mental instability

deserción *f* desertion

desertar *tr* & *intr* to desert

desertor *m* deserter

deservicio *m* disservice

desesperación *f* despair; **ser una desesperación** to be unbearable

desespera·do -da *adj* despairing, desperate ‖ *mf* desperate person

desesperanza *f* hopelessness

desesperanza·do -da *adj* hopeless

desesperanzar §60 *tr* to discourage ‖ *ref* to lose hope

desesperar *tr* to drive to despair; (coll) to exasperate ‖ *intr* to lose hope; (coll) to be exasperated ‖ *ref* to be desperate, lose all hope

desestancar §73 *tr* to open up, to unclog; to make free of duty; to open the market to

desestimar *tr* to hold in low regard; to refuse, reject

deséxito *m* failure

desfachata·do -da *adj* (coll) brazen, impudent

desfachatez *f* (coll) brazenness, impudence

desfalcar §73 *tr* & *intr* to embezzle

desfalco *m* embezzlement

desfallecer §22 *tr* to weaken ‖ *intr* to grow weak; to faint, faint away; to lose courage

desfalleci·do -da *adj* weak; faint

desfallecimiento *m* weakness; fainting; discouragement

desfavorable *adj* unfavorable

desfigurar *tr* to disfigure; to distort,

misrepresent; to disguise; to change, alter ‖ *ref* to look different

desfiladero *m* defile, pass

desfilar *intr* to defile, parade, file by

desfile *m* review, parade

desflorar *tr* to deflower; to mention in passing

desfogar §44 *tr* (*un horno*) to vent; (*la cal*) to slake; (*una pasión*) to give free rein to ‖ *intr* (*una tempestad*) to break into rain and wind ‖ *ref* to give vent to one's anger

desfondar *tr* to stave in; (*una nave*) to bilge; (*agr*) to trench-plow

desforestar *tr* to deforest

desgaire *m* slovenliness; disdain, scorn; **al desgaire** scornfully; carelessly, with affected carelessness

desgajar *tr* to tear off; to split off ‖ *ref* to come off, to come loose; to arise, originate; to separate, break away

desgana *f* lack of appetite; indifference; boredom; **a desgana** unwillingly, reluctantly

desgarba·do -da *adj* ungainly, uncouth

desgarrar *tr* to tear, rend; (*la flema*) to cough up ‖ *ref* to tear oneself away

desgarro *m* tear, rent; brazenness, effrontery; boasting, bragging; (Chile, Col) phlegm, mucus

desgastar *tr* to wear away, wear down; to weaken, spoil ‖ *ref* to wear away; to grow weak, decline

desgaste *m* wear, wearing away

desgoberna·do -da *adj* ungovernable, uncontrollable

desgobernar §2 *tr* to misgovern; (*un hueso*) to dislocate ‖ *intr* (naut) to steer poorly ‖ *ref* to twist and turn in dancing

desgobierno *m* misgovernment; dislocation

desgonzar §60 *tr* to unhinge; to disconnect

desgracia *f* misfortune; (*acontecimiento adverso*) mishap; (*pérdida de favor*) disfavor, disgrace; (*aspereza en el trato*) gruffness; (*falta de gracia*) lack of charm; **correr con desgracia** to have no luck; **por desgracia** unfortunately

desgracia·do -da *adj* unfortunate; unattractive, unpleasant; disagreeable ‖ *mf* wretch, unfortunate

desgraciar *tr* to displease; to spoil ‖ *ref* to spoil; to fail; to fall out, to disagree

desgranar *tr* (*el maíz*) to shell; (*un racimo*) to pick the grapes from ‖ *ref* (*piezas ensartadas*) to come loose

desgreñar *tr* to dishevel ‖ *ref* to get disheveled; to pull each other's hair

deshabita·do -da *adj* unoccupied

deshabituar §21 *tr* to break of a habit

deshacer §39 *tr* to undo; to untie; to take apart; to wear away, consume, destroy; to melt; to put to flight, to rout; (*un tratado o negocio*) to violate ‖ *ref* to get out of order; to vanish, disappear; **deshacerse de** to get rid of; **deshacerse en** (*cumplidos*) to lavish; (*lágrimas*) to burst into; **deshacerse por** to strive hard to

desharrapa·do -da *adj* ragged, in rags

deshebillar *tr* to unbuckle

deshebrar *tr* to unravel, unthread

deshecha *f* sham, pretense; dismissal; **hacer la deshecha** to feign, pretend; (Mex) to pretend lack of interest

deshelar §2 *tr* to thaw, melt; to defrost; (aer) to deice ‖ *intr* to thaw, melt

deshereda·do -da *adj* disinherited; underprivileged

desheredar *tr* to disinherit ‖ *ref* to be a disgrace to one's family

desherrar §2 *tr* to unchain, unshackle; (*a una caballería*) to unshoe

desherrumbrar *tr* to remove the rust from

deshidratar *tr* to dehydrate

deshielo *m* thaw, melting; defrosting

deshilachar *ref* to fray

deshila·do -da *adj* in a file; **a la deshilada** in single file; secretly ‖ *m* openwork, drawn work

deshilar *tr* to unweave; (*reducir a hilos*) to shred ‖ *ref* to fray; to get thin

deshilvana·do -da *adj* disconnected, desultory

deshincar §73 *tr* to pull up, to pull out

deshinchar *tr* to deflate; (*la cólera*) to give vent to ‖ *ref* (*un tumor*) to go down; (*una persona orgullosa*) (coll) to become deflated

deshojar *tr* to strip of leaves; to tear the pages out of ‖ *ref* to lose the leaves

deshollejar *tr* to peel, skin; (*las habichuelas*) to shell

deshollina·dor -dora *mf* chimney sweep; (coll) curious observer ‖ *m* long-handled brush or broom

deshones·to -ta *adj* immodest, indecent; improper

deshonor *m* dishonor; disgrace

deshonorar *tr* to dishonor; to degrade; to disfigure

deshonra *f* dishonor; disrespect; **tener a deshonra** to consider improper

deshonrabue·nos *m* (*pl* -nos) (coll) slanderer; (coll) black sheep

deshonrar *tr* to disgrace; (*a una mujer*) to seduce; to insult

deshonro·so -sa *adj* disgraceful, improper, discreditable

deshora *f* wrong time; **a deshora** at the wrong time, inopportunely; suddenly, unexpectedly

deshuesar *tr* (*la carne de un animal*) to bone; (*la fruta*) to stone, to take the pits out of

deshumedecer §22 *tr* to dehumidify

desidia *f* laziness, indolence

desidio·so -sa *adj* lazy, indolent ‖ *mf* lazy person

desier·to -ta *adj* desert; deserted ‖ *m* desert; wilderness

designar *tr* to designate; (*un trabajo*) to plan

designio *m* design, plan, scheme

desigual *adj* unequal; unlike; rough, uneven; difficult; inconstant

desigualar *tr* to make unequal ‖ *ref* to become unequal; (*aventajarse*) to get ahead

desigualdad *f* inequality; roughness, unevenness

desilusión *f* disillusionment; disappointment

desilusionar *tr* to disillusion; to disappoint || *ref* to become disillusioned; to be disappointed

desimanar or **desimantar** *tr* to demagnetize

desimpresionar *tr* to undeceive

desinclina·do -da *adj* disinclined

desinencia *f* (gram) termination, ending

desinfectante *adj* & *m* disinfectant

desinfectar or **desinficionar** *tr* to disinfect

desinflación *f* deflation

desinflamar *tr* to take the soreness out of

desinflar *tr* to deflate; to let the air out of; (*a una persona*) (coll) to deflate

desintegración *f* disintegration

desintegrar *tr* & *ref* to disintegrate

desinterés *m* disinterestedness

desinteresa·do -da *adj* (*imparcial*) disinterested; (*poco interesado*) uninterested

desinteresar *ref* to lose interest

desintonizar §60 *tr* (rad) to tune out; (rad) to put out of tune

desistir *intr* to desist

desjarretar *tr* to hamstring; (coll) to bleed to excess

desjuicia·do -da *adj* lacking judgment, senseless

desjuntar *tr* to disjoin, separate

deslabonar *tr* to unlink; to disconnect || *ref* to come loose; to withdraw

deslastrar *tr* to unballast

deslava·do -da *adj* faded, colorless; barefaced || *mf* barefaced person

deslavar *tr* to wash superficially; to fade, to take the life out of

desleal *adj* disloyal; unfair

deslealtad *f* disloyalty

deslechar *tr* (Col) to milk

desleír §58 *tr* to dissolve; to dilute; (*los colores, la pintura*) to thin; (*sus pensamientos*) to express too diffusely || *ref* to dissolve; to become diluted

deslenguа·do -da *adj* foul-mouthed, shameless

desliar §77 *tr* to untie, undo; to unravel || *ref* to come untied

desligar §44 *tr* to untie, unbind; to disentangle; to excuse || *ref* to come untied, come loose

deslindar *tr* to mark the boundaries of; to distinguish; to define, explain

des·liz *m* (*pl* **-lices**) sliding; (*superficie lisa*) slide; slip, blunder; peccadillo, indiscretion

deslizade·ro -ra *adj* slippery || *m* slippery place; launching way

deslizadi·zo -za *adj* slippery

deslizador *m* (aer) glider

deslizar §60 *tr* to slide; (*decir por descuido*) to let slip || *intr* to slide; to slip; to glide || *ref* to slide; to slip; to glide; to slip away, sneak away; (*un reparo*) to slip out; (*caer en una flaqueza*) to slide back, to backslide

deslomar *tr* to break or strain the back of || *ref* to break or strain one's back;

no deslomarse (coll) to not strain oneself

desluci·do -da *adj* quiet, lackluster; dull, undistinguished

deslucir §45 *tr* to tarnish; to deprive of charm, deprive of distinction; to discredit

deslumbramiento *m* dazzle, glare; bewilderment, confusion

deslumbrante *adj* dazzling; bewildering, confusing

deslumbrar *tr* to dazzle; to bewilder, confuse

deslustra·do -da *adj* dull, flat, dingy; (*vidrio*) ground, frosted

deslustrar *tr* to tarnish; to dull, dim; (*el vidrio*) to frost; to discredit || *ref* to tarnish

deslustre *m* tarnishing; dulling, dimming; discredit; (*del vidrio*) frosting

deslustro·so -sa *adj* ugly, unbecoming

desmadejar *tr* to enervate, weaken

desmagnetizar §60 *tr* to demagnetize

desmán *m* excess, misconduct; misfortune, mishap

desmanchar *tr* (Chile) to clean of spots

desmanda·do -da *adj* disobedient, unruly

desmandar *tr* to cancel, countermand || *ref* to misbehave; to go away, keep apart; to get out of control

desmanear *tr* to unfetter, unshackle

desmantela·do -da *adj* dilapidated

desmantelar *tr* to dismantle; (naut) to unmast; (naut) to unrig

desmaña *f* awkwardness, clumsiness

desmaña·do -da *adj* awkward, clumsy

desmaya·do -da *adj* faint, languid, weak; unconscious; (*color*) dull

desmayar *tr* to depress, discourage || *intr* to lose heart, be discouraged; to falter || *ref* to faint

desmayo *m* depression, discouragement; faint, fainting fit; weeping willow

desmedi·do -da *adj* excessive; boundless, limitless

desmedir §50 *ref* to go too far, be impudent

desmedra·do -da *adj* weak, run-down

desmedrar *tr* to impair || *intr* & *ref* to decline, deteriorate

desmejorar *tr* to impair, spoil || *intr* & *ref* to decline, go into a decline

desmelenar *tr* to muss, dishevel, rumple

desmembrar §2 *tr* to dismember

desmemoria *f* forgetfulness

desmemoria·do -da *adj* forgetful

desmemoriar *ref* to become forgetful

desmentida *f* contradiction; **dar una desmentida a** to give the lie to

desmentir §68 *tr* to belie, give the lie to; to conceal || *intr* to be out of line || *ref* to contradict oneself

desmenudear *tr* & *intr* (Col) to sell at retail

desmenuzar §60 *tr* to crumble; to chop up; to examine in detail; to criticize harshly || *ref* to crumb, crumble

desmerece·dor -dora *adj* unworthy

desmerecer §22 *tr* to be unworthy of || *intr* to decline in value; **desmerecer de** to compare unfavorably with

desmesura *f* excess, lack of restraint

desmesura·do -da *adj* excessive, disproportionate; insolent ‖ *mf* insolent person

desmigajar *tr & ref* to crumble, break up

desmigar §44 *tr & ref* to crumble, crumb

desmilitarizar §60 *tr* to demilitarize

desmirria·do -da *adj* (coll) exhausted, emaciated, run-down

desmochar *tr* (*un árbol*) to top; (*al toro*) to dehorn; (*una obra artística*) to cut

desmodular *tr* to demodulate

desmola·do -da *adj* toothless

desmontable *adj* demountable

desmontar *tr* (*un terreno*) to level; (*un bosque*) to clear; to dismantle, dismount, take apart, knock down; (*las piezas de artillería del enemigo*) to knock out; (*el jinete el caballo*) to unhorse, to throw; (*un arma de fuego*) to uncock ‖ *ref* to dismount, alight

desmoralizar §60 *tr* to demoralize

desmoronadi·zo -za *adj* crumbly

desmoronar *tr* to wear away ‖ *ref* to wear away; to crumble, decline

desmotadera *f* burler; **desmotadera de algodón** cotton gin

desmotar *tr* (*la lana*) to burl; (*el algodón*) to gin

desmovilizar §60 *tr* to demobilize

desmurador *m* mouser

desnatadora *f* cream separator

desnatar *tr* to skim; to remove the slag from; to take the choicest part of

desnaturalizar §60 *tr* to denaturalize; (*el alcohol*) to denature; to alter, pervert

desnivel *m* unevenness; difference of level

desnivelar *tr* to make uneven ‖ *ref* to become uneven

desnudar *tr* to undress; to strip, lay bare; (*la espada*) to draw ‖ *ref* to undress, get undressed; to become evident; **desnudarse de** to get rid of

desnudez *f* nakedness; bareness

desnu·do -da *adj* naked, nude; bare; destitute, penniless ‖ **el desnudo** the nude

desnutrición *f* undernourishment, malnutrition

desnutri·do -da *adj* undernourished

desobedecer *tr & intr* to disobey

desobediencia *f* disobedience

desobediente *adj* disobedient

desocupación *f* unemployment; idleness, leisure

desocupa·do -da *adj* unemployed; idle; free, unoccupied, vacant, empty ‖ *mf* unemployed person

desocupar *tr* to empty, vacate ‖ *intr* (*una mujer*) (coll) to be delivered ‖ *ref* to become empty, vacated; to become unemployed, become idle

desodorante *adj & m* deodorant

desodorizar §60 *tr* to deodorize

desoír §48 *tr* to not hear, to pretend not to hear

desolación *f* desolation

desola·do -da *adj* desolate, disconsolate

desolar §61 *tr* to desolate, lay waste ‖ *ref* to be desolate, be disconsolate

desoldar §61 *tr* to unsolder ‖ *ref* to come unsoldered

desolla·do -da *adj* (coll) brazen, impudent

desollar §61 *tr* to skin, flay; to harm, hurt; **desollar vivo** (*hacer pagar mucho más de lo justo*) (coll) to fleece, to skin alive; (*murmurar acerbamente de*) (coll) to flay

desopilar *ref* to roar with laughter

desopinar *tr* to defame, discredit

desorbita·do -da *adj* (Am) popeyed; (Am) crazy

desorbitar *ref* to pop wide-open

desorden *m* disorder

desordena·do -da *adj* disorderly, unruly

desordenar *tr* to put out of order ‖ *ref* to get out of order; to be unruly; to go too far

desoreja·do -da *adj* (coll) infamous, degraded; (*que canta mal*) (Peru) off tune; (Cuba) shameless; (Cuba) spendthrift, prodigal; (Guat) stupid; (Chile) without handles

desorganizar §60 *tr* to disorganize

desorientar *tr* to lead astray; to confuse

desovar *intr* to spawn

desove *m* spawning; spawning season

desovillar *tr* to unravel, disentangle; to encourage

desoxidar *tr* to deoxidize; to clean of rust

despabiladeras *fpl* snuffers

despabila·do -da *adj* wide-awake

despabilar *tr* (*una candela*) to snuff, to trim; (*la hacienda*) to dissipate; (*una comida*) to dispatch; (*robar*) to snitch; (*matar*) to dispatch ‖ *ref* to brighten up; to wake up; (Am) to leave, disappear

despacio *adv* slow, slowly; at leisure; (Arg, Chile) in a low voice

despacio·so -sa *adj* slow, easy-going

despachaderas *fpl* (coll) surly reply; (coll) resourcefulness

despacha·do -da *adj* (coll) brazen, impudent; (coll) quick, resourceful

despachante *m* (Arg) clerk; **despachante de aduana** (Arg) customhouse broker

despachar *tr* to send, to ship; to dispatch, expedite; to discharge, dismiss; to decide, settle; to sell; (*a los parroquianos*) to wait on; (*la correspondencia*) to attend to; to hurry; (*matar*) (coll) to dispatch, to kill ‖ *intr* to hurry; to make up one's mind; to work, be employed ‖ *ref* to hurry; (*una mujer*) to be delivered; to speak out

despacho *m* shipping; dispatch, expedition; discharge, dismissal; (*tienda*) store, shop; (*aposento para el estudio*) study; (*aposento para los negocios*) office; (*comunicación por telégrafo o teléfono*) dispatch; (Chile) attic; **despacho de billetes** ticket office; **despacho de localidades** box office; **estar al despacho** to be pending; **tener buen despacho** to be expeditious

despachurrar *tr* to crush, smash, squash; (*dejar sin tener que replicar*) (coll) to squelch; (*lo que uno trata de decir*) (coll) to butcher, murder

despampanante *adj* (coll) stunning, terrific

despampanar *tr* (*las vides*) to prune, to trim; (coll) to astound ‖ *intr* (coll) to give vent to one's feelings ‖ *ref* to fall and hurt oneself

despancar §73 *tr* to husk (*corn*)

desparejar *tr* (*dos cosas que forman pareja*) to break, separate (*a pair*)

desparpajar *tr* to tear apart ‖ *intr* (coll) to rant, rave ‖ *ref* (coll) to rant, rave; (CAm, Mex, W-I) to wake up

desparramar *tr* to scatter, spread; (*el agua*) to spill; (*la hacienda*) to squander ‖ *ref* to scatter, spread; to make merry

despartir *tr* to divide, part, separate; to reconcile

despatarrada *f* (coll) split (*in dancing*); **hacer la despatarrada** (coll) to stretch out on the floor pretending to be ill or injured

despatarrar *tr* to dumbfound ‖ *ref* (coll) to open one's legs wide, to fall down with legs outspread; (coll) to lie motionless; to be dumbfounded

despavori·do -da *adj* terrified

despea·do -da *adj* footsore

despear *ref* to get sore feet

despecti·vo -va *adj* contemptuous; (gram) pejorative

despecha·do -da *adj* spiteful, enraged

despechar *tr* to spite, enrage; (*destetar*) (coll) to wean ‖ *ref* to be enraged; to despair, lose hope

despecho *m* spite; despair; (Am) weaning; **a despecho de** despite, in spite of; **por despecho** out of spite

despechugar §44 *tr* to carve the breast of ‖ *ref* (coll) to go with bare breast, to bare one's breast

despedazar §60 *tr* to break to pieces; (*la honra de uno*) to ruin; (*el alma de una persona*) to break ‖ *ref* to break to pieces; **despedazarse de risa** (coll) to split one's sides laughing

despedida *f* farewell, leave-taking; (*de una carta*) close, conclusion; (*copla final*) envoi

despedir §50 *tr* to throw; to emit, send forth; to discharge, dismiss; (*al que sale de la casa*) to see off; (*un mal pensamiento*) to banish; **despedir en la puerta** to see to the door ‖ *ref* to take leave, say good-by; to give up one's job; **despedirse a la francesa** to take French leave; **despedirse de** to take leave of, say good-by to

despega·do -da *adj* (coll) gruff, surly

despegar §44 *tr* to loosen, unglue, unseal; to open; to separate, detach ‖ *intr* (aer) to take off ‖ *ref* to come off; **despegarse con** to be unbecoming to

despego *m* dislike, indifference

despegue *m* (aer) take-off

despeina·do -da *adj* unkempt

despeja·do -da *adj* (*frente*) wide; (*día,*

cielo) clear, cloudless; bright, sprightly; (*en el trato*) unconstrained

despejar *tr* to clarify, explain; to free; (*una incógnita*) (math) to find ‖ *ref* to brighten up, cheer up; (*el cielo, el tiempo; una situación dificultosa*) to clear up; (*un borracho*) to sober up

despejo *m* ease, naturalness; talent, intelligence, understanding

despeluzar §60 *tr* to muss the hair of; to make the hair of (*a person*) stand on end ‖ *ref* (*el pelo*) to stand on end

despeluznante *adj* hair-raising, horrifying

despellejar *tr* to skin, flay; (coll) to slander, malign

despenar *tr* to console; (coll) to kill; (Chile) to deprive of hope

despender *tr* to spend, squander; (*el tiempo*) to waste

despensa *f* pantry; food supplies; day's marketing; stewardship; (naut) storeroom

despensero *m* butler, steward; (naut) storekeeper

despeñade·ro -ra *adj* precipitous ‖ *m* precipice; danger, risk

despeñadi·zo -za *adj* precipitous

despeñar *tr* to hurl, throw, push ‖ *ref* to hurl oneself, jump; to fall headlong; (*en vicios, pecados, pasiones*) to plunge downward

despeño *m* plunge; headlong fall; ruin, failure, collapse; (coll) loose bowels

despepitar *tr* to seed, remove the seeds from ‖ *ref* to rush around madly, to go around screaming; **despepitarse por** (coll) to be mad about

desperdicia·do -da *adj* wasteful, prodigal ‖ *mf* spendthrift, prodigal

desperdiciar *tr* to waste, squander; (*la ocasión de aprovechar una cosa*) to miss, to lose

desperdicio *m* waste, squandering; **desperdicios** waste; waste products; by-products; rubbish; **no tener desperdicio** (coll) to be excellent, be useful

desperdigar §44 *tr* to separate, scatter

desperecer §22 *ref* to long eagerly

desperezar §60 *ref* to stretch, to stretch one's arms and legs

desperfecto *m* blemish, flaw, imperfection

desperna·do -da *adj* footsore, weary

desperta·dor -dora *mf* awakener ‖ *m* alarm clock; warning

despertar §2 *tr* to awaken; to arouse, stir ‖ *intr & ref* to awaken, wake up

despestañar *tr* to pluck the eyelashes of ‖ *ref* to look hard, strain one's eyes

despiada·do -da *adj* cruel, pitiless

despichar *tr* to squeeze dry; (Col, Chile) to crush, flatten ‖ *intr* (coll) to croak, die

despidiente *m* stick placed between a hanging scaffold and wall; **despidiente de agua** flashing

despido *m* layoff, discharge

despier·to -ta *adj* wide-awake, alert; **soñar despierto** to daydream

despilfarra·do -da *adj* wasteful; ragged ‖ *mf* prodigal; raggedy person

despilfarrar tr to squander, waste || ref (coll) to spend recklessly

despilfarro m squandering, waste, extravagance; slovenliness

despintar tr to remove the paint from; to disfigure, distort, spoil; **no despintarle a uno los ojos** to not take one's eyes from a person || intr to decline, slip back; **despintar de** to be unworthy of || ref to fade, wash off; **no despintársele a uno** (coll) to not fade from one's memory

despiojar tr to delouse; (coll) to free from poverty

despique m revenge

despistar tr to outwit, to throw off the track || ref to run off the track, run off the road

desplacer m displeasure || §22 tr to displease

desplantar tr to uproot; to throw out of plumb || ref to get out of plumb; to lose one's upright posture

desplaya·do -da adj broad, open, wide || m (Arg) wide sandy beach

desplayar tr to widen, spread out || ref (el mar) to recede from the beach

desplaza·do -da adj displaced || mf displaced person

desplazar §60 tr (cierto peso de agua) to displace; to move, to transport || ref to move

desplegar §66 tr to unfold, spread; to display; to explain; (mil) to deploy || ref to unfold, spread out; (mil) to deploy

despliegue m unfolding, spreading out; display; (mil) deployment

desplomar tr to throw out of plumb || ref to get out of plumb; to collapse, tumble; to fall down in a faint; (un trono) to crumble; (aer) to pancake

desplome m leaning; collapse, tumbling; falling in a faint; downfall; (aer) pancaking

desplumar tr to pluck; (dejar sin dinero) (coll) to fleece || ref to molt

despoblado m wilderness, deserted spot

despoblar §61 tr to depopulate; to lay waste; to clear, lay bare

despojar tr to strip, despoil, divest; to dispossess || ref to undress; **despojarse de** to divest oneself of; (ropa) to take off

despojo m dispoilment; dispossession; booty, plunder, spoils; prey, victim; **despojos** scraps, leavings; mortal remains; second-hand building materials

despolarizar §60 tr to depolarize

despolvar tr to dust

despolvorear tr to dust, dust off; to scatter

desportillar tr to chip, nick || ref to chip, chip off

desposa·do -da adj handcuffed; newly married || mf newlywed

desposar tr to marry || ref to be betrothed, get engaged; to get married

desposeer §43 tr to dispossess || ref — **desposeerse de** to divest oneself of

desposorios mpl betrothal, engagement; marriage, nuptials

déspota m despot

despóti·co -ca adj despotic

despotismo m despotism

despotricar §73 intr & ref to rave, rant

despreciable adj contemptible, despicable

despreciar tr to scorn, despise; to slight, snub; to overlook, forgive; to reject || ref — **despreciarse de** to not deign to

despreciati·vo -va adj contemptuous, scornful

desprecio m scorn, contempt; slight, snub

desprender tr to loosen, unfasten, detach; to emit, give off; (chem) to liberate || ref to come loose, to come off; to issue, come forth; **desprenderse de** to give up, part with; to be deduced from

desprendi·do -da adj generous, disinterested

desprendimiento m loosening, detachment; emission, liberation; generosity, disinterestedness; landslide; (chem) liberation

despreocupación f relaxation; impartiality

despreocupa·do -da adj relaxed, unconcerned; impartial; indifferent

despreocupante adj relaxing

despreocupar ref to relax; **despreocuparse de** to forget about, be unconcerned about

desprestigiar tr to disparage, run down || ref to lose caste, lose one's standing, to lose face

desprestigio m disparagement; loss of standing, discredit

despreveni·do -da adj off one's guard; **coger a uno desprevenido** to catch someone unawares

desproporciona·do -da adj disproportionate

despropósito m absurdity, nonsense

desproveer §43 & §83 tr to deprive

desprovis·to -ta adj destitute; **desprovisto de** lacking, devoid of

después adv after, afterwards; **después de** after; **después (de) que** after

despuli·do -da adj ground (glass)

despumar tr to skim

despuntar tr to dull, blunt; (un cabo o punta) (naut) to double, round || intr to begin to sprout; (empezar a amanecer) to dawn; to stand out || ref to get dull

desquiciar tr to unhinge; to shake loose, upset; to unsettle, perturb; to overthrow, undermine

desquitar tr to recover, retrieve; to compensate || ref to retrieve a loss; to get revenge, get even

desquite m recovery, retrieval; retaliation, revenge; (sport) return match

desrazonable adj unreasonable

desrielar intr (Am) to jump the track

destaca·do -da adj outstanding, distinguished

destacamiento m (mil) detachment; (mil) detail

destacar §73 tr to highlight, point up; to emphasize; to make stand out;

(mil) to detach; (mil) to detail ‖ *intr* to stand out, be conspicuous ‖ *ref* to stand out, to project; (fig) to stand out

destajar *tr* to arrange for, establish the terms for; (*la baraja*) to cut; (Am) to carve up

destaje·ro -ra or **destajista** *mf* pieceworker, jobber; free lance

destajo *m* piecework; job, contract; **a destajo** by the piece, by the job; freelancing; **hablar a destajo** (coll) to talk too much

destapar *tr* to open, uncover, take the lid off; to uncock, unplug; to reveal ‖ *ref* to get uncovered; to throw off the covers; to unbosom oneself

destaponar *tr* to uncock, unplug; (*una botella; las fosas nasales*) to unstop

destartala·do -da *adj* tumble-down, ramshackle

destazar §60 *tr* to carve up

destechar *tr* to unroof

destejar *tr* to remove the tiles from; to leave unprotected

destejer *tr* to unbraid, unknit, unweave; to upset, disturb

destellar *tr & intr* to flash

destello *m* flash, beam, sparkle

destempla·do -da *adj* disagreeable, unpleasant; inharmonious, out of tune; indisposed; (*clima; pulso*) irregular

destemplanza *f* unpleasantness; discord; indisposition; (*del pulso*) irregularity; (*del tiempo*) inclemency; excess

destemple *m* dissonance; indisposition; disorder, disturbance

desteñir §72 *tr* to discolor ‖ *intr & ref* to fade

desternillante *adj* sidesplitting

desternillar *ref* — **desternillarse de risa** to split one's sides with laughter

desterra·do -da *adj* exiled ‖ *mf* exile

desterrar §2 *tr* to exile, to banish; (fig) to banish

destetar *tr* to wean ‖ *ref* — **destetarse con** to have known since childhood

destete *m* weaning

destiempo *m* — **a destiempo** untimely

destiento *m* surprise, shock

destierro *m* exile; backwoods

destilación *f* distillation

destiladera *f* still; scheme, stratagem

destilar *tr* to distill; to filter; to exude ‖ *intr* to drip

destilatorio *m* distillery; (*alambique*) still

destilería *f* distillery

destinación *f* destination

destinar *tr* to destine; to assign, designate

destinata·rio -ria *mf* addressee; consignee; (*de homenaje, aplausos*) recipient

destino *m* (*lugar a donde va una persona o una remesa*) destination; (*suerte, encadenamiento fatal de los sucesos*) fate, destiny; employment; place of employment; **con destino a** bound for

destituir §20 *tr* to deprive; to dismiss, discharge

destorcer §74 *tr* to untwist, straighten ‖

ref to become untwisted; (naut) to drift

destornilla·do -da *adj* rash, reckless, out of one's head

destornillador *m* screwdriver

destornillar *tr* to unscrew ‖ *ref* to lose one's head, go berserk

destoser *ref* to cough (*artificially, to attract attention*)

destrabar *tr* to loosen, untie, detach

destraillar §4 *tr* to unleash

destral *m* hatchet

destreza *f* skill, dexterity

destripacuen·tos *m* (*pl* **-tos**) (coll) butter-in

destripar *tr* to disembowel, to gut; to crush, mangle; (coll) to spoil (*a story by telling its outcome*)

destripaterro·nes *m* (*pl* **-nes**) (coll) clodhopper

destriunfar *tr* to force to play trump

destrocar §81 *tr* to swap back again

destronar *tr* to dethrone; to overthrow

destroncar §73 *tr* to chop down; to chop off; to ruin; to exhaust, wear out

destrozar §60 *tr* to shatter, break to pieces; to destroy; to squander; (*al ejército enemigo*) to wipe out

destrozo *m* havoc, destruction; rout, annihilation, defeat

destrucción *f* destruction

destructi·vo -va *adj* destructive

destructor *m* (nav) destroyer

destruir §20 *tr* to destroy ‖ *ref* (alg) to cancel each other

desuellaca·ras *m* (*pl* **-ras**) (coll) sloppy barber; (coll) scoundrel

desuello *m* skinning, flaying; shamelessness; (*precio excesivo*) (coll) highway robbery

desuncir §36 *tr* to unyoke

desunir *tr* to disunite; to take apart ‖ *ref* to disunite; to come apart

desusa·do -da *adj* obsolete, out of use; uncommon, unusual; **estar desusado** (*perder la práctica*) to be rusty

desuso *m* disuse; **caído en desuso** obsolete

desvaí·do -da *adj* lank, ungainly; (*color*) dull

desvainar *tr* to shell

desvali·do -da *adj* helpless, destitute

desvalijar *tr* (*una valija, baúl, etc.*) to rifle; to rob, wipe out

desvalorar *tr* to devalue

desvalorizar §60 *tr* to devalue

desván *m* garret, loft

desvanecedor *m* (phot) mask

desvanecer §22 *tr* to dispel, dissipate; (*una conspiración*) to break up; (*la sospecha*) to banish; (phot) to mask ‖ *ref* to disappear, vanish, evanesce; to evaporate; to faint, faint away, swoon; (rad) to fade

desvanecimiento *m* disappearance, evanescence; dissipation; pride, vanity; faintness, fainting spell; (phot) masking; (rad) fading, fadeout

desvaria·do -da *adj* delirious, raving

desvariar §77 *intr* to be delirious, to rave, to rant

desvarío *m* delirium, raving; absurdity,

nonsense, extravagance; whim, caprice; inconstancy

desvela·do -da *adj* wakeful, sleepless; watchful, vigilant; anxious, worried

desvelar *tr* to keep awake, not let sleep || *ref* to keep awake, go without sleep; to be watchful, be vigilant; **desvelarse por** to be anxious about, be worried about

desvelo *m* wakefulness, sleeplessness; watchfulness, vigilance; anxiety, worry, concern

desvenar *tr* to strip (*tobacco*)

desvencija·do -da *adj* rickety, ramshackle

desvencijar *tr* to break, tear apart || *ref* to go to rack and ruin

desvendar *tr* to unbandage, to undress

desventaja *f* disadvantage

desventajo·so -sa *adj* disadvantageous

desventura *f* misfortune

desventura·do -da *adj* unfortunate; faint-hearted; stingy

desvergonza·do -da *adj* shameless, impudent

desvergüenza *f* shamelessness, impudence

desvestir §50 *tr & ref* to undress

desviación *f* deviation, deflection; detour; (rad, telv) drift

desviacionismo *m* deviationism

desviacionista *mf* deviationist

desviadero *m* (rr) siding, turnout

desvia·do -da *adj* devious

desviar §77 *tr* to deviate, deflect; to turn aside; to dissuade; to parry, ward off; (rr) to switch || *ref* to deviate, deflect; to turn aside; to branch off; to be dissuaded

desvío *m* deviation, deflection; coldness, indifference; detour; (rr) siding, sidetrack

desvirgar §44 *tr* to deflower, ravish

desvirtuar §21 *tr* to weaken, spoil, impair

desvivir *ref* — **desvivirse por** to be crazy about; **desvivirse por** + *inf* to be eager to + *inf,* to do one's best to + *inf*

desvolvedor *m* wrench

desvolver §47 & §83 *tr* to alter, change; (*la tierra*) to turn up; (*una tuerca o tornillo*) to loosen, unscrew

detall *m* — **al detall** at retail

detalladamente *adv* in detail

detallar *tr* to detail, tell in detail; to retail, sell at retail

detalle *m* detail; (Am) retail; **ahí está el detalle** that's the point

detallista *mf* retailer; person fond of details

detección *f* detection

detectar *tr* to detect

detective *m* detective

detector *m* detector; **detector de mentiras** lie detector

detención *f* detention, detainment; delay; care, thoroughness

detener §71 *tr* to detain; to stop; to arrest; to keep, retain; (*el aliento*) to hold || *ref* to stop; to linger, tarry

detenidamente *adv* carefully, thoroughly

deteni·do -da *adj* careful, thorough;

hesitant, timid; stingy, mean || *mf* person held in custody

detenimiento *m* var of **detención**

detergente *adj & m* detergent

deteriorar *tr & ref* to deteriorate

deterioro *m* deterioration

determinación *f* determination; decision

determina·do -da *adj* determined, resolute; (*artículo*) (gram) definite

determinar *tr* to determine; to cause, to bring about || *ref* to decide

detestar *tr* to detest; to curse; **detestar** + *inf* to hate to + *inf*

detonar *intr* to detonate

detraer §75 *tr* to withdraw, take away, detract; to defame, vilify

detrás *adv* behind; **detrás de** behind, back of; **por detrás** behind; behind one's back; **por detrás de** behind the back of

detrimento *m* harm, detriment

deuda *f* debt; indebtedness

deu·do -da *mf* relative || *m* kinship || *f* see **deuda**

deu·dor -dora *adj* indebted || *mf* debtor; **deudor hipotecario** mortgagor; **deudor moroso** delinquent (*in payment*)

devalar *intr* (naut) to drift from the course

devaluación *f* devaluation

devanar *tr* to wind, to roll; (*un cuento*) to unfold || *ref* (CAm, Mex, W-I) to roll with laughter; (CAm, Mex, W-I) to writhe in pain

devanear *intr* to talk nonsense; to loaf around

devaneo *m* nonsense; loafing; flirtation

devastación *f* devastation

devastar *tr* to devastate

develar *tr* to reveal; (*p.ej., una estatua*) to unveil

devengar §44 *tr* (*salarios*) to earn; (*intereses*) to draw, to earn

devoción *f* devotion

devolución *f* return, restitution

devolver §47 & §83 *tr* to return, give back, send back; to pay back; (coll) to vomit || *ref* (Am) to return, come back

devorar *tr* to devour

devo·to -ta *adj* devout; devoted; devotional || *mf* devotee; devout person || *m* object of worship

D.F. *abbr* **Distrito Federal**

d/f *abbr* **días fecha**

dho. *abbr* **dicho**

día *m* day; daytime; daylight; **al día** per day; up to date; **al otro día** on the following day; **buenos días** good morning; **dar los días a** to wish (*someone*) many happy returns of the day; **de día** in the daytime, in the daylight; **día de años** birthday; **día de ayuno** fast day; **día de carne** meat day; **día de engañabobos** December 28th, day when practical jokes are played on unsuspecting people; **día de inauguración** (fa) private view; **día de la raza** Columbus Day; **día del juicio** judgment day; **día de los caídos** Memorial Day; **día de los difuntos**

All Souls' Day; **día de ramos** Palm Sunday; **día de Reyes** Epiphany; **día de todos los santos** All Saints' Day; **día de trabajo** workday; weekday; **día de vigilia** fast day; **día festivo** holiday; **día laborable** workday, weekday; **día lectivo** school day; **día puente** day off between two holidays; **el día de Año Nuevo** New Year's Day; **el día menos pensado** (coll) when least expected; **el mejor día** some fine day; **en cuatro días** in a few days; **en pleno día** in broad daylight; **en su día** in due time; **ocho días** a week; **poner al día** to bring up to date; **quince días** two weeks, a fortnight; **tener sus días** to be up in years; **un día sí y otro no** every other day; **vivir al día** to live from hand to mouth

diabetes f diabetes
diabéti·co -ca adj & mf diabetic
diablillo m imp
diablo m devil; (Chile) ox-drawn log drag; **ahí será el diablo** (coll) there will be the devil to pay; **diablo cojuelo** tricky devil; **diablos azules** (Am) delirium tremens
diablura f devilment, deviltry, mischief
diabóli·co -ca adj devilish, diabolical
diaconisa f deaconess
diácono m deacon
diacríti·co -ca adj diacritical
diadema f diadem; (*adorno femenino*) tiara
diáfa·no -na adj diaphanous
diafragma m diaphragm
diagno·sis f (*pl* **-sis**) diagnosis
diagnosticar §73 tr to diagnose
diagonal adj diagonal ǁ f diagonal, bias
diagrama m diagram
dialecto m dialect
diálogo m dialogue
diamante m diamond
diametral or **diamétri·co -ca** adj diametrical
diámetro m diameter
diana f bull's-eye; (mil) reveille; **hacer diana** to hit the bull's-eye
diantre m (coll) devil ǁ *interj* (coll) the devil!, the deuce!
diapasón m tuning fork; pitch pipe; (*p.ej., del violín*) finger board; **bajar el diapasón** (coll) to lower one's voice, to change one's tune
diapositiva f slide, lantern slide
dia·rio -ria adj daily ǁ m diary; daily, daily paper; **diario hablado** newscast
diarismo m (Am) journalism
diarrea f diarrhea
diástole f diastole
diatermia f diathermy
dibujante mf sketcher, illustrator ǁ m draftsman
dibujar tr to draw, sketch, design; to outline ǁ *ref* to be outlined; to appear, show
dibujo m drawing, sketch, design; outline; **dibujo al carbón** charcoal drawing; **dibujo animado** animated cartoon; **no meterse en dibujos** (coll) to attend to one's business
di·caz adj (*pl* **-caces**) sarcastic, witty

dicción f diction; word
diccionario m dictionary
diciembre m December
dicloruro m dichloride
dicotomía f dichotomy; (*entre médicos*) split fee
dictado m dictation; **escribir al dictado** to take dictation; (*lo que otro dicta*) to take down
dictador m dictator
dictadura f dictatorship
dictáfono m dictaphone
dictamen m dictum, judgment, opinion
dictar tr to dictate; (*una ley*) to promulgate; to inspire, suggest; (*una conferencia*) (Am) to give, deliver (*a lecture*)
dicterio m taunt, insult
dicha f happiness; luck; **por dicha** by chance
dicharache·ro -ra adj (coll) obscene, vulgar
dicharacho m (coll) obscenity, vulgarity; (coll) wisecrack
di·cho -cha adj said; **dicho y hecho** no sooner said than done; **mejor dicho** rather; **tener por dicho** to consider settled ǁ m saying; promise of marriage, one's word; witticism; (coll) insult; **dicho de las gentes** (coll) talk, hearsay, gossip ǁ f see **dicha**
dicho·so -sa adj happy; lucky, fortunate; annoying, tiresome
didácti·co -ca adj didactic
diecinueve adj & pron nineteen ǁ m nineteen; (*en las fechas*) nineteenth
diecinueva·vo -va adj & m nineteenth
dieciocha·vo -va adj & m eighteenth
dieciocho adj & pron eighteen ǁ m eighteen; (*en las fechas*) eighteenth
dieciséis adj & pron sixteen ǁ m sixteen; (*en las fechas*) sixteenth
dieciseisa·vo -va adj & m sixteenth
diecisiete adj & pron seventeen ǁ m seventeen; (*en las fechas*) seventeenth
diecisietea·vo -va adj & m seventeenth
diente m tooth; (*de elefante y otros animales*) tusk, fang; (*de peine, sierra, rastrillo*) tooth; (*de rueda dentada*) cog; **dar diente con diente** (coll) to shake all over; **decir entre dientes** (coll) to mutter, to mumble; **diente canino** eyetooth, canine tooth; **diente de león** dandelion; **estar a diente** (coll) to be famished; **tener buen diente** (coll) to be a hearty eater; **traer entre dientes** (coll) to have a grudge against; (coll) to talk about
dière·sis f (*pl* **-sis**) diaeresis; (*señal que indica la metafonía*) umlaut
dies·tro -tra adj right; handy, skillful; shrewd, sly; favorable; **a diestro y siniestro** wildly, right and left ǁ m expert fencer; bullfighter on foot; matador; halter, bridle ǁ f right hand; **juntar diestra con diestra** to join forces
dieta f diet; **dietas** per diem; **estar a dieta** to diet, be on a diet
dietario m family budget
dietista mf dietitian

diez *adj & pron* ten; **las diez** ten o'clock ‖ *m* ten; (*en las fechas*) tenth
diezmar *tr* (*causar gran mortandad en*) to decimate; (*pagar el diezmo de*) to tithe
diezmo *m* tithe
difamación *f* defamation, vilification
difamar *tr* to defame, to vilify
diferencia *f* difference; **a diferencia de** unlike; **partir la diferencia** to split the difference
diferenciar *tr* to differentiate ‖ *intr* (*discordar*) to differ, dissent ‖ *ref* (*distinguirse una cosa de otra*) to differ, be different
diferente *adj* different
diferir §68 *tr* to defer, postpone, put off ‖ *intr* to differ, be different
difícil *adj* difficult, hard; hard to please
difícilmente *adv* with difficulty
dificultad *f* difficulty; (*reparo que se opone a una opinión*) objection
dificultar *tr* to make difficult; to consider difficult ‖ *intr* to raise objections ‖ *ref* to become difficult
dificulto·so -sa *adj* difficult, troublesome; objecting; (coll) ugly, homely
difidencia *f* distrust
difidente *adj* distrustful
difteria *f* diphtheria
difundir *tr* to diffuse; to spread, disseminate; to divulge, publish; to broadcast ‖ *ref* to diffuse; to spread
difun·to -ta *adj & mf* deceased; **difunto de taberna** dead-drunk ‖ *m* corpse
difu·so -sa *adj* diffuse; extended; wordy
digerible *adj* digestible
digerir §68 *tr* to digest; **no digerir** to not bear, to not stand ‖ *intr* to digest
digestible *adj* digestible
digestión *f* digestion
digesti·vo -va *adj & m* digestive
digesto *m* (law) digest
dígito *m* digit
dignación *f* condescension
dignar *ref* to deign, to condescend
dignatario *m* dignitary, official
dignidad *f* dignity; bishop, archbishop
dignificar §73 *tr* to dignify
dig·no -na *adj* worthy; fitting, suitable; (*grave, decoroso*) dignified
digresión *f* digression
dije *m* amulet, charm, trinket; (*persona de excelentes cualidades*) (coll) jewel; (coll) person all dressed-up; (coll) handy person
dilacerar *tr* to tear to pieces; (*la honra, el orgullo*) to damage
dilación *f* delay
dilapidar *tr* to squander
dilatación *f* expansion; serenity
dilatar *tr* to dilate, expand; to defer, postpone; (*p.ej., la fama*) to spread ‖ *ref* to dilate, expand; to spread; to be wordy; (Am) to delay
dilección *f* true love
dilec·to -ta *adj* dearly beloved
dilema *m* dilemma
diletante *adj & mf* dilettante
diligencia *f* diligence; step, démarche; errand; dispatch, speed; stagecoach; **hacer una diligencia** to do an errand; (coll) to have a bowel movement

diligente *adj* diligent; quick, ready
dilucidar *tr* to elucidate, explain
dilución *f* dilution
dilu·do -da *adj* dilute
diluir §20 *tr* to dilute; to thin ‖ *ref* to dilute; to melt; to dissolve
diluviar *intr* to rain hard, to pour
diluvio *m* deluge
dimanar *intr* to spring up; **dimanar de** to spring from, originate in
dimensión *f* dimension
dimes *mpl* — **andar en dimes y diretes con** (coll) to bicker with
diminuti·vo -va *adj & m* (gram) diminutive
diminu·to -ta *adj* tiny, diminutive; defective
dimisión *f* resignation
dimisorias *fpl* — **dar dimisorias a** (coll) to discharge, to fire
dimitir *tr* to resign, resign from ‖ *intr* to resign
din *m* (coll) dough, money
Dinamarca *f* Denmark
dinamar·qués -quesa *adj* Danish ‖ *mf* Dane ‖ *m* Danish (*language*)
dinámi·co -ca *adj* dynamic
dinamita *f* dynamite
dinamitar *tr* to dynamite
dínamo *f* dynamo
dinasta *m* dynast
dinastía *f* dynasty
dindán *m* ding-dong
dinerada *f* or **dineral** *m* large sum of money
dinero *m* money; currency; wealth; **dinero contante** cash; **dinero contante y sonante** ready cash, spot cash; **dinero de bolsillo** pocket money
dinero·so -sa *adj* moneyed, wealthy
dintel *m* lintel, doorhead
dióce·si *f* or **dióce·sis** *f* (*pl* -sis) diocese
diodo *m* diode
dios *m* god; **Dios mediante** God willing; **¡por Dios!** goodness!, for heaven's sake; **¡válgame Dios!** bless me!; **¡vaya con Dios!** off with you!
diosa *f* goddess
diploma *m* diploma
diplomacia *f* diplomacy
diploma·do -da *adj & mf* graduate
diplomar *tr & ref* (Am) to graduate
diplomáti·co -ca *adj* diplomatic ‖ *mf* diplomat
diptongar §44 *tr & ref* to diphthongize
diptongo *m* diphthong
diputación *f* congress; commission
diputa·do -da *mf* deputy, representative
diputar *tr* to commission, delegate; to designate
dique *m* dike, jetty; dry dock; check, stop; **dique seco** dry dock
dirección *f* direction; (*señas en una carta*) address; administration, management; directorship; (aut) steering; **de dirección única** one-way; **dirección a la derecha** right-hand drive; **dirección a la izquierda** left-hand drive; **perder la dirección** to lose control of the car
directi·vo -va *adj* managing ‖ *mf* director, manager ‖ *f* management
direc·to -ta *adj* direct; straight

diréc·tor -tora adj directing, guiding; managing, governing || mf director, manager; (de un periódico) editor; (de una escuela) principal; (de una orquesta) conductor; **director de escena** stage manager; **director de funeraria** funeral director; **director gerente** managing director

directorio m directorship; directory

dirigente mf leader, head, executive

dirigible adj & m dirigible

dirigir §27 tr to direct; to manage; (un automóvil) to steer; (una carta; la palabra) to address; (una obra) to dedicate || ref to go, to betake oneself; to turn; **dirigirse a** to address; to apply to

dirimir tr to dissolve, annul; (una dificultad) to solve; (una controversia) to settle, mediate

discar §73 tr & intr to dial

disceptar intr to discuss, debate

discerniente adj discerning

discernir §28 tr to discern; to distinguish

disciplina f discipline; **disciplinas** scourge, whip

disciplina·do -da adj disciplined; (flores) many-colored

disciplinar tr to discipline; to teach; to scourge, whip

disciplinazo m lash

discípu·lo -la mf disciple; pupil

disco m disk; (del gramófono) record, disk; (sport) discus; **disco de cola** (rr) taillight; **disco de goma** (para un grifo) washer (for a spigot); **disco de identificación** identification tag; **disco de larga duración** long-playing record; **disco de señales** (rr) semaphore; **disco selector** (telp) dial; **siempre el mismo disco** (coll) the same old song

discóbolo m discus thrower

discófi·lo -la mf record lover, discophile

dísco·lo -la adj ungovernable, wayward

disconforme adj disagreeing

discontinuar §21 tr to discontinue

discordancia f discordance

discordar §61 intr to be out of tune; to disagree

discorde adj discordant, disagreeing; (mus) discordant, out of tune

discordia f discord

discoteca f discotheque, disco; record cabinet; record library

discreción f discretion; wit; witticism; **a discreción** at discretion; (mil) unconditionally

discrepancia f discrepancy; dissent

discrepar intr to differ, to disagree

discretear intr to try to be clever, to try to sparkle

discre·to -ta adj (juicioso) discreet; (discontinuo) discrete; witty

discrimen m risk, hazard; difference

discriminación f discrimination

discriminar tr to discriminate against || intr to discriminate

discriminato·rio -ria adj discriminatory

disculpa f excuse, apology

disculpar tr to excuse; (coll) to pardon, overlook || ref to apologize; **disculparse con** to apologize to; **disculparse de** to apologize for

discurrir tr to contrive, invent; to guess, conjecture || intr to ramble, roam; to occur, take place; to discourse; to reason; to pass, elapse

discursi·vo -va adj meditative

discurso m discourse, speech; (paso del tiempo) course; **discurso de sobremesa** after-dinner speech

discusión f discussion

discutible adj debatable

discutir tr to discuss || intr to discuss; to argue

disecar §73 tr to dissect; (un animal muerto) to stuff; (una planta) to mount

diseminar tr to disseminate; to scatter || ref to scatter

disensión f (oposición) dissent; (contienda) dissension

disentería f dysentery

disentir §68 intr to dissent

diseñar tr to draw, sketch; to design, outline

diseño m drawing, sketch; design, outline

disertar intr to discourse, discuss

diser·to -ta adj fluent, eloquent

disfavor m disfavor

disforme adj formless; monstrous, ugly

disforzar §35 ref (Peru) to be prudish, be finical

dis·fraz m (pl **-fraces**) disguise; (traje de máscara) costume, fancy dress

disfrazar §60 tr to disguise || ref to disguise oneself; to wear fancy dress, to masquerade, to dress in costume

disfrutar tr to enjoy, to use || intr — **disfrutar de** to enjoy, to use; **disfrutar con** to enjoy, take enjoyment in

disfrute m enjoyment, use

disgregar §44 tr & intr to disintegrate, break up

disgusta·do -da adj tasteless, insipid; sad, sorrowful; disagreeable; (Mex) hard to please

disgustar tr to displease || ref to be displeased; to fall out, become estranged

disgusto m displeasure; annoyance, unpleasantness; grief, sorrow; difference, quarrel; **a disgusto** against one's will

disidencia f dissidence; (de una doctrina) dissent

disidente adj dissident || mf dissident, dissenter

disidir intr to dissent

disíla·bo -ba adj dissyllabic || m dissyllable

disimil adj dissimilar

disimilar tr & ref to dissimilate

disimula·do -da adj sly, underhanded; **a lo disimulado** or **a la disimulada** underhandedly; **hacer la disimulada** (coll) to feign ignorance

disimular tr to dissemble, dissimulate, hide, conceal; to overlook, pardon || intr to dissemble, dissimulate

disimulo m dissembling, dissimulation; indulgence

di
di

disipación *f* dissipation
disipa·do -da *adj* dissipated; spendthrift ‖ *mf* debauchee; spendthrift
disipar *tr* to dissipate ‖ *ref* to be dissipated; to disappear, evanesce
dislate *m* nonsense
dislocar §73 *tr* to dislocate ‖ *ref* to dislocate; to be dislocated
disloque *m* (coll) tops, top notch
disminuir §20 *tr, intr & ref* to diminish
disociar *tr* to dissociate
disolución *f* dissolution; disbandment; (*relajación de costumbres*) dissoluteness, dissipation
disolu·to -ta *adj* dissolute ‖ *mf* debauchee
disolver §47 & §83 *tr* to dissolve; to disband; to destroy, ruin ‖ *intr & ref* to dissolve
disonancia *f* dissonance
disonar §61 *intr* to be dissonant, lack harmony, disagree; to cause surprise; to sound bad
dispar *adj* unlike, different; (*que no hace juego*) odd
disparada *f* (Am) sudden flight; **a la disparada** (Am) like a shot, in mad haste; **de una disparada** (Arg) right away; **tomar la disparada** (Arg) to take to one's heels
disparadero *m* trigger
disparador *m* trigger; (*de reloj*) escapement; **poner en el disparador** (coll) to drive mad
disparar *tr* to throw, hurl; to shoot, to fire ‖ *intr* to rant, talk nonsense ‖ *ref* to dash away, rush away; (*un caballo*) to run away; (*una escopeta*) to go off; to be beside oneself
disparata·do -da *adj* absurd, nonsensical; frightful
disparatar *intr* to talk nonsense; to act foolishly
disparate *m* folly, nonsense; blunder, mistake; (coll) outrage
dispare·jo -ja *adj* unequal, different, uneven, disparate; rough, broken
disparidad *f* disparity
disparo *m* shot, discharge; nonsense; (mach) release, trip; **cambiar disparos** to exchange shots
dispendio *m* waste, extravagance
dispendio·so -sa *adj* expensive
dispensar *tr* to excuse, to pardon; to exempt; to dispense; to dispense with
dispensario *m* dispensary; **dispensario de alimentos** soup kitchen
dispepsia *f* dyspepsia
dispersar *tr & ref* to disperse
displicente *adj* disagreeable; cross, fretful, peevish
disponer §54 *tr* to dispose, arrange; to direct, order ‖ *intr* to dispose; **disponer de** to dispose of, have at one's disposal ‖ *ref* to prepare, get ready; to get ready to die, make one's will
disponible *adj* available, disposable
disposición *f* disposition, arrangement, layout; inclination; preparation; disposal; predisposition; state of health; elegance; **estar a la disposición de** to be at the disposal of, be at the service

of; **última disposición** last will and testament
dispositivo *m* appliance, device
dispues·to -ta *adj* ready, prepared; comely, graceful; clever, skillful; **bien dispuesto** well-disposed; well, in good health; **mal dispuesto** ill-disposed, unfavorable; (*un reloj*) ill, indisposed
disputa *f* dispute; fight, struggle; **sin disputa** beyond dispute
disputar *tr* to dispute, to question; to argue over; to fight for ‖ *intr* to dispute; to debate, to argue; to fight
disque·ro -ra *mf* record dealer
distancia *f* distance; **a distancia** at a distance; **a larga distancia** long-distance; **tomar distancia** to stand aside, to stand off
distante *adj* distant
distar *intr* to be distant, be far; to be different
distender §51 *tr* to distend; (*p.ej., las piernas*) to stretch ‖ *ref* to distend; to relax; (*un reloj*) to run down
distensión *f* distension; relaxation of tension
distinción *f* (*honor, prerrogativa*) distinction; (*diferencia*) distinctness; **a distinción de** unlike
distingui·do -da *adj* distinguished; refined, urbane, smooth
distinguir §29 *tr* to distinguish; to give distinction to; to make out
distinti·vo -va *adj* distinctive ‖ *m* badge, insignia; distinction; distinctive mark
distin·to -ta *adj* distinct; different; **distintos** various, several
distorsión *f* distortion
distracción *f* distraction; (*licencia en las costumbres*) dissipation; (*substracción de fondos*) embezzlement
distraer §75 *tr* to distract; to amuse, divert, entertain; to seduce; to embezzle
distraí·do -da *adj* absent-minded, distracted; licentious, dissolute; (Chile, Mex) untidy, careless
distribución *f* distribution; electric supply system; timing gears, valve gears
distribui·dor -dora *adj* distributing ‖ *mf* distributor ‖ *m* (aut) distributor; slide valve; **distribuidor automático** vending machine
distribuir §20 *tr* to distribute
distrito *m* district; (rr) section; **distrito electoral** precinct; **distrito postal** zone, postal zone
disturbar *tr* to disturb
disturbio *m* disturbance
disuadir *tr* to dissuade
disyunti·vo -va *adj* disjunctive ‖ *f* dilemma
disyuntor *m* circuit breaker
dita *f* bond, surety
diuca *m* (Arg, Chile) teacher's pet ‖ *f* (Arg, Chile) finch (*Fringilla diuca*)
diur·no -na *adj* day, daytime
diva *f* goddess; (mus) diva
divagación *f* digression; wandering
divagar §44 *intr* to digress; to ramble, wander
diván *m* divan

divergir §27 *intr* to diverge
diversidad *f* diversity; abundance
diversificación *f* diversification
diversificar §73 *tr* & *ref* to diversify
diversión *f* diversion
diver·so -sa *adj* diverse, different; **diversos** several, various, divers
diverti·do -da *adj* amusing, funny; (Am) tipsy
divertimiento *m* diversion, amusement
divertir §68 *tr* to divert; to amuse ‖ *ref* to enjoy oneself, have a good time
dividendo *m* dividend
dividir *tr* to divide ‖ *ref* to divide, be divided; to separate
divieso *m* boil
divinidad *f* divinity; (*persona dotada de gran belleza*) beauty
divinizar §60 *tr* to deify; to exalt, extol
divi·no -na *adj* divine
divisa *f* badge; emblem; motto; goal, ideal; currency, foreign exchange
divisar *tr* to descry, espy
división *f* division
divisor *m* (math) divisor; **máximo común divisor** greatest common divisor; **divisor de voltaje** (rad) voltage divider
divisoria *f* dividing line; (geog) divide
di·vo -va *adj* godlike, divine ‖ *m* god; (mus) opera star ‖ *f* see **diva**
divorciar *tr* to divorce ‖ *ref* to divorce, get divorced
divorcio *m* divorce; divergency (*in opinion*); (Col) jail for women
divulgación *f* divulging, disclosure; popularization
divulgar §44 *tr* to divulge, disclose; to popularize
D.ⁿ *abbr* **don**
dobladillar *tr* to hem
dobladillo *m* hem
dobla·do -da *adj* rough, uneven; stocky, thickset; double-dealing ‖ *m* (mov) dubbing
doblaje *m* (mov) dubbing
doblar *tr* to double; to fold, to crease; to bend; (*una esquina*) to turn, to round; (*un promontorio*) to double; (*una película, generalmente en otro idioma*) to dub; (bridge) to double; (Mex) to shoot down ‖ *intr* to turn; (*tocar a muerto*) to toll; (mov, theat) to double, stand in; (bridge) to double ‖ *ref* to double; to fold, to crease; to bend; to bow, to stoop; to give in, yield
doble *adj* double; heavy, thick; stocky, thickset; deceitful, two-faced ‖ *adv* double, doubly ‖ *mf* (mov, theat) double, stand-in ‖ *m* double; fold, crease; (*toque de difuntos*) toll, knell; (*suma que se paga por la prórroga de una operación a plazos en la bolsa*) margin; **al doble** doubly
doblegar §44 *tr* to fold; to bend; (*una espada*) to brandish, flourish; to sway, dominate ‖ *ref* to fold; to bend; to give in, to yield
doblete *adj* medium ‖ *m* (*piedra falsa; cada una de dos palabras que poseen un mismo origen*) doublet; (bridge) doubleton

do·blez *m* (*pl* **-bleces**) fold, crease; (*del pantalón*) cuff; duplicity, double-dealing
doce *adj* & *pron* twelve; **las doce** twelve o'clock ‖ *m* twelve; (*en las fechas*) twelfth
docea·vo -va *adj* & *m* twelfth
docena *f* dozen; **docena del fraile** baker's dozen
docencia *f* (Arg) teaching; (Arg) teaching staff
docente *adj* educational, teaching
dócil *adj* docile; soft, ductile
doc·to -ta *adj* learned ‖ *mf* scholar
doc·tor -tora *mf* doctor ‖ *f* (coll) blue-stocking
doctorado *m* doctorate
doctoran·do -da *mf* candidate for the doctor's degree
doctorar *tr* to grant the doctor's degree to ‖ *ref* to get the doctor's degree
doctrina *f* doctrine; teaching, instruction; learning; catechism; preaching the Gospel
doctrinar *tr* to teach, instruct
doctrino *m* orphan (*in orphanage*); **parecer un doctrino** (coll) to look scared
documentación *f* documentation; **documentación del buque** ship's papers
documental *adj* documentary ‖ *m* (mov) documentary
documentar *tr* to document
documento *m* document; **documento de prueba** (law) exhibit
dogal *m* (*para atar las caballerías*) halter; (*para ahorcar a un reo*) noose, halter, hangman's rope; **estar con el dogal a la garganta** or **al cuello** (coll) to be in a tight spot
dogmáti·co -ca *adj* dogmatic
do·go -ga *mf* bulldog
dolamas *fpl* or **dolames** *mpl* hidden defects of a horse; (Am) complaints, aches and pains
dolar §61 *tr* to hew
dólar *m* dollar
dolencia *f* ailment, complaint
doler §47 *tr* to ache, to pain; to grieve, distress; **dolerle a uno el dinero** (coll) to hate to spend money ‖ *intr* to ache, to hurt, to pain ‖ *ref* to complain; to feel sorry; to repent
doliente *adj* sick, ill; aching, suffering; sad, sorrowful ‖ *mf* sufferer, patient ‖ *m* mourner
dolo *m* deceit, fraud, guile
dolor *m* ache, pain; grief, sorrow; regret, repentance; **dolor de cabeza** headache; **dolor de muelas** toothache; **dolor de oído** earache; **dolor de yegua** (CAm) lumbago; **estar con dolores** to be in labor
dolori·do -da *adj* sore, painful; grieving, disconsolate
doloro·so -sa *adj* painful; sorrowful, sad
dolo·so -sa *adj* deceitful, guileful
domador *m* horsebreaker; animal tamer
domar *tr* to tame, to break; to master
domeñar *tr* to master, subdue
domesticar §73 *tr* to domesticate; to tame

domésti·co -ca adj domestic, household || mf domestic, servant

domiciliar tr to domicile, settle; (una carta) (Mex) to address || ref to be domiciled, to take up one's residence

domicilio m domicile, home; dwelling, house; **domicilio social** home office, company office

dominación f domination; (mil) eminence, high ground

dominante adj dominant; (mandón) domineering || f (mus) dominant

dominar tr to dominate; to check, restrain, subdue; (una ciencia, un idioma) to master || intr to dominate; (mandar imperiosamente) to domineer || ref to restrain oneself

dómine m (coll) schoolmaster, Latin teacher; (coll) pedant

domingo m Sunday; **domingo de ramos** Palm Sunday; **domingo de resurrección** Easter Sunday; **guardar el domingo** to keep the Sabbath

dominguillo m tumbler

dominica·no -na adj & mf Dominican

dominio m dominion; domain; (de una ciencia, de un idioma) mastery; (del aire) supremacy

domi·nó m (pl -nós) (traje) domino; (juego) dominoes; (fichas) set of dominoes

dom.° abbr **domingo**

domo m dome

dompedro m four-o'clock

don m gift, present; talent, natural gift; Don (Spanish title used before masculine Christian names); **don de acierto** knack for doing the right thing; **don de errar** knack for doing the wrong thing; **don de gentes** charm, social grace; **don de lenguas** linguistic facility; **don de mando** ability to lead, generalship

dona f gift, present; **donas** wedding presents from the bridegroom to the bride

donación f gift, bequest; endowment

donada f lay sister

donado m lay brother

dona·dor -dora mf donor

donaire m charm, grace; witticism; cleverness

donairo·so -sa adj charming, graceful; witty; clever

donar tr to donate, to give

doncel adj mild, mellow || m (joven noble aun no armado caballero) bachelor; (hombre virgen) virgin

doncella f maiden, virgin; housemaid; lady's maid; maid of honor; (Col, Ven) felon, whitlow

doncellez f maidenhood, virginity

doncellona or **doncellueca** f spinster, maiden lady

donde conj where; wherever; in which; **donde no** otherwise; **por donde quiera** anywhere, everywhere || prep (Am) at or to the house, office, or store of

dónde adv where; **a dónde** where, whither; **de dónde** from where, whence; **por dónde** which way; for what cause, for what reason

dondequiera adv anywhere; **dondequiera que** wherever

dondiego m four-o'clock; **dondiego de día** morning-glory; **dondiego de noche** four-o'clock

donillero m sharper, smoothy

donjuán m four-o'clock

donosidad f charm, grace, wit

dono·so -sa adj charming, graceful, witty

donostiarra adj San Sebastian || mf native or inhabitant of San Sebastian

donosura f charm, grace, wit

doña f Doña (Spanish title used before feminine Christian names)

doñear intr (coll) to hang around women

doquier or **doquiera** conj wherever; **por doquier** everywhere

dorada f (ichth) gilthead

doradillo m fine brass wire

dora·do -da adj golden; gilt || m gilt, gilding; **dorados** bronze trimmings (on furniture) || f see **dorada**

dorar tr to gold-plate; to gild; (tostar ligeramente) to brown; (paliar) to sugar-coat || ref to turn golden; to turn brown

dormi·lón -lona adj (coll) sleepy || m (coll) sleepyhead || f reclining armchair; (Mex) headrest; (Ven) sleeping gown; (Am) mimosa; **dormilonas** pearl earrings

dormir §30 tr to put to sleep; (p.ej., una borrachera) to sleep off || intr to sleep; to spend the night || ref to sleep; to fall asleep; (entorpecerse, p.ej., el pie) to go to sleep

dormirlas m hide-and-seek

dormitar intr to doze, nap

dormitorio m bedroom; (muebles propios de esta habitación) bedroom suit

dorsal m (sport) number (worn on shirt)

dorso m back

dos adj & pron two; **las dos** two o'clock || m two; (en las fechas) second

dosal·bo -ba adj (horse) with two white feet

doscien·tos -tas adj & pron two hundred || **doscientos** m two hundred

dosel m canopy, dais

doselera f valance, drapery

dosificación f dosage

dosificar §73 tr (un medicamento) to dose, to give in doses

do·sis f (pl -sis) dose

dos-pie·zas m (pl -zas) two-piece bathing suit

dotación f (de una mujer; de una fundación) endowment; (nav) complement; (aer) crew; (de remeros) (sport) crew; staff, personnel

dotar tr to give a dowry to; to endow; (un buque) to man; (una oficina) to staff; to equip; to fix the wages for

dote m & f dowry, marriage portion || m (en el juego de naipes) stack of chips || f endowment, talent, gift; **dotes de mando** leadership

dovela f voussoir

doza·vo -va adj & m twelfth

d/p abbr **días plazo**

dracma *f* (*moneda griega*) drachma; (*peso farmacéutico*) dram

draga *f* dredge; (*barco*) dredger

dragado *m* dredging

dragami·nas *m* (*pl* -nas) mine sweeper

dragar §44 *tr* to dredge

dragón *m* dragon; (*planta*) snapdragon; (*soldado*) dragoon

dragonear *intr* (Am) to flirt; (Am) to boast; **dragonear de** (Am) to boast of being; (Am) to pretend to be, to pass oneself off as

drama *m* drama

dramáti·co -ca *adj* dramatic || *mf* (*autor*) dramatist; actor || *f* (*arte y género*) drama

dramatizar §60 *tr* to dramatize

dramaturgo *m* dramatist

drásti·co -ca *adj* drastic

dren *m* drain

drenaje *m* drainage

drenar *tr* to drain

driblar *tr & intr* to dribble

dril *m* drill; duck; **dril de algodón** denim

driza *f* (naut) halyard

dro. *abbr* **derecho**

droga *f* drug; annoyance, bother; deceit, trick; (Chile, Mex, Peru) bad debt; (Cuba) drug on the market; **drogas milagrosas** wonder drugs

drogado *m* doping

drogar §44 *tr* to dope

droguería *f* drug store; drug business; (*comercio de substancias usadas en química, industria, medicina, bellas artes*) drysaltery (Brit)

drogue·ro -ra *mf* druggist; drysalter (Brit)

droguista *mf* druggist; (coll) crook, cheat; (Arg) toper, drunk

droláti·co -ca *adj* droll, snappy

dromedario *m* dromedary; big heavy animal; (coll) brute (*person*)

druida *m* druid

dúa *f* (min) gang of workmen

dual *adj & m* dual

dualidad *f* duality; (Chile) tie vote

ducado *m* duchy, dukedom; (*moneda antigua*) ducat; **gran ducado** grand duchy

dúctil *adj* ductile; easy to handle

ducha *f* (*chorro de agua en una cavidad del cuerpo*) douche; (*chorro de agua sobre el cuerpo entero*) shower bath; (*lista en los tejidos*) stripe; **ducha en alfileres** needle bath

duchar *tr* to douche; to give a shower bath to || *ref* to douche; to take a shower bath

du·cho -cha *adj* experienced, expert, skillful || *f see* **ducha**

duda *f* doubt; **sin duda** doubtless, no doubt, without doubt

dudable *adj* doubtful

dudar *tr* to doubt; to question || *intr* to hesitate; **dudar de** to doubt

dudo·so -sa *adj* doubtful; dubious

duela *f* stave (*of barrel*)

duelista *m* duelist

duelo *m* (*combate entre dos*) duel; grief, sorrow; bereavement, mourning; (*los que asisten a los funerales*) mourners; **batirse en duelo** to duel, to fight a duel; **duelos** hardships; **sin duelo** in abundance

duende *m* elf, goblin; gold cloth, silver cloth; (coll) restless daemon; **tener duende** (coll) to be burning within

due·ño -ña *mf* owner, proprietor; **dueño de sí mismo** one's own master; **ser dueño de** to be master of; to be at liberty to, be free to || *m* master, landlord || *f* mistress, landlady, housekeeper; (*duenna*; matron; **dueña de casa** housewife

duermevela *f* (coll) doze, light sleep; (*sueño fatigoso o interrumpido*) fitful sleep

dula *f* common pasture land; land irrigated from common ditch

dulce *adj* sweet; (*agua*) fresh; (*metal*) soft, ductile; gentle, mild, pleasant; (*manjar*) tasteless, insipid || *m* candy; piece of candy; preserves; **dulce de almíbar** preserved fruit; **dulces** candy

dulcera *f* candy dish, preserve dish

dulcería *f* candy store, confectionery store

dulce·ro -ra *adj* (coll) sweet-toothed || *mf* confectioner || *f see* **dulcera**

dulcificar §73 *tr* to sweeten; to appease, mollify || *ref* to sweeten, turn sweet

dulcinea *f* (coll) sweetheart; (coll) ideal

dulzaina *f* flageolet

dulza·rrón -rrona *adj* (coll) cloying, sickening

dulzura *f* sweetness; pleasantness, kindliness; (*del clima*) mildness; endearment, sweet word

duna *f* dune

dun·do -da *adj* (CAm, Col) simple, stupid || *mf* (CAm, Col) simpleton

dúo *m* duet, duo

duodéci·mo -ma *adj & m* twelfth

duodeno *m* duodenum

duplica·do -da *adj & m* duplicate; **por duplicado** in duplicate

duplicar §73 *tr* to duplicate; to double; to repeat

duplicata *f* duplicate

duplicidad *f* (*falsedad*) duplicity; (*calidad de doble*) doubleness

du·plo -pla *adj & m* double

duque *m* duke; **gran duque** grand duke

duquesa *f* duchess; **gran duquesa** grand duchess

dura *f* (coll) durability; **de dura** or **de mucha dura** (coll) strong, durable

durable *adj* durable, lasting

duración *f* duration, endurance; (*espacio de tiempo del uso de una cosa*) life

durade·ro -ra *adj* durable, lasting

durante *prep* during, for

durar *intr* to last; to remain; (*la ropa*) to last, to wear, to wear well

durazno *m* peach; peach tree

dureza *f* hardness; harshness, roughness; **dureza de corazón** hardheartedness; **dureza de oído** hardness of hearing; **dureza de vientre** constipation

durmiente *adj* sleeping || *mf* sleeper || *m* girder, sleeper, stringer; (Am) tie, railroad tie; (Ven) steel bar

do
du

du·ro -ra *adj* hard; *(huevo)* hard-boiled; harsh, rough; cruel; stubborn, obstinate; unbearable; strong, tough; stingy; *(tiempo)* stormy; **duro de corazón** hard-hearted; **duro de oído** hard of hearing; **estar muy duro con** to be hard on; **ser duro de pelar** (coll) to be hard to put across; (coll) to be hard to deal with ‖ *m* dollar *(Spanish coin worth five pesetas)* ‖ *f* see **dura** ‖ **duro** *adv* hard

dux *m* (*pl* **dux**) doge

d/v *abbr* **días vista**

E

E, e (e) *f* sixth letter of the Spanish alphabet

e *conj* (used before words beginning with *i* or *hi* not followed by a vowel) and

ea *interj* hey!

ebanista *m* cabinetmaker, woodworker

ebanistería *f* cabinetmaking, woodwork; cabinetmaker's shop

ébano *m* ebony

ebriedad *f* drunkenness

e·brio -bria *adj* drunk; *(p.ej., de ira)* blind ‖ *mf* drunk

ebrio·so -sa *adj* drinking ‖ *mf* drinker

ebulición *f* boiling

eccema *m* & *f* eczema

eclécti·co -ca *adj* & *mf* eclectic

eclesiásti·co -ca *adj* & *m* ecclesiastic

eclipsar *tr* to eclipse; (fig) to outshine ‖ *ref* to be in eclipse; (fig) to disappear

eclipse *m* eclipse

eclip·sis *f* (*pl* **-sis**) var of **elipsis**

eclisa *f* (rr) fishplate

eco *m* echo; *(del tambor)* rumbling; **hacer eco** to echo; to attract attention; **tener eco** to be well received, to catch on

economato *m* stewardship; commissary, company store, coöperative store

economía *f* economy; want, poverty; **economía política** economics; **economías** savings

económi·co -ca *adj* economic; *(que gasta poco; poco costoso)* economical; cheap; miserly, niggardly

economista *mf* economist

economizar §60 *tr* to economize, to save; to avoid ‖ *intr* to economize, save; to skimp

ecónomo *m* steward, trustee; supply priest

ecuación *f* equation

ecuador *m* equator ‖ **el Ecuador** Ecuador

ecuánime *adj* calm, composed; impartial

ecuanimidad *f* equanimity; impartiality

ecuatoria·no -na *adj* & *mf* Ecuadoran, Ecuadorian

ecuestre *adj* equestrian

ecuméni·co -ca *adj* ecumenic(al)

eczema *m* & *f* eczema

echacan·tos *m* (*pl* **-tos**) (coll) good-for-nothing

echacuer·vos *m* (*pl* **-vos**) (coll) pimp, procurer; (coll) cheat

echada *f* cast, throw; man's length; (Arg, Mex) boast, hoax

echadero *m* place to stretch out

echadi·zo -za *adj* discarded, waste; spying ‖ *mf* foundling ‖ *m* spy

echa·do -da *adj* stretched out; (C-R) lazy, indolent ‖ *f* see **echada**

echar *tr* to throw, throw away, throw out; to issue, emit; to publish; to discharge, dismiss; to swallow; *(p.ej., agua)* to pour; *(p.ej., un cigarrillo)* to smoke; *(la baraja)* to deal; *(una partida de cartas)* to play; *(una llave)* to turn; *(un discurso)* to deliver; *(un drama)* to put on; *(maldiciones)* to utter; *(pelo, dientes, renuevos)* to grow, put forth; *(impuestos)* to impose, to levy; *(la buenaventura)* to tell; *(precio, distancia, edad, etc.)* to ascribe, attribute; *(una mirada)* to cast; *(sangre)* to shed; *(la culpa)* to lay; *(una mano)* to lend; **echar abajo** to demolish, destroy; to overthrow; **echar a pasear** (coll) to dismiss unceremoniously; **echar a perder** to spoil, to ruin; **echar a pique** to sink; **echar de menos** to miss; **echarla de** (coll) to claim to be, boast of being; **echarlo todo a rodar** (coll) to upset everything; (coll) to hit the ceiling ‖ *intr* — **echar a** to begin to; to burst out *(e.g., crying)*; **echar a perder** to spoil, to ruin; **echar de ver** to notice, to happen to see; **echar por** *(un empleo, un oficio)* to go into, take up; *(la derecha, la izquierda)* to turn toward; *(un camino)* to go down ‖ *ref* to throw oneself; to lie down, stretch out; *(el viento)* to fall; *(un abrigo)* to throw on; *(una gallina)* to set; **echarse a** to begin to; **echarse a morir** (coll) to give up in despair; **echarse a perder** to spoil, to be ruined; **echarse atrás** to back out; **echarse de ver** to be easy to see; **echárselas de** to claim to be, to boast of being; **echarse sobre** to rush at, fall upon

echazón *f* jettison, jetsam

echiquier *m* Exchequer

ecología *f* ecology

edad *f* age; **edad crítica** change of life; **edad de quintas** draft age; **Edad Media** Middle Ages; **edad viril** prime of life; **mayor edad** majority; **menor edad** minority

edecán *m* aide-de-camp

edición *f* edition; publication; **la segun-**

da edición de (coll) the spit and image of
edicto *m* edict
edificación *f* construction, building; buildings; (*inspiración con el buen ejemplo*) edification, uplift
edificante *adj* edifying
edificar §73 *tr* to construct, build; (*dar buen ejemplo a*) to edify, to uplift
edificio *m* edifice, building
editar *tr* to publish
edi·tor -tora *adj* publishing || *mf* publisher
editorial *adj* publishing; editorial || *m* editorial || *f* publishing house
editorialista *mf* (Am) editorial writer
editorializar §60 *intr* (Urug) to editorialize
edredón *m* eider down
educación *f* education
educacional *adj* educational
educa·dor -dora *mf* educator
educan·do -da *mf* pupil, student
educar §73 *tr* to educate; (*los sentidos*) to train; (*al niño o el adolescente*) to rear, to bring up
educati·vo -va *adj* educational
EE.UU. *abbr* **Estados Unidos**
efectismo *m* sensationalism
efectista *adj* sensational, theatrical || *mf* sensationalist
efectivamente *adv* actually, really; as a matter of fact
efecti·vo -va *adj* actual, real; (*empleo, cargo*) regular, permanent; (*vigente*) effective; **hacer efectivo** to carry out; (*un cheque*) to cash; **hacerse efectivo** to become effective || *m* cash; **efectivo en caja** cash on hand
efecto *m* effect; end, purpose; article; (*en el juego de billar*) English; **a ese efecto** for that purpose; **al efecto** for the purpose; **con efecto** or **en efecto** indeed, as a matter of fact; **efecto útil** efficiency, output; **llevar a efecto** or **poner en efecto** to put into effect, to carry out; **surtir efecto** to work, to have the desired effect
efectuar §21 *tr* to carry out, to effect, to effectuate || *ref* to take place
efervescencia *f* effervescence
efervescente *adj* effervescent
eficacia *f* efficacy
efi·caz *adj* (*pl* **-caces**) efficacious, effectual; efficient
eficiencia *f* efficiency
eficiente *adj* efficient
efigie *f* effigy
efíme·ro -ra *adj* ephemeral
efugio *m* evasion, subterfuge
efusión *f* effusion; (*manifestación de afectos muy viva*) warmth, effusiveness; **efusión de sangre** bloodshed
efusi·vo -va *adj* effusive
égida *f* aegis
egip·cio -cia *adj* & *mf* Egyptian
Egipto *m* Egypt
eglantina *f* sweetbriar
eglefino *m* haddock
égloga *f* eclogue
egoísmo *m* egoism
egoísta *adj* egoistic || *mf* egoist
egotismo *m* egotism

egotista *adj* egotistic(al) || *mf* egotist
egre·gio -gia *adj* distinguished, eminent
egresar *intr* (Am) to graduate
egreso *m* departure; (Am) graduation
eje *m* (*pieza alrededor de la cual gira un cuerpo*) axle, shaft; (*línea que divide en dos mitades; línea recta alrededor de la cual se supone que gira un cuerpo*) axis; (fig) core, crux; **eje de balancín** rocker, rockershaft; **eje de carretón** axletree; **eje motor** drive shaft
ejecución *f* execution
ejecutante *mf* performer
ejecutar *tr* to execute; to perform
ejecutivamente *adv* expeditiously
ejecuti·vo -va *adj* urgent, pressing; insistent; executive || *m* (Am) executive
ejecu·tor -tora *adj* executive || *mf* executor; **ejecutor de la justicia** executioner; **ejecutor testamentario** executor (*of a will*) || *f* — **ejecutora testamentaria** executrix
ejemplar *adj* exemplary || *m* pattern, model; (*de una obra impresa*) copy; precedent; (*caso que sirve de escarmiento*) example; **ejemplar de cortesía** complimentary copy; **ejemplar muestra** sample copy; **sin ejemplar** unprecedented; as a special case
ejemplarizar §60 *tr* (Am) to set an example to; (Am) to exemplify
ejemplificar §73 *tr* to exemplify
ejemplo *m* example, instance; **por ejemplo** for example, for instance; **sin ejemplo** unexampled
ejercer §78 *tr* (*la medicina*) to practice; (*la caridad*) to show, exercise; (*una fuerza*) to exert || *intr* to practice; **ejercer de** to practice as, to work as
ejercicio *m* exercise; drill, practice; (*de un cargo u oficio*) tenure; (*uso constante*) exertion; (*año económico*) fiscal year; **hacer ejercicio** to take exercise; (mil) to drill
ejercitar *tr* to exercise; to practice; to drill, to train || *ref* to exercise; to practice
ejército *m* army; **ejército permanente** standing army; **los tres ejércitos** the three arms of the service
ejido *m* commons
ejote *m* (CAm, Mex) string bean
el, la (*pl* **los, las**) *art def* the || *pron dem* that, the one; **el que** who, which, that; he who, the one that
él *pron pers masc* he, it; him, it
elabora·do -da *adj* elaborate; finished
elaborar *tr* to elaborate; (*una teoría*) to work out; (*el metal, la madera*) to fashion, to work
elación *f* magnanimity, nobility; (*de estilo y lenguaje*) pomposity
elástica *f* knit undershirt; **elásticas** (Ven) suspenders
elasticidad *f* elasticity
elásti·co -ca *adj* elastic || *m* elastic; (Am) bedspring || *f* see **elástica**
eléboro *m* hellebore
elección *f* election; choice
electi·vo -va *adj* elective
elec·to -ta *adj* elect
electorado *m* electorate

du
el

electorero *m* henchman, heeler
electricidad *f* electricity
electricista *mf* electrician
eléctrico -ca *adj* electric(al)
electrificar §73 *tr* to electrify
electrizar §60 *tr* to electrify
electro *m* electromagnet
electroafeitadora *f* electric shaver
electrocutar *tr* to electrocute
electrodo *m* electrode
electrodoméstí·co -ca *adj* electric-household
electróge·no -na *adj* generating electricity ‖ *m* electric generator
electroimán *m* electromagnet
electrólisis *f* electrolysis
electrólito *m* electrolyte
electromagnéti·co -ca *adj* electromagnetic
electromo·tor -tora or **-triz** *adj* (*pl* **-tores -toras -trices**) electromotive
electrón *m* electron
electróni·co -ca *adj* electronic ‖ *f* electronics
electrostáti·co -ca *adj* electrostatic
electrotecnia *f* electrical engineering
electrotipo *tr* to electrotype
electrotipo *m* electrotype
elefante *m* elephant; **elefante blanco** (fig) (SAm) white elephant
elegancia *f* elegance; style, stylishness
elegante *adj* elegant; stylish ‖ *mf* fashion plate
elegía *f* elegy
elegía·co -ca *adj* elegiac
elegible *adj* eligible
elegir §57 *tr* to elect; to choose, select
elemental *adj* (*primordial; simple, no compuesto*) elemental; (*que se refiere a los principios de una ciencia o arte; de fácil comprensión*) elementary
elemento *m* element; (*de una pila o batería*) cell; **elemento de compuestos** (gram) combining form; **estar en su elemento** to be in one's element
elenco *m* catalogue, list, table; (theat) (Am) cast
elevación *f* elevation; **elevación a potencias** (math) involution
eleva·do -da *adj* elevated, high; lofty, sublime
elevador *m* (Am) elevator; **elevador de granos** (Am) grain elevator
elevar *tr* to elevate, to lift; (math) to raise ‖ *ref* to ascend, rise; to be exalted; to become conceited
elfo *m* elf
elidir *tr* to eliminate; (*una vocal*) to elide
eliminar *tr* to eliminate; to strike out
elipse *f* (geom) ellipse
elip·sis *f* (*pl* **-sis**) (gram) ellipsis
elípti·co -ca *adj* (geom & gram) elliptic(al)
elisión *f* elision
elocución *f* public speaking, elocution
elocuencia *f* eloquence
elocuente *adj* eloquent
elogiable *adj* praiseworthy
elogiar *tr* to praise, eulogize
elogio *m* praise, eulogy

elogio·so -sa *adj* (Am) laudatory, glowing
elote *m* (Mex, Guat) ear of corn; **coger asando elotes** (CAm) to catch in the act; **pagar los elotes** (CAm) to be the goat
elucidar *tr* to elucidate
eludir *tr* to elude, evade, avoid
ella *pron pers fem* she, it; her, it; (coll) the trouble
ello *pron pers neut* it; (coll) the trouble; **ello es que** the fact is that ‖ *m* (psychoanalysis) id
E.M. *abbr* **Estado Mayor**
emancipar *tr* to emancipate
embadurnamiento *m* daub, daubing
embadurnar *tr* to daub
embaír §1 *tr* to deceive, take in, hoax
embajada *f* embassy; ambassadorship; (iron) fine proposition
embajador *m* ambassador; **embajadores** ambassador and wife
embajadora *f* ambassadress
embalaje *m* packing; package; (sport) sprint
embalar *tr* to pack ‖ *intr* (sport) to sprint ‖ *ref* (*el motor*) to race; (sport) to sprint
embaldosado *m* tile paving
embaldosar *tr* to pave with tile
embalsamar *tr* to embalm; to perfume
embalsar *tr* to dam, to dam up
embalse *m* dam; damming; backwater
embanastar *tr* to put in a basket; to pack, jam, overcrowd
embanquetar *tr* (Mex) to line with sidewalks
embarazada *adj fem* pregnant ‖ *f* pregnant woman
embarazar §60 *tr* (*estorbar*) to embarrass; to obstruct; to make pregnant ‖ *ref* to be embarrassed, be encumbered; to become pregnant
embarazo *m* embarrassment; obstruction; awkwardness; pregnancy
embarazo·so -sa *adj* embarrassing, troublesome
embarbillar *tr* to rabbet
embarcación *f* boat, ship; embarkation (*of passengers*)
embarcadero *m* pier, wharf; (rr) (Am) platform; **embarcadero de ganado** (Arg) loading chute; **embarcadero flotante** landing stage
embarcador *m* shipper
embarcar §73 *tr* to ship ‖ *intr* to entrain ‖ *ref* to embark, to ship; to get involved
embarco *m* embarkation (*of passengers*)
embargar §44 *tr* to embargo; to paralyze; (law) to seize, attach
embargo *m* embargo; indigestion; (law) seizure, attachment; **sin embargo** however, nevertheless
embarnizar §60 *tr* to varnish
embarque *m* shipment, embarkation (*of freight*)
embarrada *f* (Am) blunder
embarrancar §73 *tr, intr & ref* to run into a ditch; (*una nave*) to run aground
embarrar *tr* to splash with mud; to

smear, stain; (CAm, Mex) to involve in a shady deal; **embarrarla** (Arg) to spoil the whole thing

embarrilar *tr* to barrel, put in barrels

embarullar *tr* (coll) to muddle, make a mess of; (coll) to bungle, botch

embastar *tr* to baste, to stitch

embate *m* blow, attack; (*del mar*) beating, dashing; (*de viento*) gust; **embates de la fortuna** hard knocks

embaucar §73 *tr* to trick, bamboozle, swindle

embaula·do -da *adj* crowded, packed, jammed

embaular §8 *tr* to put in a trunk; (coll) to jam, pack in

embayar *ref* (Ecuad) to fly into a rage

embazar §60 *tr* to dye brown; to hinder, obstruct; to astound, dumbfound ‖ *ref* to get bored; to be upset, get sick at the stomach

embebecer §22 *tr* to entertain, amuse, fascinate, enchant

embeber *tr* to absorb, soak up; to soak; to contain, include; to embed; to contract, shrink ‖ *intr* to contract, shrink ‖ *ref* to be enchanted, be enraptured; to become absorbed or immersed; to become well versed

embebi·do -da *adj* (*vocal*) elided; (*columna*) engaged

embelecar §73 *tr* to cheat, dupe, bamboozle

embeleco *m* cheating, fraud; (coll) bore; **embelecos** cuteness

embeleñar *tr* to dope, stupefy; to enchant, bewitch

embelesar *tr* to charm, enrapture, fascinate

embeleso *m* charm, fascination, delight

embellece·dor -dora *adj* embellishing, beautifying ‖ *m* (aut) hubcap ‖ *f* beautician

embellecer §22 *tr* to embellish, beautify

embellecimiento *m* embellishment, beautification

embermejecer §22 *tr* to dye red; to make blush ‖ *ref* to blush

emberrinchar *ref* (coll) to fly into a rage

embestida *f* attack, assault; (*detención intempestiva*) (coll) buttonholing

embesti·dor -dora *mf* (coll) beat, sponger

embestir §50 *tr* to attack, assail; to strike; (coll) to buttonhole, waylay ‖ *intr* to attack, to charge, to rush

embetunar *tr* to blacken; to cover with tar

embicar §73 *tr* (Mex) to turn upside down, to tilt ‖ *intr* (Arg, Chile) to run aground

embocadero *m* mouth, outlet

embocadura *f* nozzle; (*de río*) mouth; (*del freno; de instrumento de viento*)

mouthpiece; (*de cigarrillo*) tip; (*del vino*) taste; stage entrance

embocar §73 *tr* to catch in the mouth; to put in the mouth; to take on, undertake; (coll) to gulp down; (coll) to try to put over ‖ *intr* & *ref* to enter, pass

embolada *f* stroke

embolado *m* bull with wooden balls on horns; (theat) minor role; (coll) trick, hoax

embolar *tr* (*los cuernos del toro*) to put wooden balls on; (*el calzado*) to shine

embolia *f* embolism

émbolo *m* (mach) piston; **émbolo buzo** (mach) plunger

embolsar *tr* to pocket, take in

embonar *tr* (Am) to fertilize; (Am) to suit, be becoming to

emboquillar *tr* (*los cigarrillos*) to put tips on; (*una galería o túnel*) to cut an entrance in; (*las junturas entre los ladrillos*) (Chile) to point, to chink

emborrachar *tr* to intoxicate ‖ *ref* to get drunk; (*los colores de una tela*) to run

emborrar *tr* to stuff, pad, wad; (coll) to gulp down

emborrascar §73 *tr* to stir up, irritate ‖ *ref* to get stormy; (*un negocio*) to fail; (*la veta de una mina*) (Arg, CAm, Mex) to peter out

emborronar *tr* to blot; to scribble

emboscada *f* ambush, ambuscade

emboscado *m* draft dodger

emboscar §73 *tr* (*tropas para sorprender al enemigo*) to ambush ‖ *ref* to ambush, lie in ambush; to shirk, take an easy way out

embota·do -da *adj* blunt, dull; (Chile) black-pawed

embotadura *f* bluntness, dullness

embotar *tr* to blunt, to dull; to dull, weaken; (*el tabaco*) to put in a jar

embotellamiento *m* bottling; traffic jam

embotellar *tr* to bottle; (*un negocio*) to tie up; (nav) to bottle up

embotijar *tr* (*un suelo*) to underlay with jugs ‖ *ref* (coll) to swell up with anger

embovedar *tr* to vault, vault over; to put in a vault

emboza·do -da *adj* muffled up ‖ *mf* person muffled up to eyes

embozar §60 *tr* to muffle up to the eyes; (*p.ej., a un perro*) to muzzle; to disguise ‖ *ref* to muffle oneself up to the eyes

embozo *m* muffler, cloak held over the face; fold back (*of bed sheet*); cunning, dissimulation; **quitarse el embozo** (coll) to drop one's mask

embragar §44 *tr* (*el motor*) to engage ‖ *intr* to throw the clutch in

embrague *m* clutch; engagement

embravecer §22 *tr* to enrage, make angry ‖ *ref* to get angry; (*el mar*) to get rough

el
em

embraveci·do -da *adj* angry; rough, wild
embrear *tr* to tar, cover with tar; to calk with tar
embregar §44 *ref* to wrangle
embriagar §44 *tr* to intoxicate, make drunk; to enrapture ‖ *ref* to get drunk
embriaguez *f* drunkenness; rapture
embridar *tr* to bridle; to check, restrain
embriología *f* embriology
embrión *m* embryo
embroca *f* poultice
embrocar §73 *tr* to empty; (*el toro al torero*) to catch between the horns ‖ *ref* (C-R) to fall on one's face; (Mex) to put on over the head
embrollar *tr* to tangle, muddle, embroil
embrollo *m* entanglement, muddle, embroilment; deception, trick
embromar *tr* to joke with, play jokes on; (Am) to bore, annoy ‖ *ref* (Am) to be bored, be annoyed
embrujar *tr* to bewitch
embrutecer §22 *tr* to brutify, stupefy
embuchado *m* pork sausage; subterfuge; (*de la urna electoral*) stuffing (of ballot box)
embudar *tr* to put a funnel in; to trick, trap
embudista *adj* tricky, scheming ‖ *mf* schemer
embudo *m* funnel; trick; (mil) shell hole; **embudo de bomba** (mil) bomb crater
embullar *tr* to stir up, excite, key up ‖ *ref* to become excited, keyed up
emburujar *tr* to jumble, pile up ‖ *ref* (Am) to wrap oneself up
embuste *m* lie, falsehood, trick; **embustes** baubles, trinkets; (*del niño*) cuteness
embuste·ro -ra *adj* lying, false, tricky ‖ *mf* liar, cheat
embuti·do -da *adj* inlaid, flush ‖ *m* inlay, marquetry; pork sausage; (Am) lace insertion
embutir *tr* to stuff, pack tight; to insert; to inlay; to set flush; (*una hoja de metal*) to fashion, to hammer into shape ‖ *ref* to squeeze in; (coll) to stuff oneself
emergencia *f* emergence; incident
emerger §17 *intr* to emerge; (*un submarino*) to surface
emersión *f* emersion; (*de un submarino*) surfacing
eméti·co -ca *adj* & *m* emetic
emigración *f* emigration; migration
emigra·do -da *mf* émigré
emigrante *adj* & *mf* emigrant
emigrar *intr* to emigrate; to migrate
eminencia *f* eminence
eminente *adj* eminent
emisa·rio -ria *mf* emissary ‖ *m* outlet
emisión *f* (*acción de exhalar; acción de lanzar ondas luminosas, etc.*) emission; (*títulos creados de una vez*) (com) issue; (*acción de emitir títulos nuevos*) (com) issuance; (rad) broadcast; **emisión seriada** (rad) serial
emi·sor -sora *adj* emitting; broadcast-

ing ‖ *m* (rad) transmitter ‖ *f* broadcasting station
emitir *tr* to emit, send forth; to issue, give out; (*p.ej., opiniones*) to utter, express; (com) to issue; (rad) to broadcast
emoción *f* emotion
emocional *adj* emotional
emocionante *adj* moving, touching; thrilling, exciting
emocionar *tr* to move, stir; to thrill
emoti·vo -va *adj* emotional
empacadi·zo -za *adj* (Arg) touchy
empaca·do -da *adj* (Arg) gruff, grim
empacar §73 *tr* to pack, to crate ‖ *ref* to be stubborn; (*un animal*) (Am) to balk, get balky
empa·cón -cona *adj* (Am) stubborn; (Am) balky
empacha·do -da *adj* backward, fumbling
empachar *tr* to hinder, embarrass; to disguise; to surfeit, upset the stomach of ‖ *ref* to blush, be embarrassed; to be upset, have indigestion
empacho *m* hindrance; embarrassment, bashfulness; indigestion
empacho·so -sa *adj* sickening; shameful
empadronar *tr* to register, to take the census of ‖ *ref* to register, be registered in the census
empalagar §44 *tr* to cloy, pall, surfeit; to bore, to weary
empalago·so -sa *adj* cloying, sickening, mawkish; boring, annoying; fawning
empalar *tr* impale
empalizada *f* palisade, stockade, fence
empalizar §60 *tr* to fence in
empalmar *tr* to splice, connect, join, couple; to combine ‖ *intr* to connect, make connections; **empalmar con** to connect with; to follow, succeed
empalme *m* splice, connection, joint, coupling; combination; (elec) joint; (rr) connection, junction
empanada *f* pie; fraud
empanadilla *f* pie
empana·do -da *adj* unlighted, unventilated ‖ *f* see **empanada**
empanar *tr* to crumb, to bread; (*las tierras*) to sow with wheat
empantanar *tr* to flood; to obstruct
empañar *tr* (*a las criaturas*) to swaddle; to blur, fog, dim, dull; to tarnish, sully ‖ *ref* to blur, fog, dim, dull
empañe·do -da *adj* dim, misty; blurred, fogged; (*voz*) flat
empañetar *tr* (Am) to plaster
empapar *tr* to soak; to soak up, absorb; to drench ‖ *ref* to soak; to be soaked; to become imbued; (coll) to be surfeited
empapelado *m* papering, paper hanging; wallpaper; paper lining
empapela·dor -dora *mf* paper hanger
empapelar *tr* to wrap in paper; to paper, line with paper; to wallpaper; (coll) to bring a criminal charge against
empaque *m* packing; (coll) look, appearance, mien; stiffness, stuffiness; (Am) brazenness
empaquetadura *f* gasket

empaquetar *tr* to pack; to jam, stuff ‖ *ref* to pack; to pack in; (coll) to dress up

empareda·do -da *mf* recluse ‖ *m* sandwich

emparedar *tr* to wall in, to confine

emparejar *tr* to pair, to match; to smooth, make level; to even, make even; (*una puerta*) to close flush ‖ *intr* to come up, come abreast; **emparejar con** to catch up with ‖ *ref* to pair, to match

emparentar §2 *intr* to become related by marriage; **emparentar con** (*buena gente*) to marry into the family of; (*una familia rica*) to marry into

emparrado *m* arbor, bower

emparrillar *tr* to grill

empasta·dor -dora *mf* (Am) bookbinder

empastadura *f* (Am) binding

empastar *tr* (*un diente*) to fill; (*un libro*) to bind with stiff covers; (Am) to convert into pasture land ‖ *ref* (Chile) to be overgrown with weeds

empaste *m* (*de diente*) filling; stiff binding

empastelar *tr* (typ) to pie

empatar *tr* (*en la votación y los juegos*) to tie; (Am) to join, connect; (Am) to tie, fasten ‖ *intr* to tie ‖ *ref* to tie; **empatársela a una persona** to be a match for someone; **empatárselo a una persona** (Guat, Hond) to put it over on someone

empate *m* tie, draw; (Col) penholder; (Ven) waste of time

empavar *tr* (Ecuad) to annoy; (Peru) to kid, to razz

empavesado *m* (naut) dressing, bunting

empavesar *tr* to bedeck with flags and bunting; (*un buque*) to dress; (*un monumento*) to veil ‖ *ref* to become overcast

empavonar *tr* to blue; (Am) to grease, spread grease over ‖ *ref* (CAm) to dress up

empecina·do -da *adj* (Am) stubborn

empederni·do -da *adj* hardened, inveterate; hard-hearted

empedra·do -da *adj* cloud-flecked; pock-marked; (*caballo*) dark-spotted ‖ *m* stone paving

empedrar §2 *tr* to pave with stones; to bespatter

empegado *m* tarpaulin

empegar §44 *tr* to coat with pitch, to dip in pitch; (*el ganado lanar*) to mark with pitch

empeine *m* instep; (*de la bota*) vamp; (*enfermedad cutánea*) tetter; (*región central del hipogastrio*) pubes

empelotar *ref* (coll) to get all tangled up; (coll) to get into a row; (Am) to take all one's clothes off; (Mex, W-I) to fall madly in love

empella *f* vamp

empellar *tr* to push, shove

empeller §31 *tr* to push, shove

empellón *m* push, shove; **a empellones** pushing, roughly

empenachar *tr* to adorn with plumes

empeña·do -da *adj* (*disputa*) bitter, heated; **no empeñado** noncommitted

empeñar *tr* (*dar en prenda*) to pawn; (*una lucha*) to launch, begin; (*prendar, hipotecar*) to pledge; (*la palabra*) to pledge; to force, compel ‖ *ref* to commit oneself, bind oneself; to go into debt; (*una lucha, una disputa*) to begin, to start; **empeñarse** in to engage in; to persist in, insist on

empeñe·ro -ra *mf* (Mex) pawnbroker

empeño *m* pledge, engagement, commitment; (*prenda*) pawn; pawnshop; persistence, insistence; eagerness, perseverance; effort, endeavor; pledge, backer, patron; favor, protection; **con empeño** eagerly

empeño·so -sa *adj* (Am) eager, persistent

empeorar *tr* to impair, make worse ‖ *intr & ref* to get worse, deteriorate

empequeñecer §22 *tr* (*hacer más pequeño*) to make smaller, to dwarf; (*amenguar la importancia de*) to belittle ‖ *ref* to get smaller, to dwarf

emperador *m* emperor; **los emperadores** the emperor and empress

empera·triz *f* (*pl* -**trices**) empress

emperchar *tr* to hang on a clothes rack

emperejilar *tr & ref* (coll) to dress up, to spruce up

emperezar §60 *tr* to delay, put off ‖ *intr & ref* to get lazy

empericar §73 *ref* (Col, Ecuad) to get drunk; (Mex) to blush

emperifollar *tr & ref* to dress up gaudily

empernar *tr* to bolt

empero *conj* but, however, yet

emperrar *ref* (coll) to get stubborn

empezar §18 *tr & intr* to begin

empicar §73 *ref* to become infatuated

empicotar *tr* to pillory

empiema *m* empyema

empina·do -da *adj* high, lofty; steep; stiff, stuck-up ‖ *f* (aer) zoom, zooming; **irse a la empinada** (*un caballo*) to rear

empinar *tr* to raise, lift; to tip over; (aer) to zoom; (*el codo*) (coll) to crook ‖ *intr* to be a toper ‖ *ref* to stand on tiptoe; (*un caballo*) to rear; to tower, rise high; (aer) to zoom

empingorota·do -da *adj* influential; (coll) proud, haughty

empingorotar *tr* (coll) to put on top ‖ *ref* (coll) to climb up, get up; (coll) to be stuck-up

empíre·o -a *adj & m* empyrean

empíri·co -ca *adj* empiric(al) ‖ *mf* empiricist

empizarrado *m* slate roof

empizarrar *tr* to roof with slate

emplastar *tr* to put a plaster on; to put make-up on; (*un negocio*) to tie up, obstruct ‖ *ref* to put make-up on; to smear oneself up

emplásti·co -ca *adj* sticky

emplasto *m* plaster, poultice

emplazamiento *m* emplacement, location; (law) summons

emplazar §60 *tr* to place, locate; to summon, to summons

emplea·do -da *mf* employee; (*de ofi-*

cina, de tienda) clerk; **empleado público** civil servant

emplear *tr* to employ; to use; (*el dinero*) to invest; **estarle a uno bien empleado** (coll) to serve someone right || *ref* to be employed; to busy oneself; **empleárselo mal** (coll) to act up, to misbehave

empleo *m* employ, employment; use; job, position, occupation

empleomanía *f* (coll) eagerness to hold public office

empleóma·no -na *mf* (Am) public officeholder, bureaucrat

emplomar *tr* to lead; to line with lead; (*un techo*) to cover with lead; to put a lead seal on; (*un diente*) (Arg) to fill

emplumar *tr* to put a feather on; to adorn with feathers; to tar and feather; (Hond) to thrash; **emplumarlas** (Col) to beat it || *intr* to fledge, grow feathers

emplumecer §22 *intr* to fledge, grow feathers

empobrecer §22 *tr* to impoverish || *intr & ref* to become poor

empodrecer §22 *intr & ref* to rot

empolva·do -da *adj* (Mex) rusty

empolvar *tr* to cover with dust; (*el rostro*) to powder || *ref* to get dusty; (*el rostro*) (Mex) to get rusty

empolla·do -da *adj* primed for an examination

empollar *tr* (*huevos*) to brood, hatch; (*estudiar con mucha detención*) (coll) to bone up on || *intr* to grind, be a grind; **empollar sobre** (coll) to bone up on || *ref* to hatch; to bone up on

empo·llón -llona *mf* (coll) grind

emponcha·do -da *adj* (SAm) poncho-wearing; (SAm) crafty, hypocritical; (SAm) suspicious-looking

emponzoñar *tr* to poison; to corrupt

emporcar §81 *tr* to soil, to dirty

empotra·do -da *adj* built-in; recessed

empotrar *tr* to embed, recess, fasten in a wall || *intr & ref* to fit, interlock

emprende·dor -dora *adj* enterprising

emprender *tr* to undertake; **emprenderla con** (coll) to squabble with, have it out with; **emprenderla para** (coll) to set out for

empreñar *tr* to make pregnant || *ref* to become pregnant

empresa *f* enterprise, undertaking; company, concern, firm; device, motto; (*la parte patronal*) management; **empresa anunciadora** advertising agency; **empresa de tranvías** traction company; **pequeña empresa** small business

empresarial *adj* managerial

empresa·rio -ria *mf* contractor; business leader, industrialist; manager; promoter; theatrical manager; **empresario de circo** showman; **empresario de pompas fúnebres** undertaker; **empresario de publicidad** advertising man; **empresario de teatro** impresario, theater manager

emprestar *tr* to borrow

empréstito *m* loan, government loan

empujar *tr* to push, to shove; to replace || *intr* to push, to shove

empujatierra *f* bulldozer

empuje *m* push; (*fuerza o presión ejercidas por una cosa sobre otra*) thrust; (*espíritu emprendedor*) enterprise, push

empujón *m* hard push, shove; **tratar a empujones** (coll) to push around

empuñadura *f* (*de la espada*) hilt; (coll) first words of a story; (*de bastón o paraguas*) (Am) handle

empuñar *tr* to seize, grasp, clutch; (*un empleo o puesto*) to obtain; (*la mano*) (Chile) to clench; (Bol) to punch; **empuñar el bastón** (fig) to seize the reins

emular *tr & intr* to emulate; **emular con** to emulate, vie with

ému·lo -la *adj* emulous || *mf* rival

emulsión *f* emulsion

emulsionar *tr* to emulsify

en *prep* at; in; into; by; on; of, e.g., **pensar en** to think of

enaceitar *tr* to oil || *ref* to get oily, get rancid

enagua *f* petticoat; (Am) skirt; **enaguas** petticoat

enagüillas *fpl* kilt, short skirt

enajenación *f* alienation; estrangement; rapture; (*distracción*) absent-mindedness; **enajenación mental** mental derangement

enajenar *tr* (*la propiedad, el dominio; a un amigo*) to alienate, estrange; to enrapture, to transport || *ref* to be enraptured, to be transported; **enajenarse de** to dispossess oneself of; (*un amigo*) to become alienated from

enaltecer §22 *tr* to exalt, extol

enamoradi·zo -za *adj* susceptible

enamora·do -da *adj* lovesick; (*propenso a enamorarse*) susceptible || *mf* sweetheart || *m* lover

enamorar *tr* to make love to; to enamor, captivate || *ref* to fall in love

enamoricar §73 *ref* (coll) to trifle in love

enangostar *tr & ref* to narrow

ena·no -na *adj* dwarfish || *mf* dwarf

enarbolar *tr* to hoist, hang out; (*una espada*) to brandish || *ref* to get angry; (*el caballo*) to rear

enarcar §73 *tr* to arch; (*los toneles*) to hoop || *ref* to become confused, be bashful; (*el caballo*) (Mex) to rear

enardecer §22 *tr* to inflame, excite || *ref* to get excited; (*una parte del cuerpo*) to become inflamed, get sore

enarenar *tr* to throw sand on || *ref* (naut) to run aground

enastar *tr* (*una herramienta*) to put a handle on; (*una bandera*) to put a shaft on

encabalgamiento *m* gun carriage; trestlework; (*en el verso*) enjambment

encabalgar §44 *tr* to provide with horses || *intr* to lean, to rest

encaballar *tr* to overlap; (typ) to pie

encabezamiento *m* heading; (*fórmula con que comienza un documento*) opening words; tax list; tax rate; **encabezamiento de factura** billhead

encabezar §60 *tr* (*un escrito*) to put a heading or title on; to head; to register; (*vinos*) to fortify

encabritar *ref* (*un caballo*) to rear; (*un buque*) to shoot up, pitch up; (*un avión*) to nose up

encadenar *tr* to chain, put in chains; to brace, buttress; to bind, tie together; to tie down

encajar *tr* to fit, fit in, make fit; to insert, put in; (*un golpe*) to give, let go; (*dinero*) to put away; (*un chiste*) to tell at the wrong time; to palm off; to throw, hurl; **encajar una cosa a uno** to foist something on someone, to palm something off on someone || *intr* to fit; (*una puerta*) to close right || *ref* to squeeze one's way; (*una prenda de vestir*) to put on; (coll) to butt in, to intrude

encaje *m* (*tejido de mallas*) lace; (*labor de taracea*) inlay, mosaic; recess, groove; fitting, matching; insertion; appearance, look

encaje·ro -ra *mf* lacemaker; lace dealer

encajonado *m* cofferdam

encajonar *tr* to box, crate, case; to squeeze in || *ref* (*un río*) to narrow, narrow down; to squeeze in, squeeze through

encalambrar *ref* (Am) to get cramps

encalar *tr* (*espolvorear con cal*) to lime, sprinkle with lime; (*blanquear con cal*) to whitewash

encalma·do -da *adj* (*mercado de valores*) dull, quiet; (*mar, viento*) becalmed

encalvecer §22 *intr* to get bald

encalladero *m* sand bank, shoal

encallar *intr* to run aground; to fail, get stuck

encallecer §22 *intr* (*la piel*) to become callous || *ref* to become callous; (fig) to become callous, become hardened

encamar *tr* to spread out on the ground || *ref* (coll) to take to bed; (*el grano*) to droop, bend over

encaminar *tr* to direct, show the way to; (*sus esfuerzos, su atención*) to direct || *ref* to set out

encanalar *tr* to channel, to pipe

encandecer §22 *tr* to make white-hot

encandila·do -da *adj* (*sombrero*) cocked; (coll) stiff, erect

encandilar *tr* to daze, befuddle; (*un fuego*) to stir || *ref* (*los ojos*) to flash

encanecer §22 *intr* & *ref* to turn gray; to get old; to become moldy

encanta·do -da *adj* (coll) absent-minded, distracted; (*casa*) (coll) rambling

encanta·dor -dora *adj* charming, enchanting || *mf* charmer || *f* enchantress

encantamiento *m* charm, enchantment

encantar *tr* to charm, enchant, bewitch

encante *m* auction sale; auction house

encanto *m* charm, enchantment, spell

encantusar *tr* (coll) to coax, wheedle

encañada *f* gorge, ravine

encañar *tr* (*el agua*) to pipe; (*las tie-*

rras) to drain; (*las plantas*) to prop up; to wind on a spool

encañizada *f* reed fence; weir

encañonar *tr* to pipe; to wind on a spool; (*un pliego*) (typ) to tip in

encaperuzar §60 *tr* to put a hood on || *ref* to put on one's hood

encapotar *tr* to cloak || *ref* to frown; to cloud over, become overcast

encaprichar *ref* to insist on getting one's way; to become infatuated

encaracolado *m* spiral ornament, spiral work

encara·do -da *adj* — **bien encarado** well-featured; **mal encarado** ill-featured

encaramar *tr* to raise up, lift up; to praise, extol; (coll) to elevate, exalt || *ref* to climb, get on top; to rise, to tower; (Am) to blush

encarar *tr* to aim, point; (*una dificultad*) to face || *intr* & *ref* to come face to face

encarcelar *tr* to incarcerate, imprison, jail; (*piezas de madera recién encoladas*) to clamp; to plaster in || *ref* to stay indoors

encarecer §22 *tr* (*el precio*) to raise; to raise the price of; to extol; to urge; to overrate || *intr* & *ref* to rise, to rise in price

encarecidamente *adv* earnestly, insistently, eagerly

encarga·do -da *mf* agent, representative; **encargado de negocios** chargé d'affaires

encargar §44 *tr* (*mercancías*) to order; (*confiar*) to entrust; to urge, to warn || *ref* to take charge, be in charge

encargo *m* assignment, job, charge; (*pedido*) order; warning; **como de encargo** or **ni de encargo** (coll) just the thing, as if made to order

encariñar *tr* to awaken love in || *ref* — **encariñarse con** to become fond of, become attached to

encarnación *f* incarnation, embodiment

encarna·do -da *adj* red; flesh-colored; (*de forma humana*) incarnate

encarnar *tr* to incarnate, to embody; (*el anzuelo*) to bait || *intr* to become incarnate; (*una herida*) to heal over

encarnecer §22 *intr* to put on flesh

encarniza·do -da *adj* bloodshot; bloody, fierce, bitter, hard-fought

encarnizar §60 *tr* to anger, provoke || *ref* to get angry; to become fierce; **encarnizarse con** or **en** to be merciless to

encaro *m* aim; stare; blunderbuss

encarrilar *tr* to put back on the rails; to set right, to put on the right track; to guide, direct

encarruja·do -da *adj* wrinkled; (*pelo*) kinky; (*terreno*) (Mex) rough

encartar *tr* to enroll, register; to outlaw; (*un naipe*) to slip in || *ref* to be unable to discard

encartonar *tr* to cover with cardboard; (*libros*) to bind in boards

encasar *tr* (*un hueso dislocado*) to set (*a broken bone*)

encasillado *m* set of pigeonholes; (*lista*

em
en

de candidatos apoyados por el gobierno) government slate; (SAm) checkerwork

encasillar *tr* to pigeonhole; to sort out, classify; (*el gobierno a un candidato*) to slate

encasquetar *tr* (*un sombrero*) to stick on the head; (*una idea*) to drive in; to force on

encasquillar *tr* to put a tip on; (*un caballo*) (Am) to shoe ‖ *ref* to stick, get stuck

encastilla·do -da *adj* haughty, proud

encastillar *tr* to fortify with castles; to pile up ‖ *ref* to stick, get stuck; to take to the hills; to stick to one's opinion

encastrar *tr* to engage, to mesh

encastre *m* engaging, meshing; groove, socket; insert

encauchar *tr* to cover with rubber, line with rubber

encausar *tr* to prosecute, to sue, to bring to trial

encausticar §73 *tr* to wax

encáustico *m* floor wax, furniture polish

encauzar §60 *tr* (*una corriente*) to channel; to guide, direct

encavar *ref* to hide, burrow

encebollado *m* beef stew with onions

encelar *tr* to make jealous ‖ *ref* to get jealous; to be in rut

encella *f* cheese mold

encenagar §44 *ref* to get covered with mud; to wallow in vice

encencerrar *tr* (*al ganado*) to put a bell on

encendada *f* kindling, brush

encendedor *m* lighter; **encendedor de bolsillo** pocket lighter

encender §51 *tr* to light, kindle; to ignite, set fire to; (*la luz, la radio*) to turn on; (*la lengua*) to burn; to stir up, excite ‖ *ref* to catch fire, to ignite; to become excited; to blush

encendi·do -da *adj* bright, high-colored; red, flushed; boiled; keen, enthusiastic ‖ *m* ignition

encenizar §60 *tr* to cover with ashes ‖ *ref* to get covered with ashes

encepar *tr* to put in the stocks ‖ *intr* & *ref* to take deep root

encera·do -da *adj* wax, wax-colored; (*huevo*) boiled ‖ *m* oilcloth; tarpaulin; (*pizarra*) blackboard

encerar *tr* to wax ‖ *intr* & *ref* (*el grano*) to ripen, turn yellow

encerotar *tr* (*el hilo*) to wax

encerradero *m* sheepfold; (taur) bull pen

encerrar §2 *tr* to shut in; to lock in, lock up; to contain, include; to encircle; to imply ‖ *ref* to lock oneself in; to go into seclusion; **encerrarse con** to be closeted with

encespedar *tr* to sod

encía *f* gum

encíclica *f* encyclical

enciclopedia *f* encyclopedia

enciclopédi·co -ca *adj* encyclopedic

encierro *m* locking up, confinement; inclusion; encirclement; lockup, prison;

solitary confinement; retirement, retreat; (taur) bull pen

encima *adv* above, overhead, on top; at hand, here now; besides, in addition; **de encima** (Chile) in the bargain; **echarse encima** to take upon oneself; **encima de** on, upon; above, over; **por encima** hastily, superficially; **por encima de** above, over; in spite of; **quitarse de encima** to get rid of, to shake off

encina *f* holm oak, evergreen oak

encinta *adj* pregnant

encintado *m* curb

encintar *tr* to trim with ribbons; to provide with curbs

enclaustrar *tr* to cloister; to hide away

enclavar *tr* to nail; to pierce, transfix; (*el pie del caballo*) to prick; (coll) to cheat

enclave *m* enclave

enclavijar *tr* to dowel; (*un instrumento*) to peg

enclenque *adj* sickly, feeble

enclíti·co -ca *adj* & *m* enclitic

enclocar §81 *intr* & *ref* to brood

encofrado *m* planking, timbering; (*para el hormigón*) form

encoger §17 *tr* to shrink, shrivel; to discourage; to draw in ‖ *intr* to shrink, shrivel ‖ *ref* to shrink, shrivel; to be discouraged; to be bashful; (*humillarse*) to cringe; (*en la cama*) to curl up; **encogerse de hombros** to shrug one's shoulders

encogi·do -da *adj* bashful, timid

encogimiento *m* shrinkage; crouch; bashfulness, timidity; **encogimiento de hombros** shrug

encojar *tr* to cripple, to lame ‖ *ref* to become lame; (coll) to feign illness

encolar *tr* to glue; (*la superficie que ha de pintarse*) to size; (*el vino*) to clarify; (*p.ej., una pelota*) to throw out of reach

encolerizar §60 *tr* to anger ‖ *ref* to get angry

encomendar §2 *tr* to commend, entrust, commit; to knight ‖ *ref* to commend oneself; to send regards

encomiar *tr* to praise, extol

encomienda *f* charge, commission; commendation, praise; favor, protection; knight's cross; royal land grant (*with Indian inhabitants*); (Am) parcel post; (Mex) fruit stand

encomio *m* encomium

enconamiento *m* soreness; rancor, ill will

enconar *tr* to make sore, inflame; to aggravate, irritate ‖ *ref* to get sore, become inflamed; (*una herida; el ánimo de uno*) to rankle, to fester

encono *m* rancor, ill will; (Col, Chile, Mex, W-I) soreness

encono·so -sa *adj* sore, sensitive; harmful; rancorous

encontra·do -da *adj* opposite, facing; contrary; hostile; **estar encontrados** to be at odds

encontrar *tr* to encounter, to meet; (*ha-*

llar) to find ‖ *intr* to meet; to collide ‖ *ref* to meet, meet each other; to be, be situated; to find oneself; **encontrarse con** to meet, run into

encontrón *m* bump, jolt, collision

encopeta·do -da *adj* aristocratic, of noble descent; conceited, boastful

encorajar *tr* to encourage ‖ *ref* to fly into a rage

encorajinar *ref* (coll) to fly into a rage; (Chile) to break up, go to ruin

encorchar *tr* (*botellas*) to cork; (*abejas*) to hive

encordar §61 *tr* (*un violín, una raqueta*) to string; to wrap, wind up with string

encordelar *tr* to string; to tie with strings

encornudar *tr* to cuckold, make a cuckold of ‖ *intr* to grow horns

encorralar *tr* to corral

encortinar *tr* to curtain

encorvada *f* stoop, bending over; **hacer la encorvada** (coll) to malinger

encorvar *tr* to bend over ‖ *ref* to stoop, bend over; to be partial, be biased

encovar §61 *tr & ref* to hide away

encrespar *tr* to curl; (*el pelo*) to make stand on end; (*plumas*) to ruffle; (*las olas*) to stir up; to irritate, anger ‖ *ref* to curl; to bristle, stand on end; (*el mar, las olas*) to get rough; to get involved; to bristle, get angry

encresta·do -da *adj* proud, haughty

encrucijada *f* crossroads, street intersection; ambush, snare, trap

encrudecer §22 *tr* to make raw; to aggravate

encuadernación *f* bookbinding; (*taller*) bindery; **encuadernación a la holandesa** half binding

encuaderna·dor -dora *mf* bookbinder

encuadernar *tr* to bind; **sin encuadernar** unbound

encuadrar *tr* (*encerrar en un marco o cuadro*) to frame; (*incluir dentro de sí*) to encompass; (*encajar*) to insert, fit in; (Arg) to summarize

encuadre *m* film adaptation; (mov & telv) frame

encubar *tr* to put in a cask or vat; (min) to shore up

encubierta *f* fraud, deception

encubrimiento *m* concealment; (law) complicity

encubrir §83 *tr* to hide, conceal ‖ *ref* to hide; to disguise oneself

encuentro *m* encounter, meeting; clash, collision; (*hallazgo*) find; (sport) game, match; **encuentro fronterizo** border clash; **llevarse de encuentro** (CAm, Mex, W-I) to knock down, run over; (CAm, Mex, W-I) to drag down to ruin; **mal encuentro** foul play; **salir al encuentro a** to go to meet; to get ahead of; to take a stand against

encuerar *tr* (Am) to strip of clothes; (Am) to fleece ‖ *ref* (Am) to strip, get undressed

encuesta *f* inquiry; (*cuestionario para conocer la opinión pública*) poll, survey

encuitar *ref* to grieve

encumbra·do -da *adj* high, lofty; sublime; influential

encumbramiento *m* height, elevation; exaltation

encumbrar *tr* to raise, elevate; to exalt ‖ *ref* to rise; to be exalted; to be proud; to be flowery, use flowery speech; (*subir una cosa a mucha altura*) to tower

encunar *tr* to cradle; to catch between the horns

encurtido *m* pickle

encurtir *tr* to pickle

enchapado *m* veneer

enchapar *tr* to veneer

encharcar §73 *tr* to make a puddle of; (*el estómago*) to upset ‖ *ref* to turn into a puddle; to wallow in vice

enchavetar *tr* to key

enchilada *f* (Guat, Mex) corn cake with tomato sauce seasoned with chili

enchilado *m* (Cuba, Mex) shellfish stew with chili sauce

enchinar *tr* to pave with pebbles; (Mex) to curl ‖ *ref* (Mex) to get goose flesh

enchispar *tr* (Am) to make drunk ‖ *ref* (Am) to get drunk

enchivar *ref* (Col, Ecuad, CAm) to fly into a rage

enchufar *tr* (*un tubo o caño*) to fit; (*dos tubos o caños*) to connect, connect together; (*dos negocios*) to merge; (elec) to connect, plug in ‖ *intr* to fit ‖ *ref* to merge

enchufe *m* fitting; (*de tubo o caño*) male end; (*de dos tubos*) joint; (elec) connector; (elec) plug; (elec) receptacle; (coll) sinecure, easy job; **tener enchufe** (coll) to have pull, to have a drag

enchufismo *m* (coll) spoils system

enchufista *m* (coll) spoilsman

ende *adv* — **por ende** therefore

endeble *adj* feeble, weak; worthless

endecha *f* dirge

endechadera *f* hired mourner

endemia *f* endemic

endémi·co -ca *adj* endemic

endemonia·do -da *adj* possessed of the devil; furious, wild; (coll) devilish

endentar §2 *tr & intr* to mesh

endentecer §22 *intr* to teethe

enderezar §60 *tr* to stand up; to straighten; to direct; to put in order; to regulate ‖ *intr* to go straight ‖ *ref* to stand up, straighten up; to head, make one's way; to go straight; (aer) to flatten out, to level off

endeuda·do -da *adj* indebted

endeudar *ref* to run into debt; to acknowledge one's indebtedness

endevota·do -da *adj* pious, devout; fond, devoted

endiabla·do -da *adj* devilish; deformed, ugly; mean, wicked; (Arg) difficult, complicated

endilgar §44 *tr* (coll) to send, direct; (coll) to spring, unload

endiosar *tr* to deify ‖ *ref* to get stuck-up; to get absorbed

endominga·do -da *adj* Sunday; all dressed up

endomingar §44 *ref* to get dressed in one's Sunday best
endosante *mf* endorser
endosar *tr* (*un documento de crédito*) to endorse; (*una cosa poco grata*) to unload
endosata·rio -ria *mf* endorsee
endoso *m* endorsement
endriago *m* fabulous monster
endri·no -na *adj* sloe-colored ‖ *m* (*arbusto*) sloe, blackthorn ‖ *f* (*fruto*) sloe
endrogar §44 *ref* (Am) to run into debt
endulzar §60 *tr* to sweeten; to make bearable
endura·dor -dora *adj* saving, stingy
endurar *tr* to harden; to delay, put off; (*tolerar*) to endure; to save, spare ‖ *ref* to get hard
endurecer §22 *tr* to harden; (*robustecer, acostumbrar*) to inure
endureci·do -da *adj* hard, strong; inured; hard-hearted; tenacious, obstinate
enebrina *f* juniper berry
enebro *m* juniper
enecha·do -da *adj & mf* foundling
eneldo *m* dill
enema *f* enema
enemiga *f* enmity, hatred
enemi·go -ga *adj* enemy; hostile ‖ *mf* enemy, foe; **el enemigo malo** the Evil One ‖ *f* see **enemiga**
enemistad *f* enmity
enemistar *tr* to make an enemy of; to make enemies of ‖ *ref* to become enemies
energía *f* energy; power
enérgi·co -ca *adj* energetic
energúme·no -na *adj* fiendish ‖ *mf* crazy person, wild person
enero *m* January
enervar *tr* to enervate; to weaken
enési·mo -ma *adj* nth
enfadadi·zo -za *adj* peevish, irritable
enfadar *tr* to annoy, bother; to anger
enfado *m* annoyance, bother; anger
enfado·so -sa *adj* annoying, disagreeable
enfaldar *ref* to tuck up one's skirt
enfardar *tr* to bale, to pack
énfa·sis *m* (*pl* **-sis**) emphasis; bombast, affected speech
enfasizar §60 *tr* to emphasize
enfáti·co -ca *adj* emphatic; affected
enfermar *tr* to make sick ‖ *intr* to get sick
enfermedad *f* sickness, illness, disease
enfermera *f* nurse; **enfermera ambulante** visiting nurse
enfermería *f* infirmary
enfermero *m* male nurse
enfermi·zo -za *adj* sickly; (*clima*) unhealthy
enfer·mo -ma *adj* sick, ill; (*enfermizo*) sickly; **enfermo de amor** lovesick ‖ *mf* patient
enfermo·so -sa *adj* (Am) sickly
enfiestar *ref* (Am) to have a good time
enfilar *tr* to line up; (*p.ej., perlas*) to string; to aim; to go down, to go up; (mil) to enfilade ‖ *intr* to bear
enfisema *m* emphysema

enflaquecer §22 *tr* to make thin; to weaken ‖ *intr* to get thin; to flag, slacken ‖ *ref* to get thin, lose weight
enflauta·do -da *adj* (coll) pompous, inflated
enflautar *tr* to blow up, inflate; (coll) to cheat
enfocar §73 *tr* to focus; (fig) to size up
enfoque *m* focus, focusing; (fig) approach (*to a problem*)
enfoscar §73 *tr* to trim with mortar; to patch with mortar; to darken, make dark ‖ *ref* to become sullen, become grouchy; to become absorbed in business; to become overcast
enfrailar *tr* to make a friar or monk of ‖ *ref* to become a friar or monk
enfranque *m* shank
enfrascar §73 *tr* to bottle ‖ *ref* to become involved, intangled; to be sunk in work; to have a good time
enfrenar *tr* (*un caballo*) to bridle; (*un tren*) to brake; to check
enfrentar *tr* to put face to face; (*p.ej., al enemigo*) to face ‖ *intr* to be facing ‖ *ref* to meet face to face; **enfrentarse con** to stand up to; to cope with
enfrente *adv* opposite, in front; **enfrente de** opposite, in front of; opposed to
enfriadera *f* bottle cooler, ice pail
enfriar §77 *tr* to cool, to chill; (Am) to kill ‖ *intr & ref* to cool off
enfundar *tr* to sheathe, to put in a case; to stuff; (*un tambor*) to muffle
enfurecer §22 *tr* to infuriate, anger ‖ *ref* to rage
enfurruñar *ref* (coll) to sulk
engalanar *tr* to adorn, deck out, dress
engalla·do -da *adj* straight, erect; haughty
engallador *m* checkrein
enganchar *tr* to hook; (*un caballo*) to hitch; (*un coche de ferrocarril*) to couple; to recruit; to inveigle ‖ *intr* to get caught ‖ *ref* to get caught; (mil) to enlist
enganche *m* hook; hooking; hitching; coupling; inveigling; recruiting; enlisting; (rr) coupler
engañabo·bos *mf* (*pl* **-bos**) (coll) bamboozler
engaña·dor -dora *adj* deceptive; (*simpático*) winsome
engañar *tr* to deceive, cheat, fool; (*el tiempo*) to while away; (*el sueño, el hambre*) to ward off; to wheedle ‖ *ref* to be mistaken
engañifa *f* (coll) deception, trick
engaño *m* deception, deceit, fraud; mistake; falsehood; **llamarse a engaño** to back out because of fraud
engaño·so -sa *adj* deceptive
engargantar *tr* (*un ave*) to stuff the throat of ‖ *intr & ref* to mesh, to engage
engarzar §60 *tr* to link, string, wire; to curl; to enchase; (Col) to hook
engastar *tr* to enchase, mount, set
engaste *m* enchasing, mounting, setting
engatusar *tr* (coll) to coax, wheedle; to inveigle

engendrar *tr* to beget, engender; (geom) to generate

engendro *m* foetus; botch, bungle; (*criatura informe*) runt, stunt; **mal engendro** (coll) young tough

engolfar *intr* to go far out in the ocean || *ref* to go far out in the ocean; to become deeply involved; to be lost in thought

engoma·do -da *adj* (Chile) all dressed up || *m* (CAm) hangover

engomar *tr* to gum || *ref* (Am) to have a hangover

engorda *f* (Am) fattening; (Am) animals being fattened

engordar *tr* to fatten || *intr* to get fat; (coll) to get fat, get rich

engorro *m* bother, nuisance, obstacle

engorro·so -sa *adj* annoying

engoznar *tr* to hinge, to hang on a hinge

engranaje *m* gear, gears, teeth; (fig) link, connection; **engranaje de distribución** (aut) timing gears; **engranaje de tornillo sin fin** worm gear

engranar *tr* to gear, to mesh; to throw into gear || *intr* to gear, to mesh

engrandecer §22 *tr* to amplify, enlarge, magnify; to exalt, extol; to enhance

engrane *m* gear; mesh

engranerar *tr* (*el grano*) to store

engrapar *tr* to clamp, to cramp

engrasador *m* grease cup; **engrasador de pistón** grease gun

engrasar *tr* to grease; to smear with grease

engrase *m* greasing; grease

engravar *tr* to spread gravel over

engredar *tr* to chalk, to clay

engreí·do -da *adj* conceited, vain

engreimiento *m* conceit, vanity

engreír §58 *tr* to make conceited; (Am) to spoil, pamper || *ref* to become conceited

engreña·do -da *adj* disheveled

engrescar §73 *tr* to incite to fight; to incite to merriment || *ref* to pick a fight; to join in the fun

engrifar *tr* to curl, to crisp || *ref* to curl up; to stand on end; (*un caballo*) to rear

engrillar *tr* to shackle, fetter || *ref* (*las patatas*) to sprout

engringar §44 *ref* to act like a foreigner

engrosar §61 *tr* to broaden; to enlarge || *intr* to get fat || *ref* to broaden; to swell, get bigger

engrudar *tr* to paste

engrudo *m* paste

engualdrapar *tr* to caparison

enguapear *ref* (Mex) to get drunk

enguirnaldar *tr* to garland, to wreathe; to trim, bedeck

engullir §13 *tr* to gulp down

engurrio *m* sadness, melancholy

enhebrar *tr* (*una aguja*) to thread; (*perlas*) to string; (*mentiras*) (coll) to rattle off

enhestar §2 *tr* to stand upright, to erect; to hoist, lift up

enhies·to -ta *adj* upright, straight, erect

enhilar *tr* to thread; to direct; to line up; (*ideas*) to marshal || *intr* to set out

enhorabuena *adv* safely, luckily; **enhorabuena que** thank heavens that || *f* congratulations; **dar la enhorabuena a** to congratulate

enhoramala *adv* unluckily, under an unlucky star; **nacer enhoramala** to be born under an unlucky star; **vete enhoramala** go to the devil

enhornar *tr* to put into the oven

enigma *m* enigma, riddle, puzzle

enigmáti·co -ca *adj* enigmatic(al)

enjabonar *tr* to soap, to lather; (*adular*) (coll) to soft-soap; (*reprender*) (coll) to upbraid

enjaezar §60 *tr* to harness, put trappings on

enjalbegado *m* whitewashing

enjalbegar §44 *tr* to whitewash; (*el rostro*) to paint || *ref* to paint the face

enjambrar *intr* (*las abejas*) to swarm; to multiply in great numbers

enjambre *m* swarm

enjaretado *m* grating, lattice work

enjarrar *ref* (C-R, Mex) to stand with arms akimbo

enjaular *tr* to cage; (coll) to jail, lock up

enjergar §44 *tr* (coll) to launch, get started, to start on a shoestring

enjoyar *tr* to adorn with jewels; to set with precious stones; to adorn

enjuagadien·tes *m* (*pl* **-tes**) mouthwash

enjuagar §44 *tr* to rinse, rinse out

enjuague *m* rinse; rinsing water; mouthwash; rinsing cup; (coll) plot

enjugador *m* drier; clotheshorse

enjugama·nos *m* (*pl* **-nos**) towel, hand towel

enjuagaparabri·sas *m* (*pl* **-sas**) windshield wiper

enjugar §44 *tr* (*secar*) to dry; (*el sudor*) to wipe, wipe off; (*lágrimas*) to wipe away; (*deudas, un déficit*) to wipe out || *ref* to lose weight

enjuiciamiento *m* procedure; prosecution, suit; trial; judgment, sentence

enjuiciar *tr* to prosecute, to sue; to try; to judge

enjundio·so -sa *adj* fatty, greasy; solid, substantial

enju·to -ta *adj* (*tiempo, clima; ojos*) dry; lean, skinny; quiet, stolid || **enjutos** *mpl* brushwood; (*para excitar la gana de beber*) tidbits

enlabiar *tr* to entice, take in; to press one's lips against

enlace *m* connection, linking; relationship; betrothal, engagement; marriage; (mil, phonet) liaison; (rr) connection, junction

enlaciar *tr, intr & ref* to wither, wilt, shrivel; to rumple

enladrillado *m* brickwork; bricklaying; brick paving

enladrillar *tr* to pave with bricks

enlajado *m* (Ven) flagstone

enlajar *tr* (Ven) to pave with flagstones

enlardar *tr* to baste

enlatado *m* canning

enlatar *tr* to can; (Am) to roof with tin, to line with tin

enlazar §60 *tr* to connect, to link; to lace; (*un animal con el lazo*) to lasso

|| *intr* (*p.ej., dos trenes*) to connect || *ref* to be connected, to be linked; to connect; to get married; to become related by marriage

enlechar *tr* to grout

enlistonado *m* lathing, lath

enlistonar *tr* to lath

enlodar *tr* to muddy, smear with mud; to plaster with mud; to seal with mud; (fig) to sling mud at

enloquecer §22 *tr* to drive crazy || *intr* to go crazy

enloquecimiento *m* insanity, madness

enlosado *m* flagstone paving

enlosar *tr* to pave with flagstone

enlozar §60 *tr* (Am) to enamel

enlozado *m* (Am) enamelware

enlucido *m* plaster, coat (*of plaster*)

enlucir §45 *tr* (*una pared*) to plaster; (*la plata*) to polish

enlutar *tr* to put in mourning, to hang with crape; to darken, sadden || *ref* to dress in mourning

enmaderar *tr* to cover with boards; to build the framework for

enmagrecer §22 *tr* to make thin || *intr* & *ref* to get thin

enmalecer §22 *tr* to spoil || *ref* to get full of weeds, to be overgrown with weeds

enmarañar *tr* to entangle; to confuse || *ref* to become entangled; to become overcast, get cloudy

enmarcar §73 *tr* to frame

enmarchitar *tr* & *ref* to wither

enmaridar *intr* & *ref* to take a husband

enmarillecer §22 *ref* to turn yellow, to turn pale

enmasar *tr* (*tropas*) to mass

enmascarar *tr* to mask; to camouflage || *ref* to put on a mask; to masquerade

enmasillar *tr* to putty

enmendación *f* emendation

enmendar §2 *tr* (*corregir*) to emend; (*reformar*) to amend; (*resarcir*) to make amends for || *ref* to amend, to mend one's ways, to go straight

enmienda *f* (*corrección*) emendation; (*propuesta de variante*) amendment; (*satisfacción del daño hecho*) amends

enmohecer §22 *tr* to make moldy; to rust; to neglect || *ref* to get moldy; to rust; (*la memoria*) to get rusty; to fade away

enmontar *ref* (CAm, Mex, Col, Ven) to become overgrown with brush

enmudecer §22 *tr* to hush, to silence || *intr* to hush up, keep quiet; to become dumb, lose one's voice

enmuescar §73 *tr* to notch; (carp) to mortise

ennegrecer §22 *tr* to blacken, dye black || *ref* to turn black; (*el porvenir*) to be black

ennoblecer §22 *tr* to ennoble; to glorify, enhance

ennoblecimiento *m* ennoblement; glory, splendor; (*grandeza de alma*) nobility

enodio *m* fawn, young deer

enojada *f* (Mex) fit of anger

enojadi·zo -za *adj* irritable, ill-tempered

enojar *tr* to anger; to annoy, vex || *ref* to get angry; **enojarse con** or **contra** to get angry with (*a person*); **enojarse de** to get angry at (*a thing*)

enojo *m* anger; annoyance, bother

eno·jón -jona *adj* (Chile, Ecuad, Mex) irritable, ill-tempered

enojo·so -sa *adj* annoying, bothersome

enorgullecer §22 *tr* to fill with pride, make proud || *ref* to be proud; **enorgullecerse de** to pride oneself on

enorme *adj* enormous, huge

enquiciar *tr* (*una puerta, una ventana*) to hang; to fasten, make firm

enrabiar *tr* to enrage || *intr* to have rabies || *ref* to become enraged

enramar *tr* (*ramos*) to intertwine; to adorn with branches || *intr* to sprout branches || *ref* to hide in the branches

enranciar *tr* to make rancid || *ref* to get rancid

enrarecer §22 *tr* to rarefy; to make scarce || *intr* to become scarce || *ref* to rarefy; to become scarce

enrarecimiento *m* (*p.ej., del aire*) thinness; scarceness, scarcity

enrasar *tr* to make flush; to grade, to level || *intr* to be flush

enratonar *ref* (coll) to get sick from eating mice; (Ven) to have a hangover

enredadera *adj* (*planta*) climbing || *f* climbing plant, vine

enreda·dor -dora *mf* (coll) gossip, busybody

enredar *tr* to catch in a net; (*redes, una trampa*) to set; to tangle up; to involve, to entangle; (*una pelea*) to start; to intertwine, interweave; to endanger, compromise || *intr* to romp around, be frisky || *ref* to get tangled up; to get involved, become entangled; (coll) to have an affair

enredijo *m* entanglement

enredo *m* tangle; involvement, entanglement, complication; restlessness; friskiness; mischievous lie; (*de una novela, un drama*) plot; (*trato ilícito de hombre y mujer*) liaison

enre·dón -dona *adj* scheming || *mf* schemer

enredo·so -sa *adj* entangled, complicated, difficult

enrejado *m* grating, trellis, latticework; iron railing; grill; openwork embroidery

enrejar *tr* to grate, lattice; (*una ventana*) to put a grate on; to fence with an iron grating; (*ladrillos, tablas*) to pile alternately crosswise; (Mex) to darn

enrielar *tr* to make into ingots; (Am) to lay rails on; (Am) to put on the tracks; (Am) to put on the right track

enriquecer §22 *tr* to enrich || *intr* & *ref* to get rich

enrisca·do -da *adj* craggy, full of cliffs

enrizar §60 *tr* & *ref* to curl

enrocar §73 *tr* & *intr* (chess) to castle

enrodrigar §44 *tr* to prop, prop up

enrojar *tr* to redden, make red; (*el*

horno) to heat up ‖ *ref* to redden, turn red

enrojecer §22 *tr* to make red; to make red-hot; to make blush ‖ *intr* to blush ‖ *ref* to turn red; to get red-hot; to flush; to get sore, get inflamed

enromar *tr* to make dull, make blunt

enronquecer §22 *tr* to make hoarse ‖ *intr & ref* to get hoarse

enronquecimiento *m* hoarseness

enroque *m* (chess) castling

enroscar §73 *tr* to coil, twist; to screw in ‖ *ref* to coil, twist

enrubiar *tr* to bleach, make blond ‖ *ref* to turn blond

enrubio *m* bleaching; bleaching lotion

enrular *tr & ref* (Arg) to curl

ensacar §73 *tr* to bag, put in a bag

ensaimada *f* twisted coffee cake

ensalada *f* salad; hodgepodge; fiasco, flop

ensaladera *f* salad bowl

ensalmar *tr* (*un hueso*) to set; to treat or heal by incantation

ensalmo *m* incantation, spell; **como por ensalmo** as if by magic

ensalzar §60 *tr* to exalt, elevate, extol

ensamblar *tr* to assemble, join, fit together; **ensamblar a cola de milano** or **a cola de pato** to dovetail

ensanchador *m* glove stretcher

ensanchar *tr* to widen, to enlarge; (*una prenda ajustada*) to ease, let out; (*el corazón*) to unburden ‖ *intr & ref* to be proud and haughty

ensanche *m* widening, extension; (*de una calle*) extension; suburban development; allowance (*for enlargement of garment*)

ensandecer §22 *intr* to go crazy

ensangrenta·do -da *adj* bloody, gory

ensangrentar §2 *tr* to bathe in blood; to stain with blood ‖ *ref* to rage, to go wild; (*p.ej., las manos*) to bloody, make bloody

ensañar *tr* to anger, enrage ‖ *ref* to be cruel, be merciless; (*una enfermedad*) to rage

ensartar *tr* (*una aguja*) to thread; (*cuentas*) to string; to stick; (coll) to rattle off ‖ *ref* to squeeze in

ensayar *tr* to try, try on, try out; (*un espectáculo*) to rehearse; (*minerales*) to assay; to teach, train; to test ‖ *ref* to practice

ensaye *m* assay

ensayista *mf* essayist; (Chile) assayer

ensayo *m* trying, trial; testing, test; (*género literario*) essay; (*de minerales*) assay; exercise, practice; (theat) rehearsal; **ensayo general** dress rehearsal

ensenada *f* inlet, cove

enseña *f* standard, ensign

enseña·do -da *adj* trained, informed; (*perro de caza*) trained

enseñanza *f* teaching; education, instruction; (*ejemplo que sirve de experiencia*) lesson; **enseñanza superior** higher education

enseñar *tr* to teach; to train; to show, point out ‖ *intr* to teach

enseñorear *ref* to control oneself; **enseñorearse de** to take possession of

enseres *mpl* utensils, equipment, household goods

enseriar *ref* (Am) to become serious

ensillar *tr* to saddle

ensimismamiento *m* absorption in thought, deep thought

ensimismar *ref* to become absorbed in thought; (Chile, Ecuad, Peru) to be proud, be boastful

ensoberbecer §22 *tr* to make proud ‖ *ref* to become proud; (*el mar, las olas*) to swell, get rough

ensoberbecimiento *m* haughtiness

ensombrecer §22 *tr* to darken ‖ *ref* to get dark; to become sad and gloomy

ensoña·dor -dora *adj* dreamy ‖ *mf* dreamer

ensopar *tr* to dip, to dunk; (Am) to soak, to drench

ensordece·dor -dora *adj* deafening

ensordecer §22 *tr* to deafen; (*una consonante sonora*) to unvoice ‖ *intr* to become deaf; to play deaf, to not answer ‖ *ref* to unvoice

ensortijar *tr* to curl, make curly; (*la nariz de un animal*) to ring, put a ring in ‖ *ref* to curl

ensuciar *tr* to dirty, soil; to stain, smear; to defile, sully ‖ *ref* to soil oneself; to take bribes

ensueño *m* dream; daydream

entablado *m* flooring; wooden framework

entablar *tr* to board, board up; (*un hueso roto*) to splint; (*una conversación*) to start; (*p.ej., una batalla*) to launch; (*un pleito*) to bring; (*las piezas del ajedrez y de las damas*) to set up ‖ *ref* (*el viento*) to settle

entable *m* boarding; (*en los juegos de ajedrez y damas*) position of men; (Col) business, undertaking

entablillar *tr* (*un hueso roto*) to splint

enta·blón -blona *adj* (Peru) blustering, bragging ‖ *mf* (Peru) bully

entalegar §44 *tr* to bag, put in a bag; (*dinero*) to hoard

entalladura *f* carving, sculpture; engraving; slot, groove, mortise; cut, incision (*in a tree*)

entallar *tr* to carve, to sculpture; to engrave; to notch; to groove, mortise; (*un traje*) to fit, to tailor ‖ *intr* to take shape; (*el vestido*) to fit; (coll) to go well, be fitting

entallecer §22 *intr & ref* to shoot, to sprout

entapizar §60 *tr* to tapestry, to hang with tapestry; to cover with a fabric; to overgrow, to spread over

entarimado *m* parquet, inlaid floor, hardwood floor

entarimar *tr* to parquet, to put an inlaid floor on ‖ *ref* (coll) to put on airs

entarugar §44 *tr* to pave with wooden blocks ‖ *ref* (*el sombrero*) (Ven) to stick on

ente *m* being; (coll) guy, queer duck

enteca·do -da or **ente·co -ca** *adj* sickly, frail

enteleri·do -da *adj* shaking with cold, shaking with fright; (Am) sickly, frail
entena *f* lateen yard
entenado -da *mf* stepchild ‖ *m* stepson ‖ *f* stepdaughter
entendederas *fpl* (coll) brains; **tener malas entendederas** (coll) to have no brains
entende·dor -dora *adj* understanding, intelligent ‖ *mf* understanding person; **al buen entendedor, pocas palabras** a word to the wise is enough
entender *m* understanding, opinion ‖ §51 *tr* to understand; to intend, mean ‖ *intr* — **entender de** to be a judge of; to be experienced as; **entender de razón** to listen to reason; **entender en** to be familiar with, to deal with ‖ *ref* to be understood; to be meant; to have a secret understanding; **entenderse con** to get along with; to concern; (*una mujer*) to have an affair with
entendi·do -da *adj* expert, skilled; informed; **no darse por entendido** to take no notice, to pretend not to understand; **los entendidos** informed sources; **un entendido en** a well-informed person in
entendimiento *m* understanding
entenebrecer §22 *tr* to darken; to confuse ‖ *ref* to get dark; to become confused
entera·do -da *adj* informed, posted; (Chile) conceited; (Chile) intrusive, meddlesome ‖ *mf* insider
enterar *tr* to inform, acquaint; (Am) to pay; (Arg, Chile) to complete ‖ *intr* (Chile) to get better; (Chile) to drift along ‖ *ref* to find out; (Am) to recover; **enterarse de** to find out about, to become aware of
entereza *f* entirety, completeness; wholeness; perfection; fairness; constancy, fortitude; strictness
enteri·zo -za *adj* in one piece
enternece·dor -dora *adj* moving, touching
enternecer §22 *tr* to move, to touch ‖ *ref* to be moved to pity
enternecimiento *m* pity, compassion
ente·ro -ra *adj* entire, whole, complete; honest, upright; firm, energetic; sound, vigorous; (*tela*) strong, heavy ‖ *m* (arith) integer; (Am) payment; (Chile) balance; **por entero** entirely, wholly, completely
enterrador *m* gravedigger
enterramiento *m* burial, interment; (*hoyo*) grave; (*monumento*) tomb
enterrar §2 *tr* to bury, inter; to outlive, survive ‖ *ref* to hide away
entesar §2 *tr* to stretch, make taut
entibar *tr* to prop up, shore up ‖ *intr* to rest, lean
entibiar *tr* to cool off; to temper, moderate ‖ *ref* to cool off, cool down
entidad *f* entity; importance, consequence, moment; body, organization
entierro *m* burial, interment; (*hoyo*) grave; (*monumento*) tomb; funeral; funeral cortege; buried treasure

entintar *tr* to ink; to ink in; to stain with ink; to dye
entoldar *tr* to cover with awnings; to adorn with hangings ‖ *ref* to get cloudy, become overcast; to swell with pride
entomología *f* entomology
entonación *f* intonation; blowing of bellows
entona·do -da *adj* arrogant; haughty; harmonious, in tune
entonar *tr* to intone; to sing in tune; (*el órgano*) to blow; (*colores*) to harmonize; to tone, tone up; (*alabanzas*) to sound ‖ *intr* to sing in tune ‖ *ref* to be puffed up with pride
entonces *adv* then ‖ *m* — **por aquel entonces** at that time
entonelar *tr* to put in barrels, put in casks
entongar §44 *tr* (Mex, W-I) to pile up, pile in rows; (Col) to drive crazy
entono *m* intoning; arrogance, haughtiness
entontecer §22 *tr* to make foolish, make stupid ‖ *intr* & *ref* to become foolish, become stupid
entorchado *m* bullion; **ganar los entorchados** to win one's stripes
entorna·do -da *adj* ajar, half-closed
entornar *tr* to half-close; (*los ojos*) to squint; (*una puerta*) to leave ajar; (*volcar*) to upset ‖ *ref* to upset
entornillar *tr* to twist, to screw up
entorpecer §22 *tr* to stupefy; to obstruct, delay; to benumb; (*una cerradura, una ventana*) to make stick ‖ *ref* to stick, get stuck
entortar §61 *tr* to bend, make crooked; to knock out the eye of ‖ *ref* to bend, get crooked
entrada *f* entrance, entry; admission; arrival; income, receipts; admission ticket; entrance hall; (*número de personas que asisten a un espectáculo*) house; (*producto de cada función*) gate; (*amistad en alguna casa*) entree; (*naipes que guarda un jugador*) hand; (*de una comida*) entree; (*visita breve*) (coll) short call; (Col) down payment; (Mex) attack, onslaught; (elec) input; **dar entrada a** to admit; to give an opening to; (*un buque*) to give the right of entry to; **entrada de taquilla** gate; **entrada general** top gallery; **entrada llena** full house; **mucha entrada** good house, good turnout; **se prohibe la entrada** no admittance
entra·do -da *adj* (Chile) officious, self-assertive; **entrado en años** advanced in years ‖ *f* see **entrada**
entra·dor -dora *adj* (Mex) lively, energetic; (*enamoradizo*) (Am) susceptible; (Chile) officious, self-assertive
entrama·do -da *adj* half-timbered ‖ *m* timber framework
entram·bos -bas *adj* & *pron indef* both; **entrambos a dos** both
entrampar *tr* to ensnare, trap; to trick, deceive; (coll) to overload with debt ‖ *ref* to get trapped; to be tricked; (coll) to run into debt

entrante _adj_ entering; (_p.ej._, _tren_) inbound, incoming; (_próximo_, _que viene_) next ‖ _mf_ entrant; **entrantes y salientes** (coll) hangers-on

entraña _f_ internal organ; (fig) heart, center; **entrañas** entrails; (fig) heart, feeling; (fig) disposition, temper

entrañable _adj_ close, intimate

entrañar _tr_ to put away deep, bury deep; to involve; (_malos pensamientos_) to harbor ‖ _ref_ to go deep into; to be buried deep; to be close, be intimate

entrapajar _tr_ to wrap up, to bandage

entrar _tr_ to bring in; to overrun, invade; to influence ‖ _intr_ to enter, go in, come in; (_un río_) to empty; (_el viento_, _la marea_) to rise; to attack; to begin; **entrar a matar** (taur) to go in for the kill; **entrar en** to enter, enter into, go into; to fit into; to adopt, take up; **que entra** next

entre _prep_ (_en medio de_) between; (_en el número de_) among; (_en el intervalo de_) in the course of; **entre manos** at hand; **entre mí** to myself; **entre que** while; **entre tanto** meanwhile; **entre Vd. y yo** between you and me

entreabier·to -ta _adj_ half-open; (_puerta_) ajar

entreabrir §83 _tr_ to half-open; to leave ajar

entreacto _m_ entr'acte

entreca·no -na _adj_ graying, grayish

entrecarril _m_ (Elev) gauge

entrecejo _m_ space between the eyebrows; frown; **fruncir el entrecejo** to frown; **mirar con entrecejo** to frown at

entrecoger §17 _tr_ to catch, seize; to press hard, to hold down

entrecoro _m_ chancel

entrecorta·do -da _adj_ broken, intermittent

entrecortar _tr_ to break in on, keep interrupting

entre·cruz _m_ (_pl_ **-cruces**) interweaving

entrecruzar §60 _tr_ & _ref_ to intercross; to interweave, interlace; to interbreed

entrecubiertas _fpl_ between-decks

entrechocar §73 _ref_ to collide, to clash

entredicho _m_ interdiction, prohibition; (law) injunction; (Bol) alarm bell; **poner en entredicho** to cast doubt upon

entredós _m_ (_tira de encaje_) insertion; (typ) long primer

entrefilete _m_ short feature, special item

entrefi·no -na _adj_ medium

entrega _f_ delivery; (_p.ej._, _de una plaza fuerte_) surrender; (_cuaderno de un libro que se vende suelto_) fascicle; (_de una revista_) issue, number; **por entregas** in instalments

entregar §44 _tr_ to deliver; to hand over, surrender; to fit in, insert; **entregarla** (coll) to die ‖ _ref_ to give in, surrender; to abandon oneself; to devote oneself; **entregarse de** to take possession of, take charge of

entrehierro _m_ (elec) spark gap; (phys) air gap

entrelazar §60 _tr_ to interlace, interweave

entremediar _tr_ to put between

entremedias _adv_ in between; in the meantime; **entremedias de** between; among

entremés _m_ hors d'œuvre, side dish; short farce (_inserted in an auto or performed between two acts of a comedia_)

entremesear _tr_ (_una conversación_) to enliven

entremeter _tr_ to put in, to insert ‖ _ref_ to meddle, intrude, butt in

entremeti·do -da _adj_ meddling, meddlesome ‖ _mf_ meddler, intruder, busybody

entremezclar _tr_ & _ref_ to intermingle, intermix

entremorir §30 & §83 _intr_ to flicker, die out

entrenador _m_ (sport) coach, trainer, handler

entrenamiento _m_ (sport) coaching, training

entrenar _tr_ & _ref_ (sport) to coach, to train

entrepaño _m_ (_de una puerta_) panel; (_espacio entre dos columnas, etc._) pier; shelf

entreparecer §60 _ref_ to show through

entrepiernas _fpl_ crotch; patches in the crotch of trousers; (Chile) bathing trunks

entrepuentes _mpl_ between-decks; (naut) steerage

entrerrenglonar _tr_ to write between the lines

entrerriel _m_ gauge

entrerrisa _f_ giggle

entrerrosca _f_ (mach) nipple

entresacar §73 _tr_ to pick, pick out, select; to cull, sift; (_árboles_; _el pelo_) to thin out

entresijo _m_ secret; mystery; **tener muchos entresijos** to be mysterious, to be hard to figure out

entresuelo _m_ mezzanine, entresol

entretallar _tr_ to carve, to engrave; to carve in bas-relief; to do openwork in; to intercept

entretanto _adv_ meantime, meanwhile ‖ _m_ meanwhile; **en el entretanto** in the meantime

entretecho _m_ (Arg, Chile, Urug) attic, garret

entretejer _tr_ to interweave

entretela _f_ interlining

entretelar _tr_ to interline

entretención _f_ (Am) amusement, entertainment

entretener §71 _tr_ to amuse, entertain; (_el tiempo_) to while away; to maintain, keep up; to put off, delay; (_el dolor_) to allay; (_el hambre_) to stave off (_by taking a bite before mealtime_); to try to get one's mind off ‖ _ref_ to amuse oneself, to be amused

entreteni·do -da _adj_ amusing, entertaining; (rad) continuous, undamped ‖ _f_ kept woman; **dar la entretenida a** or **dar con la entretenida a** to stall off by constant talk

entretenimiento *m* amusement, entertainment; upkeep, maintenance

entretiempo *m* in-between season; **de entretiempo** spring-and-fall (*coat*)

entreventana *f* pier

entrever §80 *tr* to glimpse, descry, catch a glimpse of; to guess, suspect

entreverar *tr* to mix || *ref* (Arg) to get all mixed together; (*dos grupos de caballería*) (Arg) to clash in hand-to-hand combat

entrevía *f* gauge

entrevista *f* interview

entrevistar *ref* to have an interview

entristecer §22 *tr* to sadden, make sad || *ref* to sadden, become sad

entrojar *tr* to store in a granary

entrometer *tr* & *ref* var of **entremeter**

entrometi·do -da *adj* & *mf* var of **entremetido**

entronar *tr* to enthrone

entroncamiento *m* connection, relationship; (*de caminos, ferrocarriles*) (Am) junction

entroncar §73 *tr* to prove relationship between || *intr* to be related; (*dos caminos, ferrocarriles, etc.*) (Am) to connect

entronerar *tr* (*una bola de billar*) to pocket

entronizar §60 *tr* to enthrone; to exalt; to popularize || *ref* to be puffed up with pride

entronque *m* connection, relationship; (*de caminos, ferrocarriles*) (Am) junction

entruchar *tr* (coll) to decoy, to trick

entru·chón -chona *adj* (coll) tricky || *mf* (coll) trickster

entuerto *m* wrong, harm, injustice

entumecer §22 *tr* to make numb || *ref* (*un miembro*) to get numb, go to sleep; (*el mar*) to swell, get rough

entupir *tr* to stop up, clog; to pack tight || *ref* to get stopped up, get clogged

enturbiar *tr* to stir up, make muddy; to confuse, upset

entusiasmar *tr* to enthuse, make enthusiastic || *ref* to enthuse, become enthusiastic

entusiasmo *m* enthusiasm; inspiration

entusiasta *adj* enthusiastic || *mf* enthusiast

entusiásti·co -ca *adj* enthusiastic

enumerar *tr* to enumerate

enunciar *tr* to enunciate, to enounce

enunciati·vo -va *adj* (gram) declarative

envainar *tr* to sheathe

envalentonar *tr* to embolden, make bold || *ref* to pluck up, take courage

envanecer §22 *tr* to make vain || *ref* to become vain, get conceited

envanecimiento *m* vanity, conceit

envarar *tr* to make numb, to stiffen

envasar *tr* (*p.ej., trigo*) to pack, to sack; (*p.ej., vino*) to bottle; (*p.ej., pescado*) to can; (*una espada*) to thrust, poke; (*mucho vino*) to put away || *intr* to tipple

envase *m* container; bottle, jar; can; packing; bottling; canning; **envase de hojalata** tin can

envedijar *ref* to get tangled; (coll) to come to blows

envejecer §22 *tr* to age, make old || *intr* & *ref* to age, grow old; to get out of date

envejeci·do -da *adj* old, aged; experienced, tried

envenenar *tr* to poison; (*llenar de amargura*) to envenom, embitter; (*las palabras o conducta de una persona*) to put an evil interpretation on || *ref* to take poison

enverdecer §22 *intr* to turn green

envergadura *f* (*de las alas abiertas del ave*) spread; (*ancho de una vela*) breadth; (aer) span, wingspread; (fig) compass, spread, reach

envés *m* wrong side; (*del cuerpo humano*) back

enviado *m* envoy

enviar §77 *tr* to send; (*mercancías*) to ship; **enviar a buscar** to send for; **enviar a paseo** (coll) to send on his way, to dismiss without ceremony; **enviar por** to send for

enviciar *tr* to corrupt, vitiate; (*mimar*) to spoil || *intr* to have many leaves and little fruit || *ref* to become addicted; **enviciarse con** or **en** to addict oneself to, become addicted to

envidar *tr* to bid against, to bet against || *intr* to bid, to bet

envidia *f* envy; desire

envidiable *adj* enviable

envidiar *tr* to envy, to begrudge; to desire, want

envidio·so -sa *adj* envious; greedy, covetous || *mf* envious person

envilecer §22 *tr* to debase, vilify, revile || *ref* to degrade oneself

envío *m* sending; (*de mercancías*) shipment; (*de dinero*) remittance; (*en una obra*) autograph, inscription

envirota·do -da *adj* stiff, stuck-up

envite *m* bet; bid, offer, invitation; push, shove; (*apuesta adicional a un lance o suerte*) side bet; **al primer envite** right off, at the start

enviudar *intr* (*una mujer*) to become a widow; (*un hombre*) to become a widower

envoltorio *m* bundle; (*defecto en el paño*) knot

envoltura *f* cover, wrapper, envelope; swaddling clothes

envolver §47 & §83 *tr* to wrap, wrap up; (*hilo, cinta*) to wind, roll up; (*al niño*) to swaddle; to imply, mean; to involve; to envelop; (*dejar cortado y sin salida en la disputa*) to floor; (mil) to encircle || *ref* to become involved; to have an affair

enyerbar *tr* (Col, Chile, Mex) to bewitch || *ref* (Am) to be covered with grass; (Mex) to fall madly in love; (Mex) to take poison

enyesar *tr* to plaster; to put in a plaster cast; (*la tierra, el vino*) to gypsum

enyugar §44 *tr* to yoke

enzima *f* enzyme

enzolvar *tr* (Mex) to clog, stop up

epazote *m* (CAm, Mex) Mexican tea

E.P.D. *abbr* **en paz descanse**

epénte·sis f (pl -sis) epenthesis

eperlano m smelt

épica f epic poetry

epice·no -na adj (gram) epicene, common

épi·co -ca adj epic || m epic poet || f see **épica**

epicúre·o -a adj epicurean || mf epicurean, epicure

epidemia f epidemic

epidémi·co -ca adj epidemic

epidemiología f epidemiology

epidermis f epidermis; **tener la epidermis fina** or **sensible** (coll) to be touchy

Epifanía f Epiphany, Twelfth-day

epígrafe m epigraph; inscription; headline, title; device, motto

epigrama m epigram

epilepsia f epilepsy

epilépti·co -ca adj & mf epileptic

epilogar §44 tr to sum up, summarize

episcopalista adj & mf Episcopalian

episodio m episode

epistemología f epistemology

epístola f epistle

epitafio m epitaph

epíteto m epithet

epitomar tr to epitomize

epítome m epitome

E.P.M. abbr **en propia mano**

época f epoch; **hacer época** to be epoch-making

epopeya f epic, epic poem

equidad f equity; (templanza habitual) equableness; (moderación en el precio) reasonableness

equiláte·ro -ra adj equilateral

equilibrar tr to balance, equilibrate; (el presupuesto) to balance || ref to balance, equilibrate

equilibrio m equilibrium, balance, equipoise; (del presupuesto) balancing; **equilibrio político** balance of power

equilibrista mf balancer, ropedancer

equinoccial adj equinoctial

equinoccio m equinox

equipaje m baggage; piece of baggage; equipment; (naut) crew; **equipaje de mano** hand baggage

equipar tr to equip

equiparar tr to compare

equi·pier m (pl -piers) teammate

equipo m equipment, outfit; crew, gang; (sport) team; **equipo de novia** trousseau; **equipo de urgencia** first-aid kit

equitación f horsemanship, riding

equitati·vo -va adj fair, equitable; (tranquilo) equable

equivalente adj & m equivalent

equivaler §76 intr to be equal, be equivalent

equivocación f mistake; mistakenness

equivoca·do -da adj mistaken, wrong

equivocar §73 tr (una cosa por otra) to mistake, to mix || ref to be mistaken, to make a mistake; to be wrong; **equivocarse con** to be mistaken for; **equivocarse de** to be wrong in, take the wrong ...

equívo·co -ca adj equivocal, ambiguous || m equivocation, ambiguity; pun

equivoquista mf equivocator; punster

era f era, age; threshing floor; vegetable patch, garden bed

eral m two-year-old bull

erario m state treasury

erección f erection; foundation, establishment

eremita m hermit

ergástulo m dungeon, slave prison

ergio m erg

erguir §33 tr to raise; to straighten up || ref to straighten up; to swell with pride

erial adj unplowed, uncultivated || m unplowed land, uncultivated land

erigir §27 tr to erect, build; to found, establish; (a nueva condición) to elevate || ref — **erigirse en** to be elevated to; to set oneself up as

eriza·do -da adj bristling, bristly, spiny

erizar §60 tr to make stand on end, cause to bristle || ref to stand on end, to bristle

erizo m (mamífero) hedgehog; (zurrón espinoso de la castaña) bur, thistle; (púas de hierro que coronan lo alto de una muralla) cheval-de-frise; (persona de carácter áspero) (coll) curmudgeon; **erizo de mar** (zool) sea urchin

ermita f hermitage

ermita·ño -ña mf hermit

erogación f (de bienes o caudales) distribution; (Am) expenditure; (Peru, Ven) gift, charity; (Mex) outlay

erogar §44 tr to distribute; (Ecuad) to contribute; (Mex) to cause

erosión f erosion

erosionar tr & ref to erode

erradicar §73 tr to eradicate

erra·do -da adj mistaken, wrong

errar §34 tr to miss || intr to err, to be mistaken, to be wrong; to wander || ref to be mistaken, to be wrong

errata f erratum; printer's error

erróne·o -a adj erroneous

error m error, mistake; **error de pluma** clerical error; **salvo error u omisión** barring error or omission

eructar intr to belch; (coll) to brag

eructo m belch, belching

erudición f erudition, learning

erudi·to -ta adj erudite, learned || mf scholar, savant; **erudito a la violeta** egghead, highbrow

erugino·so -sa adj rusty

erumpir intr (un volcán) to erupt

erupción f eruption

esbel·to -ta adj slender, lithe, willowy

esbirro m bailiff, constable; (el que ejecuta órdenes injustas) myrmidon, henchman

esbozar §60 tr to sketch, outline

esbozo m sketch, outline

escabechar tr to pickle; (el pelo, la barba) to dye; (reprobar en un examen) (coll) to flunk; (coll) to stab to death || ref to dye one's hair; (el pelo, la barba) to dye

escabeche m pickle; pickled fish; hair dye

en
es

escabel *m* stool; footstool; (*para medrar*) stepping stone
escabio·so -sa *adj* mangy
escabro·so -sa *adj* scabrous, risqué; scabrous, uneven, rough, harsh
escabuche *m* weeding hoe
escabullir §13 *ref* to slip away, sneak away; to slip out, wiggle out
escafandra *f* diving suit; **escafandra espacial** space suit
escafandrista *mf* diver
escala *f* (*escalera de mano*) ladder, stepladder; (*línea graduada de instrumento*) scale; (*de buque*) call; (*de avión*) stop; (*puerto donde toca una embarcación*) port of call; (*serie de las notas musicales*) scale; **en escala de** on a scale of; **en grande escala** on a large scale; **escala móvil** (*de salarios*) sliding scale; **hacer escala** (naut) to call
escalada *f* scaling, climbing; breaking in; escalation
escalador *m* climber; (*ladrón*) burglar, housebreaker
escalación *f* escalation
escalafón *m* roster, roll, register
escalar *tr* (*subir, trepar*) to scale; to break in, to burglarize; (*la compuerta de la acequia*) to open ‖ *intr* to climb; (naut) to call ‖ *ref* to escalate
escalato·rres *m* (*pl* **-rres**) steeplejack, human fly
escalda·do -da *adj* (coll) cautious, scared, wary; (*mujer*) (coll) lewd, loose
escaldar *tr* to scald; to make red hot ‖ *ref* to get scalded; to chafe
escalera *f* stairs, stairway; (*la portátil*) ladder; (*de naipes*) sequence; (*en el póker*) straight; **de escalera abajo** from below stairs, from the servants; **escalera de caracol** winding stairway; **escalera de escape** fire escape; **escalera de husillo** winding stairway; **escalera de incendios** fire escape; **escalera de mano** ladder; **escalera de salvamento** fire escape; **escalera de tijera** or **escalera doble** ladder; **escalera excusada** or **falsa** private stairs; **escalera extensible** extension ladder; **escalera hurtada** secret stairway; **escalera mecánica, móvil** or **rodante** escalator, moving stairway
escalerilla *f* low step; car step; (*en las medias*) runner; (*de naipes*) sequence; thumb index
escalfar *tr* (*huevos*) to poach; (*el pan*) to bake brown
escalinata *f* stone steps, front steps
escalo *m* burglary, breaking in
escalofria·do -da *adj* chilly
escalofrío *m* chill
escalón *m* step, rung; (*grada de la escalera*) tread; (fig) step, echelon, grade; (*paso con que uno adelanta sus pretensiones*) (fig) stepping stone; (mil) echelon; (rad) stage
escalonar *tr* to space out, spread out; (*las horas de trabajo*) to stagger; (mil) to echelon
escalope *m* (*loncha delgada de carne*) scallop (*thin slice of meat*)

escalpar *tr* to scalp
escalpelo *m* scalpel
escama *f* scale; fear, suspicion
escamar *tr* (*los peces*) to scale; (coll) to frighten ‖ *ref* to be frightened
escamondar *tr* to trim, to prune
escamo·so -sa *adj* scaly
escamotea·dor -dora *mf* prestidigitator; swindler
escamotear *tr* to whisk out of sight, cause to vanish; (*una carta*) to palm; to swipe, to snitch
escampada *f* (coll) clear spell, break in rain
escampar *tr* to clear out ‖ *intr* to stop raining; to ease up; **¡ya escampa!** (coll) there you go again! ‖ *ref* — **escamparse del agua** (Am) to get in out of the rain
escampavía *f* (naut) cutter, revenue cutter
escamujar *tr* (*un árbol, esp. un olivo*) to prune; (*ramas*) to clear out
escanciar *tr* (*vino*) to pour, to serve, to drink ‖ *intr* to drink wine
escandalizar §60 *tr* to scandalize ‖ *ref* to be scandalized; to be outraged, be exasperated
escándalo *m* scandal; **causar escándalo** to make a scene
escandalo·so -sa *adj* scandalous; noisy, riotous; (Am) loud, flashy
escandallo *m* (naut) sounding lead; (*del contenido de varios envases*) testing, sampling; cost accounting
escandina·vo -va *adj* & *mf* Scandinavian
escandir *tr* (*versos*) to scan
escansión *f* scansion; (telv) scanning
escaño *m* settle, bench with a back; (*en las Cortes*) seat; (Am) park bench; (Guat) nag
escañuelo *m* footstool
escapada *f* escape, flight; short trip, quick trip
escapar *tr* to free, to save; (*un caballo*) to drive hard ‖ *intr* to escape; to flee, run away; **escapar en una tabla** to have a narrow escape ‖ *ref* to escape; to flee, run away; (*el gas, el agua*) to leak; **escapársele a uno** to let slip; to not notice
escaparate *m* show window; (*armario con cristales*) cabinet; (Am) wardrobe, clothes closet
escaparatista *mf* window dresser
escapatoria *f* escape, getaway; (*de atenciones, deberes, etc.*) (fig) escape; (*efugio, pretexto*) (coll) evasion, subterfuge
escape *m* escape; flight; (*de gas, agua*) leak; (*de reloj*) escapement; (aut) exhaust valve; (aut) exhaust, exhaust pipe; **a escape** at full speed, on the run; **escape de rejilla** (rad) grid leak; **escape libre** (aut) cutout
escápula *f* shoulder blade, scapula
escaque *m* square; **escaques** chess
escarabajear *tr* (coll) to bother, worry, harass ‖ *intr* to swarm, crawl; to scrawl, scribble
escarabajo *m* black beetle; (*imperfec-*

ción en los tejidos) flaw; *(persona pequeña)* (coll) runt

escaramuza f skirmish

escaramuzar §60 *intr* to skirmish

escarapela f *(divisa en forma de lazo)* cockade; dispute ending in hair pulling

escarapelar *intr & ref* to quarrel, to wrangle

escarbadien·tes m (pl -tes) toothpick

escarbar *tr (el suelo)* to scratch, scratch up; *(la lumbre)* to poke; *(los dientes, los oídos)* to pick; to pry into

escarcha f frost, hoarfrost

escarchar *tr (confituras)* to frost, put frosting on; *(la tierra del alfarero)* to dilute with water; to spangle || *intr —* **escarcha** there is frost

escardar or **escardillar** *tr* to weed, weed out

escardillo m weeding hoe

escariar *tr* to ream

escarlata adj scarlet || f scarlet fever

escarlatina f scarlet fever

escarmentar §2 *tr* to make an example of || *intr* to learn one's lesson

escarmiento m example, lesson, warning; caution; wisdom; punishment

escarnecer §22 *tr* to scoff at, make fun of

escarnio m scoff, scoffing

escarola f endive

escarpa f scarp, escarpment; (Mex) sidewalk

escarpa·do -da adj steep; abrupt, craggy

escarpia f hooked spike

escarpín m pump

escasear *tr* to give sparingly; to cut down on, to avoid; to bevel || *intr* to be scarce

escase·ro -ra adj sparing; saving, frugal; stingy || mf skinflint

escasez f *(falta de una cosa)* scarcity; *(pobreza)* need, want; *(mezquindad)* stinginess

esca·so -sa adj *(poco abundante)* scarce; *(no cabal)* scant; *(muy económico)* parsimonious, frugal; *(tacaño)* stingy; *(oportunidad)* dim, slim, slight; **estar escaso de** to be short of

escatimar *tr & intr* to scrimp

escena f *(parte del teatro donde se representan las obras)* stage; *(subdivisión de un acto)* scene; incident, episode; **poner en escena** to stage

escenario m stage; *(disposición de la representación)* setting; *(guión de un cine)* scenario; *(antecedentes de una persona o cosa)* background

escenarista mf scenarist

escéni·co -ca adj scenic

escenificar §73 *tr* to adapt for the stage

escépti·co -ca adj sceptic(al) || mf sceptic

Escila f Scylla; **entre Escila y Caribdis** between Scylla and Charybdis

Escipión m Scipio

escisión f (biol) fission; (surg) excision

esclarecer §22 *tr* to light up, brighten; to explain, elucidate; to ennoble || *intr* to dawn

esclareci·do -da adj noble, illustrious

esclavitud f slavery

esclavización f enslavement

esclavizar §60 *tr* to enslave

escla·vo -va adj & mf slave

escla·vón -vona adj & mf Slav

esclusa f lock; floodgate; **esclusa de aire** caisson

esclusero m lock tender

escoba f broom

escobada f sweep; sweeping

escobar *tr* to sweep with a broom

escobazar §60 *tr* to sprinkle with a wet broom

escobén m (naut) hawse

escobilla f brush, whisk; gold and silver sweepings; (elec) brush

escocer §16 *intr* to smart, sting || *ref* to hurt; to chafe, become chafed

esco·cés -cesa adj Scotch, Scottish || mf Scot || m Scotchman; *(whisky; dialecto)* Scotch; **los escoceces** the Scotch, the Scottish

Escocia f Scotland; **la Nueva Escocia** Nova Scotia

escofina f rasp

escofinar *tr* to rasp

escoger §17 *tr* to choose, pick out

escogi·do -da adj choice, select

escolar adj school || m pupil

escolaridad f schooling, school attendance; curriculum

escolimo·so -sa adj (coll) impatient, gruff, restless

escolta f escort

escoltar *tr* to escort

escollar *intr* (Arg) to run aground on a reef; (Arg, Chile) to fail

escollera f jetty, breakwater

escollo m *(peñasco a flor de agua)* reef, rock; *(peligro)* pitfall; *(obstáculo)* stumbling block

escombrar *tr* to clear out

escombro m *(pez)* mackerel; **escombros** debris, rubble, rubbish

esconder *tr* to hide, conceal; to harbor, contain || *ref* to hide; to lurk

escondi·do -da adj hidden; **a escondidas** secretly; **a escondidas de** without the knowledge of

escondite m hiding place; *(juego de muchachos)* hide-and-seek; **jugar al escondite** to play hide-and-seek

escondrijo m hiding place

escopeta f shotgun; **escopeta blanca** gentleman hunter; **escopeta de caza** fowling piece; **escopeta de viento** air rifle; **escopeta negra** professional hunter

escopetazo m gunshot; gunshot wound; bad news, blow

escoplear *tr* to chisel

escoplo m chisel

escorbuto m scurvy

escoria f dross, scoria, slag; (fig) dross, dregs

escorial m cinder bank, slag dump

escorpión m scorpion

escorzar §60 *tr* to foreshorten

escorzo m foreshortening

escota f (naut) sheet

escota·do -da adj low-neck || m low neck

escotadura f low neck, low cut in neck

escotar *tr* to cut to fit; to draw water

from, to drain; to cut low in the neck || *intr* to go Dutch

escote *m* low neck; (*encajes en el cuello de una vestidura*) tucker; **ir a escote** or **pagar a escote** to go Dutch

escotilla *f* (naut) hatchway, scuttle

escotillón *m* hatch, trap door, scuttle; (theat) trap door

escozor *m* burning, smarting, stinging; grief, sorrow

escriba *m* scribe

escribanía *f* court clerkship; desk; writing materials

escribano *m* court clerk; lawyer's clerk

escribiente *mf* clerk, office clerk; **escribiente a máquina** typist

escribir §83 *tr* & *intr* to write || *ref* to enroll, enlist; to write to each other; **no escribirse** to be impossible to describe

escriño *m* casket, jewel case; straw basket

escri•to -ta *adj* streaked || *m* writing; (law) brief, writ; **poner por escrito** to write down, put in writing

escri•tor -tora *mf* writer

escritorio *m* writing desk; office; **escritorio ministro** kneehole desk, office desk; **escritorio norteamericano** roll-top desk

escritura *f* writing; script, handwriting, longhand; (law) deed, indenture; (law) sworn statement; **escritura al tacto** touch typewriting || **Escritura** *f* Scripture; **Sagrada Escritura** Holy Scripture, Holy Writ

escriturar *tr* to notarize; (*p.ej., a un actor*) to book || *ref* (taur) to sign up for a fight

escrnía. *abbr* **escribanía**

escrno. *abbr* **escribano**

escrófula *f* scrofula

escrúpulo *m* scruple

escrupulo•so -sa *adj* scrupulous; exact

escrutar *tr* to scrutinize; (*los votos*) to count

escrutinio *m* scrutiny; counting of votes

escuadra *f* (*pequeño número de personas o de soldados*) squad; (*pieza de metal para asegurar las ensambladuras*) angle iron; (*de carpintero*) square; (*de dibujante*) triangle; (nav) squadron

escuadrar *tr* (carp) to square

escuadrilla *f* (aer) squadron

escuadrón *m* (mil) squadron

escualidez *f* squalor

escuáli•do -da *adj* squalid

escualor *m* squalor

escucha *mf* listener || *m* (mil) scout, vedette || *f* listening; (*en un convento*) chaperon; **estar de escucha** (coll) to eavesdrop

escuchar *tr* to listen to; (*atender a*) to heed; (*radiotransmisiones*) to monitor || *intr* to listen || *ref* to like the sound of one's own voice

escudar *tr* to shield

escudero *m* esquire; nobleman; lady's page

escudete *m* escutcheon; (*refuerzo en la ropa*) gusset; (*planchuela delante de*

la cerradura) escutcheon, escutcheon plate

escudilla *f* bowl

escudo *m* shield; buckler; (*delante de la cerradura*) escutcheon plate; **escudo de armas** coat of arms; **escudo térmico** (*de una cápsula espacial*) heat shield

escudriñar *tr* to scrutinize

escuela *f* school; **escuela de artes y oficios** trade school; **escuela de párvulos** kindergarten; **escuela de verano** summer school; **escuela dominical** Sunday school; **Escuela Naval Militar** Naval Academy; **hacer escuela** to be the leader of a school (*of thought*)

escuelante *mf* (Mex) schoolteacher || *m* (Mex) schoolboy || *f* (Mex) schoolgirl

escuerzo *m* toad

escue•to -ta *adj* free, unencumbered; bare, unadorned

escuintle *adj* (Mex) sickly || *m* (*perro*) (Mex) mutt; (Mex) brat

esculpir *tr* & *intr* to sculpture, to carve; to engrave

escultismo *m* outdoor activities

escultista *m* outdoorsman

escultor *m* sculptor

escultora *f* sculptress

escultura *f* sculpture

escultural *adj* scuptural; statuesque

escupidera *f* cuspidor; (Am) chamber pot

escupidura *f* spit; fever blister

escupir *tr* & *intr* to spit

escurrepla•tos *m* (*pl* -**tos**) dish rack

escurridero *m* drainpipe; drainboard; slippery spot

escurridi•zo -za *adj* slippery

escurri•do -da *adj* narrow-hipped; (Am) abashed, confused

escurridor *m* colander

escurriduras *fpl* dregs, lees

escurrir *tr* (*una vasija; un líquido; la vajilla*) to drain; to wring, wring out; **escurrir el bulto** (coll) to duck || *intr* to drip, ooze, trickle; to slide, to slip || *ref* to drip, ooze, trickle; to slide, to slip; to slip away; (*un reparo*) to slip out

esdrúju•lo -la *adj* accented on the syllable next to the last || *m* word or verse accented on syllable next to the last

ese, esa *adj dem* (*pl* **esos, esas**) that (*near you*) || **ese** *f* sound hole (*of violin*); **hacer eses** to reel, stagger

ése, ésa *pron dem* (*pl* **ésos, ésas**) that (*near you*); **ésa** your city

esencia *f* essence; **esencia de pera** banana oil; **quinta esencia** quintessence

esencial *adj* & *m* essential

esfera *f* sphere; (*del reloj*) dial

esféri•co -ca *adj* spherical || *m* football

esfinge *f* sphinx; spiteful woman

esforza•do -da *adj* brave, vigorous, enterprising

esforzar §35 *tr* to strengthen, to invigorate; to encourage || *ref* to exert oneself; to strive

esfuerzo *m* effort, exertion, endeavor; courage, vigor, spirit

esfumar tr to stump || ref to disappear, fade away

esgarrar tr (la flema) to try to cough up || intr to clear the throat

esgrima f fencing

esgrimidura f fencing

esgrimir tr to wield, to brandish; (un argumento) to swing || intr to fence

esgrimista mf (Arg, Chile, Peru) fencer; (Chile) swindler, panhandler

esguazar §60 tr to ford

esguazo m fording; ford

esguince m dodge, duck; (gesto de disgusto) frown; twist, sprain, wrench

eslabón m (de cadena) link; (hierro acerado para sacar fuego de un pedernal; cilindro de acero para afilar cuchillos) steel

eslabonar tr to link; to link together, to string together || intr to link

eslálom m slalom

esla·vo -va adj Slav, Slavic || mf Slav || m (idioma) Slavic

esla·vón -vona adj & mf Slav

eslogan m (consigna usada en fórmulas publicitarias) slogan

eslora f (naut) length

eslova·co -ca adj & mf Slovak

esmaltar tr to enamel; to embellish

esmalte m enamel; **esmalte para las uñas** nail polish

esmera·do -da adj careful, painstaking

esmeralda f emerald

esmerar tr to polish, to shine; to examine, to check || ref to take pains, to do one's best

esmeril s emery

esmeriladora f emery wheel

esmerilar tr to grind or polish with emery

esmero m care, neatness

esmoladera f grindstone

esmoquin m tuxedo, dinner coat

esnob adj snobbish || mf (pl **esnobs**) snob

esnobismo m snobbery, snobbishness

esnobista adj snobbish

eso pron dem that; **a eso de** about; **eso es** that's it; that is; **por eso** for that reason; therefore

esófago m esophagus

espaciador m space bar

espacial adj space, spatial

espaciar §77 (Arg, Chile) & regular tr to space; to spread, scatter || ref to expatiate; to amuse oneself, to relax

espacio m space; **espacio de chispa** spark gap; **espacio exterior** outer space; **espacio libre** (entre dos cosas) clearance; **espacio muerto** (en el cilindro de un motor) clearance; **por espacio de** in the space of

espacio·so -sa adj spacious, roomy; slow, deliberate

espada m swordsman; (taur) matador || f sword; playing card (representing a sword) equivalent to spade; **entre la espada y la pared** between the devil and the deep blue sea

espadachín m swordsman; (amigo de pendencias) bully

espadaña f cattail, bulrush, reed mace; (campanario) bell gable

espadilla f (remo que se usa como timón) scull; (aguja para sujetar el pelo) bodkin; red insignia of Order of Santiago

espadín m rapier

espadón m (coll) brass hat

espalar tr to shovel

espalda f back; **a espaldas de uno** behind one's back; **de espaldas a** with one's back to; **tener buenas espaldas** to have broad shoulders; **volver las espaldas a** to turn a cold shoulder to

espaldar m (de silla) back; (enrejado para plantas) trellis, espalier

espaldarazo m slap on the back; (ceremonia para armar caballero) accolade; **dar el espaldarazo a** to accept, approve

espalera f trellis, espalier

espantada f (de un animal) sudden flight; (desistimiento ocasionado por el miedo) cold feet

espantadi·zo -za adj shy, skittish, scary

espantajo m scarecrow; (persona fea) fright

espantamos·cas m (pl -cas) (para poner a los caballos) fly net; (aparato para asustar y alejar las moscas) fly chaser

espantapája·ros m (pl -ros) scarecrow

espantar tr to scare, frighten; to scare away || ref to get scared; to be surprised, to marvel

espanto m fright, terror; (amenaza) threat; (Am) ghost

espanto·so -sa adj frightening, terrifying

España f Spain; **la Nueva España** New Spain (Mexico in the early days)

espa·ñol -ñola adj Spanish; **a la española** in the Spanish manner || mf Spaniard || m (idioma) Spanish; **los españoles** the Spanish || f Spanish woman

españolizar §60 tr to make Spanish, to Hispanicize; to translate into Spanish || ref to become Spanish

esparadrapo m sticking plaster

esparaván m spavin

esparavel m mortarboard

esparcimiento m spreading, scattering, dissemination; diversion, relaxation; frankness, openness

esparcir §36 tr to spread, scatter; to divert, relax || ref to spread, scatter; to disperse; to take it easy, to relax

espárrago m asparagus; (perno) stud bolt; awning pole

esparrancar §73 ref to spread one's legs wide apart

esparta·no -na adj & mf Spartan

esparto m esparto grass

espasmo m spasm

espasmódi·co -ca adj spasmodic

espásti·co -ca adj spastic

espato m spar; **espato flúor** fluor spar

espátula f spatula; putty knife

especia f spice

especia·do -da adj spicy

especial adj especial, special

especialidad f speciality; (ramo a que se consagra una persona o negocio) specialty

especialista mf specialist

especializar §60 *tr, intr & ref* to specialize

especiar *tr* to spice

especie *f (categoría de la clasificación biológica)* species; *(clase, género)* sort, kind; *(caso, asunto)* matter; *(chisme, cuento)* news, rumor; appearance, pretext, show; remark; **en especie** in kind; **soltar una especie** to try to draw someone out

especie·ro -ra *mf* spice dealer ‖ *m* spice box

especificar §73 *tr* to specify; to itemize

especifi·co -ca *adj* specific ‖ *m* specific; patent medicine

especimen *m (pl especímenes)* specimen

especio·so -sa *adj (engañoso)* specious; nice, neat, perfect

especiota *f (coll)* hoax, wild idea

espectáculo *m* spectacle; **dar un espectáculo** to make a scene; **espectáculo de atracciones** side show

especta·dor -dora *mf* witness; spectator

espectral *adj* ghostly

espectro *m* specter, phantom, ghost; (phys) spectrum

especular *tr* to check, examine; to contemplate ‖ *intr* to speculate

espejear *intr* to sparkle

espejismo *m* mirage

espejo *m* mirror, looking glass; model; **espejo de cuerpo entero** full-length mirror, pier glass; **espejo de retrovisión** rear-view mirror; **espejo de vestir** full-length mirror, pier glass; **espejo retrovisor** rear-view mirror

espelunca *f* cave, cavern

espeluznante *adj* hair-raising

espera *f* wait, waiting; *(puesto para cazar)* blind, hunter's blind; composure, patience, respite; delay; stay; **no tener espera** to be of the greatest urgency

esperanza *f* hope; **tener puesta su esperanza en** to pin one's faith on

esperanza·do -da *adj* hopeful *(having hope)*

esperanza·dor -dora hopeful *(giving hope)*

esperanzar §60 *tr* to give hope to

esperanzo·so -sa *adj* hopeful, full of hope

esperar *tr (aguardar)* to wait for, to await; *(tener esperanza de conseguir)* to expect, to hope for; **ir a esperar** to go to meet ‖ *intr* to wait; to hope; **esperar + inf** to hope to + *inf*; **esperar a que** to wait until; **esperar desesperando** to hope against hope; **esperar en** to put one's hope in; **esperar que** to hope that; **esperar sentado** to have a good wait

esperinque *m* smelt

esperma *f* sperm

espesar *m* depth, thickness *(of woods)* ‖ *tr* to thicken; *(un tejido)* to weave tighter ‖ *ref* to thicken, to get thick or thicker

espe·so -sa *adj* thick; dirty, greasy

espesor *m* thickness; *(de un flúido, gas, masa)* density

espesura *f* thickness; *(matorral)* thicket;

(cabellera muy espesa) shock of hair; dirtiness, greasiness

espetar *tr* to skewer; to pierce, pierce through; **espetar algo a** to spring something on ‖ *ref* to be solemn, be pompous; (coll) to settle down

espetón *m (hurgón)* poker; *(asador)* skewer, spit; jab, poke

espía *mf* spy; (coll) squealer ‖ *f* (naut) warping; *(cuerda)* (naut) warp

espiar §77 *tr* to spy on ‖ *intr* to spy; (naut) to warp

espichar *tr* to prick; *(dinero)* (Chile) to cough up; (Chile, Peru) to tap ‖ *intr* (coll) to die ‖ *ref* (Mex, W-I) to get thin

espiche *m (arma o instrumento puntiagudo)* prick; (naut) peg, bung

espichón *m* stab, prick

espiga *f* (bot) ear, spike; peg, pin, tenon; *(clavo sin cabeza)* brad; *(badajo)* clapper; *(de una llave)* stem

espigar §44 *tr* to glean; to tenon, to dowel ‖ *intr (los cereales)* to form ears ‖ *ref* to grow tall, to shoot up

espigón *m* sharp point, spur; *(mazorca)* ear of corn; *(cerro puntiagudo)* peak; breakwater

espina *f* thorn, spine; *(de los peces)* fishbone; doubt, uncertainty; sorrow; (anat) spine; **dar mala espina a** (coll) to worry; **espina de pescado** herringbone; **espina de pez** fishbone; **espina dorsal** spinal column; **estar en espinas** (coll) to be on pins and needles

espinaca *f* spinach; **espinacas** spinach

espinal *adj* spinal

espinapez *m* herringbone; thorny matter, difficulty

espinar *m* thorny spot; (fig) thorny matter ‖ *tr* to prick; *(árboles)* to protect with thornbushes; to hurt, offend

espinazo *m* backbone; *(de un arco)* keystone

espinel *m* trawl, trawl line

espineta *f* spinet

espinilla *f (de la pierna)* shin, shinbone; *(granillo en la piel)* blackhead

espino *m* hawthorn; **espino artificial** barbed wire; **espino negro** blackthorn

espinochar *tr (el maíz)* to husk

espino·so -sa *adj* thorny; *(pez)* bony; *(difícil)* (fig) thorny, knotty

espiocha *f* pickaxe

espión *m* spy

espionaje *m* spying, espionage

espira *f* turn

espiración *f* breathing; exhalation

espiral *adj* spiral ‖ *f (línea curva que da vueltas alrededor de un punto)* spiral; *(del reloj)* hairspring; *(de humo)* curl, wreath

espirar *tr* to breath; to encourage ‖ *intr* to breathe; to exhale, expire; *(el viento)* (poet) to blow gently

espiritismo *m* spiritualism

espirito·so -sa *adj* spirited, lively; *(licor)* spirituous

espíritu *m* spirit; *(mente)* mind; *(aparecido, fantasma)* ghost, spirit; **espíritu de equipo** teamwork; **Espíritu Santo** Holy Ghost, Holy Spirit; **dar, despe-**

dir, **exhalar** or **rendir el espíritu** to give up the ghost
espiritual *adj* spiritual; sharp, witty
espiritualismo *m* spiritualism
espita *f* tap, cock; (coll) tippler
espitar *tr* to tap
esplendidez *f* splendor, magnificence
esplén·dido -da *adj* splendid, magnificent; generous, open-handed; (poet) brilliant, radiant
esplendor *m* splendor
esplendoro·so -sa *adj* resplendent
espliego *m* lavender
esplín *m* melancholy
espolada *f* prick with spur; **espolada de vino** (coll) shot of wine
espolear *tr* to spur, to spur on
espoleta *f* fuse; (*hueso*) wishbone
espolón *m* (*del gallo, una montaña, un buque de guerra*) spur; dike, jetty, mole, cutwater; (*prominencia córnea de las caballerías*) fetlock; (*sabañón*) chilblain
espolvorear *tr* (*quitar el polvo de*; *esparcir el polvo sobre*) to dust; (*el azúcar*) to sprinkle
esponja *f* sponge; (*sablista*) (coll) sponge, sponger; **beber como una esponja** (coll) to drink like a fish; **tirar la esponja** (coll) to throw in (or up) the sponge
esponja·do -da *adj* proud, puffed-up; (coll) fresh, healthy
esponjar *tr* to puff up, make fluffy ‖ *ref* to puff up, become fluffy; (coll) to be puffed up, be conceited; (coll) to look fresh and healthy
esponjo·so -sa *adj* spongy
esponsales *mpl* betrothal, engagement
espontanear *ref* to make a clean breast of it; to open one's heart
espontáne·o -a *adj* spontaneous ‖ *m* (taur) spectator who jumps into the ring to take on the bull
espora *f* spore
esporádi·co -ca *adj* sporadic
esposa *f* wife; **esposas** handcuffs, manacles
esposar *tr* to handcuff, to manacle
espo·so -sa *mf* spouse ‖ *m* husband ‖ *f* see **esposa**
espuela *f* spur; **echar la espuela** (coll) to take a nightcap; **espuela de caballero** delphinium, rocket larkspur; **espuela de galán** nasturtium
espuerta *f* two-handled esparto basket
espulgar §44 *tr* to delouse; to scrutinize
espuma *f* foam; (*en un vaso de cerveza*; *saliva parecida a la espuma*) froth; (*película de impurezas en la superficie de un líquido*) scum; **crecer como espuma** (coll) to grow like weeds; (coll) to have a meteoric rise; **espuma de caucho** foam rubber; **espuma de jabón** lather; **espuma de mar** meerschaum
espumadera *f* skimmer
espumajear *intr* to froth at the mouth
espumajo·so -sa *adj* foamy, frothy
espumante *adj* foaming; (*vino*) sparkling
espumar *tr* to skim ‖ *intr* to foam, to

froth; (*el jabón*) to lather; (*el vino*) to sparkle; to increase rapidly
espumarajo *m* froth, frothing at the mouth
espumilla *f* voile; (CAm, Ecuad) meringue
espumo·so -sa *adj* foamy, frothy; (*cubierto de una película*) scummy; (*jabonoso*) lathery; (*vino*) sparkling
espu·rio -ria *adj* spurious
espurrear or **espurriar** *tr* to squirt with water from the mouth
esputar *tr & intr* to spit
esputo *m* spit, saliva
esq. *abbr* **esquina**
esqueje *m* cutting, slip
esquela *f* note; announcement; death notice; **esquela amorosa** billet-doux
esqueléti·co -ca *adj* skeleton; skeletal, thin, wasted
esqueleto *m* skeleton; (CAm, Mex) blank form; (Chile) sketch, outline
esquema *m* scheme, diagram
es·quí *m* (*pl* -**quís**) ski; skiing; **esquí acuático** water ski; water skiing; **esquí remolcado** skijoring
esquia·dor -dora *adj* ski ‖ *mf* skier
esquiar §77 *intr* to ski
esquiciar *tr* to sketch
esquicio *m* sketch
esquifar *tr* (naut) to fit out, to man
esquife *m* skiff
esquiismo *m* skiing
esquila *f* sheepshearing; hand bell
esquilar *tr* to shear, to fleece
esquilimo·so -sa *adj* (coll) fastidious, squeamish
esquilmar *tr* to harvest; (*las plantas el jugo de la tierra*) to drain, exhaust; (*una fuente de riqueza*) to drain, squander, use up; to carry away, steal
esquilmo *m* harvest, farm produce; (Mex) farm scrapings
esquilmo·so -sa *adj* (coll) fastidious
esquimal *adj & mf* Eskimo
esquina *f* corner; (SAm) corner store; **a la vuelta de la esquina** around the corner; **doblar la esquina** to turn the corner; **hacer esquina** (*un edificio*) to be on the corner; **las cuatro esquinas** puss in the corner
esquina·do -da *adj* sharp-cornered; difficult, unsociable
esquinar *tr* to be on the corner of; to put in the corner; to alienate ‖ *intr* — **esquinar con** to be on the corner of ‖ *ref* — **esquinarse con** to fall out with
esquinazo *m* (coll) corner; (Arg, Chile) serenade; **dar esquinazo a** (coll) to give the slip to, to shake off
esquinencia *f* quinsy
esquinera *f* (Am) corner piece (*of furniture*)
esquirla *f* splinter
esquirol *m* scab, strikebreaker
esquisto *m* schist
esquite *m* (CAm, Mex) popcorn
esquivar *tr* to avoid, evade, shun; to dodge ‖ *ref* to withdraw; to dodge
esquivez *f* aloofness, gruffness
esqui·vo -va *adj* aloof, gruff

es
es

estable *adj* stable, permanent; full-time ‖ *mf* regular guest, permanent guest

establecer §22 *tr* to establish, to institute ‖ *ref* to settle, take up residence; to start a business, to open an office

establecimiento *m* establishment; place of business; decree, ordinance, statute

establo *m* stable

estaca *f* stake, picket, pale; cudgel, club; (*clavo largo*) spike; (hort) cutting

estacada *f* stockade, palisade; dueling ground; **dejar en la estacada** to leave in the lurch; **quedarse en la estacada** to succumb on the field of battle, to fall in a duel; to fail; to lose out

estacar §73 *tr* to stake, to stake off; to tie to a stake ‖ *ref* to stand stiff

estación *f* (*cada una de las cuatro divisiones del año*) season; (*sitio en que paran los trenes; radioemisora*) station; (*lugar en que se hace alto en un paseo, etc.*) stop; **estación balnearia** bathing resort; **estación de cabeza** (rr) terminal; **estación de carga** freight station; **estación de empalme** junction; **estación de gasolina** gas station, filling station; **estación de la seca** dry season; **estación de paso** (rr) way station; **estación de radiodifusión** broadcasting station; **estación de seguimiento** tracking station; **estación de servicio** service station; **estación difusora** or **emisora** broadcasting station; **estación gasolinera** gas station, filling station; **estación telefónica** telephone exchange

estacional *adj* seasonal

estacionamiento *m* stationing; parking; parking lot

estacionar *tr* to station; to stand, to park ‖ *intr* to stand, to park ‖ *ref* to station oneself; to be stationary; to stand, to park; **se prohibe estacionarse** no standing, no parking

estaciona·rio -ria *adj* stationary

estada *f* stay, stop

estadía *f* (*ante un pintor*) sitting; (com) demurrage; (Am) stop, stay

estadio *m* stadium; phase, stage; (*longitud*) furlong

estadista *mf* (*perito en estadística*) statistician ‖ *m* statesman

estadística *f* statistics

estadísti·co -ca *adj* statistical ‖ *m* (Am) statistician ‖ *f* see **estadística**

estadiunense *adj* American, United States ‖ *mf* American

estadi·zo -za *adj* (*aire*) heavy, stifling; (*agua*) stagnant

estado *m* state; state, condition, status; statement, report; **en estado de buena esperanza** or **en estado interesante** in the family way; **estado civil** marital status; **estado de ánimo** state of mind; **estado de cuentas** (com) statement; **estado libre asociado** commonwealth; **estado llano** commons, common people; **estado mayor** (mil) staff; **estado mayor conjunto** joint chiefs of staff; **estado mayor general** general staff; **Estados Unidos** *msg* the United States; **estado tapón** buffer state; **estar en estado de guerra** to be under martial law; **los Estados Unidos** *mpl* the United States; **tomar estado** to take a wife; to go into the church

estado-policía *m* (*pl* **estados-policías**) police state

estadounidense or **estadunidense** *adj* American, United States ‖ *mf* American

estafa *f* swindle, trick; (*estribo*) stirrup

estafar *tr* to swindle, trick; to overcharge

estafeta *f* post, courier; post office; diplomatic mail

estallar *intr* to burst; to explode; (*un incendio, una revolución; la guerra*) to break out; (*la ira*) to break forth

estallido *m* report, crash, explosion; crack; (*p.ej., de la guerra*) outbreak; **dar un estallido** to crash, explode

estambre *m* (*hebras de lana e hilo formado de ellas*) worsted; (bot) stamen; **estambre de la vida** course or thread of life

estampa *f* stamp, print, engraving; press, printing; footstep, track; aspect, appearance; **dar a la estampa** to publish, bring out; **parecer la estampa de la herejía** (coll) to be a sight, be a mess; **la propia estampa de** the very image of

estampado *m* printing, stamping; printed fabric, cotton print

estampar *tr* to stamp, to print, to engrave; (*en el ánimo*) to fix, engrave; (*p.ej., el pie*) to leave a mark of; (bb) to tool; (*arrojar con fuerza*) (coll) to dash, to slam

estampida *f* report, crash, explosion; (Am) stampede

estampido *m* report, crash, explosion; **estampido sónico** (aer) sonic boom

estampilla *f* (*sello con letrero para estampar*) stamp; (*sello con una firma en facsímile*) rubber stamp; (*sello de correos o fiscal*) (Am) stamp

estampillar *tr* to stamp; to rubberstamp

estanca·do -da *adj* stagnant; (fig) stagnant, dead

estancar §73 *tr* to stanch; to stem, check; (*un negocio*) to suspend, hold up; to corner; to monopolize ‖ *ref* to become stagnant, to become choked up

estancia *f* stay, sojourn; (*aposento*) living room; day in hospital; cost of day in hospital; (estrofa) stanza; (mil) bivouac; (Arg, Urug, Chile) cattle ranch; (Col) small country place; (Ven) truck farm

estanciero *m* (Am) rancher, cattle raiser

estan·co -ca *adj* stanch, watertight ‖ *m* government monopoly; cigar store, government store (*for sale of tobacco, matches, postage stamps, etc.*); archives; (Ecuad) liquor store

estándar *m* standard

estandardizar §60 or **estandarizar** §60 *tr* to standardize

estandarte *m* banner, standard

estandartizar §60 *tr* to standardize
estanque *m* basin, reservoir; pond, pool
estanque·ro -ra *mf* storekeeper, tobacconist; (Ecuad) saloonkeeper ‖ *m* reservoir tender
estanquillo *m* cigar store, government store (*for sale of tobacco, matches, postage stamps, etc.*); (Col, Ecuad) bar, saloon; (Mex) booth, stand
estante *adj* located, being; settled, permanent ‖ *m* shelf; shelving; bookcase, open bookcase
estantería *f* shelves, shelving; book stack
estañar *tr* to tin; to tin-plate; to solder; (Ven) to hurt, injure; (Ven) to fire
estaño *m* tin
estaquilla *f* peg, dowel, pin; (*clavo pequeño sin cabeza*) brad; (*clavo largo*) spike
estaquillar *tr* to peg, dowel; to nail
estar §37 *v aux* (*to form progressive form*) to be, e.g., **están aprendiendo el español** they are learning Spanish ‖ *intr* to be; to be in, be home; to be ready; **¿a cuántos estamos?** what day of the month is it?; **¡está bien!** O.K.!, all right!; **estar a** to cost, sell at; **estar bien** to be well; **estar bien con** to be on good terms with; **estar de** to be (*on a temporary basis*); **estar de más** (coll) to be in the way; (coll) to be unnecessary; (coll) to be idle; **estar de viaje** to be on a trip; **estar mal** to be sick, be ill; **estar mal con** to be on bad terms with; **estar para** to be about to; **estar por** to be for, be in favor of; to be about to; to have a mind to; to remain to be + *pp*; **estar sobre sí** to be wary, be on one's guard ‖ *ref* (*p.ej., en casa*) to stay; (*p.ej., quieto*) to keep
estarcido *m* stencil
estarcir §36 *tr* to stencil
estatal *adj* state
estáti·co -ca *adj* static; dumbfounded, speechless
estatificar §73 *tr* to nationalize
estatizar §60 *tr* (Am) to nationalize
estatua *f* statue; **quedarse hecho una estatua** (coll) to stand aghast
estatuir §20 *tr* to order, decree; to establish, prove
estatura *f* stature
estatuta·rio -ria *adj* statutory
estatuto *m* statute
estay *m* (naut) stay; **estay mayor** (naut) mainstay
este, esta *adj dem* (*pl* **estos, estas**) this ‖ *m* east; east wind
éste, ésta *pron dem* (*pl* **éstos, éstas**) this one, this one here; the latter; **ésta** this city
estela *f* (*de un buque*) wake; (*de cohete, humo, cuerpo celeste, etc.*) trail
estepa *f* steppe
estera *f* mat; matting; **cargado de esteras** (coll) out of patience
esterar *tr* to cover with matting ‖ *intr* (coll) to bundle up for the cold

estercolar *m* dunghill ‖ §61 *tr* to dung, to manure
estercolero *m* manure pile, dunghill; manure collector
estereofóni·co -ca *adj* stereophonic, stereo
estereoscópi·co -ca *adj* stereoscopic, stereo
estereotipa·do -da *adj* stereotyped
estéril *adj* (*que no produce nada*) sterile; (*inútil, vano*) futile
esterilizar §60 *tr* to sterilize ‖ *ref* to become sterile
esterlina *adj fem* (*libra*) sterling (*pound*)
esternón *m* breastbone
estero *m* tideland; estuary; (Arg) swamp, marsh; (Chile) stream; (Col, Ven) pool, puddle
esterto *m* death rattle; (*ruido en ciertas enfermedades, perceptible por la auscultación*) stertor, râle; **estertor agónico** death rattle
esteta *mf* aesthete ‖ *f* beautician
estéti·co -ca *adj* aesthetic ‖ *f* aesthetics
estetoscopio *m* stethoscope
estiaje *m* low water
estiba *f* (naut) stowage
estibador *m* stevedore, longshoreman
estibar *tr* to pack, to stuff; (naut) to stow
estiércol *m* dung, manure
esti·gio -gia *adj* Stygian ‖ **Estigia** *f* Styx
estigma *m* stigma
estigmatizar §60 *tr* to stigmatize
estilar *tr* (*una escritura*) to draw up in proper form; to be given to ‖ *intr* & *ref* to be in fashion
estilete *m* (*puñal*) stiletto
estilo *m* style; **por el estilo** like that, of the kind; **por el estilo de** like; **estilo directo** (gram) direct discourse; **estilo indirecto** (gram) indirect discourse
estilográfica *f* fountain pen
estima *f* esteem; (naut) dead reckoning
estimable *adj* estimable; considerable; appreciable, computable; esteemed
estimación *f* esteem, estimation; estimate, evaluation
estimar *tr* (*tener en buen concepto*) to esteem; (*apreciar, valuar*) to estimate; to think, believe; to appreciate, thank; to be fond of, to like; **estimar en poco** to hold in low esteem
estimativa *f* judgment; instinct
estimulante *adj & m* stimulant
estimular *tr* to stimulate
estímulo *m* stimulus
estío *m* summer
estipendio *m* stipend; wages
estípti·co -ca *adj* styptic; constipated; mean, stingy
estipular *tr* to stipulate
estiradamente *adv* scarcely, hardly; violently
estira·do -da *adj* conceited, stuck-up; prim, neat; tight, closefisted
estirar *tr* to stretch; (*alambre, metal*) to draw; (*planchar ligeramente*) to iron lightly; (*un escrito, discurso, cargo, etc.*) (fig) to stretch out; (*el dinero*) (fig) to stretch ‖ *ref* to stretch; to put on airs

estirón *m* jerk, tug; **dar un estirón** (coll) to grow up in no time

estirpe *f* race, stock, lineage; (*linaje*) strain, pedigree

estival *adj* summer

esto *pron dem* that; **en esto** at this point; **por esto** for this reason

estocada *f* thrust, stab, lunge; (*herida*) stab, stab wound; (*cosa que ocasiona dolor*) blow

Estocolmo *f* Stockholm

estofa *f* brocade; quality, kind

estofado *m* stew

estoi·co -ca *adj & mf* stoic

estóli·do -da *adj* stupid, imbecile

estómago *m* stomach; **estómago de avestruz** iron digestion; **tener buen estómago** or **mucho estómago** (coll) to be thick-skinned; (coll) to have an easy conscience

estopa *f* (*de lino o cáñamo*) tow; (*de calafatear*) (naut) oakum; **estopa de acero** steel wool; **estopa de algodón** cotton waste

estopilla *f* (*tela muy sutil*) lawn; (*tela ordinaria de algodón*) cheesecloth

estoque *m* rapier; sword lily, gladiola

estoquear *tr* to stab with a rapier

estor *m* blind, blockade, window shade

estorbar *tr* to hinder, obstruct; to inconvenience, bother, annoy ‖ *intr* (coll) to be in the way

estorbo *m* hindrance, obstruction; inconvenience, bother, annoyance

estorbo·so -sa *adj* hindering; bothersome, annoying

estornino *m* starling; **estornino de los pastores** grackle, myna

estornudar *intr* to sneeze

estornudo *m* sneeze, sneezing

estrado *m* (*tarima del trono*) dais; lecture platform; (archaic) lady's drawing room; **estrados** courtrooms, law courts; **citar para estrados** to subpoena

estrafala·rio -ria *adj* (coll) queer, eccentric, odd; (coll) sloppy, sloppily dressed ‖ *mf* (coll) screwball

estragar §44 *tr* to spoil, damage, vitiate

estrago *m* damage, ruin, havoc

estrambote *m* tail (*of sonnet*)

estrambóti·co -ca *adj* (coll) odd, queer

estrangul *m* (mus) reed, mouthpiece

estrangular *tr & ref* to strangle, to choke

estraperlear *intr* to deal in the black market

estraperlista *adj* black-market ‖ *mf* black-market dealer

estraperlo *m* black market

estrapontín *m* folding seat, jump seat

estratagema *f* stratagem; craftiness

estratega *m* strategist

estrategia *f* strategy; **alta estrategia** grand strategy

estratégi·co -ca *adj* strategic(al) ‖ *m* strategist

estratificar §73 *tr & ref* to stratify

estrato *m* stratum, layer

estratosfera *f* stratosphere

estraza *f* rag; brown paper

estrechar *tr* (*reducir a menor ancho*) to narrow; (*apretar*) to tighten; to press,

pursue; to force, compel; to hug, embrace; to squeeze; **estrechar la mano a** to shake hands with ‖ *ref* to narrow down; to contract; to hug, embrace; (*reducir los gastos*) to retrench; **estrecharse en** to squeeze in; **estrecharse la mano** (*dos personas*) to shake hands

estrechez *f* narrowness; rightness; (*amistad íntima*) closeness, intimacy; austerity, strictness; poverty, want, need; trouble, jam; **estrechez de miras** narrow outlook, narrow-mindedness; **hallarse en gran estrechez** to be in dire straits

estre·cho -cha *adj* narrow; tight; close, intimate; austere, strict; stingy, tight; poor, needy; mean ‖ *m* (*paso angosto en el mar*) strait; fix, predicament

estrechura *f* narrowness; tightness; closeness, intimacy; austerity, strictness; trouble, predicament

estregar §66 *tr* to rub hard; to scour

estregón *m* hard rub

estrella *f* star; (typ) asterisk, star; (mov & theat) star; (*hado, destino*) (fig) star; **estrella de los Alpes** edelweiss; **estrella de mar** starfish; **estrella de rabo** comet; **estrella filante** or **fugaz** shooting star; **estrella fulgurante** (astr) flare star; **estrella polar** polestar; **estrella vespertina** evening star; **ver las estrellas** (coll) to see stars

estrella·do -da *adj* (*cielo*) starry; starspangled; star-shaped; (*huevos*) fried

estrellamar *m* starfish

estrellar *adj* star ‖ *tr* to star, to spangle with stars; (*huevos*) to fry; to shatter, dash to pieces ‖ *ref* to be spangled with stars; to crash; **estrellarse con** to clash with

estrellón *m* large star; (*fuego artificial*) star; (Am) smash-up

estremecer §22 *tr* to shake; (*el aire*) to rend; (fig) to shake, upset ‖ *ref* to shake, tremble, shiver, shudder

estrena *f* (*regalo que se da en señal de agradecimiento*) handsel; first use

estrenar *tr* to use for the first time, to wear for the first time; (*un drama*) to perform for the first time; (*un cine*) to show for the first time; to try out for the first time ‖ *ref* to make the day's first transaction; to appear for the first time; (*un drama, un cine*) to open

estrenista *mf* first-nighter

estreno *m* beginning, debut; première, first performance; first use

estre·nuo -nua *adj* strenuous, vigorous, enterprising

estreñimiento *m* constipation

estreñir §72 *tr* to constipate

estrépito *m* racket, crash; fuss, show

estrepito·so -sa *adj* loud, noisy, boisterous; notorious; shocking

estría *f* flute, groove

estriar §77 *tr* to flute, groove

estribar *intr* to lean, rest; to be based, to depend

estriberón *m* stepping stone

estribillo *m* (*de un poema*) burden, refrain; pet word, pet phrase

estribo *m* (*de coche*) step; (*de auto-móvil*) running board; (*apoyo para el pie*) footboard; (*para el pie del jinete*) stirrup; abutment, buttress; (fig) foundation, support; **perder los estribos** to fly off the handle, to lose one's head

estribor *m* starboard

estricnina *f* strychnine

estricote *m* (Ven) riotous living; **al estricote** hither and thither

estric·to -ta *adj* strict, severe, rigorous; proper, punctual; (*sentido de una palabra*) narrow

estrictura *f* (pathol) stricture

estrige *f* barn owl; (*Athene noctua*) little owl

estro *m* poetic inspiration; (*de animal*) rut, heat

estrofa *f* strophe

estroncio *m* strontium

estropajo *m* mop; dishcloth; **servir de estropajo** (coll) to be forced to do the dirty work; (coll) to be treated with indifference

estropajo·so -sa *adj* (coll) raggedy, slovenly; (*carne*) (coll) tough, leathery; (coll) spluttering

estropear *tr* to spoil, ruin, damage; to abuse, mistreat; to cripple, maim ‖ *ref* to spoil, go to ruin; to fail

estropicio *m* (coll) breakage; (coll) havoc, ruin; (coll) fracas, rumpus

estructura *f* structure

estruendo *m* noise, crash, boom; confusion, uproar; pomp, show; fame

estruendo·so -sa *adj* noisy, booming

estrujar *tr* to squeeze; to press, crush, mash; to bruise; to rumple; (coll) to drain, exhaust

estuante *adj* hot, burning

estuario *m* estuary; tideland

estucar §73 *tr* to stucco

estuco *m* stucco; **estuco de París** plaster of Paris

estuche *m* case, box; (*caja y utensilios que se guardan en ella*) kit; casket, jewel case; (*para tijeras*) sheath; **estuche de afeites** compact, vanity case; **ser un estuche** (coll) to be a handy fellow

estudia·do -da *adj* affected, studied

estudiantado *m* student body

estudiante *mf* student

estudiantil *adj* student

estudiar *tr* to study; (*la lección a una persona*) to hear (*someone's lesson*) ‖ *intr* to study; **estudiar para . . .** to study to become . . .

estudio *m* study; (*aposento*) studio; (mus) étude; **altos estudios** advanced studies

estudio·so -sa *adj* studious ‖ *m* student, scholar

estufa *f* stove; steam cabinet, steam room; foot stove; (*invernáculo*) hothouse

estul·to -ta *adj* stupid, silly, foolish

estupefac·to -ta *adj* stupefied, dumbfounded

estupen·do -da *adj* stupendous; (coll) famous, distinguished

estúpi·do -da *adj* stupid ‖ *mf* dolt

estupor *m* stupor; surprise, amazement

estuprar *tr* to rape, violate

estupro *m* rape, violation

estuque *m* stucco

esturión *m* sturgeon

etapa *f* stage; **a etapas pequeñas** by easy stages

éter *m* ether

etére·o -a *adj* ethereal

eternidad *f* eternity

eternizar §60 *tr* to prolong endlessly ‖ *ref* to be endless, be interminable

eter·no -na *adj* eternal

éti·co -ca *adj* ethical ‖ *f* ethics

etileno *m* ethylene

etilo *m* ethyl

étimo *m* etymon

etimología *f* etymology

etíope *adj* & *mf* Ethiopian

etiópi·co -ca *adj* & *m* Ethiopic

etiqueta *f* (*marbete*) tag, label; (*ceremonial que se debe observar*) etiquette; (*ceremonia en la manera de tratarse*) formality; **de etiqueta** formal, full-dress; **de etiqueta menor** semiformal; **estar de etiqueta** to have become cool toward each other

etiquetar *tr* to tag, to label

etiquete·ro -ra *adj* formal, ceremonious; full of compliments

etiquez *f* (pathol) consumption

étni·co -ca *adj* ethnic(al); (gram) gentilic

etnografía *f* ethnography

etnología *f* ethnology

E.U.A *abbr* **Estados Unidos de América**

eucalipto *m* eucalyptus

Eucaristía *f* Eucharist

eufemismo *m* euphemism

eufemísti·co -ca *adj* euphemistic

eufonía *f* euphony

eufóni·co -ca *adj* euphonic, euphonious

euforia *f* euphoria; endurance, fortitude

eufuísmo *m* euphuism

eufuísti·co -ca *adj* euphuistic

eugenesia *f* eugenics

eunuco *m* eunuch

euritmia *f* regular pulse

euro *m* east wind

Europa *f* Europe

europe·o -a *adj* & *mf* European

eutanasia *f* euthanasia

eutrapelia *f* moderation; lightheartedness; simple pastime

evacuación *f* evacuation; **evacuación de basuras** garbage disposal

evacuar §21 & regular *tr* to evacuate; (*un trámite*) to transact; (*una visita*) to pay; (*un encargo, un asunto*) to do, carry out; **evacuar el vientre** to have a movement of the bowels ‖ *intr* to evacuate; to have a movement of the bowels

evadi·do -da *adj* escaped ‖ *mf* escapee

evadir *tr* to avoid, evade, elude ‖ *ref* to evade; to escape, to flee

evaluar §21 *tr* to evaluate; to value

evangéli·co -ca *adj* evangelic(al)

evangelio *m* (coll) gospel, gospel truth ‖ **Evangelio** *m* Gospel, Evangel

evangelista *m* Gospel singer or chanter;

(Mex) public writer, penman || **Evangelista** *m* Evangelist

evaporar *tr* & *ref* to evaporate

evaporizar §60 *tr, intr* & *ref* to vaporize

evasión *f* (*efugio, evasiva*) evasion; (*fuga*) escape

evasi•vo -va *adj* evasive || *f* loophole, pretext, excuse

evento *m* chance, happening, contingency; (Col) sports event; **a todo evento** in any event

eventual *adj* contingent; (*emolumentos; gastos*) incidental

eventualidad *f* eventuality, contingency; uncertainty

evidencia *f* evidence, obviousness; (*prueba judicial*) (Am) evidence; **evidencia moral** moral certainty

evidenciar *tr* to show, make evident

evidente *adj* evident, obvious

evitable *adj* avoidable

evitación *f* avoidance; prevention

evitar *tr* to avoid, shun; (*p.ej., el polvo*) to keep off; to prevent; **evitar** + *inf* to avoid + *ger*; to save from + *ger*, e.g., **la luz de la luna nos evitó tener que encender los faroles** the light of the moon saved us from having to light the lights

evo *m* (poet) age, aeon; (theol) eternity

evocar §73 *tr* to evoke; (*p.ej., los demonios*) to invoke

evolución *f* evolution; change, development (*of one's point of view, plans, conduct, etc.*)

evolucionar *intr* to evolve; to change, develop; (mil & nav) to maneuver

ex *adj* ex- (*former*), e.g., **el ex presidente** the ex-president

ex abrupto *adv* brashly || *m* brash remark

exacción *f* (*de impuestos, deudas, multas, etc.*) exaction, levy; (*cobro injusto*) extortion

exacerbar *tr* to exacerbate, aggravate

exactitud *f* exactness; punctuality

exac•to -ta *adj* exact; punctual, faithful || **exacto** *interj* right!

exactor *m* tax collector

exagerar *tr* to exaggerate

exalta•do -da *adj* exalted; extreme, hotheaded; wrought-up; radical

exaltar *tr* to exalt; to extol || *ref* to be wrought-up, get excited

examen *m* examination; **examen de ingreso** entrance examination; **sufrir un examen** to take an examination

examinar *tr* to examine; to inspect || *ref* to take an examination; **examinarse de ingreso** to take entrance examinations

exangüe *adj* bloodless; (coll) weak, exhausted; (coll) dead

exánime *adj* (*sin vida*) lifeless; (*desmayado*) faint, in a faint, lifeless

exasperar *tr* to exasperate

Exc.ª *abbr* **Excelencia**

excandecer §22 *tr* to incense, enrage

excarcelación *f* release

excarcelar *tr* (*a un preso*) to release

excavadora *f* power shovel

excavar *tr* to excavate; to loosen soil around

excedente *adj* excess; excessive; on leave || *m* excess, surplus

exceder *tr* (*ser mayor que*) to exceed; (*aventajar*) to excel || *ref* to go too far, go to extremes; **excederse a sí mismo** to outdo oneself

excelencia *f* excellence, excellency; **por excelencia** par excellence; **Su Excelencia** Your Excellency

excelente *adj* excellent

excel•so -sa *adj* lofty, sublime || **el Excelso** the Most High

excéntrica *f* eccentric

excentricidad *f* eccentricity

excéntri•co -ca *adj* eccentric; (*barrio*) outlying || *mf* eccentric || *f* see **excéntrica**

excepción *f* exception; **a excepción de** with the exception of

excepcional *adj* exceptional

excepto *prep* except

exceptuar §21 *tr* to except; (*eximir*) to exempt

excerpta or **excerta** *f* excerpt

excesi•vo -va *adj* excessive; excess

exceso *m* excess; **exceso de equipaje** excess baggage; **exceso de peso** excess weight; **exceso de velocidad** speeding

excitable *adj* excitable

excitación *f* excitement; excitation

excitante *adj* & *m* stimulant

excitar *tr* to excite, stir up, stimulate || *ref* to become excited

exclamación *f* exclamation

exclamar *tr* & *intr* to exclaim

exclaustrar *tr* (*a un religioso*) to secularize

excluir §20 *tr* to exclude

exclusión *f* exclusion; **con exclusión de** to the exclusion of

exclusiva *f* rejection, turndown; sole right, monopoly; (*anticipación de una noticia por un periódico*) news beat

exclusive *adv* exclusively || *prep* exclusive of, not counting

exclusivista *adj* exclusive, clannish || *mf* snob

exclusi•vo -va *adj* exclusive || *f* see **exclusiva**

Exc.mo *abbr* **Excelentísimo**

ex combatiente *m* ex-serviceman

excomulgar §44 *tr* to excommunicate; (coll) to ostracize, banish

excomunión *f* excommunication

excoriar *tr* to skin || *ref* to skin oneself; (*p.ej., el codo*) to skin

excrementar *intr* to have a bowel movement

excremento *m* excrement

exculpar *tr* to exculpate, exonerate

excursión *f* excursion, outing

excursionista *mf* excursionist, tourist

excusa *f* excuse; **a excusa** secretly; **excusa es decir** it is unnecessary to say

excusabaraja *f* basket with lid

excusable *adj* excusable; avoidable

excusadamente *adv* unnecessarily

excusa•do -da *adj* exempt; unnecessary; private, set apart; (*puerta*) side || *m* toilet

excusa•lí *m* (*pl* **-líes**) small apron

excusar _tr_ to excuse; to exempt; to avoid; to prevent; to make unnecessary; **excusar + inf** to not have to + inf ‖ _ref_ to excuse oneself; to apologize; **excusarse de + inf** to decline to + inf

exención _f_ exemption

exencionar _tr_ to exempt

exentamente _adv_ freely; frankly, simply

exentar _tr_ to exempt

exen·to -ta _adj_ exempt; open, unobstructed; free, disengaged

exequias _fpl_ obsequies

exfolia·dor -dora _adj_ (Am) tear-off

exhalación _f_ exhalation; flash of lightning; shooting star; fume, vapor; **como una exhalación** (coll) like a flash of lightning

exhalar _tr_ to exhale, emit; (_suspiros, quejas_) to breathe forth; **exhalar el último suspiro** to breathe one's last ‖ _ref_ to exhale; (_con el ejercicio violento del cuerpo_) to breathe hard; to hurry; to crave

exhausti·vo -va _adj_ exhaustive

exhaus·to -ta _adj_ exhausted; (coll) wasted away

exheredar _tr_ to disinherit

exhibición _f_ exhibition; exhibit

exhibir _tr_ to exhibit; (Mex) to pay ‖ _ref_ (coll) to make oneself evident

exhilarante _adj_ exhilarating; (_gas_) laughing

exhortar _tr_ to exhort

exhumar _tr_ to exhume

exigencia _f_ exigency, requirement

exigente _adj_ exigent, demanding

exigir §27 _tr_ to exact, require, demand

exi·guo -gua _adj_ meager, scanty

exila·do -da _adj & mf_ (Am) exile

exi·mio -mia _adj_ choice, select, superior; distinguished

eximir _tr_ to exempt

existencia _f_ existence; **en existencia** in stock; **existencias** (com) stock

existente _adj_ existing, extant; in stock

existir _intr_ to exist

exitazo _m_ smash hit

exitista _adj_ (Arg) me-too ‖ _mf_ (Arg) me-tooer

éxito _m_ (_resultado feliz_) success; (_canción, cine, etc. que ha tenido mucho éxito_) hit; (_resultado de un negocio_) outcome, result; **éxito de librería** best seller; **éxito de taquilla** box-office hit, good box office; **éxito de venta** best seller; **éxito rotundo** smash hit

exito·so -sa _adj_ (Arg) successful

ex li·bris _m_ (_pl_ -bris) bookplate

éxodo _m_ exodus; **éxodo de técnicos** brain drain

exonerar _tr_ to exonerate, to relieve; to discharge, dismiss; **exonerar el vientre** to have a movement of the bowels

exorar _tr_ to beg, entreat

exorbitante _adj_ exorbitant

exorcizar §60 _tr_ to exorcise

exornar _tr_ to adorn, embellish

exóti·co -ca _adj_ exotic; striking, stunning, glamorous

expandir _tr & ref_ (Arg, Chile) to expand, extend, spread

expansión _f_ expansion; (_manifestación_

efusiva) expansiveness; (_difusión de una opinión_) spread; rest, recreation

expansionar _ref_ to expand; to open one's heart; to relax, take it easy

expansi·vo -va _adj_ expansive

expatria·do -da _adj & mf_ expatriate

expectación _f_ expectancy

expectativa _f_ expectation; **estar en la expectativa de** to be expecting, to be on the lookout for

expectorar _tr & intr_ to expectorate

expedición _f_ (_excursión para realizar una empresa_) expedition; (_remesa_) shipment; (_de un certificado, títulos, etc._) issuance; (_agilidad, facilidad_) expedition

expedi·dor -dora _mf_ sender, shipper

expediente _m_ expedient; makeshift, apology; (_agilidad, facilidad_) expedition; (_todos los papeles correspondientes a un asunto_) dossier; (law) action, proceedings; **expediente académico** (educ) record

expedienteo _m_ red tape

expedir §50 _tr_ to send, ship, remit; (_títulos_) to issue; (_despachar, cursar_) to expedite

expeditar _tr_ (Am) to expedite

expediti·vo -va _adj_ expeditious

expedi·to -ta _adj_ ready; clear, open, unencumbered

expeler _tr_ to expel, eject

expende·dor -dora _mf_ dealer, retailer; ticket agent; **expendedor de moneda falsa** distributor of counterfeit money

expendeduría _f_ cigar store (_for sale of state-monopolized articles_)

expender _tr_ to spend; to dispense; to sell at retail; (_moneda falsa_) to circulate

expendio _m_ (Am) shop, store; (Am) retail; (Mex) cigar store

expensar _tr_ (Chile, Guat, Mex) to pay the cost of

expensas _fpl_ expenses

experiencia _f_ (_enseñanza que se adquiere con la práctica o con el vivir; suceso en que uno ha participado, cosa que uno ha experimentado_) experience; (_ensayo, experimento_) experiment

experimenta·do -da _adj_ experienced

experimentar _tr_ to experience, undergo, feel; to test, try, try out ‖ _intr_ to experiment

experimento _m_ experiment

exper·to -ta _adj & m_ expert

expiación _f_ expiation, atonement; purification

expiar §77 _tr_ to expiate, atone for; to purify

expirar _intr_ to expire

explanación _f_ grading, leveling; explanation

explanada _f_ esplanade

explanar _tr_ to grade, to level; to explain

explayar _tr_ to enlarge, extend ‖ _ref_ to spread out, extend; to go for an outing; to expatiate, talk at length; **explayarse con** to unbosom oneself to

explicación _f_ explanation

ev
ex

explicar §73 *tr* to explain; (*exponer*) to expound; (*exculpar*) to explain away; (*una clase*) to teach ‖ *intr* to explain ‖ *ref* to explain oneself; to understand, make out

explicati·vo -va *adj* explanatory

explíci·to -ta *adj* explicit

exploración *f* exploration; (mil) scouting; (telv) scanning

explora·dor -dora *mf* explorer ‖ *m* boy scout; (mil) scout

explorar *tr* to explore; (mil) to scout; (telv) to scan

explosión *f* explosion; (*de gases en un motor*) combustion

explosi·vo -va *adj & m* explosive ‖ *f* (phonet) explosive

explotación *f* operation, running; exploitation

explotar *tr* to operate, to run; (*una mina*) to work; to exploit ‖ *intr* to explode

exponente *m* exponent

exponer §54 *tr* to expose; (*explicar*) to expound; (*a un niño recién nacido*) to abandon ‖ *intr* to display, show, exhibit; (eccl) to expose the Host ‖ *ref* to expose oneself; to be on view

exportación *f* exportation, export; (*mercaderías que se exportan*) exports

exporta·dor -dora *mf* exporter

exportar *tr & intr* to export

exposición *f* exposition; (*a un peligro; con relación a los puntos cardinales*) exposure; (phot) exposure; (rhet) exposition; **exposición universal** world's fair

exposímetro *m* light meter

expósi·to -ta *mf* foundling

exposi·tor -tora *mf* exhibitor

exprés *m* express train; (Mex) express company

expresa·do -da *adj* above-mentioned

expresamente *adv* express, expressly

expresar *tr* to express ‖ *ref* to express oneself

expresión *f* expression; (*acción de exprimir*) squeezing; (*zumo exprimido*) juice; **expresiones** regards

expresi·vo -va *adj* expressive; kind, affectionate

expre·so -sa *adj* express ‖ *m* (*tren muy rápido; correo extraordinario*) express; (Am) express company

exprimidera *f* squeezer; **exprimidera de naranjas** orange squeezer

exprimi·do -da *adj* lean, skinny; stiff, stuck-up; affected, prim, prudish

exprimidor *m* wringer; squeezer; **exprimidor de ropa** clothes wringer

exprimir *tr* to squeeze, press; (*p.ej., la ropa blanca*) to wring, wring out; (*extraer apretando*) to express

ex profeso *adv* on purpose

expropiar *tr* to expropriate

expues·to -ta *adj* dangerous, hazardous

expugnar *tr* to take by storm

expulsanie·ves *m* (*pl* -ves) snowplow

expulsar *tr* to expel

expulsión *f* expulsion

expurgar §44 *tr* to expurgate

exquisi·to -ta *adj* exquisite

extasiar §77 & **regular** *ref* to go into ecstasy

éxta·sis *m* (*pl* -sis) ecstasy

extáti·co -ca *adj* ecstatic

extemporal *adj* unseasonable

extemporáne·o -a *adj* unseasonable; untimely, inopportune

extender §51 *tr* to extend, to stretch out, to spread out; to spread; (*un documento*) to draw up ‖ *ref* to extend, to stretch out; to spread; **extenderse a** or **hasta** to amount to

extendidamente *adv* at length, in detail

extensión *f* extension; (*vasta superficie, p.ej., del océano*) expanse; (*alcance, importancia*) extent; extending

extensi·vo -va *adj* extensive; **hacer extensivos a** to extend (*e.g., good wishes*) to

exten·so -sa *adj* extensive, extended, vast; **por extenso** at length, in detail

extenuar §21 *tr* to weaken, emaciate

exterior *adj* exterior, outer, outside; foreign ‖ *m* exterior, outside; appearance, bearing; **al exterior** or **a lo exterior** on the outside; outwardly; **del exterior** from abroad; **en el exterior** on the outside; abroad; **en exteriores** (mov) on location

exterioridad *f* externals, outward appearance; **exterioridades** pomp, show

exteriorista *adj* outgoing, outgiving ‖ *mf* extrovert

exteriorizar §60 *tr* to reveal ‖ *ref* to unbosom one's heart

exterminar *tr* to exterminate

exterminio *m* extermination

exter·no -na *adj* external ‖ *mf* day pupil

extinción *f* extinction; cancellation, elimination

extinguir §29 *tr* to extinguish, put out; to wipe out, put an end to; to fulfil, carry out; (*un plazo, un tiempo*) to spend, to serve ‖ *ref* to be extinguished, go out; to come to an end

extin·to -ta *adj* (*volcán*) extinct; (Am) deceased ‖ *mf* (Am) deceased

extintor *m* fire extinguisher; **extintor de espuma** foam extinguisher; **extintor de granada** fire grenade

extirpar *tr* to extirpate, to eradicate

extorno *m* premium adjustment (*based on change in policy*)

extorsión *f* extortion; harm, damage

extorsionar *tr* to harm, damage; (Am) to extort

extra *adj* extra; **extra de** (coll) in addition to, besides ‖ *mf* (theat) extra ‖ *m* (*de un periódico*) extra; (coll) extra, bonus

extracción *f* extraction; (*en la lotería*) drawing numbers; **extracción de raíces** (math) evolution

extractar *tr* (*un escrito*) to abstract

extracto *m* (*de un escrito*) abstract; (pharm) extract

extracurricular *adj* extracurricular

extradición *f* extradition

extraer §75 *tr* to extract; to pull; (*la raíz*) (math) to extract

extrafuerte *adj* heavy-duty

extralimitar *ref* to go too far

extramural *adj* extramural

extranjerismo *m* borrowing
extranje·ro -ra *adj* foreign, alien ‖ *mf* foreigner, alien; **extranjero enemigo** enemy alien ‖ *m* foreign country; **al extranjero** abroad; **del extranjero** from abroad; **en el extranjero** abroad
extrañar *tr* to banish, expatriate; to surprise; to find strange; (*Am*) to miss ‖ *ref* to be surprised; to refuse
extrañeza *f* strangeness, peculiarity; (*desavenencia*) estrangement; wonder, surprise
extra·ño -ña *adj* foreign; (*raro, singular*) strange; extraneous; **extraño a** unconnected with ‖ *mf* foreigner
extraoficial *adj* unofficial
extraordina·rio -ria *adj* extraordinary; extra, special ‖ *m* extra dish; special mail; (*de un periódico*) extra
extrapla·no -na *adj* extra-flat
extrapolar *tr & intr* to extrapolate
extrarradio *m* outer edge of town
extrasensorial *adj* extrasensory
extravagancia *f* (*singularidad, ridiculez*) extravagance, wildness, folly
extravagante *adj* (*singular, ridículo*) extravagant, wild, foolish; (*correspondencia en la casa de correos*) in transit
extravia·do -da *adj* lost, misplaced; astray, gone astray; (*lugar*) out-of-the-way
extraviar §77 *tr* to lead astray, mislead; to mislay, misplace ‖ *ref* to get lost, go astray; to go wrong; to get out of line

extravío *m* going astray; loss; misleading; misconduct; misplacement
extrema *f* (*escasez grande*) (coll) extremity; (*de la vida*) (coll) end, last moment
extremar *tr* to carry far, carry to the limit ‖ *ref* to strive hard
extremaunción *f* extreme unction
extreme·ño -ña *adj* frontier
extremidad *f* extremity; end, tip; **extremidades** (*pies y manos*) extremities; **la última extremidad** one's last moment
extremista *mf* extremist
extre·mo -ma *adj* extreme; utmost; critical, desperate ‖ *m* extremity; (*de la calle*) end; (*del dedo*) tip; (*punto último*) extreme; great care; (*de una conversación, una carta*) point; winter pasture; **al extremo de** to the point of; **de extremo a extremo** from one end to the other; **hacer extremos** to be demonstrative, to gush ‖ *f* see **extrema**
extremo·so -sa *adj* extreme, forthright; effusive, gushy, demonstrative
extrínse·co -ca *adj* extrinsic
extroverti·do -da *mf* extrovert
exuberante *adj* exuberant; luxuriant
exudar *tr & intr* to exude
exultante *adj* exultant
exultar *intr* to exult
exvoto *m* votive offering
eyacular *tr & intr* to ejaculate

ex
fa

F

F, f (efe) *f* seventh letter of the Spanish alphabet
f.a.b. *abbr* franco a bordo
fabada *f* pork-and-bean stew (*in Asturias*)
fábrica *f* factory, plant; building, masonry; (eccl) vestry
fabricación *f* manufacture; **fabricación en serie** mass production
fabricante *mf* manufacturer
fabricar §73 *tr* to manufacture; to devise, invent; to fabricate
fabril *adj* factory
fabriquero *m* manufacturer; charcoal burner; churchwarden
fábula *f* fable; (*p.ej., de un drama*) plot, story; rumor, gossip; (*mentira*) story, lie; (*objeto de murmuración*) talk of the town
fabulario *m* book of fables
fabulo·so -sa *adj* fabulous
facción *f* faction; feature; battle; **estar de facción** (mil) to be on duty; **facciones** features
facciona·rio -ria *adj* factional
faceta *f* facet
facetada *f* (Mex) flat joke
face·to -ta *adj* (Mex) affected; (Mex) finicky ‖ *f* see **faceta**

facial *adj* facial
fácil *adj* easy; pliant, yielding; likely; loose, wanton
facilidad *f* facility, ease, easiness; **facilidades de pago** easy payments
facilitar *tr* to facilitate, to expedite; to furnish, supply
facili·tón -tona *adj* (coll) bumbling, brash ‖ *mf* (coll) bumbler
facinero·so -sa *adj* wicked ‖ *mf* villain
facistol *m* choir desk
facón *m* (Arg, Urug) gaucho knife
facsímile *m* facsimile
factible *adj* feasible
factor *m* factor; commission merchant; baggageman; freight agent
factoría *f* trading post; (Ecuad, Peru) foundry; (Mex) factory
factura *f* invoice, bill; workmanship; **factura simulada** pro forma invoice; **según factura** as per invoice
facturación *f* invoicing, billing; (*del equipaje*) checking
facturar *tr* to invoice, to bill; (*el equipaje*) to check
facultad *f* faculty; (*de la universidad*) school; knowledge, skill; power; **facultad de altos estudios** graduate school

facultar *tr* to empower, to authorize
facultati·vo -va *adj* faculty; optional ‖ *m* doctor, physician
facundia *f* eloquence, fluency
facun·do -da *adj* eloquent, fluent
facha *mf* (*adefesio*) (coll) sight ‖ *f* look, appearance; **facha a facha** face to face
fachada *f* façade; (*de un libro*) title page; (coll) look, build, bearing; **hacer fachada con** to overlook, to look out on
facha·do -da *adj* — **bien fachado** good-looking ‖ *f* see **fachada**
fachenda *m* (coll) boaster, show-off ‖ *f* (coll) boasting
fachendear *intr* (coll) to boast, to show off
fachendista, fachen·dón -dona, fachen-do·so -sa *adj* (coll) boastful ‖ *mf* (coll) boaster, show-off
fachinal *m* (Arg) marshland
fada *f* fairy, witch
faena *f* work; toil; chore, task, job; (taur) windup; (taur) stunt, trick; (mil) fatigue, fatigue duty; (Guat, Mex, W-I) extra work, overtime; (Ecuad) morning work in the field; (Chile) gang of farm hands
faenero *m* (Chile) farm hand
Faetón *m* Phaëthon
fagot *m* bassoon
faisán *m* pheasant
faja *f* sash, girdle; bandage; band, strip; newspaper wrapper; (*de carretera*) lane; (*de tierra*) strip; **faja central** or **divisoria** median strip; **faja medical** supporter
fajar *tr* to wrap; to bandage; to swaddle; (*un periódico o revista*) to put a wrapper on; (Am) to beat, thrash; (Am) to attack ‖ *ref* to put on a sash
fajardo *m* meat pie
fajín *m* sash
fajina *f* fagot; fire wood; (mil) call to quarters
fajo *m* bundle; (*de papel moneda*) roll; (Am) swig; (Mex) blow; (Mex) leather belt; **fajos** swaddling clothes
falacia *f* deception; deceitfulness
falange *f* phalanx
falangia *f* daddy-longlegs
fa·laz *adj* (*pl* **-laces**) deceitful; deceptive
falba·lá *m* (*pl* **-laes**) gore; flounce, ruffle
falce *m* sickle; falchion
falda *f* skirt, dress; (*regazo*) lap; flap, fold; (*del sombrero*) brim; foothill; (*mujer*) (coll) skirt; **cosido a las faldas de** tied to the apron strings of
falde·ro -ra *adj* skirt; (*perro*) lap; lady-loving ‖ *m* lap dog
faldillas *fpl* skirts, coattails
faldón *m* coattail; shirttail; saddle flap
falible *adj* fallible
falsada *f* swoop (*of bird of prey*)
falsa·rio -ria *adj* lying ‖ *mf* falsifier, crook; liar
falsear *tr* to falsify; to counterfeit; to forge; (*la verdad*) to distort; (*una cerradura*) to pick; to bevel ‖ *intr* to sag, to buckle; to give, give way
falsedad *f* falsity; (*mentira*) falsehood

falsete *m* falsetto; plug, tap; door (*between rooms*)
falsetista *f* falsetto
falsía *f* falsity, treachery; unsteadiness
falsificación *f* falsification; fake; counterfeit; forgery
falsificar §73 *tr* to falsify; to fake; to counterfeit; to forge
falsilla *f* guide lines
fal·so -sa *adj* false; counterfeit; (*caballo*) vicious ‖ *m* patch; **coger en falso** (Mex) to catch in a lie; **enviar en falso** to bluff
falta *f* fault; lack, want; misdeed; absence; (*ausencia de la clase*) cut; (sport) fault; **a falta de** for want of; **echar en falta** to miss; **falta de ortografía** misspelling; **hacer falta** to be needed; to be lacking; **hacerle falta a uno** to need, e.g., **le hacen falta a Juan estos libros** John needs these books; to miss, e.g., **Vd. me hace mucha falta** I miss you very much; **sin falta** without fail
faltar *intr* to be missing, be lacking, be wanting; to fall short; to run out; to be absent; to fail; to die; to lack, to need, e.g., **me falta dinero** I lack money, I need money; **faltar a la clase** to cut class; **faltar a la verdad** to fail to tell the truth; **faltar a una cita** to fail to keep an appointment; **faltar . . . para** to be . . . to, e.g., **faltan cinco minutos para las dos** it is five minutes to two; **faltar poco para** to come near; **faltar por** to remain to be, e.g., **faltan por escribir dos cartas** two letters remain to be written
fal·to -ta *adj* short, lacking; (*peso o medida*) short; (Arg) dull, stupid; (Col) proud, vain; **falto de** short of ‖ *f* see **falta**
fal·tón -tona *adj* (coll) dilatory, remiss; (Arg) simple-minded
falto·so -sa *adj* (coll) addlebrained; (Col) quarrelsome; (CAm, Mex) disrespectful
faltriquera *f* pocket; handbag; **faltriquera de reloj** watch fob; **rascarse la faltriquera** (coll) to cough up
falúa *f* barge, tender
falucho *m* felucca
falla *f* failure, breakdown; defect; (geol) fault; (Mex) baby's bonnet
fallar *tr* to trump; to judge, pass judgment on ‖ *intr* to fail, to miss; to misfire; to sag, weaken; to break down; to judge, pass judgment
falleba *f* espagnolette
fallecer §22 *intr* to die; to fail, expire
falleci·do -da *adj* deceased, late
falli·do -da *adj* unsuccessful; bankrupt; (*deuda*) uncollectible
fallir §13 *intr* to fail; (Ven) to go bankrupt
fa·llo -lla *adj* (Chile) silly, simple; **estar fallo a** to be out of (*cards of a suit*) ‖ *m* short suit; decision; judgment, verdict; **tener fallo a** or **de** to be out of ‖ *f* see **falla**
fama *f* fame; reputation; rumor; (Chile) bull's-eye; **correr fama** to be ru-

mored; **es fama** it is said, it is rumored

faméli·co -ca *adj* famished, starving

familia *f* family

familiar *adj* familiar; family; (*sin ceremonia*) informal; (*lenguaje, estilo*) colloquial ‖ *m* member of the family; member of the household; acquaintance; **familiar dependiente** dependent

familiaridad *f* familiarity

familiarizar §60 *tr* to familiarize ‖ *ref* to become familiar; to become too familiar; to familiarize oneself

famo·so -sa *adj* famous; (*excelente*) (coll) famous; (*formidable*) (coll) some, e.g., **famoso sujeto** some guy

fámu·lo -la *mf* (coll) servant

fanal *m* beacon, lighthouse; lantern; bell glass, bell jar; lamp shade

fanáti·co -ca *adj* fanatic(al) ‖ *mf* fanatic; (sport) fan

fanatismo *m* fanaticism

fanega *f* 1.58 bu.; **fanega de tierra** 1.59 acres

fanfarria *f* fanfare; (coll) blustering

fanfa·rrón -rrona *adj* (coll) blustering, bragging; (coll) flashy ‖ *mf* (coll) blusterer, braggart

fanfarronada *f* (coll) bluster, bravado

fanfarronnear *intr* (coll) to bluster, to brag

fanfarronería *f* (coll) blustering, bragging, sword rattling

fanfurriña *f* (coll) pet, peeve

fango *m* mud, mire; **llenar de fango** (fig) to sling mud at

fango·so -sa *adj* muddy; sticky, gooey

fantasear *tr* to dream of ‖ *intr* to fancy, to daydream; **fantasear de** to boast of being

fantasía *f* fantasy; fancy; conceit, vanity; imagery; **con fantasía** (Arg) hard; **de fantasía** fancy, imitation; **tocar por fantasía** (Ven) to play by ear

fantasio·so -sa *adj* (coll) vain, conceited

fantasma *m* phantom, ghost; stuffed shirt; (telv) ghost; **fantasma magnético** magnetic curves ‖ *f* scarecrow, hobgoblin

fantas·món -mona *adj* (coll) conceited ‖ *mf* (coll) conceited person ‖ *m* (coll) stuffed shirt; (coll) scarecrow

fantásti·co -ca *adj* fantastic; fancy; conceited

fantoche *m* puppet, marionette; (coll) nincompoop, whippersnapper

faquín *m* street porter, errand boy

fara·lá *m* (*pl* **-laes**) ruffle, flounce; (coll) frill

faramalla *mf* (coll) cheat, swindler ‖ *f* (coll) jabber, claptrap; (coll) bluff, fake; (Chile) bragging

faramalle·ro -ra *or* **farama·llón -llona** *adj* (coll) scheming, swindling ‖ *mf* (coll) schemer, swindler

farándula *f* (*baile*) farandole; (coll) gossip, scheming; (coll) theater people; (*de gente*) (Arg) crush, milling

farandulear *intr* (coll) to boast, to show off

Faraón *m* Pharaoh

faraute *m* herald, messenger; interpreter; (*actor*) prologue; (coll) busybody

fardel *m* bag, bundle; (coll) sloppy person

fardo *m* bundle, package

farfa·lá *m* (*pl* **-laes**) ruffle, flounce

farfullar *tr* (*p.ej., una lección*) (coll) to sputter through; (*p.ej., una tarea*) (coll) to stumble through ‖ *intr* (coll) to sputter

faringe *f* pharynx

fariseo *m* pharisee; Pharisee; (coll) lanky good-for-nothing

farmacéuti·co -ca *adj* pharmaceutical ‖ *mf* pharmacist

farmacia *f* pharmacy, drug store; **farmacia de guardia** drug store open all night

fármaco *m* drug, medicine

faro *m* lighthouse, beacon; floodlight; (aut) headlight; (fig) beacon; **faro piloto** (aut) spotlight; **faros de carretera** (aut) bright lights; **faros de cruce** (aut) dimmers; **faros de población** *or* **de situación** (aut) parking lights

farol *m* lamp, light; lantern; street light; (rr) headlight; (coll) conceited fellow; (Bol) bay window; **farol de tope** (naut) headlight

farola *f* lighthouse; street lamp, lamppost

farolear *intr* (coll) to boast, brag

farole·ro -ra *adj* (coll) boasting ‖ *mf* (coll) boaster ‖ *m* lamplighter

farolillo *m* heartseed; Canterbury bell; **farolillo veneciano** Chinese lantern, Japanese lantern

farota *f* (coll) minx, vixen

farotear *intr* (Col) to romp around, make a racket

faro·tón -tona *adj* (coll) brazen, cheeky ‖ *mf* (coll) cheeky person

farra *f* salmon trout; (SAm) revelry

fárrago *m* hodgepodge

farro *m* grits

farru·co -ca *adj* (coll) bold, fearless; (coll) ill-humored ‖ *mf* (coll) Galician abroad, Asturian abroad

farru·to -ta *adj* (Arg, Bol, Chile) sickly

farsa *f* farce; humbug

farsante *adj & mf* (coll) fake, fraud, humbug

fas — por fas o por nefas rightly or wrongly, in any event

fascinante *adj* fascinating

fascinar *tr* to fascinate, to bewitch; to cast a spell on, cast the evil eye on

fascismo *m* fascism

fascista *adj & mf* fascist

fase *f* phase

fastidiar *tr* to bore, annoy; to cloy, sicken; to disappoint ‖ *ref* to get bored; to suffer, be a victim

fastidio *m* boredom, annoyance; distaste, nausea

fastidio·so -sa *adj* boring, annoying; cloying, sickening; annoyed, displeased

fas·to -ta *adj* happy, blessed ‖ *m* pomp, show

fa
fa

fastuo·so -sa *adj* vain, pompous; magnificent
fatal *adj* fatal; bad, evil; (law) unextendible
fatalidad *f* fatality; misfortune
fatalismo *m* fatalism
fatalista *mf* fatalist
fatalmente *adv* fatally; inevitably; unfortunately; badly, poorly
fatídi·co -ca *adj* ominous, fateful
fatiga *f* fatigue; hard breathing; **fatigas** hardship
fatigar §44 *tr* to fatigue, tire, weary; to annoy, bother || *ref* to get tired
fatigo·so -sa *adj* fatiguing, tiring; (coll) trying, tedious
fa·tuo -tua *adj* fatuous; conceited || *mf* simpleton
fauces *fpl* (anat) fauces; (fig) jaws, mouth
fauna *f* fauna
fauno *m* faun
faus·to -ta *adj* happy, fortunate || *m* pomp, magnificence
fausto·so -sa *adj* magnificent
fau·tor -tora *mf* abettor; accomplice
favor *m* favor; **a favor de** under cover of; by means of; in favor of; **hágame Vd. el favor de** do me the favor to; **por favor** please; **vender favores** to peddle influence
favorable *adj* favorable
favorecer §22 *tr* to favor; to flatter
favoritismo *m* favoritism
favori·to -ta *adj & mf* favorite
fayanca *f* unstable posture
faz *f* (*pl* **faces**) face; aspect, look; (*de monedas o medallas*) obverse; **faces** cheeks; **faz a faz** face to face
F.C. *abbr* **ferrocarril**
fe *f* faith; testimony, witness; certificate; **¡a fe mía!** upon my faith!; **dar fe de** to certify; **en fe de lo cual** in witness whereof; **fe de erratas** list of errata; **hacer fe** to be valid; **la fe del carbonero** simple faith
fealdad *f* ugliness
Febe *f* Phoebe
feble *adj* weak, sickly; (*moneda, aleación*) lacking in weight or fineness
Febo *m* Phoebus
febrero *m* February
febril *adj* feverish
fécula *f* starch
feculen·to -ta *adj* starchy; fecal
fecundar *tr* to fecundate, to fertilize
fecun·do -da *adj* fecund, fertile
fecha *f* date; **con fecha de** under date of; **de larga fecha** of long standing; **hasta la fecha** to date
fechador *m* (Chile, Mex) canceler, postmark
fechar *tr* to date
fechoría *f* misdeed, villainy
federación *f* federation
federal *adj & mf* federal
federar *tr & ref* to federate
Federico *m* Frederick
feéri·co -ca *adj* fairy
fehaciente *adj* authentic
feldespato *m* feldspar
felicidad *f* felicity, happiness; luck

felicitar *tr* to felicitate, congratulate, wish happiness to
feli·grés -gresa *mf* parishioner, church member
feligresía *f* parish; congregation
Felipe *m* Philip
fe·liz *adj* (*pl* **-lices**) happy; lucky; (*oportuno*) felicitous
fe·lón -lona *adj* perfidious, treacherous || *mf* wicked person
felonía *f* perfidy, treachery
felpa *f* plush; (coll) drubbing; (coll) severe reprimand
felpu·do -da *adj* plushy, downy || *m* mat, door mat
femenil *adj* feminine, womanly
femeni·no -na *adj* feminine; (*sexo*) female || *m* feminine
fementi·do -da *adj* false, treacherous
feminismo *m* feminism
fenecer §22 *tr* to finish, to close || *intr* to come to an end; to die
Fenicia *f* Phoenicia
feni·cio -cia *adj & mf* Phoenician || *f* see **Fenicia**
fé·nix *m* (*pl* **-nix** or **-nices**) phoenix
fenobarbital *m* phenobarbital
fenomenal *adj* phenomenal
fenómeno *m* phenomenon; (coll) monster, freak
fe·o -a *adj* ugly || *m* (coll) slight; **hacer un feo a** (coll) to slight || **feo** *adv* (Arg, Col, Mex) bad, e.g., **oler feo** to smell bad
feo·te -ta *adj* ugly, hideous
feral *adj* cruel, bloody
fe·raz *adj* (*pl* **-races**) fertile
féretro *m* bier
feria *f* weekday; market; fair; day off; (Mex) change; (CAm) extra; **revolver la feria** (coll) to upset the applecart
ferial *adj* week (*day*); market (*day*) || *m* market; fair
feriante *adj* fair-going || *mf* fairgoer
feriar *tr* to buy, to sell; to give, present; (Mex) to give change for
feri·no -na *adj* wild, savage; (*tos*) whooping (*cough*)
fermentación *f* ferment; fermentation
fermentar *tr & intr* to ferment
fermento *m* ferment
ferocidad *f* ferocity, fierceness
feróst·co -ca *adj* (coll) irritable; (coll) hideous
fe·roz *adj* (*pl* **-roces**) ferocious, fierce
férre·o -a *adj* iron
ferrería *f* ironworks, foundry
ferretear *tr* to trim with iron; to work in iron
ferretería *f* ironworks; hardware; hardware store
ferrete·ro -ra *mf* hardware dealer
ferrocarril *m* railroad, railway; **ferrocarril de cremallera** rack railway, mountain railroad
ferrocarrile·ro -ra *adj* (Am) railroad, rail || *m* (Am) railroader
ferrotipo *m* tintype
ferrovia·rio -ria *adj* railroad, rail || *m* railroader
fértil *adj* fertile
fertilizar §60 *tr* to fertilize

férula f flexible splint; ferule; **estar bajo la férula de** to be under the thumb of
férvi‧do -da adj fervid; (*fiebre; sed*) burning
ferviente adj fervent
fervor m fervor, zeal
fervoro‧so -sa adj ardent, zealous
festejar tr to fete, honor, entertain; to celebrate; to court, to woo; (Mex) to beat, thrash
festejo m feast, entertainment; celebration; courting, wooing; (Peru) revelry; **festejos** public festivities
festín m feast, banquet
festinar tr (Am) to hurry through; (CAm) to entertain
festival m festival, music festival
festividad f festivity; feast day; witticism
festi‧vo -va adj festive, gay; witty; (*digno de celebrarse*) solemn
festón m festoon
festonear tr to festoon
fetiche m fetish
féti‧do -da adj fetid, foul
feto m fetus
feú‧co -ca or **feú‧cho -cha** adj hideous, repulsive
feudal adj feudal
feudalismo m feudalism
feudo m fief; **feudo franco** freehold
fiable adj trustworthy
fiado m — **al fiado** on credit; **en fiado** on bail
fia‧dor -dora mf bail; **salir fiador por** to go bail for || m fastener; catch, pawl; (Chile, Ecuad) chin strap
fiambre adj cold, cold-served; (*noticias*) old, stale || m cold lunch, cold food; stale news; (Arg) dull party; **fiambres** cold cuts
fiambrera f dinner pail, lunch basket
fiambrería f (Arg) delicatessen store
fianza f guarantee, surety; bond; bail; **fianza carcelera** bail
fiar §77 tr to entrust, confide; to guarantee; to give credit to; to sell on credit || intr & ref to trust
fiasco m fiasco
fibra f fiber; (fig) fiber, strength, vigor; **fibras del corazón** heartstrings
fibro‧so -sa adj fibrous
ficción f fiction
ficciona‧rio -ria adj fictional
fice m (ichth) hake
ficti‧cio -cia adj fictitious
ficha f chip; counter; domino; filing card; police record; (elec) plug; **ficha catalográfica** index card; **llevar ficha** to have a police record; **ser una buena ficha** (Am) to be a sly fox
ficha‧dor -dora mf file clerk
fichar tr to file; to play, to move; (coll) to black-list; (Cuba) to cheat || intr (Col) to die
fichero m card index, filing cabinet
fidedig‧no -na adj reliable, trustworthy
fideicomisa‧rio -ria mf trustee
fideicomiso m trusteeship
fidelería f (Arg, Ecuad, Peru) vermicelli factory, noodle factory
fidelidad f fidelity; punctiliousness; **alta fidelidad** (rad) high fidelity

fideo m (coll) skinny person; (Arg) joke; (Arg) confusion, disorder; **fideos** vermicelli
Fidias m Phidias
fiducia‧rio -ria adj & mf fiduciary
fiebre f fever; **fiebre del heno** hay fever; **fibre tifoidea** typhoid fever
fiel adj faithful; exact; punctilious; honest, trustworthy || m inspector of weights and measures; (*en las balanzas*) pointer; (*de las tijeras*) pin; **fiel de romana** inspector of weights in a slaughterhouse; **los fieles** the faithful
fielato m inspector's office; octroi
fieltro m felt; felt hat; felt rug
fiera f wild animal; (*persona*) fiend; (taur) bull; **ser una fiera para** (coll) to be a fiend for
fierabrás m (coll) spitfire, little terror
fierecilla f shrew
fiereza f fierceness; cruelty; deformity
fie‧ro -ra adj fierce, wild; cruel; deformed, ugly; huge, tremendous; **echar** or **hacer fieros** to bluster || f see **fiera**
fiesta f feast, holy day; holiday; celebration, festivity; **estar de fiesta** (coll) to be in a holiday mood; **fiesta de la hispanidad** or **fiesta de la raza** Columbus Day; **fiesta de todos los santos** All Saints' Day; **fiesta onomástica** saint's day, birthday; **fiestas** holiday, vacation; **hacer fiesta** to take off (*from work*); **hacer fiestas a** to act up to, to fawn on; **la fiesta brava** bullfighting; **no estar para fiestas** (coll) to be in no mood for joking; **por fin de fiestas** to top it off; **se acabó la fiesta** (coll) let's drop it
fieste‧ro -ra adj merry, gay || mf merrymaker, party-goer
figón m cheap restaurant
figura f figure; face, countenance; (*naipe*) face card; (mus) note; (theat) character; **figura retórica** figure of speech; **hacer figura** to cut a figure
figuración f representation; (Arg) status, social standing
figura‧do -da adj figurative
figurar tr to depict, trace, represent; to feign || intr to figure, to be in the limelight || ref to figure, to imagine
figurati‧vo -va adj figurative, representative
figurería f face, grimace
figurilla mf (coll) silly little runt || f figurine
figurín m dummy, model; fashion plate
figurina f figurine
figurita f (coll) silly little runt
figurón m (coll) stuffed shirt; **figurón de proa** (naut) figurehead
fija f hinge; trowel; (*caballo*) (Peru) sure bet; **la fija** (coll) sure thing
fijacarte‧les m (pl **-les**) billposter
fijación f fixing, fastening; posting; **fijación de precios** price fixing
fijado m (phot) fixing
fija‧dor -dora adj fixing || m carpenter who installs doors and windows; fixing bath; sprayer; (mas) pointer; hair set, hair spray
fijamárge‧nes m (pl **-nes**) margin stop

fijapeina·dos m (pl **-dos**) hair set, hair spray

fijar tr to fix; to fasten; (*carteles*) to post; (*una fecha; los cabellos; una imagen fotográfica; los precios; la atención; una hora, una cita*) to fix; (*residencia*) to establish; to paste, glue ‖ ref to settle; to notice; **fijarse en** to notice; to pay attention to; to be intent on

fijeza f firmness, stability; steadfastness; **mirar con fijeza** to stare at

fi·jo -ja adj fixed; firm, solid, secure, fast; sure, determined; **de fijo** surely ‖ f see **fija**

fil m — **estar en fil** or **en un fil** to be alike; **fil derecho** leapfrog

fila f row, line; file; (*linea que los soldados forman de frente*) rank; (coll) dislike, hatred; **cerrar las filas** (mil) to close ranks; **en fila** in single file; **en filas** (mil) in active service; **fila india** single file, Indian file; **llamar a filas** (mil) to call to the colors; **pasarse a las filas de** to go over to; **romper filas** (mil) to break ranks

filamento m filament

filantropía f philanthropy

filántro·po -pa mf philanthropist

filar tr (naut) to pay out slowly

filarmóni·co -ca adj philharmonic

filatelia f philately

filatelista mf philatelist

filatería f fast talking; wordiness

filate·ro -ra adj fast-talking; wordy ‖ mf fast talker; great talker

file·no -na adj (coll) cute, tiny

filete m (*de carne o pescado*) filet or fillet; (*asador*) spit; edge, rim; narrow hem; (*de tornillo*) thread; snaffle bit; (archit, bb) fillet; (typ) rule, fancy rule

filetear tr to fillet; (*un tornillo*) to thread; (bb) to tool

filiación f filiation; description, characteristics; (mil) regimental register

filial adj filial ‖ f affiliate, branch

filiar §77 tr to register ‖ ref to enroll

filibustero m filibuster, buccaneer

filigrana f filigree; (*en el papel*) watermark

filipi·no -na adj Filipine, Filipino ‖ mf Filipino ‖ **Filipinas** fpl Philippines

Filipo m Philip (*of Macedonia*)

Filis f Phyllis

filiste·o -a adj & mf Philistine ‖ m tall, fat fellow

film m (pl **films** or **filmes**) film

filmar tr to film

filo m edge; ridge; dividing line; (CAm, Mex) hunger; **al filo de** at, at about; **dar filo a** to sharpen; **filo del viento** direction of the wind; **pasar al filo de la espada** to put to the sword; **por filo** exactly

filobús m trolley bus, trackless trolley

filocomunista adj & mf procommunist

filología f philology

filólo·go -ga mf philologist

filón m seam, vein; (fig) gold mine

filo·so -sa adj (Am) sharp

filosofía f philosophy

filosófi·co -ca adj philosophic(al)

filóso·fo -fa mf philosopher

filote m (Col) corn silk; (Col) ear of green corn

filtración f filtering; leak; (fig) leak, loss

filtrado m filtrate

filtrar tr to filter ‖ intr to leak; to ooze ‖ ref to filter; (*el dinero*) to leak away, to disappear

filtro m filter; (*brebaje para conciliar el amor*) philter, love potion

filu·do -da adj (SAm) sharp-edged

filván m featheredge

fimo m dung, manure

fin m end; aim, purpose, end; **a fin de** to, in order to; **a fin de que** in order that, so that; **a fines de** toward the end of, late in; **al fin** finally; **al fin del mundo** far, far away; **al fin y a la postre** or **al fin y al cabo** after all, in the end; **dar fin a** to put an end to; **fin de semana** weekend; **por fin** finally, in short; **sin fin** endless; endlessly; **un sin fin de** no end of

fina·do -da adj deceased, late ‖ mf deceased

final adj final ‖ m end; (mus) finale; **por final** finally ‖ f (sport) finals; **final de partido** windup

finalidad f end, purpose

finalista mf finalist

finalizar §60 tr to end, terminate; (*una escritura*) (law) to execute ‖ intr to end, terminate

financiación f financing

financiar tr to finance

financie·ro -ra adj financial ‖ mf financier

finanzas fpl finances

finar intr to die ‖ ref to yearn

finca f property, piece of real estate; farm, ranch; **buena finca** (coll) sly fellow

fincar §73 tr (P-R) to cultivate, to farm ‖ intr to buy up real estate; (Col) to reside, rest, be based ‖ ref to buy up real estate

fincha·do -da adj (coll) vain, conceited

fi·nés -nesa adj Finnic; Finnish ‖ mf Finn ‖ m (*idioma uraliano*) Finnic; (*idioma de Finlandia*) Finnish

fineza f fineness; kindness, courtesy; token of affection, favor

fingi·do -da adj fake, sham; false, deceitful

fingir §27 tr & intr to feign, pretend, fake ‖ ref to pretend to be

finiquitar tr (*una cuenta*) to settle, to close; (coll) to finish, wind up

finiquito m settlement, closing; **dar finiquito a** to settle, close; (coll) to finish, wind up

finíti·mo -ma adj bordering, neighboring

fini·to -ta adj finite

finlan·dés -desa adj Finnish ‖ mf Finn, Finlander ‖ m Finnish

Finlandia f Finland

fi·no -na adj fine; (*ligero, casi transparente*) sheer; (*esbelto*) thin, slender; (*paño, papel, etc.*) thin; (*agua*) pure; polite, courteous; shrewd, cunning

finta *f* feint

finura *f* fineness, excellence; politeness, courtesy

finústi·co -ca *adj* (coll) overobsequious

firma *f* signature; signing; firm; firm name; mail to be signed; **con mi firma** under my hand; **firma en blan-co** blank check

firmamento *m* firmament

firmante *adj* signatory ‖ *mf* signer, signatory

firmar *tr & intr* to sign

firme *adj* firm, steady; solid; hard; staunch, unswerving ‖ *adv* firmly, steadily ‖ *m* roadbed; **de firme** hard, e.g., **llover de firme** to rain hard

firmeza *f* firmness; constancy, fortitude

firmón *m* shyster who signs anything

fiscal *adj* fiscal, treasury ‖ *m* treasurer; district attorney; busybody

fiscalizar §60 *tr* to control, inspect; to prosecute; to pry into

fisco *m* state treasury, exchequer

fisga *f* fish spear; prying, snooping; banter, raillery

fisgar §44 *tr* to harpoon, fish with a spear; to pry into ‖ *intr* to pry, to snoop; to mock, to jeer ‖ *ref* to mock, to jeer

fis·gón -gona *mf* (coll) mocker, jester; (coll) snooper, busybody

físi·co -ca *adj* physical; (Mex, W-I) finicky, prudish ‖ *mf* physicist ‖ *m* physique ‖ *f* physics

fisiología *f* physiology

fisiológi·co -ca *adj* physiological

fisión *f* fission

fisionable *adj* fissionable

fisonomía *f* physiognomy

fistol *m* sly fellow; (Mex) necktie pin

fisura *f* (anat, min) fissure; **fisura del paladar** cleft palate

fla·co -ca *adj* thin, skinny; feeble, weak, frail; insecure, unstable ‖ *m* weak spot

flacu·cho -cha *adj* (coll) skinny

flagrante *adj* occurring, actual; **en fla-grante** in the act

flamante *adj* bright, flaming; brand-new, spick-and-span

flameante *adj* flamboyant

flamear *intr* to flame; to flare up (*with anger*); to flutter, to wave

flamen·co -ca *adj* Flemish; buxom; Andalusian gypsy; (coll) flashy, snappy, gypsyish ‖ *mf* Fleming ‖ *m* (*idioma*) Flemish; Andalusian gypsy dance, song, or music; (orn) flamingo

fláme·o -a *adj* flamelike

flamíge·ro -ra *adj* (poet) flaming; (archit) flamboyant

flan *m* custard

flanco *m* side, flank; **coger por el flanco** to catch off guard

Flandes *f* Flanders

flanquear *tr* to flank

flaquear *intr* to weaken, flag; to become faint; to become discouraged

flaqueza *f* thinness, skinniness; weakness; instability

flato *m* gas; (Am) gloominess, melancholy

flato·so -sa *adj* flatulent, windy; (Am) gloomy, melancholy

flauta *f* flute

flautín *m* piccolo

flautista *mf* flautist, flutist

flebitis *f* phlebitis

fleco *m* fringe; ragged edge; **flecos** bangs

flecha *f* arrow; (aer) sweepback

flechar *tr* (*el arco*) to draw; (*a una persona*) to wound with an arrow, to kill with an arrow; (coll) to infatuate

flechero *m* archer, bowman

fleje *m* iron strap, iron hoop

flema *f* phlegm

flemáti·co -ca *adj* phlegmatic(al)

flemón *m* gumboil

flequillo *m* bangs

Flesinga *f* Flushing

fletante *m* shipowner; (Arg, Chile, Ecuad) conveyancer

fletar *tr* (*una nave*) to charter; (*ganado*) to load; (*bestias de carga, carros, etc.*) (Arg, Chile, Ecuad, Mex) to hire ‖ *ref* (Arg) to sneak in, slip in; (Cuba, Mex) to beat it, clear out

flete *m* (naut) freight, cargo; (Arg, Bol, Col, Urug) race horse; **salir sin flete** (Col, Ven) to beat it

flexible *adj* flexible; (*sombrero*) soft ‖ *m* soft hat; (elec) flexible cord

flexo *m* gooseneck lamp

flinflanear *intr* to tinkle

flirt *m* flirting

flirtear *intr* to flirt

flojear *intr* to ease up, to idle; to flag, weaken

flojedad *f* slackness, looseness; limpness; laziness; weakness

flojel *m* fluff, nap; down, soft feathers

flo·jo -ja *adj* slack, loose; limp; languid, lazy; weak; (*precios*) sagging; (*viento*) light; lax, careless

flor *f* flower; (*de árbol frutal*) blossom; (*del cuero*) grain; (fig) compliment, bouquet; **a flor de** even with, flush with; **a flor de agua** at water level; **decir flores a** to flatter; to flirt with; **flor de la edad** bloom of youth; **flor de la vida** prime of life; **flor del campo** wild flower; **flor de lis** (*escudo de armas de Francia*) lily, fleur-de-lis; **flor de mano** paper flower, artificial flower; **la flor de la canela** the tops; **la flor y nata de** the cream of

flora *f* flora

floral *adj* floral

florcita *f* (Am) little flower; **andar de florcita** (Arg, Bol, Chile, Urug) to stroll around with a flower in one's buttonhole, to take it easy

florear *tr* to flower, decorate with flowers; (*los naipes*) to stack; (*harina*) to bolt ‖ *intr* (*la punta de la espada*) to quiver; to twang away on a guitar; (coll) to throw bouquets

florecer §22 *intr* to flower, to blossom, to bloom; (*prosperar*) to flourish ‖ *ref* to become moldy

floreciente *adj* flowering, florescent; flourishing

florenti·no -na adj & mf Florentine
floreo m idle talk; bright remark; (de la punta de la espada) quivering; (de la guitarra) twanging; (mus) flourish; **andarse con floreos** (coll) to beat about the bush
florera f flower girl
florería f (Am) flower shop
flore·ro -ra adj flattering, jesting || mf flatterer, jester; florist || m (vaso para flores) vase; (maceta con flores) flowerpot; flower stand, jardiniere; (cuadro, pintura) flower piece || f see **florera**
florescencia f florescence
floresta f woods, woodland; grove; rural setting; anthology
florete m (esgrima) fencing; (espadín) foil
floretear tr to decorate with flowers || intr to fence
flori·do -da adj flowery, full of flowers; choice, select
florilegio m anthology
floripondio m (SAm) angel's-trumpet
florista mf florist
floristería f flower shop
florón m large flower; finial; rosette; (typ) tailpiece, vignette
flota f fleet
flotación f buoyancy
flotador m float
flotaje m log driving
flotante adj floating; (barba) flowing || m (Col) braggart
flotar intr to float; (una bandera) to wave
flote m floating; **a flote** afloat
fluctuar §21 intr to fluctuate; to bob up and down; to wave; to waver; to be in danger
fluente adj fluent, flowing; (hemorroides) bleeding
fluidez f fluidity
fluí·do -da adj fluid; (estilo, lenguaje) fluent || m fluid
fluir §20 intr to flow
flujo m flow, flux; (acceso de la marea) floodtide; **flujo de risa** fit of noisy laughter; **flujo de vientre** loose bowels; **flujo y reflujo** ebb and flow
flúor m fluorine
fluorescencia f fluorescence
fluorescente adj fluorescent
fluorhídri·co -ca adj hydrofluoric
fluorización f fluoridation
fluorizar §60 tr to fluoridate
fluoroscopio m fluoroscope
fluoruro m fluoride
flux m (en el póker) flush; (Am) suit of clothes; **estar en flux** (Am) to be penniless; **hacer flux** (coll) to blow in everything without settling accounts; **tener flux** (Am) to be lucky
fluxión f (acumulación morbosa de humores) congestion; (enrojecimiento de la cara y el cuello) flush; (constipado de narices) cold in the head; **fluxión de muelas** swollen cheek; **fluxión de pecho** pneumonia
foca f seal
focal adj focal

foco m focus; (de vicios) center; (de un absceso) core; electric light
fodo·lí adj (pl -líes) meddlesome
fodon·go -ga adj (Mex) dirty, slovenly
fo·fo -fa adj soft, fluffy, spongy
fogaje m (contribución) hearth money; (Arg) fire, blaze; (Arg, Mex) rash, eruption; (Am) blush, flush
fogata f blaze, bonfire
fogón m cooking stove; (de máquina de vapor) firebox
fogonazo m powder flash
fogonero m fireman, stoker
fogosidad f fire, spirit, dash
fogo·so -sa adj fiery, spirited
fol. abbr **folio**
folgo m foot muff
foliar tr to folio
folio m folio; **al primer folio** right off; **de a folio** (coll) enormous; **en folio** folio
folklore m folklore
follaje m foliage; gaudy ornament; (palabrería) fustian
follar tr to shape like a leaf || §61 tr to blow with bellows
folletín m newspaper serial (printed at bottom of page); pamphlet
folleto m brochure, pamphlet, tract
fo·llón -llona adj careless, indolent, lazy; arrogant, cowardly || mf lazy loafer, knave || m noiseless rocket
fomentar tr to foment; to foster, encourage, promote; to warm
fonda f inn, restaurant; (Chile) refreshment stand
fondeadero m anchorage
fondea·do -da adj (Am) well-heeled
fondear tr (un buque) to search; to scrutinize, examine closely || intr to cast anchor || ref (Am) to save up for a rainy day
fondillos mpl seat (of trousers)
fondista mf innkeeper
fondo m bottom; (de un cuarto, una tienda) back, rear; (del mar, de una piscina, etc.) floor; (de un cilindro, barril, etc.) head; background; (de una casa) depth; (de un paño) ground; (caudal) fund; (lo esencial) bottom; **a fondo** thoroughly; **bajos fondos sociales** underworld, scum of the earth; **colar a fondo** to sink; **dar fondo** to cast anchor; **echar a fondo** to sink; **en el fondo** at bottom; **estar en fondos** to have funds available; **fondo de amortización** sinking fund; **fondos** (caudales, dinero) funds; **irse a fondo** (un negocio) to go to the bottom; (un negocio) to fail; **tener buen fondo** to be good-natured
fonducho m cheap eating house
fonéti·co -ca adj phonetic
fono m (Chile) earphone
fonocaptor s pickup
fonógrafo m phonograph
fonología f phonology
fontanería f plumbing; water-supply system
fontane·ro -ra adj fountain || m plumber, tinsmith
foque m (naut) jib; (coll) piccadilly collar

foraji·do -da *adj* fugitive ‖ *mf* fugitive, outlaw, bandit
foráne·o -a *adj* foreign, strange; off-shore
foraste·ro -ra *adj* outside, strange; foreign ‖ *mf* outsider, stranger
forbante *m* freebooter
forcejar or **forcejear** *intr* to struggle, resist, contend
forceju·do -da *adj* strong, husky, robust
fór·ceps *m* (*pl* **-ceps**) forceps
forestal *adj* forest
forja *f* forge; forging; silversmith's forge; foundry, ironworks; mortar
forjar *tr* to forge; to build with stone and mortar; to roughcast; (*mentiras*) to forge ‖ *ref* to forge; to hatch, think up
forma *f* form, shape; way; (*de un libro*) format; **de forma que** so that, with the result that; **tener buenas formas** to have a good figure
formación *f* formation; **formación de palabras** word formation
formal *adj* formal, ceremonious; express, definite; reliable; sedate; serious
formalidad *f* formality; reliability; seriousness
formar *tr* to form; to shape, to fashion; to train, educate ‖ *intr* to form; to form a line, to stand in line ‖ *ref* to form; to form a line, to stand in line; to take form, to grow, to develop
formato *m* format
formidable *adj* formidable
formidolo·so -sa *adj* scared, frightened; frightful, horrible
fórmula *f* formula; prescription; **por fórmula** as a matter of form
formular *tr* to formulate
formulario *m* form, blank; **formulario de pedido** order blank
forni·do -da *adj* husky, sturdy, robust
foro *m* forum; (*abogacía*) bar; (*del escenario*) back, rear
forraje *m* forage, fodder
forrajear *tr & intr* to forage
forrar *tr* to line; (*un vestido*) to face; (*un libro, un paraguas*) to cover; (*un lienzo*) to stretch ‖ *ref* (Guat, Mex) to stuff oneself
forro *m* lining; cover, covering; (naut) sheathing, planking; **forro de freno** brake lining; **ni por el forro** (coll) not by a long shot
fortalecer §22 *tr* to fortify, strengthen
fortaleza *f* fortitude; strength, vigor; fortress, stronghold
fortificación *f* fortification
fortificante *m* tonic
fortificar §73 *tr* to fortify
fortín *m* small fort; bunker
fortui·to -ta *adj* fortuitous
fortuna *f* fortune; **correr fortuna** (naut) to ride the storm; **de fortuna** makeshift; **por fortuna** fortunately; **probar fortuna** to try one's luck
fortunón *m* (coll) windfall
forza·do -da *adj* forced; (*p.ej., entrada*) forcible; (*sonrisa*) (fig) forced; (*trabajos*) hard ‖ *m* galley slave
forzar §35 *tr* to force

forzo·so -sa *adj* unavoidable; strong, husky; (*trabajos*) hard; (*aterrizaje; marcha*) forced ‖ *f* — **hacer la forzosa a** (coll) to put the squeeze on
forzu·do -da *adj* strong, husky, robust
fosa *f* grave; (aut) pit; **fosa de los leones** (Bib) lions' den
fosar *tr* to dig a ditch around
fos·co -ca *adj* dark; cross, sullen; (*tiempo*) threatening
fosfato *m* phosphate
fosforera *f* matchbox
fosforescente *adj* phosphorescent
fósforo *m* (*cuerpo simple*) phosphorus; match; **fósforo de seguridad** safety match
fósil *adj & m* fossil
foso *m* hole, pit; (*que rodea un castillo o fortaleza*) moat; (theat & aut) pit
fotingo *m* (Am) jalopy, jitney
foto *f* (coll) photo; **foto fija** (phot) still
fotodrama *m* photoplay
fotofija *m* photo-finish camera
fotogéni·co -ca *adj* photogenic
fotograbado *m* photoengraving
fotografía *f* (*arte*) photography; (*imagen, retrato*) photograph; photograph gallery
fotografiar §77 *tr & intr* to photograph
fotógra·fo -fa *mf* photographer
fotómetro *m* light meter
fotoperiodismo *m* photojournalism
fotopila *f* solar battery
fotostatar *tr & intr* to photostat
fotóstato *m* photostat
fototubo *m* phototube
fra. *abbr* **factura**
frac *m* (*pl* **fraques**) full-dress coat, tails, swallow-tailed coat
fracasar *intr* to fail; to break to pieces
fracaso *m* failure; breakdown, crash
fracción *f* fraction
fraccionar *tr* to divide up; to break up
fracciona·rio -ria *adj* fractional
fractura *f* fracture; breaking open, breaking in
fracturar *tr* to fracture; to break open, break in ‖ *ref* (*p.ej., un brazo*) to fracture
fragancia *f* fragrance; good reputation
fragante *adj* fragrant; **en fragante** (archaic) in the act
fragata *f* frigate; **fragata ligera** corvette
frágil *adj* fragile; (*quebradizo; que cae fácilmente en el pecado*) frail; (Mex) poor, needy
fragmento *m* fragment
fragor *m* crash, roar, thunder
fragoro·so -sa *adj* noisy, thundering
fragosidad *f* roughness, unevenness; (*de un bosque*) thickness, denseness; rough road
frago·so -sa *adj* rough, uneven; thick, dense; noisy, thundering
fragua *f* forge
fraguar §10 *tr* to forge; to hatch, scheme; (*mentiras*) to forge ‖ *intr* to forge; (*la cal, el cemento*) to set
fraile *m* friar, monk; **fraile de misa y olla** (coll) friarling; **fraile rezador** praying mantis
frambesia *f* (pathol) yaws

frambuesa _f_ raspberry

frambueso _m_ raspberry bush

francachela _f_ (coll) feast, spread; (coll) carousal, high time; (Arg) excessive familiarity

francalete _m_ strap with buckle

fran·cés ·cesa _adj_ French; **despedirse a la francesa** (coll) to take French leave ‖ _m_ Frenchman; (_idioma_) French ‖ _f_ Frenchwoman

francesada _f_ French remark; French invasion of Spain in 1808

francesilla _f_ French roll; (bot) turban buttercup

Francia _f_ France

Francisca _f_ Frances

francisca·no -na _adj_ & _mf_ Franciscan

Francisco _m_ Francis

francmasón _m_ Freemason

francmasonería _f_ Freemasonry

fran·co -ca _adj_ generous, liberal; outspoken, candid, frank; (_camino_) free, open; (_suelo_) loamy; free, gratis; Frankish; **franco a bordo** free on board; **franco de porte** postpaid ‖ _mf_ Frank ‖ _m_ franc; (_idioma_) Frankish

francolín _m_ black partridge

franco·te -ta _adj_ (coll) frank, wholehearted

francotirador _m_ sniper

franela _f_ flannel

frangente _m_ accident, mishap

frangir §27 _tr_ to break up, break to pieces

frangollar _tr_ (coll) to bungle, to botch

frangollo _m_ porridge; mash for cattle; (coll) bungle, botch

franja _f_ fringe; strip, band; (opt) fringe

franjar _tr_ to fringe

franquear _tr_ to exempt; to cross, go over; to grant; to free, enfranchise; (_un camino_) to open, to clear; (_una carta_) to frank, pay the postage for; **a franquear en destino** postage will be paid by addressee ‖ _ref_ to yield; **franquearse con** to open one's heart to

franqueo _m_ freeing, liberation; postage; **franqueo concertado** postage permit

franqueza _f_ generosity; candidness, frankness; freedom

franquía _f_ (naut) sea room; **en franquía** (naut & fig) in the open

franquicia _f_ franchise; exemption, tax exemption; **franquicia postal** franking privilege

franquista _mf_ Francoist

frasca _f_ leaves, twigs, brush; (Guat, Mex) high jinks

frasco _m_ flask; (_p.ej., de aceitunas_) jar

frase _f_ phrase; (_oración cabal_) sentence; idiom; **frase hecha** saying, proverb; cliché; **gastar frases** (coll) to talk all around the subject

frasear _tr_ to phrase ‖ _intr_ (coll) to talk all around the subject

frasquera _f_ bottle frame, liquor case

fratás _m_ plastering trowel

fraternal _adj_ brotherly, fraternal

fraternidad _f_ fraternity, brotherhood

fraternizar §60 _intr_ to fraternize

frater·no -na _adj_ brotherly, fraternal

fraude _m_ fraud

fraudulen·to -ta _adj_ fraudulent

fray _m_ Fra

frecuencia _f_ frequency; **alta frecuencia** high frequency; **baja frecuencia** low frequency; **con frecuencia** frequently

frecuentar _tr_ (_ir con frecuencia a_) to frequent; to keep up, repeat

frecuente _adj_ frequent; (_usual_) common

fregadero _m_ sink, kitchen sink

frega·do -da _adj_ (Am) annoying, bothersome; (SAm) stubborn; (Am) cunning; (P-R) brazen ‖ _m_ scrubbing; mopping; (coll) mess

frega·dor -dora _mf_ dishwasher

fregar §66 _tr_ (_restregar_) to rub; (_restregar para limpiar_) to scrub, to scour; (_el pavimento_) to mop; (_los platos_) to wash; (Am) to annoy, bother

fregasue·los _m_ (_pl_ -los) mop, floor mop

frega·triz _f_ (_pl_ -trices) var of fregona

fre·gón -gona _adj_ (Am) annoying, bothersome; (Am) brazen ‖ _f_ (_criada que friega el pavimento_) scrub woman; (_criada que lava la vajilla_) dishwasher, scullery maid

freiduría _f_ fried-fish shop

freír §58 & §83 _tr_ to fry; (coll) to bore to death ‖ _intr_ to fry; **dejarle a uno freír en su aceite** (coll) to let someone stew in his own juice ‖ _ref_ to fry; (coll) to be bored to death; **freírsele a** to try to fool, to scheme to deceive

fréjol _m_ kidney bean

frenar _tr_ to bridle, to check, hold back; (_un automóvil, tren_) to brake

frene·sí _m_ (_pl_ -síes) frenzy

frenéti·co -ca _adj_ frantic; mad, furious; wild

frenillo _m_ muzzle; **no tener frenillo en la lengua** (coll) to not mince one's words

freno _m_ (_parte de la brida_) bit; (_aparato para parar el movimiento de los vehículos_) brake; (fig) brake, check, curb; **freno de contrapedal** coaster brake; **morder el freno** to champ the bit

frenología _f_ phrenology

frentazo _m_ (Mex) rebuff

frente _m_ & _f_ (_de un edificio_) front ‖ _m_ (mil) front, front line; **al frente de** at the head of, in charge of ‖ _f_ brow, forehead; face, front; head; **a frente** straight ahead; **arrugar la frente** to knit the brow; **de frente** straight ahead; abreast; **en frente de** in front of; against, opposed to; **frente a** in front of; compared with

freo _m_ channel, strait

fresa _f_ strawberry; (_de fresadora_) cutter

fresado _m_ milling, millwork

fresadora _f_ milling machine

fresal _m_ strawberry patch

fresar _tr_ to mill

fresca _f_ fresh air; cool part of the day; (coll) blunt remark, piece of one's mind

fresca·chón -chona _adj_ bouncing, buxom; (_viento_) fresh

fresca·les _mf_ (_pl_ -les) (coll) forward sort of person

frescamente *adv* recently; cheekily, brazenly
fres·co -ca *adj* (*acabado de hacer o suceder*) fresh; (*moderadamente frío*) cool; (*pintura*) fresh, wet; (*tela, vestido*) light; calm, unruffled; buxom, ruddy; (coll) cheeky, fresh; **estar fresco** (coll) to be in a fine pinch; **quedarse tan fresco** (coll) to show no offense, to be indifferent or unconcerned || *m* coolness; fresh air; fresh bacon; (fa) fresco; (Am) cool drink; **al fresco** in the open air; in the night air; **hace fresco** it is cool; **tomar el fresco** to go out for some fresh air || *f* see **fresca**
frescor *m* freshness; cool, coolness
fresco·te -ta *adj* (coll) plump and rosy
frescura *f* freshness; cool, coolness; unconcern, offhand manner; sharp reply; (coll) cheek, impudence
fresno *m* ash tree; (*madera*) ash
fresquera *f* meat closet, food cabinet, icebox
fresquería *f* (Am) ice-cream parlor, soft-drink store
fresque·ro -ra *mf* fish dealer; (Peru) soft-drink vendor || *f* see **fresquera**
freudismo *m* Freudianism
freza *f* dung; spawning; hole made by game
frialdad *f* coldness; carelessness, laxity; stupidity; (pathol) frigidity; (pathol) impotence; (fig) coolness, coldness
friáti·co -ca *adj* chilly; awkward, stupid; (*ropa*) cold
fricar §73 *tr* to rub
fricasé *m* fricassee
fricción *f* rubbing; massage; (pharm) rubbing liniment; (phys) friction
friccionar *tr* to rub; to massage
friega *f* rubbing, massage; (Am) annoyance, bother; (Am) flogging, whipping
frigidez *f* frigidity; coldness
frígi·do -da *adj* frigid; cold
frigorífero *m* freezing chamber
frigorífi·co -ca *adj* refrigerating; cold-storage || *m* refrigerator; (Arg, Urug) packing house, cold-storage plant
fríjol *m* bean, kidney bean; **fríjol de media luna** Lima bean; **¡fríjoles!** (W-I) absolutely no!
frijolear *tr* (Guat) to annoy, molest
frijolizar §60 *tr* (Peru) to bewitch
frí·o -a *adj* cold; dull, weak, colorless; (fig) cold, cool || *m* cold; (Am) chills and fever; **coger frío** to catch cold; **hace frío** it is cold; **tener frío** (*una persona*) to be cold; **tomar frío** to catch cold
friole·ro -ra *adj* chilly || *f* trifle, trinket; snack, bite
frisar *tr* to rub; to fit, fasten; (naut) to calk || *intr* to agree, get along; **frisar con** or **en** to border on
friso *m* dado, wainscot; (archit) frieze
fri·són -sona *adj* & *mf* Frisian
fritada *f* fry
fri·to -ta *adj* fried; (coll) bored to death || *m* fry; (Ven) daily bread
fritura *f* fry
frívo·lo -la *adj* frivolous; trifling

fronda *f* leaf; (*del helecho*) frond; sling-shaped bandage; **frondas** frondage, foliage
frondo·so -sa *adj* leafy; woodsy
frontalera *f* yoke pad
frontera *f* frontier, border; front, façade
fronteri·zo -za *adj* frontier, border; facing, opposite
fronte·ro -ra *adj* frontier, border; facing, opposite; front || *f* see **frontera**
frontín *m* (Mex) flip, fillip
fron·tis *m* (*pl* -**tis**) front, façade
frontispicio *m* frontispiece; (coll) face
frontón *m* (*encima de puertas o ventanas*) gable, pediment; pelota court; pelota wall; handball court
frotamiento *m* rubbing; (phys) friction
frotar *tr* to rub; to chafe || *ref* to rub
fro·tis *m* (*pl* -**tis**) (bact) smear
fructuo·so -sa *adj* fruitful
frugal *adj* (*en comer y beber*) temperate; (*no muy abundante*) frugal
fruición *f* enjoyment, satisfaction; (*del mal ajeno*) evil satisfaction
fruiti·vo -va *adj* enjoyable
frunce *m* shirr, shirring, gathering
frunci·do -da *adj* grim, gruff, stern; (Chile) temperate; (Chile) sad, gloomy || *m* shirr, shirring, gathering
fruncir §36 *tr* to wrinkle, pucker, pleat; (*la frente*) to knit; (*los labios*) to curl, to purse; (*la verdad*) to twist, disguise; to shirr, to gather || *ref* to affect modesty, to be shocked
fruslería *f* trifle, trinket; (coll) futility, triviality
frusle·ro -ra *adj* futile, trivial, trifling || *m* rolling pin
frustrar *tr* to frustrate, to thwart
fruta *f* fruit; **fruta del tiempo** fruit in season; **fruta de sartén** fritter, pancake; **frutas** fruit; **frutas agrias** citrus fruit
frutal *adj* fruit || *m* fruit tree
frutería *f* fruit store
frute·ro -ra *adj* fruit || *mf* fruit dealer || *m* fruit dish; tray of imitation fruit
frutilla *f* (*del rosario*) bead; Chilean strawberry; gumdrop
fruto *m* (bot & fig) fruit; **fruto de bendición** legitimate offspring; **frutos** produce; **sacar fruto de** to derive benefit from
fu *interj* faugh!, fie!; (*del gato*) spit!; **ni fu ni fa** (coll) neither this nor that
fucilazo *m* heat lightning, sheet lightning
fuego *m* fire; (*para encender un cigarrillo*) light; (*de arma de fuego*) firing; lighthouse, beacon; hearth, home; rash, eruption; sore, fever blister; **abrir fuego** to open fire; **echar fuego** (coll) to blow up, hit the ceiling; **¡fuego!** fire!; **fuego fatuo** will-o'-the-wisp; **fuego graneado** or **nutrido** drumfire; **fuegos artificiales** fireworks; **hacer fuego** to fire, to shoot; **marcar a fuego** to brand; **pegar fuego a** to set fire to, to set on fire; **poner a fuego y sangre** to lay waste; **prenderse fuego** to catch on fire; **romper fuego** to open fire; to

stir up a row; **tocar a fuego** to sound the fire alarm

fuelle *m* fold, pucker, wrinkle; (*instrumento para soplar*) bellows; (*cubierta de coche*) folding carriage top; wind clouds; (*persona soplona*) (coll) gossip, talebearer

fuente *f* fountain, spring; public hydrant; font, baptismal font; platter, tray; (fig) source; **beber en buenas fuentes** (coll) to have good sources of information; **fuente de gasolina** gasoline pump; **fuente de sodas** soda fountain; **fuente para beber** drinking fountain; **fuentes termales** hot springs

fuer *m* — **a fuer de** as a, by way of

fuera *adv* out, outside; away, out of town; **desde fuera** from the outside; **fuera de** outside of; away from; out of; aside from; in addition to; **fuera de que** aside from the fact that; **fuera de sí** beside oneself; **por fuera** on the outside

fuere·ño -ña *mf* (Mex) hick, stranger

fuero *m* law, statute; code of laws; jurisdiction; exemption, privilege; **fuero interior** conscience, inmost heart; **fueros** (coll) pride, arrogance

fuerte *adj* strong; hard; loud; heavy; **hacerse fuerte** to stick to one's guns; (mil) to hole up, to dig in || *adv* hard; loud || *m* fort, fortress; forte, strong point

fuerza *f* force, strength, power; (*de un ejército*) main body; literal meaning; (phys) force; **a fuerza de** by dint of, by force of; **a la fuerza** forcibly, by force; **a viva fuerza** by main strength; **fuerza aérea** air force; **fuerza de agua** water power; **fuerza de sangre** animal power; **fuerza mayor** (law) force majeure, act of God; **fuerza motriz** motive power; **fuerza pública** police; **fuerza viva** kinetic energy; **hacer fuerza** to strain, struggle; to carry weight; **por fuerza** perforce, necessarily; **ser fuerza** + *inf* to be necessary to + *inf*

fuete *m* (Am) whip

fufar *intr* (*el gato*) to spit

fuga *f* flight; (*salida de un gas o líquido*) leak; ardor, vigor; (mus) fugue; **darse a la fuga** to take flight, to run away; **poner en fuga** to put to flight

fugar §44 *ref* to flee, escape, run away

fu·gaz *adj* (*pl* **-gaces**) fleeting, passing; (*estrella*) shooting

fugiti·vo -va *adj & mf* fugitive

fugui·llas *m* (*pl* **-llas**) (coll) hustler

fula·no -na *mf* so-and-so

fulcro *m* fulcrum

fulgor *m* brilliance, radiance

fulgurar *intr* to flash

fulmicotón *m* guncotton

fulminar *tr* to strike with lightning; to strike dead; (*censuras, amenazas, etc.*) to thunder; (*balas o bombas*) to hurl

fullería *f* trickery, cheating

fulle·ro -ra *adj* crooked, cheating || *mf* crook, cheat; **fullero de naipes** cardsharp

fumada *f* puff, whiff

fumadero *m* smoking room; **fumadero de opio** opium den

fuma·dor -dora *adj* smoking || *mf* smoker

fumar *tr* to smoke || *intr* to smoke; **fumar en pipa** to smoke a pipe; **se prohibe fumar** no smoking || *ref* (coll) to squander; (coll) to stay away from; (*la clase*) (coll) to cut

fumarada *f* (*de humo*) puff; (*de tabaco*) pipeful

fumigación *f* fumigation; **fumigación aérea** crop dusting

fumigar §44 *tr* to fumigate

fumista *m* stove or heater repairman; stove or heater dealer

fumistería *f* stove or heater shop

fumo·so -sa *adj* smoky

funámbu·lo -la *mf* ropewalker

función *f* function; duty, office, function; (*espectáculo teatral*) show, performance; **entrar en funciones** to take office, take up one's duties; **función benéfica** charitable performance; **función de aficionados** amateur performance; **función de títeres** puppet show; **función secundaria** side show

funcional *adj* functional

funcionario *m* functionary, public official, civil servant

funcione·ro -ra *adj* (coll) officious, fussy

fund. *abbr* **fundador**

funda *f* case, sheath, envelope, slip; (*para una espada*) scabbard; (*para proteger los muebles*) slip cover; **funda de almohada** pillowcase; **funda de asientos** seat cover; **funda de gafas** spectacle case

fundación *f* foundation

fundadamente *adv* with good reason; on good authority

funda·dor -dora *adj* founding || *mf* founder

fundamental *adj* fundamental

fundamentar *tr* to lay the foundations of

fundamento *m* foundation; (*razón, motivo*) grounds, reason; basis; reliability, sense; (Col) skirt

fundar *tr* to found, to base || *ref* — **fundarse en** to be based on; to base one's opinion on

fundente *adj* molten || *m* flux

fundería *f* foundry

fundible *adj* fusible

fundición *f* (*acción de fundir*) founding; (*fábrica*) foundry; (*herrería*) forge; (*hierro colado*) cast iron; (typ) font

fundidor *m* founder, foundryman

fundir *tr* (*p.ej., metales*) to found; (*campanas, estatuas*) to cast; (*derretir para purificar*) to smelt; (*colores*) to mix; (*un filamento eléctrico*) to burn out || *intr* to smelt || *ref* to melt; to fuse; (*un filamento eléctrico*) to burn out; (fig) to fuse, merge; (Am) to fail, founder

fúnebre *adj* (*marcha, procesión*) funereal; (*triste*) funereal

funeral *adj* funeral; (*triste, lúgubre*)

funereal ‖ *m* funeral; **funerales** funeral
funerala — **a la funerala** (mil) with arms inverted (*as a token of mourning*)
funera·rio -ria *adj* funeral ‖ *m* mortician, funeral director ‖ *f* (*empresa*) undertaking establishment; (*local*) funeral home, funeral parlor
funes·to -ta *adj* ill-fated; sad, sorrowful; (*p.ej., influencia*) baneful
fungir §27 *intr* (CAm, Mex) to act, function
fungo *m* (pathol) fungus
fungo·so -sa *adj* fungous
funicular *adj* & *m* funicular
fuñique *adj* awkward; dull, tiresome
furgón *m* wagon, truck; (rr) freight car, boxcar; (rr) caboose
furgoneta *f* light truck, delivery truck
furia *f* fury
furibun·do -da *adj* furious, frenzied
furio·so -sa *adj* furious; (*muy grande*) terrific, tremendous
furor *m* rage, furor; **hacer furor** to be all the rage
furti·vo -va *adj* furtive; sneaky; poaching
furúnculo *m* boil
fusa *f* (mus) demisemiquaver
fus·co -ca *adj* dark

fuséla·do -da *adj* streamlined
fuselaje *m* fuselage
fusible *adj* fusible ‖ *m* (elec) fuse
fusil *m* gun, rifle
fusilar *tr* to shoot, execute; (coll) to plagiarize
fusilazo *m* (*tiro de fusil*) gunshot, rifle shot; (*relámpago sin ruido*) heat lightning, sheet lightning
fusilería *f* rifle corps; rifles, guns; (*descarga*) fusillade
fusión *f* fusion; melting; **fusión de empresas** (com) merger
fusionar *tr* & *ref* to fuse, to merge
fusta *f* brushwood, twigs; teamster's whip
fustán *m* fustian; (Am) cotton petticoat; (Ven) skirt
fuste *m* wood, timber; shaft, stem; (fig) importance, substance
fustigar §44 *tr* to whip, lash; to rebuke harshly
fútbol *m* football; soccer; **fútbol asociación** soccer
fútil *adj* futile, trifling, inconsequential
futilidad *f* futility
futre *m* (SAm) dandy, dude
futu·ro -ra *adj* future ‖ *m* future; (gram) future; (coll) fiancé; **futuros** (com) futures ‖ *f* fiancée

fu
ga

G

G, g (ge) *f* eighth letter of the Spanish alphabet
G. *abbr* **gracia**
gaba·cho -cha *adj* & *mf* Pyrenean; (coll) Frenchy ‖ *m* (coll) Frenchified Spanish (*language*)
gabán *m* overcoat
gabardina *f* gabardine; raincoat with belt
gabarra *f* barge, lighter
gabarro *m* (*en una piedra*) nodule; (*en un tejido*) flaw, defect; mistake
gabinete *m* cabinet; (*de médico, abogado, etc.*) office; studio, study; laboratory; (Col) glassed-in balcony; **de gabinete** armchair, theoretical; **gabinete de aseo** washroom; **gabinete de lectura** reading room
gablete *m* gable
gacela *f* gazelle
gaceta *f* government journal; (Am) newspaper; **mentir más que la gaceta** to lie like a trooper
gacetilla *f* town talk, gossip column; short item
gacetillero *m* gossip columnist
gacetista *mf* newspaper reader; newsmonger
gacha *f* watery mass; (Col, Ven) earthenware bowl; **gachas** mush, pap; porridge; (coll) mud; **gachas de avena** oatmeal; **hacerse unas gachas** to be mushy
ga·cho -cha *adj* turned down; flopping;

(*sombrero*) slouch; **a gachas** on all fours ‖ *f* see **gacha**
gachumbo *m* (SAm) hard fruit shell
gachu·pín -pina *mf* (CAm, Mex) Spanish settler in Latin America
gaéli·co -ca *adj* Gaelic ‖ *mf* Gael ‖ *m* Gaelic (*language*)
gafa *f* clamp; (*enganche de los anteojos*) temple; **gafas** glasses; **gafas de sol** or **gafas para sol** sunglasses
gafe *m* (coll) jinx, hoodoo
ga·fo -fa *adj* claw-handed; (Am) footsore ‖ *f* see **gafa**
gaguear *intr* (Am) to stutter
gaita *f* hornpipe; hurdy-gurdy; (coll) chore, hard task; (coll) neck; **gaita gallega** bagpipe
gaite·ro -ra *adj* (coll) flashy, gaudy ‖ *m* piper, bagpipe player
gajes *mpl* wages, salary; **gajes del oficio** cares of office, occupational annoyances
gajo *m* broken branch; (*de un racimo de uvas*) small stem; (*división interior de ciertas frutas*) slice; (*de horca*) tine, prong; (*ramal de montes*) spur; (Am) curl
gala *f* fine clothes; (*lo más selecto*) choice, cream; (Am) tip, fee; **de gala** full-dress; **hacer gala de** to glory in; **llevarse la gala** to win approval
galafate *m* slick thief
galai·co -ca *adj* Galician
galán *m* good-looking fellow; lover,

gallant, ladies' man; (*el que sirve de escolta a una dama*) escort, cavalier; (theat) leading man; **galán joven** (theat) juvenile; **primer galán** (theat) leading man

galancete *m* (theat) juvenile

gala·no -na *adj* elegant, graceful; spruce, smartly dressed; rich, tasteful

galante *adj* (*con las damas*) gallant; (*con los caballeros*) flirtatious; (*mujer*) wanton, loose

galantear *tr* to court, woo, make love to; to sue, entreat

galantería *f* gallantry; charm, elegance; generosity

galanura *f* charm, elegance

galápago *m* pond tortoise; (*del arado*) moldboard; light saddle; ingot

galardón *m* reward, recompense

galardonar *tr* to reward, recompense

galaxia *f* galaxy

galeón *m* (naut) galleon

galeote *m* galley slave

galera *f* covered wagon; women's jail; (*de hospital*) ward; (naut & typ) galley

galerada *f* wagonload; (typ) galley; (typ) galley proof

galería *f* gallery; **galería de tiro** shooting gallery; **galerías** department store; **hablar para la galería** (coll) to play to the gallery

galerna *f* stormy wind from the northwest (*on the northern coast of Spain*)

Gales *f* Wales; **el país de Gales** Wales; **la Nueva Gales del Sur** New South Wales

ga·lés -lesa *adj* Welsh || *m* Welshman; Welsh (*language*) || *f* Welsh woman

gal·go -ga *adj* (Col) sweet-toothed || *m* greyhound || *f* greyhound bitch; rolling stone; mange, rash

Galia, la Gaul

gálibo *m* template, pattern; (rr) gabarit

galicismo *m* Gallicism

gáli·co -ca *adj* Gallic || *m* syphilis; syphilitic

galillo *m* uvula; (coll) gullet

galimatí·as *m* (*pl* -as) (coll) gibberish, nonsense; (coll) confusion

galiparla *f* Frenchified Spanish

ga·lo -la *adj* Gaulish || *mf* Gaul || *m* Gaulish (*language*)

galocha *f* clog, wooden shoe

galón *m* braid, galloon; (*medida para líquidos*) gallon; (mil) chevron, stripe

galopar *intr* to gallop

galope *m* gallop; **a galope** at a gallop; in great haste; **a galope tendido** on the run

galopea·do -da *adj* (coll) hasty, sketchy || *m* (coll) beating, punching

galopear *intr* to gallop

galopillo *m* scullion, kitchen boy

galopín *m* ragamuffin; (*hombre taimado*) wise guy; (naut) cabin boy

galpón *m* (SAm) iron shed; (Col) tile works

galvanizar §60 *tr* to electroplate; to galvanize

galvanoplastia *f* electroplating

galladura *f* tread (*of egg*)

gallardete *m* streamer, pennant

gallardía *f* gallantry; elegance; nobility; generosity

gallar·do -da *adj* gallant; elegant; noble; generous; (*temporal*) fierce

gallear *intr* to stand out, excel; (coll) to shout, yell, threaten

galle·go -ga *adj & mf* Galician

gallera *f* cockpit

galleta *f* hardtack, ship biscuit; cracker; little pitcher; (coll) slap

gallina *adj* chicken-hearted || *mf* chicken-hearted person || *f* hen; **estar como gallina en corral ajeno** (coll) to be like a fish out of water; **gallina ciega** blindman's buff; **gallina de Guinea** guinea fowl

gallinería *f* poultry shop; cowardice

galline·ro -ra *mf* poultry dealer || *m* hencoop, henhouse; poultry basket; top gallery; babel, madhouse

gallipavo *m* turkey; (coll) sour note

gallito *m* (*el que figura sobre los demás*) somebody; **gallito del lugar** cock of the walk

gallo *m* cock, rooster; (coll) false note, sour note; (coll) boss; frog in the throat; **gallo de bosque** wood grouse; **gallo de pelea** gamecock; **tener mucho gallo** (coll) to be cocky

gallofa *f* vegetables; French roll; talk, gossip

gallofear *intr* to beg, bum, loaf around

gallofe·ro -ra *adj* begging, loafing || *mf* beggar, loafer

gama *f* doe, female fallow deer; (mus & fig) gamut

gamberrismo *m* gangsterism, rowdyism

gambe·rro -rra *adj & mf* libertine || *m* hoodlum, tough, rowdy

gambeta *f* crosscaper; caper, prance

gambito *m* gambit

gamo *m* buck, male fallow deer

gamón *m* asphodel

gamonal *m* field of asphodel; (Am) boss

gamuza *f* chamois

gana *f* desire; will; **darle a uno la gana de** to feel like, e.g., **le da la gana de trabajar** he feels like working; **de buena gana** willingly; **de gana** in earnest; willingly; **de mala gana** unwillingly; **tener ganas de** to feel like, to have a mind to

ganadería *f* cattle, livestock; brand, stock; cattle raising; cattle ranch

ganade·ro -ra *adj* cattle, livestock || *mf* cattle breeder; cattle dealer || *m* cattleman

ganado *m* cattle, livestock; **ganado caballar** horses; **ganado cabrío** goats; **ganado lanar** sheep; **ganado mayor** large farm animals (*cows, bulls, horses, and mules*); **ganado menor** small farm animals (*sheep, goats, pigs*); **ganado menudo** young cattle; **ganado moreno** swine; **ganado ovejuno** sheep; **ganado porcino** swine; **ganado vacuno** cattle

gana·dor -dora *adj* winning; earning; (coll) hard-working || *mf* winner; earner

ganancia *f* gain, profit; (Guat, Mex)

extra, bonus; **ganancias y pérdidas** profit and loss

ganancial *adj* profit

ganancio·so -sa *adj* gainful, profitable; earning || *mf* earner

ganapán *m* errand boy; (coll) boor

ganapierde *m & f* giveaway

ganar *tr* (*dinero trabajando*) to earn; (*la victoria luchando*) to win; (*beneficios en los negocios*) to gain; (*a una persona en una contienda*) to beat, defeat; (*aventajar*) to excel; (*la voluntad de una persona*) to win over; (*alcanzar*) to reach; **ganar algo a alguien** to win something from someone; **ganar de comer** to earn a living || *intr* to earn; (*mejorar*) to improve ¶ *ref* to win over; **ganarse la vida** to earn a livelihood

ganchero *m* log driver; (Chile) odd-jobber; (Ecuad) gentle mount

ganchillo *m* crochet needle; crochet, crochet work; **hacer ganchillo** to crochet

gancho *m* hook; shepherd's crook; coaxer; procurer, pimp; (Am) hairpin; (Col, Ecuad) lady's saddle; **gancho de botalones** (naut) gooseneck; **echar el gancho a** (coll) to hook in, to land; **tener gancho** (*una mujer*) (coll) to have a way with the men

gandaya *f* (coll) bumming, loafing

gandujar *tr* to pleat, shirr

gan·dul ·dula *adj* (coll) loafing, idling || *mf* (coll) loafer, idler

gandulear *intr* (coll) to loaf, idle

ganfo·rro -rra *mf* (coll) scoundrel

ganga *f* bargain

ganglio *m* ganglion

gangocho *m* (Am) burlap

gango·so -sa *adj* snuffling, nasal

gangrena *f* gangrene

gangrenar *tr & ref* to gangrene

ganguear *intr* to snuffle, talk through the nose

gangue·ro -ra *adj* (coll) bargain-hunting; (coll) self-seeking || *mf* (coll) bargain hunter

gano·so -sa *adj* desirous; (*caballo*) (Chile) spirited, fiery

gan·so -sa *mf* (coll) dope, dullard || *m* goose; gander; **ganso bravo** wild goose || *f* female goose

Gante Ghent

ganzúa *f* (*garfio*) picklock, lock pick; (*persona*) picklock; (coll) pumper (*of secrets*)

gañán *m* farm hand; rough, husky fellow

gañido *m* yelp; croak

gañir §12 *intr* (*el perro*) to yelp; (*p.ej., el cuervo*) to croak

garabatear *tr* to scribble || *intr* to hook; to beat about the bush; to scribble

garabato *m* hook; pothook; scribbling; weeding hoe; (*bozal*) muzzle; (*de una mujer*) (coll) winsomeness; **garabato de carnicero** meathook; **garabatos** wiggling of hands and fingers

garabato·so -sa *adj* full of scrawls; (coll) winsome

garage *m* or **garaje** *m* garage

garagista *m* garage man

garambaina *f* gaudy trimming; **garambainas** simpering, smirking; (coll) scribble

garante *adj* responsible || *mf* guarantor, voucher

garantía *f* guarantee, guaranty

garantir §1 *tr* to guarantee

garantizar §60 *tr* to guarantee

garañón *m* stud jackass; stud camel; (Am) stallion

garapiña *f* icing, sugar-coating; (Am) iced pineapple drink

garapiñar *tr* to ice, to sugar-coat; to candy

garapiñera *f* ice-cream freezer

garbanzo *m* chickpea; **garbanzo negro** (fig) black sheep

garbillar *tr* to sieve, screen, riddle

garbillo *s* sieve, screen; riddled ore

garbo *m* jauntiness, grace, fine bearing; generosity

garbo·so -sa *adj* jaunty, graceful, spruce, sprightly; generous

gardu·ño -ña *mf* (archaic) sneak thief || *f* stone marten, beech marten

garete *m* — **al garete** (naut) adrift

garfa *f* claw

garfio *m* hook, gaff

gargajear *intr* to cough up phlegm, to hawk

gargajo *m* phlegm

garganta *f* throat; (*de un río, una vasija, etc.*) neck, throat; (*del pie*) instep; (*entre montañas*) ravine, gorge; (*del arado*) sheath; (*de una polea*) groove; (archit) shaft; **tener buena garganta** to have a good voice

gargantear *intr* to warble

gargantilla *f* necklace

gárgara *f* gargling; **gárgaras** (*líquido*) (Am) gargle; **hacer gárgaras** to gargle

gargarear *intr* (Am) to gargle

gargarismo *m* gargling; (*líquido*) gargle

gargarizar §60 *intr* to gargle

gárgola *f* gargoyle

garguero *m* gullet; (*caña del pulmón*) windpipe

garita *f* sentry box; porter's lodge; (*de una fortificación*) watchtower; railroad-crossing box; privy (*with one seat*); **garita de centinela** sentry box; **garita de señales** (rr) signal tower

garito *m* gambling den

garlito *m* fish trap; (coll) trap, snare

garlopa *f* jack plane, trying plane

garra *f* claw, talon; catch, hook; **caer en las garras de** (coll) to fall into the clutches of

garrafa *f* carafe, decanter; **garrafa corchera** demijohn

garrafal *adj* awful, terrible

garrafiñar *tr* (coll) to snatch

garrafón *m* carboy, demijohn

garramar *tr* (coll) to snitch

garranchuelo *m* crab grass

garrapata *f* cattle tick, sheep tick; (mil) disabled horse; (Chile) little runt; (Mex) slut

garrapatear *intr* to scrawl, scribble

garrapato *m* pothook, scrawl; **garrapatos** scrawl

garri·do -da *adj* handsome, elegant

garroba *f* carob bean

ga
ga

garrocha *f* goad; (sport) pole

garrotazo *m* blow with a club

garrote *m* club, cudgel; garrote (*method of execution; iron collar used for such execution*); (Mex) brake; **dar garrote a** to garrote

garrote·ro -ra *adj* (Chile) stingy ‖ *m* (Mex) brakeman

garrotillo *m* croup

garrucha *f* pulley, sheave

gárru·lo -la *adj* chirping; (*hablador*) garrulous; (*arroyo*) babbling; (*viento*) rustling

garúa *f* (Am) drizzle

garuar §21 *intr* (Am) to drizzle

garulla *f* (coll) mob, rabble

garza *f* heron; **garza real** gray heron

gar·zo -za *adj* blue ‖ *f* see **garza**

garzón *m* boy, youth; suitor; woman chaser

gas *m* gas; **gas de alumbrado** illuminating gas; **gas exhilarante** or **hilarante** laughing gas; **gas lacrimógeno** tear gas

gasa *f* gauze, chiffon; (*tira de gasa negra con que se rodea el sombrero en señal de luto*) hatband

Gascuña *f* Gascony

gasear *tr* to gas

gaseo·so -sa *adj* gaseous ‖ *f* soda water, carbonated water

gasificar §73 *tr* to gasify; to exalt, elate ‖ *ref* to gasify

gasista *m* gas fitter; (Chile) gasworker

gasoducto *m* gas pipe line

gasógeno *m* gas generator, gas producer; mixture of benzine and alcohol used for lighting and cleaning

gas-oil *m* diesel oil

gasolina *f* gasoline

gasolinera *f* motor boat; gas station, filling station

gasómetro *m* gasholder, gas tank

gastadero *m* waste

gasta·do -da *adj* worn-out; used up; spent; (*chiste*) (coll) crummy, corny

gasta·dor -dora *adj* & *mf* spendthrift ‖ *m* convict; (mil) sapper, pioneer

gastadura *f* worn spot

gastar *tr* (*dinero, tiempo*) to spend; (*en cosas inútiles*) to waste; (*echar a perder con el uso*) to wear out; (*consumir*) to use up; (*p.ej., una barba*) to wear; (*un coche*) to keep; **gastarlas** (coll) to act, behave ‖ *intr* to spend ‖ *ref* to wear; to wear out; to become used up; to waste away

gasto *m* cost, expense; wear; **gastos de conservación** or **de entretenimiento** upkeep; **gastos de explotación** operating expenses; **gastos menudos** petty expenses; **hacer el gasto** (coll) to do most of the talking; (coll) to be the subject of conversation; **hacer frente a los gastos** to meet expenses; **meterse en gastos con** to go to the expense of

gasto·so -sa *adj* wasteful, extravagant

gástri·co -ca *adj* gastric

gastronomía *f* gastronomy

gastróno·mo -ma *mf* gourmet

gata *f* she-cat; low-hanging cloud; (coll) Madrid woman; (Mex) maid, servant

girl; **a gatas** on all fours, on hands and knees

gatada *f* catty act

gatatumba *f* (coll) faked attention, fake emotion, faked pain

gatazo *m* (coll) gyp

gatea·do -da *adj* catlike; grained, striped ‖ *m* crawling, climbing; (coll) scratching, clawing

gatear *tr* (coll) to scratch, claw; (coll) to snitch ‖ *intr* to crawl, to climb

gatera *f* cathole; (naut) hawsehole

gatería *f* (coll) cats; (coll) gang of toughs; (coll) fake humility

gate·ro -ra *adj* full of cats ‖ *mf* cat lover ‖ *f* see **gatera**

gates·co -ca *adj* (coll) catlike, feline

gatillo *m* (*de arma de fuego*) trigger; (coll) little pickpocket

gato *m* cat; tomcat; (*instrumento para levantar pesos*) jack, lifting jack; (coll) sly fellow; (coll) sneak thief; (coll) native of Madrid; **gato montés** wildcat; **gato rodante** dolly; **vender gato por liebre** (coll) to gyp, cheat

gauchada *f* (SAm) sly trick; (SAm) good turn

gauchaje *m* (SAm) gathering of Gauchos

gauches·co -ca *adj* Gaucho

gau·cho -cha *adj* (SAm) Gaucho; (Arg, Chile) sly, crafty ‖ *m* (SAm) Gaucho; (SAm) good horseman ‖ *f* (Arg) mannish woman; (Arg) loose woman

gaultería *f* wintergreen

gaveta *f* drawer, till

gavia *f* ditch, drain; (ave) gull; (min) gang of basket passers; (naut) topsail

gavilán *m* sparrow hawk; (*de la pluma*) nib; (*en la escritura*) hair stroke; (Am) ingrowing nail

gavilla *f* sheaf, bundle; gang

gaviota *f* sea gull

gavota *f* gavotte

gaya *f* colored stripe; (ave) magpie

gayar *tr* to trim with colored stripes

ga·yo -ya *adj* gay, bright, showy ‖ *m* (orn) jay ‖ *f* see **gaya**

gayola *f* cage; (coll) jail

gayomba *f* Spanish broom

gazapa *f* (coll) lie

gazapatón *m* (coll) blunder, slip

gazapera *f* rabbit warren; (coll) gang, gang of thugs; (coll) brawl, row

gazapo *m* young rabbit; sly fellow; slip, boner, blunder; (*de actor*) fluff

gazmiar *tr* (*oliendo*) to sniff; (*comiendo*) to nibble ‖ *ref* (coll) to complain

gazmoñada or **gazmoñería** *f* prudishness, priggishness

gazmoñe·ro -ra or **gazmo·ño -ña** *adj* prudish, priggish, strait-laced, demure ‖ *mf* prude, prig

gaznápiro *m* gawk, boob, bumpkin

gaznate *m* gullet; (Mex) fritter

gazpacho *m* cold vegetable soup; (Hond) leftovers

gazuza *f* (coll) hunger

Gedeón *m* Gideon

gehena *f* Gehenna

géiser *m* geyser

gel *m* gel

gelatina *f* gelatine

gema *f* gem; (bot) bud

geme·lo -la *adj* & *mf* twin; gemelos twins; binoculars; cuff links; gemelos de campo field glasses; gemelos de teatro opera glasses || Gemelos *mpl* (astr) Gemini

gemido *m* moan, groan; wail, whine; howl, roar

Géminis *m* (astr) Gemini

gemiquear *intr* (Chile) to whine

gemir §50 *intr* to moan, groan; to wail, whine; to howl, roar

gen *m* gene

genciana *f* gentian

gendarme *m* (Am) policeman

genealogía *f* genealogy

generación *f* generation

genera·dor -dora *adj* generating || *m* generator

general *adj* general; common, usual; en general or por lo general in general || *m* general; general de brigada brigadier, brigadier general; general de división major general || generales *fpl* general information, personal data

generala *f* general's wife; call to arms

generalato *m* generalship

generalidad *f* generality; majority; la generalidad de the general run of

generalísimo *m* generalissimo

generalizar §60 *tr* & *intr* to generalize || *ref* to become generalized

generar *tr* to generate

genéri·co -ca *adj* generic; (*artículo*) definite; (*nombre*) common; showing gender

género *m* kind, sort; way, manner; cloth, material; (biol, log) genus; (gram) gender; de género genre; género chico one-act play, one-act operetta; género de punto knit goods, knitwear; género humano humankind; género ínfimo light vaudeville; género novelístico fiction; género picaresco burlesque; géneros goods, merchandise, material; géneros de pieza yard goods; géneros para vestidos dress goods

genero·so -sa *adj* generous; highborn; noble, magnanimous; (*vino*) rich, full

géne·sis *f* (*pl* -sis) genesis || el Génesis (Bib) Genesis

genéti·co -ca *adj* genetic || *f* genetics

genial *adj* inspired, genius-like; pleasant, agreeable; temperamental

geniazo *m* (coll) fiery temper

genio *m* (*índole, carácter*) temperament, disposition; (*don altísimo de invención; persona que lo posee; espíritu tutelar, deidad pagana*) genius; fire, spirit

genital *adj* genital || genitales *mpl* genitals

geniti·vo -va *adj* & *m* genitive

genocida *adj* genocidal || *mf* genocide

genocidio *m* genocide

Génova *f* Genoa

geno·vés -vesa *adj* & *mf* Genoese

gente *f* people; (*parentela, familia*) folks; race, nation; troops; gente baja lower classes, rabble; gente bien nice people; gente de bien decent people; gente de capa parda country people; gente de coleta (coll) bullfighters; gente de color colored people; gente de la cuchilla (coll) butchers; gente de la vida airada bullies; underworld; gente del bronce bright, lively people; gente del rey convicts; gente de mal vivir toughs, underworld; gente de mar seafaring people; gente de paz (*palabras con las cuales se contesta al que pregunta ¿quién?*) friend; gente de pluma (coll) clerks; gente de su majestad convicts; gente de trato tradespeople; gente forzada convicts; gente menuda (coll) small fry; (coll) common people

gentecilla *f* (coll) mob, rabble

gentil *adj* heathen, gentile; elegant, genteel; noble || *mf* heathen, pagan

gentileza *f* elegance, gentility, courtesy; gallantry; show, splendor; (*hidalguía*) nobility

gentilhombre *m* (*pl* gentileshombres) gentleman; messenger to the king; my good man; gentilhombre de cámara gentleman in waiting

gentili·cio -cia *adj* national; family; (gram) gentile

gentilidad *f* heathendom

gentío *m* crowd, mob

gentualla or gentuza *f* (coll) rabble, riffraff

genui·no -na *adj* genuine

geofísi·co -ca *adj* geophysical || *mf* geophysicist || *f* geophysics

geografía *f* geography

geográfi·co -ca *adj* geographic(al)

geógra·fo -fa *mf* geographer

geología *f* geology

geológi·co -ca *adj* geologic(al)

geólo·go -ga *mf* geologist

geómetra *mf* geometrician

geometría *f* geometry; geometría del espacio solid geometry

geométri·co -ca *adj* geometric(al)

geopolíti·co -ca *adj* geopolitical || *f* geopolitics

geranio *m* geranium

gerencia *f* management; manager's office

gerente *m* manager, director; gerente de publicidad advertising manager; gerente de ventas sales manager

geriatría *f* geriatry

geriatra *adj* geriatrical || *mf* geriatrician

geriátri·co -ca *adj* geriatrical

germanía *f* gypsy slang, cant of thieves

germanizar §60 *tr* to Germanize

germen *m* germ; germen plasma germ plasm

germicida *adj* germicidal || *m* germicide

germinal *adj* germ; germinal

germinar *intr* to germinate

gerontología *f* gerontology

gerundio *m* gerund; present participle; bombastic writer or speaker

gestación *f* gestation

gestear *intr* to make faces

gesticular *intr* to make a face, to make faces; (*hacer ademanes*) to gesticulate

ga
ge

gestión f step, measure; management; action, proceeding, negotiation

gestionar tr to promote, pursue; to manage; to negotiate

gesto m face; wry face, grimace; look, appearance; (*movimiento, ademán*) gesture

ges·tor -tora adj managing || m manager

gestu·do -da adj (coll) cross-looking

ghetto m ghetto

giba f hump; (coll) annoyance

giga f jig

giganta f giantess

gigante adj giant || m giant; (*en las procesiones*) giant figure

gigantes·co -ca adj gigantic

gigantez f giant size

gigantilla f large-headed masked figure; little fat woman

gigan·tón -tona mf huge giant || m giant figure

gigote m chopped-meat stew; **hacer gigote** (coll) to chop up

gimnasia f gymnastics; **gimnasia sueca** Swedish movements, setting-up exercises

gimnasio m gymnasium; secondary school, academy

gimnasta mf gymnast

gimnásti·co -ca adj gymnastic || f gymnastics

gimotear intr (coll) to whine

gimoteo m (coll) whining

ginebra f gin; (*de voces*) buzz, din; confusion, disorder || **Ginebra** f Geneva

ginebri·no -na adj & mf Genevan

ginecología f gynecology

ginecólo·go -ga mf gynecologist

ginesta f Spanish broom

gira f var of jira

gira·do -da mf drawee

gira·dor -dora mf drawer

giralda f weathercock (*in the form of person or animal*)

girándula f girandole

girar tr (*una visita*) to pay; (com) to draw || intr to turn; to rotate, gyrate; to trade; (com) to draw

girasol m sunflower; sycophant

girato·rio -ria adj revolving || f revolving bookcase

gi·ro -ra adj (Guat) drunk; (Mex) cocky || m turn; rotation; revolution; course, trend, turn; turn of phrase; boast, threat; gash, slash; line of business; trade; (com) draft; **giro a la vista** sight draft; **giro postal** money order || f see **gira**

giroflé m clove

giroscopio m gyroscope

gis m (Col) slate pencil

gitana f gypsy woman, gypsy girl

gitanada f gypsy trick; fawning, flattery

gitanería f band of gypsies; gypsy life; fawning, flattery

gitanes·co -ca adj gypsyish

gita·no -na adj gypsy; flattering; sly, tricky || mf gypsy || m Gypsy (*language*) || f see **gitana**

glacial adj glacial; (*zona*) frigid; (fig) cold, indifferent

glaciar m glacier

glándula f gland; **glándula cerrada** ductless gland

glasé m glacé silk

glasea·do -da adj glossy, shiny

glicerina f glycerin

global adj total; global, world-wide

globo m globe; (*aparato que, lleno de un gas, se eleva en el aire*) balloon; (*bomba de lámpara*) globe, lamp shade; **globo del ojo** eyeball; **globo sonda** trial balloon; **lanzar un globo sonda** (fig) to send up a trial balloon

glóbulo m globule; (physiol) corpuscle; **glóbulo rojo** red cell

gloria f glory; **ganar la gloria** to go to glory; **oler a gloria** (coll) to smell heavenly; **saber a gloria** (coll) to taste heavenly

gloriar §77 tr to glorify || intr to recite the rosary || ref to glory

glorieta f arbor, bower, summerhouse; public square; traffic circle

glorificar §73 tr to glorify || ref to glory

glorio·so -sa adj glorious; boastful

glosa f gloss

glosa·dor -dora adj commenting || mf commentator

glosar tr to gloss; to audit; (Col) to scold || intr to find fault

glosario m glossary

glóti·co -ca adj glottal

glo·tón -tona adj gluttonous || mf glutton

glotonería f gluttony

glucosa f glucose

gluglú m (*del agua*) gurgle, glug; (*del pavo*) gobble; **hacer gluglú** to gurgle, to glug

gluglutear intr to gobble

gnomo m gnome

gob. abbr **gobierno**

gobernación f governing; government; department of the interior; (Arg) territory

goberna·dor -dora adj governing || m governor

gobernalle m rudder, helm

gobernante adj governing || mf ruler || m (coll) self-appointed head

gobernar §2 tr to govern; to guide, direct; to control, rule; (*un buque*) to steer || intr to govern; to steer

goberno·so -sa adj (coll) orderly

gobierno m government; governor's office, governorship; management; control, rule; guidance; (*de un buque*) navigability; **de buen gobierno** (*buque*) navigable; **gobierno de monigotes** puppet government; **gobierno doméstico** housekeeping; **gobierno exilado** government in exile; **para su gobierno** for your guidance; **servir de gobierno** (coll) to serve as a guide

goce m enjoyment

go·do -da adj Gothic || mf Goth; Spanish noble; (Arg, Chile) Spaniard

gofio m (Am) roasted corn meal

gol m goal

gola f gullet

goldre m quiver

goleta f schooner

golf m golf

golfán *m* white water lily

golfista *mf* golfer

gol·fo -fa *mf* ragamuffin ‖ *m* gulf; open sea; golfo de Méjico Gulf of Mexico; golfo de Vizcaya Bay of Biscay

Gólgota, el (Bib) Golgotha

golilla *f* gorget, ruff; magistrate's collar; pipe flange; (de los caños de barro) collar, sleeve; (del gallo) (Am) erectile bristles

golondrina *f* swallow

golosina *f* delicacy, tidbit; eagerness, appetite; trifle

golosinear *intr* to go around eating candy

golo·so -sa *adj* sweet-toothed; (glotón) gluttonous; (apetitoso) tasty

golpe *m* blow, stroke, hit; bump, bruise; heartbeat; crowd, throng, flock; (del bolsillo) flap; (pestillo) bolt, latch; (de licor) shot; surprise, wonder; (infortunio) blow; witticism; dar golpe to make a hit; de golpe all at once, suddenly; de golpe y porrazo slambang; de un golpe at one stroke; golpe de ariete water hammer; golpe de estado coup d'état; golpe de fortuna stroke of fortune; golpe de gracia coup de grâce; golpe de mano surprise attack; golpe de mar surge; golpe de ojo glance; golpe de teatro dramatic turn of events; golpe de tos fit of coughing; golpe de vista, glance, look; view; golpe en vago miss, flop; golpe mortal deathblow; no dar golpe to not raise a hand, not do a stroke of work

golpear *tr* to strike, hit, beat; to bump, bruise ‖ *intr* to beat, strike; (el reloj) to tick; (el motor de combustión interna) to knock

golpete *m* door catch, window catch

golpetear *tr & intr* to beat; to rattle

golpismo *m* government by coup d'état

gollería *f* delicacy, dainty; pedir gollerías (coll) to ask for too much

gollete *m* throat, neck; (de botella) neck

goma *f* gum, rubber; (tira de goma elástica) rubber band; (neumático) tire; goma arábiga gum arabic; goma de borrar eraser, rubber; goma de mascar chewing gum; goma espumosa foam rubber; goma laca shellac

gomecillo *m* (coll) blind man's guide

gomia *f* bugaboo; (coll) waster; (coll) glutton

gomo·so -sa *adj* gum; gummy ‖ *m* dude, dandy

góndola *f* gondola

gondolero *m* gondolier

gongo *m* gong

gonorrea *f* gonorrhea

gordal *adj* large-size

gordia·no -na *adj* Gordian

gordi·flón -flona or gordin·flón -flona *adj* (coll) chubby, pudgy, fatty ‖ *mf* (coll) fatty

gor·do -da *adj* fat, plump; fatty, greasy; coarse; big, large; whopping big; (agua) hard ‖ *m* fat, suet; (coll) first prize (in lottery) ‖ gordo *adv* — hablar gordo (coll) to talk big

gordura *f* fatness, plumpness, stoutness, corpulence; fat, grease

gorgojo *m* grub, weevil; (coll) dwarf, runt; gorgojo del algodón boll weevil

gorgojo·so -sa *adj* grubby

gorgón *m* (Col) concrete

gorgonear *intr* (el pavo) to gobble

gorgoritear *intr* (coll) to trill

gorgorito *m* (coll) trill

gorgotear *intr* to burble, gurgle

gorgotero *m* peddler, hawker

gorigori *m* (coll) lugubrious funeral chant

gorila *f* gorilla

gorjear *intr* to warble, trill ‖ *ref* (el niño) to gurgle

gorra *f* cap; bumming, sponging; andar de gorra to sponge; colarse de gorra (coll) to crash the gate; gorra de visera cap; vivir de gorra to live on other people

gorrada *f* tipping the hat

gorrear *intr* (Ecuad) to sponge

gorretada *f* tipping the hat

gorrión *m* sparrow; gorrión triguero bunting

gorrista *adj* sponging ‖ *mf* sponger

gorro *m* cap, bonnet; baby's bonnet; gorro de dormir nightcap

go·rrón -rrona *adj* sponging ‖ *mf* sponger ‖ *m* pivot; journal, gudgeon

gota *f* drop; (pathol) gout; gotas touch of rum or brandy in coffee; sudar la gota gorda (coll) to work one's head off

gotear *intr* to drip, dribble; (llover a gotas espaciadas) to sprinkle

gotera *f* drip, dripping; mark left by dripping; (en el techo) leak; (adorno de una cama) valance; estar lleno de goteras (coll) to be full of aches and pains; es una gotera (coll) it's a constant drain; goteras (coll) aches, pains; (Col) environs, outskirts

góti·co -ca *adj* Gothic; noble, illustrious ‖ *m* Gothic

goto·so -sa *adj* gouty ‖ *mf* gout sufferer

gozar §60 *tr* (poseer) to enjoy ‖ *intr* to enjoy oneself; gozar de (poseer) to enjoy ‖ *ref* to enjoy oneself; to rejoice

gozne *m* hinge

gozo *m* joy, enjoyment; no caber en sí de gozo (coll) to be beside oneself with joy; saltar de gozo to leap with joy

gozo·so -sa *adj* joyful; gozoso con or de joyful over

gozque *m* or gozquejo *m* little yapping dog

grabación *f* (de disco) recording; grabación sobre cinta tape recording

grabado *m* engraving; print, cut, picture; (de disco) recording; grabado en madera wood engraving, woodcut; grabado fuera de texto inset, insert

graba·dor -dora *adj* recording ‖ *mf* engraver ‖ *f* recorder; grabadora de cinta tape recorder

grabadura *f* engraving

grabar *tr* to engrave; (un sonido, una canción, un disco, etc.) to record;

grabar en or **sobre cinta** to tape-record || *ref* to become engraved
gracejada *f* (CAm, Mex) cheap comedy, clownishness
gracejar *intr* to be engaging, be witty; to joke
gracejo *m* lightness, winsome manner, charm; (CAm, Mex) clown
gracia *f* witticism, witty remark, joke; grace; gracefulness; favor; pardon; (*de un chiste*) point; (coll) name; **caer en gracia a** to be pleasing to; **de gracia** gratis; **decir dos gracias a** (coll) to tell someone a thing or two; **en gracia a** because of; **gracia de Dios** daily bread; air and sunshine; **gracias** thanks; **¡gracias!** thanks!; **gracias a** thanks to; **¡gracias a Dios!** thank heavens!; **hacer gracia** to be pleasing; **hacer gracia de algo a uno** to exempt or free someone from something; **hacerle a uno gracia** to strike someone as funny; **¡linda gracia!** nonsense!; **tener gracia** to be funny, be surprising
graciable *adj* kind, gracious; easy to grant
grácil *adj* thin, small, slender
gracio·so -sa *adj* (*que tiene donaire, gracia*) graceful; (*afable, fino*) gracious; (*agudo, chistoso*) funny, witty; (*que se da de balde*) free, gratis || *mf* comic || *m* gracioso (*gay, comic character in Spanish comedy*)
grada *f* step, stair; row of seats; grandstand; altar step; (agr) harrow; (*plano inclinado sobre el cual se construyen los barcos*) slip; **gradas** stone steps; (Chile, Peru) atrium; **gradas al aire libre** bleachers
gradar *tr* (agr) to harrow
gradería *f* stone steps; row of seats; bleachers; **gradería cubierta** grandstand
gradiente *m* (phys) gradient || *f* (Am) slope, gradient
grado *m* step; grade; degree; (*título que se da en las universidades*) degree; (*sección en las escuelas*) grade, form, class; (mil) rank; **de buen grado** willingly; **de grado en grado** by degrees; **de grado o por fuerza** willy-nilly; **de mal grado** unwillingly; **en sumo grado** to a great extent; **mal de mi grado** unwillingly, against my wishes
graduación *f* graduation; (*de las bebidas espirituosas*) strength; (mil) rank
gradual *adj* gradual
graduan·do -da *mf* (*persona próxima a graduarse en la universidad*) graduate (*candidate for a degree*)
graduar §21 *tr* to graduate, to grade; (*un grifo, una válvula, etc.*) to regulate; to appraise, estimate || *ref* to graduate
grafía *f* graph
gráfi·co -ca *adj* graphic(al); printing; illustrated; picture, camera || *m* diagram || *f* graph
grafito *m* graphite
grafospasmo *m* writer's cramp

gragea *f* colored candy; sugar-coated pill
grajear *intr* (*los cuervos*) to caw; (*los niños*) to gurgle
grajien·to -ta *adj* (Am) foul-smelling
gra·jo -ja *mf* rook, crow; (coll) chatter-box || *m* (Am) body odor
gral. *abbr* **general**
gramática *f* grammar; **gramática parda** (coll) shrewdness, mother wit
gramatical *adj* grammatical
gramáti·co -ca *adj* grammatical || *mf* grammarian || *f* see **gramática**
gramil *m* marking gauge, gauge
gramo *m* gram
gramófono *m* gramophone
gramola *f* console phonograph; portable phonograph
gran *adj* apocopated form of **grande**, used only before nouns of both genders in the singular
grana *f* seed; seeding; seeding time; red; **dar en grana** to go to seed
granada *f* pomegranate; (*proyectil explosivo*) grenade; **granada de mano** hand grenade; **granada de metralla** shrapnel; **granada extintora** fire extinguisher, fire grenade
granadero *m* grenadier
granadilla *f* passionflower
granadina *f* grenadine
grana·do -da *adj* choice, select; mature, expert || *m* pomegranate; **granado blanco** rose of Sharon || *f* see **granada**
granalla *f* filings
granangular *adj* wide-angle
granate *m adj invar* & *m* garnet
Gran Bretaña, la Great Britain
grande *adj* big, large; great || *m* grandee
grandeza *f* bigness, largeness; greatness; (*tamaño*) size; (*magnificencia*) grandeur; grandees; grandeeship
grandi·llón -llona *adj* (coll) oversize, overgrown
grandio·so -sa *adj* grandiose, grand
grandor *m* size
granea·do -da *adj* spattered; (*fuego*) heavy and continuous
granear *tr* to sow; (*la pólvora; una piedra litográfica*) to grain; to stipple
granel — a granel in bulk, loose; at random; lavishly
granelar *tr* (*el cuero*) to grain
granero *m* granary
granete *m* center punch
granífu·go -ga *adj* hail-dispersing
granito *m* granite
granizada *f* hailstorm; (Arg, Chile) iced drink
granizar §60 *tr* (p.ej., golpes) to hail; to sprinkle || *intr* to hail
granizo *m* hail
granja *f* farm, grange; dairy; country place
granjear *tr* to earn, gain; to win, win over || *ref* to win, win over
granjería *f* husbandry; gain, profit
granje·ro -ra *mf* farmer; merchant, trader
grano *m* grain; (*baya*) berry; (*baya de la uva*) grape; (*tumorcillo en la piel*)

pimple; (*peso*) grain; **grano de belleza** beauty spot; **grano de café** coffee bean; **granos** (*fruto de los cereales*) grain; **ir al grano** (coll) to come to the point

granuja *m* scoundrel; (*muchacho vagabundo*) (coll) waif ‖ *f* loose grape; grapeseed

granujo *m* (coll) pimple

granular *adj* granular; pimply ‖ *tr & ref* to granulate

gránulo *m* granule

grapa *f* clamp, clip, staple

grasa *f* fat, grease; (*polvo*) pounce; (Mex) shoe polish; **grasa de ballena** blubber; **grasas** slag

grasien·to -ta *adj* greasy

grasilla *f* pounce

gra·so -sa *adj* fatty, greasy ‖ *m* fattiness, greasiness ‖ *f* see **grasa**

grasones *mpl* wheat porridge

graso·so -sa *adj* greasy; (pathol) fatty

grata *f* wire brush; (*carta*) favor

gratificar §73 *tr* to gratify; to reward, recompense; to tip, to fee

gratín *m* — **al gratín** au gratin

gratis *adv* gratis

gratisda·to -ta *adj* free, gratis

gratitud *f* gratitude

gra·to -ta *adj* pleasing; free; (Bol, Chile) grateful ‖ *f* see **grata**

gratui·to -ta *adj* gratuitous; free, gratis

grava *f* gravel; crushed stone

gravamen *m* burden, obligation; encumbrance, lien; assessment

gravar *tr* to burden, encumber; to assess

grave *adj* grave, serious, solemn; hard, difficult; (*que pesa*) heavy; (*sonido*) grave, deep, low; (*música*) majestic, noble; (*negocio*) important; (*enfermedad*) serious; (*acento*) grave; paroxytone

gravedad *f* gravity; seriousness; **de gravedad** seriously; gravely; **gravedad nula** weightlessness, zero gravity

gravedo·so -sa *adj* heavy, pompous

gravidez *f* pregnancy

grávi·do -da *adj* pregnant

gravitación *f* gravitation

gravitar *intr* to gravitate; **gravitar sobre** to weigh down on

gravo·so -sa *adj* burdensome, onerous, costly; boring, tiresome

graznar *intr* to caw, to croak; to cackle; (*al cantar*) (fig) to cackle

graznido *m* caw, croak; cackle; (*canto que disuena mucho*) (fig) cackle

Grecia *f* Greece

grecia·no -na *adj* Grecian

gre·co -ca *adj & mf* Greek

greda *f* clay, fuller's earth

grega·rio -ria *adj* (*que vive confundido con otros*) gregarious; slavish, servile

gregoria·no -na *adj* Gregorian

gremial *adj* guild; trade-union, union ‖ *m* guildsman; union member

gremio *m* guild, corporation; trade union, union; association, society

greña *f* confusion, entanglement; (*de cabello*) shock, tangled mop; **andar a la greña** (coll) to get into a hot argu-

ment; (*dos mujeres*) (coll) to pull each other's hair

greñu·do -da *adj* bushy-headed, shock-headed

gres *m* sandstone; stoneware

gresca *f* tumult, uproar; row, quarrel

grey *f* (*de ganado menor*) flock; group, party; nation, people; (*de fieles*) flock, congregation

grie·go -ga *adj* Greek ‖ *mf* Greek ‖ *m* (idioma) Greek; **hablar en griego** (coll) to not make sense

grieta *f* crack, crevice, chink; (*en la piel*) chap

grieta·do -da *adj* crackled ‖ *m* crackleware

grietar *ref* to crack, split; (*la piel*) to become chapped

gri·fo -fa *adj* (*pelo*) kinky, tangled; (*letra*) script; (W-I) colored; (Mex) drunk; (Col) conceited ‖ *mf* (W-I) colored person; (Mex) drunk ‖ *m* faucet, spigot, tap, cock; (myth) griffin; (Peru) gas station

grilla *f* female cricket; (rad) grid; (Col) fight, quarrel; (SAm) annoyance, bother; **¡ésa es grilla!** (coll) you expect me to believe that!

grillar *intr* (*el grillo*) to chirp ‖ *ref* (*las semillas, bulbos, etc.*) to sprout

grillete *m* fetter, shackle

grillo *m* (*insecto*) cricket; (*brote tierno*) sprout, shoot; **grillos** fetters, shackles

grima *f* fright, horror; **dar grima** to grate on the nerves

grin·go -ga *mf* (disparaging) foreigner; (*anglosajón*) (Am) gringo ‖ *m* (coll) gibberish

griñón *m* (*toca de monja*) wimple; (*melocotón*) nectarine

gripe *f* grippe

gris *adj* gray; dull, gloomy ‖ *m* gray; **hacer gris** (*el tiempo*) (coll) to be sharp, be brisk

grisáce·o -a *adj* grayish

gri·sú *m* (*pl* -súes) firedamp

grita *f* shouting; hubbub, uproar; **dar grita a** (coll) to hoot at

gritar *intr* to shout, cry out

gritería *f* shouting, outcry, uproar

grito *m* cry, shout; scream, shriek; **el último grito** (coll) the latest thing, all the rage; **poner el grito en el cielo** (coll) to raise the roof, to scream wildly

gro. *abbr* **género**

Groenlandia *f* Greenland

grosella *f* currant; **grosella silvestre** gooseberry

grosellero *m* currant bush; **grosellero silvestre** gooseberry bush

grosería *f* grossness, coarseness; churlishness, rudeness; stupidity; vulgarity

grose·ro -ra *adj* gross, coarse; churlish, rude; stupid; vulgar ‖ *mf* churl, boor

grosor *m* thickness, bulk

grosura *f* fat, suet, tallow; meat diet; coarseness, vulgarity

grotes·co -ca *adj* grotesque

grúa *f* crane, derrick; **grúa de bote** (naut) davit; **grúa de auxilio** wrecking crane; **grúa de caballete** gantry crane

gr
gr

grúa-remolque m tow truck

grue·so -sa adj big, thick, bulky, heavy; coarse, ordinary; stout, fat; (mar) rough, heavy; en grueso in gross, in bulk ‖ f (doce docenas) gross

grulla f (orn) crane

grumete m ship's boy, cabin boy

grumo m clot, curd; bunch, cluster

grumo·so -sa adj clotty, curdly

gruñido m (de cerdo) grunt; (de perro cuando amenaza) growl; (de persona) grumble; (de puerta) creak; (coll) grumble, scolding

gruñir §12 intr (el cerdo) to grunt; (el perro) to growl; (una persona) to grumble; (una puerta) to creak

gru·ñón -ñona adj (coll) grumpy, grumbly ‖ mf (coll) crosspatch

grupa f croup, rump

grupada f squall

grupal adj group

grupo m group; (mach & elec) unit

gruta f grotto

grutes·co -ca adj & m (fa) grotesque

Gruyère m Swiss cheese

gte. abbr gerente

guaca f (Bol, Peru) Indian tomb; (Am) hidden treasure

guacal m (Am) crate

guacama·yo -ya adj (P-R) flashy, sporty ‖ m (Am) macaw

guachapear tr to splash with the feet; to bungle, botch ‖ intr to clank, clatter

guachinan·go -ga adj (Am) flattering, sly ‖ mf (disparaging term used by Cubans) Mexican

gua·cho -cha adj (SAm) homeless, orphan; (SAm) odd, unmatched

guadal m (Am) bog, swamp; (Am) sand hill, dune

Guadalupe f Guadeloupe

guadama·cí m (pl -cíes) embossed leather

guadaña f scythe

guadañadora f mowing machine

guadañar tr to cut with a scythe

guadarnés m harness room; harness man

guagua f trifle; (SAm) baby; (W-I) bus; (Col) paca

guajada f (Mex) nonsense, folly

guaje adj (Hond, Mex) foolish, stupid ‖ m (Hond, Mex) calabash, gourd; (CAm) piece of junk

guaji·ro -ra mf (W-I) peasant, yokel

guajolote m (Am) turkey; (Mex) simpleton

gualda f (bot) weld, dyer's rocket

gual·do -da adj yellow ‖ f see gualda

gualdrapa f housing, trappings; (coll) dirty rag hanging from clothes

gualdrapear tr to line up head to tail ‖ intr (las velas) to flap

Gualterio m Walter

guanaco m (SAm) dope, simpleton; (SAm) tall lanky fellow; (zool) guanaco

guanajo m (W-I) boob, dunce; (Am) turkey

guano m (Am) palm tree; (Am) bird manure

guante m glove; arrojar el guante to throw down the gauntlet; echar un

guante to pass the hat; guantes tip, fee; recoger el guante to take up the gauntlet; salvo el guante (coll) excuse my glove

guantelete m gauntlet

guantería f glove shop

guapear intr (coll) to bluster, to swagger; (coll) to dress to kill

guape·tón -tona adj (coll) handsome; (coll) flashy, sporty; (coll) bold, fearless ‖ m (coll) bully, tough

guapeza f (coll) good looks; (coll) flashiness, sportiness; (coll) boldness, daring; (coll) bravado

gua·po -pa adj (coll) handsome, good-looking; (coll) flashy, sporty; (coll) bold, daring ‖ m (hombre pendenciero) bully; gallant, lady's man

guapura f (coll) good looks

guarache m (Mex) leather sandal; (Mex) tire patch

guarapo m sugar-cane juice; (Am) fermented juice of sugar cane

guarda mf guard, custodian ‖ m (Arg) trolley-car conductor; guarda de la aduana customhouse officer; guarda forestal forest ranger ‖ f guard, custody; (de la ley) observance; (de la espada) guard; (de la cerradura) ward; (bb) flyleaf

guardabarrera mf (rr) gatekeeper

guardaba·rros m (pl -rros) fender, mudguard, dashboard

guardabosque m gamekeeper; forest ranger; (Am) shortstop

guardabrisa m windshield; (naut) glass candle shade

guardacantón m spur stone

guardacarril m (rr) railguard

guardacar·tas m (pl -tas) letter file

guardaco·ches m (pl -ches) car watcher

guardacos·tas m (pl -tas) revenue cutter, coast guard cutter; guardacostas mpl (servicio) coast guard

guarda·dor -dora adj guarding, protecting; mindful, observant; stingy ‖ m guardian, keeper; observer

guardaespal·das m (pl -das) bodyguard

guardafango m fender, mudguard

guardafre·nos m (pl -nos) (rr) brakeman, flagman

guardafuego m fender, fireguard

guardagu·jas m (pl -jas) (rr) switchman

guardajo·yas m (pl -yas) jewel case

guardalado m railing, parapet

guardalmacén m warehouseman; (Cuba) country station master

guardamalleta f valance

guardameta m goalkeeper

guardamue·bles m (pl -bles) warehouse, furniture warehouse

guardanieve m snowshed

guardapelo m locket

guardapolvo m (sobretodo ligero) duster; (resguardo para preservar del polvo) cover, cloth; (del reloj) inner lid; (sobre una puerta o ventana) hood

guardapuerta f storm door

guardar tr to guard; to watch over; to protect; to put away; to show, observe; to save, e.g., ¡Dios guarde a

la Reina God save the Queen ‖ *intr* to keep, to save; **¡guarda!** look out!, watch out! ‖ *ref* to be on one's guard; **guardarse de** to look out for, watch out for, guard against

guardarraya *f* (CAm, W-I) boundary line, property line

guardarropa *mf* keeper of the wardrobe ‖ *m* (*armario donde se guarda la ropa*) wardrobe; (*local destinado a la custodia de ropa en establecimientos públicos*) checkroom, cloakroom; check boy ‖ *f* check girl, hat girl

guardarropía *f* (theat) wardrobe

guardasilla *f* chair rail

guardaventana *f* storm window

guardavía *m* (rr) trackwalker, lineman

guardavida *mf* lifeguard

guardavien·tos *m* (*pl* **-tos**) (*abrigo contra los vientos*) windbreak; (*mitra de chimenea*) chimney pot

guardavivo *m* bead, corner bead

guardería *f* guard, guardship; **guardería infantil** day nursery

guardesa *f* woman guard

guardia *m* guard, guardsman; **guardia civil** rural policeman; **guardia marina** midshipman, middy; **guardia urbano** policeman ‖ *f* (*cuerpo de hombres armados; manera de defenderse en la esgrima*) guard; (naut) watch; **de guardia** on duty; on guard; **guardia civil** rural police; **guardia de asalto** shock troops; **guardia de corps** (mil) bodyguard; **guardia de cuartillo** (naut) dogwatch; **guardia suiza** Swiss Guards

guar·dián -diana *mf* guardian ‖ *m* watchman

guardilla *f* attic; attic room

guardo·so -sa *adj* careful, neat, tidy; (*que ahorra mucho*) thrifty; (*mezquino*) stingy

guarecer §22 *tr* to take in, give shelter to; to keep, preserve; (*a un enfermo*) to treat ‖ *ref* to take refuge, take shelter

guarida *f* den, lair; shelter; haunt, hangout, hide-out

guarismo *m* cipher, figure

guarnecer §22 *tr* to trim, adorn; to equip, provide; to bind, to edge; (*joyas*) to set; to stucco, to plaster; (*frenos*) to line; (*un cojinete*) to bush; (*una plaza fuerte*) to man, garrison; (culin) to garnish

guarnición *f* trimming; equipping; binding, edging; (*de joyas*) setting; stuccoing, plastering; (*de la espada*) guard; (*de frenos*) lining; (*del émbolo*) packing; (*tropa que guarnece un lugar*) garrison; (culin) garnish; **guarniciones** fixtures, fittings; (*de la caballería*) harness

guarnicionar *tr* to garrison

guarnicionero *m* harness maker

gua·rro -rra *mf* hog

guasa *f* (coll) heaviness, churlishness; (coll) joking, kidding

guasca *f* (Am) rawhide; (Am) whip; **dar guasca a** (Am) to whip, thrash

guasería *f* (SAm) coarseness, crudity; (Chile) timidity

gua·so -sa *adj* (SAm) coarse, crude, uncouth ‖ *mf* (Chile) peasant ‖ *f* see **guasa**

gua·són -sona *adj* (coll) heavy, churlish; (coll) funny, comical ‖ *mf* (coll) dullard, churl; (coll) joker, kidder

guata *f* wadding, padding; (Arg, Chile, Peru) belly, paunch; (*de una pared*) (Chile) bulging, warping; (Ecuad) boon companion; **echar guata** (Chile) to prosper

guatemalte·co -ca *adj* & *mf* Guatemalan

guáter *m* (coll) toilet, water closet

guau *m* (*ladrido del perro*) bowwow; (bot) woodbine, Virginia creeper; **guau guau** (*perro*) bowwow ‖ *interj* bowwow!

guay *interj* — **¡guay de mí!** (poet) woe is me!

guayaba *f* guava, guava apple

guayabo *m* guava tree; (Am) lie, trick

guayaco *m* lignum vitae

Guayana *f* Guiana

gubernamental *adj* governmental; (*defensor*) strong-government

gubernati·vo -va *adj* governmental

gubia *f* gouge

guedeja *f* shock of hair; lion's mane

guerra *f* war, warfare; billiards; **Gran guerra** Great War; **guerra a muerte** war to the death; **guerra bacteriológica** germ warfare; **guerra de guerrillas** guerrilla warfare; **guerra de las dos Rosas** War of the Roses; **guerra de los Cien Años** Hundred Years' War; **guerra del Transvaal** Boer War; **guerra de ondas** radio jamming; **guerra de Troya** Trojan War; **guerra fría** cold war; **Guerra Mundial** World War; **guerra relámpago** blitzkrieg; **hacer la guerra** to wage war

guerrea·dor -dora *adj* warring ‖ *mf* warrior

guerrear *intr* to war, wage war, fight; to struggle, resist

guerre·ro -ra *adj* war, warlike; warring; (coll) mischievous ‖ *mf* fighter ‖ *m* warrior, soldier, fighting man ‖ *f* tight-fitting military jacket

guerrilla *f* band of skirmishers; guerrilla band; guerrilla warfare

guerrillear *intr* to skirmish; to wage guerrilla warfare

guerrillero *m* guerrilla

guía *mf* guide, leader; adviser ‖ *m* (mil) guide ‖ *f* guide; guidance; directory; (*del viajero*) guidebook; (*caballo*) leader; (*de la bicicleta*) handle bar; (*del bigote*) turned-up end; (*de la sierra*) fence; marker; shoot, sprout; (mach) guide; (rr) timetable; **guías** reins; **guía sonora** sound track; **guía telefónica** telephone directory

guiadera *f* (mach) guide

guiar §77 *tr* to guide, to lead; (*un automóvil*) to steer, to drive; to pilot; (*una planta, una vid*) to train ‖ *intr* to shoot, to sprout ‖ *ref* — **guiarse por** to be guided by, to go by

guija *f* pebble; grass pea

guijarro *m* cobble, cobblestone

guije·ño -ña *adj* pebbly; hard-hearted

guijo m gravel
guijo·so -sa adj gravelly; pebbly
guillame m rabbet plane
Guillermo m William
guillotina f guillotine; paper cutter
guillotinar tr to guillotine
guimbalete m pump handle
guinda f sour cherry
guindal m sour cherry tree
guindaleza f (naut) hawser
guindar tr to hoist, raise; (coll) to win; (ahorcar) (coll) to hang, to string up
guindilla m (coll) policeman, cop; Guinea pepper
guindo m sour cherry tree
guindola f (naut) boatswain's chair; (naut) life buoy
guinea f (moneda) guinea
guineo m small banana
guinga f gingham
guiña f (Col, Ven) bad luck
guiñada f wink; (naut) yaw
guiñapo m rag, tatter; ragamuffin
guiñar tr (el ojo) to wink || intr to wink; (naut) to yaw || ref to wink at each other
guiño m wink; hacer guiños a to make eyes at; hacerse guiños to make faces at each other
guión m banner, standard; cross (carried before prelate in procession); (signo ortográfico) hyphen; (signo ortográfico largo) dash; (mil) guidon; (mov & theat) scenario; (rad & telv) script; (mus) repeat sign; guión de montaje (mov) cutter's script; guión de rodaje (mov) shooting script
guionista mf (mov) scenarist; (mov) scriptwriter; (mov) subtitle writer
guirigay m (coll) gibberish; (coll) confusion, hubbub
guirindola f frill, jabot
guirlache m almond brittle, peanut brittle
guirnalda f garland, wreath
guisa f way, manner, wise; a guisa de in the manner of, like
guisado m stew, meat stew

guisante m pea; guisante de olor sweet pea
guisar tr to cook; to stew; to arrange, prepare || intr to cook
guiso m dish
guisote m hash
guita f twine; (coll) dough, money
guitarra f guitar
guitarrista mf guitarist
gui·tón -tona mf tramp, bum
gula f gluttony; gorging, guzzling
gulo·so -sa adj gluttonous; guzzling
gumía f Moorish poniard
gurrumi·no -na adj weak, puny || m henpecked husband || f uxoriousness
gusanear intr to swarm
gusanera f nest of worms; (coll) ruling passion
gusanien·to -ta adj wormy, grubby
gusanillo m small worm; twist stitch; (de la barrena) spur; matar el gusanillo (coll) to take a shot of liquor before breakfast
gusano m worm; gusano de luz glowworm; gusano de seda silk worm; gusano de tierra earthworm
gusano·so -sa adj wormy, grubby
gusarapo m waterworm, vinegar worm
gustación f tasting; taste
gustar tr to taste; to try, sample; to please, be pleasing to; to like, e.g., me gustan estas peras I like these pears || intr to like, e.g., como Vd. guste as you like; gustar de to like; to like to
gustillo m slight taste, touch
gusto m taste; flavor; liking; caprice, whim; pleasure; a gusto as you like it; con mucho gusto with pleasure, gladly; encontrarse a gusto or estar a gusto to like it (e.g., in the country); tanto gusto so glad to meet you
gusto·so -sa adj tasty; agreeable, pleasant; ready, willing, glad
gutapercha f gutta-percha
gutural adj guttural

H

H, h (hache) f ninth letter of the Spanish alphabet
haba f bean, broad bean; (simiente del café y el cacao) bean; ser habas contadas (coll) to be a sure thing
Habana, La Havana
haber m salary, wages; credit, credit side; haberes property, wealth || v §38 tr to have; to get, get hold of || v aux to have, e.g., lo he visto a menudo I have seen it often; haber de + inf to be to + inf, e.g., ha de llegar a mediodía he is to arrive at noon || v impers there to be, e.g., ha habido tres personas allí there were three people there; haber que + inf to be necessary to + inf; no hay de qué

you're welcome, don't mention it || ref to behave oneself; habérselas con to deal with; to have it out with
habichuela f kidney bean; habichuela verde string bean
hábil adj skillful, capable; (día) work
habilidad f skill, ability, capability; (lo que se ejecuta con gracia) feat; (enredo, embuste) scheme, trick
habilido·so -sa adj skillful
habilitación f qualification; backing, financing; equipping, outfitting; habilitaciones fixtures
habilitar tr to qualify; to back, finance; to equip, fit out; (en un examen) to pass
habitable adj inhabitable

habitación f habitation; (*edificio donde se habita*) house, home, dwelling; (*aposento de la casa o el hotel*) room; (*donde vive una especie vegetal o animal*) habitat
habitante mf (*de una casa*) dweller, occupant; (*de una población*) inhabitant
habitar tr to inhabit, live in; (*una casa, un piso*) to occupy || intr to live
hábito m garment, dress; habit, custom; **ahorcar los hábitos** (coll) to doff the cassock, to leave the priesthood; (coll) to change jobs; **el hábito no hace al monje** clothes don't make the man
habitua·do -da mf habitué
habitual adj habitual; regular, usual
habituar §21 tr to accustom || ref to become accustomed
habitud f relationship, connection; custom, habit
habla f speech; **al habla** speaking
habla·dor -dora adj talkative; gossipy || mf talker, chatterbox; gossip
habladuría f cut, sarcasm; **andar con habladurías** to go around gossiping
hablante adj speaking || mf speaker
hablar tr (*una lengua*) to speak, to talk; (*disparates*) to talk || intr to speak, to talk; **es hablar por demás** it's wasted talk; **estar hablando** (*una pintura, una estatua*) to be almost alive; **hablar claro** to talk straight from the shoulder
hablilla f story, piece of gossip
hablista mf speaker, good speaker
hacede·ro -ra adj feasible, practicable
hacenda·do -da adj landed, property-owning || mf landholder, property owner; (Am) cattle rancher; (Am) plantation owner
hacendar §2 tr (*el dominio de bienes raíces*) to pass on || ref to buy property in order to settle down
hacende·ro -ra adj thrifty
hacendista m economist, fiscal expert; man of independent means
hacendo·so -sa adj hard-working, thrifty
hacer §39 tr (*crear, producir, formar*) to make; (*ejecutar, llevar a cabo*) to do; (*un baúl*) to pack; (*un papel*) to play; (*un mandato*) to give; (*un drama*) to act, perform; to pretend to be; (*una pregunta*) to ask; **hace ago**, e.g., **hace un mes** a month ago; **hacer + inf** to have + inf, e.g., **le hice tomar un libro en la biblioteca** I had him get a book at the library; to make + inf, e.g., **el médico me hizo guardar cama** the doctor made me stay in bed; to have + pp, e.g., **hará construir una casa** he will have a house built; **hacer . . . que** to be . . . since, e.g., **hace un año que yo estuve aquí** it is a year since I was here; to be for . . ., e.g., **hace un año que estoy aquí** I have been here for a year; for expressions like **hacer frío** to be cold, see the noun || intr to act; **hacer a** to fit; **hacer al caso** (coll) to be to the purpose; **hacer como que + ind** to pretend to + inf; **hacer de to**

act as, to work as; **hacer por** to try to || ref to become, get to be, grow; **hacerse a** to become accustomed to; **hacerse a un lado** to step aside; **hacerse con** to make off with; **hacerse chiquito** (coll) to sing small; **hacérsele a uno difícil** to strike one as difficult; **hacerse viejo** to grow old; (coll) to kill time
hacia prep toward; (*cierta hora o época*) about, near; **hacia abajo** downward; **hacia adelante** forward; **hacia arriba** upward; **hacia atrás** backward; (coll) the wrong way; **hacia dentro** inward; **hacia fuera** outward
hacienda f farmstead, landed estate, country property; property, possessions; (Arg) cattle, livestock; (Am) ranch; **hacienda pública** public finance, federal income; **haciendas** household chores
hacina f pile, heap; shock, stack
hacinar tr to pile, heap, stack
hacha f axe; (*hacha pequeña*) hatchet; torch, firebrand; four-wick wax candle; **hacha de armas** battleaxe
hachazo m blow with an axe
hachear tr & intr to hew, hack, or chop with an axe
hachero m torchbearer; (*candelero*) torch stand; (*leñador*) woodcutter
hachich m or **hachís** m hashish
hacho m torch; (*sitio elevado cerca de la costa*) beacon, beacon hill
hada f fairy; (*mujer que encanta por su belleza, gracia, etc.*) charmer; **hada madrina** fairy godmother
hadar tr (*determinar el hado*) to predestine, foreordain; (*pronosticar*) to foretell; (*encantar*) to charm, cast a spell on
hado m fate, destiny
haiga m (slang) flashy auto; (slang) sport
halagar §44 tr (*lisonjear*) to flatter; (*demostrar cariño a*) to cajole, fawn on; (*agradar*) to gratify, please
halago m flattery; cajolery; gratification; **halagos** flattery, blandishments
halagüe·ño -ña adj flattering; fawning; gratifying, pleasing; bright, rosy, promising
halar tr (naut) to haul, to pull
halcón m falcon
halconear intr (*la mujer*) to chase after men
halconería f falconry
halconero m falconer
halda f skirt; **poner haldas en cinta** (coll) to pull up one's skirts to run; (coll) to roll up one's sleeves
halieto m fish hawk, osprey
hálito m breath; vapor; (poet) gentle breeze
halitosis f halitosis
halo m halo
halógeno m halogen
halterio m dumbbell
haluro m halide
hallar tr to find; (*averiguar*) to find out, discover || ref to find oneself; to be; **hallarse bien con** to be satisfied with; **hallárselo todo hecho** to never

gu
ha

have to turn a hand; **no hallarse** to feel uncomfortable, to not like it

hallazgo m (*cosa hallada*) find; (*acción de hallar*) finding, discovery; (*premio al que ha hallado una cosa perdida*) reward, finder's reward, e.g., **diez dólares de hallazgo** ten dollars reward

hallulla f bread baked on embers or hot stones; (Chile) fine bread

hamaca f hammock

hamamelina f witch hazel

hambre f hunger; (*escasez general de comestibles*) famine; **matar de hambre** to starve to death; **morir de hambre** to starve to death, die of starvation; **pasar hambre** to go hungry; **tener hambre** to be hungry

hambrear tr & intr to starve, to famish

hambrien-to -ta adj hungry, starving

hambruna f (SAm) mad hunger; (Ecuad) starvation

hamburguesa f hamburger sandwich

hamo m fishhook

hampa f underworld life; denizens of the underworld

hampes-co -ca adj underworld

hampón m bully, tough

hangar m (aer) hangar

hara·gán -gana adj idling, loafing, lazy || mf idler, loafer

haraganear intr to idle, to loaf, to hang around

harapien-to -ta adj ragged, tattered

harapo m rag, tatter; **andar** or **estar hecho un harapo** (coll) to go around in rags

harapo·so -sa adj ragged, tattered

harén m harem

harina f (*especialmente del trigo*) flour; (*de cualquier grano*) meal; **estar metido en harina** (coll) to be deeply absorbed; (coll) to be fat and heavy; **harina de avena** oatmeal; **harina de maíz** corn meal; **ser harina de otro costal** (coll) to be a horse of another color

harine·ro -ra adj flour || m flour dealer; flour bin

harino·so -sa adj floury, mealy

harnear tr (Col, Chile) to sift

harnero m sieve

ha·rón -rona adj lazy || mf lazy loafer

harpillera f burlap, sackcloth

hartar tr to stuff, to cram; to satisfy, to satiate; to tire, to bore; to overwhelm, deluge || intr to have one's fill || ref to stuff; to be satiated; to tire, be bored

hartazgo or **hartazón** m fill, bellyful; **darse un hartazgo** (coll) to eat one's fill; **darse un hartazgo de** (coll) to have or to get one's fill of

har·to -ta adj full, fed up; very much; **harto de** full of, fed up with, sick of || **harto** adv enough; very, quite

hartura f fill, satiety; full satisfaction; abundance

hasta adv even || prep until, till; to, as far as; down to, up to; as much as; **hasta ahora** up till now; **hasta aquí** so far; **hasta después** (coll) so long, good-by; **hasta la vista** or **hasta luego**

so long, good-by; **hasta mañana** see you tomorrow; **hasta más no poder** to the utmost; **hasta no más** to the utmost; **hasta que** until, till

hastial m gable end; (*hombrón rústico*) bumpkin

hastiar §77 tr to surfeit, sicken, cloy; (*fastidiar*) to bother, annoy, bore

hastío m surfeit, loathing, disgust; bother, annoyance, boredom

hataca f large wooden ladle; (*cilindro para extender la masa*) rolling pin

hatajo m small herd, small flock; (*p.ej., de disparates*) (coll) lot, flock

hato m (*de ganado vacuno*) herd; (*de ovejas*) flock; (*de ropa*) pack, bundle; (*de gente*) clique, ring; (*de gente malvada*) gang; everyday outfit; (*de disparates*) flock, lot; (Am) cattle ranch; **liar el hato** (coll) to pack up, pack one's baggage; **revolver el hato** (coll) to stir up trouble

haya f beech tree; (*madera*) beech || **La Haya** The Hague

hayaca f (Ven) mince pie

hayo m (Col) coca; (Col) coca leaves (*mixed for chewing*)

hayuco m beechnut, mast

haz m (pl **haces**) bunch, bundle; (*de leña*) fagot; (*de mieses*) sheaf; (*de rayos*) beam, pencil; (*de soldados*) file || f (pl **haces**) face; (*de la tierra*) surface; (*de paño o tela*) right side; (*de un edificio*) façade, front; **a sobre haz** on the surface; **ser de dos haces** to be two-faced

hazaña f feat, exploit, deed

hazañería f fuss

hazañe·ro -ra adj fussy

hazaño·so -sa adj gallant, courageous

hazmerreír m (coll) laughingstock, butt

he adv behold, lo and behold; **he aquí** here is, here are; **he allí** there is, there are

hebilla f buckle

hebra f thread; fiber; (*en la madera*) grain; (*del discurso*) (fig) thread; **de una hebra** (Chile) all at once; **pegar la hebra** (coll) to strike up a conversation; (coll) to keep on talking

hebre·o -a adj & mf Hebrew || m (*idioma*) Hebrew; (coll) usurer

hebro·so -sa adj fibrous, stringy

hecatombe f hecatomb

hechicera f witch, sorceress; (*mujer que por su belleza cautiva*) enchantress

hechicería f witchcraft, sorcery, wizardry; (fig) fascination, charm

hechice·ro -ra adj bewitching, charming, enchanting; magic || mf sorcerer, magician; charmer, enchanter || m wizard, sorcerer || f see **hechicera**

hechizar §60 tr to bewitch, cast a spell on; (fig) to bewitch, charm, enchant || intr to practice sorcery; (fig) to be charming, to enchant

hechi·zo -za adj fake, artificial; (*de quita y pon*) detachable; made, manufactured; (*producto*) (Am) local, home || m spell, charm; magic, sorcery; (fig) magic, sorcery, glamour; (fig) charmer; **hechizos** (*de una mujer*) charms

he·cho -cha *adj* accustomed; finished; turned into; (*traje*) ready-made; (*llegado a la edad adulta*) full-grown || *m* act, deed; fact; event; (*hazaña*) feat; **de hecho** in fact; **en hecho de verdad** as a matter of fact; **estar en el hecho de** to catch on to; **hecho consumado** fait accompli || **hecho** *interj* all right!, OK!

hechura *f* form, shape, cut, build; creation, creature; workmanship; (Chile) drink, treat; **hechuras** cost of making; **no tener hechura** to be impracticable

heder §51 *tr* to bore, annoy, tire || *intr* to stink, to reek

hediondez *f* stench, stink

hedion·do -da *adj* stinking, smelly; annoying, boring; obscene, filthy, dirty || *m* bean trefoil; skunk

hedor *m* stench, stink

helada *f* freezing; (*escarcha*) frost; **helada blanca** hoarfrost

heladera *f* refrigerator; (Chile) ice-cream tray

heladería *f* (Am) ice-cream parlor

hela·do -da *adj* cold, icy; (*pasmado por el miedo, la sorpresa, etc.*) frozen; (*esquivo, indiferente*) cold, chilly; (*cubierto de azúcar*) (Ven) iced || *m* cold drink; (*manjar*) water ice; (*sorbete*) ice cream; **helado al corte** brick ice cream || *f* see **helada**

hela·dor -dora *adj* freezing || *f* ice-cream freezer

helar §2 *tr* to freeze; to harden, congeal; to dumbfound; to discourage || *intr* to freeze || *ref* to freeze; to harden, congeal, set; (*cubrirse de hielo*) to ice

helecho *m* fern

heléni·co -ca *adj* Hellenic

hele·no -na *adj* Hellenic || *mf* Hellene

helero *m* glacier

hélice *f* helix; (*de un buque*) screw, propeller; (*de un avión*) propeller

helicóptero *m* helicopter

helio *m* helium

heliotropo *m* heliotrope

helipuerto *m* heliport

hematíe *m* red cell

hembra *adj invar* (*animal, planta, herramienta*) female; weak, thin, delicate || *f* female; (*del corchete*) eye; (*tuerca*) nut; **hembra de terraja** (mach) die

hembraje *m* (SAm) females of a flock or herd

hembrilla *f* (mach) female part or piece; (*armella*) eyebolt

hemeroteca *f* periodical library

hemiciclo *m* (*semicírculo*) hemicycle; (*gradería semicircular*) amphitheater; (*espacio central del salón de sesiones de las Cortes*) floor

hemisferio *m* hemisphere

hemistiquio *m* hemistich

hemofilia *f* hemophilia

hemoglobina *f* hemoglobin

hemorragia *f* hemorrhage

hemorroides *fpl* hemorrhoids

hemóstato *m* hemostat

henal *m* hayloft

henar *m* hayfield

henchir §50 *tr* to fill; (*un colchón*) to stuff; (*a una persona, p.ej., de favores*) to heap, to shower || *ref* to be filled; to stuff, to stuff oneself

hendedura *f* crack, split, cleft

hender §51 *tr* to crack, split, cleave; (*el aire, las ondas*) to cleave; to make one's way through || *ref* to crack, to split

hendidura *f* crack, split, cleft

henil *m* hayloft, haymow

henna *f* henna

heno *m* hay

heñir §72 *tr* to knead; **hay mucho que heñir** (coll) there's still a lot of work to do

heraldía *f* heraldry

heráldi·co -ca *adj* heraldic || *f* heraldry

heraldo *m* herald

herbáce·o -a *adj* herbaceous

herbajar *tr & intr* to graze

herbaje *m* herbage

herba·rio -ria *adj* herbal || *m* (*libro*) herbal; (*colección*) herbarium

herbicida *m* weed killer

herbo·so -sa *adj* grassy

hercúle·o -a *adj* herculean

heredad *f* country estate

heredar *tr & intr* to inherit; **heredar a** to inherit from

herede·ro -ra *mf* heir, inheritor; owner of an estate; **heredero forzoso** heir apparent || *m* heir || *f* heiress

heredita·rio -ria *adj* hereditary

hereje *mf* heretic

herejía *f* heresy; insult, outrage; (coll) outrageous price

herencia *f* heritage, inheritance; (*transmisión de caracteres biológicos*) heredity; (*patrimonio de un difunto*) estate

heréti·co -ca *adj* heretic(al)

herida *f* injury, wound; insult, outrage; **renovar la herida** to open an old sore; **tocar en la herida** to sting to the quick

heri·do -da *adj* hurt, wounded; (*ofendido*) hurt || *mf* injured person, wounded person; **los heridos** the injured, the wounded || *f* see **herida**

herir §68 *tr* to injure, hurt, wound; (*ofender*) (fig) to hurt; (*golpear*) to strike; (*el sol sobre*) to beat down upon; (*un instrumento de cuerda*) to play; (*la cuerda de un instrumento*) to pluck; to touch, to move

hermana *f* sister; **hermana de leche** foster sister; **hermana política** sister-in-law; **media hermana** half sister

hermanar *tr* to match, to mate; to combine, join; to harmonize || *ref* to match; to become attached as brothers or sisters or brother and sister

hermanastra *f* stepsister

hermanastro *m* stepbrother

hermandad *f* brotherhood; sisterhood; close friendship; close relationship

herma·no -na *adj* (p.ej., *idioma*) sister || *mf* companion, mate || *m* brother; **hermano de leche** foster brother; **hermano político** brother-in-law; **hermanos** brother and sister; brothers and sisters; **hermanos siameses** Siamese twins; **medio hermano** half brother; **primo hermano** first cousin || *f* see **hermana**

hermét·i·co -ca *adj* hermetic(al); airtight; impenetrable; tight-lipped

hermosear *tr* to beautify, to embellish

hermo·so -sa *adj* beautiful; (*caballero*) handsome

hermosura *f* beauty; (*mujer hermosa*) belle, beauty

hernia *f* hernia

héroe *m* hero

heroi·co -ca *adj* heroic; (*remedio*) desperate

heroína *f* heroine; (pharm) heroin

heroísmo *m* heroism

herrada *f* wooden bucket

herrador *m* horseshoer

herradura *f* horseshoe; **mostrar las herraduras** (*un caballo*) to kick, be vicious; (coll) to show one's heels

herraje *m* hardware, ironwork

herramental *adj* tool || *m* toolbox, tool bag

herramienta *f* tool; set of tools; (coll) teeth; (coll) horns

herrar §2 *tr* (*guarnecer con hierro*) to fit with hardware; (*un caballo*) to shoe; (*marcar con hierro candente*) to brand; (*un barril*) to hoop

herrería *f* forge, blacksmith shop; blacksmithing; ironworks; rumpus

herrero *m* blacksmith; **herrero de grueso** ironworker; **herrero de obra** steelworker

herrete *m* tip, metal tip

herretear *tr* to tip, put a metal tip on

herrín *m* rust

herrón *m* (*tejo de hierro horadado*) quoit; (*arandela*) washer

herrumbre *f* rust; (*honguillo parásito*) rust, plant rot

herrumbro·so -sa *adj* rusty

herventar §2 *tr* to boil

hervidero *m* boiling; bubbling spring; (*en el pecho*) rattle; (*de gente*) swarm

hervidor *m* boiler, cooker

hervir §68 *intr* to boil; (*el mar; una persona encolerizada*) to boil, to seethe; to swarm, to teem

hervor *m* boil, boiling; (*de la juventud*) fire, restlessness; **alzar el hervor** to begin to boil

hervoro·so -sa *adj* ardent, fiery, impetuous

heterócli·to -ta *adj* irregular; unconventional

heterodinar *tr* to heterodyne

heterodi·no -na *adj* heterodyne

heterodo·xo -xa *adj* heterodox

heterogeneidad *f* heterogeneity

heterogéne·o -a *adj* heterogeneous

hexámetro *m* hexameter

hez *f* (*pl* **heces**) (fig) scum, dregs; **heces** lees, dregs; feces, excrement

hiato *m* hiatus

hibisco *m* hibiscus

hibridación *f* hybridization

hibridar *tr & intr* to hybridize

híbri·do -da *adj & m* hybrid

hidal·go -ga *adj* noble, illustrious || *m* nobleman || *f* noblewoman

hidalguez *f* or **hidalguía** *f* nobility

hidra *f* hydra

hidratar *tr & ref* to hydrate

hidrato *m* hydrate

hidráuli·co -ca *adj* hydraulic || *f* hydraulics

hidroala *m* (*vehículo mixto de buque y avión*) hydrofoil

hidroaleta *f* (*miembro alar del hidroala*) hydrofoil

hidroavión *m* hydroplane

hidrocarburo *m* hydrocarbon

hidroeléctri·co -ca *adj* hydroelectric

hidrófi·lo -la *adj* (*algodón*) absorbent (*cotton*)

hidrofobia *f* hydrophobia

hidrófu·go -ga *adj* waterproof

hidrógeno *m* hydrogen

hidropesía *f* dropsy

hidróxido *m* hydroxide

hiedra *f* ivy

hiel *f* bile, gall; (fig) gall, bitterness, sorrow; **echar la hiel** (coll) to strain, to overwork

hielo *m* ice; (fig) coldness, coolness; **hielo flotante** drift ice, ice pack; **hielo seco** dry ice; **romper el hielo** (*quebrantar la reserva*) to break the ice

hiena *f* hyena

hienda *f* dung

hierba *f* grass; (*especialmente la que tiene propiedades medicinales*) herb; **hierba de la plata** honesty; **hierba del asno** evening primrose; **hierba de París** truelove; **hierba gatera** catnip; **hierba pastel** woad; **hierbas** grass, pasture; herb poison; (coll) years of age (*said of animals*); **mala hierba** weed; (coll) wayward young fellow

hierbabuena *f* mint

hierro *m* iron; (*marca candente que se pone a los ganados*) brand; **hierro colado** cast iron; **hierro colado en barras** pig iron; **hierro de desecho** scrap iron; **hierro de marcar** branding iron; **hierro dulce** wrought iron; **hierro fundido** cast iron; **hierro galvanizado** galvanized iron; **hierro ondulado** corrugated iron; **hierros** irons, fetters; **llevar hierro a Vizcaya** to carry coals to Newcastle

higa *f* baby's fist-shaped amulet; (coll) scorn, contempt; **dar higa** to miss fire; **no dar dos higas por** (coll) to not give a rap for

hígado *m* liver; **echar los hígados** (coll) to strain, to overwork; **hígados** (coll) guts, courage; **malos hígados** (coll) hatred, grudge

higiene *f* hygiene

higiéni·co -ca *adj* hygienic

higo *m* fig; **higo chumbo** prickly pear; **higo paso** dried fig; **no valer un higo** (coll) to be not worth a continental

higuera *f* fig tree; **higuera chumba** prickly pear

hija *f* daughter; **hija política** daughter-in-law

hijas·tro -tra *m* stepchild || *m* stepson || *f* stepdaughter

hi·jo -ja *mf* child; (*de un animal*) young; **hijo de bendición** legitimate child; good child; **hijo de la cuna**

foundling; **hijo del amor** love child; **hijo de leche** foster child || *m* son; **cada hijo de vecino** (coll) every man Jack, every mother's son; **hijo del agua** good sailor; good swimmer; **hijo de su padre** (coll) chip off the old block; **hijo de sus propias obras** self-made man; **hijo político** son-in-law; **hijos** children; descendants || *f* see **hija**

hijodalgo *m* (*pl* **hijosdalgo**) nobleman

hijuela *f* little girl, little daughter; (*tira de tela*) gore; branch drain; side path

hijuelero *m* rural postman

hijuelo *m* shoot, sucker

hila *f* row, line; (*acción de hilar*) spinning; **a la hila** in single file; **hilas** (*hebras para curar heridas*) lint

hilacha *f* shred, fraying; **hilacha de acero** steel wool; **hilacha de algodón** cotton waste; **hilacha de vidrio** spun glass; **hilachas** lint; **mostrar la hilacha** (Arg) to show one's worst side

hilachos *mpl* (Mex) rags, tatters

hilacho·so -sa *adj* frayed, raggedy

hilada *f* row, line; (mas) course

hilado *m* spinning; (*hilo*) yarn, thread

hila·dor -dora *adj* spinning || *mf* spinner || *f* spinning machine

hilandería *f* spinning; spinning mill

hilande·ro -ra *adj* spinning || *m* spinning mill

hilar *tr & intr* to spin; **hilar delgado** to hew close to the line; **hilar largo** to drag on

hilarante *adj* laughable; (*gas*) laughing

hilaza *f* yarn, thread; lint; **descubrir la hilaza** (coll) to show one's true nature

hilera *f* row, line; fine thread, fine yarn; (*parhilera*) ridgepole; (mil) file

hilo *m* thread; (*hebras retorcidas*) yarn; (*alambre*) wire; (*de perlas*) string; (*de agua*) thin stream; (*de luz*) beam; linen, linen fabric; (*de un discurso, de la vida*) (fig) thread; **hilo bramante** twine; **hilo de la muerte** end of life; **hilo de masa** (aut) ground wire; **hilo de medianoche** midnight sharp; **hilo dental** dental floss; **hilo de tierra** (elec) ground wire; **irse al hilo** or **tras el hilo de la gente** to follow the crowd; **manejar los hilos** to pull strings; **perder el hilo de** to lose the thread of

hilván *m* basting, tacking; basting stitch; (Chile) basting thread; (Ven) hem; **hablar de hilván** (coll) to jabber along

hilvanar *tr* to baste, to tack; to sketch, outline; (*hacer con precipitación*) (coll) to hurry; (Ven) to hem || *intr* to baste, to tack

himnario *m* hymnal, hymn book

himno *m* hymn; **himno nacional** national anthem

hin *m* neigh, whinny

hincadura *f* driving, thrusting, sticking

hincapié *m* stamping the foot; **hacer hincapié en** (coll) to lay great stress on, to emphasize

hincar §73 *tr* to drive, thrust, stick, sink; (*la rodilla*) to go down on, to

fall on || *ref* to kneel, kneel down; **hincarse de rodillas** to go down on one's knees

hincha *mf* (sport) fan, rooter || *f* (coll) grudge, ill will

hinchable *adj* inflatable; (*goma de mascar*) bubble

hincha·do -da *adj* swollen; swollen with pride; (*estilo, lenguaje*) pompous, high-flown || *m* (*de un neumático*) inflation || *f* (sport) fans, rooters

hinchar *tr* to swell; to inflate; (*un neumático*) to pump up; to exaggerate, embroider || *ref* to swell; to swell up, become puffed up (*with pride*)

hinchazón *f* swelling; vanity, conceit; (*del estilo, lenguaje*) bombast

hinchismo *m* (sport) fans, rooters

hin·dú -dúa (*pl* **-dúes -dúas**) *adj & mf* Hindoo, Hindu

hiniesta *f* Spanish broom

hinojo *m* fennel; **de hinojos** on one's knees

hipar *intr* to hiccup; (*los perros cuando siguen la caza*) to pant, to snuffle; (*gimotear*) to whimper; to be worn out; **hipar por** to long for; to long to

hiperacidez *f* hyperacidity

hipérbola *f* (geom) hyperbola

hipérbole *f* (rhet) hyperbole

hiperbóli·co -ca *adj* (geom & rhet) hyperbolic

hipersensible *adj* (*alérgico*) hypersensitive

hipertensión *f* hypertension, high blood pressure

hípi·co -ca *adj* horse, equine

hipnosis *f* hypnosis

hipnóti·co -ca *adj* hypnotic || *mf* hypnotic || *m* (*medicamento que provoca el sueño*) hypnotic

hipnotismo *m* hypnotism

hipnotista *mf* hypnotist

hipnotizar §60 *tr* to hypnotize

hipo *m* hiccup; longing, desire; **tener hipo contra** to have a grudge against; **tener hipo por** to desire eagerly

hipocondría·co -ca *adj & mf* hypochondriac

hipocresía *f* hypocrisy

hipócrita *adj* hypocritical || *mf* hypocrite

hipodérmi·co -ca *adj* hypodermic

hipódromo *m* hippodrome, race track

hipopótamo *m* hippopotamus

hiposulfito *m* hyposulfite

hipoteca *f* mortgage; **¡buena hipoteca!** (coll) you may believe it, if you want to!

hipotecar §73 *tr* to mortgage

hipoteca·rio -ria *adj* mortgage

hipotenusa *f* hypotenuse

hipóte·sis *f* (*pl* **-sis**) hypothesis

hipotéti·co -ca *adj* hypothetic(al)

hiriente *adj* cutting, stinging

hirsu·to -ta *adj* hairy, bristly; (fig) brusque, gruff

hirviente *adj* boiling

hisopear *tr* to sprinkle with holy water

hisopo *m* (bot) hyssop; aspergillum, sprinkler of holy water; (Am) paint brush, shaving brush

hispalense *adj & mf* Sevillian

hispáni·co -ca adj Hispanic
hispanista mf Hispanist
hispa·no -na adj Spanish; Spanish American ‖ mf Spaniard; Spanish American
hispanohablante adj Spanish-speaking ‖ mf speaker of Spanish
híspi·do -da adj bristly, spiny
histéri·co -ca adj hysteric(al)
histerismo m hysteria
histología f histology
historia f history; story, tale; **de historia** (coll) notorious, infamous; **dejarse de historias** (coll) to come to the point; **historia de lagrimitas** (coll) sob story; **historias** (coll) gossip, meddling; **pasar a la historia** to become a thing of the past; **picar en historia** to turn out to be serious
historia·do -da adj richly adorned; overadorned; (cuadro, dibujo) storied
historial adj historical ‖ m record, dossier
historiar §77 & regular tr to tell the history of; to tell the story of; (un suceso histórico) (fa) to depict
históri·co -ca adj historic(al)
historieta f anecdote, brief story; **historieta gráfica** comic strip
histrión m actor; juggler, buffoon
histrióni·co -ca adj histrionic
hita f brad; landmark, milestone
hi·to -ta adj fixed, firm; (casa, calle) next; (caballo) black ‖ m (clavo fijado en la tierra) peg, hob; (juego) quoits; (blanco) target; (mojón) landmark, milestone; **dar en el hito** to hit the nail on the head; **mirar de hito en hito** to eye up and down ‖ f see **hita**
Hno. abbr **Hermano**
hoba·chón -chona adj (coll) lumpish
hocicar §73 tr to nuzzle, to root; (coll) to keep on kissing ‖ intr to nuzzle, to root; to run into a snag; (la proa) (naut) to dip
hocico m snout; (de una persona) (coll) snout; sour face; **caer de hocicos** (coll) to fall on one's face; **meter el hocico en todo** (coll) to poke one's nose into everything; **poner hocico** (coll) to make a face
hogaño adv (coll) this year; (coll) at the present time
hogar m fireplace, hearth; furnace; home; family life; (hoguera) bonfire
hogare·ño -ña adj home-loving ‖ mf homebody, stay-at-home
hogaza f large loaf of bread
hoguera f bonfire
hoja f (de planta, libro, mesa, muelle, puerta plegadiza, etc.) (pétalo de flor) leaf; (de planta acuática) pad; (de papel) sheet; blank sheet; (de cuchillo, sierra, espada, etc.) blade; (hojuela de metal) foil; (de persiana) slat; (del patín) runner; **doblar la hoja** (coll) to change the subject; **hoja clínica** clinical chart; **hoja de afeitar** razor blade; **hoja de embalaje** packing slip; **hoja de encuadernador** (bb) end paper; **hoja de estaño** tin foil; **hoja de estudios** tran-

script; **hoja de guarda** (bb) flyleaf; **hoja del anunciante** tear sheet; **hoja de lata** tin, tin plate; **hoja de nenúfar** lily pad; **hoja de paga** pay roll; **hoja de parra** fig leaf; **hoja de pedidos** order blank; **hoja de rodaje** (mov) shooting record; **hoja de ruta** waybill; **hoja de servicios** service record; **hoja de trébol** cloverleaf (intersection); **hoja maestra** master blade (of spring); **hojas del autor** (typ) advance sheets; **hoja suelta** leaflet, handbill; (bb) flyleaf; **hoja volante** leaflet, handbill
hojalata f tin, tin plate
hojalatería f tinsmith's shop; tinwork
hojalatero m tinsmith, tinner
hojaldre m & f puff paste
hojarasca f dead leaves; trash, rubbish; bluff, vain show
hojear tr to leaf through ‖ intr to scale off; (las hojas de los árboles) to flutter
hojita f leaflet; **hojita de afeitar** razor blade
hojo·so -sa adj leafy
hojuela f (hoja de otra compuesta) leaflet; (fruta de sartén) pancake; (hoja muy delgada de metal) foil; **hojuela de estaño** tin foil
hola interj hey!, hello!
Holanda f Holland
holan·dés -desa adj Dutch; **a la holandesa** (bb) half-bound ‖ mf Hollander ‖ m Dutchman; (idioma) Dutch ‖ f Dutch woman
holga·chón -chona adj (coll) lazy, idle ‖ mf (coll) loafer, idler
holgadero m hangout
holga·do -da adj idle, unoccupied; (vestido) loose, full, roomy; (que vive con bienestar) fairly well-off
holganza f idleness, leisure; pleasure, enjoyment
holgar §63 intr to idle, be idle; to take it easy, to rest up; to not fit, be too loose; to be unnecessary, be of no use; to be glad ‖ ref to be glad; to be amused
holga·zán -zana adj idle, lazy ‖ mf idler, loafer
holgazanear intr to idle, loaf, bum around
hol·gón -gona adj pleasure-loving ‖ mf loafer, lizard
holgorio m (coll) fun, merriment
holgura f looseness, fulness; enjoyment, merriment; comfort, easy circumstances; (mach) play
holocausto m holocaust
hollar §61 tr to tread on, to trample on
hollejo m hull, peel, skin
hollín m soot
hollinar tr (Chile) to cover with soot
hollinien·to -ta adj sooty
hombracho m big husky fellow
hombrada f manly act
hombradía f manliness, courage
hombre m man; (coll) husband, man; (coll) my boy, old chap; **buen hombre** good-natured fellow; **¡hombre al agua!** or **¡hombre a la mar!** man overboard!; **hombre bueno** arbiter,

referee; **hombre de bien** honorable man; **hombre de buenas prendas** man of parts; **hombre de dinero** man of means; **hombre de letras** man of letters; **hombre de mundo** man of the world; **hombre de suposición** man of straw; **hombre hecho** grown man || *interj* man alive!, upon my word!
hombre-anuncio *m* sandwich man
hombrear *tr* (Arg) to carry on the shoulders; (Mex) to aid, back || *intr* to try to be somebody; (*una mujer*) to be mannish; **hombrear con** to try to equal
hombrecillo *m* little man; (*lúpulo*) hop
hombrera *f* (*del vestido*) shoulder; shoulder pad; epaulet
hombre-rana *m* (*pl* **hombres-ranas**) frogman
hombría *f* manliness; **hombría de bien** honor, probity
hombrillo *m* (*de la camisa*) yoke; shoulder piece
hombro *m* shoulder; **arrimar el hombro** to lend a hand, put one's shoulder to the wheel; **encoger los hombros** to let one's shoulders droop; **encogerse de hombros** to shrug one's shoulders; to crouch, to shrink with fear; to not answer; **mirar por encima del hombro** to look down upon; **salir en hombros** to be carried off on the shoulders of the crowd
hombru‧no -na *adj* (coll) mannish
homenaje *m* homage; (feud) homage; (Chile) gift, favor; **homenaje de boca** lip service; **rendir homenaje a** to swear allegiance to
homeópata *mf* homeopath
homeopatía *f* homeopathy
homicida *adj* homicidal || *mf* homicide
homicidio *m* homicide
homilía *f* homily
homogeneidad *f* homogeneity
homogeneizar §60 *tr* to homogenize
homogéne‧o -a *adj* homogeneous
homologación *f* confirmation, ratification; (sport) validation
homologar §44 *tr* to confirm, ratify; (*un récord*) (sport) to validate
homóni‧mo -ma *adj* homonymous; of the same name || *mf* namesake || *m* homonym
homosexual *adj* & *mf* homosexual; (coll) gay
homúnculo *m* (coll) guy, little runt
honda *f* sling
hondazo *m* blow with a sling
hondear *tr* (naut) to sound
hondillos *mpl* patches in the crotch of pants
hon‧do -da *adj* deep; (*terreno*) low || *m* bottom || *f* see **honda** || **hondo** *adv* deep
hondón *m* (*de la aguja*) eye; (*de un vaso*) bottom; lowland
hondonada *f* lowland, ravine
hondura *f* depth, profundity; **meterse en honduras** (coll) to go beyond one's depth
hondure‧ño -ña *adj* & *mf* Honduran
honestidad *f* decency; chastity; mod-

esty; honesty, probity; fairness, reasonableness
hones‧to -ta *adj* decent; chaste, pure; modest; honest, upright; (*precio*) fair, reasonable
hongo *m* fungus, mushroom; (*sombrero*) bowler, derby
honor *m* honor; **en honor a la verdad** as a matter of fact, to tell the truth; **hacer honor a** to do honor to; (*la firma*) to honor
honorable *adj* honorable
honora‧rio -ria *adj* honorary || *s* fee, honorarium
honorífi‧co -ca *adj* honorific
honra *f* honor; **tener a mucha honra** to be proud of
honradez *f* honesty, integrity
honra‧do -da *adj* honorable
honrar *tr* to honor || *ref* to feel honored
honrilla *f* — **por la negra honrilla** out of concern for what people will say
honro‧so -sa *adj* honorable
hopo *m* tuft, shock (*of hair*); bushy tail; **seguir el hopo a** (coll) to keep right after
hora *f* hour; (*momento determinado para algo*) time; **a la hora** on time; **a la hora de ahora** right now; **a la hora en punto** on the hour; **a las pocas horas** within a few hours; **dar hora** to fix a time; **dar la hora** (*el reloj*) to strike; **de última hora** up-to-date; most up-to-date; (*noticias*) late; **en buen hora** or **en hora buena** safely, luckily; all right; **en mal hora** or **en hora mala** unluckily, in an evil hour; **fuera de horas** after hours; **hasta altas horas** until late into the night; **hora de acostarse** bedtime; **hora de aglomeración** rush hour; **hora de comer** mealtime; **hora deshorada** fatal hour; **hora de verano** daylight-saving time; **hora de verdad** (taur) kill; **hora legal** or **oficial** standard time; **hora punta** peak hour; rush hour; **horas de consulta** office hours (*of a doctor*); **horas de ocio** leisure hours; **horas de punta** rush hours; **horas extraordinarias de trabajo** overtime
horadar *tr* to drill, bore, pierce
hora‧rio -ria *adj* hour || *m* hour hand; clock; (*de ferrocarriles*) timetable; **horario escolar** roster
horca *f* (*para levantar la paja*) pitchfork; (*para ahorcar a un condenado*) gallows, gibbet; (*de ajos, cebollas, etc.*) string
horcajadas — **a horcajadas** astride, astraddle
horcajadillas — **a horcajadillas** astride, astraddle
horcajadura *f* crotch
horcajo *m* (*confluencia de dos ríos*) fork; (*para mulas*) yoke
horcón *m* pitchfork; forked prop (*for fruit trees*); (Am) upright, prop
horchata *f* orgeat
horda *f* horde
horizontal *adj* & *f* horizontal
horizonte *m* horizon

horma *f* form, mold; shoe tree; hat block; **hallar la horma de su zapato** (coll) to meet one's match

hormiga *f* ant; (*enfermedad que causa comezón*) itch

hormigón *m* concrete; **hormigón armado** reinforced concrete

hormigonera *f* concrete mixer

hormigo•so -sa *adj* ant; full of ants; ant-eaten; (*picante*) itchy

hormiguear *intr* (*ponerse en movimiento gente o animales*) to swarm; (*experimentar una sensación de hormigas corriendo por el cuerpo*) to crawl, to creep; to abound, to teem

hormiguero *m* anthill; (*de gente*) swarm, mob

hormillón *m* hat block

hormón *m* or **hormona** *f* hormone

hornacina *f* niche

hornada *f* (*cantidad que se cuece de una vez en un horno*) batch, bake; (*conjunto de individuos de una misma promoción*) crop

hornazo *m* Easter cake filled with hard-boiled eggs; Easter gift to Lenten preacher

horne•ro -ra *mf* baker

hornilla *f* kitchen grate; pigeonhole

hornillo *m* kitchen stove; hot plate; (*de la pipa de fumar*) bowl

horno *m* oven, furnace; (*para cocer ladrillos*) kiln; **alto horno** blast furnace; **horno de cal** limekiln; **horno de fundición** smelting furnace; **horno de ladrillero** brickkiln

horóscopo *m* horoscope; **sacar un horóscopo** to cast a horoscope

horqueta *f* pitchfork; fork, prop; (*ángulo agudo en un río*) (Arg) bend

horquilla *f* pitchfork; (*de bicicleta*) fork; (*de microteléfono*) cradle; (*alfiler para sujetar el pelo*) hairpin

hórreo *m* granary; (in Asturias and Galicia) crib or granary raised on pillars (*to protect grain from mice and dampness*)

horrible *adj* horrible

horripilante *adj* hair-raising, blood-curdling

horror *m* horror; **tener horror a** to have a horror of

horrorizar §60 *tr* to horrify

horroro•so -sa *adj* horrid; (coll) hideous, ugly

hortaliza *f* vegetable

hortela•no -na *adj* garden ǁ *mf* gardener

hortera *m* (coll) clerk, helper ǁ *f* wooden bowl

hortícola *adj* horticultural

horticul•tor -tora *mf* horticulturist

horticultura *f* horticulture

hos•co -ca *adj* dark, dark-skinned; sullen, grim, gloomy

hospedaje *m* lodging

hospedar *tr* to lodge ǁ *ref* to lodge, stop, put up

hospedería *f* hospice; inn, hostelry

hospede•ro -ra *mf* innkeeper

hospicio *m* hospice; poorhouse; orphan asylum

hospital *m* hospital; **estar hecho un hos**-pital (*una persona*) (coll) to be full of aches and pains; (*una casa*) (coll) to be turned into a hospital; **hospital de la sangre** poor relations; **hospital de primera sangre** (mil) field hospital; **hospital robado** (coll) bare house

hospitala•rio -ria *adj* hospitable

hospitalidad *f* hospitality; (*estancia del enfermo en el hospital*) hospitalization

hospitalizar §60 *tr* to hospitalize

hosquedad *f* darkness; sullenness, grimness, gloominess

hostería *f* inn, hostelry

hostia *f* sacrificial victim; wafer; (eccl) wafer, Host

hostigar §44 *tr* to scourge; to harass; to pester; (Am) to cloy, surfeit

hostigo•so -sa *adj* (Am) cloying, sickening

hostil *adj* hostile

hostilidad *f* hostility

hostilizar §60 *tr* to antagonize; (*al enemigo*) to harry, harass

hotel *m* (*establecimiento donde se da comida y alojamiento por dinero*) hotel; (*casa particular lujosa*) mansion

hotele•ro -ra *adj* hotel ǁ *mf* hotelkeeper

hoy *adv & s* today; de hoy a mañana any time now; **de hoy en adelante** from now on; **hoy día** nowadays

hoya *f* hole, pit, ditch; (*sepultura*) grave; valley; (*almáciga*) seedbed; (Am) river basin

hoyanca *f* potter's field

hoyo *m* hole; grave; pockmark

hoyo•so -sa *adj* full of holes

hoyuelo *m* dimple; (*juego de muchachos*) pitching pennies

hoz *f* (*pl* **hoces**) sickle; narrow pass, defile; **de hoz y de coz** (coll) headlong, recklessly

hozar §60 *tr & intr* to nuzzle, to root

hta. *abbr* **hasta**

huacal *m* var of **guacal**

huachinango *m* (Mex) red snapper

hucha *f* workingman's chest; (*alcancía*) toy bank; (*dinero ahorrado*) savings, nest egg

huchear *intr* to cry, shout

hue•co -ca *adj* hollow; (*mullido*) soft, fluffy, spongy; (*voz*) deep, resounding; vain, conceited; (*estilo, lenguaje*) affected, pompous ǁ *m* hollow; interval; (*en un muro, una hilera de coches, etc.*) opening; (*empleo sin proveer*) (coll) opening; **hueco de la axila** armpit; **hueco de escalera** stairwell

huélfago *m* (vet) heaves

huelga *f* (*ocio*) rest, leisure, idleness; recreation; pleasant spot; (*cesación del trabajo en señal de protesta*) strike; (mach) play; **huelga de brazos caídos** sit-down strike; **huelga de hambre** hunger strike; **huelga patronal** lockout; **huelga sentada** sit-down strike; **ir a la huelga** or **ponerse en huelga** to go on strike

huelguista *mf* striker

huella *f* track, footprint; trace, mark; rut; (*acción de hollar*) tread, treading; (peldaño en que se asienta el pie) tread; **huella dactilar** or **digital** fingerprint; **huella de sonido** sound track; **seguir las huellas de** to follow in the footsteps of

huérfa·no -na adj orphan; orphaned; alone, deserted ‖ mf orphan; (Chile, Peru) foundling

hue·ro -ra adj rotten; (fig) empty, hollow; (Guat, Mex) blond; **salir huero** (coll) to flop, to turn out bad ‖ mf (Guat, Mex) blond

huerta f vegetable garden; fruit garden; irrigated region

huerte·ro -ra mf (Arg, Peru) gardener

huerto m (de árboles frutales) orchard; (de verduras) kitchen garden

huesa f grave

huesillo m (Chile, Peru) sun-dried peach

hueso m bone; (de ciertas frutas) stone, pit; drudgery; **a otro perro con ese hueso** (coll) tell that to the marines; **calarse hasta los huesos** to get soaked to the skin; **hueso de la alegría** crazy bone, funny bone; **hueso de la suerte** wishbone; **hueso duro de roer** (coll) a hard nut to crack; **la sin hueso** (coll) the tongue; **no dejarle a uno un hueso sano** (coll) to beat someone up; (coll) to pick someone to pieces; **no poder con sus huesos** (coll) to be all in; **soltar la sin hueso** (coll) to talk too much; (coll) to pour forth insults; **tener los huesos molidos** (coll) to be all fagged out

hueso·so -sa adj bony

hués·ped -peda mf (persona alojada en casa ajena) guest; (persona que hospeda a otra en su casa) host; (mesonero) innkeeper, host

hueste f followers; (ejército) army, host

huesu·do -da adj bony, big-boned

hueva f roe, fish roe

hueve·ro -ra mf egg dealer ‖ f eggcup; oviduct

huevo m egg; **huevo a la plancha** fried egg; **huevo al plato** shirred egg; **huevo del té** tea ball; **huevo de zurcir** darning egg or gourd; **huevo duro** hard-boiled egg; **huevo escalfado** poached egg; **huevo estrellado** or **frito** fried egg; **huevo pasado por agua** soft-boiled egg; **huevos revueltos** scrambled eggs

huída f flight; (de un líquido) leak; (ensanche en un agujero) flare, splay; (de caballo) shying

huidi·zo -za adj fugitive; evasive

huincha f (SAm) tape; (SAm) tape measure

huipil m (Mex) colorful poncho worn by Indian women

huir §20 tr to flee, avoid, shun; (el cuerpo) to duck ‖ intr to flee; (el tiempo) to fly; (de la memoria) to slip ‖ ref to flee

hule m (tela impermeable) oilcloth; rubber; (taur) blood, goring

hulear intr (CAm) to gather rubber

hulla f coal; **hulla azul** tide power; wind

power; **hulla blanca** white power, water power

hullera f colliery, coal mine

humanidad f humanity; (coll) fatness

humanista adj & mf humanist

humanita·rio -ria adj & mf humanitarian

huma·no -na adj (perteneciente al hombre) human; (compasivo, misericordioso; civilizador) humane

humareda f cloud of smoke

humeante adj smoking, smoky; steamy; reeking

humear tr (SAm) to fumigate ‖ intr to smoke; to steam, to reek; to put on airs; (reliquias de un alboroto, enemistad, etc.) to last, persist

humectador m humidifier

humedad f humidity, dampness, moisture

humedecer §22 tr to humidify, dampen, moisten, wet

húme·do -da adj humid, damp, moist

humero m smokestack, chimney

húmero m humerus

humildad f humility

humilde adj humble

humilladero m calvary, road shrine; prie-dieu

humillante adj humiliating

humillar tr (abatir el orgullo de) to humble; (avergonzar) to humiliate; (la cabeza) to bow; (el cuerpo, las rodillas) to bend ‖ ref to humble oneself; to cringe, grovel

humo m smoke; steam, fume; **a humo de pajas** (coll) lightly, thoughtlessly; **bajar los humos a** (coll) to humble, take down a peg; **echar más humo que una chimenea** to smoke like a chimney; **humos** airs, conceit; hearths, homes; **irse todo en humo** to go up in smoke; **tragar el humo** to inhale; **vender humos** to peddle influence

humor m humor; **de mal humor** out of humor; **estar de humor para** to be in the humor for; **seguir el humor a** to humor

humorismo m humor, humorousness

humorista mf humorist

humorísti·co -ca adj humorous

humo·so -sa adj smoky

hundible adj sinkable

hundir tr to sink; to plunge; (abrumar) to overwhelm; to confound, confute; to destroy, ruin ‖ ref to sink; to collapse; to settle, cave in; to come to ruin; (coll) to disappear, vanish

húnga·ro -ra adj & mf Hungarian ‖ m (idioma) Hungarian

Hungría f Hungary

hupe m punk

huracán m hurricane

huraña f shyness, unsociability

hura·ño -ña adj shy, unsociable

hurgar §44 tr to poke; (fig) to stir up, incite; **peor es hurgallo** (i.e., hurgarlo) better keep hands off ‖ intr to poke ‖ ref (la nariz) to pick

hurgón m poker; (coll) thrust, stab

hurgonazo m (con hurgón) poke; (coll) jab, stab, thrust

ho
hu

hurgonear *tr* to poke; (*coll*) to jab, to stab at

hurgonero *m* poker

hu·rón -rona *adj* (*coll*) shy, diffident ‖ *mf* (*coll*) prier, snooper; (*coll*) shy person, diffident person ‖ *m* ferret

huronear *tr* to ferret, hunt with a ferret; (*coll*) to ferret out

huronera *f* ferret hole; (*coll*) lair, hiding place

hurtadillas — a hurtadillas by stealth, on the sly; a hurtadillas de unbeknown to

hurtar *tr* to steal; (*en pesos y medidas*) to cheat; (*el suelo*) to wear away; to plagiarize; hurtar el cuerpo to dodge, to duck ‖ *ref* to withdraw, to hide

hurto *m* thieving; theft; a hurto stealthily, on the sly; coger con el hurto en las manos to catch with the goods

husma *f* snooping; andar a la husma to go around snooping

husmear *tr* to scent, to smell out; (*coll*) to pry into ‖ *intr* (*la carne*) to smell bad, to become gamy

husmo *m* gaminess, high odor; estar al husmo (*coll*) to wait for a chance

huso *m* (*para hilar*) spindle; (*para devanar*) bobbin; (*cilindro del torno*) drum; huso horario time zone; ser más derecho que un huso (*coll*) to be as straight as a ramrod

huta *f* hunter's blind

huy *interj* ouch!

huyente *adj* (*frente*) receding; (*ojeada*) shifty

I

I, i (i) *f* tenth letter of the Spanish alphabet

ib. *abbr* ibídem

íbéri·co -ca *adj* Iberian

íbe·ro -ra *adj* & *mf* Iberian

íbice *m* ibex

ice·berg *m* (*pl* -bergs) iceberg

iconoclasia *f* or **iconoclasmo** *m* iconoclasm

iconoclasta *mf* iconoclast

iconoscopio *m* (*telv*) iconoscope

ictericia *f* jaundice

icterícia·do -da *adj* jaundiced

ictiología *f* ichthyology

ida *f* going; departure; rashness; sally; trail; de ida y vuelta round-trip; idas y venidas comings and goings

idea *f* idea; mudar de idea to change one's mind

ideal *adj* & *m* ideal

idealista *adj* & *mf* idealist

idealizar §60 *tr* to idealize

idear *tr* to think up, to devise

idemista *adj* yes-saying ‖ *mf* yes sayer

idénti·co -ca *adj* identic(al); (*muy parecido*) very similar

identidad *f* identity, sameness

identificación *f* identification

identificar §73 *tr* to identify

ideología *f* ideology

idíli·co -ca *adj* idyllic

idilio *m* idyll

idioma *m* language; (*modo particular de hablar*) idiom, speech

idiomáti·co -ca *adj* idiomatic; language, linguistic

idiosincrasia *f* idiosyncrasy

idiota *adj* idiotic ‖ *mf* idiot

idiotez *f* idiocy

idiotismo *m* ignorance; (*idiotez*) idiocy; (*gram*) idiom

í·do -da *adj* wild, scatterbrained; (*Am*) drunk ‖ los idos the dead ‖ *f* see ida

idolatrar *tr* to idolize

idolatría *f* idolatry; (*amor excesivo a una persona*) idolization

ídolo *m* idol

idoneidad *f* fitness, suitability

idóne·o -a fit, suitable

idus *mpl* ides

iglesia *f* church; entrar en la iglesia to go into the church; llevar a la iglesia to lead to the altar

iglesie·ro -ra *adj* (*Arg*) church-going ‖ *mf* (*Arg*) church goer

igna·ro -ra *adj* ignorant

ignominio·so -sa *adj* ignominious

ignorancia *f* ignorance

ignorante *adj* ignorant ‖ *mf* ignoramus

ignorar *tr* to not know, be ignorant of

igno·to -ta *adj* unknown

igual *adj* equal; (*liso, llano*) smooth, even, level; (*no variable*) firm, constant, equable; indifferent; me es igual it makes no difference to me ‖ *m* equal; equal sign; al igual de like, after the fashion of; al igual que as; while, whereas; en igual de instead of

iguala *f* equalization; agreement

igualación *f* equalization; agreement

igualar *tr* to equal; (*alisar, allanar*) to smooth, to even, to level; to make equal, to match; to deem equal ‖ *intr* & *ref* to be equal

igualdad *f* equality; smoothness, evenness; igualdad de ánimo equanimity

igualmente *adv* likewise; igualmente que the same as

ijada *f* (*de animal*) flank; (*del cuerpo humano*) loin; (*dolor en estas partes*) stitch; tener su ijada to have its weak side or point

ijadear *intr* to pant

ijar *m* flank; loin

ilegal *adj* illegal

ilegible *adj* illegible

ilegíti·mo -ma *adj* illegitimate

ile·so -sa *adj* unscathed, unharmed

iletra·do -da *adj* unlettered, uncultured

ilíci·to -ta *adj* illicit, unlawful

ilimita·do -da *adj* limitless

ilitera·to -ta *adj* illiterate

ilógi·co -ca *adj* illogical

iludir *tr* to elude, evade

iluminación f illumination
iluminar tr to illuminate, light, light up
|| ref to light up, brighten
ilusión f illusion; (esperanza infundada)
delusion; enthusiasm, zeal; dream;
forjarse or hacerse ilusiones to kid
oneself, to indulge in wishful thinking
ilusionar tr to delude || ref to have
illusions, to indulge in wishful thinking; to be enraptured, be beguiled
ilusionista mf prestidigitator, magician
ilusi·vo -va adj illusive
ilu·so -sa adj deluded, misguided; (propenso a ilusionarse) visionary
iluso·rio -ria adj illusory
ilustración f illustration; enlightenment;
illustrated magazine
ilustra·do -da adj illustrated; learned,
informed; enlightened
ilustrar tr (adornar con grabados alusi-
vos al texto) to illustrate; to make
illustrious, make famous; to explain,
elucidate; to enlighten || ref to be-
come famous; to be enlightened
ilustre adj illustrious
imagen f image; picture
imaginación f imagination
imaginar tr, intr & ref to imagine
imagina·rio -ria adj imaginary
imaginati·vo -va adj imaginative || f
imagination; understanding
imaginería f fancy colored embroidery;
carving or painting of religious
images
imán m magnet; (fig) loadstone; imán
de herradura horseshoe magnet;
imán inductor (elec) field magnet
imanar or imantar tr to magnetize
imbatible adj unbeatable
imbécil adj & mf imbecile
imbecilidad f imbecility
imberbe adj beardless
imbornal m drain hole
imborrable adj indelible; ineffaceable;
unforgettable
imbuir §20 tr to imbue
imitación adj invar imitation || f imita-
tion; a imitación de in imitation of;
de imitación imitation, fake
imita·do -da adj imitated; mock, sham;
imitation
imitar tr to imitate
impaciencia f impatience
impacientar tr to make impatient || ref
to get impatient
impaciente adj impatient
impacto m impact, hit; (señal que deja
el proyectil) mark; impacto directo
direct hit
impar adj odd, uneven; (que no tiene
igual) unmatched || m odd number
imparcial adj impartial; (que no entra
en ningún partido) nonpartisan
impartir tr to distribute, impart
impás m finesse
impasible adj impassible, impassive
impávi·do -da adj dauntless, fearless,
intrepid
impecable adj impeccable
impedancia f impedance
impedi·do -da adj disabled, crippled,
paralytic

impedimento m impediment, obstacle,
hindrance
impedir §55 tr to hinder, prevent
impeler tr to impel; to spur, incite
impenetrable adj impenetrable
impenitente adj & mf impenitent
impensable adj unthinkable
impensa·do -da adj unexpected
imperar intr to rule, reign, command
imperati·vo -va adj & m imperative
imperceptible adj imperceptible
imperdible m safety pin
imperdonable adj unpardonable, unforgivable
imperecede·ro -ra adj imperishable, undying
imperfección f imperfection
imperfec·to -ta adj & m imperfect
imperial adj imperial || f imperial, roof
(of a coach or bus)
imperialista adj & mf imperialist
impericia f unskillfulness, inexpertness
imperio m empire; dominion, sway
imperio·so -sa adj (que manda con
imperio) imperious; (indispensable)
imperative
imperi·to -ta adj unskilled, inexpert
impermeable adj impermeable; water-
proof || m raincoat
impersonal adj impersonal
impertérri·to -ta adj dauntless, intrepid
impertinencia f impertinence; irrelevance; fussiness
impertinente adj impertinent; (que no
viene al caso) irrelevant; (nimiamente
susceptible) fussy || impertinentes
mpl lorgnette
impetrar tr to beg, beg for; to obtain by
entreaty
ímpetu m impetus; force; haste
impetuo·so -sa adj impetuous
impiedad f (falta de religión) impiety;
(falta de compasión) pitilessness
impí·o -a adj (irreligioso) impious;
(falto de compasión) pitiless
impla f wimple
implacable adj relentless
implantar tr to implant; to introduce
implicar §73 tr (envolver) to implicate;
(incluir en esencia) to imply || intr
to stand in the way
implíci·to -ta adj implicit, implied
implorar tr to implore
implume adj featherless
imponente adj imposing || mf depositor,
investor
imponer §54 tr (la voluntad de uno,
silencio, tributos) to impose; (dinero
a rédito) to invest; (dinero en depósito) to deposit; to instruct; to im-
pute falsely || intr to dominate, com-
mand respect || ref (responsabilida-
des) to assume; to command attention, command respect; imponerse a
to dominate, command the respect
of; imponerse de to learn, to find out
imponible adj taxable
impopular adj unpopular
impopularidad f unpopularity
importación f importation; import; im-
ports
importa·dor -dora mf importer
importancia f importance; (extensión,

hu
im

tamaño size; **ser de la importancia de** to be the concern of
importante *adj* important; large
importar *tr* (*introducir en un país*) to import; to amount to; to involve, imply; to concern ‖ *intr* to import; to be important; to matter
importe *m* amount
importunar *ir* to importune
importu·no -na *adj* (*molesto*) importunate; (*fuera de sazón*) inopportune
imposibilita·do -da *adj* paralyzed, disabled
imposibilitar *tr* to make impossible ‖ *ref* to become paralyzed, become disabled
imposible *adj* impossible
imposición *f* (*de la voluntad de uno*) imposition; burden; imposture; (*de dinero*) deposit; (*typ*) make-up
impos·tor -tora *mf* impostor; slanderer
impostura *f* imposture
impotable *adj* undrinkable
impotencia *f* impotence
impotente *adj* impotent
impracticable *adj* impracticable, impassable; impractical
impregnar *tr* to impregnate, to saturate
impremedita·do -da *adj* unpremeditated
imprenta *f* printing; printing shop; (*lo que se publica impreso*) printed matter; (*máquina para imprimir o prensar; conjunto de periódicos o periodistas*) press
imprentar *tr* (*la ropa*) (Chile) to press, to iron; (Ecuad) to mark
imprescindible *adj* indispensable, essential
impresentable *adj* unpresentable
impresión *f* (*efecto producido en el ánimo; señal que una cosa deja en otra por presión*) impression; (*acción de imprimir*) printing; (*los ejemplares de una edición*) edition, issue; (*phot*) print; **impresión dactilar** or **digital** fingerprint
impresionable *adj* impressionable
impresionante *adj* impressive
impresionar *tr* to impress; (*un disco fonográfico*) to record; (*phot*) to expose ‖ *intr* to make an impression ‖ *ref* to be impressed
impreso *m* printed paper or book; **impresos** printed matter
impre·sor -sora *mf* printer
imprevisible *adj* unforeseeable
imprevisión *f* improvidence, lack of foresight
imprevi·sor -sora *adj* improvident
imprevis·to -ta *adj* unforeseen, unexpected ‖ **imprevistos** *mpl* emergencies, unforeseen expenses
imprimar *tr* to prime
imprimir *tr* (*respeto, miedo; movimiento*) to impart ‖ §83 *tr* to stamp, imprint, impress; (*un disco fonográfico*) to press; (typ) to print
improbable *adj* improbable
improbar §61 *tr* to disapprove
improbidad *f* dishonesty; hardness, arduousness
ímpro·bo -ba *adj* dishonest; (*trabajo*) arduous

improcedente *adj* wrong; untimely
improducti·vo -va *adj* unproductive; unemployed
impronunciable *adj* unpronounceable
improperar *tr* to insult, revile
improperio *m* insult, affront
impropi·cio -cia *adj* unpropitious
impro·pio -pia *adj* improper; (*ajeno*) foreign
impróspe·ro -ra *adj* unsuccessful
imprôvi·do -da *adj* unprepared
improvisación *f* improvisation; meteoric rise; (mus) impromptu
improvisadamente *adv* suddenly, unexpectedly; extempore
improvisar *tr & intr* to improvise
improvi·so -sa *adj* unforeseen, unexpected
imprudencia *f* imprudence; **imprudencia temeraria** criminal negligence
imprudente *adj* imprudent
impudicia *f* immodesty
impúdi·co -ca *adj* immodest
impues·to -ta *adj* informed ‖ *m* tax; **impuesto al valor agregado** value-added tax; **impuesto sobre la renta** income tax
impugnar *tr* to impugn, to contest
impulsar *tr* to impel; to drive
impulsión *f* impulse, drive
impulsi·vo -va *adj* impulsive
impulso *m* impulse
impune *adj* unpunished
impunidad *f* impunity
impureza *f* impurity
impu·ro -ra *adj* impure
imputar *tr* to impute; to credit on account
inabordable *adj* unapproachable
inacabable *adj* endless, interminable
inaccesible *adj* inaccessible
inacción *f* inaction
inacentua·do -da *adj* unaccented
inactividad *f* inactivity
inacti·vo -va *adj* inactive
inadecua·do -da *adj* inadequate; unsuited
inadvertencia *f* inadvertence, oversight
inadverti·do -da *adj* inadvertent, unwitting; careless, thoughtless; unseen
inagotable *adj* inexhaustible
inaguantable *adj* unbearable
inalámbri·co -ca *adj* wireless
inalcanzable *adj* unattainable
inamisto·so -sa *adj* unfriendly
inamovible *adj* irremovable; undetachable; (*incorporado*) built-in
inamovilidad *f* irremovability; tenure, permanent tenure
inane *adj* inane
inanición *f* starvation
inanima·do -da *adj* inanimate, lifeless
inapelable *adj* unappealable; unavoidable
inapetencia *f* loss of appetite
inapreciable *adj* inappreciable; imperceptible
inarmóni·co -ca *adj* unharmonious
inarrugable *adj* wrinkle-free
inarticula·do -da *adj* inarticulate
inartísti·co -ca *adj* inartistic
inasequible *adj* unattainable; unobtainable

inastillable *adj* nonshatterable, shatter-proof

inatacable *adj* unattackable; **inatacable por** resistant to

inaudi·to -ta *adj* unheard-of; outrageous

inauguración *f* inauguration; (*de una estatua*) unveiling

inaugural *adj* inaugural

inaugurar *tr* to inaugurate; (*p.ej., una estatua*) to unveil

inaveriguable *adj* unascertainable

inca *mf* Inca

incai·co -ca *adj* Inca, Incan

incalificable *adj* unqualifiable; (*infame, atroz*) unspeakable

incambiable *adj* unchangeable

incandescente *adj* incandescent

incansable *adj* untiring, indefatigable

incapacitar *tr* to incapacitate; (law) to declare incompetent

inca·paz *adj* (*pl* -**paces**) incapable, unable; not large enough; stupid; (law) incompetent; (coll) frightful, unbearable

incasable *adj* unmarriageable; opposed to marriage; (*por su fealdad*) unable to find a husband

incautar *ref* — **incautarse de** to hold until claimed; (law) to seize, to attach

incau·to -ta *adj* unwary, heedless

incendajas *fpl* kindling

incendiar *tr* to set on fire || *ref* to catch fire

incendia·rio -ria *adj* incendiary || *mf* incendiary, firebug

incendio *m* fire; (fig) fire, passion

incensar §2 *tr* to incense, to burn incense before; (fig) to flatter

incensario *m* censer, incense burner

incenti·vo -va *adj* & *m* incentive

inceremonio·so -sa *adj* unceremonious

incertidumbre *f* uncertainty, incertitude

incesante *adj* unceasing

incesto *m* incest

incestuo·so -sa *adj* incestuous

incidencia *f* incidence; **por incidencia** by chance

incidente *adj* incident; incidental || *m* incident

incidir *tr* to make an incision in || *intr* — **incidir en culpa** to fall into guilt; **incidir en** or **sobre** to strike, to impinge on

incienso *m* incense; (*olíbano*) frankincense

incier·to -ta *adj* uncertain

incineración *f* incineration; (*de cadáveres*) cremation

incinerar *tr* to incinerate; (*cadáveres*) to cremate

incipiente *adj* incipient

incisión *f* incision; (*mordacidad en el lenguaje*) incisiveness, sarcasm

incisi·vo -va *adj* incisive; biting, sarcastic

inci·so -sa *adj* (*estilo del escritor*) choppy || *m* comma; clause; sentence

incitar *tr* to incite

incivil *adj* rude, impolite

inciviliza·do -da *adj* uncivilized

inclemencia *f* inclemency; **a la inclemencia** in the open, without shelter

inclemente *adj* inclement

inclinación *f* inclination; bent, leaning, propensity; nod, bow

inclinar *tr, intr* & *ref* to incline; to bend, to bow

ínclí·to -ta *adj* illustrious, renowned

incluir §20 *tr* to include; (*en una carta*) to inclose

inclusa *f* foundling home

incluse·ro -ra *mf* (coll) foundling

inclusión *f* inclusion; friendship

inclusive *adv* inclusive, inclusively || *prep* including

inclusi·vo -va *adj* inclusive

inclu·so -sa *adj* inclosed || *f* see **inclusa** || **incluso** *adv* inclusively; (*hasta, aun*) even || **incluso** *prep* including

incobrable *adj* uncollectible; irrecoverable

incógni·to -ta *adj* (*no conocido*) unknown; (*que no se da a conocer*) incognito || *mf* (*persona*) incognito || *m* (*condición de no ser conocido*) incognito; **de incógnito** (*sin ser conocido*) incognito || *f* (math & fig) unknown quantity

incoherente *adj* incoherent

íncola *m* inhabitant

incolo·ro -ra *adj* colorless

incólume *adj* unharmed, safe

incombustible *adj* incombustible, fireproof; cold, indifferent

incomerciable *adj* unmarketable

incomible *adj* uneatable, inedible

incomodar *tr* to inconvenience, to disturb

incomodidad *f* inconvenience; annoyance, discomfort

incómo·do -da *adj* inconvenient; annoying, uncomfortable || *m* inconvenience; discomfort

incomparable *adj* incomparable

incompartible *adj* unsharable

incompasi·vo -va *adj* pitiless, unsympathetic

incompatible *adj* incompatible; (*acontecimientos, citas, horas de clase, etc.*) conflicting

incompetente *adj* incompetent

incompetible *adj* unmatchable

incomple·to -ta *adj* incomplete

incomponible *adj* unmendable, beyond repair

incomprable *adj* unpurchasable

incomprensible *adj* incomprehensible

incomunicación *f* isolation, solitary confinement

inconcebible *adj* inconceivable

inconclu·so -sa *adj* unfinished

inconcluyente *adj* inconclusive

inconcu·so -sa *adj* undeniable

incondicional *adj* unconditional

incone·xo -xa *adj* unconnected; (*inaplicable*) irrelevant

inconfidente *adj* distrustful

inconfundible *adj* unmistakable

incon·gruo -grua *adj* incongruous

inconocible *adj* unknowable

inconquistable *adj* unconquerable; (*que no se deja vencer con ruegos y dádivas*) unbending, unyielding

inconsciencia *f* unconsciousness; unawareness

inconsciente *adj* unconscious; unaware; **lo inconsciente** the unconscious

inconsecuencia *f* (*falta de consecuencia o correspondencia en dichos y hechos*) inconsistency

inconsecuente *adj* inconsistent; (*que no se deduce de otra cosa*) inconsequential

inconsidera·do -da *adj* inconsiderate

inconsiguiente *adj* inconsequential, illogical

inconsistencia *f* (*falta de cohesión*) inconsistency

inconsistente *adj* inconsistent

inconsolable *adj* inconsolable

inconstante *adj* inconstant

inconstitucional *adj* unconstitutional

inconsútil *adj* seamless

incontable *adj* countless, innumerable

incontenible *adj* irrepressible

incontestable *adj* incontestable

incontinente *adj* incontinent ‖ *adv* at once, instantly

incontrastable *adj* invincible; inconvincible; (*argumento*) unanswerable

incontrovertible *adj* incontrovertible

inconveniencia *f* inconvenience; unsuitability; impoliteness; impropriety

inconveniente *adj* inconvenient; unsuitable; impolite; improper ‖ *m* drawback, disadvantage; objection

incordio *m* (coll) bore, nuisance

incorporación *f* incorporation, embodiment

incorpora·do -da *adj* (*el que estaba echado*) sitting up; (*montado en la construcción*) built-in

incorporar *tr* to incorporate, embody ‖ *ref* to incorporate; (*el que estaba echado*) to sit up; **incorporarse a** to join

incorrec·to -ta *adj* incorrect

incrédu·lo -la *adj* incredulous ‖ *mf* disbeliever, doubter

increíble *adj* incredible

incremento *m* increment, increase

increpar *tr* to chide, to rebuke

incriminar *tr* to incriminate; (*un delito, falta, defecto*) to exaggerate the gravity of

incruen·to -ta *adj* bloodless

incrustar *tr* to incrust; (*embutir por adorno*) to inlay

incubadora *f* incubator

incubar *tr* & *intr* to incubate ‖ *ref* (fig) to be brewing

incuestionable *adj* unquestionable

inculcar §73 *tr* to inculcate ‖ *ref* to become obstinate

inculpable *adj* blameless, guiltless

inculpar *tr* to accuse, to blame

incultivable *adj* untillable

incul·to -ta *adj* uncultivated, untilled; uncultured; (*estilo*) coarse, sloppy

incumbencia *f* incumbency, duty, obligation, province

incumbir *intr* — **incumbir a** to be incumbent on

incumplimiento *m* nonfulfillment

incunable *m* incunabulum

incurable *adj* & *mf* incurable

incuria *f* carelessness, negligence

incurio·so -sa *adj* careless, negligent

incurrir *intr* — **incurrir en** to incur

incursión *f* incursion, inroad, raid

indagación *f* investigation, research

indagar §44 *tr* to investigate

indebidamente *adv* unduly

indebi·do -da *adj* undue; wrong

indecencia *f* indecency

indecente *adj* indecent

indecible *adj* unspeakable, unutterable

indeci·so -sa *adj* undecided, indecisive; (*contorno, forma*) vague, obscure

indeclinable *adj* unavoidable; (gram) indeclinable

indecoro·so -sa *adj* improper

indefectible *adj* unfailing

indefendible *adj* indefensible

indefen·so -sa *adj* defenceless, undefended

indefinible *adj* indefinable

indefini·do -da *adj* indefinite; limitless; vague

indeleble *adj* indelible

indelibera·do -da *adj* unpremeditated

indelica·do -da *adj* indelicate

indemne *adj* unharmed, undamaged

indemnidad *f* (*seguridad contra un daño*) indemnity

indemnización *f* (*compensación*) indemnity, indemnification; **indemnización por despido** severance pay

indemnizar §60 *tr* to indemnify

independencia *f* independence

independiente *adj* & *mf* independent

independizar §60 *tr* to free, to emancipate ‖ *ref* to become independent

indescriptible *adj* indescribable

indeseable *adj* & *mf* undesirable

indesea·do -da *adj* unwanted

indesmallable *adj* runproof

indestructible *adj* indestructible

indetermina·do -da *adj* indeterminate; (gram) indefinite

indevo·to -ta *adj* impious; not fond, not devoted

india *f* wealth, riches; **Indias Occidentales** West Indies; **la India** India

indiana *f* printed calico

india·no -na *adj* & *mf* Spanish American; East Indian; West Indian ‖ *m* man back from America with great wealth; **indiano de hilo negro** (coll) skinflint ‖ *f* see **indiana**

indicación *f* indication; **por indicación de** at the direction of

indica·do -da *adj* appropriate, advisable; **muy indicado** just the thing, just the person

indica·dor -dora *adj* indicating, pointing ‖ *m* indicator; gauge; (*de tránsito*) traffic signal

indicar §73 *tr* to indicate

indicati·vo -va *adj* & *m* indicative

índice *m* index; **índice de libros prohibidos** (eccl) Index; **índice de materias** table of contents; **índice en el corte** thumb index

indiciar *tr* to betoken, indicate; to surmise, suspect

indicio *m* sign, token, indication; **indicios vehementes** circumstantial evidence

indiferente *adj* indifferent; (*que no importa*) immaterial

indígena *adj* indigenous || *mf* native
indigente *adj* indigent
indigestar *ref* to be indigestible; (coll) to be disliked, to be unbearable
indigestible *adj* indigestible
indigestión *f* indigestion
indignación *f* indignation
indigna·do -da *adj* indignant
indignar *tr* to anger, to provoke || *ref* to become indignant
indignidad *f* (*falta de mérito*) unworthiness; (*acción reprobable*) indignity
indig·no -na *adj* unworthy
índigo *m* indigo
in·dio -dia *adj* & *mf* Indian || *f* see **india**
indirec·to -ta *adj* indirect || *f* hint, innuendo; **indirecta del padre Cobos** broad hint
indiscernible *adj* indiscernible
indiscre·to -ta *adj* indiscreet
indisculpable *adj* inexcusable
indiscutible *adj* undeniable
indisoluble *adj* indissoluble
indispensable *adj* unpardonable; indispensable
indisponer §54 *tr* (*alterar la salud de*) to indispose, upset; to disturb, to upset; **indisponer a uno con** to set someone against, to prejudice someone against || *ref* to become indisposed; **indisponerse con** to fall out with
indisponible *adj* unavailable
indispues·to -ta *adj* indisposed
indistintamente *adv* indistinctly; indiscriminately, without distinction
indistin·to -ta *adj* indistinct
individual *adj* individual; (*habitación en un hotel; partido de tenis*) single
individualidad *f* individuality
indivi·duo -dua *adj* individual; indivisible || *mf* (*persona indeterminada*) (coll) individual || *m* (*cada persona*) individual; (*miembro de una corporación*) member, fellow
indócil *adj* unteachable; headstrong, unruly
indocumenta·do -da *adj* unidentified; unqualified || *mf* nobody (*person of no account*)
indochi·no -na *adj* & *mf* Indo-Chinese || **la Indochina** Indochina
indoeurope·o -a *adj* & *m* Indo-European
índole *f* kind, class; nature, disposition, temper
indolente *adj* stolid, impassive; (*perezoso*) indolent
indolo·ro -ra *adj* painless
indoma·do -da *adj* untamed
indone·sio -sia *adj* & *mf* Indonesian || **la Indonesia** Indonesia
inducción *f* induction
inducido *m* (*de dínamo o motor*) (elec) armature
inducir §19 *tr* to induce
inductor *m* (*de dínamo o motor*) (elec) field
indudable *adj* doubtless
indulgente *adj* indulgent
indultar *tr* to pardon; to free, exempt
indulto *m* pardon; exemption

indumentaria *f* clothing, dress; historical study of clothing
indumento *m* clothing, dress
industria *f* industry; **de industria** on purpose
industrial *adj* industrial || *m* industrialist
industrializar §60 *tr* to industrialize
industriar *tr* to teach, instruct, train || *ref* to get along, to manage
industrio·so -sa *adj* industrious
inédi·to -ta *adj* unpublished; new, novel, unknown
inefable *adj* ineffable
ineficacia *f* inefficacy
inefi·caz *adj* (*pl* -**caces**) inefficacious, ineffectual
inelegible *adj* ineligible
ineludible *adj* inescapable
inenarrable *adj* indescribable
inencogible *adj* unshrinkable
inencontrable *adj* unobtainable
inequidad *f* inequity
inequívo·co -ca *adj* unmistakable
inercia *f* inertia
inerme *adj* unarmed
inerte *adj* inert; slow, sluggish
inescrupulo·so -sa *adj* unscrupulous
inescrutable or **inescudriñable** *adj* inscrutable
inespera·do -da *adj* unexpected, unforeseen; unhoped-for
inestable *adj* unstable
inevitable *adj* unavoidable, inevitable
inexactitud *f* inaccuracy, inexactness
inexac·to -ta *adj* inaccurate, inexact
inexcusable *adj* inexcusable, unpardonable; unavoidable; indispensable
inexorable *adj* inexorable
inexperiencia *f* inexperience
inexplicable *adj* inexplicable, unexplainable
inexplica·do -da *adj* unexplained, unaccounted-for
inexplora·do -da *adj* unexplored; (*mar*) uncharted
inexpresable *adj* inexpressible
inexpues·to -ta *adj* (phot) unexposed
inexpugnable *adj* impregnable; firm, unshakable
inextinguible *adj* unextinguishable; perpetual, lasting; (*sed*) unquenchable; (*risa*) uncontrollable
inextirpable *adj* ineradicable
infalible *adj* infallible
infamación *f* defamation
infamar *tr* to defame, discredit
infame *adj* infamous; (coll) vile, frightful || *mf* scoundrel
infamia *f* infamy
infancia *f* infancy
infan·do -da *adj* odious, unmentionable
infanta *f* female child; infanta (*any daughter of a king of Spain; wife of an infante*)
infante *m* male child; infante (*any son of a king of Spain who is not heir to the throne*); (mil) infantryman; **infante de coro** choirboy
infantería *f* infantry; **infantería de marina** marines, marine corps
infantil *adj* infant, infantile, childlike; innocent

infatigable *adj* indefatigable
infatuar §21 *tr* to make vain ‖ *ref* to become vain
infaus·to -ta *adj* fatal, unlucky
infección *f* infection
infeccionar *tr* to infect
infeccio·so -sa *adj* infectious
infectar *tr* to infect
infec·to -ta *adj* foul, corrupt; infected; fetid
infecun·do -da *adj* sterile, barren
infe·liz (*pl* **-lices**) *adj* unhappy; (coll) simple, good-hearted ‖ *m* wretch, poor soul
inferior *adj* inferior; lower; **inferior a** inferior to; lower than; less than; smaller than ‖ *m* inferior
inferioridad *f* inferiority
inferir §68 *tr* to infer; to lead to, to entail; (*una herida*) to inflict; (*una ofensa*) to cause, offer
infernáculo *m* hopscotch
infernal *adj* infernal
infernar §2 *tr* to damn; to irritate, annoy
infernillo *m* chafing dish
infestar *tr* infest ‖ *ref* to become infested
inficionar *tr* to infect ‖ *ref* to become infected
infidelidad *f* infidelity; (*conjunto de infieles*) unbelievers
infidente *adj* faithless, disloyal
infiel *adj* (*falto de fidelidad*) unfaithful; (*no exacto*) inaccurate, inexact; (*no cristiano*) infidel ‖ *mf* infidel
infierno *m* hell; **en el quinto infierno** or **en los quintos infiernos** (coll) far, far away
infijo *m* (gram) infix
infiltrar *tr & ref* to infiltrate
ínfi·mo -ma *adj* lowest; humblest, most abject; meanest, vilest
infinidad *f* infinity
infiniti·vo -va *adj & m* infinitive
infini·to -ta *adj* infinite ‖ *m* infinite; (math) infinity ‖ **infinito** *adv* greatly, very much
infirme *adj* infirm
inflación *f* inflation; (*vanidad*) conceit
inflado *m* inflation (*of a tire*)
inflamable *adj* inflammable, flammable
inflamación *f* ignition, inflammation; ardor, enthusiasm; (pathol) inflammation
inflamar *tr* to set on fire; to inflame ‖ *ref* to catch fire; to become inflamed
inflar *tr* to inflate; to exaggerate; to puff up with pride ‖ *ref* to inflate; to be puffed up with pride
inflexible *adj* inflexible; unyielding, unbending
inflexión *f* inflection; **inflexión vocálica** (*metafonía*) umlaut
inflexionar *tr* to umlaut
infligir §27 *tr* to inflict
influencia *f* influence
influenciar *tr* to influence
influenza *f* influenza
influir §20 *intr* to have influence; to have great weight; **influir en** or **sobre** to influence
influjo *m* influence; rising tide

influyente *adj* influential
información *f* information; (law) judicial inquiry, investigation; **informaciones testimonial**
informal *adj* (*que no se ajusta a las reglas debidas*) informal; unreliable
informar *tr & intr* to inform ‖ *ref* to inquire, find out
informati·vo -va *adj* informational; (*sección de un periódico*) news
informe *adj* shapeless, formless; misshapen ‖ *m* piece of information; report; **informes** information; **informes confidenciales** inside information
infortuna·do -da *adj* unfortunate, unlucky
infortunio *m* misfortune; (*acaecimiento desgraciado*) mishap
infracción *f* infraction, infringement
infraconsumo *m* underconsumption
infrac·to -ta *adj* unperturbable
infraestructura *f* substructure; (rr) roadbed
inframundo *m* underworld
infrarro·jo -ja *adj & m* infrared
infrascri·to -ta *adj* undersigned; hereinafter mentioned
infrecuente *adj* infrequent
infringir §27 *tr* to infringe, to break, to violate
infructuo·so -sa *adj* fruitless, unfruitful
ínfulas *fpl* conceit, airs; **darse ínfulas** to put on airs
infunda·do -da *adj* unfounded, groundless, baseless
infundio *m* (coll) lie, fib
infundir *tr* to infuse, to instill
infusión *f* infusion; (*acción de echar agua sobre el que se bautiza*) sprinkling; **estar en infusión para** (coll) to be all set for
ingeniar *tr* to think up ‖ *ref* to manage; **ingeniarse a** or **para** to manage to; **ingeniarse para ir viviendo** to manage to get along
ingeniería *f* engineering
ingeniero *m* engineer; **ingeniero de caminos, canales y puertos** government civil engineer
ingenio *m* talent, creative faculty; talented person; cleverness, skill, wit; (*artificio mecánico*) apparatus, device; (*del encuadernador*) paper cutter; engine of war; **afilar** or **aguzar el ingenio** to sharpen one's wits; **ingenio de azúcar** sugar refinery
ingeniosidad *f* ingenuity; wittiness
ingenio·so -sa *adj* (*dotado de ingenio; hecho con ingenio*) ingenious; (*agudo, sutil*) witty
ingéni·to -ta *adj* innate, inborn
ingente *adj* huge, enormous
ingenuidad *f* ingenuousness
inge·nuo -nua *adj* ingenuous
ingerir §68 *tr & ref* var of **injerir**
Inglaterra *f* England; **la Nueva Inglaterra** New England
ingle *f* groin
in·glés -glesa *adj* English; **a la inglesa** in the English manner ‖ *m* Englishman; (*idioma*) English; **el inglés medio** Middle English; **los ingleses** the English ‖ *f* Englishwoman

ingramatical *adj* ungrammatical
ingratitud *f* ingratitude, ungratefulness
ingra•to -ta *adj* (*desagradecido*) ungrateful; (*desagradecido; desagradable, áspero; improductivo*) thankless ‖ *mf* ingrate
ingravidez *f* lightness, tenuousness; (*gravedad nula*) weightlessness
ingrávi•do -da *adj* light, tenuous; weightless
ingrediente *m* ingredient
ingresa•do -da *mf* new student
ingresar *tr* to deposit ‖ *intr* to enter, become a member; (*beneficios*) to come in ‖ *ref* (Mex) to enlist
ingreso *m* entrance; admission; ingresos income, revenue
íngri•mo -ma *adj* (Am) solitary, alone
inhábil *adj* unable; unskillful; unfit, unqualified
inhabilidad *f* inability; unskillfulness; unfitness
inhabilitar *tr* to disable, to disqualify, to incapacitate
inhabita•do -da *adj* uninhabited
inhabitua•do -da *adj* unaccustomed
inherente *adj* inherent
inhibir *tr* to inhibit
inhospitala•rio -ria *adj* inhospitable
inhóspi•to -ta *adj* inhospitable
inhumanidad *f* inhumanity
inhuma•no -na *adj* inhuman, inhumane; (Chile) filthy
iniciación *f* initiation
inicial *adj* & *f* initial
iniciar *tr* to initiate ‖ *ref* to be initiated
iniciativa *f* initiative
ini•cuo -cua *adj* wicked, iniquitous
inigualа•do -da *adj* unequaled
inteligente *adj* unintelligent
ininteligible *adj* unintelligible
ininterrumpi•do -da *adj* uninterrupted
iniquidad *f* iniquity
injerencia *f* interference, meddling
injerir §68 *tr* to insert, introduce; (hort) to graft; (*alimentos*) (Am) to take in ‖ *ref* to interfere, meddle, intrude
injertar *tr* (hort & surg) to graft
injerto *m* (hort & surg) graft
injuria *f* offense, insult; abuse, wrong; damage, harm
injuriar *tr* to offend, insult; to abuse, to wrong; to harm, damage
injurio•so -sa *adj* offensive, insulting; abusive; harmful; (*lenguaje*) profane
injusticia *f* injustice
injustifica•do -da *adj* unjustified
injus•to -ta *adj* unjust
inmacula•do -da *adj* immaculate
inmanejable *adj* unmanageable; unhandy
inmarcesible *adj* unfading
inmaterial *adj* immaterial
inmaturo -ra *adj* immature
inmediación *f* immediacy; proximity, nearness; inmediaciones neighborhood, outskirts
inmediatamente *adv* immediately; inmediatamente que as soon as
inmedia•to -ta *adj* immediate; close, adjoining, next; next above; next below; (*pago*) prompt; venir a las in-

mediatas (coll) to get into the thick of the fight
inmejorable *adj* superb, unsurpassable
inmemorial *adj* immemorial
inmen•so -sa *adj* immense
inmensurable *adj* immesurable
inmereci•do -da *adj* undeserved
inmergir §27 *tr* to immerse
inmersión *f* immersion
inmigración *f* immigration
inmigrante *mf* immigrant
inmigrar *intr* to immigrate
inminente *adj* imminent
inmiscuir §20 & regular *tr* to mix ‖ *ref* to meddle, to interfere
inmobila•rio -ria *adj* real-estate
inmoble *adj* motionless; firm, constant
inmodera•do -da *adj* immoderate
inmodes•to -ta *adj* immodest
inmódi•co -ca *adj* excessive
inmoral *adj* immoral
inmortal *adj* immortal, deathless ‖ *mf* immortal
inmortalizar §60 *tr* to immortalize
inmovilizar §60 *tr* to immobilize; (*un caudal*) to tie up
inmueble *m* property, piece of real estate; inmuebles real estate
inmun•do -da *adj* dirty, filthy
inmune *adj* immune
inmunizar §60 *tr* to immunize
inmutar *tr* to change, alter; to disturb, upset ‖ *ref* to change, alter; to change countenance; sin inmutarse without batting an eye
inna•to -ta *adj* innate, inborn; natural
innatural *adj* unnatural
innavegable *adj* (*río*) unnavigable; (*embarcación*) unseaworthy
innecesa•rio -ria *adj* unnecessary
innegable *adj* undeniable
innoble *adj* ignoble
inno•cuo -cua *adj* harmless
innovación *f* innovation
innovar *tr* to innovate
innumerable *adj* innumerable
inocencia *f* innocence
inocentada *f* (coll) simpleness; (coll) blunder; (Ecuad) April Fools' joke
inocente *adj* & *mf* innocent; coger por inocente to make an April fool of
inocen•tón -tona *adj* (coll) simple, gullible ‖ *mf* (coll) gull, dupe
inoculación *f* inoculation
inocular *tr* to inoculate; to contaminate, to pervert
inodo•ro -ra *adj* odorless ‖ *m* deodorizer; (*excusado que funciona con agua corriente*) toilet
inofensi•vo -va *adj* inoffensive
inolvidable *adj* unforgettable
inope *adj* impecunious
inopia *f* indigence
inoportu•no -na *adj* inopportune, untimely
inorgáni•co -ca *adj* inorganic
inortodo•xo -xa *adj* unorthodox
inoxidable *adj* (*acero*) stainless; inoxidizable
inquietante *adj* disquieting, upsetting
inquietar *tr* to disquiet, to worry; to stir up, excite
inquie•to -ta *adj* anxious, worried

inquietud f disquiet, worry, concern
inquili·no -na mf tenant, renter
inquina f aversion, dislike, ill will
inquirir §40 tr to inquire, inquire into
inquisición f inquiry; inquisition
insabible adj unknowable
insaciable || mf insatiable
insania f insanity
insa·no -na adj insane; imprudent
insatisfe·cho -cha adj unsatisfied
inscribir §83 tr to inscribe; (law) to record || ref to enroll, register
inscripción f inscription; enrollment, registration
insecticida adj & m insecticide
insecto m insect
insegu·ro -ra adj insecure, unsafe; uncertain
insensa·to -ta adj foolish, stupid
insensible adj callous, hard-hearted, unfeeling; imperceptible
inseparable adj inseparable; undetachable || mf inseparable || m lovebird
insepul·to -ta adj unburied
inserción f insertion
inserir §68 tr to insert; (injertar) to graft, engraft
insertar tr to insert
inservible adj useless
insidia f snare, ambush; plotting
insidiar tr to ambush, to waylay; to trap, to trick
insidio·so -sa adj insidious
insigne adj noted, famous, renowned
insignia f badge, decoration, insignia; banner, standard
insignificante adj insignificant
insince·ro -ra adj insincere
insinuación f insinuation, hint
insinuante adj engaging, slick, crafty
insinuar §21 tr to insinuate; to suggest, to hint at || ref to creep in, to slip in; to ingratiate oneself; to flow, to run; insinuarse en to work one's way in
insípi·do -da adj insipid, vapid
insistir intr to insist
ínsi·to -ta adj inbred, innate
insociable adj unsociable
insolencia f insolence
insolentar tr to make insolent || ref to become insolent
insolente adj insolent
insóli·to -ta adj unusual
insoluble adj insoluble
insolvencia f insolvency
insomne adj sleepless
insomnio m insomnia
insondable adj fathomless; inscrutable
insonorizar §60 tr to soundproof
insono·ro -ra adj soundproof
insospecha·do -da adj unsuspected
insostenible adj untenable
inspección f inspection; inspectorship
inspeccionar tr to inspect
inspiración f inspiration; inhalation
inspirante adj inspiring
inspirar tr & intr to inspire; (atraer a los pulmones) to inhale, to breathe in || ref to be inspired
instalación f plant, factory; outfit, equipment; arrangements, fittings; installment; **instalación sanitaria** plumbing

instalar tr to install || ref to settle
instantáne·o -a adj instantaneous || f snapshot
instante m instant, moment; **al instante** right away, immediately; **por instantes** uninterruptedly; any time
instantemente adv insistently, urgently
instar tr to press, to urge || intr to be pressing, to be urgent
instaurar tr to restore; to reëstablish
instigar §44 tr to instigate
instilar tr to instill
instinti·vo -va adj instinctive
instinto m instinct
institución f institution; **instituciones** (de un Estado) constitution; (de una ciencia, arte, etc.) principles
instituir §20 tr to institute, found
instituto m institute; (de una orden religiosa) rule, constitution; **instituto de segunda enseñanza** or **de enseñanza media** high school
institu·triz f (pl -trices) governess
instrucción f instruction; education
instructi·vo -va adj instructive
instruc·tor -tora mf teacher, instructor || m (mil) drillmaster || f instructress
instruí·do -da adj well-educated; well-posted
instruir §20 tr to instruct; (un proceso o expediente) to draw up
instrumentar tr to instrument
instrumentista mf instrumentalist
instrumento m instrument; (persona que se emplea para alcanzar un resultado) tool; **instrumento de cuerda** (mus) stringed instrument; **instrumento de viento** (mus) wind instrument
insubordina·do -da adj insubordinate
insubstituible adj irreplaceable
insudar intr to drudge
insuficiente adj insufficient
insufrible adj insufferable
ínsula f island; one-horse town
insular adj insular || mf islander
insulina f insulin
insulsez f tastelessness; dullness, heaviness
insul·so -sa adj tasteless; dull, heavy
insultar tr to insult || ref to faint, swoon
insulto m insult; fainting spell
insume adj expensive
insumergible adj unsinkable
insuperable adj insurmountable
insurgente adj & mf insurgent
insurrección f insurrection
intac·to -ta adj intact, untouched
intachable adj blameless, irreproachable
integración f integration
integridad f integrity; virginity
ínte·gro -gra adj integral, whole; honest
intelecto m intellect
intelectual adj & mf intellectual
intelectualidad f intellectuality; (conjunto de los intelectuales de un país o región) intelligentsia
inteligencia f intelligence; **estar en inteligencia con** to be in collusion with
inteligente adj intelligent; trained, skilled
inteligible adj intelligible

intemperancia f intemperance
intemperante adj intemperate
intemperie f inclement weather; **a la intemperie** in the open, unsheltered
intempesti•vo -va adj unseasonable, inopportune, untimely
intención f intention; (*cautelosa advertencia*) caution; (*instinto dañino de un animal*) viciousness; **con intención** deliberately, knowingly; **de intención** on purpose
intendencia f intendance; (SAm) mayoralty
intendente m intendant; quartermaster general; (SAm) mayor
intensar tr & ref to intensify
intensidad f intensity
intensificar §73 tr & ref to intensify
intensión f intensity
intensi•vo -va adj intensive
inten•so -sa adj intense
intentar tr to try, to attempt; to intend; to try out
intento m intent, purpose; **de intento** on purpose
intentona f (coll) rash attempt (*e.g., to rob, escape, etc.*)
interacción f interaction
interamerica•no -na adj inter-American
intercalar tr to intercalate, to insert
intercambiar tr & ref to interchange
intercambio m interchange, exchange
interceder intr to intercede
interceptar tr to intercept
intercep•tor -tora mf interceptor ‖ m trap; separator; (aer) interceptor
interdecir §24 tr to interdict, forbid
interés m interest; **intereses creados** vested interests; **poner a interés** to put out at interest
interesa•do -da adj interested ‖ mf interested party
interesante adj interesting
interesar tr to interest; to involve ‖ intr to be interesting ‖ ref — **interesarse en or por** to be interested in, take an interest in
interescolar adj interscholastic, intercollegiate
interfec•to -ta adj murdered ‖ mf victim of murder
interferencia f interference
interferir §68 tr to interfere with ‖ intr to interfere
interfono m intercom
ínterin adv meanwhile ‖ conj (coll) while, as long as ‖ s (pl **ínterines**) temporary incumbency
interinar tr to fill temporarily, to fill in an acting capacity
interi•no -na adj temporary, acting, interim
interior adj interior, inner, inside; home, domestic ‖ m interior, inside; mind, soul; **interiores** entrails, insides
interioridad f inside; **interioridades** inside story, private matters
interjección f interjection
interlinear tr to interline; (typ) to space, to lead
interlocu•tor -tora mf speaker, party; interviewer

intermedia•rio -ria adj & mf intermediary ‖ m (com) middleman
interme•dio -dia adj intermediate ‖ m interval, interim; (mus) intermezzo; (theat) intermission, entr'acte
intermitente adj intermittent
internacional adj international
internacionalizar §60 tr to internationalize
interna•do -da mf (mil) internee ‖ m boarding school
internamiento m internment
internar tr to send inland; to intern ‖ intr to move inland ‖ ref to move inland; to take refuge, to hide; to insinuate oneself; **internarse en** to go deeply into
internista mf internist
inter•no -na adj internal; inside ‖ mf boarding-school student; **interno de hospital** intern
interpelar tr to seek the protection or aid of; to interrogate; to interpellate
interpolar tr to interpolate; to interpose; to interrupt briefly
interponer §54 tr to interpose; to appoint as mediator ‖ ref to intervene, intercede
interprender tr to take by surprise
interpresa f surprise action; surprise seizure
interpretar tr to interpret
intérprete mf interpreter
interrogación f interrogation; question mark
interrogar §44 tr & intr to question, interrogate
interrumpir tr to interrupt
interruptor m (elec) switch; **interruptor automático** (elec) circuit breaker; **interruptor del encendido** (aut) ignition switch; **interruptor de resorte** (elec) snap switch
intersección f (geom) intersection
intersticio m interstice; interval
intervalo m interval
intervención f intervention; inspection; (*de cuentas*) audit, auditing; (surg) operation; **intervención de los precios** price control; **no intervención** nonintervention
intervenir §79 tr to take up, work on; to inspect, supervise; (*cuentas*) to audit; (*un teléfono*) to tap; (surg) to operate on ‖ intr to mediate, intervene, intercede; to participate; to happen
interventor m election supervisor; (com) auditor
inter•view m (pl **-views**) interview
intervievar tr to interview
intesta•do -da adj & mf intestate
intesti•no -na adj internal; domestic ‖ m intestine; **intestino delgado** small intestine; **intestino grueso** large intestine
intimación f announcement, notification
intimar tr to announce ‖ intr & ref to become well-acquainted, to become intimate
intimidad f intimacy; (*parte íntima o personal*) privacy
intimidar tr intimidate

ínti·mo -ma *adj* intimate; (*más interno*) innermost
intitular *tr* to entitle ‖ *ref* to use a title; to be called
intocable *mf* untouchable
intolerante *adj & mf* intolerant
inton·so -sa *adj* unshorn; ignorant; (*libro o revista*) uncut ‖ *mf* ignoramus
intoxicar §73 *tr* to poison, intoxicate
intracruzamiento *m* inbreeding
intraquilidad *f* uneasiness, worry
intraquilizar §60 *tr* to make uneasy, worry
intranqui·lo -la *adj* uneasy, worried
intransigente *adj & mf* intransigent, diehard
intransiti·vo -va *adj* intransitive
intratable *adj* unmanageable; impassable; unsociable
intrepidez *f* intrepidity
intrépi·do -da *adj* intrepid
intriga *f* intrigue
intrigar §44 *tr* (*excitar la curiosidad de*) to intrigue ‖ *intr* to intrigue ‖ *ref* to be intrigued
intrinca·do -da *adj* intricate
intrincar §73 *tr* to complicate; to confuse, bewilder
intríngu·lis *m* (*pl* -lis) (coll) hidden motive, mystery
intrínse·co -ca *adj* intrinsic(al)
introducción *f* introduction
introducir §19 *tr* to introduce; to insert, put in ‖ *ref* to gain access; to meddle, interfere, intrude
introito *m* (*de un escrito o una oración*) introduction; (*de un poema dramático*) prologue; (eccl) introit
introspecti·vo -va *adj* introspective
introverti·do -da *mf* introvert
intruso -sa *adj* intrusive ‖ *mf* intruder, interloper
intuición *f* intuition
intuir §20 *tr* to guess, to sense
intuito *m* view, glance, look; **por intuito de** in view of
inundación *f* flood, inundation
inundar *tr* to flood, to inundate
inurba·no -na *adj* discourteous, unmannerly
inusita·do -da *adj* (*no ordinario*) unusual; obsolete, out of use
inusual *adj* unusual
inútil *adj* useless
invadir *tr* to invade
invalidar *tr* to invalidate
invalidez *f* invalidity
inváli·do -da *adj & mf* invalid
invariable *adj* invariable
invasión *f* invasion
inva·sor -sora *mf* invader
invectiva *f* invective
invectivar *tr* to inveigh against
invencible *adj* invincible
invención *f* invention; finding, discovery; deception
invendible *adj* unsalable
inventar *tr* to invent
inventariar §77 & regular *tr* to inventory
inventario *m* inventory

inventi·vo -va *adj* inventive ‖ *f* inventiveness
invento *m* invention
inven·tor -tora *adj* inventive ‖ *mf* inventor
inverecun·do -da *adj* shameless, brazen
inverisímil *adj* improbable, unlikely
invernáculo *m* greenhouse, hothouse, conservatory
invernada *f* wintertime; (SAm) pasture land; (Ven) torrential rain
invernadero *m* greenhouse, hothouse; winter resort; winter pasture
invernal *adj* winter ‖ *m* cattle shed (*in winter-pasture land*)
invernar §2 *intr* to winter; to be winter
inverni·zo -za *adj* winter; wintery
inverosímil *adj* improbable, unlikely
inversión *f* inversion; (*de dinero*) investment; (gram) inverted order
inversionista *adj* investment ‖ *mf* investor
inver·so -sa *adj* inverse, opposite; **a or por la inversa** on the contrary
invertebra·do -da *adj & m* invertebrate
inverti·do -da *adj* inverted ‖ *mf* invert
invertir §68 *tr* to invert; (*dinero*) to invest; (*tiempo*) to spend; to reverse
investidura *f* investment, investiture; station, standing
investigación *f* investigation, research
investigar §44 *tr* to investigate ‖ *intr* to research
investir §50 *tr* — **investir con** or **de** (*poner en posesión de*) to invest with
invetera·do -da *adj* inveterate, confirmed
invic·to -ta *adj* unconquered
invidencia *f* blindness
invidente *adj* blind ‖ *mf* blind person
invierno *m* winter; (Am) rainy season
invisible *adj* invisible ‖ *m* (Mex) hair net; **en un invisible** in an instant
invitación *f* invitation
invita·do -da *mf* guest
invitar *tr* to invite
invocar §73 *tr* to invoke
involunta·rio -ra *adj* involuntary
invulnerable *adj* invulnerable
inyección *f* injection
inyecta·do -da *adj* bloodshot, inflamed
inyectar *tr* to inject ‖ *ref* to become congested; to become inflamed
ionizar §60 *tr* to ionize ‖ *ref* to be ionized
ir §41 *intr* to go; to be becoming, to fit, to suit; to be at stake; **ir a** + *inf* to be going to + *inf* (*to express futurity*); **ir a buscar** to go get, to go for; **ir a parar en** to end up in; **ir con cuidado** to be careful; **ir con miedo** to be afraid; **ir con tiento** to watch one's step; **ir de caza** to go hunting; **ir de pesca** to go fishing; **lo que va de** so far (as); **¡qué va!** of course not!; **¡vaya!** the deuce!; what a . . .! ‖ *ref* to go away; to leak; to wear away; to get old; to break to pieces
ira *f* anger, wrath, ire
iracun·do -da *adj* angry, wrathful, irate
Irak, el Irak or Iraq
Irán, el Iran

ira·nés -nesa or **ira·nio -nia** *adj & mf* Iranian

ira·qués -quesa or **iraquiano -na** *adj & mf* Iraqui

iris *m* (*pl* **iris**) (*del ojo*) iris; rainbow

Irlanda *f* Ireland

irlan·dés -desa *adj* Irish ‖ *m* Irishman; (*idioma*) Irish; **los irlandeses** the Irish ‖ *f* Irishwoman

ironía *f* irony

iróni·co -ca *adj* ironic(al)

ironizar §60 *tr* to ridicule

irracional *adj* irrational

irradiar *tr* to radiate, to irradiate; (*difundir*) to broadcast ‖ *intr* to radiate

irrazonable *adj* unreasonable

irreal *adj* unreal

irrealidad *f* unreality

irrebatible *adj* irrefutable

irreconocible *adj* unrecognizable

irrecuperable *adj* irretrievable

irrecusable *adj* unimpeachable

irredimible *adj* irredeemable

irreemplazable *adj* irreplaceable

irreflexión *f* rashness, thoughtlessness

irreflexi·vo -va *adj* rash, thoughtless

irregular *adj* irregular ‖ *m* (mil) irregular

irregularidad *f* irregularity; embezzlement

irreligio·so -sa *adj* irreligious

irrellenable *adj* nonrefillable

irremediable *adj* irremediable

irremisible *adj* unpardonable

irreparable *adj* irreparable

irreprimible *adj* irrepressible

irreprochable *adj* irreproachable

irresistible *adj* irresistible

irresoluble *adj* unworkable, unsolvable

irrespetuo·so -sa *adj* disrespectful

irresponsable *adj* irresponsible

irresuel·to -ta *adj* hesitant, wavering

irreverente *adj* irreverent

irrigación *f* irrigation

irrigar §44 *tr* to irrigate

irrisible *adj* laughable, absurd

irrisión *f* derision, ridicule; (coll) laughingstock

irritante *adj & m* irritant

irritar *tr* to irritate ‖ *ref* to become exasperated

irrompible *adj* unbreakable

irrumpir *intr* to burst in; **irrumpir en** to burst into

irrupción *f* sudden attack; invasion

isi·dro -dra *mf* (coll) hick, jake, yokel

isla *f* island; (*manzana de casas*) block; **isla de seguridad** safety island, safety zone; **islas Baleares** Balearic Islands; **islas Canarias** Canary Islands; **islas de Barlovento** Windward Islands; **islas de Sotavento** Leeward Islands; **Islas Filipinas** Philippine Islands

Islam, el Islam

islan·dés -desa *adj* Icelandic ‖ *mf* Icelander ‖ *m* (*idioma*) Icelandic

Islandia *f* Iceland

isle·ño -ña *adj* island ‖ *mf* islander; (Cuba) Canarian

isleta *f* isle

isósce·les *adj* (*pl* **-les**) isosceles

isótopo *m* isotope

israe·lí (*pl* **-líes**) *adj & mf* Israeli

israelita *adj & mf* Israelite

istmo *m* isthmus

Italia *f* Italy

italia·no -na *adj & mf* Italian

itáli·co -ca *adj* Italic; (typ) italic ‖ *f* (typ) italics

itinera·rio -ria *adj & m* itinerary

izar §60 *tr* (naut) to hoist, to haul up

izquierda *f* left hand; left-hand side; (pol) left; **a la izquierda** left, on the left, to the left

izquierdear *intr* to go wild, to go astray, to go awry

izquierdista *adj* leftist ‖ *mf* leftist, leftwinger

izquierdizante *adj* leftish

izquier·do -da *adj* left; left-hand; left-handed; crooked; **levantarse del izquierdo** to get out of bed on the wrong side ‖ *f* see **izquierda**

in
ja

J

J, j (jota) *f* eleventh letter of the Spanish alphabet

jabalcón *m* strut, brace

jaba·lí *m* (*pl* **-líes**) wild boar

jabalina *f* javelin; wild sow

jabardillo *m* (*de insectos*) noisy swarm; (coll) noisy throng

jabeque *m* (naut) xebec; (coll) gash in the face

jabón *m* soap; cake of soap; **dar jabón a** (coll) to softsoap; **dar un jabón a** (coll) to upbraid, to reprimand; **jabón de afeitar** shaving soap; **jabón de Castilla** Castile soap; **jabón de tocador** or **de olor** toilet soap; **jabón de sastre** soapstone, French chalk; **jabón en polvo** soap powder

jabonado *m* soaping; (*ropa lavada o por lavar*) wash

jabonadura *f* soaping; **dar una jabonadura a** (coll) to lambaste, to upbraid; **jabonaduras** soapy water; soapsuds

jabonar *tr* to soap; (coll) to reprimand

jaboncillo *m* cake of toilet soap; **jaboncillo de sastre** soapstone, French chalk

jabone·ro -ra *adj* soap; (*toro*) yellowish, dirty-white ‖ *mf* soapmaker; soap dealer ‖ *f* soap dish

jabonete *m* cake of toilet soap

jabono·so -sa *adj* soapy, lathery

jaca *f* pony, jennet

jacal *m* (Guat, Mex, Ven) hut, shack

jácara *f* merry ballad; gay song and

dance; night revelers; (coll) story, argument; (coll) fake, hoax, lie; (coll) annoyance, bother

jacarear intr (coll) to go serenading, to go singing in the street; (coll) to be disagreeable

jáca·ro -ra adj & m braggart || f see **jácara**

jacinto m hyacinth

jaco m nag, jade; gray parrot

jactancia f boasting, bragging

jactancio·so -sa adj boastful, bragging

jactar ref to boast, to brag; **jactarse de** to boast of

jade m jade

jadeante adj panting

jadear intr to pant

jadeo m panting

ja·ez m (pl -eces) harness, piece of harness; ilk, stripe, kind; **jaeces** trappings

jaguar m jaguar

jagüel m (Arg) reservoir

jaharrar tr to plaster

jalar tr (coll) to pull; (Am) to flirt with || intr (Am) to get out, to beat it || ref (Am) to get drunk

jalbegar tr to whitewash; (el rostro) to paint || ref to paint the face

jalbegue m whitewash; whitewashing; paint, make-up

jalda·do -da adj bright-yellow

jalea f jelly; **hacerse una jalea** (coll) to be madly in love

jalear tr (a los que bailan y cantan) to animate with clapping and shouting; (a los perros) to incite, urge on; (Chile) to tease, pester || intr to dance the jaleo || ref to have a noisy time; to swing and sway

jaleo m cheering, shouting; jamboree; jaleo (vivacious Spanish solo dance)

jalis·co -ca adj (Guat, Mex) drunk || m (Mex) straw hat

jalma f small packsaddle

jalón m surveying rod, range pole; (Guat, Mex) swig of liquor; (CAm) beau; **jalón de mira** leveling rod

jalonar tr to stake out, mark out

jalonear tr (Mex) to pull, to jerk

jalonero m (surv) rodman

jamaica m Jamaica rum || f (Mex) charity fair

jamaica·no -na adj & mf Jamaican

jamaiqui·no -na adj & mf (Am) Jamaican

jamar tr (coll) to eat

jamás adv never; ever

jamba f jamb

jambaje m doorframe, window frame

jamelgo m (coll) jade, nag

jamete m samite

jamón m ham

jamona f (coll) fat middle-aged woman

jamugas fpl mule chair

jánda·lo -la adj & mf Andalusian

Jantipa or **Jantipe** f Xanthippe

Japón, el Japan

japo·nés -nesa adj & mf Japanese || m (idioma) Japanese

jaque m (lance del ajedrez) check; (coll) bully; **dar jaque a** to check; **dar jaque mate a** to checkmate; en

jaque in check; **estar muy jaque** (coll) to be full of pep; **jaque mate** checkmate; **tener en jaque** to hold a threat over the head of || interj check!

jaquear tr to check; (al enemigo) to harass

jaqueca f sick headache; **dar una jaqueca a** (coll) to bore to death

jaqueco·so -sa adj boring, tiresome

jaquemar m jack (figure which strikes a clock bell)

jarabe m syrup; sweet drink; **jarabe de pico** (coll) lip service, idle promise

jarana f (coll) merrymaking; (coll) rumpus; (coll) carousal, spree; (coll) trick, deceit; (Am) jest, joke; (Am) small guitar; **ir de jarana** (coll) to go on a spree

jaranear tr (CAm, Col) to swindle, cheat || intr (coll) to go on a spree; (coll) to raise a rumpus; (Am) to joke

jarane·ro -ra adj merrymaking; gay, merry || mf merrymaker, reveler

jarano m sombrero

jarcia f fishing tackle; (coll) jumble, mess; **jarcias** tackle, rigging; **jarcia trozada** junk (old cable)

jardín m garden, flower garden; (baseball) field, outfield; (naut) privy, latrine; **jardín central** (baseball) center field; **jardín de la infancia** kindergarten; **jardín derecho** (baseball) right field; **jardín izquierdo** (baseball) left field

jardinera f jardiniere, flower stand; basket carriage; summer trolley car, open trolley car

jardinería f gardening

jardine·ro -ra mf gardener; **jardinero adornista** landscape gardener || m (baseball) fielder, outfielder || f see **jardinera**

jardinista mf landscape gardener

jarea f (Mex) hunger

jarear intr (Bol) to stop for a rest || ref (Mex) to flee, run away; (Mex) to swing, to sway; (Mex) to die of starvation

jareta f (sew) casing

jari·fa -fa adj showy, spruce, natty

jaro·cho -cha adj brusk, bluff || m insulting fellow; Veracruz peasant

jarope m syrup; (coll) nasty potion

jarra f jug, jar, water pitcher; **de jarras** or **en jarras** with arms akimbo

jarrete m hock, gambrel

jarretera f garter

jarro m pitcher; **echar un jarro de agua (fría) a** to pour cold water on

jarrón m (vaso para adornar chimeneas, consolas, etc.) vase; (sobre un pedestal) urn

jaspe m jasper

jaspea·do -da adj marbled, speckled || m marbling, speckling

jaspear tr to marble, speckle

jateo m foxhound

ja·to -ta mf calf

Jauja f Cockaigne; **¿estamos aquí o en Jauja?** (coll) where do you think you are?; **vivir en Jauja** (coll) to live in the lap of luxury

jaula f cage; (*embalaje de listones de madera*) crate; (Mex) open freight car; (Cuba, P-R) police wagon; **jaula de locos** insane asylum, madhouse
jauría f pack (*of hounds*)
java‧nés -nesa adj & mf Javanese ‖ m (*idioma*) Javanese
Javier m Xavier
jazmín m jasmine; **jazmín de la India** gardenia
jazz m jazz
J.C. abbr **Jesucristo**
jebe m alum; (SAm) rubber
jedive m khedive
jefa f female head or leader; **jefa de ruta** hostess (*on a bus*)
jefatura f headship, leadership; (*de policía*) headquarters
jefe m chief, head, leader; (*de una tribu*) chieftain; **jefe de cocina** chef; **jefe de coro** choirmaster; **jefe de equipajes** (rr) baggage master; **jefe de estación** stationmaster; **jefe del estado** chief of state; **jefe del gobierno** chief executive; **jefe de redacción** editor in chief; **jefe de ruta** guide; **jefe de tren** (rr) conductor; **quedar jefe** (Chile) to gamble away everything
jején m gnat, sandfly
jenabe m or **jenable** m mustard
jengibre m ginger
Jenofonte m Xenophon
jeque m sheik
jerarca m hierarch, head
jerarquía f hierarchy; **de jerarquía** important
jeremiada f jeremiad
jerez m sherry
jerga f coarse cloth; straw mattress; (*lenguaje especial de ciertos oficios; lenguaje difícil de entender*) jargon
jergón m straw mattress; (coll) ill-fitting clothes; (*persona torpe y estúpida*) (coll) lummox
Jericó Jericho
jerife m shereef
jerigonza f (*lenguaje especial de ciertos oficios; lenguaje difícil de entender*) jargon; (*lenguaje vulgar, caló*) slang; (coll) piece of folly
jeringa f syringe; (*para inyectar materias blandas en una máquina*) gun; (coll) annoyance, plague; **jeringa de engrase** or **grasa** grease gun
jeringar §44 tr to syringe; to inject; to give an enema to; (coll) to plague
jeringazo m injection, shot; squirt
jeringuilla f (*jeringa pequeña*) syringe; (bot) mock orange
Jerjes m Xerxes
jeroglífi‧co -ca adj & m hieroglyphic
Jerónimo m Jerome
jer‧sey m (pl -seis) jersey, sweater
Jerusalén Jerusalem
Jesucristo m Jesus Christ
jesuíta adj & m Jesuit
jesuíti‧co -ca adj Jesuitic(al)
Jesús m Jesus; (*imagen del niño Jesús*) bambino; **en un decir Jesús** in an instant; **¡Jesús, María y José!** my gracious!
jeta f hog's snout, pig face; (*rostro de una persona*) (coll) phiz, mug; **estar con tanta jeta** (coll) to make a long face; **poner jeta** (coll) to pucker one's lips
jetu‧do -da adj thick-lipped; (coll) grim, gruff
Jhs. abbr **Jesús**
jíba‧ro -ra mf (W-I) white peasant
jibia f cuttlefish
jícara f chocolate cup; (CAm, Mex, W-I) calabash cup
jifia f swordfish
jilguero m linnet, goldfinch
jineta f (zool) genet
jinete m rider, horseman
jinetear tr (*caballos cerriles*) (Am) to break in ‖ intr to show off one's horsemanship
jinglar intr to swing, to rock
jingoísmo m jingoism
jingoísta adj & mf jingo
jipa‧to -ta adj (Am) pale, wan; (Am) insipid, tasteless; (Guat) drunk
jipijapa m Panama hat ‖ f jipijapa; strip of jipijapa straw
jira f strip of cloth; outing, picnic; trip, tour; swing, political trip
jirón m rag, tatter, shred; (*de una falda*) facing; pennant; bit, drop, shred; **hacer jirones** to tear to shreds
jitomate m (Mex) tomato
joco‧so -sa adj jocose, jocular
jocotal m (CAm, Mex) Spanish plum (*tree*)
jocote m (CAm, Mex) Spanish plum (*fruit*)
jocoyote m (Mex) baby (*youngest child*)
jofaina f washbowl, basin
jolgorio m (coll) fun, merriment
jonrón m (baseball) home run
Jordán m Jordan (*river*); **ir al Jordán** (coll) to be born again
Jordania f Jordan (*country*)
jorda‧no -na adj & mf Jordanian
jorguín m sorcerer, wizard
jorguina f sorceress, witch
jorguinería f sorcery, witchcraft
jornada f journey, trip, stage; day's journey; (*horas del trabajo diario del obrero*) workday; (*tiempo que dura la vida de un hombre*) lifetime; battle; (*muerte*) passing; summer residence of diplomat or diplomatic corps; event, occasion; undertaking; (mil) expedition; (*de un drama*) (archaic) act; **a grandes** or **largas jornadas** by forced marches; **al fin de la jornada** in the end; **caminar por sus jornadas** to proceed with circumspection; **hacer mala jornada** to get nowhere; **jornada ordinaria** full time
jornal m day's work; day's pay; **a jornal** by the day; **jornal mínimo** minimum wage
jornalero m day laborer
joroba f hump; (coll) annoyance, bother
joroba‧do -da adj humpbacked, hunchbacked; (coll) annoyed, bothered ‖ mf humpback, hunchback
jorobar tr (coll) to annoy, pester
jorongo m (Mex) poncho; (Mex) woolen blanket

jota f (letra del alfabeto) J; jota (Spanish folk dance and music); jot, iota, tittle; vegetable soup; **sin faltar una jota** (coll) with not a whit left out

joven adj young; **ser joven de esperanzas** (coll) to have a bright future ‖ mf youth, young person; **de joven** as a youth, as a young man, as a young woman

jovial adj jovial

joya f jewel; (brocamantón) diamond brooch; (agasajo) gift, present; (persona o cosa de mucha valía) (fig) jewel, gem; **joya de familia** heirloom; **joyas** jewelry; trousseau; **joyas de fantasía** costume jewelry

joyante adj glossy

joyelero m jewel case, casket

joyería f (conjunto de joyas) jewelry; jewelry shop; jewelry trade

joye·ro -ra mf jeweler ‖ m jewel case, casket

Juan m John; **Buen Juan** (coll) sap, easy mark; **Juan Español** the Spanish people, the typical Spaniard; **San Juan Bautista** John the Baptist

Juana f Jane, Jean, Joan; **Juana de Arco** Joan of Arc, Jeanne d'Arc; **juanas** glove stretcher

juanete m bunion; high cheekbone

jubilación f retirement; (renta de la persona jubilada) pension, retirement annuity

jubila·do -da adj retired ‖ mf retired person, pensioner

jubilar tr to retire, to pension; (coll) to throw out ‖ intr to rejoice; to retire, be pensioned ‖ ref to rejoice; to retire, be pensioned; (Col) to decline, go to pieces; (CAm, Ven) to play hooky; (Cuba, Mex) to become a past master

jubileo m (coll) much coming and going, great doings; (eccl) jubilee; **por jubileo** (coll) once in a long time

júbilo m jubilation

jubilo·so -sa adj jubilant, joyful

jubón m jerkin

judaísmo m Judaism

judería f (raza judaica) Jewry; (barrio de los judíos) ghetto

judía f Jewess; kidney bean, string bean; **judía de careta** black-eyed bean; **judía de la peladilla** Lima bean

judicatura f judicature; (cargo de juez) judgeship

judicial adj judicial, judiciary

judí·o -a adj Jewish ‖ mf Jew ‖ f see **judía**

juego m (acción de jugar) play, playing; (ejercicio recreativo en el cual se gana o se pierde) game; (vicio de jugar) gambling; (lugar donde se ejecutan ciertos juegos): (bowling) alley; (tennis) court; (baseball) field; (tantos necesarios para ganar la partida) game; (de muebles) suit, suite; (de café) service; (de vajilla) set; (de luces, colores, aguas) play; (mach) play; (p.ej., de diplomacia) (fig) game; **a juego** to match, e.g., **una silla a juego** a chair to match; **conocer el**

juego de to see through, to have the number of; **en juego** at hand; **hacer juego** to match; **hacer juego con** to match, to go with; **juego de alcoba** bedroom suit; **juego de azar** game of chance; **juego de bolas** (mach) ball bearing; **juego de campanas** chimes; **juego de comedor** dining-room suit; **juego de envite** gambling game, game played for money; **juego de escritorio** desk set; **juego de la cuna** cat's cradle; **juego de la pulga** tiddlywinks; **juego del corro** ring-around-a-rosy; **juego del salto** leapfrog; **juego del tres en raya** tick-tack-toe played with movable counters or pebbles; **juego de manos** legerdemain, sleight of hand; (coll) roughhousing; **juego de niños** (cosa muy fácil) child's play; **juego de palabras** play on words, pun; **juego de pelota** ball game; pelota; **juego de piernas** footwork; **juego de por ver** (Chile) game played for fun; **juego de prendas** game of forfeits, forfeits; **juego de suerte** game of chance; **juego de tejo** shuffleboard; **juego de timbres** glockenspiel; **juego de vocablos** or **voces** play on words, pun; **juego limpio** fair play; **juego público** gambling house; **juegos de sociedad** parlor games; **juegos malabares** juggling; flimflam; **juego sucio** foul play; **no ser cosa de juego** to be no laughing matter; **por juego** in fun, for fun; **verle a uno el juego** to be on to someone

juerga f (coll) carousal, spree; **juerga de borrachera** (coll) drinking bout, binge; **ir de juerga** (coll) to go on a spree

juerguista mf (coll) carouser, reveler

jue·ves m (pl -ves) Thursday; **Jueves Santo** Maundy Thursday

juez m (pl jueces) judge; **juez de guardia** coroner; **juez de instrucción** examining magistrate; **juez de paz** justice of the peace; **juez de salida** (sport) starter; **juez de tiempo** (sport) timekeeper

jugada f (lance) play, throw, stroke, move; **mala jugada** dirty trick

juga·dor -dora mf player; gambler; **jugador de manos** prestidigitator; **jugador de ventaja** sharper

jugar §42 tr (p.ej., un naipe, una partida de juego) to play; (una espada) to wield; (arriesgar) to stake, to risk; (las manos, los dedos) to move; **jugarle a uno las bebidas** to match someone for the drinks ‖ intr to play; to gamble; (hacer jugar dos cosas) to match; (intervenir) to figure, participate; **jugar a** (p.ej., los naipes, el tenis) to play; **jugar con** (un contrario) to play; (una persona; los sentimientos de una persona) to toy with; to match; **jugar en** to have a hand in ‖ ref (p.ej., la vida) to risk; to be at stake; **jugarse el todo por el todo** to stake all, to shoot the works

jugarreta f (coll) bad play, poor play; (coll) mean trick, dirty trick

juglar *m* minstrel, jongleur; (*bufón*) (archaic) juggler

juglaría *f* minstrelsy

jugo *m* (*p.ej., de la naranja*) juice; (*de la carne*) gravy; (*líquido orgánico*) juice; (fig) gist, essence, substance; **en su jugo** (culin) au jus; **jugo de muñeca** (coll) elbow grease

jugo·so -sa *adj* juicy; substantial, important

juguete *m* toy, plaything; (*burla*) joke, jest; (theat) skit; **de juguete** toy, e.g., **soldado de juguete** toy soldier; **juguete de movimiento** mechanical toy; **por juguete** for fun, in fun

juguetear *intr* to frolic, romp, sport

juguete·ro -ra *adj* toy || *mf* toy dealer || *m* whatnot, étagère

juguete-sorpresa *m* (*pl* **juguetes-sorpresa**) jack-in-the-box

jugue·tón -tona *adj* playful, frolicsome, frisky

juicio *m* judgment; (law) trial; **estar en su cabal juicio** to be in one's right mind; **estar fuera de juicio** to be out of one's mind; **juicio de Dios** (hist) ordeal; **pedir en juicio** (law) to sue

juicio·so -sa *adj* judicious, wise

julepe *m* julep; (coll) scolding; (Am) scare, fright

julepear *tr* (coll) to scold; (coll) to whip; (SAm) to scare, frighten; (Mex) to weary, tire out

julio *m* July

julo *m* lead cow, lead mule

jumen·to -ta *mf* ass, donkey

juncal *adj* willowy, rushy; (fig) willowy, lissome

juncia *f* sedge; **vender juncia** (coll) to boast, brag

junco *m* (*embarcación china*) junk; (bot) rush, bulrush; **junco de Indias** (bot) rattan; **junco de laguna** (bot) rush, bulrush

junco·so -sa *adj* rushy, full of rushes

jungla *f* jungle

junio *m* June

junípero *m* juniper

junquera *f* rush, bulrush

junquillo *m* jonquil

junta *f* meeting, conference; board, council; junction, union; joint, seam; (*empaquetadura*) gasket; (*arandela*) washer; **junta de comercio** board of trade; **junta de charnela** (mach) knuckle; **junta de sanidad** board of health; **junta universal** (mach) universal joint

juntamente *adv* together; at the same time

juntar *tr* to join, unite; to gather, gather together; (*una puerta*) to half-close || *ref* to gather together; to go along; to copulate

jun·to -ta *adj* joined, united; **jun·tos -tas** together || *f* see **junta** || **junto** *adv* together; at the same time; **junto a** near, close to; **junto con** along with, together with; **todo junto** at the same time, all at once

juntura *f* junction; (*p.ej., de una cañería; de un hueso*) joint; connection, coupling

jura *f* oath

jura·do -da *adj* (*enemigo*) sworn || *m* (*conjunto de ciudadanos encargados de determinar la culpabilidad del acusado; conjunto de examinadores de un certamen*) jury; (*cada uno de los expresados individuos*) juror, juryman

juramentar *tr* to swear in || *ref* to take an oath, to be sworn in

juramento *m* oath; (*voto, reniego*) curse, swearword; **prestar juramento a** to swear to; **tomar juramento a** to swear in

jurar *tr* to swear; (*la verdad de una cosa*) to swear to; to swear allegiance to || *intr* (*pronunciar un juramento*) to swear, take an oath; (*echar votos o reniegos*) to swear, to curse; **jurar + *inf*** to swear to + *inf* || *ref* to swear; **jurársela** or **jurárselas a uno** (coll) to have it in for someone, to swear to get even with someone

jure·ro -ra *mf* (SAm) false witness

jurídi·co -ca *adj* juridical

jurisconsulto *m* (*el que escribe sobre el derecho*) jurist; (*jurisperito*) legal expert

jurisdicción *f* jurisdiction

jurisperito *m* jurist, legal expert

jurisprudencia *f* jurisprudence

jurista *mf* jurist

juro *m* right of perpetual ownership; **de juro** inevitably, for sure

justa *f* joust, tournament

justamente *adv* just, just at that time; justly; (*ajustadamente*) tightly

justar *intr* to joust, to tilt

justicia *f* justice; (*castigo de muerte*) execution; **de justicia** justly, deservedly; **hacer justicia a** to do justice to; **ir por justicia** to go to court, to bring suit

justicie·ro -ra *adj* just, fair; stern, righteous

justificable *adj* justifiable

justifica·do -da *adj* (*hecho*) just, right; (*persona*) just, upright

justificante *m* voucher, proof

justificar §73 *tr* to justify; (typ) to justify

justillo *m* jerkin, waist

justipreciar *tr* to estimate, appraise

jus·to -ta *adj* just; right, exact; (*apretado*) tight || *mf* just person || *f* see **justa** || **justo** *adv* just; right, in tune; tight; (*con estrechez*) in straitened circumstances

Jutlandia *f* Jutland

ju·to -ta *mf* Jute

juvenil *adj* juvenile, youthful

juventud *f* youth; young people

juzgado *m* court of law; courtroom; court of one judge

juzgar §44 *tr & intr* to judge; **a juzgar por** judging by; **juzgar de** to judge, pass judgment on

jo
ju

K

K, k (ka) *f* twelfth letter of the Spanish alphabet
kermesse *f* var of **quermés**
keroseno *m* kerosene, coal oil
kg. *abbr* **kilogramo**
kilate *m* var of **quilate**
kilo *m* kilo, kilogram
kilociclo *m* kilocycle
kilogramo *m* kilogram
kilometraje *m* kilometrage, distance in kilometers
kilométri·co -ca *adj* kilometric; (coll) interminable, long-drawn-out

kilómetro *m* kilometer
kilovatio *m* kilowatt
kilovatio-hora *m* (*pl* **kilovatios-hora**) kilowatt-hour
kimono *m* var of **quimono**
kinescopio *m* (telv) kinescope
kiosco *m* var of **quiosco**
kirieleisón *m* (coll) dirge; **cantar el kirieleisón** (coll) to beg mercy
km. *abbr* **kilómetro**
kph. *abbr* **kilómetros por hora**
kv. *abbr* **kilovatio**
kv-h *abbr* **kilovatio-hora**

L

L, l (ele) *f* thirteenth letter of the Spanish alphabet
la *art def fem* of **el** ‖ *pron pers fem* her, it; you ‖ *pron dem* that, the one; **la que** who, which, that; she who, the one that
laberinto *m* labyrinth, maze
labia *f* (coll) fluency, smoothness
labial *adj & f* labial
labio *m* lip; (fig) edge, lip; **chuparse los labios** to smack one's lips; **labio leporino** harelip; **leer en los labios** to lip-read
labiolectura *f* lip reading
labio·so -sa *adj* (Am) fluent, smooth
labor *f* labor, work; (*cultivo de los campos*) farming, tilling; (*obra de coser, bordar, etc.*) needlework, fancywork, embroidery; **hacer labor** to match; **labor blanca** linen work, linen embroidery; **labor de ganchillo** crocheting
laborable *adj* workable; arable, tillable; (*día*) work
laborante *m* journeyman; political henchman
laborar *tr* to work ‖ *intr* to scheme
laboratorio *m* laboratory
laborio·so -sa *adj* (*trabajador*) laborious, industrious; (*trabajoso*) laborious, arduous
laborismo *m* British Labour Party
laborista *adj* Labour ‖ *mf* Labourite
labra *f* carving
labrada *f* fallow ground (*to be sown the following year*)
labrade·ro -ra *adj* arable, tillable
labra·do -da *adj* wrought, fashioned; carved; figured, embroidered ‖ *m* carving; **labrado de madera** wood carving ‖ *f* see **labrada**
labra·dor -dora *adj* work; farm ‖ *mf* farmer; (*campesino*) peasant ‖ *m* plowman; **el Labrador** Labrador
labrantí·o -a *adj* farm ‖ *m* farmland
labranza *f* farming; farm, farmland
labrar *tr* to work, to fashion; (*la piedra, la madera*) to carve; (*arar*) to

plow; (*construir o mandar construir*) to build; to till, to cultivate; to cause, bring about ‖ *intr* to make a lasting impression
labrie·go -ga *mf* peasant
laca *f* lacquer; shellac; **laca de uñas** nail polish; **lacas** lacquer ware
lacayo *m* lackey, footman
lacear *tr* to tie with a bow; to adorn with bows; (*la caza*) to drive within shot; (*la caza menor*) to trap, to snare
lacería *f* poverty, want; trouble, bother; leprosy
lacerio·so -sa *adj* poor, needy
lacero *m* lassoer; poacher; dogcatcher
la·cio -cia *adj* faded, withered; languid; (*cabello*) lank, straight
lacóni·co -ca *adj* laconic
lacra *f* fault, defect; (*señal dejada por una enfermedad*) mark, remains; (Am) sore; (Am) scab
lacrimóge·no -na *adj* tear, tear-producing
lacrimo·so -sa *adj* lachrymose, tearful
lactar *tr* to suckle
lácte·o -a *adj* milky
lacustre *adj* lake
ladear *tr* to tip, to tilt; to bend, to lean; (*un avión*) to bank ‖ *intr* to tip, to tilt; to bend, to lean; to turn away, turn off; (*la aguja de brújula*) to deviate ‖ *ref* to tip, to tilt; to bend, to lean; to be equal, be even; (Chile) to fall in love; **ladearse a** (*un dictamen, un partido*) to lean to or toward
ladeo *m* tipping, tilting; bending, leaning; inclination, bent
lade·ro -ra *adj* side, lateral ‖ *f* hillside
ladilla *f* crab louse; **pegarse como ladilla** (coll) to stick like a leech
ladi·no -na *adj* crafty, sly, cunning; polyglot
lado *m* side; direction; (*del hilo telefónico*) end; **al lado** nearby; **dejar a un lado** to leave aside; **de lado** square, e.g., **diez centímetros de lado** ten centimeters square; **de otro lado**

on the other hand; **de un lado** on the one hand; **echar a un lado** to cast aside; to finish up; **hacer lado** to make room; **hacerse a un lado** to step aside; **lados** backers, advisers; **mirar de lado** or **de medio lado** to look askance at; to sneak a look at; **ponerse al lado de** to take sides with; **por el lado de** in the direction of; **tirar por su lado** to pull for oneself

ladrar *tr* (*p.ej.*, *injurias*) to bark ‖ *intr* to bark

ladrido *m* bark, barking; (coll) slander, blame

ladrillador *m* bricklayer

ladrillal *m* brickyard

ladrillo *m* brick; (*azulejo*) tile; (*p.ej.*, *de chocolate*) cake; **ladrillo de fuego** or **ladrillo refractario** firebrick

la·drón -drona *adj* thievish, thieving ‖ *mf* thief ‖ *m* sluice gate; **ladrón de corazones** heartbreaker, lady-killer

ladronera *f* den of thieves; thievery; (*alcancía*) child's bank

ladronería *m* (Arg) gang of thieves; (Arg) wave of thieving

ladronzue·lo -la *mf* petty thief

lagaña *f* var of legaña

lagar *m* wine press; olive press; (*establecimiento*) winery

lagarta *f* female lizard; (ent) gypsy moth; (coll) sly woman

lagartija *f* green lizard; wall lizard

lagarto *m* lizard; (coll) sly fellow; **lagarto de Indias** alligator

lago *m* lake

lagotear *tr & intr* to flatter, to wheedle

lágrima *f* tear; (*de cualquier licor*) drop; **beberse las lágrimas** (coll) to hold back one's tears; **deshacerse en lágrimas** to weep one's eyes out; **lágrimas de cocodrilo** crocodile tears; **llorar a lágrima viva** to shed bitter tears

lagrimear *intr* to weep easily, to be tearful; (*los ojos*) to fill

lagrimo·so -sa *adj* tearful; (*ojos*) watery

laguna *f* (*lago pequeño*) lagoon; (*hueco, omisión*) lacuna, gap

laical *adj* lay

laicismo *m* secularism

laja *f* slab, flagstone

lama *f* mud, ooze, slime; pond scum

lambrija *f* earthworm; (coll) skinny person

lamedero *m* salt lick

lame·dor -dora *adj* licking ‖ *mf* licker ‖ *m* syrup; **dar lamedor** (coll) to lose at first in order to take in one's opponent

lamedura *f* lick, licking

lamentable *adj* lamentable

lamentación *f* lamentation

lamentar *tr, intr & ref* to lament, to mourn

lamento *m* lament

lamento·so -sa *adj* lamentable; plaintive

lamer *tr* to lick; to lap, lap against; (*las llamas un tejado*) to lick ‖ *ref* (*p.ej.*, *los dedos*) to lick

lame·rón -rona *adj* (coll) sweet-toothed

lametada *f* lap, lick

lámina *f* sheet, plate, strip; (*plancha grabada*) engraving; (*pintura en cobre*) copper plate; (*figura estampada*) cut, picture, illustration

laminador *m* rolling mill

laminar *tr* to laminate; (*el hierro, el acero*) to roll

lampadario *m* floor lamp

lámpara *f* lamp, light; (*mancha en la ropa*) grease spot, oil spot; (rad) vacuum tube; **atizar la lámpara** (coll) to fill up the glasses again; **lámpara de alcohol** spirit lamp; **lámpara de arco** arc lamp, arc light; **lámpara de bolsillo** flashlight; **lámpara de carretera** (aut) bright light; **lámpara de cruce** (aut) dimmer; **lámpara de pie** floor lamp; **lámpara de sobremesa** table lamp; **lámpara de socorro** trouble light; **lámpara de soldar** blowtorch; **lámpara de techo** ceiling light; (aut) dome light; **lámpara inundante** floodlight; **lámpara testigo** pilot light

lamparilla *f* rushlight; aspen

lampi·ño -ña *adj* beardless; hairless

lampista *mf* lamplighter ‖ *m* tinsmith, plumber, glazier, electrician

lana *f* wool; **lana de acero** steel wool; **lana de ceiba** kapoc; **lana de escorias** mineral wool, rock wool; **lana de vidrio** glass wool

lance *m* cast, throw; (*en la red*) catch, haul; (*accidente en el juego*) play, move, stroke; (*ocasión crítica*) chance, pass, juncture; incident, event; (*riña*) row, quarrel; (taur) capework; **de lance** cheap; secondhand; **echar buen lance** (coll) to have a break; **lance de honor** affair of honor, duel; **tener pocos lances** (coll) to be dull and uninteresting

lancero *m* lancer, spearman, pikeman

lanceta *f* (surg) lancet

lancinante *adj* piercing

lancha *f* barge, lighter; flagstone, slab; (naut) longboat; (nav) launch; (Ecuad) mist, fog; (Ecuad) frost; **lancha automóvil** launch, motor launch; **lancha de auxilio** lifeboat (*stationed on shore*); **lancha de carreras** speedboat; **lancha de desembarco** (nav) landing craft; **lancha salvavidas** lifeboat (*on shipboard*)

lanchar *intr* (Ecuad) to get foggy; (Ecuad) to freeze

lan·dó *m* (*pl* -**dós**) landau

landre *f* swollen gland; hidden pocket

lanería *f* wool shop; **lanerías** woolens, woolen goods

langosta *f* (*insecto*) locust; (*crustáceo*) lobster, spiny lobster

langostera *f* lobster pot

langostín *m* or **langostino** *m* prawn (*Peneus*)

langostón *m* green grasshopper

languidecer §22 *intr* to languish

languidez *f* languor

lángui·do -da *adj* languid, languorous

lano·so -sa *adj* woolly

lanu·do -da *adj* woolly; (Ecuad, Ven) coarse, ill-bred

lanza *f* lance, pike; (*de la manguera*) nozzle; (*palo de coche*) wagon pole

k
la

lanzabom·bas *m* (*pl* **-bas**) (aer) bomb release; (mil) trench mortar

lanzacohe·tes *m* (*pl* **-tes**) rocket launcher

lanzadera *f* shuttle; **parecer una lanzadera** (coll) to buzz around

lanza·do -da *adj* sloping; (*salida de una carrera*) (sport) running (*start*)

lanza·dor -dora *mf* thrower; **lanzador de lodo** (fig) mudslinger || *m* launcher; (aer) jettison gear; (baseball) pitcher

lanzaespu·mas *m* (*pl* **-mas**) foam extinguisher

lanzalla·mas *m* (*pl* **-mas**) flame thrower

lanzamiento *m* throw, hurl, fling, launch; (*de un buque*) launching; (*de un cohete*) shot, launch; (*p.ej., de víveres*) (aer) airdrop; (*de bombas*) (aer) release; (*de paracaidistas*) (aer) jump; (law) dispossession; (naut) steeve

lanzami·nas *m* (*pl* **-nas**) (nav) mine layer

lanzapla·tos *m* (*pl* **-tos**) trap

lanzar §60 *tr* to throw, hurl, fling; (*un proyecto, un cohete, maldiciones, una ofensiva, un producto nuevo, un buque*) to launch; (*una mirada*) to cast; to vomit, to throw up; (*flores, hojas una planta*) to put forth; (*una advertencia*) to toss, toss out; (aer) to airdrop; (*bombas*) (aer) to release; (law) to dispossess || *ref* to launch, launch forth; to throw oneself; to dash, to rush; (aer) to jump; (sport) to sprint

lanzatorpe·dos *m* (*pl* **-dos**) (nav) torpedo tube

laña *f* clamp; rivet

lañar *tr* to clamp; (*objetos de porcelana*) to rivet

lapicero *m* pencil holder; mechanical pencil

lápida *f* tablet, stone; **lápida sepulcral** gravestone

lapidar *tr* to stone to death

lá·piz *m* (*pl* **-pices**) (*grafito*) black lead; (*barrita que sirve para escribir*) pencil, lead pencil; **lápiz de labios** lipstick; **lápiz de pizarra** slate pencil; **lápiz de plomo** graphite; **lápiz estíptico** styptic pencil; **lápiz labial** lipstick

lapizar §60 *tr* to mark or line with a pencil

la·pón -pona *adj* Lapp || *mf* Lapp, Laplander || *m* (*idioma*) Lapp

Laponia *f* Lapland

lapso *m* lapse

laquear *tr* to lacquer

lardo·so -sa *adj* greasy, fatty

larga *f* long billiard cue; **dar largas a** to postpone, to put off

largamente *adv* at length, extensively; in comfort; generously; long, for a long time

largar §44 *tr* to get go, release; to ease, slack; (naut) to unfurl; (coll) to utter; (*un golpe*) to deal, strike, give; (Col) to give || *ref* to move away; to get away, sneak away, beat it; to take to sea; (*el ancla*) to come loose

lar·go -ga *adj* long; abundant; liberal, generous; quick, ready; (coll) shrewd, cunning; (naut) loose, slack; **a la larga** in the long run, in the end; **a lo largo** lengthwise; at great length; far away; **a lo largo de** along; along with; throughout; in the course of; (*el mar*) far out in; **a lo más largo** at most; **hacerse a lo largo** to get out in the open sea; **largo de lengua** loosetongued; **largo de uñas** light-fingered; **pasar de largo** to pass without stopping; to take a quick look; to miss; **ponerse de largo** to come out, make one's debut; **vestir de largo** to wear long clothes || *m* length || *f* see **larga** || **largo** *adv* at length, at great length; abundantly || **largo** *interj* get out of here!

largometraje *m* full-featured film, full-length movie

largor *m* length

larguero *m* (*palo, madero*) stringer; (*almohada larga*) bolster; (aer) longeron

largueza *f* length; liberality, generosity

larguiru·cho -cha *adj* (coll) gangling, lanky

largura *f* length

lárice *m* larch tree

laringe *f* larynx

larínge·o -a *adj* laryngeal

laringitis *f* laryngitis

laringoscopio *m* laryngoscope

larva *f* larva; mask; (*duende*) hobgoblin

lascar §73 *tr* (naut) to pay out, to slacken; (Mex) to scratch, to bruise; (*un objeto de porcelana*) (Mex) to chip

lascivia *f* lasciviousness

lasci·vo -va *adj* lascivious; playful

láser *m* laser

la·so -sa *adj* tired, exhausted; weak

lástima *f* pity; (*quejido*) complaint; **contar lástimas** to tell a hard-luck story; **dar lástima** to be pitiful; **es lástima (que)** it is a pity (that); **estar hecho una lástima** to be a sorry sight; **hacer lástima** to be pitiful; **llorar lástimas** (coll) to put on a show of tears; **poner lástima** to be pitiful; ¡**qué lástima**! what a pity!, what a shame!; ¡**qué lástima de saliva!** (coll) what a waste of breath!

lastimar *tr* to hurt, injure; to hurt, offend; to bruise || *ref* to hurt oneself; to bruise oneself; to complain

lastime·ro -ra *adj* hurtful, injurious; pitiful, sad, doleful

lastimo·so -sa *adj* pitiful

lastra *f* slab, flagstone

lastrar *tr* (aer & naut) to ballast

lastre *m* (aer & naut) ballast; (fig) wisdom, maturity; (coll) food; (rr) (Chile) ballast

lat. *abbr* **latín, latitud**

lata *f* (*hojalata*) tin, tin plate; (*envase*) tin can; (*madero sin pulir*) log; (*tabla delgada*) lath; (coll) annoyance, bore; **dar la lata a** (coll) to pester; **estar en la lata** (Col) to be penniless

latebra *f* hiding place

latebro·so -sa *adj* furtive, secretive
latente *adj* latent
lateral *adj* lateral
latido *m* (*del perro*) yelp; (*del corazón*) beat, throb; (*dolor*) pang, twinge
latifundio *m* large neglected landed estate
latigazo *m* lash; crack of whip; (*represión áspera*) lashing
látigo *m* whip, horsewhip; cinch strap
latiguear *tr* (*Am*) to lash, to whip || *intr* to crack a whip
latiguillo *m* small whip; (*del actor u orador*) claptrap
latín *m* Latin; **latín de cocina** dog Latin, hog Latin; **latín rústico** or **vulgar** Vulgar Latin; **saber latín** or **mucho latín** (*coll*) to be very shrewd
latinajo *m* (*coll*) dog Latin, hog Latin; (*coll*) Latin word or phrase (*slipped into the vernacular*)
latinar or **latinear** *intr* to use Latin
lati·no -na *adj* Latin; (*naut*) lateen || *mf* Latin
Latinoamérica *f* Latin America
latinoamerica·no -na *adj* Latin-American || *mf* Latin American
latir *tr* (*Ven*) to annoy, bore, molest || *intr* (*el perro*) to bark, yelp; (*el corazón*) to beat, throb; **me late que** (*Mex*) I have a hunch that
latitud *f* latitude
la·to -ta *adj* broad || *f* see **lata**
latón *m* brass; (*Cuba*) garbage pail
lato·so -sa *adj* annoying, boring || *mf* bore
latrocinio *m* thievery; thievishness
laucha *f* (*Arg, Chile*) mouse
laúd *m* (*mus*) lute; (*zool*) leatherback turtle
laudable *adj* laudable
láudano *m* laudanum
laudato·rio -ria *adj* laudatory
laudo *m* (*law*) finding, decision
láurea *f* laurel wreath
laurea·do -da *adj* & *mf* laureate
laurean·do -da *mf* graduate, candidate for a degree
laurear *tr* to trim or adorn with laurel; to crown with laurel; to decorate, honor, reward
laurel *m* laurel; (*de la victoria*) laurels; **dormirse sobre sus laureles** to rest or sleep on one's laurels
láure·o -a *adj* laurel || *f* see **láurea**
lauréola *f* crown of laurel, laurel wreath; (*aureola*) halo
lava *f* lava; (*min*) washing
lavable *adj* washable
lavabo *m* washstand; washroom, lavatory
lavaca·ras *mf* (*pl -ras*) (*coll*) fawner, flatterer, bootlicker
lavaco·ches *m* (*pl -ches*) car washer
lavade·dos *m* (*pl -dos*) finger bowl
lavadero *m* laundry; (*tabla de lavar*) washboard; (*a orillas de un río*) washing place; (*Guat, Mex, SAm*) placer
lava·do -da *adj* (*coll*) brazen, fresh, impudent || *m* wash, washing; **lavado a seco** dry cleaning; **lavado cerebral**

or **de cerebro** brain-washing; **lavado químico** dry cleaning
lava·dor -dora *mf* washer || *m* (*phot*) washer || *f* washing machine; **lavadora de platos** or **de vajilla** dishwasher
lavadura *f* washing; (*agua sucia; rozadura de una cuerda*) washings
lavafru·tas *m* (*pl -tas*) fruit bowl, finger bowl
lavama·nos *m* (*pl -nos*) (*pila con caño y llave*) washstand; (*jofaina*) washbowl
lavanda *f* lavender
lavandera *f* laundress, laundrywoman, washerwoman; (*orn*) sandpiper
lavandero *m* launderer, laundryman
lavándula *f* lavender
lavao·jos *m* (*pl -jos*) eyecup
lavaparabri·sas *m* (*pl -sas*) windshield washer
lavapla·tos (*pl -tos*) *mf* (*persona*) dishwasher || *m* (*aparato*) dishwasher; (*Chile*) kitchen sink
lavar *tr* & *ref* to wash
lavativa *f* enema; (*coll*) annoyance, bore
lavatorio *m* washing; washstand; toilet; (*ceremonia de lavar los pies*) maundy; (*med*) wash, lotion; (*Am*) washroom
lavazas *fpl* dirty water, wash water
laxante *adj* & *m* laxative
laxar *tr* to ease, to slack; (*el vientre*) to loosen
la·xo -xa *adj* lax, slack; (*fig*) lax, loose
laya *f* spade; kind, quality
layar *tr* to spade, dig with a spade
lazada *f* bowknot
lazar §60 *tr* to lasso
lazarillo *m* blind man's guide
lazari·no -na *adj* leprous || *mf* leper
lázaro *m* raggedy beggar; **estar hecho un lázaro** to be full of sores
lazo *m* bow, knot, tie; lasso, lariat, snare, trap; bond, tie; **armar lazo a** (*coll*) to set a trap for; **caer en el lazo** (*coll*) to fall into the trap; **lazo de amor** truelove knot; **lazo de unión** (*fig*) tie, bond
Ldo. *abbr* **Licenciado**
le *pron pers* to him, to her, to it; to you; him; you
leal *adj* loyal, faithful; reliable, trustworthy || *m* loyalist
lealtad *f* loyalty; reliability, trustworthiness
le·brel -brela *mf* whippet, small greyhound
lebrillo *m* earthen washtub
lebrón *m* large hare; (*coll*) coward; (*Mex*) slicker
lección *f* lesson; (*interpretación de un pasaje*) reading; **dar la lección** to recite one's lesson; **echar** or **señalar lección** to assign the lesson; **tomar una lección a** to hear the lesson of
leccionista *mf* private tutor
lecti·vo -va *adj* school (*e.g., day*)
lec·tor -tora *adj* reading || *mf* reader || *m* foreign-language teacher; (*empleado que anota el consumo registrado por el contador de agua, gas o*

electricidad) meter reader; **lector mental** mind reader

lectura *f* reading; broad culture; public lecture; college subject; (*interpretación de un pasaje*) reading; (elec) playback; (typ) pica; **lectura de la mente** mind reading

lechada *f* grout; whitewash; (*para hacer papel*) pulp; (CAm, Mex, W-I) whitewash

lechar *tr* (Am) to milk; (CAm, Mex, W-I) to whitewash

leche *f* milk; **estar con la leche en los labios** to lack experience, to be young and inexperienced; **leche de manteca** buttermilk; **leche desnatada** skim milk; **leche en polvo** milk powder

lechecillas *fpl* sweetbread

lechera *f* milkmaid, dairymaid; (*vasija para guardar la leche*) milk can; (*vasija para servir la leche*) milk pitcher

lechería *f* dairy, creamery

leche·ro -ra *adj* (*que da leche*) milch; (*perteneciente a la leche*) milk; (*cicatero*) (coll) stingy || *m* milkman, dairyman || *f see* **lechera**

lecho *m* bed; (*especie de sofá*) couch; (*cauce de río*) bed; layer, stratum; **abandonar el lecho** to get up (*from illness*); **lecho de plumas** (fig) feather bed

le·chón -chona *adj* (coll) filthy, sloppy || *mf* suckling pig; (*persona sucia, desaseada*) (coll) pig || *m* pig || *f* sow

lecho·so -sa *adj* milky || *m* papaya (*tree*) || *f* papaya (*fruit*)

lechuga *f* lettuce; head of lettuce; (*fuelle formado en la tela*) frill; **lechuga romana** romaine lettuce

lechugui·no -na *adj* stylish, sporty || *m* dandy || *f* stylish young lady

lechuza *f* barn owl, screech owl; (coll) owllike woman

lechu·zo -za *adj* owlish; (*muleto*) yearling || *m* bill collector; summons server; (coll) owllike fellow || *f see* **lechuza**

leer §43 *tr* to read || *intr* to read; to lecture; **leer en** to read (*someone's thoughts*) || *ref* to read, e.g., **este libro se lee con facilidad** this book reads easily

leg. *abbr* legal, legislatura

lega *f* lay sister

legación *f* legation

legado *m* (*don que se hace por testamento*) legacy; (*enviado diplomático*) legate

legajo *m* file, docket, dossier

legal *adj* legal; faithful, prompt, right

legalidad *f* legality; faithfulness, promptness

legalizar §60 *tr* to legalize; to authenticate

légamo *m* slime, ooze

legamo·so -sa *adj* slimy, oozy

legaña *f* gum (*on edge of eyelids*)

legaño·so -sa *adj* gummy

legar §44 *tr* to bequeath, to will

legata·rio -ria *mf* legatee

legenda·rio -ria *adj* legendary

legible *adj* legible

legión *f* legion

legislación *f* legislation

legisla·dor -dora *adj* legislating || *mf* legislator

legislar *intr* to legislate

legislati·vo -va *adj* legislative

legislatura *f* session of a legislature; (Am) legislature

legista *m* law professor; law student

legitimar *tr* to legitimate; to legitimize

legitimidad *f* legitimacy

legíti·mo -ma *adj* legitimate

le·go -ga *adj* lay; uninformed || *m* layman; lay brother || *f see* **lega**

legua *f* league; **a leguas** far, far away

leguleyo *m* pettifogger

legumbre *f* (*hortaliza*) vegetable; (bot) legume; (Chile) vegetable stew

leíble *adj* legible, readable

leída *f* reading

leí·do -da *adj* well-read; **leído y escribido** (coll) posing as learned || *f see* **leída**

lejanía *f* distance, remoteness

leja·no -na *adj* distant, remote; (*pariente*) distant

lejía *f* lye; wash water; (coll) severe rebuke

lejiadora *f* washing machine

lejos *adv* far; **a lo lejos** in the distance; **de lejos** or **desde lejos** from a distance || *m* glimpse; look from afar; **tener buen lejos** to look good at a distance

le·lo -la *adj* stupid, inane

lema *m* motto, slogan; theme

len *adj* soft, flossy

lena *f* spirit, vigor; breathing

lencería *f* linen goods, dry goods; linen closet; dry-goods store

lence·ro -ra *mf* linen dealer, dry-goods dealer

lendrera *f* fine-toothed comb

lendro·so -sa *adj* nitty, lousy

lene *adj* (*suave al tacto*) soft; (*ligero*) light; kind, agreeable

lengua *f* (anat) tongue; (*idioma*) language, tongue; (*de tierra, de fuego, de zapato; badajo de campana; lengua de un animal usada como alimento*) tongue; **buscar la lengua a** (coll) to pick a fight with; **dar la lengua** (coll) to chew the rag; **hacerse lenguas de** (coll) to rave about; **írsele a** (*uno*) **la lengua** (coll) to blab; **lengua madre** or **materna** mother tongue (*language from which another is derived*); **lengua materna** mother tongue (*language acquired by reason of nationality*); **morderse la lengua** to hold one's tongue; **tener en la lengua** (coll) to have on the tip of one's tongue; **tener la lengua gorda** (coll) to talk thick; (coll) to be drunk; **tener mala lengua** (coll) to be blasphemous; (coll) to have an evil tongue; **tener mucha lengua** (coll) to be a great talker; **tirar de la lengua a** (coll) to draw out; **tomar en lenguas** (coll) to gossip about; **tomar lengua** or **lenguas** to pick up news

lenguado *m* sole

lenguaje *m* language

lengua·raz (*pl* **-races**) *adj* foul-mouthed, scurrilous; polyglot || *mf* linguist
len·guaz *adj* (*pl* **-guaces**) garrulous
lengüeta *f* (*de la balanza*) pointer, needle; (*del zapato*) tongue; (anat) epiglottis; (carp) tongue; (*de un instrumento de viento*) (mus) reed; (Chile) paper cutter; (Mex) petticoat fringe; (SAm) chatterbox
lengüetada *f* licking, lapping
lengüetear *intr* to stick the tongue out; to flicker, to flutter; (Am) to jabber, to rant
lengüilar·go -ga *adj* (coll) foul-mouthed, scurrilous
lengüisu·cio -cia *adj* (Mex, P-R) foul-mouthed, scurrilous
lenidad *f* lenience
lenocinio *m* pandering, procuring
lente *m* & *f* lens; **lente de aumento** magnifying glass; **lente de contacto** or **lente invisible** contact lens; **lentes** *mpl* nose glasses; **lentes de nariz** or **de pinzas** pince-nez
lenteja *f* lentil; (*del reloj*) bob, pendulum bob
lentejuela *f* sequin, spangle
lentitud *f* slowness
len·to -ta *adj* slow; sticky; (*fuego*) low
leña *f* firewood, kindling wood; **cargar de leña** (coll) to give a drubbing to; **llevar leña al monte** to carry coals to Newcastle
leña·dor -dora *mf* woodcutter || *m* woodsman
leñame *m* lumber, timber; stock of firewood
leñero *m* wood merchant; wood purchaser; (*sitio donde se guarda la leña*) woodshed
leño *m* (*madera*) wood; (*tronco de árbol, limpio de ramas*) log; (coll) sap, blockhead; (poet) ship, vessel; **dormir como un leño** to sleep like a log
leño·so -sa *adj* woody
león *m* lion
leona *f* lioness
leona·do -da *adj* tawny, fulvous
leonera *f* lion cage, den of lions; (coll) dive, gambling joint; (coll) junk room, lumber room
leonero *m* lion keeper; (coll) keeper of a gambling joint
leontina *f* watch chain
leopardo *m* leopard
leopoldina *f* watch fob; (mil) Spanish shako
leotardo *m* leotard
lepe *m* (Ven) flip in the ear; **saber más que Lepe** to be wide-awake
leperada *f* (CAm, Mex) coarseness, vulgarity
lepisma *f* (ent) silver fish, fish moth
lepori·no -na *adj* hare, harelike
lepra *f* leprosy
leprosería *f* leper house
lepro·so -sa *adj* leprous || *mf* leper
ler·do -da *adj* slow, dull; coarse, crude
lesbianismo *m* lesbianism
les·bio -bia *adj* & *mf* Lesbian || *f* (*mujer homosexual*) Lesbian, lesbian
lesión *f* harm, hurt; (pathol) lesion

lesionar *tr* to harm, hurt, injure
lesi·vo -va *adj* harmful, injurious
lesna *f* awl
le·so -sa *adj* hurt, harmed, injured; wounded; offended; perverted; (SAm) simple, foolish
leste *m* (naut) east
letal *adj* lethal, deadly
letame *m* manure
letanía *f* litany; (*enumeración seguida*) (coll) litany
letárgi·co -ca *adj* lethargic
letargo *m* lethargy
letargo·so -sa *adj* lethargic
le·tón -tona *adj* Lettish || *mf* Lett || *m* (*idioma*) Lettish, Lett
Letonia *f* Latvia
letra *f* (*del alfabeto*) letter; (*modo de escribir propio de una persona*) hand, handwriting; (*de una canción*) words, lyric; (com) draft; (typ) type; (*sentido material*) (fig) letter; **a la letra** (*al pie de la letra*) to the letter; **a letra vista** (com) at sight; **bellas letras** belles lettres; **cuatro letras** or **dos letras** (*esquela, cartita*) a line; **en letras de molde** in print; **escribir en letra de molde** to print; **las letras y las armas** the pen and the sword; **letra a la vista** (com) sight draft; **letra de cambio** (com) bill of exchange; **letra de mano** handwriting; **letra de imprenta** (typ) type; **letra de mano** handwriting; **letra de molde** printed letter; **letra menuda** fine print; (fig) cunning; **letra muerta** dead letter; **letra negrilla** (typ) boldface; **letra redonda** or **redondilla** (typ) roman; **letras** (*literatura*) letters; (coll) a few words, a line; **primeras letras** elementary education, three R's
letra·do -da *adj* learned, lettered; (coll) pedantic || *m* lawyer
letrero *m* sign, notice; (*p.ej., en una botella*) label
letrina *f* privy, latrine; (*cloaca*) sewer; (*cosa sucia*) (fig) cesspool
letrista *mf* lyricist, writer of lyrics (*for songs*); calligrapher, engrosser
leucemia *f* leukemia
leucorrea *f* leucorrhea
leudar *tr* to leaven, to ferment with yeast || *ref* (*la masa con la levadura*) to rise
leu·do -da *adj* leavened, fermented
leva *f* weighing anchor; (mach) cam; (mil) levy
levada *f* (*de la espada, el florete, etc.*) flourish; (*de los astros*) rise; (*del émbolo*) stroke
levadi·zo -za *adj* (*puente*) lift
levadura *f* leaven; leavening; yeast; (*tabla*) board; **levadura comprimida** yeast cake; **levadura de cerveza** brewer's yeast; **levadura en polvo** baking powder
levantaco·ches *m* (*pl* **-ches**) auto jack
levantada *f* rising, getting up (*from bed or from sickbed*)
levantamiento *m* rise, elevation; insurrection, revolt, uprising; **levantamiento del cadáver** inquest; **levantamiento del censo** census taking; **le-**

le
le

vantamiento de planos surveying

levantar *tr* to raise, to lift, to elevate; to agitate, rouse, stir up; (*una sesión*) to adjourn; (*la mesa*) to clear; (*la voz*) to raise; (*el campo*) to break; (*gente para el ejército; un sitio; fondos*) to raise; (*el ancla*) to weigh; to straighten up; to build, construct, erect; to establish, found; **levantar casa** to break up housekeeping; **levantar planos** to make a survey || *ref* to rise; (*de la cama*) to get up; (*de una silla*) to stand up; to straighten up; (*sublevarse*) to rise up, rebel

levantaválvu·las *m* (*pl* **-las**) valve lifter

levantaventana *m* sash lift

levante *m* east; (*viento*) levanter || **Levante** *m* (*países de la parte oriental del Mediterráneo*) Levant; northeastern Mediterranean shores of Spain, especially around Valencia, Alicante, and Murcia

levanti·no -na *adj* Levantine; of the northeastern Mediterranean shores of Spain || *mf* Levantine; native or inhabitant of the northeastern Mediterranean shores of Spain

levar *tr* (*el ancla*) to weigh || *ref* to set sail

leve *adj* (*de poco peso*) light; slight, trivial, trifling

levedad *f* lightness; trivialness

leviatán *m* (Bib & fig) leviathan

levita *m* deacon || *f* coat, frock coat

levitón *m* heavy frock coat

léxi·co -ca *adj* lexical || *m* lexicon; (*caudal de voces de un autor*) vocabulary; (*conjunto de vocablos de una lengua o dialecto*) wordstock

lexicografía *f* lexicography

lexicográfi·co -ca *adj* lexicographic(al)

lexicógra·fo -fa *mf* lexicographer

lexicología *f* lexicology

lexicón *m* lexicon

ley *f* law; loyalty, devotion; norm, standard; (*de un metal*) fineness; **a ley de caballero** on the word of a gentleman; **de buena ley** sterling, genuine; **ley de la selva** law of the jungle; **ley del menor esfuerzo** line of least resistance; **ley marcial** martial law; **ley seca** dry law; **tener** or **tomar ley a** to become devoted to; **venir contra una ley** to break a law

leyenda *f* legend

leyente *adj* reading || *mf* reader

lezna *f* awl

lía *f* plaited esparto rope; **lías** lees, dregs

lianza *f* (Chile) account, credit (*in a store*)

liar §77 *tr* to tie, bind; to tie up, wrap up; (*un cigarrillo*) to roll; (coll) to embroil, to involve; **liarlas** (coll) to beat it; (coll) to kick the bucket || *ref* to join together, to be associated; to have a liaison; (coll) to become embroiled, become involved; **liárselos** (coll) to roll one's own (*i.e., cigarrettes*)

libación *f* libation; (*acción de beber vino u otro licor*) libation

liba·nés -nesa *adj* & *mf* Lebanese

Líbano, el Lebanon

libar *tr* to suck; to taste, to sip || *intr* to pour out a libation; to imbibe

libelo *m* lampoon, libel; (law) petition

libélula *f* dragonfly

liberación *f* liberation; (*cancelación de la carga que grava un inmueble*) redemption; (*de una cuenta*) settlement, closing; quittance

liberal *adj* liberal; (*expedito*) quick, ready; (pol) liberal; (*de amplias miras*) (Arg) liberal-minded || *mf* (pol) liberal

liberalidad *f* liberality

liberar *tr* to free

libertad *f* liberty, freedom; **libertad de cátedra** academic freedom; **libertad de cultos** freedom of worship; **libertad de empresa** free enterprise; **libertad de enseñanza** academic freedom; **libertad de imprenta** freedom of the press; **libertad de los mares** freedom of the seas; **libertad de palabra** freedom of speech, free speech; **libertad de reunión** freedom of assembly; **libertad vigilada** probation; **plena libertad** free hand; **tomarse la libertad de** to take the liberty to

liberta·do -da *adj* bold, daring; free, brash, unrestrained

liberta·dor -dora *mf* liberator

libertar *tr* to liberate, to set free; (*de un peligro, la muerte, etc.*) to save

liberta·rio -ria *adj* anarchistic

libertinaje *m* licentiousness; impiety

liberti·no -na *adj* & *mf* libertine

liber·to -ta *mf* (law) probationer || *m* freedman || *m* freedwoman

libídine *f* lewdness, lust; (*impulso a las actividades sexuales*) libido

libidino·so -sa *adj* libidinous

libido *f* libido

libra *f* pound; **libra esterlina** pound sterling

libraco or **libracho** *m* (coll) trashy book

libra·do -da *mf* (com) drawee

libra·dor -dora *mf* (com) drawer

libranza *f* (com) draft; **libranza postal** money order

librar *tr* to free; to save, to spare; (*la esperanza*) to place; (*batalla*) to give, to join; (com) to draw || *intr* to be delivered, to give birth; (*una religiosa*) to receive a visitor in the locutory; (com) to draw; **librar bien** to come off well, to succeed; **librar mal** to come off badly, to fail || *ref* to free oneself; to escape

libre *adj* free; free, brash, outspoken; free, unmarried; free, loose, licentious; innocent, guiltless; **libre de culpa** no-fault (*divorce, insurance*); **libre de porte** postage prepaid

librea *f* livery

librecambio *m* free trade

librecambista *m* freetrader

librepensa·dor -dora *adj* freethinking || *mf* freethinker

librería *f* bookstore, bookshop; book business; (*mueble*) bookshelf; **librería de viejo** second-hand bookshop

libreril *adj* book

librero *m* bookseller; (*encuadernador*) bookbinder; (Cuba, Mex) bookshelf
libres·co -ca *adj* bookish
libreta *f* notebook; **libreta de banco** bankbook
libreto *m* (mus) libretto
librillo *m* earthen washtub; (*de papel de fumar, de sellos, etc.*) book
libro *m* book; **ahorcar los libros** (coll) to become a dropout; **a libro abierto** at sight; **hacer libro nuevo** (coll) to turn over a new leaf; **libro a la rústica** paperbound book; **libro de caballerías** romance of chivalry; **libro de cocina** cookbook; **libro de cheques** checkbook; **libro de chistes** joke book; **libro de lance** second-hand book; **libro de mayor venta** best seller; **libro de memoria** memo book; **libro de oro** guest book; **libro de recuerdos** scrapbook; **libro de teléfonos** telephone book; **libro de texto** textbook; **libro diario** day book; **libro en rústica** paperbound book; **libro mayor** (com) ledger; **libro talonario** checkbook, stub book
libro-registro *m* (com) book
licencia *f* license; leave of absence; (mil) furlough; **licencia absoluta** (mil) discharge; **licencia por enfermedad** sick leave
licencia·do -da *adj* pedantic || *mf* licenciate || *m* lawyer; (mil) discharged soldier; (coll) university student (*wearing the long student gown*)
licenciar *tr* to license; to allow, permit; to confer the degree of licenciate or master on; (mil) to discharge || *ref* to receive the degree of licenciate or master; to become dissolute; (mil) to be discharged
licenciatura *f* licenciate, master's degree; graduation with a licenciate or master's degree; work leading to a licenciate or master's degree
licencio·so -sa *adj* licentious
liceo *m* (*sociedad literaria, establecimiento de enseñanza popular*) lyceum; (*instituto de segunda enseñanza*) (Chile) lycée; (Mex) primary school
licitación *f* bidding
licita·dor -dora *mf* bidder
licitar *tr* to bid on; (Arg) to buy at auction, to sell at auction || *intr* to bid
líci·to -ta *adj* fair, just; licit, legal
licor *m* (*bebida espirituosa; cuerpo líquido*) liquor; (*bebida espirituosa preparada por mezcla de azúcar y substancias aromáticas*) liqueur
licorera *f* cellaret
licorista *mf* distiller; liquor dealer
licoro·so -sa *adj* spirituous, alcoholic; (*vino*) rich, generous
licuar §21 & *regular tr* to liquefy
lid *f* fight, combat; dispute, argument; **en buena lid** by fair means
líder *m* leader
lidia *f* fight; bullfight
lidiadera *f* (Ecuad) quarreling, bickering

lidia·dor -dora *mf* fighter || *m* bullfighter
lidiar *tr* (*un toro*) to fight || *intr* to fight; **lidiar con** to fight with; to have to put up with
liebre *f* hare; (*hombre cobarde*) (coll) coward
liendre *f* nit
lien·to -ta *adj* damp, dank
lienza *f* strip of cloth
lienzo *m* linen, linen cloth; linen handkerchief; (*de edificio o pared*) face, front; (*pintura sobre lienzo*) canvas; **lienzo de la Verónica** veronica (*representing face of Christ*)
liga *f* (*cinta elástica para asegurar las medias*) garter; (*aleación*) alloy; (*materia pegajosa para cazar pájaros*) birdlime; (*confederación, alianza*) league; (*muérdago*) mistletoe; band; **liga de goma** rubber band
ligado *m* (mus & typ) ligature
ligadura *f* tie, bond; (mus) ligature, glide; (surg) ligature
ligamento *m* ligament
ligar §44 *tr* to tie, bind; to join, combine; to alloy; (*bebidas*) to mix; (surg) to ligate || *ref* to league together; to be committed; to be bound or attached (*e.g., in friendship*)
ligereza *f* lightness; speed, rapidity; fickleness, inconstancy; tactlessness
lige·ro -ra *adj* light; (*té*) weak; (*tejido*) light, thin; quick; slight; **a la ligera** lightly; quickly; unceremoniously; **de ligero** thoughtlessly, rashly; **ligero de cascos** light-headed, scatter-brained; **ligero de lengua** loose-tongued; **ligero de pies** light-footed; **ligero de ropa** scantily clad || **ligero** *adv* (Am) fast, rapidly
lignito *m* lignite
ligustro *m* privet
lija *f* (*pez*) dogfish; (*papel que sirve para pulir*) sandpaper; **darse lija** (W-I) to boast, brag, pat oneself on the back
lijar *tr* to sand, to sandpaper
lila *adj* (coll) silly, simple || *m* lilac (*color*) || *f* lilac (*plant and flower*)
li·lac *f* (*pl* **-laques**) lilac
liliputiense *adj* & *mf* Lilliputian
lima *f* (*herramienta*) file; sweet lime; sweet-lime tree; (*del tejado*) hip; hip rafter; correcting, polishing; **lima de uñas** nail file; **lima hoya** valley (*of roof*)
limadura *f* filing; (*partecillas*) filings
limalla *f* filings
limar *tr* to file; to file down; to polish, touch up; to smooth, smooth over; (*cercenar*) to curtail
limaza *f* (*babosa*) slug; (Ven) large file
limazo *m* slime, sliminess
limbo *m* (*borde*) edge; (theol) limbo; **estar en el limbo** (coll) to be quite distraught
limen *m* (physiol, psychol & fig) threshold
limenso *m* (Chile) honeydew melon
lime·ño -ña *adj* & *mf* Limean
limero *m* sweet-lime tree
limita·do -da *adj* limited; dull-witted

limitador _m_ — **limitador de corriente**
clock meter; slot meter
limitar _tr_ to limit; to cut down, reduce
‖ _intr_ — **limitar con** to border on
límite _m_ limit; boundary, border
limítrofe _adj_ bordering
limo _m_ slime, mud
limón _m_ lemon; lemon tree; (_de un
coche o carro_) shaft
limonada _f_ lemonade
limoncillo _m_ citronella
limonera _f_ shaft
limonero _m_ lemon tree
limosna _f_ alms
limosnear _intr_ to beg
limosne·ro -ra _adj_ almsgiving, charitable ‖ _mf_ almsgiver; (Am) beggar ‖
_m_ alms box
limo·so -sa _adj_ slimy, muddy
limpia _f_ cleaning
limpiaba·rros _m_ (_pl_ **-rros**) scraper, foot
scraper
limpiabo·tas _m_ (_pl_ **-tas**) bootblack
limpiacrista·les _m_ (_pl_ **-les**) windshield
washer
limpiachimene·as _m_ (_pl_ **-as**) chimney
sweep
limpiadien·tes _m_ (_pl_ **-tes**) toothpick
limpia·dor -dora _adj_ cleaning ‖ _mf_
cleaner
limpiadura _f_ cleaning; **limpiaduras**
cleanings, dirt
limpiama·nos _m_ (_pl_ **-nos**) (Guat, Hond)
towel
limpiamente _adv_ in a clean manner;
with ease, skillfully; simply, sincerely;
unselfishly
limpiameta·les _m_ (_pl_ **-les**) metal polish
limpianieve _m_ snowplow
limpiaparabri·sas _m_ (_pl_ **-sas**) windshield
wiper
limpia·piés _m_ (_pl_ **-piés**) (Mex) door mat
limpiapi·pas _m_ (_pl_ **-pas**) pipe cleaner
limpiaplu·mas _m_ (_pl_ **-mas**) penwiper
limpiar _tr_ to clean; (_purificar_) to
cleanse; (_de culpas_) to exonerate; (_un
árbol_) to clean out, to prune; (_zapa-
tos_) to shine; (_hurtar_) (coll) to
snitch; (_a una persona en el juego_)
(coll) to clean out; (_dinero en el
juego_) (coll) to clean up; (mil) to
mop up; **limpiarle a uno de** to clean
someone out of ‖ _ref_ to clean, to
clean oneself
limpiau·ñas _m_ (_pl_ **-ñas**) nail cleaner,
orange stick
limpiaví·as _m_ (_pl_ **-as**) track cleaner
limpieza _f_ (_acción de limpiar_) cleaning;
(_calidad de limpio_) cleanness; (_hábito
del aseo_) cleanliness; neatness, tidiness; honesty; chastity; ease, skill;
(_observancia de las reglas en los
juegos_) fair play; **limpieza de bolsa**
(coll) emptiness of the pocketbook;
limpieza de la casa house cleaning;
limpieza en seco dry cleaning
lim·pio -pia _adj_ clean; (_que tiene el
hábito del aseo_) cleanly; neat, tidy;
honest, chaste; clear, free; **dejar limpio** (coll) to clean out; **en limpio**
(com) net; **limpio de polvo y paja**
(coll) free, for nothing; (coll) net,
after deducting expenses; **poner en**

limpio to make a clear or fair copy
of; **quedar limpio** (coll) to be cleaned
out; **sacar en limpio** to make a clear
or clean copy of; to deduce, to understand ‖ _f_ see **limpia** ‖ **limpio** _adv_
fair; cleanly; **jugar limpio** to play
fair
limpión _m_ (_limpiadura ligera_) lick;
(coll) cleaner; (Col) scolding; (Col,
Ven) dustcloth; (Ecuad) dishcloth
limusina _f_ limousine
lín. _abbr_ **línea**
lina _f_ (Chile) coarse wool
linaje _m_ lineage; class, description;
linaje humano mankind
linaju·do -da _adj_ highborn ‖ _mf_ highborn person
linaza _f_ flaxseed, linseed
lince _adj_ keen, shrewd, discerning;
(_ojos_) keen ‖ _m_ lynx; (fig) keen person
lincear _tr_ (coll) to see into
linchamiento _m_ lynching
linchar _tr_ to lynch
lindante _adj_ bordering, adjoining
lindar _intr_ to border, be contiguous;
lindar con to border on
linde _m_ & _f_ limit, boundary
linde·ro -ra _adj_ bordering, adjoining ‖
_m_ edge; (Am) boundary stone, landmark ‖ _f_ limit, boundary; (bot) spice-
bush
lindeza _f_ prettiness, niceness; elegance;
witticism, funny remark; (coll) flirting; **lindezas** (coll) insults
lin·do -da _adj_ pretty, nice; fine, perfect; **de lo lindo** (coll) a lot, a great
deal; wonderfully ‖ _m_ (coll) dude,
sissy
lindura _f_ prettiness, niceness
línea _f_ line; (_contorno de una figura,
un vestido_) lines; figure, waistline;
conservar la línea to keep one's
figure; **leer entre líneas** to read between the lines; **línea de agua** water
line; **línea de batalla** line of battle;
línea de empalme (rr) branch line;
línea de flotación water line; **línea de
fuego** firing line; **línea de fuerza**
(elec) power line; (phys) line of
force; **línea del partido** party line;
línea de mira line of sight; **línea de
montaje** assembly line; **línea de puntos** dotted line; **línea de tiro** (mil) line
of fire; **línea férrea** railway; **línea internacional de cambio de fecha** international date line; **línea suplementaria** (mus) added line, ledger
line
lineal _adj_ linear
lineamentos _mpl_ lineaments
linfa _f_ lymph; (poet) water
linfáti·co -ca _adj_ lymphatic
lingote _m_ ingot, slug; (naut) ballast bar
lingual _adj_ & _f_ lingual
lingüista _mf_ linguist
lingüísti·co -ca _adj_ linguistic ‖ _f_ linguistics
linimento _m_ liniment
lino _m_ flax; (_tela_) linen; (poet) sail
linóleo _m_ linoleum
linón _m_ lawn
linotipia _f_ linotype

linotípi·co -ca adj linotype
linotipista mf linotype operator
linotipo m linotype
linterna f lantern; **linterna eléctrica** flashlight
lío m bundle; (de papeles) batch; (coll) muddle, mess; (coll) liaison, affair; **armar un lío** (coll) to raise a row; **hacerse un lío** (coll) to get into a jam
liofilizar tr to freeze-dry
lionesa — a la lionesa (culin) lyonnaise
liorna f (coll) hubbub, uproar ‖ **Liorna** f Leghorn
lio·so -sa adj (coll) trouble-making; (coll) knotty, troublesome
liq.ⁿ abbr **liquidación**
líq.º abbr **líquido**
liquen m lichen
liquidar tr to liquefy; (com) to liquidate ‖ intr (com) to liquidate ‖ ref to liquefy
liquidez f liquidity
líqui·do -da adj & m liquid; (com) net ‖ f (phonet) liquid
lira f (mus) lyre; (numen de un poeta) inspiration; poems, poetry
lírica f lyric poetry
líri·co -ca adj lyric(al); (músico, operístico) lyric; (Am) fantastic, utopian ‖ m lyric poet; (Arg, Ven) visionary ‖ f see **lírica**
lirio m (bot) iris; **lirio blanco** (azucena) Madonna lily; **lirio de agua** (bot) calla, calla lily; **lirio de los valles** (bot) lily of the valley
lirismo m lyricism; spellbinding; (Am) fancy, illusion
lirón m (bot) water plantain; (zool) dormouse; (coll) sleepyhead
lis m (bot) lily ‖ f (bot) iris; (heral) fleur-de-lis
Lisboa f Lisbon
lisia·do -da adj hurt, injured; crippled; (muy deseoso) eager ‖ mf cripple
lisiar tr to hurt, injure; to cripple ‖ ref to become crippled
lisimaquia f loosestrife
li·so -sa adj even, smooth; (vestido) plain, unadorned; (franco, sincero) simple, plain-dealing; (Am) brash, insolent; **liso y llano** (coll) simple, easy
lisonja f flattery
lisonjear tr to flatter; to please ‖ intr to flatter
lisonje·ro -ra adj flattering; pleasing ‖ mf flatterer
lista f list; (tira) strip; (en un tejido) colored stripe; (recuento en alta voz de las personas que deben estar en un lugar) roll call; **lista de bajas** casualty list; **lista de comidas** bill of fare; **lista de correos** general delivery; **lista de espera** waiting list; **lista de frecuencia** frequency list; **lista de pagos** payroll
listar tr to list
listero m roll keeper, timekeeper
lis·to -ta adj ready; quick, prompt; alert, wide-awake; **estar listo** to be ready; to be finished; **listo de manos** (coll) light-fingered; **pasarse de listo** to be shrewd, to be clever ‖ f see **lista**
listón m (cinta) ribbon, tape; (pedazo de tabla angosta) lath, strip of wood
listonado m lath, lathing
lisura f evenness, smoothness; plainness; simpleness, candor; (Am) brashness, insolence
lit. abbr **literalmente**
lite f lawsuit
litera f (vehículo llevado por hombres o por animales) litter; (cama fija en los camarotes) berth; **litera alta** upper berth; **litera baja** lower berth
literal adj literal
litera·rio -ria adj literary
litera·to -ta adj literary ‖ mf literary person; **literatos** literati
literatura f literature; **literatura de escape** or **de evasión** escape literature
litigación s litigation
litigante adj & mf litigant
litigar §44 tr & intr to litigate
litigio m litigation, lawsuit; argument, dispute
litigio·so -sa adj litigious
litina s (chem) lithia
litio m (chem) lithium
litisexpensas fpl (law) costs
litografía f (arte de grabar en piedra para la reproducción en estampa) lithography; (estampa) lithograph
litografiar §77 tr to lithograph
litógra·fo -fa mf lithographer
litoral adj coastal, littoral ‖ m coast, shore
litro m liter
liturgia f liturgy
litúrgi·co -ca adj liturgic(al)
liviandad f lightness; inconstancy, fickleness; lewdness
livia·no -na adj light; inconstant, fickle; lewd ‖ m leading donkey; **livianos** lights, lungs
lívi·do -da adj livid
liza f combat, fight; (campo para lidiar) lists; **entrar en liza** to enter the lists
lo art def neut (used with masc sg form of adj) the, e.g., **lo bueno** the good; what is, e.g., **lo útil** what is useful; **lo mío** what is mine; (used with adv or inflected adj) the + noun, e.g., **lo aprisa que habla** the speed with which he speaks; **lo tacaños que son** the stinginess of them; how, e.g., **Vd., no sabe lo felices que son** you do not know how happy they are; **lo más** as . . . as, e.g., **lo más temprano posible** as early as possible ‖ pron pers masc him, it; you; (with estar, ser, parecer, and the like, it stands for an adjective or noun understood and is either not translated or is translated by 'so'), e.g., **Vd. está preparado pero ella no lo está** you are ready but she is not ‖ pron dem that; **de lo que** + verb than + verb, e.g., **ese libro ha costado más dinero de lo que vale** that book cost more money than it is worth; **lo de** the matter of, the question of, e.g., **lo de sus deudas** the matter of your debts; **lo de que** the fact that, the statement that; **lo de siempre** the same old story; **lo que** what, that which; **todo lo que** all

(that), e.g., **me dió todo lo que tenía** he gave me all he had

loa *f* praise; (*del teatro antiguo*) prologue; short dramatic poem

loable *adj* laudable, praiseworthy

loar *tr* to praise

loba *f* she-wolf; ridge

lobagante *m* lobster (*Homarus*)

lobanillo *m* wen, cyst

lobato *m* wolf cub

lo·bo -ba *adj & mf* (Mex) half-breed || *m* wolf; **coger** or **pillar un lobo** (coll) to go on a jag; **desollar** or **dormir un lobo** (coll) to sleep off a drunk; **lobo de mar** (ichth) sea wolf; (coll) old salt, sea dog; **lobo solitario** (fig) lone wolf || *f* see **loba**

lóbre·go -ga *adj* dark, dismal; gloomy

lobreguez *f* darkness; gloominess

lobu·no -na *adj* wolf, wolfish

locación *f* lease

local *adj* local || *m* quarters, place

localidad *f* (*lugar, sitio*) location, locality; (*plaza en un tren*) accommodations; (theat) seat

localización *f* localization; location; **localización de averías** trouble shooting

localizar §60 *tr* (*limitar a un punto determinado*) to localize; (*determinar el lugar de*) to locate

locería *f* (Am) pottery

loción *f* wash; (pharm) lotion

lo·co -ca *adj* crazy, insane, mad; terrific, wonderful; **estar loco por** (coll) to be crazy about, to be mad about; **loco de amor** madly in love; **loco de atar** (coll) raving mad; **loco perenne** insane, demented; (coll) full of fun; **loco rematado** (coll) stark-mad; **volver loco** to drive crazy || *mf* crazy person, lunatic || *m* (*bufón*) fool

locomotora *f* engine, locomotive; **locomotora de maniobras** shifting engine

locro *m* (SAm) meat and vegetable stew

lo·cuaz *adj* (*pl* **-cuaces**) loquacious

locución *f* expression, locution; idiomatic phrase, idiom

locuela *f* speech, way of speaking

locue·lo -la *adj* (coll) wild, frisky || *f* see **locuela**

locura *f* insanity, madness; folly, madness

locu·tor -tora *mf* announcer, commentator

locutorio *m* (*en un convento de monjas*) parlor, locutory; telephone booth

lodazal *m* mudhole

lodo *m* mud, mire; (*substancia que sirve para cerrar junturas, tapar grietas, etc.*) (chem) lute

lodo·so -sa *adj* muddy

logaritmo *m* logarithm

logia *f* (*p.ej., de francmasones*) lodge; (archit) loggia

lógi·co -ca *adj* logical || *mf* logician || *f* logic

logísti·co -ca *adj* logistic(al) || *f* logistics

logrado -da *adj* successful

lograr *tr* to get, to obtain; to achieve, attain; **lograr + inf** to succeed in + ger || *ref* to be successful

logrear *intr* to be a moneylender; to profiteer

logre·ro -ra *adj* moneylending; profiteering || *mf* moneylender; profiteer; (Chile) sponger

logro *m* attainment, success; gain, profit; usury; **dar** or **prestar a logro** to lend at usurious rates

loma *f* low hill, elevation

Lombardía *f* Lombardy

lombar·do -da *adj & mf* Lombard

lombriguera *f* wormhole in the ground; (bot) tansy

lom·briz *f* (*pl* **-brices**) worm, earthworm; (pathol) worm; (*persona muy alta y delgada*) (coll) beanpole; **lombriz de tierra** earthworm; **lombriz solitaria** tapeworm

lomera *f* (*de la guarnición*) backstrap; (*del tejado*) ridgepole; (bb) backing

lominhies·to -ta *adj* high-backed; (coll) conceited

lomo *m* (*de animal, libro, cuchillo*) back; (*tierra que levanta el arado*) ridge; (*carne de lomo del animal*) loin; (*pliegue del tejido*) crease; spine; **lomos** ribs

lona *f* canvas; sailcloth; (Mex) burlap

loncha *f* slab, flagstone; slice, strip

londinense *adj* London || *mf* Londoner

Londres *m* London; **el Gran Londres** Greater London

longáni·mo -ma *adj* long-suffering

longaniza *f* pork sausage

longevidad *f* longevity

longe·vo -va *adj* long-lived

longitud *f* length; (astr & geog) longitud

lonja *f* exchange, commodity exchange; grocery store; wool warehouse; (*de carne*) slice; (*de cuero*) strip; (*a la entrada de un edificio*) elevated parvis; (Arg) rawhide

lonjeta *f* bower, summerhouse

lonjista *mf* grocer

lontananza *f* (*de una pintura*) background; **en lontananza** in the distance, on the horizon

loor *m* praise

loquear *intr* to talk nonsense, to play the fool; to carry on, to have a high time

loquería *f* (Chile) madhouse, insane asylum

loque·ro -ra *mf* guard in a mental hospital || *m* (Arg) confusion, pandemonium; (Arg) insane asylum

loques·co -ca *adj* crazy; funny, jolly

lord *m* (*pl* **-lores**) lord

lo·ro -ra *adj* dark-brown || *m* parrot; cherry laurel; (Chile) spy; (Chile) glass bedpan; (Chile) third degree

losa *f* slab, flagstone; tomb

losange *m* lozenge; (baseball) diamond

lote *m* lot, share, portion; lottery prize; (Cuba, Mex) remnant; (Arg) dunce, simpleton; (Col) swallow, swig; (*de terreno*) (Cuba, Mex) lot

lotear *tr* (Chile) to divide up, divide into lots

lotería *f* lottery; (*juego casero*) lotto; (*cosa insegura, riesgo*) gamble

lote·ro -ra *mf* vendor of lottery tickets

lotizar §60 *tr* (Peru) to divide into lots

loto *m* lotus

loza *f* (*barro cocido y barnizado*) porcelain; crockery, earthenware; **loza fina** china, chinaware

lozanear *intr* to be luxuriant; to be full of life || *ref* (*deleitarse*) to luxuriate

lozanía *f* luxuriance, verdure; exuberance, vigor; pride, haughtiness

loza·no -na *adj* luxuriant, verdant; exuberant, vigorous; proud, haughty

lubricante *adj & m* lubricant

lubricar §73 *tr* to lubricate

lúbri·co -ca *adj* (*resbaladizo; lascivo*) lubricous (*slippery; lewd*)

lubrificar §73 *tr* to lubricate

lucera *f* skylight

lucerna *f* large chandelier; (*abertura, tronera*) loophole

lucero *m* bright star; (*planeta*) Venus; (*ventanillo en un muro*) light; **lucero del alba** or **de la mañana** morning star; **lucero de la tarde** evening star; **luceros** (poet) eyes

luci·do -da *adj* generous, magnificent; brilliant, successful; sumptuous; (Arg) striking, dashing

lúci·do -da *adj* lucid

luciente *adj* bright, shining

luciérnaga *f* glowworm, firefly

lucifer *m* overbearing fellow || **Lucifer** *m* Lucifer

lucífe·ro -ra *adj* (poet) bright, dazzling || *m* morning star; (Col) match

lucimiento *m* brilliance, luster; show, dash; success; **quedar** or **salir con lucimiento** to come off with flying colors

lu·cio -cia *adj* shiny || *m* salt pool; (*pez*) pike, luce

lucir §45 *tr* to light, light up; to show, display; (*p.ej., un traje nuevo*) to sport; to help; to plaster || *intr* to shine || *ref* to dress up; to come off with great success; (*sobresalir, distinguirse*) to shine; (coll) to flop, e.g., **lucido me quedé** I was a flop

lucrar *tr* to get, obtain || *intr & ref* to profit, make money

lucrati·vo -va *adj* lucrative

lucro *m* gain, profit; **lucros y daños** profit and loss

lucro·so -sa *adj* lucrative

luctuo·so -sa *adj* sad, mournful, gloomy

lucha *f* fight; (*disputa*) quarrel; (*actividad forzada*) struggle; (*combate cuerpo a cuerpo*) wrestling; **lucha de la cuerda** (sport) tug of war; **lucha por la vida** struggle for existence

lucha·dor -dora *mf* fighter; wrestler

luchar *intr* (*combatir*) to fight; (*disputar*) to quarrel; (*esforzarse*) to struggle; (*pelear cuerpo a cuerpo*) to wrestle

ludibrio *m* derision, mockery, scorn

ludir *tr, intr & ref* to rub, rub together

luego *adv* next, then; therefore; soon; **desde luego** right away; of course; **hasta luego** good-bye, so long; **luego como** as soon as; **luego de** after, right after; **luego que** as soon as

luen·go -ga *adj* long

lúes *f* pestilence; **lúes canina** distemper; **lúes venérea** syphilis

lugano *m* (orn) siskin

lugar *m* place; site, spot; job, position; (*espacio*) room, space; (*asiento*) seat; village, hamlet; (geom) locus; **dar lugar** to make room; **dar lugar a** to give cause for; to give rise to; **en lugar de** instead of, in place of; **hacer lugar** to make room; **lugar común** (*expresión trivial*) commonplace; (*retrete*) toilet, water closet; **lugar de cita** tryst; **lugares estrechos** close quarters; **lugar geométrico** locus; **lugar religioso** place of burial

lugarejo *m* hamlet

lugare·ño -ña *adj* village || *mf* villager

lugarteniente *m* lieutenant

luge *m* sled

lúgubre *adj* dismal, gloomy, lugubrious

luir §20 *tr* (naut) to gall, to wear; (Chile) to muss, to rumple; (*vasijas de barro*) (Chile) to polish || *ref* (Chile) to rub, wear away

luisa *f* (bot) lemon verbena

lujo *m* luxury; **de lujo** de luxe; **gastar mucho lujo** to live in high style; **lujo de** abundance of, excess of

lujo·so -sa *adj* luxurious

lujuria *f* lust, lechery

lujuriante *adj* (*lozano*) luxuriant, lush; (*libidinoso*) lustful

lujuriar *intr* to lust, be lustful; (*los animales*) to copulate

lujurio·so -sa *adj* lustful, lecherous || *mf* lecher

lu·lo -la *adj* (Chile) lank, slender || *m* (Chile) bundle

lu·lú *m* (*pl* **-lúes**) spitz dog

lumbago *m* lumbago

lumbre *f* light; fire; (*para encender el cigarrillo*) light; (*hueco en un muro por donde entra la luz*) light; brightness, brilliance; knowledge, learning; **echar lumbre** (coll) to blow one's top; **lumbre del agua** surface of the water; **lumbres** tinderbox; **ni por lumbre** (coll) not for love or money; **ser la lumbre de los ojos de** to be the light of the eyes of

lumbrera *f* lantern, source of light; light, lamp; (*abertura por donde entran el aire y la luz*) louver; sky light; dormer window; air duct, ventilating shaft; (*persona insigne*) light, luminary; (mach) port; **lumbreras** eyes

luminar *m* luminary

luminiscente *adj* luminescent

lumino·so -sa *adj* luminous; (*idea*) bright

luminotecnia *f* lighting engineering

lun. *abbr* **lunes**

luna *f* moon; moonlight; (*tabla de cristal*) plate glass; (*espejo*) mirror; (*de los anteojos*) lens, glass; (coll) caprice, whim; **estar de buena luna** to be in a good mood; **estar de mala luna** to be in a bad mood; **luna de miel** honeymoon; **luna llena** full moon; **luna menguante** waning moon; **luna nueva** new moon; **media luna** half moon; (*figura de cuarto de luna creciente o menguante*) crescent; **quedarse a la luna de Valencia** (coll) to be disappointed

lunar adj lunar ‖ m (mancha de la piel) mole; (punto en un diseño de puntos) polka dot; (fig) stain, blot, stigma; **lunar postizo** beauty spot

lunáti·co -ca adj & mf lunatic

lu·nes m (pl -nes) Monday; **hacer San Lunes** (Am) to knock off on Monday

luneta f (de los anteojos) lens, glass; orchestra seat; (aut) rear window

lunfardo m (Arg) thief; (Am) underworld slang

lupa m magnifying glass

lupanar m brothel, bawdyhouse

lupia mf (Hond) quack, healer ‖ f wen, cyst; **lupias** (Col) small amount of money, small change

lúpulo m (vid) hop; (flores desecadas de la vid) hops

luquete m slice of orange or lemon used to flavor wine; (Chile) bald spot; (en la ropa) (Chile) spot, hole

lu·rio -ria adj (Mex) mad, crazy

lusitanismo m Lusitanism

lusitano -na adj & mf Lusitanian, Portuguese

lustrabo·tas m (pl -tas) (Am) bootblack

lustrar tr to shine, to polish ‖ intr to wander, roam

lustre m shine, polish; luster, gloss; (fama, gloria) (fig) luster

lustrina f (Chile) shoe polish

lustro m five years; chandelier

lustro·so -sa adj shining, bright, lustrous

lutera·no -na adj & mf Lutheran

luto m (señal exterior de duelo) mourning; (duelo, aflicción) sorrow, bereavement; **estar de luto** to be in mourning; **lutos** crape; **luto riguroso** deep mourning

lutocar m (Chile) trash cart

luz f (pl luces) light; window, light; guiding light; (dinero) (coll) money, cash; **a primera luz** at dawn; **a toda luz** or **a todas luces** everywhere; by all means; **dar a luz** to have a child; to give birth to; to bring out, to publish; **entre dos luces** at twilight; (coll) half-seas over; **luces de carretera** (aut) bright lights; **luces de cruce** (aut) dimmers; **luz de balizaje** (aer) marker light; **luz de magnesio** magnesium light; (phot) flash bulb, flashlight; **luz de matrícula** license-plate light; **luz de parada** stop light; **luz trasera** tail light; **sacar a luz** to bring to light; **salir a luz** to come to light; to come out, be published; to take place; **ver la luz** to see the light, see the light of day

Luzbel m Lucifer

Ll

Ll, ll (elle) f fourteenth letter of the Spanish alphabet

llaga f sore, ulcer; sorrow, grief; (entre dos ladrillos) (mas) seam, joint

llagar §44 tr to make sore; to hurt

llama f flame, blaze; marsh, swamp; (zool) llama; (fig) fire, passion; **saltar de las llamas y caer en las brasas** to jump out of the frying pan into the fire

llamada f call; (movimiento con que se llama la atención de uno) sign, signal; knock, ring; reference, reference mark; (mil) call, call to arms; **batir** or **tocar a llamada** (mil) to sound the call to arms; **llamada a filas** (mil) call to the colors; **llamada a quintas** draft call; **llamada por cobrar** collect call

llamadera f goad

llama·do -da adj so-called ‖ f see llamada

llama·dor -dora mf caller ‖ m messenger; door knocker; push button

llamamiento m call; calling, vocation

llamar tr to call; (dar nombre a) to name, to call; to summon; to invoke, call upon; (la atención) to attract ‖ intr to call; (golpear en la puerta) to knock; (hacer sonar la campanilla) to ring; (el viento) (naut) to veer ‖ ref to be called, to be named; **se llama Juan** his name is John

llamarada f blaze, flare-up; (encendimiento repentino del rostro) flush; (fig) flare-up, outburst

llamarón m (Am) flare-up

llamati·vo -va adj showy, loud, flashy, gaudy; (manjar) thirst-raising

llamazar m swamp, marsh

llame m (Chile) bird net, bird trap

llamear intr to blaze, flame, flash

llampo m (Chile) ore

llana f trowel, float; plain; **dar de llana** to smooth with the trowel

llanada f plain

llanero m (Am) ranger, plainsman

llaneza f plainness, simplicity; familiarity; sincerity

lla·no -na adj even, level, smooth; (parecido a un plano geométrico) plane; (sencillo) plain, simple; clear, evident; (palabras) frank; accented on the next to last syllable ‖ m plain; (de la escalera) landing ‖ f see llana

llanque m (Peru) rawhide sandal

llanta f (cerco exterior de la rueda) tire (of iron or rubber); (borde exterior de la rueda) rim; (pieza de hierro más ancha que gruesa) iron flat; **llanta de goma** rubber tire; **llanta de oruga** (de un tractor de oruga) track

llanto m weeping, crying; **en llanto** in tears

llanura f evenness, level, smoothness; (terreno extenso y llano) plain

llapan·go -ga adj (Ecuad) barefooted

llares m pothanger

llave *adj* key ‖ *f* (*pieza para abrir y cerrar las cerraduras*) key; (*herramienta*) wrench; (*grifo*) faucet, spigot, cock; (*de arma de fuego*) cock; (elec) switch; (*de un instrumento de viento*) (mus) key; (*de un enigma, secreto, traducción, cifra; lugar estratégico más propicio*) key; **bajo llave** under lock and key; **echar la llave a** to lock; **llave de caja** socket wrench; **llave de caño** pipe wrench; **llave de cubo** socket wrench; **llave de chispa** flintlock; **llave de estufa** damper; **llave de mandíbulas dentadas** alligator wrench; **llave de paso** stopcock; passkey; **llave de purga** drain cock; **llave espacial** space key; **llave inglesa** monkey wrench; **llave maestra** master key, skeleton key; **llave para tubos** pipe wrench

llave·ro -ra *mf* keeper of the keys; (*carcelero*) turnkey ‖ *m* key ring

llavín *m* latchkey

llegada *f* arrival

llegar §44 *tr* to bring up, bring close ‖ *intr* to arrive; to happen; **llegar a** to arrive at; to reach; to amount to; to be equal to; **llegar a** + *inf* to come to + *inf*; to succeed in + *ger*; **llegar a ser** to become ‖ *ref* to come close

llena *f* flood

llenado *m* filling

llena·dor -dora *adj* (*alimento*) (Chile) filling

llenar *tr* to fill; (*un formulario*) to fill out; (*ciertas condiciones*) to fulfill; to satisfy; (*colmar*) to overwhelm ‖ *intr* (*la luna*) to be full ‖ *ref* to fill, fill up; (coll) to stuff oneself; **llenarse a rebosar** to be filled to overflowing

llene *m* filling; full tank

lle·no -na *adj* full; **lleno a rebosar** full to overflowing; **lleno de goteras** (coll) full of aches and pains ‖ *m* fill, plenty; fulness, full enjoyment; completeness; full moon; (*en el teatro*) full house ‖ *f* see **llena**

lleva or **llevada** *f* carrying, conveying; ride; **lleva gratuita** free ride

llevade·ro -ra *adj* bearable, tolerable

llevar *tr* (*transportar*) to carry; (*traer consigo*) to take; (*conducir*) to lead; to carry away, to take away; (*cuentas, libros; la anotación en los naipes*) to keep; (*la correspondencia con una persona*) to carry on; (*un drama a la pantalla*) to put on; (*buena o mala vida*) to lead; (*aguantar*) to bear, to stand for; (*castigo*) to suffer; to get, obtain; to win; (*cierto precio*) to charge; (*traje, vestido*) to wear; (*armas*) to bear; (*cierto tiempo*) to have been, e.g., **llevo ocho días en cama** I have been in bed for a week; (*ropa*) **a todo llevar** for all kinds of wear; **llevar** (*cierto tiempo*) **a** (*uno*) to be older than (*someone*) by (*a certain age*); (*cierta distancia*) **a** (*uno*) to be ahead of (*someone*) by (*a certain distance*); (*cierto peso*) **a** (*uno*) to be heavier than (*someone*) by (*a certain weight*); **llevarla hecha** (coll) to have it all figured out; **llevar puesto** to wear, to have on; **llevar** + *pp* to have + *pp*, e.g., **lleva conseguidas muchas victorias** he has won many victories ‖ *ref* to carry away; to take, take away; to carry off; to win; to get along; **llevarse algo a alguien** to take something away from someone

lloradue·los *mf* (*pl* -los) crybaby, sniveler

lloralásti·mas *mf* (*pl* -mas) (coll) poverty-crying skinflint

llorar *tr* to weep over; to mourn, lament ‖ *intr* to weep, to cry; (*los ojos*) to water, to run

lloriquear *intr* to whine, to whimper

lloriqueo *m* whining, whimpering

lloro *m* weeping, crying; tears

llo·rón -rona *adj* weeping, crying ‖ *mf* weeper, crybaby ‖ *m* weeping willow; pendulous plume ‖ *f* hired mourner

lloro·so -sa *adj* weepy; sad, tearful

llovedi·zo -za *adj* (*agua*) rain; (*techo*) leaky

llover §47 *tr* (*enviar como lluvia*) to rain ‖ *intr* to rain; **como llovido** unexpectedly; **llueva o no** rain or shine; **llueve** it is raining ‖ *ref* (*el techo*) to leak

llovido *m* stowaway

llovizna *f* drizzle

lloviznar *intr* to drizzle

llovizno·so -sa *adj* moist, damp (*from drizzle*); (Am) drizzly

lluvia *f* rain; rain water; (*copia, muchedumbre*) (fig) shower, downpour; **lluvia radiactiva** fallout, radioactive fallout

lluvio·so -sa *adj* rainy

M

M, m (eme) *f* fifteenth letter of the Spanish alphabet

m. *abbr* **mañana, masculino, meridiano, metro, minuto, muerto**

maca *f* flaw, blemish; bruise (*on fruit*); spot, stain; hammock

maca·co -ca *adj* (Am) ugly, misshapen ‖ *m* — **macaco de la India** rhesus

macadamizar §60 *tr* to macadamize

macadán *m* macadam

macana *f* cudgel, club; drug on the market; (Am) nonsense; (Arg) botch; (Arg) lie, trick

macanu·do -da *adj* (Am) terrific, swell, grand; (Col, Ecuad) strong, husky

macarrón *m* macaroon; **macarrones** macaroni

macear *tr* to mace, hammer ‖ *intr* to pester, to bore

macelo *m* slaughterhouse

macero *m* macebearer

maceta *f* stone hammer; flowerpot; flower vase; (*de herramienta*) handle; (*de cantero*) hammer; (Mex) head

macfarlán *m* inverness cape

macilen·to -ta *adj* pale, wan, gaunt

macillo *m* hammer (*of piano*)

macis *m* mace (*spice*)

macizar §60 *tr* to fill in, fill up

maci·zo -za *adj* solid; massive ‖ *m* solid; flower bed; bulk, mass; massif; wall space

macu·co -ca *adj* (Chile) sly, cunning; (Arg, Chile, Ven) important, notable; (Ecuad) old, worthless; (Arg, Chile, Peru) strong, husky ‖ *m* (Arg, Bol, Col) overgrown boy

mácula *f* spot; stain; blemish; (coll) trick, deception

macha *f* (Bol) drunkenness; (Arg) joke; (Bol) mannish woman

machaca *mf* (coll) pest, bore ‖ *f* crusher

machacar §73 *tr* to crush, mash, pound ‖ *intr* to pester, bore

macha·cón -cona *adj* boring, tiresome, importunate ‖ *mf* bore

machada *f* flock of billy goats; (coll) stupidity

machado *m* hatchet

machamartillo — a machamartillo (coll) solidly, firmly, lastingly

machaque·ro -ra *adj* (coll) tiresome, boring ‖ *mf* (coll) bore

machar *tr* to crush, grind, pound ‖ *ref* (Bol, Ecuad) to get drunk

machete *m* machete, cane knife

machi *mf* (Chile) quack, healer

machihembrar *tr* (*ensamblar a ranura y lengüeta*) to feather; (*ensamblar a caja y espiga*) to mortise

machina *f* derrick, crane; pile driver; (P-R) merry-go-round

macho *adj invar* (*animal, planta, herramienta*) male; strong, robust; dull, stupid ‖ *m* sledge hammer; abutment, pillar; male; he-mule; dullard; (*del corchete*) hook; (mach) male piece; (coll) he-man; (C-R) blond foreigner; **macho cabrío** he-goat, billy goat; **macho de aterrajar** or **macho de terraja** (mach) tap, screw tap

machona *f* (Arg, Bol, Ecuad, Guat) mannish woman

macho·rro -rra *adj* barren, sterile ‖ *f* barren woman; (Mex) mannish woman

machucar §73 *tr* to beat, pound, bruise

machu·cho -cha *adj* sedate, judicious; elderly

madamita *m* (coll) sissy

madeja *f* hank, skein; tangle of hair; (*hombre flojo*) (coll) jellyfish; **madeja sin cuenda** (coll) hopeless tangle

madera *m* Madeira wine ‖ *f* wood; piece of wood; (coll) knack, flair; (coll) makings; **madera aserradda** lumber; **madera contrachapada** plywood; **madera de sierra** lumber; **madera laminada** plywood

maderada *f* raft, float

maderaje *m* or **maderamen** *m* woodwork

maderería *f* lumberyard

madere·ro -ra *adj* lumber ‖ *m* lumberman; carpenter; log driver

madero *m* log, beam; ship, vessel; (coll) blockhead

madrastra *f* stepmother; bother

madraza *f* (coll) doting mother

madre *adj* mother ‖ *f* mother; matron; womb; main sewer; river bed; dregs, sediment; **madre adoptiva** foster mother; **madre de leche** wet nurse; **madre patria** mother country, old country; **madre política** mother-in-law; stepmother; **sacar de madre** (coll) to annoy, to upset

madreperla *f* (*molusco*) pearl oyster; (*nácar*) mother-of-pearl

madreselva *f* honeysuckle

madriga·do -da *adj* twice-married; (*toro*) that has sired; (coll) worldly-wise

madriguera *f* burrow, lair, den

madrile·ño -ña *adj* Madrid ‖ *mf* native or inhabitant of Madrid

madrina *f* godmother; patroness, protectress; prop, shore, brace; joke; leading mare; **madrina de boda** bridesmaid; **madrina de guerra** war mother

madrugada *f* early morning, dawn; early rising

madruga·dor -dora *adj* early-rising ‖ *mf* early riser

madrugar §44 *intr* to get up early; to be out in front

madurar *tr* to ripen; to mature; to think out ‖ *intr* to ripen; to mature

madurez *f* ripeness; maturity

madu·ro -ra *adj* ripe; mature

maestra *f* teacher; elementary girls' school; **maestra de escuela** schoolmistress

maestranza *f* arsenal, armory; navy yard; order of equestrian knights

maestría *f* mastery; mastership

maes·tro -tra *adj* master; masterly; chief, main; (*perro*) trained ‖ *m* master; teacher; (*en la música y la pintura*) maestro; **maestro de capilla** choirmaster; **maestro de ceremonias** master of ceremonies; **maestro de equitación** riding master; **maestro de escuela** elementary schoolteacher; **maestro de esgrima** fencing master; **maestro de obras** master builder ‖ *f* see **maestra**

Magallanes *m* Magellan

magancear *intr* (Col, Chile) to loaf around

magan·to -ta *adj* dull, spiritless

magia *f* magic

magiar *adj* & *mf* Magyar

mági·co -ca *adj* magic ‖ *mf* magician, wizard ‖ *f* magic

magín *m* (coll) fancy, imagination

magisterio *m* teaching; teachers

magistrado *m* magistrate

magistral *adj* masterly

magnáni·mo -ma *adj* magnanimous

magnesio *m* magnesium; (phot) flash-light

magnetismo *m* magnetism

magnetizar §60 *tr* magnetize

magneto *m* & *f* magneto

magnetofón *m* or **magnetófono** *m* tape recorder, wire recorder
magnificar §73 *tr* to magnify; to exalt
magnífi·co -ca *adj* magnificent
magnitud *f* magnitude
mag·no -na *adj* great, e.g., **Alejandro Magno** Alexander the Great
mago *m* magician; soothsayer; (fig) wizard, expert; **Magos de Oriente** Wise Men of the East
ma·gro -gra *adj* lean, thin ‖ *m* (coll) loin of pork ‖ *f* slice of ham
maguar §10 *ref* (Ven, W-I) to be disappointed
magüeta *f* heifer
magüeto *m* young bull
maguey *m* century plant
magullar *tr* to bruise ‖ *ref* to get bruised
mahometa·no -na *adj & mf* Mohammedan
mahometismo *m* Mohammedanism
mahonesa *f* mayonnaise
maído *m* meow
maitines *mpl* matins
maíz *m* maize, Indian corn; **maíz en la mazorca** corn on the cob
maizal *m* cornfield
maja *f* flashy dame
majada *f* sheepfold; dung, manure
majadería *f* piece of folly, nonsensical remark
majade·ro -ra *adj* pestiferous, stupid ‖ *mf* bore, dunce ‖ *m* pestle
majar *tr* to crush, mash, grind, pound; (coll) to annoy, bother
majestad *f* majesty
majestuo·so -sa *adj* majestic
ma·jo -ja *adj* sporty; handsome, dashing; pretty, nice; (coll) all dressed up ‖ *mf* sport ‖ *m* bully ‖ *f* see **maja**
mal *adj* apocopated form of **malo**, used only before nouns in masculine singular ‖ *adv* badly, poorly; wrong; hardly, scarcely; **mal de** short of; **mal que le pese** in spite of him ‖ *m* evil; damage, harm; wrong; sickness; misfortune; **mal de altura** mountain sickness; **mal de la tierra** homesickness; **mal de mar** seasickness; **mal de piedra** (pathol) stone; **mal de rayos** radiation sickness; **mal de vuelo** airsickness; **por mal de mis pecados** to my sorrow; **tener a mal** to object to; **¡mal haya . . .!** curses on . . .!
mala *f* mail; mailbag; mailboat
malabarista *mf* juggler; (Am) sneak thief
malacate *m* whim; (*hoisting machine*) (Mex, Hond) spindle
malaconseja·do -da *adj* ill-advised
malagradeci·do -da *adj* (Am) ungrateful
malandante *adj* unlucky, unfortunate
malandanza *f* bad luck, misfortune
malan·drín -drina *adj* evil, wicked ‖ *mf* scoundrel, rascal
malaria *f* malaria
malaventura *f* misfortune
mala·yo -ya *adj & mf* Malay
malbaratar *tr* to undersell; to squander
malcasa·do -da *adj* mismated; undutiful
malcasar *tr* to mismate ‖ *intr & ref* to be mismated
malcaso *m* treachery

malconten·to -ta *adj & mf* malcontent
malcria·do -da *adj* ill-bred
malcriar §77 *tr* to spoil, pamper
maldad *f* evil, wickedness
maldecir §11 *tr* to curse ‖ *intr* to curse, to damn; **maldecir de** to slander, to vilify
maldición *f* malediction, curse; (coll) oath, curse
maldispues·to -ta *adj* ill, indisposed; unwilling, ill-disposed
maldi·to -ta *adj* damned, accursed; wicked; (Mex) coarse, crude, indecent; **no saber maldita la cosa de** (coll) to not know a single thing about ‖ **el Maldito** the Evil One ‖ *f* (coll) tongue; **soltar la maldita** (coll) to talk too much
maleante *adj* wicked, evil ‖ *mf* crook, hoodlum, rowdy
malear *tr* to spoil; to corrupt ‖ *ref* to spoil, get spoiled; to be corrupted
malecón *m* levee, dike, mole, jetty
maledicencia *f* calumny, slander
maleficiar *tr* to damage, harm; to curse, bewitch, cast a spell on
maleficio *m* curse, spell; witchcraft
maléfi·co -ca *adj* evil, mischievous
malentender §51 *tr* to misunderstand
malentendido *m* misunderstanding, misapprehension
malestar *m* malaise, indisposition
maleta *m* (coll) bungler; (coll) ham bullfighter ‖ *f* valise; **hacer la maleta** to pack up
maletín *m* satchel
malevolencia *f* malice, malevolence
malévo·lo -la *adj* malevolent
maleza *f* thicket, underbrush; weeds
malgasta·do -da *adj* ill-spent
malgastar *tr* to waste, squander
malgenio·so -sa *adj* (Am) ill-tempered, irritable
malhabla·do -da *adj* foul-mouthed
malhada·do -da *adj* ill-starred
malhe·cho -cha *adj* deformed ‖ *m* misdeed
malhe·chor -chora *mf* malefactor ‖ *f* malefactress
malherir §68 *tr* to injure badly
malhumora·do -da *adj* ill-humored
malicia *f* (*maldad*) evil; (*bellaquería, malevolencia*) malice; insidiousness, trickiness; (coll) suspicion
malicio·so -sa *adj* evil; malicious; insidious, tricky
malignar *tr* to corrupt, vitiate; to spoil
malignidad *f* malignity
malig·no -na *adj* (*malévolo; pernicioso*) malign; (*malicioso; perjudicial*) malignant; (pathol) malignant
malintenciona·do -da *adj* ill-disposed, evil-minded
malmaridada *f* (coll) faithless wife
malmeter *tr* to lead astray, misguide; to alienate, estrange
ma·lo -la *adj* bad, poor, evil; (*travieso*) naughty, mischievous; (*enfermo*) sick, ill; (*que no es como debiera ser*) wrong; (*inflamado, dolorido*) sore; **estar de malas** to be out of luck; **lo malo es que** the trouble is that; **malo con** or **para con** mean to; **por malas o por buenas** willingly or unwillingly;

ser **malo de engañar** to be hard to trick ‖ **el Malo** the Evil One ‖ *f* see **mala**

malogra·do -da *adj* late, ill-fated

malograr *tr* to miss ‖ *ref* to fail; to come to an untimely end

malogro *m* failure; disappointment

maloliente *adj* malodorous, foul-smelling

malón *m* mean trick; (SAm) Indian incursion; (Chile) surprise party

malpara·do -da *adj* hurt; **salir malparado (de)** to fail (in), to come out worsted (in)

malparar *tr* to mistreat

malparir *intr* to miscarry, have a miscarriage

malparto *m* miscarriage

malquerencia *f* dislike

malquerer §55 *tr* to dislike

malquistar *tr* to alienate, estrange ‖ *ref* to become alienated

malquis·to -ta *adj* disliked, unpopular

malrotar *tr* to squander

malsa·no -na *adj* unhealthy

malsín *m* mischief-maker

malsonante *adj* obnoxious, odious

malsufri·do -da *adj* impatient

malta *m* malt ‖ *f* asphalt, tar; (Am) dark beer; (Chile) premium beer

maltraer §75 *tr* to abuse, ill-treat; to call down, scold

maltratar *tr* to abuse, ill-treat, maltreat; to damage, spoil

maltre·cho -cha *adj* battered, damaged

malu·co -ca *or* **malu·cho -cha** *adj* (coll) sickish, upset

malva *f* mallow; **malva arbórea** hollyhock, rose mallow; **ser como una malva** (coll) to be meek and mild

malvado -da *adj* evil, wicked ‖ *mf* evildoer

malvarrosa *f* hollyhock, rose mallow

malvavisco *m* marsh mallow

malvender *tr* to sell at a loss

malversación *f* graft, embezzlement, misappropriation

malversar *tr & intr* to graft, embezzle

malvezar §60 *tr* to give bad habits to ‖ *ref* to acquire bad habits

malla *f* mesh, meshing; (*de la armadura*) mail; (*traje*) tights; bathing suit

mallete *m* mallet

Mallorca *f* Majorca

mallor·quín -quina *adj & mf* Majorcan

mama *f* mamma

ma·má *f* (*pl* -**más**) mamma

mamada *f* suck; sucking; (Am) cinch

mama·lón -lona *adj* (Ven, W-I) loafing ‖ *mf* (Cuba) sponger

mamama *f* (Hond) granny

mamamama *f* (Peru) granny

mamar *tr* to suck; to learn as a child; (coll) to swallow; (coll) to wangle; **mamóla** (coll) he was taken in ‖ *intr* to suck ‖ *ref* (coll) to swallow; (*obtener sin mérito*) (coll) to wangle; (SAm) to get drunk; **mamarse a uno** (coll) to get the best of someone; (coll) to take someone in; (Col, Chile, Peru) to do away with someone

mamarracho *m* (coll) mess, sight; (*hombre ridículo*) milksop

mamelón *m* knoll, mound

mamífe·ro -ra *adj* mammalian ‖ *m* mammal, mammalian

mamola *f* chuck (*under the chin*); **hacer la mamola a** to chuck under the chin; (coll) to take in, make a fool of

ma·món -mona *adj* sucking; fond of sucking ‖ *mf* suckling ‖ *m* shoot, sucker; (Guat, Hond) club; (Mex) soft cake ‖ *f* chuck (*under chin*)

1amonear *tr* (Guat, Hond) to beat, cudgel; (S-D) to put off, delay; (*el tiempo*) (S-D) to waste

mamotreto *m* memo book; (coll) batch of papers; (coll) hulk, bulk

mampara *f* screen; folding screen; (Peru) glass door

mamparo *m* bulkhead

mampostería *f* rubble, rubblework; masonry, stone masonry

ma·mut *m* (*pl* -**muts**) mammoth

manada *f* (*de ganado vacuno*) herd, drove; (*de ganado lanar*) flock; (*de lobos*) pack; (*de gente*) gang, troop; (*de hierba, trigo, etc.*) handful

manade·ro -ra *adj* flowing ‖ *m* spring, source; shepherd

manantial *adj* flowing, running ‖ *m* spring, source; (fig) source

manar *tr* to run with ‖ *intr* to pour forth, to run; to abound

manaza *f* big hand

mancar §73 *tr* to maim, cripple ‖ *intr* (*el viento*) (naut) to abate, subside

manca·rrón -rrona *adj* (*caballería*) skinny, worn-out; (Chile) tired out, exhausted ‖ *m* old nag; (Chile, Peru) dam, dike

manceba *f* mistress, concubine

mancebía *f* bawdyhouse, brothel; wild oats; youth

mance·bo -ba *adj* youthful ‖ *m* youngster; youth, young man; (*en una farmacia, barbería, etc.*) helper ‖ *f* see **manceba**

mancerina *f* saucer with hook to hold chocolate cup

mancilla *f* spot, blemish

mancillar *tr* to spot, blemish

man·co -ca *adj* armless, one-armed; one-handed; defective, faulty ‖ *mf* cripple ‖ *m* (Chile) old nag

mancomún — de mancomún jointly, in common

mancomunar *tr* to unite, combine; (*fuerzas, caudales, etc.*) to pool ‖ *ref* to unite, combine

mancomunidad *f* association, union; (*asociación de provincias*) commonwealth

mancornar §61 *tr* (*un novillo*) to throw and hold on the ground; (*una res vacuna*) to tie a horn and front leg of; (*dos reses*) to tie together by the horns; (coll) to join, bring together

mancuernas *fpl* (Mex) cuff links

mancuernillas *fpl* (Guat, Hond) cuff links

mancha *f* spot, stain; (*de vegetación*) patch; speckle; (fig) stain, blot; **mancha solar** sunspot

manchar *tr* to spot, stain; to speckle;

(fig) to stain, disgrace || *intr* to spot; ¡**mancha**! wet paint!

manda *f* gift, offer; bequest, legacy

mandade·ro -ra *mf* messenger || *m* errand boy

mandado *m* order, command; errand; **hacer un mandado** to run an errand

manda·más *m* (*pl* **-mases**) (slang) big shot; (*jefe político*) (slang) boss

mandamiento *m* order, command; (Bib) commandment; (law) writ; **los cinco mandamientos** (coll) the five fingers of the hand

mandar *tr* to order, command; (*legar*) to bequeath; (*enviar*) to send; **mandar + inf** to have + *inf*, e.g., **la mandé leer en voz alta** I had her read aloud || *intr* to be in command, be the boss; **mandar llamar** to send for; **mandar por** to send for; **mande Vd.** I beg your pardon || *ref* (*un enfermo*) to manage to get around; (*dos piezas*) to be communicating; **mandarse con** (*otra pieza*) to communicate with; (Am) to be rude to

mandarina *f* tangerine

mandatario *m* agent, proxy; (Am) chief executive

mandato *m* mandate; (Am) term (*of office*)

mandíbula *f* jaw, jawbone; **reír a mandíbula batiente** (coll) to roar with laughter

mandil *m* apron

mando *m* command; control, drive; **alto mando** (mil) high command; **mando a distancia** remote control; **mando a punta de dedo** finger-tip control; **mando de las válvulas** timing gears; **mando por botón** push-button control; **tener el mando y el palo** (coll) to be the boss, rule the roost

mandolina *f* mandolin

man·dón -dona *adj* bossy || *mf* domineering person || *m* (en las minas) (Am) boss, foreman; (*en las carreras de caballos*) (Chile) starter

mandrágora *f* mandrake

mandril *m* (mach) chuck

mandrilar *tr* to bore

manea *f* hobble

manear *tr* to hobble

manecilla *f* (*de reloj*) hand; clasp, book clasp; (bot) tendril; (typ) fist, index

manejable *adj* manageable

manejar *tr* to manage; to handle, wield; (*un automóvil*) (Am) to drive || *ref* to behave; to get around, move about

manejo *m* management; handling; intrigue, scheming; horsemanship; (Am) driving; **manejo a distancia** remote control; **manejo doméstico** housekeeping

manera *f* manner, way; **a la manera de** in the manner of; like; **de manera que** so that; **en gran manera** to a great extent; extremely; **sobre manera** exceedingly

manga *f* (*parte del vestido*) sleeve; (*tubo de caucho*) hose; waterspout; (bridge) game; **en mangas de camisa** in shirt sleeves; **ir de manga** (coll) to be in cahoots; **manga de agua** water-

spout; cloudburst; **manga de camisa** shirt sleeve; **manga de riego** watering hose; **manga de viento** whirlwind; **manga marina** waterspout; **mangas** extras, profits

mangana *f* lasso

manganear *tr* to lasso; (Peru) to annoy, bother

manganeso *m* manganese

mango *m* handle; **mango de escoba** broomstick; (aer) stick, control stick

mangonear *tr* (Am) to plunder || *intr* (coll) to loaf around; (coll) to meddle; (coll) to dabble

mangosta *f* mongoose

mangote *m* sleeve protector

manguera *f* hose; (*tubo de ventilación*) funnel

mangueta *f* fountain syringe; door jamb

manguitero *m* furrier

manguito *m* muff; sleeve guard; coffee cake; (mach) sleeve

ma·ní *m* (*pl* **-níes** or **-nises**) peanut

manía *f* mania; craze, whim; (coll) grudge; **tener manía a** (coll) to dislike

maniabier·to -ta *adj* open-handed

maní·co -ca *adj* maniac(al) || *mf* maniac

maniatar *tr* to tie the hands of

maniáti·co -ca *adj* stubborn; queer, eccentric; (*entusiasta*) crazy || *mf* crank, eccentric

manicomio *m* madhouse, insane asylum

manicor·to -ta *adj* closefisted, tight

manicu·ro -ra *mf* manicure, manicurist || *f* manicure, manicuring

mani·do -da *adj* shabby, worn; hackneyed; (culin) high || *f* haunt, hangout

manifestación *f* manifestation; (*reunión pública para dar a conocer un sentimiento u opinión*) demonstration

manifestante *mf* demonstrator

manifestar §2 *tr* to manifest; (*el Santísimo Sacramento*) to expose || *intr* to demonstrate || *ref* to become manifest

manifies·to -ta *adj* manifest || *m* manifesto; (eccl) exposition of the Host; (naut) manifest

manigua *f* (Mex, W-I) thicket, jungle; **irse a la manigua** (W-I) to revolt

manija *f* handle; clamp; crank

manilar·go -ga *adj* ready-fisted; generous

manilla *f* bracelet; handcuff, manacle

manillar *m* handle bar

maniobra *f* handling; lever; maneuver; (naut) gear, tackle

maniobrar *intr* to work with the hands; to maneuver; (rr) to shift

maniota *f* hobble

manipula·dor -dora *mf* manipulator || *m* (telg) key

manipular *tr* to manipulate

mani·quí (*pl* **-quíes**) *m* manikin, mannequin; (*para exponer prendas de ropa*) dress form; (*de pintores y escultores*) lay figure; (fig) puppet; **ir hecho un maniquí** to be a fashion plate || *f* (*mujer joven que luce los trajes de última moda*) mannequin, model

manirro·to -ta *adj* lavish, prodigal

manivaci·o -a adj empty-handed
manivela f crank; **manivela de arranque** starting crank
manjar m dish, food, tidbit, delicacy; lift, recreation
mano m first to play, e.g., **soy mano** I'm first ‖ f hand; (de cuadrúpedo) forefoot; (de pintura) coat; (de papel) quire; (saetilla de reloj u otro instrumento) hand; (lance en un juego) round, hand; (del elefante) trunk; pestle, masher; **a la mano** at hand, on hand; within reach; understandable; **a mano airada** violently; **asidos de la mano** hand in hand; **bajo mano** underhandedly; **caer en manos de** to fall into the hands of; **¡dame esa mano!** put it here!; **dar la mano** to lend a hand; **darse las manos** to join hands; to shake hands; **de las manos** hand in hand; **de primera mano** at first hand; first-hand; **de segunda mano** second-hand; **echar mano de** to resort to; **echar una mano** to lend a hand; to play a game; **en buena mano está** (coll) after you, you drink first; **escribir a la mano** to take dictation; **escribir a manos de** to write in care of; **estrecharse la mano** to shake hands; **ganarle a uno por la mano** to steal a march on someone; **lavarse las manos de** to wash one's hands of; **llegar a las manos** to come to blows; **malas manos** awkwardness; **mano de gato** cat's-paw; master hand, master touch; **mano de obra** labor; **mano derecha** right-hand man; **mano de santo** (coll) sure cure; **¡manos a la obra!** let's get to work!; **manos libres** outside work; **manos limpias** extras, perquisites; (coll) clean hands; **manos puercas** (coll) graft; **probar la mano** to try one's hand; **tener mano con** to have a pull with; **tener mano izquierda** (coll) to be on one's toes; **untar la mano a** (coll) to grease the palm of; **venir a las manos** to come to blows; **vivir de la mano a la boca** to live from hand to mouth
manojo m bunch, bundle, handful; **a manojos** in abundance
manopla f gauntlet; postilion's whip; (Chile) knuckles, brass knuckles
manosear tr to finger, to paw; to muss, to rumple; to fiddle with; (Am) to pet ‖ ref (Am) to spoon, to neck
manotada f slap
manotear tr to slap, to smack ‖ intr to gesticulate
manquedad f lack of one or both hands or arms; disability; deficiency
mansalva — **a mansalva** without risk; without warning; **a mansalva de** safe from
mansarda f mansard, mansard roof
mansedumbre f gentleness, mildness, meekness; tameness
mansión f stay, sojourn; abode, dwelling; **hacer mansión** to stop, stay
man·so -sa adj gentle, mild, meek; tame ‖ m bellwether; farm
manta f blanket; heavy shawl; (coll)

beating, thrashing; (Chile, Ecuad) poncho; (Col, Mex, Ven) coarse cotton cloth; **a manta de Dios** copiously; **dar una manta a** to toss in a blanket; **manta de coche** lap robe; **manta de viaje** steamer rug; **tirar de la manta** (coll) to let the cat out of the bag
mantear tr to toss in a blanket; (Am) to abuse, mistreat
manteca f (grasa de los animales, esp. la del cerdo) lard; butter; pomade; (dinero) (slang) dough; **como manteca** smooth as butter; **manteca de puerco** lard; **manteca de vaca** butter
mantecado m custard ice cream, French ice cream
mantecón m (coll) mollycoddle, milksop
mantel m tablecloth; altar cloth
mantelería f table linen
mantelillo m embroidered centerpiece
mantelito m lunch cloth
mantener §71 tr to maintain; to keep; to keep up; to sustain, defend ‖ ref to keep, remain, continue
mantenida f (Am) kept woman
mantenido m (hombre que vive a expensas de su mujer) (Guat, Mex, W-I) gigolo; (Guat, Mex, W-I) sponger
mantenimiento m maintenance; food, support, living
manteo m mantle, cloak
mantequera f churn, butter churn; butter dish
mantequería f creamery; delicatessen
mantequilla f butter; **mantequilla azucarada** hard sauce; **mantequilla derretida** drawn butter
mantilla f mantilla (silk or lace head scarf); **mantillas** swaddling clothes
mantillo m humus, mold
manto m mantle, cloak; (de chimenea) mantel; (ropa talar de algunos religiosos, catedráticos, alumnos) robe, gown; (fig) cloak
mantón m shawl, kerchief
manuable adj handy
manual adj (que se hace con las manos) hand; (fácil de manejar) handy; easy; easy to understand; easy-going; manual ‖ m manual, handbook; notebook
manubrio m handle; crank; winch
manuela f open hack (in Madrid)
manufactura f (fábrica) factory; (obra fabricada) manufacture
manufacturar tr to manufacture
manuscribir §83 tr to write by hand
manuscri·to -ta adj & m manuscript
manutención f maintenance; care, upkeep; shelter, protection
manutener §71 tr (law) to maintain, support
manzana f apple; (conjunto aislado de varias casas contiguas) block, city block; (remate en un mueble) knob, finial; **manzana de Adán** (Chile) Adam's apple
manzanar m apple orchard
manzanilla f camomile; (aceituna pequeña; vino blanco) manzanilla (small olive; white wine); (remate en un mueble) knob, finial

manzano *m* apple tree

maña *f* skill, dexterity; cunning, craftiness; bad habit, vice; (*de lino, cáñamo, etc.*) bunch; (Am) sister; **darse maña** to manage, contrive; **hacer maña** (Col) to fool around

mañana *adv* tomorrow; ¡**hasta mañana!** see you tomorrow!; **pasado mañana** the day after tomorrow ‖ *m* tomorrow; (*tiempo venidero*) morrow ‖ *f* morning; **de mañana** in the morning; **muy de mañana** very early in the morning; **por la mañana** in the morning; **tomar la mañana** to get up early; (coll) to have a shot of liquor before breakfast

mañanear *intr* to be in the habit of getting up early

mañane·ro -ra *adj* morning; early-rising

mañanica *f* early morning, break of day

mañanita *f* woman's bed jacket

mañear *tr* to manage craftily ‖ *intr* to act with cunning

mañerear *intr* (Arg) to dawdle, dilly-dally

mañería *f* sterility

mañe·ro -ra *adj* clever, shrewd; simple, easy; (Am) skittish

ma·ño -ña *mf* (coll) Aragonese ‖ *m* (Am) brother ‖ *f* see **maña**

maño·so -sa *adj* skillful, clever; crafty, tricky; vicious

mañuela *f* craftiness, trickiness

mañue·las *mf* (*pl* **-las**) (coll) tricky person

mapa *m* map; **mapa itinerario** road map ‖ *f* — **llevarse la mapa** (coll) to take the prize

mapache *m* coon, raccoon

mapamundi *m* map of the world; (coll) buttocks, behind

mapurite *m* (CAm) skunk

maque *m* lacquer

maquear *tr* to lacquer; (Mex) to varnish

maqueta *f* (*en tamaño reducido*) maquette; (*en tamaño natural*) mock-up; (*de un libro*) dummy

maquillador *m* (theat) make-up man

maquillaje *m* (theat) make-up

maquillar *tr* & *ref* to make up

máquina *f* machine; (*motor*) engine; locomotive; plan, project; (fig) machinery; (coll) heap, pile, lot; (Cuba) auto; (Chile) ganging up; **escribir a máquina** to typewrite; **máquina de afeitar** safety razor; **máquina de apostar** gambling machine; **máquina de componer** typesetter; **máquina de coser** sewing machine; **máquina de escribir** typewriter; **máquina de lavar** washing machine; **máquina de sumar** adding machine; **máquina de volar** flying machine; **máquina fotográfica** camera; **máquina parlante** talking machine; **máquina sacaperras** slot machine

maquinación *f* machination, scheming

máquina-herramienta *f* (*pl* **máquinas-herramientas**) machine tool

maquinal *adj* mechanical

maquinar *tr* to plot, to scheme

maquinaria *f* machinery; applied mechanics

maquinilla *f* windlass, winch; clippers; **maquinilla cortapelos** clippers, hair clippers; **maquinilla de afeitar** safety razor; **maquinilla de rizar** curling iron

maquinista *mf* (*persona que fabrica máquinas*) machinist; (*persona que dirige una máquina o locomotora*) engineer; **segundo maquinista** (naut) machinist

mar *m* & *f* sea; tide, flood; **alta mar** high seas; **a mares** abundantly, copiously; **arrojarse a la mar** to plunge, take great risks; **baja mar** low tide; **correr los mares** to follow the sea; **hablar de la mar** (coll) to talk wildly, to talk on and on; **hacerse a la mar** to put to sea; **la mar de** (fig) oceans of, large numbers of; **mar alta** rough sea; **mar ancha** high seas; **mar bonanza** calm sea; **mar Caribe** Caribbean Sea, Caribbean; **mar de las Antillas** Caribbean Sea; **mar de las Indias** Indian Ocean; **mar de nubes** cloud bank; **mar Latino** Mediterranean Sea; **mar llena** high tide; **meter la mar en un pozo** to attempt the impossible; **meterse mar adentro** (fig) to go beyond one's depth

maraña *f* undergrowth, thicket; silk waste; (*de hilo, pelo, etc.*) tangle; trick, scheme; puzzle

marañón *m* cashew

maraño·so -sa *adj* scheming ‖ *mf* schemer

maravilla *f* wonder, marvel; (bot) marigold, calendula; **a las maravillas** or **a las mil maravillas** magnificently; **a maravilla** wonderfully well; **por maravilla** rarely, occasionally

maravillar *tr* to astonish ‖ *ref* to wonder, to marvel; **maravillarse con** or **de** to marvel at, to wonder at

maravillo·so -sa *adj* wonderful, marvelous

marbete *m* label, tag; baggage check; edge, border; **marbete engomado** sticker

marca *f* mark; (*tipo de producto*) make, brand; (*de tamaño*) standard; score; record; height-measuring device; **de marca** outstanding; **marca de agua** watermark; **marca de fábrica** trademark; **marca de reconocimiento** (naut) landmark, seamark; **marca de taquilla** box-office record; **marca registrada** registered trademark

marca·do -da *adj* marked, pronounced

marcaje *m* (sport) scoring; (sport) interfering; (telp) dialing

marcapaso *m* pacemaker

marcar §73 *tr* to mark; to brand; to embroider; (*p.ej., un pañuelo*) to initial; (*la hora un reloj*) to show; (*un tanto*) to make, to score; (*el número telefónico*) to dial ‖ *ref* (*un buque*) to take bearings

marcear *tr* to shear ‖ *ref* to be March-like

marcial *adj* martial; gallant, noble

marco *m* frame; framework; (*de pesas y medidas*) standard

marcha *f* march; (*funcionamiento*) running, operation; (*p.ej., de los astros*) course, path; (*desenvolvimiento de un asunto*) course, march, progress; (*grado de velocidad*) rate of speed; (*de los engranajes*) (aut) speed; **cambiar de marcha** to shift gears; **en marcha** on the march; underway; in motion; **marcha atrás** reverse; **marcha del hambre** hunger march; **marcha directa** high gear; **marcha forzada** (mil) forced march

marchamo *m* customhouse mark; (Arg, Bol) tax on slaughtered cattle

marchante *adj* commercial ‖ *m* dealer, merchant; (Am) customer

marchapié *m* running board

marchar *intr* to march; to run, work, go; to leave, go away; to come along, proceed; **marchar en vacío** to idle ‖ *ref* to leave, go away

marchitar *tr* to wilt, wither ‖ *ref* to wilt, wither; to languish

marchi·to -ta *adj* withered, faded; (fig) languid

marea *f* tide; tideland; gentle sea breeze; dew; drizzle; **marea alta** high tide; **marea baja** low tide; **marea creciente** or **entrante** flood tide; **marea menguante** ebb tide; **marea muerta** neap tide; **marea viva** spring tide; **rendir la marea** to stem the tide

marea·do -da *adj* nauseated, sick, lightheaded; seasick

mareaje *m* navigation, seamanship; (*de un buque*) course

marear *tr* to sail; (coll) to annoy, pester ‖ *intr* (coll) to be annoying ‖ *ref* to get sick, to get giddy; to get seasick; to be damaged at sea; (Am) to fade

marejada *f* heavy sea; (*de desorden*) stirring, undercurrent; **marejada de fondo** ground swell

maremagno or **maremágnum** *m* (coll) big mess

mareo *m* nausea, dizziness, sickness; seasickness; (coll) annoyance

marfil *m* ivory

marfile·ño -ña *adj* ivory

mar·fuz -fuza *adj* (*pl* **-fuces -fuzas**) cast aside, rejected; deceptive

marga *f* marl

margar §44 *tr* to marl

margarita *f* pearl; (bot) daisy; **margarita de los prados** English daisy

margen *m* & *f* margin; border, edge; marginal note; **al margen de** aloof from; outside of; independent of; aside from; **dar margen para** to give occasion for; **dejar al margen** to leave out; **quedar al margen de** to be left out of

marginal *adj* marginal

mariache *m* Mexican band and singers

marica *m* (coll) sissy, milksop ‖ *f* magpie

maricón *m* (coll) sissy

maridable *adj* marital

maridaje *m* married life; (fig) union

maridar *tr* to combine, unite ‖ *intr* to get married; to live as man and wife

marido *m* husband

mariguana *f* marihuana

mariguanza *f* (Chile) hocus-pocus; (Chile) pirouette; **mariguanzas** (Chile) clowning; (Chile) powwowing

marimacho *m* (coll) mannish woman

marimandona *f* (coll) queen bee, bossy woman

marimarica *m* (coll) sissy

marimorena *f* (coll) fight, row

marina *f* navy; (*conjunto de buques*) marine, fleet; (*cuadro o pintura*) seascape; shore, seaside; sailing, navigation; **marina de guerra** navy; **marina mercante** merchant marine

marinar *tr* to marinate, to salt; (*un buque*) to man ‖ *intr* to be a sailor

marinera *f* sailor blouse; (*blusa de niño*) middy, middy blouse

marinería *f* sailoring; sailors

marine·ro -ra *adj* sea, marine; seaworthy; seafaring ‖ *m* mariner, seaman, sailor; **marinero de agua dulce** (*el que ha navegado poco*) landlubber (*person unacquainted with the sea*); **marinero matalote** (*hombre de mar, rudo y torpe*) landlubber (*awkward and unskilled seaman*) ‖ *f* see **marinera**

marines·co -ca *adj* sailor; sailorly

mari·no -na *adj* marine, sea ‖ *m* mariner, seaman, sailor ‖ *f* see **marina**

marioneta *f* marionette

mariposa *f* butterfly; butterfly valve; wing nut; rushlight; (Col) blindman's buff; **mariposa nocturna** moth

mariposear *intr* to flit about; to be fickle

mariposón *m* (Cuba, Guat, Mex) fickle flirt

mariquita *m* (coll) sissy, milksop, popinjay ‖ *f* (ent) ladybird

marisabidilla *f* (coll) bluestocking

mariscal *m* blacksmith; (mil) marshal; **mariscal de campo** (mil) field marshal

marisco *m* shellfish; **mariscos** seafood

marisma *f* swamp, marsh, salt marsh

marisquería *f* seafood store, seafood restaurant

maríti·mo -ma *adj* maritime; marine, sea

maritor·nes *f* (*pl* **-nes**) (coll) mannish maidservant, wench

marmita *f* pot, boiler, kettle

marmitón *m* kitchen scullion

mármol *m* marble

marmóre·o -a *adj* marble

marmosete *m* vignette

marmota *f* marmot; sleepyhead; worsted cap; **marmota de Alemania** hamster; **marmota de América** ground hog, woodchuck

maroma *f* hemp rope, esparto rope; (Am) acrobatic stunt

maromear *intr* (Am) to perform acrobatic stunts, to walk the tight rope; (Am) to wobble, to sway from side to side (*e.g., in politics*); (Am) to hesitate

marome·ro -ra *mf* (Am) acrobat, tightrope walker; (Am) weaseler

marqués *m* marquis; **los marqueses** the marquis and marchioness

marquesa *f* marchioness, marquise; (*sobre la puerta de un hotel*) marquee

marquesina *f* cover over field tent; (*sobre la puerta de un hotel*) marquee; locomotive cab

marquetería *f* cabinetwork, woodwork; (*taracea*) marquetry

marra·jo -ja *adj* sly, tricky; (*toro*) vicious

marrana *f* sow; (coll) slattern, slut

marranada *f* (coll) piggishness, filth

marranalla *f* (coll) rabble, riffraff

marra·no -na *adj* base, vile; (coll) dirty, sloppy ǁ *mf* hog ǁ *m* male hog, boar; filthy person, hog; cad, cur ǁ *f* see **marrana**

marrar *intr* to miss, fail; to go astray

marras *adv* (coll) long ago; **hacer marras que** (Bol, Ecuad) to be a long time since

marro *m* game resembling quoits and played with a stone; (*juego de muchachos*) tag; (*ladeo*) dodge, duck; slip, miss

marrón *adj invar* maroon (*dark-red*); tan (*shoes*) ǁ *m* maroon; candied chestnut; stone (*used as a sort of quoit*)

marro·quí (*pl* **-quíes**) *adj & mf* Moroccan ǁ *m* morocco, morocco leather

marro·quín -quina *adj & mf* var of **marroquí**

marrubio *m* horehound

marrue·co -ca *adj & mf* Moroccan

Marruecos *m* Morocco

marrulle·ro -ra *adj* cajoling, wheedling ǁ *mf* cajoler, wheedler

Marsella *f* Marseille

marsopa *or* **marsopla** *f* porpoise

mart. *abbr* **martes**

marta *f* pine marten; **marta cebellina** sable, Siberian sable; **marta del Canadá** fisher

Marte *m* Mars

mar·tes *m* (*pl* **-tes**) Tuesday; **martes de carnaval** *or* **carnestolendas** Shrove Tuesday

martillar *tr* to hammer; to pester, worry ǁ *intr* to hammer

martillazo *m* blow with a hammer

martillear *tr & intr* var of **martillar**

martillero *m* (Chile) auctioneer

martillo *m* hammer; auction house; (*persona*) scourge; (mus) tuning hammer; (*de arma de fuego*) cock

martín *m* — **martín pescador** (*pl* **martín pescadores**) kingfisher

martinete *m* drop hammer; pile driver; (*del piano*) hammer

martínico *m* (coll) ghost, goblin

mártir *mf* martyr

martirio *m* martyrdom

márts. *abbr* **mártires**

marullo *m* surge, swell

marxista *adj & mf* Marxist or Marxian

marzo *m* March

mas *conj* but

más *adv* more; most; **a lo más** at most, at the most; **a más de** besides, in addition to; **como el que más** as the next one, as well as anybody; **cuando**

más at the most; **de más** extra; too much, too many; **estar de más** to be in the way; to be unnecessary; to be superfluous; **los más de** most of, the majority of; **más bien** rather; **más de** + *número* more than; **más de lo que** + *verbo* more than; **más que** more than; better than; **no . . . más** no longer; **no . . . más nada** nothing more; **no . . . más que** only ǁ *prep* plus ǁ *m* more; (*signo de adición*) plus

masa *f* mass; (*pasta que se forma con agua y harina*) dough; (*masa aplastada*) mash; nature, disposition; (Chile, Ecuad) puff paste; (*p.ej., de un automóvil*) (elec) ground; **las masas** the masses

masada *f* farm

masadero *m* farmer

masaje *m* massage; **masaje facial** facial

masajear *tr* to massage

masajista *m* masseur ǁ *f* masseuse

masar *tr* to knead; to massage

mascar §73 *tr* to chew; (coll) to mumble, mutter ǁ *ref* (*un cabo*) (naut) to gall

máscara *mf* (*persona*) mask, mummer ǁ *f* mask; (*traje, disfraz*) masquerade; **máscara antigás** gas mask

mascarada *f* masquerade

mascarilla *f* half mask; false face; death mask

mascarón *m* false face; (*persona fea*) fright; (archit) mask; **mascarón de proa** (naut) figurehead

mascota *f* mascot

mascujar *tr & intr* (coll) to chew with difficulty; (coll) to mumble

masculi·no -na *adj* masculine; (*sexo*) male; (*traje*) men's ǁ *m* masculine

mascullar *tr & intr* (coll) to mumble, mutter; (coll) to chew with difficulty

masera *f* kneading trough

masilla *f* putty

masita *f* (mil) money withheld for clothing; (Arg, Bol) cake

masón *m* Mason

masonería *f* Masonry

mastelero *m* (naut) topmast

masticar §73 *tr* to chew, masticate; to meditate on; to mumble

mástil *m* (*de una embarcación*) mast; (*de un violín o guitarra*) neck; stalk; (*de pluma*) shaft, stem; upright

mas·tín -tina *mf* mastiff; **mastín danés** Great Dane

mastodonte *m* mastodon

masturzo *m* (bot) cress; (coll) dolt

masturbar *ref* to masturbate

mat. *abbr* **matemática**

mata *f* bush, shrub; blade, sprig; brush, underbrush; **mata de pelo** crop of hair, head of hair; **mata parda** chaparro (*oak*); **saltar de la mata** (coll) to come out of hiding

mataca·bras *m* (*pl* **-bras**) cold blast from the north

matacán *m* dog poison

matacande·las *m* (*pl* **-las**) candle snuffer

matadero *m* abattoir, slaughterhouse; (coll) drudgery

mata·dor -dora *mf* killer ‖ *m* matador; **matador de mujeres** lady-killer

matadura *f* sore, gall

matafue·gos *m* (*pl* **-gos**) fire extinguisher; (*oficial*) fireman

matalo·bos *m* (*pl* **-bos**) wolf's-bane

mata·lón -lona *mf* (coll) skinny old nag

matalotaje *m* (naut) ship stores; (coll) mess, hodgepodge

matamale·zas *m* (*pl* **-zas**) weed killer

matamari·dos *f* (*pl* **-dos**) (coll) many times a widow

matamo·ros *m* (*pl* **-ros**) (coll) bully

matamos·cas *m* (*pl* **-cas**) fly swatter; flypaper

matanza *f* slaughter, massacre; butchering; pork products; (CAm) butcher shop; (Ven) slaughterhouse

matape·rros *m* (*pl* **-rros**) (coll) harum-scarum, street urchin

matar *tr* to kill; to butcher; (*el fuego, la luz*) to put out; (*la cal*) to slack; (*el metal*) to mat; (*un color*) to tone down; (*un naipe*) to spot; to play a card higher than; (*a un caballo*) to gall; to bore to death; (*el tiempo, el hambre, etc.*) (fig) to kill ‖ *intr* to kill ‖ *ref* to kill oneself; to drudge, overwork; to be disappointed; **matarse con** to quarrel with; **matarse por** to struggle for; to struggle to

matarratas *m* rat poison; (*aguardiente de mala calidad*) (coll) rotgut

matarro·tos *m* (*pl* **-tos**) (Chile) pawnshop

matasa·nos *m* (*pl* **-nos**) quack doctor

matasellar *tr* to cancel, to postmark

matase·llos *m* (*pl* **-llos**) postmark

matasie·te *m* (*pl* **-te**) (coll) bully, swashbuckler

matatí·as *m* (*pl* **-as**) (coll) moneylender, pawnbroker

matazar·zas *m* (*pl* **-zas**) weed killer

mate *adj* dull, flat ‖ *m* checkmate; (SAm) maté; (SAm) maté gourd; **dar mate a** to checkmate; to make fun of; **dar mate ahogado a** to stalemate; **mate ahogado** stalemate

matear *tr* to plant at regular intervals; to make dull; (Chile) to checkmate ‖ *ref* (*el trigo*) to sprout; (*un perro de caza*) to hunt through the bushes

matemáti·co -ca *adj* mathematical ‖ *mf* mathematician ‖ *f* mathematics; **matemáticas** mathematics

materia *f* matter; material, stuff; **materia colorante** dyestuff; **materia prima** or **primera materia** raw material

material *adj* material; (*grosero*) crude ‖ *m* material; (*conjunto de objetos necesario para un servicio*) matériel; (typ) matter, copy; **material de guerra** matériel; **material fijo** (rr) permanent way; **material móvil** or **rodante** (rr) rolling stock; **ser material** (coll) to be immaterial

materialismo *m* materialism

materializar §60 *tr* (*beneficios*) to realize

maternal *adj* maternal, mother; (*afectos, cuidados, etc.*) motherly

maternidad *f* maternity; motherhood

mater·no -na *adj* maternal, mother

matinal *adj* morning

matinée *f* matinée; dressing gown, wrapper

ma·tiz *m* (*pl* **-tices**) shade, hue, nuance

matizar §60 *tr* (*diversos colores*) to blend; (*un color, un sonido*) to shade; (*en cuanto al color*) to match

matón *m* (coll) bully, browbeater

matorral *m* thicket, underbrush

matraca *f* rattle, noisemaker; taunting; bantering; bore, pest; **dar matraca a** (coll) to taunt, to tease

matraquear *intr* (coll) to make a racket; (coll) to taunt, to tease

ma·traz *m* (*pl* **-traces**) flask

matre·ro -ra *adj* cunning, shrewd ‖ *m* (SAm) cheat, swindler

matriarca *f* matriarch

matricida *adj* matricidal ‖ *mf* matricide

matricidio *m* matricide

matrícula *f* register, roster, roll; licence; registry

matricular *tr* & *ref* to matriculate

matrimonialmente *adv* as husband and wife

matrimoniar *intr* to marry, get married

matrimonio *m* marriage, matrimony; (*marido y mujer*) (coll) married couple; **matrimonio consensual** common-law marriage

ma·triz (*pl* **-trices**) *adj* main, first, mother ‖ *f* matrix; (*del libro talonario*) stub; screw nut; first draft

matrona *f* matron; (coll) matronly lady

matronal *adj* matronly

matun·go -ga *adj* (Am) skinny, full of sores ‖ *m* (Am) old nag

maturran·go -ga *adj* (SAm) poor, clumsy ‖ *m* (SAm) stranger; (SAm) old nag ‖ *f* (coll) trickery

Matusalén *m* Methuselah; **vivir más años que Matusalén** to be as old as Methuselah

matute *m* smuggling; smuggled goods; gambling den

matutear *intr* to smuggle

matute·ro -ra *mf* smuggler

matutinal or **matuti·no -na** *adj* morning

maula *mf* (coll) lazy loafer; (coll) poor pay; (coll) tricky person, cheat ‖ *f* junk, trash; remnant; trickery

maulería *f* remnant shop; trickiness

maullar §8 *intr* to meow

maullido or **maúllo** *m* meow

mausoleo *m* mausoleum

máxima *f* maxim; principle

máxime *adv* chiefly, mainly, especially

máxi·mo -ma *adj* maximum; top; superlative ‖ *m* maximum ‖ *f* see **máxima**

may. *abbr* **mayúscula**

maya *f* May queen; English daisy

mayal *m* flail

mayear *intr* to be Maylike

mayestáti·co -ca *adj* royal

mayido *m* meow

mayo *m* May; Maypole

mayonesa *f* mayonnaise

mayor *adj* greater; larger; older, elder; greatest; largest; oldest, eldest; major; elderly; (*calle*) main; (*altar, misa*) high; **hacerse mayor de edad**

to come of age; **ser mayor de edad** to be of age ‖ *m* chief, head, superior; **al por mayor** wholesale; **mayor de edad** (*persona de edad legal*) major; **mayores** elders; ancestors, forefathers; **mayor general** staff officer

mayoral *m* boss, foreman; head shepherd; stagecoach driver; (Arg) streetcar conductor

mayorazgo *m* primogeniture; entailed estate descending by primogeniture; first-born son

mayordoma *f* stewardess, housekeeper

mayordomo *m* steward, butler, majordomo

mayoreo *m* (Am) wholesale

mayoría *f* (*mayor edad; el mayor número, la mayor parte*) majority; superiority; **alcanzar su mayoría de edad** to come of age; **mayoría de edad** majority

mayoridad *f* majority

mayorista *adj* (Arg, Chile) wholesale ‖ *mf* (Arg, Chile) wholesaler

mayorita·rio -ria *adj* majority

mayormente *adv* chiefly, mainly, mostly

mayúscu·lo -la *adj* (*letra*) capital; (coll) awful, tremendous ‖ *f* capital, capital letter

maza *f* mace; heavy drumstick; (coll) bore, pedant; **la maza y la mona** constant companions; **maza de gimnasia** Indian club

mazacote *m* barilla; concrete, cement; botched job; (coll) tough, doughy food; (coll) bore

mazar §60 *tr* to churn

mazmorra *f* dungeon

mazo *m* mallet, maul; bunch; (*de la campana*) clapper; (*hombre fastidioso*) bore, pest

mazonería *f* stone masonry; (*obra de relieve*) relief; gold or silver embroidery

mazorca *f* ear of corn; cocoa bean; (*husada*) spindleful; (*de un balustre*) spindle; **comer maíz de** or **en la mazorca** to eat corn on the cob

mazorral *adj* coarse, crude

m/c *abbr* mi cargo, mi cuenta, moneda corriente

m/cta *abbr* mi cuenta

m/cte *abbr* moneda corriente

me (used as object of verb) *pron pers* me, to me ‖ *pron reflex* myself, to myself

meada *f* urination, water; urine stain

meadero *m* urinal

meados *mpl* urine

meaja *f* crumb; **meaja de huevo** tread

meandro *m* meander; wandering speech, wandering whine

mear *tr* to urinate on ‖ *intr* & *ref* to urinate

Meca, La Mecca

mecáni·co -ca *adj* mechanical; (coll) low, mean ‖ *m* (*obrero perito en el arreglo de las máquinas*) mechanic; (*obrero que fabrica y compone máquinas*) machinist; workman, repairman; driver, chauffeur ‖ *f* mechanics; (*aparato que da movimiento a un artefacto*) machinery, works; (coll)

meanness; **mecánicas** (coll) household chores

mecanismo *m* mechanism, machinery

mecanizar §60 *tr* to mechanize; to motorize

mecanografía *f* typewriting; **mecanografía al tacto** touch typewriting

mecanografiar §77 *tr* & *intr* to typewrite

mecanógra·fo -fa *mf* typist, typewriter

mecapale·ro -ra *m* (Mex) messenger, porter

mece·dor -dora *adj* swinging, rocking ‖ *m* stirrer; (*columpio*) swing ‖ *f* rocker, rocking chair

mecer §46 *tr* (*un líquido*) to stir; (*la cuna*) to rock ‖ *ref* to rock, swing

mecha *f* (*de vela o bujía*) wick; (*tubo de pólvora*) fuse; lock of hair; (*para mechar carne*) slice of bacon; bundle of thread; (Col, Ecuad, Ven) joke

mechar *tr* (*la carne*) to lard, interlard

mechera *f* (coll) shoplifter

mechero *m* (*p.ej., de cigarrillos*) lighter, pocket lighter; (*de aparato de alumbrado*) burner; (*de candelero*) socket; **mechero encendedor** pilot, pilot light

mechón *m* cowlick; (Guat) torch

medalla *f* medal; medallion

medallón *m* medallion; (*joya en que se colocan retratos, etc.*) locket

médano *m* dune, sandbank

media *f* stocking; (math) mean; **media corta** (Arg) sock; **media media** (Arg, Ecuad, Ven) sock; **y media** half past, e.g., **las dos y media** half past two

mediación *f* mediation

media·do -da *adj* half over; half-full; **a mediados de** about the middle of; **mediada la tarde** in the middle of the afternoon

media·dor -dora *mf* mediator

mediana *f* long billiard cue

medianería *f* party wall; party fence

mediane·ro -ra *adj* middle; mediating ‖ *mf* mediator; partner; owner of a row house

medianía *f* average; (*persona que carece de dotes relevantes*) mediocrity

media·no -na *adj* middling, medium; average, fair; (coll) mediocre ‖ *f* see **mediana**

medianoche *f* midnight; small meat pie

mediante *adj* interceding ‖ *prep* by means of, by virtue of

mediar *intr* to be half over; to be in the middle; to intercede, mediate; to elapse; to take place

mediatinta *f* half-tone

medible *adj* measurable

medical *adj* medical

medicamento *m* medicine

medicamento·so -sa *adj* medicinal

medicastro *m* quack

medicina *f* medicine

medicinar *tr* to treat ‖ *ref* to take medicine

medición *f* measurement; metering

médi·co -ca *adj* medical ‖ *mf* doctor, physician; **médico de cabecera** family physician

medida *f* measurement; measure; caution, moderation; **a medida de** in proportion to; according to; **a medida que** in proportion as; **en la medida que** to the extent that; **hecho a la medida** custom-made; **medida para áridos** dry measure; **medida para líquidos** liquid measure; **tomarle a uno las medidas** to take someone's measure, to size up someone

medidamente *adv* with moderation

medidor *m* measurer; (Mex, SAm) meter

medie·ro -ra *mf* hosier; partner

medieval *adj* medieval

medievalista *mf* medievalist

medievo *m* Middle Ages

me·dio -dia *adj* middle; medium; medieval; half; a half, e.g., **media libra** a half pound; half a, e.g., **media naranja** half an orange; average, mean; mid, in the middle of, e.g., **a media tarde** in mid afternoon, in the middle of the afternoon; **a medias** half; half-and-half; **ir a medias (con)** to go halves (with), to go fifty-fifty (with) ‖ *m* middle; medium, environment; step, measure; means; (*en el espiritismo*) medium; (baseball) shortstop; (arith) half; (*del ruedo*) (taur) center; **a medio** half; **en medio de** in the middle of; in the midst of; **justo medio** happy medium, golden mean; **por medio de** by means of; **quitarse de en medio** (coll) to get out of the way ‖ *f* see **media** ‖ **medio** *adv* half

mediocre *adj* mediocre

mediocridad *f* mediocrity

mediodía *m* noon, midday; south; **en pleno mediodía** at high noon; **hacer mediodía** to stop for the noon meal

mediquillo *m* quack

medir §50 *tr* to measure ‖ *intr* to measure ‖ *ref* to act with moderation

meditabun·do -da *adj* meditative

meditar *tr* to meditate; to plan, contemplate ‖ *intr* to meditate

mediterráne·o -na *adj* inland ‖ **Mediterráne·o -na** *adj* & *m* Mediterranean

mé·dium *m* (*pl* **-dium** or **-diums**) medium

medra *f* growth, prosperity

medrana *f* fear

medrar *intr* to thrive, prosper, improve

medro *m* growth, prosperity; **medros** progress

medro·so -sa *adj* fearful, scared; frightful, terrible

médula or **medula** *f* marrow, medulla; (bot) pith; (fig) pith, gist, essence; **médula espinal** spinal cord

medular *adj* pithy

medusa *f* jellyfish

mefistoféli·co -ca *adj* Mephistophelian

megaciclo *m* megacycle

megáfono *m* megaphone

me·go -ga *adj* meek, gentle, mild

megohmio *m* megohm

Méj. *abbr* Méjico

mejica·no -na *adj* & *mf* Mexican

Méjico *m* Mexico; **Nuevo Méjico** New Mexico

meji·do -da *adj* beaten with sugar and milk

mejilla *f* cheek

mejor *adj* better; best; (*licitador*) highest; **a lo mejor** (coll) unexpectedly; (coll) worse luck; (coll) perhaps, maybe; **el mejor día** some fine day ‖ *adv* better; best; **mejor dicho** rather

mejora *f* growth, improvement; higher bid; alteration

mejoramiento *m* improvement

mejorana *f* sweet marjoram

mejorar *tr* to improve; (*los licitadores el precio de una cosa*) to raise; **mejorando lo presente** present company excepted ‖ *intr* & *ref* to improve, get better, recover; to make progress; (*el tiempo*) to clear up

mejoría *f* improvement; (*en una enfermedad*) betterment, recovery

mejunje *m* brew, potion, mixture

mela·do -da *adj* honey-colored ‖ *m* (Am) thick cane syrup

melancolía *f* (*tristeza vaga*) melancholy; (*depresión moral*) melancholia

melancóli·co -ca *adj* melancholy

melaza *f* molasses

melcocha *f* taffy, molasses candy

melchor *m* German silver

melena *f* hair falling over the eyes; long hair, loose hair; (*del león*) mane; (*del caballo*) forelock; **andar a la melena** (coll) to pull each other's hair; (coll) to get into a fight; **estar en melena** (coll) to have one's hair down

melga *f* (Am) ridge made by plow; (Col, Chile) plot of ground to be sown; (Hond) small piece of work to be finished

melindre *m* honey fritter; (*dulce de pasta de mazapán*) ladyfinger; narrow ribbon; prudery, finickiness

melindrear *intr* to be prudish, be finicky

melindro·so -sa *adj* prudish, finicky

melocotón *m* peach tree; peach

melocotonero *m* peach tree

melodía *f* melody

melodio·so -sa *adj* melodious

melodramáti·co -ca *adj* melodramatic

melón *m* melon; (*Cucumis melo*) muskmelon; (coll) blockhead; (coll) bald head; **melón de agua** watermelon

melo·so -sa *adj* sweet, honeyed; gentle, mild, mellow

mella *f* dent, nick, notch; gap, hollow; harm, injury; **hacer mella a** to have an effect on; **hacer mella en** to harm

mellar *tr* to dent, nick, notch; to harm

melli·zo -za *adj* & *mf* twin

membrana *f* membrane; (*del teléfono, micrófono*) diaphragm

membrete *m* note, memo; letterhead; heading; written invitation

membrillero *m* quince tree

membrillo *m* quince; quince tree

membru·do -da *adj* brawny, burly

memeches — a memeches (CAm) on horseback

memela *f* (CAm, Mex) cornmeal pancake

me·mo -ma *adj* foolish, simple ‖ *mf* fool, simpleton

memorán·dum *m* (*pl* **-dum**) memorandum book, notebook; (*sección en los*

periódicos) professional services;
(*papel con membrete*) letterhead

memorar *tr* & *ref* to remember

memoria *f* memory; (*exposición de ciertos hechos*) memoir; account, record; **de memoria** by heart; **encomendar a la memoria** to commit to memory; **hablar de memoria** (coll) to say the first thing that comes to one's mind; **hacer memoria de** to bring up; **memorias** memoirs; regards

memorial *m* memorandum book; memorial, petition; (law) brief

memorizar §60 *tr* to memorize

mena *f* ore

menaje *m* household furniture; school supplies

mención *f* mention

mencionar *tr* to mention

men·daz (*pl* **-daces**) *adj* mendacious ‖ liar

mendicante *adj* & *mf* mendicant

mendigante *adj* begging, mendicant ‖ *mf* beggar, mendicant

mendigar §44 *tr* to beg for ‖ *intr* to beg, go begging

mendi·go -ga *mf* beggar

mendiguez *f* begging

mendo·so -sa *adj* false, wrong

mendrugo *m* crumb, crust

menear *tr* to stir, to shake; to wiggle; (*la cola*) to wag; (*un negocio*) to manage; **peor es meneallo** (i.e., **menearlo**) better keep hands off ‖ *ref* to shake; to wiggle; to wag; (coll) to hustle, bestir oneself

meneo *m* stirring, shaking; wagging; hustling; (coll) drubbing, thrashing

menester *m* need; want, lack; job, occupation; **haber menester** to be necessary, to be need for; **menesteres** bodily needs; property; (coll) implements, tools; **ser menester** to be necessary

menestero·so -sa *adj* needy ‖ *mf* needy person

menestra *f* vegetable soup

menes·tral -trala *mf* mechanic

meng. *abbr* **menguante**

mengua *f* want, lack; poverty; decline; decrease, diminution; **en mengua de** to the discredit of

mengua·do -da *adj* timid, cowardly; simple, silly; mean, stingy; wretched, miserable; poor, needy; fatal

menguante *adj* decreasing; declining; waning ‖ *f* decrease; decline; low water; ebb tide; **menguante de la luna** wane, waning of the moon

menguar §10 *tr* to diminish, lessen; to discredit ‖ *intr* to diminish, lessen; to decline; to decrease; (*la luna*) to wane; (*la marea*) to fall

mengue *m* (coll) devil

menina *f* young lady in waiting

menino *m* noble page of the royal family

menor *adj* less, lesser; smaller; younger; least; smallest; youngest; slightest; minor ‖ *m* minor; **al por menor** retail; **menor de edad** minor; **por menor** retail; in detail, minutely ‖ *f* minor premise

Menorca *f* Minorca

menoría *f* inferiority, subordination; (*tiempo de menor edad*) minority

menorista *adj* (Arg, Chile) retail ‖ *mf* (Arg, Chile) retailer

menor·quín -quina *adj* & *mf* Minorcan

menos *adv* less; fewer; least; fewest; **al menos** at least; **a lo menos** at least; **a menos que** unless; **echar de menos** to miss; **¡menos mal!** lucky break!; **menos mal que** it is a good thing that; **no poder menos de** + *inf* to not be able to help + *ger;* **por lo menos** at least; **tener en menos** to think little of; **venir a menos** to decline; to become poor ‖ *prep* less, minus; (*al decir la hora*) of, to, e.g., **las tres menos diez** ten minutes of (or to) three ‖ *m* less; (*signo de resta o sustracción*) minus, minus sign

menoscabar *tr* to lessen, diminish, reduce; to damage; to discredit

menoscabo *m* lessening, reduction; damage; discredit; **con menoscabo de** to the detriment of

menoscuenta *f* part payment

menospreciable *adj* despicable, contemptible

menospreciar *tr* to underestimate, underrate; to scorn, despise

menosprecio *m* underestimation; scorn

mensaje *m* message

mensajería *f* public conveyance; **mensajerías** transportation company; shipping line

mensaje·ro -ra *mf* messenger ‖ *m* harbinger

men·so -sa *adj* (Mex) foolish, stupid

menstruar §21 *intr* to menstruate

menstruo *m* menses

mensual *adj* monthly

mensualidad *f* monthly pay, monthly instalment

ménsula *f* bracket; elbow rest

mensurar *tr* to measure

menta *f* mint; **menta piperita** peppermint; **menta romana** or **verde** spearmint

menta·do -da *adj* famous, renowned

mentar §2 *tr* to mention

mente *f* mind

mentecatería or **mentecatez** *f* simpleness, folly

menteca·to -ta *adj* simple, foolish ‖ *mf* simpleton, fool

mentidero *m* (coll) hangout; (coll) gossip column

mentir §68 *tr* to disappoint ‖ *intr* to lie; to be misleading; (*un color*) to clash; **¡miento!** my mistake!

mentira *f* lie; error, mistake; **mentira inocente** or **oficiosa** white lie; **parece mentira** it's hard to believe

mentirilla *f* fib, white lie; **de mentirillas** for fun

mentirón *m* whopper

mentiro·so -sa *adj* lying; false, deceptive; full of errors ‖ *mf* liar

men·tís (*pl* **-tís**) insulting contradiction; **dar un mentís a** to give the lie to

mentón *m* chin

me·nú *m* (*pl* **-nús**) menu

me
me

menudamente *adv* in detail; at retail

menudear *tr* to make frequently; to tell in detail; (Col) to sell at retail ‖ *intr* to happen frequently, to be frequent; to go into detail; (Arg) to grow, increase

menudencia *f* smallness; trifle; meticulousness; **menudencias** pork products; (Col, Mex) giblets

menudeo *m* constant repetition; detailed accounting; **al menudeo** at retail

menudillos *mpl* giblets

menu·do -da *adj* small, slight, minute; futile, worthless; meticulous; common, vulgar; petty ‖ *m* innards (*of fowl and other animals*); rice coal; **al menudo** at retail; **a menudo** often; **menudos** small change; **por menudo** in detail; at retail

meñique *adj* little, tiny; (*dedo*) little ‖ *m* little finger

meollo *m* marrow; pith; (*seso*) brain; brains, intelligence; gist, marrow, essence

me·ón -ona *adj* (*niño*) piddling; (*niebla*) dripping

mequetrefe *m* (coll) whippersnapper, jackanapes

mercachifle *m* peddler; small dealer

mercadear *intr* to deal, to trade

merca·der -dera *mf* merchant; **mercader de grueso** wholesale merchant

mercadería *f* merchandise, commodity; **mercaderías** goods, merchandise

mercado *m* market; **lanzar al mercado** to put on the market; **mercado de valores** stock market; **mercado negro** black market

mercaduría *f* commodity

mercancía *f* trade, commerce; merchandise; piece of merchandise; **mercancías** goods, merchandise ‖ **mercancías** *msg* (*pl* **-as**) freight train

mercante *adj* & *m* merchant

mercantil *adj* mercantile

mercar §73 *tr* to buy ‖ *intr* to trade, deal

merced *f* pay, wages; favor, grace; **a merced de** at the mercy of; **merced a** thanks to; **merced de agua** distribution of irrigating water; **vuestra merced** your grace

mercena·rio -ria *adj* mercenary ‖ *m* mercenary; day laborer, hireling

mercería *f* haberdashery, notions store; (Am) dry-goods store; (Chile) hardware store

mercología *f* marketing

mercurio *m* mercury

merecer §22 *tr* to deserve, merit; (*lo que se desea*) to attain; (*alabanza*) to win; (*cierta suma*) to be worth; **merecer la pena** to be worth while ‖ *intr* to be deserving; **merecer bien de** to deserve the gratitude of

mereci·do -da *adj* deserved ‖ *m* just deserts; **llevar su merecido** to get what's coming to one

mereciente *adj* deserving

merecimiento *m* desert, merit

merendar §2 *tr* to lunch on, have for lunch; to keep an eye on, to peep at

‖ *intr* to lunch ‖ *ref* to manage to get; (*en el juego*) (Chile) to clean out

merendero *m* lunchroom; picnic grounds

merendona *f* fine spread

merengar §44 *tr* to whip (*cream*)

merengue *m* meringue

mere·triz *f* (*pl* **-trices**) harlot

meridiana *f* lounge, couch; afternoon nap; meridian line; **a la meridiana** at noon

meridia·no -na *adj* meridian; bright, dazzling ‖ *m* meridian ‖ *f* see **meridiana**

meridional *adj* southern ‖ *mf* southerner

merienda *f* lunch, snack; (coll) hunchback

meri·no -na *adj* merino; (*cabello*) thick and curly ‖ *mf* merino ‖ *m* merino shepherd; merino wool

mérito *m* merit, desert; value, worth; **hacer mérito de** to make mention of; **hacer méritos** to try to please, to put one's best foot forward

merito·rio -ria *adj* meritorious ‖ *m* volunteer worker; unpaid learner, apprentice

merluza *f* (*pez*) hake; (coll) drunk, spree

merma *f* decrease, reduction; leakage, shrinkage

mermar *tr* to decrease, reduce ‖ *intr* to decrease, shrink, dwindle

mermelada *f* marmalade

me·ro -ra *adj* mere, pure; (Col, Ven) alone ‖ *m* grouper, jewfish ‖ **mero** *adv* (CAm) almost, soon

merodea·dor -dora *adj* marauding ‖ *m* marauder

merodear *intr* to maraud

mes *m* month; monthly pay; menses; **caer en el mes del obispo** (coll) to come at the right time

mesa *f* table; (*mostrador*) counter; (*escritorio*) desk; (*de arma blanca o herramienta*) flat side; (*de escalera*) landing; (*comida*) fare, food; (*conjunto de dirigentes*) board; **alzar la mesa** to clear the table; **hacer mesa limpia** to clean up (*in gambling*); **levantar la mesa** to clear the table; **mesa de batalla** sorting table; **mesa de extensión** extension table; **mesa de juego** gambling table; **mesa de milanos** (coll) scanty fare; **mesa de trucos** pool table; **mesa perezosa** drop table; **poner la mesa** to set or lay the table; **tener a mesa y mantel** to feed, to support; **tener mesa** to keep open house

mesana *f* (naut) mizzen

mesar *tr* (*los cabellos*) to tear, pull out ‖ *ref* — **mesarse los cabellos** to pull out one's hair; to pull out each other's hair

mescolanza *f* (coll) jumble, hodgepodge, medley

meseguería *f* harvest watch

mesera *f* (Am) waitress

mesero *m* journeyman on monthly pay; (Am) waiter

meseta *f* plateau, tableland; (*de escalera*) landing

Mesías _m_ Messiah

mesilla _f_ mantel, mantelpiece; (_de escalera_) landing; window sill

mesita _f_ stand, small table; **mesita portateléfono** telephone table

mesnada _f_ armed retinue; band, company

mesón _m_ inn, tavern; (Chile) bar; (Chile) counter

mesone·ro -ra _adj_ inn, tavern ‖ _mf_ innkeeper, tavern keeper

mester _m_ (archaic) craft, trade; (archaic) literary genre; **mester de clerecía** clerical verse of the Middle Ages; **mester de juglaría** popular minstrelsy of the Middle Ages

mesti·zo -za _adj_ & _mf_ half-breed; (_perro_) mongrel

mesura _f_ dignity, gravity; calm, restraint; courtesy, civility

mesura·do -da _adj_ dignified, sedate; calm, restrained; polite; moderate, temperate

mesurar _tr_ to temper, moderate ‖ _ref_ to act with restraint

meta _f_ goal

metafonía _f_ umlaut

metáfora _f_ metaphore

metafóri·co -ca _adj_ metaphorical

metal _m_ metal; money; (_de la voz_) timbre; condition, quality; (mus) brass; **el vil metal** (coll) filthy lucre; **metal blanco** nickel silver; **metal de imprenta** type metal

metale·ro -ra _adj_ (Bol, Chile, Peru) metal ‖ _m_ (Bol, Chile, Peru) metalworker

metáli·co -ca _adj_ metallic ‖ _m_ metalworker; cash, coin

metalistería _f_ metalwork

metalizar §60 _tr_ to make metallic; to put a metal coating on; to turn into cash ‖ _ref_ to become mercenary

metaloide _m_ nonmetal

metalurgia _f_ metallurgy

metamorfo·sis _f_ (_pl_ -sis) metamorphosis

metano _m_ methane

metate _m_ (CAm, Mex) flat stone on which corn is ground

metáte·sis _f_ (_pl_ -sis) metathesis

mete·dor -dora _mf_ smuggler

metedería _f_ smuggling

metemuer·tos _m_ (_pl_ -tos) stagehand; busybody, meddler

meteo _f_ weather bureau, weather report

meteóri·co -ca _adj_ meteoric

meteoro or **metéoro** _m_ meteor; atmospheric phenomenon

meteorología _f_ meteorology

meter _tr_ to put, to place; to insert; (_un ruido_) to make; (_miedo_) to cause; (_mentiras_) to tell; (_chismes, enredos_) to start; (_dinero en el juego_) to stake; to smuggle; (_un golpe_) (Am) to strike ‖ _ref_ to project; to meddle, butt in; **meterse a** to set oneself up as; to take it upon oneself to; **meterse con** to pick a quarrel with; **meterse en** to get into; to plunge into; to empty into

meticulo·so -sa _adj_ meticulous; shy, timid

meti·do -da _adj_ close, tight; rich, abundant; (Am) meddlesome; **muy metido con** on close terms with; **muy metido en** deeply involved in ‖ _m_ push; punch; strong lye; loose leaf; (_tela sobrante en las costuras de una prenda_) seam

metódi·co -ca _adj_ methodic(al)

metodista _adj_ & _mf_ Methodist

método _m_ method

metraje _m_ distance or length in meters; (_cine_) **de corto metraje** short; (_cine_) **de largo metraje** full-length

metralla _f_ scrap iron; grapeshot; shrapnel

métri·co -ca _adj_ metric(al) ‖ _f_ prosody

metro _m_ meter; ruler; tape measure; subway; **metro plegadizo** folding rule

metrónomo _m_ metronome

metrópoli _f_ metropolis; mother country

metropolita·no -na _adj_ metropolitan ‖ _m_ subway; (eccl) metropolitan

Méx. _abbr_ México

mexica·no -na _adj_ & _mf_ (Am) Mexican

México _m_ (Am) Mexico; **Nuevo México** New Mexico

mezcla _f_ mixture; (_argamasa_) mortar; (_tejido_) tweed

mezclar _tr_ to mix; to blend ‖ _ref_ to mix; (_introducirse uno entre otros_) to mingle; to intermarry; to meddle

mezclilla _f_ light tweed

mezcolanza _f_ jumble, hodgepodge, medley

mezquinar _tr_ (Am) to be stingy with ‖ _intr_ (Am) to be stingy

mezquindad _f_ meanness, stinginess; need, poverty; smallness, tininess; wretchedness

mezqui·no -na _adj_ mean, stingy; needy, poor; small, tiny; wretched

mezquita _f_ mosque

mi _adj poss_ my

mí (used as object of a preposition) _pron pers_ me ‖ _pron reflex_ myself

miar §77 _intr_ to meow

miau _m_ meow

mica _f_ mica; (Guat) flirt; **ponerse una mica** (CAm) to go on a jag

mico _m_ long-tailed monkey; libertine; (coll) hoodlum; **dar mico** (coll) to not keep a date

microbio _m_ microbe

microbiología _f_ microbiology

microbús _m_ (Chile) jitney

microfaradio _m_ microfarad

microficha _f_ microcard

micro·film _m_ (_pl_ -films o -filmes) microfilm

microfilmar _tr_ to microfilm

micrófono _m_ microphone

microonda _f_ microwave

micropelícula _f_ microfilm

microscópi·co -ca _adj_ microscopic

microscopio _m_ microscope

microsurco _adj invar_ microgroove ‖ _m_ microgroove

microteléfono _m_ handset, French telephone

mi·cho -cha _mf_ (coll) pussy cat

miedo _m_ fear, dread; **miedo cerval**

great fear; **por miedo de** for fear of; **por miedo (de) que** for fear that; **tener miedo (a)** to be afraid (of); **tener miedo de** to be in fear of, be afraid of; to be afraid to

miedo·so -sa *adj* (coll) fearful, afraid

miel *f* honey; (*jarabe saturado*) molasses; **dejar con la miel en los labios** to spoil the fun for; **hacerse de miel** to be peaches and cream

mielga *f* lucerne

miembro *m* member; (*extremidad del hombre y los animales*) member, limb

mientes *fpl* mind, thought; wish, desire; **caer en las mientes** or **en mientes** to come to mind; **parar** or **poner mientes en** to reflect on; **venírsele a uno a las mientes** to come to one's mind

mientras *conj* while; whereas; **mientras que** while; whereas; **mientras tanto** meanwhile

miérco·les *m* (*pl* **-les**) Wednesday; **miércoles de ceniza** Ash Wednesday

mies *f* cereal, grain; harvest time; **mieses** grain fields

miga *f* (*porción pequeña*) bit; (*parte más blanda del pan*) crumb; (fig) substance; **hacer buenas migas con** to get along well with; **migas** fried crumbs

migaja *f* bit, piece; (*de inteligencia*) smattering; **migajas** crumbs; leavings

migajón *m* crumb; (coll) substance

migar §44 *tr* (*el pan*) to crumb; (*p.ej., la leche*) to put crumbs in

migrato·rio -ria *adj* migratory

miguelear *tr* (CAm) to make love to

miguele·ño -ña *adj* (Hond) impolite, discourteous

mijo *m* millet

mil *adj* & *m* thousand, a thousand, one thousand; **a las mil quinientas** (coll) at an unearthly hour

milagre·ro -ra *adj* superstitious; miracle-working

milagro *m* (*hecho sobrenatural*) miracle; (*cosa rara*) wonder; votive offering; **colgar el milagro a** (coll) to put the blame on; **vivir de milagro** to have a hard time getting along; to have had a narrow escape

milagrón *m* (coll) fuss, excitement

milagro·so -sa *adj* miraculous; marvelous, wonderful

milano *m* burr, down; (orn) kite

mil·deu *m* (*pl* **-deues**) mildew

milena·rio -ria *adj* millennial || *m* millennium

milenio *m* millennium

milenrama *f* yarrow

milési·mo -ma *adj* & *m* thousandth

miliamperio *m* milliampere

milicia *f* militia; soldiery; warfare; military service

milicia·no -na *adj* military || *m* militiaman

miligramo *m* milligram

milímetro *m* millimeter

militante *adj* militant

militar *adj* military; army || *m* soldier, military man || *intr* to fight, go to

war; to struggle; to serve in the army; (*surtir efecto*) to militate

militarismo *m* militarism

militarista *adj* & *mf* militarist

militarizar §60 *tr* to militarize

mílite *m* soldier

milpa *f* (CAm, Mex) cornfield

milla *f* mile

millar *m* thousand

millarada *f* about a thousand; **echar millaradas** to boast about one's wealth

millo *m* millet

millón *m* million

millona·rio -ria *adj* of a million or more inhabitants || *mf* millionaire

mimar *tr* to fondle, to pet; to pamper, indulge, spoil

mimbre *m* & *f* (bot) osier; osier, wicker, withe

mimbrear *intr* & *ref* to sway

mimbre·ño -ña *adj* willowy

mimbrera *f* (bot) osier, osier willow

mimbro·so -sa *adj* osier; (*hecho de mimbre*) wicker

mimeografiar §77 *tr* to mimeograph

mimeógrafo *m* mimeograph

mímica *f* mimicry; sign language

mimo *m* (*entre los griegos y romanos*) mime; fondling, petting; pampering

mimo·so -sa *adj* delicate, tender; finicky, fussy

mina *f* mine; (*de lápiz*) lead; (fig) mine, gold mine, storehouse; underground passage; (SAm) moll; **beneficiar una mina** to work a mine; **mina de carbón** or **mina hullera** coal mine

minado *m* mine work; (nav) mining

mina·dor -dora *adj* (nav) mine-laying || *m* (mil) miner; (nav) mine layer

minar *tr* to mine; to undermine; to consume; to plug away at || *intr* to mine

minarete *m* minaret

mineraje *m* mining; **mineraje a tajo abierto** (Hond) strip mining

mineral *adj* & *m* mineral

mineralogía *f* mineralogy

minería *f* mining; mine operators

mine·ro -ra *adj* mining || *m* miner; mine operator; (fig) source, origin

mingitorio *m* street urinal

min·gón -gona *adj* (Ven) spoiled, pampered

miniar *tr* to paint in miniature; (*un manuscrito*) to illuminate

miniatura *f* miniature

miniaturización *f* miniaturization

minifalda *f* miniskirt

míni·mo -ma *adj* minimum; tiny, small, minute; least, smallest || *m* minimum || *f* tiny bit

mini·no -na *mf* (coll) kitty, pussy

ministerial *adj* ministerial

ministerio *m* ministry, cabinet, government; **formar ministerio** to form a government; **ministerio de Hacienda** Treasury Department (U.S.A.); Treasury (Brit); **ministerio de la Gobernación** Department of the Interior (U.S.A.); Home Office (Brit); **ministerio del Ejército** Department of the Army (U.S.A.); War Office (Brit); **ministerio de Marina** Department of the Navy (U.S.A.); Board of Admiralty (Brit)

ministrar *tr* to administer; to furnish

ministro *m* minister; bailiff, constable; **ministro de asuntos exteriores** foreign minister; **ministro de Gobernación** Home Secretary (Brit); **ministro de Hacienda** Secretary of the Treasury (U.S.A.); Chancellor of the Exchequer (Brit); **ministro de Justicia** Attorney General (U.S.A.); **primer ministro** prime minister, premier

minorar *tr* to diminish, reduce; to weaken

minorati·vo -va *adj & m* laxative

minoría *f* minority

minoridad *f* minority

minorita·rio -ria *adj* minority

minucia *f* trifle; **minucias** minutiae

minucio·so -sa *adj* minute, meticulous

minué *m* or **minuete** *m* minuet

minúscu·lo -la *adj* (*letra*) small; (coll) small, tiny ǁ *f* small letter

minuta *f* first draft, rough draft; memorandum; menu, bill of fare; roll, list

minutero *m* minute hand

minu·to -ta *adj* minute ǁ *m* minute ǁ *f* see **minuta**

mí·o -a *adj poss* mine; of mine, e.g., **un amigo mío** a friend of mine ǁ *pron poss* mine

miope *adj* near-sighted ǁ *mf* near-sighted person

miopía *f* near-sightedness

mira *f* (*de arma de fuego, telescopio, etc.*) sight; aim, object, purpose; target; watchtower; **estar a la mira** to be on the lookout; **poner la mira en** to have designs on

mirada *f* glance, look; **apuñalar con la mirada** to look daggers at; **mirada de soslayo** side glance

miradero *m* (*lugar desde donde se mira*) lookout; (*persona o cosa que es objeto de la atención pública*) cynosure

mira·do -da *adj* cautious, circumspect; **bien mirado** highly regarded ǁ *f* see **mirada**

mirador *m* belvedere; bay window, oriel

miramiento *m* considerateness, courtesy, regard; look; **miramientos** (coll) fuss, bother

miranda *f* eminence, vantage point

mirar *tr* to look at, to watch; to consider, contemplate; **mirar bien** to look with favor on; **mirar por encima** to glance at ǁ *intr* to look, to glance; **¡mira!** look out!; **mirar a** to look at, glance at; to face, overlook; to aim at; to aim to; **mirar por** to look after ǁ *ref* to look at oneself; to look at each other; **mirarse en ello** to watch one's step; **mirarse en una persona** to be all wrapped up in a person

mirasol *m* sunflower

miríada *f* myriad

mirilla *f* peephole; (*para dirigir visuales*) target; (phot) finder

miriñaque *m* hoop skirt, crinoline; bauble, trinket; (Arg) cowcatcher

mirística *f* nutmeg tree

mirlar *ref* (coll) to try to look important

mirlo *m* blackbird; (coll) solemn look; **mirlo blanco** (coll) rare bird; **soltar el mirlo** (coll) to start to jabber

mirmidón *m* tiny fellow, nincompoop

mi·rón -rona *adj* onlooking; nosy ǁ *mf* onlooker; (*de una partida de juego*) kibitzer; busybody

mirra *f* myrrh

mirto *m* myrtle

misa *f* mass; **cantar misa** to say mass; **como en misa** in dead silence; **misa cantada** High Mass; **misa de prima** early mass; **misa mayor** High Mass; **misa rezada** Low Mass

misal *m* missal

misantropía *f* misanthropy

misántropo *m* misanthrope

misar *intr* (coll) to say mass; (coll) to hear mass

misario *m* acolyte

misceláne·o -na *adj* miscellaneous ǁ *f* miscellany

miserable *adj* miserable, wretched; mean, stingy; despicable, vile ǁ *mf* cur, cad; wretch; miser

miseran·do -da *adj* pitiful

miserear *intr* (coll) to be stingy

miseria *f* misery, wretchedness; poverty; stinginess; (coll) trifle, pittance; **comerse de miseria** (coll) to live in great poverty

misericordia *f* compassion, mercy, pity

misericordio·so -sa *adj* merciful

mise·ro -ra *adj* miserable, wretched ǁ *mf* wretch

misión *f* mission; ration for harvesters; **ir a misiones** to go away as a missionary

misional *adj* missionary

misionario *m* missionary; envoy, messenger

misionero *m* missionary

misi·vo -va *adj & f* missive

mismísi·mo -ma *adj* very same, self-same

mis·mo -ma *adj & pron indef* same; own, very; -self, e.g., **ella misma** herself; myself, e.g., **yo mismo** I myself; yourself, himself, herself, itself; **así mismo** likewise, also; **casi lo mismo** much the same; **lo mismo** just the same; **lo mismo me da** (coll) it's all the same to me; **mismo . . . que** same . . . as; **por lo mismo** for that very reason ǁ *mismo adv* right, e.g., **ahora mismo** right now; **aquí mismo** right here

mistela *f* flavored brandy; needled must, spiked must

misterio *m* mystery; **hablar de misterio** to talk mysteriously

misterio·so -sa *adj* mysterious

misticismo *m* mysticism

místi·co -ca *adj* mystic(al) ǁ *mf* mystic

mistificación *f* hoax, mystification

mistificar §73 *tr* to hoax, to mystify

mistifori *m* (coll) hodgepodge

misturera *f* (Peru) flower girl

mita *f* mite, cheese mite; (SAm) Indian slave labor; (*turno en el trabajo*) (Arg, Chile) shift, turn

mi
mi

mitad *f* half; middle; **a (la) mitad de** halfway through; **cara mitad** (coll) better half; **en la mitad de** in the middle of; **la mitad de** half the; **mitad y mitad** half-and-half; **por la mitad** in half, in the middle

míti·co -ca *adj* mythical

mitigar §44 *tr* to mitigate, appease, allay

mitin *m* (*pl* **mitins** or **mítines**) meeting, rally

mito *m* myth

mitología *f* mythology

mitológi·co -ca *adj* mythological

mitón *m* mitten

mitra *f* chimney pot; (eccl) miter

mixtificación *f* hoax, mystification

mixtificar §73 *tr* to hoax, to mystify

mixtifori *m* (coll) hodgepodge

mixtión *f* mixture

mix·to -ta *adj* mixed || *m* compound number; sulphur match; explosive compound

mixtura *f* mixture

mixturar *tr* to mix

mixturera *f* (Peru) flower girl

miz *interj* here, pussy!, here, kitty!

mízcalo *m* edible milk mushroom

m/l *abbr* **mi letra**

m/n *abbr* **moneda nacional**

mobilia·rio -ria *adj* personal (*property*) || *m* furniture, suit of furniture

moblaje *m* furniture, suit of furniture

moblar §61 *tr* to furnish

moca *f* Mocha coffee || *f* (Ecuad) mudhole; (Mex) wineglass

mocador *m* handkerchief

mocar §73 *tr* to blow the nose of || *ref* to blow one's nose

mocarro *m* (coll) snot

mocasín *m* moccasin

mocear *intr* to act young; to sow one's wild oats

mocedad *f* youth; wild oats

mocerío *m* young people

mocero *adj masc* woman-crazy

mocetón *m* strapping young fellow

mocetona *f* buxom young woman

mocil *adj* youthful

moción *f* motion, movement; (*en junta deliberante*) motion; **hacer** or **presentar una moción** to make a motion

mocionante *mf* (Am) mover

mocionar *tr & intr* (Am) to move

moci·to -ta *adj* young || *mf* youngster

moco *m* (*humor segregado por una membrana mucosa*) mucus; (*mocarro*) snot; (*extremo del pabilo de una vela*) snuff; **a moco de candil** by candle light; **llorar a moco tendido** (coll) to cry like a baby; **moco de pavo** crest of a turkey; (bot) cockscomb; (col) trifle

moco·so -sa *adj* snotty, snively; rude, ill-bred; flip, saucy; mean, worthless || *mf* brat

mochar *tr* to butt; (Arg) to rob; (Am) to chop off; (Col) to fire

mochil *m* errand boy for farmers in the field

mochila *f* knapsack, haversack; tool bag; (mil) ration

mochín *m* (slang) executioner

mo·cho -cha *adj* blunt, stub, flat; (*árbol*) topped; stub-horned || *m* butt end

mochuelo *m* (orn) little owl; (*de una o más palabras*) omission; **cargar con el mochuelo** or **tocarle a** (*uno*) **el mochuelo** (coll) to get the worst of a deal

moda *f* fashion, mode, style; **a la moda de** after the fashion of, in the style of; **alta moda** haute couture; **de moda** in fashion; **fuera de moda** out of fashion; **pasar de moda** to go out of fashion

modales *mpl* manners

modalidad *f* manner, way, nature, kind

modelar *tr* to model; to form, shape; to mold || *ref* to model; **modelarse sobre** to pattern oneself after

modelo *adj invar* model, e.g., **ciudad modelo** model city || *mf* model, mannequin, fashion model || *m* model, pattern; form, blank; equal, peer; style

modera·do -da *adj* moderate

moderador *m* regulator; (*para retardar el efecto de los neutrones*) moderator

moderar *tr* to moderate, control, restrain || *ref* to moderate, control oneself, restrain oneself

modernizar §60 *tr* to modernize

moder·no -na *adj* modern

modestia *f* modesty

modes·to -ta *adj* modest

modicidad *f* moderateness, reasonableness

módi·co -ca *adj* moderate, reasonable

modificante *adj* modifying || *m* (gram) modifier

modificar §73 *tr* to modify

modismo *m* idiom

modista *f* dressmaker; **modista de sombreros** milliner

modistería *f* dressmaking; (Am) ladies' dress shop

modistilla *f* (coll) dressmaker's helper; (coll) unskilled dressmaker

modisto *m* ladies' tailor

modo *m* manner, mode, way; (gram) mood, mode; **al** or **a modo de** like, on the order of; **de buen modo** politely; **de ese modo** at that rate; **de tal modo que** with the result that; **de modo que** so that; and so; **de ningún modo** by no means; **de todos modos** anyhow, at any rate; **en cierto modo** after a fashion; **modo de ser** nature, disposition; **por modo de** as, by way of; **sobre modo** extremely; **uno a modo de** a sort of, a kind of

modorra *f* drowsiness, heaviness

modorrar *tr* to make drowsy || *ref* to get drowsy, fall asleep; (*la fruta*) to get squashy

modo·rro -rra *adj* drowsy, heavy; dull, stupid; (*fruta*) squashy || *f* see **modorra**

modo·so -sa *adj* quiet, well-behaved

modrego *m* (coll) boor, awkward fellow

modulación *f* modulation; **modulación de altura** or **de amplitud** amplitude modulation; **modulación de frecuen-cia** frequency modulation

modular tr & intr to modulate

modulo·so -sa adj harmonious

mofa f jeering, scoffing, mockery

mofeta f skunk; (gas pernicioso que se desprende de las minas) blackdamp, firedamp

moflete m (coll) fat cheek, jowl

mofletu·do -da adj fat-cheeked

mo·gol -gola adj & mf Mongol, Mongolian

mogollón m — **comer de mogollón** (coll) to sponge

mo·gón -gona adj one-horned, broken-horned

mogote m knoll, hilloc.:; stack of sheaves; budding antler

mohatra f fake sale; cheating

mohien·to -ta adj moldy, musty; (hierro) rusty

mohín m face, grimace

mohina f annoyance, displeasure

mohi·no -na adj sad, melancholy, moody; (caballo, buey, vaca) black, black-nosed || mf hinny || m blue magpie || f see **mohina**

moho m mold, must; (del hierro) rust; sloth, laziness; **no dejar criar moho** (coll) to keep in constant use, to use up quickly

moho·so -sa adj moldy, musty; (hierro) rusty; (chiste) stale

Moisés m Moses

moja·do -da adj wet; (p.ej., por la lluvia) drenched, soaked; (húmedo) moist; (phonet) liquid || m (Mex) wetback

mojar tr to wet; (la lluvia a una persona) to drench, soak; (humedecer) to dampen, to moisten; (ensopar) to dunk; (coll) to stab || intr — **mojar en** to get mixed up in || ref to get wet; to get drenched, get soaked

mojarrilla mf (coll) jolly person

moje m sauce, gravy

mojicón m muffin, bun; (coll) slap in the face

mojiganga f masquerade, mummery; clowning

mojigatería or **mojigatez** f hypocrisy, prudery, sanctimoniousness

mojiga·to -ta adj hypocritical; prudish, sanctimonious || mf hypocrite; prude, sanctimonious person

mojinete m (de un muro) coping; (de un tejado) ridge; (Arg) gable; (Chile) gable end

mojón m boundary stone, landmark; (montón sin orden) pile, heap; (guía en desplobado) road mark; (porción de excremento humano) turd

moldar tr to mold; to put molding on

molde m mold; pattern; cast, stamp, matrix; (persona) model, ideal; (letra) **de molde** printed; **venir de molde** to be just right

moldear tr to mold; (vaciar) to cast; to put molding on

moldura f molding

moldurar tr to put molding on

mole adj soft || m (Mex) stew seasoned with chili sauce || f bulk, mass

molécula f molecule

molende·ro -ra mf miller, grinder || m chocolate grinder; (CAm) grinding table

moler §47 tr (granos) to grind, to mill; to annoy, harass, weary; to tire out, fatigue; (coll) to chew; **moler a palos** (coll) to beat up

molesquina f moleskin

molestar tr to disturb, molest; to bother, annoy; to tire, weary || ref to bother; to be annoyed; **molestarse en** to take the trouble to

molestia f disturbance, discomfort; annoyance, bother, nuisance

moles·to -ta adj bothersome, troublesome; boring, tedious; bored, tired

molesto·so -sa adj (Am) bothersome

moleteado m knurl

moletear tr to knurl

molibdeno m molybdenum

molicie f softness; effeminacy, voluptuous living

moli·do -da adj exhausted, worn out

molienda f grinding, milling; (cantidad que se muele de una vez) grist; (molino) mill; (coll) bore, annoyance; (coll) fatigue, weariness

molimiento m grinding; weariness

moline·ro -ra adj mill || m miller || f miller's wife

molinete m little mill; ventilating fan; (juguete de papel) windmill; (movimiento que se hace con el bastón) twirl; (con la espada) flourish; (naut) windlass; (rueda de cohetes) (Mex) pinwheel

molinillo m hand mill; **molinillo de café** coffee grinder

molino m mill; **luchar con los molinos de viento** to tilt at windmills; **molino de sangre** animal-driven mill; **molino de viento** windmill; **molino harinero** gristmill, flour mill

moloc m (Ecuad) mashed potatoes

molondrón m (coll) lazy bum; (Ven) large inheritance, large amount of money

molusco m mollusk

mollar adj soft, tender; mushy, squashy; (carne) lean; profitable; (coll) gullible, easily taken in

mollear intr to give, to yield; to bend

molleja f gizzard; **criar molleja** (coll) to get lazy; **mollejas** sweetbread

mollejón m grindstone; (coll) big fat loafer; (coll) good-natured fellow

mollera f crown (of the head); (coll) brains, sense; **cerrado de mollera** (coll) stupid; **duro de mollera** (coll) stubborn

mollete m muffin

molli·no -na adj drizzly || f drizzle

mollizna f drizzle

momentáne·o -a adj momentary

momento m moment; **al momento** at once; **de un momento a otro** at any moment

momería f clowning

mome·ro -ra adj clowning || mf clown

momia f mummy

momificar §73 tr to mummify

mi
mo

mo·mio -mia *adj* lean, skinny ‖ *m* extra; (*ganga*) bargain; sinecure ‖ *f* see **momia**

momo *m* face, grimace; (coll) caress

mona *f* female monkey; Barbary ape; (coll) ape, copycat; (coll) drunkenness; (*persona*) (coll) drunk; (taur) guard for right leg; **dormir la mona** (coll) to sleep off a drunk; **pillar una mona** (coll) to go on a jag; **pintar la mona** (coll) to put on airs

monacal *adj* monachal

monacato *m* monkhood

monacillo *m* altar boy, acolyte

monada *f* monkeyshine; (*gesto*) face, grimace, monkey face; darling; cuteness; flattery; folly, childishness

monaguillo *m* altar boy, acolyte

monaquismo *m* monasticism

monarca *m* monarch

monarquía *f* monarchy

monárqui·co -ca *adj* monarchic(al) ‖ *mf* monarchist

monasterio *m* monastery

monásti·co -ca *adj* monastic

monda *f* pruning, trimming; parings, peelings; (Am) beating, whipping

mondadien·tes *m* (*pl* -tes) toothpick

mondadura *f* pruning, trimming; **mondaduras** peelings

mondar *tr* to clean; to prune, to trim; to peel, pare, hull, husk; (*quitar con engaño los bienes a*) to fleece; (Am) to beat, whip

mon·do -da *adj* clean; pure; **mondo y lirondo** (coll) pure, unadulterated ‖ *f* see **monda**

mondonga *f* (coll) kitchen wench

mondongo *m* intestines, insides; (*del hombre*) (coll) guts

monear *intr* (coll) to act like a monkey; (Am) to boast ‖ *ref* (Hond) to plug away; (Hond) to punch each other

moneda *f* coin; (coll) money; **la Moneda** the government of Chile; **moneda corriente** currency; (coll) common knowledge; **moneda falsa** counterfeit; **moneda menuda** change; **moneda metálica** or **sonante** specie; **moneda suelta** change; **pagar en la misma moneda** to pay back in one's own coin

monedar *tr* to coin, to mint

monedero *m* moneybag; **monedero falso** counterfeiter

monería *f* monkeyshine; cuteness; childishness

mones·co -ca *adj* (coll) apish

moneta·rio -ria *adj* monetary

mon·gol -gola *adj* & *mf* Mongol, Mongolian

monigote *m* lay brother; rag figure, stuffed form; botched painting, botched statue; (coll) sap, boob

monipodio *m* (coll) collusion, deal, plot

monís *m* trinket; **monises** (coll) money, dough

mónita *f* (coll) cunning, smoothness, slickness

monitor *m* monitor

monja *f* nun; **monjas** lingering sparks in burning paper

monje *m* monk

monjía *f* monkhood

monjil *adj* nunnish ‖ *m* nun's dress

mono -na *adj* (coll) cute, nice; (Am) blond; (*cabello*) (Am) red ‖ *m* monkey, ape; (*traje de faena*) coveralls; whippersnapper, squirt; (taur) attendant of picador; (Chile) pyramid of fruit or vegetables; **estar de monos** (coll) to be on the outs; **mono de Gibraltar** Barbary ape ‖ *f* see **mona**

monóculo *m* monocle

monogamia *f* monogamy

monografía *f* monograph

monograma *m* monogram

monolíti·co -ca *adj* monolithic

monologar §44 *intr* to soliloquize

monólogo *m* monologue

monomanía *f* monomania

monomio *m* monomial

mono·no -na *adj* (coll) cute, sweet

monopatín *m* scooter

monoplano *m* monoplane

monopolio *m* monopoly

monopolizar §60 *tr* to monopolize

monorriel *m* monorail

monosabio *m* (taur) attendant of picador

monosílabo *m* monosyllable

monoteísta *adj* monotheistic ‖ *mf* monotheist

monotipia *f* monotype

monotipista *mf* monotype operator

monotipo *m* monotype

monotonía *f* monotony

monóto·no -na *adj* monotonous

monóxido *m* monoxide

monseñor *m* monseigneur; (eccl) monsignor

monserga *f* (coll) gibberish

monstruo *m* monster

monstruosidad *f* monstrosity

monstruo·so -sa *adj* monstrous

monta *f* sum, total; **de poca monta** of little account

montacar·gas *m* (*pl* -gas) hoist, freight elevator

montadero *m* horse block

montadura *f* mounting; (*de una caballería de silla*) harness; (*engaste*) setting, mount

montaje *m* montage; setting up; (mach) assembly; (tel) hookup

montanero *m* forest ranger

montante *m* post, upright; (*suma*) amount; (*hueco cuadrilongo sobre una puerta*) transom; (*espadón*) broadsword ‖ *f* flood tide

montaña *f* mountain; mountain country; **la Montaña** the Province of Santander, Spain; **montaña de hielo** iceberg; **montaña rusa** roller coaster

monta·ñés -ñesa *adj* mountain ‖ *mf* mountaineer, highlander

montaño·so -sa *adj* mountainous

montapla·tos *m* (*pl* -tos) dumbwaiter

montar *tr* to mount, to get on; (*un caballo, una bicicleta, los hombros de una persona*) to ride; (*un servicio*) to set up, establish; (*un fusil*) to cock; (*una piedra preciosa*) to set, to mount; (*el caballo a la yegua*) to cover; (*un reloj*) to wind; (elec) to hook up; (mach) to assemble, to mount; *(la guardia)* (mil) to mount; *(un cabo)* (naut) to round; *(un buque)* (naut) to command; *(importar)* to amount to || *intr* to mount; to get on top; to weigh, to be important; **tanto monta** it's all the same || *ref* to mount; to get on top; **montarse en cólera** to fly into a rage

monta·raz *(pl* **-races)** *adj* backwoods; wild, untamed || *m* forester, warden

monte *m* mountain, mount; woods, woodland; obstruction, interference; backwoods, wilds; bank, kitty; (coll) dirty head of hair; **andar al monte** (coll) to take to the woods; **monte alto** forest; **monte bajo** thicket, brushwood; **monte de piedad** pawnshop; **monte pío** pension fund for widows and orphans; mutual benefit society; **monte tallar** tree farm

montear *tr* to hunt, to track down; to make a working drawing of; to arch, to vault

montecillo *m* mound, hillock

montepío *m* pension fund for widows and orphans; mutual benefit society

montera *f* cloth cap; glass roof; wife of hunter; bullfighter's black bicorne; (Hond) drunk, jag

montería *f* hunting, big-game hunting; hunting party; (Bol, Ecuad) canoe to shoot the rapids; (Mex) lumbermen's camp

monterilla *f* (naut) moonsail

montero *m* hunter, huntsman

montés or **montesi·no -na** *adj* wild *(e.g., goat)*

montículo *m* mound, hillock

montilla *f* montilla *(a pale dry sherry)*

monto *m* sum, total

montón *m* pile, heap; *(de gente)* crowd; (coll) lot, great deal, great many; **a, de,** or **en montón** (coll) taken together; **a montones** (coll) in abundance; **ser del montón** (coll) to be quite ordinary

montonera *f* (Am) heap, pile; (Am) band of mounted rebels

montu·no -na *adj* wooded; (Am) wild, untamed, rustic

montuo·so -sa *adj* wooded, woody; rugged, hilly

montura *f* *(cabalgadura)* mount; *(de una cabalgadura)* harness; seat, saddle; *(de una piedra preciosa, de un instrumento astronómico)* mounting; *(de gafas)* frame

monumento *m* monument

monzón *m* monsoon

moña *f* doll; mannequin; ribbon, hair ribbon; (coll) drunk, jag

moño *m* topknot; crest, top; (Col) caprice, whim; *(de caballo)* (Chile) forelock; **moños** frippery

moquear *intr* to snivel

moqueo *m* snivel, sniveling

moquero *m* handkerchief

moquete *m* punch in the nose

moquillo *m* runny nose; (vet) distemper

moquita *f* mucus, snivel

mor *m* — **por mor de** for love of; because of

mora *f* black mulberry; blackberry; brambleberry; white mulberry

morada *f* dwelling; stay, sojourn

mora·do -da *adj* purple, mulberry || *f* see **morada**

moral *adj* moral || *m* black mulberry tree || *f* *(ciencia de la conducta; conducta)* morals; *(espíritu, confianza)* morale; *(p.ej., de una fábula)* (coll) moral

moraleja *f* moral

moralidad *f* morality; *(de una fábula)* moral

morar *intr* to live, dwell

moratoria *f* moratorium

mórbi·do -da *adj* *(perteneciente a la enfermedad)* morbid; soft, delicate, mellow

morbo *m* sickness, illness; **morbo gálico** syphilis; **morbo regio** jaundice

morbo·so -sa *adj* morbid, diseased

morcilla *f* blood pudding, black pudding; *(añadidura que mete un actor en su papel)* gag

mor·daz *adj* *(pl* **-daces)** mordant, mordacious, sharp, caustic

mordaza *f* *(pañuelo o instrumento que se pone en la boca para impedir el hablar)* gag; *(aparato que sirve para apretar)* clamp, jaw; pipe vise; **poner la mordaza a** to gag

mordedura *f* bite

morder §47 *tr* to bite; to nibble at; to wear away; to gossip about, ridicule; (Mex, Ven, W-I) to cheat || *intr* to bite; to take hold

mordicar §73 *tr* & *intr* to bite, sting

mordida *f* (Am) bite; *(para eludir una multa)* (Mex) payoff

mordiente *m* mordant

mordiscar §73 *tr* to nibble at || *intr* to nibble, gnaw away; to champ

mordisco *m* nibble, bite; champ

more·no -na *adj* brown, dark-brown; dark, dark-complexioned; *(de la raza negra)* (coll) colored; (Am) mulato || *mf* (coll) colored person; (Am) mulato || *m* brunet || *f* brunette; loaf of brown bread; rick of new-mown hay

morería *f* Moorish quarter; Moorish land

moretón *m* (coll) black-and-blue mark

morfina *f* morphine

morfinomanía *f* morphine habit, drug habit

morfinóma·no -na *adj* addicted to morphine, addicted to drugs || *mf* morphine addict, drug addict

morfología *f* morphology

moribun·do -da *adj* moribund, dying || *mf* dying person

morillo *m* andiron, firedog

morir §30 & §83 *intr* to die; *(el fuego, la luz, etc.)* to die away; **morir ahogado** to drown; **morir de risa** to die laughing; **morir de viejo** to die of old age; **morir helado** to freeze to death; **morir quemado** to burn to death; **morir vestido** (coll) to die a violent death || *ref* to die; to be dying; to die away, die out; *(una pierna, un brazo)* to go to sleep; **morirse por** to be crazy about; to be dying to

mo
mo

moris·co -ca adj Morisco, Moorish ‖ mf Moor converted to Christianity (after the Reconquest); (descendiente de mulato y española o de mulata y español) (Mex) Morisco

mo·ro -ra adj Moorish; (vino) unwatered ‖ mf Moor; **hay moros en la costa** (coll) there's trouble brewing; **moro de paz** man of peace ‖ f see **mora**

moro·cho -cha adj (Am) strong, robust; (SAm) dark

morón m mound, knoll; moron

moron·do -da adj bare, stripped

moro·so -sa adj slow, tardy; (retrasado en el pago de deudas) delinquent

morra f (de la cabeza) top, crown; (de gato) purr; **andar a la morra** to come to blows

morrada f slap, punch; (golpe dado con la cabeza) butt

morral m nose bag; (saco de cazador) game bag; (de soldado, viandante, etc.) knapsack; (coll) boor, lout

morralla f small fish; (gente de escaso valor) rabble, trash; (mezcla de cosas inútiles) junk, trash; (Mex) change, small change

morriña f (coll) blues, melancholy; **morriña de la tierra** (coll) homesickness

morriño·so -sa adj sickly; (coll) blue, melancholy

morrión m helmet; (mil) bearskin

morro m (cosa redonda) knob; (monte redondo) knoll; (guijarro) pebble; (saliente que forman los labios) snout; **beber a morro** (slang) to drink out of the bottle; **estar de morro or de morros** (coll) to be on the outs; **poner morro** to make a snout

morrocotu·do -da adj (coll) strong, thick, heavy; (asunto, negocio) (coll) weighty; (Am) big, enormous; (Col) rich, wealthy; (Chile) graceless, monotonous

morsa f walrus

mortaja f shroud, winding sheet; (carp) mortise; (Am) cigarette paper

mortal adj mortal; deadly; mortally ill; deathly pale; sure, conclusive ‖ m mortal

mortalidad f mortality; death rate

mortandad f massacre, mortality, butchery

morteci·no -na adj dead; dying; failing, weak; **hacer la mortecina** (coll) to play dead, to play possum

mortero m (vaso que sirve para machacar; argamasa) mortar; (en los molinos de aceite) nether stone; (arti) mortar

mortífe·ro -ra adj deadly

mortificar §73 tr to vex, annoy, bother; to mortify ‖ ref (Mex) to be mortified, be embarrassed

mortuo·rio -ria adj mortuary, funeral; (casa) of the deceased ‖ m (archaic) funeral

morueco m ram

moru·no -na adj Moorish

mosai·co -ca adj Mosaic ‖ m tile, paving tile; mosaic; **mosaico de madera** marquetry

mosca f fly; (barba) imperial; (coll) cash, dough; (coll) disappointment; (coll) bore, nuisance; **aflojar la mosca** (coll) to shell out, to fork out; **mosca borriquera** horsefly; **mosca de las frutas** fruit fly; **mosca del vinagre** fruit fly; **mosca muerta** (coll) hypocrite; **moscas** sparks; **moscas volantes** spots before the eyes; **papar moscas** (coll) to gape, gawk

moscareta f (orn) flycatcher

moscona f hussy, brazen woman

Moscú Moscow

mosquear tr (moscas) to shoo; to beat, to whip; to answer sharply ‖ intr (Mex) to sneak a ride ‖ ref to shake off annoyances; to take offense

mosquero m flytrap; fly swatter

mosquete m musket

mosquetear intr (Arg, Bol) to snoop

mosquete·ro -ra adj idle ‖ mf (Arg, Bol) bystander, snooper ‖ m musketeer ‖ f wallflower

mosquetón m snap hook

mosquitera f or **mosquitero** m mosquito net; fly net

mosquito m (Culex pungens) mosquito; (insecto parecido al anterior) gnat; (coll) tippler

mostacera f mustard jar

mostacho m mustache; (coll) spot on the face

mostachón m macaroon

mostaza f mustard; (semilla; munición) mustard seed; **subírsele a (uno) la mostaza a las narices** (coll) to fly into a rage

mosto m must; **mosto de cerveza** wort

mostrador m (en las tiendas) counter; (en las tabernas) bar; (de reloj) dial

mostrar §61 tr to show ‖ ref to show; to show oneself to be

mostrear tr to spot, to splash

mostren·co -ca adj ownerless, unclaimed; (que no tiene casa ni hogar) (coll) homeless; (animal) (coll) stray; (coll) slow, dull; (coll) fat, heavy ‖ mf (coll) dolt, dullard

mota f mote, speck; (en el paño) burl, knot; hill, rise; defect, fault; (Mex, W-I) powder puff

mote m device, emblem, riddle; (apodo) nickname; (Chile) mistake; (SAm) stewed corn

motear tr to speck, speckle; to dapple, mottle ‖ intr (Peru) to eat stewed corn

motejar tr to call names; to scoff at, make fun of; **motejar de** to brand as

motín m mutiny, riot

motinista mf (Peru) rioter

motivar tr to explain, account for; to rationalize

moti·vo -va adj motive ‖ m motive, reason; (mus) motif; **con motivo de** because of; on the occasion of; **de su motivo propio** on his own accord; **motivo conductor** (mus) leitmotif; **motivos** grounds, reasons; (Chile) finickiness, prudery

moto *m* guidepost, landmark ‖ *f* (coll) motorcycle
motobomba *f* fire truck, fire engine
motocarro *m* three-wheel delivery truck
motocicleta *f* motorcycle
motogrúa *f* truck crane
motolí·to -ta *adj* simple, stupid; **vivir de motolito** to be a sponger, to live on other people ‖ *f* (orn) wagtail; (Ven) decent woman
motón *m* (naut) block, pulley
motonáuti·co -ca *adj* motorboat ‖ *f* motorboating
motonautismo *m* (sport) motorboating
motonave *f* motor launch; motor ship
motoneta *f* motor scooter; light three-wheel delivery truck
mo·tor -tora *adj* motor, motive ‖ *m* motor, engine; **motor a chorro** jet engine; **motor de arranque** (aut) starter, starting motor; **motor de cuatro tiempos** four-cycle engine; **motor de dos tiempos** two-cycle engine; **motor de explosión** internal-combustion engine; **motor fuera de borda** outboard motor; **motor térmico** heat engine ‖ *f* small motor boat
motorista *mf* motorist; motorcyclist; motorcycle racer ‖ *m* motorcycle policeman; (Am) motorman
motorizar §60 *tr* to motorize
motosegadora *f* power mower
motovelero *m* (naut) motor sailer
motriz *adj fem* (fuerza) motive
movedi·zo -za *adj* shaky, unsteady; fickle, inconstant; (arena) quick, shifting
mover §47 *tr* to move; (la cola el perro) to wag; (discordia) to stir up ‖ *intr* to move; to abort, miscarry; to bud, sprout ‖ *ref* to move; to be moved
movible *adj* movable; fickle, inconstant, changeable
móvil *adj* movable, mobile; fickle, changeable; moving ‖ *m* moving body; cause, motive
movilizar §60 *tr* to mobilize
movimiento *m* movement, motion
moza *f* girl, lass; mistress, concubine; maid, kitchen maid; (en algunos juegos de naipes) last hand; wash bat; **buena moza** or **real moza** good-looking girl or woman; **moza de fortuna** or **del partido** prostitute; **moza de taberna** barmaid
mozalbete *m* lad, young fellow
mozárabe *adj* Mozarabic ‖ *mf* Mozarab
mo·zo -za *adj* young, youthful; single, unmarried ‖ *m* youth, lad; (camarero) waiter; (criado) servant; porter; (cuelgacapas) cloak hanger; **buen mozo** or **real mozo** handsome fellow; **mozo de caballerías** hostler, stable boy; **mozo de café** waiter; **mozo de cámara** (naut) cabin boy; **mozo de ciego** blind man's guide; **mozo de cordel** street porter, public errand boy; **mozo de cuadra** stable boy; **mozo de cuerda** public errand boy; **mozo de espuelas** groom who walks in front of master's horse; **mozo de esquina** street porter, public errand boy; **mozo de estación** station porter;

mozo de estoques (taur) sword handler; **mozo de hotel** bellboy, bellhop; **mozo de paja y cebada** hostler (at an inn); **mozo de restaurante** waiter ‖ *f* see **moza**
mozue·lo -la *mf* youngster ‖ *m* lad, young fellow ‖ *f* lass, young girl
m/p *abbr* **mi pagaré**
m/r *abbr* **mi remesa**
Mro. *abbr* **Maestro**
M.S. *abbr* **manuscrito**
mtd. *abbr* **mitad**
mu *m* moo ‖ *f* bye-bye; **ir a la mu** to go bye-bye
muaré *adj invar* & *m* moiré
muca·mo -ma *mf* (Arg, Urug) house servant ‖ *f* (Arg, Chile, Urug) servant girl
muceta *f* (de los doctores en los actos universitarios) hood; (eccl) mozzetta
muco·so -sa *adj* mucous ‖ *f* mucous membrane
múcura *f* (Bol, Col, Ven, W-I) water pitcher; (Col) thickhead
muchacha *f* girl; maid, servant girl
muchachada *f* youthful prank
muchachez *f* boyishness, girlishness
mucha·cho -cha *adj* young, youthful ‖ *mf* youth, young person; servant ‖ *m* boy ‖ *f* see **muchacha**
muchedumbre *f* crowd, multitude, flock
mu·cho -cha *adj* much, a lot of, a great deal of; (tiempo) a long ‖ *pron* much, a lot, a great deal ‖ **mu·chos -chas** *adj* & *pron* many ‖ **mucho** *adv* much; (más de lo regular) hard; often; a long time; **con mucho** by far; **ni con mucho** or **ni mucho menos** not by a long shot; **por mucho que** however much; **sentir mucho** to be very sorry; **tener mucho de** to take after
muda *f* change; change of voice; change of clothes; (cambio de plumas o de piel) molt, molting; molting season; **estar de muda** to be changing one's voice; **estar en muda** (coll) to keep too quiet; **hacer la muda** to molt; **muda de ropa** change of clothing
mudable *adj* fickle, inconstant
mudada *f* (Am) change of clothing; (Am) move, change of residence
mudadi·zo -za *adj* fickle, inconstant
mudanza *f* change; (cambio de domicilio) moving; fickleness, inconstancy; (en el baile) figure
mudar *tr* to change ‖ *intr* to change; **mudar de** to change ‖ *ref* to change; to change clothing; to move; to move away; to have a movement of the bowels; **mudarse de** to change
mudez *f* muteness, dumbness; continued silence
mu·do -da *adj* dumb, mute; (phonet) voiceless, surd ‖ *mf* mute ‖ *f* see **muda**
mueblaje *m* furniture, suit of furniture
mueble *adj* movable ‖ *m* piece of furniture; (p.ej., de un aparato de radio) cabinet; **muebles** furniture
mueblería *f* furniture shop
mueblista *mf* furniture dealer
mueca *f* face, grimace

mo
mu

muela f grindstone; knoll, mound; back tooth, grinder; **muela cordal** wisdom tooth; **muela de esmeril** emery wheel; **muela del juicio** wisdom tooth; **muela de molino** millstone

muellaje m dockage, wharfage

muelle adj soft; voluptuous ‖ m (pieza elástica de metal) spring; (obra en la orilla del mar o de un río) dock, wharf, pier; (rr) freight platform; **muelle real** mainspring

muérdago m mistletoe

muérgano m (Col, Ven) piece of junk, drug on the market; (Col, Ecuad, Ven) boor, nobody

muermo m (vet) glanders

muerte f death; **cada muerte de obispo** once in a blue moon; **dar la muerte a** to put to death; **de mala muerte** (coll) crummy, not much of a; **estar a la muerte** to be at death's door; **muerte chiquita** (coll) nervous shudder

muer·to -ta adj dead; (apagado, marchito) flat, dull; (cal, yeso) slaked; **muerto de** dying of; **muerto por** crazy about ‖ mf corpse, dead person ‖ m (en los naipes) dummy; **hacerse el muerto** to play possum; to play deaf; **tocar a muerto** to toll

muesca f nick, notch; (carp) mortise

muestra f (porción de un producto que sirve para conocer su calidad) sample; model, specimen; (rótulo sobre una tienda u hotel) sign; show, exhibition, indication; (esfera de reloj) dial, face; (parada del perro para levantar la caza) set; (ademán, porte) bearing; **dar muestras de** to show signs of

mugido m moo, low; bellow, roar

mugir §27 intr (la res vacuna) to moo, to low; (con ira) to bellow; (el viento, el mar) to roar

mugre f dirt, filth, grime

mugrien·to -ta adj dirty, filthy, grimy

muguete m lily of the valley

mujer f woman; (esposa) wife; **mujer de gobierno** housekeeper; **mujer de su casa** good manager; **mujer fatal** vamp; **ser mujer** to be a grown woman

mujeren·go -ga adj (Arg, Urug, CAm) effeminate

mujerie·go -ga adj feminine, womanly; effeminate, womanish; fond of women; **a mujeriegas** sidesaddle ‖ m flock of women

mujeril adj womanly; womanish

mújol m mullet, striped mullet

mula f mule, she-mule; junk, trash; (Arg) ingrate, traitor; (Arg) hoax; (C-R) jag, drunk; (Guat, Hond) anger, rage; (Mex) drug on the market; (Ven) flask; **devolver la mula** (CAm) to pay back in one's own coin; **echar la mula a** (Mex) to rake over the coals; **en mula de San Francisco** on shank's mare

mulada f drove of mules

muladar m dungheap, dunghill; dump, trash heap; filth

mula·to -ta adj & mf mulatto

muleta f (palo para apoyarse al andar) crutch; muleta (cloth attached to a stick, used by matador); support, prop; snack

muletilla f cross-handle cane; pet word, pet phrase; (taur) muleta

mulo m mule

multa f fine

multar tr to fine

multicopista m duplicating machine, copying machine

multigrafiar §77 tr to multigraph

multigrafo m multigraph

multilateral adj multilateral

multiláte·ro -ra adj multilateral

múltiple adj multiple, manifold ‖ m manifold; **múltiple de admisión** intake manifold; **múltiple de escape** exhaust manifold

multiplicar §73 tr, intr, & ref to multiply

multiplicidad f multiplicity

múlti·plo -pla adj multiple, manifold ‖ m (math) multiple

multitud f multitude

mulli·do -da adj soft, fluffy ‖ m stuffing (for cushions, pillows, etc.) ‖ f bedding, litter (for animals)

mullir §13 tr to soften, fluff up; (la cama) to beat up, shake up; (la tierra) to loosen around a stalk ‖ ref to get fluffy

munda·no -na adj mundane, worldly; (mujer) loose

mundial adj world-wide, world

mundillo m arched clotheshorse; cushion for making lace; warming pan; guelder-rose, cranberry tree; world (of artists, scholars, etc.)

mundo m world; **así va el mundo** so it goes; **desde que el mundo es mundo** (coll) since the world began; **echar al mundo** to bring into the world; to bring forth; **el otro mundo** the other world; **gran mundo** high society; **medio mundo** (mucha gente) (coll) half the world; **tener mucho mundo** (coll) to know one's way around; **todo el mundo** everybody; **ver mundo** to see the world, to travel

mundonuevo m peep show

munición f munition, ammunition; **de munición** (mil) government issue; (coll) done hurriedly

municionar tr to supply with munition

municipal adj municipal ‖ m policeman

munícipe m citizen

municipio m municipality; town council

munidad f susceptibility to infection

munífi·co -ca adj munificent

muñeca f (figurilla infantil con que juegan las niñas) doll; (parte del cuerpo humano en donde se articula la mano con el brazo) wrist; manikin, dress form; tea bag; (mujer linda; mozuela frívola) (coll) doll; **muñeca de trapo** rag doll, rag baby; **muñeca parlante** talking doll

muñeco m doll (representing a male child or animal); dummy, manikin, fop, effeminate fellow; (fig) puppet; (coll) lad, little fellow

muñequera *f* strap for wrist watch
muñequilla *f* (mach) chuck; (Arg, Chile) young ear of corn
muñidor *m* heeler, henchman
muñir §12 *tr* to convoke, summon; (pol) to fix, to rig
muñón *m* (*p.ej., de un brazo cortado*) stump; (mach) journal, gudgeon; **muñón de cola** dock
mural *adj* mural
muralla *f* wall, rampart
murar *tr* to surround with a wall
murciélago *m* bat
murga *f* (coll) tin-pan band
muriente *adj* dying, faint
murmujear *tr & intr* (coll) to mumble
murmullar *intr* to murmur
murmullo *m* murmur; whisper; (*de aguas corrientes*) ripple; (*del viento*) rustle
murmurar *tr* to murmur, to mutter; to murmur at || *intr* to murmur, to mutter; to whisper; (*las aguas corrientes*) to ripple, to purl; (*el viento*) to rustle; (coll) to gossip
muro *m* wall
murria *f* (coll) blues, dejection
musa *f* muse; **las Musas** the Muses; **soplarle a uno la musa** (coll) to be inspired to write poetry; (coll) to be lucky at games of chance
musaraña *f* shrew, shrewmouse; bug, worm; **mirar a las musarañas** (coll) to stare vacantly
músculo *m* muscle
musculo·so -sa *adj* muscular
muselina *f* muslin
museo *m* museum; **museo de cera** waxworks
muserola *f* noseband
mus·go -ga *adj* dark-brown || *m* moss
musgo·so -sa *adj* mossy, moss-covered
música *f* music; (*músicos que tocan juntos*) band; (coll) noise, racket; **con**

la música a otra parte (coll) don't bother me, get out; **música celestial** (coll) nonsense, piffle; **música de fondo** background music; **poner en música** to set to music
musical *adj* musical
musicalidad *f* musicianship
music-hall *s* vaudeville theater, burlesque show
músi·co -ca *adj* musical || *mf* musician; **músico mayor** bandmaster || *f* see **música**
musicología *f* musicology
musicólo·go -ga *mf* musicologist
musiquero *m* music cabinet
musitar *tr & intr* to mutter, mumble
muslime *adj & mf* Moslem
muslo *m* thigh; (*de ave cocida*) (coll) leg, drumstick
mustiar *ref* to wither
mus·tio -tia *adj* sad, gloomy; (*marchito*) withered; (Mex) hypocritical; (Mex) stand-offish
musul·mán -mana *adj & mf* Mussulman
mutación *f* mutation; unsettled weather, change of weather; (biol) mutation, sport; (theat) change of scene
mutila·do -da *adj* crippled || *mf* cripple
mutilar *tr* to mutilate; to cripple
múti·lo -la *adj* mutilated; crippled
mutis *m* (theat) exit; **hacer mutis** (theat) to exit; to keep quiet
mutual *adj* mutual
mutualidad *f* mutuality; mutual benefit; mutual benefit association
mutualista *mf* member of a mutual benefit association
mu·tuo -tua *adj* mutual, reciprocal
muy *adv* very; very much; too, e.g., **es muy tarde para dar un paseo tan largo** it is too late to take such a long walk; **muy de noche** late at night; **Muy señor mío** Dear Sir

mu
na

N

N, n (ene) *f* sixteenth letter of the Spanish alphabet
n/ *abbr* **nuestro**
N. *abbr* **Norte**
nabo *m* turnip; (naut) mast
Nabucodonosor *m* Nebuchadnezzar
nácar *m* mother-of-pearl
nacara·do -da *adj* mother-of-pearl
nacatamal *m* (CAm, Mex) meat-filled tamale
nacela *f* nacelle
nacencia *f* birth; growth, tumor
nacer §22 *intr* to be born; to bud, take rise, originate, appear; to dawn || *ref* to bud, to shoot, to sprout; (*abrirse la ropa por las costuras*) to split
naci·do -da *adj* natural, innate; apt, proper, fit; **nacida** née or nee || *m* human being; growth, boil
naciente *adj* incipient; resurgent; (*sol*) rising || *m* east

nacimiento *m* birth; origin, beginning, fountainhead; descent, lineage; (*de agua*) spring, fountainhead; crèche
nación *f* nation
nacional *adj* national; domestic || *mf* national || *m* militiaman
nacionalidad *f* nationality
nacionalismo *m* nationalism
nacionalista *adj & mf* nationalist
nacionalizar §60 *tr* to nationalize || *ref* to be naturalized; to become a citizen
nacista *adj & mf* Nazi
naco *m* (Arg, Bol, Urug) black rolled leaf of chewing tobacco; (Arg) fear, scare; (Col) stewed corn; (Col) mashed potatoes
nada *pron indef* nothing, not . . . anything; **de nada** don't mention it, you're welcome || *adv* not at all
nadaderas *fpl* water wings
nada·dor -dora *adj* swimming, floating

|| *mf* swimmer || *m* (Chile) fishnet float

nadar *intr* to swim; to float; to fit loosely or too loosely; **nadar en** (*riqueza*) to be rolling in; (*suspiros*) to be full of; (*sangre*) to be bathed in

nadear *tr* to destroy, wipe out

nadería *f* trifle

nadie *pron indef* nobody, not . . . anybody; **nadie más** nobody else; **nadie más que** nobody but || *m* nobody; **un don nadie** a nonentity

nado — a nado swimming, floating; **echarse a nado** to dive in; **pasar a nado** to swim across

nafta *f* naphtha

nagual *m* (Guat, Hond) (*dícese de un animal*) inseparable companion; (Mex) sorcerer, wizard; (Mex) lie

nagualear *intr* (Mex) to lie; (Mex) to be out looking for trouble all night

naguás *fpl* petticoat

naipe *m* playing card; deck of cards; **naipe de figura** face card; **tener buen naipe** to be lucky

naire *m* mahout

nalgada *f* shoulder, ham; blow on or with the buttocks

nalgas *fpl* buttocks, rump

nana *f* grandma; lullaby, cradlesong; (CAm, Mex, W-I) child's nurse; (Arg, Chile, Urug) child's complaint

nao *f* ship, vessel

napoleóni·co -ca *adj* Napoleonic

Nápoles *f* Naples

napolita·no -na *adj & mf* Neapolitan

naranja *f* orange; **media naranja** (coll) sidekick, better half; **naranja cajel** Seville orange, sour orange; **¡naranjas!** nonsense!

naranjada *f* orangeade; orange juice; orange marmalade

naranjal *m* orange grove

naranjo *m* orange tree; (coll) boob, simpleton

narciso *m* narcissus; fop, dandy; **narciso trompón** daffodil || **Narciso** *m* Narcissus

narcóti·co -ca *adj & m* narcotic

narcotizar §60 *tr* to dope, to drug

narguile *m* hookah

narigada *f* (SAm) pinch of snuff

nari·gón -gona *adj* big-nosed || *m* big nose

narigu·do -da *adj* big-nosed; nose-shaped

nariguera *f* nose ring

na·riz (*pl* -**rices**) *f* nose; nostril; sense of smell; (*del vino*) bouquet; **nariz de pico de loro** hooknose; **sonarse las narices** to blow one's nose; **tabicarse las narices** to hold one's nose; **tener agarrado por las narices** to lead by the nose

narración *f* narration

narra·dor -dora *adj* narrating || *mf* narrator

narrar *tr* to narrate

narrati·vo -va *adj* narrative || *f* (*relato; habilidad en narrar*) narrative

narria *f* sled, sledge, drag

nasal *adj & f* nasal

nasalizar §60 *tr* to nasalize

nata *f* cream; whipped cream; élite, choice; skim, scum

natación *f* swimming

natal *adj* natal; native || *m* birth; birthday

natali·cio -cia *adj* birth || *m* birthday

natalidad *f* birth rate

naterón *m* cottage cheese

natillas *fpl* custard

natividad *f* birth; Christmas; (*día; festividad; pintura*) Nativity

nati·vo -va *adj* native; natural; natural-born; innate

na·to -ta *adj* born, e.g., **criminal nato** born criminal || *f* see **nata**

natural *adj* natural; native; (mus) natural || *mf* native || *m* temper, disposition, nature; **al natural** au naturel; rough, unfinished; live; **del natural** from life, from nature

naturaleza *f* nature; disposition, temperament; nationality; **naturaleza muerta** still life

naturalidad *f* naturalness; nationality

naturalismo *m* naturalism

naturalista *mf* naturalist

naturalización *f* naturalization

naturalizar §60 *tr* to naturalize; to acclimatize || *ref* to become naturalized; to go native

naturalmente *adv* naturally; easily, readily

naufragar §44 *intr* to be shipwrecked; to fail

naufragio *m* shipwreck; failure, ruin

náufra·go -ga *adj* shipwrecked || *m* shipwrecked person || *m* shark

náusea *f* nausea; **dar náuseas a** to nauseate; to sicken, disgust; **tener náuseas** to be nauseated, to be sick at one's stomach

nauseabun·do -da *adj* nauseating, nauseous, loathsome, sickening

nauta *m* mariner, sailor

náuti·co -ca *adj* nautical || *f* sailing, navigation

nava *f* hollow plain between mountains

navaja *f* folding knife; razor; penknife; tusk of wild boar; razor clam; (coll) evil tongue; **navaja barbera** straight razor

navajada *f* or **navajazo** *m* slash, gash

navajero *m* razor case; razor cloth

naval *adj* naval; nautical; **naval militar** naval

nava·rro -rra *adj & mf* Navarrese || **Navarra** *f* Navarre

navazo *m* garden in sandy marshland

nave *f* ship, vessel; (*de un taller, fábrica, tienda, iglesia, etc.*) aisle; commercial ground floor; hall, shed, bay, building; **nave central** or **principal** (archit) nave; **nave lateral** (archit) aisle

navegable *adj* navigable

navegación *f* navigation; sailing; sea voyage; **navegación a vela** sailing

navega·dor -dora or **navegante** *adj* navigating || *mf* navigator

navegar §44 *tr* to sail || *intr* to navigate, to sail; to move around

navel *f* (*pl* -**vels**) navel orange

Navidad *f* Christmas; Christmas time;

¡**Felices Navidades!** Merry Christmas!; **contar** or **tener muchas Navidades** to be pretty old

navidal *m* Christmas card

navide·ño -ña *adj* Christmas

navie·ro -ra *adj* ship, shipping ‖ *m* shipowner; outfitter

navío *m* ship, vessel; **navío de guerra** warship

náyade *f* naiad

nazare·no -na *adj & mf* Nazarene ‖ *m* penitent in Passion Week procession ‖ **nazarenas** *fpl* (SAm) large gaucho spurs

nazi *adj & mf* Nazi

N.B. *abbr* nota bene (Lat) note well

nébeda *f* catnip

neblina *f* fog, mist

neblino·so -sa *adj* foggy, misty

nebulo·so -sa *adj* nebulous, cloudy, misty, hazy, vague; gloomy, sullen ‖ *f* nebula

necedad *f* foolishness, stupidity, nonsense

necesa·rio -ria *adj* necessary ‖ *f* water closet, privy

neceser *m* toilet case; sewing kit; **neceser de belleza** vanity case; **neceser de costura** workbasket

necesidad *f* necessity; need, want; starvation; **de necesidad** from weakness, of necessity; **necesidad mayor** bowel movement; **necesidad menor** urination

necesita·do -da *adj* necessitous, poor, needy; **estar necesitado de** to be in need of ‖ *mf* needy person

necesitar *tr* to necessitate; to need; **necesitar** + *inf* to have to, to need to + *inf* ‖ *intr* to be in need; **necesitar de** to be in need of, to need ‖ *ref* to be needed, to be necessary

ne·cio -cia *adj* foolish, stupid; imprudent; stubborn; (Am) touchy ‖ *mf* fool

necrología *f* necrology

necromancia *f* necromancy

néctar *m* nectar

neerlan·dés -desa *adj* Netherlandish, Dutch ‖ *mf* Netherlander ‖ *m* Dutchman; (*idioma*) Netherlandish or Dutch ‖ *f* Dutchwoman

nefalista *mf* teetotaler

nefan·do -da *adj* base, infamous

nefas·to -ta *adj* ominous, fatal, tragic

negable *adj* deniable

negación *f* negation; denial; refusal

nega·do -da *adj* unfit, incompetent; dull, indifferent

negar §66 *tr* to deny; to refuse; to prohibit; to disown; to conceal ‖ *intr* to deny ‖ *ref* to avoid; to refuse; to deny oneself to callers; **negarse a** to refuse; **negarse a** + *inf* to refuse to + *inf*

negati·vo -va *adj* negative ‖ *f* negative; denial; refusal

negligencia *f* negligence

negligente *adj* negligent

negociable *adj* negotiable

negociación *f* negotiation; deal, matter

negociado *m* department, bureau; affair, business; (SAm) illegal dealing; (Chile) store

negociante *m* dealer, trader

negociar *tr* to negotiate ‖ *intr* to negotiate; to deal, to trade

negocio *m* business; affair, deal, transaction; profit; (SAm) store

negocio·so -sa *adj* businesslike

negrear *intr* to turn black; to look black

negre·ro -ra *adj* slave-trading; (fig) slave-driving ‖ *mf* slave trader; (fig) slave driver

negrilla *f* (typ) boldface

ne·gro -gra *adj* black; dark; gloomy, dismal; fatal, evil, wicked; Negro; (coll) broke ‖ *mf* Negro; (Am) dear, darling ‖ *m* black; **negro de humo** lampblack

negror *m* or **negrura** *f* blackness

negruz·co -ca *adj* blackish

néme·sis *f* (*pl* **-sis**) (*justo castigo; castigador*) nemesis ‖ **Némesis** *f* Nemesis

nemoro·so -sa *adj* (poet) woody, sylvan

ne·ne -na *mf* baby; dear, darling ‖ *m* rascal, villain

nenúfar *m* white water lily

neo *m* neon

neocelan·dés -desa *adj* New Zealand ‖ *mf* New Zealander

neoesco·cés -cesa *adj & mf* Nova Scotian

neófi·to -ta *mf* neophyte

neologismo *m* neologism

neomejica·no -na *adj & mf* New Mexican

neomicina *f* neomycin

neón *m* neon

neoyorki·no -na *adj* New York ‖ *mf* New Yorker

Nepal, el Nepal

nepa·lés -lesa *adj & mf* Nepalese

nepente *m* nepenthe

nepote *m* relative and favorite of the Pope ‖ **Nepote** *m* Nepos

neptunio *m* neptunium

Neptuno *m* Neptune

nereida *f* Nereid

Nerón *m* Nero

nervio *m* nerve; (*del ala del insecto*) rib; strength, vigor

nerviosidad *f* nervousness

nervio·so -sa *adj* nervous; energetic, vigorous, sinewy; (*célula; centro; tónico*) nerve; (*sistema; enfermedad; postración, colapso*) nervous

nervosidad *f* nervosity; ductility, flexibility; (*de un argumento*) force, cogency

nervo·so -sa *adj* var of **nervioso**

nervu·do -da *adj* vigorous, sinewy

nervura *f* backbone (*of book*)

nesga *f* gore

nesgar §44 *tr* to gore

ne·to -ta *adj* net

neumáti·co -ca *adj* pneumatic; air ‖ *m* tire

neumonía *f* pneumonia

neuralgia *f* neuralgia

neurología *f* neurology

neuro·sis *f* (*pl* **-sis**) neurosis; **neurosis de guerra** shell shock

neuróti·co -ca *adj & mf* neurotic

neutral *adj & mf* neutral

neutralidad *f* neutrality

neutralismo *m* neutralism

neutralista *adj & mf* neutralist

neutralizar §60 *tr* to neutralize

neu·tro -tra *adj* neuter; (*que no es de un color ni de otro*) neutral; (bot, chem, elec, phonet, zool) neutral; (*verbo*) intransitive

neutrón *m* neutron

neva·do -da *adj* snow-covered; snow-white ‖ *f* snowfall

nevar §2 *tr* to make snow-white ‖ *intr* to snow

nevasca *f* snowfall; snowstorm, blizzard

nevazón *f* (SAm) snowfall

nevera *f* icebox, refrigerator; icehouse; (P-R) jail

nevería *f* ice-cream parlor

neve·ro -ra *mf* ice-cream dealer ‖ *m* place of perpetual snow; perpetual snow ‖ *f* see **nevera**

nevisca *f* snow flurry

neviscar §73 *intr* to snow lightly

nevo *m* mole; **nevo materno** birth mark

nevo·so -sa *adj* snowy

ni *conj* neither, nor; **ni . . . ni** neither . . . nor; **ni . . . siquiera** not even

niacina *f* niacin

nicaragüense or **nicaragüe·ño -ña** *adj & mf* Nicaraguan

Nicolás *m* Nicholas

nicotina *f* nicotine

nicho *m* niche

nidada *f* (*huevos en el nido*) nestful of eggs; (*pajarillos en el nido*) nest, brood, hatch

nidal *m* (*donde la gallina pone sus huevos*) nest; nest egg; haunt; source; basis, foundation

nido *m* nest; haunt; home; source; (*de ladrones*) nest, den

niebla *f* fog, mist, haze; mildew; fog, confusion; **hay niebla** it is foggy; **niebla artificial** smoke screen

nie·to -ta *mf* grandchild ‖ *m* grandson; **nietos** grandchildren ‖ *f* granddaughter

nieve *f* snow; (Am) water ice

nigromancia *f* necromancy

nihilismo *m* nihilism

nihilista *mf* nihilist

Nilo *m* Nile; **Nilo Azul** Blue Nile

nilón *m* nylon

nimbo *m* nimbus; halo

nimiedad *f* excess; fussiness, fastidiousness; (coll) timidity

ni·mio -mia *adj* excessive; fussy, fastidious; (Am) tiny

ninfa *f* nymph; **ninfa marina** mermaid

ninfea *f* white water lily

ningún *adj indef* apocopated form of **ninguno**, used only before masculine singular nouns and adjectives

ningu·no -na *adj indef* no, not any ‖ *pron indef* none, not any; neither, neither one; **ninguno de los dos** neither one ‖ **ninguno** *pron indef* nobody, no one

niña *f* child, girl; (*del ojo*) pupil; **niña del ojo** (coll) apple of one's eye; **niña exploradora** girl scout

niñada *f* childishness

niñera *f* nursemaid

niñería *f* childishness; trifle

niñero -ra *adj* fond of children ‖ *f* see **niñera**

niñez *f* childhood; childishness; (fig) infancy

ni·ño -ña *adj* childlike, childish; young, inexperienced ‖ *mf* child; (*persona joven e inexperta*) babe; **desde niño** from childhood; **niño expósito** foundling; **niño travieso** imp ‖ *m* child, boy; **niño bonito** playboy; **niño de coro** choirboy; **niño de la bola** child Jesus; (coll) lucky fellow; **niño explorador** boy scout; **niño gótico** playboy ‖ *f* see **niña**

ni·pón -pona *adj & mf* Nipponese

níquel *m* nickel

niquelar *tr* to nickel-plate

nirvana, el nirvana

níspero *m* medlar (*tree and fruit*)

níspola *f* medlar (*fruit*)

nitidez *f* brightness, clearness; sharpness

níti·do -da *adj* bright, clear; sharp

nitrato *m* nitrate

nítri·co -ca *adj* nitric

nitro *m* niter; **nitro de Chile** saltpeter

nitrógeno *m* nitrogen

nitro·so -sa *adj* nitrous

nitruro *m* nitride

nivel *m* level; **nivel de burbuja** spirit level; **nivel de vida** standard of living

nivelar *tr* to level; to even, make even; to grade; to survey

no *adv* not; no; ¿**cómo no?** why not?; of course, certainly; **creer que no** to think not, to believe not; ¿**no?** is it not so?; **no bien** no sooner; **no más que** not more than; only; **no sea que** lest; **no . . . sino** only; **ya no** no longer

nobabia *f* (aer) dope

noble *adj* noble ‖ *m* noble, nobleman

nobleza *f* nobility

noción *f* notion, idea; rudiment

noci·vo -va *adj* noxious, harmful

noctur·no -na *adj* nocturnal; lonely, sad, melancholy; night, nighttime

noche *f* night, nighttime; darkness; **buenas noches** good evening; good night; **de la noche a la mañana** overnight; unexpectedly, suddenly; **de noche** at night, in the nighttime; **esta noche** tonight; **hacer noche en** to spend the night in; **hacerse de noche** to grow dark; **muy de noche** late at night; **por la noche** at night, in the nighttime; **noche buena** Christmas Eve; **noche de estreno** (theat) first night; **noche de uvas** New Year's Eve; **noche vieja** New Year's Eve; watch night

nochebuena *f* Christmas Eve

nochebueno *m* Christmas cake; Yule log

nodo *m* (astr, med, phys) node

No-Do *m* (acronym for **Noticiario y Documentales**) newsreel; newsreel theater

nodriza *f* wet nurse; vacuum tank

Noé *m* Noah

nogal *m* walnut; **nogal de la brujería** witch hazel

nómada or **nómade** *adj & mf* nomad

nomádi·co -ca *adj* nomadic
nombradía *f* fame, renown, reputation
nombra·do -da *adj* famous
nombramiento *m* naming; appointment
nombrar *tr* to name; to appoint
nombre *m* name; fame, reputation; nickname; watchword; noun; **del mismo nombre** (elec) like; **de nombres contrarios** (elec) unlike; **nombre comercial** firm name; **nombre de lugar** place name; **nombre de pila** first name, Christian name; **nombre de soltera** maiden name; **nombre substantivo** noun; **nombre supuesto** alias
nomeolvi·des *f* (*pl* -des) forget-me-not; German madwort
nómina *f* list, roll; pay roll
nominal *adj* nominal; noun
nominar *tr* to name; to appoint
nominati·vo -va *adj & m* nominative
non *adj* odd, uneven ‖ *m* odd number
nonada *f* trifle, nothing
no·na -na *adj & m* ninth
nopal *m* prickly pear
norcorea·no -na *adj & mf* North Korean
nordestada *f* or **nordeste** *m* (*viento*) northeaster (*wind*)
noria *f* chain pump; (*pozo*) draw well; Ferris wheel; (coll) treadmill, drudgery
norma *f* norm, standard; rule, method; (carp) square
normal *adj* normal; standard; perpendicular
Normandía *f* Normandy
norman·do -da *adj & mf* Norman ‖ *m* Norseman
norte *m* north; north wind; (*guía*) (fig) polestar, lodestar
Norteamérica *f* North America; America, the United States
norteamerica·no -na *adj & mf* North American; (*estadunidense*) American
norte·ño -ña *adj* northern
norue·go -ga *adj & mf* Norwegian ‖ Noruega *f* Norway
nos (used as object of verb) *pron pers* us; to us ‖ *pron reflex* ourselves, to ourselves; each other, to each other
noso·tros -tras *pron pers* we; us; ourselves
nostalgia *f* nostalgia
nota *f* note; (*en la escuela*) mark, grade; (*en el restaurante*) check; (mus) note; **nota de adorno** grace note; **nota tónica** keynote
notar *tr* to note; to dictate; **to annotate**; to criticize; to discredit
notario *m* notary, notary public
noticia *f* news; notice, information; notion, rudiment; knowledge; **noticias de actualidad** news of the day; **noticias de última hora** late news; **una noticia** a piece of news, a news item
noticiar *tr* to notify; to give notice of
noticia·rio -ria *adj* news ‖ *m* up-to-the-minute news; newsreel; newscast; **noticiario gráfico** picture page; **noticiario teatral** theater page
noticie·ro -ra *adj* news ‖ *m* newsman, reporter; late news

noticio·so -sa *adj* informed; learned; well-informed; (Am) newsy ‖ *m* (Am) news item
notificar §73 *tr* to notify; to report on
no·to -ta *adj* known, well-known ‖ *m* south wind ‖ *f* see **nota**
notoriedad *f* general knowledge; fame
noto·rio -ria *adj* manifest, well-known
nov. *abbr* noviembre
novatada *f* hazing; beginner's blunder
nova·to -ta *adj* beginning ‖ *mf* beginner; freshman
novecien·tos -tas *adj & pron* nine hundred ‖ **novecientos** *m* nine hundred
novedad *f* newness, novelty; news; fashion; happening; change; failing health; **sin novedad** as usual; safe; well; without anything happening
novel *adj* new, inexperienced, beginning ‖ *m* beginner
novela *f* novel; story, lie; **novela caballista** novel of western life; **novela policíaca** or **policial** detective story; **novela por entregas** serial
novele·ro -ra *adj* fond of novelty; fond of fiction; gossipy; fickle
noveles·co -ca *adj* novelistic, fictional; romantic, fantastic
novelista *mf* novelist
novelísti·co -ca *adj* fictional ‖ *f* fiction
novelizar §60 *tr* to fictionalize
nove·no -na *adj & m* ninth
noventa *adj, pron & m* ninety
noventa·vo -va *adj & m* ninetieth
novia *f* fiancée; bride; **novia de guerra** war bride
noviazgo *m* engagement, courtship
novi·cio -cia *adj & mf* novice
noviembre *m* November
novilunio *m* new moon
novilla *f* heifer
novillada *f* drove of young bulls; (taur) fight with young bulls by aspiring bullfighters
novillero *m* herdsman of young cattle; (taur) aspiring fighter, untrained fighter; (coll) truant
novillo *m* young bull; (coll) cuckold; **hacer novillos** (coll) to play truant
novio *m* suitor; fiancé; bridegroom; **novios** engaged couple; bride and groom, newlyweds
novocaína *f* novocaine
nro. *abbr* nuestro
N.S. *abbr* Nuestro Señor
ntro. *abbr* nuestro
nubada *f* local shower; abundance
nubarrón *m* storm cloud
nube *f* cloud; **andar** (*los precios*) **por las nubes** to be sky-high; **bajar de las nubes** to come back to or down to earth; **poner en** or **sobre las nubes** to praise to the skies
nube-hongo *f* mushroom cloud
nubla·do -da *adj* cloudy ‖ *m* storm cloud; impending danger; abundance; **aguantar el nublado** to suffer resignedly
nublar *tr* to cloud, cloud over ‖ *ref* to become cloudy
nu·blo -bla *adj* cloudy ‖ *m* storm cloud
nublo·so -sa *adj* cloudy; adverse, unfortunate

nubo·so -sa *adj* cloudy
nuca *f* nape
nuclear *adj* nuclear
núcleo *m* nucleus; core; (*de nuez*) kernel; (*de la fruta*) stone; (*de un electroimán*) core
nudillo *m* knuckle; stocking stitch; plug (*in wall*)
nudo *m* knot; bond, tie, union; crux; tangle, plot; difficulty; (*en el drama*) crisis; center, juncture; (*bot*) node; (*naut*) knot; **cortar el nudo gordiano** to cut the Gordian knot; **hacérsele a** (*uno*) **un nudo en la garganta** to get a lump in one's throat
nudo·so -sa *adj* knotted, knotty
nuera *f* daughter-in-law
nues·tro -tra *adj poss* our ‖ *pron poss* ours
nueva *f* news; piece of news; **nuevas** *fpl* news
Nueva York *m & f* New York; **el Gran Nueva York** Greater New York
Nueva Zelanda New Zealand
nueve *adj & pron* nine; **las nueve** nine o'clock ‖ *m* nine; (*en las fechas*) ninth
nue·vo -va *adj* new; **de nuevo** again, anew; **nuevo flamante** brand-new; **¿qué hay de nuevo?** what's new? ‖ *mf* novice; freshman ‖ *f* see **nueva**
nuevomejica·no -na *adj & mf* New Mexican
Nuevo Méjico *m* New Mexico
nuez *f* (*pl* **nueces**) nut; walnut; Adam's apple; **nuez dura** (*árbol*) hickory; hickory nut; **nuez moscada** nutmeg
nulidad *f* nullity; incapacity; (*coll*) nobody

nu·lo -la *adj* null, void, worthless
núm. *abbr* **número**
numen *m* deity; inspiration
numeral *adj* numeral
numerar *tr* to number; to count; to numerate
numerario *m* cash, coin, specie
numéri·co -ca *adj* numerical
número *m* number; (*de un periódico*) copy, issue; (*de zapatos*) size; lottery ticket; **cargar or cobrar al número llamado** (telp) to reverse the charges; **de número** (*dícese de los individuos de una sociedad*) regular; **mirar por el número uno** to look out for number one; **número de serie** series number; **número equivocado** (telp) wrong number
numero·so -sa *adj* numerous
nunca *adv* never; **no . . . nunca** not . . . ever, never **nunca jamás** never more
nupcial *adj* nuptial
nupcialidad *f* marriage rate
nupcias *fpl* nuptials, marriage; **casarse en segundas nupcias** to marry the second time
nutria *f* otter
nutrición *f* nutrition
nutri·do -da *adj* great, intense, robust, vigorous, steady; full, abounding, rich, heavy; (*carácter, letra*) thick; (*cañoneo*) heavy, sustained
nutrimento or **nutrimiento** *m* nourishment, nutriment
nutrir *tr* to nourish, to feed; to supply, to stock; to support, back up; to fill to overflowing
nu·triz *f* (*pl* **-trices**) wet nurse

Ñ

Ñ, ñ (eñe) *f* seventeenth letter of the Spanish alphabet
ñadi *m* (Chile) broad, shallow swamp
ñajú *m* (Am) okra, gumbo
ñámbar *m* Jamaica rosewood
ñame *m* yam; (W-I) blockhead, dunce
ñan·dú·m (*pl* **-dúes**) nandu, American ostrich
ñaño -ña *adj* (Am) close, intimate; (Am) spoiled, overindulged ‖ *m* (Am) elder brother ‖ *f* (Am) elder sister; (Am) nursemaid; (Am) dear
ñapa *f* (Am) something thrown in; **de ñapa** (Am) in the bargain
ñaque *m* junk, pile of junk
ña·to -ta *adj* (Am) pug-nosed; (Arg) ugly, deformed

ñeque *adj* (Am) strong, vigorous; (*dícese de los ojos*) (Am) drooping ‖ *m* (Am) slap, blow; (Am) pep
ñiqueñaque *m* (coll) trash
ñisca *f* (Am) bit, fragment; (Am) excrement
ñoclo *m* macaroon
ñolombre *m* (Am) old peasant; **¡viene ñolombre!** (Am) here comes the bogeyman
ñon·go -ga *adj* (Am) slow, lazy; (Am) foolish, stupid; (Am) tricky; (Am) suspicious
ñoñería or **ñoñez** *f* timidity; inanity; dotage
ño·ño -ña *adj* timid; inane; doting

O

O, o (o) *f* eighteenth letter of the Spanish alphabet
o *conj* or; **o . . . o** either . . . or
oa·sis *m* (*pl* **-sis**) oasis
ob. *abbr* **obispo**

obduración *f* obduracy
obedecer §22 *tr* (with personal **a**) to obey ‖ *intr* to obey; **obedecer a** to yield to, be due to, be in keeping with, arise from

obediencia *f* obedience
obediente *adj* obedient
obelisco *m* obelisk; (typ) dagger
obertura *f* (mus) overture
obesidad *f* obesity
obe·so -sa *adj* obese
obispo *m* bishop
óbito *m* decease, demise
obituario *m* (Am) obituary
objeción *f* objection
objetable *adj* objectionable (*open to objection*)
objetar *tr* to object; (*dudas*) to raise; (*una razón contraria*) to set up, offer, present; to object to
objeti·vo -va *adj & m* objective
objeto *m* object; subject matter; **objetos de cotillón** favors
oblea *f* wafer; pill, tablet; **hecho una oblea** (coll) nothing but skin and bones
obli·cuo -cua *adj* oblique
obligación *f* obligation, duty; bond, debenture; **obligaciones** *fpl* family responsibilities
obligacionista *mf* bondholder
obliga·do -da *adj* obliged, grateful; submissive; (mus) obbligato ‖ *m* (mus) obbligato
obligar §44 *tr* to obligate; to oblige
obliterar *tr* to cancel
oblon·go -ga *adj* oblong
oboe *m* oboe; oboist
oboísta *mf* oboist
óbolo *m* mite
obra *f* work; **obra de** a matter of; **obra de consulta** reference work; **obra maestra** masterpiece; **obra pía** charity; (coll) useful effort; **obra prima** shoemaking; **obras** construction, repairs, alterations; **obra segunda** shoe repairing; **poner por obra** to undertake, set to work on
obrera *f* workingwoman
obrerismo *m* labor; labor movement
obre·ro -ra *adj* working; labor ‖ *m* workman; **los obreros** labor ‖ *f* see **obrera**
obrero-patronal *adj* labor-management
obscenidad *f* obscenity
obsce·no -na *adj* obscene
obscurecer §22 *tr* to darken; to dim; to discredit; to cloud, confuse ‖ *intr* to grow dark ‖ *ref* to cloud over; to become dimmed; (coll) to fade away
obscuridad *f* obscurity; darkness
obscu·ro -ra *adj* obscure; dark; gloomy; uncertain, dangerous; **a obscuras** in the dark ‖ *m* dark; (paint) shading
obsequia·do -da *mf* recipient; guest of honor
obsequiar *tr* to fawn over, flatter; to present, to give; to court, to woo

obsequio *m* flattery; gift; attention, courtesy; **en obsequio de** in honor of
obsequio·so -sa *adj* obsequious; obliging, courteous
observación *f* observation
observa·dor -dora *adj* observant ‖ *mf* observer
observancia *f* observance; deference, respectfulness
observar *tr* to observe
observatorio *m* observatory
obsesión *f* obsession
obsesionar *tr* to obsess
obstaculizar §60 *tr* to prevent; to obstruct
obstáculo *m* obstacle
obstante *adj* standing in the way; **no obstante** however, nevertheless; in spite of
obstar *intr* to stand in the way; **obstar a** or **para** to hinder, check, oppose
obstetricia *f* obstetrics
obstétri·co -ca *adj* obstetrical ‖ *mf* obstetrician
obstinación *f* obstinacy
obstina·do -da *adj* obstinate
obstinar *ref* to be obstinate
obstrucción *f* obstruction
obstruir §20 *tr* to obstruct; to block; to stop up
obtención *f* obtaining
obtener §71 *tr* to obtain; to keep
obtenible *adj* obtainable
obturador *m* stopper, plug; (aut) choke; (aut) throttle; (phot) shutter; **obturador de guillotina** drop shutter
obtu·so -sa *adj* obtuse
obús *m* howitzer; shell; (*de válvula de neumático*) plunger
obvención *f* extra, bonus, incidental
obvencional *adj* incidental
obviar §77 & *regular tr* to obviate, prevent ‖ *intr* to stand in the way
ob·vio -via *adj* obvious; unnecessary
oca *f* goose
ocasión *f* occasion; opportunity, chance; danger, risk; **aprovechar la ocasión** to improve the occasion; **aprovechar la ocasión de** to avail oneself of the opportunity to; **asir la ocasión por la melena** to take time by the forelock; **de ocasión** secondhand
ocasiona·do -da *adj* dangerous, risky; exposed, subject, liable; annoying
ocasionar *tr* to occasion, to cause; to stir up; to endanger
ocasional *adj* occasional; causal; causing; (*causa*) responsible; accidental
ocaso *m* west; (*de un cuerpo celeste*) setting; sunset; decline; end, death
occidental *adj* western; occidental
occidente *m* occident
oceáni·co -ca *adj* oceanic
océano *m* ocean
ocio *m* idleness, leisure; distraction, pastime; spare time
ocio·so -sa *adj* idle; useless, needless
oclusión *f* occlusion
oclusi·vo -va *adj & f* occlusive
ocote *m* (Mex) torch pine
octava *f* octave
octavilla *f* handbill; eight-syllable verse

octavín *m* piccolo

octa·vo -va *adj* eighth ‖ *mf* octoroon ‖ *m* eighth ‖ *f* see **octava**

oct.ᵉ *abbr* octubre

octogési·mo -ma *adj & m* eightieth

octubre *m* October

ocular *adj* ocular, eye ‖ *m* eyepiece, eyeglass, ocular

oculista *mf* oculist; (Am) fawner, flatterer

ocultar *tr & ref* to hide

ocul·to -ta *adj* hidden, concealed; (*misterioso, sobrenatural*) occult

ocupación *f* occupation; occupancy; employment

ocupa·do -da *adj* busy; occupied; **ocupada** pregnant

ocupante *adj* occupying ‖ *mf* occupant ‖ **ocupantes** *mpl* occupying forces

ocupar *tr* to occupy; to busy, keep busy; to employ; to bother, annoy; to attract the attention of ‖ *ref* to be occupied; to be busy; to be preoccupied; to bother

ocurrencia *f* occurrence; witticism; bright idea

ocurrente *adj* witty

ocurrir *intr* to occur, happen; to come; (*venir a la mente*) to occur

ocha·vo -va *adj* eighth; octagonal ‖ *m* eighth; octagon

ochenta *adj, pron & m* eighty

ochenta·vo -va *adj & m* eightieth

ocho *adj & pron* eight; **las ocho** eight o'clock ‖ *m* eight; (*en las fechas*) eighth

ochocien·tos -tas *adj & pron* eight hundred ‖ **ochocientos** *m* eight hundred

oda *f* ode

odiar *tr* to hate

odio *m* hate, hatred

odio·so -sa *adj* odious, hateful

Odisea *f* Odyssey

Odiseo *m* Odysseus

odontología *f* odontology, dentistry

odontólo·go -ga *mf* odontologist, dentist

odre *m* goatskin wine bag; (coll) toper

OEA *f* OAS

oeste *m* west; west wind

ofender *tr & intr* to offend ‖ *ref* to take offense

ofensa *f* offense

ofensi·vo -va *adj & f* offensive

ofen·sor -sora *adj* offending ‖ *mf* offender

oferta *f* offer; gift, present; **oferta y demanda** supply and demand

oficial *adj* official ‖ *m* official, officer; skilled workman; clerk, office worker; journeyman; commissioned officer; **oficial de derrota** navigator

oficiar *tr* to announce officially in writing; (*la misa*) to celebrate; to officiate at ‖ *intr* to officiate; **oficiar de** (coll) to act as

oficina *f* office; shop; pharmacist's laboratory; **oficina de objetos perdidos** lost-and-found department

oficines·co -ca *adj* office, clerical; bureaucratic

oficinista *mf* clerk, office worker

oficio *m* office, occupation; function,

rôle; craft, trade; memo, official note; (eccl) office, service; **de oficio** officially; professionally; **hacer oficios de** to function as; **tomar por oficio** (coll) to take to, to keep at

oficio·so -sa *adj* diligent; obliging; officious, meddlesome; profitable; unofficial

ofrecer *tr & intr* to offer; (*una recepción*) to give ‖ *ref* to offer; to offer oneself; to happen

ofrecimiento *m* offer, offering; **ofrecimiento de presentación** introductory offer

ofrenda *f* offering; gift

ofrendar *tr* to make offerings of; to contribute

oftalmología *f* ophthalmology

oftalmólo·go -ga *mf* ophthalmologist

ofuscar §73 *tr* to obfuscate; to dazzle

ogro *m* ogre

Oh *interj* O!, Oh!

ohmio *m* ohm

oíble *adj* audible

oída *f* hearing; **de** or **por oídas** by hearsay

oído *m* hearing; ear; **abrir tanto oído** to be all ears; **al oído** by listening; confidentially; **decir al oído** to whisper; **hacer** or **tener oídos de mercader** to turn a deaf ear

oír §48 *tr* to hear; to listen to; (*una conferencia*) to attend; **oír + inf** to hear + *inf*, e.g., **oí entrar a mi hermano** I heard my brother come in; to hear + *ger*, e.g., **oí cantar a la muchacha** I heard the girl singing; to hear + *pp*, e.g., **oí tocar la campana** I heard the bell rung; **oír decir que** to hear that; **oír hablar de** to hear about ‖ *intr* to hear; to listen; **¡oiga!** say!, listen!; the idea!, the very idea!

ojada *f* (Col) skylight

ojal *m* buttonhole; eyelet; grommet

ojalá *interj* God grant . . . !, would to God . . . !; **¡ojalá que . . . !** would that . . . !, I hope that . . . !

ojeada *f* glimpse, glance; **buena ojeada** eyeful

ojear *tr* to eye, stare at; to hoodoo, to cast the evil eye on; (*la caza*) to start, to rouse; to frighten, to startle

ojera *f* eyecup, eyeglass; **ojeras** (*bajo los párpados inferiores*) rings, circles

ojeriza *f* grudge, ill will

ojero·so -sa *adj* with rings or circles under the eyes

ojete *m* eyelet, eyehole

ojienju·to -ta *adj* dry-eyed, tearless

ojituer·to -ta *adj* cross-eyed

ojiva *f* ogive, pointed arch

ojo *m* eye; (*de la escalera*) opening, well; (*del puente*) bay, span; (*de agua*) spring; **a ojos vistas** visibly, openly; **costar un ojo de la cara** to cost a mint, to cost a fortune; **dar los ojos de la cara por** to give one's eyeteeth for; **hasta los ojos** up to one's ears; **mirar con ojos de carnero degollado** to make sheep's eyes at; **no pegar el ojo** to not sleep a wink; **ojo de buey** (archit, meteor, naut) bull's-eye; (bot) oxeye; **ojo de la cerradura**

keyhole; **poner los ojos en blanco** to roll one's eyes; **saltar a los ojos** to be self-evident; **valer un ojo de la cara** to be worth a mint || *interj* beware!; look out!; attention!; **¡mucho ojo!** be careful!, watch out!; **¡ojo con . . .!** look out for . . .!; **¡ojo, mancha!** fresh paint!

ojota *f* (SAm) sandal; (SAm) tanned llama hide

ola *f* wave; (*de gente apiñada*) surge

ole *m* or **olé** *m* bravo || *interj* bravo!

oleada *f* big wave; (*de gente apiñada*) surge, swell

oleaje *m* surge, rush of waves

óleo *m* oil; holy oil; oil painting; **los santos óleos** extreme unction

oleoducto *m* pipe line

oler §49 *tr* to smell; to pry into; to sniff out || *intr* to smell, to smell fragrant, to smell bad; **no oler bien** (coll) to look suspicious; **oler a** to smell of, to smell like; to smack of

olfatear *tr* to smell, scent, sniff; (coll) (*p.ej., un buen negocio*) to scent, to sniff out

olfato *m* smell, sense of smell; scent; keen insight

olíbano *m* frankincense

oliente *adj* smelling, odorous

oligarquía *f* oligarchy

Olimpíada *f* Olympiad

olímpi·co -ca *adj* Olympian; Olympic; haughty

oliscar §73 *tr* to smell, scent, sniff; to investigate || *intr* to smell bad

oliva *f* olive; olive tree; barn owl; olive branch, peace

olivar *m* olive grove

olivillo *m* mock privet

olivo *m* olive tree; **tomar el olivo** (taur) to duck behind the barrier; (coll) to beat it

olmeda *f* or **olmedo** *m* elm grove

olmo *m* elm tree

olor *m* odor; promise, hope; trace, suspicion; **olores** (Chile, Mex) spice, condiment

oloro·so -sa *adj* odorous, fragrant

olote *m* (CAm & Mex) cob, corncob

olvidadi·zo -za *adj* forgetful; ungrateful

olvida·do -da *adj* forgetful; ungrateful

olvidar *tr & intr* to forget; **olvidar** + *inf* to forget to + *inf* || *ref* to forget oneself; **olvidarse de** to forget; **olvidarse de** + *inf* to forget to + *inf*; **olvidársele a uno** to forget, e.g., **se me olvidó mi pasaporte** I forgot my passport; **olvidársele a uno** + *inf* to forget to + *inf*, e.g., **se me olvidó cerrar la ventana** I forgot to close the window

olvido *m* forgetfulness; oblivion

olla *f* pot, kettle; stew; eddy, whirlpool; **olla a** or **de presión** pressure cooker

ombligo *m* navel; (*centro, punto medio*) (fig) navel

omino·so -sa *adj* ominous

omisión *f* omission; oversight, neglect

omi·so -sa *adj* neglectful, remiss

omitir *tr* to omit; to overlook, neglect

ómni·bus *adj* (tren) accommodation || *m* (*pl* **-bus**) bus, omnibus; **ómnibus de dos pisos** double-decker

omnímo·do -da *adj* all-inclusive

omnipotente *adj* omnipotent

omnisciente or **omnis·cio -cia** *adj* omniscient

omnívo·ro -ra *adj* omnivorous

omóplato *m* shoulder blade

once *adj & pron* eleven; **las once** eleven o'clock || *m* eleven; (*en las fechas*) eleventh

oncea·vo -va *adj & m* eleventh

once·no -na *adj & m* eleventh

onda *f* wave; flicker; (*en el pelo*) wave; **onda portadora** (rad) carrier wave; **ondas entretenidas** (rad) continuous waves

ondear *tr* (*el pelo*) to wave || *intr* to wave; to ripple; to flow; to flicker; to be wavy || *ref* to wave, sway, swing

ondo·so -sa *adj* wavy

ondulación *f* undulation; wave; wave motion

ondula·do -da *adj* wavy, ripply; rolling; corrugated || *m* (*en el pelo*) wave

ondular *tr* (*el pelo*) to wave || *intr* to undulate; (*una bandera*) to wave, flutter; (*las ondas del mar*) to billow; (*una culebra*) to wriggle

onero·so -sa *adj* onerous, burdensome

ónice *m*, **ónique** *m* or **ónix** *m* onyx

onomásti·co -ca *adj* of proper names || *m* name day || *f* study of proper names

ONU *f* UN

onza *f* ounce; (zool) snow leopard

onza·vo -va *adj & m* eleventh

opa·co -ca *adj* opaque; sad, gloomy

ópalo *m* opal

opción *f* option, choice

ópera *f* opera; **ópera semiseria** light opera; **ópera seria** grand opera

operación *f* operation; transaction

operar *tr* to operate on || *intr* to operate; to work || *ref* to occur, come about; to be operated on

opera·rio -ria *mf* worker || *m* workman || *f* working woman

opereta *f* operetta

operista *mf* opera singer

operísti·co -ca *adj* operatic

opia·to -ta *adj, m & f* opiate

opinable *adj* moot

opinar *intr* to opine; to think; to pass judgment

opinión *f* opinion, view; reputation, public image

opio *m* opium

opípa·ro -ra *adj* sumptuous, lavish

oponer §54 *tr* to oppose; (*resistencia*) to offer, put up || *ref* to oppose each other; to face each other; **oponerse a** to oppose, be opposed to; to be against, to resist; to compete for

oporto *m* port, port wine

oportunidad *f* opportunity; opportuneness; **oportunidades** *fpl* witticisms

oportunista *adj* opportunistic || *mf* opportunist

oportu·no -na *adj* opportune, timely; proper; witty

oposición *f* opposition; competitive examination

oposi·tor -tora *adj* rivaling, competing || *mf* opponent; competitor

opresión *f* oppression

opresi·vo -va *adj* oppressive

opre·sor -sora *adj* oppressive || *mf* oppressor

oprimir *tr* to oppress; to squeeze, to press

oprobiar *tr* to defame, to revile

oprobio *m* opprobrium

oprobio·so -sa *adj* opprobrious

optar *tr* to choose, to select; *intr* — **optar entre** to choose between; **optar por** to choose to

ópti·co -ca *adj* optical || *mf* optician || *f* optics

óptimamente *adv* to perfection

optimismo *m* optimism

optimista *adj* optimistic || *mf* optimist

ópti·mo -ma *adj* fine, excellent

optometrista *mf* optometrist

opues·to -ta *adj* opposite, contrary

opugnar *tr* to attack; to lay siege to; to contradict

opulen·to -ta *adj* opulent

opúsculo *m* short work, opuscule

oquedad *f* hollow; hollowness

ora *conj* — **ora . . . ora** now . . . now, now . . . then

oración *f* oration, speech; prayer; sentence; **oración dominical** Lord's prayer; **ponerse en oración** to get down on one's knees

oráculo *m* oracle

ora·dor -dora *mf* orator, speaker; **orador de plazuela** soapbox orator; **orador de sobremesa** after-dinner speaker

oraje *m* rough weather, storm

oral *adj* oral

orangután *m* orang-outang

orar *intr* to pray; to make a speech

orato·rio -ria *adj* oratorical || *m* oratorio; *(capilla privada)* oratory || *f (arte de la elocuencia)* oratory

orbe *m* orb; world

órbita *f* orbit

orca *f* killer whale

órcadas *fpl* Orkney Islands

órdago — **de órdago** (coll) swell, real

orden *m & f* order; **hasta nueva orden** until further notice; **orden** *f* **de allanamiento** search warrant; **orden** *m* **de colocación** word order

ordenancista *adj* strict, severe || *mf* taskmaster, disciplinarian, martinet

ordenanza *m* errand boy; (mil) orderly || *f* ordinance; order, system; command; **ser de ordenanza** (coll) to be the rule

ordenar *tr* to order; to put in order; to ordain || *ref* to be ordained, to take orders

ordeñadero *m* milk pail

ordeñar *tr* to milk

ordeño *m* milking

ordinal *adj* orderly; ordinal || *m* ordinal

ordinariez *f* (coll) coarseness, crudeness

ordina·rio -ria *adj* ordinary || *m* daily household expenses; delivery man

orear *tr* to air || *ref* to be aired; to dry in the air; to take an airing

orégano *m* pot or wild marjoram, winter sweet

oreja *f* ear; *(del zapato)* flap; *(de martillo)* claw; lug, flange, ear; **aguzar las orejas** to prick up one's ears; **con las orejas caídas** crestfallen; **con las orejas tan largas** all ears; **descubrir** or **enseñar las orejas** (coll) to give oneself away

oreja·no -na *adj (res)* unbranded; *(animal)* (Am) skittish; (Am) shy; (Am) cautious

orejera *f* earflap, earmuff

orejeta *f* lug

ore·jón -jona *adj* (Am) coarse, uncouth; (Mex) skinny || *m* strip of dried peach; pull on the ear; *(de la hoja de un libro)* dog's-ear

oreju·do -da *adj* big-eared

oreo *m* breeze

orfanato *m* orphanage

orfandad *f* orphanage, orphanhood

orfebre *m* goldsmith; silversmith

Orfeo *m* Orpheus

orfeón *m* glee club, choral society

organ·dí *m* (pl -díes) organdy

orgáni·co -ca *adj* organic

organillero -ra *mf* organ-grinder

organillo *m* barrel organ, hand organ, hurdy-gurdy

organismo *m* organism; organization

organista *mf* organist

organizar §60 *tr* to organize

órgano *m* organ; *(de una máquina)* part; *(medio, conducto)* organ; (mus) organ

orgía *f* orgy

orgullo *m* haughtiness; pride

orgullo·so -sa *adj* haughty; proud

oriental *adj* eastern; oriental

orientar *tr* to orient; to guide, direct; *(una vela)* to trim || *ref* to orient oneself; to find one's bearings

oriente *m* east; source, origin; east wind; youth || **Oriente** *m* Orient; **el Cercano Oriente** the Near East; **el Extremo Oriente** the Far East; **el Lejano Oriente** the Far East; **el Oriente Medio** the Middle East; **el Próximo Oriente** the Near East; **gran oriente** *(logia masónica central)* grand lodge

orificar §73 *tr* to fill with gold

orífice *m* goldsmith

orificio *m* orifice, aperture, hole

origen *m* origin; source

original *adj* original; queer, odd, quaint || *m* original; character, queer duck; **de buen original** on good authority; **original de imprenta** copy

originar *tr & ref* to originate, to start

orilla *f* border, edge; margin; bank, shore; sidewalk; breeze; **orillas** (Arg, Mex) outskirts; **salir a la orilla** to manage to get through

orillar *tr* to put a border or edge on; to trim || *intr* to come up to the shore

orillo *m* selvage, list

orín *m* rust; **orines** urine; **tomarse de orines** to get rusty

orina *f* urine

orinal *m* chamber pot

orinar *tr* to pass, to urinate ‖ *intr &
ref* to urinate
oriun·do -da *adj & mf* native; **ser
oriundo de** to come from, to hail
from
orla *f* border, edge; trimming, fringe
orlar *tr* to border, to put an edge on;
to trim, to trim with a fringe
orn. *abbr* **orden**
ornamentar *tr* to ornament, adorn
ornamento *m* ornament, adornment
ornar *tr* to adorn
ornato *m* adornment, show
oro *m* gold; playing card (*representing a gold coin*) equivalent to diamond; **de oro y azul** (coll) all dressed
up; **oro batido** gold leaf; **oro de ley**
standard gold; **poner de oro y azul**
(coll) to rake over the coals; **ponerle
colores al oro** to gild the lily
oron·do -da *adj* big-bellied; (coll) hollow, spongy, puffed up; (coll) pompous, self-satisfied
oropel *m* tinsel; **gastar mucho oropel**
(coll) to put up a big front
oropéndola *f* golden oriole
orozuz *m* licorice
orquesta *f* orchestra; **orquesta típica**
regional orchestra
orquestar *tr* to orchestrate
órquide *f* or **orquídea** *f* orchid
ortiga *f* nettle; **ser como unas ortigas**
(coll) to be a grouch
orto *m* rise (*of sun or star*)
ortodo·xo -xa *adj* orthodox
ortografía *f* orthography; spelling
ortografiar §77 *tr & intr* to spell
oruga *f* caterpillar
orujo *m* bagasse of grapes or olives
orzuelo *m* sty
os *pron pers & reflex* (used as object of
verb and corresponding to **vos** and
vosotros) you, to you; yourself, to
yourself; yourselves, to yourselves;
each other, to each other
osa *f* she-bear; **Osa mayor** Great Bear;
Osa menor Little Bear
osadía *f* boldness, daring
osa·do -da *adj* bold, daring
osamenta *f* skeleton; bones
osar *intr* to dare
osario *m* ossuary, charnel house
oscilar *intr* to oscillate; to fluctuate;
to waver, hesitate
ósculo *m* kiss
oscurecer §22 *tr, intr & ref* var of
obscurecer
oscuridad *f* var of **obscuridad**
oscu·ro -ra *adj & m* var of **obscuro**
osera *f* bear's den
osificar §73 *tr & ref* to ossify
oso *m* bear; **hacer el oso** (coll) to make
a fool of oneself; (coll) to make love
in the open; **oso blanco** polar bear;
oso hormiguero ant bear, anteater;
oso lavador raccoon
ostensorio *m* (eccl) monstrance
ostentar *tr* to show; to make a show of
‖ *ref* to show off; to boast

ostentati·vo -va *adj* ostentatious
ostento *m* portent, prodigy
ostento·so -sa *adj* magnificent, showy
osteópata *mf* osteopath
osteopatía *f* osteopathy
ostión *m* large oyster
ostra *f* oyster; **ostras en su concha**
oyster cocktail, oysters on the half
shell
ostracismo *m* ostracism
ostral *m* oyster bed, oyster farm
ostrería *f* oysterhouse
ostre·ro -ra *adj* oyster ‖ *m* oysterman;
oyster bed, oyster farm
osu·do -da *adj* bony
osu·no -na *adj* bearish, bearlike
O.T.A.N., la Nato
O.T.A.S.E., la Seato
otate *m* Mexican giant grass (*Guadua
amplexifolia*); otate stick
otero *m* hillock, knoll
otomán *m* ottoman
otoma·no -na *adj & mf* Ottoman ‖ *f*
ottoman
otoñal *adj* autumnal
otoño *m* autumn, fall
otorgar §44 *tr* to agree to; to grant, to
confer; (law) to execute
o·tro -tra *adj indef* other, another ‖
pron indef other one, another one;
como dijo el otro as someone said
ovación *f* ovation
ovacionar *tr* to give an ovation to
oval *adj* oval
óvalo *m* oval
ovante *adj* victorious, triumphant
ovario *m* ovary
oveja *f* ewe, female sheep; **oveja negra**
(fig) black sheep; **oveja perdida** (fig)
lost sheep
oveje·ro -ra *adj* sheep ‖ *mf* sheep raiser
oveju·no -na *adj* sheep, of sheep
ove·ro -ra *adj* blossom-colored; egg-
colored
Ovidio *m* Ovid
ovillar *tr* to wind up; to sum up ‖ *intr*
to form into a ball ‖ *ref* to curl up
into a ball
ovillo *m* ball of yarn; ball, heap; tangled ball; **hacerse un ovillo** (coll) to
cower, to recoil; (*hablando*) (coll) to
get all tangled up
oxear *tr & intr* to shoo
oxiacanta *f* hawthorn
oxidar *tr* to oxidize ‖ *ref* to oxidize; to
get rusty
óxido *m* oxide; **óxido de carbono** carbon monoxide; **óxido de mercurio**
mercuric oxide
oxígeno *m* oxygen
oxíto·no -na *adj* oxytone
oxte *interj* get out!, beat it!; **sin decir
oxte ni moxte** (coll) without opening
one's mouth
oyente *mf* hearer; (*a la radio*) listener;
(*en la escuela*) auditor
ozono *m* ozone

op
oz

P

P, p (pe) *f* nineteenth letter of the Spanish alphabet

P. *abbr* **Padre, Papa, Pregunta**

pabellón *m* pavilion; bell tent; flag, banner; *(de fusiles)* stack; canopy; summerhouse; *(de instrumento de viento)* bell

pabilo *or* **pábilo** *m* wick

Pablo *m* Paul

pábulo *m* food; support, encouragement, fuel

pacana *f* pecan

paca·to -ta *adj* mild, gentle

pacer §22 *tr* to pasture, graze; to gnaw, eat away ‖ *intr* to pasture, graze

paciencia *f* patience

paciente *adj* & *mf* patient

pacienzu·do -da *adj* long-suffering

pacificar §73 *tr* to pacify ‖ *intr* to sue for peace ‖ *ref* to calm down

pacífi·co -ca *adj* pacific

pacifismo *m* pacifism

pacifista *adj* & *mf* pacifist

pa·co -ca *adj* (Chile) bay, reddish ‖ *m* paco, alpaca; Moorish sniper; sniper ‖ **Paco** *m* Frank

pacotilla *f* trash, junk; (Chile) rabble, mob; **hacer su pacotilla** (coll) to make a cleanup; **ser de pacotilla** to be shoddy, to be poorly made

pacotille·ro -ra *mf* (Chile, Ven) peddler

pactar *tr* to agree upon ‖ *intr* to come to an agreement

pacto *m* pact, covenant

pacha·cho -cha *adj* (Chile) short-legged; (Chile) lax, lazy; (Chile) chubby

pa·chón -chona *adj* (CAm) shaggy, hairy, wooly ‖ *m* *(perro)* pointer; *(hombre flemático)* (coll) sluggard

pachorra *f* (coll) sluggishness, indolence

padecer §22 *tr* to suffer; to be victim of ‖ *intr* to suffer

padrastro *m* stepfather; hangnail

padre *adj* (Am) huge; (Peru) terrific ‖ *m* father; stallion, sire; **padres** parents; ancestors; **tener el padre alcalde** to have pull, to have a friend at court

padrina *f* godmother

padrinazgo *m* godfathership; sponsorship, patronage

padrino *m* godfather; sponsor; *(en un desafío)* second; **padrino de boda** best man; **padrinos** godparents

padrón *m* poll, census; pattern, model; memorial column; (coll) indulgent father; (Am) stallion; (Col) stock bull

padrote *m* (Am) stock animal; (Mex) pimp, procurer

paella *f* saffron-flavored stew of chicken, seafood, and rice with vegetables

paf *interj* bang!

pág. *abbr* **página**

paga *f* pay, payment; wages; fine

paga-alquiler *f* rent, rent money

pagadero -ra *adj* payable

paga·do -da *adj* pleased, cheerful; **estamos pagados** we are quits; **pagado de sí mismo** self-satisfied, conceited

paga·dor -dora *adj* paying ‖ *mf* payer ‖ *m* paymaster

paganismo *m* paganism

paga·no -na *adj* & *mf* pagan ‖ *m* (coll) easy mark

pagar §44 *tr* to pay; to pay for; *(una bondad, una visita)* to return ‖ *intr* to pay ‖ *ref* to become fond; to be flattered; to boast; to be satisfied

pagaré *m* promissory note, I.O.U.

página *f* page

paginar *tr* to page

pago *m* payment; *(de viñas u olivares)* district, region

pagote *m* (coll) easy mark

paila *f* large pan

pairar *intr* (naut) to lie to

país *m* country, land; landscape; **el país de Gales** Wales; **los Países Bajos** *(Bélgica, Holanda y Luxemburgo)* the Low Countries; *(Holanda)* The Netherlands

paisaje *m* landscape

paisajista *mf* landscape painter

paisa·no -na *adj* of the same country ‖ *mf* peasant; civilian; (Mex) Spaniard ‖ *m* fellow countryman; **de paisano** in civies

paja *f* straw; chaff; trash, rubbish; **no dormirse en las pajas** to not let the grass grow under one's feet; **no levantar paja del suelo** to not lift a hand, to not do a stroke of work

pájara *f* paper kite; paper rooster; bird; crafty female

pajarera *f* aviary; large bird cage

pajarería *f* flock of birds; bird store; pet shop

pajare·ro -ra *adj* (coll) bright, cheerful; (coll) bright-colored, gaudy ‖ *m* bird dealer; bird fancier ‖ *f* see **pajarera**

pajarita *f* paper kite; bow tie; wing collar, piccadilly

pájaro *m* bird; crafty fellow; expert; **pájaro bobo** penguin; (Am) motmot; **pájaro carpintero** woodpecker; **pájaro de cuenta** (coll) big shot; **pájaro mosca** hummingbird

pajarota *or* **pajarotada** *f* hoax, canard

paje *m* page; valet; dressing table; (naut) cabin boy

pajilla *f* cornhusk cigarette; **pajilla de madera** excelsior

paji·zo -za *adj* straw; straw-colored; straw-thatched

pajuela *f* short straw; sulfur match or fuse; (Am) toothpick; (Bol) match

Pakistán, el var of **Paquistán**

pakista·ní *(pl -níes) adj* & *mf* var of **paquistaní**

pala *f* shovel; *(de remo, de la azada, etc.)* blade; *(del panadero)* peel; scoop; racket; *(del calzado)* upper; *(de excavadora)* bucket; shoulder strap; (coll) cunning, craftiness

palabra *f* word; speech; *(de una canción)* words; *(derecho para hablar en asambleas)* floor; **palabras mayores**

words, angry words; **remojar la pala-bra** (coll) to wet one's whistle; **usar de la palabra** to speak, make a speech
palabre·ro -ra adj wordy, windy || mf windbag
palabrota f vulgarity, obscenity
palacie·go -ga adj palace, court || m courtier
palacio m palace; mansion; **palacio municipal** city hall
palada f shovelful; (de remo) stroke
paladar m palate; taste; gourmet
paladear tr to taste, to relish
paladín m champion, hero
palafrén m palfrey
palanca f lever; pole; crowbar; **palanca de mando** (aer) control stick; **palanca de mayúsculas** shift key
palancada f leverage
palangana f washbowl, basin
palanganero m washstand
palangre m trawl, trawl line
palanqueta f jimmy; **palanquetas** (Arg) dumbbell
palatal adj & f palatal
palco m (theat) box
palear tr to beat, to pound; (Am) to shovel
palenque m paling, palisade; (SAm) hitching post; (C-R) Indian ranch; (Chile) pandemonium
paleta f palette; small shovel; trowel; (de una rueda) paddle; blade, bucket, vane; shoulder blade; (dulce con un palito que sirve de mango) lollipop
paletilla f shoulder blade
paleto m fallow deer; rustic, yokel
palia f altar cloth; (eccl) pall
paliacate m (Mex) bandanna
paliar §77 & regular tr to palliate
palidecer §22 intr to pale, to turn pale
palidez f paleness, pallor
páli·do -da adj pale, pallid
palillo m toothpick; drumstick; bob-bin; **palillos** chopsticks; castanets; (coll) rudiments; (coll) trifles
palinodia f backdown; **cantar la pali-nodia** to eat crow, eat humble pie
palique m (coll) chit-chat, small talk
paliquear intr (coll) to chat, to gossip
paliza f beating, thrashing
palizada f fenced-in enclosure; stock-ade; embankment
palma f (de la mano) palm; (árbol y hoja) palm; **batir palmas** to clap, to applaud; **llevarse la palma** to carry off the palm
palmada f slap; hand, applause, clap-ping; **dar palmadas** to clap hands
palma·rio -ria adj clear, evident
palmatoria f candlestick
palmera f date palm
palmito m palmetto; (coll) woman's face; (coll) slender figure
palmo m span, palm; **dejar con un palmo de narices** (coll) to disappoint
palmotear tr to pat; to clap, applaud || intr to clap, applaud
palo m stick; pole; staff; handle; (golpe) whack; (madera) wood; (gru-po de naipes de la baraja) suit; (naut) mast; (Am) tree; **dar palos de ciego** to lay about, to swing wildly;

de tal palo tal astilla like father like son; **palo de escoba** broomstick; **palo en alto** (fig) big stick; **palo mayor** (naut) mainmast; **servir del palo** to follow suit
paloma f pigeon, dove; prostitute; (fig) dove, meek person; **paloma mensa-jera** carrier pigeon; **palomas** white-caps
palomar m pigeon house, dovecot
palomilla f doveling; small butterfly; white horse; (del caballo) back; pil-low block, journal bearing; **palomi-llas** whitecaps
palomita f doveling; (baseball) fly; **palomitas** (Am) popcorn
palpable adj palpable
palpar tr to touch, to feel; to grope through || intr to grope
palpitante adj throbbing; thrilling; (cuestión) burning
palpitar intr to palpitate, to throb; (un afecto) to flash, break forth
pálpito m (SAm) hunch
palta f (SAm) alligator pear, avocado (fruit)
palto m (SAm) alligator pear, avocado (tree)
palúdi·co -ca adj marshy; malarial
paludismo m malaria
palur·do -da adj rustic, boorish || mf rustic, boor
pallador m (SAm) Gaucho minstrel
pampa f pampa; **La Pampa** the Pampas
pámpana f vine leaf
pámpano m tendril; vine leaf
pan m bread; loaf; loaf of bread; wheat; food; livelihood; pie dough; (de jabón, cera, etc.) cake; gold foil or leaf; silver foil or leaf; **como el pan bendito** (coll) as easy as pie; **de pan llevar** arable, tillable; **llamar al pan pan y al vino vino** to call a spade a spade; **panes** grain, bread-stuff; **venderse como pan bendito** to sell like hot cakes || **Pan** m Pan
pana f corduroy; (aut) breakdown
panacea f panacea
panadería f bakery; baking business
panade·ro -ra mf baker; (Chile) flat-terer
panadizo m felon; (coll) sickly person
panal m honeycomb
pana·má m (pl -maes) Panama hat
paname·ño -ña adj & mf Panamanian
panamerica·no -na adj Pan-American
pancarta f placard, poster
pancista adj weaseling || mf weaseler
páncre·as m (pl -as) pancreas
pancho m (coll) paunch, belly
pandear intr & ref to warp, to bulge, to buckle, to sag, to bend
pandereta f tambourine
pandilla f party, faction; gang, band; picnic, excursion
pan·do -da adj bulging; slow-moving; slow, deliberate
pandorga f kite; (coll) fat, lazy woman
panecillo m roll, crescent
panfleto m pamphlet
paniaguado m servant, minion; protégé, favorite

páni·co -ca adj panic, panicky ‖ m panic

panizo m Italian millet; (Chile) gangue; (Chile) abundance

panocha f ear of grain; ear of corn; (Am) pancake made of corn and cheese; (Mex) panocha (*brown sugar*)

panoja f ear of grain; ear of corn

panorama m panorama

pano·so -sa adj mealy

panqué m or **panqueque** m pancake

pantalán m pier, wooden pier

pantalón m trousers; **calzarse los pantalones** to wear the pants; **pantalones** trousers, pants

pantalla f lamp shade; fire screen; motion-picture screen; television screen; (*persona que encubre a otra*) blind; (*cine, arte del cine*) screen; (Am) fan; **llevar a la pantalla** to put on the screen; **pantalla de plata** silver screen; **servir de pantalla a** to be ? blind for

pantano m bog, marsh, swamp; dam, reservoir; trouble, obstacle

pantano·so -sa adj marshy, swampy; muddy; knotty, difficult

panteísmo m pantheism

panteón m pantheon; cemetery

pantera f panther

pantomima f pantomime

pantoque m (naut) bilge

pantorrilla f calf (*of leg*)

pantufla f or **pantuflo** m house slipper

panza f paunch, belly

panzu·do -da adj paunchy, big-bellied

pañal m diaper; shirttail; **pañales** swaddling clothes; infancy; early stages

pañe·ro -ra adj dry-goods, cloth ‖ mf dry-goods dealer, clothier

paño m cloth; rag; (*de agujas*) paper; (*ancho de la tela*) breadth; (*mancha en el rostro*) spot; (*en, p.ej., un espejo*) blur; sailcloth, canvas; **al paño** off-stage; **conocer el paño** (coll) to know one's business, to know the ropes; **paño de adorno** doily; **paño de cocina** washrag, dishcloth; **paño de lágrimas** helping hand, stand-by; **paño de mesa** tablecloth; **paño de tumba** crape; **paño mortuorio** pall; **paños menores** underclothing

pañuelo m handkerchief; shawl; **pañuelo de hierbas** bandanna

papa m pope ‖ f (coll) potato; (coll) fake, hoax; (coll) food, grub; (Am) snap, cinch; **ni papa** (Am) nothing

pa·pá m (pl **-pás**) papa, daddy

papada f double chin; (*de animal*) dewlap; (Guat) stupidity

papado m papacy

papagayo m parrot

papalina f sunbonnet; (coll) drunk

papana·tas m (pl **-tas**) (coll) simpleton, gawk

paparrucha f (coll) hoax; (coll) trifle

papel m paper; piece of paper; rôle, part; character, figure; **desempeñar** or **hacer un papel** to play a rôle; **papel alquitranado** tar paper; **papel cebolla** onionskin; **papel de empapelar** wallpaper; **papel de esmeril** emery paper; **papel de estaño** tin foil;

papel de excusado toilet paper; **papel de fumar** cigarette paper; **papel de lija** sandpaper; **papel de oficio** foolscap; **papel de seda** tissue paper; **papel de segundón** (fig) second fiddle; **papel de tornasol** litmus paper; **papel filtrante** filter paper; **papel higiénico** toilet paper; **papel moneda** paper money; **papel pintado** wallpaper; **papel secante** blotting paper; **papel viejo** waste paper; **papel volante** handbill, printed leaflet

papeleo m red tape

papelera f paper case; writing desk; wastebasket; paper factory

papelería f stationery store; mess of papers, litter

papele·ro -ra adj paper; boastful, showy ‖ mf stationer; paper manufacturer; (Mex) paperboy ‖ f see **papelera**

papeleta f slip of paper; card, file card; ticket; **papeleta de empeño** pawn ticket

papelista m paper maker, paper manufacturer; stationer; paper hanger

pape·lón -lona adj (coll) bluffing, four-flushing ‖ mf (coll) bluffer, four-flusher ‖ m thin cardboard

papelonear intr (coll) to bluff, to four-flush

papelote m worthless piece of paper; (Am) paper kite

papel-prensa m newsprint

papera f goiter; mumps

papilla f pap; guile, deceit

papiro m papyrus

papirote m fillip, flick; (coll) nincompoop

paq. abbr **paquete**

paquear tr to snipe at ‖ intr to snipe

paque·te -ta adj (Arg) chic, dolled-up; (Am) self-important, pompous ‖ m package, parcel, bundle, bale; (coll) sport, dandy; **darse paquete** (Guat, Mex) to put on airs; **en paquete aparte** under separate cover, in a separate package; **paquetes postales** parcel post

Paquistán, el Pakistan

paquista·ní (pl **-níes**) or **paquistano -na** adj & mf Pakistani

Paquita f Fanny

par adj like, similar, equal; (math) even ‖ m pair, couple; peer; (elec, mech) couple; (math) even number; **a pares** in twos; **de par en par** wide-open; completely; overtly; **¿pares o nones?** odd or even? ‖ f par; **a la par** equally; jointly; at the same time; at par; **bajo la par** below par, under par; **sobre la par** above par

para prep to, for; towards; compared to; (*antes de*) by; **para + inf** in order to + inf; about to + inf; **para con** towards; **para que** in order that, so that

parabién m congratulation

parábola f parable

parabri·sa m or **parabri·sas** m (pl **-sas**) windshield

paracaí·das m (pl **-das**) parachute; **lanzarse en paracaídas** to parachute; **sal-**

varse en paracaídas to parachute to safety
paracaidismo *m* parachute jumping; (sport) sky diving
paracaidista *mf* parachutist ‖ *m* paratrooper
parachis·pas *m* (*pl* **-pas**) spark arrester
paracho·ques *m* (*pl* **-ques**) bumper
parada *f* stop; end; stay; shutdown; (*en el juego*) stake; dam; (*para el ganado*) stall; stud farm; (*en la esgrima*) parry; (*tiro de caballerías de reemplazo*) relay; (mil) parade, dress parade, review; **parada de taxi** taxi stand
paradero *m* end; whereabouts; stopping place; (Am) wayside station
para·do -da *adj* slow, spiritless, witless; idle, unemployed; closed; (Am) proud, stiff ‖ *f* see **parada**
paradoja *f* paradox
paradóji·co -ca *adj* paradoxical
parador *m* inn, wayside inn; motel
parafina *f* paraffin
paragol·pes *m* (*pl* **-pes**) buffer, bumper
para·guas *m* (*pl* **-guas**) umbrella
Paraguay, el Paraguay
paraguaya·no -na or **paragua·yo -ya** *adj* & *mf* Paraguayan
paragüero *m* umbrella man; umbrella stand
paraíso *m* paradise
paraje *m* place, spot; state, condition
paralela *f* parallel, parallel line; **paralelas** parallel bars
paralelizar §60 *tr* to parallel, compare
parale·lo -la *adj* parallel ‖ *m* (geog) parallel ‖ *f* see **paralela**
paráli·sis *f* (*pl* **-sis**) paralysis
paralíti·co -ca *adj* & *mf* paralytic
paralizar §60 *tr* to paralyze ‖ *ref* to become paralyzed
páramo *m* high barren plain; bleak windy spot; (Bol, Col, Ecuad) cold drizzle
paranie·ves *m* (*pl* **-ves**) snow fence
paraninfo *m* assembly hall, auditorium
paranoi·co -ca *adj* & *mf* paranoiac
parapeto *m* parapet
parar *tr* to stop; to check; to change; to prepare; to put up, to stake; to parry; to order; to get, acquire; (*la atención*) to fix; (*la caza*) to point; (typ) to set ‖ *intr* to stop; (*en un hotel*) to put up; **parar en** to become; to run to, to run as far as ‖ *ref* to stop; to stop work; to turn, to become; (*el perro de muestra*) to point; (*el pelo*) to stand on end; (Am) to stand; **pararse en** to pay attention to
pararra·yo or **pararra·yos** *m* (*pl* **-yos**) (*barra metálica que sirve para preservar los edificios del rayo*) lightning rod; (*dispositivo que sirve para preservar una instalación eléctrica de la electricidad atmosférica o de las chispas que produce*) lightning arrester
parasíti·co -ca *adj* parasitic
parási·to -ta *adj* parasitic; (elec) stray ‖ *m* parasite; **parásitos atmosféricos** atmospherics, static
parasol *m* parasol

parato·pes *m* (*pl* **-pes**) bumper
Parcas *fpl* Fates
parcela *f* particle; plot of ground
parcelar *tr* to parcel, to divide into lots
parcial *adj* partial; partisan ‖ *mf* partisan
par·co -ca *adj* frugal, sparing; moderate
parchar *tr* (Am) to mend, patch
parche *m* plaster, sticking plaster; patch; drum; drumhead; daub, botch, splotch; **parche poroso** porous plaster
pardal *m* linnet; (coll) sly fellow
pardiez *interj* (coll) by Jove!
pardillo *m* linnet
par·do -da *adj* brown, drab; dark; cloudy; (*voz*) dull, flat; (*cerveza*) dark; (Am) mulatto ‖ *mf* (Am) mulatto ‖ *m* brown, drab; leopard
pardus·co -ca *adj* dark-brown, drabbish
parea·do -da *adj* rhymed ‖ *m* couplet
parear *tr* to pair; to match ‖ *ref* to pair off
parecer *m* opinion; look, mien, countenance ‖ *v* §22 *intr* to appear; to show up; to look, to seem; **me parece que . . .** I think that . . . ‖ *ref* to look alike, to resemble each other; **parecerse a** to look like
pareci·do -da *adj* like, similar; **bien parecido** good-looking; **parecido a** like, e.g., **esta casa es parecida a la otra** this house is like the other one; **parecidos** alike, e.g., **estas casas son parecidas** these houses are alike ‖ *m* similarity, resemblance, likeness; **tener un gran parecido** to be a good likeness
pared *f* wall; **dejar pegado a la pared** to nonplus; **paredes** house
pareja *f* pair, couple; dancing partner; **correr parejas** or **a las parejas** to be abreast, arrive together; to go together, match, be equal; **correr parejas con** to keep up with, to keep abreast of; **parejas** (*de naipes*) pair
pareje·ro -ra *adj* even, equal; (Am) servile, fawning; (Am) forward, overfamiliar ‖ *m* (Am) race horse
pare·jo -ja *adj* equal, like; even, smooth ‖ *m* (CAm) dancing partner ‖ *f* see **pareja**
parentela *f* kinsfolk, relations
parentesco *m* relationship; bond, tie
parénte·sis *m* (*pl* **-sis**) parenthesis; break, interval
parhilera *f* ridgepole
paria *mf* pariah, outcast
paridad *f* par, parity; comparison
parien·te -ta *adj* related ‖ *mf* relative; (coll) spouse
parihuela *f* handbarrow; (*camilla*) stretcher
parir *tr* to bear, give birth to, bring forth ‖ *intr* to give birth; to come forth, to come to light; to talk well
parisiense *adj* & *mf* Parisian
parlamentar *intr* to talk, chat; to parley
parlamento *m* parliament; parley; speech; (theat) speech
parlan·chín -china *adj* (coll) jabbering ‖ *mf* (coll) chatterbox
parlar *intr* to speak with facility; to

chatter, talk too much; (*el loro*) to talk

parle·ro -ra *adj* loquacious, garrulous; gossipy; (*ave*) singing, song; (*ojos*) expressive; (*arroyo, fuente*) babbling

parlotear *intr* (coll) to prattle, jabber, chin

parloteo *m* (coll) jabber, prattle

parnaso *m* (*colección de poesías*) Parnassus; **el Parnaso** Parnassus, Mount Parnassus

paro *m* shutdown, work stoppage; lockout; titmouse; (*de dados*) (SAm) throw; **paro forzoso** layoff

parodia *f* parody, travesty

parodiar *tr* to parody, to travesty, to burlesque

paroxíto·no -na *adj* & *m* paroxytone

parpadear *intr* to blink, wink; to flicker

parpadeo *m* blinking, winking; flicker

párpado *m* eyelid

parque *m* park; parking; parking lot; **parque de atracciones** amusement park

parqué *m* floor, inlaid floor

parqueadero *m* (Col) parking lot

parquear *tr* to park

parquímetro *m* parking meter

parra *f* grapevine; earthen jug

párrafo *m* paragraph; (coll) chat

parral *m* grape arbor

parranda *f* (coll) spree, party; (Col) large number; **andar de parranda** (coll) to go out on a spree, go out to celebrate

parricida *mf* patricide, parricide

parricidio *m* patricide, parricide

parrilla *f* grill, gridiron, broiler; grate, grating; grillroom, grill; **asar a la parrilla** to broil

párroco *m* parish priest

parroquia *f* parish; parish church; customers, clientele

parroquial *adj* parochial

parroquia·no -na *mf* parishioner; customer

parte *m* dispatch, communiqué; **parte meteorológico** weather report || *f* part; share; party; side; direction; (*papel de un actor*) role; (law) party; **de un mes a esta parte** for about a month past; **en ninguna otra parte** nowhere else; **en ninguna parte** nowhere; **ir a la parte** to go shares; **la mayor parte** most, the majority; **parte del león** lion's share; **parte de por medio** (theat) bit part, walk-on; **partes** parts, gifts, talent; faction; parts, genitals; **por otra parte** in another direction; elsewhere; on the other hand; **por todas partes** everywhere; **salva sea la parte** excuse me for not mentioning where

partea·guas *m* (*pl* **-guas**) divide, ridge

partear *tr* to deliver

parte·luz *m* (*pl* **-luces**) mullion, sash bar

Partenón *m* Parthenon

partera *f* midwife

partición *f* partition, division

participar *tr* to notify, to inform; to give notice of || *intr* to participate; to partake

participio *m* participle

partícula *f* particle

particular *adj* particular; peculiar; private, personal; **particular a particular** (telp) person-to-person || *m* particular; matter, subject; individual

particularizar §60 *tr* to itemize || *ref* to stand out; to specialize

partida *f* departure; entry, item; certificate; party, group, band; band of guerrillas; game; (*de cartas*) hand; (*de tenis*) set; lot, shipment; (coll) behavior; **mala partida** (coll) mean trick; **partida de campo** picnic; **partida doble** (com) double entry; **partida sencilla** (com) single entry

partida·rio -ria or **partidista** *adj* & *mf* partisan

parti·do -da *adj* generous, open-handed || *m* (pol) party; decision; profit; advantage; step, measure; deal, agreement; protection, support; (*casamiento que elegir*) match; district, county; (sport) team; (sport) game, match; **partido de desempate** play-off; **tomar partido** to take a stand, to take sides || *f* see **partida**

partir *tr* to divide; to distribute; to share; to split, split open; to break, crack; (coll) to upset, disconcert || *intr* to start, depart, leave, set out; **a partir de** beginning with || *ref* to become divided; to crack, to split

partisa·no -na *mf* (mil) partisan

partitura *f* (mus) score

parto *m* childbirth, confinement; newborn child; offspring; **estar de parto** to be in labor, to be confined; **parto del ingenio** brain child

parva *f* light breakfast (*on fast days*); heap of unthreshed grain; heap, pile

parvulista *mf* kindergarten teacher

párvu·lo -la *adj* small, tiny; simple, innocent; humble || *mf* child, tot; (*niño*) kindergartner

pasa *f* raisin; **pasa de Corinto** currant

pasada *f* passage; passing; **de pasada** in passing, hastily; **mala pasada** (coll) mean trick

pasade·ro -ra *adj* passable || *f* stepping stone; walkway, catwalk

pasadizo *m* passage, corridor, hallway, alley; catwalk

pasa·do -da *adj* past; gone by; overripe; spoiled; overdone; stale; burned out; antiquated; faded || *m* past; **pasados** ancestors || *f* see **pasada**

pasa·dor -dora *mf* smuggler || *m* door bolt; bolt, pin; hatpin; brooch; stickpin; safety pin; strainer

pasaje *m* passage; fare; fares; passengers; **cobrar el pasaje** to collect fares

pasaje·ro -ra *adj* passing, fleeting; (*camino, calle*) common, traveled || *mf* passenger; **pasajero colgado** straphanger; **pasajero no presentado** no-show

pasamano *m* lace trimming; (*baranda*) handrail; (naut) gangway

pasamonta·ña *m* or **pasamonta·ñas** *m* (*pl* **-ñas**) ski mask, storm hood

pasaporte *m* passport

pasar *m* livelihood || *tr* to pass; to

cross; to take across; to send, transfer, transmit; (*contrabando*) to slip in; to spend; to swallow; to excel; to overlook, stand for; to undergo, suffer; (*un libro*) to go through; (*una película*) to show; to dry in the sun; to tutor; to study with or under; **pasarlo** to get along; to live; (*dícese de la salud*) to be; **pasar por alto** to disregard; to omit, leave out, skip || *intr* to pass; to go; to pass away; to pass over; to happen; to last; to spread; to get along; to yield; to come in, e.g., **pase Vd.** come in; **pasar de** to go beyond, to exceed; to go above; to be more than; **pasar por** to pass by, down, through, over, etc.; to pass as, pass for; to stop or call at; **pasar sin** to do without || *ref* to pass; to go; to excel; to pass over; to get along; to pass away; to take an examination; to leak; to go too far; to become overripe, become overcooked; to rot; to melt; to burn out; (*una llave, un tornillo*) to not fit, to be loose; to forget; **pasarse por** to stop or call at; **pasarse sin** to do without

pasarela *f* footbridge; catwalk; gangplank

pasatiempo *m* pastime

pascua *f* Passover; Easter; Twelfthnight; Pentecost; Christmas; **dar las pascuas** to wish a Happy New Year; **estar como una pascua** or **unas pascuas** (coll) to be bubbling over with joy; **¡Felices Pascuas!** Merry Christmas!; **Pascua de flores** Easter; **Pascua del Espíritu Santo** Pentecost; **Pascua de Navidad** Christmas; **Pascua de Resurrección** or **Pascua florida** Easter; **Pascuas navideñas** Christmas

pase *m* (*permiso; billete gratuito; movimiento de las manos del mesmerista, el torero*) pass; (*en la esgrima*) feint; **pase de cortesía** complimentary ticket

paseante *adj* strolling || *mf* stroller

pasear *tr* to walk; to promenade, show off || *intr* to take a walk; to go for a ride || *ref* to take a walk; to go for a ride; to wander, ramble; to take it easy

paseíllo *m* processional entrance of bullfighters

paseo *m* walk, stroll, promenade; ride; drive; avenue; **dar un paseo** to take a walk; to take a ride; **enviar a paseo** (coll) to send on his way, to dismiss without ceremony; **paseo de caballos** bridle path; **paseo de la cuadrilla** processional entrance of the bullfighters

pasillo *m* short step; passage, corridor; (theat) short piece, sketch

pasión *f* passion

pasi·vo -va *adj* passive; (*pensión*) retirement || *m* liabilities; debit side

pasmar *tr* to chill; to frostbite; to stun, benumb; to dumbfound, astound || *ref* to chill; to become frostbitten; to be astounded; to get lockjaw; (*los colores*) to become dull or flat

pasmo *m* cold; lockjaw, tetanus; astonishment; wonder, prodigy

pasmo·so -sa *adj* astounding; awesome

paso *m* step; pace; (*de la escalera*) step; gait; walk; passing; passage; step, measure, démarche; pass, permit; strait; footstep, footprint; incident, happening; (*de hélice, tornillo*) pitch; (elec) pitch; (rad) stage; (theat) short piece, sketch, skit; **al paso** in passing, on the way; **al paso que** at the rate that; (*a la vez que, mientras*) while, whereas; **ceder el paso** to make way; to keep clear; **de paso** in passing; at the same time; **paso a nivel** grade crossing; **paso de ganado** cattle crossing; **paso de ganso** goose step

paspa *f* (SAm) crack in the lips

pasquín *m* lampoon

pasquinar *tr* to lampoon

pasta *f* paste, dough, pie crust, soup paste; mash; (*para hacer papel*) pulp; cardboard; board binding; (*de un diente*) filling; (*dinero*) (coll) dough; **pasta dentífrica** tooth paste; **pasta española** marbled leather binding, tree calf; **pastas** noodles, macaroni, spaghetti, etc.; **pasta seca** cookie

pastar *tr & intr* to graze

pastel *m* pie; pastry roll; pastel; settlement, pacification; cheat, trick; (typ) pi; (typ) smear; (coll) plot, deal; **pastel de cumpleaños** birthday cake

pastelería *f* pastry; pastry shop

pastele·ro -ra *mf* pastry cook

pastelillo *m* tart, cake; (*de mantequilla*) pat

pasterizar §60 *tr* to pasteurize

pastilla *f* tablet, lozenge, drop; (*pequeña masa pastosa*) dab; (*de jabón, chocolate, etc.*) cake

pasto *m* pasture; grass; food, nourishment; **a pasto** to excess; in abundance; **a todo pasto** freely, without restriction; **de pasto** ordinary, everyday

pastor *m* shepherd; pastor

pastora *f* shepherdess

pastoral *adj & f* pastoral

pastorear *tr* (*a las ovejas o los fieles*) to shepherd; (Am) to lie in ambush for; (Am) to spoil, pamper; (Arg, Urug) to court

pasto·so -sa *adj* pasty, doughy; (*voz*) mellow; (Arg, Chile) grassy

pastura *f* pasture; fodder

pasu·do -da *adj* (Am) kinky

pata *f* paw, foot, leg; (*de un mueble*) leg; duck; **a cuatro patas** (coll) on all fours; **estirar la pata** (coll) to kick the bucket; **meter la pata** (coll) to butt in, to put one's foot in it; **pata de gallo** crow's-foot; (coll) blunder; (coll) piece of nonsense; **pata de palo** peg leg, wooden leg; **pata galana** (coll) game leg; (coll) lame person; **patas arriba** (coll) on one's back, upside down; (coll) topsy-turvy

patada *f* kick; stamp, stamping; (coll) step; (coll) footstep, track; **en dos patadas** (Am) in a jiffy

patalear *intr* to kick; to stamp the feet

pataleta _f_ (coll) fit; (coll) feigned fit or convulsion; (dial) tantrum
patán _m_ (coll) churl, boor, lout; (coll) peasant
pataplún _interj_ kerplunk!
patata _f_ potato
patear _tr_ (coll) to kick; (coll) to trample on ‖ _intr_ (coll) to stamp one's foot; (coll) to bustle around; (Am) to kick
patentar _tr_ to patent
patente _adj_ patent, clear, evident ‖ _f_ grant, privilege, warrant; patent; **de patente** (Chile) excellent, first-class; **patente de circulación** owner's license; **patente de invención** patent; **patente de sanidad** bill of health
paternal _adj_ paternal, fatherly
paternidad _f_ paternity, fatherhood; **paternidad literaria** authorship
pater·no -na _adj_ paternal
pateta _m_ (coll) the devil; (coll) cripple
patéti·co -ca _adj_ pathetic
patetismo _m_ pathos
patibula·rio -ria _adj_ hair-raising
patíbulo _m_ scaffold
patiesteva·do -da _adj_ bowlegged
patilla _f_ small paw or foot; pocket flap; (naut) compass; (Am) watermelon; **patillas** sideburns, side whiskers
patín _m_ small patio; skate; skid, slide, runner; (_ave marina_) petrel; **patín de cuchilla** or **de hielo** ice skate; **patín de ruedas** roller skate
patinadero _m_ skating rink
patina·dor -dora _mf_ skater
patinaje _m_ skating; skidding; **patinaje artístico** figure skating; **patinaje de fantasía** fancy skating; **patinaje de figura** figure skating
patinar _intr_ to skate; to skid; to slip
patinazo _m_ skid; slip; (coll) slip, blunder
patinete _m_ scooter
patio _m_ patio, court, yard; campus; (rr) yard, switchyard; **patio de recreo** playground
patituer·to -ta _adj_ crooked-legged; (coll) crooked, lopsided
patizam·bo -ba _adj_ knock-kneed
pato _m_ duck, drake; **pagar el pato** (coll) to be the goat; **pato de flojel** eider duck
patochada _f_ (coll) blunder, stupidity
patología _f_ pathology
patota _f_ (Arg, Urug) teen-age gang
patraña _f_ fake, humbug, hoax
patria _f_ country; mother country, fatherland, native land; birthplace; (_p.ej., de las artes_) home; **patria chica** native heath
patriarca _m_ patriarch
patri·cio -cia _adj_ & _mf_ patrician
patrimonio _m_ patrimony
pa·trio -tria _adj_ native, home; paternal ‖ _f_ see **patria**
patriota _mf_ patriot
patrióti·co -ca _adj_ patriotic
patriotismo _m_ patriotism
patrocinar _tr_ to sponsor, patronize
patrocinio _m_ sponsorship
patrón _m_ sponsor, protector; patron saint; patron; landlord; owner, master; boss, foreman; host; (_de un barco_) skipper; pattern; standard; **patrón oro** gold standard; **patrón picado** stencil
patrona _f_ patroness; landlady; owner, mistress; hostess
patronal _adj_ management, employers'
patronato _m_ employers' association; foundation; board of trustees; patronage
patronear _tr_ to skipper
patro·no -na _mf_ sponsor, protector; employer ‖ _m_ patron; landlord; boss, foreman; lord of the manor; **los patronos** the management ‖ _f_ see **patrona**
patrulla _f_ patrol; gang, band
patrullar _tr_ & _intr_ to patrol
paulati·no -na _adj_ slow, gradual
Paulo _m_ Paul
pausa _f_ pause; slowness, delay; (mus) rest
pausa·do -da _adj_ slow, calm, deliberate ‖ **pausado** _adv_ slowly, calmly
pausar _tr_ & _intr_ to slow down
pauta _f_ ruler; guide lines; guideline, rule, guide, standard, model
pava _f_ turkey hen; **pelar la pava** (coll) to make love at a window
pavesa _f_ ember, cinder, spark
pavimentar _tr_ to pave
pavimento _m_ pavement
pavo _m_ turkey; turkey cock; **comer pavo** (coll) to be a wallflower; **pavo real** peacock
pavón _m_ bluing; peacock
pavonar _tr_ to blue
pavonear _intr_ & _ref_ to strut, swagger
pavor _m_ fear, terror, dread
pavoro·so -sa _adj_ frightful, dreadful
payador _m_ (SAm) gaucho minstrel
payasada _f_ clownishness, clownish remark
payaso _m_ clown; laughingstock
paz _f_ (_pl_ **paces**) peace; peacefulness; **dejar en paz** to leave alone, stop pestering; **estar en paz** to be even; to be quits; **hacer las paces con** to make peace with, to come to terms with; **salir en paz** to break even
pazgua·to -ta _adj_ simple, doltish ‖ _mf_ simpleton, dolt
pazpuerca _f_ (coll) slut, slattern
P.D. _abbr_ posdata
peaje _m_ toll
peatón _m_ pedestrian; rural postman
pebete _m_ punk, joss stick; fuse; (_cosa hedionda_) (coll) stinker
peca _f_ freckle
pecado _m_ sin
peca·dor -dora _adj_ sinning, sinful ‖ _mf_ sinner
pecamino·so -sa _adj_ sinful
pecar §73 _intr_ to sin; **pecar de** to be too, e.g., **pecar de confiado** to be too trusting
pecera _f_ fish globe, fish bowl
pecino·so -sa _adj_ slimy
pecio _m_ flotsam
pecíolo _m_ leafstalk
pécora _f_ head of sheep; **buena pécora** or **mala pécora** (coll) schemer, scheming woman

peco·so -sa _adj_ freckly, freckle-faced
peculado _m_ embezzlement, peculation
peculiar _adj_ peculiar
pecunia·rio -ria _adj_ pecuniary
pechada _f_ (Am) bump or push with the chest; (Am) tossing an animal (_with a bump of horse's chest_); (Am) bumping contest between two horsemen
pechar _tr_ to pay as a tax; _to_ fulfill; to take on; (Am) to drive one's horse against; (Am) to bump with the chest; (Am) to strike for a loan ‖ _ref_ (_dos jinetes_) (Am) to vie in a bumping contest
pechera _f_ shirt front, shirt bosom; chest protector; (_del delantal_) bib; breast strap; (coll) bosom; **pechera postiza** dickey
pecho _m_ chest; breast, bosom; heart, courage; **dar el pecho** to nurse, to suckle; (coll) to face it out; **de dos pechos** double-breasted; **de un solo pecho** single-breasted; **echar el pecho al agua** (coll) to put one's shoulder to the wheel; (coll) to speak out; **en pechos de camisa** (Am) in shirt sleeves; **tomar a pecho** to take to heart; **¡pecho al agua!** take heart!, put your shoulder to the wheel!
pechuga _f_ (_del ave_) breast; (coll) breast, bosom; (coll) slope, hill; (Am) brass, cheek; (Am) treachery, perfidy
pechu·gón -gona _adj_ (coll) big-chested; (Am) brazen ‖ _mf_ (Am) sponger ‖ _m_ slap or blow on the chest; fall on the chest
pedagogía _f_ pedagogy
pedal _m_ pedal, treadle
pedalear _intr_ to pedal
pedante _adj_ pedantic ‖ _mf_ pedant
pedantería _f_ pedantry
pedantes·co -ca _adj_ pedantic
pedantismo _m_ pedantry
pedazo _m_ piece; **hacer pedazos** (coll) to break to pieces; **hacerse pedazos** (coll) to fall to pieces; (coll) to strain, to wear oneself out; **pedazo de alcornoque, de animal** or **de bruto** (coll) dolt, imbecile, good-for-nothing; **pedazo del alma, de las entrañas** or **del corazón** (_niño_) (coll) darling, apple of one's eye; **pedazo de pan** (_pequeña cantidad_) crumb; (_precio bajo_) (coll) song
pedernal _m_ flint; flintiness; flint-hearted person
pedestal _m_ pedestal
pedestre _adj_ pedestrian
pedestrismo _m_ pedestrianism; walking; foot racing; cross-country racing
pediatría _f_ pediatrics
pedido _m_ request; (_encargo de mercancías_) order
pedigüe·ño -ña _adj_ insistent, demanding, bothersome
pedir §50 _tr_ to ask, to ask for; to request; to demand, require; to need; to ask for the hand of; (_mercancías_) to order; (gram) to govern; **pedir prestado** a to borrow from ‖ _intr_ to ask; to beg; to bring suit; **a pedir de boca** opportunely; as desired

pedorre·ro -ra _adj_ flatulent ‖ _f_ flatulence; (orn) tody; **pedorreras** tights
pedrada _f_ stoning; hit or blow with a stone; (coll) hint, taunt
pedregal _m_ rocky ground; pile of rocks
pedrego·so -sa _adj_ stony, rocky; suffering from gallstones ‖ _mf_ sufferer from gallstones
pedrejón _m_ boulder
pedrera _f_ quarry, stone quarry
pedrería _f_ precious stones, jewelry
Pedro _m_ Peter
pedrusco _m_ boulder
pedúnculo _m_ stem, stalk
peer §43 _intr_ & _ref_ to break wind
pega _f_ sticking; pitch varnish; drubbing; (_en un examen_) catch question; (coll) trick, joke; (W-I) work, jobs; **de pega** (coll) fake
pegadi·zo -za _adj_ sticky; catching, contagious; sponging; fake, imitation
pegajo·so -sa _adj_ sticky; contagious; tempting; (coll) soft, gentle; (coll) mushy
pegar §44 _tr_ to stick, to paste; to fasten, attach, tie; (_carteles_) to post; (_fuego_) to set; (_una enfermedad_) to transmit; (_un botón_) to sew on; (_un grito_) to let out; (_un salto_) to take; (_un golpe, una bofetada_) to let go; to beat; **no pegar el ojo** to not sleep a wink ‖ _intr_ to stick, to catch; to take root, take hold; to cling; to join; to fit, to match; to be fitting; to pass, be accepted; to beat; to knock ‖ _ref_ to stick, to catch; to take root, take hold; to hang on, stick around; (_una enfermedad_) to be catching; **pegár-sela a uno** (coll) to make a fool of someone
pegotear _intr_ (coll) to hang around, to sponge
peina·do -da _adj_ groomed; effeminate ‖ _m_ hairdo, coiffure; (_manera de componer el pelo_) hairstyle; **peinado al agua** finger wave
peina·dor -dora _mf_ hairdresser ‖ _m_ wrapper, dressing gown
peinar _tr_ to comb ‖ _ref_ to comb oneself, comb one's hair
peine _m_ comb; (coll) sly fellow
peineta _f_ back comb
pelada _f_ pelt, sheepskin
peladilla _f_ sugar almond; small pebble
peladillo _m_ clingstone peach
pela·do -da _adj_ bare; bald; barren; penniless; (_decena, centena, etc._) even ‖ _m_ raggedy fellow; (W-I) haircut ‖ _f_ see **pelada**
pelafus·tán -tana _mf_ (coll) derelict, good-for-nothing
pelaga·tos _m_ (_pl_ -tos) (coll) wretch, ragamuffin
pelaje _m_ coat, fur; (_especie, calidad_) (coll) sort, stripe
pelar _tr_ (_pelo_) to cut; (_pelo, plumas_) to pluck, pull out; to peel, skin, husk, hull, shell; (_los dientes_) to show; (_en el juego_) (coll) to clean out; (Am) to beat, thrash ‖ _ref_ to peel off; to lose one's hair; to get a haircut; (Am) to clear out, make a getaway; **pelárselas por** (coll) to crave; (coll) to crave to

peldaño *m* step

pelea *f* fight; quarrel; struggle; **pelea de gallos** cockfight

pelear *intr* to fight; to quarrel; to struggle || *ref* to fight, fight each other

pele·ón -ona *adj* (coll) pugnacious, quarrelsome; (*vino*) (coll) cheap, ordinary || *mf* (coll) quarrelsome person || *m* (coll) cheap wine || *f* row, scuffle, fracas

peletería *f* furriery; fur shop; (Cuba) shoe store

pelete·ro -ra *mf* furrier; (Cuba) shoe dealer

peliagu·do -da *adj* furry, long-haired; (coll) arduous, ticklish

película *f* film; motion picture; **película de dibujos** animated cartoon; **película del Oeste** western; **película sonora** sound film

pelicule·ro -ra *adj* moving-picture || *mf* scenario writer || *m* movie actor || *f* movie actress

peligrar *intr* to be in danger

peligro *m* danger, peril, risk; **ponerse en peligro de paz** to be alerted for war

peligro·so -sa *adj* dangerous

pelillo *m* (coll) trifle; **echar pelillos a la mar** (coll) to bury the hatchet; **no pararse en pelillos** (coll) to not bother about trifles, to pay no attention to small matters; **no tener pelillos en la lengua** (coll) to speak right out

pelirro·jo -ja *adj* red-haired, redheaded || *mf* redhead

pelo *m* hair; (*en las frutas y el cuerpo humano*) down; (*del paño*) nap; (*de la madera*) grain; (*de un animal*) coat; (*en las piedras preciosas*) flaw; (*del caballo*) color; (*en el billar*) kiss; (*del reloj*) hairspring; hair trigger; fiber, filament; raw silk; **al pelo** with the hair, with the nap; (coll) perfectly, to the point; **con todos sus pelos y señales** chapter and verse; **en pelo** bareback; **escapar por un pelo** to escape by a hairbreadth, to have a narrow escape; **no tener pelos en la lengua** (coll) to be outspoken, to not mince words; **ponerle a uno los pelos de punta** to make one's hair stand on end; **tomar el pelo a** (coll) to make fun of, make a fool of; **venir a pelo** to come in handy

pe·lón -lona *adj* bald, hairless; (coll) dull, stupid; (coll) penniless

Pélope *m* Pelops

peloponense *adj* & *mf* Peloponnesian

Peloponeso *m* Peloponnesus

pelo·so -sa *adj* hairy

pelota *f* ball; ball game; handball; **en pelota** stripped; stark-naked; **pelota acuática** water polo; **pelota rodada** (baseball) grounder; **pelota vasca** pelota, jai alai

pelotari *mf* pelota player

pelotear *intr* to knock a ball around; to wrangle, to argue

pelotera *f* (coll) row, brawl

pelotón *m* large ball; gang, crowd; platoon; **pelotón de fusilamiento** firing squad; **pelotón de los torpes** awkward squad

peltre *m* pewter

peluca *f* wig

pelu·do -da *adj* hairy, furry; bushy

peluquería *f* hairdresser's, barbershop

peluque·ro -ra *mf* hairdresser, barber; wigmaker

pelusa *f* down; lint, fuzz; nap; (coll) jealousy, envy

pellejo *m* skin; pelt, rawhide; peel, rind; wineskin; (*la vida de uno*) (coll) hide, skin; (coll) sot, drunkard; **dar, dejar** or **perder el pellejo** (coll) to die

pellizcar §73 to pinch; to nip; to take a pinch of || *ref* (coll) to long, to pine

pellizco *m* pinch; nip; bit, pinch

pena *f* punishment; penalty; pain, hardship, toil; sorrow, grief; effort, trouble; **a duras penas** hardly, with great difficulty; **de pena** of a broken heart; **¡qué pena!** what a pity!; **so pena de** on pain of, under penalty of; **valer la pena** to be worth while (to)

penacho *m* crest; tuft, plume; arrogance; (bot) tassel

pena·do -da *adj* afflicted, grieved; difficult || *mf* convict

penalidad *f* trouble, hardship; (law) penalty

penar *tr* to penalize; to punish || *intr* to suffer; to linger; **penar por** to pine for, long for || *ref* to grieve

penca *f* pulpy leaf; cowhide; **coger una penca** (Am) to get a jag on

penco *m* nag, jade; (Am) boor

pendejo *m* pubes; (coll) coward

pendencia *f* dispute, quarrel, fight; pending litigation

pendencie·ro -ra *adj* quarrelsome || *mf* wrangler

pender *intr* to hang, dangle; to depend; to be pending

pendiente *adj* pendent, hanging, dangling; pending; under way; expecting; **estar pendiente de** (*las palabras de una persona*) to hang on; to depend on; to be in the process of || *m* earring, pendant; watch chain || *f* slope, grade; dip, pitch

péndola *f* feather; pendulum; clock; pen, quill; queen post

pendolón *m* king post

pendón *m* banner, standard, pennon

péndulo *m* pendulum; clock

penetrar *tr* to penetrate; to pierce; to grasp, fathom || *intr* to penetrate || *ref* to grasp, fathom; to realize; to become convinced

penicilina *f* penicilin

península *f* peninsula

peninsular *adj* & *mf* peninsular; (*ibero*) Peninsular

penique *m* penny

penitencia *f* penitence; penance; **hacer penitencia** to do penance; to eat sparingly; to take potluck

penitente *adj* & *mf* penitent

penol *m* (naut) yardarm

peno·so -sa *adj* arduous, difficult; suffering; (coll) conceited; (Am) shy

pensa·dor -dora adj thinking ‖ mf thinker

pensamiento m thought; (planta y flor) pansy

pensar §2 tr to think; to think over; (un naipe, un número, etc.) to think of; to intend to; **pensar de** to think of, e.g., ¿qué piensa Vd. de este libro? what do you think of this book? ‖ intr to think; **pensar en** (dirigir sus pensamientos a) to think of (to turn one's thoughts to)

pensati·vo -va adj pensive, thoughtful

pensión f pension; annuity; allowance; boardinghouse; (para ampliar estudios) fellowship; **pensión completa** board and lodging

pensionar tr to pension

pensionista mf pensioner; boarder; boarding-school pupil; **medio pensionista** day boarder

pentagrama m staff, musical staff

Pentecostés, el Pentecost

penúlti·mo -ma adj penultimate; next to last ‖ f penult

penumbra f penumbra; semidarkness, half-light

penuria f shortage

peña f rock, boulder; cliff; club, group, circle

peñasco m pinnacle; crag

peñasco·so -sa adj rocky, craggy

peñón m rock, spire; **peñón de Gibraltar** rock of Gibraltar

peón m laborer; pedestrian; foot soldier; (en el ajedrez) pawn; (en las damas) man; top, peg top; spindle, axle; (taur) attendant; (Am) farm hand; **peón de albañil** or **de mano** hod carrier

peor adj & adv worse; worst

pepa f (de la manzana) (Col) seed; (del durazno) (Arg) stone; (canica) (Arg) marble; (Col) lie, cheat, trick

Pepe m Joe

pepinillo m gherkin

pepino m cucumber

pepita f seed, pip; nugget; (vet) pip

peque m tot

pequén m (Chile) burrowing owl

pequeñez f (pl -ñeces) smallness; infancy; trifle

peque·ño -ña adj little, small; young; low, humble

Pequín m Peking

pequi·nés -nesa adj & mf Pekinese

pera f pear; goatee; cinch, sinecure; pear-shaped bulb; pear-shaped switch

peral m pear tree

perca f (ichth) perch

percance m mischance, misfortune; **percances** perquisites

percatar ref — **percatarse de** to be aware of; to beware of, guard against

percebe m barnacle; (coll) fool, sap

percepción f perception; collection

percibir tr to perceive; to collect

percudir tr to tarnish, to dull; to spread through

percha f perch, pole, roost; clothes tree; coat hanger; coat hook; barber pole

perchero m rack, clothes rack, clothes hanger

perde·dor -dora adj losing ‖ mf loser

perder §51 tr to lose; to waste, squander; (un tren, una ocasión) to miss; (una asignatura) to flunk; to ruin; to spoil ‖ intr to lose; to fade ‖ ref to get lost; to miscarry; to sink; to become ruined; to spoil; to go to the dogs

perdición f perdition; loss; outrage; ruination

pérdida f loss; waste; ruination; **no tener pérdida** (coll) to be easy to find

perdi·do -da adj (bala) stray, wild; (manga) wide, loose; fruitless; (horas) off, spare, idle; distracted; inveterate; madly in love ‖ m profligate, rake

perdido·so -sa adj unlucky; easily lost

perdigón m young partridge; (coll) profligate; (coll) heavy loser; (alumno) (coll) failure; **perdigones** (granos de plomo) shot; **perdigón zorrero** buckshot

per·diz f (pl -dices) partridge

perdón m pardon, forgiveness; **con perdón** by your leave

perdonable adj pardonable

perdonar tr to pardon, forgive, excuse; **no perdonar** to not miss, to not omit

perdula·rio -ria adj careless, sloppy; incorrigible, vicious ‖ mf good-for-nothing, profligate

perdurable adj long-lasting; everlasting

perdurar intr to last, last a long time, survive

perecede·ro -ra adj perishable; mortal ‖ m (coll) extreme want

perecer §22 intr to perish; to suffer; to be in great want ‖ ref to pine; **perecerse por** to be dying for; (una mujer) to be mad about

peregrinación f peregrination; pilgrimage

peregri·no -na adj wandering, traveling; foreign; rare, strange; beautiful; mortal; (ave) migratory ‖ mf pilgrim

perejil m parsley; (coll) frippery

perenne adj perennial

pereza f laziness; slowness

perezo·so -sa adj lazy; slow, dull, heavy ‖ mf lazybones; sleepyhead ‖ m (zool) sloth

perfección f perfection

perfeccionar tr to perfect, to improve

perfec·to -ta adj & m perfect

perfidia f perfidy

pérfi·do -da adj perfidious

perfil m profile; side view; cross section; thin stroke; outline, sketch; **perfil aerodinámico** streamlining; **perfiles** finishing touches; courtesies

perfila·do -da adj (cara) long and thin; (nariz) well-formed; (facciones) delicate; streamlined

perfilar tr to profile, outline; to perfect, polish, finish ‖ ref to be outlined; to show one's profile, to stand sidewise; to stand out; (coll) to dress up

perfora·dor -dora adj perforating; drilling ‖ f pneumatic drill, rock drill

perforar *tr* to perforate; to drill, to bore; to puncture; (*una tarjeta*) to punch

perforista *mf* keypuncher

perfumar *tr* to perfume

perfume *m* perfume

pergamino *m* parchment

pericia *f* skill, expertness

periclitar *intr* to be in jeopardy, to be shaky

perico *m* (*pelo postizo*) periwig; parakeet; (*slang*) chamber pot; **perico entre ellas** (coll) lady's man

periferia *f* periphery; surroundings

perifollos *mpl* finery, frippery, chiffons

perilla *f* pear-shaped ornament; goatee; knob, doc. knob; (*del arzón*) pommel; (*de la oreja*) lobe; **de perilla** (coll) apropos, to the point

periodísti·co -ca *adj* newspaper, journalistic

periódi·co -ca *adj* periodic ‖ *m* newspaper; periodical

periodismo *m* journalism

periodista *mf* journalist ‖ *m* newspaperman ‖ *f* newspaperwoman

período *m* period; compound sentence; (phys) cycle; **período lectivo** (*en la escuela*) term

peripues·to -ta *adj* (coll) dudish, all spruced up, sporty

periquete *m* (coll) jiffy; **en un periquete** (coll) in a jiffy

periquito *m* parakeet; **periquito de Australia** budgerigar

periscopio *m* periscope

peri·to -ta *adj* skilled, skillful; expert ‖ *m* expert

perjudicar §73 *tr* to damage, impair, hurt, prejudice

perjudicial *adj* harmful, injurious, detrimental, prejudicial

perjuicio *m* harm, injury, damage, prejudice; **en perjuicio de** to the detriment of

perjurar *intr* to commit perjury; to swear, be profane ‖ *ref* to commit perjury; to perjure oneself

perjurio *m* perjury

perla *f* pearl; **de perlas** perfectly

perlesía *f* palsy

permanecer §22 *intr* to stay, to remain

permanencia *f* permanence; stay, sojourn

permanente *adj* permanent ‖ *f* permanent wave

permiso *m* permission; permit; time off; (*en el monedaje*) tolerance; leave; **con permiso** excuse me; **permiso de circulación** owner's license; **permiso de conducir** driver's license

permitir *tr* to permit, to allow ‖ *ref* to be permitted

permutar *tr* to interchange; to barter; to permute

pernear *intr* to kick; (coll) to hustle; (coll) to fuss, fret

pernera *f* trouser leg

pernicio·so -sa *adj* pernicious

pernil *m* trouser leg; (*anca y muslo*) ham

perno *m* bolt; **perno con anillo** ring-bolt; **perno roscado** screw bolt

pernoctar *intr* to spend the night

pero *conj* but, yet ‖ *m* (coll) but; (coll) fault, defect; **poner pero a** (coll) to find fault with

perogrullada *f* (coll) platitude, inanity

peroración *f* peroration; (coll) harangue

perorar *intr* to perorate; (coll) to orate

peróxido *m* peroxide; **peróxido de hidrógeno** hydrogen peroxide

perpendicular *adj* & *f* perpendicular

perpetrar *tr* to perpetrate

perpetuar §21 *tr* to perpetuate

perpe·tuo -tua *adj* perpetual; life

perplejidad *f* perplexity; worry, anxiety

perple·jo -ja *adj* perplexed; worried, anxious; baffling, perplexing

perra *f* bitch; tantrum; drunkenness

perrada *f* pack of dogs; (coll) dirty trick

perrera *f* kennel, doghouse; tantrum; toil, drudgery

perro *m* dog; **el perro del hortelano** dog in the manger; **perro caliente** (slang) hot dog; **perro cobrador** retriever; **perro de aguas** spaniel; **perro de lanas** poodle; **perro de muestra** pointer; **perro faldero** lap dog; **perro marino** dogfish, shark; **perro raposero** foxhound; **perro viejo** (coll) wise old owl

perro-lazarillo *m* (*pl* **perros-lazarillos**) Seeing Eye dog

persa *adj* & *mf* Persian

persecución *f* persecution; pursuit; annoyance, harassment

perseguir §67 *tr* to persecute; to pursue; to annoy, harass

perseverar *intr* to persevere

persiana *f* slatted shutter; flowered silk; louver; Venetian blind; **persiana del radiador** (aut) louver

persistir *intr* to persist

persona *f* person; personage; **persona desplazada** displaced person; **personas** people; **por persona** per capita

personaje *m* personage; (theat) character; person of importance

personal *adj* personal ‖ *m* personnel, staff, force

personalidad *f* personality

personificar §73 *tr* to personify

perspectiva *f* perspective; outlook, prospect; appearance

perspi·caz *adj* (*pl* **-caces**) perspicacious, discerning; keen-sighted

persuadir *tr* to persuade

persuasión *f* persuasion

pertenecer §22 *intr* to belong; to pertain ‖ *ref* to be independent, be free

perteneciente *adj* pertaining

pértiga *f* pole, rod, staff

perti·naz *adj* (*pl* **-naces**) pertinacious; (*dolor de cabeza*) persistent

pertinente *adj* pertinent, relevant

pertrechos *mpl* supplies, provisions, equipment; tools; **pertrechos de guerra** ordnance

perturbar *tr* to perturb; to disturb; to upset, disconcert; to confuse, interrupt

Perú, el Peru

perua·no -na *adj* & *mf* Peruvian

perversidad *f* perversity

perversión f perversion
perver·so -sa adj perverse; wicked, depraved ‖ mf profligate
perverti·do -da mf pervert
pervertir §68 tr to pervert ‖ ref to become perverted; to go to the bad
pesa f weight
pesacar·tas m (pl -tas) letter scales
pesadez f heaviness; slowness; tiresomeness; harshness; (phys) gravity
pesadilla f nightmare
pesa·do -da adj heavy; slow; tiresome; harsh; boring
pesadumbre f sorrow, grief; trouble; weight, heaviness
pesaje m weighing; (sport) weigh-in
pésame m condolence; **dar el pésame a** to extend one's sympathy to
pesantez f (phys) gravity
pesar m sorrow, regret; **a pesar de** in spite of ‖ tr to weigh; to make sorry ‖ intr to weigh; to be heavy; to cause regret, cause sorrow
pesaro·so -sa adj sorrowful, regretful
pesca f fishing; catch; **ir de pesca** to go fishing; **pesca de bajura** off-shore fishing; **pesca de gran altura** deep-sea fishing
pescadería f fish market; fish store; fish stand
pescade·ro -ra mf fish dealer, fishmonger
pescado m fish (that has been caught)
pesca·dor -dora adj fishing ‖ m fisherman ‖ f fisherwoman, fishwife
pescante m coach box; (de una grúa) jib; (aut) front seat; (naut) davit; (theat) trap door
pescar §73 tr to fish; to fish for; to fish out; (peces) to catch; (coll) to manage to get ‖ intr to fish
pescozón m slap on the neck or head
pescuezo m neck
pesebre m crib, rack, manger; (Am) crèche
pesimismo m pessimism
pesimista adj pessimistic ‖ mf pessimist
pési·mo -ma adj very bad, abominable
peso m weight; scale, balance; burden, load; judgment, good sense; (unidad monetaria) (Am) peso; **peso atómico** atomic weight; **caerse de su peso** to be self-evident; **llevar el peso de la batalla** to bear the brunt of the battle
pespuntar tr & intr to backstitch
pespunte m backstitch
pesquera f fishery; fishing grounds; (presa para detener los peces) weir
pesquería f fishing; fishery
pesque·ro -ra adj fishing ‖ m fishing boat ‖ f see **pesquera**
pesquis m acumen, keenness
pesquisa m (Arg) detective ‖ f inquiry, investigation
pesquisar tr to investigate, inquire into
pestaña f eyelash; flange; fringe, edging; index tab
pestañear intr to wink, blink; **sin pestañear** without batting an eye
peste f pest, plague; epidemic; stink, stench; (coll) abundance; (Col, Peru) head cold; (Chile) smallpox; **pestes** (coll) insults

pesticida m pesticide
pestífe·ro -ra adj pestiferous; stinking
pestilencia f pestilence
pestillo m bolt; doorlatch
petaca f cigar case; cigarette case; tobacco pouch; leather-covered hamper
pétalo m petal
petardear tr to swindle ‖ intr (aut) to backfire
petardeo m swindling; (aut) backfire
petardo m petard; bomb; swindle, cheat
petate m sleeping bag; bedding; (coll) luggage; (coll) cheat; (coll) poor soul; **liar el petate** (coll) to pack up and get out; (coll) to kick the bucket
petición f petition; request; plea; (law) claim, bill; **a petición de** at the request of; **petición de mano** formal betrothal
petimetre m dude, sport, dandy
petirrojo m redbreast, robin
Petrarca m Petrarch
petrificar §73 tr & ref to petrify
petróleo m petroleum; **petróleo combustible** fuel oil
petrole·ro -ra adj oil, petroleum ‖ mf oil dealer ‖ m oil tanker
petulancia f flippancy, pertness
petulante adj flippant, pert
pez m (pl **peces**) fish; (coll) reward, just desert; **como un pez en el agua** (coll) snug as bug in a rug; **pez de plata** (ent) silverfish **salga pez o salga rana** (coll) blindly, hit or miss ‖ f pitch, tar
pezón m stem; nipple, teat
pezonera f linchpin
pezuña f hoof
piado·so -sa adj merciful; pitiful; pious
piafar intr (el caballo) to paw, to stamp
piano m piano; **piano de cola** grand piano; **piano de media cola** baby grand
piar §77 intr to peep, to chirp
pica f pike; pikeman; picador's goad; (Col) pique, resentment
picada f peck; bite; (Bol) knock at the door; (Arg, Bol, Urug) narrow ford; (SAm) path, trail
picadillo m (carne, verduras, ajos, etc. reducidos a pequeños trozos) hash; (carne picada) mincemeat
pica·do -da adj perforated; pitted; (tabaco) cut; (hielo) cracked; (mar) choppy; piqued ‖ m mincemeat; (aer) dive; **picado con motor** (aer) power dive ‖ f see **picada**
picador m horsebreaker; (torero de a caballo) picador (mounted bullfighter); chopping block
picadura f bite, prick, sting; nick; puncture; cut tobacco; (en un diente) cavity
picaflor m hummingbird
picahie·los m (pl -los) ice pick
picamade·ros m (pl -ros) green woodpecker
picante adj biting, pricking, stinging; piquant, juicy, racy; (SAm) highly seasoned ‖ m mordancy; piquancy
picapedrero m stonecutter
picaplei·tos m (pl -tos) (coll) troublemaker; (coll) shyster, pettifogger

picaporte *m* latch; latchkey; door knocker

picar §73 *tr* to prick, pierce, puncture; to sting; to bite; to burn; to peck; to nibble; to pit, to pock; to mince, chop up, cut up; to stick, poke; to spur; to goad; to perforate; (*hielo*) to crack; to harass, pursue; to tame; to pique, annoy ‖ *intr* to itch; (*el sol*) to burn; to nibble; to have a smattering; to be catching; (*los negocios*) to pick up; (aer) to dive; (*caer en el lazo*) (coll) to bite; **picar en** to nibble at; to dabble in; **picar muy alto** (coll) to aim high, expect too much ‖ *ref* to rot; (*la ropa*) to be moth-eaten; (*el vino*) to turn sour; (*un diente*) to be decayed; (*el mar*) to get rough; to be offended; (Am) to get drunk; **picarse de** to boast of being

picardía *f* roguishness, knavery; crudeness, coarseness; mischief

picares·co -ca *adj* roguish, rascally; picaresque; rough, coarse, crude; (coll) witty, humorous, gay

píca·ro -ra *adj* roguish; scheming, tricky; low, vile; mischievous ‖ *mf* rogue; schemer

picaza *f* magpie

picazón *f* itch, itching; (coll) annoyance

pícea *f* spruce tree

pick-up *m* pickup; phonograph

pico *m* beak, bill; (*de jarra*) spout; (*del yunque*) beak; (*del pañuelo*) corner; nib, tip; (*de la pluma de escribir*) point; peak; (*herramienta*) pick; (*de dinero*) pile, lot; talkativeness; (elec) peak; (naut) bow, prow; **callar el pico** (coll) to shut up; **darse el pico** (*las palomas*) to bill; **pico de oro** silver-tongue; **tener mucho pico** (coll) to talk too much; **y pico** odd, e.g., **trescientos y pico** three hundred odd; a little after, e.g., **a las tres y pico** a little after three o'clock

picor *m* (*del paladar*) smarting; itch, itching, burning

pico·so -sa *adj* pock-marked

picota *f* pillory; peak, point, spire

picotazo *m* peck

picotear *tr* to peck ‖ *intr* (*el caballo*) to toss the head; (coll) to chatter, jabber, gab; (*las mujeres*) (coll) to wrangle

pichel *m* pewter tankard

pi·chón -chona *mf* (coll) darling ‖ *m* young pigeon; **pichón de barro** clay pigeon

pie *m* foot; footing; foothold; base, stand; (*de copa*) stem; (*de la cama*) footboard; cause, origin, reason; (*de la página*) foot, bottom; (theat) cue; (Chile) down payment; **a cuatro pies** on all fours; **al pie de fábrica** (coll) at the factory; **al pie de la letra** literally; **al pie de la obra** (com) delivered; **a pie** on foot, walking; **buscar cinco** (or **tres**) **pies al gato** (coll) to be looking for trouble; **de pie** standing; up and about; firm, steady; firmly, steadily; **en pie de guerra** on a war footing; **ir a pie** to go on foot, to walk; **morir al pie del cañón** to

die in the harness, to die with one's boots on; **nacer de pie** or **de pies** to be born with a silver spoon in one's mouth; **pie de atleta** athlete's foot; **pie de cabra** crowbar; **pie de imprenta** imprint, printer's mark; **pie derecho** upright, stanchion; **pie marino** sea legs; **pie quebrado** (*de verso*) short line; **vestirse por los pies** (coll) to be a man

piedad *f* (*devoción a las cosas santas*) piety; (*misericordia*) pity, mercy

piedra *f* stone; rock; (*pedernal*) flint; heavy hailstone; (pathol) stone; **piedra angular** cornerstone; (fig) cornerstone, keystone; **piedra arenisca** sandstone; **piedra azul** (chem) bluestone; **piedra de albardilla** copestone; **piedra de amolar** grindstone; **piedra de chispa** flint; **piedra de pipas** meerschaum; **piedra imán** loadstone; **piedra miliar** or **miliaria** milestone; **piedra movediza** rolling stone; **piedra pómez** pumice, pumice stone

piel *f* skin; hide, pelt; fur; leather; (*de las frutas*) peel, skin; **piel de cabra** goatskin; **piel de foca** sealskin; **piel de gallina** goose flesh; **piel roja** *m* (*pl* **pieles rojas**) (*indio norteamericano*) redskin

pienso *m* feed, feeding; **ni por pienso** by no means, don't think of it

pierna *f* leg; post, upright; **dormir a pierna suelta** or **tendida** (coll) to sleep like a log; **estirar la pierna** (coll) to lie down on the job; (coll) to kick the bucket; **estirar** or **extender las piernas** (coll) to stretch one's legs, go for a walk; **ser buena pierna** (Arg, Urug) to be a good-natured fellow

pieza *f* (*órgano de una máquina o artefacto*; *obra dramática*; *composición suelta de música*; *cañón*; *figura que sirve para jugar a las damas, al ajedrez, etc.*; *moneda*) piece; (*objeto*; *mueble*; *porción de tela*) piece or article; (*habitación, cuarto*) room; **buena pieza** hussy; sly fox; **pieza de recambio** or **de repuesto** spare part; **quedarse en una pieza** or **hecho una pieza** to be dumbfounded, to stand motionless

pífano *m* fife; fifer

pifia *f* (billiards) miscue; (coll) miscue, slip

pifiar *intr* to miscue

pigmentar *tr* & *ref* to pigment

pigmento *m* pigment

pigme·o -a *adj* & *mf* pygmy

pijama *f* pajamas

pila *f* basin; trough; sink; font; pile, heap; (elec) battery, cell; (elec & phys) pile; **pila de linterna** flashlight battery

pilar *m* (*de una fuente*) basin, bowl; pillar; stone post, milestone; (*persona*) (fig) pillar ‖ *tr* (*el grano*) to crush, to pound

Pilatos *m* Pilate

píldora *f* pill; (coll) bad news; **píldora para dormir** sleeping pill

pileta *f* sink; basin; bowl; font; swimming pool

pilón m pylon; drinking trough; loaf of sugar; counterpoise; drop hammer

pilotar tr to pilot

pilote m pile

piloto m pilot; first mate; (Chile) hail fellow well met

pillar tr to pillage, plunder; to catch

pi·llo -lla adj (coll) roguish, rascally; (coll) sly, crafty ‖ m (coll) rogue, rascal; (coll) crafty fellow

pilluelo m (coll) scamp, little scamp

pimentero m pepper, black pepper; pepperbox

pimentón m cayenne pepper, red pepper; (condimento preparado moliendo pimientos encarnados secos) paprika

pimienta f pepper, black pepper; allspice, pimento; allspice tree

pimiento m (planta) pepper, black pepper; Guinea pepper

pimpante adj smart, spruce

pimpollo m sucker, shoot, sprout; rosebud; (árbol nuevo) sapling; (coll) handsome child; (coll) handsome young person

pina f felloe

pinacoteca f picture gallery

pináculo m pinnacle

pincel m brush; painter; painting; (de luz) pencil, beam

pincelada f brush stroke; touch, finish, flourish

pincelar tr to paint; to picture; (med) to pencil

pincia·no ·na adj Valladolid ‖ mf native or inhabitant of Valladolid

pincha f kitchenmaid

pinchar tr to prick, jab, pierce, puncture; to stir up, prod, provoke ‖ intr to have a puncture; **no pinchar ni cortar** to have no say

pinchazo m prick, jab, puncture; provocation; **a prueba de pinchazos** puncture-proof

pinche m scullion, kitchen boy; helper

pincho m thorn, prick; snack; spike

Píndaro m Pindar

pingajo m (coll) rag, tatter

pingo m (coll) rag, tatter; (coll) ragamuffin; (coll) horse; **andar** or **ir de pingo** (una mujer) (coll) to gad about

pingüe adj oily, greasy, fat; abundant, rich; fertile; profitable

pingüino m penguin

pinito m first step, little step; **hacer pinitos** to begin to walk; (fig) to take the first steps

pino m pine tree; first step; **hacer pinos** to begin to walk; (fig) to take the first steps

pinocha f pine needle

pinta m (coll) scoundrel ‖ f spot, mark, sign; dot; pint

pintacilgo m goldfinch

pintada f Guinea hen

pinta·do -da adj spotted, mottled; tipsy; accented; **el más pintado** (coll) the aptest one; (coll) the shrewdest one; (coll) the best one; **venir como pintado** to be just the thing ‖ m (acto de pintar) painting ‖ f see **pintada**

pintar tr to paint; (una letra, un acento, etc.) to draw; to picture, depict; to put an accent mark on; **pintarla** (coll) to put it on, to put on airs ‖ intr to paint; to begin to turn red, begin to ripen; (coll) to show, to turn out ‖ ref to paint, put on make-up; to begin to turn red, begin to ripen

pintarrajear tr to daub, to smear

pin·to -ta adj (Am) speckled, spotted ‖ f see **pinta**

pin·tor -tora mf painter; **pintor de brocha gorda** painter, house painter; (coll) dauber

pintores·co -ca adj picturesque

pintura f (color preparado para pintar) paint; (arte; obra pintada) painting; **hacer pinturas** (coll) to prance; **no poder ver ni en pintura** to not be able to stand the sight of

pinture·ro -ra adj (coll) showy, conceited ‖ mf (coll) show-off

pinza f clothespin; (de langosta, cangrejo, etc.) claw; **pinzas** pliers; pincers; tweezers; forceps

pinzón m pump handle; (orn) finch

piña f fir cone, pine cone; knob; plug; cluster, knot; pineapple

piñonear intr (un arma de fuego) to click; (coll) to reach the age of puberty; (coll) to be an old goat

piñoneo m click (of a firearm)

pi·o -a adj pious; merciful, compassionate; (caballo) pied, dappled ‖ m peeping, chirping; (coll) keen desire

piocha f jeweled head adornment; artificial flower made of feathers; pick

piojo m louse

piojo·so -sa adj lousy; mean, stingy

pione·ro -ra adj & mf pioneer

pipa f (para fumar tabaco) pipe; (medida para vinos) butt; wine cask; (simiente) pip; (mus) pipe, reed; **pipa de espuma de mar** meerschaum pipe; **pipa de riego** watering cart; **pipa de tierra** clay pipe

pique m pique, resentment; eagerness; (insecto) chigger; (naipe) spade; **a pique** steep; **a pique de** in danger of; on the verge of; **echar a pique** to sink; to ruin; **irse a pique** to sink; to go to ruin, be ruined

piquera f bung, bunghole; (Mex) dive, joint

piquete m sharp jab; small hole; stake, picket; (de soldados, de huelguistas) picket; **piquete de ejecución** firing squad; **piquete de salvas** firing squad

pira f pyre

piragua f pirogue; (sport) single shell

piragüista m (sport) crewman

pirámide f pyramid

pirata m pirate

piratear intr to pirate, be a pirate

pirca f (SAm) dry stone wall

pirco m (Chile) succotash

Pireo, el Piraeus

pirine·o -a adj Pyrenean ‖ **Pirineos** mpl Pyrenees

pirita f pyrites

piró·fa·go -ga adj fire-eating ‖ mf fire-eater

piropear tr (coll) to flatter, flirt with

pi
pi

piropo *m* garnet, carbuncle; (coll) flattery, compliment, flirtatious remark
piróscafo *m* steamship
pirotecnia *f* pyrotechnics
pirotécni·co -ca *adj* pyrotechnical || *m* powder maker, fireworks manufacturer
pirueta *f* pirouette; somersault; caper
piruetear *intr* to pirouette
pisada *f* tread; footstep; footprint; trampling
pisapape·les *m* (*pl* -les) paperweight
pisar *tr* to trample, tread on, step on; to tamp, pack down; (*p.ej., uvas*) to tread; to cover part of; to ram; (*una tecla*) to strike; (mus) to pluck; (coll) to abuse, tread all over; **pisar algo a alguien** (coll) to snitch something from someone || *intr* to be right above; to step || *ref* (Arg) to guess wrong, come out wrong
pisaverde *m* (coll) fop, dandy
piscina *f* swimming pool; fishpond
pisco *m* Peruvian brandy
pisicorre *f* (W-I) station wagon
piso *m* tread; floor; flooring; (*de una carretera*) surface; flat, apartment; **buscar piso** to be looking for a place to live; **piso alto** top floor; **piso bajo** street floor, ground floor; **piso principal** main floor, second floor
pisón *m* ram, tamper
pisotear *tr* to trample, to tread on, to tread under foot; (coll) to abuse, tread all over
pisotón *m* stamp, tread
pista *f* track; trace, trail; clew; race track; (*de bolera*) alley; (*de cabaret*) floor; (aer) runway; **pista de esquí** ski run; **pista de patinar** skating rink
pisto *m* (*para los enfermos*) chicken broth; vegetable cutlet; jumbled speech or writing; mess
pistola *f* pistol; sprayer; rock drill; **pistola de arzón** horse pistol; **pistola engrasadora** grease gun
pistolera *f* holster
pistolerismo *m* gangsterism
pistolero *m* gangster, gunman
pistón *m* piston
pistonear *intr* to knock
pistoneo *m* knock
pistonu·do -da *adj* (coll) stunning, swank
pita *f* century plant; hiss, hissing; glass marble
pitar *tr* to pay, pay off; (*a un torero*) to whistle disapproval of || *intr* to blow a whistle, to whistle; to blow the horn, to honk; (coll) to talk nonsense; **no pitar** (coll) to not be popular; **salir pitando** to run away, dash away
pitazo *m* blast, toot, honk
pitillera *f* cigarette maker; cigarette case
pitillo *m* cigarette
pito *m* whistle; horn; fife; fifer; cigarette; jackstone; (*insecto*) tick; woodpecker; (coll) continental, straw, tinker's dam
pitón *m* lump, sprig; tenderling; (*del cuerno*) tip; nozzle, spout; python

pitonisa *f* witch, siren; pythoness
pitu·so -sa *adj* tiny, cute || *mf* tot
piular *intr* to peep, to chirp
pivotar *intr* to pivot
pivote *m* pivot; **pivote de dirección** (aut) kingpin
píxide *f* pyx
pizarra *f* slate; blackboard
pizarrero *m* roofer, slater
pizarrín *m* slate pencil
pizca *f* (coll) mite, whit, jot
placa *f* plaque, tablet; badge; plate; slab, sheet; (anat, elec, electron, phot, zool) plate; (Am) scab; **placa de matrícula** license plate; **placa giratoria** (*de ferrocarril; de gramófono*) turntable
placaminero *m* persimmon
placebo *m* placebo
pláceme *m* congratulation
placente·ro -ra *adj* pleasant, agreeable
placer *m* pleasure; sandbank, reef; a placer at one's convenience || *v* §52 *tr* to please
place·ro -ra *adj* public || *mf* market vendor; loafer, town gossip
pláci·do -da *adj* placid; pleasing
plaga *f* plague; pest; scourge; abundance; sore; clime, region
plagar §44 *tr* to plague, infest; (*de minas*) to sow
plagiar *tr* to plagiarize
plagio *m* plagiarism; (Am) abduction, kidnaping
plan *m* plan; level, height; **plan de estudios** or **plan escolar** curriculum
plana *f* plain, flat country; trowel; cooper's plane; page
plancha *f* plate, sheet; iron, flatiron; gangplank; (coll) blunder; **a la plancha** grilled; (*huevo*) fried; **plancha de blindaje** armor plate
planchado *m* ironing; pressing
planchar *tr* (*la ropa interior blanca*) to iron; (*un traje de hombre*) to press || *intr* (Am) to be a wallflower
planchear *tr* to plate
planear *tr* to plan, to outline; (*una tabla*) to plane || *intr* to hover; (aer) to volplane, to glide
planeta *m* planet
planicie *f* plain
planificar §73 *tr* to plan
planilla *f* (Am) list, roll, schedule; (*de candidatos para un puesto público*) (Mex) panel; (Mex) ballot; (Mex) commutation ticket
pla·no -na *adj* plane; level, smooth, even; flat || *m* plan; map; (*superficie*) plane; (aer) plane; **de plano** clearly, plainly, flatly; flat; **levantar un plano** to make a survey; **primer plano** foreground || *f* see **plana**
planta *f* (*del pie*) sole; foot; plan; project; floor plan; (*del personal de una oficina*) roster; plant, factory; (bot) plant; (sport) stance; **de planta** from the ground up; **echar plantas** to swagger, to bully; **planta baja** ground floor; **planta del sortilegio** (bot) witch hazel; **tener buena planta** (coll) to make a fine appearance
plantar *tr* to plant; to establish, to

found; (*un golpe*) (coll) to plant; (coll) to jilt; (*en la calle, en la cárcel*) (coll) to throw ‖ *ref* to take a stand; to gang together; (*un animal*) (coll) to balk; (coll) to land, to arrive

plantear *tr* to plan, to outline; to establish, execute, carry out; to state, set up, expound, pose

plantel *m* nursery garden; educational establishment

plantificar §73 *tr* to plan, to outline; (*un golpe*) (coll) to plant; (*en la calle, la cárcel*) (coll) to throw ‖ *ref* (coll) to land, to arrive

plantilla *f* plantlet, young plant; insole; reinforced sole; model, pattern, template; (*de empleados*) staff; (*del personal de una oficina*) roster; plan, design; (*bizcocho*) (Am) ladyfinger

plantío *m* planting; garden patch; tree nursery

plantón *m* (*que ha de ser transplantado*) shoot; graft; guard, watchman; waiting, standing around

plañide·ro -ra *adj* mournful, plaintive ‖ *f* hired mourner

plañir §12 *tr* to lament, grieve over ‖ *intr* to lament, grieve, bewail

plasmar *tr* to mold, shape

plasta *f* paste, soft mass; flattened object; (coll) poor job, bungle

plástica *f* (*arte de plasmar*) plastic; plastic arts

plásti·co -ca *adj* plastic ‖ *m* (*substancia*) plastic ‖ *f* see **plástica**

plata *f* silver; (*moneda o monedas*) silver; wealth; money; **en plata** (coll) briefly, to the point; (coll) plainly; **plata de ley** sterling silver

plataforma *f* platform; platform car; (*del ferrocarril*) roadbed; (*programa político*) platform; (*de lanzamiento de cohete*) pad; **plataforma giratoria** (rr) turntable

platanal *m* or **platanar** *m* banana plantation

plátano *m* banana; banana tree; plane tree; **plátano de occidente** buttonwood tree

platea *f* (theat) orchestra, parquet

platear *tr* to silver, coat or plate with silver

platero *m* silversmith; jeweler

plática *f* talk, chat; talk, informal lecture; sermon

platicar §73 *tr* to talk over, to discuss ‖ *intr* to talk, to chat; to discuss; to preach

platillo *m* plate; saucer; (*de la balanza*) pan; (mus) cymbal; **platillo volador** or **volante** flying saucer

platino *m* platinum

plato *m* dish; plate; (*de una comida*) course; daily fare; **plato fuerte** main course; **plato giratorio** (*del gramófono*) turntable

pla·tó *m* (*pl* -tós) (mov) set

Platón *m* Plato

plausible *adj* praiseworthy; acceptable

playa *f* beach, shore, strand; **playa infantil** sand pile

playera *f* fishwoman; beach shoe

plaza *f* plaza, square; market place;

town, city; fortified town; space, room; yard; office, employment; character, reputation; seat; **sentar plaza** to enlist; **plaza de armas** parade ground; (Am) public square; **plaza de gallos** cockpit; **plaza de toros** bullring; **plaza mayor** main square

plazo *m* term; time; time limit; date of payment; instalment; **a plazo** on credit, on time; **en plazos** in instalments

pleamar *f* high tide, high water

plebe *f* common people

plebe·yo -ya *adj & mf* plebeian

plegadi·zo -za *adj* folding; pliable

plegar §66 *tr* to fold; to crease; to pleat ‖ *ref* to yield, to give in

plegaria *f* prayer; noon call to prayer

pleito *m* litigation, lawsuit; dispute, quarrel; fight; **pleito de acreedores** bankruptcy proceedings; **pleito homenaje** (feud) homage; **pleito viciado** mistrial

plenilunio *m* full moon

plenitud *f* fullness, abundance

ple·no -na *adj* full; **en plena marcha** in full swing; **en pleno rostro** right in the face

pleuresía *f* pleurisy

pliego *m* (*de papel*) sheet; folder; cover, envelope; bid, specification; sealed letter; printer's proof

pliegue *m* fold, crease, pleat; **pliegue de tabla** box pleat

plisar *tr* to pleat

plomada *f* carpenter's lead pencil; plummet; plumb bob; sinker, sinkers; scourge tipped with lead balls

plomar *tr* to seal with lead

plomazo *m* (Guat, Mex, W-I) gunshot

plomería *f* lead roofing; leadwork, plumbing

plomero *m* lead worker; plumber

plomi·zo -za *adj* lead, leaden

plomo *m* lead; (*pedazo de plomo; bala*) lead; (elec) fuse; (coll) bore; **a plomo** plumb, perpendicularly; straight down; (coll) just right

pluma *f* feather; quill; plume; pen; (Am) faucet; (CAm) hoax; (Chile) crane, derrick; **pluma esferográfica** (Am) ball-point pen; **pluma estilográfica** or **pluma fuente** fountain pen

plumaje *m* plumage

plúmbe·o -a *adj* lead

plumero *m* (*caja o vaso para las plumas*) penholder; feather duster

plumife·ro -ra *adj* (*escritor*) (coll) hack, second-rate; (poet) feathered ‖ *m* padded or quilted jacket, ski jacket; (coll) hack writer; (coll) newshound

plumilla *f* small feather; (*de la pluma fuente*) point, tip

plumón *m* down; feather bed

plumo·so -sa *adj* downy, feathery

plural *adj & m* plural

pluriempleo *m* moonlighting

plus *m* extra, bonus

plusmarca *f* (sport) record

plusmarquista *mf* (sport) record breaker

pl
pl

plusvalía *f* appreciation (*in value*)
Plutarco *m* Plutarch
plutonio *m* plutonium
población *f* population; village, town, city
poblada *f* (SAm) riot, mob
pobla·do -da *adj* thick, bushy || *m* town, community || *f* see **poblada**
poblar §61 *tr* to people, to populate; to found, settle, colonize; (*un estanque, una colmena*) to stock; (*con árboles*) to plant || *intr* to settle, colonize; to multiply, be prolific || *ref* to become full, covered, or crowded
pobre *adj* poor || *mf* pauper; beggar
pobreza *f* poverty, want; poorness
pocilga *f* pigpen
poción *f* potion, dose
po·co -ca *adj & pron* (*comp & super* **menos**) little; few, e.g., **poca gente** few people; **pocos** few; **unos pocos** a few || **poco** *adv* little; **a poco** shortly afterwards; **a poco de** shortly after; **dentro de poco** shortly; **por poco** almost, nearly; **tener en poco** to hold in low esteem, to think little of; **un poco (de)** a little
po·cho -cha *adj* faded, discolored; overripe; rotten; (Chile) chubby
podar *tr* to prune, to trim
podenco *m* hound
poder *m* power; power of attorney, proxy; **el cuarto poder** the fourth estate; **obra en mi poder** I have at hand, I have in my possession; **poder adquisitivo** purchasing power || *v* §53 *intr* to be possible; to be able, to have power or strength; **a más no poder** as hard as possible; **no poder con** to not be able to stand, to not be able to manage; **no poder más** to be exhausted, to be all in; **no poder menos de** to not be able to keep from, to not be able to help || *v aux* to be able to, may, can, might, could; **no poder ver** to not be able to stand
poderhabiente *mf* attorney, proxy
poderío *m* power, might; wealth, riches; sway, dominion
podero·so -sa *adj* powerful, mighty; wealthy, rich
podre *f* pus
podredumbre *f* corruption, putrefaction; pus; deep grief
poema *m* poem
poesía *f* poetry; poem; **bella poesía** (fig) fairy tale
poeta *m* poet
poéti·co -ca *adj* poetic(al) || *f* poetics
poetisa *f* poetess
pola·co -ca *adj* Polish || *mf* Pole || *m* (*idioma*) Polish
polaina *f* legging
polar *adj* pole; polar || *f* polestar
polarizar §60 *tr* to polarize
polea *f* pulley
poleame *m* (naut) tackle
polen *m* pollen
policía *m* policeman || *f* police; policing; politeness; cleanliness, neatness; **policía urbana** street cleaning
policía·co -ca or **policial** *adj* police; (*novela*) detective

polifacéti·co -ca *adj* many-sided
políga·mo -ma *adj* polygamous || *mf* polygamist
poligло·to -ta *adj* polyglot || *mf* polyglot, linguist
polígono *m* polygon
polígrafo *m* prolific writer; copying machine; ball-point pen; lie detector
polilla *f* moth
polinizar §60 *tr* to pollinate
polinomio *m* polynomial
polio *f* (path) polio
pólipo *m* polyp
polisón *m* bustle
polista *mf* poloist, polo player
politeísta *adj* polytheistic || *mf* polytheist
política *f* politics; policy; manners, politeness, courtesy; **política de café** parlor politics; **política del buen vecino** Good Neighbor Policy
políti·co -ca *adj* political; politic, tactful; polite, courteous; -in-law, e.g., **padre político** father-in-law || *mf* politician || *f* see **política**
póliza *f* policy, contract; draft, check; customhouse permit; **póliza de seguro** insurance policy
polizón *m* bum, tramp; stowaway
polizonte *m* (coll) cop; policeman
polo *m* pole; popsicle; (*juego*) polo; **polo de agua** water polo; **polo de atracción popular** drawing card
Polonia *f* Poland
pol·trón -trona *adj* idle, lazy, comfortloving || *f* easy chair
polución *f* (*del ambiente*) pollution
polvareda *f* cloud of dust; rumpus
polvera *f* compact, powder case
polvo *m* dust; powder; pinch of snuff; **polvo dentífrico** tooth powder; **polvos** dust; powder; **polvos de la madre Celestina** (coll) hocus-pocus; **polvos de talco** talcum powder
pólvora *f* powder, gunpowder; fireworks; (*persona avispada*) (coll) live wire; **correr como pólvora en reguero** to spread like wildfire
polvorear *tr* to dust, sprinkle with dust or powder
polvorien·to -ta *adj* dusty; powdery
polvorín *m* powder magazine; powder flask; (*insecto*) (Am) tick; (Chile) spitfire
polvoro·so -sa *adj* dusty; **poner pies en polvorosa** (coll) to take to one's heels
polla *f* pullet; (*puesta en juegos de naipes*) stake, kitty; (coll) lassie
pollera *f* poultry woman; chicken coop; poultry yard; gocart; (Arg, Chile) skirt
pollero *m* poulterer; poultry yard
polli·no -na *mf* donkey, ass
polli·to -ta *mf* chick; (*persona joven*) (coll) chick, chicken
pollo *m* chicken; (*persona joven*) chicken
pomada *f* pomade
pómez *f* pumice stone
pomo *m* pome; (*de la guarnición de la espada*) pommel; (*bola aromática*) pomander; (*frasco para perfume*) flacon; **pomo de puerta** doorknob

pompa f pomp; soap bubble; swell, bulge; (de la ropa) billowing, ballooning; (de las alas del pavo real) spread; (naut) pump; **pompa fúnebre** funeral

pompo·so -sa adj pompous; high-flown, highfalutin

pómulo m cheekbone

ponche m (bebida) punch; **ponche de huevo** eggnog

ponchera f punch bowl

pon·cho -cha adj lazy, careless, easygoing; (Col) chubby ‖ m poncho; greatcoat

ponderar tr to weigh; to ponder, ponder over; to exaggerate; to praise to the skies; to balance; to weight

ponencia f paper, report

poner §54 tr to put, place, lay, set; to arrange, dispose; (una observación) to put in; (una pieza dramática) to put on; (la mesa) to set; to assume, suppose; (una ley, un impuesto) to impose; to wager, to stake; (huevos) to lay; (por escrito) to set down, put down; (tiempo) to take; (p.ej., miedo) to cause; to make, to turn; (la luz, la radio) to turn on; (marcha directa) (aut) to go in; **poner en limpio** to make a clean copy of; **poner por encima** to prefer, to put ahead ‖ ref to put or place oneself; to become, to get, to turn; (el sol, los astros) to set; (sombrero, saco, etc.) to put on; to dress, dress up; to get spotted; to get, reach, arrive; **ponerse a** to set out to, to begin to; **ponerse tan alto** to take offense, to become hoity-toity

poniente m west; west wind

ponqué m (Am) poundcake

pontífice m pontiff

pontón m pontoon; pontoon bridge; (buque viejo) hulk

ponzoña f poison

ponzoño·so -sa adj poisonous

popa f poop, stern

popote m (Mex) straw for brooms; (para tomar refrescos) (Mex) straw

populache·ro -ra adj popular; cheap, vulgar; rabble-rousing ‖ mf rabble rouser

populacho m populace, mob, rabble

popular adj popular

popularizar §60 tr to popularize

populo·so -sa adj populous

popu·rrí m (pl -rríes) medley

poquedad f paucity, scantiness; scarcity; timidity; trifle

poqui·to -ta adj very little; (Am) timid, shy, backward

por prep by; through; over; via, by way of; in, e.g., **por la mañana** in the morning; for; because of; for the sake of; on account of; in exchange for; in order to; as; about, e.g., **por Navidad** about Christmastime; out of, e.g., **por ignorancia** out of ignorance; times, e.g., **tres por cuatro** four times three; **estar por** to be on the point of, to be ready to; to be still to be, e.g., **la carta está por escribir** the letter is still to be written; **ir por** to go for, to go after; to follow; **por ciento** per cent; **por entre** among, between; **por que** because; in order that; **por qué** why; **por + adj** or adv **+ que** however

porcelana f porcelain, chinaware; (usado por los plateros) enamel; (Mex) washbowl

porcentaje m percentage

porción f portion

porche m porch, portico

pordiosear intr to beg, to go begging

pordiose·ro -ra mf beggar

porfía f persistence, stubbornness, obstinacy; **a porfía** in emulation; insistently

porfia·do -da adj persistent, stubborn, obstinate; opinionated

porfiar §77 intr to persist; to argue stubbornly

pórfido m porphyry

pormenor m detail, particular

pormenorizar §60 tr to detail, tell in detail; to itemize

poro m pore

poro·so -sa adj porous

poroto m (SAm) bean, string bean; (Chile) little runt

porque conj because; in order that

porqué m (coll) why; (coll) quantity, share; (coll) wherewithal, money

porquería f (coll) dirt, filth; (coll) trifle; (coll) crudity; (alimento dañoso a la salud) (coll) junk

porra f club, bludgeon; (coll) bore, nuisance; (coll) boasting; (pelos enredados) (Arg, Bol) knot, tangle; (Mex) claque

porrazo m clubbing; blow, bump, thump

porta f porthole

portaavio·nes m (pl -nes) aircraft carrier, flattop

portacandado m hasp

portada f front, façade; portal; title page; (de una revista) cover; **falsa portada** half title

portadis·cos m (pl -cos) turntable

porta·dor -dora adj (onda) (rad) carrier ‖ mf bearer; carrier ‖ m waiter's tray

portaequipaje m (aut) trunk

portaequipa·jes m (pl -jes) baggage rack

portaguan·tes m (pl -tes) (aut) glove compartment

portal m vestibule, entrance hall; porch, portico; arcade; city gate; (de un túnel) portal m; (Am) crèche

portalámpa·ras m (pl -ras) (elec) socket

portalón m gate, portal; (en el costado del buque) gangway

portamira m (surv) rodman

portamone·das m (pl -das) pocketbook

portanue·vas m (pl -vas) newsmonger

portañuela f (de los pantalones) fly; (Col, Mex) carriage door

portapape·les m (pl -les) brief case

portaplu·mas m (pl -mas) penholder

portar tr (Am) to carry, to bear; (hunt) to retrieve ‖ ref to behave, conduct oneself

portase·nos m (pl -nos) brassière

portátil adj portable

pl
po

portatinte·ro *m* inkstand
portavian·das *m* (*pl* **-das**) dinner pail
porta·voz *m* (*pl* **-voces**) megaphone; mouthpiece, spokesman
portazgo *m* toll, road toll
portazo *m* bang, slam
porte *m* portage; carrying charge, freight; postage; behavior, conduct; dress, bearing; size, capacity; (Chile) birthday present; **porte concertado** mailing permit; **porte pagado** postage prepaid, freight prepaid
portear *tr* to carry, transport || *intr* to slam || *ref* (*las aves*) to migrate
portento *m* prodigy, wonder
portento·so -sa *adj* portentous, extraordinary
porte·ño -ña *adj* Buenos Aires; Valparaíso; pertaining to any large South American city with a port || *mf* native or inhabitant of Buenos Aires, Valparaíso or any large South American city with a port
porte·ro -ra *mf* doorkeeper; gatekeeper; (sport) goalkeeper || *m* porter, janitor; doorman || *f* portress, janitress
portezuela *f* small door; (*de un coche o automóvil*) door; pocket flap
pórtico *m* portico, porch; little gate
portilla *f* porthole; private cart road, private cattle pass
portillo *m* gap, opening; nick, notch; (*puerta chica en otra mayor*) wicket; gate; narrow pass; side entrance
portorrique·ño -ña *adj & mf* Puerto Rican
portua·rio -ria *adj* port, harbor, dock || *m* dock hand, dock worker
Portugal *m* Portugal
portu·gués -guesa *adj & mf* Portuguese
porvenir *m* future
pos — en pos de after, behind; in pursuit of
posa *f* knell, toll
posada *f* inn, wayside inn; lodging; boarding house; home, dwelling; camp; **posadas** (Mex) pre-Christmas celebration
posadero -ra *mf* innkeeper; **posaderas** buttocks
posar *tr* to put down || *intr* to put up, lodge; to alight, to perch; to pose || *ref* to alight, to perch; to settle; to rest
posbéli·co -ca *adj* postwar
posdata *f* postscript
pose *f* pose; (phot) exposure
poseer §43 *tr* to own, possess, hold; to have a mastery of || *ref* to control oneself
posesión *f* possession; **tomar posesión de** (*un cargo*) to take up
posesionar *tr* to give possession to || *ref* to take possession
posfecha *f* postdate
posguerra *f* postwar period
posible *adj* possible; **hacer todo lo posible** to do one's best || **posibles** *mpl* means, income, property
posición *f* position; standing
positi·vo -va *adj* positive || *f* (phot) print, positive

poso *m* sediment, dregs; grounds; rest, quiet; **poso del café** coffee grounds
posponer §54 *tr* to subordinate; to think less of
posta *f* (*de caballos*) relay; posthouse; stage; stake, wager; slice; **a posta** (coll) on purpose; **por la posta** (coll) posthaste; **postas** buckshot
postal *adj* postal || *f* post card; **postal ilustrada** picture post card
poste *m* post, pilar, pole; **poste de alumbrado** or **de farol** lamppost; **poste de telégrafo** telegraph pole; (*persona muy alta y delgada*) beanpole; **poste indicador** road sign
postergar §44 *tr* to delay, postpone; to pass over
posteridad *f* posterity; posthumous fame
posterior *adj* back, rear; later, subsequent
postigo *m* (*puerta chica en otra mayor*) wicket; (*puertecilla en una ventana*) peep window; (*puerta excusada*) postern; shutter
posti·zo -za *adj* false, artificial; (*cuello*) detachable || *m* switch, false hair, false piece
postóni·co -ca *adj* posttonic
postor *m* bidder; **el mejor postor** the highest bidder
postración *f* prostration
postrar *tr* to prostrate; to weaken, exhaust || *ref* to collapse, be prostrated; to prostrate oneself
postre *adj* last, final; **a la postre** at last; afterwards || *m* dessert; **postres** dessert
postulación *f* postulation; nomination
postulante *mf* applicant, candidate
póstu·mo -ma *adj* posthumous
postura *f* posture; attitude, stand; stake, wager; agreement, pact; egg, eggs; (*de huevos*) laying; **postura del sol** sunset
potabilizar §60 *tr* to make drinkable
potable *adj* drinkable
potaje *m* pottage; jumble; (*bebida*) mixture; (Am) scheme; **potajes** vegetables
potasa *f* potash
potasio *m* potassium
pote *m* pot, jug; flowerpot; **a pote** (coll) in abundance
potencia *f* potency; power; **potencia de choque** striking power
potenciación *f* (math) involution
potencial *adj & m* potential
potenciar *tr* (*las aguas de un río; el entusiasmo de una persona*) to harness; (*elevar a una potencia*) (math) to raise
potentado *m* potentate
potente *adj* powerful; (coll) big, huge
potestad *f* power
potista *mf* (coll) toper, soak
potosí *m* great wealth, gold mine
potra *f* filly; (coll) hernia, rupture
potranca *f* young mare
potro *m* colt; pest, annoyance
pozal *m* bucket, pail
pozo *m* well; pit; whirlpool; (min) shaft; (naut) hold; (Chile, Col) pool, puddle; (Ecuad) spring, fountain;

pozo de ciencia fountain of knowledge; **pozo de lanzamiento** launching silo; **pozo de lobo** (mil) foxhole; **pozo negro** cesspool

P.P. *abbr* **porte pagado, por poder**

p.p.ᵈᵒ *abbr* **próximo pasado**

práctica *f* practice; method; skill; **prácticas** studies, training

prácticamente *adv* through practice, by experience

practicar §73 *tr* to practice; to bring about; (*un agujero*) to make, to cut

prácti·co -ca *adj* practical; skillful, practiced; practicing ‖ *m* medical practitioner; (naut) pilot ‖ *f* see **práctica**

pradera *f* meadowland; prairie

prado *m* meadow, pasture; promenade

Praga *f* Prague

pral. *abbr* **principal**

pralte. *abbr* **principalmente**

prángana — estar en la prángana (Mex, W-I) to be broke; (P-R) to be naked

preámbulo *m* preamble; evasion; **no andarse en preámbulos** (coll) to come to the point

prebéli·co -ca *adj* prewar

prebenda *f* prebend; (coll) sinecure

preca·rio -ria *adj* precarious

precaución *f* precaution

precaver *tr* to stave off, head off ‖ *intr* & *ref* to be on one's guard; **preca-verse contra** or **de** to guard against

precavido -da *adj* cautious

precedente *adj* preceding ‖ *m* precedent

preceder *tr* & *intr* to precede

precepto *m* precept; order, injunction; **los preceptos** the Ten Commandments

preces *fpl* devotions; supplications

precia·do -da *adj* esteemed, valued; precious, valuable; boastful, proud

preciar *tr* to appraise, estimate ‖ *ref* to boast

precintar *tr* to bind, strap; to seal

precio *m* price; value, worth; esteem, credit; **a precio de quemazón** (coll) at a giveaway price; **precios de cierre** closing prices; **precio tope** ceiling price

preciosidad *f* preciousness; beauty, gem, jewel

precio·so -sa *adj* precious; valuable; witty; (coll) beautiful

precipicio *m* precipice; destruction

precipitación *f* precipitation; **precipitación acuosa** rainfall; **precipitación radiactiva** fallout

precipitar *tr* to precipitate; to rush, hurl, throw headlong ‖ *ref* to rush, throw oneself headlong

precipito·so -sa *adj* precipitous, rash, reckless; risky, dangerous

precisar *tr* to state precisely, to specify; to fix; to need; to oblige, to force ‖ *intr* to be necessary; to be important; to be urgent; **precisar de** to need

precisión *f* precision; necessity, obligation; (Chile) haste; **precisiones** data

preci·so -sa *adj* necessary; precise; (Ven) haughty

precita·do -da *adj* above-mentioned

precla·ro -ra *adj* illustrious, famous

preconizar §60 *tr* to proclaim, commend publicly

pre·coz *adj* (*pl* **-coces**) precocious

predato·rio -ria *adj* predatory

predecir §24 *tr* to predict, foretell

prédica *f* protestant sermon; harangue

predicar §73 *tr* to preach; to praise to the skies; to scold, preach to

predicción *f* prediction; **predicción del tiempo** weather forecasting

predilec·to -ta *adj* favorite, preferred

predio *m* property, estate

predisponer §54 *tr* to predispose

predominante *adj* predominant

preeminente *adj* preëminent

preestreno *m* (mov) preview

prefabricar §73 *tr* to prefabricate

prefacio *m* preface

preferencia *f* preference; **de preferencia** preferably

preferente *adj* preferable; favored; (*acciones*) preferred

preferible *adj* preferable

preferir §68 *tr* to prefer

prefigurar *tr* to foreshadow

prefijar *tr* to prefix; to prearrange

prefijo *m* prefix

pregón *m* proclamation, public announcement (*by town crier*)

pregonar *tr* to proclaim, announce publicly; to hawk; to reveal; to outlaw; to praise openly

pregonero *m* auctioneer; town crier

preguerra *f* prewar period

pregunta *f* question; **hacer una pregunta** to ask a question

preguntar *tr* to ask; to question ‖ *intr* to ask, to inquire; **preguntar por** to ask after or for ‖ *ref* to ask oneself; to wonder

pregun·tón -tona *adj* (coll) inquisitive ‖ *mf* (coll) inquisitive person

prejudicio or **prejuicio** *m* prejudgment; prejudice

prelado *m* prelate

preliminar *adj* & *m* preliminary; **preliminares** (*de un libro*) front matter

preludio *m* prelude

premeditar *tr* to premeditate

premiar *tr* to reward; to give an award to

premio *m* reward, prize; premium; **a premio** at a premium; **premio de enganche** (mil) bounty; **premio gordo** first prize

premio·so -sa *adj* tight, close; bothersome; strict, rigid; slow, dull

premisa *f* premise; mark, token, clue

premura *f* pressure, haste, urgency

premuro·so -sa *adj* pressing, urgent

prenda *f* pledge; security; pawn; jewel, household article; garment, article of clothing; gift, talent; darling, loved one; **en prenda** in pawn; **en prenda de** as a pledge of; **prenda perdida** forfeit; **prendas** (*juego*) forfeits

prendar *tr* to pawn; to pledge; to charm, captivate ‖ *ref* — **prendarse de** to take a liking for, fall in love with

prendedero *m* fillet, brooch; stickpin

prender *tr* to seize, grasp; to catch; to imprison; to dress up; to pin; to

po
pr

fasten || *intr* to catch; to catch fire;
to take root; to turn out well || *ref*
to dress up; to be fastened; to catch
hold
prendería *f* second-hand shop
prende•ro -ra *mf* second-hand dealer
prensa *f* press; printing press; vise;
press, newspapers; press, frame; **entrar en prensa** to go to press; **meter
en prensa** (coll) to put the squeeze
on; **prensa taladradora** drill press
prensado *m* pressing; (*lustre de los
tejidos prensados*) sheen
prensar *tr* to press; to squeeze
preña•do -da *adj* pregnant; sagging,
bulging; full, charged
preñez *f* pregnancy; fullness; impending danger; inherent confusion
preocupación *f* (*posesión anticipada;
cuidado, desvelo*) preoccupation; (*posesión anticipada*) preoccupancy;
bias, prejudice
preocupar *tr* to preoccupy, to worry ||
ref to become preoccupied, to be
worried
preparación *f* preparation
prepara•do -da *adj* ready, prepared ||
m (pharm) preparation
preparar *tr* to prepare || *ref* to prepare,
to get ready
preparati•vo -va *adj* preparatory || *m*
preparation, readiness
preponderante *adj* preponderant
preposición *f* preposition
prepóste•ro -ra *adj* reversed, upset, out
of order, inopportune
prerrogativa *f* prerogative
presa *f* capture, seizure; catch, prey;
booty, spoils; dam; trench, ditch,
flume; bit, morsel; fang, tusk, claw;
fishweir; (sport) hold; **hacer presa**
to seize; **ser presa de** to be a victim
of; to be prey to
presagiar *tr* to presage, forebode
presagio *m* presage, omen, token
présbita or **présbite** *adj* far-sighted ||
mf presbyte
presbiteria•no -na *adj* & *mf* Presbyterian
prescindir *intr* — **prescindir de** to leave
aside, leave out, disregard; to do
without, dispense with; to avoid
prescribir §83 *tr* & *intr* to prescribe
presencia *f* presence; show, display;
presencia de ánimo presence of mind
presenciar *tr* to witness, be present at
presentación *f* presentation; (*de una
persona en el trato de otra u otras*)
introduction; (*de un nuevo automóvil, libro, etc.*) appearance
presentar *tr* to present; to introduce ||
ref to present oneself; to appear,
show up; to introduce oneself
presente *adj* present; **hacer presente** to
notify of, to remind of; **tener presente**
to bear or keep in mind || *interj* here!,
present! || *m* present, gift; person
present
presentimiento *m* presentiment, premonition
presentir §68 *tr* to have a presentiment
of
preservar *tr* to preserve, protect

preservati•vo -va *adj* & *m* preventive;
preservative
presidencia *f* presidency; chairmanship
presidente *m* president; chairman; pre-
siding judge
presidiario *m* convict
presidio *m* garrison; fortress; citadel;
penitentiary; imprisonment; hard labor; aid, help
presidir *tr* to preside over; to dominate
|| *intr* to preside
presilla *f* loop, fastener; clip; shoulder
strap
presión *f* pressure; (*cerveza*) **a presión**
on draught; **presión de inflado** tire
pressure
presionar *tr* to press; to put pressure
on || *intr* to press; **presionar sobre** to
put pressure on
pre•so -sa *adj* seized; imprisoned || *mf*
prisoner; convict; *f* see **presa**
presta•do -da *adj* lent, loaned; **dar
prestado** to lend; **pedir** or **tomar prestado** to borrow
prestamista *mf* moneylender; pawnbroker
préstamo *m* loan; **préstamo lingüístico**
loan word, borrowing
prestar *tr* to lend, to loan; (*oído;
ayuda; noticias*) to give; (*atención*)
to pay; (*un favor*) to do; (*un servicio*) to render; (*juramento*) to take;
(*silencio*) to keep; (*paciencia*) to
show || *intr* (*un paño, la ropa*) to
give, to yield; to be useful || *ref* to
lend oneself, to lend itself
prestatar•rio -ria *mf* borrower
presteza *f* speed, promptness, readiness
prestidigitación *f* sleight of hand
prestidigita•dor -dora *adj* captivating ||
mf magician; faker, impostor
prestigio *m* prestige; good standing;
spell; illusion
prestigio•so -sa *adj* captivating, spellbinding; famous, renowned; illusory
pres•to -ta *adj* quick, prompt, ready;
nimble || **presto** *adv* right away
presumi•do -da *adj* conceited, vain ||
mf would-be
presumir *tr* to presume || *intr* to boast,
be conceited
presunción *f* presumption; conceit
presuntuo•so -sa *adj* conceited, vain
presuponer §54 *tr* to presuppose; to
budget
presupuestar *tr* to budget; (*el coste de
una obra*) to estimate
presupuesto *m* budget; reason, motive;
supposition; estimate
presuro•so -sa *adj* speedy, quick, hasty;
zealous, persistent
pretencio•so -sa *adj* pretentious, showy;
conceited, vain
pretender *tr* to claim, to pretend to; to
try for, to try to do; to be a suitor for
|| *intr* to insist; **pretender + inf** to try
to + *inf*
pretendiente *mf* pretender, claimant;
office seeker || *m* suitor
pretensión *f* pretension; claim; pretense; presumption; effort, pursuit
pretéri•to -ta *adj* & *m* past

pretil *m* parapet, railing; walk along a parapet

pretina *f* girdle, belt; waistband

pretóni·co -ca *adj* pretonic

prevalecer §22 *intr* to prevail; to take root; to thrive

prevaler §76 *ref* — **prevalerse de** to avail oneself of, take advantage of

prevaricar §73 *intr* to collude, connive; to play false; to transgress; (coll) to rave, be delirious

prevención *f* preparation; prevention; foresight; warning; prejudice; stock, supply; jail, lockup; guardhouse; **a or de prevención** spare, emergency

preveni·do -da *adj* prepared, ready; foresighted, forewarned; stocked, full

prevenir §79 *tr* to prepare, make ready; to forestall, prevent, anticipate; to overcome; to warn; to prejudice ‖ *intr* (*una tempestad*) to come up ‖ *ref* to get ready; to come to mind

prever §80 *tr* to foresee

pre·vio -via *adj* previous; preliminary; after, with previous, subject to, e.g., **previo acuerdo** subject to agreement

previsión *f* prevision, foresight; foresightedness; forecast; **previsión del tiempo** weather forecasting

prie·to -ta *adj* dark, blackish; stingy, mean; tight, compact; (Am) dark-complexioned ‖ *mf* (W-I) darling

prima *f* early morning; bonus, bounty; (ins) premium; (mil) first quarter of the night; (*cuerda*) (mus) treble

pri·mal -mala *adj & mf* yearling

prima·rio -ria *adj* primary ‖ *m* (elec) primary

primavera *f* spring, springtime; cowslip, primrose; robin

primer *adj* apocopated form of **primero**, used only before masculine singular nouns and adjectives

prime·ro -ra *adj* first; former; early; primary; prime; (*materia*) raw ‖ *m* first; **a primeros de** around the beginning of ‖ **primero** *adv* first

primicia *f* first fruits

primige·nio -nia *adj* original, primitive

primiti·vo -va *adj* primitive

pri·mo -ma *adj* first; prime, excellent; skillful; (*materia*) raw ‖ *mf* cousin; (coll) sucker, dupe; **primo carnal or primo hermano** first cousin, cousin-german ‖ *f see* **prima** ‖ **primo** *adv* in the first place

primogéni·to -ta *adj & mf* first-born

primor *m* care, skill, elegance; beauty

primoro·so -sa *adj* careful, skillful, elegant; fine, exquisite

princesa *f* princess; **princesa viuda** dowager princess

principal *adj* principal, main, chief; first, foremost; essential, important; famous, illustrious; (*piso*) second ‖ *m* principal, head, chief

príncipe *m* prince; **portarse como un príncipe** to live like a prince; **príncipe de Asturias** heir apparent of the King of Spain; **príncipe de Gales** prince of Wales; **príncipes** prince and princess

principiante *adj* beginning ‖ *mf* beginner, apprentice, novice

principiar *tr, intr & ref* to begin

principio *m* start, beginning; principle; origin, source; (culin) entree; **a principios de** around the beginning of; **en un principio** at the beginning; **principio de admiración** inverted exclamation point; **principio de interrogación** inverted question mark

pringar §44 *tr* to dip or soak in grease or fat; to spot or stain with grease: (coll) to make bleed; (coll) to slander, run down; (Am) to splash ‖ *intr* (coll) to meddle; (CAm, Mex) to drizzle ‖ *ref* to peculate

pringo·so -sa *adj* greasy, fatty

prioridad *f* priority; **de máxima prioridad** of the highest priority

prisa *f* hurry, haste; urgency; crush, crowd; **darse prisa** to hurry, make haste; **estar de prisa** or **tener prisa** to be in a hurry

prisión *f* seizure, capture; imprisonment; prison; **prisión celular** cell house; **prisiones** shackles, fetters

prisione·ro -ra *mf* prisoner; (*cautivo de una pasión o afecto*) captive ‖ *m* setscrew; studbolt

prisma *m* prism

prismáticos *mpl* binoculars

priva·do -da *adj* private ‖ *m* (*de un alto personaje*) favorite ‖ *f* cesspool

privar *tr* to deprive; to forbid, prohibit ‖ *intr* to be in vogue; to prevail; to be in favor ‖ *ref* to deprive oneself; **privarse de** to give up

privilegiar *tr* to grant a privilege to

privilegio *m* privilege

pro *m & f* profit, advantage; **¡buena pro!** good appetite!; **de pro** of note, of worth; **el pro y el contra** the pros and the cons; **en pro de** on behalf of

proa *f* (aer) nose; (naut) prow

probable *adj* probable, likely

probar §61 *tr* to prove; to test; to try; (*clothing*) to try on; to try out; to sample; to fit; to suit; (*vino*) to touch ‖ *intr* to taste; **probar de** to take a taste of ‖ *ref* to try on

probidad *f* probity, integrity, honesty

problema *m* problem

pro·caz *adj* (*pl* **-caces**) impudent, insolent, bold

procedencia *f* origin, source; point of departure

procedente *adj* coming, originating; proper

proceder *m* conduct, behavior ‖ *intr* to proceed; to originate; to behave; to be proper

procedimiento *m* procedure; proceeding; process

procelo·so -sa *adj* tempestuous, stormy

prócer *adj* high, lofty ‖ *m* hero, leader

procesar *tr* to sue, prosecute; to indict; to try

procesión *f* procession; origin, emergence

proceso *m* process; progress; suit, lawsuit; **proceso verbal** (Am) minutes

proclama *f* proclamation; marriage banns

proclamar *tr* to proclaim; to acclaim
proclíti·co -ca *adj & m* proclitic
procurador *m* attorney, solicitor; proxy
procurar *tr* to strive for; to manage as attorney; to yield, produce; to try to
prodigar §44 *tr* to lavish; to squander; to waste || *ref* to be a show-off
prodigio *m* prodigy
prodigio·so -sa *adj* prodigious, marvelous; fine, excellent
pródigo -ga *adj* prodigal; lavish || *mf* prodigal
producción *f* production; crop, yield, produce; **producción en masa** or **en serie** mass production
producir §19 *tr* to produce; to yield, to bear; to cause, bring about || *ref* to explain oneself; to come about; to take place
producto *m* product; produce; proceeds
proeza *f* prowess; feat, stunt
profanar *tr* to profane
profa·no -na *adj* profane; indecent, immodest; worldly; lay || *mf* profane; worldly person; layman
profecía *f* prophecy || **las Profecías** (Bib) the Prophets
proferir §68 *tr* to utter
profesar *tr & intr* to profess
profesión *f* profession; **profesión de fe** confession of faith
profe·sor -sora *mf* teacher; professor
profeta *m* prophet
profetisa *f* prophetess
profetizar §60 *tr* to prophesy
profilácti·co -ca *adj & m* prophylactic; preventive || *f* hygiene
prófu·go -ga *adj & mf* fugitive || *m* slacker, draft dodger
profundidad *f* profundity; depth
profundizar §60 *tr* to deepen; to fathom, get to the bottom of
profun·do -da *adj* profound; deep
progenie *f* descent, lineage, parentage
progno·sis *f* (*pl* **-sis**) prognosis; (*del tiempo*) forecast
programa *m* program; **programa continuo** (mov) continuous showing; **programa de estudios** curriculum; **programa para computadora** program(me); (coll) software
programar *tr* to program
progresar *intr* to progress
progresista *adj & mf* (pol) progressive
progreso *m* progress; **hacer progresos** to make progress
prohibir *tr* to prohibit, forbid || *ref* **se prohibe fijar carteles** post no bills
prohijar *tr* to adopt
prohombre *m* (*en los gremios de los artesanos*) master; leader, head; (coll) big shot
prójimo *m* fellow man, fellow creature, neighbor; (coll) fellow
prole *f* progeny, offspring
proletariado *m* proletariat
proleta·rio -ria *adj & m* proletarian
proliferar *intr* to proliferate
prolífi·co -ca *adj* prolific
proli·jo -ja *adj* tedious, too long; fussy, fastidious; long-winded; tiresome

prologar §44 *tr* to preface, write a preface for
prólogo *m* prologue; preface
prolongar §44 *tr* to prolong, extend; (geom) to produce
promediar *tr* to divide into two equal parts; to average || *intr* to mediate; to be half over
promedio *m* average, mean; middle
promesa *f* promise
promete·dor -dora *adj* promising
prometer *tr & intr* to promise || *ref* to become engaged
prometi·do -da *adj* engaged, betrothed || *m* promise; fiancé || *f* fiancée
prominente *adj* prominent
promiso·rio -ria *adj* promissory
promoción *f* promotion; advancement; (*conjunto de individuos que obtienen un grado en un mismo año*) class, year, crop
promontorio *m* promontory, headland; unwieldy thing
promover §47 *tr* to promote; to advance, to further
promulgar §44 *tr* to promulgate
pronombre *m* pronoun
pronosticar §73 *tr* to prognosticate, to foretell
pronóstico *m* prognostic, forecast; almanac; (med) prognosis
pron·to -ta *adj* quick, speedy; prompt; ready || *m* jerk; (coll) sudden impulse, fit of anger || **pronto** *adv* right away, soon; early; promptly; **lo más pronto posible** as soon as possible; **tan pronto como** as soon as
pronunciación *f* pronunciation
pronuncia·do -da *adj* marked; (*curva*) sharp; (*pendiente*) steep; bulky
pronunciamiento *m* insurrection, uprising; (*golpe de estado militar*) pronunciamento; (law) decree
pronunciar *tr* to pronounce; to utter; (*un discurso*) to make, to deliver; to decide on || *ref* to rebel; to declare oneself
propaganda *f* propaganda; advertising
propagar §44 *tr* to propagate; to spread; to broadcast
propalar *tr* to divulge, to spread
proparoxíto·no -na *adj & m* proparoxytone
propasar *ref* to go too far, to take undue liberty
propender *intr* to tend, to incline, to be inclined
propensión *f* propensity; predisposition
propen·so -sa *adj* inclined, disposed, prone
propiciar *tr* to propitiate; (Am) to support, favor, sponsor
propi·cio -cia *adj* propitious, favorable
propiedad *f* property; ownership; naturalness, likeness; **es propiedad** copyrighted; **propiedad horizontal** one-floor ownership in an apartment house; **propiedad literaria** copyright
propieta·rio -ria *mf* owner || *m* proprietor || *f* proprietress
propina *f* tip, fee, gratuity
propinar *tr* (*algo a beber*) to offer; (*medicamentos*) to prescribe or ad-

minister; (*palos, golpes, etc.*) (coll) to give || *ref* (*una bebida*) to treat oneself to

propin·cuo -cua *adj* near, close at hand

pro·pio -pia *adj* proper, suitable; peculiar, characteristic; natural; same; himself, herself, etc.; own || *m* messenger; native; **propios** public lands

proponer §54 *tr* to propose; to propound; (*a una persona para un empleo*) to name, to present || *ref* to plan; to propose

proporción *f* proportion; opportunity

proporciona·do -da *adj* proportionate; fit, suitable

proporcionar *tr* to furnish, provide, supply, give; to proportion; to adapt, adjust

proposición *f* proposition; **proposición dominante** main clause

propósito *m* aim, purpose, intention; subject matter; **a propósito** by the way; apropos, fitting; in place; **a propósito de** apropos of; **de propósito** on purpose; **fuera de propósito** irrelevant, beside the point

propuesta *f* proposal, proposition

propulsar *tr* to propel, to drive

propulsión *f* propulsion; **propulsión a chorro** jet propulsion; **propulsión a cohete** rocket propulsion

pror. *abbr* procurador

prorratear *tr* to prorate

prórroga *f* extension, renewal

prorrogar §44 *tr* to defer, postpone, extend

prorrumpir *intr* to spurt, shoot forth; to break forth, burst out

prosa *f* prose; (coll) chatter, idle talk

prosai·co -ca *adj* prose; prosaic, dull

proscribir §83 *tr* to outlaw, to proscribe

proscrip·to -ta *mf* exile, outlaw

prosecución *f* continuation, prosecution; pursuit

proseguir §67 *tr* to continue, carry on || *intr* to continue

prosélito *m* proselyte

prosista *mf* prose writer; (coll) chatterbox

prosódi·co -ca *adj* (*acento*) stress

prospectar *tr & intr* to prospect

prosperar *tr* to make prosper || *intr* to prosper, to thrive

prosperidad *f* prosperity

próspe·ro -ra *adj* prosperous, thriving, successful

prosternarse *ref* to prostrate oneself

prostituir §20 *tr* to prostitute || *ref* to prostitute oneself; to become a prostitute

prostituta *f* prostitute

prosu·do -da *adj* (Chile, Ecuad, Peru) pompous, solemn

protagonista *mf* protagonist

protagonizar §60 *tr* to play the leading rôle of

protección *f* protection; **protección aduanera** protective tariff; **protección a la infancia** child welfare

proteger §17 *tr* to protect

protegida *f* protégée

protegido *m* protégé

proteína *f* protein

proter·vo -va *adj* perverse

protesta *f* protest; pledge, promise

protestante *adj & mf* protestant; Protestant

protestar *tr* to protest, asseverate; (*la fe*) to profess || *intr* to protest; **protestar de** (*aseverar con ahinco*) to protest (*to state positively*); **protestar contra** (*negar la validez de*) to protest (*to deny forcibly*)

protocolo *m* protocol

protoplasma *m* protoplasm

prototipo *m* prototype

protozoario or **protozoo** *m* protozoön

provec·to -ta *adj* old, ripe

provecho *m* advantage, benefit; profit, gain; advance, progress; **¡buen provecho!** good luck!; good appetite!; **de provecho** useful; **provechos** perquisites

provecho·so -sa *adj* advantageous, beneficial; profitable; useful

proveedor -dora *mf* supplier, provider, purveyor; steward

proveer §43 & §83 *tr* to provide, furnish; to supply; to resolve, settle || *intr* to provide; **proveer a** to provide for || *ref* to supply oneself; to have a movement of the bowels

provenir §79 *intr* to come, arise

Provenza, la Provence

provenzal *adj & mf* Provençal

proverbio *m* proverb

providencia *f* providence, foresight; step, measure

providencial *adj* providential

provincia *f* province

provisión *f* provision; supply, stock; **provisiones de boca** foodstuffs

proviso·rio -ria *adj* provisory, provisional

provocar §73 *tr* to provoke; to promote, bring about; to incite, to tempt, to move || *intr* to provoke; (coll) to vomit

proxeneta *mf* go-between

proximidad *f* proximity; **proximidades** neighborhood

próxi·mo -ma *adj* next; near; neighboring, close; early; **próximo pasado** last

proyección *f* projection; influence

proyectar *tr* to project; to cast; to design || *ref* to project, stick out; (*una sombra*) to be projected, to fall

proyectil *m* projectile; **proyectil buscador del blanco** homing missile; **proyectil dirigido** or **teleguiado** guided missile

proyecto *m* project; **proyecto de ley** bill

proyector *m* projector, searchlight; projection machine

prudencia *f* prudence

prudente *adj* prudent

prueba *f* proof; trial, test; examination; (*de un traje*) fitting; (*de un alimento o una bebida*) sample, sampling; evidence; (sport) event; (Am) acrobatics; (Am) sleight of hand; **a prueba** on approval, on trial; **a prueba de** proof against, -proof, e.g., **a prueba de escaladores** burglarproof;

pruebas de planas page proof; **pruebas de primeras** first proof (*for proofreader*); **pruebas de segundas** galley proof (*for author*)
pruebista *mf* (Am) acrobat
prurito *m* itching; eagerness, itch
psicoanálisis *m* psychoanalysis
psicoanalizar §60 *tr* to psychoanalyze
psicología *f* psychology
psicológi·co -ca *adj* psychologic(al)
psicólo·go -ga *mf* psychologist
psicópata *mf* psychopath
psico·sis *f* (*pl* **-sis**) psychosis; **psicosis de guerra** war psychosis, war scare
psicóti·co -ca *adj & mf* psychotic
psique *f* cheval glass || **Psique** *f* Psyche
psiquiatra *mf* psychiatrist
psiquiatría *f* psychiatry
psíqui·co -ca *adj* psychic
P.S.M. *abbr* **por su mandato**
pte. *abbr* **parte, presente**
púa *f* point; prick, barb; tine, prong; (*del fonógrafo*) needle; (*del peine*) tooth; thorn; (*del puerco espín*) spine, quill; sting; graft; plectrum; (coll) tricky person
pubertad *f* puberty
publicación *f* publication
publicar §73 *tr* to publish; to publicize
publicidad *f* publicity; advertising; **publicidad de lanzamiento** advance publicity
publicita·rio -ria *adj* publicity; advertising
públi·co -ca *adj & m* public
pucha *f* (W-I) small bouquet; (Mex) crescent roll
puchero *m* pot, kettle; stew; (coll) daily bread; (coll) pouting; **hacer pucheros** to pout, screw up one's face
pucho *m* (Am) fag end, remnant; (*de cigarro*) (Am) stump; (Am) trifle, trinket; (*el hijo menor*) (Am) baby
puden·do -da *adj* ugly, shameful; obscene; (*partes*) private
pudiente *adj* powerful; well-off, well-to-do
pudín *m* pudding
pudor *m* modesty, shyness; chastity
pudoro·so -sa *adj* modest, shy; chaste
pudrición *f* rot, rotting
pudrir §83 *tr* to rot; to worry || *intr* to be dead and buried || *ref* to rot; to be worried; (*en la cárcel*) to languish
pueblo *m* people; common people; town, village; **pueblo de Dios o de Israel** children of God
puente *m* bridge; (dent, mus) bridge; (aut) axle, rear axle; **hacer puente** to take the intervening day off; **puente aéreo** airlift, air bridge; **puente colgante** suspension bridge; **puente de engrase** grease lift; **puente levadizo** drawbridge, lift bridge
puer·co -ca *adj* piggish, hoggish; dirty, filthy; slovenly; coarse, mean; lewd || *m* hog; **puerco espín o espino** porcupine || *f* sow; slattern, slut
puericia *f* childhood
pueril *adj* puerile, childish
puerilidad *f* puerility, childishness
puerro *m* leek

puerta *f* door, doorway; gate, gateway; **a puerta cerrada** or **a puertas cerradas** behind closed doors
puerto *m* harbor, port; haven; mountain pass; **puerto aéreo** airport; **puerto brigantino** Corunna; **puerto de arribada** port of call; **puerto de mar** seaport; **puerto franco** free port; **puerto marítimo** dock, port; **puerto seco** frontier customhouse
puertorrique·ño -ña *adj & mf* Puerto Rican
pues *adv* then, well; yes, certainly; why; anyhow; **pues bien** well then; **pues que** since || *conj* for, since, because, inasmuch as || *interj* well!, then!
puesta *f* setting; laying; putting; (*dinero apostado*) stake; **a puesta del sol** or **a puestas del sol** at sunset; **puesta a punto** adjustment; carrying out, completion; **puesta a tierra** (elec) grounding; **puesta de largo** coming out, social debut
pues·to -ta *adj* dressed; **puesto que** since, inasmuch as || *m* place; booth, stand; office; station; barracks; (*para cazadores*) blind; **puesto de socorros** first-aid station || *f* see **puesta**
púgil *m* pugilist
pugilato *m* boxing; fist fight
pugilismo *m* pugilism
pugna *f* fight, battle; struggle, conflict; **en pugna** at issue; **en pugna con** at odds with
pugnar *intr* to fight; to struggle; to strive, persist
pug·naz (*pl* **-naces**) pugnacious
pujante *adj* powerful, mighty, vigorous
pujar *tr* (*un proyecto*) to push; (*un precio*) to raise, bid up || *intr* to struggle, strain; to falter; (*por decir una cosa*) to grope; (coll) to snivel; **pujar para adentro** (CAm, W-I) to keep silent, say nothing
pul·cro -cra *adj* neat, tidy, trim; circumspect
pulga *f* flea; **de malas pulgas** peppery, hot-tempered; **hacer de una pulga un camello** or **un elefante** (coll) to make a mountain out of a molehill; **no aguantar pulgas** (coll) to stand for no nonsense
pulgada *f* inch
pulgar *m* thumb
puli·do -da *adj* pretty; neat; polished; clean, spotless
pulimentar *tr* to polish
pulimento *m* polish
pulir *tr* to polish; to finish; to give a polish to
pulmón *m* lung; **pulmón de acero** or **de hierro** iron lung
pulmonía *f* pneumonia
púlpito *m* pulpit
pulpo *m* octopus
pulsación *f* pulsation, throb; beat; strike, striking; (*del pianista, el mecanógrafo*) touch
pulsar *tr* (*un botón*) to push; (*un piano, arpa, guitarra*) to play; (*una tecla*) to strike; to feel or take the pulse

of; to sound out, examine ‖ *intr* to pulsate, throb, beat

pulsear *intr* to hand-wrestle

pulsera *f* bracelet; wristlet, watch strap; **pulsera de pedida** engagement bracelet

pulso *m* pulse; steadiness, steady hand; tact, care, caution; (Am) bracelet; (Am) wrist watch; **a pulso** with hand and wrist; by main strength; (*dibujo*) freehand; **sacar a pulso** (coll) to carry out against odds; **tomar el pulso a** to feel or take the pulse of

pulular *intr* to swarm; to bud, to sprout

pulverizar §60 *tr* to pulverize; to atomize; to spray

pulla *f* dig, cutting remark; filthy remark; witticism

pum *interj* bang!

puma *m* cougar

puna *f* (SAm) bleak tableland in the Andes; (SAm) mountain sickness

pundonor *m* point of honor; face

pundonoro·so -sa *adj* punctilious, scrupulous; haughty, dignified

pungir §27 *tr* to prick; to sting

punta *f* (*extremo agudo*) point; tip, end; (*del cigarro*) butt; nail; point, cape, headland; (*del toro*) horn; (*del asta del ciervo*) tine, prong; style, graver; touch, tinge, trace; (*del vino*) souring; (elec) point; **de punta** on end; on tiptoe; **de punta en blanco** in full armor; (coll) in full regalia; **estar de punta (con)** to be at odds (with); **punta de combate** (*del torpedo*) warhead; **punta de lanza** spearhead; **punta de París** wire nail; **sacar punta a** to put a point on, to sharpen; **tener en la punta de la lengua** (coll) to have on the tip of one's tongue

puntada *f* hint; (sew) stitch; (*dolor agudo*) (Am) stitch, sharp pain

puntal *m* prop, support; stay, stanchion; (naut) depth of hold; backing, support; (Am) bite, snack

puntapié *m* kick; **echar a puntapiés** (coll) to kick out

puntear *tr* to dot, mark with dots; (*guitarra*) to pluck; to stipple; to stitch ‖ *intr* (naut) to tack

puntera *f* toe, toe patch; leather tip; (coll) kick

puntería *f* aim, aiming; marksmanship

puntero *m* pointer; (*del reloj*) hand; stonecutter's chisel; punch; (Am) leading animal

puntiagu·do -da *adj* sharp-pointed

puntilla *f* brad; narrow lace edging; (*de la pluma fuente*) point; (carp) tracing point; dagger; **de puntillas** on tiptoe; **puntilla francesa** finishing nail

puntillero *m* bullfighter who delivers coup de grace with dagger

puntillo·so -sa *adj* punctilious

punto *m* (*señal de dimensiones poco perceptibles*) point, dot; stitch, loop; mesh; (*rotura en un tejido de punto*) break; jot; cabstand, hackstand; (gram) period; (math, typ, sport, fig)

point; **a buen punto** opportunely; **al punto** at once; **a punto de** on the point of; **a punto fijo** for certain; **de punto** knitted; **dos puntos** (gram) colon; **en punto** sharp, on the dot; **poner punto final a** to wind up, to bring to an end; **punto de admiración** exclamation mark or point; **punto de aguja** knitting; **punto de Hungría** herringbone; **punto de media** knitwork; **punto de mira** aim; center of attraction; **¡punto en boca!** mum's the word!; **punto interrogante** question mark; **punto menos** almost; **puntos y rayas** dots and dashes; **punto y coma** *msg* semicolon

puntuación *f* punctuation; mark, grade; scoring

puntual *adj* punctual; certain, sure; exact, accurate

puntualizar §60 *tr* to fix in the memory; to give a detailed account of; to finish; to draw up

puntuar §21 *tr* & *intr* to punctuate; to score

puntura *f* puncture, prick

punzada *f* prick; shooting pain; (*del remordimiento*) pang

punzante *adj* sharp, pricking; barbed, biting, caustic

punzar §60 *tr* to prick, puncture, punch; to sting; to grieve ‖ *intr* to sting

punzón *m* punch; pick; burin, graver; budding horn, tenderling; **punzón de marcar** center punch

puñada *f* punch

puñado *m* handful, bunch

puñal *m* dagger, poniard

puñalada *f* stab; blow, sudden sorrow; **puñalada de misericordia** coup de grâce; **puñalada trapera** stab in the back

puñetazo *m* punch; bang with the fist

puño *m* fist; cuff; wristband; grasp; fistful, handful; hilt; (*p.ej., del paraguas*) handle; (*del bastón*) head; punch; **como un puño** (coll) whopping big; (coll) tiny, microscopic; (coll) close-fisted; **de su propio puño** or **de su puño y letra** in his own hand, in his own writing

pupa *f* pimple; fever blister

pupila *f* (*del ojo*) pupil

pupi·lo -la *mf* boarder; orphan, ward; pupil ‖ *f* see **pupila**

pupitre *m* writing desk

puquio *m* (SAm) spring or pool of fresh, clear water

puré *m* purée; **puré de patatas** mashed potatoes; **puré de tomates** stewed tomatoes

pureza *f* purity

purga *f* purge; purgative; drain valve

purgante *adj* & *m* purgative

purgar §44 *tr* to purge; to physic; to drain; to purify, refine; to expiate; (*pasiones*) to control, to check; (*sospechas*) to clear away ‖ *ref* to take a physic; to unburden oneself

puridad *f* purity

purificar §73 *tr* to purify

pr
pu

purita·no -na *adj* & *mf* puritan; Puritan
pu·ro -ra *adj* pure; sheer; (*cielo*) clear; out-and-out, outright; **de puro** completely, totally; because of being ‖ *m* cigar
púrpura *f* purple
purpura·do -da *adj* purple ‖ *m* (eccl) cardinal
purpúre·o -a *adj* purple

pusilánime *adj* pusillanimous
pústula *f* pustule
puta *f* whore
putañear or **putear** *intr* (coll) to whore around, to chase after lewd women
putati·vo -va *adj* spurious
putrefac·to -ta *adj* rotten, putrid
pútri·do -da *adj* putrid, rotten
puya *f* steel point; (*del gallo*) spur

Q

Q, q (cu) *f* twentieth letter of the Spanish alphabet
q.b.s.m. *abbr* **que besa su mano**
q.b.s.p. *abbr* **que besa sus pies**
q.e.p.d. *abbr* **que en paz descanse**
q.e.s.m. *abbr* **que estrecha su mano**
quántum *m* (*pl* **quanta**) quantum
que *pron rel* that, which; who, whom; **el que** he who; which, the one which; who, the one who ‖ *adv* than ‖ *conj* that; for, because; let, e.g., **que entre** let him come in; **a que** (coll) I'll bet that
qué *adj* & *pron interr* what, which; **¿qué tal?** how?; hello, how's everything? ‖ *interj* what!; what a!; how!
quebrada *f* gorge, ravine, gap; failure, bankruptcy; (Am) brook
quebradi·zo -za *adj* brittle, fragile; frail
quebra·do -da *adj* weakened; bankrupt; ruptured; rough; winding; fractional ‖ *m* (math) fraction; (Am) tobacco leaf full of holes ‖ *f* see **quebrada**
quebrantable *adj* breakable
quebrantar *tr* to break; to break open; to break out of; to grind, crush; to soften, mollify; (*un contrato; la ley; un hábito; un testamento; el corazón de una persona*) to break ‖ *ref* to break; to become broken
quebrantaterro·nes *m* (*pl* **-nes**) (coll) clodhopper
quebranto *m* break, breaking; heavy loss; great sorrow; discouragement
quebrar §2 *tr* to break; to bend, twist; to crush; to overcome; to temper, soften ‖ *intr* to break; to fail; to weaken, give in ‖ *ref* to break; to weaken; to become ruptured
queda *f* curfew
quedar *intr* to remain; to stay; to be left; to be left over; to stop, leave off; to turn out; to be; to be found, be located; **quedar en** to agree on; to agree to; **quedar por** + *inf* or **sin** + *inf* to remain to be + *pp* ‖ *ref* to remain; to stay; to stop; to be; to be left; to put up; **quedarse con** to keep, to take; **quedarse tan fresco** (coll) to show no offense
que·do -da *adj* quiet, still; gentle ‖ *f* see **queda** ‖ **quedo** *adv* softly, in a low voice; gropingly
quehacer *m* work, task, chore
queja *f* complaint, lament; whine, moan

quejar *ref* to complain, lament; to whine, moan
quejido *m* complaint, whine, moan
quejumbre *f* complaining, whine, moan
quejumbro·so -sa *adj* complaining; whining, whiny
quema *f* fire; burning; **a quema ropa** point-blank; **de quema** distilled; **hacer quema** (Arg, Bol) to hit the mark
quemada *f* burnt brush; (Mex) fire
quemadero *m* incinerator; (*poste destinado para quemar a los condenados a la pena de fuego*) stake
quema·do -da *adj* burned; burnt out; (Am) angry ‖ *m* burnt brush; **oler a quemado** (coll) to smell of fire; **saber a quemado** (coll) to taste burned ‖ *f* see **quemada**
quema·dor -dora *adj* burning; incendiary ‖ *m* burner
quemadura *f* burn; (agr) smut
quemar *tr* to burn; to scald; to set on fire; to scorch; to frostbite; to sell too cheap ‖ *intr* to burn, be hot ‖ *ref* to burn; to be burning up; (coll) to fret; (*estar cercano a lo que se busca*) (coll) to be warm, to be hot; **quemarse las cejas** (coll) to burn the midnight oil
quemarropa — a quemarropa point-blank
quemazón *f* burn; burning; intense heat; (*de un fusible*) blowout; (coll) itch; (coll) cutting remark; (coll) pique, anger; (hum) bargain sale; (Arg, Bol, Chile) mirage on the pampas
que·pis *m* (*pl* **-pis**) kepi
querella *f* complaint; dispute, quarrel
querellar *ref* to complain; to whine
querencia *f* liking, affection; attraction; love of home; (*de animales*) haunt; favorite spot
querencio·so -sa *adj* homing; (*sitio*) favorite
querer *m* love, affection; liking, fondness ‖ *v* §55 *tr* to wish, want, desire; to like; to love; **como quiera** anyhow; anyway; **como quiera que** whereas; inasmuch as; no matter how; **cuando quiera** any time; **donde quiera** anywhere; **querer bien** to love; **sin querer** unwillingly; unintentionally ‖ *v aux* to wish to, to want to, to desire to; will; to be about to, to be trying to,

e.g., **quiere llover** it is trying to rain; **querer decir** to mean; **querer más** to prefer to, would rather

queri·do -da adj dear ‖ mf lover; paramour; (coll) dearie ‖ f mistress

quermés f or **quermese** f bazaar; village or country fair

queroseno m var of **keroseno**

querubín m cherub

quesadilla f cheesecake; sweet pastry

quese·ro -ra adj cheesy ‖ mf cheesemonger; cheesemaker ‖ f cheese board; cheese mold; cheese dish

queso m cheese; **queso de cerdo** headcheese; **queso helado** brick ice cream

quevedos mpl nose glasses

quiá interj oh, no!

quicio m pivot hole (of hinge); **fuera de quicio** out of order; **sacar de quicio** to put out of order; to unhinge

quiebra f crack; damage, loss; bankruptcy

quien pron rel who, whom; he who, she who; someone who, anyone who

quién pron interr who, whom

quienquiera pron indef anyone, anybody; **quienquiera que** whoever; **a quienquiera que** whomever

quie·to -ta adj quiet, calm; virtuous

quietud f quiet, calm, stillness

quijada f jaw, jawbone

quijotes·co -ca adj quixotic

quilate m carat

quilo m kilogram; **sudar el quilo** (coll) to slave, to be a drudge

quilla f keel; (de ave) breastbone; **dar de quilla** (naut) to keel over

quimera f chimera; dispute, quarrel

química f chemistry

quími·co -ca adj chemical ‖ mf chemist ‖ f see **química**

quimicultura f tank farming

quimono m kimono

quimoterapia f chemotherapy

quina f cinchona, Peruvian bark

quincalla f hardware

quincallería f hardware store; hardware business; hardware factory

quincalle·ro -ra mf hardware merchant

quince adj & pron fifteen ‖ m fifteen; (en las fechas) fifteenth

quincea·vo -va adj & m fifteenth

quince·no -na adj & m fifteenth ‖ f fortnight; two weeks; two weeks' pay

quincuagési·mo -ma adj & m fiftieth

quiniela f pelota game of five; soccer lottery; daily double; (Arg, Urug) numbers game

quinien·tos -tas adj & pron five hundred ‖ **quinientos** m five hundred

quinina f quinine

quinqué m student lamp, oil lamp

quinquenal adj five-year

quinta f villa, country house; draft, induction; **ir a quintas** to be drafted; **redimirse de las quintas** to be exempted from the draft

quintal m quintal, hundredweight

quintar tr to draft

quinteto m quintet

quintilla f five-line stanza of eight syllables and two rhymes; any five-line stanza with two rhymes

quintilli·zo -za mf quint, quintuplet

Quintín — armar la de San Quintín to raise a rumpus, raise a row

quin·to -ta adj fifth ‖ m fifth; lot; pasture; draftee ‖ f see **quinta**

quinza·vo -va adj & m fifteenth

quiosco m kiosk, summerhouse; stand; **quiosco de música** bandstand; **quiosco de necesidad** comfort station; **quiosco de periódicos** newsstand

quiquiri·quí m (pl **-quíes**) cock-a-doodle-doo; (coll) cock of the walk

quirófano m operating room

quiromancia or **quiromancía** f palmistry

quiropodista mf chiropodist

quiroprácti·co -ca adj chiropractic ‖ mf chiropractor

quirúrgi·co -ca adj surgical

quirurgo m surgeon

quiscal m grackle

quisicosa f puzzler

quisqui·do -da adj (Arg) constipated

quisquilla f trifle, triviality; **pararse en quisquillas** to bicker, to make a fuss over trifles; **quisquillas** hairsplitting, quibbling

quisquillo·so -sa adj trifling; touchy; fastidious; hairsplitting

quiste m cyst

quis·to -ta adj — **bien quisto** well-liked, welcome; **mal quisto** disliked, unwelcome

quitaesmalte m nail-polish remover

quitaman·chas (pl **-chas**) mf (persona) clothes cleaner, spot remover ‖ m (substancia) clothes cleaner, spot remover

quitamo·tas mf (pl **-tas**) (coll) bootlicker, apple polisher

quitanie·ve m or **quitanie·ves** m (pl **-ves**) snowplow

quitapie·dras m (pl **-dras**) cowcatcher

quitapintura m paint remover

quitapón m pompon for draft mules; **de quitapón** detachable, removable

quitar tr to remove; to take away; (la mesa) to clear; (esfuerzo, trabajo) to save; (tiempo) to take; to free; to parry; **quitar algo a algo** to take something off something, to remove something from something; **quitar algo a uno** to remove something from someone; to take something away from someone ‖ intr — **de quita y pon** detachable, removable ‖ ref (el sombrero, una prenda de vestir) to take off; (el sombrero en señal de cortesía) to tip; (una mancha) to come out, to come off; (un vicio) to give up; to withdraw

quitasol m parasol

quite m removal; hindrance; dodge; (en la esgrima) parry; (taur) passes made with the cape to draw the bull away from the man in danger

quizá or **quizás** adv maybe, perhaps

quó·rum m (pl **-rum**) quorum

pu
qu

R

R, r (ere) *f* twenty-first letter of the Spanish alphabet

R. *abbr* **respuesta, Reverencia, Reverendo**

rabada *f* hind quarter, rump

rabadilla *f* base of the spine

rábano *m* radish; **rábano picante** or **rusticano** horseradish; **tomar el rábano por las hojas** (coll) to be on the wrong track

ra·bí *m* (*pl* **-bíes**) rabbi

rabia *f* anger, rage; (*hidrofobia*) rabies; **tener rabia a** (coll) to have a grudge against

rabiar *intr* to rage, to rave; to get mad; to go mad, to have rabies; **que rabia** like the deuce; **rabiar por** to be dying for; to be dying to

rabieta *f* (coll) tantrum

rabillo *m* leafstalk; flower stalk; (*en los cereales*) mildew spot; (*del ojo*) corner

rabio·so -sa *adj* mad, rabid

rabo *m* tail; (*del ojo*) corner; (fig) tail, train; **rabo verde** (CAm) old rake

ra·bón -bona *adj* bobtail; (Chile) bare, naked; (Mex) mean, wretched || *f* (Am) camp follower; **hacer rabona** (coll) to play hooky

rabotada *f* swish of the tail; (coll) coarse remark

rabu·do -da *adj* long-tailed

racial *adj* racial

racimar *ref* to cluster, to gather together

racimo *m* bunch; cluster; (*de perlas*) string

raciocinio *m* reasoning

ración *f* ration; allowance; **ración de hambre** starvation wages

racional *adj* rational

racionar *tr* to ration

racha *f* split, crack; chip; squall, gust of wind; streak of luck

rada *f* (naut) road, roadstead

radar *m* radar

radiación *f* radiation

radiacti·vo -va *adj* radioactive

radia·dor -dora *adj* radiating || *m* radiator

radiante *adj* radiant; (*alegre, sonriente*) radiant

radiar *tr* to radiate; to radio; to broadcast; to cross out, erase || *intr* to radiate

radicación *f* taking root; (math) evolution

radical *adj* & *m* radical

radicar §73 *intr* to take root; to be located || *ref* to take root; to settle; (*un negocio*) to be based

radio *m* edge, outskirts; (*de una rueda*) spoke, rung; (*de acción*) radius; (chem) radium; (math) radius || *m* & *f* radio

radioafïciona·do -da *mf* radio amateur, radio fan

radiodifundir *tr* & *intr* to broadcast

radiodifusión *f* broadcasting

radioemisora *f* broadcasting station

radioescucha *mf* radio listener; radio monitor

radiofrecuencia *f* radio frequency

radiografiar §77 *tr* to X-ray; to radio, to wireless

radiograma *m* X ray (*photograph*)

radioperturbación *f* jamming

radioyente *mf* radio listener

raer §56 *tr* to scrape, scrape off; to smooth, to level; to wipe || *ref* to become frayed, to wear away

ráfaga *f* gust, puff; gust of wind; flash of light; (*de ametralladora*) burst

raí·do -da *adj* threadbare; barefaced

ra·íz *f* (*pl* **-íces**) root; **a raíz de** close to the root of; even with; right after, hard upon; **de raíz** by the root; completely; **echar raíces** to take root

raja *f* crack, split; splinter, chip; slice

rajar *tr* to crack, to split; to splinter, chip; to slice || *intr* (coll) to boast; (coll) to chatter || *ref* to crack, to split; to splinter, chip; (Mex, CAm, W-I) to back down, to break one's promise

rajatabla — a rajatabla (coll) desperately, ruthlessly

ralea *f* kind, quality; breed, ilk

ralear *intr* to thin out; to be true to form

ra·lo -la *adj* sparse, thin

rallador *m* grater

rallar *tr* to grate; (coll) to grate on, annoy

rallo *m* grater; scraper; rasp; (*de la regadera*) spout, nozzle; unglazed porous jug (*for cooling water by evaporation*)

rama *f* branch, bough; **andarse por las ramas** (coll) to beat about the bush; **en rama** raw; unbound, in sheets; in the grain

ramaje *m* branches, foliage

ramal *m* (*de una cuerda*) strand; halter; branch; (rr) branch line

ramalazo *m* lash; (*señal en el cutis por un golpe o enfermedad*) spot, pock; sharp pain; blow, sudden sorrow

rambla *f* dry ravine; avenue, boulevard

ramera *f* whore, harlot

ramificar §73 *tr* & *ref* to ramify

ramillete *m* bouquet; centerpiece, epergne; (bot) cluster

ramo *m* branch, limb; bouquet, cluster; (*de géneros, negocios, etc.*) line; (*p.ej.,* *de una ciencia*) branch; (*de una enfermedad*) touch, slight attack

ramojo *m* brushwood, dead wood

ramonear *intr* to trim twigs; to browse

rampa *f* ramp; cramp; (aer) apron; (Bol) litter, stretcher

ram·plón -plona *adj* (*zapato*) heavy, coarse; common, vulgar

ramplonería *f* coarseness, vulgarity

rana *f* frog; **no ser rana** (coll) to be a past master; **rana toro** bullfrog

ran·cio -cia *adj* rank, rancid, stale;

(vino) old; old, ancient; old, old-fashioned

ranchar *ref* (Col, Ven) to balk

ranchear *tr* (Am) to sack, pillage ‖ *intr & ref* to build huts, form a settlement

ranchero *m* messman; (Am) rancher, ranchman

rancho *m* mess; meeting, gathering; camp; thatched hut; (naut) stock of provisions; (Am) ranch; (Arg) straw hat; **hacer rancho** (coll) to make room; **hacer rancho aparte** (coll) to be a lone wolf, to go one's own way

randa *m* (coll) pickpocket ‖ *f* lace trimming

rango *m* rank; class, nature; (Am) pomp, splendor; (elevada condición social) (Am) status, standing

ranura *f* groove; slot

rapagón *m* stripling

rapar *tr* to shave; to crop; to scrape; (coll) to snatch, filch ‖ *ref* to shave; (una vida regalada) to lead

ra·paz (*pl* **-paces**) *adj* thievish; rapacious ‖ *m* young boy, lad

rapaza *f* young girl, lass

rapé *m* snuff

rápi·do -da *adj* rapid ‖ *m* (rr) express; **rápidos** (de un río) rapids

raposa *f* fox; female fox; (persona) (coll) fox

raposo *m* male fox; (coll) foxy fellow; (coll) slipshod fellow

raptar *tr* to abduct; to kidnap

rapto *m* abduction; kidnaping; rapture; faint, swoon

raque *m* beachcombing; **andar al raque** to go beachcombing

raquear *intr* to beachcomb

raquero *m* pirate; beachcomber

raqueta *f* racket; battledore; badminton; snowshoe; **raqueta y volante** battledore and shuttlecock

raquíti·co -ca *adj* (que padece raquitis) rickety; flimsy, weak, miserable

raquitis *f* rickets

raramente *adv* rarely, seldom; oddly

rareza *f* rareness; rarity; oddness, strangeness; peculiarity

ra·ro -ra *adj* rare; odd, strange; thin, sparse

ras *m* evenness; **a ras** close, even, flush; **a ras de** even with, flush with; **ras con ras** flush, at the same level; grazing

rasar *tr* to graze, to skim ‖ *ref* to clear up

rascacie·los *m* (*pl* **-los**) skyscraper

rascamoño *m* fancy hairpin; (bot) zinnia

rascar §73 *tr* to scrape; to scuff; to scratch; to scrape clean ‖ *ref* (una cicatriz, un grano) to pick; (Am) to get drunk

rasete *m* satinet

rasga·do -da *adj* (boca; ventana) wide-open; (ojos) large; (Am) outspoken; (Col) generous ‖ *m* tear, rip, rent

rasgar §44 *tr* to tear, to rip ‖ *ref* to become torn

rasgo *m* (de una pluma de escribir) flourish, stroke; trait, characteristic;

feat, deed; flash of wit, bright remark; **a grandes rasgos** in bold strokes; **rasgos** (de la cara) features

rasguear *tr* to thrum on ‖ *intr* to make a flourish

rasgón *m* tear, rip, rent

rasguñar *tr* to scratch; to sketch, outline

rasguño *m* scratch; sketch, outline

ra·so -sa *adj* smooth, flat, level, even; common, plain; clear, cloudless; (coll) brazen, shameless ‖ *m* flat country; satin; **al raso** in the open

raspa *f* stalk, stem; (de mazorca de maíz) beard; (de pez) spine, backbone; shell, rind

raspadura *f* scraping; erasure; (Am) pan sugar

raspar *tr* to scrape, scrape off; to scratch, scratch out; to graze; (el vino) to bite; to take, to steal; (W-I) to dismiss, fire; (W-I) to scold ‖ *intr* (Ven) to go away; (Ven) to die

raspear *tr* (SAm) to scold ‖ *intr* (una pluma) to scratch

rastra *f* rake; harrow; drag; track, trail; (p.ej., de cebollas) string; (naut) drag; **pescar a la rastra** to trawl

rastracuero *m* (Am) show-off; (Am) upstart; (Am) sharper, adventurer

rastreador *m* dredge; (nav) mine sweeper

rastrear *tr* to trail, track, trace; to drag; to dredge; to check into ‖ *intr* to rake; to skim the ground, fly low

rastre·ro -ra *adj* dragging, trailing; creeping; low-flying; groveling, cringing; low, vile

rastrillar *tr* to rake; (cáñamo, lino) to hatchel, to comb; (Arg, Col) to shoot, to fire; (un fósforo) (Arg, Col) to strike (a match)

rastrillo *m* rake; hackle, hatchel, flax comb; (de cerradura o llave) ward; grating, iron grate; (rr) cowcatcher

rastro *m* rake; harrow; track, trail; scent; trace, vestige; slaughterhouse; wholesale meat market; rag fair; **rastro de condensación** (aer) contrail

rastrojo *m* stubble

rasura *f* shaving; scraping

rasurar *tr & ref* to shave

rata *f* rat; female rat; **rata del trigo** hamster

ratear *tr* to apportion; to snitch

ratería *f* baseness, meanness, vileness; petty thievery; petty theft

rate·ro -ra *adj* thievish; trailing, dragging; base, vile ‖ *mf* sneak thief

ratificar §73 *tr* to ratify

rato *m* time, while, little while; **a ratos** from time to time; **a ratos perdidos** in spare time, in one's leisure hours; **buen rato** pleasant time; (coll) large amount; **pasar el rato** (coll) to waste one's time; **un rato** awhile

ratón *m* mouse; (Ven) hangover; **ratón de biblioteca** (coll) bookworm

ratonera *f* (trampa) mousetrap; (agujero) mousehole; nest of mice; (Am) hut, shop

raudal *m* stream, torrent; abundance

·do -da *adj* rapid, swift, impetuous

raya *f* stripe; (*línea fina; pez*) ray; (*en la imprenta, la escritura y la telegrafía*) dash; (*de los pantalones*) crease; (*en los cabellos*) part; boundary line, limit; (*para impedir la comunicación del incendio en los campos*) firebreak; (*del espectro*) (phys) line; (Mex) pay, wages; **a rayas** striped; **hacerse la raya** to part one's hair; **pasar de la raya** to go too far; **tener a raya** to keep within bounds

raya·no -na *adj* bordering; borderline

rayar *tr* (*papel*) to rule, to line; to stripe; to scratch, score, mark; to cross out; to underscore ‖ *intr* to border; to stand out; (*el alba, el día, la luz, el sol*) to begin, arise, come forth; **rayar en** to verge on, to border on ‖ *ref* (Col) to get rich

rayo *m* (*de luz*) ray; (*de rueda*) spoke; lightning, flash of lightning, stroke of lightning, thunderbolt; (*persona*) (fig) live wire; **echar rayos** (coll) to blow up, hit the ceiling; **rayo mortífero** death ray; **rayos X** X rays

rayón *m* rayon

raza *f* race; breed, stock; crack, slit; quality; ray of light (*coming through a crack*)

razón *f* reason; right, justice; account, story; (*cantidad o grado medidos por otra cosa tomada como unidad*) rate; (math) ratio; **a razón de** at the rate of; **con razón o sin ella** right or wrong; **hacer la razón** to return a toast; to join at table; **meterse en razón** to listen to reason; **no tener razón** to be wrong; **razón social** firm name, trade name; **tener razón** to be right; to be in the right

razonable *adj* reasonable

razonar *tr* to reason, reason out; to itemize ‖ *intr* to reason

reabrir §83 *tr & ref* to reopen

reacción *f* reaction; **reacción en cadena** chain reaction

reaccionar *intr* to react

reacciona·rio -ria *adj & mf* reactionary

rea·cio -cia *adj* stubborn, obstinate

reactivo *m* reagent

real *adj* real; royal; fine, splendid ‖ *m* army camp; fairground; real (*old Spanish coin; Spanish money of account equal to a quarter of a peseta*)

realce *m* embossment, raised work; enhancement, lustre; emphasis; **bordar de realce** to embroider in relief; (fig) to embroider, to exaggerate

realeza *f* royalty

realidad *f* reality; truth; **hecho realidad** come true, e.g., **un sueño hecho realidad** a dream come true

realismo *m* realism

realista *mf* (*persona que tiende a ver las cosas como son*) realist; (*partidario de la monarquía*) royalist

realización *f* realization, fulfillment; achievement; sale; **realización de beneficios** profit taking

realizar §60 *tr* to fulfill; to carry out; to turn into cash ‖ *ref* to become fulfilled; to be carried out

realquilar *tr* to sublet

realzar §60 *tr* to raise, elevate; to emboss; to enhance, set off; to emphasize

reanimar *tr* to revive, restore; to cheer, encourage ‖ *ref* to revive, recover one's spirits

reanudar *tr* to renew, to resume

reaparecer §22 *intr* to reappear

reata *f* rope to keep animals in single file; single file; **de reata** in single file; (coll) in blind submission; (coll) next, following

rebaba *f* burr, fin

rebaja *f* rebate; diminution

rebajar *tr* to lower; to diminish, reduce; to rebate; (*precios*) to mark down; (*a una persona*) to deflate; (carp) to rabbet ‖ *ref* to stoop; to humble oneself

rebajo *m* rabbet, groove; offset, recess

rebalsar *tr* to dam ‖ *ref* to become dammed up; to be checked; to pile up, accumulate

rebanada *f* slice

rebanar *tr* to slice; to cut through

rebañadera *f* grapnel

rebaño *m* flock

rebarbati·vo -va *adj* crabbed, surly

rebasar *tr* to exceed; to overflow; to sail past

rebatiña *f* grabbing, scramble; **andar a la rebatiña** (coll) to scramble

rebatir *tr* to repel, drive back; to check; to resist; to strengthen; to rebut, refute; to deduct, rebate; to beat hard

rebato *m* alarm, call to arms; alarm, excitement; (mil) surprise attack

rebeca *f* cardigan

rebelar *ref* to revolt, rebel; to resist; to break away

rebelde *adj* rebellious; stubborn ‖ *mf* rebel

rebeldía *f* rebelliousness; defiance, stubbornness

rebelión *f* rebellion, revolt

rebe·lón -lona *adj* balky, restive

reborde *m* flange, rim, collar

rebosar *tr* to cause to overflow ‖ *intr* to overflow, run over; to be in abundance; **rebosar de** or **en** to overflow with, to burst with; to be rich in; to have an abundance of ‖ *ref* to overflow, run over

rebotar *tr* to bend back; to repel; (coll) to annoy, worry ‖ *intr* to bounce; to bounce back, rebound ‖ *ref* (coll) to become annoyed, become worried

rebote *m* bounce; rebound

rebozar §60 *tr* (*la cara*) to muffle up; to cover with batter ‖ *ref* to muffle up, to muffle oneself up

rebozo *m* muffling; muffler; shawl; **de rebozo** secretly; **sin rebozo** frankly, openly

rebulta·do -da *adj* bulky, massive

rebullicio *m* hubbub, loud uproar

rebullir §13 *intr* to stir, begin to move; to give signs of life ‖ *ref* to stir, begin to move

rebusca *f* seeking, searching; gleaning; leavings, refuse

rebusca·do -da *adj* affected, unnatural, recherché

rebuscar §73 *tr* to seek after; to search into; to glean

rebuznar *intr* to bray; (coll) to talk nonsense

rebuzno *m* braying; (coll) nonsense

recade·ro -ra *mf* messenger ‖ *m* errand boy

recado *m* errand; message; gift, present; daily marketing; compliments, regards; safety, security; equipment, outfit; **mandar recado** to send word; **recado de escribir** writing materials

recaer §15 *intr* to fall again; to fall back; to relapse; **recaer en** to fall to; **recaer sobre** to fall upon, devolve upon

recaída *f* relapse; backsliding

recalar *tr* to soak, saturate ‖ *intr* to sight land

recalcar §73 *tr* to press, squeeze; to cram, pack, stuff; (*sus palabras*) to stress ‖ *intr* (naut) to list, to heel; **recalcar en** to lay stress on ‖ *ref* (coll) to harp on the same string; (coll) to sprawl; (*p.ej., la muñeca*) (coll) to sprain

recalentar §2 *tr* to overheat; (*la comida*) to warm over

recalmón *m* (naut) lull

recamado *m* embroidery

recamar *tr* to embroider

recámara *f* dressing room; (*de un arma de fuego*) breech, chamber; (coll) reserve, caution; (Mex) bedroom

recamarera *f* (Mex) chambermaid

recambio *m* spare part; (*parte, rueda, etc.*) **de recambio** spare

recapacitar *tr* to run over in one's mind ‖ *intr* to refresh one's memory; to reflect

recargar §44 *tr* to reload; to overload; to recharge; to overcharge; to overadorn; (*una cuota de impuesto*) to increase; (elec) to recharge ‖ *ref* to become more feverish

recargo *m* new burden; extra charge; new charge; (*que paga el contribuyente moroso*) penalty; (pathol) rise in temperature; **recargo de tarifa** extra fare

recata·do -da *adj* cautious, circumspect; modest; shy

recatar *tr* to hide, conceal ‖ *ref* to hide; to be afraid to take a stand

recato *m* caution, reserve; modesty

recauchutaje *m* recapping, retreading

recauchutar *tr* to recap, to retread

recaudar *tr* (*impuestos, tributos*) to gather, collect; to guard, watch over

recaudo *m* tax collecting; care, precaution; bail, surety; **a buen recaudo** under guard, in safety

recelar *tr* to fear, distrust ‖ *intr & ref* to fear, be afraid

recelo *m* fear, distrust

recelo·so -sa *adj* fearful, distrustful

recensión *f* review, book review

recepción *f* reception; reception desk

recepcionista *m* room clerk ‖ *f* receptionist

receptáculo *m* receptacle; shelter; refuge

receptar *tr* to receive, welcome; (*delincuentes*) to hide, conceal; (*cosas robadas*) to receive

recepti·vo -va *adj* receptive; susceptible

receptor *m* receiver; **receptor de cabeza** headpiece; **receptor telefónico** receiver

receta *f* recipe; (pharm) prescription

recetar *tr* (*un medicamento*) to prescribe; (coll) to request

recibí *m* receipt; received payment

recibi·dor -dora *mf* receiver; receiving teller; ticket collector ‖ *m* reception room

recibimiento *m* reception; welcome; reception room; (*visita en que una persona recibe a sus amistades*) at-home

recibir *tr* to receive; (*visitas*) to entertain ‖ *intr* to receive; to entertain ‖ *ref* to be received, be admitted; **recibirse de** to be admitted to practice as; to be graduated as

recibo *m* reception; receipt; hall; parlor; at-home; **acusar recibo de** to acknowledge receipt of; **estar de recibo** to be at home; **ser de recibo** to be acceptable

recién *adv* (used before past participles) recently, just, newly, e.g., **recién llegado** newly arrived; (Am) just now, recently

reciente *adv* recently

recinto *m* area, inclosure, place

re·cio -cia *adj* strong; thick, coarse, heavy; harsh; hard, bitter, arduous; (*tiempo*) severe; swift, impetuous ‖ **recio** *adv* strongly; swiftly; hard; loud

reciprocidad *f* reciprocity

recípro·co -ca *adj* reciprocal

recital *m* (*de música o poesía*) recital

recitar *tr* to recite; (*un discurso*) to deliver

reclamación *f* claim, demand; objection; protest, complaint

reclamar *tr* to claim, demand; (*un ave*) to decoy, lure ‖ *intr* to cry out, protest, complain

reclamo *m* bird call; decoy bird; (*para aves*) lure; allurement, attraction; advertisement; blurb, puff; reference; (typ) catchword

reclinar *tr* (*p.ej., la cabeza*) to lean, to bend ‖ *ref* to recline

reclinatorio *m* prie-dieu; couch, lounge

recluir §20 *tr* to seclude, shut in; to imprison ‖ *ref* to go into seclusion

reclusión *f* seclusion; imprisonment

reclu·so -sa *adj* secluded; imprisoned ‖ *mf* prisoner; inmate

recluta *m* recruit ‖ *f* recruiting; (*del ganado disperso*) (Arg) roundup

reclutar *tr* to recruit; (Arg) to round up

recobrar *tr* to recover ‖ *ref* to recover; to come to

recobro *m* recovery; (*de un motor*) pickup

recodar *intr* to lean; to bend, twist, turn, wind

recodo *m* bend, twist, turn

recoger §17 *tr* to pick up; to gather,

collect; to harvest; to shorten, draw in; to keep; to welcome; to lock up || *ref* to take shelter, take refuge; to withdraw; *(echarse en la cama)* to retire; to go home; to cut down expenses

recogida *f* collection; withdrawal; suspension

recogimiento *m* gathering, collecting; harvesting; seclusion, retreat; concentration; self-communion

recolectar *tr* to gather, gather in; *(el algodón)* to pick

recombinado *adj (genética)* recombinant

recomendable *adj* commendable

recomendar §2 *tr* to recommend; to commend

recompensa *f* recompense, reward

recompensar *tr* to recompense, reward

recomprar *tr* to buy back, to repurchase

reconcentrar *tr* to bring together; *(un sentimiento o afecto)* to conceal, disguise || *ref* to come together; to be absorbed in thought

reconciliar *tr* to reconcile || *ref* to become reconciled

recóndi·to -ta *adj* hidden, concealed

reconfortar *tr* to comfort, to cheer

reconocer §22 *tr* to recognize; to admit, to acknowledge; to examine; (mil) to reconnoiter || *intr* (mil) to reconnoiter || *ref* to be clear

reconoci·do -da *adj* grateful

reconocimiento *m* recognition; admission, acknowledgment; gratitude; reconnaissance; **reconocimiento médico** inquest

reconsiderar *tr* to reconsider

reconstruir §20 *tr* to reconstruct, to rebuild, to recast

recontar §61 *tr (volver a contar; narrar)* to recount *(to count again; to narrate)*

reconvenir §79 *tr* to expostulate with, to remonstrate with

reconversión *f* reconversion

recopilar *tr* to compile

re·cord *m (pl* **-cords)** (sport) record; **batir un record** to break a record; **establecer un record** to make a record

recordar §61 *tr* to remember; to remind || *intr* to remember; to get awake; to come to; **si mal no recuerdo** (coll) if I remember correctly

recordati·vo -va *adj* reminding, reminiscent || *m* reminder

recordatorio *m* reminder; memento

record·man *(pl* **-men)** record holder

recorrer *tr* to go over, to go through; to look over, look through; *(un libro)* to run through; to overhaul

recorrido *m* trip, run, route; *(del émbolo)* stroke; repair

recortado *m* cutout

recortar *tr* to trim, to cut off; *(figuras en una tela, en un papel)* to cut out; to outline || *ref* to stand out

recorte *m* cutting; *(de un periódico)* clipping; dodge, duck; **recortes** cuttings, trimmings

recostar §61 *tr* to lean || *ref* to lean, lean back, sit back

recova *f* poultry business; poultry stand; (Arg) portico; (SAm) food market

recoveco *m* bend, turn, twist; subterfuge, trick

recreación *f* recreation

recreo *m* recreation; place of amusement

recrudecer §22 *intr & ref* to flare up, get worse

rectángu·lo -la *adj* right-angled || *m* rectangle

rectificar §73 *tr* to rectify; *(un cilindro de motor)* to rebore

rec·to -ta *adj* straight; *(ángulo)* right; right, just, righteous || *m* rectum

rec·tor -tora *adj* governing, managing || *mf* principal, superior || *m* rector; *(de una universidad)* rector, president

recua *f* drove; *(de personas o cosas)* (coll) string, line

recuadro *m* panel, square; *(sección de un impreso encerrada dentro de un marco)* box

recubrir §83 *tr* to cover, cap, coat

recuento *m* count; recount; inventory

recuerdo *m* memory, remembrance; keepsake, souvenir

recuero *m* muleteer

recular *intr* to back up; *(un arma de fuego)* to recoil; (coll) to back down

reculón *m* (Am) backing; **a reculones** (coll) backing away, recoiling

recuperar *tr & ref* to recuperate, to recover

recurrir *intr* to resort, have recourse; to revert

recurso *m* recourse; resource; resort; appeal, petition

recusar *tr* to refuse, reject; (law) to challenge

rechazar §60 *tr* to refuse, to reject; to repel, drive back

rechazo *m* rejection; rebound, recoil

rechifla *f* catcall

rechiflar *tr & intr* to catcall, to hiss || *ref* to make fun

rechinar *intr* to creak, grate, squeak; to act with bad grace

rechon·cho -cha *adj* (coll) chubby, tubby, plump

rechupete — de rechupete (coll) fine, wonderful

red *f* net; netting; network, system; baggage netting; (fig) net, snare, trap; **a red barredera** with a clean sweep; **red barredera** dragnet

redacción *f* writing; editing; editorial staff; newspaper office, city room

redactar *tr* to write up; to edit

redac·tor -tora *mf* writer; editor, newspaper editor; **redactor publicitario** copy writer

redada *f (de peces)* catch, netful; *(p.ej., de criminales)* (coll) haul, roundup

redecilla *f* hair net

rededor *m* surroundings; **al rededor (de)** around

redención *f* redemption; help, recourse

reden·tor -tora *mf* redeemer

redición *f* constant repetition

redi·cho -cha *adj* (coll) overprecise

redil *m* sheepfold

redimir *tr* to redeem; to ransom; to buy back

rédito *m* income, revenue, yield

redituar §21 *tr* to yield, produce

redobla·do -da *adj* stocky, heavy-built; heavy, strong; (mil) double-quick

redoblar *tr* to double; to clinch; to repeat ‖ *intr* (*un tambor*) to roll

redoble *m* doubling; clinching; repeating; roll of a drum

redoma *f* phial, flask

redoma·do -da *adj* sly, crafty

redonda *f* district, neighborhood; (mus) semibreve; **a la redonda** around, roundabout

redondear *tr* to round, make round; to round off; to round out ‖ *ref* to be well-off; to be out of debt

redondel *m* circle; round cloak; (*espacio destinado a la lidia*) (taur) ring

redondilla *f* eight-syllable quatrain with rhyme abba or abab

redon·do -da *adj* round; straightforward; (*terreno*) pasture; (Am) honest; (Am) stupid ‖ *m* ring, circle; (coll) cash ‖ *f* see **redonda**

redopelo *m* (coll) row, scuffle; **al redopelo** against the grain, the wrong way; (coll) roughly, violently

reducir §19 *tr & ref* to reduce; **reducirse a** to come to, to amount to; to be obliged to

reducto *m* (fort) redoubt

redundante *adj* redundant

redundar *intr* to redound; to overflow; **redundar en** to redound to

reelección *f* reëlection

reembarcar §73 *tr, intr & ref* to reship, to reëmbark

reembarco *m* reshipment (*of persons*), reëmbarkation

reembarque *m* reshipment (*of goods*)

reembolsar *tr* to reimburse; to refund ‖ *ref* to collect a debt, to be reimbursed

reembolso *m* reimbursement; refund; **contra reembolso** collect on delivery; cash on delivery

reemplazar §60 *tr* to replace

reemplazo *m* replacement; (mil) replacements; (*hombre que sirve en lugar de otro*) (mil) replacement

reencuadernar *tr* (bb) to rebind

reencuentro *m* collision; (*de tropas*) clash

reenganchar *tr & ref* to reënlist

reentrada *f* reëntry

reestrenar *tr* (theat) to revive

reestreno *m* (theat) revival

reexamen *m* or **reexaminación** *f* reëxamination

reexpedición *f* forwarding, reshipment

reexpedir §50 *tr* to forward, reship

refacción *f* refreshment; allowance; repair, repairs; (coll) extra, bonus; (Am) spare part

refajo *m* underskirt, slip

referencia *f* reference; account, report

referi·do -da *adj* above-mentioned

referir §68 *tr* to refer; to tell, report ‖ *ref* to refer

refinamiento *m* refinement

refinar *tr* to refine; to polish, perfect

refinería *f* refinery

reflejar *tr* to reflect; to reflect on; to show, reveal ‖ *intr* to reflect

reflejo *m* glare; reflection; reflex; **reflejo patelar** or **rotuliano** knee jerk

reflexión *f* reflection

reflexionar *tr* to reflect on or upon ‖ *intr* to reflect

reflujo *m* ebb

refocilar *tr* to cheer; to strengthen ‖ *intr* (Arg, Urug) to lighten ‖ *ref* to be cheered; to take it easy

reforma *f* reform; reformation; alteration, renovation ‖ **la Reforma** the Reformation

reformación *f* reformation

reformar *tr* to reform; to mend, repair; to alter, renovate; to revise; to reorganize ‖ *ref* to reform; to hold oneself in check

reforzar §35 *tr* to reinforce; to strengthen; to encourage

refracción *f* refraction

refracta·rio -ria *adj* rebellious, unruly, stubborn

refrán *m* proverb, saying

refregar §66 *tr* to rub; (coll) to upbraid

refrenar *tr* to curb, to rein; to check, restrain

refrendar *tr* to countersign; to authenticate; to visé; (coll) to repeat

refrescar §73 *tr* to refresh; to cool, to refrigerate ‖ *intr & ref* to refresh; to refresh oneself; to cool off; to go out for fresh air; (*el viento*) (naut) to blow up

refresco *m* refreshment; cold drink, soft drink

refriega *f* fray, scuffle

refrigerador *m* refrigerator; ice bucket

refrigerio *m* coolness; relief; pick-me-up, light lunch

refuerzo *m* reinforcement

refugia·do -da *mf* refugee

refugiar *tr* to shelter ‖ *ref* to take refuge

refugio *m* refuge; hospice; shelter; haunt; (*para peatones en medio de la calle*) safety zone; **refugio antiaéreo** air-raid shelter; **refugio antiatómico** fallout shelter

refundición *f* recast; revision; (*de una pieza dramática*) adaptation

refundir *tr* to recast; to revise; (*una pieza dramática*) to adapt ‖ *intr* to redound

refunfuñar *intr* to grumble, to growl

refutar *tr* to refute

regadera *f* watering can; street sprinkler

regadí·o -a or **regadi·zo -za** *adj* irrigable ‖ *m* irrigated land

regala *f* gunwale

regala·do -da *adj* dainty, delicate; pleasing, pleasant; (*vida*) of ease

regalar *tr* to give; to regale, entertain; to treat; to caress, fondle; to indulge

regalía *f* privilege, perquisite; bonus; (Arg, Chile) muff; (Am) royalty

regaliz *m* licorice

regalo *m* gift, present; treat; joy, pleasure; **regalos de fiesta** favors

rega·lón -lona *adj* (coll) comfort-loving, pampered; (*vida*) (coll) soft, easy

regañar *tr* (coll) to scold ‖ *intr* to

growl, snarl; to grumble; to quarrel; (coll) to scold

regaño m (coll) scolding; growl, snarl; grumble

regar §66 tr to water, sprinkle; to irrigate; to spread, sprinkle, strew

regate m dodge, duck; (fig) dodge, subterfuge

regatear tr to haggle over; to sell at retail; (coll) to avoid, to shun || intr to haggle, to bargain; (naut) to race; (coll) to duck, to dodge

regazo m lap

regenerar tr & ref to regenerate

regente m director, manager; registered pharmacist; (typ) foreman

regicida mf regicide

regicidio m regicide

regi·dor -dora adj ruling, governing || m alderman, councilman

régimen m (pl **regímenes**) regime; diet; rate; management; (gram) government; **régimen de hambre** starvation diet; **régimen de justicia** rule of law

regimental adj regimental

regimentar §2 tr to regiment

regimiento m regiment; rule, government; city council

re·gio -gia adj regal, royal; magnificent

región f region

regir §57 tr to rule, govern; to control, manage; to guide, steer; (gram) to govern || intr to prevail, to be in force

registra·dor -dora adj registering; recording || m registrar, recorder; inspector || f cash register

registrar tr to register; to record; to examine, inspect || ref to register; to be recorded; to take place

registro m registration, registry; recording; examination, inspection; entry, record; bookmark; manhole; (de chimenea) damper; (de reloj) regulator; (de órgano) (mus) stop; (de piano) (mus) pedal

regla f rule; (para trazar líneas) ruler; measure, moderation; order; menstruation; **regla de cálculo** slide rule; **reglas** monthlies, menses

reglamenta·rio -ria adj prescribed, statutory

reglamento m rules, regulations

reglar tr to regulate; (papel) to rule || ref to guide oneself, be guided

regleta f (typ) lead

regletear tr (typ) to lead, to space

regocijar tr to cheer, delight || ref to rejoice

regocijo m cheer, delight, rejoicing

regoldar §3 intr to belch

regolfar intr & ref to surge back, flow back, back up

regorde·te -ta adj dumpy, plump

regresar intr to return

regreso m return; **estar de regreso** to be back

regüeldo m belch, belching

reguero m drip, trickle; (señal que deja una cosa que se va vertiendo) track; irrigating ditch; **ser un reguero de pólvora** to spread like wildfire

regulador m regulator; (de locomotora) throttle; (mach) governor

regular adj regular; fair, moderate, medium; **por lo regular** as a rule || tr to regulate; to put in order; to throttle

rehacer §39 tr to remake, make over, do over; to mend, repair, renovate || ref to recover, to rally

rehén m hostage; **llevarse en rehenes** to carry off as a hostage

rehilandera f pinwheel

rehilar intr to quiver; to whiz by

rehilete m shuttlecock; (que se lanza por diversión) dart; dig, cutting remark; (taur) banderilla

rehuir §20 tr to avoid, shun; to shrink from; to refuse; to dislike || intr & ref to flee

rehusar tr to refuse, turn down

reimpresión f reprint

reimprimir §83 tr to reprint

reina f queen; **reina Margarita** aster, China aster; **reina viuda** queen dowager

reinado m reign

reinar intr to reign; to prevail

reincidir intr to backslide; to repeat an offense

reingreso m reëntry

reino m kingdom; **Reino Unido** United Kingdom

reinstalar tr to reinstate, reinstall

reintegrar tr to refund, pay back

reintegro m refund, payment

reír §58 tr to laugh at || intr & ref to laugh; **reír de** or **reírse de** to laugh at

reja f grate, grating, grille; plowshare, colter; **entre rejas** behind bars

rejilla f screen; grating; lattice, latticework; cane, cane upholstery; foot brasier; fire grate; (electron) grid; (de acumulador) (elec) grid; (rr) baggage rack

rejón m spear; dagger; (taur) lance

rejonear tr (el jinete al toro) (taur) to jab with a lance made to break off in the bull's neck

rejuvenecimiento m rejuvenation

relación f relation; account; list; (en un drama) speech; **relación de ciego** blind man's ballad; **relaciones** betrothal, engagement

relacionar tr to relate || ref to be related

relai m or **relais** m (elec) relay

relajación f or **relajamiento** m relaxation; slackening; laxity; rupture, hernia

relajar tr to relax; to slacken; to debauch || intr to relax || ref to relax, become relaxed; to become debauched; to be ruptured

relamer ref to lick one's lips; to gloat; to relish; to boast; to slick oneself up

relami·do -da adj prim, overnice

relámpago m flash of lightning; flash of wit; **relámpago fotogénico** flash bulb, flashlight; **relámpagos** lightning

relampaguear intr to lighten; to flash

relatar tr to relate, report

relati·vo -va adj relative

relato m story; statement, report

relé m (elec) relay

releer §43 tr to reread

relegar §44 *tr* to relegate; to banish, exile; to shelve, lay aside

relente *m* night dew, light drizzle

relevador *m* (elec) relay

relevante *adj* outstanding

relevar *tr* to emboss; to make stand out; to relieve; to release; to absolve; to replace ‖ *intr* to stand out in relief

relevo *m* (elec) relief; (mil) relief; **relevos** (sport) relay race

relicario *m* shrine; (*medallón*) (Am) locket

relieve *m* relief; merit, distinction; **en relieve** in relief; **poner de relieve** to point out; to make stand out; **relieves** scraps, leftovers

religión *f* religion

religio·so -sa *adj* religious

relinchar *intr* to neigh

relincho *m* neigh, neighing; cry of joy

reliquia *f* relic; trace, vestige; **reliquia de familia** heirloom

reloj *m* watch; clock; meter; **como un reloj** like clockwork; **conocer el reloj** to know how to tell time; **reloj de caja** grandfather's clock; **reloj de carillón** chime clock; **reloj de cuclillo** cuckoo clock; **reloj de ocho días cuerda** eight-day clock; **reloj de pulsera** wrist watch; **reloj de sol** sundial; **reloj despertador** alarm clock; **reloj registrador** time clock; **reloj registrador de tarjetas** punch clock

relojera *f* watch case; watch pocket

relojería *f* watchmaking, clockmaking; watchmaker's shop

reloje·ro -ra *mf* watchmaker, clock-maker ‖ *f* see **relojera**

reluciente *adj* shining, brilliant, flashing

relucir §45 *intr* to shine

relumbrar *intr* to shine, dazzle, glare

relumbre *m* beam, sparkle; flash; dazzle, glare

relumbrón *m* flash, glare; tinsel; **de relumbrón** showy, tawdry

rellano *m* (*en la pendiente de un terreno*) level stretch; (*de escalera*) landing

rellenar *tr* to refill; to fill up; to stuff; to pad; to fill out; (coll) to cram, to stuff ‖ *ref* to fill up; (coll) to cram, stuff oneself

relle·no -na *adj* full, packed; stuffed ‖ *m* refill; filling, stuffing; padding, wadding; (*en un escrito*) filler

remachar *tr* (*un clavo ya clavado*) to clinch; (*un roblón*) to rivet; to stress, emphasize ‖ *ref* (Col) to maintain strict silence

remache *m* clinching; riveting; rivet

remanso *m* dead water, backwater

remar *intr* to row; to toil, struggle

rema·do -da *adj* hopeless; **loco rematado** (coll) raving mad

rematar *tr* to finish, put an end to; to finish off, kill off; (*en una subasta*) to knock down ‖ *intr* to end ‖ *ref* to come to ruin

remate *m* end; crest, top, finial; closing; highest bid; (*en una subasta*) sale; **de remate** hopelessly

remecer §46 *tr & ref* to shake, swing, rock

remedar *tr* to copy, imitate; to ape, mimic; to mock

remediar *tr* to remedy; to help; to prevent; (*del peligro*) to free, to save

remediava·gos *m* (*pl* -gos) short cut

remedio *m* remedy; help; recourse; **no hay remedio or no hay más remedio** it can't be helped; **no tener remedio** to be unavoidable

remedión *m* (theat) substitute performance

remedo *m* copy, imitation; poor imitation

remendar §2 *tr* to patch, mend, repair; to darn; to emend, correct; to touch up

remen·dón -dona *mf* mender, repairer; shoe mender; tailor (*who does mending*)

reme·ro -ra *mf* rower ‖ *m* oarsman

remesa *f* remittance; shipment

remesar *tr* to remit; to ship

remezón *m* (Am) hard shake; (Am) tremor

remiendo *m* patch; mending, repair; retouching; emendation, correction; job printing, job work; **a remiendos** (coll) piecemeal

remilga·do -da *adj* prim and finicky; affected, smirking

remilgar §44 *intr* to be prim and finicky, to smirk

remilgo *m* primness, affectation

remira·do -da *adj* circumspect, discreet

remisión *f* remission; reference

remitente *mf* sender, shipper

remitido *m* (*noticia de un particular a un periódico*) personal; letter to the editor

remitir *tr* to remit; to forward, send, ship; to refer; to defer, postpone; to pardon, forgive ‖ *intr* to remit, let up; to refer ‖ *ref* to remit, let up; to defer, yield

remo *m* oar; leg, arm, wing; toil, labor; (sport) rowing; **aguantar los remos** to lie or rest on one's oars

remoción *f* discharge, dismissal; removal

remojar *tr* to soak, to steep, to dip; to celebrate with a drink; **remojar la palabra** (coll) to wet one's whistle

remojo *m* soaking, steeping; **poner en remojo** (coll) to put off to a more suitable time

remolacha *f* beet; **remolacha azucarera** sugar beet

remolcador *m* tug, tugboat; towboat; tow car

remolcar §73 *tr* to tow; to take in tow

remoler §47 *tr* to grind up; (coll) to bore

remolinear *tr, intr & ref* to eddy, whirl about

remolino *m* eddy, whirlpool; swirl, whirl; disturbance, commotion; throng, crowd; cowlick

remo·lón -lona *adj* lazy, indolent ‖ *mf* shirker, quitter

remolonear *intr* to refuse to budge

remolque *m* tow; towing; trailer; **a remolque** in tow

remontar *tr* to mend, repair; to frighten

away; to elevate, raise up; *(p.ej., un río)* to go up ‖ *intr (en el tiempo)* to go back ‖ *ref* to rise, rise up; to soar; *(en el tiempo)* to go back

remontuar *m* stem-winder

remoquete *m* punch; nickname; sarcasm; (coll) flirting

rémora *f* hindrance, obstacle

remordimiento *m* remorse

remo·to -ta *adj* remote; unlikely; **estar remoto** to be rusty

remover §47 *tr* to remove; to shake; to stir; to disturb, upset; to dismiss, to discharge ‖ *ref* to move away

remozar §60 *tr* to rejuvenate ‖ *ref* to become rejuvenated

rempujar *tr* (coll) to push, jostle

rempujón *m* (coll) push, jostle

remuda *f* change, replacement; change of clothes

remudar *tr* to change, replace; to move around

remuneración *f* remuneration; **remuneración por rendimiento** piece wage

renacer §22 *intr* to be reborn, to be born again; to recover

renacimiento *m* rebirth; renaissance

renacuajo *m* tadpole; (coll) shrimp, little squirt

Renania *f* Rhineland

ren·co -ca *adj* lame

rencor *m* rancor; **guardar rencor** to bear malice

rendición *f* surrender; submission; fatigue, exhaustion; yield

rendi·do -da *adj* tired, worn-out; submissive

rendija *f* crack, split, slit

rendimiento *m* submission; exhaustion; yield; output; (mech) efficiency

rendir §50 *tr* to conquer; to subdue; to surrender; to exhaust, wear out; to return, give back; to yield, produce; *(gracias, obsequios, homenaje)* to render ‖ *intr* to yield ‖ *ref* to surrender; to yield, give in; to be exhausted, to be worn out

renegar §66 *tr* to deny vigorously; to abhor, detest ‖ *intr* to curse; (coll) to be insulting; **renegar de** to deny; to curse; to abhor, detest

renegociación *f* renegotiation

Renfe, la acronym for **la Red Nacional de los Ferrocarriles Españoles** the Spanish National Railroad System

renglón *m* line; **a renglón seguido** right below; **leer entre renglones** to read between the lines

reniego *m* curse

reno *m* reindeer

renombra·do -da *adj* renowned, famous

renombre *m* renown, fame

renovar §61 *tr* to renew; to renovate; to transform, restore; to remodel

renquear *intr* to limp

renta *f* income; private income; annuity; public debt; rent; **renta nacional** gross national product

rentar *tr* to produce, yield

rentista *mf* bondholder; financier; person of independent means

renuente *adj* reluctant, unwilling

renuevo *m* sprout, shoot; renewal

renuncia *f* renunciation; resignation; (law) waiver

renunciar *tr* to renounce; to resign ‖ *intr* to renounce; *(no servir al palo que se juega)* to renege; **renunciar a** to give up, to renounce, to waive

renuncio *m* slip, mistake; *(en juegos de naipes)* renege; (coll) lie

reñi·do -da *adj* on bad terms; bitter, hard-fought

reñir §72 *tr (regañar)* to scold; *(una batalla, un desafío)* to fight ‖ *intr* to fight; to be at odds, to fall out

re·o -a *adj* guilty, criminal ‖ *reo mf* offender, criminal; (law) defendant

reojo — de reojo askance, out of the corner of one's eye; hostilely

reorganizar §60 *tr & ref* to reorganize

reóstato *m* rheostat

repanchigar or **repantigar** §44 *ref* to sprawl, to loll

reparar *tr* to repair, to mend; to make amends for; to notice, observe; *(un golpe)* to parry ‖ *intr* to stop; **reparar en** to notice, pay attention to ‖ *ref* to stop; to refrain

reparo *m* repairing, repairs; notice, observation; doubt, objection; shelter; bashfulness

repa·rón -rona *adj* (coll) faultfinding ‖ *mf* (coll) faultfinder

repartir *tr* to distribute; *(naipes)* to deal

reparto *m* distribution; *(de naipes)* deal; (theat) cast; **reparto de acciones gratis** stock dividend

repasar *tr* to repass; to retrace; to review; to revise; *(la ropa)* to mend

repasata *f* (coll) scolding, reprimand

repaso *m* revision; *(de una lección)* review; mending; (coll) reprimand

repatriar §77 *tr* to repatriate; to send home ‖ *intr & ref* to be repatriated; to go or come home

repeler *tr* to repel, to repulse

repente *m* start, sudden movement; **de repente** suddenly

repenti·no -na *adj* sudden, unexpected

repentista *mf* (mus) improviser; (mus) sight reader

repentizar §60 *intr* to improvise; (mus) to sight-read, perform at sight

repercutir *intr* to rebound; to reëcho, reverberate

repertorio *m* repertory

repetición *f* repetition; (mus) repeat

repetir §50 *tr & intr* to repeat

repicar §73 *tr* to mince, to chop up; to ring, to sound; to sting again ‖ *intr* to peal, ring out, resound ‖ *ref* to boast, be conceited

repique *m* chopping, mincing; peal, ringing; (coll) squabble, quarrel

repiqueteo *m* pealing, ringing; beating, rapping

repisa *f* shelf, ledge; bracket; **repisa de chimenea** mantelpiece; **repisa de ventana** window sill

replantear *tr* to lay out again; to reaffirm, to reimplement

replegar §66 *tr* to fold over and over ‖ *ref* to fold, fold up; (mil) to fall back

reple·to -ta *adj* replete, full, loaded; fat, chubby

réplica *f* answer, retort; replica

replicar §73 *tr* to argue against ‖ *intr* to answer back, retort

repli·cón -cona *adj* (coll) saucy, flip

repliegue *m* fold, crease; (mil) falling back

repollo *m* cabbage; (*p.ej., de lechuga, col*) head

reponer §54 *tr* to replace, put back; to restore; (*una pieza dramática*) to revive; **repuso** he replied ‖ *ref* to recover; to calm down

reportaje *m* reporting; news coverage; report

reportar *tr* to check, restrain; to get, obtain; to bring, carry; to report ‖ *ref* to restrain or control oneself

reporte *m* report, news report; gossip

repórter *m* reporter

reporte·ro -ra *mf* reporter

reposar *intr* & *ref* to rest, repose; to take a nap; (*en la sepultura*) to lie, be at rest; (*poso, sedimento*) to settle

reposición *f* replacement; (*de la salud*) recovery; (theat) revival

reposo *m* rest, repose

repostar *tr, intr* & *ref* to stock up; to refuel

repostería *f* pastry shop, confectionery; pantry

reposte·ro -ra *mf* pastry cook, confectioner

repregunta *f* (law) cross-examination

repreguntar *tr* (law) to cross-examine

reprender *tr* to reprehend, to scold

represa *f* dam; damming; repression, check; (*de un buque*) recapture

represalia *f* reprisal; retaliation

represar *tr* to dam; to repress, to check; (*un buque*) to recapture

representación *f* representation; dignity, standing; performance; **en representación de** representing

representante *adj* representing ‖ *mf* representative; actor, player; (com) agent, representative

representar *tr* to represent; to show, express; to state, declare; to act, perform, play; (*determinada edad*) to appear to be ‖ *ref* to imagine

representati·vo -va *adj* representative

reprimenda *f* reprimand

reprimir *tr* to repress

reprobación *f* reproof; flunk, failure

reprobar §61 *tr* to reprove; to flunk, to fail

reprochar *tr* to reproach

reproche *m* reproach

reproducción *f* reproduction; breeding

reproducir §19 *tr* & *ref* to reproduce

repro·pio -pia *adj* balky

reptar *intr* to crawl; to cringe

reptil *m* reptile

república *f* republic

republica·no -na *adj* & *mf* republican ‖ *m* patriot

repudiar *tr* to repudiate, to disown, to disavow

repues·to -ta *adj* secluded; spare, extra ‖ *m* stock, supply; serving table; pantry; **de repuesto** spare, extra

repugnante *adj* repugnant, disgusting

repugnar *tr* to conflict with; to contra-

dict; to object to, to avoid; to revolt, be repugnant to ‖ *intr* to be repugnant

repujar *tr* to emboss

repulgar §44 *tr* to hem, to border

repulgo *m* hem, border

repuli·do -da *adj* highly polished; all dolled up

repulsar *tr* to reject, refuse

repulsi·vo -va *adj* repulsive

repuntar *tr* (*animales dispersos*) (Arg, Chile, Urug) to round up ‖ *intr* to begin to appear; (naut) to begin to rise; (naut) to begin to ebb ‖ *ref* to begin to turn sour; (coll) to fall out

repuso see **reponer**

reputación *f* reputation, repute

reputar *tr* to repute; to esteem

requebra·dor -dora *adj* flirtatious ‖ *mf* flirt

requebrar §2 *tr* to break into smaller pieces; to flatter, to flirt with

requemar *tr* to burn again; to parch; to overcook; to inflame; to bite, sting ‖ *ref* to become tanned or sunburned; to smolder, burn within

requerir §68 *tr* to notify; to summon; to request; to urge; to check, examine; to require; to seek, look for; to reach for; to court, make love to

requesón *m* cottage cheese

requiebro *m* fine crushing; flattery, flattering remarks, flirtation

requisi·to -ta *adj* requisite ‖ *m* requisite, requirement; accomplishment; **requisito previo** prerequisite

res *f* head of cattle; beast; **reses** cattle

resabio *m* unpleasant aftertaste; bad habit, vice

resabio·so -sa *adj* (Am) sly, crafty; (*caballo*) (Am) vicious

resaca *f* surge, surf; undertow; (com) redraft; (slang) hangover

resalir §65 *intr* to jut out, project

resaltar *tr* to emphasize ‖ *intr* to bounce, rebound; to jut out, project; to stand out

resanar *tr* to retouch, patch, repair

resarcir §36 *tr* to indemnify, to make amends to; (*un daño, un agravio*) to repay; (*una pérdida*) to make good; to mend, repair ‖ *ref* — **resarcirse de** to make up for

resbaladi·zo -za *adj* slippery; skiddy; risky; (*memoria*) shaky

resbalar *intr* to slide; to skid; to slip ‖ *ref* to slide; to slip; (fig) to slip, to misstep

rescatar *tr* to ransom, redeem; to rescue; (*el tiempo perdido*) to make up for; to relieve; to atone for

rescate *m* ransom, redemption; rescue; salvage; ransom money

rescindir *tr* to rescind

rescoldera *f* heartburn

rescoldo *m* embers; smoldering; doubt, scruple; **arder en rescoldo** to smolder

resenti·do -da *adj* resentful

resentimiento *m* resentment; sorrow, disappointment

resentir §68 *ref* to be resentful; **resentirse de** to feel the bad effects of; to resent; to suffer from

reseña *f* outline; book review; newspaper account; (mil) review

reseñar *tr* to outline; (*un libro*) to review; (mil) to review

reserva *f* reserve; reservation; **con** or **bajo la mayor reserva** in strictest confidence; **reserva de caza** game preserve

reservar *tr* to reserve; to put aside; to postpone; to exempt; to keep secret ‖ *ref* to save oneself, to bide one's time; to beware, be distrustful

resfriado *m* cold

resfriar §77 *tr* to cool, chill ‖ *intr* to turn cold ‖ *ref* to catch cold; to cool off, grow cold

resguardar *tr* to defend; to protect, shield ‖ *ref* to take shelter; to protect oneself

resguardo *m* defense; protection; check, voucher; collateral; (naut) wide berth, sea room

residencia *f* residence; impeachment

residenciar *tr* to call to account; to impeach

residir *intr* to reside

residuo *m* residue, remains; remainder

resignación *f* resignation

resignar *tr* to resign ‖ *ref* to resign, become resigned; **resignarse con** (*p.ej., su suerte*) to be resigned to

resina *f* resin

resistencia *f* resistance; strength; **resistencia de rejilla** (electron) grid leak

resistente *adj* resistant; strong; (hort) hardy

resistir *tr* to bear, to stand; (*la tentación*) to resist ‖ *intr* to resist; to hold out; **resistir a** (*la violencia; la risa*) to resist; to refuse to ‖ *ref* to resist; to struggle; **resistirse a** to refuse to

resma *f* ream

resobrina *f* grandniece, greatniece

resobrino *m* grandnephew, greatnephew

resolución *f* resolution; **en resolución** in brief, in a word

resolver §47 & §83 *tr* to resolve; to solve; to decide on; to dissolve; ‖ *ref* to resolve; to make up one's mind

resollar §61 *intr* to breathe; to breathe hard, pant; to stop for a rest

resonar §61 *intr* to resound, to echo

resoplar *intr* to puff; to snort

resoplido *m* puffing; snort

resorte *m* spring; springiness; means; province, scope; (Am) rubber band; **resorte espiral** coil spring; **tocar resortes** to pull wires, to pull strings

respailar *intr* — **ir respailando** (coll) to scurry along

respaldar *m* back ‖ *tr* to back; to indorse ‖ *ref* to lean back; to sprawl

respaldo *m* back; backing; indorsement

respectar *tr* (with personal **a**) to concern; **por lo que respecta a . . .** as far as . . . is concerned

respecti‧vo -va *adj* respective

respecto *m* respect, reference, relation; **al respecto** in the matter; **respecto a** or **de** with respect to, in or with regard to

respetable *adj* respectable

respetar *tr* to respect

respeto *m* respect; consideration; **campar por sus respetos** (coll) to be inconsiderate, to go one's (his, her, etc.) own way; **de respeto** spare, extra

respetuo‧so -sa *adj* respectful; awesome, impressive; humble, obedient

respigón *m* hangnail

respingar §44 *intr* to balk, to shy; (*elevarse el borde, p.ej., de la falda*) to curl up; (coll) to give in unwillingly

respin‧gón -gona *adj* (*nariz*) snubby, upturned; (Am) surly, churlish

respirar *tr* to breathe ‖ *intr* to breathe; to breath freely; to breathe a sigh of relief; to catch one's breath, to stop for a rest; **no respirar** (coll) to not breathe a word; **sin respirar** without respite, without letup

respiro *m* breathing; respite, breather, breathing spell; (*para el pago de una deuda*) extension of time

resplandecer §22 *intr* to shine; to flash, glitter

resplandeciente *adj* brilliant; resplendent

resplandor *m* brilliance, radiance; resplendence; glare

responder *tr* to answer ‖ *intr* to answer, respond; to correspond; to answer back; **responder de** (*una cosa*) to answer for; **responder por** (*una persona*) to answer for

respon‧dón -dona *adj* (coll) saucy

responsable *adj* responsible; **responsable de** responsible for

respuesta *f* answer, response

resquebrajar *tr* & *ref* to crack, to split

resquemar *tr* & *intr* to bite, to sting ‖ *ref* to be parched; (*resentirse sin manifestarlo*) to smolder

resquemo *m* bite, sting

resquicio *m* crack, chink; chance, opportunity

restablecer §22 *tr* to reëstablish, to restore ‖ *ref* to recover

restañar *tr* to retin; (*sangre*) to stanch, stop the flow of

restar *tr* to deduct; to reduce; to take away; (*una pelota*) to return; to subtract ‖ *intr* to remain, be left

restaurante *m* restaurant; **restaurante automático** automat

restaurar *tr* to restore; to recover

restitución *f* restitution, return

restituir §20 *tr* to return, give back; to restore ‖ *ref* to return, come back

resto *m* rest, remainder, residue; (*en juegos de naipes*) stakes; (*de una pelota*) return; **a resto abierto** (coll) without limit; **echar el resto** to stake all, to shoot the works; **restos remains**, mortal remains; **restos de serie** remnants

restregar §66 *tr* to rub hard; to scrub hard

restringir §27 *tr* to restrict; to constrict, to contract

resucitar *tr* & *intr* to resuscitate; to resurrect; (coll) to revive

resuel‧to -ta *adj* resolute, resolved, determined; prompt, quick

resuello *m* breathing; hard breathing, panting

resulta *f* result; outcome; vacancy; **de resultas de** as a result of

resultado *m* result

resultar *intr* to result; to prove to be, to turn out to be; to be, to become

resumen *m* summary, résumé; **en resumen** in brief, in a word

resumir *tr* to summarize, to sum up ‖ *ref* to be reduced, be transformed

resurrección *f* resurrection

retaguardia *f* rearguard

retal *m* piece, remnant

retama *f* Spanish broom; **retama de escoba** furze

retar *tr* to challenge, to dare; (coll) to blame, find fault with

retardar *tr* to retard, slow down

retardo *m* retard, delay

retazo *m* piece, remnant; scrap, fragment

retén *m* store, stock, reserve; catch, pawl; (mil) reserve

retener §71 *tr* to retain, keep, withhold; to detain, arrest; (*el pago de un haber*) to stop

reticente *adj* deceptive, misleading; noncommittal

retintín *m* jingle, tinkling; (*en el oído*) ringing; (coll) tone of reproach, sarcasm, mockery

retiñir §12 *intr* to jingle, to tinkle; (*los oídos*) to ring

retirada *f* retirement, withdrawal; place of refuge; (mil) retreat, retirement; (*toque*) (mil) retreat; **batirse en retirada** to beat a retreat

retirar *tr* to retire, to withdraw; to take away; to pull back ‖ *ref* to retire, to withdraw; (mil) to retire

reto *m* challenge, dare; threat

retocar §73 *tr* to retouch; to touch up; (*un disco de fonógrafo*) to play back

retoño *m* sprout, shoot, sucker

retorcer §74 *tr* to twist; to twist together; (*las manos*) to wring; (fig) to twist, misconstrue ‖ *ref* to twist; to writhe

retórico -ca *adj* rhetorical ‖ *f* rhetoric

retornar *tr* to return, give back; to back, back up ‖ *intr & ref* to return, go back

retorno *m* return; barter, exchange; reward, requital; **retorno terrestre** (elec) ground

retorta *f* (chem) retort

retozar §60 *intr* to frolic, gambol, romp

retozo *m* frolic, gambol, romping; **retozo de la risa** giggle, titter

reto·zón -zona *adj* frolicsome, frisky

retractar *tr & ref* to retract

retraer §75 *tr* to bring again, to bring back; to dissuade ‖ *ref* to withdraw, retire; to take refuge

retraí·do -da *adj* solitary; reserved, shy

retransmisión *f* rebroadcasting

retransmitir *tr* to rebroadcast

retrasar *tr* to delay, retard; to put off; (*un reloj*) to set or turn back ‖ *intr* to be too slow; (*en los estudios*) to be or fall behind ‖ *ref* to delay, be late, be slow, be behind time; (*un reloj*) to go or be slow

retraso *m* delay; **tener retraso** to be late

retratar *tr* to portray; to photograph; to imitate ‖ *ref* to sit for a portrait; to have one's picture taken

retrato *m* portrait; photograph; copy, imitation; description; **el vivo retrato de** the living image of

retrepar *ref* to lean back, to lean back in the chair

retreta *f* (mil) retreat, tattoo; (Am) outdoor band concert

retrete *m* toilet, lavatory

retribuir §20 *tr* to repay, to pay back

retroacti·vo -va *adj* retroactive

retroceder *intr* to retrogress; to back away; to back down, back out

retroceso *m* retrogression; (*de un arma de fuego*) recoil; (*de una enfermedad*) flare-up; (mach, mov) rewind

retrocohete *m* retrorocket

retrodisparo *m* retrofiring

retropropulsión *f* (aer) jet propulsion

retrospecti·vo -va *adj* retrospective ‖ *f* (mov) flashback

retrovisor *m* rear-view mirror

retrucar §73 *intr* to answer, reply; (billiards) to kiss

retruco *m* (billiards) kiss

retruécano *m* pun

retumbar *intr* to resound, to rumble

retumbo *m* resounding, rumble, echo

reumáti·co -ca *adj & mf* rheumatic

reumatismo *m* rheumatism

reunificación *f* reunification

reunión *f* reunion, gathering, meeting; assemblage

reunir §59 *tr* to join, unite; to assemble, gather together, bring together; to reunite; (*dinero*) to raise ‖ *ref* to unite; to assemble, gather together, come together, meet; to reunite

reválida *f* final examination (*for a higher degree*)

revejecer §22 *intr & ref* to grow old before one's time

revelación *f* revelation

revelado *m* (phot) development

revelador *m* (phot) developer

revelar *tr* to reveal; (phot) to develop

revender *tr* to resell; to retail

reventa *f* resale

reventar §2 *tr* to smash, crush; to burst, blow out, explode; to ruin; to annoy, bore; (*a una persona*) to work to death; (*a un caballo*) to run to death ‖ *intr* to burst, blow out, explode; (*las olas*) to break; (*morir*) (coll) to croak; (*de ira*) (coll) to blow up, hit the ceiling; **reventar por** to be dying to ‖ *ref* to burst, blow out, explode; to be worked to death; (*un caballo*) to be run to death

reventón *m* burst; (aut) blowout

rever §80 *tr* to revise, to review; (*un caso legal*) to retry

reverberar *intr* to reverberate

reverbero *m* reflector; street lamp; (Am) chafing dish

reverencia *f* reverence; bow, curtsy

reverenciar *tr* to revere, to reverence ‖ *intr* to bow, to curtsy

reveren·do -da *adj & m* reverend

reverso *m* back; wrong side; reverse

revertir §68 *intr* to revert

revés *m* back, reverse; wrong side; backhand; (*desgracia, contratiempo*) reverse, setback; **al revés** wrong side out; inside out; upside down; backwards

revestir §50 *tr* to put on, to don; to cover, coat, face, line, surface; to assume, take on; to disguise; (*un cuento*) to adorn; to invest ‖ *ref* to put on vestments; to be haughty; to gird oneself

revirar *tr* to turn, twist; to turn over

revisar *tr* to revise, review, check; to audit

revisión *f* revision, review, check

revisionismo *m* revisionism

revisionista *adj & mf* revisionist

revisor *m* inspector, examiner; (rr) conductor, ticket collector

revista *f* review; (mil) review; (theat) review, revue; (law) new trial

revistar *tr* (mil) to review

revivir *tr & intr* to revive

revocar §73 *tr* to revoke; to dissuade; to drive back, drive away; to plaster, to stucco

revolar §61 *intr & ref* to flutter, to flutter around

revolcar §81 *tr* to knock down; (*a un adversario*) (coll) to floor; (*a un alumno en un examen*) (coll) to flunk, to fail ‖ *ref* to wallow, roll around; to be stubborn

revolotear *tr* to fling up ‖ *intr* to flutter, flutter around, flit

revoltijo or **revoltillo** *m* mess, jumble; (Am) stew

revolto·so -sa *adj* rebellious, riotous; (*niño*) unruly, mischievous; complicated; winding ‖ *mf* troublemaker, rioter

revolución *f* revolution

revoluciona·rio -ria *adj & mf* revolutionary

revolver §47 & §83 *tr* to shake; to stir; to turn around; to turn upside down; to wrap up; to mess up; to disturb; (*sus pasos*) to retrace; to alienate, estrange ‖ *intr* to retrace one's steps ‖ *ref* to retrace one's steps; to turn around; to toss and turn; (*un astro en su órbita*) to revolve; (*el mar*) to get rough

revólver *m* revolver

revuelco *m* upset, tumble; wallowing

revuelo *m* whirl, flying around; stir, commotion

revuelta *f* revolution, revolt; disturbance; turning point; fight, row

rey *m* king; (coll) swinehard; **los Reyes Católicos** Ferdinand and Isabella; **los Reyes Magos** the Three Wise Men; **ni rey ni roque** (coll) nobody; **rey de zarza** wren; **reyes** king and queen; **Reyes** Twelfth-night

reyerta *f* quarrel, wrangle

reyezuelo *m* (orn) kinglet; **reyezuelo moñudo** goldcrest

rezaga·do -da *mf* straggler, laggard

rezagar §44 *tr* to outstrip, leave behind; to postpone ‖ *ref* to fall behind

rezar §60 *tr* (*una oración*) to pray; (*una oración; la misa*) to say; (coll) to say, to read; (*anunciar*) (coll) to call for ‖ *intr* to pray; (coll) to grumble; (coll) to say, to read; **rezar con** (coll) to concern

rezo *m* prayer; devotions

rezón *m* grapnel

rezongar §44 *tr* (CAm) to scold ‖ *intr* to grumble, growl

rezumar *intr* to ooze, seep ‖ *ref* to ooze, seep; to leak; (*una especie*) (coll) to leak out

ría *f* estuary, fiord

riachuelo *m* rivulet, streamlet

riada *f* flood, freshet

ribazo *m* slope, embarkment

ribera *f* bank, shore; riverside

ribere·ño -ña *adj* riverside

ribero *m* levee, dike

ribete *m* edge, trimming, border; (*a un cuento*) embellishment

ribetear *tr* to edge, trim, border, bind

ri·co -ca *adj* rich; dear, darling

ridiculizar §60 *tr* to ridicule

ridícu·lo -la *adj* ridiculous; touchy ‖ *m* ridiculous situation; **poner en ridículo** to ridicule, to expose to ridicule

riego *m* irrigation; watering

riel *m* ingot; curtain rod; rail

rielar *intr* to shimmer, gleam; (poet) to twinkle

rienda *f* rein; **a rienda suelta** swiftly, violently; with free rein

riente *adj* laughing; bright, cheerful

riesgo *m* risk, danger; **correr riesgo** to run or take a risk

rifa *f* raffle; fight, quarrel

rifar *tr* to raffle, to raffle off ‖ *intr* to raffle; to fight, quarrel

rígi·do -da *adj* rigid, stiff; strict, severe

riguro·so -sa *adj* rigorous; severe

rima *f* rhyme; **rimas** poems, poetry

rimar *tr & intr* to rhyme

rimbombante *adj* resounding; flashy

rimero *m* heap, pile

Rin *m* Rhine

rincón *m* corner; nook; piece of land; (coll) home

rinconera *f* corner piece of furniture; corner table; corner cupboard

ringla *f*, **ringle** *m* or **ringlera** *f* row, tier

ringorrango *m* (coll) curlicue; (coll) frill, frippery

rinoceronte *m* rhinoceros

riña *f* fight, scuffle

riñón *m* kidney; (fig) heart, center, interior; **tener bien cubierto el riñón** (coll) to be well-heeled

río *m* river; **pescar en río revuelto** to fish in troubled waters

riostra *f* brace, stay; guy wire

riostrar *tr* to brace, stay

ripia *f* shingle

ripio *m* debris; rubble; (*palabras inútiles empleadas para completar el verso*) padding; **no perder ripio** (coll) not to miss a trick

riqueza *f* riches, wealth; richness

risa *f* laugh, laughter

risco *m* cliff, crag; honey fritter

risible adj laughable

risotada f guffaw, horse laugh

ristra f string of onions, string of garlic; (coll) string, row, file

ristre m lance rest

risue·ño -ña adj smiling

rítmi·co -ca adj rhythmic(al)

ritmo m rhythm; **a gran ritmo** at great speed

rito m rite

rival mf rival

rivalidad f rivalry; enmity

rivalizar §60 intr to vie, compete; **rivalizar con** to rival

riza·do -da adj curly; ripply || m curl, curling; rippling

rizador m curling iron, hair curler

rizar §60 tr & ref to curl; (la superficie del agua) to ripple

ri·zo -za adj curly || m curl, ringlet; ripple; (aer) loop; **rizar el rizo** (aer) to loop the loop

ro interj — **¡ro ro!** hushaby!, bye-bye!

roba·dor -dora mf robber, thief

róbalo or **robalo** m (Labrax lupus) bass; (Centropomus undecimalis) snook

robar tr to rob, steal; (un naipe o ficha de dominó) to draw || intr & ref to steal

robinete m faucet, spigot, cock

roblar tr to clinch, to rivet

roble m oak; (Quercus robur) British oak tree; (coll) husky fellow

roblón m rivet

robo m robbery, theft; (naipe tomado del monte) draw; **robo con escalamiento** burglary

ro·bot m (pl -bots) robot

robus·to -ta adj robust

roca f rock

rocalla f pebbles; stone chips; large glass bead

rocallo·so -sa adj stony, pebbly

roce m rubbing; close contact

rociada f sprinkling; dew; (de balas, piedras, etc.) shower; (de invectivas) volley

rociadera f sprinkling can

rociar §77 tr to sprinkle; to spray; to bedew; to scatter || intr to drizzle; **rocía** there is dew

rocín m hack, nag; work horse, draft horse; (coll) rough fellow; (Am) riding horse

rocío m dew; drizzle; sprinkling

roco·so -sa adj rocky

rodada f rut, track

roda·do -da adj (fácil, flúido) rounded, fluent; (tránsito) vehicular || f see **rodada**

rodadura f rolling; rut; (de neumático) tread

rodaja f disk, caster; round slice

rodaje m wheels; (de una película cinematográfica) shooting, filming; **en rodaje** (aut) being run in; (mov) being filmed

rodamiento m bearing; (de un neumático) tread; **rodamientos** running gear

Ródano m Rhone

rodante adj rolling; on wheels; (Chile) wandering

rodapié m baseboard, washboard

rodar §61 tr to roll; (una película cinematográfica) to shoot, to film, to take; to screen, to project; to drag along; (una llave) to turn; (la escalera) to roll down; (un nuevo coche) to run in; (válvulas de un motor) to grind || intr to roll, roll along; to roll down; to rotate, revolve; to tumble; to roam, wander about; (por medio de ruedas) to run; to prowl

Rodas f Rhodes

rodear tr to surround; (Am) to round up || intr to go around; to go by a roundabout way; to beat about the bush || ref to turn, twist, toss about

rodela f buckler, target; padded ring

rodeo m detour, roundabout way; dodge, duck; rodeo, roundup; **andar con rodeos** to beat about the bush; **dar un rodeo** to go a roundabout way

rodilla f knee; floor rag, mop; padded ring; **de rodillas** kneeling, on one's knees

rodillera f kneepad; baggy knee; (de prenda de vestir) knee; (del órgano) (mus) knee swell

rodillo m roller; rolling pin; road roller; inking roller; (de la máquina de escribir) platen

rodrigar §44 tr to prop, prop up, stake

rodrigón m prop, stake

roer §62 tr to gnaw, to gnaw away at; (un hueso) to pick; to wear down

rogar §63 tr & intr to beg; to pray; **hacerse de rogar** to like to be coaxed

roí·do -da adj (coll) miserly, stingy

ro·jo -ja adj red; ruddy; red-haired; Red || mf (comunista) Red || m red; **al rojo** to a red heat

rollar tr to roll, roll up

rolli·zo -za adj round, cylindrical; plump, stocky || m round log

rollo m roll, coil; roller, rolling pin; round log; yoke pad; rôle; (de tela) bolt

romadizo m cold in the head

romance adj (neolatino) Romance || m Romance language; Spanish language; romance of chivalry; octosyllabic verse with alternate lines in assonance; narrative poem in octosyllabic verse; ballad; **romance heroico** hendecasyllabic verse with alternate lines in assonance

romancero m collection of Old Spanish romances

romancillo m verse of less than eight syllables with alternate lines in assonance

románi·co -ca adj (neolatino) Romance, Romanic; (arquitectura) Romanesque || m Romanesque

roma·no -na adj & mf Roman

romanticismo m romanticism

románti·co -ca adj romantic

romanza f (mus) romance, romanza

romería f pilgrimage; crowd, gathering

rome·ro -ra mf pilgrim || m rosemary

ro·mo -ma adj blunt, dull; flat-nosed

rompeáto·mos m (pl -mos) atom smasher

rompecabe·zas m (pl -zas) riddle, puzzle; *(figura que ha sido cortada en trozos menudos y que hay que recomponer)* jigsaw puzzle

rompehie·los *m* *(pl* **-los)** iceboat, icebreaker

rompehuel·gas *m* *(pl* **-gas)** strikebreaker

rompeo·las *m* *(pl* **-las)** mole, breakwater

romper §83 *tr* to break; to break through; to break up; to tear ‖ *intr* to break; *(las flores)* to break open, to burst open; to break down; **romper a** to start to, to burst out

rompiente *m* reef, shoal; *(oleaje que choca contra las rocas)* breaker

rompope *m* (Am) eggnog

ron *m* rum; **ron de laurel** or **de malagueta** bay rum

ronca *f (época del celo)* rut; cry of buck in rutting season; (coll) bullying

roncar §73 *intr* to snore; *(el viento, el mar)* to roar; to cry in rutting season; (coll) to bully

ronce·o -ra *adj* slow, poky; grouchy

ron·co -ca *adj* hoarse; harsh ‖ *f* see **ronca**

roncha *f* weal, welt; black-and-blue mark

ronchar *tr* to crunch

ronda *f (de un policía; de visitas; de cigarros o bebidas)* round; *(juego del corro)* (Chile) ring-around-a-rosy

rondar *tr* to go around; to fly around; to patrol; (coll) to hang around; (coll) to court ‖ *intr* to patrol by night; to gad about at nighttime; to go serenading; to prowl; (mil) to make the rounds

ronquedad *f* hoarseness; harshness

ronquera *f* hoarseness

ronquido *m* snore; rasping sound

ronronear *intr* to purr

ronroneo *m* purr, purring

ronzal *m* halter

ronzar §60 *tr* to crunch, to munch

roña *f* scab, mange; sticky dirt; pine bark; stinginess; (Col) malingering; (Am) spite, ill will; **jugar a roña** (Peru) to play for fun

roño·so -sa *adj* scabby, mangy; dirty, filthy; stingy; (Am) spiteful

ropa *f* clothing, clothes; dry goods; **a quema ropa** point-blank; **ropa blanca** linen; **ropa de cama** bed linen; bedclothes; **ropa dominguera** Sunday best; **ropa hecha** ready-made clothing; **ropa interior** underwear; **ropa sucia** laundry

ropaje *m* clothes, clothing; gown, robe; drapery

ropaveje·ro -ra *mf* old-clothes dealer

rope·ro -ra *mf* ready-made clothier; wardrobe keeper ‖ *m* wardrobe, clothes closet

roque *m* rook, castle

roque·ño -ña *adj* rocky; hard, flinty

rorro *m* baby; (Mex) doll

rosa *f* rose; **rosa de los vientos** or **rosa náutica** (naut) compass card; **rosas** popcorn; **verlo todo de color de rosa** to see everything through rose-colored glasses

rosa·do -da *adj* rose-colored, rosy; pink; flushed ‖ *f* frost

rosaleda or **rosalera** *f* rose garden

rosario *m* rosary; *(de sucesos)* string; chain pump

ros·bif *m* *(pl* **-bifs)** roast beef

rosca *f* coil, spiral; *(de una espiral)* turn; twisted roll; *(de un tornillo)* thread; (Chile) padded ring

roscar §73 *tr* to thread

roseta *f* sprinkling spout or nozzle; red spot on cheek; **rosetas** popcorn

rosetón *m* rose window

rosita *f* little rose; (Chile) earring; **rositas** popcorn

rosquilla *f* coffeecake, doughnut, cruller

rostro *m* face; snout; beak; *(retrato)* de **rostro entero** full-faced

rostropáli·do -da *mf* paleface

rota *f* rout, defeat; (naut) route, course

rotograbado *m* rotogravure

rótula *f* lozenge; kneecap; knuckle

rotular *tr* to label, title, letter

rótulo *m* label, title; poster, show bill

rotun·do -da *adj* round; rotund, sonorous, full; peremptory

rotura *f* break, breaking; breach, opening; tear, tearing

roya *f* (agr) blight, rust

rozamiento *m* rubbing; friction; *(desavenencia)* (fig) friction

rozar §60 *tr* to graze; to scrape; to border on; to grub, to stub; *(las tierras)* to clear; *(la hierba)* to nibble; *(leña menuda)* to cut and gather ‖ *intr* to graze by ‖ *ref* to be on close terms, to rub elbows, to hobnob; to falter, stammer; to be alike

roznar *tr* to crunch ‖ *intr* to bray

roznido *m* crunch, crunching noise; bray, braying

Rte. *abbr* **Remite**

ru·bí *m* *(pl* **-bíes)** ruby; *(de un reloj)* ruby, jewel

rubia *f* blonde; station wagon; (coll) peseta; **rubia oxigenada** peroxide blonde; **rubia platino** platinum blonde

rubia·les *mf* *(pl* **-les)** (coll) goldilocks

ru·bio -bia *adj* blond, fair; golden ‖ *m* blond ‖ *f* see **rubia**

rubor *m* bright red; blush, flush; bashfulness

ruborizar §60 *tr* to make blush ‖ *ref* to blush

rúbrica *f* title, heading; *(rasgo después de la firma de uno)* flourish

ru·bro -bra *adj* red ‖ *m* (Am) title, heading; (Chile) (com) entry

rudimento *m* rudiment

ru·do -da *adj* coarse, rough; rude, crude; dull, stupid; hard, severe

rueca *f* distaff

rueda *f* wheel; caster, roller; *(de gente)* ring, circle; round slice; pinwheel; *(de la cola del pavo)* spread; sunfish; **hacer la rueda** *(el pavo)* to spread its tail; **hacer la rueda a** (coll) to play up to; **rueda de andar** treadmill; **rueda de cadena** sprocket, sprocket wheel; **rueda de escape** escapement wheel; **rueda de fuego** pinwheel; **rueda dentada** gearwheel; **rueda de paletas** paddle wheel; **rueda de pre-**

sos line-up; **rueda de recambio** spare wheel; **rueda de tornillo sin fin** worm wheel; **rueda motriz** drive wheel

ruedo *m* turn, rotation; round mat; selvage; hemline; (*taur*) ring; **a todo ruedo** at all events

ruego *m* request, entreaty; prayer

ru·fián -fiana *mf* bawd, go-between ‖ *m* cur, cad

ru·fo -fa *adj* sandy, sandy-haired; curly-haired

rugido *m* roar; (*de las tripas*) rumble

rugir §27 *intr* to roar; to rumble

rugo·so -sa *adj* rugged, wrinkled

ruibarbo *m* rhubarb

ruido *m* noise; rumor; row, rumpus

ruido·so -sa *adj* noisy; loud; sensational

ruin *adj* base, mean, vile; stingy; (*animal*) vicious

ruina *f* ruin

ruindad *f* baseness, meanness, vileness; stinginess; viciousness

ruino·so -sa *adj* tottery, run-down

ruiseñor *m* nightingale

ruleta *f* roulette; (CAm, Arg) tape measure

ruletero *m* (Mex) cruising taxi driver (*in search of fares*)

ruma·no -na *adj & mf* Rumanian

rumbo *m* bearing, course, direction; (coll) pomp, show; (coll) generosity; **por aquellos rumbos** in those parts; **rumbo a** bound for

rumbo·so -sa *adj* pompous, magnificent; (coll) generous

rumiar *tr & intr* to ruminate

rumor *m* rumor; (*de voces*) murmur, buzz; rumble

rumorear *tr* to rumor, to circulate by a rumor ‖ *intr* to murmur, buzz, rumble ‖ *ref* to be rumored; **se rumorea que** it is rumored that

rumoro·so -sa *adj* noisy, loud, rumbling

runfla or **runflada** *f* (coll) string, row; (*en los naipes*) (coll) sequence

ruptor *m* (elec) contact breaker

ruptura *f* rupture, break; crack, split; (*cesación de relaciones*) rupture

Rusia *f* Russia; **la Rusia Soviética** Soviet Russia

ru·so -sa *adj & mf* Russian

rúst. *abbr* **rústica**

rústi·co -ca *adj* rustic; coarse, crude, clumsy; (*latín*) Vulgar; **en rústica** paper-bound ‖ *m* rustic, peasant

ruta *f* route; **ruta aérea** air lane

rutilante *adj* shining, sparkling

rutina *f* routine

rutina·rio -ria *adj* routine

S

S, s (ese) *f* twenty-second letter of the Spanish alphabet

S. *abbr* **San, Santo, sobresaliente, sur**

sábado *m* (*de los cristianos*) Saturday; (*de los judíos*) Sabbath

sábalo *m* shad

sabana *f* (Am) savanna, pampa; **ponerse en la sabana** (Ven) to get rich overnight

sábana *f* sheet; altar cloth

sabandija *f* insect, bug, worm; (*persona*) vermin; **sabandijas** (*animales o personas*) vermin

sabanilla *f* kerchief; altar cloth

sabañón *m* chilblain

sabe·dor -dora *adj* aware, informed

sabelotodo *m* (*pl* **sabelotodo**) know-it-all, wise guy

saber *m* knowledge, learning ‖ *v* §64 *tr & intr* to know; to find out; to taste; **a saber** namely, to wit; **no saber dónde meterse** to not know which way to turn; **que yo sepa** as far as I know; **saber a** to taste of; to smack of; **saber a poco** to be just a taste, to taste like more; **saber de** to be aware of; to hear from ‖ *ref* to know; to be or become known

sabidi·llo -lla *adj & mf* (coll) know-it-all

sabi·do -da *adj* well-informed; learned; **de sabido** certainly, surely

sabiduría *f* wisdom; knowledge, learning

sabiendas — **a sabiendas** knowingly, consciously; **a sabiendas de que** knowing that, aware that

sabihon·do -da *adj & mf* (coll) know-it-all

sa·bio -bia *adj* wise; learned; (*animal*) trained ‖ *mf* wise person, scholar, scientist ‖ *m* wise man, sage

sablazo *m* stroke with a saber, wound made by a saber; (coll) sponging; **dar un sablazo a** (coll) to hit for a loan

sable *m* saber, cutlass; (coll) sponging

sablear *tr* (coll) to hit for a loan, to sponge on ‖ *intr* (coll) to go around sponging

sablista *mf* (coll) sponger

sabor *m* taste, flavor

saborcillo *m* slight taste, touch

saborear *tr* to flavor; to taste; to savor; to entice ‖ *ref* to smack one's lips; **saborearse de** to taste; to savor

sabotaje *m* sabotage

sabotear *tr & intr* to sabotage

sabro·so -sa *adj* tasty, savory, delicious

sabueso *m* bloodhound; sleuth

saburro·so -sa *adj* (*boca*) foul; (*lengua*) coated

sacaboca·do or **sacaboca·dos** *m* (*pl* -**dos**) ticket punch; (coll) sure thing

sacabotas *m* (*pl* -**tas**) bootjack

sacacor·chos *m* (*pl* -**chos**) corkscrew

sacaman·chas *mf* (*pl* -**chas**) clothes cleaner, spot remover; dry cleaner; dyer

sacamue·las *mf* (*pl* **-las**) (coll) tooth puller; (coll) quack, cheat
sacamuer·tos *m* (*pl* **-tos**) stagehand
sacapintura *m* paint remover
sacapun·tas *m* (*pl* **-tas**) pencil sharpener
sacar §73 *tr* (*un clavo, una espada, agua, una conclusión*) to draw; to pull out; to pull up; to take out; to extract, remove; to show; to bring out, publish; to find out, to solve; (*un secreto*) to elicit, draw out; to copy; (*una fotografía*) to take; to except, exclude; to get, obtain; to produce, invent, imitate; (*un premio*) to win; (*una pelota*) to serve; (*el pecho*) to stick out; **sacar a bailar** (coll) to drag in; **sacar a relucir** (coll) to bring up unexpectedly; **sacar en claro** or **en limpio** to recopy clearly; to deduce, to clear up
sacarina *f* saccharin
sacasi·llas *m* (*pl* **-llas**) stagehand
sacerdocio *m* priesthood
sacerdote *m* priest
saciar *tr* to satiate
saco *m* bag, sack; coat, jacket; sack, plunder, pillage; (*de mentiras*) pack; **saco de dormir** sleeping bag; **saco de noche** overnight bag
sacramento *m* sacrament
sacrificar §73 *tr* to sacrifice; to slaughter ‖ *intr* to sacrifice ‖ *ref* to sacrifice; to sacrifice onself
sacrificio *m* sacrifice; **sacrificio del altar** Sacrifice of the Mass
sacrilegio *m* sacrilege
sacríle·go -ga *adj* sacrilegious
sacristán *m* sacristan; sexton; **sacristán de amén** yes man
sacristía *f* sacristy, vestry
sa·cro -cra *adj* sacred
sacudida *f* shake, jar, jolt, jerk, bump; (elec) shock
sacudi·do -da *adj* intractable; determined ‖ *f* see **sacudida**
sacudir *tr* to shake; to beat; to jar, jolt; to rock; to shake off ‖ *ref* to shake, to shake oneself; to rock; **sacudirse bien** (coll) to wangle one's way out
sádi·co -ca *adj* sadistic ‖ *mf* sadist
saeta *f* arrow, dart; (*del reloj*) hand; magnetic needle
saetilla *f* small arrow; (*del reloj*) hand; magnetic needle; (bot) arrowhead
saetín *m* flume, millrace
sa·gaz *adj* (*pl* **-gaces**) sagacious; keen-scented
sagra·do -da *adj* sacred ‖ *m* asylum, haven, sanctuary; **acogerse a sagrado** to take sanctuary
sagrario *m* sanctuary, shrine; ciborium
sahariana *f* tight-fitting military jacket
sahornar *ref* to skin oneself
sahumar *tr* to perfume with smoke or incense; (Chile) to gold-plate, to silver-plate
sainete *m* one-act farce; flavor, relish, spice, zest; sauce, seasoning; tidbit
sa·jón -jona *adj* & *mf* Saxon
sal *f* salt; grace, charm; wit; (CAm) misfortune; **sal de sosa** washing soda;

sales aromáticas smelling salts; **sal gema** rock salt
sala *f* hall; drawing room, living room, sitting room; **sala de batalla** sorting room; **sala de calderas** boiler room; **sala de enfermos** infirmary; **sala de espera** waiting room; **sala de estar** living room, sitting room; **sala de fiestas** night club; **sala del cine** moving-picture house; **sala de máquinas** engine room
saladillo *m* salted peanut
Salamina *f* Salamis
salar *tr* to salt; (Am) to spoil, ruin; (Am) to bring bad luck to
salario *m* wages, pay; **salario de hambre** starvation wages
salcochar *tr* to boil in salt water
salcocho *m* (Am) food boiled in salt water
salchicha *f* sausage
salchiche·ro -ra *mf* pork butcher
saldar *tr* to settle, liquidate; to sell out
saldo *m* settlement; balance; remnant; bargain; **saldo de mercancías** job lot; **saldo deudor** debit balance
salero *m* saltshaker, saltcellar; salt lick; (coll) grace, charm, wit
salero·so -sa *adj* (coll) charming, winsome, lively; (coll) salty, witty
salgar §44 *tr* (*el ganado*) to salt
salida *f* start; departure; exit; outcome, result; subterfuge; pretext; outlay, expenditure; projection; outlying fields; (elec) output; (sport) start; (mil) sally, sortie; (coll) witticism, sally; **salida de baño** bathrobe; **salida del sol** sunrise; **salida de teatro** evening wrap; **salida de teatros** after-theater party; **salida de tono** (coll) irrelevancy, impropriety; **salida lanzada** (sport) running start; **tener salida** to sell well; (*una muchacha*) to be popular with the boys
saliente *adj* projecting; (*p.ej., tren*) outbound; (*sol*) rising ‖ *m* east ‖ *f* projection; (*de la carretera*) shoulder
salir §65 *intr* to go out, come out; to leave, go away, depart; to sail; to run out, come to an end; to appear, show up; (*una mancha*) to come out, come off; (*p.ej., el sol*) to rise; to shoot, spring, come up; to project, stick out; to make the first move; to result, turn out; to be elected; **salga lo que saliere** (coll) come what may; **salir a** to amount to; to open into; to resemble, look like; **salir al encuentro a** to go to meet; to take a stand against; to get ahead of; **salir bien en un examen** to pass an examination; **salir con bien** to be successful; **salir de** to depart from; to cease being; to get rid of; (*p.ej., su juicio, sentido*) to lose; **salir disparado** to start like a shot; **salir pitando** (coll) to start off on a mad run; (coll) to blow up, hit the ceiling; **salir reprobado** (*en un examen*) to fail ‖ *ref* to slip out, escape; to slip off, run off; to leak; to boil over; **salirse con la suya** to have one's own way; to carry one's point
salitre *m* saltpeter

saliva *f* saliva; **gastar saliva** (coll) to rattle along; (coll) to waste one's breath

salmo *m* psalm

salmón *m* salmon

salmuera *f* brine, pickle; salty food or drink

salobre *adj* brackish, saltish

salón *m* salon, drawing room; (*de un buque*) saloon; meeting room; **salón de actos** auditorium; **salón de baile** ballroom; **salón de belleza** beauty parlor; **salón del automóvil** automobile show; **salón de refrescos** ice-cream parlor; **salón de tertulia** or **salón** social lounge

saloncillo *m* (*p.ej., de un teatro*) rest room

salpicar §73 *tr* to splash; to sprinkle

salpimentar §2 *tr* to salt and pepper, season with salt and pepper; (fig) to sweeten

salpullido *m* rash, eruption

salpullir §13 *tr* to cause a rash in; to splotch ‖ *ref* to break out

salsa *f* sauce, dressing, gravy; **salsa de ají** chili sauce; **salsa de tomate** catsup, ketchup; **salsa inglesa** Worcestershire sauce

salsera *f* gravy dish; small saucer (*to mix paints*)

saltaban·co or **saltaban·cos** *m* (*pl* -cos) quack, mountebank; prestidigitator; (coll) nuisance

saltamon·tes *m* (*pl* -tes) grasshopper

saltar *tr* to jump, jump over; to skip, skip over ‖ *intr* to jump, leap, hop, skip; to bounce; to shoot up, spurt; to come loose, come off; to crack, break, burst; to chip; to project, stick out; **saltar a la vista** or **los ojos** to be self-evident; **saltar por** to jump over, to jump out of ‖ *ref* to skip; to come off

saltatum·bas *m* (*pl* -bas) (coll) burying parson

salteador *m* highwayman, holdup man

saltear *tr* to attack, hold up, waylay; to take by surprise

saltimbanco *m* var of **saltabanco**

salto *m* jump, leap, bound; skip; dive; fall, waterfall; leapfrog; **salto de altura** high jump; **salto de ángel** swan dive; **salto de cama** morning wrap, dressing gown; **salto de carpa** jackknife; **salto de esquí** ski jump; **salto de viento** (naut) sudden shift in the wind; **salto mortal** somersault; **salto ornamental** fancy dive

salubre *adj* healthful, salubrious

salud *f* health; welfare; salvation; greeting; **gastar, vender** or **verter salud** (coll) to radiate health ‖ *interj* greetings!; **¡salud y pesetas!** health and wealth!

saludar *tr* to greet, salute, hail, bow to; to give regards to ‖ *intr* to salute; to bow

saludo *m* greeting, salute, bow; salutation; **saludo final** conclusion

salutación *f* salutation, greeting, bow

salva *f* greeting, welcome; salvo; oath;

tray; (*de aplausos; de una batería de artillería*) round

salvado *m* bran

salva·dor -dora *mf* savior, saver, rescuer ‖ **el Salvador** the Saviour; (*país de la América Central*) El Salvador

salvadore·ño -ña *adj & mf* Salvadoran

salvaguardar *tr* to safeguard

salvaguardia *m* bodyguard, escort ‖ *f* safeguard, safe-conduct; protection, shelter

salvaje *adj* wild, uncultivated; savage; stupid ‖ *mf* savage; dolt

salvaji·no -na *adj* wild; (*de la carne de los animales monteses*) gamy ‖ *f* wild animal; wild animals

salvamante·les *m* (*pl* -les) coaster

salvamento *m* salvation; lifesaving; rescue; salvage; place of safety

salvar *tr* to save, rescue; to salvage; (*una dificultad*) to avoid, overcome; (*un obstáculo*) to clear, get around; (*una distancia*) to cover, get over; to rise above; to jump over; to make an exception of; **salvar apariencias** to save face ‖ *ref* to save onself, escape danger; to be saved; **sálvese el que pueda** every man for himself

salvavi·das *m* (*pl* -das) life preserver; lifeboat; (*empleado de una estación de salvamento*) lifeguard

salvedad *f* reservation, exception

salvia *f* (bot) sage

sal·vo -va *adj* safe; omitted; **a salvo** safe, out of danger; **a salvo de** safe from ‖ **salvo** *prep* save, except for; **salvo error u omisión** barring error or omission; **salvo que** unless ‖ *f* see **salva**

salvoconducto *m* safe-conduct

sámara *f* (bot) key, key fruit

san *adj* apocopated and unstressed form of **santo**

sanaloto·do *m* (*pl* -do) cure-all

sanar *tr* to cure, heal ‖ *intr* to heal; to recover

sanción *f* (*aprobación*) sanction; (*castigo, pena*) penalty

sancionar *tr* (*aprobar*) to sanction; (*imponer pena a*) to penalize

sancochar *tr* to parboil

sandalia *f* sandal

sándalo *m* (yellow) sandalwood

san·dez *f* (*pl* -deces) folly, nonsense; piece of folly

sandía *f* watermelon

san·dio -dia *adj* foolish, nonsensical

saneamiento *m* sanitation, drainage; guarantee

sanear *tr* to guarantee; to indemnify; to make sanitary, to drain, dry up

sangrar *tr* to bleed; to drain; to tap; (typ) to indent; (coll) to rob ‖ *intr* to bleed; **estar sangrando** to be new or recent; to be plain or obvious ‖ *ref* to have oneself bled; (*los colores*) to run

sangre *f* blood; **a sangre** by horsepower; **a sangre fría** in cold blood; **pura sangre** *m* thoroughbred; **sangre torera** bullfighting in the blood

sangría *f* bleeding; outlet, draining;

ditch, trench; (*bebida*) sangaree; tap; tapping; (typ) indentation

sangrien·to -ta *adj* bloody; bleeding; cruel, sanguinary

sangüesa *f* raspberry

sangüeso *m* raspberry bush

sanguijuela *f* leech

sanguina·rio -ria *adj* sanguinary, bloodthirsty

sanidad *f* healthiness; healthfulness; health; sanitation; **sanidad pública** health department

sanita·rio -ria *adj* sanitary

sa·no -na *adj* hale, healthy; healthful; sound; sane; earnest, sincere; safe, sure; (coll) whole, untouched, unharmed; **sano y salvo** safe and sound

santiague·ro -ra *adj* Santiago de Cuba || *mf* native or inhabitant of Santiago de Cuba

santia·gués -guesa *adj* Santiago de Compostela || *mf* native or inhabitant of Santiago de Compostela

santiagui·no -na *adj* Santiago de Chile || *mf* native or inhabitant of Santiago de Chile

santiamén *m* (coll) jiffy; **en un santiamén** (coll) in the twinkling of an eye

santidad *f* holiness, sanctity, saintliness; **su Santidad** his Holiness

santificar §73 *tr* to sanctify, to hallow, to consecrate; (*las fiestas*) to keep; (coll) to excuse, justify

santiguar §10 *tr* to bless, make the sign of the cross over; (coll) to punish, slap, abuse || *ref* to cross oneself, make the sign of the cross

san·to -ta *adj* holy, saintly, blessed; (*día*) live-long; (coll) artless, simple; **santo y bueno** well and good || *mf* saint || *m* name day; image of a saint; a santo de because of; **desnudar a un santo para vestir a otro** to rob Peter to pay Paul; **írsele a uno el santo al cielo** (coll) to forget what one was up to; **santo y seña** password, watchword

Santo Domingo Hispaniola

santuario *m* sanctuary, shrine; (Col) buried treasure; (Col, Ven) Indian idol

santu·rrón -rrona *adj* sanctimonious || *mf* sanctimonious person

saña *f* fury, rage; cruelty

sañu·do -da *adj* furious, enraged; cruel

sapiente *adj* wise, intelligent

sapo *m* toad; (coll) stuffed shirt; (Chile) little runt

saque *m* (*en el tenis*) serve; service; server; service line; (Col) distillery; **tener buen saque** (coll) to be a heavy eater and drinker

saquear *tr* to sack, plunder, pillage, loot

sarampión *m* measles

sarao *m* soirée, evening party

sarape *m* (Guat, Mex) bright-colored woolen poncho

sarcásti·co -ca *adj* sarcastic

sardina *f* sardine; **como sardinas en banasta** or **en lata** (coll) packed in like sardines

sar·do -da *adj & mf* Sardinian

sarga *f* serge

sargento *m* sergeant

sarmiento *m* vine shoot, running stem

sarna *f* itch, mange

sarno·so -sa *adj* itchy, mangy

sarrace·no -na *adj & mf* Saracen

sarracina *f* scuffle, free fight; bloody brawl

sarro *m* crust; (*p.ej., en la lengua*) fur; (*en los dientes*) tartar

sarta *f* string; line, file, series

sartén *f* frying pan; **saltar de la sartén y dar en las brasas** (coll) to jump from the frying pan into the fire

sastre *m* tailor

satélite *m* satellite

satelizar §60 *tr* to put into orbit; (pol) to make a satellite of || *ref* to go into orbit

satén *m* sateen

satíri·co -ca *adj* satiric(al) || *mf* satirist

satirizar §60 *tr & intr* to satirize

satisfacción *f* satisfaction

satisfacer §39 *tr & intr* to satisfy || *ref* to satisfy oneself, be satisfied, take satisfaction

satisfacto·rio -ria *adj* satisfactory

saturar *tr* to saturate; to satiate

sauce *m* willow tree; **sauce de Babilonia** or **sauce llorón** weeping willow

saúco *m* elder, elderberry

savia *f* sap

saxofón *m* or **saxófono** *m* saxophone

saya *f* skirt; petticoat

sayo *m* smock frock, tunic; (coll) garment

sazón *f* ripeness, season; time, occasion; taste, seasoning; **a la sazón** at that time; **en sazón** in season, ripe; on time, opportunely

sazonar *tr* to ripen; to season || *ref* to ripen, mature

s/c *abbr* su cuenta

S.E. *abbr* Su Excelencia

se *pron reflex* himself, to himself; herself, to herself; itself, to itself; themselves, to themselves; yourself, to yourself; yourselves, to yourselves; oneself, to oneself; each other, to each other || *pron pers* (used before the pronouns **lo, la, le,** etc.) to him, to her, to it, to them, to you

sebo *m* tallow; fat, suet

seca *f* drought; dry season

secador *m* drier, hair drier

secadora *f* clothes dryer

secafir·mas *m* (pl -mas) blotter

secano *m* dry land, unwatered land

secansa *f* sequence

secante *m* blotting paper

secar §73 *tr* to dry, wipe dry; to annoy, bore || *ref* to dry, get dry; to dry oneself; to wither; to be dry, be thirsty; (*un pozo*) to run dry

secarropa *f* clothes dryer; **secarropa de travesaños** clotheshorse

sección *f* section; cross section; **sección de fondo** editorial section

secesión *f* secession

se·co -ca *adj* dry; dried up, withered; lank, lean; harsh, sharp; (*bebida*) straight; indifferent; plain, unadorned || *f* see **seca**

secreta·rio -ria *adj* confidential, trusted || *mf* secretary

secreter *m* secretary (*writing desk*)

secre·to -ta *adj* secret || *m* secret; secrecy; hiding place, secret drawer; (*mecanismo oculto para abrir una cerradura*) key; **en el secreto de las cosas** on the inside

secta *f* sect

secta·rio -ria *adj & mf* sectarian

sector *m* sector; **sector de distribución** house current, power line

se·cuaz (*pl* **-cuaces**) *adj* partisan || *mf* partisan, follower

secuela *f* sequel, result

secuencia *f* sequence

secuestrar *tr* to kidnap; (law) to sequester

secular *adj* secular

secundar *tr* to second, to back

secunda·rio -ria *adj* secondary || *m* (elec) secondary

sed *f* thirst; drought; **tener sed** to be thirsty

seda *f* silk; **como una seda** smooth as silk; easy as pie; sweet-natured; **seda encerada** dental floss

sedal *m* fish line

sedán *m* sedan; **sedán de reparto** delivery truck

sede *f* (*p.ej., del gobierno*) seat; (eccl) see; **Santa Sede** Holy See

sedenta·rio -ria *adj* sedentary

sede·ño -ña *adj* silk, silken

sedición *f* sedition

sedicio·so -sa *adj* seditious

sedien·to -ta *adj* thirsty; (*terreno*) dry; anxious, eager

sedimento *m* sediment

sedo·so -sa *adj* silky

seducción *f* seduction; charm, captivation

seducir §19 *tr* to seduce; to tempt, lead astray; to charm, captivate

seducti·vo -va *adj* seductive; tempting; charming, captivating

seduc·tor -tora *adj* seductive; tempting; charming || *mf* seducer; tempter; charmer

sefar·dí (*pl* **-fíes**) *adj* Sephardic || *mf* Sephardi

sega·dor -dora *adj* harvesting || *m* harvestman || *f* harvester; mowing machine; **segadora de césped** lawn mower; **segadora trilladora** combine

segar §66 *tr* to reap, harvest, mow; to mow down || *intr* to reap, harvest, mow

segazón *f* harvest; harvest time

seglar *adj* secular, lay || *m* layman || *f* laywoman

segmento *m* segment; **segmento de émbolo** piston ring

segregacionista *mf* segregationist

segregar §44 *tr* to segregate

seguida *f* series, succession; **de seguida** without interruption, continuously; at once; in a row; **en seguida** at once, immediately

seguidilla *f* Spanish stanza made up of a quatrain and a tercet; **seguidillas** seguidilla (*Spanish dance and music*)

segui·do -da *adj* continued, successive; straight, direct; running, in a row; **todo seguido** straight ahead || *f* see **seguida**

seguimiento *m* chase, hunt, pursuit; continuation; (*de vehículos espaciales*) tracking

seguir §67 *tr* to follow; to pursue; to continue; to dog, to hound || *intr* to go on, to continue; to still be, to be now; to keep + *ger* || *ref* to follow, ensue; to issue, to spring

según *prep* according to, as per; **según que** according as || *conj* as, according as

segunda *f* double meaning; (aut & mus) second

segundero *m* second hand; **segundero central** sweep-second, center-second

segun·do -da *adj* second || *m* second; **ser sin segundo** to be second to none || *f* see **segunda**

segur *f* axe; sickle

segurador *s* security, bondsman

seguridad *f* security; safety; surety; certainty; assurance; confidence

segu·ro -ra *adj* sure, certain; secure, safe; reliable; constant; steady, unfailing || *m* assurance, certainty; safety; confidence; insurance; **a buen seguro** surely, truly; **seguro contra accidentes** accident insurance; **seguro de desempleo** or **desocupación** unemployment insurance; **seguro de enfermedad** health insurance; **seguro de incendios** fire insurance; **seguro sobre la vida** life insurance; **sobre seguro** without risk || **seguro** *adv* surely

seis *adj & pron* six; **las seis** six o'clock || *m* six; (*en las fechas*) sixth

seiscien·tos -tas *adj & pron* six hundred || **seiscientos** *m* six hundred

selección *f* selection

seleccionar *tr* to select, to choose

selec·to -ta *adj* select, choice

selva *f* forest, woods; jungle

selváti·co -ca *adj* woodsy; rustic, wild

sellar *tr* to seal; to stamp; to close; to finish up

sello *m* seal; stamp; signet; wafer; **sello aéreo** air-mail stamp; **sello de correo** postage stamp; **sello de urgencia** special-delivery stamp; **sello fiscal** revenue stamp

semáforo *m* semaphore; traffic light

semana *f* week; week's pay; **semana inglesa** working week of five and a half days

semanal *adj* weekly

semanalmente *adv* weekly

semana·rio -ria *adj & m* weekly

semánti·co -ca *adj* semantic || *f* semantics

semblante *m* face, mien, countenance; appearance, expression, look

semblanza *f* biographical sketch, portrait

sembrado *m* sown ground, grain field

sembrar §2 *tr* to seed, to sow; to scatter, to spread; to sprinkle

semejante *adj* like, similar; such; **semejante a** like; **semejantes** alike, e.g., **estas sillas son semejantes** these

sa
se

chairs are alike ‖ *m* resemblance, likeness; fellow, fellow man

semejanza *f* similarity, resemblance; simile; **a semejanza de** like

semejar *tr* to resemble, to be like ‖ *intr* & *ref* to be alike; **semejar a** or **semejarse a** to resemble, to be like

semen *m* semen

semental *adj* (*animal*) stud, breeding ‖ *m* sire; stallion; stock bull

semestral *adj* semester

semestre *m* semester

semibola *f* little slam

semibreve *f* (mus) whole note

semiconductor *m* semiconductor

semiconsciente *adj* semiconscious

semicul·to -ta *adj* semilearned

semidifun·to -ta *adj* half-dead

semidormi·do -da *adj* half-asleep

semifinal *adj* & *f* (sport) semifinal

semilla *f* seed; **semilla de césped** grass seed

semillero *m* seedbed

seminario *m* seminary; seminar; nursery

semi-remolque *m* semitrailer

semita *mf* Semite ‖ *m* (*idioma*) Semitic

semíti·co -ca *adj* Semitic

semivi·vo -va *adj* half-alive

semovientes *mpl* stock, livestock

sempiter·no -na *adj* everlasting

Sena *m* Seine

senado *m* senate

senador *m* senator

senaduría *f* senatorship

sencillez *f* simplicity, plainness, candor

senci·llo -lla *adj* simple, plain, candid; single ‖ *m* change, loose change

senda *f* path, footpath

sendero *m* path, footpath, byway

sen·dos -das *adj pl* one each, one to each, e.g., **les dio sendos libros** he gave one book to each of them, he gave each of them a book

senectud *f* age, old age

senil *adj* senile

senilidad *f* senility

senilismo *m* (pathol) senility

seno *m* bosom, breast; lap; heart; womb; bay, gulf; cavity, hollow, recess; asylum, refuge

sensación *f* sensation

sensatez *f* good sense

sensa·to -ta *adj* sensible

sensibilizar §60 *tr* to sensitize

sensible *adj* appreciable, perceptible, noticeable, sensible; considerable; sensitive; deplorable, regrettable

sensiblería *f* mawkishness

sensible·ro -ra *adj* mawkish

sensiti·vo -va *adj* (*de los sentidos*) sense, sensitive; sentient; stimulating

senso·rio -ria *adj* sensory

sensual *adj* sensual, sensuous

sentada *f* sitting; **de una sentada** at one sitting

senta·do -da *adj* seated; settled; stable, permanent; sedate; **dar por sentado** to take for granted ‖ *f* see **sentada**

sentar §2 *tr* to seat; to settle; to fit, to suit; to agree with ‖ *ref* to sit, to sit down; to settle, settle down

sentencia *f* maxim; (law) sentence

sentenciar *tr* to sentence; (*una cuestión*) to decide; (*p.ej., un libro a la hoguera*) (coll) to consign

senti·do -da *adj* felt; deep-felt; sensitive; eloquent; **darse por sentido** to take offense ‖ *m* sense, meaning; direction; consciousness; **sentido común** common sense

sentimiento *m* sentiment; feeling; sorrow, regret

sentir *m* feeling; opinion; judgment ‖ §68 *tr* to feel; to hear; to be or feel sorry for; to sense ‖ *intr* to feel; to be sorry, to feel sorry ‖ *ref* to feel; to feel oneself to be; to be resentful; to crack, be cracked; **sentirse de** to feel; to have a pain in; to resent

seña *f* sign, mark, token; password, watchword; **por las señas** (coll) to all appearances; **por más señas** or **por señas** (coll) as a greater proof; **señas** address; description

señal *f* sign, mark, token; landmark; bookmark; trace, vestige; scar; signal; traffic light; representation; reminder; pledge; brand; down payment; **señal de ocupado** (telp) busy signal; **señal de tramo** (rr) block signal; **señal de vídeo** video signal; **señal digital** fingerprint; **señal para marcar** (telp) dial tone

señala *f* (Chile) earmark (*on livestock*)

señala·do -da *adj* noted, distinguished

señalar *tr* to mark; to show, indicate; to point at, point out; to signal; to brand; to determine, fix; to appoint; to sign and seal; to scar; to threaten ‖ *ref* to distinguish oneself, to excel

señalizar §60 *tr* to signal

señor *m* sir, mister; lord, master, owner; **muy señor mío** Dear Sir; **señores** Mr. and Mrs.; ladies and gentlemen

señora *f* madam, missus; mistress, owner; wife; **muy señora mía** Dear Madam; **Nuestra Señora** our Lady; **señora de compañía** chaperon

señorear *tr* to dominate, to rule; to master, to control; to seize, take control of; to tower over; to excel ‖ *intr* to strut, to swagger ‖ *ref* to strut, to swagger; to control oneself; **señorearse de** to seize, take control of

señoría *f* lordship; ladyship; rule, sway

señoril *adj* lordly; haughty; majestic

señorío *m* dominion, sway, rule; mastery; arrogance, lordliness, majesty; gentry, nobility

señorita *f* young lady; miss

señorito *m* master; young gentleman; (coll) playboy

señuelo *m* decoy, lure; bait; enticement

separa·do -da *adj* separate; separated; apart; **por separado** separately; under separate cover

separar *tr* to separate; to dismiss, discharge ‖ *ref* to separate; to resign

separata *f* reprint, offprint

sept.e *abbr* **septiembre**

septeto *m* septet

sépti·co -ca *adj* septic

septiembre *m* September

sépti·mo -ma *adj* & *m* seventh

sepulcro *m* sepulcher, tomb, grave; **santo sepulcro** Holy Sepulcher

sepultar *tr* to bury; to hide away

sepultura *f* burial; grave; **estar con un pie en la sepultura** to have one foot in the grave

sepulturero *m* gravedigger

sequedad *f* dryness, drought; gruffness, surliness

sequía *f* drought

séquito *m* retinue, suite; following, popularity

ser *m* being; essence; life ‖ *v* §69 *v aux* (to form passive voice) to be, e.g., **el discurso fue aplaudido por todos** the speech was applauded by everybody ‖ *intr* to be; **a no ser por** if it were not for; **a no ser que** unless; **érase que se era** (coll) once upon a time there was; **es decir** that is to say; **sea lo que fuere** be that as it may; **ser de** to belong to; to become of; to be, e.g., **el reloj es de oro** the watch is gold; **ser de ver** to be worth seeing; **soy yo** it is I

serafín *m* seraph; great beauty (*person*)

serena *f* night love song; (coll) night dew, night air

serenar *tr* to calm; to pacify; to cool; to settle

serenata *f* serenade

serenidad *f* serenity; **serenidad del espíritu** peace of mind

sere‧no -na *adj* serene, calm; clear, cloudless ‖ *m* night watchman; night dew, night air ‖ *f see* **serena**

serial *adj* serial ‖ *m* (rad) serial; **serial lacrimógeno** soap opera; **serial radiado** (rad) serial

serie *f* series; **de serie** stock, e.g., **coche de serie** stock car; **en serie** mass; **fuera de serie** custom-built, special; outsize

seriedad *f* seriousness; reliability; sternness, severity; solemnity

se‧rio -ria *adj* serious; reliable; stern; solemn

sermón *m* sermon

sermonear *tr & intr* to sermonize

serpear or **serpentear** *intr* to wind, meander; to wriggle, squirm

serpentín *m* coil

serpiente *f* serpent, snake; **serpiente de cascabel** rattlesnake

serranía *f* range of mountains, mountainous country

serra‧no -na *adj* highland, mountain ‖ *mf* highlander, mountaineer

serrar §2 *tr* to saw

serrería *f* sawmill

serrín *m* sawdust

serrucho *m* handsaw

Servia *f* Serbia

servicial *adj* accommodating, obliging

servicio *m* service; (tennis) service, serve; (Am) toilet; **libre servicio** self-service; **servicio de grúa** (aut) towing service

servi‧dor -dora *mf* servant; humble servant; (tennis) server; **servidor de Vd.** your servant, at your service ‖ *m* waiter; suitor ‖ *f* waitress

servidumbre *f* servitude; servants, help;

compulsion; (law) easement; **servidumbre de la gleba** serfdom; **servidumbre de paso** (law) right of way; **servidumbre de vía** (rr) right of way

servil *adj* servile

servilleta *f* napkin

servilletero *m* napkin ring

ser‧vio -via *adj & mf* Serbian ‖ *f see* **Servia**

servir §50 *tr* to serve; to help, wait on; (*un pedido*) to fill; (tennis) to serve; **para servir a Vd.** at your service ‖ *intr* to serve; (*en los naipes*) to follow suit; **servir de** to serve as; to be used as; **servir para** to be good for, to be used for ‖ *ref* to help oneself, to serve oneself; to have the kindness to, to deign to; **servirse de** to use, to make use of; **sírvase** please

serv.º *abbr* servicio

servocroata *adj & mf* Serbo-Croatian

servodirección *f* (aut) power steering

servoembrague *m* (aut) automatic clutch

sésamo *m* sesame; **sésamo ábrete** open sesame

sesenta *adj, pron & m* sixty

sesenta‧vo -va *adj & m* sixtieth

sesgar §44 *tr* (*el paño*) to cut on the bias; to bevel, slant, slope

ses‧go -ga *adj* beveled, slanting, sloped; oblique; stern; calm ‖ *m* bevel; bias; slant, slope; turn; compromise; **al sesgo** obliquely; on the bias

sesión *f* session; sitting; meeting; (*cada representación de un drama o película*) show; **sesión continua** (mov) continuous showing; **sesión de espiritistas** séance, spiritualistic séance

sesionar *intr* to be in session

seso *m* brain; brains, intelligence; **calentarse** or **devanarse los sesos** to rack one's brain

sestear *intr* to take a siesta; (*el ganado*) to rest in the shade

sesu‧do -da *adj* brainy; (Chile) stubborn

seta *f* bristle; toadstool

setecien‧tos -tas *adj & pron* seven hundred ‖ **setecientos** *m* seven hundred

setenta *adj, pron & m* seventy

setenta‧vo -va *adj & m* seventieth

seto *m* fence; **seto vivo** hedge, quickset

seudónimo *m* pseudonym, pen name

s.e.u.o. *abbr* salvo error u omisión

seve‧ro -ra *adj* severe; stern; strict

sevicia *f* ferocity, cruelty

sexo *m* sex; **el bello sexo** the fair sex; **el sexo feo** the sterner sex

sextante *m* sextant

sex‧to -ta *adj & m* sixth

sexual *adj* sexual, sex

si *conj* if; whether; I wonder if; **por si acaso** just in case; **si acaso** if by chance; **si no** otherwise

sí *adv* yes; indeed; (gives emphasis to verb and is often equivalent to English auxiliary verb) **él sí habla español** he does speak Spanish ‖ *pron reflex* himself, herself, itself, themselves; yourself, yourselves; oneself; each other ‖ *m* (*pl* **síes**) yes; **dar el sí** to say yes

sia·més -mesa adj & mf Siamese
siberia·no -na adj & mf Siberian
sibila f sibyl
sicalipsis f spiciness, suggestiveness
sicalípti·co -ca adj spicy, suggestive, sexy
Sicilia f Sicily
sicilia·no -na adj & mf Sicilian
sicoanálisis m var of psicoanálisis
sicoanalizar §60 tr var of psicoanalizar
sicodélico adj psychedelic
sicología f var of psicología
sicológi·co -ca adj var of psicológico
sicólo·go -ga mf var of psicólogo
sicópata mf var of psicópata
sico·sis f (pl -sis) psychosis; (afección de la piel) sycosis
sicóti·co -ca adj var of psicótico
sideral or **sidére·o -a** adj sidereal
siderurgia f iron and steel industry
sidra f cider; **sidra achampañada** hard cider
siega f reaping, mowing; harvest; crop
siembra f sowing; seeding; seedtime; sown field
siempre adv always; **de siempre** usual; **para siempre** or **por siempre** forever; **por siempre jamás** forever and ever; **siempre que** whenever; provided
siempreviva f everlasting flower
sien f temple
sierpe f serpent, snake
sierra f saw; sierra, mountain range; **sierra circular** buzz saw; **sierra continua** band saw; **sierra de armero** hacksaw; **sierra de bastidor** bucksaw; **sierra de hilar** ripsaw; **sierra de vaivén** jig saw; **sierra sin fin** band saw
sier·vo -va mf slave; servant; **siervo de la gleba** serf
siesta f siesta; hot time of day; **siesta del carnero** nap before lunch
siete adj & pron seven; **las siete** seven o'clock || m seven; (en las fechas) seventh; (coll) V-shaped tear or rip
sífilis f syphilis
sifón m siphon; siphon bottle; (tubo doblemente acodado) trap
sig.ᵉ abbr **siguiente**
sigilar tr to seal, to stamp; to conceal, keep silent
sigilo m seal; concealment, reserve; **sigilo sacramental** inviolable secrecy of the confessional
sigilo·so -sa adj tight-lipped; reserved
sigla f initial; abbreviation, symbol
siglo m (cien años) century; (comercio de los hombres) world; (largo tiempo) age; **siglo de la ilustración** or **de las luces** Age of Enlightenment
signar tr to mark; to sign; to make the sign of the cross over
signatura f library number; (mus & typ) signature
significado m meaning
significar §73 tr to signify, to mean; to point out || intr to be important
signo m sign; mark; sign of the cross; fate, destiny; **signo de admiración** exclamation mark; **signo de interrogación** question mark
siguiente adj following; next

sílaba f syllable; **última sílaba** ultima
silbar tr (p.ej., una canción) to whistle; (un silbato) to blow; (a un actor) to hiss || intr to whistle; (ir zumbando por el aire) to whiz, to whiz by
silbato m whistle
silbido m whistle, whistling, hiss; (rad) howling, squealing; **silbido de oídos** ringing in the ears
silbo m whistle, hiss
silenciador m silencer; (aut) muffler
silencio m silence; (toque que manda que cada cual se acueste) (mil) taps; (mus) rest
silencio·so -sa adj silent, noiseless, quiet, still || m (aut) muffler
sílfide f sylph
silo m silo; cave, dark place
silogismo m syllogism
silueta f silhouette
siluetear tr to silhouette
silva f (materias escritas sin orden) miscellany; verse of iambic hendecasyllables intermingled with seven-syllable lines
silvestre adj wild; rustic, uncultivated
silvicultura f forestry
silla f chair; **silla alta** high chair; **silla de balanza** (Am) rocking chair; **silla de cubierta** deck chair; **silla de junco** rush-bottomed chair; **silla de manos** sedan chair; **silla de montar** saddle, riding saddle; **silla de ruedas** wheel chair; **silla de tijera** folding chair; **silla giratoria** swivel chair; **silla hamaca** (Arg) rocking chair; **silla plegadiza** folding chair; **silla poltrona** armchair, easy chair
sillar m ashlar
silleta f bedpan
sillico m chamber pot, commode
sillín m saddle (of bicycle)
sillón m armchair, easy chair; **sillón de orejas** wing chair
sima f chasm, abyss
simbóli·co -ca adj symbolic(al)
simbolizar §60 tr to symbolize
símbolo m symbol; **Símbolo de la fe** or **de los Apóstoles** Apostles' Creed
simetría f symmetry
simétri·co -ca adj symmetric(al)
simiente f seed
símil adj like, similar || m similarity; (rhet) simile
similar adj similar
similigrabado m (typ) half-tone
similor m ormolu, similor; **de similor** fake, sham
simón m cab, hack (in old Madrid); hackman
simpatía f affection, attachment, fondness, liking; friendliness; congeniality; **tomar simpatía a** to take a liking for
simpáti·co -ca adj agreeable, pleasant, likeable, congenial
simpatizar §60 intr to be congenial, to get on well together; **simpatizar con** to get on well with
simple adj simple; single || mf simpleton || m (planta medicinal) simple
simpleza f simpleness; stupidity
simulacro m phantom, vision; idol,

image; semblance, show; pretense; sham battle; **simulacro de ataque aéreo** air-raid drill; **simulacro de combate** sham battle

simula·do -da *adj* fake; (com) pro forma

simular *tr* to simulate, feign, fake ‖ *intr* to malinger; to pretend

simultáne·o -a *adj* simultaneous

sin *prep* without; **sin embargo** nevertheless, however; **sin que** + *subj* without + *ger*

sinagoga *f* synagogue

sinapismo *m* mustard plaster; (coll) bore, nuisance

sincerar *tr* to vindicate, justify

sinceridad *f* sincerity

since·ro -ra *adj* sincere

síncopa *f* (phonet) syncope

síncope *m* fainting spell

sincróni·co -ca *adj* synchronous

sincronizar §60 *tr & intr* to synchronize

sindicar §73 *tr & ref* to syndicate

sindicato *m* syndicate; labor union

síndico *m* trustee; (*en una quiebra*) receiver

sin·diós (*pl* **-diós**) *adj* godless ‖ *mf* atheist

sinecura *f* sinecure

sinfín *m* endless amount, number

sinfonía *f* symphony

sinfóni·co -ca *adj* symphonic

singladura *f* (naut) day's run; (*de mediodía a mediodía*) (naut) day

singular *adj* singular; special; single ‖ *m* singular; **en singular** in particular

singularizar §60 *tr* to distinguish, to single out ‖ *ref* to distinguish oneself, to stand out

sinhueso *f* (coll) tongue

sinies·tro -tra *adj* evil, perverse; calamitous, disastrous ‖ *m* calamity, disaster ‖ *f* left hand, left-hand side

sinnúmero *m* great amount, great number

sino *conj* but, except; **no . . . sino** only; **no . . . sino que** only; **no solo . . . sino que** not only . . . but also ‖ *m* fate, destiny

sinóni·mo -ma *adj* synonymous ‖ *m* synonym

sinop·sis *f* (*pl* **-sis**) synopsis

sinrazón *f* wrong, injustice

sinsabor *m* displeasure; anxiety, trouble, worry

sinsonte *m* mockingbird

sintaxis *f* syntax

sínte·sis *f* (*pl* **-sis**) synthesis

sintéti·co -ca *adj* synthetic(al)

sintetizar §60 *tr* to synthesize

síntoma *m* symptom; **síntoma de abstinencia** withdrawal symptom

sintonía *f* (rad) tuning; (rad) theme song

sintonizar §60 *tr* (*el aparato receptor*) to tune; (*la estación emisora*) to tune in

sinuo·so -sa *adj* sinuous, winding; wavy; evasive

sinvergüenza *adj* (coll) brazen, shameless ‖ *mf* (coll) scoundrel, rascal

sionismo *m* Zionism

siquiatra *mf* var of **psiquiatra**

siquiatría *f* var of **psiquiatría**

síqui·co -ca *adj* var of **psíquico**

siquiera *adv* even; at least ‖ *conj* although, even though

sirena *f* siren; mermaid; **sirena de la playa** bathing beauty; **sirena de niebla** foghorn

sirga *f* towrope, towline

sirgar §44 *tr* to tow

Siria *f* Syria

si·rio -ria *adj & mf* Syrian ‖ **Sirio** *m* (astr) Sirius ‖ *f* see **Siria**

sirvienta *f* maid, servant girl

sirviente *m* servant; waiter

sisa *f* petty theft; (*para fijar los panes de oro*) sizing

sisar *tr* to filch, to snitch; (*lo que se ha de dorar*) to size

sisear *tr* to hiss ‖ *intr* to hiss; to sizzle

siseo *m* hiss, hissing; sizzle, sizzling

Sísifo *m* Sisyphus

sismógrafo *m* seismograph

sismología *f* seismology

sistema *m* system

sistematizar §60 *tr* to systematize

sístole *f* systole

sitiar *tr* to surround, hem in; to siege, besiege

sitio *m* place, spot, room; location, site; country place; seat; (mil) siege; (Am) cattle ranch; (Am) taxi stand

si·to -ta *adj* situated, located

situación *f* situation, position; **pedir situación** (aer) to ask for bearings

situar §21 *tr* to situate, locate, place; (*dinero*) to place, invest; (*un pedido*) to place ‖ *ref* to take a position; to settle; (aer) to get one's bearings

s.l. *abbr* **sin lugar**

S.M. *abbr* **Su majestad**

smo·king *m* (*pl* **-kings**) tuxedo, dinner coat

so *prep* under, e.g., **so pena de** under penalty of ‖ *interj* whoa!; (coll) you **. . . !**, e.g., **¡so animal!** you beast!

sobaco *m* armpit

sobajar *tr* to crush, to rumple; (Am) to humiliate

sobaquera *f* (*en el vestido*) armhole; (*para resguardar del sudor la parte del vestido correspondiente al sobaco*) shield

sobar *tr* to knead; to massage; to beat, slap; to paw, pet, feel; to annoy, be fresh to; (Am) to flatter; (*un hueso dislocado*) (CAm) to set; (*la caballadura*) (Arg) to tire out; (Col) to flay, to skin; (P-R) to bribe

sobarba *f* noseband

soberanía *f* sovereignty

sobera·no -na *adj* sovereign; superb ‖ *mf* sovereign ‖ *m* (*moneda*) sovereign

sober·bio -bia *adj* proud, haughty; arrogant; magnificent, superb ‖ *f* pride, haughtiness; arrogance; magnificence

so·bón -bona *adj* (coll) malingering; (coll) fresh, mushy, spoony

sobornar *tr* to bribe

soborno *m* bribery; (SAm) extra load; **de soborno** (Bol) in addition; **soborno de testigo** (law) subornation of perjury

sobra *f* extra, surplus; **sobras** leftovers, leavings; trash

sobradillo *m* penthouse

sobra·do -da *adj* excessive, superfluous; bold, daring; rich, wealthy ǁ *m* attic, garret ǁ **sobrado** *adv* too

sobrante *adj* remaining, leftover, surplus ǁ *m* leftover, surplus

sobrar *tr* to exceed, surpass ǁ *intr* to be more than enough; to be in the way; to be left, to remain

sobre *prep* on, upon; over; above; about; near; after; in addition to; out of, e.g., **en nueve casos sobre diez** in nine out of ten cases ǁ *m* envelope; **sobre de ventanilla** window envelope

sobrealimentar *tr* to overfeed; to supercharge

sobrecama *f* bedspread

sobrecarga *f* overload, extra load; overcharge; surcharge

sobrecargar §44 *tr* to overload, to overburden; to overcharge; to surcharge

sobrecargo *m* (naut) supercargo; (Am) purser ǁ *f* (Am) air hostess, stewardess

sobrecejo *m* frown

sobreceño *m* frown

sobrecoger §17 *tr* to surprise, catch; to scare, terrify ǁ *ref* to be surprised; to be scared; **sobrecogerse de** to be seized with

sobrecubierta *f* extra cover; (*de un libro*) jacket, dust jacket

sobredi·cho -cha *adj* above-mentioned

sobreexcitar *tr* to overexcite ǁ *ref* to become overexcited

sobreexponer §54 *tr* to overexpose

sobreexposición *f* overexposure

sobregirar *tr & intr* to overdraw

sobregiro *m* overdraft

sobrehombre *m* superman

sobrehuma·no -na *adj* superhuman

sobrellevar *tr* to bear, carry; (*la carga de otra persona*) to ease; (*los trabajos o molestias de la vida*) to share; (*molestias*) to suffer with patience

sobremanera *adv* exceedingly, beyond measure

sobremesa *f* tablecloth, table cover; **de sobremesa** desk, e.g., **reloj de sobremesa** desk clock; after-dinner, e.g., **discurso de sobremesa** after-dinner speech

sobremodo *adv* var of **sobremanera**

sobrenadar *intr* to float

sobrenatural *adj* supernatural

sobrenombrar *tr* to surname; to nickname

sobrenombre *m* surname; nickname

sobrentender §51 *tr* to understand ǁ *ref* to be understood, be implied

sobrepasar *tr* to excel, surpass, outdo; to exceed; to overtake ǁ *ref* to outdo each other; to go too far

sobrepe·lliz *f* (*pl* **-llices**) surplice

sobreponer §54 *tr* to superpose, put on top; to superimpose ǁ *ref* to control oneself; to triumph over adversity; **sobreponerse a** to overcome

sobreprecio *m* extra charge, surcharge

sobreproducción *f* overproduction

sobrepujar *tr* to excel, surpass

sobresaliente *adj* projecting; conspicuous, outstanding; (*en un examen*) distinguished ǁ *mf* substitute; understudy

sobresalir §65 *intr* to project, jut out; to stand out, excel

sobresaltar *tr* to assail, to rush upon; to startle, frighten ǁ *intr* to stand out clearly ǁ *ref* to be startled, be frightened; to start, to wince

sobresalto *m* fright, scare; start, shock, wince; **de sobresalto** suddenly, unexpectedly

sobrescribir §83 *tr* to address

sobrescrito *m* address

sobrestante *m* boss, foreman

sobresueldo *m* extra wages, extra pay

sobretiro *m* offprint

sobretodo *adv* especially ǁ *m* overcoat, topcoat

sobrevenir §79 *intr* to happen, take place; to supervene, to set in; **sobrevenir a** to overtake

sobrevidriera *f* window screen; window grill; storm window

sobrevivencia *f* (Ecuad) survival

sobreviviente *adj* surviving ǁ *mf* survivor

sobrevivir *intr* to survive; **sobrevivir a** to survive, to outlive

sobrevolar §61 *tr* to overfly

sobriedad *f* sobriety, moderation

sobrina *f* niece

sobrino *m* nephew

so·brio -bria *adj* sober, moderate, temperate

socaire *m* (naut) lee; **al socaire de** (naut) under the lee of; (coll) under the shelter of; **estar al socaire** (coll) to shirk

socapa *f* subterfuge; **a socapa** clandestinely

socarrén *m* eaves

socarrar *tr* to singe, scorch

soca·rrón -rrona *adj* crafty, cunning, sly; sneering; roguish

socavar *tr* to undermine, to dig under

socavón *m* cave-in; cave; (min) gallery

sociable *adj* sociable

social *adj* social; company, e.g., **edificio social** company building

socialismo *m* socialism

socialista *mf* socialist

sociedad *f* society; company, firm; **buena sociedad** (*mundo elegante*) society; **sociedad anónima** stock company; **sociedad de control** holding company; **Sociedad de las Naciones** League of Nations

so·cio -cia *mf* partner; companion; member ǁ *m* fellow; (scornful) fellow, guy

sociología *f* sociology

socorrer *tr* to aid, help, succor

socorri·do -da *adj* ready; handy, useful; hackneyed, trite, worn; well stocked

socorro *m* aid, help, succor

socoyote *m* (Mex) baby, youngest son

soda *f* soda; soda water

sodio *m* sodium

so·ez *adj* (*pl* **-eces**) base, mean, vile

so·fá *m* (*pl* **-fás**) sofa; **sofá cama** day bed

soflama _f_ glow, flicker; blush; deceit, cheating

soflamar _tr_ to flimflam; to make blush ‖ _ref_ to become scorched

sofocar §73 _tr_ to choke, suffocate, stifle, smother; to quench, extinguish; to make blush; (coll) to bother, harass ‖ _ref_ to choke, suffocate; to blush; to get excited; to get out of breath

sofoco _m_ blush, embarrassment

sofrenar _tr_ (un caballo) to check suddenly; (una pasión) to control; to chide, reprimand

soga _m_ sly fellow ‖ _f_ rope, cord; **dar soga a** (coll) to make fun of; **hacer soga** (coll) to lag behind

soja _f_ soy, soy bean

sojuzgar §44 _tr_ to subjugate, subdue

sol _m_ sun; sunlight; sunny side; **de sol a sol** from sunrise to sunset; **hacer sol** to be sunny; **soles** (poet) eyes

solamente _adv_ only

solana _f_ sunny spot; sun porch

solapa _f_ lapel; pretext, pretense; flap

solapa·do -da _adj_ overlapping; cunning, underhanded, sneaky

solapar _tr_ to put lapels on; to overlap; to conceal, cover up ‖ _intr_ to overlap

solapo _m_ lapel; flap; (coll) chuck under chin

solar _adj_ solar; ancestral ‖ _m_ ground, plot; manor house, ancestral mansion; noble lineage; (Cuba) tenement ‖ _v_ §61 _tr_ to pave, to floor; (zapatos) to sole

solarie·go -ga _adj_ ancestral; manorial

so·laz _m_ (_pl_ -laces) solace, consolation; recreation; **a solaz** with pleasure

soldada _f_ wages, pay

soldadera _f_ (Mex) camp follower

soldadesca _f_ soldiery; undisciplined troops

soldado _m_ soldier; **soldado de a pie** foot soldier; **soldado de juguete** toy soldier; **soldado de marina** marine; **soldado de plomo** tin soldier; **soldado de primera** private first class; **soldado raso** buck private

soldadura _f_ solder; soldering; weld; welding; **soldadura al arco** arc welding; **soldadura autógena** welding; **soldadura a tope** butt welding; **soldadura por puntos** spot welding

soldar §61 _tr_ to solder; (sin materia extraña) to weld ‖ _ref_ (los huesos) to knit

solear _tr_ to sun ‖ _ref_ to sun, sun oneself

soledad _f_ solitude, loneliness; longing, grieving; lonely spot

soledo·so -sa _adj_ solitary, lonely; longing, grieving

solemne _adj_ solemn; (error, mentira, etc.) (coll) downright

soler §47 _intr_ to be accustomed to

solera _f_ crossbeam; lumber, timber; mother liquor, mother of the wine; blend of sherry; old vintage sherry; tradition, standing; (Chile) curb; (Mex) brick, tile, stone; **de solera** or **de rancia solera** of the good old school, of the good old times

solevantar _tr_ to raise up; to rouse up, incite ‖ _ref_ to rise up; to revolt

solevar _tr_ to raise up; to incite to rebellion ‖ _ref_ to rise up; to revolt

solicitante _mf_ petitioner; applicant

solicitar _tr_ to solicit, ask for; to apply for; to woo, to court; to drive, to pull; (la atención) to attract; (phys) to attract

solíci·to -ta _adj_ solicitous; careful, diligent; obliging; (coll) fond, affectionate

solicitud _f_ solicitude; petition, request; application

solidar _tr_ to harden; to establish, to prove

solida·rio -ria _adj_ jointly liable; jointly binding; **solidario con** or **de** integral with

solidez _f_ solidity; strength, soundness; constancy

sóli·do -da _adj_ solid; strong, sound ‖ _m_ solid

soliloquio _m_ soliloquy

solista _adj_ (p.ej., instrumento) (mus) solo ‖ _mf_ (mus) soloist

solita·rio -ria _adj_ solitary; lonely ‖ _mf_ hermit, recluse, solitary ‖ _m_ (juego y diamante) solitaire ‖ _f_ tapeworm

sóli·to -ta _adj_ accustomed, customary

soliviantar _tr_ to rouse, stir up, incite

soliviar _tr_ to lift, lift up

so·lo -la _adj_ only, sole; alone; lonely; (p.ej., whisky) straight; (café) black; **a mis solas** alone, all by myself; **a solas** alone, unaided ‖ _pron_ only one ‖ _m_ (mus) solo

sólo _adv_ only, solely

solomillo _m_ sirloin

solomo _m_ sirloin; loin of pork

solsticio _m_ solstice

soltador _m_ release; **soltador del margen** margin release

soltar §61 _tr_ to untie, unfasten, loosen; to let go; to let go of; (una observación) to drop, to let slip; (el agua) to turn on ‖ _ref_ to get loose or free; to come loose, come off; to loosen up; to burst out; to thaw out, let oneself go

solte·ro -ra _adj_ single, unmarried ‖ _m_ bachelor ‖ _f_ spinster, maiden lady

solterona _f_ (coll) old maid

soltura _f_ looseness; agility, ease, freedom; fluency; dissoluteness; release

solución _f_ solution

solucionar _tr_ to solve, to resolve

solventar _tr_ (lo que uno debe) to settle, to pay up; (una dificultad) to solve

solvente _adj_ & _m_ solvent

sollastre _m_ scullion

sollozar §60 _intr_ to sob

sollozo _m_ sob

sombra _f_ (falta de luz brillante) shade; (imagen obscura que proyecta un cuerpo opaco) shadow; shady side; darkness; parasol; ignorance; ghost, spirit; grace, charm, wit; favor, protection; (coll) luck; **a la sombra** in the shade; (coll) in jail; **a sombra de tejado** (coll) stealthily, sneakingly; **ni por sombra** by no means; without any notice; **no ser su sombra** to be but a shadow of one's former self; **tener buena sombra** (coll) to be likeable; (coll) to bring good luck

sombrear *tr* to shade; (*un dibujo*) to hatch

sombrerera *f* bandbox, hatbox

sombrerería *f* hat store, hat factory; millinery shop

sombrere·ro -ra *mf* hatter, hat maker ‖ *f* see **sombrerera**

sombrero *m* hat; **sombrero de copa** high hat, top hat; **sombrero de muelles** opera hat; **sombrero de paja** straw hat; **sombrero de pelo** (Am) high hat; **sombrero de tres picos** three-cornered hat; **sombrero gacho** slouch hat; **sombrero hongo** derby; **sombrero jarano** (Am) sombrero

sombrilla *f* parasol, sunshade; **sombrilla de playa** beach umbrella; **sombrilla protectora** (mil) umbrella

sombrí·o -a *adj* shady; somber; gloomy

sombro·so -sa *adj* shadowy, full of shadows; shady

some·ro -ra *adj* brief, summary; slight; superficial, shallow

someter *tr* to subdue, to subject; (*razones, reflexiones; un negocio*) to submit ‖ *ref* to yield, submit, surrender

someti·do -da *adj* humble, submissive

sometimiento *m* subjection

somier *m* bedspring, spring mattress

somorgujar *tr* to plunge, to submerge ‖ *intr* to dive ‖ *ref* to plunge

son *m* sound; news, rumor; pretext, motive; manner, mode; **en son de** in the manner of, by way of; as

sona·do -da *adj* talked-about; famous, noted

sonaja *f* jingle

sonajero *m* rattle, child's rattle

sonámbu·lo -la *mf* sleepwalker, somnambulist

sonar §61 *tr* to sound, to ring; (*un instrumento de viento, un silbato*) to blow; (*un instrumento de viento*) to play ‖ *intr* to sound, to ring; (*un reloj*) to strike; to seem; (coll) to sound familiar; **sonar a** to sound like, have the appearance of ‖ *ref* to be rumored; (*las narices*) to blow

sonda *f* sounding; plummet, lead; drill; (surg) probe, sound

sondar or **sondear** *tr* & *intr* to sound, to probe

sonetizar §60 *intr* to sonneteer

soneto *m* sonnet

sóni·co -ca *adj* sonic

sonido *m* sound; report, rumor

sonoridad *f* sonority

sonorizar §60 *tr* (*una película cinematográfica*) to record sound effects on; (*una consonante sorda*) to voice ‖ *ref* to voice

sono·ro -ra *adj* sound; clear, loud, resounding

sonreír §58 *intr* & *ref* to smile

sonriente *adj* smiling

sonrisa *f* smile

sonrojar or **sonrojear** *tr* to make blush ‖ *ref* to blush

sonrojo *m* blush; word that causes blushing

sonrosar or **sonrosear** *tr* to rose-color; to make blush ‖ *ref* to become rose-colored; to blush

sonsacar §73 *tr* to pilfer; to entice away; to elicit, draw out

sonsonete *m* rhythmical tapping; singsong

soña·dor -dora *adj* dreamy ‖ *mf* dreamer

soñar §61 *tr* to dream; **ni soñarlo** (coll) not even in a dream, by no means ‖ *intr* to dream; **soñar con** to dream of; **soñar despierto** to daydream

soñolien·to -ta *adj* sleepy, dozy, drowsy; somnolent; lazy

sopa *f* (*pan u otra cosa empapada en un líquido*) sop; soup; **hecho una sopa** (coll) soaked to the skin, sopping wet; **sopa de pastas** noodle soup

sopapo *m* chuck under the chin; (coll) blow, slap

sopetear *tr* to dip, to dunk; to abuse

sopetón *m* slap, box; **de sopetón** suddenly

sopista *mf* beggar

soplar *tr* to blow; to blow away; to blow up, inflate; to snitch, swipe; to inspire; to prompt; to tip off; (*la dama a un rival*) to cut out; (coll) to squeal on ‖ *intr* to blow; (coll) to squeal ‖ *ref* to be puffed up, be conceited; (coll) to swill, gulp, gobble

soplete *m* blowpipe

soplillo *m* blower, fan; chiffon, silk gauze; light sponge cake

soplo *m* blowing, blast; breath; gust of wind; instant, moment; (*informe dado en secreto*) tip; (coll) squealing; (coll) squealer

so·plón -plona *adj* (coll) tattletale ‖ *mf* (coll) tattletale, squealer

sopor *m* sleepiness, drowsiness; stupor

soportal *m* porch, portico, arcade

soportar *tr* to support, hold up, bear; to endure, suffer

soporte *m* support, bearing, rest, standard; base, stand

soprano *mf* (*persona*) soprano ‖ *m* (*voz*) soprano

sor *f* (used before names of nuns) Sister

sorber *tr* to sip; to absorb, soak up

sorbete *m* sherbet, water ice

sorbetera *f* ice-cream freezer; (coll) high hat

sorbo *m* sip; gulp

sordera *f* deafness

sórdi·do -da *adj* sordid

sordina *f* silencer; (mus) mute; (mus) damper; **a la sordina** silently, on the quiet

sor·do -da *adj* deaf; silent, mute; muffled, dull; (*dolor, ruido*) dull ‖ *mf* deaf person; **hacerse el sordo** to pretend to be deaf; to turn a deaf ear

sordomu·do -da *adj* deaf and dumb ‖ *mf* deaf-mute

sorgo *m* sorghum, broomcorn

sorna *f* slowness; sluggishness; cunning

sorochar *ref* (SAm) to become mountain-sick; (Am) to blush

soroche *m* (SAm) mountain sickness; (Am) flush, blush; (Bol, Chile) silver-bearing galena

sorprendente *adj* surprising

sorprender *tr* to surprise; to catch; (*un secreto*) to discover

sorpresa *f* surprise; surprise package
sortear *tr* to draw or cast lots for; to choose by lot; to dodge; to duck through ‖ *intr* to draw or cast lots
sorteo *m* drawing, casting of lots; choosing by lot; dodging; (taur) workout, performance
sortija *f* ring; curl; hoop; **sortija de sello** signet ring
sortilegio *m* sorcery, witchery
sortíle·go -ga *adj* fortuneteller ‖ *m* sorcerer ‖ *f* sorceress
sosa *f* soda
sosega·do -da *adj* calm, quiet, peaceful
sosegar §66 *tr* to calm, quiet, allay ‖ *intr* to become calm, to rest ‖ *ref* to calm down, to quiet down
sosiega *f* nightcap
sosiego *m* calm, quiet, serenity
sosla·yo -ya *adj* slanting, oblique; **al soslayo** or **de soslayo** slantingly; askance
so·so -sa *adj* insipid; tasteless; dull, inane ‖ *f* see **sosa**
sospecha *f* suspicion
sospechar *tr* to suspect
sospecho·so -sa *adj* suspicious; suspect ‖ *m* suspect
sostén *m* support; (*de un buque*) steadiness; brassière
sostener §71 *tr* to support, hold up; to sustain; to maintain; to bear, to stand ‖ *ref* to remain
sosteni·do -da *adj & m* (mus) sharp
sota *m* (Chile) boss, foreman ‖ *f* (*en los naipes*) jack; jade, hussy
sotana *f* soutane, cassock
sótano *m* basement, cellar
sotavento *m* (naut) leeward
soterrar §2 *tr* to bury; to hide away
soto *m* grove; brush, thicket, copse
so·viet *m* (*pl* -**viets**) soviet
soviéti·co -ca *adj* soviet, sovietic
sovietizar §60 *tr* to sovietize
sovoz — a sovoz sotto voce, in a low tone
Sr. *abbr* **Señor**
Sra. *abbr* **Señora**
Srta. *abbr* **Señorita**
S.S.S. *abbr* **su seguro servidor**
ss. ss. *abbr* **seguros servidores**
su *adj poss* his, her, its, their, your, one's
suave *adj* suave, smooth, soft; gentle, mild, meek
suavizador *m* razor strop
suavizar §60 *tr* to smooth, ease, sweeten, soften, mollify; (*una navaja de afeitar*) to strop
subalter·no -na *adj & mf* subaltern, subordinate
subasta *f* auction, auction sale; **sacar a pública subasta** to sell at auction
subastar *tr* to auction, sell at auction
subcampe·ón -ona *mf* (sport) runner-up
subcentral *f* (elec) substation
subconsciencia *f* subconscious, subconsciousness
subconsciente *adj* subconscious
subdesarrolla·do -da *adj* underdeveloped
súbdi·to -ta *adj & mf* subject

subentender §51 *tr* to understand ‖ *ref* to be understood, be implied
subestimar *tr* to underestimate
subfusil *m* submachine gun
subi·do -da *adj* high, fine, superior; strong, intense; (*color*) bright; high, high-priced ‖ *f* rise; ascent; (*p.ej., al trono*) accession
subir *tr* to raise; to lift; to carry up; (*p.ej., una escalera*) to go up; (mus) to raise the pitch of ‖ *intr* to go up, to come up; to rise; to get worse; to spread; **subir a** to climb; to climb on; to get in or into; to get on, to mount ‖ *ref* to rise
súbi·to -ta *adj* sudden, unexpected; hurried; hasty, impetuous ‖ **súbito** *adv* suddenly
subjeti·vo -va *adj* subjective
subjunti·vo -va *adj & m* subjunctive
sublevación *f* uprising, revolt
sublevado *m* rebel, insurrectionist
sublevar *tr* to incite to rebellion ‖ *ref* to revolt
submarinista *mf* (sport) skin diver ‖ *m* (nav) submariner
submari·no -na *adj & m* submarine
suboficial *m* sergeant major; noncommissioned officer
subordina·do -da *adj & mf* subordinate
subordinar *tr* to subordinate
subproducto *m* by-product
subrayar *tr* to underline; to emphasize
subrepti·cio -cia *adj* surreptitious
subsanar *tr* to excuse, overlook; to correct, repair
subscribir §83 *tr* to subscribe; to subscribe to, to endorse; to subscribe to or for; to sign; to sign up ‖ *ref* to subscribe
subseguir §67 *intr & ref* to follow next
subsidiar *tr* to subsidize
subsidio *m* subsidy; aid, help
subsiguiente *adj* subsequent
subsistencia *f* subsistence, sustenance
subsistir *intr* to subsist
substancia *f* substance
substanciar *tr* to abstract, to abridge
substanti·vo -va *adj & m* substantive
substitución *f* replacement; (chem, law, math) substitution
substitui·dor -dora *adj & mf* substitute
substituir §20 *tr* to replace; to substitute for, take the place of ‖ *intr* to take someone's place ‖ *ref* to be replaced; to relieve each other
substituti·vo -va *adj & m* substitute
substitu·to -ta *mf* substitute
substraer §75 *tr* to remove; to deduct; to rob, steal; to subtract ‖ *ref* to withdraw; **substraerse a** to evade, avoid, slip away from
subte *m* (Arg, Urug) subway
subteniente *m* second lieutenant
subterrán·e·o -a *adj* subterranean, underground ‖ *m* subterranean; (Arg) subway
subtitular *tr* to subtitle
subtítulo *m* subtitle, subheading
suburbio *m* suburb; outlying slum
subvención *f* subvention, subsidy
subvencionar *tr* to subvention, to subsidize

subvenir §79 *intr* to provide; **subvenir a** to provide for; (*gastos*) to defray

subvertir §68 *tr* to subvert

subyugar §44 *tr* to subjugate, to subdue

sucedáne·o -a *adj & m* substitute

suceder *tr* to succeed, follow ‖ *intr* to happen; **suceder a** (*p.ej., el trono*) to succeed to ‖ *ref* to follow one another

sucesi·vo -va *adj* successive; **en lo sucesivo** in the future

suceso *m* event, happening; issue, outcome; **sucesos de actualidad** current events

suciedad *f* dirt, filth; dirtiness, filthiness

su·cio -cia *adj* dirty, filthy; base, low; tainted; blurred; (sport) foul ‖ **sucio** *adv* (sport) foully, unfairly

sucumbir *intr* to succumb

sucursal *f* branch, branch office

Sudamérica *f* South America

sudamerica·no -na *adj & mf* South American

sudar *tr* to sweat; (coll) to cough up ‖ *intr* to sweat; (*trabajar mucho*) (coll) to sweat

sudario *m* shroud, winding sheet

sudcorea·no -na *adj & mf* South Korean

sudor *m* sweat; (fig) sweat, toil; **chorrear de sudor** to swelter

sudoro·so -sa *adj* sweaty

Suecia *f* Sweden

sue·co -ca *adj* Swedish ‖ *mf* Swede ‖ *m* (*idioma*) Swedish

suegra *f* mother-in-law

suegro *m* father-in-law

suela *f* sole; sole leather; (*fish*) sole

sueldacostilla *f* grape hyacinth

sueldo *m* salary, pay

suelo *m* ground, soil, land; floor, flooring; pavement; (*p.ej., de una botella*) bottom; **no pisar en el suelo** to walk on air; **suelo franco** loam; **suelo natal** home country

suel·to -ta *adj* loose; free; easy; swift, agile, nimble; fluent; bold, daring; (*ejemplar*) single; (*verso*) blank; odd, separate; spare; bulk; **suelto de lengua** loose-tongued ‖ *m* small change; news item

sueñecillo *m* nap; **descabezar un sueñecillo** to take a nap

sueño *m* sleep; dream; (*cosa de gran belleza*) (fig) dream; **conciliar el sueño** to manage to go to sleep; **ni por sueños** by no means; **no dormir sueño** to not sleep a wink; **tener sueño** to be sleepy; **último sueño** (*muerte*) last sleep; **sueño hecho realidad** dream come true; **sueños dorados** daydreams

suero *m* serum

suerte *f* fortune, luck; piece of luck; fate, lot; kind, sort; way, manner; feat, trick; (taur) play, suerte; (Peru) lottery ticket; **de esta suerte** in this way; **de suerte que** so that, with the result that; **la suerte está echada** the die is cast; **suerte de capa** (taur) capework

suerte·ro -ra *adj* (Am) fortunate, lucky

sué·ter *m* (*pl* **-ters**) sweater

suficiente *adj* sufficient; adequate; fit, competent

sufijo *m* suffix

sufragar §44 *tr* to help, support, favor; to defray ‖ *intr* (SAm) to vote

sufragio *m* help, succor; benefit; (*voto*) suffrage

sufragismo *m* woman suffrage

sufragista *mf* woman-suffragist ‖ *f* suffragette

sufri·do -da *adj* long-suffering; (*color*) serviceable; (*marido*) complaisant

sufrir *tr* to suffer; to undergo, experience; to support, hold up; to tolerate; (*un examen*) to take ‖ *intr* to suffer

sugerencia *f* suggestion

sugerir §68 *tr* to suggest

sugestión *f* suggestion

sugestionar *tr* to influence by suggestion

sugesti·vo -va *adj* suggestive; stimulating, striking, conspicuous

suicida *adj* suicidal ‖ *mf* suicide

suicidar *ref* to commit suicide

suicidio *m* suicide

Suiza *f* Switzerland

sui·zo -za *adj & mf* Swiss ‖ *f* see **Suiza**

sujeción *f* subjection; surrender; fastening; fastener

sujetahilo *m* (elec) binding post

sujetapape·les *m* (*pl* **-les**) paper clip

sujetar *tr* to subject; to subdue; to fasten, tighten ‖ *ref* to subject oneself, to submit; to stick, adhere

suje·to -ta *adj* subject, liable; (Am) able, capable ‖ *m* subject; fellow, individual; **buen sujeto** good egg

sulfato *m* sulfate

sulfito *m* sulfite

sulfúri·co -ca *adj* sulfuric

sulfuro *m* sulfide; **sulfuro de hidrógeno** hydrogen sulfide

sulfuro·so -sa *adj* sulfurous

sultán *m* sultan; (*galanteador*) (coll) sheik

suma *f* sum, addition; summary; sum and substance; **en suma** in short, in a word

sumadora *f* adding machine

sumamente *adv* extremely, exceedingly

sumar *tr* to add; to sum up; to amount to ‖ *intr* to add; to amount; **suma y sigue** add and carry ‖ *ref* to add up; to adhere

suma·rio -ria *adj & m* summary

sumergir §27 *tr* to submerge ‖ *ref* to submerge; (*un submarino*) to dive

sumersión *f* submersion; (*de un submarino*) dive

sumidad *f* top, apex, summit

sumidero *m* drain, sewer; sink

suministrar *tr* to provide, to supply

suministro *m* provision, supply; **suministros** supplies

sumir *tr* to sink; to press down; to overwhelm ‖ *ref* to sink; (*p.ej., los carrillos, el pecho*) to be sunken; (Am) to shrink, to shrivel; (Am) to cower; (*p.ej., el sombrero*) (Am) to pull down

sumisión *f* submission; (*sometimiento*) subjection

sumi·so -sa *adj* submissive

su·mo -ma *adj* high, great, extreme;

supreme; **a lo sumo** at most, at the most ‖ *f* see **suma**

suncho *m* hoop

suntuo·so -sa *adj* sumptuous

supeditar *tr* to hold down, oppress

superar *tr* to surpass, excel; to conquer

superávit *m* (com) surplus

supercarburante *m* high-test fuel

superchería *f* fraud, deceit

superficial *adj* superficial; surface

superficie *f* surface; exterior, outside; area; **superficie de sustentación** (aer) airfoil

super·fluo -flua *adj* superfluous

superhombre *m* superman

superintendente *mf* superintendent, supervisor; **superintendente de patio** (rr) yardmaster

superior *adj* superior; upper; higher; **superior a** superior to; higher than; more than; larger than ‖ *m* superior

superiora *f* mother superior

superioridad *f* superiority; authorities

superlati·vo -va *adj* & *m* superlative

supermercado *m* supermarket

super·no -na *adj* highest, supreme

superpoblar §61 *tr* to overpopulate

superponer §54 *tr* to superpose

superproducción *f* overproduction

supersóni·co -ca *adj* supersonic ‖ *f* supersonics

superstición *f* superstition

supersticio·so -sa *adj* superstitious

supervisar *tr* to supervise

supervivencia *f* survival; (law) survivorship

súpi·to -ta *adj* sudden; (coll) impatient; (Col) dumbfounded

suplantar *tr* to supplant by treachery; (*un documento*) to alter fraudulently

suplefal·tas *mf* (*pl* -tas) substitute, fill-in

suplemento *m* supplement; excess fare

súplica *f* entreaty, supplication; request

suplicante *adj* & *mf* suppliant

suplicar §73 *tr* & *intr* to entreat, implore; (law) to petition

suplicio *m* torture; punishment, execution; anguish

suplir *tr* to supplement, make up for; to replace, take the place of; (*un defecto de otra persona*) to cover up; (gram) to understand

suponer §54 *tr* to suppose; to presuppose, imply; to entail ‖ *intr* to have weight, have authority

suposición *f* supposition; distinction; falsehood, imposture

supositorio *m* suppository

supradi·cho -cha *adj* above-mentioned

supre·mo -ma *adj* supreme

supresión *f* suppression, elimination, omission; cancellation; deletion

suprimir *tr* to suppress, eliminate, do away with; to cancel; to delete

supues·to -ta *adj* supposed, assumed, hypothetical; **supuesto que** since, inasmuch as ‖ *m* assumption, hypothesis; **dar por supuesto** to take for granted; **por supuesto** of course, naturally

supurar *intr* suppurate, discharge pus

sur *m* south; south wind

Suramérica *f* South America

surcar §73 *tr* to furrow; to plough; to cut through; to streak through

surco *m* furrow; wrinkle, rut, cut; (*del disco gramofónico*) groove; **echarse en el surco** (coll) to lie down on the job

surcorea·no -na *adj* & *mf* South Korean

sure·ño -ña *adj* (Am) southern ‖ *mf* (Am) southerner

surestada *f* (Arg) southeaster

surgir §27 *intr* to spout, spurt; to come forth, spring up; to arise, appear

suripanta *f* (hum) chorine; (scornful) slut, jade

surti·do -da *adj* assorted ‖ *m* assortment; supply, stock

surtidor *m* jet, spout, fountain; **surtidor de gasolina** gasoline pump

surtir *tr* to furnish, provide, supply ‖ *intr* to spout, spurt, shoot up

susceptible *adj* susceptible; touchy

suscitar *tr* to stir up, provoke; (*dudas, una cuestión*) to raise

susodi·cho -cha *adj* above-mentioned

suspender *tr* to hang; to suspend; to astonish; to postpone; to fail, to flunk ‖ *ref* to be suspended

suspensión *f* suspension; astonishment; **suspensión de fuegos** cease fire

suspen·so -sa *adj* suspended, hanging; baffled, bewildered; (theat) closed ‖ *m* flunk, condition

suspensores *mpl* (Am) suspenders

suspensorio *m* jockstrap, supporter

suspi·caz *adj* (*pl* -caces) suspicious, distrustful

suspirar *intr* to sigh

suspiro *m* sigh; ladyfinger; (mus) quarter rest

sustentación *f* support, prop; (aer) lift

sustentar *tr* to sustain, support, feed; to maintain; (*una tesis*) to defend

sustento *m* sustenance, support, food; maintenance

susto *m* scare, fright

susurrar *tr* to whisper ‖ *intr* to whisper; to murmur, rustle, purl, hum; to be bruited about ‖ *ref* to be bruited about

susurro *m* whisper; murmur, rustle, purling, hum

susu·rrón -rrona *adj* (coll) whispering ‖ *mf* (coll) whisperer

sutil *adj* subtle; keen, observant; thin, delicate

su·yo -ya *adj poss* of his, of hers, of yours, of theirs, e.g., **un amigo suyo** a friend of his; *pron poss* his, hers, yours, theirs, its, one's; **hacer de las suyas** (coll) to be up to one's old tricks; **salirse con la suya** to have one's way; to carry one's point

T

T, t (te) *f* twenty-third letter of the Spanish alphabet

t. *abbr* **tarde**

taba *f* anklebone; (*del carnero*) knucklebone; (*juego*) knucklebones

tabaco *m* tobacco; cigar; snuff; (Cuba, CAm, Mex) punch; **tabaco en rama** leaf tobacco

tabalada *f* (coll) bump, thump, heavy fall; (coll) slap

tabalear *tr* to rock, to sway ‖ *intr* to drum with the fingers

tabanazo *m* (coll) slap; (coll) slap in the face

tabanco *m* stand, stall, booth

tábano *m* horsefly, gadfly

tabanque *m* treadle wheel

tabaola *f* noise, hubbub

tabaquera *f* snuffbox; (*de la pipa de fumar*) bowl; (Arg, Chile) tobacco pouch

tabaquería *f* tobacco store, cigar store

tabaque·ro -ra *adj* tobacco ‖ *mf* tobacconist; cigar maker ‖ *m* (Bol) pocket handkerchief ‖ *f* see **tabaquera**

tabardete *m* or **tabardillo** *m* (coll) sunstroke; (coll) harum-scarum

tabarra *f* (coll) bore, tiresome talk

taberna *f* tavern, saloon, barroom, pub

tabernáculo *m* tabernacle

tabernera *f* barmaid

tabernero *m* tavern keeper; bartender

tabica *f* (*para cubrir un hueco*) board; (*del frente de un escalón*) riser

tabicar §73 *tr* to close up, to shut up; to wall up

tabique *m* thin wall; partition wall, partition

tabla *f* (*de madera*) board; (*de metal*) sheet; (*de piedra*) slab; (*de tierra*) strip; (*cuadro pintado en una tabla*) panel; (*lista, catálogo; índice de materias*) table; **escapar** or **salvarse en una tabla** to have a narrow escape; **tabla de lavar** washboard; **tabla de planchar** ironing board; **tabla de salvación** lifesaver, helping hand; **tablas** draw, tie; (*escenario del teatro*) stage; (*de la plaza de toros*) barrier; **tener tablas** to have stage presence

tablado *m* flooring; scaffold; (*escenario del teatro*) stage

tablear *tr* to cut into boards; to divide into plots or patches; to level, to grade

tablero *m* boarding; timber; table top; gambling table; cutting board; checkerboard, chessboard; counter; blackboard; **poner al tablero** to risk; **tablero de instrumentos** (aer) control panel; (aut) dashboard

tableta *f* small board; (*taco de papel; comprimido, pastilla*) tablet

tabletear *intr* to rattle

tablilla *f* tablet; splint; bulletin board

tablón *m* plank; beam

tabloncillo *m* (taur) seat in last row

ta·bú *m* (*pl* **-búes**) taboo

tabuco *m* hovel

tabulador *m* tabulator

tabular *tr* to tabulate

taburete *m* stool

tac *m* tick

tacada *f* stroke (*of a billiard cue*)

taca·ño -ña *adj* stingy

táci·to -ta *adj* tacit; silent

tacitur·no -na *adj* taciturn; melancholy

taco *m* bung, plug; wad, wadding; billiard cue; pad, tablet; drumstick; (coll) snack, bite; (coll) drink; (coll) oath, curse; (Am) heel; (Am) muddle, mess

tacón *m* heel

taconear *tr* (Chile) to fill, to stuff ‖ *intr* to click the heels; to strut

taconeo *m* click, clicking (*of heels*)

tácti·co -ca *adj* tactical ‖ *m* tactician ‖ *f* tactics

tacto *m* (sense of) touch; (*del dactilógrafo, el pianista, el instrumento*) touch; skill; tact

tacha *f* defect, fault, flaw

tachar *tr* to erase; to strike out; to blame, find fault with

tacho *m* (Arg) garbage can; (Arg) watch; (Arg, Chile) boiler; (Cuba) sugar pan; (Am) tin sheet

tachón *m* scratch, erasure; ornamental tack or nail; trimming

tachonar *tr* to adorn with ornamental tacks; to trim with ribbon; to spangle, to stud

tachuela *f* tack; hobnail; (Chile, Mex) runt, half pint; (SAm) drinking cup

Tadeo *m* Thaddeus

tafetán *m* taffeta; **tafetanes** flags, colors; (coll) finery; **tafetán inglés** court plaster

tafilete *m* morocco leather; (Am) sweatband

tagarote *m* sparrow hawk; scrivener; (coll) lout; (coll) gentleman sponger

tagua *f* (Chile) mud hen; (*arbusto*) (SAm) ivory palm; (*fruto*) (SAm) ivory nut

taha·lí *m* (*pl* **-líes**) baldric

tahona *f* horse-driven flour mill; bakery

ta·hur -hura *adj* gambling; cheating ‖ *mf* gambler; cheat; cardsharp

tailan·dés -desa *adj* & *mf* Thai

Tailandia *f* Thailand

taima·do -da *adj* sly, crafty; (Arg, Ecuad) lazy; (Chile) gruff, sullen

tajada *f* cut; slice; (coll) hoarseness; (coll) drunk

tajadero *m* chopping block

tajalá·piz *m* (*pl* **-pices**) pencil sharpener

tajamar *m* cutwater; (Am) dike, dam

tajar *tr* to cut; to slice; (*un lápiz*) to sharpen

tajo *m* cut; cutting edge; chopping block; execution block; steep cliff ‖ **Tajo** *m* Tagus

tal *adj indef* such; such a ‖ *pron indef* so-and-so; such a thing; someone ‖ *adv* so; in such a way; **con tal (de) que** provided (that); **¿qué tal?** how?; hello!, how's everything?

talabarte *m* sword belt
talabartero *m* saddler, harness maker
talache *m* or **talacho** *m* (Mex) mattock
taladrar *tr* to bore, drill, pierce, perforate; (*un billete*) to punch; (*un problema*) to get to the bottom of
taladro *m* drill; auger; drill hole; drill press
tálamo *m* bridal bed
talán *m* ding-dong
talante *m* countenance, mien; desire, will, pleasure; way, manner
talar *adj* (*traje, vestidura*) long || *tr* (*árboles*) to fell; to destroy, lay waste
talco *m* tinsel; talc; **talco en polvo** talcum powder
talega *f* bag, sack; **talegas** (coll) money, wealth
talego *m* big bag, sack; (coll) slob; **tener talego** (coll) to have money tucked away
taleguilla *f* small bag; bullfighter's breeches
talento *m* talent
talento·so -sa *adj* talented
Tales *m* Thales
Talía *f* Thalia
talismán *m* talisman
talón *m* heel; (aut) lug, flange; check, voucher, coupon; (*de un cheque*) stub
talona·rio -ria *adj* stub || *m* stub book, checkbook
talonear *intr* (coll) to dash along
talud *m* slope
talla *f* cut; carving; height, stature; size; ransom; reward; (Arg) chatting, prattle; (CAm) fraud, lie; (Col) beating, thrashing
tallar *tr* to carve; (*una piedra preciosa*) to cut; (*naipes*) to deal; to appraise; to engrave; to grind; to size up; (Col) to beat, to thrash || *intr* (Arg) to chat, converse; (Chile) to make love
tallarín *m* noodle
talle *m* shape, figure, stature; waist; fit; appearance, outline; (Am) bodice
taller *m* shop, workshop; factory, mill; atelier; studio; laboratory; **taller agremiado** closed shop; **taller franco** open shop; **taller penitenciario** workhouse
tallo *m* stem, stalk; shoot, sprout; (Col) cabbage
tamal *m* (CAm, Mex) tamale; (Am) intrigue; (Chile) bundle
tamañi·to -ta *adj* so small; very small; confused, disconcerted
tama·ño -ña *adj* so big; such a big; very big, very large; so small; **abrir tamaños ojos** to open one's eyes wide || *m* size
tambaleante *adj* staggering
tambalear *intr* & *ref* to stagger, reel, totter
también *adv* also, too
tambo *m* (Arg, Chile) brothel; (SAm) roadside inn; (Arg, Urug) dairy
tambor *m* drum; (*persona que toca el tambor*) drummer; sieve, screen; eardrum; coffee roaster; **a tambor batiente** with drums beating; in triumph; **tambor mayor** drum major

tamborilear *tr* to praise to the skies || *intr* to drum
Támesis *m* Thames
ta·miz *m* (*pl* **-mices**) sieve
tamizar §60 *tr* to sift, to sieve
tamo *m* fuzz, fluff
tampoco *adv* neither, not either; **ni yo tampoco** nor I either
tampón *m* stamp pad
tan *adv* so; **tan . . . como** or **cuan** as . . . as; **tan siquiera** at least; **un tan + adj** such a + *adj* || *m* boom (*of a drum*)
tanda *f* turn; shift, relay; task; coat, layer; game, match; flock, lot, pack; (Am) show; (Am) habit, bad habit
tangente *adj* & *f* tangent; **escaparse, irse** or **salir por la tangente** (coll) to evade the issue
Tánger *f* Tangier
tanguista *f* hostess (*in a night club*)
ta·no -na *adj* & *mf* (Arg) Neapolitan, Italian
tanque *m* tank; (dial) dipper, drinking cup
tantán *m* tom-tom; clanging; boom
tantear *tr* to compare; to size up; to probe, test, feel out; to sketch, outline; to keep the score of || *intr* to keep score; (Am) to grope; **¡tantee Vd.!** just imagine!, fancy that!
tanteo *m* comparison; careful consideration; test, probe, trial; trial and error; score
tan·to -ta *adj* & *pron indef* so much; as much; **tanto . . . como** as much . . . as; both . . . and; **tan·tos -tas** so many; as many; **tantos . . . como** as many . . . as; **y tantos** odd, or more, e.g., **veinte y tantos** twenty odd, twenty or more || *m* copy; counter, chip; point; (Am) portion, part; **apuntar los tantos** to keep score; **entre tanto** in the meantime; **estar al tanto de** to be aware of, to be or keep informed about; **poner al tanto de** to make aware of, to keep informed of; **por lo tanto** or **por tanto** therefore || **tanto** *adv* so much; so hard; so often; so long; as much
tañer §70 *tr* (*un instrumento músico*) to play; (*una campana*) to ring || *intr* to drum with the fingers
tañido *m* sound, tone; twang; ring, tang
tapa *f* lid, cover, top, cap; (*de un cilindro, un barril*) head; (*de una compuerta*) gate; (*de un libro*) board cover; shirt front; (aut) valve cap; **levantarse** or **saltarse la tapa de los sesos** to blow one's brains out; **tapas** appetizer, free lunch
tapabalazo *m* (Am) fly (*of trousers*)
tapabarro *m* (Chile) mudguard
tapaboca *f* slap in the mouth; muffler; (coll) squelch, squelcher
tapacu·bo or **tapacu·bos** *m* (*pl* **-bos**) (aut) hubcap
tapadera *f* lid, cover, cap
tapagote·ras *m* (*pl* **-ras**) (Arg) roofing cement; (Col) roofer
tapaguje·ros *m* (*pl* **-ros**) (coll) bungling mason; (coll) substitute, replacement
tapar *tr* to cover; to cover up, to hide;

to plug, stop, stop up; to conceal; to obstruct; to wrap up; (*un diente*) (Chile) to fill

tapara *f* (Ven) gourd; **vaciarse como una tapara** (Ven) to spill all one knows

taparrabo *m* loincloth; bathing trunks

tapera *f* (SAm) ruins; (SAm) shack

tapete *m* rug; runner; table scarf; **estar sobre el tapete** to be on the carpet, be under discussion; **tapete verde** card table, gambling table

tapia *f* mud wall, adobe wall

tapiar *tr* to wall up, wall in; to close up

tapicería *f* tapestries; upholstery; tapestry shop; upholstery shop

tapicero *m* tapestry maker; upholsterer; carpet maker; carpet layer

ta·piz *m* (*pl* **-pices**) tapestry

tapizar §60 *tr* to tapestry; to upholster; to carpet; to cover

tapón *m* stopper, cork; cap; bottle cap; bung, plug; (elec) fuse; (surg) tampon; **tapón de algodón** (surg) swab; **tapón de cubo** (aut) hubcap; **tapón de desagüe** drain plug; **tapón de tráfico** traffic jam; **tapón de vaciado** (aut) drain plug

taponar *tr* to plug, stop up; (surg) to tampon

taponazo *m* pop

taque *m* click; knock, rap

taqué *m* (aut) tappet

taquigrafía *f* shorthand, stenography

taquigrafiar §77 *tr* to take down in shorthand ‖ *intr* to take shorthand

taquígra·fo -fa *mf* stenographer

taquilla *f* ticket rack; ticket window; ticket office; box office; gate, take; file; (C-R) inn, tavern

taquille·ro -ra *adj* box-office ‖ *mf* ticket agent

taquimeca *mf* (coll) shorthand-typist

taquimecanógra·fo -fa *mf* shorthand-typist

tarabilla *f* millclapper; catch; turnbuckle; (*de la hebilla de la correa*) tongue; (coll) chatterbox; (coll) jabber; **soltar la tarabilla** (coll) to talk a blue streak

tarabita *f* (*clavillo de la hebilla*) tongue; (SAm) rope of rope bridge

taracea *f* marquetry, inlaid work

tarambana *adj & mf* (coll) crackpot

tararear *tr & intr* to hum

tarasca *f* dragon (*in Corpus Christi procession*); (*mujer fea*) (coll) hag

tarascada *f* bite; (coll) tart reply

tardanza *f* slowness, delay, tardiness

tardar *intr* to be long, to be slow; to be late; **a más tardar** at the latest; **tardar en** + *inf* to be late in + *ger* ‖ *ref* to be long, to be slow; to be late

tarde *adv* late; too late; **hacerse tarde** to grow late; **tarde o temprano** sooner or later ‖ *f* afternoon; evening; **de la tarde a la mañana** overnight; suddenly, in no time; unexpectedly

tardecer §22 *intr* to grow dark, to grow late

tardí·o -a *adj* late, delayed; dilatory; tardy; slow

tar·do -da *adj* slow; late; slow, dull; dense

tar·dón -dona *mf* (coll) poke, slow poke

tarea *f* task, job; care, worry

tarifa *f* tariff; price list; rate; fare (telp) toll; **tarifa recargada** extra fare

tarima *f* platform; stand; stool; low bench; (*entablado para dormir*) bunk

tarjeta *f* card; **tarjeta de buen deseo** or **de felicitación** greeting card; **tarjeta de visita** calling card, visiting card; **tarjeta navideña** Christmas card; **tarjeta perforada** punch card; **tarjeta postal** post card, postal card

tarjetero *m* card case; card index

tarquín *m* mire, slime, mud

tarro *m* jar; milk pail; (Am) horn; (SAm) top hat

tarta *f* tart, cake; pan

tartajear *intr* to stutter

tartalear *intr* (coll) to stagger, to sway; (coll) to be speechless

tartamudear *intr* to stutter, to stammer

tartamudeo *m* stuttering, stammering

tartamu·do -da *mf* stutterer, stammerer

tartán *m* Scotch plaid

tartana *f* tartana (*two-wheeled round-top carriage of Valencia*)

tarugo *m* wooden plug; wooden paving block; (Guat, Mex) dolt, blockhead

tasa *f* appraisal; measure, standard; rate; ceiling price

tasación *f* appraisal; regulation

tasajo *m* jerked beef

tasar *tr* to appraise; to regulate; to hold down, keep within bounds; to grudge

tasca *f* dive, joint; tavern; (Peru) surf, breakers

tata *m* (coll) daddy ‖ *f* (coll) nursemaid; (Am) little sister

tato *m* (Am) little brother

tatuaje *m* tattoo, tattooing

tatuar §21 *tr & ref* to tattoo

tauri·no -na *adj* bullfighting

taurófi·lo -la *mf* bullfight fan

tauromaquia *f* bullfighting

taxear *intr* (aer) to taxi

taxi *m* taxi, taxicab ‖ *f* taxi dancer

taxista *mf* taxi driver

taza *f* cup; (*de la fuente*) basin; (*del inodoro*) bowl

te *pron pers & reflex* thee, to thee; you, to you; thyself, to thyself; yourself, to yourself

té *m* tea; **té bailable** tea dance

tea *f* torch, firebrand

teatral *adj* theatrical

teatre·ro -ra *mf* (Am) theater-goer

teatro *m* theater; **dar teatro a** to ballyhoo; **teatro de estreno** first-run house; **teatro de repertorio** stock company

teatrólo·go -ga *mf* theater critic ‖ *m* actor ‖ *f* actress

Tebas *f* Thebes

tebe·o -a *adj & mf* Theban ‖ *m* comic book, funny paper

teca *f* teak

tecla *f* (*de piano, máquina de escribir, etc.*) key; touchy subject; **dar en la tecla** (coll) to get the knack of it; **tecla de cambio** shift key; **tecla de escape** margin release; **tecla de espa-**

cios space bar; **tecla de retroceso** backspacer

teclado *m* keyboard; **teclado manual** (mus) manual

teclear *tr* (coll) to feel out ‖ *intr* to run over the keys; to drum, to thrum; (Chile) to be at death's door; (*un jugador*) (Chile) to be losing one's last cent

tecleo *m* fingering; touch; (*de la máquina de escribir*) click

técni·co -ca *adj* technical ‖ *m* technician; expert ‖ *f* technique; technics

tecolote *m* eagle owl (*of Central America*); (Mex) night policeman

techado *m* roof; **bajo techado** indoors

techar *tr* to roof

techo *m* ceiling; roof; (*sombrero*) (coll) hat; **techo de paja** thatched roof

techumbre *f* ceiling; roof

tedio *m* ennui, boredom

tedio·so -sa *adj* tedious, boresome

teja *f* roofing tile; shovel hat; yew tree; linden tree; **a toca teja** (coll) for cash; **teja de madera** shingle

tejadillo *m* cover, top; (*de coche*) roof

tejado *m* tile roof; roof; **tejado de vidrio** (fig) glass house

tejama·ní *m* (*pl* -níes) (Am) shake (*long shingle*)

tejar *m* tile works ‖ *tr* to tile, roof with tiles

teja·roz *m* (*pl* -roces) eaves

teje·dor -dora *adj* weaving; (coll) scheming ‖ *mf* weaver; (coll) schemer

tejer *tr* & *intr* to weave

tejido *m* weave, texture; web; fabric, textile, tissue; (biol & fig) tissue; **tejido adhesivo** friction tape; **tejido de saco** (Mex) burlap; **tejido de punto** knitted fabric, jersey

tejo *m* disk; quoit; yew tree

tejón *m* badger

tela *f* cloth, fabric; (*de cebolla*) skin; (*del insecto*) web; film; (bb) cloth; (paint) canvas; (*dinero*) (slang) dough; **poner en tela de juicio** to question, to doubt; **tela de alambre** wire screen; **tela de araña** spider web, cobweb; **tela emplástica** court plaster; **tela metálica** chicken wire; wire screen

telar *m* loom; frame; embroidery frame; (bb) sewing press

telaraña *f* spider web, cobweb

telecontrol *m* remote control

teledifundir *tr* & *intr* to telecast

teledifusión *f* telecasting; telecast

telefonar *tr* & *intr* (Am) to telephone

telefonazo *m* (coll) telephone call

telefonear *tr* & *intr* to telephone

telefonema *m* telephone message

telefonista *mf* telephone operator

teléfono *m* telephone; **teléfono automático** dial telephone; **teléfono público** pay station

teleg. *abbr* **telégrafo, telegrama**

telegrafiar §77 *tr* & *intr* to telegraph

telegrafista *mf* telegrapher

telégrafo *m* telegraph; **telégrafo de banderas** wigwagging; **telégrafo de máquinas** (naut) engine-room tele-graph; **telégrafo sin hilos** wireless telegraph

telegrama *m* telegram

teleimpresor *m* teletype, teleprinter

Telémaco *m* Telemachus

telemando *m* remote control

telemetrar *tr* to telemeter

telemetría *f* telemetry

telémetro *m* telemeter; (mil) range finder

telen·do -da *adj* sprightly, lively

telerreceptor *m* television set

telescopar *tr* & *ref* to telescope

telescopio *m* telescope

telesilla *f* chair lift

telespecta·dor -dora *mf* viewer, televiewer

telesquí *m* ski lift, ski tow

teleta *f* blotter, blotting paper

teletipo *m* teletype

teletubo *m* (telv) picture tube

televidente *mf* viewer, televiewer

televisar *tr* to televise

televisión *f* television; **televisión en circuito cerrado** closed-circuit television; **televisión en colores** color television

televi·sor -sora *adj* televising; television ‖ *m* television set ‖ *f* television transmitter

telón *m* drop curtain; **telón de acero** (fig) iron curtain; **telón de boca** (theat) front curtain; **telón de fondo** or **foro** (theat) backdrop

tema *m* theme, subject; exercise; (gram) stem; (mus) theme ‖ *f* fixed idea; persistence; grudge; **a tema** in emulation

temario *m* agenda

temblar §2 *intr* to tremble, shake, quiver, shiver; **estar temblando** to teeter

tem·blón -blona *adj* (coll) shaking, tremulous ‖ *m* aspen tree

temblor *m* tremor, shaking, trembling; **temblor de tierra** earthquake

tembloro·so -sa *adj* trembling, shaking, tremulous

tem·bo -ba *adj* (Col) silly, stupid

temer *tr* & *intr* to fear

temera·rio -ria *adj* rash, reckless, foolhardy

temeridad *f* rashness, recklessness, foolhardiness, temerity

temero·so -sa *adj* frightful, dread; timid; fearful

temible *adj* dreadful, terrible, fearful

temor *m* fear, dread

témpano *m* small drum; drumhead; (*de barril*) head; (*de tocino*) flitch; (*de hielo*) iceberg, floe; (archit) tympan; (mus) kettledrum

temperamental *adj* temperamental

temperamento *m* temperament; conciliation, compromise; weather

temperar *tr* to temper, soften, moderate, calm; to tune ‖ *intr* (Am) to go to a warmer climate

temperatura *f* temperature; weather

temperie *f* weather, state of the weather

tempestad *f* storm, tempest; **tempestad de arena** sandstorm; **tempestades de risas** gales of laughter

ta
te

tempesti·vo -va *adj* opportune, timely
tempestuo·so -sa *adj* stormy, tempestuous

templa·do -da *adj* temperate; moderate; lukewarm, medium; (coll) brave, courageous; (SAm) in love; (Am) drunk, tipsy; (CAm, Mex) clever
templanza *f* temperance; mildness
templar *tr* to temper; to soften; to ease; to dilute; (*colores*) to blend; (*velas*) to trim || *intr* (*el tiempo*) to warm up || *ref* to temper; to moderate; (Am) to fall in love; (Am) to die
temple *m* weather, state of the weather; temper, disposition; humor; average; dash, boldness; (*del acero, el vidrio, etc.*) temper
templo *m* temple
témpora *f* Ember days
temporada *f* season; period; (*p.ej., de buen tiempo*) spell; **de temporada** temporarily; vacationing
temporal *adj* temporal; temporary || *m* weather; storm, tempest; spell of rainy weather
temporáne·o -a or **tempora·rio -ria** *adj* temporary
temporizar §60 *intr* to temporize; to putter around
temprane·ro -ra *adj* early
tempra·no -na *adj* early || **temprano** *adv* early
tenacidad *f* tenacity; persistence
tenacillas *fpl* sugar tongs; hair curler; tweezers; snuffers
te·naz *adj* (*pl* **-naces**) tenacious; persistent
tenazas *fpl* pincers, pliers; tongs
tenazón — a or **de tenazón** without taking aim; offhand
tenazuelas *fpl* tweezers
tendedera *f* (Am) clothesline; (Am) litter
tendedero *m* drier, frame for drying clothes; drying ground
tendencia *f* tendency
tender §51 *tr* to spread; to stretch out; to extend; to reach out; to offer, to tender; (*la ropa*) to hang out; (*con una capa de cal o yeso*) to coat; (*un puente*) to throw, build; (*una trampa*) to set; (*conductores eléctricos, vías de ferrocarril, cañerías*) to lay; (*la cama*) (Am) to make; (*un cadáver*) (Am) to lay out || *intr* to tend || *ref* to stretch out; to throw one's cards on the table; to run at full gallop
ténder *m* tender
tenderete *m* stand, booth
tende·ro -ra *adj* shopkeeper, storekeeper || *m* tent maker
tendido -da *adj* (*p.ej., de un cable*) laying; (*de una cortina de humo*) spreading; (*de alambres*) hanging, stretching; wires; (*trecho de ferrocarril*) stretch; (*ropa que tiende la lavandera*) wash; (*de cal o yeso*) coat; (*del tejado*) slope; (*de panes*) batch; (taur) uncovered stand; (Col) bedclothes
tendón *m* tendon
tenducha *f* or **tenducho** *m* miserable old store

tenebro·so -sa *adj* dark, gloomy; (*negocio*) dark, shady; (*estilo*) obscure
tenedor *m* holder, bearer; fork, tabl⟨ fork; **tenedor de acciones** stock holder; **tenedor de bonos** bondholder **tenedor de libros** bookkeeper
teneduría *f* bookkeeping
tenencia *f* tenure, tenancy; (mil & nav⟨ lieutenancy
tener §71 *tr* to have; to hold; to keep to own, possess; to consider; (*recibir* to get; to esteem; to stop; **no tenerla todas consigo** (coll) to be alarmed dismayed; **no tener nada que ver co⟨** to have nothing to do with; **no tene⟨ sobre qué caerse muerto** (coll) to no have a cent to one's name; **tener qu⟨** to have to; for expressions like **tene⟨ hambre** to be hungry, see the noun || *ref* to stop; to catch oneself, to kee⟨ from falling; to consider oneself; t⟨ fit, to go
tenería *f* tannery
tenida *f* (Am) meeting, session
teniente *adj* holding, owning; unripe mean, miserly; (coll) hard of hearin⟨ || *m* lieutenant; **teniente coronel** lieu tenant colonel; **teniente de navío** (nav) lieutenant
tenis *m* tennis
tenista *mf* tennis player
tenor *m* tenor, character, import, drif⟨ tenor; **a tenor de** in accordance wit⟨
tenorio *m* lady-killer
tensión *f* tension, stress; (elec) tension voltage; (mech) stress; **tensión arte rial** or **sanguínea** blood pressure
ten·so -sa *adj* tense, tight, taut
tentación *f* temptation
tentáculo *m* tentacle, feeler
tenta·dor -dora *adj* tempting || *n⟨* tempter
tentar §2 *tr* to touch; (*el camino*) t⟨ feel; to try, to attempt; to examine to try out, to test; to tempt; to prob⟨
tentati·vo -va *adj* tentative || *f* attempt trial, feeler
tentempié *m* (coll) snack, bite, pick me-up; (*juguete*) (coll) tumbler
tenue *adj* tenuous; light, soft; faint, sub dued; (*estilo*) simple
teñir §72 *tr* to dye; to stain; to tinge shade, color
teología *f* theology; **no meterse en teo logías** (coll) to keep out of deep wa ter
teorema *m* theorem
teoría *f* theory
tepe *m* turf, sod
tequila *m* (Mex) tequila (*distilled liquor*)
terapéuti·co -ca *adj* therapeutic(al) || *f⟨* therapeutics
terapia *f* therapy
tercena *f* government tobacco warehouse; (Ecuad) butcher shop
terce·ro -ra *adj* third || *mf* third; mediator; go-between || *m* procurer, bawd; referee, umpire
Tercero Mundo *m* Third World
terceto *m* tercet; trio
terciar *tr* to place diagonally; to divide into three parts; (*p.ej., la capa, el*

fusil) to swing over one's shoulder; (*licor*) (Am) to water ‖ *intr* to intercede, mediate ‖ *ref* to happen; to be opportune

tercia·rio -ria *adj* tertiary

ter·cio -cia *adj* third ‖ *m* third; (mil) corps; **hacer buen tercio a** to do a good turn

terciopelo *m* velvet

ter·co -ca *adj* stubborn; hard, resistant

Teresa *f* Theresa

tergiversar *tr* to slant, to twist, to distort

terliz *m* ticking

termal *adj* thermal; steam

termas *fpl* hot baths

térmi·co -ca *adj* temperature; steam; steam-generated

terminación *f* termination

terminal *adj* terminal ‖ *m* (elec) terminal

terminante *adj* final, definitive, peremptory

terminar *tr* to end, terminate; to finish ‖ *intr* to end, terminate

término *m* end, limit; boundary; bearing, manner; term; **medio término** subterfuge, evasion; compromise; **primer término** foreground; (mov) close-up; **segundo término** middle distance; **término medio** average; **último término** background

termistor *m* (elec) thermistor

termite *m* termite

termodinámi·co -ca *adj* thermodynamic ‖ *f* thermodynamics

termómetro *m* thermometer; **termómetro clínico** clinical thermometer

termonuclear *adj* thermonuclear

termopar *m* (elec) thermocouple

Termópilas, las Thermopylae

ter·mos *m* (*pl* **-mos**) thermos bottle; hot-water heater; **termos de acumulación** (elec) off-peak heater

termosifón *m* hot-water boiler

termóstato *m* thermostat

terna *f* trio

terne·jo -ja *adj* (Ecuad, Peru) peppy, energetic

ternera *f* calf; (*carne*) veal

terneza *f* tenderness; fondness; love; **ternezas** flirting, flirtation

ternilla *f* gristle

terno *m* suit of clothes; oath, curse; trio; (coll) piece of luck; (Col) cup and saucer; (W-I) set of jewelry

ternura *f* tenderness; fondness, love

terquedad *f* stubbornness; hardness, resistance

terraja *f* diestock

terral *adj* (*viento*) land ‖ *m* land breeze

Terranova *m* (*perro*) Newfoundland (dog) ‖ *f* (*isla y provincia*) Newfoundland (*island and province*)

terraplén *m* fill; embankment; terrace, platform; earthwork, rampart

terrateniente *mf* landholder, landowner

terraza *f* terrace; veranda; flat roof; (*de jardín*) border, edge; sidewalk cafe; glazed jar with two handles

terremoto *m* earthquake

terrenal *adj* earthly, mundane, worldly

terre·no -na *adj* terrestrial; mundane,

worldly ‖ *m* land, ground, terrain; lot, plot; (sport) field; (fig) field, sphere; **sobre el terreno** on the spot; with data in hand; **terreno echadizo** refuse dump

terre·ro -ra *adj* earthly; of earth; humble ‖ *m* pile, heap; mark, target; terrace; public square; (min) dump

terrestre *adj* terrestrial; ground, land

terrible *adj* terrible; gruff, surly, ill-tempered

territorio *m* territory

terromontero *m* hill, butte

terrón *m* clod; lump, cake

terror *m* terror

terrorismo *m* terrorism, frightfulness

terro·so -sa *adj* earthly; dirty

terruño *m* piece of ground; soil; country, native soil

ter·so -sa *adj* smooth, glossy, polished; smooth, limpid, flowing

tertulia *f* party, social gathering; literary gathering; game room; **estar de tertulia** to sit around and talk

tertulia·no -na *mf* party-goer; regular member

Tesalia, la Thessaly

te·sis *f* (*pl* **-sis**) thesis

te·so -sa *adj* taut, tight, tense ‖ *m* top of hill; (*en superficie lisa*) rough spot

tesón *m* grit, pluck, tenacity

tesone·ro -ra *adj* (Am) obstinate, stubborn, tenacious

tesorería *f* treasury

tesore·ro -ra *mf* treasurer

tesoro *m* treasure; treasury; treasure house; thesaurus

Tespis *m* Thespis

testa *f* head; front; (coll) head, brains; **testa coronada** crowned head

testaferro *m* (coll) dummy, figurehead, straw man

testamento *m* testament, will; **Antiguo Testamento** Old Testament; **Nuevo Testamento** New Testament; **Viejo Testamento** Old Testament

testar *tr* (Ecuad) to cross out ‖ *intr* to make a will

testaru·do -da *adj* stubborn, pig-headed

testera *f* front; (*de animal*) forehead; (*de coche*) back seat

testículo *m* testicle

testificar §73 *tr* & *intr* to testify

testigo *mf* witness; **testigo de vista, testigo ocular,** or **testigo presencial** eyewitness ‖ *m* (*evidencia*) witness; (*en un experimento*) control

testimoniar *tr* to attest, to testify to, to bear witness to

testimonio *m* testimony; affidavit; false witness

tes·tuz *m* (*pl* **-tuces**) (*p.ej., de caballo*) face; nape

teta *f* teat; breast

tetera *f* teapot, teakettle

tetilla *f* nipple

tétri·co -ca *adj* dark, gloomy; sad, sullen, gloomy

textil *adj* & *m* textile

texto *m* text; **fuera de texto** tipped-in

textura *f* texture

tez *f* complexion

ti *pron pers* thee; you

tía *f* aunt; old lady, old woman; (coll) bawd; **no hay tu tía** (coll) there's no chance; **tía abuela** grandaunt

tiara *f* tiara

tibante *adj* (Col) haughty, proud

tibia *f* shinbone; pipe, flute

ti·bio -bia *adj* tepid, lukewarm; (SAm) angry ‖ *f* see **tibia**

tibor *m* large porcelain vase; (Am) chamber pot

tiburón *m* shark

Ticiano, El Titian

tictac *m* tick-tock

tiemblo *m* aspen tree

tiempo *m* time; weather; (gram) tense; *(de un motor de combustión interna)* cycle; *(de una sinfonía)* (mus) movement; (mus) tempo; **darse buen tiempo** to have a good time; **de cuatro tiempos** (mach) four-cycle; **de dos tiempos** (mach) two-cycle; **de un tiempo a esta parte** for some time now; **el Tiempo** Father Time; **fuera de tiempo** untimely, at the wrong time; **hacer buen tiempo** to be clear; **mucho tiempo** a long time; **tomarse tiempo** to bide one's time

tienda *f* store, shop; tent; **ir de tiendas** to go shopping; **tienda de campaña** army tent; camping tent; **tienda de modas** ladies' dress shop; **tienda de objetos de regalo** gift shop; **tienda de raya** (Mex) company store

tienta *f* cleverness; probe; (taur) testing the mettle of a young bull; **andar a tientas** to grope in the dark; to feel one's way

tiento *m* touch; blind man's stick; ropewalker's pole; steady hand; care, caution; mahlstick; (coll) blow, hit; (coll) swig; **andarse con tiento** to watch one's step; **perder el tiento** to lose one's touch

tier·no -na *adj* tender; loving; tearful; soft

tierra *f* earth; ground; land; dirt; (elec) ground; **dar en tierra con** to upset, overthrow, ruin; **echar tierra a** to hush up; **en tierra, mar y aire on** land, on sea, and in the air; **irse a tierra** to topple, to collapse; **la tierra de nadie** (mil) no man's land; **tierra adentro** inland; **tierra de pan llevar** wheat land, cereal-growing land; **tierra firme** mainland; land, terra firma; **Tierra Firme** Spanish Main; **Tierra Santa** Holy Land; **tomar tierra** to land; to find one's way around; **venir** or **venirse a tierra** to topple, to collapse; **ver tierras** to see the world, to go traveling

tierral *m* (Am) cloud of dust

tie·so -sa *adj* stiff; tight, taut, tense; stubborn; bold, enterprising; strong, well; stiff, stuck-up; **tenérselas tiesas a** or **con** to stand up to ‖ **tieso** *adv* hard

ties·to -ta *adj* stiff; tight, taut, tense; stubborn ‖ *m* flowerpot; *(pedazo roto)* potsherd ‖ **tiesto** *adv* hard

tiesura *f* stiffness

ti·fo -fa *adj* (coll) full, satiated ‖ *m* typhus; **tifo de América** yellow fever; **tifo de Oriente** bubonic plague

tifón *m* waterspout; typhoon

tigra *f* tigress; (Am) female jaguar

tigre *m* tiger; (Am) jaguar

tijera *f* scissors, shears; sawbuck; **buena tijera** (coll) good cutter; (coll) good eater; (coll) gossip; **tijeras** scissors, shears

'ijeretear *tr* to snip, clip, cut; (coll) to meddle with ‖ *intr* (Am) to gossip

tila *f* linden tree; linden-blossom tea

tildar *tr* to put a tilde or dash over; to erase, strike out; **tildar de** to brand as

tilde *m* & *f* tilde; accent mark; superior dash; blemish, flaw; censure ‖ *f* jot, tittle

tiliche *m* (CAm, Mex) trinket

tiliche·ro -ra *mf* (CAm, Mex) peddler

tilín *m* ting-a-ling

tilo *m* linden tree; (Am) linden-blossom tea

tilo·so -sa *adj* (CAm) dirty, filthy

timar *tr* to snitch; to swindle ‖ *ref* (coll) to make eyes at each other

timba *f* (coll) game of chance; (coll) gambling den; (CAm, Mex) belly

timbal *m* kettledrum; *(pastel relleno)* casserole

timbrar *tr* to stamp

timbre *m* stamp, seal; tax stamp; stamp tax; deed of glory; (phonet & phys) timbre; **timbre nasal** twang; **timbres** glockenspiel

tími·do -da *adj* timid, bashful

timo *m* (coll) theft, swindle ‖ *m* (coll) lie; (coll) catch phrase

timón *m* *(del arado)* beam; rudder; (fig) helm; **timón de dirección** (aer) vertical rudder; **timón de profundidad** (aer) elevator

timonel *m* helmsman, steersman

timonera *f* (naut) pilot house, wheelhouse

timora·to -ta *adj* God-fearing; chickenhearted

tímpano *m* eardrum; kettledrum

tina *f* large earthen jar; wooden vat; bathtub

tinaja *f* large earthen jar

tincazo *m* (Arg, Ecuad) fillip

tinglado *m* shed; intrigue, trick; (zool) leatherback

tinieblas *fpl* darkness

tino *m* feel *(for things)*; good aim; knack; insight, wisdom; **coger el tino** to get the knack of it

tinta *f* ink; tint, hue; dyeing; **de buena tinta** (coll) on good authority; **tinta china** India ink; **tinta simpática** invisible ink

tinte *m* dye; dyeing; dyer's shop; (fig) coloring, false appearance

tinterillo *m* (coll) clerk, lawyer's clerk; (Am) pettifogger

tintero *m* inkstand, inkwell

tintín *m* clink; jingle

tintinear *intr* to clink; to jingle

tin·to -ta *adj* red ‖ *m* red table wine ‖ *f* see **tinta**

tintorería *f* dyeing; dyeing establishment; dry-cleaning establishment

tintore·ro -ra *mf* dyer; dry cleaner

tintura f dye; dyeing; rouge; tincture; (fig) smattering; **tintura de tornasol** litmus, litmus solution; **tintura de yodo** iodine

tiña f ringworm; (coll) stinginess

tiño·so -sa adj scabby, mangy; (coll) stingy

tío m uncle; old man; (coll) guy, fellow; **tío abuelo** granduncle; **tíos** uncle and aunt

tiovivo m merry-go-round, carrousel

tipiadora f (máquina) typewriter; (mujer) typist

tipiar tr & intr to type, to typewrite

tipicista adj regional, local

típi·co -ca adj typical; regional; quaint

tipismo m quaintness

tipista mf typist, typewriter

tiple mf soprano (person); treble-guitar player ǁ m soprano (voice); treble guitar

tipo m type; (de descuento, de interés, de cambio) rate; shape, figure, build; (coll) fellow, guy, specimen; **tener buen tipo** to have a good figure; **tipo de ensayo or prueba** eye-test chart; **tipo de impuesto** tax rate; **tipo de letra** typeface; **tipo menudo** small print

tipografía f typography

típula f (ent) daddy-longlegs

tira m (Arg, Chile, Col) detective ǁ f strip; **hecho tiras** (Chile) in rags; **tira emplástica** (Arg) court plaster; **tira proyectable** film strip; **tiras cómicas** comics, funnies

tirabala f popgun

tirabuzón m corkscrew; corkscrew curl

tirada f throw; distance, stretch; time, period; printing; edition, issue; shooting party, hunting party; tirade; **de or en una tirada** at one stroke; **tirada aparte** reprint

tira·do -da adj dirt-cheap; (letra) cursive ǁ f see **tirada**

tira·dor -dora mf shot, good shot ǁ m knob; doorknob; pull chain; **tirador certero** sharpshooter; **tirador emboscado** sniper

tirafondo m wood screw

tiraje m draft; printing, edition

tiramira f long, narrow mountain range; (de personas o cosas) string; distance, stretch

tiranía f tyranny

tiráni·co -ca adj tyrannic(al)

tira·no -na adj tyrannous ǁ mf tyrant

tirante adj tense, taut, tight; (fig) tense, strained ǁ m (de los arreos de una caballería) trace; **tirantes** suspenders

tirantez f tenseness, tautness, tightness; strain

tirar tr to throw, cast, fling; to throw away; to shoot, fire; (alambre) to draw, pull, stretch; (una línea) to draw; (una coz, un pellizco) to give; to print; to attract; to tear down, knock down; (phot) to print ǁ intr to pull; to last; to appeal, have an appeal; (una chimenea) to draw; (a la derecha, a la izquierda) to bear, to turn; **ir tirando** (coll) to get along; **tirar a** to shoot at; (la espada) to

handle; to shade into; to tend to; to aspire to; **tirar de** to pull, pull on; (una espada) to draw; to attract; to boast of being; **tira y afloja** (coll) give and take; (coll) hot and cold ǁ ref to rush, throw oneself; to give oneself over; to lie down

tirilla f neckband; **tirilla de bota** bootstrap; **tirilla de camisa** collarband

tiritar intr to shiver

tiro m throw; shot; charge, load; (estampido) report; rifle range; (p.ej., de chimenea) draft; (de caballos) team; (de escalera) flight; (de las guarniciones) trace; (de un paño) length; pull cord, pull chain; reach; hurt, damage; trace; theft; (min) shaft; (sport) drive, shot; (alusión desfavorable) shot; (fig) shot, marksman; **a tiro de fusil** within gunshot; **a tiro de piedra** within a stone's throw; **matar a tiros** to shoot to death; **ni a tiros** not for love nor money; **poner el tiro muy alto** to hitch one's wagon to a star; **tiro al blanco** target practice; **tiro al vuelo** trapshooting; **tiro de la pesa** (sport) shot-put

tirón m tyro, novice; jerk; tug, pull; **de un tirón** all at once; at a stretch

tirotear tr to snipe at, to blaze away at ǁ ref to fire at each other; to bicker

tirria f (coll) dislike, grudge; **tener tirria a** (coll) to have it in for

tisana f tea, infusion

tisis f consumption, tuberculosis

titanio m titanium

tít. abbr **título**

títere m marionette, puppet; fixed idea; (coll) whipper-snapper, nincompoop; **no dejar títere con cabeza or cara** (coll) to upset the applecart; **títeres** puppet show

titilar tr to titillate ǁ intr to flutter, quiver; to twinkle

titubear intr to stagger, totter; to stammer, stutter; to waver, hesitate

titular m bearer, holder; incumbent; headline ǁ f capital letter ǁ tr to title, entitle ǁ intr to receive a title ǁ ref to be called; to call oneself

titulillo m running head

título m title; titled person; regulation; bond; certificate; degree; diploma; headline; **a título de** as a, by way of, on the score of; **títulos** credentials

tiza f chalk

tiznar tr to soil with soot; to spot, stain; to defame ǁ ref to become soiled, to get spotted or stained; (Arg, Chile, CAm) to get drunk

tizne m & f soot ǁ m firebrand

tiznón m smudge, spot of soot

tizón m brand, firebrand; wheat smut; brand, dishonor

tizonear intr to stir up the fire

tlapalería f (Mex) paint store

toalla f towel; **toalla rusa** Turkish towel; **toalla sin fin** roller towel

toallero m towel rack

toar tr (naut) to tow

tobar tr (Col) to tow

tobillera f anklet; (sport) ankle support; (coll) subdeb; (coll) flapper

tobillo *m* ankle

tobo *m* (Ven) bucket

tobogán *m* toboggan; chute, slide

toca *f* toque; headdress

tocadis·cos *m* (*pl* -cos) record player; **tocadiscos automático** record changer

toca·do -da *adj* (*echado a perder; medio loco*) touched; **tocado de la cabeza** (coll) touched in the head || *m* hairdo, coiffure

toca·dor -dora *mf* performer, player || *m* boudoir; dressing table; dressing case, toilet case

tocante *adj* touching; **tocante a** concerning, with reference to

tocar §73 *tr* to touch; to touch on; to feel; to ring; to toll; to strike; to come to know, to suffer, to feel; (*el cabello*) to do; (*un tambor*) to beat; (mus) to play; (paint) to touch up || *intr* to touch; **tocar a** to knock at; to pertain to, to concern; to fall to the lot of; to be the turn of; (*el fin*) to approach; **tocar en** (*un puerto*) to touch at; (*tierra*) to touch; to touch on; to approach, border on || *ref* to put one's hat on, to cover one's head; to touch each other; to be related; to make one's toilet; to become mentally unbalanced; (*el sombrero*) to tip; **tocárselas** (coll) to beat it

toca·yo -ya *mf* namesake

tocino *m* bacon; salt pork

tocón *m* stump

tocuyo *m* (SAm) coarse cotton cloth

tochimbo *m* (Peru) smelting furnace

to·cho -cha *adj* rough, coarse, crude

todavía *adv* still, yet; **todavía no** not yet

to·do -da *adj* all, whole, every; any || *m* whole; everything; **con todo** still, however; **del todo** wholly, entirely; **jugar el todo por el todo** to stake everything, to shoot the works; **sobre todo** above all, especially; **todo el que** everybody who; **todo lo que** all that; **todos all, everybody; todos cuantos** all those who

todopodero·so -sa *adj* all-powerful, almighty

toga *f* (academic) gown

toldilla *f* poop, poop deck

toldería *f* (SAm) Indian camp, Indian village

toldo *m* awning; pride, haughtiness; (SAm) Indian hut

tole *m* hubbub, uproar; **tole tole** gossip, talk; **tomar el tole** (coll) to run away

tolerancia *f* tolerance; **por tolerancia** on sufferance

tolerar *tr* to tolerate

tolete *m* (Am) club, cudgel; (Am) raft; (Cuba) dunce

toletole *m* (Col) persistence, obstinacy; (Ven) merry life of a wanderer

tolon·dro -dra *adj* scatterbrained || *mf* scatterbrain || *m* bump, lump

tolva *f* hopper; chute

tolvanera *f* dust storm

tolla *f* quagmire; (Cuba) watering trough

tom. *abbr* **tomo**

toma *f* taking; seizure, capture; tap; in-

take, inlet; (elec) tap, outlet; (elec) plug; (elec) terminal; (*de rapé*) pinch; **toma de posesión** installation, induction; inauguration; **toma de tierra** (aer) landing; (rad) ground connection; **toma directa** high gear

toma-corrien·te *m* or **toma-corrien·tes** *m* (*pl* -tes) (elec) current collector; (elec) tap, outlet; (elec) plug

tomadero *m* handle; intake, inlet

toma·dor -dora *mf* (com) drawee; (coll) thief; (Am) drinker, toper

tomar *tr* to take; to get; to seize; to take on; (*un resfriado*) to catch; (*p.ej., el desayuno*) to have, to eat; (*el café, un trago*) to take, to drink; **tomar a bien** to take in the right spirit; **tomar a mal** to take offense at; **tomarla con** to pick a quarrel with; to have a grudge against; **tomar prestado** to borrow; **tomar sobre sí** to take upon oneself || *intr* to take, to turn || *ref* to take; (*p.ej., el desayuno*) to have, to eat; (*el café*) to take, to drink; to get rusty

tomate *m* tomato; (*en medias, calcetines, etc.*) (coll) tear, run

tomavis·tas *m* (*pl* -tas) motion-picture camera; cameraman

tómbola *f* raffle, charity raffle

tomillo *m* thyme

tomo *m* volume; bulk; importance, consequence; **de tomo y lomo** of consequence; (coll) bulky and heavy

ton. *abbr* **tonelada**

ton *m* — **sin ton ni son** without rhyme or reason

tonada *f* air, melody, song; (Cuba) hoax; (*pronunciación particular*) (Arg, Chile) accent; (Am) singsong

tonel *m* cask, barrel

tonelada *f* (*unidad de peso; unidad de volumen; unidad de desplazamiento*) ton; (*medida de capacidad para el vino*) tun

tonelaje *m* tonnage

tonele·ro -ra *mf* barrelmaker, cooper

tonga *f* coat, layer; (Arg, Col) task; (Col) sleep; (Cuba) heap, pile

tongonear *ref* (Am) to strut, swagger

tóni·co -ca *adj & m* tonic || *f* (mus) keynote

tonillo *m* singsong; (*pronunciación particular*) accent

tono *m* tone; tune; (mus) pitch; (mus) key; (*de un instrumento de bronce*) (mus) slide; **dar el tono** to set the standard; **darse tono** (coll) to put on airs; **de buen tono** stylish, elegant; **estar a tono** (coll) to be in style; **poner a tono** (*un motor de automóvil*) to tune up; **tono mayor** (mus) major key; **tono menor** (mus) minor key

tonsila *f* tonsil

tonsilitis *f* tonsilitis

tonsurar *tr* to shear, to clip

tontear *intr* to talk nonsense, to act foolishly

tontería *f* foolishness, nonsense

ton·to -ta *adj* foolish, stupid, silly; **a tontas y a locas** wildly, recklessly; in disorder, haphazardly || *mf* fool, dolt; **tonto de capirote** (coll) blatant fool

tonu·do -da adj (Arg) magnificent, showy, conceited

topacio m topaz

topar tr to butt; to bump; to run into, encounter || intr to butt; to succeed; to lie, be found; **topar con** or **en** to run into, encounter

tope adj (precio) top; (fecha) last || m butt; bumper; bump, collision; rub, difficulty; scuffle; masthead; **al tope** or **a tope** end to end; flush; **estar hasta el tope** or **los topes** to be loaded to the gunwales; (coll) to be fed up; **tope de puerta** doorstop

topera f molehill

topetada f butt

topetar tr to butt || intr to butt; **topetar con** (coll) to bump, bump into; (coll) to run across

topetón m butt; bump, collision

tópi·co -ca adj local || m topic; (med) external application

topinera f molehill; **beber como una topinera** to drink like a fish

topo m mole; (coll) blunderer; (coll) stumbler, awkward person

topografía f topography

toque m touch; (de una campana) ringing; (del tambor) beat; sound; knock; stroke; check, test; (punto esencial) gist; (paint) touch; (coll) blow; **dar un toque a** (coll) to put to the test; (coll) to feel out, to sound out; **toque a muerto** knell, toll; **toque de diana** reveille; **toque de queda** curfew; **toque de retreta** (mil) tattoo; **toque de tambor** drumbeat

torada f drove of bulls

tó·rax m (pl -rax) thorax

torbellino m whirlwind; (persona bulliciosa) (coll) harum-scarum

torcecuello m (orn) wryneck

torcedura f twist; sprain; dislocation

torcer §74 tr to twist; to bend; to turn; to sprain; (la cara) to screw up; (el tobillo) to wrench; to turn; (interpretar mal) to distort, to misconstrue || intr to turn || ref to twist; to bend; to sprain, dislocate; to turn sour; to go crooked; to fail

torci·do -da adj twisted; crooked; bent; (ojos) cross; (persona o conducta) crooked; (Guat) unlucky || f wick, lampwick; curlpaper

tor·do -da adj dapple-gray || mf dapple-gray horse || m thrush; (Am) starling

torear tr (toros) to fight; to banter, tease, string along || intr to fight bulls, be a bullfighter

toreo m bullfighting; (taur) performance

tore·ro -ra adj (coll) bullfighting || mf bullfighter

toril m (taur) bull pen

tormenta f storm; adversity, misfortune

tormento m torment, torture; anguish

tormento·so -sa adj stormy; (barco) storm-ridden

torna f return; dam; tap; **se han vuelto las tornas** the luck has changed; **volver las tornas** to give tit for tat

tornar tr to return, give back; to turn, to make || intr to return; to turn; **tornar a** + inf verb + again, e.g., **tornó a abrir la puerta** he opened the door again || ref to turn, to become

tornasol m sunflower; litmus; iridescence

tornasola·do -da adj changeable, iridescent

tornavía m (rr) turntable

torna·voz m (pl -voces) sounding board; **hacer tornavoz** to cup one's hands to one's mouth

tornear tr to turn, turn up || intr to go around; to tourney; to muse, meditate

torneo m tourney; match, tournament; **torneo radiofónico** quiz program

tornillo m (cilindro que entra en la tuerca) screw; (clavo con resalto helicoidal) bolt; (instrumento con dos mandíbulas) vise; (mil) desertion; (CAm, Ven) screw tree; **apretar los tornillos a** (coll) to put the screws on; **tener flojos los tornillos** (coll) to have a screw loose; **tornillo de mariposa** or **de orejas** thumbscrew; **tornillo de presión** setscrew; **tornillo para metales** machine screw

torniquete m (para contener hemorragias) tourniquet; (torno para cerrar un paso) turnstile; **dar torniquete a** to twist the meaning of

torno m turn, revolution; (máquina simple que consiste en un cilindro que gira sobre su eje) winch, windlass; (de alfarero) potter's wheel; (instrumento con dos mandíbulas) vise; (máquina herramienta que sirve para labrar metal o madera) lathe; (de coche) brake; (de un río) bend, turn; revolving server; **en torno a** or **de** around; **torno de alfarero** potter's wheel; **torno de banco** bench vise; **torno de hilar** spinning wheel

toro m bull; **toro corrido** (coll) smart fellow; **toros** bullfight

torón m strand

toronja f grapefruit

toronjo m grapefruit (tree)

torpe adj slow, heavy; clumsy, awkward; stupid; lewd; crude, ugly

torpedear tr to torpedo

torpedo m torpedo; touring car

torpeza f torpidity, slowness; clumsiness, awkwardness; stupidity; lewdness; turpitude; crudeness, ugliness

torrar tr to toast

torre f tower; watchtower; (en el ajedrez) castle, rook; **torre del homenaje** donjon, keep; **torre de lanzamiento** launching tower; **torre de marfil** (fig) ivory tower; **torre de vigía** (naut) crow's-nest; **torre maestra** donjon, keep; **torre reloj** clock tower

torreja f (dial, Am) French toast

torrentada f flash flood

torrente m torrent

torreón m (archit) turret

torreta f (nav) turret

tórri·do -da adj torrid

torrija f French toast

torta f cake; (typ) font; (coll) slap; **ser tortas y pan pintado** (coll) to be a cinch; **torta a la plancha** hot cake, griddle cake

torticolis *m* or **torticolis** *m* wryneck, stiff neck

tortilla *f* omelet; (CAm, Mex) tortilla (*corn-meal cake*); **tortilla a la española** potato omelet; **tortilla a la francesa** plain omelet; **tortilla de tomate** Spanish omelet

tórtola *f* turtledove

tortuga *f* tortoise, turtle

tortuo·so -sa *adj* winding; (fig) devious

tortura *f* torture

torturar *tr* to torture

tor·vo -va *adj* grim, stern

tos *f* cough; **tos ferina** whooping cough

tosca·no -na *adj* Tuscan ‖ **la Toscana** Tuscany

tos·co -ca *adj* coarse, rough; uncouth

toser *intr* to cough

tósigo *m* poison; sorrow

tosiguero *m* poison ivy

tosquedad *f* coarseness, roughness; uncouthness

tostada *f* piece of toast; toast; **dar** or **pegar la tostada** or **una tostada a** (coll) to cheat, to trick; **tostadas** toast

tosta·do -da *adj* brown; tan, sunburned ‖ *m* toasting; roasting ‖ *f* see **tostada**

tostador *m* toaster, roaster

tostar §61 *tr* & *ref* to toast; to roast; to tan, to burn

tostón *m* roasted chickpea; toast dipped in olive oil; roast pig; scorched food

total *adj* & *m* total ‖ *adv* (coll) in a word

totalidad *f* totality; entirety; **en su totalidad** in its entirety

tóxi·co -ca *adj* & *m* toxic

toxicomanía *f* drug addiction

toxicóma·no -na *adj* drug-addicted ‖ *mf* drug addict

tozu·do -da *adj* stubborn

tpo. *abbr* **tiempo**

traba *f* bond, tie; clasp, lock; hobble, clog; obstacle, hindrance

traba·do -da *adj* tied, fastened; joined, connected; robust, sinewy; (*sílaba*) checked; (Am) tongue-tied; (*ojos*) (Col) cross

trabaja·do -da *adj* overworked, worn-out; strained, forced, labored; busy

trabaja·dor -dora *adj* working; industrious, hard-working ‖ *mf* worker, toiler ‖ *m* workman, workingman ‖ *f* workingwoman

trabajar *tr* to work; to till; to bother, disturb; (*a una persona*) to work, to drive ‖ *intr* to work; to strain; to warp; **trabajar en** or **por** to strive to ‖ *ref* to strive, to exert oneself

trabajo *m* work; trouble; (*en contraposición de capital*) labor; **costar trabajo** + *inf* to be hard to + *inf*; **trabajo a destajo** piecework; **trabajo a domicilio** homework; **trabajo a jornal** timework; **trabajo de menores** child labor; **trabajo de oficina** clerical work; **trabajo de taller** shopwork; **trabajos** hardships, tribulations; **trabajos forzados** or **forzosos** hard labor, penal labor

trabajo·so -sa *adj* arduous, laborious; (*magano*) wan, languid; (*falto de espontaneidad*) labored; (Am) unpleasant, annoying

trabalen·guas *m* (*pl* **-guas**) tongue twister, jawbreaker

trabar *tr* to join, unite; to catch, seize; to fasten; to fetter; to lock; to begin; (*una batalla*) to join; (*una conversación, amistad*) to strike up ‖ *intr* to take hold ‖ *ref* to become entangled; to jam; to foul; **trabársele a uno la lengua** to become tongue-tied

trabe *f* beam

trabilla *f* gaiter strap; belt loop; end stitch, loose stitch

trabuco *m* blunderbuss; popgun

trac *m* stage fright

tracale·ro -ra *adj* (CAm, Mex, W-I) cheating, tricky ‖ *mf* (CAm, Mex, W-I) cheat, trickster

tracción *f* traction; **tracción delantera** front drive; **tracción trasera** rear drive

tractor *m* tractor; **tractor de oruga** caterpillar tractor

tradición *f* tradition

tradicionista *mf* folklorist

traducción *f* translation; **traducción automática** machine translation

traducir §19 *tr* to translate; to change

traduc·tor -tora *mf* translator

traer §75 *tr* to bring; to bring on; to draw, pull; to make, keep; to wear; to have, carry; **traer a mal traer** (coll) to abuse, mistreat ‖ *intr* — **traer y llevar** to gossip ‖ *ref* to dress; to behave; **traérselas** (coll) to get worse and worse, to cause a lot of trouble

tráfago *m* traffic, trade; toil, drudgery

trafa·gón -gona *adj* (coll) hustling, lively; (coll) slick, tricky ‖ *mf* hustler, live wire

traficante *mf* dealer, merchant

traficar §73 *intr* to deal, trade, traffic; to travel about

tráfico *m* trade; traffic

tragaderas *fpl* (coll) gullibility; (coll) tolerance; **tener buenas tragaderas** (coll) to be too gullible

tragalda·bas *mf* (*pl* **-bas**) (coll) glutton; (coll) easy mark

tragale·guas *mf* (*pl* **-guas**) (coll) great walker

traga·luz *m* (*pl* **-luces**) skylight, bull's-eye; cellar window

tragamone·das *m* (*pl* **-das**) or **tragape·rras** *m* (*pl* **-rras**) (coll) slot machine

tragar §44 *tr* to swallow; to swallow up; to gulp down; (*creer fácilmente*) to swallow; to overlook; **no poder tragar** (coll) to not be able to stomach ‖ *intr* & *ref* to swallow

tragasable *m* sword swallower

tragavenado *m* (SAm) anaconda

tragaviro·tes *m* (*pl* **-tes**) (coll) stuffed shirt

tragedia *f* tragedy

trági·co -ca *adj* tragic(al) ‖ *m* tragedian

trago *m* swallow; swig; (coll) misfortune; **a tragos** (coll) slowly

tra·gón -gona *adj* (coll) gluttonous ‖ *mf* (coll) glutton

traición *f* treachery, betrayal; *(delito contra la patria)* treason; treacherous act; **alta traición** high treason; **a traición** treacherously; **hacer traición a** to betray

traicionar *tr* to betray

traicione·ro -ra *adj* treacherous; treasonable ‖ *mf* traitor

traída *f* conveyance, transfer; (Guat) sweetheart; **traída de aguas** water supply

traí·do -da *adj* worn, threadbare ‖ *f* see **traída**

traí·dor -dora *adj* treacherous; treasonable ‖ *mf* traitor; betrayer ‖ *m* villain ‖ *f* traitress

traílla *f* leash; road scraper

traje *m* suit; clothes; dress; gown; **cortar un traje a** (coll) to gossip about; **traje a la medida** suit made to order; **traje de baño** bathing suit; **traje de calle** street clothes; **traje de ceremonia** or **de etiqueta** dress suit; full dress; evening clothes; **traje de faena** (mil) fatigue clothes; **traje de luces** bullfighter's costume; **traje de malla** tights; **traje de montar** riding habit; **traje de paisano** civilian clothes; **traje hecho** ready-made suit; **traje sastre** lady's tailor-made suit; **traje serio** formal dress; **vestir su primer traje largo** to come out, to make one's debut

trajear *tr* to dress, clothe

trajín *m* carrying, transfer, conveyance; going and coming; bustle, commotion

trajinar *tr* to carry, convey; (Arg, Chile) to poke into; (Arg, Chile) to deceive; (Pan) to annoy ‖ *intr* to bustle around

tralla *f* lash, whiplash, whipcord

trama *f* weft, woof; plot, scheme, machination; *(de un drama o novela)* plot

tramar *tr* to weave; to plot, to scheme; *(un enredo)* to hatch *(a plot)*

trambucar §73 *intr* (Col, Ven) to be shipwrecked; (Col, Ven) to go out of one's mind

tramitación *f* transaction, negotiation; procedure, steps; **tramitación automática de datos** data processing

tramitar *tr* to transact, to negotiate

trámite *m* step, procedure; proceeding; transaction

tramo *m* tract; stretch; *(de una escalera)* flight; *(de un puente)* span; *(de un canal entre dos esclusas)* level

tramontana *f* north; north wind; pride, haughtiness

tramoya *f* stage machinery; scheme

tramoyista *adj* scheming, tricky ‖ *mf* schemer, impostor ‖ *m* stagehand

trampa *f* trap; trap door; *(de un mostrador)* flap; *(de los pantalones)* fly; **armar una trampa a** (coll) to lay a trap for; **trampa explosiva** (mil) booby trap

trampear *tr* (coll) to trick, to swindle ‖ *intr* (coll) to cheat; (coll) to manage to get along

trampilla *f* peephole in the floor; *(de los pantalones)* fly; *(de un secreter)* top, lid; *(de una mesa)* leaf, hinged leaf

trampolín *m* diving board; springboard; ski jump

trampo·so -sa *adj* tricky, crooked ‖ *mf* cheat, swindler

tranca *f* beam, pole; crossbar; (Arg, Chile) drunk, spree; (P-R) dollar; **a trancas y barrancas** (coll) through fire and water

trancar §73 *tr* to bar ‖ *intr* (coll) to stride along

trance *m* crisis; peril; trance; **a todo trance** at any cost; **último trance** *(de la vida)* last stage, end

tranco *m* long stride; threshold

tranquera *f* palisade, fence

tranquilidad *f* tranquillity

tranquilizante *m* tranquilizer

tranquilizar §60 *tr, intr & ref* to tranquilize, to calm down

tranqui·lo -la *adj* tranquil, calm

tranquilla *f* feeler

tranquillo *m* knack

transacción *f* settlement, compromise; transaction

transaéreo *m* air liner

transar *tr* (Am) to settle ‖ *intr* (Am) to yield, give in, compromise

transatlánti·co -ca *adj & m* transatlantic

transbordador *m* ferry

transbordar *tr* to transship; to transfer ‖ *intr* to transfer, to change trains

transbordo *m* transshipment; transfer

transcribir §83 *tr* to transcribe

transcripción *f* transcription

transcurrir *intr* to pass, elapse

transcurso *m* course *(of time)*

transepto *m* transept

transeúnte *adj* transient ‖ *mf* transient; passer-by

transferencia *f* transfer

transferir §68 *tr* to transfer; to postpone

transformador *m* transformer

transformar *tr* to transform ‖ *ref* to transform, be transformed

tránsfuga *mf* turncoat; fugitive

transfusión *f* transfusion; **transfusión de sangre** transfusion, blood transfusion

transgredir §1 *tr* to transgress

transgresión *f* transgression

transi·do -da *adj* overcome, paralyzed; mean, cheap, stingy

transigencia *f* compromise; compromising

transigente *adj* compromising

transigir §27 *tr* to settle, to compromise ‖ *intr* to settle, to compromise; to agree

transistor *m* transistor

transitable *adj* passable, practicable

transitar *intr* to go, walk; to travel

transiti·vo -va *adj* transitive

tránsito *m* transit; traffic; stop; passage; transfer

transito·rio -ria *adj* transitory

translúci·do -do *adj* translucent

transmisión *f* transmission; **transmisión del pensamiento** thought transference

transmisor *m* transmitter; **transmisor de órdenes** (naut) engine-room telegraph

transmitir *tr & intr* to transmit

transmudar *tr* to transfer; to persuade, convince

transmutar *tr, intr & ref* to transmute

transparecer §22 *intr* to show through
transparencia *f* transparency; slide
transparentar *ref* to show through
transparente *adj* transparent ‖ *m* curtain, window curtain; **transparente de resorte** window blind or shade
transpirar *intr* to transpire; (*dejarse conocer una cosa secreta*) to transpire
transplantar *tr* to transplant
transponer §54 *tr* to transpose; to disappear behind ‖ *ref* (*ocultarse detrás del horizonte*) to set; to get sleepy
transportar *tr* to transport; (mus) to transpose
transporte *m* transport; transportation; (aer & naut) transport
transportista *mf* transport worker
tranvía *m* trolley, trolley car, streetcar; **tranvía de sangre** horsecar
tranzar §60 *tr* to cut off, rip off; to plait, braid
trapacear *tr* to cheat, swindle
trapacería *f* cheating, swindling
trapace·ro -ra *adj* cheating, swindling ‖ *mf* cheat, swindler
trapajo *m* rag, tatter
trápala *adj* (coll) chattering; (coll) cheating ‖ *mf* (coll) chatterbox; (coll) cheat ‖ *m* loquacity ‖ *f* noise, uproar; (*del trote de un caballo*) clatter; (coll) cheating
trapear *tr* (Am) to mop
trapecio *m* (geom) trapezoid; (sport) trapeze
trapecista *mf* trapeze performer
trape·ro -ra *mf* ragpicker; junk dealer
trapiche *m* sugar mill; olive press; ore crusher
trapien·to -ta *adj* raggedy, in rags
trapío *m* (coll) flipness, pertness; (*del toro de lidia*) spirit
trapisonda *f* (coll) brawl, row; (coll) scheming
trapisondista *mf* (coll) schemer
trapo *m* rag; (naut) canvas, sails; bullfighter's bright-colored cape; (*de la muleta*) cloth; **a todo trapo** full sail; **poner como un trapo** (coll) to rake over the coals; **sacar los trapos a la colada, a relucir** or **al sol** (coll) to wash one's dirty linen in public; **soltar el trapo** (coll) to burst out crying, to burst out laughing; **trapos** (coll) rags, duds; **trapos de cristianar** (coll) Sunday best
trapo·so -sa *adj* (Am) raggedy, in rags
tráquea *f* trachea, windpipe
traquea·do -da *adj* (*sendero*) (Arg) beaten
traquear *tr* to shake, to rattle; (coll) to fool with ‖ *intr* to crackle; to rattle, to chatter
traqueo *m* shake, rattle
traquetear *tr & intr* to rattle; to jerk
tras *prep* after; behind; **tras de** behind; in addition to
trasatlánti·co -ca *adj & m* var of **trasatlántico**
trasbordador *m* var of **transbordador**
trasbordar *tr & intr* var of **trasbordar**
trasbordo *m* var of **trasbordo**
trascendencia *f* penetration, keenness; importance

trascendente *adj* penetrating; important
trascender §51 *tr* to go into, dig up ‖ *intr* to smell; to come to be known, to leak out
trascendi·do -da *adj* keen, perspicacious
trascocina *f* scullery
trascorral *m* back yard; (coll) backside
trascribir §83 *tr* var of **transcribir**
trascripción *f* var of **transcripción**
trascuarto *m* back room
trascurrir *intr* var of **transcurrir**
trascurso *m* var of **transcurso**
trasegar §66 *tr* to upset, turn topsy-turvy; to decant, to draw off
trase·ro -ra *adj* back, rear ‖ *m* buttock, rump
trasferir §68 *tr* var of **transferir**
trasformador *m* var of **transformador**
trasformar *tr & intr* var of **transformar**
trásfuga *mf* var of **tránsfuga**
trasfusión *f* var of **transfusión**
trasgo *m* goblin, hobgoblin; imp
trashojar *tr* to leaf through
trasiego *m* upset, disorder; decantation
trasladar *tr* to transfer; to postpone; to copy, transcribe; to transmit; to move ‖ *intr* to go; to move
traslado *m* transfer; copy, transcript; moving
traslapar *tr, intr & ref* to overlap
traslapo *m* lap, overlap
traslúci·do -da *adj* var of **translúcido**
traslucir §45 *tr* to guess ‖ *intr* to leak out ‖ *ref* to be translucent; to leak out
traslumbrar *tr* to dazzle ‖ *ref* to be dazzled; to vanish
trasluz *m* diffused light; glint, gleam; **al trasluz** against the light
trasmisión *f* var of **transmisión**
trasmisor *m* var of **transmisor**
trasmitir *tr & intr* var of **transmitir**
trasmóvil *m* (Col) mobile unit, radio pickup
trasmudar *tr* var of **transmudar**
trasmundo *m* afterlife, future life
trasmutar *tr, intr & ref* var of **transmutar**
trasnocha·do -da *adj* stale; haggard, run-down; hackneyed ‖ *f* last night; sleepless night; (mil) night attack
trasnocha·dor -dora *mf* night owl
trasnochar *tr* (*un problema*) to sleep over ‖ *intr* to spend the night; to spend a sleepless night; to stay up late
trasoír §48 *tr* to hear wrong
traspapelar *tr* to mislay ‖ *ref* to become mislaid
trasparecer §22 *intr* var of **transparecer**
trasparencia *f* var of **transparencia**
trasparente *adj & m* var of **transparente**
traspasar *tr* to cross, cross over; to send; to transfer; to move; to pierce, to transfix; to pain, grieve ‖ *ref* to go too far
traspié *m* slip, stumble; trip
traspirar *intr* var of **transpirar**
trasplantar *tr* var of **transplantar**
trasponer §54 *tr & ref* var of **transponer**
trasportar *tr* var of **transportar**
trasporte *m* var of **transporte**
trasportista *mf* var of **transportista**

traspunte *m* (theat) callboy

traspuntín *m* flap seat, folding seat, jump seat

trasquilar *tr* to crop, to lop; *(las ovejas)* to shear; (coll) to curtail

trastazo *m* (coll) whack, blow

traste *m* fret; **dar al traste con** to throw away, ruin, spoil

trastera *f* attic, junk room

trastienda *f* back room

trasto *m* piece of furniture; piece of junk; (coll) good-for-nothing; **trastos** tools, implements, utensils; arms, weapons; junk; muleta and sword

trastornar *tr* to upset, overturn; to disturb; to perplex; to daze, to make dizzy; to persuade

trastorno *m* upset; disturbance

trastrocar §81 *tr* to turn around, to reverse, to change

trasudor *m* cold sweat

trasueño *m* blurred dream, vague recollection

trasuntar *tr* to copy; to abstract, to sum up

trasunto *m* copy; record; likeness

trasverter §51 *intr* to run over, to overflow

trasvolar §61 *tr* to fly over

trata *f* traffic, trade, slave trade; **trata de blancas** white slavery; **trata de esclavos** slave trade

tratado *m* *(escrito, libro)* treatise; *(convenio entre gobiernos)* treaty; agreement

tratamiento *m* treatment; title; **apear el tratamiento** to leave off the title

tratante *mf* dealer, retailer

tratar *tr* to handle; to deal with; to treat; **tratar a uno de** to address someone as; to charge someone with being || *intr* to deal; to treat; to try; **tratar de** to deal with; to treat of; to come in contact with; to try to || *ref* to deal; to behave; *(bien o mal)* to live; **tratarse de** to deal with; to be a question of

trate·ro -ra *mf* (Chile) pieceworker

trato *m* treatment; deal, agreement; manner; business; title; friendly relations; **tener buen trato** to be very nice, to be very pleasant; **trato colectivo** collective bargaining; **trato doble** double-dealing; **¡trato hecho!** it's a deal!

través *m* bend, bias, turn; reverse, misfortune; (naut) beam; **al or a través de** through, across; **dar al través con** to do away with; **mirar de través** to squint; to look at out of the corner of one's eye

travesaño *m* crosspiece; *(de cama)* bolster; *(p.ej., de una silla)* rung

travesear *intr* to romp, carry on; to sparkle, be witty; to lead a wild life

travesía *f* crossing, voyage; crossroad; distance, passage; cross wind; (Arg, Bol) wasteland; (Chile) west wind

travesura *f* prank, antic, caper; mischief; sparkle, wit; slick trick

traviesa *f* crossing, voyage; rafter; side bet; (rr) tie

travie·so -sa *adj* cross; keen, shrewd;

restless, fidgety; naughty, mischievous; debauched || *f* see **traviesa**

trayecto *m* journey, passage, course; stretch, run

trayectoria *f* trajectory; path

traza *f* plan, design; scheme; means; appearance; mark, trace; footprint; streak, trait; **tener trazas de** to show signs of; to look like

trazar §60 *tr* to plan, design; to outline; to trace; *(una línea)* to draw; to lay out, to plot

trazo *m* line, stroke; trace; outline

trebejo *m* implement; chessman

trébol *m* clover; *(naipe que corresponde al basto)* club

trece *adj & pron* thirteen || *m* thirteen; *(en las fechas)* thirteenth; **estarse, mantenerse** or **seguir en sus trece** (coll) to stand firm

trecea·vo -va *adj & m* thirteenth

trecho *m* stretch; while; **a trechos** at intervals

tregua *f* truce; respite, letup

treinta *adj & pron* thirty || *m* thirty; *(en las fechas)* thirtieth

treinta·vo -va *adj & m* thirtieth

tremar *intr* to tremble, to shake

tremen·do -da *adj* frightful, terrible, tremendous; *(muy grande)* (coll) tremendous

trementina *f* turpentine

tremer *intr* to tremble, shake

tremolar *tr & intr* to wave

tren *m* *(de coches o vagones; de ondas)* train; outfit, equipment; following, retinue; show, pomp; *(de la vida)* way; **tren aerodinámico de lujo** (rr) streamliner; **tren ascendente** (rr) up train; **tren correo** (rr) mail train; **tren de aterrizaje** (aer) landing gear; **tren de laminadores** rolling mill; **tren de lavado** (Am) laundry; **tren de mercancías** freight train; **tren de mudadas** (Am) moving company; **tren descendente** (rr) down train; **tren de viajeros** passenger train; **tren ómnibus** (rr) accommodation train; **tren rápido** (rr) flyer

treno *m* dirge

trenza *f* braid, plait; tress; *(p.ej., de ajos)* (Am) string; **en trenzas** with her hair down

trenzar §60 *tr* to braid, plait || *intr* to caper; to prance

trepa·dor -dora *adj* climbing || *mf* climber || *f* (bot) climber

trepar *tr* to climb; to drill, bore || *intr* to climb; **trepar por** to climb up || *ref* to lean back

trepidar *intr* to shake, vibrate; (Chile) to hesitate, waver

tres *adj & pron* three; **las tres** three o'clock || *m* three; *(en las fechas)* third

trescien·tos -tas *adj & pron* three hundred || **trescientos** *m* three hundred

tresillo *m* ombre; three-piece living-room suit; (mus) triplet

tresnal *m* (agr) shock

treta *f* trick, scheme; *(del esgrimidor)* feint

treza·vo -va *adj & m* thirteenth

triángulo m triangle

triar §77 tr to sort

tribu f tribe

tribuna f tribune, rostrum, platform; grandstand; (en la iglesia) gallery; **tribuna de la prensa** press box; **tribuna del órgano** (mus) organ loft; **tribuna de los acusados** (law) dock

tribunal m tribunal, court; **tribunal tutelar de menores** juvenile court

tributar tr (contribuciones, impuestos, etc.) to pay; (admiración, gratitud, etc.) to render

tributa·rio -ria adj tributary; tax; **ser tributario de** to be indebted to ‖ m tributary

tributo m tribute; tax

tricornio m tricorn, three-cornered hat

trifocal adj trifocal

trifulca f (coll) wrangle, squabble

trigési·mo -ma adj & m thirtieth

trigo m wheat; (slang) dough, money; **trigo sarraceno** buckwheat

trigonometría f trigonometry

trigue·ño -ña adj swarthy, olive-skinned

trilogía f trilogy

trilla f threshing

trilla·do -da adj (sendero) beaten; trite, commonplace

trilladora f threshing machine

trillar tr to thresh; to mistreat; (coll) to frequent

trilli·zo -za mf triplet

trillón m British trillion; quintillion (in U.S.A.)

trimestral adj quarterly

trimestre m quarter

trinado m trill, warble

trinar intr to trill, warble, quaver; (coll) to get angry

trinca f trinity

trincar §73 tr to bind, to lash, to tie fast; to crush; (slang) to kill ‖ intr to take a drink

trinchar tr to carve, to slice

trinchera f cut; trench; trench coat

trineo m sleigh, sled

Trinidad f Trinity

trino m trill

trinquete m pawl, ratchet; (naut) foresail

trin·quis m (pl **-quis**) drink, swig

trío m sorting; trio; (mus) trio

tripa f gut, intestine; belly; (del cigarro) filler; **hacer de tripas corazón** (coll) to pluck up courage

triple adj & m triple

triplica·do -da adj & m triplicate; **por triplicado** in triplicate

triplicar §73 tr to triplicate ‖ intr to treble

trípode m tripod

tríptico m triptych

tripu·do -da adj big-bellied, potbellied

tripulación f crew

tripulante m crew member

tripular tr to man; to fit out, equip

trique m crack, swish; **a cada trique** (coll) at every turn; **triques** (Mex) tools, implements

triquiñuela f (coll) chicanery, subterfuge

triquitraque m clatter; firecracker

tris m crackle; (coll) shave, inch; (coll) trice

trisar tr (Chile) to crack, to chip ‖ intr to chirp

triscar §73 tr to mix; (una sierra) to set ‖ intr to stamp the feet; to romp, frisk around; (Col) to gossip

trismo m lockjaw

triste adj sad; dismal, gloomy; (despreciable, ridículo) sorry

tristeza f sadness; gloominess

tris·tón -tona adj wistful, melancholy

tritón m eft, newt, triton; (hombre experto en la natación) merman

trituradora f crushing machine

triturar tr to grind, crush; to abuse

triunfal adj triumphal

triunfante adj triumphant

triunfar intr to triumph; to trump; **triunfar de** to triumph over; to trump

triunfo m triumph; trump; **sin triunfo** no trump

trivial adj trivial; trite, commonplace; (sendero) beaten

trivialidad f triviality; triteness

triza f shred; **hacer trizas** to tear to pieces

trizar §60 tr to tear to pieces

trocar §81 tr to exchange, to swap; to barter; to confuse, to twist, to distort ‖ intr to swap ‖ ref to change; to change seats

trocha f trail, narrow path; (Am) gauge

trofeo m trophy; victory

troj f or **troje** f granary; olive bin

trole m trolley pole

trolebús m trolley bus, trackless trolley

tromba f (de polvo, agua, etc.) whirl, column; **tromba marina** waterspout; **tromba terrestre** tornado

trombón m trombone

trompa f (del elefante) trunk; waterspout; top; nozzle; (anat) duct, tube; (mus) horn; (Col, Chile) cowcatcher; **trompa de armonía** French horn; **trompa de Eustaquio** Eustachian tube

trompada f (coll) bump, collision; (coll) punch

trompar intr to spin a top

trompeta f trumpet; bugle, clarion; (coll) good-for-nothing; (Am) drunkenness

trompetear intr (coll) to trumpet, to sound the trumpet

trompetilla f ear trumpet; (Am) Bronx cheer

trompicar §44 tr to trip, make stumble ‖ intr to stumble

trompicón m stumble

trompiza f (Am) fist fight

trompo m (juguete) top; (en el ajedrez) man; (buque malo y pesado) tub

tronada f thunderstorm

tronar §61 tr (Mex) to shoot ‖ intr to thunder; (coll) to fail, collapse; **por lo que pueda tronar** (coll) just in case

troncar §44 tr to cut off the head of; (un escrito) to cut, shorten

tronco m (del cuerpo, del árbol, de una familia, del ferrocarril) trunk; (leño) log; (de caballerías) team; (coll) sap, fathead; **estar hecho un tronco** (coll) to be knocked out; (coll) to be sound asleep

troncha f (Am) slice; (Am) cinch

tronchar tr to smash, split; to chop off

tronera m madcap, roisterer ‖ f embrasure, loophole; louver; (de la mesa de billar) pocket

tronido m thunderclap

trono m throne

tronquista m driver, teamster

tronzar §60 tr to shatter, break to pieces; to pleat; to wear out

tropa f troop; (Am) herd, drove; **en tropa** straggling, without formation; **tropas de asalto** shock troops, storm troops

tropel m crowd, throng; rush, hurry; jumble; **de** or **en tropel in** a mad rush

tropelía f mad rush; outrage

tropero m (Arg) cowboy

tropezar §18 tr to strike ‖ intr to stumble; to slip, to blunder; **tropezar con** or **en** to stumble over, to trip over; to run into; to come upon

trope·zón -zona adj stumbly ‖ m stumble; stumbling place; **a tropezones** by fits and starts; falteringly; **dar un tropezón** to stumble, to trip

tropical adj tropic(al)

trópico m tropic

tropiezo m stumble; stumbling block; slip, blunder, fault; obstacle; quarrel

tropilla f (Arg, Urug) drove of horses following a leading mare

troposfera f troposphere

troquel m die

trotaconven·tos f (pl -tos) (coll) procuress, bawd

trotamun·dos m (pl -dos) globetrotter

trotar intr to trot; (coll) to hustle

trote m trot; (coll) chore; **al trote** (coll) right away; **para todo trote** (coll) for everyday wear; **trote de perro** jog trot

trotona f chaperone

trovador m troubadour

trovadores·co -ca adj troubadour

trovero m trouvère

Troya f Troy; **ahí fué Troya** (coll) it's a shambles; **¡arda Troya!** (coll) come what may!

troya·no -na adj & mf Trojan

troza f log

trozar §60 tr to break to pieces; (un tronco) to cut into logs

trozo m piece, fragment; block; excerpt, selection

truco m contrivance, device; trick; pocketing of ball; **truco de naipes** card trick; **trucos** pool

truculen·to -ta adj truculent

trucha f trout

trueno m thunder, thunderclap; shot, report; (coll) rake, roué; **trueno gordo** finale (of fireworks); big scandal; **truenos** (Ven) heavy shoes

trueque m barter; exchange, swap; trade-in; **a trueque de** in exchange for; **trueques** (Col) change

trufa f truffle; fib, lie

tru·hán -hana adj crooked; clownish ‖ mf crook; clown

trujal m wine press; oil press

trulla f noise, bustle; crowd; trowel

truncar §73 tr to cut off the head of; (palabras o frases) to cut, slash; to cut off, interrupt

trusas fpl trunk hose; (Am) trunks

tu adj poss thy, your

tú pron pers thou, you

tubérculo m (rizoma engrosado, p.ej., de la patata) tuber; (protuberancia) tubercle

tuberculosis f tuberculosis

tubería f tubing; piping

tubo m tube; pipe; **tubo de desagüe** drainpipe; **tubo de ensayo** test tube; **tubo de humo** flue; **tubo de imagen** picture tube; **tubo de vacío** vacuum tube; **tubo digestivo** alimentary canal; **tubo sonoro** chime

tuerca f nut; **tuerca de aletas** wing nut

tuer·to -ta adj crooked, bent; one-eyed; **a tuertas** upside down; crosswise; **a tuertas o a derechas** rightly or wrongly; thoughtlessly ‖ mf one-eyed person ‖ m wrong, harm, injustice; **tuertos** afterpains

tuétano m marrow; pith; **hasta los tuétanos** (coll) through and through; (coll) head over heels

tufi·llas mf (pl -llas) (coll) touchy person

tufillo m whiff, smell

tufo m fume, vapor; sidelock; foul odor, foul breath; **tufos** (coll) airs, conceit

tugurio m shepherd's hut; hovel

tuición f protection, custody

tulipán m tulip

tullecer §22 tr to abuse, mistreat ‖ intr to be crippled

tulli·do -da adj paralyzed, crippled ‖ mf paralytic, cripple

tullir §13 tr to cripple, to paralyze; to abuse, mistreat ‖ ref to become crippled or paralyzed

tumba f grave, tomb; tombstone; arched top; (Am) felling of trees

tumbacuartí·llos mf (pl -llos) (coll) old toper, rounder

tumbar tr to knock down; to catch, to trick; (coll) to stun ‖ intr to tumble; to capsize ‖ ref (coll) to lie down

tumbo m fall, tumble; boom, rumble; crisis; rise and fall of sea; rough surf

tumbona f hammock

tumor m tumor

túmulo m catafalque

tumulto m tumult

tuna f loafing, bumming

tunante adj bumming, loafing; crooked, tricky ‖ mf bum, loafer; crook

tundidora f lawn mower

tuneci·no -na adj & mf Tunisian

túnel m tunnel

tunes mpl (Col) little steps, first steps

Túnez (ciudad) Tunis; (país) Tunisia

tungsteno m tungsten

túnica f tunic

tu·no -na adj crooked, tricky ‖ mf crook ‖ f see tuna

tupé m toupee; (coll) nerve, cheek, brass

tupi·do -da adj thick, dense, compact; dull, stupid; (Am) clogged up

tupir *tr* to pack tight ‖ *ref* to stuff, stuff oneself

turba *f* crowd, mob; peat

turbamulta *f* (coll) mob, rabble

turbar *tr* to disturb, trouble; to stir up ‖ *ref* to be confused

turbiedad *f* muddiness; confusion

turbina *f* turbine

tur·bio -bia *adj* turbid, muddy, cloudy; confused; obscure

turbión *m* squall, thunderstorm; (*p.ej., de balas*) (fig) hail

turbopropulsor *m* turboprop (*engine*)

turborreactor *m* turbojet (*engine*)

turbulen·to -ta *adj* turbulent

tur·co -ca *adj* Turkish ‖ *mf* Turk ‖ *m* (*idioma*) Turkish

turfista *adj* horsy ‖ *m* turfman

turismo *m* touring; touring car

turista *mf* tourist

turísti·co -ca *adj* tourist; touring

turnar *intr* to alternate, take turns

tur·nio -nia *adj* (*ojos*) cross; cross-eyed; (*que mira con ceño*) cross-looking

turno *m* turn, shift; **aguardar turno** to wait one's turn; **por turno** in turn; **turno diurno** day shift

turón *m* polecat

turquesa *s* turquoise

Turquía *s* Turkey

turrón *m* nougat; (coll) plum

tusa *f* (Am) corncob; (Am) corn silk; (Chile) mane; (Col) pockmark; (CAm, W-I) trollop

tusar *tr* to shear, clip, cut

tutear *tr* to thou, to address familiarly ‖ *ref* to thou each other, to address each other familiarly

tutela *f* guardianship; protection

tutelar *adj* guardian; protecting ‖ *tr* to protect, shelter, guide

tu·tor -tora or **-triz** (*pl* **-trices**) *mf* guardian, tutor

tu·yo -ya *adj poss* of thee ‖ *pron poss* thine, yours

tuza *f* gopher

U

U, u (u) *f* twenty-fourth letter of the Spanish alphabet

u *conj* (used before words beginning with *o* or *ho*) or

U. *abbr* usted

ubicar §73 *tr* (Am) to locate, place ‖ *intr & ref* to be situated

ubi·cuo -cua *adj* ubiquitous

ubre *f* udder

Ucrania *f* Ukraine

ucrania·no -na *adj & mf* Ukrainian

ucra·nio -nia *adj & mf* Ukrainian ‖ *f* see **Ucrania**

Ud. *abbr* usted

Uds. *abbr* ustedes

ufanar *ref* — **ufanarse con** or **de** to boast of, be proud of

ufanía *f* pride, conceit; cheer, satisfaction; ease, smoothness

ufa·no -na *adj* proud, conceited; cheerful, satisfied; easy, smooth

ujier *m* doorman, usher

úlcera *f* ulcer, fester, sore; **úlcera de decúbito** bedsore

ulcerar *tr & ref* to ulcerate, to fester

ulterior *adj* ulterior; subsequent

ulteriormente *adv* subsequently, later

últimamente *adv* finally; lately, recently

ultimar *tr* to finish, end, conclude, wind up; (Am) to kill, finish off

ultimátum *m* (*pl* **-tums**) ultimatum; (coll) definite decision

últi·mo -ma *adj* last, latest; final; excellent, superior; (*precio*) lowest, final; most remote; (*piso*) top; (*hora*) late; **a la última** in the latest fashion; **a última hora** at the eleventh hour; **a últimos de** toward the end of, in the latter part of; **de última hora** last-minute; **estar a lo último** or **en las últimas** to be up to date, to be well-informed; to be on one's last legs; **por último** at last, finally; **último suplicio** capital punishment

ultraatmosféri·co -ca *adj* outer (*space*)

ultraeleva·do -da *adj* (rad) ultrahigh

ultrajar *tr* to outrage, to offend

ultraje *m* outrage, offense

ultrajo·so -sa *adj* outrageous, offensive

ultramar *m* country overseas

ultramari·no -na *adj* overseas ‖ **ultramarinos** *mpl* groceries, delicatessen

ultranza — **a ultranza** to the death; unflinchingly

ultrarro·jo -ja *adj & m* infrared

ultratumba *adv* beyond the grave

ultraviola·do -da or **ultravioleta** *adj & m* ultraviolet

ululación *f* howl; whoop; (*del buho*) hoot; (*del disco del fonógrafo*) wow

ulular *intr* to howl; to whoop; (*el buho*) to hoot

ululato *m* howl; (*del buho*) hoot

umbilical *adj* umbilical

umbral *m* threshold, doorsill; (*madero que sostiene el muro encima de un vano*) lintel; (physiol, psychol & fig) threshold; **atravesar** or **pisar los umbrales** to cross the threshold; **estar en los umbrales de** to be on the threshold of

umbralada *f* (Col) threshold

umbrí·o -a *adj* shady ‖ *f* shady side

umbro·so -sa *adj* shady

un, una (the apocopated form **un** is used before masculine singular nouns and adjectives and before feminine singular nouns beginning with stressed *a* or *ha*) *art indef* a ‖ *adj* one

unánime *adj* unanimous

unanimidad *f* unanimity

unción *f* unction

uncir §36 *tr* (*bueyes*) to yoke, to hitch
undéci·mo -ma *adj & m* eleventh
undo·so -sa *adj* wavy
ungir §27 *tr* to smear with ointment or with oil; to anoint
ungüento *m* unguent, ointment, salve
únicamente *adv* only, solely
úni·co -ca *adj* only, sole; (*sin otro de su especie*) unique; one, e.g., **precio único** one price
unicornio *m* unicorn
unidad *f* (*concepto de una sola cosa o persona; cantidad que se toma como medida común de todas las demás de su clase; el número entero más pequeño*) unit; (*indivisión; armonía de conjunto; el número uno*) unity
uni·do -da *adj* united; smooth, even; close-knit
unificar §73 *tr* to unify
uniformar *tr* to make uniform; to provide with a uniform
uniforme *adj* uniform ‖ *m* uniform; **uniforme de gala** (mil) full dress
uniformidad *f* uniformity
unilateral *adj* unilateral
unión *f* union; double ring
unir *tr & ref* to unite
unisonancia *f* (mus) unison; (*de un orador*) monotony
unísono — **al unísono** in unison; unanimously; **al unísono de** in unison with
unita·rio -ria *adj* unit
universal *adj* universal; (*teclado de máquina de escribir*) standard
universidad *f* university
universita·rio -ria *adj* university ‖ *mf* (Am) university student, college student ‖ *m* university professor
universo *m* universe
u·no -na *pron* one, someone; **a una** of one accord; **la una** one o'clock; **somos uno** we are one; **uno a otro, unos a otros** each other, one another; **uno que otro** one or more, a few; **u·nos -nas** some; a pair of, e.g., **unas gafas** a pair of glasses; **unas tijeras** a pair of scissors; **unos cuantos** some; **uno y otro** both ‖ *pron indef* one, e.g., **uno no sabe qué hacer aquí** one does not know what to do here ‖ *m* (*unidad y signo que la representa*) one
untar *tr* to smear, to grease; to anoint; (coll) to bribe ‖ *ref* to get smeared; to grease oneself; (coll) to peculate
unto *m* grease; (*gordura del cuerpo del animal*) fat; (Chile) shoe polish; **unto de Méjico** or **de rana** (coll) bribe money
untuo·so -sa *adj* unctuous, greasy, sticky
uña *f* nail, fingernail, toenail; (*pezuña*) hoof; (*del ancla*) fluke, bill; (mach) claw, gripper; **enseñar** or **mostrar las uñas** to show one's teeth; **ser largo de uñas** to have long fingers; **ser uña y carne** (coll) to be hand in glove; **tener en la uña** to have on the tip of one's fingers
uñada *f* scratch, nail scratch; (*impulso dado con la uña*) flip
uñero *m* ingrowing nail; (*inflamación*

del dedo en la raíz de la uña) whitlow
ural *adj* Ural ‖ **Urales** *mpl* Urals
uranio *m* uranium
urbanidad *f* urbanity
urbanismo *m* city planning
urbanista *mf* city planner
urbanísti·co -ca *adj* city-planning ‖ *f* city planning
urbanizar §60 *tr* (*convertir en poblado*) to urbanize; to refine, polish
urba·no -na *adj* urban, city; (*atento, cortés*) urbane ‖ *m* policeman
urbe *f* metropolis
urdema·las *mf* (*pl* -las) (coll) schemer
urdimbre *f* warp; scheme, scheming; **estar en la urdimbre** (Chile) to be thin, be emaciated
urdir *tr* (*los hilos*) to beam; (*una conspiración*) to hatch
urente *adj* burning, smarting
uretra *f* urethra
urgencia *f* urgency; **de urgencia** special-delivery
urgente *adj* urgent; (*correo*) special-delivery
urgir §27 *intr* to be urgent
urina·rio -ria *adj* urinary ‖ *m* urinal
urna *f* glass case; ballot box; (*para guardar las cenizas de los cadáveres*) urn; **acudir** or **ir a las urnas** to go to the polls
urología *f* urology
urraca *f* magpie
U.R.S.S. *abbr* **Unión de Repúblicas Socialistas Soviéticas**
urticaria *f* hives
Uruguay, el Uruguay
urugua·yo -ya *adj & mf* Uruguayan
usa·do -da *adj* (*empleado; gastado por el uso; acostumbrado*) used; skilled, experienced; (*vocablo*) **poco usado** rare
usanza *f* use, usage, custom
usar *tr* to use, make use of; (*un cargo, un oficio*) to follow ‖ *intr* — **usar +** *inf* to be accustomed to + *inf*; **usar de** to use, to have recourse to; **usar de la palabra** to speak, make a speech ‖ *ref* to be the custom
usina *f* (Am) factory, plant; (Am) powerhouse; (*estación de tranvía*) (Arg) carbarn
uso *m* use; custom, usage; wear, wear and tear; habit, practice; **al uso** according to custom; **en buen uso** (coll) in good condition; **hacer uso de la palabra** to speak, make a speech
usted *pron pers* you
usual *adj* (*de uso común*) usual; (*que se usa con facilidad*) usable; sociable
usualmente *adv* usually
usua·rio -ria *mf* user
usufructo *m* use, enjoyment
usufructuar §21 *tr* to enjoy the use of
usura *f* usury; profit; **pagar con usura** to pay back a thousandfold
usurero *m* loan shark; profiteer
usurpar *tr* to usurp
utensilio *m* utensil
útero *m* uterus, womb
útil *adj* useful ‖ **útiles** *mpl* utensils, tools, equipment

utilería f (Arg) properties, stage equipment

utilero m (Arg) property man

utilidad f utility, usefulness; profit, earnings

utilita·rio -ria adj utilitarian

utilizable adj usable

utilizar §60 tr to utilize, to use ‖ ref — **utilizarse con, de** or **en** to make use of; **utilizarse para** to be good for

utopía f utopia

utopista adj & mf utopian

UU. abbr **ustedes**

uva f grape; wart on eyelid; (*baya*) berry; **estar hecho una uva** (coll) to have a load on; **uva crespa** gooseberry; **uva de Corinto** currant; **uva de raposa** nightshade; **uva espín** or **espina** gooseberry; **uva pasa** raisin; **uvas verdes** (*de la fábula de Esopo*) sour grapes

uve f (*letra del alfabeto*) V

uxoricida m uxoricide (*husband*)

uxoricidio m uxoricide (*act*)

uxo·rio -ria adj uxorious

V

V, v (ve *or* uve) f twenty-fifth letter of the Spanish alphabet

V. abbr **usted, véase, venerable**

V.A. abbr **Vuestra Alteza**

vaca f cow; (*cuero*) cowhide; (*carne de vaca o de buey*) beef; **hacer vaca** (Peru) to play truant; **vaca de la boda** (coll) goat, laughingstock; (coll) friend in need; **vaca de leche** milch cow; **vaca de San Antón** (ent) ladybird

vacación f (*cargo que está sin proveer*) vacancy; **de vacaciones** on vacation; **vacaciones** vacation; **vacaciones retribuidas** vacation with pay

vacacionista mf vacationist

vacancia f vacancy

vacante adj vacant ‖ f vacancy

vacar §73 intr (*un empleo, un cargo*) to be vacant, be unfilled; to take off, take a vacation; **vacar a** to attend to; **vacar de** to lack, be devoid of

vacia·do -da adj hollow-ground ‖ m cast, casting; plaster cast

vaciante f ebb tide

vaciar §77 & regular tr to empty, to drain; to cast, to mold; (*formar un hueco en*) to hollow out; to sharpen on a grindstone; to copy, transcribe; to explain in detail ‖ intr to empty; to flow; (*el agua en el río*) to fall, go down ‖ ref (coll) to blab

vacilación f vacillation; flickering; hesitancy, hesitation

vacilada f (Mex) spree, high time; (Mex) drunk

vacilante adj vacillating; (*luz*) flickering; (*irresoluto*) hesitant

vacilar intr to vacillate; (*la luz*) to flicker; to shake, wobble; (*estar irresoluto*) to hesitate, to waver

vací·o -a adj empty; (*hueco*) hollow; idle; useless, unsuccessful; (*vaca*) barren; presumptuous ‖ m emptiness; (*laguna, abertura; vacante*) vacancy; (*espacio que no contiene ninguna materia*) void; (*espacio de que se ha extraído el aire*) vacuum; (*ijada*) side, flank; **de vacío** light, unloaded; **hacer el vacío a** to isolate

vacuidad f vacuity, emptiness

vacuna f (*enfermedad de las vacas*) cowpox; (*virus cuya inoculación preserva de una enfermedad determinada*) vaccine

vacunación f vaccination

vacunar tr to vaccinate

vacu·no -na adj bovine; cowhide ‖ f see **vacuna**

va·cuo -cua adj vacant ‖ m cavity, hollow

vadear tr (*un río*) to ford; to wade through; to overcome; to sound out ‖ ref to behave; to manage

vado m ford; expedient, resource; **al vado o a la puente** (coll) one way or another; **no hallar vado** to see no way out; **tentar el vado** to feel one's way

vagabundaje m vagrancy

vagabundear intr to wander, to roam; to loaf around

vagabun·do -da adj vagabond ‖ mf vagabond, tramp; wanderer

vagancia f loafing, vagrancy

vagar m leisure; **con vagar** slowly; **estar de vagar** to have nothing to do ‖ §44 intr to wander, to roam; to be idle; to have plenty of leisure; (*una cosa*) to lie around; (*p.ej., una sonrisa por los labios*) to play

vagido m cry of a newborn baby

vagneria·no -na adj & mf Wagnerian

va·go -ga adj wandering, roaming; idle, loafing; lax, loose; hesitating, wavering; (*indefinido, indeciso*) vague; (*mirada*) blank ‖ m vagabond; idler, loafer; en vago shakily; in vain; in the air; **poner en vago** to tilt

vagón m car, railroad car; **vagón cama** sleeping car; **vagón carbonero** coal car; **vagón cerrado** boxcar; **vagón cisterna** tank car; **vagón de carga** freight car; **vagón de cola** caboose; **vagón de mercancías** freight car; **vagón de plataforma** flatcar; **vagón frigorífico** refrigerator car; **vagón salón** chair car; **vagón tolva** hopper-bottom car; **vagón volquete** dump car

vagoneta f tip car; station wagon

vaguear intr to wander-around

vaguedad f vagueness; vague remark

vaguido m faintness, fainting spell

vaharada f breath, exhalation

vahear *intr* to emit odors, to give forth an aroma

vahido *f* faintness, fainting spell

vaho *m* odor, aroma, vapor, fume

vaina *f* sheath; scabbard; knife case; (*de ciertas semillas*) pod, husk; (Am) annoyance, bother; (Col) luck, stroke of luck

vainica *f* hemstitch

vainilla *f* vanilla

vainita *f* (Ven) string bean

vaivén *m* swing, seesaw, backward and forward motion; unsteadiness, inconstancy; risk, chance

vajilla *f* dishes, set of dishes; **lavar la vajilla** to wash the dishes; **vajilla de oro** gold plate; **vajilla de plata** silver plate, silverware; **vajilla de porcelana** chinaware

vale *m* promissory note; voucher; farewell; (Ven) chum, pal; **vale respuesta** reply coupon

valede·ro -ra *adj* valid, effective

vale·dor -dora *mf* defender, protector; (Mex) friend, companion

valedura *f* (Mex) favor, protection

valencia *f* (chem) valence

valentía *f* bravery, valor; feat, exploit; dash, boldness; boast; **pisar de valentía** to strut, swagger

valen·tón -tona *adj* arrogant, boastful ‖ *mf* braggart, boaster ‖ *f* bragging

valer *m* worth, merit, value ‖ §76 *tr* to defend, protect; to favor, patronize; to avail; to yield; to be worth, be valued at; to be equal to; to suit; **valer la pena** to be worth while (to); **valerle a uno** + *inf* to help someone to + *inf*, to get someone to + *inf*; **valer lo que pesa** (coll) to be worth its (his, her, etc.) weight in gold; **valga lo que valiere** come what may; **¡válgame Dios!** bless my soul!, so help me God! ‖ *intr* to have worth; to be worthy; to be valuable; to be valid; to prevail; to hold, to count; to have influence; **hacer valer** (*sus derechos*) to assert; to make felt; to make good; to turn to account; **más vale** it is better (to); **vale** O.K.; **valer para** to be useful for; **valer por** to be equal to ‖ *ref* to help oneself, to defend oneself; **valerse de** to make use of, to avail oneself of

valero·so -sa *adj* valorous, brave; strong, active, effective

va·let *m* (*pl* -lets) (cards) jack

valía *f* value, worth; favor, influence; **mayor valía** or **plus valía** appreciation, increased value; unearned increment

validación *f* validation

validar *tr* to validate

validez *f* validity; strength, vigor

vali·do -da *adj* highly esteemed, influential ‖ *m* court favorite; prime minister

váli·do -da *adj* valid; strong, robust

valiente *adj* valiant; strong, robust; fine, excellent; (*grande y excesivo*) terrific ‖ *m* brave fellow; bully

valija *f* satchel, brief case; mailbag, mailpouch; mail; **valija diplomática** diplomatic pouch

valimiento *m* favor, protection; favor at court, favoritism

valio·so -sa *adj* valuable; influential; wealthy

va·lón -lona *adj* & *mf* Walloon

valor *m* value, worth; valor, courage; meaning, import; efficacy; equivalence; (*rédito*) income, return; effrontery; (*persona, cosa o cualidad dignas de ser poseídas*) (fig) asset; **¿cómo va ese valor?** (coll) how are you?; **valor de rescate** (ins) surrender value; **valores** securities

valoración *f* valuation, appraisal

valorar or **valorear** *tr* (*poner precio a*) to value, to appraise; to enhance the value of

valorizar §60 *tr* to value; to enhance the value of; (Am) to sell off (*for quick realization*)

vals *m* waltz

valsar *intr* to waltz

valuación *f* valuation, appraisal

valuar §21 *tr* to estimate

válvula *f* valve; **válvula corrediza** slide valve; **válvula de admisión** intake valve; **válvula de escape** exhaust valve; **válvula de escape libre** cutout; **válvula de seguridad** safety valve; **válvula en cabeza** valve in the head, overhead valve

valla *f* fence, railing; barricade; hindrance, obstacle; (sport) hurdle; (W-I) cockpit; **valla paranieves** snow fence

vallado *m* barricade, stockade

valle *m* valley; river bed; valley dwellings; **valle de lágrimas** vale of tears

vampiresa *f* vampire

vampíri·co -ca *adj* vampire; ghoulish

vampiro *m* vampire; (*persona que se deleita con cosas horribles*) ghoul

vanadio *m* vanadium

vanagloriar §77 & regular *ref* to boast

vanaglorio·so -sa *adj* vainglorious, conceited, boastful

vanamente *adv* vainly

vandalismo *m* vandalism

vánda·lo -la *adj* & *mf* Vandal; (fig) vandal

vanguardia *f* (mil & fig) vanguard, van; **a vanguardia** in the vanguard

vanguardismo *m* avant-garde

vanguardista *adj* avant-garde ‖ *mf* avant-gardist

vanidad *f* vanity; (*fausto*) pomp, show; **ajar la vanidad de** (coll) to take down a peg; **hacer vanidad de** to boast of

vanido·so -sa *adj* vain, conceited

va·no -na *adj* vain; hollow, empty; **en vano** in vain ‖ *m* opening in a wall

vapor *m* steam; (*el visible: exhalación, vaho, niebla, etc.*) vapor; steamer, steamboat; **al vapor** at full speed; **vapores** gas (*belched*); blues; **vapor volandero** tramp steamer

vaporar *tr* & *ref* to evaporate

vaporizador *m* atomizer, sprayer

vaporizar §60 *tr* to vaporize; to spray ‖ *ref* to vaporize

vaporo·so -sa *adj* vaporous

ut
va

vapular or **vapulear** *tr* whip, to flog

vaquería *f* drove of cattle; dairy; (Mex) party

vaqueri·zo -za *adj* cattle ‖ *f* winter stable for cattle

vaque·ro -ra *adj* cattle ‖ *mf* cattle tender; (Peru) truant ‖ *m* cow hand; cowboy

vaqueta *f* leather; (P-R) strop; **zurrarle a uno la vaqueta** (Am) to tan someone's hide

vaquillona *f* (Arg, Chile) heifer

vara *f* pole, rod, staff; (*de carruaje*) shaft; (*bastón de mando*) wand; measuring stick; (taur) thrust with goad; **tener vara alta** to have the upper hand; **vara alcándara** shaft; **vara alta** upper hand; **vara buscadora** divining rod (*ostensibly to discover water or metals*); **vara de adivinar** divining rod; **vara de oro** goldenrod; **vara de pescar** fishing rod; **vara de San José** goldenrod

vara-alta *m* (coll) boss

varada *f* beaching; running aground

varadero *m* repair dock

varapalo *m* long pole; (coll) setback, disappointment, reverse

varar *tr* (*una embarcación*) to beach ‖ *intr* to run aground; (*un negocio*) to come to a standstill

varear *tr* (*los frutos de los árboles*) to beat down, knock down; to beat, strike; (taur) to goad; (*los caballos de carreras*) (SAm) to exercise, to train ‖ *ref* to lose weight, get thin

varec *m* (bot) wrack

varenga *f* (naut) floor, floor timber

vareta *f* twig, stick; lime twig for catching birds; colored stripe; (coll) cutting remark; (coll) hint; **irse de vareta** (coll) to have diarrhea

variable *adj* & *f* variable

variación *f* variation

varia·do -da *adj* varied; variegated

variante *adj* & *f* variant

variar §77 *tr* to vary, to change ‖ *intr* to vary, to change; to be different; **variar de** or **en opinión** to change one's mind

varice *f* or **várice** *f* varicose veins

varicela *f* chicken pox

varico·so -sa *adj* varicose

variedad *f* variety; **variedades** variety show, vaudeville

varilla *f* rod, stem, twig; (*bastón de mando*) wand; (*de paraguas, abanico, etc.*) rib; (*del corsé*) stay; (*de rueda*) wire spoke; (coll) jawbone; (Mex) peddler's wares; **varilla de nivel** dipstick; **varilla de virtudes** wand, magician's wand

varillaje *m* ribs, ribbing; (*de máquina de escribir*) type bars

varille·ro -ra *adj* (*caballo*) (Ven) race ‖ *m* (Mex) peddler

va·rio -ria *adj* (*de diversos colores; que tiene variedad*) various, varied; fickle, inconstant; **varios** various; several

varón *adj* male, e.g., **hijo varón** male child ‖ *m* man, male; grown man, adult male; man of standing; **santo varón** (coll) plain artless fellow

varonía *f* male issue

varonil *adj* manly, virile; courageous

Varsovia *f* Warsaw

vasa·llo -lla *adj* & *mf* vassal

vas·co -ca *adj* & *mf* Basque (*of Spain and France*) ‖ *m* Basque (*language*)

vas·cón -cona *adj* & *mf* Basque (*of old Spain*)

vasconga·do -da *adj* & *mf* Basque (*of Spain*) ‖ *m* Basque (*language*) ‖ **las Vascongadas** the Basque Provinces

vascuence *adj* & *m* Basque (*language*) ‖ *m* (coll) gibberish

vaselina *f* vaseline

vasera *f* kitchen shelf; bottle rack, tumbler rack

vasija *f* container, vessel

vaso *m* tumbler, glass; vase, flower jar; (anat) duct, vessel; vase de engrase (mach) grease cup; **vaso de noche** pot, chamber pot; **vaso graduado** measuring glass; **vaso sanguíneo** blood vessel

vástago *m* shoot, sapling; scion, offspring; rod, stem; **vástago de émbolo** piston rod; **vástago de válvula** valve stem

vastedad *f* vastness

vas·to -ta *adj* vast

vate *m* bard, seer, poet

váter *m* (coll) toilet, water closet

vatiaje *m* wattage

vaticinar *tr* to prophesy, predict

vaticinio *m* prophecy, prediction

vatídi·co -ca *adj* prophetical ‖ *mf* prophet

vatímetro *m* wattmeter

vatio *m* watt

vatio-hora *m* (*pl* **vatios-hora**) watt-hour

vaya *f* jest, jeer

Vd. *abbr* **usted**

Vds. *abbr* **ustedes**

V.E. *abbr* **Vuestra Excelencia**

vece·ro -ra *adj* alternating; yielding in alternate years ‖ *mf* person waiting his turn

vecinamente *adv* nearby

vecindad *f* neighborhood, vicinity; residency; residents; **hacer mala vecindad** to be a bad neighbor

vecindario *m* neighborhood, community; people, population

veci·no -na *adj* neighboring; like, similar ‖ *mf* resident, citizen

veda *f* prohibition; (*de la caza y la pesca*) closed season

vedado *m* game preserve

vedar *tr* to forbid, prohibit; to hinder, stop; to veto

vedija *f* fleece, tuft of wool; mat of hair; matted hair

vee·dor -dora *adj* curious, spying ‖ *mf* busybody ‖ *m* supervisor, overseer

vega *f* fertile plain; (Cuba) tobacco plantation

vegetación *f* vegetation; **vegetaciones adenoideas** adenoids

vegetal *adj* & *m* vegetable

vegetaria·no -na *adj* & *mf* vegetarian

vego·so -sa *adj* (Chile) damp, wet

vehemencia *f* vehemence

vehemente *adj* vehement

vehículo *m* vehicle; **vehículo espacial** space vehicle

veinta·vo -va *adj & m* twentieth

veinte *adj & pron* twenty; **a las veinte** (coll) late, untimely || *m* twenty; (*en las fechas*) twentieth

veintena *f* score, twenty

veintiún *adj* this apocopated form of **veintiuno** is used before masculine singular nouns and adjectives

veintiu·no -na *adj & pron* twenty-one || *m* twenty-one; (*en las fechas*) twenty-first || *f* (*juego de naipes*) twenty-one

vejación *f* vexation, annoyance

vejamen *m* vexation, annoyance; bantering, taunting

vejar *tr* to vex, annoy; to taunt

vejestorio *m* (coll) old dodo

vejete *m* (coll) little old fellow

vejez *f* old age; oldness; dotage; platitude, old story; **a la vejez, viruelas** there's no fool like an old fool

vejiga *f* (*órgano que recibe la orina de los riñones*) bladder; (*ampolla*) blister; (*saco hecho de piel, goma, etc.*) bag, pouch, bladder; **vejiga de la bilis** or **de la hiel** gall bladder

vela *f* wakefulness; pilgrimage; evening; work in the evening; sail; sailboat; (*cilindro que recibe una torcida que sirve para alumbrar*) candle; vigil (*before Eucharist*); awning; (Mex) scolding; **a toda vela** full sail; **a vela** under sail; **a vela llena** under full sail; **en vela** awake; **estar entre dos velas** to be half-seas over, to have a sheet in the wind; **hacerse a la vela** to set sail; **vela latina** lateen sail; **vela mayor** mainsail; **vela romana** Roman candle

velada *f* evening party, soirée; vigil, watch

vela·do -da *adj* veiled, hidden; (phot) light-struck || *f* see **velada**

velador *m* pedestal table, gueridon; wooden candlestick; watchman; (SAm) night table; (Mex) lamp globe

velaje *m* or **velamen** *m* (naut) canvas, sails

velar *adj & f* velar || *tr* to watch over; to guard; (*la guardia*) to keep; to hold a wake over; (*cubrir con un velo*) to veil; (phot) to fog; (fig) to veil, hide, conceal || *intr* to stay awake; to stay awake working; to keep vigil; (*el viento*) to keep up all night; (*un escollo, un peñasco*) to stick up out of the water; **velar por** or **sobre** to watch over || *ref* (phot) to fog, to be light-struck

velatorio *m* wake

veleidad *f* whim, caprice; fickleness, flightiness

veleido·so -sa *adj* whimsical, capricious; fickle, flighty

vele·ro -ra *adj* swift-sailing || *m* sailboat

veleta *mf* (*persona inconstante*) (coll) weathercock || *f* vane, weathervane, weathercock; (*de un molino*) rudder vane; (*de la caña de pescar*) bob; streamer, pennant; **veleta de manga** (aer) air sleeve, air sock

velís *m* (Mex) valise

velita *f* little candle

velo *m* veil; taking the veil; confusion, perplexity; (*disfraz*) veil; (*de lágrimas*) mist; (phot) fog; **correr el velo** to pull aside the curtain, to dispel the mystery; **tomar el velo** to take the veil; **velo del paladar** soft palate

velocidad *f* (*rapidez*) speed, velocity; (mech) velocity; **en gran velocidad** (rr) by express; **en pequeña velocidad** (rr) by freight; **primera velocidad** (aut) low gear; **segunda velocidad** (aut) second; **tercera velocidad** (aut) high gear; **velocidad con respecto al suelo** (aer) ground speed; **velocidad permitida** speed limit

velocímetro *m* speedometer

velón *m* brass olive-oil lamp

velorio *m* evening party or bee; wake; wake for a dead child; (Am) dull party; (Am) come-on

ve·loz *adj* (*pl* **-loces**) swift, speedy; agile, quick

vello *m* down, fuzz

vellocino *m* fleece; **vellocino de oro** Golden Fleece

vellón *m* fleece; unsheared sheepskin; lock of wool; copper coin; copper-silver alloy

vello·so -sa *adj* downy, hairy, fuzzy

velludillo *m* velveteen

vellu·do -da *adj* shaggy, hairy, fuzzy || *m* (*felpa*) plush; (*terciopelo*) velvet

vena *f* vein; (*en piedras*) grain; (fig) poetical inspiration; **estar en vena** (coll) to be all set, to be inspired; (coll) to sparkle with wit; **vena de loco** fickle disposition

venablo *m* dart, javelin; **echar venablos** to burst forth in anger

venado *m* deer, stag; **pintar el venado** (Mex) to play hooky

venáti·co -ca *adj* (coll) fickle, unsteady; (coll) daffy, nutty

vence·dor -dora *adj* conquering, victorious || *mf* conqueror, victor

vencejo *m* band, string; (orn) European swift, black martin

vencer §78 *tr* to vanquish, conquer; to excel, outdo; to overcome, to surmount || *intr* to conquer, be victorious; (*un plazo*) to be up; (*un contrato*) to expire; (*una letra*) to mature, fall due || *ref* to control oneself; (*un camino*) to bend, turn; (Chile) to wear out, become useless

vencetósigo *m* milkweed, tame poison

venci·do -da *adj* conquered; (com) due, mature, payable

vencimiento *m* (*acción de vencer*) victory; (*hecho de ser vencido*) defeat; (com) expiration, maturity

venda *f* (*para ligar un miembro herido*) bandage; (*para tapar los ojos*) blindfold

vendaje *m* bandage, dressing; **vendaje enyesado** plaster cast

vendar *tr* (*un miembro, una herida*) to bandage; (*los ojos*) to blindfold; (*cegar*) (fig) to blind; (*engañar*) (fig) to hoodwink

vendaval *m* strong southeasterly wind from the sea; strong wind, gale

vendedera *f* saleswoman, saleslady

vende‧dor -dora *adj* selling ‖ *m* salesman ‖ *f* saleslady, sales girl
vendehu‧mos *mf* (*pl* **-mos**) (coll) influence peddler
vendeja *f* public sale
vender *tr* to sell; to betray, sell out; **vender salud** to be the picture of health ‖ *intr* to sell; **¡vendo, vendo, vendí!** going, going, gone! ‖ *ref* to sell oneself; to sell, be for sale; to betray oneself, to give oneself away; **venderse caro** to be hard to see; to be quite a stranger; **venderse en** (*p.ej.,* **cien pesetas**) to sell for; **venderse por** to pass oneself off as
ven‧di *m* (*pl* **-dies**) certificate of sale
vendible *adj* salable, marketable
vendimia *f* vintage; (fig) big profit
vendimia‧dor -dora *mf* vintager
vendimiar *tr* (*la uva*) to gather, to harvest; (*las viñas*) to gather the grapes of; to make off with; (coll) to kill
venduta *f* (Am) public sale; (W-I) greengrocery
Venecia *f* (*ciudad*) Venice; (*provincia*) Venetia
venecia‧no -na *adj & mf* Venetian
veneno *m* poison, venom
veneno‧so -sa *adj* poisonous, venomous
venera *f* scallop shell; (*manantial de agua*) spring; **empeñar la venera** (coll) to go all out, spare no expense
venerable *adj* venerable
venerar *tr* to venerate, revere; to worship
venére‧o -a *adj* venereal ‖ *m* venereal disease
venero *m* (*de agua*) spring; (*filón de mineral*) lode, vein; (fig) source
venezola‧no -na *adj & mf* Venezuelan
Venezuela *f* Venezuela
venga‧dor -dora *adj* avenging ‖ *mf* avenger
venganza *f* vengeance, revenge
vengar §44 *tr* to avenge ‖ *ref* to take revenge; **vengarse de** to take revenge on
vengati‧vo -va *adj* vengeful, vindictive
venia *f* forgiveness, pardon; leave, permission; bow, greeting
venida *f* coming; return; flood, freshet
venide‧ro -ra *adj* coming, future ‖ **venideros** *mpl* successors, posterity
venir §79 *intr* to come; **que viene** coming, next; **venga lo que viniere** come what may; **venir** + *ger* to be + *ger*; **venir a** + *inf* to come to + *inf*; to amount to + *ger*; to happen to + *inf*; to finally + *inf*, e.g., **después de una larga enfermedad, vino a morir** after a long illness he finally died; **venir a ser** to turn out to be ‖ *ref* to ferment; **venirse abajo** to collapse
veno‧so -sa *adj* venous
venta *f* sale; roadside inn; (Chile) refreshment stand; (S-D) grocery store; **de venta** or **en venta** on sale, for sale; **ser una venta** (coll) to be an expensive place; **venta al descubierto** short sale
ventaja *f* advantage; (*en juegos o apuestas*) odds; extra pay
ventajo‧so -sa *adj* advantageous

ventalla *f* valve
ventana *f* window; (*de la nariz*) nostril; **echar la casa por la ventana** (coll) to go to a lot of expense; **ventana batiente** casement; **ventana de guillotina** sash window; **ventana salediza** bay window
ventanal *m* church window; picture window
ventanear *intr* (coll) to be at the window all the time
ventanilla *f* (*de coche, de banco, de sobre*) window; ticket window; (*de la nariz*) nostril
ventanillo *m* (*postigo de puerta o ventana*) wicket; (*mirilla*) peephole
ventar §2 *tr* to sniff ‖ *impers* — **vienta** it is windy
ventarrón *m* gale, windstorm
ventear *tr* to sniff; to dry in the wind; to snoop into ‖ *intr* to snoop, pry around ‖ *impers* — **ventea** it is windy ‖ *ref* (*henderse*) to split; (coll) to break wind; (Am) to spend a lot of time in the open
vente‧ro -ra *mf* innkeeper
ventilador *m* ventilator; fan; (naut) funnel; **ventilador aspirador** exhaust fan
ventilar *tr* to ventilate; (fig) to air, ventilate
ventisca *f* drift, snowdrift; (*borrasca*) blizzard
ventiscar §73 *intr* to snow and blow; (*la nieve*) to drift
ventisquero *m* snowdrift; blizzard; snow-capped mountain; glacier
ventolera *f* blast of wind; (*molinete*) pinwheel; vanity, pride; (coll) wild idea; (Mex) wind
ventosa *f* vent, air hole; **pegar una ventosa a** (coll) to swindle
ventosear *intr* to break wind
vento‧so -sa *adj* windy ‖ *f* see **ventosa**
ventregada *f* brood, litter; outpouring, abundance
ventrículo *m* ventricle
ventrílo‧cuo -cua *mf* ventriloquist
ventriloquia *f* or **ventriloquismo** *m* ventriloquism
ventura *f* happiness; luck, chance; danger, risk; **a la ventura** at random; **al azar**; **por ventura** perhaps, perchance; **probar ventura** to try one's luck
venture‧ro -ra *adj* adventurous; fortunate, lucky ‖ *mf* adventurer
ventu‧ro -ra *adj* future, coming ‖ *f* see **ventura**
venturón *m* stroke of luck
venturo‧so -sa *adj* fortunate, lucky
Venus *m* (astr) Venus ‖ *f* (myth) Venus; (*mujer de gran belleza*) Venus
venus‧to -ta *adj* beautiful, graceful
venza *f* goldbeater's skin
ver *m* (*vista*) sight; (*apariencia*) appearance; opinion; **a mi ver** in my opinion ‖ §80 *tr* to see; to look at; (law) to hear, to try; **no poder ver** to not be able to bear; **no tener nada que ver con** to have nothing to do with; **ver** + *inf* to see + *inf*, e.g., **ví entrar a mi hermano** I saw my

brother come in; **to see** + **ger,** e.g., **ví bailar a la muchacha** I saw the girl dancing; **to see** + **pp,** e.g., **ví ahorcar al criminal** I saw the criminal hanged; **ver venir a uno** to see what someone is up to ‖ *intr* to see; **a más ver** so long; **a ver** let's see; **hasta más ver** good-bye, so long; **ver de** to try to; **ver y creer** seeing is believing ‖ *ref* to be seen; **to be obvious;** to see oneself; to see each other; to meet; (*encontrarse*) to be, to find oneself; **verse con** to see, have a talk with; **ya se ve** of course, certainly

vera *f* edge, border; **a la vera de** near, beside; **de veras** in truth; **jugar de veras** to play for keeps; **veras** truth, reality; earnestness

veracidad *f* veracity, truthfulness

veranda *f* verandah; bay window, closed porch

veraneante *mf* summer vacationist, summer resident

veranear *intr* to summer

veranie·go -ga *adj* summer; unimportant, insignificant

veranillo *m* Indian summer; **veranillo de San Martín** Indian summer

ve·raz *adj* (*pl* **-races**) veracious, truthful

verbena *f* fair, country fair, night festival; (bot) verbena

verbigracia *adv* for example

verbo *m* verb ‖ **Verbo** *m* (theol) Word

verbo·so -sa *adj* verbose, wordy

verdacho *m* green earth

verdad *f* truth; **a la verdad** in truth, as a matter of fact; **de verdad** really; **la verdad desnuda** the plain truth; **¿no es verdad?** or **¿verdad?** isn't that so? La traducción al inglés de esta pregunta depende generalmente de la aseveración que la precede. Si la aseveración es afirmativa, la pregunta es negativa, p.ej., **Vd. vivió aquí. ¿No es verdad?** You lived here. Did you not?; Si la aseveración es negativa, la pregunta es afirmativa, p.ej., **Vd. no vivió aquí. ¿No es verdad?** You did not live here? Did you? Si el sujeto de la aseveración es un nombre sustantivo, va representado en la pregunta con un pronombre personal, p.ej., **Juan no estuvo aquí anoche. ¿No es verdad?** John was not here last evening. Was he?; **ser verdad** to be true; **verdad trillada** truism

verdade·ro -ra *adj* true; real; (*que dice siempre la verdad*) truthful

verde *adj* green; young, youthful; (*viuda*) merry; (*viejo*) gay; (*cuento*) shady, off-color; **están verdes** (coll) they're hard to reach ‖ *m* green; foliage, verdure

verdear *intr* to turn green, to look green

verdecer §22 *intr* to turn green, to grow green again

verdecillo *m* (orn) greenfinch

verdemar *m* sea green

verdete *m* verdigris

verdín *m* fresh green; (*capa verde de*

aguas estancadas) mold, pond scum; (*cardenillo*) verdigris

verdise·co -ca *adj* half-dry

verdor *m* verdure; youth

verdo·so -sa *adj* greenish

verdugado *m* hoop skirt

verdugo *m* shoot, sucker; (*estoque*) rapier; (*azote*) scourge; (*roncha*) welt; executioner, hangman; torment; butcher bird, shrike

verdugón *m* wale, weal

verdulería *f* greengrocery

verdule·ro -ra *mf* greengrocer ‖ *f* fishwife

verdura *f* greenness; (*color verde de las plantas*) verdure; (*obscenidad*) smuttiness; **verduras** vegetables, greens

verecundia *f* bashfulness, shyness

verecun·do -da *adj* bashful, shy

vereda *f* path, lane; (Am) sidewalk

veredicto *m* verdict

verga *f* (naut) yard

vergel *m* flower and fruit garden

vergonzo·so -sa *adj* (*que causa vergüenza*) shameful; (*que tiene vergüenza*) ashamed; (*que se avergüenza con facilidad*) bashful, shy; (*que causa humillación*) embarrassing; shabby, wretched ‖ *mf* bashful person ‖ *m* armadillo

vergüenza *f* (*arrepentimiento*) shame; (*oprobio*) shamefulness; (*pudor, timidez*) bashfulness, shyness; (*desconcierto, humillación*) embarrassment; (*pundonor*) dignity, face; public punishment; **¡qué vergüenza!** shame on you!; **tener vergüenza** to be ashamed; **vergüenzas** privates, genitals

vericueto *m* rough, rocky ground

verídi·co -ca *adj* truthful

verificación *f* verification; checking, testing, inspection

verifica·dor -dora *adj* verifying ‖ *m* meter inspector

verificar §73 *tr* to verify, to check; (*llevar a cabo*) to carry out; (*los contadores de agua, gas y electricidad*) to inspect ‖ *ref* to prove true; to take place

verja *f* iron gate, iron fence, grating

ver·mú *m* (*pl* **-mús**) vermouth; (Am) matinée

vernácu·lo -la *adj* vernacular

verónica *f* (bot) veronica; (taur) veronica (*graceful pass in which the bullfighter waits for the bull with open cape*)

veroniquear *intr* (taur) to perform veronicas

verosímil *adj* likely, probable

verraco *m* male hog, boar

verraquear *intr* (coll) to grunt, grumble; (coll) to cry hard

verruga *f* wart; (coll) bore, nuisance

verrugo *m* (coll) miser

versal *adj* & *f* capital

versalilla *f* or **versalita** *f* small capital

Versalles Versailles

versar *intr* — **versar acerca de** or **sobre** to deal with, to treat of ‖ *ref* — **versarse en** to be or become versed in

versátil *adj* fickle

versículo *m* verse (*in the Bible*)

versificación *f* versification

versificar §73 *tr & intr* to versify

versión *f* version; translation

verso *m* verse; (typ) verso; **versos pareados** rhymed couplet

vertebra•do -da *adj & m* vertebrate

vertedero *m* dump; weir, spillway

verter §51 *tr* (*un líquido, un polvo*) to pour; (*un recipiente*) to empty; (*lágrimas; luz; sangre*) to shed; (*descargar*) to dump; to translate || *intr* to flow || *ref* to run, to empty

vertical *adj & f* vertical

vértice *m* vertex

vertiente *m & f* (*declive*) slope; (*colina por donde corre el agua*) shed || *f* (Arg, Col, Chile) spring, fountain

vertigino•so -sa *adj* dizzy

vértigo *m* vertigo, dizziness; fit of insanity

vesícula *f* vesicle; **vesícula biliar** gall bladder

veso *m* polecat

Véspero *m* Vesper

vesperti•no -na *adj* evening || *m* evening sermon

vestíbulo *m* vestibule; (theat) foyer, lobby

vestido *m* clothing, dress; (*de mujer*) gown, dress; (*de hombre*) suit; costume; **vestido de ceremonia** dress suit; **vestido de etiqueta** evening clothes; **vestido de etiqueta de mujer** or **vestido de noche** evening gown; **vestido de gala** (mil) full dress; **vestido de serio** evening clothes; **vestido de tarde-noche** cocktail dress

vestidura *f* clothing; (*del sacerdote*) vestment

vestigio *m* vestige, trace; track, footprint

vestir §50 *tr* to dress, to clothe; to adorn; to cover up; to disguise; (*tal o cual vestido*) to wear; to put on; **vestir el cargo** to look the part || *intr* to dress; (*una prenda o la materia*) to be dressy; **vestir de** (*p.ej., blanco*) to dress in; **vestir de etiqueta** to dress in evening clothes; **vestir de paisano** to dress in civilian clothes || *ref* to dress, to get dressed; to dress oneself; (*de una enfermedad*) to be up, to be about; **vestirse de** (*nubes, flores, hierba, etc.*) to be covered with; (*importancia, humildad, etc.*) to assume

vestuario *m* (*las prendas de uno*) wardrobe; dressing room; bathhouse; checkroom, cloakroom; (mil) uniform; (theat) dressing room

Vesubio, el Vesuvius

veta *f* vein; streak, stripe; **descubrir la veta de** (coll) to be on to

vetar *tr* to veto

vetea•do -da *adj* veined, striped || *m* graining || *f* (Ecuad) whipping

vetear *tr* to grain, to stripe; (Ecuad) to whip, to flog

veteranía *f* experience, know-how

vetera•no -na *adj & mf* veteran

veterina•rio -ria *adj* veterinary || *mf* veterinarian || *f* veterinary medicine

vetus•to -ta *adj* old, ancient

vez *f* (*pl* **veces**) time; (*tiempo de hacer una cosa por turno*) turn; **a la vez** at the same time; **a la vez que** while; **alguna vez** sometimes; ever; **a su vez** in turn; on his part; **a veces** at times, sometimes; **cada vez** every time; **cada vez más** more and more; **cuántas veces** how often; **de una vez** at one time; once and for all; **de vez en cuando** once in a while; **dos veces** twice; **en vez de** instead of; **esperar vez** to wait one's turn; **hacer las veces de** to take the place of; **las más veces** most of the time; **muchas veces** often; **otra vez** again; **raras veces** or **rara vez** seldom, rarely; **repetidas veces** over and over again; **tal vez** perhaps; **tomar la vez** (coll) to get ahead of; **una que otra vez** once in a while; **una vez** once

veza *f* vetch, spring vetch

v.g. or **v.gr.** *abbr* **verbigracia**

vía *f* road, route, way; (*par de rieles y el suelo en que se asientan*) (rr) track; (*el mismo carril*) (rr) rail, track; (anat) passage, tract; (fig) way; **por la vía de** via; **por vía aérea** by air; **por vía bucal** by mouth; **vía aérea** airway; **vía ancha** (rr) broad gauge; **vía de agua** waterway; (naut) leak; **vía estrecha** (rr) narrow gauge; **vía férrea** railway; (fig) railroad; **vía fluvial** waterway; **Vía Láctea** Milky Way; **vía muerta** (rr) siding; **vía normal** (rr) standard gauge; **vía pública** thoroughfare; **vías de hecho** (law) assault and battery || *prep* via

viable *adj* feasible

viaducto *m* viaduct

viajante *adj* traveling || *mf* traveler || *m* drummer, traveling salesman

viajar *tr* to sell on the road; (*ciertas comarcas*) to cover as salesman || *intr* to travel, to journey

viaje *m* trip, journey; travel book; water supply; **¡buen viaje!** bon voyage!; **viaje de ida y vuelta** or **viaje redondo** round trip

viaje•ro -ra *adj* traveling || *mf* traveler; passenger

vial *adj* road, highway || *m* tree-lined road

vianda *f* food, viand; meal

viandante *mf* traveler; itinerant

viático *m* travel allowance; (eccl) viaticum

víbora *f* viper

vibración *f* vibration

vibrar *tr* to vibrate; (*la voz; la r*) to roll; (*una lanza*) to hurl || *intr* to vibrate || *ref* to be thrilled

vicaría *f* vicarage

vicario *m* vicar

vicealmirante *m* vice-admiral

vicepresiden•te -ta *mf* vice-president

viceversa *adv* vice versa

viciar *tr* to vitiate; (*una proposición*) to slant || *ref* to become vitiated; to give oneself up to vice; to become addicted; (*una tabla*) to warp

vicio *m* vice; pampering, spoiling; luxuriance, overgrowth; **hablar de**

vicio (coll) to talk all the time, to talk too much; **quejarse de vicio** (coll) to be a chronic complainer

vicio·so -sa *adj* vicious; faulty, defective; strong, robust; luxuriant, overgrown; dissolute; (*niño*) (coll) spoiled

víctima *f* victim, **víctima propiciatoria** scapegoat

victimar *tr* (Am) to kill, murder

victoria *f* victory

victorio·so -sa *adj* victorious

vid *f* vine, grapevine

vida *f* life; living, livelihood; **darse buena vida** to live high; to live in comfort; **de por vida** for life; **en mi vida** never; **escapar con vida** to have a narrow escape; **ganar** or **ganarse la vida** to earn one's livelihood, to make a living; **hacer por la vida** (coll) to get a bite to eat; **mudar de vida** to mend one's ways; **¡por vida mía!** upon my soul!; **vida airada** licentious living; **vida ancha** loose living; **vida de familia** or **de hogar** home life; **vida mía** my darling

vidalita *f* (Arg, Chile, Urug) mournful love song

vidente *mf* clairvoyant ‖ *m* prophet, seer ‖ *f* seeress

videograbación *f* video-tape recording

videoseñal *f* picture signal

vidria·do -da *adj* glazed; brittle ‖ *m* glaze, glazing; glazed pottery; dishes

vidriar §77 & regular *tr* to glaze ‖ *ref* (*los ojos*) to become glassy

vidriera *f* glass window, glass door; (Am) shopwindow, store window; **vidriera de colores** or **vidriera pintada** stained-glass window

vidriería *f* glassworks; glass store

vidriero *m* glass blower, glassworker; glazier; glass dealer

vidrio *m* glass; piece of glass; windowpane; **pagar los vidrios rotos** (coll) to take the blame, to be the goat; **vidrio cilindrado** plate glass; **vidrio de aumento** magnifying glass; **vidrio de color** stained glass; **vidrio deslustrado** ground glass; **vidrio tallado** cut glass

vidrio·so -sa *adj* glassy, vitreous; (*quebradizo*) brittle; (*resbaladizo*) slippery; (*que se resiente fácilmente*) (coll) touchy; (*mirada, ojos*) (fig) glassy

vie·jo -ja *adj* old ‖ *m* old man; **viejo verde** old goat, old rake ‖ *f* old woman

vie·nés -nesa *adj* & *mf* Viennese

viento *m* wind; course, direction; (*cuerda que mantiene una cosa derecha*) guy; (*gases intestinales*) (coll) wind; **ceñir el viento** (naut) to sail close to the wind; **viento de cola** (aer) tail wind; **viento en popa** (naut) tail wind; **vientos alisios** trade winds

vientre *m* belly; (*parte de la ondulación entre dos nodos*) (phys) loop; **evacuar** or **exonerar el vientre** to have a bowel movement; **vientre flojo** loose bowels

vier·nes *m* (*pl* -nes) Friday; **Viernes santo** Good Friday

viertea·guas *m* (*pl* -guas) *m* flashing

vietna·més -mesa *adj* & *mf* Vietnamese

viga *f* beam, girder, rafter; **estar contando las vigas** (coll) to gaze blankly at the ceiling; **viga de celosía** lattice girder

vigencia *f* force, operation; (*de una póliza de seguro*) life; **en vigencia** in force, in effect

vigente *adj* effective, in force

vigési·mo -ma *adj* & *m* twentieth

vigía *m* lookout, watch; **vigía de incendios** firewarden ‖ *f* watch; watchtower; (naut) rock, reef

vigiar §77 *tr* to watch over.

vigilancia *f* vigilance, watchfulness; **bajo vigilancia médica** under the care of a physician

vigilante *adj* vigilant, watchful ‖ *m* guard, watchman; **vigilante nocturno** night watchman

vigilar *tr* to watch over; to look out for ‖ *intr* to watch, keep guard

vigilia *f* vigil; wakefulness; night work, night study; (*víspera*) eve; (mil) guard, watch; **comer de vigilia** to fast, to abstain from meat

vigor *m* vigor; **en vigor** in force; into effect

vigoriza·dor -dora *adj* invigorating ‖ *m* tonic; **vigorizador del cabello** hair tonic

vigorizante *adj* invigorating

vigorizar §60 *tr* to invigorate; to encourage

vigoro·so -sa *adj* vigorous

vigueta *f* small beam, small girder

vihuela *f* Spanish lute

vil *adj* vile, base, mean ‖ *mf* scoundrel

vilano *m* bur, down

vileza *f* vileness, baseness

vilipendiar *tr* to scorn, despise

vilipendio·so -sa *adj* contemptible

vilo — **en vilo** in the air; (fig) up in the air

vilorta *f* reed hoop; (*arandela*) washer

villa *f* town; (*casa de recreo en el campo*) villa; **la Villa** the city (*Madrid*)

villancico *m* carol, Christmas carol

villanes·co -ca *adj* boorish, crude, rustic

villanía *f* humbleness, humble birth; vileness, meanness; foul remark

villa·no -na *adj* base, vile; rude, impolite ‖ *mf* peasant; knave, scoundrel

villorrio *m* small country town

vinagre *m* vinegar; (*persona de genio áspero*) (coll) grouch

vinagrera *f* vinaigrette; (bot) sorrel; (SAm) heartburn; **vinagreras** cruet stand

vinagreta *f* French dressing, vinaigrette sauce

vinagro·so -sa *adj* vinegary

vinariego *m* vineyardist

vinatería *f* wine business; wine shop

vinate·ro -ra *adj* wine ‖ *m* wine dealer, vintner

vincular *tr* to bind, to tie, to unite; to continue, to perpetuate; (*esperanzas*) to found, to base; (law) entail

vínculo *m* bond, tie; (law) entail

vindicar §73 *tr* (*vengar*) to avenge; (*exculpar*) to vindicate

vindicta *f* revenge

ve
vi

vinicul·tor -tora *mf* winegrower
vinicultura *f* winegrowing
vinilo *m* vinyl
vino *m* wine; sherry reception, wine party; **tener mal vino** to be a quarrelsome drunk; **vino cubierto** dark-red wine; **vino de Jerez** sherry; **vino del terruño** local wine; **vino de mesa** table wine; **vino de Oporto** port wine; **vino de pasto** table wine; **vino de postre** after-dinner wine; **vino de segunda** second-run wine; **vino de solera** solera sherry; **vino tinto** red table wine
vinolen·to -ta *adj* too fond of wine
viña *f* vineyard; **ser una viña** (coll) to be a mine; **tener una viña** (coll) to have a sinecure
viña·dor -dora *mf* vineyardist, vinedresser ‖ *m* guard of a vineyard
viñedo *m* vineyard
viñeta *f* vignette, headpiece
viola·do -da *adj & m* violet (*color*)
violar *m* bed of violets ‖ *tr* to violate; to ravish, rape; to profane, desecrate; to tamper with
violencia *f* violence
violentar *tr* to do violence to; (*p.ej.*, *una casa*) to break into ‖ *ref* to force oneself
violen·to -ta *adj* violent
violeta *m* (*color; colorante*) violet ‖ *f* (bot) violet
violín *m* violin; (billiards) bridge, cue rest; **embolsar el violín** (Arg, Ven) to cower, to slink away
violinista *mf* violinist
violón *m* (mus) bass viol; **tocar el violón** (coll) to talk nonsense
violoncelista *mf* cellist, violoncellist
violoncelo *m* (mus) cello, violoncello
violonchelista *mf* cellist, violoncellist
violonchelo *m* (mus) cello, violoncello
vira *f* welt; (*saetilla*) dart
virada *f* turn, change of direction; (naut) tack
virago *f* mannish woman
viraje *m* turn, swerve; (phot) toning
virar *tr* (naut) to wind; (naut) to tack, to veer; (phot) to tone ‖ *intr* to turn, to swerve; (naut) to tack, to veer
virgen *adj* virgin ‖ *f* virgin, maiden
virginidad *f* virginity
vírgula *f* rod; thin line, light dash
virgulilla *f* fine line; diacritic mark
virilidad *f* virility
virin·go -ga *adj* (Col) naked
virolen·to -ta *adj* pock-marked; having smallpox
virología *f* virology
virote *m* (*saeta*) bolt; (coll) sporty young fellow; (coll) stuffed shirt
virrey *m* viceroy
virtual *adj* virtual
virtud *f* virtue
virtuosísimo *m* virtuosity
virtuo·so -sa *adj* virtuous ‖ *m* virtuoso
viruela *f* smallpox; pock mark; **viruelas locas** chicken pox
virulencia *f* virulence
virulen·to -ta *adj* virulent
vi·rus *m* (pl -rus) virus
viruta *f* shaving

virutilla *f* thin shaving; **virutillas de acero** steel wool
visado *m* visa
visaje *m* face, grimace
visar *tr* to visa; to O.K.; (arti & surv) to sight
vísceras *fpl* viscera
visco *m* birdlime
viscosa *f* viscose
viscosilla *f* rayon thread
visco·so -sa *adj* viscous ‖ *f* see **viscosa**
visera *f* (*del yelmo, de las gorras, del parabrisas del automóvil, etc.*) visor; (*pequeña pantalla que se pone en la frente para resguardar la vista*) eyeshade; (W-I) blinder, blinker
visible *adj* visible; (*manifiesto*) evident; (*que llama la atención*) conspicuous
visigo·do -da *adj* Visigothic ‖ *mf* Visigoth
visillo *m* window curtain, window shade
visión *f* vision; view; (*persona fea y ridícula*) (coll) sight, scarecrow; **ver visiones** (coll) to be seeing things; **visión negra** (*del aviador*) blackout
visionar *tr* to contemplate, to look at
visiona·rio -ria *adj & mf* visionary
visir *m* vizier; **gran visir** grand vizier
visita *f* visit; visitor, caller; inspection; **ir de visitas** to go calling; **pagar la visita a** to return the call of; **tener visita** to have callers; **visita de cumplido** formal call; **visita de médico** (coll) short call
visita·dor -dora *mf* frequent caller ‖ *m* inspector ‖ *f* (Hond, Ven) enema
visitante *adj* visiting ‖ *mf* visitor
visitar *tr* to visit; to inspect
visite·ro -ra *adj* (coll) visiting; (*médico*) (coll) fond of making calls ‖ *mf* (coll) visitor
vislumbrar *tr* to descry, to glimpse; to surmise, suspect ‖ *ref* (*verse confusamente por la distancia*) to glimmer; (*aparecer en la distancia*) to loom
vislumbre *f* glimpse, glimmer; vislumbres inkling, notion
viso *m* sheen, gleam; (*de ciertas telas*) luster; streak, strain; appearance, thin veneer; elevation, height; colored material worn under transparent outer garment; **a dos visos** with a double purpose; **de viso** conspicuous; **hacer visos** to be iridescent
visón *m* mink
visor *m* (aer) bombsight; (phot) finder
víspera *f* eve, day before; **en vísperas de** on the eve of; **víspera de año nuevo** New Year's Eve; **víspera de Navidad** Christmas Eve; **vísperas** (eccl) vespers, evensong
vista *m* custom-house inspector ‖ *f* (*sentido del ver*) vision, sight; (*paisaje que se ve desde un punto; estampa que representa un lugar*) view; (*panorama, perspectiva*) vista; comparison; purpose, design; (*ojeada*) glance, look; interview; eye; eyes; (law) hearing, trial; **a la vista** (com) at sight; **a vista de** in view of; compared with; **con vistas a** with a view to; **de vista** by sight; **doble vista** second sight; **hacer la vista gorda**

ante to shut one's eyes to; **hasta la vista** good-bye, so long; **medir con la vista** to size up; **saltar a la vista** to be self-evident; **tener a la vista** to keep one's eyes on; (*p.ej., una carta*) to have at hand; **torcer la vista** to squint; **vista a ojo de pájaro** bird's-eye view; **vistas** (*aberturas de un edificio*) lights, openings; view, outlook; visible parts, parts that show

vistazo m look, glance

vistillas *fpl* eminence, height; **irse a las vistillas** (coll) to try to get a look at one's opponent's cards

vis•to -ta *adj* evident, obvious; in view of; **bien visto** looked upon with approval; **mal visto** looked upon with disapproval; **no visto** or **nunca visto** unheard-of; **por lo visto** apparently, judging from the facts; **visto bueno** approved, O.K.; **visto que** whereas, inasmuch as ‖ *m* whereas ‖ *f* see **vista**

visto•so -sa *adj* showy, flashy, loud

visual *adj* visual ‖ *f* line of sight

vital *adj* vital

vitali•cio -cia *adj* life, lifetime ‖ *m* life-insurance policy; life annuity

vitalidad *f* vitality

vitalizar §60 *tr* to vitalize

vitamina *f* vitamin

vitan•do -da *adj* hateful, odious; to be shunned

vitela *f* vellum

viticul•tor -tora *mf* grape grower, vineyardist

viticultura *f* grape growing

vitola *f* cigar size; mien, appearance; (Cuba) cigar band

vítor *interj* hurray! ‖ *m* panegyric tablet; triumphal pageant

vitorear *tr* to cheer, to acclaim

vitral *m* stained-glass window

vítre•o -a *adj* vitreous, glassy

vitrina *f* showcase, glass cabinet; (Am) shopwindow

vitrióli•co -ca *adj* (chem) vitriolic

vituallas *fpl* victuals

vituperable *adj* vituperable

vituperar *tr* to vituperate

viuda *f* widow; **viuda de marido vivo** or **viuda de paja** grass widow

viudedad *f* widowhood; dower, widow's pension

viudez *f* (*estado de viuda*) widowhood; (*estado de viudo*) widowerhood

viu•do -da *adj* left a widow; left a widower ‖ *m* widower ‖ *f* see **viuda**

viva *interj* viva!, long live! ‖ *m* viva

vivacidad *f* longevity; vivacity, liveliness; brightness, brilliance

vivande•ro -ra *mf* (mil) sutler, camp follower

vivaque *m* bivouac; guardhouse; (Am) police headquarters; **estar al vivaque** to bivouac

vivaquear *intr* to bivouac

vivar *m* warren, burrow; aquarium ‖ *tr* (Am) to cheer, acclaim

vivara•cho -cha *adj* (coll) vivacious, lively

vi•vaz *adj* (*pl* **-vaces**) long-lived; viva-

cious, lively; keen, perceptive; (bot) perennial

víveres *mpl* food, provisions, victuals

vivero *m* tree nursery; fishpond; (*origen de cosas perjudiciales*) (fig) hotbed

viveza *f* agility, briskness; ardor, vehemence; sharpness, keenness; perception; brightness, brilliance; witticism; (*de los ojos*) sparkle; (*acción o palabra poco considerada*) thoughtlessness

vivide•ro -ra *adj* livable

viví•do -da *adj* quick, perceptive; lively

vivienda *f* dwelling; life, way of life

viviente *adj* living, alive

vivificar §73 *tr* to vivify, to enliven

vivir *m* life, living ‖ *tr* (*una experiencia o ventura*) to live; (*toda la vida; la vejez*) to live out; (*habitar*) to live in ‖ *intr* to live; **¿quién vive?** (mil) who goes there? **vivir de** (*p.ej., carne*) to live on; **vivir para ver** to live and learn; **vivir y dejar vivir** to live and let live

vivisección *f* vivisection

vi•vo -va *adj* living, alive, live; (*lleno de vida; intenso*) live; (*sutil, agudo*) sharp, keen; (*dolor*) acute; (*carne*) raw; active, effective; (*luz*) bright, intense; (*pronto y ágil*) quick; (*idioma*) living, modern; **de viva voz** viva voce, by word of mouth; **herir en lo vivo** to cut or to sting to the quick ‖ *mf* living person; **los vivos y los muertos** the quick and the dead ‖ *m* edging, border; (vet) mange

Vizcaya *f* Biscay; **llevar hierro a Vizcaya** to carry coals to Newcastle

vizconde *m* viscount

vizcondesa *f* viscountess

V.M. *abbr* **Vuestra Majestad**

V.ºB.º *abbr* **visto bueno**

vocablista *mf* punster

vocablo *m* word; **jugar del vocablo** to pun

vocabulario *m* vocabulary

vocación *f* vocation, calling

vocal *adj* vocal ‖ *mf* director ‖ *f* vowel

vocalista *mf* singer, vocalist

vocativo *m* vocative

voceador *m* town crier; (Col, Ecuad) paper boy

vocear *tr* to cry, shout; to cheer, acclaim; to call, to page; (coll) to boast about publicly ‖ *intr* to shout

vocería *f* shouting, outcry; spokesmanship

vocerío *m* shouting, outcry

vocero *m* spokesman, mouthpiece

vociferar *tr* (*injurias*) to shout; to boast loudly about ‖ *intr* to vociferate, to shout

vocingle•ro -ra *adj* loudmouthed; loud, talkative

vo•dú *m* (*pl* **-dúes**) voodoo

voduísta *adj & mf* voodoo

vol. *abbr* **volumen, voluntad**

volada *f* short flight; (*del jugador de billar*) (Arg) stroke; (Col, Ecuad) trick; (*noticia inventada*) (Mex) hoax

voladi•zo -za *adj* projecting ‖ *m* projection

vola·do -da *adj* (typ) superior ‖ *f* see **volada**

vola·dor -dora *adj* flying; hanging, dangling; swift, fast ‖ *m* rocket; flying fish

voladura *f* blast, explosion

volandas — en volandas in the air; fast

volante *adj* flying; unsettled ‖ *m* shuttlecock; battledore and shuttlecock; *(rueda que regula el movimiento de una máquina)* flywheel; *(rueda de mano para la dirección del automóvil)* steering wheel; *(pieza del reloj movida por la espiral)* balance wheel; flunkey, lackey; *(criado que iba a pie delante del coche o caballo)* outrunner; *(de papel)* slip, leaflet; (sew) flounce, ruffle; **un buen volante** a good driver

volan·tín -tina *adj* unsettled ‖ *m* fish line; (Am) kite

volantista *m* (coll) driver, man at the wheel

volan·tón -tona *mf* fledgling ‖ *f* (Ven) loose woman

volapié *m* (taur) stroke in which the matador moves in for the kill; **a volapié** half running, half flying; half walking, half swimming

volar §61 *tr* *(llevar en un aparato de aviación)* to fly; to blow up, to explode; to irritate; *(una letra, tipo o signo)* (typ) to raise ‖ *intr* to fly; to fly away; to disappear; to jut out, project; *(una especie)* to spread rapidly; *(p.ej., una torre)* to rise in the air; **volar sin motor** (aer) to glide ‖ *ref* to fly away; (Am) to fly off the handle

volatería *f* fowling with decoys; **de volatería** offhand

volátil *adj* volatile

volatilizar *tr & ref* to volatilize

volatín *m* ropewalker, acrobat, tumbler

volatine·ro -ra *mf* ropewalker, acrobat, tumbler

volcán *m* volcano

volcar §81 *tr* to upset, overturn, dump; to tip, to tilt; *(a una persona un olor fuerte)* to make dizzy; to change the mind of; to irritate, tease ‖ *intr* to upset ‖ *ref* to turn upside down

volear *tr* (tennis) to volley

voleo *m* (tennis) volley; reeling punch; **del primer voleo** or **de un voleo** (coll) with a smash, all at once; **sembrar al voleo** to sow broadcast

volframio *m* wolfram

volibol *m* volleyball

volquete *m* dumpcart, dump truck

voltai·co -ca *adj* voltaic

voltaje *m* voltage

volta·rio -ria *adj* fickle, inconstant; (Chile) willful; (Chile) sporty

voltea·do -da *mf* (Col) turncoat, deserter

voltear *tr* to upset, turn over; to turn around; to move, to transform ‖ *intr* to roll over, to tumble

volteo *m* upset, overturning; tumbling; (P-R) scolding

voltereta *f* tumble; turning up card to determine trump

voltímetro *m* voltmeter

voltio *m* volt

volti·zo -za *adj* curled, twisted; fickle

voluble *adj* easily turned; fickle, inconstant

volumen *m* volume; **volumen sonoro** volume; (geom) volume

volumino·so -sa *adj* voluminous

voluntad *f* will; *(amor, cariño)* fondness, love; **a voluntad** at will; **buena voluntad** willingness; **de buena voluntad** willingly; **de mala voluntad** unwillingly; **de su propia voluntad** of one's own volition; **última voluntad** last will and testament; last wish; **voluntad de hierro** iron will

voluntariedad *f* willfulness

volunta·rio -ria *adj* *(que se hace por espontánea voluntad)* voluntary; *(que tiene voluntad obstinada)* willful; *(que se presta voluntariamente a hacer algo)* volunteer ‖ *mf* volunteer

voluntario·so -sa *adj* willful

voluptuo·so -sa *adj* *(que inspira complacencia en los placeres sensuales)* voluptuous; *(dado a los placeres sensuales)* voluptuary ‖ *mf* voluptuary

voluta *f* (archit) scroll, volute; *(p.ej., de humo)* ring

volvedor *m* screwdriver; (Col) extra, something thrown in; **volvedor de machos** tap wrench

volver §47 & §83 *tr* to turn; to turn upside down; to turn inside out; to return, send back, give back; *(una puerta)* to push to, to pull to; to translate; to vomit ‖ *intr* to turn; to return, come back; **volver a** + *inf* verb + again, e.g., **volvió a abrir la puerta** he opened the door again; **volver en sí** to come to; **volver por** to defend, to stand up for ‖ *ref* to become; to turn around; to return, come back; to change one's mind; to turn, turn sour; **volverse atrás** to back out; **volverse contra** to turn on

vomitar *tr* to vomit, throw up; *(fuego los cañones)* to belch forth; *(maldiciones)* to utter; *(un secreto)* to let out; *(lo que uno retiene indebidamente)* (coll) to cough up ‖ *intr* to vomit, throw up; (coll) to come across, disgorge

vómito *m* vomit, vomiting; **provocar a vómito** (coll) to nauseate; **vómitos del embarazo** morning sickness

voracidad *f* voracity

vorágine *f* whirlpool, vortex

vo·raz *adj* (pl **-races**) voracious

vormela *f* polecat

vórtice *m* vortex

vos *pron pers* (subject of verb and object of preposition; takes plural form of verb but is singular in meaning; used in addressing the Deity, the Virgin, etc., and distinguished persons; in Spanish America is much used instead of **tú**) you

voso·tros -tras *pron pers* (plural of **tú**) you

votación *f* vote, voting

votante *adj* voting ‖ *mf* voter

votar *tr* to vote for; (*sí, no*) to vote; (*p.ej., un cirio a la Virgen*) to vow ‖ *intr* to vote; to vow; to swear, curse

voti•vo -va *adj* votive

voto *m* (*sufragio; derecho de votar; persona que da su voto*) vote; (*promesa solemne*) vow; (*exvoto*) votive offering; (*blasfemia*) oath, curse; wish, desire; **echar votos** to swear, to curse; **regular los votos** to tally the votes; **voto de amén** (coll) vote of a yes man; (coll) yes man; **voto de calidad** casting vote; **voto informativo** straw vote; **votos** good wishes; **¡voto va!** come now!

voz *f* (*pl* **voces**) voice; (*vocablo*) word; **aclarar la voz** to clear one's throat; **a una voz** with one voice; **a voces** shouting; **a voz en cuello** or **en grito** at the top of one's voice; **correr la voz que** to be rumored that; **dar voces** to shout, to cry out; **de viva voz** viva voce, by word of mouth; **en alta voz** aloud, in a loud voice; **en voz baja** in a low voice; **llevar la voz cantante** (coll) to have the say, to be the boss; **voces** outcry

vro. *abbr* **vuestro**

V.S. *abbr* **Vueseñoría**

vuelco *m* upset, overturn; **darle a uno un vuelco el corazón** (coll) to have a presentiment

vuelo *m* flight; flying; (*de una falda*) flare, fullness; projection; lace cuff trimming; **al vuelo** at once; on the wing; scattered at random; (chess) **en passant**; **alzar el vuelo** to take flight; (coll) to dash away; **echar a vuelo las campanas** to ring a full peal; **tirar al vuelo** to shoot on the wing; **tocar a vuelo las campanas** to ring a full peal; **vuelo a ciegas** (aer) blind flying; **vuelo de distancia** (aer) long-distance flight; **vuelo de ensayo** or **de prueba** (aer) test flight; **vuelo espacial tripulado** manned space flight; **vuelo planeado** (aer) volplane; **vuelo rasante** (aer) hedgehopping; **vuelo sin escala** (aer) nonstop flight; **vuelo sin motor** (aer) glide, gliding

vuelta *f* turn; (*regreso; devolución*) return; (*dinero sobrante de un pago*) change; (*de un camino*) bend, turn; (*del pantalón*) cuff; cuff trimming; (*paseo corto*) stroll; (*revés*) other side; (*paliza*) beating, whipping; (*en un cabo*) loop; (*en la media*) clock; (*mudanza*) change; **a la vuelta** on returning; please turn the page; **a la vuelta de** at the end of; at the turn of; (*la esquina*) around; **a vuelta de** about; **a vuelta de correo** by return mail; **dar cien vueltas a** to run rings around, be away ahead of; **dar la vuelta de campana** to turn somersault; **darse una vuelta a la redonda** (coll) to tend to one's own business; **dar una vuelta** to take a stroll, take a walk; to take a look; to change one's ways; **dar vuelta** to turn around; (*el vino*) to turn sour; **dar vuelta a** to reverse, to turn around; **estar de vuelta** to be back; **quedarse con la vuelta** to keep the change; **vuelta de campana** somersault; **vuelta del mundo** trip around the world

vuelto *m* (Am) change

vues•tro -tra (corresponds to **vos** and **vosotros**) *adj poss* your ‖ *pron poss* yours

vulcanizar §60 *tr* to vulcanize

vulgacho *m* (coll) populace, mob

vulgar *adj* vulgar, popular, common, vernacular

vulgarismo *m* popular expression; (philol) popular word, popular form

vulgarizar §60 *tr* to popularize; to translate into the vernacular ‖ *ref* to associate with the people

Vulgata *f* Vulgate

vulgo *adv* commonly ‖ *m* common people; (*personas que en una materia sólo conocen la parte superficial*) laity

vulnerable *adj* vulnerable

vulnerar *tr* to hurt, injure; (*la reputación de una persona*) to damage; (*una ley, un precepto*) to break

vulpeja *f* she-fox, vixen

V.V. or **VV** *abbr* **ustedes**

X

X, x (equis) *f* twenty-sixth letter of the Spanish alphabet

xenia *f* xenia

xenofobia *f* xenophobia

xenófo•bo -ba *mf* xenophobe

xenón *m* xenon

xilófono *m* (mus) xylophone

xilografía *f* (*arte*) xylography; (*grabado*) xylograph

xpiano *abbr* **cristiano**

Xpo *abbr* **Cristo**

xptiano *abbr* **cristiano**

Xpto *abbr* **Cristo**

xunde *m* (Mex) reed basket, palm basket

Y

Y, y (ye) *f* twenty-seventh letter of the Spanish alphabet

y *conj* and

ya *adv* already; right away; now; no

ya not only; **ya no** no longer; **ya que** since, inasmuch as

yac *m* (*bandera de proa*) (naut) jack; (*bóvido del Tibet*) yak

yacer §82 *intr* to lie

yacija *f* bed, couch; (*sepultura*) grave

yacimiento *m* bed, field, deposit

yámbi·co -ca *adj* iambic

yambo *m* iamb, iambus

yanqui *adj & mf* Yankee

Yanquilandia *f* Yankeedom

yapa *f* (Am) bonus, extra, allowance; **de yapa** (Am) in the bargain, extra

yarda *f* yard; yardstick

yate *m* yacht

yedra *f* ivy

yegua *f* mare; (CAm) cigar butt

yeguada *f* stud

yelmo *m* helmet

yema *f* (*de huevo*) yolk; candied yolk; (*del invierno*) dead; (*renuevo*) bud; (fig) cream; **dar en la yema** (coll) to put one's finger on the spot; **yema del dedo** finger tip; **yema mejida** eggnog

yente — **yentes y vinientes** *mpl* habitués, frequenters

yerba *f* var of **hierba**

yer·mo -ma *adj* deserted, uninhabited; (*suelo*) unsown; (*mujer*) not pregnant ‖ *m* desert, wilderness

yerno *m* son-in-law

yerro *m* error, mistake; **yerro de cuenta** miscalculation; **yerro de imprenta** printer's error

yer·to -ta *adj* stiff, rigid

yesca *f* punk, tinder; (*cosa que excita una pasión*) fuel; **echar una yesca to** strike a light

yeso *m* gypsum; plaster cast

yo *pron pers* I; **soy yo** it is I

yodhídri·co -ca *adj* hydriodic

yodo *m* iodine

yoduro *m* iodide

yola *f* (sport) shell

yugo *m* yoke; **sacudir el yugo** to throw off the yoke

Yugoeslavia *f* Yugoslavia

yugoesla·vo -va *adj & mf* Yugoslav

yugular *adj & f* jugular ‖ *tr* to cut off, to nip in the bud

yunque *m* anvil; (fig) drudge, work horse

yunta *f* yoke, team

yute *m* jute

yuxtaponer §54 *tr* to juxtapose

yuyo *m* (Arg, Chile) weed; **yuyos** (Col, Ecuad, Peru) greens

Z

Z, z (zeda or zeta) *f* twenty-eighth letter of the Spanish alphabet

zabordar *intr* (naut) to run aground

zabullir §13 *tr* (*p.ej., a un perro*) to duck, give a ducking to; (coll) to throw, to hurl ‖ *ref* (*meterse debajo del agua con ímpetu*) to dive; (*esconderse rápidamente*) to duck

zacapela or **zacapella** *f* row, rumpus

zacate *m* (CAm, Mex) hay, fodder; **zacate de empaque** (Am) excelsior

zacateca *m* (Cuba) undertaker, grave-digger

zacatín *m* old-clothes market

zacear *tr* (*al perro*) to chase away ‖ *intr* to lisp

zafaduría *f* (Arg) brazenness, effrontery

zafar *tr* to adorn, bedeck; to loosen, untie; to clear, to free; (*un buque*) to lighten ‖ *ref* to slip away; to slip off, come off; **zafarse de** to get out of

zafarrancho *m* (naut) clearing the decks; (coll) havoc, ravage; (coll) scuffle, row; **zafarrancho de combate** (naut) clearing the deck for action

za·fio -fia *adj* rough, uncouth, boorish

zafiro *m* sapphire

za·fo -fa *adj* unhurt, intact; (naut) free, clear ‖ **zafo** *prep* (Col) except

zafra *f* olive-oil can; drip jar; sugar crop; sugar making; sugar-making season; (min) rubbish, muck

zaga *f* rear; load carried in the rear; (mil) rearguard; **a la zaga, a zaga** or **en zaga** behind, in the rear; **no ir en zaga a** (coll) to not be behind, to be as good as

zagal *m* young fellow; strapping young fellow; shepherd boy; footboy

zagala *f* lass, maiden; young shepherdess

zaguán *m* vestibule, hall, entry

zague·ro -ra *adj* back, rear ‖ *m* (sport) back, backstop

zaherir §68 *tr* to upbraid, reproach; to scold shamefully

zahones *mpl* chaps, hunting breeches

zaho·rí *m* (*pl* **-ríes**) keen observer; seer, clairvoyant

zahurda *f* pigpen

zai·no -na *adj* treacherous, false; (*caballo*) vicious; (*caballo*) dark-chestnut; **mirar a lo zaino** or **de zaino** to look askance at

za·lá *f* (*pl* **-laes**) Mohammedan prayer; **hacer la zalá a** (coll) to fawn on

zalagarda *f* ambush; skirmish; (*trampa para cazar animales*) trap; (coll) trick; (coll) row, rumpus; (coll) mock fight

zalamería *f* flattery, cajolery

zalame·ro -ra *adj* flattering, fawning ‖ *mf* flatterer, fawner

zalea *f* unsheared sheepskin

zalear *tr* to drag around, to shake; (*al perro*) to chase away

zalema *f* salaam

zamacuco *m* (coll) blockhead; (coll) sullen fellow; (coll) drunkenness

zamacueca *f* cueca (*Chilean courtship dance*)

zamarra *f* undressed sheepskin; sheepskin jacket

zam·bo -ba *adj* knock-kneed

zambra *f* merrymaking, celebration; Moorish boat

zambucar §73 *tr* (coll) to slip away, hide away

zambullida f dive, plunge; (fencing) thrust to the breast

zambulli·dor -dora adj diving, plunging || mf diver, plunger || m (orn) diver, loon

zambullir §13 tr (p.ej., a un perro) to duck, to give a ducking to; (coll) to throw, to hurl || ref (meterse debajo del agua con ímpetu) to dive; (esconderse rápidamente) to duck

zampa f pile, bearing pile

zampacuarti·llos mf (pl -llos) (coll) toper, soak

zampalimos·nas mf (pl -nas) (coll) bum, ordinary bum

zampar tr to slip away, hide away; to gobble down || ref to slip away, hide away

zampator·tas mf (pl -tas) (coll) glutton; (coll) boor

zampear tr (el terreno) to strengthen with piles and rubble

zampoña f shepherd's pipe, rustic flute; (coll) nonsense, folly

zampuzar §60 tr to duck, give a ducking to; (coll) to slip away, hide away

zanahoria f carrot

zanca f long leg; (de la escalera) horse

zancada f long stride; **en dos zancadas** (coll) in a flash, in a jiffy

zancadilla f (coll) booby trap; **echar la zancadilla a** to stick out one's foot and trip

zancajo m heel; **no llegar a los zancajos a** (coll) to not come up to, to not be equal to

zancajo·so -sa adj duck-toed; down-at-the-heel

zancarrón m (coll) dirty old fellow

zanco m stilt; **en zancos** (coll) from a vantage point

zancu·do -da adj long-legged; (orn) wading || m mosquito || f wading bird

zanfonía f hurdy-gurdy

zangala f buckram

zangamanga f (coll) trick

zanganada f (coll) impertinence, impudence

zanganear intr (coll) to loaf around

zángano m (ent) drone; (fig) drone, loafer; (CAm) scoundrel

zangarrear intr (coll) to thrum a guitar

zangolotear tr (coll) to jiggle || intr (coll) to fuss around || ref (coll) to jiggle, to flop around, to rattle

zangoloteo m (coll) jiggle, jiggling, rattle; (coll) fuss, bother

zanguanga f (coll) malingering; (coll) flattery; **hacer la zanguanga** (coll) to malinger

zanguan·go -ga adj (coll) slow, lazy || mf (coll) loafer || f see **zanguanga**

zanja f ditch, trench; (SAm) gully; **abrir las zanjas** to lay the foundations

zanquear intr to waddle; to rush around

zanquilar·go -ga adj leggy, long-legged

zanquituer·to -ta adj bandy-legged

zapa f spade; sharkskin, shagreen; (mil) sap

zapapico m mattock, pickax

zapar tr (mil) to sap, mine, excavate

zaparrastrar intr — **ir zaparrastrando**

(coll) to go along trailing one's clothes on the ground

zapateado m clog dance, tap dance

zapatear tr to hit with the shoe; to tap with the feet; (coll) to abuse, ill-treat || intr to tap-dance; (las velas) to flap || ref — **zapatearse con** to hold out against

zapatería f shoemaking; shoemaker's shop; (tienda) shoe store

zapate·ro -ra adj poorly cooked || mf shoemaker; shoe dealer; **quedarse zapatero** (coll) to not take a trick; **¡zapatero, a tus zapatos!** stick to your last!; **zapatero de viejo** or **zapatero remendón** cobbler, shoemaker

zapatilla f slipper; (escarpín) pump; (del grifo) washer; (del florete) leather tip or button; cloven hoof

zapato m shoe, low shoe; **andar con zapatos de fieltro** to gumshoe; **como tres en un zapato** (coll) hard up; (coll) like sardines; **zapato de goma** overshoe; **zapato inglés** low shoe

zapatón m (Guat, SAm) overshoe

zapear tr (al gato) to scare away, chase away

zaque m wineskin; (coll) tippler, drunk

zaquiza·mí m (pl -míes) attic, garret; hovel, pigpen

zar m czar

zarabanda f (mus) saraband; (coll) noise, confusion, uproar; (Mex) beating, thrashing

zaragata f (coll) scuffle, row; **zaragatas** (W-I) flattery

Zaragoza f Saragossa

zaranda f sieve, screen; colander; (Ven) horn; (Ven) top

zarandajas fpl (coll) odds and ends, trinkets

zarandar tr to sift, to screen; to winnow, pick out, select; (coll) to jiggle || ref (coll) to jiggle; (Am) to swagger, strut

zaraza f chintz, printed cotton

zarcillo m eardrop; (bot) tendril

zarigüeya f opossum

zarina f czarina

zarpa f claw, paw; (naut) weighing anchor

zarpar tr (el ancla) (naut) to weigh (anchor); intr (naut) to weigh anchor, to set sail

zarpo·so -sa adj mud-splashed

zarracatería f (coll) cajolery, insincere flattery

zarracatín m (coll) sharp trader

zarramplín m (coll) botcher, bungler

zarrien·to -ta adj mud-splashed

zarza f blackberry, bramble (bush)

zarzamora f blackberry (fruit)

zarzaparrilla f sarsaparilla

zarzo m hurdle, wattle

zarzo·so -sa adj brambly

zarzuela f small bramble; (theat) zarzuela (Spanish musical comedy); **zarzuela grande** three-act zarzuela

zas interj bang!; **¡zas, zas!** bing, bang!

zascandilear intr (coll) to meddle, to scheme

zepelín m zeppelin

Zeus m Zeus

ya
ze

zigzag *m* zigzag

zigzaguear *intr* to zigzag

zinc *m* (*pl* zinces) zinc

zipizape *m* (coll) scuffle, row, rumpus

ziszás *m* zigzag

zoca *f* public square

zócalo *m* (archit) socle; (*de una pared*) dado; (rad) socket; (Mex) public square, center square

zoca·to -ta *adj* (*fruto*) corky, pithy; (coll) left; (coll) left-handed ‖ *mf* (coll) left-handed person

zoclo *m* clog, wooden shoe

zo·co -ca *adj* (coll) left; (coll) left-handed ‖ *mf* (coll) left-handed person ‖ *m* clog, wooden shoe; Moroccan market place; (archit) socle; **andar de zocos en colodros** (coll) to jump from the frying pan into the fire ‖ *f* see **zoca**

zodíaco *m* zodiac

zofra *f* Moorish carpet, Moorish rug

zolo·cho -cha *adj* (coll) stupid, simple ‖ *mf* (coll) simpleton

zollipar *intr* (coll) to sob

zollipo *m* (coll) sob

zona *m* (pathol) shingles ‖ *f* zone; (*banda, faja*) belt, girdle; **zona a batir** target area

zon·zo -za *adj* tasteless, insipid; dull, inane ‖ *mf* dolt, dimwit

zoófito *m* zoöphyte

zoología *f* zoölogy

zoológi·co -ca *adj* zoölogic(al)

zoólo·go -ga *mf* zoölogist

zopen·co -ca *adj* (coll) dull, stupid ‖ *mf* (coll) dullard, blockhead

zopilote *m* (Mex, CAm) turkey buzzard, turkey vulture

zo·po -pa *adj* crippled; awkward, gauche ‖ *mf* cripple

zoquete *m* (*de madera*) block, chunk, end; (*de pan*) bit, crust; (coll) chump, lout

zoquetu·do -da *adj* coarse, crude

zorra *f* fox; female fox; (coll) foxy person; (coll) prostitute; (coll) drunkenness; dray, truck; **pillar una zorra** (coll) to get drunk

zorrería *f* (coll) foxiness

zorre·ro -ra *adj* (coll) sly, foxy; (coll) slow, heavy, tardy ‖ *f* see **zorrera**

zorrillo *m* (Am) skunk

zorro *m* male fox; (*piel*) fox; (*hombre taimado*) (coll) fox; **estar hecho un zorro** (coll) to be overwhelmed with sleep; (coll) to be dull and sullen; **zorros** duster

zorzal *m* (orn) fieldfare; sly fellow; (Chile) simpleton

zozobra *f* capsizing, sinking; anxiety

zozobrar *tr* (*un buque*) to sink; (*un negocio*) to wreck ‖ *intr* to capsize, sink; (*la embarcación en la tempestad*) to wallow; (*un negocio*) to be in great danger; to be greatly worried ‖ *ref* to capsize, sink

zueco *m* clog, wooden shoe, sabot

zulacar §73 *tr* to waterproof

zulaque *m* waterproofing

zulú (*pl* **-lús** o **-lúes**) *adj* & *mf* Zulu

zullar *ref* (coll) to have a movement of the bowels; (coll) to break wind

zullen·co -ca *adj* (coll) windy, flatulent

zumaque *m* sumach; (coll) wine

zumaya *f* (*autillo*) tawny owl; (*chotacabras*) goatsucker

zumba *f* bell worn by leading mule; (Mex) drunkenness; **hacer zumba a** to make fun of; **sin zumba** (Mex) in a rush, in a hurry

zumbador *m* buzzer; (Mex) pauraque; (Mex, CAm, W-I) hummingbird

zumbar *tr* to make fun of; (*un golpe, una bofetada*) to let have ‖ *intr* to buzz; to zoom; (*los oídos*) to ring; **zumbar a** (*frisar con*) to be close to, to border on ‖ *ref* (Cuba) to go too far, to forget oneself; (P-R) to rush ahead; **zumbarse de** to make fun of

zumbido *m* buzz; zoom; (coll) blow, smack; **zumbido de ocupación** (telp) busy signal; **zumbido de oídos** ringing in the ears

zum·bón -bona *adj* waggish, playful ‖ *mf* wag, jester

zumien·to -ta *adj* juicy

zumo *m* juice; advantage, profit; **zumo de cepas** or **de parras** (coll) fruit of the vine

zumo·so -sa *adj* juicy

zunchar *tr* to band, to hoop

zuncho *m* band, hoop

zupia *f* (*del vino*) dregs; slop, wine full of dregs; (fig) junk, trash

zurcido *m* darning; darn; invisible mending

zurcir §36 *tr* to darn; (*una mentira*) (coll) to hatch, concoct; (*unas mentiras*) (coll) to weave (*a tissue of lies*)

zurdazo *m* (box) left, blow with the left

zur·do -da *adj* left; left-handed; **a zurdas** with the left hand; the wrong way ‖ *mf* left-handed person

zurear *intr* to coo

zuro *m* stripped corncob

zurra *f* dressing, currying; scuffle, quarrel; drubbing, thrashing; (*trabajo o estudio continuados*) grind

zurrapa *f* thread, filament; (coll) trash, rubbish; **con zurrapas** (coll) in a sloppy manner

zurrar *tr* (*el cuero*) to dress, to curry; to get the best of; (*censurar con dureza*) to dress down; (*castigar con azotes*) to drub, to thrash ‖ *ref* (*hacer sus necesidades involuntariamente*) to have an accident; (coll) to be scared to death; (Arg) to break wind noiselessly

zurriagar §44 *tr* to whip, to horsewhip

zurriago *m* whip, lash

zurribanda *f* (coll) rain of blows; (coll) rumpus, scuffle

zurrir *intr* to buzz, to grate

zurrón *m* shepherd's leather bag; leather bag; (*cáscara*) husk

zurrona *f* (coll) loose, evil woman

zurullo *m* (coll) soft roll; (coll) turd

zurupeto *m* (coll) unregistered broker; (coll) shyster notary

zuta·no -na *mf* (coll) so-and-so

MODEL VERBS

ORDER OF TENSES

(a) gerund
(b) past participle
(c) imperative
(d) present indicative

(e) present subjunctive
(f) imperfect indicative
(g) future indicative
(h) preterit indicative

All simple tenses are shown in these tables if they contain one irregular form or more, except the conditional (which can always be derived from the stem of the future indicative) and the imperfect and future subjunctive (which can always be derived from the third plural preterit indicative minus the last syllable **-ron**). The tenses are identified with the letters (a) to (h) as shown above.

---

§1 abolir: defective verb used only in forms whose endings contain the vowel **i**

§2 acertar
  (c) **acierta,** acertad
  (d) **acierto, aciertas, acierta,** acertamos, acertáis, **aciertan**
  (e) **acierte, aciertes, acierte,** acertemos, acertéis, **acierten**

§3 agorar: like §61 but with diaeresis on the **u** of **ue**
  (c) **agüera,** agorad
  (d) **agüero, agüeras, agüera,** agoramos, agoráis, **agüeran**
  (e) **agüere, agüeres, agüere,** agoremos, agoréis, **agüeren**

§4 airar
  (c) **aíra,** airad
  (d) **aíro, aíras, aíra,** airamos, airáis, **aíran**
  (e) **aíre, aíres, aíre,** airemos, airéis, **aíren**

§5 andar
  (h) **anduve, anduviste, anduvo, anduvimos, anduvisteis, anduvieron**

§6 argüir: like §20 but with diaeresis on **u** in forms with accented **i** in the ending
  (a) **arguyendo**
  (b) **argüido**
  (c) **arguye,** argüid
  (d) **arguyo, arguyes, arguye,** argüimos, argüís, **arguyen**
  (e) **arguya, arguyas, arguya, arguyamos, arguyáis, arguyan**
  (h) argüí, argüiste, **arguyó,** argüimos, argüisteis, **arguyeron**

§7 asir
  (d) **asgo,** ases, ase, asimos, asís, asen
  (e) **asga, asgas, asga, asgamos, asgáis, asgan**

§8 aunar
  (c) **aúna,** aunad
  (d) **aúno, aúnas, aúna,** aunamos, aunáis, **aúnan**
  (e) **aúne, aúnes, aúne,** aunemos, aunéis, **aúnen**

§9 avergonzar: combination of §3 and §60
  (c) **avergüenza,** avergonzad

(d) **avergüenzo, avergüenzas, avergüenza,** avergonzamos, avergonzáis, **avergüenzan**

(e) **avergüence, avergüences, avergüence, avergoncemos, avergoncéis, avergüencen**

(h) **avergoncé,** avergonzaste, avergonzó, avergonzamos, avergonzasteis, avergonzaron

§10 averiguar

(e) **averigüe, averigües, averigüe, averigüemos, averigüéis, averigüen**

(h) **averigüé,** averiguaste, averiguó, averiguamos, averiguasteis, averiguaron

§11 bendecir

(a) **bendiciendo**

(c) **bendice,** bendecid

(d) **bendigo, bendices, bendice,** bendecimos, bendecís, **bendicen**

(e) **bendiga, bendigas, bendiga, bendigamos, bendigáis, bendigan**

(h) **bendije, bendijiste, bendijo, bendijimos, bendijisteis, bendijeron**

§12 bruñir

(a) **bruñendo**

(h) bruñí, bruñiste, **bruñó,** bruñimos, bruñisteis, **bruñeron**

§13 bullir

(a) **bullendo**

(h) bullí, bulliste, **bulló,** bullimos, bullisteis, **bulleron**

§14 caber

(d) **quepo,** cabes, cabe, cabemos, cabéis, caben

(e) **quepa, quepas, quepa, quepamos, quepáis, quepan**

(g) **cabré, cabrás, cabrá, cabremos, cabréis, cabrán**

(h) **cupe, cupiste, cupo, cupimos, cupisteis, cupieron**

§15 caer

(a) **cayendo**

(b) **caído**

(d) **caigo,** caes, cae, caemos, caéis, caen

(e) **caiga, caigas, caiga, caigamos, caigáis, caigan**

(h) caí, **caíste, cayó, caímos, caísteis, cayeron**

§16 cocer: combination of §47 and §78

(c) **cuece,** coced

(d) **cuezo, cueces, cuece,** cocemos, cocéis, **cuecen**

(e) **cueza, cuezas, cueza, cozamos, cozáis, cuezan**

§17 coger

(d) **cojo,** coges, coge, cogemos, cogéis, cogen

(e) **coja, cojas, coja, cojamos, cojáis, cojan**

§18 comenzar: combination of §2 and §60

(c) **comienza,** comenzad

(d) **comienzo, comienzas, comienza,** comenzamos, comenzáis, **comienzan**

(e) **comience, comiences, comience, comencemos, comencéis, comiencen**

(h) **comencé,** comenzaste, comenzó, comenzamos, comenzasteis, comenzaron

§19 conducir
    (d) **conduzco,** conduces, conduce, conducimos, conducís, conducen
    (e) **conduzca, conduzcas, conduzca, conduzcamos, conduzcáis, conduzcan**
    (h) **conduje, condujiste, condujo, condujimos, condujisteis, condujeron**

§20 construir
    (a) **construyendo**
    (b) **construído**
    (c) **construye,** construid
    (d) **construyo, construyes, construye,** construimos, construís, **construyen**
    (e) **construya, construyas, construya, construyamos, construyáis, construyan**
    (h) construí, construiste, **construyó,** construimos, construisteis, **construyeron**

§21 continuar
    (c) **continúa,** continuad
    (d) **continúo, continúas, continúa,** continuamos, continuáis, **continúan**
    (e) **continúe, continúes, continúe,** continuemos, continuéis, **continúen**

§22 crecer
    (d) **crezco,** creces, crece, crecemos, crecéis, crecen
    (e) **crezca, crezcas, crezca, crezcamos, crezcáis, crezcan**

§23 dar
    (d) **doy,** das, da, damos, dais, dan
    (e) **dé,** des, **dé,** demos, deis, den
    (h) **dí,** diste, dio, dimos, disteis, dieron

§24 decir
    (a) **diciendo**
    (b) **dicho**
    (c) **di,** decid
    (d) **digo, dices, dice,** decimos, decís, **dicen**
    (e) **diga, digas, diga, digamos, digáis, digan**
    (g) **diré, dirás, dirá, diremos, diréis, dirán**
    (h) **dije, dijiste, dijo, dijimos, dijisteis, dijeron**

§25 delinquir
    (d) **delinco,** delinques, delinque, delinquimos, delinquís, delinquen
    (e) **delinca, delincas, delinca, delincamos, delincáis, delincan**

§26 desosar: like **§61** but with **h** before **ue**
    (c) **deshuesa,** desosad
    (d) **deshueso, deshuesas, deshuesa,** desosamos, desosáis, **deshuesan**
    (e) **deshuese, deshueses, deshuese,** desosemos, desoséis, **deshuesen**

§27 dirigir
    (d) **dirijo,** diriges, dirige, dirigimos, dirigís, dirigen
    (e) **dirija, dirijas, dirija, dirijamos, dirijáis, dirijan**

§28 discernir
  (c) **discierne,** discernid
  (d) **discierno, disciernes, discierne,** discernimos, discernís, **disciernen**
  (e) **discierna, disciernas, discierna,** discernamos, discernáis, **disciernan**

§29 distinguir
  (d) **distingo,** distingues, distingue, distinguimos, distinguís, distinguen
  (e) **distinga, distingas, distinga, distingamos, distingáis, distingan**

§30 dormir
  (a) **durmiendo**
  (c) **duerme,** dormid
  (d) **duermo, duermes, duerme,** dormimos, dormís, **duermen**
  (e) **duerma, duermas, duerma, durmamos, durmáis, duerman**
  (h) dormí, dormiste, **durmió,** dormimos, dormisteis, **durmieron**

§31 empeller
  (a) **empellendo**
  (h) empellí, empelliste, **empelló,** empellimos, empellisteis, **empelleron**

§32 enraizar: combination of §4 and §60
  (c) **enraíza,** enraizad
  (d) **enraízo, enraízas, enraíza,** enraizamos, enraizáis, **enraízan**
  (e) **enraíce, enraíces, enraíce, enraicemos, enraicéis, enraícen**
  (h) **enraicé,** enraizaste, enraizó, enraizamos, enraizasteis, enraizaron

§33 erguir: combination of §29 and §50 or §68
  (a) **irguiendo**
  (c) **irgue** or **yergue,** erguid
  (d) **irgo, irgues, irgue,**
      yergo, yergues, yergue, } erguimos, erguís, { **irguen**
                                                        { **yerguen**
  (e) **irga, irgas, irga,**
      yerga, yergas, yerga, } **irgamos, irgáis,** { **irgan**
                                                        { **yergan**
  (h) erguí, erguiste, **irguió,** erguimos, erguisteis, **irguieron**

§34 errar: like §2 but with initial ye for ie
  (c) **yerra,** errad
  (d) **yerro, yerras, yerra,** erramos, erráis, **yerran**
  (e) **yerre, yerres, yerre,** erremos, erréis, **yerren**

§35 esforzar: combination of §60 and §61
  (c) **esfuerza,** esforzad
  (d) **esfuerzo, esfuerzas, esfuerza,** esforzamos, esforzáis, **esfuerzan**
  (e) **esfuerce, esfuerces, esfuerce,** esforcemos, esforcéis, **esfuercen**
  (h) **esforcé,** esforzaste, esforzó, esforzamos, esforzasteis, esforzaron

§36 esparcir
  (d) **esparzo,** esparces, esparce, esparcimos, esparcís, esparcen
  (e) **esparza, esparzas, esparza, esparzamos, esparzáis, esparzan**

348

§37 estar
  (c) **está,** estad
  (d) **estoy, estás, está,** estamos, estáis, **están**
  (e) **esté, estés, esté,** estemos, estéis, **estén**
  (h) **estuve, estuviste, estuvo, estuvimos, estuvisteis, estuvieron**

§38 haber
  (c) **hé,** habed
  (d) **he, has, ha, hemos,** habéis, **han** (*v impers*) **hay**
  (e) **haya, hayas, haya, hayamos,** hayáis, **hayan**
  (g) **habré, habrás, habrá, habremos, habréis, habrán**
  (h) **hube, hubiste, hubo, hubimos, hubisteis, hubieron**

§39 hacer
  (b) **hecho**
  (c) **haz,** haced
  (d) **hago, haces, hace, hacemos, hacéis, hacen**
  (e) **haga, hagas, haga, hagamos, hagáis, hagan**
  (g) **haré, harás, hará, haremos, haréis, harán**
  (h) **hice, hiciste, hizo, hicimos, hicisteis, hicieron**

§40 inquirir
  (c) **inquiere,** inquirid
  (d) **inquiero, inquieres, inquiere,** inquirimos, inquirís, **inquie-
        ren**
  (e) **inquiera, inquieras, inquiera,** inquiramos, inquiráis, **inquie-
        ran**

§41 ir
  (a) **yendo**
  (c) **vé, vamos,** id
  (d) **voy, vas, va, vamos, vais, van**
  (e) **vaya, vayas, vaya, vayamos, vayáis, vayan**
  (f) **iba, ibas, iba, íbamos, ibais, iban**
  (h) **fui, fuiste, fue, fuimos, fuisteis, fueron**

§42 jugar: like **§63** but with radical **u**
  (c) **juega,** jugad
  (d) **juego, juegas, juega,** jugamos, jugáis, **juegan**
  (e) **juegue, juegues, juegue, juguemos, juguéis, jueguen**
  (h) **jugué,** jugaste, jugó, jugamos, jugasteis, jugaron

§43 leer
  (a) **leyendo**
  (b) **leído**
  (h) **leí, leíste, leyó, leímos, leísteis, leyeron**

§44 ligar
  (e) **ligue, ligues, ligue, liguemos, liguéis, liguen**
  (h) **ligué,** ligaste, ligó, ligamos, ligasteis, ligaron

§45 lucir
  (d) **luzco,** luces, luce, lucimos, lucís, lucen
  (e) **luzca, luzcas, luzca, luzcamos, luzcáis, luzcan**

§46 mecer
  (d) **mezo,** meces, mece, mecemos, mecéis, mecen
  (e) **meza, mezas, meza, mezamos, mezáis, mezan**

§47 mover

(c) mueve, moved
(d) muevo, mueves, mueve, movemos, movéis, mueven
(e) mueva, muevas, mueva, movamos, mováis, muevan

§48 oír

(a) oyendo
(b) oído
(c) oye, oíd
(d) oigo, oyes, oye, oímos, oís, oyen
(e) oiga, oigas, oiga, oigamos, oigáis, oigan
(h) oí, oíste, oyó, oímos, oísteis, oyeron

§49 oler: like §47 but with h before ue

(c) huele, oled
(d) huelo, hueles, huele, olemos, oléis, huelen
(e) huela, huelas, huela, olamos, oláis, huelan

§50 pedir

(a) pidiendo
(c) pide, pedid
(d) pido, pides, pide, pedimos, pedís, piden
(e) pida, pidas, pida, pidamos, pidáis, pidan
(h) pedí, pediste, pidió, pedimos, pedisteis, pidieron

§51 perder

(c) pierde, perded
(d) pierdo, pierdes, pierde, perdemos, perdéis, pierden
(e) pierda, pierdas, pierda, perdamos, perdáis, pierdan

§52 placer

(d) plazco, places, place, placemos, placéis, placen
(e) plazca, plazcas, plazca, plazcamos, plazcáis, plazcan
(h) plací, placiste, plació (or plugo), placimos, placisteis, placieron

§53 poder

(a) pudiendo
(c) (puede, poded)
(d) puedo, puedes, puede, podemos, podéis, pueden
(e) pueda, puedas, pueda, podamos, podáis, puedan
(g) podré, podrás, podrá, podremos, podréis, podrán
(h) pude, pudiste, pudo, pudimos, pudisteis, pudieron

§54 poner

(b) puesto
(c) pon, poned
(d) pongo, pones, pone, ponemos, ponéis, ponen
(e) ponga, pongas, ponga, pongamos, pongáis, pongan
(g) pondré, pondrás, pondrá, pondremos, pondréis, pondrán
(h) puse, pusiste, puso, pusimos, pusisteis, pusieron

§55 querer

(c) quiere, quered
(d) quiero, quieres, quiere, queremos, queréis, quieren
(e) quiera, quieras, quiera, queramos, queráis, quieran
(g) querré, querrás, querrá, querremos, querréis, querrán
(h) quise, quisiste, quiso, quisimos, quisisteis, quisieron

§56 raer
- (a) **rayendo**
- (b) **raído**
- (d) **raigo** (or **rayo**), raes, rae, raemos, raéis, raen
- (e) **raiga** (or **raya**), **raigas, raiga, raigamos, raigáis, raigan**
- (h) raí, **raíste, rayó, raímos, raísteis, rayeron**

§57 regir: combination of §27 and §50
- (a) **rigiendo**
- (c) **rige,** regid
- (d) **rijo, riges, rige,** regimos, regís, **rigen**
- (e) **rija, rijas, rija, rijamos, rijáis, rijan**
- (h) regí, registe, **rigió,** regimos, registeis, **rigieron**

§58 reír
- (a) **riendo**
- (b) **reído**
- (c) **ríe, reíd**
- (d) **río, ríes, ríe, reímos,** reís, **ríen**
- (e) **ría, rías, ría, riamos, riáis, rían**
- (h) reí, **reíste, rió, reímos, reísteis, rieron**

§59 reunir
- (c) **reúne,** reunid
- (d) **reúno, reúnes, reúne,** reunimos, reunís, **reúnen**
- (e) **reúna, reúnas, reúna,** reunamos, reunáis, **reúnan**

§60 rezar
- (e) **rece, reces, rece, recemos, recéis, recen**
- (h) **recé,** rezaste, rezó, rezamos, rezasteis, rezaron

§61 rodar
- (c) **rueda,** rodad
- (d) **ruedo, ruedas, rueda,** rodamos, rodáis, **ruedan**
- (e) **ruede, ruedes, ruede,** rodemos, rodéis, **rueden**

§62 roer
- (a) **royendo**
- (b) **roído**
- (d) roo (**roigo,** or **royo**), roes, roe, roemos, roéis, roen
- (e) roa (**roiga,** or **roya**), roas, roa, roamos, roáis, roan
- (h) roí, **roíste, royó, roímos, roísteis, royeron**

§63 rogar: combination of §44 and §61
- (c) **ruega,** rogad
- (d) **ruego, ruegas, ruega,** rogamos, rogáis, **ruegan**
- (e) **ruegue, ruegues, ruegue, roguemos, roguéis, rueguen**
- (h) **rogué,** rogaste, rogó, rogamos, rogasteis, rogaron

§64 saber
- (d) **sé,** sabes, sabe, sabemos, sabéis, saben
- (e) **sepa, sepas, sepa, sepamos, sepáis, sepan**
- (g) **sabré, sabrás, sabrá, sabremos, sabréis, sabrán**
- (h) **supe, supiste, supo, supimos, supisteis, supieron**

§65 salir
- (c) **sal,** salid
- (d) **salgo,** sales, sale, salimos, salís, salen
- (e) **salga, salgas, salga, salgamos, salgáis, salgan**
- (g) **saldré, saldrás, saldrá, saldremos, saldréis, saldrán**

§66 segar: combination of §2 and §44
   (c) siega, segad
   (d) siego, siegas, siega, segamos, segáis, siegan
   (e) siegue, siegues, siegue, seguemos, seguéis, sieguen
   (h) segué, segaste, segó, segamos, segasteis, segaron

§67 seguir: combination of §29 and §50
   (a) siguiendo
   (c) sigue, seguid
   (d) sigo, sigues, sigue, seguimos, seguís, siguen
   (e) siga, sigas, siga, sigamos, sigáis, sigan
   (h) seguí, seguiste, siguió, seguimos, seguisteis, siguieron

§68 sentir
   (a) sintiendo
   (c) siente, sentid
   (d) siento, sientes, siente, sentimos, sentís, sienten
   (e) sienta, sientas, sienta, sintamos, sintáis, sientan
   (h) sentí, sentiste, sintió, sentimos, sentisteis, sintieron

§69 ser
   (c) sé, sed
   (d) soy, eres, es, somos, sois, son
   (e) sea, seas, sea, seamos, seáis, sean
   (f) era, eras, era, éramos, erais, eran
   (h) fui, fuiste, fue, fuimos, fuisteis, fueron

§70 tañer
   (a) tañendo
   (h) tañí, tañiste, tañó, tañimos, tañisteis, tañeron

§71 tener
   (c) ten, tened
   (d) tengo, tienes, tiene, tenemos, tenéis, tienen
   (e) tenga, tengas, tenga, tengamos, tengáis, tengan
   (g) tendré, tendrás, tendrá, tendremos, tendréis, tendrán
   (h) tuve, tuviste, tuvo, tuvimos, tuvisteis, tuvieron

§72 teñir: combination of §12 and §50
   (a) tiñendo
   (c) tiñe, teñid
   (d) tiño, tiñes, tiñe, teñimos, teñís, tiñen
   (e) tiña, tiñas, tiña, tiñamos, tiñáis, tiñan
   (h) teñí, teñiste, tiñó, teñimos, teñisteis, tiñeron

§73 tocar
   (e) toque, toques, toque, toquemos, toquéis, toquen
   (h) toqué, tocaste, tocó, tocamos, tocasteis, tocaron

§74 torcer: combination of §47 and §78
   (c) tuerce, torced
   (d) tuerzo, tuerces, tuerce, torcemos, torcéis, tuercen
   (e) tuerza, tuerzas, tuerza, torzamos, torzáis, tuerzan

§75 traer
   (a) trayendo
   (b) traído
   (d) traigo, traes, trae, traemos, traéis, traen
   (e) traiga, traigas, traiga, traigamos, traigáis, traigan
   (h) traje, trajiste, trajo, trajimos, trajisteis, trajeron

§76 valer
    (d) valgo, vales, vale, valemos, valéis, valen
    (e) valga, valgas, valga, valgamos, valgáis, valgan
    (g) valdré, valdrás, valdrá, valdremos, valdréis, valdrán

§77 variar
    (c) varía, variad
    (d) varío, varías, varía, variamos, variáis, varían
    (e) varíe, varíes, varíe, variemos, variéis, varíen

§78 vencer
    (d) venzo, vences, vence, vencemos, vencéis, vencen
    (e) venza, venzas, venza, venzamos, venzáis, venzan

§79 venir
    (a) viniendo
    (c) ven, venid
    (d) vengo, vienes, viene, venimos, venís, vienen
    (e) venga, vengas, venga, vengamos, vengáis, vengan
    (g) vendré, vendrás, vendrá, vendremos, vendréis, vendrán
    (h) vine, viniste, vino, vinimos, vinisteis, vinieron

§80 ver
    (b) visto
    (d) veo, ves, ve, vemos, veis, ven
    (e) vea, veas, vea, veamos, veáis, vean
    (f) veía, veías, veía, veíamos, veíais, veían

§81 volcar: combination of **§61** and **§73**
    (c) vuelca, volcad
    (d) vuelco, vuelcas, vuelca, volcamos, volcáis, vuelcan
    (e) vuelque, vuelques, vuelque, volquemos, volquéis, vuelquen
    (h) volqué, volcaste, volcó, volcamos, volcasteis, volcaron

§82 yacer
    (c) yaz (or yace), yaced
    (d) yazco (yazgo, or yago), yaces, yace, yacemos, yacéis, yacen
    (e) yazca (yazga, or yaga), yazcas, yazca, yazcamos, yazcáis, yazcan

§83 The following verbs, some of which are included in the foregoing table, and their compounds have irregular past participles:

abrir	abierto	morir	muerto
cubrir	cubierto	poner	puesto
decir	dicho	proveer	provisto
escribir	escrito	pudrir	podrido
freír	frito	romper	roto
hacer	hecho	solver	suelto
imprimir	impreso	ver	visto
		volver	vuelto

PART TWO

Gramática Inglesa

GRAMÁTICA INGLESA
para el uso de este diccionario

Índice de materias

1. PRONUNCIACIÓN DEL INGLÉS

Los símbolos siguientes representan aproximadamente todos los sonidos del idioma inglés.

VOCALES

SÍMBOLO	SONIDO	EJEMPLO
[æ]	Más cerrado que la a de caro.	hat [hæt]
[ɑ]	Como la a de bajo.	father ['fɑðər] proper ['prɑpər]
[ɛ]	Como la e de perro.	met [mɛt]
[e]	Más cerrado que la e de canté. Suena como si fuese seguido de [ɪ].	fate [fet] they [ðe]
[ə]	Como la e de la palabra francesa le.	heaven ['hɛvən] pardon ['pɑrdən]
[i]	Como la i de nido.	she [ʃi] machine [mə'ʃin]
[ɪ]	Menos cerrado que la i de nido. Como la i de tilde.	fit [fɪt] beer [bɪr]
[o]	Más cerrado que la o de habló. Suena como si fuese seguido de [ʊ].	nose [noz] road [rod]
[ɔ]	Menos cerrado que la o de torre.	bought [bɔt] law [lɔ]

SÍMBOLO	SONIDO	EJEMPLO
|ʌ|	Más o menos como **eu** en la palabra francesa **peur.**	**cup** |kʌp| **come** |kʌm| **mother** |'mʌðər|
|u|	Menos cerrado que la **u** de **bulto.**	**pull** |pʊl| **book** |bʊk| **wolf** |wʊlf|
\[u\]	Como la **u** de **agudo.**	**rude** |rud| **move** |muv| **tomb** |tum|

DIPTONGOS

SÍMBOLO	SONIDO	EJEMPLO
\[aı\]	Como **ai** de **amáis.**	**night** |naıt| **eye** |aı|
|aʊ|	Como **au** de **causa.**	**found** |faʊnd| **cow** |kaʊ|
\[ɔı\]	Como **oy** de **estoy.**	**voice** |vɔıs| **oil** |ɔıl|

CONSONANTES

SÍMBOLO	SONIDO	EJEMPLO
\[b\]	Como la **b** de **hombre.** Sonido bilabial oclusivo sonoro.	**bed** |bed| **robber** |'rʌbər|
\[d\]	Como la **d** de **conde.** Sonido dental oclusivo sonoro.	**dead** |ded| **add** |æd|
\[dʒ\]	Como la **y** de **cónyuge.** Sonido palatal africado sonoro.	**gem** |dʒem| **jail** |dʒel|
\[ð\]	Como la **d** de **nada.** Sonido interdental fricativo sonoro.	**this** \[ðıs\] **father** |'fɑðər|
\[f\]	Como la **f** de **fecha.** Sonido labiodental sordo.	**face** |fes| **phone** |fon|
\[g\]	Como la **g** de **gato.** Sonido velar oclusivo sonoro.	**go** \[go\] **get** |get|
\[h\]	Sonido más aspirado pero menos áspero que el sonido velar fricativo sordo de la **j** de **junto.**	**hot** |hat| **alcohol** |'ælkə,hɔl|
\[j\]	Como la **y** de **cuyo.** Sonido palatal semiconsonántal sonoro.	**yes** |jes| **unit** |'junıt|
\[k\]	Como la **c** de **cama.** Sonido velar oclusivo sordo.	**cat** |kæt| **chord** |kɔrd| **kill** |kıl|
\[l\]	Como la **l** de **lado.** Sonido alveolar fricativo lateral sonoro.	**late** |let| **allow** |ə'laʊ|
\[m\]	Como la **m** de **madre.** Sonido bilabial nasal sonoro.	**more** |mor| **command** |kə'mænd|
\[n\]	Como la **n** de **carne.** Sonido alveolar nasal sonoro.	**nest** |nest| **manner** |'mænər|
\[ŋ\]	Como la **n** de **banco.** Sonido velar nasal sonoro.	**king** |kıŋ| **conquer** |'kaŋkər|
\[p\]	Como la **p** de **tapar.** Sonido bilabial oclusivo sordo.	**pen** \[pen\] **cap** |kæp|
\[r\]	La **r** más común en muchas partes de Inglaterra y en la mayor parte de los Estados Unidos y en Canadá es un sonido semivocal que se articula con la punta de la lengua elevada más hacia el paladar duro	**run** |rʌn| **far** |fɑr| **art** |ɑrt| **carry** |'kæri|

MBOLO	SONIDO	EJEMPLO
	que en la r fricativa española y aun doblada hacia atrás. Intervocálica y al final de sílaba, es muy débil y casi no se puede oír.	
	La r, precedida de los sonidos [ʌ] o [ə], da colorido propio a estos sonidos y desaparece completamente como sonido consonantal.	burn [bʌrn] learn [lʌrn] weather [ˈwɛðər]
s]	Como la s de clase. Sonido alveolar fricativo sordo.	send [sɛnd] cellar [ˈsɛlər]
ʃ]	Como ch de la palabra francesa chose. Sonido palatal fricativo sordo.	shall [ʃæl] machine [məˈʃin] nation [ˈneʃən]
t]	Como la t de arte. Sonido dental oclusivo sordo.	ten [tɛn] dropped [drɑpt]
ʃ]	Como la ch de mucho. Sonido palatal africado sordo.	child [tʃaild] much [mʌtʃ] nature [ˈnetʃər]
θ]	Como la z de zapato en la pronunciación de Castilla. Sonido interdental fricativo sordo.	think [θiŋk] truth [truθ]
v]	Como la v de la palabra francesa avant. Sonido labiodental fricativo sonoro.	vest [vɛst] over [ˈovər] of [ɑv]
w]	Como la u de hueso. Sonido labiovelar fricativo sonoro.	work [wʌrk] tweed [twid] queen [kwin]
z]	Como la s de mismo. Sonido alveolar fricativo sonoro.	zeal [zil] busy [ˈbizi] his [hiz]
ʒ]	Como la j de la palabra francesa jardin. Sonido palatal fricativo sonoro.	azure [ˈɛʒər] measure [ˈmɛʒər]

2. PRONUNCIACIÓN DE LA S DEL PLURAL

La s del plural en general es sorda ([s]) como la s de ser después de los sonidos rdos, representados por los consonantes f, k, p, t, th[θ] etc.; p.ej.:

[f]	roofs [rufs], laughs [læfs], triumphs [ˈtraɪ·əmfs]		[p]	maps [mæps]
[k]	looks [lʊks], cliques [kliks]		[t]	hats [hæts]
			[θ]	lengths [lɛŋθs]

La s del plural es sonora ([z]) como la s de mismo después de los sonidos sonoros, representados por el mayor número de las consonantes y por las vocales; p.ej.:

[b]	robes [robz]		[e]	days [dez]
[d]	heads [hedz]		[i]	knees [niz]
[g]	dogs [dɔgz], rogues [rogz]		[o]	toes [toz]
[l]	halls [hɔlz]		[u]	shoes [ʃuz]
[m]	arms [ɑrmz]		[aɪ]	lies [laɪz], sighs [saɪz]
[n]	pins [pɪnz]		[aʊ]	cows [kaʊz]
[ŋ]	things [θiŋz]		[ɔɪ]	boys [bɔɪz]
[r]	furs [fʌrz]		[ə]	sofas [ˈsofəz]
[v]	stoves [stovz]			
[ð]	lathes [leðz]			

or consiguiente, wife se pronuncia [waɪf], pero wives se pronuncia [waɪvz].)

La terminación es que se añade después de los sibilantes se pronuncia [ɪz]; p.ej.:

[s]	kisses [ˈkɪsɪz]		[tʃ]	watches [ˈwɑtʃɪz]
[z]	roses [ˈrozɪz]		[ʒ]	garages [gəˈrɑʒɪz]
[ʃ]	wishes [ˈwɪʃɪz]		[dʒ]	pages [ˈpedʒɪz]

Véase también sección 4, p. vii.

3. PRONUNCIACIÓN DE LOS PARTICIPIOS PASADOS

La terminación del participio pasado ed se pronuncia [d] si el infinitivo termi
en el sonido de una vocal o en el sonido de una consonante sonora, excep
[d]: [b], [g], [l], [m], [n], [ŋ], [r], [v], [z], [ð], [ʒ] o [dʒ]

ÚLTIMO SONIDO	INFINITIVO	PARTICIPIO PASADO Y PRETÉRITO
[b]	ebb [ɛb]	ebbed [ɛbd]
[g]	sag [sæg]	sagged [sægd]
[l]	mail [mel]	mailed [meld]
[m]	storm [stɔrm]	stormed [stɔrmd]
[n]	tan [tæn]	tanned [tænd]
[ŋ]	hang [hæŋ]	hanged [hæŋd]
[r]	fear [fɪr]	feared [fɪrd]
[v]	save [sev]	saved [sevd]
[z]	buzz [bʌz]	buzzed [bʌzd]
[ð]	smooth [smuð]	smoothed [smuðd]
[ʒ]	massage [mə'sɑʒ]	massaged [mə'sɑʒd]
[dʒ]	page [pedʒ]	paged [pedʒd]
sonido de vocal	key [ki]	keyed [kid]
	sigh [saɪ]	sighed [saɪd]

La terminación del participio pasado ed se pronuncia [t] si el infinitivo termi
en el sonido de una consonante sorda: [f], [k], [p], [s], [θ], [ʃ] o [tʃ]

ÚLTIMO SONIDO	INFINITIVO	PARTICIPIO PASADO Y PRETÉRITO
[f]	loaf [lof]	loafed [loft]
[k]	back [bæk]	backed [bækt]
[p]	wipe [waɪp]	wiped [waɪpt]
[s]	hiss [hɪs]	hissed [hɪst]
[θ]	lath [læθ]	lathed [læθt]
[ʃ]	mash [mæʃ]	mashed [mæʃt]
[tʃ]	match [mætʃ]	matched [mætʃt]

La terminación del participio pasado ed se pronuncia [ɪd] o [əd] si el infinit
termina en el sonido de una consonante dental: [t] o [d]

ÚLTIMO SONIDO	INFINITIVO	PARTICIPIO PASADO Y PRETÉRITO
[t]	wait [wet]	waited ['wetɪd]
	mate [met]	mated ['metɪd]
[d]	mend [mɛnd]	mended ['mɛndɪd]
	wade [wed]	waded ['wedɪd]

4. PLURAL DE LOS SUBSTANTIVOS

Por regla general, la terminación de la palabra en plural es una s que se aña
a la forma propia del singular: program, programs; syllable, syllables; toe, t

La mayor parte de los substantivos terminados en f o fe forman el plural c
ves: leaf, leaves; wife, wives; half, halves
Excepciones: dwarfs; gulfs; safes; still-lifes; cliffs; roofs etc.

Los substantivos que terminan en y precedida de consonante (o y precedida
qu) forman el plural cambiando la y en ies: fly, flies; family, families; oddi
oddities; colloquy, colloquies
Excepciones con los nombres propios: Mary, Marys; Kennedy, Kennedys
(Nótese que day/days, key/keys, monkey/monkeys etc. tienen la for
regular.)

Los substantivos que terminan en o precedida de consonante forman el plu
añadiendo es [z]: potato, potatoes; tomato, tomatoes
Excepciones: radio, radios; memo, memos etc.

Los substantivos que terminan en un sibilante ([s], [z], [ʃ], [tʃ], [ʒ] o [dʒ]) forman el plural añadiendo es [ɪz] o s [ɪz] (después de una e muda): miss, misses; buzz, buzzes; wish, wishes; arch, arches ['ɑrtɪz]; garage, garages; judge, judges

(Nótese que cuando **ch** se pronuncia [k] se añade s: **monarch, monarchs** | 'mɑnərks| etc.)

Algunos substantivos que terminan en is forman el plural cambiando is en es |iz|: crisis, crises; synopsis, synopses etc.

Plurales irregulares: **child, children; die, dice; foot, feet; goose, geese; louse, lice; mouse, mice; man, men; ox, oxen; tooth, teeth; woman, women**

Substantivos invariables: **craft, craft; deer, deer; fish, fish** (o **fishes**); **grouse, grouse; salmon, salmon; sheep, sheep; swine, swine; trout, trout**

Véase también sección 2, p. v.

5. GÉNERO

A diferencia de los substantivos en español, los nombres de cosas en inglés usualmente no tienen género.

NEUTROS:
Los nombres de cosas concretos o abstractos: **chair, idea** etc. (**the chair and** *its* **legs**)
Los de animales cuando no se especifica su sexo: **dog, kitten** etc. (**the dog and** *its* **tail**)
Los que significan niño o niño de pecho: **child, baby** etc. (**the baby and** *its* **smile**)

MASCULINOS: Los nombres que significan varón o animal macho: **actor, boy, buck, father, knight** etc. (**the actor and** *his* **voice**)

FEMININOS: Los nombres que significan mujer o animal hembra: **girl, cow, actress, mother, heroine** etc. (**the actress and** *her* **speech**) (también los nombres de barcos, máquinas y países)

COMUNES: **acquaintance, chairperson, poet, nurse, president, dentist** etc. (**Dr. Paul Miller is a dentist;** *his* **office is closed. Dr. Mary Miller is also a dentist;** *her* **office is open.**)

6. LA S DE POSESIÓN

Es posible expresar la «posesión» de los nombres substantivos utilizando un apóstrofe + s('s): **my friend's car** el coche de mi amigo; **a month's vacation** unas vacaciones de un mes

Cuando el substantivo es plural, se añade s + un apóstrofe (s'): **the birds' nests** los nidos de los pájaros; **my friends' house** la casa de mis amigos

Pero se puede también expresar la posesión utilizando of: **the main street of Newark** o **Newark's main street** la calle principal de Newark; **the cover of the book** o **the book's cover** la cubierta del libro.

Cuando se usa el nombre propio de una persona hay que añadir siempre un apóstrofe + s ('s) para expresar la posesión (o solamente un apóstrofe si el nombre propio de la persona termina en s): **Philip's brother** el hermano de Felipe; **Mary's book** el libro de María; **Williams' dictionary** el diccionario de Williams

7. REGLAS GENERALES PARA EL ADJETIVO Y EL ADVERBIO

LUGAR DEL ADJETIVO. Por regla general, el adjetivo (cuando no tiene función de predicado) precede al substantivo que califica o determina: **an intelligent student, a great country**

LUGAR DEL ADVERBIO. Por regla general, el adverbio va delante de la palabra que modifica: **seriously ill, very well**

GÉNERO Y NÚMERO. Los adjetivos y adverbios en inglés no tienen género o número; son invariables: **the very intelligent boy, the very intelligent girls**

8. FORMACIÓN DEL ADVERBIO

Por regla general, los adverbios se forman añadiendo **ly** al adjetivo: **quick, quickly; luxurious, luxuriously; faithful, faithfully**

Hay irregularidades:
- (a) Los adjetivos terminados en **y** precedida de consonante cambian la **y** en **i** antes de añadir **ly: easy, easily**
- (b) Los terminados en **ble** cambian la **e** en **y: probable, probably**
- (c) Los terminados en **ue** pierden la **e** final antes de añadir **ly: true, truly**
- (d) Muchos adjetivos que terminan en **ic** añaden **ally: poetic, poetically.** (Pero otros añaden **ly: public, publicly**)

9. FORMACIÓN DEL COMPARATIVO Y DEL SUPERLATIVO

Para construir el comparativo y el superlativo de los adjetivos y de los adverbios de una sílaba se añaden **er** para el comparativo y **est** para el superlativo: **fast, faster, fastest**

Los adjetivos y adverbios que terminan en **e** muda omiten la **e** antes de añadir **er** o **est: late, later, latest**

Los adjetivos que terminan en una consonante precedida de una vocal corta acentuada doblan la consonante: **big, bigger, biggest**

Los adjetivos y adverbios que terminan en **y** precedida de consonante cambian la **y** en **i: early, earlier, earliest**

Para construir el comparativo y el superlativo de los adjetivos y de los adverbios de dos o más sílabas debe emplearse las palabras **more** y **most: faithful, more faithful, most faithful; faithfully, more faithfully, most faithfully**

10. FORMAS IRREGULARES DEL COMPARATIVO Y DEL SUPERLATIVO

bad, ill, badly	worse	worst
good, well	better	best
little, small	less, lesser	least
far	farther, further	farthest, furthest
much, many	more	most
old	older, elder	oldest, eldest

11. SUPERLATIVO ABSOLUTO

El superlativo absoluto se construye con **very** o **most** + adjetivo o adverbio: **very cold,** friísimo; **very slowly,** despacísimo; **most excellent,** excelentísimo

12. CONSTRUCCIÓN DE FRASES COMPARATIVAS Y SUPERLATIVAS

El comparativo de superioridad:
> This train is *later than* the other one. (más . . . que)
> This train arrives *later than* the other one.
> My friends are *more faithful than* yours.
> This student copies *more faithfully than* the others.

El superlativo de superioridad:
> This train is *the latest.* (el más . . .)
> This train arrives *the latest.* (lo más . . .)
> My friends are *the most faithful.*
> This student copies *the most faithfully.*

El comparativo de inferioridad:
> My friends are *less faithful than* yours. (menos . . . que)
> This student copies *less faithfully than* the others.

El superlativo de inferioridad:

My friends are *the least faithful.* (los menos . . .)
This student copies *the least faithfully.* (lo menos . . .)

El comparativo de igualdad:

This train is *as late as* the other one. (tan . . . como)
This train arrives *as late as* the other one.
My friends are *as faithful as* yours.
This student copies *as faithfully as* the others.

13. PRONOMBRES PERSONALES

SUJETO	COMPLEMENTO	REFLEXIVO	POSESIVO
I	me	myself	mine
you	you	yourself	yours
he	him	himself	his
she	her	herself	hers
it	it	itself	its own
we	us	ourselves	ours
you	you	yourselves	yours
they	them	themselves	theirs

Los *adjetivos posesivos* son: my, your, his, her, its, our, your, their

Ejemplo del uso de pronombres personales y adjetivos posesivos: *We gave her his book* (o *We gave his book to her*), but *I told myself that she wanted theirs.* Le dimos *su* libro, pero *me* dije que *ella* quería *los suyos.*

El pronombre complemento indirecto puede usarse sin o con una preposición. Cuando no tiene una preposición, va delante del objeto directo (his book): *We gave her his book.* Cuando tiene una preposición, va después del objeto directo (his book): *We gave his book to her.*

Si el pronombre complemento es directo, no puede usarse una preposición: *We saw her.* La veíamos.

(Nótese que la misma regla se aplica cuando el objeto indirecto es un substantivo. Sin preposición: *We gave our father the book.* Con una preposición: *We gave the book to our father.* Dimos el libro a nuestro padre.)

14. CONJUGACIÓN REGULAR

PRESENTE Simple present (llego etc.)	PRETÉRITO Simple past (llegué etc.)	PRETÉRITO PERFECTO COMPUESTO Present perfect (he llegado etc.)	PRETÉRITO PLUSCUAM- PERFECTO Past perfect (había llegado etc.)
I arrive	I arrived	I have arrived	I had arrived
you arrive	you arrived	you have arrived	you had arrived
he arrives	he arrived	he *has* arrived	he had arrived
she arrives	she arrived	she *has* arrived	she had arrived
it arrives	it arrived	it *has* arrived	it had arrived
we arrive	we arrived	we have arrived	we had arrived
you arrive	you arrived	you have arrived	you had arrived
they arrive	they arrived	they have arrived	they had arrived

FUTURO Future (llegaré etc.)	CONDICIONAL Conditional (llegaría etc.)	CONJUGACIÓN CONTINUA Present progressive (estoy llegando etc.)
I will arrive	I would arrive	I am arriving
you will arrive	you would arrive	you are arriving (etc.)
he will arrive	he would arrive	
she will arrive	she would arrive	Past progressive (estaba llegando etc.)
it will arrive	it would arrive	
we will arrive	we would arrive	I was arriving
you will arrive	you would arrive	you were arriving (etc.)
they will arrive	they would arrive	

arrive! ¡llega! ¡llegad! ¡llegue Vd.! ¡lleguen Vds.!
let us arrive! ¡lleguemos!
let him arrive! ¡que él llegue! **let her arrive!** ¡que ella llegue! **let it arrive!**
¡que llegue! **let them arrive!** ¡que lleguen!

Nótese que algunas veces en inglés la misma forma del verbo sirve para el pretérito y el imperfecto: **I arrived** llegaba, **you arrived** llegabas etc. Otras veces el imperfecto se expresa en inglés por medio de la conjugación continua: **I was arriving** estaba llegando etc.

15. FORMACIÓN DEL GERUNDIO

Por regla general, los verbos del inglés forman el gerundio añadiendo **ing** al infinitivo: **to land, landing**

Si el verbo termina en una **e** muda, se omite la **e**: **to arrive, arriving.** (Excepciones están indicadas para los verbos irregulares, p. xi.)

Si el verbo termina en una consonante simple precedida de una vocal corta acentuada, en general se dobla la consonante: **to star, starring; to rebel, rebelling.** (Estas consonantes dobladas están indicadas para los verbos irregulares, p. xi.)

Si el verbo termina en **ic**, el infinitivo en general añade **k** antes de añadir **ing**: **to picnic, picnicking; to panic, panicking**

16. FORMACIÓN DE LA TERCERA PERSONA DEL SINGULAR

Por regla general, la tercera persona del singular (presente) se forma añadiendo **s** al infinitivo: **to land, he lands; to arrive, she arrives.** (La pronunciación de esta **s** sigue las reglas para el plural de los substantivos, p. v.)

Si el verbo termina en un sibilante ([s], [z], [ʃ], [tʃ] o [dʒ]), se añade **es** [ɪz]: **to guess, she guesses; to match, he matches**

Si el verbo termina en una **o** precedida de consonante, en general se añade **es** [z]: **to echo, it echoes.** (Excepciones son los verbos irregulares **to do** y **to go**, p. xii.)

Si el verbo termina en **y** precedida de consonante, en general cambia la **y** en **i** antes de añadir **es**: **to dry, it dries.** (Excepciones están indicados para los verbos irregulares, p. xi.)

17. FORMACIÓN DEL PRETÉRITO Y PARTICIPIO PASADO

Por regla general, el pretérito y participio pasado (o pasivo) se forma añadiendo **ed** al infinitivo: **to land, they landed** y **they have landed.** (Véase sección 3, p. vi, para la pronunciación de **ed**.)

Si el verbo termina en una **e** muda, pierde la **e** antes de añadir **ed**: **to arrive, she arrived** y **she has arrived**

Si el verbo termina en una consonante simple precedida de una vocal corta acentuada, en general se dobla la consonante: **to star, you starred** y **you have starred**

Si el verbo termina en **y** precedida de consonante, cambia la **y** en **i** antes de añadir **ed**: **to dry, it dried** y **it has dried**

Si el verbo termina en **ic**, el infinitivo en general añade **k** antes de añadir **ed**: **to picnic, we picnicked** y **we have picnicked; to panic, they panicked** y **they have panicked**

18. CONJUGACIÓN DEL VERBO *TO BE*

Nótese que los verbos *ser* y *estar* son expresados por un solo verbo en inglés: to be

I am	I was	I have been	Gerundio:
you are	you were	you have been	being
he is	he was	he has been	
she is	she was	she has been	
it is	it was	it has been	
we are	we were	we have been	
you are	you were	you have been	
they are	they were	they have been	

19. VERBOS IRREGULARES

Indicados después del infinitivo están las formas irregulares
(a) del gerundio (véase p. x.)
(b) de la tercera persona del singular, dentro de paréntesis (véase p. x.)

Marcados con un asterisco (*) están los participios pasados (o pasivos) que han caído en desuso como formas del verbo, pero que son utilizados como adjetivos en algunas expresiones corrientes (p.ej., **burnt almonds** almendras tostadas; a **drunken driver** un conductor embriagado).

INFINITIVO	PRETÉRITO	PARTICIPIO PASADO
abide	abode	abode
arise	arose	arisen
awake	awoke	awaked
be (SECCIÓN 18)	was, were	been
bear	bore	borne, *born
beat	beat	beat, beaten
become	became	become
begin/-ning	began	begun
bend	bent	bent, *bended
bereave	bereaved, bereft	bereaved, *bereft
beseech (-es)	beseeched, besought	beseeched, besought
bet/-ting	bet, betted	bet, betted
bid/-ding	bade, bid	bidden
bide	bode, bided	bided
bind	bound	bound, *bounden
bite	bit	bit, bitten
bleed	bled	bled
blend	blended, blent	blended, blent
blow	blew	blown
break	broke	broken
breed	bred	bred
bring	brought	brought
build	built	built
burn	burned, burnt	burned, *burnt
burst	burst	burst
buy	bought	bought
can (AUXILIAR MODAL, INVARIABLE)		
canoe/-ing	canoed (REGULAR)	canoed
cast	cast	cast
catch (-es)	caught	caught
chide	chided, chid	chided, chid, chidden
choose	chose	chosen
cleave	cleaved, cleft	cleaved, *cleft, *cloven
cling	clung	clung
clothe	clothed	clothed, *clad
come	came	come
cost	cost	cost
could (AUXILIAR MODAL, INVARIABLE)		
creep	crept	crept

xi

INFINITIVO	PRETÉRITO	PARTICIPIO PASADO
cut/-ting	cut	cut
deal	dealt	dealt
dig/-ging	dug, digged	dug, digged
dive	dived, dove	dived
do (-es) [dʌz]	did	done
draw	drew	drawn
dream	dreamed, dreamt	dreamed, dreamt
drink	drank	drunk, *drunken
drive	drove	driven
dwell	dwelled, dwelt	dwelled, dwelt
dye/-ing	dyed (REGULAR)	dyed
eat	ate	eaten
fall	fell	fallen
feed	fed	fed
feel	felt	felt
fight	fought	fought
find	found	found
flee/-ing	fled	fled
fling	flung	flung
fly (flies)	flew	flown
forbear	forbore	forborne
forbid/-ding	forbade, forbad	forbidden
forget/-ting	forgot	forgot, forgotten
forsake	forsook	forsaken
freeze	froze	frozen
get/-ting	got	got, gotten
gild	gilded, gilt	gilded, *gilt
gird	girt	girded
give	gave	given
go (-es)	went	gone
grind	ground	ground
grow	grew	grown
hang (colgar)	hung	hung
hang (ahorcar)	hanged (REGULAR)	hanged
have (has)	had	had
hear	heard	heard
heave	heaved, hove	heaved, hove
hew	hewed	hewed, hewn
hide	hid	hid, hidden
hit/-ting	hit	hit
hold	held	held
hurt	hurt	hurt
keep	kept	kept
kneel	knelt, kneeled	knelt, kneeled
knit/-ting	knitted, knit	knitted, *knit
know	knew	known
lade	laded	laded, *laden
lay (poner)	laid	laid
lead (conducir)	led	led
lean	leaned, leant	leaned, leant
leap	leaped, leapt	leaped, leapt
learn	learned, learnt	learned, learnt
leave	left	left
lend	lent	lent
let/-ting	let	let
lie/lying (yacer)	lay	lain
lie/lying (mentir)	lied (REGULAR)	lied
light	lighted, lit	lighted, lit
lose	lost	lost
make	made	made
may (AUXILIAR MODAL, INVARIABLE)		
mean	meant	meant
meet	met	met

INFINITIVO	PRETÉRITO	PARTICIPIO PASADO
t	melted	melted, *molten
ht (AUXILIAR MODAL, INVARIABLE)		
v	mowed	mowed, *mown
st (AUXILIAR MODAL, INVARIABLE)		
ht (AUXILIAR MODAL, INVARIABLE)		
	paid	paid
/-ning	penned, pent	penned, *pent
ad	pleaded, pled	pleaded, pled
/-ting	put	put
t/-ting	quit, quitted	quit, quitted
1	read	read
1	rent	rent
-ding	rid	rid
	rode	ridden
	rang	rung
	rose	risen
/-ning	ran	run
	sawed	sawed, sawn
	said	said
-ing	saw	seen
k	sought	sought
	sold	sold -
d	sent	sent
-ting	set	set
ke	shook	shaken
l (AUXILIAR MODAL, INVARIABLE)		
ve	shaved	shaved, *shaven
ar	sheared	sheared, *shorn
d/-ding	shed	shed
ae (brillar)	shone	shone
ae (pulir)	shined (REGULAR)	shined
e/-ing	shod	shod
ot	shot	shot
uld (AUXILIAR MODAL, INVARIABLE)		
w	showed	showed, shown
ed/-ding	shredded, shred	shredded, shred
ink	shrank, shrunk	shrunk, shrunken
t/-ting	shut	shut
g	sang	sung
ge/-ing	singed (REGULAR)	singed
k	sank, sunk	sunk, *sunken
-ting	sat	sat
r	slew	slain
p	slept	slept
e	slid	slid
g	slung	slung
k	slunk	slunk
/-ting	slit	slit
ll	smelled, smelt	smelled, smelt
te	smote	smit, *smitten
	sowed	sowed, sown
ak	spoke	spoken
ed	sped	sped
ll	spelled, spelt	spelled, spelt
nd	spent	spent
l	spilled, spilt	spilled, spilt
a/-ning	spun	spun
/-ting	spit, spat	spit, spat
t/-ting	split	split
il	spoiled, spoilt	spoiled, spoilt
ead	spread	spread
ng	sprang, sprung	sprung
ad	stood	stood

xiii

INFINITIVO	PRETÉRITO	PARTICIPIO PASADO
stave	staved, stove	staved, stove
steal	stole	stolen
stick	stuck	stuck
sting	stung	stung
stink	stank, stunk	stunk
strew	strewed	strewed, strewn
stride	strode	stridden
strike	struck	struck
string	strung	strung
strive	strove	striven
swear	swore	sworn
sweat/-ing	sweat, sweated	sweat, sweated
sweep	swept	swept
swell	swelled	swelled, swollen
swim/-ming	swam	swum
swing	swung	swung
take	took	taken
teach (-es)	taught	taught
tear	tore	torn
tell	told	told
think	thought	thought
thrive	thrived, throve	thrived, thriven
throw	threw	thrown
thrust	thrust	thrust
tread	trod	trod, *trodden
understand	understood	understood
vie (vying)	vied (REGULAR)	vied
wake	waked, woke	waked
wear	wore	worn
weave (tejer)	wove	woven, wove
weave (zigzaguear)	weaved (REGULAR)	weaved
wed/-ding	wed, wedded	wed, wedded
weep	wept	wept
wet/-ting	wet, wetted	wet, wetted
will (AUXILIAR MODAL, INVARIABLE)		
win/-ning	won	won
wind	wound	wound
work	worked, wrought	worked, *wrought
would (AUXILIAR MODAL, INVARIABLE)		
wring	wrung	wrung
write	wrote	written

20. CONSTRUCCIÓN DE LA ORACIÓN INTERROGATIVA

La oración interrogativa en general se construye con el auxiliar **to do**, que
delante del sujeto; el verbo toma la forma invariable del infinitivo sin **to**:
you see this tree? ¿ves este árbol? **did your country win?** ¿ganó su país?

Si el verbo es **to be** o un auxiliar modal (**can, could, may, might, must, ou
shall, should, will, would**), la oración interrogativa se construye sin **to do**
sujeto va inmediatamente después del verbo: **are the students ready?** ¿e
listos los estudiantes? **shall we go?** ¿nos vamos?

21. CONSTRUCCIÓN DE LA NEGACIÓN

La negación en general se construye con el auxiliar **to do** seguido de **not**
verbo toma la forma invariable del infinitivo sin **to: I do not see it** no lo v
he does not play él no juega; **her father did not come** su padre no vino

Si el verbo es **to be** o un auxiliar modal (**can, could, may, might, must, ou
shall, should, will, would**), la negación se construye sin **to do**, poniendo
inmediatamente después del verbo: **they are not here** no están aquí; **John
not win** Juan no ganará

22. CONTRACCIONES

Las contracciones son muy corrientes en inglés, especialmente en el lenguaje coloquial y la escritura familiar.

Contracciones del pronombre y del verbo:

I am = I'm [aɪm]   I have = I've [aɪv]
you are = you're [jur]   you have = you've [juv]
he is = he's [hiz]   he has = he's [hiz]
she is = she's [ʃiz]   she has = she's [ʃiz]
it is = it's [ɪts]   it has = it's [ɪts]
we are = we're [wir]   we have = we've [wiv]
they are = they're [ðer]   they have = they've [ðev]
who is = who's [huz]   who has = who's [huz]

I will = I'll [aɪl]   I would = I'd [aɪd]
you will = you'll [jul]   you would = you'd [jud]
he will = he'll [hil]   he would = he'd [hid]
she will = she'll [ʃil]   she would = she'd [ʃid]
it will = it'll [ɪtl]
we will = we'll [wil]   we would = we'd [wid]
they will = they'll [ðel]   they would = they'd [ðed]
who will = who'll [hul]   who would = who'd [hud]

Nótese que se usan las contracciones del pronombre y del verbo **to have** solamente con los participios pasados, p.ej., she's written a book. (No se usa la contracción en casos como she has a book.)

Negaciones:

are not = aren't [ɑrnt]   do not = don't [dont]
is not = isn't [ɪznt]   does not = doesn't [dʌznt]
was not = wasn't [wɑznt]   did not = didn't [dɪdnt]
were not = weren't [wʌrnt]   can not (o cannot) = can't [kænt]
have not = haven't [hævnt]   could not = couldn't [kʊdnt]
has not = hasn't [hæznt]   might not = mightn't [maɪtnt]
had not = hadn't [hædnt]   must not = mustn't [mʌsnt]
will not = won't [wont]   shall not = shan't [ʃænt]
would not = wouldn't [wʊdnt]   should not = shouldn't [ʃʊdnt]

Nótese: he is not = he's not o he isn't
          you are not = you're not o you aren't
          you have not = you've not o you haven't

También es posible hacer contracciones de un adverbio y un verbo o de un substantivo y un verbo:

there is = there's [ðerz]   three is = three's [θriz]
there will = there'll [ðerl]   (three's a crowd aquí sobra uno)
there would = there'd [ðerd]   John is = John's [dʒɑnz]
here is = here's [hirz]   (John's sick Juan está enfermo)

23. NÚMEROS CARDINALES Y ORDINALES

NÚMEROS CARDINALES (uno etc.)		NÚMEROS ORDINALES (primero, etc.)
1	one	first
2	two	second
3	three	third
4	four	fourth
5	five	fifth
6	six	sixth
7	seven	seventh
8	eight	eighth
9	nine	ninth
10	ten	tenth
11	eleven	eleventh

NÚMEROS CARDINALES		NÚMEROS ORDINALES
12	twelve	twelfth
13	thirteen	thirteenth
14	fourteen	fourteenth
15	fifteen	fifteenth
16	sixteen	sixteenth
17	seventeen	seventeenth
18	eighteen	eighteenth
19	nineteen	nineteenth
20	twenty	twentieth
21	twenty-one	twenty-first
30	thirty	thirtieth
40	forty	fortieth
50	fifty	fiftieth
60	sixty	sixtieth
70	seventy	seventieth
80	eighty	eightieth
90	ninety	ninetieth
99	ninety-nine	ninety-ninth
100	one (o a) hundred	(one o a) hundredth
101	one hundred and one	(one) hundred and first
200	two hundred	two-hundredth
1000	one (o a) thousand	(one o a) thousandth
1001	one thousand and one	(one) thousand and first
1981	one thousand nine hundred and eighty-one	(one) thousand nine hundred and eighty-first
100,000	one (o a) hundred thousand	(one o a) hundred thousandth
1,000,000	one (o a) million	(one o a) millionth

Nótese que en inglés se usa el número cardinal para los tomos (**volume three** tomo tercero) y el número ordinal para las fechas (**July Fourth** el cuatro de julio). Si la fecha es un año, se dice, p.ej., **nineteen eighty-two** o **nineteen hundred eighty-two** (1982).

24. MEDIDAS DE LOS ESTADOS UNIDOS

UNIDAD USA	EQUIVALENTE MÉTRICO	UNIDAD MÉTRICA	EQUIVALENTE USA
LARGURA:			
1 mile	1,6 kilómetros	1 kilómetro	.6 miles
1 yard	0,9 metros	1 metro	39.37 inches
		1 metro	3.28 feet
1 foot	30,5 centímetros	1 centímetro	.39 inches
1 inch	25,4 milímetros	1 milímetro	.039 inches
SUPERFICIE:			
1 acre	0,4 hectáreas	1 hectárea	2.5 acres
1 square mile	259 hectáreas	1 kilómetro cuadrado	.39 square miles
VOLUMEN:			
1 cubic foot	0,028 metros cúbicos	1 metro cúbico	35.315 cubic feet
CAPACIDAD:			
1 quart	0,95 litros	1 litro	1.057 quarts
1 gallon	3,8 litros	1 litro	.26 gallons
PESO:			
1 pound	0,45 kilogramos	1 kilogramo	2.2 pounds
1 ounce	28,35 gramos	100 gramos	3.53 ounces
1 (net) ton (2000 pounds)	907,2 kilogramos	1 gramo	15.432 grains

foot (ft.) pie; **gallon** (gal.) galón; **grain** (gr.) grano; **inch** (in.) pulgada; **mile** (mi.) milla; **ounce** (oz.) onza; **pound** (lb.) libra; **quart** (qt.) cuarto de galón (líquido)

PART THREE

Inglés-Español

Abreviaturas y calificativos

Marcados con un asterisco (*) están los calificativos regionales.

abbr abreviatura
(acronym) acrónimo—palabra formada de las letras o sílabas iniciales de una serie de palabras (por ej., NATO ['neto])
adj adjetivo
adv adverbio
(aer) aeronáutica
(agr) agricultura
(alg) álgebra
*(Am) hispanoamericano
(anat) anatomía
(archaic) arcaico
(archeol) arqueología
(archit) arquitectura
*(Arg) argentino
(arith) aritmética
art artículo
(arti) artillería
(astr) astronomía
(aut) automóviles
(bact) bacteriología
(bb) encuadernación
(Bib) bíblico
(billiards) billar
(biochem) bioquímica
(biol) biología
*(Bol) boliviano
(bowling) bolos
(bot) botánica
(box) boxeo
(Brit) británico
*(CAm) centroamericano
(cards) naipes
(carp) carpintería
(chem) química
(chess) ajedrez
*(Chile) chileno
*(Col) colombiano
(coll) familiar
(com) comercial
comp comparativo
cond condicional
conj conjunción
*(C-R) costarriqueño
*(Cuba) cubano
(culin) cocina

def definido
dem demostrativo
(dent) odontología
(dial) dialectal
(eccl) eclesiástico
(econ) economía
*(Ecuad) ecuatoriano
(educ) educación
(elec) electricidad
(electron) electrónica
*(El Salv) El Salvador
(ent) entomología
f nombre femenino
(fa) bellas artes
fem femenino
(fencing) esgrima
(feud) feudalismo
(fig) figurado
fpl nombre femenino plural
fsg nombre femenino singular
fut futuro
(geog) geografía
(geol) geología
(geom) geometría
ger gerundio
(gram) gramática
*(Guat) guatemalteco
(heral) heráldica
(hist) historia
*(Hond) hondureño
(hort) horticultura
(hum) jocoso
(hunt) caza
(ichth) ictiología
imperf imperfecto
impers impersonal
impv imperativo
ind indicativo
indecl indeclinable
indef indefinido
inf infinitivo
(ins) seguros
interj interjección
interr interrogativo
intr verbo intransitivo
invar invariable
(iron) irónico

3

(Lat) latín
(law) derecho
(letterword) palabra en forma de abreviatura la cual se pronuncia haciendo sonar el nombre de cada letra consecutivamente y que funciona como parte del discurso (por ej., UN ['ju'en])
(log) lógica
m nombre masculino
(mach) maquinaria
(mas) albañilería
masc masculino
(math) matemática
(mech) mecánica
(med) medicina
(metal) metalurgia
(meteor) meteorología
*(Mex) mejicano
mf nombre masculino o nombre femenino según el sexo
(mil) militar
(min) minería
(mineral) mineralogía
(mountaineering) alpinismo
(mov) cine
mpl nombre masculino plural
msg nombre masculino singular
(mus) música
(myth) mitología
m & f nombre masculino y femenino sin tener en cuenta el sexo
(naut) náutico
(nav) naval militar
neut neutro
(obs) desusado
(obstet) obstetricia
(opt) óptica
(orn) ornitología
(paint) pintura
*(Pan) panameño
*(Para) paraguayo
(pathol) patología
pers personal
*(Peru) peruano
(pharm) farmacia
(philol) filología
(philos) filosofía
(phonet) fonética
(phot) fotografía
(phys) física

(physiol) fisiología
pl plural
(poet) poético
(pol) política
poss posesivo
pp participio pasado
*(P-R) puertorriqueño
prep preposición
pres presente
pret pretérito
pron pronombre
(psychol) sicología
(rad) radio
ref verbo reflexivo
reflex reflexivo
rel relativo
(rhet) retórica
(rr) ferrocarril
s substantivo
*(SAm) sudamericano
(scornful) despreciativo
(sculp) escultura
*(S-D) República Dominicana
(sew) costura
sg singular
(slang) jerga
spl substantivo plural
ssg substantivo singular
subj subjuntivo
super superlativo
(surg) cirugía
(surv) agrimensura
(taur) tauromaquia
(telg) telegrafía
(telp) telefonía
(telv) televisión
(tennis) tenis
(theat) teatro
(theol) teología
tr verbo transitivo
(typ) imprenta
*(Urug) uruguayo
v verbo
var variante
v aux verbo auxiliar
*(Ven) venezolano
(vet) veterinaria
(vulg) grosero
*(W-I) antillano
(zool) zoología

Véase también los preliminares de este diccionario, páginas x–xi.

INGLÉS–ESPAÑOL

A

A, a [e] primera letra del alfabeto inglés

a [e] *art indef* un

aback [ə'bæk] *adv* atrás; **to be taken aback** quedar desconcertado; **to take aback** desconcertar

abaft [ə'bæft] o [ə'bɑft] *adv* a popa, en popa; *prep* detrás de

abandon [ə'bændən] *s* abandono ‖ *tr* abandonar

abase [ə'bes] *tr* degradar, humillar

abash [ə'bæʃ] *tr* avergonzar

abate [ə'bet] *tr* disminuir, reducir; deducir ‖ *intr* disminuir, moderarse

aba·tis ['æbətɪs] *s* (*pl* -**tis**) abatida

abattoir ['æbə,twɑr] *s* matadero

abba·cy ['æbəsi] *s* (*pl* -**cies**) abadía

abbess ['æbɪs] *s* abadesa

abbey ['æbi] *s* abadía

abbot ['æbət] *s* abad *m*

abbreviate [ə'brivɪ,et] *tr* abreviar

abbreviation [ə,brivɪ'eʃən] *s* (*shortening*) abreviación; (*shortened form*) abreviatura

A B C [,e,bi'si] *s* abecé *m*; **A B C's** abecedario

abdicate ['æbdɪ,ket] *tr & intr* abdicar

abdomen ['æbdəmən] o [æb'domən] *s* abdomen *m*

abduct [æb'dʌkt] *tr* raptar, secuestrar

abed [ə'bɛd] *adv* en cama, acostado

abet [ə'bɛt] *v* (*pret & pp* abetted; *ger* abetting) *tr* incitar (*a una persona, esp. al mal*); fomentar (*el crimen*)

abeyance [ə'be-əns] *s* suspensión; **in abeyance** en suspenso

ab·hor [æb'hɔr] *v* (*pret & pp* -horred; *ger* -horring) *tr* aborrecer, detestar

abhorrent [æb'hɑrənt] o [æb'hɔrənt] *adj* aborrecible, detestable

abide [ə'baɪd] *v* (*pret & pp* abode o abided) *tr* esperar; tolerar ‖ *intr* permanecer; **to abide by** cumplir con; atenerse a

abili·ty [ə'brlɪti] *s* (*pl* -**ties**) habilidad, capacidad; talento

abject [æb'dʒɛkt] *adj* abyecto, servil

ablative ['æblətɪv] *s* ablativo

ablaut ['æblaʊt] *s* apofonía

ablaze [ə'blez] *adj* brillante; ardiente; encolerizado ‖ *adv* en llamas, ardiendo

able ['ebəl] *adj* hábil, capaz; **to be able to** poder

able-bodied ['ebəl'badid] *adj* sano; fornido; experto

abloom [ə'blum] *adj* floreciente ‖ *adv* en flor

abnormal [æb'nɔrməl] *adj* anormal

aboard [ə'bord] *adv* a bordo; al bordo; **all aboard!** ¡señores viajeros

al tren!; **to go aboard** ir a bordo; **to take aboard** embarcar ‖ *prep* a bordo de; (*a train*) en

abode [ə'bod] *s* domicilio, residencia

abolish [ə'balɪʃ] *tr* eliminar, suprimir

A-bomb ['e,bɑm] *s* bomba atómica

abomination [ə,bamɪ'neʃən] *s* abominación

aborigines [,æbə'rɪdʒɪ,niz] *spl* aborígenes *mf*

abort [ə'bɔrt] *tr & intr* abortar

abortion [ə'bɔrʃən] *s* aborto

abound [ə'baʊnd] *intr* abundar

about [ə'baʊt] *adv* casi; aquí; **to be about to** estar a punto de, estar para ‖ *prep* acerca de; con respecto a; cerca de; hacia, a eso de; **to be about** tratar de

above [ə'bʌv] *adj* antedicho ‖ *adv* arriba, encima ‖ *prep* sobre, encima de, más alto que; superior a; **above all** sobre todo

above-mentioned [ə'bʌv'menʃənd] *adj* sobredicho, antedicho, susodicho

abrasive [ə'bresɪv] o [ə'breziv] *adj & s* abrasivo

abreast [ə'brɛst] *adj & adv* de frente; **to be abreast of** correr parejas con; estar al corriente de

abridge [ə'brɪdʒ] *tr* abreviar; disminuir; condensar, resumir

abroad [ə'brɔd] *adv* al extranjero; en el extranjero; fuera de casa

abrupt [ə'brʌpt] *adj* brusco; repentino; áspero; abrupto, escarpado

abscess ['æbsɛs] *s* absceso

abscond [æb'skand] *intr* irse a hurtadillas; **to abscond with** alzarse con

absence ['æbsəns] *s* ausencia

absent ['æbsənt] *adj* ausente ‖ [æb'sɛnt] *tr*—**to absent oneself** ausentarse

absentee [,æbsən'ti] *s* ausente *mf*

absent-minded ['æbsənt'maɪndɪd] *adj* distraído, absorto

absinth ['æbsɪnθ] *s* (*plant*) absintio, ajenjo; (*drink*) absenta, ajenjo

absolute ['æbsə,lut] *adj & s* absoluto

absolutely ['æbsə,lutli] *adv* absolutamente ‖ [,æbsə'lutli] *adv* (coll) positivamente

absolve [æb'salv] *tr* absolver

absorb [æb'sɔrb] *tr* absorber; **to be become absorbed** ensimismarse

absorbent [æb'sɔrbənt] *adj* absorbente; (*cotton*) hidrófilo

absorbing [æb'sɔrbɪŋ] *adj* absorbente

abstain [æb'sten] *intr* abstenerse

abstemious [æb'stimɪ·əs] *adj* abstemio, sobrio

abstinent ['æbstɪnənt] *adj* abstinente

abstract ['æbstrækt] *adj* abstracto ‖ *s* resumen *m*, sumario, extracto ‖ *tr* resumir, compendiar, extractar ‖ [æb'strækt] *tr* abstraer; quitar

abstruse [æb'strus] *adj* abstruso

absurd [æb'sʌrd] o [æb'zʌrd] *adj* absurdo

absurdi·ty [æb'sʌrditi] o [æb'zʌrditi] *s* (*pl* -ties) absurdidad, absurdo

abundant [ə'bʌndənt] *adj* abundante

abuse [ə'bjus] *s* maltrato; injuria, insulto; (*bad practice; injustice*) abuso ‖ [ə'bjuz] *tr* maltratar; injuriar, insultar; (*to misapply, take unfair advantage of*) abusar de

abusive [ə'bjusɪv] *adj* injurioso, insultante; abusivo

abut [ə'bʌt] *v* (*pret & pp* **abutted;** *ger* **abutting**) *intr*—**to abut on** confinar con, terminar en

abutment [ə'bʌtmənt] *s* confinamiento; estribo, contrafuerte *m*

abyss [ə'bɪs] *s* abismo

academic [,ækə'dɛmɪk] *adj* académico

academic costume *s* toga, traje *m* de catedrático

academic freedom *s* libertad de cátedra, libertad de enseñanza

academician [ə,kædə'mɪʃən] *s* académico

academic subjects *spl* materias no profesionales

academic year *s* año escolar

acade·my [ə'kædəmi] *s* (*pl* -mies) academia

accede [æk'sid] *intr* acceder; **to accede to** acceder a, condescender a; (*e.g., the throne*) ascender a, subir a

accelerate [æk'sɛlə,ret] *tr* acelerar ‖ *intr* acelerarse

accelerator [æk'sɛlə,retər] *s* acelerador *m*

accent ['æksɛnt] *s* acento ‖ ['æksɛnt] o [æk'sɛnt] *tr* acentuar

accent mark *s* acento ortográfico

accentuate [æk'sɛntʃu,et] *tr* acentuar

accept [æk'sɛpt] *tr* aceptar

acceptable [æk'sɛptəbəl] *adj* aceptable

acceptance [æk'sɛptəns] *s* aceptación

access ['æksɛs] *s* acceso

accessible [æk'sɛsɪbəl] *adj* accesible

accession [æk'sɛʃən] *s* accesión; (*to a dignity*) ascenso; (*of books in a library*) adquisición

accesso·ry [æk'sɛsəri] *adj* accesorio ‖ *s* (*pl* -ries) accesorio; (*to a crime*) cómplice *mf*

accident ['æksɪdənt] *s* accidente *m;* **by accident** por casualidad

accidental [,æksɪ'dɛntəl] *adj* accidental

acclaim [ə'klem] *s* aclamación ‖ *tr & intr* aclamar

acclimate ['æklɪ,met] *tr* aclimatar ‖ *intr* aclimatarse

accolade [,ækə'led] *s* acolada; elogio, premio

accommodate [ə'kamə,det] *tr* acomodar; alojar

accommodating [ə'kamə,detɪŋ] *adj* acomodadizo, servicial

accommodation [ə,kamə'deʃən] *s* acomodación; **accommodations** facilidades, comodidades; (*in a train*) localidad; (*in a hotel*) alojamiento

accommodation train *s* tren *m* ómnibus

accompaniment [ə'kʌmpənɪmənt] *s* acompañamiento

accompanist [ə'kʌmpənɪst] *s* acompañante *m*

accompa·ny [ə'kʌmpəni] *v* (*pret & pp* -nied) *tr* acompañar

accomplice [ə'kamplɪs] *s* cómplice *mf*, codelincuente *mf*

accomplish [ə'kamplɪʃ] *tr* realizar, llevar a cabo

accomplished [ə'kamplɪʃt] *adj* realizado; culto, talentoso; (*fact*) consumado

accomplishment [ə'kamplɪʃmənt] *s* realización; **accomplishments** prendas, talentos

accord [ə'kɔrd] *s* acuerdo; **in accord with** de acuerdo con: **of one's own accord** de buen grado, voluntariamente; **with one accord** de común acuerdo ‖ *tr* conceder, otorgar ‖ *intr* concordar, avenirse

accordance [ə'kɔrdəns] *s* conformidad; **in accordance with** de acuerdo con

according [ə'kɔrdɪŋ] *adj* — **according as** según que; **according to** según

accordingly [ə'kɔrdɪŋli] *adv* en conformidad; por consiguiente

accordion [ə'kɔrdɪən] *s* acordeón *m*

accost [ə'kɔst] o [ə'kast] *tr* abordar, acercarse a

accouchement [ə'kuʃmənt] *s* alumbramiento, parto

account [ə'kaunt] *s* informe *m*, relato; cuenta; estado de cuenta; importancia; **by all accounts** según el decir general; **of no account** de poca importancia; **on account of** a causa de; **to bring to account** pedir cuentas a; **to buy on account** comprar a plazos; **to turn to account** sacar provecho de, hacer valer ‖ *intr*—**to account for** explicar; responder de

accountable [ə'kauntəbəl] *adj* responsable; explicable

accountant [ə'kauntənt] *s* contador *m*, contable *m*

accounting [ə'kauntɪŋ] *s* arreglo de cuentas; contabilidad

accouterments [ə'kutərmənts] *spl* equipo, avíos

accredit [ə'krɛdɪt] *tr* acreditar

accrue [ə'kru] *intr* acumularse; resultar

acct. *abbr* account

accumulate [ə'kjumjə,let] *tr* acumular ‖ *intr* acumularse

accuracy ['ækjərəsi] *s* exactitud, precisión

accurate ['ækjərɪt] *adj* exacto

accusation [,ækjə'zeʃən] *s* acusación

accusative [ə'kjuzətɪv] *adj & s* acusativo

accuse [ə'kjuz] *tr* acusar

accustom [ə'kʌstəm] *tr* acostumbrar

ace [es] *s* as *m;* **to be within an ace of** estar a dos dedos de

acetate ['æsɪ‚tet] s acetato

acetic acid [ə'sitɪk] s ácido acético

aceti·fy [ə'setɪ‚faɪ] v (pret & pp -fied) tr acetificar ‖ intr acetificarse

acetone ['æsɪ‚ton] s acetona

acetylene [ə'setɪ‚lin] s acetileno

acetylene torch s soplete oxiacetilénico

ache [ek] s achaque m, dolor m ‖ intr doler

achieve [ə'tʃiv] tr llevar a cabo; alcanzar, ganar, lograr

achievement [ə'tʃivmənt] s realización; (feat) hazaña

Achilles' heel [ə'kɪliz] s talón m de Aquiles

acid ['æsɪd] adj ácido; agrio, mordaz ‖ s ácido

acidi·fy [ə'sɪdɪ‚faɪ] v (pret & pp -fied) tr acidificar ‖ intr acidificarse

acidi·ty [ə'sɪdɪti] s (pl -ties) acidez f

acid test s prueba decisiva

ack-ack ['æk'æk] s (slang) artillería antiaérea; (slang) fuego antiaéreo

acknowledge [æk'nɑlɪdʒ] tr reconocer; acusar (recibo de una carta); agradecer (p. ej., un favor)

acknowledgment [æk'nɑlɪdʒmənt] s reconocimiento; (of receipt of a letter) acuse m; (of a favor) agradecimiento

acme ['ækmi] s auge m, colmo

acolyte ['ækə‚laɪt] s acólito

acorn ['ekɔrn] o ['ekɑrn] s bellota

acoustic [ə'kustɪk] adj acústico ‖ acoustics ssg acústica

acquaint [ə'kwent] tr informar, poner al corriente; **to be acquainted** conocerse; **to be acquainted with** conocer; estar al corriente de

acquaintance [ə'kwentəns] s conocimiento; (person) conocido

acquiesce [‚ækwɪ'ɛs] intr consentir, condescender, asentir

acquiescence [‚ækwɪ'ɛsəns] s consentimiento, condescendencia, aquiescencia

acquire [ə'kwaɪr] tr adquirir

acquisition [‚ækwɪ'zɪʃən] s adquisición

acquit [ə'kwɪt] v (pret & pp acquitted; ger acquitting) tr absolver, exculpar; **to acquit oneself** conducirse, portarse

acquittal [ə'kwɪtəl] s absolución, exculpación

acrid ['ækrɪd] adj acre, acrimonioso

acrobat ['ækrə‚bæt] s acróbata mf

acrobatic [‚ækrə'bætɪk] adj acrobático ‖ acrobatics ssg (profession) acrobatismo; spl (stunts) acrobacia

acronym ['ækrənɪm] s acrónimo

acropolis [ə'krɑpəlɪs] s acrópolis f

across [ə'krɔs] o [ə'krɑs] prep a través de; al otro lado de; **to come across** encontrarse con; **to go across** atravesar

across'-the-board' adj comprensivo, general

acrostic [ə'krɔstɪk] o [ə'krɑstɪk] s acróstico

act [ækt] s acto; (law) decreto; **in the act** en flagrante ‖ tr representar;

desempeñar (un papel); **to act the fool** hacer el bufón; **to act the part of** hacer o desempeñar el papel de ‖ intr actuar; funcionar, obrar; conducirse; **to act as if** hacer como que; **to act for** representar; **to act up** travesear; **to act up to** hacer fiestas a

acting ['æktɪŋ] adj interino ‖ s actuación

action ['ækʃən] s acción; **to take action** tomar medidas

activate ['æktɪ‚vet] tr activar

active ['æktɪv] adj activo

activi·ty [æk'tɪvɪti] s (pl -ties) actividad

act of God s fuerza mayor

actor ['æktər] s actor m

actress ['æktrɪs] s actriz f

actual ['ækt∫u-əl] adj real, efectivo

actually ['ækt∫u-əli] adv en realidad

actuar·y ['ækt∫u‚ɛri] s (pl -ies) actuario (de seguros)

actuate ['ækt∫u‚et] tr actuar; estimular, mover

acuity [ə'kju‚ɪti] s agudeza

acumen [ə'kjumən] s cacumen m, perspicacia

acute [ə'kjut] adj agudo

A.D. abbr anno Domini (Lat) in the year of our Lord

ad [æd] s (coll) anuncio

adage ['ædɪdʒ] s adagio, refrán m

Adam ['ædəm] s Adán m; **the old Adam** la inclinación al pecado

adamant ['ædəmənt] adj firme, inexora‫le

Adam's apple s nuez f

adapt [ə'dæpt] tr adaptar; refundir (un drama)

adaptation [‚ædæp'teʃən] s adaptación; (of a play) refundición

add [æd] tr agregar, añadir; sumar ‖ intr sumar; **to add up to** subir a; (coll) querer decir

added line s (mus) línea suplementaria

adder ['ædər] s víbora; serpiente f

addict ['ædɪkt] s enviciado; adicto, partidario ‖ [ə'dɪkt] tr enviciar; entregar; **to addict oneself** enviciarse con o en; entregarse a

addiction [ə'dɪkʃən] s enviciamiento; adhesividad

adding machine s sumadora, máquina de sumar

addition [ə'dɪʃən] s adición; **in addition to** además de

additive ['ædɪtɪv] adj & s aditivo

address [ə'drɛs] o ['ædrɛs] s dirección; consignación ‖ [ə'drɛs] s alocución, discurso; **to deliver an address** hacer uso de la palabra ‖ tr dirigirse a; dirigir (p. ej., una alocución, una carta); consignar

addressee [‚ædrɛ'si] s destinatario; (com) consignatario

addressing machine s máquina para dirigir sobres

adduce [ə'djus] o [ə'dus] tr aducir

adenoids ['ædə‚nɔɪdz] spl vegetaciones adenoides

adept [ə'dɛpt] adj & s experto, perito

adequate ['ædɪkwɪt] adj suficiente

adhere [æd'hɪr] *intr* adherir, adherirse; conformarse

adherence [æd'hɪrəns] *s* adhesión

adherent [æd'hɪrənt] *adj & s* adherente *m*

adhesion [æd'hiʒən] *s* (*sticking*) adherencia; (*support, loyalty*) adhesión; (pathol) adherencia; (phys) adherencia o adhesión

adhesive [æd'hisɪv] o [æd'hizɪv] *adj* adhesivo

adhesive tape *s* tafetán adhesivo

adieu [ə'dju] o [ə'du] *interj* ¡adiós! ‖ *s* (*pl* **adieus** o **adieux**) adiós *m; to bid adieu to* despedirse de

adjacent [ə'dʒesənt] *adj* adyacente

adjective ['ædʒɪktɪv] *adj & s* adjetivo

adjoin [ə'dʒɔɪn] *tr* lindar con ‖ *intr* colindar

adjoining [ə'dʒɔɪnɪŋ] *adj* colindante, contiguo

adjourn [ə'dʒʌrn] *tr* prorrogar, suspender ‖ *intr* prorrogarse, suspenderse; (coll) ir

adjournment [ə'dʒʌrnmənt] *s* prorrogación, suspensión

adjust [ə'dʒʌst] *tr* ajustar, arreglar; corregir, verificar; (ins) liquidar

adjustable [ə'dʒʌstəbəl] *adj* ajustable, arreglable

adjustment [ə'dʒʌstmənt] *s* ajuste *m*, arreglo; (ins) liquidación de la avería

adjutant ['ædʒətənt] *s* ayudante *m*

ad-lib [,æd'lɪb] *v* (*pret & pp* **-libbed**; *ger* **-libbing**) *tr & intr* improvisar

Adm. *abbr* **Admiral**

administer [æd'mɪnɪstər] *tr* administrar; *to administer an oath* tomar juramento ‖ *intr* — *to administer to* cuidar de

administrator [æd'mɪnɪs,tretər] *s* administrador *m*

admiral ['ædmɪrəl] *s* almirante *m*; buque *m* almirante

admiral·ty ['ædmɪrəlti] *s* (*pl.* **-ties**) almirantazgo

admire [æd'maɪr] *tr* admirar

admirer [æd'maɪrər] *s* admirador *m*; enamorado

admissible [æd'mɪsɪbəl] *adj* admisible

admission [æd'mɪʃən] *s* admisión; (*in a school*) ingreso; precio de entrada; *to gain admission* lograr entrar

ad·mit [æd'mɪt] *v* (*pret & pp* **-mitted**; *ger* **-mitting**) *tr* admitir ‖ *intr* dar entrada; *to admit of* admitir, permitir

admittance [æd'mɪtəns] *s* admisión; derecho de entrar; **no admittance** acceso prohibido, se prohíbe la entrada

admonish [æd'mɑnɪʃ] *tr* amonestar

ado [ə'du] *s* bulla, excitación

adobe [ə'dobi] *s* adobe *m; casa de adobe*

adolescence [,ædə'lɛsəns] *s* adolescencia

adolescent [,ædə'lɛsənt] *adj & s* adolescente *mf*

adopt [ə'dɑpt] *tr* adoptar

adoption [ə'dɑpʃən] *s* adopción

adorable [ə'dorəbəl] *adj* adorable

adore [ə'dor] *tr* adorar

adorn [ə'dɔrn] *tr* adornar

adornment [ə'dɔrnmənt] *s* adorno

adrenal gland [æd'rinəl] *s* glándula suprarrenal

Adriatic [,edrɪ'ætɪk] o [,ædrɪ'ætɪk] *adj & s* Adriático

adrift [ə'drɪft] *adj & adv* al garete, a la deriva

adroit [ə'drɔɪt] *adj* diestro

adult [ə'dʌlt] o ['ædʌlt] *adj & s* adulto

adulterate [ə'dʌltə,ret] *tr* adulterar

adulterer [ə'dʌltərər] *s* adúltero

adulteress [ə'dʌltər:s] *s* adúltera

adulter·y [ə'dʌltəri] *s* (*pl* **-ies**) adulterio

advance [æd'væns] o [æd'vɑns] *adj* adelantado; anticipado ‖ *s* adelanto, avance *m;* aumento, subida; **advances** propuestas; requerimiento amoroso; propuesta indecente; préstamo; **in advance** de antemano, por anticipado ‖ *tr* adelantar ‖ *intr* adelantar; adelantarse

advanced [æd'vænst] o [æd'vɑnst] *adj* avanzado; **advanced in years** avanzado de edad, entrado en años

advanced standing *s* traspaso de matrículas, traspaso de crédito académico

advanced studies *spl* altos estudios

advancement [æd'vænsmənt] o [æd-'vɑnsmənt] *s* adelanto, avance *m;* subida; promoción

advance publicity *s* publicidad de lanzamiento

advantage [æd'væntɪdʒ] o [æd'vɑntɪdʒ] *s* ventaja; **to take advantage of** aprovecharse de; abusar de, engañar

advantageous [,ædvən'tedʒəs] *adj* ventajoso

advent ['ædvɛnt] *s* advenimiento ‖ **Advent** *s* (eccl) Adviento

adventure [æd'vɛntʃər] *s* aventura ‖ *tr* aventurar ‖ *intr* aventurarse

adventurer [æd'vɛntʃərər] *s* aventurero

adventuresome [æd'vɛntʃərsəm] *adj* aventurero

adventuress [æd'vɛntʃərɪs] *s* aventurera

adventurous [æd'vɛntʃərəs] *adj* aventurero

adverb ['ædvʌrb] *s* adverbio

adversar·y ['ædvər,sɛri] *s* (*pl* **-ies**) adversario

adversi·ty [æd'vʌrsɪti] *s* (*pl* **-ties**) adversidad

advertise ['ædvər,taiz] o [,ædvər'taɪz] *tr & intr* anunciar

advertisement [,ædvər'taɪzmənt] o [æd'vɑrtɪzmənt] *s* anuncio

advertiser ['ædvər,taɪzər] o [,ædvər-'taɪzər] *s* anunciante *mf*

advertising ['ædvər,taɪzɪŋ] *s* propaganda, publicidad, anuncios

advertising agency *s* empresa anunciadora

advertising campaign *s* campaña de publicidad

advertising man *s* empresario de publicidad

advertising manager *s* gerente *m* de publicidad

advice [æd'vais] *s* consejo; aviso, noticia; **a piece of advice** un consejo

advisable [æd'vaizəbəl] *adj* aconsejable

advise [æd'vaiz] *tr* aconsejar, asesorar; advertir, avisar

advisement [æd'vaizmənt] *s* consideración; **to take under advisement** someter a consideración

advisory [æd'vaizəri] *adj* consultivo

advocate ['ædvə,ket] *s* defensor *m*; abogado || *tr* abogar por

Aegean Sea [i'dʒi·ən] *s* Archipiélago; (*of the ancients*) mar Egeo

aegis ['idʒis] *s* égida

aerate ['eret] o ['e·ə,ret] *tr* airear

aerial ['eri·əl] *adj* aéreo || *s* antena

aerialist ['eri·əlist] *s* volatinero

aerodrome ['erə,drom] *s* aeródromo

aerodynamic [,erodai'næmik] *adj* aerodinámico || **aerodynamics** *ssg* aerodinámica

aeronaut ['erə,nɔt] *s* aeronáuta *mf*

aeronautic [,erə'nɔtik] *adj* aeronáutico || **aeronautics** *ssg* aeronáutica

aerosol ['erə,sɔl] *s* aerosol *m*

aerospace ['ero,spes] *adj* aeroespacial

aesthete ['esθit] *s* esteta *mf*

aesthetic [es'θetik] *adj* estético || **aesthetics** *ssg* estética

afar [ə'far] *adv* lejos

affable ['æfəbəl] *adj* afable

affair [ə'fer] *s* asunto, negocio; lance *m*; amorío; encuentro, combate *m*; **affairs** negocios

affect [ə'fɛkt] *tr* influir en; impresionar, enternecer; (*to assume; to pretend*) afectar; aficionarse a

affectation [,æfɛk'teʃən] *s* afectación

affected [ə'fɛktɪd] *adj* afectado

affection [ə'fɛkʃən] *s* afecto, cariño, afección; (pathol) afección

affectionate [ə'fɛkʃənɪt] *adj* afectuoso, cariñoso

affidavit [,æfɪ'devɪt] *s* declaración jurada, acta notarial

affiliate [ə'fɪlɪ,et] *adj* afiliado || *s* afiliado; filial *f* || *tr* afiliar || *intr* afiliarse

affini·ty [ə'fɪnɪtɪ] *s* (*pl* -ties) afinidad

affirm [ə'fɑrm] *tr* & *intr* afirmar

affirmative [ə'fɑrmətɪv] *adj* afirmativo || *s* afirmativa

affix ['æfɪks] *s* añadidura; (gram) afijo || [ə'fɪks] *tr* añadir; atribuir (*p.ej., culpa*); poner (*una firma, sello, etc.*)

afflict [ə'flɪkt] *tr* afligir; **to be afflicted with** sufrir de, adolecer de

affliction [ə'flɪkʃən] *s* aflicción, desgracia; achaque *m*

affluence ['æflu·əns] *s* (*abundance*) afluencia; (*wealth*) opulencia

afford [ə'ford] *tr* proporcionar; **to be able to afford (to)** poder darse el lujo de, poder permitirse

affray [ə'fre] *s* pendencia, riña

affront [ə'frʌnt] *s* afrenta || *tr* afrentar

Afghan ['æfgən] o ['æfgæn] *adj* & *s* afgano

Afghanistan [æf'gænɪ,stæn] *s* el Afganistán

---

afire [ə'faɪr] *adj* & *adv* ardiendo

aflame [ə'flem] *adj* & *adv* en llamas

afloat [ə'flot] *adj* & *adv* a flote; a bordo; inundado; sin rumbo; (*rumor*) en circulación

afoot [ə'fʊt] *adj* & *adv* a pie; en marcha

afoul [ə'faʊl] *adj* & *adv* enredado; en colisión; **to run afoul of** enredarse con

afraid [ə'fred] *adj* asustado; **to be afraid** tener miedo

Africa ['æfrɪkə] *s* África

African ['æfrɪkən] *adj* & *s* africano

aft [æft] o [ɑft] *adj* & *adv* en popa

after ['æftər] o ['ɑftər] *adj* siguiente || *adv* después || *prep* después de; según; **after all** al fin y al cabo || *conj* después de que

af'ter-din'ner speaker *s* orador *m* de sobremesa

after-dinner speech *s* discurso de sobremesa

af'ter-hours' *adv* después del trabajo

af'ter-life' *s* vida venidera; resto de la vida

aftermath ['æftər,mæθ] o ['ɑftər,mæθ] *s* segunda siega; consecuencias, consecuencias desastrosas

af'ter-noon' *s* tarde *f*

af'ter-taste' *s* dejo, gustillo, resabio

af'ter-thought' *s* idea tardía, expediente tardío

afterward ['æftərwəd] o ['ɑftərwərd] *adv* después, luego

af'ter-while' *adv* dentro de poco

again [ə'gen] *adv* otra vez, de nuevo; además; **to + *inf* + again** volver a + *inf*, p.ej., **he will come again** volverá a venir

against [ə'genst] *prep* contra; cerca de; en contraste con; por; para

agape [ə'gep] *adj* abierto de par en par || *adv* con la boca abierta

age [edʒ] *s* edad; (*old age*) vejez *f*; (*one hundred years; a long time*) siglo; edad mental; **of age** mayor de edad; **to come of age** alcanzar su mayoría de edad, llegar a mayor edad; **under age** menor de edad || *tr* envejecer || *intr* envejecer, envejecerse

aged [edʒd] *adj* de la edad de || ['edʒɪd] *adj* anciano, viejo

ageless ['edʒlɪs] *adj* eternamente joven

agen·cy ['edʒənsɪ] *s* (*pl* -cies) agencia; mediación

agenda [ə'dʒendə] *s* agenda, temario

agent ['edʒənt] *s* agente *m*

Age of Enlightenment *s* siglo de las luces

agglomeration [ə,glɒmə'reʃən] *s* aglomeración

aggrandizement [ə'grændɪzmənt] *s* engrandecimiento

aggravate ['ægrə,vet] *tr* agravar; (coll) exasperar, irritar

aggregate ['ægrɪ,get] *adj* & *s* agregado || *tr* agregar, juntar; ascender a

aggression [ə'grɛʃən] *s* agresión

aggressive [ə'grɛsɪv] *adj* agresivo
aggressor [ə'grɛsər] *s* agresor *m*
aghast [ə'gæst] o [ə'gɑst] *adj* horrorizado
agile ['ædʒɪl] *adj* ágil
agitate ['ædʒɪ,tet] *tr & intr* agitar
aglow [ə'glo] *adj & adv* fulgurante
agnostic [æg'nɑstɪk] *adj & s* agnóstico
ago [ə'go] *adv* hace, p.ej., **two days ago** hace dos días
ago·ny ['ægənɪ] *s (pl* **-nies)** angustia, congoja; *(anguish; death struggle)* agonía
agrarian [ə'grɛrɪ·ən] *adj* agrario || *s* agrariense *mf*
agree [ə'gri] *intr* estar de acuerdo, ponerse de acuerdo; sentar bien; *(gram)* concordar
agreeable [ə'gri·əbəl] *adj (to one's liking)* agradable; *(willing to consent)* acorde, conforme
agreement [ə'grimənt] *s* acuerdo, convenio; concordancia; **in agreement** de acuerdo
agric. *abbr* **agriculture**
agriculture ['ægrɪ,kʌltʃər] *s* agricultura
agronomy [ə'grɑnəmɪ] *s* agronomía
aground [ə'graund] *adv* encallado, varado; **to run aground** encallar, varar
agt. *abbr* **agent**
ague ['egju] *s* escalofrío; fiebre *f* intermitente
ahead [ə'hed] *adj & adv* delante, al frente; **ahead of** antes de; delante de; al frente de; **to get ahead (of)** adelantarse (a)
ahoy [ə'hɔɪ] *interj* — **ship ahoy!** ¡ah del barco!
aid [ed] *s* ayuda, auxilio; *(mil)* ayudante *m* || *tr* ayudar, auxiliar; **to aid and abet** ayudar e incitar, ser cómplice de || *intr* ayudar
aide-de-camp ['eddə'kæmp] *s (pl* **aides-de-camp)** ayudante *m* de campo, edecán *m*
ail [el] *tr* inquietar; **what ails you?** ¿qué tiene Vd.? || *intr* sufrir, estar enfermo
aileron ['elə,rɑn] *s* alerón *m*
ailing ['elɪŋ] *adj* enfermo, achacoso
ailment ['elmənt] *s* enfermedad, achaque *m*
aim [em] *s* puntería; intento; punto de mira || *tr* apuntar, encarar; dirigir *(p.ej., una observación)* || *intr* apuntar
air [ɛr] *s* aire *m*; **by air** por vía aérea; **in the open air** al aire libre; **on the air** en antena, en la radio; **to let the air out of** desinflar; **to put on airs** darse aires; **to put on the air** llevar a las antenas; **to walk on air** no pisar en el suelo || *tr* airear, ventilar; radiodifundir; *(fig)* ventilar
air'-a·tom'ic *adj* aeroatómico
air'-borne' *adj* aerotransportado
air brake *s* freno de aire comprimido
air castle *s* castillo en el aire
air'-condi'tion *tr* climatizar
air conditioner *s* acondicionador *m* de aire

air conditioning *s* acondicionamiento del aire, clima *m* artificial
air corps *s* cuerpo de aviación
air'craft *ssg* máquina de volar; *spl* máquinas de volar
aircraft carrier *s* portaaviones *m*
airdrome ['ɛr,drom] *s* aeródromo
air'drop' *s* lanzamiento || *tr* lanzar
air field *s* campo de aviación
air'foil' *s* superficie *f* de sustentación
air force *s* fuerza aérea, ejército del aire
air gap *s* (phys) entrehierro
air'-ground' *adj* aeroterrestre
air hostess *s* aeromoza, azafata
air lane *s* ruta aérea
air'lift' *s* puente aéreo
air liner *s* transaéreo, avión *m* de travesía
air mail *s* correo aéreo, aeroposta
air'-mail' **letter** *s* carta aérea, carta por avión
air-mail pilot *s* aviador *m* postal
air-mail stamp *s* sello aéreo
air·man ['ermən] o ['ɛr,mæn] *s (pl* **-men** [mən] o [,mɛn]) aviador *m*
air'plane' *s* avión *m*
airplane carrier *s* portaaviones *m*
air pocket *s* bache aéreo
air pollution *s* contaminación atmosférica
air'port' *s* aeropuerto
air raid *s* ataque aéreo
air'-raid' **drill** *s* simulacro de ataque aéreo
air-raid shelter *s* abrigo antiaéreo
air-raid warning *s* alarma aérea
air rifle *s* escopeta de viento, escopeta de aire comprimido
air'ship' *s* aeronave *f*
air'sick' *adj* mareado en el aire
air sleeve o **sock** *s* veleta de manga
air'strip' *s* pista de despegue, pista de aterrizaje
air'tight' *adj* herméticamente cerrado, estanco al aire
air'waves' *spl* ondas de radio
air'way' *s* aerovía, vía aérea
airway lighting *s* balizaje *m*
air·y ['eri] *adj (comp* **-ier;** *super* **-iest)** airoso; aireado; alegre; impertinente; *(coll)* afectado
aisle [aɪl] *s (in theater, movie, etc.)* pasillo; *(in a store, factory, etc.)* nave *f*; *(archit)* nave *f* lateral; *(any of the long passageways of a church)* (archit) nave *f*
ajar [ə'dʒɑr] *adj* entreabierto, entornado
akimbo [ə'kɪmbo] *adj & adv* — **with arms akimbo** en jarras
akin [ə'kɪn] *adj* emparentado; semejante
alabaster ['ælə,bæstər] o ['ælə,bɑstər] *s* alabastro
alarm [ə'lɑrm] *s* alarma || *tr* alarmar
alarm clock *s* reloj *m* despertador
alarmist [ə'lɑrmɪst] *s* alarmista *mf*
alas [ə'læs] o [ə'lɑs] *interj* ¡ay!, ¡ay de mí!
Albanian [æl'benɪ·ən] *adj & s* albanés *m*

albatross [ˈælbəˌtrɔs] o [ˈælbəˌtrɑs] s albatros m

album [ˈælbəm] s álbum m

albumen [ælˈbjumən] s albumen m; albúmina

alchemy [ˈælkɪmi] s alquimia

alcohol [ˈælkəˌhɔl] o [ˈælkəˌhɑl] s alcohol m

alcoholic [ˌælkəˈhɔlɪk] o [ˌælkəˈhɑlɪk] adj & s alcohólico

alcove [ˈælkov] s gabinete m, rincón m; (in a bedroom) trasalcoba; (in a garden) cenador m

alder [ˈɔldər] s aliso

alder·man [ˈɔldərmən] s (pl -men [mən]) concejal m

ale [el] s ale f (cerveza inglesa, obscura, espesa y amarga)

alembic [əˈlɛmbɪk] s alambique m

alert [əˈlʌrt] adj listo, vivo; vigilante ‖ s (aer) alarma; (mil) alerta m; **to be on the alert** estar sobre aviso, estar alerta ‖ tr alertar

Aleutian Islands [əˈluʃən] spl islas Aleutas, islas Aleutianas

Alexandrine [ˌælɪɡˈzændrɪn] adj & s alejandrino

alg. abbr **algebra**

algae [ˈældʒi] spl algas

algebra [ˈældʒɪbrə] s álgebra

algebraic [ˌældʒɪˈbre·ɪk] adj algebraico

Algeria [ælˈdʒɪrɪ·ə] s Argelia

Algerian [ælˈdʒɪrɪ·ən] adj & s argelino

Algiers [ælˈdʒɪrz] s Argel f

alias [ˈelɪ·əs] adv alias ‖ s alias m, nombre supuesto

ali·bi [ˈælɪˌbaɪ] s (pl -bis) coartada; (coll) excusa

alien [ˈeljən] o [ˈelɪ·ən] adj & s extranjero

alienate [ˈeljəˌnet] o [ˈelɪ·əˌnet] tr enajenar, alienar

alight [əˈlaɪt] v (pret & pp alighted o alit [əˈlɪt]) intr bajar, apearse; posarse (un ave)

align [əˈlaɪn] tr alinear ‖ intr alinearse

alike [əˈlaɪk] adj semejantes; **to look alike** parecerse ‖ adv igualmente

alimentary canal [ˌælɪˈmɛntəri] s canal alimenticio, tubo digestivo

alimony [ˈælɪˌmoni] s alimentos

alive [əˈlaɪv] adj vivo, viviente; animado; **alive to** despierto para, sensible a; **alive with** hormigueante en

alka·li [ˈælkəˌlaɪ] s (pl -lis o -lies) álcali m

alkaline [ˈælkəˌlaɪn] o [ˈælkəlɪn] adj alcalino

all [ɔl] adj indef todo, todos; todo el, todos los ‖ pron indef todo; todos, todo el mundo; **after all** sin embargo; **all of** todo el, todos los; **all that** todo lo que, todos los que; **for all I know** que yo sepa; a lo mejor; **not at all** nada; no hay de qué ‖ adv enteramente; **all along** desde el principio; a lo largo de; **all at once** de golpe; **all right** bueno, corriente; **all too** excesivamente

Allah [ˈælə] s Alá m

allay [əˈle] tr aliviar, calmar

all-clear [ˈɔlˈklɪr] s cese m de alarma

allege [əˈlɛdʒ] tr alegar

allegiance [əˈlidʒəns] s fidelidad, lealtad; homenaje m; **to swear allegiance to** jurar fidelidad a; rendir homenaje a

allegoric(al) [ˌælɪˈɡɑrɪk(əl)] o [ˌælɪˈɡɔrɪk(əl)] adj alegórico

allego·ry [ˈælɪˌɡori] s (pl -ries) alegoría

aller·gy [ˈælərdʒi] s (pl -gies) alergia

alleviate [əˈlivɪˌet] tr aliviar

alley [ˈæli] s callejuela; paseo arbolado, paseo de jardín; (bowling) pista; (tennis) espacio lateral

All Fools' Day s var of **April Fools' Day**

Allhallows [ˌɔlˈhæloz] s día m de todos los santos

alliance [əˈlaɪ·əns] s alianza

alligator [ˈælɪˌɡetər] s caimán m

alligator pear s aguacate m

alligator wrench s llave f de mandíbulas dentadas

alliteration [əˌlɪtəˈreʃən] s aliteración

all-knowing [ˈɔlˈno·ɪŋ] adj omnisciente

allocate [ˈæləˌket] tr asignar, distribuir

allot [əˈlɑt] v (pret & pp allotted; ger allotting) tr asignar, distribuir

all'-out' adj acérrimo

allow [əˈlaʊ] tr alegar, permitir; admitir; conceder ‖ intr — **to allow for** tener en cuenta; **to allow of** permitir; admitir

allowance [əˈlaʊ·əns] s permiso; concesión; ración; descuento, rebaja; tolerancia; **to make allowance for** tener en cuenta

alloy [ˈælɔɪ] o [əˈlɔɪ] s aleación, liga ‖ [əˈlɔɪ] tr alear, ligar

all-powerful [ˈɔlˈpaʊ·ərfəl] adj todopoderoso

All Saints' Day s día m de todos los santos

All Souls' Day s día m de los difuntos

allspice [ˈɔlˌspaɪs] s pimienta inglesa

all'-star' game s (sport) juego de estrellas

allude [əˈlud] intr aludir

allure [əˈlʊr] s tentación, encanto, fascinación ‖ tr tentar, encantar

alluring [əˈlʊrɪŋ] adj tentador, encantador, fascinante

allusion [əˈluʒən] s alusión

al·ly [ˈælaɪ] o [əˈlaɪ] s (pl -lies) aliado ‖ [əˈlaɪ] v (pret & pp -lied) tr aliar ‖ intr aliarse

almanac [ˈɔlməˌnæk] s almanaque m

almighty [ɔlˈmaɪti] adj todopoderoso, omnipotente

almond [ˈɑmənd] o [ˈæmənd] s almendra

almond brittle s crocante m

almond tree s almendro

almost [ˈɔlmost] o [ɔlˈmost] adv casi

alms [ɑmz] s limosna

alms'house s casa de beneficencia

aloe [ˈælo] s áloe m

aloft [əˈlɔft] o [əˈlɑft] adv arriba; (aer) en vuelo; (naut) en la arboladura

alone [əˈlon] adj solo; **let alone** sin

mencionar; y mucho menos; **to let alone** no molestar; no mezclarse en ‖ *adv* solamente

along [ə'lɔŋ] o [ə'laŋ] *adv* conmigo, consigo, etc.; **all along** desde el principio; **along with** junto con ‖ *prep* a lo largo de

along'side' *adv* a lo largo; (naut) al costado; **to bring alongside** acostar ‖ *prep* a lo largo de; (naut) al costado de

aloof [ə'luf] *adj* apartado; reservado ‖ *adv* lejos, a distancia

aloud [ə'laud] *adv* alto, en voz alta

alphabet ['ælfə,bet] *s* alfabeto

alpine ['ælpaɪn] *adj* alpestre, alpino

Alps [ælps] *spl* Alpes *mpl*

already [ɔl'redɪ] *adv* ya

Alsace [æl'ses] o ['ælsæs] *s* Alsacia

Alsatian [æl'seʃən] *adj & s* alsaciano

also ['ɔlso] *adv* también

alt. *abbr* **alternate**, **altitude**

altar ['ɔltər] *s* altar *m*; **to lead to the altar** conducir al altar

altar boy *s* acólito, monaguillo

altar cloth *s* sabanilla, palia

al'tar-piece' *s* retablo

altar rail *s* comulgatorio

alter ['ɔltər] *tr* alterar ‖ *intr* alterarse

alteration [,ɔltə'reʃən] *s* alteración; (*in a building*) reforma; (*in clothing*) arreglo

alternate ['ɔltərnɪt] o ['ɔltərnɪt] *adj* alterno ‖ ['ɔltər,net] o ['æltər,net] *tr & intr* alternar

alternating current *s* corriente alterna o alternativa

although [ɔl'ðo] *conj* aunque

altimetry [æl'tɪmɪtrɪ] *s* altimetría

altitude ['æltɪ,tjud] o ['æltɪ,tud] *s* altitud, altura

al·to ['ælto] *s* (*pl* -**tos**) contralto

altogether [,ɔltə'geðər] *adv* enteramente; en conjunto

altruist ['æltru·ɪst] *s* altruísta *mf*

altruistic [,æltru'ɪstɪk] *adj* altruísta

alum ['æləm] *s* alumbre *m*

aluminum [ə'lumɪnəm] *s* aluminio

alum·na [ə'lʌmnə] *s* (*pl* -**nae** [ni]) graduada

alum·nus [ə'lʌmnəs] *s* (*pl* -**ni** [naɪ]) graduado

alveo·lus [æl'vi·ələs] *s* (*pl* -**li** [,laɪ]) alvéolo

always ['ɔlwɪz] o ['ɔlwez] *adv* siempre

A.M. *abbr* **ante meridiem,** i.e., **before noon; amplitude modulation**

Am. *abbr* **America, American**

amalgam [ə'mælgəm] *s* amalgama *f*

amalgamate [ə'mælgə,met] *tr* amalgamar ‖ *intr* amalgamarse

amass [ə'mæs] *tr* amontonar; amasar (*dinero*)

amateur ['æmət∫ər] *adj & s* chapucero, principiante *mf*; aficionado

amateur performance *s* función de aficionados

amaze [ə'mez] *tr* asombrar, maravillar

amazing [ə'mezɪŋ] *adj* asombroso, maravilloso

Amazon ['æmə,zɑn] o ['æməzən] *s* Amazonas *m*

ambassador [æm'bæsədər] *s* embajador *m*

ambassadress [æm'bæsədrɪs] *s* embajadora

amber ['æmbər] *adj* ambarino ‖ *s* ámbar *m*

ambigui·ty [,æmbɪ'gju·ɪtɪ] *s* (*pl* -**ties**) ambigüidad

ambiguous [æm'bɪgju·əs] *adj* ambiguo

ambition [æm'bɪ∫ən] *s* ambición

ambitious [æm'bɪ∫əs] *adj* ambicioso

amble ['æmbəl] *s* ambladura ‖ *intr* amblar

ambulance ['æmbjələns] *s* ambulancia

ambush ['æmbu∫] *s* emboscada; **to lie in ambush** estar emboscado ‖ *tr* (*to station in ambush*) emboscar; (*to lie in wait for and attack*) insidiar ‖ *intr* emboscarse

amelioration [ə,miljə're∫ən] *s* mejoramiento

amen ['e'men] o ['ɑ'men] *interj* ¡amén! ‖ *s* amén *m*

amenable [ə'minəbəl] o [ə'menəbəl] *adj* dócil; responsable

amend [ə'mend] *tr* enmendar ‖ *intr* enmendarse ‖ **amends** *spl* enmienda; **to make amends for** enmendar

amendment [ə'mendmənt] *s* enmienda

ameni·ty [ə'mɪnɪtɪ] o [ə'menɪtɪ] *s* (*pl* -**ties**) amenidad

America [ə'merɪkə] *s* América

American [ə'merɪkən] *adj & s* americano; norteamericano, estadounidense

Americanize [ə'merɪkə,naɪz] *tr* americanizar

amethyst ['æmɪθɪst] *s* amatista

amiable ['emɪ·əbəl] *adj* amable, bonachón

amicable ['æmɪkəbəl] *adj* amigable

amid [ə'mɪd] *prep* en medio de

amidship [ə'mɪd/ɪp] *adv* en medio del navío

amiss [ə'mɪs] *adj* inoportuno; malo ‖ *adv* inoportunamente; mal; **to take amiss** llevar a mal, tomar en mala parte

ami·ty ['æmɪtɪ] *s* (*pl* -**ties**) amistad

ammeter ['æm,mitər] *s* amperímetro

ammonia [ə'monɪ·ə] *s* amoníaco; agua amoniacal

ammunition [,æmjə'nɪ∫ən] *s* munición

amnes·ty ['æmnɪstɪ] *s* (*pl* -**ties**) amnistía ‖ *v* (*pret & pp* -**tied**) *tr* amnistiar

amoeba [ə'mibə] *s* amiba

among [ə'mʌŋ] *prep* entre, en medio de, en el número de

amorous ['æmərəs] *adj* amoroso; erótico, sensual, voluptuoso

amortize ['æmər,taɪz] *tr* amortizar

amount [ə'maunt] *s* cantidad, importe *m* ‖ *intr* — **to amount to** ascender a; significar

amp. *abbr* **ampere, amperage**

ampere ['æmpɪr] *s* amperio

am'pere-hour' *s* amp·rio-hora *m*

amphibious [æm'fɪbɪ·əs] *adj* anfibio

amphitheater ['æmfɪ,θi·ətər] *s* anfiteatro

ample ['æmpəl] amplio; bastante, suficiente; abundante

amplifier ['æmplɪ,faɪ·ər] s amplificador m

ampli·fy ['æmplɪ,faɪ] v (pret & pp -fied) tr amplificar ‖ intr espaciarse

amplitude ['æmplɪ,tjud] o ['æmplɪ,tud] s amplitud

amplitude modulation s modulación de amplitud

amputate ['æmpjə,tet] tr amputar

amt. abbr amount

amuck [ə'mʌk] adv frenéticamente; **to run amuck** atacar a ciegas

amulet ['æmjəlɪt] s amuleto

amuse [ə'mjuz] tr divertir, entretener

amusement [ə'mjuzmənt] s diversión, entretenimiento; pasatiempo, recreación; (in a park or circus) atracción

amusement park s parque m de atracciones

amusing [ə'mjuzɪŋ] adj divertido, gracioso

an [æn] o [ən] art indef (antes de sonido vocal) un

anachronism [ə'nækrə,nɪzəm] s anacronismo

anaemia [ə'nimɪ·ə] s anemia

anaemic [ə'nimɪk] adj anémico

anaesthesia [,ænɪs'θiʒə] s anestesia

anaesthetic [,ænɪs'θetɪk] adj & s anestésico

anaesthetize [æ'nɛsθɪ,taɪz] tr anestesiar

analogous [ə'næləɡəs] adj análogo

analo·gy [ə'nælədʒɪ] s (pl -gies) analogía

analyse ['ænə,laɪz] tr analizar

analy·sis [ə'nælɪsɪs] s (pl -ses [,siz]) análisis m & f

analyst ['ænəlɪst] s analista mf

analytic(al) [,ænə'lɪtɪk(əl)] adj analítico

analyze ['ænə,laɪz] tr analizar

anarchist ['ænərkɪst] s anarquista mf

anarchy ['ænərkɪ] s anarquía

anathema [ə'næθɪmə] s anatema m & f

anatomic(al) [,ænə'tɑmɪk(əl)] adj anatómico

anato·my [ə'nætəmɪ] s (pl -mies) anatomía

ancestor ['ænsɛstər] s antecesor m, antepasado

ances·try ['ænsɛstrɪ] s (pl -tries) abolengo, alcurnia

anchor ['æŋkər] s ancla, áncora; (fig) áncora; **to cast anchor** echar anclas; **to weigh anchor** levar anclas ‖ tr sujetar con el ancla ‖ intr anclar, ancorar

ancho·vy ['æntʃovɪ] s (pl -vies) anchoa

ancient ['enʃənt] adj antiguo

and [ænd] o [ənd] conj y; **and so forth** y así sucesivamente

Andalusia [,ændə'luʒə] s Andalucía

Andalusian [,ændə'luʒən] adj & s andaluz m

Andean [æn'di·ən] o ['ændɪ·ən] adj & s andino

Andes ['ændiz] spl Andes mpl

andirons ['ænd,aɪ·ərnz] spl morillos

anecdote ['ænɪk,dot] s anécdota

anemia [ə'nimɪ·ə] s anemia

anemic [ə'nimɪk] adj anémico

aneroid barometer ['ænə,rɔɪd] s barómetro aneroide

anesthesia [,ænɪs'θiʒə] s anestesia

anesthetic [,ænɪs'θetɪk] adj & s anestésico

anesthetize [æ'nɛsθɪ,taɪz] tr anestesiar

aneurysm ['ænjə,rɪzəm] s aneurisma m

anew [ə'nju] o [ə'nu] adv de nuevo, nuevamente

angel ['endʒəl] s ángel m; (financial backer) caballo blanco

angelic(al) [æn'dʒelɪk(əl)] adj angélico, angelical

anger ['æŋɡər] s cólera, ira ‖ tr encolerizar, airar

angina pectoris [æn'dʒaɪnə 'pɛktərɪs] s angina de pecho

angle ['æŋɡəl] s ángulo; punto de vista ‖ intr pescar con caña; intrigar

angle iron s ángulo de hierro, hierro angular

angler ['æŋɡlər] s pescador m de caña; intrigante mf

Anglo-Saxon [,æŋɡlo'sæksən] adj & s anglosajón m

an·gry ['æŋɡrɪ] adj (comp -grier; super -griest) encolerizado, airado; (pathol) inflamado, irritado; **to become angry at** enojarse de; **to become angry with** enojarse con o contra

anguish ['æŋɡwɪʃ] s angustia, congoja

angular ['æŋɡjələr] adj angular; (features) anguloso

anhydrous [æn'haɪdrəs] adj anhidro

aniline dyes ['ænɪlɪn] o ['ænɪ,laɪn] s colores mpl de anilina

animal ['ænɪməl] adj & s animal m

animal spirits spl ardor m, vigor m, vivacidad

animated cartoon ['ænɪ,metɪd] s película de dibujos, dibujo animado

animation [,ænɪ'meʃən] s animación

animosi·ty [,ænɪ'mɑsɪtɪ] s (pl -ties) animosidad

anion ['æn,aɪ·ən] s anión m

anise ['ænɪs] s anís m

aniseed ['ænɪ,sid] s grano de anís

anisette [,ænɪ'zɛt] s anisete m

ankle ['æŋkəl] s tobillo

an'kle·bone s hueso del tobillo

ankle support s tobillera

anklet ['æŋklɪt] s ajorca; (sock) tobillera

annals ['ænəlz] spl anales mpl

anneal [ə'nil] tr recocer

annex ['ænɛks] s anexo; (of a building) pabellón m ‖ [ə'nɛks] tr anexar

annihilate [ə'naɪ·ɪ,let] tr aniquilar

anniversa·ry [,ænɪ'vʌrsərɪ] adj aniversario ‖ s (pl -ries) aniversario

annotate ['ænə,tet] tr anotar

announce [ə'naʊns] tr anunciar

announcement [ə'naʊnsmənt] s anuncio

announcer [ə'naʊnsər] s anunciador m; (rad) locutor m

annoy [ə'nɔɪ] tr fastidiar, molestar

annoyance [ə'nɔɪ·əns] s fastidio, molestia

annoying [ə'nɔɪ·ɪŋ] adj fastidioso, molesto

annual ['ænjʊ·əl] adj anual ‖ s publicación anual; planta anual

annui·ty [ə'nju·ɪtɪ] o [ə'nu·ɪtɪ] s (*pl* -ties) anualidad; renta vitalicia

an·nul [ə'nʌl] v (*pret & pp* -nulled; *ger* -nulling) *tr* anular, invalidar

anode ['ænod] s ánodo

anoint [ə'nɔɪnt] *tr* ungir, untar

anomalous [ə'nɑməLəs] *adj* anómalo

anoma·ly [ə'nɑməlɪ] s (*pl* -lies) anomalía

anon. *abbr* anonymous

anonymity [ˌænə'nɪmɪtɪ] s anónimo; **to preserve one's anonymity** guardar o conservar el anónimo

anonymous [ə'nɑnɪməs] *adj* anónimo

another [ə'nʌðər] *adj & pron indef* otro

ans. *abbr* answer

answer ['ænsər] o ['ɑnsər] s contestación, respuesta; (*to a problem or puzzle*) solución ‖ *tr* contestar, responder; resolver (*un problema o un enigma*) ‖ *intr* contestar, responder; **to answer for** responder de (*una cosa*); responder por (*una persona*)

ant [ænt] s hormiga

antagonism [æn'tægə͵nɪzəm] s antagonismo

antagonize [æn'tægə͵naɪz] *tr* oponerse a; enemistar, enajenar

antarctic [ænt'ɑrktɪk] *adj* antártico ‖ **the Antarctic** las Tierras Antárticas

antecedent [ˌæntɪ'sidənt] *adj* antecedente ‖ s antecedente m; **antecedents** antecedentes *mpl*; antepasados

antechamber ['æntɪ͵tʃembər] s antecámara

antedate ['æntɪ͵det] *tr* antedatar; preceder

antelope ['æntɪ͵lop] s antílope m

anten·na [æn'tɛnə] s (*pl* -nae [ni]) (ent) antena ‖ s (*pl* -nas) (rad) antena

antepenult [ˌæntɪ'pinʌlt] s antepenúltima

anteroom ['æntɪ͵rum] o ['æntɪ͵rʊm] s antecámara

anthem ['ænθəm] s himno; antífona

ant'hill s hormiguero

antholo·gy [æn'θɑlədʒɪ] s (*pl* -gies) antología

anthracite ['ænθrə͵saɪt] s antracita

anthrax ['ænθræks] s ántrax m

anthropology [ˌænθrə'pɑlədʒɪ] s antropología

anti-aircraft [ˌæntɪ'er͵kræft] o [ˌæntɪ'er͵krɑft] *adj* antiaéreo

antibiotic [ˌæntɪbaɪ'ɑtɪk] *adj & s* antibiótico

antibod·y ['æntɪ͵bɑdɪ] s (*pl* -ies) anticuerpo

anticipate [æn'tɪsɪ͵pet] *tr* esperar, prever; anticipar; (*to get ahead of*) anticiparse a; impedir; prometerse (*p. ej., un placer*); temerse (*algo desagradable*)

antics ['æntɪks] *spl* cabriolas, gracias, travesuras

antidote ['æntɪ͵dot] s antídoto

antifreeze [ˌæntɪ'friz] s anticongelante m

antiglare [ˌæntɪ'gler] *adj* antideslumbrante

antiknock [ˌæntɪ'nɑk] *adj & s* antidetonante m

antilabor [ˌæntɪ'lebər] *adj* antiobrero

Antilles [æn'tɪlɪz] *spl* Antillas

antimissile [ˌæntɪ'mɪsɪl] *adj* antiproyectil

antimony ['æntɪ͵moni] s antimonio

antipas·to [ˌæntɪ'pɑsto] s (*pl* -tos) aperitivo, entremés m

antipa·thy [æn'tɪpəθɪ] s (*pl* -thies) antipatía

antiquar·y ['æntɪ͵kweri] s (*pl* -ies) anticuario

antiquated ['æntɪ͵kwetɪd] *adj* anticuado

antique [æn'tik] *adj* antiguo ‖ s antigüedad

antique dealer s anticuario

antique store s tienda de antigüedades

antiqui·ty [æn'tɪkwɪtɪ] s (*pl* -ties) antigüedad

anti-Semitic [ˌæntɪsɪ'mɪtɪk] *adj* antisemítico

antiseptic [ˌæntɪ'septɪk] *adj & s* antiséptico

antislavery [ˌæntɪ'slevərɪ] *adj* antiesclavista

anti-Soviet [ˌæntɪ'sovɪ͵ɛt] *adj* antisoviético

antitank [ˌæntɪ'tæŋk] *adj* antitanque

antithe·sis [æn'tɪθɪsɪs] s (*pl* -ses [͵siz]) antítesis f

antitoxin [ˌæntɪ'tɑksɪn] s antitoxina

antitrust [ˌæntɪ'trʌst] *adj* anticartel

antiwar [ˌæntɪ'wɔr] *adj* antibélico

antler ['æntlər] s cuerna

antonym ['æntənɪm] s antónimo

Antwerp ['æntwərp] s Amberes f

anvil ['ænvɪl] s yunque m

anxie·ty [æŋ'zaɪ·ətɪ] s (*pl* -ties) ansiedad, inquietud; ansia, anhelo

anxious ['æŋk/əs] *adj* ansioso, inquieto; anhelante; **to be anxious to** tener ganas de

any ['eni] *adj indef* algún, cualquier; todo; **any place** dondequiera; **any time** cuando quiera; alguna vez ‖ *pron indef* alguno, cualquiera ‖ *adv* algo

an'y·bod'y *pron indef* alguno, alguien, cualquiera, quienquiera; todo el mundo; **not anybody** nadie

an'y·how' *adv* de cualquier modo; de todos modos; sin embargo

an'y·one' *pron indef* alguno, alguien, cualquiera

an'y·thing *pron indef* algo, alguna cosa; cualquier cosa; todo cuanto; **anything at all** cualquier cosa que sea; **anything else** cualquier otra cosa; **anything else?** ¿algo más?; **not anything** nada

an'y·way' *adv* de cualquier modo; de todos modos; sin embargo; sin esmero, sin orden ni concierto

an'y·where' *adv* dondequiera; adondequiera; **not anywhere** en ninguna parte

apace [ə'pes] *adv* aprisa

apart [ə'pɑrt] *adv* aparte; en pedazos; **to fall apart** caerse a pedazos; desunirse; ir al desastre; **to live apart**

vivir separados; **vivir aislado**; **to stand apart** mantenerse apartado; **to take apart** descomponer, desarmar, desmontar; **to tell apart** distinguir
apartment [ə'partmənt] s apartamento
apartment house s casa de pisos
apathetic [‚æpə'θetɪk] adj apático
apa·thy ['æpəθi] s (pl -ties) apatía
ape [ep] s mono ‖ tr imitar, remedar
aperture ['æpərtʃər] s abertura, orificio
apex ['epɛks] s (pl **apexes** o **apices** ['æpɪ‚siz]) ápex m, ápice m
aphorism ['æfə‚rɪzəm] s aforismo
aphrodisiac [‚æfrə'dɪzɪ‚æk] adj & s afrodisíaco
apiar·y ['epɪ‚ɛri] s (pl -ies) abejar m, colmenar m
apiece [ə'pis] adv cada uno; por persona
apish ['epɪʃ] adj monesco; tonto
aplomb [ə'plam] s aplomo, sangre fría
apogee ['æpə‚dʒi] s apogeo
apologetic [ə‚palə'dʒɛtɪk] adj lleno de excusas
apologize [ə'palə‚dʒaɪz] intr excusarse, disculparse; **to apologize for** disculparse de; **to apologize to** disculparse con
apolo·gy [ə'palədʒi] s (pl -gies) excusa; (makeshift) expediente m
apoplectic [‚æpə'plɛktɪk] adj & s apopléctico
apoplexy ['æpə‚plɛksi] s apoplejía
apostle [ə'pasəl] s apóstol m
apostrophe [ə'pastrəfi] s (written sign) apóstrofo; (words addressed to absent person) apóstrofe m & f
apothecar·y [ə'paθɪ‚kɛri] s (pl -ies) boticario
apothecary's jar s bote m de porcelana
apothecary's shop s botica
appall [ə'pɔl] tr espantar, pasmar
appalling [ə'pɔlɪŋ] adj aterrador, espantoso, pasmoso
appara·tus [‚æpə'retəs] o [‚æpə'rætəs] s (pl -tus o -tuses) aparato
apparel [ə'pærəl] s indumentaria, vestido
apparent [ə'pærənt] o [ə'perənt] adj aparente
apparition [‚æpə'rɪʃən] s aparición
appeal [ə'pil] s súplica, instancia, solicitud; atracción, interés m; (law) apelación ‖ intr ser atrayente; **to appeal to** (to make an entreaty to) suplicar; (to be attractive to) atraer, interesar; (law) apelar a
appear [ə'pɪr] intr (to come into sight; to be in sight; to be published) aparecer; (to come into sight; to be in sight; to look; to seem) parecer; (to come before the public) presentarse; (to come before a court) comparecer
appearance [ə'pɪrəns] s (act of appearing) aparición; (outward look) apariencia, aspecto; (law) comparecencia
appease [ə'piz] tr apaciguar
appeasement [ə'pizmənt] s apaciguamiento

appendage [ə'pɛndɪdʒ] s apéndice m
appendicitis [ə‚pɛndɪ'saɪtɪs] s apendicitis f
appen·dix [ə'pɛndɪks] s (pl -dixes o -dices [dɪ‚siz]) apéndice m
appertain [‚æpər'ten] intr relacionarse
appetite ['æpɪ‚tart] s apetito
appetizer ['æpɪ‚taɪzər] s aperitivo, apetite m
appetizing ['æpɪ‚taɪzɪŋ] adj apetitoso
applaud [ə'plɔd] tr & intr aplaudir
applause [ə'plɔz] s aplauso, aplausos
apple ['æpəl] s manzana
ap'ple·jack' s aguardiente m de manzana
apple of the eye s niña del ojo
apple pie s pastel m de manzana
apple polisher s (slang) quitamotas mf
ap'ple·sauce' s compota de manzanas; (slang) música celestial
apple tree s manzano
appliance [ə'plaɪ‚əns] s artificio, dispositivo, aparato; aplicación
applicant ['æplɪkənt] s aspirante mf, pretendiente mf, solicitante mf
ap·ply [ə'plaɪ] v (pret & pp -plied) tr aplicar ‖ intr aplicarse; dirigirse; **to apply for** pedir, solicitar
appoint [ə'pɔɪnt] tr designar, nombrar; señalar; amueblar
appointment [ə'pɔɪntmənt] s designación, nombramiento; empleo, puesto; cita; **appointments** instalación, accesorios, adornos; **by appointment** cita previa
apportion [ə'porʃən] tr prorratear
appraisal [ə'prezəl] s tasación, valoración, apreciación
appraise [ə'prez] tr tasar, valorar, apreciar
appreciable [ə'priʃɪ‚əbəl] adj apreciable; sensible
appreciate [ə'priʃɪ‚et] tr apreciar; aprobar; comprender; estar agradecido por ‖ intr subir de valor
appreciation [ə‚priʃɪ'eʃən] s aprecio; agradecimiento; plusvalía, aumento de valor
appreciative [ə'priʃɪ‚etɪv] adj apreciador; agradecido
apprehend [‚æprɪ'hɛnd] tr aprehender, prender; comprender; temer
apprehension [‚æprɪ'hɛnʃən] s aprehensión; (fear, worry) aprensión; comprensión
apprehensive [‚æprɪ'hɛnsɪv] adj (fearful, worried) aprehensivo, aprensivo
apprentice [ə'prɛntɪs] s aprendiz m, meritorio ‖ tr poner de aprendiz
apprenticeship [ə'prɛntɪs‚ʃɪp] s aprendizaje m
apprise o **apprize** [ə'praɪz] tr informar; apreciar, tasar
approach [ə'protʃ] s acercamiento; vía de entrada; proposición; (to a problem) enfoque m ‖ tr abordar, acercarse a; (to bring closer) acercar ‖ intr acercarse, aproximarse
approbation [‚æprə'beʃən] s aprobación
appropriate [ə'proprɪ‚ɪt] adj apropiado, a propósito ‖ [ə'proprɪ‚et] tr

apropiarse; asignar, destinar (el parlamento determinada suma a un determinado fin)

approval [ə'pruvəl] s aprobación; **on approval** a prueba

approve [ə'pruv] tr & intr aprobar

approximate [ə'praksɪmɪt] adj aproximado || [ə'praksɪ,met] tr aproximar || intr aproximarse

apricot [ˈeprɪ,kɑt] o [ˈæprɪ,kɑt] s albaricoque m

apricot tree s albaricoquero

April [ˈeprɪl] s abril m

April fool s — **to make an April fool of** coger por inocente

April Fools' Day s día m de engañabobos, primer día de abril, en que se coge por inocente a la gente

apron [ˈeprən] s delantal m; (of a workman) mandil m; **tied to the apron strings of** cosido a las faldas de

apropos [,æprə'po] adj oportuno || adv a propósito; **apropos of** a propósito de

apse [æps] s ábside m

apt [æpt] adj apto; a propósito; dispuesto, inclinado

aptitude [ˈæptɪ,tjud] o [ˈæptɪ,tud] s aptitud

aquamarine [ˈækwəmə'rin] s aguamarina

aquaplane [ˈækwə,plen] s acuaplano || intr correr en acuaplano

aquari·um [ə'kwɛrɪ·əm] s (pl -ums o -a [ə]) acuario

aquatic [ə'kwætɪk] o [ə'kwɑtɪk] adj acuático || **aquatics** spl deportes acuáticos

aqueduct [ˈækwə,dʌkt] s acueducto

aquiline nose [ˈækwɪ,laɪn] s nariz aguileña

Arab [ˈærəb] adj árabe || s árabe mf; caballo árabe

Arabia [ə'rebɪ·ə] s la Arabia

Arabian [ə'rebɪ·ən] adj árabe; arábigo || s árabe mf

Arabic [ˈærəbɪk] adj arábigo || s árabe m, arábigo

Aragon [ˈærə,gɑn] s Aragón m

Arago·nese [,ærəgə'niz] adj aragonés || s (pl -nese) aragonés m

arbiter [ˈarbɪtər] s árbitro

arbitrary [ˈarbɪ,treri] adj arbitrario

arbitrate [ˈarbɪ,tret] tr & intr arbitrar

arbitration [,arbɪ'tre/ən] s arbitraje m

arbor [ˈarbər] s emparrado, glorieta

arbore·tum [,arbə'ritəm] s (pl -tums o -ta [tə]) jardín botánico de árboles

arbor vitae [ˈarbər 'vaɪti] s árbol m de la vida

arbutus [ar'bjutəs] s madroño

arc [ɑrk] s arco

arcade [ar'ked] s arcada, galería

arch. abbr archaic, archaism, archipelago, architect

arch [ɑrt/] adj astuto; travieso; principal || s arco || tr arquear, enarcar; atravesar

archaeology [,arkɪ'alədʒi] s arqueología

archaic [ar'ke·ɪk] adj arcaico

archaism [ˈarke,ɪzəm] o [ˈarki,ɪzəm] s arcaísmo

archangel [ˈark,endʒəl] s arcángel m

archbishop [ˈart/'bɪ/əp] s arzobispo

archduke [ˈart/'djuk] o [ˈart/'duk] s archiduque m

archene·my [ˈart/,ɛnimi] s (pl -mies) archienemigo

archeology [,arkɪ'alədʒi] s arqueología

archer [ˈart/ər] s arquero, flechero

archery [ˈart/əri] s tiro de flechas

archipela·go [,arkɪ'peləgo] s (pl -gos o -goes) archipiélago

architect [ˈarkɪ,tɛkt] s arquitecto

architectural [,arkɪ'tɛkt/ərəl] adj arquitectónico, arquitectural

architecture [ˈarkɪ,tɛkt/ər] s arquitectura

archives [ˈarkaɪvz] spl archivo

arch'way' s arcada

arc lamp s lámpara de arco

arctic [ˈarktɪk] adj ártico || **the Arctic** las Tierras Árticas

arc welding s soldadura de arco

ardent [ˈardənt] adj ardiente

ardor [ˈardər] s ardor m

arduous [ˈardʒʊ·əs] o [ˈardʒʊ·əs] adj arduo, difícil; enérgico; (steep) escarpado

area [ˈɛrɪ·ə] s área, superficie f; comarca, región; zona; patio

ar'ea·way' s entrada baja de un sótano

Argentina [,ardʒən'tinə] s la Argentina

Argentine [ˈardʒən,tin] o [ˈardʒən,taɪn] adj & s argentino || **the Argentine** la Argentina

Argentinean [,ardʒən'tɪnɪ·ən] adj & s argentino

Argonaut [ˈargə,nɔt] s argonauta m

argue [ˈargju] tr argüir; **to argue into** persuadir a + inf; **to argue out of** disuadir de + inf || intr argüir

argument [ˈargjəmənt] s argumento; disputa

argumentative [,argjə'mentətɪv] adj argumentativo

aria [ˈarɪ·ə] o [ˈɛrɪ·ə] s (mus) aria

arid [ˈærɪd] adj árido

aridity [ə'rɪdɪti] s aridez f

aright [ə'raɪt] adv acertadamente; **to set aright** rectificar

arise [ə'raɪz] v (pret **arose** [ə'roz]; pp **arisen** [ə'rɪzən]) intr levantarse; subir; aparecer; **to arise from** provenir de

aristocra·cy [,ærɪs'takrəsi] s (pl -cies) aristocracia

aristocrat [ə'rɪstə,kræt] s aristócrata mf

aristocratic [ə,rɪstə'krætɪk] adj aristocrático

Aristotelian [,ærɪstə'tilɪ·ən] adj & s aristotélico

Aristotle [ˈærɪ,tatəl] s Aristóteles m

arith. abbr arithmetic

arithmetic [ə'rɪθmətɪk] s aritmética

arithmetical [,ærɪθ'metɪkəl] adj aritmético

arithmetician [ə,rɪθmə'tɪ/ən] s aritmético

ark [ɑrk] s arca de Noé

ark of the covenant *s* arca de la alianza

arm [ɑrm] *s* brazo; (*weapon*) arma; **arm in arm** de bracero, asidos del brazo; **in arms** de pecho, de teta; **the three arms of the service** los tres ejércitos; **to be up in arms** estar en armas; **to keep at arm's length** mantener a distancia; mantenerse a distancia; **to lay down one's arms** rendir las armas; **to rise up in arms** alzarse en armas; **under arms** sobre las armas || *tr* armar || *intr* armarse

armament ['ɑrməmənt] *s* armamento

armature ['ɑrmə,tʃər] *s* armadura; (*of a dynamo or motor*) (elec) inducido

arm'chair' *adj* de gabinete || *s* butaca, sillón *m*, silla de brazos

Armenian [ɑr'mini·ən] *adj & s* armenio

armful ['ɑrm,ful] *s* brazado

arm'hole' *s* (*in clothing*) sobaquera

armistice ['ɑrmɪstɪs] *s* armisticio

armor ['ɑrmər] *s* armadura; coraza, blindaje *m* || *tr* acorazar, blindar

armored car *s* carro blindado

armorial bearings [ɑr'mori·əl] *spl* blasón *m*, escudo de armas

armor plate *s* plancha de blindaje

ar'mor-plate' *tr* acorazar, blindar

armor·y ['ɑrməri] *s* (*pl* -ies) arsenal *m*; (*arms factory*) armería

arm'pit' *s* sobaco, hueco de la axila

arm'rest' *s* apoyabrazos *m*

ar·my ['ɑrmi] *adj* militar, castrense || *s* (*pl* -mies) ejército

army corps *s* cuerpo de ejército

aroma [ə'romə] *s* aroma *m*, fragancia

aromatic [,ærə'mætɪk] *adj* aromático

around [ə'raʊnd] *adv* alrededor, a la redonda; en la dirección opuesta || *prep* alrededor de, en torno a o de; cerca de; (*the corner*) a la vuelta de

arouse [ə'raʊz] *tr* despertar, excitar, incitar

arpeg·gio [ɑr'pedʒo] *s* (*pl* -gios) arpegio

arraign [ə'ren] *tr* acusar; presentar al tribunal

arrange [ə'rendʒ] *tr* arreglar, disponer; (mus) adaptar, refundir

array [ə're] *s* orden *m*; orden *m* de batalla; adorno, atavío || *tr* poner en orden; poner en orden de batalla; adornar, ataviar

arrears [ə'rɪrz] *spl* atrasos; **in arrears** atrasado en pagos

arrest [ə'rest] *s* arresto, prisión; detención; **under arrest** bajo arresto || *tr* arrestar; detener; atraer (*la atención*)

arresting [ə'restɪŋ] *adj* impresionante

arrival [ə'raɪvəl] *s* llegada; (*person*) llegado

arrive [ə'raɪv] *intr* llegar; tener éxito

arrogance ['ærəgəns] *s* arrogancia

arrogant ['ærəgənt] *adj* arrogante

arrogate ['ærə,get] *tr* — **to arrogate to oneself** arrogarse

arrow ['æro] *s* flecha

ar'row·head' *s* punta de flecha; (bot) saetilla

arsenal ['ɑrsənəl] *s* arsenal *m*

arsenic ['ɑrsnɪk] *s* arsénico

arson ['ɑrsən] *s* incendio premeditado, delito de incendio

art [ɑrt] *s* arte *m & f*

arter·y ['ɑrtəri] *s* (*pl* -ies) arteria

artful ['ɑrtfəl] *adj* astuto, mañoso; diestro, ingenioso

arthritic [ɑr'θrɪtɪk] *adj & s* artrítico

arthritis [ɑr'θraɪtɪs] *s* artritis *f*

artichoke ['ɑrtɪ,tʃok] *s* alcachofa

article ['ɑrtɪkəl] *s* artículo; **an article of clothing** una prenda de vestir

articulate [ɑr'tɪkjəlɪt] *adj* claro, distinto; capaz de hablar || [ɑr'tɪkjə,let] *tr* articular

artifact ['ɑrtɪ,fækt] *s* artefacto

artifice ['ɑrtɪfɪs] *s* artificio

artificial [,ɑrtɪ'fɪʃəl] *adj* artificial

artillery [ɑr'tɪləri] *s* artillería

artillery·man [ɑr'tɪlərimən] *s* (*pl* -men [mən]) artillero

artisan ['ɑrtɪzən] *s* artesano

artist ['ɑrtɪst] *s* artista *mf*

artistic [ɑr'tɪstɪk] *adj* artístico

artistry ['ɑrtɪstri] *s* habilidad artística

artless ['ɑrtlɪs] *adj* sencillo, natural; ingenuo, inocente; (*crude, clumsy*) chabacano

arts and crafts *spl* artes y oficios

art·y ['ɑrti] *adj* (*comp* -ier; *super* -iest) (coll) ostentosamente artístico

Aryan ['eri·ən] o ['ɑrjən] *adj & s* ario

as [æz] o [əz] *pron rel* que; **the same as** el mismo que || *adv* tan; **as . . . as** tan . . . como; **as for** en cuanto a; **as long as** mientras que; ya que; **as many as** tantos como; **as much as** tanto como; **as regards** en cuanto a; **as soon as** tan pronto como; **as soon as possible** cuanto antes, lo más pronto posible; **as though** como si; **as to** en cuanto a; **as well** también; **as yet** hasta ahora a; **|| conj** como; que; ya que; a medida que; **as it seems** por lo visto, según parece || *prep* por, como; **as a rule** por regla general

asbestos [æs'bestəs] *s* asbesto, amianto

ascend [ə'send] *tr* subir a (*p.ej., el trono*) || *intr* ascender

ascendancy [ə'sendənsi] *s* ascendiente *m*

ascension [ə'senʃən] *s* ascensión

Ascension Day *s* fiesta de la Ascensión

ascent [ə'sent] *s* ascensión, subida; ascenso, promoción

ascertain [,æsər'ten] *tr* averiguar

ascertainable [,æsər'tenəbəl] *adj* averiguable

ascetic [ə'setɪk] *adj* ascético || *s* asceta *mf*

ascorbic acid [ə'skɔrbɪk] *s* ácido ascórbico

ascribe [ə'skraɪb] *tr* atribuir

aseptic [ə'septɪk] o [e'septɪk] *adj* aséptico

ash [æʃ] *s* ceniza; (*tree; wood*) fresno; **ashes** ceniza, cenizas; (*mortal remains*) cenizas

ashamed [ə'ʃemd] *adj* avergonzado; **to be ashamed** tener vergüenza

ashlar ['æʃlər] *s* sillar *m*

ashore [ə'ʃor] *adv* en tierra, a tierra

ash tray *s* cenicero
Ash Wednesday *s* miércoles *m* de ceniza
Asia ['eʒə] o ['eʃə] *s* Asia
Asia Minor *s* el Asia Menor
Asian ['eʒən] o ['eʃən] o **Asiatic** [,eʒɪ'ætɪk] o [,eʃɪ'ætɪk] *adj* & *s* asiático
aside [ə'saɪd] *adv* aparte; **aside from** además de; **to step aside** hacerse a un lado ‖ *s* (theat) aparte *m*
asinine ['æsɪ,naɪn] *adj* tonto, necio
ask [æsk] *tr* (*to request*) pedir; (*to inquire of*) preguntar; hacer (*una pregunta*); invitar; **to ask in** invitar a entrar ‖ *intr* — **to ask about, after,** or **for** preguntar por; **to ask for** pedir
askance [ə'skæns] *adv* al sesgo, de soslayo; con desdén, sospechosamente
asleep [ə'slip] *adj* dormido; **to fall asleep** dormirse
asp [æsp] *s* áspid *m*
asparagus [ə'spærəgəs] *s* espárrago
aspect ['æspekt] *s* aspecto
aspen ['æspən] *s* tiemblo, álamo temblón
aspersion [ə'spʌrʒən] o [ə'spʌrʃən] *s* calumnia, difamación
asphalt ['æsfɔlt] o ['æsfælt] *s* asfalto ‖ *tr* asfaltar
asphyxiate [æs'fɪksɪ,et] *tr* asfixiar
aspirant [ə'spaɪrənt] o ['æspɪrənt] *s* pretendiente *mf*, candidato
aspire [ə'spaɪr] *intr* aspirar
aspirin ['æspɪrɪn] *s* aspirina
ass [æs] *s* asno
assail [ə'sel] *tr* asaltar, acometer
assassin [ə'sæsɪn] *s* asesino
assassinate [ə'sæsɪ,net] *tr* asesinar
assassination [ə,sæsɪ'neʃən] *s* asesinato
assault [ə'sɔlt] *s* asalto ‖ *tr* asaltar
assault and battery *s* vías de hecho, violencias
assay [ə'se] o ['æse] *s* ensaye *m*; muestra de ensaye ‖ [ə'se] *tr* ensayar; apreciar
assemble [ə'sembəl] *tr* reunir; (mach) armar, montar ‖ *intr* reunirse
assem·bly [ə'semblɪ] *s* (pl **-blies**) asamblea; reunión; (mach) armadura, montaje *m*
assembly hall *s* aula magna, paraninfo; salón *m* de sesiones
assembly line *s* línea de montaje
assembly plant *s* fábrica de montaje
assembly room *s* sala de reunión; (mach) taller *m* de montaje
assent [ə'sɛnt] *s* asentimiento, asenso ‖ *intr* asentir
assert [ə'sʌrt] *tr* afirmar, aseverar, declarar; **to assert oneself** imponerse, hacer valer sus derechos
assertion [ə'sʌrʃən] *s* aserción, aseveración
assess [ə'sɛs] *tr* amillarar, gravar; fijar (*daños y perjuicios*); apreciar, estimar
assessment [ə'sɛsmənt] *s* amillaramiento, gravamen *m*; fijación; apreciación, estimación

asset ['æsɛt] *s* posesión, ventaja; (*person, thing,* or *quality worth having*) (fig) valor *m*; **assets** (com) activo
assiduous [ə'sɪdʒu·əs] o [ə'sɪdju·əs] *adj* asiduo
assign [ə'saɪn] *tr* asignar
assignment [ə'saɪnmənt] *s* asignación, cometido; lección
assimilate [ə'sɪmɪ,let] *tr* asimilarse (*los alimentos, el conocimiento*) ‖ *intr* asimilarse
assist [ə'sɪst] *tr* ayudar, asistir, auxiliar
assistant [ə'sɪstənt] *adj* & *s* auxiliar *mf*, ayudante *mf*
assn. *abbr* **association**
associate [ə'soʃɪ·ɪt] o [ə'soʃɪ,et] *adj* asociado ‖ *s* asociado, socio ‖ [ə'soʃɪ,et] *tr* asociar ‖ *intr* asociarse
association [ə,soʃɪ'eʃən] *s* asociación
assort [ə'sɔrt] *tr* clasificar, ordenar
assortment [ə'sɔrtmənt] *s* surtido; clase *f*, grupo
asst. *abbr* **assistant**
assume [ə'sum] o [ə'sjum] *tr* asumir (*p.ej., responsabilidades*); arrogarse; suponer, dar por sentado
assumption [ə'sʌmpʃən] *s* asunción; suposición
assurance [ə'ʃurəns] *s* aseguramiento; seguridad, confianza; (com) seguro
assure [ə'ʃur] *tr* asegurar; (com) asegurar
Assyria [ə'sɪrɪ·ə] *s* Asiria
Assyrian [ə'sɪrɪ·ən] *adj* & *s* asirio
astatine ['æstə,tin] *s* ástato
aster ['æstər] *s* (bot) aster *m*; (*China aster*) reina Margarita
asterisk ['æstə,rɪsk] *s* asterisco
astern [ə'stʌrn] *adv* por la popa
asthma ['æzmə] o ['æsmə] *s* asma *f*
astonish [ə'stɑnɪʃ] *tr* asombrar
astonishing [ə'stɑnɪʃɪŋ] *adj* asombroso
astound [ə'staund] *tr* pasmar
astounding [ə'staundɪŋ] *adj* pasmoso
astraddle [ə'strædəl] *adv* a horcajadas
astray [ə'stre] *adv* por mal camino; **to go astray** extraviarse; **to lead astray** extraviar
astride [ə'straɪd] *adv* a horcajadas ‖ *prep* a horcajadas de
astrology [ə'strɑlədʒɪ] *s* astrología
astronaut ['æstrə,nɔt] *s* astronauta *m*
astronautic [,æstrə'nɔtɪk] *adj* astronáutico ‖ **astronautics** *s* astronáutica
astronomer [ə'strɑnəmər] *s* astrónomo
astronomic(al) [,æstrə'nɑmɪk(əl)] *adj* astronómico
astronomy [ə'strɑnəmɪ] *s* astronomía
Asturian [æs'stʊrɪ·ən] *adj* & *s* asturiano
astute [ə'stjut] o [ə'stut] *adj* astuto, sagaz
asunder [ə'sʌndər] *adv* a pedazos, en dos
asylum [ə'saɪləm] *s* asilo
asymmetry [ə'sɪmɪtrɪ] *s* asimetría
at [æt] o [ət] *prep* en, por; **I saw her at the library** la ví en la biblioteca; a, p.ej., **at five o'clock** a las cinco; de, p.ej., **to be surprised at** estar sorprendido de; **to laugh at** reírse de; en casa de, p.ej., **at John's** en casa de Juan

atheism ['eθɪ,ɪzəm] s ateísmo
atheist ['eθɪ·ɪst] s ateísta *mf*, ateo
mf
Athenian [ə'θinɪ·ən] *adj* & s ateniense
Athens ['æθɪnz] s Atenas *f*
athlete ['æθlit] s atleta *mf*
athlete's foot s pie *m* de atleta
athletic [æθ'letɪk] *adj* atlético ‖ **ath-**
letics s atletismo
Atlantic [æt'læntɪk] *adj* & s Atlántico
atlas ['ætləs] s atlas *m*
atmosphere ['ætməs,fɪr] s atmósfera
atmospheric [,ætməs'ferɪk] *adj* atmos-
férico ‖ **atmospherics** *spl* parásitos
atmosféricos
atom ['ætəm] s átomo
atom bomb s bomba atómica
atomic [ə'tamɪk] *adj* atómico
atomic bomb s bomba atómica
atomic weight s peso atómico
atomize ['ætə,maɪz] *tr* atomizar
atomizer ['ætə,maɪzər] s pulverizador
m, vaporizador *m*
atom smasher s rompeátomos *m*
atone [ə'ton] *intr* dar reparación; **to**
atone for dar reparación por, expiar
atonement [ə'tonmənt] s reparación,
expiación
atop [ə'tap] *adv* encima ‖ *prep* encima
de
atrocious [ə'troʃəs] *adj* atroz; (coll)
abominable, muy malo
atroci·ty [ə'trasɪti] s *pl* **-ties**) atrocidad
atro·phy ['ætrəfɪ] s atrofia ‖ *v* (*pret*
& *pp* **-phied**) *tr* atrofiar ‖ *intr* atro-
fiarse
attach [ə'tætʃ] *tr* atar, ligar; atribuir
(*p.ej., importancia*); (law) embargar;
to be attached to aficionarse a; (*to*
be officially associated with) depender de
attaché [,ætə'ʃe] o [ə'tæʃe] s agregado
attachment [ə'tætʃmənt] s atadura,
enlace *m*; atribución; apego, cariño;
accesorio; (law) embargo
attack [ə'tæk] s ataque *m* ‖ *tr* & *intr*
atacar
attain [ə'ten] *tr* alcanzar, lograr
attainment [ə'tenmənt] s consecución,
logro; **attainments** dotes *fpl*, prendas
attempt [ə'tempt] s tentativa; (*assault*)
atentado, conato ‖ *tr* procurar, intentar; (*e.g., the life of a person*)
atentar a o contra
attend [ə'tend] *tr* atender, asistir; asistir a (*p.ej., la escuela*); auxiliar (*a*
un moribundo) ‖ *intr* atender; **to at-**
tend to atender a
attendance [ə'tendəns] s asistencia,
concurrencia; **to dance attendance**
hacer antesala
attendant [ə'tendənt] *adj* & s asistente
mf; concomitante *m*
attention [ə'tenʃən] s atención; **to at-**
tract attention llamar la atención; **to**
call attention to hacer presente; **to**
pay attention to hacer caso de
attentive [ə'tentɪv] *adj* atento
attenuate [ə'tenju,et] *tr* adelgazar; debilitar ‖ *intr* debilitarse; desaparecer

attest [ə'test] *tr* atestiguar; juramentar
‖ *intr* dar fe; **to attest to** dar fe de
attic ['ætɪk] s buharda, guardilla, desván *m*
attire [ə'taɪr] s atavío, traje *m* ‖ *tr*
ataviar, vestir
attitude ['ætɪ,tjud] o ['ætɪ,tud] s actitud, ademán *m*
attorney [ə'tʌrni] s abogado; procurador *m*
attract [ə'trækt] *tr* atraer; llamar (*la*
atención)
attraction [ə'trækʃən] s atracción;
(*personal charm*) atractivo
attractive [ə'træktɪv] *adj* atractivo;
(*agreeable, interesting*) atrayente
attribute ['ætrɪ,bjut] s atributo ‖
[ə'trɪbjut] *tr* atribuir
atty. *abbr* **attorney**
auburn ['ɔbərn] *adj* & s castaño rojizo
auction ['ɔkʃən] s almoneda, remate
m, subasta ‖ *tr* rematar, subastar
auctioneer [,ɔkʃən'ɪr] s subastador *m*
‖ *tr* & *intr* rematar, subastar
auction house s martillo
audacious [ə'deʃəs] *adj* audaz
audaci·ty [ə'dæsɪti] s (*pl* **-ties**) audacia
audience ['ɔdɪ·əns] s (*hearing; formal*
interview) audiencia; público, auditorio
audio frequency ['ɔdɪ,o] s audiofrecuencia
audiometer [,ɔdɪ'amɪtər] s audiómetro
audit ['ɔdɪt] s intervención ‖ *tr* intervenir
audition [ə'dɪʃən] s audición ‖ *tr* dar
audición a
auditor ['ɔdɪtər] s oyente *mf*; (com)
interventor *m*
auditorium [,ɔdɪ'torɪ·əm] s auditorio,
anfiteatro, paraninfo
auger ['ɔgər] s barrena
augment [ɔg'ment] *tr* & *intr* aumentar
augur ['ɔgər] s augur *m* ‖ *tr* & *intr*
augurar; **to augur well** ser de buen
agüero
augu·ry ['ɔgərɪ] s (*pl* **-ries**) augurio
august [ɔ'gʌst] *adj* augusto ‖ **August**
['ɔgəst] s agosto
aunt [ænt] o [ɑnt] s tía
aurora [ə'rorə] s aurora
auspice ['ɔspɪs] s auspicio; **under the**
auspices of bajo los auspicios de
austere [ɔs'tɪr] *adj* austero
Australia [ɔ'streljə] s Australia
Australian [ɔ'streljən] *adj* & s aus-
traliano
Austria ['ɔstrɪ·ə] s Austria
Austrian ['ɔstrɪ·ən] *adj* & s austríaco
authentic [ɔ'θentɪk] *adj* auténtico
authenticate [ɔ'θentɪ,ket] *tr* autenticar
author ['ɔθər] s autor *m*
authoress ['ɔθərɪs] s autora
authoritarian [ɑ,θɑrɪ'terɪ·ən] o [ə-
,θɑrɪ'terɪ·ən] *adj* & s autoritario
authoritative [ə'θɑrɪ,tetɪv] o [ə'θɑrɪ-
,tetɪv] *adj* autorizado; (*dictatorial*)
autoritario
authori·ty [ə'θɑrɪti] o [ə'θɔrɪti] s (*pl*
-ties) autoridad; **on good authority**
de buena tinta, de fuente fidedigna
authorize ['ɔθə,raɪz] *tr* autorizar

authorship ['ɔθər ˌʃɪp] s paternidad literaria

au·to ['ɔto] s (pl **-tos**) (coll) auto, coche m

autobiogra·phy [ˌɔtobar'ɑgrəfi] u [ˌɔtobɪ'ɑgrəfi] s (pl **-phies**) autobiografía

autobus ['ɔto ˌbʌs] s autobús m

autocratic(al) [ˌɔtə'krætɪk(əl)] adj autocrático

autograph ['ɔtə ˌgræf] u ['ɔtə ˌgrɑf] adj & s autógrafo || tr autografiar

autograph seeker s cazaautógrafos m

automat ['ɔtə ˌmæt] s restaurante automático

automatic [ˌɔtə'mætɪk] adj automático

automatic clutch s servoembrague m

automation [ˌɔtə'meʃən] s automación, automatización

automa·ton [ɔ'tamə ˌtɑn] s (pl **-tons** o **-ta** [tə]) autómata

automobile [ˌɔtəmo'bil] u [ˌɔtə'mobil] s automóvil m

automobile show s salón m del automóvil

autonomous [ɔ'tɑnəməs] adj autónomo

autonomy [ɔ'tɑnəmi] s autonomía

autop·sy ['ɔtapsi] s (pl **-sies**) autopsia

autumn ['ɔtəm] s otoño

autumnal [ɔ'tʌmnəl] adj otoñal

auxilia·ry [ɔg'zɪljəri] adj auxiliar || s (pl **-ries**) auxiliar mf; **auxiliaries** tropas auxiliares

av. abbr avenue, average, avoirdupois

avail [ə'vel] s provecho, utilidad || tr beneficiar; **to avail oneself of** aprovecharse de, valerse de || intr aprovechar

available [ə'veləbəl] adj disponible; **to make available to** poner a la disposición de

avalanche ['ævə ˌlæntʃ] o ['ævə ˌlantʃ] s alud m, avalancha

avant-garde [avã'gard] adj vanguardista || s vanguardismo

avant-guardist [avã'gardɪst] s vanguardista mf

avarice ['ævərɪs] s avaricia

avaricious [ˌævə'rɪʃəs] adj avaricioso, avariento

Ave. abbr **Avenue**

avenge [ə'vendʒ] tr vengar; **to avenge oneself on** vengarse en

avenue ['ævə ˌnju] o ['ævə ˌnu] s avenida

aver [ə'vʌr] v (pret & pp **averred;** ger **averring**) tr afirmar, declarar

average ['ævərɪdʒ] adj común, mediano, ordinario || s promedio, término medio; (naut) avería || tr calcular el término medio de; prorratear; ser de un promedio de

averse [ə'vʌrs] adj renuente, contrario

aversion [ə'vʌrʒən] s aversión, antipatía; cosa aborrecida

avert [ə'vʌrt] tr apartar, desviar; impedir

aviar·y ['evi ˌeri] s (pl **-ies**) avería, pajarera

aviation [ˌevi'eʃən] s aviación

aviation medicine s aeromedicina

aviator ['evi ˌetər] s aviador m

avid ['ævɪd] adj ávido

avidity [ə'vɪdɪti] s avidez f

avocation [ˌævə'keʃən] s distracción, diversión

avoid [ə'vɔid] tr evitar

avoidable [ə'vɔidəbəl] adj evitable

avoidance [ə'vɔidəns] s evitación

avow [ə'vau] tr admitir, confesar

avowal [ə'vau-əl] s admisión, confesión

await [ə'wet] tr aguardar, esperar

awake [ə'wek] adj despierto || v (pret & pp **awoke** [ə'wok] o **awaked**) tr & intr despertar

awaken [ə'wekən] tr & intr despertar

awakening [ə'wekənɪŋ] s despertamiento; desilusión

award [ə'wɔrd] s premio; condecoración; adjudicación || tr conceder; adjudicar

aware [ə'wer] adj enterado; **to become aware of** enterarse de, darse cuenta de

awareness [ə'wernɪs] s conciencia

away [ə'we] adj ausente; distante || adv lejos; a lo lejos; **away from** lejos de; **to do away with** deshacerse de; **to get away** escapar; **to go away** irse; **to make away with** robar, hurtar; **to run away** fugarse; **to send away** enviar; despedir; **to take away** llevarse; quitar

awe [ɔ] s temor m reverencial || tr infundir temor reverencial a

awesome ['ɔsəm] adj imponente

awestruck ['ɔ ˌstrʌk] adj espantado

awful ['ɔfəl] adj atroz, horrible; impresionante; (coll) muy malo, muy feo, enorme

awfully ['ɔfəli] adv atrozmente, horriblemente; (coll) muy, excesivamente

awhile [ə'hwaɪl] adv un rato, algún tiempo

awkward ['ɔkwərd] adj desmañado, torpe, lerdo; embarazoso, delicado

awkward squad s pelotón m de los torpes

awl [ɔl] s alesna, lezna

awning ['ɔnɪŋ] s toldo

ax [æks] s hacha

axiom ['æksɪ·əm] s axioma m

axiomatic [ˌæksɪ·ə'mætɪk] adj axiomático

axis ['æksɪs] s (pl **axes** ['æksiz]) s eje m

axle ['æksəl] s eje m, árbol m

ax'le·tree' s eje m de carretón

ay [aɪ] adv & s sí || [e] adv siempre; **for ay por siempre** || [e] interj ¡ay!

aye [aɪ] adv & s sí || [e] adv siempre; **for aye por siempre**

azimuth ['æzɪməθ] s acimut m

Azores [ə'zorz] o ['ezorz] spl Azores fpl

Aztec ['æztek] adj & s azteca mf

azure ['æʒər] o ['eʒər] adj & s azul m

au
ba

B

B, b [bi] segunda letra del alfabeto inglés

b. *abbr* **bass, bay, born, brother**

baa [bɑ] *s* be *m*, balido ‖ *intr* balar

babble ['bæbəl] *s* barboteo; charla; *(of a brook)* murmullo ‖ *tr* barbotar; decir indiscretamente ‖ *intr* barbotar; murmurar *(un arroyo)*

babe [beb] *s* rorro, criatura; *(innocent, gullible person)* niño; *(slang)* chica, chica hermosa

baboon [bæ'bun] *s* babuíno

ba·by ['bebi] *s (pl* **-bies)** rorro, criatura, bebé *m; (the youngest child)* benjamín *m* ‖ *v (pret & pp* **-bied)** *tr* mimar; tratar como niño

baby carriage *s* cochecillo para niños

baby grand *s* piano de media cola

babyhood ['bebɪ,hʊd] *s* primera infancia, niñez *f*

babyish ['bebi·ɪʃ] *adj* aniñado, infantil

Babylon ['bæbɪlən] o ['bæbɪ,lɑn] *s* Babilonia *(ciudad)*

Babylonia [,bæbɪ'loni·ə] *s* Babilonia *(imperio)*

Babylonian [,bæbɪ'loni·ən] *adj & s* babilonio

baby sitter *s* niñera tomada por horas

baccalaureate [,bækə'lɔrɪ·ɪt] *s* bachillerato

bachelor ['bætʃələr] *s (unmarried man)* soltero; *(holder of bachelor's degree)* bachiller *mf; (apprentice knight)* doncel *m*

bachelorhood ['bætʃələr,hʊd] *s* celibato, soltería *(del hombre)*

bacil·lus [bə'sɪləs] *s (pl* **-li** [laɪ]) bacilo

back [bæk] *adj* trasero, posterior; atrasado ‖ *adv* atrás, detrás; de vuelta; *(ago)* hace; **back of** detrás de; **to go back to** remontarse a; **to send back** devolver ‖ *s* espalda; dorso; *(of a coin)* reverso; *(of a chair)* espaldar *m*, respaldo; *(of an animal, of a book)* lomo; *(of a hall, a room)* fondo; *(of a writing, a book)* final *m;* **behind one's back** a espaldas de uno; **on one's back** postrado, en cama; a cuestas ‖ *tr* mover hacia atrás; apoyar, respaldar ‖ *intr* moverse hacia atrás; **to back down** u **out** volverse atrás, echarse atrás; **to back up** retroceder; regolfar *(el agua)*

back'ache' *s* dolor *m* de espalda

back'bone' *s* espinazo; *(of a book)* nervura; firmeza, resistencia

back'break'ing *adj* deslomador

back'down' *s* palinodia, retractación

back'drop' *s* telón *m* de fondo o de foro

backer ['bækər] *s* sostenedor *m*, defensor *m; (of a business venture)* impulsador *m*

back'fire' *s* (aut) petardeo ‖ *intr* (aut) petardear

back'ground' *s* fondo; antecedentes

mpl; conocimientos, educación; *(of a painting)* lontananza

background music *s* música de fondo

backing ['bækɪŋ] *s* apoyo, sostén *m;* garantía, respaldo; (bb) lomera

back'lash' *s* (mach) contragolpe *m;* (mach) juego; (fig) reacción violenta

back'log' *s* (com) reserva de pedidos pendientes; *(e.g., of work)* acumulación

back number *s* número atrasado; (coll) persona anticuada

back pay *s* sueldo retrasado

back seat *s* puesto secundario; **to take a back seat** perder influencia

back'side' *s* espalda; trasero

back'slide' *v (pret & pp* **-slid** [,slɪd]) *intr* reincidir

backspacer ['bæk ,spesər] *s* tecla de retroceso

back'stage' *adv* detrás del telón; entre bastidores

back'stairs' *adj* indirecto, secreto

back stairs *spl* escalera trasera; medios indirectos

back'stitch' *s* pespunte *m* ‖ *tr & intr* pespuntar

back'stop' *s* reja o red *f* para detener la pelota

back'swept' wing *s* (aer) ala en flecha

back talk *s* respuesta insolente

backward ['bækwərd] *adj* atrasado, tardío; tímido ‖ *adv* de atrás; de espaldas; al revés; cada vez peor; para atrás, hacia atrás

back'wa'ter *s* remanso; (fig) atraso, yermo

back'woods' *spl* monte *m*, región alejada de los centros de población

back yard *s* patio trasero, corral trasero

bacon ['bekən] *s* tocino

bacteria [bæk'tɪrɪ·ə] *pl de* **bacterium**

bacterial [bæk'tɪrɪ·əl] *adj* bacteriano

bacteriologist [bæk,tɪrɪ'ɑlədʒɪst] *s* bacteriólogo

bacteriology [bæk,tɪrɪ'ɑlədʒi] *s* bacteriología

bacteri·um [bæk'tɪrɪ·əm] *s (pl* **-a** [ə]) bacteria

bad [bæd] *adj (comp* **worse** [wʌrs]; *super* **worst** [wʌrst]) malo; *(money)* falso; *(debt)* incobrable; **from bad to worse** de mal en peor; **to be in bad** (coll) caer en desgracia; **to be too bad** ser lástima; **to go to the bad** (coll) ir por mal camino; (coll) arruinarse; **to look bad** tener mala cara

bad breath *s* mal aliento

badge [bædʒ] *s* divisa, insignia

badger ['bædʒər] *s* tejón *m*

badly ['bædli] *adv* mal; con urgencia; gravemente

badly off *adj* malparado; muy enfermo

badminton ['bædmɪntən] *s* juego del volante

baffle ['bæfəl] *s* deflector *m;* (rad)

pantalla acústica ‖ *tr* confundir; burlar, frustrar

baffling ['bæflɪŋ] *adj* perplejo, desconcertador

bag [bæg] *s* saco; saquito de mano; (*in clothing*) bolsa; (*purse*) bolso; (*take of game*) caza; **to be in the bag** (slang) ser cosa segura ‖ *v* (*pret & pp* **bagged**; *ger* **bagging**) *tr* ensacar; coger, cazar ‖ *intr* hacer bolsa (*un vestido*)

baggage ['bægɪdʒ] *s* equipaje *m*; (mil) bagaje *m*

baggage car *s* furgón *m* de equipajes

baggage check *s* contraseña de equipajes

baggage rack *s* red *f* de equipajes

baggage room *s* sala de equipajes

bag'pipe' *s* gaita, cornamusa

bag'pi'per *s* gaitero

bail [bel] *s* caución, fianza; **to go bail for** salir fiador por ‖ *tr* caucionar, afianzar; achicar (*la embarcación; el agua*); **to bail out** salir fiador por; achicar ‖ *intr* achicar; **to bail out** lanzarse en paracaídas

bailiff ['belɪf] *s* alguacil *m*, corchete *m*

bailiwick ['belɪwɪk] *s* alguacilazgo; **to be in the bailiwick of** ser de la pertenencia de

bait [bet] *s* carnada, cebo; señuelo; **to swallow the bait** tragar el anzuelo ‖ *tr* cebar, encarnar (*el anzuelo*); tentar, seducir; (*to pester*) hostigar

baize [bez] *s* bayeta

bake [bek] *tr* cocer al horno; cocer (*loza, gres, etc.*)

bakelite ['bekə,laɪt] *s* baquelita

baker ['bekər] *s* panadero, hornero

baker's dozen *s* docena del fraile

baker•y ['bekəri] *s* (*pl* **-ies**) panadería

baking powder ['bekɪŋ] *s* levadura en polvo

baking soda *s* bicarbonato de sosa

bal. *abbr* **balance**

balance ['bæləns] *s* (*instrument for weighing*) balanza; (*state of equilibrium*) equilibrio; (*amount left over*) resto; (*amount still owed*) saldo; (*statement of debits and credits*) balance *m*; **to lose one's balance** perder el equilibrio; **to strike a balance** hacer o pasar balance ‖ *tr* balancear; equilibrar; equilibrar, nivelar (*el presupuesto*) ‖ *intr* equilibrarse; (*to waver*) balancear

balance of payments *s* balanza de pagos

balance of power *s* equilibrio político

balance sheet *s* balance *m*, avanzo

balco•ny ['bælkəni] *s* (*pl* **-nies**) balcón *m*; (*in a theater*) galería, paraíso

bald [bɔld] *adj* calvo; franco, directo

baldness ['bɔldnɪs] *s* calvicie *f*

baldric ['bɔldrɪk] *s* tahalí *m*

bale [bel] *s* bala ‖ *tr* embalar

Balearic [,bælɪ'ærɪk] *adj* balear

Balearic Islands *spl* islas Baleares

baleful ['belfəl] *adj* funesto, maligno

balk [bɔk] *tr* burlar, frustrar ‖ *intr* emperrarse, resistirse

Balkan ['bɔlkən] *adj* balcánico ‖ **the Balkans** los Balcanes

balk•y ['bɔki] *adj* (*comp* **-ier;** *super* **-iest**) rebelón, repropio

ball [bɔl] *s* bola, pelota; esfera, globo; (*of wool, yarn*) ovillo; (*of finger*) yema; (*projectile*) bala; (*dance*) baile *m*

ballad ['bæləd] *s* balada

ballade [bə'lɑd] *s* (mus) balada

ballast ['bæləst] *s* (aer, naut) lastre *m*; (rr) balasto ‖ *tr* lastrar; balastar

ball bearing *s* cojinete *m* de bolas

ballerina [,bælə'rinə] *s* bailarina

ballet ['bæle] *s* ballet *m*, baile *m*

ballistic [bə'lɪstɪk] *adj* balístico

balloon [bə'lun] *s* globo

ballot ['bælət] *s* balota; sufragio ‖ *intr* balotar

ballot box *s* urna electoral

ball'play'er *s* pelotari *m*; beisbolero

ball'-point' pen *s* polígrafo, bolígrafo, pluma esferográfica

ball'room' *s* salón *m* de baile

ballyhoo ['bælɪ,hu] *s* alharaca, bombo ‖ *tr* dar teatro a, dar bombo a

balm [bɑm] *s* bálsamo

balm•y ['bɑmi] *adj* (*comp* **-ier;** *super* **-iest**) bonancible, suave

balsam ['bɔlsəm] *s* bálsamo

Baltic ['bɔltɪk] *adj* báltico

Baltimore oriole ['bɔltɪ,mor] *s* cacique veranero

baluster ['bæləstər] *s* balaustre *m*

bamboo [bæm'bu] *s* bambú *m*

bamboozle [bæm'buzəl] *tr* (coll) embaucar, engañar

bamboozler [bæm'buzlər] *s* (coll) embaucador *m*, engañabobos *mf*

ban [bæn] *s* prohibición; excomunión, entredicho; (*of marriage*) amonestación ‖ *v* (*pret & pp* **banned**; *ger* **banning**) *tr* prohibir; excomulgar

banana [bə'nænə] *s* banana, plátano; (*tree*) banano, bananero, plátano

banana oil *s* esencia de pera

band [bænd] *s* banda; (*of people*) cuadrilla; (*of a hat*) cintillo; (*of a cigar*) anillo; liga de goma; (mus) banda, música, charanga ‖ *intr* abanderizarse

bandage ['bændɪdʒ] *s* venda ‖ *tr* vendar

bandanna [bæn'dænə] *s* pañuelo de hierbas

band'box' *s* sombrerera

bandit ['bændɪt] *s* bandido

band'mas'ter *s* músico mayor

bandoleer [,bændə'lɪr] *s* bandolera

band saw *s* sierra continua, sierra sin fin

band'stand' *s* quiosco de música

baneful ['benfəl] *adj* nocivo, venenoso; (*e.g., influence*) funesto

bang [bæŋ] *adv* de golpe ‖ *interj* ¡pum! ‖ *s* golpazo; (*of a door*) portazo; **bangs** flequillo ‖ *tr* golpear con ruido; cerrar (*p.ej., una puerta*) de golpe ‖ *intr* hacer estrépito

banish ['bænɪʃ] *tr* desterrar; despedir (*p.ej., miedo*)

banishment ['bænɪʃmənt] *s* destierro

banister ['bænɪstər] *s* balaustre *m*

bank [bæŋk] *s* banco; (*in certain games*) banca; (*small container for* *coins*) alcancía; (*of a river*) ribera, orilla; (*of earth, snow, clouds*) montón *m* || *tr* depositar o guardar (*dinero*) en un banco; amontonar; cubrir (*un fuego*) con cenizas || *intr* depositar dinero; **to bank on** (coll) contar con

bank account *s* cuenta de banco

bank'book' *s* libreta de banco

banker ['bæŋkər] *s* banquero

banking ['bæŋkɪŋ] *adj* bancario || *s* banca

bank note *s* billete *m* de banco

bank roll *s* lío de papel moneda

bankrupt ['bæŋkrʌpt] *adj & s* bancarrotero; **to go bankrupt** hacer bancarrota || *tr* hacer quebrar; arruinar

bankrupt·cy ['bæŋkrʌptsi] *s* (*pl* -cies) bancarrota

banner ['bænər] *s* bandera, estandarte *m*

banner cry *s* grito de combate

banquet ['bæŋkwɪt] *s* banquete *m* || *tr & intr* banquetear

banter ['bæntər] *s* burla, chanza || *intr* burlar, chancear

baptism ['bæptɪzəm] *s* bautizo tizo

Baptist ['bæptɪst] *adj & s* baptista *mf*, bautista *mf*

baptister·y ['bæptɪstəri] *s* (*pl* -ies) baptisterio, bautisterio

baptize [bæp'taɪz] o ['bæptaɪz] *tr* bautizar

bar. *abbr* **barometer, barrel, barrister**

bar [bar] *s* barra; (*of door or window*) tranca; (*of jail*) reja; barrera; (*legal profession*) abogacía; (*members of legal profession*) curia; (*of public opinion*) tribunal *m*; (mus) barra; (*unit between two bars*) (mus) compás *m*; **behind bars** entre rejas || *prep* salvo; **bar none** sin excepción || *v* (*pret & pp* **barred;** *ger* **barring**) *tr* barrear, atrancar; impedir; prohibir; excluir

bar association *s* colegio de abogados

barb [barb] *s* púa, lengüeta; (*of a pen*) barbilla

Barbados [bar'bedoz] *s* la Barbada

barbarian [bar'bɛrɪ·ən] *s* bárbaro

barbaric [bar'bærɪk] *adj* bárbaro

barbarism ['barbə,rɪzəm] *s* barbaridad *f*; (gram) barbarismo

barbari·ty [bar'bærɪti] *s* (*pl* -ties) barbarie *f*

barbarous ['barbərəs] *adj* bárbaro

Barbary ape ['barbəri] *s* mono de Gibraltar

barbed [barbd] *adj* armado de púas; mordaz, punzante

barbed wire *s* alambre *m* de espino, alambre de púas

barber ['barbər] *adj* barberil || *s* barbero, peluquero

barber pole *s* percha de barbero

bar'ber·shop' *s* barbería, peluquería

bard [bard] *s* bardo; (*horse armor*) barda || *tr* bardar

bare [bɛr] *adj* desnudo; (*head*) descubierto; (*unfurnished*) desamueblado; (*wire*) sin aislar; mero, sencillo, puro || *tr* desnudar; descubrir

bare'back' *adj & adv* en pelo, sin silla

barefaced ['bɛr,fest] *adj* desvergonzado

bare'foot' *adj* descalzo || *adv* con los pies desnudos

bareheaded ['bɛr,hɛdɪd] *adj* descubierto || *adv* con la cabeza descubierta

barelegged ['bɛr,lɛgɪd] o ['bɛr,lɛgd] *adj* con las piernas desnudas

barely ['bɛrli] *adv* apenas

bargain ['bargɪn] *s* (*deal*) convenio, trato; (*cheap purchase*) ganga; **in the bargain** de añadidura || *tr* — to **bargain away** vender regalado || *intr* negociar; (*to haggle*) regatear

bargain counter *s* baratillo

bargain sale *s* venta de saldos

barge [bardʒ] *s* gabarra, lanchón *m* || *intr* moverse pesadamente; **to barge in** entrar sin pedir permiso, entrar sin llamar a la puerta

barium ['bɛrɪ·əm] *s* bario

bark [bark] *s* (*of tree*) corteza; (*of dog*) ladrido; (*boat*) barca || *tr* ladrar (*p.ej., injurias*) || *intr* ladrar

barley ['barli] *s* cebada

barley water *s* hordiate *m*

bar magnet *s* barra imantada

bar'maid' *s* moza de taberna

barn [barn] *s* granero, troje *m*; caballeriza, establo; cochera

barnacle ['barnəkəl] *s* cirrópodo

barn owl *s* lechuza, oliva

barn'yard' *s* corral *m*

barnyard fowl *spl* aves *fpl* de corral

barometer [bə'ramɪtər] *s* barómetro

baron ['bærən] *s* barón *m*

baroness ['bærənɪs] *s* baronesa

baroque [bə'rok] *adj & s* barroco

barracks ['bærəks] *spl* cuartel *m*

barrage [bə'raʒ] *s* (*dam*) presa; (mil) barrera de fuego

barrel ['bærəl] *s* barril *m*, tonel *m*; (*of a gun, pen, etc.*) cañón *m*

barrel organ *s* organillo

barren ['bærən] *adj* árido, estéril

barricade [,bærɪ'ked] *s* barrera || *tr* barrear

barrier ['bærɪ·ər] *s* barrera

barrier reef *s* barrera de arrecifes

barrister ['bærɪstər] *s* (Brit) abogado

bar'room' *s* bar *m*, cantina

bar'tend'er *s* cantinero, tabernero

barter ['bartər] *s* trueque *m* || *tr* trocar

base [bes] *adj* bajo, humilde; infame, vil; (*metal*) bajo de ley || *s* base *f*; (*of electric light or vacuum tube; of projectile*) culote *m*; (mus) bajo || *tr* basar

base'ball' *s* béisbol *m*; pelota de béisbol

base'board' *s* rodapié *m*

Basel ['bazəl] *s* Basilea

baseless ['besLɪs] *adj* infundado

basement ['besmənt] *s* sótano

bashful ['bæʃfəl] *adj* encogido, tímido

basic ['besɪk] *adj* básico

basic commodities *spl* artículos de primera necesidad

basilica [bə'sɪlɪkə] *s* basílica

basin ['besɪn] *s* jofaina, palangana;

(*of a fountain*) tazón m; (*of a river*) cuenca; (*of a harbor*) dársena

ba·sis ['besɪs] s (pl -ses [siz]) base f; **on the basis of** a base de

bask [bæsk] o [bɑsk] intr asolearse, calentarse

basket ['bæskɪt] o ['bɑskɪt] s cesta; (*large basket*) cesto; (*with two handles*) canasta; (*with lid*) excusabaraja; (*sport*) cesto, red f

bas'ket·ball' s baloncesto, basquetbol m

Basle [bɑl] s Basilea

Basque [bæsk] adj & s (*of Spain*) vascongado; (*of Spain and France*) vasco; (*of old Spain*) vascón m

bas-relief [,bɑrɪ'lif] o [,bærɪ'lif] s bajo relieve

bass [bæs] adj & s (mus) bajo ‖ [bæs] s (ichth) róbalo; (ichth) micróptero

bass drum s bombo

bass horn s tuba

bas·so ['bæso] o ['bɑso] s (pl -sos o -si [si]) (mus) bajo

bassoon [bə'sun] s bajón m

bass viol ['vaɪ·əl] s violón m, contrabajo

bastard ['bæstərd] adj & s bastardo

bastard title s anteportada

baste [best] tr (*to sew slightly*) hilvanar; (*to moisten with drippings while roasting*) enlardar; (*to thrash*) azotar; (*to scold*) regañar

bat. abbr battalion, battery

bat [bæt] s palo; (coll) golpe m; (zool) murciélago ‖ v (pret & pp batted; ger batting) tr golpear; batear (*una pelota*); **without batting an eye** sin inmutarse, sin pestañear ‖ intr golpear

batch [bætʃ] s (*of bread*) hornada; (*of papers*) lío

bath [bæθ] o [bɑθ] s baño

bathe [beð] tr bañar ‖ intr bañarse; **to go bathing** ir a bañarse

bather ['beðər] s bañista mf

bath'house' s casa de baños; caseta de baños

bathing beach s playa de baños

bathing beauty s sirena de la playa

bathing resort s estación balnearia

bathing suit s traje m de baño, bañador m

bathing trunks spl taparrabo

bath'robe' s albornoz m, bata de baño; bata, peinador m

bath'room' s baño, cuarto de baño

bathroom fixtures spl aparatos sanitarios

bath'tub' s bañera, baño

baton [bæ'tɑn] o ['bætən] s bastón m; (mus) batuta

battalion [bə'tæljən] s batallón m

batter ['bætər] s pasta, batido; (baseball) bateador m ‖ tr magullar, estropear

battering ram s ariete m

batter·y ['bætərɪ] s (pl -ies) batería; (*primary*) (elec) pila; (*secondary*) (elec) acumulador m; (law) violencia

battle ['bætəl] s batalla; **to do battle** librar batalla ‖ tr batallar

battle array s orden m de batalla

battle cry s grito de combate

battledore ['bætəl,dor] s raqueta; **battledore and shuttlecock** raqueta y volante

bat'tlefield' s campo de batalla

battle front s frente m de combate

battlement ['bætəlmənt] s almenaje m

battle piece s (paint) batalla

bat'tle·ship' s acorazado

battue [bæ'tu] o [bæ'tju] s batida

bauble ['bɔbəl] s chuchería; cetro de bufón

Bavaria [bə'vɛrɪ·ə] s Baviera

Bavarian [bə'vɛrɪ·ən] adj & mf bávaro

bawd [bɔd] s alcahuete m, alcahueta

bawd·y ['bɔdɪ] adj (comp -ier; super -iest) indecente, obsceno

bawd'y·house' s mancebía, lupanar m

bawl [bɔl] s voces fpl, gritos ‖ tr — **to bawl out** (slang) regañar ‖ intr vocear, gritar; llorar ruidosamente

bay [be] adj bayo ‖ s bahía; aullido, ladrido; caballo bayo; (bot) laurel m; **to keep at bay** tener a raya ‖ intr aullar, ladrar

Bay of Biscay s golfo de Vizcaya

bayonet ['be·ənɪt] s bayoneta ‖ tr herir o matar con bayoneta

bay rum s ron m de laurel, ron de malagueta

bay window s ventana saladiza, mirador m

bazooka [bə'zukə] s bazuca

bbl. abbr barrel, barrels

B.C. abbr before Christ

bd. abbr board

be [bi] v (pres am [æm], is [ɪz], are [ɑr]; pret was [wɑz] o [wʌz], were [wʌr]; pp been [bɪn]) intr estar; ser; tener, p.ej., **to be cold** tener frío; **to be wrong** no tener razón; tener la culpa; **here is** o **here are** aquí tiene Vd.; **there is** o **there are** hay ‖ v aux estar, p.ej., **he is studying** está estudiando; ser, p.ej., **she was hit by a car** fué atropellada por un coche; deber, p.ej., **what am I to do?** ¿qué debo hacer? ‖ v impers ser, p.ej., **it is necessary to get up early** es necesario levantarse temprano; haber, p.ej., **it is sunny** hay sol; hacer, p.ej., **it is cold** hace frío

beach [bitʃ] s playa

beach'comb' intr raquear; **to go beachcombing** andar al raque

beach'comb'er s raquero; vago de playa

beach'head' s cabeza de playa

beach robe s albornoz m

beach shoe s playera

beach umbrella s sombrilla de playa

beach wagon s rubia, coche m rural

beacon ['bikən] s señal luminosa; (*lighthouse*) faro; (*hill overlooking sea*) hacho; radiofaro; (*guide*) faro ‖ tr iluminar, guiar ‖ intr brillar

bead [bid] s cuenta; (*of glass*) abalorio; (*of sweat*) gota; (*moulding on corner of wall*) guardavivo; **to say o tell one's beads** rezar el rosario

beadle ['bidəl] s bedel m

beagle ['bigəl] s sabueso

beak [bik] s pico; cabo, promontorio

beam [bim] s (of wood) viga; (of light, heat, etc.) rayo; (naut) bao; (direction perpendicular to the keel) (naut) través m; (of hope) (fig) rayo; **on the beam** siguiendo el haz del radiofaro; (coll) siguiendo el buen camino || tr emitir (luz, ondas) || intr brillar; sonreír alegremente

bean [bin] s haba (Vicia faba); alubia, judía (Phaseolus vulgaris); (of coffee, cocoa) haba; (slang) cabeza

bean'pole' s rodrigón m para frijoles; (tall, skinny person) (coll) poste m de telégrafo

bear [ber] s oso; (in stock market) bajista mf || v (pret **bore** [bor]; pp **borne** [born]) tr cargar; traer; llevar (armas); apoyar; aguantar; sentir, experimentar; producir, rendir (frutos; interés); (to give birth to) parir; tener (amor, odio); **to bear out** confirmar || intr dirigirse, volver; **to bear on** referirse a; **to bear up** no perder la esperanza; **to bear with** ser indulgente para con

beard [bɪrd] s barba; (of wheat) arista

beardless [ˈbɪrdlɪs] adj imberbe

bearer [ˈberər] s portador m

bearing [ˈberɪŋ] s porte m, presencia; referencia, relación; (mach) cojinete m; **bearings** orientación; **to lose one's bearings** desorientarse

bearish [ˈberɪʃ] adj bajista

bear'skin' s piel f de oso; (military cap) morrión m

beast [bist] s bestia

beast·ly [ˈbistli] adj (comp **-lier**; super **-liest**) bestial; (coll) muy malo || adv (coll) muy mal

beast of burden s bestia de carga, acémila

beat [bit] s golpe m; (of heart) latido; (of rhythm) compás m; marca del compás; (mus) tiempo; (phys) batimiento; (rad) batido; (of a policeman) ronda; (sponger) (slang) embestidor m || v (pret **beat**; pp **beat** o **beaten**) tr azotar, pegar; batir; sacudir (una alfombra); aventajar; llevar (el compás); tocar (un tambor); (a una persona en una contienda) ganar; **to beat it** (slang) largarse; **to beat up** batir (p.ej., huevos); (slang) aporrear || intr batir; latir (el corazón); **to beat against** azotar

beaten path [ˈbitən] s camino trillado

beater [ˈbitər] s batidor m; (mixer) batidora

beautician [bjuˈtɪʃən] s embellecedora, esteta mf, esteticista mf

beati·fy [biˈætɪˌfaɪ] v (pret & pp **-fied**) tr beatificar

beating [ˈbitɪŋ] s golpeo; (of wings) aleteo; (with a whip) paliza; (defeat) derrota

beau [bo] s (pl beaus o beaux [boz]) galán m, cortejo; novio; elegante m

beautiful [ˈbjutɪfəl] adj bello, hermoso

beauti·fy [ˈbjutɪˌfaɪ] v (pret & pp **-fied**) tr hermosear, embellecer

beau·ty [ˈbjuti] s (pl **-ties**) beldad f, belleza

beauty contest s concurso de belleza

beauty parlor s salón m de belleza

beauty queen s reina de la belleza

beauty sleep s primer sueño (antes de medianoche)

beauty spot s lunar postizo; sitio pintoresco

beaver [ˈbivər] s castor m; piel f de castor

becalm [bɪˈkɑm] tr calmar, serenar

because [bɪˈkɔz] conj porque; **because of** por, por causa de

beck [bɛk] s seña (con la cabeza o la mano); **at the beck and call of** a la disposición de

beckon [ˈbɛkən] s seña (con la cabeza o la mano) || tr llamar por señas; atraer, tentar || intr hacer señas

be·come [bɪˈkʌm] v (pret **-came**; pp **-come**) tr convenir, sentar bien || intr hacerse; llegar a ser; ponerse, volverse; convertirse en; **to become of** ser de, p.ej., **what will become of the soldier?** ¿qué será del soldado?; hacerse, p.ej., **what became of his pencil?** ¿qué se ha hecho su lápiz?

becoming [bɪˈkʌmɪŋ] adj conveniente, decente; que sienta bien

bed [bed] s cama; (of a river) cauce m; (of flower garden) macizo; **to go to bed** acostarse; **to take to bed** encamarse

bed and board s pensión completa, casa y comida

bed'bug' s chinche f

bed'cham'ber s alcoba, cuarto de dormir

bed'clothes' spl ropa de cama

bed'cov'er s cubrecama, cobertor m

bedding [ˈbedɪŋ] s ropa de cama; (for animals) cama

bedev·il [bɪˈdevəl] v (pret & pp **-iled** o **-illed**; ger **-iling** o **-illing**) tr atormentar, confundir

bed'fast' adj postrado en cama

bed'fel'low s compañero o compañera de cama

bedlam [ˈbedləm] s confusión, desorden m, tumulto

bed linen s ropa de cama

bed'pan' s silleta

bed'post' s pilar m de cama

bedridden [ˈbedˌrɪdən] adj postrado en cama

bed'room' s alcoba, cuarto de dormir

bed'side' s cabecera

bed'sore' s úlcera de decúbito; **to get bedsores** decentarse

bed'spread' s sobrecama, cobertor m

bed'spring' s colchón m de muelles, somier m

bed'stead' s cuja

bed'straw' s paja de jergón

bed'tick' s cutí m

bed'time' s hora de acostarse

bed warmer s calientacamas m

bee [bi] s abeja

beech [bitʃ] s haya

beech'nut' s hayuco

beef [bif] s carne f de vaca; ganado vacuno de engorde; (coll) fuerza muscular; (slang) queja || tr — to

beef up (coll) reforzar ‖ *intr* (slang) quejarse; (slang) soplar
beef cattle *s* ganado vacuno de engorde
beef'steak' *s* biftec *m*
bee'hive' *s* colmena
bee'line' *s* — **to make a beeline for** ir en línea recta hacia, ir derecho a
beer [bɪr] *s* cerveza; **dark beer** cerveza parda, cerveza negra; **light beer** cerveza clara
beeswax ['biz,wæks] *s* cera de abejas ‖ *tr* encerar
beet [bit] *s* remolacha
beetle ['bitəl] *s* escarabajo
beetle-browed ['bitəl,braud] *adj* cejijunto; (*sullen*) ceñudo
beet sugar *s* azúcar *m* de remolacha
be·fall [bɪ'fɔl] *v* (*pret* **-fell** ['fɛl]; *pp* **-fallen** ['fɔlən]) *tr* acontecer a ‖ *intr* acontecer
befitting [bɪ'fɪtɪŋ] *adj* conveniente; decoroso
before [bɪ'for] *adv* antes; delante, enfrente ‖ *prep* (*in time*) antes de; (*in place*) delante de; (*in the presence of*) ante ‖ *conj* antes (de) que
before'hand' *adv* de antemano, con anticipación
befriend [bɪ'frɛnd] *tr* ofrecer amistad a, amparar, proteger
befuddle [bɪ'fʌdəl] *tr* aturdir, confundir
beg [bɛg] *v* (*pret & pp* **begged;** *ger* **begging**) *tr* pedir, rogar, solicitar; mendigar ‖ *intr* mendigar; **to beg off** excusarse
be·get [bɪ'gɛt] *v* (*pret* **-got** ['gɑt]; *pp* **-gotten** o **-got;** *ger* **-getting**) *tr* engendrar
beggar ['bɛgər] *s* mendigo; pobre *mf*; pícaro, bribón *m*; sujeto, tipo
be·gin [bɪ'gɪn] *v* (*pret* **-gan** ['gæn]; *pp* **-gun** ['gʌn]; *ger* **-ginning**) *tr & intr* comenzar, empezar; **beginning with** a partir de
beginner [bɪ'gɪnər] *s* principiante *mf*; iniciador *m*
beginning [bɪ'gɪnɪŋ] *s* comienzo, principio
begrudge [bɪ'grʌdʒ] *tr* dar de mala gana; envidiar
beguile [bɪ'gaɪl] *tr* engañar; divertir, entretener; engañar (*el tiempo*)
behalf [bɪ'hæf] o [bɪ'haf] *s* — **on behalf of** en nombre de; a favor de
behave [bɪ'hev] *intr* conducirse, comportarse; portarse bien; funcionar
behavior [bɪ'hevjər] *s* conducta, comportamiento; funcionamiento
behead [bɪ'hɛd] *tr* decapitar, descabezar
behind [bɪ'haɪnd] *adv* detrás; hacia atrás; con retraso; **to stay behind** quedarse atrás ‖ *prep* detrás de; **behind the back of** a espaldas de; **behind the times** atrasado de noticias; **behind time** tarde ‖ *s* (slang) trasero
behold [bɪ'hold] *v* (*pret & pp* **-held** ['hɛld]) *tr* contemplar ‖ *interj* ¡he aquí!
behoove [bɪ'huv] *tr* convenir, tocar
being ['bi·ɪŋ] *adj* existente; **for the**

time being por ahora, por el momento ‖ *s* ser, ente *m*
belch [bɛltʃ] *s* eructo, regüeldo ‖ *tr* vomitar (*p.ej.*, *llamas, injurias*) ‖ *intr* eructar, regoldar
beleaguer [bɪ'ligər] *tr* sitiar, cercar
bel·fry ['bɛlfri] *s* (*pl* **-fries**) campanario
Belgian ['bɛldʒən] *adj & s* belga *mf*
Belgium ['bɛldʒəm] *s* Bélgica
be·lie [bɪ'laɪ] *v* (*pret & pp* **-lied** ['laɪd]; *ger* **-lying** ['laɪ·ɪŋ]) *tr* desmentir
belief [bɪ'lif] *s* creencia
believable [bɪ'livəbəl] *adj* creíble
believe [bɪ'liv] *tr & intr* creer
believer [bɪ'livər] *s* creyente *mf*
belittle [bɪ'lɪtəl] *tr* empequeñecer, despreciar
bell [bɛl] *s* campana; (*electric bell*) timbre *m*, campanilla; (*ring of bell*) campanada ‖ *intr* bramar, berrear
bell'boy' *s* botones *m*
belle [bɛl] *s* beldad *f*, belleza
belles-lettres [,bɛl'lɛtrə] *spl* bellas letras
bell gable *s* espadaña
bell glass *s* fanal *m*
bell'hop' *s* (slang) botones *m*
bellicose ['bɛlɪ,kos] *adj* belicoso
belligerent [bə'lɪdʒərənt] *adj & s* beligerante *mf*
bellow ['bɛlo] *s* bramido; **bellows** fuelle *m*, barquín *m* ‖ *tr* gritar ‖ *intr* bramar
bell ringer *s* campanero
bellwether ['bɛl,wɛðər] *s* manso
bel·ly ['bɛli] *s* (*pl* **-lies**) barriga, vientre *m*; estómago ‖ *v* (*pret & pp* **-lied**) *intr* hacer barriga; hacer bolso (*las velas*)
bel'ly·ache' *s* (slang) dolor *m* de barriga ‖ *intr* (slang) quejarse
belly button *s* (coll) ombligo
belly dance *s* (coll) danza del vientre
bellyful ['bɛli,ful] *s* (slang) panzada
bel'ly·land' *intr* (aer) aterrizar de panza
belong [bɪ'lɔŋ] o [bɪ'lɑŋ] *intr* pertenecer; deber estar
belongings [bɪ'lɔŋɪŋz] o [bɪ'lɑŋɪŋz] *spl* pertenencias, efectos
beloved [bɪ'lʌvɪd] o [bɪ'lʌvd] *adj & s* querido, amado
below [bɪ'lo] *adv* abajo; (*in a text*) más abajo; bajo cero, p.ej., **ten below** diez grados bajo cero ‖ *prep* debajo de; inferior a
belt [bɛlt] *s* cinturón *m*; (aer, mach) correa; (geog) faja, zona; **to tighten one's belt** ceñirse
bemoan [bɪ'mon] *tr* deplorar, lamentar
bench [bɛntʃ] *s* banco; (law) tribunal *m*
bend [bɛnd] *s* curva; (*in a road, river, etc.*) recodo, vuelta ‖ *v* (*pret & pp* **bent** [bɛnt]) *tr* encorvar; doblar (*un tubo; la rodilla*); inclinar (*la cabeza*); dirigir (*sus esfuerzos*) ‖ *intr* encorvarse; doblarse; inclinarse
beneath [bɪ'niθ] *adv* abajo ‖ *prep* debajo de; inferior a

benediction [‚benɪ'dɪkʃən] s bendición f

benefaction [‚benɪ'fækʃən] s beneficio

benefactor ['benɪ‚fæktər] o [‚benɪ'fæktər] s bienhechor m

benefactress ['benɪ‚fæktrɪs] o [‚benɪ'fæktrɪs] s bienhechora

beneficence [bɪ'nefɪsəns] s beneficencia

beneficent [bɪ'nefɪsənt] adj bienhechor

beneficial [‚benɪ'fɪʃəl] adj beneficioso

beneficiar·y [‚benɪ'fɪʃɪ‚erɪ] s (pl -ies) beneficiario

benefit ['benɪfɪt] s beneficio; **for the benefit of** a beneficio de ‖ tr beneficiar

benefit performance s beneficio

benevolence [bɪ'nevələns] s benevolencia

benevolent [bɪ'nevələnt] adj benévolo; (e.g., institution) benéfico

benign [bɪ'naɪn] adj benigno

benigni·ty [bɪ'nɪgnɪtɪ] s (pl -ties) benignidad

bent [bent] adj encorvado, doblado, torcido; **bent on** resuelto a, empeñado en; **bent over** cargado de espaldas ‖ s encorvadura; inclinación f, propensión f

benzine [ben'zin] s bencina

bequeath [bɪ'kwið] o [bɪ'kwiθ] tr legar

bequest [bɪ'kwest] s manda, legado

berate [bɪ'ret] tr regañar, reñir

be·reave [bɪ'riv] v (pret & pp -reaved o -reft ['reft]) tr despojar, privar; desconsolar

bereavement [bɪ'rivmənt] s despojo, privación f; desconsuelo

berkelium [bər'kilɪ‚əm] s berkelio

Berliner [bər'lɪnər] s berlinés m

ber·ry ['berɪ] s (pl -ries) baya; (of coffee plant) grano, haba

berserk ['bʌrsʌrk] adj frenético ‖ adv frenéticamente

berth [bʌrθ] s (bed) litera; (room) camarote m; (for a ship) amarradero; (coll) empleo, puesto

beryllium [bə'rɪlɪ‚əm] s berilio

be·seech [bɪ'sitʃ] v (pret & pp -sought ['sɔt] o -seeched) tr suplicar

be·set [bɪ'set] v (pret & pp -set; ger -setting) tr acometer, acosar; cercar, sitiar

beside [bɪ'saɪd] adv además, también ‖ prep cerca de, junto a; en comparación de; excepto; **beside oneself** fuera de sí; **beside the point** incongruente

besiege [bɪ'sidʒ] tr asediar, sitiar

besmirch [bɪ'smʌrtʃ] tr ensuciar, manchar

bespatter [bɪ'spætər] tr salpicar

be·speak [bɪ'spik] v (pret -spoke ['spok], -pp -spoken) tr apalabrar, pedir de antemano

best [best] adj super mejor; óptimo ‖ adv super mejor; **had best** debería ‖ s (lo) mejor; (lo) más; **at best** a lo más; **to do one's best** hacer lo mejor posible; **to get the best of** aventajar,

sobresalir; **to make the best of** sacar el mejor partido de

best girl s (coll) amiga preferida, novia

be·stir [bɪ'stʌr] v (pret & pp -stirred; ger -stirring) tr excitar, incitar; **to bestir oneself** esforzarse, afanarse

bestow [bɪ'sto] tr otorgar, conferir; dedicar

best man s padrino de boda

best seller s éxito de venta, campeón m de venta; éxito de librería

bet. abbr **between**

bet [bet] s apuesta ‖ v (pret & pp bet o betted; ger betting) tr & intr apostar; **I bet a que,** apuesto a que; **to bet on** apostar por; **you bet** (slang) ya lo creo

be·take [bɪ'tek] v (pret -took ['tʊk]; pp -taken) tr — **to betake oneself** dirigirse; darse, entregarse

be·think [bɪ'θɪŋk] v (pret & pp -thought ['θɔt]) tr — **to bethink oneself of** considerar, acordarse de

Bethlehem ['beθlɪ‚əm] o ['beθlɪ‚hem] s Belén m

betide [bɪ'taɪd] tr presagiar; acontecer a ‖ intr acontecer

betoken [bɪ'tokən] tr anunciar, indicar, presagiar

betray [bɪ'tre] tr traicionar; descubrir, revelar

betrayal [bɪ'tre·əl] s traición; descubrimiento, revelación

betroth [bɪ'troð] o [bɪ'troθ] tr prometer en matrimonio; **to become betrothed** desposarse

betrothal [bɪ'troðəl] o [bɪ'trɔθəl] s desposorios, esponsales mpl

betrothed [bɪ'troðd] o [bɪ'trɔθt] s prometido, novio

better ['betər] adj comp mejor; **it is better to** más vale; **to grow better** mejorarse; **to make better** mejorar ‖ adv comp mejor; más; **had better** debería; **to like better** preferir ‖ s superior; ventaja; **to get the better of** llevar la ventaja a ‖ tr aventajar; mejorar; **to better oneself** mejorar su posición

better half s (coll) cara mitad

betterment ['betərmənt] s mejoramiento; (in an illness) mejoría

between [bɪ'twin] adv en medio, entremedias ‖ prep entre; **between you and me** entre Vd. y yo; acá para los dos

be·tween'-decks' s entrecubiertas, entrepuentes mpl

between decks adv entrecubiertas

bev·el ['bevəl] adj biselado ‖ s (instrument) cartabón m; (sloping part) bisel m ‖ v (pret & pp -eled o -elled; ger -eling o -elling) tr biselar

beverage ['bevərɪdʒ] s bebida

bev·y ['bevɪ] s (pl -ies) (of birds) bandada; (of girls) grupo

bewail [bɪ'wel] tr & intr lamentar

beware [bɪ'wer] tr guardarse de ‖ intr tener cuidado; **beware of ...!** ¡ojo con ...!, ¡cuidado con ...!; **to beware of** guardarse de

bewilder [bɪ'wɪldər] *tr* aturdir, dejar perplejo, desatinar

bewilderment [bɪ'wɪldərmənt] *s* aturdimiento, perplejidad

beyond [bɪ'jɑnd] *adv* más allá, más lejos || *prep* más allá de; además de; no capaz de; **beyond a doubt** fuera de duda; **beyond the reach of** fuera del alcance de || *s* — **the great beyond** el más allá, el otro mundo

bg. *abbr* bag

bias ['baɪ·əs] *s* sesgo, diagonal *f*; prejuicio; (electron) polarización de rejilla || *tr* predisponer, prevenir

Bib. *abbr* Bible, Biblical

bib [bɪb] *s* babero; (*of apron*) pechera

Bible ['baɪbəl] *s* Biblia

Biblical ['bɪblɪkəl] *adj* bíblico

bibliographer [,bɪblɪ'ɑgrəfər] *s* bibliógrafo

bibliogra·phy [,bɪblɪ'ɑgrəfi] *s* (*pl* -phies) bibliografía

bibliophile ['bɪblɪ·ə,faɪl] *s* bibliófilo

bicameral [baɪ'kæmərəl] *adj* bicameral

bicarbonate [baɪ'kɑrbə,net] *s* bicarbonato

bicker ['bɪkər] *s* discusión ociosa || *intr* discutir ociosamente

bicycle ['baɪsɪkəl] *s* bicicleta

bid [bɪd] *s* oferta, postura; (*in bridge*) declaración || *v* (*pret* bade [bæd] o **bid**; *ger* bidden ['bɪdən] *tr & intr* ofrecer, pujar, licitar; (*in bridge*) declarar

bidder ['bɪdər] *s* postor *m*; (*in bridge*) declarante *mf*; **the highest bidder** el mejor postor

bidding ['bɪdɪŋ] *s* mandato, orden *f*; postura; (*in bridge*) declaración

bide [baɪd] *tr* — **to bide one's time** esperar la hora propicia

biennial [baɪ'ɛnɪ·əl] *adj* bienal

bier [bɪr] *s* féretro, andas

bifocal [baɪ'fokəl] *adj* bifocal || **bifocals** *spl* anteojos bifocales

big [bɪg] *adj* (*comp* bigger; *super* biggest) grande; (*considerable*) importante; (*grown-up*) adulto; **big with child** preñada || *adv* (coll) con jactancia; **to talk big** (coll) hablar gordo

bigamist ['bɪgəmɪst] *s* bígamo

bigamous ['bɪgəməs] *adj* bígamo

bigamy ['bɪgəmi] *s* bigamia

big-bellied ['bɪg,bɛlɪd] *adj* panzudo

Big Dipper *s* Carro mayor

big game *s* caza mayor

big-hearted ['bɪg,hɑrtɪd] *adj* magnánimo, generoso

bigot ['bɪgət] *s* intolerante *mf*, fanático

bigoted ['bɪgətɪd] *adj* intolerante, fanático

bigot·ry ['bɪgətri] *s* (*pl* -ries) intolerancia, fanatismo

big shot *s* (slang) pájaro de cuenta, señorón *m*

big stick *s* palo en alto

big toe *s* dedo gordo o grande (*del pie*)

bile [baɪl] *s* bilis *f*

bilge [bɪldʒ] *s* pantoque *m* || *tr* desfondar

bilge pump *s* bomba de sentina

bilge water *s* agua de pantoque

bilge ways *spl* anguilas

bilingual [baɪ'lɪŋgwəl] *adj* bilingüe

bilious ['bɪljəs] *adj* bilioso

bilk [bɪlk] *tr* estafar, trampear

bill [bɪl] *s* (*statement of charges for goods or service*) cuenta, factura; (*paper money*) billete *m*; (*poster*) cartel *m*, aviso; cartel de teatro; (*draft of law*) proyecto de ley; (*handbill*) hoja suelta; (*of bird*) pico; (com) giro, letra de cambio || *tr* facturar; cargar en cuenta a; anunciar por carteles || *intr* darse el pico (*las palomas*); acariciarse (*los enamorados*); **to bill and coo** acariciarse y arrullarse

bill'board' *s* cartelera

billet ['bɪlɪt] *s* (mil) boleta; (mil) alojamiento || *tr* (mil) alojar

billet-doux ['bɪle'du] *s* (*pl* billets-doux ['bɪle'duz]) esquela amorosa

bill'fold' *s* cartera de bolsillo, billetero

bill'head' *s* encabezamiento de factura

billiards ['bɪljərdz] *s* billar *m*

billion ['bɪljən] *s* (U.S.A.) mil millones; (Brit) billón *m*

bill of exchange *s* letra de cambio

bill of fare *s* lista de comidas, menú *m*

bill of lading *s* conocimiento de embarque

bill of sale *s* escritura de venta

billow ['bɪlo] *s* oleada, ondulación || *intr* ondular, hincharse

bill'post'er *s* fijacarteles *m*, fijador *m* de carteles

bil·ly ['bɪli] *s* (*pl* -lies) cachiporra

billy goat *s* macho cabrío

bin [bɪn] *s* arcón *m*, hucha

bind [baɪnd] *v* (*pret & pp* bound [baʊnd] *tr* ligar, atar; juntar, unir; (*with a garland*) enguirlandar; ribetear (*la orilla del vestido*); agavillar (*las mieses*); vendar (*una herida*); encuadernar (*un libro*)

binder·y ['baɪndəri] *s* (*pl* -ies) taller *m* de encuadernación

binding ['baɪndɪŋ] *s* atadura; (*of a book*) encuadernación

binding post *s* borne *m*, sujetahilo

binge [bɪndʒ] *s* (slang) borrachera; **to go on a binge** (slang) pegarse una mona

binnacle ['bɪnəkəl] *s* bitácora

binoculars [bɪ'nɑkjələrz] o [baɪ'nɑkjələrz] *spl* gemelos, prismáticos

biochemical [,baɪ·ə'kɛmɪkəl] *adj* bioquímico

biochemist [,baɪ·ə'kɛmɪst] *s* bioquímico

biochemistry [,baɪ·ə'kɛmɪstri] *s* bioquímica

biodegradable [,baɪ·ədɪ'gredəbəl] *adj* biodegradable

biographer [baɪ'ɑgrəfər] *s* biógrafo

biographic(al) [,baɪ·ə'græfɪk(əl)] *adj* biográfico

biogra·phy [baɪ'ɑgrəfi] *s* (*pl* -phies) biografía

biologist [bar'aladʒɪst] *s* biólogo
biology [bar'aladʒi] *s* biología
biophysical [,bar-ə'fɪzɪkəl] *adj* biofísico
biophysics [,bar-ə'fɪzɪks] *s* biofísica
birch [bʌrtʃ] *s* abedul *m* ‖ *tr* azotar, varear
bird [bʌrd] *s* ave *f*, pájaro
bird cage *s* jaula
bird call *s* reclamo
bird'lime' *s* liga
bird of passage *s* ave *f* de paso
bird of prey *s* ave *f* de rapiña
bird'seed' *s* alpiste *m*, cañamones *mpl*
bird's'-eye' view *s* vista a ojo de pájaro
bird shot *s* perdigones *mpl*
birth [bʌrθ] *s* nacimiento; (*childbirth*) parto; origen *m*
birth certificate *s* partida de nacimiento
birth control *s* limitación de la natalidad
birth'day' *s* cumpleaños *m*, natal *m*; (*of any event*) aniversario; **to have a birthday** cumplir años
birthday cake *s* pastel *m* de cumpleaños
birthday present *s* regalo de cumpleaños
birth'mark' *s* antojo, nevo materno
birth'place' *s* suelo natal, patria, lugar *m* de nacimiento
birth rate *s* natalidad
birth'right' *s* derechos de nacimiento; primogenitura
Biscay [ˈbɪske] *s* Vizcaya
biscuit [ˈbɪskɪt] *s* panecillo redondo; bizcocho
bisect [barˈsɛkt] *tr* bisecar ‖ *intr* empalmar (*dos caminos*)
bishop [ˈbɪʃəp] *s* obispo; (*in chess*) alfil *m*
bismuth [ˈbɪzməθ] *s* bismuto
bison [ˈbaɪsən] o [ˈbaɪzən] *s* bisonte *m*
bit [bɪt] *s* poquito, pedacito; (*of food*) bocado; (*of time*) ratito; (*part of bridle*) bocado, freno; (*for drilling*) barrena; **a good bit** una buena cantidad
bitch [bɪtʃ] *s* (*dog*) perra; (*fox*) zorra; (*wolf*) loba; (*vulg*) mujer *f* de mal genio
bite [baɪt] *s* mordedura; (*of bird or insect*) picadura; (*burning sensation on tongue*) resquemo; (*of food*) bocado; (*snack*) (coll) tentempié *m*, refrigerio *m* ‖ *v* (*pret* **bit** [bɪt]; *pp* **bit** o **bitten** [ˈbɪtən]) *tr* morder; picar (*los peces, los insectos*); resquemar (*la lengua los alimentos*); comerse (*las uñas*) ‖ *intr* morder; picar; resquemar; (*to be caught by a trick*) (slang) picar
biting [ˈbaɪtɪŋ] *adj* penetrante; mordaz, picante
bitter [ˈbɪtər] *adj* amargo; (*e.g., struggle*) encarnizado; **to the bitter end** hasta el extremo; hasta la muerte
bitter almond *s* almendra amarga
bitterness [ˈbɪtərnɪs] *s* amargura
bitumen [bɪˈtjumən] o [bɪˈtumən] *s* betún *m*

bivou·ac [ˈbɪvʊ·æk] o [ˈbɪvwæk] *s* vivaque *m* ‖ *v* (*pret & pp* **-acked;** *ger* **-acking**) *intr* vivaquear
bizarre [bɪˈzɑr] *adj* original, raro
bk. *abbr* **bank, block, book**
bl. *abbr* **barrel**
b.l. *abbr* **bill of lading**
blabber [ˈblæbər] *tr & intr* barbullar
black [blæk] *adj* negro ‖ *s* negro; luto; **to wear black** ir de luto
black'-and-blue' *adj* encardenalado, amoratado
black'-and-white' *adj* en blanco y negro
black'ber'ry *s* (*pl* **-ries**) (*bush*) zarza; (*fruit*) zarzamora
black'bird' *s* mirlo
black'board' *s* encerado, pizarra
black'damp' *s* mofeta
blacken [ˈblækən] *tr* ennegrecer; (*to defame*) desacreditar, denigrar
blackguard [ˈblægərd] *s* bribón *m*, canalla *m* ‖ *tr* injuriar, vilipendiar
black'head' *s* espinilla, comedón *m*
black hole *s* (astr) agujero negro
blackish [ˈblækɪʃ] *adj* negruzco
black'jack' *s* (*club*) cachiporra; (*flag*) bandera negra (*de pirata*) ‖ *tr* aporrear
black'mail' *s* chantaje *m* ‖ *tr* amenazar con chantaje
blackmailer [ˈblæk,melər] *s* chantajista *mf*
Black Maria [məˈraɪ·ə] *s* (coll) coche *m* celular
black market *s* estraperlo, mercado negro
blackness [ˈblæknɪs] *s* negror *m*, negrura
black'out' *s* (*in wartime*) apagón *m*; (*in theater*) apagamiento de luces; (*of aviators*) visión negra; pérdida de la memoria
black sheep *s* (fig) oveja negra, garbanzo negro
black'smith' *s* (*man who works with iron*) herrero; (*man who shoes horses*) herrador *m*
black'thorn' *s* espino negro, endrino
black tie *s* corbata de smoking; smoking *m*
bladder [ˈblædər] *s* vejiga
blade [bled] *s* (*of a knife, sword*) hoja; (*of a propeller*) aleta; (*of a fan*) paleta; (*of an oar*) pala; (*of an electric switch*) cuchilla; (*sword*) espada; tallo de hierba; (coll) gallardo joven
blame [blem] *s* culpa ‖ *tr* culpar
blameless [ˈblemlɪs] *adj* inculpable, irreprochable
blanch [blæntʃ] o [blɑntʃ] *tr* blanquear ‖ *intr* palidecer
bland [blænd] *adj* apacible; suave; (*character; weather*) blando
blandish [ˈblændɪʃ] *tr* engatusar, lisonjear
blank [blæŋk] *adj* en blanco; blanco, vacío; (*stare, look*) vago ‖ *s* blanco; papel blanco; formulario
blank check *s* firma en blanco; (fig) carta blanca

blanket ['blæŋkɪt] *adj* general, comprensivo || *s* manta, frazada; (fig) capa, manto || *tr* cubrir con manta; cubrir, obscurecer

blasé [blɑ'ze] *adj* hastiado

blaspheme [blæs'fim] *tr* blasfemar contra || *intr* blasfemar

blasphemous ['blæsfɪməs] *adj* blasfemo

blasphe•my ['blæsfɪmi] *s* (*pl* -mies) blasfemia

blast [blæst] o [blɑst] *s* (*of wind*) ráfaga; (*of air, sand, water*) chorro; (*of bellows*) soplo; (*of a horn*) toque *m*; carga de pólvora; voladura, explosión; **full blast** en plena marcha || *tr* (*to blow up*) volar; arruinar; infamar, maldecir

blast furnace *s* alto horno

blast′off′ *s* lanzamiento de cohete

blatant ['bletənt] *adj* ruidoso; vocinglero; intruso; chillón, cursi

blaze [blez] *s* llamarada; (*fire*) incendio; (*bonfire*) hoguera; luz *f* brillante || *tr* encender, inflamar; **to blaze a trail** abrir una senda || *intr* encenderse; resplandecer

bldg. *abbr* **building**

bleach [blitʃ] *s* blanqueo || *tr* blanquear; colar (*la ropa*)

bleachers ['blitʃərz] *spl* gradas al aire libre

bleak [blik] *adj* desierto, yermo, frío, triste

bleat [blit] *s* balido || *intr* balar

bleed [blid] *v* (*pret & pp* **bled** [bled]) *tr & intr* sangrar

blemish ['blemɪʃ] *s* mancha || *tr* manchar

blend [blend] *s* mezcla; armonía || *v* (*pret & pp* **blended** o **blent** [blent]) *tr* mezclar; armonizar; fusionar || *intr* mezclarse; armonizar; fusionarse

bless [bles] *tr* bendecir; **to be blessed with** estar dotado de

blessed ['blesɪd] *adj* bendito, santo

blessedness ['blesɪdnɪs] *s* bienaventuranza

blessing ['blesɪŋ] *s* bendición

blight [blaɪt] *s* niebla, roya; ruina || *tr* anublar; arruinar

blimp [blɪmp] *s* dirigible pequeño

blind [blaɪnd] *adj* ciego || *s* (*window shade*) estor *m*, transparente *m* de resorte; (*Venetian blind*) persiana; pretexto, subterfugio || *tr* cegar; (*to dazzle*) deslumbrar; (*to deceive*) cegar, vendar

blind alley *s* callejón *m* sin salida

blind date *s* cita a ciegas

blinder ['blaɪndər] *s* anteojera

blind flying *s* (aer) vuelo a ciegas

blind′fold′ *adj* vendado de ojos || *s* venda || *tr* vendar los ojos a

blind landing *s* aterrizaje *m* a ciegas

blind man *s* ciego

blind′man′s′ buff *s* gallina ciega

blindness ['blaɪndnɪs] *s* ceguedad

blink [blɪŋk] *s* guiñada, parpadeo || *tr* guiñar (*el ojo*) || *intr* guiñar, parpadear, pestañear; oscilar (*la luz*)

blip [blɪp] *s* bache *m*

bliss [blɪs] *s* bienaventuranza, felicidad

blissful ['blɪsfəl] *adj* bienaventurado, feliz

blister ['blɪstər] *s* ampolla, vejiga || *tr* ampollar || *intr* ampollarse

blithe [blaɪð] *adj* alegre, animado

blitzkrieg ['blɪts,krig] *s* guerra relámpago

blizzard ['blɪzərd] *s* ventisca, chubasco de nieve

bloat [blot] *tr* hinchar || *intr* hincharse, abotagarse

block [blɑk] *s* bloque *m*; (*of hatter*) horma; (*of houses*) manzana; (*for chopping meat*) tajo; estorbo, obstáculo || *tr* cerrar, obstruir; conformar (*un sombrero*)

blockade [blɑ'ked] *s* bloqueo || *tr* bloquear

blockade runner *s* forzador *m* de bloqueo

block and tackle *s* aparejo de poleas

block′bust′er *s* (coll) bomba rompedora

block′head′ *s* tonto, zoquete *m*

block signal *s* (rr) señal *f* de tramo

blond [blɑnd] *adj* rubio, blondo || *s* rubio (*hombre rubio*)

blonde [blɑnd] *s* rubia (*mujer rubia*)

blood [blʌd] *s* sangre *f*; **in cold blood** a sangre fría

bloodcurdling ['blʌd,kʌrdlɪŋ] *adj* horripilante

blood′hound′ *s* sabueso

blood poisoning *s* envenenamiento de la sangre

blood pressure *s* presión arterial

blood pudding *s* morcilla

blood relation *s* pariente consanguíneo

blood′shed′ *s* efusión de sangre

blood′shot′ *adj* inyectado en sangre, encarnizado

blood test *s* análisis *m* de sangre

blood′thirst′y *adj* sanguinario

blood transfusion *s* transfusión de sangre

blood vessel *s* vaso sanguíneo

blood•y ['blʌdi] *adj* (*comp* -ier; *super* -iest) sangriento || *v* (*pret & pp* -ied) *tr* ensangrentar

bloom [blum] *s* florecimiento; flor *f* || *intr* florecer

blossom ['blɑsəm] *s* brote *m*, flor *f*; **in blossom** en cierne || *intr* cerner, florecer

blot [blɑt] *s* borrón *m* || *v* (*pret & pp* **blotted**; *ger* **blotting**) *tr* (*to smear*) borrar; secar con papel secante; **to blot out** borrar || *intr* borrarse; echar borrones (*una pluma*)

blotch [blɑtʃ] *s* manchón *m*; (*in the skin*) erupción

blotter ['blɑtər] *s* teleta, secafirmas *m*

blotting paper *s* papel *m* secante

blouse [blaus] *s* blusa

blow [blo] *s* (*hit, stroke*) golpe *m*; (*blast of air*) soplo, soplido; (*blast of wind*) ventarrón *m*; (*of horn*) toque *m*, trompetazo; (*sudden sorrow*) estocada, ramalazo; (*boaster*) (slang) fanfarrón *m*; **to come to blows** venir a las manos || *v* (*pret* **blew** [blu]; *pp*

blown' ‖ *tr* soplar; sonar, tocar (*un instrumento de viento*); silbar (*un silbato*); sonarse (*las narices*); quemar (*un fusible*); (*slang*) malgastar (*dinero*); **to blow out** apagar soplando; quemar (*un fusible*); **to blow up** (*with air*) inflar; (*e.g., with dynamite*) volar, hacer saltar; ampliar (*una foto*) ‖ *intr* soplar; (*to pant*) jadear, resoplar; fundirse (*un fusible*); (*slang*) fanfarronear; **to blow out** apagarse con el aire; quemarse, fundirse (*un fusible*); reventar (*un neumático*); **to blow up** volarse; (*to fail*) fracasar; (*with anger*) (*slang*) estallar, reventar

blow'out' *s* (aut) reventón *m*; (*of a fuse*) quemazón *f*; (*slang*) tertulia concurrida, festín *m*

blowout patch *s* parche *m* para neumático

blow'pipe' *s* (*torch*) soplete *m*; (*peashooter*) cerbatana

blow'torch' *s* antorcha a soplete, lámpara de soldar

blubber ['blʌbər] *s* grasa de ballena; lloro ruidoso ‖ *intr* llorar ruidosamente

bludgeon ['blʌdʒən] *s* cachiporra ‖ *tr* aporrear; intimidar

blue [blu] *adj* azul; abatido, triste ‖ *s* azul *m*; **the blues** la murria, la morriña ‖ *tr* azular; añilar (*la ropa blanca*) ‖ *intr* azularse

blue chip *s* valor *m* de primera fila

blue'ber'ry *s* (*pl* **-ries**) mirtilo

blue'jay' *s* cianocita

blue moon *s* cosa muy rara; **once in a blue moon** cada muerte de obispo, de Pascuas a Ramos

Blue Nile *s* Nilo Azul

blue'-pen'cil *tr* marcar o corregir con lápiz azul

blue'print' *s* cianotipo ‖ *tr* copiar a la cianotipia

blue'stock'ing *s* (coll) marisabidilla

blue streak *s* (coll) rayo; **to talk a blue streak** (coll) soltar la tarabilla

bluff [blʌf] *adj* escarpado ‖ *s* risco, peñasco escarpado; (*deception*) farol *m*; **to call someone's bluff** cogerle la palabra a uno ‖ *intr* farolear, papelonear

blunder ['blʌndər] *s* disparate *m*, desatino ‖ *intr* disparatar, desatinar

blunt [blʌnt] *adj* despuntado, embotado; brusco, franco, directo ‖ *tr* despuntar, embotar

bluntness ['blʌntnɪs] *s* embotadura; brusquedad, franqueza

blur [blʌr] *s* borrón *m*, mancha ‖ *v* (*pret & pp* **blurred**) (*of sight*) empañar; obscurecer (*la vista*) ‖ *intr* empañarse

blurb [blʌrb] *s* anuncio efusivo

blurt [blʌrt] *tr* — **to blurt out** soltar abrupta e impulsivamente

blush [blʌʃ] *s* rubor *m*, sonrojo ‖ *intr* ruborizarse, sonrojarse

bluster ['blʌstər] *s* tumulto, gritos; jactancia ‖ *intr* soplar con furia (*el viento*); bravear, fanfarronear

blustery ['blʌstəri] *adj* tempestuoso; (*wind*) violento; (*swaggering*) fanfarrón

blvd. *abbr* **boulevard**

boar [bor] *s* (*male swine*) verraco; (*wild hog*) jabalí *m*

board [bord] *s* tabla; (*to post announcements*) tablillo; (*table with meal*) mesa; (*daily meals*) pensión; (*organized group*) junta, consejo; (naut) bordo; **in boards** (bb) en cartoné; **on board** en el tren; (naut) a bordo ‖ *tr* entablar; subir a (*un tren*); embarcarse en (*un buque*) ‖ *intr* hospedarse; estar de pupilo

board and lodging *s* mesa y habitación, pensión completa

border ['bordər] *s* pensionista *mf*, pupilo

boarding house *s* pensión, casa de huéspedes

boarding school *s* escuela de internos

board of health *s* junta de sanidad

board of trade *s* junta de comercio

board of trustees *s* consejo de administración

board'walk' *s* paseo entablado a la orilla del mar

boast [bost] *s* jactancia, baladronada ‖ *intr* jactarse, baladronear

boastful ['bostfəl] *adj* jactancioso

boat [bot] *s* barco, buque *m*, nave *f*; (*small boat*) bote *m*; **to be in the same boat** correr el mismo riesgo

boat hook *s* bichero

boat'house' *s* casilla para botes

boating ['botɪŋ] *s* paseo en barco

boat-man ['botmən] *s* (*pl* **-men** [mən]) barquero, lanchero

boat race *s* regata

boatswain *s* ['bosən] o ['bot‚swən] *s* contramaestre *m*

boatswain's chair *s* guindola

boatswain's mate *s* segundo contramaestre

bob [bab] *s* (*of pendulum of clock*) lenteja; (*of plumb line*) plomo; (*of a fishing line*) corcho; (*of a horse*) cola cortada; (*of a girl*) pelo cortado corto; (*jerky motion*) sacudida ‖ *v* (*pret & pp* **bobbed**; *ger* **bobbing**) *tr* cortar corto ‖ *intr* agitarse, menearse; **to bob up and down** subir y bajar con sacudidas cortas

bobbin ['babɪn] *s* broca, canilla, bobina

bobby pin ['babi] *s* horquillita para el pelo

bob'by-socks' *spl* (coll) tobilleras (*de jovencita*)

bobbysoxer ['babi ‚saksər] *s* (coll) tobillera

bobolink ['babə‚lɪŋk] *s* chambergo

bob'sled' *s* doble trineo articulado

bob'tail' *s* animal *m* rabón; cola corta; cola cortada

bob'white' *s* colín *m* de Virginia

bock beer [bak] *s* cerveza de marzo

bode [bod] *tr* & *intr* anunciar, presagiar; **to bode ill** ser un mal presagio; **to bode well** ser un buen presagio

bodice ['badɪs] s jubón m, corpiño
bodily ['badɪli] adj corporal, corpóreo
 ‖ adv en persona; en conjunto
bodkin ['badkɪn] s (needle) aguja
 roma; (for lady's hair) espadilla; (to
 make holes in cloth) punzón m
bod·y ['badi] s (pl -ies) cuerpo; (of a
 carriage or auto) caja, carrocería
bod'y-guard' s (mil) guardia de corps;
 guardaespaldas m
Boer [bor] o [bʊr] s bóer mf
Boer War s guerra del Transvaal
bog [bag] s pantano ‖ v (pret & pp
 bogged; ger **bogging**) intr — to bog
 down atascarse, hundirse
bogey ['bogi] s duende m, coco
bo'gey-man' s (pl -men [,men]) duende m, espantajo
bogus ['bogəs] adj (coll) fingido, falso
bo·gy ['bogi] s (pl -gies) duende m,
 demonio, coco
Bohemian [bo'himɪ·ən] adj & s bo-
 hemio
boil [bɔɪl] s hervor m, ebullición;
 (pathol) divieso, furúnculo ‖ tr hacer hervir, herventar ‖ intr hervir,
 bullir; **to boil over** salirse (un líquido) al hervir
boiler ['bɔɪlər] s caldera; (for cooking) marmita, olla
boil'er-mak'er s calderero
boiler room s sala de calderas
boiling ['bɔɪlɪŋ] adj hirviente, hir-
 viendo ‖ s hervor m, ebullición
boiling point s punto de ebullición
boisterous ['bɔɪstərəs] adj bullicioso,
 ruidoso, estrepitoso
bold [bold] adj audaz, arrojado, osado; descarado, impudente; temerario
bold'face' s negrilla
boldness ['boldnɪs] s audacia, arrojo,
 osadía; descaro, impudencia; temeridad
Bolivia [bo'lɪvɪ·ə] s Bolivia
Bolivian [bo'lɪvɪ·ən] adj & s boliviano
boll weevil [bol] s gorgojo del algodón
Bologna [bə'lonjə] s Bolonia
Bolshevik ['bal/əvɪk] o ['bol/əvɪk]
 adj & s bolchevique mf
Bolshevism ['bal/ə,vɪzəm] o ['bol/ə-
 ,vɪzəm] s bolchevismo
bolster ['bolstər] s (of bed) larguero,
 travesaño; refuerzo, soporte m ‖ tr
 apoyar, sostener; animar, alentar
bolt [bolt] s perno; (to fasten a door)
 cerrojo, pasador m; (arrow) cuadrillo; (of lightning) rayo; (of cloth
 or paper) rollo ‖ tr empernar; acerrojar; deglutir de una vez; cribar,
 tamizar; disidir de (un partido político) ‖ intr salir de repente; disidir;
 desbocarse (un caballo)
bolter ['boltər] s disidente mf; (sieve)
 criba, tamiz m
bolt from the blue s rayo en cielo sin
 nubes; suceso inesperado
bomb [bam] s bomba ‖ tr bombear,
 bombardear
bombard [bam'bard] tr bombardear;
 (e.g., with questions) asediar
bombardment [bam'bardmənt] s bombardeo

bombast ['bambæst] s ampulosidad
bombastic [bam'bæstɪk] adj ampuloso
bomb crater s (mil) embudo de bomba
bomber ['bamər] s bombardero
bomb'proof' adj a prueba de bombas
bomb release s lanzabombas m
bomb'shell' s bomba; **to fall like a
 bombshell** caer como una bomba
bomb shelter s refugio antiaéreo
bomb'sight' s mira de bombardeo, visor m
bona fide ['bonə ,faɪdə] adj & adv de
 buena fe
bonbon ['ban ,ban] s bombón m, confite m
bond [band] s (tie, union) enlace m,
 vínculo, lazo de unión; (interest-
 bearing certificate) bono, obligación; (surety) fianza; (mas) aparejo; **bonds** cadenas, grillos; **in bond**
 en depósito bajo fianza
bondage ['bandɪdʒ] s cautiverio, servidumbre
bonded warehouse s depósito comercial
bond'hold'er s obligacionista mf, tenedor m de bonos
bonds·man ['bandzmən] s (pl -men
 [mən]) fiador m
bone [bon] s hueso; (of fish) espina;
 bones esqueleto; (mortal remains)
 huesos; castañuelas; (dice) (coll)
 dados; **to have a bone to pick with**
 tener una queja con; **to make no
 bones about** no andarse con rodeos
 en ‖ tr desosar; quitar la espina a;
 emballenar (un corsé) ‖ intr — to
 bone up on (coll) empollar, estudiar
 con ahinco
bone'head' s (coll) mentecato, zopenco
boneless ['bonlɪs] adj mollar, des-
 osado; (fish) sin espinas
boner ['bonər] s (coll) patochada,
 plancha, gazapo
bonfire ['ban ,faɪr] s hoguera
bonnet ['banɪt] s gorra; (sunbonnet)
 papalina; (of auto) cubierta, capó m
bonus ['bonəs] s prima, plus m; dividendo extraordinario
bon·y ['boni] adj (comp -ier; super
 -iest) osudo; descarnado; (fish) espinoso
boo [bu] s rechifla; **not to say boo** no
 decir ni chus ni mus ‖ tr & intr abuchear, rechiflar
boo·by ['bubi] s (pl -bies) bobalicón
 m, zopenco; el peor jugador
booby prize s premio al peor jugador
booby trap s (mine) trampa explosiva;
 (trick) zancadilla
boogie-woogie ['bugi'wʊgi] s bugui-
 bugui m
book [bʊk] s libro; (bankbook) libreta; (book containing records of
 business transactions) libro-registro;
 (of cigaret paper, stamps, etc.) librillo; **to keep books** llevar libros ‖
 tr reservar (un pasaje); escriturar (a
 un actor)
bookbinder ['bʊk ,baɪndər] s encuadernador m

bo
bo

book′bind′er·y *s* (*pl* **-ies**) encuadernación (*taller*)

book′bind′ing *s* encuadernación (*acción, arte*)

book′case′ *s* armario para libros, estante *m* para libros

book end *s* apoyalibros *m*

bookie [′bʊki] *s* (coll) corredor *m* de apuestas

booking [′bʊkɪŋ] *s* (*of passage*) reservación; (*of an actor*) escritura

booking clerk *s* taquillero (*que despacha pasajes o localidades*)

bookish [′bʊkɪʃ] *adj* libresco

book′keep′er *s* tenedor *m* de libros

book′keep′ing *s* teneduría de libros, contabilidad

book′mak′er *s* corredor *m* de apuestas

book′mark′ *s* registro

book′plate′ *s* ex libris *m*

book review *s* reseña

book′sell′er *s* librero

book′shelf′ *s* (*pl* **-shelves** [‚ʃelvz]) estante *m* para libros

book′stand′ *s* (*rack*) atril *m*; mostrador *m* para libros; puesto de venta para libros

book′store′ *s* librería

book′worm′ *s* polilla que roe los libros; (fig) ratón *m* de biblioteca

boom [bum] *s* (*sudden prosperity*) auge *m*; (*noise*) estampido, trueno; (*of a crane*) aguilón *m*; (naut) botalón *m* || *intr* hacer estampido, tronar; estar en auge

boomerang [′bumə‚ræŋ] *s* bumerán *m*

boom town *s* pueblo en bonanza

boon [bun] *s* bendición, dicha

boon companion *s* buen compañero

boor [bʊr] *s* patán *m*, rústico

boorish [′bʊrɪʃ] *adj* rústico, zafio

boost [bust] *s* empujón *m* hacia arriba; (*in price*) alza; alabanza; ayuda || *tr* empujar hacia arriba; alzar (*el precio*); alabar; ayudar

booster [′bustər] *s* cohete *m* lanzador; primera etapa de un cohete lanzador; (*enthusiastic backer*) bombista *mf*; (med) inyección secundaria

boot [but] *s* bota; **to boot** de añadidura, además; **to die with one′s boots on** morir al pie del cañón || *tr* dar un puntapié a; **to boot out** (slang) poner en la calle

boot′black′ *s* limpiabotas *m*

booth [buθ] *s* casilla, quiosco; (*to telephone, to vote, etc.*) cabina; (*at a fair or market*) puesto

boot′jack′ *s* sacabotas *m*

boot′leg′ *adj* contrabandista; de contrabando || *s* contrabando de licores || *v* (*pret & pp* **-legged**; *ger* **-legging**) *tr* pasar de contrabando || *intr* contrabandear en bebidas alcohólicas

bootlegger [′but‚lɛgər] *s* destilador *m* clandestino, contrabandista *m*

boot′leg′ging *s* contrabando en bebidas alcohólicas

bootlicker [′but‚lɪkər] *s* (slang) quitamotas *mf*, lavacaras *mf*

boot′strap′ *s* tirilla de bota

boo·ty [′buti] *s* (*pl* **-ties**) botín *m*, presa

booze [buz] *s* (coll) bebida alcohólica || *intr* borrachear

bor. *abbr* **borough**

borax [′boræks] *s* bórax *m*

Bordeaux [bɔr′do] *s* Burdeos

border [′bɔrdər] *adj* frontero, fronterizo || *s* borde *m*, margen *m & f*; frontera; **borders** bambalinas || *tr* bordear; deslindar || *intr* confinar

border clash *s* encuentro fronterizo

bor′der·line′ *adj* incierto, indefinido || *s* frontera

bore [bor] *s* (*drill hole*) barreno; (*size of hole*) calibre *m*; (*of firearm*) alma, ánima; (*of cylinder*) alesaje *m*; (*wearisome person*) latoso, machaca *mf*; fastidio || *tr* aburrir, fastidiar; barrenar, hacer (*un agujero*)

boredom [′bordəm] *s* aburrimiento, fastidio

boring [′borɪŋ] *adj* aburrido, pesado

born [bɔrn] *adj* nacido; (*natural, by birth*) nato, innato; **to be born** nacer

borough [′bʌro] *s* (*town*) villa; distrito electoral de municipio

borrow [′baro] *o* [′boro] *tr* pedir o tomar prestado; apropiarse (*p.ej., una idea*); incorporar (*un elemento lingüístico extranjero*); **to borrow trouble** tomarse una molestia sin motivo alguno

borrower [′baro·ər] *o* [′boro·ər] *s* prestatario

borrowing [′baro·ɪŋ] *o* [′boro·ɪŋ] *s* préstamo; préstamo lingüístico, extranjerismo

bosom [′bʊzəm] *s* seno; (*of shirt*) pechera; corazón *m*, pecho

bosom friend *s* amigo de la mayor confianza

Bosporus [′bɑspərəs] *s* Bósforo

boss [bɔs] *o* [bɑs] *s* (coll) amo, capataz *m*, mandamás, *m*, jefe *m*; (*in politics*) (coll) cacique *m*; protuberancia || *tr* (coll) mandar, dominar

boss·y [′bɔsi] *o* [′bɑsi] *adj* (*comp* **-ier**; *super* **-iest**) mandón

botanical [bə′tænɪkəl] *adj* botánico

botanist [′bɑtənɪst] *s* botánico

botany [′bɑtəni] *s* botánica

botch [bɑtʃ] *s* remiendo chapucero || *tr* remendar chapuceramente

both [boθ] *adj & pron* ambos || *adv* igualmente || *conj* a la vez; **both ... and** tanto ... como, así ... como

bother [′bɑðər] *s* incomodidad, molestia || *tr* incomodar, molestar || *intr* molestarse

bothersome [′bɑðərsəm] *adj* incómodo, molesto, fastidioso

bottle [′bɑtəl] *s* botella, frasco || *tr* embotellar; **to bottle up** (nav) embotellar

bot′tle·neck′ *s* gollete *m*; (*in traffic*) embotellamiento

bottle opener [′opənər] *s* abrebotellas *m*

bottom [′bɑtəm] *adj* (*price*) (el) más bajo; (*e.g., dollar*) último || *s* fondo; (*of a chair*) asiento; (*of jar*) culo;

(coll) trasero; **at bottom** en el fondo; **to go to the bottom** irse a pique
bottomless [ˈbɑtəmlɪs] *adj* sin fondo, insondable
boudoir [buˈdwɑr] *s* tocador *m*
bough [bau] *s* rama
bouillon [ˈbuljɑn] *s* caldo
boulder [ˈboldər] *s* pedrejón *m*
boulevard [ˈbulə‚vɑrd] *s* bulevar *m*
bounce [bauns] *s* rebote *m* ‖ *tr* hacer botar; (slang) despedir ‖ *intr* botar, rebotar; saltar; **to bounce along** dar saltos al andar
bouncer [ˈbaunsər] *s* cosa grande; (slang) apagabroncas *m*
bouncing [ˈbaunsɪŋ] *adj* frescachón, vigoroso; (*baby*) gordinflón
bound [baund] *adj* atado, ligado; (*book*) encuadernado; dispuesto, propenso; puesto en aprendizaje; **bound for** con destino a, con rumbo a; **bound in boards** (bb) encartonado, en cartoné; **bound up in** entregado a, muy adicto a; absorto en ‖ *s* salto; (*of a ball*) bote *m*; límite *m*, confín *m*; **bounds** región, comarca; **out of bounds** fuera de los límites; **within bounds** a raya
bounda‧ry [ˈbaundəri] *s* (*pl* **-ries**) límite *m*, frontera
boundary stone *s* mojón *m*
bounder [ˈbaundər] *s* persona vulgar y malcriada
boundless [ˈbaundlɪs] *adj* ilimitado, inmenso, infinito
bountiful [ˈbauntɪfəl] *adj* generoso, liberal; abundante
boun‧ty [ˈbaunti] *s* (*pl* **-ties**) generosidad, liberalidad; don *m*, favor *m*; galardón *m*, premio; (*bonus*) prima; (mil) premio de enganche
bouquet [buˈke] o [boˈke] *s* ramillete *m*; (*aroma of a wine*) nariz *f*
bourgeois [ˈburʒwɑ] *adj* & *s* burgués *m*
bourgeoisie [‚burʒwɑˈzi] *s* burguesía
bout [baut] *s* encuentro; rato; (*of an illness*) ataque *m*
bow [bau] *s* inclinación, reverencia; (*of a ship*) proa ‖ *tr* inclinar (*la cabeza*) ‖ *intr* inclinarse; **to bow and scrape** hacer reverencias obsequiosas; **to bow to** saludar, inclinarse delante ‖ [bo] *s* (*for shooting an arrow*) arco; lazo, nudo; (mus) arco; (*stroke of bow*) (mus) arqueada ‖ *tr* (mus) tocar con arco ‖ *intr* arquearse
bowdlerize [ˈbaudlə‚raɪz] *tr* expurgar
bowel [ˈbau‧əl] *s* intestino; **bowels** intestinos; (*inner part*) entrañas
bowel movement *s* evacuación del vientre; **to have a bowel movement** evacuar el vientre
bower [ˈbau‧ər] *s* emparrado, glorieta
bower‧y [ˈbau‧əri] *adj* frondoso, sombreado ‖ *s* (*pl* **-ies**) finca, granja
bowknot [ˈbo‚nɑt] *s* lazada
bowl [bol] *s* (*for soup or broth*) escudilla, cuenco; (*for washing hands*) jofaina, palangana; (*of toilet*) cubeta, taza; (*of fountain*) tazón *m*; (*of spoon*) paleta; (*of pipe*) hornillo;

(*hollow place*) concavidad, cuenco ‖ *tr* — **to bowl over** tumbar ‖ *intr* jugar a los bolos; **to bowl along** rodar
bowlegged [ˈbo‚lɛgd] o [ˈbo‚lɛgɪd] *adj* patiestevado
bowler [ˈbolər] *s* jugador *m* de bolos; (Brit) sombrero hongo
bowling [ˈbolɪŋ] *s* juego de bolos, boliche *m*
bowling alley *s* bolera, boliche *m*
bowling green *s* bolera encespada
bowshot [ˈbo‚ʃɑt] *s* tiro de flecha
bowsprit [ˈbausprɪt] o [ˈbosprɪt] *s* bauprés *m*
bow tie [bo] *s* corbata de mariposa, pajarita
bowwow [ˈbau‚wau] *interj* ¡guau! ‖ *s* guau guau *m*
box [bɑks] *s* caja; (*slap*) bofetada; (*plant*) boj *m*; (*in newspaper*) recuadro; (theat) palco ‖ *tr* encajonar; (*to slap*) abofetear; (naut) cuartear (*la aguja*) ‖ *intr* boxear
box‧car *s* vagón *m* de carga cerrado
boxer [ˈbɑksər] *s* embalador *m*; (sport) boxeador *m*
boxing [ˈbɑksɪŋ] *s* embalaje *m*; (sport) boxeo
boxing gloves *spl* guantes *mpl* de boxeo
box office *s* taquilla, despacho de localidades; boletería (Am)
box'-of'fice hit *s* éxito de taquilla
box-office record *s* marca de taquilla
box-office sale *s* venta de localidades en taquilla
box pleat *s* pliegue *m* de tabla
box seat *s* asiento de palco
box'wood' *s* boj *m*
boy [bɔɪ] *s* muchacho; (*servant*) mozo; (coll) compadre *m*
boycott [ˈbɔɪkɑt] *s* boicoteo ‖ *tr* boicotear
boyhood [ˈbɔɪhud] *s* muchachez *f*; muchachería
boyish [ˈbɔɪ‧ɪʃ] *adj* amuchachado, muchachil
boy scout *s* niño explorador
Bp. *abbr* bishop
b.p. *abbr* bills payable, boiling point
br. *abbr* brand, brother
b.r. *abbr* bills receivable
bra [brɑ] *s* (coll) portasenos *m*, sostén *m*
brace [bres] *s* riostra; berbiquí *m*; **braces** (Brit) tirantes *mpl* ‖ *tr* arriostrar; asegurar, vigorizar; **to brace oneself** (coll) cobrar ánimo ‖ *intr* — **to brace up** (coll) cobrar ánimo
brace and bit *s* berbiquí y barrena
bracelet [ˈbreslɪt] *s* brazalete *m*, pulsera
bracer [ˈbresər] *s* (coll) trago de licor
bracing [ˈbresɪŋ] *adj* fortificante, tónico
bracket [ˈbrækɪt] *s* puntal *m*, soporte *m*; ménsula, repisa; (*mark used in printing*) corchete *m*; clase *f*, categoría ‖ *tr* acorchetar; agrupar
brackish [ˈbrækɪʃ] *adj* salobre
brad [bræd] *s* clavito, estaquilla
brag [bræg] *s* jactancia ‖ *v* (*pret & pp* **bragged**; *ger* **bragging**) *intr* jactarse

braggart ['brægərt] *s* fanfarrón *m*
braid [bred] *s* (*flat strip of cotton, silk, etc.*) cinta, galón *m;* (*something braided*) trenza ‖ *tr* encintar, galonear; trenzar
brain [bren] *s* cerebro; **brains** cerebro, inteligencia; **to rack one's brains** devanarse los sesos ‖ *tr* descerebrar
brain child *s* parto del ingenio
brain drain *s* (coll) éxodo de técnicos
brainless ['brenlɪs] *adj* tonto, sin seso
brain power *s* capacidad mental
brain'storm' *s* acceso de locura; (coll) confusión mental; (coll) buena idea, hallazgo
brain trust *s* grupo de peritos
brain'wash'ing *s* lavado cerebral
brain wave *s* onda encefálica; (coll) buena idea, hallazgo
brain'work' *s* trabajo intelectual
brain·y ['breni] *adj* (*comp* **-ier;** *super* **-iest**) (coll) inteligente, sesudo
braise [brez] *tr* soasar y cocer (*la carne*) a fuego lento en vasija bien tapada
brake [brek] *s* freno; (*for dressing flax*) agramadera; (*thicket*) matorral *m;* (*fern*) helecho común ‖ *tr* frenar; agramar (*el lino o el cáñamo*)
brake band *s* cinta de freno
brake drum *s* tambor *m* de freno
brake lining *s* forro o cinta de freno
brake·man ['brekmən] *s* (*pl* **-men** [mən]) guardafrenos *m*
brake shoe *s* zapata de freno
bramble ['bræmbəl] *s* frambueso, zarza
bram·bly ['bræmblɪ] *adj* (*comp* **-blier;** *super* **-bliest**) zarzoso
bran [bræn] *s* afrecho, salvado
branch [brænt∫] *s* (*of tree*) rama; (*smaller branch; branch cut from tree; of a science, etc.*) ramo; (*of vine*) sarmiento; (*of road, railroad*) ramal *m;* (*of candlestick, river, etc.*) brazo; (*of a store, bank*) sucursal *f* ‖ *intr* ramificarse; **to branch out** extender sus actividades
branch line *s* ramal *m,* línea de empalme
branch office *s* sucursal *f*
brand [brænd] *s* (*kind, make*) marca; (*trademark*) marca de fábrica; (*branding iron*) hierro de marcar; (*mark stamped with hot iron*) hierro; (*dishonor*) tizón *m* ‖ *tr* poner marca de fábrica en; herrar con hierro candente; tiznar (*la reputación de una persona*); **to brand as** tildar de
brandied ['brændid] *adj* macerado en aguardiente
branding iron *s* hierro de marcar
brandish ['brændɪ∫] *tr* blandear
brand'-new' *adj* nuevecito, flamante
bran·dy ['brændɪ] *s* (*pl* **-dies**) aguardiente *m*
brash [bræ∫] *adj* atrevido, impetuoso; descarado, respondón ‖ *s* acceso, ataque *m*
brass [bræs] *o* [brɑs] *s* latón *m;* (*in army and navy*) (slang) los mandamases; (coll) descaro; **brasses** (mus) cobres *mpl*

brass band *s* banda, charanga
brass hat *s* (slang) espadón *m,* mandamás *m*
brassière [brə'zɪr] *s* portasenos *m,* sostén *m*
brass knuckles *s* llave inglesa, bóxer *m*
brass tack *s* clavito dorado de tapicería; **to get down to brass tacks** (coll) entrar en materia
brass winds *spl* (mus) cobres *mpl,* instrumentos músicos de metal
brass·y ['bræsi] *o* ['brɑsi] *adj* (*comp* **-ier;** *super* **-iest**) hecho de latón; metálico; descarado
brat [bræt] *s* rapaz *m,* mocoso, braguillas *m*
brava·do [brə'vɑdo] *s* (*pl* **-does** *o* **-dos**) bravata
brave [brev] *adj* bravo, valiente ‖ *s* valiente *m;* guerrero indio norteamericano ‖ *tr* hacer frente a, arrostrar; desafiar, retar
bravery ['brevəri] *s* bravura, valor *m*
bra·vo ['bravo] *interj* ¡bravo! ‖ *s* (*pl* **-vos**) bravo
brawl [brɔl] *s* pendencia, reyerta; alboroto ‖ *intr* armar pendencia; alborotar
brawler ['brɔlər] *s* pendenciero; alborotador *m*
brawn [brɔn] *s* fuerza musculosa
brawn·y ['brɔni] *adj* (*comp* **-ier;** *super* **-iest**) fornido, musculoso
bray [bre] *s* rebuzno ‖ *intr* rebuznar
braze [brez] *tr* soldadura de latón ‖ *tr* soldar con latón; cubrir de latón; adornar con latón
brazen ['brezən] *adj* de latón; descarado ‖ *tr* — **to brazen through** llevar a cabo descaradamente
brazier [brə'zɪr] *s* brasero
Brazil [brə'zɪl] *s* el Brasil
Brazilian [brə'zɪljən] *adj & s* brasileño
Brazil nut *s* castaña de Pará
breach [brit∫] *s* (*opening*) abertura; (*in a wall*) brecha; abuso, violación ‖ *tr* abrir brecha en
breach of faith *s* falta de fidelidad
breach of peace *s* perturbación del orden público
breach of promise *s* incumplimiento de la palabra de matrimonio
breach of trust *s* abuso de confianza
bread [brɛd] *s* pan *m* ‖ *tr* empanar
bread and butter *s* pan *m* con mantequilla; (coll) pan de cada día
bread crumbs *spl* pan rallado
breaded ['brɛdɪd] *adj* empanado
bread line *s* cola del pan
breadth [brɛdθ] *s* anchura; alcance *m,* extensión; (*e.g., of judgment*) amplitud *f*
bread'win'ner *s* sostén *m* de la familia
break [brek] *s* rompimiento; interrupción; intervalo, pausa; (*split*) hendidura, grieta; (*in prices*) baja; (*in clouds*) claro; (*from jail*) evasión, huída; (*among friends*) ruptura; (*luck, good or bad*) (slang) suerte *f;* (slang) disparate *m;* **to give someone a break** abrirle a uno la puerta ‖ *v* (*pret* **broke** [brok]; *pp* **broken**) *tr*

romper, quebrar; **cambiar** (*un billete*); comunicar (*una mala noticia*); suspender (*relaciones*); faltar a (*la palabra*); batir (*un récord*); cortar (*un circuito*); quebrantar (*un testamento*; *un hábito*); romper (*una ley*); levantar (*el campo*); (mil) degradar; **to break in** forzar (*una puerta*); **to break open** abrir por la fuerza ‖ *intr* romperse, quebrarse; reventar; aclarar (*el tiempo*); bajar (*los precios*); quebrantarse (*la salud*); **to break down** perder la salud; prorrumpir en llanto; **to break even** salir sin ganar ni perder; **to break in** entrar por fuerza; irrumpir en; **to break loose** desprenderse; escaparse; desbocarse (*un caballo*); desencadenarse (*una tempestad*); **to break out** estallar, declararse; (*in laughter, weeping*) romper; (*on the skin*) brotar granos; **to break through** abrirse paso; abrir paso por entre; **to break up** desmenuzarse; levantarse (*una reunión*); **to break with** romper con

breakable ['brekǝbǝl] *adj* rompible

breakage ['brekɪdʒ] *s* estropicio; indemnización por objetos rotos

break′down′ *s* mal éxito; avería, pana; (*in health*) colapso; (*in negotiations*) ruptura; análisis *m*

breaker ['brekǝr] *s* cachón *m*, rompiente *m*

breakfast ['brɛkfǝst] *s* desayuno ‖ *intr* desayunar

breakfast food *s* cereal *m* para el desayuno

break′neck′ *adj* vertiginoso; **at breakneck speed** a mata caballo

break of day *s* alba, amanecer *m*

break′through′ *s* (mil) brecha, ruptura; (fig) descubrimiento sensacional

break′up′ *s* disolución, dispersión; desplome *m*; (*in health*) postración

break′wa′ter *s* rompeolas *m*, escollera

breast [brɛst] *s* pecho, seno; (*of fowl*) pechuga; (*of garment*) pechera; **to make a clean breast of it** confesarlo todo

breast′bone′ *s* esternón *m*; (*of fowl*) quilla

breast drill *s* berbiquí *m* de pecho

breast′pin′ *s* alfiler *m* de pecho

breast stroke *s* brazada de pecho

breath [brɛθ] *s* aliento, respiración; **out of breath** sin aliento; **short of breath** corto de resuello; **to gasp for breath** respirar anhelosamente; **under one's breath** por lo bajo, en voz baja

breathe [brið] *tr* respirar; **to breathe one's last** dar el último suspiro ‖ *intr* respirar; **to breathe freely** cobrar aliento; **to breathe in** aspirar; **to breathe out** espirar

breathing spell *s* respiro, rato de descanso

breathless ['brɛθlɪs] *adj* falto de aliento, jadeante; intenso, vivo; sin aliento

breath′tak′ing *adj* conmovedor, imponente

breech [britʃ] *s* culata, recámara; **breeches** ['brɪtʃɪz] calzones *mpl*; (coll) pantalones *mpl*; **to wear the breeches** (coll) calzarse los pantalones

breed [brid] *s* casta, raza; clase *f*, especie *f* ‖ *v* (*pret & pp* **bred** [brɛd]) *tr* criar ‖ *intr* criar; criarse

breeder ['bridǝr] *s* (*of animals*) criador *m*; (*animal*) reproductor *m*

breeding ['bridɪŋ] *s* cría; crianza, modales *mpl*; **bad breeding** mala crianza; **good breeding** buena crianza

breeze [briz] *s* brisa

breez·y ['brizi] *adj* (*comp* **-ier;** *super* **-iest**) airoso; animado, vivo; (coll) desenvuelto, vivaracho

brevi·ty ['brɛvɪti] *s* (*pl* **-ties**) brevedad

brew [bru] *s* caldereada de cerveza; mezcla ‖ *tr* fabricar (*cerveza*); preparar (*té*); (fig) tramar, urdir ‖ *intr* amenazar (*una tormenta*)

brewer ['bruǝr] *s* cervecero

brewer's yeast *s* levadura de cerveza

brewer·y ['bruǝri] *s* (*pl* **-ies**) cervecería, fábrica de cerveza

bribe [braɪb] *s* soborno ‖ *tr* sobornar

briber·y ['braɪbǝri] *s* (*pl* **-ies**) soborno

bric-a-brac ['brɪkǝ‚bræk] *s* chucherías, curiosidades *fpl*

brick [brɪk] *s* ladrillo; (coll) buen sujeto ‖ *tr* enladrillar

brick′bat′ *s* pedazo de ladrillo; (coll) palabra hiriente

brick ice cream *s* queso helado, helado al corte

brickkiln ['brɪk‚kɪl] *s* horno de ladrillero

bricklayer ['brɪk‚le·ǝr] *s* ladrillador *m*

brick′yard′ *s* ladrillal *m*

bridal ['braɪdǝl] *adj* nupcial; de novia

bridal wreath *s* corona nupcial

bride [braɪd] *s* desposada, novia

bride′groom′ *s* desposado, novio

bridesmaid ['braɪdz‚med] *s* madrina de boda

bridge [brɪdʒ] *s* puente *m*; (*of nose*) caballete *m*; (*card game*) bridge *m* ‖ *tr* tender un puente sobre; salvar (*un obstáculo*); colmar, llenar (*un vacío*)

bridge′head′ *s* (mil) cabeza de puente

bridle ['braɪdǝl] *s* brida ‖ *tr* embridar ‖ *intr* engallarse, erguirse

bridle path *s* camino de herradura

brief [brif] *adj* breve, corto, conciso; *s* resumen *m*; (law) escrito; **in brief** en resumen ‖ *tr* resumir; dar consejos anticipados a; dar informes a

brief case *s* cartera

brier ['braɪ·ǝr] *s* zarza; brezo blanco

brig [brɪg] *s* (naut) bergantín *m*; prisión en buque de guerra

brigade [brɪ'ged] *s* brigada

brigadier [‚brɪgǝ'dɪr] *s* general *m* de brigada

brigand ['brɪgǝnd] *s* bandolero

brigantine ['brɪgǝn‚tin] *o* ['brɪgǝn‚taɪn] *s* (naut) bergantín *m* goleta

bright [braɪt] *adj* brillante; (*e.g., day*) claro; (*color*) subido; listo, inteligente; despierto; (*idea, thought*) luminoso; (*disposition*) alegre, vivo

brighten ['braɪtən] *tr* abrillantar; alegrar, avivar || *intr* avivarse; alegrarse; despejarse (*el cielo*)

bright lights *spl* luces *fpl* brillantes; (aut) faros o luces de carretera

brilliance ['brɪljəns] o **brilliancy** ['brɪljənsɪ] *s* brillantez *f*, brillo

brilliant ['brɪljənt] *adj* brillante

brim [brɪm] *s* borde *m*; (*of hat*) ala

brim'stone' *s* azufre *m*

brine [braɪn] *s* salmuera, agua salobre

bring [brɪŋ] *v* (*pret & pp* **brought** [brɔt]) *tr* traer; llevar; **to bring about** efectuar; **to bring back** devolver; **to bring down** abatir; **to bring forth** sacar a luz; **to bring in** traer a colación; servir (*una comida*); introducir, presentar; **to bring into play** poner en juego; **to bring on** causar, producir; **to bring out** sacar; presentar al público; **to bring suit** poner pleito; **to bring to** sacar de un desmayo; **to bring together** reunir; confrontar; reconciliar; **to bring to pass** efectuar, llevar a cabo; **to bring up** arrimar (*p.ej., una silla*); educar, criar; traer a colación; **to bring upon oneself** atraerse (*un infortunio*)

bringing-up ['brɪŋɪŋ'ʌp] *s* educación, crianza

brink [brɪŋk] *s* borde *m*, margen *m*; **on the brink of** al borde de

brisk [brɪsk] *adj* animado, vivo, vivaz

bristle ['brɪsəl] *s* cerda || *intr* erizarse, encresparse; (*to be visibly annoyed*) encresparse

bris·tly ['brɪslɪ] *adj* (*comp* **-tlier;** *super* **-tliest**) cerdoso, erizado

Britannic [brɪ'tænɪk] *adj* británico

British ['brɪtɪʃ] *adj* británico || **the British** los britanos

Britisher ['brɪtɪʃər] *s* britano

Briton ['brɪtən] *s* britano

Brittany ['brɪtənɪ] *s* Bretaña

brittle ['brɪtəl] *adj* quebradizo, frágil

bro. *abbr* **brother**

broach [brotʃ] *s* (*skewer*) asador *m*, espetón *m*; (*ornamental pin*) broche *m*, prendedero || *tr* sacar a colación

broad [brɔd] *adj* ancho; liberal, tolerante; (*day, noon, etc.*) pleno

broad'cast' *s* radiodifusión; audición, programa radiotelefónico || *v* (*pret & pp* **-cast**) *tr* difundir, esparcir || (*pret & pp* **-cast** o **-casted**) *tr* radiodifundir, radiar, emitir

broadcasting station *s* emisora, estación de radiodifusión

broad'cloth' *s* paño fino

broaden ['brɔdən] *tr* ensanchar || *intr* ensancharse

broad'loom' *adj* tejido en telar ancho y en color sólido

broad-minded ['brɔd'maɪndɪd] *adj* tolerante, de amplias miras

broad-shouldered ['brɔd'ʃoldərd] *adj* ancho de espaldas

broad'side' *s* (naut) costado; (naut) andanada; (coll) torrente *m* de injurias

broad'sword' *s* espada ancha

brocade [bro'ked] *s* brocado

broccoli ['brɑkəlɪ] *s* brécol *m*, brécoles *mpl*

brochure [bro'ʃur] *s* folleto

brogue [brog] *s* acento irlandés

broil [brɔɪl] *tr* asar a la parrilla || *intr* asarse

broiler ['brɔɪlər] *s* parrilla; pollo para asar a la parrilla

broken ['brokən] *adj* roto, quebrado; agotado; amansado; (*accent*) chapurrado; suelto

bro'ken-down' *adj* abatido; descompuesto; destartalado

broken-hearted ['brokən'hɑrtɪd] *adj* abrumado por el dolor

broker ['brokər] *s* corredor *m*

brokerage ['brokərɪdʒ] *s* corretaje *m*

bromide ['bromaɪd] *s* bromuro; (slang) trivialidad

bromine ['bromin] *s* bromo

bronchitis [brɑŋ'kaɪtɪs] *s* bronquitis *f*

bron·co ['brɑŋko] *s* (*pl* **-cos**) potro cerril

bron'co·bust'er *s* domador *m* de potros; vaquero

bronze [brɑnz] *adj* bronceado || *s* bronce *m* || *tr* broncear || *intr* broncearse

brooch [brotʃ] o [brutʃ] *s* alfiler *m* de pecho, prendedero, pasador *m*

brood [brud] *s* cría; nidada; casta, raza || *tr* empollar || *intr* enclocar; **to brood on** meditar con preocupación

brook [bruk] *s* arroyo || *tr* — **to brook no** no tolerar, no aguantar

broom [brum] o [brum] *s* escoba; (bot) hiniesta

broom'corn' *s* sorgo

broom'stick' *s* palo de escoba

bros. *abbr* **brothers**

broth [brɔθ] o [brɑθ] *s* caldo

brothel ['brɑθəl] o ['brɑðəl] *s* burdel *m*

brother ['brʌðər] *s* hermano

brotherhood ['brʌðər‚hud] *s* hermandad

broth'er-in-law' *s* (*pl* **brothers-in-law**) cuñado, hermano político; (*husband of one's wife's or husband's sister*) concuñado

brotherly ['brʌðərlɪ] *adj* fraternal

brow [brau] *s* (*forehead*) frente *f*; (*eyebrow*) ceja; **to knit one's brow** fruncir las cejas

brow'beat' *v* (*pret* **-beat;** *pp* **beaten**) *tr* intimidar con mirada ceñuda

brown [braun] *adj* pardo, castaño, moreno; (*race*) cobrizo; tostado del sol || *s* castaño, moreno || *tr* poner moreno; tostar, quemar, broncear; (culin) dorar

brownish ['braunɪʃ] *adj* que tira a moreno

brown study *s* absorción, pensamiento profundo, ensimismamiento

brown sugar *s* azúcar terciado

browse [brauz] *intr* (*to nibble at twigs*) ramonear; (*to graze*) pacer; hojear un libro ociosamente; **to browse about** o **around** curiosear

bruise [bruz] *s* contusión, magulladura

‖ *tr* contundir, magullar ‖ *intr* contundirse, magullarse

brunet [bruˈnet] *adj* moreno ‖ *s* moreno (*hombre moreno*)

brunette [bruˈnet] *s* morena (*mujer morena*)

brunt [brʌnt] *s* fuerza, choque *m*, empuje *m;* (*e.g., of a battle*) peso, (lo) más reñido

brush [brʌʃ] *s* brocha, cepillo, escobilla; (*stroke*) brochada; (*light touch*) roce *m;* (*brief encounter*) encuentro, escaramuza; (*growth of bushes*) maleza; (*elec*) escobilla ‖ *tr* acepillar; (*to graze*) rozar; **to brush aside** echar a un lado ‖ *intr* pasar ligeramente; **to brush up on** repasar

brush'-off' *s* (slang) desaire *m;* **to give the brush-off to** (slang) despedir noramala

brush'wood' *s* broza, ramojo

brusque [brʌsk] *adj* brusco, rudo

brusqueness [ˈbrʌsknɪs] *s* brusquedad

Brussels [ˈbrʌsəlz] *s* Bruselas

Brussels sprouts *spl* bretones *mpl*, col *f* de Bruselas

brutal [ˈbrutəl] *adj* brutal, bestial

brutali-ty [bruˈtælɪti] *s* (*pl* **-ties**) brutalidad, crueldad

brute [brut] *adj* bruto; (*force*) inconsciente, ciego ‖ *s* bruto

brutish [ˈbrutɪʃ] *adj* abrutado, estúpido

bu. *abbr* bushel

bubble [ˈbʌbəl] *s* burbuja; ampolla; ilusión, quimera ‖ *intr* burbujear; **to bubble over** desbordar, rebosar

buck [bʌk] *s* (*goat*) cabrón *m;* (*deer*) gamo; (*rabbit*) conejo; (*of a horse*) corveta, encorvada; (*youth*) pisaverde *m;* (slang) dólar *m;* **to pass the buck** (coll) echar la carga a otro ‖ *tr* hacer frente a, resistir a; (*to butt*) acornear, topetar; colar (*la ropa*); **to buck up** (coll) alentar, animar ‖ *intr* botarse, encorvarse; **to buck against** embestir contra

bucket [ˈbʌkɪt] *s* balde *m*, cubo; (*of a well*) pozal *m;* **to kick the bucket** (slang) estirar la pata, liar el petate

bucket seat *s* baquet *m*

buckle [ˈbʌkəl] *s* hebilla; (*bend, bulge*) alabeo, pandeo ‖ *tr* abrochar con hebilla ‖ *intr* (*to bend, bulge*) alabearse, pandear; **to buckle down to** (coll) dedicarse con empeño a

buck private *s* (slang) soldado raso

buckram [ˈbʌkrəm] *s* zangala; (bb) bocací *m*, bucarán *m*

buck'saw' *s* sierra de bastidor

buck'shot' *s* postas

buck'tooth' *s* (*pl* **-teeth**) diente *m* saliente

buck'wheat' *s* alforfón *m*, trigo sarraceno

bud [bʌd] *s* botón *m*, brote *m;* **to nip in the bud** cortar de raíz ‖ *v* (*pret & pp* **budded**; *ger* **budding**) *intr* abotonar, brotar

bud-dy [ˈbʌdi] *s* (*pl* **-dies**) (coll) camarada *m;* (coll) muchachito

budge [bʌdʒ] *tr* mover ‖ *intr* moverse

budget [ˈbʌdʒɪt] *s* presupuesto ‖ *tr* presuponer, presupuestar

budgetary [ˈbʌdʒɪˌteri] *adj* presupuestario

buff [bʌf] *adj* de ante ‖ *s* (*leather*) ante *m;* color *m* de ante; chaqueta de ante; rueda pulidora; (coll) piel desnuda; aficionado ‖ *tr* dar color de ante a; pulimentar

buffa-lo [ˈbʌfəˌlo] *s* (*pl* **-loes** o **-los**) búfalo ‖ *tr* (slang) intimidar

buffer [ˈbʌfər] *s* amortiguador *m* de choques; tope *m*, paragolpes *m;* pulidor *m*

buffer state *s* estado tapón

buffet [buˈfe] *s* (*piece of furniture*) aparador *m;* restaurante *m* de estación ‖ [ˈbʌfɪt] *tr* abofetear, golpear, pegar

buffet car [buˈfe] *s* coche *m* bar

buffet lunch [buˈfe] *s* servicio de bufet

buffet supper [buˈfe] *s* ambigú *m*, bufet *m*

buffoon [bəˈfun] *s* bufón *m*, payaso

buffoner-y [bəˈfunəri] *s* (*pl* **-ies**) bufonada, chocarrería

bug [bʌg] *s* insecto, bicho, sabandija; microbio; (*bedbug*) (Brit) chinche *f;* (coll) defecto; (slang) micrófono escondido; (slang) loco; (slang) entusiasta *mf* ‖ *v* (*pret & pp* **bugged**; *ger* **bugging**) *tr* (slang) esconder un micrófono en

bug'bear' *s* espantajo; aversión

bug-gy [ˈbʌgi] *adj* (*comp* **-gier;** *super* **-giest**) infestado de bichos; (slang) loco ‖ *s* (*pl* **-gies**) calesa

bug'house' *adj* (slang) loco ‖ *s* (slang) manicomio, casa de locos

bugle [ˈbjugəl] *s* corneta

bugle call *s* toque *m* de corneta

bugler [ˈbjuglər] *s* corneta *m*

build [bɪld] *s* forma, hechura, figura; (*of human being*) talle *m* ‖ *v* (*pret & pp* **built** [bɪlt]) *tr* construir, edificar; componer; establecer, fundar; crearse (*p.ej., una clientela*)

builder [ˈbɪldər] *s* constructor *m;* aparejador *m*, maestro de obras

building [ˈbɪldɪŋ] *s* construcción; edificio; (*one of several in a group*) pabellón *m*

building and loan association *s* sociedad *f* de crédito para la construcción

building lot *s* solar *m*

building site *s* terreno para construir

building trades *spl* oficios de edificación

build'-up' *s* acumulación, formación; (coll) propaganda anticipada

built'in' *adj* integrante, incorporado, empotrado

built'-up' *adj* armado, montado; (*land*) aglomerado

bulb [bʌlb] *s* (*of plant*) bulbo; (*of thermometer*) bola, cubeta; (*of syringe*) pera; (*of electric light*) ampolla, bombilla

Bulgaria [bʌlˈgerɪ-ə] *s* Bulgaria

Bulgarian [bʌlˈgerɪ-ən] *adj & s* búlgaro

bulge [bʌldʒ] *s* protuberancia, bulto, bombeo; **to get the bulge on** (coll) llevar la ventaja a ‖ *intr* hacer bulto, bombearse

bulk [bʌlk] *s* bulto, volumen *m*; *(main mass)* grueso; **in bulk** a granel ‖ *intr* abultar, hacer bulto; tener importancia

bulk'head' *s* mamparo; tabique hermético

bulk·y ['bʌlki] *adj* (*comp* **-ier**; *super* **-iest**) abultado, voluminoso, grueso

bull [bʊl] *s* toro; *(in stockmarket)* alcista *m*; *(papal document)* bula; disparate *m*; **to take the bull by the horns** asir al toro por las astas ‖ *tr* — **to bull the market** jugar al alza

bull'dog' *s* dogo

bulldoze ['bʊl,doz] *tr* coaccionar, intimidar con amenazas

bulldozer ['bʊl,dozər] *s* explanadora de empuje, empujatierra

bullet ['bʊlɪt] *s* bala

bulletin ['bʊlətɪn] *s* boletín *m*; comunicado; *(of a school)* anuario

bulletin board *s* tablilla

bul'let-proof' *adj* a prueba de balas, blindado

bull'fight' *s* corrida de toros

bull'fight'er *s* torero

bull'fight'ing *adj* torero ‖ *s* toreo

bull'finch' *s* (orn) camachuelo

bull'frog' *s* rana toro

bull-headed ['bʊl,hedɪd] *adj* obstinado, terco

bullion ['bʊljən] *s* oro en barras, plata en barras; *(twisted fringe)* entorchado

bullish ['bʊlɪʃ] *adj* obstinado; *(market)* en alza; *(speculator)* alcista, optimista

bullock ['bʊlək] *s* buey *m*

bull'pen' *s* (taur) toril *m*; *(jail)* (coll) prevención

bull'ring' *s* plaza de toros

bull's-eye ['bʊlz,aɪ] *s* *(of a target)* diana; (archit, meteor, naut) ojo de buey; **to hit the bull's-eye** hacer diana

bul·ly ['bʊli] *adj* (coll) excelente, magnífico ‖ *s* (*pl* **-lies**) matón *m*, valentón *m* ‖ *v* (*pret & pp* **-lied**) *tr* intimidar, maltratar

bulrush ['bʊl,rʌʃ] *s* junco; junco de laguna; *(Typha)* anea, espadaña; (Bib) papiro

bulwark ['bʊlwərk] *s* baluarte *m* ‖ *tr* abaluartar; defender, proteger

bum [bʌm] *s* (slang) holgazán *m*; (slang) vagabundo; (slang) mendigo ‖ *v* (*pret & pp* **bummed**; *ger* **bumming**) *tr* (slang) mendigar ‖ *intr* holgazanear; (slang) vagabundear; (slang) mendigar

bumblebee ['bʌmbəl,bi] *s* abejorro

bump [bʌmp] *s* *(collision)* topetón *m*; *(shake)* sacudida; *(on falling)* batacazo; *(of plane in rough air)* rebote *m*; *(swelling)* hinchazón *f*, chichón *m*; *(protuberance)* ‖ *tr* dar contra, topar; *(to bruise)* abollar ‖ *intr* chocar; dar sacudidas; **to bump into** tropezar con; encontrarse con

bumper ['bʌmpər] *adj* (coll) abun-

dante, grande ‖ *s* tope *m*, paratopes *m*; (aut) amortiguador *m*, parachoques *m*; vaso lleno

bumpkin ['bʌmpkɪn] *s* patán *m*, palurdo

bumptious ['bʌmpʃəs] *adj* engreído, presuntuoso

bump·y ['bʌmpi] *adj* (*comp* **-ier**; *super* **-iest**) *(ground)* desigual, áspero; *(air)* agitado

bun [bʌn] *s* buñuelo, bollo; *(of hair)* castaña

bunch [bʌntʃ] *s* manojo, puñado; *(of grapes, bananas, etc.)* racimo; *(of flowers)* ramillete *m*; *(of people)* grupo ‖ *tr* agrupar, juntar ‖ *intr* agruparse; arracimarse

bundle ['bʌndəl] *s* atado, bulto, lío, paquete *m*; *(of papers)* legajo; *(of wood)* haz *m* ‖ *tr* atar, liar, empaquetar, envolver; **to bundle off** despedir precipitadamente; **to bundle up** arropar ‖ *intr* — **to bundle up** arroparse

bung [bʌŋ] *s* bitoque *m*, tapón *m*

bungalow ['bʌŋgə,lo] *s* bungalow *m*, casa de una sola planta

bung'hole' *s* piquera, boca de tonel

bungle ['bʌŋgəl] *s* chapucería ‖ *tr &* *intr* chapucear

bungler ['bʌŋglər] *s* chapucero

bungling ['bʌŋglɪŋ] *adj* chapucero ‖ *s* chapucería

bunion ['bʌnjən] *s* juanete *m*

bunk [bʌŋk] *s* tarima; (slang) palabrería vana, música celestial

bunker ['bʌŋkər] *s* carbonera; (mil) fortín *m*

bun·ny ['bʌni] *s* (*pl* **-nies**) conejito

bunting ['bʌntɪŋ] *s* banderas colgadas como adorno; *(of a ship)* empavesado; (orn) gorrión triguero

buoy [bɔɪ] o ['bu·i] *s* boya; boya salvavidas, guindola ‖ *tr* — **to buoy up** mantener a flote; animar, alentar

buoyancy ['bɔɪ·ənsi] o ['bujənsi] *s* flotación; alegría, animación

buoyant ['bɔɪ·ənt] o ['bujənt] *adj* boyante; alegre, animado

bur [bʌr] *s* erizo, vilano

burble ['bʌrbəl] *s* burbujeo ‖ *intr* burbujear

burden ['bʌrdən] *s* carga; *(of a speech)* tema *m*; *(of a poem)* estribillo ‖ *tr* cargar; agobiar, gravar

burden of proof *s* peso de la prueba

burdensome ['bʌrdənsəm] *adj* gravoso, oneroso

burdock ['bʌrdɑk] *s* bardana, cadillo

bureau ['bjʊro] *s* cómoda; despacho, oficina; departamento, negociado

bureauera·cy [bju'rɑkrəsi] *s* (*pl* **-cies**) burocracia

bureaucrat ['bjʊrə,kræt] *s* burócrata *mf*

bureʋucratic [,bjʊrə'krætɪk] *adj* burocrático

burgess ['bʌrdʒɪs] *s* burgués *m*, ciudadano; alcalde *m* de un pueblo o villa

burglar ['bʌrglər] *s* escalador *m*

burglar alarm *s* alarma de ladrones

bur'glar·proof' adj a prueba de escaladores

burglar·y ['bʌrgləri] s (pl -ies) robo con escalamiento

Burgundian [bər'gʌndɪ·ən] adj & s borgoñón m

Burgundy ['bʌrgəndi] s la Borgoña; (wine) borgoña m

burial ['bɛrɪ·əl] s entierro

burial ground s cementerio

burlap ['bʌrlæp] s arpillera

burlesque [bər'lɛsk] adj burlesco, festivo ‖ s parodia ‖ tr parodiar

burlesque show s espectáculo de bailes y cantos groseros, music-hall m

bur·ly ['bʌrli] adj (comp -lier; super -liest) fornido, corpulento, membrudo

Burma ['bʌrmə] s Birmania

Bur·mese [bər'miz] adj birmano ‖ s (pl -mese) birmano

burn [bʌrn] s quemadura, quemazón f ‖ v (pret & pp **burned** o **burnt** [bʌrnt]) tr quemar ‖ intr quemar, quemarse; estar encendido (p.ej., un faro); **to burn out** quemarse (un fusible); fundirse (una bombilla); **to burn within** requemarse

burner ['bʌrnər] s (of furnace) quemador m; (of gas fixture or lamp) mechero

burning ['bʌrnɪŋ] adj ardiente ‖ s quema, incendio

burning question s cuestión palpitante

burnish ['bʌrnɪʃ] s bruñido ‖ tr bruñir ‖ intr bruñirse

burnoose [bər'nus] s albornoz m

burnt almond [bʌrnt] s almendra tostada

burr [bʌr] s (of plant) erizo; (of cut in metal) rebaba

burrow ['bʌro] s madriguera, conejera ‖ tr hacer madrigueras en; socavar ‖ intr amadrigarse; esconderse

bursar ['bʌrsər] s tesorero universitario

burst [bʌrst] s explosión, reventón m, estallido; (of machine gun) ráfaga; salida brusca ‖ v (pret & pp **burst**) tr reventar ‖ intr reventar, reventarse; partirse (el corazón); **to burst into** irrumpir en (un cuarto); desatarse en (amenazas); prorrumpir en (lágrimas); **to burst out crying** deshacerse en lágrimas; **to burst with laughter** reventar de risa

bur·y ['bɛri] v (pret & pp -ied) tr enterrar; **to be buried in thought** estar absorto en meditación; **to bury the hatchet** hacer la paz, echar pelillos a la mar

burying ground s cementerio

bus. abbr business

bus [bʌs] s (pl **busses** o **buses**) autobús m ‖ tr llevar en un autobús

bus boy s ayudante m de camarero

bus·by ['bʌzbi] s (pl -bies) morrión m de húsar, colbac m

bush [bʊʃ] s arbusto; (scrubby growth) matorral m, monte m; **to beat about the bush** andar con rodeos

bushel ['bʊʃəl] s medida para áridos (35,23 litros en E.U.A. y 36,35 litros en Inglaterra)

bushing ['bʊʃɪŋ] s buje m, forro

bush·y ['bʊʃi] adj (comp -ier; super -iest) arbustivo; peludo, lanudo; espeso

business ['bɪznɪs] adj comercial, de negocios ‖ s negocio, comercio; (company, concern) empresa; (job, employment) empleo, oficio; (matter) asunto, cuestión; (duty) obligación; (right) derecho; **on business** por negocios; **to have no business to** no tener derecho a; **to make it one's business to** proponerse; **to mean business** (coll) obrar en serio, hablar en serio; **to mind one's own business** no meterse en lo que no le importa a uno; **to send about one's business** mandar a paseo

business district s barrio comercial

businesslike ['bɪznɪs,laɪk] adj práctico, sistemático, serio

business·man ['bɪznɪs,mæn] s (pl -men [,mɛn]) comerciante m, hombre m de negocios

business suit s traje m de calle

bus·man ['bʌsmən] s (pl -men [mən]) conductor m de autobús

buss [bʌs] s (coll) beso sonado ‖ tr (coll) dar besos sonados a ‖ intr (coll) dar besos sonados; (coll) darse besos sonados

bust [bʌst] s busto; (of woman) pecho; (slang) fracaso; (slang) borrachera ‖ tr (slang) reventar, romper; (slang) arruinar; (slang) golpear, pegar ‖ intr (slang) reventar; (slang) fracasar

buster ['bʌstər] s muchachito

bustle ['bʌsəl] s (of woman's dress) polisón m; alboroto, bullicio ‖ intr ajetrearse, menearse

bus·y ['bɪzi] adj (comp -ier; super -iest) ocupado; (e.g., street) concurrido; (meddling) intruso, entremetido ‖ v (pret & pp -ied) tr ocupar; **to busy oneself with** ocuparse de

busybod·y ['bɪzɪ,badi] s (pl -ies) entremetido, fisgón m

busy signal s (telp) señal f de ocupado

but [bʌt] adv sólo, solamente, no ... más que; **but for** a no ser por; **but little** muy poco ‖ prep excepto, salvo; **all but** casi ‖ conj pero; sino, p.ej., **nobody came but John** no vino sino Juan

butcher ['bʊtʃər] s carnicero ‖ tr matar (reses para el consumo); dar muerte a; (to bungle) chapucear

butcher knife s cuchilla de carnicero

butcher shop s carnicería

butcher·y ['bʌtʃəri] s (pl -ies) (slaughterhouse) matadero; (wanton slaughter) matanza, carnicería

butler ['bʌtlər] s despensero, mayordomo

butt [bʌt] s (of gun) culata; (of cigaret) colilla, punta; (of horned animal) cabezada, topetada, topetón m; (target) blanco; hazmerreír m; (large *cask*) pipa ‖ *tr* topar, topetar; acornear ‖ *intr* dar cabezadas; **to butt against** confinar con; **to butt in** (slang) entremeterse

butter [ˈbʌtər] *s* mantequilla ‖ *tr* untar con mantequilla; **to butter up** (coll) adular, lisonjear

but′ter·cup′ *s* botón *m* de oro

butter dish *s* mantequillera

but′ter·fly′ *s* (*pl* **-flies**) mariposa

butter knife *s* cuchillo mantequillero

but′ter·milk′ *s* leche *f* de manteca

butter sauce *s* mantequilla fundida

but′ter·scotch′ *s* bombón *m* escocés, bombón hecho con azúcar terciado y mantequilla

buttocks [ˈbʌtəks] *spl* nalgas

button [ˈbʌtən] *s* botón *m* ‖ *tr* abotonar, abrocharse

but′ton·hole′ *s* ojal *m* ‖ *tr* detener con conversación

but′ton·hook′ *s* abotonador *m*

but′ton·wood′ tree *s* plátano de occidente

buttress [ˈbʌtrɪs] *s* contrafuerte *m*; (fig) apoyo, sostén *m* ‖ *tr* estribar; (fig) apoyar, sostener

butt weld *s* soldadura a tope

buxom [ˈbʌksəm] *adj* rolliza, frescachona

buy [baɪ] *s* (coll) compra; (*bargain*) (coll) ganga ‖ *v* (*pret & pp* **bought** [bɔt]) *tr* comprar; **to buy back** recomprar; **to buy off** comprar, sobornar; **to buy out** comprar la parte de (*un socio*); **to buy up** acaparar

buyer [ˈbaɪər] *s* comprador *m*

buzz [bʌz] *s* zumbido ‖ *intr* zumbar; **to buzz about** ajetrearse, cazcalear

buzzard [ˈbʌzərd] *s* alfaneque *m*

buzz bomb *s* bomba volante

buzzer [ˈbʌzər] *s* zumbador *m*

buzz saw *s* sierra circular

bx. *abbr* **box**

by [baɪ] *adv* cerca; a un lado; **by and by** luego ‖ *prep* por; cerca de, al lado de; (*not later than*) para; **by far** con mucho; **by the way** de paso; a propósito

by-and-by [ˈbaɪ·ənd′baɪ] *s* porvenir *m*

bye-bye [ˈbaɪ′baɪ] *s* mu *f*; **to go bye-bye** ir a la mu ‖ *interj* (coll) ¡adiosito!; (*to a child*) ¡ro ro!

bygone [ˈbaɪ‚gɔn] o [ˈbaɪ‚gɑn] *adj* pasado ‖ *s* pasado; **let bygones be bygones** olvidemos lo pasado

bylaw [ˈbaɪ‚lɔ] *s* reglamento, estatuto

bypass [ˈbaɪ‚pæs] o [ˈbaɪ‚pɑs] *s* desviación; tubo de paso ‖ *tr* desviar; (*a difficulty*) eludir

by′-prod′uct *s* subproducto, derivado

bystander [ˈbaɪ‚stændər] *s* asistente *mf*, circunstante *mf*

byway [ˈbaɪ‚we] *s* camino apartado

byword [ˈbaɪ‚wʌrd] *s* objeto de oprobio; refrán *m*, muletilla; apodo

Byzantine [ˈbɪzən‚tin] o [bɪˈzæntɪn] *adj & s* bizantino

Byzantium [bɪˈzænʃɪ·əm] o [bɪˈzænti·əm] *s* Bizancio

C

C, c [si] tercera letra del alfabeto inglés

c. *abbr* **cent, center, centimeter**

C. *abbr* **centigrade, Congress, Court**

cab [kæb] *s* coche *m* de plaza o de punto; taxi *m*; (*of a truck*) casilla

cabaret [‚kæbəˈre] *s* cabaret *m*

cabbage [ˈkæbɪdʒ] *s* col *f*, berza

cab driver *s* cochero de plaza; taxista *mf*

cabin [ˈkæbɪn] *s* (*hut, cottage*) cabaña; (aer) cabina; (naut) camarote *m*

cabin boy *s* mozo de cámara

cabinet [ˈkæbɪnɪt] *s* (*piece of furniture for displaying objects*) escaparate *m*, vitrina; (*for a radio*) caja, mueble *m*; (*closet*) armario; (*private room; ministry of a government*) gabinete *m*

cab′inet·ma′ker *s* ebanista *m*

cab′inet·ma′king *s* ebanistería

cable [ˈkebəl] *adj* cablegráfico ‖ *s* cable *m*; cablegrama *m* ‖ *tr & intr* cablegrafiar

cable address *s* dirección cablegráfica

cable car *s* tranvía *m* de tracción por cable

cablegram [ˈkebəl‚græm] *s* cablegrama *m*

caboose [kəˈbus] *s* (rr) furgón de cola

cab′stand′ *s* punto de coches, punto de taxis

cache [kæʃ] *s* escondrijo; víveres escondidos ‖ *tr* depositar en un escondrijo; ocultar

cachet [kæˈʃe] *s* sello

cackle [ˈkækəl] *s* (*of a hen*) cacareo; (*idle talk*) charla ‖ *intr* cacarear; charlar

cac·tus [ˈkæktəs] *s* (*pl* **-tuses** o **-ti** [taɪ]) cacto

cad [kæd] *s* sinvergüenza *mf*

cadaver [kəˈdævər] *s* cadáver *m*

cadaverous [kəˈdævərəs] *adj* cadavérico

caddie [ˈkædi] *s* caddie *m* (*muchacho que lleva los utensilios en el juego de golf*) ‖ *intr* servir de caddie

cadence [ˈkedəns] *s* cadencia

cadet [kəˈdet] *s* hermano menor, hijo menor; (*student at military school*) cadete *m*

cadmium [ˈkædmɪ·əm] *s* cadmio

cadre [ˈkædri] *s* (mil) cuadro

Caesar [ˈsizər] *s* César *m*

bu
ca

café [kæ'fe] s bar m, cabaret m; restaurante m

café society s gente f del mundo elegante que frecuenta los cabarets de moda

cafeteria [,kæfə'tɪrɪ-ə] s cafetería

cage [kedʒ] s jaula ‖ tr enjaular

cageling ['kedʒlɪŋ] s pájaro enjaulado

ca·gey ['kedʒi] adj (comp -gier; super -giest) (coll) astuto

cahoots [kə'huts] s — to be in cahoots (slang) confabularse (dos o más personas); to go cahoots (slang) entrar por partes iguales

Cain [ken] s Caín m; to raise Cain (slang) armar camorra

Cairo ['kaɪro] s El Cairo

caisson ['kesən] s cajón m de aire comprimido, esclusa de aire

cajole [kə'dʒol] tr adular, lisonjear, halagar

cajoler·y [kə'dʒoləri] s (pl -ies) adulación, lisonja, halago

cake [kek] s pastel m, bollo; (small cake) pastelillo; (sponge cake) bizcocho; (of fish) fritada; (of earth) terrón m; (of soap) pan m, pastilla; (of ice) témpano; to take the cake (coll) ser el colmo ‖ intr apelmazarse, aterronarse

calabash ['kælə,bæʃ] s calabacera; (fruit) calabaza

calamitous [kə'læmɪtəs] adj calamitoso

calami·ty [kə'læmɪti] s (pl -ties) calamidad

calci·fy ['kælsɪ,faɪ] v (pret & pp -fied) tr calcificar ‖ intr calcificarse

calcium ['kælsɪ-əm] s calcio

calculate ['kælkjə,let] tr calcular; (to reckon) (coll) calcular ‖ intr calcular; to calculate on contar con

calculating ['kælkjə,letɪŋ] adj de calcular; astuto, intrigante

calculating machine s calculadora, máquina de calcular

calcu·lus ['kælkjələs] s (pl -luses o -li [,laɪ]) (math, pathol) cálculo

caldron ['kɔldrən] s calderón m

calendar ['kæləndər] s calendario, almanaque m

calf [kæf] o [kɑf] s (pl calves [kævz] o [kɑvz]) ternero; (of the leg) pantorrilla

calf'skin' s becerro, becerrillo

caliber ['kælɪbər] s calibre m

calibrate ['kælɪ,bret] tr calibrar

cali·co ['kælɪ,ko] s (pl -coes o -cos) calicó m, indiana

California [,kælɪ'fɔrnɪ-ə] s California

calipers ['kælɪpərz] spl calibrador m, compás m de calibres

caliph ['kelɪf] o ['kælɪf] s califa m

caliphate ['kælɪ,fet] s califato

calisthenic [,kælɪs'θɛnɪk] adj calisténico ‖ calisthenics spl calistenia

calk [kɔk] tr calafatear

calking ['kɔkɪŋ] s calafateo

call [kɔl] s llamada; visita; (of a boat or airplane) escala; vocación; within call al alcance de la voz ‖ tr llamar; convocar (p.ej., una huelga); to call back mandar volver; to call down

(coll) reprender, regañar; to call in hacer entrar; (from circulation) retirar; to call off aplazar, suspender; to call out llamar (a uno) que salga; to call together convocar, reunir; to call up llamar por teléfono; evocar, recordar ‖ intr llamar, gritar; hacer una visita; (naut) hacer escala; to call on acudir a; visitar; to call out gritar; to go calling ir de visitas

calla lily ['kælə] s cala, lirio de agua

call bell s timbre m de llamada

call'boy' s (in a hotel) botones m; (theat) traspunte m

caller ['kɔlər] s visitante mf

call girl s chica de cita

calling ['kɔlɪŋ] s profesión, vocación

calling card s tarjeta de visita

calliope [kə'laɪ-əpi] o ['kælɪ·op] s (mus) órgano de vapor ‖ Calliope [kə'laɪ-əpi] s Calíope f

call number s número de teléfono; (of a book) número de clasificación

callous ['kæləs] adj calloso; (fig) duro, insensible

call to arms s — to sound the call to arms (mil) batir o tocar a llamada

call to the colors s (mil) llamada a filas

callus ['kæləs] s callo

calm [kɑm] adj tranquilo, quieto; (sea) bonancible ‖ s tranquilidad, calma ‖ tr tranquilizar, calmar ‖ intr — to calm down tranquilizarse, calmarse; abonanzar, calmar (el viento, el tiempo)

calmness ['kɑmnɪs] s tranquilidad, calma

calorie ['kæləri] s caloría

calum·ny ['kæləmni] s (pl -nies) calumnia

calva·ry ['kælvəri] s (pl -ries) (at the entrance to a town) humilladero ‖ Calvary s Calvario

calyp·so [kə'lɪpso] s (pl -sos) calipso ‖ Calypso s Calipso f

cam [kæm] s leva

cambric ['kembrɪk] s batista

camel ['kæməl] s camello

came·o ['kæmɪ·o] s (pl -os) camafeo

camera ['kæmərə] s cámara fotográfica, máquina fotográfica

camera·man ['kæmərə,mæn] s (pl -men [,mɛn]) camarógrafo, tomavistas m

camomile ['kæmə,maɪl] s manzanilla

camouflage ['kæmə,flɑʒ] s camuflaje m ‖ tr camuflar

camp [kæmp] s campamento ‖ intr acampar

campaign [kæm'pen] s campaña ‖ intr hacer campaña

campaigner [kæm'penər] s propagandista mf; veterano

camp'fire' s hoguera de campamento

camphor ['kæmfər] s alcanfor m

camp'stool' s silla de tijera, catrecillo

campus ['kæmpəs] s terrenos, recinto (de la universidad)

cam'shaft' s árbol m de levas

can [kæn] s bote m, envase m, lata ‖ v (pret & pp canned; ger canning) tr envasar, enlatar ‖ v (pret & cond could) *v aux* he can come tomorrow puede venir mañana; **can you swim?** ¿sabe Vd. nadar?

Canada ['kænədə] *s* el Canadá

Canadian [kə'nedɪ·ən] *adj & s* canadiense

canal [kə'næl] *s* canal *m*

canar·y [kə'nerɪ] *s* (*pl* -**ies**) canario ‖ **Canaries** *spl* Canarias

can·cel ['kænsəl] (*pret & pp* -**celed** o -**celled**; *ger* -**celing** o -**celling**) *tr* cancelar, eliminar, suprimir; matasellar, obliterar (*sellos de correo*)

canceler ['kænsələr] *s* matasellos *m*

cancellation [,kænsə'leʃən] *s* cancelación, eliminación, supresión; (*of stamps*) obliteración

cancer ['kænsər] *s* cáncer *m*

cancerous ['kænsərəs] *adj* canceroso

candela·brum [,kændə'lebrəm] *s* (*pl* -**bra** [brə] o -**brums**) candelabro

candid ['kændɪd] *adj* franco, sincero; imparcial

candida·cy ['kændɪdəsɪ] *s* (*pl* -**cies**) candidatura

candidate ['kændɪ,det] *s* candidato; (*for a degree*) graduando

candid camera *s* cámara indiscreta

candle ['kændəl] *s* bujía, candela, vela

can'dle·hold'er *s* candelero

can'dle·light' *s* luz *f* de vela; crepúsculo

candle power *s* bujía

can'dle·stick' *s* palmatoria

candor ['kændər] *s* franqueza, sinceridad; imparcialidad

can·dy ['kændɪ] *s* (*pl* -**dies**) bombón *m*, confite *m*, dulce *m*; dulces *mpl* ‖ *v* (*pret & pp* -**died**) *tr* almibarar, confitar, garapiñar ‖ *intr* almibararse

candy box *s* bombonera, confitera

candy store *s* confitería, dulcería

cane [ken] *s* (*plant; stem*) caña; (*walking stick*) bastón *m*; (*for chair seats*) junco, mimbre *m*, rejilla

cane seat *s* asiento de rejilla

cane sugar *s* azúcar *m* de caña

canine ['kenaɪn] *adj* canino ‖ *s* (*tooth*) canino; perro

canned goods *spl* conservas alimenticias

canner·y ['kænərɪ] *s* (*pl* -**ies**) conservera, fábrica de conservas

cannibal ['kænɪbəl] *adj & s* caníbal *mf*

canning ['kænɪŋ] *adj* conservero ‖ *s* conservería

cannon ['kænən] *s* cañón *m*; cañones

cannonade [,kænə'ned] *s* cañoneo ‖ *tr* cañonear

cannon ball *s* bala de cañón

cannon fodder *s* carne *f* de cañón

can·ny ['kænɪ] *adj* (*comp* -**nier**; *super* -**niest**) cauteloso, cuerdo; astuto

canoe [kə'nu] *s* canoa

canoeist [kə'nu·ɪst] *s* canoero

canon ['kænən] *s* canon *m*; (*priest*) canónigo

canonical [kə'nɑnɪkəl] *adj* canónico; aceptado, auténtico, establecido ‖

canonicals *spl* vestiduras sacerdotales

canonize ['kænə,naɪz] *tr* canonizar

canon law *s* cánones *mpl*, derecho canónico

canon·ry ['kænənrɪ] *s* (*pl* -**ries**) canonjía

can opener ['opənər] *s* abrelatas *m*

cano·py ['kænəpɪ] *s* (*pl* -**pies**) dosel *m*, pabellón *m*; (*over an entrance*) marquesina; (*for electrical fixtures*) campana

canopy of heaven *s* bóveda celeste

cant [kænt] *s* hipocresía; jerga, jerigonza

cantaloupe ['kæntə,lop] *s* cantalupo

cantankerous [kæn'tæŋkərəs] *adj* de mal genio, pendenciero

canteen [kæn'tin] *s* (*shop*) cantina; (*water flask*) cantimplora; (*mil*) centro de recreo

canter ['kæntər] *s* medio galope ‖ *intr* ir a medio galope

canticle ['kæntɪkəl] *s* cántico

cantilever ['kæntɪ,livər] *adj* voladizo ‖ *s* viga voladiza

cantle ['kæntəl] *s* arzón trasero

canton [kæn'tɑn] *tr* acantonar

cantonment [kæn'tɑnmənt] *s* acantonamiento

cantor ['kæntər] o ['kæntər] *s* chantre *m*; (*in a synagogue*) cantor *m* principal

canvas ['kænvəs] *s* cañamazo, lona; (*naut*) vela, lona; (*painting*) lienzo; **under canvas** (mil) en tiendas; (naut) con las velas izadas

canvass ['kænvəs] *s* pesquisa, escrutinio; (*of votes*) solicitación ‖ *tr* escrutar, solicitar; discutir detenidamente

canyon ['kænjən] *s* cañón *m*

cap. *abbr* **capital, capitalize**

cap [kæp] *s* gorra, gorra de visera; (*of academic costume*) birrete *m*; (*of bottle*) cápsula; (*e.g., of a fountain pen*) capuchón *m* ‖ *v* (*pret & pp* **capped**; *ger* **capping**) *tr* cubrir con gorra; capsular (*una botella*); **to cap the climax** ser el colmo

capabili·ty [,kepə'bɪlɪtɪ] *s* (*pl* -**ties**) habilidad, capacidad

capable ['kepəbəl] *adj* hábil, capaz

capacious [kə'peʃəs] *adj* espacioso, capaz

capaci·ty [kə'pæsɪtɪ] *s* (*pl* -**ties**) (*room, space; ability, aptitude*) capacidad; (*status, function*) calidad; **in the capacity of** en calidad de

cap and bells *spl* caperuza de bufón; cetro de la locura

cap and gown *s* birrete y toga

caparison [kə'pærɪsən] *s* caparazón *m* ‖ *tr* engualdrapar

cape [kep] *s* cabo, promontorio; (*garment*) capa, esclavina

Cape Colony *s* la Colonia del Cabo

Cape Horn *s* el Cabo de Hornos

Cape of Good Hope *s* Cabo de Buena Esperanza

caper ['kepər] *s* (*gay jump*) cabriola; (*prank*) travesura; **to cut capers** dar cabriolas; hacer travesuras ‖ *intr* cabriolear; retozar

Cape'town' o **Cape Town** *s* El Cabo, la Ciudad del Cabo

cape'work' *s* (taur) suerte *f* de capa, lance *m*

capital ['kæpɪtəl] *adj* capital ‖ *s* (*money*) capital *m*; (*city*) capital *f*; (*top of a column*) capitel *m*; **to make capital out of** sacar beneficio de

capitalism ['kæpɪtə,lɪzəm] *s* capitalismo

capitalize ['kæpɪtə,laɪz] *tr* escribir con mayúscula; capitalizar ‖ *intr* — **to capitalize on** aprovecharse de

capital letter *s* letra mayúscula

capitol ['kæpɪtəl] *s* capitolio

capitulate [kə'pɪtʃə,let] *intr* capitular

capon ['kepən] *s* capón *m*

caprice [kə'pris] *s* capricho, antojo; veleidad

capricious [kə'prɪʃəs] *adj* caprichoso, antojadizo

Capricorn ['kæprɪ,kɔrn] *s* Capricornio

capsize ['kæpsaɪz] *tr* volcar ‖ *intr* volcar; tumbar, zozobrar (*un barco*)

capstan ['kæpstən] *s* cabrestante *m*

cap'stone' *s* coronamiento

capsule ['kæpsəl] *s* cápsula

Capt. *abbr* **Captain**

captain ['kæptən] *s* capitán *m* ‖ *tr* capitanear

captain·cy ['kæptənsi] *s* (*pl* **-cies**) capitanía

caption ['kæpʃən] *s* título; (*in a movie*) subtítulo

captivate ['kæptɪ,vet] *tr* cautivar, encantar

captive ['kæptɪv] *adj* & *s* cautivo

captivi·ty [kæp'tɪvɪti] *s* (*pl* **-ties**) cautividad, cautiverio

captor ['kæptər] *s* aprenhensor *m*

capture ['kæptʃər] *s* apresamiento, captura; (*of a stronghold*) toma ‖ *tr* apresar, capturar; tomar (*una plaza*); captar (*p.ej., la atención de una persona*)

Capuchin nun ['kæpjutʃɪn] o ['kæpjuʃɪn] *s* capuchina

car [kɑr] *s* coche *m*; (*of an elevator*) caja, carro

carafe [kə'ræf] *s* garrafa

caramel ['kærəməl] o ['kɑrməl] *s* (*burnt sugar*) caramelo; bombón *m* de caramelo

carat ['kærət] *s* quilate *m*

caravan ['kærə,væn] *s* caravana

caravansa·ry [,kærə'vænsəri] *s* (*pl* **-ries**) caravanera

caraway ['kærə,we] *s* alcaravea

car'barn' *s* cochera de tranvías

carbide ['kɑrbaɪd] *s* carburo

carbine ['kɑrbaɪn] *s* carabina

carbolic acid [kɑr'bɑlɪk] *s* ácido carbólico

carbon ['kɑrbən] *s* (*chemical element*) carbono; (*pole of arc light or battery*) carbón *m*; papel *m* carbón; (*in auto cylinders*) carbonilla

carbon copy *s* copia al carbón

carbon dioxide *s* dióxido de carbono

carbon monoxide *s* óxido de carbono, monóxido de carbono

carbon paper *s* papel *m* carbón

car'boy' *s* bombona, garrafón *m*

carbuncle ['kɑrbʌŋkəl] *s* (*stone*) carbunclo, carbúnculo; (pathol) carbunclo, carbunco

carburetor ['kɑrbə,retər] o ['kɑrbjə,retər] *s* carburador *m*

car caller *s* avisacoches *m*

carcass ['kɑrkəs] *s* res muerta, cadáver *m*

card [kɑrd] *s* tarjeta; (*for playing games*) naipe *m*, carta; (*for filing*) ficha; (*person*) (coll) sujeto, tipo

card'board' *s* cartón *m*

cardboard binding *s* encuadernación en pasta

card case *s* tarjetero

card catalogue *s* catálogo de fichas

cardiac ['kɑrdɪ,æk] *adj* cardíaco ‖ *s* (*medicine; sufferer*) cardíaco

cardigan ['kɑrdɪgən] *s* albornoz *m*, rebeca

cardinal ['kɑrdɪnəl] *adj* cardinal; purpurado ‖ *s* (*prelate; bird*) cardenal *m*; número cardinal

card index *s* fichero, tarjetero

card party *s* tertulia de baraja

card'sharp' *s* fullero, tahur *m*

card trick *s* truco de naipes

care [ker] *s* (*worry*) inquietud, ansiedad; (*watchful attention*) esmero; (*charge*) cargo, custodia; **care of** suplicada en casa de; **to take care of oneself** cuidarse ‖ *intr* inquietarse, preocuparse; **to care for** cuidar de; amar, querer; **to care to** tener ganas de

careen [kə'rin] *intr* inclinarse; mecerse precipitadamente

career [kə'rɪr] *adj* de carrera ‖ *s* carrera

care'free' *adj* despreocupado, libre de cuidados

careful ['kerfəl] *adj* (*acting with care*) cuidadoso; (*done with care*) esmerado; **to be careful to** cuidarse de

careless ['kerlɪs] *adj* descuidado, negligente

carelessness ['kerlɪsnɪs] *s* descuido, negligencia

caress [kə'res] *s* caricia ‖ *tr* acariciar ‖ *intr* acariciarse

caretaker ['ker,tekər] *s* curador *m*, guardián *m*, custodio

care'worn' *adj* fatigado, rendido

car'fare' *s* pasaje *m* de tranvía o autobús

car·go ['kɑrgo] *s* (*pl* **-goes** o **-gos**) carga, cargamento

cargo boat *s* barco de carga

Caribbean [,kærɪ'biən] o [kə'rɪbiən] *adj* caribe ‖ *s* mar *m* Caribe

caricature ['kærɪkətʃər] *s* caricatura ‖ *tr* caricaturizar

caricaturist ['kærɪkətʃərɪst] *s* caricaturista *mf*

carillon ['kærɪ,lɑn] o [kə'rɪljən] *s* carillón *m*

car'load' *s* furgonada, vagonada

carnage ['kɑrnɪdʒ] s carnicería, matanza

carnation [kɑr'neʃən] adj encarnado || s clavel m, clavel reventón

carnival ['kɑrnɪvəl] adj carnavalesco || s (period before Lent) carnaval m; verbena, espectáculo de atracciones

car·ol ['kærəl] s canción alegre, villancico || v (pret & pp -oled o -olled; ger -oling o -olling); tr celebrar con villancicos || intr cantar con alegría

carom ['kærəm] s carambola || intr carambolear

carousal [kə'rauzəl] s juerga, borrachera, jarana

carouse [kə'rauz] intr emborracharse, jaranear

carp [kɑrp] s carpa || intr quejarse

carpenter ['kɑrpəntər] s carpintero

carpentry ['kɑrpəntri] s carpintería

carpet ['kɑrpɪt] s alfombra; **to be on the carpet** estar sobre el tapete || tr alfombrar

carpet sweeper s barredora de alfombras

car'-rent'al service s alquiler m de coches

carriage ['kærɪdʒ] s carruaje m; (cost of carrying) porte m, transporte m; (bearing) porte m, continente m; (mach) carro

carrier ['kærɪ·ər] s portador m, transportador m; portador de gérmenes; empresa de transportes; (mailman) cartero; vendedor m de periódicos; portaaviones m; (rad) onda portadora

carrier pigeon s paloma mensajera

carrier wave s (rad) onda portadora

carrion ['kærɪ·ən] adj carroño; inmundo || s carroña; inmundicia

carrot ['kærət] s zanahoria

carrousel [,kærə'zɛl] s caballitos, tiovivo

car·ry ['kæri] v (pret & pp -ried) tr llevar, portar, traer; transportar; sostener (una carga); **to carry away** llevarse; encantar, entusiasmar; **to carry into effect** llevar a cabo; **to carry one's point** salirse con la suya; **to carry out** llevar a cabo; **to carry the day** quedar victorioso, ganar la palma; **to carry weight** ser de peso || intr tener alcance; **to carry on** continuar, perseverar; (coll) travesear; (coll) comportarse de un modo escandaloso; (coll) hacer locuras

cart [kɑrt] s carreta, carro || tr carretear

carte blanche ['kɑrt'blɑnʃ] s carta blanca

cartel [kɑr'tɛl] s cartel m

Carthage ['kɑrθɪdʒ] s Cartago

Carthaginian [,kɑrθə'dʒɪnɪ·ən] adj & s cartaginés m

cart horse s caballo de tiro

cartilage ['kɑrtɪlɪdʒ] s cartílago

cartoon [kɑr'tun] s caricatura; (comic strip) tira cómica; (film) película de dibujos || tr caricaturizar

cartoonist [kɑr'tunɪst] s caricaturista mf

cartridge ['kɑrtrɪdʒ] s cartucho

cartridge belt s canana

carve [kɑrv] tr trinchar (carne); esculpir, tallar

carving knife ['kɑrvɪŋ] s cuchillo de trinchar

car washer s lavacoches m

caryatid [,kærɪ'ætɪd] s cariátide f

cascade [kæs'ked] s cascada

case [kes] s (instance; form of a word) caso; (box) caja; (small container) estuche m; (for cigarettes) pitillera; (sheath) vaina, funda; (law) causa, pleito; **in case** caso que; **in no case** de ninguna manera || tr encajonar, enfundar

casement ['kesmənt] s ventana batiente; bastidor m (de la ventana)

cash [kæʃ] s dinero contante; pago al contado; **cash on delivery** contra reembolso, pago contra entrega; **to pay cash** pagar al contado || tr cobrar (un cheque el portador); abonar, pagar (un cheque el banco) || intr — **to cash in on** (coll) sacar provecho de

cash and carry s pago al contado con transporte a cargo del comprador

cash'box' s caja

cashew ['kæʃu] s anacardo, marañón m

cashew nut s anacardo, nuez f de marañón

cashier [kæ'ʃɪr] s cajero || tr destruir; (in the army) degradar

cashier's check s cheque m de caja

cashier's desk s caja

cashmere ['kæʃmɪr] s casimir m, cachemir m

cash on hand s efectivo en caja

cash payment s pago al contado

cash purchase s compra al contado

cash register s caja registradora

casing ['kesɪŋ] s caja, cubierta, envoltura; (of door or window) marco, cerco; (of tire) cubierta; (sew) jareta

cask [kæsk] o [kɑsk] s casco, pipa, tonel m

casket ['kæskɪt] o ['kɑskɪt] s (box for valuables) cajita, joyero; (coffin) caja, ataúd m

casserole ['kæsə,rol] s cacerola; (dish cooked in a casserole) timbal m

cassock ['kæsək] s balandrán m, sotana

cast [kæst] o [kɑst] s echada, tiro; forma, molde m; aire m, semblante m; matiz m, tinte m; (of actors) reparto || v (pret & pp cast) tr echar, tirar; volver (los ojos); proyectar (una sombra); colar, fundir (metales); depositar (votos); echar (suertes); (theat) repartir (papeles); **to cast aside** desechar; **to cast loose** soltar; **to cast out** arrojar, echar fuera; despedir, desterrar || intr echar los dados; arrojar el sedal o el anzuelo; **to cast about** revolver proyectos; **to cast off** (naut) soltar las amarras

castanet [,kæstə'net] *s* castañuela, castañeta

cast'a·way' proscrito, réprobo; náufrago

caste [kæst] o [kɑst] *s* casta; **to lose caste** desprestigiarse

caster ['kæstər] o ['kɑstər] *s* ruedecilla de mueble; (*cruet stand*) angarillas, vinagreras; frasco

Castile [kæs'til] *s* Castilla

Castile soap *s* jabón *m* de Castilla

Castilian [kæs'tɪljən] *adj & s* castellano

casting ['kæstɪŋ] o ['kɑstɪŋ] *s* fundición, pieza fundida; (theat) reparto

casting vote *s* voto de calidad

cast iron *s* hierro colado, hierro fundido

cast'-i'ron *adj* de hierro colado; fuerte, endurecido; duro, inflexible

castle ['kæsəl] o ['kɑsəl] *s* castillo; (chess) roque *m*, torre *f* ‖ *tr & intr* (chess) enrocar

castle in Spain, castle in the air *s* castillo en el aire

cast'off' *adj* abandonado, desechado; (*clothing*) de desecho ‖ *s* desecho

castor oil ['kæstər] o [kɑstər] *s* aceite *m* de ricino

castrate ['kæstret] *tr* capar, castrar

casual ['kæʒʊ·əl] *adj* casual, fortuito; descuidado, indiferente

casual·ty ['kæʒʊ·əltɪ] *s* (*pl* -ties) desgracia, accidente *m*; accidentado, víctima; (*in war*) baja

casualty list *s* lista de bajas

cat. *abbr* catalogue, catechism

cat [kæt] *s* gato; mujer maligna; **to bell the cat** ponerle cascabel al gato; **to let the cat out of the bag** revelar el secreto

catacomb ['kætə‚kom] *s* catacumba

Catalan ['kætə‚læn] *adj & s* catalán *m*

catalogue ['kætə‚lɔg] o ['kætə‚lɑg] *s* catálogo ‖ *tr* catalogar

Catalonia [‚kætə'lonɪ·ə] *s* Cataluña

Catalonian [‚kætə'lonɪ·ən] *adj & s* catalán *m*

catapult ['kætə‚pʌlt] *s* catapulta ‖ *tr* catapultar

cataract ['kætə‚rækt] *s* catarata; (pathol) catarata

catarrh [kə'tɑr] *s* catarro

catastrophe [kə'tæstrəfɪ] *s* catástrofe *f*

cat'call' *s* rechifla ‖ *tr & intr* rechiflar

catch [kætʃ] *s* (*of a ball*) cogida; (*of fish*) pesca; (*of a lock*) cerradera, pestillo; (*booty*) botín *m*, presa; (*fastener*) broche *m*; (*good match*) buen partido ‖ *v* (*pret & pp* **caught** [kɔt]) *tr* asir, coger, atrapar; llegar a oír; coger (*un resfriado*); (*to come upon suddenly*) sorprender; comprender; capturar (*al delincuente*); **to catch fire** encenderse; **to catch hold of** agarrar, coger; apoderarse de; **to catch it** (coll) merecerse un regaño; **to catch oneself** contenerse; recobrar el equilibrio; **to catch sight of** alcanzar a ver; **to**

catch up arrebatar; coger al vuelo; (*in a mistake*) cazar ‖ *intr* pegarse (*una enfermedad*); enredarse; encenderse; **to catch at** agarrarse a, tratar de asir; **to catch on** prender en (*p.ej., un gancho*); comprender, coger el tino; **to catch up** salir del atraso; (*in one's debts*) ponerse al día; **to catch up with** emparejar con

catcher ['kætʃər] *s* (baseball) receptor, parador *m*

catching ['kætʃɪŋ] *adj* pegajoso, contagioso; atrayente, cautivador

catch question *s* pega

catchup ['kætʃəp] o ['ketʃəp] *s* salsa de tomate condimentada

catch'word' *s* lema *m*, palabra de efecto; (*actor's cue*) pie *m*; (typ) reclamo

catch·y ['kætʃɪ] *adj* (*comp* -ier; *super* -iest) (*tune*) animado, vivo; (*title of a book*) impresionante, llamativo; (*question*) intrincado; (*breathing*) espasmódico

catechism ['kætɪ‚kɪzəm] *s* catecismo

catego·ry ['kætɪ‚gorɪ] *s* (*pl* -ries) categoría

cater ['ketər] *tr & intr* abastecer, proveer; **to cater to** proveer a

cater-cornered ['kætər‚kɔrnərd] *adj* diagonal ‖ *adv* diagonalmente

caterer ['ketərər] *s* abastecedor *m*, proveedor *m* de alimentos (*esp. para fiestas caseras*)

caterpillar ['kætər‚pɪlər] *s* oruga

caterpillar tractor *s* tractor *m* de oruga

cat'fish' *s* bagre *m*

cat'gut' *s* (mus) cuerda de tripa; (surg) catgut *m*

Cath. *abbr* Catholic

cathartic [kə'θɑrtɪk] *adj & s* catártico

cathedral [kə'θidrəl] *s* catedral *f*

catheter ['kæθɪtər] *s* catéter *m*

catheterize ['kæθɪtə‚raɪz] *tr* cateterizar

cathode ['kæθod] *s* cátodo

catholic ['kæθəlɪk] *adj* católico; **Catholic** *adj & s* católico

catkin ['kætkɪn] *s* candelilla, amento

cat nap *s* sueñecito

catnip ['kætnɪp] *s* hierba gatera, nébeda

cat-o'-nine-tails [,kætə'naɪn‚telz] *s* azote *m* con nueve ramales

cat's cradle *s* juego de la cuna

cat's-paw o **catspaw** ['kæts‚pɔ] *s* mano *f* de gato, instrumento

catsup ['kætsəp] o [ketʃəp] *s* salsa de tomate condimentada

cat'tail' *s* anea, espadaña; amento

cattle ['kætəl] *s* ganado vacuno

cattle crossing *s* paso de ganado

cattle·man ['kætəlmən] *s* (*pl* -men [mən]) *s* ganadero

cattle raising *s* ganadería

cattle ranch *s* hacienda de ganado

cat·ty ['kætɪ] *adj* (*comp* -tier; *super* -tiest) (*like a cat*) felino, gatuno; (*spiteful*) malicioso; (*gossipy*) chismoso

cat'walk' *s* pasadero, pasarela

Caucasian [kɔ'keʒən] o [kɔ'keʃən] adj & s caucasiano, caucásico
Caucasus ['kɔkəsəs] s Cáucaso
caucus ['kɔkəs] s junta de políticos
cauliflower ['kɔlɪ,flau·ər] s coliflor f
cause [kɔz] s causa; (person) causante mf || tr causar
cause'way' s (highway) calzada; calzada elevada
caustic ['kɔstɪk] adj cáustico
cauterize ['kɔtə,raɪz] tr cauterizar
caution ['kɔʃən] s (carefulness) cautela; (warning) advertencia, amonestación || tr advertir, amonestar
cautious ['kɔʃəs] adj cauteloso, cauto
Cav. abbr **Cavalry**
cavalcade [,kævəl'ked] o ['kævəl,ked] s cabalgata
cavalier [,kævə'lɪr] adj (haughty) altivo, desdeñoso; (offhand) alegre, desenvuelto, inceremonioso || s (horseman) caballero; (lady's escort) galán m
caval·ry ['kævəlri] s (pl -ries) caballería
cavalry·man ['kævəlrimən] s (pl -men [mən]) soldado de caballería
cave [kev] s cueva, caverna || intr — **to cave in** hundirse; (to give in, yield) (coll) ceder, rendirse
cave'-in' s hundimiento, derrumbe m, socavón m
cave man s hombre grosero
cavern ['kævərn] s caverna
cav·il ['kævɪl] v (pret & pp -iled o -illed; ger -iling o -illing) intr buscar quisquillas
cavi·ty ['kævɪti] s (pl -ties) cavidad; (in a tooth) picadura
cavort [kə'vɔrt] intr (coll) cabriolar
caw [kɔ] s graznido || intr graznar
cc. abbr **cubic centimeter**
cease [sis] tr parar, suspender || intr cesar; cesar de, dejar de + inf
cease'fire' s cese m de fuego || intr suspender hostilidades
ceaseless ['sislɪs] adj incesante, continuo
cedar ['sidər] s cedro
cede [sid] tr ceder, traspasar
ceiling ['silɪŋ] s techo, cielo raso; (aer) techo, cielo máximo
ceiling price s precio tope
celebrant ['sɛlɪbrənt] s celebrante m
celebrate ['sɛlɪ,bret] tr celebrar || intr (to say mass) celebrar; divertirse, festejarse
celebrated ['sɛlɪ,bretɪd] adj célebre, renombrado
celebration [,sɛlɪ'breʃən] s celebración; diversión, festividad
celebri·ty [sɪ'lebrɪti] s (pl -ties) (fame; famous person) celebridad
celery ['sɛləri] s apio
celestial [sɪ'lestʃəl] adj celeste, celestial
celiba·cy ['sɛlɪbəsi] s (pl -cies) celibato
celibate ['sɛlɪ,bet] o ['sɛlɪbɪt] adj & s célibe mf
cell [sɛl] s (of convent or jail) celda; (of honeycomb) celdilla; (of elec-

tric battery) elemento; (of plant or animal; of photoelectric device; of political group) célula
cellar ['sɛlər] s sótano; (for wine) bodega
cellaret [,sɛlə'rɛt] s licorera
cell house s prisión celular
cellist o **'cellist** ['tʃɛlɪst] s violoncelista mf
cel·lo o **'cel·lo** ['tʃɛlo] s (pl -los) violoncelo
cellophane ['sɛlə,fen] s celofán m
celluloid ['sɛljə,lɔɪd] s celuloide m
Celt [sɛlt] o [kɛlt] s celta mf
Celtic ['sɛltɪk] o ['kɛltɪk] adj céltico || s (language) celta m
cement [sɪ'mɛnt] s cemento || tr revestir con cemento; (la amistad) consolidar
cemeter·y ['sɛmɪ,tɛri] s (pl -ies) cementerio
cen. abbr **central**
censer ['sɛnsər] s incensario
censor ['sɛnsər] s censor m || tr censurar
censure ['sɛnʃər] s censura || tr censurar
census ['sɛnsəs] s censo; **to take the census** levantar el censo
cent. abbr **centigrade, central, century**
cent [sɛnt] s centavo
centaur ['sɛntər] s centauro
centennial [sɛn'tɛnɪ·əl] adj & s centenario
center ['sɛntər] adj centrista || s centro || tr centrar
cen'ter·piece' s centro de mesa
center punch s granete m, punzón m de marcar
centigrade ['sɛntɪ,gred] adj centígrado
centimeter ['sɛntɪ,mitər] s centímetro
centipede ['sɛntɪ,pid] s ciempiés m
central ['sɛntrəl] adj central || s (telp) central f, central de teléfonos; (operator) telefonista mf
Central America s Centro América, la América Central
Central American adj & mf centroamericano
centralize ['sɛntrə,laɪz] tr centralizar || intr centralizarse
centu·ry ['sɛntʃəri] s (pl -ries) siglo
century plant s pita, maguey m
ceramic [sɪ'ræmɪk] adj cerámico
cereal ['sɪrɪ·əl] adj & s cereal m
ceremonious [,sɛrɪ'monɪ·əs] adj ceremonioso, etiquetero
ceremo·ny ['sɛrɪ,moni] s (pl -nies) ceremonia; **to stand on ceremony** hacer ceremonias, ser etiquetero
certain ['sʌrtən] adj cierto; **a certain** cierto; **for certain** por cierto
certainly ['sɛrtənli] adj ciertamente; (gladly) con mucho gusto
certain·ty ['sʌrtənti] s (pl -ties) certeza; **with certainty** a ciencia cierta
certificate [sər'tɪfɪkɪt] s certificación, certificado; (of birth, death, etc.) partida, fe f; (document representing financial assets) título || [sər'tɪfɪ,ket] tr certificar

ca
ce

certified public accountant [ˈsʌrtɪ-ˌfaɪd] s censor jurado de cuentas
certi·fy [ˈsʌrtɪˌfaɪ] v (pret & pp -fied) tr certificar
cervix [ˈsʌrvɪks] s (pl cervices [sərˈvaɪsiz]) cerviz f
cessation [sɛˈseʃən] s cesación
cessation of hostilities s suspensión de hostilidades
cesspool [ˈsɛsˌpul] s pozo negro; (fig) sitio inmundo
Ceylon [sɪˈlɑn] s Ceilán
Cey·lo·nese [ˌsilaˈniz] adj ceilanés || s (pl -nese) ceilanés m
cf. abbr **confer, i.e., compare**
C.F.I., c.f.i. abbr **cost, freight, and insurance**
cg. abbr **centigram**
ch. abbr **chapter, church**
chafe [tʃef] s fricción, roce m; desgaste m; irritación || tr (to rub) frotar; (to rub and make sore) escocer; (to wear) desgastar; irritar || intr escocerse; desgastarse; irritarse
chaff [tʃæf] o [tʃaf] s barcia; paja menuda; broza, desperdicio
chafing dish [ˈtʃefɪŋ] s cocinilla, infernillo
chagrin [ʃəˈgrɪn] s desazón f, disgusto || tr desazonar, disgustar
chain [tʃen] s cadena || tr encadenar
chain gang s cadena de presidiarios, collera, cuerda de presos
chain reaction s reacción en cadena
chain'smoke' intr fumar un pitillo tras otro
chain store s empresa con una cadena de tiendas; tienda de una cadena de tiendas
chair [tʃer] s silla; (de catedrático) cátedra; presidencia; **to take the chair** presidir la reunión; abrir la sesión || tr presidir (una reunión)
chair lift s telesilla
chair·man [ˈtʃermən] s (pl -men [mən]) presidente m
chairmanship [ˈtʃermənˌʃɪp] s presidencia
chair rail s guardasilla
chalice [ˈtʃælɪs] s cáliz m
chalk [tʃɔk] s (soft white limestone) creta; (piece used for writing) tiza || tr marcar o escribir con tiza; **to chalk up** apuntar; marcar (un tanto)
challenge [ˈtʃælɪndʒ] s desafío; (law) recusación || tr desafiar; (law) recusar
chamber [ˈtʃembər] s cámara; (of a gun) recámara; dormitorio; **chambers** oficina de juez
chamberlain [ˈtʃembərlɪn] s chamberlán m
cham'ber·maid' s camarera
chamber pot s orinal m
chameleon [kəˈmiljən] s camaleón m
chamfer [ˈtʃæmfər] s chaflán m || tr chaflanar
cham·ois [ˈʃæmi] s (pl -ois) gamuza
champ [tʃæmp] s mordisco; (slang) campeón m || tr & intr mordiscar; (el freno) morder
champagne [ʃæmˈpen] s champaña m

champion [ˈtʃæmpɪ·ən] s campeón m || tr defender
championess [ˈtʃæmpɪ·ənɪs] s campeona
championship [ˈtʃæmpɪ·ənˌʃɪp] s campeonato
chance [tʃæns] o [tʃans] adj casual, imprevisto || s oportunidad, ocasión; casualidad, suerte f; probabilidad; peligro, riesgo; **by chance** por casualidad; **to not stand a chance** no tener probabilidad de éxito; **to take a chance** probar fortuna; comprar un billete de lotería; **to take chances** probar fortuna; **to wait for a chance** esperar la oportunidad || intr acontecer; **to chance on** o **upon** tropezar con; **to chance to** acertar a
chancel [ˈtʃænsəl] o [ˈtʃansəl] s entrecoro
chanc/ler·y [ˈtʃænsələri] o [ˈtʃansələri] s (pl -ies) cancillería
chancellor [ˈtʃænsələr] o [ˈtʃansələr] s canciller m
chandelier [ˌʃændəˈlɪr] s araña de luces
change [tʃendʒ] s cambio, mudanza; suelto, moneda suelta; (surplus money returned with a purchase) vuelta; (of clothing) muda; **for a change** por variedad; **to keep the change** quedarse con la vuelta; || tr cambiar, mudar; cambiar de, mudar de; reemplazar; **to change clothes** cambiar de ropa; **to change gears** cambiar de velocidades; **to change hands** cambiar de dueño; **to change money** cambiar moneda; **to change one's mind** cambiar de parecer; **to change trains** cambiar de tren, transbordar || intr cambiar, mudar; corregirse
changeable [ˈtʃendʒəbəl] adj cambiable; inconstante, cambiante, mudable
change of clothing s muda de ropa
change of heart s arrepentimiento, conversión
change of life s cesación natural de las reglas
change of voice s muda
chan·nel [ˈtʃænəl] s (body of water joining two others) canal m; (bed of river) álveo, cauce m; (means of communication) vía; (passage) conducto; (groove) ranura, surco; (telv) canal m; **the Channel** el Canal de la Mancha || v (pret & pp -neled o -nelled; ger -neling o -nelling) tr acanalar; canalizar (esfuerzos, dinero, etc.)
chant [tʃænt] o [tʃant] s (song) canción; (song sung in a monotone) canto || tr & intr cantar
chanter [ˈtʃæntər] o [ˈtʃantər] s cantor m; (priest) chantre m
chanticleer [ˈtʃæntɪˌklɪr] s el gallo
chaos [ˈke·ɑs] s caos m
chaotic [keˈɑtɪk] adj caótico
chap. abbr **chaplain, chapter**
chap [tʃæp] s (jaw) mandíbula; (cheek) mejilla; (crack in the skin)

grieta; chico, tipo; **chaps** zahones *mpl* ‖ *v* (*pret & pp* **chapped;** *ger* **chapping**) *tr* agrietar, rajar ‖ *intr* agrietarse, rajarse

chapel ['tʃæpəl] *s* capilla

chaperon o **chaperone** ['ʃæpə‚ron] *s* carabina, señora de compañía ‖ *tr* acompañar (*una señora a una o más señoritas*)

chaplain ['tʃæplɪn] *s* capellán *m*

chaplet ['tʃæplɪt] *s* (*wreath for head*) guirnalda; rosario

chapter ['tʃæptər] *s* capítulo; (*of the Scriptures*) capítula; (*of a cathedral*) cabildo

chapter and verse *adv* con todos sus pelos y señales

char [tʃɑr] *v* (*pret & pp* **charred;** *ger* **charring**) *tr* carbonizar; (*to scorch*) socarrar

character ['kærɪktər] *s* carácter *m*; (*conspicuous person; person in a play or novel*) personaje *m*; (*part or role in a play*) papel *m*; (*fellow*) (coll) tipo, sujeto

characteristic [‚kærɪktə'rɪstɪk] *adj* característico ‖ *s* característica

characterize ['kærɪktə‚raɪz] *tr* caracterizar

char'coal' *s* carbón *m* de leña; (*for sketching*) carboncillo; (*sketch*) dibujo al carbón

charcoal burner *s* (*person*) carbonero; horno para hacer carbón de leña

charge [tʃɑrdʒ] *s* (*of an explosive, of electricity, of soldiers against the enemy; responsibility*) carga; (*accusation; amount owed; recording of amount owed*) cargo; (*heral*) blasón *m*; (*attack*) embestida; **in charge of** a cargo de; **to reverse the charges** (telp) cargar al número llamado; **to take charge of** hacerse cargo de ‖ *tr* cargar; cobrar (*cierto precio*); (*to order*) encargar, mandar; cargar (*un acumulador; al enemigo*); **to charge to the account of someone** cargarle a uno en cuenta; **to charge with** cargar de ‖ *intr* embestir

charge account *s* cuenta corriente

chargé d'affaires [ʃɑr'ʒe də'fer] *s* (*pl* **chargés d'affaires**) encargado de negocios

charger ['tʃɑrdʒər] *s* caballo de guerra; (*of a battery*) cargador *m*

chariot ['tʃærɪət] *s* carro romano

charioteer [‚tʃærɪ‑ə'tɪr] *s* carretero, auriga *m*

charitable ['tʃærɪtəbəl] *adj* caritativo

chari·ty ['tʃærɪti] *s* (*pl* **-ties**) caridad; asociación de beneficencia, obra pía; **charity begins at home** la caridad bien ordenada empieza por uno mismo

charity performance *s* función benéfica

charlatan ['ʃɑrlətən] *s* charlatán *m*

charlatanism ['ʃɑrlətən‚ɪzəm] *s* charlatanismo

Charlemagne ['ʃɑrlə‚men] *s* Carlomagno

Charles [tʃɑrlz] *s* Carlos *m*

charlotte ['ʃɑrlət] *s* carlota ‖ **Charlotte** *s* Carlota

charlotte russe ['ʃɑrlət 'rus] *s* carlota rusa

charm [tʃɑrm] *s* encanto, hechizo; (*trinket*) amuleto, dije *m* ‖ *tr* encantar, hechizar

charming ['tʃɑrmɪŋ] *adj* encantador

charnel ['tʃɑrnəl] *adj* cadavérico, horrible ‖ *s* carnero, osario

charnel house *s* carnero, osario

chart [tʃɑrt] *s* mapa geográfico; (naut) carta de marear; cuadro, diagrama *m* ‖ *tr* bosquejar; **to chart a course** trazar una ruta

charter ['tʃɑrtər] *s* carta (de privilegio) ‖ *tr* alquilar (*un autobús*); fletar (*un barco*)

charter member *s* socio fundador

char·woman ['tʃɑr‚wumən] *s* (*pl* **-women** [‚wɪmɪn]) alquilona, asistenta

Charybdis [kə'rɪbdɪs] *s* Caribdis *f*

chase [tʃes] *s* caza, persecución ‖ *tr* cazar, perseguir; **to chase away** ahuyentar

chasm ['kæzəm] *s* abismo

chas·sis ['tʃæsi] *s* (*pl* **-sis** [siz]) chasis *m*

chaste [tʃest] *adj* casto; (*style*) castizo

chasten ['tʃesən] *tr* castigar, corregir

chastise [tʃæs'taɪz] *tr* castigar

chastity ['tʃæstɪti] *s* castidad

chasuble ['tʃæzjubəl] *s* casulla

chat [tʃæt] *s* charla, plática ‖ *v* (*pret & pp* **chatted;** *ger* **chatting**) *intr* charlar, platicar

chatelaine ['ʃætə‚len] *s* castellana

chattels ['tʃætəlz] *spl* bienes *mpl* muebles, enseres *mpl*

chatter ['tʃætər] *s* (*talk*) cháchara; (*rattling*) traqueo; (*of teeth*) castañeteo; (*of birds*) chirrido ‖ *intr* chacharear; traquear; castañetear, dentellar (*los dientes*)

chat'ter·box' *s* charlador *m*, tarabilla

chauffeur ['ʃofər] o [ʃo'fʌr] *s* chófer *m*

cheap [tʃip] *adj* barato; (*charging low prices*) no carero, baratero; (*flashy*) cursi; **to feel cheap** sentirse avergonzado ‖ *adv* barato

cheapen ['tʃipən] *tr* abaratar

cheapness ['tʃipnɪs] *s* baratura; (*flashiness*) cursilería

cheat [tʃit] *s* trampa, fraude *m*; (*person*) trampista *mf*, defraudador *m* ‖ *tr* trampear, defraudar

check [tʃɛk] *s* (*of bank*) cheque *m*; (*for baggage*) talón *m*, contraseña; (*in a restaurant*) cuenta; (*in theater or movie*) contraseña, billete *m* de salida; (*restraint*) freno; (*to hold a door*) amortiguador *m*; (*in chess*) jaque *m*; inspección; comprobación, verificación; (*cloth*) paño a cuadros; **in check** en jaque; **to hold in check** contener, refrenar ‖ *interj* ¡jaque! ‖ *tr* parar súbitamente; contener, refrenar; amortiguar; facturar (*equipajes*); inspeccionar; comprobar, verificar; marcar, señalar; (*in chess*) jaquear, dar jaque a; **to check up** comprobar, verificar ‖ *intr* pararse súbitamente; corresponder punto por punto; **to check in** (*at a hotel*) llegar e inscribirse; **to check out** pagar la cuenta y despedirse; (*slang*) morir

check′book′ *s* talonario (de cheques)

checker ['tʃɛkər] *s* inspector *m;* cuadro; dibujo a cuadros; (*in game of checkers*) ficha, pieza; **checkers** damas, juego de damas ‖ *tr* marcar con cuadros; diversificar, variar

check′er·board′ *s* damero, tablero

check girl *s* moza de guardarropa

checking account *s* cuenta corriente

check′mate′ *s* mate *m,* jaque *m* mate ‖ *tr* dar mate a, dar jaque mate a; (fig) derrotar completamente

check′out′ *s* (*from a hotel*) salida; hora de salida; (*in a self-service retail store*) revisión y pago

checkout counter *s* mostrador *m* de revisión

check′point′ *s* punto de inspección

check′rein′ *s* engallador *m*

check′room′ *s* guardarropa *m;* (rr) consigna, depósito de equipajes

check′up′ *s* verificación rigurosa; (*of an automobile*) revisión; (med) reconocimiento general

cheek [tʃik] *s* mejilla, carrillo; (coll) descaro, frescura

cheek′bone′ *s* pómulo

cheek·y ['tʃiki] *adj* (*comp* -ier; *super* -iest) (coll) descarado, fresco

cheer [tʃɪr] *s* alegría, regocijo; (*shout*) viva *m,* aplauso; **what cheer?** ¿qué tal? ‖ *tr* alegrar, animar; aplaudir, vitorear; dar la bienvenida a, con vivas y aplausos ‖ *intr* alegrarse, animarse; **cheer up!** ¡ánimo!

cheerful ['tʃɪrfəl] *adj* alegre

cheerio ['tʃɪrɪ,o] *interj* (coll) ¡hola!, ¡qué tal!; (coll) ¡adiós!, ¡hasta la vista!

cheerless ['tʃɪrlɪs] *adj* sombrío, triste

cheese [tʃiz] *s* queso

cheese′cloth′ *s* estopilla

chef [ʃɛf] *s* primer cocinero, jefe *m* de cocina

chem. *abbr* **chemical, chemist, chemistry**

chemical ['kɛmɪkəl] *adj* químico ‖ *s* producto químico, substancia química

chemise [ʃəˈmiz] *s* camisa (de mujer)

chemist ['kɛmɪst] *s* químico

chemistry ['kɛmɪstri] *s* química

chemotherapy [,kɛmoˈθɛrəpi] *s* quimoterapia

cherish ['tʃɛrɪʃ] *tr* acariciar; (*a hope*) abrigar, acariciar

cher·ry ['tʃɛri] *s* (*pl* -ries) (*fruit; color*) cereza; (*tree*) cerezo

cher·ub ['tʃɛrəb] *s* (*pl* -ubim [əbɪm]) querubín *m* ‖ *s* (*pl* -ubs) niño angelical

chess [tʃɛs] *s* ajedrez *m*

chess′board′ *s* tablero de ajedrez

chess·man ['tʃɛs,mæn] *s* (*pl* -men [,mɛn]) pieza de ajedrez, trebejo

chess player *s* ajedrecista *mf*

chess set *s* ajedrez *m*

chest [tʃɛst] *s* (*part of body*) pecho; (*receptacle*) cajón *m,* cofre *m;* (*piece of furniture*) cómoda

chestnut ['tʃɛsnət] *s* (*tree, wood, color*) castaño; (*fruit*) castaña

chest of drawers *s* cómoda

cheval glass [ʃəˈvæl] *s* psique *f*

chevalier [,ʃɛvəˈlɪr] *s* caballero

chevron ['ʃɛvrən] *s* galón *m* en forma de V invertida

chew [tʃu] *s* mascadura ‖ *tr* mascar; **to chew the rag** (slang) dar la lengua ‖ *intr* mascar

chewing gum *s* goma de mascar, chicle *m*

chg. *abbr* **charge**

chic [ʃik] *adj & s* chic *m*

chicaner·y [ʃɪˈkɛnəri] *s* (*pl* -ies) triquiñuela

chick [tʃɪk] *s* pollito; (slang) polla

chicken ['tʃɪkən] *s* pollo; (*young person*) pollo; (*young girl*) polla

chicken coop *s* pollera

chicken feed *s* (coll) calderilla

chickenhearted ['tʃɪkən,hɑrtɪd] *adj* gallina

chicken pox *s* viruelas locas

chicken wire *s* alambrada, tela metálica

chick′pea′ *s* garbanzo

chico·ry ['tʃɪkəri] *s* (*pl* -ries) achicoria

chide [tʃaɪd] *v* (*pret* chided o chid [tʃɪd]; *pp* chided, chid o chidden ['tʃɪdən]) *tr* reprender, regañar

chief [tʃif] *adj* principal ‖ *s* jefe *m;* (*of American Indians*) cacique *m*

chief executive *s* jefe *m* del gobierno

chief justice *s* presidente *m* de sala; presidente del tribunal supremo

chiefly ['tʃifli] *adv* principalmente, mayormente

chief of staff *s* jefe *m* de estado mayor

chief of state *s* jefe *m* del estado

chieftain ['tʃiftən] *s* (*of a clan or tribe*) jefe *m;* adalid *m,* caudillo

chiffon [ʃɪˈfɑn] *s* gasa, soplillo; **chiffons** atavíos, perifollos

chiffonier [,ʃɪfəˈnɪr] *s* cómoda alta

chignon ['ʃɪnjən] *s* castaña, moño

chilblain ['tʃɪl,blen] *s* sabañón *m*

child [tʃaɪld] *s* (*pl* children ['tʃɪldrən]) *s* (*infant, youngster*) niño; (*one's offspring*) hijo; descendiente *mf;* **with child** encinta, embarazada

child′birth′ *s* alumbramiento, parto

childhood ['tʃaɪldhud] *s* niñez *f,* puericia; **from childhood** desde niño

childish ['tʃaɪldɪʃ] *adj* aniñado, pueril

childishness ['tʃaɪldɪʃnɪs] *s* puerilidad

child labor *s* trabajo de menores

childless ['tʃaɪldlɪs] *adj* sin hijos

child′like′ *adj* aniñado

child′s play *s* juego de niños

child welfare *s* protección a la infancia

Chile ['tʃɪli] *s* Chile *m*

Chilean ['tʃɪliən] *adj & s* chileno

chili sauce ['tʃɪli] *s* ají *m,* salsa de ají

chill [tʃɪl] *adj* frío ‖ *s* frío desapacible; (*sensation of cold*) escalofrío; (*lack of cordiality*) frialdad || *tr* enfriar || *intr* calofriarse

chill·y ['tʃɪli] *adj* (*comp* -ier; *super* -iest) (*causing shivering*) frío; (*sensitive to cold*) escalofriado, friolero; (*indifferent*) (fig) frío

chime [tʃaɪm] *s* campaneo, repique *m;* tubo sonoro; **chimes** juego de campanas || *tr & intr* campanear, repicar

chime clock *s* reloj *m* de carillón

chimera [kaɪ'mɪrə] o [kɪ'mɪrə] *s* quimera

chimney ['tʃɪmni] *s* chimenea; (*for a lamp*) tubo

chimney cap *s* caperuza

chimney flue *s* cañón *m* de chimenea

chimney pot *s* mitra, guardaviento *m*

chimney sweep *s* limpiachimeneas *m,* deshollinador *m*

chimpanzee [tʃɪm'pænzi] o [ˌtʃɪmpæn'zi] *s* chimpancé *m*

chin [tʃɪn] *s* barba, mentón *m; to keep one's chin up* (coll) no desanimarse || *v* (*pret & pp* **chinned;** *ger* **chinning**) *intr* (coll) charlar

china ['tʃaɪnə] *s* china, porcelana || **China** *s* China

china closet *s* chinero

China-man ['tʃaɪnəmən] *s* (*pl* -men [mən]) (offensive) chino

chi'na·ware' *s* porcelana, vajilla de porcelana

Chi·nese [tʃaɪ'niz] *adj* chino || *s* (*pl* -nese) chino

Chinese gong *s* batintín *m*

Chinese lantern *s* farolillo veneciano

Chinese puzzle *s* problema embrollado

chink [tʃɪŋk] *s* grieta, hendidura; sonido metálico

chin strap *s* barboquejo, carrillera

chintz [tʃɪnts] *s* zaraza

chip [tʃɪp] *s* astilla, brizna; (*in china*) desconchado; (*in poker*) ficha; **chip off the old block** hijo de su padre || *v* (*pret & pp* **chipped;** *ger* **chipping**) *tr* astillar (*la madera*); desconchar (*la porcelana*); **to chip in** contribuir con su cuota || *intr* astillarse; desconcharse

chipmunk ['tʃɪpˌmʌŋk] *s* ardilla listada

chipper ['tʃɪpər] *adj* (coll) alegre, jovial, vivo

chiropodist [kaɪ'rɑpədɪst] o [kɪ'rɑpədɪst] *s* quiropodista *mf*

chiropractor ['kaɪrəˌpræktər] *s* quiropráctico

chirp [tʃʌrp] *s* chirrido, gorjeo || *intr* chirriar, gorjear; hablar alegremente

chis·el ['tʃɪzəl] *s* (*for wood*) escoplo, formón *m;* (*for stone and metal*) cincel *m* || *v* (*pret & pp* **-eled** o **-elled;** *ger* **-eling** o **-elling**) *tr* escoplear; cincelar; (slang) estafar

chit-chat ['tʃɪtˌtʃæt] *s* charla, palique *m;* habilla, chismes *mpl*

chivalric ['ʃɪvəlrɪk] o [ʃɪ'vælrɪk] *adj* caballeresco

chivalrous ['ʃɪvəlrəs] *adj* caballeroso

chivalry ['ʃɪvəlri] *s* (*knighthood*) caballería; (*gallantry, gentlemanliness*) caballerosidad

chloride ['klɔraɪd] *s* cloruro

chlorine ['klɔrin] *s* cloro

chloroform ['klɔrəˌfɔrm] *s* cloroformo || *tr* cloroformizar

chlorophyll ['klɔrəfɪl] *s* clorofila

chock-full ['tʃɑk'fʊl] *adj* de bote en bote, colmado

chocolate ['tʃɑkəlɪt] o ['tʃɑkəlɪt] *s* chocolate *m*

choice [tʃɔɪs] *adj* escogido, selecto, superior || *s* elección, selección; lo más escogido; **to have no choice** no tener alternativa

choir [kwaɪr] *s* coro

choir'boy' *s* niño de coro, infante *m* de coro

choir desk *s* facistol *m*

choir loft *s* coro

choir'mas'ter *s* jefe *m* de coro, maestro de capilla

choke [tʃok] *s* estrangulación; (*of carburetor*) cierre *m,* obturador *m;* (elec) choque *m* || *tr* ahogar, sofocar, estrangular; obstruir, tapar; (aut) obturar; **to choke down** atragantar || *intr* sofocarse; atragantarse; **to choke on** atragantarse con

choke coil *s* (elec) bobina de reacción, choque *m*

cholera ['kɑlərə] *s* cólera *m*

choleric ['kɑlərɪk] *adj* colérico

cholesterol [kə'lɛstəˌrol] o [kə'lɛstəˌrɑl] *s* colesterol *m*

choose [tʃuz] *v* (*pret* **chose** [tʃoz]; *pp* **chosen** ['tʃozən]) *tr* escoger, elegir || *intr* — **to choose between** optar entre; **to choose to** optar por

chop [tʃɑp] *s* golpe *m* cortante; (*of meat*) chuleta; **chops** boca, labios || *v* (*pret & pp* **chopped;** *ger* **chopping**) *tr* cortar, tajar; picar (*la carne*); **to chop off** tronchar; **to chop up** desmenuzar

chop'house' *s* restaurante *m,* figón *m,* colmado

chopper ['tʃɑpər] *s* (*person*) tajador *m;* (*tool*) hacha; (*of butcher*) cortante *m;* (slang) helicóptero

chopping block *s* tajo

chop·py ['tʃɑpi] *adj* (*comp* -pier; *super* -piest) (*sea*) agitado, picado; (*wind*) variable; (*style*) cortado, inciso

chop'sticks' *spl* palillos

choral ['kɔrəl] *adj* coral

chorale [ko'ral] *s* coral *m*

choral society *s* orfeón *m*

chord [kɔrd] *s* (*harmonious combination of tones*) (mus) acorde *m;* (aer, anat, geom) cuerda

chore [tʃor] *s* tarea, quehacer *m*

choreography [ˌkɔri'ɑgrəfi] *s* coreografía

chorine [ko'rin] *s* (slang) corista, suripanta

chorus ['korəs] *s* coro; (*refrain of a song*) estribillo

chorus girl *s* corista, conjuntista

chorus man *s* corista *m,* conjuntista *m*

chowder ['tʃaudər] *s* estofado de almejas o pescado
Chr. *abbr* **Christian**
Christ [kraɪst] *s* Cristo
christen ['krɪsən] *tr* bautizar
Christendom ['krɪsəndəm] *s* cristiandad
christening ['krɪsənɪŋ] *s* bautismo, bautizo
Christian ['krɪstʃən] *adj* & *s* cristiano
Christianity [,krɪstʃɪ'ænɪti] *s* cristianismo
Christianize ['krɪstʃə,naɪz] *tr* cristianizar
Christian name *s* nombre *m* de pila
Christmas ['krɪsməs] *adj* navideño ‖ *s* Navidad, Pascua de Navidad
Christmas card *s* aleluya navideña
Christmas carol *s* villancico
Christmas Eve *s* nochebuena
Christmas gift *s* aguinaldo, regalo de Navidad
Christmas tree *s* árbol *m* de Navidad
Christopher ['krɪstəfər] *s* Cristóbal *m*
chrome [krom] *adj* cromado ‖ *s* cromo ‖ *tr* cromar
chromium ['kromɪ·ən] *s* cromo
chro·mo ['kromo] *s* (*pl* **-mos**) (*colored picture*) cromo; (*piece of junk*) (slang) trasto
chromosome ['kromə,som] *s* cromosoma *m*
chron. *abbr* **chronological, chronology**
chronic ['krɑnɪk] *adj* crónico
chronicle ['krɑnɪkəl] *s* crónica ‖ *tr* narrar en una crónica; narrar, contar
chronicler ['krɑnɪklər] *s* cronista *mf*
chronolo·gy [krə'nɑlədʒi] *s* (*pl* **-gies**) cronología
chronometer [krə'nɑmɪtər] *s* cronómetro
chrysanthemum [krɪ'sænθɪməm] *s* crisantemo
chub·by ['tʃʌbi] *adj* (*comp* **-bier;** *super* **-biest**) rechoncho, regordete
chuck [tʃʌk] *s* (*throw*) echada, tirada; (*under the chin*) mamola; (*of a lathe*) mandril *m* ‖ *tr* arrojar; **to chuck under the chin** hacer la mamola a
chuckle ['tʃʌkəl] *s* risa ahogada ‖ *intr* reírse con risa ahogada
chug [tʃʌg] *s* ruido explosivo sordo; (*of a locomotive*) resoplido ‖ *v* (*pret* & *pp* **chugged;** *ger* **chugging**) *intr* hacer ruidos explosivos sordos, moverse con ruidos explosivos sordos
chum [tʃʌm] *s* (coll) compinche *mf*; compañero de cuarto ‖ *v* (*pret* & *pp* **chummed;** *ger* **chumming**) *intr* (coll) ser compinche, ser compinches; (coll) compartir un cuarto
chum·my ['tʃʌmi] *adj* (*comp* **-mier;** *super* **-miest**) muy amigable, íntimo
chump [tʃʌmp] *s* tarugo, zoquete *m*; (coll) estúpido, tonto
chunk [tʃʌŋk] *s* trozo, pedazo grueso
church [tʃʌrtʃ] *s* iglesia
churchgoer ['tʃʌrtʃ,go·ər] *s* persona que frecuenta la iglesia
church·man ['tʃʌrtʃmən] *s* (*pl* **-men**

[mən]) sacerdote *m*, eclesiástico; feligrés *m*
church member *s* feligrés *m*
Church of England *s* Iglesia Anglicana
church'ward'en *s* capiller *m*
church'yard' *s* patio de iglesia; cementerio
churl [tʃʌrl] *s* palurdo, patán *m*
churlish ['tʃʌrlɪʃ] *adj* palurdo, insolente
churn [tʃʌrn] *s* mantequera ‖ *tr* mazar (*leche*); hacer (*mantequilla*) en una mantequera; agitar, revolver ‖ *intr* revolverse
chute [ʃut] *s* cascada, salto de agua; rápidos; conducto inclinado; (*e.g., into a swimming pool*) tobogán *m*; (*e.g., for grain*) tolva; paracaídas *m*
cibori·um [sɪ'borɪ·əm] *s* (*pl* **-a** [ə]) (*canopy*) ciborio, baldaquín *m*; (*cup*) copón *m*
Cicero ['sɪsə,ro] *s* Cicerón *m*
cider ['saɪdər] *s* sidra
C.I.F., c.i.f. *abbr* **cost, insurance, and freight**
cigar [sɪ'gɑr] *s* cigarro, puro
cigar band *s* anillo de cigarro
cigar case *s* cigarrera, petaca
cigar cutter *s* cortacigarros *m*
cigaret o **cigarette** [,sɪgə'rɛt] *s* cigarrillo, pitillo
cigarette case *s* pitillera
cigarette holder *s* boquilla
cigarette lighter *s* mechero, encendedor *m* de bolsillo
cigarette paper *s* papel *m* de fumar
cigar holder *s* boquilla
cigar store *s* estanco, tabaquería
cinch [sɪntʃ] *s* (*of saddle*) cincha; (*sure grip*) (coll) agarro; (*something easy*) (slang) breva ‖ *tr* cinchar; (coll) agarrar
cinder ['sɪndər] *s* ceniza; (*coal burning without flame*) pavesa
cinder bank *s* escorial *m*
Cinderella [,sɪndə'rɛlə] *s* la Cenicienta
cinder track *s* pista de cenizas
cinema ['sɪnəmə] *s* cine *m*
cinematograph [,sɪnə'mætə,græf] o [,sɪnə'mætə,grɑf] *s* cinematógrafo ‖ *tr* & *intr* cinematografiar
cinnabar ['sɪnə,bɑr] *s* cinabrio
cinnamon ['sɪnəmən] *s* canela
cipher ['saɪfər] *s* cifra; cero; (*nonentity*) cero a la izquierda; (*key to a cipher*) clave *f* ‖ *tr* cifrar; calcular
circle ['sʌrkəl] *s* círculo ‖ *tr* circundar; dar la vuelta a; girar alrededor de
circuit ['sʌrkɪt] *s* circuito
circuit breaker *s* disyuntor *m*
circuitous [sər'kju·ɪtəs] *adj* indirecto, tortuoso
circular ['sʌrkjələr] *adj* tortuoso ‖ *s* circular *f*, carta circular
circularize ['sʌrkjələ,raɪz] *tr* anunciar por circular; enviar circulares a
circulate ['sʌrkjə,let] *tr* & *intr* circular
circumcise ['sʌrkəm,saɪz] *tr* circuncidar

circumference [sər'kʌmfərəns] _s_ circunferencia

circumflex ['sʌrkəm‚flɛks] _adj_ circunflejo

circumlocution [‚sʌrkəmlo'kjuʃən] _s_ circunlocución, circunloquio

circumnavigate [‚sʌrkəm'nævɪ‚get] _tr_ circunnavegar

circumnavigation [‚sʌrkəm‚nævɪ'geʃən] _s_ circunnavegación

circumscribe [‚sʌrkəm'skraɪb] _tr_ circunscribir

circumspect ['sʌrkəm‚spɛkt] _adj_ circunspecto

circumstance ['sʌrkəm‚stæns] _s_ circunstancia; ceremonia, ostentación; **in easy circumstances** acomodado; **under no circumstances** de ninguna manera

circumstantial [‚sʌrkəm'stænʃəl] _adj_ (_derived from circumstances_) circunstancial; (_detailed_) circunstanciado

circumstantial evidence _s_ (law) indicios vehementes

circumstantiate [‚sʌrkəm'stænʃɪ‚et] _tr_ apoyar con pruebas y detalles; (_to describe in detail_) circunstanciar

circumvent [‚sʌrkəm'vɛnt] _tr_ (_to catch by a trick_) entrampar, embaucar; (_to outwit_) burlar; (_to keep away from, get around_) evitar

circus ['sʌrkəs] _s_ circo

cistern ['sɪstərn] _s_ cisterna, aljibe _m_

citadel ['sɪtədəl] _s_ ciudadela

citation [saɪ'teʃən] _s_ (_of a text_) cita; (_before a court of law_) citación; (_for gallantry_) mención

cite [saɪt] _tr_ (_to quote; to summon_) citar; (_for gallantry_) mencionar

citizen ['sɪtɪzən] _s_ ciudadano; (_civilian_) paisano

citizen‧ry ['sɪtɪzənrɪ] _s_ (_pl_ -ries) conjunto de ciudadanos

citizens band o **CB** [si'bi] _s_ banda ciudadana

citizenship ['sɪtɪzən‚ʃɪp] _s_ ciudadanía

citron ['sɪtrən] _s_ (_fruit_) cidra; (_tree_) cidro; (_candied rind_) cidrada

citronella [‚sɪtrə'nɛlə] _s_ limoncillo (_Andropogon nardus_); aceite _m_ de limoncillo

citrus fruit ['sɪtrəs] _s_ agrios, frutas cítricas

cit‧y ['sɪtɪ] _s_ (_pl_ -ies) ciudad

city clerk _s_ archivero

city council _s_ ayuntamiento

city editor _s_ redactor de periódico encargado de noticias locales

city fathers _spl_ concejales _mpl_

city hall _s_ casa consistorial

city planner _s_ urbanista _mf_

city planning _s_ urbanismo

city room _s_ redacción

civic ['sɪvɪk] _adj_ cívico ‖ **civics** _s_ estudio de los deberes y derechos del ciudadano

civies ['sɪvɪz] _spl_ (coll) traje _m_ de paisano; **in civies** (coll) de paisano

civil ['sɪvɪl] _adj_ civil

civilian [sɪ'vɪljən] _adj_ civil ‖ _s_ civil _mf_, paisano

civilian clothes _spl_ traje _m_ de paisano

civili‧ty [sɪ'vɪlɪtɪ] _s_ (_pl_ -ties) civilidad

civilization [‚sɪvɪlɪ'zeʃən] _s_ civilización

civilize ['sɪvɪ‚laɪz] _tr_ civilizar

civil servant _s_ funcionario del estado

claim [klem] _s_ demanda, pretensión, reclamación ‖ _tr_ demandar, pretender, reclamar; afirmar, declarar; **to claim to** + _inf_ pretender + _inf_

claim check _s_ comprobante _m_

clairvoyance [klɛr'vɔɪ‚əns] _s_ clarividencia

clairvoyant [klɛr'vɔɪ‚ənt] _adj_ & _s_ clarividente _mf_

clam [klæm] _s_ almeja; (_tight-lipped person_) (coll) chiticalla _m_ ‖ _intr_ — **to clam up** (coll) callarse la boca

clamber ['klæmər] _intr_ — **to clamber up** subir gateando

clamor ['klæmər] _s_ clamor _m_, clamoreo ‖ _intr_ clamorear

clamorous ['klæmərəs] _adj_ clamoroso

clamp [klæmp] _s_ abrazadera, grapa; (_vise-like device_) mordaza ‖ _tr_ agrapar, afianzar con abrazadera; sujetar en una mordaza ‖ _intr_ — **to clamp down on** (coll) apretar los tornillos a

clan [klæn] _s_ clan _m_

clandestine [klæn'dɛstɪn] _adj_ clandestino

clang [klæŋ] _s_ tantán _m_, sonido metálico resonante ‖ _tr_ hacer sonar fuertemente ‖ _intr_ sonar fuertemente

clank [klæŋk] _s_ sonido metálico seco ‖ _tr_ hacer sonar secamente ‖ _intr_ sonar secamente

clannish ['klænɪʃ] _adj_ exclusivista

clap [klæp] _s_ golpe seco; (_of the hands_) palmada; (_of thunder_) estampido ‖ _v_ (_pret & pp_ **clapped**); _ger_ **clapping**) _tr_ batir (_palmas_); palmotear, aplaudir; **to clap shut** cerrar de golpe ‖ _intr_ palmotear, dar palmadas

clap of thunder _s_ estampido de trueno

clapper ['klæpər] _s_ palmoteador _m_; (_of a bell_) badajo; (_to cause grain to slide_) tarabilla

clap'trap' _s_ faramalla; (_of an actor_) latiguillo

claque [klæk] _s_ (_paid clappers_) claque _f_; (_crush hat_) clac _m_

claret ['klærɪt] _s_ clarete _m_

clari‧fy ['klærɪ‚faɪ] _v_ (_pret & pp_ -fied) _tr_ clarificar; encolar (_el vino_)

clarinet [‚klærɪ'nɛt] _s_ clarinete _m_

clarion ['klærɪ‚ən] _adj_ claro, brillante ‖ _s_ clarín _m_

clarity ['klærɪtɪ] _s_ claridad

clash [klæʃ] _s_ choque _m_, encontrón _m_; estruendo, ruido ‖ _intr_ chocar, entrechocarse

clasp [klæsp] o [klɑsp] _s_ (_fastener_) abrazadera, cierre _m_; (_for, e.g., a necktie_) broche _m_; (_buckle_) hebilla; (_embrace_) abrazo; (_grip_) agarro ‖ _tr_ abrochar; abrazar; agarrar, apretar (*la mano*); apretarse (*la mano*)

class. *abbr* classical

class [klæs] o [klɑs] *s* clase *f*; (slang) elegancia, buen tono || *tr* clasificar || *intr* clasificarse

class consciousness *s* sentimiento de clase

classic ['klæsɪk] *adj & s* clásico; **the classics** las obras clásicas

classical ['klæsɪkəl] *adj* clásico

classical scholar *s* erudito en las lenguas clásicas

classicist ['klæsɪsɪst] *s* clasicista *mf*

classified ['klæsɪ‚faɪd] *adj* clasificado; clasificado como secreto

classified ads *spl* anuncios clasificados en secciones

classi•fy ['klæsɪ‚faɪ] *v* (*pret & pp* -fied) *tr* clasificar

class'mate' *s* compañero de clase

class'room' *s* aula, sala de clase

class struggle *s* lucha de clases

class•y ['klæsɪ] *adj* (*comp* -ier; *super* -iest) (slang) elegante

clatter ['klætər] *s* estruendo confuso; algazara, gresca; (*of hoofs*) trápala || *intr* caer o moverse con estruendo confuso; hablar rápida y ruidosamente; **to clatter down the stairs** bajar la escalera ruidosamente

clause [klɔz] *s* (*article in a legal document*) cláusula; (gram) oración dependiente

clavichord ['klævɪ‚kɔrd] *s* clavicordio

clavicle ['klævɪkəl] *s* clavícula

clavier ['klævɪ‚ər] o [klə'vɪr] *s* teclado || [klə'vɪr] *s* instrumento musical con teclado

claw [klɔ] *s* garra, uña; (*of lobster, crab, etc.*) pinza; (*of hammer, wrench, etc.*) oreja; (coll) dedos, mano *f* || *tr* (*to clutch*) agarrar; (*to scratch*) arañar; (*to tear*) desgarrar

clay [kle] *adj* arcilloso || *s* arcilla

clay pigeon *s* pichón *m* de barro

clay pipe *s* pipa de tierra

clean [klin] *adj* limpio; distinto, neto, nítido; completo || *adv* completamente; **to come clean** (slang) confesarlo todo || *tr* limpiar; (*to tidy up*) asear; **to be cleaned out** (*of money*) (slang) quedar limpio; **to clean out** limpiar; (slang) dejar limpio || *intr* limpiarse; asearse; **to clean up** limpiarse; (coll) llevárselo todo; (*in gambling*) (slang) hacer mesa limpia; **to clean up after someone** limpiar lo que alguno ha ensuciado

clean bill of health *s* patente limpia de sanidad

cleaner ['klinər] *s* limpiador *m*; (*dry cleaner*) tintorero; (*preparation*) quitamanchas *m*; **to send to the cleaners** (slang) dejar limpio

cleaning ['klinɪŋ] *s* limpieza

cleaning fluid *s* quitamanchas *m*

cleaning woman *s* criada que hace la limpieza, alquilona

cleanliness ['klɛnlɪnɪs] *s* limpieza

clean•ly ['klɛnli] *adj* (*comp* -lier; *super* -liest) limpio (*que tiene el hábito del aseo*)

cleanse [klɛnz] *tr* limpiar, lavar, depurar

clean-shaven ['klin'ʃevən] *adj* lisamente afeitado

clean'up' *s* limpieza general; **to make a cleanup** (slang) hacer su pacotilla

clear [klɪr] *adj* claro; (*cloudless*) despejado; (*of guilt, debts, annoyances*) libre || *adv* claro, claramente; **clear through** de parte a parte || *tr* despejar (*un bosque*); clarificar (*lo que estaba turbio*); (*to make less dark*) aclarar; saltar por encima de; (*to prove the innocence of*) absolver; sacar (*una ganancia neta*); abonar, acreditar; liquidar (*una cuenta*); (*in the customhouse*) despachar; salvar (*un obstáculo*); levantar (*la mesa*); desmontar (*un terreno*); **to clear the way** abrir camino || *intr* clarificarse; aclararse; **to clear away** (coll) irse, desaparecer; **to clear up** abonanzarse (*el tiempo*); despejarse (*el cielo, el tiempo*)

clearance ['klɪrəns] *s* aclaración; abono, acreditación; (*between two objects*) espacio libre; (*in a cylinder*) espacio muerto; (com) compensación

clearance sale *s* venta de liquidación

clearing ['klɪrɪŋ] *s* (*in a woods*) claro; (com) compensación

clearing house *s* cámara de compensación

clear-sighted ['klɪr'saɪtɪd] *adj* clarividente, perspicaz

clear'sto'ry *s* (*pl* -ries) var of clerestory

cleat [klit] *s* abrazadera, listón *m*

cleavage ['klivɪdʒ] *s* división, hendidura; (fig) desunión

cleave [kliv] *v* (*pret & pp* cleft [klɛft] o cleaved) *tr* rajar, partir; hender (*las aguas un buque, los aires una flecha*) || *intr* adherirse, pegarse; apegarse, ser fiel

cleaver ['klivər] *s* cortante *m*, cuchilla de carnicero

clef [klɛf] *s* (mus) clave *f*

cleft palate [klɛft] *s* fisura del paladar

clematis ['klɛmətɪs] *s* clemátide *f*

clemen•cy ['klɛmənsɪ] *s* (*pl* -cies) clemencia; (*of the weather*) benignidad

clement ['klɛmənt] *adj* clemente; (*weather*) benigno

clench [klɛntʃ] *s* agarro || *tr* agarrar; apretar, cerrar (*el puño, los dientes*)

cleresto•ry ['klɪr‚stori] *s* (*pl* -ries) claraboya

cler•gy ['klɜrdʒi] *s* (*pl* -gies) clerecía, clero

clergy•man ['klɜrdʒɪmən] *s* (*pl* -men [mən]) clérigo, pastor *m*

cleric ['klɛrɪk] *s* clérigo

clerical ['klɛrɪkəl] *adj* (*of clergy*) clerical; (*of office work*) oficinesco || *s* clérigo, eclesiático; (*supporter of power of clergy*) clerical *m*; **clericals** (coll) hábitos clericales

clerical error *s* error *m* de pluma

clerical work *s* trabajo de oficina

clerk [klʌrk] *s* (*in a store*) dependiente *mf;* (*in an office*) oficinista *mf;* (*in a city hall*) archivero; (*in a church*) lego, seglar *m;* (*in law office, in court*) escribano

clever [ˈklevər] *adj* hábil, diestro, mañoso; inteligente

cleverness [ˈklevərnɪs] *s* habilidad, destreza, maña; inteligencia

clew [klu] *s* indicio, pista

cliché [kliˈʃe] *s* (*printing plate*) clisé *m;* (*trite expression*) cliché *m*

click [klɪk] *s* golpecito; (*of typewriter*) tecleo; (*of firearm*) piñoneo; (*of heels*) taconeo; (*of tongue*) claqueo, chasquido ‖ *tr* hacer sonar con un golpecito seco; chascar (*la lengua*); **to click the heels** taconear; cuadrarse (*un soldado*) ‖ *intr* sonar con un golpecito seco; piñonear (*el gatillo de un arma de fuego*); claquear (*la lengua*)

client [ˈklaɪ.ənt] *s* cliente *mf;* cliente de abogado

clientele [ˌklaɪənˈtɛl] *s* clientela

cliff [klɪf] *s* acantilado, escarpa, risco

climate [ˈklaɪmɪt] *s* clima *m*

climax [ˈklaɪmæks] *s* colmo; **to cap the climax** ser el colmo

climb [klaɪm] *s* subida, trepa ‖ *tr & intr* escalar, subir, trepar

climber [ˈklaɪmər] *s* trepador *m;* ambicioso de figurar; (*bot*) enredadera, trepadora

clinch [klɪntʃ] *s* agarro, abrazo; (*of a nail*) remache *m* ‖ *tr* afianzar, sujetar; agarrar, abrazar; apretar (*el puño*); remachar (*un clavo ya clavado*); resolver decisivamente

cling [klɪŋ] *v* (*pret & pp* **clung** [klʌŋ]) *intr* adherirse, pegarse; **to cling to** agarrarse a, asirse de

cling'stone' peach *s* albérchigo, peladillo

clinic [ˈklɪnɪk] *s* clínica

clinical [ˈklɪnɪkəl] *adj* clínico

clinical chart *s* hoja clínica

clinician [klɪˈnɪʃən] *s* clínico

clink [klɪŋk] *s* tintín *m* ‖ *tr* hacer tintinear; chocar (*vasos, copas*) ‖ *intr* tintinear

clinker [ˈklɪŋkər] *s* escoria de hulla

clip [klɪp] *s* tijereteo, esquileo; grapa, pinza; (*to fasten papers*) sujetapapeles *m,* presilla de alambre; **at a good clip** a buen paso ‖ *v* (*pret & pp* **clipped**; *ger* **clipping**) *tr* tijeretear, esquilar; (*to fasten with a clip*) afianzar, sujetar; recortar (*p.ej., un cupón*) ‖ *intr* moverse con rapidez

clipper [ˈklɪpər] *s* tijera, cizalla; **clippers** maquinilla cortapelos; tijeras podadoras

clipping [ˈklɪpɪŋ] *s* tijereteo, esquileo; (*from a newspaper*) recorte *m*

clique [klik] *s* pandilla, corrillo ‖ *intr* — **to clique together** apandillarse

cliquish [ˈklikɪʃ] *adj* exclusivista

clk. *abbr* **clerk,** **clock**

cloak [klok] *s* capote *m;* (*disguise, excuse*) capa ‖ *tr* encapotar; disimular, encubrir

cloak-and-dagger [ˈklokənˈdægər] *adj* de capa y espada (*dícese de duelos, espionaje, etc.*)

cloak-and-sword [ˈklokənˈsord] *adj* de capa y espada (*dícese, p.ej., de las costumbres caballerescas*)

cloak hanger *s* cuelgacapas *m*

cloak'room' *s* guardarropa *m;* (Brit) excusado

clock [klɑk] *s* reloj *m* (de pared o de mesa); (*in a stocking*) cuadrado ‖ *tr* registrar; (sport) cronometrar

clock'mak'er *s* relojero

clock tower *s* torre *f* reloj

clock'wise' *adj & adv* en el sentido de las agujas del reloj

clock'work' *s* mecanismo de relojería; **like clockwork** como un reloj

clod [klɑd] *s* terrón *m*

clod'hop'per *s* destripaterrones *m,* quebrantaterrones *m;* **clodhoppers** zapatos fuertes de trabajo

clog [klɑg] *s* estorbo, obstáculo; (*wooden shoe*) zueco; (*dance*) zapateado; (*hobble on animal*) traba ‖ *v* (*pret & pp* **clogged**; *ger* **clogging**) *tr* atascar ‖ *intr* atascarse; bailar el zapateado

clog dance *s* zapateado

cloister [ˈklɔɪstər] *s* claustro ‖ *tr* enclaustrar

cloistral [ˈklɔɪstrəl] *adj* claustral

close [klos] *adj* cercano, próximo; casi igual; (*translation*) fiel, exacto; (*fabric*) compacto; (*weather, atmosphere*) pesado, sofocante; (*stingy*) tacaño; (*battle, race, election*) reñido; (*friend*) íntimo; (*shut in, enclosed*) cerrado; (*narrow*) estrecho ‖ *adv* cerca; **close to** cerca de ‖ [kloz] *s* fin *m,* terminación; (*of business, of stock market*) cierre *m;* **at the close of day** a la caída de la tarde; **to bring to a close** poner término a; **to come to a close** tocar a su fin ‖ *tr* cerrar; (*to cover*) tapar; (*to finish*) concluir; saldar (*una cuenta*); cerrar (*un trato*); **to close in** cerrar, encerrar; **to close ranks** cerrar las filas ‖ *intr* cerrar, cerrarse; **to close in on** cerrar con (*el enemigo*)

close call [klos] *s* (coll) escape *m* por un pelo

closed car [klozd] *s* coche cerrado, conducción interior

closed chapter *s* asunto concluído

closed season *s* veda

closed shop *s* taller agremiado

closefisted [ˈklosˈfɪstɪd] *adj* cicatero, tacaño, manicorto

close-fitting [ˈklosˈfɪtɪŋ] *adj* ajustado, ceñido al cuerpo

close-lipped [ˈklosˈlɪpt] *adj* callado, reservado

closely [ˈklosli] *adv* de cerca; estrechamente; fielmente; atentamente

close quarters [klos] *spl* lugar muy estrecho, lugares estrechos

close shave [klos] *s* afeitado a ras; (coll) escape *m* por un pelo

closet [ˈklɑsɪt] *s* alacena; (*wardrobe*) armario; (*small private room*) aposento, gabinete *m; (for keeping clothing)* guardarropa *m; (toilet)* retrete *m* ‖ *tr* — **to be closeted with** encerrarse con

close-up ['klos ˌʌp] *s (moving picture)* vista de cerca; fotografía de cerca

closing ['kloziŋ] *s* cerradura, cierre *m*

closing prices *spl* precios de cierre

clot [klɑt] *s* grumo, coágulo ‖ *v (pret & pp* **clotted**; *ger* **clotting**) *intr* engrumecerse, coagularse

cloth [klɔθ] o [klɑθ] *s* paño, tela; ropa clerical; *(canvas, sails)* lona, trapo, vela; *(for binding books)* tela; **the cloth** la clerecía

clothe [kloð] *v (pret & pp* **clothed** o **clad** [klæd]) *tr* trajear, vestir; cubrir; *(e.g., with authority)* investir

clothes [kloz] o [kloðz] *spl* ropa, vestidos; ropa de cama

clothes'bas'ket *s* cesto de la ropa, cesto de la colada

clothes'brush' *s* cepillo de ropa

clothes closet *s* ropero

clothes dryer *s* secadora de ropa, secarropa

clothes hanger *s* colgador *m*, perchero

clothes'horse' *s* enjugador *m*, secarropa de travesaños

clothes'line' *s* cordel *m* para tender la ropa, tendedera

clothes'pin' *s* pinza, alfiler *m* de madera

clothes tree *s* percha

clothes wringer *s* exprimidor *m* de ropa

clothier ['kloðjər] *s (person who sells ready-made clothes)* ropero; *(dealer in cloth)* pañero

clothing ['kloðiŋ] *s* ropa, vestidos, ropaje *m*

cloud [klaud] *s* nube *f* ‖ *tr* anublar ‖ *intr* — **to cloud over** anublarse

cloud bank *s* mar *m* de nubes

cloud'burst' *s* aguacero, chaparrón *m*

cloud-capped ['klaud ˌkæpt] *adj* coronado de nubes

cloudless ['klaudlɪs] *adj* despejado, sin nubes

cloud of dust *s* polvareda, nube *f* de polvo

cloud·y ['klaudi] *adj (comp* **-ier**; *super* **-iest**) nuboso, nublado; *(muddy, turbid)* turbio; confuso, obscuro; melancólico, sombrío

clove [klov] *s (flower)* clavo de especia; *(spice)* clavo

clover ['klovər] *s* trébol *m;* **to be in clover** vivir en el lujo

clo'ver·leaf' *s (pl* **-leaves** [ˌlivz]) *s* cruce *m* en trébol

clove tree *s* clavero

clown [klaun] *s* bufón *m*, payaso; *(rustic)* patán *m* ‖ *intr* hacer el payaso

clownish ['klaunɪʃ] *adj* bufonesco, rústico

cloy [klɔɪ] *tr* hastiar, empalagar

club [klʌb] *s* porra, clava; *(playing card)* basto, trébol *m;* club *m*, casino ‖ *v (pret & pp* **clubbed**; *ger*

clubbing) *tr* aporrear ‖ *intr* — **to club together** unirse; formar club

club car *s* coche *m* club, coche bar

club'house' *s* casino, club *m*

club·man ['klʌbmən] *s (pl* **-men** [mən]) clubista *m*

club·woman ['klʌb ˌwumən] *s (pl* **-women** [ˌwɪmɪn]) clubista *f*

cluck [klʌk] *s* cloqueo, clo clo ‖ *intr* cloquear, hacer clo clo

clue [klu] *s* indicio, pista

clump [klʌmp] *s (of earth)* terrón *m; (of trees or shrubs)* grupo; pisada fuerte ‖ *intr* — **to clump along** andar pesadamente

clum·sy ['klʌmzi] *adj (comp* **-sier**; *super* **-siest**) *(worker)* chapucero, desmañado, torpe; *(work)* chapucero, tosco, grosero

cluster ['klʌstər] *s* grupo; *(of grapes or other things growing or joined together)* racimo ‖ *intr* arracimarse; **to cluster around** reunirse en torno a; **to cluster together** agruparse

clutch [klʌtʃ] *s (grasp, grip)* agarro, apretón *m* fuerte; (aut) embrague *m;* (aut) pedal *m* de embrague: **to fall into the clutches of** caer en las garras de; **to throw the clutch in** embragar; **to throw the clutch out** desembragar ‖ *tr* agarrar, empuñar

clutter ['klʌtər] *tr* — **to clutter up** cubrir o llenar desordenadamente

cm. *abbr* **centimeter**

cml. *abbr* **commercial**

Co. *abbr* **Company, County**

coach [kotʃ] *s* coche *m*, diligencia; (aut) coche cerrado; (rr) coche de viajeros, coche ordinario *m;* (sport) entrenador *m* ‖ *tr* aleccionar; (sport) entrenar ‖ *intr* entrenarse

coach house *s* cochera

coaching ['kotʃɪŋ] *s* lecciones *fpl* particulares; (sport) entrenamiento

coach·man ['kotʃmən] *s (pl* **-men** [mən]) *s* cochero

coagulate [ko'ægjəˌlet] *tr* coagular ‖ *intr* coagularse

coal [kol] *s* carbón *m*, hulla ‖ *tr* proveer de carbón ‖ *intr* proveerse de carbón

coal'bin' *s* carbonera

coal bunker *s* carbonera

coal car *s* vagón carbonero

coal'deal'er *s* carbonero

coaling ['kolɪŋ] *adj* carbonero ‖ *s* toma de carbón

coalition [ˌko·ə'lɪʃən] *s* unión; *(alliance between states or factions)* coalición

coal mine *s* mina de carbón

coal oil *s* aceite *m* mineral

coal scuttle *s* cubo para carbón

coal tar *s* alquitrán *m* de hulla

coal'yard' *s* carbonería

coarse [kors] *adj (of inferior quality)* basto, burdo; *(composed of large particles)* grueso; *(crude in manners)* grosero, rudo, vulgar

coast [kost] *s* costa; **the coast is clear** ya no hay peligro ‖ *tr* costear ‖ *intr* deslizarse cuesta abajo; **to coast along** avanzar sin esfuerzo

coastal ['kostəl] *adj* costero

coaster ['kostər] *s* salvamanteles *m*

coaster brake *s* freno de contrapedal

coast guard *s* guardacostas *mpl*; guardia *m* de los guardacostas

coast guard cutter *s* escampavía de los guardacostas

coasting trade *s* cabotaje *m*

coast'land' *s* litoral *m*

coast'line' *s* línea de la costa

coast'wise' *adj* costanero ‖ *adv* a lo largo de la costa

coat [kot] *s* (*jacket*) americana, saco; (*topcoat*) abrigo, sobretodo; (*of an animal*) lana, pelo; (*of paint*) capa, mano *f* ‖ *tr* cubrir, revestir; dar una capa de pintura a

coated ['kotɪd] *adj* revestido; (*tongue*) saburroso

coat hanger *s* colgador *m*

coating ['kotɪŋ] *s* revestimiento; (*of paint*) capa; (*of plaster*) enlucido

coat of arms *s* escudo de armas

coat'room' *s* guardarropa *m*

coat'tail' *s* faldón *m*

coax [koks] *tr* engatusar

cob [kab] *s* zuro; **to eat corn on the cob** comer maíz en la mazorca

cobalt ['kobɪlt] *s* cobalto

cobbler ['kablər] *s* remendón *m*, zapatero de viejo

cob'ble·stone' *s* guijarro

cob'web' *s* telaraña

cocaine [ko'ken] *s* cocaína

cock [kak] *s* (*rooster*) gallo; (*faucet, valve*) espita, grifo; (*of firearm*) martillo; (*weathervane*) veleta; caudillo, jefe *m* ‖ *tr* amartillar (*un arma de fuego*); ladear (*la cabeza*); enderezar, levantar

cockade [ka'ked] *s* cucarda, escarapela

cock-a-doodle-doo ['kakə,dudəl'du] *s* quiquiriquí *m*

cock-and-bull story ['kakənd'bʊl] *s* cuento absurdo, cuento increíble

cocked hat [kakt] *s* sombrero de candil, sombrero de tres picos; **to knock into a cocked hat** (slang) apabullar

cockeyed ['kak,aɪd] *adj* bisojo, bizco; (coll) encorvado, torcido; (slang) disparatado, extravagante

cock'fight' *s* pelea de gallos

cockney ['kakni] *s* londinense *mf* de la clase pobre que habla un dialecto característico; dialecto de la clase pobre de Londres

cock of the walk *s* quiquiriquí *m*, gallito del lugar

cock'pit' *s* gallera; (aer) carlinga

cock'roach' *s* cucaracha

cockscomb ['kaks,kom] *s* cresta de gallo; gorro de bufón; (bot) cresta de gallo, moco de pavo

cock'sure' *adj* muy seguro de sí mismo

cock'tail' *s* coctel *m*; (*of fruit, oysters, etc.*) aperitivo

cocktail party *s* coctel *m*

cocktail shaker ['ʃekər] *s* coctelera

cock·y ['kaki] *adj* (*comp* **-ier**; *super* **-iest**) (coll) arrogante, hinchado; **to be cocky** (coll) tener mucho gallo

cocoa ['koko] *s* cacao; (*drink*) chocolate *m*

cocoanut o coconut ['kokə,nʌt] *s* coco

cocoanut palm o tree *s* cocotero

cocoon [kə'kun] *s* capullo

C.O.D., c.o.d. *abbr* **collect on delivery**; (Brit) **cash on delivery**

cod [kad] *s* abadejo, bacalao

coddle ['kadəl] *tr* consentir, mimar

code [kod] *s* (*of laws; of manners; of signals*) código; (*of telegraphy*) alfabeto; (*secret system of writing*) cifra, clave *f*; (com) cifrario; **in code** en cifra ‖ *tr* (*to put in code*) cifrar

code word *s* clave telegráfica

codex ['kodɛks] *s* (*pl* **codices** ['kodɪ,siz] o ['kadɪ,siz]) códice *m*

cod'fish' *s* abadejo, bacalao

codger ['kadʒər] *s* — **old codger** (coll) anciano, tío

codicil ['kadɪsɪl] *s* codicilo; apéndice *m*

codi·fy ['kadɪ,faɪ] o ['kodɪ,faɪ] *v* (*pret & pp* **-fied**) *tr* codificar

cod'-liv'er oil *s* aceite *m* de hígado de bacalao

coed o co-ed ['ko,ɛd] *s* alumna de una escuela coeducativa

coeducation [,ko,ɛdʒə'keʃən] *s* coeducación

coefficient [,ko·ɪ'fɪʃənt] *adj* & *s* coeficiente *m*

coerce [ko'ʌrs] *tr* forzar, coactar

coercion [ko'ʌrʃən] *s* compulsión, coacción

coeval [ko'ivəl] *adj* & *s* coetáneo

coexist [,ko·ɪg'zɪst] *intr* coexistir

coexistence [,ko·ɪg'zɪstəns] *s* coexistencia

coffee ['kɔfi] o ['kafi] *s* café *m*; (*plant*) cafeto; **black coffee** café solo

coffee bean *s* grano de café

cof'fee·cake' *s* rosquilla (que se come con el café)

coffee grinder *s* molinillo de café

coffee grounds *spl* poso del café

coffee mill *s* molinillo de café

coffee plantation *s* cafetal *m*

coffee pot *s* cafetera

coffee tree *s* cafeto

coffer ['kɔfər] o ['kafər] *s* arca, cofre *m*; **coffers** tesoro, fondos

cof'fer·dam' *s* ataguía, encajonado

coffin ['kɔfɪn] o ['kafɪn] *s* ataúd *m*

C. of S. *abbr* **Chief of Staff**

cog [kag] *s* diente *m* (*de rueda dentada*); rueda dentada; **to slip a cog** equivocarse

cogency ['kodʒənsi] *s* fuerza (*de un argumento*)

cogent ['kodʒənt] *adj* fuerte, convincente

cogitate ['kadʒɪ,tet] *tr* & *intr* cogitar, meditar

cognac ['konjæk] o ['kanjæk] *s* coñac *m*

cognizance ['kagnɪzəns] o ['kanɪzəns]

s conocimiento; **to take cognizance of** enterarse de

cognizant ['kɑgnɪzənt] o ['kɑnɪzənt] *adj* sabedor, enterado

cog'wheel' s rueda dentada

cohabit [ko'hæbɪt] *intr* cohabitar

coheir [ko'ɛr] s coheredero

cohere [ko'hɪr] *intr* adherirse, pegarse; conformarse, corresponder

coherent [ko'hɪrənt] *adj* coherente

cohesion [ko'hiʒən] s cohesión

coiffeur [kwɑ'fʌr] s peluquero

coiffure [kwɑ'fjur] s peinado, tocado

coil [kɔɪl] s (*something wound in a spiral*) rollo; (*single turn of spiral*) vuelta; (*of a still*) serpentín *m*; (*of hair*) rizo; (*of a spring*) espiral *f*; (elec) carrete *m* || *tr* arrollar, enrollar; (naut) adujar || *intr* arrollarse, enrollarse; (*like a snake*) serpentear

coil spring s resorte *m* espiral

coin [kɔɪn] s moneda; (*wedge*) cuña; **to pay back in one's own coin** pagar en la misma moneda; **to toss a coin** echar a cara o cruz || *tr* acuñar; forjar, inventar (*palabras o frases*); **to coin money** (coll) ganar mucho dinero

coincide [,ko·ɪn'saɪd] *intr* coincidir

coincidence [ko'ɪnsɪdəns] s coincidencia

coition [ko'ɪʃən] o **coitus** ['ko·ɪtəs] s coito

coke [kok] s coque *m*, cok *m*

col. *abbr* colored, colony, column

colander ['kʌləndər] o ['kɑləndər] s colador *m*, escurridor *m*

cold [kold] *adj* frío; **to be cold** (*said of a person*) tener frío; (*said of the weather*) hacer frío || s frío; (*indisposition*) resfriado; **to catch cold** resfriarse, coger un resfriado

cold blood s — **in cold blood** a sangre fría

cold chisel s cortafrío

cold comfort s poca consolación

cold cream s colcrén *m*

cold cuts *spl* fiambres *mpl*

cold feet *spl* (coll) desánimo, miedo

cold'heart'ed *adj* duro, insensible

cold meat s carne *f* fiambre

coldness ['koldnɪs] s frialdad

cold shoulder s — **to turn a cold shoulder on** (coll) tratar con suma frialdad

cold snap s corto rato de frío agudo

cold storage s conservación en cámara frigorífica

cold war s guerra fría

coleslaw ['kol,slɔ] s ensalada de col

colic ['kɑlɪk] *adj* & s cólico

coliseum [,kɑlɪ'si·əm] s coliseo

coll. *abbr* colleague, collection, college, colloquial

collaborate [kə'læbə,ret] *intr* colaborar

collaborationist [kə,læbə'reʃənɪst] s colaboracionista *mf*

collaborator [kə'læbə,retər] s colaborador *m*

collapse [kə'læps] s desplome *m*; (*in business*) fracaso; (pathol) colapso

|| *intr* desplomarse; fracasar; postrarse, sufrir colapso

collapsible [kə'læpsɪbəl] *adj* abatible, plegable, desmontable

collar ['kɑlər] s cuello; (*of dog, horse*) collar *m*; (mach) collar

col'lar·band' s tirilla de camisa

col'lar·bone' s clavícula

collate [kə'let] o ['kɑlet] *tr* colacionar, cotejar

collateral [kə'lætərəl] *adj* colateral || s (*relative*) colateral *mf*; (com) colateral *m*

collation [kə'leʃən] s (*act of comparing; light meal*) colación

colleague ['kɑlig] s colega *mf*

collect ['kɑlekt] s (eccl) colecta || [kə'lekt] *tr* acumular, reunir; colectar, recaudar (*impuestos*); coleccionar (*sellos de correo, antiguallas*); recolectar (*cosechas*); cobrar (*pasajes*); recoger (*billetes; el correo*); **to collect onself** reponerse || *intr* acumularse; **collect on delivery** contra reembolso, cobro contra entrega

collect call s llamada por cobrar

collected [kə'lektɪd] *adj* sosegado, dueño de sí mismo

collection [kə'lekʃən] s colección; (*of taxes*) recaudación; (*of mail*) recogida

collection agency s agencia de cobros de cuentas

collective [kə'lektɪv] *adj* colectivo

collector [kə'lektər] s (*of stamps, antiques*) coleccionista *mf*; (*of taxes*) recaudador *m*; (*of tickets*) cobrador *m*

college ['kɑlɪdʒ] s colegio universitario; (*of cardinals, electors, etc.*) colegio

collide [kə'laɪd] *intr* chocar

collie ['kɑli] s perro pastoril escocés

collier ['kɑljər] s barco carbonero; minero de carbón

collier·y ['kɑljəri] s (*pl* -ies) mina de carbón

collision [kə'lɪʒən] s colisión

colloid ['kɑlɔɪd] *adj* & s coloide *m*

colloquial [kə'lokwɪ·əl] *adj* coloquial, familiar

colloquialism [kə'lokwɪ·ə,lɪzəm] s coloquialismo

collo·quy ['kɑləkwi] s (*pl* -quies) coloquio

collusion [kə'luʒən] s colusión, confabulación; **to be in collusion with** estar en inteligencia con

cologne [kə'lon] s agua de colonia, colonia || **Cologne** s Colonia

colon ['kolən] s (anat) colon *m*; (gram) dos puntos

colonel ['kʌrnəl] s coronel *m*

colonel·cy ['kʌrnəlsi] s (*pl* -cies) coronelía

colonial [kə'lonɪ·əl] *adj* colonial || s colono

colonize ['kɑlə,naɪz] *tr* & *intr* colonizar

colonnade [,kɑlə'ned] s columnata

colo·ny ['kɑləni] s (*pl* -nies) colonia

colophon ['kɑlə,fɑn] s colofón *m*

color ['kʌlər] *s* color; **the colors** los colores, la bandera; **to call to the colors** llamar a filas; **to give o to lend color to** dar visos de probabilidad a; **under color of** so color de, bajo pretexto de; **with flying colors** con banderas desplegadas || *tr* colorar, colorear; (*to excuse, palliate*) colorear; (*to dye*) teñir || *intr* sonrojarse, ponerse colorado, demudarse
col'or-blind' *adj* ciego para los colores
colored ['kʌlərd] *adj* de color; (*specious*) colorado
colorful ['kʌlərfəl] *adj* colorido; pintoresco
coloring ['kʌlərɪŋ] *adj & s* colorante *m*
colorless ['kʌlərlɪs] *adj* incoloro; (fig) insulso
color photography *s* fotografía en colores
color salute *s* (mil) saludo con la bandera
color sargent *s* sargento abanderado
color screen *s* (phot) pantalla de color
color television *s* televisión en colores
colossal [kə'lɑsəl] *adj* colosal
colossus [kə'lɑsəs] *s* coloso
colt [kolt] *s* potro
Columbus [kə'lʌmbəs] *s* Colón *m*
Columbus Day *s* día *m* de la raza, fiesta de la hispanidad
column ['kɑləm] *s* columna
columnist ['kɑləmɪst] *s* columnista *mf*
com. *abbr* **comedy, commerce, common**
Com. *abbr* **Commander, Commissioner, Committee**
coma ['komə] *s* (pathol) coma *m*
comb [kom] *s* peine *m*; (*currycomb*) almohaza; (*of rooster*) cresta; cresta de ola || *tr* peinar; explorar con minuciosidad
com·bat ['kɑmbæt] *s* combate *m* || ['kɑmbæt] o [kəm'bæt] *v* (*pret & pp* -bated o -batted; *ger* -bating o -bating) *tr & intr* combatir
combatant ['kɑmbətənt] *adj & s* combatiente *m*
combat duty *s* servicio de frente
combination [,kɑmbɪ'neʃən] *s* combinación
combine ['kɑmbaɪn] *s* monopolio; segadora trilladora; (coll) combinación || [kəm'baɪn] *tr* combinar || *intr* combinarse
combining form *s* (gram) elemento de compuestos
combustible [kəm'bʌstɪbəl] *adj* combustible; (fig) ardiente, impetuoso || *s* combustible *m*
combustion [kəm'bʌstʃən] *s* combustión
come [kʌm] *v* (*pret* **came** [kem]; *pp* **come**) *intr* venir; **to come about** suceder; **to come across** encontrarse con; **to come after** venir detrás de; venir después de; venir por, venir en busca de; **to come again** volver; **to come apart** desunirse, desprenderse; **to come around** restablecerse; volver en sí; rendirse; ponerse de acuerdo; cambiar de dirección; **to come at** alcanzar; **to come back** volver; (coll) rehabilitarse; **to come before** anteponerse; **to come between** interponerse; desunir, separar; **to come by** conseguir; **to come down** bajar; (*in social position, financial status, etc.*) descender; (*from one person to another*) ser transmitido; **to come downstairs** bajar (*de un piso a otro*); **to come down with** enfermarse de; **to come for** venir por, venir en busca de; **to come forth** salir; aparecer; **to come forward** avanzar; presentarse; **to come from** venir de; provenir de; **to come in** entrar; entrar en; empezar; ponerse en uso; **to come in for** conseguir, recibir; **to come into one's own** ser reconocido; **to come off** desprenderse; acontecer; **to come out** salir; salir a luz; ponerse de largo (*una joven*); divulgarse (*una noticia*); **to come out for** anunciar su apoyo de; **to come out with** descolgarse con; **to come over** dejarse persuadir; pasar, p.ej., **what's come over him?** ¿qué le ha pasado?; **to come through** salir bien, tener éxito; ganar; **to come to** volver en sí; **to come together** juntarse, reunirse; **to come true** hacerse realidad; **to come up** subir; presentarse; **to come upstairs** subir (*de un piso a otro*); **to come up to** acercarse a; subir a; estar a la altura de; **to come up with** proponer
come'back' *s* (coll) rehabilitación; (slang) respuesta aguda; **to stage a comeback** (coll) rehabilitarse
comedian [kə'midɪ·ən] *s* cómico, comediante *m*; autor *m* de comedias
comedienne [kə,midɪ'ɛn] *s* cómica, comedianta
come'down' *s* (coll) humillación, revés *m*
com·e·dy ['kɑmədɪ] *s* (*pl* -dies) comedia cómica; (*comicalness*) comicidad
come·ly ['kʌmlɪ] *adj* (*comp* -lier; *super* -liest) (*attractive*) donairoso, gracioso; (*decorous*) conveniente, decente
comet ['kɑmɪt] *s* cometa *m*
comfort ['kʌmfərt] *s* comodidad, confort *m*; (*encouragement, consolation*) confortación; (*person*) confortador *m*; (*bed cover*) colcha, cobertor *m* || *tr* confortar
comfortable ['kʌmfərtəbəl] *adj* cómodo, confortable; (*fairly well off*) holgado; (*salary*) (coll) suficiente || *s* colcha, cobertor *m*
comforter ['kʌmfərtər] *s* confortador *m*, consolador *m*; colcha, cobertor *m*; bufanda de lana
comforting ['kʌmfərtɪŋ] *adj* confortante
comfort station *s* quiosco de necesidad
comfrey ['kʌmfrɪ] *s* consuelda
comic ['kɑmɪk] *adj* cómico || *s* cómi-

CO
CO

co; (coll) periódico cómico; **comics**
(coll) tiras cómicas
comical ['kamɪkəl] *adj* cómico
comic book *s* tebeo
comic opera *s* ópera cómica
comic strip *s* tira cómica
coming ['kamɪŋ] *adj* que viene, venidero; (coll) prometedor ‖ *s* venida
coming out *s* (*of stocks, bonds, etc.*)
emisión; (*of a young girl*) puesta de
largo, entrada en sociedad
comma ['kamə] *s* coma
command [kə'mænd] o [kə'mɑnd] *s*
(*commanding*) dominio, mando; (*order, direction*) mandato, orden *f*;
(*e.g., of a foreign language*) dominio; (mil) comando; **to be in command of** estar al mando de; **to take
command** tomar el mando ‖ *tr* mandar, ordenar; dominar (*un idioma
extranjero*); merecer (*p.ej., respeto*);
(mil) comandar ‖ *intr* mandar
commandant [,kamən'dænt] o [,kam-
ən'dɑnt] *s* comandante *m*
commandeer [,kamən'dɪr] *tr* reclutar
forzosamente; expropiar; (coll) apoderarse de
commander [kə'mændər] o [kə'mɑn-
dər] *s* comandante *m*; (*of a military
order*) comendador *m*
commandment [kə'mændmənt] o [kə-
'mɑndmənt] *s* (Bib) mandamiento
commemorate [kə'mɛmə,ret] *tr* conmemorar
commence [kə'mɛns] *tr & intr* comenzar, empezar
commencement [kə'mɛnsmənt] *s* comienzo, principio; día *m* de graduación; ceremonia de graduación
commend [kə'mɛnd] *tr* (*to entrust*)
encargar, encomendar; (*to recommend*) recomendar; (*to praise*) alabar, elogiar
commendable [kə'mɛnəbəl] *adj* recomendable
commendation [,kamən'defən] *s* encargo, encomienda; recomendación;
alabanza, elogio
comment ['kament] *s* comentario, comento ‖ *intr* comentar; **to comment
on** comentar
commentary ['kamən,tɛri] *s* (*pl* -ies)
comentario
commentator ['kamən,tetər] *s* comentarista *mf*
commerce ['kamərs] *s* comercio
commercial [kə'mʌrʃəl] *adj* comercial
‖ *s* anuncio publicitario radiofónico
o televisivo; (rad & telv) programa
publicitario
commercial traveler *s* agente viajero
commiserate [kə'mɪzə,ret] *intr* — **to
commiserate with** condolerse de
commiseration [kə,mɪzə'refən] *s* conmiseración
commissar [,kamɪ'sar] *s* comisario (*en
Rusia*)
commissary ['kamɪ,sɛri] *s* (*pl* -ies)
(*deputy*) comisario; (*store*) economato

commission [kə'mɪʃən] *s* comisión;
(mil) nombramiento; **to put in commission** poner en uso; poner (*un
buque*) en servicio activo; **to put out
of commission** inutilizar, descomponer; retirar (*un buque*) del servicio
activo ‖ *tr* comisionar; poner en
uso; poner (*un buque*) en servicio
activo; (mil) nombrar
commissioned officer *s* oficial *m*
commissioner [kə'mɪʃənər] *s* comisario; (*person authorized by a commission*) comisionado
com·mit [kə'mɪt] *v* (*pret & pp* -mitted;
ger -mitting) *tr* cometer (*un crimen,
una falta; un negocio a una persona*); (*to hand over*) confiar, entregar; dar, empeñar (*la palabra*); (*to
bind, pledge*) comprometer; internar (*a un demente*); (*to memory*)
encomendar; **to commit oneself**
comprometerse, empeñarse; **to commit to writing** poner por escrito
commitment [kə'mɪtmənt] *s* (*act of
committing*) comisión; (*to an asylum*) internación; (*written order*)
auto de prisión; compromiso, cometido, empeño
committee [kə'mɪti] *s* comité *m*, comisión
commode [kə'mod] *s* (*chest of drawers*) cómoda; (*washstand*) lavabo;
(*chamber pot*) sillico
commodious [kə'modɪ·əs] *adj* espacioso, holgado
commodi·ty [kə'madɪti] *s* (*pl* -ties)
artículo de consumo, mercancía
commodity exchange *s* lonja, bolsa
mercantil
common ['kamən] *adj* común ‖ *s*
campo común, ejido; **commons** estado llano; (*of a school*) refectorio;
the Commons (Brit) los Comunes
common carrier *s* empresa de transportes públicos
commoner ['kamənər] *s* plebeyo,
(Brit) miembro de la Cámara de los
Comunes
common law *s* derecho consuetudinario
com'mon-law' marriage *s* matrimonio
consensual
com'mon-place' *adj* común, trivial,
ordinario ‖ *s* lugar *m* común, trivialidad
common sense *s* sentido común
com'mon-sense' *adj* cuerdo, razonable
common stock *s* acción ordinaria; acciones ordinarias
commonweal ['kamən,wil] *s* bien público
com'mon·wealth' *s* estado, nación;
república; (*state of U.S.A.*) estado;
(*self-governing associated country*)
estado libre asociado; (*association
of states*) mancomunidad
commotion [kə'moʃən] *s* conmoción
commune [kə'mjun] *intr* conversar;
(eccl) comulgar
communicant [kə'mjunɪkənt] *s* comunicante *mf*; (eccl) comulgante *mf*

communicate [kə'mjunɪ‚ket] *tr* comunicar ‖ *intr* comunicarse
communicating [kə'mjunɪ‚ketɪŋ] *adj* comunicador
communicative [kə'mjunɪ‚ketɪv] *adj* comunicativo
communion [kə'mjunjən] *s* comunión; **to take communion** comulgar
communion rail *s* comulgatorio
communiqué [kə‚mjunɪ'ke] o [kə-'mjunɪ‚ke] *s* comunicado, parte *m*
communism ['kɑmjə‚nɪzəm] *s* comunismo
communist ['kɑmjənɪst] *s* comunista *mf*
communi·ty [kə'mjunɪti] *s* (*pl* **-ties**) vecindario; (*group of people living together*) comunidad
communize ['kɑmjə‚naɪz] *tr* comunizar
commutation ticket [‚kɑmjə'teʃən] *s* billete *m* de abono
commutator ['kɑmjə‚tetər] *s* (elec) colector *m*
commute [kə'mjut] *tr* conmutar ‖ *intr* viajar con billete de abono
commuter [kə'mjutər] *s* abonado al ferrocarril
comp. *abbr* **compare, comparative, composer, composition, compound**
compact [kəm'pækt] *adj* compacto; breve, preciso ‖ ['kɑmpækt] *s* convenio, pacto; estuche *m* de afeites
companion [kəm'pænjən] *s* compañero
companionable [kəm'pænjənəbəl] *adj* afable, sociable, simpático
companionship [kəm'pænjən‚ʃɪp] *s* compañerismo
companionway [kəm'pænjən‚we] *s* (naut) escalera de cámara
compa·ny ['kʌmpəni] *s* (*pl* **-nies**) compañía; visita, visitas, invitado, invitados; (naut) tripulación; **to be good company** ser compañero alegre; **to keep company** ir juntos (*un hombre y una mujer*); **to keep someone company** hacerle compañía a una persona; **to part company** separarse; enemistarse
company building *s* edificio social
company office *s* domicilio social
comparative [kəm'pærətɪv] *adj* & *s* comparativo
compare [kəm'per] *s* — **beyond compare** sin comparación, sin par ‖ *tr* comparar
comparison [kəm'pærɪsən] *s* comparación
compartment [kəm'partmənt] *s* compartimiento; (rr) departamento
compass ['kʌmpəs] *s* brújula, compás *m*; ámbito, recinto; alcance *m*, extensión; **compass** o **compasses** (*for drawing circles*) compás *m*
compass card *s* (naut) rosa náutica, rosa de los vientos
compassion [kəm'pæʃən] *s* compasión
compassionate [kəm'pæʃənɪt] *adj* compasivo
com·pel [kəm'pɛl] *v* (*pret* & *pp* **-pelled;** *ger* **-pelling**) *tr* forzar, obli-

gar, compeler; imponer (*respeto, silencio*)
compendious [kəm'pɛndɪ·əs] *adj* compendioso
compendi·um [kəm'pɛndɪ·əm] *s* (*pl* **-ums** o **-a** [ə]) compendio
compensate ['kɑmpən‚set] *tr* & *intr* compensar; **to compensate for** compensar
compensation [‚kɑmpən'seʃən] *s* compensación
compete [kəm'pit] *intr* competir
competence ['kɑmpɪtens] o **competency** ['kɑmpɪtensi] *s* (*aptitude; legal capacity*) competencia; (*sufficient means to live comfortably*) buen pasar *m*
competent ['kɑmpɪtənt] *adj* competente
competition [‚kɑmpɪ'tɪʃən] *s* (*rivalry*) competencia; (*in a match, examination, etc.*) certamen *m*, concurso; (*in business*) concurrencia
competitive examination [kəm'pɛtɪtɪv] *s* oposición
competitive prices *spl* precios de competencia
competitor [kəm'pɛtɪtər] *s* competidor *m*
compilation [‚kɑmpɪ'leʃən] *s* compilación, recopilación
compile [kəm'paɪl] *tr* compilar, recopilar
complacence [kəm'plesəns] o **complacency** [kəm'plesənsi] *s* (*quiet satisfaction*) complacencia; satisfacción de sí mismo
complacent [kəm'plesənt] *adj* (*willing to please*) complaciente; satisfecho de sí mismo
complain [kəm'plen] *intr* quejarse
complainant [kəm'plenənt] *s* (law) demandante *mf*
complaint [kəm'plent] *s* queja; (*grievance*) agravio; (*illness*) enfermedad, mal *m*; (law) demanda, querella
complaisance [kəm'plezəns] o ['kɑmplɪ‚zæns] *s* amabilidad, cortesía
complaisant [kəm'plezənt] o ['kɑmplɪ‚zænt] *adj* amable, cortés
complement ['kɑmplɪmənt] *s* complemento; (nav) dotación ‖ ['kɑmplɪ‚ment] *tr* complementar
complete [kəm'plit] *adj* completo ‖ *tr* completar, terminar, realizar
completion [kəm'pliʃən] *s* terminación, realización
complex [kəm'plɛks] o ['kɑmplɛks] *adj* (*not simple*) complejo; (*composite*) complejo; (*intricate*) complicado ‖ ['kɑmplɛks] *s* complejo; (psychol) complejo; (coll) obsesión
complexion [kəm'plɛkʃən] *s* (*constitution*) complexión; (*texture of skin, esp. of face*) tez *f*; aspecto general, índole *f*
compliance [kəm'plaɪ·əns] *s* condescendencia; sumisión, rendimiento; **in compliance with** de acuerdo con, en conformidad con
complicate ['kɑmplɪ‚ket] *tr* complicar

co
co

complicated ['kamplɪ,ketɪd] *adj* complicado

complici·ty [kəm'plɪsɪti] *s* (*pl* -ties) complicidad, codelincuencia

compliment ['kamplɪmənt] *s* (*show of courtesy*) cumplimiento; (*praise*) alabanza, halago; **compliments** saludos, recuerdos || ['kamplɪ,ment] *tr* cumplimentar; alabar, halagar

complimentary copy [,kamplɪ'mentəri] *s* ejemplar *m* de cortesía

complimentary ticket *s* billete *m* de regalo, pase *m* de cortesía

com·ply [kəm'plaɪ] *v* (*pret & pp* -plied) *intr* conformarse; **to comply with** conformarse con, obrar de acuerdo con

component [kəm'ponənt] *adj* componente || *m* componente *m;* (*mech*) componente *f*

compose [kəm'poz] *tr* componer; **to be composed of** estar compuesto de

composed [kəm'pozd] *adj* sosegado, tranquilo

composer [kəm'pozer] *s* componedor *m;* (*mus*) compositor *m;* autor *m*

composing stick *s* componedor *m*

composite [kəm'pazɪt] *adj & s* compuesto

composition [,kampə'zɪʃən] *s* composición

compositor [kəm'pazɪtər] *s* cajista *mf,* componedor *m*

composure [kəm'poʒər] *s* serenidad, sosiego

compote ['kampot] *s* (*stewed fruit*) compota; (*dish*) compotera

compound ['kampaund] *adj* compuesto || *s* compuesto; (*gram*) vocablo compuesto || [kam'paund] *tr* componer, combinar; (*interest*) capitalizar

comprehend [,kamprɪ'hend] *tr* comprender

comprehensible [,kamprɪ'hensɪbəl] *adj* comprensible

comprehension [,kamprɪ'henʃən] *s* comprensión

comprehensive [,kamprɪ'hensɪv] *adj* comprensivo, inclusivo, completo

compress ['kampres] *s* (*med*) compresa || [kəm'pres] *tr* comprimir

compression [kəm'preʃən] *s* compresión

comprise o **comprize** [kəm'praɪz] *tr* abarcar, comprender, incluir

compromise ['kamprə,maɪz] *s* (*adjustment*) componenda, transigencia, transacción; (*endangering*) comprometimiento || *tr* (*by mutual concessions*) componer, transigir; (*to endanger*) comprometer, exponer || *intr* transigir, avenirse

comptroller [kən'trolər] *s* contralor *m,* interventor *m*

compulsory [kəm'pʌlsərɪ] *adj* obligatorio

compute [kəm'pjut] *tr & intr* computar, calcular

computer [kəm'pjutər] *s* computador *m,* computadora

comrade ['kamræd] o ['kamrɪd] *s* camarada *m*

con. *abbr* **conclusion, consolidated, contra**

con [kan] *s* (*opposite opinion*) contra *m* || *v* (*pret & pp* **conned;** *ger* **conning**) *tr* leer con atención, aprender de memoria

concave ['kankev] o [kan'kev] *adj* cóncavo

conceal [kən'sil] *tr* encubrir, ocultar

concealment [kən'silmənt] *s* encubrimiento, ocultación; (*place*) escondite *m*

concede [kən'sid] *tr* conceder

conceit [kən'sit] *s* (*vanity*) orgullo, engreimiento; (*witty expression*) concepto, dicho ingenioso

conceited [kən'sitɪd] *adj* orgulloso, engreído

conceivable [kən'sivəbəl] *adj* concebible

conceive [kən'siv] *tr & intr* concebir

concentrate ['kansən,tret] *tr* concentrar || *intr* concentrarse; **to concentrate on** o **upon** reconcentrarse en

concentric [kən'sentrɪk] *adj* concéntrico

concept ['kansept] *s* concepto

conception [kən'sepʃən] *s* concepción

concern [kən'sʌrn] *s* (*business establishment*) empresa, casa comercial, razón *f* social; (*worry*) inquietud, preocupación; (*relation, reference*) concernencia; (*matter*) asunto, negocio || *tr* atañer, concernir; interesar; **as concerns** respecto de; **to whom it may concern** a quien pueda interesar, a quien corresponda

concerning [kən'sʌrnɪŋ] *prep* respecto de, tocante a

concert ['kansərt] *s* concierto || [kən'sʌrt] *tr & intr* concertar

con'cert·mas'ter *s* concertino

concer·to [kən't/erto] *s* (*pl* -tos o -ti [ti]) concierto

concession [kən'seʃən] *s* concesión

concessive [kən'sesɪv] *adj* concesivo

concierge [,kansɪ'ʌrʒ] *s* conserje *m*

conciliate [kən'sɪlɪ,et] *tr* conciliar; conciliarse (*el respeto, la estima*)

conciliatory [kən'sɪlɪ·ə,torɪ] *adj* conciliador

concise [kən'saɪs] *adj* conciso

conclude [kən'klud] *tr & intr* concluir

conclusion [kən'kluʒən] *s* conclusión; (*of a letter*) despedida

conclusive [kən'klusɪv] *adj* concluyente

concoct [kan'kakt] *tr* confeccionar; (*a story*) forjar, inventar

concomitant [kən'kamɪtənt] *adj & s* concomitante *m*

concord ['kaŋkord] *s* concordia; (*gram, mus*) concordancia

concordance [kan'kordəns] *s* concordancia

concourse ['kaŋkors] *s* (*of people*) concurso; (*of streams*) confluencia; bulevar *m,* gran vía; (*of railroad station*) gran salón *m*

concrete ['kɑnkrit] o [kən'krit] *adj* concreto; de hormigón ‖ *s* hormigón *m*

concrete block *s* bloque *m* de hormigón

concrete mixer *s* hormigonera, mezcladora de hormigón

concubine ['kɑŋkjə,baɪn] *s* concubina

con·cur [kən'kʌr] *v* (*pret & pp* **-curred;** *ger* **-curring**) *intr* concurrir

concurrence [kən'kʌrəns] *s* (*happening together*) concurrencia; (*agreement*) acuerdo

concussion [kən'kʌʃən] *s* concusión

condemn [kən'dem] *tr* condenar

condemnation [,kɑndem'neʃən] *s* condenación

condense [kən'dens] *tr* condensar ‖ *intr* condensarse

condescend [,kɑndɪ'send] *intr* dignarse

condescending [,kɑndɪ'sendɪŋ] *adj* condescendiente con inferiores

condescension [,kɑndɪ'senʃən] *s* dignación, aire *m* protector

condiment ['kɑndɪmənt] *s* condimento

condition [kən'dɪʃən] *s* condición; **on condition that** a condición (de) que ‖ *tr* acondicionar

conditional [kən'dɪʃənəl] *adj* condicional

condole [kən'dol] *intr* condolerse

condolence [kən'doləns] *s* condolencia

condone [kən'don] *tr* condonar

conduce [kən'djus] o [kən'dus] *intr* conducir

conducive [kən'djusiv] o [kən'dusiv] *adj* conducente, contribuyente

conduct ['kɑndʌkt] *s* conducta ‖ [kən'dʌkt] *tr* conducir; **to conduct oneself** conducirse, comportarse

conductor [kən'dʌktər] *s* conductor *m*, guía *mf*; (elec & phys) conductor *m*, conductora *f*; (rr) revisor *m*; (on trolley or bus) cobrador *m*

conduit ['kɑndɪt] o ['kɑndu·ɪt] *s* canal *f* para alambres o cables

cone [kon] *s* cono; (of pastry) barquillo; (of paper) cucurucho

confectioner·y [kən'fekʃə,neri] *s* (*pl* **-ies**) (*shop*) confitería; (*sweetmeats*) dulces *mpl*, confites *mpl*, confituras

confedera·cy [kən'fedərəsi] (*pl* **-cies**) confederación; (*for unlawful purpose*) conjuración

confederate [kən'fedərɪt] *s* confederado; cómplice *mf* ‖ [kən'fedə,ret] *tr* confederar ‖ *intr* confederarse

con·fer [kən'fʌr] *v* (*pret & pp* **-ferred;** *ger* **-ferring**) *tr* conferir ‖ *intr* conferenciar, consultar

conference ['kɑnfərəns] *s* conferencia, coloquio

confess [kən'fes] *tr* confesar ‖ *intr* confesar, confesarse

confession [kən'feʃən] *s* confesión

confessional [kən'feʃənəl] *s* confesonario

confession of faith *s* profesión de fe

confessor [kən'fesər] *s* (person who confesses) confesante *mf*; (Christian, esp. in spite of persecution; priest) confesor *m*

confide [kən'faɪd] *tr* confiar ‖ *intr* confiar, confiarse; **to confide in** confiarse en

confidence ['kɑnfɪdəns] *s* confianza; (secret) confidencia; **in strictest confidence** bajo la mayor reserva

confident ['kɑnfɪdənt] *adj* seguro ‖ *s* confidente *m*, confidenta

confidential [,kɑnfɪ'denʃəl] *adj* confidencial

confine ['kɑnfaɪn] *s* confín *m*; **the confines** los confines ‖ [kən'faɪn] *tr* (to keep within limits) limitar, restringir; (to keep shut in) encerrar; **to be confined** estar de parto; **to be confined to bed** tener que guardar cama

confinement [kən'faɪnmənt] *s* limitación; encierro; parto, sobreparto

confirm [kən'fʌrm] *tr* confirmar

confirmed [kən'fʌrmd] *adj* confirmado; empedernido, inveterado

confiscate ['kɑnfɪs,ket] *tr* confiscar

conflagration [,kɑnflə'greʃən] *s* conflagración

conflict ['kɑnflɪkt] *s* conflicto; (of interests, class hours, etc.) incompatibilidad ‖ [kən'flɪkt] *intr* chocar, desavenirse

conflicting [kən'flɪktɪŋ] *adj* contradictorio; (events, appointments, class hours, etc.) incompatible

confluence ['kɑnflu·əns] *s* confluencia

conform [kən'fɔrm] *intr* conformar, conformarse

conformance [kən'fɔrməns] *s* conformidad

conformi·ty [kən'fɔrmɪti] *s* (*pl* **-ties**) conformidad

confound [kɑn'faund] *tr* confundir ‖ ['kɑn'faund] *tr* maldecir; **confound it!** ¡maldito sea!

confounded [kɑn'faundɪd] o ['kɑn'faundɪd] *adj* confundido; aborrecible; maldito

confrere ['kɑnfrer] *s* colega *m*

confront [kən'frʌnt] *tr* (to face boldly) confrontarse con, hacer frente a; (to meet face to face) encontrar cara a cara; (to bring face to face; to compare) confrontar

confuse [kən'fjuz] *tr* confundir

confusion [kən'fuʒən] *s* confusión

confute [kən'fjut] *tr* confutar

Cong. *abbr* **Congregation, Congressional**

congeal [kən'dʒil] *tr* congelar ‖ *intr* congelarse

congenial [kən'dʒinjəl] *adj* simpático; agradable; compatible; (having the same nature) congenial

congenital [kən'dʒenɪtəl] *adj* congénito

conger eel ['kɑŋgər] *s* congrio

congest [kən'dʒest] *tr* congestionar ‖ *intr* congestionarse

congestion [kən'dʒestʃən] *s* congestión

congratulate [kən'grætʃə,let] *tr* congratular, felicitar

CO
CO

congratulation [kən‚græt∫ə'le∫ən] s
congratulación, felicitación
congregate ['kaŋgrɪ‚get] intr congre-
garse
congregation [‚kaŋgrɪ'ge∫ən] s congregación; feligresía, fieles mf (de
una iglesia)
congress ['kaŋgrɪs] s congreso
congress·man ['kaŋgrɪsmən] s (pl
-men [mən]) congresista m
conical ['kanɪkəl] adj cónico
conj. abbr **conjugation, conjunction**
conjecture [kən'dʒɛkt∫ər] s conjetura
|| tr & intr conjeturar
conjugal ['kandʒəgəl] adj conyugal
conjugate ['kandʒə‚get] tr conjugar
conjugation [‚kandʒə'ge∫ən] s conjugación
conjunction [kən'dʒʌŋk∫ən] s conjunción
conjuration [‚kandʒə're∫ən] s (superstitious invocation) conjuro; (magic
spell) hechizo
conjure [kən'dʒʊr] tr (to appeal to
solemnly) conjurar || ['kʌndʒər] o
['kandʒər] tr (to exorcise, drive
away) conjurar; **to conjure away**
conjurar; **to conjure up** evocar;
crear, suscitar (dificultades)
connect [kə'nɛkt] tr conectar; asociar,
relacionar || intr enlazarse; aso-
ciarse, relacionarse; empalmar, enlazar (dos trenes)
connecting rod s biela
connection [kə'nɛk∫ən] s conexión;
(relative) pariente mf; (of trains)
combinación, enlace m, empalme m;
(in subway) correspondencia; (in
connection with con respecto a;
juntamente con
conning tower ['kanɪŋ] s torreta de
mando
conniption [kə'nɪp∫ən] s pataleta, berrinche m
connive [kə'naɪv] intr confabularse,
estar en connivencia
conquer ['kaŋkər] tr vencer; (by force
of arms) conquistar || intr triunfar
conqueror ['kaŋkərər] s conquistador
m, vencedor m
conquest ['kaŋkwɛst] s conquista
conscience ['kan∫əns] s conciencia; **in
all conscience** en conciencia
conscientious [‚kan∫ɪ'ɛn∫əs] adj concienzudo
conscientious objector [əb'dʒɛktər] s
objetante m de conciencia
conscious ['kan∫əs] adj (aware of
one's own existence) consciente; (deliberate) intencional; (self-conscious)
encogido, tímido; **to become conscious** volver en sí
consciousness ['kan∫əsnɪs] s conciencia, conocimiento
conscript ['kanskrɪpt] s conscripto ||
[kən'skrɪpt] tr reclutar
conscription [kən'skrɪp∫ən] s conscripción
consecrate ['kansɪ‚kret] tr consagrar
consecutive [kən'sɛkjətɪv] adj (successive) consecutivo; (continuous)
consecuente

consensus [kən'sɛnsəs] s consenso; **the
consensus of opinion** la opinión
general
consent [kən'sɛnt] s consentimiento;
by common consent de común
acuerdo || intr consentir; **to consent
to** consentir en
consequence ['kansɪ‚kwɛns] s consecuencia; aires mpl de importancia
consequential [‚kansɪ'kwɛn∫əl] adj
consiguiente; importante; altivo,
pomposo
consequently ['kansɪ‚kwɛntlɪ] adv por
consiguiente
conservation [‚kansər've∫ən] s conservación
conservatism [kən'sʌrvə‚tɪzəm] s con-
servadurismo
conservative [kən'sʌrvətɪv] adj (preservative) conservativo; (disposed to
maintain existing views and institu-
tions) conservador; cauteloso, mo-
derado || s preservativo; conserva-
dor m
conservato·ry [kən'sʌrvə‚tori] s (pl
-ries) (school of music) conservatorio; (greenhouse) invernadero
consider [kən'sɪdər] tr considerar
considerable [kən'sɪdərəbəl] adj considerable
considerate [kən'sɪdərɪt] adj considerado
consideration [kən‚sɪdə're∫ən] s consideración; **for a consideration** por
un precio; **in consideration of** en
consideración de; en cambio de; **on
no consideration** bajo ningún concepto; **out of consideration for** por
respeto a; **without due consideration**
sin reflexión
considering [kən'sɪdərɪŋ] adv (coll)
teniendo en cuentas las circunstan-
cias || prep en vista de, en razón de
|| conj en vista de que
consign [kən'saɪn] tr consignar
consignee [‚kansaɪ'ni] s consignatario
consignment [kən'saɪnmənt] s consignación
consist [kən'sɪst] intr — **to consist in**
consistir en; **to consist of** consistir
en, constar de
consisten·cy [kən'sɪstənsɪ] s (pl -cies)
(firmness, amount of firmness) consistencia; (logical connection) consecuencia
consistent [kən'sɪstənt] adj (holding
firmly together) consistente; (agreeing with itself or oneself) consecuente; **consistent with** (in accord
with) compatible con
consisto·ry [kən'sɪstəri] s (pl -ries)
consistorio
consolation [‚kansə'le∫ən] s consolación, consuelo
console ['kansol] s consola; mesa de
consola || [kən'sol] tr consolar
consommé [‚kansə'me] s consumado,
consommé m
consonant ['kansənənt] adj & s consonante f
consort ['kansərt] s consorte mf; em-
barcación que acompaña a otra ||

[kən'sɔrt] *tr* asociar ‖ *intr* asociarse; armonizar, concordar

consorti·um [kən'sɔrʃi·əm] *s* (*pl* -a [ə]) consorcio

conspicuous [kən'spɪkju·əs] *adj* manifiesto, claro, evidente; llamativo, vistoso, sugestivo; conspicuo, notable

conspira·cy [kən'spɪrəsi] *s* (*pl* -cies) conspiración, conjuración

conspire [kən'spaɪr] *intr* conspirar, conjurar

constable ['kʌnstəbəl] o ['kʌnstəbəl] *s* policía *m*, guardia *m*, alguacil *m*

constancy ['kʌnstənsi] *s* constancia; fidelidad

constant ['kʌnstənt] *adj* constante; incesante; fiel ‖ *s* constante *f*

constellation [,kʌnstə'leʃən] *s* constelación

constipate ['kʌnstɪ,pet] *tr* estreñir

constipation [,kʌnstɪ'peʃən] *s* estreñimiento

constituen·cy [kən'stɪtʃu·ənsi] *s* (*pl* -cies) votantes *mpl*; clientela; comitentes *mpl*; distrito electoral

constituent [kən'stɪtʃu·ənt] *adj* constitutivo, componente; (*having power to create or revise a constitution*) constituyente ‖ *s* constitutivo, componente *m*; (*person who appoints another to act for him*) comitente *m*

constitute ['kʌnstɪ,tjut] o ['kʌnstɪ,tut] *tr* constituir

constitution [,kʌnstɪ'tjuʃən] o [,kʌnstɪ'tuʃən] *s* constitución

constrain [kən'stren] *tr* constreñir; detener, encerrar; restringir

construct [kən'strʌkt] *tr* construir

construction [kən'strʌkʃən] *s* construcción; interpretación

construe [kən'stru] *tr* interpretar; deducir, inferir; traducir; (*to combine syntactically*) construir; (*to explain the syntax of*) analizar

consul ['kʌnsəl] *s* cónsul *m*

consular ['kʌnsələr] o ['kʌnsjələr] *adj* consular

consulate ['kʌnsəlɪt] o ['kʌnsjəlɪt] *s* consulado

consulship ['kʌnsəl,ʃɪp] *s* consulado

consult [kən'sʌlt] *tr & intr* consultar

consultant [kən'sʌltənt] *s* consultor *m*

consultation [,kʌnsəl'teʃən] *s* (*consulting*) consulta; (*meeting*) consulta, consultación

consume [kən'sum] o [kən'sjum] *tr* consumir; (*to absorb the interest of*) preocupar; ‖ *intr* consumirse

consumer [kən'sumər] o [kən'sjumər] *s* consumidor *m*; (*of gas, electricity, etc.*) abonado

consumer credit *s* crédito consuntivo

consumer goods *spl* bienes *mpl* de consumo

consumerism *s* consumerismo

consummate [kən'sʌmɪt] *adj* consumado ‖ ['kʌnsə,met] *tr* consumar

consumption [kən'sʌmpʃən] *s* consunción, consumo; (*pathol*) consunción, tisis *f*

consumptive [kən'sʌmptɪv] *adj* con-

suntivo; (*path*) tísico ‖ *s* tísico

cont. *abbr* **contents, continued**

contact ['kʌntækt] *s* contacto; (elec) contacto; (elec) toma de corriente ‖ *tr* (coll) ponerse en contacto con ‖ *intr* contactar

contact breaker *s* (elec) ruptor *m*

contact lens *s* lente *m* de contacto, lente invisible

contagion [kən'tedʒən] *s* contagio

contagious [kən'tedʒəs] *adj* contagioso

contain [kən'ten] *tr* contener; **to contain oneself** contenerse, refrenarse

container [kən'tenər] *s* continente *m*, recipiente *m*, vaso, caja, envase *m*

containment [kən'tenmənt] *s* contención, refrenamiento

contaminate [kən'tæmɪ,net] *tr* contaminar

contamination [kən,tæmɪ'neʃən] *s* contaminación

contd. *abbr* **continued**

contemplate ['kʌntəm,plet] *tr & intr* contemplar; pensar, proyectar

contemplation [,kʌntəm'pleʃən] *s* contemplación; intención, propósito

contemporaneous [kən,tempə'reni·əs] *adj* contemporáneo

contemporar·y [kən'tempə,reri] *adj* contemporáneo, coetáneo ‖ *s* (*pl* -ies) contemporáneo, coetáneo

contempt [kən'tempt] *s* desprecio; (law) contumacia

contemptible [kən'temptɪbəl] *adj* despreciable

contemptuous [kən'temptʃu·əs] *adj* despreciativo, desdeñoso

contend [kən'tend] *tr* sostener, mantener ‖ *intr* contender

contender [kən'tendər] *s* contendiente *mf*, concurrente *mf*

content [kən'tent] *adj & s* contento ‖ ['kʌntent] *s* contenido; **contents** contenido ‖ [kən'tent] *tr* contentar

contented [kən'tentɪd] *adj* contento, satisfecho

contentedness [kən'tentɪdnɪs] *s* contentamiento, satisfacción

contention [kən'tenʃən] *s* (*strife; dispute*) contención; (*point argued for*) argumento

contentious [kən'tenʃəs] *adj* contencioso

contentment [kən'tentmənt] *s* contentamiento, contento

contest ['kʌntest] *s* (*struggle, fight*) contienda; (*competition*) competencia, concurso ‖ [kən'test] *tr* disputar; tratar de conseguir ‖ *intr* contender

contestant [kən'testənt] *s* contendiente *mf*

context ['kʌntekst] *s* contexto

contiguous [kən'tɪgju·əs] *adj* contiguo

continence ['kʌntɪnəns] *s* continencia

continent ['kʌntɪnənt] *adj & s* continente *m*; **the Continent** la Europa continental

continental [,kʌntɪ'nentəl] *adj* continental ‖ **Continental** *s* habitante *mf* del continente europeo

contingen·cy [kən'tɪndʒənsi] *s* (*pl* -cies) contingencia

contingent ['kən'tɪndʒənt] *adj & s* contingente *m*

continual [kən'tɪnjʊ-əl] *adj* continuo

continue [kən'tɪnju] *tr & intr* continuar; **to be continued** continuará

continui·ty [,kɑntɪ'nju-ɪti] o [,kɑntɪ'nu-ɪti] *s* (*pl* -ties) continuidad; (mov, rad, telv) guión *m*; (rad, telv) comentarios o anuncios entre las partes de un programa

continuous [kən'tɪnjʊ-əs] *adj* continuo

continuous showing *s* (mov) sesión continua

continuous waves *spl* (rad) ondas entretenidas

contortion [kən'tɔrʃən] *s* contorsión

contour ['kɑntʊr] *s* contorno

contr. *abbr* contracted, contraction

contraband ['kɑntrə,bænd] *adj* contrabandista || *s* contrabando

contrabass ['kɑntrə,bes] *s* contrabajo

contraceptive [,kɑntrə'sɛptɪv] *adj & s* anticonceptivo, contraceptivo

contract ['kɑntrækt] *s* contrato || ['kɑntrækt] o [kən'trækt] *tr* contraer (*p.ej.*, *matrimonio*) || *intr* (*to shrink*) contraerse; (*to enter into an agreement*) comprometerse; **to contract for** contratar

contraction [kən'trækʃən] *s* contracción

contractor [kən'træktər] *s* contratista *mf*

contradict [,kɑntrə'dɪkt] *tr* contradecir

contradiction [,kɑntrə'dɪkʃən] *s* contradicción

contradictory [,kɑntrə'dɪktəri] *adj* (*involving contradiction*) contradictorio; (*inclined to contradict*) contradictor

contrail ['kɑn,trel] *s* (aer) estela de vapor, rastro de condensación

contral·to [kən'træl̃to] *s* (*pl* -tos) (*person*) contralto *mf*; (*voice*) contralto *m*

contraption [kən'træpʃən] *s* (coll) artilugio, dispositivo

contra·ry ['kɑntreri] *adv* contrariamente || *adj* contrario || [kən'treri] *adj* obstinado, terco || ['kɑntreri] *s* (*pl* -ries) contrario; **on the contrary** al contrario

contrast ['kɑntræst] *s* contraste *m* || [kən'træst] *tr* comparar; poner en contraste || *intr* contrastar

contravene [,kɑntrə'vin] *tr* contradecir; contravenir a (*una ley*)

contribute [kən'trɪbjut] *tr* contribuir || *intr* contribuir; (*to a newspaper, conference, etc.*) colaborar

contribution [,kɑntrɪ'bjuʃən] *s* contribución; (*to a newspaper, conference, etc.*) colaboración

contributor [kən'trɪbjutər] *s* contribuidor *m*, contribuyente *mf*; colaborador *m*

contrite [kən'traɪt] *adj* contrito

contrition [kən'trɪʃən] *s* contrición

contrivance [kən'traɪvəns] *s* aparato, dispositivio; idea, plan *m*, designio

contrive [kən'traɪv] *tr* (*to devise*) idear, inventar; (*to scheme up*) maquinar, tramar; (*to bring about*) efectuar || *intr* maquinar; **to contrive to** + *inf* ingeniarse a + *inf*

con·trol [kən'trol] *s* gobierno, mando; (*of a scientific experiment*) contrarregistro, control *m*; **controls** mandos; **to get under control** conseguir dominar (*un incendio*) || *v* (*pret & pp* -trolled) *ger* -trolling) *tr* gobernar, mandar; comprobar, controlar; **to control oneself** dominarse

controlling interest *s* (el) mayor porcentaje de acciones

control panel *s* (aer) tablero de instrumentos

control stick *s* (aer) mango de escoba, palanca de mando

controversial [,kɑntrə'vʌrʃəl] *adj* controvertible, disputable; disputador

controver·sy ['kɑntrə,vʌrsi] *s* (*pl* -sies) controversia, polémica

controvert ['kɑntrə,vʌrt] o [,kɑntrə'vʌrt] *tr* (*to argue against*) contradecir; (*to argue about*) controvertir

contumacious [,kɑntju'meʃəs] o [,kɑntu'meʃəs] *adj* contumaz

contuma·cy ['kɑntjuməsi] o ['kɑntuməsi] *s* (*pl* -cies) contumacia

contume·ly ['kɑntjumɪli] o ['kɑntumɪli] *s* (*pl* -lies) contumelia

contusion [kən'tjuʒən] o [kən'tuʒən] *s* contusión

conundrum [kə'nʌndrəm] *s* acertijo, adivinanza; problema complicado

convalesce [,kɑnvə'lɛs] *intr* convalecer

convalescence [,kɑnvə'lɛsəns] *s* convalecencia

convalescent [,kɑnvə'lɛsənt] *adj & s* convaleciente *mf*

convalescent home *s* clínica de reposo

convene [kən'vin] *tr* convocar || *intr* convenir, reunirse

convenience [kən'vinjəns] *s* comodidad, conveniencia; **at your earliest convenience** a la primera oportunidad que Vd. tenga

convenient [kən'vinjənt] *adj* cómodo, conveniente; próximo

convent ['kɑnvɛnt] *s* convento; convento de religiosas

convention [kən'vɛnʃən] *s* (*agreement*) convención, conveniencia; (*accepted usage*) costumbre *f*, conveniencia social, convención; (*meeting*) congreso, convención

conventional [kən'vɛnʃənəl] *adj* convencional

conventionali·ty [kən,vɛnʃə'næliti] *s* (*pl* -ties) precedente *m* convencional

converge [kən'vʌrd] *intr* convergir

conversant [kən'vʌrsənt] *adj* familiarizado, versado

conversation [,kɑnvər'seʃən] *s* conversación

conversational [,kɑnvər'seʃənəl] *adj* conversacional

converse ['kɑnvʌrs] *adj & s* contrario || [kən'vʌrs] *intr* conversar

conversion [kən'vʌrʒən] *s* conversión;

(unlawful appropriation) malversación

convert ['kɑnvʌrt] *s* convertido, converso || [kən'vʌrt] *tr* convertir || *intr* convertirse

convertible [kən'vʌrtɪbəl] *adj* convertible || *s* (aut) convertible *m*, descapotable *m*

convex ['kɑnveks] o [kɑn'veks] *adj* convexo

convey [kən've] *tr* llevar, transportar; comunicar, participar *(informes)*; transferir, traspasar *(bienes de una persona a otra)*

conveyance [kən've·əns] *s* transporte *m*; comunicación, participación; vehículo; *(transfer of property)* traspaso; escritura de traspaso

convict ['kɑnvɪkt] *s* reo convicto, presidiario || [kən'vɪkt] *tr* probar la culpabilidad de; declarar convicto *(a un acusado)*

conviction [kən'vɪkʃən] *s* convencimiento; condena, fallo de culpabilidad

convince [kən'vɪns] *tr* convencer

convincing [kən'vɪnsɪŋ] *adj* convincente

convivial [kən'vɪvɪ·əl] *adj* jovial

convocation [‚kɑnvə'keʃən] *s* asamblea

convoke [kən'vok] *tr* convocar

convoy ['kɑnvɔɪ] *s* convoy *m*, conserva || *tr* convoyar

convulse [kən'vʌls] *tr* convulsionar; agitar; **to convulse with laughter** mover a risas convulsivas

coo [ku] *intr* arrullar

cook [kʊk] *s* cocinero || *tr* cocer, cocinar, guisar; **to cook up** (coll) falsificar; (coll) maquinar, tramar || *intr* cocer, cocinar

cook'book' *s* libro de cocina

cookie ['kʊki] *s* var de **cooky**

cooking ['kʊkɪŋ] *s* cocina, arte *m* de cocinar

cook'stove' *s* cocina económica

cook·y ['kʊki] *s* (*pl* -ies) pasta seca, pastelito dulce

cool [kul] *adj* fresco; frío, indiferente || *s* fresco || *tr* refrescar; moderar || *intr* refrescarse; moderarse; **to cool off** refrescarse; serenarse

cooler ['kulər] *s* heladera, refrigerador *m*; refrigerante *m*; (coll) cárcel *f*

cool'-head'ed *adj* sereno, tranquilo, juicioso

coolie ['kuli] *s* culí *m*

coolish ['kulɪʃ] *adj* fresquito

coolness ['kulnɪs] *s* fresco, frescura; (fig) frialdad

coon [kun] *s* mapache *m*, oso lavandero

coop [kup] *s* gallinero; *(for fattening capons)* caponera; jaula, redil *m*; *(jail)* (slang) caponera; **to fly the coop** (slang) escabullirse || *tr* encerrar en un gallinero; enjaular; **to coop up** emparedar

coöp. *abbr* **cooperative**

cooper ['kupər] *s* barrilero, tonelero

coöperate [ko'ɑpə‚ret] *intr* cooperar

coöperation [ko‚ɑpə'reʃən] *s* cooperación

coöperative [ko'ɑpə‚retɪv] *adj* cooperativo

coördinate [ko'ɔrdɪnɪt] *adj* coordenado; (gram) coordinante || *s* (math) coordenada || [ko'ɔrdɪ‚net] *tr & intr* coordinar

cootie ['kuti] *s* (slang) piojo

cop [kɑp] *s* (slang) polizonte *m* || *v* (*pret & pp* **copped**; *ger* **copping**) *tr* (slang) hurtar

copartner [ko'pɑrtnər] *s* consocio, copartícipe *mf*

cope [kop] *intr* — **to cope with** hacer frente a, enfrentarse con

cope'stone' *s* piedra de albardilla

copier ['kɑpɪ·ər] *s* (*person who copies*) copiante *mf*, copista *mf*; imitador *m*; *(apparatus)* copiador *m*

copilot ['ko‚paɪlət] *s* copiloto

coping ['kopɪŋ] *s* albardilla

copious ['kopɪ·əs] *adj* copioso

copper ['kɑpər] *adj* cobreño; (*in color*) cobrizo || *s* cobre *m*; (*coin*) calderilla, vellón *m*; (slang) polizonte *m*

cop'per·head' *s* víbora de cabeza de cobre

cop'per·smith' *s* cobrero

coppery ['kɑpəri] *adj* cobreño; (*in color*) cobrizo

coppice ['kɑpɪs] o **copse** [kɑps] *s* soto, monte bajo

copulate ['kɑpjə‚let] *intr* copularse

cop·y ['kɑpi] *s* (*pl* -ies) copia; (*of a book*) ejemplar *m*; (*of a magazine*) número; (*document to be reproduced in print*) original *m*, manuscrito || *v* (*pret & pp* -ied) *tr* copiar

cop'y·book' *s* cuaderno de escritura

copyist ['kɑpɪ·ɪst] *s* copiante *mf*, copista *mf*; imitador *m*

cop'y·right' *s* (derechos de) propiedad literaria || *tr* registrar en el registro de la propiedad literaria

copy writer *s* escritor publicitario

co·quet [ko'ket] *v* (*pret & pp* -**quetted**; *ger* -**quetting**) *intr* coquetear; burlarse

coquet·ry ['kokətri] o [ko'ketri] *s* (*pl* -ries) coquetería; burla

coquette [ko'ket] *s* coqueta

coquettish [ko'ketɪʃ] *adj* coqueta

cor. *abbr* **corner, coroner, correction, corresponding**

coral ['kɑrəl] o ['kɔrəl] *adj* coralino || *s* coral *m*

coral reef *s* arrecife *m* de coral

cord [kɔrd] *s* cordón *m* || *tr* acordonar

cordial ['kɔrdʒəl] *adj* cordial || *s* licor tónico; (*stimulating medicine*) cordial *m*

cordiali·ty [kɔr'dʒælɪti] *s* (*pl* -ties) cordialidad

corduroy ['kɔrdə‚rɔɪ] *s* pana; **corduroys** pantalones *mpl* de pana

core [kor] *s* corazón *m*; (*of an electromagnet*) núcleo

corespondent [‚korɪs'pɑndənt] *s* cómplice *mf* del demandade en juicio de divorcio

Corinth ['kɑrɪnθ] o ['kɔrɪnθ] *s* Corinto *f*

cork [kɔrk] *s* corcho; corcho, tapón *m* de corcho; tapón (*de cualquier materia*) ‖ *tr* encorchar, tapar con corcho

corking ['kɔrkɪŋ] *adj* (slang) brutal, extraordinario

cork oak *s* alcornoque *m*

cork'screw' *s* sacacorchos *m*, tirabuzón *m*

cormorant ['kɔrmərənt] *s* cormorán *m*, cuervo marino

corn [kɔrn] *s* (*in U.S.A.*) maíz *m*; (*in England*) trigo; (*in Scotland*) avena; grano (*de maíz, trigo*); (*on the foot*) callo; (coll) aguardiente *m*; (slang) trivialidad

corn bread *s* pan *m* de maíz

corn'cake' *s* tortilla de maíz

corn'cob' *s* mazorca de maíz, carozo

corncob pipe *s* pipa de fumar hecha de una mazorca de maíz

corn'crib' *s* granero para maíz

corn cure *s* callicida *m*

cornea ['kɔrnɪ·ə] *s* córnea

corner ['kɔrnər] *s* ángulo; (*esp. where two streets meet*) esquina; (*inside angle formed by two or more surfaces; secluded place; region, quarter*) rincón *m*; (*of eye*) comisura, rabillo; (*of lips*) comisura; (*awkward position*) apuro, aprieto; monopolio; **around the corner** a la vuelta de la esquina; **to turn the corner** doblar la esquina; pasar el punto más peligroso ‖ *tr* arrinconar; monopolizar

corner cupboard *s* rinconera

corner room *s* habitación de esquina

cor'ner-stone' *s* piedra angular; (*of a new building*) primera piedra

cornet [kɔr'nɛt] *s* corneta

corn exchange *s* bolsa de granos

corn'field' *s* (*in U.S.A.*) maizal *m*; (*in England*) trigal *m*; (*in Scotland*) avenal *m*

corn flour *s* harina de maíz

corn'flow'er *s* cabezuela

corn'husk' *s* perfolla

cornice ['kɔrnɪs] *s* cornisa

Cornish ['kɔrnɪʃ] *adj* & *s* córnico

corn liquor *s* chicha

corn meal *s* harina de maíz

corn on the cob *s* maíz *m* en la mazorca

corn plaster *s* emplasto para los callos

corn silk *s* cabellos, barbas del maíz

corn'stalk' *s* tallo de maíz

corn'starch' *s* almidón *m* de maíz

cornucopia [,kɔrnə'kopɪ·ə] *s* cornucopia

Cornwall ['kɔrn,wɔl] o ['kɔrnwəl] *s* Cornualles

corn·y ['kɔrni] *adj* (*comp* **-ier**; *super* **-iest**) de maíz; (coll) gastado, trivial, pesado

corollar·y ['kɑrə,lɛri] o ['kɔrə,lɛri] *s* (*pl* **-ies**) corolario

coronation [,kɑrə'neʃən] o [,kɔrə'neʃən] *s* coronación

coroner ['kɑrənər] o ['kɔrənər] *s* juez *m* de guardia

coroner's inquest *s* pesquisa dirigida por el juez de guardia

coronet ['kɑrə,nɛt] o ['kɔrə,nɛt] *s* (*worn by members of nobility*) corona; (*ornamental band of jewels worn on head*) diadema *f*

Corp. *abbr* **Corporation**

corporal ['kɔrpərəl] *adj* corporal ‖ *s* (mil) cabo

corporation [,kɔrpə'reʃən] *s* (*provincial, municipal, or service entity*) corporación; sociedad anónima por acciones

corps [kor] *s* (*pl* **corps** [korz]) cuerpo; (mil) cuerpo

corps de ballet [kɔr də bæ'lɛ] *s* cuerpo de baile

corpse [kɔrps] *s* cadáver *m*

corpulent ['kɔrpjələnt] *adj* corpulento

corpuscle ['kɔrpəsəl] *s* corpúsculo, partícula; (physiol) glóbulo

corr. *abbr* **correspondence, corresponding**

cor·ral [kə'ræl] *s* corral *m* ‖ *v* (*pret* & *pp* **-ralled**; *ger* **-ralling**) *tr* acorralar

correct [kə'rɛkt] *adj* correcto; (*proper*) cumplido ‖ *tr* corregir

correction [kə'rɛkʃən] *s* corrección

corrective [kə'rɛktɪv] *adj* & *s* correctivo

correctness [kə'rɛktnɪs] *s* corrección; cumplimiento, cumplido

correlate ['kɑrə,lɛt] o ['kɔrə,lɛt] *tr* correlacionar ‖ *intr* correlacionarse

correlation [,kɑrə'leʃən] o [,kɔrə'lɛʃən] *s* correlación

correlative [kə'rɛlətɪv] *adj* & *s* correlativo

correspond [,kɑrɪ'spɑnd] o [,kɔrɪ'spɑnd] *intr* corresponder; (*to communicate by writing*) corresponderse

correspondence [,kɑrɪ'spɑndəns] o [,kɔrɪ'spɑndəns] *s* correspondencia

correspondence school *s* escuela por correspondencia

correspondent [,kɑrɪ'spɑndənt] o [,kɔrɪ'spɑndənt] *adj* correspondiente ‖ *s* correspondiente *mf*; (*for a newspaper*) corresponsal *mf*

corresponding [,kɑrɪ'spɑndɪŋ] o [,kɔrɪ'spɑndɪŋ] *adj* correspondiente

corridor ['kɑrɪdər] o ['kɔrɪdər] *s* corredor *m*, pasillo

corroborate [kə'rɑbə,rɛt] *tr* corroborar

corrode [kə'rod] *tr* corroer ‖ *intr* corroerse

corrosion [kə'roʒən] *s* corrosión

corrosive [kə'rosɪv] *adj* & *s* corrosivo

corrugated ['kɑrə,getɪd] o ['kɔrə,getɪd] *adj* acanalado, ondulado

corrupt [kə'rʌpt] *adj* corrompido ‖ *tr* corromper ‖ *intr* corromperse

corruption [kə'rʌpʃən] *s* corrupción

corsage [kɔr'saʒ] *s* (*bodice*) corpiño, jubón *m*; (*bouquet*) ramillete *m* que se lleva en el pecho o la cintura

corsair ['kɔr,sɛr] *s* corsario

corset ['kɔrsɪt] *s* corsé *m*

corset cover *s* cubrecorsé *m*

Corsica ['kɔrsɪkə] s Córcega

Corsican ['kɔrsɪkən] adj & s corso

cortege [kɔr'teʒ] s procesión; (retinue) cortejo, séquito

cor-tex ['kɔr,teks] s (pl -tices [tɪ,siz]) corteza; corteza cerebral

cortisone ['kɔrtɪ,son] s cortisona

corvette [kɔr'vet] s corbeta

cosmetic [kaz'metɪk] adj & s cosmético

cosmic ['kazmɪk] adj cósmico

cosmonaut ['kazmə,nɔt] s cosmonauta mf

cosmopolitan [,kazmə'palɪtən] adj & s cosmopolita mf

cosmos ['kazməs] s cosmos m; (bot) cosmos

Cossack ['ka,sæk] adj & s cosaco

cost [kɔst] o [kast] s coste m, costo; **at cost** a coste y costas; **at all costs** a toda costa; **costs** (law) costas || v (pret & pp **cost**) intr costar; **cost what it may** cueste lo que cueste

cost accounting s escandallo

Costa Rican ['kastə 'rikən] o ['kɔste 'rikən] adj & s costarricense mf, costarriqueño

cost, insurance, and freight costo, seguro y flete

cost-ly ['kɔstli] o ['kastli] adj (comp -lier; super -liest) costoso, dispendioso; (lavish) pródigo; (magnificent) suntuoso

cost of living s costo de la vida, carestía de la vida

costume ['kastjum] o ['kastum] s traje m; (garb worn on stage, at balls, etc.) disfraz m, traje de época

costume ball s baile m de trajes

costume jewelry s joyas de fantasía, bisutería

cot [kat] s catre m

coterie ['kotəri] s círculo, grupo; (clique) corrillo

cottage ['katɪdʒ] s cabaña; casita de campo

cottage cheese s naterón m, requesón m

cotter pin ['katər] s chaveta

cotton ['katən] s algodón m || intr — **to cotton up to** (coll) aficionarse a

cotton field s algodonal m

cotton gin s desmotadera de algodón

cotton picker ['pɪkər] s recogedor m de algodón; máquina para recolectar el algodón

cot'ton·seed' s semilla de algodón

cottonseed oil s aceite m de algodón

cotton waste s hilacha de algodón, estopa de algodón

cot'ton·wood' s chopo del Canadá, chopo de Virginia

cottony ['katəni] adj algodonoso

couch [kautʃ] s canapé m, sofá m || tr expresar

cougar ['kugər] s puma m

cough [kɔf] o [kaf] s tos f || tr — **to cough up** arrojar por la boca; (slang) sudar, entregar || intr toser; (artificially, to attract attention) destoserse

cough drop s pastilla para la tos

cough syrup s jarabe m para la tos

could [kud] v aux pude, podía; podría

council ['kaunsəl] s (deliberative or legislative assembly) consejo; (of a municipality) concejo; (eccl) concilio

council·man ['kaunsəlmən] s (pl -men [mən]) concejal m

councilor ['kaunsələr] s consejero

coun·sel ['kaunsəl] s consejo; (advisor) consejero; (consultant) consultor m; (lawyer) abogado consultor; **to keep one's own counsel** no revelar sus intenciones || v (pret & pp -seled o -selled; ger -seling o -selling) tr aconsejar || intr aconsejarse

counselor ['kaunsələr] s consejero; abogado

count [kaunt] s (act of counting) cuenta, recuento; (result of counting) suma, total m; (nobleman) conde m; (charge) (law) cargo; **to take the count** (box) dejarse contar diez || tr contar; **to count off** separar contando; **to count out** no incluir; (sport) declarar vencido || intr contar; (to be worth consideration) valer; **to count for** valer; **to count on** contar con

countable ['kauntəbəl] adj contable

count'-down' s cuenta a cero

countenance ['kauntɪnəns] s cara, rostro, semblante m; (composure) compostura, serenidad; **to keep one's countenance** contenerse; **to lose countenance** conturbarse; **to put out of countenance** avergonzar, confundir || tr aprobar, apoyar, favorecer

counter ['kauntər] adj contrario || adv en el sentido opuesto; **counter to a** contrapelo de || s contador m; (piece of wood or metal for keeping score) ficha; (board in shop over which business is transacted) mostrador m; (box) contragolpe m || tr oponerse a; contradecir || intr (box) dar un contragolpe; **to counter with** replicar con

coun'ter·act' tr contrarrestar, contrariar

coun'ter·attack' s contraataque m || coun'ter·attack' tr & intr contraatacar

coun'ter·bal'ance s contrabalanza, contrapeso || coun'ter·bal'ance tr contrabalancear, contrapesar

coun'ter·clock'wise' adj & adv en el sentido contrario al de las agujas del reloj

coun'ter·es'pionage s contraespionaje m

counterfeit ['kauntərfɪt] adj contrahecho, falsificado || s contrahechura, falsificación; moneda falsa || tr contrahacer, falsificar

counterfeiter ['kauntər,fɪtər] s contrahacedor m, falsificador m; monedero falso

counterfeit money s moneda falsa

countermand ['kauntər,mænd] o ['kauntər,mand] s contramandato || tr contramandar; hacer volver

CO
CO

coun'ter·march' s contramarcha ‖ intr contramarchar

coun'ter·offen'sive s contraofensiva

coun'ter·pane' s cubrecama

coun'ter·part' s contraparte f; copia, duplicado

coun'ter·plot' s contratreta ‖ v (pret & pp -plotted; ger -plotting) tr complotar contra (la treta de otro u otros)

coun'ter·point' s contrapunto

Counter Reformation s Contrarreforma

coun'ter·rev'olu'sion s contrarrevolución

coun'ter·sign' s contraseña ‖ tr refrendar

coun'ter·sink' v (pret & pp -sunk) tr avellanar

coun'ter·spy' s (pl -spies) contraespía mf

coun'ter·stroke' s contragolpe m

coun'ter·weight' s contrapeso

countess ['kauntɪs] s condesa

countless ['kauntlɪs] adj incontable, innumerable

countrified ['kʌntrɪ͵faɪd] adj campesino, rústico

coun·try ['kʌntri] s (pl -tries) (territory of a nation) país m; (land of one's birth) patria; (not the city) campo

country club s club m campestre

country cousin s isidro

country estate s heredad, hacienda de campo

coun'try·folk' s gente f del campo, campesinos

country gentleman s propietario acomodado de finca rural

country house s casa de campo, quinta

country jake [dʒek] s (coll) patán m

country life s vida rural

country·man ['kʌntrimən] s (pl -men [mən]) compatriota m; campesino

country people s gente f del campo, gente de capa parda

coun'try·side' s campiña

coun'try·wide' adj nacional

country-woman ['kʌntri͵wumən] s (pl -women [͵wɪmɪn]) compatriota f: campesina

coun·ty ['kaunti] s (pl -ties) (small political unit) partido; (domain of a count) condado

county seat s cabeza de partido

coup [ku] s golpe m

coup de grâce [ku də 'grɑs] s puñalada de misericordia, golpe m de gracia

coup d'état [ku de'tɑ] s golpe m de estado

coupé [ku'pe] s cupé m

couple ['kʌpəl] s par m; (man and wife) matrimonio; (two people dancing together) pareja; (elec, mech) par m; (two more or less) (coll) par m ‖ tr acoplar, juntar, unir ‖ intr juntarse, unirse

coupler ['kʌplər] s (rr) enganche m

couplet ['kʌplɪt] s copla, pareado

coupon [ku'pɑn] o [kju'pɑn] s (of a bond) cupón m; (piece detached from larger piece) talón m

courage ['kʌrɪdʒ] s valor m, ánimo; firmeza, resolución; to have the courage of one's convictions ajustarse abiertamente con su conciencia; to pluck up courage hacer de tripas corazón

courageous [kə'redʒəs] adj valiente, animoso

courier ['kʌrɪ·ər] o ['kurɪ·ər] s estafeta, mensajero; guía m

course [kors] s (onward movement) curso; (of a ship) derrota, rumbo; (of time) transcurso; (of events) marcha; (in school) asignatura, curso; (of a meal) plato; campo de golf; (mas) hilada; in the course of en el decurso de; of course por supuesto, naturalmente

court [kort] s (of justice) tribunal m; (of a king) corte f; (open space enclosed by a building) atrio, patio; (for tennis) cancha, pista; to pay court to hacer la corte a ‖ tr cortejar; buscar, solicitar

courteous ['kʌrtɪ·əs] adj cortés

courtesan ['kʌrtɪzən] o ['kortɪzən] s cortesana

courte·sy ['kʌrtɪsi] s (pl -sies) cortesía

court'house' s palacio de justicia

courtier ['kortɪ·ər] s cortesano, palaciego

court jester s bufón m

court·ly ['kortli] adj (comp -lier; super -liest) cortés, cortesano; (pertaining to the court) cortesano

court'-mar'tial s (pl courts-martial) consejo de guerra ‖ v (pret & pp -tialed o -tialled; ger -tialing o -tialling) tr someter a consejo de guerra

court plaster s tafetán m inglés

court'room' s sala de justicia, tribunal m

courtship ['kortʃɪp] s cortejo, galanteo; noviazgo

court'yard' s atrio, patio

cousin ['kʌzɪn] s primo

cove [kov] s cala, ensenada

covenant ['kʌvənənt] s convenio, pacto; contrato; (Bib) alianza ‖ tr & intr pactar

cover ['kʌvər] s cubierta; (of a magazine) portada; (place for one person at table) cubierto; (for a bed) cobertor m; to take cover ocultarse; under cover bajo cubierto, bajo techado; oculto; disfrazado; under cover of (e.g., the night) a cubierto de; so capa de; under separate cover bajo cubierta separada, por separado ‖ tr cubrir; (to line, to coat) recubrir, revestir; recorrer (cierta distancia); cubrirse (la cabeza); tapar (una olla) ‖ intr cubrirse

coverage ['kʌvərɪdʒ] s (amount or space covered) alcance m; (of news) reportaje m; (funds to meet liabilities) cobertura

coveralls ['kʌvər͵ɔlz] s mono

cover charge s precio del cubierto

covered ['kʌvərd] adj cubierto; (wire) forrado; (bridge) cubierto

covered wagon s carromato

cover girl s (coll) muchacha hermosa en la portada de una revista

covering ['kʌvərɪŋ] s cubierta, envoltura

covert ['kʌvərt] adj disimulado, secreto

cov'er·up' s efugio, subterfugio

covet ['kʌvɪt] tr codiciar

covetous ['kʌvɪtəs] adj codicioso

covetousness ['kʌvɪtəsnɪs] s codicia

covey ['kʌvɪ] s (brood) nidada; (in flight) bandada; corro, grupo

cow [kau] s vaca || tr acobardar, intimidar

coward ['kau·ərd] s cobarde mf

cowardice ['kau·ərdɪs] s cobardía

cowardly ['kau·ərdlɪ] adj cobarde || adv cobardemente

cow'bell' s cencerro

cow'boy' s vaquero; gaucho (Arg)

cowcatcher ['kau,kætʃər] s quitapiedras m, rastrillo; trompa (Col, Chile)

cower ['kau·ər] intr agacharse

cow'herd' s vaquero, pastor m de ganado vacuno

cow'hide' s cuero; (whip) zurriago || tr zurriagar

cowl [kaul] s capucha, cogulla; (aer) cubierta del motor; (aut) cubretablero, bóveda

cow'lick' s mechón m, remolino (pelos que se levantan sobre la frente)

cowpox ['kau ,pɑks] s vacuna

coxcomb ['kɑks ,kom] s petimetre m, mequetrefe m

coxswain ['kɑksən] o ['kɑk ,swen] s timonel m; contramaestre m

coy [kɔɪ] adj recatado, modesto; coquetón

co·zy ['kozi] adj (comp -zier; super -ziest) cómodo || s (pl -zies) cubretetera

cp. abbr **compare**

c.p. abbr **candle power**

C.P.A. abbr **certified public accountant**

cpd. abbr **compound**

cr. abbr **credit, creditor**

crab [kræb] s cangrejo; (grouch) cascarrabias mf

crab apple s manzana silvestre

crabbed ['kræbɪd] adj avinagrado, ceñudo

crab grass s garranchuelo

crab louse s ladilla

crack [kræk] adj (coll) de primera clase; (shot) (coll) certero || s grieta, hendidura; (noise) crujido, estallido; (coll) instante m, momento; (joke) (slang) chiste m; **at the crack of dawn** al romper el alba || tr agrietar, hender; chasquear (un látigo); abrir (una caja fuerte) por la fuerza; cascar (nueces); descifrar (un código); (slang) decir (un chiste); (slang) descubrir (un secreto); **to crack a smile** (slang) sonreír; **to crack up**

(coll) alabar, elogiar || intr agrietarse; crujir; cascarse (la voz de una persona); enloquecerse; ceder, someterse; **to crack up** fracasar; perder la salud; estrellarse (un avión)

cracked [krækt] adj agrietado; (ice) picado; (coll) mentecato, loco

cracker ['krækər] s galleta

crack'le·ware' s grietado

crack'pot' adj & s (slang) excéntrico, tarambana mf

crack'-up' s fracaso; colisión; derrota; (aer) aterrizaje violento; (coll) colapso

cradle ['kredəl] s cuna; (of handset) horquilla || tr acunar

cra'dle·song' s canción de cuna, arrullo

craft [kræft] o [krɑft] s arte m, arte manual; astucia, maña; nave f || spl naves

craftiness ['kræftɪnɪs] o ['krɑftɪnɪs] s astucia

crafts·man ['kræftsmən] o ['krɑftsmən] s (pl -men [mən]) artesano; artista m

craftsmanship ['kræftsmən ,ʃɪp] o ['krɑftsmən ,ʃɪp] s artesanía

craft·y ['kræftɪ] o ['krɑftɪ] adj (comp -ier; super -iest) astuto, mañoso

crag [kræg] s peñasco, despeñadero

cram [kræm] v (pret & pp crammed; ger cramming) tr atascar, atracar, embutir; (coll) aprender apresuradamente || intr atracarse; (to study hard) (coll) empollar

cramp [kræmp] s (metal bar) grapa, laña; (clamp) abrazadera; (painful contraction of muscle) calambre m; **cramps** retortijón m de tripas || tr engrapar, lañar; apretar; dar calambre a

cranber·ry ['kræn ,bɛrɪ] s (pl -ries) arándano agrio

crane [kren] s (bird) grulla; (derrick) grúa || tr estirar (el cuello) || intr estirar el cuello

crani·um ['krenɪ·əm] s (pl -a [ə]) cráneo

crank [kræŋk] s manivela, manubrio; (coll) estrafalario || tr hacer girar (el motor) con la manivela

crank'case' s caja de cigüeñal, cárter m del cigüeñal

crank'shaft' s cigüeñal m

crank·y ['kræŋkɪ] adj (comp -ier; super -iest) malhumorado; (queer) estrafalario

cran·ny ['krænɪ] s (pl -nies) hendidura, grieta, rendija

crape [krep] s crespón m; crespón fúnebre, crespón negro

crape'hang'er s (slang) aguafiestas mf

craps [kræps] s juego de dados; **to shoot craps** jugar a los dados

crash [kræʃ] s caída, desplome m; colisión, choque m; estallido, estrépito; fracaso; crac financiero; lienzo grueso; (aer) aterrizaje violento || tr romper con estrépito, estrellar; **to crash a party** (slang) asistir a una fiesta sin invitación; **to crash the gate**

(slang) colarse de gorra ‖ *intr* caer, desplomarse; romperse con estrépito, estallar; (*in business*) quebrar; aterrizar violentamente, estrellarse (*un avión*); **to crash into** chocar con

crash dive *s* sumersión instantánea (*de submarino*)

crash landing *s* aterrizaje violento

crash program *s* programa intensivo

crass [kræs] *adj* espeso, tosco; (*ignorance, mistake*) craso

crate [kret] *s* (*box made of slats*) jaula; (*basket*) banasta, cuévano ‖ *tr* embalar en jaula, embalar con listones

crater ['kretər] *s* cráter *m*

cravat [krə'væt] *s* corbata

crave [krev] *tr* anhelar, ansiar; pedir (*indulgencia*) ‖ *intr* — **to crave for** anhelar, ansiar; pedir con insistencia

craven ['krevən] *adj* & *s* cobarde *mf*

craving ['krevɪŋ] *s* anhelo, ansia, deseo ardiente

craw [krɔ] *s* buche *m*

crawl [krɔl] *s* arrastre *m;* gateado ‖ *intr* reptar, arrastrarse, gatear; (*to have a feeling of insects on skin*) hormiguear; **to crawl along** andar paso a paso; **to crawl up** trepar

crayon ['kre·ən] *s* creyón *m*

craze [krez] *s* boga, moda; locura, manía ‖ *tr* enloquecer

cra·zy ['krezi] *adj* (*comp* -**zier;** *super* -**ziest**) loco; (*rickety*) desvencijado; achacoso, débil; **crazy as a bedbug** (slang) loco de atar; **to be crazy about** (coll) estar loco por; **to drive crazy** volver loco

crazy bone *s* hueso de la alegría

creak [krik] *s* crujido, rechinamiento ‖ *intr* crujir, rechinar

creak·y ['kriki] *adj* (*comp* -**ier;** *super* -**iest**) crujidero, rechinador

cream [krim] *s* crema; (*e.g., of society*) crema, nata y flor ‖ *tr* desnatar (*la leche*)

creamer·y ['kriməri] *s* (*pl* -**ies**) mantequería, quesería, lechería

cream puff *s* bollo de crema

cream separator *s* desnatadora

cream·y ['krimi] *adj* (*comp* -**ier;** *super* -**iest**) cremoso

crease [kris] *s* arruga, pliegue *m;* (*in trousers*) raya ‖ *tr* arrugar, plegar

create [kri'et] *tr* crear

creation [kri'eʃən] *s* creación

creative [kri'etɪv] *adj* creativo

creator [kri'etər] *s* creador *m*

creature ['kritʃər] *s* criatura; (*being, strange being*) ente *m;* animal *m*

credence ['kridəns] *s* creencia; **to give credence to** dar fe a

credentials [krɪ'denʃəlz] *spl* credenciales *fpl*

credible ['kredɪbəl] *adj* creíble

credit ['kredɪt] *s* crédito; **to take credit for** atribuirse el mérito de ‖ *tr* acreditar; **to credit a person with** atribuirle a una persona el mérito de

creditable ['kredɪtəbəl] *adj* honorable, estimable

credit card *s* tarjeta de crédito

creditor ['kredɪtər] *s* acreedor *m*

cre·do ['krido] o ['kredo] *s* (*pl* -**dos**) credo

credulous ['kredʒələs] *adj* crédulo

creed [krid] *s* credo

creek [krik] *s* arroyo, riachuelo

creep [krip] *v* (*pret* & *pp* **crept** [krept]) *intr* arrastrarse; (*on all fours*) gatear; (*to climb*) trepar; (*with a sensation of insects*) hormiguear; **to creep up on** acercarse insensiblemente a

creeper ['kripər] *s* planta rastrera, planta trepadora

creeping ['kripɪŋ] *adj* lento, progresivo; (*plant*) rastrero ‖ *s* arrastramiento

cremate ['krimet] *tr* incinerar

cremation [krɪ'meʃən] *s* cremación, incineración

cremato·ry ['krimə,tori] *adj* crematorio ‖ *s* (*pl* -**ries**) crematorio

crème de menthe [krem də 'mãt] *s* crema de menta

Creole ['kri·ol] *adj* & *s* criollo

crescent ['kresənt] *s* (*moon in first or last quarter*) creciente *f* de la luna; (*shape of moon in either of these phases*) media luna; panecillo (*en forma de media luna*)

cress [kres] *s* mastuerzo

crest [krest] *s* cresta

crestfallen ['krest,fɔlən] *adj* cabizbajo

Cretan ['kritən] *adj* & *s* cretense *mf*

Crete [krit] *s* Creta

cretonne [krɪ'tɑn] *s* cretona

crevice ['krevɪs] *s* grieta

crew [kru] *s* equipo; (*of a ship*) dotación, tripulación; (*group, esp. of armed men*) banda, cuadrilla

crew cut *s* corte *m* de pelo a cepillo

crib [krɪb] *s* pesebre *m;* camita de niño; (coll) plagio; (*student's pony*) (coll) chuleta ‖ *v* (*pret* & *pp* **cribbed;** *ger* **cribbing**) *tr* & *intr* (coll) hurtar

cricket ['krɪkɪt] *s* (ent) grillo; (sport) cricquet *m;* (coll) juego limpio

crier ['kraɪ·ər] *s* pregonero

crime [kraɪm] *s* crimen *m,* delito

criminal ['krɪmɪnəl] *adj* & *s* criminal *mf*

criminal code *s* código penal

criminal law *s* derecho penal

criminal negligence *s* imprudencia temeraria

crimp [krɪmp] *s* rizado, rizo; **to put a crimp in** (coll) estorbar, impedir ‖ *tr* rizar

crimple ['krɪmpəl] *tr* arrugar, rizar ‖ *intr* arrugarse, rizarse

crimson ['krɪmzən] *adj* & *s* carmesí *m* ‖ *intr* enrojecerse

cringe [krɪndʒ] *intr* arrastrarse, reptar, encogerse

crinkle ['krɪŋkəl] *s* arruga, pliegue *m;* (*in the water*) rizo u onda ‖ *tr* arrugar, plegar ‖ *intr* arrugarse

cripple ['krɪpəl] *s* zopo, lisiado ‖ *tr* lisiar, estropear; dañar, perjudicar

cri·sis ['kraɪsɪs] *s* (*pl* -**ses** [siz]) crisis *f*

crisp [krɪsp] *adj* frágil, quebradizo; (*air*, *weather*) refrescante; decisivo

criteri·on [kraɪ'tɪrɪ-ən] *s* (*pl* -**a** [ə]) u -**ons**) criterio

critic ['krɪtɪk] *s* crítico; (*faultfinder*) criticón *m*

critical ['krɪtɪkəl] *adj* crítico; (*fault-finding*) criticón

criticism ['krɪtɪ,sɪzəm] *s* crítica

criticize ['krɪtɪ,saɪz] *tr* & *intr* criticar

critique [krɪ'tik] *s* (*art of criticism*) crítica; ensayo crítico

croak [krok] *s* (*of raven*) graznido; canto de ranas ‖ *intr* graznar (*el cuervo*); croar (*la rana*); (*morir*) (slang) reventar

Croat [krot] *s* (*native or inhabitant*) croata *mf*; (*language*) croata *m*

Croatian [kro'eʃən] *adj* & *mf* croata *mf*

cro·chet [kro'ʃe] *s* croché *m* ‖ *v* (*pret* & *pp* -**cheted** ['ʃed]); *ger* -**cheting** ['ʃe-ɪŋ] *tr* trabajar con aguja de gancho ‖ *intr* hacer croché

crocheting [kro'ʃe-ɪŋ] *s* labor *f* de ganchillo

crochet needle *s* aguja de gancho

crock [krak] *s* cacharro, vasija de barro cocido

crockery ['krakərɪ] *s* loza

crocodile ['krakə,daɪl] *s* cocodrilo

crocodile tears *spl* lágrimas de cocodrilo

crocus ['krokəs] *s* azafrán *m*, croco

crone [kron] *s* vieja acartonada, vieja arrugada

cro·ny ['kronɪ] *s* (*pl* -**nies**) compinche *mf*

crook [krʊk] *s* gancho, garfio; curva; (*of shepherd*) cayado; (coll) fullero, ladrón *m* ‖ *tr* encorvar; (slang) empinar (*el codo*) ‖ *intr* encorvarse

crooked ['krʊkɪd] *adj* encorvado, torcido; (*person or his conduct*) torcido; **to go crooked** (coll) torcerse

croon [krun] *intr* cantar con voz suave, cantar con melancolía exagerada

crooner ['krunər] *s* cantor de voz suave, cantor melancólico

crop [krap] *s* cosecha; (*head of hair*) cabellera; cabello corto; (*of a bird*) buche *m*; (*whip*) látigo; (*of appointments*, *promotions*, *heroes*, *etc.*) hornada ‖ *v* (*pret* & *pp* **cropped**) *ger* **cropping**) *tr* desmochar (*un árbol*); desorejar (*a un animal*); esquilar, trasquilar ‖ *intr* — **to crop out** o **up** aflorar; asomar, dejarse ver, manifestarse inesperadamente

crop dusting *s* aerofumigación, fumigación aérea

croquet [kro'ke] *s* crocquet *m*

croquette [kro'ket] *s* croqueta

crosier ['kroʒər] *s* báculo pastoral, cayado

cross [krɔs] o [kras] *adj* transversal, travieso; (*breed*) cruzado; malhumorado, enfadado ‖ *s* cruz *f*; (*of races*, *of two roads*) cruce *m*; **to take the cross** (*to join a crusade*) cruzarse ‖ *tr* cruzar; (*to oppose*)

contrariar, frustrar; **to cross off** u **out** borrar; **to cross oneself** hacerse la señal de la cruz; **to cross one's mind** ocurrírsele a uno; **to cross one's t's** poner travesaño a las tes, poner el palo a las tes ‖ *intr* cruzar; cruzarse; **to cross over** atravesar de un lado a otro

cross'bones' *spl* huesos cruzados (*símbolo de la muerte*)

cross'bow' *s* ballesta

cross'breed' *v* (*pret* & *pp* -**bred** [,bred]) *tr* cruzar (*animales o plantas*)

cross'coun'try *adj* a campo traviesa; a través del país

cross'cur'rent *s* contracorriente *f*; (fig) tendencia encontrada

cross'-exam'i·na'tion *s* interrogatorio riguroso; (law) repregunta

cross'-ex·am'ine *tr* interrogar rigurosamente; (law) repreguntar

cross-eyed ['krɔs,aɪd] o ['kras,aɪd] *adj* bisojo, bizco, ojituerto

crossing ['krɔsɪŋ] o ['krasɪŋ] *s* (*of lines*, *streets*, *etc.*) cruce *m*; (*of the ocean*) travesía; (*of a river*) vado; (rr) crucero, paso a nivel

crossing gate *s* barrera, barrera de paso a nivel

crossing point *s* punto de cruce

cross'patch' *s* (coll) gruñón *m*

cross'piece' *s* travesaño

cross reference *s* contrarreferencia, remisión

cross'road' *s* vía transversal; **crossroads** encrucijada, cruce *m*; **at the crossroads** en el momento crítico

cross section *s* corte *m* transversal; (fig) sección representativa

cross street *s* calle traviesa, calle de travesía

cross'word' puzzle *s* crucigrama *m*

crotch [kratʃ] *s* (*forked piece*) horcajadura, bifurcación; (*between legs*) entrepierna, bragadura, horcajadura

crotchety ['kratʃɪtɪ] *adj* caprichoso, estrambótico, de mal genio

crouch [krautʃ] *s* posición agachada ‖ *intr* agacharse, acuclillarse

croup [krup] *s* garrotillo, crup *m*; (*of horse*) anca, grupa

croupier ['krupɪ·ər] *s* crupié *m*

crouton ['krutan] *s* corteza de pan

crow [kro] *s* corneja, grajo, chova; (*cry of the cock*) quiquiriquí *m*; (*crowbar*) alzaprima; **as the crow flies** a vuelo de pájaro; **to eat crow** (coll) cantar la palinodia; **to have a crow to pick with** (coll) tener que habérselas con ‖ *intr* cantar (*el gallo*); jactarse; **to crow over** jactarse de

crow'bar' *s* alzaprima, pie *m* de cabra

crowd [kraud] *s* gentío, multitud; (*flock of people*) caterva, tropel *m*; (*mob*, *common people*) populacho, vulgo; (*clique*, *set*) corrillo, grupo ‖ *tr* apiñar, apretar, atestar; (*to push*) empujar ‖ *intr* apiñarse, apretarse, atestarse; (*to mill around*) arremolinarse

crowded ['kraʊdɪd] *adj* atestado, concurrido

crown [kraʊn] *s* corona; *(of hat)* copa ‖ *tr* coronar; *(checkers)* coronar; *(slang)* golpear en la cabeza

crowned head *s* testa coronada

crown prince *s* príncipe heredero

crown princess *s* princesa heredera

crow's'-foot' *s (pl* -feet') pata de gallo

crow's'-nest' *s* (naut) cofa de vigía, torre *f* de vigía

crucial ['kruʃəl] *adj* crucial; difícil, penoso

crucible ['krusɪbəl] *s* crisol *m*

crucifix ['krusɪfɪks] *s* crucifijo

crucifixion [,krusɪ'fɪkʃən] *s* crucifixión

cruci·fy ['krusɪ,faɪ] *v (pret & pp* -fied) *tr* crucificar

crude [krud] *adj (raw, unrefined)* crudo; *(lacking culture)* grosero, tosco; *(unfinished)* basto, sin labrar

crudi·ty ['krudɪti] *s (pl* -ties) crudeza; grosería, tosquedad; bastedad

cruel ['kru·əl] *adj* cruel

cruel·ty ['kru·əlti] *s (pl* -ties) crueldad

cruet ['kru·ɪt] *s* ampolleta

cruet stand *s* angarillas, vinagreras

cruise [kruz] *s* viaje *m* por mar; (aer, naut) crucero ‖ *tr* (naut) cruzar ‖ *intr* cruzar; (coll) andar de un lado a otro

cruiser ['kruzər] *s* (nav) crucero

cruising ['kruzɪŋ] *adj* de crucero ‖ *s* (aer, naut) crucero

cruising radius *s* autonomía

cruller ['krʌlər] *s* buñuelo

crumb [krʌm] *s* migaja; *(soft part of bread)* miga; *(given to a beggar)* mendrugo ‖ *tr* desmigar *(el pan)*; (culin) empanar, cubrir con pan rallado; limpiar *(la mesa)* de migajas ‖ *intr* desmigarse, desmenuzarse

crumble ['krʌmbəl] *tr* desmenuzar ‖ *intr* desmenuzarse; *(to fall to pieces gradually)* desmoronarse

crum·my ['krʌmi] *adj (comp* -mier; *super* -miest) (slang) desaseado, sucio; (slang) de mal gusto, de mala muerte

crumple ['krʌmpəl] *tr* arrugar, ajar, chafar ‖ *intr* arrugarse, ajarse

crunch [krʌntʃ] *tr* ronchar, ronzar ‖ *intr* crujir

crusade [kru'sed] *s* cruzada ‖ *intr* hacer una cruzada

crusader [kru'sedər] *s* cruzado

crush [krʌʃ] *s* aplastamiento; *(of people)* aglomeración, bullaje *m;* **to have a crush on** (slang) estar perdido por ‖ *tr* aplastar, machacar, magullar; *(to grind)* moler; bocartear *(el mineral)*; *(to oppress, grieve)* abrumar

crush hat *s* clac *m*

crust [krʌst] *s* corteza; corteza de pan; *(scab)* costra

crustacean [krʌs'teʃən] *s* crustáceo

crustaceous [krʌs'teʃəs] *adj* crustáceo

crust·y ['krʌsti] *adj (comp* -ier; *super* -iest) *(scabby)* costroso; áspero, grosero, rudo

crutch [krʌtʃ] *s* muleta

crux [krʌks] *s* punto capital; enigma *m*

cry [kraɪ] *s (pl* cries) grito; *(weeping)* lloro; *(of peddler)* pregón *m; (of wolf)* aullido; *(of bull)* bramido; **in full cry** en plena persecución; **to have a good cry** desahogarse en lágrimas abundantes ‖ *v (pret & pp* cried) *tr* decir a gritos; *(to announce publicly)* pregonar; **to cry one's eyes o heart out** llorar amargamente; **to cry out** decir a gritos; pregonar ‖ *intr* gritar; *(to weep)* llorar; aullar *(el lobo)*; bramar *(el toro)*; **to cry for** clamar por; **to cry for joy** llorar de alegría; **to cry out** clamar; **to cry out against** clamar contra; **to cry out for** clamar, clamar por

cry'ba'by *s (pl* -bies) llorón *m*, llorona, lloraduelos *mf*

crypt [krɪpt] *s* cripta

cryptic(al) ['krɪptɪk(əl)] *adj* enigmático, misterioso

crystal ['krɪstəl] *s* cristal *m*

crystal ball *s* bola de cristal

crystalline ['krɪstəlɪn] o ['krɪstə,laɪn] *adj* cristalino

crystallize ['krɪstə,laɪz] *tr* cristalizar ‖ *intr* cristalizarse

C.S. *abbr* **Christian Science, Civil Service**

ct. *abbr* **cent**

cu. *abbr* **cubic**

cub [kʌb] *s* cachorro

Cuban ['kjubən] *adj & s* cubano

cubbyhole ['kʌbɪ,hol] *s* chiribitil *m*

cube [kjub] *adj (root)* cúbico ‖ *s* cubo; *(of ice)* cubito ‖ *tr* cubicar

cubic ['kjubɪk] *adj* cúbico

cub reporter *s* (coll) reportero novato

cuckold ['kʌkəld] *adj & s* cornudo ‖ *tr* encornudar

cuckoo ['kʊku] *adj* (slang) mentecato, loco ‖ *s* cuclillo, cuco; *(call of cuckoo)* cucú *m*

cuckoo clock *s* reloj *m* de cuclillo

cucumber ['kjukʌmbər] *s* pepino

cud [kʌd] *s* bolo alimenticio; **to chew the cud** rumiar

cuddle ['kʌdəl] *s* abrazo cariñoso ‖ *tr* abrazar con cariño ‖ *intr* estar abrazados, arrimarse cariñosamente

cudg·el ['kʌdʒəl] *s* garrote *m*, porra; **to take up the cudgels for** salir a la defensa de ‖ *v (pret & pp* -eled o -elled; *ger* -eling o -elling) *tr* apalear, aporrear

cue [kju] *s* señal *f*, indicación; *(hint)* indirecta; *(rôle)* papel *m; (rod used in billiards)* taco; *(of hair)* coleta; *(of people in line)* cola; (theat) apunte *m*

cuff [kʌf] *s (of shirt)* puño; *(of trousers)* doblez *f*, vuelta; *(blow)* bofetada ‖ *tr* abofetear

cuff links *spl* gemelos

cuirass [kwɪ'ræs] *s* coraza

cuisine [kwɪ'zin] *s* cocina *(arte culinario)*

culinary ['kjulɪ,neri] *adj* culinario

cull [kʌl] *tr (to choose, pick)* entresa-

car, escoger; (to gather, pluck) coger, recoger
culm [kʌlm] s (coal dust) cisco; (stalk
of grasses) caña, tallo
culminate ['kʌlmɪ‚net] intr culminar;
to culminate in conducir a, terminar
en
culpable ['kʌlpəbəl] adj culpable
culprit ['kʌlprɪt] s acusado; reo
cult [kʌlt] s culto; secta
cultivate ['kʌltɪ‚vet] tr cultivar
cultivated ['kʌltɪ‚vetɪd] adj culto, cultivado
cultivation [‚kʌltɪ'veʃən] s (of the
land, the arts, one's memory, etc.)
cultivo; (refinement) cultura
culture ['kʌltʃər] s cultura
cultured ['kʌltʃərd] adj culto
culvert ['kʌlvərt] s alcantarilla
cumbersome ['kʌmbərsəm] adj incómodo, molesto; (clumsy) pesado, inmanejable
cunning ['kʌnɪŋ] adj (sly) astuto;
(clever) hábil; (attractive) gracioso,
mono ‖ s astucia; habilidad, destreza
cup [kʌp] s taza; (of thermometer)
cubeta; (mach) vaso de engrase;
(sport) copa; (of sorrow) (fig) copa;
in one's cups borracho ‖ v (pret &
pp **cupped**; ger **cupping**) tr ahuecar
dando forma de taza o copa a; poner
ventosa a
cupboard ['kʌbərd] s alacena, aparador m, armario
cupidity [kju'pɪdɪti] s codicia
cupola ['kjupələ] s cúpula
cur [kʌr] s perro mestizo, perro de
mala raza; (despicable fellow) canalla m
curate ['kjurɪt] s cura m
curative ['kjurətɪv] adj curativo ‖ s
curativa
curator [kju'retər] s conservador m
curb [kʌrb] s (of sidewalk) encintado;
(of well) brocal m; (of bit) barbada;
(market) bolsín m; (check, restraint)
freno; (vet) corva ‖ tr contener, refrenar
curb'stone' s piedra de encintado; brocal m de pozo
curd [kʌrd] s cuajada ‖ tr cuajar ‖
intr cuajarse
curdle ['kʌrdəl] tr cuajar; **to curdle
the blood** horrorizar ‖ intr cuajar
cure [kjur] s cura, curación ‖ tr curar
‖ intr curar; curarse
cure'-all' s sanalotodo
curfew ['kʌrfju] s queda, cubrefuego;
toque m de queda
curi·o ['kjurɪ‚o] s (pl -os) curiosidad
curiosi·ty [‚kjurɪ'ɑsɪti] s (pl -ties)
curiosidad
curious ['kjurɪ·əs] adj curioso
curl [kʌrl] s bucle m, rizo; (spiral-
shaped curl) tirabuzón m; (of smoke)
espiral f; (curling) rizado ‖ tr encrespar, ensortijar, rizar; (to coil, to
roll up) arrollar; fruncir (los labios)
‖ intr encresparse, ensortijarse,
rizarse; arrollarse; **to curl up** arrollarse; (in bed) encogerse; (to break
up, collapse) (coll) desplomarse

curlicue ['kʌrlɪ‚kju] s ringorrango
curling iron s rizador m, maquinilla de
rizar
curl'pa'per s torcida, papelito para
rizar el pelo
curl·y ['kʌrli] adj (comp -ier; super
-iest) crespo, rizo
curmudgeon [kər'mʌdʒən] s cicatero,
tacaño, erizo
currant ['kʌrənt] s pasa de Corinto;
(Ribes alpinum) calderilla
curren·cy ['kʌrənsi] s (pl -cies) moneda corriente, dinero en circulación; uso corriente
current ['kʌrənt] adj corriente ‖ s corriente f; (elec) corriente f
current account s cuenta corriente
current events spl actualidades, sucesos
de actualidad
curricu·lum [kə'rɪkjələm] s (pl -lums o
-la [lə]) plan m de estudios
cur·ry ['kʌri] s (pl -ries) cari m ‖ v
(pret & pp -ried) tr curtir (las pieles); almohazar (el caballo); **to curry
favor** procurar complacer
cur'ry-comb' s almohaza ‖ tr almohazar
curse [kʌrs] s maldición; (profane
oath) reniego, voto; (evil, misfortune) calamidad ‖ tr maldecir ‖ intr
jurar, echar votos
cursed ['kʌrsɪd] o [kʌrst] adj maldito,
aborrecible
cursive ['kʌrsɪv] adj cursivo ‖ s cursiva
cursory ['kʌrsəri] adj apresurado,
rápido, superficial, de paso
curt [kʌrt] adj áspero, brusco; corto,
conciso
curtail [kər'tel] tr acortar, abreviar,
cercenar
curtain ['kʌrtən] s cortina; (theat)
telón m; **to draw the curtain** correr
la cortina; **to drop the curtain**
(theat) bajar el telón ‖ tr encortinar;
separar con cortina; cubrir, ocultar
curtain call s llamada a la escena para
recibir aplausos
curtain raiser ['rezər] s (theat) pieza
preliminar
curtain ring s anilla
curtain rod s riel m
curt·sy ['kʌrtsi] s (pl -sies) cortesía,
reverencia ‖ v (pret & pp -sied) intr
hacer una cortesía
curve [kʌrv] s curva ‖ tr encorvar ‖
intr encorvarse; volver, virar
curved [kʌrvd] adj curvo, encorvado;
(crooked) combo
cushion ['kuʃən] s cojín m, almohada;
(of billiard table) baranda ‖ tr
amortiguar
cusp [kʌsp] s cúspide f
cuspidor ['kʌspɪ‚dɔr] s escupidera
custard ['kʌstərd] s flan m, natillas
custodian [kəs'todɪ·ən] s custodio; (of
a house or building) casero
custo·dy ['kʌstədi] s (pl -dies) custodia; **in custody** en prisión; **to take
into custody** prender
custom ['kʌstəm] s costumbre; (cus-

cr
cu

tomers) parroquia, clientela; **customs** aduana; derechos de aduana
customary [ˈkʌstə,mɛri] *adj* acostumbrado, de costumbre
cus'tom-built' *adj* hecho por encargo, fuera de serie
customer [ˈkʌstəmər] *s* parroquiano, cliente *mf;* (*of a café or restaurant*) consumidor *m;* (coll) individuo, sujeto, tipo
cus'tom•house' *adj* aduanero ‖ *s* aduana
cus'tom-made' *adj* hecho a la medida
customs clearance *s* despacho de aduana
customs officer *s* aduanero
custom tailor *s* sastre *m* a la medida
custom work *s* trabajo hecho a la medida
cut [kʌt] *s* corte *m;* (*piece cut off*) tajada; (*wound*) cuchillada; (*for a canal, highway, etc.*) desmonte *m;* (*shortest way*) atajo; (*in prices, wages, etc.*) reducción; (*of a garment*) corte *m,* hechura; (*in winnings, earnings, etc.*) parte *f;* (typ) estampa, grabado; (tennis) golpe *m* cortante; (*absence from school*) (coll) falta de asistencia; (*snub*) (coll) desaire *m;* (coll) palabra hiriente ‖ *v* (*pret & pp* **cut;** *ger* **cutting**) *tr* cortar; practicar (*un agujero*)*;* reducir (*gastos*)*;* capar, castrar; desleír, diluir; (coll) ausentarse de, faltar a (*la clase*); (coll) desairar; (coll) herir; **to cut down** cortar; derribar cortando; castigar (*gastos*); **to cut off** cortar; desheredar; amputar (*una pierna*); (elec) cortar (*la corriente, la ignición*); cerrar (*el carburador*); **to cut open** abrir cortando; **to cut out** cortar; sacar cortando; labrar; suprimir, omitir; (*to take the place of*) desbancar; soplar (*la dama a un rival*); (slang) dejarse de (*disparates*); **to cut short** terminar de repente; interrumpir, chafar; **to cut teeth** endentecer; **to cut up** desmenuzar, despedazar; criticar severamente; (coll) afligir ‖ *intr* cortar; cortarse; salir (*los dientes*); (coll) fumarse la clase; **to cut in** entrar de repente; interrumpir; (*in a dance*) cortar o separar la pareja; **to cut under** vender a menor precio que; **to cut up** (slang) travesear, hacer travesuras; (slang) jaranear
cut-and-dried [ˈkʌtənˈdraɪd] *adj* dispuesto de antemano; monótono, poco interesante
cutaway coat [ˈkʌtə,we] *s* chaqué *m*
cut'back' *s* reducción; discontinuación, incumplimiento; (mov) retorno a una época anterior
cute [kjut] *adj* (coll) mono, monono; (coll) astuto, listo
cut glass *s* cristal tallado
cuticle [ˈkjutɪkəl] *s* cutícula
cutlass [ˈkʌtləs] *s* alfanje *m*
cutler [ˈkʌtlər] *s* cuchillero
cutlery [ˈkʌtləri] *s* cuchillería; (*knives, forks, and spoons*) cubierto
cutlet [ˈkʌtlɪt] *s* chuleta; croqueta
cut'out' *s* (*design to be cut out*) recortado; (aut) escape *m* libre, válvula de escape libre
cut'-rate' *adj* de precio reducido
cutter [ˈkʌtər] *s* cortador *m;* (*machine*) cortadora; (naut) escampavía
cut'throat' *adj* asesino; implacable ‖ *s* asesino
cutting [ˈkʌtɪŋ] *adj* cortante; hiriente, mordaz ‖ *s* corte *m;* (*from a newspaper*) recorte *m;* (hort) esqueje *m*
cutting edge *s* canto de corte
cuttlefish [ˈkʌtəl,fɪʃ] *s* jibia
cut'wa'ter *s* espolón *m,* tajamar *m*
cwt. *abbr* **hundredweight**
cyanamide [saɪˈænə,maɪd] *s* cianamida; cianamida de calcio
cyanide [ˈsaɪ•ə,naɪd] *s* cianuro
cycle [ˈsaɪkəl] *s* ciclo; bicicleta; (*of an internal-combustion engine*) tiempo; (phys) período ‖ *intr* montar en bicicleta
cyclic(al) [ˈsaɪklɪk(əl)] o [ˈsɪklɪk(əl)] *adj* cíclico
cyclone [ˈsaɪklon] *s* ciclón *m*
cyl. *abbr* **cylinder, cylindrical**
cylinder [ˈsɪlɪndər] *s* cilindro
cylinder block *s* bloque *m* de cilindros
cylinder bore *s* alesaje *m*
cylinder head *s* (*of steam engine*) tapa del cilindro; (*of gas engine*) culata del cilindro
cylindric(al) [sɪˈlɪndrɪk(əl)] *adj* cilíndrico
cymbal [ˈsɪmbəl] *s* címbalo, platillo
cynic [ˈsɪnɪk] *adj & s* cínico
cynical [ˈsɪnɪkəl] *adj* cínico
cynicism [ˈsɪnɪ,sɪzəm] *s* cinismo
cynosure [ˈsaɪnə,ʃur] o [ˈsɪnə,ʃur] *s* blanco de las miradas; guía, norte *m*
cypress [ˈsaɪprəs] *s* ciprés *m*
Cyprus [ˈsaɪprəs] *s* Chipre *f*
Cyrillic [sɪˈrɪlɪk] *adj* cirílico
Cyrus [ˈsaɪrəs] *s* Ciro
cyst [sɪst] *s* quiste *m*
czar [zɑr] *s* zar *m;* (fig) autócrata *m*
czarina [zɑˈrinə] *s* zarina
Czech [tʃɛk] *adj & s* checo
Czecho-Slovak [ˈtʃɛkoˈslovæk] *adj & s* checoeslovaco o checoslovaco
Czecho-Slovakia [,tʃɛkosloˈvækɪ•ə] *s* Checoeslovaquia o Checoslovaquia

D

D, d [di] cuarta letra del alfabeto inglés

d. *abbr* date, day, dead, degree, delete, diameter, died, dollar, denarius (penny)

D. *abbr* December, Democrat, Duchess, Duke, Dutch

D.A. *abbr* District Attorney

dab [dæb] *s* toque ligero; masa pastosa || *v* (*pret & pp* **dabbed;** *ger* **dabbing**) *tr* tocar ligeramente, frotar suavemente

dabble ['dæbəl] *tr* salpicar || *intr* chapotear; **to dabble in** meterse en; jugar a (*la Bolsa*); especular en (*granos*)

dad [dæd] *s* (coll) papá *m*

dad·dy ['dædɪ] *s* (*pl* **-dies**) (coll) papá *m*

daffodil ['dæfədɪl] *s* narciso trompón

daff·y ['dæfɪ] *adj* (*comp* **-ier;** *super* **-iest**) (coll) chiflado

dagger ['dægər] *s* daga, puñal *m*; (typ) cruz *f*, obelisco; **to look daggers at** apuñalar con la mirada

dahlia ['dæljə] *s* dalia

dai·ly ['deli] *adj* cotidiano, diario || *adv* diariamente || *s* (*pl* **-lies**) diario

dain·ty ['denti] *adj* (*comp* **-tier;** *super* **-tiest**) delicado || *s* (*pl* **-ties**) golosina

dair·y ['dɛri] *s* (*pl* **-ies**) lechería, vaquería

dais ['de·ɪs] *s* estrado

dai·sy ['dezi] *s* (*pl* **-sies**) margarita

dal·ly ['dæli] *v* (*pret & pp* **-lied**) *intr* juguetear, retozar; tardar, malgastar el tiempo

dam [dæm] *s* represa, embalse *m*; (*female quadruped*) madre *f*; (dent) dique *m* || *v* (*pret & pp* **dammed;** *ger* **damming**) *tr* represar, embalsar; cerrar, tapar, obstruir

damage ['dæmɪdʒ] *s* daño, perjuicio; (*to one's reputation*) desdoro; (com) avería; **damages** daños y perjuicios || *tr* dañar, perjudicar; averiar

damascene ['dæmə‚sin] o [‚dæmə'sin] *adj* damasquino || *s* ataujía, damasquinado || *tr* ataujiar, damasquinar

dame [dem] *s* dama, señora; (coll) mujer *f*

damn [dæm] *s* terno; **I don't give a damn** (slang) maldito lo que me importa; **that's not worth a damn** (slang) eso no vale un pito || *tr* condenar (a pena eterna); condenar; maldecir || *intr* maldecir, echar ternos

damnation [dæm'neʃən] *s* damnación; (theol) condenación

damned [dæmd] *adj* condenado (a pena eterna); abominable, detestable || **the damned** los malditos, los condenados (a pena eterna)

damp [dæmp] *adj* húmedo, mojado || *s* humedad; (*firedamp*) grisú *m* || *tr* humedecer, mojar; (*to deaden, muffle*) amortecer, amortiguar; (*to dis-*

courage) abatir, desalentar; (elec) amortiguar (*ondas electromagnéticas*)

dampen ['dæmpən] *tr* humedecer, mojar; amortecer, amortiguar; abatir, desalentar

damper ['dæmpər] *s* (*of chimney*) registro; (*of piano*) apagador *m*, sordina

damsel ['dæmzəl] *s* señorita, muchacha

dance [dæns] o [dɑns] *s* baile *m*, danza || *tr & intr* bailar, danzar

dance band *s* orquesta de jazz

dance floor *s* pista de baile

dance hall *s* salón *m* de baile

dancer ['dænsər] o ['dɑnsər] *s* bailador *m*, danzador *m*; (*professional*) bailarín *m*

dancing partner *s* pareja (de baile)

dandelion ['dændɪ‚laɪ·ən] *s* diente *m* de león

dandruff ['dændrəf] *s* caspa

dan·dy ['dændi] *adj* (*comp* **-dier;** *super* **-diest**) (coll) excelente, magnífico || *s* (*pl* **-dies**) currutaco, petimetre *m*

Dane [den] *s* danés *m*, dinamarqués *m*

danger ['dendʒər] *s* peligro

dangerous ['dendʒərəs] *adj* peligroso

dangle ['dæŋgəl] *tr & intr* colgar flojamente, colgar en el aire

Danish ['denɪʃ] *adj & s* danés *m*, dinamarqués *m*

dank [dæŋk] *adj* húmedo, liento

Danube ['dænjub] *s* Danubio

dapper ['dæpər] *adj* aseado, apuesto

dapple ['dæpəl] *adj* habado, rodado || *tr* motear

dare [dɛr] *s* desafío, reto || *tr* retar; **to dare to** (*to challenge to*) desafiar a || *intr* osar, atreverse; **I dare say** talvez; **to dare to** (*to have the courage to*) atreverse a

dare'dev'il [dɛr'dɛvil] *s* calavera *m*, temerario

daring ['dɛrɪŋ] *adj* atrevido, osado || *s* atrevimiento, osadía

dark [dɑrk] *adj* obscuro; (*in complexion*) moreno; secreto, oculto; (*gloomy*) lóbrego; (*beer*) pardo || *s* obscuridad, tinieblas; noche *f*; **in the dark** a obscuras

Dark Ages *spl* edad media; principios de la edad media

dark-complexioned [‚dɑrkkəm'plɛkʃənd] *adj* moreno

darken ['dɑrkən] *tr* obscurecer; entristecer; cegar || *intr* obscurecerse

dark horse *s* caballo desconocido; candidato nombrado inesperadamente

darkly ['dɑrkli] *adv* obscuramente; secretamente, misteriosamente

dark meat *s* carne *f* del ave que no es la pechuga

darkness ['dɑrknɪs] *s* obscuridad

dark'room' *s* (phot) cuarto obscuro

darling ['dɑrlɪŋ] *adj & s* querido, amado; predilecto

darn [dɑrn] *tr & intr* zurcir; (coll) maldecir

darnel ['dɑrnəl] *s* cizaña
darning ['dɑrnɪŋ] *s* zurcido
darning needle *s* aguja de zurcir
dart [dɑrt] *s* dardo; (*small missile used in a game*) rehilete *m* || *intr* lanzarse, precipitarse; volar como dardo
dash [dæʃ] *s* arranque *m;* (*splash*) rociada; carrera corta; (*spirit*) brío; pequeña cantidad; (*in printing, writing, telegraphy*) raya || *tr* lanzar; estrellar, romper; frustrar (*las esperanzas de uno*); rociar, salpicar; **to dash off** escribir de prisa; **to dash to pieces** hacer añicos || *intr* estrellarse (*las olas del mar*); lanzarse, precipitarse; **to dash by** pasar corriendo; **to dash in** entrar como un rayo
dash′board′ *s* tablero de instrumentos; (*on front or side of vehicle*) guardabarros *m*
dashing ['dæʃɪŋ] *adj* brioso; ostentoso, vistoso || *s* (*of waves*) embate *m*
dastard ['dæstərd] *adj & s* vil *mf,* miserable *mf,* cobarde *mf*
data bank *s* banco de datos
data processing ['detə] *s* tramitación automática de datos
date [det] *s* (*time*) fecha, data; (*palm*) datilera; (*fruit*) dátil *m;* (*appointment*) (coll) cita; **out of date** anticuado, fuera de moda; **to date** hasta la fecha; **under date of** con fecha de || *tr* fechar, datar; (coll) tener cita con || *intr* — **to date from** datar de
date line *s* línea de cambio de fecha
date palm *s* palmera (datilera)
dative ['detɪv] *adj & s* dativo
datum ['detəm] o ['dætəm] *s* (*pl* **data** ['detə] o ['dætə]) dato
daub [dɔb] *s* embadurnamiento || *tr* embadurnar
daughter ['dɔtər] *s* hija
daughter-in-law ['dɔtərɪn ˌlɔ] *s* (*pl* **daughters-in-law**) nuera, hija política
daunt [dɔnt] *tr* asustar, espantar; desanimar, acobardar
dauntless ['dɔntlɪs] *adj* atrevido, intrépido, impávido
dauphin ['dɔfɪn] *s* delfín *m*
davenport ['dævən ˌpɔrt] *s* sofá *m* cama
davit ['dævɪt] *s* (naut) pescante *m,* grúa de bote
daw [dɔ] *s* corneja
dawdle ['dɔdəl] *intr* malgastar el tiempo, haronear
dawn [dɔn] *s* amanecer *m,* alba || *intr* amanecer; despuntar (*el día, la mañana*); empezar a mostrarse; **to dawn on** empezar a hacerse patente a

day [de] *adj* diurno || *s* día *m;* (*of travel, work, worry, etc.*) jornada; (*from noon to noon*) (naut) singladura; **any day now** de un día para otro; **by day** de día; **the day after** el día siguiente; **the day after tomorrow** pasado mañana; **the day before** la víspera; **the day before yesterday** anteayer; **to call it a day** (coll) dejar de trabajar; **to win the day** ganar la jornada

day bed *s* sofá *m* cama
day′break′ *s* amanecer *m*
day coach *s* (rr) coche *m* de viajeros
day′dream′ *s* ensueño || *intr* soñar despierto
day laborer *s* jornalero
day′light′ *s* luz *f* del día; amanecer *m;* **in broad daylight** en pleno día; **to see daylight** comprender; ver el fin de una tarea difícil
day′light′-sav′ing time *s* hora de verano
day nursery *s* guardería infantil
day off *s* asueto
day of reckoning *s* día *m* de ajustar cuentas
day shift *s* turno diurno
day′time′ *adj* diurno || *s* día *m*
daze [dez] *s* aturdimiento; **in a daze** aturdido || *tr* aturdir
dazzle ['dæzəl] *s* deslumbramiento || *tr* deslumbrar
dazzling ['dæzlɪŋ] *adj* deslumbrante
deacon ['dikən] *s* diácono
deaconess ['dikənɪs] *s* diaconisa
dead [dɛd] *adj* muerto; (coll) cansado || *adv* (coll) completamente, muy || *s* — **in the dead of night** en plena noche; **the dead** los muertos; **the dead of winter** lo más frío del invierno
dead beat *s* (slang) gorrón *m;* (slang) holgazán *m*
dead bolt *s* cerrojo dormido
dead calm *s* calma chicha, calmazo
dead center *s* punto muerto
dead′drunk′ *adj* difunto de taberna
deaden ['dɛdən] *tr* amortiguar, amortecer
dead end *s* callejón *m* sin salida
dead′latch′ *s* aldaba dormida
dead′-let′ter office *s* departamento de cartas no reclamadas
dead′line′ *s* línea vedada; fin *m* del plazo
dead′lock′ *s* cerradura dormida; desacuerdo insuperable || *tr* estancar
dead-ly ['dɛdli] *adj* (*comp* **-lier;** *super* **-liest**) mortal; (*sin*) capital; abrumador
dead pan *s* (slang) semblante *m* sin expresión
dead reckoning *s* (naut) estima
dead ringer ['rɪŋər] *s* segunda edición
dead′wood′ *s* leña seca; cosa inútil, gente *f* inútil
deaf [dɛf] *adj* sordo; **to turn a deaf ear** hacerse el sordo, hacer oídos de mercader
deaf and dumb *adj* sordomudo
deafen ['dɛfən] *tr* asordar, ensordecer
deafening ['dɛfənɪŋ] *adj* ensordecedor
deaf′-mute′ *s* sordomudo
deafness ['dɛfnɪs] *s* sordera
deal [dil] *s* negocio, trato; (*of cards*) mano *f;* turno de dar; (*share*) parte *f,* porción; (coll) convenio secreto; **a good deal (of)** o **a great deal (of)** mucho; **to make a great deal of** hacer fiestas a || *v* (*pret & pp* **dealt** [dɛlt]) *tr* asestar (*un golpe*); repartir (*la baraja*) || *intr* negociar, comerciar; intervenir; (*in card games*) ser

mano; **to deal with** entender en; tratar de; tratar con
dealer ['dilər] s comerciante *mf*, concesionario; (*of cards*) repartidor *m*
dean [din] s decano; (eccl) deán *m*
deanship ['din/ɪp] s decanato
dear [dɪr] *adj* (*beloved*) caro; (*expensive*) caro; (*charging high prices*) carero; **dear me!** ¡Dios mío! ‖ *s* querido
dearie ['dɪri] s (coll) queridito
dearth [dʌrθ] s carestía
death [dɛθ] s muerte *f;* **to bleed to death** morir desangrado; **to bore to death** matar de aburrimiento; **to burn to death** morir quemado; **to choke to death** morir atragantado; **to die a violent death** morir vestido; **to freeze to death** morir helado; **to put to death** dar la muerte a; **to shoot to death** matar a tiros; **to stab to death** escabechar; **to starve to death** matar de hambre; morir de hambre
death'bed' s lecho de muerte
death'blow' s golpe *m* mortal
death certificate s fe *f* de óbito, partida de defunción
death house s capilla (*de los reos de muerte*)
deathless ['dɛθlɪs] *adj* inmortal, eterno
deathly ['dɛθli] *adj* mortal, de muerte ‖ *adv* mortalmente; excesivamente
death penalty s pena de muerte
death rate s mortalidad
death rattle s estertor agónico
death ray s rayo mortífero
death warrant s sentencia de muerte; fin *m* de toda esperanza
death'watch' s vela de un difunto; guardia de un reo de muerte
debacle [de'bakəl] s desastre *m*, ruina, derrota; (*in a river*) deshielo
de·bar [dɪ'bar] *v* (*pret & pp* **-barred;** *ger* **-barring**) *tr* excluir; prohibir
debark [dɪ'bark] *tr & intr* desembarcar
debarkation [ˌdibar'keʃən] s (*of passengers*) desembarco; (*of freight*) desembarque *m*
debase [dɪ'bes] *tr* degradar; falsificar
debatable [dɪ'betəbəl] *adj* disputable
debate [dɪ'bet] s debate *m* ‖ *tr* debatir ‖ *intr* debatir; deliberar
debauchee [ˌdebə'ʃi] o [ˌdebə't ʃi] s libertino, disoluto
debauscher·y [dɪ'bɔtʃəri] s (*pl* -ies) libertinaje *m*, crápula *f*
debenture [dɪ'bentʃər] s (*bond*) obligación; (*voucher*) vale *m*
debilitate [dɪ'bɪlɪˌtet] *tr* debilitar
debili·ty [dɪ'bɪlɪti] s (*pl* -ties) debilidad
debit ['debɪt] s debe *m;* (*entry on debit side*) cargo ‖ *tr* adeudar, cargar
debit balance s saldo deudor
debonair [ˌdebə'ner] *adj* alegre; cortés
debris [de'bri] s despojos, ruinas
debt [det] s deuda; **to run into debt** endeudarse, entramparse
debtor ['detər] s deudor *m*
debut [de'bju] o ['debju] s estreno,

debut *m;* **to make one's debut** estrenarse, debutar; ponerse de largo, entrar en sociedad (*una joven*)
debutante [ˌdebju'tɑnt] o ['debjəˌtænt] s joven *f* que se pone de largo
dec. *abbr* **deceased**
decade ['deked] s decenio, década
decadence [dɪ'kedəns] s decadencia
decadent [dɪ'kedənt] *adj & s* decadente *mf*
decanter [dɪ'kæntər] s garrafa
decapitate [dɪ'kæpɪˌtet] *tr* decapitar
decay [dɪ'ke] s (*decline*) decaimiento, descaecimiento; (*rotting*) podredumbre; (*of teeth*) caries *f* ‖ *tr* pudrir ‖ *intr* pudrirse; decaer; cariarse (*los dientes*)
decease [dɪ'sis] s fallecimiento ‖ *intr* fallecer
deceased [dɪ'sist] *adj & s* difunto
deceit [dɪ'sit] s engaño, fraude *m*
deceitful [dɪ'sitfəl] *adj* engañoso, fraudulento
deceive [dɪ'siv] *tr & intr* engañar
decelerate [dɪ'selə ˌret] *tr* desacelerar ‖ *intr* desacelerarse
December [dɪ'sembər] s diciembre *m*
decen·cy ['disənsi] s (*pl* -cies) decencia, honestidad; (*propriety*) conveniencia
decent ['disənt] *adj* decente, honesto; (*proper*) conveniente
decentralize [dɪ'sentrə ˌlaɪz] *tr* descentralizar
deception [dɪ'sepʃən] s engaño
deceptive [dɪ'septɪv] *adj* engañoso
decide [dɪ'saɪd] *tr & intr* decidir
decimal ['desɪməl] *adj & s* decimal *m*
decimal point s (*in Spanish the comma is used to separate the decimal fraction from the integer*) coma
decimate ['desɪˌmet] *tr* diezmar
decipher [dɪ'saɪfər] *tr* descifrar
decision [dɪ'sɪʒən] s decisión
decisive [dɪ'saɪsɪv] *adj* decisivo; determinado, resuelto
deck [dek] s (*of cards*) baraja; (*of ship*) cubierta; **between decks** (naut) entre cubiertas ‖ *tr* — **to deck out** adornar, engalanar
deck chair s silla de cubierta
deck hand s marinero de cubierta
deck'-land' *intr* apontizar
deck'-land'ing s apontizaje *m*
deckle edge ['dekəl] s barba
declaim [dɪ'klem] *tr & intr* declamar
declaration [ˌdeklə'reʃən] s declaración
declarative [dɪ'klærətɪv] *adj* declarativo; (gram) enunciativo
declare [dɪ'kler] *tr & intr* declarar
declension [dɪ'klenʃən] s declinación
declination [ˌdeklɪ'neʃən] s declinación
decline [dɪ'klaɪn] s bajada, declinación; (*in prices*) baja; (*in health, wealth, etc.*) bajón *m;* (*of sun*) ocaso ‖ *tr & intr* declinar; rehusar
declivi·ty [dɪ'klɪvɪti] s (*pl* -ties) declividad, declive *m*
decode [di'kod] *tr* descifrar
décolleté [ˌdekal'te] *adj* escotado

da
de

decompose [ˌdikəm'poz] *tr* descomponer ‖ *intr* descomponerse
decomposition [ˌdikɑmpə'zɪʃən] *s* descomposición
decompression [ˌdikəm'prɛʃən] *s* descompresión
decontamination [ˌdikəmˌtæmɪ'neʃən] *s* descontaminación
décor [de'kɔr] *s* decoración; (theat) decorado
decorate ['dɛkəˌret] *tr* decorar; (*with medal, badge*) condecorar
decoration [ˌdɛkə're/ən] *s* decoración; (*medal, badge*) condecoración
decorator ['dɛkəˌretər] *s* decorador *m;* (*of interiors*) adornista *mf*
decorous ['dɛkərəs] o [dɪ'korəs] *adj* decoroso
decorum [dɪ'korəm] *s* decoro
decoy [dɪ'kɔr] o ['dikɔɪ] *s* añagaza, señuelo; (*person*) entruchón *m* ‖ [dɪ'kɔɪ] *tr* atraer con señuelo; entruchar
decoy pigeon *s* cimbel *m*
decrease ['dikris] o [dɪ'kris] *s* disminución ‖ [dɪ'kris] *tr* disminuir ‖ *intr* disminuir, disminuirse
decree [dɪ'kri] *s* decreto ‖ *tr* decretar
decrepit [dɪ'krɛpɪt] *adj* decrépito
de·cry [dɪ'kraɪ] *v* (*pret & pp* **-cried**) *tr* censurar, denigrar
dedicate ['dɛdɪˌket] *tr* dedicar
dedication [ˌdɛdɪ'keʃən] *s* dedicación; (*inscription in a book*) dedicatoria
deduce [dɪ'djus] o [dɪ'dus] *tr* deducir (*inferir, concluir; derivar*)
deduct [dɪ'dʌkt] *tr* deducir (*rebajar, substraer*)
deduction [dɪ'dʌk/ən] *s* deducción
deed [did] *s* acto, hecho; (*feat, exploit*) hazaña; (law) escritura ‖ *tr* traspasar por escritura
deem [dim] *tr & intr* creer, juzgar
deep [dip] *adj* profundo; (*sound*) grave; (*color*) subido; de hondo, p.ej., **two meters deep** dos metros de hondo; **deep in debt** cargado de deudas; **deep in thought** absorto en la meditación ‖ *adv* hondo; **deep into the night** muy entrada la noche
deepen ['dipən] *tr* profundizar ‖ *intr* profundizarse
deep-laid ['dip ˌled] *adj* concebido con astucia
deep mourning *s* luto riguroso
deep-rooted ['dip ˌrutɪd] *adj* profundamente arraigado
deep'-sea' fishing *s* pesca de gran altura
deep-seated ['dip ˌsitɪd] *adj* profundamente arraigado
deer [dɪr] *s* ciervo, venado
deer'skin' *s* piel *f* de ciervo
def. *abbr* **defendant, deferred, definite**
deface [dɪ'fes] *tr* desfigurar
de facto [di'fækto] *adv* de hecho
defamation [ˌdɛfə'meʃən] o [ˌdifə'meʃən] *s* difamación
defame [dɪ'fem] *tr* difamar
default [dɪ'fɔlt] *s* falta, incumplimiento; **by default** (sport) por no

presentarse; **in default of** por falta de ‖ *tr* dejar de cumplir; no pagar ‖ *intr* faltar; (sport) perder por no presentarse
defeat [dɪ'fit] *s* derrota ‖ *tr* derrotar, vencer
defeatism [dɪ'fitɪzəm] *s* derrotismo
defeatist [dɪ'fitɪst] *adj & s* derrotista *mf*
defecate ['dɛfɪˌket] *intr* defecar
defect [dɪ'fɛkt] o ['difɛkt] *s* defecto, imperfección ‖ [dɪ'fɛkt] *intr* desertar
defection [dɪ'fɛk/ən] *s* defección; (*lack, failure*) falta
defective [dɪ'fɛktɪv] *adj* defectivo, defectuoso
defend [dɪ'fɛnd] *tr* defender
defendant [dɪ'fɛndənt] *s* (law) demandado, acusado
defender [dɪ'fɛndər] *s* defensor *m*
defense [dɪ'fɛns] *s* defensa
defenseless [dɪ'fɛnslɪs] *adj* indefenso
defensive [dɪ'fɛnsɪv] *adj* defensivo ‖ *s* defensiva
de·fer [dɪ'fɜr] *v* (*pret & pp* **-ferred;** *ger* **-ferring**) *tr* aplazar, diferir ‖ *intr* deferir
deference ['dɛfərəns] *s* deferencia
deferential [ˌdɛfə'rɛn/əl] *adj* deferente
deferment [dɪ'fʌrmənt] *s* aplazamiento, dilación
defiance [dɪ'faɪ·əns] *s* oposición; desafío, provocación; **in defiance of** sin mirar a, a despecho de
defiant [dɪ'faɪ·ənt] *adj* provocante, hostil
deficien·cy [dɪ'fɪ/ənsi] *s* (*pl* **-cies**) carencia, deficiencia; (com) descubierto
deficient [dɪ'fɪ/ənt] *adj* deficiente, defectuoso
deficit ['dɛfɪsɪt] *adj* deficitario ‖ *s* déficit *m*
defile [dɪ'faɪl] o ['difaɪl] *s* desfiladero ‖ [dɪ'faɪl] *tr* corromper, manchar ‖ *intr* desfilar
define [dɪ'faɪn] *tr* definir
definite ['dɛfɪnɪt] *adj* definido
definition [ˌdɛfɪ'nɪ/ən] *s* definición
definitive [dɪ'fɪnɪtɪv] *adj* definitivo
deflate [dɪ'flet] *tr* desinflar
deflation [dɪ'fle/ən] *s* desinflación; (*of prices*) deflación
deflect [dɪ'flɛkt] *tr* desviar ‖ *intr* desviarse
deflower [di'flau·ər] *tr* desflorar
deforest [di'fɑrɛst] o [di'fɔrɛst] *tr* desforestar, despoblar
deform [dɪ'fɔrm] *tr* deformar
deformed [dɪ'fɔrmd] *adj* deforme
deformi·ty [dɪ'fɔrmɪti] *s* (*pl* **-ties**) deformidad
defraud [dɪ'frɔd] *tr* defraudar
defray [dɪ'fre] *tr* sufragar, subvenir a
defrost [dɪ'frɔst] o [di'frɑst] *tr* descongelar, deshelar
deft [dɛft] *adj* diestro, hábil
defunct [dɪ'fʌŋkt] *adj* difunto
de·fy [dɪ'faɪ] *v* (*pret & pp* **-fied**) *tr* desafiar, provocar
deg. *abbr* **degree**

degeneracy [dɪ'dʒenərəsi] s degeneración

degenerate [dɪ'dʒenərɪt] adj & s degenerado || [dɪ'dʒenə,ret] intr degenerar

degrade [dɪ'gred] tr degradar

degrading [dɪ'gredɪŋ] adj degradante

degree [dɪ'gri] s grado; by degrees de grado en grado; to take a degree graduarse, recibir un grado o título

dehumidifier [,dihju'mɪdɪ,faɪ·ər] s deshumedecedor m

dehydrate [di'haɪdret] tr deshidratar

deice [di'aɪs] tr deshelar

dei·fy ['di·ɪ,faɪ] v (pret & pp -fied) tr deificar

deign [den] intr dignarse

dei·ty ['di·ɪti] s (pl -ties) deidad; the Deity Dios m

dejected [dɪ'dʒektɪd] adj abatido

dejection [dɪ'dʒekʃən] s abatimiento

del. abbr **delegate, delete**

delay [dɪ'le] s retraso, tardanza || tr retrasar || intr demorarse

delectable [dɪ'lektəbəl] adj deleitable

delegate ['delɪ,get] o ['delɪgɪt] s diputado, delegado; (to a convention) congresista mf || ['delɪ,get] tr delegar

delete [dɪ'lit] tr borrar, suprimir

deletion [dɪ'liʃən] s supresión

deliberate [dɪ'lɪbərɪt] adj pensado, reflexionado; (slow in deciding) cauto, circunspecto; (slow in moving) espacioso, lento || [dɪ'lɪbə,ret] tr & intr deliberar

delica·cy ['delɪkəsi] s (pl -cies) delicadeza; (choice food) golosina

delicatessen [,delɪkə'tesən] s colmado, tienda de ultramarinos || spl ultramarinos

delicious [dɪ'lɪʃəs] adj delicioso, sabroso

delight [dɪ'laɪt] s deleite m, delicia || tr deleitar || intr deleitarse

delightful [dɪ'laɪtfəl] adj deleitoso, ameno, exquisito

delinquen·cy [dɪ'lɪŋkwənsi] s (pl -cies) culpa; (in payment of debt) morosidad; (debt in arrears) atrasos

delinquent [dɪ'lɪŋkwənt] adj culpado; (in payment) moroso, atrasado; no pagado || s culpado; deudor moroso

delirious [dɪ'lɪrɪ·əs] adj delirante

deliri·um [dɪ'lɪrɪ·əm] s (pl -ums o -a [ə]) delirio

deliver [dɪ'lɪvər] tr entregar; asestar (un golpe); pronunciar, recitar (un discurso); transmitir, rendir (energía); partear (a la mujer que está de parto)

deliver·y [dɪ'lɪvəri] s (pl -ies) entrega; (of mail) distribución, reparto; (of a speech) declamación; (childbirth) alumbramiento, parto

delivery·man [dɪ'lɪvərimən] s (pl -men [mən]) mozo de reparto

delivery room s sala de alumbramiento

delivery truck s sedán m de reparto

dell [del] s vallecito

delouse [di'laus] o [di'lauz] tr despiojar

delphinium [del'fɪnɪ·əm] s (Delphinium ajacis) espuela de caballero; (Delphinium consolida) consuelda real

delude [dɪ'lud] tr deludir, engañar

deluge ['deljudʒ] s diluvio || tr inundar

delusion [dɪ'luʃən] s engaño, decepción

de luxe [dɪ'luks] o [dɪ'lʌks] adj & adv de lujo

delve [delv] intr cavar; to delve into cavar en

demagnetize [di'mægnɪ,taɪz] tr desimantar

demagogue ['demə,gag] s demagogo

demand [dɪ'mænd] o [dɪ'mɑnd] s demanda; to be in demand tener demanda || tr demandar perentoriamente

demanding [dɪ'mændɪŋ] o [dɪ'mɑndɪŋ] adj exigente

demarcate [dɪ'mɑrket] o ['dimɑr,ket] tr demarcar

démarche [de'mɑrʃ] s diligencia, gestión, paso

demeanor [dɪ'minər] s conducta, porte m

demented [dɪ'mentɪd] adj demente

demigod ['demɪ,gad] s semidiós m

demijohn ['demɪ,dʒɑn] s damajuana

demilitarize [di'mɪlɪtə,raɪz] tr desmilitarizar

demimonde ['demɪ,mɑnd] s mujeres de vida alegre

demise [dɪ'maɪz] s fallecimiento

demisemiquaver [,demɪ'semɪ,kwevər] s (mus) fusa

demitasse ['demɪ,tæs] o ['demɪ,tɑs] s taza pequeña

demobilize [di'mobɪ,laɪz] tr desmovilizar

democra·cy [dɪ'mɑkrəsi] s (pl -cies) democracia

democrat ['demə,kræt] s demócrata mf

democratic [,demə'krætɪk] adj democrático

demodulate [di'mɑdʒə,let] tr desmodular

demolish [dɪ'mɑlɪʃ] tr demoler

demolition [,demə'lɪʃən] o [,dimə-'lɪʃən] s demolición

demon ['dimən] s demonio

demoniacal [,dimə'naɪ·əkəl] adj demoníaco

demonstrate ['demən,stret] tr demostrar || intr demostrar; (to show feelings in public gatherings) manifestar

demonstration [,demən'streʃən] s demostración; (public show of feeling) manifestación

demonstrative [dɪ'mɑnstrətɪv] adj demostrativo; (giving open exhibition of emotion) extremoso

demonstrator ['demən,stretər] s demostrador m; manifestante mf

demoralize [dɪ'mɑrə,laɪz] o [dɪ'mərə,laɪz] tr desmoralizar

de
de

demote [dɪ'mot] *tr* degradar

demotion [dɪ'moʃən] *s* degradación

de·mur [dɪ'mʌr] *v* (*pret & pp* **-murred;** *ger* **-murring**) *intr* poner reparos

demure [dɪ'mjur] *adj* modesto, recatado; grave, serio

demurrage [dɪ'mʌrɪdʒ] *s* (com) estadía

den [dɛn] *s* (*of animals, thieves*) madriguera; (*dirty little room*) cuchitril *m;* lugar *m* de retiro; cuarto de estudio; (*of lions*) (Bib) fosa

denaturalize [di'nætʃərə‚laɪz] *tr* desnaturalizar

denatured alcohol [di'netʃərd] *s* alcohol desnaturalizado

denial [dɪ'naɪ‚əl] *s* denegación; negación, desmentida

denim ['dɛnɪm] *s* dril *m* de algodón

denizen ['dɛnɪzən] *s* habitante *mf,* vecino

Denmark ['dɛnmark] *s* Dinamarca

denomination [dɪ‚nɑmɪ'neʃən] *s* denominación; categoría, clase *f;* secta, confesión, comunión

denote [dɪ'not] *tr* denotar

dénoument [denu'mã] *s* desenlace *m*

denounce [dɪ'nauns] *tr* denunciar

dense [dɛns] *adj* denso; estúpido

densi·ty ['dɛnsɪti] *s* (*pl* **-ties**) densidad

dent [dɛnt] *s* abolladura, mella ‖ *tr* abollar, mellar ‖ *intr* abollarse, mellarse

dental ['dɛntəl] *adj* & *s* dental *f*

dental floss *s* hilo dental, seda encerada

dentifrice ['dɛntɪfrɪs] *s* dentífrico

dentist ['dɛntɪst] *s* dentista *mf*

dentistry ['dɛntɪstri] *s* odontología

denture ['dɛntʃər] *s* dentadura artificial

denunciation [dɪ‚nʌnsɪ'eʃən] o [dɪ‚nʌnʃɪ'eʃən] *s* denuncia

de·ny [dɪ'naɪ] *v* (*pret & pp* **-nied**) *tr* (*to declare not to be true*) negar; (*to refuse*) denegar; **to deny oneself to callers** negarse ‖ *intr* negar; denegar

deodorant [di'odərənt] *adj* & *s* desodorante *m*

deodorize [di'odə‚raɪz] *tr* desodorizar

deoxidize [di'aksɪ‚daɪz] *tr* desoxidar

dep. *abbr* department, departs, deputy

depart [dɪ'part] *intr* partir, salir, irse; desviarse

department [dɪ'partmənt] *s* departamento; (*of government*) ministerio

department store *s* grandes almacenes *mpl*

departure [dɪ'partʃər] *s* partida, salida; desviación

depend [dɪ'pɛnd] *intr* depender; **to depend on** depender de

dependable [dɪ'pɛndəbəl] *adj* confiable, fidedigno

dependence [dɪ'pɛndəns] *s* dependencia

dependen·cy [dɪ'pɛndənsi] *s* (*pl* **-cies**) dependencia; (*country, territory*) posesión

dependent [dɪ'pɛndənt] *adj* dependiente ‖ *s* carga de familia, familiar *m* dependiente

depict [dɪ'pɪkt] *tr* describir, representar, pintar

deplete [dɪ'plit] *tr* agotar, depauperar

deplorable [dɪ'plorəbəl] *adj* deplorable

deplore [dɪ'plor] *tr* deplorar

deploy [dɪ'plɔɪ] *tr* (mil) desplegar ‖ *intr* (mil) desplegarse

deployment [dɪ'plɔɪmənt] *s* (mil) despliegue *m*

depolarize [di'polə‚raɪz] *tr* despolarizar

depopulate [di'papjə‚let] *tr* despoblar

deport [dɪ'port] *tr* deportar; **to deport oneself** conducirse, portarse

deportation [‚dipor'teʃən] *s* deportación

deportee [‚dipor'ti] *s* deportado

deportment [dɪ'portmənt] *s* conducta, comportamiento

depose [dɪ'poz] *tr* & *intr* deponer

deposit [dɪ'pazɪt] *s* depósito; (*down payment*) señal *f,* pago anticipado; (min) yacimiento ‖ *tr* depositar ‖ *intr* depositarse

deposit account *s* cuenta corriente

depositor [dɪ'pazɪtər] *s* cuentacorrentista *mf,* imponente *mf*

depot ['dipo] o ['dɛpo] *s* almacén *m,* depósito; (mil) depósito; (rr) estación

depraved [dɪ'prevd] *adj* depravado

depravi·ty [dɪ'prævɪti] *s* (*pl* **-ties**) depravación

deprecate ['dɛprɪ‚ket] *tr* desaprobar

depreciate [dɪ'priʃɪ‚et] *tr* (*to lower value or price of*) depreciar; (*to disparage*) desapreciar ‖ *intr* depreciarse

depreciation [dɪ‚priʃɪ'eʃən] *s* (*drop in value*) depreciación; (*disparagement*) desaprecio

depress [dɪ'prɛs] *tr* deprimir; desanimar, desalentar; bajar (*los precios*)

depression [dɪ'prɛʃən] *s* depresión; desaliento; (*slump*) crisis *f*

deprive [dɪ'praɪv] *tr* privar

dept. *abbr* department

depth [dɛpθ] *s* profundidad; (*of a house, of a room*) fondo; **in the depth of night** en mitad de la noche; **in the depth of winter** en pleno invierno; **to go beyond one's depth** meterse en agua demasiado profunda; (fig) meterse en honduras

depth of hold *s* (naut) puntal *m*

depu·ty ['dɛpjəti] *s* (*pl* **-ties**) diputado

derail [dɪ'rel] *tr* hacer descarrilar ‖ *intr* descarrilar

derailment [dɪ'relmənt] *s* descarrilamiento

derange [dɪ'rendʒ] *tr* desarreglar, descomponer; trastornar el juicio a

derangement [dɪ'rendʒmənt] *s* desarreglo, descompostura; locura

der·by ['dʌrbi] *s* (*pl* **-bies**) sombrero hongo

derelict ['dɛrɪlɪkt] *adj* abandonado; negligente ‖ *s* pelafustán *m;* (naut) derrelicto

deride [dɪ'raɪd] *tr* burlarse de, ridiculizar

derision [dɪ'rɪʒən] *s* burla, irrisión
derive [dɪ'raɪv] *tr* & *intr* derivar
derogatory [dɪ'rɑgə,tori] *adj* despreciativo
derrick ['dɛrɪk] *s* grúa
dervish ['dʌrvɪʃ] *s* derviche *m*
desalinization [dɪ,selɪnɪ'zeʃən] *s* desalinización
desalt [di'sɔlt] *tr* desalar
descend [dɪ'sɛnd] *tr* bajar, descender (*la escalera*) ‖ *intr* bajar, descender; **to descend on** caer sobre, invadir
descendant [dɪ'sɛndənt] *adj* descendente ‖ *s* descendiente *mf*
descendent [dɪ'sɛndənt] *adj* descendente
descent [dɪ'sɛnt] *s* (*passing from higher to lower state*) descenso; (*extraction; lineage*) descendencia; cuesta, bajada; invasión
describe [dɪ'skraɪb] *tr* describir
description [dɪ'skrɪpʃən] *s* descripción
descriptive [dɪ'skrɪptɪv] *adj* descriptivo
de•scry [dɪ'skraɪ] *v* (*pret* & *pp* **-scried**) *tr* avistar, divisar; descubrir
desecrate ['dɛsɪ,kret] *tr* profanar
desegregation [di,sɛgrɪ'geʃən] *s* desegregación
desert ['dɛzərt] *adj* & *s* desierto, yermo ‖ [dɪ'zʌrt] *s* mérito; **he received his just deserts** llevó su merecido ‖ *tr* desertar de ‖ *intr* desertar
deserter [dɪ'zʌrtər] *s* desertor *m*
desertion [dɪ'zʌrʃən] *s* deserción; abandono de cónyuge
deserve [dɪ'zʌrv] *tr* & *intr* merecer
deservedly [dɪ'zʌrvɪdli] *adv* merecidamente
design [dɪ'zaɪn] *s* diseño; (*combination of details; art of designing*) dibujo; (*plan, scheme*) designio; **to have designs on** poner la mira en ‖ *tr* diseñar, dibujar; idear, proyectar ‖ *intr* diseñar, dibujar
designate ['dɛzɪg,net] *tr* designar
designing [dɪ'zaɪnɪŋ] *adj* intrigante, maquinador
desirable [dɪ'zaɪrəbəl] *adj* deseable
desire [dɪ'zaɪr] *s* deseo ‖ *tr* desear
desirous [dɪ'zaɪrəs] *adj* deseoso
desist [dɪ'zɪst] *intr* desistir
desk [dɛsk] *s* bufete *m*, escritorio; (*lectern*) atril *m*; (*clerk's counter in a hotel*) caja
desk clerk *s* cajero, recepcionista *m*
desk set *s* juego de escritorio
desolate ['dɛsəlɪt] *adj* (*hopeless*) desolado; despoblado, yermo, desierto; solitario; (*dismal*) lúgubre ‖ ['dɛsə,let] *tr* desconsolar; (*to lay waste*) desolar, devastar; despoblar
desolation [,dɛsə'leʃən] *s* (*devastation; great affliction*) desolación; (*dreariness*) lobreguez *f*
despair [dɪ'spɛr] *s* desesperación ‖ *intr* desesperar, desesperarse
despairing [dɪ'spɛrɪŋ] *adj* desesperado
despera•do [,dɛspə'redo] o [,dɛspə'rɑdo] *s* (*pl* **-does** o **-dos**) criminal dispuesto a todo

desperate ['dɛspərɪt] *adj* dispuesto a todo; (*bitter, excessive*) encarnizado; (*hopeless*) desesperado; (*remedy*) heroico
despicable ['dɛspɪkəbəl] *adj* despreciable, ruin
despise [dɪ'spaɪz] *tr* despreciar, desdeñar
despite [dɪ'spaɪt] *prep* a despecho de
desponden•cy [dɪ'spɑndənsɪ] *s* (*pl* **-cies**) abatimiento, desaliento
despondent [dɪ'spɑndənt] *adj* abatido, desalentado
despot ['dɛspɑt] *s* déspota *m*
despotic [dɛs'pɑtɪk] *adj* despótico
despotism ['dɛspə,tɪzəm] *s* despotismo
dessert [dɪ'zʌrt] *s* postre *m*
destination [,dɛstɪ'neʃən] *s* (*end of a journey or shipment*) destino; (*purpose*) destinación
destine [dɪ'stɪn] *tr* destinar
desti•ny ['dɛstɪnɪ] *s* (*pl* **-nies**) destino
destitute ['dɛstɪ,tjut] o ['dɛstɪ,tut] *adj* (*being in complete poverty*) indigente; (*lacking, deprived*) desprovisto
destitution [,dɛstɪ'tjuʃən] o [,dɛstɪ'tuʃən] *s* indigencia
destroy [dɪ'strɔɪ] *tr* destruir
destroyer [dɪ'strɔɪ•ər] *s* (nav) destructor *m*
destruction [dɪ'strʌkʃən] *s* destrucción
destructive [dɪ'strʌktɪv] *adj* destructivo
desultory ['dɛsəl,tori] *adj* deshilvanado, descosido
detach [dɪ'tætʃ] *tr* desprender, separar; (mil) destacar
detachable [dɪ'tætʃəbəl] *adj* desprendible, separable; (*collar*) postizo
detached [dɪ'tætʃt] *adj* separado, suelto; imparcial, desinteresado
detachment [dɪ'tætʃmənt] *s* desprendimiento, separación; imparcialidad, desinterés *m*; (mil) destacamento
detail [dɪ'tel] o ['ditel] *s* detalle *m*, pormenor *m*; (mil) destacamento ‖ [dɪ'tel] *tr* detallar; (mil) destacar
detain [dɪ'ten] *tr* detener; tener preso
detect [dɪ'tɛkt] *tr* detectar
detection [dɪ'tɛkʃən] *s* detección
detective [dɪ'tɛktɪv] *s* detective *m*
detective story *s* novela policíaca o policial
detector [dɪ'tɛktər] *s* detector *m*
detention [dɪ'tɛnʃən] *s* detención
de•ter [dɪ'tʌr] *v* (*pret* & *pp* **-terred**; *ger* **-terring**) *tr* impedir, refrenar
detergent [dɪ'tʌrdʒənt] *adj* & *s* detergente *m*
deteriorate [dɪ'tɪrɪ•ə,ret] *tr* deteriorar ‖ *intr* deteriorarse
determine [dɪ'tʌrmɪn] *tr* determinar
deterrent [dɪ'tʌrənt] *s* impedimento, refrenamiento
detest [dɪ'tɛst] *tr* detestar, aborrecer
dethrone [dɪ'θron] *tr* destronar
detonate ['dɛtə,net] o ['ditə,net] *tr* hacer estallar ‖ *intr* detonar
detour ['ditur] o [dɪ'tur] *s* desvío;

rodeo, vuelta; manera indirecta ‖ *tr* desviar (*el tráfico*) ‖ *intr* desviarse

detract [dɪ'trækt] *tr* detraer ‖ *intr* — **to detract from** disminuir, rebajar

detriment ['dɛtrɪmənt] *s* perjuicio, detrimento; **to the detriment of** en perjuicio de

detrimental [,dɛtrɪ'mɛntəl] *adj* perjudicial

deuce [djus] o [dus] *s* (*in cards*) dos *m*; **the deuce!** ¡demonio!

devaluation [di,væljʊ'e/ən] *s* desvalorización, devaluación

devastate ['dɛvəs,tet] *tr* devastar

devastation [,dɛvəs'te/ən] *s* devastación

develop [dɪ'vɛləp] *tr* desarrollar, desenvolver; (*phot*) revelar; explotar (*una mina*) ‖ *intr* desarrollarse, desenvolverse; evolucionar, manifestarse

developer [dɪ'vɛləpər] *s* fomentador *m*; (*phot*) revelador *m*

development [dɪ'vɛləpmənt] *s* desarrollo, desenvolvimiento; (*phot*) revelado; (*of a mine*) explotación; acontecimiento nuevo

deviate ['divɪ,et] *tr* desviar ‖ *intr* desviarse

deviation [,divɪ'e/ən] *s* desviación

deviationism [,divɪ'e/ə,nɪzəm] *s* desviacionismo

deviationist [,divɪ'e/ənɪst] *s* desviacionista *mf*

device [dɪ'vaɪs] *s* dispositivo, aparato; (*trick*) ardid *m*, treta; (*motto*) lema *m*, divisa; **to leave someone to his own devices** dejarle a uno que haga lo que se le antoje

dev•il ['dɛvəl] *s* diablo; **between the devil and the deep blue sea** entre la espada y la pared; **to raise the devil** (slang) armar un alboroto ‖ *v* (*pret & pp* **-iled** o **-illed**; *ger* **-iling** o **-illing**) *tr* condimentar con picantes; (coll) acosar, molestar

devilish ['dɛvəlɪʃ] *adj* diabólico

devilment ['dɛvəlmənt] *s* (*mischief*) diablura; (*evil*) maldad

devil•try ['dɛvəltri] *s* (*pl* **-tries**) maldad, crueldad; (*mischief*) diablura

devious ['divɪ•əs] *adj* (*straying*) desviado, extraviado; (*roundabout; shifty*) tortuoso

devise [dɪ'vaɪz] *tr* idear, inventar; (law) legar

devoid [dɪ'vɔɪd] *adj* desprovisto

devote [dɪ'vot] *tr* dedicar

devoted [dɪ'votɪd] *adj* (*zealous, ardent*) devoto; dedicado

devotee [,dɛvə'ti] *s* devoto

devotion [dɪ'vo/ən] *s* devoción; (*to study, work, etc.*) dedicación; **devotions** oraciones, preces *fpl*

devour [dɪ'vaʊr] *tr* devorar

devout [dɪ'vaʊt] *adj* devoto; cordial, sincero

dew [dju] o [du] *s* rocío

dew′drop *s* gota de rocío

dew′lap *s* papada

dew•y ['dju•i] o ['du•i] *adj* rociado

dexterity [dɛks'tɛrɪti] *s* destreza

D.F. *abbr* **Defender of the Faith**

diabetes [,daɪ•ə'bitɪs] o [,daɪ•ə'bitiz] *s* diabetes *f*

diabetic [,daɪ•ə'bɛtɪk] o [,daɪ•ə'bitɪk] *adj & s* diabético

diabolic(al) [,daɪ•ə'bɑlɪk(əl)] *adj* diabólico

diacritical [,daɪ•ə'krɪtɪkəl] *adj* diacrítico

diadem ['daɪ•ə,dɛm] *s* diadema *f*

diaere•sis [daɪ'ɛrɪsɪs] *s* (*pl* **-ses** [,siz]) diéresis *f*

diagnose [,daɪ•əg'nos] o [,daɪ•əg'noz] *tr* diagnosticar

diagno•sis [,daɪ•əg'nosɪs] *s* (*pl* **-ses** [siz]) diagnosis *f*, diagnóstico

diagonal [daɪ'ægənəl] *adj & s* diagonal *f*

diagram ['daɪ•ə,græm] *s* diagrama *m*

dial. *abbr* **dialect**

dial ['daɪ•əl] *s* (*of radio*) cuadrante *m*; (*of watch*) cuadrante *m*, esfera, muestra; (*of telephone*) disco selector ‖ *tr* sintonizar (*el radiorreceptor*); marcar (*el número telefónico*); llamar (*a una persona*) por teléfono automático ‖ *intr* (telp) marcar

dialect ['daɪ•ə,lɛkt] *s* dialecto

dialing ['daɪ•əlɪŋ] *s* (telp) marcaje *m*

dialogue ['daɪ•ə,lɔg] o ['daɪ•ə,lɑg] *s* diálogo

dial telephone *s* teléfono automático

dial tone *s* (telp) señal *f* para marcar

diam. *abbr* **diameter**

diameter [daɪ'æmɪtər] *s* diámetro

diametric(al) [,daɪ•ə'mɛtrɪk(əl)] *adj* diamétrico

diamond ['daɪmənd] *s* diamante *m*; (*figure of a rhombus*) losange *m*; (*playing card*) carró *m*, diamante *m*; (baseball) losange *m*

diaper ['daɪ•pər] *s* pañal *m*

diaphanous [daɪ'æfənəs] *adj* diáfano

diaphragm ['daɪ•ə,fræm] *s* diafragma *m*

diarrhea [,daɪ•ə'ri•ə] *s* diarrea

dia•ry ['daɪ•əri] *s* (*pl* **-ries**) diario

diastole [daɪ'æstəli] *s* diástole *f*

diathermy ['daɪ•ə,θɜrmi] *s* diatermia

dice [daɪs] *spl* dados; (*small cubes*) cubitos; **to load the dice** cargar los dados ‖ *tr* cortar en cubos

dice′box′ *s* cubilete *m*

dichloride [daɪ'klɔraɪd] *s* dicloruro

dichoto•my [daɪ'kɑtəmi] *s* (*pl* **-mies**) dicotomía

dickey ['dɪki] *s* camisolín *m*, pechera postiza; babero de niño

dict. *abbr* **dictionary**

dictaphone ['dɪktə,fon] *s* dictáfono

dictate ['dɪktet] *s* mandato ‖ ['dɪktet] o [dɪk'tet] *tr* dictar; mandar

dictation [dɪk'te/ən] *s* dictado; (*orders; giving orders*) mandato; **to take dictation** escribir al dictado

dictator ['dɪktetər] o [dɪk'tetər] *s* dictador *m*

dictatorship ['dɪktetər,/ɪp] o [dɪk'tetər/ɪp] *s* dictadura

diction ['dɪk/ən] *s* dicción

dictionar•y ['dɪk/ən,ɛri] *s* (*pl* **-ies**) diccionario

dic·tum ['dɪktəm] s (pl **-ta** [tə]) dictamen m; aforismo, sentencia

didactic(al) [daɪ'dæktɪk(əl)] o [dɪ-'dæktɪk(əl)] adj didáctico

die [daɪ] s (pl **dice** [daɪs]) dado; **the die is cast** la suerte está echada ‖ s (pl **dies**) (for stamping coins, medals, etc.) troquel m; (for cutting threads) hembra de terraja ‖ v (pret & pp **died**; ger **dying**) intr morir; **to be dying** estar agonizando; **to die laughing** morir de risa

die'-hard' adj & s intransigente mf

diesel oil ['dizəl] s gas-oil m

die'stock' s terraja

diet ['daɪət] s dieta, régimen alimenticio ‖ intr estar a dieta

dietitian [,daɪə'tɪʃən] s dietista mf

diff. abbr **difference, different**

differ ['dɪfər] intr (to be different) diferir, diferenciarse; (to dissent) diferenciar; **to differ with** desavenirse con

difference ['dɪfərəns] s diferencia; **to make no difference** no importar; **to split the difference** partir la diferencia

different ['dɪfərənt] adj diferente

differentiate [,dɪfə'renʃɪ,et] tr diferenciar ‖ intr diferenciarse

difficult ['dɪfɪ,kʌlt] adj difícil

difficul·ty ['dɪfɪ,kʌltɪ] s (pl **-ties**) dificultad

diffident ['dɪfɪdənt] adj apocado, tímido

diffuse [dɪ'fjus] adj difuso ‖ [dɪ'fjuz] tr difundir ‖ intr difundirse

dig [dɪg] s (poke) empuje m; (jibe) pulla, palabra hiriente ‖ v (pret & pp **dug** [dʌg] o **digged**; ger **digging**) tr cavar, excavar; **to dig up** desenterrar ‖ intr cavar, excavar; **to dig in** (coll) meter manos a la obra; (mil) atrincherarse; **to dig under** socavar

digest ['daɪdʒest] s compendio, resumen m; (law) digesto ‖ [dɪ'dʒest] o [daɪ'dʒest] tr & intr digerir

digestible [dɪ'dʒestɪbəl] o [daɪ'dʒestɪbəl] adj digerible, digestible

digestion [dɪ'dʒestʃən] o [daɪ'dʒestʃən] s digestión

digestive [dɪ'dʒestɪv] o [daɪ'dʒestɪv] adj & s digestivo

digit ['dɪdʒɪt] s dígito

dignified ['dɪgnɪ,faɪd] adj digno, grave, decoroso

digni·fy ['dɪgnɪ,faɪ] v (pret & pp **-fied**) tr dignificar; engrandecer el mérito de

dignitar·y ['dɪgnɪ,terɪ] s (pl **-ies**) dignatario

digni·ty ['dɪgnɪtɪ] s (pl **-ties**) dignidad; **to stand upon one's dignity** ponerse tan alto

digress [dɪ'gres] o [daɪ'gres] intr divagar

digression [dɪ'greʃən] o [daɪ'greʃən] s digresión, divagación

dike [daɪk] s dique m; (bank of earth thrown up in digging) montón m; (causeway) arrecife m, malecón m

dilapidated [dɪ'læpɪ,detɪd] adj destartalado, desvencijado

dilate [daɪ'let] tr dilatar ‖ intr dilatarse

dilatory ['dɪlə,torɪ] adj tardío

dilemma [dɪ'lemə] s dilema m, disyuntiva

dilettan·te [,dɪlə'tæntɪ] adj diletante ‖ s (pl **-tes** o **-ti** [ti]) diletante mf

diligence ['dɪlɪdʒəns] s diligencia

diligent ['dɪlɪdʒənt] adj diligente

dill [dɪl] s eneldo

dillydal·ly ['dɪlɪ,dælɪ] v (pret & pp **-lied**) intr malgastar el tiempo, haraganear

dilute [dɪ'lut] o [daɪ'lut] adj diluído ‖ [dɪ'lut] tr diluir ‖ intr diluirse

dilution [dɪ'luʃən] s dilución

dim. abbr **diminutive**

dim [dɪm] adj (comp **dimmer**; super **dimmest**) débil, indistinto, confuso; obscuro, poco claro; (chance) escaso; (not clearly understanding) torpe, lerdo; **to take a dim view of** mirar escépticamente ‖ v (pret & pp **dimmed**; ger **dimming**) tr amortiguar (la luz); poner (un faro) a media luz; disminuir ‖ intr obscurecerse

dime [daɪm] s moneda de diez centavos

dimension [dɪ'menʃən] s dimensión

diminish [dɪ'mɪnɪʃ] tr disminuir ‖ intr disminuir, disminuirse

diminutive [dɪ'mɪnjətɪv] adj (tiny) diminuto; (gram) diminutivo ‖ s diminutivo

dimi·ty ['dɪmɪtɪ] s (pl **-ties**) cotonía

dimly ['dɪmlɪ] adv indistintamente

dimmer ['dɪmər] s amortiguador m de luz; (aut) lámpara de cruce, luz f de cruce

dimple ['dɪmpəl] s hoyuelo

dimwit ['dɪm,wɪt] s (slang) mentecato, bobo

dim-witted ['dɪm,wɪtɪd] adj (slang) mentecato, bobo

din [dɪn] s estruendo, ruido ensordecedor ‖ v (pret & pp **dinned**; ger **dinning**) tr ensordecer con mucho ruido; repetir insistentemente; impresionar con repetición ruidosa ‖ intr sonar estrepitosamente

dine [daɪn] tr dar de comer a; obsequiar con una cena o comida ‖ intr cenar, comer; **to dine out** cenar fuera de casa

diner ['daɪnər] s invitado a una cena, convidado a una comida; coche-comedor m

ding-dong ['dɪŋ,dɔŋ] o ['dɪŋ,dɑŋ] s dindán m

din·gy ['dɪndʒɪ] adj (comp **-gier**; super **-giest**) deslustrado, sucio

dining car s coche-comedor m

dining room s comedor m

din'ing-room' suit s juego de comedor

dinner ['dɪnər] s cena, comida; (formal meal) banquete m

dinner coat o **jacket** s smoking m

dinner pail s fiambrera, portaviandas m

dinner set s vajilla

dinner time s hora de la cena o comida

dint [dɪnt] s abolladura; **by dint of** a fuerza de ‖ tr abollar

diocese ['daɪ·ə‚sɪs] o ['daɪ·əsɪs] s diócesi f o diócesis f

diode ['daɪ·od] s diodo

dioxide [daɪ'aksaɪd] s dióxido

dip [dɪp] s zambullida, inmersión; baño corto; (in a road) depresión; (of magnetic needle) inclinación ‖ v (pret & pp dipped; ger dipping) tr sumergir; sacar con cuchara; (bread) sopetear; **to dip the colors** saludar con la bandera ‖ intr sumergirse; inclinarse hacia abajo; desaparecer súbitamente; **to dip into** hojear (un libro); meterse en (un comercio); **to dip into one's purse** gastar dinero

diphtheria [dɪf'θɪrɪ·ə] s difteria

diphthong ['dɪfθɔŋ] o ['dɪfθaŋ] s diptongo

diphthongize ['dɪfθɔŋ‚gaɪz] o ['dɪf-θaŋ‚gaɪz] tr diptongar ‖ intr diptongarse

diploma [dɪ'plomə] s diploma m

diploma·cy [dɪ'ploməsi] s (pl -cies) diplomacia

diplomat ['dɪplə‚mæt] s diplomático

diplomatic [‚dɪplə'mætɪk] adj diplomático

diplomatic pouch s valija diplomática

dipper ['dɪpər] s cazo, cucharón m

dip'stick' s varilla de nivel

dire [daɪr] adj horrendo, espantoso

direct [dɪ'rɛkt] o [daɪ'rɛkt] adj directo; franco, sincero ‖ tr dirigir; mandar, ordenar

direct current s corriente continua

direct discourse s (gram) estilo directo

direct hit s blanco directo, impacto directo

direction [dɪ'rɛkʃən] o [daɪ'rɛkʃən] s dirección; instrucción

direct object s (gram) complemento directo

director [dɪ'rɛktər] o [daɪ'rɛktər] s director m, administrador m; (member of a governing body) vocal m

directorship [dɪ'rɛktər‚ʃɪp] o [daɪ-'rɛktər‚ʃɪp] s dirección, directorio

directo·ry [dɪ'rɛktəri] o [daɪ'rɛktəri] s (pl -ries) (list of names and addresses; board of directors) directorio; anuario telefónico, guía telefónica

dirge [dʌrdʒ] s endecha, canto fúnebre, treno; (eccl) misa de réquiem

dirigible ['dɪrɪdʒɪbəl] adj & s dirigible m

dirt [dʌrt] s (soil) tierra, suelo; (dust) polvo; (mud) barro, lodo; (excrement; accumulation of dirt) suciedad; (moral filth) suciedad, porquería, obscenidad; (gossip) chismes mpl

dirt'cheap' adj tirado, muy barato

dirt road s camino de tierra

dirt·y ['dʌrti] adj (comp -ier; super -iest) puerco, sucio; barroso, enlodado; polvoriento; (obscene) hediondo; bajo, vil ‖ v (pret & pp -tied) tr ensuciar

dirty linen s ropa sucia; **to air one's**

dirty linen in public sacar los trapos sucios a relucir

dirty trick s (slang) perrada, mala partida

disabili·ty [‚dɪsə'bɪlɪti] s (pl -ties) incapacidad, inhabilidad

disable [dɪs'ebəl] tr incapacitar, inhabilitar, lisiar; (law) descalificar

disabuse [‚dɪsə'bjuz] tr desengañar

disadvantage [‚dɪsəd'væntɪdʒ] o [‚dɪsəd'vɑntɪdʒ] s desventaja

disadvantageous [dɪs‚ædvən'tdʒəs] adj desventajoso

disagree [‚dɪsə'gri] intr desavenirse, desconvenirse; (to quarrel) altercar, contender; **to disagree with** no estar de acuerdo con; no sentar bien

disagreeable [‚dɪsə'gri·əbəl] adj desagradable

disagreement [‚dɪsə'grimənt] s desavenencia, desacuerdo; disensión

disappear [‚dɪsə'pɪr] intr desaparecer, desaparecerse

disappearance [‚dɪsə'pɪrəns] s desaparecimiento, desaparición

disappoint [‚dɪsə'pɔɪnt] tr decepcionar, desilusionar, chasquear; **to be disappointed** chasquearse, llevarse chasco

disappointment [‚dɪsə'pɔɪntmənt] s decepción, desilusión, chasco

disapproval [‚dɪsə'pruvəl] s desaprobación

disapprove [‚dɪsə'pruv] tr & intr desaprobar

disarm [dɪs'arm] tr desarmar ‖ intr desarmarse

disarmament [dɪs'arməmənt] s desarme m

disarming [dɪs'armɪŋ] adj congraciador, simpático

disarray [‚dɪsə're] s desorden m; (in apparel) desatavío ‖ tr desordenar; desataviar

disaster [dɪ'zæstər] o [dɪ'zɑstər] s desastre m, siniestro

disastrous [dɪ'zæstrəs] o [dɪ'zɑstrəs] adj desastroso, desastrado

disavow [‚dɪsə'vau] tr desconocer, negar, repudiar

disband [dɪs'bænd] tr disolver (una asamblea); licenciar (tropas) ‖ intr desbandarse

dis·bar [dɪs'bar] v (pret & pp -barred; ger -barring) tr (law) expulsar del foro

disbelief [‚dɪsbɪ'lif] s incredulidad

disbelieve [‚dɪsbɪ'liv] tr & intr descreer

disburse [dɪs'bʌrs] tr desembolsar

disbursement [dɪs'bʌrsmənt] s desembolso

disc. abbr discount, discoverer

disc [dɪsk] s disco

discard [dɪs'kard] s descarte m; **to put into the discard** desechar ‖ tr descartar; desechar

discern [dɪ'zʌrn] o [dɪ'sʌrn] tr discernir, percibir

discerning [dɪ'zʌrnɪŋ] o [dɪ'sʌrnɪŋ] adj discerniente, perspicaz

discharge [dɪs'tʃardʒ] s (of a gun, of

a battery) descarga; (*of a prisoner*) liberación; (*of a duty*) desempeño; (*of a debt, of an obligation*) descargo; (*from a job*) despedida, remoción; (mil) certificado de licencia; (pathol) derrame *m* ‖ *tr* descargar; desempeñar (*un deber*); libertar (*a un preso*); despedir, remover (*a un empleado*); (*from the hospital*) dar de alta; (mil) licenciar ‖ *intr* descargar (*un tubo, río, etc.*); descargarse (*un arma de fuego*)

disciple [dɪ'saɪpəl] *s* discípulo

disciplinarian [,dɪsɪplɪ'nɛrɪ·ən] *s* ordenancista *mf*

discipline ['dɪsɪplɪn] *s* disciplina; castigo ‖ *tr* disciplinar; castigar

disclaim [dɪs'klem] *tr* desconocer, negar

disclose [dɪs'kloz] *tr* divulgar, revelar; descubrir

disclosure [dɪs'kloʒər] *s* divulgación, revelación; descubrimiento

discolor [dɪs'kʌlər] *tr* descolorar ‖ *intr* descolorarse

discomfiture [dɪs'kʌmfɪt/ər] *s* desconcierto; frustración

discomfort [dɪs'kʌmfərt] *s* incomodidad ‖ *tr* incomodar

disconcert [,dɪskən'sʌrt] *tr* desconcertar, confundir

disconnect [,dɪskə'nɛkt] *tr* desunir, separar; desconectar

disconsolate [dɪs'kɑnsəlɪt] *adj* desconsolado, desolado

discontent [,dɪskən'tɛnt] *adj* & *s* descontento ‖ *tr* descontentar

discontented [,dɪskən'tɛntɪd] *adj* descontento

discontinue [,dɪskən'tɪnju] *tr* descontinuar

discord ['dɪskɔrd] *s* desacuerdo, discordia; discordancia

discordance [dɪs'kɔrdəns] *s* discordancia

discotheque [,dɪsko'tɛk] *s* discoteca

discount ['dɪskaʊnt] *s* descuento ‖ ['dɪskaʊnt] o [dɪs'kaʊnt] *tr* descontar; descontar por exagerado

discount rate *s* tipo de descuento; tipo de redescuento

discourage [dɪs'kʌrɪdʒ] *tr* desalentar, desanimar; desaprobar; disuadir

discouragement [dɪs'kʌrɪdʒmənt] *s* desaliento; desaprobación; disuasión

discourse ['dɪskors] o [dɪs'kors] *s* discurso ‖ [dɪs'kors] *intr* discurrir

discourteous [dɪs'kʌrtɪ·əs] *adj* descortés

discourte·sy [dɪs'kʌrtəsi] *s* (*pl* -sies) descortesía

discover [dɪs'kʌvər] *tr* descubrir

discover·y [dɪs'kʌvəri] *s* (*pl* -ies) descubrimiento

discredit [dɪs'krɛdɪt] *s* descrédito ‖ *tr* desacreditar

discreditable [dɪs'krɛdɪtəbəl] *adj* deshonroso

discreet [dɪs'krit] *adj* discreto

discrepan·cy [dɪs'krɛpənsi] *s* (*pl* -cies) discrepancia

discrete [dɪs'krit] *adj* discreto

discretion [dɪs'krɛ/ən] *s* discreción; **at discretion** a discreción

discriminate [dɪs'krɪmɪ,net] *intr* discriminar; **to discriminate against** discriminar

discrimination [dɪs,krɪmɪ'ne/ən] *s* discriminación

discriminatory [dɪs'krɪmɪnə,tori] *adj* discriminatorio

discus ['dɪskəs] *s* (sport) disco

discuss [dɪs'kʌs] *tr* & *intr* discutir

discussion [dɪs'kʌ/ən] *s* discusión

discus thrower ['θro·ər] *s* discóbolo

disdain [dɪs'den] *s* desdén *m* ‖ *tr* desdeñar

disdainful [dɪs'denfəl] *adj* desdeñoso

disease [dɪ'ziz] *s* enfermedad

diseased [dɪ'zizd] *adj* morboso

disembark [,dɪsɛm'bɑrk] *tr* & *intr* desembarcar

disembarkation [dɪs,ɛmbɑr'ke/ən] *s* (*of passengers*) desembarco; (*of freight*) desembarque *m*

disembowel [,dɪsɛm'baʊ·əl] *tr* desentrañar

disenchant [,dɪsɛn't/ænt] o [,dɪsɛn't/ant] *tr* desencantar

disenchantment [,dɪsɛn't/æntmənt] o [,dɪsɛn't/antmənt] *s* desencanto

disengage [,dɪsɛn'gedʒ] *tr* (*from a pledge*) desempeñar; (*to disconnect*) desenganchar; desembragar (*el motor*)

disengagement [,dɪsɛn'gedʒmənt] *s* desempeño; desenganche *m;* desembrague *m*

disentangle [,dɪsɛn'tæŋgəl] *tr* desenredar

disentanglement [,dɪsɛn'tæŋgəlmənt] *s* desenredo

disestablish [,dɪsɛs'tæblɪ/] *tr* separar (*la Iglesia*) del Estado

disfavor [dɪs'fevər] *s* disfavor *m*

disfigure [dɪs'fɪgjər] *tr* desfigurar

disfranchise [dɪs'fræntʃaɪz] *tr* privar de los derechos de ciudadanía

disgorge [dɪs'gɔrdʒ] *tr* & *intr* vomitar

disgrace [dɪs'gres] *s* deshonra, vergüenza; disfavor *m* ‖ *tr* deshonrar, avergonzar; despedir con ignominia

disgraceful [dɪs'gresfəl] *adj* deshonroso, vergonzoso

disgruntle [dɪs·grʌntəl] *tr* disgustar, enfadar

disguise [dɪs'gaɪz] *s* disfraz *m* ‖ *tr* disfrazar

disgust [dɪs'gʌst] *s* asco, repugnancia ‖ *tr* dar asco a, repugnar

disgusting [dɪs'gʌstɪŋ] *adj* asqueroso, repugnante

dish [dɪ/] *s* (*any container used at table*) vasija; (*shallow, circular dish; its contents*) plato; **to wash the dishes** lavar la vajilla ‖ *tr* servir en un plato; (slang) arruinar

dish'cloth *s* albero

dishearten [dɪs'hɑrtən] *tr* descorazonar, desalentar, desanimar

dishev·el [dɪ'/ɛvəl] *v* (*pret & pp* -eled o -elled) *ger* -eling o -elling) desgreñar, desmelenar

dishonest [dɪs'ɑnɪst] *adj* no honrado, ímprobo

dishones·ty [dɪs'ɑnɪsti] *s* (*pl* **-ties**) falta de honradez, improbidad

dishonor [dɪs'ɑnər] *s* deshonra, deshonor *m* || *tr* deshonrar, deshonorar; (com) no aceptar, no pagar

dishonorable [dɪs'ɑnərəbəl] *adj* ignominioso, deshonroso

dish'pan' *s* paila de lavar la vajilla

dish rack *s* escurreplatos *m*

dish'rag' *s* albero

dish'tow'el *s* paño para secar platos

dish'wash'er *s* (*person*) fregona; (*machine*) lavaplatos *m*

dish'wa'ter *s* agua de lavar platos, agua sucia

disillusion [,dɪsɪ'luʒən] *s* desilusión || *tr* desilusionar

disillusionment [,dɪsɪ'luʒənmənt] *s* desilusión

disinclination [dɪs,ɪnklɪ'neʃən] *s* aversión, desafición

disinclined [,dɪsɪn'klaɪnd] *adj* desinclinado

disinfect [,dɪsɪn'fɛkt] *tr* desinfectar, desinficionar

disinfectant [,dɪsɪn'fɛktənt] *adj* & *s* desinfectante *m*

disingenuous [,dɪsɪn'dʒɛnju·əs] *adj* insincero, poco ingenuo

disinherit [,dɪsɪn'hɛrɪt] *tr* desheredar

disintegrate [dɪs'ɪntɪ,gret] *tr* desagregar, desintegrar || *intr* desagregarse, desintegrarse

disintegration [dɪs,ɪntɪ'greʃən] *s* desagregación, desintegración

disin·ter [,dɪsɪn'tʌr] *v* (*pret* & *pp* **-terred**; *ger* **-terring**) *tr* desenterrar

disinterested [dɪs'ɪntə,rɛstɪd] o [dɪs'ɪntrɪstɪd] *adj* desinteresado

disinterestedness [dɪs'ɪntə,rɛstɪdnɪs] o [dɪs'ɪntrɪstɪdnɪs] *s* desinterés *m*

disjunctive [dɪs'dʒʌŋktɪv] *adj* disyuntivo

disk [dɪsk] *s* disco

disk jockey *s* (rad) locutor *m* de un programa de discos

dislike [dɪs'laɪk] *s* aversión, antipatía; **to take a dislike for** cobrar aversión a || *tr* desamar

dislocate ['dɪslo,ket] *tr* dislocar, dislocarse (*un hueso*)

dislodge [dɪs'lɑdʒ] *tr* desalojar

disloyal [dɪs'lɔɪ·əl] *adj* desleal

disloyal·ty [dɪs'lɔɪ·əlti] *s* (*pl* **-ties**) deslealtad

dismal ['dɪzməl] *adj* lúgubre, tenebroso; terrible, espantoso

dismantle [dɪs'mæntəl] *tr* desarmar, desmontar

dismay [dɪs'me] *s* consternación || *tr* consternar

dismember [dɪs'mɛmbər] *tr* desmembrar

dismiss [dɪs'mɪs] *tr* despedir, destituir; desechar; alejar del pensamiento, echar en olvido

dismissal [dɪs'mɪsəl] *s* despedida, destitución

dismount [dɪs'maunt] *tr* desmontar || *intr* desmontarse

disobedience [,dɪsə'bidi·əns] *s* desobediencia

disobedient [,dɪsə'bidi·ənt] *adj* desobediente

disobey [,dɪsə'be] *tr* & *intr* desobedecer

disorder [dɪs'ɔrdər] *s* desorden *m* || *tr* desordenar

disorderly [dɪs'ɔrdərli] *adj* desordenado; alborotador, revoltoso

disorderly conduct *s* conducta contra el orden público

disorderly house *s* burdel *m*, lupanar *m*

disorganize [dɪs'ɔrgə,naɪz] *tr* desorganizar

disown [dɪs'on] *tr* desconocer, repudiar

disparage [dɪs'pærɪdʒ] *tr* desacreditar, desdorar

disparagement [dɪs'pærɪdʒmənt] *s* descrédito, desdoro

disparate ['dɪspərɪt] *adj* disparejo

dispari·ty [dɪs'pærɪti] *s* (*pl* **-ties**) disparidad

dispassionate [dɪs'pæʃənɪt] *adj* desapasionado

dispatch [dɪs'pætʃ] *s* despacho || *tr* despachar; (coll) despabilar (*una comida*)

dis·pel [dɪs'pɛl] *v* (*pret* & *pp* **-pelled**; *ger* **-pelling**) *tr* desvanecer, disipar

dispensa·ry [dɪs'pɛnsəri] *s* (*pl* **-ries**) dispensario

dispense [dɪs'pɛns] *tr* dispensar (*medicamentos*); administrar (*justicia*); expender (*p.ej., gasolina*); (*to exempt*) eximir || *intr* — **to dispense with** deshacerse de; pasar sin, prescindir de

disperse [dɪs'pʌrs] *tr* dispersar || *intr* dispersarse

displace [dɪs'ples] *tr* remover, trasladar; despedir, deponer; reemplazar; desplazar (*un volumen de agua*)

displaced person *s* persona desplazada

display [dɪs'ple] *s* despliegue *m*; exhibición, exposición; ostentación || *tr* (*to unfold; to reveal*) desplegar; (*to exhibit, show*) exhibir, exponer; (*to show ostentatiously*) ostentar

display cabinet *s* vitrina, escaparate *m*

display window *s* escaparate *m* de tienda

displease [dɪs'pliz] *tr* desagradar, disgustar, desplacer

displeasing [dɪs'plizɪŋ] *adj* desagradable

displeasure [dɪs'plɛʒər] *s* desagrado, disgusto, desplacer *m*

disposable [dɪs'pozəbəl] *adj* (*available for any use*) disponible; (*made to be thrown away after serving its purpose*) desechable, descartable

disposal [dɪs'pozəl] *s* disposición; donación, liquidación, venta; **at the disposal of** a la disposición de; **to have at one's disposal** disponer de

dispose [dɪs'poz] *tr* disponer; inducir, mover || *intr* disponer; **to dispose of** disponer de; deshacerse de; dar, vender; acabar con

disposition [ˌdɪspə'zɪʃən] s disposición; índole f, genio, natural m; ajuste m, arreglo; venta

dispossess [ˌdɪspə'zɛs] tr desposeer; (to evict, oust) desahuciar

disproof [dɪs'pruf] s confutación, refutación

disproportionate [ˌdɪsprə'pɔrʃənɪt] adj desproporcionado

disprove [dɪs'pruv] tr confutar, refutar

dispute [dɪs'pjut] s disputa; **beyond dispute** sin disputa; **in dispute** disputado || tr & intr disputar

disquali·fy [dɪs'kwɑlɪˌfaɪ] v (pret & pp -fied) tr descalificar, desclasificar

disquiet [dɪs'kwaɪ·ət] s desasosiego, inquietud || tr desasosegar, inquietar

disregard [ˌdɪsrɪ'gɑrd] s desatención, desaire m || tr desatender, desairar, pasar por alto

disrepair [ˌdɪsrɪ'pɛr] s desconcierto, descompostura

disreputable [dɪs'rɛpjətəbəl] adj desacreditado, de mala fama; raído, usado, desaliñado

disrepute [ˌdɪsrɪ'pjut] s descrédito, mala fama; **to bring into disrepute** desacreditar, dar mala fama a

disrespect [ˌdɪsrɪ'spɛkt] s desacato || tr desacatar

disrespectful [ˌdɪsrɪ'spɛktfəl] adj irrespetuoso

disrobe [dɪs'rob] tr desnudar || intr desnudarse

disrupt [dɪs'rʌpt] tr romper; (to throw into disorder) desbaratar

dissatisfaction [ˌdɪssætɪs'fækʃən] s desagrado, descontento

dissatisfied [dɪs'sætɪsˌfaɪd] adj descontento

dissatis·fy [dɪs'sætɪsˌfaɪ] v (pret & pp -fied) tr descontentar

dissect [dɪ'sɛkt] tr disecar

dissemble [dɪ'sɛmbəl] tr disimular || intr disimular; obrar hipócritamente

disseminate [dɪ'sɛmɪˌnet] tr diseminar, difundir

dissension [dɪ'sɛnʃən] s disensión

dissent [dɪ'sɛnt] s disensión; (nonconformity) disidencia || intr disentir; (from doctrine or authority) disidir

dissenter [dɪ'sɛntər] s disidente mf

disservice [dɪs'sʌrvɪs] s deservicio

dissidence ['dɪsɪdəns] s disidencia

dissident ['dɪsɪdənt] adj & s disidente mf

dissimilar [dɪ'sɪmɪlər] adj disímil, desemejante

dissimilate [dɪ'sɪmɪˌlet] tr disimilar || intr disimilarse

dissimulate [dɪ'sɪmjəˌlet] tr & intr disimular

dissipate ['dɪsɪˌpet] tr disipar || intr disiparse; entregarse a la disipación

dissipated ['dɪsɪˌpetɪd] adj disipado, disoluto

dissipation [ˌdɪsɪ'peʃən] s disipación

dissociate [dɪ'soʃɪˌet] tr disociar

dissolute ['dɪsəˌlut] adj disoluto

dissolution [ˌdɪsə'luʃən] s disolución

dissolve [dɪ'zɑlv] tr disolver || intr (to have the power of dissolving) disolver; (to pass into a liquid) disolverse

dissonance ['dɪsənəns] s disonancia

dissuade [dɪ'swed] tr disuadir

dissyllabic [ˌdɪssɪ'læbɪk] adj disílabo, disilábico

dissyllable [dɪ'sɪləbəl] s disílabo

dist. abbr distance, distinguish, district

distaff ['dɪstæf] o ['dɪstɑf] s rueca

distaff side s rama femenina de la familia

distance ['dɪstəns] s distancia; **at a distance** a distancia; **in the distance** a lo lejos; **to keep at a distance** no permitir familiaridades; **to keep one's distance** mantenerse a distancia

distant ['dɪstənt] adj distante; (relative) lejano; (not familiar) frío, indiferente

distaste [dɪs'test] s aversión, repugnancia

distasteful [dɪs'testfəl] adj desagradable, repugnante

distemper [dɪs'tɛmpər] s enfermedad; (of dogs) moquillo

distend [dɪs'tɛnd] tr ensanchar, distender || intr ensancharse, distender

distension [dɪs'tɛnʃən] s ensanche m, distensión

distill [dɪs'tɪl] tr destilar

distillation [ˌdɪstɪ'leʃən] s destilación

distiller·y [dɪs'tɪləri] s (pl -ies) destilería, destilatorio

distinct [dɪs'tɪŋkt] adj distinto; cierto, indubable; (not blurred) nítido, bien definido

distinction [dɪs'tɪŋkʃən] s distinción; (distinguishing characteristic) distintivo

distinctive [dɪs'tɪŋktɪv] adj distintivo

distinguish [dɪs'tɪŋgwɪʃ] tr distinguir

distinguished [dɪs'tɪŋgwɪʃt] adj distinguido

distort [dɪs'tɔrt] tr deformar, torcer; (the truth) falsear

distortion [dɪs'tɔrʃən] s deformación, torcimiento; (of the truth) falseamiento; (rad) deformación, distorsión

distract [dɪs'trækt] tr distraer

distraction [dɪs'trækʃən] s distracción

distraught [dɪs'trɔt] adj trastornado, perplejo, aturdido

distress [dɪs'trɛs] s pena, aflicción, angustia; infortunio, peligro || tr apenar, afligir, angustiar

distressing [dɪs'trɛsɪŋ] adj penoso, angustioso

distress signal s señal f de socorro

distribute [dɪs'trɪbjut] tr distribuir, repartir

distribution [ˌdɪstrɪ'bjuʃən] s distribución, repartimiento

distributor [dɪs'trɪbjətər] s distribuidor m; (aut) distribuidor

district ['dɪstrɪkt] s comarca, región; (of a city) barrio; (administrative division) distrito || tr dividir en distritos

district attorney s fiscal m

di
di

distrust [dɪs'trʌst] *s* desconfianza ‖ *tr* desconfiar de
distrustful [dɪs'trʌstfəl] *adj* desconfiado
disturb [dɪs'tʌrb] *tr* disturbar, incomodar, molestar; desordenar, revolver; inquietar, dejar perplejo; perturbar (*el orden público*)
disturbance [dɪs'tʌrbəns] *s* disturbio, molestia; desorden *m;* inquietud; tumulto, trastorno
disuse [dɪs'jus] *s* desuso
ditch [dɪtʃ] *s* zanja ‖ *tr* zanjar; echar en una zanja; (slang) deshacerse de ‖ *intr* amarar forzosamente
ditch reed *s* carrizo
dither ['dɪðər] *s* agitación, temblor; **to be in a dither** (coll) estar muy agitado
dit•to ['dɪto] *s* (*pl* -tos) ídem *m;* (*ditto symbol*) íd.; copia, duplicado ‖ *tr* copiar, duplicar
ditto mark *s* la sigla " (*es decir:* íd.)
dit•ty ['dɪti] *s* (*pl* -ties) cancioneta
div. *abbr* **dividend, division**
diva ['divɑ] *s* (mus) diva
divan ['daɪvæn] o [dɪ'væn] *s* diván *m*
dive [daɪv] *s* zambullida; (*of a submarine*) sumersión; (aer) picado; (coll) leonera, tasca ‖ *v* (*pret & pp* **dived** o **dove** [dov]) *intr* zambullirse; (*to work as a diver*) bucear; sumergirse (*un submarino*); (aer) picar
dive'-bomb' *tr & intr* bombardear en picado
dive bombing *s* bombardeo en picado
diver ['daɪvər] *s* zambullidor *m;* (*person who works under water*) escafandrista *mf*, buzo; (orn) zambullidor *m*
diverge [dɪ'vʌrdʒ] o [daɪ'vʌrdʒ] *intr* divergir
divers ['daɪvərz] *adj* diversos, varios
diverse [dɪ'vʌrs], [daɪ'vʌrs] o ['daɪvʌrs] *adj* (*different*) diverso; (*of various kinds*) variado
diversification [dɪ͵vʌrsɪfɪ'keʃən] o [daɪ͵vʌrsɪfɪ'keʃən] *s* diversificación
diversi•fy [dɪ'vʌrsɪ͵faɪ] o [daɪ'vʌrsɪ͵faɪ] *v* (*pret & pp* -fied) *tr* diversificar ‖ *intr* diversificarse
diversion [dɪ'vʌrʒən] o [daɪ'vʌrʒən] *s* diversión
diversi•ty [dɪ'vʌrsɪti] o [daɪ'vʌrsɪti] *s* (*pl* -ties) diversidad
divert [dɪ'vʌrt] o [daɪ'vʌrt] *tr* apartar, divertir; (*to entertain*) divertir, entretener; (mil) divertir
diverting [dɪ'vʌrtɪŋ] o [daɪ'vʌrtɪŋ] *adj* divertido
divest [dɪ'vest] o [daɪ'vest] *tr* desnudar; despojar, desposeer; **to divest oneself of** desposeerse de
divide [dɪ'vaɪd] *s* (geog) divisoria ‖ *tr* dividir ‖ *intr* dividirse
dividend ['dɪvɪ͵dend] *s* dividendo
dividers [dɪ'vaɪdərz] *spl* compás *m* de división
divination [͵dɪvɪ'neʃən] *s* adivinación
divine [dɪ'vaɪn] *adj* divino ‖ *s* sacerdote *m*, clérigo ‖ *tr* adivinar

diving ['daɪvɪŋ] *s* zambullida; buceo
diving bell *s* campana de buzo
diving board *s* trampolín *m*
diving suit *s* escafandra
divining rod [dɪ'vaɪnɪŋ] *s* vara de adivinar; (*ostensibly to discover water or metals*) vara buscadora
divini•ty [dɪ'vɪnɪti] *s* (*pl* -ties) divinidad; teología; **the Divinity** Dios *m*
division [dɪ'vɪʒən] *s* división
divisor [dɪ'vaɪzər] *s* (math) divisor *m*
divorce [dɪ'vors] *s* divorcio; **to get a divorce** divorciarse ‖ *tr* divorciar (*los cónyuges*); divorciarse de (*la mujer o el marido*) ‖ *intr* divorciarse
divorcee [dɪvor'si] *s* persona divorciada; mujer divorciada
divulge [dɪ'vʌldʒ] *tr* divulgar, revelar
dizziness ['dɪzɪnɪs] *s* vértigo; confusión, perplejidad
diz•zy ['dɪzi] *adj* (*comp* -zier; *super* -ziest) (*suffering or causing dizziness*) vertiginoso; confuso, perplejo; aturdido, incauto; (coll) tonto
do. *abbr* **ditto**
do [du] *v* (*tercera persona* **does** [dʌz]; *pret* **did** [dɪd]; *pp* **done** [dʌn]) *tr* hacer; resolver (*un problema*); recorrer (*cierta distancia*); cumplir con (*un deber*); aprender (*una lección*); componer (*la cama*); tocar (*el cabello*); rendir (*homenaje*); **to do one's best** hacer todo lo posible; **to do over** volver a hacer; repetir; renovar; **to do right by** tratar bien; **to do someone out of something** (coll) defraudar algo a alguien; **to do to death** despachar, matar; **to do up** empaquetar; poner en orden; almidonar y planchar (*una camisa*) ‖ *intr* actuar, obrar; conducirse; servir, ser suficiente; estar, hallarse; **how do you do?** ¿cómo está Vd.?; **that will do** eso sirve, eso es bastante; no digas más; **to have done** haber terminado; **to have done with** no tener más que ver con; **to have nothing to do with** no tener nada que ver con; **have to do with** tratar de; **to do away with** suprimir; matar; **to do for** servir para; **to do well** salir bien; **to do without** pasar sin ‖ *v aux* úsase 1) en oraciones interrogativas: **Do you speak Spanish?** ¿Habla Vd. español?; 2) en oraciones negativas: **I do not speak Spanish** No hablo español; 3) para substituir a otro verbo en oraciones elípticas: **Did you go to church this morning? Yes, I did** ¿Fué Vd. a la iglesia esta mañana? Sí, fuí; 4) para dar más energía a la oración: **I do believe what you told me** Yo sí creo lo que me dijo Vd.; 5) en inversiones después de ciertos adverbios: **Seldom does he come to see me** él rara vez viene a verme; 6) en tono suplicante con el imperativo: **Do come in** pase Vd., por favor
docile ['dɑsɪl] *adj* dócil
dock [dɑk] *s* (*wharf*) muelle *m;* (*wa-*

terway between two piers) dársena; *(area including piers and waterways)* puerto de mar; muñón *m* de cola; (law) tribuna de los acusados ‖ *tr* (naut) atracar en el muelle; derrabar, descolar *(a an animal)*; reducir o suprimir *(el salario)* ‖ *intr* (naut) atracar

dockage ['dakɪdʒ] *s* entrada en un puerto; *(charges)* muellaje *m*

docket ['dakɪt] *s* actas, orden *m* del día; lista de causas pendientes; **on the docket** (coll) pendiente, entre manos

dock hand *s* portuario

dock'yard' *s* arsenal *m*, astillero

doctor ['daktər] *s* doctor *m*; *(physician)* médico ‖ *tr* medicinar; (coll) componer, reparar ‖ *intr* (coll) ejercer la medicina; (coll) tomar medicinas

doctorate ['daktərɪt] *s* doctorado

doctrine ['daktrɪn] *s* doctrina

document ['dakjəmənt] *s* documento ‖ ['dakjə,ment] *tr* documentar

documenta·ry [,dakjə'mentəri] *adj* documental ‖ *s (pl* -ries) documental *m*

documentation [,dakəmen'teʃən] *s* documentación

doddering ['dadərɪŋ] *adj* chocho, temblón

dodge [dadʒ] *s* esguince *m*, regate *m*; (fig) regate ‖ *tr* evitar *(un golpe)*; (fig) evitar mañosamente ‖ *intr* regatear, hurtar el cuerpo; **to dodge around the corner** voltear la esquina

do·do ['dodo] *s (pl* -dos o -does) (coll) inocente *m* de ideas anticuadas

doe [do] *s* cierva, gama, coneja

doeskin ['do,skɪn] *s* ante *m*, piel *f* de ante; tejido fino de lana

doff [daf] o [dɔf] *tr* quitarse *(el sombrero, la ropa)*

dog [dɔg] o [dag] *s* perro; **to go to the dogs** darse al abandono; **to put on the dog** (coll) darse ínfulas ‖ *v (pret & pp* **dogged; *ger* dogging)** *tr* acosar, perseguir

dog'catch'er *s* lacero

dog days *spl* canícula, caniculares *mpl*

doge [dodʒ] dux *m*

dogged ['dɔgɪd] o ['dagɪd] *adj* tenaz, terco

doggerel ['dɔgərəl] o ['dagərəl] *s* coplas de ciego

dog·gy ['dɔgi] o ['dagi] *adj (comp* -gier; *super* -giest) emperejilado ‖ *s (pl* -gies) perrito

dog'house' *s* perrera

dog in the manger *s* el perro del hortelano

dog Latin *s* latinajo, latín *m* de cocina

dogmatic [dɔg'mætɪk] o [dag'mætɪk] *adj* dogmático

dog racing *s* carreras de galgos

dog's-ear ['dɔgz,ɪr] o ['dagz,ɪr] *s* orejón *m*

dog show *s* exposición canina

dog's life *s* vida miserable

Dog Star *s* Canícula

dog'-tired' *adj* cansadísimo

dog'tooth' *s (pl* -teeth [,tiθ]) colmillo

dog track *s* galgódromo

dog'watch' *s* (naut) guardia de cuartillo

dog'wood' *s* cornejo

doi·ly ['dɔɪli] *s (pl* -lies) pañito de adorno

doings ['du·ɪŋz] *spl* acciones, obras, actividad

doldrums ['daldrəmz] *spl* (naut) calmas ecuatoriales; desanimación, inactividad

dole [dol] *s* limosna; subsidio a los desocupados ‖ *tr* — **to dole out** distribuir en pequeñas porciones

doleful ['dolfəl] *adj* triste, lúgubre

doll [dal] *s* muñeca ‖ *intr* — **to doll up** (slang) emperejilarse

dollar ['dalər] *s* dólar *m*

dollar mark *s* signo del dólar

dol·ly ['dali] *s (pl* -lies) muñequita; *(low, wheeled frame for moving heavy loads)* gato rodante

dolphin ['dalfɪn] *s* delfín *m*

dolt [dolt] *s* bobalicón *m*

doltish ['doltɪʃ] *adj* bobalicón

dom. *abbr* **domestic, dominion**

domain [do'men] *s* dominio; heredad, propiedad; *(of learning)* campo

dome [dom] *s* cúpula, domo

dome light *s* (aut) lámpara de techo

domestic [də'mestɪk] *adj & s* doméstico

domesticate [də'mestɪ,ket] *tr* domesticar

domicile ['damɪsɪl] o ['damɪ,saɪl] *s* domicilio ‖ *tr* domiciliar

dominance ['damɪnəns] *s* dominación

dominant ['damɪnənt] *adj & s* dominante *f*

dominate ['damɪ,net] *tr & intr* dominar

domination [,damɪ'neʃən] *s* dominación

domineer [,damɪ'nɪr] *intr* dominar

domineering [,damɪ'nɪrɪŋ] *adj* dominante, mandón

Dominican [də'mɪnɪkən] *adj & s* dominicano

dominion [də'mɪnjən] *s* dominio

domi·no ['damɪ,no] *s (pl* -noes o -nos) *(costume)* dominó *m*; antifaz *m*; persona que lleva dominó; ficha *(del juego de dominó)*; **dominoes** *ssg* dominó *(juego)*

don [dan] *s* caballero, señor *m*, personaje *m* de alta categoría; (coll) preceptor *m*, socio de uno de los colegios de las Universidades de Oxford y Cambridge ‖ *v (pret & pp* **donned; *ger* donning)** *tr* ponerse *(el sombrero, la ropa)*

donate ['donet] *tr* dar, donar

donation [do'neʃən] *s* donación

done [dʌn] *adj* hecho, terminado; cansado, rendido; bien asado

done for *adj* (coll) cansado, rendido, agotado; (coll) arruinado, destruído; (coll) fuera de combate; (coll) muerto

donjon ['dʌndʒən] o ['dandʒən] *s* torre *f* del homenaje

di do

donkey ['daŋki] s asno, burro
donnish ['danɪʃ] adj magistral, pedantesco
donor ['donər] s donador m
doodle ['dudəl] tr & intr borrajear
doom [dum] s ruina, perdición, muerte f; condena, juicio; juicio final; hado, destino ‖ tr condenar; sentenciar a muerte; predestinar a la ruina, a la muerte
doomsday ['dumz,de] s día m del juicio final; día del juicio
door [dor] s puerta; (of a carriage or automobile) portezuela; (one part of a double door) hoja, batiente m; **behind closed doors** a puertas cerradas; **to see to the door** acompañar a la puerta
door'bell' s campanilla de puerta, timbre m de puerta
door check s amortiguador m, cierre m de puerta
door'frame' s bastidor m de puerta, marco de puerta
door'head' s dintel m
door'jamb' s jamba de puerta
door'knob' s botón m de puerta, pomo de puerta
door knocker s aldaba
door latch s pestillo
door·man ['dormæn] s (pl -men [mən]) portero; (one who helps people in and out of cars) abrecoches m
door'mat' s felpudo de puerta
door'nail' s clavo de adorno para puertas; **dead as a doornail** (coll) muerto sin duda alguna
door'post' s jamba de puerta
door scraper s limpiabarros m
door'sill' s umbral m
door'step' s escalón m delante de la puerta; escalera exterior
door'stop' s tope m de puerta
door'way' s puerta, portal m
dope [dop] s grasa lubricante; (aer) barniz m, nobabia; (slang) bobo, tonto; (slang) informes mpl; (slang) narcótico ‖ tr (slang) narcotizar, drogar; **to dope out** (slang) descifrar
dope fiend s (slang) toxicómano
dope sheet s (slang) hoja confidencial sobre los caballos de carreras
dormant ['dormənt] adj durmiente, latente
dormer window ['dormər] s buharda, buhardilla
dormito·ry ['dormɪ,tori] s (pl -ries) dormitorio común
dor·mouse ['dor,maus] s (pl -mice [,maɪs]) lirón m
dosage ['dosɪdʒ] s dosificación
dose [dos] s dosis f; (coll) mal trago ‖ tr medicinar; dosificar (un medicamento)
dossier ['dasɪ,e] s expediente m
dot [dat] s punto; **on the dot** (coll) en punto ‖ v (pret & pp dotted; ger dotting) tr (to make with dots) puntear; poner punto a; **to dot one's i's** poner los puntos sobre las íes
dotage ['dotɪdʒ] s chochera, chochez f; **to be in one's dotage** chochear

dotard ['dotərd] s viejo chocho
dote [dot] intr chochear; **to dote on** estar chocho por
doting ['dotɪŋ] adj chocho
dots and dashes spl (telg) puntos y rayas
dotted line ['datɪd] s línea de puntos; **to sign on the dotted line** firmar ciegamente
double ['dʌbəl] adj doble ‖ adv doble; dos juntos ‖ s doble m, duplo; (mov, theat) doble mf; **doubles** (tennis) juego de dobles ‖ tr doblar; ser el doble de; (bridge) doblar ‖ intr doblarse; (mov, theat, bridge) doblar; **to double up** doblarse en dos; ocupar una misma habitación, dormir en una misma cama (dos personas)
double-barreled ['dʌbəl'bærəld] adj de dos cañones; (fig) para dos fines
double bass [bes] s contrabajo
double bassoon s contrabajón m
double bed s cama de matrimonio
double-breasted ['dʌbəl'brestɪd] adj cruzado, de dos pechos
double chin s papada
dou'ble-cross' tr traicionar (a un cómplice)
double date s cita de dos parejas
doub'le-deal'er s persona doble
double-edged ['dʌbəl'edʒd] adj de dos filos
double entry s (com) partida doble
double feature s (mov) programa m doble, programa de dos películas de largo metraje
double-header ['dʌbəl'hedər] s tren m con dos locomotoras; (baseball) dos partidos jugados sucesivamente
double-jointed ['dʌbəl'dʒɔɪntɪd] adj de articulaciones dobles
dou'ble-park' tr & intr aparcar en doble fila
dou'ble-quick' adj & adv a paso ligero ‖ s paso ligero ‖ intr marchar a paso ligero
doublet ['dʌblɪt] s (close-fitting jacket) jubón m; (counterfeit stone; each of two words having the same origin) doblete m
double talk s (coll) galimatías m; (coll) habla ambigua para engañar
double time s pago doble por horas extraordinarias de trabajo; (mil) paso redoblado
doubleton ['dʌbəltən] s doblete m
double track s doble vía
doubt [daut] s duda; **beyond doubt** sin duda; **if in doubt** en caso de duda; **no doubt** sin duda ‖ tr dudar, dudar de ‖ intr dudar
doubter ['dautər] s incrédulo
doubtful ['dautfəl] adj dudoso
doubtless ['dautlɪs] adj indudable ‖ adv sin duda; probablemente
douche [duʃ] s ducha; (instrument) jeringa ‖ tr duchar ‖ intr ducharse
dough [do] s masa, pasta; (money) (slang) pasta
dough'boy' s (coll) soldado norteamericano de infantería

dough′nut′ s rosquilla, buñuelo

dough‧ty [′dauti] adj (comp **-tier;** super **-tiest**) (hum) fuerte, valiente

dough‧y [′do‧i] adj (comp **-ier;** super **-iest**) pastoso

dour [daur] o [dur] adj triste, melancólico, austero

douse [daus] tr empapar, mojar, salpicar; (slang) apagar (la luz)

dove [dʌv] s paloma

dovecote [′dʌv‚kot] s palomar m

dove′tail′ s cola de milano, cola de pato || tr ensamblar a cola de milano, ensamblar a cola de pato; (to make fit) encajar || intr (to fit) encajar; concordar, corresponder

dowager [′dau‧ədʒər] s viuda con título o bienes que proceden del marido, p.ej., **dowager duchess** duquesa viuda; (coll) matrona, señora anciana respetable

dow‧dy [′daudi] adj (comp **-dier;** super **-diest**) desaliñado

dow‧el [′dau‧əl] s clavija || v (pret & pp **-eled** o **-elled;** ger **-eling** o **-elling**) tr enclavijar

dower [′dau‧ər] s (widow's portion) viudedad; (marriage portion) dote m & f; (natural gift) prenda || tr señalar viudedad a; dotar

down [daun] adj descendente; abatido, triste; enfermo, malo; acostado, echado; (money, payment) anticipado; (storage battery) agotado || adv abajo; hacia abajo; en tierra; al sur; por escrito; al contado; **down and out** arruinado; sin blanca; **down from** desde; **down on one's knees** de rodillas; **down to** hasta; **down under** entre los antípodas; **down with . . . !** ¡abajo . . . !; **to get down to work** aplicarse resueltamente al trabajo; **to go down** bajar; **to lie down** acostarse; **to sit down** sentarse || prep bajando; **down the river** río abajo; **down the street** calle abajo || s (of fruit and human body) vello; (of birds) plumón m; descenso; revés m de fortuna; (sand hill) duna || tr derribar; (coll) tragar

down′cast′ adj cariacontecido

down′fall′ s caída, ruina; chaparrón m; nevazo

down′grade′ adj (coll) pendiente, en declive || adv (coll) cuesta abajo || s bajada, declive m; **to be on the downgrade** decaer, declinar || tr disminuir la categoría de

downhearted [′daun‚hɑrtɪd] adj abatido, desanimado

down′hill′ adj pendiente || adv cuesta abajo; **to go downhill** ir cabeza abajo

down′pour′ s aguacero, chaparrón m

down′right′ adj absoluto, categórico; franco; claro || adv absolutamente

down′stairs′ adj de abajo || adv abajo || s piso inferior, pisos inferiores; (the help) la servidumbre

down′stream′ adv aguas abajo, río abajo

down′stroke′ s carrera descendente

down′town′ adj céntrico || adv al centro de la ciudad, en el centro de la ciudad || s barrios céntricos, calles céntricas

down train s tren m descendente

down′trend′ s tendencia a la baja

downtrodden [′daun‚trɑdən] adj pisoteado, oprimido

downward [′daunwərd] adj descendente || adv hacia abajo; hacia una época posterior

down‧y [′dauni] adj (comp **-ier;** super **-iest**) plumoso, felpudo, velloso; suave, blando

dow‧ry [′dauri] s (pl **-ries**) dote m & f

doz. abbr dozen

doze [doz] s duermevela, sueño ligero || intr dormitar

dozen [′dʌzən] s docena

dozy [′dozi] adj soñoliento

D.P. abbr displaced person

dpt. abbr department

Dr. abbr debtor, drawer, dram

Dr. abbr debtor, Doctor

drab [dræb] adj (comp **drabber;** super **drabbest**) gris amarillento; monótono || s gris amarillento; ramera; mujer desaliñada

drach‧ma [′drækmə] s (pl **-mas** o **-mae** [mi]) dracma

draft [dræft] o [drɑft] s corriente f de aire; (pulling; current of air in a chimney) tiro; (sketch, outline) bosquejo; (first form of a writing) borrador m; (drink) bebida, trago; (com) giro, letra de cambio, libranza; aire inspirado; (naut) calado; (mil) conscripción, quinta; **drafts** damas, juego de damas; **on draft** a presión; **to be exempted from the draft** redimirse de las quintas || tr dibujar; bosquejar; hacer un borrador de; redactar (un documento); (mil) quintar; **to be drafted** (mil) ir a quintas

draft age s edad f de quintas

draft beer s cerveza a presión

draft board s (mil) junta de reclutamiento

draft call s llamada a quintas

draft dodger [′dɑdʒər] s emboscado

draftee [‚dræf′ti] o [‚drɑf′ti] s conscripto, quinto

draft horse s caballo de tiro

drafting room s sala de dibujo

drafts‧man [′dræftsmən] o [′drɑftsmən] s (pl **-men** [mən]) dibujante m; (man who draws up documents) redactor m; (in checkers) peón m

draft treaty s proyecto de convenio

draft‧y [′dræfti] o [′drɑfti] adj (comp **-ier;** super **-iest**) airoso, con corrientes de aire

drag [dræg] s (sledge for conveying heavy bodies) narria; (on a cigarette) chupada; fumada; (naut) rastra; (aer) resistencia al avance; (fig) estorbo, impedimento; **to have a drag** (slang) tener buenas aldabas, tener enchufe || v (pret & pp **dragged;** ger **dragging**) tr arrastrar; (naut) rastrear || intr arrastrarse por el suelo; avanzar muy lentamente; decaer (el *interés*); **to drag on** ser interminable, prolongarse interminablemente

drag'net' *s* red barredera

dragon ['drægən] *s* dragón *m*

drag'on·fly' *s* (*pl* -**flies**) caballito del diablo, libélula

dragoon [drə'gun] *s* (*soldier*) dragón *m* ‖ *tr* tiranizar; forzar, constreñir

drain [dren] *s* dren *m*, desaguadero, desagüe *m;* (surg) dren *m;* (*source of continual expense*) (fig) desaguadero ‖ *tr* drenar, desaguar; avenar (*terrenos húmedos*); escurrir (*una vasija; un líquido*) ‖ *intr* desaguarse; escurrirse

drainage ['drenɪdʒ] *s* drenaje *m*, desagüe *m*

drain'board' *s* escurridero

drain cock *s* llave *f* de purga

drain'pipe' *s* tubo de desagüe, escurridero

drain plug *s* tapón *m* de desagüe; (aut) tapón de vaciado

drake [drek] *s* pato

dram [dræm] *s* dracma; trago de aguardiente

drama ['dramə] o ['dræmə] *s* drama *m;* (*art and genre*) dramática

dramatic [drə'mætɪk] *adj* dramático ‖ **dramatics** *ssg* representación de aficionados; *spl* obras representadas por aficionados

dramatist ['dræmətɪst] *s* dramático

dramatize ['dræmə͵taɪz] *tr* dramatizar

dram'shop' *s* bar *m*, taberna

drape [drep] *s* cortina, colgadura; (*hang of a curtain, skirt, etc.*) caída ‖ *tr* cubrir con colgaduras; adornar con colgaduras; disponer los pliegues de (*una colgadura, una prenda de vestir*)

draper·y ['drepəri] *s* (*pl* -**ies**) colgaduras, ropaje *m*

drastic ['dræstɪk] *adj* drástico

draught [dræft] o [drɑft] *s & tr* var de **draft**

draught beer *s* cerveza a presión

draw [drɔ] *s* (*in a game or other contest*) empate *m;* (*in chess or checkers*) tablas; (*in a lottery*) sorteo; (*card drawn from the bank*) robo; (*of a drawbridge*) compuerta; (*of a chimney*) tiro ‖ *v* (*pret* **drew** [dru]; *pp* **drawn** [drɔn]) *tr* tirar (*una línea; alambre*); (*to attract*) atraer; (*to pull*) tirar de; derretir (*la mantequilla*); sacar (*un clavo, una espada, agua, una conclusión*); atraerse (*aplausos*); atraer (*a la gente*); aspirar (*el aire*); llamar (*la atención*); dar (*un suspiro*); correr (*una cortina*); cobrar (*un salario*); sacarse (*un premio*); empatar (*una partida*); robar (*fichas, naipes*); levantar (*un puente levadizo*); calar (*un buque cierta profundidad*); hacer (*una comparación*); consumir (*amperios*); (*to sketch in lines*) dibujar; (*to sketch in words*) redactar; (com) girar, librar; (com) devengar (*interés*); **to draw forth** hacer salir; **to draw off** sacar, extraer; trasegar (*un líquido*);

to draw on ocasionar, provocar; ponerse (*p.ej., los zapatos*); (com) girar a cargo de; **to draw oneself up** enderezarse con dignidad; **to draw out** (*to persuade to talk*) sonsacar, tirar de la lengua a; **to draw up** redactar (*un documento*); (mil) ordenar para el combate ‖ *intr* tirar, tirar bien (*una chimenea*); empatar; echar suertes; atraer mucha gente; dibujar; **to draw aside** apartarse; **to draw back** retroceder, retirarse; **to draw near** acercarse; acercarse a; **to draw to a close** estar para terminar; **to draw together** juntarse, unirse

draw'back' *s* desventaja, inconveniente *m*

draw'bridge' *s* puente levadizo

drawee [͵drɔ'i] *s* girado, librado

drawer ['drɔ·ər] *s* dibujante *mf;* (com) girador *m*, librador *m* ‖ [drɔr] *s* cajón *m*, gaveta; **drawers** calzoncillos

drawing ['drɔ·ɪŋ] *s* dibujo; (*in a lottery*) sorteo

drawing board *s* tablero de dibujo

drawing card *s* polo de atracción popular

drawing room *s* sala, salón *m*

draw'knife' *s* (*pl* -**knives** [͵naɪvz]) cuchilla de dos mangos

drawl [drɔl] *s* habla lenta y prolongada ‖ *tr* decir lenta y prolongadamente ‖ *intr* hablar lenta y prolongadamente

drawn butter [drɔn] *s* mantequilla derretida

drawn work *s* calado, deshilado

dray [dre] *s* carro fuerte, camión *m;* (*sledge*) narria

drayage ['dre·ɪdʒ] *s* acarreo

dread [drɛd] *adj* espantoso, terrible ‖ *s* pavor *m*, terror *m* ‖ *tr & intr* temer

dreadful ['drɛdfəl] *adj* espantoso, terrible; (coll) feo, desagradable

dread'naught' *s* (nav) gran buque acorazado

dream [drim] *s* sueño, ensueño; (*thing of great beauty*) sueño; (*fancy, illusion*) ensueño; **dream come true** sueño hecho realidad ‖ *v* (*pret & pp* **dreamed** o **dreamt** [drɛmt]) *tr* soñar; **to dream up** (coll) imaginar, inventar; ‖ *intr* soñar; **to dream of** soñar con

dreamer ['drimər] *s* soñador *m*

dream'land' *s* reino del ensueño

dream world *s* tierra de la fantasía

dream·y ['drimi] *adj* (*comp* -**ier;** *super* -**iest**) soñador; visionario; vago

drear·y ['drɪri] *adj* (*comp* -**ier;** *super* -**iest**) sombrío, triste; monótono, pesado

dredge [drɛdʒ] *s* draga ‖ *tr* dragar, rastrear; (culin) enharinar

dredger ['drɛdʒər] *s* draga (*barco*)

dredging ['drɛdʒɪŋ] *s* dragado

dregs [drɛgz] *spl* heces *fpl;* (*of society*) hez *f*

drench [drɛntʃ] *tr* mojar, empapar

dress [drɛs] *s* ropa, vestidos; vestido de mujer; (*skirt*) falda; traje *m* de

etiqueta; (of a bird) plumaje m || tr
vestir; (to provide with clothing) trajear; peinar (el pelo); curar (una
herida); zurrar (el cuero); empavesar
(un barco); adornar, ataviar; aderezar, aliñar (los manjares); to dress
down (coll) reprender; to get dressed
vestirse || intr (to put one's clothing
on) vestirse; (to wear clothes) vestir;
(mil) alinearse; to dress up vestirse
de etiqueta; ponerse de veinticinco
alfileres; disfrazarse
dress ball s baile m de etiqueta
dress coat s frac m
dresser ['drɛsər] s tocador m; cómoda
con espejo; (sideboard) aparador m;
to be a good dresser vestir con elegancia
dress form s maniquí m
dress goods spl géneros para vestidos
dressing ['drɛsɪŋ] s adorno; (for food)
aliño, salsa; (stuffing for fowl) relleno; (fertilizer) abono; (for a
wound) vendaje m
dress'ing-down' s (coll) repasata, regaño
dressing gown s bata, peinador m
dressing room s cuarto de vestir;
(theat) camarín m
dressing station s (mil) puesto de socorro
dressing table s tocador m
dress'mak'er s costurera, modista
dress'mak'ing s costura, modistería
dress rehearsal s ensayo general
dress shirt s camisa de pechera almido-
nada, camisa de pechera de encaje
dress shop s casa de modas
dress suit s traje m de etiqueta
dress tie s corbata de smoking, corbata
de frac
dress-y ['drɛsi] adj (comp -ier; super
-iest) (coll) elegante; (showy) acicalado, vistoso, peripuesto
dribble ['drɪbəl] s goteo; (coll) llovizna
|| tr (sport) driblar || intr gotear; (at
the mouth) babear; (sport) driblar
driblet ['drɪblɪt] s gotita; pedacito
dried beef [draɪd] s cecina
dried fig s higo paso
dried peach s orejón m
drier ['draɪ·ər] s enjugador m; (for
hair) secador m; (for clothes) secadora; (rack for drying clothes) tendedero (de ropa)
drift [drɪft] s movimiento; (of sand,
snow) montón m; (movement of
snow) ventisca; tendencia, dirección;
intención, sentido; (aer, naut) de-
riva; (rad, telv) desviación || intr
flotar a la deriva; amontonarse (la
nieve); ventiscar; (aer, naut) derivar, ir a la deriva; (fig) vivir sin
rumbo
drift ice s hielo flotante
drift'wood' s madera flotante; madera
llevada por el agua; madera arro-
jada a la playa por el agua; (people)
vagos
drill [drɪl] s taladro; instrucción;
(fabric) dril m; (mil) ejercicio || tr
taladrar; instruir; (mil) enseñar el

ejercicio a || intr adiestrarse; (mil)
hacer el ejercicio
drill'mas'ter s amaestrador m; (mil)
instructor m
drill press s prensa taladradora
drink [drɪŋk] s bebida; the drinks are
on the house! ¡convida la casa! || v
(pret drank [dræŋk]; pp drunk
[drʌŋk]) tr beber; beberse (su sueldo); to drink down beber de una
vez; to drink in beber (las palabras
de una persona); beberse (un libro);
aspirar (el aire) || intr beber; to
drink out of beber de o en; to drink
to the health of beber a o por la
salud de
drinkable ['drɪŋkəbəl] adj bebedizo,
potable
drinker ['drɪŋkər] s bebedor m
drinking ['drɪŋkɪŋ] s (el) beber
drinking cup s taza para beber
drinking fountain s fuente f para beber
drinking song s canción báquica, canción de taberna
drinking trough s abrevadero
drinking water s agua para beber
drip [drɪp] s goteo; gotas || v (pret &
pp dripped; ger dripping) intr caer
gota a gota, gotear
drip coffee s café m de maquinilla
drip'-dry' adj de lava y pon
drip pan s colector m de aceite
drive [draɪv] s paseo en coche; calzada; fuerza, vigor m; urgencia;
campaña vigorosa; venta a bajo precio; (aut) tracción (delantera o tra-
sera); (mach) transmisión, mando ||
v (pret drove [drov]; ger driven
['drɪvən]) tr conducir, guiar, manejar (un automóvil); clavar, hincar
(un clavo); arrear (a las bestias); (in
a carriage or auto) llevar (a una
persona); empujar, impeler; estimular; forzar, compeler; obligar a trabajar mucho; (sport) golpear con
gran fuerza; to drive away ahuyentar; to drive back rechazar; to drive
mad volver loco || intr ir en coche;
to drive at aspirar a; querer decir; to
drive hard trabajar mucho; to drive
in entrar en coche; entrar en (un
sitio) en coche; to drive on the right
circular por la derecha; to drive out
salir en coche; to drive up llegar en
coche
drive-in movie theater ['draɪv,ɪn] s
auto-teatro
drive-in restaurant s restaurante m
donde los clientes no necesitan dejar sus coches
driv•el ['drɪvəl] s (slobber) baba;
(nonsense) bobería || v (pret -eled o
-elled; ger -eling o -elling) intr babear; (to talk nonsense) bobear
driver ['draɪvər] s conductor m; (of a
carriage) cochero; (of a locomotive)
maquinista m; (of pack animals)
arriero
driver's license s carnet m de chófer,
permiso de conducir
drive shaft s árbol m de mando, eje m
motor

dr
dr

drive'way' *s* calzada; camino de entrada para coches

drive wheel *s* rueda motriz

drive'-your-self' service *s* alquiler *m* sin chófer

driving school *s* auto-escuela

drizzle ['drɪzəl] *s* llovizna ‖ *intr* lloviznar

droll [drol] *adj* chusco, gracioso

dromedar·y ['drɑmə͵dɛri] *s* (*pl* -ies) dromedario

drone [dron] *s* zángano; (*buzz, hum*) zumbido; (*of bagpipe*) bordón *m*, roncón *m*; avión radiodirigido ‖ *tr* decir monótonamente ‖ *intr* hablar monótonamente; (*to live in idleness*) zanganear; (*to buzz, hum*) zumbar

drool [drul] *s* (*slobber*) baba; (*slang*) bobería ‖ *intr* babear; (*slang*) bobear

droop [drup] *s* inclinación ‖ *intr* caer, colgar; inclinarse; marchitarse; abatirse; encamarse (*el grano*)

drooping ['drupɪŋ] *adj* (*eyelid, shoulder*) caído

drop [drɑp] *s* gota; (*slope*) pendiente *f*; (*earring*) pendiente *m*; (*in temperature*) descenso; (*of supplies from an airplane*) lanzamiento; (*trap door*) escotillón *m*; (*gallows*) horca; (*lozenge*) pastilla; (*small amount*) chispa; (*slit for letters*) buzón *m*; (*curtain*) telón *m*; **a drop in the bucket** una gota en el mar ‖ *v* (*pret & pp* **dropped**; *ger* **dropping**) *tr* dejar caer; echar (*una carta*) al buzón; bajar (*una cortina*); soltar (*una indirecta*); escribir (*una esquela*); omitir, suprimir; abandonar, dejar; echar (*el ancla*); borrar de la lista (*a un alumno*); lanzar (*bombas o suministros de un avión*) ‖ *intr* caer; bajar; cesar, terminar; **to drop dead** caer muerto; **to drop in** entrar al pasar, visitar de paso; **to drop off** desaparecer; quedarse dormido; morir de repente; **to drop out** desaparecer; retirarse; darse de baja

drop curtain *s* telón *m*

drop hammer *s* martinete *m*

drop'-leaf' table *s* mesa de hoja plegadiza

drop'light' *s* lámpara colgante

drop'out' *s* fracasado, desertor *m* escolar; **to become a dropout** ahorcar los libros

dropper ['drɑpər] *s* cuentagotas *m*

drop shutter *s* obturador *m* de guillotina

dropsical ['drɑpsɪkəl] *adj* hidrópico

dropsy ['drɑpsi] *s* hidropesía

drop table *s* mesa perezosa

dross [drɔs] *o* [drɑs] *s* (*of metals*) escoria; (fig) escoria, hez *f*

drought [draut] *s* (*long period of dry weather*) sequía; (*dryness*) sequedad

drove [drov] *s* manada, rebaño, hato; gentío, multitud

drover ['drovər] *s* ganadero

drown [draun] *tr* anegar, ahogar ‖ *intr* anegarse, ahogarse

drowse [drauz] *intr* adormecerse, amodorrarse

drow·sy ['drauzi] *adj* (*comp* -sier; *super* -siest) soñoliento, modorro

drub [drʌb] *v* (*pret & pp* **drubbed**; *ger* **-drubbing**) *tr* apalear, pegar, tundir; derrotar completamente

drudge [drʌdʒ] *s* yunque *m*, esclavo del trabajo ‖ *intr* afanarse

drudger·y ['drʌdʒəri] *s* (*pl* -ies) trabajo penoso

drug [drʌg] *s* droga, medicamento; narcótico; **drug on the market** macana, artículo invendible ‖ *v* (*pret & pp* **drugged**; *ger* **drugging**) *tr* narcotizar; mezclar con drogas

drug addict *s* toxicómano

drug addiction *s* toxicomanía

druggist ['drʌgɪst] *s* boticario, farmacéutico; (*dealer in drugs, chemicals, dyes, etc.*) droguero

drug habit *s* vicio de los narcóticos

drug store *s* farmacia, botica, droguería

drug traffic *s* contrabando de narcóticos

druid ['dru·ɪd] *s* druida *m*

drum [drʌm] *s* (*cylinder; instrument of percussion*) tambor *m*; (*container for oil, gasoline, etc.*) bidón *m* ‖ *v* (*pret & pp* **drummed**; *ger* **drumming**) *tr* reunir a toque de tambor; **to drum up trade** fomentar ventas ‖ *intr* tocar el tambor; (*with the fingers*) teclear

drum'beat' *s* toque *m* de tambor

drum corps *s* banda de tambores

drum'fire' *s* fuego graneado, fuego nutrido

drum'head' *s* parche *m* de tambor

drum major *s* tambor *m* mayor

drummer ['drʌmər] *s* tambor *m*, tamborilero; agente viajero

drum'stick' *s* baqueta, palillo; (coll) muslo (*de ave cocida*)

drunk [drʌŋk] *adj* borracho; **to get drunk** emborracharse ‖ *s* (coll) borracho; (*spree*) (coll) borrachera

drunkard ['drʌŋkərd] *s* borrachín *m*

drunken ['drʌŋkən] *adj* borracho

drunken driving *s* — **to be arrested for drunken driving** ser arrestado por conducir en estado de embriaguez

drunkenness ['drʌŋkənnɪs] *s* embriaguez *f*

dry [draɪ] *adj* (*comp* **drier**; *super* **driest**) seco; (*thirsty*) sediento; (*dull, boring*) árido ‖ *s* (*pl* **drys**) (*prohibitionist*) (coll) seco ‖ *v* (*pret & pp* **dried**) *tr* secar; (*to wipe dry*) enjugar ‖ *intr* secarse; **to dry up** secarse completamente; (*slang*) callar, dejar de hablar

dry battery *s* pila seca; (*group of dry cells*) batería seca

dry cell *s* pila seca

dry'-clean' *tr* lavar en seco, limpiar en seco

dry cleaner *s* tintorero

dry cleaning *s* lavado a seco, limpieza en seco

dry'-clean'ing establishment *s* tintorería

dry dock *s* dique seco

dryer ['draɪ·ər] *s* var de **drier**

dry'-eyed' *adj* ojienjuto
dry farming *s* cultivo de secano
dry goods *spl* mercancías generales (*tejidos, lencería, pañería, sedería*)
dry ice *s* carbohielo, hielo seco
dry law *s* ley seca
dry measure *s* medida para áridos
dryness ['draɪnɪs] *s* sequedad; (*e.g., of a speaker*) aridez *f*
dry nurse *s* ama seca
dry season *s* estación de la seca
dry wash *s* ropa lavada y secada pero no planchada
d.s. *abbr* days after sight, daylight saving
D.S.T. *abbr* Daylight Saving Time
dual ['dju·əl] o ['du·əl] *adj & s* dual *m*
duali·ty [dju'ælɪti] o [du'ælɪti] *s* (*pl -ties*) dualidad
dub [dʌb] *s* (slang) jugador *m* torpe ‖ *v* (*pret & pp* **dubbed**; *ger* **dubbing**) *tr* apellidar; armar caballero; (mov) doblar
dubbing ['dʌbɪŋ] *s* doblado, doblaje *m*
dubious ['djubɪ·əs] o ['dubɪ·əs] *adj* dudoso
ducat ['dʌkət] *s* ducado
duchess ['dʌtʃɪs] *s* duquesa
duch·y ['dʌtʃɪ] *s* (*pl -ies*) ducado
duck [dʌk] *s* pato; (*female*) pata; agachada rápida; (*in the water*) zambullida; **ducks** (coll) pantalones *mpl* de dril ‖ *tr* bajar rápidamente (*la cabeza*); (*in water*) chapuzar; (coll) esquivar, evitar (*un golpe*) ‖ *intr* chapuzar; **to duck out** (coll) escabullirse
duck'-toed' *adj* zancajoso
duct [dʌkt] *s* conducto, canal *m*
ductile ['dʌktɪl] *adj* dúctil
ductless gland ['dʌktlɪs] *s* glándula cerrada
duct'work' *s* canalización
dud [dʌd] *s* (slang) bomba que no estalla; (slang) fracaso; **duds** (coll) trapos, prendas de vestir
dude [djud] o [dud] *s* caballerete *m*
due [dju] o [du] *adj* debido; aguardado, esperado; pagadero; **due to** debido a; **to fall due** vencer; **when is the train due?** ¿a qué hora debe llegar el tren? ‖ *adv* directamente, derecho ‖ *s* deuda; **dues** derechos; (*of a member*) cuota; **to get one's due** llevar su merecido; **to give the devil his due** ser justo hasta con el diablo
duel ['dju·əl] o ['du·əl] *s* duelo; **to fight a duel** batirse en duelo ‖ *v* (*pret & pp* **dueled** o **duelled**; *ger* **dueling** o **duelling**) *intr* batirse en duelo
duelist o **duellist** ['dju·əlɪst] o ['du·əlɪst] *s* duelista *m*
dues-paying ['djuz,pe·ɪŋ] o ['duz,pe·ɪŋ] *adj* cotizante
duet [dju'ɛt] o [du'ɛt] *s* dúo
duke [djuk] o [duk] *s* duque *m*
dukedom ['djukdəm] o ['dukdəm] *s* ducado
dull [dʌl] *adj* (*not sharp*) embotado, romo; (*color*) apagado; (*sound;*

pain) sordo; (*stupid*) lerdo, torpe; (*business*) inactivo, muerto; (*boring*) aburrido, tedioso; (*flat*) deslucido, deslustrado ‖ *tr* embotar, enromar; deslucir, deslustrar; enfriar (*el entusiasmo*) ‖ *intr* embotarse, enromarse; deslucirse, deslustrarse
dullard ['dʌlərd] *s* estúpido
duly ['djuli] o ['duli] *adv* debidamente
dumb [dʌm] *adj* (*lacking the power to speak*) mudo; (coll) estúpido, torpe
dumb'bell' *s* halterio; (slang) estúpido, tonto
dumb creature *s* animal *m*, bruto
dumb show *s* pantomima
dumb'wait'er *s* montaplatos *m*
dumfound [ˌdʌm'faʊnd] *tr* pasmar, dejar sin habla
dum·my ['dʌmi] *adj* falso, fingido, simulado ‖ *s* (*pl -mies*) (*dress form*) maniquí *m*; cabeza para pelucas; (*in card games*) muerto; cartas del muerto; (*figurehead, straw man*) testaferro; (*skeleton copy of a book*) maqueta; imitación, copia; (slang) estúpido
dump [dʌmp] *s* basurero, vertedero; montón *m* de basuras; (mil) depósito de municiones; (min) terrero; **to be down in the dumps** (coll) tener murria ‖ *tr* descargar, verter; vaciar de golpe; vender en grandes cantidades y a precios inferiores a los corrientes
dumping ['dʌmpɪŋ] *s* descarga; venta en grandes cantidades y a precios inferiores a los corrientes
dumpling ['dʌmplɪŋ] *s* bola de pasta rellena de fruta o carne
dump truck *s* camión *m* volquete
dump·y ['dʌmpi] *adj* (*comp -ier*; *super -iest*) regordete, rollizo
dun [dʌn] *adj* bruno, pardo, castaño ‖ *s* acreedor importuno; (*demand for payment*) apremio ‖ *v* (*pret & pp* **dunned**; *ger* **dunning**) *tr* importunar para el pago, apremiar (*a un deudor*)
dunce [dʌns] *s* zopenco, bodoque *m*
dunce cap *s* capirote *m* que se le pone al alumno torpe
dune [djun] o [dun] *s* duna, médano
dung [dʌŋ] *s* estiércol *m* ‖ *tr* estercolar
dungarees [ˌdʌŋɡə'riz] *spl* pantalones *mpl* de trabajo de tela basta de algodón
dungeon ['dʌndʒən] *s* calabozo, mazmorra; (*fortified tower of medieval castle*) torre *f* del homenaje
dung'hill' *s* estercolar *m;* lugar inmundo
dunk [dʌŋk] *tr* sopetear, ensopar
duo ['dju·o] o ['du·o] *s* dúo
duode·num [ˌdju·ə'dinəm] o [ˌdju·ə'dinəm] *s* (*pl -na* [nə]) duodeno
dupe [djup] o [dup] *s* víctima, primo, inocentón *m* ‖ *tr* embaucar, engañar
duplex house ['djupleks] o ['dupleks] *s* casa para dos familias
duplicate ['djuplɪkɪt] o ['duplɪkɪt] *adj & s* duplicado; **in duplicate** por

duplicado ‖ [ˈdjuplɪ͵ket] o [ˈduplɪ͵ket] *tr* duplicar

duplici·ty [djuˈplɪsɪti] o [duˈplɪsɪti] *s* (*pl* -ties) duplicidad

durable [ˈdjurəbəl] o [ˈdurəbəl] *adj* durable, duradero

durable goods *spl* artículos duraderos

duration [djuˈreʃən] o [duˈreʃən] *s* duración

during [ˈdjurɪŋ] o [ˈdurɪŋ] *prep* durante

dusk [dʌsk] *s* crepúsculo

dust [dʌst] *s* polvo ‖ *tr* (*to free of dust*) desempolvar; (*to sprinkle with dust*) polvorear; **to dust off** desempolvar

dust bowl *s* cuenca de polvo

dust′cloth′ *s* trapo para quitar el polvo

dust cloud *s* nube *f* de polvo, polvareda

duster [ˈdʌstər] *s* paño, plumero; (*light overgarment*) guardapolvo

dust jacket *s* sobrecubierta

dust′pan′ *s* pala para recoger la basura

dust rag *s* trapo para quitar el polvo

dust storm *s* tolvanera

dust·y [ˈdʌsti] *adj* (*comp* -ier; *super* -iest) polvoriento; (*grayish*) grisáceo

Dutch [dʌtʃ] *adj* holandés; (slang) alemán ‖ *s* (*language*) holandés *m*; (*language*) (slang) alemán *m*; **in Dutch** (slang) en la desgracia; (slang) en un apuro; **the Dutch** los holandeses; (slang) los alemanes; **to go Dutch** (coll) pagar a escote

Dutch·man [ˈdʌtʃmən] *s* (*pl* -men [mən]) holandés *m*; (slang) alemán *m*

Dutch treat *s* (coll) convite *m* a escote

dutiable [ˈdjutɪ·əbəl] o [ˈdutɪ·əbəl] *adj* sujeto a derechos de aduana

dutiful [ˈdjutɪfəl] o [ˈdutɪfəl] *adj* obediente, sumiso, solícito

du·ty [ˈdjuti] o [ˈduti] *s* (*pl* -ties) deber *m*; (*task*) faena, quehacer *m*; derechos de aduana; **off duty** libre; **on duty** de servicio, de guardia; **to do one's duty** cumplir con su deber; **to take up one's duties** entrar en funciones

du′ty-free′ *adj* libre de derechos

D.V. *abbr* **Deo volente**, i.e., **God willing**

dwarf [dwɔrf] *adj* & *s* enano ‖ *tr* achicar, empequeñecer ‖ *intr* achicarse, empequeñecerse

dwarfish [ˈdwɔrfɪʃ] *adj* enano, diminuto

dwell [dwel] *v* (*pret* & *pp* **dwelled** o **dwelt** [dwelt]) *intr* vivir, morar; **to dwell on** o **upon** hacer hincapié en

dwelling [ˈdwelɪŋ] *s* morada, vivienda

dwelling house *s* casa, domicilio

dwindle [ˈdwɪndəl] *intr* disminuir; decaer, consumirse

dwt. *abbr* pennyweight

dye [daɪ] *s* tinte *m*, tintura, color *m* ‖ *v* (*pret* & *pp* **dyed**; *ger* **dyeing**) *tr* teñir

dyed-in-the-wool [ˈdaɪdɪnðə͵wul] *adj* intransigente

dyeing [ˈdaɪ·ɪŋ] *s* tinte *m*, tintura

dyer [ˈdaɪ·ər] *s* tintorero

dye′stuff′ *s* materia colorante

dying [ˈdaɪ·ɪŋ] *adj* moribundo

dynamic [daɪˈnæmɪk] o [dɪˈnæmɪk] *adj* dinámico

dynamite [ˈdaɪnə͵maɪt] *s* dinamita ‖ *tr* dinamitar

dyna·mo [ˈdaɪnə͵mo] *s* (*pl* -mos) dínamo *f*

dynast [ˈdaɪnæst] *s* dinasta *m*

dynas·ty [ˈdaɪnəsti] *s* (*pl* -ties) dinastía

dysentery [ˈdɪsən͵teri] *s* disentería

dyspepsia [dɪsˈpɛpsɪ·ə] o [dɪsˈpɛpʃə] *s* dispepsia

dz. *abbr* dozen

E

E, e [i] quinta letra del alfabeto inglés

ea. *abbr* each

each [itʃ] *adj indef* cada ‖ *pron indef* cada uno; **each other** nos, se; uno a otro, unos a otros ‖ *adv* cada uno; por persona

eager [ˈigər] *adj* (*enthusiastic*) ardiente, celoso; **eager for** muy deseoso de; **eager to** + *inf* muy deseoso de + *inf*

eagerness [ˈigərnɪs] *s* ardor *m*, celo; deseo ardiente, empeño

eagle [ˈigəl] *s* águila

eagle owl *s* buho

ear [ɪr] *s* (*organ and sense of hearing*) oído; (*external part*) oreja; (*of corn*) mazorca; (*of wheat*) espiga; **all ears** con las orejas tan largas; **to be all ears** ser todo oídos, abrir tanto oído; **to prick up one's ears** aguzar las

orejas; **to turn a deaf ear** hacer o tener oídos de mercader

ear′ache′ *s* dolor *m* de oído

ear′drop′ *s* arete *m*

ear′drum′ *s* tímpano

ear′flap′ *s* orejera

earl [ʌrl] *s* conde *m*

earldom [ˈʌrldəm] *s* condado

ear·ly [ˈʌrli] (*comp* -lier; *super* -liest) *adj* (*occurring before customary time*) temprano; (*first in a series*) primero; (*far back in time*) primero, remoto, antiguo; (*occurring in near future*) cercano, próximo ‖ *adv* temprano; al principio; en los primeros tiempos; **as early as** (*a certain time of day*) ya a; (*a certain time or date*) ya en; **as early as possible** lo más pronto posible; **early in** (e.g., *the month of December*) ya en; **early in**

the morning muy de mañana; **early in the year** a principios del año; **to rise early** madrugar
early bird s (coll) madrugador m
early mass s misa de prima
early riser s madrugador m
ear'mark' s señal f, distintivo ‖ tr destinar, poner aparte (*para un fin determinado*)
ear'muff' s orejera
earn [ʌrn] tr ganar, ganarse; (*to get as one's due*) merecerse; (com) devengar (*intereses*) ‖ intr ganar; rendir
earnest ['ʌrnɪst] adj serio, grave; **in earnest** en serio, de buena fe ‖ s arras
earnest money s arras
earnings ['ʌrnɪŋz] s ganancia; salario
ear'phone' s audífono
ear'piece' s auricular m
ear'ring' s arete m
ear'shot' s alcance m del oído; **within earshot** al alcance del oído
ear'split'ting adj ensordecedor
earth [ʌrθ] s tierra; **to come back to o down to earth** bajar de las nubes
earthen ['ʌrθən] adj de tierra; de barro
ear'then-ware' s loza, vasijas de barro
earthly ['ʌrθli] adj terrenal; concebible, posible; **to be of no earthly use** no servir para nada
earth'quake' s terremoto, temblor m de tierra
earth'work' s terraplén m
earth'worm' s lombriz f de tierra
earth-y ['ʌrθi] adj (comp **-ier;** super **-iest**) terroso; (*worldly*) mundanal; (*unrefined*) grosero; franco, sincero
ear trumpet s trompetilla
ear'wax' s cera de los oídos
ease [iz] s facilidad; (*readiness, naturalness*) desenvoltura, soltura; (*comfort, wellbeing*) comodidad, bienestar m; **with ease** con facilidad ‖ tr facilitar; aligerar (*un peso*); (*to let up on*) aflojar, soltar; aliviar, mitigar ‖ intr aliviarse, mitigarse, disminuir; moderar la marcha
easel ['izəl] s caballete m
easement ['izmənt] s alivio; (law) servidumbre
easily ['izɪli] adj fácilmente; suavemente; sin duda; probablemente
easiness ['izɪnɪs] s facilidad; desenvoltura, soltura; (*e.g., of motion of a machine*) suavidad; indiferencia
east [ist] adj oriental, del este ‖ adv al este, hacia el este ‖ s este m
Easter ['istər] s Pascua de flores, Pascua de Resurrección, Pascua florida
Easter egg s huevo duro decorado o huevo de imitación que se da como regalo en el día de Pascua de Resurrección
Easter Monday s lunes m de Pascua de Resurrección
eastern ['istərn] adj oriental
East'er•tide' s aleluya m, tiempo de Pascua
eastward ['istwərd] adv hacia el este

eas-y ['izi] adj (comp **-ier;** super **-iest**) fácil; (*conducive to ease*) cómodo; (*not tight*) holgado; (*amenable*) manejable; (*not forced or hurried*) lento, pausado, moderado ‖ adv (coll) fácilmente; (coll) despacio; **to take it easy** (coll) descansar, holgar; (coll) ir despacio
easy chair s poltrona, silla poltrona
eas'y-go'ing adj despacioso, comodón
easy mark s (coll) víctima, inocentón m
easy money s dinero ganado sin pena; (com) dinero abundante
easy payments spl facilidades de pago
eat [it] v (pret ate [et]; pp eaten ['itən]) tr comer; **to eat away** corroer; **to eat up** comerse ‖ intr comer
eatable ['itəbəl] adj comestible ‖ **eatables** spl comestibles mpl
eaves [ivz] spl alero, socarrén m, tejaroz m
eaves'drop' v (pret & pp **-dropped;** ger **-dropping**) intr escuchar a escondidas, estar de escucha
ebb [ɛb] s reflujo; decadencia ‖ intr bajar (*la marea*); decaer
ebb and flow s flujo y reflujo
ebb tide s marea menguante
ebon-y ['ɛbəni] s (pl **-ies**) ébano
ebullient [ɪ'bʌljənt] adj hirviente; entusiasta
eccentric [ɛk'sɛntrɪk] adj excéntrico ‖ m (*odd person*) excéntrico; (*device*) excéntrica
eccentrici•ty [,ɛksɛn'trɪsɪti] s (pl **-ties**) excentricidad
ecclesiastic [ɪ,klizɪ'æstɪk] adj & s eclesiástico
echelon ['ɛʃə,lɑn] s escalón m; (mil) escalón ‖ tr (mil) escalonar
ech-o ['ɛko] s (pl **-oes**) eco ‖ tr repetir (*un sonido*); imitar ‖ intr hacer eco
éclair [e'kler] s bollo de crema
eclectic [ɛk'lɛktɪk] adj & s ecléctico
eclipse [ɪ'klɪps] s eclipse m ‖ tr eclipsar
eclogue ['ɛklɔg] o ['ɛklɑg] s égloga
ecology [ɪ'kɑlədʒi] s ecología
economic [,ikə'nɑmɪk] o [,ɛkə'nɑmɪk] adj económico (*perteneciente a la economía*)
economical [,ikə'nɑmɪkəl] o [,ɛkə'nɑmɪkəl] adj económico (*ahorrador; poco costoso*)
economics [,ikə'nɑmɪks] o [,ɛkə'nɑmɪks] s economía política
economist [ɪ'kɑnəmɪst] s economista mf
economize [ɪ'kɑnə,maɪz] tr & intr economizar
econo•my [ɪ'kɑnəmi] s (pl **-mies**) economía
ecsta•sy ['ɛkstəsi] s (pl **-sies**) éxtasis m
ecstatic [ɛk'stætɪk] adj extático
Ecuador ['ɛkwə,dɔr] s el Ecuador
Ecuadoran [,ɛkwə'dɔrən] o **Ecuadorian** [,ɛkwə'dɔrɪ•ən] adj & s ecuatoriano
ecumenic(al) [,ɛkjə'mɛnɪk(əl)] adj ecuménico
eczema ['ɛksɪmə] o [ɛg'zimə] s eczema m & f, eccema m & f

ed·dy ['edi] s (pl **-dies**) remolino ‖ v (pret & pp **-died**) tr & intr remolinear

edelweiss ['edəl,vaıs] s estrella de los Alpes

edge [edʒ] s (of a knife, sword, etc.) filo, corte m; (of a cup, glass, piece of paper, piece of cloth, an abyss, etc.) borde m; (of a piece of cloth; of a body of water) orilla; (of a table) canto; (of a book) corte m; (of clothing) ribete m; (slang) ventaja; **on edge** de canto; (fig) nervioso; **to have the edge on** (coll) llevar ventaja a; **to set the teeth on edge** dar dentera ‖ tr afilar, aguzar; bordear; ribetear (un vestido) ‖ intr avanzar de lado; **to edge in** lograr entrar

edgeways ['edʒ,wez] adv de filo, de canto; **to not let a person get a word in edgeways** no dejarle a una persona decir ni una palabra

edging ['edʒıŋ] s orla, pestaña

edgy ['edʒi] adj agudo, angular; nervioso, irritable

edible ['edıbəl] adj & s comestible m

edict ['idıkt] s edicto

edification [,edıfı'keʃən] s edificación

edifice ['edıfıs] s edificio

edi·fy ['edı,faı] v (pret & pp **-fied**) tr edificar

edifying ['edı,faı·ıŋ] adj edificante

edit. abbr **edited, edition, editor**

edit ['edıt] tr preparar para la publicación; dirigir, redactar (un periódico)

edition [ı'dıʃən] s edición

editor ['edıtər] s (of a newspaper or magazine) director m, redactor m; (of a manuscript) revisor m; (of an editorial) cronista mf

editorial [,edı'torı·əl] adj editorial ‖ editorial m, artículo de fondo

editorial staff s redacción, cuerpo de redacción

editor in chief s jefe m de redacción

educate ['edʒu,ket] tr educar, instruir

education [,edʒu'keʃən] s educación, instrucción

educational [,edʒu'keʃənəl] adj educativo, educacional

educational institution s centro docente

educator ['edʒu,ketər] s educador m

eel [il] s anguila; **to be as slippery as an eel** escurrirse como una anguila

ee·rie o ee·ry ['ıri] adj (comp **-rier;** super **-riest**) espectral, misterioso

efface [ı'fes] tr destruir; borrar; **to efface oneself** retirarse, no dejarse ver

effect [ı'fekt] s efecto; **in effect** vigente; en efecto, en realidad; **to feel the effects of** resentirse de; **to go into effect o to take effect** hacerse vigente, entrar en vigor; **to put into effect** poner en vigor ‖ tr efectuar

effective [ı'fektıv] adj eficaz; (actually in effect) efectivo; (striking) impresionante; **to become effective** hacerse efectivo, entrar en vigencia

effectual [ı'fektʃu·əl] adj eficaz

effectuate [ı'fektʃu,et] tr efectuar

effeminacy [ı'femınəsi] s afeminación

effeminate [ı'femınıt] adj afeminado

effervesce [,efər'ves] intr estar en efervescencia

effervescence [,efər'vesəns] s efervescencia

effervescent [,efər'vesənt] adj efervescente

effete [ı'fit] adj estéril, infructuoso

efficacious [,efı'keʃəs] adj eficaz

effica·cy ['efıkəsi] s (pl **-cies**) eficacia

efficien·cy [ı'fıʃənsi] s (pl **-cies**) eficiencia; (mech) rendimiento, efecto útil

efficient [ı'fıʃənt] adj eficiente, eficaz; (person) competente; (mech) de buen rendimiento

effi·gy ['efıdʒi] s (pl **-gies**) efigie f

effort ['efərt] s esfuerzo, empeño

effronter·y [ı'frʌntəri] s (pl **-ies**) desfachatez f, descaro

effusion [ı'fuʒən] s efusión

effusive [ı'fjusıv] adj efusivo, expansivo

e.g. abbr **exempli gratia, i.e., for example**

egg [eg] s huevo; (slang) buen sujeto ‖ tr — **to egg on** incitar, instigar

egg beater s batidor m de huevos

egg'cup' s huevera

egg'head' s intelectual mf, erudito

eggnog ['eg,nag] s caldo de la reina, yema mejida

egg'plant' s berenjena

egg'shell' s cascarón m, cáscara de huevo

egoism ['ego,ızəm] o ['igo,ızəm] s egoísmo

egoist ['ego·ıst] o ['igo·ıst] s egoísta mf

egotism ['ego,tızəm] o ['igo,tızəm] s egotismo

egotist ['egotıst] o ['igotıst] s egotista mf

egregious [ı'gridʒəs] adj enorme, escandaloso

egress ['igres] s salida

Egypt ['idʒıpt] s Egipto

Egyptian [ı'dʒıpʃən] adj & s egipcio

eider ['aıdər] s pato de flojel

eider down s edredón m

eight [et] adj & pron ocho ‖ s ocho; **eight o'clock** las ocho

eight'-day' clock s reloj m de ocho días cuerda

eighteen ['et'tin] adj, pron & s dieciocho, diez y ocho

eighteenth ['et'tinθ] adj & s (in a series) decimoctavo; (part) dieciochavo ‖ s (in dates) dieciocho, diez y ocho

eighth [etθ] adj & s octavo, ochavo ‖ s (in dates) ocho

eight hundred adj & pron ochocientos ‖ s ochocientos m

eightieth ['etı·ıθ] adj & s (in a series) octogésimo; (part) ochentavo

eigh·ty ['eti] adj & pron ochenta ‖ s (pl **-ties**) ochenta m

either ['iðər] o ['aıðər] adj uno u otro, cada . . . (de los dos), cual-

quier . . . de los dos; ambos ‖ *pron*
uno u otro, cualquiera de los dos ‖
adv — not either tampoco, no . . .
tampoco ‖ *conj* — either . . . or o
. . . o

ejaculate [ɪ'dʒækjə,let] *tr & intr* exclamar; (physiol) eyacular

eject [ɪ'dʒɛkt] *tr* arrojar, expulsar,
echar; *(to evict)* desahuciar

ejection [ɪ'dʒɛkʃən] *s* expulsión; *(of a
tenant)* desahucio

ejection seat *s* (aer) asiento lanzable

eke [ik] *tr* — to eke out ganarse *(la
vida)* con dificultad

elaborate [ɪ'læbərɪt] *adj (done with
great care)* elaborado; *(detailed,
ornate)* primoroso, recargado ‖
[ɪ'læbə,ret] *tr* elaborar ‖ *intr* — to
elaborate on o upon explicar con
más detalles

elapse [ɪ'læps] *intr* pasar, transcurrir

elastic [ɪ'læstɪk] *adj & s* elástico

elasticity [ɪ,læs'tɪsɪti] o [,ɪlæs'tɪsɪti]
s elasticidad

elated [ɪ'letɪd] *adj* alborozado, regocijado

elation [ɪ'leʃən] *s* alborozo, regocijo

elbow ['ɛlbo] *s* codo; *(in a river)* recodo; *(of a chair)* brazo; at one's
elbow a la mano; out at the elbows
andrajoso, enseñando los codos; to
crook the elbow empinar el codo; to
rub elbows codearse, rozarse; up to
the elbows hasta los codos ‖ *tr* —
to elbow one's way abrirse paso a
codazos ‖ *intr* codear

elbow grease *s* (coll) muñeca, jugo de
muñeca

elbow patch *s* codera

elbow rest *s* ménsula

el'bow·room *s* espacio suficiente; libertad de acción

elder ['ɛldər] *adj* mayor, más antiguo
‖ *s* mayor, señor *m* mayor; (eccl)
anciano; *(plant)* saúco

el'der·ber'ry *s (pl* -ries) saúco; baya
del saúco

elderly ['ɛldərli] *adj* viejo, anciano

elder statesman *s* veterano de la política

eldest ['ɛldɪst] *adj* (el) mayor, (el)
más antiguo

elec. *abbr* **electrical, electricity**

elect [ɪ'lɛkt] *adj (chosen)* escogido;
(selected but not yet installed) electo
‖ s elegido; the elect los elegidos ‖
tr elegir

election [ɪ'lɛkʃən] *s* elección

electioneer [ɪ,lɛkʃə'nɪr] *intr* solicitar
votos

elective [ɪ'lɛktɪv] *adj* electivo ‖ *s*
asignatura electiva

electorate [ɪ'lɛktərɪt] *s* electorado

electric(al) [ɪ'lɛktrɪk(əl)] *adj* eléctrico

electric fan *s* ventilador eléctrico

electrician [ɪ,lɛk'trɪʃən] o [,ɪlɛk-
'trɪʃən] *s* electricista *mf*

electricity [ɪ,lɛk'trɪsɪti] o [,ɛlɛk-
'trɪsɪti] *s* electricidad

electric percolator *s* cafetera eléctrica

electric shaver *s* electroafeitadora

electric tape *s* cinta aislante

electri·fy [ɪ'lɛktrɪ,faɪ] *v (pret & pp
-fied) tr (to provide with electric
power)* electrificar; *(to communicate
electricity to; to thrill)* electrizar

electrocute [ɪ'lɛktrə,kjut] *tr* electrocutar

electrode [ɪ'lɛktrod] *s* electrodo

electrolysis [ɪ,lɛk'trɑlɪsɪs] o [,ɛlɛk-
'trɑlɪsɪs] *s* electrolisis *f*

electrolyte [ɪ'lɛktrə,laɪt] *s* electrólito

electromagnet [ɪ,lɛktrə'mægnɪt] *s*
electro, electroimán *m*

electromagnetic [ɪ,lɛktrəmæg'nɛtɪk]
adj electromagnético

electromotive [ɪ,lɛktrə'motɪv] *adj*
electromotor

electron [ɪ'lɛktrɑn] *s* electrón *m*

electronic [ɪ,lɛk'trɑnɪk] o [,ɛlɛk-
'trɑnɪk] *adj* electrónico ‖ **electronics** *s* electrónica

electroplating [ɪ'lɛktrə,pletɪŋ] *s* galvanoplastia

electrostatic [ɪ,lɛktrə'stætɪk] *adj* elec-
trostático

electrotype [ɪ'lɛktrə,taɪp] *s* electrotipo ‖ *tr* electrotipar

eleemosynary [,ɛlɪ'mɑsɪ,nɛri] *adj*
limosnero

elegance ['ɛlɪgəns] *s* elegancia

elegant ['ɛlɪgənt] *adj* elegante

elegiac [,ɛlɪ'dʒaɪ·æk] o [ɪ'lidʒɪ,æk]
adj elegíaco

ele·gy ['ɛlɪdʒi] *s (pl* -gies) elegía

element ['ɛlɪmənt] *s* elemento; to be in
one's element estar en su elemento

elementary [,ɛlɪ'mɛntəri] *adj* elemental

elephant ['ɛlɪfənt] *s* elefante *m*

elevate ['ɛlɪ,vet] *tr* elevar

elevated ['ɛlɪ,vetɪd] *adj* elevado ‖ *s*
(coll) ferrocarril aéreo o elevado

elevation [,ɛlɪ've·ʃən] *s* elevación

elevator ['ɛlɪ,vetər] *s* ascensor *m*;
elevador *m* (Am); *(for freight)* mon-
tacargas *m; (for hoisting grain)* elevador de granos; *(warehouse for
storing grain)* depósito de cereales;
(aer) timón *m* de profundidad

eleven [ɪ'lɛvən] *adj & pron* once ‖ *s*
once *m;* eleven o'clock las once

eleventh [ɪ'lɛvənθ] *adj & s (in a series)*
undécimo, onceno; *(part)* onzavo ‖
s (in dates) once *m*

eleventh hour *s* último momento

elf [ɛlf] *s (pl* elves [ɛlvz]) elfo, trasgo;
enano

elicit [ɪ'lɪsɪt] *tr* sacar, sonsacar

elide [ɪ'laɪd] *tr* elidir

eligible ['ɛlɪdʒɪbəl] *adj* elegible; deseable, aceptable

eliminate [ɪ'lɪmɪ,net] *tr* eliminar

elision [ɪ'lɪʒən] *s* elisión

elite [e'lit] *adj* selecto ‖ *s* — the elite
la élite

elk [ɛlk] *s* alce *m*

ellipse [ɪ'lɪps] *s* (geom) elipse *f*

ellip·sis [ɪ'lɪpsɪs] *s (pl* -ses [siz])
(gram) elipsis *f*

elliptic(al) [ɪ'lɪptɪk(əl)] *adj* (geom &
gram) elíptico

elm tree [ɛlm] *s* olmo

ed
el

elope [ɪ'lop] *intr* fugarse con un amante

elopement [ɪ'lopmənt] *s* fuga con un amante

eloquence ['ɛləkwəns] *s* elocuencia

eloquent ['ɛləkwənt] *adj* elocuente

else [ɛls] *adj* — **nobody else** ningún otro, nadie más; **nothing else** nada más; **somebody else** algún otro, otra persona; **something else** otra cosa; **what else** qué más, qué otra cosa; **who else** quién más; **whose else** de qué otra persona ‖ *adv* de otro modo; **how else** de qué otro modo; **or else** si no, o bien; **when else** en qué otro tiempo; a qué otra hora; **where else** en otra parte

else'where' *adv* en otra parte, a otra parte

elucidate [ɪ'lusɪ,det] *tr* elucidar

elude [ɪ'lud] *tr* eludir

elusive [ɪ'lusɪv] *adj* fugaz, efímero; evasivo; (*baffling*) deslumbrador

emaciated [ɪ'meʃɪ,etɪd] *adj* enflaquecido, macilento

emancipate [ɪ'mænsɪ,pet] *tr* emancipar

embalm [ɛm'bam] *tr* embalsamar

embankment [ɛm'bæŋkmənt] *s* terraplén *m*

embar·go [ɛm'bargo] *s* (*pl* **-goes**) embargo ‖ *tr* embargar

embark [ɛm'bark] *intr* embarcarse

embarkation [,ɛmbar'keʃən] *s* (*of passengers*) embarco; (*of freight*) embarque *m*

embarrass [ɛm'bærəs] *tr* (*to make feel self-conscious*) avergonzar; (*to put obstacles in the way of*) embarazar; poner en apuros de dinero

embarrassing [ɛm'bærəsɪŋ] *adj* desconcertante, vergonzoso; embarazoso

embarrassment [ɛm'bærəsmənt] *s* desconcierto, vergüenza; (*interference; perplexity*) embarazo; (*financial difficulties*) apuros

embas·sy ['ɛmbəsi] *s* (*pl* **-sies**) embajada

em·bed [ɛm'bɛd] *s* (*pret* & *pp* **-bedded**; *ger* **-bedding**) *tr* empotrar, encajar

embellish [ɛm'bɛlɪʃ] *tr* embellecer

embellishment [ɛm'bɛlɪʃmənt] *s* embellecimiento

ember ['ɛmbər] *s* ascua, pavesa; **embers** rescoldo

Ember days *spl* témpora

embezzle [ɛm'bɛzəl] *tr* & *intr* desfalcar, malversar

embezzlement [ɛm'bɛzəlmənt] *s* desfalco, malversación

embezzler [ɛm'bɛzlər] *s* malversador *m*

embitter [ɛm'bɪtər] *tr* amargar

emblazon [ɛm'blezən] *tr* blasonar; (*fig*) blasonar

emblem ['ɛmbləm] *s* emblema *m*

emblematic(al) [,ɛmblə'mætɪk(əl)] *adj* emblemático

embodiment [ɛm'badɪmənt] *s* incorporación; personificación, encarnación

embod·y [ɛm'badi] *v* (*pret* & *pp* **-ied**) *tr* incorporar; personificar, encarnar

embolden [ɛm'boldən] *tr* envalentonar

embolism ['ɛmbə,lɪzəm] *s* embolia

emboss [ɛm'bɔs] o [ɛm'bas] *tr* (*to raise in relief*) realzar; abollonar (*metal*); repujar (*cuero*)

embrace [ɛm'bres] *s* abrazo ‖ *tr* abrazar ‖ *intr* abrazarse

embrasure [ɛm'breʒər] *s* alféizar *m*

embroider [ɛm'brɔɪdər] *tr* bordar, recamar

embroider·y [ɛm'brɔɪdəri] *s* (*pl* **-ies**) bordado, recamado

embroil [ɛm'brɔɪl] *tr* embrollar; (*to involve in contention*) envolver

embroilment [ɛm'brɔɪlmənt] *s* embrollo; (*in contention*) envolvimiento

embry·o ['ɛmbrɪ,o] *s* (*pl* **-os**) embrión *m*

embryology [,ɛmbrɪ'ɑlədʒi] *s* embriología

emend [ɪ'mɛnd] *tr* enmendar

emendation [,imɛn'deʃən] *s* enmienda

emerald ['ɛmərəld] *s* esmeralda

emerge [ɪ'mʌrdʒ] *intr* emerger

emergence [ɪ'mʌrdʒəns] *s* emergencia (*acción de emerger*)

emergen·cy [ɪ'mʌrdʒənsi] *s* (*pl* **-cies**) emergencia (*caso urgente*)

emergency exit *s* salida de auxilio

emergency landing *s* aterrizaje forzoso

emergency landing field *s* aeródromo de urgencia

emersion [ɪ'mʌrʒən] o [ɪ'mʌrʃən] *s* emersión

emery ['ɛməri] *s* esmeril *m*

emery cloth *s* tela de esmeril

emery wheel *s* esmeriladora, rueda de esmeril, muela de esmeril

emetic [ɪ'mɛtɪk] *adj* & *s* emético

emigrant ['ɛmɪgrənt] *adj* & *s* emigrante *mf*

emigrate ['ɛmɪ,gret] *intr* emigrar

émigré [emi'gre] o ['ɛmɪ,gre] *s* emigrado

eminence ['ɛmɪnəns] *s* eminencia

eminent ['ɛmɪnənt] *adj* eminente

emissar·y ['ɛmɪ,sɛri] *s* (*pl* **-ies**) emisario

emission [ɪ'mɪʃən] *s* emisión

emit [ɪ'mɪt] *v* (*pret* & *pp* **emitted**; *ger* **emitting**) *tr* emitir

emotion [ɪ'moʃən] *s* emoción

emotional [ɪ'moʃənəl] *adj* emocional, emotivo

emperor ['ɛmpərər] *s* emperador *m*

empha·sis ['ɛmfəsɪs] *s* (*pl* **-ses** [,siz]) énfasis *m*

emphasize ['ɛmfə,saɪz] *tr* acentuar, hacer hincapié en

emphatic [ɛm'fætɪk] *adj* enfático

emphysema [,ɛmfɪ'simə] *s* enfisema *m*

empire ['ɛmpaɪr] *s* imperio

empiric(al) [ɛm'pɪrɪk(əl)] *adj* empírico

empiricist [ɛm'pɪrɪsɪst] *s* empírico

emplacement [ɛm'plesmənt] *s* emplazamiento

employ [ɛm'plɔɪ] *s* empleo ‖ *tr* emplear

employee [ɛm'plɔɪ·i] o [,ɛmplɔɪ'i] *s* empleado

employer [ɛm'plɔɪ·ər] *s* patrono

employment [em'plɔɪmənt] *s* empleo, colocación
employment agency *s* agencia de colocaciones
empower [em'pau·ər] *tr* autorizar, facultar; habilitar, permitir
empress ['emprɪs] *s* emperatriz *f*
emptiness ['emptɪnɪs] *s* vaciedad, vacuidad
emp·ty ['empti] *adj* (*comp* -**tier**; *super* -**tiest**) vacío; (coll) hambriento ‖ *v* (*pret & pp* -**tied**) *tr & intr* vaciar
empty-handed ['empti'hændɪd] *adj* manivacío
empty-headed ['empti'hedɪd] *adj* tonto, ignorante
empye·ma [ˌempɪ'imə] *s* (*pl* -**mata** [mətə]) empiema *m*
empyrean [ˌempɪ'ri·ən] *adj & s* empíreo
emulate ['emjə‚let] *tr & intr* emular
emulator ['emjə‚letər] *s* émulo
emulous ['emjələs] *adj* émulo
emulsi·fy [ɪ'mʌlsɪ‚faɪ] *v* (*pret & pp* -**fied**) *tr* emulsionar
emulsion [ɪ'mʌl/ən] *s* emulsión
enable [en'ebəl] *tr* habilitar, facilitar
enact [en'ækt] *tr* decretar, promulgar; hacer el papel de
enactment [en'æktmənt] *s* ley *f*; (*of a law*) promulgación; (*of a play*) representación
enam·el [en'æməl] *s* esmalte *m* ‖ *v* (*pret & pp* -**eled** o -**elled**; *ger* -**eling** o -**elling**) *tr* esmaltar
enam′el·ware′ *s* utensilios de cocina de hierro esmaltado
enamor [en'æmər] *tr* enamorar
encamp [en'kæmp] *tr* acampar ‖ *intr* acampar, acamparse
encampment [en'kæmpmənt] *s* acampamiento
enchant [en't/ænt] o [en't/ɑnt] *tr* encantar
enchanting [en't/æntɪŋ] o [en't/ɑntɪŋ] *adj* encantador
enchantment [en't/æntmənt] o [en't/ɑntmənt] *s* encanto
enchantress [en't/æntrɪs] o [en't/ɑntrɪs] *s* encantadora
enchase [en't/es] *tr* engastar
encircle [en'sʌrkəl] *tr* encerrar, rodear; (mil) envolver
enclitic [en'klɪtɪk] *adj & s* enclítico
enclose [en'kloz] *tr* encerrar; (*in a letter*) adjuntar, incluir; **to enclose herewith** remitir adjunto
enclosure [en'kloʒər] *s* recinto; cosa inclusa, carta inclusa
encomi·um [en'komɪ·əm] *s* (*pl* -**ums** o -**a** [ə]) encomio
encompass [en'kʌmpəs] *tr* encuadrar, abarcar
encore ['ankor] *s* bis *m* ‖ *interj* ¡bis!, ¡que se repita! ‖ *tr* pedir la repetición de (*p.ej., de una pieza o canción*); pedir la repetición a (*un actor*)
encounter [en'kauntər] *s* encuentro ‖ *tr* encontrar, encontrarse con ‖ *intr* batirse, combatirse
encourage [en'kʌrɪdʒ] *tr* animar, alentar; (*to foster*) fomentar

encouragement [en'kʌrɪdʒmənt] *s* ánimo, aliento; fomento
encroach [en'krot/] *intr* — **to encroach on** o **upon** pasar los límites de; abusar de; invadir, entremeterse en
encumber [en'kʌmbər] *tr* embarazar, estorbar, impedir; (*to load with debts, etc.*) gravar
encumbrance [en'kʌmbrəns] *s* embarazo; estorbo; gravamen *m*
ency. o **encyc.** *abbr* **encyclopedia**
encyclical [en'sɪklɪkəl] o [en'saɪklɪkəl] *s* encíclica
encyclopedia [en‚saɪklə'pidɪ·ə] *s* enciclopedia
encyclopedic [en‚saɪklə'pidɪk] *adj* enciclopédico
end [end] *s* (*in time*) fin *m*; (*in space*) extremo, remate *m*; (*e.g., of the month*) fines *mpl*; (*small piece*) cabo, pieza, fragmento; (*purpose*) intento, objeto, fin, mira; **at the end of** al cabo de; a fines de; **in the end** al fin; **no end of** (coll) un sin fin de; **to make both ends meet** pasar con lo que se tiene; **to no end** sin efecto; **to stand on end** poner de punta; ponerse de punta; erizarse, encresparse (*el pelo*); **to the end that** a fin de que ‖ *tr* acabar, terminar ‖ *intr* acabar, terminar; desembocar (*p.ej., una calle*); **to end up** acabar, morir; **to end up as** acabar siendo, parar en (*p.ej., ladrón*)
endanger [en'dendʒər] *tr* poner en peligro
endear [en'dɪr] *tr* hacer querer; **to endear oneself to** hacerse querer por
endeavor [en'devər] *s* esfuerzo, empeño ‖ *intr* esforzarse, empeñarse
endemic [en'demɪk] *adj* endémico ‖ *s* endemia
ending ['endɪŋ] *s* fin *m*, terminación; (gram) desinencia, terminación
endive ['endaɪv] *s* escarola
endless ['endlɪs] *adj* interminable; (*chain, screw, etc.*) sin fin
end′most′ *adj* último, extremo
endorse [en'dɔrs] *tr* endosar; (fig) apoyar, aprobar
endorsee [ˌendɔr'si] *s* endosatario
endorsement [en'dɔrsmənt] *s* endoso; (fig) apoyo, aprobación
endorser [en'dɔrsər] *s* endosante *mf*
endow [en'dau] *tr* dotar
endowment [en'daumənt] *adj* dotal ‖ *s* (*of an institution*) dotación; (*gift, talent*) dote *f*, prenda
endurance [en'djurəns] o [en'durəns] *s* aguante *m*, paciencia; (*ability to hold out*) resistencia, fortaleza; (*lasting time*) duración
endure [en'djur] o [en'dur] *tr* aguantar, tolerar, sufrir ‖ *intr* durar; sufrir con paciencia
enduring [en'djurɪŋ] o [en'durɪŋ] *adj* duradero, permanente, resistente
enema ['enəmə] *s* enema, ayuda; (*liquid and apparatus*) lavativa
ene·my ['enəmi] *adj* enemigo ‖ *s* (*pl* -**mies**) enemigo

el
en

enemy alien *s* extranjero enemigo

energetic [ˌenərˈdʒɛtɪk] *adj* enérgico, vigoroso

ener·gy [ˈenərdʒɪ] *s* (*pl* -gies) energía

enervate [ˈenərˌvet] *tr* enervar

enfeeble [enˈfibəl] *tr* debilitar

enfold [enˈfold] *tr* arrollar, envolver

enforce [enˈfors] *tr* hacer cumplir, poner en vigor; obtener por fuerza; (*e.g., obedience*) imponer; (*an argument*) hacer valer

enforcement [enˈforsmənt] *s* compulsión; (*e.g., of a law*) ejecución

enfranchise [enˈfræntʃaɪz] *tr* franquear, libertar; conceder el derecho de sufragio a

eng. *abbr* engineer, engraving

engage [enˈgedʒ] *tr* ocupar, emplear; alquilar, reservar; atraer (*p.ej., la atención de una persona*); engranar con; trabar batalla con; **to be engaged, to be engaged to be married** estar prometido, estar comprometido para casarse; **to engage someone in conversation** entablar conversación con una persona ‖ *intr* empeñarse, comprometerse; empotrar, encajar; engranar; **to engage in** ocuparse en

engaged [enˈgedʒd] *adj* comprometido, prometido; (*column*) embebido, entregado

engagement [enˈgedʒmənt] *s* ajuste *m*, contrato, empeño; esponsales *mpl*, palabra de casamiento; (*duration of betrothal*) noviazgo; (*appointment*) cita; (mil) acción, batalla

engagement ring *s* anillo de compromiso, anillo de pedida

engaging [enˈgedʒɪŋ] *adj* agraciado, simpático

engender [enˈdʒendər] *tr* engendrar

engine [ˈendʒɪn] *s* máquina; (*of automobile*) motor *m*; (rr) máquina, locomotora

engine driver *s* maquinista *m*

engineer [ˌendʒəˈnɪr] *s* ingeniero; (*engine driver*) maquinista *m* ‖ *tr* dirigir o construir como ingeniero; llevar a cabo con acierto

engineering [ˌendʒəˈnɪrɪŋ] *s* ingeniería

engine house *s* cuartel *m* de bomberos

engine·man [ˈendʒɪnmən] *s* (*pl* -men [mən]) maquinista *m*, conductor *m* de locomotora

engine room *s* sala de máquinas; (naut) cámara de las máquinas

en'gine-room' telegraph *s* (naut) transmisor *m* de órdenes, telégrafo de máquinas

England [ˈɪŋglənd] *s* Inglaterra

Englander [ˈɪŋgləndər] *s* natural *m* inglés

English [ˈɪŋglɪʃ] *adj* inglés ‖ *s* inglés *m*; (*in billiards*) efecto; **the English** los ingleses

English Channel *s* Canal *m* de la Mancha

English daisy *s* margarita de los prados

English horn *s* (mus) corno inglés, cuerno inglés

English·man [ˈɪŋglɪʃmən] *s* (*pl* -men [mən]) inglés *m*

Eng'lish-speak'ing *adj* de habla inglesa

Eng'lish·wom'an *s* (*pl* -wom'en) inglesa

engraft [enˈgræft] o [enˈgrɑft] *tr* (hort & surg) injertar; (fig) implantar

engrave [enˈgrev] *tr* grabar; (*in the memory*) grabar

engraver [enˈgrevər] *s* grabador *m*

engraving [enˈgrevɪŋ] *s* grabado

engross [enˈgros] *tr* absorber; poner en limpio; copiar caligráficamente

engrossing [enˈgrosɪŋ] *adj* acaparador, absorbente

engulf [enˈgʌlf] *tr* hundir, inundar

enhance [enˈhæns] o [enˈhɑns] *tr* realzar

enhancement [enˈhænsmənt] o [enˈhɑnsmənt] *s* realce *m*

enigma [ɪˈnɪgmə] *s* enigma *m*

enigmatic(al) [ˌɪnɪgˈmætɪk(əl)] *adj* enigmático

enjambment [enˈdʒæmmənt] o [enˈdʒæmbmənt] *s* encabalgamiento

enjoin [enˈdʒɔɪn] *tr* encargar, ordenar

enjoy [enˈdʒɔɪ] *tr* gozar; **to enjoy** + *ger* gozarse en + *inf*; **to enjoy oneself** divertirse

enjoyable [enˈdʒɔɪ·əbəl] *adj* agradable, deleitable

enjoyment [enˈdʒɔɪmənt] *s* (*pleasure*) placer *m*; (*pleasurable use*) goce *m*

enkindle [enˈkɪndəl] *tr* encender

enlarge [enˈlɑrdʒ] *tr* agrandar, aumentar; (phot) ampliar ‖ *intr* agrandarse, aumentar; (*to talk at length*) explayarse; exagerar; **to enlarge on** o **upon** tratar con más extensión; exagerar

enlargement [enˈlɑrdʒmənt] *s* agrandamiento, aumento; (phot) ampliación

enlighten [enˈlaɪtən] *tr* ilustrar, instruir

enlightenment [enˈlaɪtənmənt] *s* ilustración, instrucción

enlist [enˈlɪst] *tr* alistar; ganar (*a una persona; el favor, los servicios de una persona*) ‖ *intr* alistarse; **to enlist in** (*a cause*) poner empeño en

enliven [enˈlaɪvən] *tr* avivar, animar

enmesh [enˈmeʃ] *tr* enredar

enmi·ty [ˈenmɪtɪ] *s* (*pl* -ties) enemistad

ennoble [enˈnobəl] *tr* ennoblecer

ennui [ˈɑnwi] *s* aburrimiento, tedio

enormous [ɪˈnɔrməs] *adj* enorme

enough [ɪˈnʌf] *adj*, *adv* & *s* bastante *m* ‖ *interj* ¡basta!, ¡no más!

enounce [ɪˈnauns] *tr* enunciar; pronunciar

en passant [ˌɑn pæˈsɑnt] *adv* (chess) al vuelo

enrage [enˈredʒ] *tr* enrabiar, encolerizar

enrapture [enˈræptʃər] *tr* embelesar, transportar, arrebatar

enrich [enˈrɪtʃ] *tr* enriquecer

enroll [enˈrol] *tr* alistar, inscribir; (*to wrap up*) envolver, enrollar ‖ *intr* alistarse, inscribirse

en route [ɑn ˈrut] *adv* en camino; **en route to** camino de, rumbo a

ensconce [enˈskɑns] *tr* esconder, abrigar; **to ensconce oneself** instalarse cómodamente

ensemble [ɑnˈsɑmbəl] *s* conjunto;

grupo de músicos que tocan o cantan juntos; traje armonioso

ensign ['ensaɪn] s (*standard*) enseña, bandera; (*badge*) divisa, insignia ‖ ['ensən] o ['ensaɪn] s (nav) alférez *m* de fragata

enslave [en'slev] *tr* esclavizar

enslavement [en'slevmənt] s esclavización

ensnare [en'sner] *tr* entrampar

ensue [en'su] o [en'sju] *intr* seguirse; resultar

ensuing [en'su·ɪŋ] o [en'sju·ɪŋ] *adj* siguiente; resultante

ensure [en'ʃur] *tr* asegurar, garantizar

entail [en'tel] s (law) vínculo ‖ *tr* acarrear, ocasionar; (law) vincular

entangle [en'tæŋgəl] *tr* enmarañar, enredar

entanglement [en'tæŋgəlmənt] s enmarañamiento, enredo

enter ['entər] *tr* entrar en (*una habitación*); entrar por (*una puerta*); (*in the customhouse*) declarar; (*to make a record of*) registrar, asentar; matricular (*a un alumno*); matricularse en; hacer miembro a; hacerse miembro de; (*to undertake*) emprender; asentar (*un pedido*); **to enter one's head** metérsele a uno en la cabeza ‖ *intr* entrar; (theat) entrar en escena, salir; **to enter into** entrar en; celebrar (*p.ej., un contrato*); **to enter on o upon** emprender

enterprise ['entər,praɪz] s (*undertaking*) empresa; (*spirit, push*) empuje *m*

enterprising ['entər,praɪzɪŋ] *adj* emprendedor

entertain [,entər'ten] *tr* entretener, divertir; (*to show hospitality to*) recibir; considerar, abrigar (*esperanzas, ideas, etc.*) ‖ *intr* recibir

entertainer [,entər'tenər] s (*host*) anfitrión *m*; (*in public*) actor *m*, bailador *m*, músico, vocalista *mf* (*esp. en un café cantante*)

entertaining [,entər'tenɪŋ] *adj* entretenido

entertainment [,entər'tenmənt] s entretenimiento, diversión; atracción, espectáculo; buen recibimiento; (*of hopes, ideas, etc.*) consideración, abrigo

enthrall [en'θrɔl] *tr* cautivar, encantar; esclavizar, sojuzgar

enthrone [en'θron] *tr* entronizar

enthuse [en'θuz] o [en'θjuz] *tr* (coll) entusiasmar ‖ *intr* (coll) entusiasmarse

enthusiasm [en'θuzɪ,æzəm] o [en'θjuzɪ,æzəm] s entusiasmo

enthusiast [en'θuzɪ,æst] o [en'θjuzɪ,æst] s entusiasta *mf*

enthusiastic [en,θuzɪ'æstɪk] o [en,θjuzɪ'æstɪk] *adj* entusiástico

entice [en'taɪs] *tr* atraer, tentar; inducir al mal, extraviar

enticement [en'taɪsmənt] s atracción, tentación; extravío

entire [en'taɪr] *adj* entero

entirely [en'taɪrli] *adv* enteramente; (*exclusively*) solamente

entire·ty [en'taɪrti] s (*pl* **-ties**) entereza; conjunto, totalidad

entitle [en'taɪtəl] *tr* dar derecho a; (*to give a name to; to honor with a title*) intitular

enti·ty ['entɪti] s (*pl* **-ties**) entidad

entomb [en'tum] *tr* sepultar

entombment [en'tummənt] s sepultura

entomology [,entə'malədʒi] s entomología

entourage [,antu'raʒ] s cortejo, séquito

entrails ['entrelz] o ['entrəlz] *spl* entrañas

entrain [en'tren] *tr* despachar en el tren ‖ *intr* embarcar, salir en el tren

entrance ['entrəns] s entrada, ingreso; (theat) entrada en escena ‖ [en'træns] o [en'trans] *tr* arrebatar, encantar

entrance examination s examen *m* de ingreso; **to take entrance examinations** examinarse de ingreso

entrancing [en'trænsɪŋ] o [en'transɪŋ] *adj* arrebatador, encantador

entrant ['entrənt] s entrante *mf*; (sport) concurrente *mf*

en·trap [en'træp] *v* (*pret* & *pp* **-trapped**; *ger* **-trapping**) *tr* entrampar

entreat [en'trit] *tr* rogar, suplicar

entreat·y [en'triti] s (*pl* **-ies**) ruego, súplica

entree ['antre] s entrada, ingreso; (culin) entrada, principio

entrench [en'trentʃ] *tr* atrincherar ‖ *intr* — **to entrench on** o **upon** infringir, violar

entrust [en'trʌst] *tr* confiar

en·try ['entri] s (*pl* **-tries**) entrada; (*item*) partida, entrada; (*in a dictionary*) artículo; (sport) concurrente *mf*

entwine [en'twaɪn] *tr* entretejer, entrelazar

enumerate [ɪ'njumə,ret] o [ɪ'numə,ret] *tr* enumerar

enunciate [ɪ'nʌnsɪ,et] o [ɪ'nʌnʃɪ,et] *tr* enunciar; pronunciar

envelop [en'veləp] *tr* envolver

envelope ['envə,lop] o ['anvə,lop] s (*for a letter*) sobre *m*; (*wrapper*) envoltura

envenom [en'venəm] *tr* envenenar

enviable ['envɪ·əbəl] *adj* envidiable

envious ['envɪ·əs] *adj* envidioso

environment [en'vaɪrənmənt] s medio ambiente; (*surroundings*) inmediaciones

environs [en'vaɪrəns] *spl* inmediaciones, alrededores *mf*

envisage [en'vɪzɪdʒ] *tr* (*to look in the face of*) encarar; considerar, representarse

envoi ['envɔɪ] s despedida (*copla al fin de una composición poética*)

envoy ['envɔɪ] s (*diplomatic agent*) enviado; (*short concluding stanza*) despedida

en·vy ['envi] s (*pl* **-vies**) envidia ‖ *v* (*pret* & *pp* **-vied**) *tr* envidiar

enzyme ['enzaɪm] o ['enzɪm] s enzima *f*

epaulet o epaulette ['epə,let] s charretera

epenthe·sis [ɛ'penθɪsɪs] s (pl -ses [,siz]) epéntesis f

epergne [ɪ'pʌrn] o [e'pern] s ramillete m, centro de mesa

ephemeral [ɪ'femərəl] adj efímero

epic ['epɪk] adj épico || s epopeya

epicure ['epɪ,kjur] s epicúreo

epicurean [,epɪkju'ri·ən] adj & s epicúreo

epidemic [,epɪ'demɪk] adj epidémico || s epidemia

epidemiology [,epɪ,dimɪ'alədʒɪ] s epidemiología

epidermis [,epɪ'dʌrmɪs] s epidermis f

epigram ['epɪ,græm] s epigrama m

epilepsy ['epɪ,lepsɪ] s epilepsia

epileptic [,epɪ'leptɪk] adj & s epiléptico

Epiphany [ɪ'pɪfənɪ] s Epifanía

Episcopalian [ɪ,pɪskə'peli·ən] adj & s episcopalista mf

episode ['epɪ,sod] s episodio

epistemology [ɪ,pɪstɪ'malədʒɪ] s epistemología

epistle [ɪ'pɪsəl] s epístola

epitaph ['epɪ,tæf] s epitafio

epithet ['epɪ,θet] s epíteto

epitome [ɪ'pɪtəmɪ] s epítome m; (fig) esencia, personificación

epitomize [ɪ'pɪtə,maɪz] tr epitomar; (fig) encarnar, personificar

epoch ['epək] o ['ipak] s época

epochal ['epəkəl] adj memorable, trascendental

ep'och-mak'ing adj que hace época

equable ['ekwəbəl] o ['ikwəbəl] adj constante, uniforme; sereno

equal ['ikwəl] adj igual; equal to a la altura de || s igual mf || v (pret & pp equaled o equalled; ger equaling o equalling) tr (to be equal to) igualarse a o con; (to make equal) igualar

equali·ty [ɪ'kwalɪtɪ] s (pl -ties) igualdad

equalize ['ikwə,laɪz] tr igualar; (to make uniform) equilibrar

equally ['ikwəlɪ] adv igualmente

equanimity [,ikwə'nɪmɪtɪ] s ecuanimidad, igualdad de ánimo

equate [i'kwet] tr poner en ecuación; considerar equivalente(s)

equation [i'kweʒən] o [i'kwefən] s ecuación

equator [i'kwetər] s ecuador m

equer·ry ['ekwərɪ] o [ɪ'kweri] s (pl -ries) caballerizo

equestrian [ɪ'kwestrɪ·ən] adj ecuestre || m jinete m, caballista m

equilateral [,ikwɪ'lætərəl] adj equilátero

equilibrium [,ikwɪ'lɪbrɪ·əm] s equilibrio

equinoctial [,ikwɪ'nakʃəl] adj equinoccial

equinox ['ikwɪ,naks] s equinoccio

equip [ɪ'kwɪp] v (pret & pp equipped; ger equipping) tr equipar

equipment [ɪ'kwɪpmənt] s equipo, avíos, pertrechos; aptitud, capacidad

equipoise ['ikwɪ,pɔɪz] o ['ekwɪ,pɔɪz]

s equilibrio; contrapeso || tr equilibrar; equipesar

equitable ['ekwɪtəbəl] adj equitativo

equi·ty ['ekwɪtɪ] s (pl -ties) (fairness) equidad; valor líquido

equivalent [ɪ'kwɪvələnt] adj & s equivalente m

equivocal [ɪ'kwɪvəkəl] adj equívoco

equivocate [ɪ'kwɪvə,ket] intr usar de equívocos para engañar, mentir

equivocation [ɪ,kwɪvə'keʃən] s equívoco

era ['ɪrə] o ['ira] s era

eradicate [ɪ'rædɪ,ket] tr erradicar

erase [ɪ'res] tr borrar

eraser [ɪ'resər] s goma de borrar; (for blackboard) cepillo

erasure [ɪ're/ər] o [ɪ'reʒər] s borradura, tachón m

ere [ɛr] prep antes de || conj antes de que; más bien que

erect [ɪ'rekt] adj derecho, enhiesto, erguido; (hair) erizado || tr (to set in upright position) erguir, enhestar; erigir (un edificio); armar, montar (una máquina)

erection [ɪ'rekʃən] s erección

erg [ʌrg] s ergio

ermine ['ʌrmɪn] s armiño; (fig) toga, judicatura

erode [ɪ'rod] tr erosionar || intr erosionarse

erosion [ɪ'roʒən] s erosión

err [ʌr] intr errar, equivocarse, marrar; pecar, marrar

errand ['erənd] s mandado, recado, comisión; to run an errand hacer un mandado

errand boy s recadero, mandadero

erratic [ɪ'rætɪk] adj irregular, inconstante, variable; excéntrico

erra·tum [ɪ'retəm] o [ɪ'ratəm] s (pl -ta [tə]) errata

erroneous [ɪ'ronɪ·əs] adj erróneo

error ['erər] s error m

erudite ['eru,daɪt] o ['erju,daɪt] adj erudito

erudition [,eru'dɪʃən] o [,erju'dɪʃən] s erudición

erupt [ɪ'rʌpt] intr hacer erupción (la piel, los dientes de un niño); erumpir (un volcán)

eruption [ɪ'rʌpʃən] s erupción

escalate ['eskə,let] intr escalarse

escalation [,eskə'leʃən] s escalada, escalación

escalator ['eskə,letər] s escalera mecánica, móvil o rodante

escallop [es'kæləp] s concha de peregrino; (on edge of cloth) festón m || tr hornear a la crema y con migajas de pan; cocer (p.ej., ostras) en su concha; festonear

escapade [,eskə'ped] s calaverada, aventura atolondrada; (flight) escapada

escape [es'kep] s (getaway) escape m, escapatoria; (from responsibilities, duties, etc.) escapatoria || tr evitar, eludir; to escape someone escapársele a uno; olvidársele a uno || intr escapar, escaparse; to escape from escaparse a (*una persona*); escaparse de (*la cárcel*)

escapee [,eskə'pi] *s* evadido

escape literature *s* literatura de escape o de evasión

escapement [es'kepmənt] *s* escape *m*

escapement wheel *s* rueda de escape

escarpment [es'kɑrpmənt] *s* escarpa

eschew [es't∫u] *tr* evitar, rehuir

escort ['eskɔrt] *s* escolta; (*man or boy who accompanies a woman or girl in public*) acompañante *m*, caballero, galán *m* ‖ [es'kɔrt] *tr* escoltar

escutcheon [es'kʌt∫ən] *s* escudo de armas; (*plate in front of lock on door*) escudo, escudete *m*

Eski·mo ['eskɪ,mo] *adj* esquimal ‖ *s* (*pl* -mos o -mo) esquimal *mf*

esopha·gus [i'safəgəs] *s* (*pl* -gi [,dʒaɪ]) esófago

esp. *abbr* especially

espalier [es'pæljər] *s* espaldar *m*, espalera

especial [es'pe∫əl] *adj* especial

espionage ['espɪ·ənɪdʒ] o [,espɪ·ə'naʒ] *s* espionaje *m*

esplanade [,esplə'ned] o [,esplə'nɑd] *s* explanada

espousal [es'pauzəl] *s* desposorios; (*of a cause*) adhesión

espouse [es'pauz] *tr* casarse con; (*to advocate, adopt*) abogar por, adherirse a

Esq. *abbr* Esquire

esquire [es'kwaɪr] o ['eskwaɪr] *s* escudero ‖ **Esquire** *s* título de cortesía que se escribe después del apellido y que se usa en vez de **Mr.**

essay ['ese] *s* ensayo

essayist ['ese·ɪst] *s* ensayista *mf*

essence ['esəns] *s* esencia

essential [e'sen∫əl] *adj* & *s* esencial *m*

est. *abbr* **established, estate, estimated**

establish [es'tæblɪ∫] *tr* establecer

establishment [es'tæblɪ∫mənt] *s* establecimiento

estate [es'tet] *s* estado; situación social; (*landed property*) finca, hacienda, heredad; (*a person's possessions*) bienes *mpl*, propiedad; (*left by a decedent*) herencia, bienes relictos

esteem [es'tim] *s* estima ‖ *tr* estimar

esthete ['esθit] *s* esteta *mf*

esthetic [es'θetɪk] *adj* estético ‖ **esthetics** *ssg* estética

estimable ['estɪməbəl] *adj* estimable

estimate ['estɪ,met] o ['estɪmɪt] *s* (*calculation of value, judgment of worth*) estimación; (*statement of cost of work to be done*) presupuesto ‖ ['estɪ,met] *tr* (*to judge, deem*) estimar; presupuestar (*el coste de una obra*)

estimation [,estɪ'me∫ən] *s* estimación

estrangement [es'trendʒmənt] *s* extrañeza

estuar·y ['est∫u,erɪ] *s* (*pl* -ies) estero

etc. *abbr* et cetera

etch [et∫] *tr* & *intr* grabar al agua fuerte

etcher ['et∫ər] *s* aguafortista *mf*

etching ['et∫ɪŋ] *s* aguafuerte *f*

eternal [ɪ'tʌrnəl] *adj* eterno

eterni·ty [ɪ'tʌrnɪti] *s* (*pl* -ties) eternidad

ether ['iθər] *s* éter *m*

ethereal [ɪ'θɪrɪ·əl] *adj* etéreo

ethical ['eθɪkəl] *adj* ético

ethics ['eθɪks] *ssg* ética

Ethiopian [,iθɪ'opɪ·ən] *adj* & *s* etíope *mf*

Ethiopic [,iθɪ'opɪk] *adj* & *s* etiópico

ethnic(al) ['eθnɪk(əl)] *adj* étnico

ethnography [eθ'nagrəfi] *s* etnografía

ethnology [eθ'nalədʒi] *s* etnología

ethyl ['eθɪl] *s* etilo

ethylene ['eθɪ,lin] *s* etileno

etiquette ['etɪ,ket] *s* etiqueta

et seq. *abbr* **et sequens, et sequentes, et sequentia** (Lat) **and the following**

étude [e'tjud] *s* (mus) estudio

etymology [,etɪ'malədʒi] *s* etimología

ety·mon ['etɪ,mɑn] *s* (*pl* -mons o -ma [mə]) étimo

eucalyp·tus [,jukə'lɪptəs] *s* (*pl* -tuses o -ti [taɪ]) eucalipto

Eucharist ['jukərɪst] *s* Eucaristía

euchre ['jukər] *s* juego de naipes ‖ *tr* (coll) ser más listo que

eugenics [ju'dʒenɪks] *s* eugenesia

eulogistic [,julə'dʒɪstɪk] *adj* elogiador

eulogize ['julə,dʒaɪz] *tr* elogiar

eulo·gy ['julədʒi] *s* (*pl* -gies) elogio

eunuch ['junək] *s* eunuco

euphemism ['jufɪ,mɪzəm] *s* eufemismo

euphemistic [,jufɪ'mɪstɪk] *adj* eufemístico

euphonic [ju'fɑnɪk] *adj* eufónico

eupho·ny ['jufəni] *s* (*pl* -nies) eufonía

euphoria [ju'forɪ·ə] *s* euforia

euphuism ['jufju,ɪzəm] *s* eufuísmo

euphuistic [,jufju'ɪstɪk] *adj* eufuístico

Europe ['jurəp] *s* Europa

European [,jurə'pi·ən] *adj* & *s* europeo

euthanasia [,juθə'neʒə] *s* eutanasia

evacuate [ɪ'vækju,et] *tr* & *intr* evacuar

evacuation [ɪ,vækju'e∫ən] *s* evacuación

evade [ɪ'ved] *tr* evadir ‖ *intr* evadirse

evaluate [ɪ'vælju,et] *tr* evaluar

Evangel [ɪ'vændʒəl] *s* Evangelio

evangelic(al) [,ivæn'dʒelɪk(əl)] o [,evən'dʒelɪk(əl)] *adj* evangélico

Evangelist [ɪ'vændʒəlɪst] *s* Evangelista *m*

evaporate [ɪ'væpə,ret] *tr* evaporar ‖ *intr* evaporarse

evasion [ɪ'veʒən] *s* evasión, evasiva

evasive [ɪ'vesɪv] *adj* evasivo

eve [iv] *s* víspera; **on the eve of** en vísperas de

even ['ivən] *adj* (*smooth*) parejo, llano, liso; (*number*) par; (*constante, uniforme, invariable*); (*temperament*) apacible, sereno; exacto, igual; **even with** al nivel de; **to be even** estar en paz; **no deber nada a nadie**; **to get even** desquitarse ‖ *adv* aun, hasta; sin embargo; también; exactamente, igualmente; **even as** así como; **even if** aunque, aun cuando; **even so** aun así; **even though** aunque, aun cuando; **even when** aun cuando; **not even** ni . . . siquiera; **to break even** salir

ep
ev

sin ganar ni perder; (in gambling) salir en paz || tr allanar, igualar

evening ['ivnɪŋ] adj vespertino || s tarde f

evening clothes spl traje m de etiqueta

evening gown s vestido de noche (de mujer)

evening primrose s hierba del asno

evening star s estrella vespertina, lucero de la tarde

evening wrap s salida de teatro

e'ven·song' s canción de la tarde; (eccl) vísperas

event [ɪ'vent] s acontecimiento, suceso; (outcome) resultado; (public function) acto; (sport) prueba; **at all events** o **in any event** en todo caso; **in the event that** en caso que

eventful [ɪ'ventfəl] adj lleno de acontecimientos; importante, memorable

eventual [ɪ'ventʃʊ·əl] adj final

eventual·ty [ɪ,ventʃʊ'ælɪti] s (pl -ties) eventualidad

eventually [ɪ'ventʃʊ·əli] adv finalmente, con el tiempo

eventuate [ɪ'ventʃʊ,et] intr concluir, resultar

ever ['evər] adv (at all times) siempre; (at any time) jamás, nunca, alguna vez; **as ever** como siempre; **as much as ever** tanto como antes; **ever since** (since that time) desde entonces; después de que; **ever so** muy; **ever so much** muchísimo; **hardly ever** o **scarcely ever** casi nunca; **not . . . ever** no . . . nunca

ev'er·glade' s tierra pantanosa cubierta de hierbas altas

ev'er·green' adj siempre verde || s planta siempre verde; **evergreens** ramas colgadas como adorno

ev'er·last'ing adj sempiterno; (lasting indefinitely) duradero; (wearisome) aburrido, cansado || s eternidad; (bot) siempreviva

ev'er·more' adv eternamente; **for evermore** para siempre jamás

every ['evri] adj indef todos los; (each) cada, todo; (being each in a series) cada, p.ej., **every three days** cada tres días; **every bit** (coll) todo, p.ej., **every bit a man** todo un hombre; **every now and then** de vez en cuando; **every once in a while** una que otra vez; **every other day** cada dos días, un día sí y otro no; **every which way** (coll) por todas partes; (coll) en desarreglo

ev'ery·bod'y pron indef todo el mundo

ev'ery·day' adj de todos los días; cotidiano, diario; común, ordinario

every man Jack o **every mother's son** s cada hijo de vecino

ev'ery·one' o **every one** pron indef cada uno, todos, todo el mundo

ev'ery·thing' pron indef todo

ev'ery·where' adv en o por todas partes; a todas partes

evict [ɪ'vɪkt] tr desahuciar

eviction [ɪ'vɪkʃən] s desahucio

evidence ['evɪdəns] s evidencia; (law) prueba

evident ['evɪdənt] adj evidente

evil ['ivəl] adj malo, malvado || s mal m, maldad

e'vil·do'er s malhechor m, malvado

e'vil·do'ing s malhecho, maldad

evil eye s mal m de ojo

evil-minded ['ivəl'maɪndɪd] adj mal pensado, malintencionado

Evil One, the el enemigo malo

evince [ɪ'vɪns] tr manifestar, mostrar

evoke [ɪ'vok] tr evocar

evolution [,evə'luʃən] s evolución; (math) extracción de raíces, radicación

evolve [ɪ'valv] tr desarrollar; desprender (olores, gases, calor) || intr evolucionar

ewe [ju] s oveja

ewer ['ju·ər] s aguamanil m

ex. abbr **examination, example, except, exchange, executive**

ex [eks] prep sin incluir, sin participación en

exact [eg'zækt] adj exacto || tr exigir

exacting [eg'zæktɪŋ] adj exigente

exaction [eg'zækʃən] s exacción

exactly [eg'zæktli] adv exactamente; (sharp, on the dot) en punto

exactness [eg'zæktnɪs] s exactitud

exaggerate [eg'zædʒə,ret] tr exagerar

exalt [eg'zɔlt] tr exaltar, ensalzar

exam [eg'zæm] s (coll) examen m

examination [eg,zæmɪ'neʃən] s examen m; **to take an examination** sufrir un examen, examinarse

examine [eg'zæmɪn] tr examinar

example [eg'zæmpəl] o [eg'zampəl] s ejemplo; (case serving as a warning to others) ejemplar m; (of mathematics) problema m; **for example** por ejemplo

exasperate [eg'zæspə,ret] tr exasperar

excavate ['ekskə,vet] tr excavar

exceed [ek'sid] tr exceder; sobrepasar (p.ej., el límite de velocidad)

exceedingly [ek'sidɪŋli] adv sumamente, sobremanera

ex·cel [ek'sel] v (pret & pp -celled; ger -celling) tr aventajar || intr sobresalir

excellence ['eksələns] s excelencia

excellen·cy ['eksələnsi] s (pl -cies) excelencia; **Your Excellency** Su Excelencia

excelsior [ek'selsɪ·ər] s pajilla de madera, virutas de madera

except [ek'sept] prep excepto; **except for** sin; **except that** a menos que || tr exceptuar

exception [ek'sepʃən] s excepción; **to take exception** poner reparos, objetar; ofenderse; **with the exception of** a excepción de

exceptional [ek'sepʃənəl] adj excepcional

excerpt ['eksʌrpt] o ['ek'sʌrpt] s excerta, selección || [ek'sʌrpt] tr escoger

excess ['ekses] o [ek'ses] adj excedente, sobrante || [ek'ses] s (amount or degree by which one thing exceeds another) exceso, excedente m; (excessive amount; immoderate indulgence, unlawful conduct) exceso; **in excess of** más que, superior a

excess baggage s exceso de equipaje
excess fare s suplemento
excessive [ɛk'sɛsɪv] adj excesivo
ex'cess-prof'its tax s impuesto sobre beneficios extraordinarios
excess weight s exceso de peso
exchange [ɛks't∫endʒ] s (of greetings, compliments, blows, etc.) cambio; (of prisoners, merchandise, newspapers, credentials, etc.) canje m; periódico de canje; (place for buying and selling) bolsa, lonja; estación telefónica, central f de teléfonos; **in exchange for** en cambio de, a trueque de || tr cambiar; canjear (prisioneros, mercancías, etc.); darse, hacerse (cortesías); **to exchange greetings** saludarse; **to exchange shots** cambiar disparos
exchequer [ɛks't∫ɛkər] o ['ɛkst∫ɛkər] s tesorería; fondos nacionales
excise tax [ɛk'saɪz] o ['ɛksaɪz] m impuesto sobre ciertas mercancías de comercio interior
excitable [ɛk'saɪtəbəl] adj excitable
excite [ɛk'saɪt] tr excitar
excitement [ɛk'saɪtmənt] s excitación
exciting [ɛk'saɪtɪŋ] adj emocionante, conmovedor; (stimulating) excitante
exclaim [ɛks'klem] tr & intr exclamar
exclamation [,ɛksklə'me∫ən] s exclamación
exclamation mark o **point** s punto de admiración
exclude [ɛks'klud] tr excluir
exclusion [ɛks'kluʒən] s exclusión; **to the exclusion of** con exclusión de
exclusive [ɛks'klusɪv] adj exclusivo; (clannish) exclusivista; (expensive) (coll) carero; (fashionable) (coll) muy de moda; **exclusive of** con exclusión de
excommunicate [,ɛkskə'mjunɪ ,ket] tr excomulgar
excommunication [,ɛkskə ,mjunɪ'ke∫ən] s excomunión
excoriate [ɛks'korɪ ,et] tr (fig) desollar, vituperar
excrement ['ɛkskrəmənt] s excremento
excruciating [ɛks'kruʃɪ ,etɪŋ] adj atroz, agudísimo, vivísimo
exculpate ['ɛkskʌl ,pet] o [ɛks'kʌlpet] tr exculpar
excursion [ɛks'kʌrʒən] o [ɛks'kʌr∫ən] s excursión
excursionist [ɛks'kʌrʒənɪst] o [ɛks'kʌr∫ənɪst] s excursionista mf
excusable [ɛks'kjusəbəl] adj excusable
excuse [ɛks'kjus] s excusa || [ɛks'kjuz] tr excusar, disculpar; dispensar, perdonar
execute ['ɛksɪ ,kjut] tr ejecutar; (law) celebrar, finalizar (una escritura)
execution [,ɛksɪ'kju∫ən] s ejecución
executioner [,ɛksɪ'kju∫ənər] s ejecutor m de la justicia, verdugo
executive [ɛg'zɛkjətɪv] adj ejecutivo || m poder ejecutivo; (of a school, business, etc.) dirigente mf
Executive Mansion s (U.S.A.) palacio presidencial
executor [ɛg'zɛkjətər] s albacea m, ejecutor testamentario

executrix [ɛg'zɛkjətrɪks] s albacea f, ejecutora testamentaria
exemplary [ɛg'zɛmpləri] o ['ɛgzəm ,plɛri] adj ejemplar
exempli-fy [ɛg'zɛmplɪ ,faɪ] v (pret & pp -fied) tr ejemplificar
exempt [ɛg'zɛmpt] adj exento || tr eximir, exentar
exemption [ɛg'zɛmp∫ən] s exención
exercise ['ɛksər ,saɪz] s ejercicio; ceremonia; **to take exercise** hacer ejercicio || tr ejercer (p.ej., caridad, influencia); ejercitar (un arte, profesión, etc.; adiestrar con el ejercicio); inquietar, preocupar; poner (cuidado) || ref ejercitarse
exert [ɛg'zʌrt] tr ejercer (una fuerza); **to exert oneself** esforzarse
exertion [ɛg'zʌr∫ən] s esfuerzo, empeño; (active use) ejercicio
exhalation [,ɛks·hə'le∫ən] s (of gas, vapors, etc.) exhalación; (of air from lungs) espiración
exhale [ɛks'hel] o [ɛg'zel] tr exhalar (gases, vapores); espirar (el aire aspirado) || intr exhalarse; espirar
exhaust [ɛg'zɔst] s escape m; tubo de escape || tr (to wear out, fatigue; to use up) agotar; hacer el vacío en; apurar (todos los medios)
exhaust fan s ventilador m aspirador
exhaustion [ɛg'zɔst∫ən] s agotamiento
exhaustive [ɛg'zɔstɪv] adj exhaustivo; comprensivo
exhaust manifold s múltiple m de escape
exhaust pipe s tubo de escape
exhaust valve s válvula de escape
exhibit [ɛg'zɪbɪt] s exhibición; (law) documento de prueba || tr exhibir
exhibition [,ɛksɪ'bɪ∫ən] s exhibición
exhibitor [ɛg'zɪbɪtər] s expositor m
exhilarating [ɛg'zɪlə ,retɪŋ] adj alegrador, regocijador, alborozador
exhort [ɛg'zɔrt] tr exhortar
exhume [ɛks'hjum] o [ɛg'zjum] tr exhumar
exigen·cy ['ɛksɪdʒənsi] s (pl -cies) exigencia
exigent ['ɛksɪdʒənt] adj exigente
exile ['ɛgzaɪl] o ['ɛksaɪl] s destierro; (person) desterrado || tr desterrar
exist [ɛg'zɪst] intr existir
existence [ɛg'zɪstəns] s existencia
existing [ɛg'zɪstɪŋ] adj existente
exit ['ɛgzɪt] o ['ɛksɪt] s salida || intr salir
exodus ['ɛksədəs] s éxodo
exonerate [ɛg'zɑnə ,ret] tr (to free from blame) exculpar; (to free from an obligation) exonerar
exorbitant [ɛg'zɔrbɪtənt] adj exorbitante
exorcise ['ɛksor ,saɪz] tr exorcizar
exotic [ɛg'zɑtɪk] adj exótico
exp. abbr **expenses, expired, export, express**
expand [ɛks'pænd] tr dilatar (un gas, el metal); (to enlarge, develop) ampliar, ensanchar; (to unfold, stretch out) desplegar, extender; (math) desarrollar (una ecuación) || intr

dilatarse; ampliarse, ensancharse; desplegarse, extenderse

expanse [ɛks'pæns] s extensión

expansion [ɛks'pænʃən] s expansión

expansive [ɛks'pænsɪv] adj expansivo

expatiate [ɛks'peʃɪ,et] intr espaciarse, explayarse

expatriate [ɛks'petrɪ·ɪt] adj & s expatriado

expect [ɛks'pɛkt] tr esperar; (coll) creer, suponer

expectan·cy [ɛks'pɛktənsɪ] s (pl -cies) expectación

expectant mother [ɛks'pɛktənt] s futura madre

expectation [,ɛkspɛk'teʃən] s expectativa

expectorate [ɛks'pɛktə,ret] tr & intr expectorar

expedien·cy [ɛks'pidɪ·ənsɪ] s (pl -cies) conveniencia, oportunidad; ventaja personal

expedient [ɛks'pidɪ·ənt] adj conveniente, oportuno; egoísta, ventajoso; (acting with self-interest) ventajista || s expediente m

expedite ['ɛkspɪ,daɪt] tr apresurar, despachar; dar curso a (un documento)

expedition [,ɛkspɪ'dɪʃən] s expedición

expeditious [,ɛkspɪ'dɪʃəs] adj expeditivo

expeditiously [,ɛkspɪ'dɪʃəslɪ] adv ejecutivamente

ex-pel [ɛks'pɛl] v (pret & pp -pelled; ger -pelling) tr expeler, expulsar

expend [ɛks'pɛnd] tr gastar, consumir

expendable [ɛks'pɛndəbəl] adj gastable; (to be thrown away after use) desechable; (soldier) sacrificable

expenditure [ɛks'pɛndɪt/ər] s gasto, consumo

expense [ɛks'pɛns] s gasto; **expenses** gastos, expensas; **to go to the expense of** meterse en gastos con; **to meet expenses** hacer frente a los gastos

expense account s cuenta de gastos

expensive [ɛks'pɛnsɪv] adj caro, costoso, dispendioso; (charging high prices) carero

experience [ɛks'pɪrɪ·əns] s experiencia || tr experimentar

experienced [ɛks'pɪrɪ·ənst] adj experimentado

experiment [ɛks'pɛrɪmənt] s experiencia, experimento || [ɛks'pɛrɪ,mɛnt] intr experimentar

expert ['ɛkspərt] adj & s experto

expiate ['ɛkspɪ,et] tr expiar

expiation [,ɛkspɪ'eʃən] s expiación

expire [ɛks'paɪr] tr expeler (el aire de los pulmones) || intr expirar (expeler el aire de los pulmones; acabarse, p.ej., un plazo; fallecer)

explain [ɛks'plen] tr explicar; **to explain away** descartar con explicaciones; (to make excuse for) explicar || intr explicar, explicarse

explanation [,ɛksplə'neʃən] s explicación

explanatory [ɛks'plænə,torɪ] adj explicativo

explicit [ɛks'plɪsɪt] adj explícito

explode [ɛks'plod] tr volar, hacer saltar; desacreditar (una teoría) || intr explotar, estallar, reventar

exploit [ɛks'plɔɪt] o ['ɛksplɔɪt] s hazaña, proeza || [ɛks'plɔɪt] tr explotar

exploitation [,ɛksplɔɪ'teʃən] s explotación

exploration [,ɛksplə'reʃən] s exploración

explore [ɛks'plor] tr explorar

explorer [ɛks'plorər] s explorador m

explosion [ɛks'ploʒən] s explosión; (of a theory) refutación

explosive [ɛks'plosɪv] adj explosivo || s explosivo; (phonet) explosiva

exponent [ɛks'ponənt] s exponente m, expositor m; (math) exponente m

export [ɛks'sport] adj de exportación || s exportación; **exports** (articles exported) exportación || [ɛks'port] o ['ɛksport] tr & intr exportar

exportation [,ɛkspor'teʃən] s exportación

exporter ['ɛksportər] o [ɛks'portər] s exportador m

expose [ɛks'poz] tr exponer; (to unmask) desenmascarar; (the Host) manifestar, exponer; (phot) impresionar

exposé [,ɛkspo'ze] s desenmascaramiento

exposition [,ɛkspə'zɪʃən] s exposición; (rhet) exposición

expostulate [ɛks'past/ə,let] intr protestar; **to expostulate with** reconvenir

exposure [ɛks'poʒər] s (to a danger; position with respect to points of compass) exposición; (unmasking) desenmascaramiento; (phot) exposición

expound [ɛks'paʊnd] tr exponer

express [ɛks'prɛs] adj expreso || adv (for a special purpose) expresamente; por expreso || s expreso; **by express** (rr) en gran velocidad || tr expresar; (to squeeze out) exprimir; enviar por expreso; **to express oneself** expresarse

express company s compañía de transportes rápidos

expression [ɛks'prɛʃən] s expresión

expressive [ɛks'prɛsɪv] adj expresivo

expressly [ɛks'prɛslɪ] adv expresamente

express·man [ɛks'prɛsmən] s (pl -men [mən]) (U.S.A.) empleado del servicio de transportes rápidos

express train s tren expreso

express'way' s carretera de vía libre

expropriate [ɛks'proprɪ,et] tr expropiar

expulsion [ɛks'pʌlʃən] s expulsión

expunge [ɛks'pʌndʒ] tr borrar, cancelar, arrasar

expurgate ['ɛkspər,get] tr expurgar

exquisite ['ɛkskwɪzɪt] o [ɛks'kwɪzɪt] adj exquisito; agudo, vivo; sensible

ex-service·man [,ɛks'sɑrvɪs,mæn] s (pl -men [,mɛn]) ex militar m, ex combatiente m

extant [ˈɛkstənt] o [ɛksˈtænt] *adj* existente

extemporaneous [ɛks͵tempəˈrenɪ·əs] *adj* sin preparación; *(made for the occasion)* provisional

extempore [ɛksˈtempəri] *adj* improvisado ‖ *adv* improvisadamente

extemporize [ɛksˈtempə͵raɪz] *tr & intr* improvisar

extend [ɛksˈtend] *tr* extender; dar, ofrecer; hacer extensivos *(p.ej., vivos deseos)*; prorrogar *(un plazo)* ‖ *intr* extenderse

extended [ɛksˈtendɪd] *adj* extenso; prolongado

extension [ɛksˈtenʃən] *s* extensión; prolongación

extension ladder *s* escalera extensible

extension table *s* mesa de extensión

extensive [ɛksˈtensɪv] *adj* *(having great extent)* extenso; *(characterized by extension)* extensivo

extent [ɛksˈtent] *s* extensión; **to a certain extent** hasta cierto punto; **to a great extent** en sumo grado; **to the full extent** en toda su extensión

extenuate [ɛksˈtenjʊ͵et] *tr (to make seem less serious)* atenuar; *(to underrate)* menospreciar, no dar importancia a

exterior [ɛksˈtɪrɪ·ər] *adj & s* exterior *m*

exterminate [ɛksˈtʌrmɪ͵net] *tr* exterminar

external [ɛksˈtʌrnəl] *adj* externo ‖ **externals** *spl* exterioridad

extinct [ɛksˈtɪŋkt] *adj* desaparecido; *(volcano)* extinto

extinguish [ɛksˈtɪŋgwɪʃ] *tr* extinguir

extinguisher [ɛksˈtɪŋgwɪʃər] *s* apagador *m*, extintor *m*

extirpate [ˈɛkstər͵pet] o [ɛksˈtʌrpet] *tr* extirpar

ex·tol [ɛksˈtol] o [ɛksˈtal] *v (pret & pp* -**tolled;** *ger* -**tolling)** *tr* ensalzar

extort [ɛksˈtɔrt] *tr* obtener por amenazas, fuerza o engaño

extortion [ɛksˈtɔrʃən] *s* extorción

extra [ˈɛkstrə] *adj* extra; *(spare)* de repuesto ‖ *adv* extraordinariamente ‖ *s (of a newspaper)* extra *m;* pieza de repuesto; *(something additional)* extra *m;* (theat) extra *mf*

extract [ˈɛkstrækt] *s* selección; (pharm) extracto ‖ [ɛksˈtrækt] *tr (to pull out, remove)* extraer; seleccionar *(pasajes de un libro);* (math) extraer

extraction [ɛksˈtrækʃən] *s* extracción

extracurricular [͵ɛkstrəkəˈrɪkjələr] *adj* extracurricular

extradition [͵ɛkstrəˈdɪʃən] *s* extradición

extra fare *s* recargo de tarifa, tarifa recargada

ex·tra-flat′ *adj* extraplano

extramural [͵ɛkstrəˈmjʊrəl] *adj* extramural

extraneous [ɛksˈtrenɪ·əs] *adj* ajeno, extraño

extraordinary [ɛksˈtrɔrdɪ͵neri] o [ɛksˈtrɔrdɪ͵neri] *adj* extraordinario

extrapolate [ɛksˈtræpə͵let] *tr & intr* extrapolar

extrasensory [͵ɛkstrəˈsensəri] *adj* extrasensorio

extravagance [ɛksˈtrævəgəns] *s* derroche *m*, prodigalidad, gasto excesivo; *(wildness, folly)* extravagancia

extravagant [ɛksˈtrævəgənt] *adj* derrochador, pródigo, gastador; *(wild, foolish)* extravagante

extreme [ɛksˈtrim] *adj & s* extremo; **in the extreme** en sumo grado; **to go to extremes** excederse, propasarse

extremely [ɛksˈtrimli] *adv* extremadamente, sumamente

extreme unction *s* extremaunción

extremi·ty [ɛksˈtremɪti] *s (pl* -**ties)** extremidad; *(great want)* extrema necesidad; **extremities** medidas extremas; *(hands and feet)* extremidades

extricate [ˈɛkstrɪ͵ket] *tr* desembarazar, desenredar

extrinsic [ɛksˈtrɪnsɪk] *adj* extrínseco

extrovert [ˈɛkstrə͵vʌrt] *s* extrovertido

extrude [ɛksˈtrud] *intr* resaltar, sobresalir

exuberant [ɛgˈzubərənt] o [ɛgˈzjubərənt] *adj* exuberante

exude [ɛgˈzud] o [ɛkˈsud] *tr & intr* exudar

exult [ɛgˈzʌlt] *intr* exultar, gloriarse

exultant [ɛgˈzʌltənt] *adj* exultante

eye [aɪ] *s* ojo; *(of hook and eye)* hembra, corcheta; **to catch one's eye** llamar la atención a uno; **to feast one's eyes on** deleitar la vista en; **to lay eyes on** alcanzar a ver; **to make eyes at** hacer guiños a; **to roll one's eyes** poner los ojos en blanco; **to see eye to eye** estar completamente de acuerdo; **to shut one's eyes to** hacer la vista gorda ante; **without batting an eye** sin pestañear, sin inmutarse ‖ *v (pret & pp* eyed**;** *ger* eying o eyeing) *tr* ojear; **to eye up and down** mirar de hito en hito

eye′ball′ *s* globo del ojo

eye′bolt′ *s* armella, cáncamo

eye′brow′ *s* ceja; **to raise one's eyebrows** arquear las cejas

eye′cup′ *s* ojera, lavaojos *m*

eyeful [ˈaɪful] *s* (coll) buena ojeada

eye′glass′ *s (of optical instrument)* ocular *m;* (eyecup) ojera, lavaojos *m;* **eyeglasses** gafas, anteojos

eye′lash′ *s* pestaña

eyelet [ˈaɪlɪt] *s* ojete *m*, ojal *m;* *(hole to look through)* mirilla

eye′lid′ *s* párpado

eye of the morning *s* sol *m*

eye opener [ˈopənər] *s* noticia asombrosa o inesperada; (coll) trago de licor

eye′piece′ *s* ocular *m*

eye′-shade′ *s* visera

eye shadow *s* crema para los párpados

eye′shot′ *s* alcance *m* de la vista

eye′sight′ *s* vista; *(range)* alcance *m* de la vista

eye socket *s* cuenca del ojo

eye′sore′ *s* cosa que ofende la vista

eye′strain′ *s* vista fatigada

eye′-test′ chart *s* escala tipográfica oftalmométrica, tipo de ensayo, tipo de prueba

eye'tooth' *s* (*pl* **teeth'**) colmillo, diente canino; **to cut one's eyeteeth** (coll) tener el colmillo retorcido; **to give one's eyeteeth for** (coll) dar los ojos de la cara por

eye'wash' *s* colirio; (slang) halago para engañar

eye'wit'ness *s* testigo ocular, testigo presencial

ey·rie o **ey·ry** [ˈɛrɪ] *s* (*pl* **-ries**) nido de águilas, nido de aves de rapiña; (fig) altura, morada elevada

F

F, f [ɛf] sexta letra del alfabeto inglés
f. *abbr* **feminine, folio**
F. *abbr* **Fahrenheit, Friday**
fable [ˈfebəl] *s* fábula
fabric [ˈfæbrɪk] *s* tejido; textura; (*structure*) fábrica
fabricate [ˈfæbrɪ͵ket] *tr* fabricar
fabrication [͵fæbrɪˈkeʃən] *s* fabricación; mentira
fabulous [ˈfæbjələs] *adj* fabuloso
façade [fəˈsad] *s* fachada
face [fes] *s* cara, rostro; (*of cloth*) haz *f;* (*of earth*) faz *f;* (*grimace*) mueca; (*of watch*) esfera, muestra; (*impudence*) descaro; **in the face of** en presencia de; **to keep a straight face** contener la risa; **to lose face** desprestigiarse; **to save face** salvar las apariencias; **to show one's face** dejarse ver ‖ *tr* volver la cara hacia; arrostrar; revestir (*un muro*); forrar (*un vestido*); **facing** cara a ‖ *intr* — **to face about** volver la mirada; dar media vuelta; cambiar de opinión; **to face on** dar a o sobre; **to face up to** encararse con
face card *s* figura, naipe *m* de figura
face lifting *s* cirugía estética
face powder *s* polvos de tocador
facet [ˈfæsɪt] *s* faceta
facial [ˈfeʃəl] *adj* facial ‖ *s* masaje *m* facial
facilitate [fəˈsɪlɪ͵tet] *tr* facilitar
facili·ty [fəˈsɪlɪtɪ] *s* (*pl* **-ties**) facilidad
facing [ˈfesɪŋ] *s* revestimiento, paramento
facsimile [fækˈsɪmɪlɪ] *s* facsímile *m*
fact [fækt] *s* hecho; **in fact** en realidad; **the fact is that** ello es que
faction [ˈfækʃən] *s* facción; discordia
factional [ˈfækʃənəl] *adj* faccionario
factionalism [ˈfækʃənə͵lɪzəm] *s* parcialidad, partidismo
factor [ˈfæktər] *s* factor *m* ‖ *tr* descomponer en factores
facto·ry [ˈfæktərɪ] *s* (*pl* **-ries**) fábrica
factual [ˈfæktʃʊ·əl] *adj* verdadero, objetivo
facul·ty [ˈfækəltɪ] *s* (*pl* **-ties**) facultad
fad [fæd] *s* afición pasajera, moda pasajera
fade [fed] *tr* desteñir ‖ *intr* desteñir, desteñirse; apagarse (*un sonido*); (rad) desvanecerse
fade'out' *s* desaparición gradual; (rad) desvanecimiento
fag [fæg] *s* (*drudge*) yunque *m;* (coll) cigarrillo ‖ *tr* — **to fag out** cansar
fagot [ˈfægət] *s* haz *m* de leña

fail [fel] *s* — **without fail** sin falta ‖ *tr* faltar a; reprobar, suspender (*a un alumno*); salir mal en (*un examen*) ‖ *intr* malograrse, fracasar; salir mal (*un alumno*); fallar (*un motor*); (com) quebrar, hacer bancarrota; **to fail to** dejar de
failure [ˈfeljər] *s* malogro, fracaso, mal éxito; (*student*) perdigón *m;* (com) quiebra
faint [fent] *adj* débil; **to feel faint** sentirse desfallecido ‖ *s* desmayo ‖ *intr* desmayarse
faint-hearted [ˈfentˈhartɪd] *adj* cobarde, tímido, apocado
fair [fer] *adj* justo, imparcial; regular, ordinario; favorable, propicio; (*hair*) rubio; (*complexion*) blanco; (*sky*) despejado; (*weather*) bueno, bonancible ‖ *adv* imparcialmente; **to play fair** jugar limpio ‖ *s* (*exhibition*) feria; (*carnival*) quermese *m*, verbena
fair'ground' *s* real *m*, campo de una feria
fairly [ˈferlɪ] *adv* justamente; bastante
fair-minded [ˈferˈmaɪndɪd] *adj* justo, imparcial
fairness [ˈfernɪs] *s* justicia, imparcialidad; (*of weather*) serenidad; (*of complexion*) blancura
fair play *s* juego limpio, limpieza
fair sex *s* bello sexo
fair to middling *adj* bastante bueno, mediano
fair'weath'er *adj* — **a fair-weather friend** amigo del buen viento
fair·y [ˈferɪ] *adj* feérico ‖ *s* (*pl* **-ies**) hada
fairy godmother *s* hada madrina
fair'y·land' *s* tierra de las hadas
fairy ring *s* corro de brujas
fairy tale *s* cuento de hadas; (fig) bella poesía
faith [feθ] *s* fe *f;* **to break faith with** faltar a la palabra dada a; **to keep faith with** cumplir la palabra dada a; **to pin one's faith on** tener puesta su esperanza en; **upon my faith!** ¡a fe mía!
faithful [ˈfeθfəl] *adj* fiel, leal ‖ **the faithful** los fieles
faithless [ˈfeθlɪs] *adj* infiel, desleal
fake [fek] *adj* (coll) falso, fingido ‖ *s* impostura, patraña; (*person*) farsante *mf* ‖ *tr* & *intr* falsificar, fingir
faker [ˈfekər] *s* (coll) impostor *m*, patrañero; (*peddler*) (coll) buhonero
falcon [ˈfɔkən] o [ˈfɔlkən] *s* halcón *m*

falconer ['fɔkənər] o ['fɔlkənər] s cetrero, halconero

falconry ['fɔkənri] o ['fɔlkənri] s cetrería, halconería

fall [fɔl] adj otoñal ‖ s caída; (of water) catarata, salto de agua; (of prices) baja; (autumn) otoño; **falls** catarata, caída de agua ‖ v (pret **fell** [fɛl]; pp **fallen** ['fɔlən]) intr caer, caerse; **to fall apart** caerse a pedazos; **to fall back** (mil) replegarse; **to fall behind** quedarse atrás; **to fall down** caerse; **to fall due** vencer (una letra); **to fall flat** caer tendido; no tener éxito; **to fall for** (slang) ser engañado por; (slang) enamorarse de; **to fall in** desplomarse (un techo); ponerse de acuerdo; **to fall in with** trabar amistades con; ponerse de acuerdo con; **to fall off** caer de; disminuir; **to fall out** desavenirse; **to fall out of caerse de; to fall out with** esquinarse con; **to fall over** caerse; (coll) adular, halagar; **to fall through** fracasar, malograrse; **to fall** tc recaer (la herencia, la elección) en; **to fall under** estar comprendido en

fallacious [fə'leʃəs] adj erróneo, engañoso

falla·cy ['fæləsi] s (pl **-cies**) error m, equivocación

fall guy s (slang) cabeza de turco

fallible ['fælɪbəl] adj falible

falling star s estrella fugaz

fall'out' s caída radiactiva, precipitación radiactiva

fallout shelter s refugio antiatómico

fallow ['fælo] adj barbechado; **to lie fallow** estar en barbecho (tierra labrantía); (fig) quedar sin emplear, quedar sin ejecutar (una cosa provechosa) ‖ s barbecho ‖ tr barbechar

false [fɔls] adj falso; (hair, teeth, etc.) postizo ‖ adv falsamente; **to play false** traicionar

false colors spl pretextos falsos

false face s mascarilla; (ugly false face) carantamaula

false-hearted ['fɔls'hɑrtɪd] adj pérfido

falsehood ['fɔls·hʊd] s falsedad

false pretenses spl impostura, falsas apariencias

false return s declaración falsa

falset·to [fɔl'sɛto] s (pl **-tos**) (voice) falsete m; (person) falsetista m

falsi·fy ['fɔlsɪ‚faɪ] v (pret & pp **-fied**) tr falsificar; (to disprove) refutar ‖ intr falsificar; mentir

falsi·ty ['fɔlsɪti] s (pl **-ties**) falsedad

falter ['fɔltər] s vacilación; (in speech) balbuceo ‖ intr vacilar; balbucear

fame [fem] s fama

famed [femd] adj afamado

familiar [fə'mɪljər] adj familiar; conocido; común; **familiar with** familiarizado con

familiari·ty [fə‚mɪlɪ'ærɪti] s (pl **-ties**) familiaridad; conocimiento

familiarize [fə'mɪljə‚raɪz] tr familiarizar

fami·ly ['fæmɪli] adj familiar; **in the family way** (coll) en estado de buena esperanza ‖ s (pl **-lies**) familia

family man s padre m de familia; hombre casero

family name s apellido

family physician s médico de cabecera

family tree s árbol genealógico

famish ['fæmɪʃ] tr & intr hambrear

famished ['fæmɪʃt] adj famélico

famous ['feməs] adj famoso; (notable, excellent) (coll) famoso

fan [fæn] s abanico; ventilador m; (slang) hincha mf, aficionado ‖ v (pret & pp **fanned**; ger **fanning**) tr abanicar; (to winnow) aventar; ahuyentar con abanico; avivar (el fuego); excitar (las pasiones); (slang) azotar ‖ intr abanicarse; **to fan out** salir (un camino) en todas direcciones

fanatic [fə'nætɪk] adj & s fanático

fanatical [fə'nætɪkəl] adj fanático

fanaticism [fə'nætɪ‚sɪzəm] s fanatismo

fancied ['fænsid] adj imaginario

fancier ['fænsɪ‚ər] s aficionado; visionario; (of animals) criador aficionado

fanciful ['fænsɪfəl] adj fantástico, extravagante; imaginativo

fan·cy ['fænsi] adj (comp **-cier**; super **-ciest**) de fantasía, de imitación; fino, de lujo, precioso; ornamental; primoroso; fantástico, extravagante ‖ s (pl **-cies**) fantasía; afición, gusto; **to take a fancy to** aficionarse a, prendarse de ‖ v (pret & pp **-cied**) tr imaginar

fancy ball s baile m de trajes

fancy dive s salto ornamental

fancy dress s traje m de fantasía

fancy foods spl comestibles mpl de lujo

fan'cy-free' adj libre del poder del amor

fancy jewelry s joyas de fantasía

fancy skating s patinaje m de fantasía

fan'cy-work' s (sew) labor f

fanfare ['fænfer] s fanfarria

fang [fæŋ] s colmillo; (of reptile) diente m

fan'light' s abanico

fantastic(al) [fæn'tæstɪk(əl)] adj fantástico

fanta·sy ['fæntəzi] o ['fæntəsi] s (pl **-sies**) fantasía

far [fɑr] adj lejano; **on the far side of** del otro lado de ‖ adv lejos; **as far as** hasta; en cuanto; **as far as I am concerned** por lo que a mí me toca; **as far as I know** que yo sepa; **by far** con mucho; **far and near** por todas partes; **far away** muy lejos; **far be it from me** no lo permita Dios; **far better** mucho mejor; **far different** muy diferente; **far from** lejos de; **far from it** ni con mucho; **far into** hasta muy adentro de; hasta muy tarde de; **far more** mucho más; **far off** a gran distancia; **how far** cuán lejos; **how far is it?** ¿cuánto hay de aquí?; **in so far as** en cuanto; **thus far** hasta ahora; **thus far this year** en lo que va del año; **to go far towards** contribuir mucho a

faraway ['fɑrə‚we] adj lejano, distante; abstraído, preocupado

ey
fa

farce [fɑrs] *s* farsa

farcical [ˈfɑrsɪkəl] *adj* ridículo

fare [fer] *s* pasaje *m*; pasajero; alimento; comida; **to collect fares** cobrar el pasaje || *intr* pasarlo, p.ej., **how did you fare?** ¿cómo lo pasó Vd.?

Far East *s* Extremo Oriente, Lejano Oriente

fare'well' *s* despedida; **to bid farewell to** o o **to take farewell of** despedirse de || *interj* ¡adiós!

far-fetched [ˈfɑrˈfɛtʃt] *adj* traído por los pelos

far-flung [ˈfɑrˈflʌŋ] *adj* de gran alcance, vasto

farm [fɑrm] *adj* agrícola; agropecuario || *s* granja; terreno agrícola || *tr* cultivar, labrar (*la tierra*) || *intr* cultivar la tierra y criar animales

farmer [ˈfɑrmər] *s* granjero; agricultor *m*, labrador *m*

farm hand *s* peón *m*, mozo de granja

farm'house' *s* alquería, cortijo

farming [ˈfɑrmɪŋ] *s* agricultura, labranza

farm'yard' *s* corral *m* de granja

far'-off' *adj* lejano, distante

far-reaching [ˈfɑrˈritʃɪŋ] *adj* de mucho alcance

far-sighted [ˈfɑrˈsaɪtɪd] *adj* longividente; precavido; présbita

farther [ˈfɑrðər] *adj* más lejano; adicional || *adv* más lejos, más allá; además, también; **farther on** más adelante

farthest [ˈfɑrðɪst] *adj* (el) más lejano; último || *adv* más lejos; más

farthing [ˈfɑrðɪŋ] *s* (Brit) cuarto de penique

Far West *s* (U.S.A.) Lejano Oeste

fascinate [ˈfæsɪˌnet] *tr* fascinar

fascinating [ˈfæsɪˌnetɪŋ] *adj* fascinante, cautivador

fascism [ˈfæsɪzəm] *s* fascismo

fascist [ˈfæsɪst] *adj* & *s* fascista *mf*

fashion [ˈfæʃən] *s* moda, boga; estilo, manera; alta sociedad; **after a fashion** en cierto modo; **in fashion de** moda; **out of fashion** fuera de moda; **to go out of fashion** pasar de moda || *tr* labrar, forjar

fashion designing *s* alta costura

fashion plate *s* figurín *m*; (*person*) (coll) figurín *m*, elegante *mf*; **to be a fashion plate** (coll) ir hecho un maniquí

fashion show *s* desfile *m* de modas

fast [fæst] o [fɑst] *adj* rápido, veloz; (*clock*) adelantado; fijado, disipado; (*friend*) fiel || *adv* aprisa, rápidamente; firmemente; (*asleep*) profundamente; **to hold fast** mantenerse firme; **to live fast** vivir de una manera disipada || *s* ayuno; **to break one's fast** romper el ayuno || *intr* ayunar

fast day *s* día *m* de ayuno

fasten [ˈfæsən] o [ˈfɑsən] *tr* fijar; atar; abrochar; cerrar con llave; (*one's belt*) ajustarse; (*blame*) aplicar || *intr* fijarse

fastener [ˈfæsənər] o [ˈfɑsənər] *s* asilla; (*snap, clasp*) cierre *m*; (*for papers*) sujetapapeles *m*

fast forward *s* (mach, mov) avance rápido

fastidious [fæsˈtɪdɪ·əs] *adj* esquilmoso, quisquilloso, descontentadizo

fasting [ˈfæstɪŋ] o [ˈfɑstɪŋ] *s* ayuno

fat [fæt] *adj* (*comp* **fatter; super fattest**) gordo; poderoso; opulento; (*profitable*) pingüe; (*spark*) caliente; **to get fat** engordar || *s* grasa; (*suet*) gordo, sebo

fatal [ˈfetəl] *adj* fatal

fatalism [ˈfetəˌlɪzəm] *s* fatalismo

fatalist [ˈfetəlɪst] *s* fatalista *mf*

fatali·ty [fəˈtælɪtɪ] *s* (*pl* **-ties**) fatalidad; (*in accidents, war*) muerte *f*

fate [fet] *s* sino, hado; **the Fates** las Parcas || *tr* condenar, predestinar

fated [ˈfetɪd] *adj* hadado, predestinado

fateful [ˈfetfəl] *adj* fatídico; fatal

fat'head' *s* (coll) tronco, estúpido

father [ˈfaðər] *s* padre *m*; (*an elderly man*) (coll) tío || *tr* servir de padre a; engendrar; inventar

fatherhood [ˈfaðərˌhud] *s* paternidad

fa'ther-in-law' *s* (*pl* **fathers-in-law**) suegro

fa'ther-land' *s* patria

fatherless [ˈfaðərlɪs] *adj* huérfano de padre, sin padre

fatherly [ˈfaðərli] *adj* paternal

Father's Day *s* día *m* del padre

Father Time *s* el Tiempo

fathom [ˈfæðəm] *s* braza || *tr* sondear; profundizar

fathomless [ˈfæðəmlɪs] *adj* insondable

fatigue [fəˈtig] *s* fatiga; (mil) faena || *tr* fatigar, cansar

fatigue clothes *spl* (mil) traje *m* de faena

fatigue duty *s* faena

fatten [ˈfætən] *tr* & *intr* engordar

fat·ty [ˈfæti] *adj* (*comp* **-tier; super -tiest**) graso; (pathol) grasoso; (*chubby*) (coll) gordiflón || *s* (*pl* **-ties**) (coll) gordiflón *m*

fatuous [ˈfætʃu·əs] *adj* fatuo; ilusivo

faucet [ˈfɔsɪt] *s* grifo

fault [fɔlt] *s* (*misdeed, blame*) culpa; (*defect*) falta; (geol) falla; (sport) falta; **it's your fault** Vd. tiene la culpa; **to a fault** excesivamente; **to find fault with** culpar, echar la culpa a; hallar defecto en

fault'find'er *s* criticón *m*, reparón *m*

fault'find'ing *adj* criticón, reparón || *s* manía de criticar

faultless [ˈfɔltlɪs] *adj* perfecto, impecable

fault·y [ˈfɔlti] *adj* (*comp* **-ier; super -iest**) defectuoso, imperfecto

faun [fɔn] *s* fauno

fauna [ˈfɔnə] *s* fauna

favor [ˈfevər] *s* favor *m*; (*letter*) atenta, grata; **do me the favor to** hágame Vd. el favor de; **by your favor** con permiso de Vd.; **favors** regalos de fiesta, objetos de cotillón; **to be in favor with** disfrutar del favor de; **to be out of favor** caer en desgracia || *tr* favorecer; (coll) parecerse a

favorable ['fevərəbəl] *adj* favorable

favorite ['fevərɪt] *adj* & *s* favorito

favoritism ['fevərɪ ˌtɪzəm] *s* favoritismo

fawn [fɔn] *s* cervato ‖ *intr* — **to fawn on** adular servilmente; hacer fiestas a

faze [fez] *tr* (coll) molestar, desanimar

FBI [ˌɛfˌbiˈaɪ] *s* (letterword) Federal Bureau of Investigation

fear [fɪr] *s* miedo; **for fear of** por miedo de, por temor de; **for fear that** por miedo (de) que; **no fear** no hay peligro; **to be in fear of** tener miedo de ‖ *tr* & *intr* temer

fearful ['fɪrfəl] *adj* medroso; (coll) enorme, muy malo

fearless ['fɪrlɪs] *adj* arrojado, intrépido

feasible [fisɪbəl] *adj* factible, viable

feast [fist] *s* fiesta; (*sumptuous meal*) festín *m*, banquete *m* ‖ *tr* & *intr* banquetear; **to feast on** regalarse con

feat [fit] *s* hazaña, proeza

feather ['feðər] *s* pluma; (*plume; arrogance*) penacho; clase *f*, género; **in fine feather** de buen humor; en buena salud ‖ *tr* emplumar; (carp) machihembrar; **to feather one's nest** hacer todo para enriquecerse

feather bed *s* colchón *m* de plumas; (*comfortable situation*) lecho de plumas

feath·er·bed'ding *s* empleo de más obreros de lo necesario (*exigido por los sindicatos*)

feath'er·brain' *s* cascabelero

feath'er·edge' *s* (*of board*) bisel *m*; (*of sharpened tool*) filván *m*

feathery ['feðərɪ] *adj* plumoso

feature ['fitʃər] *s* facción; característica, rasgo distintivo; película principal; artículo principal; **features** facciones ‖ *tr* delinear; ofrecer como cosa principal; (coll) destacar, hacer resaltar

feature writer *s* articulista *mf*

February ['febru ˌɛrɪ] *s* febrero

feces [fisiz] *spl* heces *fpl*

feckless ['fɛklɪs] *adj* abatido, sin valor; débil

federal ['fedərəl] *adj* & *s* federal *mf*

federate ['fedə ˌret] *adj* federado ‖ *tr* federar ‖ *intr* federarse

federation [ˌfedəˈreʃən] *s* federación

fedora [fɪˈdorə] *s* sombrero de fieltro suave con ala vuelta

fed up [fɛd] *adj* harto

fee [fi] *s* honorarios; (*for admission, tuition, etc.*) cuota, precio; (*tip*) propina ‖ *tr* pagar; dar propina a

feeble ['fibəl] *adj* débil

feeble-minded ['fibəlˈmaɪndɪd] *adj* imbécil; irresoluto, vacilante

feed [fid] *s* alimento, comida; (mach) dispositivo de alimentación ‖ *v* (*pret & pp* fed [fed]) *tr* alimentar ‖ *intr* alimentarse

feed'back' *s* regeneración, realimentación

feed bag *s* cebadera, morral *m*

feed pump *s* bomba de alimentación

feed trough *s* comedero

feed wire *s* (elec) conductor *m* de alimentación

feel [fil] *s* sensación; (*sense of what is right*) tino ‖ *v* (*pret & pp* felt [felt]) *tr* sentir; (*e.g., with the hands*) palpar, tentar; tomar (*el pulso*); tantear (*el camino*) ‖ *intr* (*sick, tired, etc.*) sentirse; palpar; **to feel bad** sentirse mal; condolerse; **to feel cheap** avergonzarse; **to feel comfortable** sentirse a gusto; **to feel for** buscar tentando; condolerse de; **to feel like** tener ganas de; **to feel safe** sentirse a salvo; **to feel sorry** sentir; arrepentirse; **to feel sorry for** compadecer; arrepentirse de

feeler ['filər] *s* (*something said to draw someone out*) buscapié *m*, tranquilla; **feelers** (*of insect*) anténulas, palpos; (*of mollusk*) tentáculos

feeling ['filɪŋ] *s* (*with senses*) sensación; (*impression, emotion*) sentimiento; presentimiento; parecer *m*

feign [fen] *tr* aparentar, fingir ‖ *intr* fingir; **to feign to be** fingirse

feint [fent] *s* (*threat*) finta; (*of fencer*) pase *m*, treta ‖ *intr* hacer una finta

feldspar ['feld ˌspar] *s* feldespato

felicitate [fəˈlɪsɪ ˌtet] *tr* felicitar

felicitous [fəˈlɪsɪtəs] *adj* (*opportune*) feliz; elocuente

fell [fel] *adj* cruel, feroz, mortal ‖ *tr* talar (*árboles*)

felloe ['felo] *s* aro de la rueda; (*part of this*) pina

fellow ['felo] *s* (coll) mozo, tipo, sujeto; (coll) pretendiente *m*; prójimo; (*of a society*) socio, miembro; (*holder of fellowship*) pensionista *mf*

fellow being *s* prójimo

fellow citizen *s* conciudadano

fellow countryman *s* compatriota *mf*

fellow man *s* prójimo

fellow member *s* consocio

fellowship ['felo ˌʃɪp] *s* compañerismo; (*for study*) pensión

fellow traveler *s* compañero de viaje

felon ['felən] *s* delincuente *mf* de mayor cuantía; (pathol) panadizo

felo·ny ['felənɪ] *s* (*pl* -nies) delito de mayor cuantía; **to compound a felony** aceptar dinero para no procesar

felt [felt] *s* fieltro

female ['fimel] *adj* (*sex*) femenino; (*animal, plant, piece of a device*) hembra ‖ *s* hembra

feminine ['femɪnɪn] *adj* & *s* femenino

feminism ['femɪ ˌnɪzəm] *s* feminismo

fen [fen] *s* pantano

fence [fens] *s* cerca, cercado; (*for stolen goods*) alcahuete *m*; (*of a saw*) guía; **on the fence** (coll) indeciso ‖ *tr* cercar ‖ *intr* esgrimir

fencing ['fensɪŋ] *s* (*art*) esgrima; (*act*) esgrimidura

fencing academy *s* escuela de esgrima

fend [fend] *tr* — **to fend off** apartar, resguardarse de ‖ *intr* — **to fend for oneself** (coll) tirar por su lado

fender ['fendər] *s* (*mudguard*) guardafango, guardabarros *m*; (*of locomotive*) quitapiedras *m*; (*of trolley car*)

salvavidas m; (of fireplace) guardafuego
fennel ['fɛnəl] s hinojo
ferment ['fʌrment] s fermento; fer-
mentación || [fər'mɛnt] tr & intr
fermentar
fern [fʌrn] s helecho
ferocious [fə'roʃəs] adj feroz
feroci·ty [fə'rɑsɪti] s (pl -ties) ferocidad
ferret ['fɛrɪt] s hurón m || tr — to
ferret out huronear || intr huronear
Ferris wheel ['fɛrɪs] s rueda de feria,
noria
fer·ry ['fɛri] s (pl -ries) bote m de
paso, ferry-boat m || v (pret & pp
-ried) tr pasar (viajeros, mercancías)
a través del río || intr cruzar el río
en barco
fer'ry·boat' s bote m de paso, ferryboat m
fertile ['fʌrtɪl] adj fértil
fertilize ['fʌrtɪˌlaɪz] tr abonar, fertilizar; (to impregnate) fecundar
fervid ['fʌrvɪd] adj férvido, vehemente
fervor ['fʌrvər] s fervor m
fervent ['fʌrvənt] adj ferviente, fervo-
roso
fester ['fɛstər] s úlcera || tr enconar ||
intr enconarse (una herida; el ánimo
de uno)
festival ['fɛstɪvəl] adj festivo || s
fiesta; (of music) festival m
festive ['fɛstɪv] adj festivo
festivi·ty [fɛs'tɪvɪti] s (pl -ties) festividad
festoon [fɛs'tun] s festón m || tr festo-
near
fetch [fɛtʃ] tr ir por, hacer venir, traer;
venderse a, venderse por
fetching ['fɛtʃɪŋ] adj (coll) encantador, atractivo
fete [fet] s fiesta || tr festejar
fetid ['fɛtɪd] o ['fitɪd] adj fétido
fetish ['fitɪʃ] o ['fɛtɪʃ] s fetiche m
fetlock ['fɛtlɑk] s espolón m; (tuft of
hair) cerneja
fetter ['fɛtər] s grillete m, grillo || tr
engrillar; impedir
fettle ['fɛtəl] s estado, condición; in
fine fettle en buena condición
fetus ['fitəs] s feto
feud [fjud] s odio hereditario, enemistad de larga duración
feudal ['fjudəl] adj feudal
feudalism ['fjudəˌlɪzəm] s feudalismo
fever ['fivər] s fiebre f, calentura
fever blister s escupidura, fuegos en
los labios
feverish ['fivərɪʃ] adj febril, calentu-
riento
few [fju] adj & pron pocos, no muchos; a few unos pocos, unos cuantos; quite a few muchos
fiancé [ˌfiˌɑn'se] s novio, prometido
fiancée [ˌfiˌɑn'se] s novia, prometida
fias·co [fi'æsko] s (pl -cos o -coes)
fiasco
fib [fɪb] s mentirilla || v (pret & pp
fibbed; ger fibbing) intr decir mentirillas
fiber ['faɪbər] s fibra; carácter m, índole f

fibrous ['faɪbrəs] adj fibroso
fickle ['fɪkəl] adj inconstante, veleidoso
fiction ['fɪkʃən] s (invention) ficción;
(branch of literature) novelística;
pure fiction! ¡puro cuento!
fictional ['fɪkʃənəl] adj novelesco
fictionalize ['fɪkʃənəˌlaɪz] tr novelizar
fictitious [fɪk'tɪʃəs] adj ficticio
fiddle ['fɪdəl] s violín m || tr tocar (un
aire) con el violín; to fiddle away
(coll) malgastar || intr tocar el vio-
lín; to fiddle with manosear
fiddler ['fɪdlər] s (coll) violinista mf
fiddling ['fɪdlɪŋ] adj (coll) despreciable, insignificante
fideli·ty [faɪ'dɛlɪti] o [fɪ'dɛlɪti] s (pl
-ties) fidelidad
fidget ['fɪdʒɪt] intr agitarse, menearse;
to fidget with manosear
fidgety ['fɪdʒɪti] adj inquieto, nervioso
fiduciar·y [fɪ'dju/ɪˌɛri] o [fɪ'du/ɪˌɛri]
adj fiduciario || s (pl -ies) fiduciario
fie [faɪ] interj ¡qué vergüenza!
fief [fif] s feudo
field [fild] adj (mil) de campaña || s
campo; (sown with grain) sembrado; (baseball) jardín m; (elec) campo magnético; (of motor or dynamo)
(elec) inductor m
fielder ['fildər] s (baseball) jardinero
field glasses spl gemelos de campo
field hockey s hockey m sobre hierba
field magnet s imán m inductor
field marshal s (mil) mariscal m de
campo
field'piece' s cañón m de campaña
fiend [find] s diablo; (person) fiera;
to be a fiend for ser una fiera para
fiendish ['findɪʃ] adj diabólico
fierce [fɪrs] adj feroz, fiero; (wind)
furioso; (coll) muy malo
fierceness ['fɪrsnɪs] s ferocidad, fiereza; furia
fier·y ['faɪri] o ['faɪˌəri] adj (comp
-ier; super -iest) ardiente, caliente;
brioso
fife [faɪf] s pífano
fifteen ['fɪf'tin] adj, pron & s quince
m
fifteenth ['fɪf'tinθ] adj & s (in a series)
decimoquinto; (part) quinzavo || s
(in dates) quince m
fifth [fɪfθ] adj & s quinto || s (in
dates) cinco
fifth column s quinta columna
fifth columnist s quintacolumnista mf
fiftieth ['fɪftɪ·ɪθ] adj & s (in a series)
quincuagésimo; (part) cincuentavo
fif·ty ['fɪfti] adj & pron cincuenta || s
(pl -ties) cincuenta m
fif'ty-fif'ty adv — to go fifty-fifty (coll)
ir a medias
fig. abbr figure, figuratively
fig [fɪg] s higo, breva; (tree) higuera;
(merest trifle) bledo
fight [faɪt] s lucha, pelea; (mil) batalla;
to pick a fight with meterse con,
buscar la lengua a || tr luchar con;
dar (batalla); lidiar (al toro) || intr
luchar, pelear; to fight shy of tratar
de evitar

fighter ['faɪtər] s luchador m, peleador m; (warrior) combatiente m; (game person) porfiador m; (aer) avión m de combate, caza m

fig leaf s hoja de higuera; (on statues) hoja de parra

figment ['fɪgmənt] s ficción, invención

figurative ['fɪgjərətɪv] adj figurado; (representing by a likeness) figurativo

figure ['fɪgjər] s figura; (bodily form) talle m; precio; **to be good at figures** ser listo en aritmética; **to cut a figure** hacer figura; **to have a good figure** tener buen tipo; **to keep one's figure** conservar la línea || tr adornar con figuras; figurarse, imaginar; suponer, calcular; **to figure out** descifrar || intr figurar; **to figure on** contar con

fig'ure·head' s (naut) figurón m de proa, mascarón m de proa; (straw man) testaferro

figure of speech s figura retórica

figure skating s patinaje artístico

figurine [ˌfɪgjəˈrin] s figurilla, figurina

filament ['fɪləmənt] s filamento

filch [fɪltʃ] tr birlar, ratear

file [faɪl] s fila, hilera; (tool) lima; (collection of papers) archivo; (cabinet) archivador m, fichero || tr poner en fila; limar; archivar, clasificar; anotar || intr desfilar; **to file for** solicitar

file case s fichero

file clerk s fichador m

filet [fɪˈle] o [ˈfɪle] s filete m || tr cortar en filetes

filial ['fɪlɪ·əl] o ['fɪljəl] adj filial

filiation [ˌfɪlɪˈeʃən] s filiación

filibuster ['fɪlɪˌbʌstər] s obstrucción (de la aprobación de una ley); obstruccionista mf; (buccaneer) filibustero || tr obstruir (la aprobación de una ley)

filigree ['fɪlɪˌgri] adj afiligranado || s filigrana || tr afiligranar

filing ['faɪlɪŋ] s (of documents) clasificación; limadura; **filings** limadura, limalla

filing cabinet s archivador m, clasificador m

filing card s ficha

Filipi·no [ˌfɪlɪˈpino] adj filipino || s (pl -nos) filipino

fill [fɪl] s (sufficiency) hartazgo; (place filled with earth) terraplén m; **to have o get one's fill of** darse un hartazgo de || tr llenar; rellenar; despachar (un pedido); tapar (un agujero); empastar (un diente); inflar (un neumático); llenar, ocupar (un puesto); colmar (lagunas); **to fill out** llenar (un formulario) || intr llenarse; rellenarse; **to fill in** hacer de suplente; **to fill up** ahogarse de emoción

filler ['fɪlər] s relleno; (of cigar) tripa; (sizing) aparejo; (in a writing) relleno

fillet ['fɪlɪt] s cinta, tira; (for hair) prendedero; (archit, bb) filete m || tr filetear || ['fɪle] o ['fɪlɪt] s (of

meat or fish) filete m || tr cortar en filetes

filling ['fɪlɪŋ] s (of a tooth) empaste m; (e.g., of a turkey) relleno; (of cigar) tripa

filling station s estación gasolinera

fillip ['fɪlɪp] s aguijón m, estímulo; (with finger) capirotazo

fil·ly ['fɪli] s (pl -lies) potra; (coll) muchacha retozona

film [fɪlm] s película; (mov) película, film m; (phot) película || tr filmar

film star s estrella de la pantalla

film strip s tira proyectable

film·y ['fɪlmi] adj (comp -ier; super -iest) delgadísimo, diáfano, sutil

filter ['fɪltər] s filtro || tr filtrar || intr filtrarse

filtering ['fɪltərɪŋ] s filtración

filter paper s papel m filtrante

filter tip s embocadura de filtro

filth [fɪlθ] s suciedad, porquería

filth·y ['fɪlθi] adj (comp -ier; super -iest) sucio, puerco

filthy lucre ['lukər] s (coll) el vil metal (dinero, raíz de muchos males)

filtrate ['fɪltret] s filtrado || tr filtrar || intr filtrarse

fin. abbr finance

fin [fɪn] s aleta

final ['faɪnəl] adj final; (last in a series) último; decisivo, terminante || s examen m final; **finals** (sport) final f

finale [fɪˈnɑli] s (mus) final m

finalist ['faɪnəlɪst] s finalista mf

finally ['faɪnəli] adv finalmente, por último

finance [fɪˈnæns] o ['faɪnæns] s financiación; **finances** finanzas || tr financiar

financial [fɪˈnænʃəl] o [faɪˈnænʃəl] adj financiero

financier [ˌfɪnənˈsɪr] o [ˌfaɪnənˈsɪr] s financiero

financing [fɪˈnænsɪŋ] o ['faɪnænsɪŋ] s financiación

finch [fɪntʃ] s pinzón m

find [faɪnd] s hallazgo || v (pret & pp found [faʊnd]) tr hallar, encontrar; **to find out** averiguar, darse cuenta de || intr (law) pronunciar fallo; **to find out about** informarse de

finder ['faɪndər] s (of camera) visor m; (of microscope) portaobjeto cuadriculado

finding ['faɪndɪŋ] s descubrimiento; (law) laudo, fallo

fine [faɪn] adj fino; (weather) bueno; divertido || adv (coll) muy bien; **to feel fine** (coll) sentirse muy bien de salud || s multa || tr multar

fine arts spl bellas artes

fineness s fineza; (of metal) ley f

fine print s letra menuda, tipo menudo

finer·y ['faɪnəri] s (pl -ies) adorno, galas, atavíos

fine-spun ['faɪnˌspʌn] adj estirado en hilo finísimo; (fig) alambicado

finesse [fɪˈnɛs] s sutileza; (in bridge) impás m || tr hacer el impás con || intr hacer un impás

fine-toothed comb ['faɪnˌtuθt] s lendrera, peine *m* de púas finas; **to go over with a fine-toothed comb** escudriñar minuciosamente

finger ['fɪŋgər] *s* dedo; **to burn one's fingers** cogerse los dedos; **to put one's finger on the spot** poner el dedo en la llaga; **to slip between the fingers** irse de entre los dedos; **to snap one's fingers at** tratar con desprecio; **to twist around one's little finger** manejar a su gusto || *tr* manosear; (slang) acechar, espiar; (slang) identificar

finger board *s* (*of guitar*) diapasón *m*; (*of piano*) teclado

finger bowl *s* lavadedos *m*, lavafrutas *m*

finger dexterity *s* (mus) dedeo

fingering ['fɪŋgərɪŋ] *s* manoseo; (mus) digitación

fin'ger·nail' *s* uña

fingernail polish *s* esmalte *m* para las uñas

fin'ger·print' *s* huella digital, dactilograma *m* || *tr* tomar las huellas digitales de

finger tip *s* punta del dedo; **to have at one's finger tips** tener en la punta de los dedos, saber al dedillo

finial ['fɪnɪ·əl] *s* florón *m*

finical ['fɪnɪkəl] o **finicky** ['fɪnɪki] *adj* delicado, melindroso

finish ['fɪnɪʃ] *s* acabado; fin *m*, conclusión || *tr* acabar; **to be finished** estar listo || *intr* acabar; **to finish +** *ger* acabar de + *inf*; **to finish by +** *ger* acabar por + *inf*

finishing nail *s* puntilla francesa

finishing school *s* escuela particular de educación social para señoritas

finishing touch *s* toque *m* final, última mano

finite ['faɪnaɪt] *adj* finito

finite verb *s* forma verbal flexional

Finland ['fɪnlənd] *s* Finlandia

Finlander ['fɪnləndər] *s* finlandés *m*

Finn [fɪn] *s* (*member of a Finnish-speaking group of people*) finés *m*; (*native or inhabitant of Finland*) finlandés *m*

Finnish ['fɪnɪʃ] *adj* finlandés || *s* (*language*) finlandés *m*

fir [fʌr] *s* abeto

fire [faɪr] *s* fuego; (*destructive burning*) incendio; **through fire and water** a trancos y barrancos; **to be on fire** estar ardiendo; **to be under enemy fire** estar expuesto al fuego del enemigo; **to catch fire** encenderse; **to hang fire** estar en suspensión; **to open fire** abrir fuego, romper el fuego; **to set on fire, to set fire to** pegar fuego a; **under fire** bajo el fuego del enemigo; acusado, inculpado || *interj* (mil) ¡fuego! || *tr* encender; calentar (*el horno*); cocer (*ladrillos*); disparar (*un arma de fuego*); pegar (*un tiro*); excitar (*la imaginación*); (coll) despedir (*a un empleado*) || *intr* encenderse; **to fire on** hacer fuego sobre; **to fire up** cargar el horno; calentar el horno

fire alarm *s* alarma de incendios, avisador *m* de incendios; **to sound the fire alarm** tocar a fuego

fire'arm' *s* arma de fuego

fire'ball' *s* bola de fuego; (*lightning*) rayo en bola

fire'bird' *s* cacique veranero

fire'boat' *s* buque *m* con mangueras para incendios

fire'box' *s* caja de fuego, fogón *m*

fire'brand' *s* tizón *m*; (*hothead*) botafuego

fire'break' *s* raya

fire'brick' *s* ladrillo refractario

fire brigade *s* cuerpo de bomberos

fire'bug' *s* (coll) incendiario

fire company *s* cuerpo de bomberos; compañía de seguros

fire'crack'er *s* triquitraque *m*

fire'damp' *s* grisú *m*, mofeta

fire department *s* servicio de bomberos

fire'dog' *s* morillo

fire drill *s* ejercicio para caso de incendio

fire engine *s* coche *m* bomba, bomba de incendios, motobomba

fire escape *s* escalera de salvamento

fire extinguisher *s* extintor *m*, apagafuegos *m*

fire'fly' *s* (*pl* **-flies**) luciérnaga

fire'guard' *s* guardafuego

fire hose *s* manguera para incendios

fire'house' *s* cuartel *m* de bomberos, estación de incendios

fire hydrant *s* boca de incendio

fire insurance *s* seguro contra incendios

fire irons *spl* badil *m* y tenazas

fireless cooker ['faɪrlɪs] *s* cocinilla sin fuego

fire·man ['faɪrmən] *s* (*pl* **-men** [mən]) (*man who stokes fires*) fogonero; (*man who extinguishes fires*) bombero

fire'place' *s* chimenea, chimenea francesa

fire plug *s* boca de agua

fire power *s* (mil) potencia de fuego

fire'proof' *adj* incombustible || *tr* hacer incombustible

fire sale *s* venta de mercancías averiadas en un incendio

fire screen *s* pantalla de chimenea

fire ship *s* brulote *m*

fire shovel *s* badil *m*

fire'side' *s* hogar *m*

fire'trap' *s* edificio sin medios adecuados de escape en caso de incendio

fire wall *s* cortafuego

fire'ward'en *s* vigía *m* de incendios

fire'wa'ter *s* aguardiente *m*

fire'wood' *s* leña

fire'works' *spl* fuegos artificiales

firing ['faɪrɪŋ] *s* encendimiento; (*of bricks*) cocción; (*of a gun*) disparo; (*of soldiers*) tiroteo; (*of an internal-combustion engine*) encendido; (*of an employee*) (coll) despedida

firing line *s* línea de fuego, frente *m* de batalla

firing order *s* (aut) orden *m* del encendido

firing squad *s* (*for saluting at a burial*)

piquete *m* de salvas; *(for executing)* pelotón *m* de fusilamiento, piquete *m* de ejecución

firm [fʌrm] *adj* firme ‖ *s* empresa, casa comercial

firmament ['fʌrməmənt] *s* firmamento

firm name *s* razón *f* social

firmness ['fʌrmnɪs] *s* firmeza

first [fʌrst] *adj* primero ‖ *adv* primero; **first of all** ante todo ‖ *s* primero; (aut) primera (velocidad); (mus) voz *f* principal; **at first** al principio; en primer lugar; **from the first** desde el principio

first aid *s* cura de urgencia, primeros auxilios

first'-aid' kit *s* botiquín *m*, equipo de urgencia

first-aid station *s* puesto de socorro, puesto de primera intención

first'-born' *adj & s* primogénito

first'-class' *adj* de primera, de primera clase ‖ *adv* en primera clase

first cousin *s* primo hermano

first draft *s* borrador *m*

first finger *s* dedo índice, dedo mostrador

first floor *s* piso bajo

first fruits *spl* primicia

first lieutenant *s* teniente

firstly ['fʌrstli] *adv* en primer lugar

first mate *s* (naut) piloto

first name *s* nombre *m* de pila

first night *s* (theat) noche *f* de estreno

first'-night'er *s* (theat) estrenista *mf*

first officer *s* (naut) piloto

first quarter *s* cuarto creciente (*de la luna*)

first'-rate' *adj* de primer orden; (coll) excelente ‖ *adv* (coll) muy bien

first'-run' house *s* teatro de estreno

fiscal ['fɪskəl] *adj* *(pertaining to public treasury)* fiscal; económico ‖ *s* *(public prosecutor)* fiscal *m*

fiscal year *s* año económico, ejercicio

fish [fɪʃ] *s* pez *m*; *(that has been caught, that is ready to eat)* pescado; **to be like a fish out of water** estar como gallina en corral ajeno; **to be neither fish nor fowl** no ser carne ni pescado; **to drink like a fish** beber como una topinera, beber como una esponja ‖ *tr* pescar ‖ *intr* pescar; **to fish for compliments** buscar alabanzas; **to go fishing** ir de pesca; **to take fishing** llevar de pesca

fish'bone' *s* espina de pez

fish bowl *s* pecera

fisher ['fɪʃər] *s* pescador *m*; embarcación de pesca; (zool) marta del Canadá

fisher·man ['fɪʃərmən] *s* *(pl* -men [mən]) pescador *m*; barco pesquero

fisher·y ['fɪʃəri] *s* *(pl* -ies) *(activity)* pesca; *(business)* pesquería; *(grounds)* pesquera

fish glue *s* cola de pescado

fish hawk *s* halieto

fish'hook' *s* anzuelo

fishing ['fɪʃɪŋ] *adj* pesquero ‖ *s* pesca

fishing ground *s* pesquería, pesquera

fishing reel *s* carrete *m*

fishing rod *s* caña de pescar

fishing tackle *s* aparejo de pescar, avíos de pesca

fishing torch *s* candelero

fish line *s* sedal *m*

fish market *s* pescadería

fish'plate' *s* (rr) eclisa

fish'pool' *s* piscina

fish spear *s* fisga

fish story *s* (coll) andaluzada, patraña; **to tell fish stories** (coll) mentir por la barba

fish'tail' *s* (aer) coleadura ‖ *intr* (aer) colear

fish'wife' *s* *(pl* -wives [,waɪvz]) pescadera; *(foul-mouthed woman)* verdulera

fish'worm' *s* lombriz *f* de tierra *(cebo para pescar)*

fish·y ['fɪʃi] *adj* *(comp* -ier; *super* -iest) que huele o sabe a pescado; (coll) dudoso, inverosímil

fission ['fɪʃən] *s* (biol) escisión; (phys) fisión

fissionable ['fɪʃənəbəl] *adj* fisionable

fissure ['fɪʃər] *s* hendidura, grieta; (anat, min) fisura

fist [fɪst] *s* puño; (typ) manecilla; **to shake one's fist at** amenazar con el puño

fist fight *s* pelea con los puños

fisticuff ['fɪstɪ,kʌf] *s* puñetazo; **fisticuffs** pelea a puñetazos

fit [fɪt] *adj* *(comp* -fitter; *super* -fittest) apropiado, conveniente; apto; sano; **fit to be tied** (coll) impaciente, encolerizado; **fit to eat** bueno de comer; **to feel fit** gozar de buena salud; **to see fit** juzgar conveniente ‖ *s* ajuste *m*, talle *m*; *(of one piece with another)* encaje *m*; *(of coughing)* acceso, ataque *m*; *(of anger)* arranque *m*; **by fits and starts** intermitentemente ‖ *v* *(pret & pp* -fitted; *ger* fitting) *tr* ajustar, entallar; cuadrar, sentar; encajar; cuadrar con *(p.ej., las señas de una persona)*; equipar, preparar; servir para; estar de acuerdo con *(p.ej., los hechos)*; **to fit out** o **up** pertrechar ‖ *intr* ajustar; encajar; sentar; **to fit in** caber en; encajar en

fitful ['fɪtfəl] *adj* caprichoso; intermitente, vacilante

fitness ['fɪtnɪs] *s* conveniencia; aptitud; tempestividad; buena salud

fitter ['fɪtər] *s* ajustador *m*; *(of machinery)* montador *m*; *(of clothing)* probador *m*

fitting ['fɪtɪŋ] *adj* apropiado, conveniente, justo ‖ *s* ajuste *m*; encaje *m*; *(of a garment)* prueba; tubo de ajuste; **fittings** accesorios, avíos; *(iron trimmings)* herraje *m*

five [faɪv] *adj & pron* cinco ‖ *s* cinco; **five o'clock** las cinco

five hundred *adj & pron* quinientos ‖ *s* quinientos *m*

five'-year' plan *s* plan *m* quinquenal

fix [fɪks] *s* — **in a tight fix** (coll) en calzas prietas; **to be in a fix** (coll) hallarse en un aprieto ‖ *tr* arreglar, componer, reparar; fijar *(una fecha;*

los cabellos; una imagen fotográfica; los precios; la atención; una hora, una cita); calar (la bayoneta); (coll) desquitarse con; (pol) muñir || intr fijarse; **to fix on** decidir, escoger

fixed [fɪkst] adj fijo

fixing ['fɪksɪŋ] adj fijador || s (fastening) fijación; (phot) fijado

fixing bath s fijador m

fixture ['fɪkstʃər] s accesorio, artefacto; (of a lamp) guarnición; **fixtures** (e.g., of a store) instalaciones

fizz [fɪz] s ruido sibilante; bebida gaseosa; (Brit) champaña || intr hacer un ruido sibilante

fizzle ['fɪzəl] s (coll) fracaso || intr chisporrotear débilmente; (coll) fracasar

fl. abbr **flourished, fluid**

flabbergast ['flæbər‚gæst] tr (coll) dejar sin habla, dejar estupefacto

flab·by ['flæbi] adj (comp -bier; super -biest) flojo, lacio

flag [flæg] s bandera || v (pret & pp **flagged**; ger **flagging**) tr hacer señal a (una persona) con una bandera; hacer señal de parada a (un tren) || intr aflojar, flaquear

flag captain s (nav) capitán m de bandera

flageolet [‚flædʒə'lɛt] s chirimía, dulzaina

flag·man ['flægmən] s (pl -men [mən]) (rr) guardafrenos m; (rr) guardavía m

flag of truce s bandera de parlamento

flag'pole' s asta de bandera; (surv) jalón m

flagrant ['flegrənt] adj enorme, escandaloso

flag'ship' s (nav) capitana

flag'staff' s asta de bandera

flag'stone' s losa

flag stop s (rr) apeadero

flail [flel] s mayal m || tr golpear con mayal; golpear, azotar

flair [flɛr] s instinto, perspicacia

flak [flæk] s fuego antiaéreo

flake [flek] s (thin piece) hojuela; (of snow) copo || intr desprenderse en hojuelas; caer en copos pequeños

flak·y ['fleki] adj (comp -ier; super -iest) escamoso, laminoso

flamboyant [flæm'bɔɪ‚ənt] adj flameante; llamativo; rimbombante; (archit) flameante, flamígero

flame [flem] s llama || tr (to sterilize with a flame) llamear || intr flamear

flame thrower ['θro‚ər] s lanzallamas m

flaming ['flemɪŋ] adj llameante; flamante, resplandeciente; apasionado

flamin·go [flə'mɪŋgo] s (pl -gos o -goes) flamenco

flammable ['flæməbəl] adj inflamable

Flanders ['flændərz] s Flandes f

flange [flændʒ] s pestaña

flank [flæŋk] s flanco; tr flanquear

flannel ['flænəl] s franela

flap [flæp] s (fold in clothing; of a hat) falda; (of a pocket) cartera; (of a table) hoja plegadiza; (of shoe) oreja; (of an envelope) tapa; (of

wings) aletazo; (of the counter in a store) trampa || v (pret & pp **flapped**; ger **flapping**) tr golpear con ruido seco; batir, sacudir (las alas) || intr aletear; flamear con ruido

flare [flɛr] s llamarada, destello; cohete m de señales; (aer) bengala; (outward curvature) abocinamiento; (of a dress) vuelo || tr abocinar || intr arder con gran llamarada, destellar; (to spread outward) abocinarse; **to flare up** inflamarse; recrudecer (una enfermedad); encolerizarse

flare star s (astr) estrella fulgurante

flare'-up' s llamarada; (of an illness) retroceso; (coll) llamarada, arrebato de cólera

flash [flæʃ] s (of light) relumbrón m, ráfaga; (of lightning) relámpago; (of hope) rayo; (of joy) acceso; (of insight) rasgo; mensaje m urgente || tr quemar (pólvora); enviar (un mensaje) como un rayo || intr destellar, centellear; relampaguear (los ojos); **to flash by** pasar como un rayo

flash'back' s (mov) retrospectiva

flash bulb s luz f de magnesio; bombilla de destello

flash flood s torrentada, avenida repentina

flashing ['flæʃɪŋ] s despidiente m de agua, vierteaguas m

flash'light' s linterna eléctrica, lámpara eléctrica de bolsillo; (of a lighthouse) luz f intermitente, fanal m de destellos; (for taking photographs) flash m, relámpago

flashlight battery s pila de linterna

flashlight bulb s bombilla de linterna

flashlight photography s fotografía instantánea de relámpago

flash sign s anuncio intermitente

flash·y ['flæʃi] adj (comp -ier; super -iest) chillón, llamativo

flask [flæsk] o [flɑsk] s frasco; frasco de bolsillo; (for laboratory use) matraz m, redoma

flat [flæt] adj (comp **flatter**; super **flattest**) plano; (nose; boat) chato; (surface) mate, deslustrado; (beer) muerto; (tire) desinflado; (e.g., denial) terminante; (mus) bemol || adv — **to fall flat** caer de plano; (fig) no surtir efecto, no tener éxito || s banco, bajío; (apartment) piso; (mus) bemol m; (coll) neumático desinflado

flat'boat' s chalana

flat'car' s vagón m de plataforma

flat-footed ['flæt‚fʊtɪd] adj de pies planos; (coll) inflexible

flat'head' s (of a bolt) cabeza chata; clavo, tornillo o perno de cabeza chata; (coll) tonto, mentecato

flat'i'ron s plancha

flatten ['flætən] tr allanar, aplanar; chafar, aplastar; achatar || intr allanarse, aplanarse; aplastarse; acharse, aplanarse; **to flatten out** ponerse horizontal, enderezarse

flatter ['flætər] tr lisonjear; (to make more attractive than is) favorecer || intr lisonjear

flatterer ['flætərər] *s* lisonjero
flattering ['flætərɪŋ] *adj* lisonjero
flatter·y ['flætəri] *s* (*pl* **-ies**) lisonja
flat'top' *s* portaaviones *m*
flatulence ['flæt/ələns] *s* flatulencia
flat'ware' *s* vajilla de plata; vajilla de porcelana
flaunt [flɔnt] o [flɑnt] *tr* ostentar, hacer gala de
flautist ['flɔtɪst] *s* flautista *mf*
flavor ['flevər] *s* sabor *m*, gusto; condimento, sazón *f*; (*of ice cream*) clase *f* || *tr* saborear; condimentar, sazonar; aromatizar, perfumar
flavoring ['flevərɪŋ] *s* condimento, sainete *m*
flaw [flɔ] *s* defecto, imperfección; (*crack*) grieta
flawless ['flɔlɪs] *adj* perfecto, entero
flax [flæks] *s* lino
flaxen ['flæksən] *adj* blondo, rubio
flax'seed' *s* linaza
flay [fle] *tr* desollar
flea [fli] *s* pulga
flea'bite' *s* picadura de pulga; molestia insignificante
fleck [flɛk] *s* pinta, punto; partícula, pizca || *tr* puntear
fledgling ['flɛdʒlɪŋ] *s* pajarito, volantón *m*; (fig) novato, novel *m*
flee [fli] *v* (*pret & pp* **fled** [flɛd]) *tr & intr* huir
fleece [flis] *s* (*coat of wool*) lana; (*wool shorn at one time*; *tuft of wool or hair*) vellón *m* || *tr* esquilar; (*to strip of money*) desplumar
fleec·y ['flisi] *adj* (*comp* **-ier**; *super* **-iest**) lanudo; (*clouds*) aborregado
fleet [flit] *adj* veloz || *s* armada; (*of merchant vessels, airplanes, automobiles*) flota
fleeting ['flitɪŋ] *adj* fugaz, efímero; transitorio
Fleming ['flemɪŋ] *s* flamenco
Flemish ['flemɪʃ] *adj & s* flamenco
flesh [flɛʃ] *s* carne *f*; **in the flesh** en persona; **to lose flesh** perder carnes; **to put on flesh** cobrar carnes
flesh and blood *s* (*relatives*) carne y sangre; el cuerpo humano
flesh-colored ['flɛʃ,kʌlərd] *adj* encarnado, de color de carne
fleshiness ['flɛʃɪnɪs] *s* carnosidad
fleshless ['flɛʃlɪs] *adj* descarnado
flesh'pot' *s* olla, marmita; **fleshpots** vida regalona; suntuosos nidos de vicios
flesh wound *s* herida superficial
flesh·y ['flɛʃi] *adj* (*comp* **-ier**; *super* **-iest**) carnoso
flex [flɛks] *tr* doblar || *intr* doblarse
flexible ['flɛksɪbəl] *adj* flexible
flexible cord *s* (elec) flexible *m*
flick [flɪk] *s* (*with finger*) papirote *m*; (*with whip*) latigazo; ruido seco || *tr* golpear rápida y ligeramente
flicker ['flɪkər] *s* llama trémula; (*of eyelids*) parpadeo; (*of emotion*) temblor momentáneo || *intr* flamear con llama trémula; aletear
flier ['flaɪ·ər] *s* aviador *m*; tren rápido; (coll) negocio arriesgado; (coll) hoja volante

flight [flaɪt] *s* fuga, huída; (*of an airplane*) vuelo; (*of birds*) bandada; (*of stairs*) tramo; (*of fancy*) arranque *m*; **to put to flight** poner en fuga; **to take flight** darse a la fuga
flight deck *s* (nav) cubierta de vuelo
flight·y ['flaɪti] *adj* (*comp* **-ier**; *super* **-iest**) veleidoso; casquivano
flim·flam ['flɪm,flæm] *s* (coll) engaño, trampa; (coll) tontería || *v* (*pret & pp* **-flammed**; *ger* **-flamming**) *tr* (coll) engañar, trampear
flim·sy ['flɪmzi] *adj* (*comp* **-sier**; *super* **-siest**) débil, endeble, flojo
flinch [flɪntʃ] *intr* encogerse de miedo
fling [flɪŋ] *s* echada, tiro; baile escocés muy vivo; **to go on a fling** echar una cana al aire; **to have a fling** at ensayar, probar; **to have one's fling** correrla, mocear || *v* (*pret & pp* **flung** [flʌŋ]) *tr* arrojar; (*e.g., on the floor, out the window, in jail*) echar; **to fling open** abrir de golpe; **to fling shut** cerrar de golpe
flint [flɪnt] *s* pedernal *m*
flint'lock' *s* llave *f* de chispa; trabuco de chispa
flint·y ['flɪnti] *adj* (*comp* **-ier**; *super* **-iest**) pedernalino; (fig) empedernido
flip [flɪp] *adj* (*comp* **flipper**; *super* **flippest**) (coll) petulante || *s* capirotazo || *v* (*pret & pp* **flipped**; *ger* **flipping**) *tr* echar un capirotazo, mover de un tirón; **to flip a coin** echar a cara o cruz; **to flip shut** cerrar de golpe (*p.ej., un abanico*)
flippancy ['flɪpənsi] *s* petulancia
flippant ['flɪpənt] *adj* petulante
flip side *s* contraportada del disco
flirt [flʌrt] *s* (*woman*) coqueta; (*man*) galanteador *m* || *intr* coquetear (*una mujer*); galantear (*un hombre*); **to flirt with** flirtear con; acariciar (*una idea*); jugar con (*la muerte*)
flit [flɪt] *v* (*pret & pp* **flitted**; *ger* **flitting**) *intr* revolotear, volar
flitch [flɪtʃ] *s* hoja de tocino
float [flot] *s* (*raft*) balsa; (*of fishing line*) flotador *m*; (*of mason*) llana; carroza alegórica, carro alegórico || *tr* poner a flote; lanzar (*una empresa*); emitir (*acciones, bonos, etc.*) || *intr* flotar
floating ['flotɪŋ] *adj* flotante
flock [flɑk] *s* (*of birds*) bandada; (*of sheep*) grey *f*, rebaño, manada; (*of people*) muchedumbre; (*e.g., of nonsense*) hatajo; (*of faithful*) grey *f*, rebaño || *intr* congregarse, reunirse; llegar en tropel
floe [flo] *s* banquisa, témpano
flog [flɑg] *v* (*pret & pp* **flogged**; *ger* **flogging**) *tr* azotar, fustigar
flood [flʌd] *s* inundación; (*caused by heavy rain*) diluvio; (*sudden rise of river*) crecida; (*of tide*) pleamar *f*; (*of words, etc.*) diluvio, torrente *m* || *tr* inundar; (*to overwhelm*) abrumar || *intr* desbordar, rebosar; entrar a raudales
flood'gate' *s* (*of a dam*) compuerta; (*of a canal*) esclusa

flood'light' s faro de inundación ‖ tr iluminar con faro de inundación

flood tide s pleamar f, marea montante

floor [flor] s (inside bottom surface of room) piso, suelo; (story of a building) piso, alto; (of the sea, a swimming pool, etc.) fondo; (of an assembly hall) hemiciclo; (naut) varenga; **to ask for the floor** pedir la palabra; **to have the floor** tener la palabra; **to take the floor** tomar la palabra ‖ tr entarimar; derribar, echar al suelo; (coll) confundir, envolver, revolcar (al adversario en controversia); (coll) vencer

floor lamp s lámpara de pie

floor mop s fregasuelos m, estropajo

floor plan s planta

floor show s espectáculo de cabaret

floor timber s (naut) varenga

floor'walk'er s jefe m de sección

floor wax s cera de pisos

flop [flap] s (coll) fracaso, caída; **to take a flop** (coll) caerse ‖ v (pret & pp **flopped**; ger **flopping**) intr agitarse; caerse; venirse abajo; fracasar; **to flop over** volcarse; cambiar de partido

flora [ˈflorə] s flora

floral [ˈflorəl] adj floral

Florentine [ˈflorən͵tin] o [ˈflorən͵tin] adj & s florentino

florescence [floˈresəns] s florescencia

florid [ˈflarɪd] o [ˈflorɪd] adj (complexion) encarnado; (showy, ornate) florido

Florida Keys [ˈflarɪdə] o [ˈflorɪdə] s Cayos de la Florida

florist [ˈflorɪst] s florero, florista mf

floss [flas] o [flɔs] s cadarzo; (of corn) cabellos

floss silk s seda floja sin torcer

floss·y [ˈflasi] o [ˈflɔsi] adj (comp -ier; super -iest) ligero, velloso; (slang) cursi, vistoso

flotsam [ˈflatsəm] s pecio

flotsam and jetsam s pecios, despojos; (trifles) baratijas; gente f trashumante, gente perdida

flounce [flauns] s faralá m, volante m ‖ tr adornar con faralaes o volantes ‖ intr moverse airadamente

flounder [ˈflaundər] s platija ‖ intr forcejear, obrar torpemente, andar tropezando

flour [flaur] adj harinero ‖ s harina

flourish [ˈflarɪʃ] s (with the sword) molinete m; (with the pen) plumada, rasgo; (as part of signature) rúbrica; (mus) floreo ‖ tr blandir (la espada) ‖ intr florecer, prosperar

flourishing [ˈflarɪʃɪŋ] adj floreciente, próspero

flour mill s molino de harina

floury [ˈflauri] adj harinoso

flout [flaut] tr mofarse de, burlarse de ‖ intr mofarse, burlarse

flow [flo] s flujo ‖ intr fluir; subir (la marea); ondear (el pelo en el aire); **to flow into** desaguar en, desembocar en; **to flow over** rebosar; **to flow with** nadar en, abundar en

flower [ˈflauˑər] s flor f ‖ tr florear ‖ intr florecer

flower bed s macizo, parterre m

flower garden s jardín m

flower girl s florera; (at a wedding) damita de honor

flower piece s ramillete m; (painting) florero

flow'er·pot' s tiesto, maceta

flower shop s floristería

flower show s exposición de flores

flower stand s florero

flowery [ˈflauˑəri] adj florido, cubierto de flores

flu [flu] s (coll) gripe f, influenza

fluctuate [ˈflʌktʃu͵et] intr fluctuar

flue [flu] s cañón m de chimenea; tubo de humo

fluency [ˈfluˑənsi] s afluencia, facundia

fluent [ˈfluˑənt] adj (flowing) fluente; afluente, facundo, fluido

fluently [ˈfluˑəntli] adv corrientemente

fluff [flʌf] s pelusa, tamo; vello, pelusilla; (of an actor) gazapo ‖ tr esponjar, mullir ‖ intr esponjarse

fluff·y [ˈflʌfi] adj (comp -ier; super -iest) fofo, esponjoso, mullido; velloso

fluid [ˈfluˑɪd] adj & s fluido

fluidity [fluˈɪdɪti] s fluidez f

fluke [fluk] s (of anchor) uña; (in billiards) chiripa

flume [flum] s caz m, saetín m

flunk [flʌŋk] s (coll) reprobación ‖ tr (coll) reprobar, dar calabazas a; perder (un examen o asignatura) ‖ intr (coll) fracasar, salir mal; **to flunk out** (coll) tener que abandonar los estudios por no poder aprobar

flunk·y [ˈflʌŋki] s (pl -ies) lacayo; adulador m

fluor [ˈfluˑər] s fluorita

fluorescence [͵fluˑəˈresəns] s fluorescencia

fluorescent [͵fluˑəˈresənt] adj fluorescente

fluoridate [ˈfluˑərɪ͵det] tr fluorizar

fluoridation [͵fluˑərɪˈdeʃən] s fluorización

fluoride [ˈfluˑə͵raɪd] s fluoruro

fluorine [ˈfluˑə͵rin] s flúor m

fluorite [ˈfluˑə͵raɪt] s fluorita

fluoroscope [ˈfluˑərə͵skop] s fluoroscopio

fluor spar s espato flúor

flur·ry [ˈflʌri] s (pl -ries) agitación; (of wind) racha, ráfaga; (of rain) chaparrón m; (of snow) nevisca ‖ v (pret & pp -ried) tr agitar

flush [flʌʃ] adj rasante, nivelado; (set in, in order to be flush) embutido; abundante; robusto, vigoroso; próspero, bien provisto; coloradote; (in printing) justificado; **flush with** a ras de ‖ adv ras con ras, al mismo nivel ‖ s (of water) flujo repentino; (in the cheeks) rubor m; sonrojo; (in the springtime) floración repentina; (of joy) acceso; (of youth) vigor m; chorro del inodoro; (in poker) flux m ‖ tr (to cause to blush) abochornar; limpiar con un chorro de agua; hacer saltar (una liebre) ‖ intr abochornarse, estar encendido (*el rostro*); (*to gush*) brotar

Flushing ['flʌ/ɪŋ] *s* Flesinga

flush outlet *s* (elec) caja de enchufe embutida

flush switch *s* (elec) llave embutida

flush tank *s* depósito de limpia

flush toilet *s* inodoro con chorro de agua

fluster ['flʌstər] *s* confusión, aturdimiento ‖ *tr* confundir, aturdir

flute [flut] *s* (*of a column*) estría; (mus) flauta ‖ *tr* estriar, acanalar

flutist ['flutɪst] *s* flautista *mf*

flutter ['flʌtər] *s* aleteo, revoloteo; confusión, turbación ‖ *intr* aletear, revolotear; flamear, ondear; agitarse; alterarse (*el pulso*); palpitar (*el corazón*)

flux [flʌks] *s* (*flow; flowing of tide*) flujo; (*for fusing metals*) flujo, fundente *m*

fly [flaɪ] *s* (*pl* **flies**) mosca; (*of trousers*) portañuela, braguета; (*for fishing*) mosca artificial; **flies** (theat) bambalinas; **to die like flies** morir como chinches ‖ *v* (*pret* **flew** [flu]; *pp* **flown** [flon]) *tr* hacer volar (*una cometa*); dirigir (*un avión*); (*to carry in an airship*) volar; atravesar en avión; desplegar, llevar (*una bandera*) ‖ *intr* volar; huir; ondear (*una bandera*); **to fly off** salir volando; desprenderse; **to fly open** abrirse de repente; **to fly over** trasvolar; **to fly shut** cerrarse de repente

fly ball *s* (baseball) palomita

fly'blow' *s* cresa

fly'-by-night' *adj* indigno de confianza

fly'catch'er *s* moscareta, papamoscas *m*

fly chaser *s* espantamoscas *m*

flyer ['flaɪ-ər] *s* var de **flier**

fly'-fish' *tr & intr* pescar con moscas artificiales

flying ['flaɪ-ɪŋ] *adj* volante; rápido, veloz ‖ *s* aviación

flying boat *s* hidroavión *m*

flying buttress *s* arbotante *m*

flying colors *spl* gran éxito

flying field *s* campo de aviación

flying saucer *s* platillo volante

flying sickness *s* mal *m* de altura

flying time *s* horas de vuelo

fly in the ointment *s* mosca muerta que malea el perfume

fly'leaf' *s* (*pl* **-leaves'**) guarda, hoja de guarda

fly net *s* (*for a bed*) mosquitero; (*for a horse*) espantamoscas *m*

fly'pa'per *s* papel *m* matamoscas

fly'speck' *s* mancha de mosca

fly swatter ['swatər] *s* matamoscas *m*

fly'trap' *s* atrapamoscas *m*

fly'wheel' *s* volante *m*

fm. *abbr* fathom

F.M. *abbr* frequency modulation

foal [fol] *s* potro ‖ *intr* parir (*la yegua*)

foam [fom] *s* espuma ‖ *intr* espumar

foam extinguisher *s* lanzaespumas *m*, extintor *m* de espuma

foam rubber *s* caucho esponjoso, espuma de caucho

foam·y ['fomi] *adj* (*comp* **-ier;** *super* **-iest**) espumoso, espumajoso

fob [fab] *s* faltriquera de reloj; (*chain*) leopoldina; (*ornament*) dije *m*

F.O.B. *abbr* free on board

focal ['fokəl] *adj* focal

fo·cus ['fokəs] *s* (*pl* **-cuses** o **-ci** [saɪ]) foco; **in focus** enfocado; **out of focus** desenfocado ‖ *v* (*pret & pp* **-cused** o **-cussed;** *ger* **-cusing** o **-cussing**) *tr* enfocar; fijar (*la atención*) ‖ *intr* enfocarse

fodder ['fadər] *s* forraje *m*

foe [fo] *s* enemigo

fog [fag] o [fɔg] *s* niebla; (phot) velo ‖ *v* (*pret & pp* **fogged;** *ger* **fogging**) *tr* envolver en niebla; (*to blur*) empañar; (phot) velar ‖ *intr* empañarse; (phot) velarse

fog bank *s* banco de nieblas

fog bell *s* campana de nieblas

fog'bound' *adj* atascado en la niebla, envuelto en la niebla

fog·gy ['fagi] o ['fɔgi] *adj* (*comp* **-gier;** *super* **-giest**) neblinoso, brumoso; confuso; (phot) velado; **it is foggy** hay neblina

fog'horn' *s* sirena de niebla

foible ['fɔɪbəl] *s* flaqueza, lado flaco

foil [fɔɪl] *s* (*thin sheet of metal*) hojuela, laminilla; (*of mirror*) azogado, plateado; contraste *m*, realce *m*; (*sword*) florete *m* ‖ *tr* frustrar; azogar, platear (*un espejo*)

foist [fɔɪst] *tr* — **to foist something on someone** encajar una cosa a uno

fol. *abbr* folio, following

fold [fold] *s* pliegue *m*, doblez *m*; arruga; (*for sheep*) aprisco, redil *m*; (*of the faithful*) rebaño ‖ *tr* plegar, doblar; cruzar (*los brazos*); **to fold up** doblar (*p.ej., un mapa*) ‖ *intr* plegarse, doblarse

folder ['foldər] *s* (*covers for holding papers*) carpeta; (*pamphlet*) folleto

folderol ['faldə,ral] *s* tontería, necedad; bagatela

folding ['foldɪŋ] *adj* plegadizo, plegable; plegador

folding camera *s* cámara de fuelle

folding chair *s* silla de tijera, silla plegadiza; (*of canvas*) catrecillo

folding cot *s* catre *m* de tijera

folding door *s* puerta plegadiza

folding rule *s* metro plegadizo

foliage ['foli·ɪdʒ] *s* follaje *m*

foli·o ['foli·o] *adj* en folio ‖ *s* (*pl* **-os**) (*sheet*) folio; infolio, libro en folio ‖ *tr* foliar

folk [fok] *adj* popular, tradicional, del pueblo ‖ *s* (*pl* **folk** o **folks**) gente *f*; **folks** (coll) gente (*familia*)

folk'lore' *s* folklore *m*

folk music *s* música folklórica

folk song *s* canción típica, canción tradicional

folk·sy ['foksi] *adj* (*comp* **-sier;** *super* **-siest**) (coll) sociable, tratable; (*like common people*) (coll) plebeyo

folk'way' *s* costumbre tradicional

follicle ['falɪkəl] *s* folículo

follow ['falo] *tr* seguir; seguir el hilo de; interesarse en (*las noticias del* día) ‖ *intr* seguir; resultar; **as follows** como sigue; **it follows** síguese

follower ['fɑlo·ər] *s* seguidor *m;* secuaz *mf,* partidario; imitador *m;* discípulo

following ['fɑlo·ɪŋ] *adj* siguiente ‖ *s* séquito; partidarios

fol·low-up' *adj* consecutivo; recordativo ‖ *s* carta recordativa, circular recordativa

fol·ly ['fɑli] *s* (*pl* **-lies**) desatino, locura; empresa temeraria; **follies** revista teatral

foment [fo'mɛnt] *tr* fomentar

fond [fɑnd] *adj* afectuoso, cariñoso; **to become fond of** encariñarse con, aficionarse a o de

fondle ['fɑndəl] *tr* acariciar, mimar

fondness ['fɑndnɪs] *s* afición, cariño

font [fɑnt] *s* (*source; source of water*) fuente *f;* (*for holy water*) pila; (*of type*) fundición

food [fud] *adj* alimenticio ‖ *s* comida, alimento; **food for thought** cosa en qué pensar

food store *s* tienda de comestibles, colmado

food'stuffs' *spl* comestibles *mpl,* víveres *mpl*

fool [ful] *s* tonto, necio; (*jester*) bufón *m;* (*person imposed on*) inocente *mf,* víctima; **to make a fool of** poner en ridículo; **to play the fool** hacer el tonto ‖ *tr* embaucar, engañar; **to fool away** malgastar (*tiempo, dinero*) ‖ *intr* tontear; **to fool around** (coll) malgastar el tiempo; **to fool with** (coll) ajar, manosear

fool·er·y ['fuləri] *s* (*pl* **-ies**) locura, tontería

fool'har'dy *adj* (*comp* **-dier**; *super* **-diest**) temerario

fooling ['fulɪŋ] *s* broma; engaño; **no fooling** hablando en serio

foolish ['fulɪʃ] *adj* tonto; ridículo

fool'proof' *adj* (coll) a prueba de mal trato; (coll) infalible

fools'cap' *s* gorro de bufón; papel *m* de oficio

fool's errand *s* caza de grillos

fool's scepter *s* cetro de locura

foot [fut] *s* (*pl* **feet** [fit]) pie *m;* **to drag one's feet** ir a paso de caracol; **to have one foot in the grave** estar con un pie en la sepultura; **to put one's best foot forward** (coll) hacer méritos; **to put one's foot in it** (coll) meter la pata; (coll) tirarse una plancha; **to stand on one's own feet** volar con sus propias alas; **to tread under foot** hollar ‖ *tr* pagar (*la cuenta*); **to foot it** andar a pie; bailar

footage ['futɪdʒ] *s* distancia o largura en pies

foot'ball' *s* (*game*) balompié *m,* fútbol *m;* (*ball*) balón *m*

foot'board' *s* (*support for foot*) estribo; (*of bed*) pie *m*

foot'bridge' *s* pasarela, puente *m* para peatones

foot'fall' *s* paso

foot'hill' *s* colina al pie de una montaña

foot'hold' *s* arraigo, pie *m;* **to gain a foothold** ganar pie

footing ['futɪŋ] *s* pie *m,* p.ej., **he lost his footing** perdió el pie; **on a friendly footing** en relaciones amistosas; **on an equal footing** en pie de igualdad; **on a war footing** en pie de guerra

foot'lights' *spl* candilejas, batería; (fig) tablas, escena

foot'loose' *adj* libre, no comprometido

foot·man ['futmən] *s* (*pl* **-men** [mən]) lacayo, criado de librea

foot'mark' *s* huella

foot'note' *s* nota al pie de la página

foot'path' *s* senda para peatones

foot'print' *s* huella

foot race *s* carrera a pie

foot'rest' *s* apoyapié *m,* descansapié *m*

foot rule *s* regla de un pie

foot soldier *s* soldado de a pie

foot'sore' *adj* despeado

foot'step' *s* paso; **to follow in the footsteps of** seguir los pasos de

foot'stone' *s* lápida al pie de una sepultura

foot'stool' *s* escabel *m,* escañuelo

foot warmer *s* calientapiés *m*

foot'wear' *s* calzado

foot'work' *s* juego de piernas

foot'worn' *adj* (*road*) trillado; (*person*) despeado

foozle ['fuzəl] *s* chambonada; (coll) chambón *m,* torpe *m* ‖ *tr* chafallar; errar (*un golpe*) de manera torpe ‖ *intr* chambonear

fop [fɑp] *s* currutaco, petimetre *m*

for [fɔr] *prep* para; por; como, p.ej., **he uses his living room for an office** usa la sala como oficina; de, p.ej., **time for bed** hora de acostarse; desde hace, p.ej., **he has been here for a week** está aquí desde hace una semana; en honor de; a pesar de ‖ *conj* pues, porque

for. *abbr* **foreign**

forage ['fɑrɪdʒ] o ['fɔrɪdʒ] *adj* forrajero ‖ *s* forraje *m* ‖ *tr & intr* forrajear; saquear

foray ['fɑre] o ['fɔre] *s* correría; saqueo ‖ *intr* hacer correrías

for·bear [fɔr'bɛr] *v* (*pret* **-bore** ['bor]; *pp* **-borne** ['born**]**) *tr* abstenerse de ‖ *intr* contenerse

forbearance [fɔr'bɛrəns] *s* abstención; paciencia

for·bid [fɔr'bɪd] *v* (*pret* **-bade** ['bæd] o **-bad** ['bæd]; *pp* **-bidden** ['bɪdən]; *ger* **-bidding**) *tr* prohibir

forbidding [fɔr'bɪdɪŋ] *adj* repugnante, repulsivo

force [fors] *s* fuerza; (*staff of workers*) personal *m;* (*of soldiers, police, etc.*) cuerpo; (phys) fuerza; **by force of** a fuerza de; **by main force** con todas sus fuerzas; **in force** vigente, en vigor; en gran número; **to join forces** juntar diestra con diestra ‖ *tr* forzar; obligar; **to force back** hacer retroceder; **to force open** abrir por fuerza; **to force through** llevar a cabo por fuerza

forced [forst] *adj* forzado

forced air *s* aire *m* a presión

forced landing *s* aterrizaje forzado o forzoso

forced march *s* marcha forzada

forceful ['forsfəl] *adj* enérgico, eficaz

for·ceps ['forsəps] *s* (*pl* **-ceps** o **-cipes** [sɪ‚piz]) (dent, surg) pinzas; (obstet) fórceps *m*

force pump *s* bomba impelente

forcible ['forsɪbəl] *adj* eficaz, convincente; forzado

ford [ford] *s* vado ‖ *tr* vadear

fore [for] *adj* anterior; (naut) de proa ‖ *adv* antes, anteriormente; delante; (naut) avante ‖ *interj* ¡ojo!, ¡cuidado! ‖ *s* delantera; **to the fore** destacado; a mano; vivo

fore and aft *adv* de popa a proa

fore′arm′ *s* antebrazo ‖ **fore·arm′** *tr* armar de antemano; prevenir

fore′bear′ *s* antepasado

forebode [for'bod] *tr* (*to portend*) presagiar; (*to have a presentiment of*) presentir, prever

foreboding [for'bodɪŋ] *s* presagio; presentimiento

fore′cast′ *s* pronóstico ‖ *v* (*pret & pp* **-cast** o **-casted**) *tr* pronosticar

forecastle ['foksəl], ['for‚kæsəl] o ['for‚kasəl] *s* castillo de proa

fore·close′ *tr* excluir; extinguir el derecho de redimir (*una hipoteca*); privar del derecho de redimir una hipoteca

fore·doom′ *tr* condenar de antemano, predestinar al fracaso

fore edge *s* canal *f*

fore′fa′ther *s* antepasado

fore′fin′ger *s* dedo índice, dedo mostrador

fore′front′ *s* puesto delantero; sitio de actividad más intensa; **in the forefront** a vanguardia

fore·go′ *v* (*pret* **-went′**; *pp* **-gone′**) *tr & intr* preceder

foregoing ['for‚go·ɪŋ] o [for'go·ɪŋ] *adj* anterior, precedente

fore′gone′ conclusion *s* resultado inevitable; decisión adoptada de antemano

fore′ground′ *s* primer plano, primer término

forehanded ['for‚hændɪd] *adj* (*thrifty*) ahorrado; hecho de antemano

forehead ['farɪd] o ['forɪd] *s* frente *f*

foreign ['farɪn] o ['forɪn] *adj* extranjero, exterior; **foreign to** (*not belonging to or connected with*) ajeno a

foreign affairs *spl* asuntos exteriores

for′eign-born′ *adj* nacido en el extranjero

foreigner ['farɪnər] o ['forɪnər] *s* extranjero

foreign exchange *s* cambio extranjero; (*currency*) divisa

foreign minister *s* ministro de asuntos exteriores

foreign office *s* ministerio de asuntos exteriores

foreign service *s* servicio diplomático y consular; servicio militar extranjero

foreign trade *s* comercio extranjero

fore′leg′ *s* brazo, pata delantera

fore′lock′ *s* mechón *m* de pelo sobre la frente; (*of a horse*) copete *m;* **to take time by the forelock** asir la ocasión por la melena

fore·man ['formən] *s* (*pl* **-men** [mən]) capataz *m*, mayoral *m*, sobrestante *m;* (*in a machine shop*) contramaestre *m;* presidente *m* de jurado

foremast ['forməst], ['for‚mæst] o ['for‚mast] *s* palo de trinquete

foremost ['for‚most] *adj* primero, principal, más eminente

fore′noon′ *adj* matinal ‖ *s* mañana

fore′part′ *s* parte delantera; primera parte

fore′paw′ *s* pata delantera

fore′quar′ter *s* cuarto delantero

fore′run′ner *s* precursor *m;* predecesor *m;* antepasado; anuncio, presagio

fore·sail ['forsəl] o ['for‚sel] *s* trinquete *m*

fore·see′ *v* (*pret* **-saw′**; *pp* **-seen′**) *tr* prever

foreseeable [for'si·əbəl] *adj* previsible

fore·shad′ow *tr* presagiar, prefigurar

fore·short′en *tr* escorzar

fore′short′ening *s* escorzo

fore′sight′ *s* previsión, presciencia

fore′sight′ed *adj* previsor, presciente

fore′skin′ *s* prepucio

forest ['farɪst] o ['forɪst] *adj* forestal ‖ *s* bosque *m*

fore·stall′ *tr* impedir, prevenir; anticipar; acaparar

forest ranger ['rendʒər] *s* guarda *m* forestal, montanero

forestry ['farɪstri] o ['forɪstri] *s* silvicultura, ciencia forestal

fore′taste′ *s* goce anticipado, conocimiento anticipado

fore·tell′ *v* (*pret & pp* **-told′**) *tr* predecir; presagiar

fore′thought′ *s* premeditación; providencia, previsión

forever [for'evər] *adv* por siempre; siempre

fore·warn′ *tr* prevenir, poner sobre aviso

fore′word′ *s* advertencia, prefacio

forfeit ['forfɪt] *adj* perdido ‖ *s* multa, pena; prenda perdida; **forfeits** (*game*) prendas ‖ *tr* perder el derecho a

forfeiture ['forfɪtʃər] *s* multa, pena; prenda perdida

forgather [for'gæðər] *intr* reunirse; encontrarse; **to forgather with** asociarse con

forge [fordʒ] *s* fragua; (*blacksmith shop*) herrería; ‖ *tr* fraguar, forjar; falsificar (*la firma de otra persona*); fraguar, forjar (*mentiras*) ‖ *intr* fraguar, forjar; **to forge ahead** avanzar despacio y con esfuerzo

forger·y ['fordʒəri] *s* (*pl* **-ies**) falsificación

for·get [for'get] *v* (*pret* **-got** ['gat]; *pp* **-got** o **-gotten;** *ger* **-getting**) *tr* olvidar, olvidarse de, olvidársele a uno, p.ej., he forgot his overcoat se le olvidó su abrigo; forget it! ¡no se preocupe!; to forget oneself no pensar en sí mismo; ser distraído; propasarse

forgetful [fər'gɛtfəl] adj olvidado, olvidadizo; descuidado

forgetfulness [fər'gɛtfəlnɪs] s olvido; descuido

for·get'-me-not' s nomeolvides m

forgivable [fər'gɪvəbəl] adj perdonable

for·give [fər'gɪv] v (pret -gave'; pp -giv'en) tr perdonar

forgiveness [fər'gɪvnɪs] s perdón m; misericordia

forgiving [fər'gɪvɪŋ] adj perdonador, misericordioso, clemente

for·go [fər'go] v (pret -went'; pp -gone') tr privarse de

fork [fɔrk] s horca; (of a gardener; of bicycle) horquilla; (of two rivers) horcajo; (of railroad) ramal m; (of a tree) horqueta; (for eating) tenedor m ‖ tr ahorquillar; cargar con horquilla; (in chess) amenazar (dos piezas); to fork out (slang) entregar, sudar ‖ intr bifurcarse

forked [fɔrkt] adj ahorquillado

forked lightning s relámpago en zigzag

fork'lift' truck s carretilla elevadora de horquilla

forlorn [fər'lɔrn] adj desamparado; desesperado; miserable

forlorn hope s empresa desesperada

form [fɔrm] s forma; (paper to be filled out) formulario; (construction to give shape to cement) encofrado; (type in a frame) molde m ‖ tr formar ‖ intr formarse

formal ['fɔrməl] adj formal, ceremonioso; etiquetero

formal attire s vestido de etiqueta

formal call s visita de cumplido

formali·ty [fər'mælɪti] s (pl -ties) (standard procedure) formalidad; ceremonia, etiqueta

formal party s reunión de etiqueta

formal speech s discurso de aparato

format ['fɔrmæt] s formato

formation [fɔr'meʃən] s formación

former ['fɔrmər] adj (preceding) anterior; (long past) antiguo; primero (de dos); the former aquél

formerly ['fɔrmərli] adv antes, en tiempos pasados

form'-fit'ting adj ceñido al cuerpo

formidable ['fɔrmɪdəbəl] adj formidable

formless ['fɔrmlɪs] adj informe

form letter s carta general

formu·la ['fɔrmjələ] s (pl -las o -lae [‚li]) fórmula

formulate ['fɔrmjə‚let] tr formular

for·sake [fər'sek] v (pret -sook ['suk]; pp -saken ['sekən]) tr abandonar, desamparar; dejar

fort [fɔrt] s fuerte m, fortaleza

forte [fɔrt] s (strong point) fuerte m, caballo de batalla

forth [fɔrθ] adv adelante; and so forth y así sucesivamente; from this day

forth de hoy en adelante; to go forth salir

forth'com'ing adj próximo, venidero

forth'right' adj directo, franco, sincero ‖ adv derecho; sinceramente, francamente; en seguida

forth'with' adv inmediatamente

fortieth ['fɔrtɪ·ɪθ] adj & s (in a series) cuadragésimo; (part) cuarentavo

fortification [‚fɔrtɪfɪ'keʃən] s fortificación

forti·fy ['fɔrtɪ‚faɪ] v (pret & pp -fied) tr fortificar; encabezar (vinos)

fortitude ['fɔrtɪ‚tjud] o ['fɔrtɪ‚tud] s fortaleza, firmeza

fortnight ['fɔrtnaɪt] o ['fɔrtnɪt] s quincena, dos semanas

fortress ['fɔrtrɪs] s fortaleza

fortuitous [fɔr'tju·ɪtəs] o [fɔr'tu·ɪtəs] adj fortuito

fortunate ['fɔrtʃənɪt] adj afortunado

fortune ['fɔrtʃən] s fortuna; to make a fortune enriquecerse; to tell someone his fortune decirle a uno la buenaventura

fortune hunter s cazador m de dotes

for'tune·tel'ler s adivino, agorero

for·ty ['fɔrti] adj & pron cuarenta ‖ s (pl -ties) cuarenta m

fo·rum ['fɔrəm] s (pl -rums o -ra [rə]) foro; (e.g., of public opinion) tribunal m

forward ['fɔrwərd] adj delantero; precoz; atrevido, impertinente ‖ adv hacia adelante; to bring forward pasar a cuenta nueva; to come forward adelantarse; to look forward to esperar con placer anticipado ‖ tr cursar, hacer seguir, reexpedir; fomentar, patrocinar

fossil ['fasɪl] adj & s fósil m

foster ['fastər] o ['fɔstər] adj adoptivo, de leche, de crianza ‖ tr fomentar

foster home s hogar m de adopción

foul [faul] adj sucio, puerco; (air) viciado; (wind) contrario; (weather) malo; (obscene); pérfido; (breath) fétido; (baseball) fuera del cuadro

foul-mouthed ['faul'mauðd] o ['faul'mauθt] adj deslenguado

foul play s mal encuentro; (sport) juego sucio

foul'spo'ken adj malhablado

found [faund] tr fundar; (to melt, to cast) fundir

foundation [faun'deʃən] s fundación; (endowment) dotación; (basis) fundamento; (masonry support) cimiento

founder ['faundər] s fundador m; (of metals) fundidor m ‖ intr desparese (un caballo); hundirse, irse a pique (un buque); (to fail) fracasar

foundling ['faundlɪŋ] s niño expósito

foundling hospital s casa de expósitos

found·ry ['faundri] s (pl -ries) fundición

foundry·man ['faundrɪmən] s (pl -men [mən]) fundidor m

fount [faunt] s fuente f

fountain ['fauntən] s fuente f, manantial m

foun′tain·head′ s nacimiento
fountain pen s pluma estilográfica, pluma fuente
fountain syringe s mangueta
four [for] adj & pron cuatro ‖ s cuatro; **four o′clock** las cuatro; **on all fours** a gatas
four′-cy′cle adj (mach) de cuatro tiempos
four′-cyl′inder adj (mach) de cuatro cilindros
four′-flush′ intr (coll) bravear, papelonear
fourflusher [′for‚flʌʃər] s (coll) bravucón m
four-footed [′forˈfutɪd] adj cuadrúpedo
four hundred adj & pron cuatrocientos ‖ s cuatrocientos m; **the four hundred** la alta sociedad
four′-in-hand′ s corbata de nudo corredizo; coche tirado por cuatro caballos
four′-lane′ adj cuadriviario
four′-leaf′ adj cuadrifoliado
four-legged [′forˈlegɪd] o [′forˈlegd] adj de cuatro patas; (schooner) de cuatro mástiles
four′-let′ter word s palabra impúdica de cuatro letras
four′-mo′tor plane s cuadrimotor m
four′-o′-clock′ s dondiego
four′-post′er s cama imperial
four′score′ adj cuatro veintenas de
foursome [′forsəm] s cuatrinca; cuatro jugadores; juego de cuatro
fourteen [′forˈtin] adj, pron & s catorce m
fourteenth [′forˈtinθ] adj & s (in a series) decimocuarto; (part) catorzavo ‖ s (in dates) catorce m
fourth [forθ] adj & s cuarto ‖ s (in dates) cuatro
fourth estate s cuarto poder
four′-way′ adj de cuatro direcciones; (elec) de cuatro terminales
fowl [faul] s ave f; aves; gallina; gallo; carne f de ave
fowling piece s escopeta de caza
fox [faks] s zorra; (fur) zorro; (cunning person) (fig) zorro ‖ tr (coll) engañar con astucia
fox′glove′ s dedalera
fox′hole′ s zorrera; (mil) pozo de lobo
fox′hound′ s perro raposero, perro zorrero
fox hunt s caza de zorras
fox terrier s fox-terrier m (casta de perro de talla pequeña)
fox trot s trote corto (de caballo); foxtrot m (baile de compás cuaternario)
fox·y [′faksi] adj (comp -ier; super -iest) zorrero, astuto, taimado
foyer [′fɔɪ·ər] s (of a private house) vestíbulo; (theat) salón m de entrada, vestíbulo
fr. abbr **fragment, franc, from**
Fr. abbr **Father, French, Friday**
Fra [frɑ] s fray m
fracas [′frekəs] s alboroto, riña
fraction [′frækʃən] s fracción; porción muy pequeña

fractional [′frækʃənəl] adj fraccionario; insignificante
fractious [′frækʃəs] adj reacio, rebelón; quisquilloso, regañón
fracture [′fræktʃər] s fractura ‖ tr fracturar; (e.g., an arm) fracturarse; intr fracturarse
fragile [′frædʒɪl] adj frágil
fragment [′frægmənt] s fragmento
fragrance [′fregrəns] s fragancia
fragrant [′fregrənt] adj fragante
frail [frel] adj (not robust) débil; (easily broken; morally weak) frágil ‖ s cesto de junco
frail·ty [′frelti] s (pl -ties) debilidad; (moral weakness) fragilidad
frame [frem] s (of a picture, mirror) marco; (of glasses) montura, armadura; (structure) armazón f, esqueleto; (for embroidering) bastidor m; (of government) sistema m; (mov, telv) encuadre m; (naut) cuaderna ‖ tr (to put in a frame) enmarcar; formar, forjar; construir; redactar, formular; (slang) incriminar (a un inocente)
frame house s casa de madera
frame of mind s manera de pensar
frame′-up′ s (slang) treta, trama para incriminar a un inocente
frame′work′ s armazón f, esqueleto, entramado
franc [fræŋk] s franco
France [fræns] o [frɑns] s Francia
Frances [′frænsɪs] o [′frɑnsɪs] s Francisca
franchise [′fræntʃaɪz] s franquicia, privilegio; (right to vote) sufragio
Francis [′frænsɪs] o [′frɑnsɪs] s Francisco
Franciscan [frænˈsɪskən] adj & s franciscano
frank [fræŋk] adj franco, sincero ‖ s carta franca, envío franco; franquicia postal; sello de franquicia ‖ tr franquear ‖ **Frank** s (member of a Frankish tribe) franco; (masculine name) Paco
frankfurter [′fræŋkfərtər] s salchicha de carne de vaca y de cerdo
frankincense [′fræŋkɪn‚sɛns] s olíbano
Frankish [′fræŋkɪʃ] adj & s franco
frankness [′fræŋknɪs] s franqueza, abertura, sinceridad
frantic [′fræntɪk] adj frenético
frappé [fræˈpe] adj helado ‖ s refresco helado de zumo de frutas
frat [fræt] s (slang) club m de estudiantes
fraternal [frəˈtʌrnəl] adj fraternal
fraterni·ty [frəˈtʌrnɪti] s (pl -ties) (brotherliness) fraternidad; cofradía; asociación secreta; (U.S.A.) club m de estudiantes
fraternize [′frætər‚naɪz] intr fraternizar
fraud [frɔd] s fraude m; (person) (coll) impostor m
fraudulent [′frɔdjələnt] adj fraudulento
fraught [frɔt] adj — **fraught with** cargado de, lleno de

fo
fr

fray [fre] *s* combate *m*, riña, batalla || *intr* deshilacharse, raerse

freak [frik] *s (sudden fancy)* capricho, antojo; *(person, animal)* fenómeno

freakish ['frikɪʃ] *adj* caprichoso, antojadizo; raro, fantástico

freckle ['frekəl] *s* peca

freckle-faced ['frekəl ‚fest] *adj* pecoso

freckly ['frekli] *adj* pecoso

free [fri] *adj (comp* **freer** ['fri‑ər]; *super* **freest** ['fri‑ɪst]) libre; gratis, franco; liberal, generoso; **to be free with** dar abundantemente; **to set free** libertar || *adv* libremente; en libertad; de balde, gratis || *v (pret & pp* **freed** [frid]; *ger* **freeing** ['fri‑ɪŋ]) *tr* libertar, poner en libertad; soltar; exentar, eximir

freebooter ['fri ‚butər] *s* forbante *m*, filibustero, pirata *m*

free'born' *adj* nacido libre; propio de un pueblo libre

freedom ['fridəm] *s* libertad

freedom of speech *s* libertad de palabra

freedom of the press *s* libertad de imprenta

freedom of the seas *s* libertad de los mares

freedom of worship *s* libertad de cultos

free enterprise *s* libertad de empresa

free fight *s* sarracina, riña tumultuaria

free'-for-all' *s* concurso abierto a todo el mundo; sarracina, riña tumultuaria

free hand *s* plena libertad, carta blanca

free'hand' drawing *s* dibujo a pulso

freehanded ['fri ‚hændɪd] *adj* dadivoso, generoso

free'hold' *s* (law) feudo franco

free lance *s* soldado mercenario; periodista *mf* sin empleo fijo; *(writer not on regular salary)* destajista *mf*

free lunch *s* tapas, enjutos

free‑man ['frimən] *s (pl* **-men** [mən]) hombre *m* libre; ciudadano

Free'ma'son *s* francmasón *m*

Free'ma'sonry *s* francmasonería

free of charge *adj* gratis, de balde

free on board *adj* franco a bordo

free port *s* puerto franco

free ride *s* llevada gratuita

free service *s* servicio post-venta

free'‑spo'ken *adj* franco, sin reserva

free'stone' *adj & s* abridero

free'think'er *s* librepensador *m*

free thought *s* librepensamiento

free trade *s* librecambio

free'trad'er *s* librecambista *mf*

free'way' *s* autopista

free will *s* libre albedrío

freeze [friz] *s* helada || *v (pret* **froze** [froz]; *pp* **frozen)** *tr* helar; congelar *(créditos, fondos, etc.)* || *intr* helarse; congelarse; helársele a uno la sangre *(p.ej., de miedo)*

freeze-dry *v (pret & pp* **-dried)** *tr* liofilizar

freezer ['frizər] *s* heladora, sorbetera

freight [fret] *s* carga; (naut) flete *m*; **by freight** como carga; (rr) en pequeña velocidad || *tr* enviar por carga

freight car *s* vagón *m* de carga, vagón de mercancías

freighter ['fretər] *s* buque *m* de carga, carguero

freight platform *s* (rr) muelle *m*

freight station *s* (rr) estación de carga

freight train *s* mercancías *msg*, tren *m* de mercancías

freight yard *s* (rr) patio de carga

French [frentʃ] *adj & s* francés *m;* **the French** los franceses

French chalk *s* jaboncillo de sastre

French doors *spl* puertas vidrieras dobles

French dressing *s* salsa francesa, vinagreta

French fried potatoes *spl* patatas fritas en trocitos

French horn *s* (mus) trompa de armonía

French horsepower *s* caballo de fuerza, caballo de vapor

French leave *s* despedida a la francesa; **to take French leave** despedirse a la francesa

French‑man ['frentʃmən] *s (pl* **-men** [mən]) francés *m*

French telephone *s* microteléfono

French toast *s* torrija

French window *s* puerta ventana

French'wom'an *s (pl* **-wom'en)** francesa

frenzied ['frenzid] *adj* frenético

fren‑zy ['frenzi] *s (pl* **-zies)** frenesí *m*

frequen‑cy ['frikwənsi] *s (pl* **-cies)** frecuencia

frequency list *s* lista de frecuencia

frequency modulation *s* modulación de frecuencia

frequent ['frikwənt] *adj* frecuente || [frɪ'kwent] o ['frikwənt] *tr* frecuentar

frequently ['frikwəntli] *adv* con frecuencia, frecuentemente

fres‑co ['fresko] *s (pl* **-coes** o **-cos)** fresco || *tr* pintar al fresco

fresh [freʃ] *adj* fresco; *(water)* dulce; *(wind)* fresquito; novicio, inexperto; *(cheeky)* (slang) fresco; *(toward women)* (slang) atrevido; **fresh paint!** ¡ojo mancha! || *adv* recientemente, recién; **fresh in** (coll) recién llegado, acabado de llegar; **fresh out** (coll) recién agotado

freshen ['freʃən] *tr* refrescar || *intr* refrescarse

freshet ['freʃɪt] *s* avenida, crecida

fresh‑man ['freʃmən] *s (pl* **-men** [mən]) novato; estudiante *mf* de primer año

freshness ['freʃnɪs] *s* frescura; *(cheek)* (slang) frescura

fresh'‑wa'ter *adj* de agua dulce; no acostumbrado a navegar; de poca monta

fret [fret] *s (interlaced design)* calado; (mus) ceja, traste *m*; queja || *v (pret & pp* **fretted;** *ger* **fretting)** *tr* adornar con calados || *intr* irritarse, quejarse, agitarse

fretful ['fretfəl] *adj* irritable, enojadizo, displicente

fret'work' *s* calado

Freudianism [ˈfrɔɪdɪ·ə ˌnɪzəm] s freudismo

friar [ˈfraɪ·ər] s fraile m

friar·y [ˈfraɪ·əri] s (pl -ies) convento de frailes

fricassee [ˌfrɪkəˈsi] s fricasé m

friction [ˈfrɪkʃən] s fricción, rozamiento; (fig) desavenencia, rozamiento

friction tape s cinta aislante

Friday [ˈfraɪdi] s viernes m

fried [fraɪd] adj frito

fried egg s huevo a la plancha, huevo frito o estrellado

friend [frend] s amigo; (in answer to "Who is there?") gente f de paz; to be friends with ser amigo de; to make friends trabar amistades; to make friends with hacerse amigo de

friend·ly [ˈfrendli] adj (comp -lier; super -liest) amigo, amistoso, amigable

friendship [ˈfrendʃɪp] s amistad

frieze [friz] s (archit) friso

frigate [ˈfrɪgɪt] s fragata

fright [fraɪt] s susto, espanto; (grotesque or ridiculous person) (coll) espantajo; to take fright at asustarse de

frighten [ˈfraɪtən] tr asustar, espantar; to frighten away espantar, ahuyentar || intr asustarse

frightful [ˈfraɪtfəl] adj espantoso, horroroso; (coll) feúcho, repugnante; (coll) enorme, tremendo

frightfulness [ˈfraɪtfʌlnɪs] s espanto, horror m; terrorismo

frigid [ˈfrɪdʒɪd] adj frío; (fig) frío; (zone) glacial

frigidity [frɪˈdʒɪdɪti] s frialdad; (pathol) frialdad; (fig) frialdad, frigidez f

frill [frɪl] s lechuga; (of birds and other animals) collarín m; (frippery) (coll) ringorrango; (in dress, speech, etc.) (coll) afectación

fringe [frɪndʒ] s franja, orla; (opt) franja || tr franjar, orlar

fringe benefits spl beneficios accesorios

fripper·y [ˈfrɪpəri] s (pl -ies) (flashiness) cursilería; (flashy clothes) perejil m, perifollos

frisk [frɪsk] tr (slang) cachear; (slang) registrar y robar || intr retozar

frisk·y [ˈfrɪski] adj (comp -ier; super -iest) juguetón, retozón; (horse) fogoso

fritter [ˈfrɪtər] s fruta de sartén, fragmento || tr — to fritter away desperdiciar, malgastar poco a poco

frivolous [ˈfrɪvələs] adj frívolo

friz [frɪz] s (pl frizzes) rizo, pelo rizado apretadamente || v (pret & pp frizzed; ger frizzing) tr rizar, rizar apretadamente

frizzle [ˈfrɪzəl] s rizo apretado; chirrido, siseo || tr rizar apretadamente; asar o freír en parrilla || intr chirriar, sisear

friz·zly [ˈfrɪzli] adj (comp -zlier; super -zliest) muy ensortijado

fro [fro] adv — to and fro de acá para allá; to go to and fro ir y venir

frock [frɑk] s vestido; bata, blusa; (of priest) vestido talar

frock coat s levita

frog [frɑg] o [frɔg] s rana; (button and loop on a garment) alamar m; (in throat) ronquera, gallo

frog'man' s (pl -men') hombre-rana m

frol·ic [ˈfrɑlɪk] s juego alegre, travesura; fiesta, holgorio || v (pret & pp -icked; ger -icking) intr juguetear, travesear, jaranear

frolicsome [ˈfrɑlɪksəm] adj juguetón, travieso

from [frʌm], [frəm] o [frɑm] prep de; desde; de parte de; según; a, p.ej., to take something away from someone quitarle algo a alguien

front [frʌnt] adj delantero; anterior || s frente m & f; (of a shirt) pechera; (of a book) principio; apariencia falsa (p.ej., de riqueza); además estudiado; (mil) frente m; in front of delante de, frente a, en frente de; to put on a front (coll) gastar mucho oropel; to put up a bold front (coll) hacer de tripas corazón || tr (to face) dar a; (to confront) afrontar, arrostrar; (to supply with a front) poner frente o fachada a || intr — to front on dar a; to front towards mirar hacia

frontage [ˈfrʌntɪdʒ] s fachada, frontera; terreno frontero

front door s puerta de entrada

front drive s (aut) tracción delantera

frontier [frʌnˈtɪr] adj fronterizo || s frontera

frontiers·man [frʌnˈtɪrzmən] s (pl -men [mən]) hombre m de la frontera, explorador m

frontispiece [ˈfrʌntɪsˌpis] s (of book) portada; (archit) frontispicio

front matter s preliminares mpl (de un libro)

front page s primera plana

front porch s soportal m

front room s cuarto que da a la calle

front row s primera fila

front seat s asiento delantero

front steps spl escalones mpl de acceso a la puerta de entrada

front view s vista de frente

frost [frɔst] o [frɑst] s (freezing) helada; (frozen dew) escarcha; (slang) fracaso || tr cubrir de escarcha; escarchar (confituras); helar (el frío las plantas); deslustrar (el vidrio)

frost'bit'ten adj dañado por la helada; quemado por la helada o la escarcha

frosted glass s vidrio deslustrado

frosting [ˈfrɔstɪŋ] o [ˈfrɑstɪŋ] s garapiña; (of glass) deslustre m

frost·y [ˈfrɔsti] o [ˈfrɑsti] adj (comp -ier; super -iest) cubierto de escarcha; escarchado; frío, poco amistoso; canoso, gris

froth [frɔθ] o [frɑθ] s espuma; frivolidad, vanidad || intr espumar, echar espuma; (at the mouth) espumajear

froth·y [ˈfrɔθi] o [ˈfrɑθi] adj (comp -ier; super -iest) espumoso; frívolo, vano

fr
fr

froward ['frowərd] *adj* díscolo, indócil

frown [fraun] *s* ceño, entrecejo || *intr* fruncir el entrecejo; **to frown at** u **on** mirar con ceño, desaprobar

frows·y o **frowz·y** ['frauzi] *adj* (*comp* -ier; *super* -iest) desaseado, desaliñado; maloliente; mal peinado

frozen foods ['frozən] *spl* viandas congeladas

F.R.S. *abbr* **Fellow of the Royal Society**

frt. *abbr* **freight**

frugal ['frugəl] *adj* (*moderate in the use of things*) parco; (*not very abundant*) frugal

fruit [frut] *adj* (*tree*) frutal; (*boat, dish*) frutero || *s* (*such as apple, pear, strawberry*) fruta; frutas, p.ej., **I like fruit** me gustan las frutas; (*part containing seed*) fruto; (*effect, result*) fruto

fruit cake *s* torta de frutas

fruit cup *s* compota de frutas picadas

fruit fly *s* mosca del vinagre; mosca de las frutas

fruitful ['frutfəl] *adj* fructuoso

fruition [fru'ɪʃən] *s* buen resultado, cumplimiento; **to come to fruition** lograrse cumplidamente

fruit jar *s* tarro para frutas

fruit juice *s* jugo de frutas

fruitless ['frutlɪs] *adj* infructuoso

fruit of the vine *s* zumo de cepas o de parras

fruit salad *s* ensalada de frutas, macedonia de frutas

fruit stand *s* puesto de frutas

fruit store *s* frutería

frumpish ['frʌmpɪʃ] *adj* basto, desgarbado, desaliñado

frustrate ['frʌstret] *tr* frustrar

fry [fraɪ] *s* (*pl* **fries**) fritada || *v* (*pret* & *pp* **fried**) *tr* & *intr* freír

frying pan ['fraɪɪŋ] *s* sartén *f*; **to jump from the frying pan into the fire** saltar de la sartén y dar en las brasas

ft. *abbr* **foot, feet**

fudge [fʌdʒ] *s* dulce *m* de chocolate

fuel ['fju·əl] *s* combustible *m*; (fig) pábulo || *v* (*pret* & *pp* **fueled** o **fuelled**) *ger* **fueling** o **fuelling**) *tr* aprovisionar de combustible || *intr* aprovisionarse de combustible

fuel cell *s* cámara de combustible, célula electrógena

fuel oil *s* aceite *m* combustible

fuel tank *s* depósito de combustible

fugitive ['fjudʒɪtɪv] *adj* & *s* fugitivo

fugue [fjug] *s* (mus) fuga

ful·crum ['fʌlkrəm] *s* (*pl* -**crums** o -**cra** [krə]) fulcro

fulfill [ful'fɪl] *tr* (*to carry out*) cumplir, realizar; cumplir con (*una obligación*); llenar (*una condición*)

fulfillment [ful'fɪlmənt] *s* cumplimiento, realización

full [ful] *adj* lleno; (*dress, garment*) amplio, holgado; (*formal dress*) de etiqueta; (*voice*) sonoro, fuerte; (*of food*) harto; **full of aches and pains** lleno de goteras; **full of fun** muy divertido, muy chistoso; **full of play** muy juguetón; **full to overflowing** lleno a rebosar || *adv* completamente; **full many (a)** muchísimos; **full well** muy bien, perfectamente || *s* colmo; **in full** por completo; sin abreviar; **to the full** completamente || *tr* abatanar

full-blooded ['ful'blʌdɪd] *adj* vigoroso; completo, pletórico; de raza

full-blown ['ful'blon] *adj* (*flower, blossom*) abierto; desarrollado, maduro

full-bodied ['ful'badɪd] *adj* fuerte, espeso, consistente; aromático

full dress *s* traje *m* de etiqueta; (mil) uniforme *m* de gala

full'-dress' coat *s* frac *m*

full-faced ['ful'fest] *adj* carilleno; (*view*) de cuadrado; (*portrait*) de rostro entero

full-fledged ['ful'flɛdʒd] *adj* hecho y derecho, nada menos que

full-grown ['ful'gron] *adj* crecido, completamente desarrollado

full house *s* lleno, entrada llena; (poker) fulján *m*

full'-length' mirror *s* espejo de cuerpo entero, espejo de vestir

full-length movie *s* largometraje *m*, cinta de largo metraje

full load *s* plena carga; (aer) peso total

full moon *s* luna llena, plenilunio

full name *s* nombre *m* y apellidos

full'-page' *adj* a página entera

full powers *spl* plenos poderes, amplias facultades

full sail *adv* a todo trapo

full'-scale' *adj* de tamaño natural; total, completo; pleno

full-sized ['ful'saɪzd] *adj* de tamaño natural

full speed *adv* a toda velocidad

full stop *s* parada completa; (gram) punto

full swing *s* plena actividad

full tilt *adv* a toda velocidad

full'-time' *adj* a tiempo completo

full'-view' *adj* de vista completa

full volume *s* (rad) máximo de volumen

fully ['fuli] o ['fulli] *adv* completamente; cabalmente; por lo menos

fulsome ['fulsəm] o ['fʌlsəm] *adj* bajo, craso, de mal gusto

fumble ['fʌmbəl] *tr* no coger (*la pelota*), dejar caer (*la pelota*) desmañadamente; manosear desmañadamente || *intr* revolver papeles; titubear; andar a tientas; (*in one's pockets*) buscar con las manos

fume [fjum] *s* humo, vapor *m*, gas *m*, vaho || *tr* (*to treat with fumes*) ahumar || *intr* (*to give off fumes*) humear; (*to show anger*) echar pestes; **to fume at** echar pestes contra

fumigate ['fjumɪ‚get] *tr* fumigar

fumigation [‚fjumɪ'geʃən] *s* fumigación

fun [fʌn] *s* divertimiento; broma, chacota; **to be fun** ser divertido; **to have fun** divertirse; **to make fun of** reírse de, burlarse de

function [ˈfʌŋkʃən] s función ‖ intr funcionar

functional [ˈfʌŋkʃənəl] adj funcional

functionar·y [ˈfʌŋkʃəˌnɛri] s (pl -ies) funcionario

fund [fʌnd] s fondo; **funds** fondos ‖ tr consolidar (una deuda)

fundamental [ˌfʌndəˈmɛntəl] adj fundamental ‖ s fundamento

funeral [ˈfjunərəl] adj funeral; (march, procession) fúnebre; (expense) funerario ‖ s funeral m, funerales mpl, pompa fúnebre (de cuerpo presente); **it's not my funeral** (slang) no corre a mi cuidado

funeral director s empresario de pompas fúnebres

funeral home o **parlor** s funeraria

funeral service s oficio de difuntos, misa de cuerpo presente

funereal [fjuˈnɪrɪ·əl] adj fúnebre

fungous [ˈfʌŋgəs] adj fungoso

fungus [ˈfʌŋgəs] s (pl **funguses** o **fungi** [ˈfʌndʒaɪ]) hongo; (pathol) fungo

funicular [fjuˈnɪkjələr] adj & s funicular m

funk [fʌŋk] s (coll) miedo, cobardía; (coll) cobarde mf; **in a funk** (coll) asustado

fun·nel [ˈfʌnəl] s embudo; (smoke-stack) chimenea; (tube for ventilation) manguera, ventilador m ‖ v (pret & pp -neled o -nelled; ger -neling o -nelling) tr verter por medio de un embudo

funnies [ˈfʌniz] spl páginas cómicas, tiras cómicas, tebeo

fun·ny [ˈfʌni] adj (comp -nier; super -niest) cómico; divertido, chistoso; (coll) extraño, raro; **to strike someone as funny** hacerle a uno gracia

funny bone s hueso de la alegría

funny paper s páginas cómicas

fur. abbr **furlong, furnished**

fur [fʌr] s piel f; abrigo de pieles; (on the tongue) sarro

furbelow [ˈfʌrbəˌlo] s (ruffle) faralá m; (frippery) ringorrango

furbish [ˈfʌrbɪʃ] tr acicalar, limpiar; **to furbish up** renovar

furious [ˈfjʊrɪ·əs] adj furioso

furl [fʌrl] tr enrollar; (naut) aferrar

fur-lined [ˈfʌrˌlaɪnd] adj forrado con pieles

furlong [ˈfʌrlɔŋ] o [ˈfʌrlɑŋ] s estadio

furlough [ˈfʌrlo] s licencia ‖ tr dar licencia a

furnace [ˈfʌrnɪs] s horno; (to heat a house) calorífero

furnish [ˈfʌrnɪʃ] tr amueblar; proporcionar, suministrar

furnishings [ˈfʌrnɪʃɪŋz] spl muebles mpl; (things to wear) artículos

furniture [ˈfʌrnɪtʃər] s muebles mpl, mobiliario; (naut) aparejo; **a piece of furniture** un mueble

furniture dealer s mueblista mf

furniture store s mueblería

furrier [ˈfʌrɪ·ər] s peletero

furrier·y [ˈfʌrɪ·əri] s (pl -ies) peletería

furrow [ˈfʌro] s surco ‖ tr surcar

further [ˈfʌrðər] adj adicional; nuevo; más lejano ‖ adv además; más lejos ‖ tr adelantar, promover, fomentar

furtherance [ˈfʌrðərəns] s adelantamiento, promoción, fomento

furthermore [ˈfʌrðərˌmor] adv además

furthest [ˈfʌrðɪst] adj (el) más lejano ‖ adv más lejos

furtive [ˈfʌrtɪv] adj furtivo

fu·ry [ˈfjʊri] s (pl -ries) furia

furze [fʌrz] s aulaga; retama de escoba

fuse [fjuz] s (tube or wick filled with explosive material) mecha; (device for detonating an explosive charge) espoleta; (elec) fusible m, cortacircuitos m, tapón m; **to burn out a fuse** quemar un fusible ‖ tr fundir; (to unite) fusionar ‖ intr fundirse; fusionarse

fuse box s caja de fusibles

fuselage [ˈfjuzəlɪdʒ] o [ˌfjuzəˈlɑʒ] s fuselaje m

fusible [ˈfjuzɪbəl] adj fundible, fusible

fusillade [ˌfjuzɪˈled] s fusilería; (e.g., of questions) andanada ‖ atacar o matar con una descarga de fusilería, fusilar

fusion [ˈfjuʒən] s fusión

fuss [fʌs] s alharaca, hazañería; (coll) disputa por ligero motivo; **to make a fuss** hacer alharacas; **to make a fuss over** hacer fiestas a; disputar sobre ‖ tr atolondrar, inquietar, confundir ‖ intr hacer alharacas, inquietarse por bagatelas

fuss·y [ˈfʌsi] adj (comp -ier; super -iest) alharaquiento, alborotado; descontentadizo, quisquilloso, melindroso; funcionero, hazañero; muy adornado

fustian [ˈfʌstʃən] s (coarse cloth) fustán m; (sort of velveteen) pana; (bombast) cultedad, follaje m

fust·y [ˈfʌsti] adj (comp -ier; super -iest) mohoso, rancio; que huele a cerrado; pasado de moda

futile [ˈfjutɪl] adj (unproductive) estéril; (unimportant) fútil

futili·ty [fjuˈtɪlɪti] s (pl -ties) esterilidad; futilidad

future [ˈfjutʃər] adj futuro ‖ s futuro, porvenir m; (gram) futuro; **futures** (com) futuros; **in the future** en el futuro; **in the near future** en un futuro próximo

fuze [fjuz] s (tube or wick filled with explosive material) mecha; (device for detonating an explosive charge) espoleta; (elec) fusible m ‖ tr poner la espoleta a

fuzz [fʌz] s (as on a peach) pelusa, vello; (in pockets and corners) borra, tamo

fuzz·y [ˈfʌzi] adj (comp -ier; super -iest) cubierto de pelusa, velloso; polvoriento; (indistinct) borroso

fr
fu

G

G, g [dʒi] *s* séptima letra del alfabeto inglés

G. *abbr* **German, Gulf**

g. *abbr* **gender, genitive, gram**

gab [gæb] *s* (coll) cotorreo ‖ (*pret & pp* **gabbed**; *ger* **gabbing**) *intr* (coll) cotorrear

gabardine ['gæbər,din] *s* gabardina

gabble ['gæbəl] *s* cotorreo, parloteo ‖ *intr* cotorrear, parlotear

gable ['gebəl] *s* (*of roof*) aguilón *m*; (*over a door or window*) gablete *m*, frontón *m*

gable end *s* hastial *m*

gable roof *s* tejado de dos aguas

gad [gæd] *v* (*pret & pp* **gadded**; *ger* **gadding**) *intr* callejear, andar de acá para allá; **to gad about** pindonguear (*una mujer*)

gad'a·bout' *adj* callejero ‖ *s* cirigallo; (*woman*) pindonga

gad'fly' *s* (*pl* **-flies**) tábano

gadget ['gædʒɪt] *s* adminículo, chisme *m*, artilugio

Gael [gel] *s* gaélico

Gaelic ['gelɪk] *adj & s* gaélico

gaff [gæf] *s* garfio, arpón *m*; **to stand the gaff** (slang) tener aguante

gag [gæg] *s* mordaza; (*interpolation by an actor*) morcilla; (*joke*) chiste *m*, payasada ‖ *v* (*pret & pp* **gagged**; *ger* **gagging**) *tr* amordazar; dar bascas a ‖ *intr* sentir bascas, arquear

gage [gedʒ] *s* (*pledge*) prenda; (*challenge*) desafío

gaie·ty ['ge·ɪti] *s* (*pl* **-ties**) alegría, algazara, diversión; (*of colors*) viveza

gaily ['geli] *adv* alegremente

gain [gen] *s* ganancia; (*increase*) aumento ‖ *tr* ganar; (*to reach*) alcanzar ‖ *intr* ganar terreno; mejorar (*un enfermo*); adelantarse (*un reloj*); **to gain on** ir alcanzando

gainful ['genfəl] *adj* ganancioso, provechoso

gain'say' *v* (*pret & pp* **-said** ['sed] o ['sɛd]) *tr* negar; contradecir; prohibir

gait [get] *s* paso, manera de andar

gaiter ['getər] *s* polaina corta

gal. *abbr* **gallon**

gala ['gælə] o ['gelə] *adj* de gala ‖ *s* fiesta

galax·y ['gæləksi] *s* (*pl* **-ies**) galaxia

gale [gel] *s* ventarrón *m*; **gales of laughter** tempestades de risas; **to weather the gale** correr el temporal; (fig) ir tirando

Galician [gə'lɪʃən] *adj & s* gallego

gall [gɔl] *s* bilis *f*, hiel *f*; vejiga de la bilis; (*something bitter*) (fig) hiel *f*; rencor *m*, odio; (*gallnut*) agalla; (*audacity*) (coll) descaro ‖ *tr* lastimar rozando; irritar ‖ *intr* raerse; (naut) mascarse (*un cabo*)

gallant ['gælənt] o [gə'lænt] *adj* (*attentive to women*) galante; (*pertaining to love*) amoroso ‖ ['gælənt] *adj* (*stately, grand*) gallardo; (*spirited, daring*) hazañoso; (*showy, gay*) vistoso, festivo ‖ *s* hombre *m* valiente; (*man attentive to women*) galán *m*

gallant·ry ['gæləntri] *s* (*pl* **-ries**) galantería; gallardía

gall bladder *s* vejiga de la bilis, vesícula biliar

gall duct *s* conducto biliar

galleon ['gælɪ·ən] *s* (naut) galeón *m*

galler·y ['gæləri] *s* (*pl* **-ies**) galería; (*in church, theater, etc.*) tribuna; (*cheapest seats in theater*) gallinero; **to play to the gallery** (coll) hablar para la galería

galley ['gæli] *s* (naut & typ) galera; (naut) cocina

galley proof *s* (typ) galerada, pruebas de segundas

galley slave *s* galeote *m*; (*drudge*) esclavo del trabajo

Gallic ['gælɪk] *adj* gálico

galling ['gɔlɪŋ] *adj* irritante, ofensivo

gallivant ['gælɪ,vænt] *intr* andar a placer

gall'nut' *s* agalla

gallon ['gælən] *s* galón *m* (*medida*)

galloon [gə'lun] *s* galón *m* (*cinta*)

gallop ['gæləp] *s* galope *m*; **at a gallop** a galope ‖ *tr* hacer galopar ‖ *intr* galopar; **to gallop through** (fig) hacer muy aprisa

gal·lows ['gæloz] *s* (*pl* **-lows** o **-lowses**) horca

gallows bird *s* (coll) carne *f* de horca

gall'stone' *s* cálculo biliar

galore [gə'lor] *adv* en abundancia

galosh [gə'lɑʃ] *s* chanclo alto

galvanize ['gælvə,naɪz] *tr* galvanizar

galvanized iron *s* hierro galvanizado

gambit ['gæmbɪt] *s* gambito

gamble ['gæmbəl] *s* (coll) empresa arriesgada ‖ *tr* aventurar en el juego; **to gamble away** perder en el juego ‖ *intr* jugar; (*in the stock market*) especular, aventurarse

gambler ['gæmblər] *s* jugador *m*; especulador *m*

gambling ['gæmblɪŋ] *s* juego

gambling den *s* garito

gambling house *s* casa de juego, juego público

gambling table *s* mesa de juego

gam·bol ['gæmbəl] *s* cabriola, retozo, salto ‖ *v* (*pret & pp* **-boled** o **-bolled**; *ger* **-boling** o **-bolling**) *intr* cabriolar, retozar, saltar

gambrel ['gæmbrəl] *s* corvejón *m*

gambrel roof *s* techo a la holandesa

game [gem] *adj* bravo, peleón; dispuesto, resuelto; (*leg*) cojo; de caza ‖ *s* (*form of play*) juego; (*single contest*) partida; (*score*) tantos; (*in bridge*) manga; (*any sport*) deporte *m*; (*animal or bird hunted for sport or food*) caza; (*any pursuit*) actividad; (*pursuit of diplomacy*) juego;

the game is up estamos frescos; **to make game of** burlarse de; **to play the game** jugar limpio

game bag *s* morral *m*

game bird *s* ave *f* de caza

game'cock' *s* gallo de pelea

game'keep'er *s* guardabosque *m*

game of chance *s* juego de azar

game preserve *s* vedado

game warden *s* guardabosque *m*

gamut ['gæmət] *s* (mus & fig) gama

gam·y ['gemi] *adj* (*comp* **-ier**; *super* **-iest**) (*having flavor of cooked game*) salvajino; bravo, peleón

gander ['gændər] *s* ganso

gang [gæŋ] *adj* múltiple ‖ *s* (*of workmen*) brigada, cuadrilla; (*of thugs*) pandilla ‖ *intr* — **to gang up** acuadrillarse; **to gang up against u** on atacar juntos; conspirar contra

gangling ['gæŋglɪŋ] *adj* larguirucho

gangli·on ['gæŋglɪ·ən] *s* (*pl* **-ons** o **-a** [ə]) ganglio

gang'plank' *s* plancha, pasarela

gangrene ['gæŋgrin] *s* gangrena ‖ *tr* gangrenar ‖ *intr* gangrenarse

gangster ['gæŋstər] *s* (coll) gángster *m*, pistolero

gang'way' *s* (*passageway*) pasillo; (*gangplank*) plancha, pasarela; (*in ship's side*) portalón *m* ‖ *interj* ¡abran paso!, ¡paso libre!

gantlet ['gɔntlɪt] o ['gɑntlɪt] *s* (rr) vía traslapada

gan·try ['gæntri] *s* (*pl* **-tries**) caballete *m*, poíno; (rr) puente *m* transversal de señales

gantry crane *s* grúa de caballete

gap [gæp] *s* (*break, open space*) laguna; (*in a wall*) boquete *m*; (*between mountains*) garganta, quebrada; (*between two points of view*) sima

gape [gep] o [gæp] *s* abertura, brecha; (*yawn*) bostezo; mirada de asombro; **the gapes** ganas de bostezar ‖ *intr* estar abierto de par en par; bostezar; embobarse; **to gape at** mirar embobado; **to stand gaping** embobarse

G.A.R. *abbr* Grand Army of the Republic

garage [gə'rɑʒ] *s* garage *m*

garb [gɑrb] *s* vestidura ‖ *tr* vestir

garbage ['gɑrbɪdʒ] *s* basuras, desperdicios, bazofia

garbage can *s* cubo para bazofia, latón *m* de la basura

garbage disposal *s* evacuación de basuras

garble ['gɑrbəl] *tr* mutilar (*un texto*)

garden ['gɑrdən] *s* (*of vegetables*) huerto; (*of flowers*) jardín *m*

gardener ['gɑrdənər] *s* (*of vegetables*) hortelano; (*of flowers*) jardinero

gardenia [gɑr'dini·ə] *s* gardenia, jazmín *m* de la India

gardening ['gɑrdənɪŋ] *s* horticultura; jardinería

garden party *s* fiesta que se da en un jardín o parque

gargle ['gɑrgəl] *s* gargarismo ‖ *intr* gargarizar

gargoyle ['gɑrgɔɪl] *s* gárgola

garish ['gerɪʃ] o ['gærɪʃ] *adj* charro, chillón, cursi

garland ['gɑrlənd] *s* guirnalda

garlic ['gɑrlɪk] *s* ajo

garment ['gɑrmənt] *s* prenda de vestir

garner ['gɑrnər] *tr* (*to gather, collect*) acopiar; adquirir; (*cereales*) entrojar

garnet ['gɑrnɪt] *adj* & *s* granate *m*

garnish ['gɑrnɪʃ] *s* adorno; (culin) aderezo, condimento de adorno ‖ *tr* adornar; (culin) aderezar; (law) embargar

garret ['gærɪt] *s* buhardilla, desván *m*

garrison ['gærɪsən] *s* plaza fuerte; (*troops*) guarnición ‖ *tr* guarnecer, guarnicionar (*una plaza fuerte*); guarnecer una plaza fuerte de (*tropas*)

garrote [gə'rɑt] o [gə'rot] *s* estrangulación para robar; (*method of execution*; iron collar used for such execution*) garrote *m* ‖ *tr* estrangular; estrangular para robar; agarrotar, dar garrote a

garrulous ['gærələs] o ['gærjələs] *adj* gárrulo, locuaz

garter ['gɑrtər] *s* liga, jarretera

garth [gɑrθ] *s* patio de claustro

gas [gæs] *s* gas *m*; (coll) gasolina; (coll) palabrería ‖ *v* (*pret* & *pp* **gassed**) *ger* **gassing**) *tr* abastecer de gas; (*to attack, asphyxiate, or poison with gas*) gasear; (coll) abastecer de gasolina ‖ *intr* despedir gas; (slang) charlar

gas'bag' *s* (aer) cámara de gas; (slang) charlatán *m*

gas burner *s* mechero de gas

Gascony ['gæskəni] *s* Gascuña

gas engine *s* motor *m* a gas

gaseous ['gæsɪ·əs] *adj* gaseoso

gas fitter *s* gasista *m*

gas generator *s* gasógeno

gash [gæʃ] *s* cuchillada, chirlo ‖ *tr* acuchillar

gas heat *s* calefacción por gas

gas'hold'er *s* gasómetro

gasi·fy ['gæsɪ‚faɪ] *v* (*pret* & *pp* **-fied**) *tr* gasificar ‖ *intr* gasificarse

gas jet *s* mechero de gas; llama de gas

gasket ['gæskɪt] *s* empaquetadura

gas main *s* cañería de gas

gas mask *s* careta antigás

gas meter *s* contador *m* de gas

gasohol ['gæsə‚hɔl] *s* alconafta

gasoline ['gæsə‚lin] o [‚gæsə'lin] *s* gasolina

gasoline pump *s* poste *m* distribuidor *m* de gasolina, surtidor *m* de gasolina

gasp [gæsp] o [gɑsp] *s* respiración entrecortada; (*of death*) boqueada ‖ *tr* decir con voz entrecortada ‖ *intr* boquear

gas producer *s* gasógeno

gas range *s* cocina a gas

gas station *s* estación gasolinera

gas stove *s* cocina a gas

gas tank *s* gasómetro; (aut) depósito de gasolina

gastric ['gæstrɪk] *adj* gástrico

gastronomy [gæsˈtrɑnəmi] s gastronomía

gas'works' s fábrica de gas

gate [get] s puerta; (*in fence or wall; of bird cage*) portillo; (*of sluice or lock*) compuerta; (*number of people paying admission; amount they pay*) entrada, taquilla; (rr) barrera; (fig) entrada, camino; **to crash the gate** (coll) colarse de gorra

gate'keep'er s portero; (rr) guardabarrera *mf*

gate'post' s poste *m* de una puerta de cercado

gate'way' s entrada, paso, camino

gather [ˈgæðər] *tr* recoger, reunir; recolectar (*la cosecha*); coger (*leña, flores, etc.*); cubrirse de (*polvo*); recoger (*una persona sus pensamientos*); (bb) alzar; (sew) fruncir; (*to deduce*) (fig) calcular, deducir; **to gather oneself together** componerse ‖ *intr* reunirse; amontonarse; saltar (*lágrimas*)

gathering [ˈgæðərɪŋ] s reunión; recolección; (bb) alzado; (sew) frunce *m*

gaud·y [ˈgɔdi] *adj* (*comp* -ier; *super* -iest) cursi, chillón, llamativo

gauge [gedʒ] s medida, norma; calibre *m*; (*of liquid in a container*) nivel *m*; (*of carpenter*) gramil *m*; (*of gasoline*) medidor *m*; (rr) ancho de vía, entrevía ‖ *tr* medir; calibrar; graduar; aforar (*la cantidad de agua de una corriente*); arquear (*una nave*)

gauge glass s tubo indicador, vidrio de nivel

Gaul [gɔl] s la Galia; (*native*) galo

gaunt [gɔnt] o [gɑnt] *adj* desvaído, macilento; hosco, tétrico

gauntlet [ˈgɔntlɪt] o [ˈgɑntlɪt] s guantelete *m*; guante con puño abocinado; carrera de baquetas; (rr) vía traslapada; **to run the gauntlet** correr baquetas, pasar por baquetas; **to take up the gauntlet** recoger el guante; **to throw down the gauntlet** arrojar el guante

gauze [gɔz] s gasa, cendal *m*

gavel [ˈgævəl] s mazo, martillo

gavotte [gəˈvɑt] s gavota

gawk [gɔk] s (coll) palurdo, papanatas *m* ‖ *intr* (coll) mirar de modo impertinente; papar moscas, mirar embobado

gawk·y [ˈgɔki] *adj* (*comp* -ier; *super* -iest) desgarbado, torpe, bobo

gay [ge] *adj* alegre, festivo; (*brilliant*) vistoso; amigo de los placeres; (coll) homosexual

gaye·ty [ˈge·ɪti] s var de **gaiety**

gaze [gez] s mirada fija ‖ *intr* mirar fijamente

gazelle [gəˈzɛl] s gacela

gazette [gəˈzɛt] s periódico; anuncio oficial

gazetteer [ˌgæzəˈtɪr] s diccionario geográfico

gear [gɪr] s pertrechos, utensilios; (*of transmission, steering, etc.*) mecanismo, aparato; rueda dentada; (*two or more toothed wheels meshed to-* *gether*) engranaje *m;* **out of gear** desengranado; (fig) descompuesto; **to throw into gear** engranar; **to throw out of gear** desengranar; (fig) descomponer ‖ *tr & intr* engranar

gear'box' s caja de engranajes; (aut) caja de velocidades

gear case s caja de engranajes

gear'shift' s cambio de marchas, cambio de velocidades

gearshift lever s palanca de cambio de marchas

gear'wheel' s rueda dentada

gee [dʒi] *interj* ¡caramba!; **gee up!** (*get up!, said to a horse*) ¡arre!

Gehenna [gɪˈhɛnə] s gehena *m*

gel [dʒɛl] s gel *m* ‖ *v* (*pret & pp* **gelled;** *ger* **gelling**) *intr* cuajarse en forma de gel

gelatine [ˈdʒɛlətɪn] s gelatina

geld [gɛld] *v* (*pret & pp* **gelded** o **gelt** [gɛlt]) *tr* castrar

gem [dʒɛm] s gema, piedra preciosa; (fig) joya, preciosidad

Gemini [ˈdʒɛmɪˌnaɪ] s (*constellation*) Géminis o Gemelos; (*sign of zodiac*) Géminis *m*

gen. *abbr* **gender, general, genitive, genus**

gender [ˈdʒɛndər] s (gram) género; (coll) sexo

genealo·gy [ˌdʒɛnɪˈæləd ʒi] o [ˌdʒɪnɪˈæləd ʒi] s (*pl* -gies) genealogía

general [ˈdʒɛnərəl] *adj & s* general *m;* **in general** en general o por lo general

general delivery s lista de correos

generalissi·mo [ˌdʒɛnərəˈlɪsɪmo] s (*pl* -mos) generalísimo

generali·ty [ˌdʒɛnəˈrælɪti] s (*pl* -ties) generalidad

generalize [ˈdʒɛnərəˌlaɪz] *tr & intr* generalizar

generally [ˈdʒɛnərəli] *adv* por lo general

general practitioner s médico general

generalship [ˈdʒɛnərəlˌʃɪp] s generalato; don *m* de mando

general staff s estado mayor general

generate [ˈdʒɛnəˌret] *tr* (*to beget*) engendrar; generar (*electricidad*); (geom) engendrar

generating station s central *f*

generation [ˌdʒɛnəˈreʃən] s generación

generator [ˈdʒɛnəˌretər] s generador *m*

generic [dʒɪˈnɛrɪk] *adj* genérico

generous [ˈdʒɛnərəs] *adj* generoso; abundante, grande

gene·sis [ˈdʒɛnɪsɪs] s (*pl* -ses [ˌsiz]) génesis *f* ‖ **Genesis** s (Bib) el Génesis

genetic [dʒɪˈnɛtɪk] *adj* genético ‖ **genetics** s genética

Geneva [dʒɪˈnivə] s Ginebra

Genevan [dʒɪˈnivən] *adj & s* ginebrino

genial [ˈdʒinɪ·əl] *adj* afable, complaciente

genie [ˈdʒini] s genio

genital [ˈdʒɛnɪtəl] *adj* genital ‖ **genitals** *spl* genitales *mpl*, órganos genitales

genitive [ˈdʒɛnɪtɪv] *adj & s* genitivo

genius [ˈdʒinjəs] o [ˈdʒinɪ·əs] s (*pl* **geniuses**) (*great inventive gift; person possessing it*) genio ‖ s (*pl* **geni-**

['dʒɪnɪ‚aɪ]) (*guardian spirit; pagan deity*) genio

Genoa ['dʒeno‧ə] *s* Génova

genocidal [‚dʒenə'saɪdəl] *adj* genocida

genocide ['dʒenə‚saɪd] *s* (*act*) genocidio; (*person*) genocida *mf*

Geno‧ese [‚dʒeno'iz] *adj* genovés ‖ *s* (*pl* -ese) genovés *m*

genre ['ʒɑnrə] *adj* de género

gent. o **Gent.** *abbr* **gentleman, gentlemen**

genteel [dʒen'til] *adj* gentil, elegante; cortés, urbano

gentian ['dʒenʃən] *s* genciana

gentile ['dʒentɪl] o ['dʒentaɪl] *adj* gentilicio; (*gram*) gentilicio ‖ ['dʒentaɪl] *adj & s* no judío; cristiano; (*pagan*) gentil *mf*

gentili‧ty [dʒen'tɪlɪtɪ] *s* (*pl* -ties) gentileza

gentle ['dʒentəl] *adj* apacible, benévolo; dulce, manso, suave; cortés, fino; (*e.g., tap on the shoulder*) ligero

gen'tle‧folk' *s* gente bien nacida

gentle‧man ['dʒentəlmən] *s* (*pl* -men [mən]) *s* caballero; (*attendant to a person of high rank*) gentilhombre *m*

gentleman in waiting *s* gentilhombre *m* de cámara

gentlemanly ['dʒentəlmənlɪ] *adj* caballeroso

gentleman of leisure *s* señor *m* que vive sin trabajar, caballero de vida holgada

gentleman of the road *s* salteador *m* de caminos

gentleman's agreement *s* acuerdo verbal

gentle sex *s* bello sexo, sexo débil

gentry ['dʒentrɪ] *s* gente bien nacida

genuine ['dʒenjʊ‧ɪn] *adj* genuino; sincero, franco

genus ['dʒinəs] *s* (*pl* **genera** ['dʒenərə] o **genuses**) (biol, log) género

geog. *abbr* **geography**

geographer [dʒɪ'ɑgrəfər] *s* geógrafo

geographic(al) [‚dʒi‧ə'græfɪk(əl)] *adj* geográfico

geogra‧phy [dʒɪ'ɑgrəfɪ] *s* (*pl* -phies) geografía

geol. *abbr* **geology**

geologic(al) [‚dʒi‧ə'lɑdʒɪk(əl)] *adj* geológico

geologist [dʒɪ'ɑlədʒɪst] *s* geólogo

geolo‧gy [dʒɪ'ɑlədʒɪ] *s* (*pl* -gies) geología

geom. *abbr* **geometry**

geometric(al) [‚dʒi‧ə'metrɪk(əl)] *adj* geométrico

geometrician [dʒɪ‚ɑmɪ'trɪʃən] *s* geómetra *mf*

geome‧try [dʒɪ'ɑmɪtrɪ] *s* (*pl* -tries) geometría

geophysics [‚dʒi‧ə'fɪzɪks] *s* geofísica

geopolitics [‚dʒi‧ə'pɑlɪtɪks] *s* geopolítica

George [dʒɔrdʒ] *s* Jorje *m*

geranium [dʒɪ'renɪ‧əm] *s* geranio

geriatrical [‚dʒerɪ'ætrɪkəl] *adj* geriátrico

geriatrician [‚dʒerɪ‧ə'trɪʃən] *s* geriatra *mf*

geriatrics [‚dʒerɪ'ætrɪks] *s* geriatría

germ [dʒʌrm] *s* germen *m*

German ['dʒʌrmən] *adj & s* alemán *m*

germane [dʒʌr'men] *adj* pertinente, relacionado

Germanize ['dʒʌrmə‚naɪz] *tr* germanizar

German measles *s* rubéola

German silver *s* melchor *m*, alpaca

Germany ['dʒʌrmənɪ] *s* Alemania

germ carrier *s* portador *m* de gérmenes

germ cell *s* célula germen

germicidal [‚dʒʌrmɪ'saɪdəl] *adj* germicida

germicide ['dʒʌrmɪ‚saɪd] *s* germicida *m*

germinate ['dʒʌrmɪ‚net] *intr* germinar

germ plasm *s* germen *m* plasma

germ theory *s* teoría germinal

germ warfare *s* guerra bacteriana

gerontology [‚dʒerɑn'talədʒɪ] *s* gerontología

gerund ['dʒerənd] *s* gerundio

gerundive [dʒɪ'rʌndɪv] *s* gerundio adjetivo

gestation [dʒes'teʃən] *s* gestación

gesticulate [dʒes'tɪkjə‚let] *intr* accionar, manotear

gesticulation [dʒes‚tɪkjə'leʃən] *s* ademán *m*, manoteo

gesture ['dʒestʃər] *s* ademán *m*, gesto; demostración, muestra ‖ *intr* hacer ademanes, hacer gestos

get [get] *v* (*pret* **got** [gɑt]; *pp* **got** o **gotten** ['gɑtən]; *ger* **getting**) *tr* conseguir, obtener; recibir; ir por, buscar; tomar (*p.ej., un billete*); alcanzar; encontrar, hallar; hacer (*p.ej., la comida*); resolver (*un problema*); aprender de memoria; captar (*una estación emisora*); **to get across** hacer aceptar; hacer comprender; **to get back** recobrar; **to get down** descolgar; (*to swallow*) tragar; **to get off** quitar (*p.ej., una mancha*); **to get someone to** + *inf* lograr que alguien + *subj*; **to get** + *pp* hacer + *inf*; **to have got** (coll) tener; **to have got to** + *inf* (coll) tener que + *inf* ‖ *intr* (*to become*) hacerse, ponerse, volverse; (*to arrive*) llegar; **get up!** (*to an animal*) ¡arre!; **to get about** estar levantado (*un convaleciente*); **to get along** seguir andando; irse; ir tirando; tener éxito; llevarse bien; ir de acuerdo; **to get along in years** ponerse viejo; **to get along with** congeniar con; **to get angry** enfadarse; **to get around** divulgarse; salir mucho, ir a todas partes; eludir; manejar (*a una persona*); **to get away** conseguir marcharse; evadirse; **to get away with** llevarse, escaparse con; (coll) hacer impunemente; **to get back** volver, regresar; **to get back at** (coll) desquitarse con; **to get behind** quedarse atrás; apoyar, abogar por; **to get by** lograr pasar; (*to manage to shift*) (coll) arreglárselas; **to get going** ponerse en marcha; **to get in** entrar; volver a casa; llegar (*un tren*); **to get in with**

ga
ge

llegar a ser amigo de; **to get married** casarse; **to get off** apearse; marcharse; **to get old** envejecer; **to get on** subir; llevarse bien; **to get out** salir, marcharse; divulgarse; **to get out of** bajar de (*un coche*); librarse de; perder (*la paciencia*); **to get out of the way** quitarse de en medio; **to get run over** ser atropellado; **to get through** pasar por entre; terminar; **to get to be** llegar a ser; **to get under way** ponerse en camino; **to get up** levantarse; **to not get over it** (coll) no volver de su asombro

get'a·way' s escapatoria, escape m; (*of an automobile*) arranque m

get'-to·geth'er s reunión, tertulia

get'-up' s (coll) disposición, presentación; (coll) atavío, traje m

gewgaw ['gjugɔ] adj cursi, charro, chillón || s fruslería, chuchería; adorno charro

geyser ['gaɪzər] s géiser m || ['gizər] s (Brit) calentador m de agua

ghast·ly ['gæstli] o ['gɑstli] adj (comp -lier; super -liest) cadavérico, espectral; espantoso, horrible

Ghent [gent] s Gante

gherkin ['gʌrkɪn] s pepinillo

ghet·to ['geto] s (pl -tos) ghetto

ghost [gost] s espectro, fantasma m; (telv) fantasma m; **not a ghost of a** ni sombra de; **to give up the ghost** entregar el alma, rendir el alma

ghost·ly ['gostli] adj (comp -lier; super -liest) espectral

ghost story s cuento de fantasmas

ghost writer s colaborador anónimo, escritor anónimo de obras firmadas por otra persona

ghoul [gul] s demonio que se alimenta de cadáveres; ladrón m de tumbas; (*person who revels in horrible things*) vampiro

ghoulish ['gulɪʃ] adj vampírico, horrible

G.H.Q. abbr **General Headquarters**

GI ['dʒi'aɪ] s (pl GI's) (coll) soldado raso (*del ejército norteamericano*)

giant ['dʒaɪ·ənt] adj & s gigante m

giantess ['dʒaɪ·əntɪs] s giganta

gibberish ['dʒɪbərɪʃ] o ['gɪbərɪʃ] s guirigay m

gibbet ['dʒɪbɪt] s horca || tr ahorcar; poner a la vergüenza

gibe [dʒaɪb] s remoque m, mofa || intr mofarse; **to gibe at** mofarse de

giblets ['dʒɪblɪts] spl menudillos

giddiness ['gɪdɪnɪs] s vértigo, vahido; falta de juicio

gid·dy ['gɪdi] adj (comp -dier; super -diest) vertiginoso; mareado; casquivano, ligero de cascos

Gideon ['gɪdɪ·ən] s (Bib) Gedeón m

gift [gɪft] s regalo; (*natural ability*) don m, dote f, prenda

gifted ['gɪftɪd] adj talentoso; muy inteligente

gift horse s — **never look a gift horse in the mouth** a caballo regalado no se le mira el diente

gift of gab s (coll) facundia, labia

gift shop s comercio de objetos de regalo, tienda de regalos

gift'-wrap' v (pret & pp -wrapped; ger wrapping) tr envolver en paquete regalo

gigantic [dʒaɪ'gæntɪk] adj gigantesco

giggle ['gɪgəl] s risita, risa ahogada, retozo de la risa || intr reírse bobamente

gigo·lo ['dʒɪgə,lo] s (pl -los) acompañante m profesional de mujeres; (*man supported by a woman*) mantenido

gild [gɪld] v (pret & pp gilded o gilt [gɪlt]) tr dorar

gilding ['gɪldɪŋ] s dorado

gill [gɪl] s (*of fish*) agalla; (*of cock*) barba || [dʒɪl] s cuarta parte de una pinta

gillyflower ['dʒɪlɪ,flau·ər] s alhelí m

gilt [gɪlt] adj & s dorado

gilt-edged ['gɪlt,edʒd] adj de toda confianza, de lo mejor que hay

gilt'head' s dorada

gimcrack ['dʒɪm,kræk] adj de oropel || s chuchería

gimlet ['gɪmlɪt] s barrena de mano

gimmick ['gɪmɪk] s (slang) adminículo; (slang) adminículo mágico

gin [dʒɪn] s (*alcoholic liquor*) ginebra; desmotadera de algodón; trampa; (*fish trap*) garlito; torno de izar || v (pret & pp ginned; ger ginning) tr desmotar

gin fizz s ginebra con gaseosa

ginger ['dʒɪndʒər] s jenjibre m; (coll) energía, viveza

ginger ale s cerveza de jengibre gaseosa

gin'ger·bread' s pan m de jengibre; adorno charro

gingerly ['dʒɪndʒərli] adj cauteloso, cuidadoso || adv cautelosamente

gin'ger·snap' s galletita de jengibre

gingham ['gɪŋəm] s guinga

giraffe [dʒɪ'ræf] o [dʒɪ'rɑf] s jirafa

girandole ['dʒɪrən,dol] s girándula

gird [gʌrd] v (pret & pp girt [gʌrt] o girded) tr ceñir; (*to equip*) dotar; (*to prepare*) aprestar; (*to surround, hem in*) rodear, encerrar

girder ['gʌrdər] s viga, trabe f

girdle ['gʌrdəl] s faja; corsé pequeño || tr ceñir; circundar, rodear

girl [gʌrl] s muchacha, niña, chica; (*servant*) moza

girl friend s (coll) amiguita

girlhood ['gʌrlhʊd] s muchachez f; juventud femenina

girlish ['gʌrlɪʃ] adj de muchacha; juvenil

girl scout s niña exploradora

girth [gʌrθ] s (*band*) cincha; (*waistband*) pretina; circunferencia

gist [dʒɪst] s esencia

give [gɪv] s elasticidad || v (pret gave [gev]; pp given ['gɪvən]) tr dar; ocasionar (*molestia, trabajo, etc.*); representar (*una obra dramática*); pronunciar (*un discurso*); **to give away** dar de balde; revelar; llevar (*a la novia*); (coll) traicionar; **to give back** devolver; **to give forth** despedir (*p.ej., olores*); **to give oneself up**

entregarse; **to give up** abandonar, dejar (un empleo); renunciar || intr dar; dar de sí; romperse (p.ej., una cuerda); **to give in** ceder, rendirse; **to give out** agotarse; no poder más; **to give up** darse por vencido

give'-and-take' s concesiones mutuas; conversación sazonada de burlas

give'a·way' s (coll) revelación involuntaria; (coll) traición; (e.g., in checkers) (coll) ganapierde m & f

given ['gɪvən] adj dado; (math) conocido; **given that** dado que, suponiendo que

given name s nombre m de pila

giver ['gɪvər] s dador m, donador m

gizzard ['gɪzərd] s molleja

glacial ['gleʃəl] adj glacial

glacier ['gleʃər] s glaciar m, helero

glad [glæd] adj (comp **gladder;** super **gladdest**) alegre, contento; **to be glad (to)** alegrarse (de)

gladden ['glædən] tr alegrar

glade [gled] s claro, claro herboso (en un bosque)

glad hand s (coll) acogida efusiva

gladiola [ˌglædɪˈolə] o [gləˈdaɪ·ələ] s estoque m

gladly ['glædlɪ] adv alegremente; de buena gana, con mucho gusto

gladness ['glædnɪs] s alegría, regocijo

glad rags spl (slang) trapitos de cristianar; (slang) vestido de etiqueta

glamorous ['glæmərəs] adj fascinador, elegante

glamour ['glæmər] s fascinación, elegancia, hechizo

glamour girl s belleza exótica

glance [glæns] o [glɑns] s ojeada, vistazo, golpe m de vista; **at a glance** de un vistazo; **at first glance** a primera vista || intr lanzar una mirada; **to glance at** lanzar una mirada a; examinar de paso; **to glance off** desviarse de soslayo; desviarse de, al chocar; **to glance over** mirar por encima

gland [glænd] s glándula

glanders ['glændərz] spl muermo

glare [glɛr] s fulgor m deslumbrante, luz intensa; mirada feroz, mirada de indignación || intr relumbrar; lanzar miradas feroces; **to glare at** echar una mirada feroz a

glaring ['glɛrɪŋ] adj deslumbrante, relumbrante; (look) feroz, penetrante; manifiesto, que salta a la vista

glass [glæs] o [glɑs] s vidrio, cristal m; (tumbler) vaso, copa; (mirror) espejo; (glassware) vajilla de cristal; **glasses** anteojos

glass blower ['bloˌər] s soplador m de vidrio, vidriero

glass case s vitrina

glass cutter s cortavidrios m

glass door s puerta vidriera

glassful ['glæsful] o ['glɑsful] s vaso

glass'house' s invernadero; (fig) tejado de vidrio

glassine [glæˈsin] s papel m cristal

glass'ware' s cristalería, vajilla de vidrio

glass wool s cristal hilado

glass'works' s cristalería, vidriería

glass'work·er s vidriero

glass·y ['glæsi] o ['glɑsi] adj (comp -ier; super -iest) vidrioso

glaze [glez] s vidriado, esmalte m; (of ice) capa resbaladiza || tr vidriar, esmaltar; garapiñar (golosinas)

glazier ['gleʒər] s vidriero

gleam [glim] s destello, rayo de luz; luz f tenue; (of hope) rayo || intr destellar; brillar con luz tenue

glean [glin] tr espigar; (to gather bit by bit, e.g., out of books) espigar

glee [gli] s alegría, regocijo

glee club s orfeón m

glib [glɪb] adj (comp **glibber;** super **glibbest**) locuaz; (tongue) suelto; fácil e insincero

glide [glaɪd] s deslizamiento; (aer) vuelo sin motor, planeo; (mus) ligadura || intr deslizarse; (aer) volar sin motor, planear; **to glide along** pasar suavemente

glider ['glaɪdər] s (aer) planeador m, deslizador m

glimmer ['glɪmər] s luz f tenue; (faint perception) vislumbre f || intr brillar con luz tenue; (to appear faintly) vislumbrarse

glimmering ['glɪmərɪŋ] adj tenue, trémulo || s luz f tenue; vislumbre f

glimpse [glɪmps] s vislumbre f; **to catch a glimpse of** entrever, vislumbrar || tr vislumbrar

glint [glɪnt] s destello, rayo || intr destellar

glisten ['glɪsən] s centelleo || intr centellear

glitter ['glɪtər] s resplandor m, brillo || intr resplandecer, brillar

gloaming ['glomɪŋ] s crepúsculo vespertino

gloat [glot] intr relamerse; **to gloat over** mirar con satisfacción maligna

globe [glob] s globo

globetrotter ['globˌtrɑtər] s trotamundos m

globule ['glɑbjul] s glóbulo

glockenspiel ['glɑkənˌspil] s juego de timbres, órgano de campanas

gloom [glum] s lobreguez f, tinieblas, obscuridad; abatimiento, tristeza; aspecto abatido

gloom·y ['glumi] adj (comp -ier; super -iest) (dark; sad) lóbrego; pesimista

glori·fy ['glorɪˌfaɪ] v (pret & pp -fied) tr glorificar; (to enhance) realzar

glorious ['glorɪ·əs] adj glorioso; espléndido, magnífico; (coll) alegre

glo·ry ['glorɪ] s (pl -ries) gloria; **to go to glory** ganar la gloria; (slang) fracasar || v (pret & pp -ried) intr gloriarse

gloss [glɑs] o [glɑs] s brillo, lustre m; (note, commentary) glosa; glosario || tr (to annotate) glosar; lustrar, satinar; **to gloss over** disculpar, paliar

glossa·ry ['glɑsərɪ] s (pl -ries) glosario

gloss·y ['glɑsi] o ['glɑsi] adj (comp -ier; super -iest) brillante, lustroso; (silk) joyante

ge
gl

glottal ['glɑtəl] *adj* glótico

glove [glʌv] *s* guante *m*

glove compartment *s* portaguantes *m*

glove stretcher *s* ensanchador *m*, juanas

glow [glo] *s* (*light of incandescence*) resplandor *m*; (*e.g., of sunset*) brillo, esplendor *m*; sensación de calor; color *m* en las mejillas ‖ *intr* brillar sin llama; estar encendido (*el rostro, el cielo*); estar muy animado

glower ['glau‧ər] *s* ceño, mirada ceñuda ‖ *intr* mirar con ceño

glowing ['glo‧ɪŋ] *adj* ardiente, encendido; radiante; entusiasta, elogioso

glow'worm' *s* gusano de luz, luciérnaga

glucose ['glukos] *s* glucosa

glue [glu] *s* cola ‖ *tr* encolar; pegar fuertemente

glue pot *s* cazo de cola

gluey ['glu‧i] *adj* (*comp* **gluier**; *super* **gluiest**) pegajoso; (*smeared with glue*) encolado

glug [glʌg] *s* gluglú *m* ‖ *v* (*pret & pp* **glugged**; *ger* **glugging**) *intr* hacer gluglú (*el agua*)

glum [glʌm] *adj* (*comp* **glummer**; *super* **glummest**) hosco

glut [glʌt] *s* abundancia, gran acopio; exceso; **to be a glut on the market** abarrotarse ‖ *v* (*pret & pp* **glutted**; *ger* **glutting**) *tr* hartar, saciar; inundar (*el mercado*); obstruir

glutton ['glʌtən] *adj & s* glotón *m*

gluttonous ['glʌtənəs] *adj* glotón

glutton·y ['glʌtəni] *s* (*pl* **-ies**) glotonería, gula

glycerine ['glɪsərɪn] *s* glicerina

G.M. *abbr* **general manager, Grand Master**

G-man ['dʒi ,mæn] *s* (*pl* **-men** [,mɛn]) (coll) agente *m* de la policía federal

G.M.T. *abbr* **Greenwich mean time**

gnarl [nɑrl] *s* nudo ‖ *tr* torcer ‖ *intr* gruñir

gnarled [nɑrld] *adj* nudoso, retorcido

gnash [næʃ] *tr* hacer rechinar (*los dientes*) ‖ *intr* hacer rechinar los dientes

gnat [næt] *s* jején *m*

gnaw [nɔ] *tr* roer; practicar (*un agujero*) royendo

gnome [nom] *s* gnomo

go [go] *s* (*pl* **goes**) ida; (coll) energía, ímpetu *m*; (coll) boga; (coll) ensayo; (*for traffic*) paso libre; **it's a go** (coll) es un trato hecho; **it's all the go** (coll) hace furor; **it's no go** (coll) es imposible; **on the go** (coll) en continuo movimiento; **to make a go of** (coll) lograr éxito en ‖ *v* (*pret* **went** [wɛnt]; *pp* **gone** [ɡɔn] *o* [ɡɑn]) *tr* (coll) soportar, tolerar; **to go it alone** obrar sin ayuda ‖ *intr* ir; (*to work, operate*) funcionar, marchar; andar (*p.ej., desnudo*); volverse (*p.ej., loco*); **going, going, gone!** ¡vendo, vendo, vendí!; **so it goes** así va el mundo; **to be going to** + *inf* ir a + *inf*; **to be gone** haber ido; haberse agotado; haber dejado de ser; **to go against** ir en contra de; **to go ahead** seguir adelante; **to go away** irse,

marcharse; **to go back** volver; **to go by** pasar por; guiarse por; atenerse a; **to go down** bajar; hundirse (*un buque*); **to go fishing** ir de pesca; **to go for** ir por; **to go get** ir por, ir a buscar; **to go house hunting** ir a cazar casa; **to go hunting** ir de caza; **to go in** entrar; entrar en; (*to fit in*) caber en; **to go in for** dedicarse a, interesarse por; **to go into** entrar en; investigar; (aut) poner (*p.ej., primera*); **to go in with** asociarse con; **to go off** irse, marcharse; llevarse a cabo; estallar (*p.ej., una bomba*); dispararse (*un fusil*); **to go on** seguir adelante; ir tirando; **to go on** + *ger* seguir + *ger*; **to go on with** continuar; **to go out** salir; pasar de moda; apagarse (*un fuego, una luz*); declararse en huelga; (*for entertainment, etc.*) salir; **to go over** tener éxito; releer; examinar, revisar; pasar por encima de; **to go over to** pasarse a las filas de; **to go through** pasar por; llegar al fin de; agotar (*una fortuna*); **to go with** ir con, acompañar; salir con (*una muchacha*); hacer juego con; **to go without** andarse sin, pasarse sin

goad [god] *s* aguijada, aguijón *m* ‖ *tr* aguijonear

go'-a·head' *adj* (coll) emprendedor ‖ *s* (coll) señal *f* para seguir adelante, luz *f* verde

goal [gol] *s* meta; (*in football*) gol *m*

goal'keep'er *s* guardameta *m*, portero

goal line *s* raya de la meta

goal post *s* poste *m* de la meta

goat [got] *s* cabra; (*male goat*) macho cabrío; (coll) víctima inocente; **to be the goat** (slang) pagar el pato; **to get the goat of** (slang) tomar el pelo a; **to ride the goat** (coll) ser iniciado en una sociedad secreta

goatee [go'ti] *s* perilla

goat'herd' *s* cabrero

goat'skin' *s* piel *f* de cabra

goat'suck'er *s* chotacabras *m*

gob [gɑb] *s* (coll) masa informe y pequeña; (coll) marinero de guerra

gobble ['gɑbəl] *s* gluglú *m* ‖ *tr* engullir; **to gobble up** engullirse ávidamente; (coll) asir de repente, apoderarse ávidamente de ‖ *intr* engullir; gluglutear, gorgonear (*el pavo*)

gobbledegook ['gɑbəldɪ,guk] *s* (coll) lenguaje obscuro e incomprensible, galimatías *m*

go'-be·tween' *s* (*intermediary*) medianero; (*in promoting marriages*) casamentero; (*in shady love affairs*) alcahuete *m*, alcahueta

goblet ['gɑblɪt] *s* copa

goblin ['gɑblɪn] *s* duende *m*, trasgo

go'-by' *s* (coll) desaire *m*; **to give someone the go-by** (coll) negarse al trato de alguien

go'cart' *s* andaderas; cochecito para niños; carruaje ligero

god [gɑd] *s* dios *m*; **God forbid** no lo quiera Dios; **God grant** permita Dios; **God willing** Dios mediante

god'child' s (pl **chil'dren**) ahijado, ahijada

god'daugh'ter s ahijada

goddess ['gɑdɪs] s diosa

god'fa'ther s padrino

God'-fear'ing adj timorato; devoto, pío

God'for-sak'en adj dejado de la mano de Dios; (coll) desolado, desierto

god'head' s divinidad || **Godhead** s Dios m

godless ['gɑdlɪs] adj infiel, impío; desalmado, malvado

god·ly ['gɑdlɪ] adj (comp **-lier;** super **-liest**) devoto, pío

god'moth'er s madrina

God's acre s campo santo

god'send' s cosa llovida del cielo, bendición

god'son' s ahijado

God'speed' s bienandanza, buena suerte, buen viaje m

go'-get'ter s (slang) buscavidas mf, persona emprendedora

goggle ['gɑgəl] intr volver los ojos; abrir los ojos desmesuradamente

goggle-eyed ['gɑgəl‚aɪd] adj de ojos saltones

goggles ['gɑgəlz] spl anteojos de camino, gafas contra el polvo

going ['go·ɪŋ] adj en marcha, funcionando; **going on** casi, p.ej., **it is going on nine o'clock** son casi las nueve || s ida, partida

going concern s empresa que marcha

goings on spl actividades; bulla, jarana

goiter ['gɔɪtər] s bocio

gold [gold] adj áureo, de oro; dorado || s oro

gold'beat'er s batidor m de oro, batihoja m

goldbeater's skin s venza

gold brick s — **to sell a gold brick** (coll) vender gato por liebre

gold'crest' s reyezuelo moñudo

gold digger s ['dɪgər] s (slang) extractora de oro

golden ['goldən] adj áureo, de oro; (gilt) dorado; (hair) rubio; excelente, favorable, floreciente

golden age s edad de oro, siglo de oro

golden calf s becerro de oro

Golden Fleece s vellocino de oro

golden mean s justo medio

golden plover s chorlito

gold'en·rod' s vara de oro, vara de San José

golden rule s regla de la caridad cristiana

golden wedding s bodas de oro

gold-filled ['gold‚fɪld] adj empastado en oro

gold'finch' s jilguero, pintacilgo

gold'fish' s carpa dorada, pez m de color

goldilocks ['goldɪ‚lɑks] s rubiales mf

gold leaf s pan m de oro

gold mine s mina de oro; **to strike a gold mine** (fig) encontrar una mina de oro

gold plate s vajilla de oro

gold'-plate' tr dorar

gold'smith' s orfebre m

gold standard s patrón m oro

golf [gɑlf] s golf m || intr jugar al golf

golf club s palo de golf; asociación de jugadores de golf

golfer ['gɑlfər] s golfista mf

golf links spl campo de golf

Golgotha ['gɑlgəθə] s el Gólgota

gondola ['gɑndələ] s góndola

gondolier [‚gɑndə'lɪr] s el gondolero

gone [gɔn] o [gɑn] adj agotado; arruinado; desaparecido; muerto; **gone on** (coll) enamorado de

gong [gɔŋ] o [gɑŋ] s batintín m

gonorrhea [‚gɑnə'ri·ə] s gonorrea

goo [gu] s (slang) substancia pegajosa

good [gud] adj (comp **better;** super **best**) bueno; **good and ...** (coll) muy, p.ej., **good and cheap** muy barato; **good for** bueno para; capaz de hacer; capaz de pagar; capaz de vivir (cierto tiempo); **to be good at** tener talento para; **to be no good** (coll) no servir para nada; (coll) ser un perdido; **to make good** tener éxito; cumplir (sus promesas); pagar (una deuda); responder de (los daños) || s bien m, provecho, utilidad; **for good** para siempre; **for good and all** de una vez para siempre; **goods** efectos; géneros, mercancías; **the good** lo bueno; los buenos; **to catch with the goods** (slang) coger en flagrante; **to deliver the goods** (slang) cumplir lo prometido; **to do good** hacer el bien; dar salud o fuerzas a; **to the good** de sobra, en el haber; **what is the good of ...?** ¿para qué sirve ...?

good afternoon s buenas tardes

good'-by' o **good'-bye'** s adiós m || interj ¡adiós!

good day s buenos días

good evening s buenas noches, buenas tardes

good fellow s (coll) buen chico, buen sujeto

good fellowship s compañerismo

good'-for-noth'ing adj inútil, sin valor || s pelafustán m, perdido

Good Friday s Viernes santo

good graces spl favor m, estimación

good-hearted ['gud'hɑrtɪd] adj de buen corazón

good-humored ['gud'hjumərd] o ['gud'jumərd] adj de buen humor; afable

good-looking ['gud'lukɪŋ] adj guapo, bien parecido

good looks spl hermosura, guapeza

good·ly ['gudlɪ] adj (comp **-lier;** super **-liest**) considerable; bien parecido, hermoso; bueno; excelente

good morning s buenos días

good-natured ['gud'netʃərd] adj bonachón, afable

Good Neighbor Policy s política del buen vecino

goodness ['gudnɪs] s bondad; **for goodness' sake!** ¡por Dios!; **goodness knows!** ¡quién sabe! || interj ¡válgame Dios!

good night s buenas noches

good sense s buen sentido, sensatez f

gl
go

good-sized ['gud'saɪzd] *adj* bastante grande, de buen tamaño

good speed *s* adiós *m* y buena suerte

good-tempered ['gud'tempərd] *adj* de natural apacible

good time *s* rato agradable; **to have a good time** divertirse; **to make good time** ir a buen paso; llegar en poco tiempo

good turn *s* favor *m*, servicio

good way *s* buen trecho

good will *s* buena voluntad; (com) buen nombre *m*, clientela

good·y ['gudi] *adj* (coll) beatuco, santurrón ǁ *s* (*pl* -ies) (coll) golosina ǁ *interj* (coll) ¡qué bien!, ¡qué alegría!

gooey ['gu·i] *adj* (*comp* **gooier**; *super* **gooiest**) (slang) pegajoso, fangoso

goof [guf] *s* (slang) tonto ǁ *tr* & *intr* (slang) chapucear

goof·y ['gufi] *adj* (*comp* -ier; *super* -iest) (slang) tonto, mentecato

goon [gun] *s* (*roughneck*) (coll) gamberro, canalla *m*; (coll) terrorista *m* de alquiler; (slang) estúpido

goose [gus] *s* (*pl* geese [gis]) *s* ánsar *m*, ganso, oca; **the goose hangs high** todo va a pedir de boca; **to cook one's goose** malbaratarle a uno los planes; **to kill the goose that lays the golden eggs** matar la gallina de los huevos de oro ǁ *s* (*pl* gooses) plancha de sastre

goose·ber'ry *s* (*pl* -ries) (*plant*) grosellero silvestre; (*fruit*) grosella silvestre

goose egg *s* huevo de oca; (slang) cero

goose flesh *s* carne *f* de gallina

goose'neck' *s* cuello de cisne; (naut) gancho de botalones

goose pimples *spl* carne *f* de gallina

goose step *s* (mil) paso de ganso

G.O.P. *abbr* Grand Old Party

gopher ['gofər] *s* ardilla de tierra, ardillón *m*; (*Geomys*) tuza

Gordian knot ['gɔrdɪ·ən] *s* nudo gordiano; **to cut the Gordian knot** cortar el nudo gordiano

gore [gor] *s* sangre derramada, sangre cuajada; (*insert in a piece of cloth*) cuchillo, nesga ǁ *tr* (*to pierce with a horn*) acornar; poner cuchillo o nesga a; nesgar

gorge [gɔrdʒ] *s* garganta, desfiladero; (*in a river*) atasco de hielo ǁ *tr* atiborrar ǁ *intr* atiborrarse

gorgeous ['gɔrdʒəs] *adj* primoroso, brillante, magnífico, suntuoso

gorilla [gə'rɪlə] *s* gorila

gorse [gɔrs] *s* aulaga

gor·y ['gori] *adj* (*comp* -ier; *super* -iest) ensangrentado, sangriento

gosh [gɑʃ] *interj* ¡caramba!

goshawk ['gɑs,hɔk] *s* azor *m*

gospel ['gɑspəl] *s* evangelio ǁ **Gospel** *s* Evangelio

gospel truth *s* evangelio, pura verdad

gossamer ['gɑsəmər] *s* telaraña flotante; gasa sutilísima; tela impermeable muy delgada; impermeable *m* de tela muy delgada

gossip ['gɑsɪp] *s* chismes *m*; (*person*)

chismoso; **piece of gossip** chisme *m* ǁ *intr* chismear

gossip column *s* mentidero

gossip columnist *s* gacetillero, cronista *mf* social

gossipy ['gɑsɪpi] *adj* chismoso

Goth [gɑθ] *s* godo; (fig) bárbaro

Gothic ['gɑθɪk] *adj* & *s* gótico

gouge [gaudʒ] *s* gubia; (*cut made with a gouge*) muesca; (coll) estafa ǁ *tr* excavar con gubia; (coll) estafar

goulash ['gulɑʃ] *s* puchero húngaro

gourd [gord] o [gurd] *s* calabaza

gourmand ['gurmənd] *s* gastrónomo; glotón *m*, goloso

gourmet ['gurme] *s* gastrónomo delicado

gout [gaut] *s* gota

gout·y ['gauti] *adj* (*comp* -ier; *super* -iest) gotoso

gov. *abbr* governor, government

govern ['gʌvərn] *tr* gobernar; (gram) regir ǁ *intr* gobernar

governess ['gʌvərnɪs] *s* aya, institutriz *f*

government ['gʌvərnmənt] *s* gobierno; (gram) régimen *m*

governmental [,gʌvərn'mentəl] *adj* gubernamental, gubernativo

government in exile *s* gobierno exilado

governor ['gʌvərnər] *s* gobernador *m*; (*of a jail, castle, etc.*) alcaide *m*; (mach) regulador *m*

governorship ['gʌvərnər,ʃɪp] *s* gobierno

govt. *abbr* government

gown [gaun] *s* (*of a woman*) vestido; (*of a professor, judge, etc.*) toga; (*of a priest*) traje *m* talar; (*dressing gown*) bata, peinador *m*; (*nightgown*) camisa de dormir

G.P.O. *abbr* General Post Office, Government Printing Office

gr. *abbr* gram, grams, grain, grains, gross

grab [græb] *s* asimiento, presa; (coll) robo ǁ *v* (*pret* & *pp* grabbed; *ger* grabbing) *tr* asir, agarrar; arrebatar ǁ *intr* — **to grab at** tratar de asir

grace [gres] *s* (*charm; favor; pardon*) gracia; (*prayer at table*) benedícite *m*; (*extension of time*) demora; **to be in the good graces of** gozar del favor de; **to say grace** rezar el benedícite; **with good grace** de buen talante ǁ *tr* adornar, engalanar; favorecer

graceful ['gresfəl] *adj* agraciado, gracioso

grace note *s* apoyatura, nota de adorno

gracious ['greʃəs] *adj* graciable, gracioso; misericordioso ǁ *interj* ¡válgame Dios!

grackle ['grækəl] *s* (*myna*) estornino de los pastores; (*purple grackle*) quiscal *m*

grad. *abbr* graduate

gradation [gre'deʃən] *s* (*gradual change*) paso gradual; (*arrangement in grades*) graduación; (*step in a series*) paso, grado

grade [gred] *s* grado; (*slope*) pendiente *f*; (*mark for work in class*) calificación, nota; **to make the grade**

lograr subir la cuesta; vencer los
obstáculos || *tr* graduar, calificar;
dar nota a (*un alumno*); explanar,
nivelar
grade crossing *s* (rr) paso a nivel,
cruce *m* a nivel
grade school *s* escuela elemental
gradient ['gredɪ·ənt] *adj* pendiente || *s*
pendiente *f*; (phys) gradiente *m*
gradual ['grædʒu·əl] *adj* paulatino
gradually ['grædʒu·əli] *adv* paulatinamente, gradualmente, poco a poco
graduate ['grædʒu·ɪt] *adj* graduado ||
s graduado; (*candidate for a degree*)
graduando; vasija graduada ||
['grædʒu·ˌet] *tr* graduar || *intr* gra-
duarse
graduate school *s* facultad de altos
estudios
graduate student *s* estudiante graduado
graduate work *s* altos estudios
graduation [ˌgrædʒu·'eʃən] *s* graduación; ceremonia de graduación
graft [græft] o [grɑft] *s* (hort & surg)
injerto; (coll) soborno político, ga-
nancia ilegal || *tr* & *intr* (hort &
surg) injertar; (coll) malversar
graham bread ['gre·əm] *s* pan *m* integral
graham flour *s* harina de trigo sin
cerner
grain [gren] *s* (*small seed; tiny particle of sand, etc.; small unit of
weight*) grano; (*cereal seeds*) granos;
(*in stone*) vena; (*in wood*) fibra;
against the grain a contrapelo || *tr*
granear (*la pólvora; una piedra litográfica*); crispir, vetear (*la madera*);
granular (*una piel*)
grain elevator *s* elevador *m* de granos;
(*tall building where grain is stored*)
depósito de cereales
grain'field' *s* sembrado
graining ['grenɪŋ] *s* veteado
gram [græm] *s* gramo
grammar ['græmər] *s* gramática
grammarian [grə'merɪ·ən] *s* gramático
grammar school *s* escuela pública elemental
grammatical [grə'mætɪkəl] *adj* gramático
gramophone ['græmə·ˌfon] *s* (trademark) gramófono
grana·ry ['grænəri] *s* (*pl* **-ries**) granero
grand [grænd] *adj* espléndido, grandioso; importante, principal
grand'aunt' *s* tía abuela
grand'child' *s* (*pl* **-chil'dren**) nieto,
nieta
grand'daugh'ter *s* nieta
grand duchess *s* gran duquesa
grand duchy *s* gran ducado
grand duke *s* gran duque *m*
grandee [græn'di] *s* grande *m* de
España
grandeur ['grændʒər] o ['grændʒʊr] *s*
grandeza, magnificencia
grand'fa'ther *s* abuelo; (*forefather*)
antepasado
grandfather's clock *s* reloj *m* de caja
grandiose ['grændɪ·ˌos] *adj* grandioso;
hinchado, pomposo
grand jury *s* jurado de acusación

grand larceny *s* hurto mayor
grand lodge *s* gran oriente *m*
grandma ['grænd·ˌmɑ], ['græm·ˌmɑ] o
['græmə] *s* (coll) abuela, abuelita
grand'moth'er *s* abuela
grand'neph'ew *s* resobrino
grand'niece *s* resobrina
grand opera *s* ópera seria
grandpa ['grænd·ˌpɑ], ['græn·ˌpɑ] o
['græmpə] *s* (coll) abuelo, abuelito
grand'par'ent *s* abuelo, abuela
grand piano *s* piano de cola
grand slam *s* bola
grand'son' *s* nieto
grand'stand' *s* gradería cubierta, tribuna
grand strategy *s* alta estrategia
grand total *s* gran total *m*, suma de
totales
grand'un'cle *s* tío abuelo
grand vizier *s* gran visir *m*
grange [grendʒ] *s* (*farm with barns,
etc.*) granja; (*organization of farmers*) cámara agrícola
granite ['grænɪt] *s* granito
grant [grænt] o [grɑnt] *s* concesión;
donación, otorgamiento; traspaso de
propiedad || *tr* conceder; dar (*per-
miso, perdón*); transferir (*bienes
inmuebles*); **to take for granted** dar
por sentado; tratar con indiferencia
grantee [græn'ti] o [grɑn'ti] *s* cesio-
nario
grant'-in-aid' *s* (*pl* **grants-in-aid**) subvención concedida por el gobierno
para obras de utilidad pública; pensión para estimular conocimientos
científicos, literarios, artísticos
grantor [græn'tor] o [grɑn'tor] *s* cesio-
nista *mf*, otorgante *mf*
granular ['grænjələr] *adj* granular
granulate ['grænjə·ˌlet] *tr* granular ||
intr granularse
granule ['grænjul] *s* gránulo
grape [grep] *s* (*fruit*) uva; (*vine*) vid *f*
grape arbor *s* parral *m*
grape'fruit' *s* (*fruit*) toronja; (*tree*)
toronjo
grape hyacinth *s* sueldacostilla
grape juice *s* zumo de uva
grape'shot' *s* metralla
grape'vine' *s* vid *f*, parra; **by the
grapevine** por vías secretas, por vías
misteriosas
graph [græf] o [grɑf] *s* (*diagram*)
gráfica; (gram) grafía
graphic(al) ['græfɪk(əl)] *adj* gráfico
graphite ['græfaɪt] *s* grafito
graph paper *s* papel *m* cuadriculado
grapnel ['græpnəl] *s* rebañadera; (*anchor*) rezón *m*
grapple ['græpəl] *s* asimiento, presa;
lucha cuerpo a cuerpo || *tr* asir, aga-
rrar || *intr* agarrarse; luchar a brazo
partido; **to grapple with** luchar a
brazo partido con; tratar de resolver
grappling iron *s* arpeo
grasp [græsp] o [grɑsp] *s* asimiento;
(*power, reach*) poder *m*, alcance *m*;
(fig) comprensión; **to have a good
grasp of** saber a fondo; **within the
grasp of** al alcance de || *tr* (*with
hand*) empuñar; (*to get control of*)

apoderarse de; (fig) comprender ‖
intr — **to grasp at** tratar de asir;
aceptar con avidez

grasping ['græspɪŋ] o ['grɑspɪŋ] *adj*
avaro, codicioso

grass [græs] o [grɑs] *s* hierba; (*pasture land*) pasto; (*lawn*) césped *m;*
to go to grass ir a pacer; disfrutar de
una temporada de descanso; gas-
tarse, arruinarse; morir; **to not let
the grass grow under one's feet** no
dormirse en las pajas

grass court *s* cancha de césped

grass'hop'per *s* saltamontes *m*

grass pea *s* almorta, guija

grass'-roots' *adj* (coll) de la gente
común

grass seed *s* semilla de césped

grass widow *s* viuda de paja, viuda de
marido vivo

grass·y ['græsi] o ['grɑsi] *adj* (*comp
-ier; super -iest*) herboso

grate [gret] *s* (*at a window*) reja; (*for
cooking*) parrilla ‖ *tr* (*to put a grate
on*) enrejar; rallar (*p.ej., queso*) ‖
intr crujir, rechinar; **to grate on** (fig)
rallar

grateful ['gretfəl] *adj* agradecido;
(*pleasing*) agradable

grater ['gretər] *s* rallador *m*

grati·fy ['grætɪ,faɪ] *v* (*pret & pp -fied*)
tr complacer, gratificar

gratifying ['grætɪ,faɪ·ɪŋ] *adj* grato,
satisfactorio

grating ['gretɪŋ] *adj* áspero, irritante;
(*sound*) chirriante ‖ *s* enrejado

gratis ['gretɪs] o ['grætɪs] *adj* gracioso, gratuito ‖ *adv* gratis, de balde

gratitude ['grætɪ,tjud] o ['grætɪ,tud]
s gratitud, reconocimiento

gratuitous [grə'tju·ɪtəs] o [grə'tu·ɪtəs]
adj gratuito

gratui·ty [grə'tju·ɪti] o [grə'tu·ɪti] *s*
(*pl* -ties) propina

grave [grev] *adj* (*serious, dangerous,
important*) grave; solemne; (*sound,
accent*) grave ‖ *s* sepulcro, sepultura;
to have one foot in the grave estar
con un pie en la sepultura

gravedigger ['grev,dɪgər] *s* enterrador
m, sepulturero

gravel ['grævəl] *s* grava, cascajo

graven image ['grevən] *s* ídolo

grave'stone' *s* lápida sepulcral

grave'yard' *s* camposanto

gravitate ['grævɪ,tet] *intr* gravitar;
ser atraído

gravitation [,grævɪ'teʃən] *s* gravitación

gravi·ty ['grævɪti] *s* (*pl* -ties) gravedad

gravure [grə'vjʊr] o ['grevjʊr] *s* fotograbado

gra·vy ['grevi] *s* (*pl* -vies) (*juice from
cooking meat*) jugo; (*sauce made
with this juice*) salsa; (slang) ganga,
breva

gravy dish *s* salsera

gray [gre] *adj* gris; (*gray-haired*) cano,
canoso ‖ *s* gris *m;* traje *m* gris ‖ *intr*
encanecer

gray'beard' *s* anciano, viejo

gray-haired ['gre,herd] *adj* canoso

gray'hound' *s* galgo

grayish ['gre·ɪʃ] *adj* grisáceo; (*person; hair*) entrecano

gray matter *s* substancia gris; (*intelligence*) (coll) materia gris

graze [grez] *tr* (*to touch lightly*) rozar;
(*to scratch lightly in passing*) raspar; pacer (*la hierba*); apacentar (*el
ganado*); (*to lead to the pasture*)
pastar ‖ *intr* pacer, pastar

grease [gris] *s* grasa ‖ [gris] o [griz]
tr engrasar; (slang) sobornar

grease cup [gris] *s* vaso de engrase

grease gun [gris] *s* engrasador *m* de
pistón, jeringa de engrase

grease lift [gris] *s* puente *m* de engrase

grease paint [gris] *s* maquillaje *m*

grease pit [gris] *s* fosa de engrase

grease spot [gris] *s* lámpara, mancha
de grasa

greas·y ['grisi] o ['grizi] *adj* (*comp
-ier; super -iest*) grasiento, pringoso

great [gret] *adj* grande; (coll) excelente ‖ **the great** los grandes

great'-aunt' *s* tía abuela

Great Bear *s* Osa Mayor

Great Britain ['brɪtən] *s* la Gran Bretaña

great'coat' *s* gabán *m* de mucho abrigo

Great Dane *s* mastín *m* danés

Greater London *s* el Gran Londres

Greater New York *s* el Gran Nueva
York

great'-grand'child' *s* (*pl* -chil'dren)
bisnieto, bisnieta

great'-grand'daugh'ter *s* bisnieta

great'-grand'fa'ther *s* bisabuelo

great'-grand'moth'er *s* bisabuela

great'-grand'par'ent *s* bisabuelo, bisabuela

great'-grand'son' *s* bisnieto

greatly ['gretli] *adj* grandemente

great'-neph'ew *s* resobrino

greatness ['gretnɪs] *s* grandeza

great'-niece' *s* resobrina

great'-un'cle *s* tío abuelo

Great War *s* Gran guerra

Grecian ['griʃən] *adj & s* griego

Greece [gris] *s* Grecia

greed [grid] *s* codicia, avaricia; (*in
eating and drinking*) glotonería

greed·y ['gridi] *adj* (*comp -ier; super
-iest*) codicioso, avaro; glotón

Greek [grik] *adj & s* griego

green [grin] *adj* verde; inexperto ‖ *s*
verde *m;* (*lawn*) césped *m;* **greens**
verduras

green'back' *s* (U.S.A.) billete *m* de
banco (*de dorso verde*)

green corn *s* maíz tierno

green earth *s* verdacho

greener·y ['grinəri] *s* (*pl* -ies) (*foliage*)
verdura; (*hothouse*) invernáculo

green-eyed ['grin,aɪd] *adj* de ojos
verdes; celoso

green'gage' *s* ciruela claudia

green grasshopper *s* langostón *m*

green'gro'cer *s* verdulero

green'gro'cer·y *s* (*pl* -ies) verdulería

green'horn' *s* novato; (*dupe*) primo,
inocentón *m;* (coll) papanatas *m,*
isidro

green'house' *s* invernáculo

greenish ['grinɪʃ] adj verdoso

Greenland ['grinlənd] s Groenlandia

greenness ['grinnɪs] s verdura, verdor m; falta de experiencia

green'room' s saloncillo; chismería de teatro

greensward ['grin,swɔrd] s césped m

green thumb s pulgares mpl verdes (don de criar plantas)

green vegetables spl verduras

green'wood' s bosque m verde, bosque frondoso

greet [grit] tr saludar; acoger, recibir; presentarse a (los ojos u los oídos de uno)

greeting ['gritɪŋ] s saludo; acogida, recibimiento || greetings interj ¡salud!

greeting card s tarjeta de buen deseo

gregarious [grɪ'gɛrɪ·əs] adj (living in the midst of others) gregario; (fond of the company of others) sociable

Gregorian [grɪ'gori·ən] adj gregoriano

grenade [grɪ'ned] s granada; (to put out fires) granada extintora

grenadier [,grɛnə'dɪr] s granadero

grenadine [,grɛnə'din] s granadina

grey [gre] adj, s & intr var de gray

grid [grɪd] s parrilla, rejilla; (electron) rejilla; (of a storage battery) (elec) rejilla

griddle ['grɪdəl] s plancha

grid'dle·cake' s tortada (de harina) a la plancha

grid'i'ron s parrilla; campo de fútbol

grid leak s (electron) resistencia de rejilla, escape m de rejilla

grief [grif] s aflicción, pesar m; (coll) desgracia, disgusto; to come to grief fracasar, arruinarse

grievance ['grivəns] s agravio, injusticia; despecho, disgusto; motivo de queja

grieve [griv] tr afligir, penar || intr afligirse, apenarse; to grieve over añorar

grievous ['grivəs] adj doloroso, penoso; atroz, cruel; (deplorable) lastimoso

griffin ['grɪfɪn] s (myth) grifo

grill [grɪl] s parrilla || tr emparrillar; someter (a un acusado) a un interrogatorio muy apremiante

grille [grɪl] s reja, verja; (of an automobile) parrilla, rejilla

grill'room' s parrilla

grim [grɪm] adj (comp grimmer; super grimmest) (fierce) cruel, feroz; (repellent) horrible, siniestro; (unyielding) formidable, implacable; (stern-looking) ceñudo

grimace ['grɪməs] o [grɪ'mes] s mueca, gesto || intr hacer muecas, gestear

grime [graɪm] s mugre f; (soot) tizne m & f

grim·y ['graɪmi] adj (comp -ier; super -iest) mugriento; tiznado

grin [grɪn] s sonrisa bonachona; mueca (mostrando los dientes) || v (pret & pp grinned; ger grinning) intr sonreírse bonachonamente; hacer una mueca (mostrando los dientes)

grind [graɪnd] s molienda; (long hard work or study) (coll) zurra; (student) (coll) empollón m || v (pret & pp ground [graund]) tr moler; (to sharpen) afilar, amolar, tallar (lentes); pulverizar; picar (carne); rodar (las válvulas de un motor); dar vueltas a (un manubrio) || intr hacer molienda; molerse; rechinar; (coll) echar los bofes

grinder ['graɪndər] s (to sharpen tools) muela, esmoladera; (to grind coffee, pepper, etc.) molinillo; (back tooth) muela

grind'stone' s esmoladera, piedra de amolar; to keep one's nose to the grindstone trabajar con ahinco

grin·go ['grɪŋgo] s (pl -gos) (disparaging) gringo

grip [grɪp] s (grasp) asimiento; (with hand) apretón m; (handle) asidero; saco de mano; to come to grips (with) luchar cuerpo a cuerpo (con); arrostrarse (con) || v (pret & pp gripped; ger gripping) tr asir, agarrar; tener asido; absorber (la atención); absorber la atención a (una persona)

gripe [graɪp] s (coll) queja; gripes retortijón m de tripas || intr (coll) quejarse, refunfuñar

grippe [grɪp] s gripe f

gripping ['grɪpɪŋ] adj conmovedor, impresionante

gris·ly ['grɪzli] adj (comp -lier; super -liest) espantoso, espeluznante

grist [grɪst] s (batch of grain for one grinding) molienda; (grain that has been ground) harina; (coll) acopio, acervo; to be grist to one's mill (coll) serle a uno de mucho provecho

gristle ['grɪsəl] s cartílago, ternilla

gris·tly ['grɪsli] adj (comp -tlier; super -tliest) cartilaginoso, ternilloso

grist'mill' s molino harinero

grit [grɪt] s arena, guijo fino; (fig) ánimo, valentía; grits farro, sémola || v (pret & pp gritted; ger gritting) tr hacer rechinar (los dientes); cerrar fuertemente (los dientes)

grit·ty ['grɪti] adj (comp -tier; super -tiest) arenoso; (fig) valiente, resuelto

griz·zly ['grɪzli] adj (comp -zlier; super -zliest) grisáceo; canoso || s (pl -zlies) oso gris

grizzly bear s oso gris

groan [gron] s gemido, quejido || intr gemir, quejarse; estar muy cargado, crujir por exceso de peso

grocer ['grosər] s abacero, tendero de ultramarinos

grocer·y ['grosəri] s (pl -ies) abacería, tienda de ultramarinos, colmado; groceries víveres mpl, ultramarinos

grocery store s abacería, tienda de ultramarinos, colmado

grog [grɑg] s grog m

grog·gy ['grɑgi] adj (comp -gier; super -giest) (coll) inseguro, vacilante;

gr
gr

(shaky, e.g., from a blow) (coll) atontado; (coll) borracho

groin [grɔɪn] s (anat) ingle f; (archit) arista de encuentro

groom [grum] s (bridegroom) novio; mozo de caballos || tr asear, acicalar; almohazar (caballos); enseñar (a un político) para presentarse como candidato

grooms·man ['grumzmən] s (pl -men [mən]) padrino de boda

groove [gruv] s ranura; (of a pulley) garganta; (of a phonograph record) surco; (mark left by a wheel) rodada; (coll) rutina, hábito arraigado || tr ranurar, acanalar

grope [grop] intr andar a tientas; (for words) pujar; **to grope for** buscar a tientas, buscar tentando; **to grope through** palpar (p.ej., la obscuridad)

gropingly ['gropɪŋlɪ] adv a tientas

grosbeak ['gros,bik] s pico duro

gross [gros] adj (dense, thick) denso, espeso; (coarse; vulgar) grosero; (fat, burly) grueso; (with no deductions) bruto || s conjunto, totalidad; (twelve dozen) gruesa; **in gross** en grueso || tr obtener un ingreso bruto de

grossly ['groslɪ] adv aproximadamente

gross national product s renta nacional

grotesque [gro'tɛsk] adj (ridiculous, extravagant) grotesco; (f.a.) grutesco || s (f.a.) grutesco

grot·to ['grɑto] s (pl -toes o -tos) gruta

grouch [graʊtʃ] s (coll) mal humor m; (person) (coll) cascarrabias mf, vinagre m || intr (coll) refunfuñar

grouch·y ['graʊtʃɪ] adj (comp -ier; super -iest) (coll) gruñón, malhumorado

ground [graʊnd] s (earth, soil, land) tierra; (piece of land) terreno; (basis, foundation) causa, fundamento, motivo, razón f; (elec) tierra; (body of automobile corresponding to ground) (elec) masa; (elec) borne m de tierra; **ground for complaint** motivo de queja; **grounds** terreno; jardines mpl; causa, fundamento; (of coffee) posos; **on the ground of** con motivo de; **to break ground** empezar la excavación; **to fall to the ground** fracasar, abandonarse; **to gain ground** ganar terreno; **to give ground** ceder terreno; **to lose ground** perder terreno; **to stand one's ground** mantenerse firme; **to yield ground** ceder terreno || tr establecer, fundar; (elec) poner a tierra; **to be grounded** estar sin volar (un avión); **to be well grounded** ser muy versado || intr (naut) encallar, varar

ground connection s (rad) toma de tierra

ground crew s (aer) personal m de tierra

grounder ['graʊndər] s (baseball) pelota rodada

ground floor s piso bajo

ground glass s vidrio deslustrado

ground hog s marmota de América

ground lead [lid] s (elec) conductor m a tierra

groundless ['graʊndlɪs] adj infundado

ground plan s primer proyecto; (of a building) planta

ground speed s (aer) velocidad con respecto al suelo

ground swell s marejada de fondo

ground troops spl (mil) tropas terrestres

ground wire s (rad) alambre m de tierra; (aut) hilo de masa

ground'work' s infraestructura

group [grup] adj grupal; colectivo || s grupo || tr agrupar || intr agruparse

grouse [graʊs] s perdiz blanca, bonasa americana, gallo de bosque; (slang) refunfuño || intr (slang) refunfuñar

grout [graʊt] s lechada || tr enlechar

grove [grov] s arboleda, bosquecillo

grov·el ['grʌvəl] o ['grɑvəl] v (pret & pp -eled o -elled; ger -eling o -elling) intr arrastrarse servilmente; rebajarse servilmente; deleitarse en vilezas

grow [gro] v (pret **grew** [gru]; pp **grown** [gron]) tr cultivar (plantas); criar (animales); dejarse (la barba) || intr crecer; cultivarse; criarse; brotar, nacer; (to become) hacerse, ponerse, volverse; **to grow angry** enfadarse; **to grow old** envejecerse; **to grow out of** tener su origen en; perder (p.ej., la costumbre); **to grow together** adherirse el uno al otro; **to grow up** crecer, desarrollar

growing child ['gro·ɪŋ] s muchacho de creces

growl [graʊl] s gruñido; refunfuño || intr gruñir (el perro); refunfuñar

grown'-up' adj adulto; juicioso || s (pl **grown-ups**) adulto; **grown-ups** personas mayores

growth [groθ] s crecimiento; desarrollo; aumento; (of trees, grass, etc.) cobertura; (pathol) tumor m

growth stock s acción crecedera

grub [grʌb] s (drudge) esclavo del trabajo; (larva) gorgojo; (coll) comida, alimento || v (pret & pp **grubbed**; ger **grubbing**) tr arrancar (tocones); desmalezar (un terreno) || intr cavar; trabajar como esclavo

grub·by ['grʌbɪ] adj (comp -bier; super -biest) gorgojoso; sucio, roñoso

grudge [grʌdʒ] s rencor m, inquina; **to have a grudge against** guardar rencor a, tener inquina a || tr dar de mala gana; envidiar

grudgingly ['grʌdʒɪŋlɪ] adv de mala gana

gru·el ['gru·əl] s avenate m || v (pret & pp -eled o -elled; ger -eling o -elling) tr agotar, castigar cruelmente

gruesome ['grusəm] adj espantoso, horripilante

gruff [grʌf] adj áspero, brusco, rudo; (voice, tone) ronco

grumble ['grʌmbəl] s gruñido, refunfuño; ruido sordo y prolongado || intr gruñir, refunfuñar; retumbar grump·y ['grʌmpi] adj (comp -ier; super -iest) gruñón, malhumorado

grunt [grʌnt] s gruñido || intr gruñir

G-string ['dʒiˌstrɪŋ] s (loincloth) taparrabo; (worn by women entertainers) cubresexo

gt. abbr great; gutta (Lat) drop

g.u. abbr genitourinary

Guadeloupe [ˌgwædəˈlup] s Guadalupe f

guarantee [ˌgærənˈti] s garantía; (guarantor) garante mf; persona de quien otra sale fiadora || tr garantizar

guarantor ['gærənˌtor] s garante mf

guaran·ty ['gærənti] s (pl -ties) garantía || v (pret & pp -tied) tr garantizar

guard [gard] s (act of guarding; part of handle of sword) guarda; (person who guards or takes care of something) guarda mf; (group of armed men; posture in fencing) guardia; (member of group of armed men) guardia m; (in front of trolley car) salvavidas m; (sport) coraza; (rr) guardabarrera mf; (rr) guardafrenos m; off guard desprevenido; on guard alerta, prevenido; de centinela; to mount guard montar la guardia; under guard a buen recaudo || tr guardar || intr estar de centinela; to guard against guardarse de, precaverse contra o de

guard'house' s cuartel m de la guardia; prisión militar

guardian ['gardɪ-ən] adj tutelar || s guardián m; (law) curador m, tutor m

guardian angel s ángel m custodio, ángel de la guarda

guardianship ['gardɪ-ənˌʃɪp] s amparo, protección; (law) curaduría, tutela

guard'rail' s baranda; (naut) barandilla; (rr) contracarril m

guard'room' s cuarto de guardia; cárcel f militar

guards·man ['gardzmən] s (pl -men [mən]) guardia m, soldado de guardia

Guatemalan [ˌgwatɪˈmalən] adj & s guatemalteco

guerrilla [gəˈrɪlə] s guerrillero

guerrilla warfare s guerra de guerrillas

guess [ges] s conjetura, suposición; adivinación || tr & intr conjeturar, suponer; (to judge correctly) acertar, adivinar; (coll) creer, suponer; I guess so (coll) creo que sí, me parece que sí

guess'work' s conjetura; by guesswork por conjeturas

guest [gest] s convidado; (lodger) huésped m; (of a boarding house) pensionista mf; (of a hotel) cliente mf; (caller) visita

guest book s libro de oro

guest room s cuarto de reserva

guffaw [gəˈfɔ] s risotada, carcajada || intr risotear, reír a carcajadas

Guiana [gɪˈɑnə] o [gɪˈænə] s Guayana

guidance ['gaɪdəns] s guía, gobierno;

dirección; for your guidance para su gobierno

guide [gaɪd] s (person) guía mf; (book) guía; (guidance) guía; dirección; poste m indicador; (mach) guía, guiadera; (mil) guía m || tr guiar

guide'board' s señal f de carretera

guide'book' s guía m, guía del viajero

guided missile ['gaɪdɪd] s proyectil dirigido o teleguiado

guide dog s perro-lazarillo

guide'line' s cuerda de guía; norma, pauta, directorio

guide'post' s poste m indicador

guidon ['gaɪdən] s (mil) guión m; (mil) portaguión m

guild [gɪld] s (medieval association of craftsmen) gremio; asociación benéfica

guild'hall' s casa consistorial

guile [gaɪl] s astucia, dolo, maña

guileful ['gaɪlfəl] adj astuto, doloso, mañoso

guileless ['gaɪllɪs] adj cándido, inocente, sencillo

guillotine ['gɪləˌtin] s guillotina || [ˌgɪləˈtin] tr guillotinar

guilt [gɪlt] s culpa

guiltless ['gɪltlɪs] adj inocente, libre de culpa

guilt·y ['gɪlti] adj (comp -ier; super -iest) culpable; (charged with guilt) culpado; (found guilty) reo

guimpe [gɪmp] o [gæmp] s canesú m

guinea ['gɪni] s (monetary unit) guinea; gallina de Guinea

guinea fowl s pintada, gallina de Guinea

guinea hen s pintada, gallina de Guinea (hembra)

guinea pig s conejillo de Indias

guise [gaɪz] s traje m; aspecto, semejanza; under the guise of so capa de

guitar [gɪˈtar] s guitarra

guitarist [gɪˈtarɪst] s guitarrista mf

gulch [gʌltʃ] s barranco, quebrada

gulf [gʌlf] s golfo

Gulf of Mexico s golfo de Méjico

Gulf Stream s Corriente f del Golfo

gull [gʌl] s gaviota; (coll) bobo || tr estafar, engañar

gullet ['gʌlɪt] s gaznate m, garguero; esófago

gullible ['gʌlɪbəl] adj crédulo; to be too gullible tener buenas tragaderas

gul·ly ['gʌli] s (pl -lies) barranca, arroyada; (channel made by rain water) badén m

gulp [gʌlp] s trago || tr — to gulp down engullir; reprimir (p.ej., sollozos) || intr respirar entrecortadamente

gum [gʌm] s goma; chanclo de goma; (firm flesh around base of teeth) encía; (mucous on edge of eyelid) legaña || v (pret & pp gummed; ger gumming) tr engomar || intr exudar goma

gum arabic s goma arábiga

gum'boil' s flemón m

gum boot s bota de agua

gum'drop' s frutilla

gum·my ['gʌmi] adj (comp -mier; super -miest) gomoso; (eyelid) legañoso

gumption ['gʌmpʃən] s (coll) ánimo, iniciativa, empuje m, fuerza; (coll) juicio, seso

gum'shoe' s chanclo de goma; (coll) detective m || v (pret & pp -shoed; ger -shoeing) intr (slang) andar con zapatos de fieltro

gun [gʌn] s escopeta, fusil m; cañón m; (for injections) jeringa; (coll) revólver m; **to stick to one's guns** mantenerse en sus trece || v (pret & pp gunned; ger gunning) tr hacer fuego sobre; (slang) acelerar rápidamente (un motor, un avión) || intr andar a caza; disparar; **to gun for** ir en busca de; buscar para matar

gun'boat' s cañonero

gun carriage s cureña, encabalgamiento

gun'cot'ton s fulmicotón m, algodón m pólvora

gun'fire' s fuego (de armas de fuego); cañoneo

gun·man ['gʌnmən] s (pl -men [mən]) bandido armado, pistolero

gun metal s bronce m de cañón; metal pavonado

gunnel ['gʌnəl] s (naut) borda, regala

gunner ['gʌnər] s artillero; cazador m

gunnery ['gʌnəri] s artillería

gunny sack ['gʌni] s saco de yute

gun'pow'der s pólvora

gun'run'ner s contrabandista m de armas de fuego

gun'run'ning s contrabando de armas de fuego

gun'shot' s escopetazo, tiro de fusil; alcance m de un fusil; **within gunshot** a tiro de fusil

gunshot wound s escopetazo

gun'smith' s armero

gun'stock' s caja de fusil

gunwale ['gʌnəl] s (naut) borda, regala

gup·py ['gʌpi] s (pl -pies) lebistes m

gurgle ['gʌrgəl] s gorgoteo, gluglú m; (of a child) gorjeo || intr gorgotear, hacer gluglú; gorjearse (el niño)

gush [gʌʃ] s borbollón m, chorro || intr surgir, salir a borbollones; (coll) hacer extremos, ser extremoso

gusher ['gʌʃər] s pozo de chorro de petróleo; (coll) persona extremosa

gushing ['gʌʃɪŋ] adj surgente; (coll) extremoso || s borbollón m, chorro; (coll) efusión, extremos

gush·y ['gʌʃi] adj (comp -ier; super -iest) (coll) efusivo, extremoso

gusset ['gʌsɪt] s escudete m

gust [gʌst] s (of wind) ráfaga; (of rain) aguacero; (of smoke) bocanada; (of noise) explosión; (of anger or enthusiasm) arrebato

gusto ['gʌsto] s deleite m, entusiasmo; **with gusto** con sumo placer

gust·y ['gʌsti] adj (comp -ier; super -iest) tempestuoso, borrascoso

gut [gʌt] s tripa; cuerda de tripa; **guts** tripas; (slang) agallas || v (pret & pp gutted; ger gutting) tr destripar; destruir lo interior de

gutta-percha ['gʌtə'pʌrtʃə] s gutapercha

gutter ['gʌtər] s (on side of road) cuneta; (in street) arroyo; (of roof) canal f; (ditch formed by rain water) badén m; barrios bajos

gut'ter·snipe' s pilluelo, hijo de la miseria; gamberro

guttural ['gʌtərəl] adj gutural || s sonido gutural

guy [gaɪ] s viento, cable m de retén; (coll) tipo, tío, sujeto || tr (coll) burlarse de

guy wire s cable m de retén

guzzle ['gʌzəl] tr & intr beber con exceso

guzzler ['gʌzlər] s borrachín m

gym [dʒɪm] s (coll) gimnasio

gymnasi·um [dʒɪm'nezɪ·əm] s (pl -ums o -a [ə]) gimnasio

gymnast ['dʒɪmnæst] s gimnasta mf

gymnastic [dʒɪm'næstɪk] adj gimnástico || **gymnastics** spl gimnasia, gimnástica

gynecologist [ˌgaɪnə'kalədʒɪst], [ˌdʒaɪnə'kalədʒɪst] o [ˌdʒɪnə'kalədʒɪst] s ginecólogo

gynecology [ˌgaɪnə'kalədʒi], [ˌdʒaɪnə'kalədʒi] o [ˌdʒɪnə'kalədʒi] s ginecología

gyp [dʒɪp] s (slang) estafa, timo; (person) (slang) estafador m, timador m || v (pret & pp gypped; ger gypping) tr (slang) estafar, timar

gypsum ['dʒɪpsəm] s yeso, aljez m

gyp·sy ['dʒɪpsi] adj gitano || s (pl -sies) gitano || **Gypsy** s gitano (idioma)

gypsyish ['dʒɪpsi·ɪʃ] adj gitanesco

gypsy moth s lagarta

gyrate ['dʒaɪret] intr girar

gyroscope ['dʒaɪrə‚skop] s giroscopio

H

H, h [etʃ] octava letra del alfabeto inglés

h. abbr harbor, high, hour, husband

haberdasher ['hæbər‚dæʃər] s camisero; (dealer in notions) mercero

haberdasher·y ['hæbər‚dæʃəri] s (pl -ies) camisería, tienda de artículos para hombres; artículos para hombres

habit ['hæbɪt] s costumbre f, hábito; (costume) traje m; **to be in the habit of** acostumbrar

habitat ['hæbɪ‚tæt] s habitación
habitation [‚hæbɪ'teʃən] s habitación
habit-forming ['hæbɪt‚fɔrmɪŋ] adj enviciador
habitual [hə'bɪt/ʊ-əl] adj habitual
habitué [hə‚bɪt/ʊ'e] s habituado
hack [hæk] s (cut) corte m; (notch) mella; (cough) tos seca; coche m de alquiler; caballo de alquiler; caballo de silla; (nag) rocín m; escritor m a sueldo ‖ tr cortar, machetear
hack·man ['hækmən] s (pl -men [mən]) cochero de punto
hackney ['hækni] s caballo de silla; coche m de alquiler; esclavo del trabajo
hackneyed ['hæknid] adj trillado, gastado
hack'saw' s sierra de armero, sierra de cortar metales
haddock ['hædək] s eglefino
haft [hæft] o [hɑft] s mango, puño
hag [hæg] s (ugly old woman) tarasca; (witch) bruja
haggard ['hægərd] adj ojeroso, macilento, trasnochado
haggle ['hægəl] intr regatear
Hague, The [heg] La Haya
hail [hel] s (frozen rain) granizo; (greeting) saludo; **within hail** al alcance de la voz ‖ interj ¡salud!, ¡salve! ‖ tr saludar; dar vivas a, acoger con vivas; aclamar; granizar (p.ej., golpes) ‖ intr granizar; **to hail from** venir de, ser oriundo de
hail'-fel'low well met s compañero muy afable y simpático
Hail Mary s avemaría
hail'stone' s piedra de granizo
hail'storm' s granizada
hair [her] s pelo, cabellos; **to a hair** con la mayor exactitud; **to get in one's hair** (slang) enojarle a uno; **to have one's hair down** estar en melena; **to let one's hair down** (slang) hablar con mucha desenvoltura; **to make one's hair stand on end** ponerle a uno los pelos de punta; **to not turn a hair** no inmutarse; **to split hairs** pararse en quisquillas
hair'breadth' s (el) grueso de un pelo, casi nada; **to escape by a hairbreadth** escapar por un pelo
hair'brush' s cepillo de cabeza
hair'cloth' s tela de crin; (worn as a penance) cilicio
hair curler ['kʌrlər] s rizador m, tenacillas
hair'cut' s corte m de pelo; **to get a haircut** cortarse el pelo
hair'do' s (pl -dos) peinado, tocado
hair'dress'er s peinador m, peluquero
hair dryer s secador m
hair dye s tinte m para el pelo
hairless ['herlɪs] adj pelón
hair net s redecilla
hair'pin' s horquilla
hair-raising ['her‚rezɪŋ] adj (coll) espeluznante, horripilante
hair restorer [rɪ'storər] s crecepelo
hair ribbon s cinta para el cabello
hair set s fijapeinados m

hair shirt s cilicio
hairsplitting ['her‚splɪtɪŋ] adj quisquilloso ‖ s quisquillas
hair'spring' s espiral f
hair'style' s peinado
hair tonic s vigorizador m del cabello
hair·y ['heri] adj (comp -ier; super -iest) peludo, cabelludo
hake [hek] s merluza; (genus: Urophycis) fice m
halberd ['hælbərd] s alabarda
halberdier [‚hælbər'dɪr] s alabardero
halcyon days ['hælsɪ-ən] s días tranquilos, época de paz
hale [hel] adj sano, robusto; **hale and hearty** sano y fuerte ‖ tr llevar a la fuerza
half [hæf] o [hɑf] adj medio; **a half** o **half a** medio; **half the** la mitad de ‖ adv medio, p.ej., **half asleep** medio dormido; a medio, p.ej., **half finished** a medio acabar; a medias, p.ej., **half owner** dueño a medias; **half past** y media, p.ej., **half past three** las tres y media; **half … half** medio … medio ‖ s (pl **halves** [hævz] o [hɑvz]) mitad; (arith) medio; **in half** por la mitad; **to go halves** ir a medias
half'-and-half' adj mitad y mitad; indeterminado ‖ adv a medias, en partes iguales ‖ s mezcla de leche y crema; mezcla de dos cervezas inglesas
half'back' s (football) medio
half-baked ['hæf‚bekt] o ['hɑf‚bekt] adj a medio cocer; incompleto; poco juicioso, inexperto
half binding s (bb) encuadernación a la holandesa, media pasta
half'-blood' s mestizo; medio hermano
half boot s bota de media caña
half'-bound' adj (bb) a la holandesa
half'-breed' s mestizo
half brother s medio hermano
half-cocked ['hæf'kɑkt] o ['hɑf'kɑkt] adv (coll) con precipitación
half fare s medio billete
half'-full' adj mediado
half-hearted ['hæf‚hɑrtɪd] o ['hɑf‚hɑrtɪd] adj indiferente, frío
half holiday s mañana o tarde f de asueto
half hose spl calcetines mpl
half'-hour' s media hora; **on the half-hour** a la media en punto cada media hora
half leather s (bb) encuadernación a la holandesa, media pasta
half'-length' adj de medio cuerpo
half'-mast' s — **at half-mast** a media asta
half moon s media luna
half mourning s medio luto
half note s (mus) nota blanca
half pay s media paga; medio sueldo
halfpen·ny ['hepəni] o ['hepni] s (pl -nies) medio penique
half pint s media pinta; (little runt) (slang) gorgojo, mirmidón m
half'-seas' over adj — **to be half-seas over** (slang) estar entre dos velas, estar entre dos luces

gu
ha

half shell s (*either half of a bivalve*) concha; (*oysters*) **on the half shell** en su concha

half sister s media hermana

half sole s media suela

half'-sole' tr poner media suela a

half'-staff' s — **at half-staff** a media asta

half-timbered ['hæf,tɪmbərd] o ['hɑf,tɪmbərd] adj entramado

half title s anteportada, falsa portada

half'-tone' s (phot & paint) mediatinta; (typ) similigrabado

half'-track' s media oruga, semitractor m

half'truth' s verdad a medias

half'way' adj a medio camino; incompleto, hecho a medias ‖ adv a medio camino; **halfway through** a la mitad de; **to meet halfway** partir el camino con; partir la diferencia con; hacer concesiones mutuas (*dos personas*)

half-witted ['hæf,wɪtɪd] o ['hɑf,wɪtɪd] adj imbécil; necio, tonto

halibut ['hælɪbət] s halibut m

halide ['hælaɪd] o ['helaɪd] s (chem) haluro

halitosis [,hælɪ'tosɪs] s halitosis f, aliento fétido

hall [hɔl] s (*passageway*) corredor m; (*entranceway*) vestíbulo, zaguán m; (*large meeting room*) sala, salón m; (*assembly room of a university*) paraninfo; (*building, e.g., of a university*) edificio

halleluiah o **hallelujah** [,hælɪ'lujə] s aleluya m & f ‖ interj ¡aleluya!

hall'mark' s marca de constraste; (*distinguishing feature*) (fig) sello

hal·lo [ɪ ˌo] s (pl **-los**) grito ‖ interj ¡hola!; (*to incite dogs in hunting*) ¡sus! ‖ intr gritar

hallow ['hælo] tr santificar

hallowed ['hælod] adj santo, sagrado

Halloween o **Hallowe'en** [,hælo'in] s víspera de Todos los Santos

hallucination [hə,lusɪ'neʃən] s alucinación

hall'way' s corredor m; vestíbulo, zaguán m

ha·lo ['helo] s (pl **-los** o **-loes**) halo

halogen ['hælədʒən] s halógeno

halt [hɔlt] adj cojo, renco ‖ s alto, parada; **to call a halt** mandar hacer alto; **to come to a halt** pararse, detenerse, interrumpirse ‖ tr parar, detener ‖ intr hacer alto

halter ['hɔltər] s (*for leading or fastening horse*) cabestro, ronzal m, dogal m; (*noose*) dogal m, cuerda de ahorcar; muerte f en la horca

halting ['hɔltɪŋ] adj cojo, renco; vacilante

halve [hæv] o [hɑv] tr partir en dos, partir por la mitad

halyard ['hæljərd] s (naut) driza

ham [hæm] s (*part of leg behind knee*) corva; (*thigh and buttock*) pernil m; (*cured meat from hog's hind leg*) jamón m; (slang) comicastro; (slang) aficionado (*a la radio*); **hams** nalgas

ham and eggs spl huevos con jamón

hamburger ['hæm,bʌrgər] s hamburguesa

hamlet ['hæmlɪt] s aldehuela, caserío

hammer ['hæmər] s martillo; (*of piano*) macillo, martinete m; **to go under the hammer** venderse en pública subasta ‖ tr martillar; **to hammer out** formar a martillazos; sacar en limpio a fuerza de mucho esfuerzo ‖ intr martillar; **to hammer away** trabajar asiduamente

hammock ['hæmək] s hamaca

hamper ['hæmpər] s canasto, cesto grande con tapa ‖ tr estorbar, impedir

hamster ['hæmstər] s marmota de Alemania, rata del trigo

ham·string ['hæm,strɪŋ] v (pret & pp **-strung**) tr desjarretar; (fig) estropear, incapacitar

hand [hænd] adj (*done or operated with the hands*) manual ‖ s mano f; (*workman*) obrero, peón m; (*way of writing*) escritura, puño y letra; (*signature*) firma; (*clapping of hands*) salva de aplausos; (*of clock or watch*) mano f, manecilla; (*all the cards in one's hand*) juego; (*a round of play*) mano f; (*player*) jugador m; (*source, origin*) fuente f; (*skill* destreza; **all hands** (naut) toda la tripulación; (coll) todos; **at first hand** de primera mano; directamente, de buena tinta; **at hand** disponible; **hand in glove** uña y carne; **hand in hand** asidos de la mano; juntos; **hands up!** ¡arriba las manos!; **hand to hand** cuerpo a cuerpo; **in hand** entre manos; **in his own hand** de su propio puño; **on hand** entre manos; disponible; **on hands and knees** (*crawling*) a gatas; (*beseeching*) de rodillas; **on the one hand** por una parte; **on the other hand** por otra parte; **out of hand** luego, en seguida; desmandado; **to be at hand** obrar en mi (nuestro) poder (*una carta*); **to change hands** mudar de manos; **to clap hands** batir palmas; **to eat out of one's hand** aceptar dócilmente la autoridad de uno; **to fall into the hands of** caer en manos de; **to have a hand in** tomar parte en; **to have one's hands full** estar ocupadísimo; **to hold hands** tomarse de las manos; **to hold up one's hands** (*as a sign of surrender*) alzar las manos; **to join hands** darse las manos; casarse; **to keep one's hands off** no tocar, no meterse en; **to lend a hand** echar una mano; **to live from hand to mouth** vivir al día, vivir de la mano a la boca; **to not lift a hand** no levantar paja del suelo; **to play into the hands of** hacer el caldo gordo a; **to raise one's hand** (*in taking an oath*) alzar el dedo; **to shake hands** estrecharse la mano; **to show one's hand** descubrir su juego; **to take in hand** hacerse cargo de; tratar, estudiar (*una cuestión*); **to throw up one's hands** darse por vencido; **to try one's hand** probar la mano; **to turn one's hand**

to dedicarse a, ocuparse en; **to wash one's hands of** lavarse las manos de; **under my hand** con mi firma, bajo mi firma, de mi puño y letra; **under the hand and seal of** firmado y sellado por ‖ *tr* dar, entregar; **to hand in** entregar; **to hand on** transmitir; **to hand out** repartir

hand′bag′ *s* saco de noche; bolso de señora

hand baggage *s* equipaje *m* de mano

hand′ball′ *s* pelota; juego de pelota a mano

hand′bill′ *s* hoja volante

hand′book′ *s* manual *m;* guía de turistas; registro para apuestas

hand′breadth′ *s* palmo menor

hand′car′ *s* (rr) carrito de mano

hand′cart′ *s* carretilla de mano

hand control *s* mando a mano

hand′cuff′ *s* manilla; **handcuffs** manillas, esposas ‖ *tr* poner esposas a

handful ['hænd,fʊl] *s* puñado, manojo

hand glass *s* espejo de mano; lupa

hand grenade *s* granada de mano

handi·cap ['hændɪ,kæp] *s* desventaja, obstáculo; (sport) handicap *m* ‖ *v* (*pret* & *pp* **-capped;** *ger* **-capping**) *tr* poner trabas a; (sport) handicapar

handicraft ['hændɪ,kræft] o ['hændɪ,krɑft] *s* destreza manual; arte mecánica

handiwork ['hændɪ,wʌrk] *s* hechura, trabajo; obra manual

handkerchief ['hæŋkərtʃɪf] o ['hæŋkər,tʃif] *s* pañuelo

handle ['hændəl] *s* (*of a basket, crock, pitcher*) asa; (*of a shovel, rake, etc.*) mango; (*of an umbrella, sword*) puño; (*of a door, drawer*) tirador *m;* (*of a hand organ*) manubrio; (*of a water pump*) guimbalete *m; (opportunity, pretext*) asidero; **to fly off the handle** (slang) salirse de sus casillas ‖ *tr* manosear, manipular; dirigir, manejar, gobernar; comerciar en ‖ *intr* manejarse

handle bar *s* manillar *m,* guía

handler ['hændlər] *s* (sport) entrenador *m*

hand′made′ *adj* hecho a mano

hand′maid′ o **hand′maid′en** *s* criada, sirvienta

hand′-me-down′ *s* (coll) prenda de vestir de segunda mano

hand organ *s* organillo

hand′out′ *s* comida que se da de limosna; comunicado de prensa

hand-picked ['hænd,pɪkt] *adj* escogido a mano; escogido escrupulosamente; escogido con motivos ocultos

hand′rail′ *s* barandilla, pasamano

hand′saw′ *s* serrucho, sierra de mano

hand′set′ *s* microteléfono

hand′shake′ *s* apretón *m* de manos

handsome ['hænsəm] *adj* hermoso, elegante, guapo; considerable

hand′spring′ *s* voltereta sobre las manos

hand′-to-hand′ *adj* cuerpo a cuerpo

hand′-to-mouth′ *adj* inseguro, precario; imprévido

hand′work′ *s* trabajo a mano

hand′-wres′tle *intr* pulsear

hand′-writ′ing *s* escritura; (*writing by hand which characterizes a particular person*) letra

hand·y ['hændɪ] *adj* (*comp* **-ier;** *super* **-iest**) (*easy to handle*) manuable; (*within easy reach*) próximo, a la mano; (*skillful*) diestro, hábil; **to come in handy** venir a pelo

handy man *s* dije *m,* factótum *m*

hang [hæŋ] *s* (*of a dress, curtain, etc.*) caída; (*skill; insight*) tino; **I don't care a hang** (coll) no me importa un bledo; **to get the hang of it** (coll) coger el tino ‖ *v* (*pret* & *pp* **hung** [hʌŋ]) *tr* colgar; tender (*la ropa mojada*); pegar (*el papel pintado*); fijar (*un cartel, un letrero*); enquiciar (*una puerta, una ventana*); bajar (*la cabeza*); **hang it!** (coll) ¡caramba!; **to hang up** colgar (*el sombrero*); impedir los progresos de ‖ *intr* colgar, pender; estar agarrado; vacilar; **to hang around** esperar sin hacer nada; haraganear; rondar; **to hang on** colgar de; depender de; estar pendiente de (*las palabras de una persona*); estar sin acabar de morir; agarrarse; **to hang out** asomarse; (slang) recogerse, alojarse; **to hang over** (*to threaten*) cernerse sobre; **to hang together** mantenerse unidos; **to hang up** (telp) colgar ‖ *v* (*pret* **hanged** o **hung**) *tr* ahorcar ‖ *intr* ahorcarse

hangar ['hæŋər] o ['hæŋgɑr] *s* cobertizo; (aer) hangar *m*

hang′bird′ *s* pájaro de nido colgante; (*Baltimore oriole*) cacique veranero

hanger ['hæŋər] *s* colgador *m,* suspensión; (*hook*) colgadero

hang′er·on′ *s* (*pl* **hangers-on**) secuaz *mf;* parásito; (*sponger*) pegote *m*

hanging ['hæŋɪŋ] *adj* colgante, pendiente ‖ *s* ahorcadura, muerte *f* en la horca; **hangings** colgaduras

hang·man ['hæŋmən] *s* (*pl* **-men** [mən]) verdugo

hang′nail′ *s* padrastro, respigón *m*

hang′out′ *s* guarida, querencia; (*place to loaf and gossip*) mentidero

hang′o′ver *s* (slang) resaca

hank [hæŋk] *s* madeja

hanker ['hæŋkər] *intr* sentir anhelo

Hannibal ['hænɪbəl] *s* Aníbal *m*

haphazard [,hæp'hæzərd] *adj* casual, fortuito, impensado ‖ *adv* al acaso, a la ventura

hapless ['hæplɪs] *adj* desgraciado, desventurado

happen ['hæpən] *intr* acontecer, suceder; (*to turn out*) resultar; (*to be the case by chance*) dar la casualidad; **to happen in** entrar por casualidad; **to happen on** encontrarse con; **to happen to** hacerse de; **to happen to** + *inf* por casualidad + *ind,* p.ej., **I happened to see her at the theater** por casualidad la vi en el teatro

happening ['hæpənɪŋ] *s* acontecimiento, suceso

happily ['hæpɪlɪ] *adv* felizmente

happiness ['hæpɪnɪs] *s* felicidad

hap·py ['hæpɪ] *adj* (*comp* **-pier;** *super* **-piest**) feliz; (*pleased*) contento; **to be happy to** alegrarse de, tener gusto en

hap'py-go-luck'y *adj* irresponsible, impróvido ‖ *adv* a la buenaventura

happy medium *s* justo medio

Happy New Year *interj* ¡Feliz Año Nuevo!

harangue [hə'ræŋ] *s* arenga ‖ *tr &
intr* arengar

harass ['hærəs] o [hə'ræs] *tr* acosar, hostigar; molestar, vejar

harbinger ['harbɪndʒər] *s* precursor *m;* anuncio, presagio ‖ *tr* anunciar, presagiar

harbor ['harbər] *adj* portuario ‖ *s* puerto ‖ *tr* albergar; alcahuetar, encubrir (*delincuentes u objetos robados*); guardar (*sentimientos de odio*)

harbor master *s* capitán *m* de puerto

hard [hard] *adj* duro; (*difficult*) difícil; (*water*) crudo, duro; (*solder*) fuerte; (*work*) asiduo; (*drinker*) empedernido; espiritoso, fuertemente alcohólico; **to be hard on** (*to treat severely*) ser muy duro con; (*to wear out fast*) gastar, echar a perder ‖ *adv* duro; fuerte; mucho; **hard upon** a raíz de; **to drink hard** beber de firme; **to rain hard** llover de firme

hard and fast *adj* inflexible, riguroso ‖ *adv* firmemente

hard-bitten ['hard'bɪtən] *adj* terco, tenaz, inflexible

hard-boiled ['hard'bɔɪld] *adj* (*egg*) duro, muy cocido; (coll) duro, inflexible

hard candy *s* caramelos

hard cash *s* dinero contante y sonante

hard cider *s* sidra muy fermentada

hard coal *s* antracita

hard-earned ['hard'ʌrnd] *adj* ganado a pulso

harden ['hardən] *tr* endurecer ‖ *intr* endurecerse

hardening ['hardənɪŋ] *s* endurecimiento

hard facts *spl* realidades

hard-fought ['hard'fɔt] *adj* reñido

hard-headed ['hard'hedɪd] *adj* astuto, sagaz; terco, tozudo

hard-hearted ['hard'hartɪd] *adj* duro de corazón

hardihood ['hardɪ,hud] *s* audacia, resolución; descaro, insolencia

hardiness ['hardɪnɪs] *s* fuerza, robustez; audacia, resolución

hard labor *s* trabajos forzados

hard luck *s* mala suerte

hard'-luck' story *s* (coll) cuento de penas; **to tell a hard-luck story** (coll) contar lástimas

hardly ['hardlɪ] *adv* apenas; casi no; (*with great difficulty*) a duras penas; (*grievously*) penosamente; **hardly ever** casi nunca

hardness ['hardnɪs] *s* dureza; (*of water*) crudeza

hard of hearing *adj* duro de oído, teniente

hard-pressed ['hard'prest] *adj* aco-

sado; (*for money*) apurado, alcanzado

hard rubber *s* vulcanita

hard sauce *s* mantequilla azucarada

hard'-shell' clam *s* almeja redonda

hard-shell crab *s* cangrejo de cáscara dura

hardship ['hardʃɪp] *s* penalidad, infortunio, apuro

hard'tack' *s* galleta, sequete *m*

hard times *spl* período de miseria, apuros

hard to please *adj* difícil de contentar

hard up *adj* (coll) apurado, alcanzado

hard'ware' *s* ferretería, quincalla; (*metal trimmings*) herraje *m;* (*computer*) computadora

hardware·man ['hard,wermən] *s* (*pl* **-men** [mən]) ferretero, quincallero

hardware store *s* ferretería, quincallería

hard-won ['hard,wʌn] *adj* ganado a pulso

hard'wood' *s* madera dura; árbol *m* de madera dura

hardwood floor *s* entarimado

har·dy ['hardɪ] *adj* (*comp* **-dier;** *super* **-diest**) fuerte, robusto; audaz, resuelto; (*rash*) temerario; (hort) resistente

hare [her] *s* liebre *f*

harebrained ['her,brend] *adj* atolondrado

hare'lip' *s* labio leporino

harelipped ['her,lɪpt] *adj* labiohendido

harem ['herəm] *s* harén *m*

hark [hark] *intr* escuchar; **to hark back** volver (*la jauría*) sobre la pista; **to hark back to** volver a, recordar

harken ['harkən] *intr* escuchar

harlequin ['harləkwɪn] *s* arlequín *m*

harlot ['harlət] *s* meretriz *f*

harm [harm] *s* daño, perjuicio ‖ *tr* dañar, perjudicar, hacer daño a

harmful ['harmfəl] *adj* dañoso, perjudicial; (*e.g., pests*) dañino

harmless ['harmlɪs] *adj* innocuo, inofensivo

harmonic [har'manɪk] *adj & s* armónico

harmonica [har'manɪkə] *s* armónica

harmonious [har'monɪ-əs] *adj* armonioso

harmonize ['harmə,naɪz] *tr & intr* armonizar

harmo·ny ['harmənɪ] *s* (*pl* **-nies**) armonía

harness ['harnɪs] *s* arreos, guarniciones; **to get back in the harness** volver a la rutina; **to die in the harness** morir al pie del cañón ‖ *tr* enjaezar, poner las guarniciones a; enganchar; captar (*las aguas de un río*)

harness maker *s* guarnicionero

harness race *s* carrera con sulky

harp [harp] *s* arpa ‖ *intr* — **to harp on** repetir porfiadamente

harpist ['harpɪst] *s* arpista *mf*

harpoon [har'pun] *s* arpón *m* ‖ *tr & intr* arponear

harpsichord ['harpsɪ,kɔrd] *s* clave *m*

har·py ['harpi] s (pl -pies) arpía

harrow ['hæro] s (agr) grada || tr (agr) gradar; atormentar

harrowing ['hæro·ɪŋ] adj horripilante, espantoso

har·ry ['hæri] v (pret & pp -ried) tr acosar, hostilizar, hostigar; atormentar, molestar

harsh [harʃ] adj (to touch, taste, eyes, hearing) áspero; duro, cruel

harshness ['harʃnɪs] s aspereza; dureza, crueldad

hart [hart] s ciervo

harum-scarum ['herəm'skerəm] adj atolondrado || adv atolondradamente || s mataperros m

harvest ['harvɪst] s cosecha || tr & intr cosechar

harvester ['harvɪstər] s cosechero; (helper) agostero; (machine) segadora

harvest home s entrada de los frutos; fiesta de segadores; canción de segadores

harvest moon s luna de la cosecha

has-been ['hæz,bɪn] s (coll) antigualla

hash [hæʃ] s picadillo || tr picar

hash house s bodegón m

hashish ['hæʃiʃ] s hachich m

hasp [hæsp] o [hasp] s portacandado; (of book covers) broche m

hassle ['hæsəl] s (coll) riña, disputa

hassock ['hæsək] s cojín m (para los pies o las rodillas)

haste [hest] s prisa; **in haste** de prisa; **to make haste** darse prisa

hasten ['hesən] tr apresurar; apretar (el paso) || intr apresurarse

hast·y ['hesti] adj (comp -ier; super -iest) apresurado; inconsiderado, impulsivo, colérico

hat [hæt] s sombrero; **to keep under one's hat** (coll) callar, no divulgar; **to throw one's hat in the ring** (coll) decidirse a bajar a la arena

hat'band' s cintillo; (worn to show mourning) gasa

hat block s horma, conformador m

hat'box' s sombrerera

hatch [hætʃ] s (brood) cría, nidada; (trap door) escotillón m; (lower half of door) media puerta; (opening in ship's deck) escotilla; (lid for opening in ship's deck) cuartel m || tr empollar (huevos); sombrear (un dibujo); maquinar, tramar || intr empollarse; salir del huevo

hat'-check' girl s guardarropa

hatchet ['hætʃɪt] s destral m, hacha pequeña; **to bury the hatchet** envainar la espada

hatch'way' s (trap door) escotillón m; (opening in ship's deck) escotilla

hate [het] s odio, aborrecimiento || tr & intr odiar, aborrecer, detestar

hateful ['hetfəl] adj odioso, aborrecible

hat'pin' s aguja de sombrero, pasador m

hat'rack' s percha

hatred ['hetrɪd] s odio, aborrecimiento

hatter ['hætər] s sombrerero

haughtiness ['hotɪnɪs] s altanería, altivez f

haugh·ty ['hoti] adj (comp -tier; super -tiest) altanero, altivo

haul [hol] s (pull, tug) tirón m; (amount caught) redada; (distance transported) trayecto, recorrido; (roundup, e.g., of thieves) redada || tr acarrear, transportar; (naut) halar

haunch [hontʃ] o [hantʃ] s (hip) cadera; (hind quarter of an animal) anca; (leg of animal used for food) pierna

haunt [hont] o [hant] s guarida, nidal m, querencia || tr andar por, vagar por; frecuentar; inquietar, molestar; perseguir (las memorias a una persona)

haunted house s casa de fantasmas

haute couture [ot ku'tyr] s alta moda

Havana [hə'vænə] s La Habana

have [hæv] v (pret & pp had [hæd]) tr tener; (to get, to take) tomar; **to have and to hold** (úsase sólo en el infinitivo) para ser poseído en propiedad; **to have got** (coll) tener, poseer; **to have got to** + inf tener que + inf; **to have it in for** (coll) tener tirria a; **to have it out with** (coll) habérselas con, emprenderla con; **to have on** llevar puesto; **to have** (something) **to do with** tener que ver con; **to have** + inf hacer, mandar + inf, p.ej., **I had him go out that door** le hice salir por esa puerta; **to have** + pp hacer, mandar + inf, p.ej., **I had my watch repaired** hice componer mi reloj || intr — **to have at** atacar, embestir; **to have to** + inf tener que + inf; **to have to do with** (to be concerned with) tratar de; (to have connections with) tener relaciones con || v aux haber, p.ej., **he has studied his lesson** ha estudiado su lección

havelock ['hævlak] s cogotera

haven ['hevən] s puerto; abrigo, asilo, buen puerto

have-not ['hæv,nat] s — **the haves and the have-nots** (coll) los ricos y los desposeídos

haversack ['hævər,sæk] s barjuleta; (of soldier) mochila

havoc ['hævək] s estrago, estragos; **to play havoc with** hacer grandes estragos en

haw [ho] s (of hawthorn) baya, simiente f; (in speech) vacilación || interj ¡a la izquierda! || tr & intr volver a la izquierda

haw'-haw' s carcajada

hawk [hok] s halcón m, gavilán m, cernícalo; (mortarboard) esparavel m; (sharper) (coll) fullero || tr pregonar; **to hawk up** arrojar tosiendo || intr carraspear, gargajear

hawker ['hokər] s buhonero

hawksbill turtle ['hoks,bɪl] s carey m

hawse [hoz] s (naut) muz m; (hole) (naut) escobén m; (naut) longitud de cadenas

hawse'hole' s (naut) escobén m

hawser ['hɔzər] s (naut) guindaleza

haw'thorn' s espino, oxiacanta

hay [he] s heno; **to hit the hay** (slang) acostarse; **to make hay while the sun shines** hacer su agosto

hay fever s fiebre f del heno

hay'field' s henar m

hay'fork' s horca; (machine) elevador m de heno

hay'loft' s henil m, henal m

hay'mak'er s (box) golpe m que pone fuera de combate

haymow ['he͵mau] s henil m; acopio de heno

hay'rack' s pesebre m

hayrick ['he͵rɪk] s almiar m

hay ride s paseo de placer en carro de heno

hay'seed' s simiente f de heno; (coll) patán m, campesino

hay'stack' s almiar m

hay'wire' adj (slang) descompuesto; (slang) destornillado, loco ‖ s alambre m para embalar el heno

hazard ['hæzərd] s peligro, riesgo; (chance) acaso, azar m; (golf) obstáculo; **at all hazards** por grande que sea el riesgo ‖ tr arriesgar; aventurar (una opinión)

hazardous ['hæzərdəs] adj peligroso, arriesgado

haze [hez] s calina, bruma; (fig) confusión, vaguedad ‖ tr dar novatada a

hazel ['hezəl] adj castaño claro ‖ s avellano

ha'zel·nut' s avellana

hazing ['hezɪŋ] s novatada

ha·zy ['hezi] adj (comp -zier; super -ziest) calinoso, brumoso; confuso, vago

H-bomb ['etʃ͵bɑm] s bomba de hidrógeno

H.C. abbr **House of Commons**

hd. abbr **head**

hdqrs. abbr **headquarters**

H.E. abbr **His Eminence, His Excellency**

he [hi] pron pers (pl **they**) él ‖ s (pl **hes**) macho, varón m

head [hed] s cabeza; (of a bed) cabecera; (caption) encabezamiento; (of a boil) centro; (on a glass of beer) espuma; (of a drum) parche m; (of a cane) puño; (of a barrel, cylinder, etc.) fondo, tapa; (of cylinder of automobile engine) culata; crisis f, punto decisivo; **at the head of** a la frente de; **from head to foot** de pies a cabeza; **head over heels** en un salto mortal; hasta los tuétanos; precipitadamente; **heads** (of a coin) cara; **heads or tails** a cara o cruz; **over one's head** fuera del alcance de uno; (going to a higher authority) por encima de uno; **to be out of one's head** (coll) delirar; **to come into one's head** pasarle a uno por la cabeza; **to go to one's head** subírsele a uno a la cabeza; **to keep one's head** no perder la cabeza; **to keep one's head above water** no dejarse vencer; **to put heads together** con-

sultarse entre sí; **to not make head or tail of** no ver pies ni cabeza a ‖ tr acaudillar, dirigir, mandar; estar a la cabeza de (p.ej., la clase); venir primero en (una lista) ‖ intr — **to head towards** dirigirse hacia

head'ache' s dolor m de cabeza

head'band' s cinta para la cabeza; (of a book) cabezada

head'board' s cabecera de cama

head'cheese' s queso de cerdo

head'dress' s (style of hair) tocado; prenda para la cabeza

header ['hedər] s — **to take a header** (coll) caerse de cabeza

head'first' adv de cabeza; precipitadamente

head'gear' s sombrero; (for protection) casco

head'hunt'er s cazador m de cabezas

heading ['hedɪŋ] s encabezamiento; (of a letter) membrete m; (of a chapter of a book) cabecera

headland ['hedlənd] s promontorio

headless ['hedlɪs] adj sin cabeza; sin jefe; estúpido

head'light' s (aut) faro; (naut) farol m de tope; (rr) farol m

head'line' s (of newspaper) cabecera; (of a page of a book) titulillo, título de página ‖ tr poner cabecera a; (slang) destacar, dar cartel a (un actor)

head'lin'er s (slang) atracción principal

head'long' adj de cabeza; precipitado ‖ adv de cabeza; precipitadamente

head·man ['hed͵mæn] s (pl -men [͵men]) caudillo, jefe m

head'mas'ter s director m de un colegio

head'most' adj delantero, primero

head office s oficina central

head of hair s cabellera

head'-on' adj & adv de frente; **head-on collision** colisión de frente

head'phone' s auricular m de casco, receptor m de cabeza

head'piece' s (any covering for head) casco, yelmo, morrión m; (brains, judgment) cabeza, juicio; cabecera de cama; (headset) auricular m de casco, receptor m de cabeza; (typ) cabecera, viñeta

head'quar'ters s centro de dirección; (of police) jefatura; (mil) cuartel m general

head'rest' s apoyo para la cabeza

head'set' s auricular m de casco, receptor m de cabeza

head'ship' s jefatura, dirección

head'stone' s (cornerstone) piedra angular; (on a grave) lápida sepulcral

head'stream' s afluente m principal

head'strong' adj cabezudo, terco

head'wait'er s jefe m de camareros, encargado de comedor

head'wa'ters spl cabecera

head'way' s avance m, progreso; espacio libre; **to make headway** avanzar, progresar

head'wear' s prendas de cabeza

head wind s viento de frente, viento por la proa

head'work' s trabajo intelectual

head·y ['hɛdi] adj (comp -ier; super -iest) excitante, emocionante; impetuoso, violento; (intoxicating) cabezudo; (clever) sesudo

heal [hil] tr curar, sanar; cicatrizar; remediar (un daño) || intr curar, sanar; cicatrizarse; remediarse

healer ['hilər] s curador m, sanador m

health [hɛlθ] s salud f; **to be in good health** estar bien de salud; **to be in poor health** estar mal de salud; **to drink to the health of** beber a la salud de; **to radiate health** verter salud; **to your health!** ¡a su salud!

healthful ['hɛlθfəl] adj saludable; sano

health·y ['hɛlθi] adj (comp -ier; super -iest) sano; saludable

heap [hip] s montón m || tr amontonar, apilar; (to supply with, e.g., favors) colmar; (to bestow in great quantity) dar generosamente || intr amontonarse, apilarse

hear [hɪr] v (pret & pp heard [hʌrd]) tr oír; **to hear it said** oírlo decir || intr oír; **hear! hear!** ¡bravo!; **to hear about** oír hablar de; **to hear from** tener noticias de; **to hear of** oír hablar de; **to hear tell of** oír hablar de; **to hear that** oír decir que

hearer ['hɪrər] s oyente mf

hearing ['hɪrɪŋ] s (sense) oído; (act) oída; audiencia; **in the hearing of** en presencia de; **within hearing** al alcance del oído

hearing aid s aparato auditivo

hear'say' s rumor m; **by hearsay** de o por oídas

hearse [hʌrs] s coche m fúnebre, carroza fúnebre

heart [hɑrt] s corazón m; (e.g., of lettuce) cogollo; **after one's heart** enteramente del gusto de uno; **by heart** de memoria; **heart and soul of** todo corazón; **to break the heart of** partir el corazón de; **to die of a broken heart** morir de pena; **to eat one's heart out** sufrir en silencio; **to get to the heart of** llegar al fondo de; **to have one's heart in one's work** trabajar con entusiasmo; **to have one's heart in the right place** tener buenas intenciones; **to lose heart** descorazonarse; **to open one's heart to** descubrirse con; **to take heart** cobrar aliento; **to take to heart** tomar a pecho; **to wear one's heart on one's sleeve** llevar el corazón en la mano; **with all one's heart** con toda el alma de uno; **with one's heart in one's mouth** con el credo en la boca

heart'ache' s angustia, congoja

heart attack s ataque m de corazón, ataque cardíaco

heart'beat' s latido del corazón

heart'break' s angustia, dolor m abrumador

heart'break'er s ladrón m de corazones

heartbroken ['hɑrt,brokən] adj transido de dolor, muerto de pena

heart'burn' s acedía, rescoldera; (jealousy) celos

heart disease s enfermedad del corazón

hearten ['hɑrtən] tr alentar, animar

heart failure s debilidad coronaria; (death) paro del corazón; (faintness) desfallecimiento, desmayo

heartfelt ['hɑrt,fɛlt] adj cordial, sentido, sincero

hearth [hɑrθ] s hogar m

hearth'stone' s solera del hogar; (home) hogar m

heartily ['hɑrtɪli] adv cordialmente; con buen apetito; de buena gana; bien, mucho

heartless ['hɑrtlɪs] adj cruel, inhumano

heart-rending ['hɑrt,rɛndɪŋ] adj angustioso, que parte el corazón

heart'seed' s farolillo

heart'sick' adj afligido, desconsolado

heart'strings' spl fibras del corazón, entretelas

heart'-to-heart' adj franco, sincero

heart trouble s — **to have heart trouble** enfermar del corazón

heart'wood' s madera de corazón

heart·y ['hɑrti] adj (comp -ier; super -iest) cordial, sincero; sano, fuerte; (meal) abundante; (laugh) bueno; (eater) grande

heat [hit] adj térmico || s calor m; (warming of a room, house, etc.) calefacción; (rut of animals) celo; (in horse racing) carrera de prueba; (fig) ardor m, ímpetu m; **in heat** en celo || tr calentar; calefaccionar (p.ej., una casa); (fig) acalorar, excitar || intr calentarse; (fig) acalorarse, excitarse

heated ['hitɪd] adj acalorado

heater ['hitər] s calentador m; (for central heating) calorífero; (electron) calefactor m

heater man s calefactor m

heath [hiθ] s (shrub) brezo; (tract of land) brezal m

hea·then ['hiðən] adj gentil, pagano; irreligioso || s (pl -then o -thens) gentil mf, pagano

heathendom ['hiðəndəm] s gentilidad

heather ['hɛðər] s brezo

heating ['hitɪŋ] adj calentador || s calefacción

heat lightning s fucilazo, relámpago de calor

heat shield s blindaje térmico, escudo térmico

heat'stroke' s insolación

heat wave s (phys) onda calorífica; (coll) ola de calor

heave [hiv] s esfuerzo para levantar; esfuerzo para levantarse; **heaves** (vet) huélfago || v (pret & pp heaved o hov [hov]) tr alzar, levantar; arrojar, lanzar; exhalar (un suspiro) || intr levantarse y bajar alternativamente; palpitar (el pecho); elevarse; hacer esfuerzos por vomitar

heaven ['hɛvən] s cielo; **for heaven's sake!** o **good heavens!** ¡válgame Dios!; **heavens** (firmament) cielo ||

Heaven s cielo (*mansión de los bienaventurados*)
heavenly ['hevənli] adj (*body*) celeste; (*life, home*) celestial; (*fig*) celestial
heavenly body s astro, cuerpo celeste
heav·y ['hevi] adj (*comp* -ier; *super* -iest) (*of great weight*) pesado; (*liquid*) espeso, denso; (*cloth, paper, sea, line*) grueso; (*traffic*) denso; (*crop, harvest*) abundante, copioso; (*expense*) fuerte; (*rain*) recio; (*features*) basto; (*eyes*) agravado; (*gunfire*) fragoroso; (*heart*) abatido, triste; (*drinker*) grande; (*stock market*) postrado; (*clothing*) de mucho abrigo || adv pesadamente; **to hang heavy** pasar (*el tiempo*) con gran lentitud
heav·y·du·ty adj extrafuerte
heav·y·hearted ['hevɪ'hɑrtɪd] adj afligido, acongojado
heav·y·set' adj costilludo, espalduda
heav·y·weight' s (box) peso pesado
Hebrew ['hibru] adj & s hebreo
hecatomb ['hekə,tom] o ['hekə,tum] s hecatombe f
heckle ['hekəl] tr interrumpir (*a un orador*) con preguntas impertinentes
hectic ['hektɪk] adj (coll) agitado, turbulento
hedge [hedʒ] s cercado, vallado; (*of bushes*) seto vivo; apuesta compensatoria; (*in stock market*) operación compensatoria || tr cercar con vallado; cercar con seto vivo; **to hedge in** encerrar, rodear || intr no querer comprometerse; hacer apuestas compensatorias; hacer operaciones compensatorias
hedge'hog' s erizo; (*porcupine*) puerco espín m
hedge'hop' v (*pret & pp* -hopped; *ger* -hopping) intr (aer) volar rasando el suelo
hedgehopping ['hedʒ,hɑpɪŋ] s (aer) vuelo rasante
hedge'row' s cercado de arbustos, seto vivo
heed [hid] s atención, cuidado; **to take heed** tr con cuidado || tr atender a, hacer caso de || intr atender, hacer caso
heedless ['hidlɪs] adj desatento, descuidado
heehaw ['hi,hɔ] s (*of donkey*) rebuzno; risotada || intr rebuznar; reír groseramente
heel [hil] s (*of foot*) calcañar m, talón m; (*of stocking or shoe*) talón m; (*raised part of shoe below heel*) tacón m; (slang) sinvergüenza mf; **down at the heel** desaliñado, mal vestido; **to cool one's heels** (coll) hacer antesala; **to kick up one's heels** (slang) mostrarse alegre; **to show a clean pair of heels** o **to take to one's heels** poner pies en polvorosa
heeler ['hilər] s (slang) muñidor m
heft·y ['hefti] adj (*comp* -ier; *super* -iest) (*heavy*) pesado; (*strong*) fuerte, fornido
hegemo·ny [hɪ'dʒeməni] o ['hedʒɪ,moni] s (*pl* -nies) hegemonía

hegira [hɪ'dʒaɪrə] o ['hedʒɪrə] s fuga, huída
heifer ['hefər] s novilla, vaquilla
height [haɪt] s altura; (*e.g., of folly*) colmo
heighten ['haɪtən] tr hacer más alto; (*to increase the amount of*) aumentar; (*to set off, bring out*) realzar || intr aumentarse
heinous ['henəs] adj atroz, nefando
heir [er] s heredero
heir apparent s (*pl* heirs apparent) heredero forzoso
heirdom ['erdəm] s herencia
heiress ['erɪs] s heredera
heirloom ['er,lum] s joya de familia, reliquia de familia
helicopter ['helɪ,kɑptər] s helicóptero
heliotrope ['hilɪ-ə,trop] s heliotropo
heliport ['helɪ,port] s helipuerto
helium ['hilɪ-əm] s helio
helix ['hilɪks] s (*pl* helixes o helices ['helɪ,siz]) hélice f
hell [hel] s infierno
hell-bent ['hel'bent] adj (slang) muy resuelto; **hell-bent on** (slang) empeñado en
hell'cat' s (*bad-tempered woman*) arpía, mujer perversa; (*witch*) bruja
hellebore ['helɪ,bor] s eléboro
Hellene ['helin] s heleno
Hellenic [he'lenɪk] o [he'linɪk] adj helénico
hell'fire' s fuego del infierno
hellish ['helɪʃ] adj infernal
hel·lo [he'lo] s saludo || interj ¡qué tal!; (*on telephone*) ¡diga!
hello girl s (coll) chica telefonista
helm [helm] s barra del timón; rueda del timón; (fig) timón m || tr dirigir, gobernar
helmet ['helmɪt] s casco; (*of ancient armor*) yelmo
helms·man ['helmzmən] s (*pl* -men [mən]) timonel m
help [help] s ayuda, socorro; (*of food*) ración; (*relief*) remedio, p.ej., **there's no help for it** no hay remedio; criados; empleados; obreros; **to come to the help of** acudir en socorro de || interj ¡socorro! || tr ayudar, socorrer; aliviar, mitigar; (*to wait on*) servir; **it can't be helped** no hay remedio; **so help me God!** ¡así Dios me salve!; **to help down** ayudar a bajar; **to help a person with his coat** ayudarle a una persona a ponerse el abrigo; **to help oneself** valerse por sí mismo; servirse; **to help up** ayudar a subir; ayudar a levantarse; **to not be able to help** + *ger* no poder menos de + inf, p.ej., **he can't help laughing** no puede menos de reír || intr ayudar
helper ['helpər] s ayudante mf; (*in a drug store, barbershop, etc.*) mancebo
helpful ['helpfəl] adj útil, provechoso; servicial
helping ['helpɪŋ] s ración (*de alimento*)
helpless ['helplɪs] adj (*weak*) débil; (*powerless*) impotente; (*penniless*)

desvalido; (*confused*) perplejo; (*situation*) irremediable

help'meet' s compañero; (*wife*) compañera

helter-skelter ['hɛltər'skɛltər] *adj, adv & s* cochite hervite m

hem [hɛm] s tos fingida; (*of a garment*) bastilla, dobladillo ‖ *interj* ¡ejem! ‖ *v* (*pret & pp* **hemmed**; *ger* **hemming**) *tr* bastillar, dobladillar; **to hem in** encerrar, rodear ‖ *intr* destoserse; vacilar; **to hem and haw** vacilar al hablar; ser evasivo

hemisphere ['hɛmɪ,sfɪr] s hemisferio

hemistich ['hɛmɪ,stɪk] s hemistiquio

hem'line' s ruedo de la falda, borde m de la falda

hem'lock' s (*Tsuga canadensis*) abeto del Canadá; (*herb and poison*) cicuta

hemoglobin [,hɛmə'globɪn] o [,hɪmə'globɪn] s hemoglobina

hemophilia [,hɛmə'fɪlɪ-ə] o [,hɪmə'fɪlɪ-ə] s hemofilia

hemorrhage ['hɛmərɪdʒ] s hemorragia

hemorrhoids ['hɛmə,rɔɪdz] *spl* hemorroides *fpl*

hemostat ['hɛmə,stæt] o ['hɪmə,stæt] s hemóstato

hemp [hɛmp] s cáñamo

hemstitch ['hɛm,stɪtʃ] s vainica ‖ *tr* hacer vainica en ‖ *intr* hacer vainica

hen [hɛn] s gallina

hence [hɛns] *adv* de aquí; desde ahora; por lo tanto, por consiguiente; de aquí a, p.ej., **three weeks hence** de aquí a tres semanas

hence'forth' *adv* de aquí en adelante

hench·man ['hɛntʃmən] s (*pl* **-men** [mən]) secuaz m, servidor m; (*political schemer*) muñidor m

hen'coop' s gallinero

hen'house' s gallinero

henna ['hɛnə] s alcana, alheña; (*dye*) henna f ‖ *tr* alheñarse (*el pelo*)

hen'peck' *tr* dominar (*la mujer al marido*)

henpecked husband s calzonazos m, gurrumino

hep [hɛp] *adj* (slang) enterado; **to be hep to** (slang) estar al corriente de

her [hʌr] *adj poss* su; el . . . de ella ‖ *pron pers* la; ella; **to her** le; a ella

herald ['hɛrəld] s heraldo; anunciador m ‖ *tr* anunciar; ser precursor de

heraldic [hɛ'rældɪk] *adj* heráldico

herald·ry ['hɛrəldrɪ] s (*pl* **-ries**) (*office or duty of herald*) heraldía; (*science of armorial bearings*) blasón m, heráldica; (*heraldic device; coat of arms*) blasón; pompa heráldica

herb [ʌrb] o [hʌrb] s hierba; hierba aromática; hierba medicinal

herbaceous [hʌr'beʃəs] *adj* herbáceo

herbage ['ʌrbɪdʒ] o ['hʌrbɪdʒ] s herbaje m

herbal ['ʌrbəl] o ['hʌrbəl] *adj & s* herbario

herbalist ['hʌrbəlɪst] o ['ʌrbəlɪst] s herbolario

herbari·um [hʌr'bɛrɪ-əm] s (*pl* **-ums** o **-a** [ə]) herbario

herb doctor s herbolario

herculean [hʌr'kjulɪ-ən] o [,hʌrkju-

'li·ən] *adj* (*hard to perform*) penoso, laborioso; (*strong, big*) hercúleo

herd [hʌrd] s manada, rebaño, hato; (*of people*) chusma, multitud ‖ *tr* reunir en manada; reunir ‖ *intr* reunirse en manada; reunirse, ir juntos

herds·man ['hʌrdzmən] s (*pl* **-men** [mən]) manadero; (*of sheep*) pastor m; (*of cattle*) vaquero

here [hɪr] *adj* presente ‖ *adv* aquí; **here and there** acá y allá; **here is** o **here are** aquí tiene Vd.; **that's neither here nor there** eso no viene al caso ‖ *s* — **the here and the hereafter** esta vida y la futura ‖ *interj* ¡presente!

hereabouts ['hɪrə,bauts] *adv* por aquí, cerca de aquí

here·af'ter *adv* de aquí en adelante; en lo sucesivo; en la vida futura ‖ **the hereafter** la otra vida, el más allá

here·by' *adv* por esto; por la presente

hereditary [hɪ'rɛdɪ,tɛrɪ] *adj* hereditario

heredi·ty [hɪ'rɛdɪtɪ] s (*pl* **-ties**) herencia

here·in' *adv* aquí dentro; en este asunto

here·of' *adv* de esto

here·on' *adv* en esto, sobre esto

here·sy ['hɛrəsɪ] s (*pl* **-sies**) herejía

heretic ['hɛrətɪk] *adj* herético ‖ s hereje *mf*

heretical [hɪ'rɛtɪkəl] *adj* herético

heretofore [,hɪrtu'for] *adv* antes, hasta ahora

here·u·pon' *adv* en esto, sobre esto; en seguida

here·with' *adv* adjunto, con la presente; de este modo

heritage ['hɛrɪtɪdʒ] s herencia

hermetic(al) [hʌr'mɛtɪk(əl)] *adj* hermético

hermit ['hʌrmɪt] s eremita m, ermitaño

hermitage ['hʌrmɪtɪdʒ] s ermita

herni·a ['hʌrnɪ-ə] s (*pl* **-as** o **-ae** [,i]) hernia

he·ro ['hɪro] s (*pl* **-roes**) héroe m

heroic [hɪ'ro·ɪk] *adj* heroico ‖ **heroics** *spl* verso heroico; lenguaje rimbombante

heroin ['hero·ɪn] s heroína (*polvo cristalino*)

heroine ['hero·ɪn] s heroína (*mujer*)

heroism ['hero,ɪzəm] s heroísmo

heron ['hɛrən] s garza; (*Ardea cinerea*) airón m, garza real

herring ['hɛrɪŋ] s arenque m

her'ring·bone' s (*in fabrics*) espina de pescado; (*in hardwood floors*) espinapez m, punto de Hungría

hers [hʌrz] *pron poss* el suyo, el de ella; suyo

herself [hʌr'sɛlf] *pron pers* ella misma; sí, sí misma; se, p.ej., **she enjoyed herself** se divirtió; **with herself** consigo

hesitan·cy ['hɛzɪtənsɪ] s (*pl* **-cies**) vacilación

hesitant ['hɛzɪtənt] *adj* vacilante

hesitate ['hɛzɪ͵tet] *intr* vacilar, titu-bear; (*to stutter*) titubear
hesitation [͵hɛzɪ'teʃən] *s* vacilación
heterodox ['hɛtərə͵dɑks] *adj* hetero-doxo
heterodyne ['hɛtərə͵daɪn] *adj* hetero-dino || *tr* heterodinar
heterogenei·ty [͵hɛtərədʒɪ'niˑɪtɪ] *s* (*pl* -ties) heterogeneidad
heterogeneous [͵hɛtərə'dʒɪnɪˑəs] *adj* heterogéneo
hew [hju] *v* (*pret* hewed; *pp* hewed o hewn) *tr* cortar, tajar; (*with an ax*) hachear; labrar (*madera*); picar (*piedra*); **to hew down** derribar a hachazos || *intr* — **to hew close to the line** (coll) hilar delgado
hex [hɛks] *s* (coll) bruja; (coll) hechizo || *tr* (coll) embrujar
hexameter [hɛks'æmɪtər] *s* hexámetro
hey [he] *interj* ¡oye!, ¡oiga!
hey'day' *s* época de mayor prosperi-dad
hf. *abbr* half
H.H. *abbr* His Highness, Her High-ness; His Holiness
hia·tus [haɪ'etəs] *s* (*pl* -tuses o -tus) (*gap*) abertura, laguna; (*in a text; in verse*) hiato
hibernate ['haɪbər͵net] *intr* invernar; estar inactivo
hibiscus [hɪ'bɪskəs] o [haɪ'bɪskəs] *s* hibisco
hiccough o **hiccup** ['hɪkəp] *s* hipo || *intr* hipar
hick [hɪk] *adj* & *s* (coll) campesino, palurdo
hicko·ry ['hɪkərɪ] *s* (*pl* -ries) nuez en-carcelada, nuez dura (*árbol*)
hickory nut *s* nuez encarcelada, nuez dura (*fruto*)
hidden ['hɪdən] *adj* escondido, oculto, obscuro
hide [haɪd] *s* cuero, piel *f*; hides co-rambre *f*; **neither hide nor hair** ni un vestigio; **to tan someone's hide** (coll) zurrarle a uno la badana || *v* (*pret* hid [hɪd]; *pp* hid o hidden ['hɪdən]) *tr* esconder, ocultar || *intr* esconderse, ocultarse; **to hide out** (coll) recatarse
hide-and-seek' *s* escondite *m*; **to play hide-and-seek** jugar al escondite
hide'bound' *adj* fanático, obstinado, dogmático
hideous ['hɪdɪˑəs] *adj* (*very ugly*) feote; (*heinous*) atroz, nefando; (*dis-tressingly large*) brutal, enorme
hide'-out' *s* (coll) guarida, refugio, es-condrijo
hiding ['haɪdɪŋ] *s* ocultación; (*place of concealment*) escondite *m*, escon-drijo; **in hiding** escondido, oculto; (*in ambush*) emboscado
hiding place *s* escondite *m*, escondrijo
hie [haɪ] *v* (*pret* & *pp* hied; *ger* hieing o hying) *tr* — **hie thee home** apre-súrate a volver a casa || *intr* apresu-rarse, ir volando
hierar·chy ['haɪə͵rɑrkɪ] *s* (*pl* -chies) jerarquía
hieroglyphic [͵haɪərə'glɪfɪk] *adj* & *s* jeroglífico

hi·fi ['haɪ'faɪ] *adj* (coll) de alta fide-lidad || *s* (coll) alta fidelidad
hi-fi fan *s* (coll) aficionado a la alta fidelidad
higgledy-piggledy ['hɪgəldɪ'pɪgəldɪ] *adj* confuso, revuelto || *adv* confusa-mente, revueltamente
high [haɪ] *adj* alto; (*river*) crecido; (*sound*) agudo; (*wind*) fuerte; (coll) borracho; (culin) manido; **high and dry** abandonado, desamparado; **high and mighty** (coll) muy arrogante || *adv* en sumo grado; a gran precio; **to aim high** poner el tiro muy alto; **to come high** venderse caro || *s* (aut) marcha directa; **on high** en el cielo
high altar *s* altar *m* mayor
high'ball' *s* highball *m*
high blood pressure *s* hipertensión ar-terial
high'born' *adj* linajudo, de ilustre cuna
high'boy' *s* cómoda alta con patas altas
high'brow' *adj* & *s* (slang) erudito
high chair *s* silla alta
high command *s* alto mando
high cost of living *s* carestía de la vida
higher education *s* enseñanza superior
higher-up [͵haɪˑər'ʌp] *s* (coll) su-perior jerárquico
high explosive *s* explosivo rompedor
highfalutin [͵haɪfə'lutən] *adj* (coll) pomposo, presuntuoso
high fidelity *s* alta fidelidad
high'-fre'quency *adj* de alta frecuencia
high gear *s* marcha directa, toma di-recta
high'-grade' *adj* de calidad superior
high-handed ['haɪ'hændɪd] *adj* arbi-trario
high hat *s* sombrero de copa
high'-hat' *adj* (coll) copetudo, esnob; **to be high-hat** (coll) tener mucho copete || **high'-hat'** *v* (*pret* & *pp* -hatted; *ger* -hatting) *tr* (coll) des-airar
high-heeled shoe ['haɪ͵hild] *s* zapato de tacón alto
high horse *s* ademán *m* arrogante
high'jack' *tr* var de hijack
high jinks [dʒɪŋks] *s* (slang) jarana, payasada
high jump *s* salto de altura
highland ['haɪlənd] *s* región monta-ñosa; **highlands** montañas, tierras altas
high life *s* alta sociedad, gran mundo
high'light' *s* elemento sobresaliente || *tr* destacar
highly ['haɪlɪ] *adv* altamente; en sumo grado; a gran precio; con aplauso general; **to speak highly of** decir mil bienes de
High Mass *s* misa cantada, misa mayor
high-minded ['haɪ'maɪndɪd] *adj* no-ble, magnánimo
highness ['haɪnɪs] *s* altura || **Highness** *s* Alteza
high noon *s* pleno mediodía
high-pitched ['haɪ'pɪtʃt] *adj* agudo; tenso, impresionable
high-powered ['haɪ'paʊˑərd] *adj* de alta potencia
high'-pres'sure *adj* de alta presión;

(fig) emprendedor, enérgico ‖ *tr* (coll) apremiar

high-priced ['haɪ'praɪst] *adj* de precio elevado

high priest *s* sumo sacerdote

high rise *s* edificio de muchos pisos

high'road' *s* camino real

high school *s* escuela de segunda enseñanza

high sea *s* mar gruesa; **high seas** alta mar

high society *s* alta sociedad, gran mundo

high'-speed' *adj* de alta velocidad

high-spirited ['haɪ'spɪrɪtɪd] *adj* animoso; vivaz; (*horse*) fogoso

high spirits *spl* alegría, buen humor *m*, animación

high-strung ['haɪ'strʌŋ] *adj* tenso, impresionable

high'-test' fuel *s* supercarburante *m*

high tide *s* pleamar *f*, marea alta; (fig) punto culminante

high time *s* hora, p.ej., **it is high time for you to go** ya es hora de que Vd. se marche; (slang) jarana, parranda

high treason *s* alta traición

high water *s* aguas altas; pleamar *f*, marea alta

high'way' *s* carretera

highway-man ['haɪˌwemən] *s* (*pl* **-men** [mən]) salteador *m* de caminos

hijack ['haɪˌdʒæk] *tr* (coll) robar (*a un contrabandista de licores*); (coll) robar (*el licor a un contrabandista*)

hike [haɪk] *s* caminata, marcha; (*increase, rise*) aumento ‖ *tr* elevar de un tirón; aumentar ‖ *intr* dar una caminata

hiker ['haɪkər] *s* caminador *m*, aficionado a las caminatas

hilarious [hɪ'lerɪ·əs] o [haɪ'lerɪ·əs] *adj* jubiloso, regocijado

hill [hɪl] *s* colina, collado ‖ *tr* aporcar (*las hortalizas*)

hillbil·ly ['hɪlˌbɪlɪ] *s* (*pl* **-lies**) (coll) rústico montañés (*del sur de los EE.UU.*)

hillock ['hɪlək] *s* altozano, montecillo

hill'side' *s* ladera

hill'top' *s* cumbre *f*, cima

hill·y ['hɪlɪ] *adj* (*comp* **-ier**; *super* **-iest**) colinoso; (*steep*) empinado

hilt [hɪlt] *s* empuñadura, puño; **up to the hilt** completamente

him [hɪm] *pron pers* le, lo; él; **to him** le; a él

himself [hɪm'self] *pron pers* él mismo; sí, sí mismo; se, p.ej., **he enjoyed himself** se divirtió; **with himself** consigo

hind [haɪnd] *adj* posterior, trasero ‖ *s* cierva

hinder ['hɪndər] *tr* estorbar, impedir

hindmost ['haɪndˌmost] *adj* postrero, último

Hindoo ['hɪndu] *adj* & *s* hindú *m*

hind'quar'ter *s* cuarto trasero

hindrance ['hɪndrəns] *s* estorbo, impedimento, obstáculo

hind'sight' *s* (*of a firearm*) mira posterior; percepción tardía, sabiduría tardía

Hindu ['hɪndu] *adj* & *s* hindú *m*

hinge [hɪndʒ] *s* (*of a door*) charnela, gozne *m*, bisagra; (*of a mollusk*) charnela; (bb) cartivana; punto capital ‖ *tr* engoznar ‖ *intr* — **to hinge on** depender de

hin·ny ['hɪnɪ] *s* (*pl* **-nies**) burdégano, mohino

hint [hɪnt] *s* indirecta, insinuación; **to take the hint** darse por aludido ‖ *tr* & *intr* insinuar; indicar; **to hint at** aludir indirectamente a

hinterland ['hɪntərˌlænd] *s* región interior

hip [hɪp] *s* cadera; (*of a roof*) caballete *m*, lima

hip'bone' *s* cía, hueso de la cadera

hipped [hɪpt] *adj* (*livestock*) renco; (*roof*) a cuatro aguas; **hipped on** (coll) obsesionado por

hippety-hop ['hɪpɪtɪ'hap] *adv* (coll) a coxcojita

hip·po ['hɪpo] *s* (*pl* **-pos**) (coll) hipopótamo

hippodrome ['hɪpəˌdrom] *s* hipódromo

hippopota·mus [ˌhɪpə'patəməs] *s* (*pl* **-muses** o **-mi** [ˌmaɪ]) hipopótamo

hip roof *s* tejado a cuatro aguas

hire [haɪr] *s* alquiler *m*; precio; salario; **for hire** de alquiler ‖ *tr* alquilar (*p.ej., un coche*); ajustar (*p.ej., a un criado*) ‖ *intr* — **to hire out** ajustarse

hired girl *s* criada

hired man *s* (coll) mozo de campo

hireling ['haɪrlɪŋ] *adj* & *s* alquiladizo

his [hɪz] *adj poss* su; el . . . de él ‖ *pron poss* el suyo, el de él; suyo

Hispanic [hɪs'pænɪk] *adj* hispánico

Hispaniola [ˌhɪspən'jolə] *s* Santo Domingo

hispanist ['hɪspənɪst] *s* hispanista *mf*

hiss [hɪs] *s* siseo, silbido ‖ *tr* sisear, silbar (*p.ej., una escena, a un actor por malo*) ‖ *intr* sisear, silbar

hist. *abbr* **historian, history**

histology [hɪs'talədʒɪ] *s* histología

historian [hɪs'torɪ·ən] *s* historiador *m*

historic(al) [hɪs'tarɪk(əl)] o [hɪs'torɪk(əl)] *adj* histórico

histo·ry ['hɪstərɪ] *s* (*pl* **-ries**) historia

histrionic [ˌhɪstrɪ'anɪk] *adj* histriónico; teatral ‖ **histrionics** *s* actitud teatral, modales *mpl* teatrales

hit [hɪt] *s* golpe *m*; (*of a bullet*) impacto; (*blow that hits its mark*) tiro certero; (*sarcastic remark*) censura acerba; (baseball) batazo; (coll) éxito; **to make a hit** (coll) dar golpe; **to make a hit with** caer en la gracia de (*una persona*) ‖ *v* (*pret* & *pp* **hit**; *ger* **hitting**) *tr* golpear, pegar; dar con, dar contra, chocar con; dar en (*p.ej., el blanco*); censurar acerbamente; (*to run over in a car*) atropellar; afectar mucho (*un acontecimiento a una persona*) ‖ *intr* chocar; **to hit against** dar contra; **to hit on** dar con (*lo que se busca*)

hit'-and-run' *adj* que atropella y se da a la huída

hitch [hɪtʃ] *s* (*jerk*) tirón *m*; dificultad; obstáculo; **without a hitch** a

he
hi

pedir de boca, sin tropiezo || *tr* (*to tie*) atar, sujetar; enganchar (*un caballo*); uncir (*bueyes*); (slang) casar

hitch'hike' *intr* (coll) hacer autostop, viajar en autostop

hitch'hik'er *s* autostopista *mf*

hitching post *s* poste *m* para atar a las cabalgaduras

hither ['hɪðər] *adv* acá, hacia acá; **hither and thither** acá y allá

hith'er·to' *adv* hasta ahora, hasta aquí

hit'-or-miss' *adj* descuidado, casual

hit parade *s* (rad) canciones que gozan de más popularidad en la actualidad

hit record *s* (coll) disco de mucho éxito

hit'-run' *adj* que atropella y se da a la huída

hive [haɪv] *s* (*box for bees*) colmena; (*swarm*) enjambre *m*; **hives** urticaria || *tr* encorchar (*abejas*)

H.M. *abbr* **Her Majesty, His Majesty**

H.M.S. *abbr* **Her Majesty's Ship, His Majesty's Ship**

hoard [hord] *s* (*of money, provisions, etc.*) cúmulo; tesoro escondido || *tr* acumular secretamente; atesorar (*dinero*) || *intr* guardar víveres; atesorar dinero

hoarding ['hordɪŋ] *s* acumulación secreta; atesoramiento

hoar'frost' *s* helada blanca, escarcha

hoarse [hors] *adj* ronco

hoarseness ['horsnɪs] *s* ronquedad; (*from a cold*) ronquera

hoar·y ['hori] *adj* (*comp* -**ier;** *super* -**iest**) cano, canoso; (*old*) vetusto

hoax [hoks] *s* pajarota, mistificación || *tr* mistificar

hob [hab] *s* repisa interior del hogar; **to play hob with** (coll) trastornar

hobble ['habəl] *s* (*limp*) cojera; (*rope used to tie legs of animal*) manea, traba || *tr* dejar cojo; manear, trabar; dificultar || *intr* cojear; tambalear

hobble skirt *s* falda de medio paso

hob·by ['habɪ] *s* (*pl* -**bies**) comidilla, afición favorita, trabajo preferido; **to ride a hobby** entregarse demasiado al tema favorito

hob'by·horse' *s* (*stick with horse's head*) caballito; (*rocking horse*) caballo mecedor

hob'gob'lin *s* duende *m*, trasgo; (*bogy*) bu *m*, coco

hob'nail' *s* tachuela || *tr* clavetear con tachuelas; (fig) atropellar

hob·nob ['hab‚nab] *v* (*pret* & *pp* -**nobbed;** *ger* -**nobbing**) *intr* codearse, rozarse; beber juntos

ho·bo ['hobo] *s* (*pl* -**bos** o -**boes**) vagabundo

Hobson's choice ['habsənz] *s* alternativa entre la cosa ofrecida o ninguna

hock [hak] *s* jarrete *m*, corvejón *m* || *tr* (*to hamstring*) desjarretar; (coll) empeñar

hockey ['hakɪ] *s* hockey *m*, chueca

hock'shop' *s* (slang) casa de empeños, monte *m* de piedad

hocus-pocus ['hokəs'pokəs] *s* (*mean-*

ingless formula) abracadabra *m*; burla, engaño; juego de manos

hod [had] *s* capacho, cuezo; cubo para carbón

hod carrier *s* peón *m* de albañil, peón de mano

hodgepodge ['had‚pad‚] *s* baturrillo

hoe [ho] *s* azada, azadón *m* || *tr* & *intr* azadonar

hog [hag] o [hɔg] *s* cerdo, puerco || *v* (*pret* & *pp* **hogged;** *ger* **hogging**) *tr* (slang) tragarse lo mejor de

hog'back' *s* cuchilla

hoggish ['hagɪʃ] o ['hɔgɪʃ] *adj* comilón; glotón; egoísta

hog Latin *s* latín *m* de cocina

hogs'head' *s* pipa de 63 galones o más; medida de capacidad de 63 galones

hog'wash' *s* bazofia

hoist [hɔɪst] *s* (*apparatus for lifting*) montacargas *m*, torno izador, grúa; empujón *m* hacia arriba || *tr* alzar, levantar; enarbolar (*p.ej., una bandera*); (naut) izar

hoity-toity ['hɔɪtɪ'tɔɪtɪ] *adj* frívolo, veleidoso; arrogante, altanero; **to be hoity-toity** ponerse tan alto

hokum ['hokəm] *s* (coll) música celestial, tonterías

hold [hold] *s* (*grip*) agarro; (*handle*) asa, mango; autoridad, dominio; (in *wrestling*) presa; (aer) cabina de carga; (mus) calderón *m*; (naut) bodega; **to take hold of** agarrar, coger; apoderarse de || *v* (*pret* & *pp* **held** [held]) *tr* tener, retener; (*to hold up, support*) apoyar, sostener (*e.g., with a pin*) sujetar; contener, tener cabida para; ocupar (*un cargo, puesto, etc.*); celebrar (*una reunión*); sostener (*una opinión*); (mus) sostener (*una nota*); **to hold back** detener; retener; contener; **to hold in** refrenar; **to hold one's own** mantenerse firme, no perder terreno; **to hold over** aplazar, diferir; **to hold up** apoyar, sostener; (*to rob*) (coll) atracar || *intr* ser valedero, seguir vigente; pegarse; **hold on!** ¡un momento!; **to hold back** refrenarse; **to hold forth** poner cátedra; **to hold off** esperar; mantenerse a distancia; **to hold on** agarrarse bien; **to hold on** to asirse de; **to hold out** no cejar; tirando; **to hold out for** insistir en

holder ['holdər] *s* tenedor *m*, posesor *m*; (*for a cigar or cigaret*) boquilla; (*to hold, e.g., a hot plate*) cojinillo; (*e.g., of a passport*) titular *m*; asa, mango

holding ['holdɪŋ] *s* tenencia, posesión; **holdings** valores habidos

holding company *s* sociedad de control, compañía tenedora

hold'up' *s* (*stop, delay*) detención; (coll) atraco, asalto; (coll) precio excesivo

holdup man *s* (coll) atracador *m*, salteador *m*

hole [hol] *s* agujero; (*in cheese, bread, etc.*) ojo; (*in a road*) bache *m*; (*den of animals; den of vice*) guarida; (*dirty, disorderly dwelling*) cochitril *m;* **in the hole** adeudado, perdidoso; **to burn a hole in one's pocket** írsele a uno (*el dinero*) de entre las manos; **to pick holes in** (coll) poner reparos a || *intr* — **to hole up** encovarse; buscar un rincón cómodo

holiday [ˈhɑlɪˌde] *s* día festivo; vacación

holiday attire *s* trapos de cristianar

holiness [ˈholɪnɪs] *s* santidad; **his Holiness** su Santidad

Holland [ˈhɑlənd] *s* Holanda

Hollander [ˈhɑləndər] *s* holandés *m*

hollow [ˈhɑlo] *adj* hueco; (*voice*) ahuecado, sepulcral; (*eyes, cheeks*) hundido; falso, engañoso || *adv* — **to beat all hollow** (coll) derrotar completamente || *s* hueco, cavidad; (*small valley*) vallecito || *tr* ahuecar, excavar

hol·ly [ˈhɑli] *s* (*pl* -lies) acebo

hol'ly·hock' *s* malva arbórea

holm oak [hom] *s* encina

holocaust [ˈhɑləˌkɔst] *s* holocausto

holster [ˈholstər] *s* pistolera

ho·ly [ˈholi] *adj* (*comp* -lier; *super* -liest) santo; (*e.g., writing*) sagrado; (*e.g., water*) bendito

Holy Ghost *s* Espíritu Santo

holy orders *spl* órdenes sagradas; **to take holy orders** recibir las órdenes sagradas, ordenarse

holy rood [rud] *s* crucifijo || **Holy Rood** *s* Santa Cruz

Holy Scripture *s* Sagrada Escritura

Holy See *s* Santa Sede

Holy Sepulcher *s* santo sepulcro

holy water *s* agua bendita

Holy Writ *s* Sagrada Escritura

homage [ˈhɑmɪdʒ] o [ˈɑmɪdʒ] *s* homenaje *m;* (*feud*) homenaje, pleito homenaje

home [hom] *adj* casero, doméstico; nacional || *s* casa, domicilio, hogar *m;* (*native heath*) patria chica; (*of the arts, etc.*) patria; (*for the sick, poor, etc.*) asilo; (sport) meta; **at home** en casa; en su propio país; (*ready to receive callers*) de recibo; (*at ease, comfortable*) a gusto; (sport) en campo propio; **away from home** fuera de casa; **make yourself at home** está Vd. en su casa || *adv* en casa; a casa; **to see home** acompañar a casa; **to strike home** dar en lo vivo

home'bod'y *s* (*pl* -ies) hogareño

homebred [ˈhomˌbred] *adj* doméstico; sencillo, inculto, tosco

home'-brew' *s* cerveza o vino caseros

home-coming [ˈhomˌkʌmɪŋ] *s* regreso al hogar

home country *s* suelo natal

home delivery *s* distribución a domicilio

home front *s* frente doméstico

home'land' *s* tierra natal, patria

homeless [ˈhomlɪs] *adj* sin casa, sin hogar

home life *s* vida de familia

home-loving [ˈhomˌlʌvɪŋ] *adj* casero, hogareño

home·ly [ˈhomli] *adj* (*comp* -lier; *su-*

per -liest) (*not attractive or good-looking*) feo; (*plain, not elegant*) sencillo, llano

homemade [ˈhomˈmed] *adj* casero, hecho en casa

homemaker [ˈhomˌmekər] *s* ama de casa

home office *s* domicilio social, oficina central || **Home Office** *s* (Brit) ministerio de la Gobernación

homeopath [ˈhomɪ·əˌpæθ] o [ˈhɑmɪ·əˌpæθ] *s* homeópata *mf*

homeopathy [ˌhomɪˈɑpəθi] o [ˌhɑmɪˈɑpəθi] *s* homeopatía

home plate *s* (baseball) puesto meta

home port *s* puerto de origen

home rule *s* autonomía, gobierno autónomo

home run *s* (baseball) jonrón *m*, cuadrangular *m*

home'sick' *adj* nostálgico; **to be homesick (for)** sentir nostalgia (de)

home'sick'ness *s* nostalgia, mal *m* de la tierra

homespun [ˈhomˌspʌn] *adj* hilado en casa; sencillo, llano

home'stead' *s* casa y terrenos, heredad

home stretch *s* esfuerzo final, último trecho

home town *s* ciudad natal

homeward [ˈhomwərd] *adj* de regreso || *adv* hacia casa; hacia su país

home'work' *s* trabajo a domicilio; (*of a student*) deber *m*, trabajo escolar

homey [ˈhomi] *adj* (*comp* homier; *super* homiest) (coll) íntimo, cómodo

homicidal [ˌhɑmɪˈsaɪdəl] *adj* homicida

homicide [ˈhɑmɪˌsaɪd] *s* (*act*) homicidio; (*person*) homicida *mf*

homi·ly [ˈhɑmɪli] *s* (*pl* -lies) homilía

homing [ˈhomɪŋ] *adj* (*animal*) querencioso; (*weapon*) buscador del blanco

homing pigeon *s* paloma mensajera

hominy [ˈhɑmɪni] *s* maíz molido

homogenei·ty [ˌhomədʒɪˈni·ɪti] o [ˌhɑmədʒɪˈni·ɪti] *s* (*pl* -ties) homogeneidad

homogeneous [ˌhoməˈdʒɪnɪ·əs] o [ˌhɑməˈdʒɪnɪ·əs] *adj* homogéneo

homogenize [həˈmɑdʒəˌnaɪz] *tr* homogeneizar

homonym [ˈhɑmənɪm] *s* homónimo

homonymous [həˈmɑnɪməs] *adj* homónimo

homosexual [ˌhoməˈsɛkʃʊ·əl] *adj* & *s* homosexual *mf*

hon. *abbr* honorary

Hon. *abbr* Honorable

Honduran [hɑnˈdurən] *adj* & *s* hondureño

hone [hon] *s* piedra de afilar || *tr* afilar, amolar, asentar

honest [ˈɑnɪst] *adj* honrado, probo, recto; (*money*) bien adquirido; sincero; genuino

honesty [ˈɑnɪsti] *s* honradez *f*, probidad, rectitud; (bot) hierba de la plata

hon·ey [ˈhʌni] *adj* meloso, dulce; (coll) querido || *s* miel *f;* (coll) vida mía; **it's a honey** (slang) es una preciosidad || *v* (*pret & pp* -eyed o -ied)

hi
ho

tr enmelar, endulzar con miel; adular, lisonjear

hon'ey·bee' *s* abeja doméstica, abeja de miel

hon'ey·comb' *s* panal *m* || *tr (to riddle)* acribillar; llenar, penetrar

hon'ey·dew' melon *s* melón muy dulce, blanco y terso

honeyed ['hʌnɪd] *adj* dulce, enmelado; melodioso; adulador

honey locust *s* acacia de tres espinas

hon'ey·moon' *s* luna de miel; viaje *m* de bodas || *intr* pasar la luna de miel

honeysuckle ['hʌnɪ,sʌkəl] *s* madreselva

honk [hɑŋk] o [hɔŋk] *s (of wild goose)* graznido; *(of automobile horn)* bocinazo || *tr* tocar *(la bocina)* || *intr* graznar *(el ganso silvestre)*; tocar la bocina

honkytonk ['hɑŋkɪ,tɑŋk] o ['hɔŋkɪ,tɔŋk] *s (slang)* sala de fiestas de mala muerte

honor ['ɑnər] *s (distinction; award for distinction; integrity)* honor *m; (good reputation; chastity)* honor, honra || *tr* honrar; hacer honor a *(su firma)*; aceptar y pagar *(una letra)*

honorable ['ɑnərəbəl] *adj (behaving with honor; performed with honor)* honrado; *(bringing honor; associated with honor)* honroso; *(worthy, of honor)* honorable

honorary ['ɑnə,rerɪ] *adj* honorario

honorific [,ɑnə'rɪfɪk] *adj* honorífico || *s* antenombre *m*

honor system *s* acatamiento voluntario del reglamento

hood [hʊd] *s* capilla; *(one with a point)* caperuza; *(one which covers the face)* capirote *m; (worn with academic gown)* muceta, capirote *m; (of a chimney)* sombrerete *m; (aut)* capó *m*, cubierta; *(slang)* gambero || *tr* encapirotar; ocultar

hoodlum ['hudləm] *s (coll)* gamberro, maleante *m*

hoodoo ['hudu] *s (body of primitive rites)* vudú *m; (coll)* mala suerte || *tr* traer mala suerte a

hood'wink' *tr* burlar, engañar, vendar

hooey ['hu·ɪ] *s (slang)* música celestial

hoof [huf] o [hʊf] *s* casco, pezuña; **on the hoof** *(cattle)* vivo, en pie || *tr & intr (coll)* caminar; **to hoof it** *(coll)* caminar, ir a pie; *(coll)* bailar

hoof'beat' *s* pisada, ruido de la pisada *(de animal ungulado)*

hook [hʊk] *s* gancho; *(for fishing)* anzuelo; *(to join two things)* enganche *m; (bend, curve)* ángulo, recodo; *(box)* crochet *m*, golpe *m* de gancho; *(of hook and eye)* corchete *m*, macho; **by hook or by crook** por fas o por nefas; **to swallow the hook** tragar el anzuelo || *tr* enganchar; *(to bend)* encorvar, doblar; coger, pescar *(un pez); (to wound with the horns)* acornar || *intr* engancharse; encorvarse, doblarse

hookah ['hukə] *s* narguile *m*

hook and eye *s* broche *m*, corchete *m (macho y hembra)*

hook and ladder *s* carro de escaleras de incendio

hooked rug *s* tapete *m* de crochet

hook'nose' *s* nariz *f* de pico de loro

hook'up' *s* montaje *m*

hook'worm' *s* anquilostoma *m*

hooky ['hʊkɪ] *s* — **to play hooky** hacer novillos

hooligan ['hulɪgən] *s* gamberro

hooliganism ['hulɪgən,ɪzəm] *s* gamberrismo

hoop [hup] o [hʊ·p] *s* aro || *tr* herrar, enarcar, enzunchar

hoop skirt *s* miriñaque *m*

hoot [hut] *s* resoplido, ululato; grito || *tr* reprobar a gritos; echar a gritos *(p.ej., a un cómico)* || *intr* resoplar, ulular; **to hoot at** dar grita a

hoot owl *s* autillo, cárabo

hop [hɑp] *s* saltito; *(coll)* vuelo en avión; *(coll)* sarao; *(coll)* baile *m;* lúpulo, hombrecillo; **hops** *(dried flowers of hop vine)* lúpulo || *v (pret & pp* **hopped;** *ger* **hopping)** *tr* cruzar de un salto; *(coll)* atravesar *(p.ej., el mar)* en avión; *(coll)* subir a *(un tren, taxi, etc.)* || *intr* saltar, brincar; *(on one foot)* saltar a la pata coja

hope [hop] *s* esperanza || *tr & intr* esperar; **to hope for** esperar

hope chest *s* ajuar *m* de novia

hopeful ['hopfəl] *adj (feeling hope)* esperanzado; *(giving hope)* esperanzador

hopeless ['hoplɪs] *adj* desesperanzado; *(situation)* desesperado

hopper ['hɑpər] *s (funnel-shaped container)* tolva; *(of blast furnace)* tragante *m*

hopper car *s (rr)* vagón *m* tolva

hop'scotch' *s* infernáculo

horde [hord] *s* horda

horehound ['hor,haʊnd] *s* marrubio; extracto de marrubio

horizon [hə'raɪzən] *s* horizonte *m*

horizontal [,hɑrɪ'zɑntəl] o [,hɔrɪ'zɑntəl] *adj & s* horizontal *f*

hormone ['hɔrmon] *s* hormón *m* u hormona

horn [hɔrn] *s (bony projection on head of certain animals)* cuerno; *(of bull)* asta, cuerno; *(of moon, anvil, etc.)* cuerno; *(of automobile)* bocina; *(mus)* cuerno; *(French horn)* (mus) trompa de armonía; **to blow one's own horn** cantar sus propias alabanzas; **to pull in one's horns** contenerse, volverse atrás || *intr* — **to horn in** *(slang)* entrometerse (en)

hornet ['hɔrnɪt] *s* crabrón *m*, avispón *m*

hornet's nest *s* panal *m* del avispón; **to stir up a hornet's nest** *(coll)* armar camorra, armar cisco

horn of plenty *s* cuerno de la abundancia

horn'pipe' *s* chirimía

horn-rimmed glasses ['hɔrn'rɪmd] *spl* anteojos de concha

horn·y ['hɔrnɪ] *adj (comp* **-ier;** *super*

-lest) córneo; (*callous*) calloso; (*having hornlike projections*) cornudo

horoscope ['hɑrə‚skop] o ['hɔrə‚skop] *s* horóscopo; **to cast a horoscope** sacar un horóscopo

horrible ['hɑrɪbəl] o ['hɔrɪbəl] *adj* horrible; (coll) muy desagradable

horrid ['hɑrɪd] o ['hɔrɪd] *adj* horroroso; (coll) muy desagradable

horri-fy ['hɑrɪ‚faɪ] o ['hɔrɪ‚faɪ] *v* (*pret & pp* **-fied**) *tr* horrorizar

horror ['hɑrər] o ['hɔrər] *s* horror *m;* **to have a horror of** tener horror a

hors d'oeuvre [ɔr 'dʌrv] *s* (*pl* **hors d'oeuvres** [ɔr 'dʌrvz]) *s* entremés *m*

horse [hɔrs] *s* caballo; (*of carpenter*) caballete *m;* **hold your horses** (coll) pare Vd. el carro; **to back the wrong horse** (coll) jugar a la carta mala; **to be a horse of another color** (coll) ser harina de otro costal

horse'back' *s* — **on horseback** a caballo ‖ *adv* — **to ride horseback** montar a caballo

horse blanket *s* manta para caballo

horse block *s* montadero

horse'break'er *s* domador *m* de caballos

horse'car' *s* tranvía *m* de sangre

horse chestnut *s* (*tree*) castaño de Indias; (*nut*) castaña de Indias

horse collar *s* collera

horse dealer *s* chalán *m*

horse doctor *s* veterinario

horse'fly' *s* (*pl* **-flies**) mosca borriquera, tábano

horse'hair' *s* crines *fpl* de caballo; (*fabric*) tela de crin

horse'hide' *s* cuero de caballo

horse laugh *s* risotada

horse-man ['hɔrsmən] *s* (*pl* **-men** [mən]) jinete *m*, caballista *m*

horsemanship ['hɔrsmən‚ʃɪp] *s* equitación, manejo

horse meat *s* carne *f* de caballo

horse opera *s* (U.S.A.) melodrama *m* del Oeste

horse pistol *s* pistola de arzón

horse'play' *s* chanza pesada, payasada

horse'pow'er *s* caballo de vapor inglés

horse race *s* carrera de caballos

horse'rad'ish *s* (*plant*) rábano picante o rusticano; (*condiment*) mostaza de los alemanes

horse sense *s* (coll) sentido común

horse'shoe' *s* herradura

horseshoe magnet *s* imán *m* de herradura

horseshoe nail *s* clavo de herrar

horse show *s* concurso hípico

horse'tail' *s* cola de caballo

horse thief *s* abigeo, cuatrero

horse'-trade' *intr* chalanear

horse trading *s* chalanería

horse'-trad'ing *adj* chalanesco

horse'whip' *s* látigo ‖ *v* (*pret & pp* **-whipped**; *ger* **-whipping**) *tr* dar latigazos a

horse-woman ['hɔrs‚wumən] *s* (*pl* **-women** [‚wɪmɪn]) amazona, caballista *f*

hors·y ['hɔrsi] *adj* (*comp* **-ier;** *super* **-iest**) caballar, hípico; (*interested in horses and horse racing*) carrerista, turfista; (coll) desmañado

horticultural [‚hɔrtɪ'kʌlt/ərəl] *adj* hortícola

horticulture ['hɔrtɪ‚kʌlt/ər] *s* horticultura

horticulturist [‚hɔrtɪ'kʌlt/ərɪst] *s* horticultor *m*

hose [hoz] *s* (*stocking*) media; (*sock*) calcetín *m;* (*flexible tube*) manguera ‖ **hose** *spl* calzas

hosier ['hoʒər] *s* mediero, calcetero

hosiery ['hoʒəri] *s* calcetas; calcetería

hospice ['hɑspɪs] *s* hospicio

hospitable ['hɑspɪtəbəl] o [hɑs'pɪtəbəl] *adj* hospitalario

hospital ['hɑspɪtəl] *s* hospital *m*

hospitali-ty [‚hɑspɪ'tælɪti] *s* (*pl* **-ties**) hospitalidad

hospitalize ['hɑspɪtə‚laɪz] *tr* hospitalizar

host [host] *s* anfitrión *m;* (*at an inn*) huésped *m*, mesonero; (*army*) hueste *f;* multitud, sinnúmero ‖ **Host** *s* (eccl) hostia

hostage ['hɑstɪdʒ] *s* rehén *m;* **to be held a hostage** quedar en rehenes

hostel·ry ['hɑstəlri] *s* (*pl* **-ries**) parador *m*, hostería

hostess ['hostɪs] *s* anfitriona; dueña; patrona; (*in a night club*) tanguista; (aer) azafata, aeromoza; (*e.g., on a bus*) jefa de ruta

hostile ['hɑstɪl] *adj* hostil

hostili-ty [hɑs'tɪlɪti] *s* (*pl* **-ties**) hostilidad

hostler ['hɑslər] o ['ɑslər] *s* mozo de cuadra, mozo de paja y cebada

hot [hɑt] *adj* (*comp* **hotter;** *super* **hottest**) (*water, air, coffee, etc.*) caliente; (*climate, country*) (*taste*) cálido; (*fiery, excitable*) caluroso; (*pursuit*) enérgico; (*in rut*) caliente; (coll) muy radiactivo; **to be hot** (*said of a person*) tener calor; (*said of the weather*) hacer calor; **to make it hot for** (coll) hostilizar

hot air *s* (slang) palabrería, música celestial

hot'-air' furnace *s* calorífero de aire

hot and cold running water *s* circulación de agua fría y caliente

hot baths *spl* caldas, termas

hot'bed' *s* (hort) almáciga; (*e.g., of vice*) sementera, semillero

hot-blooded ['hɑt'blʌdɪd] *adj* apasionado; temerario, irreflexivo

hot cake *s* torta a la plancha; **to sell like hot cakes** (coll) venderse como pan bendito

hot dog *s* (slang) perro caliente

hotel [ho'tɛl] *adj* hotelero ‖ *s* hotel *m*

ho·tel'-keep'er *s* hotelero

hot'head' *s* botafuego

hot-headed ['hɑt'hɛdɪd] *adj* caliente de cascos

hot'house' *s* estufa, invernáculo

hot plate *s* hornillo, calientaplatos *m*

hot springs *spl* fuentes *fpl* termales

hot-tempered ['hɑt'tempərd] adj irascible

hot water s — to be in hot water (coll) estar en calzas prietas

hot'-wa'ter boiler s termosifón m

hot-water bottle s bolsa de agua caliente

hot-water heater s calentador m de acumulación

hot-water heating s calefacción por agua caliente

hot-water tank s depósito de agua caliente

hound [haʊnd] s podenco, perro de caza; to follow the hounds o to ride to hounds cazar a caballo con jauría || tr acosar, hostigar

hour [aʊr] s hora; by the hour por horas; in an evil hour en hora mala; on the hour a la hora en punto cada hora; to keep late hours acostarse tarde; to work long hours trabajar muchas horas cada día

hour'glass' s reloj m de arena

hour hand s horario

hourly ['aʊrli] adj de cada hora; por hora || adv cada hora; muy a menudo

house [haʊs] s (pl houses ['haʊzɪz]) casa; (legislative body) cámara; teatro; (size of audience) entrada, p.ej., a good house mucha entrada; to keep house tener casa puesta; to put one's house in order arreglar sus asuntos || [haʊz] tr domiciliar, alojar, hospedar

house arrest s arresto domiciliario

house'boat' s barco vivienda

house'break'er s escalador m

housebreaking ['haʊs,brekɪŋ] s escalo, allanamiento de morada

housebroken ['haʊs,brokən] adj (perro o gato) enseñado (a hábitos de limpieza)

house cleaning s limpieza de la casa

house coat s bata

house current s sector m de distribución, canalización de consumo

house'fly' s (pl -flies) mosca doméstica

houseful ['haʊs,ful] s casa llena

house'fur'nishings spl menaje m, enseres domésticos

house'hold' adj casero, doméstico || s casa, familia

house'hold'er s dueño de la casa; jefe m de familia

house'-hunt' intr — to go house-hunting ir a buscar casa

house'keep'er s ama de llaves, mujer f de gobierno

house'keep'ing s manejo doméstico, gobierno doméstico; to set up housekeeping poner casa

housekeeping apartment s apartamento con cocina

house'maid' s criada de casa

house meter s contador m de abonado

house'moth'er s mujer encargada de una residencia de estudiantes

house of cards s castillo de naipes

house of ill fame s lupanar m, casa de prostitución

house painter s pintor m de brocha gorda

house physician s médico residente

house'top' s tejado; to shout from the housetops pregonar a los cuatro vientos

housewarming ['haʊs,wɔrmɪŋ] s fiesta para celebrar el estreno de una casa; to have a housewarming estrenar la casa

house'wife' s (pl -wives) ama de casa, madre f de familia

house'work' s quehaceres domésticos

housing ['haʊzɪŋ] s (of a house) gualdrapa; (aut) cárter m; (mach) caja, bastidor m

housing shortage s crisis f de viviendas

hovel ['hʌvəl] o ['hɑvəl] s casucha, choza; (shed for cattle, tools, etc.) cobertizo

hover ['hʌvər] o ['hɑvər] intr cernerse (un ave); (to hesitate; to be in danger) fluctuar; asomar (p.ej., una sonrisa en los labios de uno)

how [haʊ] adv cómo; (at what price) a cómo; how early cuándo, a qué hora; how else de qué otra manera; how far hasta dónde; cuánto, p.ej., how far is it to the airport? ¿cuánto hay de aquí al aeropuerto?; how long cuánto tiempo; how many cuántos; how much cuánto; lo mucho que; how often cuántas veces; how old are you? ¿cuántos años tiene Vd.?; how soon cuándo, a qué hora; how + adj qué + adj, p.ej., how beautiful she is! ¡qué hermosa es!; lo + adj, p.ej., you know how intelligent he is Vd. sabe lo inteligente que es; to know how to + inf saber + inf

howdah ['haʊdə] s castillo

how·ev'er adv no obstante, sin embargo; por muy . . . que, por mucho . . . que

howitzer ['haʊ·ɪtsər] s cañón m obús

howl [haʊl] s aullido; chillido; risa muy aguda; (of wind) bramido || tr decir a gritos; to howl down imponerse a gritos a (una persona) || intr aullar; chillar; reír a más no poder; bramar (el viento)

howler ['haʊlər] s aullador m; (coll) plancha, desacierto

hoyden ['hɔɪdən] s muchacha traviesa, tunantuela

H.P. abbr horsepower

hr. abbr hour

H.R.H. abbr Her (o His) Royal Highness

ht. abbr height

hub [hʌb] s cubo; (fig) centro, eje m

hubbub ['hʌbʌb] s gritería, alboroto

hub'cap' s tapacubo, embellecedor m

huckster ['hʌkstər] s (peddler) buhonero; vendedor m ambulante de hortalizas; vil traficante m, sujeto ruin

huddle ['hʌdəl] s (coll) reunión secreta; to go into a huddle (coll) conferenciar en secreto || intr acurrucarse, arrimarse

hue [hju] s matiz m; gritería; hue and cry vocería de indignación

huff [hʌf] s arrebato de cólera; **in a huff** encolerizado, ofendido

hug [hʌg] s abrazo || v (pret & pp **hugged;** ger **hugging**) tr abrazar, apretar con los brazos; ahogar entre los brazos; navegar muy cerca de (la costa); ceñirse a (p.ej., un muro) || intr abrazarse

huge [hjudʒ] adj enorme, descomunal

huh [hʌ] interj ¡eh!

hulk [hʌlk] s (body of an old ship) casco; (clumsy old ship) carcamán m, carraca; (old ship tied up at a wharf and used as a warehouse, prison, etc.) pontón m; (shell of an old building, piece of furniture, machine, etc.; heavy, unwieldy person) armatoste m

hulking ['hʌlkɪŋ] adj grueso, pesado

hull [hʌl] s (of ship or hydroplane) casco; (of a dirigible) armazón f; (of certain vegetables) hollejo, vaina || tr deshollejar, desvainar; mondar, pelar

hullabaloo ['hʌləbə,lu] o [,hʌləbə'lu] s alboroto, gritería, tumulto

hum [hʌm] s canturreo, tarareo; (of a bee, machine, etc.) zumbido || interj ¡ejem! || v (pret & pp **hummed;** ger **humming**) tr canturrear, tararear || intr canturrear, tararear; (to buzz) zumbar; (coll) estar muy activo

human ['hjumən] adj humano (perteneciente al hombre)

human being s ser humano

humane [hju'men] adj humano (compasivo)

humanist ['hjumənɪst] adj & s humanista mf

humanitarian [hju,mænɪ'terɪ-ən] adj & s humanitario

humani-ty [hju'mænɪti] s (pl -ties) humanidad

hu'man-kind' s género humano

humble ['hʌmbəl] o ['ʌmbəl] adj humilde || tr humillar

humble pie s — **to eat humble pie** cantar la palinodia

hum'bug' s patraña; (person) patrañero || v (pret & pp **-bugged;** ger **-bugging**) tr embaucar, engañar

hum'drum' adj monótono, tedioso

humer-us ['hjumərəs] s (pl **-i** [,aɪ]) húmero

humid ['hjumɪd] adj húmedo

humidifier [hju'mɪdɪ,faɪ-ər] s humectador m

humidi-fy [hju'mɪdɪ,faɪ] v (pret & pp **-fied**) tr humedecer

humidity [hju'mɪdɪti] s humedad

humiliate [hju'mɪlɪ,et] tr humillar

humiliating [hju'mɪlɪ,etɪŋ] adj humillante

humili-ty [hju'mɪlɪti] s (pl -ties) humildad

hummingbird ['hʌmɪŋ,bʌrd] s colibrí m, pájaro mosca

humor ['hjumər] o ['jumər] s humor m; **out of humor** de mal humor; **to be in the humor for** estar de humor para || tr seguir el humor a; manejar con delicadeza

humorist ['hjumərɪst] o ['jumərɪst] s humorista mf

humorous ['hjumərəs] o ['jumərəs] adj humorístico

hump [hʌmp] s corcova, joroba; (in the ground) montecillo

hump'back' s corcova, joroba; (person) corcovado, jorobado

humus ['hjuməs] s mantillo

hunch [hʌntʃ] s corcova, joroba; (premonition) (coll) corazonada || tr encorvar || intr encorvarse

hunch'back' s corcova, joroba; (person) corcovado, jorobado

hundred ['hʌndrəd] adj cien || s ciento, cien; **a hundred u one hundred** ciento, cien; **by the hundreds** a centenares

hundredth ['hʌndrədθ] adj & s centésimo

hun'dred-weight' s quintal m

Hundred Years' War s guerra de los Cien Años

Hungarian [hʌŋ'gerɪ-ən] adj & s húngaro

Hungary ['hʌŋgəri] s Hungría

hunger ['hʌŋgər] s hambre f || intr hambrear; **to hunger for** tener hambre de

hunger march s marcha del hambre

hunger strike s huelga de hambre

hun·gry ['hʌŋgri] adj (comp **-grier;** super **-griest**) hambriento; **to be hungry** tener hambre; **to go hungry** pasar hambre

hunk [hʌŋk] s (coll) buen pedazo, pedazo grande

hunt [hʌnt] s (act of hunting) caza; (hunting party) cacería; (a search) busca; **on the hunt for** a caza de || tr cazar; (to seek, look for) buscar || intr cazar; buscar; **to go hunting** ir de caza; **to hunt for** buscar; **to take hunting** llevar de caza

hunter ['hʌntər] s cazador m; perro de caza

hunting ['hʌntɪŋ] adj de caza || s (act) caza; (art) cacería, montería

hunting dog s perro de caza

hunting ground s cazadero

hunt'ing-horn' s cuerno de caza

hunting jacket s cazadora

hunting lodge s casa de montería

hunting season s época de caza

huntress ['hʌntrɪs] s cazadora

hunts·man ['hʌntsmən] s (pl **-men** [mən]) cazador m, montero

hurdle ['hʌrdəl] s (hedge over which horses must jump) zarzo; (wooden frame over which runners and horses must jump) valla; (fig) obstáculo; **hurdles** carrera de vallas || tr saltar por encima de

hurdle race s carrera de vallas

hurdy-gur·dy ['hʌrdi'gʌrdi] s (pl -dies) organillo

hurl [hʌrl] s lanzamiento || tr lanzar

hurrah [hu'rɑ] o **hurray** [hu're] s viva m || interj ¡viva!; **hurrah for . . . !** ¡viva . . . ! || tr aplaudir, vitorear || intr dar vivas

hurricane ['hʌrɪ,ken] s huracán m

hurried ['hʌrɪd] *adj* apresurado; hecho de prisa

hur·ry ['hʌri] *s* (*pl* -ries) prisa; **to be in a hurry** tener prisa, estar de prisa ‖ *v* (*pret & pp* -ried) *tr* apresurar, dar prisa a ‖ *intr* apresurarse, darse prisa; **to hurry after** correr en pos de; **to hurry away** marcharse de prisa; **to hurry back** volver de prisa; **to hurry up** darse prisa

hurt [hʌrt] *adj* (*injured*) lastimado, herido; (*offended*) resentido, herido ‖ *s* (*harm*) daño; (*injury*) herida; (*pain*) dolor *m* ‖ *v* (*pret & pp* **hurt**) *tr* (*to harm*) dañar, perjudicar; (*to injure*) lastimar, herir; (*to offend*) ofender, herir; (*to pain*) doler ‖ *intr* doler

hurtle ['hʌrtəl] *intr* lanzarse con violencia, pasar con gran estruendo

husband ['hʌzbənd] *s* marido, esposo ‖ *tr* manejar con economía

husband·man ['hʌzbəndmən] *s* (*pl* -men [mən]) agricultor *m*, granjero

husbandry ['hʌzbəndri] *s* agricultura, labranza; buena dirección, buen gobierno (*de la hacienda de uno*)

hush [hʌʃ] *s* silencio ‖ *interj* ¡chito! ‖ *tr* callar; **to hush up** echar tierra a (*un escándalo*) ‖ *intr* callarse

hushaby ['hʌʃə,baɪ] *interj* ¡ro ro!

hush'-hush' *adj* muy secreto

hush money *s* precio del silencio

husk [hʌsk] *s* cáscara, hollejo, vaina; (*of corn*) perfolla ‖ *tr* descascarar, deshollejar, desvainar; espinochar (*el maíz*)

husk·y ['hʌski] *adj* (*comp* -ier; *super* -iest) fortachón, fornido; (*voice*) ronco

hus·sy ['hʌzi] o ['hʌsi] *s* (*pl* -sies) buena pieza, moza descarada; mujer desvergonzada

hustle ['hʌsəl] *s* (coll) energía, vigor *m* ‖ *tr* apresurar; echar a empellones ‖ *intr* apresurarse; (coll) menearse, trabajar con gran ahínco

hustler ['hʌslər] *s* trafagón *m*, buscavidas *mf*

hut [hʌt] *s* casucha, choza

hyacinth ['haɪə·sɪnθ] *s* jacinto

hybrid ['haɪbrɪd] *adj & s* híbrido

hybridization [,haɪbrɪdɪ'zeʃən] *s* hibridación

hybridize ['haɪbrɪ,daɪz] *tr & intr* hibridar

hy·dra ['haɪdrə] *s* (*pl* -dras o -drae [dri]) hidra

hydrant ['haɪdrənt] *s* boca de agua, boca de riego; (*water faucet*) grifo

hydrate ['haɪdret] *s* hidrato ‖ *tr* hidratar ‖ *intr* hidratarse

hydraulic [haɪ'drɔlɪk] *adj* hidráulico ‖ **hydraulics** *s* hidráulica

hydraulic ram *s* ariete hidráulico

hydriodic [,haɪdrɪ'adɪk] *adj* yodhídrico

hydrobromic [,haɪdrə'bromɪk] *adj* bromhídrico

hydrocarbon [,haɪdrə'karbən] *s* hidrocarburo

hydrochloric [,haɪdrə'klorɪk] *adj* clorhídrico

hydroelectric [,haɪdro·ɪ'lektrɪk] *adj* hidroeléctrico

hydrofluoric [,haɪdrəflu'arɪk] o [,haɪdrəflu'ɔrɪk] *adj* fluorhídrico

hydrofoil ['haɪdrə,fɔɪl] *s* superficie hidrodinámica; (*wing designed to lift vessel*) hidroaleta; (*vessel*) hidroala *m*

.ydrogen ['haɪdrədʒən] *s* hidrógeno

.ydrogen bomb *s* bomba de hidrógeno

hydrogen peroxide *s* peróxido de hidrógeno

hydrogen sulfide *s* sulfuro de hidrógeno

hydrometer [haɪ'drɑmɪtər] *s* areómetro

hydrophobia [,haɪdrə'fobɪ·ə] *s* hidrofobia

hydroplane ['haɪdrə,plen] *s* hidroavión *m*

hydroxide [haɪ'drɑksaɪd] *s* hidróxido

hyena [haɪ'inə] *s* hiena

hygiene ['haɪdʒin] o ['haɪdʒɪ,in] *s* higiene *f*

hygienic [,haɪdʒɪ'enɪk] o [haɪ'dʒinɪk] *adj* higiénico

hymn [hɪm] *s* himno

hymnal ['hɪmnəl] *s* himnario

hyp. *abbr* hypotenuse, hypothesis

hyperacidity [,haɪpərə'sɪdɪti] *s* hiperacidez *f*

hyperbola [haɪ'pʌrbələ] *s* (geom) hipérbola

hyperbole [haɪ'pʌrbəli] *s* (rhet) hipérbole *f*

hyperbolic [,haɪpər'balɪk] *adj* (geom & rhet) hiperbólico

hypersensitive [,haɪpər'sensɪtɪv] *adj* extremadamente sensible; (*allergic*) hipersensible

hypertension [,haɪpər'tenʃən] *s* hipertensión

hyphen ['haɪfən] *s* guión *m*

hyphenate ['haɪfə,net] *tr* unir con guión; escribir con guión

hypno·sis [hɪp'nosɪs] *s* (*pl* -ses [siz]) hipnosis *f*

hypnotic [hɪp'natɪk] *adj* hipnótico ‖ *s* (*person; sedative*) hipnótico

hypnotism ['hɪpnə,tɪzəm] *s* hipnotismo

hypnotist ['hɪpnətɪst] *s* hipnotista *mf*

hypnotize ['hɪpnə,taɪz] *tr* hipnotizar

hypochondriac [,haɪpə'kandrɪ,æk] o [,hɪpə'kandrɪ,æk] *s* hipocondríaco

hypocri·sy [hɪ'pakrəsi] *s* (*pl* -sies) hipocresía

hypocrite ['hɪpəkrɪt] *s* hipócrita *mf*

hypocritical [,hɪpə'krɪtɪkəl] *adj* hipócrita

hypodermic [,haɪpə'dʌrmɪk] *adj* hipodérmico

hyposulfite [,haɪpə'sʌlfaɪt] *m* hiposulfito

hypotenuse [haɪ'patɪ,nus] o [haɪ'patɪ,njus] *s* hipotenusa

hypothe·sis [haɪ'paθɪsɪs] *s* (*pl* -ses [,siz]) hipótesis *f*

hypothetic(al) [,haɪpə'θetɪk(əl)] *adj* hipotético

hyssop [ˈhɪsəp] *s* (bot) hisopo
hysteria [hɪsˈtɪrɪ·ə] *s* histerismo, histeria

hysteric [hɪsˈterɪk] *adj* histérico ‖
    hysterics *s* paroxismo histérico
hysterical [hɪsˈterɪkəl] *adj* histérico

I

I, i [aɪ] novena letra del alfabeto inglés
I. *abbr* **Island**
I [aɪ] *pron pers* (*pl* **we** [wi]) yo; **it is I** soy yo
iambic [aɪˈæmbɪk] *adj* yámbico
iam·bus [aɪˈæmbəs] *s* (*pl* **-bi** [baɪ]) yambo
ib. *abbr* **ibidem**
Iberian [aɪˈbɪrɪ·ən] *adj* ibérico ‖ *s* ibero
ibex [ˈaɪbɛks] *s* (*pl* **ibexes** o **ibices** [ˈɪbɪˌsiz]) íbice *m*, cabra montés
ibid. *abbr* **ibidem**
ice [aɪs] *s* hielo; **to break the ice** (*to overcome reserve*) romper el hielo; **to cut no ice** (coll) no importar nada; **to skate on thin ice** (coll) buscar el peligro ‖ *tr* helar; enfriar con hielo; (*to cover with icing*) garapiñar ‖ *intr* helarse
ice age *s* época glacial
ice bag *s* bolsa para hielo
iceberg [ˈaɪsˌbʌrg] *s* banquisa, iceberg *m*
ice'boat' *s* cortahielos *m*, rompehielos *m*; trineo con vela para deslizarse sobre el hielo
ice'bound' *adj* rodeado de hielo; detenido por el hielo
ice'box' *s* nevera, fresquera
ice'break'er *s* cortahielos *m*, rompehielos *m*
ice'cap' *s* bolsa para hielo; manto de hielo
ice cream *s* helado
ice'-cream' cone *s* cucurucho de helado, barquillo de helado
ice-cream freezer *s* heladora, garapiñera
ice-cream parlor *s* salón *m* de refrescos, tienda de helados
ice-cream soda *s* agua gaseosa con helado
ice cube *s* cubito de hielo
ice hockey *s* hockey *m* sobre patines
Iceland [ˈaɪslənd] *s* Islandia
Icelander [ˈaɪsˌlændər] o [ˈaɪsləndər] *s* islandés *m*
Icelandic [aɪsˈlændɪk] *adj* islandés ‖ *s* islandés *m* (*idioma*)
ice·man [ˈaɪsˌmæn] *s* (*pl* **-men** [ˌmɛn]) vendedor *m* de hielo, repartidor *m* de hielo
ice pack *s* hielo flotante; bolsa de hielo
ice pail *s* enfriadera
ice pick *s* picahielos *m*
ice skate *s* patín *m* de cuchilla, patín de hielo
ice tray *s* bandejita de hielo
ice water *s* agua helada

ichthyology [ˌɪkθɪˈɑlədʒi] *s* ictiología
icicle [ˈaɪsɪkəl] *s* carámbano
icing [ˈaɪsɪŋ] *s* garapiña, capa de azúcar; (aer) formación de hielo
iconoclasm [aɪˈkɑnəˌklæzəm] *s* iconoclasia, iconoclasmo
iconoclast [aɪˈkɑnəˌklæst] *s* iconoclasta *mf*
iconoscope [aɪˈkɑnəˌskop] *s* (trademark) iconoscopio
icy [ˈaɪsi] *adj* (*comp* **icier;** *super* **iciest**) cubierto de hielo; (*slippery*) resbaladizo; (fig) frío
id. *abbr* **idem**
id [ɪd] *s* (psychoanalysis) ello
idea [aɪˈdi·ə] *s* idea
ideal [aɪˈdi·əl] *adj* & *s* ideal *m*
idealist [aɪˈdi·əlɪst] *adj* & *s* idealista *mf*
idealize [aɪˈdi·əˌlaɪz] *tr* idealizar
identic(al) [aɪˈdɛntɪk(əl)] *adj* idéntico
identification [aɪˌdɛntɪfɪˈke/ən] *s* identificación
identification tag *s* disco de identificación
identify [aɪˈdɛntɪˌfaɪ] *v* (*pret* & *pp* **-fied**) *tr* identificar
identi·ty [aɪˈdɛntɪti] *s* (*pl* **-ties**) identidad
ideolo·gy [ˌaɪdɪˈɑlədʒi] o [ˌɪdɪˈɑlədʒi] *s* (*pl* **-gies**) ideología
ides [aɪdz] *spl* idus *mpl*
idio·cy [ˈɪdɪ·əsi] *s* (*pl* **-cies**) idiotez *f*
idiom [ˈɪdɪ·əm] *s* (*expression that is contrary to the usual patterns of the language*) modismo; (*style of language*) idioma *m*, lenguaje *m*; (*style of an author*) estilo; (*character of a language*) índole *f*
idiomatic [ˌɪdɪ·əˈmætɪk] *adj* idiomático
idiosyncra·sy [ˌɪdɪ·əˈsɪnkrəsi] *s* (*pl* **-sies**) idiosincrasia
idiot [ˈɪdɪ·ət] *s* idiota *mf*
idiotic [ˌɪdɪ·ˈɑtɪk] *adj* idiota
idle [ˈaɪdəl] *adj* desocupado, ocioso; **at idle moments** a ratos perdidos; **to run idle** marchar en ralentí ‖ *tr* — **to idle away** gastar ociosamente (*el tiempo*) ‖ *intr* estar ocioso, holgar; marchar (*un motor*) en ralentí
idleness [ˈaɪdəlnɪs] *s* desocupación, ociosidad
idler [ˈaɪdlər] *s* haragán *m*, ocioso
idol [ˈaɪdəl] *s* ídolo
idola·try [aɪˈdɑlətri] *s* (*pl* **-tries**) idolatría
idolize [ˈaɪdəˌlaɪz] *tr* idolatrar
idyll [ˈaɪdəl] *s* idilio
idyllic [aɪˈdɪlɪk] *adj* idílico
if [ɪf] *conj* si; **as if** como si; **even if**

aunque; **if so** si es así; **if true** si es cierto

ignis fatuus ['ɪgnɪs'fætʃʊ·əs] s (*pl* **ignes fatui** ['ɪgniz'fætʃʊ·aɪ]) fuego fatuo

ignite [ɪg'naɪt] *tr* encender || *intr* encenderse

ignition [ɪg'nɪʃən] s inflamación; (aut) encendido

ignition switch s (aut) interruptor *m* de encendido

ignoble [ɪg'nobəl] *adj* innoble

ignominious [ˌɪgnə'mɪnɪ·əs] *adj* ignominioso

ignoramus [ˌɪgnə'reməs] s ignorante *mf*

ignorance ['ɪgnərəns] s ignorancia

ignorant ['ɪgnərənt] *adj* ignorante

ignore [ɪg'nor] *tr* no hacer caso de, pasar por alto

ilk [ɪlk] s especie *f*, jaez *m*

ill abbr **illustrated, illustration**

ill [ɪl] *adj* (*comp* **worse** [wʌrs]; *super* **worst** [wʌrst]) enfermo, malo || *adv* mal; **to take ill** tomar a mal; caer enfermo

ill-advised ['ɪləd'vaɪzd] *adj* desaconsejado, malaconsejado

ill at ease *adj* inquieto, incómodo

ill-bred ['ɪl'bred] *adj* malcriado

ill-considered ['ɪlkən'sɪdərd] *adj* desconsiderado, mal considerado

ill-disposed ['ɪldɪs'pozd] *adj* malintencionado, maldispuesto

illegal [ɪ'ligəl] *adj* ilegal

illegible [ɪ'ledʒɪbəl] *adj* ilegible

illegitimate [ˌɪlɪ'dʒɪtɪmɪt] *adj* ilegítimo

ill fame s mala fama, reputación de inmoral

ill-fated ['ɪl'fetɪd] *adj* aciago, funesto

ill-gotten ['ɪl'gɑtən] *adj* mal ganado

ill health s mala salud

ill-humored ['ɪl'hjumərd] *adj* malhumorado

illicit [ɪ'lɪsɪt] *adj* ilícito

illitera·cy [ɪ'lɪtərəsi] s (*pl* **-cies**) ignorancia; analfabetismo

illiterate [ɪ'lɪtərɪt] *adj* (*uneducated*) iliterato; (*unable to read or write*) analfabeto || s analfabeto

ill-mannered ['ɪl'mænərd] *adj* de malos modales

illness ['ɪlnɪs] s enfermedad

illogical [ɪ'lɑdʒɪkəl] *adj* ilógico

ill-spent ['ɪl'spent] *adj* malgastado

ill-starred ['ɪl'stɑrd] *adj* malhadado

ill-tempered ['ɪl'tempərd] *adj* de mal genio

ill-timed ['ɪl'taɪmd] *adj* inoportuno, intempestivo

ill'-treat' *tr* maltratar

illuminate [ɪ'lumɪˌnet] *tr* alumbrar, iluminar; miniar (*un manuscrito*)

illuminating gas s gas *m* de alumbrado

illumination [ɪˌlumɪ'neʃən] s iluminación

illusion [ɪ'luʒən] s ilusión

illusive [ɪ'lusɪv] *adj* ilusivo

illusory [ɪ'lusəri] *adj* ilusorio

illustrate ['ɪləs͵tret] o [ɪ'lʌstret] *tr* ilustrar

illustration [ˌɪləs'treʃən] s ilustración

illustrious [ɪ'lʌstrɪ·əs] *adj* ilustre

ill will s mala voluntad

image ['ɪmɪdʒ] s imagen *f;* **the very image of** la propia estampa de

image·ry ['ɪmɪdʒri] o ['ɪmɪdʒəri] s (*pl* **-ries**) (*formation of mental images; product of the imagination*) fantasía; (*images collectively*) imágenes *fpl*

imaginary [ɪ'mædʒɪˌneri] *adj* imaginario

imagination [ɪˌmædʒɪ'neʃən] s imaginación

imagine [ɪ'mædʒɪn] *tr & intr* imaginar; (*to conjecture*) imaginarse

imbecile ['ɪmbɪsɪl] *adj & s* imbécil *mf*

imbecili·ty [ˌɪmbɪ'sɪlɪti] s (*pl* **-ties**) imbecilidad

imbibe [ɪm'baɪb] *tr* (*to drink*) beber; (*to absorb*) embeber; (*to become absorbed in*) embeberse de o en || *intr* beber, empinar el codo

imbue [ɪm'bju] *tr* imbuir

imitate ['ɪmɪˌtet] *tr* imitar

imitation [ˌɪmɪ'teʃən] *adj* (*e.g., jewelry*) imitado, imitación, de imitación || s imitación; **in imitation of** a imitación de

immaculate [ɪ'mækjəlɪt] *adj* inmaculado

immaterial [ˌɪmə'tɪrɪ·əl] *adj* inmaterial; poco importante

immature [ˌɪmə'tjur] o [ˌɪmə'tur] *adj* inmaturo

immeasurable [ɪ'meʒərəbəl] *adj* inmensurable

immediacy [ɪ'midɪ·əsi] s inmediación

immediate [ɪ'midɪ·ɪt] *adj* inmediato

immediately [ɪ'midɪ·ɪtli] *adv* inmediatamente

immemorial [ˌɪmɪ'morɪ·əl] *adj* inmemorial

immense [ɪ'mens] *adj* inmenso; (coll) excelente

immerge [ɪ'mʌrdʒ] *intr* sumergirse

immerse [ɪ'mʌrs] *tr* sumergir, inmergir

immersion [ɪ'mʌrʃən] o [ɪ'mʌrʒən] s sumersión, inmersión

immigrant ['ɪmɪgrənt] *adj & s* inmigrante *mf*

immigrate ['ɪmɪˌgret] *intr* inmigrar

immigration [ˌɪmɪ'greʃən] s inmigración

imminent ['ɪmɪnənt] *adj* inminente

immobile [ɪ'mobɪl] o [ɪ'mobɪl] *adj* inmoble, inmóvil

immobilize [ɪ'mobɪˌlaɪz] *tr* inmovilizar

immoderate [ɪ'mɑdərɪt] *adj* inmoderado

immodest [ɪ'mɑdɪst] *adj* inmodesto

immoral [ɪ'mɑrəl] o [ɪ'mɔrəl] *adj* inmoral

immortal [ɪ'mɔrtəl] *adj & s* inmortal *mf*

immortalize [ɪ'mɔrtə͵laɪz] *tr* inmortalizar

immune [ɪ'mjun] *adj* inmune

immunize ['ɪmjə͵naɪz] o [ɪ'mjunaɪz] *tr* inmunizar

imp [ɪmp] s diablillo; (*child*) niño travieso

impact ['ɪmpækt] s impacto
impair [ɪm'pɛr] tr empeorar, deteriorar
impan·el [ɪm'pænəl] v (pret & pp -eled o -elled; ger -eling o -elling) tr inscribir en la lista de los jurados; elegir (un jurado)
impart [ɪm'part] tr (to make known) dar a conocer, hacer saber; (to transmit, communicate) imprimir
impartial [ɪm'parʃəl] adj imparcial
impassable [ɪm'pæsəbəl] o [ɪm'pasəbəl] adj intransitable, impracticable
impasse [ɪm'pæs] o ['ɪmpæs] s callejón m sin salida
impassible [ɪm'pæsɪbəl] adj impasible
impassioned [ɪm'pæʃənd] adj ardiente, vehemente
impassive [ɪm'pæsɪv] adj impasivo
impatience [ɪm'peʃəns] s impaciencia
impatient [ɪm'peʃənt] adj impaciente
impeach [ɪm'pitʃ] tr residenciar
impeachment [ɪm'pitʃmənt] s residencia
impeccable [ɪm'pɛkəbəl] adj impecable
impecunious [,ɪmpɪ'kjuni·əs] adj inope
impedance [ɪm'pidəns] s impedancia
impede [ɪm'pid] tr estorbar, dificultar
impediment [ɪm'pedɪmənt] s impedimento; (e.g., in speech) defecto
im·pel [ɪm'pɛl] v (pret & pp -pelled; ger -pelling) tr impeler, impulsar
impending [ɪm'pɛndɪŋ] adj inminente
impenetrable [ɪm'penətrəbəl] adj impenetrable
impenitent [ɪm'penɪtənt] adj & s impenitente mf
imperative [ɪm'perɪtɪv] adj (commanding) imperativo; (urgent, absolutely necessary) imperioso || s imperativo
imperceptible [,ɪmpər'sɛptɪbəl] adj imperceptible, inapreciable
imperfect [ɪm'pʌrfɪkt] adj & s imperfecto
imperfection [,ɪmpər'fɛkʃən] s imperfección
imperial [ɪm'pɪrɪ·əl] adj imperial; majestuoso || s (goatee) perilla; (top of coach) imperial f
imperialist [ɪm'pɪrɪ·əlɪst] adj & s imperialista mf
imper·il [ɪm'perɪl] v (pret & pp -iled o -illed; ger -iling o -illing) tr poner en peligro
imperious [ɪm'pɪrɪ·əs] adj imperioso
imperishable [ɪm'perɪʃəbəl] adj imperecedero
impersonal [ɪm'pʌrsənəl] adj impersonal
impersonate [ɪm'pʌrsə,net] tr personificar; hacer el papel de
impertinence [ɪm'pʌrtɪnəns] s impertinencia
impertinent [ɪm'pʌrtɪnənt] adj & s impertinente mf
impetuous [ɪm'pɛtʃʊ·əs] adj impetuoso
impetus ['ɪmpɪtəs] s ímpetu m

impie·ty [ɪm'paɪ·əti] s (pl -ties) impiedad
impinge [ɪm'pɪndʒ] intr — to impinge on o upon incidir en o sobre, herir; infringir, violar
impious ['ɪmpɪ·əs] adj impío
impish ['ɪmpɪʃ] adj endiablado, travieso
implant [ɪm'plænt] tr implantar
implement ['ɪmplɪmənt] s instrumento, utensilio, herramienta || ['ɪmplɪ,mɛnt] tr poner por obra, llevar a cabo; (to provide with implements) pertrechar
implicate ['ɪmplɪ,ket] tr implicar, comprometer, enredar
implicit [ɪm'plɪsɪt] adj implícito; (unquestioning) absoluto, ciego
implied [ɪm'plaɪd] adj implícito, sobrentendido
implore [ɪm'plor] tr implorar, suplicar
im·ply [ɪm'plaɪ] v (pret & pp -plied) tr dar a entender; implicar, incluir en esencia
impolite [,ɪmpə'laɪt] adj descortés
import ['ɪmport] s importación; artículo importado; importancia, significación || [ɪm'port] o ['ɪmport] tr importar; significar || intr importar
importance [ɪm'portəns] s importancia
important [ɪm'portənt] adj importante
importation [,ɪmpor'teʃən] s importación
importer [ɪm'portər] s importador m
importunate [ɪm'portʃənɪt] adj importuno
importune [,ɪmpor'tjun] o [,ɪmpor'tun] tr importunar
impose [ɪm'poz] tr imponer || intr — to impose on o upon abusar de
imposing [ɪm'pozɪŋ] adj imponente
imposition [,ɪmpə'zɪʃən] s (of someone's will) imposición; abuso, engaño
impossible [ɪm'pasɪbəl] adj imposible
impostor [ɪm'pastər] s impostor m
imposture [ɪm'pastʃər] s impostura
impotence ['ɪmpətəns] s impotencia
impotent ['ɪmpətənt] adj impotente
impound [ɪm'paʊnd] tr acorralar, encerrar; rebalsar (agua); (law) embargar, secuestrar
impoverish [ɪm'pavərɪʃ] tr empobrecer
impracticable [ɪm'præktɪkəbəl] adj impracticable; (intractable) intratable
impractical [ɪm'præktɪkəl] adj impracticable; soñador, utópico
impregnable [ɪm'pregnəbəl] adj inexpugnable
impregnate [ɪm'pregnet] tr (to make pregnant) empreñar; (to soak) empapar; (to fill the interstices of) impregnar; (to infuse, infect) imbuir
impresari·o [,ɪmprɪ'sari,o] s (pl -os) empresario, empresario de teatro
impress [ɪm'pres] tr (to have an effect on the mind or emotions of) impresionar; (to mark by using pres-

ig
im

sure) imprimir; (*on the memory*) grabar; (mil) enganchar

impression [ɪmˈprɛʃən] *s* impresión

impressionable [ɪmˈprɛʃənəbəl] *adj* impresionable

impressive [ɪmˈprɛsɪv] *adj* impresionante

imprint [ˈɪmprɪnt] *s* impresión; (typ) pie *m* de imprenta ‖ [ɪmˈprɪnt] *tr* imprimir

imprison [ɪmˈprɪzən] *tr* encarcelar

imprisonment [ɪmˈprɪzənmənt] *s* encarcelamiento

improbable [ɪmˈprɑbəbəl] *adj* improbable

impromptu [ɪmˈprɑmptju] o [ɪmˈprɑmptu] *adj* improvisado ‖ *adv* de improviso ‖ *s* improvisación; (mus) impromptu *m*

improper [ɪmˈprɑpər] *adj* impropio; (*contrary to good taste or decency*) indecoroso

improve [ɪmˈpruv] *tr* perfeccionar, mejorar; aprovechar (*la oportunidad*) ‖ *intr* perfeccionarse, mejorar; **to improve on** o **upon** mejorar

improvement [ɪmˈpruvmənt] *s* perfeccionamiento, mejoramiento; (*e.g., in health*) mejoría; (*useful employment, e.g., of time*) aprovechamiento

improvident [ɪmˈprɑvɪdənt] *adj* imprevisor

improvise [ˈɪmprəˌvaɪz] *tr & intr* improvisar

imprudent [ɪmˈprudənt] *adj* imprudente

impudence [ˈɪmpjədəns] *s* insolencia, descaro, impertinencia

impudent [ˈɪmpjədənt] *adj* insolente, descarado, impertinente

impugn [ɪmˈpjun] *tr* poner en tela de juicio

impulse [ˈɪmpʌls] *s* impulso

impulsive [ɪmˈpʌlsɪv] *adj* impulsivo

impunity [ɪmˈpjunɪti] *s* impunidad

impure [ɪmˈpjʊr] *adj* impuro

impuri·ty [ɪmˈpjʊrɪti] *s* (*pl* **-ties**) impureza, impuridad

impute [ɪmˈpjut] *tr* imputar

in [ɪn] *adj* interior ‖ *adv* dentro; en casa, en la oficina; **in here** aquí dentro; **in there** allí dentro; **to be in** estar en casa; **to be in for** estar expuesto a; **to be in with** gozar del favor de ‖ *prep* en; (*within*) dentro de; (*over, through*) por; (*a period of the day*) en su ... ; **dressed in** ... vestido de ... ; **in so far as** en tanto que; **in that** en que, por cuanto ‖ *s* — **ins and outs** recovecos, pormenores minuciosos

inability [ˌɪnəˈbɪlɪti] *s* inhabilidad, incapacidad

inaccessible [ˌɪnækˈsɛsɪbəl] *adj* inaccesible

inaccura·cy [ɪnˈækjərəsi] *s* (*pl* **-cies**) inexactitud, incorrección

inaccurate [ɪnˈækjərɪt] *adj* inexacto, incorrecto

inaction [ɪnˈækʃən] *s* inacción

inactive [ɪnˈæktɪv] *adj* inactivo

inactivity [ˌɪnækˈtɪvɪti] *s* inactividad

inadequate [ɪnˈædɪkwɪt] *adj* insuficiente, inadecuado

inadvertent [ˌɪnədˈvʌrtənt] *adj* inadvertido

inadvisable [ˌɪnədˈvaɪzəbəl] *adj* poco aconsejable, imprudente

inane [ɪnˈen] *adj* inane

inanimate [ɪnˈænɪmɪt] *adj* inanimado

inappreciable [ˌɪnəˈpriʃɪ·əbəl] *adj* inapreciable

inappropriate [ˌɪnəˈpropri·ɪt] *adj* no apropiado, no a propósito

inarticulate [ˌɪnɑrˈtɪkjəlɪt] *adj* (*sounds, words*) inarticulado; (*person*) incapaz de expresarse

inartistic [ˌɪnɑrˈtɪstɪk] *adj* antiartístico, inartístico

inasmuch as [ˌɪnəzˈmʌtʃˈæz] *conj* ya que, puesto que; en cuanto, hasta donde

inattentive [ˌɪnəˈtɛntɪv] *adj* desatento

inaugural [ɪnˈɔgjərəl] *adj* inaugural ‖ *s* discurso inaugural

inaugurate [ɪnˈɔgjəˌret] *tr* inaugurar

inauguration [ɪnˌɔgjəˈreʃən] *s* (*formal initiation or opening*) inauguración; (*investiture of a head of government*) toma de posesión

inborn [ˈɪnˌbɔrn] *adj* innato, ingénito

inbreeding [ˈɪnˌbridɪŋ] *s* intracruzamiento

inc. *abbr* **inclosure, included, including, incorporated, increase**

Inca [ˈɪŋkə] *adj* incaico ‖ *s* inca *mf*

incandescent [ˌɪnkənˈdɛsənt] *adj* incandescente

incapable [ɪnˈkepəbəl] *adj* incapaz

incapacitate [ˌɪnkəˈpæsɪˌtet] *tr* incapacitar, inhabilitar

incapaci·ty [ˌɪnkəˈpæsɪti] *s* (*pl* **-ties**) incapacidad

incarcerate [ɪnˈkɑrsəˌret] *tr* encarcelar

incarnate [ɪnˈkɑrnɪt] o [ɪnˈkɑrnet] *adj* encarnado ‖ [ɪnˈkɑrnet] *tr* encarnar

incarnation [ˌɪnkɑrˈneʃən] *s* encarnación

incendiarism [ɪnˈsɛndɪ·əˌrɪzəm] *s* incendio intencionado; incitación al desorden

incendiar·y [ɪnˈsɛndɪˌɛri] *adj* incendiario ‖ *s* (*pl* **-ies**) incendiario

incense [ˈɪnsɛns] *s* incienso ‖ *tr* (*to burn incense before*) incensar ‖ [ɪnˈsɛns] *tr* exasperar, encolerizar

incense burner *s* incensario

incentive [ɪnˈsɛntɪv] *adj & s* incentivo

inception [ɪnˈsɛpʃən] *s* principio, comienzo

incertitude [ɪnˈsʌrtɪˌtjud] o [ɪnˈsʌrtɪˌtud] *s* incertidumbre

incessant [ɪnˈsɛsənt] *adj* incesante

incest [ˈɪnsɛst] *s* incesto

incestuous [ɪnˈsɛstʃu·əs] *adj* incestuoso

inch [ɪntʃ] *s* pulgada; **to be within an inch of** estar a dos dedos de ‖ *intr* — **to inch ahead** avanzar poco a poco

incidence [ˈɪnsɪdəns] *s* incidencia; (*range of occurrence*) extensión

incident [ˈɪnsɪdənt] *adj & s* incidente *m*

incidental [ˌɪnsɪ'dɛntəl] *adj* incidente; (*incurred in addition to the regular amount*) obvencional ‖ *s* elemento incidental; **incidentals** gastos menudos

incidentally [ˌɪnsɪ'dɛntəlɪ] *adv* incidentemente; a propósito

incipient [ɪn'sɪpɪ·ənt] *adj* incipiente

incision [ɪn'sɪʒən] *s* incisión

incisive [ɪn'saɪsɪv] *adj* incisivo

incite [ɪn'saɪt] *tr* incitar

incl. *abbr* **inclosure, inclusive**

inclemen·cy [ɪn'klɛmənsɪ] *s* (*pl* **-cies**) inclemencia

inclement [ɪn'klɛmənt] *adj* inclemente

inclination [ˌɪnklɪ'neʃən] *s* inclinación

incline ['ɪnklaɪn] o [ɪn'klaɪn] *s* declive *m*, pendiente *f* ‖ [ɪn'klaɪn] *tr* inclinar ‖ *intr* inclinarse

inclose [ɪn'kloz] *tr* encerrar; (*in a letter*) adjuntar, incluir; **to inclose herewith** remitir adjunto

inclosure [ɪn'kloʒər] *s* recinto; cosa inclusa, carta inclusa

include [ɪn'klud] *tr* incluir, comprender

including [ɪn'kludɪŋ] *prep* incluso, inclusive

inclusive [ɪn'klusɪv] *adj* inclusivo; **inclusive of** comprensivo de ‖ *adv* inclusive

incogni·to [ɪn'kɑgnɪ·ˌto] *adj* incógnito ‖ *adv* de incógnito ‖ *s* (*pl* **-tos**) incógnito

incoherent [ˌɪnko'hɪrənt] *adj* incoherente

incombustible [ˌɪnkəm'bʌstɪbəl] *adj* incombustible

income ['ɪnkʌm] *s* renta, ingreso, utilidad

income tax *s* impuesto sobre rentas

in'come-tax' return *s* declaración de impuesto sobre rentas

in'com'ing *adj* de entrada, entrante; (*tide*) ascendente ‖ *s* entrada

incomparable [ɪn'kɑmpərəbəl] *adj* incomparable

incompatible [ˌɪnkəm'pætɪbəl] *adj* incompatible

incompetent [ɪn'kɑmpɪtənt] *adj* incompetente

incomplete [ˌɪnkəm'plit] *adj* incompleto

incomprehensible [ˌɪnkɑmprɪ'hɛnsɪbəl] *adj* incomprensible

inconceivable [ˌɪnkən'sivəbəl] *adj* inconcebible

inconclusive [ˌɪnkən'klusɪv] *adj* inconcluyente

incongruous [ɪn'kɑŋgru·əs] *adj* incongruo

inconsequential [ɪnˌkɑnsɪ'kwɛnʃəl] *adj* (*lacking proper sequence of thought or speech*) inconsecuente; (*trivial*) de poca importancia

inconsiderate [ˌɪnkən'sɪdərɪt] *adj* desconsiderado, inconsiderado

inconsisten·cy [ˌɪnkən'sɪstənsɪ] *s* (*pl* **-cies**) (*lack of coherence*) inconsistencia; (*lack of logical connection or uniformity*) inconsecuencia

inconsistent [ˌɪnkən'sɪstənt] *adj* (*lacking coherence of parts*) inconsistente; (*not agreeing with itself or oneself*) inconsecuente

inconsolable [ˌɪnkən'soləbəl] *adj* inconsolable

inconspicuous [ˌɪnkən'spɪkju·əs] *adj* poco impresionante, poco aparente

inconstant [ɪn'kɑnstənt] *adj* inconstante

incontinent [ɪn'kɑntɪnənt] *adj* incontinente

incontrovertible [ˌɪnkɑntrə'vʌrtɪbəl] *adj* incontrovertible

inconvenience [ˌɪnkən'vini·əns] *s* incomodidad, inconveniencia, molestia ‖ *tr* incomodar, molestar

inconvenient [ˌɪnkən'vini·ənt] *adj* incómodo, inconveniente, molesto

incorporate [ɪn'kɔrpə·ˌret] *tr* incorporar; constituir en sociedad anónima ‖ *intr* incorporarse; constituirse en sociedad anónima

incorporation [ɪnˌkɔrpə'reʃən] *s* incorporación; constitución en sociedad anónima

incorrect [ˌɪnkə'rɛkt] *adj* incorrecto

increase ['ɪnkris] *s* aumento; ganancia, interés *m;* **to be on the increase** ir en aumento ‖ [ɪn'kris] *tr* aumentar; (*by propagation*) multiplicar ‖ *intr* aumentar; multiplicarse

increasingly [ɪn'krisɪŋlɪ] *adv* cada vez más

incredible [ɪn'krɛdɪbəl] *adj* increíble

incredulous [ɪn'krɛdʒələs] *adj* incrédulo

increment ['ɪnkrɪmənt] *s* incremento

incriminate [ɪn'krɪmɪ·ˌnet] *tr* acriminar, incriminar

incrust [ɪn'krʌst] *tr* incrustar

incubate ['ɪnkjə·ˌbet] *tr* & *intr* incubar

incubator ['ɪnkjə·ˌbetər] *s* incubadora

inculcate [ɪn'kʌlket] o ['ɪnkʌl·ˌket] *tr* inculcar

incumben·cy [ɪn'kʌmbənsɪ] *s* (*pl* **-cies**) incumbencia

incumbent [ɪn'kʌmbənt] *adj* — **to be incumbent on** incumbir a ‖ *s* titular *m*

incunabula [ˌɪnkju'næbjələ] *spl* (*beginnings*) orígenes *mpl;* (*early printed books*) incunables *mpl*

in·cur [ɪn'kʌr] *v* (*pret* & *pp* **-curred;** *ger* **-curring**) *tr* incurrir en; (*a debt*) contraer

incurable [ɪn'kjurəbəl] *adj* & *s* incurable *mf*

incursion [ɪn'kʌrʒən] o [ɪn'kʌrʃən] *s* incursión, correría

ind. *abbr* **in·dependent, industrial**

indebted [ɪn'dɛtɪd] *adj* adeudado; obligado

indecen·cy [ɪn'disənsɪ] *s* (*pl* **-cies**) indecencia, deshonestidad

indecent [ɪn'disənt] *adj* indecente, deshonesto

indecisive [ˌɪndɪ'saɪsɪv] *adj* indeciso

indeclinable [ˌɪndɪ'klaɪnəbəl] *adj* (gram) indeclinable

indeed [ɪn'did] *adv* verdaderamente, claro ‖ *interj* ¡de veras!

indefatigable [ˌɪndɪ'fætɪgəbəl] *adj* incansable, infatigable

im
in

indefensible [ˌɪndɪ'fɛnsɪbəl] *adj* indefendible

indefinable [ˌɪndɪ'fainəbəl] *adj* indefinible

indefinite [ɪn'dɛfɪnɪt] *adj* indefinido

indelible [ɪn'dɛlɪbəl] *adj* indeleble

indelicate [ɪn'dɛlɪkɪt] *adj* indelicado

indemnification [ɪnˌdɛmnɪfɪ'keʃən] *s* indemnización

indemni•fy [ɪn'dɛmnɪˌfai] *v* (*pret & pp* -fied) *tr* indemnizar

indemni•ty [ɪn'dɛmnɪti] *s* (*pl* -ties) (*security against loss*) indemnidad; (*compensation*) indemnización

indent [ɪn'dɛnt] *tr* dentar, mellar; (typ) sangrar

indentation [ˌɪndɛn'teʃən] *s* mella, muesca; (typ) sangría

indenture [ɪn'dɛntʃər] *s* escritura, contrato; contrato de aprendizaje ‖ *tr* obligar por contrato

independence [ˌɪndɪ'pɛndəns] *s* independencia

independen•cy [ˌɪndɪ'pɛndənsi] *s* (*pl* -cies) independencia; país *m* independiente

independent [ˌɪndɪ'pɛndənt] *adj & s* independiente *mf*

indescribable [ˌɪndɪ'skraibəbəl] *adj* indescriptible

indestructible [ˌɪndɪ'strʌktɪbəl] *adj* indestructible

indeterminate [ˌɪndɪ'tʌrmɪnɪt] *adj* indeterminado

index ['ɪndɛks] *s* (*pl* indexes o indices ['ɪndɪˌsiz]) *s* índice *m*; (typ) manecilla ‖ *tr* poner índice a; poner en un índice ‖ **Index** *s* Índice de los libros prohibidos

index card *s* ficha catalográfica

index finger *s* dedo índice

index tab *s* pestaña

India ['ɪndɪə] *s* la India

India ink *s* tinta china

Indian ['ɪndɪən] *adj & s* indio

Indian club *s* maza de gimnasia

Indian corn *s* maíz *m*, panizo

Indian file *s* fila india ‖ *adv* en fila india

Indian Ocean *s* mar *m* de las Indias, océano Índico

Indian summer *s* veranillo de San Martín

India paper *s* papel *m* de China

India rubber *s* caucho

indicate ['ɪndɪˌket] *tr* indicar

indication [ˌɪndɪ'keʃən] *s* indicación

indicative [ɪn'dɪkətɪv] *adj & s* indicativo

indicator ['ɪndɪˌketər] *s* indicador *m*

indict [ɪn'dait] *tr* (law) acusar, procesar

indictment [ɪn'daitmənt] *s* acusación, procesamiento; auto de acusación formulado por el gran jurado

indifferent [ɪn'dɪfərənt] *adj* indiferente; (*not particularly good*) pasadero, mediano

indigenous [ɪn'dɪdʒɪnəs] *adj* indígena

indigent ['ɪndɪdʒənt] *adj* indigente

indigestible [ˌɪndɪ'dʒɛstɪbəl] *adj* indigestible

indigestion [ˌɪndɪ'dʒɛst/ən] *s* indigestión

indignant [ɪn'dɪgnənt] *adj* indignado

indignation [ˌɪndɪg'neʃən] *s* indignación

indigni•ty [ɪn'dɪgnɪti] *s* (*pl* -ties) indignidad

indi•go ['ɪndɪˌgo] *adj* azul de añil ‖ *s* (*pl* -gos o -goes) índigo

indirect [ˌɪndɪ'rɛkt] o [ˌɪndai'rɛkt] *adj* indirecto

indirect discourse *s* estilo indirecto

indiscernible [ˌɪndɪ'zʌrnɪbəl] o [ˌɪndɪ'sʌrnɪbəl] *adj* indiscernible

indiscreet [ˌɪndɪs'krit] *adj* indiscreto

indispensable [ˌɪndɪs'pɛnsəbəl] *adj* indispensable, imprescindible

indispose [ˌɪndɪs'poz] *tr* indisponer

indisposed [ˌɪndɪs'pozd] *adj* (*disinclined*) maldispuesto; (*somewhat ill*) indispuesto

indissoluble [ˌɪndɪ'saljəbəl] *adj* indisoluble

indistinct [ˌɪndɪ'stɪŋkt] *adj* indistinto

indite [ɪn'dait] *tr* redactar, poner por escrito

individual [ˌɪndɪ'vɪdʒu-əl] *adj* individual ‖ *s* individuo

individuali•ty [ˌɪndɪˌvɪdʒu'ælɪti] *s* (*pl* -ties) individualidad; (*person of distinctive character*) personaje *m*

Indochina ['ɪndo'tʃainə] *s* la Indochina

Indo-Chi•nese ['ɪndotʃai'niz] *adj* indochino ‖ *s* (*pl* -nese) indochino

indoctrinate [ɪn'dɑktrɪˌnet] *tr* adoctrinar

Indo-European ['ɪndoˌjurə'pi-ən] *adj & s* indoeuropeo

indolent ['ɪndələnt] *adj* indolente

Indonesia [ˌɪndo'niʃə] o [ˌɪndo'niʒə] *s* la Indonesia

Indonesian [ˌɪndo'niʃən] o [ˌɪndo'niʒən] *adj & s* indonesio

indoor ['ɪnˌdor] *adj* interior, de puertas adentro; (*inclined to stay in the house*) casero

indoors ['ɪn'dorz] *adv* dentro, en casa, bajo techado, bajo cubierto

indorse [ɪn'dors] *tr* endosar; (fig) apoyar, aprobar

indorsee [ˌɪndor'si] *s* endosatario

indorsement [ɪn'dorsmənt] *s* endoso; (fig) apoyo, aprobación

indorser [ɪn'dorsər] *s* endosante *mf*

induce [ɪn'djus] o [ɪn'dus] *tr* inducir; causar, ocasionar

inducement [ɪn'djusmənt] o [ɪn'dusmənt] *s* aliciente *m*, estímulo, incentivo

induct [ɪn'dʌkt] *tr* instalar; introducir, iniciar; (mil) quintar

induction [ɪn'dʌkʃən] *s* instalación; introducción; (elec & log) inducción; (mil) quinta

indulge [ɪn'dʌldʒ] *tr* gratificar (*p.ej., los deseos de uno*); mimar (*a un niño*) ‖ *intr* abandonar; **to indulge in** entregarse a, permitirse el placer de

indulgence [ɪn'dʌldʒəns] *s* gusto, inclinación; intemperancia, desenfreno; (*leniency*) indulgencia

indulgent [ɪnˈdʌldʒənt] *adj* indulgente
industrial [ɪnˈdʌstrɪ.əl] *adj* industrial
industrialist [ɪnˈdʌstrɪ.əlɪst] *s* industrial *m*
industrialize [ɪnˈdʌstrɪ.ə‚laɪz] *tr* industrializar
industrious [ɪnˈdʌstrɪ.əs] *adj* industrioso, aplicado
indus·try [ˈɪndəstri] *s* (*pl* -tries) industria
inebriation [ɪn‚ibriˈeʃən] *s* embriaguez *f*
inedible [ɪnˈedɪbəl] *adj* incomible
ineffable [ɪnˈefəbəl] *adj* inefable
ineffective [‚ɪnɪˈfɛktɪv] *adj* ineficaz; (*person*) incapaz
ineffectual [‚ɪnɪˈfɛktʃu.əl] *adj* ineficaz, fútil
inefficacy [ɪnˈefɪkəsi] *s* ineficacia
inefficient [ɪnˈfɪʃənt] *adj* de mal rendimiento
ineligible [ɪnˈelɪdʒɪbəl] *adj* inelegible
inequali·ty [‚ɪnɪˈkwɑlɪti] *s* (*pl* -ties) desigualdad
inequi·ty [ɪnˈɛkwɪti] *s* (*pl* -ties) inequidad
ineradicable [‚ɪnɪˈrædɪkəbəl] *adj* inextirpable
inertia [ɪnˈʌrʃə] *s* inercia
inescapable [‚ɪnesˈkepəbəl] *adj* ineludible
inevitable [ɪnˈevɪtəbəl] *adj* inevitable
inexact [‚ɪnegˈzækt] *adj* inexacto
inexcusable [‚ɪneksˈkjuzəbəl] *adj* indisculpable, inexcusable
inexhaustible [‚ɪnegˈzɔstɪbəl] *adj* inagotable
inexorable [ɪnˈeksərəbəl] *adj* inexorable
inexpedient [‚ɪnekˈspidi·ənt] *adj* malaconsejado, inoportuno
inexpensive [‚ɪnekˈspensɪv] *adj* barato, poco costoso
inexperience [‚ɪnekˈspɪrɪ·əns] *s* inexperiencia
inexplicable [ɪnˈeksplɪkəbəl] *adj* inexplicable
inexpressible [‚ɪnekˈspresɪbəl] *adj* inexpresable
Inf. *abbr* **Infantry**
infallible [ɪnˈfælɪbəl] *adj* infalible
infamous [ˈɪnfəməs] *adj* infame
infa·my [ˈɪnfəmi] *s* (*pl* -mies) infamia
infan·cy [ˈɪnfənsi] *s* (*pl* -cies) infancia
infant [ˈɪnfənt] *adj* infantil; (*in the earliest stage*) (fig) naciente || *s* criatura, nene *m*
infantile [ˈɪnfən‚taɪl] o [ˈɪnfəntɪl] *adj* infantil; (*childish*) aniñado
infan·try [ˈɪnfəntri] *s* (*pl* -tries) infantería
infantry·man [ˈɪnfəntrimən] *s* (*pl* -men [mən]) infante *m*, soldado de infantería
infatuated [ɪnˈfætʃu‚etɪd] *adj* apasionado, locamente enamorado
infect [ɪnˈfɛkt] *tr* inficionar, infectar; influir sobre
infection [ɪnˈfɛkʃən] *s* infección
infectious [ɪnˈfɛkʃəs] *adj* infeccioso
in·fer [ɪnˈfʌr] *v* (*pret* & *pp* -ferred; *ger* -ferring) *tr* inferir; (coll) conjeturar, suponer

inferior [ɪnˈfɪrɪ·ər] *adj* & *s* inferior *m*
inferiority [ɪn‚fɪrɪˈɑrɪti] *s* inferioridad
inferiority complex *s* complejo de inferioridad
infernal [ɪnˈfʌrnəl] *adj* infernal
infest [ɪn·fest] *tr* infestar
infidel [ˈɪnfɪdəl] *adj* & *s* infiel *mf*
infideli·ty [‚ɪnfɪˈdelɪti] *s* (*pl* -ties) infidelidad
in'field' *s* (baseball) cuadro interior
infiltrate [ɪnˈfɪltret] o [ˈɪnfɪl‚tret] *tr* infiltrar; infiltrarse en || *intr* infiltrarse
infinite [ˈɪnfɪnɪt] *adj* & *s* infinito
infinitive [ɪnˈfɪnɪtɪv] *adj* & *s* infinitivo
infini·ty [ɪnˈfɪnɪti] *s* (*pl* -ties) infinidad; (math) infinito
infirm [ɪnˈfʌrm] *adj* infirme, achacoso; (*unsteady*) inestable, inseguro; poco firme, poco sólido
infirma·ry [ɪnˈfʌrməri] *s* (*pl* -ries) enfermería
infirmi·ty [ɪnˈfʌrmɪti] *s* (*pl* -ties) achaque *m*; inestabilidad
in'fix' *s* (gram) infijo
inflame [ɪnˈflem] *tr* inflamar
inflammable [ɪnˈflæməbəl] *adj* inflamable
inflammation [‚ɪnfləˈmeʃən] *s* inflamación
inflate [ɪnˈflet] *tr* inflar || *intr* inflarse
inflation [ɪnˈfleʃən] *s* inflación; (*of a tire*) inflado
inflect [ɪnˈflekt] *tr* doblar, torcer; modular (*la voz*); (gram) modificar por inflexión
inflection [ɪnˈflekʃən] *s* inflexión
inflexible [ɪnˈfleksɪbəl] *adj* inflexible
inflict [ɪnˈflɪkt] *tr* infligir
influence [ˈɪnflu·əns] *s* influencia || *tr* influir sobre, influenciar
influential [‚ɪnfluˈenʃəl] *adj* influyente
influenza [‚ɪnfluˈenzə] *s* influenza
inform [ɪnˈfɔrm] *tr* informar, avisar, enterar || *intr* informar
informal [ɪnˈfɔrməl] *adj* (*not according to established rules*) informal; (*unceremonious; colloquial*) familiar
information [‚ɪnfərˈmeʃən] *s* información, informes *mpl*
informational [‚ɪnfərˈmeʃənəl] *adj* informativo
informed sources *spl* los entendidos
infraction [ɪnˈfrækʃən] *s* infracción
infrared [‚ɪnfrəˈred] *adj* & *s* infrarrojo
infrequent [ɪnˈfrikwənt] *adj* infrecuente
infringe [ɪnˈfrɪndʒ] *tr* infringir || *intr* — **to infringe on** o **upon** invadir, abusar de
infringement [ɪnˈfrɪndʒmənt] *s* infracción
infuriate [ɪnˈfjʊri‚et] *tr* enfurecer
infuse [ɪnˈfjuz] *tr* infundir
infusion [ɪnˈfjuʒən] *s* infusión
ingenious [ɪnˈdʒinjəs] *adj* ingenioso
ingenui·ty [‚ɪndʒɪˈnju·ɪti] o [‚ɪndʒɪˈnu·ɪti] *s* (*pl* -ties) ingeniosidad
ingenuous [ɪnˈdʒenju·əs] *adj* ingenuo
ingenuousness [ɪnˈdʒenju·əsnɪs] *s* ingenuidad
ingest [ɪnˈdʒest] *tr* injerir
in'go'ing *adj* entrante

in
in

ingot ['ɪŋgət] s lingote m
ingraft [ɪn'græft] o [ɪn'grɑft] tr (hort & surg) injertar; (fig) implantar
ingrate ['ɪngret] s ingrato
ingratiate [ɪn'greʃɪ,et] tr — to ingratiate oneself with congraciarse con
ingratiating [ɪn'greʃɪ,etɪŋ] adj atrayente, obsequioso
ingratitude [ɪn'grætɪ,tjud] o [ɪn-'grætɪ,tud] s ingratitud, desagradecimiento
ingredient [ɪn'gridɪ·ənt] s ingrediente m
in'grow'ing nail s uñero
ingulf [ɪn'gʌlf] tr hundir, inundar
inhabit [ɪn'hæbɪt] tr habitar, poblar
inhabitant [ɪn'hæbɪtənt] s habitante mf
inhale [ɪn'hel] tr aspirar, inspirar || intr aspirar, inspirar; tragar el humo
inherent [ɪn'hɪrənt] adj inherente
inherit [ɪn'herɪt] tr & intr heredar
inheritance [ɪn'herɪtəns] s herencia
inheritor [ɪn'herɪtər] s heredero
inhibit [ɪn'hɪbɪt] tr inhibir, prohibir
inhospitable [ɪn'hɑspɪtəbəl] o [,ɪn-hɑs'pɪtəbəl] adj inhospitalario; (affording no shelter or protection) inhóspito
inhuman [ɪn'hjumən] adj inhumano
inhumane [,ɪnhju'men] adj inhumano
inhumani·ty [,ɪnhju'mænɪti] s (pl -ties) inhumanidad
inimical [ɪ'nɪmɪkəl] adj enemigo
iniqui·ty [ɪ'nɪkwɪti] s (pl -ties) iniquidad
ini·tial [ɪ'nɪʃəl] adj & s inicial f || v (pret -tialed o -tialled; ger -tialing o -tialling) tr firmar con sus iniciales; marcar (p.ej., un pañuelo)
initiate [ɪ'nɪʃɪ,et] tr iniciar
initiation [ɪ,nɪʃɪ'eʃən] s iniciación
initiative [ɪ'nɪʃɪ·ətɪv] o [ɪ'nɪʃɪətɪv] s iniciativa
inject [ɪn'dʒɛkt] tr inyectar; introducir (una especie, una advertencia)
injection [ɪn'dʒɛkʃən] s inyección
injudicious [,ɪndʒu'dɪʃəs] adj imprudente
injunction [ɪn'dʒʌŋkʃən] s admonición, mandato; (law) entredicho
injure ['ɪndʒər] tr (to harm) dañar, hacer daño a; (to wound) herir, lisiar, lastimar; (to offend) agraviar
injurious [ɪn'dʒurɪ·əs] adj dañoso, perjudicial; (offensive) agravioso
inju·ry ['ɪndʒəri] s (pl -ries) (harm) daño; (wound) herida, lesión; (offense) agravio
injustice [ɪn'dʒʌstɪs] s injusticia
ink [ɪŋk] s tinta || tr entintar
inkling ['ɪŋklɪŋ] s sospecha, indicio, noción vaga, vislumbre f
ink'stand' s (cuplike container) tintero; (stand for ink, pens, etc.) portatintero
ink'well' s tintero
ink·y ['ɪŋki] adj (comp -ier; super -iest) entintado; negro
inlaid ['ɪn,led] o [,ɪn'led] adj embutido, taraceado
inland ['ɪnlənd] adj & s interior m || adv tierra adentro

in'-law' s (coll) pariente político
in·lay ['ɪn,le] s embutido || [ɪn'le] o ['ɪn,le] v (pret & pp -laid) tr embutir, taracear
inlet s ensenada, cala, caleta
in'mate' s (in a hospital or home) asilado, recluso, acogido; (in a jail) presidiario, preso
inn [ɪn] s mesón m, posada
innate [ɪ'net] o ['ɪnet] adj ingénito, innato
inner ['ɪnər] adj interior; secreto
in'ner·spring' mattress s colchón m de muelles interiores
inner tube s cámara (de neumático)
inning ['ɪnɪŋ] s mano f, entrada, turno
inn'keep'er s mesonero, posadero
innocence ['ɪnəsəns] s inocencia
innocent ['ɪnəsənt] adj & s inocente mf
innovate ['ɪnə,vet] tr innovar
innovation [,ɪnə've∫ən] s innovación
innuen·do [,ɪnju'endo] s (pl -does) indirecta, insinuación
innumerable [ɪ'njumərəbəl] o [ɪ'numərəbəl] adj innumerable, incontable
inoculate [ɪn'ɑkjə,let] tr inocular; (fig) imbuir
inoculation [ɪn,ɑkjə'le∫ən] s inoculación
inoffensive [,ɪnə'fɛnsɪv] adj inofensivo
inopportune [ɪn,ɑpər'tjun] o [ɪn-,ɑpər'tun] adj inoportuno
inordinate [ɪn'ɔrdɪnɪt] adj excesivo; (unrestrained) desenfrenado
inorganic [,ɪnɔr'gænɪk] adj inorgánico
in'put' s gasto, consumo; (elec) entrada; (mech) potencia consumida
inquest ['ɪnkwɛst] s encuesta; (of coroner) pesquisa judicial, levantamiento del cadáver
inquire [ɪn'kwaɪr] tr averiguar, inquirir || intr preguntar; to inquire about, after o for preguntar por; to inquire into averiguar, inquirir
inquir·y [ɪn'kwaɪri] o ['ɪnkwɪri] s (pl -ies) averiguación, encuesta; pregunta
inquisition [,ɪnkwɪ'zɪ∫ən] s inquisición
inquisitive [ɪn'kwɪzɪtɪv] adj curioso, preguntón
in'road' s incursión
ins. abbr insulated, insurance
insane [ɪn'sen] adj loco, insano
insane asylum s manicomio, casa de locos
insani·ty [ɪn'sænɪti] s (pl -ties) demencia, locura, insania
insatiable [ɪn'se∫əbəl] adj insaciable
inscribe [ɪn'skraɪb] tr inscribir; dedicar (una obra literaria)
inscription [ɪn'skrɪp∫ən] s inscripción; (of a book) dedicatoria
inscrutable [ɪn'skrutəbəl] adj inescrutable
insect ['ɪnsɛkt] s insecto
insecticide [ɪn'sɛktɪ,saɪd] adj & s insecticida m
insecure [,ɪnsɪ'kjur] adj inseguro

inseparable [ɪn'sepərəbəl] *adj* inseparable

insert ['ɪnsʌrt] *s* inserción || [ɪn'sʌrt] *tr* insertar

insertion [ɪn'sʌrʃən] *s* inserción; (*strip of lace*) entredós *m*

in·set ['ɪn,set] *s* intercalación || [ɪn'set] o ['ɪn,set] *v* (*pret & pp* -set; *ger* -setting) *tr* intercalar, encastrar

in'shore' *adj* cercano a la orilla || *adv* cerca de la orilla; hacia la orilla

in'side' *adj* interior; interno; secreto || *adv* dentro, adentro; **inside of** dentro de; **to turn inside out** volver al revés; volverse al revés || *prep* dentro de || *s* interior *m*; **insides** (coll) entrañas; **on the inside** (coll) en el secreto de las cosas

inside information *s* informes *mpl* confidenciales

insider [,ɪn'saɪdər] *s* persona enterada

insidious [ɪn'sɪdɪ·əs] *adj* insidioso

in'sight' *s* penetración

insigni·a [ɪn'sɪgnɪ·ə] *s* (*pl* -a o -as) insignia

insignificant [,ɪnsɪg'nɪfɪkənt] *adj* insignificante

insincere [,ɪnsɪn'sɪr] *adj* insincero

insinuate [ɪn'sɪnju,et] *tr* insinuar

insipid [ɪn'sɪpɪd] *adj* insípido

insist [ɪn'sɪst] *intr* insistir

insofar as [,ɪnso'fɑr,æz] *conj* en cuanto

insolence ['ɪnsələns] *s* insolencia

insolent ['ɪnsələnt] *adj* insolente

insoluble [ɪn'saljəbəl] *adj* insoluble

insolven·cy [ɪn'salvənsɪ] *s* (*pl* -cies) insolvencia

insomnia [ɪn'samnɪ·ə] *s* insomnio

insomuch [,ɪnso'mʌt/] *adv* hasta tal punto; **insomuch as** ya que, puesto que; **insomuch that** hasta el punto que

inspect [ɪn'spekt] *tr* inspeccionar

inspection [ɪn'spek/ən] *s* inspección

inspiration [,ɪnspɪ'reʃən] *s* inspiración

inspire [ɪn'spaɪr] *tr & intr* inspirar

inspiring [ɪn'spaɪrɪŋ] *adj* inspirante

inst. *abbr* **instant** (*i.e.,* **present month**)

Inst. *abbr* **Institute, Institution**

install [ɪn'stɔl] *tr* instalar

installment [ɪn'stɔlmənt] *s* instalación; entrega; **in installments** por entregas; a plazos

installment buying *s* compra a plazos

installment plan *s* pago a plazos, compra a plazos; **on the installment plan** con facilidades de pago

instance ['ɪnstəns] *s* caso, ejemplo; **for instance** por ejemplo

instant ['ɪnstənt] *adj* instantáneo || *s* instante *m*, momento; mes *m* corriente

instantaneous [,ɪnstən'tenɪ·əs] *adj* instantáneo

instantly ['ɪnstəntlɪ] *adv* al instante

instead [ɪn'sted] *adv* preferiblemente; en su lugar; **instead of** en vez de, en lugar de

in'step' *s* empeine *m*

instigate ['ɪnstɪ,get] *tr* instigar

in·still' *tr* instilar

instinct ['ɪnstɪŋkt] *s* instinto

instinctive [ɪn'stɪŋktɪv] *adj* instintivo

institute ['ɪnstɪ,tjut] o ['ɪnstɪ,tut] *s* instituto || *tr* instituir

institution [,ɪnstɪ'tju/ən] o [,ɪnstɪ'tu/ən] *s* institución

instruct [ɪn'strʌkt] *tr* instruir

instruction [ɪn'strʌk/ən] *s* instrucción

instructive [ɪn'strʌktɪv] *adj* instructivo

instructor [ɪn'strʌktər] *s* instructor *m*

instrument ['ɪnstrəmənt] *s* instrumento || ['ɪnstrə,ment] *tr* instrumentar

instrumentalist [,ɪnstrə'mentəlɪst] *s* instrumentista *mf*

instrumentali·ty [,ɪnstrəmən'tælɪti] *s* (*pl* -ties) agencia, mediación

insubordinate [,ɪnsə'bɔrdɪnɪt] *adj* insubordinado

insufferable [ɪn'sʌfərəbəl] *adj* insufrible

insufficient [,ɪnsə'fɪ/ənt] *adj* insuficiente

insular ['ɪnsələr] o ['ɪnsjulər] *adj* insular; (fig) de miras estrechas

insulate ['ɪnsə,let] *tr* aislar

insulation [,ɪnsə'leʃən] *s* aislación

insulator ['ɪnsə,letər] *s* aislador *m*

insulin ['ɪnsəlɪn] *s* insulina

insult ['ɪnsʌlt] *s* insulto || [ɪn'sʌlt] *tr* insultar

insurance [ɪn'ʃurəns] *s* seguro

insure [ɪn'ʃur] *tr* asegurar

insurer [ɪn'ʃurər] *s* asegurador *m*

insurgent [ɪn'sʌrdʒənt] *adj & s* insurgente *mf*

insurmountable [,ɪnsər'mauntəbəl] *adj* insuperable

insurrection [,ɪnsə'rek/ən] *s* insurrección

insusceptible [,ɪnsə'septɪbəl] *adj* insusceptible

int. *abbr* **interest, interior, internal, international**

intact [ɪn'tækt] *adj* intacto, ileso

in'take' *s* (*place of taking in*) entrada; (*act or amount*) toma; (mach) admisión

intake manifold *s* múltiple *m* de admisión, colector *m* de admisión

intake valve *s* válvula de admisión

intangible [ɪn'tændʒɪbəl] *adj* intangible; vago, indefinido

integer ['ɪntɪdʒər] *s* (arith) entero

integral ['ɪntɪgrəl] *adj* íntegro; **integral with** solidario de || *s* conjunto

integration [,ɪntɪ'greʃən] *s* integración

integrity [ɪn'tegrɪtɪ] *s* integridad

intellect ['ɪntə,lekt] *s* intelecto; (*person*) intelectual *mf*

intellectual [,ɪntə'lekt/u·əl] *adj & s* intelectual *mf*

intellectuali·ty [,ɪntə,lekt/u'ælɪti] *s* (*pl* -ties) intelectualidad

intelligence [ɪn'telɪdʒəns] *s* inteligencia; información

intelligence bureau *s* departamento de inteligencia

intelligence quotient *s* cociente *m* intelectual

intelligent [ɪn'telɪdʒənt] *adj* inteligente

intelligentsia [ɪn,telɪ'dʒentsɪ·ə] o [ɪn,telɪ'gentsɪ·ə] *s* intelectualidad (*con-*

intelligible — 174 — internship

junto de los intelectuales de un país o región)

intelligible [ɪn'tɛlɪdʒɪbəl] *adj* inteligible

intemperance [ɪn'tempərəns] *s* intemperancia

intemperate [ɪn'tempərɪt] *adj* intemperante; *(climate)* riguroso

intend [ɪn'tend] *tr* pensar, proponerse, intentar; *(to mean for a particular purpose)* destinar; *(to signify)* querer decir

intendance [ɪn'tendəns] *s* intendencia

intendant [ɪn'tendənt] *s* intendente *m*

intended [ɪn'tendɪd] *adj & s* (coll) prometido, prometida

intense [ɪn'tens] *adj* intenso

intensi·fy [ɪn'tensɪ‚faɪ] *v* (*pret & pp* -fied) *tr* intensificar, intensar; (phot) reforzar ‖ *intr* intensificarse, intensarse

intensi·ty [ɪn'tensɪti] *s* (*pl* -ties) intensidad

intensive [ɪn'tensɪv] *adj* intensivo

intent [ɪn'tent] *adj* atento; resuelto; intenso; **intent on** resuelto a ‖ *s* (*purpose*) intento; (*meaning*) acepción, sentido; **to all intents and purposes** en realidad de verdad

intention [ɪn'tenʃən] *s* intención

intentional [ɪn'tenʃənəl] *adj* intencional, deliberado

in·ter [ɪn'tʌr] *v* (*pret & pp* -terred; *ger* -terring) *tr* enterrar

interact ['ɪntər‚ækt] *s* (theat) entreacto ‖ [‚ɪntər'ækt] *intr* obrar recíprocamente

interaction [‚ɪntər'ækʃən] *s* interacción

inter-American [‚ɪntərə'merɪkən] *adj* interamericano

inter·breed [‚ɪntər'brid] *v* (*pret & pp* -bred* ['bred]) *tr* entrecruzar ‖ *intr* entrecruzarse

intercalate [ɪn'tʌrkə‚let] *tr* intercalar

intercede [‚ɪntər'sid] *intr* interceder

intercept [‚ɪntər'sept] *tr* interceptar

interceptor [‚ɪntər'septər] *s* interceptor *m*

interchange ['ɪntər‚tʃendʒ] *s* intercambio; (*on a highway*) correspondencia ‖ [‚ɪntər'tʃendʒ] *tr* intercambiar ‖ *intr* intercambiarse

intercollegiate [‚ɪntərkə'lidʒɪ‚ɪt] *adj* interescolar

intercom ['ɪntər‚kam] *s* interfono

intercourse ['ɪntər‚kors] *s* comunicación, trato; (*interchange of products, ideas, etc.*) intercambio; (*copulation*) cópula, comercio; **to have intercourse** juntarse

intercross [‚ɪntər'krɔs] o [‚ɪntər'kras] *tr* entrecruzar ‖ *intr* entrecruzarse

interdict ['ɪntər‚dɪkt] *s* entredicho ‖ [‚ɪntər'dɪkt] *tr* interdecir

interest ['ɪntərɪst] o ['ɪntrɪst] *s* interés *m*; **the interests** las grandes empresas, el grupo influyente; **to put out at interest** poner a interés ‖ ['ɪntərɪst], ['ɪntrɪst] o ['ɪntə‚rest] *tr* interesar

interested ['ɪntrɪstɪd] o ['ɪntə‚restɪd] *adj* interesado

interesting ['ɪntrɪstɪŋ] o ['ɪntə‚restɪŋ] *adj* interesante

interfere [‚ɪntər'fɪr] *intr* inmiscuirse, injerirse, interferir; (sport) parar una jugada; **to interfere with** dificultar, impedir, interferir

interference [‚ɪntər'fɪrəns] *s* injerencia, interferencia

interim ['ɪntərɪm] *adj* interino ‖ *s* intermedio, intervalo; **in the interim** entretanto

interior [ɪn'tɪrɪ·ər] *adj & s* interior *m*

interject [‚ɪntər'dʒekt] *tr* interponer ‖ *intr* interponerse

interjection [‚ɪntər'dʒekʃən] *s* interposición; exclamación; (gram) interjección

interlard [‚ɪntər'lard] *tr* interpolar; mechar (*la carne*)

interline [‚ɪntər'laɪn] *tr* interlinear; entretelar (*una prenda de vestir*)

interlining ['ɪntər‚laɪnɪŋ] *s* (*of a garment*) entretela

interlink [‚ɪntər'lɪŋk] *tr* eslabonar

interlock [‚ɪntər'lak] *tr* trabar ‖ *intr* trabarse

interlope [‚ɪntər'lop] *intr* entremeterse; traficar sin derecho

interloper ['ɪntər‚lopər] *s* intruso

interlude ['ɪntər‚lud] *s* intervalo; (mus) interludio; (theat) intermedio

intermarriage [‚ɪntər'mærɪdʒ] *s* casamiento entre parientes; casamiento entre personas de distintas razas, castas, etc.

intermediar·y [‚ɪntər'midɪ‚eri] *adj* intermediario ‖ *s* (*pl* -ies) intermediario

intermediate [‚ɪntər'midɪ·ɪt] *adj* intermedio

interment [ɪn'tʌrmənt] *s* entierro

intermez·zo [‚ɪntər'metso] o [‚ɪntər'medzo] *s* (*pl* -zos o -zi [tsi] o [dzi]) (mus) intermezzo

intermingle [‚ɪntər'mɪŋgəl] *tr* entremezclar ‖ *intr* entremezclarse

intermittent [‚ɪntər'mɪtənt] *adj* intermitente

intermix [‚ɪntər'mɪks] *tr* entremezclar ‖ *intr* entremezclarse

intern ['ɪntʌrn] *s* interno de hospital ‖ [ɪn'tʌrn] *tr* internar, recluir

internal [ɪn'tʌrnəl] *adj* interno

inter·nal-combus·tion engine *s* motor *m* de explosión

internal revenue *s* rentas internas

international [‚ɪntər'næʃənəl] *adj* internacional

international date line *s* línea internacional de cambio de fecha

internationalize [‚ɪntər'næʃənə‚laɪz] *tr* internacionalizar

internecine [‚ɪntər'nisɪn] *adj* sanguinario

internee [‚ɪntʌr'ni] *s* (mil) internado

internist [ɪn'tʌrnɪst] *s* internista *mf*

internment [ɪn'tʌrnmənt] *s* internamiento

internship ['ɪntʌrn‚ʃɪp] *s* residencia de un médico en un hospital

interpellate [ˌɪntərˈpɛlet] o [ɪnˈtʌrpɪˌlet] *tr* interpelar

interplay [ˈɪntərˌple] *s* interacción

interpolate [ɪnˈtʌrpəˌlet] *tr* interpolar

interpose [ˌɪntərˈpoz] *tr* interponer

interpret [ɪnˈtʌrprɪt] *tr* interpretar

interpreter [ɪnˈtʌrprɪtər] *s* intérprete *mf*

interrogate [ɪnˈterəˌget] *tr & intr* interrogar

interrogation [ɪnˌterəˈgeʃən] *s* interrogación

interrogation mark o **point** *s* signo de interrogación

interrupt [ˌɪntəˈrʌpt] *tr* interrumpir

interscholastic [ˌɪntərskəˈlæstɪk] *adj* interescolar

intersection [ˌɪntərˈsɛkʃən] *s* (*of streets, roads, etc.*) cruce *m;* (geom) intersección

intersperse [ˌɪntərˈspʌrs] *tr* entremezclar, esparcir

interstice [ɪnˈtʌrstɪs] *s* intersticio

intertwine [ˌɪntərˈtwaɪn] *tr* entrelazar ‖ *intr* entrelazarse

interval [ˈɪntərvəl] *s* intervalo; **at intervals** (*now and then*) de vez en cuando; (*here and there*) de trecho en trecho

intervene [ˌɪntərˈvin] *intr* intervenir

intervening [ˌɪntərˈvinɪŋ] *adj* intermedio

intervention [ˌɪntərˈvɛnʃən] *s* intervención

interview [ˈɪntərˌvju] *s* entrevista, interview *m* ‖ *tr* entrevistarse con

inter·weave [ˌɪntərˈwiv] *v* (*pret* -wove [ˈwov] o -weaved [ˈwov] o weaved) *tr* entretejer

intestate [ɪnˈtestet] o [ɪnˈtestɪt] *adj & s* intestado

intestine [ɪnˈtestɪn] *s* intestino

inthrall [ɪnˈθrɔl] *tr* cautivar, encantar; esclavizar, sojuzgar

inthrone [ɪnˈθron] *tr* entronizar

intima·cy [ˈɪntɪməsi] *s* (*pl* -cies) intimidad

intimate [ˈɪntɪmɪt] *adj* íntimo ‖ *s* amigo íntimo ‖ [ˈɪntɪˌmet] *tr* insinuar, intimar

intimation [ˌɪntɪˈmeʃən] *s* insinuación

intimidate [ɪnˈtɪmɪˌdet] *tr* intimidar

intitle [ɪnˈtaɪtəl] *tr* dar derecho a; (*to give a name to; to honor with a title*) intitular

into [ˈɪntu] o [ˈɪntu] *prep* en; hacia; hacia el interior de

intolerant [ɪnˈtalərənt] *adj & s* intolerante *mf*

intomb [ɪnˈtum] *tr* sepultar

intombment [ɪnˈtummənt] *s* sepultura

intonation [ˌɪntoˈneʃən] *s* entonación

intone [ɪnˈton] *tr* entonar

intoxicant [ɪnˈtaksɪkənt] *s* bebida alcohólica

intoxicate [ɪnˈtaksɪˌket] *tr* embriagar, emborrachar; (*to exhilarate*) alegrar, excitar; (*to poison*) envenenar, intoxicar

intoxication [ɪnˌtaksɪˈkeʃən] *s* embriaguez *f;* alegría, excitación; (*poisoning*) envenenamiento, intoxicación

intractable [ɪnˈtræktəbəl] *adj* intratable

intransigent [ɪnˈtrænsɪdʒənt] *adj & s* intransigente *mf*

intransitive [ɪnˈtrænsɪtɪv] *adj* intransitivo

intrench [ɪnˈtrentʃ] *tr* atrincherar ‖ *intr* — **to intrench on** o **upon** infringir, violar

intrepid [ɪnˈtrepɪd] *adj* intrépido

intrepidity [ˌɪntrɪˈpɪdɪti] *s* intrepidez *f*

intricate [ˈɪntrɪkɪt] *adj* intrincado

intrigue [ɪnˈtrig] o [ˈɪntrig] *s* intriga; intriga amorosa, enredo amoroso ‖ [ɪnˈtrig] *tr* (*to arouse the curiosity of*) intrigar ‖ *intr* intrigar; tener intrigas amorosas

intrinsic(al) [ɪnˈtrɪnsɪk(əl)] *adj* intrínseco

introd. *abbr* **introduction**

introduce [ˌɪntrəˈdjus] o [ˌɪntrəˈdus] *tr* introducir; (*to make acquainted*) presentar

introduction [ˌɪntrəˈdʌkʃən] *s* introducción; (*of one person to another or others*) presentación

introductory offer [ˌɪntrəˈdʌktəri] *s* ofrecimiento de presentación, oferta preliminar

introit [ˈɪntro·ɪt] *s* (eccl) introito

introspective [ˌɪntrəˈspɛktɪv] *adj* introspectivo

introvert [ˈɪntrəˌvʌrt] *s* introvertido

intrude [ɪnˈtrud] *intr* injerirse, entremeterse

intruder [ɪnˈtrudər] *s* intruso, entremetido

intrusive [ɪnˈtrusɪv] *adj* intruso

intrust [ɪnˈtrʌst] *tr* confiar

intuition [ˌɪntuˈɪʃən] o [ˌɪntjuˈɪʃən] *s* intuición

inundate [ˈɪnənˌdet] *tr* inundar

inundation [ˌɪnənˈdeʃən] *s* inundación

inure [ɪnˈjur] *tr* acostumbrar, endurecer, aguerrir ‖ *intr* ponerse en efecto; **to inure to** redundar en

inv. *abbr* **inventor, invoice**

invade [ɪnˈved] *tr* invadir

invader [ɪnˈvedər] *s* invasor *m*

invalid [ɪnˈvælɪd] *adj* inválido (*nulo, de ningún valor*) ‖ [ˈɪnvəlɪd] *adj* inválido (*por viejo o por enfermo*) ‖ [ˈɪnvəlɪd] *s*

invalidate [ɪnˈvælɪˌdet] *tr* invalidar

invalidity [ˌɪnvəˈlɪdɪti] *s* invalidez *f*

invaluable [ɪnˈvæljuˌəbəl] *adj* inestimable, inapreciable

invariable [ɪnˈvɛrɪ·əbəl] *adj* invariable

invasion [ɪnˈveʒən] *s* invasión

invective [ɪnˈvɛktɪv] *s* invectiva

inveigh [ɪnˈve] *intr* — **to inveigh against** lanzar invectivas contra

inveigle [ɪnˈvegəl] o [ɪnˈvigəl] *tr* engatusar

invent [ɪnˈvent] *tr* inventar

invention [ɪnˈvenʃən] *s* invención, invento

inventive [ɪnˈventɪv] *adj* inventivo

inventiveness [ɪnˈventɪvnɪs] *s* inventiva

inventor [ɪnˈvɛntər] s inventor m
inven·to·ry [ˈɪnvənˌtori] s (pl -ries) inventario ‖ v (pret & pp -ried) tr inventariar
inverse [ɪnˈvʌrs] adj inverso
inversion [ɪnˈvʌrʒən] o [ɪnˈvʌrʃən] s inversión
invert [ˈɪnvʌrt] s invertido ‖ [ɪnˈvʌrt] tr invertir
invertebrate [ɪnˈvʌrtɪˌbret] o [ɪnˈvʌrtɪbrɪt] adj & s invertebrado
inverted exclamation point s principio de admiración
inverted question mark s principio de interrogación
invest [ɪnˈvɛst] tr (to vest, to install) investir; invertir (dinero); (to besiege) cercar, sitiar; (to surround, envelop) cubrir, envolver
investigate [ɪnˈvɛstɪˌget] tr investigar
investigation [ɪnˌvɛstɪˈgeʃən] s investigación
investment [ɪnˈvɛstmənt] s (of money) inversión; (with an office or dignity) investidura; (siege) cerco, sitio
investor [ɪnˈvɛstər] s inversionista mf
inveterate [ɪnˈvɛtərɪt] adj inveterado, empedernido
invidious [ɪnˈvɪdɪ·əs] adj irritante, odioso, injusto
invigorate [ɪnˈvɪgəˌret] tr vigorizar
invigorating [ɪnˈvɪgəˌretɪŋ] adj vigorizador, vigorizante
invincible [ɪnˈvɪnsɪbəl] adj invencible
invisible [ɪnˈvɪzɪbəl] adj invisible
invisible ink s tinta simpática
invitation [ˌɪnvɪˈteʃən] s invitación, convite m
invite [ɪnˈvaɪt] tr invitar, convidar
inviting [ɪnˈvaɪtɪŋ] adj atractivo, seductor; (e.g., food) apetitoso
invoice [ˈɪnvɔɪs] s factura; **as per invoice** según factura ‖ tr facturar
invoke [ɪnˈvok] tr invocar; evocar, conjurar (p.ej., los demonios)
involuntary [ɪnˈvɑlənˌteri] adj involuntario
involution [ˌɪnvəˈluʃən] s (math) elevación a potencias, potenciación
involve [ɪnˈvɑlv] tr envolver, comprometer
invulnerable [ɪnˈvʌlnərəbəl] adj invulnerable
inward [ˈɪnwərd] adj interior ‖ adv interiormente, hacia dentro
iodide [ˈaɪ·əˌdaɪd] s yoduro
iodine [ˈaɪ·əˌdin] s yodo ‖ [ˈaɪ·əˌdaɪn] s tintura de yodo
ion [ˈaɪ·ən] o [ˈaɪ·ɑn] s ion m
ionize [ˈaɪ·əˌnaɪz] tr ionizar
IOU [ˈaɪˈoˈju] s (letterword) pagaré m
I.Q. [ˈaɪˈkju] abbr & s (letterword) **intelligence quotient**
Iran [ɪˈrɑn] o [aɪˈræn] s el Irán
Iranian [aɪˈrenɪ·ən] adj & s iranés m o iranio
Iraq [ɪˈrɑk] s el Irak
Ira·qi [ɪˈrɑki] adj iraqués o iraquiano ‖ s (pl -qis) iraqués m o iraquiano
irate [ˈaɪret] o [aɪˈret] adj airado
ire [aɪr] s ira, cólera
Ireland [ˈaɪrlənd] s Irlanda

iris [ˈaɪrɪs] s (of the eye) iris m; (rainbow) iris, arco iris; (bot) lirio
Irish [ˈaɪrɪʃ] adj irlandés ‖ s (language) irlandés m; whisky m de Irlanda; **the Irish** los irlandeses
Irish·man [ˈaɪrɪʃmən] s (pl -men [mən]) irlandés m
Irish stew s guisado de carne con patatas y cebollas
I'rish·wom'an s (pl -wom'en) irlandesa
irk [ʌrk] tr fastidiar, molestar
irksome [ˈʌrksəm] adj fastidioso, molesto
iron [ˈaɪ·ərn] adj férreo ‖ s hierro; (implement used to press or smooth clothes) plancha; **irons** (fetters) hierros, grilletes mpl; **strike while the iron is hot** a hierro caliente batir de repente ‖ tr planchar (la ropa); **to iron out** allanar (una dificultad)
i'ron-bound' adj zunchado con hierro; (unyielding) férreo, duro, inflexible; (rock-bound) escabroso, rocoso
ironclad [ˈaɪ·ərnˌklæd] adj acorazado, blindado; inflexible, exigente
iron curtain s (fig) telón m de hierro, cortina de hierro
iron digestion s estómago de avestruz
iron horse s (coll) locomotora
ironic(al) [aɪˈrɑnɪk(əl)] adj irónico
ironing [ˈaɪ·ərnɪŋ] s planchado; ropa planchada; ropa por planchar
ironing board s tabla de planchar
iron lung s pulmón m de acero o de hierro
i'ron·ware' s ferretería
iron will s voluntad de hierro
i'ron·work' s herraje m; **ironworks** ferrería, herrería
i'ron-work'er s herrero de grueso; (metalworker) cerrajero
iro·ny [ˈaɪrəni] s (pl -nies) ironía
irradiate [ɪˈrediˌet] tr irradiar; (med) someter a radiación ‖ intr irradiar
irrational [ɪˈræʃənəl] adj irracional
irrecoverable [ˌɪrɪˈkʌvərəbəl] adj incobrable, irrecuperable
irredeemable [ˌɪrɪˈdiməbəl] adj irredimible
irrefutable [ˌɪrɪˈfjutəbəl] o [ɪˈrɛfjutəbəl] adj irrebatible
irregular [ɪˈrɛgjələr] adj irregular ‖ s (mil) irregular m
irrelevance [ɪˈrɛləvəns] s impertinencia, inaplicabilidad
irrelevant [ɪˈrɛləvənt] adj impertinente, inaplicable
irreligious [ˌɪrɪˈlɪdʒəs] adj irreligioso
irremediable [ˌɪrɪˈmidɪ·əbəl] adj irremediable
irremovable [ˌɪrɪˈmuvəbəl] adj inamovible
irreparable [ɪˈrɛpərəbəl] adj irreparable
irreplaceable [ˌɪrɪˈplesəbəl] adj insubstituíble, irreemplazable
irrepressible [ˌɪrɪˈprɛsɪbəl] adj irreprimible, incontenible
irreproachable [ˌɪrɪˈprotʃəbəl] adj irreprochable
irresistible [ˌɪrɪˈzɪstɪbəl] adj irresistible
irrespective [ˌɪrɪˈspɛktɪv] adj — irre-

spective of sin hacer caso de, independiente de

irresponsible [ˌɪrɪ'spɑnsɪbəl] *adj* irresponsable

irretrievable [ˌɪrɪ'trivəbəl] *adj* irrecuperable

irreverent [ɪ'revərənt] *adj* irreverente

irrevocable [ɪ'revəkəbəl] *adj* irrevocable

irrigate ['ɪrɪˌget] *tr* irrigar

irrigation [ˌɪrɪ'geʃən] *s* irrigación

irritant ['ɪrɪtənt] *adj & s* irritante *m*

irritate ['ɪrɪˌtet] *tr* irritar

irruption [ɪ'rʌpʃən] *s* irrupción

is. *abbr* **island**

isinglass ['aɪzɪnˌglæs] o ['aɪzɪŋˌglɑs] *s (form of gelatine)* cola de pescado, colapez *f;* mica

isl. *abbr* **island**

Islam ['ɪsləm] o [ɪs'lɑm] *s* el Islam

island ['aɪlənd] *adj* isleño ‖ *s* isla

islander ['aɪləndər] *s* isleño

isle [aɪl] *s* isleta

isolate ['aɪsəˌlet] o ['ɪsəˌlet] *tr* aislar

isolation [ˌaɪsə'leʃən] o [ˌɪsə'leʃən] *s* aislamiento

isolationist [ˌaɪsə'leʃənɪst] o [ˌɪsə-'leʃənɪst] *s* aislacionista *mf*

isosceles [aɪ'sɑsəˌliz] *adj* isosceles

isotope ['aɪsəˌtop] *s* isótopo

Israe·li [ɪz'reli] *adj* israelí ‖ *s (pl* **-lis** [liz]*)* israelí *mf*

Israelite ['ɪzrɪ·əˌlaɪt] *adj & s* israelita *mf*

issuance ['ɪʃʊ·əns] *s* emisión, expedición

issue ['ɪʃʊ] *s (outgoing; outlet)* salida; *(result)* consecuencia, resultado; *(offspring)* descendencia, sucesión; *(of a magazine)* edición, impresión, tirada, número; *(e.g., of a bond)* emisión; *(yield, profit)* beneficios, producto; punto en disputa; *(pathol)* flujo; **at issue** en disputa; **to face the issue** afrontar la situación; **to force the issue** forzar la solución; **to take issue with** llevar la contraria a ‖ *tr* publicar, dar a luz *(un nuevo libro, una*

revista, *etc.)*; emitir, expedir *(títulos, obligaciones, etc.)*; distribuir *(ropa, alimento)* ‖ *intr* salir; **to issue from** provenir de

isthmus ['ɪsməs] *s* istmo

it [ɪt] *pron pers* (aplícase a cosas inanimadas, a niños de teta, a animales cuyo sexo no se conoce; y muchas veces no se traduce) él, ella; lo, la; **it is I** soy yo; **it is snowing** nieva; **it is three o'clock** son las tres

ital. *abbr* **italics**

Ital. *abbr* **Italian, Italy**

Italian [ɪ'tæljən] *adj & s* italiano

italic [ɪ'tælɪk] *adj* (typ) itálico ‖ **italics** *s* (typ) itálica, bastardilla ‖ **Italic** *adj* itálico

italicize [ɪ'tælɪˌsaɪz] *tr* imprimir en bastardilla; subrayar

Italy ['ɪtəli] *s* Italia

itch [ɪtʃ] *s* comezón *f;* (pathol) sarna; *(eagerness)* (fig) .comezón, prurito ‖ *tr* dar comezón a ‖ *intr* picar; **to itch to** tener prurito por

itch·y ['ɪtʃi] *adj (comp* **-ier;** *super* **-iest)** picante, hormigoso; (pathol) sarnoso

item ['aɪtəm] *s* artículo; noticia, suelto; *(in an account)* partida

itemize ['aɪtəˌmaɪz] *tr* particularizar, especificar, pormenorizar

itinerant [aɪ'tɪnərənt] o [ɪ'tɪnərənt] *adj* ambulante, errante ‖ *s* viandante *mf*

itinerar·y [aɪ'tɪnəˌreri] o [ɪ'tɪnəˌreri] *adj* itinerario ‖ *s (pl* **-ies)** itinerario

its [ɪts] *adj poss* su ‖ *pron poss* el suyo; suyo

itself [ɪt'self] *pron pers* mismo; sí, sí mismo; se

ivied ['aɪvɪd] *adj* cubierto de hiedra

ivo·ry ['aɪvəri] *adj* marfileño ‖ *s (pl* **-ries)** marfil *m;* **ivories** (slang) teclas del piano; (slang) bolas de billar; *(dice)* (slang) dados; (slang) dientes *mpl*

ivory tower *s* (fig) torre *f* de marfil

ivy ['aɪvi] *s (pl* **ivies)** hiedra

J

J. j [dʒe] décima letra del alfabeto inglés

J. *abbr* **Judge, Justice**

jab [dʒæb] *s* hurgonazo; *(prick)* pinchazo; *(with elbow)* codazo ‖ *v (pret & pp* **jabbed;** *ger* **jabbing)** *tr* hurgonear; dar un codazo a ‖ *intr* hurgonear

jabber ['dʒæbər] *s* chapurreo ‖ *tr & intr* chapurrear

jabot [dʒæ'bo] o ['dʒæbo] *s* chorrera

jack [dʒæk] *s (for lifting heavy objects)* gato, cric *m; (fellow)* mozo, sujeto; *(jackass)* asno, burro; *(in card games)* sota, valet *m; (small ball for bowling)* boliche *m; (jackstone)* cantillo; *(device for turning a*

spit) torno de asador; *(figure which strikes a clock bell)* jaquemar *m;* (to remove a boot) sacabotas *m;* marinero; *(flag at the bow)* (naut) yac *m;* (rad & telv) jack *m;* (elec) caja de enchufe; (slang) dinero; **every man Jack** cada hijo de vecino; **jacks** cantillos, juego de los cantillos ‖ *tr* — **to jack up** alzar con el gato; (coll) subir *(sueldos, precios, etc.)*; (coll) recordar su obligación a

jackal ['dʒækəl] *s* chacal *m*

jackanapes ['dʒækəˌneɪs] *s* mequetrefe *m*

jack'ass' *s* asno, burro

jack'daw' *s* corneja

jacket ['dʒækɪt] *s* chaqueta; *(folded*

paper) cubierta, envoltura; (*paper cover of a book*) sobrecubierta; (*metal casing*) camisa

jack′ham′mer *s* martillo perforador

jack′-in-the-box′ *s* caja de sorpresa, jugete-sorpresa *m*, muñeco en una caja de resorte

jack′knife′ *s* (*pl* **-knives′**) navaja de bolsillo; (*fancy dive*) salto de carpa

jack of all trades *s* hombre que hace toda clase de oficios, dije *m*

jack-o′-lantern [′dʒækə‚læntərn] *s* fuego fatuo; linterna hecha con una calabaza cortada de modo que remede una cabeza humana

jack pot *s* — **to hit the jack pot** (slang) ponerse las botas

jack rabbit *s* liebre grande norteamericana

jack′screw′ *s* cric *m* o gato de tornillo

jack′stone′ *s* cantillo; **jackstones** cantillos, juego de los cantillos

jack′-tar′ *s* (coll) marinero

jade [dʒed] *adj* verdoso como el jade ǁ *s* (*ornamental stone*) jade *m*; verde *m* de jade; (*worn-out horse*) jamelgo; picarona, mujerzuela ǁ *tr* cansar, ahitar, saciar

jaded [′dʒedɪd] *adj* ahito, saciado

jag [dʒæg] *s* diente *m*, púa; **to have a jag on** (slang) estar borracho

jagged [′dʒægɪd] *adj* dentado, mellado; rasgado en sietes

jaguar [′dʒægwar] *s* jaguar *m*

jail [dʒel] *s* cárcel *f;* **to break jail** escaparse de la cárcel ǁ *tr* encarcelar

jail′bird′ *s* (coll) preso, encarcelado; (coll) infractor *m* habitual

jail delivery *s* evasión de la cárcel

jailer [′dʒelər] *s* carcelero

jalop•y [dʒə′lɑpi] *s* (*pl* **-ies**) automóvil viejo y ruinoso

jam [dʒæm] *s* apiñadura, apretura; (*e.g., in traffic*) embotellamiento, bloqueo; (*preserve*) compota, conserva; (*difficult situation*) (coll) aprieto, apuros ǁ *v* (*pret & pp* **jammed**; *ger* **jamming**) *tr* apiñar, apretujar; machucarse (*p.ej., un dedo*); (rad) perturbar, sabotear; **to jam on the brakes** frenar de golpe

Jamaican [dʒə′mekən] *adj & s* jamaicano; jamaiquino (Am)

jamb [dʒæm] *s* jamba

jamboree [‚dʒæmbə′ri] *s* (coll) francachela, holgorio; reunión de niños exploradores

jamming [′dʒæmɪŋ] *s* radioperturbación

jam nut *s* contratuerca

jam-packed [′dʒæm′pækt] *adj* (coll) apiñado, apretujado, atestado

jam session *s* reunión de músicos de jazz para tocar improvisaciones

jangle [′dʒæŋgəl] *s* cencerreo; altercado, riña ǁ *tr* hacer sonar con ruido discordante ǁ *intr* cencerrear; reñir

janitor [′dʒænɪtər] *s* portero, conserje *m*

janitress [′dʒænɪtrɪs] *s* portera

January [′dʒænju‚ɛri] *s* enero

ja•pan [dʒə′pæn] *s* laca japonesa; obra japonesa laqueada; aceite *m* secante

(*paper*) ǁ *v* (*pret & pp* **-panned**; *ger* **-panning**) *tr* barnizar, charolar, laquear con laca japonesa ǁ **Japan** *s* el Japón

Japa•nese [‚dʒæpə′niz] *adj* japonés ǁ *s* (*pl* **-nese**) japonés *m*

Japanese beetle *s* escarabajo japonés

Japanese lantern *s* farolillo veneciano

Japanese persimmon *s* caqui *m*

jar [dʒar] *s* tarro; (*e.g., of olives*) frasco; (*of a storage battery*) recipiente *m*; (*jolt*) sacudida; ruido desapacible; sorpresa desagradable; **on the jar** (*said of a door*) entreabierto, entornado ǁ *v* (*pret & pp* **jarred**; *ger* **jarring**) *tr* sacudir; chocar; (*with a noise*) traquetear ǁ *intr* sacudirse; traquetear; disputar; **to jar on** irritar

jardiniere [‚dʒardɪ′nɪr] *s* (*stand*) jardinera; (*pot, bowl*) florero

jargon [′dʒargən] *s* jerga, jerigonza

jasmine [′dʒæsmɪn] o [′dʒæzmɪn] *s* jazmín *m*

jasper [′dʒæspər] *s* jaspe *m*

jaundice [′dʒɔndɪs] o [′dʒɑndɪs] *s* ictericia; (fig) envidia, celos, negro humor

jaundiced [′dʒɔndɪst] o [′dʒɑndɪst] *adj* ictericiado; (fig) avinagrado

jaunt [dʒɔnt] o [dʒɑnt] *s* caminata, excursión, paseo

jaun•ty [′dʒɔnti] o [′dʒɑnti] *adj* (*comp* **-tier**; *super* **-tiest**) airoso, gallardo, vivo; elegante, de buen gusto

Java•nese [‚dʒævə′niz] *adj* javanés ǁ *s* (*pl* **-nese**) javanés *m*

javelin [′dʒævlɪn] o [′dʒævəlɪn] *s* jabalina

jaw [dʒɔ] *s* mandíbula, quijada; **into the jaws of death** a las garras de la muerte; **jaws** boca, garganta ǁ *tr* (slang) regañar ǁ *intr* (slang) regañar; (slang) chacharear, chismear

jaw′bone′ *s* mandíbula, quijada

jaw′break′er *s* (*word*) (coll) trabalenguas *m;* (*candy*) (coll) hinchabocas *m;* (mach) trituradora de quijadas

jay [dʒe] *s* (orn) arrendajo; (coll) tonto, necio

jay′walk′ *intr* (coll) cruzar la calle descuidadamente

jay′walk′er *s* (coll) peatón descuidado

jazz [dʒæz] *s* (mus) jazz *m*; (coll) animación, viveza ǁ *tr* — **to jazz up** (coll) animar, dar viveza a

jazz band *s* orquesta de jazz

J.C. *abbr* **Jesus Christ, Julius Caesar**

jct. *abbr* **junction**

jealous [′dʒɛləs] *adj* celoso; envidioso; (*watchful in keeping or guarding something*) solícito, vigilante

jealous•y [′dʒɛləsi] *s* (*pl* **-ies**) celosía, celos; envidia; solicitud, vigilancia

jean [dʒin] *s* dril *m;* **jeans** pantalones *mpl* de dril

Jeanne d′Arc [‚ʒan′dark] *s* Juana de Arco

jeep [dʒip] *s* jip *m*, pequeño automóvil de propulsión total

jeer [dʒɪr] *s* befa, mofa, vaya ǁ *tr*

befar || *intr* mofarse; **to jeer at** befar, mofarse de

jelab [dʒəˈlɑb] *s* chilaba

jell [dʒɛl] *s* jalea || *intr* (*to become jellylike*) cuajarse; (*to take hold, catch on*) (fig) cuajar

jel·ly [ˈdʒɛli] *s* (*pl* **-lies**) jalea || *v* (*pret & pp*) *tr* convertir en jalea || *intr* convertirse en jalea

jel'ly·fish' *s* aguamala, medusa; (*weak person*) (coll) calzonazos *m*

jeopardize [ˈdʒɛpərˌdaɪz] *tr* arriesgar, exponer, poner en peligro

jeopardy [ˈdʒɛpərdi] *s* riesgo, peligro

jeremiad [ˌdʒɛrɪˈmaɪˌæd] *s* jeremiada

Jericho [ˈdʒɛrɪˌko] *s* Jericó

jerk [dʒʌrk] *s* arranque *m*, estirón *m*, tirón *m*; tic *m*, espasmo muscular; **by jerks** a sacudidas || *tr* mover de un tirón; arrojar de un tirón; atascajar (*carne*) || *intr* avanzar a tirones

jerked beef *s* tasajo

jerkin [ˈdʒʌrkɪn] *s* jubón *m*, justillo

jerk'wa'ter train *s* (coll) tren de ferrocarril económico

jerk·y [ˈdʒʌrki] *adj* (*comp* **-ier**; *super* **-iest**) (*road*; *style*) desigual; que va dando tumbos, que anda a tirones

Jerome [dʒəˈrom] *s* Jerónimo

jersey [ˈdʒʌrsi] *s* jersey *m*, chaqueta de punto

Jerusalem [dʒɪˈrusələm] *s* Jerusalén

jest [dʒɛst] *s* broma, chanza, chiste *m*; cosa de risa; **in jest** en broma || *intr* bromear

jester [ˈdʒɛstər] *s* bromista *mf*, burlón *m*; (*professional fool of medieval rulers*) bufón *m*

Jesuit [ˈdʒɛʒʊˌɪt] o [ˈdʒɛzjʊˌɪt] *adj & s* jesuíta *m*

Jesuitic(al) [ˌdʒɛʒʊˈɪtɪk(əl)] [ˌdʒɛzjʊˈɪtɪk(əl)] *adj* jesuítico

Jesus [ˈdʒizəs] *s* Jesús *m*

Jesus Christ *s* Jesucristo

jet [dʒɛt] *adj* de azabache; azabachado || *s* (*of a fountain*) surtidor *m*; (*of gas*) mechero; (*stream shooting forth from nozzle, etc.*) chorro; avión *m* a reacción, avión de chorro; (*hard black mineral*; *lustrous black*) azabache *m* || *v* (*pret & pp* **jetted**; *ger* **jetting**) *tr* arrojar en chorro || *intr* chorrear, salir en chorro; volar en avión de chorro

jet age *s* era de los aviones de chorro

jet'-black' *adj* azabachado

jet bomber *s* bombardero de reacción a chorro

jet coal *s* carbón *m* de bujía, carbón de llama larga

jet engine *s* motor *m* a chorro, motor de reacción

jet fighter *s* caza de reacción, cazarreactor *m*

jet'lin'er *s* avión *m* de travesía con propulsión a chorro

jet plane *s* avión *m* de chorro

jet propulsion *s* propulsión a chorro, propulsión de escape

jetsam [ˈdʒɛtsəm] *s* (naut) echazón *f*; cosas desechadas

jet stream *s* escape *m* de un motor cohete; (meteor) chorros de viento

(*que soplan de oeste a este a la altura de 10 kilómetros*)

jettison [ˈdʒɛtɪsən] *s* (naut) echazón *f* || *tr* (naut) echar al mar; desechar, rechazar

jettison gear *s* (aer) lanzador *m*

jet·ty [ˈdʒɛti] *s* (*pl* **-ties**) (*structure projecting into sea to protect harbor*) escollera, malecón *m*; (*wharf*) muelle *m*, desembarcadero

Jew [dʒu] *s* judío

jewel [ˈdʒu·əl] *s* piedra preciosa; (*valuable personal ornament*) alhaja, joya; (*of a watch*) rubí *m*; (*article of costume jewelry*) joya de imitación; (*highly prized person or thing*) alhaja, joya

jewel case *s* guardajoyas *m*, estuche *m*, joyero

jeweler o **jeweller** [ˈdʒu·ələr] *s* joyero; relojero

jewelry [ˈdʒu·əlri] *s* joyería, joyas

jewelry shop *s* joyería; relojería

Jewess [ˈdʒu·ɪs] *s* judía

jew'fish' *s* mero

Jewish [ˈdʒu·ɪʃ] *adj* judío

Jew·ry [ˈdʒu·ri] *s* (*pl* **-ries**) judería

jews'-harp o **jew's-harp** [ˈdʒuzˌhɑrp] *s* birimbao

jib [dʒɪb] *s* (*of a crane*) aguilón *m*, pescante *m*; (naut) foque *m*

jib boom *s* (naut) botalón *m* de foque

jibe [dʒaɪb] *s* remoque *m*, mofa || *intr* mofarse; (coll) concordar (*dos cosas*); **to jibe at** mofarse de

jif·fy [ˈdʒɪfi] *s* (*pl* **-fies**) — **in a jiffy** (coll) en un santiamén

jig [dʒɪg] *s* (*dance and music*) giga; **the jig is up** (slang) ya se acabó todo, estamos perdidos

jigger [ˈdʒɪgər] *s* (*for fishing*) anzuelo de cuchara; (*for separating ore*) criba de vaivén; (*flea*) nigua; (*gadget*) cosilla, chisme *m*, dispositivo; vasito para medir el licor de un coctel (*onza y media*)

jiggle [ˈdʒɪgəl] *s* zangoloteo || *tr* zangolotear || *intr* zangolotearse

jig saw *s* sierra de vaivén

jig'saw' puzzle *s* rompecabezas *m* (*figura que ha sido cortada caprichosamente en trozos menudos y que hay que recomponer*)

jilt [dʒɪlt] *tr* dar calabazas a (*un novio*)

jim·my [ˈdʒɪmi] *s* (*pl* **-mies**) palanqueta || *v* (*pret & pp* **-mied**) *tr* forzar con palanqueta; **to jimmy open** abrir con palanqueta

jingle [ˈdʒɪŋgəl] *s* (*small bell*) cascabel *m*; (*of tambourine*) sonaja; (*sound*) cascabeleo; rima infantil; (rad) anuncio rimado y cantado || *tr* hacer sonar || *intr* cascabelear

jin·go [ˈdʒɪŋgo] *adj* jingoísta || *s* (*pl* **-goes**) jingoísta *mf*; **by jingo!** (coll) ¡caramba!

jingoism [ˈdʒɪŋgoˌɪzəm] *s* jingoísmo

jinx [dʒɪŋks] *s* gafe *m* || *tr* (coll) traer mala suerte a

jitters [ˈdʒɪtərz] *spl* (coll) inquietud, nerviosidad; **to give the jitters to**

(coll) poner nervioso; **to have the jitters** (coll) ponerse nervioso

jittery ['dʒɪtəri] *adj* (coll) nervioso

Joan of Arc ['dʒon əv 'ɑrk] *s* Juana de Arco

job [dʒab] *s* (*piece of work*) trabajo; (*task, chore*) quehacer *m*, tarea; (*work done by contract*) destajo; (*employment*) empleo, oficio; (coll) robo; **by the job** a destajo; **on the job** trabajando de aprendiz; (slang) vigilante, atento a sus obligaciones; **to be out of a job** estar desocupado, estar sin trabajo; **to lie down on the job** (slang) echarse en el surco, estirar la pierna

job analysis *s* análisis *m* ocupacional

jobber ['dʒabər] *s* comerciante medianero; (*pieceworker*) destajero; (*dishonest official*) agiotista *m*

job'hold'er *s* empleado; (*in the government*) burócrata *mf*

jobless ['jablɪs] *adj* desocupado, sin empleo

job lot *s* saldo de mercancías

job printer *s* impresor *m* de remiendos

job printing *s* remiendo

jockey ['dʒaki] *s* jockey *m* ǁ *tr* montar (*un caballo*) en la pista; maniobrar; embaucar

jockstrap ['dʒak ˌstræp] *s* suspensorio (*para sostener el escroto*)

jocose [dʒo'kos] *adj* jocoso

jocular ['dʒakjələr] *adj* jocoso, festivo

jog [dʒag] *s* golpecito; (*to the memory*) estímulo; trote corto ǁ *v* (*pret & pp* jogged; *ger* jogging) *tr* empujar levemente; estimular (*la memoria*) ǁ *intr* — **to jog along** avanzar al trote corto

jog trot *s* trote *m* de perro; (fig) rutina

John [dʒan] *s* Juan *m*

John Bull *s* el inglés típico, el pueblo inglés

John Hancock ['hænkɑk] *s* (coll) la firma de uno

johnnycake ['dʒani ˌkek] *s* pan *m* de maíz

John'ny-come'-late'ly *s* (coll) recién llegado

John'ny-jump'-up' *s* (*pansy*) pensamiento, trinitaria; violeta

John'ny-on-the-spot' *s* (coll) el que está siempre presente y listo

John the Baptist *s* San Juan Bautista

join [dʒɔɪn] *tr* juntar, unir, ensamblar; asociarse a, unirse a; incorporarse a, ingresar en; abrazar (*un partido*); hacerse socio de (*una asociación*); alistarse en (*el ejército*); trabar (*batalla*); desaguar en (*el océano*) ǁ *intr* juntarse, unirse; confluir (*p.ej., dos ríos*)

joiner ['dʒɔɪnər] *s* carpintero; (coll) el que tiene la manía de incorporarse a muchas asociaciones

joint [dʒɔɪnt] *s* (*in a pipe*) empalme *m*, juntura; (*of bones*) articulación, juntura, coyuntura; (*backbone of book*) nervura; (*hinge of book*) cartivana; (*in woodwork*) emsambladura; (*of meat*) tajada; (elec) empalme *m*; (*gambling den*) (slang)

garito; (slang) restaurante *m* de mala muerte; **out of joint** desencajado, descoyuntado; (fig) en desorden, desbarajustado; **to throw out of joint** descoyuntarse (*p.ej., el brazo*)

joint account *s* cuenta en común

Joint Chiefs of Staff *spl* (U.S.A.) Estado mayor conjunto

jointly ['dʒɔɪntli] *adv* juntamente, en común

joint owner *s* condueño

joint session *s* sesión conjunta

joint'-stock' company *s* sociedad anónima, compañía por acciones

joist [dʒɔɪst] *s* viga

joke [dʒok] *s* broma, chiste *m*; (*trifling matter*) cosa de reír; (*person laughed at*) bufón *m*, hazmerreír *m*; **no joke** cosa seria; **to tell a joke** contar un chiste; **to play a joke on** gastar una broma a ǁ *tr* — **to joke one's way into** conseguir (*p.ej., un empleo*) burla burlando ǁ *intr* bromear, hablar en broma; **joking aside** o **joking** burlas aparte

joke book *s* libro de chistes

joker ['dʒokər] *s* bromista *mf*; (*wise guy*) sábelotodo; (*playing card*) comodín *m*; (*hidden provision*) cláusula engañadora

jol·ly ['dʒali] *adj* (*comp* -lier; *super* -liest) alegre, festivo ǁ *adv* (coll) muy, harto ǁ *v* (*pret & pp* -lied) *tr* (coll) candonguear

jolt [dʒolt] *s* sacudida ǁ *tr* sacudir ǁ *intr* dar tumbos

Jonah ['dʒonə] *s* Jonás *m*; (fig) ave *f* de mal agüero

jongleur ['dʒaŋglər] *s* juglar *m*, trovador *m*

jonquil ['dʒaŋkwɪl] *s* junquillo

Jordan ['dʒɔrdən] *s* (*country*) Jordania; (*river*) Jordán *m*

Jordan almond *s* almendra de Málaga

Jordanian [dʒɔr'denɪ·ən] *adj & s* jordano

josh [dʒaʃ] *tr* (coll) dar broma a ǁ *intr* dar broma

jostle ['dʒasəl] *s* empellón *m*, empujón *m* ǁ *tr* empellar, empujar ǁ *intr* chocar, encontrarse; avanzar a fuerza de empujones o codazos

jot [dʒat] *s* — **I don't care a jot for** no se me da un bledo de ǁ *v* (*pret & pp* jotted; *ger* jotting) *tr* — **to jot down** apuntar, anotar

jounce [dʒauns] *s* sacudida ǁ *tr* sacudir ǁ *intr* dar tumbos

journal ['dʒɑrnəl] *s* (*newspaper*) periódico; (*magazine*) revista; (*daily record*) diario; (com) libro diario; (naut) cuaderno de bitácora; (mach) gorrón *m*, muñón *m*

journalese [ˌdʒɑrnə'liz] *s* lenguaje periodístico

journalism ['dʒɑrnə ˌlɪzəm] *s* periodismo

journalist ['dʒɑrnəlɪst] *s* periodista *mf*

journalistic [ˌdʒɑrnə'lɪstɪk] *adj* periodístico

journey ['dʒɑrni] *s* viaje *m* ǁ *intr* viajar

journey·man ['dʒʌrnimən] s (pl -men [mən]) oficial m

joust [dʒʌst] o [dʒust] o [dʒaust] s justa ‖ intr justar

jovial ['dʒovɪəl] adj jovial

joviality [,dʒovɪ'ælɪti] s jovialidad

jowl [dʒaul] s (cheek) moflete m; (jawbone) quijada; (of cattle) papada; (of fowl) barba

joy [dʒɔɪ] s alegría, regocijo; **to leap with joy** saltar de gozo

joyful ['dʒɔɪfəl] adj alegre; **joyful over** gozoso con o de

joyless ['dʒɔɪlɪs] adj triste, sin alegría

joyous ['dʒɔɪ·əs] adj alegre

joy ride s (coll) paseo de recreo en coche; (coll) paseo alocado en coche

J.P. abbr Justice of the Peace

Jr. abbr junior

jubilant ['dʒubɪlənt] adj jubiloso

jubilation [,dʒubɪ'leʃən] s júbilo, viva alegría

jubilee ['dʒubɪ,li] s (jubilation) júbilo; aniversario; quincuagésimo aniversario; (eccl) jubileo

Judaism ['dʒude,ɪzəm] s judaísmo

judge [dʒʌdʒ] s juez m; **to be a good judge of** ser buen juez de o en ‖ tr & intr juzgar; **judging by** a juzgar por

judge advocate s (in the army) auditor m de guerra; (in the navy) auditor de marina

judgeship ['dʒʌdʒʃɪp] s judicatura

judgment ['dʒʌdʒmənt] s juicio; (legal decision) sentencia, fallo

judgment day s día m del juicio

judgment seat s tribunal m

judicature ['dʒudɪkət/ər] s judicatura

judicial [dʒu'dɪʃəl] adj judicial; (becoming a judge) crítico, juicioso

judiciar·y [dʒu'dɪʃɪ,ɛri] adj judicial ‖ s (pl -ies) (judges of a city, country, etc.) judicatura; (branch of government that administers justice) poder m judicial

judicious [dʒu'dɪʃəs] adj juicioso

jug [dʒʌg] s botija, jarra, cántaro; (jail) (slang) chirona

juggle ['dʒʌgəl] s juego de manos; (trick, deception) trampa ‖ tr hacer suertes con (p.ej., bolas); alterar fraudulentamente, falsear (cuentas, documentos, etc.); **to juggle away** escamotear ‖ intr hacer suertes; hacer trampas

juggler ['dʒʌglər] s malabarista mf; impostor m

juggling ['dʒʌglɪŋ] s juegos malabares

Jugoslav ['jugo'slav] adj & s yugoeslavo

Jugoslavia ['jugo'slavɪ·ə] s Yugoeslavia

jugular ['dʒʌgjələr] o ['dʒugjələr] adj & s yugular f

juice [dʒus] s jugo, zumo; (natural fluid of an animal body) jugo; (slang) electricidad; (slang) gasolina; **to stew in one's own juice** (coll) freír en su aceite

juic·y ['dʒusi] adj (comp -ier; super -iest) jugoso, zumoso; (interesting, spicy) picante

jukebox ['dʒuk,baks] s tocadiscos m tragamonedas

julep ['dʒulɪp] s julepe m

julienne [,dʒulɪ'en] s sopa juliana

July [dʒu'laɪ] s julio

jumble ['dʒʌmbəl] s revoltijo, masa confusa ‖ tr emburujar, revolver

jum·bo ['dʒʌmbo] adj (coll) enorme, colosal ‖ s (pl -bos) (large clumsy person) (coll) elefante m; (coll) objeto enorme

jump [dʒʌmp] s salto; (in a parachute) lanzamiento; (of prices) alza repentina; **to be always on the jump** (coll) andar siempre de aquí para allí; **to get o to have the jump on** (slang) ganar la ventaja a ‖ tr saltar; hacer saltar (a un caballo); (in checkers) comer; salir (un tren) fuera de (el carril) ‖ intr saltar; (in a parachute from an airplane) lanzarse; pasar del tope (el carro de la máquina de escribir); **to jump at** apresurarse a aceptar (un convite); apresurarse a aprovechar (la oportunidad); **to jump on** saltar a (un tren); (slang) regañar, criticar; **to jump over** saltar por, pasar de un salto; saltar (la página de un libro); **to jump to a conclusion** sacar una conclusión precipitadamente

jumper ['dʒʌmpər] s saltador m; blusa de obrero; **jumpers** traje holgado de juego para niños

jumping jack ['dʒʌmpɪŋ] s títere m

jump'ing-off' place s fin m del camino

jump seat s estrapontín m, traspuntín m

jump spark s (elec) chispa de entrehierro

jump wire s (elec) alambre m de cierre

jump·y ['dʒʌmpi] adj (comp -ier; super -iest) saltón; asustadizo, nervioso

junc. abbr junction

junction ['dʒʌŋk/ən] s juntura, unión; (of pieces of wood) ensambladura; (of two rivers) confluencia; (rail connection) empalme m; (rr) estación de empalme

juncture ['dʒʌŋkt/ər] s juntura, unión; (time, occasion) coyuntura; **at this juncture** a esta sazón, a estas alturas

June [dʒun] s junio

jungle ['dʒʌŋgəl] s jungla, selva; revoltijo, maraña

junior ['dʒunjər] adj menor, de menor edad; joven; del penúltimo año; hijo, p.ej., **John Jones, Junior** Juan Jones, hijo ‖ s menor m; socio menor; alumno del penúltimo año

junior college s escuela de estudios universitarios de primero y segundo años

junior high school s escuela intermedia entre la primaria y la secundaria

juniper ['dʒunɪpər] s enebro; (red cedar) cedro de Virginia

juniper berry s enebrina

junk [dʒʌŋk] s chatarra, hierro viejo; ropa vieja; (useless stuff) (coll) trastos viejos, baratijas viejas; (old cable) jarcia trozada; (Chinese ship) junco; (naut) carne salada ‖ tr

ji
ju

(slang) echar a la basura; reducir a hierro viejo

junk dealer *s* chatarrero, chapucero

junket ['dʒʌŋkɪt] *s* manjar *m* de leche, cuajo y azúcar; (*outing*) viaje *m* de recreo; (*trip paid out of public funds*) jira ‖ *intr* hacer un viaje de recreo; ir de jira

junk·man ['dʒʌŋk‚mæn] *s* (*pl* **-men** [‚men]) chatarrero, chapucero; ropavejero; tripulante *m* de junco

junk room *s* leonera, trastera

junk shop *s* tienda de trastos viejos

junk yard *s* chatarrería

juridical [dʒʊ'rɪdɪkəl] *adj* jurídico

jurisdiction [‚dʒʊrɪs'dɪkʃən] *s* jurisdicción

jurisprudence [‚dʒʊrɪs'prudəns] *s* jurisprudencia

jurist ['dʒʊrɪst] *s* jurista *mf*

juror ['dʒʊrər] *s* (*individual*) jurado

ju·ry ['dʒʊri] *s* (*pl* **-ries**) (*group*) jurado

jury box *s* tribuna del jurado

jury·man ['dʒʊrimən] *s* (*pl* **-men** [mən]) (*individual*) jurado

Jus. P. *abbr* **justice of the peace**

just [dʒʌst] *adj* justo ‖ *adv* justamente, justo; hace poco, apenas; sólo; (coll) absolutamente; **just** + *pp* acabado de + *inf*, p.ej., **just received** acabado de recibir; recién + *pp*, p.ej., **just arrived** recién llegado; **just as** como; en el momento en que; tal como; lo mismo que; **just beyond** un poco más allá (de); **just now** hace poco; ahora mismo; **just out** acabado de

aparecer, recién publicado; **to have just** + *pp* acabar de + *inf*, p.ej., **I have just arrived** acabo de llegar; **I had just arrived** acababa de llegar

justice ['dʒʌstɪs] *s* justicia; (*judge*) juez *m*; (*just deserts*) premio merecido; **to bring to justice** aprehender y condenar por justicia; **to do justice to** hacer justicia a; apreciar debidamente

justice of the peace *s* juez *m* de paz

justifiable ['dʒʌstɪ‚faɪ-əbəl] *adj* justificable

justi·fy ['dʒʌstɪ‚faɪ] *v* (*pret & pp* **-fied**) *tr* justificar; (typ) justificar

justly ['dʒʌstli] *adj* justamente, debidamente

jut [dʒʌt] *v* (*pret & pp* **jutted**; *ger* **jutting**) *intr* — **to jut out** resaltar, proyectarse

jute [dʒut] *s* yute *m* ‖ **Jute** *m* juto

Jutland ['dʒʌtlənd] *s* Jutlandia

juvenile ['dʒuvənɪl] o ['dʒuvə‚naɪl] *adj* juvenil; para jóvenes ‖ *s* joven *mf*, mocito; libro para niños; (theat) galán *m*, galancete *m*

juvenile court *s* tribunal *m* tutelar de menores

juvenile delinquency *s* delincuencia de menores

juvenile lead [lid] *s* (theat) papel *m* de galancete; (theat) galancete *m*

juvenilia [‚dʒuvə'nɪlɪ-ə] *spl* obras de juventud

juxtapose [‚dʒʌkstə'poz] *tr* yuxtaponer

K

K, k [ke] undécima letra del alfabeto inglés

k. *abbr* **karat, kilogram**

K. *abbr* **King, Knight**

kale [kel] *s* col *f*, berza; (slang) dinero, pasta

kaleidoscope [kə'laɪdə‚skop] *s* calidoscopio

kangaroo [‚kæŋgə'ru] *s* canguro

kapok ['kepɑk] *s* capoc *m*, lana de ceiba

katydid ['ketidɪd] *s* saltamontes *m* cuyo macho emite un sonido chillón

kc. *abbr* **kilocycle**

kedge [kedʒ] *s* (naut) anclote *m*

keel [kil] *s* quilla ‖ *intr* — **to keel over** (naut) dar de quilla; volcarse; (coll) desmayarse

keelson ['kelsən] o ['kilsən] *s* (naut) sobrequilla

keen [kin] *adj* (*having a sharp edge*) agudo, afilado; (*sharp, cutting*) mordaz, penetrante; (*sharp-witted*) sutil, astuto, perspicaz; (*eager, much interested*) intenso, vivo; (slang) maravilloso; **to be keen on** ser muy aficionado a

keep [kip] *s* manutención, subsisten-

cia; (*of medieval castle*) torre *f* del homenaje; **for keeps** (coll) de veras; (coll) para siempre; **to earn one's keep** (coll) ganarse la vida ‖ *v* (*pret & pp* **kept** [kept]) *tr* guardar, conservar; (*deciding to make a purchase*) quedarse con; cumplir, guardar (*su palabra, su promesa*); llevar (*cuentas*); apuntar (*los tantos*); tener (*criados, caballos, huéspedes*); cultivar (*una huerta*); dirigir (*un hotel, una escuela*); celebrar (*una fiesta*); hacer tardar (*a una persona*); **to keep away** tener alejado; **to keep back** retener; beberse (*las lágrimas*); reservar, no divulgar; **to keep down** reprimir; reducir (*los gastos*) al mínimo; **to keep** (*a una persona*) **from** + *ger* no dejarle (*a una persona*) + *inf*; **to keep in** no dejar salir; **to keep off** tener a distancia; no dejar penetrar (*p.ej., la lluvia*); evitar (*p.ej., el polvo*); **to keep out** no dejar entrar; no dejar penetrar; **to keep someone informed** (**about**) ponerle a uno al corriente (de); **to keep someone waiting** hacerle a uno esperar; **to keep up** mantener, conservar ‖ *intr* permanecer, quedarse; conservarse, no echarse a perder; **to keep** + *ger* seguir + *ger*; **to keep away** mantenerse a distancia; no dejarse ver; **to keep from** + *ger* abstenerse de + *inf*; **to keep informed (about)** ponerse al corriente (de); **to keep in with** (coll) congraciarse con, no perder el favor de; **to keep off** no acercarse a; no pisar (*el césped*); **to keep on** + *ger* seguir + *ger*; **to keep on with** continuar con; **to keep out** mantenerse fuera, no entrar; **to keep out of** no entrar en; no meterse en; evitar (*el peligro*); **to keep quiet** estarse quieto; **to keep to** seguir por, llevar (*la derecha, la izquierda*); **to keep to oneself** quedarse a solas; **to keep up** continuar; no rezagarse; **to keep up with** correr parejas con; llevar adelante, proseguir

keeper ['kipər] *s* guardián *m*, custodio; (*of a game preserve*) guardabosque *m*; (*of a magnet*) armadura, culata

keeping ['kipɪŋ] *s* custodia, cuidado; (*of a holiday*) celebración; **in keeping with** de acuerdo con, en armonía con; **in safe keeping** en lugar seguro, a buen recaudo; **out of keeping with** en desacuerdo con

keep'sake' *s* recuerdo

keg [kɛg] *s* cuñete *m*, cubeto

ken [kɛn] *s* alcance *m* de la vista, alcance del saber; **beyond the ken of** fuera del alcance de

kennel ['kɛnəl] *s* perrera

kep·i ['kepi] o ['kɛpi] *s* (*pl* **-is**) quepis *m*

kept woman [kɛpt] *s* entretenida, mancеba

kerchief ['kʌrtʃɪf] *s* pañuelo, mantón *m*

kerchoo [kər'tʃu] *interj* ¡ah-chís!

kernel ['kʌrnəl] *s* (*inner part of a nut or fruit stone*) almendra, núcleo; (*of wheat or corn*) grano; (fig) medula

kerosene ['kɛrə‚sin] o [‚kɛrə'sin] *s* keroseno

kerosene lamp *s* lámpara de petróleo

kerplunk [kər'plʌŋk] *interj* ¡pataplún!

ketchup ['kɛtʃəp] *s* salsa de tomate condimentada

kettle ['kɛtəl] *s* caldera, marmita; (*tea-kettle*) tetera

ket'tle·drum' *s* timbal *m*, tímpano

key [ki] *adj* clave || *s* (*of door, trunk, etc.*) llave *f*; (*of piano, typewriter, etc.*) tecla; (*wedge or cotter used to lock parts together*) clavija, cuña, chaveta; (*reef or low island*) cayo; (bot) sámara; (*tone of voice*) tono; (mus) clave *f* o llave *f*; (telg) manipulador *m*; (*to a puzzle, secret, translation, code*) (fig) clave o llave; (*place giving control to a region*) (fig) llave *f*; (fig) persona principal; **off key** desafinado; desafinadamente || *va* acuñar, enchavetar; **to key up** alentar, excitar

key'board' *s* teclado

key fruit *s* sámara

key'hole' *s* ojo de la cerradura; (*of a clock*) agujero de cuerda

key'note' *s* (mus) tónica, nota tónica; (fig) idea fundamental

keynote speech *s* discurso de apertura (*en que se expone el programa de un partido político*)

key'punch'er *s* perforista *mf*

key ring *s* llavero

key'stone' *s* clave *f*, espinazo; (fig) piedra angular

Key West *s* Cayo Hueso

key word *s* palabra clave

kg. *abbr* **kilogram**

kha·ki ['kɑki] o ['kæki] *adj* caqui || *s* (*pl* **-kis**) caqui *m*

khedive [kə'div] *s* jedive *m*

kibitz ['kɪbɪts] *intr* (coll) dar consejos molestos a los jugadores

kibitzer ['kɪbɪtsər] *s* (coll) mirón molesto (*de una partida de juego*); (coll) entremetido

kiblah ['kɪblɑ] *s* alquibla

kibosh ['kaɪbɑʃ] o [kɪ'bɑʃ] *s* (coll) música celestial; **to put the kibosh on** (coll) desbaratar, imposibilitar

kick [kɪk] *s* puntapié *m*; (*of an animal*) coz *f*; (*of a gun*) coz, culatazo; (*complaint*) (slang) queja, protesta; (*of liquor*) (slang) fuerza, estímulo; (*thrill*) gusto, placer intenso; **to get a kick out of** (slang) hallar mucho placer en || *tr* acocear, dar de puntapiés a; sacudir (*los pies*); **to kick out** (coll) echar a puntapiés a la calle; (coll) echar, despedir; **to kick up a row** (slang) armar un bochinche || *intr* cocear; dar culetazos (*un arma de fuego*); (coll) quejarse; **to kick about** (coll) quejarse de; **to kick against the pricks** dar coces contra el aguijón; **to kick off** (football) dar el golpe de salida

kick'back' *s* (coll) contragolpe *m*; (slang) devolución a un cómplice de una parte de lo robado

kick'off' *s* (football) golpe *m* de salida, puntapié *m* inicial

kid [kɪd] *s* (*young goat*) cabrito; (*leather*) cabritilla; (coll) chiquillo, chico; **kids** guantes *mpl* o zapatos de cabritilla || *v* (*pret & pp* **kidded**; *ger* **kidding**) *tr* (slang) embromar, tomar el pelo a; **to kid oneself** (slang) forjarse ilusiones || *intr* (slang) decirlo en broma

kidder ['kɪdər] *s* (slang) bromista *mf*

kid gloves *spl* guantes *mpl* de cabritilla; **to handle with kid gloves** tratar con suma discreción o cautela

kid'nap' *s* (*pret & pp* **-naped** o **-napped**; *ger* **-naping** o **-napping**) *tr* secuestrar

kidnaper o **kidnapper** ['kɪd‚næpər] *s* secuestrador *m*, ladrón *m* de niños

kidney ['kɪdni] *s* riñón *m*; (coll) clase *f*, especie *f*; (coll) carácter *m*

kidney bean *s* judía

kidney stone *s* cálculo renal

kill [kɪl] *s* matanza; (*of a wild beast, an army, a pack of hounds*) ataque *m* final; (*creek*) arroyo, riachuelo; **for the kill** para el golpe final || *tr*

ju
ki

matar; ahogar (*un proyecto de ley*); quitar (*el sabor*); producir una impresión irresistible en

killer ['kɪlər] *s* matador *m*

killer whale *s* orca

killing ['kɪlɪŋ] *adj* matador; (*exhausting*) abrumador; (coll) muy divertido, de lo más ridículo || *s* matanza; (*game killed on a hunt*) cacería, piezas; (coll) gran ganancia; **to make a killing** (coll) enriquecerse de golpe

kill'-joy' *s* aguafiestas *mf*

kiln [kɪl] o [kɪln] *s* horno

kil·o ['kɪlo] o ['kilo] *s* (*pl* -os) kilo, kilogramo; kilómetro

kilocycle ['kɪlə,saɪkəl] *s* kilociclo

kilogram ['kɪlə,græm] *s* kilogramo

kilometer ['kɪlə,mitər] o [kɪ'lɑmɪtər] *s* kilómetro

kilometric [,kɪlə'mɛtrɪk] *adj* kilométrico

kilowatt ['kɪlə,wɑt] *s* kilovatio

kilowatt-hour ['kɪlə,wɑt'aʊr] *s* (*pl* **kilowatt-hours**) kilovatio-hora

kilt [kɪlt] *s* enagüillas, falda corta

kilter ['kɪltər] *s* — **to be out of kilter** (coll) estar descompuesto

kimo·no [kɪ'monə] o [kɪ'mono] *s* (*pl* -nos) quimono

kin [kɪn] *s* (*family relationship*) parentesco; (*relatives*) deudos; **near of kin** muy allegado; **of kin** allegado; **the next of kin** el pariente más próximo, los parientes próximos

kind [kaɪnd] *adj* bueno, bondadoso; (*greeting*) afectuoso; **kind to** bueno para con || *s* clase *f*, especie *f*, suerte *f*, género; **a kind of** uno a modo de; **all kinds of** (coll) gran cantidad de; **in kind** en especie; en la misma moneda; **kind of** (coll) algo, más bien; **of a kind** de una misma clase; (*poor, mediocre*) de poco valor, de mala muerte; **of the kind** por el estilo

kindergarten ['kɪndər,gɑrtən] *s* escuela de párvulos, jardín *m* de la infancia

kindergartner ['kɪndər,gɑrtnər] *s* (*child*) párvulo; (*teacher*) parvulista *mf*

kind-hearted ['kaɪnd'hɑrtɪd] *adj* bondadoso, de buen corazón

kindle ['kɪndəl] *tr* encender || *intr* encenderse

kindling ['kɪndlɪŋ] *s* encendajas

kindling wood *s* leña

kind·ly ['kaɪndli] *adj* (*comp* -lier; *super* -liest) (*kind-hearted*) bondadoso; apacible, benigno; favorable || *adv* bondadosamente; cordialmente; con gusto; por favor; **to not take kindly to** no aceptar de buen grado

kindness ['kaɪndnɪs] *s* bondad; **have the kindness to** tenga Vd. la bondad de

kindred ['kɪndrɪd] *adj* emparentado; afín, semejante || *s* parentela; semejanza, afinidad

kinescope ['kɪnɪ,skop] *s* (trademark) cinescopio, cinescopia

kinetic [kɪ'nɛtɪk] o [kaɪ'nɛtɪk] *adj* cinético || **kinetics** *s* cinética

kinetic energy *s* fuerza viva, energía cinética

king [kɪŋ] *s* rey *m*; (cards, chess, & fig) rey; (checkers) dama

king'bolt' *s* pivote *m* central

kingdom ['kɪŋdəm] *s* reino

king'fish'er *s* martín *m* pescador

king·ly ['kɪŋli] *adj* (*comp* -lier; *super* -liest) real, regio; (*stately*) majestuoso || *adv* regiamente

king'pin' *s* (bowling) bolo delantero; pivote *m* central; (aut) pivote de dirección; (coll) persona principal

king post *s* pendolón *m*

king's evil *s* escrófula

kingship ['kɪŋ/ɪp] *s* dignidad real

king'-size' *adj* de tamaño grande

king's ransom *s* riquezas de Creso

kink [kɪŋk] *s* (*twist, e.g., in a rope*) enroscadura, cocura; (*e.g., in Negro's hair*) pasa; (*soreness in neck*) tortícolis *m*; (*flaw, difficulty*) estorbo, traba; (*mental twist*) chifladura, manía || *tr* enroscar || *intr* enroscarse

kink·y ['kɪŋki] *adj* (*comp* -ier; *super* -iest) encarrujado, ensortijado

kinsfolk ['kɪnz,fok] *s* parentela, familia, deudos

kinship ['kɪn/ɪp] *s* parentesco; semejanza, afinidad

kins·man ['kɪnzmən] *s* (*pl* -men [mən]) pariente *m*

kins·woman ['kɪnz,wʊmən] *s* (*pl* -women [,wɪmɪn]) *s* parienta

kipper ['kɪpər] *s* arenque accinado, salmón accinado || *tr* accinar (*el arenque o el salmón*)

kiss [kɪs] *s* beso; (billiards) retruco; (*confection*) dulce *m*, merengue *m* || *tr* besar; **to kiss away** borrar con besos (*las penas de una persona*) || *intr* besar; besarse; (billiards) retrucar

kit [kɪt] *s* cartera de herramientas; (*case and its contents for various purposes*) estuche *m*; (*of a soldier*) equipo, pertrechos; (*of a traveler*) equipaje *m*; (*pail, tub*) balde *m*

kitchen ['kɪt/ən] *s* cocina

kitchenette [,kɪt/ə'nɛt] *s* cocinilla

kitchen garden *s* huerto

kitch'en·maid' *s* ayudanta de cocina, pincha

kitchen police *s* (mil) trabajo de cocina; soldados que están de cocina

kitchen range *s* cocina económica

kitchen sink *s* fregadero

kitch'en·ware' *s* utensilios de cocina

kite [kaɪt] *s* cometa; (orn) milano; **to fly a kite** hacer volar una cometa

kith and kin [kɪθ] *spl* parientes *mpl*; parientes y amigos

kitten ['kɪtən] *s* gatito, minino

kittenish ['kɪtənɪ/] *adj* juguetón, retozón; (*coy, flirtatious*) coquetón

kit·ty ['kɪti] *s* (*pl* -ties) gatito, minino; (*in card games*) polla, puesta || *interj* ¡miz!

kleptomaniac [,klɛptə'meni,æk] *s* cleptómano

km. *abbr* **kilometer**

knack [næk] *s* tino, tranquillo, maña

knapsack ['næp,sæk] *s* mochila

knave [nev] *s* bribón *m*, pícaro; (cards) sota

knaver·y ['nevəri] *s* (*pl* -ies) bribonería, picardía

knead [nid] *tr* amasar, sobar

knee [ni] *s* rodilla; (*of animal*) codillo; (*e.g., of trousers*) rodillera; (mach) ángulo, codo; **to bring** (*someone*) **to his knees** rendir, vencer; **to go down on one's knees** hincarse de rodillas, caer de rodillas; **to go down on one's kness to** implorar de rodillas

knee breeches ['brɪtʃɪz] *spl* pantalones cortos

knee'cap' *s* rótula; (*protective covering*) rodillera

knee'-deep' *adj* metido hasta las rodillas

knee'-high' *adj* que llega hasta la rodilla

knee'hole' *s* hueco para acomodar las rodillas

knee jerk *s* reflejo rotuliano

kneel [nil] *v* (*pret & pp* **knelt** [nɛlt] o **kneeled**) *intr* arrodillarse; estar de rodillas

knee'pad' *s* rodillera

knee'pan' *s* rótula

knee swell *s* (*of organ*) (mus) rodillera

knell [nɛl] *s* doble *m*, toque *m* de difuntos; mal agüero; **to toll the knell of** anunciar la muerte de, anunciar el fin de ‖ *intr* doblar, tocar a muerto; sonar tristemente

knickers ['nɪkərz] *spl* pantalones *mpl* de media pierna

knickknack ['nɪk,næk] *s* chuchería, bujería, baratija

knife [naɪf] *s* (*pl* **knives** [naɪvz]) cuchillo; (*of a paper cutter or other instrument*) cuchilla; **to go under the knife** (coll) hacerse operar ‖ *tr* acuchillar; (slang) traicionar

knife sharpener *s* afilador *m*, afilón *m*

knife switch *s* (elec) interruptor *m* de cuchilla

knight [naɪt] *s* caballero; (chess) caballo ‖ *tr* armar caballero

knight-errant ['naɪt'ɛrənt] *s* (*pl* **knights-errant**) caballero andante

knight-errant·ry ['naɪt'ɛrəntri] *s* (*pl* -ries) caballería andante; (*quixotic behavior*) quijotada

knighthood ['naɪt·hʊd] *s* caballería

knightly ['naɪtli] *adj* caballeroso, caballeresco

Knight of the Rueful Countenance *s* Caballero de la triste figura (*Don Quijote*)

knit [nɪt] *v* (*pret & pp* **knitted** o **knit**; *ger* **knitting**) *tr* tejer a punto de aguja; enlazar, unir; fruncir (*las cejas*), arrugar (*la frente*) ‖ *intr* hacer calceta, hacer malla; trabarse, unirse; soldarse (*un hueso*)

knit goods *spl* géneros de punto

knitting ['nɪtɪŋ] *s* punto de media, trabajo de punto

knitting machine *s* máquina de hacer tejidos de punto

knitting needle *s* aguja de hacer media

knit'wear' *s* géneros de punto

knob [nɑb] *s* (*lump*) bulto, protuberancia; (*of a door*) botón *m*, tirador *m*; (*of a radio set*) botón, perilla; (*ornament on furniture*) manzana; colina o montaña redondeada

knock [nɑk] *s* golpe *m*; (*e.g., on a door*) toque *m*, llamada; (*with a door knocker*) aldabazo; (*of an internal-combustion engine*) pistoneo; (slang) censura, crítica ‖ *tr* golpear; (*repeatedly*) golpetear; (slang) censurar, criticar; **to knock down** (*with a blow, punch, etc.*) derribar; (*to the highest bidder*) rematar; desarmar, desmontar (*un aparato o máquina*); **to knock off** hacer saltar con un golpe; suspender (*el trabajo*); poner fin a; (slang) matar; **to knock out** agotar; (box) poner fuera de combate ‖ *intr* tocar, llamar; golpear, pistonear (*el motor de combustión interna*); (slang) censurar, criticar; **to knock about** andar vagando; **to knock against** dar contra, tropezar con; **to knock at** tocar a, llamar a (*la puerta*); **to knock off** dejar de trabajar

knocker ['nɑkər] *s* (*on a door*) aldaba; (coll) criticón *m*

knock-kneed ['nɑk,nid] *adj* patizambo, zambo

knock'out' *s* golpe decisivo, puñetazo decisivo; (box) (el) fuera de combate; (elec) destapadero; (coll) real moza

knockout drops *spl* (slang) gotas narcóticas

knoll [nol] *s* loma, otero

knot [nɑt] *s* nudo; (*worn as ornament*) lazo; corrillo, grupo; (*difficult matter; bond or tie*) nudo; nudo o lazo de matrimonio; (*protuberance in a fabric*) envoltorio; (naut) nudo; **to tie the knot** (coll) casarse ‖ *v* (*pret & pp* **knotted**; *ger* **knotting**) *tr* anudar; fruncir (*las cejas*) ‖ *intr* anudarse

knot'hole' *s* agujero en la madera (*que deja un nudo al desprenderse*)

knot·ty ['nɑti] *adj* (*comp* -tier; *super* -tiest) nudoso; (fig) espinoso, difícil

know [no] *s* — **to be in the know** estar enterado, tener informes secretos ‖ *v* (*pret* **knew** [nju] o [nu]; *pp* **known**) *tr & intr* (*by reasoning or learning*) saber; (*by the senses or by perception; through acquaintance or recognition*) conocer; **as far as I know** que yo sepa; **to know about** saber de; **to know best** ser el mejor juez, saber lo que más conviene; **to know how to** + inf saber + inf; **to know it all** (coll) sabérselo todo; **to know what one is doing** obrar con conocimiento de causa; **to know what's what** (coll) saber cuántas son cinco; **you ought to know better** deberías tener vergüenza

knowable ['noəbəl] *adj* conocible

know'-how' *s* conocimiento, destreza, habilidad

knowingly ['no·ɪŋli] *adv* a sabiendas,

con conocimiento de causa; (*on purpose*) adrede

know'-it-all' *adj* & *s* (coll) sabidillo

knowledge ['nɑlɪdʒ] *s* (*faculty*) ciencia, conocimientos, el saber; (*awareness, acquaintance, familiarity*) conocimiento; **to have a thorough knowledge of** conocer a fondo; **to my knowledge** que yo sepa; **to the best of my knowledge** según mi leal saber y entender; **with full knowledge** con conocimiento de causa; **without my knowledge** sin saberlo yo

knowledgeable ['nɑlɪdʒəbəl] *adj* (coll) conocedor, inteligente

know'-noth'ing *s* ignorante *mf*

knuckle ['nʌkəl] *s* nudillo; (*of a quadruped*) jarrete *m*; (mach) junta de charnela; **knuckles** bóxer *m* ‖ *intr* — **to knuckle down** someterse, darse

por vencido; aplicarse con empeño al trabajo

knurl [nʌrl] *s* moleteado ‖ *tr* moletear, cerrillar (*p.ej., las piezas de moneda*)

k.o. *abbr* **knockout**

Koran [ko'ran] o [ko'ræn] *s* Corán *m*

Korea [ko'ri·ə] *s* Corea

Korean [ko'ri·ən] *adj* & *s* coreano

kosher ['koʃər] *adj* autorizado por la ley judía; (coll) genuino

kowtow ['kau'tau] o ['ko'tau] *intr* arrodillarse y tocar el suelo con la frente; doblegarse servilmente, mostrarse servilmente obsequioso

Kt. *abbr* **Knight**

kudos ['kjudɑs] o ['kudɑs] *s* (coll) gloria, renombre *m*, fama

kw. *abbr* **kilowatt**

K.W.H. *abbr* **kilowatt-hour**

L

L, l [ɛl] duodécima letra del alfabeto inglés

l. *abbr* **liter, line, league, length**

L. *abbr* **Latin, Low**

la·bel ['lebəl] *s* etiqueta, marbete *m*, rótulo; (*descriptive word*) calificación ‖ *v* (*pret* & *pp* **-beled** o **-belled**; *ger* **-beling** o **-belling**) *tr* poner etiqueta o marbete a, rotular; calificar

labial ['lebɪ·əl] *adj* & *s* labial *f*

labor ['lebər] *adj* obrero ‖ *s* trabajo, labor *f*; (*job, task*) tarea, faena; (*manual work involved in an undertaking; the wages for such work*) mano *f* de obra; (*wage-earning workers as contrasted with capital and management*) los obreros; (*childbirth*) parto; **labors** esfuerzos; **to be in labor** estar de parto ‖ *intr* trabajar; (*to exert oneself*) forcejar; estar de parto; moverse penosamente; cabecear y balancear (*un buque*); **to labor under** ser víctima de

labor and management *spl* los obreros y los patronos

laborato·ry ['læbərə,tori] *s* (*pl* **-ries**) laboratorio

labored ['lebərd] *adj* penoso, dificultoso; artificial, forzado

laborer ['lebərər] *s* trabajador *m*, obrero; (*unskilled worker*) bracero, jornalero, peón *m*

laborious [lə'borɪ·əs] *adj* laborioso

la'bor-man'agement *adj* obrero-patronal

labor union *s* gremio obrero, sindicato

Labourite ['lebə,raɪt] *s* laborista *mf*

Labrador ['læbrə,dɔr] *s* el Labrador

labyrinth ['læbɪrɪnθ] *s* laberinto

lace [les] *s* encaje *m*; (*string to tie shoe, corset, etc.*) cordón *m*, lazo; (*braid*) galón *m* de oro o plata ‖ *tr*

adornar con encaje; atar (*los zapatos, el corsé*); (coll) dar una paliza a

lace trimming *s* randa

lace'work' *s* encaje *m*, obra de encaje

lachrymose ['lækrɪ,mos] *adj* lacrimoso

lacing ['lesɪŋ] *s* cordón *m*; lazo; galón *m*; (coll) paliza

lack [læk] *s* carencia, falta; (*complete lack*) defecto ‖ *tr* carecer de, necesitar ‖ *intr* (*to be lacking*) faltar

lackadaisical [,lækə'dezɪkəl] *adj* desaprovechado, indiferente

lackey ['læki] *s* lacayo; secuaz *m* servil

lacking ['lækɪŋ] *prep* sin, carente de

lack'lus'ter *adj* deslustrado, deslucido

laconic [lə'kɑnɪk] *adj* lacónico

lacquer ['lækər] *s* laca ‖ *tr* laquear

lacquer ware *s* lacas, objetos de laca

lacu·na [lə'kjunə] *s* (*pl* **-nas** o **-nae** [ni]) laguna

lac·y ['lesi] *adj* (*comp* **-ier**; *super* **-iest**) de encaje; (fig) diáfano

lad [læd] *s* muchacho, chico

ladder ['lædər] *s* escalera; (*stepladder*) escala, escalera de mano; (*two ladders fastened together at the top with hinges*) escalera de tijera; (*stepping stone*) (fig) escalón *m*

ladder truck *s* carro de escaleras de incendio

ladies' room *s* cuarto tocador

ladle ['ledəl] *s* cazo; (*for soup*) cucharón *m*; (*of tinsmith*) cucharilla ‖ *tr* servir con cucharón; sacar con cucharón

la·dy ['ledi] *s* (*pl* **-dies**) señora, dama

la'dy·bird' o **la'dy·bug'** *s* mariquita, vaca de San Antón

la'dy·fin'ger *s* melindre *m*

lady in waiting *s* camarera de la reina

la'dy·kil'ler *s* ladrón *m* de corazones

la'dy·like' *adj* elegante; **to be ladylike** ser muy dama

la'dy·love' *s* amada, amiga querida
lady of the house *s* ama de casa
ladyship ['ledɪ͵ʃɪp] *s* señoría
lady's maid *s* doncella
lady's man *s* perico entre ellas
lag [læg] *s* retraso ‖ *v* (*pret & pp* lagged; *ger* lagging) *intr* retrasarse; **to lag behind** quedarse atrás, rezagarse
lager beer ['lɑgər] *s* cerveza reposada
laggard ['lægərd] *s* perezoso, rezagado
lagoon [lə'gun] *s* laguna
laid paper [led] *s* papel vergueteado
laid up *adj* almacenado, ahorrado; (*naut*) inactivo; (coll) encamado por estar enfermo
lair [lɛr] *s* cubil *m*
lai·ty ['le·ɪtɪ] *s* legos
lake [lek] *adj* lacustre ‖ *s* lago
lamb [læm] *s* cordero; carne *f* de cordero; piel *f* de cordero; (*meek person*) cordero ‖ (fig) cordero
lambaste [læm'best] *tr* (*to thrash*) (coll) dar una paliza a; (*to reprimand harshly*) (coll) dar una jabonadura a
lamb chop *s* chuleta de cordero
lambkin ['læmkɪn] *s* corderito; (fig) nenito
lamb'skin' *s* piel *f* de cordero, corderina; (*dressed with its wool*) corderillo
lame [lem] *adj* cojo; (*sore*) dolorido; (*e.g., excuse*) débil, pobre ‖ *tr* encojar
lament [lə'mɛnt] *s* lamento; (*dirge*) elegía ‖ *tr* lamentar ‖ *intr* lamentarse
lamentable ['læməntəbəl] *adj* lamentable
lamentation [͵læmən'teʃən] *s* lamentación
laminate ['læmɪ͵net] *tr* laminar
lamp [læmp] *s* lámpara
lamp'black' *s* negro de humo
lamp chimney *s* tubo de lámpara
lamp'light' *s* luz *f* de lámpara
lamp'light'er *s* farolero
lampoon [læm'pun] *s* pasquín *m*, libelo ‖ *tr* pasquinar
lamp'post' *s* poste *m* de farol
lamp shade *s* pantalla de lámpara
lamp'wick' *s* mecha de lámpara, torcida
lance [læns] o [lɑns] *s* lanza; (surg) lanceta ‖ *tr* alancear; (surg) abrir con lanceta
lance rest *s* ristre *m*
lancet ['lænsɪt] o ['lɑnsɪt] *s* (surg) lanceta
land [lænd] *adj* terrestre; (*wind*) terral ‖ *s* tierra; **on land, on sea, and in the air** en tierra, mar y aire; **to make land** atracar a tierra; **to see how the land lies** medir el terreno, ver el cariz que van tomando las cosas ‖ *tr* desembarcar; conducir (*un avión*) a tierra; coger (*un pez*); (coll) conseguir ‖ *intr* desembarcar; (*to reach land*) arribar, aterrar; aterrizar (*un avión*); (*to arrive or come to rest*) ir a dar, ir a parar; **to land on one's**

feet caer de pies; **to land on one's head** caer de cabeza
landau ['lændɔ] o ['lændaʊ] *s* landó *m*
land breeze *s* terral *m*
landed ['lændɪd] *adj* (*owning land*) hacendado; (*real-estate*) inmobiliario; **landed property** bienes *mpl* raíces
land'fall' *s* (*sighting land*) aterrada; (*landing of ship or plane*) aterraje *m*; tierra vista desde el mar; (*landslide*) derrumbe *m*
land grant *s* donación de tierras
land'hold'er *s* terrateniente *mf*, hacendado
landing ['lændɪŋ] *s* (*of ship or plane*) aterraje *m*; (*of passengers*) desembarco; (*place where passengers and goods are landed*) desembarcadero; (*of stairway*) desembarco, descanso
landing beacon *s* (aer) radiofaro de aterrizaje
landing craft *s* (nav) lancha de desembarco
landing field *s* (aer) pista de aterrizaje
landing force *s* (nav) compañía de desembarco
landing gear *s* (aer) tren *m* de aterrizaje
landing stage *s* embarcadero flotante
landing strip *s* (aer) faja de aterrizaje
land'la'dy *s* (*pl* -dies) (*e.g., of an apartment*) casera, patrona; (*of a lodging house*) ama, patrona; (*of an inn*) mesonera, posadera
land'lord' *s* (*e.g., of an apartment*) casero, dueño; (*of a lodging house*) amo, patrón *m*; (*of an inn*) mesonero, posadero
land'lub'ber *s* (*person unacquainted with the sea*) marinero de agua dulce; (*awkward and unskilled seaman*) marinero matalote
land'mark' *s* (*boundary stone*) mojón *m*; (*feature of landscape that marks a location*) guía; suceso que hace época; (naut) marca de reconocimiento
land office *s* oficina del catastro
land'-of'fice business *s* (coll) negocio de mucho movimiento
land'own'er *s* terrateniente *mf*, hacendado
landscape ['lænd͵skep] *s* paisaje *m* ‖ *tr* ajardinar
landscape architect *s* arquitecto paisajista
landscape gardener *s* jardinero adornista, jardinista
landscape painter *s* paisajista *mf*
landscapist ['lænd͵skepɪst] *s* paisajista *mf*
land'slide' *s* derrumbe *m*, derrumbamiento de tierra, corrimiento; (fig) mayoría de votos abrumadora; (fig) victoria arrolladora
landward ['lændwərd] *adv* hacia tierra, hacia la costa
land wind *s* terral *m*
lane [len] *s* (*narrow street or passage*) callejuela; (*path*) carril *m*; (*of an*

automobile highway) faja; *(of an air or ocean route)* derrotero, vía

langsyne ['læŋ'saɪn] *adv* (Scotch) hace mucho tiempo ‖ *s* (Scotch) tiempo de antaño

language ['læŋgwɪdʒ] *s* idioma *m*, lengua; *(way of speaking or writing, style; figurative or poetic expression; communication of meaning said to be employed by flowers, birds, art, etc.)* lenguaje *m; (of a special group of people)* jerga

languid ['læŋgwɪd] *adj* lánguido

languish ['læŋgwɪʃ] *intr* languidecer; afectar languidez

languor ['læŋgər] *s* languidez *f*

languorous ['læŋgərəs] *adj* lánguido; *(causing languor)* enervante

lank [læŋk] *adj* descarnado, larguirucho; *(hair)* lacio

lank·y ['læŋki] *adj (comp* -ier; *super* -iest) descarnado, larguirucho

lantern ['læntərn] *s* linterna

lantern slide *s* diapositiva, tira de vidrio

lanyard ['lænjərd] *s* (naut) acollador *m*

lap [læp] *s (of human body or clothing)* regazo; *(loose fold)* caída, doblez *f; (overlap of garment)* traslapo; *(with the tongue)* lametada; *(of the waves)* chapaleteo; *(in a race)* (sport) etapa, vuelta; **to live in the lap of luxury** llevar una vida regalada ‖ *v (pret & pp* lapped; *ger* lapping) *tr* beber con la lengua; lamer *(las olas la playa); (to overlap)* traslapar; juntar a traslapo; **to lap up** tragar a lengüetadas; (coll) aceptar con entusiasmo ‖ *intr* traslapar; traslaparse *(dos o más cosas);* **to lap against** lamer *(las olas la playa);* **to lap over** salir fuera, rebosar

lap'board' *s* tabla faldera

lap dog *s* perro de falda

lapel [lə'pɛl] *s* solapa

Lap'land' *s* Laponia

Laplander ['læp,lændər] *s* lapón *m (habitante)*

Lapp [læp] *s* lapón *m (habitante; idioma)*

lap robe *s* manta de coche

lapse [læps] *s (passing of time; slipping into guilt or error)* lapso; *(fall, decline)* caída; caída en desuso; *(e.g., of an insurance policy)* invalidación ‖ *intr* caer en culpa o error; decaer, pasar *(p.ej., el entusiasmo);* caducar *(p.ej., una póliza de seguro)*

lap'wing' *s* ave fría

larce·ny ['larsəni] *s (pl* -nies) hurto, r bo

larch [lartʃ] *s* alerce *m,* lárice *m*

lard [lard] *s* cochevira, manteca de puerco ‖ *tr* (culin) mechar

larder ['lardər] *s* despensa

large [lardʒ] *adj* grande; **at large en** libertad

large intestine *s* intestino grueso

largely ['lardʒli] *adj* por la mayor parte

largeness ['lardʒnɪs] *s* grandeza

large'-scale' *adj* en grande escala, grande escala

lariat ['læri·ət] *s (for catching animals)* lazo; *(for tying grazing animals)* cuerda, soga

lark [lark] *s* alondra; (coll) parranda; **to go on a lark** (coll) andar de parranda, echar una cana al aire

lark'spur' *s (rocket larkspur)* espuela de caballero; *(field larkspur)* consuelda real

lar·va ['larvə] *s (pl* -vae [vi]) larva

laryngeal [lə'rɪndʒɪ·əl] o [,lærɪn'dʒɪ·əl] *adj* laríngeo

laryngitis [,lærɪn'dʒaɪtɪs] *s* laringitis *f*

laryngoscope [lə'rɪŋgə,skop] *s* laringoscopio

lar·ynx ['lærɪŋks] *s (pl* **larynxes** o **larynges** [lə'rɪndʒiz]) laringe *f*

lascivious [lə'sɪvɪ·əs] *adj* lascivo

lasciviousness [lə'sɪvɪ·əsnɪs] *s* lascivia

laser ['lezər] *s* láser *m*

lash [læʃ] *s (cord on end of whip)* tralla; *(blow with whip; scolding)* latigazo; *(e.g., of animal's tail)* coletazo; *(of waves)* embate *m; (eyelash)* pestaña ‖ *tr (to beat, whip)* azotar; *(to bind, tie)* atar; *(to shake, to switch)* agitar, sacudir; *(to attack with words)* increpar, reñir ‖ *intr* lanzarse, pasar rápidamente; **to lash out at** azotar; embestir; vituperar

lashing ['læʃɪŋ] *s* atadura; paliza, zurra; *(severe scolding)* latigazo

lass [læs] *s* muchacha, chica; amada

las·so ['læso] o [læ'su] *s (pl* -sos o -soes) lazo ‖ *tr* lazar

last [læst] *adj (after all others; the only remaining; utmost, extreme)* último; *(most recent)* pasado; **before last** antepasado; **every last one** todos sin excepción; **last but one** penúltimo ‖ *adv* después de todos; por último; por última vez ‖ *s* última persona; última cosa; fin *m; (for holding shoe)* horma; **at last** por fin; **at long last** al fin y al cabo; **stick to your last!** ¡zapatero, a tus zapatos!; **the last of the month** a fines del mes; **to breathe one's last** dar el último suspiro; **to see the last of** no volver a ver; **to the last** hasta el fin ‖ *intr* durar; resistir; dar buen resultado *(p.ej., una prenda de vestir);* seguir así

lasting ['læstɪŋ] o ['lɑstɪŋ] *adj* perdurable, duradero

lastly ['læstli] o ['lɑstli] *adv* finalmente, por último

last'-min'ute news *s* noticias de última hora

last name *s* apellido

last night *adv* anoche

last quarter *s* cuarto menguante

last sleep *s* último sueño

last straw *s* acabóse *m,* colmo

Last Supper, the la Cena

last will and testament *s* última disposición, última voluntad

last word *s* última palabra; *(latest style)* (coll) última palabra

lat. *abbr* latitude

Lat. *abbr* Latin

latch [læt∫] s picaporte m ǁ tr cerrar con picaporte
latch'key' s llavín m
latch'string' s cordón m de aldaba; **the latchstring is out** ya sabe Vd. que ésta es su casa
late [let] adj (happening after the usual time) tardío; (person) atrasado; (hour of the night) avanzado; (news) de última hora; (party, meeting, etc.) que termina tarde; (coming toward the end of a period of time) de fines de; (incumbent of an office) anterior; (deceased) difunto, fallecido; **of late** recientemente, últimamente; **to be late** ser tarde; tardar (p.ej., el tren); **to be late in** + ger tardar en + inf; **to grow late** hacerse tarde ǁ adv tarde; **late in** (the week, the month, etc.) a fines de, hacia fines de; **late in life** a una edad avanzada
late-comer ['let‚kʌmər] s recién llegado; (one who arrives late) rezagado
lateen sail [læ'tin] s vela latina
lateen yard s entena
lately ['letli] adv recientemente, últimamente
latent ['letənt] adj latente
lateral ['lætərəl] adj lateral
lath [læθ] o [laθ] s lata, listón; enlistonado ǁ tr enlistonar
lathe [leð] s torno (máquina que sirve para labrar madera, hierro, etc. con un movimiento circular)
lather ['læðər] s espuma de jabón; espuma de sudor ǁ tr enjabonar; (coll) tundir, zurrar ǁ intr espumar
lathery ['læðəri] adj espumoso, jabonoso
lathing ['læθɪŋ] o ['laθɪŋ] s enlistonado
Latin ['lætɪn] o ['lætən] adj latino ǁ s (language) latín m; (person) latino
Latin America s Latinoamérica, la América Latina
Latin American s latinoamericano
Lat'in-Amer'ican adj latinoamericano
latitude ['læti‚tjud] o ['læti‚tud] s latitud
latrine [lə'trin] s letrina
latter ['lætər] adj (more recent) posterior; segundo (de dos); **the latter** éste; **the latter part of** fines mpl de (p.ej., el siglo)
lattice ['lætɪs] s enrejado ǁ tr enrejar
lattice girder s viga de celosía
lat'tice·work' s enrejado
Latvia ['lætvɪ·ə] s Letonia, Latvia
laudable ['lɔdəbəl] adj laudable
laudanum ['lɔdənəm] o ['lɔdnəm] s láudano
laudatory ['lɔdə‚tori] adj laudatorio
laugh [læf] o [laf] s risa — tr — to **laugh away** ahogar en risas; **to laugh off** tomar a risa ǁ intr reír, reírse
laughable ['læfəbəl] o ['lafəbəl] adj risible
laughing ['læfɪŋ] o ['lafɪŋ] adj reidor; **to be no laughing matter** no ser cosa de risa ǁ s risa, (el) reír
laughing gas s gas m hilarante
laugh'ing·stock' s hazmerreír m

laughter ['læftər] o ['laftər] s risa, risas
launch [lɔnt∫] o [lant∫] s (of a ship) botadura; (of a rocket) lanzamiento; (open motorboat) lancha automóvil; (nav) lancha ǁ tr botar, lanzar (un buque); (to throw; to start, set going, send forth) lanzar ǁ intr lanzarse
launching ['lɔnt∫ɪŋ] o ['lant∫ɪŋ] s lanzamiento
launching pad s plataforma de lanzamiento
launder ['lɔndər] o ['landər] tr lavar y planchar ǁ intr resistir el lavado
launderer ['lɔndərər] o ['landərər] s lavandero
laundress ['lɔndrɪs] o ['landrɪs] s lavandera
laun·dry ['lɔndri] o ['landri] s (pl -dries) lavadero; lavado de la ropa; ropa lavada o para lavar
laundry·man ['lɔndrimən] o ['landrimən] s (pl -men [mən]) lavandero
laun'dry·wom'an s (pl -wom'en) lavandera
laureate ['lɔrɪ·ɪt] adj laureado ǁ s laureado; poeta laureado
lau·rel ['lɔrəl] o ['larəl] s laurel m; **laurels** laurel (de la victoria); **to rest o sleep on one's laurels** dormirse sobre sus laureles ǁ v (pret & pp -reled o -relled; ger -reling o -relling) tr laurear, coronar de laurel
lava ['lavə] o ['lævə] s lava
lavato·ry ['lævə‚tori] s (pl -ries) (room equipped for washing hands and face) lavabo; (bowl with running water) lavamanos m; (toilet) excusado
lavender ['lævəndər] s alhucema, espliego, lavanda
lavender water s agua de alhucema, agua de lavanda
lavish ['lævɪ∫] adj pródigo ǁ tr prodigar
law [lɔ] s (of man, of nature, of science) ley f; (branch of knowledge concerned with law; body of laws; study of law, profession of law) derecho; **to enter the law** hacerse abogado; **to go to law** recurrir a la ley; **to lay down the law** dar órdenes terminantes; **to maintain law and order** mantener la paz; **to practice law** ejercer la profesión de abogado; **to read law** estudiar derecho
law-abiding ['lɔ·ə‚baɪdɪŋ] adj observante de la ley
law'break'er s infractor m de la ley
law court s tribunal m de justicia
lawful ['lɔfəl] adj legal, legítimo
lawless ['lɔlɪs] adj ilegal; (unbridled) desenfrenado, licencioso
law'mak'er s legislador m
lawn [lɔn] s césped m; (fabric) linón m
lawn mower s cortacésped m, tundidora de césped
law office s bufete m, despacho de abogado
law of nations s derecho de gentes
law of the jungle s ley f de la selva
law student s estudiante mf de derecho

law'suit' s pleito, proceso, litigio

lawyer ['lɔjər] s abogado

lax [læks] adj (in morals, discipline, etc.) laxo, relajado; vago, indeterminado; (loose, not tense) laxo, flojo, suelto

laxative ['læksətɪv] adj & s laxante m

lay [le] adj (not belonging to clergy) lego, seglar; (not having special training) lego, profano ‖ s situación, orientación ‖ v (pret & pp laid [led]) tr poner, colocar; dejar en el suelo; tender (un cable); echar (los cimientos; la culpa); situar (la acción de un drama); asentar (el polvo); poner (huevos la gallina; la mesa una criada); formar (planes); hacer (una apuesta); to be laid in ser (la escena) en; to lay aside echar a un lado; ahorrar; to lay down afirmar, declarar; dar (la vida); deponer (las armas); to lay low abatir, derribar; obligar a guardar cama; matar; to lay off despedir (a obreros); (to mark off the boundaries of) marcar, trazar; to lay open descubrir, revelar; (to a risk or danger) exponer; to lay out extender, tender; marcar (una tarea, un trabajo); gastar (dinero); amortajar (a un difunto); to lay up obligar a guardar cama; ahorrar; (naut) desarmar ‖ intr poner (las gallinas); to lay about dar palos de ciego; to lay for acechar; to lay off (coll) dejar de trabajar; (coll) dejar de molestar; to lay over detenerse durante un viaje; to lay to (naut) capear

lay brother s donado, lego

lay day s (naut) día m de estadía

layer ['le·ər] s (e.g., of paint) capa; (e.g., of bricks) camada; (e.g., of coal, rocks) estrato, capa; (hort) codadura ‖ tr (hort) acodar

layer cake s bizcocho de varias camadas

layette [le'et] s canastilla

lay figure s maniquí m

laying ['le·ɪŋ] s colocación; (of eggs) postura; (of a cable) tendido

lay·man ['lemən] s (pl -men [mən]) (person who is not a clergyman) lego, seglar m; (person who has no special training) lego, profano

lay'off' s (dismissal of workmen) despido; (period of unemployment) paro forzoso

lay of the land s cariz m que van tomando las cosas

lay'out' s plan m; (of tools) equipo; disposición, organización; (coll) banquete m, festín m

lay'o'ver s parada en un viaje

lay sister s donada

laziness ['lezinis] s pereza

la·zy ['lezi] adj (comp -zier; super -ziest) perezoso

la'zy·bones' s (coll) perezoso

lb. abbr pound

l.c. abbr lower case; loco citato (Lat) in the place cited

Ld. abbr Lord

lea [li] s prado

lead [led] adj plomizo ‖ s plomo; (of lead pencil) mina; (for sounding depth) (naut) escandallo; (typ) interlínea, regleta ‖ [led] v (pret & pp leaded; ger leading) tr emplomar; (typ) interlinear, regletear ‖ s [lid] s (foremost place) primacía; (guidance) conducta, guía, dirección; indicación; ejemplo; (cards) salida; (leash) traílla; (of a newspaper article) primer párrafo; (elec) conductor m; (elec & mach) avance m; (min) filón m; (rad) alambre m de entrada; (theat) papel m principal; (theat) galán m; (theat) dama; to take the lead tomar la delantera ‖ [lid] v (pret & pp led [led]) tr conducir, llevar; (to command) acaudillar, mandar; estar a la cabeza de; dirigir (p.ej., una orquesta); llevar (buena o mala vida); salir con (cierto naipe); (elec & mach) avanzar; to lead someone to + inf llevar a alguien a + inf ‖ intr ir delante, enseñar el camino; ser el primero; tener el mando; (cards) salir, ser mano; (mus) llevar la batuta; to lead up to conducir a, llevar a; llevar la conversación a

leaden ['ledən] adj (of lead; like lead) plomizo; (heavy as lead) plúmbeo; (sluggish) tardo, indolente; (with sleep) cargado; triste, lóbrego

leader ['lidər] s caudillo, jefe m, líder m; (ringleader) cabecilla m; (of an orchestra) director m; (in a dance; among animals) guión m; (horse) guía; (in a newspaper) artículo de fondo

leader dog s perro-lazarillo

leadership ['lidər,ʃɪp] s caudillaje m, jefatura; dotes fpl de mando

leading ['lidɪŋ] adj primero, principal; preeminente; delantero

leading article s artículo de fondo

leading edge s (aer) borde m de ataque

leading lady s primera actriz, dama

leading man s primer actor m, primer galán m

leading question s pregunta tendenciosa

leading strings spl andadores mpl

lead-in wire ['lid,ɪn] s (rad) bajada de antena, alambre m de entrada

lead pencil s lápiz m

leaf [lif] s (pl leaves [livz]) hoja; (of vine) pámpano; (hinged leaf of table) trampilla; to shake like a leaf temblar como un azogado; to turn over a new leaf hacer libro nuevo ‖ intr echar hojas; to leaf through hojear, trashojar

leafless ['liflɪs] adj deshojado

leaflet ['liflɪt] s hoja suelta, hoja volante; (blade of compound leaf) hojuela

leaf'stalk' s pecíolo

leaf·y ['lifi] adj (comp -ier; super -iest) hojoso, frondoso

league [lig] s (unit of distance) legua; (association, alliance) liga ‖ tr asociar ‖ intr asociarse, ligarse

League of Nations s Sociedad de las Naciones

leak [lik] s (*in a roof*) gotera; (*in a ship*) agua, vía de agua; (*of water, gas, electricity, steam*) escape m, fuga, salida; agujero, grieta, raja (*por donde se escapa el agua, etc.*); (*of money, news, etc.*) filtración; **to spring a leak** tener un escape; (naut) empezar a hacer agua || *tr* dejar escapar, dejar salir (*el agua, gas, etc.*); dejar filtrar (*una noticia*) || *intr* rezumarse (*un barril*); escaparse, salirse (*el agua, gas, etc.*); (naut) hacer agua; **to leak away** filtrarse (*el dinero*); **to leak out** rezumarse (*una especie*); trascender (*un hecho que estaba oculto*)

leakage ['likɪdʒ] s escape m, fuga, salida; (com) merma

leak·y ['liki] adj (*comp* **-ier;** *super* **-iest**) agujereado, roto; (*roof*) llovedizo; (naut) que hace agua; (coll) indiscreto

lean [lin] adj magro, mollar; (*thin*) flaco; (*gasoline mixture*) pobre; **lean years** años de carestía || *v* (*pret & pp* **leaned** o **leant** [lɛnt]) *tr* inclinar, ladear, arrimar || *intr* inclinarse, ladearse, arrimarse; (fig) inclinarse, tender; **to lean against** arrimarse a, estar arrimado a; **to lean back** retreparse, recostarse; **to lean on** apoyarse en; (*with the elbows*) acodarse sobre; **to lean out (of)** asomarse (a); **to lean over backwards** (coll) extremar la imparcialidad; **to lean toward** (fig) inclinarse a, ladearse a

leaning ['linɪŋ] adj inclinado || s inclinación; (fig) inclinación, tendencia

lean'-to' s (pl **-tos**) colgadizo

leap [lip] s salto; **by leaps and bounds** a pasos agigantados; **leap in the dark** salto a ciegas, salto en vago || *v* (*pret & pp* **leaped** o **leapt** [lɛpt]) *tr* saltar || *intr* saltar; dar un salto (*el corazón de uno*)

leap day s día m intercalar

leap'frog' s fil derecho, juego del salto; **to play leapfrog** jugar a la una la mula

leap year s año bisiesto

learn [lʌrn] *v* (*pret & pp* **learned** o **learnt** [lʌrnt]) *tr* aprender; oír decir; saber (*una noticia*) || *intr* aprender

learned ['lʌrnɪd] adj docto, erudito; (*e.g., word*) culto

learned journal s revista científica

learned society s sociedad de eruditos

learned word s cultismo, voz culta

learned world s mundo de la erudición

learner ['lʌrnər] s principiante mf, aprendiz m, estudiante mf

learning ['lʌrnɪŋ] s (*act and time devoted*) aprendizaje m; (*scholarship*) erudición

lease [lis] s arrendamiento, locación; **to give a new lease on life to** renovar completamente; volver a hacer feliz || *tr* arrendar || *intr* arrendarse

lease'hold' adj arrendado || s arrendamiento; bienes raíces arrendados

leash [liʃ] s traílla; **to strain at the leash** sufrir la sujeción con impaciencia || *tr* atraillar

least [list] adj (el) menor, mínimo, más pequeño || adv menos || s (el) menor; (lo) menos; **at least o at the least** al menos, a lo menos, por lo menos; **not in the least** de ninguna manera

leather ['lɛðər] s cuero

leath'er·back' turtle s laúd m

leath'er·neck' s (slang) soldado de infantería de marina de los EE.UU.

leathery ['lɛðəri] adj correoso, coriáceo

leave [liv] s (*permission*) permiso; (*permission to be absent*) licencia; (*farewell*) despedida; **on leave** con licencia; **to give leave to** dar licencia a; **to take leave (of)** despedirse (de) || *v* (*pret & pp* **left** [lɛft]) *tr* (*to let stay; to stop, give up; to disregard*) dejar; (*to go away from*) salir de; (*to bequeath*) legar; **leave it to me!** ¡déjemelo a mí!; **to be left** quedar p.ej., **the letter was left** unanswered la carta quedó sin contestar; **to leave alone** dejar en paz, dejar tranquilo; **to leave no stone unturned** no dejar piedra por mover; **to leave off** dejar; no ponerse (*una prenda de vestir*); **to leave out** omitir; **to leave things as they are** dejarlo como está || *intr* irse, marcharse; salir (*un avión, un tren, un vapor*)

leaven ['lɛvən] s levadura; (fig) influencia || *tr* leudar; (fig) transformar

leavening ['lɛvənɪŋ] s levadura

leave of absence s licencia

leave'-tak'ing s despedida

leavings ['livɪŋz] spl desperdicios, sobras

Leba·nese [ˌlɛbə'niz] adj libanés || s (pl **-nese**) libanés m

Lebanon ['lɛbənən] s el Líbano

Lebanon Mountains spl cordillera del Líbano

lecher ['lɛtʃər] s libertino, lujurioso

lecherous ['lɛtʃərəs] adj lascivo, lujurioso

lechery ['lɛtʃəri] s lascivia, lujuria

lectern ['lɛktərn] s atril m

lecture ['lɛktʃər] s conferencia; (*tedious reprimand*) sermoneo || *tr* instruir por medio de una conferencia; sermonear || *intr* dar una conferencia, dar conferencias

lecturer ['lɛktʃərər] s conferenciante mf

ledge [lɛdʒ] s (*projection in a wall*) retallo; cama de roca; arrecife m

ledger ['lɛdʒər] s (com) libro mayor

ledger line s (mus) línea suplementaria

lee [li] s (*shelter*) (naut) socaire m; (*quarter sheltered from the wind*) sotavento; **lees** heces fpl

leech [litʃ] s sanguijuela; **to stick like a leech** pegarse como ladilla

leek [lik] s puerro

leer [lɪr] s mirada de soslayo, mirada lujuriosa || *intr* — **to leer at** mirar de soslayo, mirar lujuriosamente

la
le

leery ['lɪri] *adj* (coll) receloso, suspicaz

leeward ['liwərd] o ['lu·ərd] *adj* (naut) de sotavento ǁ *adv* (naut) a sotavento ǁ *s* (naut) sotavento

Leeward Islands ['liwərd] *spl* islas de Sotavento

lee'way' *s* (aer & naut) deriva; (coll) tiempo de sobra, espacio de sobra, dinero de sobra; (coll) libertad de acción

left [lɛft] *adj* izquierdo ǁ *adv* hacia la izquierda ǁ *s* (*left hand*) izquierda; (box) zurdazo; (pol) izquierda; **on the left** a la izquierda

left field *s* (baseball) jardín izquierdo

left'-hand' drive *s* conducción o dirección a la izquierda

left-handed ['lɛft'hændɪd] *adj* (*individual*) zurdo; (*clumsy*) desmañado, torpe; insincero; contrario a las agujas del reloj

leftish ['lɛftɪʃ] *adj* izquierdizante

leftist ['lɛftɪst] *adj* & *s* izquierdista *mf*

left'o'ver *adj* & *s* sobrante *m*; **leftovers** *spl* sobras

left'-wing' *adj* izquierdista

left-winger ['lɛft'wɪŋər] *s* (coll) izquierdista *mf*

leg. *abbr* legal, legislature

leg [lɛg] *s* (*of man or animal*) pierna; (*of animal, table, chair, etc.*) pata; (*of boot or stocking*) caña; (*of trousers*) pernera; (*of a cooked fowl*) muslo; (*of a journey*) etapa, trecho; **to be on one's last legs** estar sin recursos; estar en las últimas; **to not have a leg to stand on** (coll) no tener justificación alguna, no tener disculpa alguna; **to pull the leg of** (coll) tomar el pelo a; **to shake a leg** (coll) darse prisa; (*to dance*) (coll) bailar; **to stretch one's legs** estirar las piernas, dar un paseíto

lega·cy ['lɛgəsi] *s* (*pl* -**cies**) legado

legal ['ligəl] *adj* legal

legali·ty [lɪ'gælɪti] *s* (*pl* -**ties**) legalidad

legalize ['ligə,laɪz] *tr* legalizar

legal tender *s* curso legal

legate ['lɛgɪt] *s* legado

legatee [,lɛgə'ti] *s* legatario

legation [lɪ'geʃən] *s* legación

legend ['lɛdʒənd] *s* leyenda

legendary ['lɛdʒən,dɛri] *adj* legendario

legerdemain [,lɛdʒərdɪ'men] *s* juego de manos, prestidigitación; (*cheating, trickery*) trapacería

legging ['lɛgɪŋ] *s* polaina

leg·gy ['lɛgi] *adj* (*comp* -**gier;** *super* -**giest**) zanquilargo; de piernas largas y elegantes

leg'horn' *s* sombrero de paja de Italia ǁ **Leghorn** *s* Liorna

legible ['lɛdʒɪbəl] *adj* legible

legion ['lidʒən] *s* legión

legislate ['lɛdʒɪs,let] *tr* imponer mediante legislación ǁ *intr* legislar

legislation [,lɛdʒɪs'leʃən] *s* legislación

legislative ['lɛdʒɪs,letɪv] *adj* legislativo

legislator ['lɛdʒɪs,letər] *s* legislador *m*

legislature ['lɛdʒɪs,let/ər] *s* asamblea legislativa, cuerpo legislativo

legitimacy [lɪ'dʒɪtɪməsi] *s* legitimidad

legitimate [lɪ'dʒɪtɪmɪt] *adj* legítimo ǁ [lɪ'dʒɪtɪ,met] *tr* legitimar

legitimate drama *s* drama serio (*a distinción del cine o el melodrama*)

legitimize [lɪ'dʒɪtɪ,maɪz] *tr* legitimar

leg'work' *s* (coll) el mucho caminar

leisure ['liʒər] o ['lɛʒər] *s* desocupación, ocio; **at leisure** desocupado, libre; **at one's leisure** a la comodidad de uno, cuando uno pueda

leisure class *s* gente acomodada

leisure hours *spl* horas de ocio, ratos perdidos

leisurely ['liʒərli] o ['lɛʒərli] *adj* lento, pausado ǁ *adv* lentamente, despacio, sin prisa

lemon ['lɛmən] *s* limón *m*

lemonade [,lɛmə'ned] *s* limonada

lemon squeezer *s* exprimidera de limón

lemon verbena *s* luisa

lend [lɛnd] *s* (*pret* & *pp* **lent** [lɛnt]) *tr* prestar

lending library *s* biblioteca de préstamo

length [lɛŋθ] *s* largura, largo; (*of time*) extensión; (naut) eslora; **at length** por fin; largamente; **to go to any length** hacer cuanto esté de su parte; **to keep at arm's length** mantener a distancia; mantenerse a distancia

lengthen ['lɛŋθən] *tr* alargar ǁ *intr* alargarse

length'wise' *adj* longitudinal ǁ *adv* longitudinalmente

length·y ['lɛŋθi] *adj* (*comp* -**ier;** *super* -**iest**) muy largo, prolongado

leniency ['lini·ənsi] *s* clemencia, indulgencia, lenidad

lenient ['lini·ənt] *adj* clemente, indulgente

lens [lɛnz] *s* lente *m* & *f*; (*of the eye*) cristalino

Lent [lɛnt] *s* cuaresma *f*

Lenten ['lɛntən] *adj* cuaresmal

lentil ['lɛntəl] *s* lenteja

leopard ['lɛpərd] *s* leopardo

leotard ['li·ə,tard] *s* leotardo

leper ['lɛpər] *s* leproso

leper house *s* leprosería

leprosy ['lɛprəsi] *s* lepra

leprous ['lɛprəs] *adj* leproso; (*covered with scales*) escamoso

Lesbian ['lɛzbɪ·ən] *adj* lesbio ǁ *s* lesbio; (*female homosexual*) lesbia

lesbianism ['lɛzbɪ·ə,nɪzəm] *s* lesbianismo

lese majesty ['liz'mædʒɪsti] *s* delito de lesa majestad

lesion ['liʒən] *s* lesión

less [lɛs] *adj* menor ǁ *adv* menos; **less and less** cada vez menos; **less than** menos que; (*followed by numeral*) menos de; (*followed by verb*) menos de lo que ǁ *s* menos *m*

lessee [lɛs'i] *s* arrendatario

lessen ['lɛsən] *tr* disminuir, reducir a menos; quitar importancia a ǁ *intr* disminuirse, reducirse; amainar (*el viento*)

lesser ['lɛsər] *adj* menor, más pequeño

lesson ['lɛsən] *s* lección

lessor ['lɛsər] *s* arrendador *m*

lest [lɛst] *conj* no sea que, de miedo que

let [lɛt] *v* (*pret & pp* **let**; *ger* **letting**) *tr* dejar, permitir; alquilar, arrendar; **let** + *inf* que + *subj*, p.ej., **let him come in** que entre; **let alone** y mucho menos; **let good enough alone** bueno está lo bueno; **let us** + *inf* vamos a + *inf*, p.ej., **let us eat** vamos a comer, comamos; **to let se alquila; to let alone** dejar en paz, dejar tranquilo; **to let be** no tocar; dejar en paz; **to let by** dejar pasar; **to let down** dejar bajar; desilusionar, traicionar; dejar plantado; **to let fly** disparar; (*fig*) disparar, soltar (*palabras injuriosas*); **to let go** soltar, desasirse de; vender; **to let in** dejar entrar, dejar entrar en; **to let it go at that** no hacer o decir nada más; **to let know** hacer saber; **to let loose** soltar; **to let on** (coll) dar a entender; **to let out** dejar salir; revelar, publicar; dar, soltar (*p.ej., más cuerda*); dar (*un grito*); ensanchar (*un vestido que aprieta*); dar en arrendamiento; (coll) despedir; **to let through** dejar pasar, dejar pasar por; **to let up** dejar subir; dejar levantarse ‖ *intr* alquilarse, arrendarse; **to let down** (coll) ir más despacio; **to let go** desasirse; **to let go of** desasirse de; **to let on** (coll) fingir; **to let out** (coll) despedirse, cerrarse (*p.ej., la escuela*); **to let up** (coll) desistir; (coll) aflojar, amainar

let'down' *s* disminución; aflojamiento; desilusión, decepción; humillación

lethal ['liθəl] *adj* letal

lethargic [lɪ'θɑrdʒɪk] *adj* (*affected with lethargy*) letárgico; (*producing lethargy*) letargoso

lethar·gy ['lɛθərdʒi] *s* (*pl* **-gies**) letargo

Lett [lɛt] *s* letón *m*

letter ['lɛtər] *s* (*written message*) carta; (*of the alphabet*) letra; (*literal meaning*) (fig) letra; **letters** (*literature*) letras; **to the letter** al pie de la letra ‖ *tr* estampar o marcar con letras

letter box *s* buzón *m* (*caja*)

letter carrier *s* cartero

letter drop *s* buzón *m* (*agujero*)

letter file *s* guardacartas *m*

let'ter·head' *s* membrete *m*; (*paper with printed heading*) memorándum *m*

lettering ['lɛtərɪŋ] *s* inscripción; letras

letter of credit *s* carta de crédito

letter opener ['opənər] *s* abrecartas *m*

letter paper *s* papel *m* de cartas

let'ter·per'fect *adj* que tiene bien aprendido su papel; correcto, exacto

let'ter·press' *s* impresión tipográfica; texto (*a distinción de los grabados*)

letter scales *spl* pesacartas *m*

Lettish ['lɛtɪʃ] *adj* letón ‖ *s* letón *m*

lettuce ['lɛtɪs] *s* lechuga

let'up' *s* (coll) calma, interrupción; **without letup** (coll) sin cesar

leucorrhea [ˌlukə'riə] *s* leucorrea

leukemia [lu'kimɪə] *s* leucemia

Levant [lɪ'vænt] *s* Levante *m* (*países de la parte oriental del Mediterráneo*)

Levantine ['lɛvəntin] o [lɪ'væntin] *adj & s* levantino

levee ['lɛvi] *s* (*embankment to hold back water*) ribero; (*reception at court*) besamanos *m*

lev·el ['lɛvəl] *adj* raso, llano; nivelado; (coll) sensato, juicioso; **level with** al nivel de, a flor de, a ras de ‖ *s* (*device for determining horizontal position; degree of elevation*) nivel *m*; (*flat and even area of land*) terreno llano, llanura; (*part of a canal between two locks*) tramo; **to be on the level** obrar sin engaño, decir la pura verdad; **to find one's level** hallar su propio nivel ‖ *v* (*pret & pp* **-eled** o **-elled**; *ger* **-eling** o **-elling**) *tr* nivelar; (*to smooth, flatten out*) arrasar, allanar; (*to bring down*) derribar, echar por tierra; apuntar (*un arma de fuego*); (fig) allanar (*dificultades*) ‖ *intr* — **to level off** (aer) enderezarse para aterrizar

level-headed ['lɛvəl'hɛdɪd] *adj* sensato, juicioso

lever ['livər] o ['lɛvər] *s* palanca ‖ *tr* apalancar

leverage ['livərɪdʒ] o ['lɛvərɪdʒ] *s* palancada; poder *m* de una palanca; (fig) influencia, poder *m*

leviathan [lɪ'vaɪəθən] *s* (Bib & fig) leviatán *m*; buque *m* muy grande

levitation [ˌlɛvɪ'teʃən] *s* levitación

levi·ty ['lɛvɪti] *s* (*pl* **-ties**) frivolidad; (*fickleness*) ligereza

lev·y ['lɛvi] *s* (*pl* **-ies**) (*of taxes*) exacción, recaudación; dinero recaudado; (mil) leva, enganche *m*, recluta ‖ *v* (*pret & pp* **-ied**) *tr* exigir, recaudar (*impuestos*); (mil) enganchar, reclutar; hacer (*la guerra*)

lewd [lud] *adj* lascivo, lujurioso; obsceno

lewdness ['ludnɪs] *s* lascivia, lujuria; obscenidad

lexical ['lɛksɪkəl] *adj* léxico

lexicographer [ˌlɛksɪ'kɑgrəfər] *s* lexicógrafo

lexicographic(al) [ˌlɛksɪkə'græfɪk(əl)] *s* lexicográfico

lexicography [ˌlɛksɪ'kɑgrəfi] *s* lexicografía

lexicology [ˌlɛksɪ'kɑlədʒi] *s* lexicología

lexicon ['lɛksɪkən] *s* léxico, lexicón *m*

liabili·ty [ˌlaɪə'bɪlti] *s* (*pl* **-ties**) (*e.g., to disease*) propensión; responsabilidad, obligación; desventaja; **liabilities** deudas; (*as detailed in balance sheet*) pasivo

liability insurance *s* seguro de responsabilidad civil

liable ['laɪəbəl] *adj* (*e.g., to disease*) propenso, expuesto; responsable; **to**

be liable to + *inf* (coll) amenazar + *inf*

liaison ['li·ə‚zɑn] o [li'ezən] *s* enlace *m*, unión; (*illicit relationship between a man and woman*) amancebamiento, enredo, lío; (mil, nav & phonet) enlace *m*

liaison officer *s* (mil) oficial *m* de enlace

liar ['laɪ·ər] *s* mentiroso

lb. *abbr* **librarian, library**

libation [laɪ'beʃən] *s* libación; (*drink*) libación

li·bel ['laɪbəl] *s* calumnia, difamación; (*defamatory writing*) libelo ‖ *v* (*pret & pp* **-beled** o **-belled;** *ger* **-beling** o **-belling**) *tr* calumniar, difamar

libelous ['laɪbələs] *adj* calumniador

liberal ['lɪbərəl] *adj* (*generous; done or given generously*) liberal; (*open-minded*) tolerante, de amplias miras; (*translation*) libre; (pol) liberal ‖ *s* liberal *mf*

liberali·ty [‚lɪbə'rælɪti] *s* (*pl* **-ties**) liberalidad

liberal-minded ['lɪbərəl'maɪndɪd] *adj* tolerante, de amplias miras

liberate ['lɪbə‚ret] *tr* libertar; (*to disengage from a combination*) (chem) desprender

liberation [‚lɪbə'reʃən] *s* liberación; (chem) desprendimiento

liberator ['lɪbə‚retər] *s* libertador *m*

libertine ['lɪbər‚tin] *adj & s* libertino

liber·ty ['lɪbərti] *s* (*pl* **-ties**) libertad; **to take the liberty to** tomarse la libertad de

liberty-loving ['lɪbərti'lʌvɪŋ] *adj* amante de la libertad

libidinous [lɪ'bɪdɪnəs] *adj* libidinoso

libido [lɪ'bido] o [lɪ'baɪdo] *s* libidine *f*, libido *f*

librarian [laɪ'brɛrɪ·ən] *s* bibliotecario

librar·y ['laɪ‚brɛri] o ['laɪbrəri] *s* (*pl* **-ies**) biblioteca

library number *s* signatura

library school *s* escuela de bibliotecarios

library science *s* bibliotecnia

libret·to [lɪ'breto] *s* (*pl* **-tos**) (mus) libreto

license ['laɪsəns] *s* licencia ‖ *tr* licenciar

license number *s* número de matrícula

license plate o **tag** *s* chapa de circulación, placa de matrícula

licentious [laɪ'sɛn/əs] *adj* licencioso, disoluto

lichen ['laɪkən] *s* liquen *m*

lick [lɪk] *s* lamedura; (*place where animals go to lick*) lamedero; (*blow*) (coll) bofetón *m*; (*speed*) (coll) velocidad; (*beating*) (coll) zurra; (*quick cleaning*) (coll) limpión *m*; **to give a lick and a promise to** (coll) hacer rápida y superficialmente ‖ *tr* lamer; lamerse (*p.ej., los dedos*); lamer (*las llamas un tejado*); (*to beat, thrash*) (coll) zurrar; (*to conquer*) (coll) vencer

licorice ['lɪkərɪs] *s* regaliz *m*, orozuz *m*; dulce *m* de regaliz

lid [lɪd] *s* (*of a box, trunk, chest, etc.*) tapa, tapadera; (*of a dish, pot, etc.*) cobertera; (*eyelid*) párpado; (*hat*) (slang) techo

lie [laɪ] *s* mentira; **to catch in a lie** coger en una mentira; **to give the lie to** dar un mentís a ‖ *v* (*pret & pp* **lied**; *ger* **lying**) *tr* — **to lie oneself out of** o **to lie one's way out of** librarse de un aprieto mintiendo ‖ *intr* mentir ‖ *v* (*pret* **lay** [le]; *pp* **lain** [len]; *ger* **lying**) *intr* estar echado; hallarse, estar situado; (*e.g., in the grave*) yacer, estar enterrado; **to lie down** echarse, acostarse

lie detector *s* detector *m* de mentiras

lien [lin] o ['li·ən] *s* gravamen *m*, derecho de retención

lieu [lu] *s* — **in lieu of** en lugar de, en vez de

lieutenant [lu'tɛnənt] *s* lugarteniente *m*; (mil) teniente *m*; (nav) teniente de navío

lieutenant colonel *s* (mil) teniente coronel *m*

lieutenant commander *s* (nav) capitán *m* de corbeta

lieutenant governor *s* (U.S.A.) vicegobernador *m* (*de un Estado*)

lieutenant junior grade *s* (nav) alférez *m* de navío

life [laɪf] *adj* (*animate*) vital; (*lifelong*) perpetuo; (*annuity, income*) vitalicio; (*working from nature*) (fa) del natural ‖ *s* (*pl* **lives** [laɪvz]) vida; (*of an insurance policy*) vigencia; **for life** de por vida; **for the life of me** así me mienten; **the life and soul of** (*e.g., a party*) la alegría de; **to come to life** volver a la vida; **to depart this life** partir de esta vida; **to run for one's life** salvarse por los pies

life annuity *s* renta vitalicia

life belt *s* cinturón *m* salvavidas

life'boat' *s* bote *m* de salvamento, bote salvavidas; (*for shore-based rescue services*) lancha de auxilio

life buoy *s* boya salvavidas, guindola

life float *s* balsa salvavidas

life'guard' *s* salvavidas *m*, guardavida *m*

life imprisonment *s* cadena perpetua

life insurance *s* seguro sobre la vida

life jacket *s* chaleco salvavidas

lifeless ['laɪflɪs] *adj* muerto, sin vida; (*in a faint*) desmayado, exánime; (*dull, colorless*) deslucido

life'like' *adj* natural, vivo

life line *s* cuerda salvavidas; cuerda de buzo

life'long' *adj* perpetuo, de toda la vida

life of leisure *s* vida de ocio

life of Riley ['raɪli] *s* (slang) vida regalada

life of the party *s* (coll) alegría de la fiesta, alma de la fiesta

life preserver [prɪ'zʌrvər] *s* chaleco salvavidas

lifer ['laɪfər] *s* (slang) presidiario de por vida

life'sav'er *s* salvador *m* (*de vidas*); (*something that saves a person from* *a predicament*) (coll) tabla de salvación

lifesaving [ˈlaɪfˌsevɪŋ] *adj* de salvamento ‖ *s* salvamento (*de vidas*)

life sentence *s* condena a cadena perpetua

life'-size' *adj* de tamaño natural

life'time' *adj* vitalicio ‖ *s* vida, curso de la vida, jornada

life'work' *s* obra principal de la vida de uno

lift [lɪft] *s* elevación, levantamiento; ayuda (*para levantar una carga*); (aer) sustentación; **to give a lift to** invitar (*a un peatón*) a subir a un coche; llevar en un coche; (fig) reanimar ‖ *tr* elevar, levantar; quitarse (*el sombrero*); (naut) izar (*velas, vergas, etc.*); (fig) reanimar, exaltar; (coll) robar; (coll) plagiar ‖ *intr* elevarse, levantarse; disiparse (*las nubes, las nieblas, la obscuridad, etc.*)

lift bridge *s* puente levadizo

lift'-off' *s* despegue *m* vertical

lift truck *s* carretilla elevadora

ligament [ˈlɪgəmənt] *s* ligamento

ligature [ˈlɪgət/ər] *s* (mus & surg) ligadura; (mus & typ) ligado

light [laɪt] *adj* (*in weight*) ligero, leve, liviano; (*having illumination; whitish*) claro; (*hair*) blondo, rubio; (*complexion*) blanco; (*oil*) flúido; (*beer*) claro; (*reading*) poco serio; (*heart*) alegre, despreocupado; (*carrying a small cargo or none at all*) (naut) ligero; **light in the head** (*dizzy*) aturdido, mareado; (*simple, silly*) tonto, necio; **to make light of** no dar importancia a, no tomar en serio ‖ *adv* sin carga; sin equipaje ‖ *s* luz *f*; (*to light a cigarette*) lumbre *f*, fuego; (*to control traffic*) luz, señal *f*; (*window or other opening in a wall*) luz, claro, hueco; (*example, shining figure*) lumbrera; **according to one's lights** según Dios le da a uno a entender; **against the light** al trasluz; **in this light** desde este punto de vista; **lights** noticias; (*of sheep, etc.*) bofes *mpl*; **to come to light** salir a luz, descubrirse; **to shed o throw light on** echar luz sobre; **to strike a light** echar una yesca; encender un fósforo ‖ *v* (*pret & pp* **lighted** o **lit** [lɪt]) *tr* (*to furnish with illumination*) alumbrar, iluminar; (*to set afire, ignite*) encender; **to light up** iluminar ‖ *intr* alumbrarse, encenderse; posar (*un ave*); (*from an auto*) bajar; **to light into** (*to attack*) (slang) arremeter contra; (*to scold, berate*) (slang) poner de oro o azul; **to light out** (slang) poner pies en polvorosa; **to light upon** tropezar con, hallar por casualidad

light bulb *s* (elec) bombilla

light complexion *s* tez blanca

lighten [ˈlaɪtən] *tr* (*to make lighter in weight*) aligerar; iluminar; (*to cheer up*) alegrar, regocijar ‖ *intr* (*to become less dark*) iluminarse;

(*to give ᴜᴩ flashes of lightning*) relampaguear; (fig) iluminarse (*los ojos, la cara de una persona*)

lighter [ˈlaɪtər] *s* (*to light a cigarette*) encendedor *m*; (*flat-bottomed barge*) alijador *m*

light-fingered [ˈlaɪtˈfɪŋgərd] *adj* largo de uñas, listo de manos

light-footed [ˈlaɪtˈfʊtɪd] *adj* ligero de pies

light-headed [ˈlaɪtˈhɛdɪd] *adj* (*dizzy*) aturdido, mareado; (*simple, silly*) tonto, necio, ligero de cascos

light-hearted [ˈlaɪtˈhɑrtɪd] *adj* alegre, libre de cuidados

light'house' *s* faro

lighting [ˈlaɪtɪŋ] *s* alumbrado, iluminación

lighting fixtures *spl* artefactos de alumbrado

lightly [ˈlaɪtli] *adj* ligeramente

light meter *s* exposímetro

lightness [ˈlaɪtnɪs] *s* (*in weight*) ligereza; (*in illumination*) claridad

lightning [ˈlaɪtnɪŋ] *s* relámpagos, relampagueo ‖ *intr* relampaguear

lightning arrester [əˈrɛstər] *s* pararrayos *m*

lightning bug *s* luciérnaga

lightning rod *s* pararrayos *m*

light opera *s* opereta

light'ship' *s* buque *m* fanal, buque faro

light-struck [ˈlaɪtˌstrʌk] *adj* velado

light'weight' *adj* ligero; de entretiempo, p.ej., **lightweight coat** abrigo de entretiempo

light'-year' *s* año luz

lignite [ˈlɪgnaɪt] *s* lignito

lignum vitae [ˈlɪgnəmˈvaɪti] *s* guayaco, palo santo

likable [ˈlaɪkəbəl] *adj* simpático

like [laɪk] *adj* parecido, semejante; parecido a, semejante a, p.ej., **this hat is like mine** este sombrero es parecido al mío; (elec) del mismo nombre; **like father like son** de tal palo tal astilla; **to feel like** + *ger* tener ganas de + *inf*; **to look like** parecerse a; parecer que, p.ej., **it looks like rain** parece que va a llover ‖ *adv* como; **like enough** (coll) probablemente; **nothing like** ni con mucho ‖ *prep* a semejanza de ‖ *conj* (coll) del mismo modo que; (coll) que, p.ej., **it seems like he is right** parece que tiene razón ‖ *s* (*liking*) gusto, preferencia; (*fellow, fellow man*) prójimo, semejante *m*; **and the like** y cosas por el estilo; **to give like for like** pagar en la misma moneda ‖ *tr* gustar de, p.ej., **I like music** gusto de la música; gustar, p.ej., **Mary likes peaches** a María le gustan los melocotones; **to like best** o **better** preferir; **to like it in** encontrarse a gusto en (*p.ej., el campo*); **to like to** + *inf* gustarle a uno + *inf*, p.ej., **I like to travel** me gusta viajar; gustarle a uno que + *subj*, p.ej., **I should like him to come to see me** me gustaría que él viniese a verme ‖

intr querer, p.ej., **as you like** como Vd. quiera; **if you like** si Vd. quiere
likelihood ['laɪklɪ,hʊd] *s* probabilidad
like·ly ['laɪklɪ] *adj* (*comp* **-lier**; *super* **-liest**) probable; a propósito; prometedor; **to be likely to** + *inf* ser probable que + *ind*, p.ej., **Mary is likely to come to see us tomorrow** es probable que María vendrá a vernos mañana ‖ *adv* probablemente
like-minded ['laɪk'maɪndɪd] *adj* del mismo parecer; de natural semejante
liken ['laɪkən] *tr* asemejar, comparar
likeness ['laɪknɪs] *s* (*picture or image*) retrato; (*similarity*) semejanza, parecido; forma, aspecto, apariencia
like'wise' *adv* igualmente, asimismo; **to do likewise** hacer lo mismo
liking ['laɪkɪŋ] *s* gusto, afición, simpatía; **to be to the liking of** ser del gusto de; **to have a liking for** aficionarse a
lilac ['laɪlək] *adj* de color lila ‖ *s* lilac *m*, lila
Lilliputian [,lɪlɪ'pjuʃən] *adj & s* liliputiense *mf*
lilt [lɪlt] *s* paso airoso, movimiento airoso; canción cadenciosa, música alegre
lil·y ['lɪlɪ] *s* (*pl* **-ies**) (*Lilium candidum*) azucena, lirio blanco; cala, lirio de agua; (*fleur-de-lis, the royal arms of France*) flor *f* de lis; **to gild the lily** ponerle colores al oro
lily of the valley *s* lirio de los valles, muguete *m*
lily pad *s* hoja de nenúfar
Lima bean ['laɪmə] *s* judía de la peladilla, frijol *m* de media luna
limb [lɪm] *s* (*arm or leg*) miembro; (*of a tree*) rama; (*of a cross; of the sea*) brazo; **to be out on a limb** (coll) estar en un aprieto
limber ['lɪmbər] *adj* ágil; flexible ‖ *intr* — **to limber up** agilitarse
lim·bo ['lɪmbo] *s* (*pl* **-bos**) lugar *m* de olvido; (theol) limbo
lime [laɪm] *s* (*calcium oxide*) cal *f*; (*Citrus aurantifolia*) limero agrio; (*its fruit*) lima agria; (*linden tree*) tila o tilo
lime'kiln' *s* calera, horno de cal
lime'light' *s* — **to be in the limelight** estar a la vista del público
limerick ['lɪmərɪk] *s* quintilla jocosa
lime'stone' *adj* calizo ‖ *s* caliza, piedra caliza
limit ['lɪmɪt] *s* límite *m*; **to be the limit** (slang) ser el colmo; **to go the limit** no dejar piedra por mover ‖ *tr* limitar
lim'ited-ac'cess high'way *s* carretera de vía libre
limited monarchy *s* monarquía constitucional
limitless ['lɪmɪtlɪs] *adj* ilimitado
limousine ['lɪmə,zin] o [,lɪmə'zin] *s* (aut) limusina
limp [lɪmp] *adj* flojo, débil, flexible ‖ *s* cojera ‖ *intr* cojear
limpid ['lɪmpɪd] *adj* diáfano, cristalino

linage ['laɪnɪdʒ] *s* (typ) número de líneas
linchpin ['lɪntʃ,pɪn] *s* pezonera
linden ['lɪndən] *s* tila, tilo
line [laɪn] *s* línea; (*of people, houses, etc.*) hilera; (*rope, string*) cuerda, cordel *m*; (*wrinkle*) arruga; (*for fishing*) sedal *m*; (*written or printed line; line of goods*) renglón *m*; manera (*de pensar*); (*of the spectrum*) (phys) raya; **all along the line** por todas partes; **desde cualquier punto de vista**; **in line** alineado; dispuesto, preparado; **in line with** de acuerdo con; **out of line** desalineado; en desacuerdo; **to bring into line** poner de acuerdo; **to draw the line at** no ir más allá de; **to fall in line** conformarse; formar cola; alinearse; **to have a line on** (coll) estar enterado de; **to read between the lines** leer entre líneas; **to stand in line** hacer cola; **to toe the line** obrar como se debe; **to wait in line** hacer cola, esperar vez ‖ *tr* alinear, rayar; arrugar (*p.ej., la cara*); formar hilera a lo largo de (*la acera, la calle*); forrar (*un vestido*); guarnecer (*un freno*) ‖ *intr* — **to line up** ponerse en fila; hacer cola
lineage ['lɪnɪ·ɪdʒ] *s* linaje *m*
lineaments ['lɪnɪ·əmənts] *spl* lineamentos
linear ['lɪnɪ·ər] *adj* lineal
line·man ['laɪnmən] *s* (*pl* **-men** [mən]) (elec) celador *m*, recorredor *m* de la línea; (rr) guardavía *m*; (surv) cadenero
linen ['lɪnən] *adj* de lino ‖ *s* (*fabric*) lienzo, lino; (*yarn*) hilo de lino; ropa blanca, ropa de cama
linen closet *s* armario para la ropa blanca
line of battle *s* línea de batalla
line of fire *s* (mil) línea de tiro
line of least resistance *s* ley *f* del menor esfuerzo; **to follow the line of least resistance** seguir la corriente, no oponer resistencia
line of sight *s* visual *f*; (*of firearm*) línea de mira
liner ['laɪnər] *s* vapor *m* de travesía; (baseball) pelota rasa, lineazo
line'-up' *s* agrupación, formación; (*of prisoners*) rueda
linger ['lɪŋgər] *intr* estarse, quedarse; (*to be tardy*) demorar, tardar; tardar en marcharse; tardar en morirse; pasearse con paso lento; **to linger over** contemplar, reflexionar
lingerie [,lænʒə'ri] *s* ropa interior de mujer
lingering ['lɪŋgərɪŋ] *adj* prolongado
lingual ['lɪŋgwəl] *adj & s* lingual *f*
linguist ['lɪŋgwɪst] *s* (*person skilled in several languages*) polígloto; (*specialist in linguistics*) lingüista *mf*
linguistic [lɪŋ'gwɪstɪk] *adj* lingüístico ‖ **linguistics** *s* lingüística
liniment ['lɪnɪmənt] *s* linimento
lining ['laɪnɪŋ] *s* (*of a coat*) forro; (*of auto brake*) guarnición; (*of a fur-*

nace) camisa; *(of a wall)* revestimiento

link ['lɪŋk] *s* eslabón *m; links* campo de golf ‖ *tr* eslabonar ‖ *intr* eslabonarse

linnet ['lɪnɪt] *s* pardillo

linoleum [lɪ'nolɪ·əm] *s* linóleo

linotype ['laɪnə‚taɪp] (trademark) *adj* linotípico ‖ *s (machine)* linotipia; *(matter produced by machine)* linotipo ‖ *tr* componer con linotipia

linotype operator *s* linotipista *mf*

linseed ['lɪn‚sid] *s* linaza

linseed oil *s* aceite *m* de linaza

lint [lɪnt] *s* borra, pelusa, hilaza; *(used to dress wounds)* hilas

lintel ['lɪntəl] *s* dintel *m,* umbral *m*

lion ['laɪ·ən] *s* león *m; (man of strength and courage)* (fig) león; (fig) celebridad muy solicitada; **to beard the lion in his den** ir a desafiar la cólera de un jefe; **to put one's head in the lion's mouth** meterse en la boca del lobo

lioness ['laɪ·ənɪs] *s* leona

lion-hearted ['laɪ·ən‚hɑrtɪd] *adj* valiente

lionize ['laɪ·ə‚naɪz] *tr* agasajar

lions' den *s* (Bib) fosa de los leones

lion's share *s* (la) parte *f* del león

lip [lɪp] *s* labio; (slang) lenguaje *m* insolente; **to hang on the lips of** estar pendiente de las palabras de; **to smack one's lips** chuparse los labios

lip'-read' *v (pret & pp* **-read** [‚red]) *tr & intr* leer en los labios

lip reading *s* labiolectura

lip service *s* homenaje *m* de boca, jarabe *m* de pico

lip'stick' *s* lápiz *m* de labios, lápiz labial

liq. *abbr* **liquid, liquor**

lique·fy ['lɪkwɪ‚faɪ] *v (pret & pp* **-fied)** *tr* liquidar ‖ *intr* liquidarse

liqueur [lɪ'kʌr] *s* licor *m*

liquid ['lɪkwɪd] *adj* líquido ‖ *s* líquido; (phonet) líquida

liquidate ['lɪkwɪ‚det] *tr & intr* liquidar

liquidity [lɪ'kwɪdɪtɪ] *s* liquidez *f*

liquid measure *s* medida para líquidos

liquor ['lɪkər] *s* licor *m*

Lisbon ['lɪzbən] *s* Lisboa

lisle [laɪl] *s* hilo fino de algodón, muy retorcido, sedalina

lisp [lɪsp] *s* ceceo ‖ *intr* cecear

lissome ['lɪsəm] *adj* flexible, elástico; ágil, ligero

list [lɪst] *s* lista; *(strip)* lista, tira; *(border)* orilla; *(selvage)* orillo; (naut) ladeo; **lists** liza; **to enter the lists** entrar en liza; **to have a list** (naut) irse a la banda ‖ *tr* alistar, listar; registrar ‖ *intr* (naut) irse a la banda

listen ['lɪsən] *intr* escuchar; obedecer; **to listen in** escuchar a hurtadillas; escuchar por radio; **to listen to** escuchar; obedecer; **to listen to reason** meterse en razón

listener ['lɪsənər] *s* oyente *mf;* radioescucha *mf,* radioyente *mf*

listening post ['lɪsənɪŋ] *s* puesto de escucha

listless ['lɪstlɪs] *adj* distraído, desatento, indiferente

list price *s* precio de catálogo, precio de tarifa

lit. *abbr* **liter, literal, literature**

lita·ny ['lɪtənɪ] *s (pl* **-nies)** letanía; *(repeated series)* (fig) letanía

liter ['litər] *s* litro

literacy ['lɪtərəsɪ] *s* capacidad de leer y escribir; instrucción

literal ['lɪtərəl] *adj* literal

literary ['lɪtə‚rerɪ] *adj* literario; *(individual)* literato

literate ['lɪtərɪt] *adj* que sabe leer y escribir; *(well-read)* literato, muy leído; *(educated)* instruído ‖ *s* persona que sabe leer y escribir; literato, erudito

literati [‚lɪtə'rɑti] *spl* literatos

literature ['lɪtərət∫ər] *s* literatura; impresos, escritos de publicidad

lithe [laɪð] *adj* flexible, cimbreño

lithia ['lɪθɪ·ə] *s* (chem) litina

lithium ['lɪθɪ·əm] *s* (chem) litio

lithograph ['lɪθə‚græf] o ['lɪθə‚grɑf] *s* litografía ‖ *tr* litografiar

lithographer [lɪ'θɑɡrəfər] *s* litógrafo

lithography [lɪ'θɑɡrəfɪ] *s* litografía

litigant ['lɪtɪɡənt] *adj & s* litigante *mf*

litigate ['lɪtɪ‚ɡet] *tr & intr* litigar

litigation [‚lɪtɪ'ɡe∫ən] *s* litigación; *(lawsuit)* litigio

litigious [lɪ'tɪdʒəs] *adj* litigioso

litmus ['lɪtməs] *s* tornasol *m*

litmus paper *s* papel *m* de tornasol

litter ['lɪtər] *s* desorden *m; (scattered rubbish)* basura, papelería; *(young brought forth at one birth)* camada, ventregada; *(bedding for animals)* cama, paja; *(vehicle carried by men or animals)* litera; *(stretcher)* camilla, parihuela ‖ *tr* esparcir papeles por; esparcir *(desechos, papeles, etc.)*; cubrir *(el suelo)* con paja ‖ *intr* parir

lit'ter·bug' *s* persona que ensucia las calles tirando papeles rotos

littering ['lɪtərɪŋ] *c — no littering* se prohibe tirar papeles rotos

little ['lɪtəl] *adj (in size)* pequeño; *(in amount)* poco, p.ej., **little money** poco dinero; **a little** un poco de, p.ej., **a little money** un poco de dinero ‖ *adv* poco; **little by little** poco a poco ‖ *s* poco; **a little** un poco; *(somewhat)* algo; **to make little of** no dar importancia a, no tomar en serio; **to think little of** tener en poco; no vacilar en

Little Bear *s* Osa menor

Little Dipper *s* Carro menor

little finger *s* dedo auricular, dedo meñique; **to twist around one's little finger** manejar con suma facilidad

lit'tle·neck' *s* almeja redonda (*Venus mercenaria*)

little owl *s* mochuelo (*Athene noctua*)

little people *spl* hadas; gente menuda

Little Red Ridinghood ['raɪdɪŋ‚hud] *s* Caperucita Roja

little slam *s* (bridge) semibola

liturgic(al) [lɪ'tʌrdʒɪk(əl)] *adj* litúrgico
litur·gy ['lɪtərdʒi] *s* (*pl* **-gies**) liturgia
livable ['lɪvəbəl] *adj* habitable, vividero; llevadero, tolerable
live [laɪv] *adj* (*living; full of life; intense*) vivo; (*coals; flame*) ardiente; de actualidad; (elec) cargado ‖ [lɪv] *tr* llevar (*tal o cual vida*); vivir (*una experiencia, una aventura; un actor sus personajes*); **to live down** borrar (*una falta*); **to live out** vivir (*toda la vida*); salir con vida de (*un desastre, una guerra*) ‖ *intr* vivir; **to live and learn** vivir para ver; **to live and let live** vivir y dejar vivir; **to live high** darse buena vida; **to live on** seguir viviendo; vivir de (*p.ej., carne*); vivir a expensas de; **to live up to** cumplir (*lo prometido*); gastar (*todas sus rentas*)
live coal *s* ascua
livelihood ['laɪvlɪ,hʊd] *s* vida; **to earn one's livelihood** ganarse la vida
livelong ['lɪv,lɒŋ] o ['lɪv,lɑŋ] *adj* — **all the livelong day** todo el santo día
live·ly ['laɪvli] *adj* (*comp* **-lier;** *super* **-liest**) animado, vivaz; alegre, festivo; (*active, keen*) vivo; (*resilient*) elástico
liven ['laɪvən] *tr* animar, regocijar ‖ *intr* animarse, regocijarse
liver ['lɪvər] *s* vividor *m;* habitante *mf;* (anat) hígado
liver·y ['lɪvəri] *s* (*pl* **-ies**) librea
livery·man ['lɪvərimən] *s* (*pl* **-men** [mən]) dueño de una cochera; mozo de cuadra
livery stable *s* cochera de carruajes de alquiler
live'stock' *adj* ganadero ‖ *s* ganadería
live wire *s* (elec) alambre cargado; (slang) trafagón *m*
livid ['lɪvɪd] *adj* lívido, amoratado; encolerizado; pálido
living ['lɪvɪŋ] *adj* vivo, viviente ‖ *s* vida; **to earn** o **to make a living** ganarse la vida
living quarters *spl* aposentos, habitaciones
living room *s* sala, sala de estar
living wage *s* jornal *m* suficiente para vivir
lizard ['lɪzərd] *s* lagarto; (slang) holgón *m*
load [lod] *s* carga; **loads** (coll) muchísimo; **loads of** (coll) gran cantidad de; **to get a load of** (slang) escuchar, oír; (slang) mirar; **to have a load on** (slang) estar borracho ‖ *tr* cargar ‖ *intr* cargar; cargarse
loaded ['lodɪd] *adj* cargado; (slang) muy borracho; (slang) muy rico
loaded dice *spl* dados cargados
load'stone' *s* piedra imán; (fig) imán *m*
loaf [lof] *s* (*pl* **loaves** [lovz]) pan *m;* (*of sugar*) pilón *m* ‖ *intr* haraganear
loafer ['lofər] *s* haragán *m*
loam [lom] *s* suelo franco; (*mixture used in making molds*) tierra de moldeo
loamy ['lomi] *adj* franco
loan [lon] *s* (*among individuals*) préstamo; (*between companies or governments*) empréstito; **to hit for a loan** (coll) dar un sablazo a ‖ *tr* prestar
loan shark *s* (coll) usurero
loan word *s* préstamo lingüístico
loath [loθ] *adj* poco dispuesto; **nothing loath** de buena gana
loathe [loð] *tr* abominar, detestar
loathing ['loðɪŋ] *s* abominación, detestación
loathsome ['loðsəm] *adj* abominable, asqueroso
lob [lɑb] *v* (*pret & pp* **lobbed;** *ger* **lobbing**) *tr* (tennis) volear desde muy alto
lob·by ['lɑbi] *s* (*pl* **-bies**) salón *m* de entrada, vestíbulo; cabilderos ‖ *v* (*pret & pp* **-bied**) *intr* cabildear
lobbying ['lɑbɪɪŋ] *s* cabildeo
lobbyist ['lɑbɪɪst] *s* cabildero
lobster ['lɑbstər] *s* (*spiny lobster*) langosta; (*Homarus*) bogavante *m*
lobster pot *s* langostera
local ['lokəl] *adj* local ‖ *s* tren suburbano; (*branch of a union*) junta local; noticia de interés local
locale [lo'kæl] *s* localidad
locali·ty [lo'kælɪti] *s* (*pl* **-ties**) localidad
localize ['lokə,laɪz] *tr* localizar
local option *s* derecho local de legislar sobre la venta de bebidas alcohólicas
locate [lo'ket] o ['loket] *tr* (*to discover the location of*) localizar; (*to place, to settle*) colocar, establecer; (*to ascribe a particular location to*) situar ‖ *intr* establecerse
location [lo'keʃən] *s* (*place, position*) localidad; (*act of placing*) colocación; (*act of finding*) localización; **on location** (mov) en exteriores
loc. cit. *abbr* **loco citato** (Lat) **in the place cited**
lock [lɑk] *s* cerradura; (*of a canal*) esclusa; (*of hair*) bucle *m;* (*of a firearm*) llave *f;* **lock, stock, and barrel** (coll) del todo, por completo; **under lock and key** bajo llave ‖ *tr* echar la llave a, cerrar con llave; (*to key*) acuñar; hacer pasar (*un buque*) por la esclusa; abrazar, enlazar; **to lock in** encerrar, poner debajo de llave; **to lock out** cerrar la puerta a, dejar en la calle; dejar sin trabajo (*a los obreros*); **to lock up** encerrar, poner debajo de llave; encarcelar
locker ['lɑkər] *s* armario cerrado con llave
locket ['lɑkɪt] *s* guardapelo, medallón *m*
lock'jaw' *s* trismo, oclusión forzosa de la boca
lock nut *s* contratuerca
lock'out' *s* huelga patronal
lock'smith' *s* cerrajero
lock step *s* marcha en fila apretada
lock stitch *s* punto encadenado
lock tender *s* esclusero
lock'up' *s* cárcel *f*
lock washer *s* arandela de seguridad

locomotive [ˌlokəˈmotɪv] s locomotora

lo·cus [ˈlokəs] s (pl -ci [saɪ]) sitio, lugar m; lugar (geométrico)

locust [ˈlokəst] s (ent) langosta (*Pachytylus*); (ent) cigarra (*Cicada*); (bot) acacia falsa

lode [lod] s filón m, venero, veta

lode′star′ s (astr) estrella polar; estrella de guía; (*guide, direction*) guía, norte m

lodge [lɑdʒ] s casa de guarda; casa de campo; (*e.g., of Masons*) logia ‖ tr alojar, hospedar; depositar; colocar; presentar (*una queja*) ‖ alojarse, hospedarse; quedar colgado, ir a parar

lodger [ˈlɑdʒər] s inquilino (*en parte de una casa*)

lodging [ˈlɑdʒɪŋ] s alojamiento, hospedaje m; (*without meals*) cobijo

loft [lɔft] o [lɑft] s (*attic*) desván m, sobrado; (*hayloft*) henal m, pajar m; (*in theater or church*) galería; (*in a store or office building*) piso alto

loft·y [ˈlɔfti] o [ˈlɑfti] adj (comp **-ier**; super **-iest**) (*towering; sublime*) encumbrado; (*haughty*) altivo, orgulloso

log. abbr **logarithm**

log [lɔg] o [lɑg] s leño, tronco; (*log chip*) (naut) barquilla; (*chip and line*) (naut) corredera; (aer) diario de vuelo; **to sleep like a log** dormir como un leño ‖ v (pret & pp **logged**; ger **logging**) tr registrar; recorrer (*cierta distancia*)

logarithm [ˈlɔgəˌrɪðəm] o [ˈlɑgəˌrɪðəm] s logaritmo

log′book′ s (aer) libro de vuelo; (naut) cuaderno de bitácora

log cabin s cabaña de troncos

log chip s (naut) barquilla

log driver s ganchero, maderero

log driving s flotaje m

logger [ˈlɔgər] o [ˈlɑgər] s leñador m, maderero; grúa de troncos; tractor m

log′ger·head′ s mentecato; **at loggerheads** reñidos

loggia [ˈlɑdʒə] s (archit) logia

logic [ˈlɑdʒɪk] s lógica

logical [ˈlɑdʒɪkəl] adj lógico

logician [loˈdʒɪʃən] s lógico

logistic(al) [loˈdʒɪstɪk(əl)] adj logístico

logistics [loˈdʒɪstɪks] s logística

log′jam′ s atasco de rollizos; (fig) estancación

log line s (naut) corredera

log′roll′ intr trocar favores políticos

log′wood′ s campeche m

loin [lɔɪn] s lomo; **to gird up one's loins** apercibirse para la acción

loin′cloth′ s taparrabo

loiter [ˈlɔɪtər] tr — **to loiter away** malgastar (*el tiempo*) ‖ intr holgazanear, rezagarse

loiterer [ˈlɔɪtərər] s holgazán m, rezagado

loll [lɑl] intr colgar flojamente; arrellanarse, repantigarse

lollipop [ˈlɑliˌpɑp] s paleta (*dulce en el extremo de un palito*)

Lombard [ˈlɑmbɑrd] o [ˈlɑmbərd] adj & s lombardo

Lombardy [ˈlɑmbərdi] s Lombardía

Lombardy poplar s álamo de Italia, chopo lombardo

lon. abbr **longitude**

London [ˈlʌndən] adj londinense ‖ s Londres m

Londoner [ˈlʌndənər] s londinense mf

lone [lon] adj solo, solitario; (*sole, single*) único

loneliness [ˈlonlinɪs] s soledad

lone·ly [ˈlonli] adj (comp **-lier**; super **-liest**) soledoso

lonesome [ˈlonsəm] adj soledoso; (*spot, atmosphere*) solitario

lone wolf s (fig) lobo solitario

long. abbr **longitude**

long [lɔŋ] o [lɑŋ] s (comp **longer** [ˈlɔŋgər] o [ˈlɑŋgər]; super **longest** [ˈlɔŋgɪst] o [ˈlɑŋgɪst]) adj largo; de largo, p.ej., **two meters long** dos metros de largo ‖ adv mucho tiempo, largo tiempo; **as long as** mientras; (*provided*) con tal de que; (*inasmuch as*) puesto que; **before long** dentro de poco; **how long** cuánto tiempo; **long ago** hace mucho tiempo; **long before** mucho antes; **longer** más tiempo; **long since** desde hace mucho tiempo; **no longer** ya no; **so long!** (coll) ¡hasta luego!; **so long as** con tal de que ‖ intr anhelar, suspirar; **to long for** anhelar por, ansiar

long′boat′ s (naut) lancha

long′-dis′tance call s (telp) llamada a larga distancia

long-distance flight s (aer) vuelo a distancia

long′-drawn′-out′ adj prolongado, pesado

longeron [ˈlɑndʒərɑn] s larguero

longevity [lɑnˈdʒɛvɪti] s longevidad

long face s (coll) cara triste

long′hair′ adj & s intelectual mf; aficionado a la música clásica

long′hand′ s escritura a mano

longing [ˈlɔŋɪŋ] o [ˈlɑŋɪŋ] adj anhelante ‖ s anhelo, ansia

longitude [ˈlɑndʒɪˌtjud] o [ˈlɑndʒɪˌtud] s longitud

long-lived [ˈlɔŋˈlaɪvd], [ˈlɔŋˈlɪvd], [ˈlɑŋˈlaɪvd] o [ˈlɑŋˈlɪvd] adj longevo, de larga vida

long-playing record [ˈlɔŋˈpleɪɪŋ] o [ˈlɑŋˈpleɪɪŋ] s disco de larga duración

long primer [ˈprɪmər] s (typ) entredós m

long′-range′ adj de largo alcance

longshore·man [ˈlɔŋˈʃormən] o [ˈlɑŋˈʃormən] s (pl **-men** [mən]) s estibador m, portuario

long′-stand′ing adj que existe desde hace mucho tiempo

long′-suf′fering adj longánimo, sufrido

long suit s (cards) palo fuerte; (fig) fuerte m

long′-term′ adj a largo plazo

long′-wind′ed adj difuso, palabrero

look [lʊk] s (*appearance*) aspecto, apariencia; (*glance*) mirada; (*search*) búsqueda; **looks** aspecto, apariencia; **to take a look at** echar una mirada a ‖ *tr* expresar con la mirada; representar (*la edad que uno tiene*); **to look daggers at** apuñalar con la mirada; **to look the part** vestir el cargo; **to look up** (*e.g., in a dictionary*) buscar; ir a visitar, venir a ver ‖ *intr* mirar; buscar; parecer; **look out!** ¡cuidado!, ¡ojo!; **to look after** mirar por; ocuparse en; **to look at** mirar; **to look back** mirar hacia atrás; (fig) mirar el pasado; **to look down** mirar por encima del hombro; **to look for** buscar; creer, p.ej., **I look for rain** creo que va a llover; **to look forward to** esperar con placer anticipado; **to look ill** tener mala cara; **to look in on** pasar por la casa o la oficina de; **to look into** averiguar, estudiar; **to look like** parecerse a; amenazar, p.ej., **it looks like rain** amenaza lluvia, parece que va a llover; **to look oneself** parecer el mismo; tener buena cara; **to look out** tener cuidado; mirar por (*p.ej., la ventana*); **to look out for** mirar por, cuidar de; guardarse de; **to look out on** dar a; **to look through** mirar por; hojear (*un libro*); **to look toward** dar a; **to look up to** admirar, mirar con respeto; **to look well** tener buena cara

looker-on [ˌlʊkərˈɑn] o [ˌlʊkərˈɔn] *s* (*pl* **lookers-on**) mirón *m*, espectador *m*

looking glass [ˈlʊkɪŋ] *s* espejo

look'out' *s* vigilancia; (*tower*) atalaya; (*person keeping watch*) vigilante *mf*; (*man watching from lookout tower*) atalaya *m*; (*care, concern*) (coll) cuidado; **to be on the lookout for** estar a la mira de

loom [lum] *s* telar *m* ‖ *intr* (*to appear indistinctly*) vislumbrarse; amenazar, parecer inevitable

loon [lun] *s* tonto, bobo; (orn) zambullidor *m*

loon·y [ˈluni] *adj* (*comp* **-ier;** *super* **-iest**) (slang) loco ‖ *s* (*pl* **-ies**) (slang) loco

loop [lup] *s* lazo; (*in a cable or rope*) vuelta; (*of a river*) meandro; (*of a road*) recoveco; (*for fastening a button*) presilla; (aer) rizo; (elec) circuito cerrado; (*part of vibrating body between two nodes*) vientre *m*; **to loop the loop** (aer) rizar el rizo ‖ *tr* hacer lazos en; enlazar ‖ *intr* formar lazos; (aer) hacer el rizo

loop'hole' *s* (*narrow opening in wall*) lucerna; (*means of evasion*) efugio, escapatoria

loose [lus] *adj* (*dress, tooth, screw, bowels*) flojo; (*fitting, thread, wire, rivet, tongue, bowels*) suelto; (*sleeve*) perdido; (*earth, soil*) desmenuzado; (*unpackaged*) a granel, sin envase; (*unbound papers*) sin encuadernar; (*pulley*) loco; (*translation*) libre; (*life, morals*) relajado; (*woman*) fácil, frágil; **to become loose** desatarse, aflojarse; **to break loose** ponerse en libertad; **to turn loose** sol-

tar ‖ *s* — **to be on the loose** (coll) ser libre, estar sin trabas; (coll) estar de juerga ‖ *tr* soltar; desatar, desencadenar

loose end *s* cabo suelto; **at loose ends** desarreglado, indeciso

loose'-leaf' notebook *s* cuaderno de hojas cambiables, cuaderno de hojas sueltas

loosen [ˈlusən] *tr* desatar, aflojar, desapretar; aflojar, laxar (*el vientre*) ‖ *intr* desatarse, aflojarse, desapretarse

looseness [ˈlusnɪs] *s* flojedad, soltura; (*in morals*) relajamiento

loose'strife' *s* lisimaquia; salicaria

loose-tongued [ˈlusˈtʌŋd] *adj* largo de lengua, ligero de lengua

loot [lut] *s* botín *m*, presa ‖ *tr* saquear, pillar

lop [lɑp] *v* (*pret* & *pp* **lopped;** *ger* **lopping**) *tr* dejar caer (*p.ej., los brazos*); **to lop off** cortar; podar (*un árbol, una vid*) ‖ *intr* colgar

lopsided [ˈlɑpˈsaɪdɪd] *adj* ladeado, sesgado; desproporcionado, asimétrico, patituerto

loquacious [loˈkweʃəs] *adj* locuaz

lord [lɔrd] *s* señor *m*; (Brit) lord *m*; (hum & poet) marido ‖ *tr* — **to lord it over** dominar despóticamente, imponerse a

lord·ly [ˈlɔrdli] *adj* (*comp* **-lier;** *super* **-liest**) señoril; magnífico; despótico, imperioso; altivo, arrogante

Lord's Day, the el domingo

lordship [ˈlɔrdʃɪp] *s* señoría, excelencia

Lord's Prayer *s* oración dominical, padrenuestro

Lord's Supper *s* sagrada comunión; Cena del Señor

lore [lor] *s* ciencia, saber *m;* ciencia popular, saber *m* popular

lorgnette [lɔrnˈjet] *s* (*eyeglasses*) impertinentes *mpl;* (*opera glasses*) gemelos de teatro con manija

lor·ry [ˈlɑri] o [ˈlɔri] *s* (*pl* **-ries**) carro de plataforma; (Brit) autocamión *m;* (Brit) vagoneta

lose [luz] *v* (*pret* & *pp* **lost** [lɔst] o [lɑst]) *tr* perder; no lograr salvar (*el médico al enfermo*); **to lose heart** desalentarse; **to lose oneself** perderse, errar el camino; ensimismarse ‖ *intr* perder; quedar vencido; retrasarse (*el reloj*)

loser [ˈluzər] *s* perdedor *m*

losing [ˈluzɪŋ] *adj* perdedor ‖ **losings** *spl* pérdidas, dinero perdido

loss [lɑs] o [lɔs] *s* pérdida; **to be at a loss** estar perplejo, no saber qué hacer; **to be at a loss to** + *inf* no saber como + *inf;* **to sell at a loss** vender con pérdida

loss of face *s* pérdida de prestigio, desprestigio

lost [lɔst] o [lɑst] *adj* perdido; **lost in thought** ensimismado, abismado; **lost to** perdido para; insensible a

lost'-and-found' department *s* oficina de objetos perdidos

lost sheep *s* oveja perdida

lot [lɑt] *s* (*for building*) solar *m*, parcela; (*fate, destiny*) suerte *f*; (*portion, parcel*) lote *m*; (*of people*) grupo; (*coll*) gran cantidad, gran número; (*coll*) sujeto, tipo; **a lot** (**of**) o **lots of** (*coll*) mucho, muchos; **to cast** o **to throw in one's lot with** compartir la suerte de; **to draw** o **to cast lots** echar suertes

lotion [ˈloʃən] *s* loción

lotter·y [ˈlɑtəri] *s* (*pl* -**ies**) lotería

lotto [ˈlɑto] *s* lotería

lotus [ˈlotəs] *s* loto

loud [laud] *adj* alto; (*noisy*) ruidoso; (*voice*) fuerte; (*garish*) chillón, llamativo; (*conspicuously vulgar*) charro, cursi; (*foul-smelling*) apestoso, maloliente ‖ *adv* alto, en voz alta; ruidosamente

loudmouthed [ˈlaudˌmavθt] o [ˈlaudˌmauðd] *adj* vocinglero

loud'speak'er *s* altavoz *m*

lounge [laundʒ] *s* diván *m*, sofá *m* cama; salón *m* de descanso, salón social ‖ *intr* repantigarse a su sabor, recostarse cómodamente; **to lounge around** estar arrimado a la pared, pasearse perezosamente

lounge lizard *s* (*slang*) holgón *m*

louse [laus] *s* (*pl* **lice** [laɪs]) piojo

lous·y [ˈlauzi] *adj* (*comp* -**ier**; *super* -**iest**) piojoso; (*mean*) (*coll*) vil, ruin; (*filthy*) (*coll*) asqueroso, sucio; (*bungling*) (*coll*) chapucero; **lousy with** (*slang*) colmado de (*p.ej., dinero*)

lout [laut] *s* patán *m*

louver [ˈluvər] *s* (*opening to let in air and light*) lumbrera; tablilla de persiana; (*aut*) persiana del radiador

lovable [ˈlʌvəbəl] *adj* amable

love [lʌv] *s* amor *m*; (*tennis*) cero, nada; **not for love nor money** ni a tiros; **to be in love** (**with**) estar enamorado (de); **to fall in love** (**with**) enamorarse (de); **to make love to** cortejar, galantear ‖ *tr* amar, querer; gustar de, tener afición a

love affair *s* amores *mpl*, amorío

love'bird' *s* inseparable *m*; **lovebirds** recién casados muy enamorados

love child *s* hijo del amor

love feast *s* ágape *m*

loveless [ˈlʌvlɪs] *adj* abandonado, sin amor; (*feeling no love*) desamado

lovelorn [ˈlʌvˌlɔrn] *adj* abandonado por su amor, herido de amor

love·ly [ˈlʌvli] *adj* (*comp* -**lier**; *super* -**liest**) bello, hermoso; adorable, precioso; (*coll*) encantador, gracioso

love match *s* matrimonio de amor

love potion *s* filtro, filtro de amor

lover [ˈlʌvər] *s* amante *mf*; (*e.g., of hunting, sports*) aficionado; (*e.g., of work*) amigo

love seat *s* confidente *m*

love'sick' *adj* enfermo de amor

love'sick'ness *s* mal *m* de amor

love song *s* canción de amor

loving [ˈlʌvɪŋ] *adj* amoroso, afectuoso

lov'ing-kind'ness *s* bondad infinita, misericordia

low [lo] *adj* bajo; (*diet; visibility; opinion*) malo; (*dress, waist*) escotado; (*depressed*) abatido; gravemente enfermo; (*fire*) lento; **to lay low** dejar tendido, derribar; matar; **to lie low** no dejarse ver ‖ *adv* bajo ‖ *s* punto bajo; precio más bajo, precio mínimo; (*moo of cow*) mugido; (*aut*) primera marcha, primera velocidad; (*meteor*) depresión ‖ *intr* mugir (*la vaca*)

low'born' *adj* de humilde cuna

low'boy' *s* cómoda baja con patas cortas

low'brow' *adj* & *s* (*slang*) ignorante *mf*

low'-cost' housing *s* casas baratas

Low Countries, the los Países Bajos

low'-down' *adj* (*coll*) bajo, vil, ruin ‖ **low'-down'** *s* (*slang*) informes *mf* confidenciales, hechos verdaderos

lower [ˈlo·ər] *adj* bajo, inferior ‖ *tr* & *intr* bajar ‖ [ˈlau·ər] *intr* poner mala cara, fruncir el entrecejo; encapotarse (*el cielo*)

lower berth [ˈlo·ər] *s* litera baja, cama baja

Lower California [ˈlo·ər] *s* la Baja California

lower case [ˈlo·ər] *s* (*typ*) caja baja

lower middle class [ˈlo·ər] *s* pequeña burguesía

lowermost [ˈlo·ərˌmost] *adj* (el) más bajo

low'-fre'quency *adj* de baja frecuencia

low gear *s* primera marcha, primera velocidad

lowland [ˈlolənd] *s* tierra baja ‖ **Lowlands** *spl* Tierra Baja (*de Escocia*)

low·ly [ˈloli] *adj* (*comp* -**lier**; *super* -**liest**) humilde; (*in growth or position*) bajo

Low Mass *s* misa rezada

low-minded [ˈloˈmaɪndɪd] *adj* vil, ruin

low neck *s* escote *m*, escotado

low-necked [ˈloˈnɛkt] *adj* escotado

low-pitched [ˈloˈpɪtʃt] *adj* (*sound*) grave; (*roof*) de poco declive

low'-pres'sure *adj* de baja presión

low'-priced [ˈloˈpraɪst] *adj* barato, de precio bajo

low shoe *s* zapato inglés

low'-speed' *adj* de baja velocidad

low-spirited [ˈloˈspɪrɪtɪd] *adj* abatido

low spirits *spl* abatimiento

low tide *s* bajamar *f*, marea baja; (*fig*) punto más bajo

low visibility *s* (aer) poca visibilidad

low water *s* (*of a river*) nivel mínimo; (*because of drought*) estiaje *m*; bajamar *f*, marea baja

loyal [ˈlɔɪ·əl] *adj* leal

loyalist [ˈlɔɪ·əlɪst] *s* leal *m*

loyal·ty [ˈlɔɪ·əlti] *s* (*pl* -**ties**) lealtad

lozenge [ˈlɑzɪndʒ] *s* losange *m*; (*candy cough drop*) pastilla, tableta

LP [ˈɛlˈpi] *s* (letterword) (trademark) disco de larga duración

Ltd. *abbr* **limited**

lubricant [ˈlubrɪkənt] *adj* & *s* lubricante *m*

lubricate [ˈlubrɪˌket] *tr* lubricar

lubricous [ˈlubrɪkəs] *adj* (*slippery; lewd*) lúbrico (*resbaladizo; lascivo*); incierto, inconstante

lo
lu

lucerne [lu'sʌrn] s mielga
lucid ['lusɪd] adj claro, inteligible; (*rational, sane*) lúcido; (*bright, shining*) luciente; (*clear, transparent*) cristalino
Lucifer ['lusɪfər] s Lucifer m
luck [lʌk] s (*good or bad*) suerte f; (*good*) suerte, buena suerte; **down on one's luck** de mala suerte, de malas; **in luck** de buena suerte, de buenas; **out of luck** de mala suerte, de malas; **to bring luck** traer buena suerte; **to try one's luck** probar fortuna; **worse luck** desgraciadamente
luckily ['lʌkɪli] adv afortunadamente
luckless ['lʌklɪs] adj desgraciado
luck·y ['lʌki] adj (*comp* -ier; *super* -iest) afortunado; (*supposed to bring luck*) de buen agüero; **to be lucky** tener suerte
lucky hit s (coll) golpe m de fortuna
lucrative ['lukrətɪv] adj lucrativo
ludicrous ['ludɪkrəs] adj absurdo, ridículo
lug [lʌg] s orejeta; (*pull, tug*) estirón m, esfuerzo || v (*pret* & *pp* lugged; *ger* lugging) tr tirar con fuerza de; (*to bring up irrelevantly*) (coll) traer a colación
luggage ['lʌgɪdʒ] s equipaje m
lugubrious [lu'gubrɪ·əs] o [lu'gjubrɪ·əs] adj lúgubre
lukewarm ['luk,wɔrm] adj tibio, templado
lull [lʌl] s momento de calma, momento de silencio; (naut) recalmón m || tr adormecer; calmar, aquietar; apaciguar
lulla·by ['lʌlə,baɪ] s (*pl* -bies) arrullo, canción de cuna
lumbago [lʌm'bego] s lumbago
lumber ['lʌmbər] s madera aserrada, madera aserradiza, madera de sierra; trastos viejos || intr andar pesadamente
lum'ber·jack' s leñador m, hachero
lumber·man ['lʌmbərmən] s (*pl* -men [mən]) (*dealer*) maderero; (*man who cuts down lumber*) leñador m, hachero
lumber room s leonera, trastera
lum'ber·yard' s maderería, depósito de maderas
luminar·y ['lumɪ,nɛri] s (*pl* -ies) luminar m, lumbrera
luminescent [,lumɪ'nɛsənt] adj luminiscente
luminous ['lumɪnəs] adj luminoso
lummox ['lʌməks] s (coll) jergón m
lump [lʌmp] s terrón m; (*swelling*) chichón m, bulto, hinchazón m, f; (*stupid person*) (coll) bodoque m; **in the lump** en grueso, por junto; **to get a lump in one's throat** hacérsele (uno) un nudo en la garganta || tr juntar, mezclar; (*to make into lumps*) aterronar; (coll) aguantar, tragar (*cosa repulsiva*)
lumpish ['lʌmpɪʃ] adj hobachón, torpe, pesado
lump sum s suma global, suma total
lump·y ['lʌmpi] adj (*comp* -ier; *super*

-iest) aterronado, borujoso; torpe, pesado; (*sea*) agitado
luna·cy ['lunəsi] s (*pl* -cies) demencia, locura
lunar ['lunər] adj lunar
lunar landing s alunizaje m
lunatic ['lunətɪk] adj & s lunático, loco
lunatic asylum s manicomio
lunatic fringe s minoría fanática
lunch [lʌntʃ] s (*regular midday meal*) almuerzo; (*light meal*) colación, merienda || intr almorzar; merendar, tomar una colación
lunch basket s fiambrera
lunch cloth s mantelito
luncheon ['lʌntʃən] s almuerzo; almuerzo de ceremonia
lunch'room' s cantina, merendero
lung [lʌŋ] s pulmón m
lunge [lʌndʒ] s arremetida, embestida; (*with a sword*) estocada || intr arremeter, lanzarse; **to lunge at** arremeter contra
lurch [lʌrtʃ] s sacudida, tumbo; (naut) bandazo; **to leave in the lurch** dejar en la estacada, dejar colgado || intr dar una sacudida, dar un tumbo; (naut) dar un bandazo
lure [lur] s (*decoy*) cebo, señuelo; (fig) aliciente m, señuelo || tr atraer con cebo, atraer con señuelo; (fig) atraer, tentar, seducir; **to lure away** llevarse con señuelo; (*from one's obligations*) desviar
lurid ['lurɪd] adj sensacional; (*gruesome*) espeluznante; (*fiery*) ardiente, encendido
lurk [lʌrk] intr acechar, andar furtivamente
luscious ['lʌʃəs] adj delicioso; lujoso; voluptuoso
lush [lʌʃ] adj jugoso, lozano; lujuriante; lujoso
Lusitanian [,lusɪ'teni·ən] adj & s lusitano
lust [lʌst] s deseo vehemente; (*greed*) codicia; (*strong sexual appetite*) lujuria; entusiasmo || intr lujuriar; **to lust after** o **for** codiciar; desear con lujuria
luster ['lʌstər] s (*gloss*) lustre m; (*of certain fabrics*) viso; (*fame, glory*) (fig) lustre
lus'ter·ware' s loza con visos metálicos
lustful ['lʌstfəl] adj lujurioso
lustrous ['lʌstrəs] adj lustroso
lust·y ['lʌsti] adj (*comp* -ier; *super* -iest) fuerte, robusto, lozano
lute [lut] s (mus) laúd m; (*substance used to close or seal a joint*) (chem) lodo
Lutheran ['luθərən] adj & s luterano
luxuriance [lʌg'ʒurɪ·əns] s lozanía
luxuriant [lʌg'ʒurɪ·ənt] adj lozano, lujuriante; (*overornamented*) recargado
luxuriate [lʌg'ʒurɪ,et] o [lʌk'ʃurɪ,et] intr crecer con lozanía; entregarse al lujo; (*to find keen pleasure*) lozanearse
luxurious [lʌg'ʒurɪ·əs] o [lʌk'ʃurɪ·əs] adj lujoso

luxu·ry [ˈlʌkʃəri] o [ˈlʌgʒəri] *s* (*pl* -ries) lujo
lye [laɪ] *s* lejía
lying [ˈlaɪ·ɪŋ] *adj* mentiroso ‖ *s* el mentir
ly'ing-in' hospital *s* casa de maternidad, clínica de parturientas
lymph [lɪmf] *s* linfa
lymphatic [lɪmˈfætɪk] *adj* linfático
lynch [lɪntʃ] *tr* linchar
lynching [ˈlɪntʃ·ɪŋ] *s* linchamiento
lynch law *s* justicia de la soga

lynx [lɪŋks] *s* lince *m*
lynx-eyed [ˈlɪŋks‚aɪd] *adj* de ojos linces
lyonnaise [‚laɪ·əˈnez] *adj* (culin) a la lionesa
lyre [laɪr] *s* (mus) lira
lyric [ˈlɪrɪk] *adj* lírico ‖ *s* poema lírico; (*words of a song*) (coll) letra
lyrical [ˈlɪrɪkəl] *adj* lírico
lyricism [ˈlɪrɪ‚sɪzəm] *s* lirismo
lyricist [ˈlɪrɪsɪst] *s* (*writer of words for songs*) letrista *mf*; (*poet*) poeta lírico

M

M, m [ɛm] decimotercera letra del alfabeto inglés
m. *abbr* **married, masculine, meter, midnight, mile, minute, month**
ma'am [mæm] o [mʊm] *s* (coll) señora
macadam [məˈkædəm] *s* macadán *m*
macadamize [məˈkædə‚maɪz] *tr* macadamizar
macaro·ni [‚mækəˈroni] *s* (*pl* -nis o -nies) macarrones *mpl*
macaroon [‚mækəˈrun] *s* mostachón *m*, almendrado
macaw [məˈkɔ] *s* aracanga, guacamayo
mace [mes] *s* maza; (*spice*) macis *m*
mace'bear'er *s* macero
machination [‚mækɪˈneʃən] *s* maquinación
machine [məˈʃin] *s* máquina; automóvil *m*, coche *m*; (*of a political party*) camarilla ‖ *tr* trabajar a máquina
machine gun *s* ametralladora
ma·chine'-gun' *tr* ametrallar
ma·chine'-made' *adj* hecho a máquina
machiner·y [məˈʃinəri] *s* (*pl* -ies) maquinaria
machine screw *s* tornillo para metales
machine shop *s* taller mecánico
machine tool *s* máquina-herramienta
machine translation *s* traducción automática
machinist [məˈʃinɪst] *s* (*person who makes machines*) maquinista *mf*; (*person who operates machines*) mecánico; (naut) segundo maquinista; (theat) maquinista *mf*, tramoyista *mf*
mackerel [ˈmækərəl] *s* caballa, escombro
mackerel sky *s* cielo aborregado
mackintosh [ˈmækɪn‚tɑʃ] *s* impermeable *m*
mad [mæd] *adj* (*comp* **madder**; *super* **maddest**) (*angry*) enojado, furioso; (*crazy*) loco; (*foolish*) tonto, necio; (*rabid*) rabioso; **to be mad about** (coll) estar loco por; **to drive mad** volver loco; **to go mad** volverse loco; rabiar (*un perro*)
madam [ˈmædəm] *s* señora
mad'cap' *s* alocado, tarambana *mf*
madden [ˈmædən] *tr* (*to make angry*) enojar, enfurecer; (*to make insane*) enloquecer

made-to-order [ˈmedtəˈɔrdər] *adj* hecho de encargo; (*clothing*) hecho a la medida
made'-up' *adj* inventado, ficticio; (*artificial*) postizo; (*face*) pintado
mad'house' *s* casa de locos, manicomio
madman [ˈmæd‚mæn] *s* (*pl* -men [‚mɛn]) loco
madness [ˈmædnɪs] *s* furia, rabia; locura; (*of a dog*) rabia
Madonna lily [məˈdɑnə] *s* azucena
maelstrom [ˈmelstrəm] *s* remolino
mag. *abbr* **magazine**
magazine [ˈmægə‚zin] o [‚mægəˈzin] *s* (*periodical*) revista, magazine *m*; (*warehouse*) almacén *m*; (*for cartridges*) cámara; (*for powder*) polvorín *m*; (naut) santabárbara; (phot) almacén *m*
Magellan [məˈdʒelən] *s* Magallanes *m*
maggot [ˈmægət] *s* cresa
Magi [ˈmedʒaɪ] *spl* magos de Oriente, Reyes Magos
magic [ˈmædʒɪk] *adj* mágico ‖ *s* magia; ilusionismo, prestidigitación; **as if by magic** como por encanto
magician [məˈdʒɪʃən] *s* (*entertainer with sleight of hand*) ilusionista *mf*, prestidigitador *m*; (*sorcerer*) mágico
magistrate [ˈmædʒɪs‚tret] *s* magistrado
magnanimous [mægˈnænɪməs] *adj* magnánimo
magnesium [mægˈni/ɪ·əm] o [mægˈniʒɪ·əm] *s* magnesio
magnet [ˈmægnɪt] *s* imán *m*
magnetic [mægˈnɛtɪk] *adj* magnético; (fig) atrayente, cautivador
magnetic curves *spl* fantasma magnético
magnetism [ˈmægnɪ‚tɪzəm] *s* magnetismo
magnetize [ˈmægnɪ‚taɪz] *tr* magnetizar, imanar
magne·to [mægˈnito] *s* (*pl* -tos) magneto *m & f*
magnificent [mægˈnɪfɪsənt] *adj* magnífico
magni·fy [ˈmægnɪ‚faɪ] *v* (*pret & pp* -fied) *tr* magnificar; exagerar
magnifying glass *s* lupa, vidrio de aumento
magnitude [ˈmægnɪ‚tjud] o [ˈmægnɪ‚tud] *s* magnitud
magpie [ˈmæg‚paɪ] *s* picaza, urraca

lu
ma

Magyar ['mægjɑr] adj & s magiar mf
mahlstick ['mɑl‚stɪk] o ['mɔl‚stɪk] s tiento
mahoga‧ny [mə'hɑgəni] s (pl -nies) caoba
Mahomet [mə'hɑmɪt] s Mahoma m
mahout [mə'haut] s naire m, cornaca m
maid [med] s (female servant) criada, moza; (young girl; housemaid) doncella; (spinster) soltera
maiden ['medən] s doncella
maid'en‧hair' s (bot) cabello de Venus
maid'en‧head' s himen m
maidenhood ['medən‚hud] s doncellez f
maiden lady s soltera
maiden name s apellido de soltera
maiden voyage s primera travesía
maid'-in-wait'ing s (pl maids-in-wait-ing) dama
maid of honor s (at a wedding) primera madrina de boda; (attendant on a princess) doncella de honor; (attendant on a queen) dama de honor
maid'serv'ant s criada, doméstica
mail [mel] s correspondencia, correo; (of armor) malla; **by return mail** a vuelta de correo || tr echar al correo
mail'bag' s valija
mail'boat' s vapor m correo
mail'box' s buzón m
mail car s carro correo, coche-correo, ambulancia de correos
mail carrier s cartero
mailing list s lista de envío
mailing permit s porte concertado
mail‧man ['mel‚mæn] s (pl -men [‚men]) cartero
mail order s pedido postal
mail'-or'der house s casa de ventas por correo
mail'plane' s avión-correo
mail train s tren m correo
maim [mem] tr estropear, mutilar
main [men] adj principal, primero, maestro, mayor || s cañería maestra; **in the main** mayormente
main clause s proposición dominante
main course s plato principal, plato fuerte
main deck s cubierta principal
mainland ['men‚lænd] o ['menlənd] s continente m, tierra firme
main line s (rr) tronco, línea principal
mainly ['menli] adv principalmente, en su mayor parte
mainmast ['menmɑst], ['men‚mæst] o ['men‚mɑst] s palo mayor
mainsail ['mensəl] o ['men‚sel] s vela mayor
main'spring' s (of watch) muelle m real; (fig) móvil m, origen m
main'stay' s (naut) estay m mayor; (fig) soporte m principal
main street s calle f mayor
maintain [men'ten] tr mantener; (to support) (law) manutener
maintenance ['mentɪnəns] s mantenimiento; (upkeep) conservación; gastos de conservación
maître d'hôtel [‚metər do'tɛl] s (but-

ler) mayordomo; (headwaiter) jefe m de comedor
maize [mez] s maíz m
majestic [mə'dʒɛstɪk] adj majestuoso
majes‧ty ['mædʒɪsti] s (pl -ties) majestad
major ['medʒər] adj (greater) mayor; (elder) mayor de edad; (mus) mayor || s (educ) especialización; (mil) comandante m || intr (educ) especializarse
Majorca [mə'dʒɔrkə] s Mallorca
Majorcan [mə'dʒɔrkən] adj & s mallorquín m
major‧do‧mo [‚medʒər'domo] s (pl -mos) mayordomo
major general s general m de división
majori‧ty [mə'dʒɑrɪti] o [mə'dʒɔrɪti] adj mayoritario || s (pl -ties) (being of full age; larger number or part) mayoría; (full age) mayoridad; (mil) comandancia
make [mek] s (brand) marca; (form, build) hechura; carácter m, natural m; **on the make** (slang) buscando provecho || v (pret & pp made [med]) tr hacer; cometer (un error); efectuar (un pago); ganar (dinero); coger (un tren); dar (dinero una baza); dar (un tren); dar (dinero una empresa); pronunciar (un discurso); cerrar (un circuito); poner (a uno, p.ej., nervioso); ser, p.ej., **she will make a good wife** será una buena esposa; **to make** + inf hacer + inf, p.ej., **she made him study to help him** hizo le estudiar; **to make into** convertir en; **to make known** declarar; dar a conocer; **to make of** pensar de; **to make oneself known** darse a conocer; **to make out** distinguir, vislumbrar; descifrar; escribir (una receta); llenar (un cheque); hacer convertir; rehacer (un traje); (com) transferir; **to make up** preparar, confeccionar; inventar (un cuento); recobrar (el tiempo perdido); (theat) maquillar || intr estar (p.ej., seguro); **to make away with** llevarse; deshacerse de; matar; **to make believe** fingir, p.ej., **he made believe he knew me** fingió conocerme; **to make for** ir hacia; embestir contra; contribuir a (p.ej., mejores relaciones); **to make much of** (coll) hacer fiestas a, mostrar cariño a; **to make off** largarse; **to make off with** llevarse, hacerse con; **to make out** arreglárselas; **to make toward** encaminarse a; **to make up** maquillarse, pintarse; componerse, hacer las paces; **to make up for** suplir; compensar por (una pérdida); **to make up to** (coll) tratar de congraciarse con
make'-be‧lieve' adj simulado || s pretexto, simulación, fantasía
maker ['mekər] s constructor m, fabricante mf
make'shift' adj de fortuna, provisional || s expediente m; (person) tapagujeros m
make'-up' s composición, constitución;

afeite *m*, maquillaje *m;* (typ) imposición

make-up man *s* (theat) maquillador *m*
make'weight' *s* contrapeso; suplente *mf*
making ['mekɪŋ] *s* fabricación; material necesario; causa del éxito; **makings** elementos, materiales *mpl;* (*personal qualities necessary for some purpose*) madera
malachite ['mælə,kaɪt] *s* malaquita
maladjustment [,mælə'dʒʌstmənt] *s* desadaptación
mala·dy ['mælədi] *s* (*pl* **-dies**) dolencia, enfermedad
malaise [mæ'lez] *s* indisposición, malestar *m*
malapropos [,mæləprə'po] *adj* impropio || *adv* fuera de propósito
malaria [mə'lerɪ·ə] *s* malaria, paludismo
Malay ['mele] o [mə'le] *adj* & *s* malayo
malcontent ['mælkən,tent] *adj* & *s* malcontento
male [mel] *adj* (*sex*) masculino; (*animal, plant, piece of a device*) macho; (*human being*) varón, p.ej., **male child** hijo varón || *s* macho; varón *m*
malediction [,mælɪ'dɪkʃən] *s* maldición
malefactor ['mælɪ,fæktər] *s* malhechor *m*
male nurse *s* enfermero
malevolent [mə'levələnt] *adj* malévolo
malice ['mælɪs] *s* malicia, malevolencia; **to bear malice** guardar rencor; **with malice prepense** [prɪ'pens] (law) con malicia y premeditación
malicious [mə'lɪ/əs] *adj* malicioso, malévolo
malign [mə'laɪn] *adj* maligno || *tr* calumniar
malignant [mə'lɪgnənt] *adj* maligno
maligni·ty [mə'lɪgnɪti] *s* (*pl* **-ties**) malignidad
malinger [mə'lɪŋgər] *intr* hacer la zanguanga, fingirse enfermo
mall [mɔl] o [mæl] *s* alameda, paseo de árboles
mallet ['mælɪt] *s* (*wooden hammer*) mazo; (*for croquet and polo*) mallete *m*
mallow ['mælo] *s* malva
malnutrition [,mælnju'trɪ/ən] o [,mælnu'trɪ/ən] *s* desnutrición
malodorous [mæl'odərəs] *adj* maloliente
malt [mɔlt] *s* malta *m;* (coll) cerveza
maltreat [mæl'trit] *tr* maltratar
mamma ['mɑmə] o [mə'mɑ] *s* mama o mamá *f*
mammal ['mæməl] *s* mamífero
mammalian [mæ'melɪ·ən] *adj* & *s* mamífero
mammoth ['mæməθ] *adj* gigantesco, enorme || *s* mamut *m*
man [mæn] *s* (*pl* **men** [mɛn]) *s* hombre *m;* (*in chess*) pieza; (*in checkers*) pieza, peón *m;* **a man** uno, p.ej., **a man can't get work in this town** uno no puede obtener empleo en este

pueblo; **as one man** unánimemente; **man alive!** ¡hombre!; **man and wife** marido y mujer; **to be one's own man** no depender de nadie || *v* (*pret* & *pp* **manned**; *ger* **manning**) *tr* dotar, tripular (*un buque*); guarnecer (*una fortaleza*); servir (*los cañones*)
man about town *s* bulevardero, hombre *m* de mucho mundo
manacle ['mænəkəl] *s* manilla; **manacles** esposas || *tr* poner esposas a
manage ['mænɪdʒ] *tr* manejar || *intr* arreglárselas; **to manage to** ingeniarse a o para; **to manage to get along** ingeniarse para ir viviendo
manageable ['mænɪdʒəbəl] *adj* manejable
management ['mænɪdʒmənt] *s* manejo, dirección, gerencia; (*group who manage a business*) la empresa, la parte patronal, los patronos
manager ['mænədʒər] *s* director *m*, administrador *m*, gerente *mf;* empresario; (sport) manager *m*
managerial [,mænə'dʒɪrɪ·əl] *adj* empresarial
mandate ['mændet] *s* mandato || *tr* asignar por mandato
mandolin ['mændəlɪn] *s* mandolina
mandrake ['mændrek] *s* mandrágora
mane [men] *s* (*of horse*) crines *fpl;* (*of lion; of person*) melena
maneuver [mə'nuvər] *s* maniobra || *tr* hacer maniobrar || *intr* maniobrar
manful ['mænfəl] *adj* varonil, resuelto
manganese ['mæŋgə,nis] o ['mæŋgə,niz] *s* manganeso
mange [mendʒ] *s* sarna
manger ['mendʒər] *s* pesebre *m*
mangle ['mæŋgəl] *tr* lacerar, aplastar
man·gy ['mændʒi] *adj* (*comp* **-gier**; *super* **-giest**) sarnoso; (*dirty, squalid*) roñoso
man'han'dle *tr* maltratar
man'hole' *s* caja de registro, pozo de inspección
manhood ['mænhʊd] *s* virilidad; hombres *mpl*
man hunt *s* caza al hombre
mania ['menɪ·ə] *s* manía
maniac ['menɪ,æk] *adj* & *s* maníaco
manicure ['mænɪ,kjʊr] *s* (*care of hands*) manicura; (*person*) manicuro, manicura || *tr* hacer la manicura a (*una persona*); hacer (*las manos y las uñas*)
manicurist ['mænɪ,kjʊrɪst] *s* manicuro, manicura
manifest ['mænɪ,fest] *adj* manifiesto || *s* (naut) manifiesto || *tr* manifestar
manifes·to [,mænɪ'festo] *s* (*pl* **-toes**) manifiesto
manifold ['mænɪ,fold] *adj* múltiple, vario || *s* copia, ejemplar *m;* (*pipe with outlets or inlets*) colector *m*, múltiple *m*
manikin ['mænɪkɪn] *s* maniquí *m;* (*dwarf*) enano
man in the moon *s* cara o cuerpo de hombre imaginarios en la luna llena
manipulate [mə'nɪpjə,let] *tr* manipular

man'kind' s el género humano ‖ man'kind' s el sexo masculino, los hombres

manliness ['mænlınıs] s masculinidad, virilidad

man·ly ['mænli] adj (comp -lier; super -liest) masculino, varonil

manned spaceship [mænd] s astronave tripulada

mannequin ['mænıkın] s maniquí m; (young woman employed to exhibit clothing) maniquí f

manner ['mænər] s manera; by all manner of means de todos modos; in a manner of speaking como si dijéramos; in the manner of a la manera de; manners modales mpl, crianza; to the manner born avezado desde la cuna

mannish ['mænıʃ] adj hombruno

man of letters s hombre m de letras

man of means s hombre m de dinero

man of parts s hombre m de buenas prendas

man of straw s hombre m de suposición

man of the world s hombre m de mundo

man-of-war [‚mænəv'wɔr] s (pl men-of-war [‚mænəv'wɔr]) s buque m de guerra

manor ['mænər] s señorío

manor house s casa solariega

man overboard interj ¡hombre al agua!

man'pow'er s número de hombres; personal m competente; (mil) fuerzas nacionales

mansard ['mænsɑrd] s mansarda; piso de mansarda

man'serv'ant s (pl men'serv'ants) criado

mansion ['mænʃən] s hotel m, palacio; (manor house) casa solariega

man'slaugh'ter s (law) homicidio sin premeditación

mantel ['mæntəl] s manto (de chimenea); (shelf above it) mesilla, repisa de chimenea

man'tel·piece' s mesilla, repisa de chimenea

mantle ['mæntəl] s capa, manto ‖ tr vestir con manto; cubrir, tapar; ocultar ‖ intr encenderse (el rostro)

manual ['mænjuəl] adj manual ‖ s (book) manual m; (mil) ejercicio; (mus) teclado manual

manual training s enseñanza de los artes y oficios

manufacture [‚mænjə'fæktʃər] s fabricación; (thing manufactured) manufactura ‖ tr fabricar, manufacturar

manufacturer [‚mænjə'fæktʃərər] s fabricante m

manure [mə'njur] o [mə'nur] s estiércol m ‖ tr estercolar

manuscript ['mænjə‚skrıpt] adj & s manuscrito

many ['meni] adj & pron muchos; a good many o a great many un buen número; as many as tantos como; hasta, p.ej., as many as twenty hasta veinte; how many cuántos; many a muchos, p.ej., many a person muchas

personas; many another muchos otros; many more muchos más; so many tantos; too many demasiados; twice as many as dos veces más que

many-sided ['meni‚saıdıd] adj multilátero; (having many interests or capabilities) polifacético

map [mæp] s mapa m; (of a city) plano ‖ v (pret & pp mapped; ger mapping) tr trazar el mapa de; indicar en el mapa; to map out trazar el plan de

maple ['mepəl] s arce m

maquette [ma'ket] s maqueta

Mar. abbr March

mar [mɑr] v (pret & pp marred; ger marring) tr desfigurar, estropear; frustrar

maraud [mə'rɔd] tr saquear ‖ intr merodear

marauder [mə'rɔdər] s merodeador m

marble ['mɑrbəl] adj marmóreo ‖ s mármol m; (little ball of glass, etc.) canica; marbles (game) canica ‖ tr crispir, jaspear

march [mɑrtʃ] s marcha; (frontier, territory) marca; to steal a march on someone ganarle a uno por la mano ‖ tr hacer marchar ‖ intr marchar ‖ March s marzo

marchioness ['mɑrʃənıs] s marquesa

mare [mer] s (female horse) yegua; (female donkey) asna

margarine ['mɑrdʒərın] s margarina

margin ['mɑrdʒın] s margen m & f; (collateral deposited with a broker) doble m

marginal ['mɑrdʒınəl] adj marginal

margin release s tecla de escape

margin stop s fijamárgenes m, cierrarrenglón m, cortarrenglón m

marigold ['mærı‚gold] s clavelón m; (Calendula) maravilla, flamenquilla

marihuana o marijuana [‚mɑrı'hwɑnə] s mariguana

marinate ['mærı‚net] tr escabechar, marinar

marine [mə'rin] adj marino, marítimo ‖ s marina; soldado de infantería de marina; marines infantería de marina; tell that to the marines (coll) cuénteselo a su abuela, a otro perro con ese hueso

mariner ['mærınər] s marino

marionette [‚mærı·ə'net] s marioneta, títere m

marital status ['mærı'əl] s estado civil

maritime ['mærı‚taım] adj marítimo

marjoram ['mɑrdʒərəm] s orégano; mejorana

mark [mɑrk] s marca, señal f; (label) marbete m; (of punctuation) punto; (in an examination) calificación, nota; (used instead of signature by an illiterate person) cruz f, signo; (spot, stain) mancha; (coin) marco; (starting point in a race) raya; (target to shoot at) blanco; to be beside the mark no venir al caso; to hit the mark dar en el blanco; to leave one's mark dejar memoria de sí; to make one's mark llegar a ser célebre; to miss the mark errar el tiro; to toe the mark ponerse en la raya; obedecer rigurosamente || *tr* marcar, señalar; dar nota a (*un alumno*); calificar (*un examen*); advertir, notar; **to mark down** poner por escrito; rebajar el precio de

mark'down' *s* reducción de precio

market ['markıt] *s* mercado; **to bear the market** jugar a la baja; **to bull the market** jugar al alza; **to play the market** jugar a la bolsa; **to put on the market** lanzar al mercado || *tr* llevar al mercado; vender

marketable ['markıtəbəl] *adj* comerciable, vendible

market basket *s* cesta para compras

marketing ['markıtıŋ] *s* mercología, mercadotecnia

market place *s* plaza del mercado

market price *s* precio corriente

marking gauge ['markıŋ] *s* gramil *m*

marks·man ['marksmən] *s* (*pl* -men [mən]) tirador *m*; **a good marksman** un buen tiro

marksmanship ['marksmən,ʃıp] *s* puntería

mark'up' *s* aumento de precio

marl [marl] *s* marga || *tr* margar

marmalade ['marmə,led] *s* mermelada

marmot ['marmət] *s* marmota

maroon [mə'run] *adj* & *s* marrón *m*, castaño obscuro || *tr* dejar abandonado (*en una isla desierta*)

marquee [mar'ki] *s* marquesina

marquess ['markwıs] *s* marqués *m*

marque·try ['markıtrı] *s* (*pl* -tries) marquetería (*taracea*)

marquis ['markwıs] *s* marqués *m*

marquise [mar'kiz] *s* marquesa; (*over the entrance to a hotel*) marquesina

marriage ['mærıdʒ] *s* casamiento, matrimonio; (*married life; intimate union*) maridaje *m*

marriageable ['mærıdʒəbəl] *adj* casadero

marriage portion *s* dote *m* & *f*

marriage rate *s* nupcialidad

married life ['mærıd] *s* vida conyugal

marrow ['mæro] *s* médula, tuétano

mar·ry ['mærı] *v* (*pret* & *pp* -ried) *tr* casar (*el sacerdote o el juez a un hombre y una mujer*); (*to take in marriage*) casar con, casarse con; (*to unite intimately*) maridar; **to get married to** casar con, casarse con || *intr* casar, casarse; **to marry into** emparentar con (*p.ej., una familia rica*); **to marry the second time** casarse en segundas nupcias

Mars [marz] *s* Marte *m*

Marseille [mar'se:j] *s* Marsella

marsh [marʃ] *s* ciénaga, pantano

mar·shal ['marʃəl] *s* cursor *m* de procesiones, maestro de ceremonias; (*mil*) mariscal *m*; (U.S.A.) oficial *m* de justicia || *v* (*pret* & *pp* -shaled o -shalled; *ger* -shaling o -shalling) *tr* conducir con ceremonia; ordenar, reunir (*los hechos de una argumentación*)

marsh mallow *s* (bot) malvavisco

marsh'mal'low *s* bombón *m* de meren-

gue y gelatina; bombón de malvavisco

marsh·y ['marʃı] *adj* (*comp* -ier; *super* -iest) pantanoso, palúdico

marten ['martən] *s* (*pine marten*) marta; (*beech marten*) garduña

martial ['marʃəl] *adj* marcial

martial law *s* ley *f* marcial; **to be under martial law** estar en estado de guerra

martin ['martın] *s* (orn) avión *m*

martinet [,martı'net] o ['martı,net] *s* ordenancista *mf*

martyr ['martər] *s* mártir *mf*

martyrdom ['martərdəm] *s* martirio

mar·vel ['marvəl] *s* maravilla || *v* (*pret* & *pp* -veled o -velled; *ger* -veling o -velling) *intr* maravillarse; **to marvel at** maravillarse con o de

marvelous ['marvələs] *adj* maravilloso

Marxist ['marksıst] *adj* & *s* marxista *mf*

masc. *abbr* masculine

mascara [mæs'kærə] *s* tinte *m* para las pestañas

mascot ['mæskat] *s* mascota

masculine ['mæskjəlın] *adj* & *s* masculino

mash [mæʃ] *s* (*crushed mass*) masa; (*to form wort*) masa de cebada || *tr* machacar, majar

mashed potatoes [mæʃt] *spl* puré *m* de patatas

masher ['mæʃər] *s* (*device*) mano *f*; (slang) galanteador atrevido

mask [mæsk] o [mask] *s* máscara; (*of beekeeper*) carilla; (*made from a corpse*) mascarilla; (*person*) máscara *mf*; (phot) desvanecedor *m* || *tr* enmascarar; (phot) desvanecer || *intr* enmascararse

masked ball [mæskt] *s* baile *m* de máscaras

mason ['mesən] *s* albañil *m* || **Mason** *s* masón *m*

mason·ry ['mesənrı] *s* (*pl* -ries) albañilería || **Masonry** *s* masonería

masquerade [,mæskə'red] o [,maskə-'red] *s* mascarada; (*costume, disguise*) máscara; (*false show*) farsa || *intr* enmascararse; **to masquerade as** disfrazarse de

masquerade ball *s* baile *m* de máscaras

mass [mæs] *s* masa; gran cantidad; (*bulk, heap*) mole *f*; (*something glimpsed, e.g., in the fog*) bulto informe; (*big splotch in a painting*) gran mancha; (*celebration of the Eucharist*) misa; **the masses** las masas || *tr* juntar, reunir; enmasar (*tropas*) || *intr* juntarse, reunirse

massacre ['mæsəkər] *s* carnicería, matanza || *tr* degollar, matar

massage [mə'saʒ] *s* masaje *m* || *tr* masar, masajear

masseur [mæ'sœr] *s* masajista *m*

masseuse [mæ'sœz] *s* masajista *f*

massive ['mæsıv] *adj* macizo; sólido, imponente

mass meeting *s* mitin *m* popular

mass production *s* fabricación en serie

mast [mæst] o [mast] *s* (*for a flag*) palo; (*of a ship*) palo, mástil *m*;

(*food for swine*) bellotas, hayucos; **before the mast** como simple marinero

master ['mæstər] o ['mɑstər] *s* (*employer*) dueño, patrón *m;* (*male head of household*) amo; (*man who possesses some special skill; teacher*) maestro; (*commander of merchant vessel*) capitán *m;* (*title of respect for a boy*) señorito ‖ *tr* dominar

master bedroom *s* alcoba de respeto

master blade *s* hoja maestra (*de una ballesta*)

master builder *s* maestro de obras

masterful ['mæstərfəl] o ['mɑstərfəl] *adj* hábil, experto; dominante, imperioso

master key *s* llave maestra

masterly ['mæstərli] o ['mɑstərli] *adj* magistral ‖ *adv* magistralmente

master mechanic *s* maestro mecánico

mas'ter·mind' *s* mente directora ‖ *tr* dirigir con gran acierto

master of ceremonies *s* maestro de ceremonias; (*in a night club, radio, etc.*) animador *m*

mas'ter·piece' *s* obra maestra

master stroke *s* golpe maestro

mas'ter·work' *s* obra maestra

master·y ['mæstəri] o ['mɑstəri] *s* (*pl* -ies) (*command, as of a subject*) dominio; ventaja, superioridad; (*skill*) maestría

mast'head' *s* (*of a newspaper*) cabecera editorial; (*naut*) tope *m*

masticate ['mæstɪˌket] *tr* masticar

mastiff ['mæstɪf] o ['mɑstɪf] *s* mastín *m*

masturbate ['mæstərˌbet] *intr* masturbarse

mat [mæt] *s* (*for floor*) estera; (*for a cup, vase, etc.*) esterilla, ruedo; (*before a door*) felpudo; (*around a picture*) borde *m* de cartón ‖ *v* (*pret & pp* matting; *ger* matting) *tr* (*to cover with matting*) esterar; enmarañar ‖ *intr* enmarañarse

match [mætʃ] *s* fósforo; (*wick*) mecha; (*counterpart*) compañero; (*suitable partner in marriage*) partido; (*suitably associated pair*) pareja; (*game, contest*) match *m*, partido; **to be a match for** poder con, poder vencer; **to meet one's match** hallar la horma de su zapato ‖ *tr* igualar; aparear, emparejar; hacer juego con; **to match someone for the drinks** jugarle a uno las bebidas ‖ *intr* hacer juego, correr parejas; **to match** a juego, p.ej., **a chair to match** una silla a juego

match'box' *s* fosforera; (*of wax matches*) cerillera

matchless ['mætʃlɪs] *adj* incomparable, sin par

matchmaker ['mætʃˌmekər] *s* casamentero

mate [met] *s* compañero; (*e.g., of a shoe*) compañero, hermano; (*husband or wife*) cónyuge *mf;* (*to a female*) macho; (*to a male*) hembra; (*in chess*) mate *m;* (*naut*) piloto ‖ *tr* aparear, casar; (*in chess*) dar jaque

mate a; **to be well mated** hacer una buena pareja ‖ *intr* aparearse, casarse

material [mə'tɪrɪ·əl] *adj* material; importante ‖ *s* material *m;* (*what a thing is made of*) materia; (*cloth, fabric*) tela, género

materialism [mə'tɪrɪ·əˌlɪzəm] *s* materialismo

materialize [mə'tɪrɪ·əˌlaɪz] *intr* realizarse

matériel [mə‚tɪrɪ'el] *s* material *m;* material de guerra

maternal [mə'tʌrnəl] *adj* materno; (*motherly*) maternal

maternity [mə'tʌrnɪti] *s* maternidad

maternity hospital *s* casa de maternidad

math. *abbr* **mathematics**

mathematical [‚mæθɪ'mætɪkəl] *adj* matemático

mathematician [‚mæθɪmə'tɪʃən] *s* matemático

mathematics [‚mæθɪ'mætɪks] *s* matemática, matemáticas

matinée [‚mætɪ'ne] *s* matinée *f*, función de tarde

mating season *s* época de celo

matins ['mætɪnz] *spl* maitines *mpl*

matriarch ['metrɪˌɑrk] *s* matriarca

matricidal [‚metrɪ'saɪdəl] o [‚mætrɪ'saɪdəl] *adj* matricida

matricide ['metrɪˌsaɪd] o ['mætrɪˌsaɪd] *s* (*act*) matricidio; (*person*) matricida *mf*

matriculate [mə'trɪkjəˌlet] *tr* matricular ‖ *intr* matricularse

matrimo·ny ['mætrɪˌmoni] *s* (*pl* -nies) matrimonio

matron ['metrən] *s* matrona

matronly ['metrənli] *adj* matronal

matter ['mætər] *s* (*physical substance; pus*) materia; (*subject talked or written about*) asunto; (*reason, ground*) motivo; (*copy for printer*) material *m;* (*printed material*) impresos; **a matter of** cosa de, obra de; **for that matter** en cuanto a eso; **in the matter** al respecto; **no matter** no importa; **no matter when** cuando quiera; **no matter where** dondequiera; **what is the matter?** ¿qué hay?; **what is the matter with you?** ¿qué tiene Vd.? ‖ *intr* importar

matter of course *s* cosa de cajón; **as a matter of course** por rutina

matter of fact *s* — **as a matter of fact** en realidad, en honor a la verdad

matter-of-fact ['mætərəv‚fækt] *adj* prosaico, práctico, de poca imaginación

mattock ['mætək] *s* zapapico

mattress ['mætrɪs] *s* colchón *m*

mature [mə't(j)ur] o [mə'tur] *adj* maduro; (*due*) pagadero, vencido ‖ *tr* madurar ‖ *intr* madurar; (*to become due*) (com) vencer

maturity [mə't(j)urɪti] o [mə'turɪti] *s* madurez *f;* (*com*) vencimiento

maudlin ['mɔdlɪn] *adj* lacrimoso, sensiblero; chispo y lloroso

maul [mɔl] *tr* aporrear, maltratar

maulstick ['mɔlˌstɪk] *s* tiento

maundy ['mɔndɪ] *s* lavatorio
Maundy Thursday *s* Jueves Santo
mausole·um [,mɔsə'li·əm] *s* (*pl* **-ums** o **-a** [ə]) mausoleo
maw [mɔ] *s* (*of fowl*) buche *m*; (*of fish*) vejiga de aire
mawkish ['mɔkɪʃ] *adj* (*sickening*) empalagoso; (*sentimental*) sensiblero
max. *abbr* **maximum**
maxim ['mæksɪm] *s* máxima
maximum ['mæksɪməm] *adj* & *s* máximo
may *v aux* **it may be** puede ser; **may I come in?** ¿puedo entrar? **may you be happy!** ¡que seas feliz! ‖ **May** *s* mayo
maybe ['mebɪ] o ['meɪbɪ] *adv* acaso, quizá, tal vez
May Day *s* primero de mayo; fiesta del primero de mayo
mayhem ['mehem] o ['me·əm] *s* (*law*) mutilación criminal
mayonnaise [,me·ə'nez] *s* mayonesa
mayor ['me·ər] o [mer] *s* alcalde *m*
mayoress ['me·ərɪs] o ['merɪs] *s* alcaldesa
May'pole' *s* mayo
Maypole dance *s* danza de cintas
May queen *s* maya
maze [mez] *s* laberinto
M.C. *abbr* **Master of Ceremonies, Member of Congress**
mdse. *abbr* **merchandise**
me [mi] *pron pers* me; mí; **to me** me; a mí; **with me** conmigo
meadow ['mɛdo] *s* prado, vega
mead'ow·land' *s* pradera
meager ['migər] *adj* escaso, pobre; flaco, magro
meal [mil] *s* (*regular repast*) comida; (*edible grain coarsely ground*) harina
meal'time' *s* hora de comer
mean [min] *adj* (*intermediate*) medio; (*low in station or rank*) humilde, obscuro; (*shabby*) andrajoso, raído; (*stingy*) mezquino, tacaño; (*of poor quality*) inferior, pobre; (*small-minded*) vil, ruin, innoble; insignificante; (*vicious, as a horse*) arisco, mal intencionado; (*coll*) indispuesto; (*coll*) avergonzado; (*coll*) de mal genio; **no mean** famoso, excelente ‖ *s* promedio, término medio; **by all means** sí, por cierto, sin falta; **by means of** por medio de; **by no means** de ningún modo, en ningún caso; **means** bienes *mpl* de fortuna; (*agency*) medio, medios; **means to an end** paso para lograr un fin; **to live on one's means** vivir de sus rentas ‖ *v* (*pret & pp* **meant** [mɛnt]) *tr* significar, querer decir; **to mean to** pensar ‖ *intr* — **to mean well** tener buenas intenciones
meander [mɪ'ændər] *s* meandro ‖ *intr* serpentear; vagar
meaning ['minɪŋ] *s* sentido, significado
meaningful ['minɪŋfəl] *adj* significativo
meaningless ['minɪŋlɪs] *adj* sin sentido
meanness ['minnɪs] *s* bajeza, vileza, ruindad; (*stinginess*) mezquindad; (*lowliness*) humildad, pobreza

mean'time' *adv* entretanto, mientras tanto ‖ *s* medio tiempo; **in the meantime** entretanto, mientras tanto
mean'while' *adv* & *s* var de **meantime**
measles ['mizlz] *s* sarampión *m*; (*German measles*) rubéola
mea·sly ['mizlɪ] *adj* (*comp* **-slier;** *super* **-sliest**) sarampioso; (*slang*) despreciable, mezquino
measurable ['mɛʒərəbəl] *adj* medible
measure ['mɛʒər] *s* medida; (*step, procedure*) paso, gestión; (*legislative bill*) proyecto de ley; (*of verse*) pie *m*; (*mus*) compás *m*; **beyond measure** con exceso; **in a measure** hasta cierto punto; **in great measure** en gran parte; (*suit*) hecho a la medida; **to take measures** tomar las medidas necesarias; **to take someone's measure** tomarle a uno las medidas ‖ *tr* medir; recorrer (*cierta distancia*); **to measure out** medir; distribuir ‖ *intr* medir
measurement ['mɛʒərmənt] *s* (*act of measuring*) medición; (*measuring; dimension*) medida
measuring glass *s* vaso graduado
meat [mit] *s* carne *f*; (*food in general*) manjar *m*, vianda; (*substance, gist*) meollo
meat ball *s* albóndiga
meat'hook' *s* garabato de carnicero
meat market *s* carnicería
meat·y ['mitɪ] *adj* (*comp* **-ier;** *super* **-iest**) carnoso; (*fig*) jugoso, substancioso
Mecca ['mɛkə] *s* La Meca
mechanic [mɪ'kænɪk] *s* mecánico
mechanical [mɪ'kænɪkəl] *adj* mecánico, maquinal; (*machinelike*) (fig) maquinal
mechanical toy *s* juguete *m* de movimiento
mechanics [mɪ'kænɪks] *ssg* mecánica
mechanism ['mɛkə,nɪzəm] *s* mecanismo
mechanize ['mɛkə,naɪz] *tr* mecanizar
med. *abbr* **medicine, medieval**
medal ['mɛdəl] *s* medalla
medallion [mɪ'dæljən] *s* medallón *m*
meddle ['mɛdəl] *intr* meterse, entremeterse
meddler ['mɛdlər] *s* entremetido
meddlesome ['mɛdəlsəm] *adj* entremetido
median ['midɪ·ən] *adj* intermedio, medio ‖ *s* punto medio, número medio
median strip *s* faja central o divisoria
mediate ['midɪ,et] *tr* dirimir (*una controversia*); reconciliar ‖ *intr* (*to be in the middle*) mediar; (*to intervene to settle a dispute*) intervenir
mediation [,midɪ'e/ən] *s* mediación
mediator ['midɪ,etər] *s* mediador *m*
medical ['mɛdɪkəl] *adj* médico
medical student *s* estudiante *mf* de medicina
medicine ['mɛdɪsɪn] *s* (*science and art*) medicina; (*remedy, treatment*) medicina, medicamento
medicine cabinet *s* armario botiquín
medicine kit *s* botiquín *m*

ma
me

medicine man s curandero, hechicero (*entre los pieles rojas*)
medieval [ˌmidɪ'ivəl] o [ˌmɛdɪ'ivəl] adj medieval
medievalist [ˌmidɪ'ivəlɪst] o [ˌmɛdɪ-'ivəlɪst] s medievalista mf
mediocre ['midɪˌokər] o [ˌmidɪ'okər] adj mediocre
mediocri·ty [ˌmidɪ'ɑkrɪti] s (pl -ties) mediocridad
meditate ['mɛdɪˌtet] tr & intr meditar
Mediterranean [ˌmɛdɪtə'renɪ·ən] adj & s Mediterráneo
medi·um ['midɪ·əm] adj intermedio; a medio asar ‖ s (pl -ums o -a [ə]) medio; (*in spiritualism*) medio, médium m; (*publication*) órgano; **through the medium of** por medio de
me'dium-range' adj de alcance medio
medlar ['mɛdlər] s (*tree and fruit*) níspero; (*fruit*) níspola
medley ['mɛdli] s mescolanza; (mus) popurrí m
medul·la [mɪ'dʌlə] s (pl -lae [li]) médula
meek [mik] adj dócil, manso
meekness ['miknɪs] s docilidad, mansedumbre
meerschaum ['mɪrʃəm] s ['mɪrʃəm] s espuma de mar; pipa de espuma de mar
meet [mit] adj conveniente, a propósito ‖ s concurso deportivo ‖ v (pret & pp **met** [mɛt]) tr encontrar, encontrarse con; (*to make the acquaintance of*) conocer; empalmar con (*otro tren o autobús*); ir a esperar; honrar, pagar (*una letra*); hacer frente a (*gastos*); cumplir (*sus obligaciones*); batirse con; hallar (*la muerte*); tener (*mala suerte*); aparecer a (*la vista*) ‖ intr encontrarse; reunirse; conocerse; **till we meet again** hasta la vista; **to meet with** encontrarse con; reunirse con; empalmar (*un tren*) con (*otro tren*); tener (*un accidente*)
meeting ['mitɪŋ] s junta, sesión; reunión; encuentro; (*of two rivers or roads*) confluencia; desafío, duelo
meeting of the minds s concierto de voluntades
meeting place s lugar m de reunión
megacycle ['mɛgəˌsaɪkəl] s megaciclo
megaphone ['mɛgəˌfon] s megáfono
megohm ['mɛgˌom] s megohmio
melancholia [ˌmɛlən'kolɪ·ə] s melancolía
melanchol·y ['mɛlənˌkɑli] adj melancólico ‖ s (pl -ies) melancolía
melee ['mele] o ['mele] s refriega, reyerta
mellow ['mɛlo] adj maduro, jugoso; suave, meloso; melodioso ‖ tr suavizar ‖ intr suavizarse
melodious [mɪ'lodɪ·əs] adj melodioso
melodramatic [ˌmɛlədrə'mætɪk] adj melodramático
melo·dy ['mɛlədi] s (pl -dies) melodía
melon ['mɛlən] s melón m
melt [mɛlt] tr derretir, fundir (*metales*); ablandar, aplacar ‖ intr derretirse; fundirse; ablandarse, apla-

carse; **to melt away** desvanecerse; **to melt into** convertirse gradualmente en; deshacerse en (*lágrimas*)
melting pot s crisol m; (fig) caldero de razas
member ['mɛmbər] s miembro
membership ['mɛmbərˌʃɪp] s asociación; (*e.g., of a club*) personal m; número de miembros
membrane ['mɛmbren] s membrana
memen·to [mɪ'mɛnto] s (pl -tos o -toes) recordatorio, prenda de recuerdo
mem·o ['mɛmo] s (pl -os) (coll) apunte m, membrete m
memoir ['mɛmwɑr] s memoria; biografía; **memoirs** memorias
memoran·dum [ˌmɛmə'rændəm] s (pl -dums o -da [də]) apunte m, membrete m
memorial [mɪ'morɪ·əl] adj conmemorativo ‖ s monumento conmemorativo; (*petition*) memorial m
memorial arch s arco triunfal
Memorial Day s día m de los caídos
memorialize [mɪ'morɪ·əˌlaɪz] tr conmemorar
memorize ['mɛməˌraɪz] tr aprender de memoria
memo·ry ['mɛməri] s (pl -ries) memoria; **to commit to memory** encomendar a la memoria
menace ['mɛnɪs] s amenaza ‖ tr & intr amenazar
ménage [me'nɑʒ] s casa, hogar m; economía doméstica
menagerie [mə'næʒəri] o [mə'nædʒəri] s casa de fieras; colección de fieras
mend [mɛnd] s remiendo; **to be on the mend** ir mejorando ‖ tr (*to repair*) componer, reparar; (*to patch*) remendar; (*to improve*) reformar, mejorar ‖ intr mejorar
mendacious [mɛn'deʃəs] adj mendaz
mendicant ['mɛndɪkənt] adj & s mendicante mf
mending ['mɛndɪŋ] s remiendo, zurcido
menfolk ['mɛnˌfok] spl hombres mpl
menial ['minɪ·əl] adj bajo, servil ‖ s criado, doméstico
menses ['mɛnsiz] spl menstruo
men's furnishings spl artículos para caballeros
men's room s lavabo para caballeros
menstruate ['mɛnstrʊˌet] intr menstruar
mental illness ['mɛntəl] s enfermedad mental
mental reservation s reserva mental
mental test s prueba de inteligencia
mention ['mɛnʃən] s mención ‖ tr mencionar; **don't mention it** no hay de qué; **not to mention** sin contar
menu ['mɛnju] o ['menju] s menú m, lista de comidas; comida
meow [mɪ'aʊ] s maullido ‖ intr maullar
Mephistophelian [ˌmɛfɪstə'filɪ·ən] adj mefistofélico
mercantile ['mʌrkənˌtil] o ['mʌrkənˌtaɪl] adj mercantil

mercenar·y ['mʌrsə ˌnɛri] *adj* mercenario || *s* (*pl* **-ies**) mercenario
merchandise ['mʌrt/ən ˌdaɪz] *s* mercancías, mercaderías
merchant ['mʌrt/ənt] *adj* mercante || *s* mercante *m*, mercader *m*
merchant·man ['mʌrt/əntmən] *s* (*pl* **-men** [mən]) buque *m* mercante
merchant marine *s* marina mercante
merchant vessel *s* buque *m* mercante
merciful ['mʌrsɪfəl] *adj* misericordioso
merciless ['mʌrsɪlɪs] *adj* despiadado, cruel, implacable
mercu·ry ['mʌrkjəri] *s* (*pl* **-ries**) mercurio, azogue *m*; columna de mercurio
mer·cy ['mʌrsi] *s* (*pl* **-cies**) misericordia; (*discretionary power*) merced *f*; **at the mercy of** a merced de
mere [mɪr] *adj* mero, puro; nada más que
meretricious [ˌmɛrɪ'trɪ/əs] *adj* postizo, de oropel; cursi, llamativo
merge [mʌrdʒ] *tr* enchufar, fusionar || *intr* enchufarse, fusionarse; convergir (*p.ej., dos caminos*); **to merge into** convertirse gradualmente en
merger ['mʌrdʒər] *s* fusión de empresas
meridian [mə'rɪdɪ·ən] *adj* meridiano; (el) más elevado || *s* meridiano; (fig) auge *m*, apogeo
meringue [mə'ræŋ] *s* merengue *m*
meri·no [mə'rino] *adj* merino || *s* (*pl* **-nos**) merino
merit ['mɛrɪt] *s* mérito || *tr* merecer
merlon ['mʌrlən] *s* almena, merlón *m*
mermaid ['mʌr ˌmed] *s* sirena; (*girl who swims well*) ninfa marina
mer·man ['mʌr ˌmæn] *s* (*pl* **-men** [ˌmen]) tritón *m*; (*good swimmer*) tritón
merriment ['mɛrɪmənt] *s* alegría, regocijo
mer·ry ['mɛri] *adj* (*comp* **-rier**; *super* **-riest**) alegre, regocijado; **to make merry** divertirse
Merry Christmas *interj* ¡Felices Pascuas!, ¡Felices Navidades!
mer'ry-go-round' *s* tiovivo, caballito; serie ininterrumpida (de fiestas, tertulias, etc.)
mer'ry-mak'er *s* fiestero, jaranero
mesh [mɛ/] *s* (*net, network*) red *f*; (*each open space of net*) malla; (*engagement of gears*) engrane *m*; **meshes** celada, red *f* || *tr* enredar; (mach) engranar || *intr* enredarse; (mach) engranar
mess [mɛs] *s* (*dirty condition*) cochinería; fregado, lío, embrollo; (*meal for a group of people; such a group*) rancho; (*refuse*) bazofia; **to get into a mess** meterse en un lío; **to make a mess of** ensuciar, echar a perder || *tr* ensuciar; desarreglar; estropear, echar a perder || *intr* comer; **to mess around** (coll) ocuparse en fruslerías
message ['mɛsɪdʒ] *s* mensaje *m*; recado
messenger ['mɛsəndʒər] *s* mensajero; (*one who goes on errands*) mandadero; precursor *m*

mess hall *s* sala de rancho; comedor *m* de militares
Messiah [mə'saɪ·ə] *s* Mesías *m*
mess kit *s* utensilios de rancho
mess'mate' *s* comensal *mf*, compañero de rancho
mess of pottage ['pɑtɪdʒ] *s* (Bib) plato de lentejas; cosa de ningún valor
Messrs. ['mɛsərz] *pl* de **Mr.**
mess·y ['mɛsi] *adj* (*comp* **-ier**; *super* **-iest**) desaliñado, desarreglado; sucio
met. *abbr* **metropolitan**
metal ['mɛtəl] *adj* metálico || *s* metal *m*; (fig) brío, ánimo
metallic [mɪ'tælɪk] *adj* metálico
metallurgy ['mɛtə ˌlʌrdʒi] *s* metalurgia
metal polish *s* limpiametales *m*
met'al·work' *s* metalistería
metamorpho·sis [ˌmɛtə'mɔrfəsɪs] *s* (*pl* **-ses** [ˌsiz]) metamorfosis *f*
metaphore ['mɛtəfər] o ['mɛtə ˌfɔr] *s* metáfora
metaphorical [ˌmɛtə'fɑrɪkəl] o [ˌmɛtə'fɔrɪkəl] *adj* metafórico
metathe·sis [mɪ'tæθɪsɪs] *s* (*pl* **-ses** [ˌsiz]) metátesis *f*
mete [mit] *tr* — **to mete out** repartir
meteor ['miti·ər] *s* estrella fugaz; (*atmospheric phenomenon*) meteoro
meteorology [ˌmiti·ə'rɑlədʒi] *s* meteorología
meter ['mitər] *s* (*unit of measurement; verse*) metro; (*instrument for measuring gas, electricity, water*) contador *m*; (mus) compás *m*, tiempo || *tr* medir (con contador)
metering ['mitərɪŋ] *s* medición
meter reader *s* lector *m* (del contador)
methane ['mɛθen] *s* metano
method ['mɛθəd] *s* método
methodic(al) [mɪ'θɑdɪk(əl)] *adj* metódico
Methodist ['mɛθədɪst] *adj* & *s* metodista *mf*
Methuselah [mɪ'θuzələ] *s* Matusalén *m*; **to be as old as Methuselah** vivir más años que Matusalén
meticulous [mɪ'tɪkjələs] *adj* meticuloso, minucioso
metric(al) ['mɛtrɪk(əl)] *adj* métrico
metronome ['mɛtrə ˌnom] *s* metrónomo
metropolis [mɪ'trɑpəlɪs] *s* metrópoli *f*
metropolitan [ˌmɛtrə'pɑlɪtən] *adj* metropolitano || *s* (eccl) metropolitano
mettle ['mɛtəl] *s* ánimo, brío; **on one's mettle** dispuesto a hacer todo el esfuerzo posible
mettlesome ['mɛtəlsəm] *adj* animoso, brioso
mew [mju] *s* maullido; (orn) gaviota; **mews** (Brit) caballerizas alrededor de un corral
Mexican ['mɛksɪkən] *adj* & *s* mejicano
Mexico ['mɛksɪ ˌko] *s* Méjico
mezzanine ['mɛzə ˌnin] *s* entresuelo
mfr. *abbr* **manufacturer**
mi. *abbr* **mile**
mica ['maɪkə] *s* mica
microbe ['maɪkrob] *s* microbio
microbiology [ˌmaɪkrəbaɪ'ɑlədʒi] *s* microbiología
microcard ['maɪkrə ˌkɑrd] *s* microficha

microfarad [ˌmaɪkrəˈfæræd] s microfaradio

microfilm [ˈmaɪkrəˌfɪlm] s microfilm m, micropelícula || tr microfilmar

microgroove [ˈmaɪkrəˌgruv] adj microsurco || s microsurco; disco microsurco

microphone [ˈmaɪkrəˌfon] s micrófono

microscope [ˈmaɪkrəˌskop] s microscopio

microscopic [ˌmaɪkrəˈskɑpɪk] adj microscópico

microwave [ˈmaɪkrəˌwev] s microonda

mid [mɪd] adj medio, p.ej., **in mid course** a medio camino

mid′day′ adj del mediodía || s mediodía m

middle [ˈmɪdəl] adj medio || s centro, medio; (of the human body) cintura; **about the middle of** a mediados de; **in the middle of** en medio de

middle age s mediana edad || **Middle Ages** spl Edad Media

middle class s burguesía, clase media

Middle East s Oriente Medio

Middle English s el inglés medio

middle finger s dedo cordial, de en medio o del corazón

mid′dle·man′ s (pl **-men** [ˌmen]) intermediario

middling [ˈmɪdlɪŋ] adj mediano, regular, pasadero || adv (coll) medianamente; **fairly middling** (coll) así, así || s (coarsely ground wheat) cabezuela; **middlings** artículos de calidad o precio medianos

mid·dy [ˈmɪdi] s (pl **-dies**) (coll) aspirante m de marina; (child's blouse) marinera

middy blouse s marinera

midget [ˈmɪdʒɪt] s enano, liliputiense mf

midland [ˈmɪdlənd] adj de tierra adentro || s región central

mid′night′ adj de medianoche; **to burn the midnight oil** quemarse las cejas || s medianoche f

midriff [ˈmɪdrɪf] s (anat) diafragma m; talle m

midship·man [ˈmɪdˌʃɪpmən] s (pl **-men** [ˌmen]) guardia marina m, aspirante m de marina

midst [mɪdst] s centro; **in the midst of** en medio de; **in lo más recio de**

mid′stream′ s — **in midstream** en pleno río

mid′sum′mer s pleno verano

mid′way′ adj situado a mitad del camino || adv a mitad del camino || s mitad del camino; (of a fair or exposition) avenida central

mid′week′ s mediados de la semana

mid′wife′ s (pl **-wives**) partera, comadrona

mid′win′ter s pleno invierno

mid′year′ adj de mediados del año || s mediados del año; **midyears** (coll) examen m de mediados del año escolar

mien [min] s aspecto, semblante m, porte m

miff [mɪf] s (coll) desavenencia || tr (coll) ofender

might [maɪt] s fuerza, poder m; **with might and main** con todas sus fuerzas, a más no poder || v aux se emplea para formar el modo potencial, p.ej., **she might not come** es posible que no venga

might·y [ˈmaɪti] adj (comp **-ier;** super **-iest**) potente, poderoso; (of great size) grandísimo || adv (coll) muy

migrate [ˈmaɪgret] intr emigrar

migratory [ˈmaɪgrəˌtori] adj migratorio

mil. abbr **military, militia**

milch [mɪltʃ] adj lechero

mild [maɪld] adj blando, suave; dócil, manso; leve, ligero; (climate) templado

mildew [ˈmɪlˌdju] o [ˈmɪlˌdu] s (mold) moho; (plant disease) mildeu m

mile [maɪl] s milla inglesa

mileage [ˈmaɪlɪdʒ] s recorrido en millas

mileage ticket s billete contado por millas, semejante al billete kilométrico

mile′post′ s poste miliario

mile′stone′ s piedra miliaria; **to be a milestone** hacer época

milieu [mɪlˈju] s ambiente m, medio

militancy [ˈmɪlɪtənsi] s belicosidad

militant [ˈmɪlɪtənt] adj militante, belicoso

militarism [ˈmɪlɪtəˌrɪzəm] s militarismo

militarist [ˈmɪlɪtərɪst] adj & s militarista mf

militarize [ˈmɪlɪtəˌraɪz] tr militarizar

military [ˈmɪlɪˌteri] adj militar || s (los) militares

Military Academy s (U.S.A.) Academia General Militar

military police s policía militar

militate [ˈmɪlɪˌtet] intr militar

militia [mɪˈlɪʃə] s milicia

militia·man [mɪˈlɪʃəmən] s (pl **-men** [ˌmən]) miliciano

milk [mɪlk] adj lechero, de leche || s leche f || tr ordeñar; chupar (los bienes de uno); abusar de, explotar || intr dar leche

milk can s lechera

milk diet s régimen lácteo

milking [ˈmɪlkɪŋ] s ordeño

milk′maid′ s lechera

milk·man [ˈmɪlkˌmæn] s (pl **-men** [ˌmen]) lechero

milk of human kindness s compasión, humanidad

milk pail s ordeñadero

milk shake s batido de leche

milk′sop′ s calzonazos m, marica m

milk′weed′ s algodoncillo, vencetósigo

milk·y [ˈmɪlki] adj (comp **-ier;** super **-iest**) lechoso, lácteo

Milky Way s Vía Láctea

mill [mɪl] s (for grinding grain) molino; (for making fabrics) hilandería; (for cutting wood) aserradero; (for refining sugar) ingenio; (for produc-

ing steel) fábrica; (*to grind coffee*) molinillo; (*part of a dollar*) milésima; **to put through the mill** (coll) poner a prueba, someter a un entrenamiento riguroso ‖ *tr* moler (*granos*); acordonar, cerrillar (*monedas*); laminar (*el acero*); triturar (*mena*); (*with a milling cutter*) fresar; batir (*chocolate*) ‖ *intr* — **to mill about** o **around** arremolinarse

mill end *s* retal *m* de hilandería
millennial [mɪˈlɛnɪ·əl] *adj* milenario
millenni·um [mɪˈlɛnɪ·əm] *s* (*pl* **-ums** o **-a** [ə]) milenario, milenio
miller [ˈmɪlər] *s* molinero; (ent) polilla blanca
millet [ˈmɪlɪt] *s* mijo, millo
milliampere [ˌmɪlɪˈæmpɪr] *s* miliamperio
milligram [ˈmɪlɪˌgræm] *s* miligramo
millimeter [ˈmɪlɪˌmitər] *s* milímetro
milliner [ˈmɪlɪnər] *s* modista *mf* de sombreros
millinery [ˈmɪlɪˌnɛri] o [ˈmɪlɪnəri] *s* artículos para sombreros de señora; confección de sombreros de señora; venta de sombreros de señora
millinery shop *s* sombrerería
milling [ˈmɪlɪŋ] *s* (*of grain*) molienda; (*of coins*) acordonamiento, cordoncillo; fresado
milling machine *s* fresadora
million [ˈmɪljən] *adj* millón de, millones de ‖ *s* millón *m*
millionaire [ˌmɪljənˈɛr] *s* millonario
millionth [ˈmɪljənθ] *adj* & *s* millonésimo
millivolt [ˈmɪlɪˌvolt] *s* milivoltio
mill'pond' *s* represa de molino
mill'race' *s* caz *m*
mill'stone' *s* muela de molino; (fig) carga pesada
mill wheel *s* rueda de molino
mill'work' *s* carpintería de taller
mime [maɪm] *s* mimo *m* ‖ *tr* remedar
mimeograph [ˈmɪmɪ·əˌgræf] o [ˈmɪmɪ·əˌgrɑf] *s* (trademark) mimeógrafo ‖ *tr* mimeografiar
mim·ic [ˈmɪmɪk] *s* imitador *m*, remedador *m* ‖ *v* (*pret* & *pp* **-icked**; *ger* **-icking**) *tr* imitar, remedar
mimic·ry [ˈmɪmɪkri] *s* (*pl* **-ries**) mímica, remedo
min. *abbr* **minimum, minute**
minaret [ˌmɪnəˈrɛt] o [ˈmɪnəˌrɛt] *s* alminar *m*, minarete *m*
mince [mɪns] *tr* desmenuzar; picar (*carne*) ‖ *intr* andar remilgadamente; hablar remilgadamente
mince'meat' *s* cuajado, picadillo
mince pie *s* pastel relleno de carne picada con frutas
mind [maɪnd] *s* mente *f*, espíritu *m*; **to bear in mind** tener presente; **to be not in one's right mind** no estar en sus cabales; **to be of one mind** estar de acuerdo; **to be out of one's mind** estar fuera de juicio; **to change one's mind** mudar de parecer; **to go out of one's mind** volverse loco; **to have a mind to** tener ganas de; **to have in mind to** pensar en; **to have on one's**

mind preocuparse con; **to lose one's mind** perder el juicio; **to make up one's mind** resolverse; **to my mind** a mi parecer; **to say whatever comes into one's mind** decir lo que se le viene a la boca; **to set one's mind on** resolverse a; **to slip one's mind** escaparse de la memoria; **to speak one's mind** decir su parecer; **with one mind** unánimamente ‖ *tr* (*to take care of*) cuidar, estar al cuidado de; obedecer; fijarse en; sentir molestia por; **do you mind the smoke?** ¿le molesta el humo?; **mind your own business** no se meta Vd. en lo que no le toca ‖ *intr* tener inconveniente; tener cuidado; **never mind** no se preocupe, no se moleste
mindful [ˈmaɪndfəl] *adj* atento; **mindful of** atento a, cuidadoso de
mind reader *s* adivinador *m* del pensamiento ajeno, lector *m* mental
mind reading *s* adivinación del pensamiento ajeno, lectura de la mente
mine [maɪn] *pron poss* el mío; mío ‖ *s* mina; **to work a mine** beneficiar una mina ‖ *tr* minar; beneficiar (*un terreno*); extraer (*mineral, carbón, etc.*) ‖ *intr* minar; abrir minas
mine field *s* campo de minas
mine layer *s* buque *m* portaminas, lanzaminas *m*
miner [ˈmaɪnər] *s* minero; (mil, nav) minador *m*
mineral [ˈmɪnərəl] *adj* & *s* mineral *m*
mineralogy [ˌmɪnəˈrælədʒi] *s* mineralogía
mineral wool *s* lana de escorias
mine sweeper *s* dragaminas *m*
mingle [ˈmɪŋgəl] *tr* mezclar, confundir ‖ *intr* mezclarse; asociarse
miniature [ˈmɪnɪ·ətʃər] o [ˈmɪnɪtʃər] *s* miniatura; **to paint in miniature** miniar, pintar de miniatura
miniaturization [ˌmɪnɪ·ətʃərɪˈzeʃən] o [ˌmɪnɪtʃərɪˈzeʃən] *s* miniaturización
minimal [ˈmɪnɪməl] *adj* mínimo
minimize [ˈmɪnɪˌmaɪz] *tr* empequeñecer
minimum [ˈmɪnɪməm] *adj* & *s* mínimo
minimum wage *s* jornal mínimo
mining [ˈmaɪnɪŋ] *adj* minero ‖ *s* mineraje *m*, minería; (nav) minado
minion [ˈmɪnjən] *s* paniaguado
minion of the law *s* esbirro, polizonte *m*
miniskirt [ˈmɪnɪˌskɜrt] *s* minifalda
minister [ˈmɪnɪstər] *s* ministro; pastor *m* prostestante ‖ *tr* & *intr* ministrar
ministerial [ˌmɪnɪsˈtɪrɪ·əl] *adj* ministerial
minis·try [ˈmɪnɪstri] *s* (*pl* **-tries**) ministerio
mink [mɪŋk] *s* visón *m*
minnow [ˈmɪno] *s* pececillo; (ichth) foxino
minor [ˈmaɪnər] *adj* (*smaller*) menor; de menor importancia; (*younger*) menor de edad; (mus) menor ‖ *s* menor *m* de edad; (educ) asignatura secundaria

mi
mi

Minorca [mɪ'nɔrkə] *s* Menorca
Minorcan [mɪ'nɔrkən] *adj* & *s* menorquín *m*
minor·ty [mɪ'nɑrɪti] o [mɪ'nɔrɪti] *adj* minoritario ‖ *s* (*pl* -**ties**) (*being under age; smaller number or part*) minoría; (*less than full age*) minoridad
minstrel ['mɪnstrəl] *s* (*retainer who sang and played for his lord*) ministril *m;* (*medieval musician and poet*) juglar *m,* trovador *m;* (U.S.A.) cantor cómico disfrazado de negro
minstrel·sy ['mɪnstrəlsi] *s* (*pl* -**sies**) juglaría; compañía de juglares; poesía trovadoresca
mint [mɪnt] *s* casa de moneda; (*plant*) menta, hierbabuena; montón *m* de dinero; fuente *f* inagotable ‖ *tr* acuñar; (fig) inventar
minuet [ˌmɪnju'ɛt] *s* minué *m,* minuete *m*
minus ['maɪnəs] *adj* menos ‖ *prep* menos; falto de, sin ‖ *s* menos *m*
minute [maɪ'njut] o [maɪ'nut] *adj* diminuto, menudo ‖ ['mɪnɪt] *s* minuto; (*short space of time*) momento; **minutes** acta; **to write up the minutes** levantar acta; **up to the minute** al corriente; de última hora
minute hand ['mɪnɪt] *s* minutero
minutiae [mɪ'njuʃɪˌi] o [mɪ'nuʃɪˌi] *spl* minucias
minx [mɪŋks] *s* moza descarada
miracle ['mɪrəkəl] *s* milagro
miracle play *s* auto
miraculous [mɪ'rækjələs] *adj* milagroso
mirage [mɪ'rɑʒ] *s* espejismo
mire [maɪr] *s* fango, lodo
mirror ['mɪrər] *s* espejo; (aut) retrovisor *m* ‖ *tr* reflejar
mirth [mʌrθ] *s* alegría, regocijo
mir·y ['maɪri] *adj* (*comp* -**ier;** *super* -**iest**) fangoso, lodoso; sucio
misadventure [ˌmɪsəd'vɛntʃər] *s* desgracia, contratiempo
misanthrope ['mɪsən͵θrop] *s* misántropo
misanthropy [mɪs'ænθrəpi] *s* misantropía
misapprehension [ˌmɪsæprɪ'hɛnʃən] *s* malentendido
misappropriation [ˌmɪsə͵proprɪ'eʃən] *s* malversación
misbehave [ˌmɪsbɪ'hev] *intr* conducirse mal, portarse mal
misbehavior [ˌmɪsbɪ'hevɪ·ər] *s* mala conducta, mal comportamiento
misc. *abbr* **miscellaneous, miscellany**
miscalculation [ˌmɪskælkjə'leʃən] *s* mal cálculo
miscarriage [mɪs'kærɪdʒ] *s* aborto, malparto; fracaso, malogro; (*of a letter*) extravío
miscar·ry [mɪs'kæri] *v* (*pret* & *pp* -**ried**) *intr* abortar, malparir; malograrse; extraviarse (*una carta*)
miscellaneous [ˌmɪsə'lenɪ·əs] *adj* misceláneo
miscella·ny ['mɪsə͵leni] *s* (*pl* -**nies**) miscelánea
mischief ['mɪstʃɪf] *s* (*harm*) daño,

mal *m;* (*disposition to annoy*) malicia; (*prankishness*) travesura
mis'chief-mak'er *s* malsín *m,* cizañero
mischievous ['mɪstʃɪvəs] *adj* dañoso, malo; malicioso; travieso
misconception [ˌmɪskən'sɛpʃən] *s* concepto erróneo, mala interpretación
misconduct [mɪs'kɑndəkt] *s* mala conducta
misconstrue [ˌmɪskən'stru] o [mɪs'kɑnstru] *tr* interpretar mal
miscount [mɪs'kaunt] *s* cuenta errónea ‖ *tr* & *intr* contar mal
miscue [mɪs'kju] *s* (*in billiards*) pifia; (*slip*) pifia ‖ *intr* pifiar; (theat) equivocarse de apunte
mis·deal ['mɪs͵dil] *s* repartición errónea ‖ [mɪs'dil] *v* (*pret* & *pp* -**dealt** ['dɛlt]) *tr* & *intr* repartir mal
misdeed [mɪs'did] o ['mɪs͵did] *s* malhecho, fechoría
misdemeanor [ˌmɪsdɪ'minər] *s* mala conducta; (law) delito de menor cuantía
misdirect [ˌmɪsdɪ'rɛkt] o [ˌmɪsdaɪ'rɛkt] *tr* dirigir erradamente; hacer perder el camino
misdoing [mɪs'du·ɪŋ] *s* mala acción
miser ['maɪzər] *s* avaro, verrugo
miserable ['mɪzərəbəl] *adj* miserable; (coll) achacoso, indispuesto
miserly ['maɪzərli] *adj* avariento, mezquino
miser·y ['mɪzəri] *s* (*pl* -**ies**) miseria
misfeasance [mɪs'fizəns] *s* (law) fraude *m*
misfire [mɪs'faɪr] *s* falla de tiro; (*of internal-combustion engine*) falla de encendido ‖ *intr* fallar (*un arma de fuego, el encendido de un motor*)
mis·fit ['mɪs͵fɪt] *s* vestido mal cortado; cosa que no encaja bien; persona mal adaptada a su ambiente ‖ [mɪs'fɪt] *v* (*pret* & *pp* -**fitted;** *ger* -**fitting**) *tr* & *intr* encajar mal, sentar mal
misfortune [mɪs'fɔrtʃən] *s* desgracia
misgiving [mɪs'gɪvɪŋ] *s* mal presentimiento, rescoldo
misgovern [mɪs'gʌvərn] *tr* desgobernar
misguidance [mɪs'gaɪdəns] *s* error *m,* extravío
misguided [mɪs'gaɪdɪd] *adj* descarriado, malaconsejado
mishap ['mɪshæp] o [mɪs'hæp] *s* accidente *m,* percance *m*
misinform [ˌmɪsɪn'fɔrm] *tr* dar informes erróneos a
misinterpret [ˌmɪsɪn'tɜrprɪt] *tr* interpretar mal
misjudge [mɪs'dʒʌdʒ] *tr* & *intr* juzgar mal
mis·lay [mɪs'le] *v* (*pret* & *pp* -**laid** [͵led]) *tr* extraviar, perder; (*among one's papers*) traspapelar
mis·lead [mɪs'lid] *v* (*pret* & *pp* -**led** [͵led]) *tr* (*to lead astray*) extraviar, descaminar; (*to lead into wrongdoing*) seducir, inducir al mal; (*to deceive*) engañar
misleading [mɪs'lidɪŋ] *adj* engañoso
mismanagement [mɪs'mænɪdʒmənt] *s* mala administración, desgobierno

misnomer [mɪs'nomər] *s* nombre impropio, mal nombre
misplace [mɪs'ples] *tr* colocar fuera de su lugar; colocar mal; (*to mislay*) (coll) extraviar, perder
misprint ['mɪs,prɪnt] *s* errata de imprenta || [mɪs'prɪnt] *tr* imprimir con erratas
mispronounce [,mɪsprə'nauns] *tr* pronunciar mal
mispronunciation [,mɪsprə,nʌnsɪ'eʃən] o [,mɪsprə,nʌn/ɪ'eʃən] *s* pronunciación incorrecta
misquote [mɪs'kwot] *tr* citar equivocadamente
misrepresent [,mɪsreprɪ'zɛnt] *tr* tergiversar
miss [mɪs] *s* falta, error *m*; fracaso, malogro; tiro errado; jovencita, muchacha || *tr* echar de menos; perder (*el tren, la función, la oportunidad*); errar (*el blanco; la vocación*); no entender, no comprender; omitir; no ver; no dar con, no encontrar; librarse de (*p.ej., la muerte*); escapársele a uno, p.ej., **I missed what you said** se me escapó lo que dijo Vd.; por poco, p.ej., **the car missed hitting me** el coche por poco me atropella || *intr* fallar; errar el blanco; malograrse || **Miss** *s* señorita
missal ['mɪsəl] *s* misal *m*
misshapen [mɪs'/epən] *adj* deforme, contrahecho
missile ['mɪsɪl] *adj* arrojadizo || *s* arma arrojadiza; proyectil *m*; proyectil dirigido
missing ['mɪsɪŋ] *adj* extraviado, perdido; desaparecido; ausente; **to be missing** hacer falta; haber desaparecido
missing link *s* hombre *m* mono
missing persons *spl* desaparecidos
mission ['mɪ/ən] *s* misión; casa de misión
missionar·y ['mɪ/ən,ɛri] *adj* misional || *s* (*pl* **-ies**) (*one sent to work to propagate his faith*) misionario, misionero; (*on a political or diplomatic mission*) misionario
missive ['mɪsɪv] *adj* misivo || *s* misiva
mis·spell [mɪs'spɛl] *v* (*pret & pp* **-spelled** o **-spelt** ['spɛlt]) *tr & intr* deletrear mal, escribir mal
misspelling [mɪs'spɛlɪŋ] *s* falta de ortografía
misspent [mɪs'spɛnt] *adj* malgastado
misstatement [mɪs'stetmənt] *s* relación equivocada, relación falsa
misstep [mɪs'stɛp] *s* paso falso; (*slip in conduct*) resbalón *m*
miss·y ['mɪsi] *s* (*pl* **-ies**) (coll) señorita
mist [mɪst] *s* neblina; (*of tears*) velo; (*fine spray*) vapor *m*
mis·take [mɪs'tek] *s* error *m*, equivocación; **and no mistake** sin duda alguna; **by mistake** por descuido; **to make a mistake** equivocarse || *v* (*pret* **-took** ['tuk]; *pp* **-taken**) *tr* tomar (*por otro; por lo que no es*); entender mal; **to be mistaken for** equivocarse con
mistaken [mɪs'tekən] *adj* (*person*)

equivocado; (*idea*) erróneo; (*act*) desacertado
mistakenly [mɪs'tekənli] *adv* equivocadamente, por error
mistletoe ['mɪsəl,to] *s* (*Viscum album*) muérdago; (*Phoradendron flavescens, used in Christmas decorations in the U.S.A.*) cabellera
mistreat [mɪs'trit] *tr* maltratar
mistreatment [mɪs'tritmənt] *s* maltratamiento
mistress ['mɪstrɪs] *s* (*of a household*) ama, dueña; moza, querida, manceba; (Brit) maestra de escuela
mistrial [mɪs'traɪ·əl] *s* pleito viciado de nulidad
mistrust [mɪs'trʌst] *s* desconfianza || *tr* desconfiar de || *intr* desconfiar
mistrustful [mɪs'trʌstfəl] *adj* desconfiado
mist·y ['mɪsti] *adj* (*comp* **-ier**; *super* **-iest**) brumoso, neblinoso; indistinto
misunder·stand [,mɪsʌndər'stænd] *v* (*pret & pp* **-stood** ['stud]) *tr* no comprender, entender mal
misunderstanding [,mɪsʌndər'stændɪŋ] *s* malentendido; (*disagreement*) desavenencia
misuse [mɪs'jus] *s* abuso, mal uso; (*of funds*) malversación || [mɪs'juz] *tr* abusar de, emplear mal; malversar (*fondos*)
misword [mɪs'wʌrd] *tr* redactar mal
mite [maɪt] *s* (*small contribution*) óbolo; (*small amount*) pizca; (ent) ácaro
miter ['maɪtər] *s* mitra; (carp) inglete *m* || *tr* cortar ingletes en; juntar con junta a inglete
miter box *s* caja de ingletes
mitigate ['mɪtɪ,get] *tr* mitigar, atenuar, paliar
mitten ['mɪtən] *s* confortante *m*, mitón *m*
mix [mɪks] *tr* mezclar; amasar (*una torta*); aderezar (*ensalada*); **to mix up** equivocar, confundir || *intr* mezclarse; asociarse
mixed [mɪkst] *adj* mixto, mezclado; (*e.g., candy*) variados; (coll) confundido
mixed company *s* reunión de personas de ambos sexos
mixed drink *s* bebida mezclada
mixed feeling *s* concepto vacilante
mixer ['mɪksər] *s* (*of concrete*) mezcladora, hormigonera; **to be a good mixer** (coll) tener don de gentes
mixture ['mɪkst/ər] *s* mezcla, mixtura
mix·'up *s* confusión; enredo, lío; (*of people*) equivocación
mizzen ['mɪzən] *s* mesana
mo. *abbr* **month**
M.O. *abbr* **money order**
moan [mon] *s* gemido || *intr* gemir
moat [mot] *s* foso
mob [mɑb] *s* chusma, populacho; (*crowd bent on violence*) muchedumbre airada || *v* (*pret & pp* **mobbed**; *ger* **mobbing**) *tr* asaltar, atropellar
mobile ['mobɪl] o ['mobil] *adj* móvil
mobility [mo'bɪlɪti] *s* movilidad

mobilization [ˌmobɪlɪˈzeʃən] s movilización

mobilize [ˈmobɪˌlaɪz] tr movilizar ‖ intr movilizar, movilizarse

mob rule s gobierno del populacho

mobster [ˈmɑbstər] s (slang) gamberro, pandillero

moccasin [ˈmɑkəsɪn] s mocasín m

Mocha coffee [ˈmokə] s moca m, café m de moca

mock [mɑk] adj simulado, fingido ‖ s burla, mofa ‖ tr burlarse de, mofarse de; despreciar; engañar ‖ intr mofarse; **to mock at** mofarse de

mocker·y [ˈmɑkəri] s (pl -ies) burla, mofa, escarnio; (subject of derision) hazmerreír m; (poor imitation) mal remedo; (e.g., of justice) negación

mock'ing·bird' s burlón m, sinsonte m

mock orange s jeringuilla, celinda

mock privet s olivillo

mock turtle soup s sopa de cabeza de ternera

mock'-up' s maqueta

mode [mod] s modo, manera; (fashion) moda; (gram) modo

mod·el [ˈmɑdəl] adj modelo, p.ej., **model city** ciudad modelo ‖ s modelo ‖ v (pret & pp -eled o -elled; ger -eling o -elling) tr (to fashion in clay, wax, etc.) modelar ‖ intr modelarse; servir de modelo

model airplane s aeromodelo

mod'el-air'plane builder s aeromodelista mf

model-airplane building s aeromodelismo

model sailing s navegación de modelos a vela

moderate [ˈmɑdərɪt] adj moderado; (tiempo) templado; (precio) módico ‖ [ˈmɑdəˌret] tr moderar; presidir (una asamblea) ‖ intr moderarse

moderator [ˈmɑdəˌretər] s (over an assembly) presidente m; (mediator) árbitro; (for slowing down neutrons) moderador m

modern [ˈmɑdərn] adj moderno

modernize [ˈmɑdərˌnaɪz] tr modernizar

modest [ˈmɑdɪst] adj modesto

modes·ty [ˈmɑdɪsti] s (pl -ties) modestia

modicum [ˈmɑdɪkəm] s pequeña cantidad

modifier [ˈmɑdɪˌfaɪ·ər] s (gram) modificante m

modi·fy [ˈmɑdɪˌfaɪ] v (pret & pp -fied) tr modificar

modish [ˈmodɪʃ] adj de moda, elegante

modulate [ˈmɑdʒəˌlet] tr & intr modular

modulation [ˌmɑdʒəˈleʃən] s modulación

mohair [ˈmoˌher] s mohair m (pelo de cabra de Angora)

Mohammedan [moˈhæmɪdən] adj & s mahometano

Mohammedanism [moˈhæmɪdəˌnɪzəm] s mahometismo

moist [mɔɪst] adj húmedo, mojado; (weather) lluvioso; (eyes) lagrimoso

moisten [ˈmɔɪsən] tr humedecer ‖ intr humedecerse

moisture [ˈmɔɪstʃər] s humedad

molar [ˈmolər] s diente m molar

molasses [məˈlæsɪz] s melaza

molasses candy s melcocha

mold [mold] s molde m; cosa moldeada; (shape) forma; (fungus) moho; (humus) mantillo; (fig) carácter m, índole f ‖ tr amoldar, moldear; (to make moldy) enmohecer ‖ intr enmohecerse

molder [ˈmoldər] s moldeador m ‖ intr convertirse en polvo, consumirse

molding [ˈmoldɪŋ] s moldeado; (cornice, shaped strip of wood, etc.) moldura

mold·y [ˈmoldi] adj (comp -ier; super -iest) (overgrown with mold) mohoso; (stale) rancio, pasado

mole [mol] s (breakwater) rompeolas m; (inner harbor) dársena; (spot on skin) lunar m; (small mammal) topo

molecule [ˈmɑlɪˌkjul] s molécula

mole'hill' s topinera

mole'skin' s piel f de topo, molesquina

molest [məˈlest] tr molestar; faltar al respeto a (una mujer)

moll [mɑl] s (slang) mujer f del hampa; (slang) ramera

molli·fy [ˈmɑlɪˌfaɪ] v (pret & pp -fied) tr apaciguar, aplacar

mollusk [ˈmɑləsk] s molusco

mollycoddle [ˈmɑlɪˌkɑdəl] s mantecón m, marica m ‖ tr consentir, mimar

molt [molt] s muda ‖ intr hacer la muda

molten [ˈmoltən] adj fundido, derretido; fundido, vaciado

molybdenum [məˈlɪbdɪnəm] o [ˌmɑlɪbˈdinəm] s molibdeno

moment [ˈmomənt] s momento; **at any moment** de un momento a otro

momentary [ˈmomənˌteri] adj momentáneo

momentous [moˈmentəs] adj importante, grave

momen·tum [moˈmentəm] s (pl -tums o -ta [tə]) ímpetu m; (mech) cantidad de movimiento

monarch [ˈmɑnərk] s monarca m

monarchic(al) [məˈnɑrkɪk(əl)] adj monárquico

monarchist [ˈmɑnərkɪst] adj & s monárquico, monarquista mf

monar·chy [ˈmɑnərki] s (pl -chies) monarquía

monaster·y [ˈmɑnəsˌteri] s (pl -ies) monasterio

monastic [məˈnæstɪk] adj monástico

monasticism [məˈnæstɪˌsɪzəm] s monaquismo

Monday [ˈmʌndi] s lunes m

monetary [ˈmɑnɪˌteri] adj monetario; pecuniario

money [ˈmʌni] s dinero; **to make money** ganar dinero; dar dinero (una empresa)

mon'ey·bag' s monedero, talega; **moneybags** (wealth) (coll) talegas; (wealthy person) (coll) ricacho

moneychanger ['mʌni ˌtʃendʒər] s cambista *mf*

moneyed ['mʌnid] *adj* adinerado

moneylender ['mʌni ˌlendər] s prestamista *mf*

mon'ey·mak'er s acaudalador *m;* (fig) manantial *m* de beneficios

money order s giro postal

Mongol ['maŋgəl] o ['maŋgal] *adj* & s mogol *mf*

Mongolian [maŋ'goli·ən] *adj* & s mogol *mf*

mon·goose ['maŋgus] s (*pl* -gooses) mangosta

mongrel ['mʌŋgrəl] o ['maŋgrəl] *adj* & s mestizo

monitor ['manɪtər] s monitor *m* || *tr* controlar (*la señal*); escuchar (*radiotransmisiones*); superentender

monk [mʌŋk] s monje *m*

monkey ['mʌŋki] s mono; **to make a monkey of** tomar el pelo a || *intr* — **to monkey around** haraganear; **to monkey with** ajar, manosear

mon'key·shine' s (slang) monería, monada, payasada

monkey wrench s llave inglesa

monkhood ['mʌŋkhʊd] s monacato; los monjes

monkshood ['mʌŋks·hʊd] s cogulla de fraile

monocle ['manəkəl] s monóculo

monogamy [mə'nagəmi] s monogamia

monogram ['manə ˌgræm] s monograma *m*

monograph ['manə ˌgræf] o ['manə ˌgraf] s monografía

monolithic [ˌmanə'lɪθɪk] *adj* monolítico

monologue ['manə ˌlɔg] o ['manə ˌlag] s monólogo

monomania [ˌmanə'meni·ə] s monomanía

monomial [mə'nomi·əl] s monomio

monopolize [mə'napə ˌlaɪz] *tr* monopolizar; acaparar (*p.ej., la conversación*)

monopo·ly [mə'napəli] s (*pl* -lies) monopolio

monorail ['manə ˌrel] s monorriel *m*

monosyllable ['manə ˌsɪləbəl] s monosílabo

monotheist ['manə ˌθi·ɪst] *adj* & s monoteísta *mf*

monotonous [mə'natənəs] *adj* monótono

monotony [mə'natəni] s monotonía

monotype ['manə ˌtaɪp] s (*machine; method*) monotipia; (*machine*) monotipo

monotype operator s monotipista *mf*

monoxide [ma'naksaɪd] s monóxido

monseigneur [ˌmansen'jœr] s monseñor *m*

monsignor [man'sinjər] s (*pl* **monsignors** o **monsignori** [ˌmɔnsi'njori]) (eccl) monseñor *m*

monsoon [man'sun] s monsón *m*

monster ['manstər] *adj* monstruoso || s monstruo

monstrance ['manstrəns] s custodia, ostensorio

monstrosi·ty [man'strasɪti] s (*pl* -ties) monstruosidad

monstrous ['manstrəs] *adj* monstruoso

month [mʌnθ] s mes *m*

month·ly ['mʌnθli] *adj* mensual || *adv* mensualmente || s (*pl* -lies) revista mensual; **monthlies** (coll) reglas

monument ['manjəmənt] s monumento

moo [mu] s mugido || *intr* mugir

mood [mud] s humor *m,* genio; (gram) modo; **moods** accesos de mal humor

mood·y ['mudi] *adj* (*comp* -ier; *super* -iest) triste, hosco, melancólico; caprichoso, veleidoso

moon [mun] s luna

moon'beam' s rayo lunar

moon'light' s claror *m* de luna, luz *f* de la luna

moon'light'ing s multiempleo, pluriempleo

moon'sail' s (naut) monterilla

moon'shine' s luz *f* de la luna; (*idle talk*) cháchara, música celestial; (coll) whisky destilado ilegalmente

moon shot s lanzamiento a la Luna

moor [mʊr] s brezal *m,* páramo || *tr* (naut) amarrar || *intr* (naut) echar las amarras || **Moor** s moro

Moorish ['mʊrɪʃ] *adj* moro

moor'land' s brezal *m*

moose [mus] s (*pl* moose) alce *m* de América

moot [mut] *adj* discutible, dudoso

mop [map] s aljofifa, fregasuelos *m,* estropajo; (*of hair*) espesura || *v* (*pret* & *pp* mopped; *ger* mopping) *tr* aljofifar; enjuagarse (*la frente con un pañuelo*); **to mop up** limpiar de enemigos

mope [mop] *intr* andar abatido, entregarse a la melancolía

mopish ['mopɪʃ] *adj* abatido, melancólico

moral ['marəl] o ['mɔrəl] *adj* moral || s (*of a fable*) moraleja, moral *f*; **morals** (*ethics; conduct*) moral *f*

moral certainty s evidencia moral

morale [mo'ræl] o [mo'ral] s moral *f* (*estado de ánimo, confianza en sí mismo*)

morali·ty [mə'rælɪti] s (*pl* -ties) moralidad

morals charge s acusación por delito sexual

morass [mə'ræs] s pantano

moratori·um [ˌmɔrə'tori·əm] o [ˌmarə'tori·əm] s (*pl* -ums o -a [ə]) s moratoria

morbid ['mɔrbɪd] *adj* (*feelings, curiosity*) malsano; (*gruesome*) horripilante; (*pertaining to disease; pathologic*) morboso

mordacious [mɔr'deʃəs] *adj* mordaz

mordant ['mɔrdənt] *adj* mordaz || s mordiente *m*

more [mor] *adj* & *adv* más; **more and more** cada vez más; **more than** más que; (*followed by numeral*) más de; (*followed by verb*) más de lo que || s más *m*

more·o'ver *adv* además, por otra parte

Moresque [moˈresk] *adj* moro; (archit) árabe ‖ *s* estilo árabe

morgue [mɔrg] *s* depósito de cadáveres

moribund [ˈmɔrɪˌbʌnd] o [ˈmɑrɪˌbʌnd] *adj* moribundo

Moris·co [məˈrɪsko] *adj* morisco, moro ‖ *s* (*pl* **-cos** o **-coes**) moro; moro de España; (*offspring of mulatto and Spaniard, in Mexico*) morisco

morning [ˈmɔrnɪŋ] *adj* matinal ‖ *s* mañana; (*time between midnight and dawn*) madrugada; **in the morning** de mañana, por la mañana

morning coat *s* chaqué *m*

morn'ing-glo'ry *s* (*pl* **-ries**) dondiego de día

morning sickness *s* vómitos del embarazo

morning star *s* lucero del alba

Moroccan [məˈrɑkən] *adj* & *s* marroquí *mf* o marroquín *m*

morocco [məˈrɑko] *s* (*leather*) marroquí *m* o marroquín *m* ‖ **Morocco** *s* Marruecos *m*

moron [ˈmɔrɑn] *s* (*person of arrested intelligence*) morón *m*; (coll) imbécil *mf*

morose [məˈros] *adj* adusto, hosco, malhumorado

morphine [ˈmɔrfin] *s* morfina

morphology [mɔrˈfɑlədʒi] *s* morfología

Morris chair [ˈmɑrɪs] o [ˈmɔrɪs] *s* poltrona extensible

morrow [ˈmɑro] o [ˈmɔro] *s* (*future time*) mañana *m*; (*time following some event*) día *m* siguiente; **on the morrow** en el día de mañana; el día siguiente

morsel [ˈmɔrsəl] *s* bocadito; pedacito

mortal [ˈmɔrtəl] *adj* & *s* mortal *m*

mortality [mɔrˈtælɪti] *s* mortalidad; (*death or destruction on a large scale*) mortandad

mortar [ˈmɔrtər] *s* (*bowl used for crushing; mixture of lime, etc.*) mortero; (arti) mortero

mor'tar·board' *s* esparavel *m*; gorro académico cuadrado

mortgage [ˈmɔrgɪdʒ] *s* hipoteca ‖ *tr* hipotecar

mortgagee [ˌmɔrgɪˈdʒi] *s* acreedor hipotecario

mortgagor [ˈmɔrgɪdʒər] *s* deudor hipotecario

mortician [mɔrˈtɪʃən] *s* empresario de pompas fúnebres

morti·fy [ˈmɔrtɪˌfaɪ] *v* (*pret* & *pp* **-fied**) *tr* humillar; mortificar (*el cuerpo, las pasiones*); **to be mortified** avergonzarse

mortise [ˈmɔrtɪs] *s* mortaja, muesca ‖ *tr* amortajar, enmuescar

mortise lock *s* cerradura embutida

mortuar·y [ˈmɔrtʃʊˌɛri] *adj* mortuorio ‖ *s* (*pl* **-ies**) depósito de cadáveres; funeraria

mosaic [moˈze·ɪk] *m* mosaico

Moscow [ˈmɑskau] o [ˈmɑsko] *s* Moscú

Moses [ˈmozɪz] o [ˈmozɪs] *s* Moisés *m*

Mos·lem [ˈmɑzləm] o [ˈmɑsləm] *adj* muslime, musulmán ‖ *s* (*pl* **-lems** o **-lem**) muslime *mf*, musulmán *m*

mosque [mɑsk] *s* mezquita

mosqui·to [məsˈkito] *s* (*pl* **-toes** o **-tos**) mosquito

mosquito net *s* mosquitero

moss [mɔs] o [mɑs] *s* musgo

moss'back' *s* (coll) reaccionario; (*old-fashioned person*) (coll) fósil *m*

moss·y [ˈmɔsi] o [ˈmɑsi] *adj* (*comp* **-ier**; *super* **-iest**) musgoso

most [most] *adj* más; la mayor parte de, los más de ‖ *adv* más; muy, sumamente; (coll) casi ‖ *s* la mayor parte, el mayor número, los más; **most of** la mayor parte de, el mayor número de; **to make the most of** sacar el mejor partido de

mostly [ˈmostli] *adv* por la mayor parte, mayormente; casi

moth [mɔθ] o [mɑθ] *s* mariposa nocturna; (*clothes moth*) polilla

moth ball *s* bola de alcanfor, bola de naftalina

moth'-ball' fleet *s* (nav) flota en conserva

moth'-eat'en *adj* apolillado; (fig) anticuado

mother [ˈmʌðər] *adj* (*love*) materna'; (*tongue*) materno; (*country*) madre; (*church*) metropolitano ‖ *s* madre *f*; (*an elderly woman*) (coll) tía ‖ *tr* servir de madre a

mother country *s* madre patria

Mother Goose *s* supuesta autora o narradora de una colección de cuentos infantiles (in Spain: *Cuentos de Calleja*)

motherhood [ˈmʌðərˌhʊd] *s* maternidad

moth'er-in-law' *s* (*pl* **mothers-in-law**) suegra

moth'er·land' *s* patria

motherless [ˈmʌðərlɪs] *adj* huérfano de madre, sin madre

motherly [ˈmʌðərli] *adj* maternal

mother-of-pearl [ˈmʌðərəvˈpʌrl] *adj* nacarado ‖ *s* nácar *m*

Mother's Day *s* día *m* de la madre

mother superior *s* superiora

mother tongue *s* (*language naturally acquired by reason of nationality*) lengua materna; (*language from which another language is derived*) lengua madre, lengua matriz

mother wit *s* gracia natural, chispa

moth hole *s* apolilladura

moth·y [ˈmɔθi] o [ˈmɑθi] *adj* (*comp* **-ier**; *super* **-iest**) apolillado

motif [moˈtif] *s* motivo

motion [ˈmoʃən] *s* movimiento; (*signal, gesture*) seña, indicación; (*in a deliberating assembly*) moción ‖ *intr* hacer señas con la mano o la cabeza

motionless [ˈmoʃənlɪs] *adj* inmoble

motion picture *s* película cinematográfica

mo'tion-pic'ture *adj* cinematográfico

motivate [ˈmotɪˌvet] *tr* animar, incitar, mover

motive [ˈmotɪv] *adj* (*promoting action*) motivo; (*producing motion*) motor ‖ *s* motivo

motive power *s* fuerza motriz, potencia

motora o motriz; (rr) conjunto de locomotoras de un ferrocarril
motley ['mɑtli] adj abigarrado; mezclado, variado
motor ['motər] adj motor ‖ s motor m; motor eléctrico; automóvil m ‖ intr viajar en automóvil
mo′tor·boat′ s gasolinera, canoa automóvil
mo′tor·bus′ s autobús m
motorcade ['motər,ked] s caravana de automóviles
mo′tor·car′ s automóvil m
mo′tor·cy′cle s motocicleta
motorist ['motərɪst] s motorista mf, automovilista mf
motorize ['motə,raɪz] tr motorizar
motor launch s lancha automóvil
motor·man ['motərmən] s (pl -men [mən]) conductor m de tranvía, conductor de locomotora eléctrica
motor sailer ['selər] s motovelero
motor scooter s motoneta
motor ship s motonave f
motor truck s autocamión m
motor vehicle s vehículo motor, autovehículo
mottle ['mɑtəl] tr abigarrar, jaspear, motear
mot·to ['mɑto] s (pl -toes o -tos) lema m, divisa
mould [mold] s, tr, & intr var de **mold**
moulder ['moldər] s & intr var de **molder**
moulding ['moldɪŋ] s var de **molding**
mouldy ['moldi] adj var de **moldy**
mound [maʊnd] s montón m de tierra; montecillo
mount [maʊnt] s (hill, mountain) monte m; (horse for riding) montura; (setting for a jewel) montadura; soporte m; cartón m, tela (en que está pegada una fotografía); (mach) montaje m ‖ tr subir (una escalera, una cuesta); subir a (una plataforma); escalar (una muralla); montar (un servicio; una piedra preciosa); poner a caballo; pegar (vistas, pruebas); (mil) montar (la guardia) ‖ intr montar, montarse; aumentar, subir (los precios)
mountain ['maʊntən] s montaña; **to make a mountain out of a molehill** hacer de una pulga un camello
mountain climbing s alpinismo, montañismo
mountaineer [,maʊntə'nɪr] s montañés m
mountainous ['maʊntənəs] adj montañoso
mountain railroad s ferrocarril m de cremallera
mountain range s cordillera, sierra
mountain sickness s mal m de las montañas
mountebank ['maʊntɪ,bæŋk] s saltabanco
mounting ['maʊntɪŋ] s (of a precious stone, of an astronomical instrument) montura; papel m de soporte; papel o tela (en que está pegada una fotografía); (mach) montaje m
mourn [morn] tr llorar (p.ej., la muerte

de una persona); lamentar (una desgracia) ‖ intr lamentarse; vestir de luto
mourner ['mornər] s doliente mf; (person who makes a public profession of penitence) penitente mf; (person hired to attend a funeral) plañidera; **mourners** duelo
mourners′ bench s banco de los penitentes
mournful ['mornfəl] adj (sorrowful) doloroso; (gloomy) lúgubre
mourning ['mornɪŋ] s luto; **to be in mourning** estar de luto
mourning band s crespón m fúnebre, brazal m de luto
mouse [maʊs] s (pl mice [maɪs]) ratón m
mouse′hole′ s ratonera
mouser ['maʊzər] s desmurador m
mouse′trap′ s ratonera
moustache [məs'tæʃ] o [məs'tɑʃ] s bigote m, mostacho
mouth [maʊθ] s (pl mouths [maʊðz]) boca; (of a river) desembocadura, embocadura; **by mouth** por vía bucal; **to be born with a silver spoon in one′s mouth** nacer de pie; **to make one′s mouth water** hacérsele a uno la boca agua; **to not open one′s mouth** no decir esta boca es mía
mouthful ['maʊθ,fʊl] s bocado
mouth organ s armónica de boca
mouth′piece′ s (of wind instrument) boquilla; (of bridle) embocadura; (spokesman) portavoz m
mouth′wash′ s enjuague m, enjuagadientes m
movable ['muvəbəl] adj movible, móvil
move [muv] s movimiento; (démarche) acción, gestión, paso; (from one house to another) mudanza; **on the move** en marcha, en movimiento; **to get a move on** (slang) menearse, darse prisa; **to make a move** dar un paso; hacer una jugada ‖ tr mover; evacuar (el vientre); (to stir, excite the feelings of) conmover, enternecer; **to move up** adelantar (una fecha) ‖ intr moverse; desplazarse (un viajante; un planeta); mudarse, mudar de casa; (e.g., to another store, to another city) trasladarse; hacer una jugada; hacer una moción; venderse, tener salida (una mercancía); evacuarse, moverse (el vientre); **to move away** apartarse; marcharse; mudarse de casa; **to move in** instalarse; alternar con, frecuentar (la buena sociedad); **to move off** alejarse
movement ['muvmənt] s movimiento; aparato de relojería; (of the bowels) evacuación; (e.g., of a symphony) tiempo
movie ['muvi] s (coll) película, cinta
movie·goer ['muvi,go·ər] s (coll) aficionado al cine
movie house s (coll) cineteatro
mov′ie·land′ s (coll) cinelandia
moving ['muvɪŋ] adj conmovedor, impresionante ‖ s movimiento; (from one house to another) mudanza

moving picture *s* película cinematográfica

moving spirit *s* alma *(de una empresa)*

moving stairway *s* escalera mecánica), móvil o rodante

mow [mo] *v (pret* **mowed**; *pp* **mowed** o **mown**) *tr* segar; **to mow down** matar *(soldados)* con fuego graneado ‖ *intr* segar

mower ['mo·ər] *s* segador *m*; segadora mecánica

mowing machine *s* segadora mecánica

Mozarab [mo'zærəb] *s* mozárabe *mf*

Mozarabic [mo'zærəbɪk] *adj* mozárabe

M.P. *abbr* **Member of Parliament, Military Police**

m.p.h. *abbr* **miles per hour**

Mr. ['mɪstər] *s (pl* **Messrs.** ['mesərz]) señor *m (tratamiento)*

Mrs. ['mɪsɪz] *s* señora *(tratamiento)*

MS. o **ms.** *abbr* **manuscript**

Mt. *abbr* **Mount**

much [mʌtʃ] *adj & pron* mucho; **too much** demasiado ‖ *adv* mucho; **however much** por mucho que; **how much** cuánto; **too much** demasiado; **very much** muchísimo

mucilage ['mjusɪlɪdʒ] *s* goma para pegar; *(gummy secretion in plants)* mucílago

muck [mʌk] *s* estiércol húmedo; suciedad, porquería; (min) zafra

muck'rake' *intr* (coll) exponer ruindades

mucous ['mjukəs] *adj* mucoso

mucus ['mjukəs] *s* moco

mud [mʌd] *s* barro, fango, lodo; **to sling mud at** llenar de fango

muddle ['mʌdəl] *s* confusión, embrollo ‖ *tr* confundir, embrollar; atontar, aturdir ‖ *intr* obrar torpemente; **to muddle through** salir del paso a pesar suyo

mud'dle·head' *s* farraguista *mf*, cajón *m* de sastre

mud·dy ['mʌdi] *adj (comp* **-dier**; *super* **-diest**) barroso, fangoso, lodoso; *(obscure)* turbio ‖ *v (pret & pp* **-died**) *tr* embarrar, enturbiar

mud'guard' *s* guardabarros *m*

mud'hole' *s* atolladero, ciénaga

mudslinger ['mʌd,slɪŋər] *s* (fig) lanzador *m* de lodo

muezzin [mju'ɛzɪn] *s* almuecín *m*, almuédano

muff [mʌf] *s* manguito ‖ *tr & intr* chapucear

muffin ['mʌfɪn] *s* mollete *m*

muffle ['mʌfəl] *tr* arropar; *(about the face)* embozar; amortiguar *(un ruido)*; enfundar *(un tambor)*

muffler ['mʌflər] *s* bufanda, tapaboca; (aut) silenciador *m*, silencioso

mufti ['mʌfti] *s* traje *m* de paisano

mug [mʌg] *s* pichel *m*; (slang) jeta, hocico ‖ *v (pret & pp* **mugged**; *ger* **mugging**) *tr* (slang) fotografiar; (slang) atacar ‖ *intr* (slang) hacer muecas

mug·gy ['mʌgi] *adj (comp* **-gier**; *super* **-giest**) bochornoso, sofocante

mulat·to [mju'læto] o [mə'læto] *s (pl* **-toes**) mulato

mulber·ry ['mʌl,bɛri] *s (pl* **-ries**) *(tree)* moral *m; (fruit)* mora

mulct [mʌlkt] *tr* defraudar

mule [mjul] *s* mulo, macho; *(slipper)* babucha

mule chair *s* artolas, jamugas

muleteer [,mjulə'tɪr] *s* mulatero

mulish ['mjulɪʃ] *adj* terco, obstinado

mull [mʌl] *tr* calentar *(vino)* con especias ‖ *intr* — **to mull over** reflexionar sobre

mullion ['mʌljən] *s* parteluz *m*

multigraph ['mʌlti,græf] o ['mʌlti,graf] *s* (trademark) multígrafo ‖ *tr* multigrafiar

multilateral [,mʌlti'lætərəl] *adj (having many sides)* multilátero; *(participated in by more than two nations)* multilateral

multiple ['mʌltɪpəl] *adj* múltiple, múltiplo ‖ *s* (math) múltiplo

multiplici·ty [,mʌlti'plɪsɪti] *s (pl* **-ties**) multiplicidad

multi·ply ['mʌlti,plaɪ] *v (pret & pp* **-plied**) *tr* multiplicar ‖ *intr* multiplicar, multiplicarse

multitude ['mʌlti,tjud] o ['mʌlti,tud] *s* multitud

mum [mʌm] *adj* callado; **mum's the word!** ¡punto en boca!; **to keep mum about** callar ‖ *interj* ¡chitón!

mumble ['mʌmbəl] *tr & intr* mascullar, mascujar

mummer·y ['mʌməri] *s (pl* **-ies**) mojiganga

mum·my ['mʌmi] *s (pl* **-mies**) momia

mumps [mʌmps] *s* papera

munch [mʌntʃ] *tr* ronzar

mundane ['mʌnden] *adj* mundano

municipal [mju'nɪsɪpəl] *adj* municipal

municipali·ty [mju,nɪsɪ'pælɪti] *s (pl* **-ties**) municipio

munificent [mju'nɪfɪsənt] *adj* munífico

munition [mju'nɪʃən] *s* munición ‖ *tr* municionar

munition dump *s* depósito de municiones

mural ['mjurəl] *adj* mural ‖ *s* pintura mural; decoración mural

murder ['mʌrdər] *s* asesinato, homicidio ‖ *tr* asesinar; *(to spoil, mar)* (coll) estropear

murderer ['mʌrdərər] *s* asesino

murderess ['mʌrdərɪs] *s* asesina

murderous ['mʌrdərəs] *adj* asesino; cruel, sanguinario

murk·y ['mʌrki] *adj (comp* **-ier**; *super* **-iest**) *(hazy)* calinoso; *(gloomy)* lóbrego

murmur ['mʌrmər] *s* murmullo ‖ *tr & intr* murmurar

mus. *abbr* **museum, music**

muscle ['mʌsəl] *s* músculo; (fig) fuerza muscular

muscular ['mʌskjələr] *adj* musculoso

muse [mjuz] *s* musa; **the Muses** las Musas ‖ *intr* meditar, reflexionar; **to muse on** contemplar

museum [mju'zi·əm] *s* museo

mush [mʌʃ] *s* gachas; (coll) sentimentalismo exagerado, sensiblería

mush'room' *s* hongo, seta ‖ *intr* aparecer de la noche a la mañana; **to**

mushroom into convertirse rápidamente en
mushroom cloud s nube-hongo f
mush·y ['mʌʃi] adj (comp **-ier;** super **-iest**) mollar, pulposo; (coll) sensiblero, sobón; (with women) (coll) baboso; **to be mushy** (coll) hacerse unas gachas
music ['mjuzɪk] s música; **to face the music** (coll) afrontar las consecuencias; **to set to music** poner en música
musical ['mjuzɪkəl] adj musical, músico
musical comedy s comedia musical
musicale [,mjuzɪ'kæl] s velada musical, concierto casero
music box s caja de música
music cabinet s musiquero
music hall s salón m de conciertos; (Brit) teatro de variedades
musician [mju'zɪ/ən] s músico
musicianship [mju'zɪ/ən /ɪp] s musicalidad
musicologist [,mjuzɪ'kalədʒɪst] s musicólogo
musicology [,mjuzɪ'kalədʒi] s musicología
music rack o **music stand** s atril m
musk [mʌsk] s almizcle m; olor m de almizcle
musk deer s almizclero
musket ['mʌskɪt] s mosquete m
musketeer [,mʌskɪ'tɪr] s mosquetero
musk'mel'on s melón m
musk'rat' s almizclera
muslin ['mʌzlɪn] s muselina
muss [mʌs] tr (the hair) (coll) descabellar, desarreglar; (clothing) (coll) chafar, arrugar
Mussulman ['mʌsəlmən] adj & s musulmán m
muss·y ['mʌsi] adj (comp **-ier;** super **-iest**) desaliñado, desgreñado
must [mʌst] s mosto; (mold) moho; cosa que debe hacerse || v aux **I must study my lesson** debo estudiar mi lección; **he must work tomorrow** tiene que trabajar mañana; **she must be ill** estará enferma
mustache [məs'taʃ], [məs'taʃ] o ['mʌstæʃ] s bigote m, mostacho
mustard ['mʌstərd] s mostaza
mustard plaster s sinapismo, cataplasma f
muster ['mʌstər] s asamblea; matrícula de revista; **to pass muster** pasar revista; ser aceptable || tr llamar a

asamblea; reunir para pasar revista; reunir, acumular; **to muster in** alistar; **to muster out** dar de baja a; **to muster up courage** cobrar ánimo
muster roll s lista de revista
mus·ty ['mʌsti] adj (comp **-tier;** super **-tiest**) (moldy) mohoso; (stale) trasnochado; anticuado, pasado de moda
mutation [mju'te/ən] s mutación
mute [mjut] adj & s mudo || tr poner sordina a
mutilate ['mjutɪ,let] tr mutilar
mutineer [,mjutɪ'nɪr] s amotinado
mutinous ['mjutɪnəs] adj amotinado
muti·ny ['mjutɪni] s (pl **-nies**) motín m || v (pret & pp **-nied**) intr amotinarse
mutt [mʌt] s (slang) perro cruzado; (slang) bobo, tonto
mutter ['mʌtər] tr & intr murmurar
mutton ['mʌtən] s carnero, carne f de carnero
mutton chop s chuleta de carnero
mutual ['mut/u·əl] adj mutual, mutuo
mutual aid s apoyo mutuo
mutual benefit association s mutualidad
muzzle ['mʌzəl] s (projecting part of head of animal) hocico; (device to keep animal from biting) bozal m; (of firearm) boca || tr abozalar; (to keep from speaking) amordazar
my [maɪ] adj poss mi
myriad ['mɪrɪ·əd] s miríada
myrrh [mʌr] s mirra
myrtle ['mʌrtəl] s arrayán m, mirto
myself [maɪ'sɛlf] pron pers yo mismo; mí, mí mismo; me, p.ej., **I enjoyed myself** me divertí; **with myself** conmigo
mysterious [mɪs'tɪrɪ·əs] adj misterioso
myster·y ['mɪstəri] s (pl **-ies**) misterio
mystic ['mɪstɪk] adj & s místico
mystical ['mɪstɪkəl] adj místico
mysticism ['mɪstɪ,sɪzəm] s misticismo
mystification [,mɪstɪfɪ'ke/ən] s confusión, mistificación
mysti·fy ['mɪstɪ,faɪ] v (pret & pp **-fied**) tr rodear de misterio; (to hoax) confundir, mistificar
myth [mɪθ] s mito
mythical ['mɪθɪkəl] adj mítico
mythological [,mɪθə'ladʒɪkəl] adj mitológico
mytholo·gy [mɪ'θalədʒi] s (pl **-gies**) mitología

mo na

N

N, n [ɛn] decimocuarta letra del alfabeto inglés
n. abbr **neuter, nominative, noon, north, noun, number**
N. abbr **Nationalist, Navy, Noon, North, November**
N.A. abbr **National Academy, National Army, North America**
nab [næb] v (pret & pp **nabbed;** ger

nabbing) tr (slang) agarrar, coger; (slang) poner preso, prender
nag [næg] s caballejo, jaco; pequeño caballo de silla || v (pret & pp **nagged;** ger **nagging**) tr importunar regañando || intr regañar
naiad ['ne·æd] o ['naɪ·æd] s náyade f; (fig) nadadora
nail [nel] s (of finger) uña; (to fasten

wood, etc.) clavo; **to hit the nail on the head** dar en el clavo ‖ *tr* clavar

nail brush *s* cepillo de uñas

nail file *s* lima para las uñas

nail polish *s* esmalte *m* para las uñas, laca de uñas

nailset ['nel‚sɛt] *s* contrapunzón *m*

naïve [nɑˈiv] *adj* cándido, ingenuo

naked ['nekɪd] *adj* desnudo; **to go naked** ir desnudo, andar a la cordobana; **to strip naked** desnudar; desnudarse; **with the naked eye** a simple vista

name [nem] *s* nombre *m;* (*first name*) nombre de pila; (*last name*) apellido; fama, reputación, renombre *m;* linaje, *m,* raza; **to call someone names** maltratar a uno de palabra; **to go by the name of** ser conocido por el nombre de; **to make a name for oneself** darse a conocer, hacerse un nombre; **what is your name?** ¿cómo se llama Vd.? ‖ *tr* nombrar; fijar (*un precio*)

name day *s* santo

nameless ['nemlɪs] *adj* sin nombre, anónimo

namely ['nemlɪ] *adv* a saber, es decir

namesake ['nem‚sek] *s* homónimo, tocayo

nanny goat ['næni] *s* (coll) cabra

nap [næp] *s* lanilla, flojel *m;* sueñecillo; **to take a nap** descabezar un sueñecillo ‖ *v* (*pret & pp* **napped;** *ger* **napping**) *intr* echar un sueñecillo; estar desprevenido; **to catch napping** coger desprevenido

napalm ['nepɑm] *s* (mil) gelatina incendiaria

nape [nep] *s* cogote *m,* nuca

naphtha ['næfθə] *s* nafta

napkin ['næpkɪn] *s* servilleta; (*of a baby*) (Brit) pañal *m*

napkin ring *s* servilletero

Naples ['nepəlz] *s* Nápoles

Napoleonic [nə‚polɪˈɑnɪk] *adj* napoleónico

narcissus [nɑrˈsɪsəs] *s* (bot) narciso ‖ **Narcissus** *s* Narciso

narcotic [nɑrˈkɑtɪk] *adj & s* narcótico

narrate [næˈret] *tr* narrar

narration [næˈreʃən] *s* narración

narrative ['nærətɪv] *adj* narrativo ‖ *s* (*story, tale; art of telling stories*) narrativa

narrator [næˈretər] *s* narrador *m*

narrow ['næro] *adj* angosto, estrecho; intolerante; minucioso; (*sense of a word*) estricto ‖ **narrows** *spl* angostura, paso estrecho ‖ *tr* enangostar, estrechar; reducir, limitar ‖ *intr* enangostarse, estrecharse; reducirse, limitarse

narrow escape *s* trance *m* difícil; **to have a narrow escape** escapar por un pelo, salvarse en una tabla

narrow gauge *s* trocha angosta, vía estrecha

narrow-minded ['næro‚maɪndɪd] *adj* intolerante, de miras estrechas, poco liberal

nasal ['nezəl] *adj & s* nasal *m*

nasalize ['nezə‚laɪz] *tr* nasalizar ‖ *intr* ganguear

nasturtium [nəˈstʌrʃəm] *s* capuchina, espuela de galán

nas•ty ['næsti] o ['nɑsti] *adj* (*comp* **-tier;** *super* **-tiest**) asqueroso, sucio; desagradable; desvergonzado; amenazador; horrible

natatorium [‚netəˈtorɪ•əm] *s* piscina de natación

nation ['neʃən] *s* nación

national ['næʃənəl] *adj & s* nacional *mf*

national anthem *s* himno nacional

national hero *s* benemérito de la patria

national holiday *s* fiesta nacional

nationalism ['næʃənə‚lɪzəm] *s* nacionalismo

nationalist ['næʃənəlɪst] *adj & s* nacionalista *mf*

national•ty [‚næʃənˈælɪti] *s* (*pl* **-ties**) nacionalidad, naturaleza

nationalize ['næʃənə‚laɪz] *tr* nacionalizar

na′tion-wide′ *adj* de toda la nación

native ['netɪv] *adj* nativo, natural; indígena; (*language*) materno; **to go native** vivir como los indígenas ‖ *s* natural *mf;* indígena *mf*

native land *s* patria

nativi•ty [nəˈtɪvɪti] *s* (*pl* **-ties**) nacimiento ‖ **Nativity** *s* (*day; festival; painting*) natividad

Nato ['neto] *s* (acronym) la O.T.A.N.

nat•ty ['næti] *adj* (*comp* **-tier;** *super* **-tiest**) elegante, garboso

natural ['nætʃərəl] *adj* natural; (mus) natural ‖ *s* imbécil *mf;* (mus) tono natural, nota natural; (*sign*) (mus) becuadro; (mus) tecla blanca; (coll) cosa de éxito certero

naturalism ['nætʃərə‚lɪzəm] *s* naturalismo

naturalist ['nætʃərəlɪst] *s* naturalista *mf*

naturalization [‚nætʃərəlɪˈzeʃən] *s* naturalización

naturalization papers *spl* carta de naturaleza

naturalize ['nætʃərə‚laɪz] *tr* naturalizar

naturally ['nætʃərəli] *adv* naturalmente; claro, desde luego, por supuesto

nature ['netʃər] *s* naturaleza; **from nature** del natural

naught [nɔt] *s* nada; cero; **to bring to naught** anular, invalidar, destruir; **to come to naught** reducirse a nada, frustrarse

naugh•ty ['nɔti] *adj* (*comp* **-tier;** *super* **-tiest**) desobediente, pícaro; desvergonzado; (*story, tale*) verde

nausea ['nɔʃɪ•ə] o ['nɔʃɪ•ə] *s* náusea

nauseate ['nɔʃɪ‚et] o ['nɔsɪ‚et] *tr* dar náuseas a ‖ *intr* nausear, marearse

nauseating ['nɔʃɪ‚etɪŋ] o ['nɔsɪ‚etɪŋ] *adj* nauseabundo, asqueroso

nauseous ['nɔʃɪ•əs] o ['nɔsɪ•əs] *adj* nauseabundo

nautical ['nɔtɪkəl] *adj* náutico, marino, naval

nav. *abbr* naval, navigation

naval ['nevəl] *adj* naval, naval militar

Naval Academy *s* (U.S.A.) Escuela Naval Militar

naval officer *s* oficial *m* de marina

naval station *s* apostadero

nave [nev] *s* (*of a church*) nave *f* central, nave principal; (*of a wheel*) cubo

navel ['nevəl] *s* ombligo; (*center point, middle*) (fig) ombligo

navel orange *s* navel *f*, naranja de ombligo

navigability [,nævigə'bɪlɪti] *s* (*of a river*) navegabilidad; (*of a ship*) buen gobierno

navigable ['nævɪgəbəl] *adj* (*river, canal, etc.*) navegable; (*ship*) marinero, de buen gobierno

navigate ['nævɪ,get] *tr & intr* navegar

navigation [,nævɪ'geʃən] *s* navegación

navigator ['nævɪ,getər] *s* navegador *m*, navegante *m*; (*he who is in charge of course of ship or plane*) oficial *m* de derrota; (Brit) peón *m*

nav·vy ['nævi] *s* (*pl* **-vies**) (Brit) bracero, peón *m*

na·vy ['nevi] *adj* azul oscuro ‖ *s* (*pl* **-vies**) marina de guerra; (*personnel*) marina; azul oscuro

navy bean *s* frijol blanco común

navy blue *s* azul marino, azul oscuro

navy yard *s* arsenal *m* de puerto

Nazarene [,næzə'rin] *adj & s* nazareno

Nazi ['natsi] o ['nætsi] *adj & s* nazi *mf*, nacista *mf*

n.b. *abbr* nota bene (Lat) note well

N-bomb ['ɛn,bʌm] *s* bomba de neutrones

Neapolitan [,ni·ə'pɑlɪtən] *adj & s* napolitano

neap tide [nip] *s* marea muerta

near [nɪr] *adj* cercano, próximo; íntimo; imitado ‖ *adv* cerca; íntimamente ‖ *prep* cerca de; hacia, por ‖ *tr* acercarse a ‖ *intr* acercarse

nearby ['nɪr,baɪ] *adj* cercano, próximo ‖ *adv* cerca

Near East *s* Cercano Oriente, Próximo Oriente

nearly ['nɪrli] *adv* casi; de cerca; íntimamente; por poco, p.ej., **he nearly fell** por poco se cae

near-sighted ['nɪr'saɪtɪd] *adj* miope

near-sightedness *s* miopía

neat [nit] *adj* aseado, pulcro, pulido; diestro, primoroso; puro, sin mezcla ‖ *ssg* res vacuna ‖ *spl* ganado vacuno

neat's'-foot' oil *s* aceite *m* de pie de buey

Nebuchadnezzar [,nɛbjəkəd'nezər] *s* Nabucodonosor *m*

nebu·la ['nɛbjələ] *s* (*pl* **-lae** [,li] o **-las**) nebulosa

nebular ['nɛbjələr] *adj* nebular

nebulous ['nɛbjələs] *adj* nebuloso

necessary ['nɛsɪ,seri] *adj* necesario

necessitate [nɪ'sɛsɪ,tet] *tr* necesitar, exigir

necessitous [nɪ'sɛsɪtəs] *adj* necesitado

necessi·ty [nɪ'sɛsɪti] *s* (*pl* **-ties**) necesidad

neck [nɛk] *s* cuello; (*of a bottle*) go-

llete *m*; (*of violin or guitar*) mástil *m*; istmo, península; estrecho; **neck and neck** parejos; **to break one's neck** (coll) matarse trabajando; **to stick one's neck out** (coll) descubrir el cuerpo ‖ *intr* (slang) acariciarse (*dos enamorados*)

neck'band' *s* tirilla de camisa

necklace ['nɛklɪs] *s* gargantilla, collar *m*

necktie ['nɛk,taɪ] *s* corbata

necktie pin *s* alfiler *m* de corbata

necrology [nɛ'klɑlədʒɪ] *s* necrología

necromancy ['nɛkrə,mænsɪ] *s* necromancia, nigromancia

nectarine [,nɛktə'rin] *s* griñón *m*

née o **nee** [ne] *adj* nacida o de soltera, p.ej., **Mary Wilson, née Miller** María Wilson, nacida Miller o María Wilson, de soltera Miller

need [nid] *s* necesidad; pobreza; **in need** necesitado ‖ *tr* necesitar ‖ *intr* estar necesitado; ser necesario ‖ *v aux* — **if need be** si fuere necesario; **to need** + *inf* deber, tener que + *inf*

needful ['nidfəl] *adj* necesario ‖ **the needful** lo necesario; (slang) el dinero

needle ['nidəl] *s* aguja; **to look for a needle in a haystack** buscar una aguja en un pajar ‖ *tr* coser con aguja; (coll) aguijonear, incitar; (coll) añadir alcohol a (*la cerveza o el vino*)

needle bath *s* ducha en alfileres

needle'case' *s* alfiletero

needle point *s* bordado al pasado; encaje *m* de mano

needless ['nidlɪs] *adj* innecesario, inútil

needle'work' *s* costura, labor *f*

needs [nidz] *adv* necesariamente, forzosamente

need·y ['nidi] *adj* (*comp* **-ier;** *super* **-iest**) necesitado, indigente ‖ **the needy** los necesitados

ne'er-do-well ['nerdu,wɛl] *adj & s* holgazán, perdido

negation [nɪ'geʃən] *s* negación

negative ['nɛgətɪv] *adj* negativo ‖ *s* negativa; electricidad negativa, borne negativo; (gram) negación; (math) término negativo; (phot) prueba negativa ‖ *tr* desaprobar; anular

neglect [nɪ'glɛkt] *s* negligencia, descuido ‖ *tr* descuidar; **to neglect to** dejar de, olvidarse de

neglectful [nɪ'glɛktfəl] *adj* negligente, descuidado

négligée o **negligee** [,nɛglɪ'ʒe] *s* bata de mujer, traje *m* de casa

negligence ['nɛglɪdʒəns] *s* negligencia, descuido

negligent ['nɛglɪdʒənt] *adj* negligente, descuidado

negligible ['nɛglɪdʒɪbəl] *adj* insignificante, imperceptible

negotiable [nɪ'goʃɪ·əbəl] *adj* negociable; transitable

negotiate [nɪ'goʃɪ,et] *tr* negociar; (coll) salvar, vencer ‖ *intr* negociar

negotiation [nɪ,goʃɪ'eʃən] *s* negociación; trámite *m*

Ne·gro ['nigro] adj negro ‖ s (pl -groes) negro

neigh [ne] s relincho ‖ intr relinchar

neighbor ['nebər] adj vecino; s vecino; (fellow man) prójimo ‖ tr ser vecino de; ser amigo de ‖ intr estar cercano; tener relaciones amistosas

neighborhood ['nebər ˌhud] s vecindad, vecindario, cercanías; **in the neighborhood of** en las inmediaciones de; (coll) cerca de, aproximadamente

neighboring ['nebəriŋ] adj vecino, colindante

neighborly ['nebərli] adj buen vecino, amable, sociable

neither ['niðər] o ['naɪðər] adj indef ninguno . . . (de los dos); **neither one** ninguno de los dos ‖ pron indef ninguno (de los dos); ni uno ni otro, ni lo uno ni lo otro ‖ conj ni; tampoco, ni . . . tampoco, p.ej., **neither do I** yo tampoco, ni yo tampoco; **neither . . . nor** ni . . . ni

neme·sis ['nemɪsɪs] s (pl -ses [ˌsiz]) (someone or something that punishes) némesis f ‖ **Nemesis** s Némesis f

neologism [ni'ɑlə ˌdʒɪzəm] s neologismo

neomycin [ˌni·ə'maɪsɪn] s neomicina

neon ['ni·ɑn] s neo, neón m

neophyte ['ni·ə ˌfaɪt] s neófito

Nepal [nɪ'pɔl] s el Nepal

Nepa·lese [ˌnɛpə'liz] adj nepalés ‖ s (pl -lese) nepalés m

nepenthe [nɪ'pɛnθi] s nepente m

nephew ['nɛfju] o ['nevju] s sobrino

Nepos ['nipɑs] o ['nɛpɑs] s Nepote m

Neptune ['nɛptʃun] o ['nɛptjun] s Neptuno

neptunium [nɛp't/unɪ·əm] o [nɛp'tjunɪ·əm] s neptunio

Nereid ['nɪrɪ·ɪd] s nereida

Nero ['nɪro] s Nerón m

nerve [nʌrv] s adj (center; system; tonic; disease; prostration; breakdown) nervioso ‖ s nervio; ánimo, valor m; audacia; (coll) descaro; **nerves** excitabilidad nerviosa; **to get on one's nerves** irritar los nervios a uno; **to strain every nerve** esforzarse al máximo

nerve-racking ['nʌrv ˌrækɪŋ] adj irritante, exasperante

nervous ['nʌrvəs] adj nervioso

nervous breakdown s colapso nervioso

nervousness ['nʌrvəsnɪs] s nerviosidad

nervous shudder s muerte chiquita

nerv·y ['nʌrvi] adj (comp -ier; super -iest) (strong, vigorous) nervioso; atrevido, audaz; (coll) descarado

nest [nɛst] s nido; (where hen lays eggs) nidal m; (birds in a nest) nidada; (set of things fitting within each other) juego; (of, e.g., thieves) nido; **to feather one's nest** hacer todo para enriquecerse ‖ tr colocar en un nido ‖ intr anidar

nest egg s (eggs left in a nest to induce hen to lay more) nidal m; ahorros, hucha

nestle ['nɛsəl] tr poner en un nido;

arrimar afectuosamente ‖ intr anidar; arrimarse cómodamente; **to nestle up to** arrimarse a

net [nɛt] adj neto, líquido ‖ s red f; precio neto, peso neto, ganancia líquida ‖ v (pret & pp netted; super netting) tr enredar, tejer; coger con red; producir (cierta ganancia líquida)

nether ['nɛðər] adj inferior, más bajo

Netherlander ['nɛðər ˌlændər] o ['nɛðərləndər] s neerlandés m

Netherlandish ['nɛðər ˌlændɪʃ] o ['nɛðərləndɪʃ] adj neerlandés ‖ s neerlandés m

Netherlands, The ['nɛðərləndz] los Países Bajos (Holanda)

netting ['nɛtɪŋ] s red f

nettle ['nɛtəl] s ortiga ‖ tr irritar, provocar

net'work' s red f; (rad & telv) cadena

neuralgia [njʊ'rældʒə] o [nʊ'rældʒə] s neuralgia

neurology [njʊ'rɑlədʒi] o [nʊ'rɑlədʒi] s neurología

neuro·sis [njʊ'rosɪs] o [nʊ'rosɪs] s (pl -ses [siz]) neurosis f

neurotic [njʊ'rɑtɪk] o [nʊ'rɑtɪk] adj & s neurótico

neut. abbr **neuter**

neuter ['njutər] o ['nutər] adj neutro ‖ s género neutro

neutral ['njutrəl] o ['nutrəl] adj (on neither side in a quarrel or war) neutral; (having little or no color) neutro; (bot, chem, elec, phonet, zool) neutro ‖ s neutral mf; (aut) punto neutral, punto muerto

neutralism ['njutrə ˌlɪzəm] o ['nutrə ˌlɪzəm] s neutralismo

neutralist ['njutrəlɪst] o ['nutrəlɪst] adj & s neutralista mf

neutrality [nju'trælɪti] o [nu'trælɪti] s neutralidad

neutralize ['njutrə ˌlaɪz] o ['nutrə ˌlaɪz] tr neutralizar

neutron ['njutrɑn] o ['nutrɑn] s neutrón m

neutron bomb s bomba de neutrones, bomba neutrónica

never ['nɛvər] adv nunca; en mi vida; de ningún modo; **never fear** no hay cuidado; **never mind** no importa

nev'er·more' adv nunca más

nevertheless [ˌnɛvərðə'lɛs] adv no obstante, sin embargo

new [nju] o [nu] adj nuevo; **what's new?** ¿qué hay de nuevo?

new arrival s recién llegado; recién nacido

new'born' adj recién nacido; renacido

New Castile s Castilla la Nueva

New'cas'tle s — **to carry coals to Newcastle** echar agua al mar, llevar hierro a Vizcaya, llevar leña al monte

newcomer ['nju ˌkʌmər] o ['nu ˌkʌmər] s recién llegado, recién venido

New England s la Nueva Inglaterra

newfangled ['nju ˌfæŋgəld] o ['nu ˌfæŋgəld] adj de última moda, recién inventado

Newfoundland ['njufənd ˌlænd] o

['nufənd ‚lænd] s (*island and province*) Terranova ‖ [nju'faundlənd] o [nu'faundlənd] s (*dog*) Terranova *m*

newly ['njuli] o ['nuli] *adv* nuevamente; **newly** + *pp* recién + *pp*

new'ly·wed' s recién casado

New Mexican *adj & s* neomejicano, nuevomejicano

New Mexico *s* Nuevo Méjico

new moon s luna nueva, novilunio

news [njuz] o [nuz] *s* noticias; periódico; **a news item** una noticia; **a piece of news** una noticia

news agency s agencia de noticias

news beat s exclusiva, anticipación de una noticia por un periódico

news'boy' s vendedor de periódicos

news'cast' s noticiario radiofónico ‖ *tr* radiodifundir (*noticias*) ‖ *intr* radiodifundir noticias

news'cast'er s cronista *mf* de radio

news conference s var de **press conference**

news coverage s reportaje *m*

news·man ['njuzmən] o ['nuzmən] *s* (*pl* **-men** [mən]) noticiero

New South Wales s la Nueva Gales del Sur

news'pa'per *adj* periodístico ‖ s periódico

newspaper·man ['njuz‚pepər‚mæn] o ['nuz‚pepər‚mæn] *s* (*pl* **-men** [‚mɛn]) periodista *m*

news'print' s papel-prensa *m*

news'reel' s actualidades, noticiario cinematográfico

news'stand' s quiosco de periódicos, puesto de periódicos

news'week'ly s (*pl* **-lies**) semanario de noticias

news'wor'thy *adj* de gran actualidad, de interés periodístico

news·y ['njuzi] o ['nuzi] *adj* (*comp* **-ier**; *super* **-iest**) (coll) informativo

new'-world' *adj* del Nuevo Mundo

New Year's card s tarjeta de felicitación de Año Nuevo

New Year's Day s el Día de Año Nuevo

New Year's Eve s la noche vieja, la víspera de año nuevo

New York [jɔrk] *adj* neoyorkino ‖ s Nueva York

New Yorker ['jɔrkər] s neoyorkino

New Zealand ['ziland] *adj* neocelandés ‖ s Nueva Zelanda

New Zealander ['zilandər] *s* neocelandés *m*

next [nɛkst] *adj* próximo, siguiente; de al lado, venidero, que viene ‖ *adv* luego, después; la próxima vez; **next to** junto a; después de; **next to nothing** casi nada; **the next best** lo mejor después de eso; **to come next** venir después, ser el que sigue

next door s la casa de al lado; **next door to** en la casa siguiente; (coll) casi

next'door' *adj* siguiente, de al lado

next of kin s (*pl* **next of kin**) pariente más cercano

niacin ['naɪ·əsɪn] s niacina

Niagara Falls [naɪ'ægərə] *spl* las Cataratas del Niágara

nibble ['nɪbəl] s mordisco ‖ *tr & intr* mordiscar; picar (*un pez*); **to nibble at** picar de o en

Nicaraguan [‚nɪkə'rɑgwən] *adj & s* nicaragüense, nicaragüeño

nice [naɪs] *adj* delicado, fino, sutil; primoroso, pulido, refinado; dengoso, melindroso; atento, cortés, culto; escrupuloso, esmerado; agradable, simpático; decoroso, conveniente; complaciente; preciso; satisfactorio; (*weather*) bueno; (*attractive*) bonito; **nice and . . .** (coll) muy, mucho; **not nice** (coll) feo

nice-looking ['naɪs'lʊkɪŋ] *adj* hermoso, guapo, bien parecido

nicely ['naɪsli] *adv* con precisión; escrupulosamente; satisfactoriamente; (coll) muy bien

nice·ty ['naɪsəti] *s* (*pl* **-ties**) precisión; sutileza; finura; **to a nicety** con la mayor precisión

niche [nɪtʃ] s hornacina, nicho; colocación conveniente

Nicholas ['nɪkələs] *s* Nicolás *m*

nick [nɪk] s mella, muesca; **in the nick of time** en el momento crítico ‖ *tr* mellar, hacer muescas en; cortar

nickel ['nɪkəl] s níquel *m*; (U.S.A.) moneda de cinco centavos ‖ *tr* niquelar

nick'el-plate' *tr* niquelar

nicknack ['nɪk‚næk] s chuchería, friolera

nick'name' s apodo, mote *m* ‖ *tr* apodar

nicotine ['nɪkə‚tin] s nicotina

niece [nis] s sobrina

nif·ty ['nɪfti] *adj* (*comp* **-tier**; *super* **-tiest**) (slang) elegante; (slang) excelente

niggard ['nɪgərd] *adj & s* tacaño

night [naɪt] *adj* nocturno ‖ *s* noche *f*; **at o by night** de noche o por la noche; **night before last** anteanoche; **to make a night of it** (coll) divertirse hasta muy entrada la noche

night'cap' s gorro de dormir; trago antes de acostarse, sosiega

night club s cabaret *m*, café *m* cantante, sala de fiestas

night driving s conducción de noche

night'fall' s anochecer *m*, caída de la noche

night'gown' s camisa de dormir

nightingale ['naɪtən‚gel] s ruiseñor *m*

night latch s cerradura de resorte

night letter s carta telegráfica nocturna

night'long' *adj* de toda la noche ‖ *adv* durante toda la noche

nightly ['naɪtli] *adj* nocturno; de cada noche ‖ *adv* de noche, por la noche; cada noche

night'mare' s pesadilla

nightmarish ['naɪt‚mɛrɪʃ] *adj* espeluznante, horroroso

night owl s buho nocturno; (coll) anochecedor *m*, trasnochador *m*

night'shirt' s camisa de dormir

night'time' *adj* nocturno ‖ s noche *f*

ne
ni

night'walk'er s vagabundo nocturno; ladrón nocturno; ramera callejera nocturna; sonámbulo

night watch s guardia de noche, ronda de noche; sereno; (mil) vigilia

night watchman s vigilante nocturno

nihilism ['naɪ·ɪ,lɪzəm] s nihilismo

nihilist ['naɪ·ɪlɪst] s nihilista mf

nil [nɪl] s nada

Nile [naɪl] s Nilo

nimble ['nɪmbəl] adj ágil, ligero; listo, vivo

nim·bus ['nɪmbəs] s (pl -buses o -bi [baɪ]) nimbo

Nimrod ['nɪmrɑd] s Nemrod m

nincompoop ['nɪnkəm,pup] s badulaque m, papirote m

nine [naɪn] adj & pron nueve || s nueve m; equipo de béisbol; **nine o'clock** las nueve; **the Nine** las nueve musas

nine hundred adj & pron novecientos || s novecientos m

nineteen ['naɪn'tin] adj, pron & s diecinueve m, diez y nueve m

nineteenth ['naɪn'tinθ] adj & s (in a series) decimonono; (part) diecinueveavo || s (in dates) diecinueve m

ninetieth ['naɪntɪ·ɪθ] adj & s (in a series) nonagésimo; (part) noventavo

nine·ty ['naɪntɪ] adj & pron noventa || s (pl -ties) noventa m

ninth [naɪnθ] adj & s nono, noveno || s (in dates) nueve m

nip [nɪp] s mordisco, pellizco; helada, escarcha; traguito; **nip and tuck** a quién ganará || v (pret & pp nipped; ger nipping) tr mordiscar, pellizcar; helar, escarchar; (slang) asir, coger; **to nip in the bud** atajar en el principio || intr beborrotear

nipple ['nɪpəl] s (of female) pezón m; (of male; of nursing bottle) tetilla; (mach) tubo roscado de unión, entrerrosca

Nippon [nɪ'pɑn] o ['nɪpɑn] s el Japón

Nippon·ese [,nɪpə'niz] adj nipón || s (pl -ese) nipón m

nip·py ['nɪpɪ] adj (comp -pier; super -piest) mordaz, picante; frío, helado; (Brit) ágil, ligero

nirvana [nɪr'vɑnə] s el nirvana

nit [nɪt] s piojito; (egg of insect) liendre f

niter ['naɪtər] s nitro; (agr) nitro de Chile

nitrate ['naɪtret] s nitrato; (agr) nitrato de potasio, nitrato de sodio

nitric acid ['naɪtrɪk] s ácido nítrico

nitride ['naɪtraɪd] s nitruro

nitrogen ['naɪtrədʒən] s nitrógeno

nitroglycerin [,naɪtrə'glɪsərɪn] s nitroglicerina

nitrous oxide ['naɪtrəs] s óxido nitroso

nitwit ['nɪt,wɪt] s (slang) bobalicón m

no [no] adj indef ninguno; **no admittance** no se permite la entrada; **no matter** no importa; **no parking** se prohibe estacionarse; **no smoking** se prohibe fumar; **no thoroughfare** prohibido el paso; **no use** inútil; **with**

no sin || adv no; **no good** de ningún valor; ruin, vil; **no longer** ya no; **no sooner** no bien

Noah ['no·ə] s Noé m

nob·by ['nɑbi] adj (comp -bier; super -biest) (slang) elegante

nobili·ty [no'bɪlɪti] s (pl -ties) nobleza; (of sentiments, character, etc.) nobleza, ennoblecimiento

noble ['nobəl] adj & s noble m

noble·man ['nobəlmən] s (pl -men [mən]) noble m, hidalgo

nobod·y ['no,bɑdi] o ['nobədi] pron indef nadie, ninguno; **nobody but** nadie más que; **nobody else** nadie más, ningún otro || s (pl -ies) nadie m, don nadie

nocturnal [nɑk'tʌrnəl] adj nocturno

nod [nɑd] s inclinación de cabeza; seña con la cabeza; (of a person going to sleep) cabezada || v (pret & pp nodded; ger nodding) tr inclinar (la cabeza); indicar con una inclinación de cabeza || intr inclinar la cabeza; (in going to sleep) cabecear

node [nod] s bulto, protuberancia; nudo, enredo; (astr, med & phys) nodo; (bot) nudo

no'-fault' adj libre de culpa (divorcio, seguro)

nohow ['no,hau] adv (coll) de ninguna manera

noise [nɔɪz] s ruido || tr divulgar

noiseless ['nɔɪzlɪs] adj silencioso

nois·y ['nɔɪzi] adj (comp -ier; super -iest) ruidoso; (boisterous) estrepitoso

nom. abbr **nominative**

nomad ['nomæd] adj & s nómada mf

nomadic [no'mædɪk] adj nomádico

no man's land s terreno sin reclamar; (mil) la tierra de nadie

nominal ['nɑmɪnəl] adj nominal; (price) módico

nominate ['nɑmɪ,net] tr postular como candidato; (to appoint) nombrar, designar

nomination [,nɑmɪ'neʃən] s postulación

nominative ['nɑmɪnətɪv] adj & s nominativo

nominee [,nɑmɪ'ni] s propuesto, candidato

nonbelligerent [,nɑnbə'lɪdʒərənt] adj & s no beligerante m

nonbreakable [nɑn'brekəbəl] adj irrompible

nonchalance ['nɑnʃələns] o [,nɑnʃə'lɑns] s indiferencia, desenvoltura

nonchalant ['nɑnʃələnt] o [,nɑnʃə'lɑnt] adj indiferente, desenvuelto

noncom ['nɑn,kɑm] s (coll) clase, suboficial m

noncombatant [nɑn'kɑmbətənt] adj & s no combatiente m

noncommissioned officer [,nɑnkə'mɪʃənd] s clase, suboficial m

noncommittal [,nɑnkə'mɪtəl] adj evasivo, reticente

noncommitted [,nɑnkə'mɪtɪd] adj no empeñado

non compos mentis ['nɑn'kɑmpəs-'mentɪs] adj falto de juicio, loco

nonconformist [‚nɑnkən'fɔrmɪst] s disidente mf

nondelivery [‚nɑndɪ'lɪvəri] s falta de entrega

nondescript ['nɑndɪˌskrɪpt] adj inclasificable, indefinido

none [nʌn] pron indef nadie, ninguno, ningunos; **none** of ninguno de; nada de; **none other** ningún otro ‖ adv nada, de ninguna manera; **none the less** sin embargo, no obstante

nonenti·ty [nɑn'entɪti] s (pl -ties) cosa inexistente; (person) nulidad

nonfiction [nɑn'fɪkʃən] s literatura no novelesca

nonfulfillment [‚nɑnful'fɪlmənt] s incumplimiento

nonintervention [‚nɑnɪntər'venʃən] s no intervención

nonmetal ['nɑnˌmetəl] s metaloide m

nonpayment [nɑn'pemənt] s falta de pago

non·plus ['nɑnplʌs] o [nɑn'plʌs] s estupefacción ‖ v (pret & pp -plused o -plussed; ger -plusing o -plussing) tr dejar estupefacto, dejar pegado a la pared

nonprofit [nɑn'prɑfɪt] adj sin fin lucrativo

nonrefillable [‚nɑnrɪ'fɪləbəl] adj irrellenable

nonresident [nɑn'rezɪdənt] s transeúnte mf

nonresidential [nɑnˌrezɪ'denʃəl] adj comercial

nonscientific [nɑnˌsaɪ·ən'tɪfɪk] adj anticientífico

nonsectarian [‚nɑnsek'terɪ·ən] adj no sectario

nonsense ['nɑnsens] s disparate m, tontería

nonsensical [nɑn'sensɪkəl] adj disparatado, tonto

nonskid ['nɑn'skɪd] adj antideslizante

nonstop ['nɑn'stɑp] adj & adv sin parar, sin escala

nonsupport [‚nɑnsə'pɔrt] s falta de manutención

noodle ['nudəl] s tallarín m; (slang) mentecato, tonto; (slang) cabeza

noodle soup s sopa de pastas, sopa de fideos

nook [nuk] s rinconcito

noon [nun] s mediodía m; **at high noon** en pleno mediodía

no one o **no-one** ['no‚wʌn] pron indef nadie, ninguno; **no one else** nadie más, ningún otro

noontime ['nun‚taɪm] s mediodía m

noose [nus] s lazo corredizo; (to hang a criminal) dogal m; trampa ‖ tr lazar; hacer un lazo corredizo en

nor [nɔr] conj ni

Nordic ['nɔrdɪk] adj & s nórdico

norm [nɔrm] s norma

normal ['nɔrməl] adj normal

Norman ['nɔrmən] adj & s normando

Normandy ['nɔrməndi] s Normandía

Norse [nɔrs] adj nórdico; noruego ‖ s (ancient Scandanavian language) nórdico; (language of Norway) no-ruego; **the Norse** los nórdicos; los noruegos

Norse·man ['nɔrsmən] s (pl -men [mən]) normando

north [nɔrθ] adj septentrional, del norte ‖ adv al norte, hacia el norte ‖ s norte m

North America s Norteamérica, la América del Norte

North American adj & s norteamericano

north'east'er s (wind) nordestada, nordeste m (viento)

northern ['nɔrðərn] adj septentrional; (Hemisphere) boreal

North Korea s la Corea del Norte

North Korean adj & s norcoreano

northward ['nɔrθwərd] adv hacia el norte

north wind s norte m, aquilón m

Norway ['nɔrwe] s Noruega

Norwegian [nɔr'widʒən] adj & s noruego

nos. abbr **numbers**

nose [noz] s nariz f; (aer) proa; **to blow one's nose** sonarse las narices; **to count noses** averiguar cuántas personas hay; **to follow one's nose** seguir todo derecho; avanzar guiándose por el instinto; **to hold one's nose** tabicarse las narices; **to lead by the nose** llevar por la barba, tener agarrado por las narices; **to look down one's nose** at mirar por encima del hombro; **to pay through the nose** pagar un precio escandaloso; **to pick one's nose** hurgarse las narices; **to poke one's nose into** meter las narices en; **to speak through the nose** ganguear; **to thumb one's nose at** señalar (a una persona) poniendo el pulgar sobre la nariz en son de burla; tratar con sumo desprecio; **to turn up one's nose at** mirar con desprecio; **under the nose of** en las narices de, en las barbas de ‖ tr olfatear ‖ intr ventear; **to nose about** curiosear; **to nose over** capotar (un avión); **to nose up** encabritarse (un buque, un avión)

nose bag s cebadera, morral m

nose'band' s muserola, sobarba

nose'bleed' s hemorragia nasal

nose cone s cono de proa

nose dive s (aer) descenso de picado; (fig) descenso precipitado

nose'-dive' intr (aer) picar; (fig) descender precipitadamente

nosegay ['noz‚ge] s ramillete m

nose ring s nariguera

no'-show' s pasajero no presentado

nostalgia [nɑ'stældʒə] s nostalgia

nostril ['nɑstrɪl] s nariz f, ventana

nos·y ['nozi] adj (comp -ier; super -iest) (coll) curioso, husmeador

not [nɑt] adv no; **not at all** nada, de ningún modo; **not yet** todavía no; **to think not** creer que no; **why not?** ¿cómo no?

notable ['notəbəl] adj & s notable m

notarize ['notə‚raɪz] tr abonar con fe notarial

nota·ry ['notəri] s (pl -ries) notario

notch [nɑtʃ] s muesca, mella, corte m; (U.S.A.) desfiladero, paso; (coll) grado || tr hacer muescas en, mellar

note [not] s nota; apunte m; esquela, cartita; marca, señal f; (com) pagaré m, vale m; canto, melodía; acento, voz f; (mus) nota || tr notar, apuntar; marcar, señalar

note'book' s cuaderno, libro de apuntes

noted ['notɪd] adj afamado, conocido

note paper s papel m de cartas

note'wor'thy adj notable, digno de notarse

nothing ['nʌθɪŋ] pron indef nada; **for nothing** inútilmente; de balde, gratis; **nothing doing** (slang) ni por pienso; **nothing else** nada más; **that's nothing to me** eso nada me importa; **to make nothing of** no hacer caso de; no aprovecharse de; no entender; despreciar; **to think nothing of** no hacer caso de; tener por fácil; despreciar || adv nada, de ninguna manera; **nothing daunted** sin temor alguno || s nada; nadería, friolera

notice ['notɪs] s atención, reparo, advertencia; aviso, noticia; letrero; mención, reseña; llamada; notificación; **on short notice** con poco tiempo de aviso; **to escape one's notice** pasarle inadvertido a uno; **to serve notice** dar noticia, hacer saber || tr notar, observar, reparar, reparar en; mencionar

noticeable ['notɪsəbəl] adj sensible, perceptible; notable

noti·fy ['notɪ͵faɪ] v (pret & pp -fied) tr notificar, avisar, hacer saber

notion ['noʃən] s noción; capricho; **notions** mercería, artículos menudos; **to have a notion to** + inf pensar + inf, tener ganas de + inf

notorie·ty [͵notə'raɪ·ɪti] s (pl -ties) mala reputación; (condition of being well known) notoriedad; (person) notable mf

notorious [no'tori·əs] adj reputado, mal reputado; bien conocido

no'-trump' adj & s sin triunfo; **a no-trump hand** un sin triunfo

notwithstanding [͵nɑtwɪð'stændɪŋ] o [͵nɑtwɪθ'stændɪŋ] adv no obstante || prep a pesar de || conj a pesar de que

nougat ['nugət] s turrón m

noun [naʊn] s nombre, nombre sustantivo

nourish ['nʌrɪʃ] tr alimentar, nutrir; abrigar (p.ej., esperanzas)

nourishing ['nʌrɪʃɪŋ] adj alimenticio, nutritivo

nourishment ['nʌrɪʃmənt] s alimento, nutrimento

Nov. abbr **November**

Nova Scotia ['novə'skoʃə] s la Nueva Escocia

Nova Scotian ['novə'skoʃən] adj & s neoescocés m

novel ['nɑvəl] adj nuevo; insólito, extraño, original || s novela

novelist ['nɑvəlɪst] s novelista mf

novel·ty ['nɑvəlti] s (pl -ties) novedad,

innovación; **novelties** bisutería, baratijas

November [no'vɛmbər] s noviembre m

novice ['nɑvɪs] s novicio

novocaine ['novə͵ken] s novocaína

now [naʊ] adv ahora; ya; entonces; **from now on** de ahora en adelante; **how now?** ¿cómo?; **just now** hace un momento; **now and again** o **now and then** de vez en cuando; **now . . . now** ora . . . ora, ya . . . ya; **now that** ya que; **now then** ahora bien || interj ¡vamos! || s actualidad

nowadays ['naʊ·ə͵dez] adv hoy en día, hoy día

no'way' o **no'ways'** adv de ningún modo

no'where' adv en ninguna parte, a ninguna parte; **nowhere else** en ninguna otra parte

noxious ['nɑkʃəs] adj nocivo

nozzle ['nɑzəl] s (of hose) lanza; (of sprinkling can) rallo, roseta; (of candlestick) cubo; (slang) nariz f

N.T. abbr **New Testament**

nth [ɛnθ] adj nᵐᵒ (enésimo); **to the nth degree** elevado a la potencia n; a más no poder

nuance [nju'ɑns] o ['nju·ɑns] s matiz m

nub [nʌb] s protuberancia; pedazo; (coll) meollo

nuclear ['njuklɪ·ər] o ['nuklɪ·ər] adj nuclear

nuclear test ban s proscripción de las pruebas nucleares

nucle·us ['njuklɪ·əs] o ['nuklɪ·əs] s (pl -i [͵aɪ] o -uses) núcleo

nude [njud] o [nud] adj desnudo || s — **in the nude** desnudo; **the nude** el desnudo

nudge [nʌdʒ] s codazo suave || tr dar un codazo suave a, empujar suavemente

nugget ['nʌgɪt] s pedazo; (of, e.g., gold) pepita; preciosidad

nuisance ['njusəns] o ['nusəns] s molestia, estorbo; persona o cosa fastidiosas

null [nʌl] adj nulo; **null and void** nulo, írrito, nulo y sin valor

nulli·fy ['nʌlɪ͵faɪ] v (pret & pp -fied) tr anular, invalidar

nulli·ty ['nʌlɪti] s (pl -ties) nulidad

numb [nʌm] adj entumecido || tr entumecer

number ['nʌmbər] s número; **a number of** varios || tr numerar; ascender a (cierto número); **his days are numbered** tiene sus días contados o sus horas contadas; **to be numbered among** hallarse entre; **to number among** contar entre

numberless ['nʌmbərlɪs] adj innumerable

numeral ['njumərəl] o ['numərəl] adj numeral || s número

numerical [nju'mɛrɪkəl] o [nu'mɛrɪkəl] adj numérico

numerous ['njumərəs] o ['numərəs] adj numeroso

numskull ['nʌm͵skʌl] s (coll) bodoque m, mentecato

nun [nʌn] *s* monja, religiosa
nuptial ['nʌp/əl] *adj* nupcial ‖ **nuptials** *spl* nupcias, bodas
nurse [nʌrs] *s* enfermera; (*to suckle a child*) ama de cría, nodriza; (*to take care of a child*) niñera ‖ *tr* cuidar (*a una persona enferma*); amamantar; alimentar; criar; tratar de curarse de (*p.ej., un resfriado*); abrigar (*p.ej., odio*) ‖ *intr* ser enfermera
nurser·y ['nʌrsəri] *s* (*pl* **-ies**) cuarto de los niños; (*of plants*) criadero, plantel *m*, semillero; (fig) semillero
nursery·man ['nʌrsərimən] *s* (*pl* **-men** [mən]) cultivador *m* de semillero
nursery rhymes *spl* versos para niños
nursery tales *spl* cuentos para niños
nursing bottle *s* biberón *m*
nursing home *s* clínica de reposo
nurture ['nʌrt/ər] *s* alimentación, nutrimento; crianza, educación ‖ *tr* alimentar, nutrir; criar, educar; acariciar (*p.ej., una esperanza*)
nut [nʌt] *s* nuez *f*; (*to screw on a bolt*)

tuerca; (slang) estrafalario; **a hard nut to crack** (coll) hueso duro de roer
nut'crack'er *s* cascanueces *m*
nutmeg ['nʌt,meg] *s* nuez moscada; (*tree*) mirística
nutriment ['njutrimənt] o ['nutrimənt] *s* nutrimento
nutrition [nju'tri/ən] o [nu'tri/ən] *s* nutrición
nutritious [nju'tri/əs] o [nu'tri/əs] *adj* nutricioso, nutritivo
nut'shell' *s* cáscara de nuez; **in a nutshell** en pocas palabras
nut·ty ['nʌti] *adj* (*comp* **-tier;** *super* **-tiest**) abundante en nueces; que sabe a nueces; (slang) chiflado, loco; **nutty about** (slang) loco por
nuzzle ['nʌzəl] *tr* hocicar, hozar ‖ *intr* hocicar; arrimarse cómodamente; arroparse bien
nylon ['nailən] *s* nilón *m;* **nylons** medias de nilón
nymph [nimf] *s* ninfa

O

O, o [o] decimoquinta letra del alfabeto inglés
O *interj* ¡oh!; ¡ay!, p.ej., **O, how pretty she is!** ¡Ay qué linda!; **O that . . . !** ¡Ojalá que . . . !
oaf [of] *s* zoquete *m,* zamacuco; niño contrahecho
oak [ok] *s* roble *m*
oaken ['okən] *adj* hecho de roble
oakum ['okəm] *s* estopa, estopa de calafatear
oar [or] *s* remo; **to lie** o **rest on one's oars** aguantar los remos; aflojar en el trabajo ‖ *tr* conducir a remo ‖ *intr* remar, bogar
oars·man ['orzmən] *s* (*pl* **-men** [mən]) remero
OAS ['o'e'ɛs] *s* (letterword) OEA *f*
oa·sis [o'esis] *s* (*pl* **-ses** [siz]) oasis *m*
oat [ot] *s* avena; **oats** (*edible grain*) avena; **to feel one's oats** (slang) estar fogoso y brioso; (slang) estar muy pagado de sí mismo; **to sow one's wild oats** correrla, pasar las mocedades
oath [oθ] *s* juramento; **on oath** bajo juramento; **to take an oath** prestar juramento
oat'meal' *s* harina de avena; gachas de avena
ob. *abbr* **obiit** (Lat) died
obbligato [,abli'gato] *adj* & *s* obligado
obduracy ['abdjərəsi] *s* obduración
obdurate ['abdjərit] *adj* obstinado, terco; empedernido
obedience [o'bidi·əns] *s* obediencia
obedient [o'bidi·ənt] *adj* obediente
obeisance [o'besəns] u [o'bisəns] *s* saludo respetuoso; homenaje *m,* respeto

obelisk ['abəlisk] *s* obelisco
obese [o'bis] *adj* obeso
obesity [o'bisiti] *s* obesidad
obey [o'be] *tr* & *intr* obedecer
obfuscate [ab'fʌsket] o ['abfəs,ket] *tr* ofuscar
obituar·y [o'bit/u,eri] *adj* necrológico ‖ *s* (*pl* **-ies**) necrología
obj. *abbr* **object, objection, objective**
object ['abdʒikt] *s* objeto ‖ [ab'dʒɛkt] *tr* objetar ‖ *intr* hacer objeciones
objection [ab'dʒɛk/ən] *s* reparo, objeción; **to have no objections to make** no tener nada que objetar
objectionable [ab'dʒɛk/ənəbəl] *adj* desagradable, reprensible; (*causing disapproval*) objetable
objective [ab'dʒɛktɪv] *adj* & *s* objetivo
obl. *abbr* **oblique, oblong**
obligate ['abli,get] *tr* obligar
obligation [,abli'ge/ən] *s* obligación
oblige [ə'blaidʒ] *tr* obligar; complacer; **much obliged** muchas gracias
obliging [ə'blaidʒiŋ] *adj* complaciente, condescendiente, servicial
oblique [ə'blik] *adj* oblicuo; indirecto, evasivo
obliterate [ə'blitə,ret] *tr* borrar; arrasar, destruir
oblivion [ə'blivi·ən] *s* olvido
oblivious [ə'blivi·əs] *adj* olvidadizo
oblong ['abləŋ] o ['ablaŋ] *adj* oblongo
obnoxious [əb'nak/əs] *adj* detestable, ofensivo
oboe ['obo] *s* oboe *m*
oboist ['obo·ist] *s* oboísta *mf*
obs. *abbr* **obsolete**
obscene [ab'sin] *adj* obsceno

no
ob

obsceni‧ty [ab'seniti] o [ab'siniti] s (pl -ties) obscenidad

obscure [ab'skjur] adj obscuro; (vowel) relajado, neutro

obscuri‧ty [ab'skjuriti] s (pl -ties) obscuridad

obsequies ['absikwiz] spl exequias

obsequious [ab'sikwi‧əs] adj obsequioso, servil, rastrero

observance [ab'zʌrvəns] s observancia; ceremonia, rito

observant [ab'zʌrvənt] adj observador

observation [ˌabzər've∫ən] s observación; observancia

observato‧ry [ab'zʌrvəˌtori] s (pl -ries) observatorio

observe [ab'zʌrv] tr observar; (a holiday; silence) guardar

observer [ab'zʌrvər] s observador m

obsess [ab'ses] tr obsesionar

obsession [ab'se∫ən] s obsesión

obsolescent [ˌabsə'lesənt] adj arcaizante

obsolete ['absəˌlit] adj desusado, caído en desuso

obstacle ['abstəkəl] s obstáculo

obstetrical [ab'stetrikəl] adj obstétrico

obstetrics [ab'stetriks] ssg obstetricia

obstina‧cy ['abstinəsi] s (pl -cies) obstinación

obstinate ['abstinit] adj obstinado

obstruct [ab'strʌkt] tr obstruir

obstruction [ab'strʌk∫ən] s obstrucción

obtain [ab'ten] tr obtener || intr existir, prevalecer

obtrusive [ab'trusiv] adj entremetido, intruso

obtuse [ab'tjus] o [ab'tus] adj obtuso

obviate ['abviˌet] tr obviar

obvious ['abvi‧əs] adj obvio

occasion [ə'keʒən] s ocasión; to improve the occasion aprovechar la ocasión

occasional [ə'keʒənəl] adj raro, poco frecuente; alguno que otro; de circunstancia

occasionally [ə'keʒənəli] adv ocasionalmente, de vez en cuando

occident ['aksidənt] s occidente m

occidental [ˌaksi'dentəl] adj occidental

occlusive [ə'klusiv] adj oclusivo || s oclusiva

occult [ə'kʌlt] o ['akʌlt] adj oculto

occupancy ['akjəpənsi] s ocupación

occupant ['akjəpənt] s ocupante mf; inquilino

occupation [ˌakjə'pe∫ən] s ocupación

occu‧py ['akjəˌpaɪ] v (pret & pp -pied) tr ocupar; habitar

oc‧cur [ə'kʌr] v (pret & pp -curred; ger -curring) intr ocurrir, acontecer, suceder; encontrarse; (to come to mind) ocurrir

occurrence [ə'kʌrəns] s acontecimiento; caso, aparición

ocean ['o∫ən] s océano

oceanic [ˌo∫i'ænik] adj oceánico

ocean liner s buque transoceánico

o'clock [ə'klak] adv por el reloj; it is one o'clock es la una; it is two o'clock son las dos; what o'clock is it? ¿qué hora es?

Oct. abbr **October**

octave ['aktiv] o ['aktev] s octava

October [ak'tobər] s octubre m

octo‧pus ['aktəpəs] s (pl -puses o -pi [ˌpaɪ]) pulpo

octoroon [ˌaktə'run] s octavo

ocular ['akjələr] adj & s ocular m

oculist ['akjəlist] s oculista mf

O.D. abbr officer of the day, olive drab

odd [ad] adj suelto; (number) impar; (that doesn't match) dispar; libre, de ocio; sobrante; extraño, raro, singular; y pico, y tantos, p.ej., **two hundred odd** doscientos y pico || **odds** ssg o spl (in betting) ventaja; apuesta desigual; puntos de ventaja; **at odds de monos,** riñendo; **by all odds** muy probablemente, sin duda alguna; **it makes no odds** lo mismo da; **the odds are** lo probable es; la ventaja es; **to be at odds** estar de punta, estar encontrados; **to set at odds** enemistar, malquistar

oddi‧ty ['aditi] s (pl -ties) rareza, cosa rara

odd jobs spl pequeñas tareas

odd lot s lote m inferior al centenar

odds and ends spl pedacitos varios, cajón m de sastre

ode [od] s oda

odious ['odi‧əs] adj odioso, abominable

odor ['odər] s olor m; **to be in bad odor** tener mala fama

odorless ['odərlis] adj inodoro

odorous ['odərəs] adj oloroso

Odysseus [o'disjus] u [o'disi‧əs] s Odiseo

Odyssey ['adisi] s Odisea

Oedipus ['edipəs] o ['idipəs] s Edipo

of [av] o [əv] prep de, p.ej., **the top of the mountain** la cima de la montaña; a: **to smell of** oler a; con: **to dream of** soñar con; en: **to think of** pensar en; menos: **a quarter of two** las dos menos un cuarto

off. abbr **office, officer, official**

off [ɔf] o [af] adj malo, p.ej., **off day** día malo; (account, sum) errado; más distante; libre; sin trabajo; quitado; apagado; (electric current) cortado; de descuento, de rebaja; de la parte del mar; (season) muerto || adv fuera, a distancia, lejos; allá; **off of** (coll) de; (coll) a expensas de; **to be off** ponerse en marcha || prep de, desde; al lado de, a nivel de; fuera de; libre de; (naut) a la altura de

offal ['afəl] u ['ɔfəl] s (of butchered meat) carniza; basura, desperdicios

off and on adv unas veces sí y otras no

off′beat′ adj (slang) insólito, chocante, original

off′chance′ s posibilidad poco probable

off′-col′or adj descolorido; indispuesto; (indecent, risqué) colorado, subido de color

offend [ə'fend] tr & intr ofender

offender [ə'fendər] s ofensor m

offense [ə'fɛns] *s* ofensa; **to take offense (at)** ofenderse (de)

offensive [ə'fɛnsɪv] *adj* ofensivo ǁ *f* ofensiva

offer ['ɔfər] o ['ɑfər] *s* ofrecimiento, oferta ǁ *tr* ofrecer; rezar (*oraciones*); oponer (*resistencia*)

offering ['ɔfərɪŋ] o ['ɑfərɪŋ] *s* ofrecimiento; (*gift, present*) oferta; (*presentation in worship*) ofrenda

off'hand' *adj* hecho de improviso; brusco, desenvuelto ǁ *adv* de improviso, súbitamente; bruscamente

office ['ɔfɪs] o ['ɑfɪs] *s* oficina, despacho; función, oficio; cargo, ministerio; (*of a lawyer*) bufete *m*; (*of a doctor*) consultorio

office boy *s* mandadero

office desk *s* escritorio ministro

of'fice-hold'er *s* funcionario, burócrata *m*

office hours *spl* horas de oficina; (*of a doctor*) horas de consultorio

officer ['ɔfɪsər] o ['ɑfɪsər] *s* jefe *m*, director *m*; (*of army, an order, a society, etc.*) oficial *m*; agente *m* de policía

office seeker ['sikər] *s* aspirante *m*, pretendiente *m*

office supplies *spl* suministros para oficinas

official [ə'fɪʃəl] *adj* oficial ǁ *s* jefe *m*, director *m*; (*of a society*) dignatario

officiate [ə'fɪʃɪˌet] *intr* oficiar

officious [ə'fɪʃəs] *adj* oficioso

off'-peak' heater *s* (elec) termos *m* de acumulación

off-peak load *s* (elec) carga de las horas de valle

off'print' *s* sobretiro

off'set' *s* compensación; (typ) offset *m* ǁ **off'set'** *v* (*pret & pp* -set; *ger* -setting) *tr* compensar; imprimir por offset

off'shoot' *s* (of plant) retoño, renuevo; (*of a family or race*) descendiente *mf*; (*branch*) ramal *m*; consecuencia

off'shore' *adj* (wind) terral; (*fishing*) de bajura; (*said of islands*) costero ǁ *adv* a lo largo

off'spring' *s* descendencia, sucesión; hijo, hijos

off'-stage' *adj* de entre bastidores

off'-the-rec'ord *adj* extraoficial, confidencial

often ['ɔfən] o ['ɑfən] *adv* a menudo, muchas veces; **how often?** ¿cuántas veces?; **not often** pocas veces

ogive ['odʒaɪv] u [o'dʒaɪv] *s* ojiva

ogle ['ogəl] *tr & intr* ojear; mirar amorosamente

ogre ['ogər] *s* ogro

ohm [om] *s* ohmio

oil [ɔɪl] *adj* (burner; field; well) de petróleo; (*pump; stove*) de aceite; (*company; tanker*) petrolero; (land) petrolífero ǁ *s* aceite *m*; (*consecrated oil; painting*) óleo; **to burn the midnight oil** quemarse las cejas; **to pour oil on troubled waters** mojar la pólvora; **to strike oil** encontrar una capa de petróleo; (fig) enriquecerse de súbito ǁ *tr* aceitar; lubricar; li-

sonjear; (*to bribe*) untar ǁ *intr* proveerse de petróleo (*un buque*)

oil'can' *s* aceitera

oil'cloth' *s* encerado, hule *m*

oil gauge indicador *m* del nivel de aceite

oil pan *s* colector *m* de aceite

oil tanker *s* petrolero

oil·y ['ɔɪli] *adj* (*comp* -ier; *super* -iest) aceitoso; liso, resbaladizo; zalamero

ointment ['ɔɪntmənt] *s* ungüento

O.K. ['o'ke] *adj* (coll) aprobado, conforme ǁ *adv* (coll) muy bien, está bien ǁ *s* (coll) aprobación ǁ *v* (*pret & pp* **O.K.'d;** *ger* **O.K.'ing**) *tr* (coll) aprobar

okra ['okrə] *s* quingombó *m*

old [old] *adj* viejo; antiguo; (*wine*) añejo; **how old is . . . ?** ¿cuántos años tiene . . . ?; **of old** de antaño, antiguamente; **to be . . . years old** tener . . . años

old age *s* ancianidad, vejez *f*; **to die of old age** morir de viejo

old boy *s* viejo; graduado; **the Old Boy** (slang) el diablo

Old Castile *s* Castilla la Vieja

old-clothes·man ['old'kloðz,mæn] *s* (*pl* -men [,mɛn]) ropavejero

old country *s* madre patria

old-fashioned ['old'fæʃənd] *adj* chapado a la antigua; anticuado, fuera de moda

old fo·gey u **old fo·gy** ['fogi] *s* (*pl* -gies) persona un poco ridícula por sus ideas o costumbres atrasadas

Old Glory *s* la bandera de los Estados Unidos

Old Guard *s* (U.S.A.) bando conservador del partido republicano

old hand *s* practicón *m*, veterano

old maid *s* solterona

old master *s* (paint) gran maestro; obra de un gran maestro

old moon *s* luna menguante

old salt *s* lobo de mar

old school *s* gente chapada a la antigua

old'-time' *adj* del tiempo viejo

old-timer ['old'taɪmər] *s* (coll) antiguo residente, veterano; (coll) persona chapada a la antigua

old wives' tale *s* cuento de viejas

old'-world' *adj* del Viejo Mundo

oleander [,olɪ'ændər] *s* adelfa

oligar·chy ['alɪ,garkɪ] *s* (*pl* -chies) oligarquía

olive ['alɪv] *adj* aceitunado ǁ *s* aceituna

olive branch *s* ramo de olivo; (peace) oliva; hijo, vástago

olive grove *s* olivar *m*

olive oil *s* aceite *m*, aceite de oliva

olive tree *s* aceituno, olivo

Olympiad [o'lɪmpɪˌæd] *s* Olimpíada

Olympian [o'lɪmpɪ·ən] *adj* olímpico ǁ *s* dios griego

Olympic [o'lɪmpɪk] *adj* olímpico

omelet u **omelette** ['amlɪt] o ['amlɪt] *s* tortilla (de huevos)

omen ['omən] *s* agüero

ominous ['amɪnəs] *adj* ominoso

omission [o'mɪʃən] *s* omisión

omit [o'mɪt] *v* (*pret & pp* **omitted;** *ger* **omitting**) *tr* omitir

omnibus ['ɑmnɪ‚bʌs] o ['ɑmnɪbəs] *adj* general; (*volume*) colecticio ‖ *s* ómnibus *m*

omnipotent [ɑm'nɪpətənt] *adj* omnipotente

omniscient [ɑm'nɪʃənt] *adj* omnisciente

omnivorous [ɑm'nɪvərəs] *adj* omnívoro

on [ɑn] u [ɔn] *adj* puesto, p.ej., **with his hat on** con el sombrero puesto; principiando; en funcionamiento; encendido; conectado; **the deal is on** ya está concertado el trato; **the game is on** ya están jugando; **the race is on** allá van los corredores; **what is on at the theater this evening?** ¿qué representan esta noche? ‖ *adv* adelante; encima; **and so on** y así sucesivamente; **come on!** ¡anda, anda!; **farther on** más allá, más adelante; **later on** más tarde, después; **to be on to a person** (coll) conocerle a uno el juego; **to have on** tener puesto; **to . . . on** seguir + *ger*, **he played on** siguió tocando ‖ *prep* en, sobre, encima de; a, p.ej., **on foot** a pie; **on my arrival** a mi llegada; bajo, p.ej., **on my responsibility** bajo mi responsabilidad; contra, p.ej., **an attack on liberty** un ataque contra la libertad; de, p.ej., **on good authority** de buena tinta; **on a journey** de viaje; hacia, p.ej., **to march on the capital** marchar hacia la capital; por, p.ej., **on all sides** por todos lados; tras, p.ej., **defeat on defeat** derrota tras derrota; **on** + *ger* al + *inf*, p.ej., **on arriving** al llegar

on and on *adv* continuamente, sin cesar, sin parar

once [wʌns] *adv* una vez; antes, p.ej., **once so happy** antes tan feliz; alguna vez, p.ej., **if this once becomes known** si esto llega a saberse alguna vez; **all at once** de súbito, de repente; **at once** en seguida; a la vez, en el mismo momento; **for once** una vez por lo menos; **once and again** repetidas veces; **once in a blue moon** cada muerte de obispo; **once in a while** de vez en cuando; **once more** otra vez; una vez más; **once upon a time there was** érase una vez, érase que se era ‖ *conj* una vez que ‖ *s* una vez; vez, p.ej., **this once** esta vez

once'-o'ver *s* (slang) examen rápido; **to give a thing the once-over** (coll) examinar una cosa superficialmente

one [wʌn] *adj* un, uno; un tal, p.ej., **one Smith** un tal Smith; único, p.ej., **one price** precio único ‖ *pron* uno, p.ej., **one does not know what to do here** uno no sabe qué hacer aquí; se, p.ej., **how does one go to the station?** ¿cómo se va a la estación?; **I for one** yo por lo menos; **it's all one and the same to me** me es igual; **my little one** mi chiquito; **of one another** el uno del otro, los unos de los otros,

p.ej., **we took leave of one another** nos despedimos el uno del otro; **one and all** todos; **one another** se, p.ej., **they greeted one another** se saludaron; uno a otro, unos a otros, p.ej., **they looked at one another** se miraron uno a otro; **one by one** uno a uno; **one o'clock** la una; **one or two** unos pocos; **one's** su, el . . . de uno; **the blue book and the red one** el libro azul y el rojo; **the one and only** el único; **the one that** el que, la que; **this one** éste; **that one** ése, aquél; **to make one** unir; casar ‖ *s* uno

one'-horse' *adj* de un solo caballo, tirado por un solo caballo; (coll) insignificante, de poca monta

onerous ['ɑnərəs] *adj* oneroso

one'self' *pron* uno mismo; sí, sí mismo; se; **to be oneself** tener dominio de sí mismo; conducirse con naturalidad

one-sided ['wʌn'saɪdɪd] *adj* de un solo lado; injusto, parcial; desigual; unilateral

one'-track' *adj* de carril único; (coll) con un solo interés

one'-way' *adj* de una sola dirección, de dirección única; (*ticket*) sencillo, de ida

onion ['ʌnjən] *s* cebolla

on'ion‧skin' *s* papel *m* de seda, papel cebolla

on'look'er *s* mirón *m*, espectador *m*

only ['onlɪ] *adj* solo, único ‖ *adv* solamente, sólo, únicamente; no . . . más que; **not only . . . but also** no sólo . . . sino también ‖ *conj* sólo que, pero

on'set' *s* arremetida, embestida; (*of an illness*) principio

onward ['ɑnwərd] u **onwards** ['ɑnwərdz] *adv* adelante, hacia adelante

onyx ['ɑnɪks] *s* ónice *m* u ónix *m*

ooze [uz] *s* chorro suave; cieno, limo, lama ‖ *tr* rezumar ‖ *intr* rezumar, rezumarse; manar suavemente (*p.ej., la sangre de una herida*); agotarse poco a poco

op. *abbr* **opera, operation, opus, opposite**

opal ['opəl] *s* ópalo

opaque [o'pek] *adj* opaco; (*writer's style*) obscuro; estúpido

open ['opən] *adj* abierto; descubierto, destapado; sin tejado; vacante; (*hour*) libre; discutible, pendiente; (*hand*) liberal; (*hunting season*) legal; **to break o crack open** abrir con violencia, abrir por la fuerza; **to throw open** abrir de par en par ‖ *s* abertura; (*in the woods*) claro; **in the open** al aire libre; a campo raso; en alta mar; abiertamente ‖ *tr* abrir; desbullar (*una ostra*) ‖ *intr* abrir; abrirse; estrenarse (*un drama*); **to open into** desembocar en; **to open on** dar a; **to open up** descubrirse; descubrir el pecho

o'pen-air' *adj* al aire libre, a cielo abierto

open-eyed ['opən ‚aɪd] *adj* alerta, vigi-

lante; con ojos asombrados; hecho
con los ojos abiertos

open-handed ['opən'hændɪd] *adj* ma-
niabierto, liberal

open-hearted ['opən'hɑrtɪd] *adj* franco, sincero

open house *s* coliche *m*; **to keep open
house** recibir a todos, gustar de tener siempre convidados en casa

opening ['opənɪŋ] *s* abertura; (*of, e.g.,
school*) apertura; (*in the woods*)
claro; (*vacancy*) hueco, vacante *f*;
(*chance to say something*) ocasión

opening night *s* noche *f* de estreno

opening number *s* primer número

opening price *s* primer curso, precio de
apertura

open-minded ['opən'maɪndɪd] *adj* receptivo, razonable, imparcial

open secret *s* secreto a voces

open shop *s* taller franco

o'pen·work' *s* calado

opera ['ɑpərə] *s* ópera

opera glasses *spl* gemelos de teatro

opera hat *s* clac *m*, sombrero de
muelles

opera house *s* teatro de la ópera

operate ['ɑpə‚ret] *tr* hacer funcionar;
dirigir, manejar; explotar ‖ *intr*
funcionar; operar; **to operate on**
operar (*p.ej., una hernia; a un niño*)

operatic [‚ɑpə'rætɪk] *adj* operístico

operating expenses *spl* gastos de explotación

operating room *s* quirófano

operating table *s* mesa operatoria

operation [‚ɑpə're/ən] *s* operación;
funcionamiento; explotación

operator ['ɑpə‚retər] *s* operador *m*,
maquinista *m*; (com) empresario;
(coll) corredor *m* de bolsa; (surg,
telp) operador *m*

operetta [‚ɑpə'retə] *s* opereta

opiate ['opɪ·ɪt] *u* ['opɪ‚et] *adj & s*
opiato

opinion [ə'pɪnjən] *s* opinión; **in my
opinion a** mi parecer; **to have a high
opinion of** tener buen concepto de

opinionated [ə'pɪnjə‚netɪd] *adj* porfiado en su parecer, dogmático

opium ['opɪ·əm] *s* opio

opium den *s* fumadero de opio

opossum [ə'pɑsəm] *s* zarigüeya

opponent [ə'ponənt] *s* contrario

opportune [‚ɑpər'tjun] o [‚ɑpər'tun]
adj oportuno

opportunist [‚ɑpər'junɪst] o [‚ɑpər-
'tunɪst] *s* oportunista *mf*

opportuni·ty [‚ɑpər'junɪtɪ] o [‚ɑpər-
'tunɪtɪ] *s* (*pl* **-ties**) oportunidad,
ocasión

oppose [ə'poz] *tr* oponerse a

opposite ['ɑpəsɪt] *adj* opuesto; de enfrente, p.ej., **the house opposite** la
casa de enfrente ‖ *prep* enfrente de
‖ *s* contrario

opposite number *s* igual *mf*, doble *mf*

opposition [‚ɑpə'zɪ/ən] *s* oposición

oppress [ə'pres] *tr* oprimir

oppression [ə'pre/ən] *s* opresión

oppressive [ə'presɪv] *adj* opresivo; sofocante, bochornoso

opprobrious [ə'probrɪ·əs] *adj* opro-
bioso

opprobrium [ə'probrɪ·əm] *s* oprobio

optic ['ɑptɪk] *adj* óptico ‖ *s* (coll) ojo;
optics *ssg* óptica

optical ['ɑptɪkəl] *adj* óptico

optician [ɑp'tɪ/ən] *s* óptico

optimism ['ɑptɪ‚mɪzəm] *s* optimismo

optimist ['ɑptɪmɪst] *s* optimista *mf*

optimistic [‚ɑptɪ'mɪstɪk] *adj* optimís-
tico

option ['ɑp/ən] *s* opción

optional ['ɑp/ənəl] *adj* facultativo, po-
testativo

optometrist [ɑp'tɑmɪtrɪst] *s* optometrista *mf*

opulent ['ɑpjələnt] *adj* opulento

or [ɔr] *conj* o, u

oracle ['ɑrəkəl] *u* ['ɔrəkəl] *s* oráculo

oracular [o'rækjələr] *adj* sentencioso;
ambiguo, misterioso; fatídico; sabio

oral ['orəl] *adj* oral

orange ['ɑrɪndʒ] *u* ['ɔrɪndʒ] *adj* ana-
ranjado ‖ *s* naranja

orangeade [‚ɑrɪndʒ'ed] *u* [‚ɔrɪndʒ'ed]
s naranjada

orange blossom *s* azahar *m*

orange grove *s* naranjal *m*

orange juice *s* zumo de naranja

orange squeezer *s* exprimidera de naranjas

orange tree *s* naranjo

orang-outang [o'ræŋu‚tæŋ] *s* orangután *m*

oration [o're/ən] *s* oración, discurso

orator ['ɑrətər] *u* ['ɔrətər] *s* orador *m*

oratorical [‚ɑrə'tɑrɪkəl] *u* [‚ɔrə-
'tɔrɪkəl] *adj* oratorio

oratori·o [‚ɑrə'torɪ‚o] *u* [‚ɔrə'tɔrɪ‚o]
s (*pl* **-os**) oratorio

orato·ry ['ɑrə‚torɪ] *u* ['ɔrə‚torɪ] *s* (*pl*
-ries) (*art of public speaking*) oratoria; (*small chapel*) oratorio

orb [ɔrb] *s* orbe *m*

orbit ['ɔrbɪt] *s* órbita; **to go into orbit**
entrar en órbita ‖ *tr* poner en órbita;
moverse en órbita alrededor de ‖ *intr*
moverse en órbita

orchard ['ɔrt/ərd] *s* huerto

orchestra ['ɔrkɪstrə] *s* orquesta; (*parquet*) platea

orchestrate ['ɔrkɪs‚tret] *tr* orquestar

orchid ['ɔrkɪd] *s* orquídea

ordain [ɔr'den] *tr* (eccl) ordenar; destinar; mandar

ordeal [ɔr'dil] *u* [ɔr'di·əl] *s* prueba
rigurosa o penosa; (hist) juicio de
Dios

order ['ɔrdər] *s* (*way one thing follows another; formal or methodical
arrangement; peace, quiet; class,
category*) orden *m*; (*command;
honor society; monastic brotherhood; fraternal organization*) orden
f; tarea, p.ej., **a big order** una tarea
peliaguda; (com) pedido; (com) giro,
libranza; (*formation*) (mil) orden *m*;
(*command*) (mil) orden *f*; **in order
that** para que, a fin de que; **in order
to** + *inf* para + *inf*, a fin de + *inf*;
to get out of order descomponerse;
to give an order dar una orden;
(com) hacer un pedido ‖ *tr* ordenar;

om
or

mandar; encargar, pedir; mandar hacer; **to order around** ser muy mandón con; **to order someone away** mandar a uno que se marche

order blank s hoja de pedidos

order·ly ['ɔrdərli] adj ordenado, gobernoso; tranquilo, obediente ‖ s (pl -lies) asistente m en un hospital; (mil) ordenanza m

ordinal ['ɔrdɪnəl] adj & s ordinal m

ordinance ['ɔrdɪnəns] s ordenanza

ordinary ['ɔrdɪˌneri] adj ordinario

ordnance ['ɔrdnəns] s artillería, cañones mpl; pertrechos de guerra

ore [or] s mena, mineral metalífero

organ ['ɔrgən] s órgano

organ·dy ['ɔrgəndi] s (pl -dies) organdí m

or'gan-grind'er s organillero

organic [ɔr'gænɪk] adj orgánico

organism ['ɔrgəˌnɪzəm] s organismo

organist ['ɔrgənɪst] s organista mf

organize ['ɔrgəˌnaɪz] tr organizar

organ loft s tribuna del órgano

or·gy ['ɔrdʒi] s (pl -gies) orgía

orient ['ɔri·ənt] s oriente m ‖ **Orient** s oriente ‖ **orient** ['ɔriˌent] tr orientar

oriental [ˌɔri'entəl] adj oriental

orifice ['ɑrɪfɪs] u ['ɔrɪfɪs] s orificio

origin ['ɑrɪdʒɪn] u ['ɔrɪdʒɪn] s origen m

original [ə'rɪdʒɪnəl] adj & s original m

originate [ə'rɪdʒɪˌnet] tr originar ‖ intr originarse

oriole ['ɔri·ol] s oropéndola

Orkney Islands ['ɔrkni] spl Órcadas

ormolu ['ɔrməˌlu] s (gold powder used in gilding) oro molido; (alloy of zinc and copper) similar m; bronce dorado

ornament ['ɔrnəmənt] s ornamento ‖ ['ɔrnəˌment] tr ornamentar

ornate [ɔr'net] u ['ɔrnet] adj muy ornado; (style) florido

orphan ['ɔrfən] adj & s huérfano ‖ tr dejar huérfano

orphanage ['ɔrfənɪdʒ] s (institution) orfanato; (state, condition) orfandad

orphan asylum s asilo de huérfanos

Orpheus ['ɔrfjus] u ['ɔrfi·əs] s Orfeo

orthodox ['ɔrθəˌdɑks] adj ortodoxo

orthogra·phy [ɔr'θɑgrəfi] s (pl -phies) ortografía

oscillate ['ɑsɪˌlet] intr oscilar

osier ['oʒər] s mimbre m & f; sauce mimbrero

ossi·fy ['ɑsɪˌfaɪ] v (pret & pp -fied) tr osificar ‖ intr osificarse

ostensible [ɑs'tensɪbəl] adj aparente, pretendido, supuesto

ostentatious [ˌɑsten'teʃəs] adj (pretentious) ostentativo; (showy) ostentoso

osteopath ['ɑstɪ·əˌpæθ] s osteópata mf

osteopathy [ˌɑstɪ'ɑpəθi] s osteopatía

ostracism ['ɑstrəˌsɪzəm] s ostracismo

ostrich ['ɑstrɪtʃ] s avestruz m

O.T. abbr Old Testament

other ['ʌðər] adj & pron indef otro ‖ adv — **other than** de otra manera que

otherwise ['ʌðərˌwaɪz] adv otramente,

de otra manera; en otras circunstancias; fuera de eso; si no, de otro modo

otter ['ɑtər] s nutria

ottoman ['ɑtəmən] s (corded fabric) otomán m; (sofa) otomana; escañuelo con cojín ‖ **Ottoman** adj & s otomano

ouch [autʃ] interj ¡ax!

ought [ɔt] s alguna cosa; cero; **for ought I know** por lo que yo sepa ‖ v aux se emplea para formar el modo potencial, p.ej., **he ought to go at once** debiera salir en seguida

ounce [auns] s onza

our [aur] adj poss nuestro

ours [aurz] pron poss el nuestro; nuestro

ourselves [aur'selvz] pron pers nosotros mismos; nos, p.ej., **we enjoyed ourselves** nos divertimos

oust [aust] tr echar fuera, desposeer; desahuciar (al inquilino)

out [aut] adj ausente; apagado; exterior; divulgado; publicado; (size) poco común ‖ adv afuera, fuera; al aire libre; hasta el fin; **out for** buscando; **out of** de; entre; de entre; fuera de; más allá de; (kindness, fear, etc.) por; (money) sin; (a suit of cards) fallo a; sobre, p.ej., **in nine out of ten cases** en nueve casos sobre diez; **out to** + inf esforzándose por + inf ‖ prep por; allá en ‖ interj ¡fuera de aquí! ‖ s cesante mf; **to be at outs u on the outs** estar de monos

out and away adv con mucho

out'-and-out' adj perfecto, verdadero, rematado ‖ adv completamente

out'-and-out'er s intransigente mf; extremista m

out·bid' v (pret -bid; pp -bid o -bidden; ger -bidding) tr pujar más que (otra persona); (bridge) sobrepasar

out'board' motor s motor m fuera de borda

out'break' s tumulto, motín m; (of anger) arranque m; (of war) estallido; (of an epidemic) brote m

out'build'ing s dependencia, edificio accesorio

out'burst' s explosión, arranque m; **outburst of laughter** carcajada

out'cast' s proscripto, paria mf; vagabundo

out'come' s resultado

out'cry' s (pl -cries) grito; gritería, clamoreo

out·dat'ed adj fuera de moda, anticuado

out·do' v (pret -did; pp -done) tr exceder; **to outdo oneself** excederse a sí mismo

out'door' adj al aire libre

out'doors' adv al aire libre, fuera de casa ‖ s aire m libre, campo raso

outer space ['autər] s espacio exterior

out'field' s (baseball) jardín m

out'field'er s (baseball) jardinero

out'fit s equipo; traje m; juego de herramientas; (of soldiers) cuerpo; (of a bride) ajuar m; (com) compañía ‖

v (pret & pp -fitted; *ger* -fitting) *tr* equipar

out·go'ing *adj* de salida; cesante; *(tide)* descendente; *(nature, character)* exteriorista || *s* salida

out·grow' *v (pret* -grew; *pp* -grown) *tr* crecer más que; ser ya grande para; ser ya viejo para; ser ya más apto que; dejar *(las cosas de los niños; a los amigos de la niñez, etc.)* || *intr* extenderse

out'growth' *s* excrecencia, bulto; *(of leaves in springtime)* nacimiento; consecuencia, resultado

outing ['autɪŋ] *s* jira, excursión al campo

outlandish [aut'lændɪʃ] *adj* estrafalario; de aspecto extranjero; de acento extranjero

out·last' *tr* durar más que; sobrevivir a

out'law' *s* forajido, bandido; prófugo, proscrito || *tr* proscribir; declarar ilegal

out'lay' *s* desembolso || **out·lay'** *v (pret & pp* -laid) *tr* desembolsar

out'let' *s* salida; desaguadero; orificio de salida; (elec) caja de enchufe; *(tap)* (elec) toma-corriente *m*

out'line' *s* contorno; trazado; esquema *m;* esbozo, bosquejo; compendio || *tr* contornar; trazar; trazar el esquema de; esbozar, bosquejar; compendiar

out·live' *tr* sobrevivir a; durar más que

out'look' *s* perspectiva; expectativa; concepto de la vida, punto de vista; atalaya

out'ly'ing *adj* remoto, circundante, de las afueras

out·mod'ed *adj* fuera de moda

out·num'ber *tr* exceder en número, ser más numeroso que

out'-of-date' *adj* fuera de moda, anticuado

out'-of-door' *adj* al aire libre

out'-of-doors' *adj* al aire libre || *adv* al aire libre, fuera de casa || *s* aire *m* libre, campo raso

out'-of-print' *adj* agotado

out'-of-the-way' *adj* apartado, remoto; poco usual, poco común

out of tune *adj* desafinado || *adv* desafinadamente

out of work *adj* desempleado, sin trabajo

out'pa'tient *s* paciente *mf* de consulta externa

out'post' *s* avanzada

out'put' *s* rendimiento; (elec) salida; (mech) rendimiento de trabajo, efecto útil

out·rage *s* atrocidad; ultraje *m* || *tr* maltratar; ultrajar; escandalizar

outrageous [aut'redʒəs] *adj (grossly offensive)* ultrajoso; *(shocking, fierce)* atroz; *(extreme)* extravagante

out·rank' *tr* exceder en rango o grado

out'rid'er *s* carrerista *m;* (Brit) viajante *m* de comercio

out'right' *adj* cabal, completo; franco, sincero || *adv* enteramente; de una vez; sin rodeos; en seguida

out'run'ner *s* volante *m (criado)*

out'set' *s* principio

out'side' *adj* exterior; superficial; ajeno; *(price)* (el) máximo || *adj* fuera, afuera; **outside of** fuera de || *prep* fuera de; más allá de; (coll) a excepción de || *s* exterior *m;* superficie *f;* apariencia

outsider [aut'saɪdər] *s* forastero; intruso

out'skirts' *spl* afueras

out'spo'ken *adj* boquifresco, franco

out·stand'ing *adj* sobresaliente; prominente; sin pagar, sin cobrar

outward ['autwərd] *adj* exterior; superficial || *adv* exteriormente, hacia fuera

out·weigh' *tr* pesar más que; contrapesar, compensar

out·wit' *v (pret & pp* -witted; *ger* -witting) *tr* burlar, ser más listo que; despistar *(al perseguidor)*

oval ['ovəl] *adj* oval || *s* óvalo

ova·ry ['ovəri] *s (pl* -ries) ovario

ovation [o'veʃən] *s* ovación

oven ['ʌvən] *s* horno

over ['ovər] *adj* acabado, concluído; superior; adicional; excesivo || *adv* encima; al otro lado, a la otra orilla; hacia abajo; al revés; patas arriba; otra vez, de nuevo; de añadidura; *(at the bottom of a page)* a la vuelta; acá, p.ej., **hand over the money** déme acá el dinero; **over again** una vez más; **over against** enfrente de; a distinción de; en contraste con; **over and over** repetidas veces; **over here** acá; **over in** allá en; **over there** allá || *prep* sobre, encima de, por encima de; por, de un extremo a otro de; al otro lado de; más allá de; desde; *(a certain number)* más de; acerca de; por causa de; durante; **over and above** además de, en exceso de

o'ver·all' *adj* cabal, completo; extremo, total || **overalls** *spl* pantalones *mf* de trabajo

o'ver·bear'ing *adj* altanero, imperioso

o'ver·board' *adv* al agua; **man overboard!** ¡hombre al agua!; **to throw overboard** arrojar, echar o tirar por la borda

o'ver·cast' *adj* encapotado, nublado || *s* cielo encapotado || *v (pret & pp* -cast) *tr* nublar

o'ver·charge' *s* cargo excesivo; recargo de precio; sobrecarga; (elec) carga excesiva || **o'ver·charge'** *tr* hacer pagar más del valor, cobrar demasiado a; cargar *(p.ej., 50 pesetas)* de más; (elec) poner una carga excesiva a

o'ver·coat' *s* abrigo, gabán *m,* sobretodo

o'ver·come' *v (pret* -came; *pp* -come) *tr* vencer; rendir; superar *(dificultades)*

o'ver·crowd' *tr* atestar, apiñar; poblar con exceso

o'ver·do' *v (pret* -did; *pp* -done) *tr* exagerar; agobiar; asurar, requemar || *intr* cansarse mucho, excederse en el trabajo

o'ver·dose' *s* dosis excesiva

or
ov

o'ver-draft' s sobregiro, giro en descubierto

o'ver-draw' v (pret -drew; pp -drawn) tr & intr sobregirar

o'ver-due' adj atrasado; vencido y no pagado

o'ver-eat' v (pret -ate; pp -eaten) tr & intr comer con exceso

o'ver-exer'tion s esfuerzo excesivo

o'ver-expose' tr sobreexponer

o'ver-expo'sure s sobreexposición

o'ver-flow' s desbordamiento, rebosamiento, derrame m; caño de reboso || o'ver-flow' intr desbordar, rebosar

o'ver-fly' v (pret -flew; pp -flown) tr sobrevolar

o'ver-grown' adj demasiado grande para su edad; denso, frondoso

o'ver-hang' v (pret & pp -hung) tr sobresalir por encima de, estar pendiente o colgando sobre, salir fuera del nivel de; amenazar || intr estar pendiente, estar colgando

o'ver-haul' tr examinar, registrar, revisar; ir alcanzando, alcanzar; componer, rehabilitar, reacondicionar

o'ver-head' adj de arriba; aéreo, elevado; general, de conjunto || o'ver-head' adv por encima de la cabeza; arriba, en lo alto || o'ver-head' s gastos generales

o'ver-hear' v (pret & pp -heard) tr oír por casualidad; acertar a oír, alcanzar a oír

o'ver-heat' tr recalentar || intr recalentarse

overjoyed [,ovər'dʒɔɪd] adj lleno de alegría; to be overjoyed no caber de contento

overland ['ovər,lænd] u ['ovərlənd] adj & adv por tierra, por vía terrestre

o'ver-lap' v (pret & pp -lapped; ger -lapping) tr solapar, traslapar || intr solapar, traslapar; traslaparse (dos o más cosas); suceder (dos hechos) en parte al mismo tiempo

o'ver-load' s sobrecarga || o'ver-load' tr sobrecargar

o'ver-look' tr dominar con la vista; pasar por alto, no hacer caso de; perdonar, tolerar; espiar, vigilar; cuidar de, dirigir; dar a, p.ej., the window overlooks the garden la ventana da al jardín

o'ver-lord' s jefe supremo || o'ver-lord' tr dominar despóticamente, imponerse a

overly ['ovərli] adv (coll) excesivamente, demasiado

o'ver-night' adv toda la noche; de la tarde a la mañana; to stay overnight pasar la noche

overnight bag s saco de noche

o'ver-pass' s viaducto

o'ver-pop'u-late' tr superpoblar

o'verpow'er tr dominar, supeditar, subyugar; colmar, dejar estupefacto

overpowering adj abrumador, arrollador, irresistible

o'ver-produc'tion s superproducción, sobreproducción

o'ver-rate' tr exagerar el valor de

o'ver-run' v (pret -ran; pp -run; ger -running) tr cubrir enteramente; infestar; exceder; to overrun one's time quedarse más de lo justo; hablar más de lo justo

o'ver-sea' u o'ver-seas' adj de ultramar || o'ver-sea' u o'ver-seas' adv allende los mares, en ultramar

o'ver-seer' s director m, superintendente mf

o'ver-shad'ow tr sombrear; (fig) eclipsar

o'ver-shoe' s chanclo, zapato de goma

o'ver-shoot' v (pret & pp -shot) tr tirar por encima de o más allá de; to overshoot oneself pasarse de listo, excederse

o'ver-sight' s inadvertencia, descuido

o'ver-sleep' v (pret & pp -slept) intr dormir demasiado tarde

o'ver-step' v (pret & pp -stepped; ger -stepping) tr exceder, traspasar

o'ver-stock' tr abarrotar

o'ver-sup-ply' s (pl -plies) provisión excesiva || o'ver-sup-ply' v (pret -plied) tr proveer en exceso

overt ['ovərt] u [o'vɑrt] adj abierto, manifiesto; premeditado

o'ver-take' v (pret -took; pp -taken) tr alcanzar; sobrepasar; sorprender; sobrevenir a

o'ver-the-count'er adj vendido directamente al comprador; vendido en tienda al por mayor

o'ver-throw' s derrocamiento; trastorno || o'ver-throw' v (pret -threw; pp -thrown) tr derrocar; trastornar

o'ver-time' adj & adv en exceso de las horas regulares || s horas extraordinarias de trabajo

o'ver-trump' s contrafallo || o'ver-trump' tr & intr contrafallar

overture ['ovərtʃər] s insinuación, proposición; (mus) obertura

o'ver-turn' s vuelco; movimiento de mercancías || o'ver-turn' tr volcar; trastornar; derrocar || intr volcar; trastornarse

overweening [,ovər'winɪŋ] adj arrogante, presuntuoso

o'ver-weight' adj excesivamente gordo o grueso || s sobrepeso; exceso de peso; peso de añadidura

overwhelm [,ovər'hwelm] tr abrumar; inundar, anonadar; (with favors, gifts, etc.) colmar

o'ver-work' s trabajo excesivo, exceso de trabajo; trabajo fuera de las horas regulares || o'ver-work' tr hacer trabajar demasiado; oprimir con el trabajo || intr trabajar demasiado

Ovid ['ɑvɪd] s Ovidio

ow [au] interj ¡ax!

owe [o] tr deber, adeudar || intr tener deudas

owing ['o-ɪŋ] adj adeudado; debido, pagadero; owing to debido a, por causa de

owl [aul] s buho, lechuza, mochuelo

own [on] adj propio, p.ej., my own brother mi propio hermano || s suyo, lo suyo; on one's own (coll) por su propia cuenta; (without tak-

ing advice from anyone) por su cabeza; (*without help from anyone*) de su cabeza; **to come into one's own** entrar en posesión de lo suyo; tener el éxito merecido, recibir el honor merecido; **to hold one's own** no aflojar, no cejar, mantenerse firme ‖ *tr* poseer; reconocer ‖ *intr* confesar; **to own up to** (coll) confesar de plano (*una culpa, un delito, etc.*)

owner ['onər] *s* amo, dueño, poseedor *m*, propietario

ownership ['onər ,∫ɪp] *s* posesión, propiedad

owner's license *s* permiso de circulación, patente *f* de circulación

ox [ɑks] *s* (*pl* **oxen** ['ɑksən]) buey *m*

ox'cart' *s* carreta de bueyes

oxide ['ɑksaɪd] *s* óxido

oxidize ['ɑksɪ ,daɪz] *tr* oxidar ‖ *intr* oxidarse

oxygen ['ɑksɪdʒən] *s* oxígeno

oxygen tent *s* cámara o tienda de oxígeno

oxytone ['ɑksɪ ,ton] *adj & s* oxítono

oyster ['ɔɪstər] *adj* ostrero ‖ *s* ostra

oyster bed *s* ostrero

oyster cocktail *s* ostras en su concha

oyster fork *s* desbullador *m*

oys'ter·house' *s* ostrería

oys'ter·knife' *s* abreostras *m*

oyster·man ['ɔɪstərmən] *s* (*pl* **-men** [mən]) ostrero

oyster opener ['opənər] *s* desbullador *m*

oyster shell *s* desbulla, concha de ostra

oyster stew *s* sopa de ostras

oz. *abbr* **ounce, ounces**

ozone ['ozon] *s* ozono; (coll) aire fresco

ozs. *abbr* **ounces**

P

P, p [pi] decimosexta letra del alfabeto inglés

p. *abbr* **page, participle**

P.A. *abbr* **Passenger Agent, power of attorney, Purchasing Agent**

pace [pes] *s* paso; **to keep pace with** ir, andar o avanzar al mismo paso que; **to put through one's paces** poner (*a uno*) a prueba; dar a (*uno*) ocasión de lucirse; **to set the pace** establecer el paso; dar el ejemplo ‖ *tr* establecer el paso para; medir a pasos; recorrer a pasos; **to pace the floor** pasearse desesperadamente por la habitación ‖ *intr* andar a pasos regulares

pace'mak'er *s* (med) marcapaso

pacific [pə'sɪfɪk] *adj* pacífico ‖ **Pacific** *adj & s* Pacífico

pacifier ['pæsɪ ,faɪ·ər] *s* pacificador *m*; (*teething ring*) chupador *m*

pacifism ['pæsɪ ,fɪzəm] *s* pacifismo

pacifist ['pæsɪfɪst] *adj & s* pacifista *mf*

paci·fy ['pæsɪ ,faɪ] *v* (*pret & pp* **-fied**) *tr* pacificar

pack [pæk] *s* lío, fardo; paquete *m*; (*of hounds*) jauría; (*of cattle*) manada; (*of evildoers*) pandilla; (*of lies*) sarta, montón *m*; (*of playing cards*) baraja; (*of cigarettes*) cajetilla; (*of floating ice*) témpano; (med) compresa ‖ *tr* empaquetar; embaular; encajonar; hacer (*el baúl, la maleta*); conservar en latas; apretar, atestar; cargar (*una acémila*); escoger de modo fraudulento (*un jurado*); **to be packed in** (coll) estar como sardinas en banasta ‖ *intr* empaquetarse; hacer el baúl, hacer la maleta; consolidarse, formar masa compacta

package ['pækɪdʒ] *s* paquete *m* ‖ *tr* empaquetar

pack animal *s* acémila, animal *m* de carga

packing box o **case** *s* caja de embalaje

packing house *s* frigorífico

packing slip *s* hoja de embalaje

pack'sad'dle *s* albarda

pack'thread' *s* bramante *m*

pack train *s* recua

pact [pækt] *s* pacto

pad [pæd] *s* cojincillo, almohadilla; (*of writing paper*) bloc *m*; (*for inking*) tampón *m*; (*of an aquatic plant*) hoja; (*for launching a rocket*) plataforma *f*; (*sound of footsteps*) pisada ‖ *v* (*pret & pp* **padded**; *ger* **padding**) *tr* acolchar, rellenar; meter mucho ripio en (*un escrito*) ‖ *intr* andar, caminar; caminar despacio y pesadamente

paddle ['pædəl] *s* (*of a canoe*) canalete *m*; (*of a wheel*) pala, paleta; (*for spanking*) palo ‖ *tr* impulsar con canalete; (*to spank*) apalear ‖ *intr* remar con canalete; remar suavemente; (*to splash*) chapotear

paddle wheel *s* rueda de paletas

paddock ['pædək] *s* dehesa; (*at racecourse*) paddock *m*

pad'lock' *s* candado ‖ *tr* cerrar con candado; (*to lock up officially*) condenar (*una habitación, un teatro*)

pagan ['pegən] *adj & s* pagano

paganism ['pegə ,nɪzəm] *s* paganismo

page [pedʒ] *s* (*of a book*) página; (*boy attendant*) paje *m*; (*in a hotel or club*) botones *m* ‖ *tr* paginar; buscar llamando

pageant ['pædʒənt] *s* espectáculo público

pageant·ry ['pædʒəntri] *s* (*pl* **-ries**) pompa, fausto; (*empty display*) bambolla

pail [pel] *s* balde *m*, cubo

pain [pen] *s* dolor *m*; **on pain of** so pena de; **pains** esmero, trabajo; dolores de parto; **to take pains** esmerarse ‖ *tr & intr* doler

ov pa

painful ['penfəl] *adj* doloroso; penoso
pain'kill'er *s* (coll) remedio contra el dolor
painless ['penlɪs] *adj* sin dolor, indoloro; fácil, sin trabajo
pains'tak'ing *adj* esmerado
paint [pent] *s* pintura; (*rouge*) afeite *m*, colorete *m* || *tr* pintar || *intr* pintar; pintarse, repintarse
paint'box' *s* caja de colores
paint'brush' *s* brocha, pincel *m*
painter ['pentər] *s* pintor *m*
painting ['pentɪŋ] *s* pintura
paint remover [rɪ'muvər] *s* sacapintura *m*, quitapintura *m*
pair [per] *s* par *m*; (*of people*) pareja; (*of cards*) parejas || *tr* aparear || *intr* aparearse
pair of scissors *s* tijeras
pair of trousers *s* pantalones *mpl*
pajamas [pə'dʒɑmɑz] o [pə'dʒæməz] *spl* pijama
Pakistan [,pɑkɪ'stɑn] *s* el Paquistán
Pakistani [,pɑkɪ'stɑni] *adj & s* paquistano, paquistaní *mf*
pal [pæl] *s* (coll) compañero || *v* (*pret & pp* **palled**; *ger* **palling**) *intr* (coll) ser compañeros
palace ['pælɪs] *s* palacio
palatable ['pælətəbəl] *adj* sabroso, apetitoso
palatal ['pælətəl] *adj & s* palatal *f*
palate ['pælɪt] *s* paladar *m*
pale [pel] *adj* pálido; (*color*) claro || *s* estaca; palizada; límite *m*, término || *intr* palidecer
pale'face' *s* rostropálido
palette ['pælɪt] *s* paleta
palfrey ['pælfri] *s* palafrén *m*
palisade [,pælɪ'sed] *s* estaca; estacada; (*line of cliffs*) acantilado
pall [pɔl] *s* paño de ataúd, paño mortuorio; (eccl) palia || *tr* hartar, saciar; quitar el sabor a || *intr* perder el sabor; **to pall on** hartar, saciar
pall'bear'er *s* acompañante *m* de un cadáver; portador de del féretro
palliate ['pælɪ,et] *tr* paliar
pallid ['pælɪd] *adj* pálido
pallor ['pælər] *s* palidez *f*, palor *m*
palm [pɑm] *s* (*of the hand*) palma; (*measure*) palmo; (*tree and leaf*) palma; **to carry off the palm** llevarse la palma; **to grease the palm of** (slang) untar la mano a; **to yield the palm to** reconocer por vencedor || *tr* esconder en la mano; escamotear (*una carta*); **to palm off something on someone** encajarle una cosa a uno
palmet·to [pæl'meto] *s* (*pl* **-tos** o **-toes**) palmito
palmist ['pɑmɪst] *s* quiromántico
palmistry ['pɑmɪstri] *s* quiromancia
palm leaf *s* palma, hoja de la palmera
palm oil *s* aceite *m* de palma; (slang) propina; (slang) soborno
Palm Sunday *s* domingo de ramos
palpable ['pælpəbəl] *adj* palpable
palpitate ['pælpɪ,tet] *intr* palpitar
pal·sy ['pɔlzi] *s* (*pl* **-sies**) perlesía || *v* (*pret & pp* **-sied**) *tr* paralizar

pal·try ['pɔltri] *adj* (*comp* **-trier;** *super* **-triest**) vil, ruin, mezquino
pamper ['pæmpər] *tr* mimar, consentir
pamphlet ['pæmflɪt] *s* folleto, panfleto
pan [pæn] *s* cacerola, cazuela, sartén *f*; caldera, perol *m* || *v* (*pret & pp* **panned;** *ger* **panning**) *tr* cocer, freír; separar (*el oro*) en la gamella; (coll) criticar ásperamente || *intr* separar el oro en la gamella; dar oro; **to pan out well** (coll) tener éxito, dar buen resultado || **Pan** *s* Pan
panacea [,pænə'si·ə] *s* panacea
Panama Canal ['pænə,mɑ] *s* canal *m* de Panamá
Panama Canal Zone *s* Zona del Canal
Panama hat *s* panamá *m*
Panamanian [,pænə'meni·ən] o [,pænə'mɑni·ən] *adj & s* panameño
Pan-American [,pænə'merɪkən] *adj* panamericano
pan'cake' *s* hojuela, panqueque *m* || *intr* (aer) desplomarse
pancake landing *s* aterrizaje aplastado, aterrizaje en desplome
pancreas ['pænkrɪ·əs] *s* páncreas *m*
pander ['pændər] *s* alcahuete *m* || *intr* alcahuetear; **to pander to** gratificar
pane [pen] *s* cristal *m*, vidrio, hoja de vidrio
pan·el ['pænəl] *s* panel *m*, entrepaño, cuarterón *m*; grupo de personas en discusión cara al público; (aut, elec) tablero, panel *m*; (law) lista de personas que pueden servir como jurados || *v* (*pret & pp* **-eled** o **-elled;** *ger* **-eling** o **-elling**) *tr* adornar con cuarterones, labrar en cuarterones; artesonar (*un techo o bóveda*)
panel discussion *s* coloquio cara al público
panelist ['pænəlɪst] *s* coloquiante *mf* cara al público
panel lights *spl* luces *fpl* del tablero
pang [pæŋ] *s* dolor agudo; (*of remorse*) punzada; (*of death*) agonía
pan'han'dle *s* mango de sartén || *intr* (slang) mendigar, pedir limosna
pan·ic ['pænɪk] *adj & s* pánico || *v* (*pret & pp* **-icked;** *ger* **-icking**) *tr* sobrecoger de pánico || *intr* sobrecogerse de pánico
pan'ic-strick'en *adj* muerto de miedo, sobrecogido de terror
pano·ply ['pænəpli] *s* (*pl* **-plies**) panoplia; traje *m* ceremonial
panorama [,pænə'ræmə] o [,pænə'rɑmə] *s* panorama *m*
pan·sy ['pænzi] *s* (*pl* **-sies**) pensamiento
pant [pænt] *s* jadeo; palpitación; **pants** pantalones *mpl*; **to wear the pants** (coll) calzarse los pantalones || *intr* jadear; palpitar
pantheism ['pænθɪ,ɪzəm] *s* panteísmo
pantheon ['pænθɪ,ɑn] o ['pænθɪ·ən] *s* panteón *m*
panther ['pænθər] *s* pantera; puma
panties ['pæntiz] *spl* pantaloncillos de mujer
pantomime ['pæntə,maɪm] *s* pantomima

pan·try ['pæntri] *s* (*pl* **-tries**) despensa
pap [pæp] *s* papilla, papas
papa·cy ['pepəsi] *s* (*pl* **-cies**) papado
paper ['pepər] *s* papel *m*; (*newspaper*) periódico; (*of needles*) paño ‖ *tr* empapelar
pa'per·back' *s* libro en rústica
pa'per·boy' *s* vendedor *m* de periódicos
paper clip *s* sujetapapeles *m*
paper cone *s* cucurucho
paper cutter *s* cortapapeles *m*, guillotina
paper doll *s* muñeca de papel
paper hanger *s* empapelador *m*, papelista *mf*
paper knife *s* cortapapeles *m*
paper mill *s* fábrica de papel
paper money *s* papel *m* moneda
paper profits *spl* ganancias no realizadas sobre valores no vendidos
paper tape *s* cinta perforada
pa'per·weight' *s* pisapapeles *m*
paper work *s* preparación o comprobación de escritos
paprika [pæ'prikə] o ['pæprɪkə] *s* pimentón *m*
papy·rus [pə'paɪrəs] *s* (*pl* **-ri** [raɪ]) papiro
par. *abbr* **paragraph, parallel, parenthesis, parish**
par [pɑr] *adj* a la par; nominal; normal ‖ *s* paridad; valor *m* nominal; **above par** sobre la par; con beneficio, con premio; **below par** o **under par** bajo la par; con pérdida; (coll) indispuesto; **to be on a par with** correr parejas con
parable ['pærəbəl] *s* parábola
parachute ['pærə,ʃut] *s* paracaídas *m* ‖ *intr* lanzarse en paracaídas; **to parachute to safety** salvarse en paracaídas
parachute jump *s* salto en paracaídas
parachutist ['pærə,ʃutɪst] *s* paracaidista *mf*
parade [pə'red] *s* desfile *m*; paseo; ostentación ‖ *tr* ostentar, pasear ‖ *intr* desfilar, pasar por las calles; (mil) formar en parada
paradise ['pærə,daɪs] *s* paraíso
paradox ['pærə,dɑks] *s* paradoja; persona o cosa incomprensibles
paradoxical [,pærə'dɑksɪkəl] *adj* paradójico
paraffin ['pærəfɪn] *s* parafina
paragon ['pærə,gɑn] *s* dechado
paragraph ['pærə,græf] o ['pærə,graf] *s* párrafo
Paraguay ['pærə,gwe] o ['pærə,gwaɪ] *s* el Paraguay
Paraguayan [,pærə'gwe·ən] o [,pærə-'gwaɪ·ən] *adj* & *s* paraguayano, paraguayo
parakeet ['pærə,kit] *s* perico, periquito
paral·lel ['pærə,lɛl] *adj* paralelo ‖ *s* (línea) paralela; (plano) paralelo; (geog) paralelo; doble raya vertical ‖ *v* (*pret* & *pp* **-leled** o **-lelled**; *ger* **-leling** o **-lelling**) *tr* ser paralelo a; poner en dirección paralela; correr parejas con; (*to compare*) paralelizar

parallel bars *spl* paralelas, barras paralelas
paraly·sis [pə'rælɪsɪs] *s* (*pl* **-ses** [,siz]) parálisis *f*
paralytic [,pærə'lɪtɪk] *adj* & *s* paralítico
paralyze ['pærə,laɪz] *tr* paralizar
paramount ['pærə,maunt] *adj* capital, supremo, principalísimo
paranoiac [,pærə'nɔɪ·æk] *adj* & *s* paranoico
parapet ['pærə,pet] *s* parapeto
paraphernalia [,pærəfər'nelɪ·ə] *spl* trastos, atavíos
parasite ['pærə,saɪt] *s* parásito
parasitic(al) [,pærə'sɪtɪk(əl)] *adj* parasítico, parasitario
parasol ['pærə,sɔl] o ['pærə,sal] *s* quitasol *m*, parasol *m*
pa'ra·troop'er *s* paracaidista *m*
pa'ra·troops' *spl* tropas paracaidistas
parboil ['pɑr,bɔɪl] *tr* sancochar; calentar con exceso
par·cel ['pɑrsəl] *s* paquete *m*, atado, bulto ‖ *v* (*pret* & *pp* **-celed** o **-celled**; *ger* **-celing** o **-celling**) *tr* empaquetar; parcelar (*el terreno*); **to parcel out** repartir
parcel post *s* paquetes *mpl* postales
parch [pɑrtʃ] *tr* abrasar, tostar; **to be parched** tener mucha sed
parchment ['pɑrtʃmənt] *s* pergamino
pardon ['pɑrdən] *s* perdón *m*; (*remission of penalty by the state*) indulto; **I beg your pardon** dispense Vd. ‖ *tr* perdonar, dispensar; indultar
pardonable ['pɑrdənəbəl] *adj* perdonable
pardon board *s* junta de perdones
pare [per] *tr* mondar (*fruta*); pelar (*patatas*); cortar (*callos, uñas*); despalmar (*la palma córnea de los animales*); adelgazar; reducir (*gastos*)
parent ['perənt] *adj* madre, matriz, principal ‖ *s* padre o madre; autor *m*, fuente *f*, origen *m*; **parents** padres *mpl*
parentage ['perəntɪdʒ] *s* paternidad o maternidad; abolengo, linaje *m*
parenthe·sis [pə'renθɪsɪs] *s* (*pl* **-ses** [,siz]) paréntesis *m*
parenthood ['perənt,hud] *s* paternidad o maternidad
pariah [pə'raɪ·ə] o ['pɑrɪ·ə] *s* paria *mf*
paring knife ['perɪŋ] *s* cuchillo para mondar
parish ['pærɪʃ] *s* parroquia, feligresía
parishioner [pə'rɪʃənər] *s* parroquiano, feligrés *m*
Parisian [pə'rɪʒən] *adj* & *s* parisiense *mf*
parity ['pærɪti] *s* paridad
park [pɑrk] *s* parque *m* ‖ *tr* estacionar, parquear; (coll) colocar, dejar ‖ *intr* estacionar, parquear
parking ['pɑrkɪŋ] *s* aparcamiento, estacionamiento; **no parking** se prohibe estacionarse
parking lights *spl* (aut) faros de situación
parking lot *s* parque *m* de estacionamiento

parking meter s reloj m de estacionamiento, parquímetro

parking ticket s aviso de multa

park'way' s gran vía adornada con árboles

parley ['pɑrli] s parlamento ‖ intr parlamentar

parliament ['pɑrlɪmənt] s parlamento

parlor ['pɑrlər] s sala; parlatorio, locutorio

parlor car s coche-salón m

parlor politics spl política de café

Parnassus [pɑr'næsəs] s (collection of poems) parnaso; el Parnaso; **to try to climb Parnassus** hacer pinos en poesía

parochial [pə'rokɪ-əl] adj parroquial; estrecho, limitado

paro·dy ['pærədi] s (pl -dies) parodia ‖ v (pret & pp -died) tr parodiar

parole [pə'rol] s palabra de honor; libertad bajo palabra ‖ tr dejar libre bajo palabra

paroxytone [pær'ɑksɪˌton] adj & s paroxítono

par·quet [pɑr'ke] s entarimado; (theat) platea ‖ v (pret & pp -queted ['ked]; ger -queting ['ke-ɪŋ]) tr entarimar

parricide ['pærɪˌsaɪd] s (act) parricidio; (person) parricida mf

parrot ['pærət] s papagayo, loro; (fig) papagayo ‖ tr repetir o imitar como loro

par·ry ['pæri] s (pl -ries) parada, quite m ‖ v (pret & pp -ried) tr parar; defenderse de

parse [pɑrs] tr analizar (una oración) gramaticalmente; describir (una palabra) gramaticalmente

parsley ['pɑrsli] s perejil m

parsnip ['pɑrsnɪp] s chirivía

parson ['pɑrsən] s cura m, párroco; clérigo; pastor m protestante

part [pɑrt] s parte f; (of a machine) pieza; (of the hair) raya; (theat) parte f, papel m; **part and parcel** parte esencial, parte inseparable, elemento esencial; **parts** partes fpl; prendas, dotes fpl; **to do one's part** cumplir con su obligación; **to look the part** vestir el cargo; **to take the part of** tomar el partido de, defender; desempeñar el papel de ‖ tr dividir, partir, separar; **to part the hair** hacerse la raya ‖ intr separarse; **to part with** deshacerse de, abandonar; despedirse de

par·take [pɑr'tek] v (pret -took ['tʊk]; pp -taken) tr compartir; comer; beber ‖ intr participar

Parthenon ['pɑrθɪˌnɑn] s Partenón m

partial ['pɑrʃəl] adj parcial; aficionado

participate [pɑr'tɪsɪˌpet] intr participar

participle ['pɑrtɪˌsɪpəl] s participio

particle ['pɑrtɪkəl] s partícula, corpúsculo

particular [pər'tɪkjələr] adj particular; difícil, exigente. quisquilloso; esmerado; minucioso; **a particular . . . cierto . . .** ‖ s particular m

partisan ['pɑrtɪzən] adj & s partidario, partidista mf; (mil) partisano

partition [pɑr'tɪʃən] s partición, distribución; división; porción; tabique m ‖ tr repartir; dividir en cuartos, aposentos; tabicar

partner ['pɑrtnər] s compañero; (wife or husband) cónyuge mf; (in a dance) pareja f; (in business) socio

partnership ['pɑrtnərˌʃɪp] s asociación; consorcio, vida en común; (com) sociedad, asociación comercial

partridge ['pɑrtrɪdʒ] s perdiz f

part'-time' adj por horas, parcial

par·ty ['pɑrti] adj de partido; de gala ‖ s (pl -ties) convite m, reunión, fiesta, tertulia, recepción; (for fishing, hunting, etc.; of armed men) partida; cómplice mf, interesado; (pol) partido; (coll) persona, individuo

party girl s chica de vida alegre

party-goer ['pɑrtiˌgo·ər] s tertuliano; fiestero

party line s (between two properties) linde m, lindero; (of communist party) línea del partido; (telp) línea compartida

party politics s política de partido

pass. abbr **passenger, passive**

pass [pæs] o [pɑs] s paso; (permit; free ticket; movement of hands of mesmerist; of bullfighter) pase m; (in an examination) aprobación; nota de aprobación ‖ tr pasar; pasar de largo (una luz roja); aprobar (un proyecto de ley; un examen; a un alumno); ser aprobado en (un examen); dejar atrás; cruzarse con; expresar (una opinión); pronunciar (una sentencia); dar (la palabra); dejar sin protestar; no pagar (un dividendo); **to pass off** colar, pasar, hacer aceptar (una moneda falsa); disimular (p.ej., una ofensa con una risa); **to pass over** omitir, pasar por alto; excusar; desdeñar; dejar sin protestar; postergar (a un empleado) ‖ intr pasar; pasarse (introducirse); aprobar; **to bring to pass** llevar a cabo; **to come to pass** suceder; **to pass as** pasar por; **to pass away** pasar, pasar a mejor vida; **to pass off** pasar (una enfermedad, una tempestad, etc.); tener lugar; **to pass out** salir; (slang) desmayarse; **to pass over** pasarse a (p.ej., el enemigo)

passable ['pæsəbəl] o ['pɑsəbəl] adj pasadero; (law) promulgable

passage ['pæsɪdʒ] s pasaje m; paso; pasillo; (of time) transcurso; (of bowels) evacuación

pass'book' s cartilla, libreta de banco

passenger ['pæsəndʒər] adj de viajeros ‖ s pasajero, viajero

passer-by ['pæsər'baɪ] o ['pɑsər'baɪ] s (pl passers-by) transeúnte mf

passing ['pæsɪŋ] o ['pɑsɪŋ] adj pasajero; corriente; de aprobado ‖ s (act of passing; death) paso; (in an examination) aprobación

passion ['pæʃən] s pasión

passionate ['pæʃənɪt] adj apasionado

passive ['pæsɪv] *adj* pasivo ‖ *s* voz pasiva, verbo pasivo

pass'key' *s* llave *f* de paso

Pass'o'ver *s* pascua (*de los hebreos*)

pass'port' *s* pasaporte *m*

pass'word' *s* santo y seña

past [pæst] o [pɑst] *adj* pasado; último; que fué, p.ej., **past president** presidente que fué; acabado, concluído ‖ *adv* más allá; por delante ‖ *prep* más allá de; más de; por delante de; fuera de; después de, p.ej., **past two o'clock** después de las dos; **past belief** increíble; **past cure** incurable; **past hope** sin esperanza ‖ *s* pasado

paste [pest] *s* (*dough; spaghetti, etc.*) pasta; (*for sticking things together*) engrudo ‖ *tr* engrudar, pegar con engrudo

paste'board' *s* cartón *m*

pasteurize ['pæstə,raɪz] *tr* pasterizar

pastime ['pæs,taɪm] o ['pɑs,taɪm] *s* pasatiempo

pastor ['pæstər] o ['pɑstər] *s* pastor *m*, clérigo, cura *m*

pastoral ['pæstərəl] o ['pɑstərəl] *adj* & *s* pastoral *f*

pas·try ['pestrɪ] *s* (*pl* -tries) pastelería

pastry cook *s* pastelero, repostero

pastry shop *s* pastelería, repostería

pasture ['pæstʃər] o ['pɑstʃər] *s* pasto, pastura, dehesa ‖ *tr* apacentar, pacer ‖ *intr* apacentarse, pacer

past·y ['pesti] *adj* (*comp* -ier; *super* -iest) pastoso; flojo, fofo, pálido

pat [pæt] *s* golpecito, palmadita; ruido de pasos ligeros; (*of butter*) pastelillo ‖ *v* (*pret* & *pp* patted; *ger* patting) *tr* dar golpecitos a, golpear ligeramente; palmotear, acariciar con la mano; **to pat on the back** elogiar, cumplimentar

patch [pætʃ] *s* remiendo, parche *m*; terreno, pedazo de terreno; mancha; lunar postizo ‖ *tr* remendar; **to patch up** componer (*una desavenencia*); componer lo mejor posible (*una cosa descompuesta*); hacer aprisa y mal

patent ['petənt] *adj* patente; abierto ‖ ['pætənt] *adj* de patentes ‖ *s* patente *f*, patente de invención; propiedad industrial; **patent applied for** se ha solicitado patente ‖ *tr* patentar

patent leather ['pætənt] *s* charol *m*

patent medicine ['pætənt] *s* medicamento de patente

patent rights ['pætənt] *spl* derechos de patente

paternal [pə'tʌrnəl] *adj* paterno; (*affection*) paternal

paternity [pə'tʌrnɪti] *s* paternidad

path [pæθ] o [pɑθ] *s* senda, sendero, trayectoria

pathetic [pə'θetɪk] *adj* patético

path'find'er *s* baquiano; explorador *m*

patholo·gy [pæ'θɑlədʒi] *s* patología

pathos ['peθɑs] *s* patetismo

path'way' *s* senda, sendero

patience ['peʃəns] *s* paciencia

patient ['peʃənt] *adj* paciente ‖ *s* paciente *mf*, enfermo

patriarch ['petrɪ,ɑrk] *s* patriarca *m*

patrician [pə'trɪʃən] *adj* & *s* patricio

patricide ['pætrɪ,saɪd] *s* (*act*) parricidio; (*person*) parricida *mf*

Patrick ['pætrɪk] *s* Patricio

patrimo·ny ['pætrɪ,moni] *s* (*pl* -nies) patrimonio

patriot ['petrɪ·ət] o ['pætrɪ·ət] *s* patriota *mf*

patriotic [,petrɪ'ɑtɪk] o [,pætrɪ'ɑtɪk] *adj* patriótico

patriotism ['petrɪ·ə,tɪzəm] o ['pætrɪ·ə,tɪzəm] *s* patriotismo

pa·trol [pə'trol] *s* patrulla ‖ *v* (*pret* & *pp* -trolled o -trolled; *ger* -trolling o -trolling) *tr* & *intr* patrullar

patrol·man [pə'trolmən] *s* (*pl* -men [mən]) guardia *m* municipal, vigilante *m* de policía

patrol wagon *s* camión *m* de policía

patron ['petrən] o ['pætrən] *adj* tutelar ‖ *s* parroquiano; patrocinador *m*

patronize ['petrə,naɪz] o ['pætrə,naɪz] *tr* ser parroquiano de (*un tendero*); comprar de costumbre en; patrocinar; tratar con aire protector

patron saint *s* patrón *m*, santo titular

patter ['pætər] *s* golpeteo; (*of rain*) chapaleteo; charla, parloteo ‖ *intr* golpetear; charlar, parlotear

pattern ['pætərn] *s* patrón *m*; modelo

P.A.U. *abbr* Pan American Union

paucity ['pɔsɪti] *s* corto número; falta, escasez *f*, insuficiencia

Paul [pɔl] *s* Pablo; (*name of popes*) Paulo

paunch [pɔntʃ] *s* panza

paunchy ['pɔntʃi] *adj* panzudo

pauper ['pɔpər] *s* pobre *mf*, indigente *mf*

pause [pɔz] *s* pausa; (*mus*) calderón *m*; **to give pause (to)** dar que pensar (a) ‖ *intr* hacer pausa, detenerse brevemente; vacilar

pave [pev] *tr* pavimentar; (*with flagstones*) enlosar; (*with bricks*) enladrillar; (*with pebbles*) enchinar; **to pave the way (for)** preparar el terreno (para), abrir el camino (a)

pavement ['pevmənt] *s* pavimento; (*of brick*) enladrillado; (*of flagstone*) enlosado; (*sidewalk*) acera

pavilion [pə'vɪljən] *s* pabellón *m*

paw [pɔ] *s* pata; garra, zarpa; (*coll*) mano *f* ‖ *tr* dar zarpazos a, restregar con las uñas; golpear, patear (*el suelo los caballos*); (*coll*) manosear; (*to handle overfamiliarly*) (*coll*) sobar ‖ *intr* piafar (*el caballo*)

pawn [pɔn] *s* (*in chess*) peón *m*; (*security, pledge*) prenda; (*tool of another person*) instrumento; víctima ‖ *tr* empeñar, dar en prenda

pawn'bro'ker *s* prestamista *mf*

pawn'shop' *s* casa de empeños, monte *m* de piedad

pawn ticket *s* papeleta de empeño

pay [pe] *s* paga; recompensa; castigo merecido ‖ *v* (*pret* & *pp* paid [ped]) *tr* pagar; prestar o poner (*atención*);

pa
pa

dar (*cumplidos*); dar (*dinero una actividad comercial*); dar dinero a, ser provechoso a; pagar en la misma moneda; pagar con creces; sufrir (*el castigo de una ofensa*); hacer (*una visita*); cubrir (*los gastos*); **to pay back** devolver; pagar en la misma moneda; **to pay off** pagar y despedir (*a un empleado*); pagar todo lo adeudado a; vengarse de; redimir (*una hipoteca*) ‖ *intr* pagar; ser provechoso, valer la pena; **pay as you enter** pague a la entrada; **pay as you go** pagar el impuesto de utilidades con descuentos anticipados; **pay as you leave** pague a la salida

payable ['pe.əbəl] *adj* pagadero

pay boost *s* aumento de salario

pay′check′ *s* cheque *m* en pago del sueldo; sueldo

pay′day′ *s* día *m* de pago

payee [pe'i] *s* portador *m* o tenedor *m* (*de un giro*)

pay envelope *s* sobre *m* con el jornal; jornal *m*, salario

payer ['pe.ər] *s* pagador *m*

pay load *s* carga útil

pay′mas′ter *s* pagador *m*

payment ['pemənt] *s* pago; castigo

pay roll *s* nómina, hoja de paga

pay station *s* teléfono público

pd. *abbr* **paid**

p.d. *abbr* **per diem, potential difference**

pea [pi] *s* guisante *m*, chícharo

peace [pis] *s* paz *f*; **to make peace with** hacer las paces con

peaceable ['pisəbəl] *adj* pacífico

peaceful ['pisfəl] *adj* tranquilo, pacífico, sosegado

peace′mak′er *s* iris *m* de paz

peace of mind *s* serenidad del espíritu

peace pipe *s* pipa ceremonial (*de los pieles rojas*)

peach [pitʃ] *s* melocotón *m*; (slang) persona o cosa admirables

peach tree *s* melocotonero

peach·y ['pitʃi] *adj* (comp **-ier;** super **-iest**) (slang) estupendo, magnífico

pea′cock′ *s* pavo real, pavón *m*; (fig) pinturero

peak [pik] *s* pico, cima, cumbre *f*; punta, extremo; máximo; (*of a cap*) visera; (*of a curve*) cresta; (elec) pico

peak hour *s* hora punta

peak load *s* (elec) carga de punta

peal [pil] *s* fragor *m*; estruendo; (*of bells*) repique *m*; juego de campanas ‖ *intr* repicar; resonar

peal of laughter *s* carcajada

peal of thunder *s* trueno

pea′nut′ *s* cacahuete *m*, aráquida

pear [per] *s* pera

pearl [pʌrl] *s* margarita, perla; (*of running water*) murmullo ‖ *tr* aljofarar

pearl oyster *s* madreperla

pear tree *s* peral *m*

peasant ['pezənt] *adj* & *s* campesino, rústico

pea′shoot′er *s* cerbatana, bodoquera

pea soup *s* sopa de guisantes; (coll) neblina espesa y amarillenta

peat [pit] *s* turba

pebble ['pebəl] *s* china, guija ‖ *tr* agranelar (*el cuero*)

peck [pek] *s* medida de áridos (*nueve litros*); montón *m*; picotazo; beso dado de mala gana ‖ *tr* picotear ‖ *intr* picotear; (coll) comer melindrosamente; **to peck at** querer picar; regañar constantemente; (coll) comer melindrosamente

peculate ['pekjə͵let] *tr* & *intr* malversar

peculiar [pɪ'kjuljər] *adj* peculiar; singular, raro; excéntrico

pedagogue ['pedə͵gag] *s* pedagogo; dómine *m*, pedante *m*

pedagogy ['pedə͵godʒi] o ['pedə͵gadʒi] *s* pedagogía

ped·al ['pedəl] *s* pedal *m* ‖ *v* (*pret & pp* **-aled** o **-alled**; *ger* **-aling** o **-alling**) *tr* impulsar pedaleando ‖ *intr* pedalear

pedant ['pedənt] *s* pedante *mf*

pedantic [pɪ'dæntɪk] *adj* pedantesco

pedant·ry ['pedəntri] *s* (*pl* **-ries**) pedantería

peddle ['pedəl] *tr* ir vendiendo de puerta en puerta; traer y llevar (*chismes*); vender (*favores*) ‖ *intr* ser buhonero

peddler ['pedlər] *s* buhonero

pedestal ['pedɪstəl] *s* pedestal *m*

pedestrian [pɪ'destri.ən] *adj* pedestre ‖ *s* peatón *m*

pediatrics [͵pidɪ'ætrɪks] o [͵pedi-'ætrɪks] *ssg* pediatría

pedigree ['pedɪ͵gri] *s* árbol genealógico; ascendencia; fuente *f*, origen *m*

pediment ['pedɪmənt] *s* frontón *m*

peek [pik] *s* mirada rápida y furtiva ‖ *intr* mirar a hurtadillas

peel [pil] *s* cáscara, pellejo ‖ *tr* pelar ‖ *intr* pelarse

peep [pip] *s* mirada a hurtadillas; (*of chickens*) pío ‖ *intr* mirar a hurtadillas; piar (*los pollos*)

peep′hole′ *s* atisbadero; (*in a door*) mirilla, ventanillo

peep show *s* mundonuevo; (slang) vistas sicalípticas

peer [pɪr] *s* par *m* ‖ *intr* mirar fijando la vista de cerca; **to peer at** mirar con ojos de miope; **to peer into** mirar hacia lo interior de, escudriñar

peerless ['pɪrlɪs] *adj* sin par

peeve [piv] *s* (coll) cojijo ‖ *tr* (coll) enojar, irritar

peevish ['pivɪʃ] *adj* cojijoso, displicente

peg [pɛg] *s* clavija, claveta, estaquilla; **to take down a peg** (coll) bajar los humos a ‖ *v* (*pret & pp* **pegged;** *ger* **pegging**) *tr* enclavijar; señalar con clavijas; fijar (*precios*) ‖ *intr* trabajar con ahinco; **to peg away at** afanarse en

peg leg *s* pata de palo

peg top *s* peonza; **peg tops** pantalones anchos de caderas y perniles ajustados

Peking ['pi'kɪŋ] *s* Pequín

Peking·ese [ˌpikɪ'niz] *adj* pequinés ‖ *s* (*pl* **-ese**) pequinés *m*

pelf [pɛlf] *s* dinero mal ganado

pell-mell ['pɛl'mɛl] *adj* tumultuoso ‖ *adv* atropelladamente

Peloponnesian [ˌpɛləpə'niʃən] *adj & s* peloponense *mf*

Peloponnesus [ˌpɛləpə'nisəs] *s* Peloponeso

Pelops ['pilɑps] *s* Pélope *m*

pelota [pe'lotə] *s* pelota vasca

pelt [pɛlt] *s* pellejo; golpe violento; (*of a person*) (hum) pellejo ‖ *tr* golpear violentamente; apedrear ‖ *intr* golpear violentamente; caer con fuerza (*el granizo, la lluvia, etc.*); apresurarse

pen. *abbr* **peninsula**

pen [pɛn] *s* pluma; corral *m*, redil *m*; **the pen and the sword** las letras y las armas ‖ *v* (*pret & pp* **penned**; *ger* **penning**) *tr* escribir (*con pluma*); redactar ‖ *v* (*pret & pp* **penned** o **pent** [pɛnt]) *tr* acorralar, encerrar

penalize ['pinəˌlaɪz] *tr* penar; (sport) sancionar

penal·ty ['pɛnəlti] *s* (*pl* **-ties**) pena; (*for late payment*) recargo; (sport) sanción; **under penalty of** so pena de

penance ['pɛnəns] *s* penitencia; **to do penance** hacer penitencia

penchant ['pɛn/ənt] *s* afición, inclinación, tendencia

pen·cil ['pɛnsəl] *s* lápiz *m*; (*of light*) pincel *m*, haz *m* ‖ *v* (*pret & pp* **-ciled** o **-cilled**; *ger* **-ciling** o **-cilling**) *tr* marcar con lápiz; (med) pincelar

pencil sharpener *s* afilalápices *m*, cortalápices *m*

pendent ['pɛndənt] *adj* pendiente; sobresaliente ‖ *s* medallón *m*; (*earring*) pendiente *m*

pending ['pɛndɪŋ] *adj* pendiente ‖ *prep* hasta; durante

pendulum ['pɛndʒələm] *s* péndulo; (*of a clock*) péndola

pendulum bob *s* lenteja

penetrate ['pɛnɪˌtret] *tr & intr* penetrar

penguin ['pɛŋgwɪn] *s* pingüino, pájaro bobo

pen'hold'er *s* (*handle*) portaplumas *m*; (*box*) plumero

penicillin [ˌpɛnɪ'sɪlɪn] *s* penicilina

peninsula [pə'nɪnsələ] *s* península

peninsular [pə'nɪnsələr] *adj & s* peninsular *mf* ‖ **Peninsular** *adj & s* (*Iberian*) peninsular *mf*

penitence ['pɛnɪtəns] *s* penitencia

penitent ['pɛnɪtənt] *adj & s* penitente *mf*

pen'knife' *s* (*pl* **-knives**) navaja, cortaplumas *m*

penmanship ['pɛnmənˌʃɪp] *s* caligrafía; (*hand of a person*) letra

pen name *s* seudónimo

pennant ['pɛnənt] *s* gallardete *m*

penniless ['pɛnɪlɪs] *adj* pelón, sin dinero

pennon ['pɛnən] *s* pendón *m*

pen·ny ['pɛni] *s* (*pl* **-nies**) (U.S.A.)

centavo ‖ *s* (*pl* **pence** [pɛns]) (Brit) penique *m*

pen'ny·weight' *s* peso de 24 granos

pen pal *s* (coll) amigo por correspondencia

pen point *s* punta de la pluma; puntilla de la pluma fuente

pension ['pɛnʃən] *s* pensión, jubilación ‖ *tr* pensionar, jubilar

pensioner ['pɛnʃənər] *s* pensionista *mf*; **pensioners** clases pasivas

pensive ['pɛnsɪv] *adj* pensativo; melancólico

Pentecost ['pɛntɪˌkɑst] o ['pɛntɪˌkɔst] *s* el Pentecostés

penthouse ['pɛntˌhaʊs] *s* alpende *m*, colgadizo; casa de azotea

pent-up ['pɛntˌʌp] *adj* contenido, reprimido

penult ['pinʌlt] *s* penúltima

penum·bra [pɪ'nʌmbrə] *s* (*pl* **-brae** [bri] o **-bras**) penumbra

penurious [pɪ'nʊrɪ·əs] *adj* (*stingy*) tacaño, mezquino; (*poor*) pobre, indigente

penury ['pɛnjəri] *s* tacañería, mezquindad; pobreza, miseria

pen'wip'er *s* limpiaplumas *m*

people ['pipəl] *spl* gente *f*; personas; gente del pueblo; se, p.ej., **people say** se dice ‖ *ssg* (*pl* **peoples**) pueblo, nación ‖ *tr* poblar

pep [pɛp] *s* (slang) ánimo, brío, vigor *m* ‖ *v* (*pret & pp* **pepped**; *ger* **pepping**) *tr* — **to pep up** (slang) animar, dar vigor a

pepper ['pɛpər] *s* (*spice*) pimienta; (*plant and fruit*) pimiento ‖ *tr* sazonar con pimienta; (*with bullets*) acribillar; salpicar

pep'per·box' *s* pimentero

pep'per·mint' *s* (*plant*) menta piperita; esencia de menta; pastilla de menta

per [pʌr] *prep* por; **as per** según

perambulator [pər'æmbjəˌletər] *s* cochecillo de niño

per capita [pər 'kæpɪtə] por cabeza, por persona

perceive [pər'siv] *tr* percibir

per cent o **percent** [pər'sɛnt] por ciento

percentage [pər'sɛntɪdʒ] *s* porcentaje *m*; (slang) provecho, ventaja

perception [pər'sɛp/ən] *s* percepción; comprensión, penetración

perch [pʌrt/] *s* percha, rama, varilla; sitio o posición elevada; (*fish*) perca ‖ *tr* colocar en un sitio algo elevado ‖ *intr* sentarse en un sitio algo elevado; posar (*un ave*)

percolator ['pʌrkəˌletər] *s* cafetera filtradora

per diem [pər 'daɪ·əm] por día

perdition [pər'dɪ/ən] *s* perdición

perennial [pə'rɛnɪ·əl] *adj* perenne; (bot) vivaz ‖ *s* planta vivaz

perfect ['pʌrfɪkt] *adj & s* perfecto ‖ [pər'fɛkt] *tr* perfeccionar

perfidious [pər'fɪdɪ·əs] *adj* pérfido

perfi·dy ['pʌrfɪdi] *s* (*pl* **-dies**) perfidia

perforate ['pʌrfəˌret] *tr* perforar

perforce [pər'fors] *adv* por fuerza, necesariamente

pa
pe

perform [pər'fɔrm] *tr* ejecutar; (theat) representar || *intr* ejecutar; funcionar (*p.ej., una máquina*)

performance [pər'fɔrməns] *s* ejecución; representación; funcionamiento; (theat) función

performer [pər'fɔrmər] *s* ejecutante *mf;* actor *m;* acróbata *mf*

perfume ['pʌrfjum] *s* perfume *m* || [pər'fjum] *tr* perfumar

perfunctory [pər'fʌŋktəri] *adj* hecho sin cuidado, hecho a la ligera; indiferente, negligente

perhaps [pər'hæps] *adv* acaso, tal vez, quizá

per·il ['perəl] *s* peligro || *v* (*pret & pp* -iled o -illed; *ger* -iling o -illing) *tr* poner en peligro

perilous ['perɪləs] *adj* peligroso

period ['pɪrɪ·əd] *s* período; (*in school*) hora; (gram) punto; (sport) división

period costume *s* traje *m* de época

periodic [,pɪrɪ'ɑdɪk] *adj* periódico

periodical [,pɪrɪ'ɑdɪkəl] *adj* periódico || *s* periódico, revista periódica

peripher·y [pə'rɪfəri] *s* (*pl* -ies) periferia

periscope ['perɪ,skop] *s* periscopio

perish ['perɪʃ] *intr* perecer

perishable ['perɪʃəbəl] *adj* perecedero; (*merchandise*) corruptible

periwig ['perɪ,wɪg] *s* perico

perjure ['pʌrdʒər] *tr* hacer (*a una persona*) quebrantar el juramento; **to perjure oneself** perjurarse

perju·ry ['pʌrdʒəri] *s* (*pl* -ries) perjurio

perk [pʌrk] *tr* alzar (*la cabeza*); aguzar (*las orejas*) || *intr* pavonearse; engalanarse; **to perk up** reanimarse, sentirse mejor

permanence ['pʌrmənəns] *s* permanencia

permanen·cy ['pʌrmənənsi] *s* (*pl* -cies) permanencia; persona, cosa o posición permanentes

permanent ['pʌrmənənt] *adj* permanente || *s* permanente *f,* ondulación permanente

permanent tenure *s* inamovilidad

permanent way *s* (rr) material fijo

permeate ['pʌrmɪ,et] *tr & intr* penetrar

permission [pər'mɪʃən] *s* permisión

per·mit ['pʌrmɪt] *s* permiso; cédula de aduana || [pər'mɪt] *v* (*pret & pp* -mitted; *ger* -mitting) *tr* permitir

permute [pər'mjut] *tr* permutar

pernicious [pər'nɪʃəs] *adj* pernicioso

pernickety [pər'nɪkɪti] *adj* (coll) descontentadizo, quisquilloso

perorate ['perə,ret] *intr* perorar

peroration [,perə'reʃən] *s* peroración

peroxide [pər'ɑksaɪd] *s* peróxido; peróxido de hidrógeno

peroxide blonde *s* rubia oxigenada

perpendicular [,pʌrpən'dɪkjələr] *adj & s* perpendicular *f*

perpetrate ['pʌrpɪ,tret] *tr* perpetrar

perpetual [pər'pet/u·əl] *adj* perpetuo

perpetuate [pər'pet/u,et] *tr* perpetuar

perplex [pər'pleks] *tr* dejar perplejo

perplexed [pər'plekst] *adj* perplejo

perplexi·ty [pər'pleksɪti] *s* (*pl* -ties) perplejidad; problema *m*

per se [pər 'si] por sí mismo, en sí mismo, esencialmente

persecute ['pʌrsɪ,kjut] *tr* perseguir

persecution [,pʌrsɪ'kjuʃən] *s* persecución

persevere [,pʌrsɪ'vɪr] *intr* perseverar

Persian ['pʌrʒən] *adj & s* persa *mf*

persimmon [pər'sɪmən] *s* placaminero

persist [pər'sɪst] o [pər'zɪst] *intr* persistir

persistent [pər'sɪstənt] o [pər'zɪstənt] *adj* persistente; (*insistent*) porfiado; (*e.g., headache*) pertinaz

person ['pʌrsən] *s* persona; **no person** nadie

personage ['pʌrsənɪdʒ] *s* personaje *m;* persona

personal ['pʌrsənəl] *adj* personal; de uso personal || *s* nota de sociedad; (*in a newspaper*) remitido

personali·ty [,pʌrsə'nælɪti] *s* (*pl* -ties) personalidad

personal property *s* bienes *mpl* muebles

personi·fy [pər'sɑnɪ,faɪ] *v* (*pret & pp* -fied) *tr* personificar

personnel [,pʌrsə'nel] *s* personal *m*

person-to-person *adv* (telp) particular a particular

perspective [pər'spektɪv] *s* perspectiva

perspicacious [,pʌrspɪ'keʃəs] *adj* perspicaz

perspire [pər'spaɪr] *intr* sudar, transpirar

persuade [pər'swed] *tr* persuadir

persuasion [pər'sweʒən] *s* persuasión; creencia religiosa; creencia fuerte

pert [pʌrt] *adj* atrevido, descarado; (coll) animado, vivo

pertain [pər'ten] *intr* pertenecer; **pertaining to** perteneciente a

pertinacious [,pʌrtɪ'neʃəs] *adj* pertinaz

pertinent ['pʌrtɪnənt] *adj* pertinente

perturb [pər'tʌrb] *tr* perturbar

Peru [pə'ru] *s* el Perú

perusal [pə'ruzəl] *s* lectura cuidadosa

peruse [pə'ruz] *tr* leer con atención

Peruvian [pə'ruvɪ·ən] *adj & s* peruano

pervade [pər'ved] *tr* penetrar, esparcirse por, extenderse por

perverse [pər'vʌrs] *adj* perverso; avieso, díscolo; contumaz

perversion [pər'vʌrʒən] *s* perversión

perversi·ty [pər'vʌrsɪti] *s* (*pl* -ties) perversidad; indocilidad; contumacia

pervert ['pʌrvərt] *s* renegado, apóstata; pervertido || [pər'vʌrt] *tr* pervertir; emplear mal (*p.ej., los talentos que uno tiene*)

pes·ky ['peski] *adj* (*comp* -kier; *super* -kiest) (coll) cargante, molesto

pessimism ['pesɪ,mɪzəm] *s* pesimismo

pessimist ['pesɪmɪst] *s* pesimista *mf*

pessimistic [,pesɪ'mɪstɪk] *adj* pesimista

pest [pest] *s* peste *f;* insecto nocivo; (*misfortune*) plaga; (*annoying person, bore*) machaca *mf*

pester ['pestər] *tr* molestar, importunar

pest'house' s lazareto, hospital m de contagiosos

pesticide ['pɛstɪ ˌsaɪd] s pesticida m

pestiferous [pɛs'tɪfərəs] adj pestífero; (coll) engorroso, molesto

pestilence ['pɛstɪləns] s pestilencia

pestle ['pɛsəl] s mano f de almirez

pet [pɛt] s animal mimado, animal casero; niño mimado; favorito; enojo pasajero ‖ v (pret & pp petted; ger petting) tr acariciar, mimar ‖ intr (slang) besuquearse

petal ['pɛtəl] s pétalo

petard [pɪ'tɑrd] s petardo

pet'cock' s llave f de desagüe, llave de purga

Peter ['pitər] s Pedro; **to rob Peter to pay Paul** desnudar a un santo para vestir a otro

petition [pɪ'tɪʃən] s petición; (formal request signed by a number of people) memorial m, instancia, solicitud ‖ tr suplicar; dirigir una instancia, solicitar

pet name s nombre m de cariño

Petrarch ['pitrɑrk] s Petrarca m

petri-fy ['pɛtrɪ ˌfaɪ] v (pret & pp -fied) tr petrificar ‖ intr petrificarse

petrol ['pɛtrəl] s (Brit) gasolina

petroleum [pɪ'troli-əm] s petróleo

pet shop s pajarería

petticoat ['pɛtɪ ˌkot] s enaguas; (woman, girl) (slang) falda

pet-ty ['pɛti] adj (comp -tier; super -tiest) insignificante, pequeño; mezquino; intolerante

petty cash s caja de menores, efectivo para gastos menores

petty larceny s ratería, hurto

petty officer s (naut) suboficial m

petulant ['pɛtjələnt] adj malhumorado, enojadizo

pew [pju] s banco de iglesia

pewter ['pjutər] s peltre m; vajilla de peltre

pfd. abbr **preferred**

Phaëthon ['fe·ɪθɒn] s Faetón m

phalanx ['felæŋks] o ['fælæŋks] s falange f

phantasm ['fæntæzəm] s fantasma m

phantom ['fæntəm] s fantasma m

Pharaoh ['fero] s Faraón m

pharisee ['færɪ ˌsi] s fariseo ‖ **Pharisee** s fariseo

pharmaceutical [ˌfɑrmə'sutɪkəl] adj farmacéutico

pharmacist ['fɑrməsɪst] s farmacéutico

pharma-cy ['fɑrməsi] s (pl -cies) farmacia

pharynx ['færɪŋks] s faringe f

phase [fez] s fase f ‖ tr poner en fase; llevar a cabo a etapas uniformes; (coll) inquietar, molestar; **to phase out** deshacer paulatinamente

pheasant ['fɛzənt] s faisán m

phenobarbital [ˌfino'bɑrbɪ ˌtæl] s fenobarbital m

phenomenal [fɪ'nɑmɪnəl] adj fenomenal

phenome·non [fɪ'nɑmɪ ˌnɑn] s (pl -na [nə]) fenómeno

phial ['faɪ·əl] s frasco pequeño

Phidias ['fɪdɪ·əs] s Fidias m

philanderer [fɪ'lændərər] s galanteador m, tenorio

philanthropist [fɪ'lænθrəpɪst] s filántropo

philanthro·py [fɪ'lænθrəpi] s (pl -pies) filantropía

philatelist [fɪ'lætəlɪst] s filatelista mf

philately [fɪ'lætəli] s filatelia

Philip ['fɪlɪp] s Felipe m; (of Macedon) Filipo

Philippine ['fɪlɪ ˌpin] adj filipino ‖ **Philippines** spl Islas Filipinas

Philistine [fɪ'lɪstɪn], ['fɪlɪ ˌstin] o ['fɪlɪ ˌstaɪn] adj & s filisteo

philologist [fɪ'lɑlədʒɪst] s filólogo

philology [fɪ'lɑlədʒi] s filología

philosopher [fɪ'lɑsəfər] s filósofo

philosophic(al) [ˌfɪlə'sɑfɪk(əl)] adj filosófico

philoso·phy [fɪ'lɑsəfi] s (pl -phies) filosofía

philter ['fɪltər] s filtro

phlebitis [flɪ'baɪtɪs] s flebitis f

phlegm [flɛm] s flema f, gargajo; **to cough up phlegm** gargajear

phlegmatic(al) [flɛg'mætɪk(əl)] adj flemático

Phoebe ['fibi] s Febe f

Phoebus ['fibəs] s Febo m

Phoenicia [fɪ'nɪʃə] o [fɪ'nɪʃə] s Fenicia

Phoenician [fɪ'nɪʃən] o [fɪ'nɪʃən] adj & s fenicio

phoenix ['finɪks] s fénix m

phone [fon] s (coll) teléfono; **to come o to go to the phone** acudir al teléfono, ponerse al aparato ‖ tr & intr (coll) telefonear

phone call s llamada telefónica

phonetic [fo'nɛtɪk] adj fonético

phonograph ['fonə ˌgræf] o ['fonə ˌgrɑf] s fonógrafo

phonology [fə'nɑlədʒi] s fonología

pho·ny ['foni] adj (comp -nier; super -niest) falso, contrahecho ‖ s (pl -nies) (slang) farsa; (coll) farsante mf

phosphate ['fɑsfet] s fosfato

phosphorescent [ˌfɑsfə'rɛsənt] adj fosforescente

phospho·rus ['fɑsfərəs] s (pl -ri [ˌraɪ]) fósforo

pho·to ['foto] s (pl -tos) foto f

photoengraving [ˌfoto·ɛn'greviŋ] s fotograbado

photo finish s (sport) llegada a la meta, determinada mediante el fotofija

pho'to-fin'ish camera s fotofija m

photogenic [ˌfoto'dʒɛnɪk] adj fotogénico

photograph ['fotə ˌgræf] o ['fotə ˌgrɑf] s fotografía ‖ tr & intr fotografiar

photographer [fə'tɑgrəfər] s fotógrafo

photography [fə'tɑgrəfi] s fotografía

photojournalism [ˌfotə'dʒʌrnə ˌlɪzəm] s fotoperiodismo

pho'to-play' s fotodrama m

photostat ['fotə ˌstæt] s (trademark) fotóstato ‖ tr & intr fotostatar

phototube ['fotə ˌtjub] o ['fotə ˌtub] s fototubo

phrase [frez] s frase f ‖ tr frasear

phrenology [frɪ'nɑlədʒi] s frenología

Phyllis ['fɪlɪs] *s* Filis *f*
phys. *abbr* **physical, physician, physics, physiology**
phys·ic ['fɪzɪk] *s* medicamento; purgante *m* ‖ *v* (*pret & pp* **-icked;** *ger* **-icking**) *tr* curar; purgar
physical ['fɪzɪkəl] *adj* físico
physician [fɪ'zɪʃən] *s* médico
physicist ['fɪzɪsɪst] *s* físico
physics ['fɪzɪks] *s* física
physiognomy [ˌfɪzɪ'agnəmi] o [ˌfɪzɪ-'anəmi] *s* fisonomía
physiological [ˌfɪzɪ·ə'ladʒɪkəl] *adj* fisiológico
physiology [ˌfɪzɪ'alədʒi] *s* fisiología
physique [fɪ'zɪk] *s* físico, talle *m*, exterior *m*
pi [paɪ] *s* (math) pi *f*; (typ) pastel *m* ‖ *v* (*pret & pp* **pied;** *ger* **piing**) *tr* (typ) empastelar
pian·o [pɪ'æno] *s* (*pl* **-os**) piano
picaresque [ˌpɪkə'rɛsk] *adj* picaresco
picayune [ˌpɪkə'jun] *adj* de poca monta, mezquino
piccadil·ly [ˌpɪkə'dɪli] *s* (*pl* **-lies**) cuello de pajarita
picco·lo ['pɪkəˌlo] *s* (*pl* **-los**) flautín *m*
pick [pɪk] *s* (*tool*) pico; (*choice*) selección; (*choicest*) flor *f* ‖ *tr* escoger; recoger (*p.ej., flores*); recolectar (*p.ej., algodón*); romper (*el hielo*) con un picahielos; escarbarse (*los dientes*); descañonar, desplumar (*un ave*); hurgarse (*la nariz*); rascarse (*una cicatriz, un grano*); roer (*un hueso*); mondar (*las frutas*); falsear, forzar (*una cerradura*); armar (*una pendencia*); herir (*las cuerdas de un instrumento*); buscar (*defectos*); hurtar de (*los bolsillos*); **to pick out** entresacar; **to pick someone to pieces** (coll) no dejarle a uno un hueso sano; **to pick up** recoger; recobrar (*ánimo; velocidad*); descolgar (*el receptor*); hallar por casualidad; aprender con la práctica; aprender de oídas; invitar a subir a un coche; entablar conservación con (*sin presentación previa*); captar (*una señal de radio*) ‖ *intr* comer melindrosamente; escoger esmeradamente; **to pick at** comer melindrosamente; tomarla con, regañar; **to pick on** escoger; (coll) regañar; (coll) molestar; **to pick over** ir revolviendo y examinando; **to pick up** (coll) ir mejor, sentirse mejor; recobrar velocidad
pick'ax' *s* zapapico
picket ['pɪkɪt] *s* (*stake, pale*) piquete *m*; (*of strikers; of soldiers*) piquete *m* ‖ *tr* poner un cordón de piquetes a ‖ *intr* servir de piquete
picket fence *s* cerca de estacas
picket line *s* línea de piquetes
pickle ['pɪkəl] *s* encurtido; escabeche *m*, salmuera; (coll) apuro, aprieto ‖ *tr* encurtir; escabechar
pick-me-up ['pɪkmiˌʌp] *s* (coll) tentempié *m*; (coll) trago fortificante
pick'pock'et *s* carterista *m*, ratero
pick'up' *s* recolección; (*of a motor*) recobro; (*of an automobile*) aceleración; (elec) pick-up, fonocaptor *m*

pic·nic ['pɪknɪk] *s* jira, partida de campo ‖ *v* (*pret & pp* **-nicked;** *ger* **-nicking**) *intr* hacer una jira al campo, merendar en el campo
pictorial [pɪk'tori·əl] *adj* gráfico; ilustrado ‖ *s* revista ilustrada
picture ['pɪktʃər] *s* cuadro; retrato; imagen *f*; lámina, grabado; fotografía; película; pintura ‖ *tr* dibujar; pintar; describir; **to picture to oneself** representarse
picture gallery *s* galería de pinturas
picture post card *s* postal ilustrada
picture show *s* exhibición de pinturas; cine *m*
picture signal *s* videoseñal *f*
picturesque [ˌpɪktʃə'rɛsk] *adj* pintoresco
picture tube *s* tubo de imagen, tubo de televisión
picture window *s* ventana panorámica
piddling ['pɪdlɪŋ] *adj* de poca monta, insignificante
pie [paɪ] *s* pastel *m*; (bird) picaza; (typ) pastel *m* ‖ *v* (*pret & pp* **pied;** *ger* **pieing**) *tr* (typ) empastelar
piece [pis] *s* (*fragment; section of cloth*) pedazo; (*part of a machine; drama; single composition of music; coin; figure or block used in checkers, chess, etc.*) pieza; (*of land*) lote *m*, parcela; **a piece of advice** un consejo; **a piece of baggage** un bulto; **a piece of furniture** un mueble; **to break to pieces** despedazar, hacer pedazos; despedazarse; **to fall to pieces** desbaratarse, caer en ruina; **to give someone a piece of one's mind** decirle a uno su parecer con toda franqueza; **to go to pieces** desvenciarse; darse a la desesperación; ir al desastre (*un negocio*); sufrir un ataque de nervios; perder por completo la salud; **to pick someone to pieces** (coll) no dejarle a uno un hueso sano ‖ *tr* formar juntando piezas; remendar ‖ *intr* (coll) comer a deshora
piece'work' *s* destajo, trabajo a destajo
piece'work'er *s* destajero, destajista *mf*
pier [pɪr] *s* muelle *m*; (*of a bridge*) estribo, sostén *m*; (*of a harbor*) rompeolas *m*; (*wall between two openings*) (archit) entrepaño
pierce [pɪrs] *tr* agujerear, horadar, taladrar; atravesar, traspasar; picar, pinchar, punzar; (fig) traspasar (*de dolor*) ‖ *intr* penetrar, entrar a la fuerza
piercing ['pɪrsɪŋ] *adj* agudo, penetrante, desgarrador; (*pain*) lancinante
pier glass *s* espejo de cuerpo entero
pie·ty ['paɪ·əti] *s* (*pl* **-ties**) piedad, devoción
piffle ['pɪfəl] *s* (coll) disparates *mpl*, música celestial
pig [pɪg] *s* cerdo; (*young hog*) lechón *m*; (*domestic hog*) puerco, cochino; carne *f* de puerco; (metal) lingote *m*; (*person who acts like a pig*) (coll) marrano, cochino
pigeon ['pɪdʒən] *s* paloma

pi'geon·hole' s hornilla, casilla de paloma; casilla ‖ tr encasillar
pigeon house s palomar m
piggish ['pɪgɪʃ] adj glotón, voraz
pig'gy·back' adv a cuestas, en hombros
pig'-head'ed adj terco, cabezudo
pig iron s arrabio, hierro en lingotes
pigment ['pɪgmənt] s pigmento ‖ tr pigmentar ‖ intr pigmentarse
pig'pen' s pocilga; (fig) pocilga, corral m de vacas
pig'skin' s piel f de cerdo; (coll) balón m (con que se juega al fútbol)
pig'sty' s (pl -sties) pocilga
pig'tail' s coleta, trenza; (of tobacco) andullo
pike [paɪk] s pica; (of an arrow) punta; carretera; camino de barrera; (fish) lucio
piker ['paɪkər] s (slang) persona de poco fuste
Pilate ['paɪlət] s Pilatos m
pile [paɪl] s pila, montón m; (stake) pilote m; lanilla, pelusa; pira; (elec, phys) pila; (coll) caudal m; **piles** almorranas ‖ tr apilar, amontonar ‖ intr apilarse, amontonarse; **to pile in** o **into** entrar atropelladamente en; entrar todos en; subir todos a (p.ej., un coche)
pile driver s martinete m
pilfer ['pɪlfər] tr & intr ratear
pilgrim ['pɪlgrɪm] s peregrino, romero
pilgrimage ['pɪlgrɪmɪdʒ] s peregrinación, romería
pill [pɪl] s píldora; mal trago, sinsabor m; (coll) persona molesta
pillage ['pɪlɪdʒ] s pillaje m, saqueo ‖ tr & intr pillar, saquear
pillar ['pɪlər] s pilar m; **from pillar to post** de acá para allá sin objeto determinado
pillo·ry ['pɪləri] s (pl -ries) picota ‖ v (pret & pp -ried) tr empicotar; (fig) motejar, poner en ridículo
pillow ['pɪlo] s almohada
pil'low·case' o **pil'low·slip'** s funda de almohada
pilot ['paɪlət] s piloto; (of a harbor) práctico; (of a gas range) mechero encendedor; (rr) trompa, delantera ‖ tr pilotar; conducir
pimp [pɪmp] s alcahuete m
pimple ['pɪmpəl] s barro, grano
pim·ply ['pɪmpli] adj (comp -plier; super -pliest) granujoso
pin [pɪn] s alfiler m; (e.g., for a necktie) prendedero; (peg) clavija; (e.g., to hold scissors together) clavillo, clavito; (bowling) bolo; **to be on pins and needles** estar en espinas ‖ v (pret & pp pinned; ger pinning) tr alfilerar; clavar, fijar, sujetar; **to pin something on someone** (coll) achacarsle a uno de una cosa; **to pin up** recoger y apuntar con alfileres; fijar en la pared con alfileres
pinafore ['pɪnə,for] s delantal m de niño
pin'ball' s billar romano, bagatela
pince-nez ['pæns,ne] s lentes mpl de nariz, lentes de pinzas
pincers ['pɪnsərz] ssg o spl pinzas

pinch [pɪntʃ] s pellizco; (of hunger) tormento; (slang) arresto; (slang) hurto, robo; **in a pinch** en un aprieto; **en caso necesario** ‖ tr pellizcar; cogerse (los dedos, p.ej., en una puerta); apretar (p.ej., el zapato a una persona); contraer (el frío la cara de uno); limitar los gastos de; (slang) arrestar, prender; (slang) hurtar, robar ‖ intr apretar; economizar, privarse de lo necesario
pinchers ['pɪntʃərz] ssg o spl var of pincers
pin'cush'ion s acerico
Pindar ['pɪndər] s Píndaro
pine [paɪn] s pino ‖ intr languidecer; **to pine away** consumirse; **to pine for** penar por
pine'ap'ple s ananás m, piña
pine cone s piña
pine needle s pinocha
ping [pɪŋ] s silbido de bala ‖ intr silbar (una bala); silbar como una bala
pin'head' s cabecilla de alfiler; cosa muy pequeña o insignificante; (coll) bobalicón m
pink [pɪŋk] adj rosado, sonrosado ‖ s estado perfecto; comunistoide mf; (bot) clavel m, clavellina
pin money s alfileres mpl
pinnacle ['pɪnəkəl] s pináculo
pin'point' adj exacto, preciso ‖ s punta de alfiler ‖ tr & intr señalar con precisión
pin'prick' s alfilerazo
pinup girl ['pɪn,ʌp] s guapa
pin'wheel' s rueda de fuego, rueda giratoria de fuegos artificiales (child's toy) rehilandera, ventolera
pioneer [,paɪə'nɪr] s pionero; (mil) zapador m ‖ intr abrir nuevos caminos, explorar
pious ['paɪəs] adj pío, piadoso; mojigato; respetuoso
pip [pɪp] s (seed) pepita; (on a card, dice, etc.) punto; (vet) pepita
pipe [paɪp] s caño, conducto, tubo; (to smoke tobacco) pipa; (mus) pipa, caramillo, zampoña; (of an organ) cañón m ‖ tr conducir por medio de tubos o cañerías; proveer de tuberías o cañerías ‖ intr tocar el caramillo; **to pipe down** (slang) callarse
pipe cleaner s limpiapipas m
pipe dream s esperanza imposible, castillo en el aire
pipe line s cañería, tubería; oleoducto; fuente f de informes confidenciales
pipe organ s (mus) órgano
piper ['paɪpər] s flautista m; gaitero; **to pay the piper** pagar los vidrios rotos
pipe wrench s llave f para tubos
pippin ['pɪpɪn] s (apple) camuesa; (tree) camueso; (slang) real moza
piquancy ['pikənsi] s picante m
piquant ['pikənt] adj picante
pique [pik] s pique m, resentimiento ‖ tr picar, enojar; despertar, excitar
Piraeus [paɪ'ri·əs] s el Pireo
pirate ['paɪrɪt] s pirata m ‖ tr pillar,

robar; publicar fraudulentamente ‖ *intr* piratear

pirouette [ˌpɪruˈet] *s* pirueta ‖ *intr* piruetear

pistol [ˈpɪstəl] *s* pistola

piston [ˈpɪstən] *s* (mach) émbolo, pistón *m*; (mus) pistón *m*

piston displacement *s* cilindrada

piston ring *s* anillo de émbolo, aro de émbolo, segmento de émbolo

piston rod *s* vástago de émbolo

piston stroke *s* carrera de émbolo

pit [pɪt] *s* hoyo; (*in the skin*) cacaraña; (*of certain fruit*) hueso; (*for cockfights, etc.*) cancha, reñidero; (*of the stomach*) boca; abismo, infierno; (min) pozo; (theat) foso ‖ *v* (*pret & pp* pitted; *ger* pitting) *tr* marcar con hoyos; dejar hoyoso (*el rostro*); deshuesar (*p.ej., una ciruela*)

pitch [pɪtʃ] *s* (*black sticky substance*) pez *f*; echada, lanzamiento; cosa lanzada; pelota lanzada; (*of a boat*) arfada, cabezada; (*of a roof*) pendiente *f*; (*of, e.g., a screw*) paso; (*of a winding*) (elec) paso; (mus) tono, altura; (fig) grado, extremo; (coll) bombo, elogio ‖ *tr* echar, lanzar; elevar (*el heno*) con la horquilla; armar o plantar (*una tienda de campaña*); embrear; (mus) graduar el tono de ‖ *intr* caerse, caer de cabeza; bajar en declive, inclinarse; arfar, cabecear (*un buque*); **to pitch in** (coll) poner manos a la obra; (coll) comenzar a comer

pitch accent *s* acento de altura

pitcher [ˈpɪtʃər] *s* jarro; (*in baseball*) lanzador *m*

pitch'fork' *s* horca, horquilla; **to rain pitchforks** (coll) llover a cántaros

pitch pipe *s* (mus) diapasón *m*

pit'fall' *s* callejo, trampa; (*danger for the unwary*) escollo, atascadero

pith [pɪθ] *s* médula; (*essential part*) (fig) médula; (fig) fuerza, vigor *m*

pith·y [ˈpɪθi] *adj* (*comp* -ier; *super* -iest) medular; enérgico, expresivo

pitiful [ˈpɪtɪfəl] *adj* lastimoso; compasivo; despreciable

pitiless [ˈpɪtɪlɪs] *adj* despiadado, empedernido, incompasivo

pit·y [ˈpɪti] *s* (*pl* -ies) piedad, compasión, lástima; **for pity's sake!** ¡por piedad!; **to have o to take pity on** tener piedad de, apiadarse de; **what a pity!** ¡qué lástima!, ¡qué pena! ‖ *v* (*pret & pp* -ied) *tr* apiadarse de, compadecer

pivot [ˈpɪvət] *s* pivote *m*, gorrón *m*, eje *m* de rotación; (fig) eje *m* ‖ *intr* pivotar; **to pivot on** girar sobre; depender de

placard [ˈplækɑrd] *s* cartel *m* ‖ *tr* fijar carteles en; fijar (*un anuncio*) en sitio público; publicar por medio de carteles

place [ples] *s* sitio, lugar *m*; (*of business*) local *m*; (*job*) puesto; grado, rango; **in no place** en ninguna parte; **in place of** en lugar de; **out of place** fuera de su lugar; fuera de propósito; **to be looking for a place to live** buscar piso; **to take place** tener lugar ‖ *tr* poner, colocar; acordarse bien de; dar empleo a; prestar (*dinero*) a interés ‖ *intr* colocarse (*un caballo en las carreras*)

place·bo [pləˈsibo] *s* (*pl* -bos o -boes) placebo

place card *s* tarjetita con el nombre (*que indica la colocación de uno en la mesa*)

placement [ˈplesmənt] *s* colocación

place name *s* nombre *m* de lugar, topónimo

placid [ˈplæsɪd] *adj* plácido, tranquilo

plagiarism [ˈpledʒəˌrɪzəm] *s* plagio

plagiarize [ˈpledʒəˌraɪz] *tr* plagiar

plague [pleg] *s* peste *f*, plaga; (*great public calamity*) plaga ‖ *tr* apestar, plagar; atormentar, molestar

plaid [plæd] *s* (*cloth*) tartán *m*; cuadros a la escocesa

plain [plen] *adj* llano, claro, evidente; abierto, franco; ordinario; feo; humilde; solo, natural; **in plain English** sin rodeos; **in plain sight o view** en plena vista ‖ *s* llano, llanura

plain clothes *spl* traje *m* de calle, traje de paisano

plainclothesman [ˈplenˈkloðzˌmæn] *s* (*pl* -men [ˌmɛn]) policía *m* que lleva traje de paisano

plain omelet *s* tortilla a la francesa

plains·man [ˈplenzmən] *s* (*pl* -men [mən]) llanero

plaintiff [ˈplentɪf] *s* (law) demandante *mf*

plaintive [ˈplentɪv] *adj* quejumbroso

plan [plæn] *s* plan *m*, intento, proyecto; (*drawing, diagram*) plan *m*, plano; **to change one's plans** cambiar de proyecto ‖ *v* (*pret & pp* planned; *ger* planning) *tr* planear, planificar; **to plan to** proponerse ‖ *intr* hacer proyectos

plane [plen] *adj* plano ‖ *s* (*surface*) plano; aeroplano, avión *m*; (*of an airplane*) plano; (carp) cepillo; (*tree*) plátano ‖ *tr* cepillar ‖ *intr* viajar en aeroplano

plane sickness *s* mareo del aire, mal *m* de vuelo

planet [ˈplænɪt] *s* planeta *m*

plane tree *s* plátano

planing mill [ˈplenɪŋ] *s* taller *m* de cepillado

plank [plæŋk] *s* tabla gruesa, tablón *m*; artículo de un programa político ‖ *tr* entablar, entarimar

plant [plænt] o [plɑnt] *s* fábrica, taller *m*; (*of an automobile*) grupo motor; (*educational establishment*) plantel *m*; (bot) planta ‖ *tr* plantar; sembrar (*semillas*); inculcar (*doctrinas*); (slang) ocultar (*géneros robados*)

plantation [plænˈteʃən] *s* plantación, campo de plantas; (*estate cultivated by workers living on it*) hacienda

planter [ˈplæntər] *s* plantador *m*, cultivador *m*

plaster [ˈplæstər] o [ˈplɑstər] *s* (*gypsum*) yeso; (*mixture of lime, sand,* *water, etc.)* argamasa; *(coating)* enlucido; *(poultice)* emplasto ‖ *tr* enyesar; argamasar; enlucir; emplastar; embadurnar; pegar *(anuncios)*

plas'ter·board' *s* cartón *m* de yeso y fieltro

plaster cast *s* (surg) vendaje enyesado; (sculp) yeso

plaster of Paris *s* estuco de París

plastic ['plæstɪk] *adj* plástico ‖ *s* *(substance)* plástico; *(art of modeling)* plástica

plate [plet] *s (dish)* plato; *(sheet of metal, etc.)*, chapa, placa; vajilla de oro, vajilla de plata; dentadura postiza, base *f* de la dentadura postiza; *(baseball)* puesto meta, puesto del batter; *(anat, elec, electron, phot, zool)* placa; *(typ)* clisé *m* ‖ *tr* chapear, planchear; blindar; platear, dorar, niquelar *(por la galvanoplastia)*; *(typ)* clisar

plateau [plæ'to] *s* meseta

plate glass *s* vidrio o cristal cilindrado

platen ['plætən] *s* rodillo

platform ['plæt͵fɔrm] *s* plataforma *f*; *(of passenger station)* andén *m*; *(of freight station)* cargadero; *(of a speaker)* tribuna; *(political program)* plataforma

platform car *s* plataforma *f*

platinum ['plætɪnəm] *s* platino

platinum blonde *s* rubia platino

platitude ['plætɪ͵tjud] o ['plætɪ͵tud] *s* perogrullada, trivialidad

Plato ['pleto] *s* Platón *m*

platoon [plə'tun] *s* pelotón *m*

platter ['plætər] *s* fuente *f*; (slang) disco de fonógrafo

plausible ['plɔzɪbəl] *adj* aparente, especioso; bien hablado; (coll) creíble

play [ple] *s* juego; *(act or move in a game)* jugada; *(drama)* pieza; *(of water, colors, lights)* juego; *(mach)* huelgo, juego; **to give full play to** dar rienda suelta a ‖ *tr* jugar *(p.ej., un naipe, una partida de juego)*; jugar a *(p.ej., los naipes)*; jugar con *(un contrario)*; dar *(un chasco)*; gastar *(una broma)*; hacer *(una mala jugada)*; dirigir *(agua, una manguera)*; desempeñar *(un papel)*; desempeñar el papel de; representar *(una obra dramática, un film)*; apostar por *(un caballo)*; tocar *(un instrumento, una pieza, un disco de fonógrafo)* ‖ *intr* jugar; desempeñar un papel, representar; correr *(una fuente)*; rielar *(la luz en la superficie del agua)*; vagar *(p.ej., una sonrisa por los labios)*; **to play out** rendirse; agotarse; acabarse; **to play safe** tomar sus precauciones; **to play sick** hacerse el enfermo; **to play up to** hacer la rueda a

play'back' *s* lectura; aparato de lectura

play'bill' *s (poster)* cartel *m*; *(of a play)* programa *m*

player piano ['ple·ər] *s* autopiano

playful ['plefəl] *adj* juguetón, retozón; dicho en broma

playgoer ['ple͵go·ər] *s* aficionado al teatro

play'ground' *s* campo de juego; patio de recreo

play'house' *s* casita de muñecas; teatro

playing card ['ple·ɪŋ] *s* naipe *m*

playing field *s* campo de deportes

play'mate' *s* compañero de juego

play'-off' *s* partido de desempate

play'pen' *s* parque *m*, corral *m (para bebés)*

play'thing' *s* juguete *m*

play'time' *s* hora de recreo, hora de juego

playwright ['ple͵rait] *s* dramaturgo, autor dramático

play'writ'ing *s* dramaturgia, dramática

plea [pli] *s* ruego, súplica; disculpa, excusa; (law) contestación a la demanda

plead [plid] *v (pret & pp* **pleaded** o **pled** [pled]) *tr* defender *(una causa)* ‖ *intr* suplicar; abogar; **to plead guilty** confesarse culpable; **to plead not guilty** negar la acusación, declararse inocente

pleasant ['plɛzənt] *adj* agradable; simpático

pleasant·ry ['plɛzəntri] *s (pl* **-ries)** broma, chiste *m*, dicho gracioso

please [pliz] *tr & intr* gustar; **as you please** como Vd. quiera; **if you please** si me hace el favor; **please** + *inf* hágame Vd. el favor de + *inf*; **to be pleased** to alegrarse de, complacerse en; **to be pleased with** estar satisfecho de o con

pleasing ['plizɪŋ] *adj* agradable, grato

pleasure ['plɛʒər] *s* placer *m*, gusto; **what is your pleasure?** ¿en qué puedo servirle?, ¿qué es lo que Vd. desea?; **with pleasure** con mucho gusto

pleasure seeker ['sikər] *s* amigo de los placeres

pleat [plit] *s* pliegue *m*, plisado ‖ *tr* plegar, plisar

plebeian [plɪ'bi·ən] *adj & s* plebeyo

pledge [plɛdʒ] *s* empeño, prenda; *(vow)* voto, promesa; *(toast)* brindis *m*; **as a pledge of** en prenda de; **to take the pledge** comprometerse a no tomar bebidas alcohólicas ‖ *tr* empeñar, prendar; dar *(la palabra)*; brindar por

plentiful ['plɛntɪfəl] *adj* abundante, copioso

plenty ['plɛnti] *adv* (coll) completamente ‖ *s* abundancia, copia; suficiencia

pleurisy ['plʊrɪsi] *s* pleuresía

pliable ['plai·əbəl] *adj* flexible, plegable; dócil

pliers ['plai·ərz] *ssg* o *spl* alicates *mpl*

plight [plait] *s* estado, situación; apuro, aprieto; compromiso solemne ‖ *tr* dar o empeñar *(su palabra)*; **to plight one's troth** prometer fidelidad; dar palabra de casamiento

plod [plad] *v (pret & pp* **plodded;** *ger* **plodding)** *tr* recorrer *(un camino)* pausada y pesadamente ‖ *intr* caminar pausada y pesadamente; trabajar laboriosamente

plot [plat] *s* complot *m*, conspiración; *(of a play or novel)* argumento, trama; parcela, solar *m;* cuadro de flores; cuadro de hortalizas; plano, mapa *m* ‖ *v* (*pret & pp* **plotted;** *ger* **plotting**) *tr* fraguar, tramar, urdir, maquinar; dividir en parcelas o solares; trazar el plano de; trazar, tirar (*líneas*) ‖ *intr* conspirar

plough [plau] *s, tr & intr* var de **plow**

plover ['plʌvər] o ['plovər] *s* chorlito

plow [plau] *s* arado; quitanieve *m* ‖ *tr* arar; surcar; quitar o barrer (*la nieve*); **to plow back** reinvertir (*ganancias*) ‖ *intr* arar; avanzar como un arado

plow-man ['plaumən] *s* (*pl* **-men** [mən]) arador *m,* yuguero

plow'share' *s* reja de arado

pluck [plʌk] *s* ánimo, coraje *m,* valor *m;* tirón *m* ‖ *tr* arrancar; coger (*flores*); desplumar (*un ave*); puntear (*p.ej., una guitarra*) ‖ *intr* dar un tirón; **to pluck up** recobrar ánimo

pluck·y ['plʌki] *adj* (*comp* **-ier;** *super* **-iest**) animoso, valiente

plug [plʌg] *s* taco, tarugo; boca de agua; tableta de tabaco; (*hat*) (slang) chistera; (elec) clavija, toma, ficha; (aut) bujía; (coll) rocín; (slang) elogio incidental ‖ *v* (*pret & pp* **plugged;** *ger* **plugging**) *tr* atarugar; calar (*un melón*); **to plug in** (elec) enchufar ‖ *intr* (coll) trabajar con ahinco

plum [plʌm] *s* (*tree*) ciruelo; (*fruit*) ciruela; (slang) turrón *m,* pingüe destino

plumage ['plumidʒ] *s* plumaje *m*

plumb [plʌm] *adj* vertical; (coll) completo ‖ *adv* a plomo; (coll) verticalmente; (coll) directamente ‖ *tr* aplomar; sondear

plumb bob *s* plomada

plumber ['plʌmər] *s* fontanero; (*worker in lead*) plomero

plumbing ['plʌmiŋ] *s* instalación sanitaria; conjunto de cañerías; (*working in lead*) plomería; sondeo

plumbing fixtures *spl* artefactos sanitarios

plumb line *s* cuerda de plomada

plum cake *s* pastel aderezado con pasas de Corinto y ron

plume [plum] *s* (*of a bird*) pluma; (*tuft of feathers worn as ornament*) penacho ‖ *tr* emplumar; componerse (*las plumas*); **to plume oneself on** enorgullecerse de

plummet ['plʌmit] *s* plomada ‖ *intr* caer a plomo, precipitarse

plump [plʌmp] *adj* rechoncho, regordete; brusco, franco ‖ *adv* de golpe; francamente ‖ *s* (coll) caída pesada; (coll) ruido sordo ‖ *intr* caer a plomo

plum pudding *s* pudín *m* inglés con pasas de Corinto, corteza de limón, huevos y ron

plum tree *s* ciruelo

plunder ['plʌndər] *s* pillaje *m;* botín *m* ‖ *tr* pillar, saquear

plunge [plʌndʒ] *s* zambullida; caída a plomo; sacudida violenta; salto; baño de agua fría; (*of a boat*) cabeceo ‖ *tr* zambullir; sumergir; hun-

dir (*p.ej., un puñal*) ‖ *intr* zambullirse; sumergirse; hundirse (*p.ej., en la tristeza*); caer a plomo; arrojarse, precipitarse; cabecear (*un buque*); (slang) entregarse al juego, entregarse a las especulaciones

plunger ['plʌndʒər] *s* zambullidor *m;* émbolo buzo; (*of a tire valve*) obús *m;* (slang) jugador desenfrenado

plunk [plʌŋk] *adv* (coll) con un golpe seco, con un ruido de golpe seco ‖ *tr* (coll) arrojar, empujar o dejar caer pesadamente ‖ *intr* sonar o caer con un ruido de golpe seco

plural ['plurəl] *adj & s* plural *m*

plus [plʌs] *adj* más y pico; **to be plus** (coll) tener por añadidura ‖ *prep* más ‖ *s* (*sign*) más *m;* añadidura

plush [plʌʃ] *adj* afelpado; (coll) lujoso, suntuoso ‖ *s* felpa

Plutarch ['plutark] *s* Plutarco

plutonium [plu'toni·əm] *s* plutonio

ply [plai] *s* (*pl* **plies**) (e.g., *of a cloth*) capa, doblez *m;* (*of a cable*) cordón *m* ‖ *v* (*pret & pp* **plied**) *tr* manejar (*la aguja, etc.*); ejercer (*un oficio*); batir (*el agua con los remos*); importunar; navegar por (*p.ej., un río*) ‖ *intr* avanzar; **to ply between** hacer (*un barco*) el servicio entre

ply'wood' *s* chapeado, madera laminada

P.M. *abbr* **Postmaster; post meridiem** (Lat), **afternoon**

pneumatic [nju'mætɪk] o [nu'mætɪk] *adj* neumático

pneumatic drill *s* perforadora de aire comprimido

pneumonia [nju'moni·ə] o [nu'moni·ə] *s* neumonía o pulmonía

poach [potʃ] *tr* escalfar (*huevos*) ‖ *intr* cazar o pescar en vedado

poacher ['potʃər] *s* cazador furtivo, pescador furtivo

pock [pak] *s* cacaraña, hoyuelo

pocket ['pakit] *s* bolsillo, faltriquera; (*in billiards*) tronera; (aer) bolsa de aire; (mil) bolsón *m* ‖ *tr* embolsar; entronerar (*una bola de billar*); tragarse (*injurias*)

pock'et·book' *s* portamonedas *m; (of a woman)* bolsa

pocket calculator *s* bolsicalculadora, calculadora de bolsillo

pocket handkerchief *s* pañuelo de bolsillo o de mano

pock'et·knife' *s* (*pl* **-knives**) navaja, cortaplumas *m*

pocket money *s* alfileres *mpl* dinero de bolsillo

pock'mark' *s* cacaraña, hoyuelo

pod [pad] *s* vaina

poem ['po·im] *s* poema *m,* poesía

poet ['po·it] *s* poeta *m*

poetess ['po·itis] *s* poetisa

poetic [po'etik] *adj* poético ‖ **poetics** *ssg* poética

poetry ['po·itri] *s* poesía

pogrom ['pogrəm] *s* levantamiento contra los judíos

poignancy ['pɔinənsi] *s* picante *m,* viveza, intensidad

poignant ['pɔɪnənt] *adj* picante, vivo, intenso

point [pɔɪnt] *s (of a sword, pencil; of land)* punta; *(of pen)* pico; *(of fountain pen)* puntilla; *(mark of imperceptible dimensions)* punto; *(of a joke)* gracia; (elec) punta; (math, typ, sport, fig) punto; (coll) indirecta, insinuación; **beside the point** fuera de propósito; **on the point of** a punto de; **to carry one's point** salirse con la suya; **to come to the point** venir al caso o al grano; **to get the point** caer en la cuenta ‖ *tr* aguzar, sacar punta a; apuntar *(p.ej., un arma de fuego)*; resanar *(una pared)*; **to point one's finger** señalar con el dedo; **to point out** señalar, indicar, hacer notar ‖ *intr* apuntar; pararse *(el perro de muestra)*; **to point at** señalar con el dedo

point'blank' *adj & adv* a quemarropa

pointed ['pɔɪntɪd] *adj* puntiagudo; picante; acentuado, directo

pointer ['pɔɪntər] *s* puntero; indicador *m; (of a clock)* manecilla; perro de muestra; (mas) fijador *m;* (coll) indicación, dirección

poise [pɔɪz] *s* aplomo, equilibrio ‖ *tr* equilibrar; considerar ‖ *intr* equilibrarse; estar suspendido

poison ['pɔɪzən] *s* veneno, ponzoña ‖ *tr* envenenar

poison ivy *s* tosiguero

poisonous ['pɔɪzənəs] *adj* venenoso

poke [pok] *s (push)* empuje *m,* empujón *m; (thrust)* hurgonazo; *(with elbow)* codazo; *(slow person)* tardón *m* ‖ *tr* empujar; hacer *(un agujero)* a empujones; abrirse *(paso)* a empujones; atizar, hurgar *(el fuego);* **to poke fun at** burlarse de; **to poke one's nose into** entrometerse en ‖ *intr* fisgar, husmear; andar perezosamente

poker ['pokər] *s* hurgón *m; (card game)* póker *m,* pócar *m*

poker face *s* (coll) cara de jugador de póker; **to keep a poker face** (coll) disfrazar la expresión del rostro, mantener una expresión imperturbable

pok·y ['poki] *adj (comp* -ier; *super* -iest) (coll) tardo, roncero

Poland ['poland] *s* Polonia

polar bear ['polər] *s* oso blanco

polarize ['polə͵raɪz] *tr* polarizar

pole [pol] *s (long rod or staff)* pértiga; *(of a flag)* asta; *(upright support)* poste *m; (to push a boat)* botador *m;* (astr, biol, elec, geog, math) polo ‖ *tr* impeler *(un barco)* con botador ‖ **Pole** *s* polaco

pole'cat' *s* turón *m,* veso

pole'star' *s* estrella polar; *(guide)* norte *m; (center of interest)* miradero

pole vault *s* salto con garrocha o con pértiga

police [pə'lis] *s* policía ‖ *tr* poner o mantener servicio de policía en; (mil) limpiar

police·man [pə'lismən] *s (pl* -men [mən]) policía *m,* guardia urbano

police state *s* estado-policía *m*

police station *s* cuartel *m* o estación de policía

poli·cy ['pɑlɪsi] *s (pl* -cies) política; (ins) póliza

polio ['pɑli͵o] *s* (coll) polio *f*

polish ['pɑlɪʃ] *s* pulimento; cera de lustrar; *(for shoes)* bola, betún *m,* lustre *m;* elegancia; cultura, urbanidad ‖ *tr* pulimentar, pulir; embolar, dar betún a *(los zapatos);* **to polish off** (coll) terminar de prisa; (slang) engullir *(la comida, un trago)* ‖ **Polish** ['polɪʃ] *adj & s* polaco

polisher ['pɑlɪʃər] *s* pulidor *m; (machine)* pulidora; *(for floors, tables, etc.)* enceradora

polite [pə'laɪt] *adj* cortés, fino, urbano; culto

politeness [pə'laɪtnɪs] *s* cortesía, fineza, urbanidad; cultura

politic ['pɑlɪtɪk] *adj* prudente, sagaz; astuto; juicioso

political [pə'lɪtɪkəl] *adj* político

politician [͵pɑlɪ'tɪʃən] *s* político; *(politician seeking personal or partisan gain)* politicastro

politics ['pɑlɪtɪks] *ssg* o *spl* política

poll [pol] *s (questionnaire to determine opinion)* encuesta; votación; lista electoral; cabeza; **polls** urnas electorales; **to go to the polls** acudir a las urnas; **to take a poll** hacer una encuesta ‖ *tr* dar *(un voto);* recibir *(votos)*

pollen ['pɑlən] *s* polen *m*

pollinate ['pɑlɪ͵net] *tr* polinizar

polling booth ['polɪŋ] *s* cabina o caseta de votar

polliwog ['pɑlɪ͵wɑg] *s* renacuajo

poll tax *s* capitación, impuesto por cabeza

pollutant [pə'lutənt] *s* contaminante *m*

pollute [pə'lut] *tr* contaminar, corromper, ensuciar

pollution [pə'luʃən] *s* contaminación; *(of the environment)* polución; (fig) corrupción

polo ['polo] *s* polo

polo player *s* polista *mf,* jugador *m* de polo

polygamist [pə'lɪgəmɪst] *s* polígamo

polygamous [pə'lɪgəməs] *adj* polígamo

polyglot ['pɑlɪ͵glɑt] *adj & s* poligloto

polygon ['pɑlɪ͵gɑn] *s* polígono

Polyhymnia [͵pɑlɪ'hɪmnɪ·ə] *s* Polimnia

polynomial [͵pɑlɪ'nomɪ·əl] *s* polinomio

polyp ['pɑlɪp] *s* pólipo

polytheist ['pɑlɪ͵θi·ɪst] *s* politeísta *mf*

polytheistic [͵pɑlɪθi'ɪstɪk] *adj* politeísta

pomade [pə'med] o [pə'mɑd] *s* pomada

pomegranate ['pɑm͵grænɪt] *s (shrub)* granado; *(fruit)* granada

pom·mel ['pʌməl] o ['pɑməl] *s (on hilt of sword)* pomo; *(on saddle)* perilla ‖ *v (pret & pp* -meled o

pl
po·

-melled; *ger* **-meling** o **-melling)** *tr* apuñear, aporrear

pomp [pɑmp] *s* pompa, fausto

pompadour [ˈpɑmpəˌdor] o [ˈpɑmpəˌdur] *s* copete *m*

pompous [ˈpɑmpəs] *adj* pomposo, faustoso

pon·cho [ˈpɑntʃo] *s* (*pl* **-chos**) capote *m* de monte, poncho

pond [pɑnd] *s* estanque *m*, charca

ponder [ˈpɑndər] *tr* ponderar ‖ *intr* meditar; **to ponder over** ponderar, considerar con cuidado

ponderous [ˈpɑndərəs] *adj* pesado, inmanejable; tedioso, fastidioso

pond scum *s* lama, verdín *m*

poniard [ˈpɑnjərd] *s* puñal *m*

pontiff [ˈpɑntɪf] *s* pontífice *m*

pontoon [pɑnˈtun] *s* pontón *m*

po·ny [ˈponi] *s* (*pl* **-nies**) jaca, caballito; (*for drinking liquor*) (coll) pequeño vaso; (*translation used dishonestly in school*) (coll) chuleta

poodle [ˈpudəl] *s* perro de lanas

pool [pul] *s* (*small puddle*) charco; (*for swimming*) piscina; (*game*) trucos; (*in certain games*) polla, puesta; combinación de intereses; caudales unidos para un fin ‖ *tr* mancomunar

pool'room' *s* sala de trucos

pool table *s* mesa de trucos

poop [pup] *s* popa; (*deck*) toldilla

poor [pur] *adj* (*having few possessions; arousing pity*) pobre; (*not good, inferior*) malo

poor box *s* cepillo, caja de limosnas

poor'house' *s* asilo de pobres, casa de caridad

poorly [ˈpurli] *adv* mal

poor white *s* pobre *mf* de la raza blanca (*en el sur de los EE.UU.*)

pop. *abbr* **popular, population**

pop [pɑp] *s* estallido, taponazo; bebida gaseosa ‖ *v* (*pret & pp* **popped;** *ger* **popping**) *tr* hacer estallar; **to pop the question** (coll) hacer una declaración de amor ‖ *intr* estallar

pop'corn' *s* rosetas, palomitas (de maíz)

pope [pop] *s* papa *m*

popeyed [ˈpɑpˌaɪd] *adj* de ojos saltones; (*with fear, surprise, etc.*) desorbitado

pop'gun' *s* tirabala

poplar [ˈpɑplər] *s* álamo, chopo

pop·py [ˈpɑpi] *s* (*pl* **-pies**) amapola

pop'py-cock' *s* (coll) necedad, tontería

popsicle [ˈpɑpsɪkəl] *s* polo

populace [ˈpɑpjəlɪs] *s* populacho

popular [ˈpɑpjələr] *adj* popular

popularize [ˈpɑpjələˌraɪz] *tr* popularizar, vulgarizar

populous [ˈpɑpjələs] *adj* populoso

porcelain [ˈpɔrsəlɪn] o [ˈpɔrslɪn] *s* porcelana

porch [pɔrtʃ] *s* porche *m*, pórtico

porcupine [ˈpɔrkjəˌpaɪn] *s* puerco espín

pore [por] *s* poro ‖ *intr* — **to pore over** estudiar larga y detenidamente

pork [pɔrk] *s* carne *f* de cerdo

pork chop *s* chuleta de cerdo

porous [ˈporəs] *adj* poroso

porous plaster *s* parche poroso

porphy·ry [ˈpɔrfɪri] *s* (*pl* **-ries**) pórfido

porpoise [ˈpɔrpəs] *s* marsopa, puerco de mar; (*dolphin*) delfín *m*

porridge [ˈpɑrɪdʒ] o [ˈpɔrɪdʒ] *s* gachas

port [port] *adj* portuario ‖ *s* puerto; (*opening in ship's side*) portilla; (*left side of ship or airplane*) babor *m*; oporto, vino de Oporto; (mach) lumbrera

portable [ˈportəbəl] *adj* portátil

portal [ˈportəl] *s* portal *m*

portend [porˈtend] *tr* anunciar de antemano, presagiar

portent [ˈportɛnt] *s* augurio, presagio

portentous [porˈtɛntəs] *adj* portentoso, extraordinario; amenazante, ominoso

porter [ˈportər] *s* (*doorkeeper*) portero, conserje *m*; (*in hotels and trains*) mozo de servicio; pórter *m* (*cerveza de Inglaterra de color obscuro*)

portfoli·o [portˈfoliˌo] *s* (*pl* **-os**) cartera

port'hole' *s* porta, portilla

porti·co [ˈportɪˌko] *s* (*pl* **-coes** o **-cos**) pórtico

portion [ˈporʃən] *s* porción; (*dowry*) dote *m & f*

port·ly [ˈportli] *adj* (*comp* **-lier;** *super* **-liest**) corpulento; grave, majestuoso

port of call *s* escala

portrait [ˈportret] o [ˈportrɪt] *s* retrato; **to sit for a portrait** retratarse

portray [porˈtre] *tr* retratar

portrayal [porˈtreəl] *s* representación gráfica; retrato, descripción acertada

Portugal [ˈportʃəgəl] *s* Portugal *m*

Portu·guese [ˈportʃəˌgiz] *adj* portugués ‖ *s* (*pl* **-guese**) portugués *m*

port wine *s* vino de Oporto

pose [poz] *s* pose *f* ‖ *tr* plantear (*una pregunta, cuestión, etc.*) ‖ *intr* posar (*para retratarse; como modelo*); tomar una postura afectada; **to pose as** hacerse pasar por

posh [pɑʃ] *adj* (slang) elegante; (slang) lujoso, suntuoso

position [pəˈzɪʃən] *s* posición; empleo, puesto; opinión; **to be in a position to** estar en condiciones de

positive [ˈpɑzɪtɪv] *adj* positivo ‖ *s* positiva

possess [pəˈzɛs] *tr* poseer

possession [pəˈzɛʃən] *s* posesión

possible [ˈpɑsɪbəl] *adj* posible

possum [ˈpɑsəm] *s* zarigüeya; **to play possum** hacer la mortecina

post [post] *s* (*piece of wood, metal, etc. set upright*) poste *m*; (*position*) puesto; (*job*) puesto, cargo; casa de correos ‖ *tr* fijar (*carteles*); echar al correo; apostar, situar; tener al corriente; **post no bills** se prohíbe fijar carteles

postage [ˈpostɪdʒ] *s* porte *m*, franqueo; **postage will be paid by addressee** a franquear en destino

postage meter *s* franqueadora

postage stamp *s* sello de correo; estampilla, timbre *m* (Am)

postal ['postəl] *adj* postal ‖ *s* postal *f*
postal card *s* tarjeta postal
postal permit *s* franqueo concertado
postal savings bank *s* caja postal de ahorros
post card *s* tarjeta postal
post'date' *s* posfecha ‖ **post'date'** *tr* posfechar
poster ['postər] *s* cartel *m*, cartelón *m*, letrero
posterity [pɑs'terɪti] *s* posteridad
postern ['postərn] *s* postigo, portillo
post'haste' *adv* por la posta, a toda prisa
posthumous ['pɑstʃuməs] *adj* póstumo
post·man ['postmən] *s* (*pl* **-men** [mən]) cartero
post'mark' *s* matasellos *m*, timbre *m* de correos ‖ *tr* matasellar, timbrar
post'mas'ter *s* administrador *m* de correos
post-mortem [,post'mɔrtəm] *adj* posterior a la muerte ‖ *s* examen *m* de un cadáver
post office *s* casa de correos
post'-of'fice box *s* apartado de correos, casilla postal
postpaid ['post,ped] *adj* con porte pagado, franco de porte
postpone [post'pon] *tr* aplazar
postscript ['post,skrɪpt] *s* posdata
posttonic [post'tɑnɪk] *adj* postónico
posture ['pɑstʃər] *s* postura ‖ *intr* adoptar una postura
post'war' *adj* de la posguerra
po·sy ['pozi] *s* (*pl* **-sies**) flor *f*, ramillete *m*
pot [pɑt] *s* pote *m*; (*for flowers*) tiesto; (*for the kitchen*) caldera, olla, puchero; vaso de noche, orinal *m*; (*in gambling*) puesta; (*slang*) mariguana
potash ['pɑt,æʃ] *s* potasa
potassium [pə'tæsɪ·əm] *s* potasio
pota·to [pə'teto] *s* (*pl* **-toes**) patata, papa; (*sweet potato*) batata, buniato
potato omelet *s* tortilla a la española
potbellied ['pɑt,belid] *adj* barrigón, panzudo
poten·cy ['potənsi] *s* (*pl* **-cies**) potencia
potent ['potənt] *adj* potente
potentate ['potən,tet] *s* potentado
potential [pə'tenʃəl] *adj* & *s* potencial *m*
pot'hang'er *s* llares *fpl*
pot'hook' *s* garabato
potion ['poʃən] *s* poción
pot'luck' *s* lo que hay de comer; **to take potluck** hacer penitencia
pot shot *s* tiro a corta distancia
potter ['pɑtər] *s* alfarero ‖ *intr* ocuparse en fruslerías
potter's clay *s* arcilla figulina
potter's field *s* cementerio de los pobres, hoyanca
potter's wheel *s* torno de alfarero
potter·y ['pɑtəri] *s* (*pl* **-ies**) alfarería; cacharros (de alfarería)
pouch [pautʃ] *s* bolsa, saquillo; (*of kangaroo*) bolsa; (*for tobacco*) petaca; valija
poulterer ['poltərər] *s* pollero

poultice ['poltɪs] *s* cataplasma *f*
poultry ['poltri] *s* aves *fpl* de corral
pounce [pauns] *intr* — **to pounce on** saltar sobre, precipitarse sobre
pound [paund] *s* (*weight*) libra; (*for stray animals*) corral *m* de concejo ‖ *tr* golpear; machacar, moler; encerrar en el corral de concejo; bombardear incesantemente; (*to keep walking over*) desempedrar ‖ *intr* golpear
pound'cake' *s* pastel *m* en que entra una libra de cada ingrediente; ponqué *m* (Am)
pound sterling *s* libra esterlina
pour [por] *tr* vaciar, verter, derramar; echar, servir (*p.ej., té*); escanciar (*vino*) ‖ *intr* fluir rápidamente; llover a torrentes; **to pour out of** salir a montones de (*p.ej., el teatro*)
pout [paut] *s* mala cara, puchero ‖ *intr* poner mala cara, hacer pucheros
poverty ['pɑvərti] *s* pobreza
POW *abbr* prisoner of war
powder ['paudər] *s* polvo; (*for face*) polvos; (*explosive*) pólvora ‖ *tr* pulverizar; (*to sprinkle with powder*) empolvar, polvorear
powder puff *s* borla para empolvarse
powder room *s* cuarto tocador, cuarto de aseo
powdery ['paudəri] *adj* (*like powder*) polvoriento; (*sprinkled with powder*) empolvado; (*crumbly*) quebradizo
power ['pau·ər] *s* (*ability to act or do something; possession*) poder *m*; (*control, influence; wealth*) poderío; (*influential nation; energy, force, strength*) potencia; **the powers that be** las autoridades, los que mandan ‖ *tr* accionar, impulsar
power dive *s* (aer) picado con motor
powerful ['pau·ərfəl] *adj* poderoso
pow'er·house' *s* central eléctrica
powerless ['pau·ərlɪs] *adj* impotente
power line *s* (elec) sector *m* de distribución
power mower *s* motosegadora
power of attorney *s* poder *m*
power plant *s* (aer) grupo motopropulsor; (aut) grupo motor; (elec) central eléctrica, estación generadora
power steering *s* (aut) servodirección
power tool *s* herramienta motriz
pp. *abbr* pages
p.p. *abbr* parcel post, postpaid
pr. *abbr* pair, present, price
practical ['præktɪkəl] *adj* práctico
practically ['præktɪkəli] *adv* poco más o menos
practice ['præktɪs] *s* práctica; uso, costumbre; ensayo; (*of a profession*) ejercicio; (*of a doctor*) clientela ‖ *tr* practicar; ejercitar (*p.ej., la caridad*); ejercer (*una profesión*); estudiar (*p.ej., el piano*); tener por costumbre ‖ *intr* ejercitarse; practicar la medicina; ensayarse; entrenarse, adiestrarse; **to practice as** ejercer de (*p.ej., abogado*)
practitioner [præk'tɪʃənər] *s* (*medical doctor*) práctico
Prague [prɑg] o [preg] *s* Praga

po
pr

prairie ['preri] s pradera, llanura, pampa
prairie dog s ardilla ladradora
prairie wolf s coyote m
praise [prez] s alabanza, elogio || tr alabar, elogiar
praise'wor'thy adj laudable, plausible
pram [præm] s cochecillo de niño
prance [præns] o [prɑns] s cabriola, trenzado || intr cabriolar, trenzar
prank [præŋk] s travesura
prate [pret] intr charlar, parlotear
prattle ['prætəl] s charla, parloteo || intr charlar, parlotear; balbucear (un niño)
pray [pre] tr implorar, rogar, suplicar; rezar (una oración) || intr orar, rezar; **pray tell me** sírvase decirme
prayer [prer] s ruego, súplica; oración, rezo
prayer book s devocionario
preach [prit∫] tr predicar; aconsejar (p.ej., la paciencia) || intr predicar
preacher ['prit∫ər] s predicador m
preamble ['pri,æmbəl] s preámbulo
prebend ['prebənd] s prebenda
precarious [prɪ'keri·əs] adj precario
precaution [prɪ'kɔ∫ən] s precaución
precede [prɪ'sid] tr & intr preceder
precedent ['presɪdənt] s precedente m
precept ['prisept] s precepto
precinct ['prisɪŋkt] s barriada; distrito electoral
precious ['pre∫əs] adj precioso; caro, amado; (coll) considerable || adv (coll) muy, p.ej., **precious little** muy poco
precipice ['presɪpɪs] s precipicio
precipitate [prɪ'sɪpɪ,tet] adj & s precipitado || tr precipitar || intr precipitarse
precipitous [prɪ'sɪpɪtəs] adj empinado, escarpado; (hurried, reckless) precipitoso
precise [prɪ'saɪs] adj preciso; meticuloso
precision [prɪ'sɪʒən] s precisión
preclude [prɪ'klud] tr excluir, imposibilitar
precocious [prɪ'ko∫əs] adj precoz
predatory ['predə,tori] adj predatorio
predicament [prɪ'dɪkəmənt] s apuro, situación difícil
predict [prɪ'dɪkt] tr predecir
prediction [prɪ'dɪk∫ən] s predicción
predispose [,pridɪs'poz] tr predisponer
predominant [prɪ'dɑmɪnənt] adj predominante
preëminent [prɪ'emɪnənt] adj preeminente
preëmpt [prɪ'empt] tr apropiarse o apropiarse de
preen [prin] tr arreglarse (las plumas) con el pico; **to preen oneself** componerse, vestirse cuidadosamente
pref. abbr **preface, preferred, prefix**
prefabricate [pri'fæbrɪ,ket] tr prefabricar
preface ['prefɪs] s prefacio, advertencia || tr introducir, empezar
pre·fer [prɪ'fʌr] v (pret & pp **-ferred**; ger **-ferring**) tr preferir; presentar; promover

preferable ['prefərəbəl] adj preferible
preference ['prefərəns] s preferencia
prefix ['prifɪks] s prefijo || tr prefijar
pregnan·cy ['pregnənsi] s (pl **-cies**) preñez f, embarazo
pregnant ['pregnənt] adj preñado
prejudice ['predʒədɪs] s prejuicio; (detriment) perjuicio; **to the prejudice of** con perjuicio de; **without prejudice** (law) sin detrimento de sus propios derechos || tr predisponer, prevenir; (to harm) perjudicar
prejudicial [,predʒə'dɪ∫əl] adj perjudicial
prelate ['prelɪt] s prelado
pre-Lenten [pri'lentən] adj carnavalesco
preliminar·y [prɪ'lɪmɪ,neri] adj preliminar || s (pl **-ies**) preliminar m
prelude ['preljud] o ['prilud] s preludio || tr preludiar
premeditate [pri'medɪ,tet] tr premeditar
premier [prɪ'mɪr] o ['primi·ər] s primer ministro, presidente m del consejo
première [prə'mjer] o [prɪ'mɪr] s estreno; actriz f principal
premise ['premɪs] s premisa; **on the premises** en el local mismo; **premises** predio, local m
premium ['primi·əm] s premio; (ins) prima
premonition [,primə'nɪ∫ən] s presagio; presentimiento
preoccupancy [pri'ɑkjəpənsi] s preocupación
preoccupation [pri,ɑkjə'pe∫ən] s preocupación
preoccu·py [pri'ɑkjə,paɪ] v (pret & pp **-pied**) tr preocupar
prepaid [pri'ped] adj pagado por adelantado; con porte pagado
preparation [,prepə're∫ən] s preparación; (e.g., for a trip) preparativo; (pharm) preparado
preparatory [prɪ'pærə,tori] adj preparativo, preparatorio
prepare [prɪ'per] tr preparar || intr prepararse
preparedness [prɪ'perɪdnɪs] o [prɪ'perdnɪs] s preparación; preparación militar
pre·pay [pri'pe] v (pret & pp **-paid**) tr pagar por adelantado
preponderant [prɪ'pɑndərənt] adj preponderante
preposition [,prepə'zɪ∫ən] s preposición
prepossessing [,pripə'zesɪŋ] adj atractivo, simpático
preposterous [prɪ'pɑstərəs] adj absurdo, ridículo
prep school [prep] s (coll) escuela preparatoria
prerecorded [,priri'kɔrdɪd] adj (rad & telv) grabado de antemano
prerequisite [pri'rekwɪzɪt] s requisito previo
prerogative [prɪ'rɑgətɪv] s prerrogativa
Pres. abbr **Presbyterian, President**

presage ['prɛsɪdʒ] s presagio ‖ [prɪ-
'sedʒ] tr presagiar
Presbyterian [,prezbɪ'tɪrɪ·ən] adj & s
presbiteriano
prescribe [prɪ'skraɪb] tr & intr prescribir
prescription [prɪ'skrɪpʃən] s prescrip-
ción; (pharm) receta
presence ['prɛzəns] s presencia
present ['prɛzənt] adj presente ‖ s
presente m, regalo ‖ [prɪ'zɛnt] tr
presentar, obsequiar
presentable [prɪ'zɛntəbəl] adj bien
apersonado
presentation [,prɛzən'teʃən] o [,pri-
zən'teʃən] s presentación
presentation copy s ejemplar m de cortesía con dedicatoria del autor
presentiment [prɪ'zɛntɪmənt] s presentimiento
presently ['prɛzəntlɪ] adv luego, dentro de poco
preserve [prɪ'zʌrv] s conserva, compota; (for game) vedado ‖ tr conservar; preservar, proteger
preserved fruit s dulce m de almíbar
preside [prɪ'zaɪd] intr presidir; **to preside over** presidir
presiden·cy ['prɛzɪdənsɪ] s (pl -cies)
presidencia
president ['prɛzɪdənt] s presidente m;
(of a university) rector m
press [prɛs] s apretón m, empujón m;
(e.g., of business) urgencia; muchedumbre; (machine for printing, for
making wine; newspapers and news-
papermen) prensa; (printing) imprenta; (closet) armario; **to go to
press** entrar en prensa ‖ tr apretar
(p.ej., un botón); (in a press) prensar; planchar (la ropa); imprimir
(discos de fonógrafo); oprimir (una
tecla); apresurar; abrumar; apremiar, instar; insistir en
press agent s agente m de publicidad
press conference s conferencia de prensa
pressing ['prɛsɪŋ] adj apremiante,
urgente ‖ s planchado
press release s comunicado de prensa
pressure ['prɛʃər] s presión; premura,
urgencia
pressure cooker ['kʊkər] s olla de presión, cocina de presión
prestige [prɛs'tiʒ] o ['prɛstɪdʒ] s
prestigio
presumably [prɪ'zuməblɪ] o [prɪ-
'zjuməblɪ] adv probablemente, vero-
símilmente
presume [prɪ'zum] o [prɪ'zjum] tr
presumir; suponer; **to presume to**
tomar la libertad de ‖ intr suponer;
to presume on o **upon** abusar de
presumption [prɪ'zʌmpʃən] s presunción; pretensión
presumptuous [prɪ'zʌmptʃʊ·əs] adj
confianzudo, desenvuelto
presuppose [,prɪsə'poz] tr presuponer
pretend [prɪ'tɛnd] tr aparentar, fingir
‖ intr fingir; **to pretend to** pretender
(p.ej., el trono)
pretender [prɪ'tɛndər] s pretendiente
mf
pretense [prɪ'tɛns] o ['pritɛns] s pre-

tensión; fingimiento; **under false
pretenses** con apariencias fingidas;
under pretense of so pretexto de
pretentious [prɪ'tɛnʃəs] adj preten-
cioso, aparatoso; ambicioso, vasto
pretonic [prɪ'tɑnɪk] adj pretónico
pret·ty ['prɪtɪ] adj (comp -tier; super
-tiest) bonito, lindo; (coll) bastante,
considerable ‖ adv algo; bastante;
muy
prevail [prɪ'vel] intr prevalecer, reinar; **to prevail on** o **upon** persuadir
prevailing [prɪ'velɪŋ] adj prevale-
ciente, reinante; común, corriente
prevalent ['prɛvələnt] adj común,
corriente, en boga
prevaricate [prɪ'værɪ,ket] intr mentir
prevent [prɪ'vɛnt] tr impedir ‖ intr
obstar
prevention [prɪ'vɛnʃən] s (el) impedir;
medidas de precaución
preventive [prɪ'vɛntɪv] adj & s pre-
servativo
preview ['pri,vju] s vista anticipada;
(private showing) (mov) preestreno;
(showing of brief scenes for advertising) (mov) avance m
previous ['privɪ·əs] adj previo, anterior ‖ adv previamente; **previous to**
con anterioridad a, antes de
prewar ['pri,wɔr] adj prebélico, de
preguerra
prey [pre] s presa; víctima; **to be prey
to** ser presa de ‖ intr cazar; **to prey
on** o **upon** apresar y devorar; pillar,
robar; tener preocupado
price [praɪs] s precio ‖ tr apreciar,
estimar; fijar el precio de, poner
precio a; pedir el precio de
price control s intervención de precios
price cutting s reducción de precios
price fixing s fijación de precios
price freezing s congelación de precios
priceless ['praɪslɪs] adj inapreciable,
sin precio; (coll) absurdo, divertido
price war s guerra de precios
prick [prɪk] s (pointed weapon or instrument) espiche m; (sharp point)
púa; (small hole made with sharp
point) agujerillo; (spur) aguijón m;
(jab; sharp pain) pinchazo, punzada;
to kick against the pricks dar coces
contra el aguijón ‖ tr pinchar; marcar con agujerillos; dar una punzada
a; (to sting) punzar; **to prick up**
aguzar (las orejas)
prick·ly ['prɪklɪ] adj (comp -lier; super
-liest) espinoso, puado, punzante
prickly heat s salpullido causado por
el calor
prickly pear s (plant) chumbera; (fruit)
higo chumbo
pride [praɪd] s orgullo; arrogancia;
the pride of la flor y nata de ‖ tr —
to pride oneself on o **upon** enorgullecerse de
priest [prist] s sacerdote m
priesthood ['prist·hʊd] s sacerdocio
priest·ly ['pristlɪ] adj (comp -lier; super -liest) sacerdotal
prig [prɪg] s gazmoño, pedante mf
prim [prɪm] adj (comp primmer; super primmest) estirado, relamido

prima·ry ['praɪ ,meri] o ['praɪməri] *adj* primario ‖ *s* (*pl* **-ries**) elección preliminar; (elec) primario

prime [praɪm] *adj* primero, principal; (*of the best quality*) primo ‖ *s* flor *f*, juventud, primavera; alba, aurora; (la) flor y nata; (*of a degree*) (phys) minuto; (typ) virgulilla; **prime of life** edad viril, flor *f* de edad *f* ‖ *tr* informar de antemano; cebar (*un arma de fuego, una bomba, un car-burador*); (*for painting*) imprimar; poner la primera capa o la primera mano a; poner virgulilla a

prime minister *s* primer ministro

primer ['prɪmər] *s* cartilla ‖ ['praɪ-mər] *s* (*for paint*) aprestado *m*; (mach) cebador *m*

primitive ['prɪmɪtɪv] *adj* primitivo

primp [prɪmp] *tr* acicalar, engalanar ‖ *intr* acicalarse, engalanarse

prim′rose′ *s* primavera

primrose path *s* vida dada a los placeres de los sentidos

prin. *abbr* **principal**

prince [prɪns] *s* príncipe *m;* **to live like a prince** portarse como un príncipe

Prince of Wales *s* príncipe *m* de Gales

princess ['prɪnsɪs] *s* princesa

principal ['prɪnsɪpəl] *adj* principal ‖ *s* principal *m*, jefe *m;* (*of a school*) director *m;* criminal *mf;* (*main sum, not interest*) capital *m*

principle ['prɪnsɪpəl] *s* principio

print [prɪnt] *s* marca, impresión; (*printed cloth*) estampado; (*design in printed cloth*) diseño; grabado, lámina; letras de molde; (*act of printing*) impresión; edición, tirada; (phot) impresión; **in print** impreso, publicado; **out of print** agotado ‖ *tr* imprimir; estampar; hacer imprimir; publicar; escribir en caracteres de imprenta; (phot) tirar, imprimir; (fig) imprimir o grabar (*en la memoria*)

printed matter *s* impresos

printer ['prɪntər] *s* impresor *m*

printer's devil *s* aprendiz *m* de imprenta

printer's ink *s* tinta de imprenta

printer's mark *s* pie *m* de imprenta

printing ['prɪntɪŋ] *s* impresión; caracteres impresos; edición, tirada; letras de mano imitación de las impresas; (phot) tiraje *m*

prior ['praɪ·ər] *adj* anterior ‖ *adv* anteriormente; **prior to** antes de

priori·ty [praɪ'ɑrɪti] o [praɪ'ɔrɪti] *s* (*pl* **-ties**) prioridad; **of the highest priority** de máxima prioridad

prism ['prɪzəm] *s* prisma *m*

prison ['prɪzən] *s* cárcel *f*, prisión ‖ *tr* encarcelar

prisoner ['prɪzənər] o ['prɪznər] *s* preso; (mil) prisionero

prison van *s* coche *m* celular

pris·sy ['prɪsi] *adj* (*comp* **-sier;** *super* **-siest**) (coll) remilgado, melindroso

priva·cy ['praɪvəsi] *s* (*pl* **-cies**) aislamiento, retiro; secreto, reserva

private ['praɪvɪt] *adj* particular, pri-vado; confidencial; ‖ *s* soldado raso; **in private** privadamente; en secreto; **privates** partes pudendas

private first class *s* soldado de primera, aspirante *m* a cabo

private hospital *s* clínica, casa de salud

private property *s* bienes *mpl* particulares

private view *s* día *m* de inauguración

privet ['prɪvɪt] *s* aligustre *m*

privilege ['prɪvɪlɪdʒ] *s* privilegio

priv·y ['prɪvi] *adj* privado; **privy to** enterado secretamente de ‖ *s* (*pl* **-ies**) letrina

prize [praɪz] *s* premio; (*something captured*) presa ‖ *tr* apreciar, estimar

prize fight *s* partido de boxeo profesional

prize fighter *s* boxeador *m* profesional

prize ring *s* cuadrilátero de boxeo

pro [pro] *prep* en pro de ‖ *s* (*pl* **pros**) voto afirmativo; (coll) deportista *mf* profesional; **the pros and the cons** el pro y el contra

probabili·ty [,prɑbə'bɪlɪti] *s* (*pl* **-ties**) probabilidad; acontecimiento probable; tiempo probable

probable ['prɑbəbəl] *adj* probable

probation [pro'beʃən] *s* libertad vigilada; período de prueba

probe [prob] *s* encuesta, indagación; (*instrument*) sonda ‖ *tr* indagar; sondar

problem ['prɑbləm] *s* problema *m*

procedure [pro'sidʒər] *s* procedimiento

proceed [pro'sid] *intr* proceder ‖ **proceeds** ['prosidz] *spl* producto, ganancia

proceeding [pro'sidɪŋ] *s* procedimiento; **proceedings** actas; diligencias

process ['prɑses] *s* procedimiento; proceso, progreso; **in the process of time** con el tiempo ‖ *tr* elaborar

process server ['sʌrvər] *s* entregador *m* de la citación

proclaim [pro'klem] *tr* proclamar

proclitic [pro'klɪtɪk] *adj & s* proclítico

procommunist [pro'kɑmjənɪst] *adj & s* filocomunista *mf*

procrastinate [pro'kræstɪ ,net] *tr* diferir de un día para otro ‖ *intr* tardar, no decidirse

procure [pro'kjur] *tr* conseguir, obtener ‖ *intr* alcahuetear

prod [prɑd] *s* aguijada; empuje *m* ‖ *v* (*pret & pp* **prodded;** *ger* **prodding**) *tr* aguijar, pinchar; aguijonear, estimular

prodigal ['prɑdɪgəl] *adj & s* pródigo

prodigious [pro'dɪdʒəs] *adj* prodigioso, maravilloso; enorme, inmenso

prodi·gy ['prɑdɪdʒi] *s* (*pl* **-gies**) prodigio

produce ['prɑdjus] o ['prɑdus] *s* producto; productos agrícolas ‖ [pro-'djus] o [pro'dus] *tr* producir; presentar (*p.ej., un drama*) al público; (geom) prolongar

product ['prɑdəkt] *s* producto

production [pro'dʌkʃən] *s* producción

profane [pro'fen] *adj* profano; (*lan-*

guage) injurioso, blasfemo ‖ *s* profano ‖ *tr* profanar
profani·ty [proˈfænɪti] *s* (*pl* **-ties**) blasfemia
profess [proˈfɛs] *tr* & *intr* profesar
profession [proˈfɛʃən] *s* profesión
professor [proˈfɛsər] *s* profesor *m*, catedrático; (coll) profesor, maestro
proffer [ˈprɑfər] *s* oferta, propuesta ‖ *tr* ofrecer, proponer
proficient [proˈfɪʃənt] *adj* perito, diestro, hábil
profile [ˈprofaɪl] *s* perfil *m* ‖ *tr* perfilar
profit [ˈprɑfɪt] *s* provecho, beneficio, utilidad, ganancia; **at a profit** con ganancia ‖ *tr* servir, ser de utilidad a ‖ *intr* sacar provecho, ganar; adelantar, mejorar; **to profit by** aprovechar, sacar provecho de
profitable [ˈprɑfɪtəbəl] *adj* provechoso
profit and loss *s* ganancias y pérdidas
profiteer [ˌprɑfɪˈtɪr] *s* logrero, explotador *m* ‖ *intr* logrear, explotar
profit taking *s* realización de beneficios
profligate [ˈprɑflɪgɪt] *adj* & *s* libertino; pródigo
pro forma invoice [pro ˈfɔrmə] *s* factura simulada
profound [proˈfaʊnd] *adj* profundo
profuse [prəˈfjus] *adj* (*extravagant*) pródigo; (*abundant*) profuso
proge·ny [ˈprɑdʒəni] *s* (*pl* **-nies**) prole *f*
progno·sis [prɑgˈnosɪs] *s* (*pl* **-ses** [siz]) pronóstico
prognostic [prɑgˈnɑstɪk] *s* pronóstico
program [ˈprogræm] *s* programa *m* ‖ *tr* programar
progress [ˈprɑgrɛs] *s* progreso; progresos; **to make progress** hacer progresos ‖ [prəˈgrɛs] *intr* progresar
progressive [prəˈgrɛsɪv] *adj* progresivo; (pol) progresista ‖ *s* (pol) progresista *mf*
prohibit [proˈhɪbɪt] *tr* prohibir
project [ˈprɑdʒɛkt] *s* proyecto ‖ [prəˈdʒɛkt] *tr* proyectar ‖ *intr* proyectarse
projectile [prəˈdʒɛktɪl] *s* proyectil *m*
projection [prəˈdʒɛkʃən] *s* proyección
projector [prəˈdʒɛktər] *s* proyector *m*
proletarian [ˌprolɪˈtɛriən] *adj* & *s* proletario
proletariat [ˌprolɪˈtɛriət] *s* proletariado
proliferate [prəˈlɪfəˌret] *intr* proliferar
prolific [prəˈlɪfɪk] *adj* prolífico
prolix [ˈprolɪks] o [proˈlɪks] *adj* difuso, verboso
prologue [ˈprolɑg] o [ˈprolag] *s* prólogo
prolong [proˈlɔŋ] o [proˈlaŋ] *tr* prolongar
promenade [ˌprɑmɪˈned] o [ˌprɑmɪˈnad] *s* paseo; baile *m* de gala ‖ *intr* pasear o pasearse
promenade deck *s* (naut) cubierta de paseo
prominent [ˈprɑmɪnənt] *adj* prominente
promise [ˈprɑmɪs] *s* promesa ‖ *tr* & *intr* prometer

promising young man *s* joven *m* de esperanzas
promissory [ˈprɑmɪˌsori] *adj* promisorio
promissory note *s* pagaré *m*
promonto·ry [ˈprɑmənˌtori] *s* (*pl* **-ries**) promontorio
promote [prəˈmot] *tr* promover; fomentar
promotion [prəˈmoʃən] *s* promoción; fomento
prompt [prɑmpt] *adj* pronto, puntual; listo, dispuesto ‖ *tr* incitar, mover; inspirar, sugerir; (theat) apuntar
prompter [ˈprɑmptər] *s* (theat) apuntador *m*
prompter's box *s* (theat) concha
promulgate [ˈprɑm,ˌget] o [proˈmʌlget] *tr* promulgar
prone [pron] *adj* postrado boca abajo; extendido sobre el suelo; dispuesto, propenso
prong [prɔŋ] o [praŋ] *s* punta (*de un tenedor, horquilla, etc.*)
pronoun [ˈpronaʊn] *s* pronombre *m*
pronounce [prəˈnaʊns] *tr* pronunciar
pronouncement [prəˈnaʊnsmənt] *s* declaración; decisión, opinión
pronunciamen·to [prəˌnʌnsiəˈmɛnto] *s* (*pl* **-tos**) pronunciamiento
pronunciation [prəˌnʌnsiˈeʃən] o [prəˌnʌnsɪˈeʃən] *s* pronunciación
proof [pruf] *adj* de prueba; **proof against** a prueba de ‖ *s* prueba
proof'read'er *s* corrector *m* de pruebas
prop [prɑp] *s* apoyo, puntal *m*; (*to hold up a plant*) rodrigón *m*; **props** (theat) accesorios ‖ *v* (*pret* & *pp* **propped**; *ger* **propping**) *tr* apoyar, apuntalar; poner un rodrigón a
propaganda [ˌprɑpəˈgændə] *s* propaganda
propagate [ˈprɑpəˌget] *tr* propagar
proparoxytone [ˌpropærˈɑksɪˌton] *adj* & *s* proparoxítono
pro·pel [prəˈpɛl] *v* (*pret* & *pp* **-pelled**; *ger* **-pelling**) *tr* propulsar, impeler
propeller [prəˈpɛlər] *s* hélice *f*
propensi·ty [prəˈpɛnsiti] *s* (*pl* **-ties**) propensión
proper [ˈprɑpər] *adj* propio, conveniente; decente, decoroso; exacto, justo
proper·ty [ˈprɑpərti] *s* (*pl* **-ties**) propiedad; **properties** (theat) accesorios
property owner *s* propietario de bienes raíces
prophe·cy [ˈprɑfɪsi] *s* (*pl* **-cies**) profecía
prophe·sy [ˈprɑfɪˌsaɪ] *v* (*pret* & *pp* **-sied**) *tr* profetizar
prophet [ˈprɑfɪt] *s* profeta *m*
prophetess [ˈprɑfɪtɪs] *s* profetisa
prophylactic [ˌprofɪˈlæktɪk] *adj* & *s* profiláctico
propitiate [prəˈpɪʃɪˌet] *tr* propiciar
propitious [prəˈpɪʃəs] *adj* propicio
prop'jet' *s* turbohélice *m*
proportion [prəˈporʃən] *s* proporción; **in proportion as** a medida que; **out of proportion** desproporcionado ‖ *tr* proporcionar

pr
pr

proportionate [prə'porʃənɪt] *adj* proporcionado

proposal [prə'pozəl] *s* propuesta; oferta de matrimonio

propose [prə'poz] *tr* proponer ‖ *intr* proponer matrimonio; **to propose to** pedir la mano a; proponerse a + *inf*

proposition [,prɑpə'zɪʃən] *s* proposición, propuesta

propound [prə'paʊnd] *tr* proponer

proprietor [prə'praɪ·ətər] *s* propietario

proprietress [prə'praɪ·ətrɪs] *s* propietaria

proprie·ty [prə'praɪ·əti] *s* (*pl* -ties) corrección, conducta decorosa, conveniencia; **proprieties** cánones *mpl* sociales, convenciones

propulsion [prə'pʌlʃən] *s* propulsión

prorate [pro'ret] *tr* prorratear

prosaic [pro'ze·ɪk] *adj* prosaico

proscribe [pro'skraɪb] *tr* proscribir

prose [proz] *adj* prosaico ‖ *s* prosa

prosecute ['prɑsɪ,kjut] *tr* llevar a cabo; (law) procesar

prosecutor ['prɑsɪ,kjutər] *s* acusador *m*, demandante *mf*; (*lawyer*) fiscal *m*

proselyte ['prɑsɪ,laɪt] *s* prosélito

prose writer *s* prosista *mf*

prosody ['prɑsədi] *s* métrica

prospect ['prɑspɛkt] *s* vista; esperanza; probabilidad de éxito; cliente *mf* o comprador *m* probable ‖ *tr* & *intr* prospectar; **to prospect for** buscar (*p.ej.*, oro, petróleo)

prosper ['prɑspər] *tr* & *intr* prosperar

prosperi·ty [prɑs'pɛrɪti] *s* (*pl* -ties) prosperidad

prosperous ['prɑspərəs] *adj* próspero

prostitute ['prɑstɪ,tjut] o ['prɑstɪ,tut] *s* prostituta ‖ *tr* prostituir

prostrate ['prɑstret] *adj* postrado, prosternado ‖ *tr* postrar

prostration [prɑs'treʃən] *s* postración

Prot. *abbr* **Protestant**

protagonist [pro'tægənɪst] *s* protagonista *mf*

protect [prə'tɛkt] *tr* proteger

protection [prə'tɛkʃən] *s* protección

protégé ['protə,ʒe] *s* protegido

protégée ['protə,ʒe] *s* protegida

protein ['proti·ɪn] o ['protin] *s* proteína

pro-tempore [pro'tɛmpəri] *adj* interino

protest ['protɛst] *s* protesta ‖ [prə'tɛst] *tr* & *intr* protestar

protestant ['prɑtɪstənt] *adj* & *s* protestante *mf* ‖ **Protestant** *adj* & *s* protestante *mf*

prothonotar·y [pro'θɑnə,tɛri] *s* (*pl* -ies) escribano principal (*de un tribunal*)

protocol ['protə,kɑl] *s* protocolo

protoplasm ['protə,plæzəm] *s* protoplasma *m*

prototype ['protə,taɪp] *s* prototipo

protozoön [,protə'zo·ɑn] *s* protozoo

protract [pro'trækt] *tr* prolongar

protrude [pro'trud] *intr* resaltar

proud [praʊd] *adj* orgulloso; soberbio; glorioso

proud flesh *s* carnosidad, bezo

prove [pruv] *v* (*pret* proved; *pp* proved o proven) *tr* probar ‖ *intr* resultar; **to prove to be** venir a ser, resultar

proverb ['prɑvɜrb] *s* proverbio

provide [prə'vaɪd] *tr* proporcionar, suministrar ‖ *intr* — **to provide for** proveer a; asegurarse (*el porvenir*)

provided [prə'vaɪdɪd] *conj* a condición (de) que, con tal (de) que

providence ['prɑvɪdəns] *s* providencia

providential [,prɑvɪ'dɛnʃəl] *adj* providencial

providing [prə'vaɪdɪŋ] *conj* var de **provided**

province ['prɑvɪns] *s* provincia; (*sphere of activity or knowledge*) competencia

provision [prə'vɪʒən] *s* provisión; condición, estipulación

provi·so [prə'vaɪzo] *s* (*pl* -sos o -soes) condición, estipulación, salvedad

provoke [prə'vok] *tr* provocar

provoking [prə'vokɪŋ] *adj* provocador, irritante

prow [praʊ] *s* proa

prowess ['prau·ɪs] *s* proeza; destreza

prowl [praʊl] *intr* cazar al acecho, rodar, vagabundear

prowler ['praʊlər] *s* rondador *m*; ladrón *m*

proximity [prɑk'sɪmɪti] *s* proximidad

prox·y ['prɑksi] *s* (*pl* -ies) poder *m*, poderhabiente *mf*

prude [prud] *s* mojigato, gazmoño

prudence ['prudəns] *s* prudencia

prudent ['prudənt] *adj* prudente

pruder·y ['prudəri] *s* (*pl* -ies) mojigatería, gazmoñería

prudish ['prudɪʃ] *adj* mojigato, gazmoño

prune [prun] *s* ciruela pasa ‖ *tr* podar, escamondar

pry [praɪ] *v* (*pret* & *pp* pried) *tr* — **to pry open** forzar con la alzaprima o palanca; **to pry out of** arrancar (*p.ej.*, *un secreto*) a (*una persona*) ‖ *intr* entremeterse

P.S. *abbr* **postscript, Privy Seal**

psalm [sɑm] *s* salmo

Psalter ['sɔltər] *s* Salterio

pseudo ['sudo] o ['sjudo] *adj* supuesto, falso, fingido

pseudonym ['sudənɪm] o ['sjudənɪm] *s* seudónimo

Psyche ['saɪki] *s* Psique *f*

psychedelic [,saɪkə'dɛlɪk] *adj* sicodélico

psychiatrist [saɪ'kaɪ·ətrɪst] *s* psiquiatra *mf*

psychiatry [saɪ'kaɪ·ətri] *s* psiquiatría

psychic ['saɪkɪk] *adj* psíquico; mediúmnico ‖ *s* médium *mf*

psychoanalysis [,saɪko·ə'nælɪsɪs] *s* psicoanálisis *m*

psychoanalyze [,saɪko'ænə,laɪz] *tr* psicoanalizar

psychologic(al) [,saɪko'lɑdʒɪk(əl)] *adj* psicológico

psychologist [saɪ'kɑlədʒɪst] *s* psicólogo

psychology [saɪ'kɑlədʒi] *s* psicología

psychopath ['saɪkə,pæθ] *s* psicópata *mf*

psycho·sis [saɪˈkosɪs] s (pl **-ses** [siz]) psicosis f; estado mental
psychotic [saɪˈkɑtɪk] adj & s psicótico
pt. abbr **part, pint, point**
pub [pʌb] s (Brit) taberna
puberty [ˈpjubərti] s pubertad
public [ˈpʌblɪk] adj & s púbiico
publication [ˌpʌblɪˈkeʃən] s publicación
public conveyance s vehículo de servicio público
publicity [pʌbˈlɪsɪti] s publicidad
publicize [ˈpʌblɪˌsaɪz] tr publicar
public library s biblioteca municipal
public school s (U.S.A.) escuela pública; (Brit) internado privado con dote
public speaking s elocución, oratoria
public spirit s celo patriótico del buen ciudadano
public toilet s quiosco de necesidad
public utility s empresa de servicio público; **public utilities** acciones emitidas por empresas de servicio público
publish [ˈpʌblɪʃ] tr publicar
publisher [ˈpʌblɪʃər] s editor m
publishing house s casa editorial
pucker [ˈpʌkər] s (small fold) frunce m; pliego mal hecho || tr fruncir (una tela; la frente); plegar mal || intr plegarse mal
pudding [ˈpudɪŋ] s budín m, pudín m
puddle [ˈpʌdəl] s aguazal m, charco
pudg·y [ˈpʌdʒi] adj (comp **-ier**; super **-iest**) gordinflón, rechoncho
puerile [ˈpjuˌərɪl] adj pueril
puerili·ty [ˌpjuˌəˈrɪlɪti] s (pl **-ties**) puerilidad
Puerto Rican [ˈpwɛrto ˈrikən] adj & s puertorriqueño
puff [pʌf] s soplo vivo; (of smoke) bocanada; (in clothing) bullón m; borla de polvos; pastelillo de crema o jalea; alabanza exagerada; ráfaga, ventolera || tr soplar; hinchar; alabar exageradamente || intr soplar; hincharse; enorgullecerse exageradamente
puff paste s hojaldre m & f
pugilism [ˈpjudʒɪˌlɪzəm] s pugilismo
pugilist [ˈpjudʒɪlɪst] s pugilista m
pug-nosed [ˈpʌgˌnozd] adj braco
puke [pjuk] s (slang) vómito || tr & intr (slang) vomitar
pull [pul] s estirón m, tirón m; (on a cigar) chupada; (of a door) tirador m; (slang) enchufe m, buenas aldabas || tr tirar o; torcer (un ligamento); (typ) sacar (una impresión o prueba); **to pull down** demoler, derribar; bajar (p.ej., la cortinilla); abatir, degradar; **to pull oneself together** componerse, recobrar la calma || intr tirar; moverse despacio, moverse con esfuerzo; **to pull at** tirar de (p.ej., la corbata); chupar (p.ej., un cigarro); **to pull for** (slang) abogar por, ayudar; **to pull for oneself** tirar por su lado; **to pull in** llegar (un tren) a la estación; **to pull out** partir (un tren) de la estación; **to pull through** salir a flote; recobrar la salud

pullet [ˈpulɪt] s polla
pulley [ˈpuli] s polea
pulp [pʌlp] s pulpa; (to make paper) pasta; (of tooth) bulbo
pulpit [ˈpulpɪt] s púlpito
pulsate [ˈpʌlset] intr pulsar; vibrar
pulsation [pʌlˈseʃən] s pulsación; vibración
pulse [pʌls] s pulso; **to feel o take the pulse of** tomar el pulso a
pulverize [ˈpʌlvəˌraɪz] tr pulverizar
pumice stone [ˈpʌmɪs] s pómez f, piedra pómez
pum·mel [ˈpʌməl] v (pret & pp **-meled** o **-melled**; ger **-meling** o **-melling**) tr apuñear, aporrear
pump [pʌmp] s bomba; (slipperlike shoe) escarpín m, zapatilla || tr elevar o sacar (agua) por medio de una bomba; (coll) tirar de la lengua a (una persona); **to pump up** hinchar, inflar (un neumático)
pump handle s guimbalete m
pumpkin [ˈpʌmpkɪn] o [ˈpʌŋkɪn] s calabaza común; **some pumpkins** (coll) persona de muchas campanillas
pump-priming [ˈpʌmp ˌpraɪmɪŋ] s inyección económica (por parte del gobierno)
pun [pʌn] s equívoco, retruécano || v (pret & pp **punned**; ger **punning**) intr decir equívocos, jugar del vocablo
punch [pʌntʃ] s puñetazo; (tool) punzón m; (for tickets) sacabocado; (drink) ponche m || tr dar un puñetazo a; taladrar, perforar (un billete, una tarjeta)
punch bowl s ponchera
punch card s tarjeta perforada
punch clock s reloj m registrador de tarjetas
punch'-drunk' adj atontado (p.ej., por una tunda de golpes); completamente aturdido
punched tape s cinta perforada
punching bag s punching m, boxibalón m
punch line s broche m de oro, colofón m del artículo
punctilious [pʌŋkˈtɪlɪ·əs] adj puntilloso, pundonoroso
punctual [ˈpʌŋktʃu·əl] adj puntual
punctuate [ˈpʌŋktʃuˌet] tr puntuar; acentuar, destacar; interrumpir || intr puntuar
punctuation [ˌpʌŋktʃuˈeʃən] s puntuación
punctuation mark s signo de puntuación
puncture [ˈpʌŋktʃər] s puntura; (of a tire) picadura, pinchazo || tr pinchar, picar, perforar
punc'ture-proof' adj a prueba de pinchazos
pundit [ˈpʌndɪt] s erudito, sabio
pungent [ˈpʌndʒənt] adj picante; estimulante
punish [ˈpʌnɪʃ] tr castigar; (coll) maltratar
punishment [ˈpʌnɪʃmənt] s castigo; (coll) maltrato

pr
pu

punk [pʌŋk] *adj* (slang) malo, de mala calidad ‖ *s* yesca, pebete *m;* (*decayed wood*) hupe *m;* (slang) pillo, gamberro

punster ['pʌnstər] *s* equivoquista *mf,* vocablista *mf*

pu·ny ['pjuni] *adj* (*comp* -nier; *super* -niest) encanijado, débil; insignificante, mezquino

pup [pʌp] *s* cachorro

pupil ['pjupəl] *s* alumno; (*of the eye*) pupila

puppet ['pʌpɪt] *s* títere *m;* (*doll*) muñeca; (*person controlled by another*) maniquí *m*

puppet government *s* gobierno de monigotes

puppet show *s* función de títeres

puppy love ['pʌpi] *s* (coll) primeros amores

purchase ['pʌrtʃəs] *s* compra; agarre *m* firme ‖ *tr* comprar

purchasing power *s* poder adquisitivo

pure [pjʊr] *adj* puro

purgative ['pʌrgətɪv] *adj & s* purgante *m*

purge [pʌrdʒ] *s* purga ‖ *tr* purgar

puri·fy ['pjʊrɪ‚faɪ] *v* (*pret & pp* -fied) *tr* purificar

puritan ['pjʊrɪtən] *adj & s* puritano ‖ **Pu·ritan** *adj & s* puritano

purity ['pjʊrɪti] *s* pureza

purloin [pər'lɔɪn] *tr & intr* robar, hurtar

purple ['pʌrpəl] *adj* purpurado, rojo morado ‖ *m* púrpura, rojo morado

purport ['pʌrport] *s* significado, idea principal *m* [pər'port] *tr* significar, querer decir

purpose ['pʌrpəs] *s* intención, propósito; fin *m,* objeto; **for the purpose** al efecto; **for what purpose?** ¿con qué fin?; **on purpose** adrede, de propósito; **to good purpose** con buenos resultados; **to no purpose** sin resultado; **to serve one's purpose** servir para el caso

purposely ['pʌrpəsli] *adv* adrede, de propósito

purr [pʌr] *s* ronroneo ‖ *intr* ronronear

purse [pʌrs] *s* bolsa; (*money collected for charity*) colecta ‖ *tr* fruncir

purser ['pʌrsər] *s* contador *m* de navío, comisario de a bordo

purse snatcher ['snætʃər] *s* carterista *mf*

purse strings *spl* cordones *mpl* de la bolsa; **to hold the purse strings** tener las llaves de la caja

pursue [pər'su] o [pər'sju] *tr* perseguir (*al que huye*); proseguir (*lo empezado*); seguir (*una carrera*); dedicarse a

pursuit [pər'sut] o [pər'sjut] *s* persecución; prosecución; (*e.g., of happiness*) busca o búsqueda; empleo

pursuit plane *s* caza *m,* avión *m* de caza

purvey [pər've] *tr* proveer, suministrar

pus [pʌs] *s* pus *m*

push [pʊ/] *s* empuje *m,* empujón *m* ‖ *tr* empujar; pulsar (*un botón*); extender (*p.ej., conquistas*); **to push around** (coll) tratar a empujones; **to**

push aside hacer a un lado; **to push through** forzar (*p.ej., una resolución*) ‖ *intr* empujar; **to push off** (coll) irse, salir; (naut) desatracarse

push button *s* botón *m* de llamada, botón interruptor

push'-but'ton control *s* mando por botón

push'cart' *s* carretilla de mano

pushing ['pʊ/ɪŋ] *adj* emprendedor; entremetido, agresivo

pusillanimous [‚pjusɪ'lænɪməs] *adj* pusilánime

puss [pʊs] *interj* ¡miz! ‖ *s* micho; chica, muchacha; (slang) cara, boca

puss in the corner *s* las cuatro esquinas

puss·y ['pʊsi] *s* (*pl* -ies) michito

pussy willow *s* sauce norteamericano de amentos muy sedosos

pustule ['pʌst/ul] *s* pústula

put [pʊt] *v* (*pret & pp* **put;** *ger* **putting**) *tr* poner, colocar; arrojar, echar, lanzar; hacer (*una pregunta*); **to put across** llevar a cabo; hacer aceptar; **to put aside** poner aparte; rechazar; ahorrar (*dinero*); **to put down** anotar, apuntar; sofocar (*una insurrección*); rebajar (*los precios*); **to put off** posponer; deshacerse de; **to put on** ponerse (*la ropa*); poner en escena; llevar (*p.ej., un drama a la pantalla*); accionar (*un freno*); cargar (*impuestos*); fingir; atribuir; **to put oneself out** incomodarse, molestarse; afanarse, desvivirse; **to put out** extender (*la mano*); apagar (*el fuego, la luz*); poner en la calle; dar a luz, publicar; decepcionar; (sport) sacar fuera de la partida; **to put over o through** (coll) llevar a cabo; **to put up** construir, edificar; abrir (*un paraguas*); conservar (*fruta, legumbres*); (coll) incitar ‖ *intr* dirigirse; **to put on** fingir; **to put up** parar, hospedarse; **to put up with** aguantar, tolerar

put'-out' *adj* contrariado, enojado

putrid ['pjutrɪd] *adj* pútrido; corrompido, perverso

Putsch [pʊt/] *s* intentona de sublevación; sublevación

putter ['pʌtər] *intr* trabajar sin orden ni sistema; **to putter around** ocuparse en fruslerías, temporizar

put·ty ['pʌti] *s* (*pl* -ties) masilla ‖ *v* (*pret & pp* -tied) *tr* enmasillar

putty knife *s* cuchillo de vidriero, espátula

put'-up' *adj* (coll) premeditado con malicia

puzzle ['pʌzəl] *s* enigma *m;* acertijo, rompecabezas *m* ‖ *tr* confundir, poner perplejo; **to puzzle out** descifrar ‖ *intr* estar perplejo; **to puzzle over** tratar de descifrar

puzzler ['pʌzlər] *s* quisicosa

PW *abbr* prisoner of war

pyg·my ['pɪgmi] *adj* pigmeo ‖ *s* (*pl* -mies) pigmeo

pylon ['paɪlɑn] *s* pilón *m*

pyramid ['pɪrəmɪd] *s* pirámide *f* ‖ *tr* aumentar (*su dinero*) comprando o

vendiendo al crédito y empleando las ganancias para comprar o vender más
pyre [paɪr] s pira
Pyrenean [ˌpɪrɪˈniːən] adj pirineo
Pyrenees [ˈpɪrɪˌniz] spl Pirineos
pyrites [paɪˈraɪtiz] o [ˈpaɪraɪts] s pirita

pyrotechnical [ˌpaɪrəˈtɛknɪkəl] adj pirotécnico
pyrotechnics [ˌpaɪrəˈtɛknɪks] spl pirotecnia
python [ˈpaɪθən] o [ˈpaɪθɛn] s pitón m
pythoness [ˈpaɪθənɪs] s pitonisa
pyx [pɪks] s píxide f, copón m

Q

Q, q [kju] decimoséptima letra del alfabeto inglés
Q. abbr **quarto, queen, question, quire**
Q.M. abbr **quartermaster**
qr. abbr **quarter, quire**
qt. abbr **quantity, quart**
qu. abbr **quart, quarter, quarterly, queen, query, question**
quack [kwæk] adj falso ‖ s graznido del pato; charlatán m; medicastro, curandero ‖ intr parpar (el pato)
quacker·y [ˈkwækəri] s (pl -ies) charlatanismo
quadrangle [ˈkwɑdˌræŋgəl] s cuadrángulo; patio cuadrangular
quadrant [ˈkwɑdrənt] s cuadrante m
quadroon [kwɑdˈrun] s cuarterón m
quadruped [ˈkwɑdruˌped] adj & s cuadrúpedo
quadruple [ˈkwɑdrupəl] o [kwɑdˈrupəl] adj & s cuádruple m ‖ tr cuadruplicar ‖ intr cuadruplicarse
quadruplet [ˈkwɑdruˌplet] o [kwɑdˈruplet] s cuatrillizo
quaff [kwɑf] o [kwæf] s trago grande ‖ tr & intr beber en gran cantidad
quail [kwel] s codorniz f ‖ intr acobardarse
quaint [kwent] adj curioso, raro; afectado, rebuscado; fantástico, singular
quake [kwek] s temblor m, terremoto ‖ intr temblar
Quaker [ˈkwekər] adj & s cuáquero
Quaker meeting s reunión de cuáqueros; reunión en que hay poca conversación
quali·fy [ˈkwɑlɪˌfaɪ] v (pret & pp -fied) tr calificar; capacitar, habilitar ‖ intr capacitarse, habilitarse
quali·ty [ˈkwɑlɪti] s (pl -ties) (characteristic; virtue) calidad; (property, attribute) cualidad; (of a sound) timbre m
qualm [kwɑm] s escrúpulo de conciencia; duda, inquietud; (nausea) basca
quanda·ry [ˈkwɑndəri] s (pl -ries) incertidumbre, perplejidad
quanti·ty [ˈkwɑntɪti] s (pl -ties) cantidad
quan·tum [ˈkwɑntəm] adj cuántico ‖ s (pl -ta [tə]) cuanto, quántum m
quantum theory s teoría cuántica
quarantine [ˈkwɑrənˌtin] o [ˈkwɔrənˌtin] s cuarentena; estación de cuarentena ‖ tr poner en cuarentena
quar·rel [ˈkwɑrəl] o [ˈkwɔrəl] s disputa, riña, pelea; **to have no quarrel with** no estar en desacuerdo con; **to pick a quarrel with** tomarse con ‖ v (pret & pp -reled o -relled; ger -reling o -relling) intr disputar, reñir, pelear
quarrelsome [ˈkwɑrəlsəm] o [ˈkwɔrəlsəm] adj pendenciero
quar·ry [ˈkwɑri] o [ˈkwɔri] s (pl -ries) cantera, pedrera; caza, presa ‖ v (pret & pp -ried) tr sacar de una cantera; extraer, sacar
quart [kwort] s cuarto de galón
quarter [ˈkwortər] adj cuarto ‖ s cuarto, cuarta parte; (three months) trimestre m; moneda de 25 centavos; cuarto de luna; barrio; región, lugar m; (clemency) cuartel m; (mil) **quarters** morada, vivienda; local m; (mil) cuarteles mpl; **to take up quarters** alojarse ‖ tr descuartizar
quar'ter-deck' s alcázar m
quar'ter-hour' s cuarto de hora; **on the quarter-hour** al cuarto en punto cada cuarto de hora
quarter·ly [ˈkwortərli] adj trimestral ‖ adv trimestralmente ‖ s (pl -lies) publicación o revista trimestral
quar'ter-mas'ter s (mil) comisario; (nav) cabo de brigadas
quartet [kworˈtet] s cuarteto
quartz [kworts] s cuarzo
quasar [ˈkwesɑr] s (astr) objeto del espacio, fuente f cuasiestelar de radio
quash [kwɑʃ] tr sofocar, reprimir; anular, invalidar
quaver [ˈkwevər] s temblor m, estremecimiento; (mus) trémolo ‖ intr temblar, estremecerse
quay [ki] s muelle m, desembarcadero
queen [kwin] s reina; (in chess) dama o reina; (in cards) dama (que corresponde al caballo); abeja reina
queen bee s abeja reina, abeja maestra; (slang) marimandona, la que lleva la voz cantante
queen dowager s reina viuda
queen·ly [ˈkwinli] adj (comp -lier; super -liest) de reina; como reina; regio
queen mother s reina madre
queen olive s aceituna de la reina, aceituna gordal
queen post s péndola
queen's English s inglés castizo
queer [kwɪr] adj curioso, raro; estrambótico, estrafalario; aturdido, indispuesto; (coll) sospechoso, misterioso ‖ tr (slang) echar a perder; (slang) comprometer
quell [kwel] tr sofocar, reprimir; mitigar (una pena o dolor)

quench [kwɛntʃ] *tr* apagar (*el fuego; la sed*); sofocar, reprimir; (electron) amortiguar

que·ry [ˈkwɪri] *s* (*pl* **-ries**) pregunta; signo de interrogación; duda ‖ *v* (*pret & pp* **-ried**) *tr* interrogar; marcar con signo de interrogación; dudar

ques. *abbr* question

quest [kwɛst] *s* búsqueda; (*of the Holy Grail*) demanda; **in quest of** en busca de

question [ˈkwɛstʃən] *s* pregunta; (*problem for discussion*) cuestión; asunto, proposición; **beside the question** que no viene al caso; **beyond question** fuera de duda; **out of the question** imposible, indiscutible; **to ask a question** hacer una pregunta; **to be a question of** tratarse de, ser cuestión de; **to call in question** poner en duda; **without question** sin duda ‖ *tr* interrogar; cuestionar (*poner en tela de juicio*)

questionable [ˈkwɛstʃənəbəl] *adj* cuestionable

question mark *s* punto interrogante, signo de interrogación

questionnaire [ˌkwɛstʃənˈɛr] *s* cuestionario

queue [kju] *s* (*of hair*) coleta; (*of people*) cola ‖ *intr* hacer cola

quibble [ˈkwɪbəl] *intr* sutilizar

quick [kwɪk] *adj* rápido, veloz; ágil, vivo; despierto, listo; **the quick and the dead** los vivos y los muertos; **to cut** o **to sting to the quick** herir en lo vivo, tocar en la herida

quicken [ˈkwɪkən] *tr* acelerar, avivar; animar ‖ *intr* acelerarse; animarse

quick′lime′ *s* cal viva

quick lunch *s* servicio de la barra, servicio rápido

quick′sand′ *s* arena movediza

quick′sil′ver *s* azogue *m*

quiet [ˈkwaɪ‧ət] *adj* (*still*) quieto; silencioso; (*market*) (com) encalmado; **to keep quiet** callarse ‖ quietud; silencio; **on the quiet** a las calladas ‖ *tr* aquietar; acallar ‖ *intr* aquietarse; callarse; **to quiet down** calmarse

quill [kwɪl] *s* pluma de ave; cañón *m* de pluma; (*of hedgehog, porcupine*) púa

quilt [kwɪlt] *s* edredón *m*, colcha ‖ *tr* acolchar

quince [kwɪns] *s* membrillo

quinine [ˈkwaɪnaɪn] *s* quinina

quinsy [ˈkwɪnzi] *s* cinanquia, esquinencia

quintessence [kwɪnˈtɛsəns] *s* quintaesencia

quintet [kwɪnˈtɛt] *s* quinteto

quintuplet [kwɪnˈtjuplɛt] o [kwɪnˈtuplɛt] *s* quintillizo

quip [kwɪp] *s* chufleta, pulla ‖ *v* (*pret & pp* **quipped**; *ger* **quipping**) *tr* decir en son de burla ‖ *intr* echar pullas

quire [kwaɪr] *s* mano *f* de papel; (bb) alzado

quirk [kwʌrk] *s* excentricidad, rareza; sutileza; vuelta repentina

quit [kwɪt] *adj* libre, descargado; **to be quits** estar desquitados; **to cry quits** pedir treguas ‖ *v* (*pret & pp* **quit** o **quitted**; *ger* **quitting**) *tr* dejar ‖ *intr* irse; (coll) dejar de trabajar

quite [kwaɪt] *adv* enteramente; verdaderamente; (coll) bastante, muy

quitter [ˈkwɪtər] *s* remolón *m*; (*of a cause*) desertor *m*

quiver [ˈkwɪvər] *s* temblor *m*; (*to hold arrows*) aljaba, carcaj *m* ‖ *intr* temblar

quixotic [kwɪksˈɑtɪk] *adj* quijotesco

quiz [kwɪz] *s* (*pl* **quizzes**) examen *m*; interrogatorio ‖ *v* (*pret & pp* **quizzed**; *ger* **quizzing**) *tr* examinar; interrogar

quiz game *s* torneo de preguntas y respuestas

quiz program *s* programa *m* de preguntas y respuestas, torneo radiofónico

quiz section *s* grupo de práctica

quizzical [ˈkwɪzɪkəl] *adj* curioso; cómico; burlón

quoin [kɔɪn] o [kwɔɪn] *s* esquina; piedra angular; (*wedge*) cuña ‖ *tr* (typ) acuñar

quoit [kwɔɪt] o [kɔɪt] *s* herrón *m*, tejo; **quoits** *ssg* hito

quondam [ˈkwɑndæm] *adj* antiguo, de otro tiempo

quorum [ˈkworəm] *s* quórum *m*

quota [ˈkwotə] *s* cuota

quotation [kwoˈteʃən] *s* (*from a book*) cita; (*of prices*) cotización

quotation marks *spl* comillas

quote [kwot] *s* (coll) cita; (coll) cotización; **close quote** fin de la cita; **quotes** (coll) comillas ‖ *tr & intr* citar; cotizar; quote cito

quotient [ˈkwoʃənt] *s* cociente *m*

q.v. *abbr* **quod vide** (Lat) **which see**

R

R, r [ɑr] decimoctava letra del alfabeto inglés

r. *abbr* **railroad, railway, road, rod, ruble, rupee**

R. *abbr* **railroad, railway; Regina** (Lat), **Queen; Republican, response; Rex** (Lat), **King; River, Royal**

rabbet [ˈræbɪt] *s* barbilla, rebajo ‖ *tr* embarbillar, rebajar

rab·bi [ˈræbaɪ] *s* (*pl* **-bis** o **-bies**) rabino

rabbit [ˈræbɪt] *s* conejo

rabbit ears *spl* (rad) (coll) antena de conejo

rabble rouser [ˈrauzər] *s* populachero, alborotapueblos *mf*

rabies [ˈrebiz] o [ˈrebi ˌiz] *s* rabia

raccoon [ræˈkun] *s* mapache *m*, oso lavador

race [res] *s* (*people of same stock*) raza; (*contest in speed, etc.*) carrera; (*channel to lead water*) caz *m* || *tr* competir con, en una carrera; hacer correr de prisa; hacer funcionar (*un motor*) a velocidad excesiva || *intr* correr de prisa; correr en una carrera; competir en una carrera; embalarse (*un motor*); (naut) regatear

race horse *s* caballo de carreras

race riot *s* disturbio racista

race track *s* pista de carreras

racial ['reʃəl] *adj* racial

racing car *s* coche *m* de carreras

rack [ræk] *s* (*sort of shelf*) estante *m*; (*to hang clothes*) percha; (*for fodder for cattle*) pesebre *m*; (*for baggage*) red *f* de equipaje; (*for guns*) armero; (*bar made to gear with a pinion*) cremallera; **to go to rack and ruin** desvencijarse; ir al desastre || *tr* estirar, forzar; atormentar; despedazar; oprimir, agobiar; **to rack off** trasegar (*el vino*); **to rack one's brains** calentarse la cabeza, devanarse los sesos

racket ['rækɪt] *s* raqueta; (*noise*) baraúnda, alboroto; (slang) trapisonda, trapacería; **to raise a racket** armar un alboroto

racketeer [,rækɪ'tɪr] *s* trapisondista *mf*, trapacista *mf* || *intr* trapacear

rack railway *s* ferrocarril *m* de cremallera

rac·y ['resi] *adj* (*comp* **-ier**; *super* **-iest**) espirituoso, chispeante; perfumado; (*somewhat indecent*) picante

radar ['redər] *s* radar *m*

radiant ['redɪ·ənt] *adj* radiante, resplandeciente; (*cheerful, smiling*) radiante

radiate ['redɪˌet] *tr* radiar; difundir (*p.ej., felicidad*) || *intr* radiar, irradiar

radiation [,redɪ'eʃən] *s* radiación

radiation sickness *s* enfermedad de radiación, mal *m* de rayos

radiator ['redɪˌetər] *s* radiador *m*

radiator cap *s* tapón *m* de radiador

radical ['rædɪkəl] *adj* & *s* radical *m*

radi·o ['redɪ,o] *s* (*pl* **-os**) radio *f*; radiograma *m* || *tr* radiodifundir

radioactive [,redɪ·o'æktɪv] *adj* radiactivo

radio amateur *s* radioaficionado

radio announcer *s* locutor *m* de radio

ra'dio·broad'cast'ing *s* radiodifusión

radio frequency *s* radiofrecuencia

radio listener *s* radioescucha *mf*, radioyente *mf*

radiology [,redɪ'ɑlədʒi] *s* radiología

radio network *s* red *f* de emisoras

radio newscaster *s* cronista *mf* de radio

radio receiver *s* radiorreceptor *m*

radio set *s* aparato de radio

radish ['rædɪʃ] *s* rábano

radium ['redɪəm] *s* radio *m*

radi·us ['redɪ·əs] *s* (*pl* **-i** [,aɪ] o **-uses**) radio; (*range of operation*) radio; **within a radius of** en . . . a la redonda

raffle ['ræfəl] *s* rifa || *tr & intr* rifar

raft [ræft] o [rɑft] *s* armadía, balsa; (coll) gran número

rafter ['ræftər] o ['rɑftər] *s* cabrio, contrapar *m*, traviesa

rag [ræg] *s* trapo; **to chew the rag** (slang) dar la lengua

ragamuffin ['rægəˌmʌfɪn] *s* pelagatos *m*; golfo, chiquillo haraposo

rag baby o **rag doll** *s* muñeca de trapo

rage [redʒ] *s* rabia; **to be all the rage** estar en boga, hacer furor; **to fly into a rage** montar en cólera

ragged ['rægɪd] *adj* andrajoso; (*edge*) cortado en dientes

ragpicker ['rægˌpɪkər] *s* andrajero, trapero

rag'weed' *s* ambrosía

raid [red] *s* incursión, invasión; ataque de sorpresa; ataque aéreo || *tr* invadir; atacar inesperadamente; capturar (*p.ej., la policía un garito*)

rail [rel] *s* carril *m*, riel *m*; (*railing*) barandilla; (*of a bridge*) guardalado; (*at a bar*) apoyo para los pies; palo; **by rail** por ferrocarril; **rails** títulos o valores de ferrocarril || *tr* poner barandilla a || *intr* quejarse amargamente; **to rail at** injuriar, ultrajar

rail fence *s* cerca hecha de palos horizontales

rail'head' *s* (rr) cabeza de línea

railing ['relɪŋ] *s* barandilla, pasamano

rail'road' *adj* ferroviario || *s* ferrocarril *m* || *tr* (coll) llevar a cabo con demasiada precipitación; (slang) encarcelar falsamente || *intr* trabajar en el ferrocarril

railroad crossing *s* paso a nivel

rail'way' *adj* ferroviario || *s* ferrocarril *m*

raiment ['remənt] *s* prendas de vestir, indumentaria

rain [ren] *s* lluvia; **rain or shine** llueva o no, con buen o mal tiempo || *tr & intr* llover

rain'bow' *s* arco iris

rain'coat' *s* impermeable *m*

rain'fall' *s* lluvia repentina; precipitación acuosa

rain·y ['reni] *adj* (*comp* **-ier**; *super* **-iest**) lluvioso

rainy day *s* día lluvioso; tiempo futuro de posible necesidad

raise [rez] *s* aumento || *tr* levantar; aumentar; criar (*a niños, animales*); cultivar (*plantas*); reunir (*dinero*); suscitar (*una duda*); resucitar (*a los muertos*); dejarse (*barba, bigote*); poner (*una objeción*); plantear (*una pregunta*); levantar (*tropas; un sitio*); (math) elevar; (*to come in sight of*) (naut) avistar

raisin ['rezən] *s* pasa, uva seca

rake [rek] *s* rastro, rastrillo; (*person*) calavera *m*, libertino || *tr* rastrillar; **to rake together** acumular (*dinero*)

rake'-off' *s* (slang) dinero obtenido ilícitamente

rakish ['rekɪʃ] *adj* airoso, gallardo; listo, vivo; libertino

ral·ly ['ræli] *s* (*pl* **-lies**) reunión popular, reunión política; recuperación, recobro || *v* (*pret & pp* **-lied**) *tr* reunir; reanimar; recobrar (la fuerza, la salud, el ánimo) || intr reunirse; recobrarse (p.ej., los precios en la Bolsa); recobrar la fuerza, la salud, el ánimo; **to rally to the side of** acudir a, ir en socorro de

ram [ræm] s (male sheep) morueco, carnero padre; (device for battering, crushing, etc.) pisón m || v (pret & pp **rammed**; ger **ramming**) tr dar contra, chocar en; atestar, rellenar || intr chocar; **to ram into** chocar en

ramble ['ræmbəl] s paseo || intr pasear; serpentear (p.ej., un río); extenderse serpenteando (las enredaderas); (to wander aimlessly; to talk in an aimless way) divagar

rami·fy ['ræmɪˌfaɪ] v (pret & pp **-fied**) tr ramificar || intr ramificarse

ramp [ræmp] s rampa

rampage ['ræmpedʒ] s alboroto; **to go on a rampage** alborotar, comportarse como un loco

rampart ['ræmpɑrt] s muralla, terraplén m; amparo, defensa

ram'rod' s atacador m, baqueta

ram'shack'le adj desvencijado, destartalado

ranch [ræntʃ] s granja, hacienda

rancid ['rænsɪd] adj rancio

rancor ['ræŋkər] s rencor m

random ['rændəm] adj casual, fortuito; **at random** al azar, a la ventura

range [rendʒ] s (row, line) fila, hilera; (scope, reach) alcance m; (of speeds, prices, etc.) escala; campo de tiro; terreno de pasto; (of a boat or airplane) autonomía; (of the voice) extensión; (of colors) gama, serie f; (stove) cocina económica; **within range of** al alcance de || tr alinear; recorrer (un terreno); ir a lo largo de (la costa); arreglar, ordenar || intr fluctuar, variar (entre ciertos límites); extenderse; divagar, errar; **to range over** recorrer

range finder s telémetro

rank [ræŋk] adj exuberante, lozano; denso, espeso; grosero; maloliente; excesivo; incorregible, rematado; indecente, vulgar || s categoría, rango; condición, posición; distinción; (line of soldiers standing abreast) fila; (mil) empleo, grado || tr alinear; ordenar; tener grado o posición más alta que || intr ocupar el último grado; **to rank high** ocupar alta posición; ser tenido en alta estima; sobresalir; **to rank low** ocupar baja posición; **to rank with** estar al nivel de; tener el mismo grado que

rank and file s soldados de fila; pueblo, gente f común

rankle ['ræŋkəl] tr enconar, irritar || intr enconarse

ransack ['rænsæk] tr. registrar, escudriñar; robar, saquear

ransom ['rænsəm] s rescate m || tr rescatar

rant [rænt] intr desvariar, despotricar

rap [ræp] s golpe corto y seco; (noise) taque m; (coll) ardite m, bledo; (slang) crítica mordaz; **to take the** rap (slang) pagar la multa; sufrir las consecuencias || v (pret & pp **rapped**; ger **rapping**) tr golpear con golpe corto y seco; decir vivamente; (slang) criticar mordazmente || intr golpear con golpe corto y seco; **to rap at the door** tocar a la puerta

rapacious [rə'peʃəs] adj rapaz

rape [rep] s rapto; (of a woman) estupro, violación || tr raptar; estuprar, violar

rapid ['ræpɪd] adj rápido || **rapids** spl (of a river) rápidos

rap'id-fire' adj de tiro rápido; hecho vivamente

rapier ['repɪ·ər] s estoque m, espadín m

rapt [ræpt] adj arrebatado, extático, transportado; absorto

rapture ['ræptʃər] s embeleso, éxtasis f, rapto

rare [rer] adj raro; (word) poco usado; (meat) poco asado; (gem) precioso

rare bird s mirlo blanco

rare·fy ['rerɪˌfaɪ] v (pret & pp **-fied**) tr enrarecer || intr enrarecerse

rarely ['rerli] adv rara vez

rascal ['ræskəl] s bellaco, bribón m, pícaro

rash [ræʃ] adj temerario || s brote m, salpullido, erupción

rasp [ræsp] o [rɑsp] s escofina; (sound of a rasp) sonido áspero || tr escofinar; irritar, molestar; decir con voz ronca || intr hacer sonido áspero

raspber·ry ['ræzˌberi] o ['rɑzˌberi] s (pl **-ries**) frambuesa, sangüesa

raspberry bush s frambueso, sangüeso

rat [ræt] s rata; (false hair) (coll) postizo; **to smell a rat** (coll) olerse una trama, sospechar una intriga

ratchet ['rætʃɪt] s trinquete m

rate [ret] s (amount or degree measured in proportion to something else) razón f; (of interest) tipo; velocidad; precio; **at any rate** de todos modos; **at the rate of** a razón de || tr valuar; estimar, juzgar; clasificar || intr ser considerado, ser tenido; estar clasificado

rate of exchange s tipo de cambio

rather ['ræðər] o ['rɑðər] adv algo, un poco; bastante; antes, más bien; mejor dicho; por el contrario; muy, mucho; **rather than** antes que, más bien que || interj ¡ya lo creo!

rati·fy ['rætɪˌfaɪ] v (pret & pp **-fied**) tr ratificar

ra·tio ['reʃo] o ['reʃɪˌo] s (pl **-tios**) (math) razón f; (math) cociente m

ration ['reʃən] o ['ræʃən] s ración || tr racionar

ration book s cartilla de racionamiento

rational ['ræʃənəl] adj racional

rat poison s matarratas m

rattle ['rætəl] s (number of short, sharp sounds) traqueteo; (noise-making device) carraca, matraca; (child's toy) sonajero; baraúnda; (in the throat) estertor m || tr tabletear, traquetear; (to confuse) (coll) atortolar, desconcertar; **to rattle off**

decir rápidamente || *intr* tabletear, traquetear

rat'tle·snake' *s* serpiente *f* de cascabel

rat'trap' *s* ratonera; trance apurado, atolladero

raucous ['rɔkəs] *adj* ronco

ravage ['rævɪdʒ] *s* destrucción, estrago, ruina || *tr* destruir, estragar, arruinar

rave [rev] *intr* desvariar, delirar; bramar, enfurecerse; **to rave about** hacerse lenguas de, deshacerse en elogios de

raven ['revən] *s* cuervo

ravenous ['rævənəs] *adj* famélico, hambriento, voraz; rapaz

ravine [rə'vin] *s* cañón *m*, hondonada

ravish ['rævɪʃ] *tr* encantar, entusiasmar; raptar; violar (*a una mujer*)

ravishing ['rævɪʃɪŋ] *adj* encantador

raw [rɔ] *adj* crudo; (*cotton, silk*) en rama; inexperto, principiante; ulceroso; (*weather, day*) crudo

raw deal *s* (slang) mala pasada

raw'hide' *s* cuero en verde; látigo hecho de cuero en verde

raw material *s* primera materia, materia prima

ray [re] *s* (*of light*) rayo; (*fine line; fish*) raya

rayon ['re·ɑn] *s* rayón *m*

raze [rez] *tr* arrasar, asolar

razor ['rezər] *s* navaja de afeitar

razor blade *s* hoja u hojita de afeitar

razor strop *s* asentador *m*, suavizador *m*

razz [ræz] *s* (slang) irrisión || *tr* (slang) mofarse de

R.C. *abbr* **Red Cross, Reserve Corps, Roman Catholic**

R.D. *abbr* **Rural Delivery**

reach [ritʃ] *s* alcance *m*; extensión; **out of reach (of)** fuera del alcance (de); **within reach of** al alcance de || *tr* alcanzar; extender; entregar en con la mano; llegar a; ponerse en contacto con; influenciar; cumplir (*cierto número de años*) || *intr* alcanzar; extender la mano o el brazo; **to reach after o for** esforzarse por coger

react [rɪ'ækt] *intr* reaccionar

reaction [rɪ'ækʃən] *s* reacción

reactionar·y [rɪ'ækʃən,eri] *adj* reaccionario || *s* (*pl* **-ies**) reaccionario

read [rid] *v* (*pret & pp* read [rɛd]) *tr* leer; recitar (*poesía*); estudiar (*derecho*); leer en, adivinar (*el pensamiento ajeno*); **to read over** recorrer, repasar || *intr* leer; rezar, p.ej., **this page reads thus** esta página reza así; leerse, p.ej., **this book reads easily** este libro se lee con facilidad; **read on** seguir leyendo

reader ['ridər] *s* lector *m*; libro de lectura

readily ['rɛdɪli] *adv* de buena gana; fácilmente

reading ['ridɪŋ] *s* lectura; recitación

reading desk *s* atril *m*

reading glass *s* lente *f* para leer, vidrio de aumento; **reading glasses** anteojos para la lectura

reading lamp *s* lámpara de sobremesa

reading room *s* gabinete *m* de lectura; sala de lectura

read·y ['rɛdi] *adj* (*comp* **-ier;** *super* **-iest**) listo, preparado; pronto; ágil, diestro; vivo; disponible; **to make ready** preparar; prepararse || *v* (*pret & pp* **-ied**) *tr* preparar || *intr* prepararse

ready cash *s* dinero a la mano, dinero contante y sonante

read'y-made' clothing *s* ropa hecha

ready-made suit *s* traje hecho

reagent [rɪ'edʒənt] *s* reactivo

real ['ri·əl] *adj* real, verdadero

real estate *s* bienes *mpl* raíces, bienes inmuebles

re'al-es·tate' *adj* inmobiliario

realism ['ri·ə,lɪzəm] *s* realismo

realist ['ri·əlɪst] *s* realista *mf*

reali·ty [rɪ'ælɪti] *s* (*pl* **-ties**) realidad

realize ['ri·ə,laɪz] *tr* darse cuenta de; realizar, llevar a cabo; adquirir (*ganancias*); reportar (*ganancias*) || *intr* (*to sell property for ready money*) realizar

realm [rɛlm] *s* reino

realtor ['ri·əl,tɔr] o ['ri·əltər] *s* corredor *m* de bienes raíces

realty ['ri·əlti] *s* bienes *mpl* raíces, bienes inmuebles

ream [rim] *s* resma; **reams** (coll) montones *mpl* || *tr* escariar

reap [rip] *tr & intr* (*to cut*) segar; (*to gather*) cosechar

reaper ['ripər] *s* (*person*) segador *m*; máquina segadora

reappear [,ri·ə'pɪr] *intr* reaparecer

reapportionment [,ri·ə'pɔr/ənmənt] *s* nuevo prorrateo

rear [rɪr] *adj* posterior, trasero; de atrás || *s* espalda; (*of a room*) fondo; (*of a row; of an automobile*) cola; retaguardia; (slang) culo, trasero || *tr* levantar; edificar; criar, educar || *intr* encabritarse (*un caballo*)

rear admiral *s* contraalmirante *m*

rear drive *s* tracción trasera

rearmament [rɪ'ɑrməmənt] *s* rearme *m*

rear'-view' mirror *s* retrovisor *m*, espejo de retrovisión

rear window *s* (aut) luneta, luneta posterior

reason ['rizən] *s* razón *f*; **by reason of** con motivo de, a causa de; **to listen to reason** meterse en razón; **to stand to reason** ser razonable || *tr & intr* razonar

reasonable ['rizənəbəl] *adj* razonable

reassessment [,ri·ə'sɛsmənt] *s* nuevo amillaramiento; nueva estimación

reassure [,ri·ə'/ʊr] *tr* volver a asegurar; tranquilizar

reawaken [,ri·ə'wekən] *tr* volver a despertar || *intr* volver a despertarse

rebate ['ribet] o [rɪ'bet] *s* rebaja || *tr* rebajar

rebel ['rɛbəl] *adj & s* rebelde *mf* || **re·bel** [rɪ'bɛl] *v* (*pret & pp* **-belled;** *ger* **-belling**) *intr* rebelarse

rebellion [rɪ'bɛljən] *s* rebelión

rebellious [rɪ'bɛljəs] *adj* rebelde

re·bind [ri'baɪnd] *v* (*pret & pp* **-bound**

ra
re

['baʊnd]) *tr* reatar; *(to edge, to border)* ribetear; (bb) reencuadernar

rebirth ['rɪbʌrθ] o [rɪ'bʌrθ] *s* renacimiento

rebore [rɪ'bor] *tr* rectificar

rebound ['rɪ,baʊnd] o [rɪ'baʊnd] *s* rebote *m* ‖ [rɪ'baʊnd] *intr* rebotar

rebroad·cast [rɪ'brɔd,kæst] o [rɪ'brɔd,kɑst] *s* retransmisión ‖ *v (pret & pp -cast o -casted) tr* retransmitir

rebuff [rɪ'bʌf] *s* desaire *m*, rechazo ‖ *tr* desairar, rechazar

re·build [rɪ'bɪld] *v (pret & pp -built* ['bɪlt]) *tr* reconstruir, reedificar

rebuke [rɪ'bjuk] *s* represión ‖ *tr* reprender

re·but [rɪ'bʌt] *v (pret & pp -butted; ger -butting) tr* rebatir, refutar

rebuttal [rɪ'bʌtəl] *s* rebatimiento, refutación

rec. *abbr* **receipt, recipe, record, recorder**

recall [rɪ'kɔl] o ['rikəl] *s* llamada; recordación; revocación; *(of a diplomat)* retirada ‖ [rɪ'kɔl] *tr* hacer volver, mandar volver; recordar; revocar; retirar *(a un diplomático)*

recant [rɪ'kænt] *tr* retractar ‖ *intr* retractarse

re·cap ['ri,kæp] o [ri'kæp] *v (pret & pp -capped; ger -capping) tr* recauchutar

recapitalization [ri,kæpɪtəlɪ'zeʃən] *s* recapitalización

recapitulation [,rikə,pɪtʃə'leʃən] *s* recapitulación

re·cast ['ri,kæst] o ['ri,kɑst] *s* refundición; *(of a sentence)* reconstrucción ‖ [ri'kæst] o [ri'kɑst] *v (pret & pp -cast) tr* refundir; reconstruir *(p.ej., una frase)*

recd. o rec'd. *abbr* **received**

recede [rɪ'sid] *intr (to move back)* retroceder; *(to move away)* alejarse, retirarse; deprimirse *(p.ej., la frente de una persona)*

receipt [rɪ'sit] *s* recepción; *(acknowledgment)* recibo; *(acknowledgment of payment)* recibí *m*; *(recipe)* receta; **receipt in full** finiquito; **receipts** entradas, ingresos ‖ *tr* poner el recibí a

receive [rɪ'siv] *tr* recibir; receptar *(cosas que son materia de delito)*; **received payment** recibí ‖ *intr* recibir

receiver [rɪ'sivər] *s* receptor *m*; *(in bankruptcy)* contador *m*, síndico; receptor telefónico

receiving set *s* aparato receptor

receiving teller *s* recibidor *m (de un banco)*

recent ['risənt] *adj* reciente

recently ['risəntli] *adv* recientemente; recién, p.ej., **recently arrived** recién llegado

receptacle [rɪ'septəkəl] *s* receptáculo

reception [rɪ'sepʃən] *s* recepción; *(welcome)* recibimiento

reception desk *s* recepción

receptionist [rɪ'sepʃənɪst] *s* recepcionista *f*

receptive [rɪ'septɪv] *adj* receptivo

recess [rɪ'ses] o ['rises] *s* intermisión;

descanso; hora de recreo; *(in a surface)* depresión; *(in a wall)* hueco, nicho; escondrijo ‖ [rɪ'ses] *tr* ahuecar; empotrar; deprimir ‖ *intr* prorrogarse, suspenderse

recession [rɪ'seʃən] *s* retroceso, retirada; *(e.g., in a wall)* depresión; procesión de vuelta; contracción económica

recipe ['resɪ ,pi] *s* receta (de cocina)

reciprocal [rɪ'sɪprəkəl] *adj* recíproco

reciprocity [,resɪ'prɑsɪti] *s* reciprocidad

recital [rɪ'saɪtəl] *s* narración; *(of music or poetry)* recital *m*

recite [rɪ'saɪt] *tr* narrar; *(formally)* recitar

reckless ['reklɪs] *adj* atolondrado, temerario

reckon ['rekən] *tr* calcular; considerar; (coll) calcular, conjeturar ‖ *intr* calcular; **to reckon on** contar con; **to reckon with** tener en cuenta

reclaim [rɪ'klem] *tr* hacer utilizable; hacer labrantío *(un terreno)*; ganar *(terreno)* a la mar; recuperar *(materiales usados)*; conducir, guiar *(a los que hacen mala vida)*

recline [rɪ'klaɪn] *intr* reclinarse

recluse [rɪ'klus] o ['reklus] *s* solitario, ermitaño

recognize ['rekəg,naɪz] *tr* reconocer

recoil [rɪ'kɔɪl] *s* reculada; *(of a firearm)* reculada, culetazo ‖ *intr* recular, apartarse; recular *(un arma de fuego)*

recollect [,rekə'lekt] *tr & intr* recordar

recombinant [rɪ'kɑmbənənt] *adj (genetics)* recombinado

recommend [,rekə'mend] *tr* recomendar

recompense ['rekəm,pens] *s* recompensa ‖ *tr* recompensar

reconcile ['rekən,saɪl] *tr* reconciliar; **to reconcile oneself** resignarse

reconnaissance [rɪ'kɑnɪsəns] *s* reconocimiento

reconnoiter [,rekə'nɔɪtər] o [,rikə-'nɔɪtər] *tr & intr* reconocer

reconstruct [,rikən'strʌkt] *tr* reconstruir

reconversion [,rikən'vʌrʒən] o [,rikən'vʌrʃən] *s* reconversión

record ['rekərd] *s* anotación; ficha, historial *m*, historia personal; *(of a notary)* protocolo; *(of a phonograph)* disco; (educ) expediente académico; (sport) record *m*, plusmarca; **off the record** confidencialmente; **records** anales *mpl*, memorias; archivo; **to break a record** batir un record; **to make a record** establecer un record; grabar un disco ‖ [rɪ'kɔrd] *tr* asentar; registrar; inscribir; grabar *(un sonido, una canción, un disco fonográfico, etc.)*

record breaker *s* plusmarquista *mf*

record changer ['tʃendʒər] *s* cambiadiscos *m*, tocadiscos automático

record holder *s* (sport) recordman *m*

recording [rɪ'kɔrdɪŋ] *adj* registrador;

(*wire or tape*) magnetofónico ‖ *s* registro; (*of phonograph records*) grabación o grabado

recording secretary *s* secretario escribiente, secretario de actas

record player *s* tocadiscos *m*

recount ['ri‚kaʊnt] *s* recuento ‖ [ri-'kaʊnt] *tr* (*to count again*) recontar ‖ [ri'kaʊnt] *tr* (*to narrate*) recontar

recourse [rɪ'kors] o ['rikors] *s* recurso; (*helping hand*) paño de lágrimas; **to have recourse to** recurrir a

recover [rɪ'kʌvər] *tr* recobrar; rescatar; **to recover consciousness** recobrar el conocimiento, volver en sí ‖ *intr* recobrarse; recobrar la salud; ganar un pleito

recover·y [rɪ'kʌvəri] *s* (*pl* -ies) recobro, recuperación; **past recovery** sin remedio

recreant ['rɛkrɪ‚ənt] *adj & s* cobarde *mf*, traidor *m*

recreation [‚rɛkrɪ'eʃən] *s* recreación

recruit [rɪ'krut] *s* recluta *m* ‖ *tr* reclutar ‖ *intr* alistar reclutas; ganar reclutas; restablecerse, reponerse

rect. *abbr* **receipt, rector, rectory**

rectangle ['rɛk‚tæŋgəl] *s* rectángulo

recti·fy ['rɛktɪ‚faɪ] *v* (*pret & pp* -fied) *tr* rectificar

rec·tum ['rɛktəm] *s* (*pl* -ta [tə]) recto

recumbent [rɪ'kʌmbənt] *adj* reclinado, recostado

recuperate [rɪ'kjupə‚ret] *tr* recuperar; restablecer, reponer ‖ *intr* recuperarse, recobrarse

re·cur [rɪ'kʌr] *v* (*pret & pp* -curred; *ger* -curring) *intr* volver a ocurrir; volver a presentarse (*a la memoria*); volver (*a un asunto*)

recurrent [rɪ'kʌrənt] *adj* repetido; periódico; (*illness*) recurrente

red [rɛd] *adj* (*comp* **redder;** *super* **reddest**) rojo, colorado; (*wine*) tinto; enrojecido, inflamado ‖ *s* rojo; **in the red** (coll) endeudado; **to see red** (coll) enfurecerse ‖ **Red** *adj & s* (*communist*) rojo

red'bait' *tr* motejar (*a uno*) de rojo o comunista

red'bird' *s* cardenal *m;* piranga

red-blooded ['rɛd‚blʌdɪd] *adj* fuerte, valiente, vigoroso

red'breast' *s* petirrojo

red'bud' *s* ciclamor *m* del Canadá

red'cap' *s* (Brit) policía militar; (U.S.A.) mozo de estación

red cell *s* glóbulo rojo, hematíe *m*

red'coat' *s* (hist) soldado inglés

redden ['rɛdən] *tr* enrojecer ‖ *intr* enrojecerse

redeem [rɪ'dim] *tr* redimir; cumplir (*una promesa*)

redeemer [rɪ'dimər] *s* redentor *m*

redemption [rɪ'dɛmpʃən] *s* redención

red-haired ['rɛd‚hɛrd] *adj* pelirrojo

red'head' *s* pelirrojo

red herring *s* artificio para distraer la atención del asunto de que se trata

red'-hot' *adj* candente, calentado al rojo; ardiente, entusiasta; fresco, nuevo

rediscount rate [ri'dɪskaʊnt] *s* tipo de redescuento

rediscover [‚ridɪs'kʌvər] *tr* redescubrir

red'-let'ter day *s* día *m* memorable

red'-light' district *s* barrio de los lupanares, barrio de mala vida

red man *s* piel roja *m*

re·do ['ri'du] *v* (*pret* -did ['dɪd]; *pp* -done ['dʌn]) *tr* rehacer, repetir; refundir; reformar

redolent ['rɛdələnt] *adj* fragante, perfumado; **redolent of** que huele a

redoubt [rɪ'daʊt] *s* (fort) reducto

redound [rɪ'daʊnd] *intr* redundar; **to redound to** redundar en

red pepper *s* pimentón *m*

redress [rɪ'drɛs] o ['ridrɛs] *s* reparación; remedio ‖ [rɪ'drɛs] *tr* reparar; remediar

Red Ridinghood ['raɪdɪŋ‚hʊd] *s* Caperucita Roja

red'skin' *s* piel roja *m*

red tape *s* expedienteo, papeleo

reduce [rɪ'djus] o [rɪ'dus] *tr* reducir; (mil) degradar ‖ *intr* reducirse; reducir peso

reducing exercises *spl* ejercicios físicos para reducir peso

redundant [rɪ'dʌndənt] *adj* redundante

red'wood' *s* secoya

reed [rid] *adj* (*organ, musical instrument*) de lengüeta ‖ *s* (*stalk*) caña; (*plant*) carrizo, caña; (mus) instrumento de lengüeta; (*of instrument*) lengüeta

reëdit [ri'ɛdɪt] *tr* refundir

reef [rif] *s* arrecife *m*, escollo; (min) filón *m*, veta ‖ *tr* (naut) arrizar

reefer ['rifər] *s* chaquetón *m;* (slang) pitillo de mariguana

reek [rik] *intr* vahear, humear; estar bañado en sudor; estar mojado con sangre; **to reek of o with** oler a

reel [ril] *s* (*spool*) carrete *m; (of a shuttle*) broca; (*of motion pictures*) cinta; (*sway, staggering*) tambaleo; **off the reel** (coll) fácil y prestamente ‖ *tr* aspar, devanar; **to reel off** (coll) narrar fácil y prestamente ‖ *intr* tambalear; cejar (*p.ej., el enemigo*)

reëlection [‚ri·ɪ'lɛkʃən] *s* reelección

reënlist [‚ri·ɛn'lɪst] *tr* reenganchar ‖ *intr* reengancharse

reën·try [rɪ'ɛntri] *s* (*pl* -tries) reingreso, nueva entrada; (*return to earth's atmosphere*) reentrada

reëxamination [‚ri‚ɛg‚zæmɪ'neʃən] *s* reexaminación

ref. *abbr* **referee, reference, reformation**

re·fer [rɪ'fʌr] *v* (*pret & pp* -ferred; *ger* -ferring) *tr* referir ‖ *intr* referirse

referee [‚rɛfə'ri] *s* árbitro ‖ *tr & intr* arbitrar

reference ['rɛfərəns] *adj* (*library, book, work*) de consulta ‖ *s* referencia

referen·dum [‚rɛfə'rɛndəm] *s* (*pl* -da [də]) *s* referéndum *m*

refill ['rifɪl] *s* relleno ‖ [ri'fɪl] *tr* rellenar

refine [rɪ'faɪn] *tr* refinar

refinement [rɪ'faɪnmənt] *s* refinamiento; buena crianza, cultura

refiner·y [rɪ'faɪnəri] *s* (*pl* **-ies**) refinería

reflect [rɪ'flɛkt] *tr* reflejar || *intr* reflejar; (*to meditate*) reflexionar; **to reflect on** o **upon** reflexionar en o sobre; perjudicar

reflection [rɪ'flɛkʃən] *s* (*thinking*) reflexión; (*reflected light; image*) reflejo

reforestation [,rifɔrɪs'teʃən] o [,rifərɪs'teʃən] *s* reforestación

reform [rɪ'fɔrm] *s* reforma || *tr* reformar || *intr* reformarse

reformation [,rɛfər'meʃən] *s* reformación || **the Reformation** la Reforma

reformato·ry [rɪ'fɔrmə,tori] *s* (*pl* **-ries**) reformatorio

reform school *s* casa de corrección

refraction [rɪ'frækʃən] *s* refracción

refrain [rɪ'fren] *s* estribillo || *intr* abstenerse

refresh [rɪ'frɛʃ] *tr* refrescar || *intr* refrescarse

refreshing [rɪ'frɛʃɪŋ] *adj* confortante, restaurante

refreshment [rɪ'frɛʃmənt] *s* refresco

refrigerator [rɪ'frɪdʒə,retər] *s* heladera, nevera, refrigerador *m*

refrigerator car *s* carro o vagón frigorífico

refuel [ri'fjul] *tr & intr* repostar

refuge ['rɛfjudʒ] *s* refugio; expediente *m*, subterfugio; **to take refuge (in)** refugiarse (en)

refugee [,rɛfju'dʒi] *s* refugiado

refund ['rifʌnd] *s* reembolso || [rɪ'fʌnd] *tr* reembolsar || [ri'fʌnd] *tr* consolidar

refurnish [ri'fʌrnɪʃ] *tr* amueblar de nuevo

refusal [rɪ'fjuzəl] *s* negativa

refuse ['rɛfjus] *s* basura, desecho, desperdicios || [rɪ'fjuz] *tr* rehusar; rechazar, no querer aceptar; **to refuse to** negarse a

refute [rɪ'fjut] *tr* refutar

reg. *abbr* **register, registrar, registry, regular**

regain [rɪ'gen] *tr* recobrar, recuperar; volver a alcanzar; **to regain consciousness** recobrar el conocimiento, volver en sí

regal ['rigəl] *adj* regio

regale [rɪ'gel] *tr* regalar, agasajar

regalia [rɪ'geli·ə] *spl* (*of an office or order*) distinctivos; galas, trajes *mpl* de lujo

regard [rɪ'gard] *s* consideración, miramiento; (*esteem*) respeto; (*particular matter*) respecto; (*look*) mirada; **in regard to** respecto a o de; **regards** recuerdos; **without regard to** sin hacer caso de; **with regard to** respecto a o de || *tr* considerar; mirar; tocar a, referirse a; **as regards** en cuanto a

regarding [rɪ'gardɪŋ] *prep* tocante a, respecto a o de

regardless [rɪ'gardlɪs] *adj* desatento, indiferente || *adv* (coll) pese a quien pese, cueste lo que cueste; **regardless of** sin hacer caso de; a pesar de

regenerate [rɪ'dʒɛnə,ret] *tr* regenerar || *intr* regenerarse

regent ['ridʒənt] *s* regente *mf*

regicide ['rɛdʒɪ,saɪd] *s* (*act*) regicidio; (*person*) regicida *mf*

regime o **régime** [re'ʒim] *s* régimen *m*

regiment ['rɛdʒɪmənt] *s* regimiento || ['rɛdʒɪ,mɛnt] *tr* regimentar

regimental [,rɛdʒɪ'mɛntəl] *adj* regimental || **regimentals** *spl* uniforme *m* militar

region ['ridʒən] *s* región, comarca

register ['rɛdʒɪstər] *s* (*record; book for keeping such a record*) registro; reja regulable de calefacción; (*of the voice or an instrument*) extensión || *tr* (*to indicate by a record; to show, as on a scale*) registrar; empadronar (*los vecinos en el padrón*); manifestar, dar a conocer; certificar (*envíos por correo*); inscribir || *intr* registrarse; empadronarse; inscribirse

registered letter *s* carta certificada

registrar ['rɛdʒɪs,trar] *s* registrador *m*, archivero

registration fee [,rɛdʒɪs'treʃən] *s* derechos de matrícula

re·gret [rɪ'grɛt] *s* pesar *m*, sentimiento; pesadumbre, remordimiento; **regrets** excusas || *v* (*pret & pp* **-gretted;** *ger* **-gretting**) *tr* sentir, lamentar; lamentar la pérdida de; **to regret to** sentir

regrettable [rɪ'grɛtəbəl] *adj* lamentable

regular ['rɛgjələr] *adj* regular; (coll) cabal, completo, verdadero || *s* obrero permanente; parroquiano regular; **regulars** tropas regulares

regulate ['rɛgjə,let] *tr* regular

rehabilitate [,rihə'bɪlɪ,tet] *tr* rehabilitar

rehearsal [rɪ'hʌrsəl] *s* ensayo

rehearse [rɪ'hʌrs] *tr* ensayar || *intr* ensayarse

reign [ren] *s* reinado || *intr* reinar

reimburse [,ri·ɪm'bʌrs] *tr* reembolsar

rein [ren] *s* rienda; **to give free rein to** dar rienda suelta a || *tr* dirigir por medio de riendas; contener, refrenar, gobernar

reincarnation [,ri·ɪnkar'neʃən] *s* reencarnación

reindeer ['ren,dɪr] *s* reno

reinforce [,ri·ɪn'fors] *tr* reforzar; armar (*el hormigón*)

reinforcement [,ri·ɪn'forsmənt] *s* refuerzo

reinstate [,ri·ɪn'stet] *tr* reinstalar

reiterate [ri'ɪtə,ret] *tr* reiterar

reject [rɪ'dʒɛkt] *tr* rechazar

rejection [rɪ'dʒɛkʃən] *s* rechazamiento

rejoice [rɪ'dʒɔɪs] *intr* regocijarse

rejoinder [rɪ'dʒɔɪndər] *s* contestación; (law) contrarréplica

rejuvenation [rɪ,dʒuvɪ'neʃən] *s* rejuvenecimiento

rel. *abbr* **relating, relative, religion, religious**

relapse [rɪ'læps] *s* recaída || *intr* recaer

relate [rɪ'let] *tr* (*to establish relationship between*) relacionar; (*to narrate*) contar, relatar

relation [rɪ'leʃən] s (connection; narration) relación; (narration) relato; (relative) pariente mf; (kinship) parentesco; **in relation to** o **with** tocante a, respecto a o de

relationship [rɪ'leʃən͵ʃɪp] s (connection) relación; (kinship) parentesco

relative ['rɛlətɪv] adj relativo ‖ s deudo, pariente mf

relax [rɪ'læks] tr & intr relajar

relaxation [͵rilæks'eʃən] s relajación; despreocupación

relaxation of tension s disminución de tensión; disminución de la tirantez internacional

relaxing [rɪ'læksɪŋ] adj relajador; despreocupante, tranquilizador

relay ['rile] o [rɪ'le] s (elec) relais m, relevador m, relevo; (mil & sport) relevo; (sport) carrera de relevos ‖ v (pret & pp -layed) tr transmitir relevándose; transmitir con un relais; retransmitir (una emisión); reexpedir (un radiotelegrama) ‖ [rɪ'le] v (pret & pp -laid) tr volver a colocar, volver a tender

relay race s carrera de relevos

release [rɪ'lis] s liberación; (from jail) excarcelación; alivio; permiso de publicación, venta, etc.; obra o pieza lista para la publicación, venta, etc.; (aer) lanzamiento; (mach) escape m, disparador m ‖ tr soltar; libertar; excarcelar (a un preso); permitir la publicación, venta, etc. de; (aer.) lanzar (una bomba)

relent [rɪ'lɛnt] intr ablandarse, aplacarse

relentless [rɪ'lɛntlɪs] adj implacable

relevant ['rɛlɪvənt] adj pertinente

reliable [rɪ'laɪ·əbəl] adj confiable, fidedigno

reliance [rɪ'laɪ·ɑns] s confianza

relic ['rɛlɪk] s reliquia

relief [rɪ'lif] s alivio; caridad; (projection of figures; elevation) relieve m; (mil) relevo; **in relief** en relieve; **on relief** viviendo de socorro, recibiendo auxilio social

relieve [rɪ'liv] tr (to release from a post) relevar; aliviar; auxiliar (a los necesitados); (mil) relevar

religion [rɪ'lɪdʒən] s religión

religious [rɪ'lɪdʒəs] adj religioso

relinquish [rɪ'lɪŋkwɪʃ] tr abandonar, dejar

relish ['rɛlɪʃ] s buen sabor, gusto; condimento, sazón f; entremés m; buen apetito ‖ tr gustar de; comer o beber con placer

reluctance [rɪ'lʌktəns] s renuencia, aversión

reluctant [rɪ'lʌktənt] adj renuente, maldispuesto

re·ly [rɪ'laɪ] v (pret & pp -lied) intr depender, confiar; **to rely on** depender de, confiar en

remain [rɪ'men] intr permanecer, quedarse ‖ **remains** spl desechos, restos; restos mortales; obra póstuma

remainder [rɪ'mendər] s resto, residuo; libro casi invendible ‖ tr saldar (libros que ya no se venden)

re·make [rɪ'mek] v (pret & pp -made ['med]) tr rehacer

remark [rɪ'mɑrk] s observación ‖ tr & intr observar; **to remark on** aludir a, comentar

remarkable [rɪ'mɑrkəbəl] adj notable, extraordinario

remar·ry [rɪ'mæri] v (pret & pp -ried) intr volver a casarse

reme·dy ['rɛmɪdi] s (pl -dies) remedio ‖ v (pret & pp -died) tr remediar

remember [rɪ'mɛmbər] tr acordarse de, recordar; dar recuerdos de parte de, p.ej., **remember me to your brother** déle Vd. a su hermano recuerdos de mi parte ‖ intr acordarse, recordar; **if I remember correctly** si mal no me acuerdo

remembrance [rɪ'mɛmbrəns] s recuerdo

remind [rɪ'maɪnd] tr recordar

reminder [rɪ'maɪndər] s recordatorio, recordativo

reminisce [͵rɛmɪ'nɪs] intr entregarse a los recuerdos, contar sus recuerdos

remiss [rɪ'mɪs] adj descuidado, negligente

re·mit [rɪ'mɪt] v (pret & pp -mitted; ger -mitting) tr (to send, to ship; to pardon) remitir

remittance [rɪ'mɪtəns] s remesa

remnant ['rɛmnənt] s (something left over) remanente m; (of cloth) retal m, retazo; (piece of cloth to be sold at reduced price) saldo; vestigio

remod·el [rɪ'mɑdəl] v (pret & pp -eled o -elled; ger -eling o -elling) tr modelar de nuevo; rehacer, reconstruir; convertir, transformar

remonstrate [rɪ'mɑnstret] intr protestar; **to remonstrate with** reconvenir

remorse [rɪ'mɔrs] s remordimiento

remorseful [rɪ'mɔrsfəl] adj compungido, arrepentido

remote [rɪ'mot] adj remoto

remote control s comando a distancia, telecontrol m

removable [rɪ'muvəbəl] adj amovible

removal [rɪ'muvəl] s remoción; mudanza, traslado; (dismissal) deposición

remove [rɪ'muv] tr remover; quitar de en medio, apartar matando ‖ intr removerse

remuneration [rɪ͵mjunə'reʃən] s remuneración

renaissance [͵rɛnə'sɑns] o [rɪ'nesəns] s renacimiento

rend [rɛnd] v (pret & pp rent [rɛnt]) tr (to tear) desgarrar; (to split) hender, rajar; estremecer (un ruido el aire)

render ['rɛndər] tr rendir (gracias, obsequios, homenaje); prestar, suministrar (ayuda); pagar (tributo); desempeñar (un papel); traducir (sentimientos); (from one language to another) verter; hacer (justicia); ejecutar (una pieza de música); derretir (cera, manteca); extraer la grasa o el sebo de; poner, volver

rendezvous ['rɑndə͵vu] s (pl -vous [͵vuz] cita; (in space) encuentro, reunión ‖ *v* (*pret* & *pp* -voused [‚vud]; *ger* -vousing [‚vu·ɪŋ]) *intr* reunirse en una cita

rendition [ren'dɪʃən] *s* rendición; traducción; (mus) ejecución

renege [rɪ'nɪg] *s* renuncio ‖ *intr* renunciar; (coll) volverse atrás

renegotiation [‚rini‚goʃɪ'eʃən] *s* renegociación

renew [rɪ'nju] o [rɪ'nu] *tr* renovar ‖ *intr* renovarse

renewable [rɪ'nju·əbəl] o [rɪ'nu·əbəl] *adj* renovable

renewal [rɪ'nju·əl] o [rɪ'nu·əl] *s* renovación

renounce [rɪ'naʊns] *tr* renunciar; renunciar a (*p.ej., el mundo*) ‖ *intr* renunciar

renovate ['renə‚vet] *tr* renovar; reformar (*p.ej., una tienda, una casa*)

renown [rɪ'naʊn] *s* renombre *m*

renowned [rɪ'naʊnd] *adj* renombrado

rent [rent] *adj* desgarrado ‖ *s* alquiler *m*, arriendo; (*tear, slit*) desgarro ‖ *tr* alquilar, arrendar ‖ *intr* alquilarse, arrendarse

rental ['rentəl] *s* alquiler *m*, arriendo

renunciation [rɪ‚nʌnsɪ'eʃən] o [rɪ‚nʌnʃɪ'eʃən] *s* renunciación

reopen [ri'opən] *tr* reabrir ‖ *intr* reabrirse

reorganize [ri'ɔrgə‚naɪz] *tr* reorganizar ‖ *intr* reorganizarse

rep. *abbr* report, reporter, representative, republic

repair [rɪ'per] *s* reparación; in repair en buen estado ‖ *tr* reparar ‖ *intr* dirigirse; volver

repaper [ri'pepər] *tr* empapelar de nuevo

reparation [‚repə'reʃən] *s* reparación

repartee [‚repar'ti] *s* respuesta viva; agudeza y gracia en responder

repast [rɪ'pæst] o [rɪ'pɑst] *s* comida, comilona

repatriate [ri'petrɪ‚et] *tr* repatriar

re·pay [rɪ'pe] *v* (*pret* & *pp* -paid ['ped]) *tr* reembolsar; resarcir (*un daño, una injuria*); compensar

repayment [rɪ'pemənt] *s* reembolso; resarcimiento; compensación

repeal [rɪ'pil] *s* abrogación, revocación ‖ *tr* abrogar, revocar

repeat [rɪ'pit] *s* repetición ‖ *tr* & *intr* repetir

re·pel [rɪ'pel] *v* (*pret* & *pp* -pelled; *ger* -pelling) *tr* rechazar, repeler; repugnar

repent [rɪ'pent] *tr* arrepentirse de ‖ *intr* arrepentirse

repentance [rɪ'pentəns] *s* arrepentimiento

repentant [rɪ'pentənt] *adj* arrepentido

repertory theater ['repər‚tori] *s* teatro de repertorio

repetition [‚repɪ'tɪʃən] *s* repetición

repine [rɪ'paɪn] *intr* afligirse, quejarse

replace [rɪ'ples] *tr* (*to put back*) reponer; (*to take the place of*) reemplazar

replacement [rɪ'plesmənt] *s* reposición; reemplazo; pieza de repuesto; soldado reemplazante

replenish [rɪ'plenɪʃ] *tr* rellenar; reaprovisionar

replete [rɪ'plit] *adj* repleto

replica ['replɪkə] *s* réplica

re·ply [rɪ'plaɪ] *s* (*pl* -plies) contestación, respuesta ‖ *v* (*pret* & *pp* -plied) *tr* & *intr* contestar, responder

reply coupon *s* vale *m* respuesta

report [rɪ'port] *s* relato, informe *m*; voz *f*, rumor *m*; (*e.g., of a firearm*) detonación, tiro; denuncia ‖ *tr* relatar, informar acerca de; denunciar ‖ *intr* hacer un relato; redactar un informe; ser repórter; presentarse; to report on dar cuenta de, notificar

report card *s* certificado escolar

reportedly [rɪ'portɪdli] *adv* según se informa

reporter [rɪ'portər] *s* repórter *m*

reporting [rɪ'portɪŋ] *s* reportaje *m*

repose [rɪ'poz] *s* descanso ‖ *tr* descansar; poner (*confianza*) ‖ *intr* descansar

reprehend [‚reprɪ'hend] *tr* reprender

represent [‚reprɪ'zent] *tr* representar

representative [‚reprɪ'zentətɪv] *adj* representativo ‖ *s* representante *mf*

repress [rɪ'pres] *tr* reprimir

reprieve [rɪ'priv] *s* suspensión temporal de un castigo, suspensión temporal de la pena de muerte; respiro, alivio temporal ‖ *tr* suspender temporalmente el castigo de o la pena de muerte de; aliviar temporalmente

reprimand ['reprɪ‚mænd] o ['reprɪ‚mɑnd] *s* reprimenda ‖ *tr* reconvenir, reprender

reprint ['ri‚prɪnt] *s* reimpresión; tirada aparte ‖ [ri'prɪnt] *tr* reimprimir

reprisal [rɪ'praɪzəl] *s* represalia

reproach [rɪ'protʃ] *s* reproche *m*; oprobio ‖ *tr* reprochar; oprobiar

reproduce [‚riprə'djus] o [‚riprə'dus] *tr* reproducir ‖ *intr* reproducirse

reproduction [‚riprə'dʌkʃən] *s* reproducción

reproof [rɪ'pruf] *s* reprobación

reprove [rɪ'pruv] *tr* reprobar

reptile ['reptɪl] *s* reptil *m*

republic [rɪ'pʌblɪk] *s* república

republican [rɪ'pʌblɪkən] *adj* & *s* republicano

repudiate [rɪ'pjudɪ‚et] *tr* repudiar; no reconocer (*p.ej., una deuda*)

repugnant [rɪ'pʌgnənt] *adj* repugnante

repulse [rɪ'pʌls] *s* repulsión, rechazo ‖ *tr* repeler, rechazar

repulsive [rɪ'pʌlsɪv] *adj* repulsivo

reputation [‚repjə'teʃən] *s* reputación; buena reputación

repute [rɪ'pjut] *s* reputación; buena reputación ‖ *tr* reputar

reputedly [rɪ'pjutɪdli] *adv* según la opinión común

request [rɪ'kwest] *s* petición, solicitud; at the request of a petición de ‖ *tr* pedir

require [rɪ'kwaɪr] *tr* exigir, requerir

requirement [rɪ'kwaɪrmənt] *s* requisito; necesidad

requisite ['rekwɪzɪt] *adj* & *s* requisito

requital [rɪ'kwaɪtəl] *s* compensación, retorno

requite [rɪ'kwaɪt] tr corresponder a (los beneficios, el amor, etc.); corresponder con (el bienhechor)

re·read [ri'rid] v (pret & pp -read ['red]) tr releer

resale ['ri,sel] o [ri'sel] s reventa

rescind [rɪ'sɪnd] tr rescindir

rescue ['reskju] s salvación, rescate m, liberación; **to go to the rescue of** acudir al socorro de ‖ tr salvar, rescatar, libertar

rescue party s pelotón m de salvamento

research [rɪ'sʌrtʃ] o ['risʌrtʃ] s investigación ‖ intr investigar

re·sell [ri'sel] v (pret & pp -sold ['sold]) tr revender

resemblance [rɪ'zembləns] s parecido, semejanza

resemble [rɪ'zembəl] tr parecerse a, asemejarse a

resent [rɪ'zent] tr resentirse de o por

resentful [rɪ'zentfəl] adj resentido

resentment [rɪ'zentmənt] s resentimiento

reservation [,rezər've/ən] s reserva

reserve [rɪ'zʌrv] s reserva ‖ tr reservar

reservoir ['rezər,vwɑr] s depósito; (where water is dammed back) embalse m, pantano; (of wisdom) fondo

re·ship [ri'/ɪp] v (pret & pp -shipped; ger -shipping) tr reenviar, reexpedir; (on a ship) reembarcar ‖ intr reembarcarse

reshipment [ri'/ɪpmənt] s reenvío, reexpedición; (of persons) reembarco; (of goods) reembarque m

reside [rɪ'zaɪd] intr residir

residence ['rezɪdəns] s residencia

resident ['rezɪdənt] adj & s residente mf, vecino

residue ['rezɪ,dju] o ['rezɪ,du] s residuo

resign [rɪ'zaɪn] tr dimitir, resignar, renunciar ‖ intr dimitir; (to yield, submit) resignarse; **to resign to** resignarse con (p.ej., su suerte)

resignation [,rezɪg'ne/ən] s (from a job, etc.) dimisión; (state of being submissive) resignación

resin ['rezɪn] s resina

resist [rɪ'zɪst] tr resistir (la tentación); resistir a (la violencia; la risa) ‖ intr resistirse

resistance [rɪ'zɪstəns] s resistencia

resole [ri'sol] tr sobresolar

resolute ['rezə,lut] adj resuelto

resolution [,rezə'lu/ən] s resolución; **good resolutions** buenos propósitos

resolve [rɪ'zɔlv] s resolución ‖ tr resolver ‖ intr resolverse

resort [rɪ'zɔrt] s lugar muy frecuentado; (e.g., for vacations) estación; (for help or support) recurso; **as a last resort** como último recurso ‖ intr recurrir

resound [rɪ'zaund] intr resonar

resource [rɪ'sors] o ['risors] s recurso

resourceful [rɪ'sorsfəl] adj ingenioso

respect [rɪ'spekt] s (deference, esteem) respeto; (reference, relation; detail) respecto; **respects** recuerdos, saludos; **to pay one's respects (to)** ofre-

cer sus respetos (a); **with respect to** respecto a o de ‖ tr respetar

respectable [rɪ'spektəbəl] adj respetable; decente, presentable

respectful [rɪ'spektfəl] adj respetuoso

respectfully [rɪ'spektfali] adj respetuosamente; **respectfully yours** de Vd. atento y seguro servidor

respecting [rɪ'spektɪŋ] prep con respecto a, respecto de

respective [rɪ'spektɪv] adj respectivo

respire [rɪ'spaɪr] tr & intr respirar

respite ['respɪt] s (temporary relief) respiro; (postponement, especially of death sentence) suspensión; **without respite** sin respirar

resplendent [rɪ'splendənt] adj resplandeciente

respond [rɪ'spɑnd] intr responder

response [rɪ'spɑns] s respuesta

responsible [rɪ'spɑnsɪbəl] adj responsable; (job, position) de confianza; **responsible for** responsable de

rest [rest] s (after exertion or work; sleep) descanso; (lack of motion) reposo; (of the dead) paz f; (what remains) resto; (mus) pausa; **at rest** (not moving) en reposo; tranquilo; dormido; (dead) muerto; **the rest** lo demás; los demás; **to come to rest** venir a parar; **to lay to rest** enterrar ‖ tr descansar; parar; poner (p.ej., confianza) ‖ intr descansar; estar, hallarse; **to rest assured (that)** estar seguro, tener la seguridad (de que); **to rest on** descansar en o sobre, estribar en

restaurant ['restərənt] o ['restə,rɑnt] s restaurante m

rest cure s cura de reposo

restful ['restfəl] adj descansado, tranquilo, reposado

resting place s lugar m de descanso; (of a staircase) descansadero; (of the dead) última morada

restitution [,restɪ'tju/ən] o [,restɪ'tu/ən] s restitución

restless ['restlɪs] adj intranquilo; (sleepless) insomne

restock [ri'stak] tr reaprovisionar; repoblar (p.ej., un acuario)

restore [rɪ'stor] tr restaurar; (to give back) devolver

restrain [rɪ'stren] tr contener, refrenar; aprisionar

restraint [rɪ'strent] s restricción; comedimiento, moderación

restrict [rɪ'strɪkt] tr restringir

rest room s sala de descanso; excusado, retrete m; (of a theater) saloncillo

result [rɪ'zʌlt] s resultado; **as a result of** de resultas de ‖ intr resultar; **to result in** dar por resultado, parar en

resume [rɪ'zum] o [rɪ'zjum] tr reasumir; reanudar (el viaje, el vuelo, etc.); volver a tomar (su asiento) ‖ intr continuar; recomenzar; reanudar el hilo del discurso

résumé [,rezu'me] o [,rezju'me] s resumen m

resurface [ri'sʌrfɪs] tr dar nueva superficie a ‖ intr volver a emerger (un submarino)

re
re

resurrect [,rezə'rekt] *tr* & *intr* resucitar

resurrection [,rezə'rekʃən] *s* resurrección

resuscitate [rɪ'sʌsɪ,tet] *tr* & *intr* resucitar

retail ['ritel] *adj* & *adv* al por menor || *s* venta al por menor || *tr* detallar, vender al por menor || *intr* vender al por menor; venderse al por menor

retailer ['riteIər] *s* detallista *mf*, comerciante *mf* al por menor

retain [rɪ'ten] *tr* retener; contratar (*a un abogado*)

retaliate [rɪ'tælɪ,et] *intr* desquitarse, vengarse

retaliation [rɪ,tælɪ'eʃən] *s* desquite *m*, venganza

retard [rɪ'tard] *s* retardo || *tr* retardar

retch [retʃ] *tr* vomitar || *intr* arquear, esforzarse por vomitar

retching ['retʃɪŋ] *s* arcadas

ret'd. *abbr* returned

reticence ['retɪsəns] *s* reserva, circunspección, sigilo

reticent ['retɪsənt] *adj* reservado, circunspecto

retinue ['retɪ,nju] o ['retɪ,nu] *s* comitiva, séquito

retire [rɪ'taɪr] *tr* retirar; jubilar (*a un empleado*) || *intr* retirarse; jubilarse; (*to go to bed*) recogerse; (mil) retirarse

retirement [rɪ'taɪrmənt] *s* retiro; (*of an employee with pension*) jubilación; (mil) retirada

retirement annuity *s* jubilación

retort [rɪ'tɔrt] *s* respuesta pronta y aguda, réplica; (chem) retorta || *intr* replicar

retouch [rɪ'tʌtʃ] *tr* retocar

retrace [rɪ'tres] *tr* repasar; **to retrace one's steps** volver sobre sus pasos

retract [rɪ'trækt] *tr* retractarse de, desdecirse de (*lo que se ha dicho*) || *intr* retractarse, desdecirse

re·tread ['ri,tred] *s* neumático recauchutado; neumático ranurado || [rɪ'tred] *v* (*pret* & *pp* **-treaded**) *tr* recauchutar; volver a ranurar || *v* (*pret* **-trod** o **-trod** o **-trodden**) *tr* desandar || *intr* volverse atrás

retreat [rɪ'trit] *s* (*act of withdrawing; place of seclusion*) retiro; (eccl) retiro; (mil) retreta, retirada; (*signal*) (mil) retreta; **to beat a retreat** retirarse; (mil) batirse en retirada || *intr* retirarse

retrench [rɪ'trentʃ] *tr* cercenar || *intr* recogerse

retribution [,retrɪ'bjuʃən] *s* justo castigo; (theol) juicio final

retrieve [rɪ'triv] *tr* cobrar; reparar (*p.ej., un daño*); desquitarse de (*una pérdida, una derrota*); (hunt) cobrar, portar || *intr* (hunt) cobrar, portar

retriever [rɪ'trivər] *s* perro cobrador, perro traedor

retroactive [,retro'æktɪv] *adj* retroactivo

retrofiring [,retro'faɪrɪŋ] *s* retrodisparo

retrogress ['retrə,grɛs] *intr* retroceder; empeorar

retrorocket [,retro'rɑkɪt] *s* retrocohete *m*

retrospect ['retrə,spɛkt] *s* retrospección; **in retrospect** retrospectivamente

retrospective [,retrə'spɛktɪv] *adj* retrospectivo

re·try [rɪ'traɪ] *v* (*pret* & *pp* **-tried**) *tr* reensayar; rever (*un caso legal*); procesar de nuevo (*a una persona*)

return [rɪ'tʌrn] *adj* repetido; de vuelta; **by return mail** a vuelta de correo || *s* vuelta; devolución; recompensa; respuesta; informe *m*, noticia; ganancia, beneficio, rédito; (*of an election*) resultado; (*of income tax*) declaración; **in return (for)** en cambio (de); **many happy returns of the day!** ¡que cumpla muchos más! || *tr* devolver; dar en cambio; corresponder a (*un favor*); dar (*una respuesta, las gracias*) || *intr* volver; responder

return address *s* dirección del remitente

return bout o **engagement** *s* (box) combate *m* revancha

return game *s* desquite *m*

return ticket *s* billete *m* de vuelta; billete de ida y vuelta

return trip *s* viaje *m* de vuelta

reunification [ri,junɪfɪ'keʃən] *s* reunificación

reunion [ri'junjən] *s* reunión

reunite [,riju'naɪt] *tr* reunir || *intr* reunirse

rev. *abbr* revenue, reverse, review, revised, revision, revolution

Rev. *abbr* Revelation, Reverend

rev [rev] *s* revolución || *v* (*pret* & *pp* **revved**; *ger* **revving**) *tr* cambiar la velocidad de; **to rev up** acelerar || *intr* acelerarse

revamp [ri'væmp] *tr* componer, renovar, remendar

reveal [rɪ'vil] *tr* revelar

reveille ['revəli] *s* diana, toque *m* de diana

rev·el ['revəl] *s* jarana, regocijo tumultuoso || *v* (*pret* & *pp* **-eled** o **-elled**; *ger* **-eling** o **-elling**) *intr* jaranear; deleitarse

revelation [,revə'leʃən] *s* revelación

revel·ry ['revəlri] *s* (*pl* **-ries**) jarana, diversión tumultuosa

revenge [rɪ'vendʒ] *s* venganza || *tr* vengar

revengeful [rɪ'vendʒfəl] *adj* vengativo

revenue ['revə,nju] o ['revə,nu] *s* renta, rédito; rentas públicas

revenue cutter *s* escampavía

revenue stamp *s* sello fiscal, timbre *m* del estado

reverberate [rɪ'vʌrbə,ret] *intr* reverberar

revere [rɪ'vɪr] *tr* reverenciar, venerar

reverence ['revərəns] *s* reverencia || *tr* reverenciar

reverend ['revərənd] *adj* & *s* reverendo

reverie ['revəri] *s* ensueño

reversal [rɪ'vʌrsəl] *s* inversión; (*e.g., of opinion*) cambio

reverse [rɪ'vʌrs] *adj* invertido; contrario; de marcha atrás ‖ *s (opposite or rear)* revés *m;* contrario; contramarcha, marcha atrás; *(check, defeat)* revés *m,* contratiempo ‖ *tr* invertir; dar vuelta a; poner en marcha atrás; **to reverse oneself** cambiar de opinión; **to reverse the charges** cobrar al destinatario; (telp) cobrar al número llamado ‖ *intr* invertirse

reverse lever *s* palanca de marcha atrás

revert [rɪ'vʌrt] *intr* revertir; saltar atrás; **to revert to one's old tricks** volver a las andadas

review [rɪ'vju] *s (reëxamination; survey; magazine; musical show)* revista; *(of a book)* reseña, revista; *(of a lesson)* repaso; (mil) reseña, revista ‖ *tr* rever, revisar; reseñar *(un libro);* repasar *(una lección);* (mil) revistar

revile [rɪ'vaɪl] *tr* ultrajar, vilipendiar

revise [rɪ'vaɪz] *s* revisión; refundición; (typ) segunda prueba ‖ *tr* rever, revisar; refundir *(un libro);* enmendar

revision [rɪ'vɪʒən] *s* revisión; *(of a book)* refundición; enmienda

revisionism [rɪ'vɪʒə͵nɪzəm] *s* revisionismo

revisionist [rɪ'vɪʒənɪst] *adj & s* revisionista

revival [rɪ'vaɪvəl] *s* resucitación; reanimación; *(e.g., of learning)* renacimiento; despertamiento religioso; (theat) reestreno, reposición

revive [rɪ'vaɪv] *tr* revivir; (theat) reestrenar, reponer ‖ *intr* revivir; volver en sí, recordar

revoke [rɪ'vok] *tr* revocar

revolt [rɪ'volt] *s* rebelión, sublevación ‖ *tr* dar asco a, repugnar ‖ *intr* rebelarse, sublevarse

revolting [rɪ'voltɪŋ] *adj* asqueroso, repugnante; rebelde

revolution [͵revə'luʃən] *s* revolución

revolutionar•y [͵revə'luʃə͵nerɪ] *adj* revolucionario ‖ *s (pl* -ies) revolucionario

revolve [rɪ'valv] *tr* hacer girar; *(in one's mind)* revolver ‖ *intr* girar; revolverse *(un astro en su órbita)*

revolver [rɪ'valvər] *s* revólver *m*

revolving bookcase *s* giratoria

revolving door *s* puerta giratoria

revolving fund *s* fondo rotativo

revue [rɪ'vju] *s* (theat) revista

revulsion [rɪ'vʌlʃən] *s* aversión, repugnancia; reacción fuerte

reward [rɪ'word] *s* premio, recompensa; *(money used to recapture or recover)* rescate *m;* hallazgo, p.ej., **five dollars reward** cinco dólares de hallazgo ‖ *tr* premiar, recompensar

rewarding [rɪ'wordɪŋ] *adj* remunerador, provechoso, agradecido

rewind [rɪ'waɪnd] *s* (mach, mov) retroceso

re•write [rɪ'raɪt] *v (pret* -wrote ['rot]; *pp* -written ['rɪtən]) *tr* escribir de nuevo; refundir *(un escrito);* redactar *(un escrito de otra persona)*

R.H. *abbr* **Royal Highness**

rhapso•dy ['ræpsədɪ] *s (pl* -dies) rapsodia

rheostat ['ri-ə͵stæt] *s* reóstato

rhesus ['risəs] *s* macaco de la India

rhetoric ['retərɪk] *s* retórica

rhetorical [rɪ'tɑrɪkəl] o [rɪ'tɔrɪkəl] *adj* retórico

rheumatic [ru'mætɪk] *adj & s* reumático

rheumatism ['rumə͵tɪzəm] *s* reumatismo

Rhine [raɪn] *s* Rin *m*

Rhineland ['raɪn͵lænd] *s* Renania

rhine'stone' *s* diamante de imitación hecho de vidrio

rhinoceros [raɪ'nɑsərəs] *s* rinoceronte *m*

Rhodes [rodz] *s* Rodas *f*

Rhone [ron] *s* Ródano

rhubarb ['rubɑrb] *s* ruibarbo

rhyme [raɪm] *s* rima; **without rhyme or reason** sin ton ni son ‖ *tr & intr* rimar

rhythm ['rɪðəm] *s* ritmo

rhythmic(al) ['rɪðmɪk(əl)] *adj* rítmico

rial•to [rɪ'ælto] *s (pl* -tos) mercado ‖ **the Rialto** el puente del Rialto; el centro teatral de Nueva York

rib [rɪb] *s* costilla; *(of a fan or umbrella)* varilla; *(of a tire)* cuerda; *(in cloth)* canilla; *(of the wing on an insect)* nervio ‖ *v (pret & pp* ribbed; *ger* ribbing) *tr* proveer de costillas; hacer canillas en; (slang) tomar el pelo a

ribald ['rɪbəld] *adj* grosero y obsceno

ribbon ['rɪbən] *s* cinta

rice [raɪs] *s* arroz *m*

rich [rɪtʃ] *adj* rico; *(color)* vivo; *(voice)* sonoro; *(wine)* generoso; azucarado, condimentado; (coll) divertido; (coll) ridículo; **to strike it rich** descubrir un buen filón ‖ **riches** *spl* riquezas; **the rich** los ricos

rickets ['rɪkɪts] *s* raquitis *f*

rickety ['rɪkɪtɪ] *adj (object)* destartalado, desvencijado; *(person)* tambaleante, vacilante; *(suffering from rickets)* raquítico

rid [rɪd] *v (pret & pp* rid; *ger* ridding) *tr* desembarazar; **to get rid of** desembarazarse de, deshacerse de; matar

riddance ['rɪdəns] *s* supresión, libramiento; **good riddance!** ¡adiós, gracias!, ¡de buena me he librado!

riddle ['rɪdəl] *s* acertijo, adivinanza; *(person or thing hard to understand)* enigma *m;* criba gruesa ‖ *tr* acribillar; destruir *(un argumento; la reputación de una persona);* **to riddle with bullets** acribillar a balazos; **to riddle with questions** acribillar a preguntas

ride [raɪd] *s* paseo ‖ *v (pret* rode [rod]; *pp* ridden ['rɪdən]) *tr* montar *(un caballo);* montar sobre *(los hombros de una persona);* recorrer a caballo; flotar sobre *(las olas);* dominar, tiranizar; (coll) burlarse de; **to ride down** atropellar; vencer; **to ride out** luchar felizmente con *(una tempestad);* aguantar con buen éxito *(una desgracia)* ‖ *intr* montar; pa-

sear en coche o carruaje; **to let ride**
(slang) dejar correr; **to take riding**
llevar de paseo

rider ['raɪdər] *s* jinete *m*; pasajero

ridge [rɪdʒ] *s* (*of a roof; of earth between two furrows*) caballete *m;* (*of
a fabric*) cordoncillo; (*of mountains*)
cordillera; (*of two plane surfaces*)
arista

ridge′pole′ *s* parhilera

ridicule ['rɪdɪˌkjul] *s* irrisión; **to expose to ridicule** poner en ridículo ǁ
tr ridiculizar

ridiculous [rɪ'dɪkjələs] *adj* ridículo

riding academy *s* escuela de equitación

riding boot *s* bota de montar

riding habit *s* amazona, traje *m* de
montar

rife [raɪf] *adj* común, corriente, general; abundante, lleno; **rife with**
abundante en, lleno de

riffraff ['rɪfˌræf] *s* bahorrina, canalla

rifle ['raɪfəl] *s* rifle *m*, fusil *m* ǁ *tr*
hurtar, robar; escudriñar y robar;
desnudar, despojar

rift [rɪft] *s* abertura, raja; desacuerdo,
desavenencia

rig [rɪg] *s* equipaje *m*; carruaje *m* con
caballo o caballos; traje extraño;
(naut) aparejo ǁ *v* (*pret & pp* **rigged;**
ger **rigging**) *tr* equipar; aprestar, disponer; improvisar; vestir de una manera extraña; arreglar de una manera
fraudulenta; (naut) aparejar

rigging ['rɪgɪŋ] *s* avíos, instrumentos,
equipo; (naut) aparejo, cordaje *m*

right [raɪt] *adj* derecho; verdadero;
exacto; conveniente; favorable; sano,
normal; bien; correcto; señalado;
correspondiente; que se busca, p.ej.,
this is the right house ésta es la casa
que se busca; que se necesita, p.ej.,
this is the right train éste es el tren
que se necesita; que debe, p.ej., **he
is going the right way** sigue el camino que debe; **right or wrong** con
razón o sin ella, bueno o malo; **to
be all right** estar bien; estar bien de
salud; **to be right** tener razón ǁ *adv*
derechamente; directamente; correctamente; exactamente; favorablemente; en orden, en buen estado; hacia la derecha; completamente; (coll)
muy; mismo, p.ej., **right here** aquí
mismo; **all right** muy bien ǁ *interj*
¡bien! ǁ *s* (*justice, reason*) derecho;
(*right hand*) derecha; (box) derechazo; (com) derecho; (pol) derecha; **by right** según derecho; **on the
right** a la derecha; **to be in the right**
tener razón ǁ *tr* enderezar; corregir,
rectificar; hacer justicia a; deshacer
(*un entuerto*) ǁ *intr* enderezarse

righteous ['raɪtʃəs] *adj* recto, justo;
virtuoso

right field *s* (baseball) jardín derecho

rightful ['raɪtfəl] *adj* justo; legítimo

right′-hand′ drive *s* conducción o dirección a la derecha

right-hand man *s* mano derecha, brazo
derecho

rightist ['raɪtɪst] *adj & s* derechista
mf

rightly ['raɪtli] *adv* derechamente;
correctamente; con razón; convenien-
temente; **rightly or wrongly** con razón o sin ella; **rightly so** a justo título

right mind *s* entero juicio

right of way *s* derecho de tránsito o de
paso; (law) servidumbre de paso;
(rr) servidumbre de vía; **to yield the
right of way** ceder el paso

rights of man *s pl* derechos del hombre

right′-wing′ *adj* derechista

right-winger ['raɪt'wɪŋər] *s* (coll) derechista *mf*

rigid ['rɪdʒɪd] *adj* rígido

rigmarole ['rɪgməˌrol] *s* galimatías *m*

rigorous ['rɪgərəs] *adj* riguroso

rile [raɪl] *tr* (coll) exasperar

rill [rɪl] *s* arroyuelo

rim [rɪm] *s* canto, borde *m*; (*of a
wheel*) llanta; (*of a tire*) aro

rime [raɪm] *s* (*in verse*) rima; (*frost*)
escarcha; **without rime or reason** sin
ton ni son ǁ *tr & intr* rimar

rind [raɪnd] *s* cáscara, corteza

ring [rɪŋ] *s* (*circular band, line, or
mark*) anillo; (*for the finger*) sortija;
(*for curtains; for gymnastics*) anilla;
(*for nose of animal*) argolla; (*for
fruit jars*) círculo de goma; (*for some
sport or exhibition*) circo; (*for boxing*) cuadrilátero, ruedo; (*for bullfight*) redondel *m*, ruedo; boxeo;
(*of a group of people*) corro; (*of evildoers*) pandilla; (*under the
eyes*) ojera; (*of the anchor*) arganeo;
(*sound of a bell, of a clock*) campanada; (*of a small bell; of the glass
of glassware*) tintineo; (*to summon
a person*) llamada; (*character, nature, spirit*) tono; **to be in the ring
(for)** ser candidato (a); **to run rings
around** dar cien vueltas a ǁ *v* (*pret
& pp* **ringed**) *tr* cercar, rodear; (*to
put a ring on*) anillar ǁ *intr* formar
círculo o corro ǁ *v* (*pret* **rang** [ræŋ];
pp **rung** [rʌŋ]) *tr* tañer, tocar; (*to
peal, ring out*) repicar; llamar al
timbre; dar (*las horas la campana
del reloj*); llamar por teléfono; **to
ring up** llamar por teléfono; marcar
(*una compra*) con el timbre ǁ *intr*
sonar (*una campana, un timbre, el
teléfono*); tintinear (*el choque de
copas, una campanilla*); resonar, retumbar; llamar; zumbar (*los oídos*);
to ring for llamar, llamar al timbre;
to ring off terminar una llamada por
teléfono; **to ring up** llamar por teléfono

ring-around-a-rosy ['rɪŋəˌraʊndə'rozi]
s juego del corro

ringing ['rɪŋɪŋ] *adj* resonante, retum-
bante ǁ *s* anillamiento; campaneo,
repique *m*; (*of the glass of glassware*) tintineo; (*in the ears*) retintín
m, silbido

ring′leader *s* cabecilla *m*

ring′mas′ter *s* hombre encargado de
los ejercicios ecuestres y acrobáticos
de un circo

ring′side′ *s* lugar junto al cuadrilátero;
lugar desde el cual se puede ver de
cerca

ring′worm′ s tiña
rink [rɪŋk] s patinadero
rinse [rɪns] s aclaración, enjuague m ||
tr aclarar, enjuagar
riot [′raɪ·ət] s alboroto, tumulto; re-
gocijos ruidosos; (of colors) exhibición brillante; to run riot desen-
frenarse; crecer lozanamente (las
plantas) || intr alborotarse, amoti-
narse
rioter [′raɪ·ətər] s alborotador m,
amotinado
rip [rɪp] s rasgón m, siete m; (open
seam) descosido || v (pret & pp
ripped; ger ripping) tr desgarrar,
rasgar; descoser (lo que estaba cosi-
do) || intr desgarrarse, rasgarse;
(coll) adelantar o moverse de prisa
o con violencia; to rip out with (coll)
decir con violencia
ripe [raɪp] adj maduro; acabado, hecho; dispuesto, preparado; (boil, tumor) madurado; (olive) negro
ripen [′raɪpən] tr & intr madurar
ripple [′rɪpəl] s temblor m, rizo;
(sound) murmullo, susurro || tr rizar
|| intr rizarse; murmurar, susurrar
rise [raɪz] s (of temperature, prices, a
road) subida; (of ground, of the
voice) elevación; (of a heavenly
body) salida; (of a step) altura; (in
one's employment) ascenso; (of water) crecida; (of a source of water)
nacimiento; (of a valve) levantamiento; to get a rise out of (slang)
sacar una réplica mordaz a; to give
rise to dar origen a || v (pret rose
[roz]; pp risen [′rɪzən]) intr subir;
levantarse; salir (un astro); asomar
(un peligro); brotar (un manantial,
una planta); (in someone's esteem)
ganar; resucitar; to rise above alzarse
por encima de; mostrarse superior a;
to rise early madrugar; to rise to
ponerse a la altura de
riser [′raɪzər] s contraescalón m, contrahuella; early riser madrugador m;
late riser dormilón m
risk [rɪsk] s riesgo; to run o take a
risk correr riesgo, correr peligro ||
tr arriesgar; arriesgarse en (una empresa dudosa)
risk·y [′rɪski] adj (comp -ier; super
-iest) arriesgado; escabroso
risqué [rɪs′ke] adj escabroso
rite [raɪt] s rito; last rites honras
fúnebres
ritual [′rɪtʃʊ·əl] adj & s ritual m
riv. abbr river
ri·val [′raɪvəl] s rival mf || v (pret &
pp -valed o -valled; ger -valing o
-valling) tr rivalizar con
rival·ry [′raɪvəlrɪ] s (pl -ries) rivalidad
river [′rɪvər] s río; down the river río
abajo; up the river río arriba
river basin s cuenca de río
river bed s cauce m
river front s orilla del río
riv′er·side′ adj ribereño || s ribera
rivet [′rɪvɪt] s roblón m, remache m;
(e.g., to hold scissors together) cla-
villo || tr remachar; clavar (p.ej., los
ojos en una persona)

rm. abbr ream, room
R.N. abbr registered nurse, Royal Navy
roach [rotʃ] s cucaracha
road [rod] adj itinerario, caminero ||
s camino; (naut) rada; to be in the
road estorbar el paso; incomodar; to
get out of the road quitarse de en
medio
road′bed′ s (of a highway) firme m;
(rr) infraestructura
road′block′ s (mil) barricada; (fig)
obstáculo
road′house′ s posada en el camino
road laborer s peón caminero
road map s mapa itinerario
road service s auxilio en carretera
road′side′ s borde m del camino, borde
de la carretera
roadside inn s posada en el camino
road sign s señal f de carretera, poste
m indicador
road′stead′ s rada
road′way′ s camino, vía
roam [rom] s vagabundeo || tr vagar
por, recorrer a la ventura || intr va-
gar, andar errante
roar [ror] s bramido, rugido || intr
bramar, rugir; reírse a carcajadas
roast [rost] s asado; café tostado || tr
asar; tostar (café); (coll) despellejar
|| intr asarse; tostarse
roast beef s rosbif m
roast of beef s carne de vaca asada o
para asar
roast pork s carne de cerdo asada
rob [rab] v (pret & pp robbed; ger
robbing) tr & intr robar
robber [′rabər] s robador m, ladrón m
robber·y [′rabərɪ] s (pl -ies) robo
robe [rob] s manto; abrigo; (of a
woman) traje m, vestido; (of a professor, judge, etc.) toga, túnica; (of
a priest) traje m talar; (dressing
gown) bata; (for lap in a carriage)
manta || tr vestir || intr vestirse
robin [′rabɪn] s (in Europe) petirrojo;
(in North America) primavera
robot [′robɑt] s robot m
robust [ro′bʌst] adj robusto; vigoroso
rock [rak] s roca; (sticking out of water) escollo; (one that is thrown)
piedra; (slang) diamante m, piedra
preciosa; on the rocks arruinado, en
pobreza extrema; (said of hard
liquor) (coll) sobre hielo || tr acunar,
mecer; (to sleep) arrullar; sacudir;
to rock to sleep adormecer meciendo
|| intr mecerse; sacudirse
rock′-bot′tom adj (el) mínimo, (el)
más bajo
rock candy s azúcar m cande
rock crystal s cristal m de roca
rocker [′rakər] s (chair) mecedora;
(curved piece at bottom of rocking
chair or cradle) arco; (mach) balancín m; (mach) eje m de balancín
rocket [′rakɪt] s cohete m || intr subir
como un cohete
rocket bomb s bomba cohete
rocket launcher [′lɒntʃər] o [′lɑntʃər]
s lanzacohetes m
rocket ship s aeronave f cohete
rock garden s jardín m entre rocas

ri
ro

rocking chair s mecedora, sillón m de hamaca

rocking horse s caballo mecedor

Rock of Gibraltar [dʒɪˈbrɔltər] s peñón m de Gibraltar

rock salt s sal f de compás, sal gema

rock wool s lana mineral

rock·y [ˈrɑki] adj (comp **-ier;** super **-iest**) rocoso, roqueño; (slang) débil, poco firme

rod [rɑd] s vara; varilla; barra; (authority) vara alta; opresión, tiranía; (of the retina) bastoncillo; (elongated microörganism) bastoncito; (mach) vástago; (surv) jalón m; (Bib) linaje m, raza, vástago; (slang) revólver m, pistola; **to spare the rod** excusar la vara

rodent [ˈrodənt] adj & s roedor m

rod·man [ˈrɑdmən] s (pl **-men** [mən]) jalonero, portamira m

roe [ro] s (deer) corzo; (of fish) hueva

rogue [rog] s bribón m, pícaro

rogues' gallery s colección de retratos de malhechores para uso de la policía

roguish [ˈrogɪʃ] adj bribón, pícaro; travieso, retozón

rôle or **role** [rol] s papel m; **to play a rôle** desempeñar un papel

roll [rol] s (of cloth, film, paper, fat, etc.) rollo; (roller) rodillo; (cake of bread) panecillo; (of dice) echada; (of a boat) balance m; (of a drum) redoble m; (of thunder) retumbo m; bamboleo; ondulación; rol m; lista; (of paper money) fajo; **to call the roll** pasar lista ‖ tr hacer rodar; empujar hacia adelante; cilindrar, laminar; (to wrap up with rolling motion) arrollar; alisar con rodillo; liar (un cigarrillo); mover de un lado a otro; poner (los ojos) en blanco; tocar redobles con (el tambor); vibrar (la voz; la r); **to roll one's own** liárselos; **to roll up** arremangar (p.ej., las mangas); amontonar (p.ej., una fortuna) ‖ intr rodar; bambolear; balancear (un barco); girar; retumbar (el trueno); redoblar (un tambor); **to roll around** revolcarse

roll call s lista, (el) pasar lista

roller [ˈrolər] s rodillo; (of a piece of furniture) ruedecilla; (of a skate) rueda; ola larga y creciente

roller bearing s cojinete m de rodillos

roller coaster s montaña rusa

roller skate s patín m de ruedas

roller towel s toalla sin fin

rolling mill [ˈrolɪŋ] s taller m de laminación; tren m de laminadores

rolling pin s rodillo, hataca

rolling stock s (rr) material m móvil, material rodante

rolling stone s piedra movediza

roll'-top' desk s escritorio norteamericano, escritorio de cortina corrediza

roly-poly [ˈroliˈpoli] adj regordete, rechoncho

Rom. abbr Roman, Romance

roman [ˈromən] adj (typ) redondo ‖ s (typ) letra redonda ‖ **Roman** adj & s romano

Roman candle s vela romana

Roman Catholic adj & s católico romano

romance [roˈmæns] o [ˈromæns] s (tale of chivalry) romance m; cuento de aventuras; cuento de amor; intriga amorosa; novela sentimental; (mus) romanza ‖ [roˈmæns] intr contar o escribir romances, cuentos de aventuras o cuentos de amor; pensar o hablar de un modo romántico; exagerar, mentir ‖ **Romance** [ˈromæns] o [roˈmæns] adj (Neo-Latin) romance o románico

romance of chivalry s libro de caballerías

Roman Empire s Imperio romano

Romanesque [ˌromənˈɛsk] adj & s mánico

Roman nose s nariz aguileña

romantic [roˈmæntɪk] adj romántico; (spot, place) encantador

romanticism [roˈmæntɪˌsɪzəm] s romanticismo

romp [rɑmp] intr corretear, triscar

rompers [ˈrɑmpərz] spl traje holgado de juego

roof [ruf] o [rʊf] s (top outer covering of a house) tejado; (of a car or bus) imperial f, tejadillo; (of the mouth) paladar m; (of heaven) bóveda; (home, dwelling) (fig) techo; **to raise the roof** (slang) poner el grito en el cielo ‖ tr techar

roofer [ˈrufər] o [ˈrʊfər] s techador m, pizarrero

roof garden s (garden on the roof) pérgola; azotea de baile y diversión

rook [rʊk] s (bird) grajo; (in chess) roque m ‖ tr trampear

rookie [ˈrʊki] s (slang) bisoño, novato

room [rum] o [rʊm] s aposento, cuarto, habitación, pieza; espacio, sitio, lugar m; ocasión; **to make room** abrir paso, hacer lugar ‖ intr alojarse

room and board s pensión completa

room clerk s empleado en la recepción, encargado de las reservas

roomer [ˈrumər] o [ˈrʊmər] s inquilino

rooming house s casa donde se alquilan cuartos

room'mate' s compañero de cuarto

room·y [ˈrumi] o [ˈrʊmi] adj (comp **-ier;** super **-iest**) amplio, espacioso

roost [rust] s percha de gallinero, gallinero; lugar m de descanso; **to rule the roost** ser el amo del cotarro, tener el mando y el palo ‖ intr descansar (las aves) en la percha; estar alojado; pasar la noche

rooster [ˈrustər] s gallo

root [rut] o [rʊt] s raíz f; **to get to the root of** profundizar; **to take root** echar raíces ‖ tr hocicar, hozar ‖ intr arraigar; **to root for** (slang) gritar alentando

rooter [ˈrutər] o [ˈrʊtər] s (slang) hincha mf

rope [rop] s cuerda; (of a hangman)

dogal *m; (to catch an animal)* lazo; **to jump rope** saltar a la comba; **to know the ropes** (slang) saber todas las tretas || *tr* atar con una cuerda; coger con lazo; **to rope in** (slang) embaucar, engañar

rope'walk'er *s* funámbulo, volatinero

rosa·ry ['rozəri] *s (pl -ries)* rosario

rose [roz] *adj* de color de rosa || *s* rosa

rose'bud' *s* pimpollo, capullo de rosa

rose'bush' *s* rosal *m*

rose'-col'ored *adj* rosado; **to see everything through rose-colored glasses** verlo todo de color de rosa

rose garden *s* rosaleda, rosalera

rosemar·y ['roz,meri] *s (pl -ies)* romero

rose of Sharon ['ʃerən] *s* granado blanco, rosa de Siria

rose window *s* rosetón *m*

rose'wood' *s* palisandro

rosin ['rɑzɪn] *s* colofonia, brea seca

roster ['rɑstər] *s* catálogo, lista; horario escolar, horas de clase

rostrum ['rɑstrəm] *s* tribuna

ros·y ['rozi] *adj (comp* **-ier;** *super* **-iest)** rosado, sonrosado; alegre

rot [rɑt] *s* podredumbre; (slang) tontería || *v (pret & pp* **rotted;** *ger* **rotting)** *tr* pudrir || *intr* pudrirse

rotate ['rotet] o [ro'tet] *tr* hacer girar; alternar || *intr* girar; alternar

rote [rot] *s* rutina, repetición maquinal; **by rote** de memoria, maquinalmente

rot'gut' *s* (slang) matarratas *m*

rotogravure [,rotəgrə'vjur] o [,rotə-'grevjur] *s* rotograbado

rotten ['rɑtən] *adj* putrefacto, pútrido; corrompido

rotund [ro'tʌnd] *adj* redondo de cuerpo; *(language)* redondo

rouge [ruʒ] *s* arrebol *m*, colorete *m* || *tr* arrebolar, pintar || *intr* arrebolarse, pintarse

rough [rʌf] *adj* áspero; *(sea)* agitado, picado; *(crude, unwrought)* tosco, grosero; aproximado || *tr* — **to rough it** vivir sin comodidades, hacer vida campestre

rough'cast' *s* modelo tosco; mezcla gruesa || *v (pret & pp* **-cast)** *tr (to prepare in rough form)* bosquejar; dar a *(la pared)* una capa de mezcla gruesa

rough copy *s* borrador *m*

roughly ['rʌfli] *adv* asperamente; brutalmente; aproximadamente

roulette [ru'let] *s* ruleta

round [raund] *adj* redondo || *adv* redondamente; alrededor; de boca en boca; por todas partes || *prep* alrededor de; *(e.g., the corner)* a la vuelta de; cerca de; acá y allá en || *s* camino, circuito; *(of a policeman; of visits; of drinks or cigars)* ronda; *(of applause; discharge of guns)* salva; *(discharge of a single gun)* disparo, tiro; *(of people)* corro, círculo; *(of golf)* partido, rutina, serie *f*, sucesión; redondez *f*; revolución; (box) asalto; **to go the rounds** ir de

boca en boca; ir de mano en mano || *tr (to make round)* redondear; cercar, rodear; doblar *(una esquina, un promontorio)*; **to round off** u **out** redondear; acabar, completar, perfeccionar; **to round up** juntar, recoger; rodear *(el ganado)*

roundabout ['raundə,baut] *adj* indirecto || *s* curso indirecto; (Brit) tío vivo; (Brit) glorieta de tráfico

rounder ['raundər] *s* (coll) pródigo; (coll) catavinos *m*, borrachín habitual

round'house' *s* cocherón *m*, casa de máquinas, depósito de locomotoras

round-shouldered ['raund'ʃoldərd] *adj* cargado de espaldas

Round Table *s* Tabla Redonda

round'-trip' ticket *s* billete *m* de ida y vuelta

round'up' *s (of cattle)* rodeo; *(of criminals)* redada; *(of old friends)* reunión

rouse [rauz] *tr* despertar; excitar, provocar; levantar *(la caza)* || *intr* despertarse, despabilarse

rout [raut] *s* derrota; fuga desordenada || *tr* derrotar; poner en fuga desordenada; arrancar hozando || *intr* hozar

route [rut] o [raut] *s* ruta; itinerario || *tr* encaminar

routine [ru'tin] *adj* rutinario || *s* rutina

rove [rov] *intr* andar errante, vagar

row [rau] *s* (coll) camorra, pendencia, riña; (coll) alboroto, bullicio; **to raise a row** (coll) armar camorra || [ro] *s* fila, hilera; *(of houses)* calle *f*; **in a row** seguidos, p.ej., **five hours in a row** cinco horas seguidas || *intr* remar

rowboat ['ro,bot] *s* bote *m*, bote de remos

row·dy ['raudi] *adj (comp* **-dier;** *super* **-diest)** gamberro || *s (pl* **-dies)** gamberro

rower ['ro·ər] *s* remero

royal ['rɔɪ·əl] *adj* real; *(magnificent, splendid)* regio

royalist ['rɔɪ·əlɪst] *s* realista *mf*

royal·ty ['rɔɪ·əlti] *s (pl* **-ties)** realeza; personaje *m* real, personajes reales; derechos de autor; derechos de inventor

r.p.m. *abbr* **revolutions per minute**

R.R. *abbr* **railroad, Right Reverend**

rub [rʌb] *s* frotación, roce *m;* **there's the rub** ahí está el busilis || *v (pret & pp* **rubbed;** *ger* **rubbing)** *tr* frotar; **to rub elbows with** rozarse mucho con; **to rub out** borrar; (slang) asesinar || *intr* frotar; **to rub off** quitarse frotando; borrarse

rubber ['rʌbər] *s* caucho, goma; goma de borrar; chanclo, zapato de goma; *(in bridge)* robre *m* || *intr* (slang) estirar el cuello o volver la cabeza para ver

rubber band *s* liga de goma

rubber plant *s* árbol *m* del caucho

rubber plantation *s* cauchal *m*

rubber stamp *s* cajetín *m*, sello de goma; *(with a person's signature)*

ro
ru

estampilla; (coll) persona que aprueba sin reflexionar

rub′ber-stamp′ tr estampar con un sello de goma; (with a person's signature) estampillar; (coll) aprobar sin reflexionar

rubbish [ˈrʌbɪʃ] s basura, desecho, desperdicios; (coll) disparate m, tontería

rubble [ˈrʌbəl] s (broken stone) ripio; (masonry) mampostería

rub′down′ s masaje m, fricción

rube [rub] s (slang) isidro, rústico

ru·by [ˈrubi] s (pl -bies) rubí m

rudder [ˈrʌdər] s timón m, gobernalle m

rud·dy [ˈrʌdi] adj (comp -dier; super -diest) coloradote, rubicundo

rude [rud] adj rudo

rudiment [ˈrudɪmənt] s rudimento

rue [ru] tr lamentar, arrepentirse de

rueful [ˈrufəl] adj lamentable; triste

ruffian [ˈrʌfɪ·ən] s hombre grosero y brutal

ruffle [ˈrʌfəl] s arruga; (of drum) redoble m; (sew) volante m ‖ tr arrugar; agitar, descomponer; enojar, molestar; confundir; redoblar (el tambor); (sew) fruncir un volante en, adornar o guarnecer con volante

rug [rʌg] s alfombra; alfombrilla; (lap robe) manta

rugged [ˈrʌgɪd] adj áspero, rugoso; recio, vigoroso; tempestuoso

ruin [ˈru·ɪn] s ruina ‖ tr arruinar; estropear; echar a perder

rule [rul] s regla; autoridad, mando; regla de imprenta; (reign) reinado; (of a court of law) decisión, fallo; **as a rule** por regla general; **to be the rule** ser lo que se hace ‖ tr gobernar, regir; dirigir, guiar; contener, reprimir; (to mark with lines) reglar; (law) decidir, determinar; **to rule out** excluir, rechazar ‖ intr gobernar, regir; prevalecer; **to rule over** gobernar, regir

rule of law s régimen m de justicia

ruler [ˈrulər] s gobernante mf; soberano; (for ruling lines) regla

ruling [ˈrulɪŋ] adj gobernante, dirigente, imperante ‖ s (of a court or judge) decisión, fallo; (of paper) rayado

rum [rʌm] s ron m; (any alcoholic drink) (U.S.A.) aguardiente m

Rumanian [ruˈmenɪ·ən] adj & s rumano

rumble [ˈrʌmbəl] s retumbo; (of the intestines) rugido; (slang) riña entre pandillas ‖ intr retumbar; avanzar retumbando

ruminate [ˈrumɪˌnet] tr & intr rumiar

rummage [ˈrʌmɪdʒ] tr & intr buscar revolviéndolo todo

rummage sale s venta de prendas usadas

rumor [ˈrumər] s rumor m ‖ tr rumorear; **it is rumored that** se rumorea que

rump [rʌmp] s anca, nalga; (cut of beef) cuarto trasero

rumple [ˈrʌmpəl] s arruga ‖ tr arrugar, ajar, chafar ‖ intr arrugarse

rumpus [ˈrʌmpəs] s (coll) batahola, alboroto; **to raise a rumpus** (coll) armar la de San Quintín

run [rʌn] s carrera; clase f, tipo; arroyo; (e.g., in a stocking) carrera; (on a bank by depositors) asedio; (of consecutive performances of a play) serie f; (baseball & mus) carrera; **in the long run** a la larga; **on the run** a escape; en fuga desordenada; **the common run of people** el común de las gentes; **the general run of** la generalidad de; **to have a long run** permanecer en cartel durante mucho tiempo; **to have the run of** hallar el secreto de; tener libertad de ir y venir por ‖ v (pret **ran** [ræn]; pp **run**; ger **running**) tr hacer funcionar; dirigir, manejar; trazar, tirar (una línea); exhibir (un cine); hacer (mandados); tener como candidato; burlar, violar (un bloqueo); tener (calentura); correr (un caballo; un riesgo); **to run down** cazar y matar; derribar; atropellar (a un peatón); (coll) denigrar, desacreditar; **to run in** rodar (un nuevo coche); **to run off** tocar (una pieza de música); tirar, imprimir; **to run up** (coll) aumentar (gastos) ‖ intr correr; (on wheels) rodar; darse prisa; trepar (la vid); ir y venir (un vapor); supurar (una llaga); colar (un líquido); correrse (un color o tinte); presentar su candidatura; andar, funcionar, marchar; deshilarse (las medias); migrar (los peces); estar en fuerza; (to be worded or written) rezar; **to run across** dar con, tropezar con; **to run away** correr, huir; desbocarse (un caballo); **to run down** escurrir, gotear (un líquido); descargarse (un acumulador); distenderse (el muelle de un reloj); acabarse la cuerda, p.ej., **the watch ran down** se acabó la cuerda; **to run for** presentar su candidatura a; **to run in the family** venir de familia; **to run into** tropezar con; chocar con, topar con; **to run off the track** descarrilar (un tren); **to run out** salir; expirar, terminar; acabarse; agotarse; **to run out of** acabársele a uno, e.g., **I have run out of money** se me ha acabado el dinero; **to run over** atropellar (a un peatón); registrar a la ligera; pasar por encima; leer rápidamente; rebosar (un líquido); **to run through** disipar rápidamente (una fortuna); registrar a la ligera; estar difundido en

run′a·way′ adj fugitivo; (horse) desbocado ‖ s fugitivo; caballo desbocado; fuga

run′-down′ adj desmedrado; desmantelado; inculto; (clock spring) sin cuerda, distendido; (storage battery) descargado

rung [rʌŋ] s (of ladder or chair) travesaño; (of wheel) radio, rayo

runner [ˈrʌnər] s corredor m; caballo

de carreras; mensajero; (of an ice skate) cuchilla; (of a sleigh) patín m; (long narrow rug) pasacaminos m; (strip of cloth for table top) tapete m; (in stockings) carrera

run'ner-up' s (pl runners-up) subcampeón m

running ['rʌnɪŋ] adj corredor; (expenses; water) corriente; (knot) corredizo; (sore) supurante; (writing) cursivo; continuo; consecutivo; en marcha; (start) (sport) lanzado || s carrera, corrida; administración, dirección; marcha, funcionamiento; **to be in the running** tener esperanzas o posibilidades de ganar

running board s estribo

running head s titulillo

running start s (sport) salida lanzada

run-of-mine coal ['rʌnəv'maɪn] s carbón m tal como sale

run'proof' adj indesmallable

runt [rʌnt] s enano, hombrecillo; (little child) redrojo; animal achaparrado

run'way' s (of a stream) cauce m; senda trillada; (aer) pista de aterrizaje

rupture ['rʌptʃər] s ruptura; (pathol) quebradura; (break in relations) ruptura || tr romper; causar una hernia en || intr romperse; padecer hernia

rural free delivery ['rʊrəl] s distribución gratuita del correo en el campo

rural police s guardia civil

rural policeman s guardiacivil m

ruse [ruz] s astucia, artimaña

rush [rʌʃ] adj urgente || s prisa grande, precipitación; agolpamiento de gente;

(bot) junco; **in a rush** de prisa || tr empujar con violencia o prisa; despachar con prontitud; (slang) cortejar insistentemente (a una mujer); **to rush through** ejecutar de prisa, despachar rápidamente || intr lanzarse, precipitarse; venir de prisa, ir de prisa; actuar con prontitud; **to rush through** lanzarse a través de, lanzarse por entre

rush-bottomed chair ['rʌʃ'batəmd] s silla de junco

rush hour s hora de aglomeración, horas de punta

rush'light' s mariposa, lamparilla

rush order s pedido urgente

russet ['rʌsɪt] adj canelo

Russia ['rʌʃə] s Rusia

Russian ['rʌʃən] adj & s ruso

rust [rʌst] s orín m, moho, herrumbre; (agr) roña, roya; color rojizo o anaranjado || tr aherrumbrar || intr aherrumbrarse

rustic ['rʌstɪk] adj rústico; sencillo, sin artificio || s rústico

rustle ['rʌsəl] s susurro, crujido || tr hacer susurrar, hacer crujir; hurtar (ganado) || intr susurrar, crujir; (slang) trabajar con ahinco

rust·y ['rʌsti] adj (comp -ier; super -iest) herrumbroso, mohoso; rojizo; (out of practice) empolvado, desusado, remoto

rut [rʌt] s (track, groove in road) rodada, bache m; hábito arraigado; (sexual excitement in animals) celo; (period of this excitement) brama

ruthless ['ruθlɪs] adj despiadado, cruel

Ry. abbr railway

rye [raɪ] s centeno; whisky de centeno

S

S, s [es] decimonona letra del alfabeto inglés

s abbr second, shilling, singular

Sabbath ['sæbəθ] s (of Jews) sábado; (of Christians) dominica; **to keep the Sabbath** observar el descanso dominical, guardar el domingo

saber ['sebər] s sable m

sable ['sebəl] adj negro || s marta cebellina; **sables** vestidos de luto

sabotage ['sæbə,taʒ] s sabotaje m || tr & intr sabotear

saccharin ['sækərɪn] s sacarina

sachet [sæ'ʃe] o [sæ'ʃe] s polvo oloroso; saquito de perfumes

sack [sæk] s saco; vino blanco generoso; (mil) saqueo, saco; (of an employee) (slang) despedida || tr ensacar; saquear, pillar; (slang) despedir (a un empleado)

sack'cloth' s harpillera; (worn for penitence) cilicio

sacrament ['sækrəmənt] s sacramento

sacred ['sekrəd] adj sagrado

sacrifice ['sækrɪ,faɪs] s sacrificio; at

a sacrifice con pérdida || tr sacrificar; (to sell at a loss) malvender || intr sacrificar; sacrificarse

Sacrifice of the Mass s sacrificio del altar

sacrilege ['sækrɪlɪdʒ] s sacrilegio

sacrilegious [,sækrɪ'lɪdʒəs] o [,sækrɪ'lidʒəs] adj sacrílego

sacristan ['sækrɪstən] s sacristán m

sacris·ty ['sækrɪsti] s (pl -ties) sacristía

sad [sæd] adj (comp sadder; super saddest) triste; (slang) malo

sadden ['sædən] tr entristecer || intr entristecerse

saddle ['sædəl] s silla de montar; (of a bicycle) sillín m || tr ensillar; **to saddle with** echar a cuestas a

sad'dle·bags' spl alforjas

sad'dle·bow' [,bo] s arzón delantero

sad'dle·tree' s arzón m

sadist ['sædɪst] o ['sedɪst] s sádico

sadistic [sæ'dɪstɪk] o [se'dɪstɪk] adj sádico

sadness ['sædnɪs] s tristeza

safe [sef] adj seguro, ileso, salvo;

cierto, digno de confianza; sin peligro, a salvo; **safe and sound** sano y salvo; **safe from** a salvo de ‖ s caja fuerte, caja de caudales

safe′-con′duct s salvoconducto

safe′-depos′it box s caja de seguridad

safe′guard′ s salvaguardia, medida de seguridad ‖ tr salvaguardar

safe•ty ['sefti] adj de seguridad ‖ s (pl -ties) seguridad; **to parachute to safety** lanzarse en paracaídas; **to reach safety** ponerse a salvo, llegar a lugar seguro

safety belt s (aer, aut) correa de seguridad; (naut) cinturón m salvavidas

safety match s fósforo de seguridad

safety pin s imperdible m, alfiler m de seguridad

safety rail s guardarriel m

safety razor s maquinilla de seguridad

safety valve s válvula de seguridad

saffron ['sæfrən] adj azafranado ‖ s azafrán m ‖ tr azafranar

sag [sæg] s comba, combadura; (e.g., of a cable) flecha ‖ v (pret & pp sagged; ger sagging) intr combarse; (to slacken, yield) aflojar, ceder, doblegarse; bajar (los precios)

sagacious [sə'geʃəs] adj sagaz

sage [sedʒ] adj sabio, cuerdo ‖ s sabio; (bot) salvia; (bot) artemisa

sage′brush′ s (bot) artemisa

sail [sel] s vela; barco de vela; paseo en barco de vela; **to set sail** hacerse a la vela; **under full sail** a vela llena ‖ tr gobernar (un barco de vela); navegar (un mar, río, etc.) ‖ intr navegar, navegar a la vela; salir, salir de viaje; deslizarse, flotar, volar; **to sail into** (slang) atacar, regañar, reñir

sail′boat′ s barco de vela, buque m de vela, velero

sail′cloth′ s lona, paño

sailing ['selɪŋ] adj de salida ‖ s paseo en barco de vela; navegación; salida

sailing vessel s buque velero

sailor ['selər] s (one who makes a living sailing) marinero; (an enlisted man in the navy) marino

saint [sent] adj & s santo ‖ tr (coll) canonizar

saintliness ['sentlɪnɪs] s santidad

Saint Vitus's dance ['vaɪtəsəs] s (pathol) baile m de San Vito

sake [sek] s respeto, bien, amor m; **for his sake** por su bien; **for the sake of** por, por motivo de, por amor a; **for your own sake** por su propio bien

salaam [sə'lɑm] s zalema ‖ tr saludar con zalemas, hacer zalemas a

salable ['seləbəl] adj vendible

salad ['sæləd] s ensalada

salad bowl s ensaladera

salad oil s aceite m de comer

Salamis ['sæləmɪs] s Salamina

sala•ry ['sæləri] s (pl -ries) sueldo

sale [sel] s venta; (auction) almoneda, subasta; **for sale** de venta; **se vende(n)**

sales′clerk′ s dependiente mf de tienda

sales′la′dy s (pl -dies) vendedora

sales•man ['selzmən] s (pl -men**

[mən]) vendedor m, dependiente m de tienda

sales manager s gerente m de ventas

sales′man•ship′ s arte de vender

sales′room′ s salón m de ventas; salón de exhibición

sales talk s argumento para inducir a comprar

sales tax s impuesto sobre ventas

saliva [sə'laɪvə] s saliva

sallow ['sælo] adj cetrino

sal•ly ['sæli] s (pl -lies) paseo, viaje m; ímpetu m, arranque m; salida, ocurrencia; (mil) salida, surtida ‖ v (pret & pp -lied) intr salir, hacer una salida; ir de paseo; **to sally forth** salir, avanzar con denuedo

salmon ['sæmən] s salmón m

salon [sæ'lɑn] s salón m

saloon [sə'lun] s cantina, taberna; (on a steamer) salón m

saloon′keep′er s tabernero

salt [sɔlt] s sal f; **to be not worth one's salt** no valer (uno) el pan que come ‖ tr salar; (to preserve with salt) salpresar; marinar (el pescado); salgar (el ganado); **to salt away** (slang) ahorrar, guardar para uso futuro

salt′cel′lar s salero

salted peanuts spl saladillos

saltine [sɔl'tin] s galletita salada

salt lick s salero, lamedero

salt of the earth, the lo mejor del mundo

salt′pe′ter s (potassium nitrate) salitre m; (sodium nitrate) nitro de Chile

salt′sha′ker s salero

salt•y ['sɔlti] adj (comp -ier; super -iest) salado

salubrious [sə'lubrɪ-əs] adj salubre

salutation [ˌsæljə'teʃən] s salutación

salute [sə'lut] s saludo ‖ tr saludar

Salvadoran [ˌsælvə'dorən] o **Salvadorian** [ˌsælvə'dorɪ-ən] adj & s salvadoreño

salvage ['sælvɪdʒ] s salvamento ‖ tr salvar; recobrar

Salvation Army [sæl've/ən] s ejército de Salvación

salve [sæv] o [sɑv] s ungüento ‖ tr curar con ungüento; preservar; aliviar

sal•vo ['sælvo] s (pl -vos o -voes) salva

Samaritan [sə'mærɪtən] adj & s samaritano

same [sem] adj & pron indef mismo; **it's all the same to me** lo mismo me da; **just the same** lo mismo, sin embargo; **same . . . as** mismo . . . que

samite ['sæmaɪt] o ['semaɪt] s jamete m

sample ['sæmpəl] s muestra ‖ tr catar, probar

sample copy s ejemplar m muestra

sancti•fy ['sæŋktɪˌfaɪ] v (pret & pp -fied) tr santificar

sanctimonious [ˌsæŋktɪ'monɪ-əs] adj santurrón

sanction ['sæŋkʃən] s sanción ‖ tr sancionar

sanctuar•y ['sæŋktʃʊˌɛri] s (pl -ies)

santuario; asilo, refugio; **to take sanctuary** acogerse a sagrado
sand [sænd] *s* arena || *tr* enarenar; lijar con papel de lija
sandal ['sændəl] *s* sandalia
san'dal•wood' *s* (bot) sándalo
sand'bag' *s* saco de arena
sand'bank' *s* banco de arena
sand bar *s* barra de arena
sand'blast' *s* chorro de arena || *tr* limpiar con chorro de arena
sand'box' *s* (rr) arenero
sand dune *s* duna, médano
sand'glass' *s* reloj *m* de arena, ampolleta
sand'pa'per *s* papel *m* de lija || *tr* lijar
sand'stone' *s* piedra arenisca
sand'storm' *s* tempestad de arena
sandwich ['sændwɪtʃ] *s* emparedado, sandwich *m* || *tr* intercalar
sandwich man *s* hombre-anuncio
sand•y ['sændi] *adj* (*comp* **-ier;** *super* **-iest**) arenoso; (*hair*) rufo; cambiante, movible
sane [sen] *adj* cuerdo, sensato; (*principles*) sano
sanguinary ['sæŋgwɪn,ɛri] *adj* sanguinario
sanguine ['sæŋgwɪn] *adj* confiado, esperanzado; (*countenance*) coloradote
sanitary ['sænɪ,tɛri] *adj* sanitario
sanitary napkin *s* compresa higiénica
sanitation [,sænɪ'teʃən] *s* (*sanitary measures*) sanidad; (*drainage*) saneamiento
sanity ['sænɪti] *s* cordura, sensatez *f*
Santa Claus ['sæntə,klɔz] *s* el Papá Noel, San Nicolás
sap [sæp] *s* savia; (mil) zapa; (coll) necio, tonto || *v* (*pret* & *pp* **sapped;** *ger* **sapping**) *tr* agotar, debilitar; zapar, socavar
sap'head' *s* (coll) cabeza de chorlito
sapling ['sæplɪŋ] *s* árbol *m* muy joven, pimpollo; jovenzuelo, mozuelo
sapphire ['sæfaɪr] *s* zafiro
saraband ['særə,bænd] *s* zarabanda
Saracen ['særəsən] *adj* & *s* sarraceno
Saragossa [,særə'gɑsə] *s* Zaragoza
sardine [sɑr'din] *s* sardina; **packed in like sardines** como sardinas en banasta o en lata
Sardinia [sɑr'dɪnɪ-ə] *s* Cerdeña
Sardinian [sɑr'dɪnɪ-ən] *adj* & *s* sardo
sarsaparilla [,sɑrsəpə'rɪlə] *s* zarzaparrilla
sash [sæʃ] *s* banda, faja; (*of a window*) marco
sash window *s* ventana de guillotina
satchel ['sætʃəl] *s* maletín *m*; (*of a schoolboy*) cartapacio
sateen [sæ'tin] *s* satén *m*
satellite ['sætə,laɪt] *s* satélite *m*
satellite country *s* país *m* satélite
satiate ['seʃɪ,et] *adj* ahito, harto || *tr* saciar
satin ['sætən] *s* raso
satinet [,sætɪ'nɛt] *s* rasete *m*
satiric(al) [sə'tɪrɪk(əl)] *adj* satírico
satirist ['sætɪrɪst] *s* satírico
satirize ['sætɪ,raɪz] *tr* & *intr* satirizar
satisfaction [,sætɪs'fækʃən] *s* satisfacción

satisfactory [,sætɪs'fæktəri] *adj* satisfactorio
satis•fy ['sætɪs,faɪ] *v* (*pret* & *pp* **-fied**) *tr* & *intr* satisfacer
saturate ['sætʃə,ret] *tr* saturar
Saturday ['sætərdi] *s* sábado
sauce [sɔs] *s* salsa; (*of fruit*) compota; (*of chocolate*) crema; gracia, viveza; (coll) insolencia, lenguaje descomedido || *tr* condimentar || [sɔs] o [sæs] *tr* (coll) ser respondón con
sauce'pan' *s* cacerola
saucer ['sɔsər] *s* platillo
sau•cy ['sɔsi] *adj* (*comp* **-cier;** *super* **-ciest**) descarado, insolente; gracioso, vivo
sauerkraut ['saur,kraut] *s* chucruta
saunter ['sɔntər] *s* paseo tranquilo y alegre || *intr* dar un paseo tranquilo y alegre; pasear tranquila y alegremente
sausage ['sɔsɪdʒ] *s* salchicha, embutido
savage ['sævɪdʒ] *adj* & *s* salvaje *mf*
savant ['sævənt] *s* sabio, erudito
save [sev] *prep* salvo, excepto, menos || *tr* salvar (*p.ej., una vida, un alma*); ahorrar (*dinero*); conservar, guardar; proteger, amparar; **God save the Queen!** ¡Dios guarde a la Reina!; **to save face** salvar las apariencias
saving ['sevɪŋ] *prep* salvo, excepto; con el debido respeto a || *adj* económico || **savings** *spl* ahorros, economías
savings account *s* cuenta de ahorros
savings bank *s* banco de ahorros, caja de ahorros
Savior ['sevjər] *s* salvador *m*
Saviour ['sevjər] *s* Salvador *m*
savor ['sevər] *s* sabor *m* || *tr* saborear || *intr* oler; **to savor of** oler a, saber a
savor•y ['sevəri] *adj* (*comp* **-ier;** *super* **-iest**) sabroso; picante; fragante || *s* (*pl* **-ies**) (bot) ajedrea
saw [sɔ] *s* (*tool*) sierra; proverbio, refrán *m* || *tr* aserrar, serrar
saw'buck' *s* cabrilla, caballete *m*
saw'dust' *s* aserrín *m*, serrín *m*
saw'horse' *s* cabrilla, caballete *m*
saw'mill' *s* aserradero, serrería
Saxon ['sæksən] *adj* & *s* sajón *m*
saxophone ['sæksə,fon] *s* saxofón *m*
say [se] *s* decir *m*; **to have one's say** decir su parecer || *v* (*pret* & *pp* **said** [sed]) *tr* decir; **I should say so!** ¡ya lo creo!; **it is said** se dice; **no sooner said than done** dicho y hecho; **that is to say** es decir, esto es; **to go without saying** caerse de su peso
saying ['se•ɪŋ] *s* dicho; proverbio, refrán *m*
sc. *abbr* **scene, science, scruple, scilicet** (Lat) **namely**
scab [skæb] *s* costra; (*strikebreaker*) esquirol *m*; (slang) bribón *m*, golfo
scabbard ['skæbərd] *s* funda, vaina
scab•by ['skæbi] *adj* (*comp* **-bier;** *super* **-biest**) costroso; (coll) ruin, vil
scabrous ['skæbrəs] *adj* escabroso
scads [skædz] *spl* (slang) montones *mpl*

scaffold [ˈskæfəld] s andamio; (*to execute a criminal*) cadalso, patíbulo
scaffolding [ˈskæfəldɪŋ] s andamiaje *m*
scald [skɔld] *tr* escaldar
scale [skel] s escama; balanza; platillo de balanza; (*e.g., of a map*) escala; (mus) escala; **on a scale of** en escala de; **on a large scale** en grande escala; **scales** balanza; **to tip the scales** inclinar la balanza ‖ *tr* escamar; descortezar, descostrar; escalar, subir, trepar; graduar ‖ *intr* descamarse; descortezarse, descostrarse; subir, trepar
scallop [ˈskɑləp] o [ˈskæləp] s concha de peregrino; (*shell or dish for serving fish*) concha; (*thin slice of meat*) escalope *m*; (*on edge of cloth*) festón *m* ‖ *tr* cocer (*p.ej., ostras*) en su concha; festonear
scalp [skælp] s cuero cabelludo ‖ *tr* escalpar; comprar y revender (*billetes de teatro*) a precios extraoficiales
scalpel [ˈskælpəl] s escalpelo
scal·y [ˈskeli] *adj* (*comp* **-ier;** *super* **-iest**) escamoso
scamp [skæmp] s bribón *m*, golfo
scamper [ˈskæmpər] *intr* escaparse precipitadamente; **to scamper away** escaparse precipitadamente
scan [skæn] *tr* (*pret & pp* **scanned;** *ger* **scanning**) *tr* escudriñar; escandir (*versos*); (telv) explorar; (coll) dar un vistazo a
scandal [ˈskændəl] s escándalo
scandalize [ˈskændə͵laɪz] *tr* escandalizar
scandalous [ˈskændələs] *adj* escandaloso
Scandinavian [͵skændɪˈnevɪ·ən] *adj & s* escandinavo
scanning [ˈskænɪŋ] s (telv) escansión, exploración
scansion [ˈskænʃən] s escansión
scant [skænt] *adj* escaso, insuficiente; solo, apenas suficiente ‖ *tr* escatimar
scant·y [ˈskænti] *adj* (*comp* **-ier;** *super* **-iest**) escaso, insuficiente, poco suficiente; (*clothing*) ligero
scape′goat′ s cabeza de turco, víctima propiciatoria
scar [skɑr] s cicatriz *f*, señal *f* ‖ *v* (*pret & pp* **scarred;** *ger* **scarring**) *tr* señalar, marcar ‖ *intr* cicatrizarse
scarce [skers] *adj* escaso, raro; **to make oneself scarce** (coll) no dejarse ver
scarcely [ˈskersli] *adv* apenas; probablemente no; ciertamente no; **scarcely ever** raramente
scarci·ty [ˈskersɪti] s (*pl* **-ties**) escasez *f*, carestía
scare [sker] s susto, alarma ‖ *tr* asustar, espantar; **to scare away** espantar, ahuyentar; **to scare up** (coll) juntar, recoger (*dinero*)
scare′crow′ s espantajo, espantapájaros *m*
scarf [skɑrf] s (*pl* **scarfs** o **scarves** [skɑrvz]) bufanda; pañuelo para el cuello; (*cover for a table, bureau, etc.*) tapete *m*; corbata
scarf′pin′ s alfiler *m* de corbata

scarlet [ˈskɑrlɪt] *adj* escarlata
scarlet fever s escarlata
scar·y [ˈskeri] *adj* (*comp* **-ier;** *super* **-iest**) (*easily frightened*) (coll) asustadizo, espantadizo; (*causing fright*) (coll) espantoso
scathing [ˈskeðɪŋ] *adj* acerbo, duro
scatter [ˈskætər] *tr* esparcir, dispersar ‖ *intr* esparcirse, dispersarse
scatterbrained [ˈskætər͵brend] *adj* (coll) alegre de cascos, casquivano
scattered showers *spl* lluvias aisladas
scenari·o [sɪˈnɛrɪ͵o] o [sɪˈnɑrɪ͵o] s (*pl* **-os**) guión *m*, escenario
scenarist [sɪˈnɛrɪst] o [sɪˈnɑrɪst] s guionista *mf*, escenarista *mf*
scene [sin] s (*view*) paisaje *m*; (*in literature, art, the theater, the movie*) escena; escándalo, demostración de pasión; **behind the scenes** entre bastidores; **to make a scene** causar escándalo
scener·y [ˈsinəri] s (*pl* **-ies**) paisaje *m*; (theat) decoraciones
scene shifter s tramoyista *m*
scenic [ˈsinɪk] o [ˈsɛnɪk] *adj* pintoresco; (*representing an action graphically*) gráfico; (*pertaining to the stage*) escénico
scent [sent] s olor *m*; perfume *m*; (*sense of smell*) olfato; (*trail*) rastro, pista ‖ *tr* oler; perfumar; olfatear, ventear; sospechar
scepter [ˈsɛptər] s cetro
sceptic [ˈskɛptɪk] *adj & s* escéptico
sceptical [ˈskɛptɪkəl] *adj* escéptico
schedule [ˈskɛdjul] s catálogo, cuadro, lista; plan *m*, programa *m*; (*of trains, planes, etc.*) horario ‖ *tr* catalogar; proyectar; fijar la hora de
scheme [skim] s esquema *m*; plan *m*, proyecto; (*trick*) ardid *m*, treta; (*plot*) intriga, trama ‖ *tr & intr* proyectar; tramar
schemer [ˈskimər] s proyectista *mf*; intrigante *mf*
scheming [ˈskimɪŋ] *adj* astuto, mañoso, intrigante ‖ *s* intriga
schism [ˈsɪzəm] s cisma *m*; facción cismática
schist [ʃɪst] s esquisto
scholar [ˈskɑlər] s (*pupil*) alumno; (*scholarship holder*) becario; (*learned person*) sabio, erudito
scholarly [ˈskɑlərli] *adj* sabio, erudito
scholarship [ˈskɑlər͵ʃɪp] s erudición; (*grant to study*) beca
school [skul] s escuela; (*of a university*) facultad; (*of fish*) banco, cardume *m* ‖ *tr* enseñar, instruir, disciplinar
school age s edad escolar
school attendance s escolaridad
school board s junta de instrucción pública
school′boy′ s alumno de escuela
school day s día lectivo
school′girl′ s alumna de escuela
school′house′ s escuela
schooling [ˈskulɪŋ] s instrucción, enseñanza; experiencia
school′mate′ s compañero de escuela
school′room′ s aula, sala de clase

school'teach'er s maestro de escuela

school year s año lectivo

schooner ['skunər] s goleta

sci. abbr science, scientific

science ['saɪ·əns] s ciencia

scientific [‚saɪ·ən'tɪfɪk] adj científico

scientist ['saɪ·əntɪst] s científico, sabio, hombre m de ciencia

scil. abbr scilicet (Lat) namely

scimitar ['sɪmɪtər] s cimitarra

scintillate ['sɪntɪ‚let] intr chispear, centellear

scion ['saɪ·ən] s vástago

Scipio ['sɪpɪ‚o] s Escipión m

scissors ['sɪzərz] ssg o spl tijeras

scoff [skɔf] o [skɑf] s burla, mofa || intr burlarse, mofarse; to scoff at burlarse de, mofarse de

scold [skold] s regañón m, regañona || tr & intr regañar

scoop [skup] s (instrument like a spoon) cuchara, cucharón m; (tool like a shovel) pala; (kitchen utensil) paleta; (for water) achicador m; cucharada, palada, paletada; (hollow made by a scoop) hueco; (big haul) (coll) buena ganancia || tr sacar con cuchara, pala, paleta; achicar (agua); to scoop out ahuecar, vaciar

scoot [skut] s (coll) carrera precipitada || intr (coll) correr precipitadamente

scooter ['skutər] s monopatín m, patinete m

scope [skop] s alcance m, extensión; campo, espacio; to give free scope to dar campo libre a

scorch [skɔrtʃ] s chamusco || tr chamuscar; (to dry, wither) abrasar; criticar acerbamente || intr chamuscarse; abrasarse

scorching ['skɔrtʃɪŋ] adj abrasador; acerbo, duro, mordaz

score [skor] s (in a game) cuenta, tantos; (in an examination) nota; entalladura, muesca; línea, raya; (twenty) veintena; (mus) partitura; on the score of a título de; to keep score apuntar los tantos || tr anotar (los tantos); ganar, tantear (tantos); rayar, señalar; regañar acerbamente; (mus) instrumentar || intr ganar tantos; marcar los tantos

score board s marcador m, cuadro indicador

scorn [skɔrn] s desdén m, desprecio || tr & intr desdeñar, despreciar; to scorn to no dignarse

scornful ['skɔrnfəl] adj desdeñoso

scorpion ['skɔrpɪ·ən] s alacrán m, escorpión m

Scot [skɑt] s escocés m

Scotch [skɑtʃ] adj escocés || s (dialect) escocés m; whisky m escocés; the Scotch los escoceses

Scotch·man ['skɑtʃ/mən] s (pl -men [mən]) escocés m

Scotland ['skɑtlənd] s Escocia

Scottish ['skɑtɪʃ] adj escocés || s (dialect) escocés m; the Scottish los escoceses

scoundrel ['skaʊndrəl] s bribón m, pícaro

scour [skaʊr] tr fregar, estregar; recorrer, explorar detenidamente

scourge [skʌrdʒ] s azote m || tr azotar

scout [skaʊt] s (mil) escucha, explorador m; niño explorador, niña exploradora; exploración, reconocimiento; (slang) individuo, sujeto, tipo || tr explorar, reconocer (un territorio); observar (al enemigo); negarse a creer

scout'mas'ter s jefe m de tropa de niños exploradores

scowl [skaʊl] s ceño, semblante ceñudo || intr mirar con ceño, poner mal gesto, poner mala cara

scramble ['skræmbəl] s arrebatiña || tr arrebatar; recoger de prisa; revolver; hacer un revoltillo de (huevos); trepar || intr luchar; trepar

scrambled eggs spl revoltillo, huevos revueltos

scrap [skræp] s fragmento, pedacito; desecho; chatarra; (slang) riña, contienda; scraps desperdicios, desechos; (from the table) sobras || v (pret & pp scrapped; ger scrapping) tr desechar, descartar, echar a la basura; reducir a hierro viejo || intr (slang) reñir, pelear

scrap'book' s álbum m de recortes, libro de recuerdos

scrape [skrep] s raspadura; (place scratched) raspazo; aprieto, enredo; || tr raspar; (to gather together with much difficulty) arañar || intr raspar; to scrape along ir tirando; to scrape through aprobar justo

scrap heap s montón m de cachivaches

scrap iron s chatarra, desecho de hierro

scrap paper s papel m para apuntes; papel de desecho

scratch [skrætʃ] s arañazo, rasguño; marca, raya, garrapato; (billiards) chiripa; (sport) línea de partida; to start from scratch empezar desde el principio; up to scratch en buena condición || tr arañar, rasguñar; borrar, rasgar (lo escrito); garrapatear; (sport) borrar (a un corredor o caballo) || intr arañar, rasguñar; garrapatear; raspear (una pluma)

scratch pad s cuadernillo de apuntes

scratch paper s papel m para apuntes

scrawl [skrɔl] s garrapatos || tr & intr garrapatear

scraw·ny ['skrɔnɪ] adj (comp -nier; super -niest) huesudo, flaco

scream [skrim] s chillido, grito || tr vociferar || intr chillar, gritar; reírse a gritos

screech [skritʃ] s chillido || intr chillar

screech owl s buharro; (barn owl) lechuza

screen [skrin] s mampara, biombo; (in front of chimney) pantalla; (to keep flies out) alambrera; (to sift sand) tamiz m; (mov, phys, telv) pantalla; to put on the screen llevar a la pantalla, llevar al celuloide || tr defender, proteger; cubrir, ocultar; cinematografiar; rodar, proyectar (una película); adaptar para el cine; tamizar (p.ej., arena)

screen grid *s* (electron) rejilla blindada
screen′play′ *s* cinedrama *m*
screw [skru] *s* tornillo; (*internal or female screw*) rosca, tuerca; (*of a boat*) hélice *f;* **to have a screw loose** (slang) tener flojos los tornillos; **to put the screws on** apretar los tornillos a ‖ *tr* atornillar; (*to twist, twist in*) enroscar; **to screw up** torcer (*el rostro*); ‖ *intr* atornillarse
screw′ball′ *s* (slang) estrafalario, excéntrico
screw′driv′er *s* destornillador *m*
screw eye *s* armella
screw jack *s* gato de tornillo
screw propeller *s* hélice *f*
scribal error [′skraɪbəl] *s* error *m* de escribiente
scribble [′skrɪbəl] *s* garrapatos ‖ *tr & intr* garrapatear
scribe [skraɪb] *s* (*teacher of Jewish law*) escriba *m;* escribiente *mf;* copista *mf;* autor *m,* escritor *m* ‖ *tr* arañar, rayar; trazar con punzón
scrimp [skrɪmp] *tr & intr* escatimar
script [skrɪpt] *s* escritura, letra cursiva; manuscrito, texto; (*of a play, movie, etc.*) palabras; (rad, telv) guión *m;* (typ) plumilla inglesa
scripture [′skrɪptʃər] *s* escrito sagrado ‖ **Scripture** *s* Escritura
script′writ′er *s* guionista *mf,* cinematurgo
scrofula [′skrɑfjələ] *s* escrófula
scroll [skrol] *s* rollo de papel, rollo de pergamino; (archit) voluta
scroll′work′ *s* obra de volutas, adornos de voluta
scrub [skrʌb] *s* chaparral *m,* monte bajo; animal achaparrado; persona de poca monta; (*act of scrubbing*) fregado; (sport) jugador *m* no oficial ‖ *v* (*pret & pp* **scrubbed;** *ger* **scrubbing**) *tr* fregar, restregar
scrub oak *s* chaparro
scrub woman *s* fregona
scruff [skrʌf] *s* nuca; piel *f* que cubre la nuca; capa, superficie *f;* espuma
scruple [′skrupəl] *s* escrúpulo
scrupulous [′skrupjələs] *adj* escrupuloso
scrutinize [′skrutɪˌnaɪz] *tr* escudriñar, escrutar
scruti‧ny [′skrutɪni] *s* (*pl* **-nies**) escudriñamiento, escrutinio
scuff [skʌf] *s* rascadura, desgaste *m* ‖ *tr* rascar, desgastar
scuffle [′skʌfəl] *s* lucha, sarracina ‖ *intr* forcejear, luchar
scull [skʌl] *s* espadilla ‖ *tr* impulsar con espadilla ‖ *intr* remar con espadilla
sculler‧y [′skʌləri] *s* (*pl* **-ies**) trascocina
scullery maid *s* fregona
scullion [′skʌljən] *s* pinche *m*
sculptor [′skʌlptər] *s* escultor *m*
sculptress [′skʌlptrɪs] *s* escultora
sculpture [′skʌlptʃər] *s* escultura ‖ *tr & intr* esculpir
scum [skʌm] *s* espuma, nata; (*on metals*) escoria; (fig) escoria, canalla, gente baja ‖ *v* (*pret & pp*

scummed; *ger* **scumming**) *tr & intr* espumar
scum‧my [′skʌmi] *adj* (*comp* **-mier;** *super* **-miest**) espumoso; (fig) vil, ruin
scurf [skʌrf] *s* (*shed by the skin*) caspa; (*shed by any surface*) costra
scurrilous [′skʌrɪləs] *adj* chocarrero, grosero, insolente, difamatorio
scur‧ry [′skʌri] *v* (*pret & pp* **-ried**) *intr* echar a correr, escabullirse; **to scurry around** menearse; **to scurry away** ir respailando
scur‧vy [′skʌrvi] *adj* (*comp* **-vier;** *super* **-viest**) despreciable, ruin, vil ‖ *s* escorbuto
scuttle [′skʌtəl] *s* (*bucket for coal*) cubo, balde *m;* (*trap door*) escotillón *m;* fuga, paso acelerado; (naut) escotilla ‖ *tr* barrenar, dar barreno a ‖ *intr* echar a correr
Scylla [′sɪlə] *s* Escila; **between Scylla and Charybdis** entre Escila y Caribdis
scythe [saɪð] *s* dalle *m,* guadaña
sea [si] *s* mar *m & f;* **at sea** en el mar; confuso, perplejo; **by the sea** a la orilla del mar; **to follow the sea** correr los mares, ser marinero; **to put to sea** hacerse a la mar
sea′board′ *adj* costanero, costero ‖ *s* costa del mar, litoral *m*
sea breeze *s* brisa de mar
sea′coast′ *s* costa marítima, litoral *m*
sea dog *s* (*seal*) foca; (coll) marinero viejo, lobo de mar
seafarer [′siˌfɛrər] *s* marinero; viajero por mar
sea′food′ *s* mariscos
seagoing [′siˌgoˌɪŋ] *adj* de alta mar
sea gull *s* gaviota
seal [sil] *s* (*raised design; stamp; mark*) sello; (*sea animal*) foca ‖ *tr* sellar; cerrar herméticamente; decidir irrevocablemente; (*with sealing wax*) lacrar
sea legs *spl* pie marino
sea level *s* nivel *m* del mar
sealing wax *s* lacre *m*
seal′skin′ *s* piel *f* de foca
seam [sim] *s* costura; (*edges left after making a seam*) metido; (mark, line) arruga; (*scar*) costurón *m;* grieta, juntura; (min) filón *m,* veta
sea‧man [′simən] *s* (*pl* **-men** [mən]) marinero; (nav) marino
sea mile *s* milla náutica
seamless [′simlɪs] *adj* inconsútil, sin costura
seamstress [′simstrɪs] *s* costurera; (*dressmaker's helper*) modistilla
seam‧y [′simi] *adj* (*comp* **-ier;** *super* **-iest**) lleno de costuras; tosco, burdo; vil, soez; miserable
séance [′se‧ɑns] *s* sesión de espiritistas
sea′plane′ *s* hidroavión *m,* hidroplano
sea′port′ *s* puerto de mar
sea power *s* potencia naval
sear [sɪr] *adj* seco, marchito; gastado, raído ‖ *s* chamusco, socarra ‖ *tr* chamuscar, socarrar; quemar; marchitar; cauterizar
search [sʌrtʃ] *s* busca; pesquisa, in-

dagación; (*frisking a person*) cacheo;
in search of en busca de ‖ *tr* averiguar, explorar; registrar ‖ *intr* buscar; **to search for** buscar; **to search
into** indagar, investigar

search'light' *s* reflector *m*, proyector *m*
search warrant *s* auto de registro domiciliario, orden *f* de allanamiento
sea'scape' *s* vista del mar; (*painting*)
marina
sea shell *s* concha marina
sea'shore' *s* costa, playa, ribera del mar
sea'sick' *adj* mareado
sea'sick'ness *s* mareo
sea'side' *s* orilla del mar, ribera del
mar, playa
season ['sizən] *s* (*one of four parts of
year*) estación; (*period of the year;
period marked by certain activities*)
temporada; (*opportune time; time of
maturity, of ripening*) sazón *f*; **in
season** en sazón; **in season and out
of season** en tiempo y a destiempo;
out of season fuera de sazón ‖ *tr*
condimentar, sazonar; curar (*la madera*); moderar, templar
seasonal ['sizənəl] *adj* estacional
seasoning ['sizənɪŋ] *s* aderezo, aliño,
condimento; (*of wood*) cura; (fig) sal
f, chiste *m*
season ticket *s* billete *m* de abono
seat [sit] *s* asiento; (*of trousers*) fondillos; morada; sitio, lugar *m*; (*e.g.,
of government*) sede *f*; (*in parliament*) escaño; (*e.g., of a war*) teatro;
(*e.g., of learning*) centro; (*of a saddle*) batalla; (*of human body*) nalgas; (theat) localidad ‖ *tr* sentar; tener asientos para; poner asiento a
(*una silla*); echar fondillos a (*pantalones*); arraigar, establecer; **to be
seated** estar sentado; **to seat oneself**
sentarse
seat belt *s* cinturón *m* de asiento
seat cover *s* funda de asiento, cubreasiento
SEATO ['sito] *s* (acronym) la O.T.
A.S.E.
sea wall *s* dique marítimo
sea'way' *s* ruta marítima; avance *m* de
un buque por mar; vía de agua interior para buques de alta mar; mar
gruesa
sea'weed' *s* alga marina; plantas ma-
rinas
sea wind *s* viento que sopla del mar
sea'wor'thy *adj* marinero, en condiciones de navegar
sec. *abbr* **secant, second, secondary,
secretary, section, sector**
secede [sɪ'sid] *intr* separarse, retirarse
secession [sɪ'sɛʃən] *s* secesión
seclude [sɪ'klud] *tr* recluir
secluded [sɪ'kludɪd] *adj* aislado, apartado, solitario
seclusion [sɪ'kluʒən] *s* reclusión, soledad
second ['sɛkənd] *adj* segundo; **to be
second to none** no tan bueno como
el que más, no tener segundo ‖ *adv*
en segundo lugar ‖ *s* segundo; artículo de segunda calidad; (*in dates*)

dos *m*; (*in a challenge*) padrino;
(aut) segunda (velocidad); (mus) segunda ‖ *tr* secundar; apoyar (*una
moción*)
secondar•y ['sɛkən,dɛri] *adj* secundario ‖ *s* (*pl* -ies) (elec) secundario
sec'ond-best' *adj* (el) mejor después del
primero
sec'ond-class' *adj* de segunda clase
second hand *s* segundero
sec'ond-hand' *adj* de segunda mano, de
ocasión
second-hand bookshop *s* librería de viejo
second lieutenant *s* alférez *m*, subteniente *m*
sec'ond-rate' *adj* de segundo orden; de
calidad inferior
second sight *s* doble vista
second wind *s* nuevo aliento
secre•cy ['sikrɪsi] *s* (*pl* -cies) secreto;
in secrecy en secreto
secret ['sikrɪt] *adj* & *s* secreto; **in
secret** en secreto
secretar•y ['sɛkrɪ,tɛri] *s* (*pl* -ies) secretario; (*desk*) secreter *m*, escritorio
secrete [sɪ'krit] *tr* encubrir, esconder;
(physiol) secretar
secretive [sɪ'kritɪv] *adj* callado, reservado
sect [sɛkt] *s* secta, comunión
sectarian [sɛk'tɛrɪ•ən] *adj* & *s* sectario
section ['sɛkʃən] *s* sección; (*of a country*) región; (*of a city*) barrio; (*of a
law*) artículo; (*department, bureau*)
negociado; (rr) tramo
secular ['sɛkjələr] *adj* secular, seglar ‖
s clérigo secular
secularism ['sɛkjələ,rɪzəm] *s* laicismo
secure [sɪ'kjur] *adj* seguro ‖ *tr* asegurar; conseguir, obtener
securi•ty [sɪ'kjurɪti] *s* (*pl* -ties) seguridad; (*person*) segurador *m;* **securities**
valores *mpl*, obligaciones, títulos
secy. o **sec'y.** *abbr* **secretary**
sedan [sɪ'dæn] *s* silla de manos; (aut)
sedán *m*
sedate [sɪ'det] *adj* sentado, sosegado
sedative ['sɛdətɪv] *adj* & *s* sedativo
sedentary ['sɛdən,tɛri] *adj* sedentario
sedge [sɛdʒ] *s* juncia
sediment ['sɛdɪmənt] *s* sedimento
sedition [sɪ'dɪʃən] *s* sedición
seditious [sɪ'dɪʃəs] *adj* sedicioso
seduce [sɪ'djus] o [sɪ'dus] *tr* seducir
seducer [sɪ'djusər] o [sɪ'dusər] *s* seductor *m*
seduction [sɪ'dʌkʃən] *s* seducción
seductive [sɪ'dʌktɪv] *adj* seductivo
sedulous ['sɛdjələs] *adj* cuidadoso, diligente
see [si] *s* (eccl) sede *f* ‖ *v* (*pret* saw
[sɔ]; *pp* seen [sin]) *tr* ver; **to see off**
ir a despedir; **to see through** llevar a
cabo; ayudar en un trance difícil ‖
intr ver; **see here!** ¡mire Vd.!; **to see
into** o **to see through** conocer el
juego de
seed [sid] *s* semilla, simiente *f;* **to go to
seed** dar semilla; echarse a perder ‖
tr sembrar; (*to remove the seeds
from*) despepitar ‖ *intr* sembrar; dejar caer semillas
seed'bed' *s* semillero

seedling ['sidlɪŋ] *s* planta de semilla; árbol *m* de pie

seed·y ['sidi] *adj* (*comp* **-ier; super -iest**) lleno de granos; (coll) andrajoso, raído

seeing ['si·ɪŋ] *adj* vidente ‖ *s* vista, visión ‖ *conj* visto que

Seeing Eye dog *s* perro-lazarillo

seek [sik] *v* (*pret & pp* **sought** [sɔt]) *tr* buscar; recorrer buscando; dirigirse a ‖ *intr* buscar; **to seek after** tratar de obtener; **to seek to** esforzarse por

seem [sim] *intr* parecer

seemingly ['simɪŋli] *adv* aparentemente, al parecer

seem·ly ['simli] *adj* (*comp* **-lier; super -liest**) decente, decoroso, correcto; bien parecido

seep [sip] *intr* escurrirse, rezumarse

seer [sɪr] *s* profeta *m*, vidente *m*

see'saw' *s* balancín *m*, columpio de tabla; (*motion*) vaivén *m* ‖ *intr* columpiarse; alternar; vacilar

seethe [sið] *intr* hervir

segment ['segmənt] *s* segmento

segregate ['segrɪ ˌget] *tr* segregar

segregationist [ˌsegrɪ'geʃənɪst] *s* segregacionista *mf*

Seine [sen] *s* Sena *m*

seismograph ['saɪzmə ˌgræf] o ['saɪzme ˌgraf] *s* sismógrafo

seismology [saɪz'malədʒi] *s* sismología

seize [siz] *tr* agarrar, asir, coger; atar, prender, sujetar; apoderarse de; comprender; (law) embargar, secuestrar; aprovecharse de (*una oportunidad*)

seizure ['siʒər] *s* prendimiento, prisión; captura, toma; (*of an illness*) ataque *m*; (law) embargo, secuestro

seldom ['seldəm] *adv* raramente, rara vez

select [sɪ'lekt] *adj* escogido, selecto ‖ *tr* seleccionar

selectee [sɪ ˌlek'ti] *s* (mil) quinto

selection [sɪ'lekʃən] *s* selección; trozo escogido; (*of goods for sale*) surtido

self [self] *adj* mismo ‖ *pron* sí mismo ‖ *s* (*pl* **selves** [selvz]) uno mismo; ser *m*; yo; **all by one's self** sin ayuda de nadie

self'-abuse' *s* abuso de sí mismo; masturbación

self'-addressed' envelope *s* sobre *m* con el nombre y dirección del remitente

self'-cen'tered *adj* egocéntrico

self'-con'scious *adj* cohibido, apocado, tímido

self'-con·trol' *s* dominio de sí mismo

self'-de·fense' *s* autodefensa; **in self-defense** en defensa propia

self'-de·ni'al *s* abnegación

self'-de·ter'mi·na'tion *s* autodeterminación

self'-dis'ci·pline *s* autodisciplina

self'-ed'u·cat'ed *adj* autodidacto

self'-em·ployed' *adj* que trabaja por su propia cuenta

self'-ev'i·dent *adj* patente, manifiesto

self'-ex·plan'a·tor'y *adj* que se explica por sí mismo

self'-gov'ernment *s* autogobierno, autonomía; dominio sobre sí mismo

self'-im·por'tant *adj* altivo, arrogante

self'-in·dul'gence *s* intemperancia, desenfreno

self'-in'terest *s* egoísmo, interés *m* personal

selfish ['selfɪʃ] *adj* egoísta

selfishness ['selfɪ/nɪs] *s* egoísmo

selfless ['selflɪs] *adj* desinteresado

self'-liq'ui·dat'ing *adj* autoamortizable

self'-love' *s* amor propio, egoísmo

self'-made' man *s* hijo de sus propias obras

self'-por'trait *s* autorretrato

self'-pos·sessed' *adj* dueño de sí mismo

self'-pres'er·va'tion *s* propia conservación

self'-re·li'ant *adj* confiado en sí mismo

self'-re·spect'ing *adj* lleno de dignidad, decoroso

self'-right'eous *adj* santurrón

self'-sac'ri·fice' *s* sacrificio de sí mismo

self'same' *adj* mismísimo

self'-sat'is·fied' *adj* pagado de sí mismo

self'-seek'ing *adj* egoísta ‖ *s* egoísmo

self'-ser'vice restaurant *s* restaurante *m* de libre servicio, restaurante de autoservicio

self'-start'er *s* arranque automático

self'-sup·port' *s* mantenimiento económico propio

self'-taught' *adj* autodidacto

self'-willed' *adj* obstinado, terco

self'-wind'ing clock *s* reloj *m* de cuerda automática, reloj de autocuerda

sell [sel] *v* (*pret & pp* **sold** [sold]) *tr* vender; **to sell out** realizar, saldar; (*to betray*) vender ‖ *intr* venderse, estar de venta; **to sell for** venderse a o en (*p.ej., cien pesetas*); **to sell off** bajar (*el mercado de valores*); **to sell out** venderlo todo, realizar

seller ['selər] *s* vendedor *m*

sell'out' *s* (slang) realización, saldo; (slang) traición

Seltzer water ['seltsər] *s* agua de seltz

selvage ['selvɪdʒ] *s* orillo, vendo

semantic [sɪ'mæntɪk] *adj* semántico ‖ **semantics** *s* semántica

semaphore ['semə ˌfor] *s* semáforo; (rr) disco de señales

semblance ['sembləns] *s* apariencia, imagen *f*, simulacro

semen ['simen] *s* semen *m*

semester [sɪ'mestər] *adj* semestral ‖ *s* semestre *m*

semester hour *s* hora semestral

sem'ico'lon *s* punto y coma

sem'iconduc'tor *s* semiconductor *m*

sem'icon'scious *adj* semiconsciente

sem'ifi'nal *adj & s* (sport) semifinal *f*

sem'ilearn'ed *adj* semiculto

sem'imonth'ly *adj* quincenal ‖ *s* (*pl* **-lies**) periódico quincenal

seminar ['semɪ ˌnɑr] o [ˌsemɪ'nɑr] *s* seminario

seminar·y ['semɪ ˌneri] *s* (*pl* **-ies**) seminario

sem'ipre'cious *adj* semiprecioso, fino

Semite ['semaɪt] o ['simaɪt] *s* semita *mf*

Semitic [sɪˈmɪtɪk] *adj* semítico ‖ *s* semita *mf*; (*language*) semita *m*

sem'itrail'er *s* semi-remolque *m*

sem'iweek'ly *adj* bisemanal ‖ *s* (*pl* -lies) periódico bisemanal

sem'iyear'ly *adj* semestral

Sen. o **sen.** *abbr* **Senate, Senator, Senior**

senate [ˈsɛnɪt] *s* senado

senator [ˈsɛnətər] *s* senador *m*

senatorship [ˈsɛnətərˌʃɪp] *s* senaduría

send [sɛnd] *v* (*pret & pp* **sent** [sɛnt]) *tr* enviar, mandar; expedir, remitir; lanzar (*una bola, flecha, etc.*); **to send back** devolver, reenviar; **to send packing** despedir con cajas destempladas ‖ *intr* (*telg*) transmitir; **to send for** enviar por, enviar a buscar

sender [ˈsɛndər] *s* remitente *mf*; (*telg*) transmisor *m*

send'-off' *s* (coll) despedida afectuosa

senile [ˈsinaɪl] o [ˈsɪnɪl] *adj* senil

senility [sɪˈnɪlɪti] *s* senilidad; (pathol) senilismo

senior [ˈsinjər] *adj* mayor, de mayor edad; viejo; del último año; padre, p.ej., **John Jones, Senior** Juan Jones, padre ‖ *s* mayor *m*; socio más antiguo; alumno del último año

senior citizens *spl* gente *f* de edad

seniority [sinˈjɔrɪti] o [sinˈjɑrɪti] *s* antigüedad; precedencia, prioridad

sensation [sɛnˈseʃən] *s* sensación

sense [sɛns] *s* sentido; **to make sense out of** comprender, explicarse ‖ *tr* intuir, sentir, sospechar; (coll) comprender

senseless [ˈsɛnslɪs] *adj* falto de sentido; desmayado; insensato, necio

sense of guilt *s* cargo de conciencia

sense organ *s* órgano sensorio

sensibili·ty [ˌsɛnsɪˈbɪlɪti] *s* (*pl* -ties) sensibilidad; **sensibilities** sentimientos delicados

sensible [ˈsɛnsɪbəl] *adj* cuerdo, sensato; perceptible, sensible

sensitive [ˈsɛnsɪtɪv] *adj* sensible; (*of the senses*) sensorio, sensitivo

sensitize [ˈsɛnsɪˌtaɪz] *tr* sensibilizar

sensory [ˈsɛnsəri] *adj* sensorio

sensual [ˈsɛnʃuəl] *adj* sensual, voluptuoso

sensuous [ˈsɛnʃuəs] *adj* sensual

sentence [ˈsɛntəns] *s* (gram) frase *f*, oración; (law) sentencia ‖ *tr* sentenciar, condenar

sentiment [ˈsɛntɪmənt] *s* sentimiento

sentimentali·ty [ˌsɛntɪmɛnˈtælɪti] *s* (*pl* -ties) sentimentalismo

sentinel [ˈsɛntɪnəl] *s* centinela *m* or *f*; **to stand sentinel** estar de centinela, hacer centinela

sen·try [ˈsɛntri] *s* (*pl* -tries) centinela *m* or *f*

sentry box *s* garita de centinela

separate [ˈsɛpərɪt] *adj* separado; suelto ‖ [ˈsɛpəˌret] *tr* separar ‖ *intr* separarse

Sephardic [sɪˈfɑrdɪk] *adj* sefardí, sefardita

Sephardim [sɪˈfɑrdɪm] *spl* sefardíes *mpl*

September [sɛpˈtɛmbər] *s* septiembre *m*

septet [sɛpˈtɛt] *s* septeto

septic [ˈsɛptɪk] *adj* séptico

sepulcher [ˈsɛpəlkər] *s* sepulcro

seq. *abbr* **sequentia** (Lat) **the following**

sequel [ˈsikwəl] *s* resultado, secuela; continuación

sequence [ˈsikwəns] *s* serie *f*, sucesión; (cards) secansa, escalera, runfla; (gram, mov & mus) secuencia

sequester [sɪˈkwɛstər] *tr* apartar, separar; (law) secuestrar

sequin [ˈsikwɪn] *s* lentejuela

ser·aph [ˈsɛrəf] *s* (*pl* -aphs o -aphim [əfɪm]) serafín *m*

Serb [sʌrb] *adj & s* servio

Serbia [ˈsʌrbɪ·ə] *s* Servia

Serbian [ˈsʌrbɪ·ən] *adj & s* servio

Serbo-Croatian [ˌsʌrbokroˈeʃən] *adj & s* servocroata *mf*

sere [sɪr] *adj* seco, marchito

serenade [ˌsɛrəˈned] *s* serenata ‖ *tr* dar serenata a ‖ *intr* dar serenatas

serene [sɪˈrin] *adj* sereno

serenity [sɪˈrɛnɪti] *s* serenidad

serf [sʌrf] *s* siervo de la gleba

serfdom [ˈsʌrfdəm] *s* servidumbre de la gleba

serge [sʌrdʒ] *s* sarga

sergeant [ˈsɑrdʒənt] *s* sargento

ser'geant-at-arms' *s* (*pl* **sergeants-at-arms**) oficial *m* de orden

sergeant major *s* (*pl* **sergeant majors**) sargento mayor

serial [ˈsɪrɪ·əl] *adj* serial; publicado por entregas ‖ *s* cuento o novela por entregas; (rad) serial *m*, serial radiado, emisión seriada

serially [ˈsɪrɪ·əli] *adv* en serie, por series; por entregas

serial number *s* número de serie

se·ries [ˈsɪriz] *s* (*pl* -ries) serie *f*

serious [ˈsɪrɪ·əs] *adj* (*e.g., person, face, matter*) serio; (*e.g., condition, illness*) grave

sermon [ˈsʌrmən] *s* sermón *m*

sermonize [ˈsʌrməˌnaɪz] *tr & intr* sermonear

serpent [ˈsʌrpənt] *s* serpiente *f*

se·rum [ˈsɪrəm] *s* (*pl* -rums o -ra [rə]) suero

servant [ˈsʌrvənt] *s* criado, sirviente *m*

servant girl *s* criada, sirvienta

servant problem *s* crisis *f* del servicio doméstico

serve [sʌrv] *s* (*in tennis*) saque *m*, servicio ‖ *tr* servir; (*to supply*) abastecer, proporcionar; cumplir (*una condena*); (*in tennis*) servir; **it serves me right** bien me lo merezco ‖ *intr* servir; **to serve as** servir de

service [ˈsʌrvɪs] *s* servicio; **at your service** para servir a Vd.; **the services** las fuerzas armadas ‖ *tr* instalar; mantener, reparar

serviceable [ˈsʌrvɪsəbəl] *adj* útil; duradero; cómodo

service·man [ˈsʌrvɪsˌmæn] *s* (*pl* -men [ˌmɛn]) reparador *m*, mecánico; militar *m*

service record *s* hoja de servicios

service station *s* estación de servicio, taller *m* de reparaciones

service stripe *s* galón *m* de servicio

servile ['sʌrvɪl] *adj* servil

servitude ['sʌrvɪ,tjud] o ['sʌrvɪ,tud] *s* servidumbre; trabajos forzados

sesame ['sɛsəmɪ] *s* sésamo; **open sesame** sésamo ábrete

session ['sɛʃən] *s* sesión; **to be in session** sesionar

set [sɛt] *adj* determinado, resuelto; inflexible, obstinado; fijo, firme; estudiado, meditado ‖ *s* (*of books, chairs, etc.*) juego; (*of gears*) tren *m;* (*of horses*) pareja; (*of diamonds*) aderezo; (*of tennis*) partida; (*of dishes*) servicio; (*of kitchen utensils*) batería; clase *f,* grupo; equipo; porte *m,* postura; (*of a garment*) caída, ajuste *m;* (*of glue*) endurecimiento; (*of cement*) fraguado; (*of artificial teeth*) caja; (*mov*) plató *m;* (*rad*) aparato; (*theat*) decoración ‖ *v* (*pret & pp* set; *ger* setting) *tr* asentar; colocar, poner; establecer, instalar; arreglar, preparar; adornar; apostar; poner (*un reloj*) en hora; (*in bridge*) reenvidar; poner, meter, pegar (*fuego*); fijar (*el precio*); engastar, montar (*una piedra preciosa*); encasar (*un hueso dislocado*); disponer (*los tipos*); triscar (*una sierra*); armar, colocar (*una trampa*); fijar (*el peinado*); poner (*la mesa*); dar (*un ejemplo*); **to set back** parar; poner obstáculos a; hacer retroceder; atrasar, retrasar (*el reloj*); **to set forth** exponer, dar a conocer; **to set one's heart on** tener la esperanza puesta en; **to set store by** dar mucha importancia a; **to set up shop** poner tienda; **to set up the drinks** (coll) convidar a beber ‖ *intr* ponerse (*el Sol, la Luna, etc.*); cuajarse (*un líquido*); endurecerse (*la cola*); fraguar (*el cemento, el yeso*); empollar (*una gallina*); caer, sentar (*una prenda de vestir*); **to set about** ponerse a; **to set out** ponerse en camino; emprender un negocio; **to set out to** ponerse a; **to set to work** poner manos a la obra; **to set upon** acometer, atacar

set′back′ *s* revés *m,* contrariedad

set′screw′ *s* tornillo de presión

settee [sɛ'ti] *s* sofá *m,* canapé *m*

setting ['sɛtɪŋ] *s* (*environment*) ambiente *m;* (*of a gem*) engaste *m,* montadura; (*of cement*) fraguado; (*e.g., of the sun*) puesta, ocaso; (*theat*) escena; (*theat*) puesta en escena, decoración

set′ting-up′ exercises *spl* ejercicios sin aparatos, gimnasia sueca

settle ['sɛtəl] *tr* asentar, colocar; asegurar, fijar; componer, conciliar; calmar, moderar; matar (*el polvo*); casar; poblar, colonizar; ajustar, arreglar (*cuentas*) ‖ *intr* asentarse (*un líquido, un edificio*); establecerse; componerse; calmarse, moderarse; solidificarse ‖ **to settle down to work** ponerse seriamente a trabajar;

to settle on escoger; fijar (*p.ej., una fecha*)

settlement ['sɛtəlmənt] *s* establecimiento; colonia, caserío; decisión; (*of accounts*) arreglo, ajuste *m;* traspaso; casa de beneficencia

settler ['sɛtlər] *s* fundador *m;* poblador *m;* colono; árbitro, conciliador *m*

set′up′ *s* porte *m,* postura; (*e.g., of the parts of a machine*) disposición; (coll) organización; (slang) invitación a beber

seven ['sɛvən] *adj & pron* siete ‖ *s* siete *m;* **seven o'clock** las siete

seven hundred *adj & pron* setecientos ‖ *s* setecientos *m*

seventeen ['sɛvən'tin] *adj, pron & s* diecisiete *m,* diez y siete

seventeenth ['sɛvən'tinθ] *adj & s* (*in a series*) decimoséptimo; (*part*) diecisieteavo ‖ *s* (*in dates*) diecisiete *m*

seventh ['sɛvənθ] *adj & s* séptimo ‖ *s* (*in dates*) siete *m*

seventieth ['sɛvəntɪ.ɪθ] *adj & s* (*in a series*) septuagésimo; (*part*) setentavo

seven·ty ['sɛvəntɪ] *adj & pron* setenta ‖ *s* (*pl* -ties) setenta *m*

sever ['sɛvər] *tr* desunir, separar; romper (*relaciones*) ‖ *intr* desunirse, separarse

several ['sɛvərəl] *adj* diversos, varios; distintos, respectivos ‖ *spl* varios; algunos

severance pay ['sɛvərəns] *s* indemnización por despido

severe [sɪ'vɪr] *adj* severo; (*weather*) riguroso; recio, violento; (*look*) adusto; (*pain*) agudo; (*illness*) grave

sew [so] *v* (*pret* sewed; *pp* sewed o sewn) *tr & intr* coser

sewage ['su·ɪdʒ] o ['sju·ɪdʒ] *s* agua de albañal, aguas cloacales

sewer ['su·ər] o ['sju·ər] *s* albañal *m,* cloaca, alcantarilla ‖ *tr* alcantarillar

sewerage ['su·ərɪdʒ] o ['sju·ərɪdʒ] *s* desagüe *m;* (*system*) alcantarillado; aguas de albañal

sewing basket ['so·ɪŋ] *s* cesta de costura

sewing machine *s* máquina de coser

sex [sɛks] *s* sexo; **the fair sex** el bello sexo; **the sterner sex** el sexo feo

sex appeal *s* atracción sexual; encanto femenino

sextant ['sɛkstənt] *s* sextante *m*

sextet [sɛks'tɛt] *s* sexteto

sexton ['sɛkstən] *s* sacristán *m*

sexual ['sɛkʃu·əl] *adj* sexual

sex·y ['sɛksi] *adj* (*comp* -ier; *super* -iest) (slang) sicalíptico, erótico

shab·by ['ʃæbi] *adj* (*comp* -bier; *super* -biest) gastado, raído, usado; andrajoso, desaseado; ruin, vil

shack [ʃæk] *s* casucha, choza

shackle ['ʃækəl] *s* grillete *m;* (*to tie an animal*) maniota; (fig) impedimento, traba; **shackles** cadenas, esposas, grillos ‖ *tr* poner grilletes a, poner esposas a; encadenar; (fig) trabar

shad [ʃæd] *s* sábalo, alosa

shade [ʃed] *s* sombra; (*of a lamp*)

pantalla; *(of a window)* cortina, estor *m,* visillo, cortina de resorte; *(for the eyes)* visera; *(hue; slight difference)* matiz *m;* **the shades** las tinieblas; *(of the dead)* las sombras ‖ *tr* sombrear; obscurecer; rebajar ligeramente *(el precio)*

shadow ['ʃædo] *s* sombra ‖ *tr* sombrear; simbolizar; acechar, espiar *(a una persona)*; **to shadow forth** representar vagamente, representar de un modo profético

shadowy ['ʃædo·i] *adj* sombroso; ligero, vago; imaginario; simbólico

shad·y ['ʃedi] *adj (comp* **-ier;** *super* **-iest)** sombrío, umbroso; (coll) sospechoso; (coll) de mala fama; *(story)* (coll) verde; **to keep shady** (slang) no dejarse ver

shaft [ʃæft] o [ʃɑft] *s* dardo, flecha, saeta; *(of an arrow; of a feather)* astil *m; (of light)* rayo; *(of a wagon)* vara alcándara, limonera; *(of a mine; of an elevator)* pozo; *(of a column)* fuste *m,* caña; *(of a flag)* asta; *(of a motor)* árbol *m;* *(to make fun of someone)* dardo

shag·gy ['ʃægi] *adj (comp* **-gier;** *super* **-giest)** hirsuto, peludo, veludo; lanudo; áspero

shake [ʃek] *s* sacudida; (coll) apretón *m* de manos; (slang) instante *m,* momento ‖ *v (pret* **shook** [ʃuk]; *pp* **shaken)** *tr* sacudir; agitar; apretar, estrechar *(la mano a uno)*; inquietar, perturbar; *(to get rid of)* (slang) dar esquinazo a, zafarse de ‖ *intr* sacudirse; agitarse; temblar; inquietarse, perturbarse; *(from cold)* tiritar; **shake!** (coll) ¡choque Vd. esos cinco!, ¡vengan esos cinco!

shake'down' *s* (slang) exacción, concusión

shake'-up' *s* profunda conmoción; cambio de personal, reorganización completa

shak·y ['ʃeki] *adj (comp* **-ier;** *super* **-iest)** trémulo, vacilante, movedizo; indigno de confianza

shall [ʃæl] *v (cond* **should** [ʃud]) *v aux* empléase para formar (1) el fut de ind, p.ej., **I shall do it** lo haré; (2) el fut perf de ind, p.ej., **I shall have done it** lo habré hecho; (3) el modo potencial, p.ej., **what shall I do?** ¿qué he de hacer?, ¿qué debo hacer?

shallow ['ʃælo] *adj* bajo, poco profundo; (fig) frívolo, superficial

sham [ʃæm] *adj* falso, fingido; postizo ‖ *s* fingimiento, falsificación, engaño; *(person)* (coll) farsante *mf* ‖ *v (pret & pp* **shammed;** *ger* **shamming)** *tr & intr* fingir

sham battle *s* simulacro de combate

shambles ['ʃæmbəlz] *s* destrucción, ruina; *(confusion, mess)* lío, revoltijo

shame [ʃem] *s* vergüenza; deshonra; **shame on you!** ¡qué vergüenza!; **what a shame!** ¡qué lástima! ‖ *tr* avergonzar; deshonrar

shameful ['ʃemfəl] *adj* vergonzoso

shameless ['ʃemlɪs] *adj* descarado, desvergonzado

shampoo [ʃæm'pu] *s* champú *m* ‖ *tr* lavar *(la cabeza)*; lavar la cabeza a

shamrock ['ʃæmrɑk] *s* trébol *m* irlandés

shanghai ['ʃæŋhaɪ] o [ʃæŋ'haɪ] *tr* embarcar emborrachando, embarcar narcotizando; llevarse con violencia, llevarse con engaño

shank [ʃæŋk] *s (of the leg)* caña, canilla; *(of an animal)* pierna; *(of a bird)* zanca; *(of an anchor)* caña; *(of the sole of a shoe)* enfranque *m;* astil *m,* caña, fuste *m;* extremidad, remate *m;* **to go** o **to ride on shank's mare** caminar en coche de San Francisco

shan·ty ['ʃænti] *s (pl* **-ties)** chabola, choza

shape [ʃep] *s* forma; **in bad shape** (coll) arruinado; (coll) muy enfermo; **out of shape** deformado; descompuesto ‖ *tr* formar, dar forma a; amoldar ‖ *intr* formarse; **to shape up** tomar forma; desarrollarse bien

shapeless ['ʃeplɪs] *adj* informe

shape·ly ['ʃepli] *adj (comp* **-lier;** *super* **-liest)** bien formado, esbelto

share [ʃer] *s* parte *f,* porción; *(of stock in a company)* acción; **to go shares** ir a la parte ‖ *tr (to enjoy jointly)* compartir; *(to apportion)* repartir ‖ *intr* participar, tener parte

share'hold'er *s* accionista *mf*

shark [ʃɑrk] *s* tiburón *m; (swindler)* estafador *m;* (slang) experto, perito

sharp [ʃɑrp] *adj* afilado, agudo; anguloso; *(curve, slope, etc.)* fuerte, pronunciado; *(photograph)* nítido; *(hearing)* fino; *(step, gait)* rápido; atento, despierto; picante, mordaz; listo, vivo; (mus) sostenido; (slang) elegante; **sharp features** facciones bien marcadas ‖ *adv* agudamente; en punto, p.ej., **at four o'clock sharp** a las cuatro en punto ‖ *s* (mus) sostenido

sharpen ['ʃɑrpən] *tr* aguzar; sacar punta a *(un lápiz)* ‖ *intr* afilarse

sharper ['ʃɑrpər] *s* fullero, jugador *m* de ventaja

sharp'shoot'er *s* tirador certero; (mil) tirador distinguido

shatter ['ʃætər] *tr* hacer astillas, romper de un golpe; quebrantar *(la salud)*; destruir, destrozar; agitar, perturbar ‖ *intr* hacerse pedazos, romperse

shat'ter-proof' *adj* inastillable

shave [ʃev] *s* afeitado; rebanada delgada; **to have a close shave** (coll) escapar en una tabla ‖ *tr* afeitar *(la cara)*; raer, raspar; *(to graze; to cut close)* rozar; *(to slice thin)* rebanar; (carp) cepillar ‖ *intr* afeitarse

shaving ['ʃevɪŋ] *adj* de afeitar, para afeitar, p.ej., **shaving soap** jabón *m* de o para afeitar ‖ *s* afeitado; **shavings** acepilladuras, virutas

shawl [ʃɔl] *s* chal *m,* mantón *m*

she [ʃi] *pron pers (pl* **they)** ella ‖ *s (pl* **shes)** hembra

sheaf [ʃif] *s (pl* **sheaves** [ʃivz]) gavilla; *(of paper)* atado

se
sh

shear [ʃɪr] *s* hoja de la tijera; **shears** tijeras grandes; (*to cut metal*) cizallas || *v* (*pret* **sheared**; *pp* **sheared** or **shorn** [ʃorn]) *tr* esquilar, trasquilar (*las ovejas*); cizallar; quitar cortando; tundir (*paño*)

sheath [ʃiθ] *s* (**sheaths** [ʃiðz]) envoltura, estuche *m*, funda; (*for a sword*) funda, vaina

sheathe [ʃið] *tr* enfundar, enviainar

shed [ʃed] *s* cobertizo; (*line from which water flows in two directions*) vertiente *m* & *f* || *v* (*pret* & *pp* **shed**; *ger* **shedding**) *tr* derramar, verter (*p.ej., sangre*); dar, echar, esparcir (*luz*); mudar (*la pluma, el pellejo*)

sheen [ʃin] *s* brillo, lustre *m*; (*of pressed cloth*) prensado

sheep [ʃip] *s* (*pl* **sheep**) carnero; (*female*) oveja; tonto; **to make sheep's eyes (at)** mirar con ojos de carnero degollado

sheep dog *s* perro ovejero, perro de pastor

sheep'fold' *s* aprisco, redil *m*

sheepish [ʃipɪʃ] *adj* avergonzado, corrido; tímido, tonto

sheep'skin' *s* (*undressed*) zalea; (*dressed*) badana; (*coll*) diploma *m*

sheer [ʃɪr] *adj* delgado, fino, ligero; casi transparente; escarpado; puro, sin mezcla; completo || *intr* desviarse

sheet [ʃit] *s* (*e.g., for the bed*) sábana; (*of paper*) hoja; (*of metal*) hoja, lámina; (*of water*) extensión; hoja impresa; periódico; (*naut*) escota

sheet lightning *s* fucilazo

sheet metal *s* metal laminado

sheet music *s* música en hojas sueltas

sheik [ʃik] *s* jeque *m*; (*great lover*) (slang) sultán *m*

shelf [ʃelf] *s* (*pl* **shelves** [ʃelvz]) estante *m*, anaquel *m*; bajío, banco de arena; **on the shelf** arrinconado, desechado, olvidado

shell [ʃel] *s* (*of an egg, nut, etc.*) cáscara; (*of a crustacean*) caparazón *m*, concha; (*of a vegetable*) vaina; (*of a cartridge*) cápsula; (*of a boiler*) cuerpo; armazón *f*, esqueleto; bomba, proyectil *m*; (*long, narrow racing boat*) (sport) yola || *tr* descascarar; desgranar, desvainar (*legumbres*); bombardear, cañonear; **to shell out** (coll) entregar (*dinero*)

shel·lac [ʃə'læk] *s* laca, goma laca || *v* (*pret* & *pp* **-lacked**; *ger* **-lacking**) *tr* barnizar con goma laca; (slang) azotar, zurrar; (slang) derrotar

shell'fish' *s* marisco, mariscos

shell hole *s* (mil) embudo

shell shock *s* neurosis *f* de guerra

shelter [ʃeltər] *s* abrigo, asilo, amparo, refugio; **to take shelter** abrigarse, refugiarse || *tr* abrigar, amparar, proteger

shelve [ʃelv] *tr* poner sobre un estante; proveer de estantes; arrinconar, dejar a un lado; diferir indefinidamente

shepherd [ʃepərd] *s* pastor *m* || *tr* pastorear (*a las ovejas o los fieles*)

shepherd dog *s* perro ovejero, perro de pastor

shepherdess [ʃepərdɪs] *s* pastora

sherbet [ʃɑrbət] *s* sorbete *m*

shereef [ʃeʾrif] *s* jerife *m*

sheriff [ʃerɪf] *s* alguacil *m* mayor

sher·ry [ʃeri] *s* (*pl* **-ries**) jerez *m*, vino de Jerez

shield [ʃild] *s* escudo; (*for armpit*) sobaquera; (elec) blindaje *m* || *tr* amparar, defender, escudar; (elec) blindar

shift [ʃɪft] *s* cambio; (*order of work or other activity*) turno; (*group of workmen*) tanda; maña, subterfugio || *tr* cambiar; deshacerse de; echar (*la culpa*); dar || *intr* cambiar de (*marcha*) || *intr* cambiar, cambiar de puesto; mañear; (naut) correrse (*el lastre*); (naut) maniobrar; **to shift for oneself** ayudarse, ingeniarse

shift key *s* tecla de cambio, palanca de mayúsculas

shiftless [ʃɪftlɪs] *adj* desidioso, perezoso

shift·y [ʃɪfti] *adj* (*comp* **-ier**; *super* **-iest**) ingenioso, mañoso; evasivo, tramoyista; (*glance*) huyente

shilling [ʃɪlɪŋ] *s* chelín *m*

shimmer [ʃɪmər] *s* luz trémula || *intr* rielar

shin [ʃɪn] *s* espinilla || *v* (*pret* & *pp* **shinned**; *ger* **shinning**) *tr* & *intr* trepar

shin'bone' *s* espinilla

shine [ʃaɪn] *s* brillo, luz *f*; bruñido, lustre *m*; buen tiempo; (*on shoes*) (coll) lustre *m*; **to take a shine to** (slang) tomar simpatía a || *v* (*pret* & *pp* **shined**) *tr* pulir, lustrar; (coll) embolar, limpiar (*el calzado*) || *v* (*pret* & *pp* **shone** [ʃon]) *intr* brillar, lucir, resplandecer; hacer sol, hacer buen tiempo; (*to be distinguished, to stand out*) (fig) brillar, lucir

shingle [ʃɪŋgəl] *s* ripia, teja de madera; tejamaní *m* (Am); pelo a la garçonne; (coll) letrero de oficina; **shingles** (pathol) zona; **to hang out one's shingle** (coll) abrir una oficina; (coll) abrir un consultorio médico || *tr* cubrir con ripias; cortar (*el pelo*) a la garçonne

shining [ʃaɪnɪŋ] *adj* brillante, luciente

shin·y [ʃaɪni] *adj* (*comp* **-ier**; *super* **-iest**) brillante, lustroso; (*paper*) glaseado; (*from much wear*) brilloso

ship [ʃɪp] *s* nave *f*, buque *m*, barco, navío; (*steamer*) vapor *m*; aeronave *f* || *v* (*pret* & *pp* **shipped**; *ger* **shipping**) *tr* embarcar; enviar, remitir, remesar; armar (*los remos*); embarcar (*agua*) || *intr* embarcarse

ship'board' *s* bordo; **on shipboard** a bordo

ship'build'er *s* arquitecto naval, constructor *m* de buques

ship'build'ing *s* arquitectura naval, construcción de buques

ship'mate' *s* camarada *m* de a bordo

shipment [ʃɪpmənt] *s* embarque *m* (*por agua*); envío, expedición, remesa

shipper [ˈʃɪpər] s embarcador m; expedidor m, remitente mf
shipping memo [ˈʃɪpɪŋ] s nota de remisión
ship'shape' adj & adv en buen orden
ship'side' adj & adv al costado del buque ‖ s zona de embarque y desembarque; muelle m
ship's papers spl documentación del buque
ship's time s hora local del buque
ship'wreck' s naufragio; barco náufrago ‖ tr hacer naufragar ‖ intr naufragar
ship'yard' s astillero, varadero
shirk [ʃʌrk] tr evitar (el trabajo); faltar a (un deber) ‖ intr escurrir el hombro
shirred eggs [ʃʌrd] spl huevos al plato
shirt [ʃʌrt] s camisa; **to keep one's shirt on** (slang) quedarse sereno; **to lose one's shirt** (slang) perder hasta la camisa
shirt'band' s cuello de camisa
shirt front s pechera de camisa, camisolín m
shirt sleeve s manga de camisa; **in shirt sleeves** en mangas de camisa
shirt'tail' s faldón m, pañal m
shirt'waist' s blusa (de mujer)
shiver [ˈʃɪvər] s estremecimiento, tiritón m ‖ intr estremecerse, tiritar
shoal [ʃol] s bajío, banco de arena
shock [ʃak] s (sudden and violent blow or encounter) choque m; (sudden agitation of mind or emotions) sobresalto; temblor m de tierra; (of hair) greña; (agr) tresnal m; (elec) sacudida; (med) choque m; (profound depression) (pathol) choque m; (coll) parálisis f ‖ tr chocar; sobresaltar; dar una sacudida eléctrica a; chocar, escandalizar
shock absorber [æbˈsɔrbər] s amortiguador m
shocking [ˈʃakɪŋ] adj chocante, escandalizador
shock troops spl tropas de asalto
shod·dy [ˈʃadi] adj (comp -dier; super -diest) falso, de imitación
shoe [ʃu] s (which goes above the ankle) bota, botina; (which does not go above the ankle) zapato; (of a tire) cubierta; **to put on one's shoes** calzarse ‖ v (pret & pp shod [ʃad]) tr calzar; herrar (un caballo)
shoe'black' s limpiabotas m
shoe'horn' s calzador m
shoe'lace' s cordón m de zapato, lazo de zapato
shoe'mak'er s zapatero; zapatero remendón
shoe mender [ˈmendər] s zapatero remendón
shoe polish s betún m, bola
shoe'shine' s brillo, lustre m; limpiabotas m
shoe store s zapatería
shoe'string' s cordón m de zapato, lazo de zapato; **on a shoestring** con muy poco dinero
shoe tree s horma
shoo [ʃu] tr & intr oxear

shoot [ʃut] s (sprout, twig) renuevo, vástago; conducto inclinado; (for grain, sand, etc.) tolva; tiro al blanco, certamen m de tiradores; (hunting party) partida de caza ‖ v (pret & pp shot [ʃat]) tr tirar, disparar (un arma); herir o matar con arma; (to execute with a discharge of rifles) fusilar; fotografiar; (to take a moving picture of) rodar; echar (los dados); medir la altura de (p.ej., el Sol); **to shoot down** derribar (un avión); **to shoot up** (slang) destrozar echando balas a diestra y siniestra ‖ intr tirar; nacer, brotar; lanzarse, precipitarse, moverse rápidamente; punzar (un dolor, una llaga); **to shoot at** tirar a; (to strive for) (coll) poner el tiro en
shooting gallery s galería de tiro al blanco
shooting match s certamen m de tiro al blanco; (slang) conjunto, totalidad
shooting star s estrella fugaz, estrella filante
shop [ʃap] s (store) tienda; (workshop) taller m; **to talk shop** hablar de su oficio, hablar del propio trabajo (fuera de tiempo) ‖ v (pret & pp shopped; ger shopping) intr ir de compras, ir de tiendas; **to go shopping** ir de compras, ir de tiendas; **to send shopping** mandar a la compra; **to shop around** ir de tienda en tienda buscando gangas
shop'girl' s muchacha de tienda
shop'keep'er s tendero
shoplifter [ˈʃap‚lɪftər] s mechera, ratero de tiendas
shopper [ˈʃapər] s comprador m
shopping center s centro comercial (grupo de establecimientos minoristas, con aparcamiento)
shopping district s barrio comercial
shop'win'dow s escaparate m
shop'work' s trabajo de taller
shop'worn' adj desgastado con el trajín de la tienda
shore [ʃor] s orilla, ribera; costa, playa; **shores** (poet) clima m, regiór ‖ tr acodalar, apuntalar
shore dinner s comida de pescado y mariscos
shore leave s (nav) permiso para ir a tierra
shore line s línea de la playa; línea de buques costeros
shore patrol s (nav) patrulla en tierra
short [ʃɔrt] adj (in space, time, and quantity) corto; (in time) breve; (in stature) bajo; (fig) corto, sucinto; (fig) brusco, seco; **in a short time** dentro de poco; **in short** en fin; **on short notice** con poco tiempo de aviso; **to be short of** estar escaso de; **short of breath** corto de resuello ‖ adv brevemente; bruscamente; (without possessing the stock sold) al descubierto, p.ej., **to sell short** vender al descubierto; **to run short of** acabársele a uno, p.ej., **I am running short of gasoline** se me acaba la

sh
sh

gasolina; **to stop short** parar de repente ‖ s (elec) cortocircuito; (mov) cortometraje m; **shorts** calzones cortos, calzoncillos ‖ tr (elec) poner en cortocircuito ‖ intr (elec) ponerse en cortocircuito

shortage ['ʃɔrtɪdʒ] s carestía, escasez f, falta; déficit m; (from pilfering) substracción

short'cake' s torta de frutas; torta quebradiza

short'change' tr (coll) no devolver la vuelta debida a

short circuit s (elec) cortocircuito

short'cir'cuit tr (elec) cortocircuitar ‖ intr (elec) cortocircuitarse

short'com'ing s falta, defecto, desperfecto

short cut s atajo; (method) remedia-vagos m

shorten ['ʃɔrtən] tr acortar, abreviar ‖ intr acortarse, abreviarse

short'hand' adj taquigráfico ‖ s taquigrafía; **to take shorthand** taquigrafiar

short-lived ['ʃɔrt'laɪvd] o ['ʃɔrt'lɪvd] adj de breve vida, de breve duración

shortly ['ʃɔrtli] adv en breve, luego; descortésmente; **shortly after** poco tiempo después (de)

short'-range' adj de poco alcance

short sale s (coll) venta al descubierto

short-sighted ['ʃɔrt'saɪtɪd] adj miope; (fig) falto de perspicacia

short'stop' s (baseball) medio; guarda-bosque m, torpedero (Am)

short story s cuento

short-tempered ['ʃɔrt'tempərd] adj de mal genio

short'-term' adj a corto plazo

shot [ʃɑt] s tiro, disparo; (hit or wound made with a bullet) balazo; (distance) alcance m; (in certain games) jugada, tirada, golpe m; (of a rocket into space) lanzamiento; conjetura, tentativa; fotografía, instantánea; (small pellets of lead) perdigones mpl; munición; (marksman) tiro; (heavy metal ball) (sport) pesa; (hypodermic injection) (slang) jeringazo; (drink of liquor) (slang) trago; **not by a long shot** ni con mucho, ni por pienso; **to start like a shot** salir disparado

shot'gun' s escopeta

shot'-put' s (sport) tiro de la pesa

should [ʃʊd] v aux empléase para formar (1) el pres de cond, p.ej., **if I should wait for him, I should miss the train** si yo le esperase, perdería el tren; (2) el perf de cond, p.ej., **if I had waited for him, I should have missed the train** si yo le hubiese esperado, habría perdido el tren; y (3) el modo potencial, p.ej., **he should go at once** debiera salir en seguida; **he should have gone at once** debiera haber salido en seguida

shoulder ['ʃoldər] s hombro; (of slaughtered animal) brazuelo; (of a garment) hombrera; **across the shoulder** en bandolera; **to put one's shoulders to the wheel** arrimar el

hombro, echar el pecho al agua; **to turn a cold shoulder to** volver las espaldas a ‖ tr cargar sobre las espaldas; tomar sobre sí, hacerse responsable de; empujar con el hombro para abrirse paso

shoulder blade s escápula, omóplato

shoulder strap s (of underwear) presilla; (mil) charretera

shout [ʃaut] s grito, voz f ‖ tr gritar, vocear; **to shout down** hacer callar a gritos ‖ intr gritar, dar voces

shove [ʃʌv] s empujón m ‖ tr empujar ‖ intr dar empujones, avanzar a empujones; **to shove off** alejarse de la costa; (slang) ponerse en marcha, salir

shov-el ['ʃʌvəl] s pala ‖ v (pret & pp -eled o -elled; ger -eling o -elling) tr traspalar; espalar (p.ej., la nieve) ‖ intr trabajar con pala

show [ʃo] s exhibición, exposición, muestra; espectáculo; (in the theater) función; (each performance of a play or movie) sesión; demostración, prueba; indicación, señal f, signo; apariencia; (e.g., of confidence) alarde m; (coll) ocasión, oportunidad; ostentación; espectáculo ridículo, hazmerreír m; **to make a show of** hacer gala de; **to steal the show from** robar la obra a (otro actor) ‖ tr mostrar, enseñar; demostrar, probar; poner, proyectar (un film); (e.g., to the door) acompañar; **to show up** (coll) desenmascarar ‖ intr mostrarse, aparecer, asomar; salir (p.ej., las enaguas); **to show off** fachendear; **to show through** clarearse, transparentarse; **to show up** (coll) presentarse, dejarse ver

show bill s cartel m

show business s comercio de los espectáculos

show'case' s vitrina (de exposición)

show'down' s cartas boca arriba; (coll) revelación forzosa, arreglo terminante

shower ['ʃau·ər] s (sudden fall of rain) aguacero, chaparrón m; (shower bath) ducha; (e.g., of bullets) rociada; despedida de soltera ‖ tr regar; **to shower with** colmar de ‖ intr llover

shower bath s ducha, baño de ducha

show girl s (theat) corista f, conjuntista f

show-man ['ʃomən] s (pl -men [mən]) empresario de teatro, empresario de circo

show'-off' s (coll) pinturero

show'piece' s objeto de arte sobresaliente

show'place' s sitio o edificio que se exhibe por su belleza o lujo

show'room' s sala de muestras, sala de exhibición

show window s escaparate m de tienda

show-y ['ʃo·i] adj (comp -ier; super -iest) aparatoso, cursi, ostentoso

shrapnel ['ʃræpnəl] s granada de metralla

shred [ʃred] s jirón m, tira, triza; fragmento, pizca; **to tear to shreds** hacer trizas ‖ v (pret & pp **shredded** o **shred;** ger **shredding**) tr desmenuzar, hacer trizas; deshilar (carne)

shrew [ʃru] s (nagging woman) arpía, fierecilla; (animal) musaraña

shrewd [ʃrud] adj astuto; despierto; listo

shriek [ʃrik] s chillido, grito agudo; risotada chillona ‖ intr chillar

shrill [ʃrɪl] adj agudo, chillón

shrimp [ʃrɪmp] s camarón m; (little insignificant person) renacuajo

shrine [ʃraɪn] s relicario; sepulcro de santo; lugar sagrado

shrink [ʃrɪŋk] v (pret **shrank** [ʃræŋk] o **shrunk** [ʃrʌŋk]; pp **shrunk** o **shrunken**) tr contraer, encoger ‖ intr contraerse, encogerse; moverse hacia atrás; rehuirse, retirarse

shrinkage [ˈʃrɪŋkɪdʒ] s contracción, encogimiento; disminución, reducción; merma, pérdida

shriv·el [ˈʃrɪvəl] v (pret & pp **-eled** o **-elled;** ger **-eling** o **-elling**) tr arrugar, marchitar, fruncir ‖ intr arrugarse, marchitarse, fruncirse; **to shrivel up** avellanarse

shroud [ʃraʊd] s mortaja, sudario; cubierta, velo ‖ tr amortajar; cubrir, velar

Shrove Tuesday [ʃrov] s martes m de carnaval

shrub [ʃrʌb] s arbusto

shrubber·y [ˈʃrʌbəri] s (pl **-ies**) arbustos; plantío de arbustos

shrug [ʃrʌg] s encogimiento de hombros ‖ v (pret & pp **shrugged;** ger **shrugging**) tr contraer; **to shrug one's shoulders** encogerse de hombros ‖ intr encogerse de hombros

shudder [ˈʃʌdər] s estremecimiento ‖ intr estremecerse

shuffle [ˈʃʌfəl] s (of cards) barajadura; turno de barajar; (of feet) arrastramiento; evasiva; recomposición ‖ tr barajar (naipes); arrastrar (los pies); mezclar, revolver ‖ intr barajar; caminar arrastrando los pies; bailar arrastrando los pies; moverse rápidamente de un lado a otro; **to shuffle along** ir arrastrando los pies; ir tirando; **to shuffle off** irse arrastrando los pies

shuf·fle·board [ˈʃʌfəlˌbord] s juego de tejo

shun [ʃʌn] v (pret & pp **shunned;** ger **shunning**) tr esquivar, evitar, rehuir

shunt [ʃʌnt] tr apartar, desviar; (elec) poner en derivación; (rr) desviar

shut [ʃʌt] adj cerrado ‖ v (pret & pp **shut;** ger **shutting**) tr cerrar; **to shut in** encerrar; **to shut off** cortar (electricidad, gas, etc.); **to shut up** cerrar bien; aprisionar; (coll) hacer callar ‖ intr cerrarse; **to shut up** (coll) callarse la boca

shut'down' s cierre m, paro

shutter [ˈʃʌtər] s celosía, persiana; (outside a window) contraventana; (outside a show window) cierre metálico; (phot) obturador m

shuttle [ˈʃʌtəl] s (used in sewing) lan-

zadera ‖ intr hacer viajes cortos de ida y vuelta

shuttle train s tren m lanzadera

shy [ʃaɪ] adj (comp **shyer** o **shier;** super **shyest** o **shiest**) arisco, recatado, tímido; (fearful) asustadizo; escaso, pobre; **I am shy a dollar** me falta un dólar ‖ v (pret & pp **shied**) intr esquivarse, hacerse a un lado; espantarse, respingar; **to shy away** alejarse asustado

shyster [ˈʃaɪstər] s (coll) abogado trampista

Sia·mese [ˌsaɪ·əˈmiz] adj siamés ‖ s (pl **-mese**) siamés m

Siamese twins spl hermanos siameses

Siberian [saɪˈbɪrɪ·ən] adj & s siberiano

sibilant [ˈsɪbɪlənt] adj & s sibilante f

sibyl [ˈsɪbɪl] s sibila

Sicilian [sɪˈsɪljən] adj & s siciliano

Sicily [ˈsɪsɪli] s Sicilia

sick [sɪk] adj enfermo, malo; nauseado; **sick and tired of** (coll) harto y cansado de; **sick at heart** afligido de corazón; **to be sick at one's stomach** tener náuseas; **to take sick** caer enfermo ‖ tr azuzar (a un perro)

sick'bed' s lecho de enfermo

sicken [ˈsɪkən] tr & intr enfermar

sickening [ˈsɪkənɪŋ] adj repelente, repugnante, nauseabundo

sick headache s jaqueca con náuseas

sickle [ˈsɪkəl] s hoz f

sick leave s licencia por enfermedad

sick·ly [ˈsɪkli] adj (comp **-lier;** super **-liest**) enfermizo

sickness [ˈsɪknɪs] s enfermedad; náusea

side [saɪd] adj lateral ‖ s lado; (of a solid; of a phonograph record) cara; (of a hill) falda; (of human body, of a ship) costado; facción, partido ‖ intr tomar partido; **to side with** tomar el partido de

side arms spl armas de cinto

side'board' s aparador m

side'burns' spl patillas

side dish s plato de entrada

side door s puerta lateral; puerta excusada

side effect s efecto secundario perjudicial (de ciertos medicamentos)

side glance s mirada de soslayo

side issue s cuestión secundaria

side line s negocio accesorio; **on the side lines** sin tomar parte

sidereal [saɪˈdɪrɪ·əl] adj sidéreo

side'sad'dle adv a asentadillas, a mujeriegas

side show s función secundaria, espectáculo de atracciones

side'split'ting adj desternillante

side'track' s apartadero, desviadero, vía muerta ‖ tr desviar (un tren); echar a un lado

side view s perfil m, vista de lado

side'walk' s acera; banqueta (Guat, Mex); vereda (Arg, Cuba, Perú)

sidewalk café s terraza, café m en la acera

sideward [ˈsaɪdwərd] adj oblicuo, sesgado ‖ adv de lado, hacia un lado

sh
si

side'ways' adj oblicuo, sesgado ‖ adv de lado, hacia un lado; al través

side whiskers spl patillas

side'wise' adj oblicuo, sesgado ‖ adv de lado, hacia un lado; al través

siding ['saɪdɪŋ] s (rr) apartadero, desviadero, vía muerta

sidle ['saɪdəl] intr ir de lado; **to sidle up to** acercarse de lado a (una persona) para no ser visto

siege [sidʒ] s sitio, cerco; **to lay siege to** poner sitio o cerco a; (fig) asediar (p.ej., el corazón de una mujer)

sieve [sɪv] s cedazo, tamiz m ‖ tr cerner, tamizar

sift [sɪft] tr cerner, cribar; escudriñar, examinar; (to screen, separate) entresacar; (to scatter with or as with a sieve) empolvar

sigh [saɪ] s suspiro; **to breathe a sigh of relief** respirar ‖ tr decir con suspiros ‖ intr suspirar; **to sigh for** suspirar por

sight [saɪt] s vista; cosa digna de verse; (of a firearm, telescope, etc.) mira; (coll) gran cantidad, montón m; (coll) horror m, atrocidad; **at first sight** a primera vista; **at sight** a primera vista; (translation) a libro abierto; (com) a la vista; **out of sight** fuera del alcance de la vista; (prices) por las nubes; **to catch sight of** alcanzar a ver; **to know by sight** conocer de vista; **to not be able to stand the sight of** no poder ver ni en pintura; **to see the sights** visitar los puntos de interés ‖ tr avistar, alcanzar con la vista ‖ intr apuntar con una mira; (arti & surv) visar

sight draft s (com) giro a la vista, letra a la vista

sight'-read' v (pret & pp **-read** [,rɛd]) tr leer a libro abierto; (mus) ejecutar a la primera lectura ‖ intr leer a libro abierto; (mus) repentizar

sight reader s lector m a libro abierto; (mus) repentista mf

sight'see'ing s turismo, visita de puntos de interés; **to go sightseeing** ir a ver los puntos de interés

sightseer ['saɪt,si·ər] s turista mf, excursionista mf

sign [saɪn] s signo; señal f, marca; huella, vestigio; letrero, muestra; **to show signs of** dar muestras de, tener trazas de; **to make the sign of the cross** hacerse la señal de la cruz ‖ tr firmar; contratar; ceder, traspasar ‖ intr firmar; **to sign off** (rad) terminar la transmisión; **to sign up** (coll) firmar el contrato

sig·nal ['sɪgnəl] adj señalado, notable ‖ s señal f ‖ v (pret & pp **-naled** o **-nalled**; ger **-naling** o **-nalling**) tr señalar ‖ intr hacer señales

signal tower s (rr) garita de señales

signato·ry ['sɪgnɪ,tori] s (pl **-ries**) firmante mf

signature ['sɪgnətfər] s firma; (mus & typ) signatura

sign'board' s cartelón m, letrero

signer ['saɪnər] s firmante mf

signet ring ['sɪgnɪt] s anillo sigilar, sortija de sello

signi·fy ['sɪgnɪ,faɪ] v (pret & pp **-fied**) tr significar

sign'post' s hito, poste m de guía

silence ['saɪləns] s silencio ‖ tr acallar; (mil) apagar el fuego de; (mil) apagar (el fuego del enemigo)

silent ['saɪlənt] adj silencioso

silent movie s cine mudo

silhouette [,sɪlu'ɛt] s silueta ‖ tr siluetear

silk [sɪlk] adj sedeño ‖ s seda; **to hit the silk** (slang) lanzarse en paracaídas

silken ['sɪlkən] adj sedeño

silk hat s sombrero de copa

silk'-stock'ing adj aristocrático ‖ s aristócrata mf

silk'worm' s gusano de seda

silk·y ['sɪlki] adj (comp **-ier**; super **-iest**) sedoso, asedado

sill [sɪl] s travesaño; (of a door) umbral m; (of a window) antepecho

sil·ly ['sɪli] adj (comp **-lier**; super **-liest**) necio, tonto

si·lo ['saɪlo] s (pl **-los**) silo ‖ tr asilar

silt [sɪlt] s cieno, sedimento

silver ['sɪlvər] adj de plata; (voice) argentino; elocuente ‖ s plata ‖ tr platear; azogar (un espejo)

sil'ver·fish' s (ent) pez m de plata

silver foil s hoja de plata

silver lining s aspecto agradable de una condición desgraciada o triste

silver plate s vajilla de plata

silver screen s pantalla de plata

sil'ver·smith' s platero, orfebre m

silver spoon s riqueza heredada; **to be born with a silver spoon in one's mouth** nacer de pie

sil'ver·tongue' s (coll) pico de oro

sil'ver·ware' s plata, vajilla de plata

similar ['sɪmɪlər] adj similar, semejante, análogo

simile ['sɪmɪli] s (rhet) símil m

simmer ['sɪmər] tr cocer a fuego lento ‖ intr cocer a fuego lento; (coll) estar a punto de estallar; **to simmer down** (coll) tranquilizarse lentamente

simoon [sɪ'mun] s simún m

simper ['sɪmpər] s sonrisa boba ‖ intr sonreír bobamente

simple ['sɪmpəl] adj simple, sencillo ‖ s (medicinal plant) simple m

simple-minded ['sɪmpəl'maɪndɪd] adj candoroso, ingenuo; idiota, mentecato; estúpido, ignorante

simple substance s (chem) cuerpo simple

simpleton ['sɪmpəltən] s simple mf, bobo, mentecato

simulate ['sɪmjə,let] tr simular

simultaneous [,saɪməl'teni·əs] o [,sɪməl'teni·əs] adj simultáneo

sin [sɪn] s pecado ‖ v (pret & pp sinned; ger sinning) intr pecar

since [sɪns] adv desde entonces, después ‖ prep desde; después de ‖ conj desde que; después (de) que; ya que, puesto que

sincere [sɪn'sɪr] adj sincero

sincerity [sɪn'sɛrɪti] s sinceridad

sinecure ['saɪnɪˌkjʊr] o ['sɪnɪˌkjʊr] s sinecura

sinew ['sɪnju] s tendón m; (fig) fibra, nervio, vigor m

sinful ['sɪnfəl] adj (person) pecador; (act, intention, etc.) pecaminoso

sing [sɪŋ] v (pret sang [sæŋ] o sung [sʌŋ]; pp sung) tr cantar; **to sing to sleep** arrullar ‖ intr cantar

singe [sɪndʒ] v (ger singeing) tr chamuscar, socarrar

singer ['sɪŋər] s cantante mf; (in a night club) vocalista mf

single ['sɪŋgəl] adj solo, único; simple, sencillo; particular; (e.g., room in a hotel) individual; (copy) suelto; (unmarried) soltero; solteril, de soltero ‖ tr escoger, elegir; **to single out** singularizar

single blessedness s el bendito celibato

single-breasted ['sɪŋgəl'brɛstɪd] adj sin cruzar, de un solo pecho

single entry s (com) partida simple

single file s fila india; **in single file** de reata

single-handed ['sɪŋgəl'hændɪd] adj solo, sin ayuda

single life s vida de soltero

sin'gle-track' adj de vía única; (coll) de cortos alcances

sing'song' adj monótono ‖ s sonsonete m

singular ['sɪŋgjələr] adj & s singular m

sinister ['sɪnɪstər] adj amenazante, ominoso, funesto

sink [sɪŋk] s fregadero, pila ‖ v (pret sank [sæŋk] o sunk [sʌŋk]; pp sunk) tr hundir, sumergir; echar a pique; abrir, cavar (un pozo); hincar (los dientes); invertir (mucho dinero) perdiéndolo todo ‖ intr hundirse; irse a pique; hundirse (p.ej., el Sol en el horizonte); descender, desaparecer; decaer (un enfermo; una llama); (e.g., in a chair) dejarse caer

sinking fund s fondo de amortización

sinless ['sɪnlɪs] adj impecable

sinner ['sɪnər] s pecador m

sinuous ['sɪnjʊ·əs] adj sinuoso

sinus ['saɪnəs] s seno

sip [sɪp] s sorbo, trago ‖ v (pret & pp sipped; ger sipping) tr sorber, beber a tragos

siphon ['saɪfən] s sifón m ‖ tr sacar con sifón, trasegar con sifón

siphon bottle s sifón m

sir [sʌr] s señor m; (British title) sir m; **Dear Sir** Muy señor mío, Estimado señor

sire [saɪr] s padre m, semental m; caballo padre ‖ tr engendrar

siren ['saɪrən] s sirena

Sirius ['sɪrɪ·əs] s (astr) Sirio

sirloin ['sʌrlɔɪn] s solomillo

sirup ['sɪrəp] s var de **syrup**

sissi·fy ['sɪsɪˌfaɪ] v (pret & pp -fied) tr (coll) afeminar

sis·sy ['sɪsɪ] s (pl -sies) (coll) hermanita; (coll) maricón m, santito

sister ['sɪstər] adj (ship) gemelo; (language) hermano ‖ s hermana

sis'ter-in-law' s (pl **sisters-in-law**) cu-

ñada, hermana política; (wife of one's husband's or wife's brother) concuñada

Sisyphus ['sɪsɪfəs] s Sísifo

sit [sɪt] v (pret & pp sat [sæt]; ger sitting) intr estar sentado; sentarse; echarse (un ave sobre los huevos); reunirse, celebrar junta; descansar; **to sit down** sentarse; **to sit still** estarse quieto; **to sit up** incorporarse (el que estaba echado)

sit'-down' strike s huelga de sentados, huelga de brazos caídos

site [saɪt] s sitio, paraje m

sitting ['sɪtɪŋ] s (period one remains seated) sentada; (before a painter) estadía; (of a court or legislature) sesión; **at one sitting** de una sentada

sitting duck s pato sentado en el agua (fácil de matar a tiro de escopeta); (coll) blanco de fácil alcance

sitting room s sala de estar

situate ['sɪtʃʊˌet] tr situar

situation [ˌsɪtʃʊ'eʃən] s situación; colocación, puesto

six [sɪks] adj & pron seis ‖ s seis m; **at sixes and sevens** en confusión, en desacuerdo; **six o'clock** las seis

six hundred adj & pron seiscientos ‖ s seiscientos m

sixteen ['sɪks'tin] adj, pron & s dieciséis m, diez y seis

sixteenth ['sɪks'tinθ] adj & s (in a series) decimosexto; (part) dieciseisavo ‖ s (in dates) dieciséis m

sixth [sɪksθ] adj & s sexto ‖ s (in dates) seis m

sixtieth ['sɪkstɪ·ɪθ] adj & s (in a series) sexagésimo; (part) sesentavo

six·ty ['sɪkstɪ] adj & pron sesenta ‖ s (pl -ties) sesenta m

sizable ['saɪzəbəl] adj considerable, bastante grande

size [saɪz] s tamaño; (of a person or garment) talla; (of a pipe, a wire) diámetro; (for gilding) sisa, cola de retazo; (coll) verdadera situación ‖ tr clasificar según tamaño; sisar, encolar; **to size up** enfocar (un problema); medir con la vista

sizzle ['sɪzəl] s siseo ‖ intr sisear

S.J. abbr **Society of Jesus**

skate [sket] s patín m; (slang) adefesio, tipo ‖ intr patinar; **to skate on thin ice** buscar el peligro

skating rink s patinadero, pista de patinar

skein [sken] s madeja; enredo, maraña

skeleton ['skɛlɪtən] adj esquelético ‖ s esqueleto

skeleton key s llave maestra

skeptic ['skɛptɪk] adj & s escéptico

skeptical ['skɛptɪkəl] adj escéptico

sketch [skɛtʃ] s boceto, dibujo; bosquejo, esbozo; drama corto, pieza corta ‖ tr dibujar; bosquejar, esbozar

sketch'book' s libro de bocetos; libro de esbozos literarios

skewer ['skju·ər] s broqueta ‖ tr espetar; traspasar con aguja

ski [ski] *s* (*pl* **skis** o **ski**) esquí *m* ‖ *intr* esquiar

skid [skɪd] *s* (*of an auto*) resbalón *m*; (*of a wheel*) patinaje *m*, patinazo; calzo ‖ *v* (*pret & pp* **skidded;** *ger* **skidding**) *tr* calzar ‖ *intr* resbalar (*un coche*); patinar (*una rueda*)

skier ['ski·ər] *s* esquiador *m*

skiff [skɪf] *s* esquife *m*

skiing ['ski·ɪŋ] *s* esquiismo

ski jacket *s* plumífero

skijoring [ski'dʒorɪŋ] *s* esquí remolcado

ski jump *s* salto de esquí; cancha de esquiar; trampolín *m*

ski lift *s* telesquí *m*

skill [skɪl] *s* destreza, habilidad, pericia

skilled [skɪld] *adj* hábil, experimentado, experto

skillet ['skɪlɪt] *s* cacerola de mango largo; sartén *f*

skillful ['skɪlfəl] *adj* diestro, hábil

skim [skɪm] *v* (*pret & pp* **skimmed;** *ger* **skimming**) *tr* desnatar (*la leche*); espumar (*el caldo, el almíbar*); (*to graze*) rasar, rozar; examinar ligeramente ‖ *intr* rozar; **to skim over** pasar rozando; examinar a la ligera

ski mask *s* pasamontaña *m*

skimmer ['skɪmər] *s* (*utensil*) espumadera; (*straw hat*) canotié *m*

skim milk *s* leche desnatada

skimp [skɪmp] *tr* escatimar; chapucear ‖ *intr* economizar, apretarse; chapucear

skimp·y ['skɪmpi] *adj* (*comp* **-ier;** *super* **-iest**) escaso; tacaño, mezquino

skin [skɪn] *s* piel *f*; (*of an animal, of fruit*) pellejo; **to be nothing but skin and bones** estar hecho un costal de huesos, estar en los huesos; **to get soaked to the skin** calarse hasta los huesos; **to save one's skin** salvar el pellejo ‖ *v* (*pret & pp* **skinned;** *ger* **skinning**) *tr* pelar, desollar; escoriarse (*p.ej., el codo*); (*coll*) timar; **to skin alive** (*coll*) desollar vivo; (*coll*) vencer completamente

skin'-deep' *adj* superficial

skin diver *s* submarinista *mf*

skin'flint' *s* escasero, avaro

skin game *s* (*slang*) fullería

skin·ny ['skɪni] *adj* (*comp* **-nier;** *super* **-niest**) flaco, enjuto, magro, seco

skip [skɪp] *s* salto ‖ *v* (*pret & pp* **skipped;** *ger* **skipping**) *tr* saltar; saltar espacios (*la máquina de escribir*); moverse saltando; irse precipitadamente

skip bombing *s* (aer) bombardeo de rebote

ski pole *s* bastón de esquiar

skipper ['skɪpər] *s* caudillo, jefe *m*; (*of a boat*) patrón *m*; gusano del queso ‖ *tr* patronear

skirmish ['skɜrmɪʃ] *s* escaramuza ‖ *intr* escaramuzar

skirt [skɜrt] *s* falda; borde *m*, orilla; (*woman*) (*slang*) falda ‖ *tr* seguir el borde de; moverse a lo largo de

ski run *s* pista de esquí

ski stick *s* bastón *m* de esquiar

skit [skɪt] *s* boceto burlesco, paso cómico

skittish ['skɪtɪʃ] *adj* caprichoso; asustadizo; tímido; (*bull*) abanto

skulduggery [skʌl'dʌgəri] *s* (coll) trampa, embuste *m*

skull [skʌl] *s* cráneo, calavera

skull'cap' *s* casquete *m*

skunk [skʌŋk] *s* mofeta; (*person*) (coll) canalla *m*

sky [skaɪ] *s* (*pl* **skies**) cielo; **to praise to the skies** poner por las nubes, poner en el cielo

sky'lark' *s* alondra ‖ *intr* jaranear

sky'light' *s* tragaluz *m*, claraboya

sky'line' *s* línea del horizonte, línea de los edificios contra el cielo

sky'rock'et *s* cohete *m* ‖ *intr* subir como un cohete

sky'scrap'er *s* rascacielos *m*

sky'writ'ing *s* escritura aérea

slab [slæb] *s* losa; plancha, tabla

slack [slæk] *adj* flojo, perezoso; negligente; inactivo ‖ *s* flojedad; inactividad; estación muerta, temporada inactiva; **slacks** pantalones flojos ‖ *tr* aflojar; apagar (*la cal*) ‖ *intr* atrasarse; descuidarse; **to slack up** aflojar el paso

slacker ['slækər] *s* perezoso; (mil) prófugo

slag [slæg] *s* escoria

slake [slek] *tr* aplacar, calmar; apagar (*la cal*)

slalom ['slɑləm] *s* eslálom *m*

slam [slæm] *s* golpe *m*; (*of a door*) portazo; (coll) crítica acerba ‖ *v* (*pret & pp* **slammed;** *ger* **slamming**) *tr* cerrar de golpe; golpear o empujar estrepitosamente; (coll) criticar acerbamente ‖ *intr* cerrarse de golpe

slam'-bang' *adv* (coll) de golpe y porrazo

slander ['slændər] *s* calumnia, difamación ‖ *tr* calumniar, difamar

slanderous ['slændərəs] *adj* calumnioso, difamatorio

slang [slæŋ] *s* caló *m*, jerigonza

slant [slænt] *s* inclinación; parecer *m*, punto de vista ‖ *tr* inclinar, sesgar; deformar, tergiversar (*un informe*) ‖ *intr* inclinarse, sesgarse

slap [slæp] *s* manazo, palmada; (*in the face*) bofetada; (*in the back*) espaldarazo; desaire *m*, insulto ‖ *v* (*pret & pp* **slapped;** *ger* **slapping**) *tr* dar una palmada a; abofetear

slash [slæʃ] *s* cuchillada ‖ *tr* acuchillar; hacer fuerte rebaja de (*precios, sueldos, etc.*)

slat [slæt] *s* lámina, tablilla

slate [slet] *s* pizarra; candidatura, lista de candidatos ‖ *tr* empizarrar; designar, destinar; poner en la lista de candidatos

slate pencil *s* pizarrín *m*

slate roof *s* empizarrado

slattern ['slætərn] *s* mujer desaliñada, pazpuerca

slaughter ['slɔtər] *s* carnicería, matanza ‖ *tr* matar

slaughter house *s* matadero

Slav [slɑv] o [slæv] *adj & s* eslavo

slave 297 sloe

slave [slev] *adj* & *s* esclavo ‖ *intr* trabajar como esclavo
slave driver *s* negrero; (fig) negrero
slave'hold'er *s* dueño de esclavos
slavery ['slevəri] *s* esclavitud
slave trade *s* trata de esclavos
slave trader *s* negrero
Slavic ['slɑvɪk] o ['slævɪk] *adj* & *s* eslavo
slay [sle] *v* (*pret* **slew** [slu]; *pp* **slain** [slen]) *tr* matar
slayer ['sle·ər] *s* matador *m*
sled [sled] *s* luge *m* ‖ *v* (*pret* & *pp* **sledded**; *ger* **sledding**) *intr* deslizarse en luge o trineo
sledge hammer [sledʒ] *s* acotillo
sleek [slik] *adj* liso y brillante ‖ *tr* alisar y pulir; suavizar
sleep [slip] *s* sueño; **to be overcome with sleep** caerse de sueño; **to go to sleep** dormirse; dormirse, morirse (*un miembro*); **to put to sleep** adormecer; matar por anestesia ‖ *v* (*pret* & *pp* **slept** [slept]) *tr* pasar durmiendo; **to sleep it off** dormir la mona; **to sleep it over** consultar con la almohada; **to sleep off** dormir (*p.ej., una borrachera*) ‖ *intr* dormir
sleeper ['slipər] *s* (*person*) durmiente *mf*; (*girder*) durmiente *m*
sleeping bag *s* saco de dormir
sleeping car *s* coche-cama *m*
sleeping pill *s* píldora para dormir
sleepless ['slIplɪs] *adj* insomne, desvelado; pasado en vela
sleep'walk'er *s* sonámbulo
sleep·y ['slipi] *adj* (*comp* **-ier;** *super* **-iest**) soñoliento; **to be sleepy** tener sueño
sleep'y·head' *s* dormilón *m*
sleet [slit] *s* cellisca ‖ *intr* cellisquear
sleeve [sliv] *s* manga; (mach) manguito; **to laugh in o up one's sleeve** reírse para sí
sleigh [sle] *s* trineo ‖ *intr* pasearse en trineo
sleigh bell *s* cascabel *m*
sleigh ride *s* paseo en trineo
sleight of hand [slaɪt] *s* juego de manos, prestidigitación
slender ['slɛndər] *adj* esbelto, flaco, delgado; escaso, insuficiente
sleuth [sluθ] *s* sabueso
slew [slu] *s* (coll) montón *m*
slice [slaɪs] *s* rebanada, tajada; (*of an orange*) gajo ‖ *tr* rebanar, tajar; dividir; cortar
slick [slɪk] *adj* liso y brillante; meloso, suave; (coll) astuto, mañoso ‖ *s* lugar aceitoso y lustroso (*en el agua*)
slicker ['slɪkər] *s* impermeable *m* de hule; (coll) embaucador *m*
slide [slaɪd] *s* resbalón *m*; (*slippery place*) resbaladero; (*slippery surface*) desliz *m*; derrumbamiento de tierra; (*image for projection*) diapositiva, transparencia; (*of a microscope*) plaquilla de vidrio; (*piece of a device that slides*) cursor *m*; (*of a trombone*) corredera (tubular) ‖ *v* (*pret* & *pp* **slid** [slɪd]) *tr* deslizar ‖ *intr* deslizar, resbalar; **to let slide** dejar pasar, no hacer caso de

slide fastener *s* cierre *m* cremallera, cierre relámpago
slide rule *s* regla de cálculo
slide valve *s* corredera, válvula corrediza
sliding contact *s* cursor *m*
sliding door *s* puerta de corredera
sliding scale *s* regla de cálculo; (*of salaries*) escala móvil
slight [slaɪt] *adj* delgado; leve; pequeño; escaso ‖ *s* desatención, descuido; desaire *m*, menosprecio ‖ *tr* desatender, descuidar; desairar
slim [slɪm] *adj* (*comp* **slimmer;** *super* **slimmest**) delgado, esbelto; débil, leve, pequeño, escaso
slime [slaɪm] *s* légamo; (*of snakes, fish, etc.*) baba
slim·y ['slaɪmi] *adj* (*comp* **-ier;** *super* **-iest**) legamoso; baboso, viscoso; puerco, sucio
sling [slɪŋ] *s* (*to shoot stones*) honda; (*to hold up a broken arm*) cabestrillo ‖ *v* (*pret* & *pp* **slung** [slʌŋ]) *tr* lanzar con una honda, lanzar, tirar; poner en cabestrillo; colgar flojamente
sling'shot' *s* honda
slink [slɪŋk] *v* (*pret* & *pp* **slunk** [slʌŋk]) *intr* andar furtivamente; **to slink away** escabullirse, salir con el rabo entre piernas
slip [slɪp] *s* resbalón *m*, desliz *m*; falta, error *m*, desliz *m*; lapso; embarcadero; (*cover for a pillow, for furniture*) funda; (*piece of paper*) papeleta; (*cutting from a plant*) sarmiento; (*piece of underclothing*) combinación; (*of a dog*) traílla; huída, evasión; mozuelo, mozuela; **to give the slip to** burlar la vigilancia de ‖ *v* (*pret* & *pp* **slipped;** *ger* **slipping**) *tr* poner rápidamente; quitar rápidamente; pasar por alto; eludir, evadir; **to slip off** (coll) quitarse de prisa; **to slip on** (coll) ponerse de prisa; **to slip one's mind** olvidársele a uno ‖ *intr* deslizarse; patinar (*el embrague*); errar, equivocarse; (coll) declinar, deteriorarse; **to let slip** dejar pasar; decir inadvertidamente; **to slip away** escurrirse; **to slip by** pasar inadvertido; pasar rápidamente (*el tiempo*); **to slip out of one's hands** escurrirse de entre las manos; **to slip up** (coll) errar, equivocarse
slip cover *s* funda
slip of the pen *s* error *m* de pluma
slip of the tongue *s* error *m* de lengua
slipper ['slɪpər] *s* zapatilla, babucha
slippery ['slɪpəri] *adj* deslizadizo, resbaladizo; astuto, zorro, evasivo
slip'-up' *s* (coll) error *m*, equivocación
slit [slɪt] *s* hendidura, raja; cortada, incisión ‖ *v* (*pret* & *pp* **slit;** *ger* **slitting**) *tr* hender, rajar; cortar
slob [slɑb] *s* (slang) sujeto desaseado, puerco
slobber ['slɑbər] *s* baba; sensiblería ‖ *intr* babear; hablar con sensiblería
sloe [slo] *s* (*shrub*) endrino; (*fruit*) endrina

sk
sl

slogan ['slogən] *s* lema *m*, mote *m*; grito de combate; (*striking phrase used in advertising*) eslogan *m*

sloop [slup] *s* balandra

slop [slɑp] *s* gacha, zupia, agua sucia ‖ *v* (*pret & pp* slopped; *ger* slopping) *tr* salpicar, ensuciar ‖ *intr* derramarse; chapotear

slope [slop] *s* cuesta, pendiente *f*; (*of a container or a roof*) vertiente *m* & *f* ‖ *tr* inclinar ‖ *intr* inclinarse

slop-py ['slɑpi] *adj* (*comp* -pier; *super* -piest) mojado y sucio; (*in one's dress*) desgalichado; (*in one's work*) chapucero

slot [slɑt] *s* ranura; (*for letters*) buzón *m*

sloth [sloθ] o [slɔθ] *s* pereza; (zool) perezoso

slot machine *s* tragamonedas *m*, máquina sacaperras

slot meter *s* contador automático

slouch [slautʃ] *s* postura relajada; persona torpe de movimientos ‖ *intr* agacharse, andar caído de hombros; **to slouch in a chair** repanchigarse

slouch hat *s* sombrero gacho

slough [slau] *s* cenagal *m*, fangal *m*; estado de abandono moral ‖ [slʌf] *s* (*of a snake*) camisa; (pathol) escara ‖ *tr* mudar, echar de sí ‖ *intr* caerse, desprenderse

Slovak ['slovæk] o [slo'væk] *adj & s* eslovaco

sloven-ly ['slʌvənli] *adj* (*comp* -lier; *super* -liest) desaseado, desaliñado

slow [slo] *adj* lento; (*sluggish*) cachazudo, despacioso; (*clock, watch*) atrasado; (*in understanding*) lerdo, tardo, torpe ‖ *adv* despacio ‖ *tr* retrasar; atrasar (*un reloj*) ‖ *intr* retardarse, ir más despacio; atrasarse (*un reloj*)

slow'down' *s* huelga de brazos caídos

slow'-mo'tion *adj* a cámara lenta

slow'poke' *s* tardón *m*

slug [slʌg] *s* (*heavy piece of metal*) lingote *m*; (*metal disk used as a coin*) ficha; (zool) limaza, babosa; (coll) porrazo, puñetazo ‖ *v* (*pret & pp* slugged; *ger* slugging) *tr* (coll) aporrear, apuñear

sluggard ['slʌgərd] *s* pachón *m*, perezoso

sluggish ['slʌgɪʃ] *adj* inactivo, indolente, tardo; pachorrudo, perezoso

sluice [slus] *s* canal *m*; (*floodgate*) compuerta; (*dam; flume*) presa

sluice gate *s* compuerta de presa

slum [slʌm] *s* barrio bajo ‖ *v* (*pret & pp* slummed; *ger* slumming) *intr* visitar los barrios bajos

slumber ['slʌmbər] *s* sueño ligero, sueño tranquilo ‖ *intr* dormir; dormitar

slump [slʌmp] *s* depresión, crisis económica; (*in prices, stocks, etc.*) baja repentina ‖ *intr* hundirse, desplomarse; bajar repentinamente (*los precios, valores, etc.*)

slur [slʌr] *s* pronunciación indistinta; reparo crítico; (mus) ligado ‖ *v* (*pret & pp* slurred; *ger* slurring) *tr* co-

merse (*sonidos, sílabas*); despreciar, insultar; (mus) ligar

slush [slʌʃ] *s* fango muy blando, agua nieve fangosa, nieve *f* a medio derretir; sentimentalismo tonto

slut [slʌt] *s* perra; (*slovenly woman*) pazpuerca; ramera, mala mujer

sly [slai] *adj* (*comp* slyer o slier; *super* slyest o sliest) furtivo, secreto; astuto, socarrón; travieso; **on the sly** a hurtadillas

smack [smæk] *adv* (coll) de golpe, de sopetón ‖ *s* dejo, gustillo; palmada, manotada; golpe *m*; beso sonado; (*of a whip*) chasquido ‖ *tr* dar una manotada a; golpear; hacer chasquidos con (*un látigo*); besar sonoramente; **to smack one's lips** chuparse los labios ‖ *intr* — **to smack of** saber a, oler a

small [smɔl] *adj* pequeño, chico; (*short in stature*) bajo; pobre, obscuro, humilde; (typ) minúsculo

small arms *spl* armas ligeras

small beer *s* cerveza floja; bagatela; persona de poca monta

small business *s* pequeña empresa

small capital *s* versalilla o versalita

small change *s* suelto, dinero menudo

small fry *s* gente menuda; gente de poca monta

small'-fry' *adj* de niños, para niños; de poca monta

small hours *spl* primeras horas (*de la mañana*)

small intestine *s* intestino delgado

small-minded ['smɔl'maindɪd] *adj* tacaño, mezquino; intolerante

smallpox ['smɔl,paks] *s* viruela

small print *s* tipo menudo

small talk *s* palique *m*, charlas frívolas

small'-time' *adj* de poca monta

small'-town' *adj* lugareño, apegado a cosas lugareñas

smart [smɑrt] *adj* listo, vivo, inteligente; agudo, penetrante; astuto; elegante, majo; picante, punzante; (coll) grande, considerable ‖ *s* escozor *m*; dolor vivo ‖ *intr* escocer, picar; padecer, sufrir

smart aleck ['ælɪk] *s* (coll) fatuo, sabihondo

smart set *s* gente *f* chic, gente de buen tono

smash [smæʃ] *s* rotura violenta; fracaso, ruina, quiebra, bancarrota; (coll) choque violento, tope violento ‖ *tr* romper con fuerza; arruinar, destrozar; aplastar ‖ *intr* romperse con fuerza; arruinarse, destrozarse; aplastarse; **to smash into** chocar con, topar con

smash hit *s* (coll) éxito rotundo

smash'-up' *s* colisión violenta; ruina, desastre *m*; quiebra, bancarrota

smattering ['smætərɪŋ] *s* barniz *m*, tintura, migaja

smear [smɪr] *s* embarradura; calumnia; (bact) frotis *m* ‖ *tr* embarrar; calumniar ‖ *intr* embarrarse

smear campaign *s* campaña de calumnias

smell [smel] *s* olor *m*; (*sense*) olfato;

fragancia, perfume *m* ‖ *v* (*pret & pp* **smelled** o **smelt** [smelt]) *tr* oler, olfatear ‖ *intr* oler; heder, oler mal; **to smell of** oler a

smelling salts *spl* sales aromáticas

smell·y ['smelɪ] *adj* (*comp* **-ier;** *super* **-iest**) hediondo, maloliente

smelt [smelt] *s* (*fish*) eperlano, esperinque *m* ‖ *tr & intr* fundir

smile [smaɪl] *s* sonrisa ‖ *intr* sonreír, sonreírse

smiling ['smaɪlɪŋ] *adj* risueño

smirk [smʌrk] *s* sonrisa fatua y afectada ‖ *intr* sonreír fatua y afectadamente

smite [smaɪt] *v* (*pret* **smote** [smot]; *pp* **smitten** ['smɪtən] o **smit** [smɪt]) *tr* golpear o herir súbitamente y con fuerza; caer con fuerza sobre; apenar, afligir; castigar

smith [smɪθ] *s* forjador *m*, herrero

smith·y ['smɪθi] *s* (*pl* **-ies**) herrería

smitten ['smɪtən] *adj* afligido; (coll) muy enamorado

smock [smɑk] *s* bata

smock frock *s* blusa de obrero

smog [smɑg] *s* (coll) mezcla de humo y niebla

smoke [smok] *s* humo; **to go up in smoke** irse todo en humo ‖ *tr* (*to cure or treat with smoke*) ahumar; fumar (*tabaco*); **to smoke out** ahuyentar con humo, dar humazo a; descubrir ‖ *intr* humear; fumar; hacer humo (*una chimenea dentro de la habitación*)

smoked glasses *spl* gafas ahumadas

smokeless powder ['smoklɪs] *s* pólvora sin humo

smoker ['smokər] *s* fumador *m*; (*room*) fumadero; (rr) coche-fumador *m*; reunión de fumadores

smoke rings *spl* anillos de humo; **to blow smoke rings** sacar humo formando anillos

smoke screen *s* cortina de humo

smoke'stack' *s* chimenea

smoking ['smokɪŋ] *s* el fumar; **no smoking** se prohíbe fumar

smoking car *s* coche-fumador *m*, vagón *m* de fumar

smoking jacket *s* batín *m*

smoking room *s* fumadero, saloncito para fumadores

smok·y ['smoki] *adj* (*comp* **-ier;** *super* **-iest**) humoso; (*emitting smoke*) humeante

smolder ['smoldər] *s* fuego lento sin llama y con mucho humo ‖ *intr* arder en rescoldo, arder sin llamas; (fig) estar latente; (*to burn within*) (fig) requemarse; (fig) expresar (*p.ej., los ojos*) una ira latente

smooth [smuð] *adj* liso, terso, suave; plano, llano; igual; acaramelado, afable, blando, meloso; (*water*) tranquilo; (*style*) flúido; **smooth as butter** como manteca ‖ *tr* alisar, suavizar; allanar; facilitar; **to smooth away** quitar (*p.ej., obstáculos*) suavemente; **to smooth down** ablandar, calmar

smooth-faced ['smuð,fest] *adj* barbilampiño

smooth-spoken ['smuθ,spokən] *adj* meloso, lisonjero

smooth·y ['smuði] *s* (*pl* **-ies**) (coll) galante *m*; (coll) elegante *m*; (coll) adulador *m*

smother ['smʌðər] *tr* ahogar, sofocar; suprimir; reprimir

smudge [smʌdʒ] *s* tiznón *m*; mancha ‖ *tr* tiznar; manchar; ahumar, fumigar (*una huerta*)

smug [smʌg] *adj* (*comp* **smugger;** *super* **smuggest**) pagado de sí mismo; compuesto, pulcro; relamido

smuggle ['smʌgəl] *tr* meter de contrabando ‖ *intr* contrabandear

smuggler ['smʌglər] *s* contrabandista *mf*

smuggling ['smʌglɪŋ] *s* contrabando

smut [smʌt] *s* tiznón *m*; obscenidad; (agr) carbón *m*, tizón *m*

smut·ty ['smʌti] *adj* (*comp* **-tier;** *super* **-tiest**) tiznado, manchado; obsceno; (agr) atizonado

snack [snæk] *s* parte *f*, porción; bocadillo, tentempié *m*

snag [snæg] *s* (*of a tree*) tocón *m*; (*of a tooth*) raigón *m*; obstáculo, tropiezo; **to strike** o **to hit a snag** tropezar con un obstáculo

snail [snel] *s* caracol *m*; (*slow person*) pachón *m*; **at a snail's pace** a paso de caracol, a paso de tortuga

snake [snek] *s* culebra, serpiente *f*

snake in the grass *s* traidor *m*, amigo pérfido

snap [snæp] *s* (*crackling sound*) chasquido, estallido; (*of the fingers*) castañetazo; (*bite*) mordisco; (*cracker*) galletita; (*of cold weather*) corto período; (*catch or fastener*) broche *m* de presión; (phot) instantánea; (coll) brío, vigor *m*; (slang) breva, cosa fácil ‖ *v* (*pret & pp* **snapped**) *ger* **snapping**) *tr* asir, cerrar, etc. de golpe; castañetear (*los dedos*); chasquear (*el látigo*); fotografiar instantáneamente; tomar (*una instantánea*); **to snap one's fingers at** tratar con desprecio; **to snap up** aceptar con avidez, comprar con avidez; cortar la palabra a ‖ *intr* chasquear, estallar; (*to crack*) saltar; (*from fatigue*) estallar; tratar de querer morder; asir (*una oportunidad*); **to snap out of it** (slang) cambiarse repentinamente; **to snap shut** cerrarse de golpe

snap'drag'on *s* (bot) boca de dragón

snap fastener *s* corchete *m* de presión

snap judgment *s* decisión atolondrada

snap·py ['snæpi] *adj* (*comp* **-pier;** *super* **-piest**) mordaz; (coll) elegante, garboso; (coll) enérgico, vivo; (*food*) acre, picante

snap'shot' *s* instantánea

snap switch *s* (elec) interruptor *m* de resorte

snare [snɛr] *s* lazo, trampa; (*of a drum*) bordón *m*, tirante *m*

snare drum *s* caja clara

snarl [snɑrl] *s* gruñido; regaño; maraña, enredo ‖ *tr* decir con un gru-

sl
sn

ñido; enmarañar, enredar ‖ *intr* gruñir; regañar; enmarañarse, enredarse

snatch [snætʃ] *s* arrebatamiento; pedacito, trocito; ratito ‖ *tr & intr* arrebatar; **to snatch at** tratar de asir o agarrar; **to snatch from** arrebatar a

sneak [snik] *adj* furtivo ‖ *s* sujeto solapado ‖ *tr* mover a hurtadillas ‖ *intr* andar furtivamente, moverse a hurtadillas

sneaker ['snikər] *s* sujeto solapado; (coll) zapato blando, zapato de lona

sneak thief *s* ratero, descuidero

sneak·y ['sniki] *adj* (*comp* -ier; *super* -iest) solapado, furtivo

sneer [snɪr] *s* expresión de desprecio ‖ *intr* hablar con desprecio, echar una mirada de desprecio; **to sneer at** mofarse de

sneeze [sniz] *s* estornudo ‖ *intr* estornudar; **not to be sneezed at** (coll) no ser despreciable

snicker ['snɪkər] *s* risa tonta ‖ *intr* reírse tontamente

sniff [snɪf] *s* husmeo, venteo; sorbo por las narices ‖ *tr* husmear, ventear; sorber por las narices; (fig) husmear, averiguar; (fig) sospechar ‖ *intr* ventear; **to sniff at** husmear; menospreciar

sniffle ['snɪfəl] *s* resuelfo fuerte y repetido; **the sniffles** ataque de resoplidos ‖ *intr* resollar fuerte y repetidamente

snip [snɪp] *s* tijeretada; recorte *m*, pedacito; (coll) persona pequeña e insignificante ‖ *v* (*pret & pp* snipped; *ger* snipping) *tr* tijeretear

snipe [snaɪp] *s* agachadiza, becacín *m* ‖ *intr* paquear, tirar desde un escondite

sniper ['snaɪpər] *s* paco, tirador emboscado

snippet ['snɪpɪt] *s* recorte *m*; (coll) persona pequeña e insignificante

snip·py ['snɪpi] *adj* (*comp* -pier; *super* -piest) (coll) arrogante, desdeñoso; (coll) acre, brusco

snitch [snɪtʃ] *tr & intr* (slang) escamotear, ratear

sniv·el ['snɪvəl] *s* gimoteo, lloriqueo; moqueo ‖ *v* (*pret & pp* -eled o -elled; *ger* -eling o -elling) *intr* gimotear, lloriquear; (*to have a runny nose*) moquear

snob [snɑb] *s* esnob *mf*

snobbery ['snɑbəri] *s* esnobismo

snobbish ['snɑbɪʃ] *adj* esnob, esnobista

snoop [snup] *s* (coll) buscavidas *mf*, curioso ‖ *intr* (coll) curiosear, ventear

snoopy ['snupi] *adj* (coll) curioso, entremetido

snoot [snut] *s* (slang) cara, narices *fpl*

snoot·y ['snuti] *adj* (*comp* -ier; *super* -iest) (slang) esnob

snooze [snuz] *s* (coll) sueñecito ‖ *intr* echar un sueñecito

snore [snor] *s* ronquido ‖ *intr* roncar

snort [snɔrt] *s* bufido ‖ *intr* bufar

snot [snɑt] *s* (slang) mocarro

snot·ty ['snɑti] *adj* (*comp* -tier; *super*

-tiest) (coll) mocoso; (coll) asqueroso, sucio; (slang) engreído

snout [snaut] *s* hocico; (*something shaped like the snout of an animal*) morro; (*of a person*) (coll) hocico

snow [sno] *s* nieve *f* ‖ *intr* nevar

snow'ball' *s* bola de nieve ‖ *tr* lanzar bolas de nieve a ‖ *intr* aumentar rápidamente

snow'-blind' *adj* cegado por reflejos de la nieve

snow-capped ['sno,kæpt] *adj* coronado de nieve

snow'drift' *s* ventisquero, masa de nieve

snow'fall' *s* nevada

snow fence *s* valla paranieves

snow'flake' *s* copo de nieve, ampo

snow flurry *s* nevisca

snow line o **limit** *s* límite *m* de las nieves perpetuas

snow man *s* figura de nieve

snow'plow' *s* expulsanieves *m*, quitanieves *m*

snow'shoe' *s* raqueta de nieve

snow'storm' *s* nevasca, fuerte nevada

snow'-white' *adj* blanco como la nieve

snow·y ['sno·i] *adj* (*comp* -ier; *super* -iest) nevoso

snowy owl *s* lechuza blanca

snub [snʌb] *s* desaire *m* ‖ *v* (*pret & pp* snubbed; *ger* snubbing) *tr* desairar

snub·by ['snʌbi] *adj* (*comp* -bier; *super* -biest) (*nose*) respingona

snuff [snʌf] *s* rapé; (*of a candlewick*) moco; **up to snuff** (slang) en buena condición; (slang) difícil de engañar ‖ *tr* husmear, olfatear; sorber por la nariz; despabilar (*una candela*); **to snuff out** apagar, extinguir

snuff'box' *s* tabaquera

snuffers ['snʌfərz] *spl* despabiladeras

snug [snʌg] *adj* (*comp* snugger; *super* snuggest) cómodo; (*garment*) ajustado, ceñido; (*well-off*) acomodado; (*in hiding*) escondido

snuggle ['snʌgəl] *intr* apretarse, arrimarse; dormir bien abrigado; **to snuggle up to** arrimarse a

so [so] *adv* así; tan + *adj* o *adv*; por tanto; también; **and so** así pues; también, lo mismo; **and so on** y así sucesivamente; **or so** más o menos; **to think so** creer que sí; **so as to** + *inf* para + *inf*; **so far** hasta aquí; hasta ahora; **so long** hasta la vista; **so many tantos**; **so much** tanto; **so so** tal cual, así así; **so that** de modo que, de suerte que, así que; para que; con tal de que; **so to speak** por decirlo así ‖ *conj* así que ‖ *interj* ¡bien!; ¡verdad!

soak [sok] *s* mojada; (*toper*) (coll) potista *mf* ‖ *tr* empapar, remojar; embeber; (slang) aporrear; (slang) hacer pagar un precio exorbitante; **to soak up** absorber, embeber; (fig) entender; **soaked to the skin** calado hasta los huesos ‖ *intr* empaparse, remojarse

so'-and-so' *s* (*pl* -sos) fulano, fulano de tal; tal cosa

soap [sop] *s* jabón *m* ‖ *tr* jabonar

soap'box' s caja de jabón; tribuna callejera

soapbox orator s orador m de plazuela

soap bubble s burbuja de jabón, pompa de jabón

soap dish s jabonera

soap flakes spl copos de jabón

soap'mak'er s jabonero

soap opera s (coll) serial lacrimógeno

soap powder s jabón m en polvo, polvo de jabón

soap'stone' s jaboncillo de sastre

soap'suds' spl jabonaduras

soap·y ['sopi] adj (comp -ier; super -iest) jabonoso

soar [sor] intr encumbrarse, subir muy alto, volar a gran altura; aspirar, pretender; (aer) planear

sob [sɑb] s sollozo || v (pret & pp sobbed; ger sobbing) tr decir o expresar sollozando || intr sollozar

sober ['sobər] adj sobrio; no embriagado; grave, serio; cuerdo, sensato; sereno, tranquilo; (color) apagado || tr poner sobrio; desemborrachar || intr volverse sobrio; desemborracharse; **to sober down** calmarse, sosegarse; **to sober up** desemborracharse

sobriety [so'braɪ-əti] s sobriedad, moderación; gravedad, seriedad; cordura, sensatez; serenidad

sobriquet ['sobrɪ,ke] s apodo

sob sister s (slang) periodista llorona

sob story s (slang) historia de lagrimitas

soc. o **Soc.** abbr **society**

so'-called' adj llamado, así llamado; supuesto

soccer ['sɑkər] s fútbol m asociación

sociable ['soʃəbəl] adj sociable

social ['soʃəl] adj social || s reunión social

social climber ['klaɪmər] s ambicioso de figurar

socialism ['soʃə,lɪzəm] s socialismo

socialist ['soʃəlɪst] s socialista mf

socialite ['soʃə,laɪt] s (coll) personaje m de la buena sociedad

social register s guía m social, registro de la buena sociedad

socie·ty [sə'saɪ-əti] s (pl -ties) sociedad; (companionship or company) compañía; buena sociedad, mundo elegante

society editor s cronista mf de la vida social

sociology [,sosɪ'ɑlədʒi] o [,soʃɪ'ɑlədʒi] s sociología

sock [sɑk] s calcetín m; (slang) golpe m fuerte || tr (slang) golpear con fuerza

socket ['sɑkɪt] s (of the eyes) cuenca; (of a tooth) alvéolo; (of a candlestick) cañón m; (of a socket wrench) cubo; (elec) portalámparas; (rad) zócalo

socket wrench s llave f de caja, llave de cubo

sod [sɑd] s césped m; terrón m de césped || v (pret & pp sodded; ger sodding) tr encespedar

soda ['sodə] s soda, sosa; (drink) soda

soda fountain s fuente f de sodas

soda water s agua gaseosa

sodium ['sodɪ-əm] adj sódico, de sodio || s sodio

sofa ['sofə] s sofá m

soft [sɔft] o [sɑft] adj blando, muelle; (skin) suave; (iron) dulce; (hat) flexible; (solder) tierno; (coll) fácil

soft-boiled egg ['sɔft'bɔɪld] o ['sɑft-'bɔɪld] s huevo pasado por agua

soft coal s hulla grasa

soft drink s bebida no alcohólica

soften ['sɔfən] o ['sɑfən] tr ablandar; **to soften up** (by bombardment) ablandar || intr ablandarse

soft'-ped'al tr (mus) disminuir la intensidad de, por medio del pedal suave; (slang) moderar

soft soap s jabón blando o graso; (coll) adulación

soft'-soap' tr (coll) enjabonar, dar jabón a

soft'ware' s (computer) programa m para computadora

sog·gy ['sɑgi] adj (comp -gier; super -giest) remojado, ensopado

soil [sɔɪl] s suelo; país m, región; (spot, stain) mancha; (fig) mancha, deshonra || tr manchar, ensuciar; manchar, deshonrar; viciar, corromper || intr mancharse, ensuciarse

soil pipe s tubo de desagüe sanitario

soiree o **soirée** [swɑ're] s sarao, velada

sojourn ['sodʒʌrn] s estancia, permanencia || ['sodʒʌrn] o [so'dʒʌrn] intr estarse, permanecer

solace ['sɑlɪs] s solaz m, consuelo || tr solazar, consolar

solar ['solər] adj solar

solar battery s fotopila

solder ['sɑdər] s soldadura || tr soldar

soldering iron s cautín m, soldador m

soldier ['soldʒər] s (enlisted man as distinguished from an officer) soldado; (man in military service) militar m || intr servir como soldado

soldier of fortune s aventurero militar

soldier·y ['soldʒəri] s (pl -ies) soldadesca

sold out [sold] adj agotado; **the theater is sold out** todas las localidades están vendidas; **we are sold out of those neckties** se nos han agotado esas corbatas

sole [sol] adj solo, único; exclusivo || s (of foot) planta; (of shoe) suela; (fish) lenguado || tr solar

solely ['solli] adv solamente, únicamente

solemn ['sɑləm] adj solemne

solicit [sə'lɪsɪt] tr solicitar; intentar seducir

solicitor [sə'lɪsɪtər] s solicitador m, agente m; (law) procurador m

solicitous [sə'lɪsɪtəs] adj solícito

solicitude [sə'lɪsɪ,tjud] o [sə'lɪsɪ,tud] s solicitud

solid ['sɑlɪd] adj sólido; unánime; (sound, good) sólido, macizo; (e.g., clouds) denso; (without pause or interruption) entero; (e.g., gold) puro || s sólido

solid geometry s geometría del espacio

solidity [sə'lɪdɪti] s (pl -ties) solidez f

solid tire *s* (aut) macizo
solilo·quy [sə'lɪləkwi] *s* (*pl* **-quies**) soliloquio
solitaire ['salɪ,ter] *s* (*game and diamond*) solitario; sortija solitaria
solitar·y ['salɪ,teri] *adj* solitario ‖ *s* (*pl* **-ies**) solitario
solitary confinement *s* incomunicación, aislamiento penal
solitude ['salɪ,tjud] o ['salɪ,tud] *s* soledad
so·lo ['solo] *adj* (*instrument*) solista; a solas, hecho a solas ‖ *s* (*pl* **-los**) (mus) solo
soloist ['solo·ɪst] *s* solista *mf*
solstice ['salstɪs] *s* solsticio
solution [sə'luʃən] *s* solución
solve [salv] *tr* resolver, solucionar; adivinar (*un enigma*)
solvent ['salvənt] *adj* & *s* solvente *m*
somber ['sambər] *adj* sombrío
some [sʌm] *adj indef* algún; un poco de; unos; (coll) grande, bueno, famoso ‖ *pron indef pl* algunos, unos
some'bod'y *pron indef* alguien; **somebody else** algún otro, otra persona ‖ *s* (*pl* **-ies**) (coll) personaje *m*
some'day' *adv* algún día
some'how' *adv* de algún modo, de alguna manera; **somehow or other** de un modo u otro
some'one' *pron indef* alguien; **someone else** algún otro, otra persona
somersault ['sʌmər,sɔlt] *s* salto mortal ‖ *intr* dar un salto mortal
something ['sʌmθɪŋ] *adv* algo, un poco; (coll) muy, excesivamente ‖ *pron indef* alguna cosa, algo; **something else** otra cosa
some'time' *adj* antiguo, de otro tiempo ‖ *adv* alguna vez; antiguamente
some'times' *adv* a veces, algunas veces
some'way' *adv* de algún modo
some'what' *adv* algo, un poco ‖ *s* alguna cosa, algo
some'where' *adv* en alguna parte, a alguna parte; en algún tiempo; **somewhere else** en otra parte, a otra parte
somnambulist [sam'næmbjəlɪst] *s* sonámbulo
somnolent ['samnələnt] *adj* soñoliento
son [sʌn] *s* hijo
song [sɔŋ] o [saŋ] *s* canción, canto; **for a song** muy barato; **to sing the same old song** volver a la misma canción
song'bird' *s* ave canora
Song of Songs *s* Cantar *m* de los Cantares
sonic ['sanɪk] *adj* sónico
sonic boom *s* (aer) estampido sónico
son'-in-law' *s* (*pl* **sons-in-law**) yerno, hijo político
sonnet ['sanɪt] *s* soneto
sonneteer [,sanɪ'tɪr] *s* sonetista *mf*; poetastro ‖ *intr* sonetizar
son·ny ['sʌni] *s* (*pl* **-nies**) hijito
sonori·ty [sə'narɪti] o [sə'nɔrɪti] *s* (*pl* **-ties**) sonoridad
soon [sun] *adv* pronto, en breve; temprano; de buena gana; **as soon as** así que, en cuanto, luego que, tan

pronto como; **as soon as possible** cuanto antes, lo más pronto posible; **had sooner** preferiría; **how soon?** ¿cuándo?; **soon after** poco después, poco después de; **sooner or later** tarde o temprano
soot [sut] o [sut] *s* hollín *m*
soothe [suð] *tr* aliviar, calmar, sosegar
soothsayer ['suθ,se·ər] *s* adivino
soot·y ['suti] o ['suti] *adj* (*comp* **-ier**; *super* **-iest**) holliniento, tiznado
sop [sap] *s* (*food soaked in milk, etc.*) sopa; regalo (*para acallar, apaciguar o sobornar*) ‖ *v* (*pret & pp* **sopped**; *ger* **sopping**) *tr* empapar, ensopar; **to sop up** absorber
sophisticated [sə'fɪstɪ,ketɪd] *adj* mundano, falto de simplicidad, corrido
sophomore ['safə,mor] *s* estudiante *mf* de segundo año
sopping ['sapɪŋ] *adj* empapado; **sopping wet** hecho una sopa
soprano [sə'præno] o [sə'prano] *adj* de soprano; para soprano ‖ *s* (*pl* **-os**) soprano *mf*
sorcerer ['sɔrsərər] *s* brujo, hechicero
sorceress ['sɔrsərɪs] *s* bruja, hechicera
sorcer·y ['sɔrsəri] *s* (*pl* **-ies**) brujería, hechicería, sortilegio
sordid ['sɔrdɪd] *adj* sórdido
sore [sor] *adj* enrojecido, inflamado; (coll) resentido, picado; **to be sore at** (coll) estar enojado con ‖ *s* llaga, úlcera; pena, dolor *m*, aflicción; **to open an old sore** renovar la herida
sorely ['sorli] *adv* penosamente; con urgencia
sore throat *s* dolor *m* de garganta
sorori·ty [sə'rarɪti] o [sə'rɔrɪti] *s* (*pl* **-ties**) hermandad de estudiantas
sorrel ['sɔrəl] o ['sɔrəl] *adj* alazán
sorrow ['saro] o ['sɔro] *s* dolor *m*, pena, pesar *m*; arrepentimiento ‖ *intr* dolerse, apenarse, sentir pena; arrepentirse; **to sorrow for** añorar
sorrowful ['sarəfəl] o ['sɔrəfəl] *adj* doloroso, pesaroso, acongojado
sor·ry ['sari] o ['sɔri] *adj* (*comp* **-rier**; *super* **-riest**) afligido, apenado, pesaroso; arrepentido; malo, pésimo; despreciable, ridículo; **to be o feel sorry** sentir; arrepentirse; **to be o feel sorry for** compadecer; arrepentirse de
sort [sɔrt] *s* clase *f*, especie *f*; modo, manera; **a sort of** uno a modo de; **out of sorts** de mal humor; **sort of** (coll) algo, en cierta medida ‖ *tr* clasificar, separar; escoger, entresacar
so'-so' *adj* mediano, regular, talcualillo ‖ *adv* así así, tal cual
sot [sat] *s* borracho
sotto voce ['sato 'votʃe] *adv* a sovoz, en voz baja
soubrette [su'brɛt] *s* (theat) confidenta de comedia; (theat) doncella coqueta
soul [sol] *s* alma; **upon my soul!** ¡por vida mía!
sound [saund] *adj* sano; sólido, firme; solvente; sonoro; (*sleep*) profundo;

prudente; legal, válido ‖ *adv* profundamente ‖ *s* sonido; ruido; (*passage of water*) estrecho, brazo de mar; (surg) sonda, tienta; **within sound of** al alcance de ‖ *tr* sonar; tocar (*p.ej., campanas*); tantear, sondear; auscultar (*p.ej., los pulmones*); entonar (*p.ej., alabanzas*) ‖ *intr* sonar, resonar; sondar; parecer; **to sound like** sonar a, sonar como

sound film *s* película sonora

soundly ['saʊndlɪ] *adv* sanamente; profundamente; a fondo, completamente

sound'proof' *adj* antisonoro ‖ *tr* insonorizar

soup [sup] *s* sopa

soup kitchen *s* comedor *m* de beneficencia, dispensario de alimentos

soup spoon *s* cuchara de sopa

sour [saʊr] *adj* agrio ‖ *tr* agriar ‖ *intr* agriarse

source [sors] *s* fuente *f*, manantial *m*

source material *s* fuentes *fpl* originales

sour cherry *s* (*tree*) guindo; (*fruit*) guinda

sour grapes *interj* ¡están verdes las uvas!

south [saʊθ] *adj* meridional, del sur ‖ *adv* al sur, hacia el sur ‖ *s* sur *m*, mediodía *m*

South America *s* Sudamérica, la América del Sur

South American *adj & s* sudamericano

southern ['sʌðərn] *adj* meridional

Southern Cross *s* Cruz *f* del Sur

southerner ['sʌðərnər] *s* meridional *mf*; sureño (Am)

South Korea *s* la Corea del Sur

South Korean *adj & s* surcoreano

south'paw' *adj & s* (slang in sport) zurdo

southward ['saʊθwərd] *adv* hacia el sur

south wind *s* austro, noto

souvenir [,suvə'nɪr] o ['suvə,nɪr] *s* recuerdo, memoria

sovereign ['sʌvrɪn] o ['sʌvrɪn] *adj* soberano ‖ *s* (*king; coin*) soberano; (*queen*) soberana

sovereign-ty ['sʌvrɪntɪ] o ['sʌvrɪntɪ] *s* (*pl* -ties) soberanía

soviet ['sovɪ‚ɛt] o [‚sovɪ'ɛt] *adj* soviético ‖ *s* soviet *m*

sovietize ['sovɪ‚ɛ‚taɪz] *tr* sovietizar

Soviet Russia *s* la Rusia Soviética

Soviet Union *s* Unión Soviética

sow [saʊ] *s* puerca ‖ [so] *v* (*pret* sowed; *pp* sown o sowed) *tr* sembrar; (*with mines*) plagar

soybean ['sɔɪ‚bin] *s* soja; semilla de soja

sp. *abbr* special, species, specific, specimen, spelling

spa [spɑ] *s* caldas, balneario

space [spes] *adj* espacial, del espacio ‖ *s* espacio; **in the space of** por espacio de ‖ *tr* espaciar

space bar *s* espaciador *m*, tecla de espacios

space'craft' *s* astronave *f*

space flight *s* vuelo espacial

space key *s* llave *f* espacial

space·man ['spes‚mæn] *s* (*pl* -men [‚mɛn]) navegador *m* del espacio; visitante *m* a la Tierra del espacio exterior

space'ship' *s* nave *f* del espacio

space suit *s* escafandra espacial

space vehicle *s* vehículo espacial

spacious ['speʃəs] *adj* espacioso

spade [sped] *s* laya; (*playing card*) pique *m;* **to call a spade a spade** llamar al pan pan y al vino vino

spade'work' *s* trabajo preliminar

Spain [spen] *s* España

span [spæn] *s* palmo, cuarta, llave *f* de la mano; recuesto, lapso, trecho; (*of horses*) pareja; (*of a bridge*) ojo; (aer) envergadura ‖ *v* (*pret & pp* spanned; *ger* spanning) *tr* medir a palmos; atravesar, extenderse sobre

spangle ['spæŋgəl] *s* lentejuela ‖ *tr* adornar con lentejuelas; (*to stud with bright objects*) estrellar ‖ *intr* brillar

Spaniard ['spænjərd] *s* español *m*

spaniel ['spænjəl] *s* perro de aguas

Spanish ['spænɪʃ] *adj & s* español *m;* **the Spanish** los españoles

Spanish America *s* la América Española, Hispanoamérica

Spanish broom *s* retama

Spanish fly *s* abadejo, cantárida

Spanish Main *s* Costa Firme, Tierra Firme; mar *m* Caribe

Spanish moss *s* barba española

Spanish omelet *s* tortilla de tomate

Span'ish-speak'ing *adj* de habla española, hispanohablante

spank [spæŋk] *tr* azotar, zurrar

spanking ['spæŋkɪŋ] *adj* rápido; fuerte; (coll) muy grande, muy hermoso, extraordinario ‖ *s* azote *m*

spar *s* (mineral) espato; (naut) mástil *m*, palo, verga ‖ *v* (*pret & pp* sparred; *ger* sparring) *intr* pelear, reñir; boxear

spare [sper] *adj* sobrante; libre, disponible; de repuesto; delgado, enjuto, flaco; parco, sobrio ‖ *tr* pasar sin; perdonar; guardar, salvar; ahorrar; **to have . . . to spare** tener de sobra; **to spare oneself** ahorrarse esfuerzos

spare bed *s* cama de sobra

spare parts *spl* piezas de repuesto o de recambio

spare room *s* cuarto de reserva

sparing ['sperɪŋ] *adj* económico; (*scanty*) escaso

spark [spark] *s* chispa; (*e.g., of truth*) centellita ‖ *tr* (coll) cortejar, galantear (*a una mujer*) ‖ *intr* chispear

spark coil *s* bobina de chispas, bobina de encendido

spark gap *s* (*of induction coil*) entrehierro; (*of spark plug*) espacio de chispa

sparkle ['sparkəl] *s* chispita, destello; (*wit*) travesura; alegría, viveza ‖ *intr* chispear; ser alegre; espumar, ser efervescente

sparkling ['sparklɪŋ] *adj* centelleante, chispeante; (*wine*) espumante, espumoso; (*water*) gaseoso

spark plug s bujía

sparrow ['spæro] s gorrión m

sparse [spɑrs] adj (population) poco denso; (hair) ralo

Spartan ['spɑrtən] adj & s espartano

spasm ['spæzəm] s espasmo; esfuerzo súbito y de breve duración

spasmodic [spæz'mɑdɪk] adj espasmódico; intermitente; caprichoso

spastic ['spæstɪk] adj espástico

spat [spæt] s disputa, riña; botín m, polaina corta

spatial ['speʃəl] adj espacial

spatter ['spætər] tr salpicar; manchar || intr chorrear; chapotear

spatula ['spætʃələ] s espátula

spavin ['spævɪn] s esparaván m

spawn [spɔn] s freza; prole f; producto, resultado || tr engendrar || intr desovar, frezar (los peces)

speak [spik] v (pret **spoke** [spok]; pp **spoken**) tr hablar (un idioma); decir (la verdad) || intr hablar; **so to speak** por decirlo así; **speaking!** ¡al habla!; **to speak out** o **up** osar hablar, elevar la voz

speak'-eas'y s (pl -ies) (slang) taberna clandestina

speaker ['spikər] s hablante mf; orador m; (of a legislative assembly) presidente m; (rad) altavoz m

speaking ['spikɪŋ] adj hablante; **to be on speaking terms** hablarse || s habla; elocuencia

speaking tube s tubo acústico

spear [spɪr] s lanza; (for fishing) arpón m; (of grass) hoja || tr alancear, herir con lanza

spear'head' s punta de lanza || tr dirigir, conducir; encabezar; dar impulso a

spear'mint' s menta verde, menta romana

spec. abbr **special**

special ['speʃəl] adj especial || s tren m especial

spe'cial-deliv'ery adj urgente, de urgencia

specialist ['speʃəlɪst] s especialista mf

speciali•ty [ˌspeʃɪ'ælɪti] s (pl -ties) especialidad

specialize ['speʃəˌlaɪz] tr especializar || intr especializar o especializarse

special•ty ['speʃəlti] s (pl -ties) especialidad

spe•cies ['spisiz] s (pl -cies) especie f

specific [spɪ'sɪfɪk] adj & s específico

speci•fy ['spesɪˌfaɪ] v (pret & pp -fied) tr especificar

specimen ['spesɪmən] s espécimen m; (coll) tipo, sujeto

specious ['spiʃəs] adj especioso, engañoso

speck [spek] s mota, manchita || tr motear, manchar; salpicar de manchas

speckle ['spekəl] s mota, punto || tr motear, puntear

spectacle ['spektəkəl] s espectáculo; **spectacles** anteojos, gafas

spectator ['spektetər] o [spek'tetər] s espectador m

specter ['spektər] s espectro

spec•trum ['spektrəm] s (pl -tra [trə] o -trums) espectro

speculate ['spekjəˌlet] intr especular

speech [spitʃ] s habla; (of an actor) parlamento; (talk before an audience) conferencia, discurso

speech clinic s clínica de la palabra

speech correction s rehabilitación del habla

speechless ['spitʃlɪs] adj sin habla; estupefacto

speed [spid] s velocidad; (aut) marcha, velocidad || v (pret & pp **sped** [spɛd]) tr apresurar; despedir; ayudar || intr apresurarse; adelantar, progresar; ir con exceso de velocidad

speeding ['spidɪŋ] s exceso de velocidad

speed king s as m del volante

speed limit s velocidad permitida

speedometer [spi'dɑmɪtər] s (to indicate speed) velocímetro; velocímetro y cuentakilómetros unidos

speed record s marca de velocidad

speed•y ['spidi] adj (comp -ier; super -iest) rápido, veloz

spell [spel] s encanto, hechizo; tanda, turno; rato, poco tiempo; (e.g., of good weather) temporada; **to cast a spell on** encantar, hechizar || v (pret & pp **spelled** o **spelt** [spelt]) tr deletrear; indicar, significar; **to spell out** (coll) explicar detalladamente || intr deletrear || v (pret & pp **spelled**) tr reemplazar, relevar

spell'bind'er s (coll) orador m fascinante, orador persuasivo

spelling ['spelɪŋ] adj ortográfico || s (act) deletreo; (subject or study) ortografía; (way a word is spelled) grafía

spelunker [spɪ'lʌŋkər] s espeleólogo de afición

spend [spend] v (pret & pp **spent** [spent]) tr gastar; pasar (una hora, un día, etc.)

spender ['spendər] s gastador m

spending money s dinero para gastos menudos

spend'thrift' s derrochador m, pródigo

sperm [spʌrm] s esperma f

sperm whale s cachalote m

spew [spju] tr & intr vomitar

sp. gr. abbr **specific gravity**

sphere [sfɪr] s esfera; astro, cuerpo celeste

spherical ['sferɪkəl] adj esférico

sphinx [sfɪŋks] s (pl sphinxes o sphinges ['sfɪndʒiz]) esfinge f

spice [spaɪs] s especia; (zest, piquancy) sainete m; fragancia || tr especiar; dar gusto o picante a

spice box s especiero

spick-and-span ['spɪkənd'spæn] adj flamante; limpio, pulcro

spic•y ['spaɪsi] adj (comp -ier; super -iest) especiado; picante; aromático; sicalíptico

spider ['spaɪdər] s araña

spider web s tela de araña, telaraña

spiff·y [ˈspɪfi] *adj* (*comp* **-ier;** *super* **-iest**) (slang) guapo, elegante

spigot [ˈspɪgət] *s* grifo; (*plug to stop a vent*) espiche *m*

spike [spaɪk] *s* (*long, heavy nail*) estaca, escarpia; (*sharp projection or part*) punta, pico, púa; (bot) espiga ‖ *tr* empernar; acabar, poner fin a

spill [spɪl] *s* derrame *m;* líquido derramado; (coll) caída, vuelco ‖ *v* (*pret & pp* **spilled** o **spilt** [spɪlt]) *tr* derramar, verter; (coll) hacer caer, volcar ‖ *intr* derramarse, verterse; (coll) caer, volcarse

spill′way′ *s* bocacaz *m,* canal *m* de desagüe

spin [spɪn] *s* vuelta, giro muy rápido; (coll) paseo en coche, etc.; **to go into a spin** (aer) entrar en barrena ‖ *v* (*pret & pp* **spun** [spʌn]; *ger* **spinning**) *tr* hacer girar; hilar (*p.ej., lino*); bailar (*un trompo*); **to spin out** extender, prolongar; **to spin yarns** contar cuentos increíbles ‖ *intr* dar vueltas, girar; hilar; bailar (*un trompo*); (aer) entrar en barrena

spinach [ˈspɪnɪtʃ] o [ˈspɪnɪdʒ] *s* espinaca; (*leaves used as food*) espinacas

spinal [ˈspaɪnəl] *adj* espinal

spinal column *s* espina dorsal, columna vertebral

spinal cord *s* médula espinal

spindle [ˈspɪndəl] *s* (*rounded rod tapering toward each end*) huso; (*small shaft, axle*) eje *m;* (*turned ornament in a baluster*) mazorca

spine [spaɪn] *s* espina, púa; (*rib, ridge*) cordoncillo, loma, cerro; (anat) espina; (bb) lomo; (fig) ánimo, valor *m*

spineless [ˈspaɪnlɪs] *adj* sin espinas, sin espinazo; sin firmeza de carácter

spinet [ˈspɪnɪt] *s* espineta

spinner [ˈspɪnər] *s* hilandero; máquina de hilar

spinning [ˈspɪnɪŋ] *adj* hilador ‖ *s* (*act*) hila; (*art*) hilandería

spinning wheel *s* torno de hilar

spinster [ˈspɪnstər] *s* solterona

spi·ral [ˈspaɪrəl] *adj & s* espiral *f* ‖ *v* (*pret & pp* **-raled** o **-ralled**; *ger* **-raling** o **-ralling**) *intr* dar vueltas como una espiral; (aer) volar en espiral

spiral staircase *s* escalera de caracol

spire [spaɪr] *s* cima, ápice *m;* (*of a steeple*) aguja, chapitel *m;* (*e.g., of grass*) tallo

spirit [ˈspɪrɪt] *s* espíritu *m;* humor *m,* temple *m;* personaje *m;* licor *m* ‖ *tr* — **to spirit away** llevarse misteriosamente

spirited [ˈspɪrɪtɪd] *adj* fogoso, espiritoso

spirit lamp *s* lámpara de alcohol

spiritless [ˈspɪrɪtlɪs] *adj* apocado, tímido, sin ánimo

spirit level *s* nivel *m* de burbuja

spiritual [ˈspɪrɪtʃʊ·əl] *adj* espiritual

spiritualism [ˈspɪrɪtʃʊə‚lɪzəm] *s* espiritismo; (*belief that all reality is spiritual*) espiritualismo

spirituous liquors [ˈspɪrɪtʃʊ·əs] *spl* licores espirituosos

spit [spɪt] *s* esputo, saliva; (*for roasting*) asador *m,* espetón *m;* punta o lengua de tierra; **the spit and image of** la segunda edición de, el retrato de ‖ *v* (*pret & pp* **spat** [spæt] o **spit;** *ger* **spitting**) *tr* escupir ‖ *intr* escupir; lloviznar; neviscar; fufar (*el gato*)

spite [spaɪt] *s* despecho, rencor *m,* inquina; **in spite of** a pesar de, a despecho de; **out of spite** por despecho ‖ *tr* despechar, molestar, picar

spiteful [ˈspaɪtfəl] *adj* despechado, rencoroso

spit′fire′ *s* fierabrás *m;* mujer *f* de mal genio

spittoon [spɪˈtun] *s* escupidera

splash [splæʃ] *s* rociada, salpicadura; (*e.g., with the hands*) chapaleo, chapoteo; **to make a splash** (coll) hacer impresión, llamar la atención ‖ *tr & intr* salpicar; chapotear

splash′down′ *s* acuatizaje *m*

spleen [splin] *s* mal humor *m;* (anat) bazo; **to vent one's spleen** descargar la bilis

splendid [ˈsplɛndɪd] *adj* espléndido; (coll) magnífico, maravilloso

splendor [ˈsplɛndər] *s* esplendor *m*

splice [splaɪs] *s* empalme *m,* junta ‖ *tr* empalmar, juntar

splint [splɪnt] *s* (*splinter*) astilla, tablilla; (surg) tablilla ‖ *tr* entablillar (*un hueso roto*)

splinter [ˈsplɪntər] *s* astilla; (*of stone, glass, bone*) esquirla ‖ *tr* astillar ‖ *intr* astillarse, hacerse astillas

splinter group *s* grupo disidente

split [splɪt] *adj* hendido, partido; dividido ‖ *s* división, fractura; (slang) porción ‖ *v* (*pret & pp* **split;** *ger* **splitting**) *tr* dividir, partir; **to split one's sides with laughter** desternillarse de risa ‖ *intr* dividirse a lo largo; **to split away (from)** separarse (de)

split fee *s* dicotomía (*entre médicos*)

split personality *s* personalidad desdoblada

splitting [ˈsplɪtɪŋ] *adj* partidor; fuerte, violento; (*headache*) enloquecedor

splotch [splɑtʃ] *s* borrón *m,* mancha grande ‖ *tr* salpicar, manchar

splurge [splʌrdʒ] *s* (coll) fachenda, ostentación ‖ *intr* (coll) fachendear

splutter [ˈsplʌtər] *s* chisporroteo; (*manner of speaking*) farfulla ‖ *tr* farfullar ‖ *intr* chisporrotear; farfullar

spoil [spɔɪl] *s* botín *m,* presa; **spoils** (*taken from an enemy*) botín, despojos; (*of political victory*) enchufes *mpl* ‖ *v* (*pret & pp* **spoiled** o **spoilt** [spɔɪlt]) *tr* echar a perder, estropear; mimar (*a un niño*); amargar (*una tertulia*) ‖ *intr* echarse a perder

spoiled [spɔɪld] *adj* (*child*) consentido, mimado; (*food*) pasado, podrido

spoils·man [ˈspɔɪlzmən] *s* (*pl* **-men** [mən]) enchufista *m*

spoils system *s* enchufismo

spoke [spok] *s* (*of a wheel*) radio, rayo; (*of a ladder*) escalón *m*

spokes·man ['spoksmən] s (pl **-men** [mən]) portavoz m, vocero

sponge [spʌndʒ] s esponja; **to throw in** (o up) **the sponge** (coll) tirar la esponja ‖ tr limpiar con esponja; borrar; absorber ‖ intr ser absorbente; **to sponge on** (coll) vivir a costa de

sponge cake s bizcocho muy ligero

sponger ['spʌndʒər] s esponja (gorrón, parásito)

sponge rubber s caucho esponjoso

spon·gy ['spʌndʒi] adj (comp **-gier;** super **-giest**) esponjoso

sponsor ['spʌnsər] s patrocinador m; (godfather) padrino; (godmother) madrina ‖ tr patrocinar

sponsorship ['spʌnsər‚ʃɪp] s patrocinio

spontaneous [spɑn'teni·əs] adj espontáneo

spoof [spuf] s (slang) mistificación, engaño; (slang) broma ‖ tr (slang) mistificar, engañar ‖ intr (slang) bromear, burlar; (slang) parodiar

spook [spuk] s (coll) aparecido, espectro

spook·y ['spuki] adj (comp **-ier;** super **-iest**) (coll) espectral, espeluznante; (horse) (coll) asustadizo

spool [spul] s carrete m, bobina

spoon [spun] s cuchara ‖ tr cucharear ‖ intr (slang) besuquearse (los enamorados)

spoonful ['spun‚ful] s cucharada

spoon·y ['spuni] adj (comp **-ier;** super **-iest**) (coll) baboso, sobón

sporadic(al) [spə'rædɪk(əl)] adj esporádico

spore [spor] s espora

sport [sport] adj deportivo, de deporte ‖ s deporte m; deportista mf; (person or thing controlled by some power or passion) juguete m; (laughingstock) hazmerreír m; (gambler) (coll) tahur m, jugador m; (in gambling or playing games) (coll) buen perdedor; (flashy fellow) (coll) guapo, majo; (biol) mutación; **to make sport of** burlarse de, reírse de ‖ tr (coll) lucir (p.ej., un traje nuevo) ‖ intr divertirse; estar de burla, juguetear

sport clothes spl trajes mpl de sport

sport fan s (slang) aficionado al deporte, deportista mf

sporting chance s (coll) riesgo de buen perdedor

sporting goods spl artículos de deporte

sporting house s (coll) casa de juego; (coll) casa de rameras

sports'cast'er s locutor deportivo

sports·man ['sportsmən] s (pl **-men** [mən]) deportista m; jugador honrado

sports news s noticiario deportivo

sports'wear' s trajes deportivos

sports writer s cronista deportivo

sport·y ['sporti] adj (comp **-ier;** super **-iest**) (coll) elegante, guapo; (coll) alegre, brillante; (coll) magnánimo; (coll) disipado, libertino

spot [spɑt] s mancha; sitio, lugar m; (coll) poquito; **on the spot** allí mis-

mo; al punto; (slang) en dificultad; (slang) en peligro de muerte; **to hit the spot** tener razón; (coll) dar completa satisfacción ‖ v (pret & pp **spotted;** ger **spotting**) tr manchar; (coll) descubrir, reconocer ‖ intr mancharse, tener manchas

spot cash s dinero contante

spotless ['spɑtlɪs] adj inmaculado, sin manchas

spot'light' s proyector m orientable; luz concentrada; (aut) faro piloto, faro giratorio; (fig) atención del público

spot remover [rɪ'muvər] s (person) quitamanchas mf; (material) quitamanchas m

spot welding s soldadura por puntos

spouse [spauz] o [spaus] s cónyuge mf, consorte mf

spout [spaut] s (to carry off water from roof) canalón m; (of a jar, pitcher, etc.) pico; (of a sprinkling can) rallo, roseta; (jet) chorro; **up the spout** (slang) acabado, arruinado ‖ tr echar en chorro; (coll) declamar ‖ intr chorrear; (coll) declamar

sprain [spren] s torcedura, esguince m ‖ tr torcer, torcerse

sprawl [sprɔl] intr arrellanarse

spray [spre] s rociada; (of the sea) espuma; (device) pulverizador m; (twig) ramita ‖ tr & intr rociar

sprayer ['spre·ər] s rociador m, pulverizador m, vaporizador m

spread [spred] s extensión; amplitud, anchura; difusión; diferencia; cubrecama, sobrecama; mantel m, tapete m; (of the wings of a bird; of the wings of an airplane) envergadura; (coll) festín m, comilona ‖ v (pret & pp **spread**) tr extender; difundir, propagar; esparcir; escalonar; abrir, separar; poner (la mesa) ‖ intr extenderse; difundirse; esparcirse; abrirse, separarse

spree [spri] s juerga, parranda; borrachera; **to go on a spree** ir de juerga; pillar una mona

sprig [sprɪg] s ramita

spright·ly ['spraɪtli] adj (comp **-lier;** super **-liest**) alegre, animado, vivo

spring [sprɪŋ] adj primaveral; de manantial; de muelle, de resorte ‖ s (season of the year) primavera; (issue of water from earth) fuente f, manantial m; (elastic device) muelle m, resorte m; (of an automobile or wagon) ballesta; (leap, jump) brinco, salto; abertura, grieta; tensión, tirantez f ‖ v (pret **sprang** [spræŋ] o **sprung** [sprʌŋ]; pp **sprung**) tr soltar (un muelle o resorte); torcer, combar, encorvar; hacer saltar (una trampa, una mina) ‖ intr saltar; saltar de golpe; brotar, nacer, proceder; torcerse, combarse, encorvarse; **to spring at** abalanzarse sobre; **to spring forth** precipitarse; brotar; **to spring up** levantarse de un salto; brotar, nacer; presentarse a la vista

spring'board' s trampolín m

spring chicken s polluelo; (young person) (coll) pollita

spring fever s (hum) ataque m primaveral, galbana

spring mattress s colchón m de muelles, somier m

spring′time′ s primavera

sprinkle ['sprɪŋkəl] s rociada; llovizna; pizca ‖ tr regar, rociar; salpicar, sembrar; espolvorear (p.ej., azucar) ‖ intr rociar; lloviznar, gotear

sprinkling can s regadera, rociadera

sprint [sprɪnt] s (sport) embalaje m ‖ intr (sport) embalarse, lanzarse

sprite [spraɪt] s duende m, trasgo

sprocket ['sprɑkɪt] s diente m de rueda de cadena; rueda de cadena

sprout [spraʊt] s brote m, renuevo, retoño ‖ intr brotar, germinar, echar renuevos; crecer rápidamente

spruce [sprus] adj apuesto, elegante, garboso ‖ s abeto del Norte, abeto falso, pícea ‖ tr ataviar, componer ‖ intr ataviarse, componerse; **to spruce up** emperifollarse

spry [spraɪ] adj (comp **spryer** o **sprier**; super **spryest** o **spriest**) activo, ágil

spud [spʌd] s (chisel) escoplo; (agr) escoda; (coll) patata

spun glass [spʌn] s vidrio hilado, cristal hilado

spunk [spʌŋk] s (coll) ánimo, coraje m, corazón m, valor m

spun silk s seda cardada o hilada

spur [spʌr] s espuela; (central point of an auger) gusanillo; (of a cock, mountain, warship) espolón m; (rr) ramal corto; (goad, stimulus) (fig) espuela; **on the spur of the moment** impulsivamente, sin la reflexión debida ‖ v (pret & pp **spurred**; ger **spurring**) tr espolear; **to spur on** espolear, aguijonear

spurious ['spjʊrɪ·əs] adj espurio

spurn [spʌrn] s desdén m, menosprecio ‖ tr desdeñar, menospreciar; rechazar con desdén

spurt [spʌrt] s chorro repentino; esfuerzo repentino; arranque m ‖ intr salir en chorro, salir a borbotones

sputter ['spʌtər] s (manner of speaking) farfulla; (sizzling) chisporroteo ‖ tr farfullar ‖ intr farfullar; chisporrotear

spy [spaɪ] s (pl **spies**) espía mf ‖ v (pret & pp **spied**) tr columbrar, divisar ‖ intr espiar; **to spy on** espiar

spy′glass′ s catalejo, anteojo

sq. abbr **square**

squabble ['skwɑbəl] s reyerta, riña ‖ intr reñir, disputar

squad [skwɑd] s escuadra

squadron ['skwɑdrən] s (aer) escuadrilla; (of cavalry) (mil) escuadrón m; (nav) escuadra

squalid ['skwɑlɪd] adj escuálido

squall [skwɔl] s grupada, turbión m; (quarrel) (coll) riña; (upset, commotion) (coll) chubasco

squalor ['skwɑlər] s escualidez f

squander ['skwɑndər] tr despilfarrar, malgastar

square [skwɛr] adj cuadrado, p.ej., **eight square inches** ocho pulgadas cuadradas; en cuadro, de lado, p.ej., **eight inches square** ocho pulgadas en cuadro, ocho pulgadas de lado; rectangular; justo, recto; honrado, leal; saldado; fuerte, sólido; (coll) abundante, completo; **to get square with** (coll) hacérselas pagar a ‖ adv en cuadro; en ángulo recto; honradamente, lealmente ‖ s cuadrado; (of checkerboard or chessboard) casilla, escaque m; (city block) manzana; (open area in town or city) plaza; (carpenter's tool) escuadra; **to be on the square** (coll) obrar de buena fe ‖ tr cuadrar; dividir en cuadros; ajustar, nivelar, conformar; saldar (una cuenta); (carp) escuadrar ‖ intr cuadrarse; **to square off** (coll) colocarse en posición de defensa

square dance s danza de figuras

square deal s (coll) trato equitativo

square meal s (coll) comida abundante

square shooter ['ʃutər] s (coll) persona leal y honrada

squash [skwɑʃ] s aplastamiento; (bot) calabaza; (sport) frontón m con raqueta; ‖ tr aplastar, despachurrar; confutar (un argumento); acallar con un argumento, respuesta, etc. ‖ intr aplastarse

squash·y ['skwɑʃi] adj (comp **-ier**; super **-iest**) mojado y blando; (muddy) lodoso; (fruit) modorro

squat [skwɑt] adj en cuclillas; rechoncho ‖ v (pret & pp **squatted**; ger **squatting**) intr acuclillarse, agacharse; sentarse en el suelo; establecerse en terreno ajeno sin derecho; establecerse en terreno público para crear un derecho

squatter ['skwɑtər] s advenedizo, intruso, colono usurpador

squaw [skwɔ] s india norteamericana; mujer, esposa, muchacha

squawk [skwɔk] s graznido; (slang) queja chillona ‖ intr graznar; (slang) quejarse chillando

squaw man s blanco casado con india

squeak [skwik] s chillido; chirrido ‖ intr dar chillidos; chirriar

squeal [skwil] s chillido ‖ intr dar chillidos; (slang) delatar, soplar; **to squeal on** (slang) delatar, soplar (a una persona)

squealer ['skwilər] s (coll) soplón m

squeamish ['skwimɪʃ] adj escrupuloso, remilgado; excesivamente modesto; (easily nauseated) asqueroso

squeeze [skwiz] s apretón m; **to put the squeeze on someone** (coll) hacer a uno la forzosa, meter en prensa a uno ‖ tr apretar; agobiar, oprimir; exprimir ‖ intr apretar; **to squeeze through** abrirse paso a estrujones por entre; salir de un aprieto a duras penas

squeezer ['skwizər] s exprimidera

squelch [skwɛltʃ] s (coll) tapaboca ‖ tr apabullar, despachurrar

squid [skwɪd] s calamar m

sp
sq

squint [skwɪnt] *s* mirada bizca; mirada furtiva; (*strabismus*) bizquera ‖ *tr* achicar, entornar (*los ojos*) ‖ *intr* bizquear; torcer la vista; tener los ojos medio cerrados

squint-eyed [ˈskwɪntˌaɪd] *adj* bisojo, bizco; malévolo, sospechoso

squire [skwaɪr] *s* acompañante *m* (*de una señora*); (Brit) terrateniente *m* de antigua heredad; (U.S.A.) juez *m* de paz, juez local ‖ *tr* acompañar (*a una señora*)

squirm [skwʌrm] *s* retorcimiento ‖ *intr* retorcerse; **to squirm out of** escaparse de (*p.ej., un aprieto*) haciendo mucho esfuerzo

squirrel [ˈskwʌrəl] *s* ardilla

squirt [skwʌrt] *s* chorro; jeringazo; (coll) mono, presuntuoso ‖ *tr* arrojar a chorros ‖ *intr* salir a chorros

Sr. *abbr* **senior, Sir**

S.S. *abbr* **Secretary of State, steamship, Sunday school**

St. *abbr* **Saint, Strait, Street**

stab [stæb] *s* puñalada; (coll) tentativa; **to make a stab at** (slang) esforzarse por hacer ‖ *v* (*pret & pp* **stabbed**; *ger* **stabbing**) *tr* apuñalar, traspasar ‖ *intr* apuñalar

stab in the back *s* puñalada trapera

stable [ˈstebəl] *adj* estable ‖ *s* establo, cuadra, caballeriza

stack [stæk] *s* montón *m*, pila; (*of rifles*) pabellón *m*; (*of books in a library*) estantería, depósito; (*of a chimney*) cañón *m*; (*of straw*) niara; (*of firewood*) hacina; (coll) montón *m*, gran número ‖ *tr* amontonar, apilar; florear (*el naipe*); hacinar (*leña*)

stadi·um [ˈstedɪəm] *s* (*pl* **-ums** o **-a** [ə]) estadio

staff [stæf] o [stɑf] *s* bastón *m*, apoyo, sostén *m*; personal *m*; (mil) estado mayor; (mus) pentagrama *m* ‖ *tr* dotar, proveer de personal, nombrar personal para

stag [stæg] *adj* exclusivo para hombres, de hombres solos ‖ *s* (*male deer*) ciervo; varón *m*; varón solo (*no acompañado de mujeres*)

stage [stedʒ] *s* escena; etapa, jornada; (*coach*) diligencia; (*scene of an event*) teatro; (*of a microscope*) portaobjeto; (rad) etapa; **by easy stages** a pequeñas etapas; lentamente; **to go on the stage** hacerse actor ‖ *tr* poner en escena, representar; preparar, organizar

stage'coach' *s* diligencia

stage'craft' *s* arte *f* teatral

stage door *s* (theat) entrada de los artistas

stage fright *s* trac *m*, miedo al público

stage'hand' *s* tramoyista *m*, metemuertos *m*, metesillas *m*

stage manager *s* director *m* de escena

stage'-struck' *adj* loco por el teatro

stage whisper *s* susurro en voz alta

stagger [ˈstæɡər] *tr* sorprender; asustar; escalonar (*las horas de trabajo*) ‖ *intr* tambalear, hacer eses al andar

staggering *adj* **tambaleante**; sorprendente

stagnant [ˈstæɡnənt] *adj* estancado; (fig) estancado, inactivo, paralizado

staid [sted] *adj* grave, serio, formal

stain [sten] *s* mancha; tinte *m*, tintura; materia colorante ‖ *tr* manchar; teñir; colorar ‖ *intr* mancharse; hacer manchas

stained glass *s* vidrio de color

stained'glass' window *s* vidriera de colores, vidriera pintada, vitral *m*

stainless [ˈstenlɪs] *adj* inmanchable; (*steel*) inoxidable; inmaculado

stair [ster] *s* escalera; (*step of a series*) escalón *m*; **stairs** escalera

stair'case' *s* escalera

stair'way' *s* escalera

stair well *s* hueco de escalera

stake [stek] *s* estaca; (*of a cart or truck*) telero; (*to hold up a plant*) rodrigón *m*; (*in gambling*) puesta; premio del vencedor; **at stake** en juego; **en gran peligro; to die at the stake** morir en la hoguera; **to pull up stakes** (coll) irse; (coll) mudarse de casa ‖ *tr* estacar; atar a una estaca; rodrigar (*plantas*); apostar; arriesgar, aventurar; **to stake all** jugarse el todo por el todo; **to stake off** o **to stake out** estacar, señalar con estacas

stale [stel] *adj* añejo, rancio, viejo; (*air*) viciado; (*joke*) mohoso; anticuado

stale'mate' *s* mate ahogado; **to reach a stalemate** llegar a un punto muerto ‖ *tr* dar mate ahogado a; estancar, paralizar

stalk [stɔk] *s* tallo ‖ *tr* cazar al acecho; acechar, espiar ‖ *intr* cazar al acecho; andar con paso majestuoso; andar con paso altivo; **to stalk out** salir con paso airado

stall [stɔl] *s* cuadra, establo; pesebre *m*; (*booth in a market*) puesto; (*at a fair*) caseta; (Brit) butaca; (slang) pretexto ‖ *tr* encerrar en un establo; poner trabas a; parar (*un motor*); **to stall off** (coll) eludir, evitar ‖ *intr* atascarse, atollarse; pararse (*un motor*); (slang) eludir para engañar o demorar; **to stall for time** (slang) tardar para ganar tiempo

stallion [ˈstæljən] *s* caballo padre, caballo semental

stalwart [ˈstɔlwərt] *adj* fornido, forzudo; valiente; leal, constante ‖ *s* persona fornida; partidario leal

stamen [ˈstemən] *s* estambre *m*

stamina [ˈstæmɪnə] *s* fuerza, nervio, vigor *m*, resistencia

stammer [ˈstæmər] *s* balbuceo, tartamudeo ‖ *tr* balbucear (*p.ej., excusas*) ‖ *intr* balbucear, tartamudear

stamp [stæmp] *s* (*device used for making an impression; mark made with it; piece of paper or mark used to show payment of postage*) sello; (*tool used for crushing or marking*) pisón *m*; (*tool for stamping coins and medals*) cuño, troquel *m*; marca, impresión; clase *f*, tipo ‖ *tr* sellar; troquelar; estampar, imprimir; hollar;

pisotear; indicar, señalar; poner el sello a; bocartear (*el mineral*); **to stamp out** apagar pateando; extinguir por la fuerza; suprimir; **to stamp the feet** dar patadas ‖ *intr* patalear

stampede [stæm'pid] *s* fuga precipitada; estampida (Am) ‖ *tr* hacer huir en desorden; provocar a pánico ‖ *intr* huir en tropel; obrar por común impulso

stamping grounds *spl* (slang) guarida (*sitio frecuentado por una persona*)

stamp pad *s* tampón *m*

stamp'-vend'ing machine *s* máquina expendedora de sellos

stance [stæns] *s* (sport) postura, planta

stanch [stɑnt∫] *adj* firme, fuerte; constante, leal; (*watertight*) estanco ‖ *tr* estancar; restañar (*la sangre de una herida*)

stand [stænd] *s* parada; alto para defenderse; postura, posición; resistencia; estrado, tribuna; sostén *m*, soporte *m*, pie *m*; puesto, quiosco ‖ *v* (*pret & pp* **stood** [stʊd]) *tr* poner, colocar; poner derecho; soportar, tolerar, resistir; (coll) aguantar (*a una persona*); (coll) sufragar (*un gasto*); **to stand off** tener a raya; **to stand one's ground** mantenerse firme ‖ *intr* estar, estar situado; estar parado; estacionarse; estar de pie, estar derecho; ponerse de pie, levantarse; resultar; persistir; mantenerse; **to stand aloof, apart** o **aside** mantenerse apartado; **to stand back of** respaldar; **to stand for** significar, representar; apoyar, defender; apadrinar; mantener (*p.ej., una opinión*); presentarse como candidato de; navegar hacia; (coll) tolerar; **to stand in line** hacer cola; **to stand out** sobresalir; destacarse, resaltar; **to stand up** ponerse de pie, levantarse; durar; **to stand up to** hacer resueltamente frente a

standard ['stændərd] *adj* normal; (*typewriter keyboard*) universal; corriente, regular; legal; clásico ‖ *s* patrón *m;* norma, regla establecida; bandera, estandarte *m;* emblema *m,* símbolo; soporte *m,* pilar *m*

standardize ['stændər‚daiz] *tr* normalizar, estandardizar

standard of living *s* nivel *m* de vida

standard time *s* hora legal, hora oficial

standee [stæn'di] *s* (coll) espectador *m* que asiste de pie; (coll) pasajero de pie

stand'-in' *s* (theat & mov) doble *mf;* (coll) buenas aldabas

standing ['stændiŋ] *adj* derecho, en pie; de pie; parado, inmóvil; (*water*) encharcado, estancado; (*army; committee*) permanente; vigente ‖ *s* condición, posición; reputación; parada; **in good standing** en posición acreditada; **of long standing** de mucho tiempo, de antigua fecha

standing army *s* ejército permanente

standing room *s* sitio para estar de pie

stand'point' *s* punto de vista

stand'still' *s* detención, parada; alto; descanso, inactividad; **to come to a standstill** cesar, pararse

stanza ['stænzə] *s* estancia, estrofa

staple ['stepəl] *adj* primero, principal; corriente, establecido ‖ *s* (*to fasten papers*) grapa; artículo o producto de primera necesidad; materia prima; fibra textil ‖ *tr* sujetar con grapas

stapler ['steplər] *s* engrapador *m,* cosepapeles *m*

star [stɑr] *s* (*heavenly body*) astro; (*heavenly body except sun and moon; figure that represents a star*) estrella; (mov & theat) estrella; (*of football*) as *m;* (typ) estrella o asterisco; (*fate, destiny*) (fig) estrella; **to see stars** (coll) ver las estrellas; **to thank one's lucky stars** estar agradecido por su buena suerte ‖ *v* (*pret & pp* **starred**) *ger* **starring**) *tr* estrellar, adornar o señalar con estrellas; marcar con asterisco; presentar como estrella (*a un actor*) ‖ *intr* ser la estrella; lucirse; sobresalir

starboard ['stɑrbərd] o ['stɑr‚bɔrd] *adj* de estribor ‖ *adv* a estribor ‖ *s* estribor *m*

starch [stɑrt∫] *s* almidón *m,* fécula; arrogancia, entono; (slang) fuerza, vigor *m* ‖ *tr* almidonar

stare [ster] *s* mirada fija ‖ *intr* mirar fijamente; **to stare at** clavar la vista en, mirar con fijeza

star'fish' *s* estrella de mar, estrellamar *m*

star'gaze' *intr* mirar las estrellas; ser distraído, soñar despierto

stark [stɑrk] *adj* cabal, completo, puro; rígido, tieso; duro, severo ‖ *adv* completamente, enteramente; rígidamente, severamente

stark'-na'ked *adj* en pelota, en cueros

star'light' *s* luz *f* de las estrellas

starling ['stɑrliŋ] *s* estornino

Star'-Span'gled Banner *s* bandera estrellada (*bandera de los EE.UU.*)

start [stɑrt] *s* comienzo, principio; salida, partida; lugar *m* de partida; (*scare*) sobresalto; (*sudden start*) arranque *m;* (*advantage*) ventaja ‖ *tr* empezar, principiar; poner en marcha; hacer arrancar; dar la señal de partida a; entablar (*una conversación*); levantar (*la caza*) ‖ *intr* empezar, principiar; ponerse en marcha; arrancar; (*to be startled*) sobresaltar; nacer, provenir; **starting from** o **with** a partir de; **to start after** salir en busca de

starter ['stɑrtər] *s* iniciador *m;* (*of a series*) primero; (aut) arranque *m,* motor *m* de arranque; (sport) juez *m* de salida

starting ['stɑrtiŋ] *adj* de salida; de arranque ‖ *s* puesta en marcha

starting crank *s* manivela de arranque

starting point *s* punto de partida, arrancadero

startle ['stɑrtəl] *tr* asustar, sorprender, sobrecoger ‖ *intr* asustarse, sorprenderse, sobrecogerse

startling ['stɑrtliŋ] *adj* alarmante, asombroso

sq
st

starvation [star'veʃən] s hambre f, inanición

starvation diet s régimen m de hambre, cura de hambre

starvation wages spl salario de hambre

starve [starv] tr hambrear; hacer morir de hambre; **to starve out** hacer rendirse por hambre || intr hambrear; morir de hambre; (coll) tener hambre

starving ['starvɪŋ] adj hambriento, famélico

stat. abbr **statuary, statute, statue**

state [stet] adj de estado; del estado; estatal; público; de gala, de lujo || s estado; fausto, ceremonia, pompa; **to lie in state** estar expuesto en capilla ardiente, estar de cuerpo presente; **to live in state** gastar mucho lujo; **to ride in state** pasear en carruaje de lujo || tr afirmar, declarar; exponer, manifestar; plantear (un problema)

state-ly ['stetli] adj (comp **-lier**; super **-liest**) imponente, majestuoso

statement ['stetmənt] s declaración, exposición, informe m, relación; (com) estado de cuentas

state of mind s estado de ánimo

state'room' s camarote m; (rr) compartimiento particular

states-man ['stetsmən] s (pl **-men** [mən]) estadista m, hombre m de estado

static ['stætɪk] adj estático; (rad) atmosférico || s (rad) parásitos atmosféricos

station ['steʃən] s estación; condición, situación || tr estacionar, apostar

station agent s jefe m de estación

stationary ['steʃən‚ɛri] adj estacionario

station break s (rad) descanso, intermedio

stationer ['steʃənər] s papelero

stationery ['steʃən‚ɛri] s efectos de escritorio; papel m para cartas

stationery store s papelería

station house s cuartelillo de policía

station identification s (rad & telv) indicativo de la emisora

sta'tion·mas'ter s jefe m de estación

station wagon s rubia, coche m rural, vagoneta

statistical [stə'tɪstɪkəl] adj estadístico

statistician [‚stætɪs'tɪʃən] s estadístico

statistics [stə'tɪstɪks] ssg (science) estadística; spl (data) estadística o estadísticas

statue ['stætʃʊ] s estatua

statuesque [‚stætʃʊ'ɛsk] adj escultural

stature ['stætʃər] s estatura, talla; carácter m, habilidad

status ['stetəs] s condición, estado; situación social, legal o profesional; (prestige or superior rank) categoría

status seeking s esfuerzo por adquirir categoría

status symbol s símbolo de categoría social

statute ['stætʃʊt] s estatuto, ley f

statutory ['stætʃʊ‚tɔri] adj estatutario, legal

staunch [stɔntʃ] o [stɑntʃ] adj & tr var de **stanch**

stave [stev] s (of a barrel) duela; (of a ladder) peldaño; (mus) pentagrama m || v (pret & pp **staved** o **stove** [stov]) tr romper, destrozar; (to break a hole in) desfondar; **to stave off** mantener a distancia; evitar, impedir, diferir

stay [ste] s morada, permanencia, estancia; suspensión; (of a corset) ballena, varilla; apoyo, sostén m; (law) espera; (naut) estay m || tr aplazar, detener; poner freno a || intr quedar, quedarse, permanecer; pararse, hospedarse; habitar; **to stay up** no acostarse, velar

stay'-at-home' adj & s hogareño

stead [sted] s lugar m; in his stead en su lugar, en lugar de él; **to stand in good stead** ser de provecho, ser ventajoso

stead'fast' adj fijo; resuelto; constante

stead-y ['stedi] adj (comp **-ier**; super **-iest**) constante, fijo, firme, seguro; regular, uniforme; resuelto; asentado, serio || v (pret & pp **-ied**) tr estabilizar, reforzar; calmar (los nervios) || intr estabilizarse; calmarse

steak [stek] s lonja, tajada; biftec m

steal [stil] s (coll) hurto, robo || v (pret **stole** [stol]; pp **stolen**) tr hurtar, robar; atraer, cautivar || intr hurtar, robar; **to steal away** escabullirse; **to steal into** meterse a hurtadillas en; **to steal upon** aproximarse sin ruido a

stealth [stelθ] s cautela, recato; **by stealth** a hurtadillas

steam [stim] adj de vapor || s vapor m; vaho, humo; **to get up steam** dar presión; **to let off steam** descargar vapor; (fig) desahogarse || tr cocer al vapor; saturar de vapor; empañar (p.ej., las ventanas) || intr echar vapor, emitir vapor; evaporarse; funcionar o marchar a vapor; **to steam ahead** avanzar por medio del vapor; (fig) hacer grandes progresos

steam'boat' s buque m de vapor

steamer ['stimər] s vapor m

steamer rug s manta de viaje

steamer trunk s baúl m de camarote

steam heat s calefacción por vapor

steam roller s apisonadora movida a vapor; (coll) fuerza arrolladora

steam'ship' s vapor m, buque m de vapor

steam shovel s pala mecánica de vapor

steam table s plancha caliente

steed [stid] s caballo; (high-spirited horse) corcel m

steel [stil] adj acerado; (business, industry) siderúrgico; (fig) duro, frío || s acero; (for striking fire from flint; for sharpening knives) eslabón m || tr acerar; **to steel oneself** acerarse

steel wool s virutillas de acero, estopa de acero

steelyard ['stil‚jard] o ['stiljərd] s romana

steep [stip] adj escarpado, empinado;

(*price*) alto, excesivo ‖ *tr* empapar, remojar; **steeped in** absorbido en

steeple ['stipəl] *s* aguja, campanario

stee·ple·chase' *s* carrera de campanario, carrera de obstáculos

stee·ple·jack' *s* escalatorres *m*

steer [stɪr] *s* buey *m* ‖ *tr* conducir, gobernar, guiar ‖ *intr* conducirse; **to steer clear of** (coll) evitar, eludir

steerage ['stɪrɪdʒ] *s* dirección; (naut) proa, entrepuente *m*

steerage passenger *s* (naut) pasajero de entrepuente

steering wheel *s* (aut) volante *m;* (naut) rueda del timón

stem [stɛm] *s* (*of a goblet*) pie *m;* (*of a pipe, of a feather*) cañón *m;* (*of a column*) fuste *m;* (*of a watch*) botón *m;* (*of a key*) espiga, tija; (*of a word*) tema *m;* (bot) tallo, vástago; **from stem to stern** de proa a popa ‖ *v* (*pret & pp* **stemmed;** *ger* **stemming**) *tr* (*to remove the stem from*) desgranar; (*to check*) detener, refrenar; (*to plug*) estancar; hacer frente a; rendir (*la marea*) ‖ *intr* nacer, provenir; **to stem from** originarse en, provenir de

stem'-wind'er *s* remontuar *m*

stench [stɛntʃ] *s* hedor *m,* hediondez *f*

sten·cil ['stɛnsəl] *s* cartón picado; (*work produced by it*) estarcido ‖ *v* (*pret & pp* **-ciled** o **-cilled;** *ger* **-ciling** o **-cilling**) *tr* estarcir

stenographer [stə'nɑgrəfər] *s* estenógrafo

stenography [stə'nɑgrəfi] *s* estenografía

step [stɛp] *s* paso; (*of staircase*) grada, peldaño; (*footprint*) huella, pisada; (*of carriage*) estribo; (*measure, démarche*) gestión, medida; (mus) intervalo; **step by step** paso a paso; **to watch one's step** proceder con cautela, andarse con tiento ‖ *v* (*pret & pp* **stepped;** *ger* **stepping**) *tr* escalonar; **to step off** medir a pasos ‖ *intr* dar un paso, dar pasos; caminar, ir; (coll) andar de prisa; **to step on it** (coll) acelerar la marcha, darse prisa; **to step on the starter** pisar el arranque

step'broth'er *s* medio hermano, hermanastro

step'child' *s* (*pl* **-children** [,tʃɪldrən]) hijastro

step'daugh'ter *s* hijastra

step'fa'ther *s* padrastro

step'lad'der *s* escala, escalera de tijera

step'moth'er *s* madrastra

steppe [stɛp] *s* estepa

stepping stone *s* estriberón *m,* pasadera; (fig) escalón *m,* escabel *m*

step'sis'ter *s* media hermana, hermanastra

step'son' *s* hijastro

stere·o ['stɛri ,o] o ['stɪri ,o] *adj* (coll) estereofónico; (coll) estereoscópico ‖ *s* (*pl* **-os**) (coll) música estereofónica, disco estereofónico; (coll) radiodifusión estereofónica; (coll) fotografía estereoscópica

stereotyped ['stɛri·ə ,taɪpt] o ['stɪri·ə ,taɪpt] *adj* estereotipado

sterile ['stɛrɪl] *adj* estéril

sterilize ['stɛri ,laɪz] *tr* esterilizar

sterling ['stɑrlɪŋ] *adj* fino, de ley; verdadero, genuino, puro, excelente ‖ *s* libras esterlinas; plata de ley; vajilla de plata

stern [stʌrn] *adj* austero, severo; decidido, firme ‖ *s* popa

stethoscope ['stɛθə ,skop] *s* estetoscopio

stevedore ['stivə ,dor] *s* estibador *m*

stew [stju] o [stu] *s* guisado, estofado ‖ *tr* guisar, estofar ‖ *intr* abrasarse; (coll) estar apurado

steward ['stju·ərd] o ['stu·ərd] *s* mayordomo; administrador *m;* (*of ship or plane*) camarero

stewardess ['stju·ərdɪs] o ['stu·ərdɪs] *s* mayordoma; (*of ship or plane*) camarera; (*of plane*) azafata, aeromoza

stewed fruit *s* compota de frutas

stewed tomatoes *spl* puré *m* de tomates

stick [stɪk] *s* palo, palillo; bastón *m,* vara; (*of dynamite*) barra; (naut) mástil *m,* verga; (typ) componedor *m* ‖ *v* (*pret & pp* **stuck** [stʌk]) *tr* picar, punzar; apuñalar; clavar, hincar; pegar; (coll) confundir; **to stick out** asomar (*la cabeza*); sacar (*la lengua*); **to stick up** (*in order to rob*) (slang) asaltar, atracar ‖ *intr* estar prendido, estar hincado; pegarse; agarrarse (*la pintura*); encastillarse (*p.ej., una ventana*); resaltar, sobresalir; continuar, persistir; permanecer; atascarse; **to stick out** salir (*p.ej., el pañuelo del bolsillo*); sobresalir, proyectarse; velar (*un escollo*); resultar evidente; **to stick together** (coll) quedarse unidos, no abandonarse; **to stick up** destacarse; estar de punta (*el pelo*); **to stick up for** (coll) defender

sticker ['stɪkər] *s* etiqueta engomada, marbete engomado; punta, espina; (coll) problema arduo

sticking plaster *s* esparadrapo

stick'pin' *s* alfiler *m* de corbata

stick'-up' *s* (slang) asalto, atraco

stick·y ['stɪki] *adj* (*comp* **-ier;** *super* **-iest**) pegajoso; (coll) húmedo, mojado; (*weather*) bochornoso

stiff [stɪf] *adj* tieso; entorpecido, entumecido; arduo, difícil; (*price*) (coll) excesivo ‖ *s* (slang) cadáver *m*

stiff collar *s* cuello almidonado

stiffen ['stɪfən] *tr* atiesar; endurecer; espesar ‖ *intr* atiesarse; endurecerse; espesarse; obstinarse

stiff neck *s* torticolis *m;* obstinación

stiff-necked ['stɪf ,nɛkt] *adj* terco, obstinado

stiff shirt *s* camisola

stifle ['staɪfəl] *tr* ahogar, sofocar; apagar, suprimir

stig·ma ['stɪgmə] *s* (*pl* **-mas** o **-mata** [mətə]) estigma *m*

stigmatize ['stɪgmə ,taɪz] *tr* estigmatizar

stilet·to [stɪ'lɛto] *s* (*pl* **-tos**) estilete *m,* puñal *m*

still [stɪl] *adj* inmóvil, quieto, tranquilo; callado, silencioso; (*wine*) no espumoso ‖ *adv* tranquilamente; silenciosamente; aún, todavía ‖ *conj* con todo, sin embargo ‖ *s* alambique *m*, destiladera; destilería; fotografía de lo inmóvil; (poet) silencio ‖ *tr* acallar; amortiguar; calmar ‖ *intr* callar; calmarse

still'birth' *s* parto muerto

still'born' *adj* nacido muerto

still life *s* (*pl* **still lifes** o **still lives**) bodegón *m*, naturaleza muerta

stilt [stɪlt] *s* zanco; (*in the water*) pilote *m*

stilted ['stɪltɪd] *adj* elevado; hinchado, pomposo, tieso

stimulant ['stɪmjələnt] *adj & s* estimulante *m*, excitante *m*

stimulate ['stɪmjə,let] *tr* estimular

stimu·lus ['stɪmjələs] *s* (*pl* -li [,laɪ]) estímulo

sting [stɪŋ] *s* picadura; aguijón *m* ‖ *v* (*pret & pp* **stung** [stʌŋ]) *tr* picar; aguijonear ‖ *intr* picar

stin·gy ['stɪndʒi] *adj* (*comp* -gier; *super* -giest) mezquino, tacaño

stink [stɪŋk] *s* hedor *m*, mal olor *m* ‖ *v* (*pret* **stank** [stæŋk] o **stunk** [stʌŋk]; *pp* **stunk**) *tr* dar mal olor a ‖ *intr* heder, oler muy mal; **to stink of** heder a; (slang) poseer (*p.ej., dinero*) en un grado que da asco

stint [stɪnt] *s* faena, tarea ‖ *tr* limitar, restringir ‖ *intr* ser económico, ahorrar con mezquindad

stipend ['staɪpənd] *s* estipendio

stipulate ['stɪpjə,let] *tr* estipular

stir [stʌr] *s* agitación, meneo; alboroto, tumulto; **to create a stir** meter ruido ‖ *v* (*pret & pp* **stirred**; *ger* **stirring**) *tr* agitar, mover; revolver; conmover, excitar; atizar, avivar (*el fuego*); remover (*un líquido*); **to stir up** revolver; despertar; conmover; fomentar (*discordias*) ‖ *intr* bullirse, moverse

stirring ['stʌrɪŋ] *adj* conmovedor, emocionante

stirrup ['stʌrəp] o ['stɪrəp] *s* estribo

stitch [stɪtʃ] *s* puntada, punto; pedazo de tela; punzada, dolor *m* punzante; (coll) poquito; **to be in stitches** (coll) desternillarse de risa ‖ *tr* coser, bastear, hilvanar ‖ *intr* coser

stock [stak] *adj* común, regular; banal, vulgar; bursátil; ganadero, del ganado; (theat) de repertorio ‖ *s* surtido; capital *f* comercial; acciones, valores *mpl*; (*of meat*) caldo; (*of a tree*) tronco; (*of an anvil*) cepo; (*of a rifle*) caja, culata; (*of a tree; of a family*) cepa; mango, manija; palo, madero; leño; (*livestock*) ganado; (theat) programa *m*, repertorio; **in stock** en existencia; **out of stock** agotado; **to take stock** hacer el inventario; **to take stock in** (coll) dar importancia a, confiar en ‖ *tr* abastecer, surtir; tener existencias de; acopiar, acumular; poblar (*un estanque, una colmena, etc.*)

stockade [sta'ked] *s* estacada, empalizada ‖ *tr* empalizar

stock'breed'er *s* criador *m* de ganado

stock'bro'ker *s* bolsista *mf*, corredor *m* de bolsa

stock car *s* (aut) coche *m* de serie; (rr) vagón *m* para el ganado

stock company *s* (com) sociedad anónima; (theat) teatro de repertorio

stock dividend *s* acción liberada

stock exchange *s* bolsa

stock'hold'er *s* accionista *mf*, tenedor *m* de acciones

stockholder of record *s* accionista *mf* que como tal figura en el libro-registro de la compañía

Stockholm ['stakhom] *s* Estocolmo

stocking ['stakɪŋ] *s* media

stock market *s* bolsa, mercado de valores; **to play the stock market** jugar a la bolsa

stock'pile' *s* reserva de materias primas ‖ *tr* acumular (*materias primas*) ‖ *intr* acumular materias primas

stock raising *s* ganadería

stock'room' *s* almacén *m*; sala de exposición

stock split *s* reparto de acciones gratis

stock·y ['staki] *adj* (*comp* -ier; *super* -iest) bajo, grueso y fornido

stock'yard' *s* corral *m* de concentración de ganado

stoic ['sto·ɪk] *adj & s* estoico

stoke [stok] *tr* atizar, avivar (*el fuego*); alimentar, cebar (*el horno*)

stoker ['stokər] *s* fogonero

stolid ['stalɪd] *adj* impasible, insensible

stomach ['stʌmək] *s* estómago; apetito; deseo, inclinación ‖ *tr* tragar; **to not be able to stomach** (coll) no poder tragar

stone [ston] *s* piedra; (*of fruit*) hueso; (pathol) mal *m* de piedra ‖ *tr* lapidar, apedrear; deshuesar (*la fruta*)

stone'-broke' *adj* arrancado, sin blanca

stone'-deaf' *adj* sordo como una tapia

stone'ma'son *s* albañil *m*

stone quarry *s* cantera, pedrera

stone's throw *s* tiro de piedra; **within a stone's throw** a tiro de piedra

ston·y ['stoni] *adj* (*comp* -ier; *super* -iest) pedregoso; duro, empedernido

stool [stul] *s* escabel *m*, taburete *m*; sillico, retrete *m*; (*bowel movement*) cámara, evacuación

stoop [stup] *s* encorvada, inclinación; escalinata de entrada ‖ *intr* doblarse, inclinarse, encorvarse; andar encorvado; humillarse, rebajarse

stoop-shouldered ['stup'ʃoldərd] *adj* cargado de espaldas

stop [stap] *s* parada, alto; estada, estancia; cesación, fin *m*, suspensión; cerradura, tapadura; impedimento, obstáculo; freno; tope *m*, retén *m*; (*in writing; in telegrams*) punto; (*of a guitar*) llave *f*, traste *m*; **to put a stop to** poner fin a ‖ *v* (*pret & pp* **stopped**; *ger* **stopping**) *tr* parar, detener; acabar, terminar; estorbar, obstruir; interceptar; suspender; cerrar, tapar; rechazar (*un golpe*); retener (*un sueldo o parte de él*); **to stop up** cegar, obstruir, tapar ‖ *intr* parar, pararse, detenerse; quedarse; permanecer; alojarse, hospedarse; acabarse, terminarse; **to stop** + *ger* cesar de + *inf*, dejar de + *inf*

stop'cock' s llave f de cierre, llave de paso

stop'gap' *adj* provisional ‖ s substituto provisional

stop light s luz f de parada

stop'o'ver s parada intermedia, escala; billete m de parada intermedia

stoppage ['stɑpɪdʒ] s parada, detención; (*of work*) paro; interrupción; suspensión; obstáculo; (*of wages*) retención; (*pathol*) obstrucción

stopper ['stɑpər] s tapón m; taco, tarugo

stop sign o **stop signal** s señal f de alto, señal de parada

stop watch s reloj m de segundos muertos, cronómetro

storage ['storɪdʒ] s almacenaje m; (*costs*) derechos de almacenaje

storage battery s (elec) acumulador m

store [stor] s tienda, almacén m; **I know what is in store for you** sé lo que le espera; **to set store by** dar mucha importancia a ‖ *tr* abastecer; tener guardado, almacenar; **to store away** acumular

store'house' s almacén m, depósito; (*e.g., of wisdom*) (fig) mina

store'keep'er s tendero, almacenista mf

store'room' s cuarto de almacenar; (*for furniture*) guardamuebles m; (naut) despensa

stork [stɔrk] s cigüeña; **to have a visit from the stork** recibir a la cigüeña

storm [stɔrm] s borrasca, tempestad, tormenta; (mil) asalto; (naut) borrasca; (fig) tempestad, tumulto; **to take by storm** tomar por asalto ‖ *tr* asaltar ‖ *intr* tempestear; precipitarse

storm cloud s nubarrón m

storm door s contrapuerta, guardapuerta

storm sash s contravidriera

storm troops *spl* tropas de asalto

storm window s guardaventana, sobrevidriera

storm·y ['stɔrmi] *adj* (*comp* **-ier**; *super* **-iest**) borrascoso, tempestuoso; (*session, meeting, etc.*) tumultuoso

sto·ry ['stori] s (*pl* **-ries**) historia, cuento, anécdota; enredo, trama; (coll) mentira; piso, alto ‖ *v* (*pret & pp* **-ried**) *tr* historiar

sto'ry·tel'ler s narrador m; (coll) mentiroso

stout [staut] *adj* corpulento, gordo, robusto; animoso; leal; terco ‖ s cerveza obscura fuerte

stove [stov] s (*for heating a house or room*) estufa; (*for cooking*) hornillo, cocina de gas, cocina eléctrica

stove'pipe' s tubo de estufa, tubo de hornillo; (*hat*) (coll) chistera, chimenea

stow [sto] *tr* guardar, meter, esconder; (naut) arrumar, estibar ‖ *intr* — **to stow away** embarcarse clandestinamente, esconderse en un barco o avión

stowage ['sto·ɪdʒ] s arrumaje m, estiba

stow'a·way' s llovido, polizón m

str. *abbr* strait, steamer

straddle ['strædəl] s esparrancamiento ‖ *tr* montar a horcajadas; (coll) tratar de favorecer a ambas partes en (*p.ej., un pleito*) ‖ *intr* ponerse a horcajadas; (coll) tratar de favorecer a ambas partes

strafe [straf] o [stref] s (slang) bombardeo violento ‖ *tr* (slang) bombardear violentamente

straggle ['strægəl] *intr* errar, vagar; andar perdido, extraviarse; separarse; estar esparcido

straight [stret] *adj* derecho; recto; erguido; (*hair*) lacio; continuo, seguido; honrado, sincero; correcto; decidido, intransigente; (*e.g., whiskey*) solo; **to set a person straight** mostrar el camino a una persona; dar consejo a una persona; mostrar a una persona el modo de proceder ‖ *adv* derecho; sin interrupción; sinceramente; exactamente; en seguida; **straight ahead** todo seguido, derecho; **to go straight** (coll) enmendarse

straighten ['stretən] *tr* enderezar; poner en orden ‖ *intr* enderezarse

straight face s cara seria

straight razor s navaja barbera

straight'way' *adv* luego, en seguida

strain [stren] s tensión, tirantez f; esfuerzo muy grande; fatiga excesiva, agotamiento; (*of a muscle*) torcedura; aire m, melodía; (*of a family or lineage*) cepa; linaje m, raza; rasgo racial; genio, vena; huella, rastro ‖ *tr* estirar; torcer o torcerse (*p.ej., la muñeca*); forzar (*p.ej., los nervios, la vista*); apretar; deformar; colar, tamizar ‖ *intr* esforzarse; deformarse; colarse, tamizarse; filtrarse; exprimirse (*un jugo*); resistirse; **to strain at** hacer grandes esfuerzos por

strained [strend] *adj* (*smile*) forzado; (*friendship*) tirante

strainer ['strenər] s colador m

strait [stret] s estrecho; **straits** estrecho; **to be in dire straits** estar en el mayor apuro, hallarse en gran estrechez

strait jacket s camisa de fuerza

strait-laced ['stret,lest] *adj* gazmoño

strand [strænd] s playa; filamento; (*of rope or cable*) torón m, ramal m; (*of pearls*) hilo; pelo ‖ *tr* deshebrar; retorcer, trenzar (*cuerda, cable, etc.*); dejar extraviado; (naut) varar

stranded ['strændɪd] *adj* desprovisto, desamparado; (*ship*) encallado; (*rope or cable*) trenzado, retorcido

strange [strendʒ] *adj* extraño, singular; nuevo, desconocido; novel, no acostumbrado

stranger ['strendʒər] s forastero; visi-

tador *m;* intruso; desconocido; principiante *mf*
strangle ['stræŋgǝl] *tr* estrangular;
reprimir, suprimir || *intr* estrangu-
larse
strap [stræp] *s (of leather)* correa; *(of
cloth, metal, etc.)* banda, tira; *(to
sharpen a razor)* asentador *m* || *v
(pret & pp* **strapped;** *ger* **strapping)**
tr atar o liar con correa, banda o
tira; azotar con una correa; fajar,
vendar; asentar *(una navaja)*
strap'hang'er *s* (coll) pasajero colgado
stratagem ['strætǝdʒǝm] *s* estratagema
f
strategic(al) [strǝ'tidʒɪk(ǝl)] *adj* estratégico
strategist ['strætɪdʒɪst] *s* estratega *m*
strate·gy ['strætɪdʒɪ] *s (pl* **-gies)** estrategia
strati·fy ['strætɪ,faɪ] *v (pret & pp*
-fied) *tr* estratificar || *intr* estratifi-
carse
stratosphere ['strætǝ,sfɪr] o ['stretǝ-
,sfɪr] *s* estratosfera
stra·tum ['stretǝm] o ['strætǝm] *s (pl*
-ta [tǝ] o **-tums)** estrato; *(e.g., of
society)* clase *f*
straw [strǝ] *adj* pajizo; baladí, de poca
importancia; falso; ficticio || *s* paja;
(for drinking) pajita; **I don't care a
straw** no se me da un bledo; **to be
the last straw** ser el colmo, no faltar
más
straw'ber'ry *s (pl* **-ries)** fresa
straw hat *s* sombrero de paja; *(with
low flat crown)* canotié *m*
straw man *s* figura de paja; *(figurehead)* testaferro; testigo falso
straw vote *s* voto informativo
stray [stre] *adj* extraviado, perdido;
aislado, suelto || *s* animal extraviado
o perdido || *intr* extraviarse, perderse
streak [strik] *s* lista, raya; vena, veta;
rasgo, traza; *(of light)* rayo; *(of good
luck)* racha; (coll) tiempo muy
breve; **like a streak** (coll) como un
rayo || *tr* listar, rayar; abigarrar ||
intr rayarse; (coll) andar o pasar
como un rayo
stream [strim] *s (current)* corriente *f;*
arroyo, río; chorro, flujo; *(of people)*
torrente *m;* (e.g., *of automobiles)*
desfile *m* || *intr* correr, manar *(un
líquido);* chorrear; flotar, ondear;
salir a torrentes
streamer ['strimǝr] *s* flámula, banderola; cinta ondeante; rayo de luz
streamlined ['strim,laɪnd] *adj* aerodinámico, perfilado
stream'lin'er *s* tren aerodinámico de
lujo
street [strit] *adj* callejero || *s* calle *f*
street'car' *s* tranvía *m*
street cleaner *s* basurero; *(device)* barredera
street clothes *spl* traje *m* de calle
street floor *s* piso bajo
street lamp *s* farol *m* (de la calle)
street sprinkler ['sprɪŋklǝr] *s* carricuba, carro de riego, regadera
street'walk'er *s* cantonera, carrerista
strength [strɛŋθ] *s* fuerza; intensidad;

(of spirituous liquors) graduación;
(com) tendencia a la subida; (mil)
número; **on the strength of** fundán-
dose en, confiando en
strengthen ['strɛŋθǝn] *tr* fortificar, re-
forzar; confirmar || *intr* fortificarse,
reforzarse
strenuous ['strɛnjʊ·ǝs] *adj* estrenuo,
enérgico, vigoroso; arduo, difícil
stress [strɛs] *s* tensión, fuerza; compulsión; acento; (mech) tensión; **to
lay stress on** hacer hincapié en || *tr*
someter a esfuerzo; hacer hincapié
en; acentuar
stress accent *s* acento prosódico
stretch [strɛtʃ] *s* estiramiento, estirón
m; (distance in time or space) trecho; *(section of road)* tramo; extensión; *(of the imagination)* esfuerzo;
(confinement in jail) (slang) con-
dena; **at a stretch** de un tirón || *tr*
estirar; extender; tender; forzar, violentar; (fig) estirar *(el dinero);* **to
stretch a point** hacer una concesión;
to stretch oneself desperezarse || *intr*
estirarse; extenderse; tenderse; des-
perezarse; **to stretch out** (coll)
echarse
stretcher ['strɛtʃǝr] *s (for gloves)* ensanchador *m; (for a painting)* bastidor *m; (to carry sick or wounded)*
camilla
stretch'er-bear'er *s* camillero
strew [stru] *v (pret* **strewed;** *pp*
strewed o **strewn)** *tr* derramar, esparcir; sembrar, salpicar; polvorear
stricken ['strɪkǝn] *adj* afligido; inhabilitado; herido; **stricken in years**
debilitado por los años
strict [strɪkt] *adj* estricto, riguroso;
(exacting) severo
stricture ['strɪktʃǝr] *s* crítica severa;
(pathol) estrictura
stride [straɪd] *s* zancada, tranco; **to
hit one's stride** alcanzar la actividad
o velocidad acostumbrada; **to make
great (o rapid) strides** avanzar a
grandes pasos; **to take in one's stride**
hacer sin esfuerzo || *v (pret* **strode**
[strod]; *pp* **stridden** ['strɪdǝn]) *tr*
cruzar de un tranco; montar a horca-
jadas || *intr* dar zancadas, caminar a
paso largo, andar a trancos
strident ['straɪdǝnt] *adj* estridente
strife [straɪf] *s* contienda; rivalidad
strike [straɪk] *s (blow)* golpe *m; (stopping of work)* huelga; *(discovery of
ore, oil, etc.)* descubrimiento repentino; golpe *m* de fortuna; **to go on
strike** ir a la huelga || *v (pret & pp*
struck [strʌk]) *tr* golpear; pulsar
(una tecla); herir, percutir; topar, dar
con; acuñar *(monedas);* echar *(raíces);* frotar, rayar, encender *(un
fósforo);* descubrir repentinamente
(mineral, aceite, etc.); cerrar *(un
trato);* arriar *(las velas);* dar *(la
hora);* asumir, tomar *(una postura);*
borrar, cancelar; impresionar; atraer
(la atención); **to strike it rich** descubrir un buen filón, tener un golpe de
fortuna || *intr* dar, sonar *(una cam-
pana, un reloj);* declararse en huelga;

(mil) dar el asalto; **to strike out** ponerse en marcha, echar camino adelante

strike′break′er s rompehuelgas m, esquirol m

striker ['straɪkər] s golpeador m; huelguista mf

striking ['straɪkɪŋ] adj impresionante, llamativo, sorprendente; en huelga

striking power s potencia de choque

string [strɪŋ] s cuerdecilla; (of pearls; of lies) sarta; (of beans) hebra; (of onions or garlic) ristra; (row) hilera; (mus) cuerda; (limitation, proviso) (coll) condición; **strings** instrumentos de cuerda; **to pull strings** tocar resortes ‖ v (pret & pp **strung** [strʌŋ]) tr enhebrar, ensartar; atar con cuerdas; proveer de cuerdas; colgar de una cuerda; tender (un cable, un alambre); encordar (un violín, una raqueta); colocar en fila; (slang) engañar, burlar; **to string along** (slang) traer al retortero; **to string up** (coll) ahorcar

string bean s habichuela verde, judía verde

stringed instrument [strɪŋd] s instrumento de cuerda

stringent ['strɪndʒənt] adj riguroso, severo, estricto; convincente

string quartet s cuarteto de cuerdas

strip [strɪp] s tira; (of metal) lámina; (of land) faja ‖ v (pret & pp **stripped**; ger **stripping**) tr desnudar; despojar; desforrar; deshacer (la cama); estropear (el engranaje, un tornillo); desvenar (tabaco); descortezar; **to strip of** despojar de ‖ intr desnudarse; despojarse; descortezarse

stripe [straɪp] s banda, lista, raya; gaya; cinta, franja; (mil & nav) galón m; índole f, tipo; **to win one's stripes** ganar los entorchados ‖ tr listar, rayar; gayar

strip mining s mineraje m a tajo abierto

strive [straɪv] v (pret **strove** [strov]; pp **striven** ['strɪvən]) intr esforzarse; luchar

stroke [strok] s golpe m; (of bell or clock) campanada; (of pen) plumada; (of brush) pincelada, brochada; (of arms in swimming) brazada; (in a game) jugada; (caress with hand) caricia; (with a racket) raquetazo; (of a piston) carrera, embolada; (of a paddle) palada; (of an oar) remada; (of lightning) rayo; (line, mark) raya; (of good luck) golpe m; (of wit) agudeza, chiste m; (of genius) rasgo; ataque m de parálisis; **at the stroke of** (e.g., five) al dar las (p.ej., cinco); **to not do a stroke of work** no dar golpe, no levantar paja del suelo ‖ tr frotar suavemente, acariciar con la mano

stroll [strol] s paseo; **to take a stroll** dar un paseo ‖ intr pasear, pasearse; callejear, errar, vagar

stroller ['strolər] s paseante mf; cochecito para niños

strong [strɔŋ] o [straŋ] adj fuerte,

resistente; recio, robusto; intenso; (stock market) firme; enérgico; marcado; picante; rancio

strong′box′ s cofre m fuerte, caja de caudales

strong drink s bebida alcohólica, bebida fuerte

strong′hold′ s plaza fuerte

strong man s (e.g., in a circus) hércules m; (leader, good planner) alma, promotor m; (dictator) hombre m fuerte

strong-minded ['strɔŋ‚maɪndɪd] o [straŋ‚maɪndɪd] adj independiente; de inteligencia vigorosa; (e.g., woman) hombruna

strontium ['strɑnfɪ·əm] s estroncio

strop [strɑp] s suavizador m ‖ v (pret & pp **stropped**; ger **stropping**) tr suavizar, afilar

strophe ['strofi] s estrofa

structure ['strʌktʃər] s estructura; edificio

struggle ['strʌgəl] s lucha; esfuerzo, forcejeo ‖ intr luchar; esforzarse, forcejear

strum [strʌm] v (pret & pp **strummed**; ger **strumming**) tr arañar (un instrumento músico) sin arte ‖ intr cencerrear; **to strum on** rasguear

strumpet ['strʌmpɪt] s ramera

strut [strʌt] s (brace, prop) riostra, tornapunta; contoneo, pavoneo ‖ v (pret & pp **strutted**; ger **strutting**) intr contonearse, pavonearse

strychnine ['strɪknaɪn] o ['strɪknɪn] s estricnina

stub [stʌb] s fragmento, trozo; (of a cigar) colilla; (of a tree) tocón m; (of a pencil) cabo; (of a check) talón m ‖ v (pret & pp **stubbed**; ger **stubbing**) tr — **to stub one's toe** dar un tropezón

stubble ['stʌbəl] s rastrojo; (of beard) cañón m

stubborn ['stʌbərn] adj terco, testarudo, obstinado; porfiado; intratable

stuc·co ['stʌko] s (pl **-coes** o **-cos**) estuco ‖ tr estucar

stuck′-up′ adj (coll) estirado, orgulloso

stud [stʌd] s tachón m; botón m de camisa; montante m, pie derecho; clavo de adorno; (bolt) espárrago; caballeriza; (of mares) yeguada ‖ v (pret & pp **studded**; ger **studding**) tr tachonar

stud bolt s espárrago

stud′book′ s registro genealógico de caballos

student ['stjudənt] o ['studənt] adj estudiantil ‖ s estudiante mf; (person who investigates) estudioso

student body s estudiantado, alumnado

stud′horse′ s caballo padre, caballo semental

studied ['stʌdid] adj premeditado, hecho adrede; (affected) estudiado

studi·o ['stjudɪ‚o] o ['studɪ‚o] s (pl **-os**) estudio, taller m; (mov & rad) estudio

studious ['stjudɪ·əs] o ['studɪ·əs] adj estudioso; asiduo, solícito

stud·y ['stʌdi] s (pl **-ies**) estudio; solicitud; meditación profunda; (e.g.,

of a professor) gabinete *m*, estudio ‖
v (*pret & pp* **-ied**) *tr & intr* estudiar
stuff [stʌf] *s* materia; género, paño,
tela; muebles *mpl*, baratijas; medicina; fruslerías; cosa, cosas ‖ *tr* rellenar; henchir, llenar; atascar, cerrar, tapar; embutir; (*with food*)
atracar; meter sin orden, llenar sin
orden; disecar (*un animal muerto*) ‖
intr atracarse, hartarse
stuffed shirt *s* (slang) tragavirotes *m*
stuffing [ˈstʌfɪŋ] *s* relleno
stuff·y [ˈstʌfi] *adj* (*comp* **-ier;** *super*
-iest) sofocante, mal ventilado; aburrido, sin interés; (*prim*) (coll) relamido
stumble [ˈstʌmbəl] *intr* tropezar, dar
un traspié; moverse a tropezones;
hablar a tropezones; **to stumble on** o
upon tropezar con
stumbling block *s* escollo, tropezadero
stump [stʌmp] *s* (*of a tree, arm, etc.*)
tocón *m*; (*of an arm*) muñón *m*; (*of
a tooth*) raigón *m*; (*of a cigar*) colilla; (*of a tail*) rabo; paso pesado;
fragmento, resto; tribuna pública;
(*for shading drawings*) esfumino ‖
tr recorrer (*el país*) pronunciando
discursos políticos; (coll) confundir,
dejar sin habla; esfumar
stump speaker *s* orador callejero
stump speech *s* arenga electoral
stun [stʌn] *v* (*pret & pp* **stunned;** *ger*
stunning) *tr* atolondrar, aturdir
stunning [ˈstʌnɪŋ] *adj* (coll) pasmoso,
estupendo, pistonudo, elegante
stunt [stʌnt] *s* atrofia; (*underdeveloped
creature*) engendro; (coll) suerte
acrobática; (coll) faena, hazaña,
proeza ‖ *tr* atrofiar ‖ *intr* (coll) hacer suertes acrobáticas
stunt flying *s* vuelo acrobático
stunt man *s* (mov) doble *m* que hace
suertes peligrosas
stupe·fy [ˈstjupɪˌfaɪ] o [ˈstupɪˌfaɪ] *v*
(*pret & pp* **-fied**) *tr* dejar estupefacto, pasmar; causar estupor a
stupendous [stjuˈpɛndəs] o [stuˈpɛndəs] *adj* estupendo; enorme
stupid [ˈstjupɪd] o [ˈstupɪd] *adj* estúpido
stupor [ˈstjupər] o [ˈstupər] *s* estupor
m, modorra
stur·dy [ˈstʌrdi] *adj* (*comp* **-dier;** *super* **-diest**) fuerte, robusto, fornido;
firme, tenaz
sturgeon [ˈstʌrdʒən] *s* esturión *m*
stutter [ˈstʌtər] *s* tartamudeo ‖ *tr* decir tartamudeando ‖ *intr* tartamudear
sty [staɪ] *s* (*pl* **sties**) pocilga, zahurda;
(pathol) orzuelo
style [staɪl] *s* estilo; moda; elegancia;
to live in great style vivir en gran
lujo ‖ *tr* intitular, nombrar
stylish [ˈstaɪlɪʃ] *adj* de moda, elegante
styptic pencil [ˈstɪptɪk] *s* lápiz estíptico
Styx [stɪks] *s* Estigia
suave [swɑv] o [swɛv] *adj* suave;
afable, fino, zalamero, pulido
sub. *abbr* **subscription, substitute,
suburban**

subaltern [səbˈɔltərn] *adj & s* subalterno
subconscious [sʌbˈkɑnʃəs] *adj* subconsciente ‖ *s* subconsciencia
subconsciousness [sʌbˈkɑnʃəsnɪs] *s*
subconsciencia
subdeb [ˈsʌbˌdɛb] *s* tobillera
subdivide [ˈsʌbdɪˌvaɪd] o [ˌsʌbdɪ
ˈvaɪd] *tr* subdividir ‖ *intr* subdividirse
subdue [səbˈdju] o [səbˈdu] *tr* sojuzgar, subyugar; amansar, dominar;
suavizar
subdued [səbˈdjud] o [səbˈdud] *adj*
sojuzgado; sumiso; (*e.g., light*) suave
subheading [ˈsʌbˌhɛdɪŋ] *s* subtítulo
subject [ˈsʌbdʒɪkt] *adj* sujeto; súbdito
‖ *s* asunto, materia, tema *m*; (*person
in his relationship to a ruler or government*) súbdito; (gram, med,
philos) sujeto ‖ [səbˈdʒɛkt] *tr* sujetar, someter, sojuzgar
subject index *s* índice *m* de materias
subjection [səbˈdʒɛkʃən] *s* sumisión,
sometimiento
subjective [səbˈdʒɛktɪv] *adj* subjetivo
subject matter *s* asunto, materia
subjugate [ˈsʌbdʒəˌɡet] *tr* subyugar
subjunctive [səbˈdʒʌŋktɪv] *adj & s*
subjuntivo
sub·let [ˈsʌbˈlɛt] o [ˈsʌbˌlɛt] *v* (*pret &
pp* **-let;** *ger* **-letting**) *tr* realquilar,
subarrendar
submachine gun [ˌsʌbməˈʃin] *s* subfusil *m* ametrallador
submarine [ˈsʌbməˌrin] *adj & s* submarino ‖ *tr* (coll) atacar o hundir
con un submarino
submarine chaser [ˈtʃesər] *s* cazasubmarinos *m*
submerge [səbˈmʌrdʒ] *tr* sumergir ‖
intr sumergirse
submersion [səbˈmʌrʒən] o [səb
ˈmʌrʃən] *s* sumersión
submission [səbˈmɪʃən] *s* sumisión
submissive [səbˈmɪsɪv] *adj* sumiso
sub·mit [səbˈmɪt] *v* (*pret & pp* **-mitted;**
ger **-mitting**) *tr* someter; proponer,
permitirse decir ‖ *intr* someterse
subordinate [səbˈɔrdɪnɪt] *adj & s* subordinado ‖ [səbˈɔrdɪˌnet] *tr* subordinar
subornation of perjury [ˌsʌbərˈneʃən]
s (law) soborno de testigo
subplot [ˈsʌbˌplɑt] *s* trama secundaria
subpoena o **subpena** [sʌbˈpinə] o [sə
ˈpinə] *s* comparendo ‖ *tr* mandar
comparecer
sub rosa [sʌbˈrozə] *adv* en secreto, en
confianza
subscribe [səbˈskraɪb] *tr* subscribir ‖
intr subscribir; subscribirse, abonarse; **to subscribe to** subscribirse a,
abonarse a (*una publicación periódica*); subscribir (*una opinión*)
subscriber [səbˈskraɪbər] *s* abonado
subsequent [ˈsʌbsɪkwənt] *adj* subsiguiente, posterior
subservient [səbˈsʌrvɪ·ənt] *adj* servil;
subordinado; útil
subside [səbˈsaɪd] *intr* calmarse; acabarse, cesar; bajar (*el nivel del
agua*); amainar (*el viento*)

subsidize ['sʌbsɪ‚daɪz] *tr* subsidiar, subvencionar; (*to bribe*) sobornar

subsi‧dy ['sʌbsɪdɪ] *s* (*pl* **-dies**) subsidio, subvención

subsist [səb'sɪst] *intr* subsistir

subsistence [səb'sɪstəns] *s* subsistencia

substance ['sʌbstəns] *s* substancia

substandard [sʌb'stændərd] *adj* inferior al nivel normal

substantial [səb'stænʃəl] *adj* considerable, importante; fuerte, sólido; acomodado, rico; esencial; (*food*) substancial

substantiate [səb'stænʃɪ‚et] *tr* comprobar, establecer, verificar

substantive ['sʌbstəntɪv] *adj & s* substantivo

substation ['sʌb‚steʃən] *s* (elec) subcentral *f*

substitute ['sʌbstɪ‚tjut] o ['sʌbstɪ‚tut] *adj* substitutivo || *s* (*person*) substituto; (*thing, substance*) substitutivo; (mil) reemplazo || *tr* poner (*a una persona o cosa*) en lugar de otra || *intr* actuar de substituto; **to substitute for** substituir (*with personal* a)

substitution [‚sʌbstɪ'tjuʃən] o [‚sʌbstɪ'tuʃən] *s* empleo o uso (de una persona o cosa en lugar de otra); (chem, law, math) substitución; (coll) imitación fraudulenta

subterranean [‚sʌbtə'renɪ‑ən] *adj & s* subterráneo

subtitle ['sʌb‚taɪtəl] *s* subtítulo || *tr* subtitular

subtle ['sʌtəl] *adj* sutil; astuto; insidioso

subtle‧ty ['sʌtəltɪ] *s* (*pl* **-ties**) sutileza; agudeza; distinción sutil

subtract [səb'trækt] *tr* substraer; (math) substraer, restar

suburb ['sʌbʌrb] *s* suburbio, arrabal *m;* **the suburbs** las afueras, los barrios externos

subvention [səb'venʃən] *s* subvención || *tr* subvencionar

subversive [səb'vʌrsɪv] *adj* subversivo || *s* subversor *m*

subvert [səb'vʌrt] *tr* subvertir

subway ['sʌb‚we] *s* galería subterránea; metro, ferrocarril subterráneo

succeed [sək'sid] *tr* suceder (*a una persona o cosa*) || *intr* tener buen éxito

success [sək'ses] *s* buen éxito

successful [sək'sesfəl] *adj* feliz, próspero; acertado; logrado

succession [sək'seʃən] *s* sucesión; **in succession** seguidos, uno tras otro

successive [sək'sesɪv] *adj* sucesivo

succor ['sʌkər] *s* socorro || *tr* socorrer

succotash ['sʌkə‚tæʃ] *s* guiso de maíz tierno y habas

succumb [sə'kʌm] *intr* sucumbir

such [sʌtʃ] *adj & pron indef* tal, semejante; **such a** tal, semejante; **such a + adj** un tan + adj; **such as** quienes, los que

suck [sʌk] *s* chupada; mamada || *tr* chupar; mamar; aspirar (*el aire*)

sucker ['sʌkər] *s* chupador *m;* mamón

m; (bot & mach) chupón *m;* (coll) bobo, primo

suckle ['sʌkəl] *tr* lactar; criar, educar

suckling pig ['sʌklɪŋ] *s* lechón *m,* cerdo de leche

suction ['sʌkʃən] *adj* aspirante || *s* succión

sudden ['sʌdən] *adj* súbito, repentino; **all of a sudden** de repente

suds [sʌdz] *spl* jabonadura; (coll) espuma, cerveza

sue [su] o [sju] *tr* demandar; pedir; (law) procesar || *intr* (law) poner pleito, entablar juicio; **to sue for damages** demandar por daños y perjuicios; **to sue for peace** pedir la paz

suede [swed] *s* gamuza, ante *m*

suet ['su‧ɪt] o ['sju‧ɪt] *s* sebo

suffer ['sʌfər] *tr & intr* sufrir, padecer

sufferance ['sʌfərəns] *s* tolerancia; paciencia; **on sufferance** por tolerancia

suffering ['sʌfərɪŋ] *adj* doliente || *s* dolencia, sufrimiento

suffice [sə'faɪs] *intr* bastar, ser suficiente

sufficient [sə'fɪʃənt] *adj* suficiente

suffix ['sʌfɪks] *s* sufijo

suffocate ['sʌfə‚ket] *tr* sofocar || *intr* sofocarse

suffrage ['sʌfrɪdʒ] *s* sufragio; aprobación, voto favorable

suffragette [‚sʌfrə'dʒet] *s* sufragista (*mujer*)

suffuse [sə'fjuz] *tr* saturar, bañar

sugar ['ʃugər] *adj* azucarero || *s* azúcar *m* || *tr* azucarar

sugar beet *s* remolacha azucarera

sugar bowl *s* azucarero

sugar cane *s* caña de azúcar

sug'ar-coat' *tr* azucarar; (fig) endulzar, dorar

suggest [səg'dʒest] *tr* sugerir

suggestion [səg'dʒestʃən] *s* sugestión, sugerencia; sombra, traza ligera

suggestive [səg'dʒestɪv] *adj* sugestivo; sicalíptico

suicidal [‚su‧ɪ'saɪdəl] o ['sju‧ɪ‚saɪdəl] *adj* suicida

suicide ['su‧ɪ‚saɪd] o ['sju‧ɪ‚saɪd] *s* (*act*) suicidio; (*person*) suicida *mf*; **to commit suicide** suicidarse

suit [sut] o [sjut] *s* traje *m,* terno; (*of a lady*) traje *m* sastre; (*group forming a set*) juego; (*of cards*) palo; petición, súplica; cortejo, galanteo; (law) pleito, proceso; **to follow suit** servir del palo; seguir la corriente || *tr* adaptar, ajustar; adaptarse a; sentar, ir o venir bien a; favorecer, satisfacer; **to suit oneself** hacer (*uno*) lo que le guste || *intr* convenir, ser a propósito

suitable ['sutəbəl] o ['sjutəbəl] *adj* apropiado, conveniente, adecuado

suit'case' *s* maleta, valija

suite [swit] *s* comitiva, séquito; (*group forming a set*) juego; serie *f;* (*of rooms*) crujía; habitación salón; (mus) suite *f*

suiting ['sutɪŋ] o ['sjutɪŋ] *s* corte *m* de traje

suit of clothes *s* traje completo (*de hombre*)

suitor ['sutər] o ['sjutər] s pretendiente m; (law) demandante mf
sulfa drugs ['sʌlfə] spl medicamentos
sulfas
sulfate ['sʌlfet] s sulfato
sulfide ['sʌlfaɪd] s sulfuro
sulfite ['sʌlfaɪt] s sulfito
sulfur ['sʌlfər] s (chem) azufre m;
véase **sulphur**
sulfuric [sʌl'fjurɪk] adj sulfúrico
sulfur mine s azufrera
sulfurous ['sʌlfərəs] adj sulfuroso ||
['sʌlfərəs] o [sʌl'fjurəs] adj (chem)
sulfuroso
sulk [sʌlk] s murria || intr amorrarse,
enfurruñarse
sulk·y ['sʌlki] adj (comp -ier; super
-iest) enfurruñado, murrio, resentido
sullen ['sʌlən] adj hosco, malhumorado, taciturno, triste
sul·ly ['sʌli] v (pret & pp -lied) tr empañar, manchar
sulphur ['sʌlfər] adj azufrado || s
azufre m; color de azufre || tr azu-
frar
sultan ['sʌltən] s sultán m
sul·try ['sʌltri] adj (comp -trier; super
-triest) bochornoso, sofocante
sum [sʌm] s suma; (coll) problema m
de aritmética || v (pret & pp
summed; ger summing) tr sumar; **to
sum up** sumar, resumir
sumac o **sumach** ['ʃumæk] o ['sumæk]
s zumaque m
summarize ['sʌmə raɪz] tr resumir
summa·ry ['sʌməri] adj sumario || s
(pl -ries) sumario, resumen m
summer ['sʌmər] adj estival, veraniego
|| s verano, estío || intr veranear
summer resort s lugar m de veraneo
summersault ['sʌmər sɔlt] s salto mor-
tal || intr dar un salto mortal
summer school s escuela de verano
summery ['sʌməri] adj estival, veraniego
summit ['sʌmɪt] s cima, cumbre f
summit conference s conferencia en la
cumbre
summon ['sʌmən] tr convocar, llamar;
evocar; (law) citar, emplazar
summons ['sʌmənz] s orden f, señal f;
(law) citación, emplazamiento || tr
(coll) citar, emplazar
sumptuous ['sʌmptʃu·əs] adj suntuoso
sun [sʌn] s sol m; **to have a place in
the sun** ocupar su puesto en el mun-
do || v (pret & pp sunned; ger sun-
ning) tr asolear || intr asolearse
sun bath s baño de sol
sun'beam' s rayo de sol
sun'bon'net s papalina
sun'burn' s quemadura de sol || v (pret
& pp -burned o burnt) tr quemar al
sol || intr quemarse al sol
sundae ['sʌndi] s helado con frutas,
jarabes o nueces
Sunday ['sʌndi] adj dominical; (used
or worn on Sunday) dominguero || s
domingo
Sunday best s (coll) trapos de cristianar, ropa dominguera
Sunday's child s niño nacido de pies,
niño mimado de la fortuna

Sunday school s escuela dominical,
doctrina dominical
sunder ['sʌndər] tr separar; romper
sun'di'al s reloj m de sol, cuadrante m
solar
sun'down' s puesta del sol
sundries ['sʌndriz] spl artículos diversos
sundry ['sʌndri] adj diversos, varios
sun'flow'er s girasol m, tornasol m
sun'glass'es spl gafas de sol, gafas para
el sol
sunken ['sʌŋkən] adj hundido, sumido
sun lamp s lámpara de rayos ultra-
violetas
sun'light' s luz f del sol
sun'lit' adj iluminado por el sol
sun·ny ['sʌni] adj (comp -nier; super
-niest) de sol; asoleado; brillante,
resplandeciente; alegre, risueño; **to
be sunny** hacer sol
sunny side s sol m; (fig) lado bueno,
lado favorable
sun porch s solana
sun'rise' s salida del sol; **from sunrise
to sunset** de sol a sol
sun'set' s puesta del sol
sun'shade' s quitasol m, sombrilla;
toldo; visera contra el sol
sun'shine' s claridad del sol; alegría;
in the sunshine al sol
sun'spot' s mancha solar
sun'stroke' s insolación
sup. abbr superior, supplement
sup [sʌp] v (pret & pp supped; ger
supping) intr cenar
superannuated [supər'ænju etɪd] adj
jubilado, inhabilitado por ancianidad
o enfermedad; fuera de moda
superb [su'pʌrb] o [sə'pʌrb] adj soberbio, estupendo, magnífico
supercar·go ['supər kargo] s (pl -goes
o -gos) (naut) sobrecargo
supercharge [supər'tʃardʒ] tr sobrealimentar
supercilious [supər'sɪlɪ·əs] adj arrogante, altanero, desdeñoso
superficial [supər'fɪʃəl] adj superficial
superfluous [su'pʌrflu·əs] adj superfluo
superhuman [supər'hjumən] adj so-
brehumano
superimpose [supərɪm'poz] tr sobreponer
superintendent [supərɪn'tendənt] s
superintendente mf
superior [sə'pɪrɪ·ər] o [su'pɪrɪ·ər] adj
superior; indiferente, sereno; arro-
gante; (typ) volado || s superior m
superiority [sə pɪrɪ'arɪti] o [su pɪrɪ-
'arɪti] s superioridad; indiferencia,
serenidad; arrogancia
superlative [sə'pʌrlətɪv] o [su'pʌrlə-
tɪv] adj & s superlativo
super·man ['supər mæn] s (pl -men
[men]) sobrehombre m, superhombre m
supermarket ['supər markɪt] s supermercado
supernatural [supər'nætʃərəl] adj sobrenatural
superpose [supər'poz] tr sobreponer,
superponer

supersede [ˌsupərˈsid] *tr* reemplazar; desalojar
supersonic [ˌsupərˈsɑnɪk] *adj* supersónico ǁ **supersonics** *ssg* supersónica
superstitious [ˌsupərˈstɪʃəs] *adj* supersticioso
supervene [ˌsupərˈvin] *intr* sobrevenir
supervise [ˈsupərˌvaɪz] *tr* superintender, supervisar, dirigir
supervisor [ˈsupərˌvaɪzər] *s* superintendente *mf*, supervisor *m*, dirigente *mf*
supp. *abbr* **supplement**
supper [ˈsʌpər] *s* cena
supplant [səˈplænt] *tr* reemplazar
supple [ˈsʌpəl] *adj* flexible; dócil
supplement [ˈsʌplɪmənt] *s* suplemento ǁ [ˈsʌplɪˌment] *tr* suplir, completar
suppliant [ˈsʌplɪənt] *adj & s* suplicante *mf*
supplication [ˌsʌplɪˈkeʃən] *s* súplica
sup·ply [səˈplaɪ] *s* (*pl* **-plies**) suministro, provisión; surtido, repuesto; oferta, existencia; **supplies** pertrechos, provisiones, víveres *mf*; artículos, efectos ǁ *v* (*pret & pp* **-plied**) *tr* suministrar, aprovisionar; reemplazar
supply and demand *spl* oferta y demanda
support [səˈport] *s* apoyo, soporte *m*, sostén *m*; sustento ǁ *tr* apoyar, soportar, sostener; sustentar; aguantar
supporter [səˈportər] *s* partidario; (*jockstrap*) suspensorio; faja abdominal, faja medical
suppose [səˈpoz] *tr* suponer; creer; **to be supposed to** deber; **to suppose so** creer que sí
supposed [səˈpozd] *adj* supuesto
supposition [ˌsʌpəˈzɪʃən] *s* suposición
supposito·ry [səˈpɑzɪˌtori] *s* (*pl* **-ries**) supositorio
suppress [səˈpres] *tr* suprimir
suppression [səˈpreʃən] *s* supresión
suppurate [ˈsʌpjəˌret] *intr* supurar
supreme [səˈprim] o [suˈprim] *adj* supremo
supt. *abbr* **superintendent**
surcharge [ˈsʌrˌtʃɑrdʒ] *s* sobrecarga ǁ [ˌsʌrˈtʃɑrdʒ] o [ˈsʌrˌtʃɑrʒ] *tr* sobrecargar
sure [ʃur] *adj* seguro; **to be sure** seguramente, sin duda ǁ *adv* (coll) seguramente, claro; **sure enough** efectivamente
sure thing *adv* (slang) seguramente ǁ *interj* ¡claro!, ¡seguro! ǁ *s* (slang) sacabocados *m*
sure·ty [ˈʃʊrti] o [ˈʃʊrɪti] *s* (*pl* **-ties**) seguridad, garantía, fianza
surf [sʌrf] *s* cachones *mpl*, olas que rompen en la playa
surface [ˈsʌrfɪs] *adj* superficial ǁ *s* superficie *f* ǁ *tr* alisar, allanar; recubrir ǁ *intr* emerger (*p.ej., un submarino*)
surface mail *s* correo por vía ordinaria
surf'board *s* patín *m* de mar
surfeit [ˈsʌrfɪt] *s* exceso; hartura, hastío; empacho, indigestión *f*; *tr* atracar, hastiar; encebadar (*las bestias*) ǁ *intr* atracarse, hastiarse; encebadarse

surf'-rid'ing *s* patinaje *m* sobre las olas
surge [sʌrdʒ] *s* oleada; (elec) sobretensión ǁ *intr* agitarse, ondular
surgeon [ˈsʌrdʒən] *s* cirujano
surger·y [ˈsʌrdʒəri] *s* (*pl* **-ies**) cirugía; sala de operaciones
surgical [ˈsʌrdʒɪkəl] *adj* quirúrgico
sur·ly [ˈsʌrli] *adj* (*comp* **-lier;** *super* **-liest**) áspero, rudo, hosco, insolente
surmise [sərˈmaɪz] o [ˈsʌrmaɪz] *s* conjetura, suposición ǁ [sərˈmaɪz] *tr & intr* conjeturar, suponer
surmount [sərˈmaunt] *tr* levantarse sobre; aventajar, sobrepujar; superar; coronar
surname [ˈsʌrˌnem] *s* apellido; (*added name*) sobrenombre *m* ǁ *tr* apellidar; sobrenombrar
surpass [sərˈpæs] o [sərˈpɑs] *tr* aventajar, sobrepasar
surplice [ˈsʌrplɪs] *s* sobrepelliz *f*
surplus [ˈsʌrplʌs] *adj* sobrante, excedente ǁ *s* sobrante *m*, exceso; (com) superávit *m*
surprise [sərˈpraɪz] *adj* inesperado, improviso ǁ *s* sorpresa; **to take by surprise** coger por sorpresa ǁ *tr* sorprender
surprise package *s* sorpresa
surprise party *s* reunión improvisada para felicitar por sorpresa a una persona
surprising [sərˈpraɪzɪŋ] *adj* sorprendente
surrender [səˈrendər] *s* rendición ǁ *tr* rendir ǁ *intr* rendirse
surrender value *s* (ins) valor *m* de rescate
surreptitious [ˌsʌrepˈtɪʃəs] *adj* subrepticio
surround [səˈraund] *tr* cercar, rodear, circundar; (mil) sitiar
surrounding [səˈraundɪŋ] *adj* circundante, circunstante ǁ **surroundings** *spl* alrededores *mpl*, contornos; ambiente *m*, medio
surtax [ˈsʌrˌtæks] *s* impuesto complementario
surveillance [sərˈveləns] o [sərˈveljəns] *s* vigilancia
survey [ˈsʌrve] *s* estudio, examen *m*, inspección, reconocimiento; agrimensura, medición, plano; levantamiento de planos; (*of opinion*) encuesta; (*of literature*) bosquejo ǁ [sʌrˈve] o [ˈsʌrve] *tr* estudiar, examinar, inspeccionar, reconocer; medir; levantar el plano de ǁ *intr* levantar el plano
surveyor [sərˈve·ər] *s* inspector *m*; agrimensor *m*
survival [sərˈvaɪvəl] *s* supervivencia
survive [sərˈvaɪv] *tr* sobrevivir a (*otra persona; algún acontecimiento*) ǁ *intr* sobrevivir
surviving [sərˈvaɪvɪŋ] *adj* sobreviviente
survivor [sərˈvaɪvər] *s* sobreviviente *mf*
survivorship [sərˈvaɪvərˌʃɪp] *s* (law) sobrevivencia
susceptible [səˈseptɪbəl] *adj* susceptible; (*to love*) enamoradizo
suspect [ˈsʌspekt] o [səsˈpekt] *adj &*

su
su

s sospechoso || *tr* sospechar

suspend [səs'pɛnd] *tr* suspender || *intr* dejar de obrar; suspender pagos

suspenders [səs'pɛndərz] *spl* tirantes *mpl*

suspense [səs'pɛns] *s* suspenso, suspensión; duda, incertidumbre; indecisión, irresolución; ansiedad

suspension bridge [səs'pɛn/ən] *s* puente *m* colgante

suspicion [səs'pɪ/ən] *s* sospecha, suspicacia; sombra, traza ligera

suspicious [səs'pɪ/əs] *adj* (*inclined to suspect*) suspicaz; (*subject to suspicion*) sospechoso

sustain [səs'ten] *tr* sostener, sustentar; apoyar, defender; confirmar, probar; sufrir (*p.ej., un daño, una pérdida*)

sustenance ['sʌstɪnəns] *s* sustento, alimentos; sostenimiento

sutler ['sʌtlər] *s* (mil) vivandero

swab [swɑb] *s* escobón *m*, estropajo; (naut) lampazo; (surg) tapón *m* de algodón || *v* (pret & pp **swabbed**; ger **swabbing**) *tr* fregar, limpiar; (naut) lampacear; (surg) limpiar con algodón

swaddle ['swɑdəl] *tr* empañar, fajar

swaddling clothes *spl* pañales *mpl*

swagger ['swægər] *adj* (coll) muy elegante || *s* fanfarronada; contoneo, paso jactancioso || *intr* fanfarronear; contonear

swain [swen] *s* (*lad*) zagal; galán *m*, amante *m*

swallow ['swɑlo] *s* trago; (orn) golondrina || *tr* tragar, deglutir; (fig) tragar, tragarse || *intr* tragar, deglutir

swallow-tailed coat ['swɑlo,teld] *s* frac *m*

swal'low-wort' *s* vencetósigo

swamp [swɑmp] *s* pantano, marisma || *tr* encharcar, inundar; (*e.g., with work*) abrumar

swamp-y ['swɑmpi] *adj* (comp **-ier;** super **-iest**) pantanoso

swan [swɑn] *s* cisne *m*

swan dive *s* salto de ángel

swank [swæŋk] *adj* (slang) elegante, vistoso || *s* (slang) elegancia vistosa

swan knight *s* caballero del cisne

swan's-down ['swɑnz,daun] *s* plumón *m* de cisne; moletón *m*, paño de vicuña

swan song *s* canto del cisne

swap [swɑp] *s* (coll) trueque *m*, cambalache *m* || *v* (pret & pp **swapped**; ger **swapping**) *tr* & *intr* trocar, cambalachear

swarm [swɔrm] *s* enjambre *m* || *intr* enjambrar; volar en enjambres; hormiguear (*una multitud de gente o animales*)

swarth-y ['swɔrði] o ['swɔrθi] *adj* (comp **-ier;** super **-iest**) atezado, carinegro, moreno

swashbuckler ['swɑʃ,bʌklər] *s* espadachín *m*, matasiete *m*, valentón *m*

swat [swɑt] *s* (coll) golpe violento || *v* (pret & pp **swatted**; ger **swatting**) *tr* (coll) golpear con fuerza; (coll) aporrear, aplastar (*una mosca*)

sway [swe] *s* oscilación, vaivén *m;* dominio, imperio || *tr* hacer oscilar; conmover; disuadir; gobernar, dominar || *intr* oscilar; desviarse; tambalear, flaquear

swear [swɛr] *v* (pret **swore** [swor]; pp **sworn** [sworn]) *tr* jurar; juramentar; prestar (*juramento*); **to swear in** to mar juramento a; **to swear off** jurar renunciar a; **to swear out** obtener mediante juramento || *intr* jurar; **to swear at** maldecir; **to swear by** jurar por; poner toda su confianza en; **to swear to** prestar juramento a; declarar bajo juramento; jurar + *inf*

sweat [swɛt] *s* sudor *m* || *v* (pret & pp **sweat** o **sweated**) *tr* sudar (*agua por los poros; la ropa*); (slang) hacer sudar; **to sweat it out** (slang) aguantarlo hasta el fin || *intr* sudar

sweater ['swɛtər] *s* suéter *m*

sweat-y ['swɛti] *adj* (comp **-ier;** super **-iest**) sudoroso

Swede [swid] *s* sueco

Sweden ['swidən] *s* Suecia

Swedish ['swidɪʃ] *adj* & *s* sueco

sweep [swip] *s* barrido; alcance *m*, extensión; (of wind) soplo; (of a well) cigoñal *m* || *v* (pret & pp **swept** [swɛpt]) *tr* barrer; arrastrar; rozar, tocar; recorrer con la mirada, los dedos, etc. || *intr* barrer; pasar rápidamente; extenderse; precipitarse; andar con paso majestuoso

sweeper ['swipər] *s* (person) barrendero; (machine for sweeping streets) barredera; barredera de alfombra; (nav) dragaminas *m*

sweeping ['swipɪŋ] *adj* arrebatador; comprensivo, extenso, vasto || **sweepings** *spl* barreduras

sweep'-sec'ond *s* segundero central

sweep'stakes' *ssg* o *spl* lotería en la cual una persona gana todas las apuestas; carrera que decide todas las apuestas; premio en las carreras de caballos

sweet [swit] *adj* dulce; oloroso; melodioso, grato al oído; fresco; bonito, lindo; amable; querido; **to be sweet on** (coll) estar enamorado de || *adv* dulcemente; **to smell sweet** tener buen olor || **sweets** *spl* dulces *mpl,* golosinas

sweet'bread' *s* lechecillas, mollejas

sweet'bri'er *s* eglantina

sweeten ['switən] *tr* azucarar, endulzar; suavizar; purificar || *intr* azucararse, endulzarse; suavizarse

sweet'heart' *s* enamorado o enamorada; amiga querida; galán *m*, cortejo

sweet marjoram *s* mejorana

sweet'meats' *spl* dulces *mpl,* confites *mpl,* confitura

sweet pea *s* guisante *m* de olor

sweet potato *s* batata, camote *m*

sweet-scented ['swit,sentɪd] *adj* oloroso, perfumado

sweet tooth *s* gusto por los dulces

sweet-toothed ['swit,tuθt] *adj* dulcero, goloso

sweet william s clavel m de ramillete, minutisa

swell [swel] adj (coll) muy elegante; (slang) de órdago, magnífico ‖ s hinchazón f; bulto; marejada; oleaje m; (of a crowd of people) oleada; (coll) petimetre m, pisaverde m ‖ v (pret **swelled**; pp **swelled** o **swollen** ['swolən]) tr hinchar, inflar; abultar, aumentar; elevar, levantar; (fig) hinchar, engreír ‖ intr hincharse; abultarse, aumentar, crecer; elevarse, levantarse; embravecerse (el mar); (fig) hincharse, engreírse

swelled head s entono; **to have a swelled head** estar muy pagado de sí mismo, creerse gran cosa

swelter ['sweltər] intr sofocarse de sudor

swept'back' wing s (aer) ala en flecha

swerve [swʌrv] s viraje m, desvío brusco ‖ tr desviar ‖ intr desviarse, torcer

swift [swɪft] adj rápido, veloz; pronto; repentino ‖ adv rápidamente, velozmente ‖ s vencejo

swig [swɪg] s (coll) chisguete, tragantada ‖ v (pret & pp **swigged**; ger **swigging**) tr & intr (coll) beber a grandes tragos

swill [swɪl] s basura, inmundicia; tragantada ‖ tr beber a grandes tragos; emborrachar ‖ intr beber a grandes tragos; emborracharse

swim [swɪm] s natación; **the swim** (in affairs, society, etc.) (coll) la corriente ‖ v (pret **swam** [swæm]; pp **swum** [swʌm]; ger **swimming**) tr pasar a nado ‖ intr nadar; deslizarse, escurrirse; padecer vahídos; dar vueltas (la cabeza); **to swim across** atravesar a nado

swimmer ['swɪmər] s nadador m

swimming pool s piscina

swimming suit s traje m de baño

swindle ['swɪndəl] s estafa, timo ‖ tr & intr estafar, timar

swine [swaɪn] s cerdo, puerco; spl ganado porcino

swing [swɪŋ] s balance m, oscilación, vaivén m; (device used for recreation) columpio; hamaca; turno, período; fuerza, ímpetu m; (trip) jira; (box) golpe m de lado; (mus) ritmo constantemente repetido; **in full swing** en plena marcha ‖ v (pret & pp **swung** [swʌŋ]) tr blandir (p.ej., un arma); menear (los brazos); hacer oscilar; columpiar; manejar con éxito ‖ intr oscilar; balancearse; columpiar; estar colgado; dar una vuelta; **to swing open** abrirse de pronto (una puerta)

swinging door ['swɪŋɪŋ] s batiente m oscilante, puerta de vaivén

swinish ['swaɪnɪʃ] adj porcuno; (fig) cochino, puerco

swipe [swaɪp] s (coll) golpe m fuerte ‖ tr (coll) dar un golpe fuerte a; (slang) hurtar, robar

swirl [swʌrl] s remolino, torbellino ‖ tr hacer girar ‖ intr arremolinarse, remolinar; girar

swish [swɪʃ] s (e.g., of a whip) chasquido; (of a dress) crujido ‖ tr chasquear (el látigo) ‖ intr chasquear; crujir (un vestido)

Swiss [swɪs] adj & s suizo

Swiss chard [tʃɑrd] s acelga

Swiss cheese s Gruyère m, queso suizo

Swiss Guards spl guardia suiza

switch [swɪtʃ] s bastoncillo, latiguillo; latigazo; coletazo; (false hair) trenza postiza, moño postizo; (elec) llave f, interruptor m, conmutador m; (rr) agujas ‖ tr azotar, fustigar; (elec) conmutar; (rr) desviar; **to switch off** (elec) cortar, desconectar; **to switch on** (elec) cerrar (el circuito); (elec) encender, poner (la luz, la radio, etc.) ‖ intr cambiarse, moverse; desviarse

switch'back' s vía en zigzag

switch'board' s cuadro de distribución

switching engine s locomotora de maniobras

switch·man ['swɪtʃmən] s (pl -men [mən]) agujetero, guardagujas m

switch'yard' s patio de maniobras

Switzerland ['swɪtsərlənd] s Suiza

swiv·el ['swɪvəl] s eslabón giratorio ‖ v (pret & pp -eled o -elled; ger -eling o -elling) intr girar sobre un eje

swivel chair s silla giratoria

swoon [swun] s desmayo ‖ intr desmayarse

swoop [swup] s descenso súbito; (of a bird of prey) calada ‖ intr bajar rápidamente, precipitarse; abatirse (p.ej., el ave de rapiña)

sword [sord] s espada; **at swords' points** enemistados a sangre y fuego; **to put to the sword** pasar al filo de la espada, pasar a cuchillo

sword belt s cinturón m

sword'fish' s pez m espada

sword handler s (taur) mozo de estoques

sword rattling s fanfarronería

swords·man ['sordzmən] s (pl -men [mən]) espada m; esgrimidor m

sword swallower ['swɑlo·ər] s tragasable m

sword thrust s estocada, golpe m de espada

sworn [sworn] adj (enemy) jurado

sycophant ['sɪkəfənt] s adulador m; parásito

sycosis [saɪ'kosɪs] s (pathol) sicosis f

syll. abbr **syllable**

syllable ['sɪləbəl] s sílaba

syllogism ['sɪlədʒɪzəm] s silogismo

sylph [sɪlf] s sílfide f

sym. abbr **symbol, symmetrical, symphony, symptom**

symbol ['sɪmbəl] s símbolo

symbolic(al) [sɪm'bɑlɪk(əl)] adj simbólico

symbolize ['sɪmbə,laɪz] tr simbolizar

symmetric(al) [sɪ'metrɪk(əl)] adj simétrico

symme·try ['sɪmɪtri] s (pl -tries) simetría

sympathetic [,sɪmpə'θetɪk] adj compasivo; favorablemente dispuesto

sympathize ['sɪmpə,θaɪz] intr compa-

su
sy

decerse; **to sympathize with** compadecerse de; comprender

sympa·thy ['sɪmpəθi] *s* (*pl* **-thies**) compasión, conmiseración; **to be in sympathy with** estar de acuerdo con, ser partidario de; **to extend one's sympathy to** dar el pésame a

symphonic [sɪm'fɑnɪk] *adj* sinfónico

sympho·ny ['sɪmfəni] *s* (*pl* **-nies**) sinfonía

symposi·um [sɪm'pozɪ·əm] *s* (*pl* **-a** [ə]) coloquio

symptom ['sɪmptəm] *s* síntoma *m*

syn. *abbr* **synonym, synonymous**

synagogue ['sɪnə‚gɔg] o ['sɪnə‚gɑg] *s* sinagoga

synchronize ['sɪŋkrə‚naɪz] *tr* & *intr* sincronizar

synchronous ['sɪŋkrənəs] *adj* sincrónico

syncope ['sɪŋkə‚pi] *s* (phonet) síncopa

syndicate ['sɪndɪkɪt] *s* sindicato || ['sɪndɪ‚ket] *tr* sindicar || *intr* sindicarse

synonym ['sɪnənɪm] *s* sinónimo

synonymous [sɪ'nɑnɪməs] *adj* sinónimo

synop·sis [sɪ'nɑpsɪs] *s* (*pl* **-ses** [siz]) sinopsis *f*

syntax ['sɪntæks] *s* sintaxis *f*

synthe·sis ['sɪnθɪsɪs] *s* (*pl* **-ses** [‚siz]) síntesis *f*

synthesize ['sɪnθɪ‚saɪz] *tr* sintetizar

synthetic(al) [sɪn'θɛtɪk(əl)] *adj* sintético

syphilis ['sɪfɪlɪs] *s* sífilis *f*

Syria ['sɪrɪ·ə] *s* Siria

Syrian ['sɪrɪ·ən] *adj* & *s* sirio

syringe [sɪ'rɪndʒ] o ['sɪrɪndʒ] *s* jeringa; (*fountain syringe*) mangueta; (*syringe fitted with needle for hypodermic injections*) jeringuilla || *tr* jeringar

syrup ['sɪrəp] o ['sʌrəp] *s* almíbar *m*; (*with fruit juices or medicinal substances*) jarabe *m*

system ['sɪstəm] *s* sistema *m*

systematic(al) [‚sɪstə'mætɪk(əl)] *adj* sistemático

systematize ['sɪstəmə‚taɪz] *tr* sistematizar

systole ['sɪstəli] *s* sístole *f*

T

T, t [ti] vigésima letra del alfabeto inglés

t. *abbr* **teaspoon, temperature, tenor, tense, territory, town**

T. *abbr* **Territory, Testament**

tab [tæb] *s* apéndice *m*, proyección; marbete *m*; **to keep tab on** (coll) tener a la vista; **to pick up the tab** (coll) pagar la cuenta

tab·by ['tæbi] *s* (*pl* **-bies**) gato atigrado; gata; solterona; chismosa

tabernacle ['tæbər‚nækəl] *s* tabernáculo

table ['tebəl] *s* mesa; (*list, catalogue; index of a book*) tabla; **to set the table** poner la mesa; **to turn the tables** volver las tornas; **under the table** completamente emborrachado || *tr* aplazar la discusión de

tab·leau ['tæblo] *s* (*pl* **-leaus** o **-leaux** [loz]) cuadro vivo

ta'ble·cloth' *s* mantel *m*

table d'hôte ['tabəl'dot] *s* mesa redonda; comida a precio fijo

ta'ble·land' *s* meseta

table linen *s* mantelería

table manners *spl* modales *mpl* que uno tiene en la mesa

table of contents *s* índice *m* de materias, tabla de materias

ta'ble·spoon' *s* cuchara de sopa

tablespoonful ['tebəl‚spun‚ful] *s* cucharada

tablet ['tæblɪt] *s* (*writing pad*) bloc *m*; (*slab*) lápida, placa; (*lozenge, pastille*) comprimido, tableta

table talk *s* conversación de sobremesa

table tennis *s* tenis de mesa

ta'ble·ware' *s* servicio de mesa, artículos para la mesa

tabloid ['tæblɔɪd] *s* periódico sensacional

taboo [tə'bu] *adj* prohibido || *s* tabú *m* || *tr* prohibir

tabulate ['tæbjə‚let] *tr* tabular

tabulator ['tæbjə‚letər] *s* tabulador *m*

tacit ['tæsɪt] *adj* tácito

taciturn ['tæsɪ‚tʌrn] *adj* taciturno

tack [tæk] *s* tachuela; nuevo plan de acción; (naut) virada; (sew) hilván *m* || *tr* clavar con tachuelas; añadir; unir; (naut) virar; (sew) hilvanar || *intr* cambiar de plan; (naut) virar

tack·y ['tæki] *adj* (*comp* **-ier**; *super* **-iest**) pegajoso; (coll) desaliñado

tact [tækt] *s* tacto, juicio, tino

tactful ['tæktfəl] *adj* discreto, político

tactical ['tæktɪkəl] *adj* táctico

tactician [tæk'tɪʃən] *s* táctico

tactics ['tæktɪks] *ssg* (mil) táctica || *spl* táctica

tactless ['tæktlɪs] *adj* indiscreto

tad'pole' *s* renacuajo

taffeta ['tæfɪtə] *s* tafetán *m*

taffy ['tæfi] *s* arropía, melcocha; (coll) lisonja, zalamería

tag [tæg] *s* etiqueta, marbete *m*; herrete *m*; pingajo; mechón *m*; vedija; (*curlicue in writing*) ringorrango; **to play tag** jugar al tócame tú || *v* (*pret* & *pp* **tagged**; *ger* **tagging**) *tr* pegar un marbete a; marcar con marbete || *intr* (coll) seguir de cerca

tag end *s* cabo flojo; retal *m*, retazo

Tagus ['tegəs] *s* Tajo

tail [tel] *adj* de cola || *s* cola; **tails** (*of a coin*) cruz *f*; (coll) frac *m*; **to turn**

tail mostrar los talones ‖ *tr* atar, juntar ‖ *intr* formar cola; **to tail after** pisar los talones a

tail assembly *s* (aer) empenaje *m*, planos de cola

tail end *s* cola, extremo; conclusión; **at the tail end** al final

tail'light' *s* faro trasero; (rr) disco de cola

tailor ['telər] *s* sastre *m* ‖ *tr* entallar (*un traje*) ‖ *intr* ser sastre

tailoring ['telərɪŋ] *s* sastrería, costura

tai'lor-made' suit *s* traje *m* de sastre, traje hecho a la medida

tail'piece' *s* apéndice *m*, cabo; (*of stringed instrument*) (mus) cordal *m;* (typ) florón *m*

tail'race' *s* cauce *m* de salida; (min) canal *m* de desechos

tail spin *s* (aer) barrena picada

tail wind *s* (aer) viento de cola; (naut) viento en popa

taint [tent] *s* mancha; corrupción, infección ‖ *tr* manchar; corromper, inficionar

take [tek] *s* toma; presa, redada; (mov) toma; (slang) entradas, ingresos *m* ‖ *v* (*pret* **took** [tʊk]; *pp* **taken**) *tr* tomar; (*to carry off with one*) llevarse; (*to remove*) quitar; quedarse con (*p.ej., una compra en una tienda*); comer (*una pieza, en el juego de ajedrez y en el de damas*); dar (*un paso, un salto, un paseo*); hacer (*un viaje; ejercicio*); seguir (*un consejo; una asignatura*); sacar (*una fotografía*); calzar, usar (*cierto tamaño de zapatos o guantes*); estudiar (*p.ej., historia, francés, matemáticas*); echar (*una siesta*); tomar (*un tren, autobús, tranvía*); aguantar, tolerar; soportar; **to take amiss** llevar a mal; **to take apart** descomponer, desarmar, desmontar; **to take down** bajar; descolgar; poner por escrito, tomar nota de; desmontar; (*to humble*) quitar los humos a; **to take for** tomar por, p.ej., **I took you for someone else** le tomé por otra persona; **to take from** quitar a; **to take in** acoger, admitir; (*to welcome into one's home, one's company*) recibir; (*to encompass*) abarcar, comprender; ganar (*dinero*); visitar (*los puntos de interés*); (*to win over by flattery or deceit*) cazar; meter (*p.ej., las costuras de una prenda de vestir*); **to take it that** suponer que; **to take off** quitarse (*p.ej., el sombrero*); descontar; (coll) imitar, parodiar; **to take on** tomar, contratar; empezar; cargar con, tomar sobre sí; desafiar; **to take out** sacar; pasear (*p.ej., a un niño, un caballo*); omitir; extraer, separar; **to take place** tener lugar; **to take up** subir; levantar; apretar; coger; recoger; emprender, comenzar; tomar posesión de (*un cargo, un puesto*); tomar, estudiar; ocupar, llenar (*un espacio*) ‖ *intr* arraigar, prender; cuajar; actuar, obrar; salir, resultar; adherirse; pegar; (coll) tener éxito; **to take after** parecerse a; **to take off**

levantarse; salir; (aer) despegar; to take up with (coll) estrechar amistad con; (coll) vivir con; **to take well** (coll) sacar buen retrato

take'-off' *s* (aer) despegue *m;* (coll) imitación burlesca, parodia

talcum powder ['tælkəm] *s* polvos de talco; talco en polvo

tale [tel] *s* cuento, relato; embuste *m*, mentira

tale'bear'er *s* chismoso, cuentista *mf*

talent ['tælənt] *s* talento; gente *f* de talento

talented ['tæləntɪd] *adj* talentoso

talent scout *m* buscador *m* de nuevas figuras

talk [tɔk] *s* charla, plática; (*gossip*) fábula, comidilla; (*lecture*) conferencia; **to cause talk** dar que hablar ‖ *tr* hablar; convencer hablando; **to talk up** ensalzar ‖ *intr* hablar; parlar (*el loro*); **to talk on** discutir (*un asunto*); hablar sin parar; continuar hablando; **to talk up** elevar la voz, osar hablar

talkative ['tɔkətɪv] *adj* hablador, locuaz

talker ['tɔkər] *s* hablador *m;* orador *m;* charlatán *m*, parlón *m*

talkie ['tɔki] *s* (coll) cine hablado

talking doll ['tɔkɪŋ] *s* muñeca parlante

talking film *s* película hablada

talking machine *s* máquina parlante

talking picture *s* cine hablado, cine parlante

tall [tɔl] *adj* alto; (coll) exagerado

tallow ['tælo] *s* sebo

tal·ly ['tæli] *s* (*pl* **-lies**) cuenta ‖ *v* (*pret & pp* **-lied**) *tr* echar la cuenta de ‖ *intr* echar la cuenta; concordar, corresponder, conformarse

tally sheet *s* hoja en que se anota una cuenta

talon ['tælən] *s* garra

tambourine [,tæmbə'rin] *s* pandereta

tame [tem] *adj* manso, domesticado; dócil, sumiso; insípido ‖ *tr* amansar, domesticar; domar (*a un animal salvaje*); someter; captar (*una caída de agua*)

tamp [tæmp] *tr* atacar (*un barreno*); apisonar

tamper ['tæmpər] *s* (*person*) apisonador *m;* (ram) pisón *m* ‖ *intr* entremeterse; **to tamper with** manosear, tocar ajando; tratar de forzar (*una cerradura*); falsificar (*un documento*); corromper (*p.ej., a un testigo*)

tampon ['tæmpɑn] *s* (surg) tapón *m* ‖ *tr* (surg) taponar

tan [tæn] *adj* requemado, tostado; de color de canela; marrón; café (Am) ‖ *v* (*pret & pp* **tanned**; *ger* **tanning**) *tr* adobar, curtir, zurrar; quemar, tostar; (coll) zurrar, dar una paliza a

tang [tæŋ] *s* sabor *m* u olor *m* fuerte y picante; dejo, gustillo; (*ringing sound*) tañido

tangent ['tændʒənt] *adj* tangente ‖ *s* tangente *f;* **to fly off at a tangent** tomar súbitamente nuevo rumbo, cambiar de repente

tangerine [ˌtændʒəˈrin] s mandarina

tangible [ˈtændʒɪbəl] adj palpable, tangible

Tangier [tænˈdʒɪr] s Tánger f

tangle [ˈtæŋgəl] s enredo, maraña, lío ‖ tr enredar, enmarañar ‖ intr enredarse, enmarañarse

tank [tæŋk] s tanque m, depósito; (mil) tanque, carro de combate; (rr) ténder m; (heavy drinker) (slang) bodega

tank car s (rr) carro cuba, vagón m tanque

tanker [ˈtæŋkər] s barco tanque, buque m cisterna; avión-nodriza m

tank farming s quimicultura, cultivo hidropónico

tank truck s camión m tanque

tanner [ˈtænər] s curtidor m

tanner·y [ˈtænəri] s (pl -ies) curtiduría, tenería

tantalize [ˈtæntəˌlaɪz] tr atormentar con falsas promesas

tantamount [ˈtæntəˌmaʊnt] adj equivalente

tantrum [ˈtæntrəm] s berrinche m, rabieta

tap [tæp] s golpecito, palmadita; canilla, espita; grifo; (elec) toma; (mach) macho de terraja; **on tap** sacado del barril, servido al grifo; listo, a mano; **taps** (signal to put out lights) (mil) silencio ‖ v (pret & pp **tapped;** ger **tapping**) tr dar golpecitos o un golpecito a o en; espitar, poner la espita o; sacar o tomar (quitando la espita); sangrar (un árbol); intervenir (un teléfono); derivar (electricidad); aterrajar (tuercas) ‖ intr dar golpecitos

tap dance s zapateado

tap'-dance' intr zapatear

tape [tep] s cinta ‖ tr proveer de cinta; medir con cinta; (coll) grabar en cinta magnetofónica

tape measure s cinta de medir

taper [ˈtepər] s cerilla, velita larga y delgada ‖ tr ahusar ‖ intr ahusarse; ir disminuyendo

tape'-re·cord' tr grabar sobre cinta

tape recorder [rɪˈkɔrdər] s magnetófono, grabadora de cinta

tapes·try [ˈtæpɪstri] s (pl -tries) tapiz m ‖ v (pret & pp **-tried**) tr tapizar

tape'worm' s solitaria, lombriz solitaria

tappet [ˈtæpɪt] s (aut) alzaválvulas m, taqué m

tap'room' s bodegón m, taberna

tap water s agua de grifo

tap wrench s volvedor m de machos

tar [tɑr] s alquitrán m; (coll) marinero ‖ v (pret & pp **tarred;** ger **tarring**) tr alquitranar; **to tar and feather** embrear y emplumar

tar·dy [ˈtɑrdi] adj (comp **-dier;** super **-diest**) tardío

target [ˈtɑrgɪt] s blanco

target area s zona a batir

target practice s tiro al blanco

tariff [ˈtærɪf] adj arancelario ‖ s (duties) arancel m; (rates in general) tarifa

tarnish [ˈtɑrnɪʃ] s deslustre m ‖ tr deslustrar ‖ intr deslustrarse

tar paper s papel alquitranado

tarpaulin [tɑrˈpɔlɪn] s alquitranado, encerado, empegado

tar·ry [ˈtɑri] adj alquitranado, embreado ‖ [ˈtæri] v (pret & pp **-ried**) intr detenerse, quedarse; tardar

tart [tɑrt] adj acre, agrio; (fig) áspero, mordaz ‖ s tarta; (coll) puta

task [tæsk] o [tɑsk] s tarea; **to bring** o **take to task** llamar a capítulo

task'mas'ter s amo, superintendente mf; ordenancista mf, tirano

tassel [ˈtæsəl] s borla; (bot) penacho

taste [test] s gusto, sabor m; sorbo, trago; muestra; gusto, buen gusto; **in bad taste** de mal gusto; **in good taste** de buen gusto; **to acquire a taste for** tomar gusto a ‖ tr gustar; (to sample) probar ‖ intr saber; **to taste of** saber a

tasteless [ˈtestlɪs] adj desabrido, insípido; de mal gusto

tast·y [ˈtesti] adj (comp **-ier;** super **-iest**) (coll) sabroso; (coll) de buen gusto

tatter [ˈtætər] s andrajo, harapo, guiñapo ‖ tr hacer andrajos

tattered [ˈtætərd] adj andrajoso, haraposo

tattle [ˈtætəl] s charla; habladuría ‖ intr charlar; chismear, murmurar

tat'tle·tale' adj revelador ‖ s cuentista mf, chismoso

tattoo [tæˈtu] s tatuaje m; (mil) retreta ‖ tr tatuar o tatuarse

taunt [tɔnt] o [tɑnt] s mofa, pulla ‖ tr provocar con insultos

taut [tɔt] adj tieso, tirante

tavern [ˈtævərn] s taberna; mesón m, posada

taw·dry [ˈtɔdri] adj (comp **-drier;** super **-driest**) cursi, charro, vistoso

taw·ny [ˈtɔni] adj (comp **-nier;** super **-niest**) leonado

tax [tæks] s contribución, impuesto ‖ tr poner impuestos a (una persona); poner impuestos sobre (la propiedad); abrumar, cargar; agotar (la paciencia de uno)

taxable [ˈtæksəbəl] adj imponible

taxation [tækˈseʃən] s imposición de contribuciones; contribuciones, impuestos

tax collector s recaudador m de impuestos

tax cut s reducción de impuestos

tax evader [ɪˈvedər] s burlador m de impuestos

tax'-ex·empt' adj exento de impuesto

tax·i [ˈtæksi] s (pl **-is**) taxi m ‖ v (pret & pp **-ied;** ger **-iing** o **-ying**) tr (aer) carretear ‖ intr ir en taxi; (aer) carretear, taxear

tax'i·cab' s taxi m

taxi dancer s taxi f

taxi driver s taxista mf

tax'i·plane' s avioneta de alquiler

taxi stand s parada de taxis

tax'pay'er s contribuyente mf

tax rate s tipo impositivo

t.b. abbr **tuberculosis**

tbs. o **tbsp.** *abbr* **tablespoon, table-spoons**
tea [ti] *s* té *m; (medicinal infusion)* tisana; caldo de carne
tea bag *s* muñeca
tea ball *s* huevo del té
tea'cart' *s* mesita de té *(con ruedas)*
teach [titʃ] *v (pret & pp* **taught** [tɔt]) *tr & intr* enseñar
teacher ['titʃər] *s* maestro, instructor *m; (such as adversity)* (fig) maestra
teacher's pet *s* alumno mimado
teaching ['titʃɪŋ] *adj* docente ‖ *s* enseñanza; doctrina
teaching aids *spl* material *m* auxiliar de instrucción
teaching staff *s* personal *m* docente
tea'cup' *s* taza para té
tea dance *s* té *m* bailable
teak [tik] *s* teca
tea'ket'tle *s* tetera
team [tim] *s (e.g., of horses)* tiro, tronco; *(of oxen)* yunta; *(sport)* equipo ‖ *tr* enganchar, uncir, enyugar ‖ *intr —* **to team up** asociarse, unirse; formar un equipo
team'mate' *s* compañero de equipo, equipier *m*
teamster ['timstər] *s (of horses)* tronquista *m; (of a truck)* camionista *m*
team'work' *s* espíritu de equipo; trabajo de equipo
tea'pot' *s* tetera
tear [tɪr] *s* lágrima; **to burst into tears** romper a llorar; **to fill with tears** arrasarse *(los ojos)* de o en lágrimas; **to hold back one's tears** beberse las lágrimas; **to laugh away one's tears** convertir las lágrimas en risas ‖ [ter] *s* desgarro, rasgón *m* ‖ [ter] *v (pret* **tore** [tor]; *pp* **torn** [tɔrn]) *tr* desgarrar, rasgar; acongojar, afligir; mesarse *(los cabellos);* **to tear apart** romper en dos; **to tear down** derribar *(un edificio);* desarmar *(una máquina);* **to tear off** desgajar; **to tear up** romper *(p.ej., un papel)* ‖ *intr* desgarrarse, rasgarse; **to tear along** correr a toda velocidad
tear bomb [tɪr] *s* bomba lacrimógena
tearful ['tɪrfəl] *adj* lacrimoso
tear gas [tɪr] *s* gas lacrimógeno
tear-jerker ['tɪr ˌdʒɜrkər] *s* (slang) drama *m* o cine *m* que arrancan lágrimas
tear-off ['ter ˌɔf] o ['ter ˌɑf] *adj* exfoliador
tea'room' *s* salón *m* de té
tear sheet [ter] *s* hoja del anunciante
tease [tiz] *tr* embromar, azuzar
tea'spoon' *s* cucharilla, cuchara
teaspoonful ['ti ˌspun ˌful] *s* cucharadita
teat [tit] *s* teta, pezón *m*
tea time *s* hora del té
technical ['tɛknɪkəl] *adj* técnico
technicali·ty [ˌtɛknɪˈkælɪti] *s (pl* **-ties)** detalle técnico
technician [tɛkˈnɪʃən] *s* técnico
technics ['tɛknɪks] *ssg* técnica
technique [tɛkˈnik] *s* técnica
Teddy bear ['tɛdi] *s* oso de juguete, oso de trapo

tedious ['tidɪ·əs] o ['tidʒəs] *adj* tedioso, enfadoso
teem [tim] *intr* hormiguear; llover a cántaros; **to teem with** hervir de
teeming ['timɪŋ] *adj* hormigueante; *(rain)* torrencial
teen age [tin] *s* edad de 13 a 19 años
teen-ager ['tin ˌedʒər] *s* joven *mf* de 13 a 19 años de edad
teens [tinz] *spl* números ingleses que terminan en -teen (de 13 a 19); edad de 13 a 19 años; **to be in one's teens** tener de 13 a 19 años
tee·ny ['tini] *adj (comp* **-nier;** *super* **-niest)** (coll) diminuto, pequeñito
teeter ['titər] *s* vaivén *m,* balanceo ‖ *intr* balancear, oscilar
teethe [tið] *intr* endentecer
teething ['tiðɪŋ] *s* dentición
teething ring *s* chupador *m*
teetotaler [tiˈtotələr] *s* teetotalista *mf,* nefalista *mf,* abstemio
tel. *abbr* **telegram, telegraph, telephone**
tele-cast ['tɛlɪ ˌkæst] o ['tɛlɪ ˌkɑst] *s* teledifusión ‖ *v (pret & pp* **-cast** o **-casted)** *tr & intr* teledifundir
telegram ['tɛlɪ ˌgræm] *s* telegrama *m*
telegraph ['tɛlɪ ˌgræf] o ['tɛlɪ ˌgrɑf] *s* telégrafo ‖ *tr & intr* telegrafiar
telegrapher [tɪˈlɛgrəfər] *s* telegrafista *mf*
telegraph pole *s* poste *m* de telégrafo
Telemachus [tɪˈlɛməkəs] *s* Telémaco
telemeter [tɪˈlɛmɪtər] *s* telémetro ‖ *tr* telemetrar
telemetry [tɪˈlɛmɪtri] *s* telemetría
telephone ['tɛlɪ ˌfon] *s* teléfono ‖ *tr & intr* telefonear
telephone booth *s* locutorio, cabina telefónica
telephone call *s* llamada telefónica
telephone directory *s* anuario telefónico, guía telefónica
telephone exchange *s* estación telefónica, central *f* de teléfonos
telephone operator *s* telefonista *mf*
telephone receiver *s* receptor telefónico
telephone table *s* mesita portateléfono
teleprinter ['tɛlɪ ˌprɪntər] *s* teleimpresor *m*
telescope ['tɛlɪ ˌskop] *s* telescopio ‖ *tr* telescopar ‖ *intr* telescoparse
teletype ['tɛlɪ ˌtaɪp] *s* teletipo ‖ *tr & intr* transmitir por teletipo
teleview ['tɛlɪ ˌvju] *tr & intr* ver por televisión
televiewer ['tɛlɪ ˌvju·ər] *s* televidente *mf,* telespectador *m*
televise ['tɛlɪ ˌvaɪz] *tr* televisar
television ['tɛlɪ ˌvɪʃən] *adj* televisor ‖ *s* televisión
television screen *s* pantalla televisora
television set *s* televisor *m,* telerreceptor *m*
tell [tɛl] *v (pret & pp* **told** [told]) *tr* decir; *(to narrate; to count)* contar; determinar; conocer, distinguir; **I told you so!** ¡por algo te lo dije!; **to tell someone to +** *inf* decirle a uno que **+** *subj* ‖ *intr* hablar; surtir efecto; **to tell on** dejarse ver en *(p.ej., la salud de uno);* (coll) denunciar

ta
te

teller ['tɛlər] s narrador m; (of a bank) cajero; (of votes) escrutador m

temper ['tɛmpər] s temple m, natural m, genio; cólera, mal genio; (of steel, glass, etc.) temple m; **to keep one's temper** dominar su mal genio; **to lose one's temper** encolerizarse, perder la paciencia || tr templar || intr templarse

temperament ['tɛmpərəmənt] s disposición; temperamento sensible o excitable

temperamental [,tɛmpərə'mɛntəl] adj temperamental

temperance ['tɛmpərəns] s templanza

temperate ['tɛmpərɪt] adj templado

temperature ['tɛmpərətʃər] s temperatura

tempest ['tɛmpɪst] s tempestad

tempestuous [tɛm'pɛstʃu‧əs] adj tempestuoso

temple ['tɛmpəl] s (place of worship) templo; (of forehead) sien f; (sidepiece of spectacles) gafa

tem‧po ['tɛmpo] s (pl -pos o -pi [pi]) (mus) tiempo; (fig) ritmo (p.ej., de la vida)

temporal ['tɛmpərəl] adj temporal

temporary ['tɛmpə,rɛri] adj temporáneo, temporario, provisional, interino

temporize ['tɛmpə,raɪz] intr contemporizar, temporizar

tempt [tɛmpt] tr tentar

temptation [tɛmp'teʃən] s tentación

tempter ['tɛmptər] s tentador m

tempting ['tɛmptɪŋ] adj tentador

ten [tɛn] adj & pron diez || s diez m; **ten o'clock** las diez

tenable ['tɛnəbəl] adj defendible

tenacious [tɪ'neʃəs] adj tenaz

tenacity [tɪ'næsɪti] s tenacidad

tenant ['tɛnənt] s arrendatario, inquilino; morador m, residente mf

tend [tɛnd] tr cuidar, vigilar; servir || intr tender, dirigirse; **to tend to** atender a; **to tend to** + inf tender a + inf

tenden‧cy ['tɛndənsi] s (pl -cies) tendencia

tender ['tɛndər] adj tierno; (painfully sensitive) dolorido || n oferta; (naut) alijador m, falúa; (rr) ténder m || tr ofrecer, tender

tender-hearted ['tɛndər,hɑrtɪd] adj compasivo, tierno de corazón

ten'der‧loin' s filete m || **Tenderloin** s barrio de mala vida

tenderness ['tɛndərnɪs] s ternura, terneza; sensibilidad

tendon ['tɛndən] s tendón m

tendril ['tɛndrɪl] s zarcillo

tenement ['tɛnɪmənt] s habitación, vivienda; casa de vecindad

tenement house s casa de vecindad

tenet ['tɛnɪt] s dogma m, credo, principio

tennis ['tɛnɪs] s tenis m

tennis court s campo de tenis

tennis player s tenista mf

tenor ['tɛnər] s tenor m, carácter m, curso, tendencia; (mus) tenor

tense [tɛns] adj tenso, tieso; (person; situation) (fig) tenso; (relations) tirante || s (gram) tiempo

tension ['tɛnʃən] s tensión; ansia, congoja, esfuerzo mental; (in personal or diplomatic relations) tirantez f

tent [tɛnt] s tienda; tienda de campaña

tentacle ['tɛntəkəl] s tentáculo

tentative ['tɛntətɪv] adj tentativo

tenth [tɛnθ] adj & s décimo || s (in dates) diez m

tenuous ['tɛnju‧əs] adj tenue; (thin in consistency) raro

tenure ['tɛnjər] s (of property) tenencia; (of an office) ejercicio; (protection from dismissal) inamovilidad

tepid ['tɛpɪd] adj tibio

tercet ['tʌrsɪt] s terceto

term [tʌrm] s término; (of imprisonment) condena; semestre m, período escolar; (of the presidency of the U.S.A.) mandato, período; **terms** condiciones || tr llamar, nombrar

termagant ['tʌrməgənt] s mujer regañona, mujer de mal genio

terminal ['tʌrmɪnəl] adj terminal || s término, fin m; (elec) terminal m; (rr) estación de fin de línea

terminate ['tʌrmɪ,net] tr & intr terminar

termination [,tʌrmɪ'neʃən] s terminación

terminus ['tʌrmɪnəs] s término; (rr) estación de cabeza, estación extrema

termite ['tʌrmaɪt] s termite m, comején m

terrace ['tɛrəs] s terraza; (flat roof of a house) azotea

terra firma ['tɛrə 'fʌrmə] s tierra firme; **on terra firma** sobre suelo firme

terrain [tɛ'ren] s terreno

terrestrial [tə'rɛstrɪ‧əl] adj terrestre

terrible ['tɛrɪbəl] adj terrible; muy desagradable

terrific [tə'rɪfɪk] adj terrífico; (coll) enorme, intenso, brutal

terri‧fy ['tɛrɪ,faɪ] v (pret & pp -fied) tr aterrorizar, atemorizar

territo‧ry ['tɛrɪ,tori] s (pl -ries) territorio

terror ['tɛrər] s terror m

terrorize ['tɛrə,raɪz] tr aterrorizar; imponerse a, mediante el terror

terry cloth ['tɛri] s albornoz m

terse [tʌrs] adj breve, sucinto

tertiary ['tʌrʃɪ,ɛri] o ['tʌrʃəri] adj terciario

Test. abbr **Testament**

test [tɛst] s prueba, ensayo; examen m || tr probar, poner a prueba; examinar

testament ['tɛstəmənt] s testamento

test flight s vuelo de ensayo

testicle ['tɛstɪkəl] s testículo

testi‧fy ['tɛstɪ,faɪ] v (pret & pp -fied) tr & intr testificar

testimonial [,tɛstɪ'monɪ‧əl] s recomendación, certificado; (expression of esteem, gratitude, etc.) homenaje m

testimo‧ny ['tɛstɪ,moni] s (pl -nies) testimonio

test pilot s (aer) piloto de pruebas

test tube s probeta, tubo de ensayo

tether [ˈtɛðər] s atadura, traba; **at the end of one's tether** al límite de las posibilidades o la paciencia de uno || *tr* apersogar

tetter [ˈtɛtər] s empeine m

text [tɛkst] s texto; tema m, lema m

text'book' s libro de texto

textile [ˈtɛkstɪl] o [ˈtɛkstaɪl] adj & s textil m

texture [ˈtɛkstʃər] s textura

Thai [ˈtɑ·i] o [ˈtaɪ] adj & s tailandés m

Thailand [ˈtaɪlənd] s Tailandia

Thales [ˈθeliz] s Tales m

Thalia [θəˈlaɪ·ə] s Talía

Thames [tɛmz] s Támesis m

than [ðæn] *conj* que, p.ej., **he is richer than I** es más rico que yo; (*before a numeral*) de, p.ej., **more than twenty** más de veinte; (*before a verb*) de lo que, p.ej., **the crop is larger than was expected** la cosecha es mayor de lo que se esperaba; (*before a verb with direct object understood*) del (de la, de los, de las) que, p.ej., **they sent us more coffee than we ordered** nos enviaron más café del que pedimos

thank [θæŋk] *tr* agradecer, dar las gracias a; **to thank someone for something** agradecerle a uno una cosa || **thanks** *spl* gracias; **thanks to** gracias a, merced a || **thanks** *interj* ¡gracias!

thankful [ˈθæŋkfəl] adj agradecido

thankless [ˈθæŋklɪs] adj ingrato

thanksgiving [ˌθæŋksˈɡɪvɪŋ] s acción de gracias

Thanksgiving Day s (U.S.A.) día m de acción de gracias

that [ðæt] adj *dem* (*pl* those) ese; aquel; **that one** ése; aquél || *pron dem* (*pl* those) ése; aquél; eso; aquello || *pron rel* que, quien, el cual, el que || *adv* tan; **that far** tan lejos; hasta allí; **that many** tantos; **that much** tanto || *conj* que; para que

thatch [θætʃ] s barda, paja; techo de paja || *tr* cubrir de paja, techar con paja, bardar

thaw [θɔ] s deshielo, derretimiento || *tr* deshelar, derretir || *intr* deshelarse, derretirse

the [ðə], [ðɪ] o [ði] *art def* el || *adv* cuanto, p.ej., **the more the merrier** cuanto más mejor; **the more . . . the more** cuanto más . . . tanto más

theater [ˈθi·ətər] s teatro

the'ater-go'er s teatrero

theater news s actualidad escénica

theater page s noticiario teatral

theatrical [θiˈætrɪkəl] adj teatral

Thebes [θibz] s Tebas f

thee [ði] *pron pers* (archaic, poet, Bib) te; ti; **with thee** contigo

theft [θɛft] s hurto, robo

their [ðɛr] adj *poss* su; el . . . de ellos

theirs [ðɛrz] *pron poss* el suyo, el de ellos

them [ðɛm] *pron pers* los; ellos; **to them** les; a ellos

theme [θim] s tema m; (mus) tema m

theme song s (mus) tema m central; (rad) sintonía

them·selves' *pron pers* ellos mismos; sí, sí mismos; se, p.ej., **they enjoyed themselves** se divirtieron; **with themselves** consigo

then [ðɛn] *adv* entonces; después, luego, en seguida; además, también; **by then** para entonces; **from then on** desde entonces, de allí en adelante; **then and there** ahí mismo

thence [ðɛns] *adv* desde allí; desde entonces; por eso

thence'forth' *adv* de allí en adelante; desde entonces

theolo·gy [θiˈɑlədʒi] s (*pl* -gies) teología

theorem [ˈθi·ərəm] s teorema m

theo·ry [ˈθi·əri] s (*pl* -ries) teoría

therapeutic [ˌθɛrəˈpjutɪk] adj terapéutico || **therapeutics** *ssg* terapéutica

thera·py [ˈθɛrəpi] s (*pl* -pies) terapia

there [ðɛr] *adv* allí, allá; **there is** o **there are** hay; aquí tiene Vd.

there'a·bouts' *adv* por allí; cerca, aproximadamente

there·af'ter *adv* de allí en adelante, después de eso

there·by' *adv* con eso; así, de tal modo; por allí cerca

therefore [ˈðɛrfor] *adv* por lo tanto, por consiguiente

there·in' *adv* en esto, en eso; en ese respecto

there·of' *adv* de ello, de eso

Theresa [təˈrisə] o [təˈresə] s Teresa

there·u·pon' *adv* sobre eso, encima de eso; por consiguiente; en seguida

thermistor [θərˈmɪstər] s (elec) termistor m

thermocouple [ˈθɑrmoˌkʌpəl] s (elec) termopar m

thermodynamic [ˌθɑrmodaɪˈnæmɪk] adj termodinámico || **thermodynamics** *ssg* termodinámica

thermometer [θərˈmɑmɪtər] s termómetro

thermonuclear [ˌθɑrmoˈnjuklɪ·ər] o [ˌθɑrmoˈnuklɪ·ər] adj termonuclear

Thermopylae [θərˈmɑpɪˌli] s las Termópilas

thermos bottle [ˈθɑrməs] s termos m, botella termos

thermostat [ˈθɑrməˌstæt] s termóstato

thesau·rus [θɪˈsɔrəs] s (*pl* -ri [raɪ]) tesoro; (*dictionary or the like*) tesauro, tesoro

these [ðiz] *pl de* this

the·sis [ˈθisɪs] s (*pl* -ses [siz]) tesis f

Thespis [ˈθɛspɪs] s Tespis m

Thessaly [ˈθɛsəli] s la Tesalia

they [ðe] *pron pers* ellos, ellas

thick [θɪk] adj espeso, grueso; denso; (coll) estúpido; (coll) íntimo || s espesor m; **the thick of** (*e.g., a crowd*) lo más denso de; (*e.g., a battle*) lo más reñido de; **through thick and thin** contra viento y marea

thicken [ˈθɪkən] *tr* espesar || *intr* espesarse; complicarse (*el enredo*)

thicket [ˈθɪkɪt] s espesura, matorral m, soto

thick-headed [ˈθɪkˈhɛdɪd] adj (coll) torpe, estúpido

thick'-set' adj grueso, rechoncho

thief [θif] s (pl **thieves** [θivz]) ladrón m

thieve [θiv] intr hurtar, robar

thiev·y ['θivəri] s (pl -**ies**) latrocinio, hurto, robo

thigh [θaɪ] s muslo

thigh'bone' s hueso del muslo, fémur m

thimble ['θɪmbəl] s dedal m

thin [θɪn] adj (comp **thinner**; super **thinnest**) delgado, flaco, tenue; (cloth, paper, sole of shoe, etc.) fino; (hair) ralo; (broth) aguado; (excuse) débil; claro, ligero, escaso ‖ v (pret & pp **thinned**; ger **thinning**) tr adelgazar, enflaquecer; enrarecer; aclarar; aguar; desleír (los colores) ‖ intr adelgazarse, enflaquecerse; enrarecerse; **to thin out** ralear (el pelo)

thine [δaɪn] adj poss (archaic & poet) tu ‖ pron poss (archaic & poet) tuyo; el tuyo

thing [θɪŋ] s cosa; **of all things!** ¡qué sorpresa!; **to be the thing** ser la última moda; **to be the thing to do** ser lo que debe hacerse; **to see things** ver visiones, padecer alucinaciones

think [θɪŋk] v (pret & pp **thought** [θɔt]) tr pensar; **to think it over** pensarlo; **to think nothing of** tener en poco; creer fácil; no dar importancia a; **to think of** pensar de, p.ej., **what do you think of this book?** ¿qué piensa Vd. de este libro?; **to think up** imaginar; inventar (p.ej., una excusa) ‖ intr pensar; **to think not** creer que no; **to think of** (to turn one's thoughts to) pensar en; pensar (un número, un naipe, etc.); **to think so** creer que sí; **to think well of** tener buena opinión de

thinker ['θɪŋkər] s pensador m

third [θʌrd] adj tercero ‖ s (in a series) tercero; (one of three equal parts) tercio; (in dates) tres m

third degree s (coll) interrogatorio bajo tortura

third rail s (rr) tercer carril m, carril de toma

Third World n Tercero Mundo

thirst [θʌrst] s sed f ‖ intr tener sed; **to thirst for** tener sed de

thirst·y ['θʌrsti] adj (comp -**ier**; super -**iest**) sediento; **to be thirsty** tener sed

thirteen ['θʌr'tin] adj, pron & s trece m

thirteenth ['θʌr'tinθ] adj & s (in a series) decimotercero; (part) trezavo ‖ s (in dates) trece m

thirtieth ['θʌrtɪ·ɪθ] adj & s (in a series) trigésimo; (part) treintavo ‖ s (in dates) treinta m

thir·ty ['θʌrti] adj & pron treinta ‖ s (pl -**ties**) treinta m

this [δɪs] adj dem (pl **these**) este; **this one** éste ‖ pron dem (pl **these**) éste; esto ‖ adv tan

thistle ['θɪsəl] s cardo

thither ['θɪðər] o ['δɪðər] adv allá, hacia allá

thong [θɔŋ] o [θɑŋ] s correa

tho·rax ['θoræks] s (pl -**raxes** o -**races** [rə,siz]) tórax m

thorn [θɔrn] s espina

thorn·y ['θɔrni] adj (comp -**ier**; super -**iest**) espinoso; (difficult) (fig) espinoso

thorough ['θʌro] adj cabal, completo; concienzudo, cuidadoso

thor'ough·bred' adj de pura sangre; bien nacido ‖ s pura sangre m; persona bien nacida

thor'ough·fare' s vía pública; **no thoroughfare** se prohibe el paso

thor'ough·go'ing adj cabal, completo, esmerado, perfecto

thoroughly ['θʌroli] adv a fondo

those [δoz] pl de **that**

thou [δaʊ] pron pers (archaic, poet & Bib) tú ‖ tr & intr tutear

though [δo] adv sin embargo ‖ conj aunque, bien que; **as though** como si

thought [θɔt] s pensamiento

thoughtful ['θɔtfəl] adj pensativo; atento, considerado

thoughtless ['θɔtlɪs] adj irreflexivo; descuidado; inconsiderado

thought transference s transmisión del pensamiento

thousand ['θaʊzənd] adj & s mil m; **a thousand u one thousand** mil m

thousandth ['θaʊzəndθ] adj & s milésimo

thralldom ['θrɔldəm] s esclavitud, servidumbre

thrash [θræʃ] tr (agr) trillar; azotar, zurrar; **to thrash out** decidir después de una discusión cabal ‖ intr trillar; agitarse, menearse

thread [θred] s hilo; (mach) filete m, rosca; (of a speech, of life) hilo; **to lose the thread of** perder el hilo de ‖ tr enhebrar, enhilar; ensartar (p.ej., cuentas); (mach) aterrajar, filetear

thread'bare' adj raído; gastado, usado, viejo

threat [θret] s amenaza

threaten ['θretən] tr & intr amenazar

threatening ['θretənɪŋ] adj amenazante

three [θri] adj & pron tres ‖ s tres m; **three o'clock** las tres

three'-cor'nered adj triangular; (hat) de tres picos

three hundred adj & pron trescientos ‖ s trescientos m

threepence ['θrepəns] o ['θrɪpəns] s suma de tres peniques; moneda de tres peniques

three'-ply' adj de tres capas

three R's [arz] spl lectura, escritura y aritmética, primeras letras

three'score' adj tres veintenas de

thre·no·dy ['θrenədi] s (pl -**dies**) treno

thresh [θreʃ] tr (agr) trillar; **to thresh out** decidir después de una discusión cabal ‖ intr trillar; agitarse, menearse

threshing machine s máquina trilladora

threshold ['θreʃold] s umbral m; (physiol, psychol & fig) umbral, limen m; **to be on the threshold of** estar en los umbrales de; **to cross the threshold** atravesar o pisar los umbrales

thrice [θraɪs] adv tres veces; repetidamente, sumamente

thrift [θrɪft] *s* economía, parquedad

thrift·y ['θrɪfti] *adj* (*comp* **-ier**; *super* **-iest**) económico, parco; próspero

thrill [θrɪl] *s* emoción viva ‖ *tr* emocionar, conmover ‖ *intr* emocionarse, conmoverse

thriller ['θrɪlər] *s* cuento o pieza de teatro espeluznante

thrilling ['θrɪlɪŋ] *adj* emocionante; espeluznante

thrive [θraɪv] *v* (*pret* **thrived** o **throve** [θrov]; *pp* **thrived** o **thriven** ['θrɪvən]) *intr* medrar, prosperar

throat [θrot] *s* garganta; **to clear one's throat** aclarar la voz

throb [θrɑb] *s* latido, palpitación, pulsación ‖ *v* (*pret & pp* **throbbed**; *ger* **throbbing**) *intr* latir, palpitar, pulsar

throe [θro] *s* congoja, dolor *m*; **throes** angustia, agonía; esfuerzo penoso

throne [θron] *s* trono

throng [θrɔŋ] o [θrɑŋ] *s* gentío, tropel *m*, muchedumbre ‖ *intr* agolparse, apiñarse

throttle ['θrɑtəl] *s* válvula reguladora; (*of a locomotive*) regulador *m*; (*of an automobile*) acelerador *m* ‖ *tr* ahogar, sofocar; impedir, suprimir; (*mach*) regular; **to throttle down** reducir la velocidad de

through [θru] *adj* directo, sin paradas; acabado, terminado; **to be through with** haber terminado; no querer ocuparse más de ‖ *adv* a través, de un lado a otro; completamente ‖ *prep* por, a través de; por medio de; a causa de; todo lo largo de

through·out' *adv* por todas partes; en todos respectos; desde el principio hasta el fin ‖ *prep* por todo . . .; durante todo . . .; a lo largo de

through'way' *s* carretera de peaje de acceso limitado

throw [θro] *s* echada, tirada, lance *m*; cobertor ligero ‖ *v* (*pret* **threw** [θru]; *pp* **thrown**) *tr* arrojar, echar, lanzar; tirar (*los dados*); lanzar (*una mirada*); desazonar (*a un jinete*); proyectar (*una sombra*); tender (*un puente*); perder con premeditación (*un juego, una carrera*); **to throw away** tirar; malgastar; perder, no aprovechar; **to throw in** añadir, dar de más; **to throw out** arrojar, botar, desechar; echar a la calle; **to throw over** abandonar, dejar ‖ *intr* arrojar, echar, lanzar; **to throw up** vomitar

thrum [θrʌm] *v* (*pret & pp* **thrummed**; *ger* **thrumming**) *intr* teclear; zangarrear; **to thrum on** rasguear

thrush [θrʌʃ] *s* tordo

thrust [θrʌst] *s* empuje *m*; acometida; (*with horns*) cornada; (*with dagger*) puñalada; (*with sword*) estocada; (*with knife*) cuchillada ‖ *v* (*pret & pp* **thrust**) *tr* empujar; acometer; clavar, hincar; atravesar, traspasar

thud [θʌd] *s* baque *m*, ruido sordo ‖ *v* (*pret & pp* **thudded**; *ger* **thudding**) *tr & intr* golpear con ruido sordo

thug [θʌg] *s* ladrón *m*, asesino

thumb [θʌm] *s* pulgar *m*, dedo gordo;

all thumbs (coll) desmañado, chapucero, torpe; **to twiddle one's thumbs** menear ociosamente los pulgares; no hacer nada; **under the thumb of** bajo la férula de ‖ *tr* manosear sin cuidado; ensuciar con los dedos; hojear (*un libro*) con el pulgar; **to thumb a ride** pedir ser llevado en automóvil indicando la dirección con el pulgar; **to thumb one's nose at** (coll) señalar (*a una persona*) poniendo el pulgar sobre la nariz en son de burla; (coll) tratar con sumo desprecio

thumb index *s* escalerilla, índice *m* con pestañas

thumb'print' *s* impresión del pulgar ‖ *tr* marcar con impresión del pulgar

thumb'screw' *s* tornillo de mariposa, tornillo de orejas

thumb'tack' *s* chinche *m*

thump [θʌmp] *s* golpazo, porrazo ‖ *tr* golpear, aporrear ‖ *intr* caer con golpe pesado; andar con pasos pesados; latir (*el corazón*) con golpes pesados

thumping ['θʌmpɪŋ] *adj* (coll) enorme, pesado

thunder ['θʌndər] *s* trueno; (*of applause*) estruendo; amenaza ‖ *tr* fulminar (*p.ej., censuras, amenazas*) ‖ *intr* tronar; **to thunder at** tronar contra

thun'der·bolt' *s* rayo

thun'der·clap' *s* tronido

thunderous ['θʌndərəs] *adj* atronador, tronitoso

thun'der·show'er *s* chubasco con truenos

thun'der·storm' *s* tronada

thun'der·struck' *adj* atónito, estupefacto, pasmado

Thursday ['θʌrsdi] *s* jueves *m*

thus [ðʌs] *adv* así; **thus far** hasta aquí, hasta ahora

thwack [θwæk] *s* golpe *m*, porrazo ‖ *tr* golpear, pegar

thwart [θwɔrt] *adj* transversal, oblicuo ‖ *adv* de través ‖ *tr* desbaratar, impedir, frustrar

thy [ðaɪ] *adj poss* (archaic & poet) tu

thyme [taɪm] *s* tomillo

thyroid gland ['θaɪrɔɪd] *s* glándula tiroides

thyself [ðaɪ'self] *pron* (archaic & poet) tú mismo; ti mismo; te; ti

tiara [taɪ'ɑrə] o [taɪ'ɛrə] *s* (*papal miter*) tiara; (*female adornment*) diadema *f*

tick [tɪk] *s* tictac *m*; funda (*de almohada o colchón*); (coll) crédito; (ent) garrapata; **on tick** (coll) al fiado ‖ *intr* hacer tictac; latir (*el corazón*)

ticker ['tɪkər] *s* teleimpresor *m* de cinta; (slang) reloj *m*; (slang) corazón *m*

ticker tape *s* cinta de teleimpresor

ticket ['tɪkɪt] *s* billete *m*; boleto (Am); (theat) entrada, localidad; (*for wrong parking*) (coll) aviso de multa; (*of a political party*) (U.S.A.) lista de candidatos; **that's the ticket** (coll) eso es, eso es lo que se necesita

ticket agent *s* taquillero
ticket collector *s* revisor *m*
ticket office *s* taquilla, despacho de billetes
ticket scalper [ˈskælpər] *s* revendedor *m* de billetes de teatro
ticket window *s* taquilla, ventanilla
ticking [ˈtɪkɪŋ] *s* cutí *m*, terliz *m*
tickle [ˈtɪkəl] *s* cosquillas || *tr* cosquillear; gustar, satisfacer; divertir || *intr* cosquillear
ticklish [ˈtɪklɪʃ] *adj* cosquilloso; difícil, delicado; inseguro
tick-tock [ˈtɪk͵tak] *s* tictac *m*
tidal wave [ˈtaɪdəl] *s* aguaje *m*, ola de marea; (*e.g., of popular indignation*) ola
tidbit [ˈtɪd͵bɪt] *s* buen bocado, bocadito
tiddlywinks [ˈtɪdli͵wɪŋks] *s* juego de la pulga
tide [taɪd] *s* marea; temporada; **to go against the tide** ir contra la corriente; **to stem the tide** rendir la marea || *tr* llevar, hacer flotar; **to tide over** ayudar un poco; superar (*una dificultad*)
tide'wa'ter *adj* costanero || *s* agua de marea; orilla del mar
tidings [ˈtaɪdɪŋz] *spl* noticias, informes *mpl*
ti·dy [ˈtaɪdi] *adj* (*comp* **-dier;** *super* **-diest**) aseado, limpio, pulcro, ordenado || *s* (*pl* **-dies**) pañito bordado, cubierta de respaldar || *v* (*pret & pp* **-died**) *tr* asear, limpiar, arreglar, poner en orden || *intr* asearse
tie [taɪ] *s* atadura; lazo, nudo; (*worn on neck*) corbata; (*in games and elections*) empate *m*; (mus) ligado; (rr) traviesa || *v* (*pret & pp* **tied;** *ger* **tying**) *tr* atar, liar; enlazar; hacer (*la corbata*); confinar, limitar; empatar (*p.ej., una elección*); empatársela a (*una persona*); **to be tied up** estar ocupado; **to tie down** confinar, limitar; **to tie up** atar; envolver; obstruir (*el tráfico*) || *intr* atar; empatar o empatarse (*dos candidatos, dos equipos*)
tie'pin' *s* alfiler *m* de corbata
tier [tɪr] *s* fila, ringlera; (theat) fila de palcos
tiger [ˈtaɪgər] *s* tigre *m*
tiger lily *s* azucena atigrada
tight [taɪt] *adj* apretado, estrecho, ajustado; bien cerrado, hermético; compacto, denso; fijo, firme, sólido; (com) escaso; (sport) casi igual; (coll) agarrado, tacaño; (slang) borracho || *adv* firmemente; **to hold tight** mantener fijo; agarrarse bien || **tights** *spl* traje *m* de malla
tighten [ˈtaɪtən] *tr* apretar; atiesar, estirar || *intr* apretarse; atiesarse, estirarse
tight-fisted [ˈtaɪtˈfɪstɪd] *adj* agarrado, tacaño
tight'-fit'ting *adj* ceñido, muy ajustado
tight'rope' *s* cuerda tirante
tight squeeze *s* (coll) brete *m*, aprieto
tigress [ˈtaɪgrɪs] *s* tigresa
tile [taɪl] *s* azulejo; (*for floors*) bal-

dosa; (*for roofs*) teja || *tr* azulejar; embaldosar; tejar
tile roof *s* tejado (de tejas)
till [tɪl] *prep* hasta || *conj* hasta que || *s* cajón *m* o gaveta del dinero || *tr* labrar, cultivar
tilt [tɪlt] *s* inclinación; justa, torneo; **full tilt** a toda velocidad || *tr* inclinar; asestar (*una lanza*) || *intr* inclinarse; justar, tornear; luchar; **to tilt at** luchar con, arremeter contra; protestar contra
timber [ˈtɪmbər] *s* madera de construcción; madero, viga; bosque *m*, árboles *mpl* de monte
tim'ber·land' *s* bosque *m* maderable
timber line *s* límite *m* de la vegetación, límite del bosque maderable
timbre [ˈtɪmbər] *s* (phonet & phys) timbre *m*
time [taɪm] *s* tiempo; hora, p.ej., vez, p.ej., **five times** cinco veces; rato, p.ej., **a nice time** un buen rato; (*period for payment*) plazo; horas de trabajo; sueldo; tiempo de parir, término del embarazo; última hora; (phot) tiempo de exposición; **for the time being** por ahora, por el momento; **on time** a tiempo, a la hora debida; (*in installments*) a plazos; **to bide one's time** esperar la hora propicia; **to do time** (coll) cumplir una condena; **to have a good time** darse buen tiempo; **to have no time for** no poder tolerar; **to lose time** atrasarse (*el reloj*); **to make time** avanzar con rapidez; **to pass the time of day** saludarse (*dos personas*); **to take one's time** no darse prisa, ir despacio; **what time is it?** ¿qué hora es? || *tr* calcular el tiempo de; medir el tiempo de; (sport) cronometrar
time bomb *s* bomba-reloj *f*
time'card' *s* hoja de presencia, tarjeta registradora
time clock *s* reloj *m* registrador
time exposure *s* exposición de tiempo
time fuse *s* espoleta de tiempos
time'keep'er *s* alistador *m* de tiempo; reloj *m*; (sport) cronometrador *m*, juez *m* de tiempo
time·ly [ˈtaɪmli] *adj* (*comp* **-lier;** *super* **-liest**) oportuno
time'piece' *s* reloj *m*
time signal *s* señal horaria
time'ta'ble *s* horario, itinerario
time'work' *s* trabajo a jornal
time'worn' *adj* gastado por el tiempo
time zone *s* huso horario
timid [ˈtɪmɪd] *adj* tímido
timing gears [ˈtaɪmɪŋ] *spl* engranaje *m* de distribución, mando de las válvulas
timorous [ˈtɪmərəs] *adj* tímido, miedoso
tin [tɪn] *s* (*element*) estaño; (*tin plate*) hojalata; (*cup, box, etc.*) lata || *v* (*pret & pp* **tinned;** *ger* **tinning**) *tr* estañar; (*to pack in cans*) enlatar; recubrir de hojalata
tin can *s* lata, envase *m* de hojalata
tincture [ˈtɪŋktʃər] *s* tintura

tin cup s taza de hojalata
tinder ['tɪndər] s yesca
tin'der·box' s lumbres fpl, yesquero; persona muy excitable; semillero de violencia
tin foil s hojuela de estaño, papel m de estaño
ting-a-ling ['tɪŋə,lɪŋ] s tilín m
tinge [tɪndʒ] s matiz m, tinte m; dejo, gustillo || v (ger tingeing o tinging) tr matizar, teñir; dar gusto o sabor a
tingle ['tɪŋɡəl] s comezón f, picazón f || intr sentir comezón; zumbar (los oídos); (e.g., with enthusiasm) estremecerse
tin hat s (coll) yelmo de acero
tinker ['tɪŋkər] s calderero remendón; chapucero || intr ocuparse vanamente
tinkle ['tɪŋkəl] s retintín m || tr hacer retiñir || intr retiñir
tin plate s hojalata
tin roof s tejado de hojalata
tinsel ['tɪnsəl] s oropel m; (e.g., for a Christmas tree) lentejuelas de hojas de estaño
tin'smith' s hojalatero
tin soldier s soldadito de plomo
tint [tɪnt] s tinte m, matiz m || tr teñir, matizar, colorar ligeramente
tin'type' s ferrotipo
tin'ware' s objetos de hojalata
ti·ny ['taɪni] adj (comp -nier; super -niest) diminuto, menudo, pequeñito
tip [tɪp] s extremo, extremidad; (of shoestring) herrete m; (of arrow) casquillo; (of umbrella) regatón m; (of tongue) punta; (of shoe) puntera; (of cigarette) embocadura; inclinación; golpecito; soplo, aviso confidencial; (fee) propina || v (pret & pp tipped; ger tipping) tr herretear; inclinar, ladear; volcar; golpear ligeramente; dar propina a; informar por debajo de cuerda; tocarse (el sombrero) con los dedos; quitarse (el sombrero en señal de cortesía); to tip in (bb) encañonar (un pliego) || intr dar una propina o propinas; inclinarse, ladearse; volcarse
tip'cart' s volquete m
tip'-off' s (coll) informe dado por debajo de cuerda
tipped'-in' adj (bb) fuera de texto
tipple ['tɪpəl] intr beborrotear
tip'staff' s vara de justicia; alguacil m de vara
tip·sy ['tɪpsi] adj (comp -sier; super -siest) achispado
tip'toe' s punta del pie; on tiptoe de puntillas; alerta; furtivamente || v (pret & pp -toed; ger -toeing) intr andar de puntillas
tirade ['taɪred] s diatriba, invectiva
tire [taɪr] s neumático, llanta de goma; (of metal) calce m, llanta || tr cansar; aburrir, fastidiar || intr cansar; (to be tiresome) cansar; (to get tired) cansarse; aburrirse, fastidiarse
tire chain s cadena de llanta, cadena antirresbaladiza
tired [taɪrd] adj cansado, rendido
tire gauge s indicador m de presión de inflado

tireless ['taɪrlɪs] adj incansable, infatigable
tire pressure s presión de inflado
tire pump s bomba para inflar neumáticos
tiresome ['taɪrsəm] adj cansado, aburrido, pesado
tissue ['tɪʃu] s tejido fino; papel m de seda; (biol & fig) tejido
tissue paper s papel m de seda
titanium [tai'teni·əm] o [tɪ'teni·əm] s titanio
tithe [taɪð] s décimo, décima parte; (tax paid to church) diezmo || tr diezmar
Titian ['tɪʃən] adj castaño rojizo || s el Ticiano
title ['taɪtəl] s título; (sport) campeonato || tr titular
title deed s título de propiedad
ti'tle-hold'er s titulado; (sport) campeón m
title page s portada, frontispicio
title rôle s (theat) papel m principal (el que corresponde al título de la obra)
titter ['tɪtər] s risita ahogada, risita disimulada || intr reír a medias, reír con disimulo
titular ['tɪtʃələr] adj titular; nominal
tn. abbr **ton**
to [tu], [tʊ] o [tə] adv hacia adelante; **to and fro** de una parte a otra, de aquí para allá; **to come to** volver en sí || prep a, p.ej., **he is going to Madrid** va a Madrid; **they gave something to the beggar** dieron algo al pobre; **we are learning to dance** aprendemos a bailar; para, p.ej., **he is reading to himself** lee para sí; por, p.ej., **work to do** trabajo por hacer; hasta, p.ej., **to a certain extent** hasta cierto punto; en, p.ej., **from door to door** de puerta en puerta; con, p.ej., **kind to her** amable con ella; segun, p.ej., **to my way of thinking** según mi modo de pensar; menos, p.ej., **five minutes to ten** las diez menos cinco
toad [tod] s sapo
toad'stool' s agárico, seta; seta venenosa
to-and-fro ['tu·ənd'fro] adj alternativo, de vaivén
toast [tost] s tostadas; (drink) brindis m; **a piece of toast** una tostada || tr tostar; brindar a o por || intr tostarse; brindar
toaster ['tostər] s (of bread) tostador m; brindador m
toast'mas'ter s el que presenta a los oradores en un banquete, maestro de ceremonias
tobac·co [tə'bæko] s (pl -cos) tabaco
tobacco pouch s petaca
toboggan [tə'bɑɡən] s tobogán m || intr deslizarse en tobogán
tocsin ['tɑksɪn] s campana de alarma; campanada de alarma
today [tu'de] adv & s hoy
toddle ['tɑdəl] s pasitos vacilantes || intr andar con pasitos vacilantes; hacer pinitos (un niño o un enfermo)

ti
to

tod·dy ['tɑdi] s (pl **-dies**) ponche m
to-do [tə'du] s (coll) alharaca, alboroto
toe [to] s dedo del pie; (of stocking) punta || v (pret & pp **toed**; ger **toeing**) tr — **to toe the line** o **the mark** ponerse a la raya; obrar como se debe
toe'nail' s uña del dedo del pie
tog [tɑg] s (coll) prenda de vestir
together [tu'gɛðər] adv juntamente; juntos; al mismo tiempo; sin interrupción; de acuerdo; **to bring together** reunir; confrontar; reconciliar; **to call together** convocar; **to go together** ir juntos; ser novios; hacer juego; **to stick together** (coll) quedarse unidos, no abandonarse
toil [tɔɪl] s afán m, fatiga; faena, obra laboriosa; **toils** red f, lazo || intr atrafagar; moverse con fatiga
toilet ['tɔɪlɪt] s tocado, atavío; (dressing table) tocador m; retrete m, inodoro, excusado; **to make one's toilet** asearse, acicalarse
toilet articles spl artículos de tocador
toilet paper s papel higiénico
toilet powder s polvos de tocador
toilet soap s jabón m de olor, jabón de tocador
toilet water s agua de tocador
token ['tokən] s señal f, prueba; prenda, recuerdo; (used as money) ficha, tanto; **by the same token** por el mismo motivo; **in token of** en señal de
tolerance ['tɑlərəns] s tolerancia
tolerate ['tɑlə‚ret] tr tolerar
toll [tol] s (of bells) doble m; (to pass along a road or over a bridge) peaje m; (to use a canal) derechos de paso; (to use a telephone) tarifa; (number of victims) baja, mortalidad || tr tocar a muerto (una campana); llamar con toque de difuntos || intr doblar
toll bridge s puente m de peaje
toll call s (telp) llamada a larga distancia
toll'gate' s barrera de peaje
toma·to [tə'meto] o [tə'mɑto] s (pl **-toes**) (plant) tomatera o tomate m; (fruit) tomate m
tomb [tum] s tumba, sepulcro
tomboy ['tɑm‚bɔɪ] s moza retozona, muchacha traviesa
tomb'stone' s piedra o lápida sepulcral
tomcat ['tɑm‚kæt] s gato macho
tome [tom] s tomo; libro grueso
tomorrow [tu'mɑro] o [tu'mɔro] adv mañana || s mañana m; **the day after tomorrow** pasado mañana
tom-tom ['tɑm‚tɑm] s tantán m
ton [tʌn] s tonelada; **tons** (coll) montones mpl
tone [ton] s tono || tr entonar || intr armonizar; **to tone down** moderarse; **to tone up** reforzarse
tone poem s poema sinfónico
tongs [tɔŋz] o [tɑŋz] spl tenazas; (e.g., for sugar) tenacillas
tongue [tʌŋ] s (anat) lengua; (of a wagon) vara, lanza; (of a belt buckle) tarabilla; (of shoe) lengua, lengüeta; (language) lengua, idioma

m; **to hold one's tongue** morderse la lengua
tongue twister ['twɪstər] s trabalenguas m
tonic ['tɑnɪk] adj & s tónico
tonic accent s acento prosódico
tonight [tu'naɪt] adv & s esta noche
tonnage ['tʌnɪdʒ] s tonelaje m
tonsil ['tɑnsəl] s tonsila, amígdala
tonsillitis [‚tɑnsɪ'laɪtɪs] s tonsilitis f, amigdalitis f
ton·y ['toni] adj (comp -ier; super -iest) (slang) elegante, aristocrático
too [tu] adv (also) también; (more than enough) demasiado; **too bad!** ¡qué lástima!; **too many** demasiados; **too much** demasiado
tool [tul] s herramienta; (person used for one's own ends) instrumento || tr trabajar con herramienta; (bb) filetear, estampar
tool bag s bolsa de herramientas
tool'mak'er s tallador m de herramientas, herrero de herramientas
toot [tut] s (of horn) toque m; (of klaxon) bocinazo; (of locomotive) pitazo; (coll) parranda || tr sonar; **to toot one's own horn** cantar sus propias alabanzas || intr sonar
tooth [tuθ] s (pl **teeth** [tiθ]) diente m
tooth'ache' s dolor m de muelas
tooth'brush' s cepillo de dientes
toothless ['tuθlɪs] adj desdentado
tooth paste s pasta dentífrica
tooth'pick' s limpiadientes m, mondadientes m, palillo
tooth powder s polvo dentífrico
top [tɑp] s (of a mountain, tree, etc.) cima; (of a mountain; high point) cumbre f; (of a tree) copa; (of a barrel, box, etc.) tapa; (of a page) principio; (of a table) tablero; (of a wall) coronamiento; (of a bathing suit) camiseta; (of a carriage or auto) capota; (toy) peón m, peonza; (naut) cofa; **at the top of** en lo alto de; (e.g., one's class) a la cabeza de; **at the top of one's voice** a voz en grito; **from top to bottom** de arriba abajo; de alto a bajo; completamente; **on top of** en lo alto de; encima de; **the tops** (slang) la flor de la canela; **to sleep like a top** dormir como un leño || v (pret & pp **topped**; ger **topping**) tr coronar, rematar; cubrir; aventajar, superar; descopar (p.ej., un árbol)
topaz ['topæz] s topacio
top billing s cabecera de cartel
top'coat' s sobretodo; abrigo de entretiempo
toper ['topər] s borrachín m
top hat s chistera, sombrero de copa
top'-heav'y adj más pesado arriba que abajo
topic ['tɑpɪk] s asunto, materia, tema m
top'knot' s moño
top'mast' s (naut) mastelero
top'most adj (el) más alto
topogra·phy [tə'pɑgrəfi] s (pl **-phies**) topografía
topple ['tɑpəl] tr derribar, volcar ||

intr derribarse, volcarse; caerse, venirse abajo

top priority *s* máxima prioridad

topsail ['tɑpsəl] o ['tɑp,sel] *s* (naut) gavia

top'soil' *s* capa superficial del suelo

topsy-turvy ['tɑpsi'tʌrvi] *adj* desbarajustado || *adv* en cuadro, patas arriba || *s* desbarajuste *m*

torch [tɔrtʃ] *s* antorcha; lámpara de bolsillo; **to carry the torch for** (slang) amar desesperadamente

torch'bear'er *s* hachero; (fig) adicto, partidario

torch'light' *s* luz *f* de antorcha

torch song *s* canción lenta y melancólica de amor no correspondido

torment ['tɔrment] *s* tormento || [tɔr-'ment] *tr* atormentar

torna·do [tɔr'nedo] *s* (*pl* -does o -dos) tornado, tromba terrestre

torpe·do [tɔr'pido] *s* (*pl* -does) torpedo || *tr* torpedear

torrent ['tɑrənt] o ['tɔrənt] *s* torrente *m*

torrid ['tɑrɪd] o ['tɔrɪd] *adj* tórrido

tor·so ['tɔrso] *s* (*pl* -sos) torso

tortoise ['tɔrtəs] *s* tortuga

tortoise shell *s* carey *m*

torture ['tɔrtʃər] *s* tortura || *tr* torturar, atormentar

toss [tɔs] o [tɑs] *s* echada; alcance *m* de una echada || *tr* arrojar, echar; lanzar al aire; agitar, menear; levantar airosamente (*la cabeza*); lanzar (*p.ej., un comentario*); echar a cara o cruz; **to toss off** hacer muy rápidamente; tragar de un golpe || *intr* agitarse, menearse; **to toss and turn** (*in bed*) revolverse, dar vueltas

toss'-up' *s* cara o cruz; probabilidad igual

tot [tɑt] *s* párvulo, peque *m*, chiquitín *m*

to·tal ['totəl] *adj* total; (*e.g., loss*) completo || *s* total *m* || *v* (*pret & pp* -taled o -talled; *ger* -taling o -talling) *tr* ascender a, sumar

totter ['tɑtər] *s* tambaleo || *intr* tambalear; estar para desplomarse

touch [tʌtʃ] *s* (*act*) toque *m*; (*sense*) tacto, tiento; (*of piano, pianist, typewriter, typist*) tacto; (*of an illness*) ramo, ataque ligero; pizca, poquito; **to get in touch with** ponerse en comunicación o contacto con; **to lose one's touch** perder el tiento || *tr* tocar; conmover, enternecer; probar (*vino, licor*); (*for a loan*) (slang) pedir prestado a, dar un sablazo a; **to touch up** retocar || *intr* tocar; **to touch at** tocar en (*un puerto*)

touching ['tʌtʃɪŋ] *adj* conmovedor, enternecedor || *prep* tocante a

touch typewriting *s* escritura al tacto

touch·y ['tʌtʃi] *adj* (*comp* -ier; *super* -iest) quisquilloso, enojadizo

tough [tʌf] *adj* correoso; tenaz; difícil; gamberro; (*e.g., luck*) malo || *s* gamberro, guapetón *m*

toughen ['tʌfən] *tr* hacer correoso; hacer tenaz; dificultar || *intr* ponerse

correoso; hacerse tenaz; hacerse difícil

tour [tʊr] *s* jira, paseo, vuelta; viaje largo; **on tour** de jira, de viaje || *tr* viajar por, recorrer || *intr* viajar por distracción o diversión

touring car ['tʊrɪŋ] *s* coche *m* de turismo

tourist ['tʊrɪst] *adj* turístico || *s* turista *mf*

tournament ['tʊrnəmənt] o ['tʌrnəmənt] *s* torneo

tourney ['tʊrni] o ['tʌrni] *s* torneo || *intr* tornear

tourniquet ['tʊrnɪ,ket] o ['tʌrnɪ,ke] *s* torniquete *m*

tousle ['tauzəl] *tr* despeinar, enmarañar

tow [to] *s* remolque *m*; (*e.g., of hemp*) estopa; **to take in tow** dar remolque a; (fig) encargarse de || *tr* remolcar

towage ['to·ɪdʒ] *s* remolque *m*; derechos de remolque

toward(s) [tord(z)] o [tə'word(z)] *prep* (*in the direction of*) hacia; (*with regard to*) para con; (*a certain hour*) cerca de, a eso de

tow'boat' *s* remolcador *m*

tow·el ['tau·əl] *s* toalla || *v* (*pret & pp* -eled o -elled; *ger* -eling o -elling) *tr* secar con toalla

towel rack *s* toallero

tower ['tau·ər] *s* torre *f* || *intr* encumbrarse, empinarse

towering ['tau·ərɪŋ] *adj* encumbrado; sobresaliente; excesivo

towing service ['to·ɪŋ] *s* servicio de grúa

tow'line' *s* cable *m* de remolque, sirga

town [taun] *s* población, pueblo, villa; **in town** a la ciudad, en la ciudad

town clerk *s* escribano municipal

town council *s* concejo municipal

town crier *s* pregonero público

town hall *s* ayuntamiento, casa de ayuntamiento

towns'folk' *spl* vecinos del pueblo

township ['taun/ɪp] *s* sexmo; terreno público de seis millas en cuadro

towns·man ['taunzmən] *s* (*pl* -men [mən]) ciudadano, vecino; conciudadano, paisano

towns'peo'ple *spl* vecinos del pueblo

town talk *s* comidilla o hablillas del pueblo

tow'path' *s* camino de sirga

tow plane *s* avión *m* de remolque

tow'rope' *s* cuerda de remolque

tow truck *s* camión-grúa *m*

toxic ['tɑksɪk] *adj & s* tóxico

toy [tɔɪ] *adj* de juguete || *s* juguete *m*; (*trifle*) bagatela; (*trinket*) dije *m*, bujería || *intr* jugar; divertirse; **to toy with** jugar con (*los sentimientos de una persona*); acariciar (*una idea*)

toy bank *s* alcancía, hucha

toy soldier *s* soldado de juguete

trace [tres] *s* huella, rastro; indicio, vestigio; (*of harness*) tirante *m*; pizca || *tr* rastrear; trazar (*p.ej., una curva; los rasgos de una persona o cosa*); averiguar el paradero de; remontar al origen de

to
tr

trache·a ['trekɪ·ə] *s* (*pl* **-ae** [ˌi]) tráquea

track [træk] *s* (*of. foot*) huella; (*of a wheel*) rodada, carril *m;* (*of a boat*) estela; (*of railroad*) vía; (*of an airplane, a hurricane*) trayectoria; (*of a tractor*) llanta de oruga; camino, senda; (*course followed by a boat*) derrota; (*of ideas, events, etc.*) sucesión; (sport) pista; **to keep track of** no perder de vista; no olvidar; **to lose track of** perder de vista; olvidar; **to make tracks** dejar pisadas; irse muy de prisa ‖ *tr* rastrear; seguir la huella o la pista de; dejar pisadas en, manchar pisando; **to track down** seguir y capturar; averiguar el origen de

tracking ['trækɪŋ] *s* seguimiento (*de vehículos espaciales*)

tracking station *s* estación de seguimiento

trackless trolley ['træklɪs] *s* filobús *m,* trolebús *m*

track meet *s* concurso de carreras y saltos

track'walk'er *s* guardavía *m*

tract [trækt] *s* espacio, tracto; folleto; (anat) canal *m,* sistema *m*

traction ['trækʃən] *s* tracción

traction company *s* empresa de tranvías

tractor ['træktər] *s* tractor *m*

trade [tred] *s* comercio; negocio, trato; trueque *m,* canje *m;* (*calling, job*) oficio; clientela, parroquia; (*e.g., in slaves*) trata ‖ *tr* cambiar, trocar; **to trade in** dar como parte del pago; **to trade off** cambalachear; ‖ *intr* comerciar; comprar; **to trade in** comerciar en; **to trade on** aprovecharse de

trade'mark' *s* marca de fábrica, marca registrada

trade name *s* nombre *m* comercial, razón *f* social; nombre de fábrica

trader ['tredər] *s* traficante *mf*

trade school *s* escuela de artes y oficios

trades·man ['tredzmən] *s* (*pl* **-men** [mən]) tendero; comerciante *m;* (Brit) artesano

trades union o **trade union** *s* sindicato, gremio de obreros

trade unionist *s* sindicalista *mf*

trade winds *spl* vientos alisios

trading post ['tredɪŋ] *s* factoría; (*in stock exchange*) puesto de compraventa

trading stamp *s* sello de premio, sello de descuento

tradition [trə'dɪʃən] *s* tradición

traduce [trə'djus] o [trə'dus] *tr* calumniar

traf·fic ['træfɪk] *s* tráfico, comercio; tráfico, circulación; (*e.g., in slaves*) trata ‖ *v* (*pret & pp* **-ficked**) *ger* **-ficking**) *intr* traficar

traffic circle *s* glorieta de tráfico

traffic court *s* juzgado de tráfico

traffic jam *s* embotellamiento, tapón *m* de tráfico

traffic light *s* luz *f* de tráfico, semáforo

traffic sign o **signal** *s* señal *f* de tráfico

traffic ticket *s* aviso de multa

tragedian [trə'dʒidɪ·ən] *s* trágico

trage·dy ['trædʒɪdi] *s* (*pl* **-dies**) tragedia

tragic ['trædʒɪk] *adj* trágico

trail [trel] *s* rastro, huella, pista; (*path through rough country*) trocha, senda, vereda; (*of a gown*) cola; (*of smoke, a rocket, etc.*) estela ‖ *tr* arrastrar; seguir la pista de; andar detrás de; llevar (*p.ej., barro*) con los pies ‖ *intr* arrastrar; rezagarse; arrastrarse, trepar (*una planta*); **to trail off** desaparecer poco a poco

trailer ['trelər] *s* remolque *m,* coche-habitación *m,* casa rodante; planta rastrera

trailing arbutus ['trelɪŋ] *s* epigea rastrera

train [tren] *s* (*of railway cars; of waves*) tren *m;* (*of thought*) hilo ‖ *tr* adiestrar; guiar (*las plantas*); (sport) entrenar ‖ *intr* adiestrarse; (sport) entrenarse

trained nurse *s* enfermera graduada

trainer ['trenər] *s* (sport) entrenador *m*

training ['trenɪŋ] *s* adiestramiento; instrucción; (sport) entrenamiento

training school *s* escuela práctica; reformatorio

training ship *s* buque *m* escuela

trait [tret] *s* característica, rasgo

traitor ['tretər] *s* traidor *m*

traitress ['tretrɪs] *s* traidora

trajecto·ry [trə'dʒektəri] *s* (*pl* **-ries**) trayectoria

tramp [træmp] *s* vagabundo; marcha pesada, ruido de pisadas ‖ *tr* pisar con fuerza; recorrer a pie ‖ *intr* andar a pie; vagabundear

trample ['træmpəl] *tr* pisotear ‖ *intr* — **to trample on** o **upon** pisotear

tramp steamer *s* vapor volandero

trance [træns] o [trɑns] *s* arrobamiento, rapto; estado hipnótico

tranquil ['træŋkwɪl] *adj* tranquilo

tranquilize ['træŋkwɪˌlaɪz] *tr & intr* tranquilizar

tranquilizer ['træŋkwɪˌlaɪzər] *s* tranquilizante *m*

tranquillity [træŋ'kwɪlɪti] *s* tranquilidad

transact [træn'zækt] o [træns'ækt] *tr* tramitar; llevar a cabo

transaction [træn'zækʃən] o [træns-'ækʃən] *s* tramitación, transacción

transatlantic [ˌtrænsət'læntɪk] *adj & s* transatlántico

transcend [træn'sɛnd] *tr* exceder, superar ‖ *intr* sobresalir

transcribe [træn'skraɪb] *tr* transcribir

transcript ['trænskrɪpt] *s* trasunto, traslado; (educ) hoja de estudios, certificado de estudios

transcription [træn'skrɪpʃən] *s* transcripción

transept ['trænsɛpt] *s* crucero, transepto

trans·fer ['trænsfər] *s* traslado; transbordo; contraseña o billete *m* de transferencia ‖ [træns'fʌr] o ['trænsfər] *v* (*pret & pp* **-ferred;** *ger*

-ferring) *tr* trasladar, transferir; transbordar ‖ *intr* cambiar de tren, tranvía, etc.

transfix [træns'fɪks] *tr* espetar, traspasar; dejar atónito

transform [træns'fɔrm] *tr* transformar ‖ *intr* transformarse

transformer [træns'fɔrmər] *s* transformador *m*

transfusion [træns'fjuʒən] *s* transfusión; (med) transfusión de la sangre

transgress [træns'grɛs] *tr* transgredir, violar; exceder, traspasar (*p.ej., los límites de la prudencia*) ‖ *intr* pecar, prevaricar

transgression [træns'grɛʃən] *s* transgresión; pecado, prevaricación

transient ['trænʃənt] *adj* pasajero, transitorio; de tránsito ‖ *s* transeúnte *mf*

transistor [træn'zɪstər] *s* transistor *m*

transit ['trænsɪt] o ['trænzɪt] *s* tránsito

transitive ['trænsɪtɪv] *adj* transitivo ‖ *s* verbo transitivo

transitory ['trænsɪ‚tori] *adj* transitorio

translate [træns'let] o ['trænslet] *tr* (*from one language to another*) traducir; (*from one place to another*) trasladar ‖ *intr* traducir

translation [træns'leʃən] *s* traducción; traslación

translator [træns'letər] *s* traductor *m*

transliterate [træns'lɪtə‚ret] *tr* transcribir

translucent [træns'lusənt] *adj* translúcido

transmission [træns'mɪʃən] *s* transmisión; (aut) cambio de marchas, cambio de velocidades

transmis'sion-gear' box *s* caja de cambio de marchas, caja de velocidades

trans·mit [træns'mɪt] *v* (*pret & pp* -mitted; *ger* -mitting) *tr & intr* transmitir

transmitter [træns'mɪtər] *s* transmisor *m*

transmitting set *s* aparato transmisor

transmitting station *s* estacion transmisora, emisora

transmute [træns'mjut] *tr & intr* transmutar

transom ['trænsəm] *s* (*crosspiece*) travesaño; (*window over door*) montante *m*; (*of ship*) yugo de popa

transparen·cy [træns'pɛrənsi] *s* (*pl* -cies) transparencia

transparent [træns'pɛrənt] *adj* transparente

transpire [træns'paɪr] *intr* transpirar; (*to become known, leak out*) transpirar; (coll) acontecer, tener lugar

transplant [træns'plænt] o [træns'plɑnt] *tr* transplantar ‖ *intr* transplantarse

transport ['trænsport] *s* transporte *m*; (aer & naut) transporte *m*; rapto, éxtasis *m*, transporte *m* ‖ [træns'port] *tr* transportar

transportation [‚trænspɔr'teʃən] *s* transporte *m*; (U.S.A.) pasaje *m*, billete *m* de viaje

transport worker *s* transportista *mf*

transpose [træns'poz] *tr* transponer; (mus) transportar

trans·ship [træns'ʃɪp] *v* (*pret & pp* -shipped; *ger* -shipping) *tr* transbordar

transshipment [træns'ʃɪpmənt] *s* transbordo

trap [træp] *s* trampa; (*double-curved pipe*) sifón *m*; coche ligero de dos ruedas; (sport) lanzaplatos *m* ‖ *v* (*pret & pp* trapped; *ger* trapping) *tr* entrampar; atrapar (*a un ladrón*)

trap door *s* escotillón *m*, trampa; (theat) escotillón *m*, pescante *m*

trapeze [trə'piz] *s* trapecio

trapezoid ['træpɪ‚zɔɪd] *s* trapecio

trapper ['træpər] *s* cazador *m* de alforja

trappings ['træpɪŋz] *spl* (*adornments*) adornos, atavíos; (*of a horse's harness*) jaeces *mpl*

trap'shoot'ing *s* tiro al vuelo

trash [træʃ] *s* broza, basura, desecho; (*junk*) cachivaches *mpl*; (*nonsense*) disparates *mpl*; (*worthless people*) gentuza

trash can *s* basurero

travail ['trævel] o [trə'vel] *s* afán *m*, labor *f*, pena; dolores *mpl* del parto

trav·el ['trævəl] *s* viaje *m*; el viajar; (mach) recorrido ‖ *v* (*pret & pp* -eled o -elled; *ger* -eling o -elling) *tr* viajar por; recorrer ‖ *intr* viajar; andar, recorrer

travel bureau *s* oficina de turismo

traveler ['trævələr] *s* viajero; (*salesman*) viajante *m*

traveler's check *s* cheque *m* de viajeros

traveling expenses *spl* gastos de viaje

traveling salesman *s* viajante *m*, agente viajero

traverse ['trævərs] o [trə'vʌrs] *tr* atravesar; recorrer, pasar por

traves·ty ['trævɪsti] *s* (*pl* -ties) parodia ‖ *v* (*pret & pp* -tied) *tr* parodiar

trawl [trɔl] *s* red barredera, espinel *m*, palangre *m* ‖ *tr & intr* pescar a la rastra

tray [tre] *s* bandeja; (chem & phot) cubeta

treacherous ['trɛtʃərəs] *adj* traicionero, traidor; incierto, poco seguro

treacher·y ['trɛtʃəri] *s* (*pl* -ies) traición, alevosía

tread [trɛd] *s* (*stepping*) pisada; (*of stairs*) grada, huella, peldaño; (*of stilts*) horquilla; (*of a tire*) banda de rodamiento; (*of shoe*) suela; (*of an egg*) meaje, galladura ‖ *v* (*pret* trod [trad]; *pp* trodden ['tradən] o trod) *tr* pisar, pisotear; abrumar, agobiar ‖ *intr* andar, caminar

treadle ['trɛdəl] *s* pedal *m*

tread'mill' *s* rueda de andar; (*futile drudgery*) noria

treas. *abbr* treasurer, treasury

treason ['trizən] *s* traición

treasonable ['trizənəbəl] *adj* traicionero, traidor

treasure ['trɛʒər] *s* tesoro ‖ *tr* atesorar

treasurer ['trɛʒərər] *s* tesorero

treasur·y ['trɛʒəri] *s* (*pl* -ies) tesorería; tesoro

tr
tr

treat [trit] *s* convite *m; (to a drink)* convidada; *(something providing particular enjoyment)* regalo, deleite *m* ‖ *tr* tratar; convidar, regalar; curar *(a un enfermo)* ‖ *intr* tratar; convidar, regalar; **to treat of** tratar de

treatise ['tritɪs] *s* tratado

treatment ['tritmənt] *s* tratamiento

trea·ty ['triti] *s (pl -ties)* tratado

treble ['trɛbəl] *adj (threefold)* tresdoble, triple; sobreagudo; (mus) atiplado; (mus) de tiple ‖ *s (person)* tiple *mf; (voice)* tiple *m* ‖ *tr* triplicar ‖ *intr* triplicarse

tree [tri] *s* árbol *m*

tree farm *s* monte *m* tallar

treeless ['trilɪs] *adj* pelado, sin árboles

tree'top' *s* copa, cima de árbol

trellis ['trɛlɪs] *s* enrejado, espaldera; emparrado

tremble ['trɛmbəl] *s* temblor *m*, estremecimiento ‖ *intr* temblar, estremecerse

tremendous [trɪ'mɛndəs] *adj* tremendo

tremor ['trɛmər] o ['trimər] *s* temblor *m*

trench [trɛntʃ] *s* foso, zanja; *(for irrigation)* acequia; (mil) trinchera

trenchant ['trɛntʃənt] *adj* mordaz, punzante; enérgico, bien definido

trench coat *s* trinchera

trench mortar *s* (mil) lanzabombas *m*

trench'-plow' *tr* (agr) desfondar

trend [trɛnd] *s* curso, dirección, tendencia ‖ *intr* dirigirse, tender

trespass ['trɛspəs] *s* entrada sin derecho; infracción, violación; culpa, pecado ‖ *intr* entrar sin derecho; pecar; **no trespassing** prohibida la entrada; **to trespass against** pecar contra; **to trespass on** entrar sin derecho en; infringir, violar; abusar de *(p.ej., la paciencia de uno)*

tress [trɛs] *s (braid of hair)* trenza; *(curl)* bucle *m*, rizo

trestle ['trɛsəl] *s* caballete *m;* puente *m* o viaducto de caballetes

trial ['traɪəl] *s* ensayo, prueba; aflicción, desgracia; (law) juicio, proceso, vista; **on trial** a prueba; (law) en juicio; **to bring to trial** encausar

trial and error *s* método de tanteos

trial balloon *s* globo sonda; **to send up a trial balloon** (fig) lanzar un globo sonda

trial by jury *s* juicio por jurado

trial jury *s* jurado procesal

trial order *s* (com) pedido de ensayo

triangle ['traɪ͵æŋɡəl] *s* triángulo

tribe [traɪb] *s* tribu *f*

tribunal [trɪ'bjunəl] o [traɪ'bjunəl] *s* tribunal *m*

tribune ['trɪbjun] *s* tribuna

tributar·y ['trɪbjə͵teri] *adj* tributario ‖ *s (pl -ies)* tributario

tribute ['trɪbjut] *s* tributo

trice [traɪs] *s* momento, instante *m;* **in a trice** en un periquete

trick [trɪk] *s* ardid *m*, artimaña; *(knack)* maña; *(feat)* suerte *f; (prank)* travesura, burla, chasco; tanda, turno; ilusión; *(feat with*

cards) truco; *(cards in one round)* baza; (coll) chiquita; **to be up to one's old tricks** hacer de las suyas; **to play a dirty trick on** hacer una mala jugada a ‖ *tr* trampear; burlar, engañar; ataviar

tricker·y ['trɪkəri] *s (pl -ies)* trampería, malas mañas

trickle ['trɪkəl] *s* chorro delgado, goteo ‖ *intr* escurrir, gotear; pasar gradual e irregularmente

trickster ['trɪkstər] *s* tramposo, embustero

trick·y ['trɪki] *adj (comp -ier; super -iest)* tramposo, engañoso; difícil; *(animal)* vicioso; *(ticklish to deal with)* delicado

tricorn ['traɪkɔrn] *adj & s* tricornio

tried [traɪd] *adj* fiel, probado, seguro

trifle ['traɪfəl] *s* bagatela, friolera, fruslería; *(trinket)* bagatela, baratija ‖ *tr* — **to trifle away** malgastar ‖ *intr* estar ocioso, holgar; **to trifle with** manosear; jugar con, burlarse de

trifling ['traɪflɪŋ] *adj* frívolo, fútil, ligero; insignificante, trivial

trifocal [traɪ'fokəl] *adj* trifocal ‖ *s* lente *f* trifocal; **trifocals** anteojos trifocales

trig. *abbr* **trigonometric, trigonometry**

trigger ['trɪɡər] *s (e.g., of a gun)* disparador *m*, gatillo; *(of any device)* disparador ‖ *tr* poner en movimiento, provocar

trigonometry [͵trɪɡə'nɑmɪtri] *s* trigonometría

trill [trɪl] *s* trinado, trino; *(made with voice, esp. of birds)* gorjeo; (phonet) vibración ‖ *tr* decir o cantar gorjeando; pronunciar con vibración ‖ *intr* trinar; gorjear

trillion ['trɪljən] *s* (U.S.A.) billón *m;* (Brit) trillón *m*

trilo·gy ['trɪlədʒi] *s (pl -gies)* trilogía

trim [trɪm] *adj (comp* **trimmer;** *super* **trimmest)** acicalado, compuesto, elegante ‖ *s* condición, estado; buena condición; adorno, atavío; traje *m*, vestido; *(of sails)* orientación ‖ *v (pret & pp* **trimmed;** *ger* **trimming)** *tr* ajustar, adaptar; arreglar, componer; adornar, decorar; decorar, enguirnaldar *(el árbol de Navidad);* recortar; cortar ligeramente *(el pelo);* despabilar *(una lámpara o vela);* mondar, podar *(árboles, plantas);* acepillar, desbastar; (naut) orientar *(las velas);* (coll) derrotar, vencer; (coll) regañar

trimming ['trɪmɪŋ] *s* adorno, guarnición; franja, orla; (coll) paliza, zurra; (coll) derrota; **trimmings** accesorios, arreuvres *mpl;* recortes *mpl*

trini·ty ['trɪnɪti] *s (pl -ties) (group of three)* trinca ‖ **Trinity** *s* Trinidad

trinket ['trɪŋkɪt] *s (small ornament)* dije *m; (trivial object)* baratija, bujería, chuchería

tri·o ['tri·o] *s (pl -os) (group of three)* terna, trío; (mus) trío

trip [trɪp] *s* viaje *m;* jira, recorrido;

(*stumble*) tropiezo; (*act of causing a person to stumble*) traspié *m*, zancadilla; (*blunder*) desliz *m* ‖ *v* (*pret & pp* tripped; *ger* tripping) *tr* trompicar, echar la zancadilla a; detener, estorbar; inclinar; coger en falta; coger en una mentira ‖ *intr* ir con paso rápido y ligero; brincar, saltar, correr; tropezar; to trip over tropezar con, contra o en

tripe [traɪp] *s* callos, mondongo; (slang) disparate *m*, barbaridad

trip'ham'mer *s* martillo pilón

triphthong ['trɪfθɒŋ] o ['trɪfθɑŋ] *s* triptongo

triple ['trɪpəl] *adj & s* triple *m* ‖ *tr* triplicar ‖ *intr* triplicarse

triplet ['trɪplɪt] *s* (*offspring*) trillizo; (*stanza of three lines*) terceto; (mus) terceto, tresillo

triplicate ['trɪplɪkɪt] *adj & s* triplicado; in triplicate por triplicado ‖ ['trɪplɪ,ket] *tr* triplicar

tripod ['traɪpɒd] *m* trípode *m*

triptych ['trɪptɪk] *s* tríptico

trite [traɪt] *adj* gastado, trillado, trivial

triumph ['traɪ·əmf] *s* triunfo ‖ *intr* triunfar; to triumph over triunfar de

triumphal arch [traɪ'ʌmfəl] *s* arco triunfal

triumphant [traɪ'ʌmfənt] *adj* triunfante

trivia ['trɪvɪ·ə] *spl* bagatelas, trivialidades

trivial ['trɪvɪ·əl] *adj* trivial, insignificante

triviali·ty [,trɪvɪ'ælɪti] *s* (*pl* -ties) trivialidad

Trojan ['trodʒən] *adj & s* troyano

Trojan horse *s* caballo de Troya

Trojan War *s* guerra de Troya

troll [trol] *tr & intr* pescar a la cacea

trolley ['trɑli] *s* polea o arco de trole; tranvía *m*

trolley bus *s* trolebús *m*

trolley car *s* coche *m* de tranvía

trolley pole *s* trole *m*

trolling ['trolɪŋ] *s* cacea, pesca a la cacea

trollop ['trɑləp] *s* (*slovenly woman*) cochina; mujer *f* de mala vida

trombone ['trɑmbon] *s* trombón *m*

troop [trup] *s* tropa; (*of actors*) compañía; (*of cavalry*) escuadrón *m* ‖ *intr* agruparse; marcharse en tropel

trooper ['trupər] *s* soldado de caballería; corcel *m* de guerra; policía *m* de a caballo; (*ship*) transporte *m*; to swear like a trooper jurar como un carretero

tro·phy ['trofi] *s* (*pl* -phies) trofeo; (*any memento*) recuerdo

tropic ['trɑpɪk] *adj* tropical ‖ *s* trópico

tropical ['trɑpɪkəl] *adj* tropical

tropics o Tropics ['trɑpɪks] *spl* zona tropical

troposphere ['trɑpə,sfɪr] *s* troposfera

trot [trɑt] *s* trote *m* ‖ *v* (*pret & pp* trotted; *ger* trotting) *tr* hacer trotar; to trot out (slang) sacar para mostrar ‖ *intr* trotar

troth [troθ] o [troθ] *s* fe *f*; verdad;

esponsales *mpl*; in troth en verdad; to plight one's troth prometer fidelidad; dar palabra de casamiento

troubadour ['trubə,dor] o ['trubə,dʊr] *adj* trovadoresco ‖ *s* trovador *m*

trouble ['trʌbəl] *s* apuro, dificultad; confusión, estorbo; conflicto; inquietud, preocupación; pena, molestia; mal *m*, enfermedad; (*of a mechanical nature*) avería, falla, pana; not to be worth the trouble no valer la pena; that's the trouble ahí está el busilis; the trouble is that . . . lo malo es que . . .; to be in trouble estar en un aprieto; to be looking for trouble buscar tres pies al gato; to get into trouble enredarse, meterse en líos; to take the trouble to tomarse la molestia de ‖ *tr* apurar; confundir, estorbar; inquietar, preocupar; apenar, afligir; incomodar, molestar; dar que hacer a; to be troubled with padecer de; to trouble oneself molestarse ‖ *intr* apurarse; inquietarse, preocuparse; molestarse, darse molestia; to trouble to molestarse en

trouble lamp *s* lámpara de socorro

trou'ble-mak'er *s* perturbador *m*, alborotador *m*

troubleshooter ['trʌbəl,ʃutər] *s* localizador *m* de averías; (*in disputes*) componedor *m*

troubleshooting ['trʌbəl,ʃutɪŋ] *s* localización de averías; (*of disputes*) composición, arbitraje *m*

troublesome ['trʌbəlsəm] *adj* molesto, pesado, gravoso; impertinente; perturbador

trouble spot *s* lugar *m* de conflicto

trough [trɔf] o [traf] *s* (*e.g., to knead bread*) artesa; (*for water for animals*) abrevadero; (*for feeding animals*) comedero; (*under eaves*) canal *f*; (*between two waves*) seno

troupe [trup] *s* compañía de actores o de circo

trousers ['trauzərz] *spl* pantalones *mpl*

trous·seau [tru'so] o ['truso] *s* (*pl* -seaux o -seaus) ajuar *m* de novia, equipo de novia

trout [traut] *s* trucha

trouvère [tru'ver] *s* trovero

trowel ['trau·əl] *s* paleta, llana

Troy [trɔɪ] *s* Troya

truant ['tru·ənt] *s* novillero; to play truant hacer novillos

truce [trus] *s* tregua

truck [trʌk] *s* carro; vagoneta; camión *m*; autocamión *m*; (*to be moved by hand*) carretilla; (*of locomotive or car*) carretón *m*; hortalizas para el mercado; (coll) desperdicios; (coll) negocio, relaciones ‖ *tr* acarrear

truck driver *s* camionista *mf*

truck garden *s* huerto de hortalizas (*para el mercado*)

truculent ['trʌkjələnt] o ['trukjələnt] *adj* truculento

trudge [trʌdʒ] *intr* caminar, ir a pie; to trudge along marchar con pena y trabajo

true [tru] *adj* verdadero; exacto; constante, uniforme; fiel, leal; alineado; a plomo, a nivel; **to come true** hacerse realidad; **true to life** conforme a la realidad

true copy *s* copia fiel

true-hearted ['tru,hɑrtɪd] *adj* fiel, leal, sincero

true'love' *s* fiel amante *mf*; (bot) hierba de París

truelove knot *s* lazo de amor

truffle ['trʌfəl] *o* ['trufəl] *s* trufa

truism ['tru·ɪzəm] *s* perogrullada, verdad trillada

truly ['truli] *adv* verdaderamente; efectivamente; fielmente; **truly yours** de Vd. atto. y S.S., su seguro servidor

trump [trʌmp] *s* triunfo; (coll) buen chico, buena chica; **no trump** sin triunfo ‖ *tr* matar con un triunfo; aventajar, sobrepujar; **to trump up** forjar, inventar (*para engañar*) ‖ *intr* triunfar

trumpet ['trʌmpɪt] *s* trompeta; trompeta acústica; **to blow one's own trumpet** cantar sus propias alabanzas ‖ *tr* pregonar a son de trompeta ‖ *intr* trompetear

truncheon ['trʌntʃən] *s* cachiporra; bastón *m* de mando

trunk [trʌŋk] *s* (*of living body, tree, family, railroad*) tronco; (*chest for clothes, etc.*) baúl *m*; (*of an automobile*) portaequipaje *m*; (*of elephant*) trompa; **trunks** taparrabo

trunk hose *spl* trusas

truss [trʌs] *s* (*framework*) armadura; haz *m*, paquete *m*, lío; (*for holding back a hernia*) braguero ‖ *tr* armar; empaquetar; espetar; apretar (*barriles*)

trust [trʌst] *s* confianza; esperanza; cargo, custodia; depósito; crédito; obligación; (econ) trust *m*, cartel *m*; (law) fideicomiso; **in trust** en confianza; en depósito; **on trust** a crédito, al fiado ‖ *tr* confiar; confiar en; vender a crédito a ‖ *intr* confiar; fiar; **to trust in** fiarse a o de

trust company *s* banco fideicomisario, banco de depósitos

trustee [trʌs'ti] *s* administrador *m*, comisario; regente (universitario); (*of an estate*) fideicomisario

trusteeship [trʌs'ti·ʃɪp] *s* cargo de administrador, fideicomisario; (*of the UN*) fideicomiso

trustful ['trʌstfəl] *adj* confiado

trust'wor'thy *adj* confiable, fidedigno

trust·y ['trʌsti] *adj* (*comp* **-ier;** *super* **-iest**) honrado, fidedigno ‖ *s* (*pl* **-ies**) presidiario fidedigno (*que se ha merecido ciertos privilegios*)

truth [truθ] *s* verdad; **in truth** a la verdad, en verdad

truthful ['truθfəl] *adj* verídico, veraz

try [traɪ] *s* (*pl* **tries**) ensayo, intento, prueba ‖ *v* (*pret & pp* **tried**) *tr* ensayar, intentar, probar; comprobar, verificar; cansar; exasperar, irritar; (law) procesar (*a una persona*); (law) ver (*un pleito*); **to try on** probarse (*una prenda de vestir*) ‖ *intr*

ensayar, probar; esforzarse; **to try to** tratar de, intentar

trying ['traɪ·ɪŋ] *adj* cansado, molesto, irritante; penoso

tryst [trɪst] *o* [traɪst] *s* cita; lugar *m* de cita

tub [tʌb] *s* cuba, tina; (coll) baño; (*clumsy boat*) (coll) carcamán *m*, trompo; (*fat person*) (coll) cuba

tube [tjub] *o* [tub] *s* tubo; túnel *m*; (*of a tire*) cámara; (coll) ferrocarril subterráneo

tuber ['tjubər] *o* ['tubər] *s* tubérculo

tubercle ['tjubərkəl] *o* ['tubərkəl] *s* tubérculo

tuberculosis [tju,bɑrkjə'losɪs] *o* [tu,bɑrkjə'losɪs] *s* tuberculosis *f*

tuck [tʌk] *s* alforza ‖ *tr* alforzar; **to tuck away** encubrir, ocultar; **to tuck in** arropar, enmantar; remeter (*p.ej., la ropa de cama*); **to tuck up** arremangar (*un vestido*); guarnecer (*un cama*)

tucker ['tʌkər] *s* escote *m* ‖ *tr* — **to tucker out** (coll) agotar, cansar

Tuesday ['tjuzdi] *o* ['tuzdi] *s* martes *m*

tuft [tʌft] *s* (*of feathers, hair, etc.*) penacho, copete *m;* manojo, racimo, ramillete *m;* borla ‖ *tr* empenachar ‖ *intr* crecer formando mechones

tug [tʌg] *s* estirón *m*, tirón *m;* (*boat*) remolcador *m* ‖ *v* (*pret & pp* **tugged;** *ger* **tugging**) *tr* arrastrar, tirar con fuerza de; remolcar (*un barco*) ‖ *intr* tirar con fuerza; esforzarse, luchar

tug'boat' *s* remolcador *m*

tug of war *s* lucha de la cuerda

tuition [tju'ɪʃən] *o* [tu'ɪʃən] *s* enseñanza; precio de la enseñanza

tulip ['tjulɪp] *o* ['tulɪp] *s* tulipán *m*

tumble ['tʌmbəl] *s* caída, tumbo; (*somersault*) voltereta, tumba; confusión, desorden *m* ‖ *intr* caerse, rodar; voltear; derribarse, volcarse; brincar, dar saltos; (*into bed*) echarse; (*to catch on*) (slang) caer, comprender; **to tumble down** desplomarse, hundirse, venirse abajo

tum'ble-down' *adj* destartalado, desvencijado

tumbler ['tʌmblər] *s* (*for drinking*) vaso; (*person who performs bodily feats*) volatinero; (*self-righting toy*) dominguillo, tentemozo

tumor ['tjumər] *o* ['tumər] *s* tumor *m*

tumult ['tjumʌlt] *o* ['tumʌlt] *s* tumulto

tun [tʌn] *s* barril *m*, tonel *m;* (*measure of capacity for wine*) tonelada

tuna ['tunə] *s* atún *m*

tune [tjun] *o* [tun] *s* tonada, aire *m;* (*manner of acting or speaking*) tono; **in tune** afinado; afinadamente; **out of tune** desafinado; desafinadamente; **to change one's tune** mudar de tono ‖ *tr* acordar, afinar; (rad) sintonizar; **to tune in** (rad) sintonizar; **to tune out** (rad) desintonizar; **to tune up** poner a punto; poner a tono (*un motor de automóvil*)

tungsten ['tʌŋstən] *s* tungsteno

tunic ['tjunɪk] *o* ['tunɪk] *s* túnica

tuning coil *s* (rad) bobina de sintonía

tuning fork s diapasón m

Tunis ['tjunɪs] o ['tunɪs] s Túnez (ciudad)

Tunisia [tju'nɪʒə] o [tu'nɪʒə] s Túnez (país)

Tunisian [tju'nɪʒən] o [tu'nɪʒən] adj & s tunecino

tun·nel ['tʌnəl] s túnel m; (min) galería || v (pret & pp -neled o -nelled; ger -neling o -nelling) tr construir un túnel a través de o debajo de

turban ['tʌrbən] s turbante m

turbid ['tʌrbɪd] adj turbio

turbine ['tʌrbɪn] o ['tʌrbaɪn] s turbina

turbojet ['tʌrbo‚dʒɛt] s turborreactor m; avión m de turborreacción

turboprop ['tʌrbo‚prɑp] s turbopropulsor m; avión m de turbopropulsión

turbulent ['tʌrbjələnt] adj turbulento

tureen [tu'rin] o [tju'rin] s sopera

turf [tʌrf] s (surface layer of grassland) césped m; terrón m de césped; (peat) turba; **the turf** el hipódromo; las carreras de caballos

turf·man ['tʌrfmən] s (pl -men [mən]) turfista m

Turk [tʌrk] s turco

turkey ['tʌrki] s pavo || **Turkey** s Turquía

turkey vulture s aura

Turkish ['tʌrkɪʃ] adj & s turco

Turkish towel s toalla rusa

turmoil ['tʌrmɔɪl] s alboroto, disturbio, tumulto

turn [tʌrn] s vuelta; (time of action) turno; (change of direction) virada; (bend) recodo; (walk) paseo corto; (of a spiral, roll of wire, etc.) espira; aspecto; inclinación; vahído, vértigo; giro, expresión; servicio; (coll) sacudida, susto; **at every turn** a cada paso; **in turn** por turno; **to be one's turn** tocarle a uno, p.ej., **it's your turn** le toca a Vd.; **to take turns** alternar, turnar; **to wait one's turn** aguardar turno, esperar vez || tr volver; dar vuelta a (p.ej., una llave); torcer (p.ej., el tobillo); doblar (la esquina); dirigir (p.ej., los ojos); (to make sour) agriar; (on a lathe) tornear; tener (p.ej., veinte años cumplidos); **to turn against** predisponer en contra de; **to turn around** volver; voltear; torcer (las palabras de una persona); **to turn aside** desviar; **to turn away** desviar; despedir; **to turn back** devolver; hacer retroceder; retrasar (el reloj); **to turn down** doblar hacia abajo; invertir; rechazar, rehusar; bajar (p.ej., el gas); **to turn in** doblar hacia adentro; entregar; **to turn off** apagar (la luz, la radio); cortar (el agua, gas, etc.); cerrar (la llave del agua, gas, etc.; la radio, la televisión); interrumpir (la corriente eléctrica); **to turn on** encender (la luz); poner (la luz, la radio, etc.); abrir (la llave del agua, gas, etc.); establecer (la corriente eléctrica); **to turn out** despedir; echar al campo (a los animales); volver al revés; apa-

gar (la luz); hacer, fabricar; **to turn up** doblar hacia arriba; levantar; arremangar (p.ej., las mangas); volver (un naipe); poner más alto o más fuerte (la radio); abrir la llave de (p.ej., el gas) || intr volver, p.ej., **the road turns to the right** el camino vuelve a la derecha, virar (un automóvil, un avión, etc.); (to revolve) girar; volverse (p.ej., la conversación; la opinión; ciertos licores); **to turn against** cobrar aversión a; rebelarse contra; **to turn around** dar vuelta; **to turn aside o away** desviarse; alejarse; **to turn back** volver, regresar; retroceder; **to turn down** doblarse hacia abajo; invertirse; **to turn in** doblarse hacia adentro; replegarse; recogerse, volver a casa; (coll) recogerse, acostarse; **to turn into** entrar en; convertirse en; **to turn on** volverse contra; depender de; versar sobre; ocuparse de; **to turn out badly** salir mal; **to turn out right** acabar bien; **to turn out to be** venir a ser; resultar, salir; **to turn over** volcar, derribarse (un vehículo); **to turn up** doblarse hacia arriba; levantarse; acontecer; aparecer

turn'coat' s tránsfuga mf, apóstata mf, renegado; **to become a turncoat** volver la casaca, cambiarse la camisa

turn'down' adj (collar) caído || s rechazamiento

turning point s punto de transición; punto decisivo

turnip ['tʌrnɪp] s nabo; (cheap watch) (slang) calentador m; (slang) tipo

turn'key' s carcelero, llavero de cárcel

turn of life s menopausia

turn'out' s (gathering of people) concurrencia; (number attending a show, etc.) entrada; (side track or passage) apartadero; (amount produced) producción; (array, outfit) equipaje m; carruaje m de lujo

turn'o'ver s (spill, upset) vuelco; cambio de personal; movimiento de mercancías; ciclo de compra y venta

turn'pike' s carretera de peaje

turnstile ['tʌrn‚staɪl] s torniquete m

turn'ta'ble s (of phonograph) placa giratoria, plato giratorio; (rr) placa giratoria, plataforma giratoria

turpentine ['tʌrpən‚taɪn] s trementina

turpitude ['tʌrpɪ‚tjud] o ['tʌrpɪ‚tud] s torpeza, infamia, vileza

turquoise ['tʌrkɔɪz] o ['tʌrkwɔɪz] s turquesa

turret ['tʌrɪt] s torrecilla; (archit) torreón m; (nav) torreta

turtle ['tʌrtəl] s tortuga; **to turn turtle** derribarse patas arriba

tur'tle·dove' s tórtola

Tuscan ['tʌskən] adj & s toscano

Tuscany ['tʌskəni] s la Toscana

tusk [tʌsk] s colmillo

tussle ['tʌsəl] s agarrada || intr agarrarse, asirse, reñir

tutor ['tjutər] o ['tutər] s maestro particular; (guardian) tutor m || intr dar enseñanza particular a || intr dar enseñanza particular; (coll) tomar lecciones particulares

tuxe·do [tʌk'sido] s (pl **-dos**) esmoquin m, smoking m

TV abbr television

twaddle ['twadəl] s charla, tonterías, música celestial ‖ intr charlar, decir tonterías

twang [twæŋ] s (of musical instrument) tañido; (of voice) timbre m nasal ‖ tr tocar con un tañido; decir con timbre nasal ‖ intr hablar por la nariz

twang·y ['twæŋi] adj (comp **-ier;** super **-iest**) (device) tañente; (person, voice) gangoso

tweed [twid] s mezcla de lana; traje m de mezcla de lana; **tweeds** ropa de mezcla de lana

tweet [twit] s pío ‖ intr piar

tweeter ['twitər] s altavoz m para audiofrecuencias elevadas

tweezers ['twizərz] spl bruselas, pinzas, tenacillas

twelfth [twelfθ] adj & s (in a series) duodécimo; (part) dozavo ‖ s (in dates) doce m

Twelfth'-night' s la víspera del día de Reyes; la noche del día de Reyes

twelve [twelv] adj & pron doce ‖ s doce m; **twelve o'clock** las doce

twentieth ['twentι·ιθ] adj & s (in a series) vigésimo; (part) veintavo ‖ s (in dates) veinte m

twen·ty ['twenti] adj & pron veinte ‖ s (pl **-ties**) veinte m

twice [twais] adv dos veces

twice'-told' adj dicho dos veces; trillado, sabido

twiddle ['twidəl] tr menear o revolver ociosamente

twig [twig] s ramito; **twigs** leña menuda

twilight ['twai‚lait] adj crepuscular ‖ s crepúsculo

twill [twil] s tela cruzada; (pattern of weave) cruzado ‖ tr cruzar

twin [twin] adj & s gemelo

twine [twain] s guita, cuerda, bramante m ‖ tr enroscar, retorcer ‖ intr enroscarse, retorcerse

twinge [twindʒ] s punzada, dolor agudo

twin'jet' plane s avión m birreactor

twinkle ['twiŋkəl] s centelleo; (of eye) pestañeo; instante m ‖ intr centellear; pestañear; moverse rápidamente

twin'-screw' adj (naut) de doble hélice

twirl [twʌrl] s vuelta, giro ‖ tr hacer girar; (baseball) lanzar (la pelota) ‖ intr dar vueltas, girar; piruetear

twist [twist] s torcedura; enroscadura; curva, recodo; giro, vuelta; propensión, prejuicio; (of mind or disposition) sesgo ‖ tr torcer; retorcer; enroscar; hacer girar; entrelazar; desviar; (to give a different meaning to) torcer ‖ intr torcerse; retorcerse; enroscarse; dar vueltas; entrelazarse;

desviarse; serpentear; **to twist and turn** (in bed) dar vueltas

twit [twit] v (pret & pp **twitted;** ger **twitting**) tr reprender (a uno) recordando algo desagradable o poniéndole en ridículo

twitch [twitʃ] s crispatura; ligero temblor ‖ intr crisparse; temblar (p.ej., los párpados)

twitter ['twitər] s gorjeo; risita sofocada; inquietud ‖ intr gorjear; reír sofocadamente; temblar de inquietud

two [tu] adj & pron dos ‖ s dos m; **to put two and two together** atar cabos, sacar la conclusión evidente; **two o'clock** las dos

two'-cy'cle adj (mach) de dos tiempos

two'-cyl'inder adj (mach) de dos cilindros

two-edged ['tu‚edʒd] adj de dos filos

two hundred adj & pron doscientos ‖ s doscientos m

twosome ['tusəm] s pareja; pareja de jugadores; juego de dos

two'-time' tr (slang) engañar en amor, ser infiel a (una persona del otro sexo)

tycoon [tai'kun] s (coll) magnate m

type [taip] s tipo; (piece) (typ) tipo, letra; (pieces collectively) (typ) letra; letras impresas, letras escritas a máquina ‖ tr escribir a máquina, tipiar; representar, simbolizar ‖ intr escribir a máquina

type'face' s tipo de letra

type'script' s material escrito a máquina

typesetter ['taip‚setər] s (typ) cajista mf; (typ) máquina de componer

type'write' v (pret **-wrote** [‚rot]; pp **-written** [‚ritən]) tr & intr escribir a máquina, tipiar

type'writ'er s máquina de escribir; tipista mf

typewriter ribbon s cinta para máquinas de escribir

type'writ'ing s mecanografía; trabajo hecho con máquina de escribir

typhoid fever ['taifəid] s fiebre tifoidea

typhoon [tai'fun] s tifón m

typical ['tipikəl] adj típico

typi·fy ['tipi‚fai] v (pret & pp **-fied**) tr simbolizar; ser ejemplo o modelo de

typist ['taipist] s mecanógrafo, tipista mf

typographic(al) [‚taipə'græfik(əl)] adj tipográfico

typographical error s error m de imprenta

typography [tai'pagrəfi] s tipografía

tyrannic(al) [ti'rænik(əl)] o [tai-'rænik(əl)] adj tiránico

tyrannous ['tirənəs] adj tirano

tyran·ny ['tirəni] s (pl **-nies**) tiranía

tyrant ['tairənt] s tirano

ty·ro ['tairo] s (pl **-ros**) tirón m, novicio

U

U, u [ju] vigésima primera letra del alfabeto inglés

U. *abbr* **University**

ubiquitous [ju'bɪkwɪtəs] *adj* ubicuo

udder ['ʌdər] *s* ubre *f*

ugliness ['ʌglɪnɪs] *s* fealdad; (coll) malhumor *m*

ug·ly ['ʌgli] *adj* (*comp* **-lier;** *super* **-liest**) feo; (coll) malhumorado

ugly mug *s* (slang) carantamaula

Ukraine ['jukren] o [ju'kren] *s* Ucrania

Ukrainian [ju'krenɪ·ən] *adj & s* ucraniano, ucranio

ulcer ['ʌlsər] *s* llaga, úlcera; (*corrupting influence*) (fig) llaga

ulcerate ['ʌlsə.ret] *tr* ulcerar ‖ *intr* ulcerarse

ulterior [ʌl'tɪrɪ·ər] *adj* ulterior; (*concealed*) escondido, oculto

ultimate ['ʌltɪmɪt] *adj* último

ultima·tum [.ʌltɪ'metəm] *s* (*pl* **-tums** o **-ta** [tə]) ultimátum *m*

ultimo ['ʌltɪ.mo] *adv* de o en el mes próximo pasado

ultrahigh [.ʌltrə'haɪ] *adj* (electron) ultraelevado

ultraviolet [.ʌltrə'vaɪ·əlɪt] *adj & s* ultravioleta, ultraviolado

umbilical cord [ʌm'bɪlɪkəl] *s* cordón *m* umbilical

umbrage ['ʌmbrɪdʒ] *s* — **to take umbrage at** resentirse de o por

umbrella [ʌm'brelə] *s* paraguas *m*; (mil) sombrilla protectora

umbrella man *s* paragüero

umbrella stand *s* paragüero

umlaut ['umlaut] *s* inflexión vocálica, metafonía; (*mark*) diéresis *f* ‖ *tr* inflexionar; escribir con diéresis

umpire ['ʌmpaɪr] *s* árbitro *m* ‖ *tr & intr* arbitrar

UN ['ju'ɛn] *s* (letterword) ONU *f*

unable [ʌn'ebəl] *adj* incapaz, imposibilitado; **to be unable to** no poder

unabridged [.ʌnə'brɪdʒd] *adj* sin abreviar, íntegro

unaccented [ʌn'æksɛntɪd] o [.ʌnæk-'sɛntɪd] *adj* inacentuado

unaccountable [.ʌnə'kauntəbəl] *adj* inexplicable; irresponsable

unaccounted-for [.ʌnə'kauntɪd.fɔr] *adj* inexplicado; no hallado

unaccustomed [.ʌnə'kʌstəmd] *adj* (*unusual*) desacostumbrado; inhabituado

unafraid [.ʌnə'fred] *adj* sin miedo

unaligned [.ʌnə'laɪnd] *adj* no empeñado

unanimity [.junə'nɪmɪti] *s* unanimidad

unanimous [ju'nænɪməs] *adj* unánime

unanswerable [ʌn'ænsərəbəl] *adj* incontestable; (*argument*) incontrastable

unappreciative [.ʌnə'priʃɪ.etɪv] *adj* ingrato, desagradecido

unapproachable [.ʌnə'protʃəbəl] *adj* inabordable; incomparable, único

unarmed [ʌn'armd] *adj* desarmado, inerme

unascertainable [ʌn.æsər'tenəbəl] *adj* inaveriguable

unasked [ʌn'æskt] o [ʌn'askt] *adj* no solicitado; no convidado

unassembled [.ʌnə'sɛmbəld] *adj* desmontado, desarmado

unassuming [.ʌnə'sumɪŋ] o [.ʌnə-'sjumɪŋ] *adj* modesto, sencillo

unattached [.ʌnə'tæt/t] *adj* independiente; (*loose*) suelto; (*not engaged to be married*) no prometido; (law) no embargado; (mil & nav) de reemplazo

unattainable [.ʌnə'tenəbəl] *adj* inasequible, inalcanzable

unattractive [.ʌnə'træktɪv] *adj* poco atrayente, desairado

unavailable [.ʌnə'veləbəl] *adj* indisponible

unavailing [.ʌnə'velɪŋ] *adj* ineficaz, inútil, vano

unavoidable [.ʌnə'vɔɪdəbəl] *adj* inevitable, ineluctable

unaware [.ʌnə'wɛr] *adj* — **to be unaware of** no estar al corriente de ‖ *adv* de improviso; sin saberlo

unawares [.ʌnə'wɛrz] *adv* (*unexpectedly*) de improviso; (*unknowingly*) sin saberlo

unbalanced [ʌn'bælənst] *adj* desequilibrado

unbandage [ʌn'bændɪdʒ] *tr* desvendar

un·bar [ʌn'bar] *v* (*pret & pp* **-barred;** *ger* **-barring**) *tr* desatrancar

unbearable [ʌn'berəbəl] *adj* inaguantable

unbeatable [ʌn'bitəbəl] *adj* imbatible

unbecoming [.ʌnbɪ'kʌmɪŋ] *adj* inconveniente, indecente; que sienta mal

unbelievable [.ʌnbɪ'livəbəl] *adj* increíble

unbending [ʌn'bendɪŋ] *adj* inflexible

unbiased o **unbiassed** [ʌn'baɪ·əst] *adj* imparcial

un·bind [ʌn'baɪnd] *v* (*pret & pp* **-bound** ['baund]) *tr* desatar

unbleached [ʌn'blit/t] *adj* sin blanquear

unbolt [ʌn'bolt] *tr* desatrancar (*p.ej., una puerta*); (*to remove the bolts from*) desempernar

unborn [ʌn'bɔrn] *adj* no nacido, por nacer, futuro

unbosom [ʌn'buzəm] *tr* confesar, descubrir (*sus pensamientos, sus secretos*); **to unbosom oneself** abrir su pecho, desahogarse

unbound [ʌn'baund] *adj* (*book*) sin encuadernar

unbreakable [ʌn'brekəbəl] *adj* irrompible

unbuckle [ʌn'bʌkəl] *tr* deshebillar

unburden [ʌn'bʌrdən] *tr* descargar; **to unburden oneself of** desahogarse de

unburied [ʌn'berid] *adj* insepulto

unbutton [ʌn'bʌtən] *tr* desabotonar

uncalled-for [ʌn'kɔld.fɔr] *adj* inne-

tu
un

cesario, no justificado; insolente

uncanny [ʌnˈkæni] *adj* espectral, misterioso; extraordinario, maravilloso

uncared-for [ʌnˈkerd ˌfɔr] *adj* desamparado, descuidado, abandonado

unceasing [ʌnˈsisiŋ] *adj* incesante

unceremonious [ˌʌnserɪˈmoni‧əs] *adj* inceremonioso

uncertain [ʌnˈsʌrtən] *adj* incierto

uncertain‧ty [ʌnˈsʌrtənti] *s* (*pl* -ties) incertidumbre

unchain [ʌnˈtʃen] *tr* desencadenar

unchangeable [ʌnˈtʃendʒəbəl] *adj* incambiable, inmutable

uncharted [ʌnˈtʃɑrtɪd] *adj* inexplorado

unchecked [ʌnˈtʃekt] *adj* no verificado; no refrenado; desenfrenado

uncivilized [ʌnˈsɪvɪ ˌlaɪzd] *adj* incivilizado

unclad [ʌnˈklæd] *adj* desvestido

unclaimed [ʌnˈklemd] *adj* sin reclamar; (*mail*) rechazado, sobrante

unclasp [ʌnˈklæsp] o [ʌnˈklɑsp] *tr* desabrochar

unclassified [ʌnˈklæsɪ ˌfaɪd] *adj* no clasificado; no clasificado como secreto

uncle [ˈʌŋkəl] *s* tío

unclean [ʌnˈklin] *adj* desaseado, sucio

un‧clog [ʌnˈklɑg] *v* (*pret & pp* -clogged; *ger* -clogging) *tr* desatrancar

unclouded [ʌnˈklaʊdɪd] *adj* despejado

uncollectible [ˌʌnkəˈlektɪbəl] *adj* incobrable

uncomfortable [ʌnˈkʌmfərtəbəl] *adj* incómodo

uncommitted [ˌʌnkəˈmɪtɪd] *adj* no empeñado, no comprometido

uncommon [ʌnˈkamən] *adj* raro, poco común

uncompromising [ʌnˈkɑmprə ˌmaɪzɪŋ] *adj* intransigente

unconcerned [ˌʌnkənˈsʌrnd] *adj* despreocupado, indiferente

unconditional [ˌʌnkənˈdɪʃənəl] *adj* incondicional

uncongenial [ˌʌnkənˈdʒini‧əl] *adj* antipático; incompatible; desagradable

unconquerable [ʌnˈkɑŋkərəbəl] *adj* inconquistable

unconquered [ʌnˈkɑŋkərd] *adj* invicto

unconscionable [ʌnˈkɑnʃənəbəl] *adj* inescrupuloso; desrazonable, excesivo

unconscious [ʌnˈkɑnʃəs] *adj* inconsciente; (*temporarily deprived of consciousness*) desmayado; (*unintentional*) involuntario

unconsciousness [ʌnˈkɑnʃəsnɪs] *s* inconsciencia; desmayo

unconstitutional [ˌʌnkɑnstɪˈtjuʃənəl] o [ˌʌnkɑnstɪˈtuʃənəl] *adj* inconstitucional

uncontrollable [ˌʌnkənˈtroləbəl] *adj* ingobernable; (*laughter*) inextinguible

unconventional [ˌʌnkənˈvenʃənəl] *adj* no convencional

uncork [ʌnˈkɔrk] *tr* destapar, descorchar

uncouth [ʌnˈkuθ] *adj* desgarbado, torpe, rústico

uncover [ʌnˈkʌvər] *tr* descubrir

unction [ˈʌŋkʃən] *s* (*anointing*) unción; suavidad hipócrita

unctuous [ˈʌŋktʃʊ‧əs] *adj* untuoso; zalamero

uncultivated [ʌnˈkʌltɪ ˌvetɪd] *adj* inculto (*que no está cultivado*; *rústico, grosero*)

uncultured [ʌnˈkʌltʃərd] *adj* inculto, rústico, grosero

uncut [ʌnˈkʌt] *adj* sin cortar; (*book or magazine*) intonso

undamaged [ʌnˈdæmɪdʒd] *adj* indemne, ileso

undaunted [ʌnˈdɔntɪd] *adj* impávido, denodado

undecided [ˌʌndɪˈsaɪdɪd] *adj* indeciso

undefeated [ˌʌndɪˈfitɪd] *adj* invicto

undefended [ˌʌndɪˈfendɪd] *adj* indefenso

undefiled [ˌʌndɪˈfaɪld] *adj* inmaculado, impoluto

undeniable [ˌʌndɪˈnaɪ‧əbəl] *adj* innegable

under [ˈʌndər] *adj* inferior; (*clothing*) interior || *adv* debajo; más abajo; **to go under** hundirse; (*to fail*) fracasar || *prep* bajo, debajo de; inferior a; **under full sail** a vela llena; **under lock and key** bajo llave; **under oath** bajo juramento; **under penalty of death** so pena de muerte; **under sail** a vela; **under separate cover** por separado, bajo cubierta separada; **under steam** bajo presión; **under the hand and seal of** firmado y sellado por; **under the nose of** (coll) en las barbas de; **under the weather** (coll) algo indispuesto; **under way** en camino

un'der‧age' *adj* menor de edad

un'der‧bid' *v* (*pret & pp* -bid; *ger* -bidding) *tr* ofrecer menos que

un'der‧brush' *s* maleza

un'der‧car'riage *s* carro inferior; (aer) tren *m* de aterrizaje

un'der‧clothes' *s* ropa interior

un'der‧con‧sump'tion *s* infraconsumo

un'der‧cov'er *adj* secreto

underdeveloped [ˌʌndərdɪˈveləpt] *adj* subdesarrollado

un'der‧dog' *s* víctima, perdidoso; **the underdogs** los de abajo

underdone [ˈʌndərˌdʌn] *adj* a medio asar, soasado

un'der‧es'ti‧mate' *tr* subestimar

un'der‧gar'ment *s* prenda de vestir interior

un'der‧go' *v* (*pret* -went; *pp* -gone) *tr* experimentar; sufrir, padecer

un'der‧grad'uate *adj* no graduado; (*course*) para el bachillerato || *s* alumno no graduado de universidad

un'der‧ground' *adj* subterráneo; clandestino || *adv* bajo tierra; ocultamente || *s* ferrocarril subterráneo; movimiento de resistencia

un'der‧growth' *s* maleza

underhanded [ˈʌndərˈhændɪd] *adj* clandestino, taimado, disimulado

un'der‧line' o **underline** *tr* subrayar

underling [ˈʌndərlɪŋ] *s* subordinado, secuaz *m* servil

un'der‧mine' *tr* socavar, minar

underneath [ˌʌndərˈniθ] adj inferior, más bajo || adv debajo || prep debajo de || s parte baja, superficie f inferior

undernourished [ˌʌndərˈnʌrɪʃt] adj desnutrido

un'der·nour'ish·ment s desnutrición

un'der·pass' s paso inferior

un'der·pay' s pago insuficiente || v (pret & pp -paid) tr & intr pagar insuficientemente

un'der·pin' v (pret & pp -pinned; ger -pinning) tr apuntalar, socalzar

underprivileged [ˌʌndərˈprɪvɪlɪdʒd] adj desheredado, desamparado

un'der·rate' tr menospreciar

un'der·score' tr subrayar

un'der·sea' adj submarino || **un'der·sea'** adv debajo de la superficie del mar

un'der·sec're·tar'y s (pl -ies) subsecretario

un'der·sell' v (pret & pp -sold) tr vender a menor precio que; (for less than the actual value) malbaratar

un'der·shirt' s camiseta

undersigned [ˈʌndərˌsaɪnd] adj infrascrito, subscrito

un'der·skirt' s enaguas, refajo

un'der·stand' v (pret & pp -stood) tr entender, comprender; sobrentender, subentender (una cosa que no está expresa) || intr entender, comprender

understandable [ˌʌndərˈstændəbəl] adj comprensible

understanding [ˌʌndərˈstændɪŋ] adj entendedor; (tolerant, sympathetic) comprensivo || s comprensión; (intellectual faculty, mind) entendimiento; (agreement) acuerdo; **to come to an understanding** llegar a un acuerdo

un'der·stud'y s (pl -ies) sobresaliente mf

un'der·take' v (pret -took; pp -taken) tr emprender; (to agree to perform) comprometerse a

undertaker [ˌʌndərˈtekər] o [ˈʌndərˌtekər] s empresario || [ˈʌndərˌtekər] s empresario de pompas fúnebres, director m de funeraria

undertaking [ˌʌndərˈtekɪŋ] s (task) empresa; (pledge) empeño || [ˈʌndərˌtekɪŋ] s (business of funeral director) funeraria

un'der·tak'ing establishment s funeraria, empresa de pompas fúnebres

un'der·tone' s voz baja; (background sound) fondo; color apagado

un'der·tow' s (countercurrent below surface) contracorriente f; (on the beach) resaca

un'der·wear' s ropa interior

un'der·world' s (criminal world) inframundo, bajos fondos sociales; (the earth) mundo terrenal; (pagan world of the dead) averno, infierno; (world under the water) mundo submarino; (opposite side of earth) antípodas

un'der·write' o **un'der·write'** v (pret -wrote; pp -written) tr subscribir; (to insure) asegurar

un'der·writ'er s subscritor m; asegurador m; compañía aseguradora

undeserved [ˌʌndɪˈzʌrvd] adj inmerecido

undesirable [ˌʌndɪˈzaɪrəbəl] adj & s indeseable mf

undetachable [ˌʌndɪˈtætʃəbəl] adj inamovible

undignified [ʌnˈdɪgnɪˌfaɪd] adj poco digno, poco grave, indecoroso

undiscernible [ˌʌndɪˈzʌrnɪbəl] o [ˌʌndɪˈsʌrnəbəl] adj imperceptible, invisible

un·do' v (pret -did; pp -done) tr deshacer; anular, borrar; arruinar

undoing [ʌnˈduɪŋ] s destrucción, pérdida, ruina

undone [ʌnˈdʌn] adj sin hacer, por hacer; **to come undone** deshacerse, desatarse; **to leave nothing undone** no dejar nada por hacer

undoubtedly [ʌnˈdautɪdli] adv indudablemente, sin duda

undramatic [ˌʌndrəˈmætɪk] adj poco dramático

undress [ˈʌnˌdrɛs] o [ʌnˈdrɛs] s traje m de casa; vestido de calle; (mil) traje de cuartel || [ʌnˈdrɛs] tr desnudar; desvendar (una herida) || intr desnudarse

undrinkable [ʌnˈdrɪŋkəbəl] adj impotable

undue [ʌnˈdju] o [ʌnˈdu] adj indebido

undulate [ˈʌndjəˌlet] intr ondular

unduly [ʌnˈdjuli] o [ʌnˈduli] adv indebidamente

undying [ʌnˈdaɪ·ɪŋ] adj imperecedero

unearned increment [ʌnˈʌrnd] s plusvalía

unearth [ʌnˈʌrθ] tr desenterrar

unearthly [ʌnˈʌrθli] adj sobrenatural; fantástico, espectral; extraordinario

uneasy [ʌnˈizi] adj (worried) inquieto; (constrained) encogido, embarazado

uneatable [ʌnˈitəbəl] adj incomible

uneconomic(al) [ˌʌnikəˈnamɪk(əl)] o [ˌʌnekəˈnamɪk(əl)] adj antieconómico

uneducated [ʌnˈedjəˌketɪd] adj ineducado, sin instrucción

unemployed [ˌʌnɛmˈplɔɪd] adj desocupado, desempleado; improductivo

unemployment [ˌʌnɛmˈplɔɪmənt] s desocupación, desempleo

unemployment insurance s seguro de desempleo o desocupación, seguro contra el paro obrero

unending [ʌnˈendɪŋ] adj interminable

unequal [ʌnˈikwəl] adj desigual; **to be unequal to** (a task) no estar a la altura de

unequaled o **unequalled** [ʌnˈikwəld] adj inigualado

unerring [ʌnˈʌrɪŋ] o [ʌnˈɛrɪŋ] adj infalible, seguro

unessential [ˌʌneˈsɛnʃəl] adj no esencial

uneven [ʌnˈivən] adj desigual; (number) impar

unexceptionable [ˌʌnɛkˈsɛpʃənəbəl] adj intachable, irreprensible

unexpected [ˌʌnɛkˈspɛktɪd] adj inesperado

unexplained [ˌʌnɛkˈsplend] adj inexplicado

unexplored [ˌʌnɛk'splɔrd] *adj* inexplorado

unexposed [ˌʌnɛk'spozd] *adj* (phot) inexpuesto

unfading [ʌn'fedɪŋ] *adj* inmarcesible

unfailing [ʌn'felɪŋ] *adj* indefectible; (*inexhaustible*) inagotable

unfair [ʌn'fer] *adj* injusto; desleal, doble, falso; (sport) sucio

unfaithful [ʌn'feθfəl] *adj* infiel

unfamiliar [ˌʌnfə'mɪljər] *adj* poco familiar; poco familiarizado

unfasten [ʌn'fæsən] o [ʌn'fɑsən] *tr* desatacar, desatar, soltar

unfathomable [ʌn'fæðəməbəl] *adj* insondable

unfavorable [ʌn'fevərəbəl] *adj* desfavorable

unfeathered [ʌn'feðərd] *adj* implume

unfeeling [ʌn'filɪŋ] *adj* insensible

unfetter [ʌn'fetər] *tr* desencadenar

unfilled [ʌn'fɪld] *adj* no lleno; por cumplir, pendiente

unfinished [ʌn'fɪnɪʃt] *adj* sin acabar; imperfecto, mal acabado; (*business*) pendiente

unfit [ʌn'fɪt] *adj* impropio, incapaz, inhábil; inservible, inútil

unfold [ʌn'fold] *tr* desplegar ‖ *intr* desplegarse

unforeseeable [ˌʌnfor'si·əbəl] *adj* imprevisible

unforeseen [ˌʌnfor'sin] *adj* imprevisto

unforgettable [ˌʌnfər'getəbəl] *adj* inolvidable

unforgivable [ˌʌnfər'gɪvəbəl] *adj* imperdonable

unfortunate [ʌn'fɔrtjənɪt] *adj* & *s* desgraciado

unfounded [ʌn'faʊndɪd] *adj* infundado

unfreeze [ʌn'friz] *tr* deshelar; desbloquear (*el crédito*)

unfriendly [ʌn'frendli] *adj* inamistoso; desfavorable

unfruitful [ʌn'frutfəl] *adj* infructuoso

unfulfilled [ˌʌnfəl'fɪld] *adj* incumplido

unfurl [ʌn'fʌrl] *tr* desplegar, extender

unfurnished [ʌn'fʌrnɪʃt] *adj* desamueblado

ungainly [ʌn'genli] *adj* desgarbado, desmañado

ungentlemanly [ʌn'dʒɛntəlmənli] *adj* poco caballeroso, descortés

ungird [ʌn'gʌrd] *tr* desceñir

ungodly [ʌn'gɑdli] *adj* impío, irreligioso; (*dreadful*) (coll) atroz

ungracious [ʌn'greʃəs] *adj* descortés; desagradable

ungrammatical [ˌʌngrə'mætɪkəl] *adj* ingramatical

ungrateful [ʌn'gretfəl] *adj* ingrato, desagradecido

ungrudgingly [ʌn'grʌdʒɪŋli] *adj* de buena gana, sin quejarse

unguarded [ʌn'gɑrdɪd] *adj* indefenso, descuidado; (*moment*) de inadvertencia

unguent ['ʌŋgwənt] *s* ungüento

unhandy [ʌn'hændi] *adj* inmanejable; (*awkward*) desmañado

unhappiness [ʌn'hæpɪnɪs] *s* infelicidad

unhap·py [ʌn'hæpi] *adj* (*comp* -**pier;**

super -**piest**) infeliz; (*unlucky*) desgraciado; (*fateful*) aciago

unharmed [ʌn'hɑrmd] *adj* indemne

unharmonious [ˌʌnhɑr'moni·əs] *adj* inarmónico

unharness [ʌn'hɑrnɪs] *tr* desenjaezar, desguarnecer; desenganchar

unhealthy [ʌn'helθi] *adj* malsano

unheard-of [ʌn'hɑrd‚av] *adj* inaudito

unhinge [ʌn'hɪndʒ] *tr* desgonzar; (fig) desequilibrar, trastornar

unhitch [ʌn'hɪtʃ] *tr* desenganchar

unho·ly [ʌn'holi] *adj* (*comp* -**lier;** *super* -**liest**) impío, malo, profano

unhook [ʌn'huk] *tr* desabrochar; desenganchar; (*to take down from a hook*) descolgar

unhoped-for [ʌn'hopt‚fər] *adj* inesperado, no esperado

unhorse [ʌn'hors] *tr* desarzonar

unhurt [ʌn'hʌrt] *adj* incólume, ileso

unicorn ['juni‚kɔrn] *s* unicornio

unification [ˌjunɪfɪ'keʃən] *s* unificación

uniform ['juni‚fɔrm] *adj* & *s* uniforme *m* ‖ *tr* uniformar

uniformi·ty [ˌjuni'fɔrmɪti] *s* (*pl* -**ties**) uniformidad

uni·fy ['juni‚fai] *v* (*pret* & *pp* -**fied**) *tr* unificar

unilateral [ˌjuni'lætərəl] *adj* unilateral

unimpeachable [ˌʌnɪm'pitʃəbəl] *adj* irrecusable, intachable

unimportant [ˌʌnɪm'pɔrtənt] *adj* poco importante

uninhabited [ˌʌnɪn'hæbɪtɪd] *adj* inhabitado

uninspired [ˌʌnɪn'spaɪrd] *adj* sin inspiración; aburrido, fastidioso

unintelligent [ˌʌnɪn'tɛlɪdʒənt] *adj* ininteligente

unintelligible [ˌʌnɪn'tɛlɪdʒɪbəl] *adj* ininteligible

uninterested [ʌn'ɪntrɪstɪd] o [ʌn'ɪntə‚rɛstɪd] *adj* desinteresado

uninteresting [ʌn'ɪntrɪstɪŋ] o [ʌn'ɪntə‚rɛstɪŋ] *adj* poco interesante

uninterrupted [ˌʌnɪntə'rʌptɪd] *adj* ininterrumpido

union ['junjən] *s* unión; (*organization of workmen*) gremio obrero, sindicato; unión matrimonial

unionize ['junjə‚naɪz] *tr* agremiar ‖ *intr* agremiarse

union shop *s* taller *m* de obreros agremiados

union suit *s* traje *m* interior de una sola pieza

unique [ju'nik] *adj* único

unison ['junɪsən] o ['junɪzən] *s* unisonancia; **in unison (with)** al unísono (de)

unit ['junɪt] *adj* unitario ‖ *s* unidad; (mach & elec) grupo

unite [ju'naɪt] *tr* unir ‖ *intr* unirse

united [ju'naɪtɪd] *adj* unido

United Kingdom *s* Reino Unido

United Nations *spl* Naciones Unidas

United States *adj* estadounidense ‖ **the United States** *s* los Estados Unidos *mpl;* Estados Unidos *msg*

uni·ty ['junɪti] *s* (*pl* -**ties**) unidad

univ. *abbr* universal, university

universal [ˌjunɪ'vʌrsəl] *adj* universal

universal joint *s* cardán *m*, junta universal

universal product code o **UPC** [ˌjuˌpi'si] *s* códico universal de producto

universe ['junɪˌvʌrs] *s* universo

universi•ty [ˌjunɪ'vʌrsɪti] *adj* universitario ‖ *s* (*pl* -ties) universidad

unjust [ʌn'dʒʌst] *adj* injusto

unjustified [ʌn'dʒʌstɪˌfaɪd] *adj* injustificado

unkempt [ʌn'kempt] *adj* despeinado

unkind [ʌn'kaɪnd] *adj* poco amable; duro, despiadado

unknowable [ʌn'no·əbəl] *adj* inconocible, insabible

unknowingly [ʌn'no·ɪŋli] *adv* desconocidamente, sin saberlo

unknown [ʌn'non] *adj* desconocido, ignoto, incógnito ‖ *s* desconocido; (math) incógnita

unknown quantity *s* (math & fig) incógnita

unknown soldier *s* soldado desconocido

unlace [ʌn'les] *tr* desenlazar; desatar (*los cordones del zapato*)

unlatch [ʌn'lætʃ] *tr* abrir levantando el picaporte

unlawful [ʌn'lɔfəl] *adj* ilegal

unleash [ʌn'liʃ] *tr* destraillar; soltar, desencadenar

unleavened [ʌn'levənd] *adj* ázimo

unless [ʌn'les] *conj* a menos que, a no ser que

unlettered [ʌn'letərd] *adj* iletrado, indocto; sin rotular; (*illiterate*) analfabeto

unlike [ʌn'laɪk] *adj* desemejante; desemejante de; (*poles of a magnet*) (elec) de nombres contrarios; (elec) de signo contrario ‖ *prep* a diferencia de

unlikely [ʌn'laɪkli] *adj* improbable

unlimber [ʌn'lɪmbər] *tr* preparar para la acción ‖ *intr* prepararse para la acción

unlined [ʌn'laɪnd] *adj* (*coat*) sin forro; (*paper*) sin rayar; (*face*) sin arrugas

unload [ʌn'lod] *tr* descargar; (coll) deshacerse de ‖ *intr* descargar

unloading [ʌn'lodɪŋ] *s* descarga, descargue *m*

unlock [ʌn'lɑk] *tr* abrir (*p.ej., una puerta*); (typ) desapretar

unloose [ʌn'lus] *tr* aflojar, soltar, desatar

unloved [ʌn'lʌvd] *adj* desamado

unlovely [ʌn'lʌvli] *adj* desgraciado

unluck•y [ʌn'lʌki] *adj* (*comp* -ier; *super* -iest) desgraciado, desdichado; aciago, nefasto; de mala suerte

un•make [ʌn'mek] *v* (*pret & pp* -made ['med]) *tr* deshacer; destruir

unmanly [ʌn'mænli] *adj* afeminado; bajo, cobarde

unmannerly [ʌn'mænərli] *adj* descortés, malcriado

unmarketable [ʌn'mɑrkɪtəbəl] *adj* incomerciable

unmarriageable [ʌn'mærɪdʒəbəl] *adj* incasable

unmarried [ʌn'mærɪd] *adj* soltero

unmask [ʌn'mæsk] o [ʌn'mɑsk] *tr* desenmascarar ‖ *intr* desenmascararse

unmatchable [ʌn'mætʃəbəl] *adj* incomparable, sin igual; (*price*) incompetible

unmerciful [ʌn'mʌrsɪfəl] *adj* despiadado, inclemente

unmesh [ʌn'meʃ] *tr* desengranar ‖ *intr* desengranarse

unmindful [ʌn'maɪndfəl] *adj* desatento, descuidado; **to be unmindful of** olvidar, no pensar en

unmistakable [ˌʌnmɪs'tekəbəl] *adj* inequívoco, inconfundible

unmixed [ʌn'mɪkst] *adj* puro, sin mezcla

unmoor [ʌn'mur] *tr* desamarrar (*un buque*); desaferrar (*las áncoras*)

unmoved [ʌn'muvd] *adj* fijo, inmoto; impasible

unmuzzle [ʌn'mʌzəl] *tr* desbozalar

unnatural [ʌn'nætʃərəl] *adj* innatural; (*artificial, forced*) afectado; anormal; inhumano

unnecessary [ʌn'nesəˌseri] *adj* innecesario

unnerve [ʌn'nʌrv] *tr* acobardar, trastornar

unnoticeable [ʌn'notɪsəbəl] *adj* imperceptible

unnoticed [ʌn'notɪst] *adj* inadvertido

unobliging [ˌʌnə'blaɪdʒɪŋ] *adj* poco servicial, poco amable

unobserved [ˌʌnəb'zʌrvd] *adj* inadvertido, sin ser visto

unobtainable [ˌʌnəb'tenəbəl] *adj* inencontrable, inasequible

unobtrusive [ˌʌnəb'trusɪv] *adj* discreto, reservado

unoccupied [ʌn'ɑkjəˌpaɪd] *adj* libre, vacante; (*not busy*) desocupado

unofficial [ˌʌnə'fɪʃəl] *adj* extraoficial, oficioso

unopened [ʌn'opənd] *adj* sin abrir; (*book*) no cortado

unorthodox [ʌn'ɔrθəˌdɑks] *adj* inortodoxo

unpack [ʌn'pæk] *tr* desembalar, desempaquetar

unpalatable [ʌn'pælətəbəl] *adj* desabrido, ingustable

unparalleled [ʌn'pærəˌleld] *adj* incomparable, sin par, sin igual

unpardonable [ʌn'pɑrdənəbəl] *adj* imperdonable

unpatriotic [ˌʌnpætrɪ'ɑtɪk] o [ˌʌnpætrɪ'ɑtɪk] *adj* antipatriótico

unperceived [ˌʌnpər'sivd] *adj* inadvertido

unperturbable [ˌʌnpər'tʌrbəbəl] *adj* infracto, imperturbable

unpleasant [ʌn'plezənt] *adj* antipático, desagradable

unpopular [ʌn'pɑpjələr] *adj* impopular

unpopularity [ʌn ˌpɑpjə'lærɪti] *s* impopularidad

unprecedented [ʌn'presɪˌdentɪd] *adj* sin precedente, inaudito

unprejudiced [ʌn'predʒədɪst] *adj* sin prejuicios, imparcial

unpremeditated [ˌʌnprɪ'medɪˌtetɪd] *adj* impremeditado

un
un

unprepared [ˌʌnprɪˈpɛrd] adj desprevenido; falto de preparación

unprepossessing [ˌʌnpripəˈzɛsɪŋ] adj poco atrayente

unpresentable [ˌʌnprɪˈzɛntəbəl] adj impresentable

unpretentious [ˌʌnprɪˈtɛnʃəs] adj modesto, sencillo

unprincipled [ʌnˈprɪnsɪpəld] adj sin principios, sin conciencia

unproductive [ˌʌnprəˈdʌktɪv] adj improductivo

unprofitable [ʌnˈprɑfɪtəbəl] adj no provechoso, inútil

unpronounceable [ˌʌnprəˈnaʊnsəbəl] adj impronunciable

unpropitious [ˌʌnprəˈpɪʃəs] adj impropicio

unpublished [ʌnˈpʌblɪʃt] adj inédito

unpunished [ʌnˈpʌnɪʃt] adj impune

unpurchasable [ʌnˈpʌrtʃəsəbəl] adj incomparable

unquenchable [ʌnˈkwɛntʃəbəl] adj inextinguible

unquestionable [ʌnˈkwɛstʃənəbəl] adj incuestionable

unrav·el [ʌnˈrævəl] v (pret & pp -eled o -elled; ger -eling o -elling) tr deshebrar; desenredar, desenmarañar || intr desenredarse, desenmarañarse

unreachable [ʌnˈritʃəbəl] adj inalcanzable

unreal [ʌnˈri·əl] adj irreal

unreali·ty [ˌʌnrɪˈælɪti] s (pl -ties) irrealidad

unreasonable [ʌnˈrizənəbəl] adj irrazonable, desrazonable

unrecognizable [ʌnˈrɛkəɡˌnaɪzəbəl] adj irreconocible

unreel [ʌnˈril] tr desenrollar || intr desenrollarse

unrefined [ˌʌnrɪˈfaɪnd] adj no refinado, impuro; grosero, rudo, tosco

unrelenting [ˌʌnrɪˈlɛntɪŋ] adj inexorable, inflexible, implacable

unreliable [ˌʌnrɪˈlaɪ·əbəl] adj indigno de confianza, informal

unremitting [ˌʌnrɪˈmɪtɪŋ] adj constante, incesante; infatigable

unrenewable [ˌʌnrɪˈnju·əbəl] o [ˌʌnrɪˈnu·əbəl] adj irrenovable; (com) improrrogable

unrented [ʌnˈrɛntɪd] adj desalquilado

unrepentant [ˌʌnrɪˈpɛntənt] adj impenitente

unrequited love [ˌʌnrɪˈkwaɪtɪd] s amor no correspondido

unresponsive [ˌʌnrɪˈspɑnsɪv] adj insensible, frío, desinteresado

unrest [ʌnˈrɛst] s intranquilidad, inquietud; alboroto, desorden m

un·rig [ʌnˈrɪɡ] v (pret & pp -rigged; ger -rigging) tr (naut) desaparejar

unrighteous [ʌnˈraɪtʃəs] adj injusto, malvado, vicioso

unripe [ʌnˈraɪp] adj inmaturo, verde; prematuro, precoz

unrivaled o **unrivalled** [ʌnˈraɪvəld] adj sin rival, sin par

unroll [ʌnˈrol] tr desenrollar, desplegar

unromantic [ˌʌnroˈmæntɪk] adj poco romántico

unruffled [ʌnˈrʌfəld] adj tranquilo, sereno

unruly [ʌnˈruli] adj ingobernable, indómito, revoltoso

unsaddle [ʌnˈsædəl] tr desensillar (un caballo); desarzonar (al jinete)

unsafe [ʌnˈsef] adj inseguro, peligroso

unsaid [ʌnˈsɛd] adj callado, no dicho

unsalable [ʌnˈseləbəl] adj invendible

unsanitary [ʌnˈsænɪˌtɛri] adj antihigiénico, insalubre

unsatisfactory [ʌnˌsætɪsˈfæktəri] adj insatisfactorio, poco satisfactorio

unsatisfied [ʌnˈsætɪsˌfaɪd] adj insatisfecho

unsavory [ʌnˈsevəri] adj desabrido; (fig) infame, deshonroso

unscathed [ʌnˈskeðd] adj ileso, sano y salvo

unscientific [ˌʌnsaɪ·ənˈtɪfɪk] adj anticientífico

unscrew [ʌnˈskru] tr destornillar || intr destornillarse

unscrupulous [ʌnˈskrupjələs] adj inescrupuloso

unseal [ʌnˈsil] tr desellar; (fig) abrir

unseasonable [ʌnˈsizənəbəl] adj intempestivo, inoportuno

unseaworthy [ʌnˈsiˌwʌrði] adj innavegable

unseemly [ʌnˈsimli] adj impropio, indecoroso, indigno

unseen [ʌnˈsin] adj invisible, oculto

unselfish [ʌnˈsɛlfɪʃ] adj desinteresado, generoso, altruísta

unsettled [ʌnˈsɛtəld] adj inhabitado, despoblado; sin residencia fija; indeciso; descompuesto; (bills) por pagar

unshackle [ʌnˈʃækəl] tr desherrar, desencadenar

unshaken [ʌnˈʃekən] adj imperturbado

unshapely [ʌnˈʃepli] adj desproporcionado, mal formado

unshatterable [ʌnˈʃætərəbəl] adj inastillable

unshaven [ʌnˈʃevən] adj sin afeitar

unsheathe [ʌnˈʃið] tr desenvainar

unshod [ʌnˈʃɑd] adj descalzo; (horse) desherrado

unshrinkable [ʌnˈʃrɪŋkəbəl] adj inencogible

unsightly [ʌnˈsaɪtli] adj feo, de aspecto malo, repugnante

unsinkable [ʌnˈsɪŋkəbəl] adj insumergible

unskilled [ʌnˈskɪld] adj inexperto

unskilled laborer s bracero, peón m

unskillful [ʌnˈskɪlfəl] adj desmañado

unsnarl [ʌnˈsnɑrl] tr desenredar

unsociable [ʌnˈsoʃəbəl] adj insociable, huraño

unsold [ʌnˈsold] adj invendido

unsolder [ʌnˈsɑdər] tr desoldar; (fig) desunir, separar

unsophisticated [ˌʌnsəˈfɪstɪˌketɪd] adj ingenuo, natural, sencillo

unsound [ʌnˈsaʊnd] adj poco firme; falso, erróneo; (decayed) podrido; (sleep) ligero

unsown [ʌnˈson] adj yermo, no sembrado

unspeakable [ʌnˈspikəbəl] adj indecible, inefable; *(atrocious, infamous)* incalificable

unsportsmanlike [ʌn'spɔrtsmən ˌlaɪk] *adj* antideportivo

unstable [ʌn'stebəl] *adj* inestable

unsteady [ʌn'stedi] *adj* inseguro, inestable; irresoluto, inconstante; poco juicioso

unstinted [ʌn'stɪntɪd] *adj* no escatimado, generoso, liberal

unstitch [ʌn'stɪtʃ] *tr* descoser

un·stop [ʌn'stɑp] *v* (*pret & pp* -stopped; *ger* -stopping) *tr* destaponar

unstressed [ʌn'strest] *adj* sin énfasis; *(syllable)* inacentuado

unstrung [ʌn'strʌŋ] *adj* nervioso, trastornado

unsuccessful [ˌʌnsək'sesfəl] *adj* (*person*) desairado; *(undertaking)* impróspero; **to be unsuccessful** no tener éxito

unsuitable [ʌn'sutəbəl] o [ʌn'sjutəbəl] *adj* inadecuado, inconveniente

unsurpassable [ˌʌnsər'pæsəbəl] o [ˌʌnsər'pɑsəbəl] *adj* insuperable

unsuspected [ˌʌnsəs'pɛktɪd] *adj* insospechado

unswerving [ʌn'swʌrvɪŋ] *adj* firme, inmutable, resoluto

unsymmetrical [ˌʌnsɪ'metrɪkəl] *adj* asimétrico, disimétrico

unsympathetic [ˌʌnsɪmpə'θetɪk] *adj* incompasivo, indiferente

unsystematic(al) [ˌʌnsɪstə'mætɪk(əl)] *adj* poco sistemático, sin sistema

untactful [ʌn'tæktfəl] *adj* indiscreto, falto de tacto

untamed [ʌn'temd] *adj* indomado, bravío

untangle [ʌn'tæŋgəl] *tr* desenredar, desenmarañar

unteachable [ʌn'titʃəbəl] *adj* indócil

untenable [ʌn'tenəbəl] *adj* insostenible

unthankful [ʌn'θæŋkfəl] *adj* ingrato, desagradecido

unthinkable [ʌn'θɪŋkəbəl] *adj* impensable

unthinking [ʌn'θɪŋkɪŋ] *adj* irreflexivo, desatento; irracional, instintivo

untidy [ʌn'taɪdi] *adj* desaseado, desaliñado

un·tie [ʌn'taɪ] *v* (*pret & pp* -tied; *ger* -tying) *tr* desatar; deshacer (*un nudo, una cuerda*); *(to free from restraint)* soltar; resolver || *intr* desatarse

until [ʌn'tɪl] *prep* hasta || *conj* hasta que; **to wait until** aguardar a que, esperar a que

untillable [ʌn'tɪləbəl] *adj* incultivable

untimely [ʌn'taɪmli] *adj* intempestivo

untiring [ʌn'taɪrɪŋ] *adj* incansable

untold [ʌn'told] *adj* nunca dicho; *(uncounted)* innumerable, incalculable

untouchable [ʌn'tʌtʃəbəl] *adj* intangible || *s* intocable *mf*

untouched [ʌn'tʌtʃt] *adj* intacto; íntegro; impasible; no mencionado

untoward [ʌn'tord] *adj* desfavorable; indecoroso

untrammeled o **untrammelled** [ʌn'træməld] *adj* libre, sin trabas

untried [ʌn'traɪd] *adj* no probado, no ensayado

untroubled [ʌn'trʌbləd] *adj* tranquilo, sosegado

untrue [ʌn'tru] *adj* falso; infiel

untrustworthy [ʌn'trʌst ˌwɔrði] *adj* indigno de confianza

untruth [ʌn'truθ] *s* falsedad, mentira

untruthful [ʌn'truθfəl] *adj* falso, mentiroso

untwist [ʌn'twɪst] *tr* destorcer || *intr* destorcerse

unused [ʌn'juzd] *adj* inutilizado, no usado; nuevo; **unused to** [ʌn'juzdtu] o [ʌn'justu] *adj* no acostumbrado a

unusual [ʌn'juʒu-əl] *adj* inusual, insólito

unutterable [ʌn'ʌtərəbəl] *adj* indecible, inexpresable

unvanquished [ʌn'væŋkwɪʃt] *adj* invicto

unvarnished [ʌn'vɑrnɪʃt] *adj* sin barnizar; (fig) sencillo, sin adornos

unveil [ʌn'vel] *tr* quitar el velo a; descubrir, develar, inaugurar (*una estatua*) || *intr* quitarse el velo

unveiling [ʌn'velɪŋ] *s* develación, inauguración

unventilated [ʌn'venti ˌletɪd] *adj* sin ventilar

unvoice [ʌn'vɔɪs] *tr* afonizar, ensordecer || *intr* afonizarse, ensordecerse

unwanted [ʌn'wɑntɪd] *adj* indeseado

unwarranted [ʌn'wɑrəntɪd] *adj* injustificado; no autorizado; sin garantía

unwary [ʌn'weri] *adj* incauto, imprudente

unwavering [ʌn'wevərɪŋ] *adj* firme, determinado, resuelto

unwelcome [ʌn'welkəm] *adj* mal acogido; importuno, molesto

unwell [ʌn'wel] *adj* indispuesto, enfermo; (coll) menstruante

unwholesome [ʌn'holsəm] *adj* insalubre

unwieldy [ʌn'wildi] *adj* inmanejable, abultado, pesado

unwilling [ʌn'wɪlɪŋ] *adj* desinclinado, maldispuesto, renuente

unwillingly [ʌn'wɪlɪŋli] *adv* de mala gana

un·wind [ʌn'waɪnd] *v* (*pret & pp* -wound* ['waʊnd]) *tr* desenvolver || *intr* desenvolverse; distenderse (*el muelle del reloj*)

unwise [ʌn'waɪz] *adj* indiscreto, malaconsejado

unwished-for [ʌn'wɪʃt ˌfɔr] *adj* indeseado

unwitting [ʌn'wɪtɪŋ] *adj* inadvertido, inconsciente

unwonted [ʌn'wʌntɪd] *adj* poco común, raro, insólito

unworldly [ʌn'wʌrldli] *adj* no terrenal, no mundano, espiritual

unworthy [ʌn'wʌrði] *adj* indigno, desmerecedor

un·wrap [ʌn'ræp] *v* (*pret & pp* -wrapped; *ger* -wrapping) *tr* desenvolver, desempapelar

unwrinkle [ʌn'rɪŋkəl] *tr* desarrugar || *intr* desarrugarse

un
un

unwritten [ʌn'rɪtən] *adj* no escrito; (*blank*) en blanco; oral

unyielding [ʌn'jildɪŋ] *adj* firme, inflexible; terco, reacio

unyoke [ʌn'jok] *tr* desuncir

up [ʌp] *adj* ascendente; alto, elevado; derecho, en pie; terminado; cumplido; levantado de la cama; **to be up and about** estar levantado (*el que estaba enfermo*) || *s* subida; **ups and downs** altibajos, vicisitudes || *adv* arriba; en el aire; hacia arriba; al norte; **to be up** estar levantado; vencer (*un plazo*); **to be up in arms** estar sobre las armas; protestar vehementemente; **to be up to a person** tocarle a una persona; **to get up** levantarse; **to go up** subir; **to keep up** mantener; continuar; mantenerse firme; **to keep up with** correr parejas con; **up above** allá arriba; **up against it** (slang) en apuros; **up to** hasta; (*capable of*) a la altura de; (*informed of*) al corriente de; (*scheming*) armando, tramando; **what is up?** ¿qué pasa? || *prep* subiendo; **up the river** río arriba; **up the street** calle arriba

up-and-coming [ʌpən'kʌmɪŋ] *adj* (coll) prometedor

up-and-doing [ʌpən'duɪŋ] *adj* (coll) emprendedor

up-and-up [ʌpən'ʌp] *s* — **on the up-and-up** (coll) mejorándose; (coll) abiertamente, sin dolo

up·braid' *tr* regañar, reprender

upbringing [ʌp,brɪŋɪŋ] *s* educación, crianza

up'coun'try *adv* (coll) hacia el interior, tierra adentro || *s* (coll) interior *m* del país

up·date' *tr* poner al día

upheaval [ʌp'hivəl] *s* trastorno, cataclismo

up'hill' *adj* ascendente; arduo, difícil, penoso || **up'hill'** *adv* cuesta arriba

up·hold' *v* (*pret & pp* **-held**) *tr* levantar; apoyar, sostener; defender

upholster [ʌp'holstər] *tr* tapizar

upholsterer [ʌp'holstərər] *s* tapicero

upholster·y [ʌp'holstəri] *s* (*pl* **-ies**) tapicería

up'keep' *s* conservación, manutención; gastos de conservación, gastos de entretenimiento

upland [ʌplənd] o [ʌplænd] *adj* alto, elevado || *s* tierra alta, terreno elevado

up'lift' *s* (*lifting*) elevación, levantamiento; mejora social; (*moral or spiritual improvement*) edificación || **up·lift'** *tr* elevar, levantar; edificar

upon [ə'pɑn] *prep* en, sobre, encima de; **upon** + *ger* al + *inf*, p.ej., **upon arriving** al llegar; **upon my word!** ¡por mi palabra!

upper [ʌpər] *adj* alto, superior; (*country*) interior; (*clothing*) exterior || *s* (*of shoe*) pala; **on one's uppers** con las suelas gastadas; (coll) andrajoso, pobre, sin blanca

upper berth *s* litera alta, cama alta

upper case *s* (typ) caja alta

upper classes *spl* altas clases

upper hand *s* dominio, ventaja; **to have the upper hand** tener vara alta

upper middle class *s* alta burguesía

up'per·most' *adj* (el) más alto; (el) principal || *adv* en lo más alto; primero, en primer lugar

uppish [ʌpɪʃ] *adj* (coll) copetudo, arrogante

up·raise' *tr* levantar

up'right' *adj* derecho, vertical; probo, recto || *adv* verticalmente || *s* montante *m*

uprising [ʌp'raɪzɪŋ] o [ʌp,raɪzɪŋ] *s* insurrección, levantamiento

up'roar' *s* alboroto, conmoción, tumulto

uproarious [ʌp'rorɪ·əs] *adj* tumultuoso; (*noisy*) ruidoso; (*funny*) muy cómico

up·root' *tr* desarraigar

up·set' o **up'set'** *adj* (*overturned*) volcado; trastornado; indispuesto || **up'set'** *s* (*overturn*) vuelco; (*unexpected defeat*) contratiempo; (*disturbance*) trastorno; (*illness*) indisposición, enfermedad || **up·set'** *v* (*pret & pp* **-set**; *ger* **-setting**) *tr* volcar; trastornar; indisponer || *intr* volcar

upset price *s* precio mínimo fijado en una subasta

upsetting [ʌp'setɪŋ] *adj* desconcertante

up'shot' *s* conclusión, resultado; esencia, quid *m*

up'side' *s* parte *f* superior, lado superior; **on the upside** (*said of prices*) subiendo

upside down *adv* al revés, lo de arriba abajo, patas arriba; en confusión, revuelto; **to turn upside down** volcar; trastornar; volcarse; trastornarse

up'stage' *adj* situado al fondo de la escena; (coll) altanero, arrogante || *adv* al fondo de la escena || **up'stage'** *tr* (coll) mirar por encima del hombro, desairar

up'stairs' *adj* de arriba || *adv* arriba || *s* piso superior, pisos superiores

upstanding [ʌp'stændɪŋ] *adj* derecho; gallardo; probo, recto

up'start' *adj & s* advenedizo

up'stream' *adv* aguas arriba, río arriba

up'stroke' *s* carrera ascendente

up'swing' *s* movimiento hacia arriba; mejora notable; **on the upswing** mejorando notablemente

up'-to-date' *adj* corriente; reciente, moderno; de última hora, de última moda

up'-to-the-min'ute *adj* al día, de actualidad

up'town' *adj* de la parte alta de la ciudad || *adv* en la parte alta de la ciudad

up train *s* tren *m* ascendente

up'trend' *s* tendencia al alza

up'turn' *s* alza, subida, mejora

upturned [ʌp'tʌrnd] *adj* revuelto; (*part of clothing*) arremangado; (*nose*) respingada

upward [ʌpwərd] *adj* ascendente || *adv* hacia arriba; **upward of** más de

Ural ['jurəl] *adj* ural ‖ **Urals** *spl* Urales *mpl*

uranium [ju'reni·əm] *s* uranio

urban ['ʌrbən] *adj* urbano (*perteneciente a la ciudad*)

urbane [ʌr'ben] *adj* urbano (*atento, cortés*)

urbanite ['ʌrbə,naɪt] *s* ciudadano

urbanity [ʌr'bænɪti] *s* urbanidad

urbanize ['ʌrbə,naɪz] *tr* urbanizar

urchin ['ʌrtʃɪn] *s* pilluelo, galopín *m*

ure·thra [ju'riθrə] *s* (*pl* -**thras** o -**thrae** [θri]) uretra

urge [ʌrdʒ] *s* impulso, estímulo ‖ *tr* apremiar, impeler, estimular; pedir instantemente; (*to try to persuade*) instar ‖ *intr* instar

urgen·cy ['ʌrdʒənsi] *s* (*pl* -**cies**) urgencia; instancia, apremio

urgent ['ʌrdʒənt] *adj* urgente; apremiante

urinal ['jurɪnəl] *s* (*receptacle*) orinal *m*; (*place*) urinario

urinary ['juri,neri] *adj* urinario

urinate ['juri,net] *tr* orinar (*p.ej., sangre*) ‖ *intr* orinar, orinarse

urine ['jurɪn] *s* orina, orines *mpl*

urn [ʌrn] *s* (*decorative vase*) jarrón *m*; cafetera o tetera con grifo; (*to hold ashes of the dead after cremation*) urna

urology [ju'rolədʒi] *s* urología

Uruguay ['jurə,gwe] o ['jurə,gwaɪ] *s* el Uruguay

Uruguayan [,jurə'gwe·ən] o [,jurə-'gwaɪ·ən] *adj & s* uruguayo

us [ʌs] *pron pers* nos; nosotros; **to us** nos; a nosotros

U.S.A. *abbr* **United States of America, United States Army, Union of South Africa**

usable ['juzəbəl] *adj* aprovechable, utilizable

usage ['jusɪdʒ] o ['juzɪdʒ] *s* usanza; (*e.g., of a language*) uso

use [jus] *s* uso, empleo; utilidad; **in use** en uso; **out of use** desusado; **to be of no use** no servir para nada; **to have no use for** no necesitar; no servirse de; (*coll*) tener en poco; **to make use of** servirse de ‖ [juz] *tr* usar, emplear, servirse de; **to use badly**

maltratar; **to use up** agotar, consumir ‖ *intr* (empléase sólo en el pretérito y se traduce al español con el pretérito imperfecto o el verbo **soler**), p.ej., **I used to go out for a walk every evening** salía de paseo todas las tardes o solía salir de paseo todas las tardes

used [juzd] *adj* (*customarily employed; worn, partly worn-out; accustomed*) usado; **used to** ['juzdtu] o ['justu] acostumbrado a

useful ['jusfəl] *adj* útil

usefulness ['jusfəlnɪs] *s* utilidad

useless ['juslɪs] *adj* inservible, inútil

user ['juzər] *s* usuario

usher ['ʌʃər] *s* (*in a theater*) acomodador *m*; (*doorkeeper*) ujier *m*, portero ‖ *tr* acomodar; **to usher in** anunciar, introducir

U.S.S.R. *abbr* **Union of Soviet Socialist Republics**

usual ['juʒu·əl] *adj* usual, acostumbrado; **as usual** como de costumbre

usually ['juʒu·əli] *adv* usualmente, de ordinario

usurp [ju'zʌrp] *tr* usurpar

usu·ry ['juʒəri] *s* (*pl* -**ries**) usura

utensil [ju'tensɪl] *s* utensilio

uter·us ['jutərəs] *s* (*pl* -**i** [,aɪ]) útero

utilitarian [,jutɪlɪ'tɛrɪ·ən] *adj* utilitario

utili·ty [ju'tɪlɪti] *s* (*pl* -**ties**) utilidad; empresa de servicio público

utilize ['juti,laɪz] *tr* utilizar

utmost ['ʌt,most] *adj* sumo, extremo, último; más grande, mayor posible; más lejano ‖ *s* — **the utmost** lo sumo, lo mayor, lo más; **to the utmost** a lo sumo, a más no poder; **to do one's utmost** hacer todo lo posible

utopia [ju'topɪ·ə] *s* utopía

utopian [ju'topɪ·ən] *adj* utópico, utopista ‖ *s* utopista *mf*

utter ['ʌtər] *adj* total, absoluto ‖ *tr* proferir, pronunciar; dar (*un suspiro*)

utterance ['ʌtərəns] *s* expresión, pronunciación; declaración

utterly ['ʌtərli] *adj* completamente, totalmente, absolutamente

uxoricide [ʌk'sorɪ,saɪd] *s* (*husband*) uxoricida *m*; (*act*) uxoricidio

uxorious [ʌk'sorɪ·əs] *adj* uxorio

V

V, v [vi] vigésima segunda letra del alfabeto inglés

v. *abbr* **verb, verse, versus, vide** (Lat) **see, voice, volt, volume**

V. *abbr* **Venerable, Vice, Viscount, Volunteer**

vacan·cy ['vekənsi] *s* (*pl* -**cies**) (*emptiness; gap, opening*) vacío; (*unfilled position or job*) vacancia, vacante *f*, vacío; piso vacante; cargo

vacant ['vekənt] *adj* (*empty*) vacío; (*having no occupant; untenanted*)

vacante; (*expression, look*) vago; distraído

vacate ['veket] *tr* dejar vacante; anular, invalidar, revocar ‖ *intr* (*to move out*) desalojar; (*coll*) irse, marcharse

vacation [ve'keʃən] *s* vacaciones *pl*; **on vacation** de vacaciones ‖ *intr* tomar vacaciones

vacationist [ve'keʃənɪst] *s* vacacionista *mf*

vacation with pay *s* vacaciones retribuídas

un va

vaccinate ['væksɪ͵net] *tr* vacunar
vaccination [͵væksɪ'neʃən] *s* vacunación
vaccine [væk'sin] *s* vacuna
vacillate ['væsɪ͵let] *intr* vacilar
vacillating ['væsɪ͵letɪŋ] *adj* vacilante
vacui·ty [væ'kjuˌɪti] *s* (*pl* -ties) vacuidad
vacu·um ['vækjuˌəm] *s* (*pl* -ums o -a [ə]) vacío || *tr* (coll) limpiar
vacuum cleaner *s* aspirador *m* de polvo
vacuum tank *s* (aut) aspirador *m* de gasolina, nodriza
vacuum tube *s* tubo de vacío
vagabond ['vægə͵bɑnd] *adj* & *s* vagabundo
vagar·y [və'geri] *s* (*pl* -ies) capricho
vagran·cy ['vegrənsi] *s* (*pl* -cies) vagabundaje *m*
vagrant ['vegrənt] *adj* & *s* vagabundo
vague [veg] *adj* vago
vain [ven] *adj* vano; (*conceited*) vanidoso; in vain en vano
vainglorious [ven'gloriˌəs] *adj* vanaglorioso
valance ['væləns] *s* (*across the top of a window*) guardamalleta; (*drapery*) doselera
vale [vel] *s* valle *m*
valedictorian [͵vælɪdɪk'toriˌən] *s* alumno que pronuncia el discurso de despedida al fin del curso
valedicto·ry [͵vælɪ'dɪktəri] *adj* de despedida || *s* (*pl* -ries) discurso de despedida
valence ['veləns] *s* (chem) valencia
valentine ['vælən͵taɪn] *s* tarjeta amorosa o jocosa del día de San Valentín
Valentine Day *s* día *m* de los corazones, día de los enamorados (*14 de febrero*)
vale of tears *s* valle *m* de lágrimas
valet ['vælɪt] o ['vælе] *s* ayuda *m*, paje *m*
valiant ['væljənt] *adj* valiente, valeroso
valid ['vælɪd] *adj* válido, valedero
validate ['vælɪ͵det] *tr* validar; (sport) homologar
validation [͵vælɪ'deʃən] *s* validación; (sport) homologación
validi·ty [və'lɪdɪti] *s* (*pl* -ties) validez *f*
valise [və'lis] *s* maleta
valley ['væli] *s* valle *m*; (*of roof*) lima hoya
valor ['vælər] *s* valor *m*, ánimo
valorous ['vælərəs] *adj* valeroso
valuable ['væljuˌəbəl] o ['væljəbəl] *adj* (*having monetary value*) valioso; (*highly thought of*) estimable || valuables *spl* alhajas, objetos de valor
value ['vælju] *s* valor *m*; (*return for one's money in a purchase*) (coll) adquisición, inversión, p.ej., an excellent value una adquisición excelente || *tr* (*to think highly of*) estimar; (*to set a price for*) valorar, valuar
value-added tax *s* impuesto al valor agregado
valueless ['væljuˌl̄ɪs] *adj* sin valor
valve [vælv] *s* válvula; (*of mollusk*) valva; (mus) llave *f*
valve cap *s* capuchón *m*
valve gears *spl* distribución

valve lifter ['lɪftər] *s* levantaválvulas *m*
valve seat *s* asiento de válvula
valve spring *s* muelle *m* de válvula
valve stem *s* vástago de válvula
vamp [væmp] *s* (*of shoe*) empella; (*patchwork*) remiendo; (*woman who preys on men*) (slang) mujer *f* fatal, vampiresa || *tr* poner empella a (*un zapato*); remendar; (*to concoct*) componer, enmendar; (jazz) improvisar (*un acompañamiento*); (slang) seducir (*una mujer mundana a un hombre*)
vampire ['væmpaɪr] *s* vampiro; (*woman who preys on men*) mujer *f* fatal, vampiresa
van [væn] *s* carro de carga, camión *m* de mudanzas; (mil & fig) vanguardia; (Brit) furgón *m* de equipajes
vanadium [və'nedɪˌəm] *s* vanadio
vandal ['vændəl] *adj* & *s* vándalo || Vandal *adj* & *s* vándalo
vandalism ['vændə͵lɪzəm] *s* vandalismo
vane [ven] *s* (*weathervane*) veleta; (*of windmill*) aspa; (*of propeller or turbine*) paleta; (*of feather*) barba
vanguard ['væn͵gɑrd] *s* (mil & fig) vanguardia; in the vanguard a vanguardia
vanilla [və'nɪlə] *s* vainilla
vanish ['vænɪʃ] *intr* desvanecerse
vanishing cream ['vænɪ/ɪŋ] *s* crema desvanecedora
vani·ty ['vænɪti] *s* (*pl* -ties) vanidad; (*dressing table*) tocador *m*; (*vanity case*) estuche *m* de afeites
vanity case *s* estuche *m* de afeites, neceser *m* de belleza
vanquish ['væŋkwɪʃ] *tr* vencer, rendir
vantage ground ['væntɪdʒ] *s* posición ventajosa
vapid ['væpɪd] *adj* insípido
vapor ['vepər] *s* vapor *m* (*el visible; exhalación, vaho, niebla, etc.*)
vaporize ['vepə͵raɪz] *tr* vaporizar || *intr* vaporizarse
vaporous ['vepərəs] *adj* vaporoso
vapor trail *s* (aer) estela de vapor, rastro de condensación
var. *abbr* variant
variable ['verɪˌəbəl] *adj* & *s* variable *f*
variance ['verɪˌəns] *s* diferencia, variación; at variance with en desacuerdo con
variant ['verɪˌənt] *adj* & *s* variante *f*
variation [͵verɪ'eʃən] *s* variación
varicose ['værɪ͵kos] *adj* varicoso
varicose vein *s* (pathol) varice *f*
varied ['verid] *adj* variado, vario
variegated ['verɪˌə͵getɪd] o ['verɪˌɡetɪd] *adj* abigarrado, variado
varie·ty [və'raɪˌɪti] *s* (*pl* -ties) variedad
variety show *s* variedades
variola [və'raɪˌələ] *s* (pathol) viruela
various ['verɪˌəs] *adj* (*several; of different kinds*) varios; (*many-sided; many-colored*) vario
varnish ['vɑrnɪʃ] *s* barniz *m*; (fig) capa, apariencia || *tr* barnizar; (fig) dar apariencia falsa a
varsi·ty ['vɑrsɪti] *adj* (sport) universi-

tario ‖ s (pl -ties) (sport) equipo principal de la universidad

var·y ['veri] v (pret & pp -ied) tr & intr variar

vase [ves] o [vez] s florero, jarrón m

vaseline ['væsə,lin] s (trademark) vaselina

vassal ['væsəl] adj & s vasallo

vast [væst] o [vɑst] adj vasto

vastly ['væstli] o ['vɑstli] adv enormemente

vastness ['væstnɪs] o ['vɑstnɪs] s vastedad

vat [væt] s cuba, tina

vaudeville ['vodvɪl] o ['vɔdəvɪl] s variedades; (light theatrical piece interspersed with songs) zarzuela

vault [vɔlt] s (underground chamber) bodega; (of a bank) cámara acorazada; (burial chamber) sepultura, tumba; (firmament) bóveda celeste; (leap) salto; (archit) bóveda ‖ tr abovedar; saltar ‖ intr saltar

vaunt [vɔnt] o [vɑnt] s jactancia ‖ tr jactarse de ‖ intr jactarse

veal [vil] s ternera, carne f de ternera

veal chop s chuleta de ternera

vedette [vɪ'dɛt] s buque m escucha; centinela m de avanzada

veer [vɪr] s viraje m ‖ tr virar ‖ intr virar; (naut) llamar (el viento)

vegetable ['vɛdʒɪtəbəl] adj vegetal ‖ s (plant) vegetal m; (edible part of plant) hortaliza, legumbre f

vegetable garden s huerto de hortalizas, huerto de verduras

vegetable soup s menestra, sopa de hortalizas

vegetarian [,vɛdʒɪ'tɛrɪ·ən] adj & s vegetariano

vehemence ['vi·ɪməns] s vehemencia

vehement ['vi·ɪmənt] adj vehemente

vehicle ['vi·ɪkəl] s vehículo

vehicular traffic [vɪ'hɪkjələr] s circulación rodada

veil [vel] s velo; **to take the veil** tomar el velo ‖ tr velar (cubrir con un velo; cubrir, disimular)

vein [ven] s vena; (streak) veta; (distinctive quality) rasgo ‖ tr vetear

velar ['vilər] adj & s velar f

vellum ['vɛləm] s vitela; papel m vitela

veloci·ty [vɪ'lɑsɪti] s (pl -ties) velocidad

velvet ['vɛlvɪt] adj de terciopelo ‖ s terciopelo; (slang) ganancia limpia

velveteen [,vɛlvɪ'tin] s velludillo

velvety ['vɛlvɪti] adj aterciopelado

Ven. abbr **Venerable**

vend [vɛnd] tr vender como buhonero

vending machine s distribuidor automático

vendor ['vɛndər] s vendedor m, buhonero

veneer [və'nɪr] s chapa, enchapado; (fig) apariencia ‖ tr enchapar

venerable ['vɛnərəbəl] adj venerable

venerate ['vɛnə,ret] tr venerar

venereal [vɪ'nɪrɪ·əl] adj venéreo

Venetia [vɪ'niʃɪ·ə] o [vɪ'niʃə] s Venecia (provincia)

Venetian [vɪ'niʃən] adj & s veneciano

Venetian blind s persiana

Venezuela [,vɛnɪ'zwilə] s Venezuela

Venezuelan [,vɛnɪ'zwilən] adj & s venezolano

vengeance ['vɛndʒəns] s venganza; **with a vengeance** con furia, con violencia; excesivamente, con creces

vengeful ['vɛndʒfəl] adj vengativo

Venice ['vɛnɪs] s Venecia (ciudad)

venire [vɪ'naɪri] s (law) auto de convocación del jurado

venison ['vɛnɪsən] o ['vɛnɪzən] s carne f de venado

venom ['vɛnəm] s veneno

venomous ['vɛnəməs] adj venenoso

vent [vɛnt] s agujero, orificio; (outlet) salida; **to give vent to** dar libre curso a ‖ tr proveer de abertura; desahogar, expresar; **to vent one's spleen** descargar la bilis

vent'hole' s respiradero

ventilate ['vɛntɪ,let] tr ventilar

ventilator ['vɛntɪ,letər] s ventilador m

ventricle ['vɛntrɪkəl] s ventrículo

ventriloquism [vɛn'trɪlə,kwɪzəm] s ventriloquia

ventriloquist [vɛn'trɪləkwɪst] s ventrílocuo

venture ['vɛntʃər] s empresa arriesgada; **at a venture** a la buena ventura ‖ tr aventurar ‖ intr aventurarse; **to venture on** arriesgarse en

venturesome ['vɛntʃərsəm] adj (bold, daring) aventurero; (hazardous) aventurado

venturous ['vɛntʃərəs] adj (bold, daring) aventurero; (hazardous) aventurado, arriesgado

venue ['vɛnju] s (law) lugar m del crimen; (law) lugar donde se reúne el jurado; **change of venue** (law) traslado de jurisdicción

Venus ['vinəs] s (astr) Venus m; (myth) Venus f; (very beautiful woman) Venus f

veracious [vɪ'reʃəs] adj veraz

veraci·ty [vɪ'ræsɪti] s (pl -ties) veracidad

veranda o **verandah** [və'rændə] s terraza, veranda, galería

verb [vʌrb] adj verbal ‖ s verbo

verbatim [vər'betɪm] adj textual ‖ adv palabra por palabra, al pie de la letra

verbena [vər'binə] s (bot) verbena

verbiage ['vʌrbɪ·ɪdʒ] s palabrería, verbosidad

verbose [vər'bos] adj verboso

verdant ['vʌrdənt] adj verde; cándido, sencillo

verdict ['vʌrdɪkt] s veredicto, fallo

verdigris ['vʌrdɪ,gris] s verdete m

verdure ['vʌrdʒər] s verdor m

verge [vʌrdʒ] s borde m, límite m; (of a column) fuste m; báculo; (eccl) cetro; **on the verge of** al borde de; a punto de; **within the verge of** al alcance de ‖ intr — **to verge on** o **upon** llegar casi hasta, rayar en

verification [,vɛrɪfɪ'keʃən] s verificación

veri·fy ['vɛrɪ,faɪ] v (pret & pp -fied) tr verificar, comprobar; (law) afirmar bajo juramento

va
ve

verily ['vɛrɪli] *adv* verdaderamente, en verdad

veritable ['vɛrɪtəbəl] *adj* verdadero

vermicelli [,vʌrmɪ'sɛli] *s* fideos

vermilion [vər'mɪljən] *adj* bermejo ‖ *s* bermellón *m*

vermin ['vʌrmɪn] *ssg* (*objectionable person*) sabandija ‖ *spl* (*objectionable animals or persons*) sabandijas

vermouth [vər'muθ] o ['vʌrmuθ] *s* vermú *m*

vernacular [vər'nækjələr] *adj* vernáculo ‖ *s* lenguaje vernáculo; idioma *m* corriente; (*language peculiar to a class or profession*) jerga

veronica [vɛ'rɑnɪkə] *s* (bot & taur) verónica; lienzo de la Verónica

Versailles [vɛr'saɪ] *s* Versalles

versatile ['vʌrsətɪl] *adj* (*person*) de muchas habilidades; (*informed on many subjects*) polifacético, universal; (*device or tool*) útil para muchas cosas

verse [vʌrs] *s* verso; (*in the Bible*) versículo

versed [vʌrst] *adj* versado; **to become versed in** versarse en

versification [,vʌrsɪfɪ'keʃən] *s* versificación

versi·fy ['vʌrsɪ ,faɪ] *v* (*pret & pp* **-fied**) *tr & intr* versificar

version ['vʌrʒən] *s* versión

ver·so ['vʌrso] *s* (*pl* **-sos**) (*e.g., of a coin*) reverso; (typ) verso

versus ['vʌrsəs] *prep* contra

verte·bra ['vʌrtɪbrə] *s* (*pl* **-brae** [,bri] o **-bras**) vértebra

vertebrate ['vʌrtɪ ,bret] *adj & s* vertebrado

ver·tex ['vʌrtɛks] *s* (*pl* **-texes** o **-tices** [tɪ ,siz]) (*top, summit*) ápice *m*; (geom) vértice *m*

vertical ['vʌrtɪkəl] *adj & s* vertical *f*

vertical hold *s* (telv) bloqueo vertical

vertical rudder *s* (aer) timón *m* de dirección

verti·go ['vʌrtɪ ,go] *s* (*pl* **-gos** o **-goes**) vértigo

verve [vʌrv] *s* brío, ánimo, vigor *m*

very ['vɛri] *adj* mismísimo; (*sheer, utter*) mero, puro; (*actual*) verdadero ‖ *adv* muy; mucho, p.ej., **to be very hungry** tener mucha hambre

vesicle ['vɛsɪkəl] *s* vesícula

vesper ['vɛspər] *s* tarde *f*, caída de la tarde; oración de la tarde; canción de la tarde; **vespers** (eccl) vísperas ‖ **Vesper** *s* Véspero

vesper bell *s* campana que llama a vísperas

vessel ['vɛsəl] *s* vasija, recipiente *m*; (*ship*) bajel *m*, embarcación, buque *m*; (anat) vaso

vest [vɛst] *s* (*of man's suit*) chaleco; (*jabot*) chorrera; (*undershirt*) camiseta ‖ *tr* vestir; **to vest in** conceder (*p.ej., poder*) a; **to vest with** investir de ‖ *intr* vestirse; **to vest in** pasar a

vested interests *spl* intereses creados

vestibule ['vɛstɪ ,bjul] *s* vestíbulo, zaguán *m*

vestige ['vɛstɪdʒ] *s* vestigio

vestment ['vɛstmənt] *s* vestidura

vest'-pock'et *adj* de bolsillo, en miniatura; diminuto

ves·try ['vɛstri] *s* (*pl* **-tries**) sacristía; (*chapel*) capilla; junta parroquial; reunión de la junta parroquial

vestry·man ['vɛstrimən] *s* (*pl* **-men** [mən]) miembro de la junta parroquial

Vesuvius [vɪ'suvɪ·əs] o [vɪ'sjuvɪ·əs] *s* el Vesubio

vet. *abbr* **veteran, veterinary**

vetch [vɛtʃ] *s* arveja, veza; (*grass pea*) almorta

veteran ['vɛtərən] *adj & s* veterano

veterinarian [,vɛtərɪ'nɛrɪ·ən] *s* veterinario

veterinar·y ['vɛtərɪ ,nɛri] *adj* veterinario ‖ *s* (*pl* **-ies**) veterinario

veterinary medicine *s* veterinaria, medicina veterinaria

ve·to ['vito] *s* (*pl* **-toes**) veto ‖ *tr* vetar

vex [vɛks] *tr* vejar, molestar

vexation [vɛk'seʃən] *s* vejación, molestia

v.g. *abbr* **verbi gratia** (Lat) **for example**

via ['vaɪ·ə] *prep* vía, p.ej., **via Lisbon** vía Lisboa

viaduct ['vaɪ·ə ,dʌkt] *s* viaducto

vial ['vaɪ·əl] *s* redoma, frasco pequeño

viati·cum ['vaɪ'ætɪkəm] *s* (*pl* **-cums** o **-ca** [kə]) (eccl) viático

viand ['vaɪ·ənd] *s* vianda, manjar *m*

vibrate ['vaɪbret] *tr & intr* vibrar

vibration [vaɪ'breʃən] *s* vibración

vicar ['vɪkər] *s* vicario

vicarage ['vɪkərɪdʒ] *s* casa del vicario; (*duties of vicar*) vicaría

vicarious [vaɪ'kɛrɪ·əs] o [vɪ'kɛrɪ·əs] *adj* substituto; (*punishment*) sufrido por otro; (*power, authority*) delegado; (*enjoyment*) reflejado

vice [vaɪs] *s* vicio

vice'-ad'miral *s* vicealmirante *m*

vice'-pres'ident *s* vicepresidente *m*

viceroy ['vaɪsrɔɪ] *s* virrey *m*

vice versa ['vaɪsi 'vʌrsə] o ['vaɪs 'vʌrsə] *adv* viceversa

vicini·ty [vɪ'sɪnɪti] *s* (*pl* **-ties**) vecindad

vicious ['vɪʃəs] *adj* vicioso; (*dog*) bravo; (*horse*) arisco

victim ['vɪktɪm] *s* víctima

victimize ['vɪktɪ ,maɪz] *tr* hacer víctima; engañar, estafar

victor ['vɪktər] *s* vencedor *m*

victorious [vɪk'torɪ·əs] *adj* victorioso

victo·ry ['vɪktəri] *s* (*pl* **-ries**) victoria

victuals ['vɪtəlz] *spl* vituallas, provisiones de boca

vid. *abbr* **vide** (Lat) **see**

video signal ['vɪdɪ ,o] *s* señal *f* de vídeo

video tape *s* cinta grabada de televisión

vid'eo-tape' recording *s* videograbación

vie [vaɪ] *v* (*pret & pp* **vied;** *ger* **vying**) *intr* competir, emular, rivalizar

Vien·nese [,vi·ə'niz] *adj* vienés ‖ *s* (*pl* **-nese**) vienés *m*

Vietnam·ese [vɪ ,ɛtnə'miz] *adj* vietnamés ‖ *s* (*pl* **-ese**) vietnamés *m*

view [vju] *s* vista; (*purpose*) propósito, vista; **to be on view** estar expuesto (*p.ej., un cadáver*); **to keep in view** no perder de vista; no olvidar, tener presente; **to take a dim view of** no entusiasmarse por, mirar escépticamente; **with a view to** con vistas a ‖ *tr* ver, mirar; considerar, contemplar; examinar, inspeccionar

viewer ['vju.ər] *s* espectador *m;* telespectador *m,* televidente *mf;* proyector *m* de transparencias; mirador *m* de transparencias

view finder *s* (phot) visor *m*

view'point' *s* punto de vista

vigil ['vɪdʒɪl] *s* vigilia; **to keep vigil** velar

vigilance ['vɪdʒɪləns] *s* vigilancia

vigilant ['vɪdʒɪlənt] *adj* vigilante

vignette [vɪn'jɛt] *s* viñeta

vigor ['vɪgər] *s* vigor *m*

vigorous ['vɪgərəs] *adj* vigoroso

vile [vaɪl] *adj* vil; *(disgusting)* asqueroso, repugnante; *(weather)* muy malo

vili·fy ['vɪlɪˌfaɪ] *v* (*pret & pp* **-fied**) *tr* difamar, denigrar

villa ['vɪlə] *s* villa, quinta

village ['vɪlɪdʒ] *s* aldea

villager ['vɪlɪdʒər] *s* aldeano

villain ['vɪlən] *s* malvado; *(of a play)* malo, traidor *m*

villainous ['vɪlənəs] *adj* malvado

villain·y ['vɪləni] *s* (*pl* **-ies**) maldad, perfidia

vim [vɪm] *s* fuerza, brío, vigor *m*

vinaigrette [ˌvɪnə'grɛt] *s* vinagrera

vinaigrette sauce *s* vinagreta

vindicate ['vɪndɪˌket] *tr* vindicar, exculpar

vindictive [vɪn'dɪktɪv] *adj* vengativo

vine [vaɪn] *s* *(creeping or climbing plant)* enredadera; *(grape plant)* vid *f,* parra

vine'dress'er *s* viñador *m,* viticultor *m*

vinegar ['vɪnɪgər] *s* vinagre *m*

vinegarish ['vɪnɪgərɪʃ] *adj* avinagrado

vinegary ['vɪnɪgəri] *adj* vinagroso

vineyard ['vɪnjərd] *s* viña, viñedo

vineyardist ['vɪnjərdɪst] *s* viñador *m,* viticultor *m*

vintage ['vɪntɪdʒ] *s* vendimia; vino de buena cosecha; (coll) categoría, clase *f*

vintager ['vɪntɪdʒər] *s* vendimiador *m*

vintage wine *s* vino de buena cosecha

vintage year *s* año de buen vino

vintner ['vɪntnər] *s* vinatero

vinyl ['vaɪnɪl] *s* vinilo

violate ['vaɪ·əˌlet] *tr* violar

violence ['vaɪ·ələns] *s* violencia

violent ['vaɪ·ələnt] *adj* violento

violet ['vaɪ·əlɪt] *adj* violado ‖ *s* *(color)* violeta *m,* violado; *(dye)* violeta *m;* (bot) violeta *f*

violin [ˌvaɪ·ə'lɪn] *s* violín *m*

violinist [ˌvaɪ·ə'lɪnɪst] *s* violinista *mf*

violoncellist [ˌvaɪ·ələn't'ʃɛlɪst] o [ˌvi·ələn't'ʃɛlɪst] *s* violoncelista *mf*

violoncel·lo [ˌvaɪ·ələn't'ʃɛlo] o [ˌvi·ələn't'ʃɛlo] *s* (*pl* **-los**) violoncelo

viper ['vaɪpər] *s* víbora

vira·go [vɪ'rego] *s* (*pl* **-goes** o **-gos**) mujer de mal genio

virgin ['vʌrdʒɪn] *adj & s* virgen *f*

virgin birth *s* parto virginal de María Santísima; (zool) partenogénesis *f*

Virginia creeper [vər'dʒɪnɪ·ə] *s* (bot) guau *m*

virginity [vər'dʒɪnɪti] *s* virginidad

virility [vɪ'rɪlɪti] *s* virilidad

virology [vaɪ'rɑlədʒi] *s* virología

virtual ['vʌrtʃu·əl] *adj* virtual

virtue ['vʌrtʃu] *s* virtud

virtuosi·ty [ˌvʌrtʃu'ɑsɪti] *s* (*pl* **-ties**) virtuosismo

virtuo·so [ˌvʌrtʃu'oso] *s* (*pl* **-sos** o **-si** [si]) virtuoso

virtuous ['vʌrtʃu·əs] *adj* virtuoso

virulence ['vɪrjələns] *s* virulencia

virulent ['vɪrjələnt] *adj* virulento

virus ['vaɪrəs] *s* virus *m*

Vis. *abbr* **Viscount**

visa ['vizə] *s* visa ‖ *tr* visar

visage ['vɪzɪdʒ] *s* cara, semblante *m;* aspecto, apariencia

vis-à-vis [ˌvizə'vi] *adj* enfrentados ‖ *adv* frente a frente ‖ *prep* enfrente de; respecto de

viscera ['vɪsərə] *spl* vísceras

viscount ['vaɪkaunt] *s* vizconde *m*

viscountess ['vaɪkauntɪs] *s* vizcondesa

viscous ['vɪskəs] *adj* viscoso

vise [vaɪs] *s* tornillo, torno

visé ['vize] o [vi'ze] *s & tr* var de **visa**

visible ['vɪzɪbəl] *adj* visible

Visigoth ['vɪzɪˌgɑθ] *s* visigodo

vision ['vɪʒən] *s* visión; *(sense of sight)* vista

visionar·y ['vɪʒəˌnɛri] *adj* visionario ‖ *s* (*pl* **-ies**) visionario

visit ['vɪzɪt] *s* visita ‖ *tr* visitar; afligir, acometer; enviar *(p.ej., castigo, venganza)* ‖ *intr* hacer visitas; visitarse *(dos o más personas)*

visitation [ˌvɪzɪ'teʃən] *s* visitación; gracia del cielo, castigo del cielo

visiting card *s* tarjeta de visita

visiting hours *spl* horas de visita

visiting nurse *s* enfermera ambulante

visitor ['vɪzɪtər] *s* visitante *mf*

visor ['vaɪzər] *s* visera; *(disguise)* máscara

vista ['vɪstə] *s* vista, panorama *m*

visual ['vɪʒu·əl] *adj* visual

visual acuity *s* agudeza visual

visualize ['vɪʒu·əˌlaɪz] *tr* representarse en la mente; hacer visible

vital ['vaɪtəl] *adj* vital; *(deadly)* mortal ‖ **vitals** *spl* partes *fpl* vitales, órganos vitales

vitality [vaɪ'tælɪti] *s* vitalidad

vitalize ['vaɪtəˌlaɪz] *tr* vitalizar

vitamin ['vaɪtəmɪn] *s* vitamina

vitiate ['vɪʃɪˌet] *tr* viciar

vitreous ['vɪtrɪ·əs] *adj* vítreo

vitriolic [ˌvɪtrɪ'ɑlɪk] *adj* (chem) vitriólico; (fig) cáustico, mordaz

vituperable [vaɪ'tupərəbəl] o [vaɪ'tjupərəbəl] *adj* vituperable

vituperate [vaɪ'tupəˌret] o [vaɪ'tjupəˌret] *tr* vituperar

viva ['viva] *interj* ¡viva! ‖ *s* viva *m*

vivacious [vɪ've·əs] o [vaɪ've·əs] *adj* vivaz, vivaracho

vivaci·ty [vɪ'væsɪti] o [vaɪ'væsɪti] *s* (*pl* **-ties**) vivacidad, animación

viva voce ['vaɪvə 'vosi] *adv* de viva voz

vivid ['vɪvɪd] adj vivo (intenso; brillante; expresivo)

vivi·fy ['vɪvɪ,faɪ] v (pret & pp **-fied**) tr vivificar

vivisection [,vɪvɪ'sɛkʃən] s vivisección

vixen ['vɪksən] s vulpeja; mujer regañona y colérica

viz. abbr **videlicet** (Lat) namely, to wit

vizier [vɪ'zɪr] o ['vɪzjər] s visir m

vocabular·y [vo'kæbjə,lɛri] s (pl **-ies**) vocabulario

vocal ['vokəl] adj vocal; (inclined to express oneself freely) expresivo

vocalist ['vokəlɪst] s vocalista mf

vocation [vo'keʃən] s vocación; empleo, ocupación

vocative ['vakətɪv] s vocativo

vociferate [vo'sɪfə,ret] intr vociferar

vociferous [vo'sɪfərəs] adj clamoroso, vocinglero

vogue [vog] s boga, moda; **in vogue** en boga, de moda

voice [vɔɪs] s voz f; **in a loud voice** en alta voz; **in a low voice** en voz baja; **with one voice** a una voz || tr expresar; sonorizar (una consonante sorda) || intr sonorizarse

voiceless ['vɔɪslɪs] adj sin voz; mudo; silencioso; (phonet) sordo

void [vɔɪd] adj (empty) vacío; (useless) vano; (law) inválido, nulo; **void of** desprovisto de || s vacío; (gap) hueco || tr vaciar; evacuar (el vientre); anular || intr excretar

voile [vɔɪl] s espumilla

vol. abbr **volume**

volatile ['valətɪl] adj volátil

volatilize ['valətɪ,laɪz] tr volatilizar || intr volatilizarse

volcanic [val'kænɪk] adj volcánico

volca·no [val'keno] s (pl **-noes** o **-nos**) volcán m

volition [və'lɪʃən] s voluntad; **of one's own volition** por su propia voluntad

volley ['vali] s (of stones, bullets, etc.) descarga, lluvia; (mil) descarga; (tennis) voleo || tr & intr volear

vol'ley·ball' s volibol m

volplane ['val,plen] s vuelo planeado || intr planear

volt [volt] s voltio

voltage ['voltɪdʒ] s voltaje m

voltage divider s (rad) divisor m de voltaje

voltaic [val'te·ɪk] adj voltaico

volte-face [volt'fas] s cambio de dirección; cambio de opinión

volt'me'ter s voltímetro

voluble ['valjəbəl] adj locuaz, hablador

volume ['valjəm] s (book; bulk; mass, e.g., of water) volumen m; (each book in a set) tomo; (degree of loudness) volumen sonoro; (geom) volumen m; **to speak volumes** ser muy significativo; ser muy expresivo

voluminous [və'lumɪnəs] adj voluminoso

voluntar·y ['valən,tɛri] adj voluntario || s (pl **-ies**) (eccl) solo de órgano

volunteer [,valən'tɪr] adj & s voluntario || tr ofrecer (sus servicios) || intr ofrecerse; servir como volunta-

rio; **to volunteer to** + inf ofrecerse a + inf

voluptuar·y [və'lʌptʃu,ɛri] adj voluptuoso || s (pl **-ies**) voluptuoso, sibarita mf

voluptuous [və'lʌptʃu·əs] adj voluptuoso

volute [və'lut] s voluta

vomit ['vamɪt] s vómito; (emetic) vomitivo || tr & intr vomitar

voodoo ['vudu] adj voduísta || s (practice) vodú m; (person) voduísta mf

voracious [və'reʃəs] adj voraz

voracity [və'ræsɪti] s voracidad

vor·tex ['vɔrtɛks] s (pl **-texes** o **-tices** [tɪ,siz]) vórtice m

vota·ry ['votəri] s (pl **-ries**) persona ligada por votos solemnes; aficionado, partidario

vote [vot] s (formal expression of choice; right to vote; person who votes) voto; (act of voting; votes considered together) votación; **to put to the vote** poner a votación; **to tally the votes** regular los votos || tr votar (sí, no); **to vote down** derrotar por votación; **to vote in** elegir por votación || intr votar

vote getter ['gɛtər] s acaparador m de votos; (slogan) consigna que gana votos

voter ['votər] s votante mf

voting machine ['votɪŋ] s máquina registradora de votos

votive ['votɪv] adj votivo

votive offering s voto, exvoto

vouch [vautʃ] tr garantizar || intr — **to vouch for** responder de (una cosa); responder por (una persona)

voucher ['vautʃər] s garante mf; (certificate) comprobante m

vouch·safe' tr conceder, otorgar; permitir || intr — **to vouchsafe to** + inf dignarse + inf

voussoir [vu'swar] s dovela

vow [vau] s voto; **to take vows** tomar el hábito religioso || tr votar (p.ej., un cirio a la Virgen); jurar (venganza) || intr votar; **to vow to** hacer votos de

vowel ['vau·əl] s vocal f

voyage ['vɔɪ·ɪdʒ] s travesía, trayecto; (any journey) viaje m || tr atravesar (p.ej., el mar) || intr viajar

voyager ['vɔɪ·ɪdʒər] s pasajero, navegante mf, viajero

V.P. abbr **Vice-President**

vs. abbr **versus**

Vul. abbr **Vulgate**

vulcanize ['vʌlkə,naɪz] tr vulcanizar

vulg. abbr **vulgar**

Vulg. abbr **Vulgate**

vulgar ['vʌlgər] adj grosero; (popular, common; vernacular) vulgar

vulgari·ty [vʌl'gærɪti] s (pl **-ties**) grosería

Vulgar Latin s latín vulgar, latín rústico

Vulgate ['vʌlget] s Vulgata

vulnerable ['vʌlnərəbəl] adj vulnerable

vulture ['vʌltʃər] s buitre m; (American vulture) catartes m, aura (buitre americano)

W

W, w ['dʌbəl ,ju] vigésima tercera letra del alfabeto inglés

w *abbr* **watt**

w. *abbr* **week, west, wide, wife**

W. *abbr* **Wednesday, west**

wad [wɑd] *s* (*of cotton*) bolita, tapón *m;* (*of papers*) fajo, lío; (*in a gun*) taco ‖ *v* (*pret & pp* **wadded;** *ger* **wadding**) *tr* emborrar, rellenar; atacar (*una escopeta*)

waddle ['wɑdəl] *s* anadeo ‖ *intr* anadear

wade [wed] *intr* andar sobre terreno cubierto de agua; andar descalzo por la orilla; chapotear (*los niños*) con los pies desnudos; **to wade into** (coll) embestir con violencia; (coll) meter el hombro a; **to wade through** (coll) avanzar con dificultad por; (coll) leer con dificultad

wading bird ['wedɪŋ] *s* ave zancuda

wafer ['wefər] *s* (*for sealing letters; pill*) oblea; (*thin, crisp cake*) hostia; (eccl) hostia

waffle ['wɑfəl] *s* barquillo

waffle iron *s* barquillero

waft [wæft] o [wɑft] *tr* llevar por el aire; llevar por encima del agua ‖ *intr* flotar

wag [wæg] *s* (*of head*) meneo; (*of tail*) coleada; (*jester*) bromista *mf* ‖ *v* (*pret & pp* **wagged;** *ger* **wagging**) *tr* menear (*la cabeza, la cola*) ‖ *intr* menearse

wage [wedʒ] *s* salario; **wages** galardón *m,* premio ‖ *tr* hacer (*la guerra*)

wage earner ['ʌrnər] *s* asalariado

wager ['wedʒər] *s* apuesta; **to lay a wager** hacer una apuesta ‖ *tr & intr* apostar

wage′work′er *s* asalariado

waggish ['wægɪʃ] *adj* divertido, gracioso; (*person*) bromista

Wagnerian [vɑg'nɪrɪ·ən] *adj & s* vagneriano

wagon ['wægən] *s* carro, furgón *m,* carretón *m;* **on the wagon** (slang) sin tomar bebidas alcohólicas; **to hitch one's wagon to a star** poner el tiro muy alto

wag′tail′ *s* aguanieves *m,* aguzanieves *m*

waif [wef] *s* (*foundling*) expósito; animal extraviado o abandonado; (*stray child*) granuja *m*

wail [wel] *s* gemido, lamento ‖ *intr* gemir, lamentar

wain·scot ['wenskət] o ['wenskɑt] *s* arrimadillo, friso de madera ‖ *v* (*pret & pp* **-scoted** o **-scotted;** *ger* **-scoting** o **-scotting**) *tr* poner arrimadillo o friso de madera a

waist [west] *s* (*of human body; corresponding part of garment*) talle *m,* cintura; (*garment*) corpiño, jubón *m,* blusa

waist′band′ *s* pretina

waist′cloth′ *s* taparrabo

waistcoat ['west ,kot] o ['weskət] *s* chaleco

waist′line′ *s* cintura

wait [wet] *s* espera; **to have a good wait** (coll) esperar sentado; **to lie in wait for** acechar emboscado ‖ *tr* — **to wait one's turn** esperar vez ‖ *intr* esperar, aguardar; **to wait for** esperar, aguardar; **to wait on** atender, despachar (*a los parroquianos en una tienda*); servir (*a una persona a la mesa*); **to wait until** esperar a que

waiter ['wetər] *s* camarero, mozo de restaurante; (*tray*) bandeja

waiting list *s* lista de espera

waiting room *s* (*of station*) sala de espera; (*of doctor's office*) antesala

waitress ['wetrɪs] *s* camarera, moza de restaurante

waive [wev] *tr* renunciar a (*un derecho*); diferir, poner a un lado

waiver ['wevər] *s* renuncia

wake [wek] *s* (*watch by the body of a dead person*) velatorio; (*of a boat or other moving object*) estela; **in the wake of** siguiendo inmediatamente; de resultas de ‖ *v* (*pret* **waked** o **woke** [wok]; *pp* **waked**) *tr* despertar ‖ *intr* — **to wake to** darse cuenta de; **to wake up** despertar

wakeful ['wekfəl] *adj* desvelado

wakefulness ['wekfəlnɪs] *s* desvelo

waken ['wekən] *tr & intr* despertar

wale [wel] *s* verdugón *m*

Wales [welz] *s* Gales, el país de Gales

walk [wɔk] *s* (*act*) paseo; (*distance*) caminata; (*way of walking, bearing*) andar *m,* paso; (*of a horse*) andadura; (*place to walk animals*) cercado; empleo, cargo, carrera; **at a walk** al paso de una persona; **to go for a walk** salir a pasear; **to take a walk** dar un paseo ‖ *tr* pasear (*a un niño, un caballo*); caminar (*recorrer caminando*); hacer ir al paso (*un caballo*); **to walk off** quitarse (*p.ej., un dolor de cabeza*) caminando ‖ *intr* andar, caminar, ir a pie; (*to stroll*) pasear; **to walk away from** alejarse caminando de; **to walk off with** cargar con, llevarse; **to walk out** salir repentinamente; declararse en huelga; **to walk out on** (coll) dejar airadamente

walkaway ['wɔkə ,we] *s* (coll) triunfo fácil

walker ['wɔkər] *s* caminante *mf;* (*pedestrian*) peatón *m;* (*gocart*) andaderas

walkie-talkie ['wɔki'tɔki] *s* (rad) transmisor-receptor *m* portátil

walking papers *spl* (coll) despedida de un empleo

walking stick *s* bastón *m*

walk′-on′ *s* (theat) parte *f* de por medio

walk′out′ *s* (coll) huelga

walk′o′ver *s* (coll) triunfo fácil

wall [wɔl] *s* muro; (*between rooms; of a pipe, boiler, etc.*) pared *f;* (*of a* *fortification)* muralla; **to drive to the wall** poner entre la espada y la pared; **to go to the wall** rendirse; fracasar || *tr* murar, amurallar *(una ciudad, un castillo)*; emparedar *(a un criminal)*; **to wall up** cerrar con muro

wall′board′ *s* cartón *m* tabla

wallet ['walɪt] *s* cartera de bolsillo

wall′flow′er *s* alhelí *m;* **to be a wall-flower** (coll) comer pavo, planchar el asiento

Walloon [wɑ'lun] *adj & s* valón *m*

wallop ['waləp] *s* (coll) golpazo, puñetazo || *tr* (coll) golpear fuertemente; (coll) vencer cabalmente

wallow ['walo] *s* revuelco; *(place)* revolcadero || *intr* revolcarse; *(e.g., in wealth)* nadar

wall′pa′per *s* papel *m* de empapelar, papel pintado || *tr* empapelar

walnut ['wɔlnʌt] *s (tree and wood)* nogal *m;* nuez *f* de nogal

walrus ['wɔlrəs] o ['wɑlrəs] *s* morsa

Walter ['wɔltər] *s* Gualterio

waltz [wɔlts] *s* vals *m* || *tr* hacer valsar; (coll) conducir directamente || *intr* valsar

wan [wɑn] *adj (comp* **wanner;** *super* **wannest)** pálido, macilento; débil

wand [wɑnd] *s* vara; *(of deviner or magician)* varilla de virtudes

wander ['wɑndər] *tr* recorrer a la ventura || *intr* errar, vagar; extraviarse, perderse; **to wander around** errar de una parte a otra

wanderer ['wɑndərər] *s* vagabundo; peregrino

wan′der·lust′ *s* ansia de viajar

wane [wen] *s* decadencia, declinación; menguante *f* de la luna; **on the wane** decayendo, declinando; menguando *(la luna)* || *intr* decaer, declinar; menguar *(la luna)*

wangle ['wæŋgəl] *tr (to obtain by scheming)* (coll) mamar o mamarse; (coll) adulterar, falsear *(cuentas)* || **to wangle one's way out of** (coll) salir con maña de || *intr (to get along by scheming)* (coll) sacudirse

want [wɑnt] o [wɔnt] *s* deseo; necesidad; carencia; **for want of** a falta de; **to be in want** pasar necesidad || *tr* desear; necesitar; carecer de || *intr* desear; **to want for** necesitar; carecer

want ad *s* anuncio clasificado

wanton ['wɑntən] *adj* inconsiderado, desconsiderado; insensible, perverso; disoluto, licencioso; lascivo; cabezudo

war [wɔr] *s* guerra; **to go to war** declarar la guerra; *(as a soldier)* ir a la guerra; **to wage war** hacer la guerra || *v (pret & pp* **warred;** *ger* **warring)** *intr* guerrear; **to war on** guerrear con, hacer la guerra a

warble ['wɔrbəl] *s* gorjeo, trino || *intr* gorjear, trinar

warbler ['wɔrblər] *s* pájaro cantor; curruca de cabeza negra

war cloud *s* amenaza de guerra

ward [wɔrd] *s (person, usually a minor, under protection of another)* pupilo; *(guardianship)* custodia, tutela; *(of a city)* barrio, distrito; *(of a hospital)* cuadra, crujía; *(of a lock)* guarda || *tr* — **to ward off** parar, desviar

warden ['wɔrdən] *s* guardián *m;* *(of a jail)* alcaide *m,* carcelero; *(of a church)* capiller *m;* *(in charge of fire prevention)* vigía *m*

ward heeler *s* muñidor *m*

ward′robe′ *s (closet or cabinet for holding clothes)* guardarropa *m;* *(stock of clothing for a person)* vestuario; (theat) guardarropía

wardrobe trunk *s* baúl ropero

ward′room′ *s* (nav) cámara de oficiales

ware [wer] *s* loza; **wares** efectos, artículos de comercio, mercancías

war effort *s* esfuerzo bélico

ware′house′ *s* almacén *m;* *(for furniture)* guardamuebles *m*

warehouse·man ['wer,hausmən] *s (pl* **-men** [mən]) almacenista *m;* guarda-almacén *m*

war′fare′ *s* guerra

war′head′ *s* punta de combate

war horse *s* corcel *m* de guerra; (coll) veterano

warily ['werɪli] *adv* cautelosamente

wariness ['werɪnɪs] *s* cautela

war′like′ *adj* guerrero

war loan *s* empréstito de guerra

war lord *s* jefe *m* militar

warm [wɔrm] *adj (being moderately hot)* caliente; *(neither hot nor cold)* templado; *(clothing)* abrigador; *(climate, region)* caluroso; *(color)* cálido; (fig) caluroso, cordial; **to be warm** *(said of a person)* tener calor; *(said of the weather)* hacer calor || *tr* calentar, acalorar; (fig) animar, acalorar; **to warm up** recalentar *(p.ej., la comida)*; hacer más amistoso || *intr* calentarse; **to warm up** templar *(el tiempo)*; *(with work or exercise)* acalorarse; **to warm up to** cobrar afecto a

warm-blooded ['wɔrm'blʌdɪd] *adj* apasionado, ardiente; *(animals)* de sangre caliente

war memorial *s* monumento a los caídos

warmer ['wɔrmər] *s* calentador *m*

warm-hearted ['wɔrm'hɑrtɪd] *adj* afectuoso, de buen corazón

warming pan *s* mundillo

warmonger ['wɔr,mʌŋgər] *s* belicista *mf*

war mother *s* madrina de guerra

warmth [wɔrmθ] *s* calor *m;* ardor *m,* entusiasmo; cordialidad

warm′-up′ *s* calentón *m*

warn [wɔrn] *tr* advertir, avisar; *(to exhort)* amonestar; *(to advise)* aconsejar

warning *adj* de aviso || *s* advertencia, aviso

War of the Roses *s* guerra de las dos Rosas

warp [wɔrp] *s (of a fabric)* urdimbre *f;* *(of a board)* comba, alabeo; aberración mental; (naut) espía || *tr* combar, alabear; pervertir *(el juicio* *de una persona*); (naut) mover con espía || *intr* combarse, alabearse; (naut) espiar

war'path' *s* — **to be on the warpath** prepararse para la guerra; estar buscando pendencia

war'plane' *s* avión *m* de guerra

warrant ['wɑrənt] o ['wɔrənt] *s* garantía, promesa; (*for arrest*) orden *f* de prisión; (*before a judge*) citación; cédula, certificado || *tr* garantizar, prometer; autorizar; justificar

warrantable ['wɑrəntəbəl] o ['wɔrəntəbəl] *adj* garantizable; justificable

warrant officer *s* suboficial *m* de las clases

warren ['wɑrən] o ['wɔrən] *s* (*where rabbits breed*) conejera; barrio densamente poblado

warrior ['wɔrjər] o ['wɑrjər] *s* guerrero

Warsaw ['wɔrsɔ] *s* Varsovia

war'ship' *s* buque *m* de guerra

wart [wɔrt] *s* verruga

war'time' *s* tiempo de guerra

war'-torn' *adj* devastado por la guerra

war to the death *s* guerra a muerte

war·y ['weri] *adj* (*comp* -ier; *super* -iest) cauteloso

wash [wɑʃ] o [wɔʃ] *s* lavado; (*clothes washed or to be washed*) jabonado; (*dirty water*) lavazas; loción; (*place where surf breaks*) batiente *m*; (aer) estela turbulenta || *tr* lavar; fregar (*los platos*); bañar, mojar; **to wash away** quitar lavando; derrubiar (*las aguas corrientes la tierra de las riberas*) || *intr* lavarse; lavar la ropa; batir (*el agua*); derrubiarse

washable ['wɑʃəbəl] o ['wɔʃəbəl] *adj* lavable

wash and wear *adj* de lava y pon

wash'ba'sin *s* jofaina, palangana

wash'bas'ket *s* cesto de la colada

wash'board' *s* lavadero, tabla de lavar; (*baseboard*) rodapié *m*

wash'bowl' *s* jofaina, palangana

wash'cloth' *s* paño para lavarse

wash'day' *s* día *m* de la colada

washed-out ['wɑʃt ,aut] o ['wɔʃt ,aut] *adj* desteñido; (coll) debilitado, rendido

washed-up ['wɑʃt ,ʌp] o ['wɔʃt ,ʌp] *adj* (coll) agotado, deslomado

washer ['wɑʃər] o ['wɔʃər] *s* lavador *m*; (*machine*) lavadora; (*ring of metal placed under head of bolt*) arandela; (*ring of rubber, etc. to keep a spigot from leaking*) zapatilla; (phot) lavador

wash'er·wom'an *s* (*pl* -wom'en) lavandera

wash goods *spl* tejidos lavables

washing ['wɑʃɪŋ] o ['wɔʃɪŋ] *s* (*act of washing; washed clothes or clothes to be washed*) lavado; **washings** (*dirty water; abraded material*) lavadura

washing machine *s* lejiadora, lavadora mecánica

washing soda *s* sal *f* de sosa

wash'out' *s* derrubio; derrumbe *m*; (coll) desilusión, fracaso

wash'rag' *s* paño para lavarse; paño de cocina

wash'room' *s* gabinete *m* de aseo, lavabo

wash'stand' *s* lavamanos *m*

wash'tub' *s* cuba de colada, tina de lavar

wash water *s* lavazas

wasp [wɑsp] *s* avispa

waste [west] *s* derroche *m*, desgaste *m*; (*garbage*) basura, despojo; (*wild region*) despoblado, yermo; (*of time*) pérdida; (*useless by-products*) desperdicios; excremento; (*for wiping machinery*) hilacha de algodón; **to lay waste** devastar, poner a fuego y sangre || *tr* malgastar, perder || *intr* — **to waste away** consumirse

waste'bas'ket *s* papelera

wasteful ['westfəl] *adj* derrochador, manirroto; devastador, destructivo

waste paper *s* papeles usados, papel de desecho, papel viejo

waste pipe *s* tubo de desagüe

waste products *spl* desperdicios; materia excretada

wastrel ['westrəl] *s* derrochador *m*, malgastador *m*; pródigo, desalmado

watch [wɑtʃ] *s* reloj *m* (*de bolsillo o de pulsera*); (*lookout*) vigía *m*; (mil) vigilia; (naut) guardia; **to be on the watch for** estar a la mira de; **to keep watch over** velar || *tr* (*to look at*) mirar; (*to oversee*) velar, vigilar; guardar; tener cuidado con || *intr* mirar; (*to keep awake*) velar; **to watch for** acechar; **to watch out** tener cuidado; **to watch out for** estar a la mira de; tener cuidado con; guardarse de; **to watch over** velar, vigilar

watch'case' *s* caja de reloj

watch charm *s* dije *m*

watch crystal *s* cristal *m* de reloj

watch'dog' *s* perro de guarda, perro guardián; (fig) guardián *m* fiel

watchful ['wɑtʃfəl] *adj* desvelado, vigilante

watchfulness ['wɑtʃfəlnɪs] *s* desvelo, vigilancia

watch'mak'er *s* relojero

watch·man ['wɑtʃmən] *s* (*pl* -men [mən]) vigilante *m*, velador *m*

watch night *s* noche vieja; oficio de noche vieja

watch pocket *s* relojera

watch strap *s* pulsera

watch'tow'er *s* atalaya, vigía

watch'word' *s* santo y seña; (*slogan*) lema *m*

water ['wɔtər] o ['wɑtər] *s* agua; **of the first water** de lo mejor; **to back water** ciar; **to carry water on both shoulders** nadar entre dos aguas; **to fish in troubled waters** pescar en río revuelto; **to hold water** (coll) ser bien fundado; **to make water** (*to urinate*) hacer aguas; (naut) hacer agua; **to pour o throw cold water on** echar un jarro de agua (fría) a || *tr* regar, rociar; abrevar (*el ganado*); aguar (*el vino*); proveer de agua || *intr* abrevarse (*el ganado*); tomar agua (*una locomotora*); llorar (*los ojos*)

water carrier *s* aguador *m*

water closet *s* excusado, retrete *m*, váter *m*

water color *s* acuarela

wa′ter·course′ *s* corriente *f* de agua; lecho de corriente

water cress *s* berzo

water cure *s* cura de aguas

wa′ter·fall′ *s* cascada, caída de agua

water front *s* terreno ribereño

water gap *s* garganta, hondonada

water hammer *s* golpe *m* de ariete

water heater *s* calentador *m* de agua

water ice *s* sorbete *m*

watering can *s* regadera

watering place *s* aguadero; balneario

watering pot *s* regadera

watering trough *s* abrevadero

water jacket *s* camisa de agua

water lily *s* ninfea, nenúfar *m*

water line *s* línea de agua, línea de flotación; nivel *m* de agua

water main *s* cañería de agua

wa′ter·mark′ *s* (*in paper*) filigrana; marca de nivel de agua

wa′ter·mel′on *s* sandía

water meter *s* contador *m* de agua

water pipe *s* cañería de agua

water polo *s* polo de agua

water power *s* fuerza de agua, hulla blanca

wa′ter·proof′ *adj & s* impermeable *m*

wa′ter·shed′ *s* divisoria de aguas; (*drainage area*) cuenca

water ski *s* esquí acuático

wa′ter·spout′ *s* (*to carry water from roof*) canalón *m*; (*funnel of wet air extending from cloud to surface of water*) manga de agua, tromba marina

wa′ter·sup·ply′ system *s* fontanería

wa′ter·tight′ *adj* estanco, hermético; (fig) seguro

water tower *s* arca de agua

water wagon *s* (mil) carro de agua; **on the water wagon** (slang) sin tomar bebidas alcohólicas

wa′ter·way′ *s* vía de agua, vía fluvial; (naut) canalizo

water wheel *s* rueda de agua; turbina de agua; (*of steamboat*) rueda de paletas

water wings *spl* nadaderas

wa′ter·works′ *s* estación de bombas

watery [′wɔtəri] o [′wɑtəri] *adj* acuoso; (*said of the eyes*) lagrimoso, lloroso; insípido; húmedo, mojado

watt [wɑt] *s* vatio

wattage [′wɑtɪdʒ] *s* vatiaje *m*

watt′-hour′ *s* (*pl* **watt-hours**) vatio-hora

wattle [′wɑtəl] *s* (*of bird*) barba; (*of fish*) barbilla

watt′me′ter *s* vatímetro

wave [wev] *s* onda; (*of hair*) onda, ondulación; (*e.g., of heat or cold*) ola; (*e.g., of strikes*) oleaje *m*; señal hecha con la mano ‖ *tr* blandir (*la espada*); ondear, ondular (*el cabello*); hacer señal con (*la mano*); decir (*adiós*) con la mano; **to wave**

aside rechazar ‖ *intr* ondear u ondearse; hacer señal con la mano

wave motion *s* movimiento ondulatorio

waver [′wevər] *intr* oscilar; (*to hesitate*) vacilar, titubear; (*to totter*) tambalear

wav·y [′wevi] *adj* (*comp* **-ier**; *super* **-iest**) undoso, ondoso; (*water*) ondulado; (*hair*) ondeado

wax [wæks] *s* cera; **to be wax in one's hands** ser como una cera ‖ *tr* encerar; cerotear (*el hilo*) ‖ *intr* hacerse, volverse; crecer (*la luna*)

wax paper *s* papel encerado, papel parafinado

wax taper *s* cerilla

wax′works′ *s* museo de cera

way [we] *s* vía, camino; dirección, sentido; manera, modo; costumbre, hábito; **across the way** enfrente; **a good way** un buen trecho; **all the way** hasta el fin del camino; **any way** de cualquier modo; **by the way** a propósito; **in a way** hasta cierto punto; **in every way** en todos respectos; **in this way** de este modo; **on the way to** camino de, rumbo a; **on the way out** saliendo; desapareciendo; **out of the way** hecho, despachado; inconveniente, impropio; a un lado, apartado; fuera de lo común; **that way** por allí; de ese modo; **this way** por aquí; de este modo; **to be in the way** estorbar; **to feel one's way** tantear el camino; proceder con tiento; **to force one's way** abrirse paso por fuerza; **to get out of the way** quitarse de en medio; (*to finish*) quitarse de encima; **to give way** ceder, retroceder; romperse (*una cuerda*); fracasar; **to give way to** entregarse a; **to go out of one's way** dar un rodeo; dar un rodeo innecesario; darse molestia; **to have one's way** salirse con la suya; **to keep out of the way** no obstruir el paso; **to know one's way around** saber entendérselas; **to know one's way to** conocer el camino a, saber ir a; **to lead the way** enseñar el camino; ir o entrar primero; **to lose one's way** perder el camino, extraviarse; **to make one's way** avanzar; hacer carrera, acreditarse; **to make way for** dar paso a, hacer lugar para; **to mend one's ways** mudar de vida; **to not know which way to turn** no saber dónde meterse; **to put out of the way** alejar, apartar; quitar de en medio; **to see one's way to** ver el modo de; **to take one's way** irse, marcharse; **to wend one's way** seguir camino; **to wind one's way through** serpentear por; **to wing one's way** ir volando; **under way** en marcha, en camino; vaya en entrada; **way out** salida; **ways** maneras, modales *mpl*; (*for launching a ship*) anguilas; **which way?** ¿por dónde?; ¿cómo?

way′bill′ *s* hoja de ruta

wayfarer [′we‚ferər] *s* caminante *mf*

way′lay′ *v* (*pret & pp* **-laid′**) *tr* detener de improviso; (*to attack from ambush*) insidiar, asaltar way'side' s borde m del camino; to fall by the wayside (to disappear) caer en el camino; fracasar

way station s apeadero

way train s tren m ómnibus

wayward ['wewərd] adj díscolo, voluntarioso; voltario, caprichoso

w.c. abbr water closet, without charge

we [wi] pron pers nosotros

weak [wik] adj débil, flaco; (vowel; verb) débil

weaken ['wikən] tr debilitar, enflaquecer || intr debilitarse, enflaquecerse

weakling ['wiklɪŋ] s alfeñique m, canijo

weak-minded ['wik'maɪndɪd] adj irresoluto; simple, mentecato

weakness ['wiknɪs] s debilidad, flaqueza; lado débil; afición, gusto

weal [wil] s verdugón m

wealth [welθ] s riqueza

wealth·y ['welθi] adj (comp -ier; super -iest) rico

wean [win] tr destetar; to wean away from apartar gradualmente de

weanling ['winlɪŋ] adj & s destetado

weapon ['wepən] s arma

wear [wer] s (act of wearing) uso; (clothing) ropa; estilo, moda; (wasting away from use) desgaste m, deterioro; (lasting quality) durabilidad; for all kinds of wear a todo llevar; for everyday wear para todo trote || v (pret wore [wor]; pp worn [worn]) tr llevar, traer, llevar puesto; calzar (cierto tamaño de zapato o guante); (to waste away by use) desgastar, deteriorar; (to tire) agotar, cansar; to wear out consumir, gastar; agotar, cansar; abusar de (la hospitalidad de una persona) || intr desgastarse, deteriorarse; to wear off pasar, desaparecer; to wear out gastarse, usarse; to wear well durar, ser duradero

wear and tear s uso y desgaste

weariness ['wɪrɪnɪs] s cansancio; aburrimiento

wearing apparel ['werɪŋ] s ropaje m, prendas de vestir

wearisome ['wɪrɪsəm] adj aburrido, cansado, fastidioso

wea·ry ['wɪri] adj (comp -rier; super -riest) cansado || v (pret & pp -ried) tr cansar || intr cansarse

weasel ['wizəl] s comadreja

weaseler ['wizələr] s pancista mf

weasel words spl palabras ambiguas

weather ['weðər] s tiempo; mal tiempo; to be under the weather (coll) no estar muy católico; (coll) estar borracho || tr aguantar (el temporal, la adversidad)

weather-beaten ['weðər,bitən] adj curtido por la intemperie

weather bureau s meteo f, servicio meteorológico

weath'er·cock' s veleta; (fickle person) (fig) veleta

weather forecasting s pronóstico del tiempo, previsión del tiempo

weather·man ['weðər,mæn] s (pl -men [,men]) meteorologista m, pronosticador m del tiempo

weather report s parte meteorológico

weather stripping ['strɪpɪŋ] s burlete m, cierre hermético

weather vane s veleta

weave [wiv] s tejido || v (pret wove [wov] o weaved; pp wove o woven ['wovən]) tr tejer; to weave one's way avanzar zigzagueando || intr tejer; zigzaguear

weaver ['wivər] s tejedor m

web [web] s tejido, tela; (of spider) tela; (between toes of birds and other animals) membrana; (of an iron rail) alma; (fig) tejido, tela; enredo

web-footed ['web,futɪd] adj palmípedo, de pie palmeado

wed [wed] v (pret & pp wed o wedded; ger wedding) tr (to join in marriage) casar; casarse con || intr casarse

wedding ['wedɪŋ] adj nupcial || s bodas, nupcias, matrimonio

wedding cake s pastel m de boda

wedding day s día m de bodas

wedding march s marcha nupcial

wedding night s noche f de bodas

wedding ring s anillo nupcial

wedge [wedʒ] s cuña || tr acuñar, apretar con cuña

wed'lock' s matrimonio

Wednesday ['wenzdi] s miércoles m

wee [wi] adj pequeñito, diminuto

weed [wid] s mala hierba; (coll) tabaco; weeds ropa de luto (especialmente, de una viuda) || tr desherbar, escardar

weeding hoe s escardillo

weed killer s matamalezas m, herbicida m

week [wik] s semana; week in week out semana tras semana

week'day' s día m laborable

week'end' s fin m de semana || intr pasar el fin de semana

week·ly ['wikli] adj semanal || adv cada semana || s (pl -lies) revista semanal, semanario

weep [wip] v (pret & pp wept [wept]) tr llorar (p.ej., la muerte de una persona); derramar (lágrimas) || intr llorar

weeper ['wipər] s llorón m; (hired mourner) llorona, plañidera

weeping willow s sauce m llorón

weep·y ['wipi] adj (comp -ier; super -iest) (coll) lloroso

weevil ['wivəl] s gorgojo

weft [weft] s (yarns running across warp) trama; (fabric) tejido

weigh [we] tr pesar; (naut) levantar (el ancla) || intr pesar; to weigh in pesarse (un jockey)

weight [wet] s peso; (of scales, clock, gymnasium, etc.) pesa; to lose weight rebajar de peso; to put on weight ponerse gordo; to throw one's weight around (coll) hacer valer su poder || tr cargar, gravar; (statistically) ponderar

weightless ['wetlɪs] adj ingrávido

weightlessness ['wetlɪsnɪs] s ingravidez f

weight·y ['weti] adj (comp -ier; super

-iest) (*heavy*) pesado; (*troublesome*) gravoso; importante, influyente

weir [wɪr] *s* presa, vertedero; (*for catching fish*) pescadera

weird [wɪrd] *adj* misterioso, sobrenatural, espectral; extraño, raro

welcome [ˈwɛlkəm] *adj* bienvenido; grato, agradable; **you are welcome** (*i.e., gladly received*) sea Vd. bienvenido; (*in answer to thanks*) no hay de qué; **you are welcome to it** está a la disposición de Vd.; **you are welcome to your opinion** piense Vd. lo que quiera || *interj* ¡bienvenido! || *s* bienvenida, buena acogida || *tr* dar la bienvenida a; acoger con gusto, recibir con amabilidad

weld [wɛld] *s* autógena; (bot) gualda || *tr* soldar con autógena; (fig) unir || *intr* soldarse

welder [ˈwɛldər] *s* soldador *m*; (*machine*) soldadora

welding [ˈwɛldɪŋ] *s* autógena, soldadura autógena

wel'fare' *s* bienestar *m*; (*effort to improve living conditions of the underprivileged*) asistencia, beneficencia; **to be on welfare** vivir de la asistencia pública

welfare state *s* gobierno socializante, estado de beneficencia

well [wɛl] *adj* bien; bien de salud || *adv* bien; pues; pues bien; **as well** también; **as well as** así como; **as well as** además de || *interj* ¡vaya! || *s* pozo; (*natural source of water*) fuente *f*, manantial *m* || *intr* — **to well up** salir a borbotones

well-appointed [ˈwɛləˈpɔɪntɪd] *adj* bien amueblado, bien equipado

well-attended [ˈwɛləˈtɛndɪd] *adj* muy concurrido

well-behaved [ˈwɛlbɪˈhevd] *adj* de buena conducta

well'-be'ing *s* bienestar *m*

well'born' *adj* bien nacido

well-bred [ˈwɛlˈbrɛd] *adj* cortés, bien criado

well-disposed [ˈwɛldɪsˈpozd] *adj* bien dispuesto

well-done [ˈwɛlˈdʌn] *adj* bien hecho; (*meat*) bien asado

well-fixed [ˈwɛlˈfɪkst] *adj* (coll) acaudalado

well-formed [ˈwɛlˈfɔrmd] *adj* bien formado; (*nose*) perfilado

well-founded [ˈwɛlˈfaʊndɪd] *adj* bien fundado

well-groomed [ˈwɛlˈgrumd] *adj* de mucho aseo, atildado

well-heeled [ˈwɛlˈhild] *adj* (coll) acomodado; **to be well-heeled** (coll) tener bien cubierto el riñón

well-informed [ˈwɛlɪnˈfɔrmd] *adj* versado, bien enterado

well-intentioned [ˈwɛlɪnˈtɛnʃənd] *adj* bien intencionado

well-kept [ˈwɛlˈkɛpt] *adj* bien cuidado, bien atendido; (*secret*) bien guardado

well-known [ˈwɛlˈnon] *adj* bien conocido; familiar

well-meaning [ˈwɛlˈminɪŋ] *adj* bien intencionado

well-nigh [ˈwɛlˈnaɪ] *adv* casi

well'-off' *adj* adinerado, acaudalado

well-preserved [ˈwɛlprɪˈzɜrvd] *adj* bien conservado

well-read [ˈwɛlˈrɛd] *adj* leído, muy leído

well-spent [ˈwɛlˈspɛnt] *adj* (*money, youth, life*) bien empleado

well-spoken [ˈwɛlˈspokən] *adj* (*person*) bienhablado; (*word*) bien dicho

well'spring' *s* fuente *f*, manantial *m*; fuente inagotable

well sweep *s* cigoñal *m*

well-tempered [ˈwɛlˈtɛmpərd] *adj* bien templado

well-thought-of [ˈwɛlˈθɔt ˌʌv] *adj* bien mirado

well-timed [ˈwɛlˈtaɪmd] *adj* oportuno

well-to-do [ˈwɛltəˈdu] *adj* adinerado, acaudalado

well-wisher [ˈwɛlˈwɪʃər] *s* amigo, favorecedor *m*

well-worn [ˈwɛlˈworn] *adj* trillado, vulgar

welsh [wɛlʃ] *intr* (slang) dejar de cumplir; **to welsh on** (slang) dejar de cumplir con || **Welsh** *adj* galés || *s* (*language*) galés *m*; **the Welsh** los galeses

Welsh-man [ˈwɛlʃmən] *s* (*pl* -men [mən]) galés *m*

Welsh rabbit *o* **rarebit** [ˈrɛrbɪt] *s* tostada cubierta de queso derretido en cerveza

welt [wɛlt] *s* (*finish along a seam*) ribete *m*; (*of a shoe*) vira; (*wale from a blow*) verdugón *m*

welter [ˈwɛltər] *s* confusión, conmoción; (*a tumbling about*) revuelco || *intr* revolcar

wel'ter-weight' *s* (box) peso mediano ligero

wen [wɛn] *s* lobanillo

wench [wɛntʃ] *s* muchacha, jovencita; moza, criada

wend [wɛnd] *tr* — **to wend one's way** dirigir sus pasos, seguir su camino

west [wɛst] *adj* occidental, del oeste || *adv* al oeste, hacia el oeste || *s* oeste *m*

western [ˈwɛstərn] *adj* occidental || *s* película del Oeste

West Indies [ˈɪndiz] *spl* Indias Occidentales

westward [ˈwɛstwərd] *adv* hacia el oeste

wet [wɛt] *adj* (*comp* **wetter;** *super* **wettest**) mojado; (*damp*) húmedo; (*paint*) fresco; (*weather*) lluvioso; (coll) antiprohibicionista || *s* (coll) antiprohibicionista *mf* || *v* (*pret & pp* **wet** *o* **wetted;** *ger* **wetting**) *tr* mojar || *intr* mojarse

wet'back' *s* mojado

wet battery *s* pila húmeda

wet blanket *s* aguafiestas *mf*

wet goods *spl* caldos

wet nurse *s* ama de cría o de leche

w.f. *abbr* wrong font

w.g. *abbr* wire gauge

whack [hwæk] *s* (coll) golpe ruidoso;

(coll) prueba, tentativa ‖ *tr* (coll) golpear ruidosamente

whale [hwel] *s* ballena; (*sperm whale*) cachalote *m;* **a whale at** (coll) un as de; **a whale for** (coll) un genio para; **a whale of a difference** (coll) una enorme diferencia; **a whale of a meal** (coll) una comida brutal ‖ *tr* (coll) azotar ‖ *intr* pescar ballenas

whale'bone' *s* ballena

wharf [hwɔrf] *s* (*pl* **wharves** [hwɔrvz] o **wharfs**) muelle *m*, embarcadero

what [hwɑt] *pron interr* qué; cuál; **what else?** ¿qué más?; **what if . . .?** ¿y si . . .?, ¿qué le parece si?; **what of it?** ¿qué importa? ‖ *pron rel* lo que; **what's what** lo que hay, toda la verdad ‖ *adj interr* qué ‖ *adj rel* el . . . que, la . . . que, etc. ‖ *interj* qué; **what a . . .!** qué . . . más o tan, p.ej., **what a beautiful day!** ¡qué día más (o tan) hermoso!

what·ev'er *pron* cualquiera; todo lo que ‖ *adj* cualquier; cualquier . . . que

what'not' *s* juguetero

what's-his-name ['hwɑtsɪz,nem] *s* (coll) el señor fulano

wheal [hwil] *s* roncha

wheat [hwit] *s* trigo

wheedle ['hwidəl] *tr* engatusar; conseguir por medio de halagos

wheel [hwil] *s* rueda; (coll) bicicleta; **at the wheel** en el volante ‖ *tr* pasear (*a un niño*) en un cochecito; conducir (*a un enfermo*) en una silla de ruedas ‖ *intr* (coll) ir en bicicleta; **to wheel about** o **around** dar una vuelta; cambiar de opinión

wheelbarrow ['hwil,bæro] *s* carretilla

wheel base *s* batalla, paso, distancia entre ejes

wheel chair *s* silla de ruedas, cochecillo para inválidos

wheeler-dealer ['hwilər'dilər] *s* (slang) negociante *m* de gran influencia e independencia

wheel horse *s* caballo de varas; (fig) esclavo (*el que trabaja mucho y cumple con sus obligaciones*)

wheelwright ['hwil,raɪt] *s* carpintero de carretas

wheeze [hwiz] *s* resuello ruidoso ‖ *intr* resollar produciendo un silbido

whelp [hwɛlp] *s* cachorro ‖ *intr* parir

when [hwɛn] *adv* cuándo ‖ *conj* cuando

whence [hwɛns] *adv* de dónde; por lo tanto ‖ *conj* de donde

when·ev'er *conj* siempre que, cada vez que

where [hwɛr] *adv* dónde; adónde ‖ *conj* donde; adonde

whereabouts ['hwɛrə,bauts] *s* paradero

whereas [hwɛr'æz] *conj* mientras que, al paso que; considerando ‖ *s* considerando

where·by' *adv* por medio del cual

wherefore ['hwɛrfor] *adv* por qué, para qué; por eso, por tanto ‖ *conj* por lo cual ‖ *s* motivo, razón *f*

where·from' *adv* de donde

where·in' *adv* dónde, en qué ‖ *conj* donde; en el que; en lo cual

where·of' *adv* de qué ‖ *conj* de que; de lo cual

where·up·on' *adv* con lo cual, después de lo cual

wherever [hwɛr'ɛvər] *conj* dondequiera que

wherewithal ['hwɛrwɪð,ɔl] *s* cumquibus *m*, medios

whet [hwet] *v* (*pret & pp* **whetted;** *ger* **whetting**) *tr* afilar, aguzar; despertar, estimular; abrir (*el apetito*)

whether ['wɛðər] *conj* si; **whether or no** en todo caso, de todas maneras; **whether or not** si . . . o no, ya sea que . . . o no

whet'stone' *s* piedra de afilar

whey [hwe] *s* suero de la leche

which [hwɪtʃ] *pron interr* cuál; **which is which** cuál es el uno y cuál el otro ‖ *pron rel* que, el (la, etc.) que ‖ *adj interr* qué, cuál, cuál de los (las) ‖ *adj rel* el (la, etc.) . . . que

which·ev'er *pron rel* cualquiera ‖ *adj rel* cualquier; **whichever ones** cualesquiera

whiff [hwɪf] *s* soplo; fumada; olorcillo; acceso, arranque *m;* **to get a whiff of** percibir un olor fugaz de ‖ *intr* soplar (*el viento*); echar bocanadas (*el que fuma*)

while [hwaɪl] *conj* mientras, mientras que ‖ *s* rato; **a long while** largo rato; **a while ago** hace un rato; **between whiles** de vez en cuando ‖ *tr* — **to while away** entretener (*el tiempo*); pasar (*p.ej., la tarde*) de un modo entretenido

whim [hwɪm] *s* capricho, antojo

whimper ['hwɪmpər] *s* lloriqueo ‖ *tr* decir lloriqueando ‖ *intr* lloriquear

whimsical ['hwɪmzɪkəl] *adj* caprichoso, extravagante, fantástico

whine [hwaɪn] *s* gimoteo, quejido ‖ *intr* gimotear, quejarse

whin·ny ['hwɪni] *s* (*pl* **-nies**) relincho ‖ *v* (*pret & pp* **-nied**) *intr* relinchar

whip [hwɪp] *s* látigo, zurriago; huevos batidos con nata ‖ *v* (*pret & pp* **whipped** o **whip**.; *ger* **whipping**) *tr* azotar, zurriagar, fustigar; batir (*huevos y nata*); (coll) derrotar, vencer; **to whip off** (coll) escribir de prisa; **to whip out** sacar de repente; **to whip up** (coll) preparar de prisa; (coll) avivar, excitar

whip'cord' *s* tralla; tejido fuerte con costurones diagonales

whip hand *s* mano *f* del látigo; (*upper hand*) vara alta

whip'lash' *s* tralla

whipped cream *s* nata, crema batida

whipper-snapper ['hwɪpər,snæpər] *s* arrapiezo, mequetrefe *m*

whippet ['hwɪpɪt] *s* perro lebrel

whipping boy ['hwɪpɪŋ] *s* cabeza de turco, víctima inocente

whipping post *s* poste *m* de flagelación

whippoorwill [,hwɪpər'wɪl] *s* chotacabras norteamericano (*Caprimulgus vociferus*)

whir [hwʌr] *s* zumbido ‖ *v* (*pret & pp*

whirred; *ger* whirring) *intr* girar zumbando

whirl [hwʌrl] *s* vuelta, giro; remolino; (*of events, parties, etc.*) serie *f* interminable || *tr & intr* remolinear; my head whirls siento vértigo

whirligig ['hwʌrlɪ,gɪg] *s* (ent) escribano del agua; tíovivo; (*pinwheel*) rehilandera, molinete *m*; peonza

whirl'pool' *s* remolino, vorágine *f*

whirl'wind' *s* torbellino, manga de viento

whirlybird ['hwʌrlɪ,bʌrd] *s* (coll) helicóptero

whish [hwɪʃ] *s* zumbido suave || *intr* zumbar suavemente

whisk [hwɪsk] *s* escobilla; toque ligero || *tr* barrer, cepillar; to whisk out of sight escamotear || *intr* moverse rápidamente

whisk broom *s* escobilla

whiskers ['hwɪskərz] *spl* barbas; (*on side of face*) patillas; (*of cat*) bigotes *mpl*

whiskey ['hwɪskɪ] *adj* (*voice*) (coll) aguardentoso || *s* whisky *m*

whisper ['hwɪspər] *s* cuchicheo; (*of leaves*) susurro; in a whisper en voz baja || *tr* susurrar, decir al oído || *intr* cuchichear, hablar al oído; susurrar (*p.ej., las hojas*); (*to gossip*) susurrar, murmurar

whisperer ['hwɪspərər] *s* susurrón *m*

whispering ['hwɪspərɪŋ] *adj & s* (*gossiping*) susurrón *m*

whist [hwɪst] *s* whist *m* (*juego de naipes*)

whistle ['hwɪsəl] *s* (*sound*) silbido, silbo; (*device*) silbato, pito; to wet one's whistle (coll) remojar la palabra || *tr* silbar (*p.ej., una canción*) || *intr* silbar; to whistle for llamar con un silbido; (coll) tener que componérselas sin

whistle stop *s* apeadero, pueblecito

whit [hwɪt] *s* — not a whit ni pizca; to not care a whit no importarle a (*uno*) un bledo

white [hwaɪt] *adj* blanco || *s* blanco; (*of an egg*) clara; whites (pathol) pérdidas blancas, flujo blanco

white'caps' *spl* cabrillas, palomas

white coal *s* hulla blanca

white'-col'lar *adj* oficinesco

white feather *s* — to show the white feather mostrarse cobarde

white goods *spl* tejidos de algodón; ropa blanca; aparatos electrodomésticos

white-haired ['hwaɪt,hɛrd] *adj* de pelo blanco; (*gray-haired*) cano; (coll) favorito, predilecto

white heat *s* blanco, calor blanco; (fig) viva agitación

white lead [lɛd] *s* albayalde *m*

white lie *s* mentirilla, mentira inocente u oficiosa

white meat *s* pechuga, carne *f* de la pechuga del ave

whiten ['hwaɪtən] *tr* blanquear, emblanquecer || *intr* blanquear, emblanquecerse; palidecer

whiteness ['hwaɪtnɪs] *s* blancura

white plague *s* peste blanca (*tuberculosis*)

white slavery *s* trata de blancas

white tie *s* corbatín blanco; traje *m* de etiqueta

white'wash' *s* jalbegue *m*, lechada; (*e.g., of a scandal*) encubrimiento || *tr* jalbegar, enjalbegar, encalar; absolver sin justicia; encubrir (*un escándalo*)

whither ['hwɪðər] *adv* adónde || *conj* adonde

whitish ['hwaɪtɪʃ] *adj* blanquecino, blancuzco

whitlow ['hwɪtlo] *s* panadizo, uñero

Whitsuntide ['hwɪtsən,taɪd] *s* semana de Pentecostés

whittle ['hwɪtəl] *tr* sacar pedazos a (*un trozo de madera*); to whittle away o down reducir poco a poco

whiz o whizz [hwɪz] *s* silbido, zumbido; (slang) perito, fenómeno || *v* (*pret & ger* whizzed; *ger* whizzing) *intr* — to whiz by rehilar, silbar; pasar como una flecha

who [hu] *pron interr* quién; who else? ¿quién más?; who goes there? (mil) ¿quién vive?; who's who quién es el uno y quién el otro; quiénes son gente de importancia || *pron rel* que, quien; el (la, etc.) que

whoa [hwo] o [wo] *interj* ¡so!

who·ev'er *pron rel* quienquiera que, cualquiera que

whole [hol] *adj* todo, entero; (*intact*) ileso; (*not scattered or dispersed*) único, p.ej., the whole interest for him was the child he was raising el único interés para él era el niño que educaba; made out of the whole cloth enteramente falso o imaginario || *s* conjunto, todo; as a whole en conjunto; on the whole en general; por la mayor parte

wholehearted ['hol,hɑrtɪd] *adj* sincero, cordial

whole note *s* (mus) semibreve *f*

whole'sale' *adj & adv* al por mayor || *s* venta al por mayor || *tr* vender al por mayor || *intr* vender al por mayor; venderse al por mayor

wholesaler ['hol,selər] *s* comerciante *mf* al por mayor

wholesome ['holsəm] *adj* (*conducive to good health*) saludable; (*in good health*) fresco, rollizo

wholly ['holi] *adv* enteramente, completamente

whom [hum] *pron interr* a quién || *pron rel* que, a quien; al (a la, etc.) que

whom·ev'er *pron rel* a quienquiera que

whoop [hup] o [hwup] *s* ululato || *tr* — to whoop it up (slang) armar una gritería || *intr* ulular

whooping cough ['hupɪŋ] o ['hwupɪŋ] *s* tos ferina, tos convulsiva

whopper ['hwɑpər] *s* (coll) enormidad; (coll) mentirón *m*

whopping ['hwɑpɪŋ] *adj* (coll) enorme, grandísimo

whore [hor] *s* puta || *intr* — to whore around putañear, putear

whortleber·ry ['hwʌrtəl,bɛri] s (pl -ries) arándano

whose [huz] pron interr de quién || pron rel de quien, cuyo

why [hwaɪ] adv por qué; **why not?** ¿cómo no? || s (pl **whys**) porqué m || interj ¡toma!; **why, certainly!** ¡desde luego!, ¡por supuesto!; **why, yes!** ¡claro!, ¡pues sí!

wick [wɪk] s mecha, pabilo

wicked ['wɪkɪd] adj malo; (mischievous) travieso, revoltoso; (vicious) arisco; ofensivo

wicker ['wɪkər] adj mimbroso || s mimbre m & f

wicket ['wɪkɪt] s (small door in a larger one) portillo, postigo; (small opening in a door) ventanillo; (ticket window) taquilla; (gate to regulate flow of water) compuerta; (cricket) meta; (croquet) aro

wide [waɪd] adj ancho; de ancho; (sense of a word) amplio, lato || adv de par en par; enteramente; lejos; **wide of the mark** lejos del blanco; fuera de propósito

wide'-an'gle adj granangular

wide'-a-wake' adj despabilado

widen ['waɪdən] tr ensanchar || intr ensancharse

wide'-o'pen adj abierto de par en par; **to be wide-open** estar (p.ej., una ciudad) abierta a los jugadores

wide'spread' adj (arms, wings) extendido; difundido, extenso

widow ['wɪdo] s viuda; (cards) baceta || tr dejar viuda

widower ['wɪdo·ər] s viudo

widowhood ['wɪdo,hud] s viudez f

widow's mite s limosna que da un pobre

widow's pension s viudedad

widow's weeds spl luto de viuda

width [wɪdθ] s anchura

wield [wild] tr esgrimir, manejar (la espada); ejercer (el poder)

wife [waɪf] s (pl **wives** [waɪvz]) esposa, mujer f

wig [wɪg] s peluca

wiggle ['wɪgəl] s meneo rápido || tr menear rápidamente || intr menearse rápidamente

wig'wag' s comunicación con banderas || v (pret & pp -wagged; ger -wagging) tr menear; mandar (informes) moviendo banderas || intr menearse; señalar con banderas

wigwam ['wɪgwɑm] s choza cónica (de los pieles rojas)

wild [waɪld] adj (not domesticated; growing without cultivation; uncivilized) salvaje; (unrestrained) descabellado; (frantic, mad) frenético; (riotous) desenfrenado, revoltoso; extravagante; (bullet, shot) perdido; **wild about** loco por || adv disparatadamente; **to run wild** crecer locamente; estar sin gobierno || s desierto, yermo; **wilds** monte m, despoblado

wild boar s jabalí m

wild card s comodín m

wild'cat' s gato montés; lince m; empresa arriesgada

wildcat strike s huelga no autorizada por el sindicato

wilderness ['wɪldərnɪs] s desierto, yermo

wild'fire' s fuego fatuo; fucilazo; **to spread like wildfire** ser un reguero de pólvora, correr como pólvora en reguero

wild flower s flor f del campo

wild goose s ganso bravo

wild'-goose' chase s caza de grillos

wild'life' s animales mf salvajes

wild oats spl excesos de la juventud, mocedad; **to sow one's wild oats** llevar (los mozos) una vida de excesos

wild olive s acebuche m

wile [waɪl] s ardid m, engaño; (cunning) astucia || tr engatusar; **to wile away** entretener (el tiempo); pasar (p.ej., la tarde)

will [wɪl] s voluntad; (law) testamento; **at will** a voluntad || tr querer; (to bequeath) legar || intr querer; **do as you will** haga Vd. lo que quiera || v (pret & cond **would**) v aux **he will arrive at six o'clock** llegará a las seis; **he will go for days without smoking** pasa días enteros sin fumar

willful ['wɪlfəl] adj voluntarioso

willfulness ['wɪlfəlnɪs] s voluntariedad

William ['wɪljəm] s Guillermo

willing ['wɪlɪŋ] adj dispuesto; gustoso, pronto; espontáneo; **willing or unwilling** que quiera, que no quiera

willingly ['wɪlɪŋli] adv de buena gana, de buena voluntad

willingness ['wɪlɪŋnɪs] s buena gana, buena voluntad

will-o'-the-wisp ['wɪləðə'wɪsp] s fuego fatuo; ilusión, quimera

willow ['wɪlo] s sauce m

willowy ['wɪlo·i] adj (pliant) juncal, mimbreño; (slender, graceful) juncal, cimbreño, esbelto; lleno de sauces

will power s fuerza de voluntad

willy-nilly ['wɪli'nɪli] adv de grado o por fuerza

wilt [wɪlt] tr marchitar || intr marchitarse

wil·y ['waɪli] adj (comp -ier; super -iest) artero, engañoso; astuto

wimple ['wɪmpəl] s griñón m, impla

win [wɪn] s (coll) éxito, triunfo || v (pret & pp **won** [wʌn]; ger **winning**) tr ganar; **to win over** ganar, conquistar || intr ganar; **to win out** ganar; (coll) tener éxito

wince [wɪns] s sobresalto || intr sobresaltarse

winch [wɪntʃ] s maquinilla, torno; (handle, crank) manubrio

wind [wɪnd] s viento; (breath) respiración, resuello; **to break wind** ventosear; **to get wind of** saber de, tener noticia de; **to sail close to the wind** (naut) ceñir el viento; **to take the wind out of one's sails** apagarle a uno los fuegos || tr dejar sin aliento || [waɪnd] v (pret & pp **wound**

[waund]) *tr* (*to coil; to wrap up*) arrollar, envolver; devanar (*alambre*); ovillar (*hilo*); torcer (*hebras*); hacer girar (*un manubrio*); dar cuerda a (*un reloj*); **to wind one's way through** serpentear por; **to wind up** arrollar, envolver; (coll) poner punto final a ‖ *intr* serpentear (*un camino*)

windbag ['wɪnd‚bæg] *s* (*of bagpipe*) odre *m;* (coll) charlatán *m,* palabrero

windbreak ['wɪnd‚brek] *s* guardavientos *m*

wind cone [wɪnd] *s* (aer) cono de viento

winded ['wɪndɪd] *adj* falto de respiración, sin resuello

windfall ['wɪnd‚fɔl] *s* fruta caída del árbol; fortunón *m,* cosa llovida del cielo

winding sheet ['waɪndɪŋ] *s* sudario, mortaja

winding stairs *spl* escalera de caracol

wind instrument [wɪnd] *s* (mus) instrumento de viento

windlass ['wɪndləs] *s* maquinilla, torno

windmill ['wɪnd‚mɪl] *s* (*mill operated by wind*) molino de viento; (*modern wind-driven source of power*) aeromotor *m;* (*pinwheel*) molinete *m;* **to tilt at windmills** luchar con los molinos de viento

window ['wɪndo] *s* ventana; (*of ticket office; of envelope*) ventanilla; (*of coach, automobile*) ventanilla, portezuela

window dresser *s* escaparatista *mf*

window dressing *s* adorno de escaparates

window frame *s* marco de ventana

win'dow‚pane' *s* cristal *m* o vidrio de ventana

window screen *s* alambrera, sobrevidriera

window shade *s* visillo, transparente *m* de resorte

win'dow-shop' *v* (*pret & pp* **-shopped;** *ger* **-shopping**) *intr* mirar los escaparates sin comprar

window shutter *s* contraventana

window sill *s* repisa de ventana

windpipe ['wɪnd‚paɪp] *s* tráquea

windshield ['wɪnd‚ʃild] *s* parabrisa *m*

windshield washer *s* lavaparabrisas *m*

windshield wiper *s* limpiaparabrisas *m*

wind sock *s* (aer) cono de viento

windstorm ['wɪnd‚stɔrm] *s* ventarrón *m*

wind-up ['waɪnd‚ʌp] *s* conclusión; (sport) final *f* de partido

windward ['wɪndwərd] *s* barlovento; **to turn to windward** barlovento

Windward Islands *spl* islas de Barlovento

Windward Passage *s* paso de los Vientos

wind·y ['wɪndɪ] *adj* (*comp* **-ier;** *super* **-iest**) ventoso; (*unsubstantial*) vacío; palabrero, ampuloso; **it is windy** hace viento

wine [waɪn] *s* vino ‖ *tr* obsequiar con vino ‖ *intr* beber vino

wine cellar *s* bodega

wine'glass' *s* copa para vino

winegrower ['waɪn‚gro·ər] *s* vinicultor *m*

winegrowing ['waɪn‚gro·ɪŋ] *s* vinicultura

wine press *s* lagar *m*

winer·y ['waɪnərɪ] *s* (*pl* **-ies**) lagar *m*

wine'skin' *s* odre *m*

winetaster ['waɪn‚testər] *s* catavinos *m*

wing [wɪŋ] *s* ala; facción, bando; (theat) bastidor *m;* **to take wing** alzar el vuelo ‖ *tr* herir en el ala; **to wing one's way** avanzar volando

wing chair *s* sillón *m* de orejas

wing collar *s* cuello de pajarita

wing nut *s* tuerca de aletas

wing'spread' *s* envergadura

wink [wɪŋk] *s* guiño; **to not sleep a wink** no pegar los ojos; **to take forty winks** (coll) descabezar el sueño ‖ *tr* guiñar (*el ojo*) ‖ *intr* guiñar; (*to blink*) parpadear, pestañear; **to wink at** guiñar el ojo a; fingir no ver

winner ['wɪnər] *s* ganador *m,* vencedor *m;* premiado

winning ['wɪnɪŋ] *adj* triunfante, victorioso; atrayente, simpático ‖ **winnings** *spl* ganancias

winnow ['wɪno] *tr* aventar; entresacar ‖ *intr* aletear

winsome ['wɪnsəm] *adj* atrayente, simpático, engañador; alegre

winter ['wɪntər] *adj* invernal ‖ *s* invierno ‖ *intr* invernar

win'ter·green' *s* gaulteria, té *m* del Canadá; esencia de gaulteria

win·try ['wɪntrɪ] *adj* (*comp* **-trier;** *super* **-triest**) invernal, invernizo; helado, frío

wipe [waɪp] *tr* frotar para limpiar; enjugar (*la cara, el sudor, las manos*); **to wipe away** enjugar (*lágrimas*); **to wipe off** quitar frotando; **to wipe out** (coll) borrar, cancelar; (coll) aniquilar, destruir; (coll) enjugar (*deudas, un déficit*)

wiper ['waɪpər] *s* paño, trapo; (elec) contacto deslizante

wire [waɪr] *s* (*thread of metal*) alambre *m;* telégrafo; telegrama *m;* teléfono; **to pull wires** (coll) tocar resortes ‖ *tr* alambrar; telegrafiar ‖ *intr* telegrafiar

wire cutter *s* cortaalambres *m*

wire entanglement *s* (mil) alambrado

wire gauge *s* calibrador *m* de alambre

wire-haired ['waɪr‚herd] *adj* de pelo áspero

wireless ['waɪrlɪs] *adj* inalámbrico, sin hilos

wire nail *s* punta de París, clavo de alambre

wire pulling ['pʊlɪŋ] *s* (coll) empleo de resortes

wire recorder *s* grabadora de alambre

wire screen *s* alambrera, tela de alambre

wire'tap' *v* (*pret & pp* **-tapped;** *ger* **-tapping**) *tr* intervenir (*una conversación telefónica*)

wiring ['waɪrɪŋ] *s* (elec) alambraje *m*

wir·y ['waɪrɪ] *adj* (*comp* **-ier;** *super*

-iest) alambrino; cimbreante; nervudo; vibrante

wisdom ['wɪzdəm] s sabiduría, cordura

wisdom tooth s muela cordal, muela del juicio

wise [waɪz] adj sabio, cuerdo; (step, decision) acertado, juicioso; **to be wise to** (slang) conocer el juego de; **to get wise** (coll) caer en el chiste ‖ s modo, manera; **in no wise** de ningún modo

wiseacre ['waɪz‚ekər] s sabihondo

wise′crack′ s (slang) cuchufleta ‖ intr (slang) cuchufletear

wise guy s (slang) sabelotodo

wish [wɪʃ] s deseo; **to make a wish** pensar algo que se desea ‖ tr desear; dar (los buenos días) ‖ intr desear; **to wish for** desear, anhelar

wish′bone′ s espoleta, hueso de la suerte

wishful ['wɪʃfəl] adj deseoso

wishful thinking s optimismo a ultranza; **to indulge in wishful thinking** forjarse ilusiones

wistful ['wɪstfəl] adj melancólico, tristón, pensativo

wit [wɪt] s agudeza; (person) chistoso; (keen mental power) juicio; **to be at one's wits' end** no saber qué hacer; **to have the wit to** tener el tino de; **to live by one's wits** vivir del cuento

witch [wɪtʃ] s bruja, hechicera; (old hag) bruja

witch′craft′ s brujería

witches' Sabbath s aquelarre m

witch hazel s (shrub) nogal m de la brujería, planta del sortilegio; (liquid) hamamelina, hazelina

with [wɪð] o [wɪθ] prep con; de

with·draw′ v (pret **-drew**; pp **-drawn**) tr retirar ‖ intr retirarse

withdrawal [wɪð'drɔ·əl] o [wɪθ'drɔ·əl] s retirada

withdrawal symptom s síntoma m de abstinencia

wither ['wɪðər] tr marchitar; (fig) aplastar, confundir ‖ intr marchitarse; confundirse

with·hold′ v (pret & pp **-held**) tr retener; suspender (pago); negar (un permiso)

withholding tax s impuesto deducido del sueldo

with·in′ adv dentro ‖ prep dentro de; al alcance de; poco menos de; con un margen de

with·out′ adv fuera ‖ prep fuera de; (lacking, not with) sin; **to do without** pasar sin; **without** + ger sin + inf, p.ej., **he left without saying goodbye** salió sin despedirse; sin que + subj, p.ej., **he came in without anyone seeing him** entró sin que nadie le viese

with·stand′ v (pret & pp **-stood**) tr aguantar, resistir

witness ['wɪtnɪs] s testigo mf; **in witness whereof** en fe de lo cual; **to bear witness** dar testimonio ‖ tr (to be present at) presenciar; (to attest) atestiguar, testimoniar; firmar como testigo

witness stand s banquillo o estrado de los testigos

witticism ['wɪtɪ‚sɪzəm] s agudeza, dicho agudo, ocurrencia

wittingly ['wɪtɪŋli] adv a sabiendas

wit·ty ['wɪti] adj (comp **-tier**; super **-tiest**) agudo, ingenioso; (person) ocurrente, chistoso

wizard ['wɪzərd] s brujo, hechicero; (coll) as m, experto

wizardry ['wɪzərdri] s hechicería, magia

wizened ['wɪzənd] adj acartonado, arrugado

woad [wod] s hierba pastel

wobble ['wɑbəl] s bamboleo, tambaleo ‖ intr bambolear, tambalear; bailar (una silla); (fig) vacilar, ser inconstante

wob·bly ['wɑbli] adj (comp **-blier**; super **-bliest**) bamboleante, inseguro; vacilante

woe [wo] s aflicción, miseria, infortunio ‖ interj — **woe is me!** ¡ay de mí!

woebegone ['wobɪ‚gɔn] o ['wobɪ‚gɑn] adj cariacontecido, triste

woeful ['wofəl] adj triste, miserable; (of poor quality) malo, pésimo

wolf [wʊlf] s (pl **wolves** [wʊlvz]) lobo; persona cruel, persona mañosa; (coll) tenorio; **to cry wolf** dar falsa alarma; **to keep the wolf from the door** ponerse a cubierto del hambre ‖ tr & intr comer vorazmente, engullir

wolf′hound′ s galgo lobero

wolfram ['wʊlfrəm] s (element) volframio; (mineral) volframita

wolf's-bane o **wolfsbane** ['wʊlfs‚ben] s matalobos m

woman ['wʊmən] s (pl **women** ['wɪmɪn]) mujer f

womanhood ['wʊmən‚hʊd] s el sexo femenino; las mujeres

womanish ['wʊmənɪʃ] adj mujeril; (effeminate) afeminado

wom′an-kind′ s el sexo femenino

womanly ['wʊmənli] adj (comp **-lier**; super **-liest**) femenil, mujeriego

woman suffrage s sufragismo

woman-suffragist ['wʊmən's‚ʌfrədʒɪst] s sufragista mf

womb [wum] s útero; (fig) seno

womenfolk ['wɪmɪn‚fok] spl las mujeres

wonder ['wʌndər] s (something strange or surprising) maravilla; (feeling of surprise) admiración; (something strange, miracle) milagro; **for a wonder** cosa extraña; **no wonder that . . .** no es mucho que . . .; **to work wonders** hacer milagros ‖ tr preguntarse ‖ intr admirarse, maravillarse; **to wonder at** admirarse de, maravillarse con o de

wonder drugs spl drogas milagrosas

wonderful ['wʌndərfəl] adj maravilloso

won′der·land′ s tierra de las maravillas; reino de las hadas

wonderment ['wʌndərmənt] s asombro, sorpresa

wont [wʌnt] o [wɔnt] adj acostum-

brado; **to be wont to** acostumbrar ‖
s costumbre, hábito
wonted ['wʌntɪd] o ['wɔntɪd] *adj*
acostumbrado, habitual
woo [wu] *tr* cortejar (*a una mujer*);
tratar de conquistar; tratar de persuadir
wood [wʊd] *s* madera; (*for making a
fire*) leña; barril *m* de madera; **out
of the woods** (coll) fuera de peligro;
(coll) libre de dificultades; **to take to
the woods** andar a monte; **woods**
bosque *m*
woodbine ['wʊd,baɪn] *s* (*honeysuckle*)
madreselva; (*Virginia creeper*) guau
m
wood carving *s* labrado de madera
wood'chuck' *s* marmota de América
wood'cock' *s* becada, coalla, chocha
wood'cut' *s* (typ) grabado en madera
wood'cut'ter *s* leñador *m*
wooded ['wʊdɪd] *adj* arbolado, enselvado
wooden ['wʊdən] *adj* de madera, hecho de madera; torpe, estúpido; sin
ánimo
wood engraving *s* (typ) grabado en
madera
wooden-headed ['wʊdən,hɛdɪd] *adj*
(coll) torpe, estúpido
wooden leg *s* pata de palo
wooden shoe *s* zueco
wood grouse *s* gallo de bosque
woodland ['wʊdlənd] *adj* selvático ‖ *s*
bosque *m*, monte *m*
woodland scene *s* (paint) boscaje *m*
wood·man ['wʊdmən] *s* (*pl* **-men**
[mən]) leñador *m*
woodpecker ['wʊd,pɛkər] *s* carpintero, pájaro carpintero; (*green woodpecker*) picamaderos *m*
wood'pile' *s* montón *m* de leña
wood screw *s* tirafondo
woods·man ['wʊdzmən] *s* (*pl* **-men**
[mən]) leñador *m*
wood'wind' *s* (mus) instrumento de
viento de madera
wood'work' *s* (*working in wood*) ebanistería, obra de carpintería; (*things
made of wood*) maderaje *m*
wood'work'er *s* ebanista *mf*, carpintero
wood'worm' *s* carcoma
wood·y ['wʊdɪ] *adj* (*comp* **-ier;** *super*
-iest) arbolado, enselvado; (*like
wood*) leñoso
wooer ['wu·ər] *s* pretendiente *m*,
galán *m*
woof [wuf] *s* (*yarns running across
warp*) trama; (*fabric*) tejido
woofer ['wʊfər] *s* altavoz *m* para audiofrecuencias bajas
wool [wʊl] *s* lana
woolen ['wʊlən] *adj* de lana, hecho de
lana ‖ *s* tejido de lana; **woolens** lanerías
woolgrower ['wʊl,gro·ər] *s* criador *m*
de ganado lanar
wool·ly ['wʊli] *adj* (*comp* **-lier;** *super*
-liest) lanoso, lanudo; borroso, confuso
word [wʌrd] *s* palabra; **to be as good
as one's word** cumplir lo prometido;

to have a word with hablar cuatro
palabras con; **to have word from**
recibir noticias de; **to keep one's
word** cumplir su palabra; **to leave
word** dejar dicho; **to send word that**
mandar decir que; **words** (*a quarrel*)
palabras mayores; (*text of a song*)
letra ‖ *tr* redactar, formular ‖ **Word**
s (theol) Verbo
word count *s* recuento de vocabulario
word formation *s* (gram) formación de
palabras
wording ['wʌrdɪŋ] *s* fraseología, estilo
word order *s* (gram) orden *m* de colocación
word'stock' *s* vocabulario, léxico
word·y ['wʌrdɪ] *adj* (*comp* **-ier;** *super*
-iest) verboso
work [wʌrk] *s* (*exertion; labor, toil*)
trabajo; (*result of exertion; human
output; engineering structure*) obra;
(sew) labor *f*; **at work** trabajando;
(*not at home*) en la oficina, en el
taller, en la tienda; **out of work** sin
trabajo, desempleado; **to shoot the
works** (slang) echar el resto; **works**
fábrica; mecanismo; (*of clock*) movimiento ‖ *tr* hacer trabajar; trabajar, obrar (*la madera, el hierro*);
obrar (*un milagro*); explotar (*una
mina*); **to work up** preparar; estimular, excitar ‖ *intr* trabajar; funcionar,
marchar (*un aparato, un motor*);
obrar (*p.ej., un remedio*); **to work
loose** aflojarse; **to work out** resolverse
workable ['wʌrkəbəl] *adj* (*feasible*)
practicable; (*that can be worked*)
laborable
work'bench' *s* banco de trabajo, banco
de taller
work'book' *s* (*manual of instructions*)
libro de reglas; libro de ejercicios
work'box' *s* caja de herramientas; (*for
needlework*) caja de labor
work'day' *s* día de cada día; ordinario,
vulgar ‖ *s* día *m* de trabajo; (*number of hours of work*) jornada
worked-up ['wʌrkt'ʌp] *adj* muy conmovido, sobreexcitado, exaltado
worker ['wʌrkər] *s* trabajador *m*,
obrero
work force *s* mano *f* de obra, personal
obrero
work'horse' *s* caballo de carga; (*tireless worker*) yunque *m*
work'house' *s* taller penitenciario;
(Brit) asilo de pobres
working class *s* clase obrera
work'ing-girl' *s* trabajadora joven
working hours *spl* horas de trabajo
working-man ['wʌrkɪŋ,mæn] *s* (*pl*
-men [,mɛn]) obrero, trabajador *m*
working·woman ['wʌrkɪŋ,wʊmən] *s*
(*pl* **-women** [,wɪmɪn]) obrera, trabajadora
work·man ['wʌrkmən] *s* (*pl* **-men**
[mən]) obrero, trabajador *m;* (*skilled
worker*) artífice *m*
workmanship ['wʌrkmən,ʃɪp] *s* destreza en el trabajo; (*work executed*)
hechura, obra
work of art *s* obra de arte

work'out' s ensayo, prueba; (*physical exercise*) ejercicio
work'room' s (*for manual work*) obrador m, taller m; (*study*) gabinete m de trabajo
work'shop' s obrador m, taller m
work stoppage s paro
world [wʌrld] adj mundial ‖ s mundo; **a world of** la mar de; **half the world** (*a lot of people*) medio mundo; **since the world began** desde que el mundo es mundo; **the other world** el otro mundo; **to bring into the world** echar al mundo; **to see the world** ver mundo; **to think the world of** tener un alto concepto de
world affairs spl asuntos internacionales
world'ly ['wʌrldli] adj (comp **-lier;** super **-liest**) mundano
world'ly-wise' adj que tiene mucho mundo
world's fair s exposición mundial
World War s Guerra Mundial
world'-wide' adj global, mundial
worm [wʌrm] s gusano; **worms** (pathol) lombrices fpl ‖ tr limpiar de lombrices; **to worm a secret out of a person** arrancar mañosamente un secreto a una persona; **to worm one's way into** insinuarse en
worm-eaten ['wʌrm‚itən] adj carcomido; (fig) decaído, desgastado
worm gear s engranaje m de tornillo sin fin
worm'wood' s (Artemisia) ajenjo; (*Artemisia absinthium*) ajenjo del campo o ajenjo mayor; (*something bitter or grievous*) (fig) ajenjo
worm·y ['wʌrmi] adj (comp **-ier;** super **-iest**) gusaniento, gusanoso; (*worm-eaten*) carcomido; (*groveling*) rastrero, servil
worn [worn] adj roto, raído, gastado
worn'-out' adj muy gastado, inservible; (*by toil, illness*) consumido, rendido
worrisome ['wʌrisəm] adj inquietante; (*inclined to worry*) aprensivo, inquieto
wor·ry ['wʌri] s (pl **-ries**) inquietud, preocupación; (*cause of anxiety*) molestia ‖ v (pret & pp **-ried**) tr inquietar, preocupar; (*to harass, pester*) acosar, molestar; **to be worried** estar inquieto ‖ intr inquietarse, preocuparse; **don't worry** pierda Vd. cuidado
worse [wʌrs] adj & adv comp peor; **worse and worse** de mal en peor
worsen ['wʌrsən] tr & intr empeorar
wor·ship ['wʌrʃip] s adoración, culto; **your worship** vuestra merced ‖ v (pret & pp **-shiped** o **-shipped;** ger **-shiping** o **-shipping**) tr & intr adorar, venerar
worshiper o **worshipper** ['wʌrʃipər] s adorador m, devoto
worst [wʌrst] adj & adv super peor ‖ s (lo) peor; **at worst** en las peores circunstancias; **if worst comes to worst** si pasa lo peor; **to get the worst of** llevar la peor parte, salir perdiendo

worsted ['wʊstid] adj de estambre ‖ s estambre m; tela de estambre
wort [wʌrt] s (bot) hierba, planta; mosto de cerveza
worth [wʌrθ] adj del valor de; digno de; **to be worth** valer; tener una fortuna de; **to be worth** + ger valer la pena de + inf; **to be worth while** valer la pena; ser de mérito ‖ s valor m; mérito; **a dollar's worth of** un dólar de
worthless ['wʌrθlis] adj sin valor, inútil, inservible; (*person*) despreciable
worth'while' adj de mérito, digno de atención
wor·thy ['wʌrði] adj (comp **-thier;** super **-thiest**) digno; benemérito, meritorio ‖ s (pl **-thies**) benemérito; (*hum & iron*) personaje m
would [wʊd] v aux **she said she would do it** dijo que lo haría; **he would come if he could** vendría si pudiese; **he would go for days without smoking** pasaba días enteros sin fumar; **would that . . .!** ¡ojalá que . . .!
would'-be' adj llamado; supuesto ‖ s presumido
wound [wund] s herida ‖ tr herir
wounded ['wundid] adj herido ‖ **the wounded** los heridos
wow [waʊ] s (*of phonograph record*) ululación; (slang) éxito rotundo ‖ tr (slang) entusiasmar
wrack [ræk] s naufragio; vestigio; (*fucaceous seaweed*) varec m; **to go to wrack and ruin** desvencijarse; ir al desastre
wraith [reθ] s fantasma m, espectro
wrangle ['ræŋgəl] s pendencia, riña ‖ intr pelotear, reñir
wrap [ræp] s abrigo, manto ‖ v (pret & pp **wrapped;** ger **wrapping**) tr envolver; **to be wrapped up in** (fig) estar prendado de; **to wrap up** envolver; (*in clothing*) arropar; (coll) concluir ‖ intr — **to wrap up** arroparse
wrapper ['ræpər] s bata, peinador m; (*of newspaper or magazine*) faja; (*of tobacco*) capa
wrapping paper ['ræpiŋ] s papel m de envolver, papel de embalar
wrath [ræθ] o [rɑθ] s cólera, ira; venganza
wrathful ['ræθfəl] o ['rɑθfəl] adj colérico, iracundo
wreak [rik] tr descargar (*la cólera*); infligir (*venganza*)
wreath [riθ] s (pl **wreaths** [riðz]) guirnalda; corona funeraria; (*worn as a mark of honor or victory*) corona de laurel; (*of smoke*) espiral f
wreathe [rið] tr enguirnaldar; ceñir, envolver; tejer (*una guirnalda*) ‖ intr elevarse en espirales (*el humo*)
wreck [rek] s destrucción, ruina; naufragio; catástrofe f, desastre m; despojos, restos; (*of one's hopes*) naufragio; **to be a wreck** estar hecho un cascajo, estar hecho una ruina ‖ tr destruir, arruinar; hacer

naufragar; hacer chocar, descarrilar (*un tren*)

wrecking ball *s* bola rompedora

wrecking car *s* (aut) camión *m* de auxilio; (rr) carro de grúa

wrecking crane *s* grúa de auxilio

wren [ren] *s* buscareta, coletero, rey *m* de zarza

wrench [rentʃ] *s* llave *f*; (*pull*) arranque *m*, tirón *m*; (*twist of a joint*) esguince *m* ‖ *tr* torcerse (*p.ej., la muñeca*); (fig) torcer (*el sentido de una oración*)

wrest [rest] *tr* arrebatar, arrancar violentamente

wrestle ['resəl] *s* lucha; partido de lucha ‖ *intr* luchar

wrestling match ['reslɪŋ] *s* partido de lucha

wretch [retʃ] *s* miserable *mf*

wretched ['retʃɪd] *adj* miserable; (*poor, worthless*) malísimo, pésimo

wriggle ['rɪgəl] *s* culebreo, meneo serpentino ‖ *tr* menear rápidamente ‖ *intr* culebrear, ondular; **to wriggle out of** escabullirse de

wrig‧gly ['rɪglɪ] *adj* (*comp* **-glier;** *super* **-gliest**) retorciéndose; (fig) evasivo, tramoyista

wring [rɪŋ] *v* (*pret & pp* **wrung** [rʌŋ]) *tr* torcer; retorcer (*las manos*); exprimir (*el zumo, la ropa, etc.*); sacar por fuerza (*la verdad*); arrancar (*dinero*); **to wring out** exprimir (*la ropa*)

wringer ['rɪŋər] *s* exprimidor *m*

wrinkle ['rɪŋkəl] *s* arruga; (*clever trick or idea*) (coll) ardid *m*, truco ‖ *tr* arrugar ‖ *intr* arrugarse

wrin‧kly ['rɪŋklɪ] *adj* (*comp* **-klier;** *super* **-kliest**) arrugado

wrist [rɪst] *s* muñeca

wrist'band' *s* bocamanga, puño

wrist watch *s* reloj *m* de pulsera

writ [rɪt] *s* escrito, escritura; (law) mandato, orden *f*

write [raɪt] *v* (*pret* **wrote** [rot]; *pp* **written** ['rɪtən]) *tr* escribir; **to write down** poner por escrito; bajar el precio de; **to write off** cancelar (*una deuda*); **to write up** describir extensamente por escrito; (*to ballyhoo*) dar bombo a ‖ *intr* escribir; **to write back** contestar por carta

writer ['raɪtər] *s* escritor *m*

writer's cramp *s* grafospasmo

write'-up' *s* (*favorable report*) bombo; (com) valoración excesiva

writhe [raɪð] *intr* contorcerse, retorcerse

writing ['raɪtɪŋ] *s* el escribir; (*something written*) escrito; profesión de escritor; **at this writing** al escribir ésta; **in one's own writing** de su puño y letra; **to put in writing** poner por escrito

writing desk *s* escritorio

writing materials *spl* recado de escribir

writing paper *s* papel *m* de escribir, papel de cartas

written accent ['rɪtən] *s* acento ortográfico

wrong [rɔŋ] o [rɑŋ] *adj* injusto; malo; erróneo, equivocado; impropio; no . . . que se busca, p.ej., **this is the wrong house** ésta no es la casa que se busca; no . . . que se necesita, p.ej., **this is the wrong train** éste no es el tren que se necesita; no . . . que debe, p.ej., **he is going the wrong way** no sigue el camino que debe; **in the wrong place** mal colocado; **to be wrong** no tener razón; tener la culpa; **to be wrong with** pasar algo a, p.ej., **something is wrong with the motor** algo le pasa al motor ‖ *adv* mal; sin razón; al revés; **to go wrong** ir por mal camino; darse a la mala vida ‖ *s* daño, perjuicio; agravio, injusticia; error *m*; **to be in the wrong** no tener razón; tener la culpa; **to do wrong** obrar mal ‖ *tr* agraviar, hacer daño a, ofender, ser injusto con

wrongdoer ['rɔŋ‚du‧ər] o ['rɑŋ‚du‧ər] *s* malhechor *m*

wrongdoing ['rɔŋ‚du‧ɪŋ] o ['rɑŋ‚du‧ɪŋ] *s* malhecho, maldad

wrong number *s* (telp) número equivocado

wrong side *s* contrahaz *f*, revés *m*; (*of the street*) lado contrario; **to get out of bed on the wrong side** levantarse del lado izquierdo; **wrong side out** al revés

wrought iron [rɔt] *s* hierro dulce

wrought'-up' *adj* muy conmovido, sobreexcitado, exaltado

wry [raɪ] *adj* (*comp* **wrier;** *super* **wriest**) torcido; desviado, pervertido; irónico, burlón

wry'neck' *s* (orn) torcecuello; (pathol) torticolis *m*

wt. *abbr* **weight**

X

X, x [eks] vigésima cuarta letra del alfabeto inglés

Xanthippe [zæn'tɪpɪ] *s* Jantipa

Xavier ['zævi‧ər] o ['zcvɪ‧ər] *s* Javier *m*

xebec ['zibek] *s* (naut) jabeque *m*

xenia ['zɪnɪ‧ə] *s* xenia

xenon ['zinɑn] o ['zenɑn] *s* xenón *m*

xenophobe ['zenə‚fob] *s* xenófobo

xenophobia [‚zenə'fobɪ‧ə] *s* xenofobia

Xenophon ['zenəfən] *s* Jenofonte *m*

Xerxes ['zʌrksiz] *s* Jerjes *m*

Xmas ['krɪsməs] *s* Navidad

X ray s rayo X; (*photograph*) radiograma m

X-ray ['ɛks‚re] *adj* radiográfico || ['ɛks're] *tr* radiografiar; tratar por medio de los rayos X

xylograph ['zaɪlə‚græf] o ['zaɪlə‚gruf] s xilografía

xylography [zaɪ'lugrəfi] s xilografía

xylophone ['zaɪlə‚fon] s (mus) xilófono

Y

Y, y [waɪ] vigésima quinta letra del alfabeto inglés

y. *abbr* **yard, year**

yacht [jɑt] s yate m

yacht club s club náutico

yak [jæk] s (zool) yac m

yam [jæm] s ñame m; (*sweet potato*) boniato, camote m

yank [jæŋk] s (coll) tirón m || *tr* (coll) sacar de un tirón || *intr* (coll) dar un tirón

Yankee ['jæŋki] *adj* & s yanqui mf

Yankeedom ['jæŋkidəm] s Yanquilandia; los yanquis

yap [jæp] s ladrido corto; (slang) charla necia y ruidosa || v (*pret* & *pp* **yapped**; *ger* **yapping**) *intr* ladrar con ladrido corto; (slang) charlar necia y ruidosamente

yard [jɑrd] s cercado, patio; (*measure*) yarda; (naut) verga; (rr) patio

yard'arm' s (naut) penol m

yard goods spl géneros de pieza

yard'mas'ter s (rr) superintendente m de patio

yard'stick' s yarda, vara de medir; (fig) criterio, norma

yarn [jɑrn] s hilado, hilaza; (coll) cuento increíble, burlería

yarrow ['jæro] s milenrama

yaw [jɔ] s (naut) guiñada; **yaws** (pathol) frambesia || *intr* (naut) guiñar

yawl [jɔl] s (naut) bote m; (naut) queche m

yawn [jɔn] s bostezo || *intr* bostezar; abrirse desmesuradamente

yd. *abbr* **yard**

yea [je] *adv* & s sí m

yean [jin] *intr* parir (*la oveja, la cabra, etc.*)

year [jɪr] s año; **to be . . . years old** cumplir . . . años; **year in, year out** año tras año

year'book' s anuario

yearling ['jɪrlɪŋ] *adj* & s primal m

yearly ['jɪrli] *adj* anual || *adv* anualmente

yearn [jʌrn] *intr* suspirar; **to yearn for** suspirar por, anhelar por

yearning ['jʌrnɪŋ] s anhelo, deseo ardiente

yeast [jist] s levadura

yeast cake s levadura comprimida, pastilla de levadura

yell [jɛl] s grito, voz f || *tr* decir a gritos || *intr* gritar, dar voces

yellow ['jɛlo] *adj* amarillo; (*cowardly*) (coll) blanco; (*journalism*) sensacional || s amarillo; yema de huevo || *intr* amarillecer

yellowish ['jɛlo·ɪʃ] *adj* amarillento

yellow jacket s avispón m

yellowness ['jɛlonɪs] s amarillez f

yellow streak s vena de cobarde

yelp [jɛlp] s gañido || *intr* gañir

yeo·man ['jomən] s (*pl* **-men** [mən]) (naut) pañolero; (naut) oficinista m de a bordo; (Brit) labrador acomodado

yeoman of the guard s (Brit) alabardero de palacio, continuo

yeoman's service s ayuda leal

yes [jes] *adv* sí || s sí m; **to say yes** dar el sí || v (*pret* & *pp* **yessed**; *ger* **yessing**) *tr* decir sí a || *intr* decir sí

yes man s (coll) sacristán m de amén

yesterday ['jɛstərdɪ] o ['jɛstər‚de] *adj* & s ayer m

yet [jet] *adv* todavía, aún; **as yet** hasta ahora; **not yet** todavía no || *conj* sin embargo

yew tree [ju] s tejo

yield [jild] s producción, rendimiento; (*crop*) cosecha; (*income produced*) rédito || *tr* producir, rendir, redituar || *intr* entregarse, rendirse, someterse; acceder, ceder, consentir; producir

yodeling o **yodelling** ['jodəlɪŋ] s tirolesa

yoke [jok] s (*pair of draft animals*) yunta; (*device to join a pair of draft animals*) yugo; (fig) yugo; (*of a shirt*) hombrillo; (elec) culata; **to throw off the yoke** sacudir el yugo || *tr* uncir

yokel ['jokəl] s patán m

yolk [jok] s yema

yonder ['jɑndər] *adj* aquel, de más allá || *adv* allá, más allá

yore [jor] s — **of yore** antaño, antiguamente

you [ju] *pron pers* usted, ustedes; te, la, les; **with you** consigo || *pron indef* se, p.ej., **you go in this way** se entra por aquí

young [jʌŋ] *adj* (*comp* **younger** ['jʌŋgər]; *super* **youngest** ['jʌŋgɪst]) joven || **the young** los jóvenes, la gente joven

young hopeful s joven m de esperanzas

young people spl jóvenes mpl, gente f joven

youngster ['jʌŋstər] s jovencito; (*child*) chico, chiquillo

your [jur] *adj poss* su, el (o su) de Vd. o de Vds.

yours [jurz] *pron poss* suyo; de Vd., de Vds.; el suyo; el de Vd., el de Vds.; **of yours** suyo; de Vd., de

Vds.; **yours truly** su seguro servidor; (coll) este cura (*yo*)
your·self [jʊr'sɛlf] *pron pers* (*pl* **-selves** ['sɛlvz]) usted mismo; sí, sí mismo; se, p.ej., **you enjoyed yourself** se divirtió Vd.
youth [juθ] *s* (*pl* **youths** [juθs] o [juðz]) juventud; (*person*) jovenzuelo; jovenzuelos, jóvenes *mpl*
youthful ['juθfəl] *adj* juvenil, mocil
yowl [jaʊl] *s* aullido, alarido ‖ *intr* aullar, dar alaridos

yr. *abbr* year
Yugoslav ['jugo'slɑv] *adj & s* yugoeslavo
Yugoslavia ['jugo'slɑvɪ·ə] *s* Yugoeslavia
Yule [jul] *s* la Navidad; la pascua de Navidad
Yule log *s* nochebueno, leño de nochebuena
Yuletide ['jul͵taɪd] *s* la pascua de Navidad

Z

Z, z [zi] vigésima sexta letra del alfabeto inglés
za·ny ['zeni] *adj* (*comp* **-nier**; *super* **-niest**) cómico, gracioso, chiflado ‖ *s* (*pl* **-nies**) bufón *m*, payaso; mentecato
zeal [zil] *s* celo, entusiasmo
zealot ['zɛlət] *s* fanático, entusiasta *mf*
zealotry ['zɛlətri] *s* fanatismo
zealous ['zɛləs] *adj* celoso, entusiasta
zebra ['zibrə] *s* cebra
zebu ['zibju] *s* cebú *m*
zenith ['zinɪθ] *s* cenit *m*
zephyr ['zɛfər] *s* céfiro
zeppelin ['zɛpəlɪn] *s* zepelín *m*
ze·ro ['zɪro] *s* (*pl* **-ros** o **-roes**) cero
zero gravity *s* gravedad nula
zest [zɛst] *s* entusiasmo; (*agreeable and piquant flavor*) gusto, sabor *m*
Zeus [zus] *s* Zeus *m*
zig·zag ['zɪɡ͵zæɡ] *adj & adv* en zigzag ‖ *s* zigzag *m*, ziszas *m* ‖ *v* (*pret & pp* **-zagged**; *ger* **-zagging**) *intr* zigzaguear
zinc [zɪŋk] *s* cinc *m*
zinc etching *s* cincograbado
zinnia ['zɪnɪ·ə] *s* rascamoño

Zionism ['zaɪ·ə͵nɪzəm] *s* sionismo
zip [zɪp] *s* (coll) silbido, zumbido; (coll) energía, brío ‖ *v* (*pret & pp* **zipped**; *ger* **zipping**) *tr* cerrar con cierre relámpago, abrir con cierre relámpago; (coll) llevar con rapidez; **to zip up** dar gusto a ‖ *intr* silbar, zumbar; (coll) moverse con energía; **to zip by** (coll) pasar rápidamente
zipper ['zɪpər] *s* cierre *m* relámpago, cierre cremallera; chanclo con cierre relámpago
zircon ['zɑrkɑn] *s* circón *m*
zirconium [zər'konɪ·əm] *s* circonio
zither ['zɪθər] *s* (mus) cítara
zodiac ['zodɪ͵æk] *s* zodíaco
zone [zon] *s* zona; distrito postal ‖ *tr* dividir en zonas
zoölogic(al) [͵zo·ə'lɑdʒɪk(əl)] *adj* zoológico
zoölogist [zo'ɑlədʒɪst] *s* zoólogo
zoölogy [zo'ɑlədʒi] *s* zoología
zoom [zum] *s* zumbido; (aer) empinada ‖ *tr* (aer) empinar ‖ *intr* zumbar; (aer) empinarse
zoöphyte ['zo·ə͵faɪt] *s* zoófito
Zu·lu ['zulu] *adj* zulú ‖ *s* (*pl* **-lus**) zulú *mf*